ACCOUNTING FORMAT GUIDE

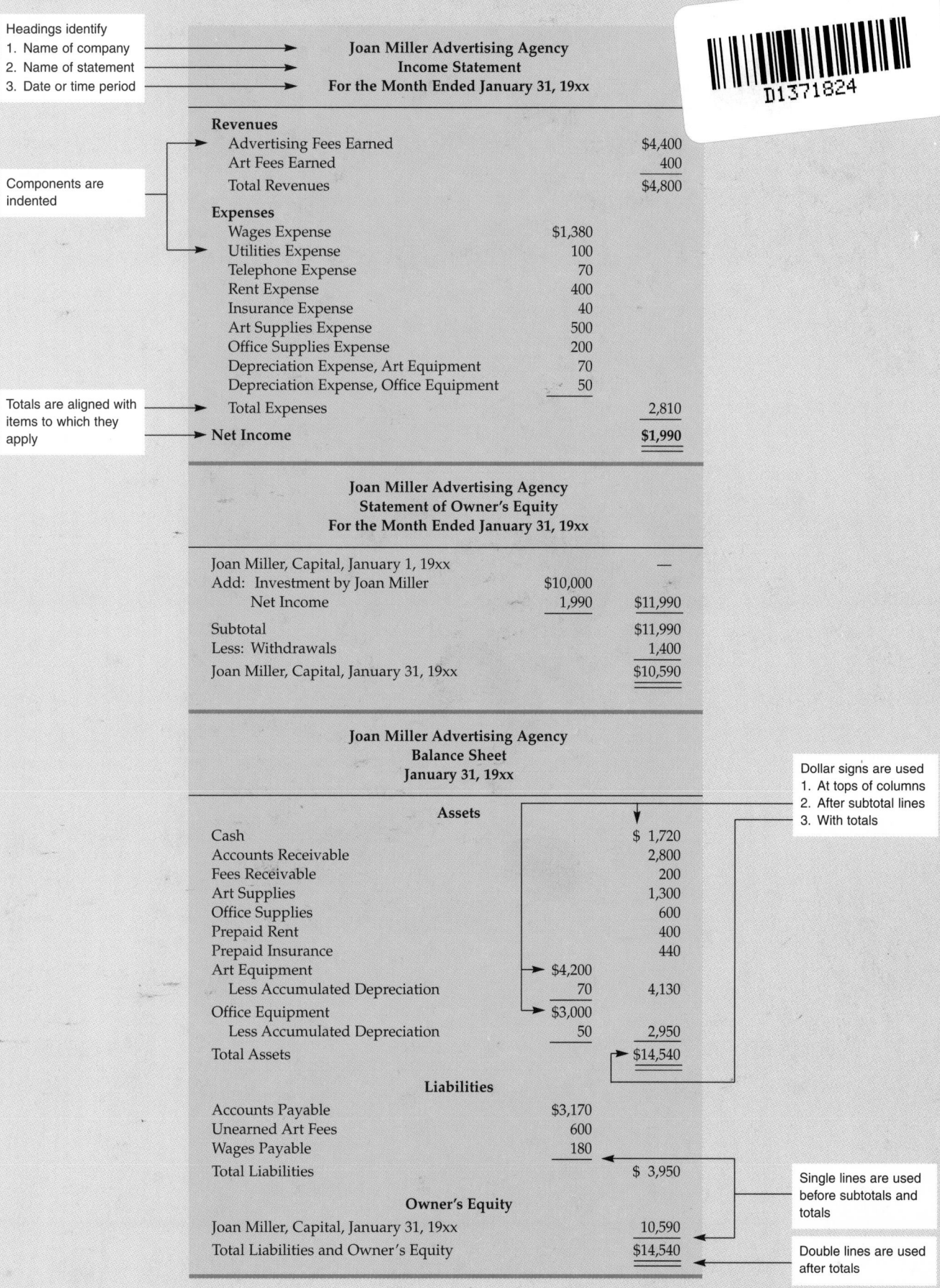

Headings identify
1. Name of company
2. Name of statement
3. Date or time period

Joan Miller Advertising Agency
Income Statement
For the Month Ended January 31, 19xx

Components are indented

Revenues

Advertising Fees Earned		$4,400
Art Fees Earned		400
Total Revenues		$4,800

Expenses

Wages Expense	$1,380	
Utilities Expense	100	
Telephone Expense	70	
Rent Expense	400	
Insurance Expense	40	
Art Supplies Expense	500	
Office Supplies Expense	200	
Depreciation Expense, Art Equipment	70	
Depreciation Expense, Office Equipment	50	
Total Expenses		2,810
Net Income		**$1,990**

Totals are aligned with items to which they apply

Joan Miller Advertising Agency
Statement of Owner's Equity
For the Month Ended January 31, 19xx

Joan Miller, Capital, January 1, 19xx		—
Add: Investment by Joan Miller	$10,000	
Net Income	1,990	$11,990
Subtotal		$11,990
Less: Withdrawals		1,400
Joan Miller, Capital, January 31, 19xx		$10,590

Joan Miller Advertising Agency
Balance Sheet
January 31, 19xx

Dollar signs are used
1. At tops of columns
2. After subtotal lines
3. With totals

Assets

Cash		$ 1,720
Accounts Receivable		2,800
Fees Receivable		200
Art Supplies		1,300
Office Supplies		600
Prepaid Rent		400
Prepaid Insurance		440
Art Equipment	$4,200	
Less Accumulated Depreciation	70	4,130
Office Equipment	$3,000	
Less Accumulated Depreciation	50	2,950
Total Assets		$14,540

Liabilities

Accounts Payable	$3,170	
Unearned Art Fees	600	
Wages Payable	180	
Total Liabilities		$ 3,950

Owner's Equity

Joan Miller, Capital, January 31, 19xx		10,590
Total Liabilities and Owner's Equity		$14,540

Single lines are used before subtotals and totals

Double lines are used after totals

To Professor Reginald R. Rushing, Texas Tech University
To Professor S. James Galley, Augustana College, Illinois
To Professor W. Baker Flowers, University of Alabama
To Professor James H. Bullock, New Mexico State University

SPONSORING EDITOR: Karen Natale
ASSOCIATE SPONSORING EDITOR: Margaret E. Monahan
EDITORIAL PRODUCTION MANAGER: Nancy Doherty Schmitt
SENIOR PROJECT EDITORS: Paula Kmetz, Margaret M. Kearney
SENIOR PRODUCTION/DESIGN COORDINATOR: Sarah Ambrose
SENIOR MANUFACTURING COORDINATOR: Priscilla Bailey

COVER DESIGN: Edda V. Sigurdardottir, Greenwood Design Studio
COVER IMAGE: Timothy Hursley, The Arkansas Office, Inc.

PHOTO CREDITS: Page 2, Deborah Davis/PhotoEdit; page 14, Tony Huchings/Tony Stone Images; page 46, The Boeing Company; page 63, Charles Gupton/Tony Stone Images; page 92, Tony Freeman/PhotoEdit; page 107, G. & M. David DeLossy/The Image Bank; page 134, Ecolab Inc.; page 176, Steve Neidorf; page 180, David Pollack, The Stock Market; page 222, Lawrence Migdale; page 244, Chris Jones/The Stock Market; page 272, Churchill & Klehr; page 293, Andy Sacks/Tony Stone Images; page 328, Zigy Kaluzny/Tony Stone Images; page 339, Jon Feingersh/The Stock Market; page 406, Gabriel M. Covian/The Image Bank; Page 385, Bob Thomason/Tony Stone Images; page 412, Bruce Herman/Tony tone Images; page 434, Ulf Sjostedt/FPG International; page 462, David Joel/Tony Stone Images; page 473, Pal Chesley/Tony Stone Images; page 502, Arthur Sacks/Tony Stone Images; page 512, Rhoda Sidney/The Image Works; page 542, Stephen Studd/Tony Stone Images; page 559, Courtesy of Pennzoil Co.; page 586, Am Reichman/Envision; page 607, Vanessa Vick/Photo Researchers; page 634, Laurent Dardelet/The Image Bank; page 651, Jeff Corwin/Tony Stone Images; page 674, Keith Wood/Tony Stone Images; page 696, Alan Levenson/Tony Stone Images; page 724, David Tejada/Tony Stone Images; page 734, Ted Horowitz/The Stock Market; page 766, William Delzell/Tony Stone Images; page 783, David Carriere/Tony Stone Images; page 8 David Falconer/Folio, Inc.; page 826 Gabe Palmer/The Stock Market; page 854, Jim Goldsmith/Photoni age 878, Billy E. Barnes/PhotoEdit; page 904, Hewlett-Packard Company; page 914, Analog Devices, Inc e 952, Schneider Studio/The Stock Market; page 968, Telegraph Colour Library/FPG International; page 9 oug Menuez/Reportage; page 1005, Brian Blauser/Tony Stone Images; page 1036, Ralph Mercer/Tony Ston ges; page 1056, Mason Morfit/FPG International; page 1076, Peter Poulides/Tony Stone Images; page 10 Will & Deni McIntyre/Tony Stone Images; page 1124, Hughes Electronics Corporation; page 1133, Charles on/Tony Stone Images; page 1180, Marriott International, Inc.; page 1189, Brett Froomer/The Image Ban e 1238, Dave Schaefer/Uniphoto; page 1243, Karen Leeds/The Stock Market.

Toys "R" Us Annual Report (excerpts and complete) year ended January 95 reprinted by permission.

Printed in the U.S.A.

Library of Congress Catalog Card Number: 95-76963

Student text ISBN: 0-395-74565-9

Exam copy ISBN: 0-395-76597-8

23456789-VH-99 98 97 96

FOURTH EDITION

Financial & Managerial

Accounting

A SOLE PROPRIETORSHIP APPROACH

Belverd E. Needles, Jr.
Ph.D., C.P.A., C.M.A.
Arthur Andersen & Alumni
Distinguished Profes of Accounting
DePaul University

Henry R. Anderson
Ph.D., C.P.A., C.M.A.
KPMG Peat Marwick Professor of Accounting
University of Central Florida

James C. Cavell
Ph.D., C.P.A.
Managing Partne
Andersen Consu
Dallas/Fort Wor

Sherry K. Mills
Ph.D., C.P.A.
Associate Professor of Accounting
New Mexico State University

Houghton Mifflin Company

Boston   Toronto   Geneva, Illinois   Palo Alto   Princeton, New Jersey

CONTENTS IN BRIEF

CONTENTS

This textbook is intended for use in the first course in accounting, at the undergraduate or graduate level. It is designed for both business and accounting majors, and requires no previous training in either area. It is part of a well-integrated learning package that includes numerous print and computerized supplements. It has proven successful in a variety of quarter or semester course sequences.

FOCUS ON DECISION MAKING AND THE USES OF ACCOUNTING INFORMATION

Through the previous editions, we approached the writing of this book with the recognition that the majority of students who take the beginning accounting course are business and management majors who will read, analyze, and interpret financial statements and internal managerial documents throughout their careers, and that the fundamental purpose of accounting is to provide information for decision making. While not neglecting topics important for accounting majors, our goal was for all students to become intelligent *users* of financial as well as nonfinancial information. We have striven to make the content authoritative, practical, and contemporary and to apply rigorously a system of integrated learning objectives that enhances the role of the overall package, and particularly that of the textbook, by fostering complete and thorough coordination between the instructor and the student. The success of the previous editions has justified our confidence in this fundamental approach. In fact, this approach is being adopted at more and more colleges and universities.

DESIGNED TO DEVELOP A BROAD SKILL SET IN STUDENTS

This edition represents a major expansion of the fundamental ideas upon which the book is built. The pedagogical system underlying the text is the Learning Improvement Model, which encompasses an enlarged set of instructional strategies designed to achieve a broad skill set in students. This model, which includes the Teaching/Learning Cycle™, cognitive levels of learning, output skills, instructional strategies, and evaluation and feedback, is described in the special new Course Manual that accompanies this text. Among the goals of this edition that result from the application of this model are to (1) develop a much stronger user orientation and reduce the procedural detail, (2) increase the real-world emphasis, (3) reorganize and expand the assignment material to develop a broad set of skills, including critical thinking, communication, interpersonal, financial statement analysis, and interpretation of nonfinancial information skills, and (4) make the book more visually interesting. How these goals are achieved is described in the following sections.

A MUCH STRONGER USER ORIENTATION

We have always emphasized the use of accounting information by both internal and external users. This edition places additional emphasis on the uses of accounting information by management and on decisions that management makes regarding accounting information.

FINANCIAL ACCOUNTING TOPICS

New Management Sections   New sections on management's use of accounting information appear at or near the beginning of chapters covering the following topics:

- Uses of accounting information
- Accounting for merchandising operations
- Short-term liquid assets
- Inventories
- Long-term assets
- Current liabilities
- Long-term liabilities

Financial Ratios   Beginning with Chapter 6, financial analysis ratios are introduced and are integrated in subsequent chapters at appropriate points. These ratios are usually discussed in the "management issues" section at the beginning of the chapters.

Reduced Procedural Detail   Many chapters have been substantially revised to reduce procedural detail. Unnecessary topics are deleted, and procedures that are not essential to conceptual understanding are treated as supplemental objectives at chapter's end. The extent of change resulting from increased emphasis on management's use of accounting information and decreased emphasis on procedural detail throughout the text can be seen in the following detailed descriptions of the revisions in two sample chapters:

■ *CHAPTER 1 Uses of Accounting Information and the Financial Statements* Rewritten and reorganized to reflect its new title, this chapter contains new material that emphasizes business and management uses of accounting information. All-new illustrations highlight the business goals of profitability and liquidity and the activities of financing, investing, and operating. A new section discusses the use of accounting information in all management functions. The section on the basic financial statements has been rewritten and is accompanied by a new illustration to underscore the interrelationship of the statements. The section on GAAP and organizations that influence GAAP has been moved toward the end of the chapter to smooth the flow of information earlier in the chapter. The section on professional ethics and the accounting profession has been rewritten and, through more concise writing, shortened.

■ CHAPTER 5 *Accounting for Merchandising Operations* Rewritten to focus on the merchandising income statement, to provide increased coverage of the perpetual inventory system, and to remove much of the procedural detail usually associated with the topic of merchandising, Chapter 5 now contains a new opening section that focuses on management issues related to merchandising businesses, including the concept of the operating cycle and its relationship to cash flows. The structure of the merchandising income statement is presented early in the chapter, and a new illustration of the components of cost of goods sold is included. The chapter now offers equal and parallel coverage of the periodic and perpetual inventory systems. Since sales discounts and purchases discounts are usually immaterial and add procedural complexity to the problems, these topics have been transferred from the discussion of merchandising transactions to the end of the chapter and treated as a supplemental objective.

Eliminated Procedural Topics Other examples of eliminated procedural topics are:

- Sum-of-the-years'-digits method
- Methods of computing goodwill
- Accounting for assets of low unit cost
- Employee payroll records

New or Revised Conceptual and Analytical Topics Examples of new or substantially revised conceptual or analytical topics are:

- The use of the chart of accounts as a data base for accounting information
- The relationships of cash flows to accrual accounting
- Management's responsibility for ethical reporting
- Components of an annual report (using Toys "R" Us)
- Parallel presentation of inventory pricing methods for both the periodic and the perpetual inventory systems
- Integration of the concepts of capital and revenue expenditures into the section on acquisition cost
- Analysis of cash flows
- Nature of nonoperating items under quality of earnings
- Comprehensive illustration of ratio analysis using the financial statements of Apple Computer, Inc.
- Ratios related to cash flow adequacy

Sections about accounting for marketable securities and bond investments have been updated for the effects of SFAS No. 115.

Supplemental Objectives Some topics are treated under supplemental objectives so they can be covered at the instructor's discretion. Exercises and problems that cover supplemental topics are identified and placed at the end of their respective assignment sets. Examples of topics that have been made supplemental objectives include:

- Sales discounts and purchases discounts
- Merchandising work sheet and closing entries
- Credit card sales
- Valuing inventories by estimation
- Special problems of depreciating plant assets
- Workbook approach to statement of cash flows

MANAGERIAL ACCOUNTING TOPICS

New Management Sections   In this edition, we continue to develop our coverage of the usefulness of accounting in helping managers. Every managerial accounting chapter begins with a learning objective that stresses the importance and use of the chapter's subject matter in the day-to-day responsibilities of managers. For example, we explain how managers obtain and use decision support information. We also describe how changes in managers' information needs cause management accounting systems to adapt in a globally competitive environment.

This emphasis on managers' uses of accounting information is apparent in the chapter assignment materials. Specific questions, short exercises, exercises, and skills development exercises are designed to make students think about and discuss the importance and use of internal accounting information.

In addition to being the focal point of the opening learning objective in each chapter, uses of internal accounting information are also highlighted throughout the managerial chapters. Students learn how to create accounting analyses and reports and how to interpret business information. Each chapter offers short cases designed specifically to help students formulate and interpret managerial accounting reports and analyses. These cases point out that most business problems have several answers, depending on how the manager interprets the circumstances.

Reduced Procedural Detail   Procedural aspects have been lessened to yield a more relevant exposure of managerial accounting to the nonaccounting major. Emphasis on the development of analyses needed to identify and provide information to managers has been increased. The use of journal entries has been reduced but not eliminated because all business students should be aware of how business data enter the accounting records. Entries also provide the link between internal accounting analyses and external financial reporting.

New or Revised Conceptual and Analytical Topics   Service types of businesses are featured in discussions of appropriate managerial topics, as well as in the exercise, problem, and case materials. One integrated decision case, *McHenry Hotels, Inc.*, deals with the hotel service business and can be used over a four- to six-week time span during the last half of the managerial accounting portion of the principles course.

Managerial accounting can no longer be studied without linking it to the changes resulting from global competition. As management philosophies evolve, so must the information supporting management decisons. The new operating environment has had a significant impact on managerial accounting practices, and so influences from the globally competitive business environment have been intregrated into all of the managerial accounting chapters. In addition, specific chapters focus on the just-in-time operating environment, activity-based costing, and total quality management and measures of quality.

INCREASE IN REAL-WORLD EMPHASIS

Many steps have been taken to increase the real-world emphasis of the text, including the following:

Decision Points   Every chapter contains at least one Decision Point based on a real company. Decision Points present a situation requiring a decision by management or other users of accounting information and then show how the decision can be made using accounting information.

Business Bulletins   Also new in this edition are features called Business Bulletins—short items related to chapter topics that show the relevance of accounting in four areas: Business Practice, International Practice, Technology in Practice, and Ethics in Practice.

Other Real-World Topics   Information from actual annual reports and articles from such periodicals as *Business Week*, *Forbes*, the *Wall Street Journal*, and *Management Accounting* enhances students' appreciation for the usefulness and relevance of accounting information. In total, more than one hundred fifty publicly held companies have been used as examples. In addition, the financial statements of Apple Computer, Inc. are presented to demonstrate comprehensive financial statement analysis. Among the real-world topics introduced in this edition are:

- Business strategies, goals, and activities
- Complete and parallel coverage of the perpetual and the periodic inventory systems
- Banking and electronic funds transfer
- Relationship of interest rates to length of maturities and risk for U.S. Treasury debt and corporate debt
- Financial leverage
- Initial public offerings and "tombstone" advertisements
- The segment information of PepsiCo, Inc.
- Target costing approach to pricing
- Linking the accounting system to automated production facilities
- Activity-based costing practices
- Nonfinancial performance measures such as throughput time, flexibility, and quality
- Just-in-time operating environment, total quality management, and continuous improvement

Real Companies in Assignments   The use of real companies in the assignment materials has been greatly increased.

International Accounting   In recognition of the global economy in which all businesses operate today, international accounting examples are introduced in Chapter 1 and integrated throughout the text. Among the foreign companies mentioned in the text and assignments are Takashimaya Co. (Japanese), Wellcome (British), Mitsubishi (Japanese), and Groupe Michelin (French).

REORGANIZED AND EXPANDED ASSIGNMENT MATERIAL TO EMPHASIZE CRITICAL THINKING, COMMUNICATION, FINANCIAL STATEMENT ANALYSIS, INTERPERSONAL, AND INTERPRETATION OF NONFINANCIAL INFORMATION SKILLS

To accommodate students' need for an expanded skill set and instructors' need for greater pedagogical flexibility, the assignments and accompanying materials have been reorganized and greatly expanded. Our objective has been to provide the most comprehensive and flexible set of assignments available and to include more cases that involve real companies. Because students need to be better prepared in writing and communication skills, we have provided ample assignments to enhance student communication skills. In the new organization, each type of assignment has a specific title and purpose. The assignments and principal accompanying materials are as follows:

QUESTIONS, SHORT EXERCISES, AND EXERCISES

Questions   Fifteen to twenty-five review questions that cover the essential topics of the chapter.

Short Exercises   Eight to ten brief exercises suitable for classroom use that cover the key points of the chapter.

Exercises   Ten to fifteen single-topic exercises that stress the application of all topics in the chapter.

SKILLS DEVELOPMENT EXERCISES

Conceptual Analysis   Designed so a written solution is appropriate, but usable in other communication modes, these short cases address conceptual accounting issues and are based on real companies and situations.

Ethical Dilemma   In recognition that accounting and business students need to be exposed in all their courses to ethical considerations, every chapter has a short case, often based on a real company, in which students must address an ethical dilemma directly related to the chapter content.

Research Activity   These exercises are designed to acquaint students with the use of business periodicals, annual reports and business references, and the library. Through field activities at actual businesses, students can improve interviewing and observation skills.

Decision-Making Practice   In the role of decision maker, the student is asked to extract relevant data from a longer case, make computations as necessary, and arrive at a determination. The decision maker may be a manager, an investor, an analyst, or a creditor.

PROBLEMS

Problem Set A   Five or more extensive applications of chapter topics, often covering more than one learning objective. Selected problems in each chapter contain writing components.

Problem Set B   An alternative set of problems.

FINANCIAL AND MANAGERIAL REPORTING AND ANALYSIS CASES

Interpreting Financial and Management Reports   Short cases abstracted from business articles and annual reports of well-known corporations and organizations such as Kmart, Sears, IBM, Toys "R" Us, Chrysler, and UAL (United Airlines), as well as specially designed internal management scenarios, that require students to extract relevant data, make computations, and interpret the results.

Formulating Management Reports   Students strengthen analytical, critical thinking, and written communication skills with these cases. They teach students how to examine, synthesize, and organize information with the object of preparing reports such as a memo to a company president identifying sources of waste, outlining performance measures to account for the waste, and estimating the current costs associated with the waste.

International Company   Short cases similar to the Interpreting Financial and Management Reports, but involving companies from other countries.

Toys "R" Us Annual Report   Cases that emphasize the reading and analysis of the actual annual report of Toys "R" Us contained in an appendix at the end of the book.

COMPUTER ASSIGNMENTS

Exercises, cases, and problems that can be solved with Lotus® or General Ledger Software are identified by icons in the text.

SUPPLEMENTARY LEARNING AIDS

Study Guide

Business Readings in Financial and Managerial Accounting

Working Papers for Exercises and A Problems

Blank Working Papers

Accounting Transaction Tutor

General Ledger Software

Lotus® Templates with Student Manual

Moody's Company Data™ **Software and Assignment Booklet**

Student Resource Videos

Financial Decision Cases and Practice Cases:
  Micro-Tec, Fourth Edition
  Collegiate Ts
  College Words and Sounds Store, Fourth Edition
  General Mills, Inc. Annual Report, Second Edition
  Heartland Airways, Inc., Third Edition
  Richland Home Centers, Inc., Third Edition
  Soft-Tec, Inc., Fifth Edition

Managerial Decision Cases:
  Aspen Food Products Company
  McHenry Hotels, Inc., Second Edition
  The Windham Company, Second Edition
  Callson Industries, Inc.

INSTRUCTOR'S SUPPORT MATERIALS

Instructor's Solutions Manual
Course Manual
Test Bank
Computerized Test Bank
E.L.M.: Electronic Lecture Manager
Solutions Transparencies
Teaching Transparencies
Videodisc
Master Teacher Videos
Business Bulletin Videos

ACKNOWLEDGMENTS

Preparing an accounting text is a long and demanding project that cannot really succeed without the help of one's colleagues. We are grateful to a large number of professors, other professional colleagues, and students for their many constructive comments on the text. Unfortunately, any attempt to list all who have helped risks slighting some by omission. Nonetheless, some effort must be made to mention those who have been so helpful.

We wish to express our deep appreciation to our colleagues at DePaul University, the University of Central Florida, and New Mexico State University who have been extremely supportive and encouraging.

The thoughtful and meticulous work of Edward Julius (California Lutheran University) is reflected not only in the Study Guide, but also in many other ways. We also would like to thank Janice Ammons (New Mexico State University) for her work on the Course Manual, Marion Taube (University of Pittsburgh) for her contribution to the Working Papers, and Mark Dawson (Duquesne University) for revising the Test Bank.

We wish to thank Marian Powers for her constant assistance, contribution, and support for this book. Also very important to the quality of this book is the supportive collaboration of our sponsoring editor, Karen Natale. We further benefited from the ideas and guidance of our associate sponsoring editor, Peggy Monahan, and our developmental editors, Cynthia Fostle and Sharon Kaufman. Thanks also go to Fred Shafer, Laurie Grano, Jenny Taylor, and Cristi Atkins for their help with the preparation of the manuscript.

Others, who have been supportive and have had an impact on this book throughout their reviews, suggestions, and class testing are:

Professor Charles D. Adkins
Casper College

Professor Marilyn L. Allan
Central Michigan University

Professor Vicky Arnold
University of Hartford

Professor Gerald Ashley
Grossmont College

Professor Sue Atkinson
Tarleton State University

Professor Dale Bandy
University of Central Florida

Professor Abdul K. Baten
Northern Virginia Community College—Manassas Campus

Professor Robert H. Bauman
Alan Hancock College

Professor Cindi S. Bearden
University of North Alabama

Professor Lon Behmer
Northeast Community College

Professor Frank R. Beigbeder
Rancho Santiago Community College

Professor Teri Bernstein
Santa Monica College

Professor Marvin L. Bouillon
Iowa State University

Professor Richard Bowden
Oakland Community College—Auburn Hills Campus

Professor Gary R. Bower
Community College of Rhode Island

Professor Russell L. Breslauer
Chabot College

Professor Sarah Brown
University of North Alabama

Professor Roy Broxterman
Hutchinson Community College

Professor Lois D. Bryan
Robert Morris College

Professor JoAnn Buchmann
Rockland Community College

Professor Edward F. Callanan
DeKalb College—North Campus

Professor Lee Cannell
El Paso Community College

Professor Eric Carlsen
Kean College of New Jersey

Professor John A. Caspari
Grand Valley State University

Professor Donna M. Chadwick
Sinclair Community College

Professor B. Lynette Chapman
Southwest Texas State University

Professor William C. Chapman
East Central University

Professor Stanley Chu
Borough of Manhattan Community College

Professor Judith Cook
Grossmont College

Ann Cosby

Professor Sharon A. Cotton
Schoolcraft College

Professor Mickey W. Cowan
East Central University

Professor Robert L. Dan
San Antonio College

Professor Elizabeth Davis
Baylor University

Professor Jo Ann DeVries
University of Central Oklahoma

Professor Walter A. Doehring
Genesee Community College

Professor Margaret Douglas
University of Arkansas

Professor John Elfrink
Central Missouri State University

Professor Richard F. Emery
Linfield College

Professor Estelle Faier
Metropolitan Community College (Fort)

Professor Robert E. Fellowes
Christopher Newport College

Professor Albert Fisher
Community College of Southern Nevada

Professor Ronald E. Fisher
Camden County College

Professor E. A. Fornstrom
University of Wyoming

Professor Jeanne C. Franco
Paradise Valley Community College

Professor Victoria A. Fratto
Robert Morris College

Professor Mark L. Frigo
DePaul University

Professor Ralph B. Fritzsch
Midwestern State University

Professor Larry Goode
Missouri Southern State College

Professor Debra Goorbin
Westchester Community College

Professor Parker Granger
Jacksonville State University

Professor Dennis Greer
Utah Valley Community College

Professor Barbara Saar-Gregorio
Nassau Community College

Professor Robert B. Gronstal
Metropolitan Community College

Professor Beverly J. Grunder
Cowley County Community College

Professor Lawrence Gulley
Norfolk State University

Professor Rama R. Guttikonda
Auburn University at Montgomery

Professor Dennis A. Gutting
Orange County Community College

Professor Carolyn B. Harris
University of Texas at San Antonio

Professor Darrell D. Haywood
North Harris County College

Professor Paula E. Hegner
Heald College

Professor Alene G. Helling
Stark Technical Community College

Professor Linda Hemmingway
Athens State College

Professor Paul E. Holt
Texas A&I University

Professor Anita Hope
Tarrant County Junior College—Northeast Campus

Professor Charles W. Hope
Tarrant County Junior College—Northwest Campus

Professor Bambi A. Hora
University of Central Oklahoma

Professor Kendra Huff
Texas A&I University

Professor Samuel J. Hughson
New York City Technical College

Professor Sid N. Hyder
Indiana University of Pennsylvania

Professor Anthony W. Jackson
Central State University

Professor Gloria M. Jackson
San Antonio College

Professor Sharon S. Jackson
Auburn University at Montgomery

Professor John S. Jeter
Cameron University

Professor David M. Johnson
Pepperdine University

Professor Herbert J. Johnson
Blinn College

Professor David T. Jones
California University of Pennsylvania

Professor Richard W. Jones
Lamar University

Professor Rita C. Jones
Georgia College

Professor Peter B. Kenyon
Humboldt State University

Professor Roberta L. Klein
SUNY, Brockport

Professor Jack L. Kockentiet
Columbus State Community College

Professor Cynthia Kreisner
Austin Community College

Professor Linda Kropp
Modesto Junior College

Professor Cathy Xanthaky Larson
Middlesex Community College

Professor William C. Lathen
Boise State University

Professor Paul J. Lisowski
Edinboro University of Pennsylvania

Professor Lenard T. Long
Fisher College

Professor Katherine A. Longbotham
Richland College

Professor George Loughron
Tomball College

Professor Nancy Pennoyer Lynch
West Virginia University

Professor L. Kevin McNelis
Eastern New Mexico University

Professor Donald L. Madden
University of Kentucky

Professor Lois Mahoney
University of Central Florida

Professor James P. Makofske
Fresno City College

Professor Gary L. Merz
Clarion University of Pennsylvania

Michael F. Monahan

Professor Doug Morrison
Clark College

Jenine Moscove

Professor Susan Murphy
Monroe Community College

Professor C. Lynn Murray
Florida Community College at Jacksonville

Professor Leila Newkirk
Garland County Community College

Professor Terry J. Nunley
University of North Carolina at Charlotte

Professor Harris M. O'Brien
North Harris County College

Professor Marilyn Okleshen
Mankato State University

Professor Anne M. Oppegard
Augustana College

Professor Lynn Mazzola Paluska
Nassau Community College

Professor Rukshad Patel
College of DuPage

Professor Ralph L. Peck
Utah State University

Professor Paul E. Pettit
Snead State Junior College

Professor Wayne E. Pfingsten
Belleville Area College

Professor Orrel E. Picklesimer
University of Texas at San Antonio

Professor Elden Price
Bee County College

Professor LaVonda Ramey
Schoolcraft College

Professor Robert Randall
Moorpark College

Professor Edward R. Rayfield
Suffolk County Community College—Western Campus

Professor David A. Reese
Southern Utah University

Professor Sara Reese
Virginia Union University

Professor Cheri Reither
Midwestern State University

Professor Harold F. Ripley
Orange County Community College

Professor Jep Robertson
New Mexico State University

Professor Margo Rock
Hillsborough Community College

Professor Marilyn Salter
University of Central Florida

Professor Dennis Schirf
Quincy College

Professor Donal R. Schmidt, Jr.
Tarleton State University

Professor James Seivwright
Hillsborough Community College—Dale Mabry Campus

Professor Gary C. Sell
Madison Area Technical College

Professor Robbie Sheffy
Tarrant County Junior College—South Campus

Professor Margaret L. Shelton
University of Houston—Downtown Campus

Professor Arthur Silva
Community College of Rhode Island

Professor S. Murray Simons
Northeastern University

Professor Jill M. Smith
Idaho State University

Professor Ron Stunda
Samford University

Professor Ellen L. Sweatt
DeKalb College—North Campus

Professor Beverly B. Terry
Central Piedmont Community College

Professor Kathryn Verrault
University of Massachusetts—Lowell

Professor Mike Watters
New Mexico State University

Professor Robert R. Wennagel
College of the Mainland

Professor Kathleen A. Wessman
Montgomery College—Rockville

Professor Dale Westfall
Midland College

Professor Kenneth Winter
University of Wisconsin—La Crosse

Professor Stanley J. Yerep
Indiana University of Pennsylvania

Glenn Young

Professor Marilyn J. Young
Tulsa Junior College

Professor Thomas E. Zaher
Bucks County Community College

How to Study Accounting Successfully

Whether you are majoring in accounting or in another business discipline, your introductory accounting course is one of the most important classes you will take, because it is fundamental to the business curriculum and to your success in the business world beyond college. The course has multiple purposes because its students have diverse interests, backgrounds, and purposes for taking it. What are your goals in studying accounting? Being clear about your goals can contribute to your success in this course.

Success in this class also depends on your desire to learn and your willingness to work hard. And it depends on your understanding of how the text complements the way your instructor teaches and the way you learn. A familiarity with how this text is structured will help you to study more efficiently, make better use of classroom time, and improve your performance on examinations and other assignments.

To be successful in the business world after you graduate, you will need a broad set of skills, which may be summarized as follows:

Technical/Analytical Skills   A major objective of your accounting course is to give you a firm grasp of the essential business and accounting terminology and techniques that you will need to succeed in a business environment. With this foundation, you then can begin to develop the higher-level perception skills that will help you to acquire further knowledge on your own.

An even more crucial objective of this course is to help you develop analytical skills that will allow you to evaluate data. Well-developed analytical and decision-making skills are among the professional skills most highly valued by employers, and will serve you well throughout your academic and professional careers.

Communication Skills   Another skill highly prized by employers is the ability to express oneself in a manner that is understood correctly by others. This can include writing skills, speaking skills, and presentation skills. Communication skills are developed through particular tasks and assignments and are improved through constructive criticism. Reading skills and listening skills support the direct communication skills.

Interpersonal Skills   Effective interaction between two people requires a solid foundation of interpersonal skills. The success of such interaction depends on empathy, or the ability to identify with and understand the problems, concerns, and motives of others. Leadership, supervision, and interviewing skills also facilitate a professional's interaction with others.

Personal/Self Skills   Personal/self skills form the foundation for growth in the use of all other skills. To succeed, a professional must take initiative, possess self-confidence, show independence, and be ethical in all areas of life. Personal/self skills can be enhanced significantly by the formal learning process and by peers and mentors who provide models upon which you can build. Accounting is just one course in your entire curriculum, but it can play an important role in your development of the above skills. Your instructor is interested in helping you gain both a knowledge of accounting and the more general skills you will need to succeed in the business world. The following sections describe how you can get the most out of this course.

THE TEACHING/LEARNING CYCLE™

Both teaching and learning have natural, parallel, and mutually compatible cycles. This teaching/learning cycle, as shown in Figure 1, interacts with the basic structure of learning objectives in this text.

The Teaching Cycle   The inner (blue) circle in Figure 1 shows the steps an instructor takes in teaching a chapter. Your teacher *assigns* material, *presents* the subject in lecture, *explains* by going over assignments and answering questions, *reviews* the subject prior to an exam, and *tests* your knowledge and understanding using examinations and other means of evaluation.

The Learning Cycle   Moving outward, the next circle (pink) in Figure 1 shows the steps you should take in studying a chapter. You should *preview* the material, *read* the chapter, *apply* your understanding by working the assignments, *review* the chapter, and *recall* and *demonstrate* your knowledge and understanding of the material on examinations and other assessments.

Integrated Learning Objectives   Your textbook supports the teaching/learning cycle through the use of integrated learning objectives. Learning objectives are simply statements of what you should be able to do after you have completed a chapter. In Figure 1, the outside (green) circle shows how learning objectives are integrated into your text and other study aids and how they interact with the teaching/learning cycle.

1. Learning objectives appear at the beginning of the chapter, as an aid to your teacher in making assignments and as a preview of the chapter for you.
2. Each learning objective is repeated in the text at the point where that subject is covered to assist your teacher in presenting the material and to help you organize your thoughts as you read the material.
3. Every exercise, problem, and case in the chapter assignments shows the applicable learning objective(s) so you can refer to the text if you need help.
4. A summary of the key points for each learning objective, a list of new concepts and terms referenced by learning objectives, and a review problem covering key learning objectives assist you in reviewing each chapter. Your Study Guide, also organized by learning objectives, provides for additional review.

Why Students Succeed   Students succeed in their accounting course when they coordinate their personal learning cycle with their instructor's cycle. Students who do a good job of previewing their assignments, reading the chapters before the instructor is ready to present them, preparing homework assignments before they are discussed in class, and reviewing carefully will ultimately achieve their potential on exams. Those who get out of phase with their instructor, for whatever reason, will do poorly or fail. To ensure that your learning cycle is synchronized with your instructor's teaching cycle, check your study habits against these suggestions.

Figure 1. The Teaching/Learning Cycle™ with Integrated Learning Objectives

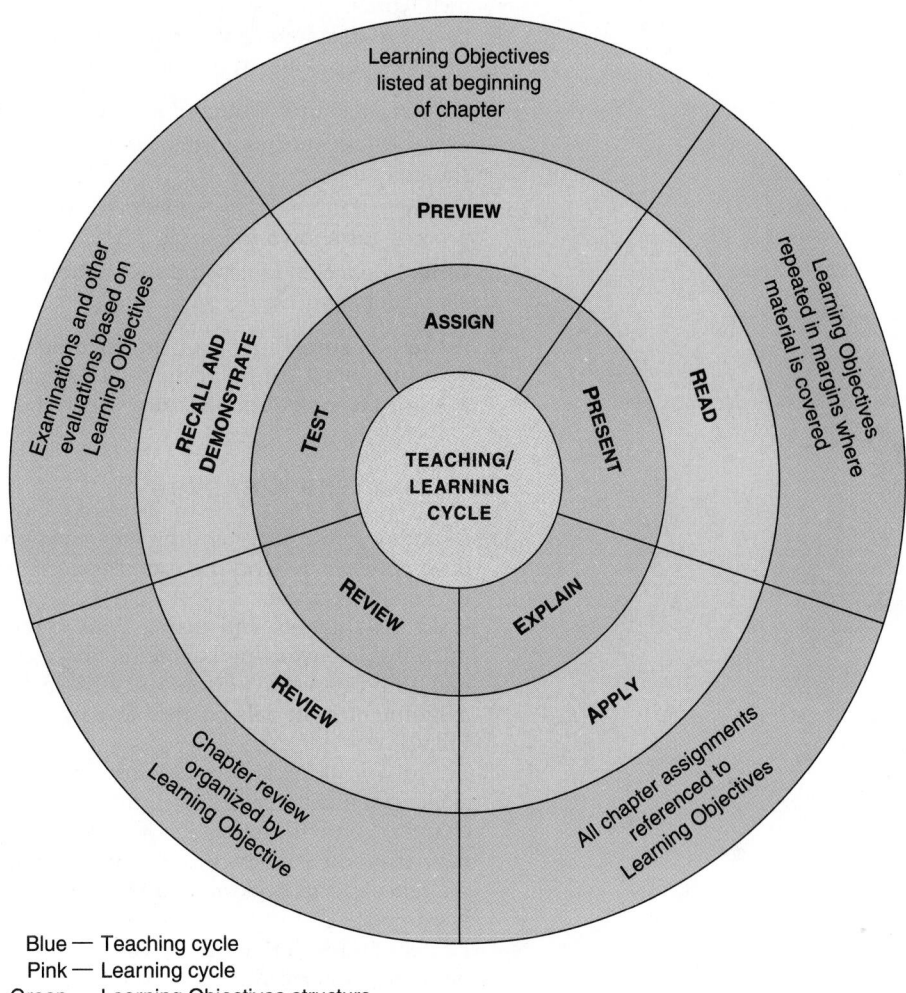

Blue — Teaching cycle
Pink — Learning cycle
Green — Learning Objectives structure

PREVIEWING THE CHAPTER

1. Read the learning objectives at the beginning of the chapter. These learning objectives specifically describe what you should be able to do after completing the chapter.
2. Study your syllabus. Know where you are in the course and where you are going. Know the rules of the course.
3. Realize that in an accounting course, each assignment builds on previous ones. If you do poorly in Chapter 1, you may have difficulty in Chapter 2 and be lost in Chapter 3.

READING THE CHAPTER

1. As you read each chapter, be aware of the learning objectives in the margins. They will tell you why the material is relevant.
2. Allow yourself plenty of time to read the text. Accounting is a technical subject. Accounting books are so full of information that almost every sentence is important.
3. Strive to understand why as well as how each procedure is done. Accounting is

logical and requires reasoning. If you understand why something is done in accounting, there is little need to memorize.

4. Relate each new topic to its learning objective and be able to explain it in your own words.

5. Be aware of colors as you read. They are designed to help you understand the text. (See the chart on the back of your textbook.)

    Yellow: All source documents and inputs are in yellow.

    Aqua: All accounting forms, working papers, and accounting processes are shown in aqua.

    Purple: All financial statements, the output or final product of the accounting process, are shown in purple.

    Gray: In selected tables and illustrations, gray is used to heighten contrasts and aid understanding.

6. If there is something you do not understand, prepare specific questions for your instructor. Pinpoint the topic or concept that confuses you. Some students keep a notebook of points with which they have difficulty.

APPLYING THE CHAPTER

1. In addition to understanding why each procedure is done, you must be able to do it yourself by working exercises, problems, and cases. Accounting is a "do-it-yourself" course.

2. Read assignments and instructions carefully. Each assignment has a specific purpose. The wording is precise, and a clear understanding of it will save time and improve your performance. Acquaint yourself with the end-of-chapter assignment materials in this text by reading the description of them in the Preface.

3. Try to work exercises, problems, and cases without referring to their discussions in the chapter. If you cannot work an assignment without looking in the chapter, you will not be able to work a similar problem on an exam. After you have tried on your own, refer to the chapter (based on the learning objective reference) and check your answer. Try to understand any mistakes you may have made.

4. Be neat and orderly. Sloppy calculations, messy papers, and general carelessness cause most errors on accounting assignments.

5. Allow plenty of time to work the chapter assignments. You will find that assignments seem harder and that you make more errors when you are feeling pressed for time.

6. Keep up with your class. Check your work against the solutions presented in class. Find your mistakes. Be sure you understand the correct solutions.

7. Note the part of each exercise, problem, or case that causes you difficulty so you can ask for help.

8. Attend class. Most instructors design classes to help you and to answer your questions. Absence from even one class can hurt your performance.

REVIEWING THE CHAPTER

1. Read the summary of learning objectives in the chapter review. Be sure you know the definitions of all the words in the review of concepts and terminology.

2. Review all assigned exercises, problems, and cases. Know them cold. Be sure you can work the assignments without the aid of the book.

3. Determine the learning objectives for which most of the problems were assigned. They refer to topics that your instructor is most likely to emphasize

on an exam. Scan the text for such learning objectives and pay particular attention to the examples and illustrations.
4. Look for and scan other similar assignments that cover the same learning objectives. They may be helpful on an exam.
5. Review quizzes. Similar material will often appear on longer exams.
6. Attend any labs or visit any tutors your school provides, or see your instructor during office hours to get assistance. Be sure to have specific questions ready.

TAKING EXAMINATIONS

1. Arrive at class early so you can get the feel of the room and make a last-minute review of your notes.
2. Have plenty of sharp pencils and your calculator (if allowed) ready.
3. Review the exam quickly when it is handed out to get an overview of your task. Start with a part you know. It will give you confidence and save time.
4. Allocate your time to the various parts of the exam, and stick to your schedule. Every exam has time constraints. You need to move ahead and make sure you attempt all parts of the exam.
5. Read the questions carefully. Some may not be exactly like your homework assignments. They may approach the material from a slightly different angle to test your understanding and ability to reason, rather than your ability to memorize.
6. To avoid unnecessary errors, be neat, use good form, and show calculations.
7. Relax. If you have followed the above guidelines, your effort will be rewarded.

PREPARING OTHER ASSIGNMENTS

1. Understand the assignment. Written assignments, term papers, computer projects, oral presentations, case studies, group activities, individual field trips, video critiques, and other activities are designed to enhance skills beyond your technical knowledge. It is essential to know exactly what your instructor expects. Know the purpose, audience, scope, and expected end product.
2. Allow plenty of time. "Murphy's Law" applies to such assignments: If anything can go wrong, it will.
3. Prepare an outline of each report, paper, or presentation. A project that is done well always has a logical structure.
4. Write a rough draft of each paper and report, and practice each presentation. Professionals always try out their ideas in advance and thoroughly rehearse their presentations. Good results are not accomplished by accident.
5. Make sure that each paper, report, or presentation is of professional quality. Instructors appreciate attention to detail and polish. A good rule of thumb is to ask yourself: Would I give this work to my boss?

Accounting as an Information System

CHAPTER 1
Uses of Accounting Information and the Financial Statements

explores the nature and environment of accounting, with special emphasis on the users and uses of accounting information. It introduces the four basic financial statements, the concept of accounting measurement, and the effects of business transactions on financial position. This chapter concludes with a discussion of ethical considerations in accounting.

CHAPTER 2
Measuring Business Transactions

continues the exploration of accounting measurement by focusing on the problems of recognition, valuation, and classification and how they are solved in the measuring and recording of business transactions.

CHAPTER 3
Measuring Business Income

defines the accounting concept of business income, discusses the role of adjusting entries in the measurement of income, and demonstrates the preparation of financial statements.

CHAPTER 4
Completing the Accounting Cycle

focuses on the preparation of closing entries and the completion of the accounting cycle. A discussion of the work sheet concludes the chapter.

Uses of Accounting Information and the Financial Statements

LEARNING OBJECTIVES

1. Define *accounting*, identify business goals and activities, and describe the role of accounting in making informed decisions.

2. Identify the many users of accounting information in society.

3. Explain the importance of business transactions, money measure, and separate entity to accounting measurement.

4. Identify the three basic forms of business organization.

5. Define *financial position*, state the accounting equation, and show how the two are affected by simple transactions.

6. Identify the four basic financial statements.

7. State the relationship of generally accepted accounting principles (GAAP) to financial statements and the independent CPA's report, and identify the organizations that influence GAAP.

8. Define *ethics* and describe the ethical responsibilities of accountants.

General Electric Co.

General Electric Co., the giant electronics, media, and financial services company, is considered one of the world's most successful companies. Why is General Electric considered successful? The ordinary person sees the quality products and services the company offers, but the investment community and others with a financial stake in the company evaluate the company and its management in financial terms. For example, General Electric's performance was recently summed up as follows:

> Any way you parse them, GE's numbers are awe-inspiring. Return on stockholders' equity for 1994: a projected 21 percent. Net return on sales after taxes: pushing 9 percent. Free cash flow after capital spending and dividends: about $2 billion. Dividends could be up 15 percent this year, GE's eighteenth straight annual boost.[1]

This excerpt contains a number of terms for common financial goals of all companies, large or small—goals by which a company's management is evaluated and by which others can evaluate a company in relation to other companies. What financial knowledge do GE's managers need to achieve these and other financial goals? What financial knowledge does anyone who is evaluating GE in relation to other companies need to understand these terms?

GE's managers must have a thorough knowledge of accounting to understand how the operations for which they are responsible contribute to the firm's overall financial health. People with a financial stake in the company, such as owners, investors, creditors, employees, attorneys, and government regulators, must also know accounting to evaluate the financial performance of a business. Anyone who aspires to any of these roles in a business requires a mastery of the terminology and concepts that underlie accounting, the way in which financial information is generated, and the way in which that information is interpreted and analyzed. The purpose of this course and this textbook is to assist you in acquiring that mastery. ⋮⋮⋮⋮⋮

1. James R. Norman, "A Very Nimble Elephant," *Forbes,* October 10, 1994.

ACCOUNTING AS AN INFORMATION SYSTEM

OBJECTIVE

1 *Define account-ing, identify business goals and activities, and describe the role of accounting in making informed decisions*

Today's accountant focuses on the ultimate needs of decision makers who use accounting information, whether those decision makers are inside or outside the business. Accounting "is not an end in itself,"[2] but is an information system that measures, processes, and communicates financial information about an identifiable economic entity. An economic entity is a unit that exists independently—for example, a business, a hospital, or a governmental body. The central focus of this book is on business entities and business activities, although other economic units, such as hospitals and governmental units, will be mentioned at appropriate points in the text and assignment material.

Accounting provides a vital service by supplying the information that decision makers need to make "reasoned choices among alternative uses of scarce resources in the conduct of business and economic activities."[3] As shown in Figure 1, accounting is a link between business activities and decision makers. First, accounting measures business activities by recording data about them for future use. Second, the data are stored until needed and then processed to become useful information. Third, the information is communicated, through reports, to decision makers. We might say that data about business activities are the input to the accounting system and that useful information for decision makers is the output.

Figure 1. Accounting as an Information System

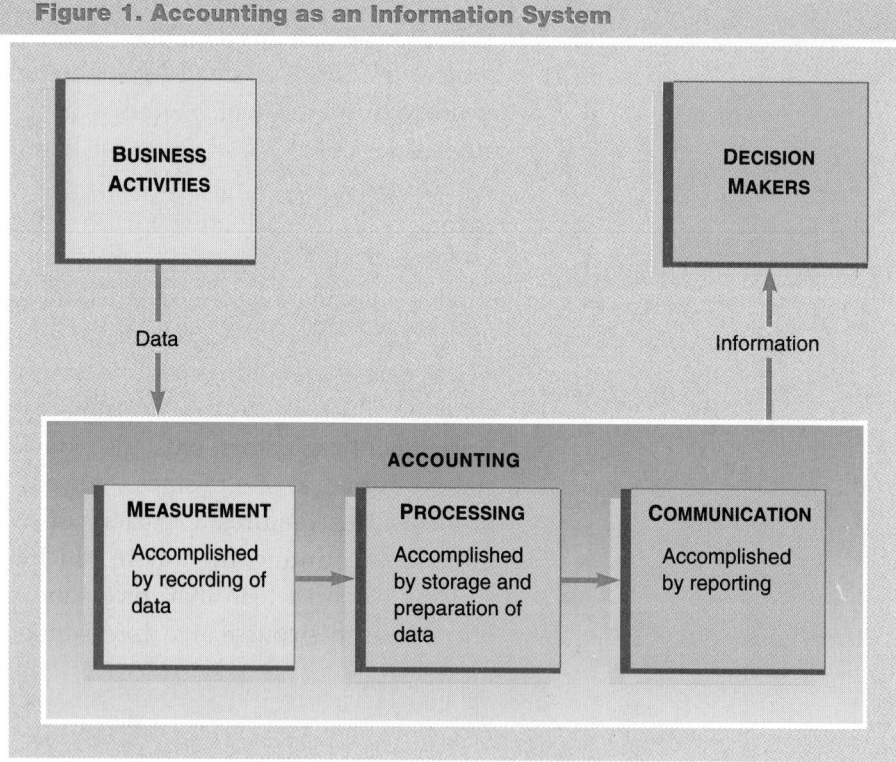

2. *Statement of Financial Accounting Concepts No. 1*, "Objectives of Financial Reporting by Business Enterprises" (Stamford, Conn.: Financial Accounting Standards Board, 1978), par. 9.

3. Ibid.

BUSINESS BULLETIN: BUSINESS PRACTICE

 Accounting is a very old discipline. Forms of it have been essential to commerce for more than five thousand years. Accounting, in a version close to what we know today, came into widespread use in the 1400s, especially in Italy, where it was instrumental to the development of shipping, trade, construction, and other forms of commerce. This system of double-entry bookkeeping was documented by the famous Italian mathematician, scholar, and philosopher Fra Luca Pacioli. In 1494, Pacioli published his most important work, *Summa de Arithmetica, Geometrica, Proportioni et Proportionalita,* which contained a detailed description of accounting as practiced in that age. This book became the most widely read book on mathematics in Italy and firmly established Pacioli as the "Father of Accounting." =====

BUSINESS GOALS AND ACTIVITIES

A business is an economic unit that aims to sell goods and services to customers at prices that will provide an adequate return to its owners. For example, listed below are some companies and the principal goods or services they sell.

General Mills	Food products and restaurants
Reebok International Ltd.	Athletic footwear and clothing
Sony Corp.	Consumer electronics
Wendy's International, Inc.	Food service
Hilton Hotels Corp.	Hotels and resorts service
Southwest Airlines, Inc.	Passenger airline service

Despite their differences, all these businesses have similar goals and engage in similar activities, as shown in Figure 2. Each must take in enough money from customers to pay all the costs of doing business, with enough left over as profit for the owners to want to stay in the business. This need to earn enough income to attract and hold investment capital is the goal of profitability. In addition, businesses must meet the goal of liquidity. Liquidity means having enough funds on hand to pay debts when they are due. For example, Toyota may meet the goal of profitability by selling many cars at a price that earns a profit, but if its customers do not pay for their cars quickly enough to enable Toyota to pay its suppliers and employees, the company may fail to meet the goal of liquidity. Both goals must be met if a company is to survive and be successful.

All businesses pursue their goals by engaging in similar activities. First, each business must engage in financing activities to obtain adequate funds, or capital, to begin and to continue operating. Financing activities include obtaining capital from owners and from creditors, such as banks and suppliers. They also include repaying creditors and paying a return to the owners. Second, each business must engage in investing activities to spend the capital it receives in ways that are productive and will help to achieve its objectives. Investing activities include buying land, buildings, equipment, and other

Figure 2. Business Goals and Activities

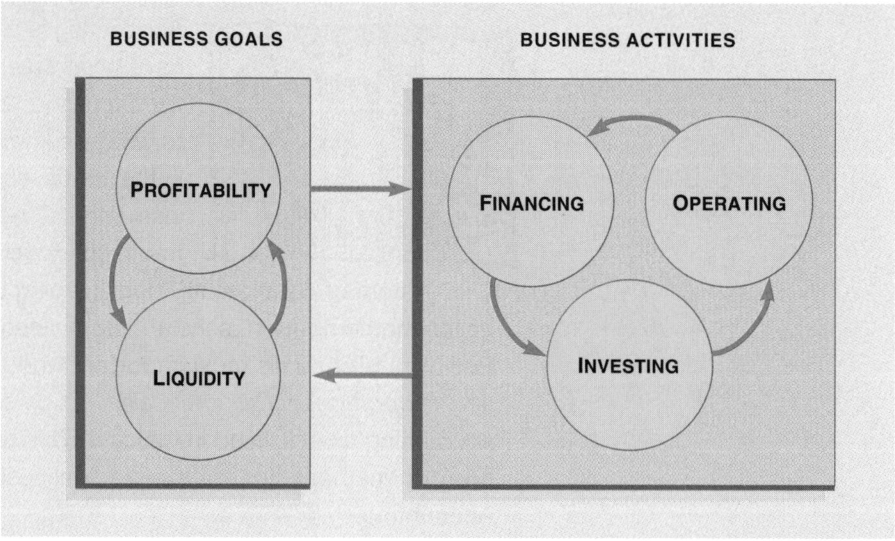

BUSINESS GOALS

PROFITABILITY

LIQUIDITY

BUSINESS ACTIVITIES

FINANCING

OPERATING

INVESTING

long-lived resources needed in the operation of the business, and selling these resources when they are no longer needed. Third, each business must engage in operating activities. In addition to the selling of goods and services to customers, operating activities include such actions as employing managers and workers, buying and producing goods and services, and paying taxes to the government.

FINANCIAL AND MANAGEMENT ACCOUNTING

Accounting's role of assisting decision makers by measuring, processing, and communicating information is usually divided into the categories of management accounting and financial accounting. Although there is considerable overlap in the functions of management accounting and financial accounting, the two can be distinguished by who the principal users of their information will be. Management accounting provides internal decision makers who are charged with achieving the goals of profitability and liquidity with information about financing, investing, and operating activities. Managers and employees who conduct the activities of the business need information that tells them how they have done in the past and what they can expect in the future. For example, The Gap needs an operating report on each mall outlet that tells how much was sold at that outlet and what costs were incurred, and it needs a budget for each outlet that projects the sales and costs for the next year. Financial accounting generates reports and communicates them to external decision makers so that they can evaluate how well the business has achieved its goals. These reports are called financial statements. The Gap, for instance, will send its financial statements to its owners (called *stockholders*), its banks and other creditors, and government regulators. Financial statements report directly on the goals of profitability and liquidity and are used extensively both inside and outside a business to evaluate the business's success. It is important for every person involved with a business to understand financial statements. They are a central feature of accounting and are the primary focus of this book.

PROCESSING ACCOUNTING INFORMATION

To avoid misunderstandings, it is important to distinguish accounting itself from the ways in which accounting information is processed by bookkeeping, the computer, and management information systems.

People often fail to understand the difference between accounting and bookkeeping. Bookkeeping is the process of recording financial transactions and keeping financial records. Mechanical and repetitive, bookkeeping is only a small—but important—part of accounting. Accounting, on the other hand, includes the design of an information system that meets the users' needs. The major goals of accounting are the analysis, interpretation, and use of information.

The computer is an electronic tool that is used to collect, organize, and communicate vast amounts of information with great speed. Accountants were among the earliest and most enthusiastic users of computers, and today they use microcomputers in all aspects of their work. It may appear that the computer is doing the accountant's job; in fact, it is only a tool that is instructed to do routine bookkeeping and to perform complex calculations.

With the widespread use of the computer today, a business's many information needs are organized into what is called a management information system (MIS). A management information system consists of the interconnected subsystems that provide the information needed to run a business. The accounting information system is the most important subsystem because it plays the key role of managing the flow of economic data to all parts of a business and to interested parties outside the business.

DECISION MAKERS: THE USERS OF ACCOUNTING INFORMATION

OBJECTIVE

2 *Identify the many users of accounting information in society*

The people who use accounting information to make decisions fall into three categories: (1) those who manage a business; (2) those outside a business enterprise who have a direct financial interest in the business; and (3) those people, organizations, and agencies that have an indirect financial interest in the business, as shown in Figure 3. These categories apply to government and not-for-profit organizations as well as to profit-oriented ventures.

MANAGEMENT

Management, collectively, is the people who have overall responsibility for operating a business and for meeting its profitability and liquidity goals. In a small business, management may include the owners. In a large business, management more often consists of people who have been hired. Managers must decide what to do, how to do it, and whether the results match their original plans. Successful managers consistently make the right decisions based on timely and valid information. To make good decisions, managers need answers to such questions as: What was the company's net income during the past quarter? Is the rate of return to the owners adequate? Does the company have enough cash? Which products are most profitable? What is the cost of manufacturing each product? Because so many key decisions are based on accounting data, management is one of the most important users of accounting information.

Figure 3. The Users of Accounting Information

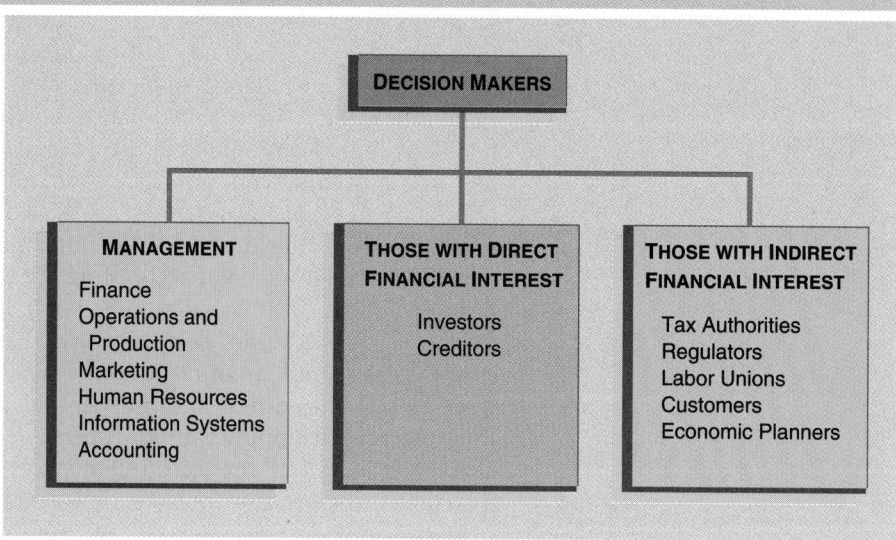

In carrying out its decision-making process, management performs a set of functions essential to the operation of the business. Although larger businesses will have more elaborate operations, the same basic functions must be accomplished in all cases, and each requires accounting information for decision making. The basic management functions are:

Financing the business   Financial management obtains financial resources so that the company can begin and continue operating.

Investing the resources of the business   Asset management invests the financial resources of the business in productive assets that support the company's goals.

Producing goods and services   Operations and production management develops and produces products and services.

Marketing goods and services   Marketing management sells, advertises, and distributes goods and services.

Managing employees   Human resource management encompasses the hiring, evaluation, and compensation of employees.

Providing information to decision makers   Information management captures data about all aspects of the company's operations, organizes the data into usable information, and provides reports to internal managers and appropriate outside parties. Accounting plays a key role in this function.

USERS WITH A DIRECT FINANCIAL INTEREST

Another group of decision makers who need accounting information are those with a direct financial interest in a business. They depend on accounting to measure and report information about how a business has performed. Most businesses periodically publish a set of general-purpose financial statements that report their success in meeting the goals of profitability and liquidity. These statements show what has happened in the past and are important indicators of what is going to happen in the future. Many people outside the company carefully study these financial reports. The two most important outside groups are investors and creditors.

Investors Those who invest or may invest in a business and acquire a part ownership are interested in its past success and its potential earnings. A thorough study of a company's financial statements helps potential investors judge the prospects for a profitable investment. After investing in a company, investors must continually review their commitment, again by examining the company's financial statements.

Creditors Most companies borrow money for both long- and short-term operating needs. Creditors, those who lend money or deliver goods and services before being paid, are interested mainly in whether a company will have the cash to pay interest charges and repay debt at the appropriate time. They study a company's liquidity and cash flow as well as its profitability. Banks, finance companies, mortgage companies, securities firms, insurance firms, suppliers, and other lenders must analyze a company's financial position before they make a loan.

USERS WITH AN INDIRECT FINANCIAL INTEREST

In recent years, society as a whole, through government and public groups, has become one of the biggest and most important users of accounting information. Users who need accounting information to make decisions on public issues include (1) tax authorities, (2) regulatory agencies, and (3) other groups.

Tax Authorities Government at every level is financed through the collection of taxes. Under federal, state, and local laws, companies and individuals pay many kinds of taxes, including federal, state, and city income taxes, social security and other payroll taxes, excise taxes, and sales taxes. Each tax requires special tax returns and often a complex set of records as well. Proper reporting is generally a matter of law and can be very complicated. The Internal Revenue Code, for instance, contains thousands of rules governing the preparation of the accounting information used in computing federal income taxes.

Regulatory Agencies Most companies must report to one or more regulatory agencies at the federal, state, and local levels. For example, all public corporations must report periodically to the Securities and Exchange Commission (SEC). This body, which was set up by Congress to protect the public, regulates the issuing, buying, and selling of stocks in the United States. Companies that are listed on a stock exchange also must meet the special reporting requirements of their exchange.

Other Groups Labor unions study the financial statements of corporations as part of preparing for contract negotiations. A company's income and costs often play an important role in these negotiations. Those who advise investors and creditors—financial analysts and advisers, brokers, underwriters, lawyers, economists, and the financial press—also have an indirect interest in the financial performance and prospects of a business. Consumers' groups, customers, and the general public have become more concerned about the financing and earnings of corporations as well as the effects that corporations have on inflation, the environment, social problems, and the quality of life. And economic planners, among them members of the President's Council of Economic Advisers and the Federal Reserve Board, use aggregated accounting information to set economic policies and evaluate economic programs.

GOVERNMENT AND NOT-FOR-PROFIT ORGANIZATIONS

More than 30 percent of the U.S. economy is generated by government and not-for-profit organizations (examples of these entities include hospitals, universities, professional organizations, and charities). The managers of these diverse entities need to understand and to use accounting information to perform the same functions as managers in businesses. They need to raise funds from investors, creditors, tax payers, and donors, and to deploy scarce resources. They need to plan to pay for operations and repay creditors on a timely basis. Moreover, they have an obligation to report their financial performance to legislators, boards, and donors, as well as deal with tax authorities, regulators, and labor unions. Although most of the examples in this text focus on business enterprises, the same basic principles apply to government and not-for-profit organizations.

ACCOUNTING MEASUREMENT

OBJECTIVE

3 *Explain the importance of business transactions, money measure, and separate entity to accounting measurement*

Accounting is an information system that measures, processes, and communicates financial information. In this section, you begin the study of the measurement aspects of accounting. Here you learn what accounting actually measures and study the effects of certain transactions on a company's financial position.

To make an accounting measurement, the accountant must answer four basic questions.

1. What is measured?
2. When should the measurement be made?
3. What value should be placed on what is measured?
4. How should what is measured be classified?

All these questions deal with basic assumptions and generally accepted accounting principles, and their answers establish what accounting is and what it is not. Accountants in industry, professional associations, public accounting, government, and academic circles debate the answers to these questions constantly, and the answers change as new knowledge and practice require. But the basis of today's accounting practice rests on a number of widely accepted concepts and conventions, which are described in this book. Here we focus on question **1**: What is measured?

WHAT IS MEASURED?

The world contains an unlimited number of things to measure and ways to measure them. For example, consider a machine that makes bottle caps. How many measurements of this machine could you make? You might start with size and then go on to location, weight, cost, or one of many other units of measurement. Some of these measurements are relevant to accounting; some are not. Every system must define what it measures, and accounting is no exception. Basically, financial accounting uses money measures to gauge the impact of business transactions on separate business entities. The concepts of business transactions, money measure, and separate entity are discussed in the next sections.

BUSINESS TRANSACTIONS AS THE OBJECT OF MEASUREMENT

Business transactions are economic events that affect the financial position of a business entity. Business entities can have hundreds or even thousands of transactions every day. These business transactions are the raw material of accounting reports.

A transaction can be an exchange of value (a purchase, sale, payment, collection, or loan) between two or more independent parties. A transaction also can be an economic event that has the same effect as an exchange transaction but does not involve an exchange. Some examples of "nonexchange" transactions are losses from fire, flood, explosion, and theft; physical wear and tear on machinery and equipment; and the day-by-day accumulation of interest.

To be recorded, a transaction must relate directly to a business entity. For example, suppose a customer buys a shovel from Ace Hardware but has to buy a hoe from a competing store because Ace is out of hoes. The transaction in which the shovel was sold is entered in Ace's records. However, the purchase of the hoe from the competitor is not entered in Ace's records because, even though it indirectly affects Ace economically, it does not involve a direct exchange of value between Ace and the customer.

MONEY MEASURE

All business transactions are recorded in terms of money. This concept is termed money measure. Information of a nonfinancial nature may be recorded, but it is from the recording of monetary amounts that the transactions and activities of a business are measured. Money is the only factor that is common to all business transactions, and thus it is the only practical unit of measure that can produce financial data that are alike and comparable.

The monetary unit a business uses depends on the country in which the business resides. For example, in the United States, the basic unit of money is the dollar. In Japan, it is the yen; in France, the franc; in Germany, the mark; and in the United Kingdom, the pound. If there are transactions between countries, exchange rates must be used to translate from one currency to another. An exchange rate is the value of one currency in terms of another. For example, a British person purchasing goods from a U.S. company and paying in U.S. dollars must exchange British pounds for U.S. dollars before making payment. In effect, the currencies are goods that can be bought and sold. Table 1 illustrates the exchange rates for several currencies in terms of

Table 1. Partial Listing of Foreign Exchange Rates

Country	Price in $ U.S.	Country	Price in $ U.S.
Britain (pound)	1.56	Italy (lira)	0.0006
Canada (dollar)	0.714	Japan (yen)	0.0101
France (franc)	0.19	Mexico (peso)	0.18
Germany (mark)	0.66	Philippines (peso)	0.04
Hong Kong (dollar)	0.13	Taiwan (dollar)	0.038

Source: Data from *Wall Street Journal*, February 13, 1995; *New York Times*, February 15, 1995.

the U.S. dollar. It shows the exchange rate for British pounds as $1.56 per pound on a particular date. Like the price of any good or service, these prices change daily according to supply and demand for the currencies. For example, a few years earlier the exchange rate for British pounds was $1.20. Although our discussion in this book focuses on dollars, selected examples and assignments will be in foreign currencies.

THE CONCEPT OF SEPARATE ENTITY

For accounting purposes, a business is a separate entity, distinct not only from its creditors and customers but also from its owner or owners. It should have a completely separate set of records, and its financial records and reports should refer only to its own financial affairs.

For example, the Jones Florist Company should have a bank account that is separate from the account of Kay Jones, the owner. Kay Jones may own a home, a car, and other property, and she may have personal debts, but these are not the Jones Florist Company's resources or debts. Kay Jones also may own another business, say a stationery shop. If she does, she should have a completely separate set of records for each business.

FORMS OF BUSINESS ORGANIZATION

OBJECTIVE

4 *Identify the three basic forms of business organization*

There are three basic forms of business organization: sole proprietorships, partnerships, and corporations. Accountants recognize each form as an economic unit separate from its owners, although legally only the corporation is considered separate from its owners. Other legal differences among the three forms are summarized in Table 2 and discussed briefly in the following sections. In this book, we begin with accounting for the sole proprietorship

Table 2. Comparative Features of the Forms of Business Organization

	Sole Proprietorship	Partnership	Corporation
1. Legal status	Not a separate legal entity	Not a separate legal entity	Separate legal entity
2. Risk of ownership	Owner's personal resources at stake	Partners' personal resources at stake	Limited to investment in corporation
3. Duration or life	Limited by choice or death of owner	Limited by choice or death of any partner	Indefinite, possibly unlimited
4. Transferability of ownership	Sale by owner establishes new company	Changes in any partner's percentage of interest requires new partnership	Transferable by sale of stock
5. Accounting treatment	Separate economic unit	Separate economic unit	Separate economic unit

because it is the simplest form of accounting. At critical points, however, we call attention to its essential differences from accounting for partnerships and corporations.

SOLE PROPRIETORSHIPS

A sole proprietorship is a business owned by one person. This form of organization gives the individual a means of controlling the business apart from his or her personal interests. Legally, however, the proprietorship is the same economic unit as the individual. The individual receives all profits or losses and is liable for all obligations of the business. Proprietorships represent the largest number of businesses in the United States, but typically they are the smallest in size. The life of a sole proprietorship ends when the owner wants it to or when the owner dies or becomes incapacitated.

PARTNERSHIPS

A partnership is like a proprietorship in most ways except that it has more than one owner. A partnership is not a legal entity separate from the owners but an unincorporated association that brings together the talents and resources of two or more people. The partners share the profits and losses of the partnership according to an agreed-on formula. Generally, any partner can bind the partnership to another party, and, if necessary, the personal resources of each partner can be called on to pay the obligations of the partnership. In some cases, one or more partners limit their liability, but at least one partner must have unlimited liability. A partnership must be dissolved when ownership changes—for example, when a partner leaves or dies. For the business to continue as a partnership, a new partnership must be formed.

CORPORATIONS

A corporation is a business unit that is legally separate from its owners (the stockholders). The owners, whose ownership is represented by shares of stock in the corporation, do not control the operations of the corporation directly. Instead, they elect a board of directors, which appoints managers to run the corporation for the benefit of the stockholders. In exchange for limited involvement in the corporation's actual operations, stockholders enjoy limited liability. That is, their risk of loss is limited to the amount they paid for their shares. If they want, stockholders can sell their shares to other people, without affecting corporate operations. Because of this limited liability, stockholders often are willing to invest in riskier, but potentially more profitable, activities. Also, because ownership can be transferred without dissolving the corporation, the life of the corporation is unlimited; it is not subject to the whims or health of a proprietor or partner.

Corporations have several important advantages over proprietorships and partnerships that make them very efficient in amassing capital for the formation and growth of very large companies. Even though corporations are fewer in number than proprietorships and partnerships, they contribute much more to the U.S. economy in monetary terms (see Figure 4). For example, in 1994 General Motors generated more revenue than all but fifteen of the world's countries.

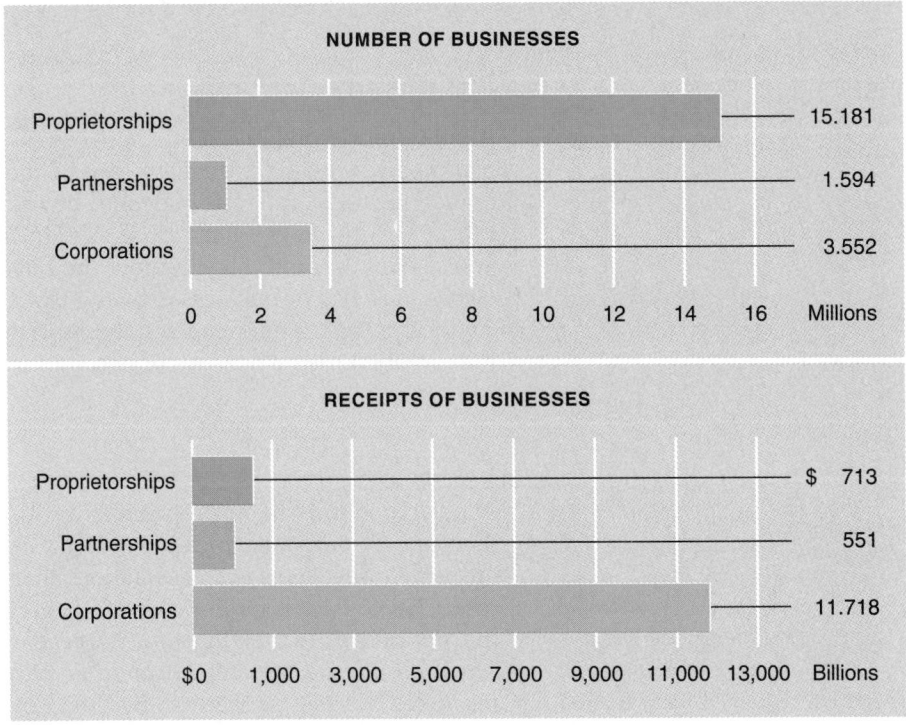

Figure 4. Number and Receipts of U.S. Proprietorships, Partnerships, and Corporations, 1992

NUMBER OF BUSINESSES

Proprietorships	15.181
Partnerships	1.594
Corporations	3.552

0   2   4   6   8   10   12   14   16   Millions

RECEIPTS OF BUSINESSES

Proprietorships	$ 713
Partnerships	551
Corporations	11.718

$0   1,000   3,000   5,000   7,000   9,000   11,000   13,000   Billions

Source: U.S. Treasury Department, Internal Revenue Service, *Statistics of Income Bulletin,* Winter 1993–1994, pp. 74, 83, 187–190.

Santini Tours Company

DECISION POINT

Carlos Santini has worked seven years for a successful travel agency that operates in Chicago. Santini has decided to leave the travel agency and start his own travel business that will specialize in organizing incentive tours, such as tours a business can give its salespeople when they exceed their sales goals. Santini has saved enough money to start the business on a small scale and hopes to grow larger by bringing in partners and investors in future years. He is deliberating on the best way to organize his business. Considering the differences between a sole proprietorship, a partnership, and a corporation, how should he structure the new business?

Because Santini is starting small and using his own capital, it is probably best to organize the business as a sole proprietorship at the beginning. A sole proprietorship is flexible and easy to establish. As Santini's business grows and other people and investors become involved, it will be advisable to change to a partnership or corporation because such forms of business are more suitable to handling the relationships of multiple owners. :: :: ::

Most people think of corporations as large national or global companies whose shares of stock are held by thousands of people and institutions. Indeed, corporations can be huge and have many stockholders. However, of the approximately 3.7 million corporations in the United States, only about 15,000 have stock that is publicly bought and sold. The vast majority of corporations are small businesses that are privately held by a few stockholders. In Illinois alone, there are more than 250,000 corporations. For this reason, the study of corporations is just as relevant to small businesses as it is to large ones. ▬▬▬

FINANCIAL POSITION AND THE ACCOUNTING EQUATION

OBJECTIVE

5 *Define* financial position, *state the accounting equation, and show how the two are affected by simple transactions*

Financial position refers to the economic resources that belong to a company and the claims against those resources at a point in time. Another term for claims is *equities*. Therefore, a company can be viewed as composed of economic resources and equities.

$$\text{Economic Resources} = \text{Equities}$$

Every company has two types of equities: creditors' equities and owner's equity. Thus,

$$\text{Economic Resources} = \text{Creditors' Equities} + \text{Owner's Equity}$$

In accounting terminology, economic resources are called *assets* and creditors' equities are called *liabilities*. So, the equation can be written like this:

$$\text{Assets} = \text{Liabilities} + \text{Owner's Equity}$$

This equation is known as the accounting equation. The two sides of the equation always must be equal, or "in balance."

ASSETS

Assets are economic resources owned by a business that are expected to benefit future operations. Certain kinds of assets—for example, cash and money owed to the company by customers (called *accounts receivable*)—are monetary items. Other assets—inventories (goods held for sale), land, buildings, and equipment—are nonmonetary, physical things. Still other assets—the rights granted by patent, trademark, or copyright—are nonphysical.

LIABILITIES

Liabilities are present obligations of a business to pay cash, transfer assets, or provide services to other entities in the future. Among these obligations are debts of the business, amounts owed to suppliers for goods or services bought on credit (called *accounts payable*), borrowed money (for example, money owed on loans payable to banks), salaries and wages owed to employees, taxes owed to the government, and services to be performed.

As debts, liabilities are claims recognized by law. That is, the law gives creditors the right to force the sale of a company's assets if the company fails to pay its debts. Creditors have rights over owners and must be paid in full before the owners receive anything, even if payment of a debt uses up all the assets of a business.

OWNER'S EQUITY

Owner's equity represents the claims by the owner of a business to the assets of the business. It equals the residual interest, or residual equity, in the assets of an entity that remains after deducting the entity's liabilities. Theoretically, it is what would be left if all the liabilities were paid, and it is sometimes said to equal net assets. By rearranging the accounting equation, we can define owner's equity this way:

$$\text{Owner's Equity} = \text{Assets} - \text{Liabilities}$$

The four types of transactions that affect owner's equity are shown in Figure 5. Two of these transactions, owner's investments and owner's withdrawals, are assets that the owner either puts into the business or takes out of the business. For instance, if the owner of Shannon Realty, John Shannon, takes cash out of his personal bank account and deposits it in the business bank account, he has made an owner's investment. The assets (cash) of the business increase, and John Shannon's equity in those assets also increases. Conversely, if John Shannon takes cash out of the business bank account and deposits it in his personal bank account, he has made a withdrawal from the business. The assets of the business decrease, and John Shannon's equity in the business also decreases.

The other two types of transactions that affect owner's equity are revenues and expenses. Simply stated, revenues and expenses are the increases and decreases in owner's equity that result from operating a business. For example, the cash a customer pays (or agrees to pay in the future) to Shannon Realty in return for a service provided by the company is a revenue. The assets (cash or accounts receivable) of Shannon Realty increase, and the owner's equity in those assets also increases. On the other hand, the cash Shannon Realty pays out (or agrees to pay in the future) in the process of providing a service is an expense. Now the assets (cash) decrease or the liabilities (accounts payable) increase, and the owner's equity in the assets decreases. Generally speaking, a company is successful if its revenues exceed its expenses. When revenues exceed expenses, the difference is called net income; when expenses exceed revenues, the difference is called net loss.

Figure 5. Four Types of Transactions That Affect Owner's Equity

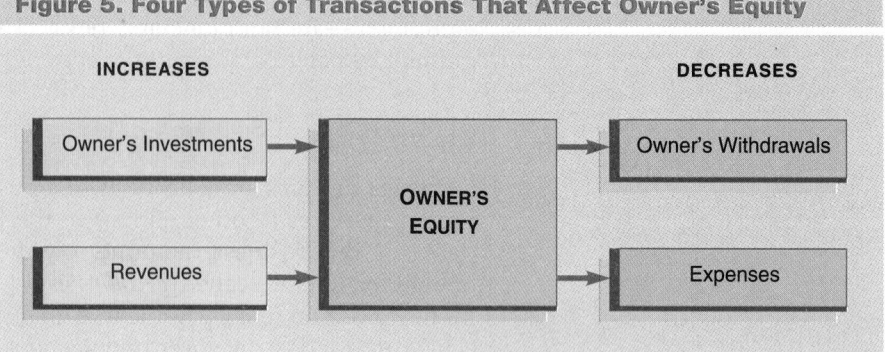

SOME ILLUSTRATIVE TRANSACTIONS

Let us now examine the effect of some of the most common business transactions on the accounting equation. Suppose that John Shannon opens a real estate agency called Shannon Realty on December 1. During December, his business engages in the transactions described in the following paragraphs. Exhibit 1 (page 21) presents a summary of these eleven illustrative transactions.

Owner's Investments   John starts his business by depositing $50,000 in a bank account in the name of Shannon Realty. The transfer of cash from his personal account to the business account is an owner's investment. The first balance sheet of the new company would show the asset Cash and the owner's equity (John Shannon, Capital):

	Assets	=	Owner's Equity (OE)	
	Cash		John Shannon, Capital	Type of OE Transaction
1.	$50,000		$50,000	Owner's Investment

At this point, the company has no liabilities, and assets equal the owner's equity. The labels Cash and John Shannon, Capital are called accounts and are used by accountants to accumulate amounts that result from similar transactions. Transactions that affect owner's equity are identified by type so that similar types may later be grouped together on accounting reports.

Purchase of Assets with Cash   John finds a good location and pays cash to purchase the lot for $10,000 and a small building on the lot for $25,000. This transaction does not change the total assets, liabilities, or owner's equity of Shannon Realty, but it does change the composition of the assets—it decreases Cash and increases Land and Building:

	Assets			=	Owner's Equity	
	Cash	Land	Building		John Shannon, Capital	Type of OE Transaction
bal.	$50,000				$50,000	
2.	−35,000	+$10,000	+$25,000			
bal.	$15,000	$10,000	$25,000		$50,000	
		$50,000				

Purchase of Assets by Incurring a Liability   Assets do not always have to be purchased with cash. They may also be purchased on credit, that is, on the basis of an agreement to pay for them later. Suppose Shannon Realty buys some office supplies for $500 on credit. This transaction increases the assets (Supplies) and increases the liabilities of Shannon Realty. This liability is designated by an account called Accounts Payable:

	Assets				= Liabilities +	Owner's Equity	
	Cash	Supplies	Land	Building	Accounts Payable	John Shannon, Capital	Type of OE Transaction
bal.	$15,000		$10,000	$25,000		$50,000	
3.		+$500			+$500		
bal.	$15,000	$500	$10,000	$25,000	$500	$50,000	
		$50,500				$50,500	

Notice that this transaction increases both sides of the accounting equation to $50,500.

Payment of a Liability   If Shannon Realty later pays $200 of the $500 owed for the supplies, both assets (Cash) and liabilities (Accounts Payable) decrease, but Supplies is unaffected:

	Assets				= Liabilities +	Owner's Equity	
	Cash	Supplies	Land	Building	Accounts Payable	John Shannon, Capital	Type of OE Transaction
bal.	$15,000	$500	$10,000	$25,000	$500	$50,000	
4.	−200				−200		
bal.	$14,800	$500	$10,000	$25,000	$300	$50,000	
		$50,300				$50,300	

Notice that both sides of the accounting equation are still equal, although now at a total of $50,300.

Revenues   Shannon Realty earns revenues in the form of commissions by selling houses for clients. Sometimes these commissions are paid to Shannon Realty immediately in the form of cash, and sometimes the client agrees to pay the commission later. In either case, the commission is recorded when it is earned and Shannon Realty has a right to a current or future receipt of cash. First, assume that Shannon Realty sells a house and receives a commission of $1,500 in cash. This transaction increases both assets (Cash) and owner's equity (John Shannon, Capital):

	Assets				= Liabilities +	Owner's Equity	
	Cash	Supplies	Land	Building	Accounts Payable	John Shannon, Capital	Type of OE Transaction
bal.	$14,800	$500	$10,000	$25,000	$300	$50,000	
5.	+1,500					+$1,500	Commissions Earned
bal.	$16,300	$500	$10,000	$25,000	$300	$51,500	
		$51,800				$51,800	

Now assume that Shannon Realty sells a house, in the process earning a commission of $2,000, and agrees to wait for payment of the commission. Because the commission has been earned now, a bill or invoice is sent to the client, and the transaction is recorded now. This revenue transaction increases both assets and owner's equity as before, but a new asset account, Accounts Receivable, shows that Shannon Realty is awaiting receipt of the commission:

		Assets				= Liabilities +	Owner's Equity	
	Cash	Accounts Receiv- able	Supplies	Land	Building	Accounts Payable	John Shannon, Capital	Type of OE Transaction
bal.	$16,300		$500	$10,000	$25,000	$300	$51,500	
6.		+$2,000					+2,000	Commissions Earned
bal.	$16,300	$2,000	$500	$10,000	$25,000	$300	$53,500	
		$53,800					$53,800	

As you progress in your study of accounting, you will be shown the use of separate accounts for revenues, like Commissions Earned.

Collection of Accounts Receivable   Let us assume that a few days later Shannon Realty receives $1,000 from the client in transaction **6.** At that time, the asset Cash increases and the asset Accounts Receivable decreases:

		Assets				= Liabilities +	Owner's Equity	
	Cash	Accounts Receiv- able	Supplies	Land	Building	Accounts Payable	John Shannon, Capital	Type of OE Transaction
bal.	$16,300	$2,000	$500	$10,000	$25,000	$300	$53,500	
7.	+1,000	−1,000						
bal.	$17,300	$1,000	$500	$10,000	$25,000	$300	$53,500	
		$53,800					$53,800	

Notice that this transaction does not affect owner's equity because the commission revenue was already recorded in transaction **6.** Also notice that the balance of Accounts Receivable is $1,000, indicating that $1,000 is still to be collected.

Expenses   Just as revenues are recorded when they are earned, expenses are recorded when they are incurred. Expenses can be paid in cash when they occur, or they can be paid later. If payment is going to be made later, a liability—for example, Accounts Payable or Wages Payable—increases. In both cases, owner's equity decreases. Assume that Shannon Realty pays $1,000 to rent some equipment for the office and $400 in wages to a part-time helper. These transactions reduce assets (Cash) and owner's equity (John Shannon, Capital):

		Assets				= Liabilities +	Owner's Equity	
	Cash	Accounts Receiv- able	Supplies	Land	Building	Accounts Payable	John Shannon, Capital	Type of OE Transaction
bal.	$17,300	$1,000	$500	$10,000	$25,000	$300	$53,500	
8.	−1,000						−1,000	Equipment Rental Expense
9.	−400						−400	Wages Expense
bal.	$15,900	$1,000	$500	$10,000	$25,000	$300	$52,100	

$52,400 $52,400

Now assume that Shannon Realty has not paid the $300 bill for utilities expense incurred for December. In this case, the effect on owner's equity is the same as when the expense is paid in cash, but instead of a reduction in assets, there is an increase in liabilities (Accounts Payable):

		Assets				= Liabilities +	Owner's Equity	
	Cash	Accounts Receiv- able	Supplies	Land	Building	Accounts Payable	John Shannon, Capital	Type of OE Transaction
bal.	$15,900	$1,000	$500	$10,000	$25,000	$300	$52,100	
10.						+300	−300	Utilities Expense
bal.	$15,900	$1,000	$500	$10,000	$25,000	$600	$51,800	

$52,400 $52,400

As you progress in your study of accounting, you will be shown the use of separate accounts for expenses, like Equipment Rental Expense, Wages Expense, and Utilities Expense.

Owner's Withdrawals   John now withdraws $600 in cash from Shannon Realty and deposits it in his personal account. This transaction reduces assets (Cash) and owner's equity (John Shannon, Capital). Although, as can be seen below, withdrawals have the same effect on the accounting equation as expenses (see transactions **8** and **9**), it is important not to confuse them. Withdrawals are not expenses: Withdrawals are personal distributions of assets to the owner; expenses are incurred by the business in its operations.

		Assets				= Liabilities +	Owner's Equity	
	Cash	Accounts Receiv- able	Supplies	Land	Building	Accounts Payable	John Shannon, Capital	Type of OE Transaction
bal.	$15,900	$1,000	$500	$10,000	$25,000	$600	$51,800	
11.	−600						−600	Owner's Withdrawal
bal.	$15,300	$1,000	$500	$10,000	$25,000	$600	$51,200	

$51,800 $51,800

Exhibit 1. Summary of Effects of Illustrative Transactions on the Accounting Equation

	Assets					=	Liabilities	+	Owner's Equity	
	Cash	Accounts Receivable	Supplies	Land	Building		Accounts Payable		John Shannon, Capital	Type of Owner's Equity Transaction
1.	$50,000								$50,000	Owner's Investment
2.	−35,000			+$10,000	+$25,000					
bal.	$15,000			$10,000	$25,000				$50,000	
3.			+$500				+$500			
bal.	$15,000		$500	$10,000	$25,000		$500		$50,000	
4.	−200						−200			
bal.	$14,800		$500	$10,000	$25,000		$300		$50,000	
5.	+1,500								+$1,500	Commissions Earned
bal.	$16,300		$500	$10,000	$25,000		$300		$51,500	
6.		+$2,000							+2,000	Commissions Earned
bal.	$16,300	$2,000	$500	$10,000	$25,000		$300		$53,500	
7.	+1,000	−1,000								
bal.	$17,300	$1,000	$500	$10,000	$25,000		$300		$53,500	
8.	−1,000								−1,000	Equip. Rental Expense
9.	−400								−400	Wages Expense
bal.	$15,900	$1,000	$500	$10,000	$25,000		$300		$52,100	
10.							+300		−300	Utilities Expense
bal.	$15,900	$1,000	$500	$10,000	$25,000		$600		$51,800	
11.	−600								−600	Owner's Withdrawal
bal.	$15,300	$1,000	$500	$10,000	$25,000		$600		$51,200	
	$51,800								$51,800	

COMMUNICATION THROUGH FINANCIAL STATEMENTS

OBJECTIVE

6 *Identify the four basic financial statements*

COMMUNICATION THROUGH FINANCIAL STATEMENTS

Financial statements are the primary means of communicating important accounting information to users. It is helpful to think of these statements as models of the business enterprise because they show the business in financial terms. As is true of all models, however, financial statements are not perfect pictures of the real thing, but rather the accountant's best effort to represent what is real. Four major financial statements are used to communicate accounting information about a business: the income statement, the statement of owner's equity, the balance sheet, and the statement of cash flows.

Exhibit 2 illustrates the relationships among the four financial statements by showing how they would appear for Shannon Realty after the eleven sample transactions shown in Exhibit 1. It is assumed that the time period covered is the month of December 19xx. Notice that each statement is headed in a similar way. Each heading identifies the company and the kind of statement. The income statement, the statement of owner's equity, and the statement of cash flows give the time period to which they apply; the balance sheet gives the specific date to which it applies. Much of this book deals with developing, using, and interpreting more complete versions of these basic statements, including statements for partnerships and corporations.

THE INCOME STATEMENT

The income statement summarizes the revenues earned and expenses incurred by a business over a period of time. Many people consider it the most important financial report because it shows whether or not a business achieved its profitability goal of earning an acceptable income. In Exhibit 2, Shannon Realty had revenues in the form of commissions earned of $3,500 ($2,000 of revenue earned on credit and $1,500 in cash). From this amount, total expenses of $1,700 were deducted (equipment rental expense of $1,000, wages expense of $400, and utilities expense of $300), to arrive at a net income of $1,800. To show that it applies to a period of time, the statement is dated "For the Month Ended December 31, 19xx."

THE STATEMENT OF OWNER'S EQUITY

The statement of owner's equity shows the changes in the owner's capital account over a period of time. In Exhibit 2, the beginning capital is zero because the company was started during this accounting period. During the month, John Shannon made an investment in the business of $50,000, and the company earned income (as shown on the income statement) of $1,800, for a total increase of $51,800. Deducted from this amount are the withdrawals for the month of $600, leaving an ending balance of $51,200 in the capital account.

THE BALANCE SHEET

The purpose of a balance sheet is to show the financial position of a business on a certain date, usually the end of the month or year. For this reason, it often is called the *statement of financial position* and is dated as of a certain date. The balance sheet presents a view of the business as the holder of resources, or assets, that are equal to the sources of those assets. The sources consist of the company's liabilities and the owner's equity in the company. In Exhibit 2,

Exhibit 2. Income Statement, Statement of Owner's Equity, Balance Sheet, and Statement of Cash Flows for Shannon Realty

Shannon Realty
Income Statement
For the Month Ended December 31, 19xx

Revenues		
Commissions Earned		$3,500
Expenses		
Equipment Rental Expense	$1,000	
Wages Expense	400	
Utilities Expense	300	
Total Expenses		1,700
Net Income		$1,800

Shannon Realty
Statement of Owner's Equity
For the Month Ended December 31, 19xx

John Shannon, Capital, December 1, 19xx		$ 0
Add: Investments by John Shannon	$50,000	
Net Income for the Month	1,800	51,800
Subtotal		$51,800
Less Withdrawals by John Shannon		600
John Shannon, Capital, December 31, 19xx		$51,200

Shannon Realty
Statement of Cash Flows
For the Month Ended December 31, 19xx

Cash Flows from Operating Activities		
Net Income		$ 1,800
Noncash Expenses and Revenues		
Included in Income		
Increase in Accounts Receivable	($ 1,000)*	
Increase in Supplies	(500)	
Increase in Accounts Payable	600	(900)
Net Cash Flows from Operating		
Activities		$ 900
Cash Flows from Investing Activities		
Purchase of Land	($10,000)	
Purchase of Building	(25,000)	
Net Cash Flows from		
Investing Activities		(35,000)
Cash Flows from Financing Activities		
Investments by John Shannon	$50,000	
Withdrawals by John Shannon	(600)	
Net Cash Flows from		
Financing Activities		49,400
Net Increase (Decrease) in Cash		$15,300
Cash at Beginning of Month		0
Cash at End of Month		$15,300

Shannon Realty
Balance Sheet
December 31, 19xx

Assets		Liabilities	
Cash	$15,300	Accounts Payable	$ 600
Accounts			
Receivable	1,000		
Supplies	500	**Owner's Equity**	
Land	10,000	John Shannon, Capital	51,200
Building	25,000	Total Liabilities and	
Total Assets	$51,800	Owner's Equity	$51,800

No Testing

*Parentheses indicate a negative impact or cash outflow.

Shannon Realty has several categories of assets, which total $51,800. These assets equal the total liabilities of $600 (Accounts Payable) plus the ending balance of owner's equity of $51,200 (John Shannon, Capital). Notice that the amount in the account on the balance sheet comes from the ending balance on the statement of owner's equity.

THE STATEMENT OF CASH FLOWS

Whereas the income statement focuses on a company's profitability goal, the statement of cash flows is directed toward the company's liquidity goal. Cash flows are the inflows and outflows of cash into and out of a business. Net cash flows are the difference between the inflows and outflows. The statement of cash flows shows the cash produced by operating a business as well as important investing and financing transactions that take place during an accounting period. Exhibit 2 shows the statement of cash flows for Shannon Realty. Notice that the statement explains how the Cash account changed during the period. Cash increased by $15,300. Operating activities produced net cash flows of $900, and financing activities produced net cash flows of $49,400. Investment activities used cash flows of $35,000.

This statement is related directly to the other three statements. Notice that net income comes from the income statement and that investments and withdrawals by John Shannon come from the statement of owner's equity. The other items in the statement represent changes in the balance sheet accounts: Accounts Receivable, Supplies, Accounts Payable, Land, and Building.

GENERALLY ACCEPTED ACCOUNTING PRINCIPLES

To ensure that financial statements will be understandable to their users, a set of practices, called generally accepted accounting principles, has been developed to provide guidelines for financial accounting. Although the term has several meanings in the literature of accounting, perhaps this is the best definition: "Generally accepted accounting principles encompass the conventions, rules, and procedures necessary to define accepted accounting practice at a particular time."[4] In other words, GAAP arise from wide agreement on the theory and practice of accounting at a particular time. These "principles" are not like the unchangeable laws of nature found in chemistry or physics. They are developed by accountants and businesses to serve the needs of decision makers, and they can be altered as better methods evolve or as circumstances change.

In this book, we present accounting practice, or GAAP, as it is today. We also try to explain the reasons or theory on which the practice is based. Both theory and practice are part and parcel of the study of accounting. However, you should realize that accounting is a discipline that is always growing, changing, and improving. Just as years of research are necessary before a new surgical method or lifesaving drug can be introduced, it may take years for research and new discoveries in accounting to become common practice. As a result, you may come across practices that seem contradictory. In some cases, we point out new directions in accounting. Your instructor also may mention certain weaknesses in current theory or practice.

FINANCIAL STATEMENTS, GAAP, AND THE INDEPENDENT CPA'S REPORT

Because financial statements are prepared by the management of a company and could be falsified for personal gain, all companies that sell ownership to

---

4. *Statement of the Accounting Principles Board No. 4,* "Basic Concepts and Accounting Principles Underlying Financial Statements of Business Enterprises" (New York: American Institute of Certified Public Accountants, 1970), par. 138.

the public and many companies that apply for sizable loans have their financial statements audited by an independent certified public accountant. Certified public accountants (CPAs) are licensed by the individual states for the same reason that lawyers and doctors are—to protect the public by ensuring the quality of professional service. One important attribute of CPAs is independence: They have no financial or other compromising ties with the companies they audit. This gives the public confidence in their work. The firms listed in Table 3 employ about 25 percent of all CPAs.

An independent CPA makes an audit, which is an examination of a company's financial statements and the accounting systems, controls, and records that produced them. The purpose of the audit is to ascertain that the financial statements have been prepared in accordance with generally accepted accounting principles. If the independent accountant is satisfied that this standard has been met, his or her report contains the following language:

> In our opinion, the financial statements . . . present fairly, in all material respects . . . in conformity with generally accepted accounting principles.

This wording emphasizes the fact that accounting and auditing are not exact sciences. Because the framework of GAAP provides room for interpretation and the application of GAAP necessitates the making of estimates, the auditor can render an opinion or judgment only that the financial statements *present fairly* or conform *in all material respects* to GAAP. The accountant's report does not preclude minor or immaterial errors in the financial statements. However, it does imply that, on the whole, investors and creditors can rely on those statements. Historically, auditors have enjoyed a strong reputation for competence and independence. As a result, banks, investors, and creditors are willing to rely on an auditor's opinion when deciding to invest in a company or to make loans to a firm that has been audited. The independent audit is an important factor in the worldwide growth of financial markets.

ORGANIZATIONS THAT INFLUENCE CURRENT PRACTICE

Many organizations directly or indirectly influence GAAP and so influence much of what is in this book. The Financial Accounting Standards Board

Table 3. Large International Certified Public Accounting Firms

Firm	Home Office	Some Major Clients
Arthur Andersen & Co.	Chicago	ITT, Texaco, United Airlines
Coopers & Lybrand	New York	AT&T, Ford
Deloitte & Touche	New York	General Motors, Procter & Gamble, Sears
Ernst & Young	New York	Coca-Cola, McDonald's, Mobil
KPMG Peat Marwick	New York	General Electric, Xerox
Price Waterhouse	New York	Du Pont, Exxon, IBM
Grant Thornton	Chicago	Fretter, Grainger, Home Shopping Network

(FASB) is the most important body for developing and issuing rules on accounting practice. This independent body issues Statements of Financial Accounting Standards. The American Institute of Certified Public Accountants (AICPA) is the professional association of certified public accountants and influences accounting practice through the activities of its senior technical committees. The Securities and Exchange Commission (SEC) is a federal agency that has the legal power to set and enforce accounting practices for companies whose securities are offered for sale to the general public. As such, it has enormous influence on accounting practice. The Governmental Accounting Standards Board (GASB), established in 1984 under the same governing body as the Financial Accounting Standards Board, is responsible for issuing accounting standards for state and local governments.

With the growth of financial markets throughout the world, worldwide cooperation in the development of accounting principles has become a priority. The International Accounting Standards Committee (IASC) has approved more than thirty international standards, which have been translated into six languages.

U.S. tax laws that govern the assessment and collection of revenue for operating the federal government also influence accounting practice. Because a major source of the government's revenue is the income tax, these laws specify the rules for determining taxable income. These rules are interpreted and enforced by the Internal Revenue Service (IRS). In some cases, these rules conflict with good accounting practice, but they still are an important influence on that practice. Businesses use certain accounting practices simply because they are required by the tax laws. Sometimes companies follow an accounting practice specified in the tax laws to take advantage of rules that can help them financially. Cases where the tax laws affect accounting practice are noted throughout this book.

PROFESSIONAL ETHICS AND THE ACCOUNTING PROFESSION

OBJECTIVE

8 *Define* ethics *and describe the ethical responsibilities of accountants*

Ethics is a code of conduct that applies to everyday life. It addresses the question of whether actions are right or wrong. Ethical actions are the product of individual decisions. You are faced with many ethical situations every day. Some may be potentially illegal—the temptation to take office supplies from your employer to use when you do homework, for example. Others are not illegal but are equally unethical—for example, deciding not to tell a fellow student who missed class that a test has been announced for the next class meeting. When an organization is said to act ethically or unethically, it means that individuals within the organization have made a decision to act ethically or unethically. When a company uses false advertising, cheats customers, pollutes the environment, treats employees poorly, or misleads investors by presenting false financial statements, members of management and other employees have made a conscious decision to act unethically. In the same way, ethical behavior within a company is a direct result of the actions and decisions of the company's employees.

Professional ethics is a code of conduct that applies to the practice of a profession. Like the ethical conduct of a company, the ethical actions of a profession are a collection of individual actions. As members of a profession, accountants have a responsibility, not only to their employers and clients but to society as a whole, to uphold the highest ethical standards. Historically, accountants have been held in high regard. For example, a survey of over one thousand prominent people in business, education, and government ranked the accounting profession second only to the clergy as having the highest ethical standards.[5] It is the responsibility of every person who becomes an accountant to uphold the high standards of the profession, regardless of which field of accounting the individual enters.

To ensure that accountants understand the responsibilities of their profession, the AICPA and each state have adopted codes of professional conduct that must be followed by certified public accountants. Fundamental to these codes is responsibility to the public, including clients, creditors, investors, and anyone else who relies on the work of the public accountant. In resolving conflicts among these groups, the accountant must act with integrity, even to the sacrifice of personal benefit. Integrity means that the accountant is honest and candid, and subordinates personal gain to service and the public trust. The accountant must also be objective. Objectivity means that he or she is impartial and intellectually honest. Furthermore, the accountant must be independent. Independence means avoiding all relationships that impair or even appear to impair the accountant's objectivity. One way in which the auditor of a company maintains independence is by having no direct financial interest in the company and not being an employee of the company. The accountant must exercise due care in all activities, carrying out professional responsibilities with competence and diligence. For example, an accountant must not accept a job for which he or she is not qualified, even at the risk of losing a client to another firm, and careless work is not acceptable. These broad principles are supported by more specific rules that public accountants must follow. (For instance, with certain exceptions, client information must be kept confidential.) Accountants who violate the rules can be disciplined or suspended from practice.

The Institute of Management Accountants (IMA) has adopted the Code of Professional Conduct for Management Accountants. This ethical code emphasizes that management accountants have a responsibility to be competent in their jobs, to keep information confidential except when authorized or legally required to disclose it, to maintain integrity and avoid conflicts of interest, and to communicate information objectively and without bias.[6]

BUSINESS BULLETIN: ETHICS IN PRACTICE

One survey showed that 45 percent of the 1,000 largest U.S. companies have ethics programs or workshops. NYNEX, for example, has appointed an ethics officer, written a new code of conduct, put more than 1,500 managers through a formal training program, and provided its 94,000 employees with a whistle blowers' hot line. Companies with such comprehensive programs tend to receive significantly lower fines from federal judges if their employees are caught in illegal acts because the judges want to reward companies that are trying to be good corporate citizens.[7]

5. Touche Ross & Co., "Ethics in American Business" (New York: Touche Ross & Co., 1988), p. 7.

6. *Statement Number IC,* "Standards of Ethical Conduct for Management Accountants" (Montvale, N.J.: Institute of Management Accountants, June 1, 1983).

7. *Business Week,* Sept. 23, 1991, p. 65

CHAPTER REVIEW

REVIEW OF LEARNING OBJECTIVES

1. **Define *accounting*, identify business goals and activities, and describe the role of accounting in making informed decisions.** Accounting is an information system that measures, processes, and communicates information, primarily financial in nature, about an identifiable entity for the purpose of making economic decisions. Management accounting focuses on the preparation of information primarily for internal use by management. Financial accounting is concerned with the development and use of accounting reports that are communicated to those external to the business organization as well as to management. Accounting is not an end in itself but a tool that provides the information that is necessary to make reasoned choices among alternative uses of scarce resources in the conduct of business and economic activities.

2. **Identify the many users of accounting information in society.** Accounting plays a significant role in society by providing information to managers of all institutions and to individuals with a direct financial interest in those institutions, including present or potential investors or creditors. Accounting information is also important to those with an indirect financial interest in the business—for example, tax authorities, regulatory agencies, and economic planners.

3. **Explain the importance of business transactions, money measure, and separate entity to accounting measurement.** To make an accounting measurement, the accountant must determine what is measured, when the measurement should be made, what value should be placed on what is measured, and how what is measured should be classified. Generally accepted accounting principles define the objects of accounting measurement as business transactions, money measure, and separate entities. Relating these three concepts, financial accounting uses money measure to gauge the impact of business transactions on a separate business entity.

4. **Identify the three basic forms of business organization.** The three basic forms of business organization are sole proprietorships, partnerships, and corporations. Legally, sole proprietorships, which are formed by one individual, and partnerships, which are formed by more than one individual, are not economically separate from their owners. In accounting, however, they are treated separately. Corporations, whose ownership is represented by shares of stock, are separate entities for both legal and accounting purposes.

5. **Define *financial position*, state the accounting equation, and show how the two are affected by simple transactions.** Financial position is the economic resources that belong to a company and the claims against those resources at a point in time. The accounting equation shows financial position in the equation form Assets = Liabilities + Owner's Equity. Business transactions affect financial position by decreasing or increasing assets, liabilities, or owner's equity in such a way that the accounting equation is always in balance.

6. **Identify the four basic financial statements.** Financial statements are the means by which accountants communicate the financial condition and activities of a business to those who have an interest in the business. The four basic financial statements are the income statement, the statement of owner's equity, the balance sheet, and the statement of cash flows.

7. **State the relationship of generally accepted accounting principles (GAAP) to financial statements and the independent CPA's report, and identify the organizations that influence GAAP.** Acceptable accounting practice consists of the conventions, rules, and procedures that make up generally accepted accounting principles at a particular time. GAAP are essential to the preparation and interpretation of financial statements and the independent CPA's report. Among the organizations that influence the formulation of GAAP are the Financial Accounting Standards Board, the American Institute of Certified Public Accountants, the Securities and Exchange Commission, and the Internal Revenue Service.

8. **Define *ethics* and describe the ethical responsibilities of accountants.** All accountants are required to follow a code of professional ethics, the foundation of

which is responsibility to the public. Accountants must act with integrity, objectivity, and independence, and they must exercise due care in all their activities.

REVIEW OF CONCEPTS AND TERMINOLOGY

The following concepts and terms were introduced in this chapter.

L O 1 **Accounting:** An information system that measures, processes, and communicates financial information about an identifiable economic entity.

L O 5 **Accounting equation:** Assets = Liabilities + Owner's Equity or Owner's Equity = Assets − Liabilities.

L O 5 **Accounts:** The labels used by accountants to accumulate the amounts that result from similar transactions.

L O 7 **American Institute of Certified Public Accountants (AICPA):** The professional association of certified public accountants.

L O 5 **Assets:** Economic resources owned by a business that are expected to benefit future operations.

L O 7 **Audit:** An examination of a company's financial statements to render an independent professional opinion that they have been presented fairly and prepared in conformity with generally accepted accounting principles.

L O 6 **Balance sheet:** The financial statement that shows the assets, liabilities, and owner's equity of a business at a point in time. Also called a *statement of financial position*.

L O 1 **Bookkeeping:** The process of recording financial transactions and keeping financial records.

L O 1 **Business:** An economic unit that aims to sell goods and services to customers at prices that will provide an adequate return to its owners.

L O 3 **Business transactions:** Economic events that affect the financial position of a business entity.

L O 6 **Cash flows:** The inflows and outflows of cash into and out of a business.

L O 7 **Certified public accountant (CPA):** A public accountant who has met the stringent licensing requirements set by the individual states.

L O 1 **Computer:** An electronic tool for the rapid collection, organization, and communication of large amounts of information.

L O 4 **Corporation:** A business unit granted a state charter recognizing it as a separate legal entity having its own rights, privileges, and liabilities distinct from those of its owners.

L O 8 **Due care:** The act of carrying out professional responsibilities competently and diligently.

L O 8 **Ethics:** A code of conduct that addresses whether everyday actions are right or wrong.

L O 3 **Exchange rate:** The value of one currency in terms of another.

L O 5 **Expenses:** Decreases in owner's equity that result from operating a business.

L O 1 **Financial accounting:** The process of generating and communicating accounting information in the form of financial statements to those outside the organization.

L O 7 **Financial Accounting Standards Board (FASB):** The most important body for developing and issuing rules on accounting practice, called *Statements of Financial Accounting Standards*.

L O 5 **Financial position:** The economic resources that belong to a company and the claims against those resources (equities) at a point in time.

L O 1 **Financial statements:** The primary means of communicating important accounting information to users. They include the income statement, statement of owner's equity, balance sheet, and statement of cash flows.

L O 1 **Financing activities:** Activities undertaken by management to obtain adequate funds to begin and to continue operating a business.

L O 7   **Generally accepted accounting principles (GAAP):** The conventions, rules, and procedures that define accepted accounting practice at a particular time.

✗L O 7   **Governmental Accounting Standards Board (GASB):** The board responsible for issuing accounting standards for state and local governments.

✗L O 6   **Income statement:** The financial statement that summarizes the revenues earned and expenses incurred by a business over a period of time.

✗L O 8   **Independence:** The avoidance of all relationships that impair or appear to impair an accountant's objectivity.

✗L O 8   **Institute of Management Accountants (IMA):** A professional organization made up primarily of management accountants.

L O 8   **Integrity:** Honesty, candidness, and the subordination of personal gain to service and the public trust.

L O 7   **Internal Revenue Service (IRS):** The federal agency that interprets and enforces the tax laws governing the assessment and collection of revenue for operating the federal government.

✗L O 7   **International Accounting Standards Committee (IASC):** The organization that encourages worldwide cooperation in the development of accounting principles; it has approved more than thirty international standards of accounting.

L O 1   **Investing activities:** Activities undertaken by management to spend capital in ways that are productive and will help to achieve the business's objectives.

L O 5   **Liabilities:** Present obligations of a business to pay cash, transfer assets, or provide services to other entities in the future.

L O 1   **Liquidity:** Having enough funds on hand to pay debts when they are due.

L O 2   **Management:** Collectively, the people who have overall responsibility for operating a business and meeting its profitability and liquidity goals.

L O 1   **Management accounting:** The process of producing accounting information for the internal use of a company's management.

L O 1   **Management information system (MIS):** The interconnected subsystems that provide the information needed to run a business.

L O 3   **Money measure:** The recording of all business transactions in terms of money.

L O 5   **Net assets:** Owner's equity, or assets minus liabilities.

L O 5   **Net income:** The difference between revenues and expenses when revenues exceed expenses.

L O 5   **Net loss:** The difference between expenses and revenues when expenses exceed revenues.

L O 8   **Objectivity:** Impartiality and intellectual honesty.

L O 1   **Operating activities:** Activities undertaken by management in the course of running a business.

L O 5   **Owner's equity:** The residual interest in the assets of a business entity that remains after deducting the entity's liabilities. Also called *residual equity.*

L O 5   **Owner's investments:** The assets that the owner puts into the business.

L O 5   **Owner's withdrawals:** The assets that the owner takes out of the business.

L O 4   **Partnership:** A business owned by two or more people.

L O 8   **Professional ethics:** A code of conduct that applies to the practice of a profession.

L O 1   **Profitability:** The ability to earn enough income to attract and hold investment capital.

L O 5   **Revenues:** Increases in owner's equity that result from operating a business.

✗L O 2   **Securities and Exchange Commission (SEC):** An agency of the federal government set up by the U.S. Congress to protect the public by regulating the issuing, buying, and selling of stocks. It has the legal power to set and enforce accounting practices for firms whose securities are sold to the general public.

L O 3   **Separate entity:** A business that is treated as distinct from its creditors, customers, and owners.

L O 4 **Sole proprietorship:** A business owned by one person.

L O 6 **Statement of cash flows:** The financial statement that shows the inflows and out-flows of cash from operating activities, investing activities, and financing activities over a period of time.

L O 6 **Statement of owner's equity:** The financial statement that shows the changes in the owner's capital account over a period of time.

REVIEW PROBLEM

EFFECT OF TRANSACTIONS ON THE ACCOUNTING EQUATION

L O 5 Charlene Rudek finished law school in June and immediately set up her own law practice. During the first month of operation, she completed these transactions.

a. Began the practice by placing $2,000 in a bank account established for the business.
b. Purchased a law library for $900 cash.
c. Purchased office supplies for $400 on credit.
d. Accepted $500 in cash for completing a contract.
e. Billed clients $1,950 for services rendered during the month.
f. Paid $200 of the amount owed for office supplies.
g. Received $1,250 in cash from one client who had been billed previously for services rendered.
h. Paid rent expense for the month in the amount of $1,200.
i. Withdrew $400 from the practice for personal use.

REQUIRED Show the effect of each of these transactions on the balance sheet equation by completing a table similar to Exhibit 1. Identify each owner's equity transaction.

ANSWER TO REVIEW PROBLEM

	Assets				= Liabilities +	Owner's Equity	
	Cash	Accounts Receivable	Office Supplies	Law Library	Accounts Payable	C. Rudek, Capital	Type of OE Transaction
a.	$2,000					$2,000	Owner's Investment
b.	−900			+$900			
bal.	$1,100			$900		$2,000	
c.			+$400		+$400		
bal.	$1,100		$400	$900	$400	$2,000	
d.	+500					+500	Legal Fees Earned
bal.	$1,600		$400	$900	$400	$2,500	
e.		+$1,950				+1,950	Legal Fees Earned
bal.	$1,600	$1,950	$400	$900	$400	$4,450	
f.	−200				−200		
bal.	$1,400	$1,950	$400	$900	$200	$4,450	
g.	+1,250	−1,250					
bal.	$2,650	$ 700	$400	$900	$200	$4,450	
h.	−1,200					−1,200	Rent Expense
bal.	$1,450	$ 700	$400	$900	$200	$3,250	
i.	−400					−400	Owner's Withdrawal
bal.	$1,050	$ 700	$400	$900	$200	$2,850	

$3,050 $3,050

CHAPTER ASSIGNMENTS

QUESTIONS

1. Why is accounting considered an information system?
2. What is the role of accounting in the decision-making process, and what broad business goals and activities does it help management to achieve and manage?
3. Distinguish between management accounting and financial accounting.
4. Distinguish among these terms: *accounting, bookkeeping,* and *management information systems.*
5. Which decision makers use accounting information?
6. A business is an economic unit whose goal is to sell goods and services to customers at prices that will provide an adequate return to the business owner. What functions must management perform to achieve that goal?
7. Why are investors and creditors interested in reviewing the financial statements of a company?
8. Among those who use accounting information are people and organizations with an indirect interest in the business entity. Briefly describe these people and organizations.
9. Why has society as a whole become one of the largest users of accounting information?
10. Use the terms *business transaction, money measure,* and *separate entity* in a single sentence that demonstrates their relevance to financial accounting.
11. How do sole proprietorships, partnerships, and corporations differ?
12. Define *assets, liabilities,* and *owner's equity.*
13. Arnold Smith's company has assets of $22,000 and liabilities of $10,000. What is the amount of his owner's equity?
14. What four elements affect owner's equity? How?
15. Give examples of the types of transactions that (a) increase assets and (b) increase liabilities.
16. What is the function of the statement of owner's equity?
17. Why is the balance sheet sometimes called the statement of financial position?
18. Contrast the purpose of the balance sheet with that of the income statement.
19. A statement for an accounting period that ends in June can be headed "June 30, 19xx" or "For the Year Ended June 30, 19xx." Which heading is appropriate for (a) a balance sheet and (b) an income statement?
20. How does the income statement differ from the statement of cash flows?
21. What are GAAP? Why are they important to the readers of financial statements?
22. What do auditors mean by the phrase "in all material respects" when they state that financial statements "present fairly, in all material respects . . . in conformity with generally accepted accounting principles"?
23. Which organization has the most influence on GAAP?
24. Discuss the importance of professional ethics in the accounting profession.

SHORT EXERCISES

SE 1. *Accounting*
L O 3, 4 *Concepts*
Check Figures: b, c, a, b, a

Tell whether each of the following words or phrases relates most closely to (a) a business transaction, (b) a separate entity, or (c) a money measure.

1. Partnership *b*
2. U.S. dollar *c*
3. Payment of an expense *a*
4. Corporation *b*
5. Sale of an asset *a*

SE 2. *The Accounting*
L O 5 *Equation*
Check Figures: $60,000, $36,000, $50,000

Determine the amount missing from each accounting equation below.

	Assets	=	Liabilities	+	Owner's Equity
1.	?		$25,000		$35,000
2.	$ 78,000		$42,000		?
3.	$146,000		?		$96,000

SE 3. *The Accounting*
L O 5 *Equation*
Check Figures: $120,000, $20,000

Use the accounting equation to answer each question below.

1. The assets of Cruse Company are $480,000, and the liabilities are $360,000. What is the amount of the owner's equity?
2. The liabilities of Nabors Company equal one-fifth of the total assets. The owner's equity is $80,000. What is the amount of the liabilities?

SE 4. *The Accounting*
L O 5 *Equation*
Check Figures: $150,000, $83,000

Use the accounting equation to answer each question below.

1. At the beginning of the year, Gilbert Company's assets were $180,000, and its owner's equity was $100,000. During the year, assets increased $60,000 and liabilities increased $10,000. What was the owner's equity at the end of the year?
2. At the beginning of the year, Sailor Company had liabilities of $50,000 and owner's equity of $48,000. If assets increased by $20,000 and liabilities decreased by $15,000, what was the owner's equity at the end of the year?

SE 5. *The Accounting*
L O 5 *Equation and Net Income*
Check Figures: $10,000, $0, $12,000

Use the following information and the accounting equation to determine the net income for the year for each alternative below.

	Assets	Liabilities
Beginning of the year	$ 70,000	$30,000
End of the year	100,000	50,000

1. No investments were made in the business and the owner made no withdrawals during the year.
2. Investments of $10,000 were made in the business, but the owner made no withdrawals during the year.
3. No investments were made in the business, but the owner withdrew $2,000 during the year.

SE 6. *The Accounting*
L O 5 *Equation and Net Income*
Check Figure: $54,000

Murillo Company had assets of $140,000 and liabilities of $60,000 at the beginning of the year, and assets of $200,000 and liabilities of $70,000 at the end of the year. During the year, the owner invested $20,000 in the business and withdrew $24,000. What amount of net income was earned during the year?

SE 7. *Effect of*
L O 5 *Transactions on the Accounting Equation*
No check figure

On a sheet of paper, list the numbers **1** through **6,** with columns labeled Assets, Liabilities, and Owner's Equity. In the columns, indicate whether each transaction below caused an increase (+), a decrease (−), or no change (NC) in assets, liabilities, and owner's equity.

1. Purchased equipment on credit.
2. Purchased equipment for cash.
3. Billed customers for services performed.
4. Received and immediately paid a utility bill.
5. Received payment from a previously billed customer.
6. The owner made an additional investment.

SE 8. *Effect of*
L O 5 *Transactions on the Accounting Equation*
No check figure

On a sheet of paper, list the numbers **1** through **6,** with columns labeled Assets, Liabilities, and Owner's Equity. In the columns, indicate whether each transaction below caused an increase (+), a decrease (−), or no change (NC) in assets, liabilities, and owner's equity.

1. Purchased supplies on credit.
2. Paid for previously purchased supplies.
3. Paid employee's weekly wages.
4. The owner made a cash withdrawal.
5. Purchased a truck with cash.
6. Received a telephone bill to be paid next month.

SE 9. *Preparation of a*
L O 6 *Balance Sheet*
Check Figure: Total assets: $6,100

Use the following accounts and balances to prepare a balance sheet for Jay Company at December 31, 19x1, using Exhibit 2 as a model.

Accounts Payable	$2,500
K. Jay, Capital	3,600
Cash	1,200
Equipment	3,300
Accounts Receivable	1,600

SE 10. *Preparation and*
L O 6 *Completion of a*
Balance Sheet
Check Figure: Total assets: $14,000

Use the following accounts and balances to prepare a balance sheet for DeLay Company at June 30, 19x1, using Exhibit 2 as a model.

Accounts Receivable	$ 800
Wages Payable	250
B. DeLay, Capital	13,750
Building	10,000
Cash	?

EXERCISES

E 1. *The Nature of*
L O 1, 2, 7 *Accounting*
Check Figures: b, c, a, d, c or d, e, a, c or d, c, a, c, b

Match the terms on the left with the descriptions on the right.

1. Bookkeeping
2. Creditors
3. Measurement
4. Financial Accounting Standards Board (FASB)
5. Tax authorities
6. Computer
7. Communication
8. Securities and Exchange Commission (SEC)
9. Investors
10. Processing
11. Management
12. Management information system

a. Function of accounting
b. Often confused with accounting
c. User(s) of accounting information
d. Organization that influences current practice
e. Tool that facilitates the practice of accounting

E 2. *Business*
L O 3 *Transactions*
No check figure

Theresa owns and operates a minimart. State which of the actions below are business transactions. If an action would not be considered a business transaction, explain why not.

1. Theresa reduces the price of a gallon of milk to match the price offered by a competitor.
2. Theresa pays a high school student cash for cleaning up the driveway behind the market.
3. Theresa fills her son's car with gasoline in payment for restocking the vending machines and the snack food shelves.
4. Theresa pays interest to herself on a loan she made to the business three years ago.

E 3. *Accounting*
L O 3, 4 *Concepts*
Check Figures: b, c, a, a, b, c, b, a, c, a

Financial accounting uses money measures to gauge the impact of business transactions on a separate business entity. Tell whether each of the following words or phrases relates most closely to (a) a business transaction, (b) a separate entity, or (c) a money measure.

1. Corporation
2. French franc
3. Sale of products
4. Receipt of cash
5. Sole proprietorship
6. U.S. dollar
7. Partnership
8. Owner's investments
9. Japanese yen
10. Purchase of supplies

E 4. *Money Measure*
L O 3

No check figure

You have been asked to compare the sales and assets of four companies that make computer chips and determine which company is the largest in each category. You have gathered the following data, but they cannot be directly compared because each company's sales and assets are in its own currency.

Company (Currency)	Sales	Assets
Inchip (U.S. dollar)	20,000,000	13,000,000
Wong (Taiwan dollar)	50,000,000	24,000,000
Mitzu (Japanese yen)	3,500,000,000	2,500,000,000
Works (German mark)	35,000,000	39,000,000

Assuming that the exchange rates in Table 1 are current and appropriate, convert all the figures to U.S. dollars and determine which company is the largest in sales and which is the largest in assets.

E 5. *The Accounting*
L O 5 *Equation*
Check Figures: $290,000, $127,000, $60,000, $170,000

Use the accounting equation to answer each question below. Show any calculations you make.

1. The assets of Newport Company are $650,000, and the owner's equity is $360,000. What is the amount of the liabilities?
2. The liabilities and owner's equity of Fitzgerald Company are $95,000 and $32,000, respectively. What is the amount of the assets?
3. The liabilities of Emerald Company equal one-third of the total assets, and the owner's equity is $120,000. What is the amount of the liabilities?
4. At the beginning of the year, Pickett Company's assets were $220,000 and its owner's equity was $100,000. During the year, assets increased $60,000 and liabilities decreased $10,000. What is the owner's equity at the end of the year?

E 6. *Owner's Equity*
L O 5 *Transactions*
Check Figures: R, W, NOE, I, E, R, NOE, E

Identify the following transactions by marking each as an owner's investment (I), owner's withdrawal (W), revenue (R), expense (E), or not an owner's equity transaction (NOE).

a. Received cash for providing a service. R
b. Withdrew cash for personal expenses. W
c. Received cash from a customer previously billed for a service. NOE
d. Transferred assets to the business from a personal account. I
e. Paid a service station for gasoline for a business vehicle. E
f. Performed a service and received a promise of payment. R
g. Paid cash to purchase equipment. NOE
h. Paid cash to an employee for services performed. E

E 7. *Effect of*
L O 5 *Transactions on the Accounting Equation*
No check figure

During the month of April, Grissom Company had the following transactions.

a. Paid salaries for April, $5,400. –
b. Purchased equipment on credit, $9,000. NC
c. Purchased supplies with cash, $300. –
d. Additional investment by owner, $12,000. +
e. Received payment for services performed, $1,800. +
f. Made partial payment on equipment purchased in transaction **b**, $3,000. –
g. Billed customers for services performed, $4,800. +
h. Withdrew cash for personal expenses, $4,500. –
i. Received payment from customers billed in transaction **g**, $900. +
j. Received utility bill, $210, to be paid next month. NC

On a sheet of paper, list the letters **a** through **j**, with columns labeled Assets, Liabilities, and Owner's Equity. In the columns, indicate whether each transaction caused an increase (+), a decrease (−), or no change (NC) in assets, liabilities, and owner's equity.

E 8. *Examples of*
L O 5 *Transactions*
No check figure

For each of the following categories, describe a transaction that would have the required effect on the elements of the accounting equation.

1. Increase one asset and decrease another asset.
2. Decrease an asset and decrease a liability.
3. Increase an asset and increase a liability.
4. Increase an asset and increase owner's equity.
5. Decrease an asset and decrease owner's equity.

E 9. *Effect of*
L O 5 *Transactions on the Accounting Equation*

Check Figures: $15,000, $37,000, $2,000, $27,000

The total assets and liabilities at the beginning and end of the year for Pizarro Company are as follows.

	Assets	Liabilities
Beginning of the year	$110,000	$ 45,000
End of the year	200,000	120,000

Determine Pizarro Company's net income for the year under each of the following alternatives.

1. The owner made no investments in or withdrawals from the business during the year.
2. The owner made no investments in the business but withdrew $22,000 during the year.
3. The owner made an investment of $13,000 but made no withdrawals during the year.
4. The owner made an investment of $10,000 in the business and withdrew $22,000 during the year.

E 10. *Identification of*
L O 5, 6 *Accounts*

Check Figures: A, L, A, OE, A, L, A; IS, BS, IS, BS, IS, BS, OE

1. Indicate whether each of the following accounts is an asset (A), a liability (L), or a part of owner's equity (OE).

   a. Cash
   b. Salaries Payable
   c. Accounts Receivable
   d. J. Johnson, Capital
   e. Land
   f. Accounts Payable
   g. Supplies

2. Indicate whether each account would be shown on the income statement (IS), the statement of owner's equity (OE), or the balance sheet (BS).

   a. Repair Revenue
   b. Automobile
   c. Fuel Expense
   d. Cash
   e. Rent Expense
   f. Accounts Payable
   g. J. Johnson, Withdrawals

E 11. *Preparation of a*
L O 6 *Balance Sheet*

Check Figure: Total assets: $210,000

Listed in random order below are the balance sheet figures for the Herron Company as of December 31, 19xx.

Accounts Payable	$ 40,000
Building	90,000
T. Herron, Capital	170,000
Supplies	10,000
Accounts Receivable	50,000
Cash	20,000
Equipment	40,000

Sort the balances and prepare a balance sheet similar to the one in Exhibit 2.

E 12. *Completion of*
L O 6 *Financial Statements*

Check Figures: a. $400; b. $150; c. $150; d. $2,300; e. $1,500; f. $2,300

Determine the amounts that correspond to the letters by completing the following independent sets of financial statements. (Assume no new investments by the owner.)

Income Statement	Set A	Set B	Set C
Revenues	$ 550	$ g	$120
Expenses	a	2,600	m
Net Income	$ b	$ h	$ 40
Statement of Owner's Equity			
Beginning Balance	$1,450	$ 7,700	$100
Net Income	c	800	n
Withdrawal by Owner	(100)	i	o
Ending Balance	$1,500	$ j	$ p

Balance Sheet

Total Assets	$ d	$10,500	$ q
Liabilities	$ 800	$ 2,500	$ r
Owner's Equity	e	k	140
Total Liabilities and Owner's Equity	$ f	$ l	$240

E 13. *Preparation of*
L O 6 *Financial Statements*
Check Figures: Net income: $2,960;
Total assets: $6,800

Kingsley Company engaged in the following activities during the year: Service Revenue, $26,400; Rent Expense, $2,400; Wages Expense, $16,540; Advertising Expense, $2,700; Utilities Expense, $1,800; and Walter Kingsley, Withdrawals, $1,400. In addition, the year-end balances of selected accounts were as follows: Cash, $3,100; Accounts Receivable, $1,500; Supplies, $200; Land, $2,000; Accounts Payable, $900; and Walter Kingsley, Capital, $4,340.

Using good form, prepare the income statement, statement of owner's equity, and balance sheet for Kingsley Company (assume the year ends on December 31, 19x3). (**Hint:** The amount given for Walter Kingsley, Capital is the beginning balance.)

E 14. *Revenues, Expenses,*
L O 6 *and Cash Flows*
Check Figures: $16,000, $3,400,
$15,600, $3,240

Tamara Longstreet, an attorney, bills her clients at a rate of $100 per hour. During July, she worked 160 hours for clients and billed them appropriately. By the end of July, 60 of these hours remained unpaid. At the beginning of the month, clients owed Longstreet $8,000, of which $5,600 was paid during July.

Longstreet has one employee, a secretary who is paid $20 per hour. During July, the secretary worked 170 hours, of which 16 hours were to be paid in August. The rest were paid in July. Also, Longstreet paid the secretary for 8 hours worked in June.

Determine the following for the month of July: (1) the amount of revenue from clients, (2) wages expense for the secretary, (3) cash received from clients, and (4) cash paid to the secretary.

E 15. *Statement of Cash*
L O 6 *Flows*
Check Figure: Cash at End of Year:
$68,000

Erez Company began the year 19x3 with cash of $92,000. In addition to earning a net income of $60,000 and making an owner's withdrawal of $30,000, Erez borrowed $120,000 from the bank and purchased equipment for $180,000 with cash. Also, Accounts Receivable increased by $12,000 and Accounts Payable increased by $18,000.

Determine the amount of cash on hand at December 31, 19x3, by preparing a statement of cash flows similar to the one in Exhibit 2.

E 16. *Accounting*
L O 7 *Abbreviations*
No check figure

Identify the accounting meaning of each of the following abbreviations: AICPA, SEC, GAAP, FASB, IRS, GASB, IASC, IMA, and CPA.

SKILLS DEVELOPMENT EXERCISES

Conceptual Analysis

SDE 1. *Business Activities*
L O 1, 2 *and Management*
Functions

No check figure

Aetna Life and Casualty Co. is a leading insurance company. According to its letter to shareholders, 1992 financial results were completely unsatisfactory, and the company would work hard to revitalize itself.

> Our strategy centers on four key elements: sharp focus on core businesses, disciplined financial programs to improve earnings and reduce expenses, reengineering to radically improve our business processes, and targeted programs to give Aetna's people the tools, training, and support they need to succeed. Our strategy is to allocate key resources—capital, people, time, technology—to those businesses that offer the best profit potential.[8]

To achieve its strategy, Aetna must organize its management into functions that relate to the principal activities of a business. Discuss the three basic activities Aetna will engage in to achieve its goals, and suggest some examples of each. What is the role of Aetna's management, and what functions must its management perform to accomplish these activities?

8. Aetna Life and Casualty Co., *Annual Report*, 1992.

SDE 2. *Users of Accounting Information*
L O 2

No check figure

Public companies report annually on their success or failure in making a net income. Suppose that the following item appeared in the newspaper.

New York, Commonwealth Power Company, a major electric utility, reported yesterday that its net income for the year just ended represented a 50 percent increase over last year. . . .

Discuss why each of the following individuals or groups might be interested in seeing the accounting reports that support this statement.

1. The management of Commonwealth Power
2. The stockholders of Commonwealth Power
3. The creditors of Commonwealth Power
4. Potential stockholders of Commonwealth Power
5. The Internal Revenue Service
6. The Securities and Exchange Commission
7. The electrical workers' union
8. A consumers' group called Public Cause
9. An economic adviser to the President of the United States

SDE 3. *Concept of an Asset*
L O 5

No check figure

Foote, Cone & Belding is one of the largest and most successful advertising agencies in the world. Its annual report carried the following statement: "Our principal asset is our people. Our success depends in large part on our ability to attract and retain personnel who are competent in the various aspects of our business."[9] Are personnel considered assets in financial statements? Discuss in what sense Foote, Cone & Belding considers its employees its principal asset.

Ethical Dilemma

SDE 4. *Professional Ethics*
L O 8

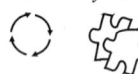

No check figure

Discuss the ethical choices in the situations below. In each instance, determine the alternative courses of action and tell what you would do.

1. You are the payroll accountant for a small business. A friend asks you how much another employee is paid per hour.
2. As an accountant for the branch office of a wholesale supplier, you discover that several of the receipts the branch manager has submitted for reimbursement as selling expense actually stem from nights out with his spouse.
3. You are an accountant in the purchasing department of a construction company. When you arrive home from work on December 22, you find a large ham in a box marked "Happy Holidays—It's a pleasure to work with you." The gift is from a supplier who has bid on a contract your employer plans to award next week.
4. As an auditor with one year's experience at a local CPA firm, you are expected to complete a certain part of an audit in twenty hours. Because of your lack of experience, you know you cannot finish the job within that time. Rather than admit this, you are thinking about working late to finish the job and not telling anyone.
5. You are a tax accountant at a local CPA firm. You help your neighbor fill out her tax return, and she pays you $200 in cash. Because there is no record of this transaction, you are considering not reporting it on your tax return.
6. The accounting firm for which you work as a CPA has just won a new client, a firm in which you own 200 shares of stock that you received as an inheritance from your grandmother. Because it is only a small number of shares and you think the company will be very successful, you are considering not disclosing the investment.

Research Activity

SDE 5. *Need for Knowledge of Accounting*
L O 1, 2

No check figure

From the business section of your local paper or a nearby metropolitan daily, clip an article about a company. List all the financial and accounting terms used in the article. Bring the article to class and be prepared to discuss how a knowledge of accounting would help a reader understand the content of the article.

9. Foote, Cone & Belding, *Annual Report,* 1989.

Decision-Making Practice

SDE 6.
LO 6 *Effect of Transactions on the Balance Sheet*

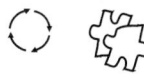

Check Figures: Total assets: $2,700, $4,645

Instead of hunting for a summer job after finishing her junior year in college, Beth Murphy started a lawn service business in her neighborhood. On June 1, she deposited $2,700 in a new bank account in the name of her company. The $2,700 consisted of a $1,000 loan from her father and $1,700 of her own money.

Using the money in this checking account, Beth rented lawn equipment, purchased supplies, and hired neighborhood high school students to mow and trim the lawns of neighbors who had agreed to pay her for the service. At the end of each month, she mailed bills to her customers.

On August 31, Beth was ready to dissolve her business and go back to school for the fall term. Because she had been so busy, she had not kept any records other than her checkbook and a list of amounts owed by customers.

Her checkbook had a balance of $3,520, and her customers owed her $875. She expected these customers to pay her during September. She planned to return unused supplies to the Lawn Care Center for a full credit of $50. When she brought back the rented lawn equipment, the Lawn Care Center also would return a deposit of $200 she had made in June. She owed the Lawn Care Center $525 for equipment rentals and supplies. In addition, she owed the students who had worked for her $100, and she still owed her father $700. Although Beth feels she did quite well, she is not sure just how successful she was.

1. Prepare one balance sheet dated June 1 and another dated August 31 for Murphy Lawn Services Company.
2. Compare the two balance sheets and comment on the performance of Murphy Lawn Services Company. Did the company have a profit or a loss? (Assume that Beth used none of the company's assets for personal purposes.)
3. If Beth wants to continue her business next summer, what kind of information from her recordkeeping system would make it easier for her to tell whether or not she is earning a profit?

PROBLEM SET A

A 1.
LO 5 *Effect of Transactions on the Accounting Equation*

Check Figure: Total assets: $8,750

Frame-It Center was started by Brenda Kuzma in a small shopping center. In the first weeks of operation, she completed the following transactions.

a. Deposited $7,000 in an account in the name of the company to start the business.
b. Paid the current month's rent, $900.
c. Purchased store equipment on credit, $3,600.
d. Purchased framing supplies for cash, $1,700.
e. Received framing revenues, $800.
f. Billed customers for services, $700.
g. Paid utilities expense, $250.
h. Received payment from customers in transaction **f,** $200.
i. Made payment on store equipment purchased in transaction **c,** $1,800.
j. Withdrew cash for personal expenses, $400.

REQUIRED

1. Arrange the following asset, liability, and owner's equity accounts in an equation similar to Exhibit 1: Cash, Accounts Receivable, Framing Supplies, Store Equipment, Accounts Payable, and Brenda Kuzma, Capital.
2. Show by addition and subtraction, as in Exhibit 1, the effects of the transactions on the accounting equation. Show new balances after each transaction, and identify each owner's equity transaction by type.

A 2.
LO 5 *Effect of Transactions on the Accounting Equation*

Check Figure: Total assets: $11,530

The Jiffy Messenger Company was founded by Hector Moreno on December 1 and engaged in the following transactions.

a. Deposited $9,000 in a bank account established in the name of Jiffy Messenger Company to start the business.
b. Purchased a motorbike on credit, $3,100.
c. Purchased delivery supplies for cash, $200.
d. Billed a customer for a delivery, $100.

e. Received delivery fees in cash, $300.
f. Made a payment on the motorbike, $700.
g. Paid repair expense, $120.
h. Received payment from customer billed in transaction **d,** $50.
i. Withdrew cash for personal expenses, $150.

REQUIRED

1. Arrange the following asset, liability, and owner's equity accounts in an equation similar to Exhibit 1: Cash, Accounts Receivable, Delivery Supplies, Motorbike, Accounts Payable, and Hector Moreno, Capital.
2. Show by addition and subtraction, as in Exhibit 1, the effects of the transactions on the accounting equation. Show new balances after each transaction, and identify each owner's equity transaction by type.

A 3. *Effect of*
L O 5 *Transactions on the Accounting Equation*
Check Figure: Total assets: $8,060

After completing her Ph.D. in management, Delia Chan set up a consulting practice. At the end of her first month of operation, Dr. Chan had the following account balances: Cash, $2,930; Accounts Receivable, $1,400; Office Supplies, $270; Office Equipment, $4,200; Accounts Payable, $1,900; and Delia Chan, Capital, $6,900. Soon thereafter, the following transactions were completed.

a. Paid current month's rent, $800.
b. Made payment toward accounts payable, $450.
c. Billed clients for services performed, $800.
d. Received payment from clients billed last month, $1,000.
e. Purchased office supplies for cash, $80.
f. Paid part-time secretary's salary, $850.
g. Paid utilities expense, $90.
h. Paid telephone expense, $50.
i. Purchased additional office equipment for cash, $400.
j. Received cash from clients for services performed, $1,200.
k. Withdrew cash for personal expenses, $500.

REQUIRED

1. Arrange the following asset, liability, and owner's equity accounts in an equation similar to Exhibit 1: Cash, Accounts Receivable, Office Supplies, Office Equipment, Accounts Payable, and Delia Chan, Capital.
2. Enter the beginning balances of the assets, liabilities, and owner's equity.
3. Show by addition and subtraction, as in Exhibit 1, the effects of the transactions on the accounting equation. Show new balances after each transaction, and identify each owner's equity transaction by type.

A 4. *Preparation of*
L O 6 *Financial Statements*
Check Figure: Total assets: $57,500

At the end of its first month of operation, June, 19xx, Lerner Plumbing Company had the following account balances.

Cash	$29,300
Accounts Receivable	5,400
Delivery Truck	19,000
Tools	3,800
Accounts Payable	4,300

In addition, during the month of June, the following transactions affected owner's equity.

Initial investment by M. Lerner	$20,000
Withdrawals by M. Lerner	2,000
Further investment by M. Lerner	30,000
Contract revenue	11,600
Repair revenue	2,800
Salaries expense	8,300
Rent expense	700
Fuel expense	200

REQUIRED

Using Exhibit 2 as a model, prepare an income statement, a statement of owner's equity, and a balance sheet for Lerner Plumbing Company. (**Hint:** The final balance of M. Lerner, Capital is $53,200.)

A 5.
L O 5, 6

Effect of Transactions on the Accounting Equation and Preparation of Financial Statements

Check Figure: Total assets: $4,620

Royal Copying Service began operations and engaged in the following transactions during July 19xx.

a. Linda Friedman deposited $5,000 in cash in an account in the name of the company to start the business.
b. Paid current month's rent, $950.
c. Purchased copier for cash, $2,500.
d. Paid cash for paper and other copier supplies, $190.
e. Copying job payments received in cash, $890.
f. Copying job billed to major customer, $680.
g. Paid wages to part-time employees, $280.
h. Purchased additional copier supplies on credit, $140.
i. Received partial payment from customer in transaction **f,** $300.
j. Paid current month's utility bill, $90.
k. Made partial payment on supplies purchased in transaction **h,** $70.
l. Withdrew cash for personal use, $700.

REQUIRED

1. Arrange the asset, liability, and owner's equity accounts in an equation similar to Exhibit 1, using these account titles: Cash, Accounts Receivable, Supplies, Copier, Accounts Payable, and L. Friedman, Capital.
2. Show by addition and subtraction, as in Exhibit 1, the effects of the transactions on the accounting equation. Show new balances after each transaction, and identify each owner's equity transaction by type.
3. Using Exhibit 2 as a guide, prepare an income statement, a statement of owner's equity, and a balance sheet for Royal Copying Service.

PROBLEM SET B

B 1.
L O 5

Effect of Transactions on the Accounting Equation

Check Figure: Total assets: $10,420

Carmen Vega, after receiving her degree in computer science, started her own business, Custom Systems Company. She completed the following transactions soon after starting the business.

a. Deposited $9,000 in the bank and contributed a systems library valued at $920 to start the business.
b. Paid current month's rent on an office, $360.
c. Purchased a minicomputer for cash, $7,000.
d. Purchased computer supplies on credit, $600.
e. Received payment from a client for programming done, $800.
f. Billed a client on completion of a short programming project, $710.
g. Paid wages, $800.
h. Received a partial payment from the client billed in transaction **f,** $80.
i. Withdrew $250 in cash for personal expenses.
j. Made a partial payment on the computer supplies purchased in transaction **d,** $200.

REQUIRED

1. Arrange the asset, liability, and owner's equity accounts in an equation similar to Exhibit 1, using the following account titles: Cash, Accounts Receivable, Supplies, Equipment, Systems Library, Accounts Payable, and Carmen Vega, Capital.
2. Show by addition and subtraction, as in Exhibit 1, the effects of the transactions on the accounting equation. Show new balances after each transaction, and identify each owner's equity transaction by type.

B 2.
L O 5

Effect of Transactions on the Accounting Equation

Check Figure: Total assets: $70,600

On June 1, Henry Redmond started a new business, the Redmond Transport Company. During the month of June, the firm completed the following transactions.

a. Deposited $66,000 in cash in a new bank account to establish the Redmond Transport Company.
b. Purchased a truck for cash, $43,000.
c. Purchased equipment on credit, $9,000.
d. Billed a customer for hauling goods, $1,200.
e. Received cash for hauling goods, $2,300.
f. Received cash payment from the customer billed in transaction **d,** $600.
g. Made a payment on the equipment purchased in transaction **c,** $5,000.
h. Paid wages expense in cash, $1,700.
i. Withdrew cash from the business for personal use, $1,200.

REQUIRED

1. Arrange the asset, liability, and owner's equity accounts in an equation similar to Exhibit 1, using the following account titles: Cash, Accounts Receivable, Trucks, Equipment, Accounts Payable, and Henry Redmond, Capital.
2. Show by addition and subtraction, as in Exhibit 1, the effects of the transactions on the accounting equation. Show new balances after each transaction, and identify each owner's equity transaction by type.

B 3.
L O 5
Effect of Transactions on the Accounting Equation
Check Figure: Total assets: $10,560

Dr. Paul Rosello, a psychologist, moved from his hometown to set up an office in St. Louis. After one month, the business had the following assets: Cash, $2,800; Accounts Receivable, $680; Office Supplies, $300; and Office Equipment, $7,500. Owner's equity—the capital account—consisted of $8,680. The Accounts Payable balance was $2,600 for purchases of office equipment on credit. During a short period of time, the following transactions were completed.

a. Paid one month's rent, $350.
b. Billed patient for services rendered, $60.
c. Made payment on accounts owed, $300.
d. Purchased and paid for office supplies, $100.
e. Paid part-time secretary's salary, $300.
f. Received payment for services rendered from patients not previously billed, $800.
g. Made payment on accounts owed, $360.
h. Withdrew $500 for living expenses.
i. Paid telephone bill for current month, $70.
j. Received payment from patients previously billed, $290.
k. Purchased additional office equipment on credit, $300.

REQUIRED

1. Arrange the asset, liability, and owner's equity accounts in an equation similar to Exhibit 1, using the following account titles: Cash, Accounts Receivable, Office Supplies, Office Equipment, Accounts Payable, and Paul Rosello, Capital.
2. Enter the beginning balances for assets, liabilities, and owner's equity.
3. Show by addition and subtraction, as in Exhibit 1, the effects of the transactions on the accounting equation. Show new balances after each transaction, and identify each owner's equity transaction by type.

B 4.
L O 6
Preparation of Financial Statements
Check Figure: Total assets: $71,900

At the end of October 19xx, the Cliff Young, Capital account of the Sunnydale Riding Club had a balance of $37,300. After operating during November, the club had the following account balances.

Cash	$ 8,700
Accounts Receivable	1,200
Supplies	1,000
Land	21,000
Building	30,000
Horses	10,000
Accounts Payable	17,800

In addition, the following transactions affected owner's equity during November.

Withdrawals by Cliff Young	$3,200
Investment by Cliff Young	16,000
Riding lesson revenue	6,200
Locker rental revenue	1,700
Salaries expense	2,300
Feed expense	1,000
Utilities expense	600

REQUIRED

Using Exhibit 2 as a model, prepare an income statement, a statement of owner's equity, and a balance sheet for Sunnydale Riding Club. (**Hint:** The final balance of Cliff Young, Capital is $54,100.)

B 5.
L O 5, 6
Effect of Transactions on the Accounting Equation and Preparation of Financial Statements

Check Figure: Total assets: $48,750

On April 1, 19xx, Dependable Taxi Service began operation. The company engaged in the following transactions during April.

a. Investment by owner, Madeline Curry, $42,000.
b. Purchase of taxi for cash, $19,000.
c. Purchase of uniforms on credit, $400.
d. Taxi fares received in cash, $3,200.
e. Paid wages to part-time drivers, $500.
f. Purchased gasoline during month for cash, $800.
g. Purchased car washes during month on credit, $120.
h. Further investment by owner, $5,000.
i. Paid part of the amount owed for the uniforms purchased in transaction **c**, $200.
j. Billed major client for fares, $900.
k. Paid for automobile repairs, $250.
l. Withdrew cash from business for personal use, $1,000.

REQUIRED

1. Arrange the asset, liability, and owner's equity accounts in an equation similar to Exhibit 1, using the following account titles: Cash, Accounts Receivable, Uniforms, Taxi, Accounts Payable, and Madeline Curry, Capital.
2. Show by addition and subtraction, as in Exhibit 1, the effects of the transactions on the accounting equation. Show new balances after each transaction, and identify each owner's equity transaction by type.
3. Using Exhibit 2 as a guide, prepare an income statement, a statement of owner's equity, and a balance sheet for Dependable Taxi Service.

FINANCIAL REPORTING AND ANALYSIS CASES

Interpreting Financial Reports

FRA 1.
L O 6
Nature of Cash, Assets, and Net Income

Check Figure: Net income in 1993: $1,069,586,000

Merrill Lynch & Co., Inc. is a U.S.-based global financial services firm. Information for 1993 and 1992 from the company's 1993 annual report is presented at the top of the next page.[10] (All numbers are in thousands.)

Three students who were looking at Merrill Lynch's annual report were overheard to make the following comments.

Student A: What a great year Merrill Lynch had in 1993! The company earned net income of $45,886,189 because its total assets increased from $107,024,173 to $152,910,362.

Student B: But the change in total assets isn't the same as net income! The company had a net income of only $531,836 because cash increased from $1,251,572 to $1,783,408.

Student C: I see from the annual report that Merrill Lynch paid cash dividends of $152,777 in 1993. Since cash dividends for a corporation are similar to withdrawals for a sole proprietorship, don't you have to take that into consideration when analyzing the company's performance?

REQUIRED

1. Comment on the interpretations of Students A and B, and then answer Student C's question.
2. Calculate Merrill Lynch's net income for 1993. (**Hint:** The first step is to find the change in owner's equity.)

---

10. Merrill Lynch & Co., Inc., *Annual Report,* 1993.

Merrill Lynch & Co., Inc.
Condensed Balance Sheets
December 31, 1993 and 1992
(in thousands)

	1993	1992
Assets		
Cash	$ 1,783,408	$ 1,251,572
Other Assets	151,126,954	105,772,601
Total Assets	$152,910,362	$107,024,173
Liabilities		
Total Liabilities	$147,424,449	$102,455,069
Owner's Equity		
Merrill Lynch, Capital	$ 5,485,913	$ 4,569,104
Total Liabilities and Owner's Equity	$152,910,362	$107,024,173

International Company

FRA 2. *The Goal of*
L O 1 *Profitability*

No check figure

The Swedish company *Volvo AB,* the largest company in Scandinavia, had a difficult year in 1992. In the company's annual report, the president said in part, "The results in 1992 for Volvo's core businesses are profoundly unsatisfactory. The operating loss in Volvo Cars was considerable and Volvo Trucks also reported a loss. . . . The measures to return Volvo to favorable profitability have the highest priority."[11] Discuss the meaning of *profitability.* What other goal must a business achieve? Why is the goal of profitability important to Volvo's president? What is the accounting measure of profitability, and on which statement is it determined?

Toys "R" Us Annual Report

FRA 3. *The Four Basic*
L O 6 *Financial Statements*

No check figure

Refer to the financial statements in the appendix on Toys "R" Us to answer the following questions. Keep in mind that every company, while following basic principles, adapts financial statements and terminology to its own special needs. Therefore, the complexity of the financial statements and the terminology in the Toys "R" Us statements will sometimes differ from those in the text.

REQUIRED

1. What names does Toys "R" Us give its four basic financial statements? (Note that the use of the word "Consolidated" in the names of the financial statements simply means that each statement combines the results of several companies owned by Toys "R" Us.)

11. Volvo AB, *Annual Report,* 1992.

2. Prove that the accounting equation works for Toys "R" Us in 1995 by finding the amounts for the following equation: Assets = Liabilities + Owners' Equity. (Note that the owner's equity section for a corporation is called stockholders' equity.)
3. What were the total revenues of Toys "R" Us for 1995?
4. Was Toys "R" Us profitable in 1995? How much was net income in that year, and did it increase or decrease from 1994?
5. Did the company's cash and equivalents increase from 1994 to 1995? By how much? In what two places in the statements can this number be found or computed?

Measuring Business Transactions

LEARNING OBJECTIVES

1. Explain, in simple terms, the generally accepted ways of solving the measurement issues of recognition, valuation, and classification.

2. Describe the chart of accounts and recognize commonly used accounts.

3. Define *double-entry system* and state the rules for double entry.

4. Apply the steps for transaction analysis and processing to simple transactions.

5. Record transactions in the general journal.

6. Post transactions from the journal to the ledger.

7. Prepare a trial balance and describe its value and limitations.

Test Questions
(Record in General Journal)

multiple choice

DECISION POINT

Southwest Airlines and The Boeing Co.

In November 1993, Southwest Airlines announced it had ordered up to 63 of Boeing's new 737X line of small airplanes. The $2.5 billion order will allow Boeing to go ahead with its program to upgrade its 737 airplanes to combat inroads by European competitors in the small jet market. For Southwest, the purchase will bring advanced airplanes at a discount price. The airplanes are scheduled for delivery between 1997 and 2001. How should this important order have been recorded, if at all, in the records of Southwest and of Boeing? When should the forthcoming purchase and sale have been recorded in the companies' records?

The order obviously was an important event, one that carried long-term consequences for both companies. But, as you will see in this chapter, it was not recorded in the accounting records of either company. At the time the order was placed, the aircraft were yet to be manufactured and would not begin to be delivered for four years. Even for the "firm" orders, Boeing cautioned in its 1994 annual report that "an economic downturn could result in airline equipment requirements less than currently anticipated resulting in requests to negotiate the rescheduling or possible cancellation of firm orders." The aircraft were not assets of Southwest, and the company had not incurred a liability. No aircraft had been delivered or even built, so Southwest was not obligated to pay at that point. And Boeing could not record any revenue until the aircraft were manufactured and delivered to Southwest, until title to the aircraft shifted from Boeing to Southwest. In 1993, some other previously firm orders were canceled or extended because of the adverse effects of the economy on the airline industry.[1]

To understand and use financial statements, it is important to know how to analyze events to determine the extent of their impact on those statements. ⁙

1. Jeff Cole and Bridget O'Brian, "Boeing Wins Huge Southwest Air Order, Giving 737 Upgrade Plans a Green Light," the *Wall Street Journal,* November 18, 1993, and The Boeing Co., *Annual Report,* 1994.

MEASUREMENT ISSUES

Business transactions are economic events that affect the financial position of a business entity. To measure a business transaction, the accountant must decide when the transaction occurred (the recognition issue), what value to place on the transaction (the valuation issue), and how the components of the transaction should be categorized (the classification issue).

These three issues—recognition, valuation, and classification—underlie almost every major decision in financial accounting today. They lie at the heart of accounting for pension plans, for mergers of giant companies, and for international transactions; and they allow the accountant to project and plan for the effects of inflation. In discussing the three basic issues, we follow generally accepted accounting principles and use an approach that promotes an understanding of the basic ideas of accounting. Keep in mind, however, that controversy does exist, and that some solutions to problems are not as cut-and-dried as they appear.

OBJECTIVE

1 *Explain, in simple terms, the generally accepted ways of solving the measurement issues of recognition, valuation, and classification*

THE RECOGNITION ISSUE

The recognition issue refers to the difficulty of deciding when a business transaction should be recorded. Often the facts of a situation are known, but there is disagreement about *when* the event should be recorded. Suppose, for instance, that a company orders, receives, and pays for an office desk. Which of the following actions constitutes a recordable event?

1. An employee sends a purchase requisition to the purchasing department.
2. The purchasing department sends a purchase order to the supplier.
3. The supplier ships the desk.
4. The company receives the desk.
5. The company receives the bill from the supplier.
6. The company pays the bill.

The answer to this question is important because amounts in the financial statements are affected by the date on which a purchase is recorded. According to accounting tradition, the transaction is recorded when title to the desk passes from the supplier to the purchaser, creating an obligation to pay. Thus, depending on the details of the shipping agreement, the transaction is recognized (recorded) at the time of either action **3** or action **4**. This is the guideline that we generally use in this book. However, in many small businesses that have simple accounting systems, the transaction is not recorded until the bill is received (action **5**) or paid (action **6**) because these are the implied points of title transfer. The predetermined time at which a transaction should be recorded is the recognition point.

The recognition issue is not always solved easily. Consider the case of an advertising agency that is asked by a client to prepare a major advertising campaign. People may work on the campaign several hours a day for a number of weeks. Value is added to the plan as the employees develop it. Should the added value be recognized as the campaign is being produced or at the time it is completed? Normally, the increase in value is recorded at the time the plan is finished and the client is billed for it. However, if a plan is going to take a long period to develop, the agency and the client may agree that the client will be billed at key points during its development. A transaction is recorded at each billing.

Not only are the accounting solutions related to recognition, valuation, and classification important for good financial reporting, but they are also designed to help management fulfill its responsibilities to company owners and the public. In its heyday, Oracle Systems Corporation was a fast-growing data base software company. In 1990, based on the fast growth of its earnings and sales, it achieved a market value of $3.8 billion. But by late 1991, the company's market value plunged to $700 million after disclosures that its management had violated the recognition point by recording sales before contracts were signed. Income was further inflated because payments for research and development had been classified as assets instead of as expenses.[2] Following proper accounting principles would have prevented management from falsely portraying the company. Subsequent management changes and improved accounting procedures have allowed Oracle to regain some of its lost credibility. ======

THE VALUATION ISSUE

Valuation is perhaps the most controversial issue in accounting. The valuation issue focuses on assigning a monetary value to a business transaction. Generally accepted accounting principles state that the appropriate value to assign to all business transactions—and therefore to all assets, liabilities, and components of owner's equity, including revenue and expenses, acquired by a business—is the original cost (often called *historical cost*). Cost is defined here as the exchange price associated with a business transaction at the point of recognition. According to this guideline, the purpose of accounting is not to account for value in terms of worth, which can change after a transaction occurs, but to account for value in terms of cost at the time of the transaction. For example, the cost of an asset is recorded when the asset is acquired, and the value is held at that level until the asset is sold, expires, or is consumed. In this context, *value* means the cost at the time of the transaction. The practice of recording transactions at cost is referred to as the cost principle.

Suppose that a person offers a building for sale at $120,000. It may be valued for real estate taxes at $75,000, and it may be insured for $90,000. One prospective buyer may offer $100,000 for the building, and another may offer $105,000. At this point, several different, unverifiable opinions of value have been expressed. Finally, suppose the seller and a buyer settle on a price and complete the sale for $110,000. All of these figures are values of one kind or another, but only the last is sufficiently reliable to be used in the records. The market value of the building may vary over the years, but it will remain on the new buyer's records at $110,000 until it is sold again. At that point, the accountant will record the new transaction at the new exchange price, and a profit or loss will be recognized.

2. Julie Pitta, "The Arrogance Was Unnecessary," *Forbes,* September 2, 1991.

The cost principle is used because the cost is verifiable. It results from the actions of independent buyers and sellers who come to an agreement on price. An exchange price is an objective price that can be verified by evidence created at the time of the transaction. It is this final price, verified by agreement of the two parties, at which the transaction is recorded.

THE CLASSIFICATION ISSUE

The classification issue has to do with assigning all the transactions in which a business engages to appropriate categories, or accounts. For example, a company's ability to borrow money can be affected by the way in which its debts are categorized. Or a company's income can be affected by whether purchases of small items such as tools are considered repair expenses (a component of owner's equity) or equipment (assets). Proper classification depends not only on correctly analyzing the effect of each transaction on the business, but also on maintaining a system of accounts that reflects that effect. The rest of this chapter explains the classification of accounts and the analysis and recording of transactions.

ACCOUNTS AND THE CHART OF ACCOUNTS

OBJECTIVE

2 *Describe the chart of accounts and recognize commonly used accounts*

In the measurement of business transactions, large amounts of data are gathered. These data require a method of storage. Business people should be able to retrieve transaction data quickly and in usable form. In other words, there should be a filing system to sort, or classify, all the transactions that occur in a business. This filing system consists of accounts. Recall that accounts are the basic storage units for accounting data and are used to accumulate amounts from similar transactions. An accounting system has a separate account for each asset, each liability, and each component of owner's equity, including revenues and expenses. Whether a company keeps records by hand or by computer, management must be able to refer to accounts so that it can study the company's financial history and plan for the future. A very small company may need only a few dozen accounts; a multinational corporation may need thousands.

In a manual accounting system, each account is kept on a separate page or card. These pages or cards are placed together in a book or file called the general ledger. In the computerized systems that most companies have today, accounts are maintained on magnetic tapes or disks. However, as a matter of convenience, accountants still refer to the all-inclusive group of company accounts as the general ledger, or simply the *ledger*.

To help identify accounts in the ledger and make them easy to find, the accountant often numbers them. A list of these numbers with the corresponding account names is called a chart of accounts. A very simple chart of accounts for an art studio business appears in Exhibit 1. Notice that the first digit refers to the major financial statement classifications. An account number that begins with the digit 1 is an asset, an account number that begins with a 2 is a liability, and so forth. The second and third digits refer to individual accounts. Notice the gaps in the sequence of numbers. The gaps allow the accountant to expand the number of accounts. The accounts in Exhibit 1 will be used in this chapter.

Exhibit 1. Chart of Accounts for a Small Business

Account Number	Account Name	Description
	Assets	
111	Cash	Money and any medium of exchange, including coins, currency, checks, postal and express money orders, and money on deposit in a bank
112	Notes Receivable	Amounts due from others in the form of promissory notes (written promises to pay definite sums of money at fixed future dates)
113	Accounts Receivable	Amounts due from others from credit sales (sales on account)
114	Fees Receivable	Amounts arising from services performed but not yet billed to customers
115	Art Supplies	Prepaid expense; art supplies purchased and not used
116	Office Supplies	Prepaid expense; office supplies purchased and not used
117	Prepaid Rent	Prepaid expense; rent paid in advance and not used
118	Prepaid Insurance	Prepaid expense; insurance purchased and not expired; unexpired insurance
141	Land	Property owned for use in the business
142	Buildings	Structures owned for use in the business
143	Accumulated Depreciation, Buildings	Sum of periodic allocations of the cost of buildings to expense
144	Art Equipment	Art equipment owned for use in the business
145	Accumulated Depreciation, Art Equipment	Sum of periodic allocations of the cost of art equipment to expense
146	Office Equipment	Office equipment owned for use in the business
147	Accumulated Depreciation, Office Equipment	Sum of periodic allocations of the cost of office equipment to expense

(continued)

Exhibit 1. Chart of Accounts for a Small Business (*continued*)

Account Number	Account Name	Description
Liabilities		
211	Notes Payable	Amounts due to others in the form of promissory notes
212	Accounts Payable	Amounts due to others for purchases on credit
213	Unearned Art Fees	Unearned revenue; advance deposits for artwork to be provided in the future
214	Wages Payable	Amounts due to employees for wages earned and not paid
221	Mortgage Payable	Amounts due on loans that are backed by the company's property and buildings
Owner's Equity		
311	Capital	Owner's investment in the company
312	Withdrawals	Assets withdrawn from the business by the owner for personal use
313	Income Summary	Temporary account used at the end of the accounting period to summarize revenues and expenses for the period
Revenues		
411	Advertising Fees Earned	Revenues derived from performing advertising services
412	Art Fees Earned	Revenues derived from performing art services
Expenses		
511	Wages Expense	Amounts earned by nonsalaried employees
512	Utilities Expense	Amounts of utilities, such as water, electricity, and gas used
513	Telephone Expense	Amounts of telephone services used
514	Rent Expense	Amounts of rent on property and buildings used
515	Insurance Expense	Amounts for insurance used
516	Art Supplies Expense	Amounts for art supplies used
517	Office Supplies Expense	Amounts for office supplies used
518	Depreciation Expense, Buildings	Amount of buildings' cost allocated to expense

(continued)

Exhibit 1. Chart of Accounts for a Small Business (*continued*)

Account Number	Account Name	Description
	Expenses (*continued*)	
519	Depreciation Expense, Art Equipment	Amount of art equipment costs allocated to expense
520	Depreciation Expense, Office Equipment	Amount of office equipment costs allocated to expense
521	Interest Expense	Amount of interest on debts

BUSINESS BULLETIN: BUSINESS PRACTICE

Today, most businesses, even the smallest, use computerized accounting systems. In small businesses, these systems are called *general ledger packages* and run on personal computers. The starting point for these systems is a chart of accounts that reflects the activities in which the business engages. Every company develops a chart of accounts for its own needs. Seldom do two companies have exactly the same chart of accounts. A small business may get by with a simple chart of accounts like that in Exhibit 1. A large, complicated business like Commonwealth Edison, the electric utility in Chicago, will have twelve or more digits in its account numbers and thousands of accounts in its chart of accounts. ▬▬

OWNER'S EQUITY ACCOUNTS

In the chart of accounts in Exhibit 1, the revenue and expense accounts are separated from the other owner's equity accounts. The relationships of these accounts to each other and to the basic financial statements are shown in Figure 1. The distinctions among them are important for legal and financial reporting purposes.

First, for income tax reporting, financial reporting, and other purposes, the law requires that capital and withdrawals accounts be separated from revenues and expenses. The capital account represents the owner's interest in the assets of the company. The withdrawals account is used to record assets taken out of the business by the owner for personal use. These withdrawals are not described as salary or wages, although the owner may think of them as such, because there is no change in the ownership of the money withdrawn. In practice, the withdrawals account often goes by other names, among them *personal* and *drawing*. Corporations do not use a withdrawals account.

Second, management needs a detailed breakdown of revenues and expenses for budgeting and operating purposes. From these accounts, which are listed on the income statement, management can identify the sources of all revenues and the nature of all expenses. In this way, accounting gives

Figure 1. Relationships of Owner's Equity Accounts

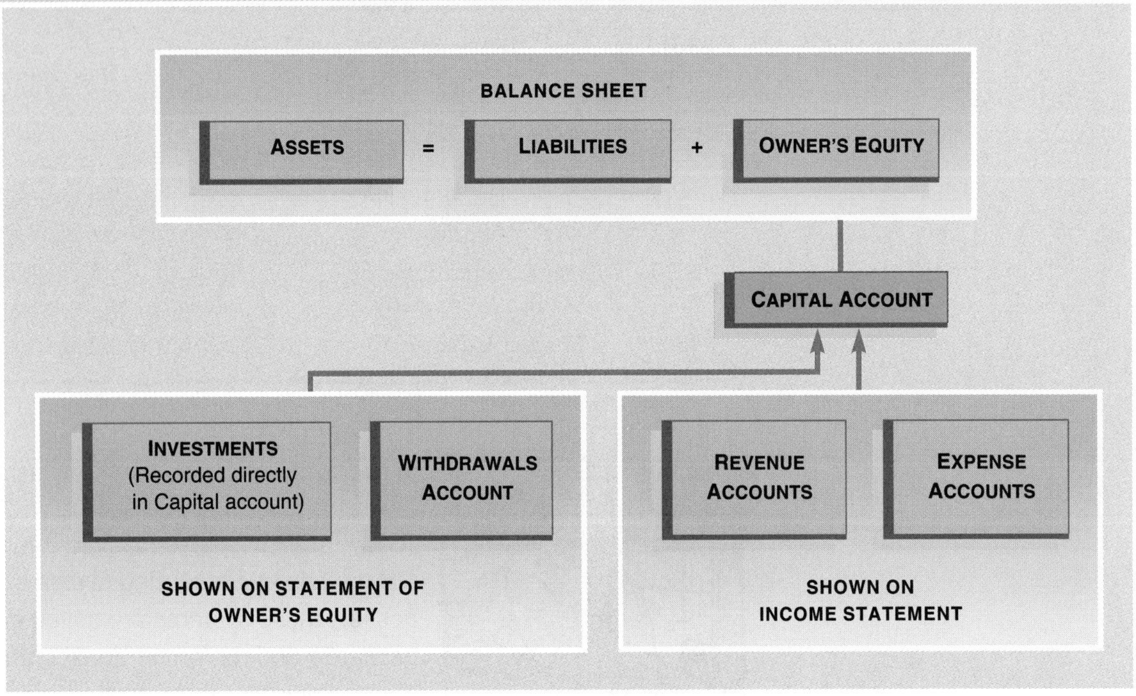

management information about how it has achieved its primary goal of earning a net income.

ACCOUNT TITLES

The names of accounts may be confusing because some of the words are new or have technical meanings. Also, the same asset, liability, or owner's equity account can have different names in different companies. (Actually, this is not so strange. People too are often called different names by their friends, families, and associates.) For example, Fixed Assets, Plant and Equipment, Capital Assets, and Long-Lived Assets are all names for long-term asset accounts. Even the most acceptable names change over time, and, out of habit, some companies use names that are out of date.

In general, an account title should describe what is recorded in the account. When you come across an account title that you do not recognize, you should examine the context of the name—whether it is classified as an asset, liability, or owner's equity component, including revenue or expense, on the financial statements—and look for the kind of transaction that gave rise to the account.

THE DOUBLE-ENTRY SYSTEM: THE BASIC METHOD OF ACCOUNTING

OBJECTIVE

3 *Define* double-entry system *and state the rules for double entry*

The double-entry system, the backbone of accounting, evolved during the Renaissance. The first systematic description of double-entry bookkeeping appeared in 1494, two years after Columbus discovered America, in a mathematics book written by Fra Luca Pacioli. Goethe, the famous German poet and dramatist, referred to double-entry bookkeeping as "one of the finest discoveries of the human intellect." And Werner Sombart, an eminent economist-sociologist, believed that "double-entry bookkeeping is born of the same spirit as the system of Galileo and Newton."

What is the significance of the double-entry system? The system is based on the *principle of duality*, which means that every economic event has two aspects—effort and reward, sacrifice and benefit, source and use—that offset, or balance, each other. In the double-entry system, each transaction must be recorded with at least one debit and one credit, so that the total dollar amount of debits and the total dollar amount of credits equal each other. Because of the way it is designed, the whole system is always in balance. All accounting systems, no matter how sophisticated, are based on the principle of duality.

THE T ACCOUNT

The T account is a good place to begin the study of the double-entry system. In its simplest form, an account has three parts: (1) a title, which describes the asset, the liability, or the owner's equity account; (2) a left side, which is called the debit side; and (3) a right side, which is called the credit side. This form of an account, called a T account because it resembles the letter *T*, is used to analyze transactions. It looks like this:

Title of Account	
Debit	Credit
(left) side	(right) side

Any entry made on the left side of the account is a debit, or debit entry, and any entry made on the right side of the account is a credit, or credit entry. The terms *debit* (abbreviated Dr., from the Latin *debere*) and *credit* (abbreviated Cr., from the Latin *credere*) are simply the accountant's words for "left" and "right" (not for "increase" or "decrease"). We present a more formal version of the T account later in this chapter, where we examine the ledger account form.

THE T ACCOUNT ILLUSTRATED

Shannon Realty had several transactions that involved the receipt or payment of cash. These transactions can be summarized in the Cash account by recording receipts on the left (debit) side of the account and payments on the right (credit) side of the account:

	Cash		
(1)	50,000	(2)	35,000
(5)	1,500	(4)	200
(7)	1,000	(8)	1,000
		(9)	400
		(11)	600
	52,500		37,200
Bal.	15,300		

The cash receipts on the left total $52,500. (The total is written in small figures so that it cannot be confused with an actual debit entry.) The cash payments on the right side total $37,200. These totals are simply working totals, or footings. Footings, which are calculated at the end of each month, are an easy way to determine cash on hand. The difference in dollars between the total debit footing and the total credit footing is called the balance, or *account balance*. If the balance is a debit, it is written on the left side. If it is a credit, it is written on the right side. Notice that Shannon Realty's Cash account has a debit balance of \$15,300 (\$52,500 − \$37,200). This is the amount of cash the business has on hand at the end of the month.

ANALYZING AND PROCESSING TRANSACTIONS

The two rules of double-entry bookkeeping are that every transaction affects at least two accounts and that the total of the debits must equal the total of the credits. In other words, for every transaction, one or more accounts must be debited and one or more accounts must be credited, and the total dollar amount of the debits must equal the total dollar amount of the credits.

Look again at the accounting equation:

$$Assets = Liabilities + Owner's\ Equity$$

You can see that if a debit increases assets, then a credit must be used to increase liabilities or owner's equity because they are on opposite sides of the equal sign. Likewise, if a credit decreases assets, then a debit must be used to decrease liabilities or owner's equity. These rules can be shown as follows:

Assets		=	Liabilities		+	Owner's Equity	
Debit for increases (+)	Credit for decreases (−)		Debit for decreases (−)	Credit for increases (+)		Debit for decreases (−)	Credit for increases (+)

1. Increases in assets are debited to asset accounts. Decreases in assets are credited to asset accounts.
2. Increases in liabilities and owner's equity are credited to liability and owner's equity accounts. Decreases in liabilities and owner's equity are debited to liability and owner's equity accounts.

One of the more difficult points to understand is the application of double-entry rules to the owner's equity components. The key is to remember that withdrawals and expenses are deductions from owner's equity. Thus, transactions that *increase* withdrawals or expenses *decrease* owner's equity. Consider this expanded version of the accounting equation:

Owner's Equity

$$Assets = Liabilities + Capital - Withdrawals + Revenues - Expenses$$

This equation may be rearranged by shifting withdrawals and expenses to the left side, as follows:

Assets		+	Withdrawals		+	Expenses		=	Liabilities		+	Capital		+	Revenues	
+ (debits)	− (credits)		+ (debits)	− (credits)		+ (debits)	− (credits)		− (debits)	+ (credits)		− (debits)	+ (credits)		− (debits)	+ (credits)

Note that the rules for double entry for all the accounts on the left of the equal sign are just the opposite of the rules for all the accounts on the right of the equal sign. Assets, withdrawals, and expenses are increased by debits and decreased by credits. Liabilities, capital, and revenues are increased by credits and decreased by debits.

With this basic information about double entry, it is possible to analyze and process transactions by following the five steps illustrated in Figure 2. To show how the steps are applied, assume that on June 1, Shell Oil Company borrows $100,000 from its bank on a promissory note. The transaction is analyzed and processed as follows:

1. *Analyze the transaction to determine its effect on assets, liabilities, and owner's equity.* In this case, both an asset (Cash) and a liability (Notes Payable) increase. A transaction is usually supported by some kind of source document—an invoice, a receipt, a check, or a contract. Here, a copy of the signed note would be the source document.
2. *Apply the rules of double entry.* Increases in assets are recorded by debits. Increases in liabilities are recorded by credits.
3. *Record the entry.* Transactions are recorded in chronological order in a journal. One form of journal, which is explained in more detail later in this chapter, records the date, the debit account, and the debit amount on one line and the credit account and the credit amount indented on the next line, as follows:

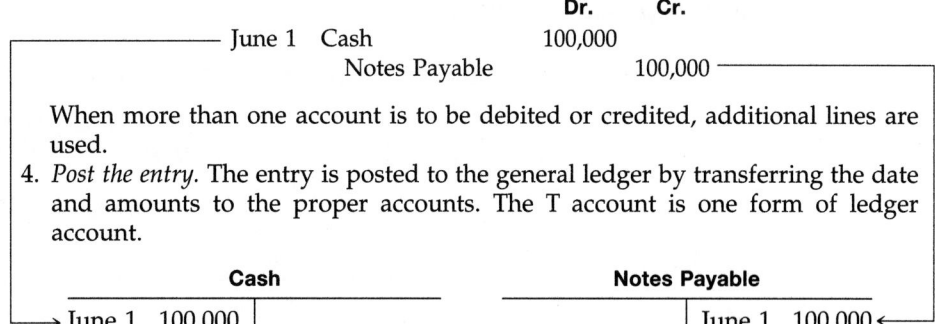

		Dr.	**Cr.**
June 1	Cash	100,000	
	Notes Payable		100,000

When more than one account is to be debited or credited, additional lines are used.

4. *Post the entry.* The entry is posted to the general ledger by transferring the date and amounts to the proper accounts. The T account is one form of ledger account.

Cash	**Notes Payable**
June 1 100,000	June 1 100,000

In formal records, step **3** is never omitted. However, for purposes of analysis, accountants often bypass step **3** and record entries directly in T accounts because doing so clearly and quickly shows the effects of transactions on the accounts. Some of the assignments in this chapter use the same approach to emphasize the analytical aspects of double entry.

5. *Prepare the trial balance to confirm the balance of the accounts.* Periodically, accountants prepare a trial balance to confirm that the accounts are still in balance after the recording and posting of transactions. Preparation of the trial balance is explained at the end of this chapter.

Figure 2. Analyzing and Processing Transactions

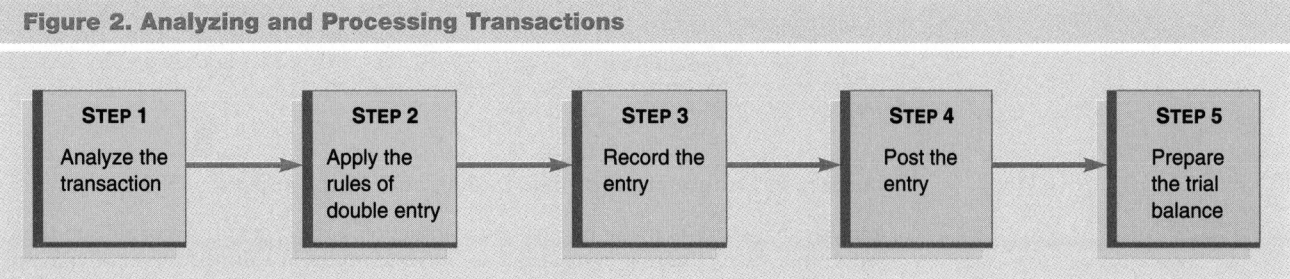

STEP 1	**STEP 2**	**STEP 3**	**STEP 4**	**STEP 5**
Analyze the transaction	Apply the rules of double entry	Record the entry	Post the entry	Prepare the trial balance

OBJECTIVE

4 *Apply the steps for transaction analysis and processing to simple transactions*

TRANSACTION ANALYSIS ILLUSTRATED

In the next few pages, we examine the transactions for Joan Miller Advertising Agency during the month of January. In the discussion, we illustrate the principle of duality and show how transactions are recorded in the accounts.

January 1: Joan Miller invests $10,000 to start her own advertising agency.

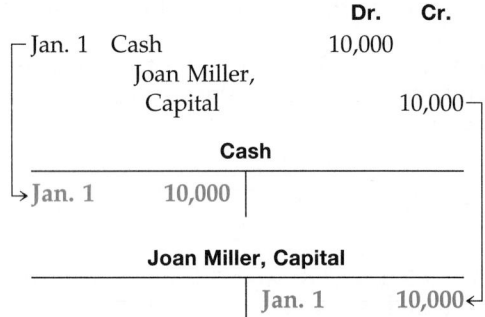

		Dr.	Cr.
Jan. 1	Cash	10,000	
	Joan Miller, Capital		10,000

Cash

| Jan. 1 | 10,000 | |

Joan Miller, Capital

| | | Jan. 1 | 10,000 |

Transaction: Owner's investment.
Analysis: Assets increase. Owner's equity increases.
Rules: Increases in assets are recorded by debits. Increases in owner's equity are recorded by credits.
Entry: The increase in assets is recorded by a debit to Cash. The increase in owner's equity is recorded by a credit to Joan Miller, Capital.

If Joan Miller had invested assets other than cash in the business, the appropriate asset accounts would have been debited.

January 2: Rents an office, paying two months' rent, $800, in advance.

		Dr.	Cr.
Jan. 2	Prepaid Rent	800	
	Cash		800

Cash

| Jan. 1 | 10,000 | Jan. 2 | 800 |

Prepaid Rent

| Jan. 2 | 800 | |

Transaction: Rent paid in advance.
Analysis: Assets increase. Assets decrease.
Rules: Increases in assets are recorded by debits. Decreases in assets are recorded by credits.
Entry: The increase in assets is recorded by a debit to Prepaid Rent. The decrease in assets is recorded by a credit to Cash.

January 3: Orders art supplies, $1,800, and office supplies, $800.

Analysis: No entry is made because no transaction has occurred. According to the recognition issue, there is no liability until the supplies are shipped or received and there is an obligation to pay for them.

January 4: Purchases art equipment, $4,200, with cash.

		Dr.	Cr.
Jan. 4	Art Equipment	4,200	
	Cash		4,200

Cash

Jan. 1	10,000	Jan. 2	800
		4	4,200

Art Equipment

| Jan. 4 | 4,200 | | |

Transaction: Purchase of equipment.
Analysis: Assets increase. Assets decrease.
Rules: Increases in assets are recorded by debits. Decreases in assets are recorded by credits.
Entry: The increase in assets is recorded by a debit to Art Equipment. The decrease in assets is recorded by a credit to Cash.

January 5: Purchases office equipment, $3,000, from Morgan Equipment; pays $1,500 in cash and agrees to pay the rest next month.

		Dr.	Cr.
Jan. 5	Office Equipment	3,000	
	Cash		1,500
	Accounts Payable		1,500

Cash

Jan. 1	10,000	Jan. 2	800
		4	4,200
		5	1,500

Office Equipment

| Jan. 5 | 3,000 | | |

Accounts Payable

		Jan. 5	1,500

Transaction: Purchase of equipment and partial payment.
Analysis: Assets increase. Assets decrease. Liabilities increase.
Rules: Increases in assets are recorded by debits. Decreases in assets are recorded by credits. Increases in liabilities are recorded by credits.
Entry: The increase in assets is recorded by a debit to Office Equipment. The decrease in assets is recorded by a credit to Cash. The increase in liabilities is recorded by a credit to Accounts Payable.

January 6: Purchases art supplies, $1,800, and office supplies, $800, from Taylor Supply Company, on credit.

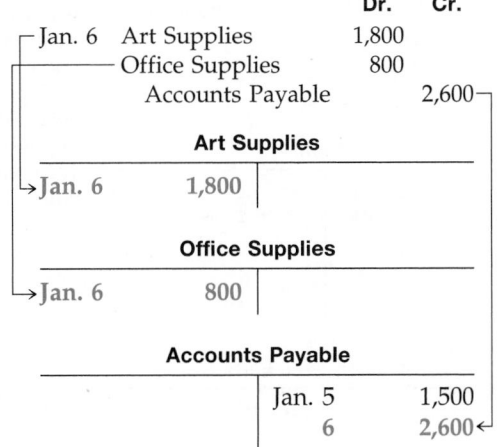

		Dr.	Cr.
Jan. 6	Art Supplies	1,800	
	Office Supplies	800	
	Accounts Payable		2,600

Art Supplies

| Jan. 6 | 1,800 | | |

Office Supplies

| Jan. 6 | 800 | | |

Accounts Payable

		Jan. 5	1,500
		6	2,600

Transaction: Purchase of supplies on credit.
Analysis: Assets increase. Liabilities increase.
Rules: Increases in assets are recorded by debits. Increases in liabilities are recorded by credits.
Entry: The increase in assets is recorded by debits to Art Supplies and Office Supplies. The increase in liabilities is recorded by a credit to Accounts Payable.

January 8: Pays for a one-year life insurance policy, $480, with coverage effective January 1.

		Dr.	Cr.
Jan. 8	Prepaid Insurance	480	
	Cash		480

Cash

Jan. 1	10,000	Jan. 2	800
		4	4,200
		5	1,500
		8	480

Prepaid Insurance

Jan. 8	480		

Transaction: Insurance coverage purchased in advance.

Analysis: Assets increase. Assets decrease.

Rules: Increases in assets are recorded by debits. Decreases in assets are recorded by credits.

Entry: The increase in assets is recorded by a debit to Prepaid Insurance. The decrease in assets is recorded by a credit to Cash.

January 9: Pays Taylor Supply Company $1,000 of the amount owed.

		Dr.	Cr.
Jan. 9	Accounts Payable	1,000	
	Cash		1,000

Cash

Jan. 1	10,000	Jan. 2	800
		4	4,200
		5	1,500
		8	480
		9	1,000

Accounts Payable

Jan. 9	1,000	Jan. 5	1,500
		6	2,600

Transaction: Partial payment on a liability.

Analysis: Assets decrease. Liabilities decrease.

Rules: Decreases in assets are recorded by credits. Decreases in liabilities are recorded by debits.

Entry: The decrease in liabilities is recorded by a debit to Accounts Payable. The decrease in assets is recorded by a credit to Cash.

January 10: Performs a service for an automobile dealer by placing advertisements in the newspaper and collects a fee, $1,400.

		Dr.	Cr.
Jan. 10	Cash	1,400	
	Advertising Fees Earned		1,400

Cash

Jan. 1	10,000	Jan. 2	800
10	1,400	4	4,200
		5	1,500
		8	480
		9	1,000

Advertising Fees Earned

		Jan. 10	1,400

Transaction: Revenue earned and cash collected.

Analysis: Assets increase. Owner's equity increases.

Rules: Increases in assets are recorded by debits. Increases in owner's equity are recorded by credits.

Entry: The increase in assets is recorded by a debit to Cash. The increase in owner's equity is recorded by a credit to Advertising Fees Earned.

January 12: Pays the secretary two weeks' wages, $600.

		Dr.	Cr.
Jan. 12	Wages Expense	600	
	Cash		600

Cash

Jan. 1	10,000	Jan. 2	800
10	1,400	4	4,200
		5	1,500
		8	480
		9	1,000
		12	600

Wages Expense

Jan. 12	600	

Transaction: Payment of wages expense.
Analysis: Assets decrease. Owner's equity decreases.
Rules: Decreases in assets are recorded by credits. Decreases in owner's equity are recorded by debits.
Entry: The decrease in owner's equity is recorded by a debit to Wages Expense. The decrease in assets is recorded by a credit to Cash.

January 15: Accepts an advance fee, $1,000, for artwork to be done for another agency.

		Dr.	Cr.
Jan. 15	Cash	1,000	
	Unearned Art Fees		1,000

Cash

Jan. 1	10,000	Jan. 2	800
10	1,400	4	4,200
15	1,000	5	1,500
		8	480
		9	1,000
		12	600

Unearned Art Fees

		Jan. 15	1,000

Transaction: Payment received for future services.
Analysis: Assets increase. Liabilities increase.
Rules: Increases in assets are recorded by debits. Increases in liabilities are recorded by credits.
Entry: The increase in assets is recorded by a debit to Cash. The increase in liabilities is recorded by a credit to Unearned Art Fees.

January 19: Performs a service by placing several major advertisements for Ward Department Stores. The fee, $2,800, is billed now but will be collected next month.

		Dr.	Cr.
Jan. 19	Accounts Receivable	2,800	
	Advertising Fees Earned		2,800

Accounts Receivable

Jan. 19	2,800	

Advertising Fees Earned

		Jan. 10	1,400
		19	2,800

Transaction: Revenue earned, to be received later.
Analysis: Assets increase. Owner's equity increases.
Rules: Increases in assets are recorded by debits. Increases in owner's equity are recorded by credits.
Entry: The increase in assets is recorded by a debit to Accounts Receivable. The increase in owner's equity is recorded by a credit to Advertising Fees Earned.

January 26: Pays the secretary two more weeks' wages, $600.

		Dr.	Cr.
Jan. 26	Wages Expense	600	
	Cash		600

Cash

Jan. 1	10,000	Jan. 2	800
10	1,400	4	4,200
15	1,000	5	1,500
		8	480
		9	1,000
		12	600
		26	600

Wages Expense

Jan. 12	600
26	600

Transaction: Payment of wages expense.
Analysis: Assets decrease. Owner's equity decreases.
Rules: Decreases in assets are recorded by credits. Decreases in owner's equity are recorded by debits.
Entry: The decrease in owner's equity is recorded by a debit to Wages Expense. The decrease in assets is recorded by a credit to Cash.

January 29: Receives and pays the utility bill, $100.

		Dr.	Cr.
Jan. 29	Utilities Expense	100	
	Cash		100

Cash

Jan. 1	10,000	Jan. 2	800
10	1,400	4	4,200
15	1,000	5	1,500
		8	480
		9	1,000
		12	600
		26	600
		29	100

Utilities Expense

Jan. 29	100

Transaction: Payment of utilities expense.
Analysis: Assets decrease. Owner's equity decreases.
Rules: Decreases in assets are recorded by credits. Decreases in owner's equity are recorded by debits.
Entry: The decrease in owner's equity is recorded by a debit to Utilities Expense. The decrease in assets is recorded by a credit to Cash.

January 30: Receives (but does not pay) the telephone bill, $70.

		Dr.	Cr.
Jan. 30	Telephone Expense	70	
	Accounts Payable		70

Accounts Payable

Jan. 9	1,000	Jan. 5	1,500
		6	2,600
		30	70

Telephone Expense

Jan. 30	70

Transaction: Expense incurred, to be paid later.
Analysis: Liabilities increase. Owner's equity decreases.
Rules: Increases in liabilities are recorded by credits. Decreases in owner's equity are recorded by debits.
Entry: The decrease in owner's equity is recorded by a debit to Telephone Expense. The increase in liabilities is recorded by a credit to Accounts Payable.

January 31: Joan Miller withdraws $1,400 from the business for personal living expenses.

		Dr.	Cr.
Jan. 31	Joan Miller,		
	Withdrawals	1,400	
	Cash		1,400

Transaction: Owner's withdrawal for personal use.

Analysis: Assets decrease. Owner's equity decreases.

Rules: Decreases in assets are recorded by credits. Decreases in owner's equity are recorded by debits.

Entry: The decrease in owner's equity is recorded by a debit to Joan Miller, Withdrawals. The decrease in assets is recorded by a credit to Cash.

Cash

Jan.	1	10,000	Jan.	2	800
	10	1,400		4	4,200
	15	1,000		5	1,500
				8	480
				9	1,000
				12	600
				26	600
				29	100
				31	1,400

Joan Miller, Withdrawals

Jan. 31	1,400	

SUMMARY OF TRANSACTIONS

In Exhibit 2, which is on the next page, the transactions for January are shown in their accounts and in relation to the accounting equation.

DECISION POINT — *American Collegiate Sales, Inc.*

American Collegiate Sales, Inc. (ACS) employed student representatives to market grooming aids, casual clothes, and other such products on college campuses. The representatives organized parties at which they displayed samples of all the products. Students who bought products paid the representative, who in turn ordered the products and paid ACS for them. When the products arrived, the student representative delivered them to the buyers. The representatives paid ACS less than they charged the buyers. The difference represented the earnings of the representatives, who were not employees of ACS. Wall Street investors admired ACS because the company had enjoyed several years of rapid growth in sales and earnings.

In 1994, the president of ACS predicted further increases of 30 percent. By December, however, it was apparent that the forecasted sales goals would not be met. So, during the last two weeks of December, ACS shipped $20 million of merchandise to the sales representatives to be held for future sales parties. The company billed the student representatives and recorded the shipments as sales. In this way, ACS was able to meet its sales goal for the year. Were these merchandise shipments properly recorded as sales?

The shipments were improperly recorded as sales. The goods had not been ordered by or sold to actual customers, and the student representatives had the right to return all the products unconditionally. In technical terms, this type of arrangement is called a *consignment*. To report consignment shipments as legitimate sales is certainly unethical and can be, as in this case, illegal when the intent is to deceive. As it turned out, most of the $20 million of products were returned during January and February, and ACS went into bankruptcy. Officials of the company were later convicted of fraud. :::::

Exhibit 2. Summary of Sample Accounts and Transactions for Joan Miller Advertising Agency

Assets		=	Liabilities		+	Owner's Equity

Cash

Jan.	1	10,000	Jan.	2	800
	10	1,400		4	4,200
	15	1,000		5	1,500
				8	480
				9	1,000
				12	600
				26	600
				29	100
				31	1,400
		12,400			10,680
Bal.		1,720			

Accounts Receivable

Jan.	19	2,800	

Art Supplies

Jan.	6	1,800	

Office Supplies

Jan.	6	800	

Prepaid Rent

Jan.	2	800	

Prepaid Insurance

Jan.	8	480	

Art Equipment

Jan.	4	4,200	

Office Equipment

Jan.	5	3,000	

Accounts Payable

Jan.	9	1,000	Jan.	5	1,500
				6	2,600
				30	70
		1,000			4,170
			Bal.		3,170

Unearned Art Fees

			Jan.	15	1,000

Joan Miller, Capital

			Jan.	1	10,000

Joan Miller, Withdrawals

Jan.	31	1,400	

Advertising Fees Earned

			Jan.	10	1,400
				19	2,800
			Bal.		4,200

Wages Expense

Jan.	12	600	
	26	600	
Bal.		1,200	

Utilities Expense

Jan.	29	100	

Telephone Expense

Jan.	30	70	

OBJECTIVE

5 *Record transactions in the general journal*

Let us now take a look at the formal processing of transactions in the general journal, the general ledger, and the trial balance.

THE GENERAL JOURNAL

As you have seen, transactions can be entered directly into the accounts. But this method makes identifying individual transactions or finding errors very difficult because the debit is recorded in one account and the credit in another. The solution is to record all transactions chronologically in a journal. The journal is sometimes called the *book of original entry* because it is where transactions first enter the accounting records. Later, the debit and credit portions of each transaction can be transferred to the appropriate accounts in the ledger.

A separate journal entry is used to record each transaction, and the process of recording transactions is called journalizing.

Most businesses have more than one kind of journal. The simplest and most flexible type is the general journal, the one we focus on in this chapter. Entries in the general journal include the following information about each transaction:

1. The date
2. The names of the accounts debited and the dollar amounts on the same lines in the Debit column
3. The names of the accounts credited and the dollar amounts on the same lines in the Credit column
4. An explanation of the transaction
5. The account identification numbers, if appropriate

Exhibit 3 displays two of the earlier transactions for Joan Miller Advertising Agency in general journal form. The procedure for recording transactions in the general journal is listed on the next page.

Exhibit 3. The General Journal

General Journal					Page 1
Date		Description	Post. Ref.	Debit	Credit
19xx Jan.	6	Art Supplies		1,800	
		Office Supplies		800	
		Accounts Payable			2,600
		Purchase of art and office supplies on credit			
	8	Prepaid Insurance		480	
		Cash			480
		Paid one-year life insurance premium			

1. Record the date by writing the year in small figures on the first line at the top of the first column, the month on the next line of the first column, and the day in the second column opposite the month. For subsequent entries on the same page for the same month and year, the month and year can be omitted.
2. Write the exact names of the accounts debited and credited in the Description column. Write the names of the accounts debited next to the left margin of the second line, and indent the names of the accounts credited. The explanation is placed on the next line and further indented. It should be brief but sufficient to explain and identify the transaction. A transaction can have more than one debit or credit entry; this is called a compound entry. In a compound entry, all debit accounts are listed before any credit accounts. (The January 6 transaction of Joan Miller Advertising Agency in Exhibit 3 is an example of a compound entry.)
3. Write the debit amounts in the Debit column opposite the accounts to be debited, and write the credit amounts in the Credit column opposite the accounts to be credited.
4. At the time the transactions are recorded, nothing is placed in the Post. Ref. (posting reference) column. (This column is sometimes called *LP* or *Folio.*) Later, if the company uses account numbers to identify accounts in the ledger, fill in the account numbers to provide a convenient cross-reference from the general journal to the ledger and to indicate that the entry has been posted to the ledger. If the accounts are not numbered, use a checkmark (✔).
5. It is customary to skip a line after each journal entry.

OBJECTIVE

6 *Post transactions from the journal to the ledger*

THE GENERAL LEDGER

The general journal is used to record the details of each transaction. The general ledger is used to update each account.

The Ledger Account Form The T account is a simple, direct means of recording transactions. In practice, a somewhat more complicated form of the account is needed to record more information. The ledger account form, with four columns for dollar amounts, is illustrated in Exhibit 4.

The account title and number appear at the top of the account form. The date of the transaction appears in the first two columns as it does in the journal. The Item column is used only rarely to identify transactions, because explanations already appear in the journal. The Post. Ref. column is used to note the journal page where the original entry for the transaction can be found. The dollar amount of the entry is entered in the appropriate Debit or

Exhibit 4. Accounts Payable in the General Ledger

General Ledger							
Accounts Payable						**Account No. 212**	
						Balance	
Date		**Item**	**Post. Ref.**	**Debit**	**Credit**	**Debit**	**Credit**
19xx Jan.	5		J1		1,500		1,500
	6		J1		2,600		4,100
	9		J1	1,000			3,100
	30		J2		70		3,170

Credit column, and a new account balance is computed in the final two columns after each entry. The advantage of this form of account over the T account is that the current balance of the account is readily available.

Posting to the Ledger   After transactions have been entered in the journal, they must be transferred to the general ledger. The process of transferring journal entry information from the journal to the ledger is called posting. Posting is usually done after several entries have been made—for example, at the end of each day or less frequently, depending on the number of transactions.

Through posting, each amount in the Debit column of the journal is transferred into the Debit column of the appropriate account in the ledger, and each amount in the Credit column of the journal is transferred into the Credit column of the appropriate account in the ledger (see Exhibit 5). The steps in the posting process are listed on the next page.

Exhibit 5. Posting from the General Journal to the Ledger

General Journal   ② Page 2

Date		Description	Post. Ref.	Debit	Credit
19xx	②	①	⑤	③	
Jan.	30	Telephone Expense	513	70	
		Accounts Payable	212		70
		Received bill for			
		telephone expense			

General Ledger

Accounts Payable   Account No. 212

Date		Item	Post. Ref.	Debit	Credit	Balance Debit	Balance Credit
19xx							
Jan.	5		J1		1,500		1,500
	6		J1		2,600		4,100
	9		J1	1,000			3,100
	30		J2		70		3,170

General Ledger

Telephone Expense   Account No. 513

Date		Item	Post. Ref.	Debit	Credit	Balance Debit	Balance Credit
19xx						④	
Jan.	30		J2	70		70	

1. In the ledger, locate the debit account named in the journal entry.
2. Enter the date of the transaction and, in the Post. Ref. column of the ledger, the journal page number from which the entry comes.
3. Enter in the Debit column of the ledger account the amount of the debit as it appears in the journal.
4. Calculate the account balance and enter it in the appropriate balance column.
5. Enter in the Post. Ref. column of the journal the account number to which the amount has been posted.
6. Repeat the same five steps for the credit side of the journal entry.

Notice that step **5** is the last step in the posting process for each debit and credit. In addition to serving as an easy reference between the journal entry and the ledger account, this entry in the Post. Ref. column of the journal indicates that all steps for the item have been completed. This allows accountants who have been called away from their work to easily find where they were before the interruption.

THE TRIAL BALANCE

OBJECTIVE

7 *Prepare a trial balance and describe its value and limitations*

For every amount debited in the ledger, an equal amount must be credited. This means that the total of debits and credits in the ledger must be equal. To test this, the accountant periodically prepares a trial balance. Exhibit 6 shows a trial balance for Joan Miller Advertising Agency. It was prepared from the accounts in Exhibit 2.

Exhibit 6. The Trial Balance

Joan Miller Advertising Agency
Trial Balance
January 31, 19xx

Cash	$ 1,720	
Accounts Receivable	2,800	
Art Supplies	1,800	
Office Supplies	800	
Prepaid Rent	800	
Prepaid Insurance	480	
Art Equipment	4,200	
Office Equipment	3,000	
Accounts Payable		$ 3,170
Unearned Art Fees		1,000
Joan Miller, Capital		10,000
Joan Miller, Withdrawals	1,400	
Advertising Fees Earned		4,200
Wages Expense	1,200	
Utilities Expense	100	
Telephone Expense	70	
	$18,370	$18,370

The trial balance may be prepared at any time but is usually prepared on the last day of the month. Here are the steps in preparing a trial balance:

1. List each ledger account that has a balance, with debit balances in the left column and credit balances in the right column. Accounts are listed in the order in which they appear in the ledger.
2. Add each column.
3. Compare the totals of the columns.

In carrying out steps **1** and **2**, remember that the account form in the ledger has two balance columns, one for debit balances and one for credit balances. In accounts in which increases are recorded by debits, the normal balance (the usual balance) is a debit balance; where increases are recorded by credits, the normal balance is a credit balance. Table 1 summarizes the normal account balances of the major account categories. According to the table, the ledger account Accounts Payable (a liability) typically has a credit balance and is copied into the trial balance as a credit balance.

Once in a while, a transaction leaves an account with a balance that is not "normal." For example, when a company overdraws its account at the bank, its Cash account (an asset) will show a credit balance instead of a debit balance. The "abnormal" balance should be copied into the trial balance columns as it stands, as a debit or a credit.

The trial balance proves whether or not the ledger is in balance. *In balance* means that the total of all debits recorded equals the total of all credits recorded. But the trial balance does not prove that the transactions were analyzed correctly or recorded in the proper accounts. For example, there is no way of determining from the trial balance that a debit should have been made in the Art Equipment account rather than in the Office Equipment account. And the trial balance does not detect whether transactions have been omitted, because equal debits and credits will have been omitted. Also, if an error of the same amount is made in both a debit and a credit, it will not be discovered by the trial balance. The trial balance proves only that the debits and credits in the accounts are in balance.

If the debit and credit columns of the trial balance are not equal, look for one or more of the following errors: (1) a debit was entered in an account as a credit, or vice versa; (2) the balance of an account was computed incorrectly; (3) an error was made in carrying the account balance to the trial balance; or (4) the trial balance was summed incorrectly.

Table 1. Normal Account Balances of Major Account Categories

Account Category	Increases Recorded by		Normal Balance	
	Debit	Credit	Debit	Credit
Asset	x		x	
Liability		x		x
Owner's Equity:				
Capital		x		x
Withdrawals	x		x	
Revenues		x		x
Expenses	x		x	

Other than simply adding the columns wrong, the two most common mistakes in preparing a trial balance are (1) recording an account with a debit balance as a credit, or vice versa, and (2) transposing two numbers when transferring an amount to the trial balance (for example, entering $23,459 as $23,549). The first of these mistakes causes the trial balance to be out of balance by an amount divisible by 2. The second causes the trial balance to be out of balance by a number divisible by 9. Thus, if a trial balance is out of balance and the addition has been verified, determine the amount by which the trial balance is out of balance and divide it first by 2 and then by 9. If the amount is divisible by 2, look in the trial balance for an amount equal to the quotient. If you find the amount, it is probably in the wrong column. If the amount is divisible by 9, trace each amount to the ledger account balance, checking carefully for a transposition error. If neither of these techniques identifies the error, first recompute the balance of each account in the ledger, then, if the error still has not been found, retrace each posting from the journal to the ledger.

BUSINESS BULLETIN: TECHNOLOGY IN PRACTICE

In computerized accounting systems, posting is done automatically and the trial balance can be easily prepared as often as needed. Any accounts with abnormal balances are highlighted for investigation. Some general ledger software packages for small businesses list the trial balance amounts in a single column, with credit balances shown as minuses. In such cases, the trial balance is in balance if the total is zero.

SOME NOTES ON PRESENTATION

A ruled line appears in financial reports before each subtotal or total to indicate that the amounts above are added or subtracted. It is common practice to use a double line under a final total to show that it has been checked, or verified.

Dollar signs ($) are required in all financial statements, including the balance sheet and income statement, and in the trial balance and other schedules. On these statements, a dollar sign should be placed before the first amount in each column and before the first amount in a column following a ruled line. Dollar signs in the same column are aligned. Dollar signs are not used in journals and ledgers.

On unruled paper, commas and decimal points are used in dollar amounts. On paper with ruled columns—like the paper in journals and ledgers—commas and decimal points are not needed. In this book, because most problems and illustrations are in whole dollar amounts, the cents column usually is omitted. When accountants deal with whole dollars, they often use a dash in the cents column to indicate whole dollars rather than take the time to write zeros.

CHAPTER REVIEW

REVIEW OF LEARNING OBJECTIVES

1. **Explain, in simple terms, the generally accepted ways of solving the measurement issues of recognition, valuation, and classification.** To measure a business transaction, the accountant must determine when the transaction occurred (the recognition issue), what value should be placed on the transaction (the valuation issue), and how the components of the transaction should be categorized (the classification issue). In general, recognition occurs when title passes, and a transaction is valued at the exchange price, the cost at the time the transaction is recognized. Classification refers to the categorizing of transactions according to a system of accounts.

2. **Describe the chart of accounts and recognize commonly used accounts.** An account is a device for storing data from transactions. There is one account for each asset, liability, and component of owner's equity, including revenues and expenses. The general ledger is a book or file consisting of all of a company's accounts arranged according to a chart of accounts. Commonly used asset accounts are Cash, Notes Receivable, Accounts Receivable, Prepaid Expenses, Land, Buildings, and Equipment. Common liability accounts are Notes Payable, Accounts Payable, Wages Payable, and Mortgages Payable. Common owner's equity accounts are Capital, Withdrawals, and revenue and expense accounts.

3. **Define double-entry system and state the rules for double entry.** In the double-entry system, each transaction must be recorded with at least one debit and one credit so that the total dollar amount of the debits equals the total dollar amount of the credits. The rules for double entry are: (1) increases in assets are debited to asset accounts, decreases in assets are credited to asset accounts; and (2) increases in liabilities and owner's equity are credited to those accounts, decreases in liabilities and owner's equity are debited to those accounts.

4. **Apply the steps for transaction analysis and processing to simple transactions.** The procedure for analyzing transactions is: (1) analyze the effect of the transaction on assets, liabilities, and owner's equity; (2) apply the rules of double entry; (3) record the entry; (4) post the entry; and (5) prepare the trial balance.

5. **Record transactions in the general journal.** The general journal is a chronological record of all transactions. That record contains the date of each transaction, the names of the accounts and the dollar amounts debited and credited, an explanation of each entry, and the account numbers to which postings have been made.

6. **Post transactions from the journal to the ledger.** After transactions have been entered in the general journal, they are posted to the general ledger. Posting is done by transferring each amount in the Debit column of the general journal to the Debit column of the appropriate account in the general ledger, and transferring each amount in the Credit column of the general journal to the Credit column of the appropriate account in the general ledger. After each entry is posted, a new balance is entered in the appropriate balance column.

7. **Prepare a trial balance and describe its value and limitations.** A trial balance is used to check that the debit and credit balances in the ledger are equal. It is prepared by listing each account with its debit or credit balance. Then, the two columns are added and compared to test their balances. The major limitation of the trial balance is that even if debit and credit balances are equal, this does not necessarily mean that the transactions were analyzed correctly or recorded in the proper accounts.

REVIEW OF CONCEPTS AND TERMINOLOGY

The following concepts and terms were introduced in this chapter.

LO 3 **Balance:** The difference in dollars between the total debit footing and the total credit footing of an account. Also called *account balance.*

L O 2   **Chart of accounts:** A scheme that assigns a unique number to each account to facilitate finding the account in the ledger; also, the list of account numbers and titles.

L O 1   **Classification:** The process of assigning transactions to the appropriate accounts.

L O 5   **Compound entry:** A journal entry that has more than one debit or credit entry.

L O 1   **Cost:** The exchange price associated with a business transaction at the point of recognition.

L O 1   **Cost principle:** The practice of recording a transaction at cost and maintaining this cost in the records until the asset, liability, or component of owner's equity is sold, expires, is consumed, is satisfied, or is otherwise disposed of.

L O 3   **Credit:** The right side of an account.

L O 3   **Debit:** The left side of an account.

L O 3   **Double-entry system:** The accounting system in which each transaction is recorded with at least one debit and one credit so that the total dollar amount of debits and the total dollar amount of credits equal each other.

L O 3   **Footings:** Working totals of columns of numbers. To *foot* means to total a column of numbers.

L O 5   **General journal:** The simplest and most flexible type of journal.

L O 2   **General ledger:** The book or file that contains all of a company's accounts arranged in the order of the chart of accounts. Also called *ledger.*

L O 5   **Journal:** A chronological record of all transactions; the place where transactions first enter the accounting records. Also called *book of original entry.*

L O 5   **Journal entry:** The notations in the journal that are used to record a single transaction.

L O 5   **Journalizing:** The process of recording transactions in a journal.

L O 6   **Ledger account form:** A form of account that has four columns: one column for debit entries, one column for credit entries, and two columns (debit and credit) for showing the balance of the account.

L O 7   **Normal balance:** The usual balance of an account; also the side (debit or credit) that increases the account.

L O 6   **Posting:** The process of transferring journal entry information from the journal to the ledger.

L O 1   **Recognition:** The determination of when a business transaction should be recorded.

L O 1   **Recognition point:** The predetermined time at which a transaction should be recorded; usually, the point at which title passes to the buyer.

L O 3   **Source document:** An invoice, check, receipt, or other document that supports a transaction.

L O 3   **T account:** The simplest form of an account; used to analyze transactions.

L O 7   **Trial balance:** A comparison of the total of debit and credit balances in the ledger to check that they are equal.

L O 1   **Valuation:** The process of assigning a monetary value to a business transaction.

REVIEW PROBLEM

TRANSACTION ANALYSIS, GENERAL JOURNAL, LEDGER ACCOUNTS, AND TRIAL BALANCE

L O 4, 5, 6, 7   After graduation from veterinary school, Laura Cox entered private practice. The transactions of the business through May 27 are as follows:

19xx

May 1   Laura Cox invested $2,000 in her business bank account.

      3   Paid $300 for two months' rent in advance for an office.

May 9 Purchased medical supplies for $200 in cash.
   12 Purchased $400 of equipment on credit, making a 25 percent down payment.
   15 Delivered a calf for a fee of $35.
   18 Made a partial payment of $50 on the equipment purchased May 12.
   27 Paid a utility bill of $40.

REQUIRED

1. Record these entries in the general journal.
2. Post the entries from the journal to the following accounts in the ledger: Cash (111); Medical Supplies (115); Prepaid Rent (117); Equipment (144); Accounts Payable (212); Laura Cox, Capital (311); Veterinary Fees Earned (411); and Utilities Expense (512).
3. Prepare a trial balance as of May 31.

ANSWER TO REVIEW PROBLEM

1. Record the journal entries.

		General Journal			Page 1
Date		**Description**	**Post. Ref.**	**Debit**	**Credit**
19xx May	1	Cash	111	2,000	
		Laura Cox, Capital	311		2,000
		Deposited $2,000 in the business bank account			
	3	Prepaid Rent	117	300	
		Cash	111		300
		Paid two months' rent in advance for an office			
	9	Medical Supplies	115	200	
		Cash	111		200
		Purchased medical supplies for cash			
	12	Equipment	144	400	
		Accounts Payable	212		300
		Cash	111		100
		Purchased equipment on credit, paying 25 percent down			
	15	Cash	111	35	
		Veterinary Fees Earned	411		35
		Collected fee for delivery of a calf			
	18	Accounts Payable	212	50	
		Cash	111		50
		Partial payment for equipment purchased May 12			
	27	Utilities Expense	512	40	
		Cash	111		40
		Paid utility bill			

2. Post the transactions to the ledger accounts.

General Ledger

Cash — Account No. 111

Date		Item	Post. Ref.	Debit	Credit	Balance Debit	Balance Credit
19xx May	1		J1	2,000		2,000	
	3		J1		300	1,700	
	9		J1		200	1,500	
	12		J1		100	1,400	
	15		J1	35		1,435	
	18		J1		50	1,385	
	27		J1		40	1,345	

Medical Supplies — Account No. 115

Date		Item	Post. Ref.	Debit	Credit	Balance Debit	Balance Credit
19xx May	9		J1	200		200	

Prepaid Rent — Account No. 117

Date		Item	Post. Ref.	Debit	Credit	Balance Debit	Balance Credit
19xx May	3		J1	300		300	

Equipment — Account No. 144

Date		Item	Post. Ref.	Debit	Credit	Balance Debit	Balance Credit
19xx May	12		J1	400		400	

Accounts Payable — Account No. 212

Date		Item	Post. Ref.	Debit	Credit	Balance Debit	Balance Credit
19xx May	12		J1		300		300
	18		J1	50			250

Laura Cox, Capital   Account No. 311

Date		Item	Post. Ref.	Debit	Credit	Balance Debit	Balance Credit
19xx May	1		J1		2,000		2,000

Veterinary Fees Earned   Account No. 411

Date		Item	Post. Ref.	Debit	Credit	Balance Debit	Balance Credit
19xx May	15		J1		35		35

Utilities Expense   Account No. 512

Date		Item	Post. Ref.	Debit	Credit	Balance Debit	Balance Credit
19xx May	27		J1	40		40	

3. Complete the trial balance.

Laura Cox, Veterinarian
Trial Balance
May 31, 19xx

Cash	$1,345	
Medical Supplies	200	
Prepaid Rent	300	
Equipment	400	
Accounts Payable		$ 250
Laura Cox, Capital		2,000
Veterinary Fees Earned		35
Utilities Expense	40	
	$2,285	$2,285

CHAPTER ASSIGNMENTS

QUESTIONS

1. What three issues underlie most accounting measurement decisions?
2. Why is recognition an issue for accountants?

3. A customer asks the owner of a store to save an item for him and says that he will pick it up and pay for it next week. The owner agrees to hold it. Should this transaction be recorded as a sale? Explain your answer.

4. Why is it practical for accountants to rely on original cost for valuation purposes?

5. Under the cost principle, changes in value after a transaction is recorded are not usually recognized in the accounts. Comment on this possible limitation of using original cost in accounting measurements.

6. What is an account, and how is it related to the ledger?

7. Tell whether each of the following accounts is an asset account, a liability account, or an owner's equity account.
   a. Notes Receivable
   b. Land
   c. Withdrawals
   d. Bonds Payable
   e. Prepaid Rent
   f. Insurance Expense
   g. Service Revenue

8. In the preparation of owner's equity accounts, how are owner's investments and withdrawals treated? Explain your answer.

9. Why is the system of recording entries called the double-entry system? What is significant about this system?

10. "Double-entry accounting refers to entering a transaction in both the journal and the ledger." Comment on this statement.

11. "Debits are bad; credits are good." Comment on this statement.

12. What are the rules of double entry for (a) assets, (b) liabilities, and (c) owner's equity?

13. Why are the rules of double entry the same for liabilities and owner's equity?

14. What is the meaning of the statement, "The Cash account has a debit balance of $500"?

15. Explain why debits, which decrease owner's equity, also increase expenses, which are a component of owner's equity.

16. What are the five steps in analyzing and processing a transaction?

17. Is it a good idea to forgo the journal and enter a transaction directly into the ledger? Explain your answer.

18. In recording entries in a journal, which is written first, the debit or the credit? How is indentation used in the general journal?

19. What is the relationship between the journal and the ledger?

20. Describe each of the following:
   a. Account
   b. Journal
   c. Ledger
   d. Book of original entry
   e. Post. Ref. column
   f. Journalizing
   g. Posting
   h. Footings
   i. Compound entry

21. What is the normal balance of Accounts Payable? Under what conditions could Accounts Payable have a debit balance?

22. What does a trial balance prove?

23. Can errors be present even though a trial balance balances? Explain your answer.

24. List the following six items in sequence to illustrate the flow of events through the accounting system.
   a. Analysis of the transaction
   b. Debits and credits posted from the journal to the ledger
   c. Occurrence of a business transaction
   d. Preparation of the financial statements
   e. Entry made in the journal
   f. Preparation of the trial balance

SHORT EXERCISES

SE 1.   *Recognition*
L O 1

No check figure

Which of the following events would be recognized and entered in the accounting records of Hawthorne Company? Why?

Jan. 10   Hawthorne Company places an order for office supplies.
Feb. 15   Hawthorne Company receives the office supplies and a bill for them.
Mar. 1   Hawthorne pays for the office supplies.

SE 2.   *Classification of*
L O 2   *Accounts*

Check Figures: Asset: b, f, h; Liability: a, g; Revenue: d; Expense: e; None of these: c

Tell whether each of the following accounts is an asset, a liability, a revenue, an expense, or none of these.

a. Accounts Payable   e. Supplies Expense
b. Supplies   f. Accounts Receivable
c. Withdrawals   g. Unearned Revenue
d. Fees Earned   h. Equipment

SE 3.   *Normal Balances*
L O 7

No check figure

Tell whether the normal balance of each account in SE 2 is a debit or a credit.

SE 4.   *Transaction Analysis*
L O 4

No check figure

For each of the following transactions, tell which account is debited and which account is credited.

May 2   Joe Hurley started a computer programming business, Hurley's Programming Service, by placing $5,000 in a bank account.
        5   Purchased a computer for $2,500 in cash.
        7   Purchased supplies on credit for $300.
      19   Received cash for programming services performed, $500.
      22   Received cash for programming services to be performed, $600.
      25   Paid the rent for May, $650.
      31   Billed a customer for programming services performed, $250.

SE 5.   *Recording*
L O 4   *Transactions in*
              T Accounts

No check figure

Set up T accounts and record each transaction in SE 4. Determine the balance of each account.

SE 6.   *Preparing a Trial*
L O 7   *Balance*

Check Figure: Trial balance: $6,650

From the T accounts created in SE 5, prepare a trial balance dated May 31, 19x1.

SE 7.   *Recording*
L O 5   *Transactions in the*
              General Journal

No check figure

Prepare a general journal form like the one in Exhibit 3 and label it Page 4. Record the following transactions in the journal.

Sept. 6   Billed a customer for services performed, $1,900.
       16   Received partial payment from the customer billed on Sept. 6, $900.

SE 8.   *Posting to the Ledger*
L O 6   *Accounts*

No check figure

Prepare ledger account forms like the one in Exhibit 4 for the following accounts: Cash (111), Accounts Receivable (113), and Service Revenue (411). Post the transactions recorded in SE 7 to the ledger accounts, being sure to make proper posting references.

SE 9.   *Preparing a Trial*
L O 7   *Balance*

Check Figure: Trial balance: $440

Using the account balances presented below, all of which are normal, prepare a trial balance for El-Tech Company at June 30, 19x1. List the accounts in proper order. Compute the balance of the Cash account.

Accounts Payable	$ 70
Accounts Receivable	140
Cash	?
D. Thomas, Capital	220
Equipment	200
Office Expense	90
Service Revenue	150

SE 10. *Correcting Errors in*
L O 7 *a Trial Balance*
Check Figure: Trial balance: $4,550

The trial balance that follows is out of balance. Assuming all balances are normal, place the accounts in proper order and correct the trial balance so that debits equal credits.

Sanders Boating Service
Trial Balance
January 31, 19x1

Cash		$2,000
Accounts Payable	$ 400	
Fuel Expense	800	
Unearned Service Revenue	250	
Accounts Receivable		1,300
Prepaid Rent		150
T. Sanders, Capital	2,150	
Service Revenue	1,750	
Wages Expense		300
	$5,350	$3,750

EXERCISES

E 1. *Recognition*
L O 1
No check figure

Which of the following events would be recognized and recorded in the accounting records of the Gugini Company on the date indicated?

Jan. 15   Gugini Company offers to purchase a tract of land for $140,000. There is a high likelihood the offer will be accepted. No

Feb.   2   Gugini Company receives notice that its rent will be increased from $500 per month to $600 per month effective March 1. R

Mar. 29   Gugini Company receives its utility bill for the month of March. The bill is not due until April 9. R

June 10   Gugini Company places a firm order for new office equipment costing $21,000. No

July   6   The office equipment ordered on June 10 arrives. Payment is not due until August 1. R

E 2. *Application of*
L O 1 *Recognition Point*
Check Figures: $5,000, $4,100

Skowron's Body Shop uses a large amount of supplies in its business. The following table summarizes selected transaction data for orders of supplies purchased.

Order	Date Shipped	Date Received	Amount
a	June 26	July 5	$ 600
b	July 10	15	1,500
c	16	22	800
d	23	30	1,200
e	27	August 1	1,500
f	August 3	7	1,000

Determine the total purchases of supplies for July alone under each of the following assumptions.

1. Skowron's Body Shop recognizes purchases when orders are shipped.
2. Skowron's Body Shop recognizes purchases when orders are received.

E 3. *Classification of Accounts*
L O 2, 7
No check figure

The following ledger accounts are for the Wonder Service Company.

a. Cash
b. Accounts Receivable
c. Reg Wonder, Capital
d. Reg Wonder, Withdrawals
e. Service Revenue
f. Prepaid Rent
g. Accounts Payable
h. Investments in Stock and Bonds
i. Bonds Payable
j. Land
k. Supplies Expense
l. Prepaid Insurance

m. Utilities Expense
n. Fees Earned
o. Unearned Revenue
p. Office Equipment
q. Rent Payable
r. Notes Receivable
s. Interest Expense
t. Notes Payable
u. Supplies
v. Interest Receivable
w. Rent Expense

Complete the following table, using Xs to indicate each account's classification and normal balance (whether a debit or credit increases the account).

| | | | Type of Account | | | | Normal Balance (increases balance) | |
| | | | Owner's Equity | | | | | |
Item	Asset	Liability	Owner's Capital	Owner's Withdrawals	Revenue	Expense	Debit	Credit
a.	x						x	

E 4. *Transaction Analysis*
L O 4
No check figure

Analyze each of the following transactions, using the form shown in the example below the list.

a. Clarence Davis established Royal Barber Shop by placing $1,200 in a bank account.
b. Paid two months' rent in advance, $420.
c. Purchased supplies on credit, $60.
d. Received cash for barbering services, $50.
e. Paid for supplies purchased in **c.**
f. Paid utility bill, $36.
g. Took cash out of the business for personal expenses, $50.

Example

a. The asset Cash was increased. Increases in assets are recorded by debits. Debit Cash $1,200. Owner's equity was increased by the investment. Increases in owner's equity are recorded by credits. Credit Clarence Davis, Capital $1,200.

E 5. *Recording Transactions in T Accounts*
L O 4
No check figure

Open the following T accounts: Cash; Repair Supplies; Repair Equipment; Accounts Payable; Michelle Donato, Capital; Michelle Donato, Withdrawals; Repair Fees Earned; Salaries Expense; and Rent Expense. Record the following transactions for the month of June directly in the T accounts; use the letters to identify the transactions in your T accounts. Determine the balance in each account.

a. Michelle Donato opened Eastmoor Repair Service by investing $4,300 in cash and $1,600 in repair equipment.
b. Paid $400 for the current month's rent.
c. Purchased repair supplies on credit, $500.
d. Purchased additional repair equipment for cash, $300.
e. Paid salary to a helper, $450.
f. Paid $200 of amount purchased on credit in **c.**
g. Withdrew $600 from the business for living expenses.
h. Accepted cash for repairs completed, $860.

E 6. *Trial Balance*
L O 7
Check Figure: Trial balance: $7,060

After recording the transactions in E 5, prepare a trial balance in proper sequence for Eastmoor Repair Service at June 30, 19xx.

E 7. *Analysis of*
L O 4 *Transactions*
No check figure

Explain each transaction (**a** through **h**) entered in the following T accounts.

Cash			
a.	60,000	b.	15,000
g.	1,500	e.	3,000
h.	900	f.	4,500

Accounts Receivable			
c.	6,000	g.	1,500

Equipment			
b.	15,000	h.	900
d.	9,000		

Accounts Payable			
f.	4,500	d.	9,000

J. Seymour, Capital			
		a.	60,000

Service Revenue			
		c.	6,000

Wages Expense	
e.	3,000

E 8. *Analysis of*
L O 4 *Transactions*
No check figure

Midway Cleanup Company provided monthly waste-removal services for Lakeshore Company, which resulted in the following transactions in Midway's records:

Cash	
Sept. 27	2,000

Accounts Receivable			
Aug. 31	3,000	Sept. 27	2,000

Waste Removal Service Revenue		
	Aug. 31	3,000

Using T accounts, prepare the corresponding entries in Lakeshore's records.

E 9. *Analysis of*
L O 4, 5 *Unfamiliar*
Transactions
No check figure

Managers and accountants often encounter transactions with which they are unfamiliar. Use your analytical skills to analyze and record in general journal form the following transactions, which have not yet been discussed in the text.

May 1 Purchased merchandise inventory on account, $2,400.
    2 Purchased marketable securities for cash, $5,600.
    3 Returned part of merchandise inventory purchased in **a** for full credit, $500.
    4 Sold merchandise inventory on account, $1,600 (record sale only).
    5 Purchased land and a building for $600,000. Payment is $120,000 cash and a thirty-year mortgage for the remainder. The purchase price is allocated $200,000 to the land and $400,000 to the building.
    6 Received an order for $24,000 in services to be provided. With the order was a deposit of $8,000.

E 10. *Recording*
L O 5, 6 *Transactions in the*
General Journal and
Posting to the Ledger
Accounts
No check figure

Open a general journal form like the one in Exhibit 3, and label it Page 10. After opening the form, record the following transactions in the journal.

Dec. 14 Purchased an item of equipment for $6,000, paying $2,000 as a cash down payment.
    28 Paid $3,000 of the amount owed on the equipment.

Prepare three ledger account forms like the one shown in Exhibit 4. Use the following account numbers: Cash, 111; Equipment, 143; and Accounts Payable, 212. Then post the two transactions from the general journal to the ledger accounts, being sure to make proper posting references.

Assume that the Cash account has a debit balance of $8,000 on the day prior to the first transaction.

E 11. *Preparing a Ledger*
L O 6 *Account*
Check Figure: Debit balance: $12,800

Below is a T account showing cash transactions for the month of March.

Cash			
Mar. 1	9,400	Mar. 2	900
7	1,200	4	200
14	4,000	8	1,700
21	200	9	5,000
28	6,400	23	600

Prepare the account in ledger form for Cash (Account 111). (Refer to Exhibit 4 for an example.)

E 12. *Preparing a Trial*
L O 7 *Balance*
Check Figure: Trial balance: $64,300

The accounts of the Emory Service Company as of March 31, 19xx, are listed below in alphabetical order. The amount of Accounts Payable is omitted.

Accounts Payable	?	Equipment	$12,000
Accounts Receivable	$ 3,000	Land	5,200
Building	34,000	Notes Payable	20,000
Cash	9,000	Prepaid Insurance	1,100
Mark Emory, Capital	$31,450		

Prepare a trial balance with the proper heading (see Exhibit 6) and with the accounts listed in the chart of accounts sequence (see Exhibit 1). Compute the balance of Accounts Payable.

E 13. *Effect of Errors on a*
L O 7 *Trial Balance*
No check figure

Which of the following errors would cause a trial balance to have unequal totals? Explain your answers.

a. A payment to a creditor was recorded as a debit to Accounts Payable for $86 and a credit to Cash for $68.
b. A payment of $100 to a creditor for an account payable was debited to Accounts Receivable and credited to Cash.
c. A purchase of office supplies of $280 was recorded as a debit to Office Supplies for $28 and a credit to Cash for $28.
d. A purchase of equipment for $300 was recorded as a debit to Supplies for $300 and a credit to Cash for $300.

E 14. *Correcting Errors in*
L O 7 *a Trial Balance*
Check Figure: Trial balance: $11,870

This was the trial balance for Engelman Services at the end of July.

Engelman Services
Trial Balance
July 31, 19xx

Cash	$ 1,920	
Accounts Receivable	2,830	
Supplies	60	
Prepaid Insurance	90	
Equipment	4,200	
Accounts Payable		$ 2,270
S. Engelman, Capital		5,780
S. Engelman, Withdrawals		350
Revenues		2,960
Salaries Expense	1,300	
Rent Expense	300	
Advertising Expense	170	
Utilities Expense	13	
	$10,883	$11,360

The trial balance does not balance because of a number of errors. Engelman's accountant compared the amounts in the trial balance with the ledger, recomputed the account balances, and compared the postings. He found the following errors:

a. The balance of Cash was understated by $200.
b. A cash payment of $210 was credited to Cash for $120.
c. A debit of $60 to Accounts Receivable was not posted.
d. Supplies purchased for $30 were posted as a credit to Supplies.
e. A debit of $90 to Prepaid Insurance was not posted.
f. The Accounts Payable account had debits of $2,660 and credits of $4,590.

g. The Notes Payable account, with a credit balance of $1,200, was not included in the trial balance.

h. The debit balance of S. Engelman, Withdrawals, was listed in the trial balance as a credit.

i. A $100 debit to S. Engelman, Withdrawals, was posted as a credit.

j. The actual balance of Utilities Expense, $130, was listed as $13 in the trial balance.

Prepare a corrected trial balance.

E 15. *Preparing a Trial*
L O 7 *Balance*

Check Figure: Trial balance: $81,300

The Viola Construction Company builds foundations for buildings and parking lots. The following alphabetical list shows the account balances as of April 30, 19xx.

Accounts Payable	$ 3,900	Prepaid Insurance	$ 4,600
Accounts Receivable	10,120	Revenue Earned	17,400
Cash	?	Supplies Expense	7,200
Construction Supplies	1,900	Utilities Expense	420
Equipment	24,500	Eric Viola, Capital	40,000
Notes Payable	20,000	Eric Viola, Withdrawals	7,800
Office Trailer	2,200	Wages Expense	8,800

Prepare a trial balance for the company with the proper heading and with the accounts in balance sheet sequence. Determine the correct balance for the Cash account on April 30, 19xx.

SKILLS DEVELOPMENT EXERCISES

Conceptual Analysis

SDE 1. *Valuation Issue*
L O 1

No check figure

Nike, Inc. manufactures and markets athletic shoes and related products. In one of the company's annual reports, under "Summary of Significant Accounting Policies," the following statement was made: "Property, plant, and equipment are recorded at cost."[3] Given that the property, plant, and equipment undoubtedly were purchased over several years and that the current value of those assets was likely to be very different from their original cost, tell what authoritative basis there is for carrying the assets at cost. Does accounting generally recognize changes in value subsequent to the purchase of property, plant, and equipment?

SDE 2. *Recognition,*
L O 1, 4 *Valuation, and*
Classification Issues

No check figure

Stauffer Chemical Company relies on agricultural chemicals, such as fertilizer and pesticides, for more than half its profits. One year, Stauffer was hammered by bad weather, depressed farm prices, and decreased farm output caused by a federal price-support program. The *Wall Street Journal* reported that Stauffer had overstated its 1982 earnings by $31.1 million by improperly accounting for certain sales. In settling a suit brought by the Securities and Exchange Commission, the company agreed, without admitting or denying the charges, to restate the 1982 financial results, lowering the 1982 profit by 25 percent. The *Wall Street Journal* summarized the situation as follows:

> In the summer of 1982, "aware that agricultural chemical sales for its 1982–83 season would probably fall off sharply," Stauffer undertook a plan to accelerate sales of certain products to dealers during fiscal 1982, according to the SEC. . . .
>
> Stauffer, the SEC charged, offered its dealers incentives to take products during the fourth quarter of 1982. As a result, the company reported $72 million of revenue that ordinarily wouldn't have been booked until early 1983. By March 1983, according to the commission, Stauffer realized that it would have to "offer its distributors relief" from the oversupply of unsaleable products. Stauffer offered dealers refunds for as much as 100% of unsold products taken in 1982, compared with 32% the previous year.
>
> Stauffer ended up refunding nearly 40% of its 1982 agricultural chemical sales, but failed to disclose the "substantial uncertainties" surrounding the sales in the annual report it filed with the SEC in April 1983. The omission was "materially false and misleading," according to the SEC.

3. Nike, Inc., *Annual Report*, 1994.

"Their business was down and they wanted to accelerate sales," said a government official familiar with the year-long SEC investigation.[4]

1. Prepare the journal entry that Stauffer made in 1982 that the SEC feels should not have been made until 1983.
2. Three issues that must be addressed when recording a transaction are recognition, valuation, and classification. Which of these issues were of most concern to the SEC in the Stauffer case? Explain how each applies to the transaction in **1.**

SDE 3.
L O 4, 5
Analysis of an Unfamiliar Transaction

No check figure

The quotations below are from the annual report of **Shelley Corporation,** a manufacturer of entertainment products.

Long-Term Obligations:
Total long-term debt increased to $160 million at December 31, 1995, from $110 million at year-end 1994. In 1995, $50 million of long-term debt, due 2008, was sold to the public.

Capital Expenditures:
Shelley plans to use the $50 million in proceeds from the sale of the long-term debt, described previously, largely for investments in buildings and equipment related to product assembly and manufacturing. Pending such use, at year-end 1995, the debt proceeds were invested in marketable securities.

1. Discuss what effect the transaction described under "Long-Term Obligations" had on Shelley's balance sheet. Prepare the entry in general journal form to record the transaction.
2. From reading the information under "Capital Expenditures," you know what Shelley did with the proceeds of the sale of long-term debt in 1995 and what the company planned to do with the proceeds in 1996. Before it can carry out these plans, what transactions must occur? Prepare three entries in general journal form to record the one transaction completed in 1995 and the two transactions planned for 1996. Use the Marketable Securities account to record entries related to the investments.

Ethical Dilemma

SDE 4.
L O 1
Recognition Point and Ethical Considerations

No check figure

One of **Penn Office Supplies Corporation**'s sales representatives, Jerry Hasbrow, is compensated on a commission basis and receives a substantial bonus for meeting his annual sales goal. The company's recognition point for sales is the day of shipment. On December 31, Jerry realizes that he needs sales of $2,000 to reach his sales goal and receive a bonus. He calls a purchaser for a local insurance company, whom he knows well, and asks him to buy $2,000 worth of copier paper today. The purchaser says, "But Jerry, that's more than a year's supply for us." Jerry says, "Buy it today. If you decide it's too much, you can return however much you want for full credit next month." The purchaser says, "Okay, ship it." The paper is shipped on December 31 and recorded as a sale. On January 15, the purchaser returns $1,750 worth of paper for full credit (okayed by Jerry) against the bill. Should the shipment on December 31 be recorded as a sale? Discuss the ethics of Jerry's action.

Research Activity

SDE 5.
L O 4, 5
Transactions in a Business Article

No check figure

Obtain a recent issue of one of the following business journals: *Barron's, Business Week, Forbes, Fortune,* or the *Wall Street Journal.* Find an article on a company you recognize or on a company in a business that interests you. Read the article carefully, noting any references to transactions that the company engages in. These may be normal transactions (sales, purchases) or unusual transactions (a merger, the purchase of another company). Bring a copy of the article to class and be prepared to describe how you would analyze and record the transactions you have noted.

---

4. Wynter, Leon E., "Stauffer Profit Overstated in '82, SEC Says in Suit," *The Wall Street Journal,* Aug. 14, 1984. Reprinted by permission of *The Wall Street Journal,* © 1984 Dow Jones and Company, Inc. All Rights Reserved Worldwide.

Decision-Making Practice

SDE 6. *Transaction Analysis*
L O 4, 5, 7 *and Evaluation of a*
Trial Balance

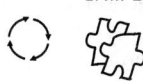

Check Figure: Trial balance: $26,425

Luis Ruiz hired an attorney to help him start Ruiz Repair Service Company. On March 1, Mr. Ruiz invested $11,500 cash in the business. When he paid the attorney's bill of $700, the attorney advised him to hire an accountant to keep his records. Mr. Ruiz was so busy that it was March 31 before he asked you to straighten out his records. Your first task is to develop a trial balance based on the March transactions.

After investing in his business and paying his attorney, Mr. Ruiz borrowed $5,000 from the bank. He later paid $260, including interest of $60, on this loan. He also purchased a used pickup truck in the company's name, paying $2,500 down and financing $7,400. The first payment on the truck is due April 15. Mr. Ruiz then rented an office and paid three months' rent, $900, in advance. Credit purchases of office equipment of $800 and repair tools of $500 must be paid by April 10.

In March, Ruiz Repair Service completed repairs of $1,300, of which $400 were cash transactions. Of the credit transactions, $300 was collected during March, and $600 remained to be collected at the end of March. Wages of $450 were paid to employees. On March 31, the company received a $75 bill for the March utilities expense and a $50 check from a customer for work to be completed in April.

1. Record the March transactions in the general journal. Label each entry alphabetically.
2. Set up T accounts. Then post the general journal entries to the T accounts. Identify each posting with the letter corresponding to the transaction.
3. Determine the balance of each account.
4. Prepare a trial balance for Ruiz Repair Service Company as of March 31.
5. Luis Ruiz is unsure how to evaluate the trial balance. His Cash account balance is $12,440, which exceeds his original investment of $11,500 by $990. Did he make a profit of $990? Explain why the Cash account is not an indicator of business earnings. Cite specific examples to show why it is difficult to determine net income by looking solely at figures in the trial balance.

PROBLEM SET A

A 1. *Transaction*
L O 4, 7 *Analysis, T*
Accounts, and Trial
Balance

Check Figure: Trial balance: $16,450

Pat McNally opened a secretarial school called VIP Secretarial Training.

a. He contributed the following assets to the business.

Cash	$5,700
Computers	4,300
Office Equipment	3,600

b. Found a location for his business and paid the first month's rent, $260.
c. Paid for an advertisement announcing the opening of the school, $190.
d. Received applications from three students for a four-week secretarial program and two students for a ten-day keyboarding course. The students will be billed a total of $1,300.
e. Purchased supplies on credit, $330.
f. Billed the enrolled students, $1,300.
g. Paid an assistant one week's salary, $220.
h. Purchased a second-hand computer, $480, and office equipment, $380, on credit.
i. Paid for the supplies purchased on credit in **e**, $330.
j. Paid cash to repair a broken computer, $40.
k. Billed new students who enrolled late in the course, $440.
l. Transferred cash to a personal checking account, $300.
m. Received partial payment from students previously billed, $1,080.
n. Paid the utility bill for the current month, $90.
o. Paid an assistant one week's salary, $220.
p. Received cash revenue from another new student, $250.

REQUIRED

1. Set up the following T accounts: Cash; Accounts Receivable; Supplies; Computers; Office Equipment; Accounts Payable; Pat McNally, Capital; Pat McNally, Withdrawals; Tuition Revenue; Salaries Expense; Utilities Expense; Rent Expense; Repair Expense; and Advertising Expense.

2. Record the transactions by entering debits and credits directly in the T accounts, using the transaction letter to identify each debit and credit.
3. Prepare a trial balance using today's date.

A 2.
L O 1, 4, 5,
6, 7

Transaction Analysis, General Journal, Ledger Accounts, and Trial Balance

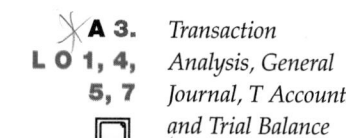

Check Figure: Trial balance: $7,400

Kwan Lee began a rug-cleaning business on October 1 and engaged in the following transactions during the month.

Oct. 1 Began business by transferring $6,000 from his personal bank account to the business bank account.
2 Ordered cleaning supplies, $500.
3 Purchased cleaning equipment for cash, $1,400.
4 Leased a van by making two months' lease payment in advance, $600.
7 Received the cleaning supplies ordered on October 2 and agreed to pay half the amount in ten days and the rest in thirty days.
9 Paid for repairs on the van with cash, $40.
12 Received cash for cleaning carpets, $480.
17 Paid half of the amount owed on supplies purchased on October 7, $250.
21 Billed customers for cleaning carpets, $670.
24 Paid cash for additional repairs on the van, $40.
27 Received $300 from the customers billed on October 21.
31 Withdrew $350 from the business for personal use.

REQUIRED

1. Prepare journal entries to record the above transactions in the general journal (Pages 1 and 2). Use the accounts listed below.
2. Set up the following ledger accounts and post the journal entries: Cash (111); Accounts Receivable (113); Cleaning Supplies (115); Prepaid Lease (116); Cleaning Equipment (141); Accounts Payable (211); Kwan Lee, Capital (311); Kwan Lee, Withdrawals (312); Cleaning Revenues (411); and Repair Expense (511).
3. Prepare a trial balance for Lee Carpet-Cleaning Service as of October 31, 19xx.

A 3.
L O 1, 4,
5, 7

Transaction Analysis, General Journal, T Accounts, and Trial Balance

Check Figure: Trial balance: $11,550

John Powers is a house painter. During the month of April, he completed the following transactions.

Apr. 2 Began his business with equipment valued at $1,230 and placed $7,100 in a business checking account.
3 Purchased a used truck costing $1,900. Paid $500 cash and signed a note for the balance.
4 Purchased supplies on account for $320.
5 Completed a painting job and billed the customer $480.
7 Received $150 in cash for painting two rooms.
8 Hired an assistant at $6 per hour.
10 Purchased supplies for $160 in cash.
11 Received a $480 check from the customer billed on April 5.
12 Paid $400 for an insurance policy for eighteen months' coverage.
13 Billed a customer $620 for a painting job.
14 Paid the assistant $150 for twenty-five hours' work.
15 Paid $40 for a tune-up for the truck.
18 Paid for the supplies purchased on April 4.
20 Purchased a new ladder (equipment) for $60 and supplies for $290, on account.
22 Received a telephone bill for $60, due next month.
23 Received $330 in cash from the customer billed on April 13.
24 Transferred $300 to a personal checking account.
25 Received $360 in cash for painting a five-room apartment.
27 Paid $200 on the note signed for the truck.
29 Paid the assistant $180 for thirty hours' work.

REQUIRED

1. Prepare journal entries to record the above transactions in the general journal. Use the accounts listed below.
2. Set up the following T accounts and post all the journal entries: Cash; Accounts Receivable; Supplies; Prepaid Insurance; Equipment; Truck; Notes Payable; Accounts Payable; John Powers, Capital; John Powers, Withdrawals; Painting Fees Earned; Wages Expense; Telephone Expense; and Truck Expense.

3. Prepare a trial balance for Powers Painting Service as of April 30, 19xx.
4. Compare how recognition applies to the transactions of April 5 and 7 and how classification applies to the transactions of April 12 and 14.

A 4. *Transaction*
L O 4, 5, *Analysis, General*
6, 7 *Journal, Ledger*
Accounts, and Trial
Balance

Check Figure: Trial balance: $10,880

The account balances for Lou's Landscaping Service at the end of July are presented in the trial balance shown below. During August, Mr. Jacobson completed the following transactions.

Aug. 1 Paid for supplies purchased on credit last month, $140.
2 Billed customers for services, $410.
3 Paid the lease on a truck, $290.
5 Purchased supplies on credit, $150.
7 Received cash from customers not previously billed, $290.
8 Purchased new equipment from Pendleton Manufacturing Company on account, $1,300.
9 Received a bill for an oil change on the truck, $40.
12 Returned a portion of the equipment that was purchased on August 8 for a credit, $320.
13 Received payments from customers previously billed, $190.
14 Paid the bill received on August 9.
16 Took cash from the business for personal use, $110.
19 Paid for the supplies purchased on August 5.
20 Billed customers for services, $270.
23 Purchased equipment from a friend who is retiring, $280. Payment was made from Lou's personal checking account, but the equipment will be used in the business. (**Hint:** Treat this as an owner's investment.)
25 Received payments from customers previously billed, $390.
27 Purchased gasoline for the truck with cash, $30.
29 Made a payment to reduce the principal of the note payable, $600.

Lou's Landscaping Service
Trial Balance
July 31, 19xx

Cash (111)	$3,100	
Accounts Receivable (113)	220	
Supplies (115)	460	
Prepaid Insurance (116)	400	
Equipment (141)	4,400	
Notes Payable (211)		$3,000
Accounts Payable (212)		700
Lou Jacobson, Capital (311)		4,200
Lou Jacobson, Withdrawals (312)	420	
Service Revenue (411)		1,490
Lease Expense (511)	290	
Truck Expense (512)	100	
	$9,390	$9,390

REQUIRED

1. Open ledger accounts for the accounts shown in the trial balance. Enter the July 31 trial balance amounts in the ledger accounts.
2. Prepare journal entries to record the August transactions in the general journal (Pages 11, 12, and 13).
3. Post the entries to the ledger accounts.
4. Prepare a trial balance as of August 31, 19xx.

A 5. *Relationship of*
L O 4, 5, *General Journal,*
6, 7 *Ledger Accounts,*
and Trial Balance

Check Figure: Trial balance: $23,515

The Other Mother Child Care Company provides babysitting and child care programs. On January 31, 19xx, the company had a trial balance as shown below. During the month of February, the company completed the following transactions.

Feb. 2 Paid this month's rent, $270.
3 Received fees for this month's services, $650.
4 Purchased supplies on account, $85.
5 Reimbursed the bus driver for gas expenses, $40.
6 Ordered playground equipment, $1,000.
7 Paid part-time assistants for two weeks' services, $230.
8 Made a payment on account, $170.
9 Received payments from customers on account, $1,200.
10 Billed customers who had not yet paid for this month's services, $700.
11 Paid for the supplies purchased on February 4.
13 Purchased playground equipment for cash, $1,000.
14 Withdrew cash for personal expenses, $110.
17 Contributed equipment to the business, $290.
19 Paid this month's utility bill, $145.
21 Paid part-time assistants for two weeks' services, $230.
22 Received payment for one month's services from customers previously billed, $500.
27 Purchased gas and oil for the bus on account, $35.
28 Paid for a one-year insurance policy, $290.

Other Mother Child Care Company
Trial Balance
January 31, 19xx

Cash (111)	$ 1,870	
Accounts Receivable (113)	1,700	
Equipment (141)	1,040	
Buses (143)	17,400	
Notes Payable (211)		$15,000
Accounts Payable (212)		1,640
Esther Clay, Capital (311)		5,370
	$22,010	$22,010

REQUIRED

1. Open accounts in the ledger for the accounts in the trial balance plus the following ones: Supplies (115); Prepaid Insurance (116); Esther Clay, Withdrawals (312); Service Revenue (411); Rent Expense (511); Bus Expense (512); Wages Expense (513); and Utilities Expense (514).
2. Enter the January 31, 19xx account balances from the trial balance.
3. Enter the above transactions in the general journal (Pages 17, 18, and 19).
4. Post the entries to the ledger accounts. Be sure to make the appropriate posting references in the journal and ledger as you post.
5. Prepare a trial balance as of February 29, 19xx.

PROBLEM SET B

B 1. *Transaction*
L O 4, 7 *Analysis, T*
Accounts, and Trial
Balance

Check Figure: Trial balance: $21,100

Diane Pastore established a small business, Pastore Training Center, to teach individuals how to use spreadsheet analysis, word processing, and other techniques on microcomputers.

a. Pastore began by transferring the following assets to the business.

Cash	$9,200
Furniture	3,100
Microcomputers	7,300

b. Paid the first month's rent on a small storefront, $580.
c. Purchased computer software on credit, $750.
d. Paid for an advertisement in the school newspaper, $100.
e. Received enrollment applications from five students for a five-day course to start next week. Each student will pay $200 if he or she actually begins the course.
f. Paid wages to a part-time helper, $150.
g. Received cash payment from three of the students enrolled in **e,** $600.
h. Billed the two other students in **e,** who attended but did not pay in cash, $400.
i. Paid the utility bill for the current month, $110.
j. Made a payment on the software purchased in **c,** $250.
k. Received payment from one student billed in **h,** $200.
l. Purchased a second microcomputer for cash, $4,700.
m. Transferred cash to personal checking account, $300.

REQUIRED

1. Set up the following T accounts: Cash; Accounts Receivable; Software; Furniture; Microcomputers; Accounts Payable; Diane Pastore, Capital; Diane Pastore, Withdrawals; Tuition Revenue; Wages Expense; Utilities Expense; Rent Expense; and Advertising Expense.
2. Record the transactions by entering debits and credits directly in the T accounts, using the transaction letter to identify each debit and credit.
3. Prepare a trial balance using the current date.

B 2.
L O 1, 4, 5, 6, 7
Transaction Analysis, General Journal, Ledger Accounts, and Trial Balance
Check Figure: Trial balance: $22,780

Vic Kostro opened a photography and portrait studio on March 1 and completed the following transactions during the month.

Mar. 1 Opened the business checking account, $17,000.
2 Paid two months' rent in advance for a studio, $900.
3 Transferred to the business personal photography equipment valued at $4,300.
4 Ordered additional photography equipment, $2,500.
5 Purchased office equipment for cash, $1,800.
8 Received and paid for the photography equipment ordered on March 4, $2,500.
10 Purchased photography supplies on credit, $700.
15 Received cash for portraits, $380.
16 Billed customers for portraits, $750.
21 Paid for half the supplies purchased on March 10, $350.
24 Paid the utility bill for March, $120.
25 Paid the telephone bill for March, $70.
29 Received payment from the customers billed on March 16, $250.
30 Paid wages to an assistant, $400.
31 Withdrew cash for personal expenses, $1,200.

REQUIRED

1. Prepare journal entries to record the above transactions in the general journal (Pages 1, 2, and 3).
2. Set up the following ledger accounts and post the journal entries: Cash (111); Accounts Receivable (113); Photography Supplies (115); Prepaid Rent (116); Photography Equipment (141); Office Equipment (143); Accounts Payable (211); Vic Kostro, Capital (311); Vic Kostro, Withdrawals (312); Portrait Revenue (411); Wages Expense (511); Utilities Expense (512); and Telephone Expense (513).
3. Prepare a trial balance for Kostro Portrait Studio as of March 31, 19xx.

B 3.
L O 1, 4, 5, 7
Transaction Analysis, General Journal, T Accounts, and Trial Balance
Check Figure: Trial balance: $10,540

Hassan Rahim won a concession to rent bicycles in the local park during the summer. During the month of June, Hassan completed the following transactions for his bicycle rental business.

June 2 Began business by placing $7,200 in a business checking account.
3 Purchased supplies on account for $150.
4 Purchased ten bicycles for $2,500, paying $1,200 down and agreeing to pay the rest in thirty days.
5 Paid $2,900 in cash for a small shed to store the bicycles and use for other operations.
6 Received $470 in cash for rentals during the first week of operation.

June 8 Paid $400 in cash for shipping and installation costs (considered an addition to the cost of the shed) to place the shed at the park entrance.
9 Hired a part-time assistant to help out on weekends at $7 per hour.
10 Paid a maintenance person $75 to clean the grounds.
13 Received $500 in cash for rentals during the second week of operation.
16 Paid the assistant $80 for a weekend's work.
17 Paid $150 for the supplies purchased on June 3.
18 Paid a $55 repair bill on bicycles.
20 Received $550 in cash for rentals during the third week of operation.
22 Paid the assistant $80 for a weekend's work.
23 Billed a company $110 for bicycle rentals for an employee outing.
25 Paid the $100 fee for June to the Park District for the right to the bicycle concession.
27 Received $410 in cash for rentals during the week.
29 Paid the assistant $80 for a weekend's work.
30 Transferred $500 to personal checking account.

REQUIRED

1. Prepare journal entries to record these transactions in the general journal.
2. Set up the following T accounts and post all the journal entries: Cash; Accounts Receivable; Supplies; Shed; Bicycles; Accounts Payable; Hassan Rahim, Capital; Hassan Rahim, Withdrawals; Rental Revenue; Wages Expense; Maintenance Expense; Repair Expense; and Concession Fee Expense.
3. Prepare a trial balance for Rahim Rentals as of June 30, 19xx.
4. Compare how recognition applies to the transactions of June 23 and 27 and how classification applies to the transactions of June 8 and 10.

B 4. *Transaction*
L O 4, 5, *Analysis, General*
6, 7 *Journal, Ledger Accounts, and Trial Balance*
Check Figure: Trial balance: $56,960

Delta Security Service provides ushers and security personnel for athletic events and other functions. Delta's trial balance at the end of April was as shown below.

Delta Security Service
Trial Balance
April 30, 19xx

Cash (111)	$13,300	
Accounts Receivable (113)	9,400	
Supplies (115)	560	
Prepaid Insurance (116)	600	
Equipment (141)	7,800	
Accounts Payable (211)		$ 5,300
Dennis Kinsella, Capital (311)		21,160
Dennis Kinsella, Withdrawals (312)	2,000	
Security Services Revenue (411)		28,000
Wages Expense (512)	16,000	
Rent Expense (513)	3,200	
Utilities Expense (514)	1,600	
	$54,460	$54,460

During May, Delta engaged in the following transactions.

May 1 Received cash from customers billed last month, $4,200.
2 Made a payment on accounts payable, $3,100.
3 Purchased a new one-year insurance policy in advance, $3,600.
5 Purchased supplies on credit, $430.
6 Billed a client for security services, $2,200.
7 Made a rent payment for May, $800.
9 Received cash from customers for security services, $1,600.
14 Paid wages for the security staff, $1,400.
16 Ordered equipment, $800.

May 17 Paid the current month's utility bill, $400.
 18 Received and paid for the equipment ordered on May 16, $800.
 19 Returned for full credit some of the supplies purchased on May 5 because they were defective, $120.
 24 Withdrew cash for personal expenses, $1,000.
 28 Paid for supplies purchased on May 5, less the return on May 19, $310.
 30 Billed a customer for security services performed, $1,800.
 31 Paid wages to the security staff, $1,050.

REQUIRED

1. Prepare journal entries to record the above transactions in the general journal (Pages 26, 27, and 28).
2. Open ledger accounts for the accounts shown in the trial balance. Enter the April 30 trial balance amounts in the ledger.
3. Post the journal entries to the ledger.
4. Prepare a trial balance as of May 31, 19xx.

B 5. *Relationship of*
L O 4, 5, *General Journal,*
6, 7 *Ledger Accounts,*
and Trial Balance
Check Figure: Trial balance: $30,710

Embassy Communications Company is a public relations firm. On July 31, 19xx, the company's trial balance was as shown below. During the month of August, the company completed the following transactions.

Aug. 2 Paid rent for August, $650.
 3 Received cash from customers on account, $2,300.
 7 Ordered supplies, $380.
 10 Billed customers for services provided, $2,800.
 12 Made a payment on accounts payable, $1,100.
 14 Received the supplies ordered on August 7 and agreed to pay for them in thirty days, $380.
 15 Paid salaries for the first half of August, $1,900.
 17 Discovered some of the supplies were not as ordered and returned them for full credit, $80.
 19 Received cash from a customer for services provided, $4,800.
 24 Paid the utility bill for August, $160.
 25 Paid the telephone bill for August, $120.
 26 Received a bill, to be paid in September, for advertisements placed in the local newspaper during the month of August to promote Embassy Communications, $700.
 29 Billed a customer for services provided, $2,700.
 30 Paid salaries for the last half of August, $1,900.
 31 Withdrew cash for personal use, $1,200.

Embassy Communications Company
Trial Balance
July 31, 19xx

Cash (111)	$10,200	
Accounts Receivable (113)	5,500	
Supplies (115)	610	
Office Equipment (141)	4,200	
Accounts Payable (211)		$ 2,600
Beth Logan, Capital (311)		17,910
	$20,510	$20,510

REQUIRED

1. Enter the above transactions in the general journal (Pages 22 and 23).
2. Open accounts in the ledger for the accounts in the trial balance plus the following accounts: Beth Logan, Withdrawals (312); Public Relations Fees (411); Salaries Expense (511); Rent Expense (512); Utilities Expense (513); Telephone Expense (514); and Advertising Expense (515).

3. Enter the July 31 account balances from the trial balance to the appropriate ledger account forms.
4. Post the entries to the ledger accounts. Be sure to make the appropriate posting references in the journal and ledger as you post.
5. Prepare a trial balance as of August 31, 19xx.

FINANCIAL REPORTING AND ANALYSIS CASES

Interpreting Financial Reports

FRA 1.
L O 2, 4, 5

Interpreting a Bank's Financial Statements

No check figure

First Chicago Corp. is the largest bank holding company in Illinois. Selected accounts from the company's 1993 annual report are as follows (in millions):[5]

Cash and Due from Banks	$ 9,953
Loans to Customers	22,420
Investment Securities	2,256
Deposits by Customers	28,186

REQUIRED

1. Indicate whether each of the accounts just listed is an asset, a liability, or a component of owner's equity on First Chicago's balance sheet.
2. Assume that you are in a position to do business with First Chicago. Prepare the general journal entry (Page 1 of First Chicago's records) to record each of the following transactions:
   a. You sell securities in the amount of $2,000 to the bank.
   b. You deposit the $2,000 received in step **a** in the bank.
   c. You borrow $5,000 from the bank.

International Company

FRA 2.
L O 5

Transaction Analysis

No check figure

United Biscuits, a United Kingdom company with operations in twenty-eight countries, is a leading producer of snack foods. Under the Keebler brand, it is the second-largest manufacturer of cookies and crackers in the United States. The following selected aggregate cash transactions were reported in the statement of cash flows in its 1992 annual report (amounts in millions).[6]

Interest paid, £42.5
Interest received, £6.4
Purchase of investments, £1.7
Proceeds from new borrowings (Loans Payable), £87.1
Repayments of borrowings (Loans Payable), £9.5

REQUIRED

Prepare journal entries to record the above transactions.

Toys "R" Us Annual Report

FRA 3.
L O 4
No check figure

Transaction Analysis

Refer to the balance sheet in the appendix on Toys "R" Us. Prepare T accounts for the accounts Cash and Cash Equivalents, Accounts and Other Receivables, Prepaid Expenses and Other, Accounts Payable, and Income Taxes Payable. Properly place the balance of the account at January 28, 1995 in the T accounts. Below are some typical transactions in which Toys "R" Us would engage. Analyze each transaction, enter it in the T accounts, and determine the balance of each account. Assume all entries are in thousands.

a. Paid cash in advance for certain expenses, $20,000.
b. Received cash from customers billed previously, $35,000.
c. Paid cash for income taxes previously owed, $24,000.
d. Paid cash to suppliers for amounts owed, $120,000.

5. First Chicago Corp., *Annual Report*, 1993.
6. United Biscuits, *Annual Report*, 1992.

Measuring Business Income

1. Define *net income* and its two major components, *revenues* and *expenses*.
2. Explain the difficulties of income measurement caused by (a) the accounting period issue, (b) the continuity issue, and (c) the matching issue.
3. Define *accrual accounting* and explain two broad ways of accomplishing it.
4. State four principal situations that require adjusting entries.
5. Prepare typical adjusting entries.
6. Prepare financial statements from an adjusted trial balance.
7. Analyze cash flows from accrual-based information.

Gannett Co., Inc.

Gannett Co., Inc. is the United States' largest newspaper publisher, with eighty-three dailies, including *USA Today*. The company also operates broadcasting stations and outdoor advertising businesses, and provides other services. Gannett has 36,500 employees, and payroll is its largest expense.[1] During most of the year, payroll is recorded as an expense when it is paid. However, at the end of the year employees may have earned compensation (wages or salaries) that will not be paid until the beginning of the next year. If these wages and salaries are not accounted for correctly, they will appear in the wrong year—the year in which they are paid instead of the year in which the company benefited from them. How does accounting solve this problem?

According to the concepts of accrual accounting and the matching rule, which you will learn in this chapter, the accountant must determine the amount of wages and salaries earned but not paid and record an adjusting entry for the amount as an expense of the current year and a liability to be paid the next year. In this way, expenses are correctly stated on the income statement and liabilities are correctly stated on the balance sheet. In the case of Gannett, the effect is significant. At the end of 1993, Gannett had a liability for compensation of $53,922,000. If an adjusting entry had not been made to record the liability and its related expense in 1993, income before taxes would have been overstated by $53,922,000. Given that income after deducting the compensation expense in 1993 was $722,374,000, without the adjusting entry, readers of the financial statements would have been misled into thinking that Gannett's income was 7.5 percent greater than it actually was. ⣿

THE MEASUREMENT OF BUSINESS INCOME

OBJECTIVE

1 *Define* net income *and its* two major components, revenues *and* expenses

For a business to succeed, or even to survive, it must earn a profit. The word profit, though, has many meanings. One is the increase in owner's equity that results from business operations. However, even this definition can be interpreted differently by economists, lawyers, business people, and the public. Because the word *profit* has more than one meaning, accountants prefer to use

1. Gannett Co., Inc., *Annual Report,* 1993.

the term *net income,* which can be precisely defined from an accounting point of view. Net income is reported on the income statement and is used by management, owners, and others to monitor business performance. Readers of income statements need to understand how the accountant defines net income and be aware of its strengths and weaknesses as a measure of company performance.

NET INCOME

Net income is the net increase in owner's equity that results from the operations of a company and that is accumulated in the Capital account. Net income, in its simplest form, is measured by the difference between revenues and expenses when revenues exceed expenses:

$$\text{Net income} = \text{revenues} - \text{expenses}$$

When expenses exceed revenues, a net loss occurs.

Revenues   Revenues are increases in owner's equity resulting from selling goods, rendering services, or performing other business activities. In the simplest case, revenues equal the price of goods sold and services rendered over a specific period of time. When a business delivers a product or provides a service to a customer, it usually receives either cash or a promise to pay cash in the near future. The promise to pay is recorded in either Accounts Receivable or Notes Receivable. The revenue for a given period equals the total of cash and receivables from goods and services provided to customers during that period.

Liabilities generally are not affected by revenues, and some transactions that increase cash and other assets are not revenues. For example, a bank loan increases liabilities and cash but does not produce revenue. The collection of accounts receivable, which increases cash and decreases accounts receivable, does not produce revenue either. Remember that when a sale on credit takes place, the asset account Accounts Receivable increases; at the same time, an owner's equity revenue account increases. So counting the collection of the receivable as revenue later would be counting the same sale twice.

Not all increases in owner's equity arise from revenues. Owner's investments increase owner's equity but are not revenue.

Expenses   Expenses are decreases in owner's equity resulting from the costs of selling goods, rendering services, or performing other business activities. In other words, expenses are the costs of the goods and services used up in the course of earning revenues. Often called the *cost of doing business,* expenses include the costs of goods sold, the costs of activities necessary to carry on a business, and the costs of attracting and serving customers. Examples are salaries, rent, advertising, telephone service, and depreciation (allocation of cost) of a building or office equipment.

Just as not all cash receipts are revenues, not all cash payments are expenses. A cash payment to reduce a liability does not result in an expense. The liability, however, may have come from incurring a previous expense, such as advertising, that is to be paid later. There may also be two steps before an expenditure of cash becomes an expense. For example, prepaid expenses or plant assets (such as machinery and equipment) are recorded as assets when they are acquired. Later, as their usefulness expires in the operation of the business, their cost is allocated to expenses. In fact, expenses sometimes are called *expired costs.*

Not all decreases in owner's equity arise from expenses. Withdrawals by the owner decrease owner's equity, but they are not expenses.

Temporary and Permanent Accounts   Revenues and expenses can be recorded directly in the owner's Capital account as increases and decreases. In practice, however, management and others want to know the details of the increases and decreases in owner's equity produced by revenues and expenses. For this reason, a separate account for each revenue and expense is needed to accumulate the amounts. Because the balances of these income statement accounts apply only to the current accounting period, they are called temporary accounts.

Temporary accounts, or *nominal accounts,* show the accumulation of revenues and expenses over one accounting period. At the end of the accounting period, their balances are transferred to owner's equity. Thus, nominal accounts start each accounting period with zero balances and then accumulate the specific revenues and expenses of that period. On the other hand, the balance sheet accounts—assets, liabilities, and the owner's Capital account—are called permanent accounts, or *real accounts,* because their balances extend beyond the end of an accounting period.

OBJECTIVE

2a *Explain the difficulties of income measurement caused by the accounting period issue*

THE ACCOUNTING PERIOD ISSUE

The accounting period issue addresses the difficulty of assigning revenues and expenses to a short period of time, such as a month or a year. Not all transactions can be easily assigned to specific time periods. Purchases of buildings and equipment, for example, have effects that extend over many years. Accountants solve this problem by estimating the number of years the buildings or equipment will be in use and the cost that should be assigned to each year. In the process, they make an assumption about periodicity: that the net income for any period of time less than the life of the business, although tentative, is still a useful estimate of the net income for the period.

Generally, to make comparisons easier, the time periods are of equal length. Financial statements may be prepared for any time period. Accounting periods of less than one year—for example, a month or a quarter—are called *interim periods.* The twelve-month accounting period used by a company is called its fiscal year. Many companies use the calendar year, January 1 to December 31, for their fiscal year. Others find it convenient to choose a fiscal year that ends during a slack season rather than a peak season. In this case, the fiscal year corresponds to the company's yearly cycle of business activity. The time period should always be noted in the financial statements.

OBJECTIVE

2b *Explain the difficulties of income measurement caused by the continuity issue*

THE CONTINUITY ISSUE

The process of measuring business income requires that certain expense and revenue transactions be allocated over several accounting periods. The number of accounting periods raises the continuity issue: How long will the business entity last? Many businesses last less than five years; in any given year, thousands go bankrupt. To prepare financial statements for an accounting period, the accountant must make an assumption about the ability of the business to survive. Specifically, unless there is evidence to the contrary, the accountant assumes that the business will continue to operate indefinitely, that the business is a going concern. Justification for all the techniques of income measurement rests on the assumption of continuity. For example, this assumption allows the costs of certain assets to be held on the balance sheet until future years, when they will become expenses on the income statement.

Another example has to do with the value of assets on the balance sheet. The accountant records assets at cost and does not record subsequent changes in their value. But the value of assets to a going concern is much higher than the value of assets to a firm facing bankruptcy. In the latter case, the accountant may be asked to set aside the assumption of continuity and to prepare financial statements based on the assumption that the firm will go out of business and sell all of its assets at liquidation value—that is, for what they will bring in cash.

BUSINESS BULLETIN: BUSINESS PRACTICE

The list below shows the diverse fiscal years used by some well-known companies.

Company	Last Month of Fiscal Year
American Greetings Corp.	February
Caesars World, Inc.	July
The Walt Disney Company	September
Eastman Kodak Company	December
Fleetwood Enterprises, Inc.	April
Lorimar	March
Mattel Inc.	December
MGM/UA Communications Co.	August
Polaroid Corp.	December

Many governmental and educational units use fiscal years that end June 30 or September 30. =====

OBJECTIVE

2c *Explain the difficulties of income measurement caused by the matching issue*

THE MATCHING ISSUE

Revenues and expenses can be accounted for on a cash received and cash paid basis. This practice is known as the cash basis of accounting. In certain cases, an individual or business may use the cash basis of accounting for income tax purposes. Under this method, revenues are reported in the period in which cash is received, and expenses are reported in the period in which cash is paid. Taxable income, therefore, is calculated as the difference between cash receipts from revenues and cash payments for expenses.

Although the cash basis of accounting works well for some small businesses and many individuals, it does not meet the needs of most businesses. As explained above, revenues can be earned in a period other than the one in which cash is received, and expenses can be incurred in a period other than the one in which cash is paid. To measure net income adequately, revenues and expenses must be assigned to the appropriate accounting period. The accountant solves this problem by applying the matching rule:

> Revenues must be assigned to the accounting period in which the goods are sold or the services performed, and expenses must be assigned to the accounting period in which they are used to produce revenue.

Direct cause-and-effect relationships seldom can be demonstrated for certain, but many costs appear to be related to particular revenues. The accountant recognizes these expenses and the related revenues in the same accounting period. Examples are the costs of goods sold and sales commissions. When there is no direct means of connecting expenses and revenues, the accountant tries to allocate costs in a systematic way among the accounting periods that benefit from the costs. For example, a building is converted from an asset to an expense by allocating its cost over the years that the company benefits from its use.

ACCRUAL ACCOUNTING

OBJECTIVE

3 *Define* accrual accounting *and explain two broad ways of accomplishing it*

To apply the matching rule, accountants have developed accrual accounting. Accrual accounting "attempts to record the financial effects on an enterprise of transactions and other events and circumstances . . . in the periods in which those transactions, events, and circumstances occur rather than only in the periods in which cash is received or paid by the enterprise."[2] That is, accrual accounting consists of all the techniques developed by accountants to apply the matching rule. It is done in two general ways: (1) by recording revenues when earned and expenses when incurred and (2) by adjusting the accounts.

RECOGNIZING REVENUES WHEN EARNED AND EXPENSES WHEN INCURRED

The first method of accrual accounting is the recognition of revenues when earned and expenses when incurred. For example, when Joan Miller Advertising Agency makes a sale on credit by placing advertisements for a client, revenue is recorded at the time of the sale by debiting Accounts Receivable and crediting Advertising Fees Earned. This is how the accountant recognizes the revenue from a credit sale before the cash is collected. Accounts Receivable serves as a holding account until payment is received. The process of determining when a sale takes place is called revenue recognition.

When Joan Miller Advertising Agency receives a telephone bill, the expense is recognized both as having been incurred and as having helped to produce revenue in the current month. The transaction is recorded by debiting Telephone Expense and crediting Accounts Payable. Until the bill is paid, Accounts Payable serves as a holding account. Notice that recognition of the expense does not depend on the payment of cash.

ADJUSTING THE ACCOUNTS

An accounting period, by definition, ends on a particular day. The balance sheet must list all assets and liabilities as of the end of that day, and the income statement must contain all revenues and expenses applicable to the period ending on that day. Although operating a business is a continuous

---

2. *Statement of Financial Accounting Concepts No. 1,* "Objectives of Financial Reporting by Business Enterprises" (Stamford, Conn.: Financial Accounting Standards Board, 1978), par. 44.

Exhibit 1. Trial Balance for Joan Miller Advertising Agency

Joan Miller Advertising Agency
Trial Balance
January 31, 19xx

Cash	$ 1,720	
Accounts Receivable	2,800	
Art Supplies	1,800	
Office Supplies	800	
Prepaid Rent	800	
Prepaid Insurance	480	
Art Equipment	4,200	
Office Equipment	3,000	
Accounts Payable		$ 3,170
Unearned Art Fees		1,000
Joan Miller, Capital		10,000
Joan Miller, Withdrawals	1,400	
Advertising Fees Earned		4,200
Wages Expense	1,200	
Utilities Expense	100	
Telephone Expense	70	
	$18,370	$18,370

process, there must be a cutoff point for the periodic reports. Some transactions invariably span the cutoff point; thus, some accounts need adjustment.

For example, some of the accounts in the end-of-the-period trial balance for Joan Miller Advertising Agency (Exhibit 1) do not show the correct balances for preparing the financial statements. The January 31 trial balance lists prepaid rent of $800. At $400 per month, this represents rent for the months of January and February. So on January 31, one-half of the $800, or $400, represents rent expense for January; the remaining $400 represents an asset that will be used in February. An adjustment is needed to reflect the $400 balance in the Prepaid Rent account on the balance sheet and the $400 rent expense on the income statement. As you will see on the following pages, several other accounts in the Joan Miller Advertising Agency trial balance do not reflect their correct balances. Like the Prepaid Rent account, they need to be adjusted.

THE ADJUSTMENT PROCESS

OBJECTIVE

4 *State four principal situations that require adjusting entries*

Accountants use adjusting entries to apply accrual accounting to transactions that span more than one accounting period. Adjusting entries have at least one balance sheet (or permanent) account entry and at least one income statement (or temporary) account entry. Adjusting entries never involve the Cash account. They are needed when deferrals or accruals exist. A deferral is the postponement of the recognition of an expense already paid or incurred, or of a revenue already received. Deferrals are used in two instances:

1. Costs have been recorded that must be apportioned between two or more accounting periods. Examples are prepaid rent, prepaid insurance, supplies, and costs of a building. The adjusting entry in this case involves an asset account and an expense account.
2. Revenues have been recorded that must be apportioned between two or more accounting periods. An example is payments collected for services yet to be rendered. The adjusting entry involves a liability account and a revenue account.

An accrual is the recognition of a revenue or expense that has arisen but has not yet been recorded. Accruals are required in two cases:

1. Revenues have been earned but not yet recorded. An example is fees earned but not yet collected or billed to customers. The adjusting entry involves an asset account and a revenue account.
2. Expenses have been incurred but are not yet recorded. Examples are the wages earned by employees in the current accounting period but after the last pay period. The adjusting entry involves an expense account and a liability account.

Once again, we use Joan Miller Advertising Agency to illustrate the kinds of adjusting entries that most businesses must make.

APPORTIONING RECORDED EXPENSES BETWEEN TWO OR MORE ACCOUNTING PERIODS (DEFERRED EXPENSES)

OBJECTIVE

5 *Prepare typical adjusting entries*

Companies often make expenditures that benefit more than one period. These expenditures are usually debited to an asset account. At the end of the accounting period, the amount that has been used is transferred from the asset account to an expense account. Two of the more important kinds of adjustments are for prepaid expenses and the depreciation of plant and equipment.

Prepaid Expenses   Some expenses customarily are paid in advance. These expenditures are called prepaid expenses. Among them are rent, insurance, and supplies. At the end of an accounting period, a portion (or all) of these goods or services will have been used up or will have expired. An adjusting entry reducing the asset and increasing the expense, as shown in Figure 1, is always required. The amount of the adjustment equals the cost of the goods or services used up or expired. If adjusting entries for prepaid expenses are

Figure 1. Adjustment for Prepaid (Deferred) Expense

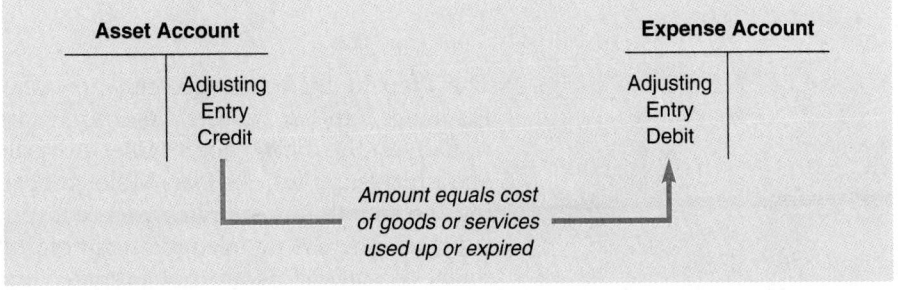

not made at the end of the period, both the balance sheet and the income statement will present incorrect information: The assets of the company will be overstated, and the expenses of the company will be understated. This means that owner's equity on the balance sheet and net income on the income statement will be overstated.

At the beginning of the month, Joan Miller Advertising Agency paid two months' rent in advance. This expenditure resulted in an asset consisting of the right to occupy the office for two months. As each day in the month passed, part of the asset's cost expired and became an expense. By January 31, one-half had expired and should be treated as an expense. Here is the analysis of this economic event.

PREPAID RENT (ADJUSTMENT A)

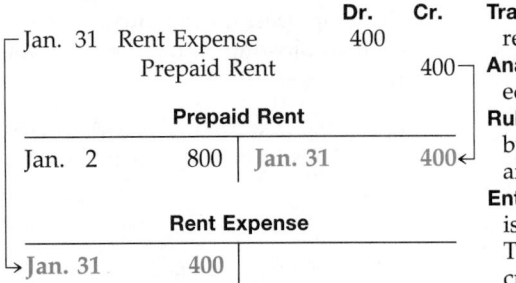

The Prepaid Rent account now has a balance of $400, which represents one month's rent paid in advance. The Rent Expense account reflects the $400 expense for the month of January.

Besides rent, Joan Miller Advertising Agency prepaid expenses for insurance, art supplies, and office supplies, all of which call for adjusting entries.

On January 8, the agency purchased a one-year life insurance policy, paying $480 for it in advance. Like prepaid rent, prepaid insurance offers benefits (in this case, protection) that expire day by day. By the end of the month, one-twelfth of the protection had expired. The adjustment is analyzed and recorded as follows:

PREPAID INSURANCE (ADJUSTMENT B)

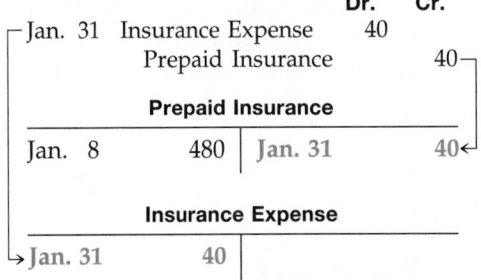

The Prepaid Insurance account now shows the correct balance, $440, and Insurance Expense reflects the expired cost, $40, for the month.

Early in the month, Joan Miller Advertising Agency purchased art supplies and office supplies. As Joan Miller prepared artwork for various clients during the month, art supplies were consumed. And her secretary used office supplies. There is no need to account for these supplies every day because the financial statements are not prepared until the end of the month and the recordkeeping would involve too much work. Instead, Joan Miller makes a careful inventory of the art and office supplies at the end of the month. The inventory records the number and cost of the supplies that are still assets of the company—that are yet to be consumed.

Suppose the inventory shows that art supplies costing $1,300 and office supplies costing $600 are still on hand. It means that of the $1,800 of art supplies originally purchased, $500 worth were used up (became an expense) in January. Of the original $800 of office supplies, $200 worth were consumed. The transactions are analyzed and recorded as follows:

ART SUPPLIES AND OFFICE SUPPLIES (ADJUSTMENTS C AND D)

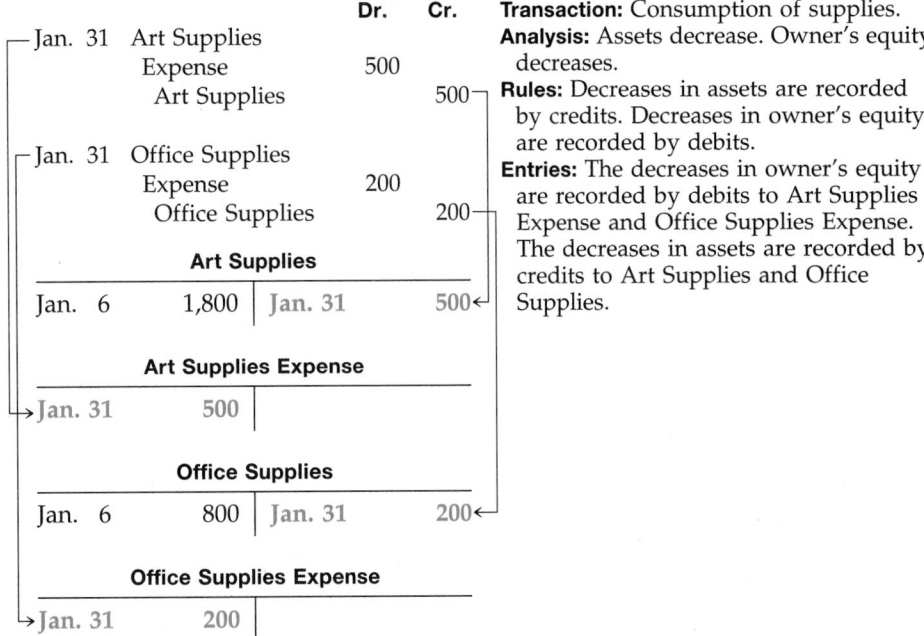

The asset accounts Art Supplies and Office Supplies now reflect the correct balances, $1,300 and $600, respectively, of supplies that are yet to be consumed. In addition, the amount of art supplies used up during the accounting period is shown as $500 and the amount of office supplies used up is shown as $200.

Depreciation of Plant and Equipment   When a company buys a long-term asset—a building, equipment, trucks, automobiles, computers, store fixtures, or office furniture—it is, in effect, prepaying for the usefulness of the asset for as long as it benefits the company. Because a long-term asset is a deferral of an expense, the accountant must allocate the cost of the asset over its estimated useful life. The amount allocated to any one accounting period is called depreciation, or *depreciation expense*. Depreciation, like other expenses, is incurred during an accounting period to produce revenue.

It is often impossible to tell how long an asset will last or how much of the asset is used in any one period. For this reason, depreciation must be estimated. Accountants have developed a number of methods for estimating depreciation and for dealing with the related complex problems. Here we look at the simplest case.

Suppose that Joan Miller Advertising Agency estimates that its art equipment and office equipment will last five years (60 months) and will be worthless at the end of that time. The monthly depreciation of art equipment and office equipment is $70 ($4,200 ÷ 60 months) and $50 ($3,000 ÷ 60 months), respectively. The amounts represent the costs allocated to each month, and they are the amounts by which the asset accounts must be reduced and the expense accounts increased (reducing owner's equity).

ART EQUIPMENT AND OFFICE EQUIPMENT (ADJUSTMENTS E AND F)

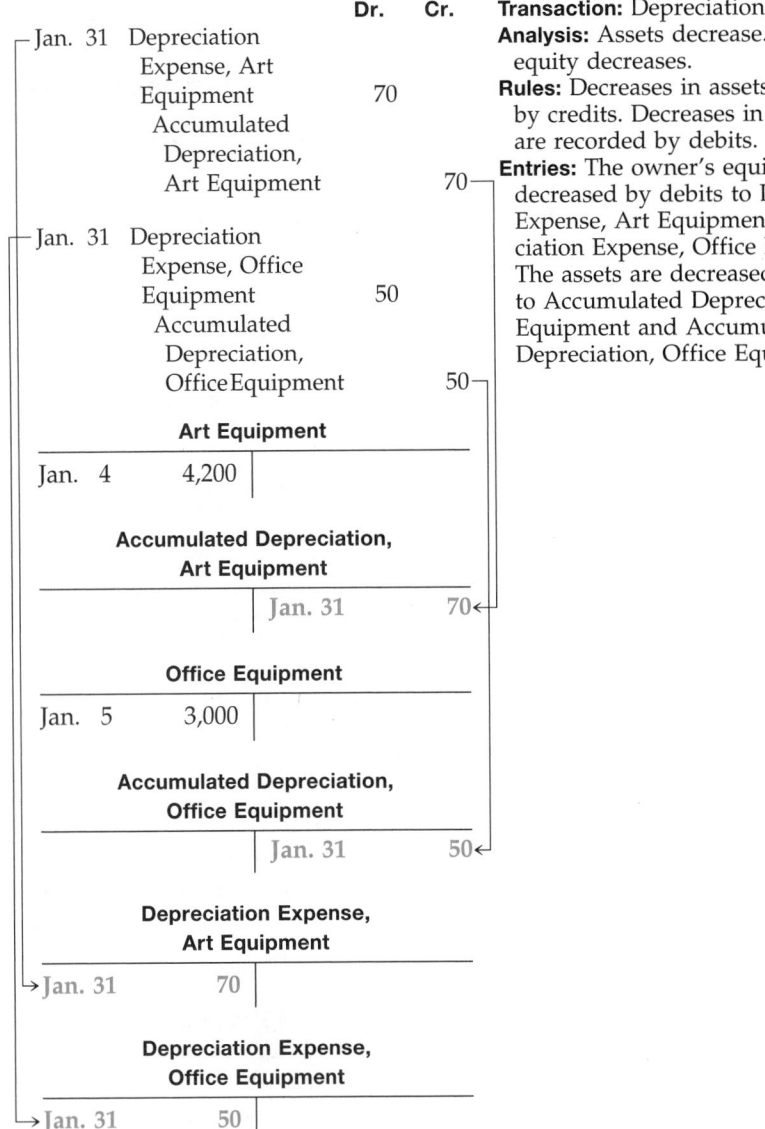

Transaction: Depreciation of equipment.

Analysis: Assets decrease. Owner's equity decreases.

Rules: Decreases in assets are recorded by credits. Decreases in owner's equity are recorded by debits.

Entries: The owner's equity is decreased by debits to Depreciation Expense, Art Equipment and Depreciation Expense, Office Equipment. The assets are decreased by credits to Accumulated Depreciation, Art Equipment and Accumulated Depreciation, Office Equipment.

Accumulated Depreciation—A Contra Account   Notice that in the previous analysis, the asset accounts are not credited directly. Instead, as shown in Figure 2, new accounts—Accumulated Depreciation, Art Equipment and Accumulated Depreciation, Office Equipment—are credited. Accumulated depreciation accounts are contra-asset accounts used to total the past depreciation expense of a specific long-term asset. A contra account is a separate account that is paired with a related account—in this case, an asset account. The balance of the contra account is shown on the financial statement as a deduction from the related account.

Figure 2. Adjustment for Depreciation

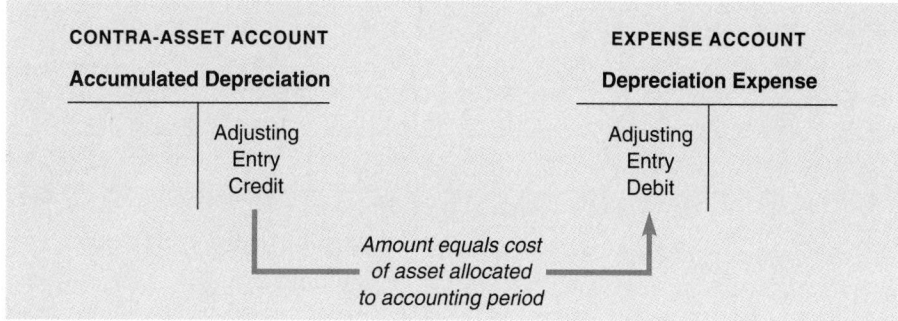

CONTRA-ASSET ACCOUNT	EXPENSE ACCOUNT
Accumulated Depreciation	**Depreciation Expense**

Adjusting Entry Credit

Adjusting Entry Debit

Amount equals cost of asset allocated to accounting period

There are several types of contra accounts. In this case, the balance of Accumulated Depreciation, Art Equipment is shown on the balance sheet as a deduction from the associated account Art Equipment. Likewise, Accumulated Depreciation, Office Equipment is shown as a deduction from Office Equipment. Exhibit 2 shows the plant and equipment section of the balance sheet for Joan Miller Advertising Agency after the two adjusting entries have been made.

A contra account is used for two very good reasons. First, it recognizes that depreciation is an estimate. Second, a contra account preserves the original cost of an asset: In combination with the asset account, it shows both how much of the asset has been allocated as an expense and the balance left to be depreciated. As the months pass, the amount of the accumulated depreciation grows, and the net amount shown as an asset declines. In six months, Accumulated Depreciation, Art Equipment will show a balance of $420; when this amount is subtracted from Art Equipment, a net amount of $3,780 will remain. The net amount is referred to as the carrying value, or *book value*, of the asset.

Exhibit 2. Plant and Equipment Section of the Balance Sheet

Joan Miller Advertising Agency Partial Balance Sheet January 31, 19xx		
Plant and Equipment		
Art Equipment	$4,200	
Less Accumulated Depreciation	70	$4,130
Office Equipment	$3,000	
Less Accumulated Depreciation	50	2,950
Total Plant and Equipment		$7,080

Other names are also used for accumulated depreciation, among them *allowance for depreciation*. But *accumulated depreciation* is the newer, better term.

APPORTIONING RECORDED REVENUES BETWEEN TWO OR MORE ACCOUNTING PERIODS (DEFERRED REVENUES)

Just as expenses can be paid before they are used, revenues can be received before they are earned. When revenues are received in advance, the company has an obligation to deliver goods or perform services. Therefore, unearned revenues are shown in a liability account. For example, publishing companies usually receive payment in advance for magazine subscriptions. These receipts are recorded in a liability account. If the company fails to deliver the magazines, subscribers are entitled to their money back. As the company delivers each issue of the magazine, it earns a part of the advance payments. This earned portion must be transferred from the Unearned Subscriptions account to the Subscription Revenue account, as shown in Figure 3.

During the month of January, Joan Miller Advertising Agency received $1,000 as an advance payment for artwork to be prepared for another agency. Assume that by the end of the month, $400 worth of the artwork was completed and accepted by the other agency. Here is the transaction analysis.

UNEARNED ART FEES (ADJUSTMENT G)

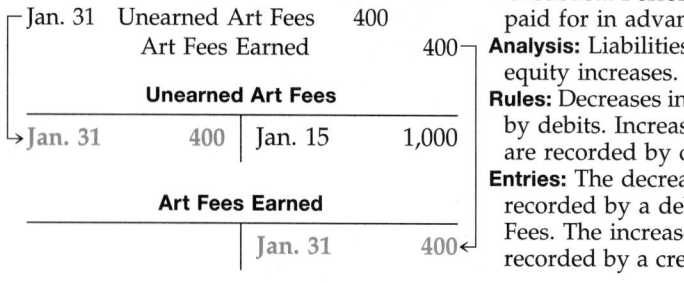

	Dr.	Cr.
Jan. 31 Unearned Art Fees	400	
Art Fees Earned		400

Unearned Art Fees

Jan. 31	400	Jan. 15	1,000

Art Fees Earned

		Jan. 31	400

Transaction: Performance of services paid for in advance.
Analysis: Liabilities decrease. Owner's equity increases.
Rules: Decreases in liabilities are recorded by debits. Increases in owner's equity are recorded by credits.
Entries: The decrease in liabilities is recorded by a debit to Unearned Art Fees. The increase in owner's equity is recorded by a credit to Art Fees Earned.

The liability account Unearned Art Fees now reflects the amount of work still to be performed, $600. The revenue account Art Fees Earned reflects the services performed and the revenue earned for them during the month, $400.

Figure 3. Adjustment for Unearned (Deferred) Revenue

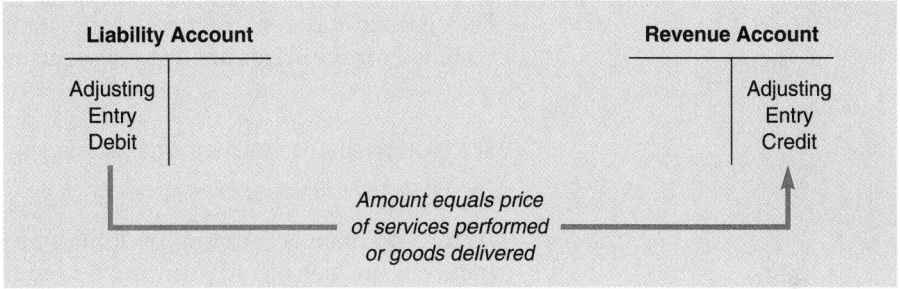

RECOGNIZING UNRECORDED REVENUES (ACCRUED REVENUES)

Accrued revenues are revenues for which a service has been performed or goods delivered but for which no entry has been recorded. Any revenues that have been earned but not recorded during the accounting period call for an adjusting entry that debits an asset account and credits a revenue account, as shown in Figure 4. For example, the interest on a note receivable is earned day by day but may not be received until another accounting period. Interest Receivable should be debited and Interest Income should be credited for the interest accrued at the end of the current period.

Suppose that Joan Miller Advertising Agency has agreed to place a series of advertisements for Marsh Tire Company and that the first appears on January 31, the last day of the month. The fee of $200 for this advertisement, which has been earned but not recorded, should be recorded this way:

ACCRUED ADVERTISING FEES (ADJUSTMENT H)

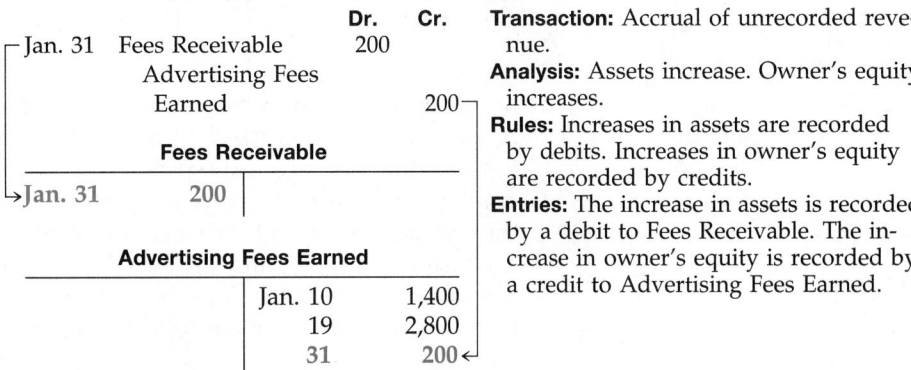

Figure 4. Adjustment for Unrecorded (Accrued) Revenues

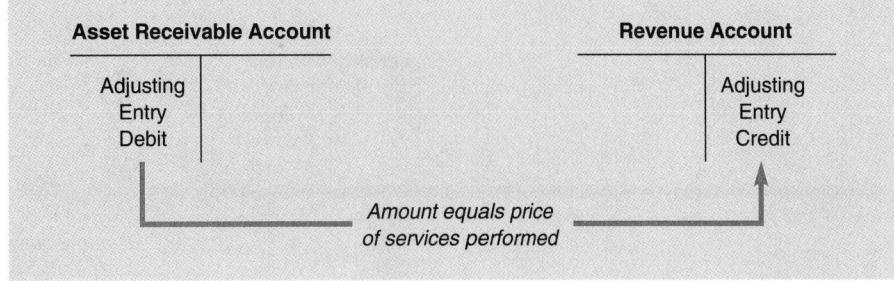

Now both the asset and the revenue accounts show the correct balance: The $200 in Fees Receivable is owed to the company, and the $4,400 in Advertising Fees Earned has been earned by the company during the month. Marsh will be billed for the series of advertisements when it is completed.

RECOGNIZING UNRECORDED EXPENSES (ACCRUED EXPENSES)

At the end of an accounting period, there are usually expenses that have been incurred but not recorded in the accounts. These expenses require adjusting entries. One such case is interest on borrowed money. Each day, interest accumulates on the debt. As shown in Figure 5, at the end of the accounting period, an adjusting entry is made to record this accumulated interest, which is an expense of the period, and the corresponding liability to pay the interest. Other unrecorded expenses are taxes, wages, and salaries. As the expense and the corresponding liability accumulate, they are said to *accrue*—hence the term accrued expenses

Accrued Wages   Suppose the calendar for January looks like this:

January

Su	M	T	W	Th	F	Sa
	1	2	3	4	5	6
7	8	9	10	11	12	13
14	15	16	17	18	19	20
21	22	23	24	25	26	27
28	29	30	31			

By the end of business on January 31, the secretary at Joan Miller Advertising Agency will have worked three days (Monday, Tuesday, and Wednesday) beyond the last biweekly pay period, which ended on January 26. The employee has earned the wages for these days, but she will not be paid until the regular payday in February. The wages for the three days are rightfully an expense for January, and the liabilities should reflect that the company owes the secretary for those days. Because the secretary's wage rate is $600 every two weeks, or $60 per day ($600 ÷ 10 working days), the expense is $180 ($60 × 3 days).

Figure 5. Adjustment for Unrecorded (Accrued) Expenses

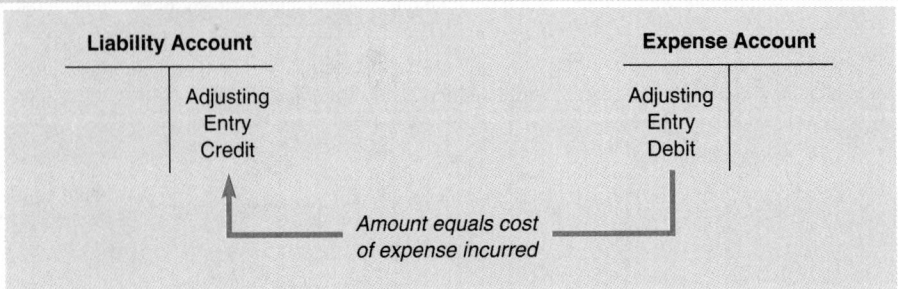

ACCRUED WAGES (ADJUSTMENT I)

		Dr.	Cr.
Jan. 31	Wages Expense	180	
	Wages Payable		180

Wages Payable

		Jan. 31	180

Wages Expense

Jan. 12	600	
26	600	
31	180	

Transaction: Accrual of unrecorded expense.
Analysis: Liabilities increase. Owner's equity decreases.
Rules: Increases in liabilities are recorded by credits. Decreases in owner's equity are recorded by debits.
Entries: The decrease in owner's equity is recorded by a debit to Wages Expense. The increase in liabilities is recorded by a credit to Wages Payable.

The liability of $180 is now reflected correctly in the Wages Payable account. The actual expense incurred for office wages during the month, $1,380, is also correct.

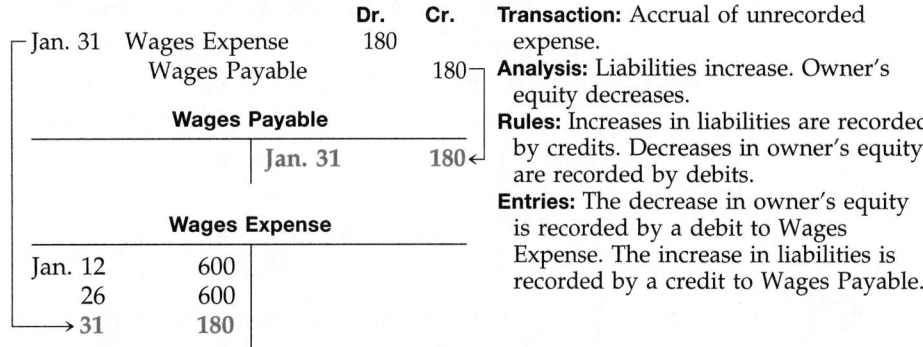

DECISION POINT

Joan Miller Advertising Agency

In the preceding wage accrual example for $180, Joan Miller might ask, "Why go to the trouble of making this adjustment? Why worry about it? Doesn't everything come out in the end, when the secretary is paid in February? Because wages expense in total is the same for the two months, isn't the net income in total unchanged?" Give three reasons why adjusting entries can help Joan Miller assess the performance of her business.

Adjusting entries are important because they help accountants compile information that is useful to management and owners. First, adjusting entries are necessary to measure income and financial position in a relevant and useful way. Joan Miller should know how much the agency earned each month and what its liabilities and assets are on the last day of the month. For instance, if the three days' accrued wages for the secretary are not recorded, the agency's income will be overstated by $180, or 9.0 percent ($180 ÷ $1,990). Second, adjusting entries allow financial statements to be compared from one accounting period to the next. Joan Miller can see whether the company is making progress toward earning a profit or if the company has improved its financial position. To return to our example, if the adjustment for accrued wages is not recorded, not only will the net income for January be overstated by $180, but the net income for February (the month when payment will be made) will be understated by $180. This error will make February's earnings, whatever they may be, appear lower than they actually are. Third, even though one adjusting entry may seem insignificant, the cumulative effect of all adjusting entries can be great. Look back over all the adjustments made by Joan Miller Advertising Agency for prepaid rent and insurance, art and office supplies, depreciation of art and office equipment, unearned art fees, accrued advertising fees, and accrued wages. These are normal adjustments. Their effect on net income in January is to increase expenses by $1,440 and revenues by $600, for a net effect of minus $840, or 42 percent ($840 ÷ $1,990) of net income. If adjusting entries had not been made, Joan Miller would have had a false impression of her company's performance. ∶ ∶ ∶ ∶ ∶

USING THE ADJUSTED TRIAL BALANCE TO PREPARE FINANCIAL STATEMENTS

OBJECTIVE

6 *Prepare financial statements from an adjusted trial balance*

After the adjusting entries have been recorded and posted, an adjusted trial balance is prepared by listing all accounts and their balances. If the adjusting entries have been posted to the accounts correctly, the adjusted trial balance should have equal debit and credit totals.

The adjusted trial balance for Joan Miller Advertising Agency is shown on the left side of Exhibit 3. Notice that some accounts, such as Cash and Accounts Receivable, have the same balances they have in the trial balance (see Exhibit 1) because no adjusting entries affected them. Some new accounts, such as Fees Receivable, depreciation accounts, and Wages Payable, appear in the adjusted trial balance, and other accounts, such as Art Supplies, Office Supplies, Prepaid Rent, and Prepaid Insurance, have different balances from those in the trial balance because adjusting entries did affect them.

From the adjusted trial balance, the financial statements can be easily prepared. The income statement is prepared from the revenue and expense accounts, as shown in Exhibit 3. Then, as shown in Exhibit 4, the statement of owner's equity and the balance sheet are prepared. Notice that the net income from the income statement is combined with investments and withdrawals on the statement of owner's equity to give the net change in the Joan Miller, Capital account. The resulting balance of Joan Miller, Capital at January 31 is used on the balance sheet, as are the asset and liability accounts.

CASH FLOWS, ACCRUAL ACCOUNTING, AND MANAGEMENT OBJECTIVES

OBJECTIVE

7 *Analyze cash flows from accrual-based information*

The purpose of accrual accounting is to measure the earnings of a business during an accounting period. This measurement of net income is directly related to management's profitability goal. A company must earn a sufficient net income to survive over the long term. Management also has the short-range goal of achieving sufficient liquidity to meet its needs for cash, to pay its ongoing obligations, and to plan for borrowing money from the bank. An important measure of liquidity is cash flow. Cash flow is the inflows and outflows of cash during an accounting period and the resulting availability of cash. It is important for managers to be able to use accrual-based financial information to analyze cash flows to plan payments to creditors and assess the need for short-term borrowing.

Every revenue or expense account on the income statement has one or more related accounts on the balance sheet. For instance, Supplies Expense is related to Supplies, Wages Expense to Wages Payable, and Service Revenues to Unearned Revenues. As shown in this chapter, these accounts are related through adjusting entries whose purpose is to apply the matching rule in the measurement of net income. The cash flows generated or paid by company

Exhibit 3. Relationship of Adjusted Trial Balance to Income Statement

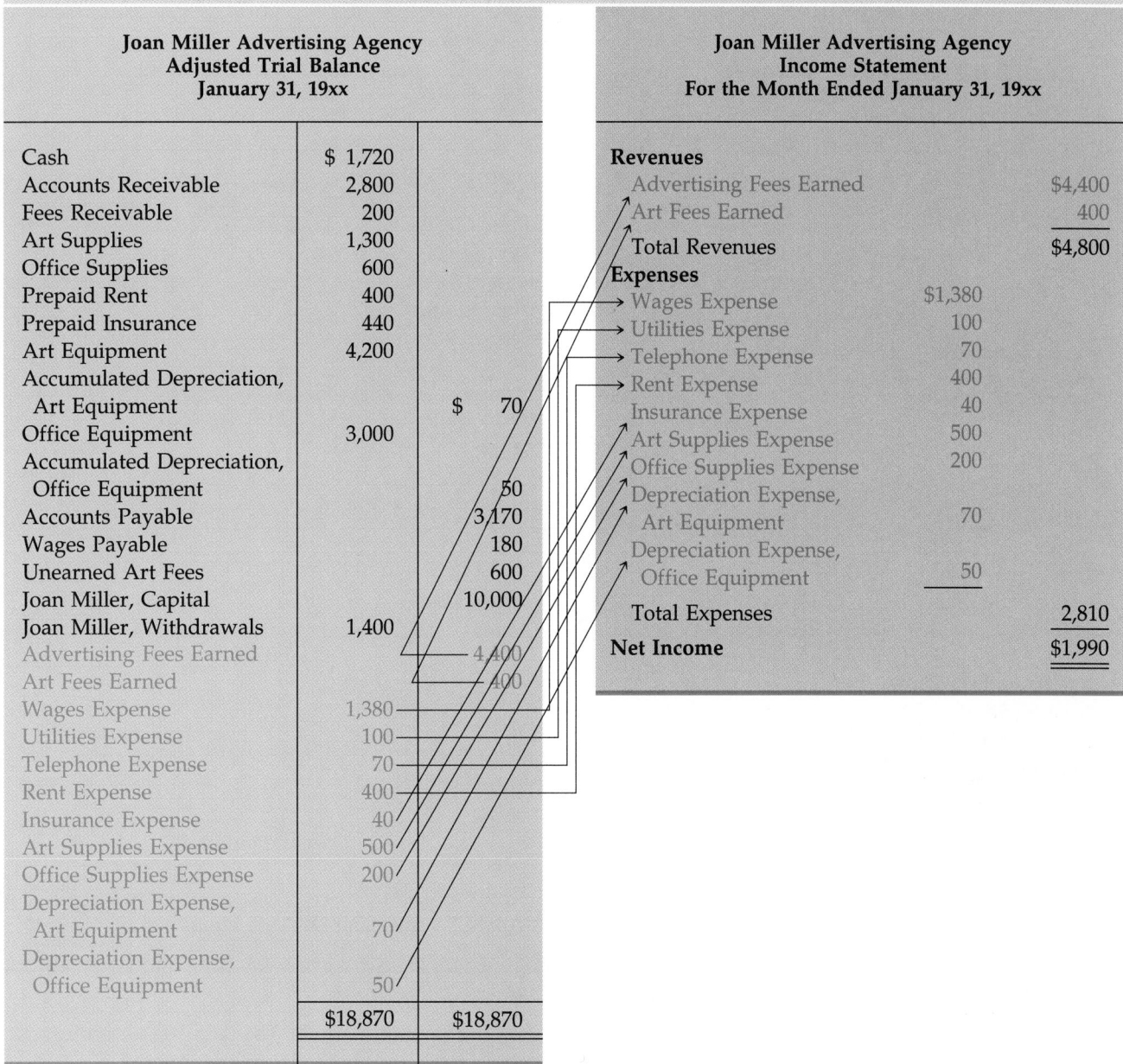

Joan Miller Advertising Agency
Adjusted Trial Balance
January 31, 19xx

Cash	$ 1,720	
Accounts Receivable	2,800	
Fees Receivable	200	
Art Supplies	1,300	
Office Supplies	600	
Prepaid Rent	400	
Prepaid Insurance	440	
Art Equipment	4,200	
Accumulated Depreciation, Art Equipment		$ 70
Office Equipment	3,000	
Accumulated Depreciation, Office Equipment		50
Accounts Payable		3,170
Wages Payable		180
Unearned Art Fees		600
Joan Miller, Capital		10,000
Joan Miller, Withdrawals	1,400	
Advertising Fees Earned		4,400
Art Fees Earned		400
Wages Expense	1,380	
Utilities Expense	100	
Telephone Expense	70	
Rent Expense	400	
Insurance Expense	40	
Art Supplies Expense	500	
Office Supplies Expense	200	
Depreciation Expense, Art Equipment	70	
Depreciation Expense, Office Equipment	50	
	$18,870	$18,870

Joan Miller Advertising Agency
Income Statement
For the Month Ended January 31, 19xx

Revenues		
Advertising Fees Earned		$4,400
Art Fees Earned		400
Total Revenues		$4,800
Expenses		
Wages Expense	$1,380	
Utilities Expense	100	
Telephone Expense	70	
Rent Expense	400	
Insurance Expense	40	
Art Supplies Expense	500	
Office Supplies Expense	200	
Depreciation Expense, Art Equipment	70	
Depreciation Expense, Office Equipment	50	
Total Expenses		2,810
Net Income		$1,990

operations may also be determined by analyzing these relationships. For example, suppose that after receiving the financial statements in Exhibits 3 and 4, Joan Miller wants to know how much cash was expended for art supplies. On the income statement, Art Supplies Expense is $500, and on the balance sheet, Art Supplies is $1,300. Because January was the first month of operation for the company, there was no prior balance of supplies, so the amount of cash expended for supplies during the month was $1,800. The cash flow used to purchase art supplies ($1,800) was much greater than the amount expensed in determining income ($500). In planning for February, Joan Miller can anticipate that the cash needed may be less than the amount expensed because, given the large inventory of art supplies, it will probably not be necessary to buy art supplies for more than a month. Understanding these cash flow effects enables Joan to better predict her business's need for cash during February.

Exhibit 4. Relationship of Adjusted Trial Balance to Balance Sheet and Statement of Owner's Equity

Joan Miller Advertising Agency
Adjusted Trial Balance
January 31, 19xx

Cash	$ 1,720	
Accounts Receivable	2,800	
Fees Receivable	200	
Art Supplies	1,300	
Office Supplies	600	
Prepaid Rent	400	
Prepaid Insurance	440	
Art Equipment	4,200	
Accumulated Depreciation, Art Equipment		$ 70
Office Equipment	3,000	
Accumulated Depreciation, Office Equipment		50
Accounts Payable		3,170
Wages Payable		180
Unearned Art Fees		600
Joan Miller, Capital		10,000
Joan Miller, Withdrawals	1,400	
Advertising Fees Earned		4,400
Art Fees Earned		400
Wages Expense	1,380	
Utilities Expense	100	
Telephone Expense	70	
Rent Expense	400	
Insurance Expense	40	
Art Supplies Expense	500	
Office Supplies Expense	200	
Depreciation Expense, Art Equipment	70	
Depreciation Expense, Office Equipment	50	
	$18,870	$18,870

Joan Miller Advertising Agency
Balance Sheet
January 31, 19xx

Assets

Cash		$ 1,720
Accounts Receivable		2,800
Fees Receivable		200
Art Supplies		1,300
Office Supplies		600
Prepaid Rent		400
Prepaid Insurance		440
Art Equipment	$4,200	
Less Accumulated Depreciation	70	4,130
Office Equipment	$3,000	
Less Accumulated Depreciation	50	2,950
Total Assets		$14,540

Liabilities

Accounts Payable	$3,170	
Wages Payable	180	
Unearned Art Fees	600	
Total Liabilities		$ 3,950

Owner's Equity

Joan Miller, Capital		10,590
Total Liabilities and Owner's Equity		$14,540

From Income Statement in Exhibit 3.

Joan Miller Advertising Agency
Statement of Owner's Equity
For the Month Ended January 31, 19xx

Joan Miller, Capital, January 1, 19xx		—
Add: Investment by Joan Miller	$10,000	
Net Income	1,990	$11,990
Subtotal		$11,990
Less Withdrawals		1,400
Joan Miller, Capital, January 31, 19xx		$10,590

The general rule for determining the cash flow received from any revenue or paid for any expense (except depreciation, which is a special case not covered here) is to determine the potential cash payments or cash receipts and deduct the amount not paid or received. The application of the general rule varies with the type of asset or liability account, as shown below.

Type of Account	Potential Payment or Receipt		Not Paid or Received	Result
Prepaid Expense	Ending Balance	+ Expense for the Period	− Beginning Balance	= Cash Payments for Expenses
Unearned Revenue	Ending Balance	+ Revenue for the Period	− Beginning Balance	= Cash Receipts from Revenues
Accrued Liability	Beginning Balance	+ Expense for the Period	− Ending Balance	= Cash Payments for Expenses
Accrued Receivable	Beginning Balance	+ Revenue for the Period	− Ending Balance	= Cash Receipts from Revenues

For instance, assume that on May 31 a company had a balance of $480 in Prepaid Insurance and that on June 30 the balance was $670. If the insurance expense during June was $120, the amount of cash expended on insurance during June can be computed as follows:

Prepaid Insurance at June 30	$670
Insurance Expense during June	120
Potential cash payments for insurance	$790
Less Prepaid Insurance at May 31	480
Cash payments for insurance during June	$310

The beginning balance is deducted because it was paid in a prior accounting period. Note that the cash payments equal the expense plus the increase in the balance of the Prepaid Insurance account [$120 + ($670 − $480) = $310]. In this case, the cash paid was almost three times the amount of insurance expense. In future months, cash payments are likely to be less than the expense.

BUSINESS BULLETIN:

In a computerized accounting system, adjusting entries may be entered just like any other transactions. However, since some adjusting entries, such as those for insurance expense and depreciation expense, may be similar for each accounting period, and others, such as those for accrued wages, may always involve the same accounts, the computer may be programmed to display the adjusting entries automatically so that all the accountant has to do is verify the amounts or enter the correct amounts. Then the adjusting entries are entered and posted, and the adjusted trial balance is prepared with the touch of a button.

A NOTE ABOUT JOURNAL ENTRIES

Thus far, we have presented a full analysis of each journal entry. The analyses showed you the thought process behind each entry. By now, you should be fully aware of the effects of transactions on the accounting equation and the rules of debit and credit. For this reason, in the rest of the book, journal entries are presented without full analysis.

CHAPTER REVIEW

REVIEW OF LEARNING OBJECTIVES

1. **Define *net income* and its two major components, *revenues* and *expenses*.** Net income is the net increase in owner's equity that results from the operations of a company. Net income equals revenues minus expenses, unless expenses exceed revenues, in which case a net loss results. Revenues equal the price of goods sold and services rendered during a specific period. Expenses are the costs of goods and services used up in the process of producing revenues.

2. **Explain the difficulties of income measurement caused by (a) the accounting period issue, (b) the continuity issue, and (c) the matching issue.** The accounting period issue recognizes that net income measurements for short periods of time are necessarily tentative. The continuity issue recognizes that even though businesses face an uncertain future, without evidence to the contrary, accountants must assume that a business will continue indefinitely. The matching issue has to do with the difficulty of assigning revenues and expenses to a period of time. It is addressed by applying the matching rule: Revenues must be assigned to the accounting period in which the goods are sold or the services performed, and expenses must be assigned to the accounting period in which they are used to produce revenue.

3. **Define *accrual accounting* and explain two broad ways of accomplishing it.** Accrual accounting consists of all the techniques developed by accountants to apply the matching rule. The two general ways of accomplishing accrual accounting are (1) by recognizing revenues when earned and expenses when incurred and (2) by adjusting the accounts.

4. **State four principal situations that require adjusting entries.** Adjusting entries are required (1) when recorded expenses have to be apportioned between two or more accounting periods, (2) when recorded revenues must be apportioned between two or more accounting periods, (3) when unrecorded revenues exist, and (4) when unrecorded expenses exist.

5. **Prepare typical adjusting entries.** The preparation of adjusting entries is summarized in the following table.

Type of Adjusting Entry	Type of Account		Examples
	Debited	**Credited**	
Deferrals			
1. Apportioning recorded expenses (expired, not recorded)	Expense	Asset (or contra asset)	Prepaid Rent Prepaid Insurance Supplies Buildings Equipment
2. Apportioning recorded revenues (earned, not recorded)	Liability	Revenue	Commissions Received in Advance
Accruals			
1. Accrued revenues (earned, not received)	Asset	Revenue	Commissions Receivable Interest Receivable
2. Accrued expenses (incurred, not paid)	Expense	Liability	Wages Payable Interest Payable

6. **Prepare financial statements from an adjusted trial balance.** An adjusted trial balance is prepared after adjusting entries have been posted to the ledger accounts. Its purpose is to test the balance of the ledger after the adjusting entries are made and before the financial statements are prepared. The income statement is prepared from the revenue and expense accounts. The balance sheet is prepared from the asset and liability accounts in the adjusted trial balance and from the statement of owner's equity.

7. **Analyze cash flows from accrual-based information.** Cash flow information bears on management's liquidity goal. The general rule for determining the cash flow effect of any revenue or expense (except depreciation, which is a special case not covered here) is to determine the potential cash payments or cash receipts and deduct the amount not paid or received.

REVIEW OF CONCEPTS AND TERMINOLOGY

The following concepts and terms were introduced in this chapter.

L O 2   **Accounting period issue:** The difficulty of assigning revenues and expenses to a short period of time.

L O 4   **Accrual:** The recognition of an expense or revenue that has arisen but has not yet been recorded.

L O 3   **Accrual accounting:** The attempt to record the financial effects of transactions and other events in the periods in which those transactions or events occur rather than only in the periods in which cash is received or paid by the business. All the techniques developed by accountants to apply the matching rule.

L O 5   **Accrued expenses:** Expenses that have been incurred but are not recognized in the accounts; unrecorded expenses.

L O 5   **Accrued revenues:** Revenues for which a service has been performed or goods delivered but for which no entry has been made; unrecorded revenues.

L O 5   **Accumulated depreciation account:** A contra-asset account used to accumulate the depreciation expense of a specific long-lived asset.

L O 6   **Adjusted trial balance:** A trial balance prepared after all adjusting entries have been recorded and posted to the accounts.

L O 4   **Adjusting entries:** Entries made to apply accrual accounting to transactions that span more than one accounting period.

L O 5   **Carrying value:** The unexpired portion of the cost of an asset. Also called *book value*.

L O 2   **Cash basis of accounting:** Accounting for revenues and expenses on a cash received and cash paid basis.

L O 2   **Continuity issue:** The difficulty associated with not knowing how long a business entity will survive.

L O 5   **Contra account:** An account whose balance is subtracted from an associated account in the financial statements.

L O 4   **Deferral:** The postponement of the recognition of an expense already paid or incurred, or of a revenue already received.

L O 5   **Depreciation:** The portion of the cost of a tangible long-term asset allocated to any one accounting period. Also called *depreciation expense*.

L O 1   **Expenses:** Decreases in owner's equity resulting from the costs of goods and services used up in the course of earning revenues.

L O 2   **Fiscal year:** Any twelve-month accounting period used by an economic entity.

L O 2   **Going concern:** The assumption, unless there is evidence to the contrary, that a business entity will continue to operate indefinitely.

L O 2   **Matching rule:** Revenues must be assigned to the accounting period in which the goods are sold or the services performed, and expenses must be assigned to the accounting period in which they are used to produce revenue.

L O 1   **Net income:** The net increase in owner's equity that results from business operations and is accumulated in the Capital account; revenues less expenses when revenues exceed expenses.

L O 1   **Net loss:** The net decrease in owner's equity that results from business operations when expenses exceed revenues. It is accumulated in the Capital account.

L O 2   **Periodicity:** The recognition that net income for any period less than the life of the business, although tentative, is still a useful estimate of net income for that period.

L O 1   **Permanent accounts:** Balance sheet accounts; accounts whose balances extend past the end of an accounting period. Also called *real accounts*.

L O 5   **Prepaid expenses:** Expenses paid in advance that have not yet expired; an asset account.

L O 1   **Profit:** The increase in owner's equity that results from business operations.

L O 3   **Revenue recognition:** In accrual accounting, the process of determining when a sale takes place.

L O 1   **Revenues:** The increases in owner's equity from selling goods, rendering services, or performing other business activities.

L O 1   **Temporary accounts:** Accounts that show the accumulation of revenues and expenses over one accounting period; at the end of the accounting period, these account balances are transferred to owner's equity. Also called *nominal accounts*.

L O 5   **Unearned revenues:** Revenues received in advance for which the goods have not yet been delivered or the services performed; a liability account.

REVIEW PROBLEM
DETERMINING ADJUSTING ENTRIES, POSTING TO T ACCOUNTS, PREPARING AN ADJUSTED TRIAL BALANCE, AND PREPARING FINANCIAL STATEMENTS

L O 5, 6   This was the unadjusted trial balance for Certified Answering Service on December 31, 19x2.

Certified Answering Service
Trial Balance
December 31, 19x2

Cash	$2,160	
Accounts Receivable	1,250	
Office Supplies	180	
Prepaid Insurance	240	
Office Equipment	3,400	
Accumulated Depreciation, Office Equipment		$ 600
Accounts Payable		700
Unearned Revenue		460
James Neal, Capital		4,870
James Neal, Withdrawals	400	
Answering Service Revenue		2,900
Wages Expense	1,500	
Rent Expense	400	
	$9,530	$9,530

The following information is also available.

a. Insurance that expired during December amounted to $40.
b. Office supplies on hand at the end of December totaled $75.
c. Depreciation for the month of December totaled $100.
d. Accrued wages at the end of December totaled $120.
e. Revenues earned for services performed but not yet billed on December 31 totaled $300.
f. Services performed in December that were paid for in advance totaled $160.

REQUIRED

1. Prepare T accounts for the accounts in the trial balance and enter the balances.
2. Determine the required adjusting entries and record them directly to the T accounts. Open new T accounts as needed.
3. Prepare an adjusted trial balance.
4. Prepare an income statement, a statement of owner's equity, and a balance sheet for the month ended December 31, 19x2. The owner made no new investments during the month.

ANSWER TO REVIEW PROBLEM

1. T accounts set up and amounts from trial balance entered
2. Adjusting entries recorded

Cash			
Bal.	2,160		

Accounts Receivable			
Bal.	1,250		

Service Revenue Receivable			
(e)	300		

Office Supplies			
Bal.	180	(b)	105
Bal.	75		

Prepaid Insurance			
Bal.	240	(a)	40
Bal.	200		

Office Equipment			
Bal.	3,400		

Accumulated Depreciation, Office Equipment			
		Bal.	600
		(c)	100
		Bal.	700

Accounts Payable			
		Bal.	700

Unearned Revenue			
(f)	160	Bal.	460
		Bal.	300

Wages Payable			
		(d)	120

James Neal, Capital			
		Bal.	4,870

James Neal, Withdrawals			
Bal.	400		

Answering Service Revenue			
		Bal.	2,900
		(e)	300
		(f)	160
		Bal.	3,360

Wages Expense			
Bal.	1,500		
(d)	120		
Bal.	1,620		

Rent Expense			
Bal.	400		

Insurance Expense			
(a)	40		

Office Supplies Expense			
(b)	105		

Depreciation Expense, Office Equipment			
(c)	100		

3. Adjusted trial balance prepared

Certified Answering Service
Adjusted Trial Balance
December 31, 19x2

Cash	$ 2,160	
Accounts Receivable	1,250	
Service Revenue Receivable	300	
Office Supplies	75	
Prepaid Insurance	200	
Office Equipment	3,400	
Accumulated Depreciation, Office Equipment		$ 700
Accounts Payable		700
Unearned Revenue		300
Wages Payable		120
James Neal, Capital		4,870
James Neal, Withdrawals	400	
Answering Service Revenue		3,360
Wages Expense	1,620	
Rent Expense	400	
Insurance Expense	40	
Office Supplies Expense	105	
Depreciation Expense, Office Equipment	100	
	$10,050	$10,050

4. Financial statements prepared

Certified Answering Service
Income Statement
For the Month Ended December 31, 19x2

Revenues

Answering Service Revenue		$3,360

Expenses

Wages Expense	$1,620	
Rent Expense	400	
Insurance Expense	40	
Office Supplies Expense	105	
Depreciation Expense, Office Equipment	100	
Total Expenses		2,265
Net Income		$1,095

Certified Answering Service
Statement of Owner's Equity
For the Month Ended December 31, 19x2

James Neal, Capital, November 30, 19x2	$4,870
Net Income	1,095
Subtotal	$5,965
Less Withdrawals	400
James Neal, Capital, December 31, 19x2	$5,565

Certified Answering Service
Balance Sheet
December 31, 19x2

Assets

Cash		$2,160
Accounts Receivable		1,250
Service Revenue Receivable		300
Office Supplies		75
Prepaid Insurance		200
Office Equipment	$3,400	
Less Accumulated Depreciation	700	2,700
Total Assets		$6,685

Liabilities

Accounts Payable	$ 700
Unearned Revenue	300
Wages Payable	120
Total Liabilities	$1,120

Owner's Equity

James Neal, Capital	5,565
Total Liabilities and Owner's Equity	$6,685

CHAPTER ASSIGNMENTS

QUESTIONS

1. Why does the accountant use the term *net income* instead of *profit*?
2. Define the terms *revenues* and *expenses*.
3. Why are income statement accounts called *temporary accounts*?
4. Why does the need for an accounting period cause problems?
5. What is the significance of the continuity assumption?

6. "The matching rule is the most significant concept in accounting." Do you agree with this statement? Explain your answer.

7. What is the difference between the cash basis and the accrual basis of accounting?

8. In what two ways is accrual accounting accomplished?

9. Why are adjusting entries necessary?

10. What are the four situations that require adjusting entries? Give an example of each.

11. "Some assets are expenses that have not expired." Explain this statement.

12. What do plant and equipment, office supplies, and prepaid insurance have in common?

13. What is the difference between accumulated depreciation and depreciation expense?

14. What is a contra account? Give an example.

15. Why are contra accounts used to record depreciation?

16. How does unearned revenue arise? Give an example.

17. Where does unearned revenue appear on the balance sheet?

18. What accounting problem does a magazine publisher who sells three-year subscriptions have?

19. Under what circumstances does a company have accrued revenues? Give an example. What asset arises when the adjustment is made?

20. What is an accrued expense? Give three examples.

21. "Why worry about adjustments? Doesn't it all come out in the wash?" Discuss these questions.

22. Why is the income statement usually the first statement prepared from the adjusted trial balance?

23. To what management goals do the measurements of net income and cash flow relate?

SHORT EXERCISES

SE 1. *Accrual Accounting*
L O 2, 3 *Concepts*
Check Figures: c, b, d, a

Match the concepts of accrual accounting on the right with the assumptions or actions on the left.

1. Assumes expenses can be assigned to the accounting period in which they are used to produce revenues
2. Assumes a business will last indefinitely
3. Assumes revenues are earned at a point in time
4. Assumes net income measured for a short period of time, such as one quarter, is a useful measure

a. periodicity
b. going concern
c. matching rule
d. revenue recognition

SE 2. *Adjustment for*
L O 5 *Prepaid Insurance*
Check Figure: $450

The Prepaid Insurance account began the year with a balance of $230. During the year, insurance in the amount of $570 was purchased. At the end of the year (December 31), the amount of insurance still unexpired was $350. Make the year-end journal entry to record the adjustment for insurance expense for the year.

SE 3. *Adjustment for*
L O 5 *Supplies*
Check Figure: $460

The Supplies account began the year with a balance of $190. During the year, supplies in the amount of $490 were purchased. At the end of the year (December 31), the inventory of supplies on hand was $220. Make the year-end journal entry to record the adjustment for supplies expense for the year.

SE 4. *Adjustment for*
L O 5 *Depreciation*
Check Figure: $800

The depreciation expense on office equipment for the month of March is $50. This is the third month that the office equipment, which cost $950, has been owned. Prepare the adjusting journal entry to record depreciation for March and show the balance sheet presentation for office equipment and related accounts after the adjustment.

SE 5. *Adjustment for*
L O 5 *Accrued Wages*
Check Figure: $115

Wages are paid each Saturday for a six-day work week. Wages are currently running $690 per week. Make the adjusting entry required on June 30, assuming July 1 falls on a Tuesday.

SE 6. *Adjustment for*
L O 5 *Unearned Revenue*
Check Figure: $380

During the month of August, deposits in the amount of $550 were received for services to be performed. By the end of the month, services in the amount of $380 had been performed. Prepare the necessary adjustment for Service Revenues at the end of the month.

SE 7. *Preparation of an*
L O 6 *Income Statement from an Adjusted Trial Balance*
Check Figure: $700

The adjusted trial balance for Cirtis Company at December 31, 19x1, contains the following accounts and balances: Sue Cirtis, Capital, $4,300; Sue Cirtis, Withdrawals, $350; Service Revenue, $2,300; Rent Expense, $400; Wages Expense, $900; Utilities Expense, $200; and Telephone Expense, $100. Prepare an income statement in proper form for the month of December.

SE 8. *Preparation of a*
L O 6 *Statement of Owner's Equity*
Check Figure: $4,650

Using the data in SE 7, prepare a statement of owner's equity for Cirtis Company.

SE 9. *Determination of*
L O 7 *Cash Flows*
Check Figure: $1,970

Wages Payable were $590 at the end of May and $920 at the end of June. Wages Expense for June was $2,300. How much cash was paid for wages during June?

SE 10. *Determination of*
L O 7 *Cash Flows*
Check Figure: $4,700

Unearned Revenue was $1,300 at the end of November and $900 at the end of December. Service Revenue was $5,100 for the month of December. How much cash was received for service provided during December?

EXERCISES

E 1. *Applications of*
L O 2, 3, 4 *Accounting Concepts Related to Accrual Accounting*
Check Figures: b, d, e, a, f, c

The accountant for Marina Company makes the assumptions or performs the activities listed below. Tell which of the following concepts of accrual accounting most directly relates to each assumption or action: (a) periodicity, (b) going concern, (c) matching rule, (d) revenue recognition, (e) deferral, and (f) accrual.

1. In estimating the life of a building, assumes that the business will last indefinitely.
2. Records a sale when the customer is billed.
3. Postpones the recognition of a one-year insurance policy as an expense by initially recording the expenditure as an asset.
4. Recognizes the usefulness of financial statements prepared on a monthly basis even though they are based on estimates.
5. Recognizes, by making an adjusting entry, wages expense that has been incurred but not yet recorded.
6. Prepares an income statement that shows the revenues earned and the expenses incurred during the accounting period.

E 2. *Revenue*
L O 5 *Recognition*
No check figure

Contemporary Life Company of Toledo, Ohio, publishes a monthly magazine featuring local restaurant reviews and upcoming social, cultural, and sporting events. Subscribers pay for subscriptions either one year or two years in advance. Cash received from subscribers is credited to an account called Magazine Subscriptions Received in Advance. On December 31, 19x3, the end of the company's fiscal year, the balance of this account was $1,000,000. Expiration of subscriptions was as follows:

During 19x3 $250,000
During 19x4   450,000
During 19x5   300,000

Prepare the adjusting journal entry for December 31, 19x3.

E 3. *Adjusting Entries for*
L O 5 *Prepaid Insurance*
Check Figure: $1,069

An examination of the Prepaid Insurance account shows a balance of $2,056 at the end of an accounting period, before adjustment. Prepare journal entries to record the insurance expense for the period under each of the following independent assumptions.

1. An examination of the insurance policies shows unexpired insurance that cost $987 at the end of the period.
2. An examination of the insurance policies shows that insurance that cost $347 has expired during the period.

E 4. *Supplies Account:*
L O 5 *Missing Data*
Check Figures: $61, $487, $157, $446

Each column below represents a Supplies account:

	a	b	c	d
Supplies on hand July 1	$132	$217	$98	$?
Supplies purchased during the month	26	?	87	964
Supplies consumed during the month	97	486	?	816
Supplies on hand July 31	?	218	28	594

1. Determine the amounts indicated by the question marks in the columns.
2. Make the adjusting entry for Column **a,** assuming supplies purchased are debited to an asset account.

E 5. *Adjusting Entry for*
L O 5 *Accrued Salaries*
Check Figure: $14,000

Photex has a five-day work week and pays salaries of $35,000 each Friday.

1. Make the adjusting entry required on May 31, assuming that June 1 falls on a Wednesday.
2. Make the entry to pay the salaries on June 3.

E 6. *Revenue and*
L O 5 *Expense Recognition*
Check Figures: $80,000, $60,000

Tampa Company produces computer software that is sold by Bond Systems Company. Tampa receives a royalty of 15 percent of sales. Royalties are paid by Bond Systems Company and received by Tampa semiannually on May 1 for sales made July through December of the previous year and on November 1 for sales made January through June of the current year. Royalty expense for Bond Systems Company and royalty income for Tampa in the amount of $12,000 were accrued on December 31, 19x2. Cash in the amounts of $12,000 and $20,000 was paid and received on May 1 and November 1, 19x3, respectively. Software sales during the July to December, 19x3 period totaled $400,000.

1. Calculate the amount of royalty expense for Bond Systems and royalty income for Tampa during 19x3.
2. Record the appropriate adjusting entry made by each company on December 31, 19x3.

E 7. *Adjusting Entries*
L O 5
No check figure

Prepare year-end adjusting entries for each of the following:

1. Office Supplies had a balance of $84 on January 1. Purchases debited to Office Supplies during the year amount to $415. A year-end inventory reveals supplies of $285 on hand.
2. Depreciation of office equipment is estimated to be $2,130 for the year.
3. Property taxes for six months, estimated at $875, have accrued but have not been recorded.
4. Unrecorded interest receivable on U.S. government bonds is $850.
5. Unearned Revenue has a balance of $900. Services for $300 received in advance have now been performed.
6. Services totaling $200 have been performed; the customer has not yet been billed.

E 8. *Accounting for*
L O 5, 6 *Revenue Received in*
Advance
No check figure

Michelle Demetri, a lawyer, was paid $24,000 on October 1 to represent a client in real estate negotiations over the next twelve months.

1. Record the entries required in Demetri's records on October 1 and at the end of the fiscal year, December 31.
2. How would this transaction be reflected in the income statement and balance sheet on December 31?

E 9. *Identification of*
L O 5 *Accruals*

No check figure

Southwest Heating Company has the following liabilities at year end.

Notes Payable	$40,000
Accounts Payable	30,000
Contract Revenue Received in Advance	18,000
Wages Payable	4,900
Interest Payable	1,400

1. Which of these accounts probably was created at the end of the fiscal year as a result of an accrual? Which probably was adjusted at year end?
2. Which adjustments probably reduced net income? Which probably increased net income?

E 10. *Preparation of*
L O 6 *Financial Statements*

Check Figures: Net income: $1,410;
Total assets: $8,637

Prepare the monthly income statement, statement of owner's equity, and balance sheet for Miracle Janitorial Service from the data provided in the following adjusted trial balance.

Miracle Janitorial Service
Adjusted Trial Balance
August 31, 19xx

Cash	$ 2,295	
Accounts Receivable	1,296	
Prepaid Insurance	190	
Prepaid Rent	100	
Cleaning Supplies	76	
Cleaning Equipment	1,600	
Accumulated Depreciation, Cleaning Equipment		$ 160
Truck	3,600	
Accumulated Depreciation, Truck		360
Accounts Payable		210
Wages Payable		40
Unearned Janitorial Revenue		460
Mae Farber, Capital		7,517
Mae Farber, Withdrawals	1,000	
Janitorial Revenue		7,310
Wages Expense	2,840	
Rent Expense	600	
Gas, Oil, and Other Truck Expenses	290	
Insurance Expense	190	
Supplies Expense	1,460	
Depreciation Expense, Cleaning Equipment	160	
Depreciation Expense, Truck	360	
	$16,057	$16,057

E 11. *Determination of*
L O 7 *Cash Flows*
Check Figures: $3,300, $20,500, $11,200

After adjusting entries had been made, the balance sheets of Target Company showed the following asset and liability amounts at the end of 19x3 and 19x4.

	19x3	19x4
Prepaid Insurance	$2,900	$2,400
Wages Payable	2,200	1,200
Unearned Fees	1,900	4,200

The following amounts were taken from the 19x4 income statement.

Insurance Expense	$ 3,800
Wages Expense	19,500
Fees Earned	8,900

Calculate the amount of cash paid for insurance and wages and the amount of cash received for fees during 19x4.

E 12. *Cash Flow Analysis*
L O 7 *of Deferrals and*
Accruals
Check Figures: $92,000, $182,000

The following amounts are taken from the balance sheets of Green Bay Company.

	December 31	
	19x1	**19x2**
Prepaid Expenses	$56,000	$ 45,000
Accrued Liabilities	88,000	103,000

During 19x2, expenses related to Prepaid Expenses were $103,000, and expenses related to Accrued Liabilities were $197,000. Determine the amount of cash payments related to Prepaid Expenses and to Accrued Liabilities for 19x2.

E 13. *Determining Cash*
L O 7 *Flows*
Check Figure: $20,000

Suburban East News Service delivers morning, evening, and Sunday city newspapers to subscribers who live in the suburbs. Customers can pay a yearly subscription fee in advance (at a savings) or pay monthly after delivery of their newspapers. The following data are available for the Subscriptions Receivable and Unearned Subscriptions accounts at the beginning and end of May 19xx:

	May 1	**May 31**
Subscriptions Receivable	$ 3,800	$4,600
Unearned Subscriptions	11,400	9,800

The income statement shows subscription revenue for May of $22,400. Determine the amount of cash received from customers for subscriptions during May. Why is it important for management to make a calculation like this?

E 14. *Relationship of*
L O 7 *Expenses to Cash*
Paid
Check Figures: $3,050, $4,500, $39,200

The income statement for Gemini Company included the following expenses for 19xx.

Rent Expense	$ 2,600
Interest Expense	3,900
Salaries Expense	41,500

Listed below are the related balance sheet account balances at year end for last year and this year.

	Last Year	**This Year**
Prepaid Rent	—	$ 450
Interest Payable	$ 600	—
Salaries Payable	2,500	4,800

1. Compute the cash paid for rent during the year.
2. Compute the cash paid for interest during the year.
3. Compute the cash paid for salaries during the year.

SKILLS DEVELOPMENT EXERCISES

Conceptual Analysis

SDE 1. *Importance of*
L O 2, 3, 4 *Adjustments*

No check figure

Never Flake Company, which operated in the northeastern part of the United States, provided a rust-prevention coating for the underside of new automobiles. The company advertised widely and offered its services through new car dealers. When a dealer sold a new car, the salesperson attempted to sell the rust-prevention coating as an option. The protective coating was supposed to make cars last longer in the severe northeastern winters. A key selling point was Never Flake's warranty, which stated that it would repair any damage due to rust at no charge for as long as the buyer owned the car.

During the 1970s and most of the 1980s, Never Flake was very successful in generating enough cash to continue operations. But in 1988 the company suddenly declared bankruptcy. Company officials said that the firm had only $5.5 million in assets against liabilities of $32.9 million. Most of the liabilities represented potential claims under the company's lifetime warranty. It seemed that owners were keeping their cars longer in the 1980s than they had in the 1970s. Therefore, more damage was being attributed to rust. Discuss what accounting decisions could have helped Never Flake to survive under these circumstances.

SDE 2. *Application of*
L O 3, 4 *Accrual Accounting*

No check figure

The *Lyric Opera of Chicago* is one of the largest and best managed opera companies in the United States. Managing opera productions requires advance planning, including the development of scenery, costumes, and stage properties; the sale of tickets; and the collection of contributions. To measure how well the company is operating in any given year, accrual accounting must be applied to these and other transactions. At year end, April 30, 1994, Lyric Opera of Chicago's balance sheet showed Deferred Production and Other Costs of $1,339,475, Deferred Revenue from Sales of Tickets of $14,263,024, and Deferred Revenue from Contributions of $4,980,560. Be prepared to discuss what accounting policies and adjusting entries are applicable to these accounts. Why are they important to Lyric Opera's management?

SDE 3. *Cash Versus Accrual*
L O 2, 3 *Accounting*

No check figure

In 1979, Jane Byrne won the mayoral election in the *City of Chicago* partly on the basis of her charge that Michael Bilandic, the former mayor, was responsible for the budget deficit. Taking office in 1980, she hired a major international accounting firm, Peat, Marwick, Mitchell & Co. (now known as KPMG Peat Marwick), to straighten things out. This excerpt appeared in an article from a leading Chicago business publication.

> [A riddle]   Q: When is a budget deficit not a deficit?
> A: When it is a surplus, of course.

> Chicago Mayor Jane Byrne was once again caught with egg on her face last week as she and her financial advisers tried to defend that riddle. On one hand, Comptroller Daniel J. Grim [a Byrne appointee], explaining $75 million in assets the mayor [Byrne] hopes to hold in reserve in the 1981 Chicago city budget, testified in hearings that the city had actually ended 1979 with a $6 million surplus, not the much-reported deficit. He said further that the modest surplus grew to $54 million as a result of tax-enrichment supplements to the 1979 balance sheet.
>
> On the other hand, the mayor stuck by the same guns she used last year on her predecessor. The city had ended 1979, under the Michael Bilandic Administration, not merely without a surplus, but with a deficit. The apparent discrepancy can be explained.[3]

Like most U.S. cities, Chicago operates under a modified accrual accounting basis. This is a combination of the straight cash basis and the accrual basis. The modified accrual basis differs from the accrual method in that an account receivable is recorded only when it is collected in the next accounting period. The collection of Chicago's parking tax, which is assessed on all city parking lots and garages, is an example.

> The tax is assessed and collected on a quarterly basis but the city doesn't collect the amount due for the last quarter of 1980 until the first quarter of 1981. Under ideal accrual methods, the parking revenues should be recorded in the 1980 financial statement. Under a cash approach, the revenues would be recorded in the 1981 budget. What the city did before was to record the money whenever it was advantageous politically. That, combined with the infamous revolving funds, allowed the city to hide the fact it was running large deficits under [former] Mayor Bilandic. That also means that no one really knew where the city stood.[4]

The auditors are now reallocating the parking revenues to the 1981 budget but are accruing other revenues by shifting the period of collection from a year in the past. Overall, more revenues were moved into earlier fiscal years than into later years, inflating those budgets. Thus, the 1979 deficit is a surplus. The article concluded:

> The upshot is that both Mayor Byrne and Mr. Grim [the comptroller] were correct. There was a deficit in the 1979 corporate or checkbook fund, but because of corrections taking place now, a surplus exists.[5]

3. Reprint permission from the December 8, 1980 issue of *Crain's Chicago Business*. Copyright 1980 by Crain Communications Inc.

4. Ibid.

5. Ibid.

1. Do you agree with the way the auditors handled parking revenues? Support your answer by explaining which method of accounting you think a city should use.
2. "Systematically applied accounting principles will allow all to know exactly where the city stands." Comment on this statement, made in another part of the article quoted above.

Ethical Dilemma

SDE 4.
L O 2, 3, 4

Importance of Adjustments

No check figure

Central Appliance Service Co., Inc. has achieved fast growth in the St. Louis area by selling service contracts on large appliances, such as washers, dryers, and refrigerators. For a fee, Central Appliance agrees to provide all parts and labor on an appliance after the regular warranty runs out. For example, by paying a fee of $200, a person who buys a dishwasher can add two years (years 2 and 3) to the regular one-year (year 1) warranty on the appliance. In 1991, the company sold service contracts in the amount of $1.8 million, all of which applied to future years. Management wanted all the sales recorded as revenues in 1991, contending that the amount of the contracts could be determined and the cash had been received. Discuss whether or not you agree with this logic. How would you record the cash receipts? What assumptions do you think should be made? Would you consider it unethical to follow management's recommendation? Who might be hurt or helped by this action?

SDE 5.
L O 4

Service Businesses and Adjusting Entries

No check figure

Research Activity

Consult the Yellow Pages of your local telephone directory. Find the names of five different kinds of service businesses. List the types of adjusting entries you think each business regularly makes. Be prepared to discuss any adjustments you think may be unique to each business.

SDE 6.
L O 1, 5

Adjusting Entries and Withdrawal Policy

Check Figures: Net income: $22,000; Total assets: $134,000

Decision-Making Practice

Karen Jamison, the owner of a newsletter for managers of hotels and restaurants, has prepared condensed amounts from the financial statements for 19x3.

Revenues	$346,000
Expenses	282,000
Net Income	$ 64,000
Total Assets	$172,000
Liabilities	$ 48,000
Owner's Equity	124,000
Total Liabilities and Owner's Equity	$172,000

Given these figures, Jamison is planning to withdraw $50,000 for personal expenses. However, Jamison's accountant has found that the following items were overlooked.

a. Although the balance of the Printing Supplies account is $32,000, only $14,000 in supplies is on hand at the end of the year.
b. Depreciation of $20,000 on equipment has not been recorded.
c. Wages in the amount of $9,400 have been earned by employees but not recognized in the accounts.
d. A liability account called Unearned Subscriptions has a balance of $16,200, although it is determined that one-third of these subscriptions have been mailed to subscribers.

1. Prepare the necessary adjusting entries.
2. Recast the condensed financial statement figures after making the necessary adjustments.
3. Discuss the performance of Jamison's business after the adjustments have been made. (**Hint:** Compare net income to revenues and total assets before and after the adjustments.) Do you think that making the withdrawal is advisable?

PROBLEM SET A

A 1. *Preparation of*
L O 5 *Adjusting Entries*

No check figure

On June 30, the end of the current fiscal year, the following information was available to aid the Sterling Company's accountants in making adjusting entries.

a. Among the liabilities of the company is a mortgage payable in the amount of $240,000. On June 30, the accrued interest on this mortgage amounted to $12,000.

b. On Friday, July 2, the company, which is on a five-day work week and pays employees weekly, will pay its regular salaried employees $19,200.

c. On June 29, the company completed negotiations and signed a contract to provide services to a new client at an annual rate of $3,600.

d. The Supplies account showed a beginning balance of $1,615 and purchases during the year of $3,766. The end-of-year inventory revealed supplies on hand of $1,186.

e. The Prepaid Insurance account showed the following entries on June 30.

Beginning Balance	$1,530
January 1	2,900
May 1	3,366

The beginning balance represents the unexpired portion of a one-year policy purchased the previous year. The January 1 entry represents a new one-year policy, and the May 1 entry represents the additional coverage of a three-year policy.

f. The following table contains the cost and annual depreciation for buildings and equipment, all of which were purchased before the current year.

Account	Cost	Annual Depreciation
Buildings	$185,000	$ 7,300
Equipment	218,000	21,800

g. On June 1, the company completed negotiations with another client and accepted a payment of $21,000, representing one year's services paid in advance. The $21,000 was credited to Services Collected in Advance.

h. The company calculated that as of June 30 it had earned $3,500 on a $7,500 contract that would be completed and billed in August.

REQUIRED

Prepare adjusting entries for each item listed above.

A 2. *Determining*
L O 5 *Adjusting Entries,*
Posting to T
Accounts, and
Preparing an Adjusted
Trial Balance

Check Figure: Adjusted trial balance: $106,167

The schedule below presents the trial balance for the Sigma Consultants Company on December 31, 19x2.

Sigma Consultants Company
Trial Balance
December 31, 19x2

Cash	$ 12,786	
Accounts Receivable	24,840	
Office Supplies	991	
Prepaid Rent	1,400	
Office Equipment	6,700	
Accumulated Depreciation, Office Equipment		$ 1,600
Accounts Payable		1,820
Notes Payable		10,000
Unearned Fees		2,860
Kevin Moriarty, Capital		29,387
Kevin Moriarty, Withdrawals	15,000	
Fees Revenue		58,500
Salaries Expense	33,000	
Utilities Expense	1,750	
Rent Expense	7,700	
	$104,167	$104,167

The following information is also available.

a. Ending inventory of office supplies, $86.
b. Prepaid rent expired, $700.
c. Depreciation of office equipment for the period, $600.
d. Interest accrued on the note payable, $600.
e. Salaries accrued at the end of the period, $200.
f. Fees still unearned at the end of the period, $1,410.
g. Fees earned but not billed, $600.

REQUIRED

1. Open T accounts for the accounts in the trial balance plus the following: Fees Receivable; Interest Payable; Salaries Payable; Office Supplies Expense; Depreciation Expense, Office Equipment; and Interest Expense. Enter account balances.
2. Determine the adjusting entries and post them directly to the T accounts.
3. Prepare an adjusted trial balance.

A 3.
L O 5, 6

Determining Adjusting Entries and Tracing Their Effects to Financial Statements

Check Figure: Adjusted trial balance: $29,778

Having graduated from college with a degree in accounting, Joyce Ozaki opened a small tax-preparation service. At the end of its second year of operation, the Ozaki Tax Service has the following trial balance.

Ozaki Tax Service
Trial Balance
December 31, 19x2

Cash	$ 2,268	
Accounts Receivable	1,031	
Prepaid Insurance	240	
Office Supplies	782	
Office Equipment	4,100	
Accumulated Depreciation, Office Equipment		$ 410
Copier	3,000	
Accumulated Depreciation, Copier		360
Accounts Payable		635
Unearned Tax Fees		219
Joyce Ozaki, Capital		5,439
Joyce Ozaki, Withdrawals	6,000	
Fees Revenue		21,926
Office Salaries Expense	8,300	
Advertising Expense	650	
Rent Expense	2,400	
Telephone Expense	218	
	$28,989	$28,989

Joyce Ozaki made no investments in her business during the year. The following information was also available.

a. Office supplies on hand, December 31, 19x2, were $227.
b. Insurance still unexpired amounted to $120.
c. Estimated depreciation of office equipment was $410.
d. Estimated depreciation of the copier was $360.
e. The telephone expense for December was $19. This bill has been received but not recorded.
f. The services for all unearned tax fees had been performed by the end of the year.

REQUIRED

1. Open T accounts for the accounts of the trial balance plus the following: Insurance Expense; Office Supplies Expense; Depreciation Expense, Office Equipment; and Depreciation Expense, Copier. Record the balances shown in the trial balance.
2. Determine the adjusting entries and post them directly to the T accounts.
3. Prepare an adjusted trial balance, an income statement, a statement of owner's equity, and a balance sheet.

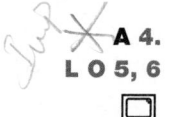

A 4. *Determining*
L O 5, 6 *Adjusting Entries*
and Tracing Their
Effects to Financial
Statements

Check Figure: Adjusted trial balance:
$209,099

At the end of its fiscal year, the trial balance for Apollo Cleaners appears as shown below. Gregory Katz, the owner, made no investments during the year. The following information is also available.

a. A study of insurance policies shows that $340 is unexpired at the end of the year.
b. An inventory of cleaning supplies shows $622 on hand.
c. Estimated depreciation for the year is $4,300 on the building and $2,100 on the delivery truck.
d. Accrued interest on the mortgage payable amounts to $500.
e. On August 1, the company signed a contract effective immediately with Stark County Hospital to dry clean, for a fixed monthly charge of $200, the uniforms used by doctors in surgery. The hospital paid for four months' service in advance.
f. Unrecorded plant wages total $982.
g. Sales and delivery wages are paid on Saturday. The weekly payroll is $480. September 30 falls on a Thursday and the company has a six-day pay week.

Apollo Cleaners
Trial Balance
September 30, 19x2

Cash (111)	$ 5,894	
Accounts Receivable (112)	13,247	
Prepaid Insurance (115)	1,700	
Cleaning Supplies (116)	3,687	
Land (141)	9,000	
Building (142)	81,000	
Accumulated Depreciation, Building (143)		$ 20,200
Delivery Truck (144)	11,500	
Accumulated Depreciation, Delivery Truck (145)		2,600
Accounts Payable (212)		10,200
Unearned Dry Cleaning Revenue (215)		800
Mortgage Payable (221)		60,000
Gregory Katz, Capital (311)		28,280
Gregory Katz, Withdrawals (312)	10,000	
Dry Cleaning Revenue (411)		60,167
Laundry Revenue (412)		18,650
Plant Wages Expense (511)	32,560	
Sales and Delivery Wages Expense (512)	18,105	
Cleaning Equipment Rent Expense (513)	3,000	
Delivery Truck Expense (514)	2,187	
Interest Expense (519)	5,500	
Other Expenses (520)	3,517	
	$200,897	$200,897

REQUIRED

1. Determine the adjusting entries and enter them in the general journal (Pages 42 and 43).
2. Open ledger accounts for each account in the trial balance plus the following: Wages Payable (213); Interest Payable (214); Insurance Expense (515); Cleaning Supplies Expense (516); Depreciation Expense, Building (517); and Depreciation Expense, Delivery Truck (518). Record the balances shown in the trial balance.
3. Post the adjusting entries to the ledger accounts, showing the correct references.
4. Prepare an adjusted trial balance.
5. Prepare an income statement, a statement of owner's equity, and a balance sheet for the year ended September 30, 19x2.
6. Give examples of how the techniques of accrual accounting affect the income statement.

A 5. *Determining*
L O 5, 6 *Adjusting Entries and Tracing Their Effects to Financial Statements*

Check Figure: Adjusted trial balance: $642,209

The Elite Livery Service was organized to provide limousine service between the airport and various suburban locations. It has just completed its second year of business. Its trial balance appears as follows.

Elite Livery Service
Trial Balance
June 30, 19x2

Cash (111)	$ 9,812	
Accounts Receivable (112)	14,227	
Prepaid Rent (117)	12,000	
Prepaid Insurance (118)	4,900	
Prepaid Maintenance (119)	12,000	
Spare Parts (141)	11,310	
Limousines (142)	200,000	
Accumulated Depreciation, Limousines (143)		$ 25,000
Notes Payable (211)		45,000
Unearned Passenger Service Revenue (212)		30,000
Raymond Lewis, Capital (311)		78,211
Raymond Lewis, Withdrawals (312)	20,000	
Passenger Service Revenue (411)		428,498
Gas and Oil Expense (511)	89,300	
Salaries Expense (512)	206,360	
Advertising Expense (513)	26,800	
	$606,709	$606,709

Raymond Lewis, the owner, made no investments during the year. The following information is also available.

a. To obtain space at the airport, Elite paid two years' rent in advance when it began business.
b. An examination of insurance policies reveals that $2,800 expired during the year.
c. To provide regular maintenance for the vehicles, a deposit of $12,000 was made with a local garage. Examination of maintenance invoices reveals that there are $10,944 in charges against the deposit.
d. An inventory of spare parts shows $1,902 on hand.
e. All of the Elite Livery Service's limousines are to be depreciated at the rate of 12.5 percent per year. There were no limousines purchased during the year.
f. A payment of $10,500 for one full year's interest on notes payable is now due.
g. Unearned Passenger Service Revenue on June 30 includes $17,815 in tickets that were purchased by employers for use by their executives and have not been redeemed.

REQUIRED

1. Determine adjusting entries and enter them in the general journal (Pages 14 and 15).
2. Open ledger accounts for the accounts in the trial balance plus the following: Interest Payable (213); Rent Expense (514); Insurance Expense (515); Spare Parts Expense (516); Depreciation Expense, Limousines (517); Maintenance Expense (518); and Interest Expense (519). Record the balances shown in the trial balance.
3. Post the adjusting entries from the general journal to the ledger accounts, showing proper references.
4. Prepare an adjusted trial balance, an income statement, a statement of owner's equity, and a balance sheet.

PROBLEM SET B

B 1. *Preparation of*
L O 5 *Adjusting Entries*
No check figure

On November 30, the end of the current fiscal year, the following information was available to assist Pinder Company's accountants in making adjusting entries.

a. The Supplies account showed a beginning balance of $2,174. Purchases during the year were $4,526. The end-of-year inventory revealed supplies on hand, $1,397.
b. The Prepaid Insurance account showed the following on November 30.

Beginning Balance	$3,580
July 1	4,200
October 1	7,272

The beginning balance represents the unexpired portion of a one-year policy purchased the previous year. The July 1 entry represents a new one-year policy, and the October 1 entry represents additional coverage in the form of a three-year policy.
c. The following table contains the cost and annual depreciation for buildings and equipment, all of which were purchased before the current year.

Account	Cost	Annual Depreciation
Buildings	$286,000	$14,500
Equipment	374,000	35,400

d. On September 1, the company completed negotiations with a client and accepted a payment of $16,800, which represented one year's services paid in advance. The $16,800 was credited to Unearned Services Revenue.
e. The company calculated that as of November 30, it had earned $4,000 on an $11,000 contract that would be completed and billed in January.
f. Among the liabilities of the company is a note payable in the amount of $300,000. On November 30, the accrued interest on this note amounted to $15,000.
g. On Saturday, December 2, the company, which is on a six-day work week, will pay its regular salaried employees $12,300.
h. On November 29, the company completed negotiations and signed a contract to provide services to a new client at an annual rate of $17,500.

REQUIRED

Prepare adjusting entries for each item listed above.

B 2. *Determining*
L O 5 *Adjusting Entries, Posting to T Accounts, and Preparing an Adjusted Trial Balance*

Check Figure: Adjusted trial balance: $121,792

The trial balance for Financial Strategies Service on December 31 is presented below.

Financial Strategies Service
Trial Balance
December 31, 19xx

Cash	$ 16,500	
Accounts Receivable	8,250	
Office Supplies	2,662	
Prepaid Rent	1,320	
Office Equipment	9,240	
Accumulated Depreciation, Office Equipment		$ 1,540
Accounts Payable		5,940
Notes Payable		11,000
Unearned Fees		2,970
Karen Howard, Capital		24,002
Karen Howard, Withdrawals	22,000	
Fees Revenue		72,600
Salaries Expense	49,400	
Rent Expense	4,400	
Utilities Expense	4,280	
	$118,052	$118,052

The following information is also available.

a. Ending inventory of office supplies, $264.
b. Prepaid rent expired, $440.
c. Depreciation of office equipment for the period, $660.
d. Accrued interest expense at the end of the period, $550.
e. Accrued salaries at the end of the month, $330.
f. Fees still unearned at the end of the period, $1,166.
g. Fees earned but unrecorded, $2,200.

REQUIRED

1. Open T accounts for the accounts in the trial balance plus the following: Fees Receivable; Interest Payable; Salaries Payable; Office Supplies Expense; Depreciation Expense, Office Equipment; and Interest Expense. Enter the balances shown in the trial balance.
2. Determine the adjusting entries and post them directly to the T accounts.
3. Prepare an adjusted trial balance.

B 3.
L O 5, 6 *Determining Adjusting Entries and Tracing Their Effects to Financial Statements*

Check Figure: Adjusted trial balance: $16,436

The Crescent Custodial Service is owned by Mike Podgorney. After six months of operation, the June 30, 19xx, trial balance for the company, presented below, was prepared. The balance of the Capital account reflects investments made by Mike Podgorney. The following information is also available.

a. Cleaning supplies of $117 are on hand.
b. Prepaid insurance represents the cost of a one-year policy purchased on January 1.
c. Prepaid rent represents a $100 payment made on January 1 toward the last month's rent of a three-year lease plus $100 rent per month for each of the six past months.
d. The cleaning equipment and the truck are depreciated at the rate of 20 percent per year (10 percent for each six-month period).
e. The unearned revenue represents a six-month payment in advance made by a customer on May 1.
f. During the last week of June, Mike completed the first stage of work on a contract that will not be billed until the contract is completed. The amount that has been earned at this stage is $400.
g. On Saturday, July 3, Mike will owe his employees $540 for one week's work (six-day work week).

Crescent Custodial Service
Trial Balance
June 30, 19xx

Cash	$ 762	
Accounts Receivable	914	
Prepaid Insurance	380	
Prepaid Rent	700	
Cleaning Supplies	1,396	
Cleaning Equipment	1,740	
Truck	3,600	
Accounts Payable		$ 170
Unearned Janitorial Fees		480
Mike Podgorney, Capital		7,095
Mike Podgorney, Withdrawals	3,000	
Janitorial Fees		7,487
Wages Expense	2,400	
Gas, Oil, and Other Truck Expenses	340	
	$15,232	$15,232

REQUIRED

1. Open T accounts for the accounts in the trial balance plus the following: Fees Receivable; Accumulated Depreciation, Cleaning Equipment; Accumulated Depreciation, Truck; Wages Payable; Rent Expense; Insurance Expense; Cleaning Supplies Expense; Depreciation Expense, Cleaning Equipment; and Depreciation Expense, Truck. Record the balances shown in the trial balance.
2. Determine the adjusting entries and post them directly to the T accounts.
3. Prepare an adjusted trial balance, an income statement, a statement of owner's equity, and a balance sheet.

B 4.

L O 5, 6

Determining Adjusting Entries and Tracing Their Effects to Financial Statements

Check Figure: Adjusted trial balance: $18,784

At the end of the first three months of operation, the trial balance of the Metropolitan Answering Service appeared as shown below. Ben Stuckey, the owner of Metropolitan, hired an accountant to prepare financial statements to determine how well the company was doing after three months. Upon examining the accounting records, the accountant found the following items of interest.

a. An inventory of office supplies reveals supplies on hand of $133.
b. The Prepaid Rent account includes the rent for the first three months plus a deposit for the last month's rent.
c. Prepaid Insurance reflects a one-year policy beginning January 1, 19x2.
d. Depreciation is $102 on the office equipment and $106 on the communications equipment for the first three months.
e. The balance of the Unearned Answering Service Revenue account represents a twelve-month service contract paid in advance on February 1.
f. On March 31, accrued wages totaled $80.

The balance of the Capital account represents investments by Ben Stuckey.

Metropolitan Answering Service
Trial Balance
March 31, 19x2

Cash (111)	$ 2,762	
Accounts Receivable (112)	4,236	
Office Supplies (115)	903	
Prepaid Rent (116)	800	
Prepaid Insurance (117)	720	
Office Equipment (141)	2,300	
Communications Equipment (143)	2,400	
Accounts Payable (211)		$ 2,673
Unearned Answering Service Revenue (213)		888
Ben Stuckey, Capital (311)		5,933
Ben Stuckey, Withdrawals (312)	2,130	
Answering Service Revenue (411)		9,002
Wages Expense (511)	1,900	
Office Cleaning Expense (513)	345	
	$18,496	$18,496

REQUIRED

1. Record the adjusting entries in the general journal (Pages 12 and 13).
2. Open ledger accounts for the accounts in the trial balance plus the following: Accumulated Depreciation, Office Equipment (142); Accumulated Depreciation, Communications Equipment (144); Wages Payable (212); Rent Expense (512); Insurance Expense (514); Office Supplies Expense (515); Depreciation Expense, Office Equipment (516); and Depreciation Expense, Communications Equipment (517). Record the balances shown in the trial balance.

3. Post the adjusting entries from the general journal to the ledger accounts, showing the correct references.
4. Prepare an adjusted trial balance.
5. Prepare an income statement, a statement of owner's equity, and a balance sheet.
6. Give examples to show how the techniques of accrual accounting affect Metropolitan's income statement.

B 5. *Determining*
L O 5, 6 *Adjusting Entries and Tracing Their Effects to Financial Statements*

Check Figure: Adjusted trial balance: $26,040

Here is the trial balance for New Wave Dance Studio at the end of its current fiscal year.

New Wave Dance Studio
Trial Balance
October 31, 19x2

Cash (111)	$ 1,028	
Accounts Receivable (112)	517	
Supplies (115)	170	
Prepaid Rent (116)	400	
Prepaid Insurance (117)	360	
Equipment (141)	4,100	
Accumulated Depreciation, Equipment (142)		$ 400
Accounts Payable (211)		380
Unearned Dance Fees (213)		900
Midge Bronson, Capital (311)		2,500
Midge Bronson, Withdrawals (312)	12,000	
Dance Fees (411)		20,995
Wages Expense (511)	3,200	
Rent Expense (512)	2,200	
Utilities Expense (515)	1,200	
	$25,175	$25,175

Midge Bronson made no investments in the business during the year. The following information is available to assist in the preparation of adjusting entries.

a. An inventory of supplies reveals $92 still on hand.
b. The prepaid rent reflects the rent for October plus the rent for the last month of the lease.
c. Prepaid insurance consists of a two-year policy purchased on May 1, 19x2.
d. Depreciation on equipment is estimated at $800.
e. Accrued wages are $65 on October 31.
f. Two-thirds of the unearned dance fees have been earned by October 31.

REQUIRED

1. Record the adjusting entries in the general journal (Page 53).
2. Open ledger accounts for the accounts in the trial balance plus the following: Wages Payable (212); Supplies Expense (513); Insurance Expense (514); and Depreciation Expense, Equipment (516). Record the balances shown in the trial balance.
3. Post the adjusting entries from the general journal to the ledger accounts, showing the correct references.
4. Prepare an adjusted trial balance, an income statement, a statement of owner's equity, and a balance sheet.

FINANCIAL REPORTING AND ANALYSIS CASES

Interpreting Financial Reports

FRA 1.
L O 2, 5

Analysis of an Asset Account

No check figure

Orion Pictures Corporation is engaged in the financing, production, and distribution of theatrical motion pictures and television programming. In Orion's 1993 annual report, the balance sheet contains an asset called Film Inventories. Film Inventories, which consist of the cost associated with producing films less the amount expensed, were $498,890,000 in 1993. The statement of cash flows reveals that the amount of film inventories expensed (amortized) during 1993 was $161,173,000 and the amount spent for new film productions was only $7,348,000 because of the company's financial problems.[6]

REQUIRED

1. What is the nature of the asset Film Inventories?
2. Prepare an entry to record the amount spent on new film production during 1993 (assume all expenditures are paid for in cash).
3. Prepare the adjusting entry that would be made to record the expense for film productions in 1993.
4. Can you suggest a method by which Orion Pictures Corporation might have determined the expense in **3** in accordance with the matching rule?

International Company

FRA 2.
L O 2, 3

Account Identification and Accrual Accounting

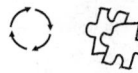

No check figure

Takashimaya Company, Limited is Japan's largest department store chain. On Takashimaya's balance sheet is an account called Gift Certificates, which contains ¥26,156 million ($176 million).[7] Is this account an asset or a liability? What transaction gives rise to the account? How is this account an example of the application of accrual accounting? Explain the conceptual issues that must be resolved for an adjusting entry to be valid.

Toys "R" Us Annual Report

FRA 3.
L O 4

Analysis of Balance Sheet and Adjusting Entries

No check figure

Refer to the balance sheet in the appendix on Toys "R" Us. Examine the accounts listed in the current assets, property and equipment, and current liabilities sections. Which accounts are most likely to have had year-end adjusting entries? Tell the nature of the adjusting entries. For more information about the property and equipment section, refer to the notes to the consolidated financial statements.

---

6. Orion Pictures Corporation, *Annual Report*, 1993.
7. Takashimaya Company, Limited, *Annual Report*, 1993.

CHAPTER 4

Completing the Accounting Cycle

LEARNING OBJECTIVES

1. State all the steps in the accounting cycle.
2. Explain the purposes of closing entries.
3. Prepare the required closing entries.
4. Prepare a post-closing trial balance.
5. Prepare reversing entries as appropriate.
6. Prepare a work sheet.
7. Use a work sheet for three different purposes.

Ecolab, Inc.

Ecolab, Inc. provides restaurants and hotels, food service and health care facilities, quick-service (fast food) restaurants, dairy plants and farms, food and beverage processors, and businesses around the world with premium products and services for cleaning, sanitizing, and maintenance. As a company whose shares are traded on the New York Stock Exchange, Ecolab is required to prepare both annual and quarterly financial statements. Whether required by law or not, the preparation of *interim* financial statements every quarter, or even every month, is a good idea for all businesses because such reports give an ongoing view of financial performance. What costs and time are involved in preparing interim financial statements?

The preparation of interim financial statements throughout the year requires more effort than the preparation of a single set of financial statements for the entire year. Each time the financial statements are prepared, adjusting entries must be determined, prepared, and recorded. Also, the ledger accounts must be prepared to begin the next accounting period. These procedures are time-consuming and costly. The advantages of preparing interim financial statements usually outweigh the costs, however, because such statements give management timely information for making decisions that improve operations. This chapter explains the procedures used to prepare financial statements at the end of an accounting period, whether that period is a month, a quarter, or a year. : : : : :

OVERVIEW OF THE ACCOUNTING CYCLE

OBJECTIVE

1 *State all the steps in the accounting cycle*

The main focus of previous chapters was on accounting measurement. This chapter emphasizes the process of accounting, or the accounting cycle. The purpose of the accounting cycle is to measure business activities in the form of transactions and to transform the transactions into financial statements that will communicate useful information to decision makers. The steps in the accounting cycle, as illustrated in Figure 1, are:

1. *Analyze* business transactions from source documents.
2. *Record* the entries in the journal.
3. *Post* the entries to the ledger and prepare a trial balance.
4. *Adjust* the accounts and prepare an adjusted trial balance.

Figure 1. Overview of the Accounting Cycle

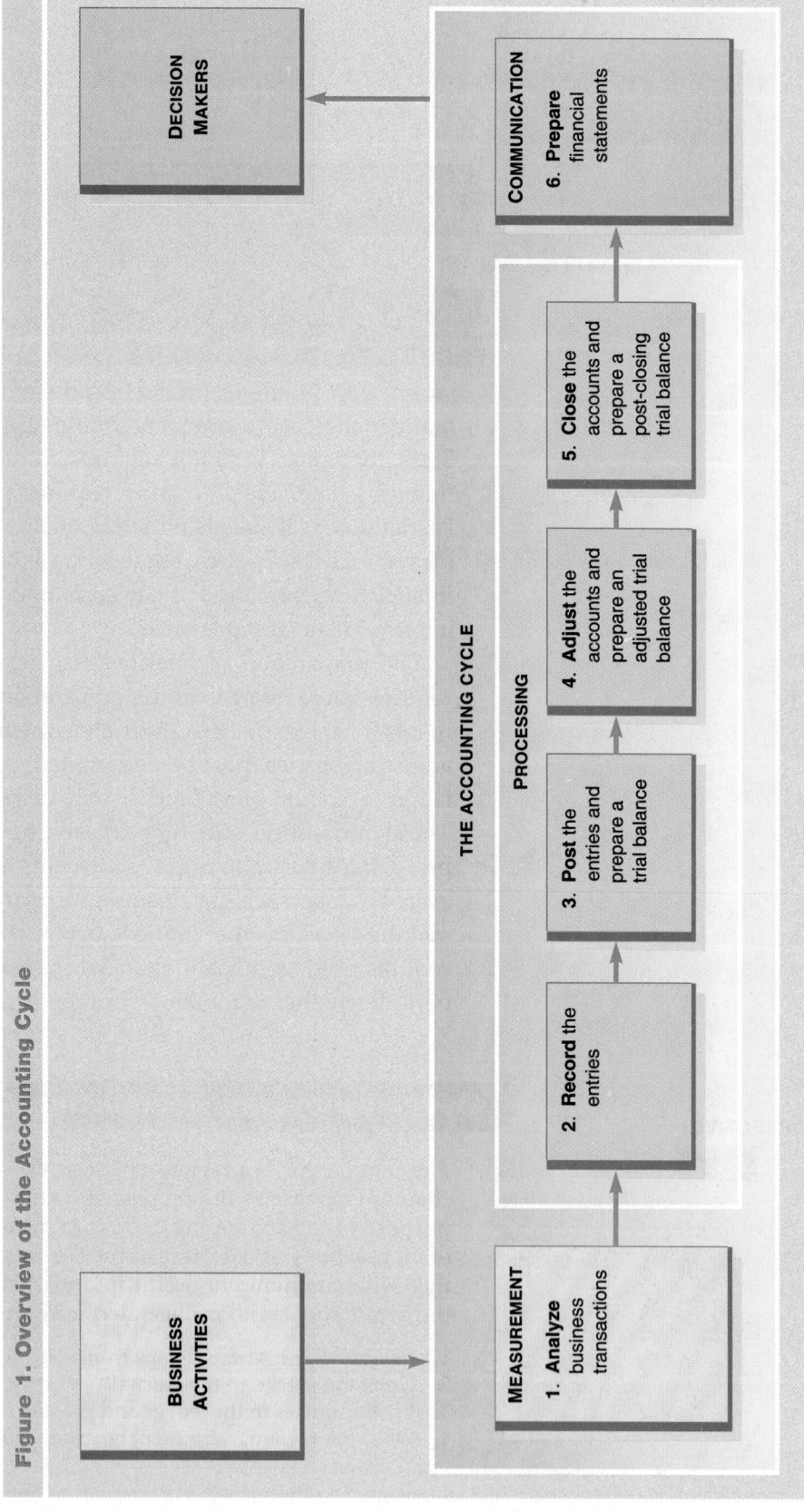

THE ACCOUNTING CYCLE

BUSINESS
ACTIVITIES

DECISION
MAKERS

MEASUREMENT

1. **Analyze**
business
transactions

2. **Record** the
entries

PROCESSING

3. **Post** the
entries and
prepare a
trial balance

4. **Adjust** the
accounts and
prepare an
adjusted trial
balance

5. **Close** the
accounts and
prepare a
post-closing
trial balance

COMMUNICATION

6. **Prepare**
financial
statements

5. *Close* the accounts and prepare a post-closing trial balance.
6. *Prepare* financial statements.

At key points during the accounting cycle, trial balances are prepared to ensure that the ledger remains in balance. You are already familiar with the first four steps, including the initial trial balance and the adjusted trial balance, and the preparation of financial statements from an adjusted trial balance. This chapter concentrates on step **5,** closing the accounts and preparing the post-closing trial balance. It also covers reversing entries, an optional first step of the next accounting period, and the work sheet, a tool accountants use to facilitate the adjusting, closing, and preparation steps in the accounting cycle.

BUSINESS BULLETIN: BUSINESS PRACTICE

Performing routine accounting functions for other companies has become big business. This practice of managing a customer's data processing operations for a fixed fee is called *outsourcing.* By leaving the data processing to an outside company, management can devote its attention to income-earning activities. Electronic Data Systems, Inc., founded by H. Ross Perot in 1962 and the source of his fortune, is the largest company in the outsourcing business (it is now owned by General Motors). EDS had revenues exceeding $8 billion in 1993 and is very profitable. ====

CLOSING ENTRIES

OBJECTIVE

2 *Explain the purposes of closing entries*

Balance sheet accounts are considered to be permanent accounts because they carry their end-of-period balances into the next accounting period. On the other hand, revenue and expense accounts are temporary, or nominal, accounts because they begin each period with a zero balance, accumulate a balance during the period, and are then cleared by means of closing entries. Closing entries are journal entries made at the end of an accounting period. They accomplish two purposes. First, closing entries set the stage for the next accounting period by clearing revenue, expense, and withdrawals accounts of their balances. Remember that the income statement reports net income (or loss) for a single accounting period and shows revenues and expenses for that period only. For the income statement to present the activity of a single accounting period, each new period must begin with zero balances in the revenue and expense accounts. The zero balances are obtained by using closing entries to clear the balances in the revenue and expense accounts at the end of each accounting period. The withdrawals account is closed in a similar manner.

Second, closing entries summarize a period's revenues and expenses. This is done by transferring the balances of revenues and expenses to the Income Summary account. This temporary account, which appears in the chart of accounts between the Withdrawals account and the first revenue account, provides a place to summarize all revenues and expenses. It is used only in the closing process and never appears in the financial statements.

The balance of the Income Summary account equals the net income or loss reported on the income statement. The net income or loss is then transferred to the Capital account. This is done because even though revenues and expenses are recorded in revenue and expense accounts, they actually represent increases and decreases in owner's equity. Closing entries transfer the net effect of increases (revenues) and decreases (expenses) to the owner's Capital account. An overview of the closing process is illustrated in Figure 2.

OBJECTIVE

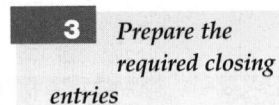

Prepare the required closing entries

REQUIRED CLOSING ENTRIES

There are four important steps in closing the accounts:

1. Closing the credit balances from the income statement accounts to the Income Summary account
2. Closing the debit balances from the income statement accounts to the Income Summary account
3. Closing the Income Summary account balance to the Capital account
4. Closing the Withdrawals account balance to the Capital account

Each of these steps is accomplished by a closing entry. All the data needed to record the closing entries are found in the adjusted trial balance. The relationships of the four kinds of entries to the adjusted trial balance are shown in Exhibit 1.

Step 1: Closing the Credit Balances from Income Statement Accounts to the Income Summary Account   On the credit side of the adjusted trial balance in Exhibit 1, two revenue accounts show balances: Advertising Fees Earned and Art Fees Earned. To close these two

Figure 2. Overview of the Closing Process

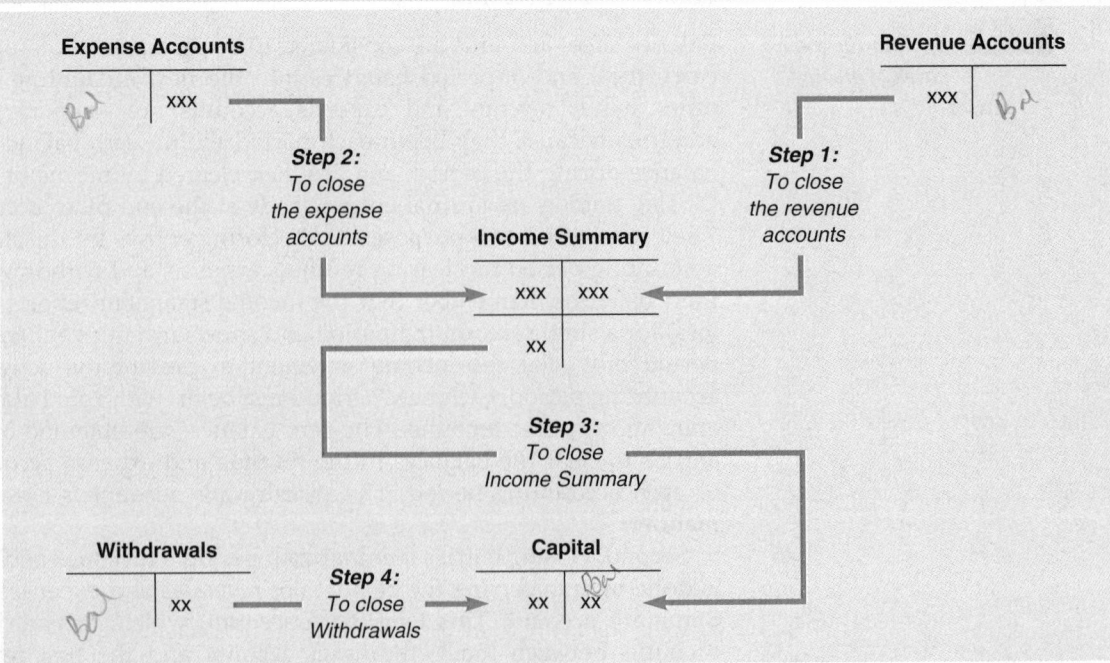

Exhibit 1. Preparing Closing Entries from the Adjusted Trial Balance

Joan Miller Advertising Agency
Adjusted Trial Balance
January 31, 19xx

Cash	$ 1,720	
Accounts Receivable	2,800	
Fees Receivable	200	
Art Supplies	1,300	
Office Supplies	600	
Prepaid Rent	400	
Prepaid Insurance	440	
Art Equipment	4,200	
Accumulated Depreciation, Art Equipment		$ 70
Office Equipment	3,000	
Accumulated Depreciation, Office Equipment		50
Accounts Payable		3,170
Wages Payable		180
Unearned Art Fees		600
Joan Miller, Capital		10,000
Joan Miller, Withdrawals	1,400	
Advertising Fees Earned		4,400
Art Fees Earned		400
Wages Expense	1,380	
Utilities Expense	100	
Telephone Expense	70	
Rent Expense	400	
Insurance Expense	40	
Art Supplies Expense	500	
Office Supplies Expense	200	
Depreciation Expense, Art Equipment	70	
Depreciation Expense, Office Equipment	50	
	$18,870	$18,870

Entry 1:

Jan. 31	Advertising Fees Earned	411	4,400	
	Art Fees Earned	412	400	
	Income Summary	313		4,800
	To close the revenue accounts			

Entry 2:

Jan. 31	Income Summary	313	2,810	
	Wages Expense	511		1,380
	Utilities Expense	512		100
	Telephone Expense	513		70
	Rent Expense	514		400
	Insurance Expense	515		40
	Art Supplies Expense	516		500
	Office Supplies Expense	517		200
	Depreciation Expense, Art Equipment	519		70
	Depreciation Expense, Office Equipment	520		50
	To close the expense accounts			

Income Summary

Jan. 31	2,810	Jan. 31	4,800
Jan. 31	**1,990**	**Bal.**	**0**

Entry 3:

Jan. 31	Income Summary	313	1,990	
	Joan Miller, Capital	311		1,990
	To close the Income Summary account			

Entry 4:

Jan. 31	Joan Miller, Capital	311	1,400	
	Joan Miller, Withdrawals	312		1,400
	To close the Withdrawals account			

accounts, a journal entry must be made debiting each in the amount of its balance and crediting the total to the Income Summary account. The effect of posting the entry is shown in Exhibit 2. Notice that the entry (1) sets the balances of the revenue accounts to zero and (2) transfers the total revenues to the credit side of the Income Summary account.

Step 2: Closing the Debit Balances from Income Statement Accounts to the Income Summary Account   Several expense accounts show balances on the debit side of the adjusted trial balance in Exhibit 1. A compound entry is needed to credit each of these expense accounts for its balance and to debit the Income Summary account for the total. The effect of

Exhibit 2. Posting the Closing Entry of the Credit Balances from the Income Statement Accounts to the Income Summary Account

Advertising Fees Earned — Account No. 411

Date	Item	Post. Ref.	Debit	Credit	Balance Debit	Balance Credit
Jan. 10		J2		1,400		1,400
19		J2		2,800		4,200
31	Adj. (h)	J3		200		4,400
31	Closing	J4	4,400			—

Income Summary — Account No. 313

Date	Item	Post. Ref.	Debit	Credit	Balance Debit	Balance Credit
Jan. 31	Closing	J4		4,800		4,800

4,400
400
4,800

Art Fees Earned — Account No. 412

Date	Item	Post. Ref.	Debit	Credit	Balance Debit	Balance Credit
Jan. 31	Adj. (g)	J3		400		400
31	Closing	J4	400			—

posting the closing entry is shown in Exhibit 3. Notice how the closing entry (1) reduces the expense account balances to zero and (2) transfers the total of the account balances to the debit side of the Income Summary account.

Step 3: Closing the Income Summary Account to the Capital Account

After the entries closing the revenue and expense accounts have been posted, the balance of the Income Summary account equals the net income or loss for the period. Since revenues are represented by the credit to Income Summary and the expenses are represented by the debit to Income Summary, a net income is indicated by a credit balance (where revenues exceed expenses), and a net loss, by a debit balance (where expenses exceed revenues). At this point, the Income Summary balance, whatever its nature, must be closed to the Capital account, as shown in Exhibit 1. The effect of posting the closing entry, when the company has a net income, is shown in Exhibit 4. Notice the dual effect of (1) closing the Income Summary account and (2) transferring the balance, net income in this case, to Joan Miller's Capital account.

Step 4: Closing the Withdrawals Account to the Capital Account

The Withdrawals account shows the amount by which capital is reduced during the period by withdrawals of cash or other assets from the business for the owner's personal use. The debit balance of the Withdrawals account is closed to the Capital account, as shown in Exhibit 1. The effect of this closing entry, as shown in Exhibit 5, is to (1) close the Withdrawals account and (2) transfer the balance to the Capital account.

THE ACCOUNTS AFTER CLOSING

After all steps in the closing process have been completed and all closing entries have been posted to the accounts, the stage is set for the next account-

Exhibit 3. Posting the Closing Entry of the Debit Balances from the Income Statement Accounts to the Income Summary Account

Wages Expense — Account No. 511

Date	Item	Post. Ref.	Debit	Credit	Balance Debit	Balance Credit
Jan. 12		J2	600		600	
26		J2	600		1,200	
31	Adj. (i)	J3	180		1,380	
31	Closing	J4		1,380	—	

Utilities Expense — Account No. 512

Date	Item	Post. Ref.	Debit	Credit	Balance Debit	Balance Credit
Jan. 29		J2	100		100	
31	Closing	J4		100	—	

Telephone Expense — Account No. 513

Date	Item	Post. Ref.	Debit	Credit	Balance Debit	Balance Credit
Jan. 30		J2	70		70	
31	Closing	J4		70	—	

Rent Expense — Account No. 514

Date	Item	Post. Ref.	Debit	Credit	Balance Debit	Balance Credit
Jan. 31	Adj. (a)	J3	400		400	
31	Closing	J4		400	—	

Insurance Expense — Account No. 515

Date	Item	Post. Ref.	Debit	Credit	Balance Debit	Balance Credit
Jan. 31	Adj. (b)	J3	40		40	
31	Closing	J4		40	—	

Art Supplies Expense — Account No. 516

Date	Item	Post. Ref.	Debit	Credit	Balance Debit	Balance Credit
Jan. 31	Adj. (c)	J3	500		500	
31	Closing	J4		500	—	

Income Summary — Account No. 313

Date	Item	Post. Ref.	Debit	Credit	Balance Debit	Balance Credit
Jan. 31	Closing	J4		4,800		4,800
31	Closing	J4	2,810			1,990

1,380
100
70
400
40
500
50
70
200
2,810

Office Supplies Expense — Account No. 517

Date	Item	Post. Ref.	Debit	Credit	Balance Debit	Balance Credit
Jan. 31	Adj. (d)	J3	200		200	
31	Closing	J4		200	—	

Depreciation Expense, Art Equipment — Account No. 519

Date	Item	Post. Ref.	Debit	Credit	Balance Debit	Balance Credit
Jan. 31	Adj. (e)	J3	70		70	
31	Closing	J4		70	—	

Depreciation Expense, Office Equipment — Account No. 520

Date	Item	Post. Ref.	Debit	Credit	Balance Debit	Balance Credit
Jan. 31	Adj. (f)	J3	50		50	
31	Closing	J4		50	—	

ing period. The ledger accounts of Joan Miller Advertising Agency, as they appear at this point, are shown in Exhibit 6. The revenue, expense, and Withdrawals accounts (temporary accounts) have zero balances. The Capital account has been increased to reflect the agency's net income and decreased for the owner's withdrawals. The balance sheet accounts (permanent accounts) show the correct balances, which are carried forward to the next period.

Exhibit 4. Posting the Closing Entry of the Income Summary Account to the Capital Account

Income Summary						Account No. 313
					Balance	
Date	Item	Post. Ref.	Debit	Credit	Debit	Credit
Jan. 31	Closing	J4		4,800		4,800
31	Closing	J4	2,810			1,990
31	Closing	J4	1,990			—

Joan Miller, Capital						Account No. 311
					Balance	
Date	Item	Post. Ref.	Debit	Credit	Debit	Credit
Jan. 1		J1		10,000		10,000
31	Closing	J4		1,990		11,990

OBJECTIVE

4 *Prepare a post-closing trial balance*

THE POST-CLOSING TRIAL BALANCE

Because it is possible to make errors in posting the closing entries to the ledger accounts, it is necessary to determine that all temporary accounts have zero balances and to double check that total debits equal total credits by preparing a new trial balance. This final trial balance, called the post-closing trial balance, is shown in Exhibit 7 for the Joan Miller Advertising Agency. Notice that only the balance sheet accounts show balances because the income statement accounts and the Withdrawals account have all been closed.

BUSINESS BULLETIN: INTERNATIONAL PRACTICE

For companies with far-flung international operations like Caterpillar, Inc., Dow Chemical, Phillips Petroleum, Gillette Co., and Bristol Myers Squibb, closing the records and preparing financial statements on a timely basis used to be a problem. It was common practice for foreign divisions of companies like these to end their fiscal year one month before the end of the fiscal year of their counterparts in the United States. This gave them the extra time they needed to perform closing procedures and mail the results back to U.S. headquarters to be used in preparation of the company's overall financial statements. Such a setup is usually unnecessary today because computers and electronic communications enable companies to close records and prepare financial statements for both foreign and domestic operations in less than a week.

Exhibit 5. Posting the Closing Entry of the Withdrawals Account to the Capital Account

Joan Miller, Withdrawals						Account No. 312
					Balance	
Date	Item	Post. Ref.	Debit	Credit	Debit	Credit
Jan. 25		J2	1,400		1,400	
31	Closing	J4		1,400	—	

Joan Miller, Capital						Account No. 311
					Balance	
Date	Item	Post. Ref.	Debit	Credit	Debit	Credit
Jan. 1		J1		10,000		10,000
31	Closing	J4		1,990		11,990
31	Closing	J4	1,400			10,590

Exhibit 6. The Accounts After Closing Entries Are Posted

Cash — Account No. 111

Date	Item	Post. Ref.	Debit	Credit	Balance Debit	Balance Credit
Jan. 1		J1	10,000		10,000	
2		J1		800	9,200	
4		J1		4,200	5,000	
5		J1		1,500	3,500	
8		J1		480	3,020	
9		J1		1,000	2,020	
10		J2	1,400		3,420	
12		J2		600	2,820	
15		J2	1,000		3,820	
26		J2		600	3,220	
29		J2		100	3,120	
31		J2		1,400	1,720	

Accounts Receivable — Account No. 113

Date	Item	Post. Ref.	Debit	Credit	Balance Debit	Balance Credit
Jan. 19		J2	2,800		2,800	

Fees Receivable — Account No. 114

Date	Item	Post. Ref.	Debit	Credit	Balance Debit	Balance Credit
Jan. 31	Adj. (h)	J3	200		200	

Art Supplies — Account No. 115

Date	Item	Post. Ref.	Debit	Credit	Balance Debit	Balance Credit
Jan. 6		J1	1,800		1,800	
31	Adj. (c)	J3		500	1,300	

Office Supplies — Account No. 116

Date	Item	Post. Ref.	Debit	Credit	Balance Debit	Balance Credit
Jan. 6		J1	800		800	
31	Adj. (d)	J3		200	600	

Prepaid Rent — Account No. 117

Date	Item	Post. Ref.	Debit	Credit	Balance Debit	Balance Credit
Jan. 2		J1	800		800	
31	Adj. (a)	J3		400	400	

Prepaid Insurance — Account No. 118

Date	Item	Post. Ref.	Debit	Credit	Balance Debit	Balance Credit
Jan. 8		J1	480		480	
31	Adj. (b)	J3		40	440	

Art Equipment — Account No. 144

Date	Item	Post. Ref.	Debit	Credit	Balance Debit	Balance Credit
Jan. 4		J1	4,200		4,200	

Accumulated Depreciation, Art Equipment — Account No. 145

Date	Item	Post. Ref.	Debit	Credit	Balance Debit	Balance Credit
Jan. 31	Adj. (e)	J3		70		70

Office Equipment — Account No. 146

Date	Item	Post. Ref.	Debit	Credit	Balance Debit	Balance Credit
Jan. 5		J1	3,000		3,000	

Accumulated Depreciation, Office Equipment — Account No. 147

Date	Item	Post. Ref.	Debit	Credit	Balance Debit	Balance Credit
Jan. 31	Adj. (f)	J3		50		50

Accounts Payable — Account No. 212

Date	Item	Post. Ref.	Debit	Credit	Balance Debit	Balance Credit
Jan. 5		J1		1,500		1,500
6		J1		2,600		4,100
9		J1	1,000			3,100
30		J2		70		3,170

Unearned Art Fees — Account No. 213

Date	Item	Post. Ref.	Debit	Credit	Balance Debit	Balance Credit
Jan. 15		J2		1,000		1,000
31	Adj. (g)	J3	400			600

Wages Payable — Account No. 214

Date	Item	Post. Ref.	Debit	Credit	Balance Debit	Balance Credit
Jan. 31	Adj. (i)	J3		180		180

(continued)

Exhibit 6. The Accounts After Closing Entries Are Posted (continued)

Joan Miller, Capital — Account No. 311

Date	Item	Post. Ref.	Debit	Credit	Balance Debit	Balance Credit
Jan. 1		J1		10,000		10,000
31	Closing	J4		1,990		11,990
31	Closing	J4	1,400			10,590

Joan Miller, Withdrawals — Account No. 312

Date	Item	Post. Ref.	Debit	Credit	Balance Debit	Balance Credit
Jan. 31		J2	1,400		1,400	
31	Closing	J4		1,400	—	

Income Summary — Account No. 313

Date	Item	Post. Ref.	Debit	Credit	Balance Debit	Balance Credit
Jan. 31	Closing	J4		4,800		4,800
31	Closing	J4	2,810			1,990
31	Closing	J4	1,990			—

Advertising Fees Earned — Account No. 411

Date	Item	Post. Ref.	Debit	Credit	Balance Debit	Balance Credit
Jan. 10		J2		1,400		1,400
19		J2		2,800		4,200
31	Adj. (h)	J3		200		4,400
31	Closing	J4	4,400			—

Art Fees Earned — Account No. 412

Date	Item	Post. Ref.	Debit	Credit	Balance Debit	Balance Credit
Jan. 31	Adj. (g)	J3		400		400
31	Closing	J4	400			—

Wages Expense — Account No. 511

Date	Item	Post. Ref.	Debit	Credit	Balance Debit	Balance Credit
Jan. 12		J2	600		600	
26		J2	600		1,200	
31	Adj. (i)	J3	180		1,380	
31	Closing	J4		1,380	—	

Utilities Expense — Account No. 512

Date	Item	Post. Ref.	Debit	Credit	Balance Debit	Balance Credit
Jan. 29		J2	100		100	
31	Closing	J4		100	—	

Telephone Expense — Account No. 513

Date	Item	Post. Ref.	Debit	Credit	Balance Debit	Balance Credit
Jan. 30		J2	70		70	
31	Closing	J4		70	—	

Rent Expense — Account No. 514

Date	Item	Post. Ref.	Debit	Credit	Balance Debit	Balance Credit
Jan. 31	Adj. (a)	J3	400		400	
31	Closing	J4		400	—	

Insurance Expense — Account No. 515

Date	Item	Post. Ref.	Debit	Credit	Balance Debit	Balance Credit
Jan. 31	Adj. (b)	J3	40		40	
31	Closing	J4		40	—	

Art Supplies Expense — Account No. 516

Date	Item	Post. Ref.	Debit	Credit	Balance Debit	Balance Credit
Jan. 31	Adj. (c)	J3	500		500	
31	Closing	J4		500	—	

Office Supplies Expense — Account No. 517

Date	Item	Post. Ref.	Debit	Credit	Balance Debit	Balance Credit
Jan. 31	Adj. (d)	J3	200		200	
31	Closing	J4		200	—	

Depreciation Expense, Art Equipment — Account No. 519

Date	Item	Post. Ref.	Debit	Credit	Balance Debit	Balance Credit
Jan. 31	Adj. (e)	J3	70		70	
31	Closing	J4		70	—	

Depreciation Expense, Office Equipment — Account No. 520

Date	Item	Post. Ref.	Debit	Credit	Balance Debit	Balance Credit
Jan. 31	Adj. (f)	J3	50		50	
31	Closing	J4		50	—	

Exhibit 7. Post-Closing Trial Balance

Joan Miller Advertising Agency
Post-Closing Trial Balance
January 31, 19xx

Cash	$ 1,720	
Accounts Receivable	2,800	
Fees Receivable	200	
Art Supplies	1,300	
Office Supplies	600	
Prepaid Rent	400	
Prepaid Insurance	440	
Art Equipment	4,200	
Accumulated Depreciation, Art Equipment		$ 70
Office Equipment	3,000	
Accumulated Depreciation, Office Equipment		50
Accounts Payable		3,170
Unearned Art Fees		600
Wages Payable		180
Joan Miller, Capital		10,590
	$14,660	$14,660

REVERSING ENTRIES: THE OPTIONAL FIRST STEP IN THE NEXT ACCOUNTING PERIOD

OBJECTIVE

5

Prepare reversing entries as appropriate

At the end of each accounting period, adjusting entries are made to bring revenues and expenses into conformity with the matching rule. A reversing entry is a general journal entry made on the first day of a new accounting period that is the exact reverse of an adjusting entry made at the end of the previous period. Reversing entries are optional. They simplify the bookkeeping process for transactions involving certain types of adjustments. Not all adjusting entries can be reversed. For the recording system used in this book, only adjustments for accruals (accrued revenues and accrued expenses) can be reversed. Deferrals cannot be reversed because such reversals would not simplify the bookkeeping process in future accounting periods.

To see how reversing entries can be helpful, consider the adjusting entry made in the records of Joan Miller Advertising Agency to accrue office wages expense:

Jan. 31	Wages Expense	180	
	Wages Payable		180
	To accrue unrecorded wages		

When the secretary is paid on the next regular payday, the accountant would make this entry:

Feb. 9	Wages Payable	180	
	Wages Expense	420	
	Cash		600
	Payment of two weeks' wages to secretary,		
	$180 of which accrued in the previous period		

Notice that when the payment is made, if there is no reversing entry, the accountant must look in the records to find out how much of the $600 applies to the current accounting period and how much is applicable to the previous period. This may seem easy in our example, but think of how difficult and time-consuming it would be if a company had hundreds of employees, especially if some were paid on different schedules. A reversing entry helps solve the problem of applying revenues and expenses to the correct accounting period. It is exactly what its name implies: a reversal made by debiting the credits and crediting the debits of a previously made adjusting entry.

For example, notice the following sequence of entries and their effects on the ledger account Wages Expense:

1. Adjusting Entry

Jan. 31   Wages Expense 180
                Wages Payable 180

2. Closing Entry

Jan. 31   Income Summary 1,380
                Wages Expense 1,380

3. Reversing Entry

Feb. 1   Wages Payable 180
                Wages Expense 180

4. Payment Entry

Feb. 9   Wages Expense 600
                Cash 600

Wages Expense					Account No. 511	
					Balance	
Date		Post. Ref.	Debit	Credit	Debit	Credit
Jan.	12	J2	600		600	
	26	J2	600		1,200	
	31	J3	180		1,380	
	31	J4		1,380	—	
Feb.	1	J5		180		180
	9	J6	600		420	

Entry 1 adjusted Wages Expense to accrue $180 in the January accounting period.

Entry 2 closed the $1,380 in Wages Expense for January to Income Summary, leaving a zero balance.

Entry 3, the reversing entry, set up a credit balance of $180 on February 1 in Wages Expense equal to the expense recognized through the adjusting entry in January (and also reduced the liability account Wages Payable to a zero balance). The reversing entry always sets up an abnormal balance in the income statement account and produces a zero balance in the balance sheet account.

Entry 4 recorded the $600 payment of two weeks' wages as a debit to Wages Expense, automatically leaving a balance of $420, which represents the correct wages expense to date in February.

The reversing entry simplified the process of making the payment entry on February 9.

Reversing entries apply to any accrued expenses or revenues. In the case of Joan Miller Advertising Agency, wages expense was the only accrued expense. However, the asset Fees Receivable was created as a result of the adjusting entry made to accrue fees earned but not yet billed. The adjusting entry for this accrued revenue would require the following reversing entry:

Feb. 1   Advertising Fees Earned 200
                Fees Receivable 200
                To reverse the adjusting entry for
                accrued fees receivable

When the series of advertisements is finished, the company can credit all the proceeds to Advertising Fees Earned without regard to the amount accrued in the previous period. The credit will automatically be reduced to the amount earned during February by the $200 debit in the account.

As noted earlier, under the system of recording used in this book, reversing entries apply only to accruals. Reversing entries do not apply to deferrals, such as those that involve supplies, prepaid rent, prepaid insurance, depreciation, or unearned art fees.

THE WORK SHEET: AN ACCOUNTANT'S TOOL

OBJECTIVE

6 *Prepare a work sheet*

As seen earlier, the flow of information that affects a business does not stop arbitrarily at the end of an accounting period. In preparing financial reports, accountants must collect relevant data to determine what should be included. For example, they need to examine insurance policies to see how much prepaid insurance has expired, examine plant and equipment records to determine depreciation, take an inventory of supplies on hand, and calculate the amount of accrued wages. These calculations, together with other computations, analyses, and preliminary drafts of statements, make up the accountants' working papers. Working papers are important for two reasons. First, they help accountants organize their work and thus avoid omitting important data or steps that affect the financial statements. Second, they provide evidence of past work so that accountants or auditors can retrace their steps and support the information in the financial statements.

A special kind of working paper is the work sheet. The work sheet is often used as a preliminary step in the preparation of financial statements. Using a work sheet lessens the possibility of leaving out an adjustment, helps the accountant check the arithmetical accuracy of the accounts, and facilitates the preparation of financial statements. The work sheet is never published and is rarely seen by management. It is a tool for the accountant.

Because preparing a work sheet is a very mechanical process, many accountants use a microcomputer. In some cases, accountants use a spreadsheet program to prepare the work sheet. In other cases, general ledger software is used to prepare financial statements from the adjusted trial balance.

PREPARING THE WORK SHEET

So far, adjusting entries have been entered directly in the journal and posted to the ledger, and the financial statements have been prepared from the adjusted trial balance. The process has been relatively simple because Joan Miller Advertising Agency is a small company. For larger companies, which may require many adjusting entries, a work sheet is essential. To illustrate the preparation of the work sheet, we continue with the Joan Miller Advertising Agency example.

A common form of work sheet has one column for account names and/or numbers and ten more columns with the headings shown in Exhibit 8. Notice that the work sheet is identified by a heading that consists of (1) the name of the company, (2) the title "Work Sheet," and (3) the period of time covered (as on the income statement).

There are five steps in the preparation of a work sheet.

1. Enter and total the account balances in the Trial Balance columns.
2. Enter and total the adjustments in the Adjustments columns.
3. Enter and total the adjusted account balances in the Adjusted Trial Balance columns.
4. Extend the account balances from the Adjusted Trial Balance columns to the Income Statement columns or the Balance Sheet columns.

5. Total the Income Statement columns and the Balance Sheet columns. Enter the net income or net loss in both pairs of columns as a balancing figure, and recompute the column totals.

1. **Enter and total the account balances in the Trial Balance columns.** The titles and balances of the accounts as of January 31 are copied directly from the ledger into the Trial Balance columns, as shown in Exhibit 8. When a work sheet is used, the accountant does not have to prepare a separate trial balance.

2. **Enter and total the adjustments in the Adjustments columns.** The required adjustments for Joan Miller Advertising Agency are entered in the Adjustments columns of the work sheet, as shown in Exhibit 9. As each adjustment is entered, a letter is used to identify its debit and credit parts. The first adjustment, identified by the letter **a,** is to recognize rent expense, which results in a debit to Rent Expense and a credit to Prepaid Rent. In practice, this letter may be used to reference supporting computations or documentation underlying the adjusting entry and may simplify the recording of adjusting entries in the general journal.

   If an adjustment calls for an account that has not been used in the trial balance, the new account is added below the accounts listed in the trial balance. The trial balance includes only the accounts that have balances. For example, Rent Expense has been added in Exhibit 9. The only exception to this rule is the Accumulated Depreciation accounts, which have a zero balance only in the initial period of operation. Accumulated Depreciation accounts are listed immediately after their associated asset accounts.

   When all the adjustments have been made, the two Adjustments columns must be totaled. This step proves that the debits and credits of the adjustments are equal and generally reduces errors in the preparation of the work sheet.

3. **Enter and total the adjusted account balances in the Adjusted Trial Balance columns.** Exhibit 10 shows the adjusted trial balance. It is prepared by combining the amount of each account in the original Trial Balance columns with the corresponding amount in the Adjustments columns and entering each result in the Adjusted Trial Balance columns.

   Some examples from Exhibit 10 illustrate crossfooting, or adding and subtracting a group of numbers horizontally. The first line shows Cash with a debit balance of $1,720. Because there are no adjustments to the Cash account, $1,720 is entered in the Debit column of the Adjusted Trial Balance columns. The second line is Accounts Receivable, which shows a debit of $2,800 in the Trial Balance columns. Again, because there are no adjustments to Accounts Receivable, the $2,800 balance is carried over to the Debit column of the Adjusted Trial Balance columns. The next line is Art Supplies, which shows a debit of $1,800 in the Trial Balance columns and a credit of $500 from adjustment **c** in the Adjustments columns. Subtracting $500 from $1,800 results in a $1,300 debit balance in the Adjusted Trial Balance columns. This process is followed for all the accounts, including those added below the trial balance totals. The Adjusted Trial Balance columns are then footed (totaled) to check the accuracy of the crossfooting.

4. **Extend the account balances from the Adjusted Trial Balance columns to the Income Statement columns or the Balance Sheet columns.** Every account in the adjusted trial balance is either a balance sheet account or an income statement account. Each account is extended to its proper place as a debit or credit in either the Income Statement columns or the Balance Sheet columns. The result of extending the accounts is shown in Exhibit 11. Revenue and expense accounts are copied to the Income Statement columns. Assets, liabilities, and the Capital and Withdrawals accounts are extended to the Balance Sheet columns. To avoid overlooking an account, extend the accounts line by line,

beginning with the first line (Cash) and not omitting any subsequent lines. For instance, the Cash debit balance of $1,720 is extended to the Debit column of the Balance Sheet columns, the Accounts Receivable debit balance of $2,800 is extended to the same Debit column, and so forth. Each amount is carried across to only one column.

5. **Total the Income Statement columns and the Balance Sheet columns. Enter the net income or net loss in both pairs of columns as a balancing figure, and recompute the column totals.** This last step, as shown in Exhibit 12, is necessary to compute net income or net loss and to prove the arithmetical accuracy of the work sheet.

Net income (or net loss) is equal to the difference between the total debits and credits of the Income Statement columns. It also equals the difference between the total debits and credits of the Balance Sheet columns.

Revenue (Income Statement Credit column total)	$4,800
Expenses (Income Statement Debit column total)	(2,810)
Net Income	$1,990

In this case, revenues (Credit column) exceed expenses (Debit column). Consequently, the company has a net income of $1,990. The same difference is shown between the total debits and credits of the Balance Sheet columns.

The $1,990 is entered in the debit side of the Income Statement columns to balance the columns, and it is entered in the credit side of the Balance Sheet columns to balance the columns. Remember that the excess of revenue over expenses (net income) increases owner's equity and that increases in owner's equity are recorded by credits.

When a net loss occurs, the opposite rule applies. The excess of expenses over revenue—net loss—is placed in the credit side of the Income Statement columns as a balancing figure. It is then placed in the debit side of the Balance Sheet columns because a net loss decreases owner's equity, and decreases in owner's equity are recorded by debits.

As a final check, the four columns are totaled again. If the Income Statement columns and the Balance Sheet columns do not balance, an account may have been extended or sorted to the wrong column, or an error may have been made in adding the columns. Of course, equal totals in the two pairs of columns are not absolute proof of accuracy. If an asset has been carried to the debit Income Statement column and a similar error involving revenues or liabilities has been made, the work sheet still balances, but the net income figure is wrong.

BUSINESS BULLETIN: TECHNOLOGY IN PRACTICE

The work sheet is a good application for electronic spreadsheet software programs like Lotus 1-2-3 and Microsoft Excel. Constructing a work sheet using spreadsheet software takes time, but once it is done, the work sheet can be used again and again. The principal advantage of electronic preparation over manual preparation is that each time a number is entered or revised, the entire electronic work sheet is updated automatically without the possibility of addition or extension mistakes. For example, if an error in an adjusting entry is corrected, the proper extensions to the other columns are made, all columns are re-added, and net income is recomputed. Of course, the software is purely mechanical. People are still responsible for inputting the correct numbers in the first place. ══════

OBJECTIVE

7 *Use a work sheet for three different purposes*

USING THE WORK SHEET

The completed work sheet assists the accountant in three principal tasks: (1) preparing the financial statements, (2) recording the adjusting entries, and (3) recording the closing entries in the general journal to prepare the records for the beginning of the next period.

Preparing the Financial Statements   Once the work sheet has been completed, preparing the financial statements is simple because the account balances have been sorted into the Income Statement and Balance Sheet columns. The income statement shown in Exhibit 13 was prepared from the account balances in the Income Statement columns of Exhibit 12. The statement of owner's equity and the balance sheet of Joan Miller Advertising Agency are presented in Exhibits 14 and 15. The account balances for these statements are drawn from the Balance Sheet columns of the work sheet shown in Exhibit 12. Notice that the total assets and the total liabilities and owner's equity in the balance sheet are not the same as the totals of the Balance Sheet columns in the work sheet. The reason is that the Accumulated Depreciation and Withdrawals accounts have normal balances that appear in

Exhibit 13. Income Statement for Joan Miller Advertising Agency

Joan Miller Advertising Agency
Income Statement
For the Month Ended January 31, 19xx

Revenues		
Advertising Fees Earned		$4,400
Art Fees Earned		400
Total Revenues		$4,800
Expenses		
Wages Expense	$1,380	
Utilities Expense	100	
Telephone Expense	70	
Rent Expense	400	
Insurance Expense	40	
Art Supplies Expense	500	
Office Supplies Expense	200	
Depreciation Expense, Art Equipment	70	
Depreciation Expense, Office Equipment	50	
Total Expenses		2,810
Net Income		$1,990

Exhibit 14. Statement of Owner's Equity for Joan Miller Advertising Agency

Joan Miller Advertising Agency
Statement of Owner's Equity
For the Month Ended January 31, 19xx

Joan Miller, Capital, January 1, 19xx		—
Add: Investment by Joan Miller	$10,000	
Net Income	1,990	$11,990
Subtotal		$11,990
Less: Withdrawals		1,400
Joan Miller, Capital, January 31, 19xx		$10,590

Exhibit 15. Balance Sheet for Joan Miller Advertising Agency

Joan Miller Advertising Agency
Balance Sheet
January 31, 19xx

Assets

Cash		$ 1,720
Accounts Receivable		2,800
Fees Receivable		200
Art Supplies		1,300
Office Supplies		600
Prepaid Rent		400
Prepaid Insurance		440
Art Equipment	$4,200	
Less Accumulated Depreciation	70	4,130
Office Equipment	$3,000	
Less Accumulated Depreciation	50	2,950
Total Assets		$14,540

Liabilities

Accounts Payable	$3,170	
Unearned Art Fees	600	
Wages Payable	180	
Total Liabilities		$ 3,950

Owner's Equity

Joan Miller, Capital, January 31, 19xx		10,590
Total Liabilities and Owner's Equity		$14,540

different columns from their associated accounts on the balance sheet. In addition, the Capital account on the balance sheet is the amount determined on the statement of owner's equity. Except for reflecting any new investments by the owner, the financial statements have been prepared from the work sheet, not from the ledger accounts. For the ledger accounts to show the correct balances, the adjusting entries must be journalized and posted to the ledger.

Recording the Adjusting Entries   For Joan Miller Advertising Agency, the adjustments were determined while completing the work sheet because they are essential to the preparation of the financial statements. The adjusting entries could have been recorded in the general journal at that point. However, it is usually convenient to delay recording them until after the work sheet and the financial statements have been prepared because this task can be done at the same time the closing entries are recorded, a process described earlier in this chapter. Recording the adjusting entries with appropriate explanations in the general journal, as shown in Exhibit 16, is an easy step. The information can simply be copied from the work sheet. Adjusting entries are then posted to the general ledger.

Recording the Closing Entries   The four closing entries for Joan Miller Advertising Agency are entered in the journal and posted to the ledger as shown in Exhibits 2 through 5. All accounts that need closing, except for Withdrawals, may be found in the Income Statement columns of the work sheet.

Exhibit 16. Adjustments from the Work Sheet Entered in the General Journal

Date		Description	Post. Ref.	Debit	Credit
19xx		General Journal			Page 3
Jan.	31	Rent Expense	514	400	
		Prepaid Rent	117		400
		To recognize expiration of one month's rent			
	31	Insurance Expense	515	40	
		Prepaid Insurance	118		40
		To recognize expiration of one month's insurance			
	31	Art Supplies Expense	516	500	
		Art Supplies	115		500
		To recognize art supplies used during the month			
	31	Office Supplies Expense	517	200	
		Office Supplies	116		200
		To recognize office supplies used during the month			

(continued)

Exhibit 16. Adjustments from the Work Sheet Entered in the General Journal (continued)

Date		Description	Post. Ref.	Debit	Credit
Jan.	31	Depreciation Expense, Art Equipment	519	70	
		Accumulated Depreciation, Art Equipment	145		70
		To record depreciation of art equipment for a month			
	31	Depreciation Expense, Office Equipment	520	50	
		Accumulated Depreciation, Office Equipment	147		50
		To record depreciation of office equipment for a month			
	31	Unearned Art Fees	213	400	
		Art Fees Earned	412		400
		To recognize performance of services paid for in advance			
	31	Fees Receivable	114	200	
		Advertising Fees Earned	411		200
		To accrue unrecorded revenue			
	31	Wages Expense	511	180	
		Wages Payable	214		180
		To accrue unrecorded wages			

(General Journal — Page 3)

CHAPTER REVIEW

REVIEW OF LEARNING OBJECTIVES

1. **State all the steps in the accounting cycle.** The steps in the accounting cycle are (1) analyze business transactions from source documents, (2) record the entries in the journal, (3) post the entries to the ledger and prepare a trial balance, (4) adjust the accounts and prepare an adjusted trial balance, (5) close the accounts and prepare a post-closing trial balance, and (6) prepare financial statements.

2. **Explain the purposes of closing entries.** Closing entries have two purposes. First, they clear the balances of all temporary accounts (revenue and expense accounts and Withdrawals) so that they have zero balances at the beginning of the next accounting period. Second, they summarize a period's revenues and expenses in the Income Summary account so that the net income or loss for the period can be transferred as a total to owner's equity.

3. **Prepare the required closing entries.** Closing entries are prepared by first transferring the revenue and expense account balances to the Income Summary account. Then the balance of the Income Summary account is transferred to the Capital

account. And, finally, the balance of the Withdrawals account is transferred to the Capital account.

4. **Prepare a post-closing trial balance.** As a final check on the balance of the ledger and to ensure that all temporary (nominal) accounts have been closed, a post-closing trial balance is prepared after the closing entries are posted to the ledger accounts.

5. **Prepare reversing entries as appropriate.** Reversing entries are optional entries made on the first day of a new accounting period to simplify routine bookkeeping procedures. They reverse certain adjusting entries made in the previous period. Under the system used in this text, they apply only to accruals.

6. **Prepare a work sheet.** There are five steps in the preparation of a work sheet: (1) Enter and total the account balances in the Trial Balance columns; (2) enter and total the adjustments in the Adjustments columns; (3) enter and total the adjusted account balances in the Adjusted Trial Balance columns; (4) extend the account balances from the Adjusted Trial Balance columns to the Income Statement or Balance Sheet columns; and (5) total the Income Statement and Balance Sheet columns, enter the net income or net loss in both pairs of columns as a balancing figure, and recompute the column totals.

7. **Use a work sheet for three different purposes.** A work sheet is useful in (1) preparing the financial statements, (2) recording the adjusting entries, and (3) recording the closing entries. The balance sheet and income statement can be prepared directly from the Balance Sheet and Income Statement columns of the completed work sheet. The statement of owner's equity is prepared using Withdrawals, net income, additional investments, and the beginning balance of the owner's Capital account. Notice that the ending balance of Capital does not appear on the work sheet. Adjusting entries can be recorded in the general journal directly from the Adjustments columns of the work sheet. Closing entries may be prepared from the Income Statement columns, except for Withdrawals, which is found in the Balance Sheet columns.

REVIEW OF CONCEPTS AND TERMINOLOGY

The following concepts and terms were introduced in this chapter.

L O 1 **Accounting cycle:** The sequence of steps followed in the accounting process to measure business transactions and transform them into financial statements.

L O 2 **Closing entries:** Journal entries made at the end of an accounting period that set the stage for the next accounting period by clearing the temporary accounts of their balances and that summarize a period's revenues and expenses.

L O 6 **Crossfooting:** Adding and subtracting numbers across a row.

L O 2 **Income Summary:** A temporary account used during the closing process that holds a summary of all revenues and expenses before the net income or loss is transferred to the Capital account.

L O 4 **Post-closing trial balance:** A trial balance prepared at the end of the accounting period after all adjusting and closing entries have been posted; a final check on the balance of the ledger.

L O 5 **Reversing entries:** Journal entries made on the first day of a new accounting period that reverse certain adjusting entries and simplify the bookkeeping process for the next accounting period.

L O 6 **Working papers:** Documents used by accountants to organize their work and to support the information in the financial statements.

L O 6 **Work sheet:** A type of working paper used as a preliminary step in the preparation of financial statements.

REVIEW PROBLEM
PREPARATION OF CLOSING ENTRIES

LO 3 At the end of the current fiscal year, the adjusted trial balance for Westwood Movers Company appeared as follows:

Westwood Movers Company
Adjusted Trial Balance
June 30, 19xx

Cash	$ 14,200	
Accounts Receivable	18,600	
Packing Supplies	10,400	
Prepaid Insurance	7,900	
Land	4,000	
Building	80,000	
Accumulated Depreciation, Building		$ 7,500
Trucks	106,000	
Accumulated Depreciation, Trucks		27,500
Accounts Payable		7,650
Unearned Storage Fees		5,400
Mortgage Payable		70,000
Art Burton, Capital		104,740
Art Burton, Withdrawals	18,000	
Moving Fees Earned		159,000
Storage Fees Earned		26,400
Drivers' Wages Expense	94,000	
Fuel Expense	19,000	
Office Wages Expense	14,400	
Office Equipment Rental Expense	3,000	
Utilities Expense	4,450	
Insurance Expense	4,200	
Depreciation Expense, Building	4,000	
Depreciation Expense, Trucks	6,040	
	$408,190	$408,190

REQUIRED Prepare the necessary closing entries.

ANSWER TO REVIEW PROBLEM

June 30	Moving Fees Earned	159,000	
	Storage Fees Earned	26,400	
	Income Summary		185,400
	To close the revenue accounts		
30	Income Summary	149,090	
	Drivers' Wages Expense		94,000
	Fuel Expense		19,000
	Office Wages Expense		14,400
	Office Equipment Rental Expense		3,000
	Utilities Expense		4,450
	Insurance Expense		4,200
	Depreciation Expense, Building		4,000
	Depreciation Expense, Trucks		6,040
	To close the expense accounts		

June 30	Income Summary	36,310	
	Art Burton, Capital		36,310
	To close the Income Summary account and transfer the balance to the Capital account		
30	Art Burton, Capital	18,000	
	Art Burton, Withdrawals		18,000
	To close the Withdrawals account		

CHAPTER ASSIGNMENTS

QUESTIONS

1. Resequence the following activities to indicate the correct order of the accounting cycle.
   a. The transactions are entered in the journal.
   b. The financial statements are prepared.
   c. The transactions are analyzed from the source documents.
   d. The adjusting entries are prepared.
   e. The closing entries are prepared.
   f. The transactions are posted to the ledger.

2. What are the two purposes of closing entries?

3. What is the difference between adjusting entries and closing entries?

4. What is the purpose of the Income Summary account?

5. Which of the following accounts do not show a balance after the closing entries are prepared and posted?
   a. Insurance Expense
   b. Accounts Receivable
   c. Commission Revenue
   d. Prepaid Insurance
   e. Withdrawals
   f. Supplies
   g. Supplies Expense
   h. Owner's Capital

6. What is the significance of the post-closing trial balance?

7. Which of the following accounts would you expect to find on the post-closing trial balance?
   a. Insurance Expense
   b. Accounts Receivable
   c. Commission Revenue
   d. Prepaid Insurance
   e. Withdrawals
   f. Supplies
   g. Supplies Expense
   h. Owner's Capital

8. How do reversing entries simplify the bookkeeping process?

9. To what types of adjustments do reversing entries apply? To what types do they not apply?

10. Why are working papers important to accountants?

11. Why are work sheets never published and rarely seen by management?

12. Can the work sheet be used as a substitute for the financial statements? Explain your answer.

13. What is the normal balance (debit or credit) of the following accounts?
    a. Cash
    b. Accounts Payable

c. Prepaid Rent
d. Sam Jones, Capital
e. Commission Revenue
f. Sam Jones, Withdrawals
g. Rent Expense
h. Accumulated Depreciation, Office Equipment
i. Office Equipment

14. Should the Adjusted Trial Balance columns of the work sheet be totaled before or after the adjusted amounts are carried to the Income Statement and Balance Sheet columns? Discuss your answer.

15. What sequence should be followed in extending the amounts in the Adjusted Trial Balance columns to the Income Statement and Balance Sheet columns? Discuss your answer.

16. Do the Income Statement columns and the Balance Sheet columns of the work sheet balance after the amounts from the Adjusted Trial Balance columns are extended?

17. Do the totals of the Balance Sheet columns of the work sheet agree with the totals on the balance sheet? Explain your answer.

18. Should adjusting entries be posted to the ledger accounts before or after the closing entries? Explain your answer.

19. At the end of the accounting period, does the posting of adjusting entries to the ledger precede or follow the preparation of the work sheet?

SHORT EXERCISES

SE 1. *Accounting Cycle*
L O 1
Check Figures: b, f, c, h, e, i, a, d, g

Resequence the following activities to indicate the correct order of the accounting cycle.

a. Close the accounts.
b. Analyze the transactions.
c. Post the entries.
d. Prepare the financial statements.
e. Adjust the accounts.
f. Record the transactions.
g. Prepare the post-closing trial balance.
h. Prepare the initial trial balance.
i. Prepare the adjusted trial balance.

SE 2. *Closing Revenue*
L O 3 *Accounts*
No check figure

Assuming credit balances at the end of the accounting period of $3,400 in Patient Services and $1,800 in Laboratory Fees, prepare the required closing entry. The accounting period ends December 31.

SE 3. *Closing Expense*
L O 3 *Accounts*
No check figure

Assuming debit balances at the end of the accounting period of $1,400 in Rent Expense, $1,100 in Wages Expense, and $500 in Other Expenses, prepare the required closing entry. The accounting period ends December 31.

SE 4. *Closing the Income*
L O 3 *Summary Account*
No check figure

Assuming total revenues were $5,200 and total expenses were $3,000, prepare the journal entry to close the Income Summary account to R. Richards's Capital account. The accounting period ends December 31.

SE 5. *Closing the*
L O 3 *Withdrawals*
Account
No check figure

Assuming that withdrawals of cash by the owner for personal expenses during the accounting period were $800, prepare the journal entry to close the Withdrawals account to R. Richards's Capital account. The accounting period ends December 31.

SE 6. *Posting Closing*
L O 3 *Entries*

Check Figure: Ending balance of
R. Richards, Capital: $2,700

Show the effects of the transactions in SE 2 through SE 5 by entering beginning balances in appropriate T accounts and recording the transactions. Assume that R. Richards's Capital account has a beginning balance of $1,300.

SE 7. *Preparation of*
L O 5 *Reversing Entries*

No check figure

Below, indicated by letters, are the adjusting entries at the end of March. Prepare the required reversing entries.

Account Name	Adjustments	
	Debit	Credit
Prepaid Insurance		(a) 180
Accumulated Depreciation, Office Equipment		(b) 1,050
Salaries Expense	(c) 360	
Insurance Expense	(a) 180	
Depreciation Expense, Office Equipment	(b) 1,050	
Salaries Payable		(c) 360
	1,590	1,590

SE 8. *Effects of Reversing*
L O 5 *Entries*

Check Figure: Ending balance of
Salaries Expense: $120

Assume that prior to the adjustment in SE 7, Salaries Expense had a debit balance of $1,800 and Salaries Payable had a zero balance. Prepare a T account for each of these accounts. Enter the beginning balance; post the adjustment for accrued salaries, the appropriate closing entry, and the reversing entry; and enter the transaction in the T accounts for a payment of $480 for salaries on April 3.

SE 9. *Preparing Closing*
L O 7 *Entries from a Work*
Sheet

No check figure

Prepare the required closing entries for the year ended December 31, using the following items from the Income Statement columns of a work sheet and assuming that withdrawals by the owner, R. Carrera, for personal expenses were $6,000.

Account Name	Income Statement	
	Debit	Credit
Repair Revenue		32,860
Wages Expense	12,260	
Rent Expense	1,800	
Supplies Expense	6,390	
Insurance Expense	1,370	
Depreciation Expense, Repair Equipment	2,020	
	23,840	32,860
Net Income	9,020	
	32,860	32,860

EXERCISES

E 1. *Preparation of*
L O 3 *Closing Entries*

No check figure

The adjusted trial balance for the Nafzger Realty Company at the end of its fiscal year is shown at the top of the next page. Prepare the required closing entries.

Nafzger Realty Company
Adjusted Trial Balance
December 31, 19xx

Cash	$ 4,275	
Accounts Receivable	2,325	
Prepaid Insurance	585	
Office Supplies	440	
Office Equipment	6,300	
Accumulated Depreciation, Office Equipment		$ 765
Automobile	6,750	
Accumulated Depreciation, Automobile		750
Accounts Payable		1,700
Unearned Management Fees		1,500
R. Nafzger, Capital		11,535
R. Nafzger, Withdrawals	7,000	
Sales Commissions Earned		31,700
Office Salaries Expense	13,500	
Advertising Expense	2,525	
Rent Expense	2,650	
Telephone Expense	1,600	
	$47,950	$47,950

E 2.   *Reversing Entries*
L O 5
Check Figure: Wages expense for January: $1,250

Selected June T accounts for Jefferson Company are presented below.

1. In which of the accounts would a reversing entry be helpful? Why?
2. Prepare the appropriate reversing entry.
3. Prepare the entry to record the payment on January 5 for wages totaling $1,570. How much of this amount represents wages expense for January?

Supplies				**Supplies Expense**			
12/1 Bal.	430	12/31 Adjust.	640	12/31 Adjust.	640	12/31 Closing	640
Dec. purchases	470			Bal.	—		
Bal.	260						

Wages Payable				**Wages Expense**			
		12/31 Adjust.	320	Dec. wages	1,970	12/31 Closing	2,290
		Bal.	320	12/31 Adjust.	320		
				Bal.	—		

E 3.   *Preparation of a*
L O 6   *Trial Balance*
Check Figure: Trial balance: $35,100

The following alphabetical list presents the accounts and balances for Sklar Realty on December 31, 19x3. All the accounts have normal balances.

Accounts Payable	$ 5,140
Accounts Receivable	2,550
Accumulated Depreciation, Office Equipment	450
Advertising Expense	600
Cash	2,545
Office Equipment	5,170
Prepaid Insurance	560
Rent Expense	2,400
Revenue from Commissions	19,300

J. Sklar, Capital	$10,210
J. Sklar, Withdrawals	9,000
Supplies	275
Wages Expense	12,000

Prepare the trial balance by listing the accounts in the correct order for work sheet preparation, with the balances in the appropriate debit or credit column.

E 4. *Completion of a*
L O 6 *Work Sheet*

Check Figure: Adjusted trial balance: $45; Net Income: $7

The following is a highly simplified alphabetical list of trial balance accounts and their normal balances for the month ended October 31, 19xx.

Trial Balance Accounts and Balances

Accounts Payable	$ 4
Accounts Receivable	7
Accumulated Depreciation, Office Equipment	1
Cash	4
Office Equipment	8
Prepaid Insurance	2
Rita Wilkins, Capital	12
Rita Wilkins, Withdrawals	6
Service Revenue	23
Supplies	4
Unearned Revenue	3
Utilities Expense	2
Wages Expense	10

1. Prepare a work sheet, entering the trial balance accounts in the order in which they would normally appear and entering the balances in the correct debit or credit column.
2. Complete the work sheet using the following information:
   a. Expired insurance, $1.
   b. Of the unearned revenue balance, $2 has been earned by the end of the month.
   c. Estimated depreciation on office equipment, $1.
   d. Accrued wages, $1.
   e. Unused supplies on hand, $1.

E 5. *Preparation of a*
L O 3, 7 *Statement of*
Owner's Equity

No check figure

The Capital, Withdrawals, and Income Summary accounts for Ruben's Barber Shop are shown in T account form below. The closing entries have been recorded for the year ended December 31, 19xx.

Ruben Ortega, Capital

12/31	9,000	1/1	26,000
		12/31	19,000
		Bal.	**36,000**

Ruben Ortega, Withdrawals

4/1	3,000	12/31	9,000
7/1	3,000		
10/1	3,000		
Bal.	—		

Income Summary

12/31	43,000	12/31	62,000
12/31	19,000		
Bal.	—		

Prepare a statement of owner's equity for Ruben's Barber Shop.

E 6.
L O 7
Derivation of Adjusting Entries from Trial Balance and Income Statement Columns

No check figure

Below is a partial work sheet of Siemons Company at June 30, 19x1, in which the Trial Balance and Income Statement columns have been completed. All amounts shown are in dollars.

Account Name	Trial Balance Debit	Trial Balance Credit	Income Statement Debit	Income Statement Credit
Cash	7			
Accounts Receivable	12			
Supplies	11			
Prepaid Insurance	8			
Building	25			
Accumulated Depreciation, Building		8		
Accounts Payable		4		
Unearned Revenue		2		
M. B., Capital		32		
Revenue		44		46
Wages Expense	27		30	
	90	90		
Insurance Expense			4	
Supplies Expense			8	
Depreciation Expense, Building			2	
			44	46
Net Income			2	
			46	46

1. Determine what adjustments have been made. (Assume that no adjustments have been made to Accounts Receivable or Accounts Payable.)
2. Prepare a balance sheet.

E 7.
L O 5, 7
Preparation of Adjusting and Reversing Entries from Work Sheet Columns

No check figure

The items below are from the Adjustments columns of a work sheet dated June 30, 19xx.

Account Name	Adjustments Debit		Adjustments Credit	
Prepaid Insurance			(a)	120
Office Supplies			(b)	315
Accumulated Depreciation, Office Equipment			(c)	700
Accumulated Depreciation, Store Equipment			(d)	1,100
Office Salaries Expense	(e)	120		
Store Salaries Expense	(e)	240		
Insurance Expense	(a)	120		
Office Supplies Expense	(b)	315		
Depreciation Expense, Office Equipment	(c)	700		
Depreciation Expense, Store Equipment	(d)	1,100		
Salaries Payable			(e)	360
		2,595		2,595

1. Prepare the adjusting entries.
2. Where required, prepare appropriate reversing entries.

E 8. *Preparation of Closing Entries from the Work Sheet*

L O 3, 7

No check figure

The items below are from the Income Statement columns of the work sheet for DiPietro Repair Shop for the year ended December 31, 19xx.

Account Name	Income Statement	
	Debit	Credit
Repair Revenue		25,620
Wages Expense	8,110	
Rent Expense	1,200	
Supplies Expense	4,260	
Insurance Expense	915	
Depreciation Expense, Repair Equipment	1,345	
	15,830	25,620
Net Income	9,790	
	25,620	25,620

Prepare entries to close the revenue, expense, Income Summary, and Withdrawals accounts. Mr. DiPietro withdrew $5,000 during the year.

SKILLS DEVELOPMENT EXERCISES

Conceptual Analysis

SDE 1. *Interim Financial Statements*

L O 1

No check figure

Ocean Oil Services Company provides services for drilling operations off the coast of Louisiana. The company has a significant amount of debt to River National Bank in Baton Rouge. The bank requires the company to provide it with financial statements every quarter. Explain what is involved in preparing financial statements every quarter.

SDE 2. *Accounting Efficiency*

L O 5

No check figure

Way Heaters Company, located just outside Milwaukee, Wisconsin, is a small, successful manufacturer of industrial heaters. The company's heaters are used, for instance, to heat chocolate for candy manufacturers. The company sells its heaters to some of its customers on credit with generous terms. The terms usually specify payment six months after purchase and an interest rate based on current bank rates. Because the interest on the loans accrues a little bit every day but is not paid until the due date of the note, it is necessary to make an adjusting entry at the end of each accounting period to debit Interest Receivable and credit Interest Income for the amount of the interest accrued but not paid to date. The company prepares financial statements every month. Keeping track of what has been accrued in the past is time-consuming because the notes carry different dates and interest rates. Discuss what the accountant can do to simplify the process of making the adjusting entry for accrued interest each month.

Ethical Dilemma

SDE 3. *Ethics and Time Pressure*

L O 2

No check figure

Jay Wheeler, the assistant accountant for *WB Company,* has made adjusting entries and is preparing the adjusted trial balance for the first six months of the year. Financial statements must be delivered to the bank by 5 o'clock to support a critical loan agreement. By noon, Jay cannot balance the adjusted trial balance. The figures are off by $1,320, so he increases the balance of the Capital account by $1,320. He closes the accounts, prepares the statements, and sends them to the bank on time. Jay hopes that no one will notice the problem and believes he can find the error and correct it by the end of next month. Are Jay's actions ethical? Why or why not? Did Jay have other alternatives?

Research Activity

Interview of a Local Business Person

Arrange to spend about an hour interviewing the owner, manager, or accountant of a local service or retail business. Your goal is to learn as much as you can about the accounting cycle of the person's business. Ask the interviewee to show you his or her accounting records and to tell you how such transactions as sales, purchases, payments, and payroll are handled. Examine the documents used to support the transactions. Look at any journals, ledgers, or work sheets. Does the business use a computer? Does it use its own accounting system, or does it use an outside or centralized service? Does it use the cash or the accrual basis of accounting? When does it prepare adjusting entries? When does it prepare closing entries? How often does it prepare financial statements? Does it prepare reversing entries? How do its procedures differ from those described in the text? When the interview is finished, organize and write up your findings and be prepared to present them to your class.

Decision-Making Practice

Conversion from Accrual to Cash Statement

Adele's Secretarial Service is a very simple business. Adele provides typing services for students at the local university. Her accountant prepared the income statement that appears below for the year ended June 30, 19x4.

Adele's Secretarial Service
Income Statement
For the Year Ended June 30, 19x4

Revenues		
Typing Services		$20,980
Expenses		
Rent Expense	$2,400	
Depreciation Expense, Office Equipment	2,200	
Supplies Expense	960	
Other Expenses	1,240	
Total Expenses		6,800
Net Income		$14,180

In reviewing this statement, Adele is puzzled. She knows she withdrew $15,600 in cash for personal expenses, yet the cash balance in the company's bank account increased from $460 to $3,100 from last June 30 to this June 30. She wants to know how her net income could be less than the cash she took out of the business if there is an increase in the cash balance.

Her accountant has completed the closing entries and shows her the balance sheets for June 30, 19x4 and June 30, 19x3. She explains that besides the change in the cash balance, accounts receivable from customers decreased by $1,480 and accounts payable increased by $380 (supplies are the only items Adele buys on credit). The only other asset or liability account that changed during the year was Accumulated Depreciation, Office Equipment, which increased by $2,200.

1. Explain to Adele why the accountant is answering her question by pointing out year-to-year changes in the balance sheet.
2. Verify the cash balance increase by preparing a statement that lists the receipts of cash and the expenditures of cash during the year.
3. How did you treat depreciation expense? Why?

PROBLEM SET A

A 1. *Closing Entries and*
L O 3 *Preparation of*
Financial Statements

Check Figure: Total assets: $56,808

Hillcrest Campgrounds, owned by Cynthia Tobin, rents out campsites in a wooded park. The adjusted trial balance for Hillcrest Campgrounds on May 31, 19x4, the end of the current fiscal year, follows.

Hillcrest Campgrounds
Adjusted Trial Balance
May 31, 19x4

Cash	$ 2,040	
Accounts Receivable	3,660	
Supplies	114	
Prepaid Insurance	594	
Land	15,000	
Building	45,900	
Accumulated Depreciation, Building		$ 10,500
Accounts Payable		1,725
Wages Payable		825
Cynthia Tobin, Capital		46,535
Cynthia Tobin, Withdrawals	18,000	
Campsite Rentals		44,100
Wages Expense	11,925	
Insurance Expense	1,892	
Utilities Expense	900	
Supplies Expense	660	
Depreciation Expense, Building	3,000	
	$103,685	$103,685

REQUIRED

1. Record the closing entries in the general journal.
2. From the information given, prepare an income statement, a statement of owner's equity, and a balance sheet. Assume no additional investments by the owner.

A 2. *Preparation of a*
L O 6, 7 *Work Sheet and*
Financial Statements

Check Figure: Net income: $103,150

The trial balance shown at the top of the next page was taken from the ledger of Deer Creek Tennis Club at the end of the company's fiscal year.

REQUIRED

1. Enter the trial balance amounts in the Trial Balance columns of a work sheet, and complete the work sheet using the following information.
   a. Expired advertising, $4,500.
   b. Inventory of unused supplies, $1,200.
   c. Estimated depreciation on building, $30,000.
   d. Estimated depreciation on equipment, $12,000.
   e. Previously unearned revenues now earned, $9,600.
   f. Accrued but unpaid property taxes, $22,500.
   g. Accrued but unpaid wages, $9,000.
2. Prepare an income statement, a statement of owner's equity, and a balance sheet. Assume no additional investments by Ruth Accardo.

Deer Creek Tennis Club
Trial Balance
June 30, 19x5

Cash	$ 26,200	
Prepaid Advertising	14,100	
Supplies	7,200	
Land	100,000	
Building	645,200	
Accumulated Depreciation, Building		$ 230,000
Equipment	156,000	
Accumulated Depreciation, Equipment		38,400
Accounts Payable		73,000
Unearned Revenue, Locker Fees		12,600
Ruth Accardo, Capital		471,150
Ruth Accardo, Withdrawals	54,000	
Revenues from Court Fees		678,100
Wages Expense	342,000	
Maintenance Expense	51,600	
Advertising Expense	35,250	
Utilities Expense	64,800	
Miscellaneous Expense	6,900	
	$1,503,250	$1,503,250

A 3. *Preparation of a*
L O 3, 5, *Work Sheet;*
6, 7 *Financial Statements; and Adjusting, Closing, and Reversing Entries*

Check Figure: Net Loss: ($713)

José Vargas opened his executive search service on July 1, 19x5. Some customers paid for his services after they were rendered, and others paid in advance for one year of service. After six months of operation, Vargas wanted to know how his business stood. The trial balance on December 31 appears below.

Vargas Executive Search Service
Trial Balance
December 31, 19x5

Cash	$ 1,713	
Prepaid Rent	1,800	
Office Supplies	413	
Office Equipment	3,750	
Accounts Payable		$ 3,173
Unearned Revenue		1,823
José Vargas, Capital		10,000
José Vargas, Withdrawals	7,200	
Search Revenue		10,140
Utilities Expense	1,260	
Wages Expense	9,000	
	$25,136	$25,136

REQUIRED

1. Enter the trial balance amounts in the Trial Balance columns of the work sheet. Remember that accumulated depreciation is listed with its asset account. Complete the work sheet using the following information.
   a. One year's rent had been paid in advance when Vargas began business.
   b. Inventory of unused office supplies, $75.
   c. One-half year's depreciation on office equipment, $300.
   d. Service rendered that had been paid for in advance, $863.

e. Executive search services rendered during the month but not yet billed, $270.

f. Wages earned by employees but not yet paid, $188.

2. From the work sheet, prepare an income statement, a statement of owner's equity, and a balance sheet.

3. From the work sheet, prepare adjusting and closing entries and, if required, reversing entries.

4. What is your evaluation of Vargas's first six months in business?

A 4.

L O 3, 5,

6, 7

Preparation of a Work Sheet; Financial Statements; and Adjusting, Closing, and Reversing Entries

Check Figure: Net income: $31,196

The following trial balance was taken from the ledger of Zolnay Package Delivery Company on August 31, 19x4, the end of the company's fiscal year.

Zolnay Package Delivery Company
Trial Balance
August 31, 19x4

Cash	$ 5,036	
Accounts Receivable	14,657	
Prepaid Insurance	2,670	
Delivery Supplies	7,350	
Office Supplies	1,230	
Land	7,500	
Building	98,000	
Accumulated Depreciation, Building		$ 26,700
Trucks	51,900	
Accumulated Depreciation, Trucks		15,450
Office Equipment	7,950	
Accumulated Depreciation, Office Equipment		5,400
Accounts Payable		4,698
Unearned Lockbox Fees		4,170
Mortgage Payable		36,000
Ruth Zolnay, Capital		64,365
Ruth Zolnay, Withdrawals	15,000	
Delivery Services Revenue		141,735
Lockbox Fees Earned		14,400
Truck Drivers' Wages Expense	63,900	
Office Salaries Expense	22,200	
Gas, Oil, and Truck Repairs Expense	15,525	
	$312,918	$312,918

REQUIRED

1. Enter the trial balance amounts in the Trial Balance columns of a work sheet and complete the work sheet using the following information.

a. Expired insurance, $1,530.

b. Inventory of unused delivery supplies, $715.

c. Inventory of unused office supplies, $93.

d. Estimated depreciation, building, $7,200.

e. Estimated depreciation, trucks, $7,725.

f. Estimated depreciation, office equipment, $1,350.

g. The company credits the lockbox fees of customers who pay in advance to the Unearned Lockbox Fees account. Of the amount credited to this account during the year, $2,815 had been earned by August 31.

h. Lockbox fees earned but unrecorded and uncollected at the end of the accounting period, $408.

i. Accrued but unpaid truck drivers' wages at the end of the year, $960.

2. Prepare an income statement, a statement of owner's equity, and a balance sheet. Assume no additional investments by Ruth Zolnay.

3. Prepare adjusting, closing, and, if required, reversing entries from the work sheet.

✗ A 5. *The Complete*
L O 3, 4, *Accounting Cycle:*
6, 7 *Two Months*
Check Figures: Net income for
October: $481; Net income for
November: $517

On October 1, 19xx, Jeff Romanoff opened Romanoff Appliance Service. During the month, he completed the following transactions for the company.

Oct. 1 Deposited $5,000 of his savings in a bank account for the company.
1 Paid the rent for a store for one month, $425.
1 Paid the premium on a one-year insurance policy, $480.
2 Purchased repair equipment from Perry Company for $4,200. The terms were $600 down and $300 per month for one year. The first payment is due November 1.
5 Purchased repair supplies from Bridger Company on credit, $468.
8 Paid cash for an advertisement in a local newspaper, $60.
15 Received cash repair revenue for the first half of the month, $400.
21 Paid Bridger Company on account, $225.
25 Withdrew cash from the company bank account to pay living expenses, $450.
31 Received cash repair revenue for the second half of October, $975.

REQUIRED FOR OCTOBER

1. Prepare journal entries to record the October transactions.
2. Open the following accounts: Cash (111); Prepaid Insurance (117); Repair Supplies (119); Repair Equipment (144); Accumulated Depreciation, Repair Equipment (145); Accounts Payable (212); Jeff Romanoff, Capital (311); Jeff Romanoff, Withdrawals (312); Income Summary (313); Repair Revenue (411); Store Rent Expense (511); Advertising Expense (512); Insurance Expense (513); Repair Supplies Expense (514); and Depreciation Expense, Repair Equipment (515). Post the October journal entries to the ledger accounts.
3. Prepare a trial balance in the Trial Balance columns of a work sheet, and complete the work sheet using the following information.
   a. One month's insurance has expired.
   b. The remaining inventory of unused repair supplies is $169.
   c. The estimated depreciation on repair equipment is $70.
4. From the work sheet, prepare an income statement, a statement of owner's equity, and a balance sheet for October.
5. From the work sheet, prepare and post adjusting and closing entries.
6. Prepare a post-closing trial balance.

During November, Jeff Romanoff completed the following transactions for Romanoff Appliance Service.

Nov. 1 Paid the monthly rent, $425.
1 Made the monthly payment to Perry Company, $300.
6 Purchased additional repair supplies on credit from Bridger Company, $863.
15 Received cash repair revenue for the first half of the month, $914.
20 Paid cash for an advertisement in the local newspaper, $60.
23 Paid Bridger Company on account, $600.
25 Withdrew cash from the company for living expenses, $450.
30 Received cash repair revenue for the last half of the month, $817.

REQUIRED FOR NOVEMBER

7. Prepare and post journal entries to record the November transactions.
8. Prepare a trial balance in the Trial Balance columns of a work sheet and complete the work sheet based on the following information.
   a. One month's insurance has expired.
   b. The inventory of unused repair supplies is $413.
   c. The estimated depreciation on repair equipment is $70.
9. From the work sheet, prepare the November income statement, statement of owner's equity, and balance sheet.
10. From the work sheet, prepare and post adjusting and closing entries.
11. Prepare a post-closing trial balance.

PROBLEM SET B

B 1. *Closing Entries and*
L O 3 *Preparation of*
Financial Statements
Check Figure: Total assets: $6,943

Quality Trailer Rental owns thirty small trailers that are rented by the day for local moving jobs. The adjusted trial balance for Quality Trailer Rental for the year ended June 30, 19x4, which is the end of the current fiscal year, is shown at the top of the next page.

Quality Trailer Rental
Adjusted Trial Balance
June 30, 19x4

Cash	$ 692	
Accounts Receivable	972	
Supplies	119	
Prepaid Insurance	360	
Trailers	12,000	
Accumulated Depreciation, Trailers		$ 7,200
Accounts Payable		271
Wages Payable		200
Elena Mota, Capital		5,694
Elena Mota, Withdrawals	7,200	
Trailer Rentals		45,546
Wages Expense	23,400	
Insurance Expense	720	
Supplies Expense	266	
Depreciation Expense, Trailers	2,400	
Other Expenses	10,782	
	$58,911	$58,911

REQUIRED

1. From the information given, record closing entries.
2. Prepare an income statement, a statement of owner's equity, and a balance sheet. Assume no additional investments by Elena Mota.

B 2. *Preparation of a*
L O 6, 7 *Worksheet and*
Financial Statements
Check Figure: Net income: $57,739

The following trial balance was taken from the ledger of Whitehead Bowling Lanes at the end of the company's fiscal year.

Whitehead Bowling Lanes
Trial Balance
December 31, 19x4

Cash	$ 16,214	
Accounts Receivable	7,388	
Supplies	1,304	
Prepaid Insurance	1,800	
Prepaid Advertising	900	
Land	5,000	
Building	100,000	
Accumulated Depreciation, Building		$ 22,400
Equipment	125,000	
Accumulated Depreciation, Equipment		22,000
Accounts Payable		15,044
Notes Payable		70,000
Unearned Revenues		2,300
Donna Webb, Capital		60,813
Donna Webb, Withdrawals	24,000	
Revenues		616,263
Wages Expense	377,114	
Advertising Expense	14,300	
Utilities Expense	42,200	
Maintenance Expense	84,100	
Miscellaneous Expense	9,500	
	$808,820	$808,820

REQUIRED

1. Enter the trial balance amounts in the Trial Balance columns of a work sheet, and complete the work sheet using the following information.
   a. Inventory of unused supplies, $156.
   b. Expired insurance, $1,500.
   c. Expired advertising, $900.
   d. Estimated depreciation on building, $4,800.
   e. Estimated depreciation on equipment, $11,000.
   f. Previously unearned revenues now earned, $2,000.
   g. Accrued but unpaid wages, $3,962.
   h. Accrued but unpaid property taxes, $10,000.
2. Prepare an income statement, a statement of owner's equity, and a balance sheet. Assume no additional investments by Donna Webb.

B 3.   *Preparation of a*
L O 3, 5,   *Work Sheet;*
6, 7   *Financial*
         Statements;
         Adjusting, Closing,
         and Reversing
         Entries

Check Figure: Net income: $8,631

Roman Patel began his consulting practice immediately after earning his M.B.A. To help him get started, several clients paid him retainers (payment in advance) for future services. Other clients paid when service was provided. After one year, the firm had the trial balance that follows.

Roman Patel, Consultant
Trial Balance
December 31, 19x5

Cash	$ 3,250	
Accounts Receivable	2,709	
Office Supplies	382	
Office Equipment	3,755	
Accounts Payable		$ 1,296
Unearned Retainers		5,000
Roman Patel, Capital		4,000
Roman Patel, Withdrawals	6,000	
Consulting Fees		18,175
Rent Expense	1,800	
Utilities Expense	717	
Wages Expense	9,858	
	$28,471	$28,471

REQUIRED

1. Enter the trial balance amounts in the Trial Balance columns of a work sheet, and complete the work sheet using the following information.
   a. Inventory of unused supplies, $58.
   b. Estimated depreciation on office equipment, $600.
   c. Services rendered during the month but not yet billed, $725.
   d. Services rendered to clients who paid in advance that should be applied against unearned retainers, $3,150.
   e. Wages earned by employees, but not yet paid, $120.
2. Prepare an income statement, a statement of owner's equity, and a balance sheet. Assume no additional investments by Roman Patel.
3. Prepare adjusting, closing, and, if required, reversing entries.
4. How would you evaluate Mr. Patel's first year in practice?

B 4. *Preparation of a*
L O 3, 5, *Work Sheet;*
6, 7 *Financial*
Statements;
Adjusting, Closing,
and Reversing
Entries

Check Figure: Net income: $49,311

At the end of the current fiscal year, the trial balance of the Esquire Theater appeared as follows:

Esquire Theater
Trial Balance
December 31, 19x5

Cash	$ 15,900	
Accounts Receivable	9,272	
Prepaid Insurance	9,800	
Office Supplies	390	
Cleaning Supplies	1,795	
Land	10,000	
Building	200,000	
Accumulated Depreciation, Building		$ 19,700
Theater Furnishings	185,000	
Accumulated Depreciation, Theater Furnishings		32,500
Office Equipment	15,800	
Accumulated Depreciation, Office Equipment		7,780
Accounts Payable		22,753
Gift Books Liability		20,950
Mortgage Payable		150,000
Mildred Brown, Capital		156,324
Mildred Brown, Withdrawals	30,000	
Ticket Sales Revenues		205,700
Theater Rental		22,600
Usher Wages Expense	92,000	
Office Wages Expense	12,000	
Utilities Expense	56,350	
	$638,307	$638,307

REQUIRED

1. Enter the trial balance amounts in the Trial Balance columns of a work sheet, and complete the work sheet using the following information.
   a. Expired insurance, $8,700.
   b. Inventory of unused office supplies, $122.
   c. Inventory of unused cleaning supplies, $234.
   d. Estimated depreciation on the building, $7,000.
   e. Estimated depreciation on the theater furnishings, $18,000.
   f. Estimated depreciation on the office equipment, $1,580.
   g. The company credits all gift books sold during the year to the Gift Books Liability account. A gift book is a booklet of ticket coupons purchased in advance as a gift. The recipient redeems the coupons at some point in the future. On December 31, it was estimated that $18,900 worth of the gift books had been redeemed.
   h. Accrued but unpaid usher wages at the end of the accounting period, $430.
2. Prepare an income statement, a statement of owner's equity, and a balance sheet. Assume no additional investments by Mildred Brown.
3. Prepare adjusting, closing, and, if required, reversing entries.

B 5. *The Complete*
L O 3, 5, *Accounting Cycle:*
6, 7 *Two Months*

Check Figures: Net Income for May: $556; Net Income for June: $189

Will Springer opened the Springer Repair Store on May 1, 19xx. During the first two months of operation, he completed the following transactions.

May 1 Began business by depositing $6,000 in a company bank account.
    1 Paid the premium on a one-year insurance policy, $600.
    1 Paid the current month's rent, $520.

May 2 Purchased repair equipment from Fisk Company for $2,200. The terms were $300 down and $100 per month for nineteen months. The first payment is due June 1.
   5 Purchased repair supplies from Cordero Company on credit, $195.
   14 Paid the utility bill for May, $77.
   15 Received cash bicycle repair revenue for the first half of May, $681.
   20 Paid Cordero Company on account, $100.
   29 Withdrew cash for personal living expenses, $400.
   31 Received cash bicycle repair revenue for the last half of May, $655.

June 1 Paid the monthly rent, $520.
   1 Made the monthly payment to Fisk Company, $100.
   9 Purchased repair supplies on credit from Cordero Company, $447.
   15 Received cash bicycle repair revenue for the first half of June, $525.
   18 Paid the utility bill for June, $83.
   19 Paid Cordero Company on account, $200.
   28 Withdrew cash for personal living expenses, $400.
   30 Received cash bicycle repair revenue for the last half of June, $687.

REQUIRED

1. Prepare journal entries to record the May transactions.
2. Open the following accounts: Cash (111); Prepaid Insurance (117); Repair Supplies (119); Repair Equipment (144); Accumulated Depreciation, Repair Equipment (145); Accounts Payable (212); Will Springer, Capital (311); Will Springer, Withdrawals (312); Income Summary (313); Bicycle Repair Revenue (411); Store Rent Expense (511); Utilities Expense (512); Insurance Expense (513); Repair Supplies Expense (514); and Depreciation Expense, Repair Equipment (515). Post the May journal entries to ledger accounts.
3. Prepare a trial balance in the Trial Balance columns of a work sheet, and complete the work sheet using the following information.
   a. One month's insurance has expired.
   b. The remaining inventory of unused repair supplies is $97.
   c. The estimated depreciation on repair equipment is $35.
4. From the work sheet, prepare an income statement, a statement of owner's equity, and a balance sheet for May.
5. From the work sheet, prepare and post adjusting and closing entries for May.
6. Prepare a post-closing trial balance for May.
7. Prepare and post the journal entries to record the June transactions.
8. Prepare a trial balance for June in the Trial Balance columns of a work sheet, and complete the work sheet based on the following information.
   a. One month's insurance has expired.
   b. The inventory of unused repair supplies is $209.
   c. The estimated depreciation on repair equipment is $35.
9. From the work sheet, prepare an income statement, a statement of owner's equity, and a balance sheet for June.
10. From the work sheet, prepare and post adjusting and closing entries for June.
11. Prepare a post-closing trial balance for June.

FINANCIAL REPORTING AND ANALYSIS CASES

Interpreting Financial Reports

FRA 1. *Closing Entries*
L O 2, 3

No check figure

H&R Block, Inc. is the world's largest tax preparation service firm. In its 1993 annual report, the statement of earnings (in thousands, without earnings per share information) for the year ended April 30, 1993, appeared as shown on the next page.[1]

1. H&R Block, Inc., *Annual Report*, 1993.

Revenues

Service Revenues	$1,382,306
Royalties	112,560
Investment Income	15,038
Other Revenues	15,426
Total Revenues	$1,525,330

Expenses

Employee Compensation and Benefits	$ 754,002
Occupancy and Equipment Expense	220,815
Marketing and Advertising Expense	52,260
Supplies, Freight, and Postage Expense	59,209
Other Operating Expenses	143,774
Total Expenses	1,230,060
Earnings Before Income Taxes	295,270
Income Taxes	114,565
Net Earnings	$ 180,705

In its statement of retained earnings, the company reported distributing cash in the amount of $103,462,000 to the owners in 1993.

REQUIRED

1. Prepare, in general journal form, the closing entries that would have been made by H&R Block on April 30, 1993. Treat income taxes as an expense, and treat cash distributions as a withdrawal.
2. Based on the way you handled expenses and cash distributions in **1** and their ultimate effect on the owners' capital, what theoretical reason can you give for not including expenses and cash distributions in the same closing entry?

International Company

FRA 2.
L O 1, 3

Accounting Cycle and Closing Entries

No check figure

Nestlé S.A., maker of such well-known products as Nescafé, Lean Cuisine, and Perrier, is one of the largest and most internationally diverse companies in the world. Only 2 percent of its $54.5 billion in revenues comes from its home country of Switzerland, with the rest coming from sales in almost every other country of the world. Nestlé has 482 factories in 69 countries[2] and is highly decentralized; that is, many of its divisions operate as separate companies in their countries. Managing the accounting operations of such a vast empire is a tremendous challenge. In what ways do you think the accounting cycle, including the closing process, would be the same for Nestlé as it is for Joan Miller Advertising Agency and in what ways would it be different?

Toys "R" Us Annual Report

FRA 3.
L O 1, 3

Fiscal Year, Closing Process, and Interim Reports

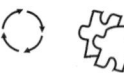

No check figure

Refer to the Notes to Consolidated Financial Statements in the appendix on Toys "R" Us. When does Toys "R" Us end its fiscal year? What reasons can you give for the company's having chosen this date? From the standpoint of completing the accounting cycle, what advantages does this date have? Does Toys "R" Us prepare interim financial statements? What are the implications of interim financial statements for the accounting cycle?

---

2. Nestlé S.A., *Annual Report,* 1992.

COMPREHENSIVE PROBLEM: JOAN MILLER ADVERTISING AGENCY

This problem continues with the Joan Miller Advertising Agency, the company used to illustrate the accounting cycle in the chapters on measuring business transactions, measuring business income, and completing the accounting cycle. It is necessary in some instances to refer to those chapters in completing this problem.

The January 31, 19xx, post-closing trial balance for the Joan Miller Advertising Agency is as follows:

Cash	$ 1,720	
Accounts Receivable	2,800	
Fees Receivable	200	
Art Supplies	1,300	
Office Supplies	600	
Prepaid Rent	400	
Prepaid Insurance	440	
Art Equipment	4,200	
Accumulated Depreciation, Art Equipment		$ 70
Office Equipment	3,000	
Accumulated Depreciation, Office Equipment		50
Accounts Payable		3,170
Unearned Art Fees		600
Wages Payable		180
Joan Miller, Capital		10,590
	$14,660	$14,660

During February, the agency engaged in the following transactions.

Feb. 1 Received an additional investment of cash from Joan Miller, $5,000.
2 Purchased additional office equipment with cash, $900.
5 Received art equipment transferred to the business from Joan Miller, $1,200.
6 Purchased additional office supplies with cash, $90.
7 Purchased additional art supplies on credit from Taylor Supply Company, $450.
8 Completed the series of advertisements for Marsh Tire Company that began on January 31, fees receivable of $200 (see page 105), and billed Marsh Tire Company for the total services performed, including the accrued revenues (fees receivable) that had been recognized in an adjusting entry in January, $800.
9 Paid the secretary for two weeks' wages, $600.
12 Paid the amount due to Morgan Equipment for the office equipment purchased last month, $1,500.
13 Accepted an advance fee in cash for artwork to be done for another agency, $1,600.
14 Purchased a copier (office equipment) from Morgan Equipment for $2,100, paying $350 in cash and agreeing to pay the rest in equal payments over the next five months.
15 Performed advertising services and received a cash fee, $950.
16 Received payment on account from Ward Department Stores for services performed last month, $2,800.
19 Paid amount due for the telephone bill that was received and recorded at the end of January, $70.
20 Performed advertising services for Ward Department Stores and agreed to accept payment next month, $3,200.
21 Performed art services for a cash fee, $580.
22 Received and paid the utility bill for February, $110.
23 Paid the secretary for two weeks' wages, $600.
26 Paid the rent for March in advance, $400.

Feb. 27 Received the telephone bill for February, which is to be paid next month, $80.

28 Paid out cash to Joan Miller as a withdrawal for personal living expenses, $1,400.

REQUIRED

1. Record in the general journal and post to the general ledger the reversing entries necessary on February 1 for Wages Payable and Fees Receivable (see pages 105–107). (Begin the general journal on Page 5.)
2. Record the transactions for February in the general journal.
3. Post the February transactions to the general ledger accounts.
4. Prepare a trial balance in the Trial Balance columns of a work sheet.
5. Prepare adjusting entries and complete the work sheet using the following information.
   a. One month's prepaid rent has expired, $400.
   b. One month's prepaid insurance has expired, $40.
   c. An inventory of art supplies reveals $600 still on hand on February 28.
   d. An inventory of office supplies reveals $410 still on hand on February 28.
   e. Depreciation on art equipment for February is calculated to be $100.
   f. Depreciation on office equipment for February is calculated to be $100.
   g. Art services performed for which payment has been received in advance total $1,300.
   h. Advertising services performed that will not be billed until March total $290.
   i. Three days' wages had accrued by the end of February.
6. From the work sheet prepare an income statement, a statement of owner's equity, and a balance sheet.
7. Record the adjusting entries in the general journal, and post them to the general ledger.
8. Record the closing entries in the general journal, and post them to the general ledger.
9. Prepare a post-closing trial balance.

This Comprehensive Problem covers all of the Learning Objectives in the chapters on measuring business transactions, measuring business income, and completing the accounting cycle.

Extensions of the

Basic

Accounting

Model

introduces the merchandising business and the merchandising income statement. The periodic and perpetual inventory systems receive equal treatment. The merchandising work sheet is included as a supplemental objective.

introduces the objectives and qualitative aspects of financial information. It demonstrates how much more useful classified financial statements are than simple financial statements in presenting information to statement users. This chapter also includes an introduction to financial statement analysis. The components of an annual report—with reference to the annual report for Toys "R" Us that appears in an appendix to this book—is presented as a supplemental objective.

addresses the goal of organizing accounting systems in order to process a large number of transactions efficiently. This chapter also describes the basic principles of internal control and then applies these principles to merchandising transactions.

Accounting for Merchandising Operations

1. Identify the management issues related to merchandising businesses.

2. Compare the income statements for service and merchandising concerns, and define the components of the merchandising income statement.

3. Distinguish between the periodic and the perpetual inventory systems, and explain the importance of taking a physical inventory.

4. Contrast and record transactions related to sales and purchases under the periodic and the perpetual inventory systems.

5. Prepare a work sheet and closing entries for a merchandising concern using the periodic inventory system.

6. Prepare a work sheet and closing entries for a merchandising concern using the perpetual inventory system.

7. Apply sales and purchases discounts to merchandising transactions.

Target Stores

DECISION POINT

The management of merchandising companies has two key decisions to make: the price at which merchandise is sold and the level of service the company provides. For instance, a department store can set the price of its merchandise at a relatively high level and provide a great deal of service. A discount store, on the other hand, may price its merchandise at a relatively low level and provide limited service. Target Stores, a division of Dayton-Hudson Corp., is a successful discount merchandiser of brand-name apparel and other products. What decisions did Target Stores make about pricing and service to achieve this success?

By emphasizing brand-name merchandise at low prices, the company chose to differentiate itself from department and specialty stores that sell at full price and from other discount chains that sell low-priced but less well-known merchandise. Target Stores decided to operate very large stores that could be controlled by a minimum number of employees. The company planned to earn income by selling a large volume of merchandise. In 1992, it operated over five hundred stores and earned income (before interest and income taxes) of $574 million on sales of $10.4 billion.[1] ⣿⣿

MANAGEMENT ISSUES IN MERCHANDISING BUSINESSES

OBJECTIVE

1 *Identify the management issues related to merchandising businesses*

Up to this point you have studied business and accounting issues related to the simplest type of business—the service business. Service businesses, such as advertising agencies and law firms, perform services for fees or commissions. Merchandising businesses, on the other hand, earn income by buying and selling products or merchandise. These companies, whether wholesale or retail, use the same basic accounting methods as do service companies, but the buying and selling of merchandise adds to the complexity of the process. As a foundation for discussing the accounting issues of merchandising businesses, we must first identify the management issues involved in running such a business.

1. Dayton-Hudson Corp., *Annual Report*, 1992.

Warehouse clubs are big business, and Sam's Clubs, a division of Wal-Mart Stores, Inc., is one of the biggest. Individuals or small businesses join a warehouse club by paying a small annual membership fee and are then allowed to shop for groceries, drugs, office supplies, and many other products at discount prices. Clubs keep prices low by minimizing overhead costs and selling on a cash-and-carry basis. Because warehouse clubs do not sell on credit, they traditionally have not sold to large companies, government agencies, or schools, which find it difficult to buy with cash. To expand into this market, a new division of Sam's Clubs, called Sam's Club Direct, will offer sales directly to big organizations. The company says, "We're tapping into a giant source of new business. . . . This is a whole new ball game for the industry."[2] Selling on credit to large organizations will affect the company's cash flow and perhaps improve its profitability. It will also affect its inventory systems and require the company to establish new controls for sales and receipts on account. ▬▬

CASH FLOW MANAGEMENT

Merchandising businesses differ from service businesses in that they have goods on hand for sale to customers, called merchandise inventory, and engage in a series of transactions called the operating cycle, as shown in Figure 1. The transactions in the operating cycle consist of (1) purchases of merchandise inventory, (2) sales of merchandise inventory for cash or on credit, and (3) collection of the cash from the sales. In the case of cash sales, sales of merchandise for cash, the cash is collected immediately. Sales on bank credit cards, such as VISA or MasterCard, are considered cash sales because funds from these sales are also available to the merchandiser immediately. In the case of credit sales, sales of merchandise on credit, the company must wait a period of time before receiving the cash. Some very small retail stores may have mostly cash sales and very few credit sales, whereas large wholesale concerns may have almost all credit sales. Most merchandising concerns, however, have a combination of cash and credit sales.

Regardless of the proportions of cash and credit sales, the operators of a merchandising business must carefully manage cash flow, or liquidity. Such cash flow management involves planning the company's receipts and payments of cash. If a company is not able to pay its bills when they are due, it may be forced out of business. Often merchandise that is purchased must be paid for before it is sold and the cash from its sale collected. For example, if a retail business must pay for its purchases in thirty days, it must have cash available or arrange for borrowing if it cannot sell and collect for the merchandise in thirty days.

The operating cycle for a merchandising firm can be 120 days, or even longer. For example, Dillard Department Stores, Inc., a successful chain of

2. John Schmeltzer, "Wal-Mart's Sam's Clubs Bend Rules for Big Firms," *Wall Street Journal,* November 2, 1993.

Figure 1. The Operating Cycle of Merchandising Concerns

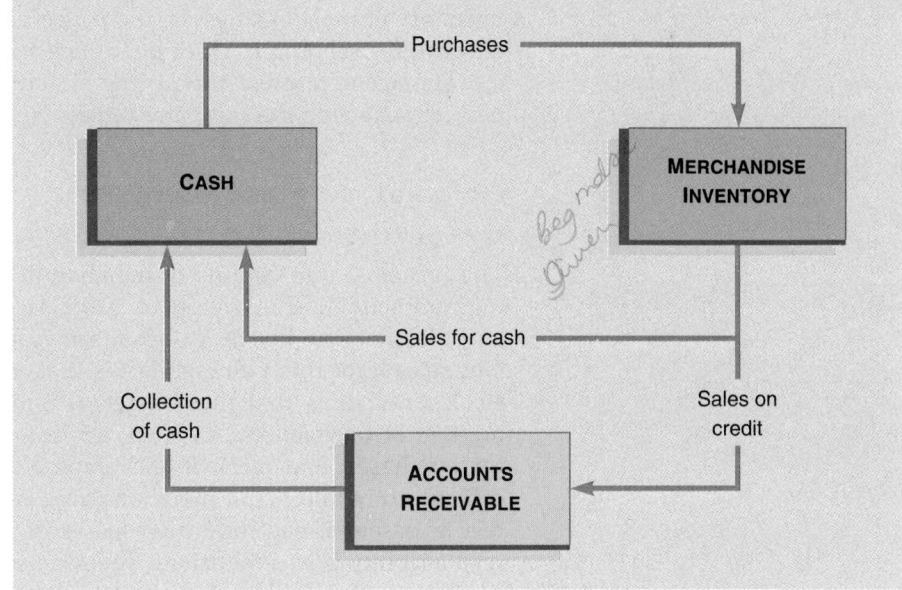

department stores in the South and Southwest, has an operating cycle of about 220 days. Its inventory is on hand on average 79 days, and it takes, on average, 141 days to collect its receivables. Since the company pays for its merchandise in an average of 65 days, a much shorter time, management must carefully plan its cash flow, including borrowing.

PROFITABILITY MANAGEMENT

In addition to managing its cash flow, management must sell its merchandise at a price that exceeds its cost by a sufficient margin to pay operating expenses, such as wages, utilities, advertising, and taxes, and have enough left over to provide sufficient income, or profitability. Profitability management is a complex activity that includes setting appropriate prices on merchandise, purchasing merchandise at favorable prices and terms, and maintaining acceptable levels of expenses. For example, Land's End, Inc., a direct merchant of casual clothing, increased its net income dramatically from 1991 to 1993 by increasing its prices and reducing its selling, general, and administrative expenses.

CHOICE OF INVENTORY SYSTEM

A third issue the management of a merchandising business must address is the choice of inventory system. There are two basic systems of accounting for the many items in the merchandise inventory. Under the periodic inventory system, the inventory on hand is counted periodically, usually at the end of the accounting period. No detailed records of the actual inventory on hand are maintained during the accounting period. Under the perpetual inventory system, continuous records are kept of the quantity and, usually, the cost of individual items as they are bought and sold. The periodic inventory system is less costly to maintain than the perpetual inventory system, but it gives management less information about the current status of merchandise inventory. Given the number and diversity of items contained in the merchandise inventory of most businesses, the perpetual inventory system is usually more effective for keeping track of quantities and ensuring optimal customer service. Management must choose the system or combination of systems that is best for achieving the company's goals.

CONTROL OF MERCHANDISING OPERATIONS

The principal transactions of merchandising businesses, which involve buying and selling, are covered by asset accounts—Cash, Accounts Receivable, and Merchandise Inventory—that are vulnerable to theft and embezzlement. One reason for this vulnerability is that cash and inventory are fairly easy to steal. Another is that these asset accounts are usually involved in a large number of transactions, such as cash receipts, receipts on account, payments for purchases, and receipts and shipments of inventory, which can become difficult to monitor. If a merchandising company does not take steps to protect its assets, it can have high losses of cash and inventory. Management's responsibility is to establish an environment, accounting systems, and control procedures that will protect these assets. These systems and procedures are called the internal control structure.

Adriana's Bazaar

DECISION POINT

Rochelle Zabarkes made all the right moves when she started her specialty food store in New York City with an unusual mix of gourmet foods and spices from around the world. She had a marketable idea, wrote a detailed business plan, lined up financing, and rented space on one of the city's busiest thoroughfares. She has been very successful in getting customers, installing a coffee bar, and starting a mail-order business. She talks of adding two more New York stores and dreams of going national. Unfortunately, Zabarkes has also defaulted on a $145,000 loan and is behind on her rent. She vows to repay the money because "I am absolutely dedicated to this business. I *will save it.*"[3] How can a merchandising business be so successful and yet be in so much trouble at the same time? What does Adriana's Bazaar need to turn its finances around?

Like most owners of small businesses, Zabarkes came up with a good idea but underestimated costs and overestimated revenues. This is the prime reason, according to the Small Business Administration, that 24 percent of all new businesses fail within two years. Zabarkes did not accurately answer the key question, How much operating capital does my business need to keep going for at least two years? As a result, her business is undercapitalized. When she started, she borrowed $250,000, but

3. Brent Bowers, "This Store Is a Hit But Somehow Cash Flow Is Missing," *Wall Street Journal,* April 13, 1993.

she really needed $350,000. As a first step in turning her business around, Zabarkes has received a reprieve on her loan from the Small Business Administration. She now needs the infusion of another $100,000 to pay off bills and finance growth. Zabarkes also needs a firm understanding of the merchandising income statement so that she appreciates the relationship of revenue, costs, and expenses to earning a sufficient net income. ⦂⦂⦂⦂⦂

INCOME STATEMENT FOR A MERCHANDISING CONCERN

OBJECTIVE

2

Compare the income statements for service and merchandising concerns, and define the components of the merchandising income statement

Service companies, as illustrated thus far in this book, require only a simple income statement. For those companies, as shown in Figure 2, net income represents the difference between revenues and expenses. But merchandising companies, because they buy and sell merchandise inventory, require a more complex income statement. As shown in Figure 2, the income statement for a merchandiser has three major parts: (1) net sales, (2) cost of goods sold, and (3) operating expenses. There are also subtotals for gross margin and net income. The main difference between a merchandiser's income statement and that of a service business is that the merchandiser must compute gross margin before operating expenses are deducted. In the following discussion, the

Figure 2. The Components of Income Statements for Service and Merchandising Companies

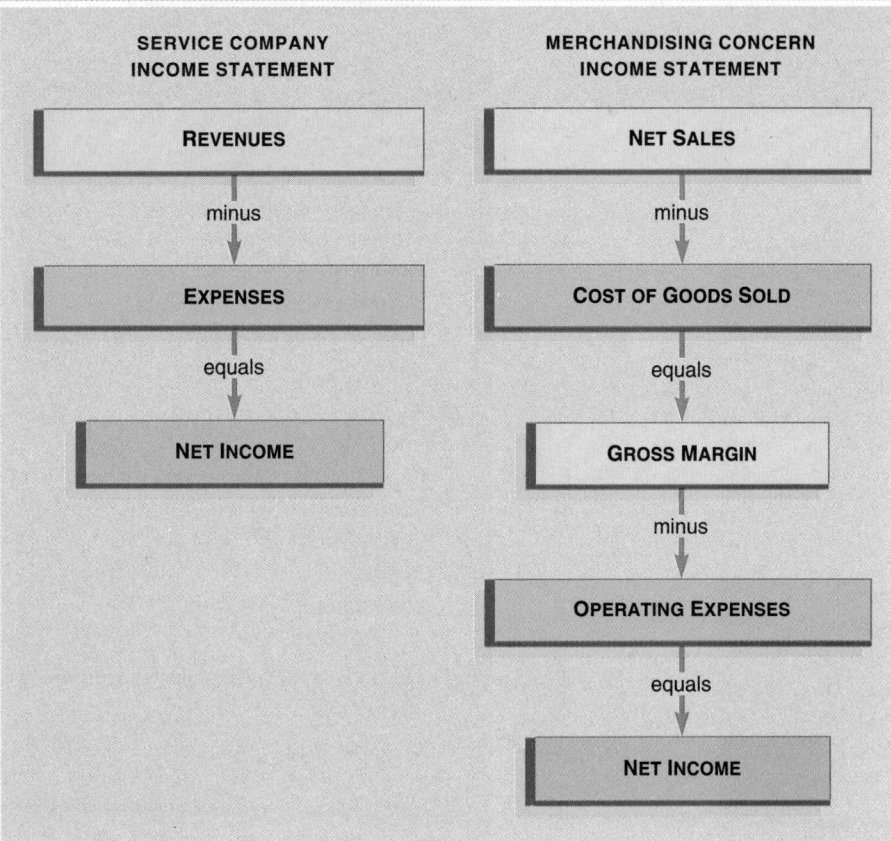

income statement for Fenwick Fashions Company, presented in Exhibit 1, will serve as an example of a merchandising income statement.

Exhibit 1. Merchandising Income Statement

Fenwick Fashions Company
Income Statement
For the Year Ended December 31, 19x2

Net Sales			
Gross Sales			$246,350
Less Sales Returns and Allowances			7,025
Net Sales			$239,325
Cost of Goods Sold			
Merchandise Inventory, December 31, 19x1		$ 52,800	
Purchases	$126,400		
Less Purchases Returns and Allowances	7,776		
Net Purchases	$118,624		
Freight In	8,236		
Net Cost of Purchases		126,860	
Goods Available for Sale		$179,660	
Less Merchandise Inventory, December 31, 19x2		48,300	
Cost of Goods Sold			131,360
Gross Margin			$107,965
Operating Expenses			
Selling Expenses			
Sales Salaries Expense	$ 22,500		
Freight Out Expense	5,740		
Advertising Expense	10,000		
Insurance Expense, Selling	1,600		
Store Supplies Expense	1,540		
Total Selling Expenses		$ 41,380	
General and Administrative Expenses			
Office Salaries Expense	$ 26,900		
Insurance Expense, General	4,200		
Office Supplies Expense	1,204		
Depreciation Expense, Building	2,600		
Depreciation Expense, Office Equipment	2,200		
Total General and Administrative Expenses		37,104	
Total Operating Expenses			78,484
Net Income			$ 29,481

NET SALES

The first major part of the merchandising income statement is net sales, or often simply *sales*. Net sales consist of the gross proceeds from sales of merchandise, or gross sales, less sales returns and allowances. Gross sales consist of total cash sales and total credit sales occurring during an accounting period. Even though the cash may not be collected until the following accounting period, revenue is recognized, under the revenue recognition rule, as being earned when title for merchandise passes from seller to buyer at the time of sale. Sales returns and allowances are cash refunds, credits on account, and allowances off selling prices made to customers who have received defective or otherwise unsatisfactory products. If other discounts or allowances are given to customers (see supplemental objective 7, for instance), they also should be deducted from gross sales.

Management, investors, and others often use the amount of sales and trends suggested by sales as indicators of a firm's progress. Increasing sales suggest growth; decreasing sales indicate the possibility of decreased future earnings and other financial problems. To detect trends, comparisons are frequently made between the net sales of different accounting periods.

COST OF GOODS SOLD

The second part of the merchandising income statement is cost of goods sold, or often simply *cost of sales*, which is the amount a merchant paid for the merchandise sold during an accounting period. The method of computing cost of goods sold is sometimes confusing because it must take into account both merchandise inventory on hand at the beginning of the accounting period, called the beginning inventory, and merchandise inventory on hand at the end of the accounting period, called the ending inventory. The ending inventory appears on the balance sheet at the end of the accounting period and becomes the beginning inventory for the next accounting period.

The computation of cost of goods sold for Fenwick Fashions based on the income statement in Exhibit 1 is illustrated in Figure 3. The goods available for sale during the year is the sum of two factors, beginning inventory and the net cost of purchases during the year. In this case, the goods available for sale is $179,660 ($52,800 + $126,860).

Figure 3. The Components of Cost of Goods Sold

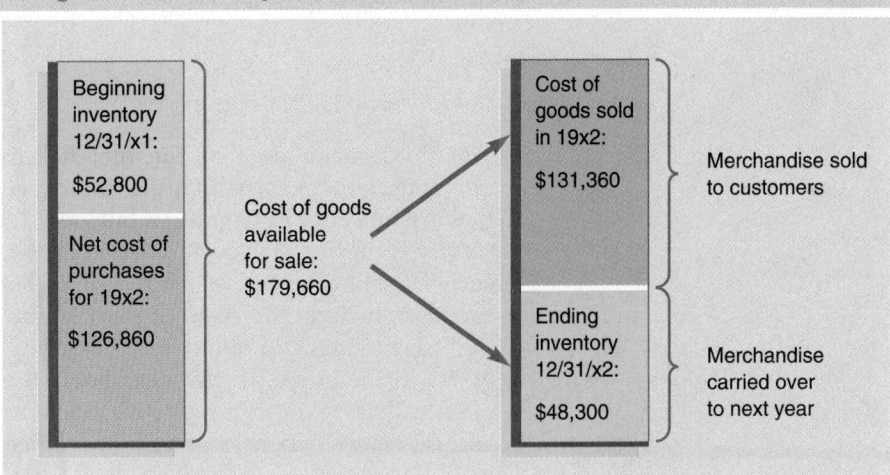

If a company sold all the goods available for sale during an accounting period, the cost of goods sold would equal the cost of goods available for sale. In most businesses, however, some merchandise will remain unsold and on hand at the end of the period. This merchandise, or ending inventory, must be deducted from the cost of goods available for sale to determine the cost of goods sold. In the case of Fenwick Fashions, the ending inventory on December 31, 19x2, is $48,300. Thus, the cost of goods sold is $131,360 ($179,660 − $48,300).

An important component of the cost of goods sold section is net cost of purchases, which consists of net purchases plus any freight charges on the purchases. Net purchases equals total purchases less any deductions, such as purchases returns and allowances and any discounts allowed by suppliers for early payment (see supplemental objective 7). Because freight charges, or freight in, are a necessary cost to receive merchandise for sale, they are added to net purchases to arrive at the net cost of purchases. Freight in may also be called *transportation in.*

GROSS MARGIN

The difference between net sales and cost of goods sold, or *gross profit,* on the merchandizing income statement is gross margin. To be successful, merchants must sell goods for an amount greater than cost—that is, gross margin must be great enough to pay operating expenses and provide an adequate income. Management is interested in both the amount and the percentage of gross margin. The percentage of gross margin is computed by dividing the dollar amount of gross margin by net sales. In the case of Fenwick Fashions, the dollar amount of gross margin is $107,965 and the percentage of gross margin is 45.1 percent ($107,965 ÷ $239,325). This information is helpful in planning business operations. For instance, management may try to increase total sales dollars by reducing the selling price. This strategy reduces the percentage of gross margin, but it will work if the total items sold increase enough to raise the absolute amount of gross margin. This is the strategy followed by a discount warehouse store like Sam's Clubs. On the other hand, management may keep a high gross margin and attempt to increase sales and the amount of gross margin by increasing operating expenses such as advertising. This is the strategy followed by upscale specialty stores like Neiman Marcus. Other strategies to increase gross margin, such as improving purchasing methods to reduce cost of goods sold, can also be explored.

OPERATING EXPENSES

The third major area of the merchandising income statement consists of operating expenses, which are the expenses other than cost of goods sold that are incurred in running a business. They are similar to the expenses of a service company. It is customary to group operating expenses into categories, such as selling expenses and general and administrative expenses. Selling expenses include the costs of storing and preparing goods for sale; displaying, advertising, and otherwise promoting sales; making sales; and delivering goods to the buyer, if the seller bears the cost of delivery. The latter cost is often called freight out expense or *delivery expense.* Among the general and administrative expenses are general office expense, which includes expenses for accounting, personnel, credit and collections, and any other expenses that apply to overall operation. Although general occupancy expenses, such as rent expense, insurance expense, and utilities expense, are often classified as general and administrative expenses, they may also be allocated between both the selling and the general and administrative categories. Careful planning and control of operating expenses can improve a company's profitability.

NET INCOME

Net income, the final figure or "bottom line" of the income statement, is what remains after operating expenses are deducted from gross margin. It is an important performance measure because it represents the amount of business earnings that accrue to the owners. It is the amount that is transferred to owner's equity from all the income-generating activities during the period. Both management and owners often use net income to measure whether a business has been operating successfully during the past accounting period.

INVENTORY SYSTEMS

OBJECTIVE

3 *Distinguish between the periodic and the perpetual inventory systems, and explain the importance of taking a physical inventory*

As we have seen, merchandise inventory is a key factor in determining the cost of goods sold. Consequently, every merchandiser needs a useful and reliable system for determining both the quantity and the cost of the goods on hand. The two basic systems of accounting for the number of items in the merchandise inventory are the periodic inventory system and the perpetual inventory system.

PERIODIC INVENTORY SYSTEM

As discussed earlier, under the periodic inventory system the inventory on hand is counted periodically, usually at the end of the accounting period. No detailed records of the actual inventory on hand are maintained during the period. Cost of goods sold under the periodic inventory system is determined according to the format shown for Fenwick Fashions in Exhibit 1 and Figure 3. In the simplest case, the cost of inventory purchased is accumulated in a Purchases account. At the end of the accounting period, the cost of the physical inventory, based on an actual count, is deducted from the cost of goods available for sale to arrive at the cost of goods sold. Entries are made at the end of the accounting period to remove the beginning inventory (the last period's ending inventory) and to enter the ending inventory of the current period. As explained later in this chapter, these are the only entries made to the Merchandise Inventory account during the period. Consequently, the figure for inventory on hand is accurate only on the balance sheet date. As soon as any purchases or sales are made, the figure becomes a historical amount and remains so until the new ending inventory is entered at the end of the next accounting period.

Some retail and wholesale businesses use periodic inventory systems because they do not require much clerical work. If a business is fairly small, management can maintain control over inventory simply by observation or by use of an off-line system of cards or computer records. On the other hand, for larger businesses, the lack of detailed records may cause inefficiencies that lead either to lost sales or to high operating costs.

BUSINESS BULLETIN: TECHNOLOGY IN PRACTICE

Many grocery stores, which traditionally used the periodic inventory system, now employ bar coding to update the physical inventory as items are sold. At the check-out counter, the cashier scans the electronic marking on each product, called a bar code or universal product code (UPC), into the cash register, which is linked to a computer. The price of the item appears on the cash register and its sale is recorded by the computer. Bar coding has become common in all types of retail companies, as well as in manufacturing firms and hospitals. It has become common for some retail businesses to use the perpetual system for keeping track of the physical flow of inventory and the periodic system for preparing the financial statements. ▬▬

PERPETUAL INVENTORY SYSTEM

Under the perpetual inventory system, records are kept of the quantity and, usually, the cost of individual items as they are bought or sold. The detailed data available under the perpetual inventory system enable management to respond to customers' inquiries about product availability, to order inventory more effectively and thus avoid running out of stock, and to control financial costs associated with investments in the inventory. Under this system, the cost of each item is recorded in the Merchandise Inventory account when it is purchased. As merchandise is sold, its cost is transferred from the Merchandise Inventory account to the Cost of Goods Sold account. Thus, at all times the balance of the Merchandise Inventory account equals the cost of goods on hand, and the balance in Cost of Goods Sold equals the cost of merchandise sold to customers. The Purchases account is not used in a perpetual inventory system.

Traditionally, the periodic inventory system has been used by companies that sell items of low value in high volume because of the difficulty and expense of accounting for the purchase and sale of each item. Examples of such companies are drugstores, automobile parts stores, department stores, discount stores, and grain companies. In contrast, companies that sell items of high unit value, such as appliances or automobiles, tend to use the perpetual inventory system. This distinction between high and low unit value for inventory systems has blurred considerably in recent years because of the widespread use of computers. Although use of the periodic inventory system is still widespread, use of the perpetual inventory system has increased greatly.

TAKING A PHYSICAL INVENTORY

Actually counting all merchandise on hand is called taking a physical inventory. This can be a difficult task because it is easy to leave items out or to count them twice. A physical inventory must be taken under both the periodic and the perpetual inventory systems.

Merchandise inventory includes all salable goods owned by a concern, regardless of where they are located—on shelves, in storerooms, in warehouses, or in trucks en route between warehouses and stores. It also includes goods in transit from suppliers if title to the goods has passed to the merchant. Ending inventory does not include merchandise sold but not yet delivered to customers or goods that cannot be sold because they are damaged or obsolete. If the damaged or obsolete goods can be sold at a reduced price, however, they should be included in ending inventory at their reduced value.

The actual count is usually taken after the close of business on the last day of the fiscal year. To facilitate taking the physical inventory, many companies end their fiscal year in a slow season, when inventories are at relatively low levels. Retail department stores often end their fiscal year in January or February, for example. After hours, at night, or on the weekend, employees count and record all items on numbered inventory tickets or sheets, following procedures to make sure that no items are missed. Sometimes a store closes for all or part of a day for inventory taking. The use of bar coding to take inventory electronically has greatly facilitated the taking of a physical inventory in many companies.

MERCHANDISING TRANSACTIONS

OBJECTIVE

4 *Contrast and record transactions related to sales and purchases under the periodic and the perpetual inventory systems*

Merchandising transactions can be divided into the two broad categories of sales transactions and purchases transactions. The ways in which these transactions are recorded differ somewhat under the periodic and the perpetual inventory systems. Before we discuss these transactions, some terms related to sales of merchandise need to be introduced.

SALES TERMS

When goods are sold on credit, both parties should understand the amount and timing of payment as well as other terms of the purchase, such as who pays delivery or freight charges and what warranties or rights of return apply. Sellers quote prices in different ways. Many merchants quote the price at which they expect to sell their goods. Others, particularly manufacturers and wholesalers, provide a price list or catalogue and quote prices as a percentage (usually 30 percent or more) off the list or catalogue prices. These discounts are called trade discounts. For example, if an article was listed at $1,000 with a trade discount of 40 percent, or $400, the seller would record the sale at $600 and the buyer would record the purchase at $600. If the seller wishes to change the selling price, the trade discount can be raised or lowered. At times the trade discount may vary depending on the quantity purchased. The list price and related trade discounts are used only to arrive at the agreed-on price; they do not appear in the accounting records.

The terms of sale are usually printed on the sales invoice and thus constitute part of the sales agreement. Customary terms differ from industry to industry. In some industries, payment is expected in a short period of time, such as ten or thirty days. In these cases, the invoice is marked "n/10" or "n/30" (read as "net ten" or "net thirty"), meaning that the amount of the invoice is due either ten days or thirty days after the invoice date. If the invoice is due ten days after the end of the month, it is marked "n/10 eom."

In some industries it is customary to give discounts for early payments. These discounts, called sales discounts, are intended to increase the seller's liquidity by reducing the amount of money tied up in accounts receivable. An invoice that offers a sales discount might be labeled "2/10, n/30," which means that the buyer either can pay the invoice within ten days of the invoice date and take a 2 percent discount or can wait thirty days and then pay the full amount of the invoice. It is almost always advantageous for a buyer to take the discount because the saving of 2 percent over a period of 20 days (from the eleventh day to the thirtieth day) represents an effective annual rate of 36 percent (360 days $\div$ 20 days $\times$ 2% = 36%). Most companies would be better off borrowing money to take the discount. The practice of giving sales discounts has been declining because it is costly to the seller and because, from the buyer's viewpoint, the amount of the discount is usually very small in relation to the price of the purchase. Accounting for sales discounts is covered in supplemental objective 7 at the end of this chapter.

In some industries, it is customary for the seller to pay transportation costs and to charge a price that includes those costs. In other industries, it is customary for the purchaser to pay transportation charges on merchandise. Special terms designate whether the supplier or the purchaser pays the freight charges. FOB shipping point means that the supplier places the merchandise "free on board" at the point of origin, and the buyer bears the shipping costs. The title to the merchandise passes to the buyer at that point. For example, when the sales agreement for the purchase of a car says "FOB factory," the buyer must pay the freight from where the car was made to wherever he or she is located, and the buyer owns the car from the time it leaves the factory. On the other hand, FOB destination means that the supplier bears the transportation costs to the place where the merchandise is delivered. The supplier retains title until the merchandise reaches its destination and usually prepays the shipping costs, in which case the buyer makes no accounting entry for freight. The effects of these special shipping terms are summarized as follows:

Shipping Term	Where Title Passes	Who Pays the Cost of Transportation
FOB shipping point	At origin	Buyer
FOB destination	At destination	Seller

TRANSACTIONS RELATED TO PURCHASES OF MERCHANDISE

The primary difference in accounting between the perpetual and the periodic inventory systems is that under the perpetual inventory system, the Merchandise Inventory account is continuously adjusted because purchases, sales, and other inventory transactions are entered in the account as they occur. Purchases increase Merchandise Inventory, and purchases returns decrease it. As sales of goods occur, the cost of the goods is transferred from Merchandise Inventory to the Cost of Goods Sold account. Under the periodic inventory system, the Merchandise Inventory account stays at its beginning balance until the physical inventory is recorded at the end of the period. A Purchases account is used to accumulate the purchases of merchandise during the accounting period, and a Purchases Returns and Allowances account is used to accumulate returns and allowances of purchases. To illustrate these differences, purchase transactions made by Fenwick Fashions follow. Differences in the two systems are shown in blue.

PURCHASES OF MERCHANDISE ON CREDIT

Oct. 3   Received merchandise purchased on credit from Neebok Company, invoice dated October 1, terms n/10, FOB shipping point, $4,890.

Periodic Inventory System			**Perpetual Inventory System**		
Oct. 3 Purchases	4,890		Merchandise Inventory	4,890	
Accounts Payable		4,890	Accounts Payable		4,890
Purchase of merchandise from Neebok Company, terms n/10, FOB shipping point, invoice dated Oct. 1			Purchased merchandise from Neebok Company, terms n/10, FOB shipping point, invoice dated Oct. 1		

Under the periodic inventory system, Purchases is a temporary account. Its sole purpose is to accumulate the total cost of merchandise purchased for resale during an accounting period. (Purchases of other assets, such as equipment, are recorded in the appropriate asset account, not in the Purchases account.) The Purchases account does not indicate whether merchandise has been sold or is still on hand. Under the perpetual inventory system, the Purchases account is not necessary, because purchases are recorded directly in the Merchandise Inventory account.

TRANSPORTATION COSTS ON PURCHASES

Oct. 4 Received bill from Transfer Freight Company for transportation costs on October 3 shipment, invoice dated October 1, terms n/10, $160.

Periodic Inventory System			**Perpetual Inventory System**		
Oct. 4 Freight In	160		Freight In	160	
Accounts Payable		160	Accounts Payable		160
Transportation charges on Oct. 3 purchase, Transfer Freight Co., terms n/10, invoice dated Oct. 1			Received freight bill from Transfer Freight Co. on Oct. 3 purchase, terms n/10, invoice dated Oct. 1		

Since most shipments contain many different items of merchandise, it is usually not practical to identify the specific cost of shipping each item. As a result, transportation costs on purchases are usually accumulated, under both the periodic and the perpetual inventory systems, in a Freight In account.

In some cases, the seller pays the freight charges and bills them to the buyer as a separate item on the invoice. When this occurs, the entries are the same as in the October 3 example, except that an additional debit is made to Freight In for the amount of the freight charges and Accounts Payable is increased by a like amount.

PURCHASES RETURNS AND ALLOWANCES

Oct. 6 Returned merchandise received from Neebok Company on October 3 for credit, $480.

Periodic Inventory System			**Perpetual Inventory System**		
Oct. 6 Accounts Payable	480		Accounts Payable	480	
Purchases Returns and Allowances		480	Merchandise Inventory		480
Merchandise from purchase of Oct. 3 returned to Neebok Company for full credit			Returned merchandise purchased on Oct. 3 to Neebok Company for full credit		

If a seller sends the wrong product or one that is otherwise unsatisfactory, the buyer may be allowed to return the item for a cash refund or credit on account, or the buyer may be given an allowance off the sales price. Under the periodic inventory system, the amount of the return or allowance is recorded in the Purchases Returns and Allowances account. This account is a contra-purchases account with a normal credit balance and is deducted from Purchases on the income statement. Under the perpetual inventory system, the returned merchandise is removed from the Merchandise Inventory account.

PAYMENTS ON ACCOUNT

Oct. 10   Paid in full the amount due to Neebok Company for the purchase of October 3, part of which was returned on October 6.

Periodic Inventory System			**Perpetual Inventory System**		
Oct. 10 Accounts Payable	4,410		Accounts Payable	4,410	
Cash		4,410	Cash		4,410
Made payment on account to Neebok Company $4,890 − $480 = $4,410			Made payment on account to Neebok Company $4,890 − $480 = $4,410		

Payments for merchandise purchased are the same under both systems.

TRANSACTIONS RELATED TO SALES OF MERCHANDISE

The primary difference in accounting for transactions related to sales under the perpetual and the periodic inventory systems pertains to the Cost of Goods Sold account. Under the perpetual inventory system, at the time of a sale, the cost of the merchandise is transferred from the Merchandise Inventory account to the Cost of Goods Sold account. In the case of a return, the cost of the merchandise is transferred from Cost of Goods Sold back to Merchandise Inventory. Under the periodic inventory system, the Cost of Goods Sold account is not used because the Merchandise Inventory account is not updated until the end of the accounting period. To illustrate these differences, transactions related to sales made by Fenwick Fashions follow. Differences in the two systems are indicated in blue.

SALES OF MERCHANDISE ON CREDIT

Oct. 7   Sold merchandise on credit to Gonzales Distributors, terms n/30, FOB destination, $1,200; the cost of the merchandise was $720.

Periodic Inventory System			**Perpetual Inventory System**		
Oct. 7 Accounts Receivable	1,200		Accounts Receivable	1,200	
Sales		1,200	Sales		1,200
Sale of merchandise to Gonzales Distributors, terms n/30, FOB destination			Sold merchandise to Gonzales Distributors, terms n/30, FOB destination		
			Cost of Goods Sold	720	
			Merchandise Inventory		720
			To transfer cost of merchandise inventory sold to Cost of Goods Sold account		

Sales of merchandise are handled in the same way under both inventory systems, except that under the perpetual inventory system, Cost of Goods Sold is updated by a transfer from Merchandise Inventory. In the case of cash sales, Cash rather than Accounts Receivable is debited for the amount of the sale.

PAYMENT OF DELIVERY COSTS

Oct. 8   Paid transportation costs for the sale on October 7, $78.

Periodic Inventory System			**Perpetual Inventory System**		
Oct. 8 Freight Out Expense	78		Freight Out Expense	78	
Cash		78	Cash		78
Delivery costs on Oct. 7 sale			Paid delivery costs on Oct. 7 sale		

A seller will often absorb delivery or freight out costs in the belief that doing so will facilitate the sale of its products. These costs are accumulated in an account called Delivery Expense or Freight Out Expense, which is shown as a selling expense on the income statement.

RETURNS OF MERCHANDISE SOLD

Oct. 9   Merchandise sold on October 7 accepted back from Gonzales Distributors for full credit and returned to merchandise inventory, $300; the cost of the merchandise was $180.

Periodic Inventory System			**Perpetual Inventory System**		
Oct. 9 Sales Returns and Allowances	300		Sales Returns and Allowances	300	
Accounts Receivable		300	Accounts Receivable		300
Return of merchandise from			Accepted return of merchandise		
Gonzales Distributors			from Gonzales Distributors		
			Mechandise Inventory	180	
			Cost of Goods Sold		180
			To transfer cost of merchandise		
			returned to the Merchandise		
			Inventory account		

Because returns and allowances to customers for wrong or unsatisfactory merchandise are often an indicator of customer dissatisfaction, such amounts are accumulated, under both methods, in a Sales Returns and Allowances account. This account is a contra-revenue account with a normal debit balance and is deducted from Sales on the income statement. Under the perpetual inventory system, the cost of the merchandise must also be transferred from the Cost of Goods Sold account back into the Merchandise Inventory account. If an allowance is made instead of accepting a return, or if merchandise cannot be returned to inventory and resold, this transfer is not made.

RECEIPTS ON ACCOUNT

Nov. 5   Received payment in full from Gonzales Distributors for sale of merchandise on Oct. 7, less the return on Oct. 9.

Periodic Inventory System			**Perpetual Inventory System**		
Nov. 5 Cash	900		Cash	900	
Accounts Receivable		900	Accounts Receivable		900
Receipt on account from			Received payment on account from		
Gonzales Distributors			Gonzales Distributors		
$1,200 − $300 = $900			$1,200 − $300 = $900		

Receipts on account are recorded in the same way under both systems.

BUSINESS BULLETIN: BUSINESS PRACTICE

In some industries a high percentage of sales returns is an accepted business practice. A book publisher like Simon & Schuster will produce and ship more copies of a bestseller than it expects to sell because, to gain the attention of potential buyers, copies must be distributed to a wide variety of outlets, such as bookstores, department stores, and discount stores. As a result, returns of unsold books may run as high as 30 to 50 percent of the books shipped. The same sales principles apply to magazines sold on newsstands, like *People,* and to popular recordings produced by companies like Motown Records. In all these businesses, management scrutinizes the Sales Returns and Allowances account for ways to reduce returns and increase profitability.

THE EFFECT OF THE PERPETUAL INVENTORY SYSTEM ON THE INCOME STATEMENT

The merchandising income statement illustrated in Exhibit 1 uses the periodic inventory system. This may be determined by the presence of the computation of net cost of purchases and the figures for beginning and ending inventory. Under the perpetual inventory system, the Cost of Goods Sold account replaces these items. The gross margin for Fenwick Fashions would be presented as shown in Exhibit 2. In this example, Freight In is included in Cost of Goods Sold. Theoretically, freight in should be allocated between ending inventory and cost of goods sold, but most companies choose not to disclose freight in on the income statement because it is a relatively small amount.

INVENTORY LOSSES

Most companies experience losses in merchandise inventory from spoilage, shoplifting, and employee pilferage. When such losses occur, the periodic inventory system provides no means of tracking them because the costs are automatically included in the cost of goods sold. For example, assume that a company has lost $1,250 in stolen merchandise during an accounting period. When the physical inventory is taken, the missing items are not in stock, so they cannot be counted. Because the ending inventory does not contain these items, the amount subtracted from cost of goods available for sale is less than it would be if the goods were in stock. The cost of goods sold, then, is overstated by $1,250. In a sense, the cost of goods sold is inflated by the amount of merchandise that has been lost.

The perpetual inventory system makes it easier to identify such losses. Because the Merchandise Inventory account is continuously updated for sales, purchases, and returns, the loss will show up as the difference between the inventory records and the physical inventory taken at the end of the accounting period. Once the amount of the loss has been identified, the ending inventory is updated by crediting the Merchandise Inventory account.

Exhibit 2. Partial Income Statement Under the Perpetual Inventory System

Fenwick Fashions Company
Partial Income Statement
For the Year Ended December 31, 19x2

Net Sales	
Gross Sales	$246,350
Less Sales Returns and Allowances	7,025
Net Sales	$239,325
Cost of Goods Sold*	131,360
Gross Margin	$107,965

*Freight In has been included in the Cost of Goods Sold.

The offsetting debit is usually listed as an increase in Cost of Goods Sold because the loss is considered a cost that reduces the company's gross margin.

THE MERCHANDISING WORK SHEET AND CLOSING ENTRIES

The work sheet for a merchandising company is basically the same as that for a service business, except that it includes the additional accounts that are needed to handle merchandising transactions. The treatment of these additional accounts differs depending on whether a company uses the periodic or the perpetual inventory system.

Supplemental
OBJECTIVE

5 *Prepare a work sheet and closing entries for a merchandising concern using the periodic inventory system*

THE PERIODIC INVENTORY SYSTEM

The accounts for a merchandising company using the periodic inventory system generally include Sales, Sales Returns and Allowances, Sales Discounts, Purchases, Purchases Returns and Allowances, Purchases Discounts, Freight In, and Merchandise Inventory. Except for Merchandise Inventory, these accounts are treated in much the same way as revenue and expense accounts for a service company. On the work sheet, they are extended to the Income Statement columns. In the closing process, they are transferred to the Income Summary account.

The Merchandise Inventory account requires special treatment because, under the periodic inventory system, purchases of merchandise are accumulated in the Purchases account, and no entries are made to Merchandise Inventory during the accounting period. As a result, at the end of the period, the balance in Merchandise Inventory is the same as it was at the beginning of the period: the beginning inventory amount. To calculate net income, the closing entries must (1) remove the beginning inventory from the Merchandise Inventory account, (2) enter the ending inventory in the Merchandise Inventory account, and (3) transfer both inventory amounts to the Income

Summary account. The following T accounts illustrate the flow of the inventory amounts at Fenwick Fashions.

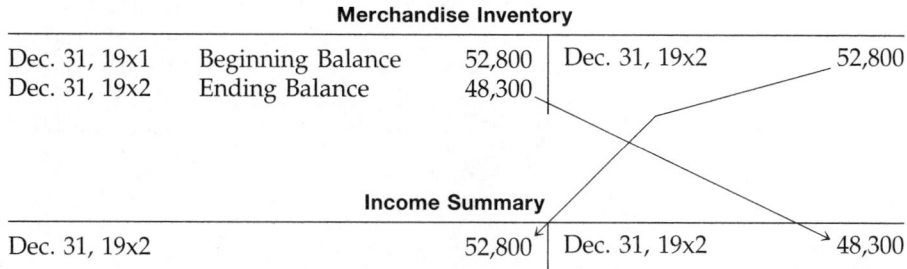

Merchandise Inventory					
Dec. 31, 19x1	Beginning Balance	52,800	Dec. 31, 19x2		52,800
Dec. 31, 19x2	Ending Balance	48,300			

Income Summary				
Dec. 31, 19x2		52,800	Dec. 31, 19x2	48,300

The beginning merchandise inventory was $52,800. This amount is removed from the Merchandise Inventory account by a credit, which leaves a zero balance, and transferred to the Income Summary account by a debit. The ending inventory was $48,300. This amount is entered in the Merchandise Inventory account by a debit and recorded in the Income Summary account by a credit. The results of the two closing entries mirror the calculation of cost of goods sold, in which beginning inventory is added to net cost of purchases and ending inventory is then subtracted. When beginning inventory is debited to the Income Summary account, it is, in effect, added to net purchases because the balance in the Purchases account is also debited to Income Summary through a closing entry. And when ending inventory is credited to Income Summary, it is, in effect, deducted from the sum of beginning inventory and net cost of purchases.

Keep these effects in mind while studying the work sheet for Fenwick Fashions Company shown in Exhibit 3. Each pair of columns in the work sheet and the closing entries are discussed in the following paragraphs.

Trial Balance Columns   The first step in the preparation of the work sheet is to enter the balances from the ledger accounts into the Trial Balance columns. You are already familiar with this procedure.

Adjustments Columns   The adjusting entries for Fenwick Fashions Company are entered in the Adjustments columns in the same way the adjusting entries were entered for service companies. Fenwick's adjusting entries involve insurance expired during the period (adjustment **a**), store and office supplies used during the period (adjustments **b** and **c**), and the depreciation of building and office equipment (adjustments **d** and **e**). No adjusting entry is made for merchandise inventory. After the adjusting entries are entered on the work sheet, the columns are totaled to prove that total debits equal total credits.

Omission of Adjusted Trial Balance Columns   These two columns, which appeared in the work sheet for a service company, can be omitted. They are optional and are used when there are many adjusting entries to record. When only a few adjusting entries are required, as is the case for Fenwick Fashions Company, these columns are not necessary and may be omitted to save time.

Income Statement and Balance Sheet Columns   After the Trial Balance columns have been totaled, the adjustments entered, and the equality of the columns proved, the balances are extended to the Income Statement and Balance Sheet columns. Again, begin with the Cash account at the top of the work sheet and move sequentially down the work sheet, one account at a

Exhibit 3. Work Sheet for Fenwick Fashions Company: Periodic Inventory System

Fenwick Fashions Company
Work Sheet
For the Year Ended December 31, 19x2

Account Name	Trial Balance Debit	Trial Balance Credit	Adjustments Debit	Adjustments Credit	Income Statement Debit	Income Statement Credit	Balance Sheet Debit	Balance Sheet Credit
Cash	29,410						29,410	
Accounts Receivable	42,400						42,400	
Merchandise Inventory	52,800				52,800	48,300	48,300	
Prepaid Insurance	17,400			(a) 5,800			11,600	
Store Supplies	2,600			(b) 1,540			1,060	
Office Supplies	1,840			(c) 1,204			636	
Land	4,500						4,500	
Building	20,260						20,260	
Accumulated Depreciation, Building		5,650		(d) 2,600				8,250
Office Equipment	8,600						8,600	
Accumulated Depreciation, Office Equipment		2,800		(e) 2,200				5,000
Accounts Payable		25,683						25,683
Gloria Fenwick, Capital		118,352						118,352
Gloria Fenwick, Withdrawals	20,000						20,000	
Sales		246,350				246,350		
Sales Returns and Allowances	7,025				7,025			
Purchases	126,400				126,400			
Purchases Returns and Allowances		7,776				7,776		
Freight In	8,236				8,236			
Sales Salaries Expense	22,500				22,500			
Freight Out Expense	5,740				5,740			
Advertising Expense	10,000				10,000			
Office Salaries Expense	26,900				26,900			
	406,611	406,611						
Insurance Expense, Selling			(a) 1,600		1,600			
Insurance Expense, General			(a) 4,200		4,200			
Store Supplies Expense			(b) 1,540		1,540			
Office Supplies Expense			(c) 1,204		1,204			
Depreciation Expense, Building			(d) 2,600		2,600			
Depreciation Expense, Office Equipment			(e) 2,200		2,200			
			13,344	13,344	272,945	302,426	186,766	157,285
Net Income					29,481			29,481
					302,426	302,426	186,766	186,766

time, entering each account balance in the correct Income Statement or Balance Sheet column.

As explained previously, the Merchandise Inventory row requires special treatment. The beginning inventory balance of $52,800 (which is already in the trial balance) is extended to the debit column of the Income Statement columns, as shown in Exhibit 3. This procedure has the effect of adding beginning inventory to net purchases because the Purchases account is also in the debit column of the Income Statement columns. The ending inventory balance of $48,300 (which is determined by the physical inventory and is not in the trial balance) is then inserted in the credit column of the Income Statement columns. This procedure has the effect of subtracting the ending inventory from goods available for sale in order to calculate the cost of goods sold. Finally, the ending merchandise inventory ($48,300) is inserted in the debit side of the Balance Sheet columns because it will appear on the balance sheet.

After all the items have been extended into the correct columns, the four columns are totaled. The net income or net loss is the difference between the debit and credit Income Statement columns. In this case, Fenwick Fashions Company has earned a net income of $29,481, which is extended to the credit side of the Balance Sheet columns. The four columns are then added to prove that total debits equal total credits.

Adjusting Entries   The adjusting entries from the work sheet are now entered into the general journal and posted to the ledger, as they would be in a service company. There is no difference in this procedure between a service company and a merchandising company.

Closing Entries   The closing entries for Fenwick Fashions Company appear in Exhibit 4. Notice that Merchandise Inventory is credited for the amount of the beginning inventory ($52,800) in the first entry and debited for the amount of the ending inventory ($48,300) in the second entry, as shown on page 194. Otherwise, these closing entries are very similar to those for a service company except that the merchandising accounts also must be closed to Income Summary. All income statement accounts with debit balances, including the merchandising accounts of Sales Returns and Allowances, Purchases, and Freight In, are credited in the first entry. The total of these accounts ($272,945) equals the total of the debit column in the Income Statement columns of the work sheet. All income statement accounts with credit balances—Sales and Purchases Returns and Allowances—are debited in the second entry. The total of these accounts ($302,426) equals the total of the Income Statement credit column in the work sheet. The third and fourth entries are used to close the Income Summary account and transfer net income to the Capital account, and to close the Withdrawals account to the Capital account.

Supplemental
OBJECTIVE

6 *Prepare a work sheet and closing entries for a merchandising concern using the perpetual inventory system*

THE PERPETUAL INVENTORY SYSTEM

Under the perpetual inventory system, the Merchandise Inventory account is up-to-date at the end of the accounting period and therefore is involved in the closing process. The account is up-to-date because, under the perpetual inventory system, purchases of merchandise are recorded directly in the Merchandise Inventory account and costs are transferred from the Merchandise Inventory account to the Cost of Goods Sold account as merchandise is sold. The work sheet for Fenwick Fashions Company, assuming the company uses the perpetual inventory system, is shown in Exhibit 5. Note that the ending

Exhibit 4. Closing Entries for Fenwick Fashions Company: Periodic Inventory System

		General Journal			Page 10
Date		Description	Post. Ref.	Debit	Credit
19x2 Dec.	31	Closing entries: Income Summary		272,945	
		Merchandise Inventory			52,800
		Sales Returns and Allowances			7,025
		Purchases			126,400
		Freight In			8,236
		Sales Salaries Expense			22,500
		Freight Out Expense			5,740
		Advertising Expense			10,000
		Office Salaries Expense			26,900
		Insurance Expense, Selling			1,600
		Insurance, Expense, General			4,200
		Store Supplies Expense			1,540
		Office Supplies Expense			1,204
		Depreciation Expense, Building			2,600
		Depreciation Expense, Office Equipment			2,200
		To close the temporary expense and revenue accounts having debit balances and to remove the beginning inventory			
	31	Merchandise Inventory		48,300	
		Sales		246,350	
		Purchases Returns and Allowances		7,776	
		Income Summary			302,426
		To close the temporary expense and revenue accounts having credit balances and to establish the ending inventory			
	31	Income Summary		29,481	
		Gloria Fenwick, Capital			29,481
		To close the Income Summary account			
	31	Gloria Fenwick, Capital		20,000	
		Gloria Fenwick, Withdrawals			20,000
		To close the Withdrawals account			

merchandise inventory is $48,300 in both the Trial Balance and the Balance Sheet columns.

The closing entries for Fenwick Fashions Company, assuming that the perpetual inventory system is used, are shown in Exhibit 6. The Cost of Goods Sold account is closed to Income Summary along with the expense accounts because the Cost of Goods Sold account has a debit balance. No closing entries affect the Merchandise Inventory account.

Exhibit 5. Work Sheet for Fenwick Fashions Company: Perpetual Inventory System

Fenwick Fashions Company
Work Sheet
For the Year Ended December 31, 19x2

Account Name	Trial Balance Debit	Trial Balance Credit	Adjustments Debit	Adjustments Credit	Income Statement Debit	Income Statement Credit	Balance Sheet Debit	Balance Sheet Credit
Cash	29,410						29,410	
Accounts Receivable	42,400						42,400	
Merchandise Inventory	48,300						48,300	
Prepaid Insurance	17,400			(a) 5,800			11,600	
Store Supplies	2,600			(b) 1,540			1,060	
Office Supplies	1,840			(c) 1,204			636	
Land	4,500						4,500	
Building	20,260						20,260	
Accumulated Depreciation, Building		5,650		(d) 2,600				8,250
Office Equipment	8,600						8,600	
Accumulated Depreciation, Office Equipment		2,800		(e) 2,200				5,000
Accounts Payable		25,683						25,683
Gloria Fenwick, Capital		118,352						118,352
Gloria Fenwick, Withdrawals	20,000						20,000	
Sales		246,350				246,350		
Sales Returns and Allowances	7,025				7,025			
Cost of Goods Sold	123,124				123,124			
Freight In	8,236				8,236			
Sales Salaries Expense	22,500				22,500			
Freight Out Expense	5,740				5,740			
Advertising Expense	10,000				10,000			
Office Salaries Expense	26,900				26,900			
	398,835	398,835						
Insurance Expense, Selling			(a) 1,600		1,600			
Insurance Expense, General			(a) 4,200		4,200			
Store Supplies Expense			(b) 1,540		1,540			
Office Supplies Expense			(c) 1,204		1,204			
Depreciation Expense, Building			(d) 2,600		2,600			
Depreciation Expense, Office Equipment			(e) 2,200		2,200			
			13,344	13,344	216,869	246,350	186,766	157,285
Net Income					29,481			29,481
					246,350	246,350	186,766	186,766

Exhibit 6. Closing Entries for Fenwick Fashions Company: Perpetual Inventory System

Date		Description	Post. Ref.	Debit	Credit
19x2		*Closing entries:*			
Dec.	31	Income Summary		216,869	
		Sales Returns and Allowances			7,025
		Cost of Goods Sold			123,124
		Freight In			8,236
		Sales Salaries Expense			22,500
		Freight Out Expense			5,740
		Advertising Expense			10,000
		Office Salaries Expense			26,900
		Insurance Expense, Selling			1,600
		Insurance Expense, General			4,200
		Store Supplies Expense			1,540
		Office Supplies Expense			1,204
		Depreciation Expense, Building			2,600
		Depreciation Expense, Office Equipment			2,200
		To close the temporary expense and revenue accounts having debit balances			
	31	Sales		246,350	
		Income Summary			246,350
		To close the temporary revenue account having a credit balance			
	31	Income Summary		29,481	
		Gloria Fenwick, Capital			29,481
		To close the Income Summary account			
	31	Gloria Fenwick, Capital		20,000	
		Gloria Fenwick, Withdrawals			20,000
		To close the Withdrawals account			

General Journal — Page 10

ACCOUNTING FOR DISCOUNTS

Supplemental OBJECTIVE 7 *Apply sales and purchases discounts to merchandising transactions*

SALES DISCOUNTS

As mentioned earlier, some industries give sales discounts for early payment. Because it usually is not possible to know at the time of the sale whether the customer will pay in time to take advantage of them, sales discounts are recorded only at the time the customer pays. For example, assume that Fenwick Fashions Company sells merchandise to a customer on September 20 for $300, on terms of 2/10, n/60. This is the entry at the time of the sale:

Sept. 20   Accounts Receivable   300
            Sales   300
                Sold merchandise on credit, terms 2/10,
                n/60

The customer can take advantage of the sales discount any time on or before September 30, ten days after the date of the invoice. If the customer pays on September 29, the entry in Fenwick's records would look like this:

Sept. 29   Cash   294
            Sales Discounts   6
                Accounts Receivable   300
                    Received payment for Sept. 20 sale;
                    discount taken

If the customer does not take advantage of the sales discount but waits until November 19 to pay for the merchandise, the entry would be as follows:

Nov. 19   Cash   300
                Accounts Receivable   300
                    Received payment for Sept. 20 sale; no
                    discount taken

At the end of the accounting period, the Sales Discounts account has accumulated all the sales discounts taken during the period. Because sales discounts reduce revenues from sales, Sales Discounts is a contra-revenue account with a normal debit balance that is deducted from gross sales in the income statement. Sales Discounts is treated the same as Sales Returns and Allowances on the work sheet and in the closing entries.

PURCHASES DISCOUNTS

Merchandise purchases are usually made on credit and sometimes involve purchases discounts for early payment. Purchases discounts are discounts taken for early payment for merchandise purchased for resale. They are to the buyer what sales discounts are to the seller. The amount of discounts taken is recorded in a separate account. Assume that Fenwick made a credit purchase of merchandise on November 12 for $1,500 with terms of 2/10, n/30 and returned $200 in merchandise on November 14. When payment is made, Fenwick's journal entry looks like this:

Nov. 22   Accounts Payable   1,300
            Purchases Discounts   26
            Cash   1,274
                Paid the invoice of Nov. 12

Purchase Nov. 12	$1,500
Less return Nov. 14	200
Net purchase	$1,300
Discount: 2%	26
Cash paid	$1,274

If the purchase is not paid for within the discount period, this is the entry:

Dec. 12   Accounts Payable   1,300
            Cash   1,300
                Paid the invoice of Nov. 12 on due date;
                no discount taken

Like Purchases Returns and Allowances, Purchases Discounts is a contra-purchases account with a normal credit balance that is deducted from Purchases on the income statement. If a company makes only a partial payment on an invoice, most creditors allow the company to take the discount applicable to the partial payment. The discount usually does not apply to freight, postage, taxes, or other charges that might appear on the invoice. Purchases Discounts is treated the same as Purchases Returns and Allowances on the work sheet and in the closing entries.

CHAPTER REVIEW

REVIEW OF LEARNING OBJECTIVES

1. **Identify the management issues related to merchandising businesses.** Merchandising companies differ from service companies in that they earn income by buying and selling products or merchandise. The buying and selling of merchandise adds to the complexity of the business and raises four issues that management must address. First, the series of transactions that merchandising companies engage in (the operating cycle) requires careful cash flow management. Second, profitability management requires the company to price goods and control costs and expenses in ways that ensure the earning of an adequate income after operating expenses have been paid. Third, the company must choose whether to use the periodic or the perpetual inventory system. Fourth, management must establish an internal control structure that protects the assets of cash, merchandise inventory, and accounts receivable.

2. **Compare the income statements for service and merchandising concerns, and define the components of the merchandising income statement.** In the simplest case, the income statement for a service company consists only of revenues and expenses. The income statement for a merchandising company has three major parts: (1) net sales, (2) cost of goods sold, and (3) operating expenses. Gross margin is the difference between revenues from net sales and the cost of goods sold. Net income is the "bottom line" after operating expenses are deducted from the gross margin. Some important relationships associated with the computation of cost of goods sold are as follows:

$$\text{Gross purchases} - \text{purchases returns and allowances} + \text{freight in} = \text{net cost of purchases}$$

$$\text{Beginning merchandise inventory} + \text{net cost of purchases} = \text{goods available for sale}$$

$$\text{Goods available for sale} - \text{ending merchandise inventory} = \text{cost of goods sold}$$

3. **Distinguish between the periodic and the perpetual inventory systems, and explain the importance of taking a physical inventory.** Merchandise inventory includes all salable goods owned, regardless of where they are located. Merchandise inventory can be determined by one of two systems. Under the *periodic inventory system*, the company usually waits until the end of an accounting period to take a physical inventory; it does not maintain detailed records of inventory on hand during the period. Under the *perpetual inventory system*, records are kept of the quantity and, usually, the cost of individual items of inventory throughout the year. The cost of goods sold is recorded as goods are transferred to customers, and the inventory balance is kept current throughout the year as items are bought and sold. Under both systems, a physical inventory, or physical count, is taken at the end of the accounting period to determine cost of goods sold under the periodic inventory system and to detect inventory losses under the perpetual inventory system.

4.   **Contrast and record transactions related to sales and purchases under the periodic and the perpetual inventory systems.** Sales terms define the amount and timing of payment, who pays delivery or freight charges, and what warranties or rights of return apply. Under the perpetual inventory system, the Merchandise Inventory account is continuously adjusted by entering purchases, sales, and other inventory transactions as they occur. Purchases increase the Merchandise Inventory account, and purchases returns decrease it. As goods are sold, their cost is transferred from the Merchandise Inventory account to the Cost of Goods Sold account. Under the periodic inventory system, in contrast, the Merchandise Inventory account stays at the beginning level until the physical inventory is recorded at the end of the period. A Purchases account is used to accumulate the purchases of merchandise during the accounting period, and a Purchases Returns and Allowances account is used to accumulate returns and allowances of purchases. Under both systems, transportation costs on purchases are accumulated in the Freight In account and transportation costs on sales are recorded as delivery expense or freight out expense.

SUPPLEMENTAL OBJECTIVES

5.   **Prepare a work sheet and closing entries for a merchandising concern using the periodic inventory system.** Preparing a work sheet for a merchandising concern is much like preparing one for a service concern, except that there are additional accounts relating to merchandising transactions, such as Sales, Sales Returns and Allowances, Purchases, Purchases Returns and Allowances, and Freight In. These accounts must be extended to the appropriate Income Statement columns. Also, the beginning merchandise inventory from the trial balance is extended to the debit column of the Income Statement columns, and the ending balance of Merchandise Inventory is inserted in both the credit column of the Income Statement columns and the debit column of the Balance Sheet columns. The closing entries for a merchandising concern under the periodic inventory system are the same as those for a service business, with one exception. The exception is that the closing entries include a credit to Merchandise Inventory for the amount of the beginning inventory and a debit to Merchandise Inventory for the amount of the ending inventory.

6.   **Prepare a work sheet and closing entries for a merchandising concern using the perpetual inventory system.** The work sheet under the perpetual inventory system is the same as the work sheet under the periodic inventory system, with two exceptions. First, since the Merchandise Inventory account is kept up-to-date, its ending balance is extended directly to the debit column of the Balance Sheet columns. There is no need to place it in the Income Statement columns. Second, the Cost of Goods Sold account replaces the Purchases and Purchases Returns and Allowances accounts and is extended to the debit column of the Income Statement columns. The closing entries for a merchandising concern under the perpetual inventory system are the same as those for a service business. There is no need to include the Merchandise Inventory account.

7.   **Apply sales and purchases discounts to merchandising transactions.** Sales discounts are discounts for early payment. Terms of 2/10, n/30 mean that the buyer can take a 2 percent discount if the invoice is paid within ten days of the invoice date. Otherwise, the buyer is obligated to pay the full amount in thirty days. Discounts on sales are recorded in the Sales Discounts account, and discounts on purchases are recorded in the Purchases Discounts account.

REVIEW OF CONCEPTS AND TERMINOLOGY

The following concepts and terms were introduced in this chapter:

L O 2   **Beginning inventory:** Merchandise on hand at the beginning of an accounting period.

L O 1   **Cash flow management:** The planning of a company's receipts and payments of cash.

L O 2   **Cost of goods sold:** The amount a merchant paid for the merchandise sold during an accounting period. Also called *cost of sales.*

L O 2   **Ending inventory:** Merchandise on hand at the end of an accounting period.

L O 4   **FOB destination:** A shipping term that means that the seller bears transportation costs to the place of delivery.

L O 4   **FOB shipping point:** A shipping term that means that the buyer bears transportation costs from the point of origin.

L O 2   **Freight in:** Transportation charges on merchandise purchased for resale. Also called *transportation in.*

L O 2   **Freight out expense:** Transportation charges on merchandise sold; an operating expense. Also called *delivery expense.*

L O 2   **Goods available for sale:** The sum of beginning inventory and the net cost of purchases during the period; the total goods available for sale to customers during an accounting period.

L O 2   **Gross margin:** The difference between net sales and cost of goods sold. Also called *gross profit.*

L O 2   **Gross sales:** Total sales for cash and on credit occurring during an accounting period.

L O 1   **Internal control structure:** A management-established environment, accounting systems, and control procedures designed to safeguard the assets of a business and provide reliable accounting records.

L O 1   **Merchandise inventory:** The goods on hand at any one time that are available for sale to customers.

L O 1   **Merchandising business:** A business that earns income by buying and selling products or merchandise.

L O 2   **Net cost of purchases:** Net purchases plus any freight charges on the purchases.

L O 2   **Net income:** For merchandising companies, what is left after deducting operating expenses from gross margin.

L O 2   **Net purchases:** Total purchases less any deductions, such as purchases returns and allowances and purchases discounts.

L O 2   **Net sales:** The gross proceeds from sales of merchandise less sales returns and allowances and any discounts. Also called *sales* on income statements.

L O 1   **Operating cycle:** A series of transactions that includes purchases of merchandise inventory, sales of merchandise inventory for cash or on credit, and collection of the cash from the sales.

L O 2   **Operating expenses:** The expenses other than cost of goods sold that are incurred in running a business.

L O 1   **Periodic inventory system:** A system for determining inventory on hand by a physical count at the end of an accounting period.

L O 1   **Perpetual inventory system:** A system for determining inventory by keeping continuous records of the quantity and, usually, the cost of individual items as they are bought and sold.

L O 3   **Physical inventory:** An actual count of all merchandise on hand at the end of an accounting period.

L O 1   **Profitability management:** The process of setting appropriate prices on merchandise, purchasing merchandise at favorable prices and terms, and maintaining acceptable levels of expenses.

L O 4   **Purchases:** A temporary account used under the periodic inventory system to accumulate the total cost of all merchandise purchased for resale during an accounting period.

S O 7   **Purchases discounts:** Discounts taken for prompt payment for merchandise purchased for resale; the Purchases Discounts account is a contra-purchases account.

L O 4   **Purchases Returns and Allowances:** A contra-purchases account used under the periodic inventory system to accumulate cash refunds, credits on account, and other allowances made by suppliers on merchandise originally purchased for resale.

L O 4 **Sales discount:** A discount given to a buyer for early payment for a sale made on credit; the Sales Discounts account is a contra-revenue account.

L O 2 **Sales Returns and Allowances:** A contra-revenue account used to accumulate cash refunds, credits on account, and other allowances made to customers who have received defective or otherwise unsatisfactory products.

L O 1 **Service business:** A business that earns income by performing a service for fees or commissions.

L O 4 **Trade discount:** A deduction (30 percent or more) off a list or catalogue price.

REVIEW PROBLEM

MERCHANDISING TRANSACTIONS: PERIODIC AND PERPETUAL INVENTORY SYSTEMS

L O 4 Dawkins Company engaged in the following transactions.

Oct. 1 Sold merchandise to Ernie Devlin on credit, terms n/30, FOB shipping point, $1,050 (cost, $630).
2 Purchased merchandise on credit from Ruland Company, terms n/30, FOB shipping point, $1,900.
2 Paid Custom Freight $145 for freight charges on merchandise received.
6 Purchased store supplies on credit from Arizin Supply House, terms n/30, $318.
9 Purchased merchandise on credit from LNP Company, terms n/30, FOB shipping point, $1,800, including $100 freight costs paid by LNP Company.
11 Accepted from Ernie Devlin a return of merchandise, which was returned to inventory, $150 (cost, $90).
14 Returned for credit $300 of merchandise received on October 2.
15 Returned for credit $100 of store supplies purchased on October 6.
16 Sold merchandise for cash, $500 (cost, $300).
22 Paid Ruland Company for purchase of October 2 less return of October 14.
23 Received full payment from Ernie Devlin for his October 1 purchase, less return on October 11.

REQUIRED

1. Prepare general journal entries to record the transactions, assuming the periodic inventory system is used.
2. Prepare general journal entries to record the transactions, assuming the perpetual inventory system is used.

ANSWER TO REVIEW PROBLEM

1. Periodic Inventory System   **2. Perpetual Inventory System**

19xx

Oct. 1 Accounts Receivable 1,050 / Sales 1,050
Sold merchandise on account to Ernie Devlin, terms n/30, FOB shipping point

Accounts Receivable 1,050 / Sales 1,050
Sale on account to Ernie Devlin, terms n/30, FOB shipping point

Cost of Goods Sold 630 / Merchandise Inventory 630
To transfer cost of merchandise sold to Cost of Goods Sold account

2 Purchases 1,900 / Accounts Payable 1,900
Purchased merchandise on account from Ruland Company, terms n/30, FOB shipping point

Merchandise Inventory 1,900 / Accounts Payable 1,900
Purchase on account from Ruland Company, terms n/30, FOB shipping point

(continued)

1. Periodic Inventory System *(continued)*

Date	Account	Debit	Credit
Oct. 2	Freight In	145	
	Cash		145
	Paid freight on previous purchase		
6	Store Supplies	318	
	Accounts Payable		318
	Purchased store supplies from Arizin Supply House, terms n/30		
9	Purchases	1,700	
	Freight In	100	
	Accounts Payable		1,800
	Purchased merchandise on account from LNP Company, terms n/30, FOB shipping point, freight paid by supplier		
11	Sales Returns and Allowances	150	
	Accounts Receivable		150
	Accepted return of merchandise from Ernie Devlin		
14	Accounts Payable	300	
	Purchases Returns and Allowances		300
	Returned portion of merchandise purchased from Ruland Company		
15	Accounts Payable	100	
	Store Supplies		100
	Returned store supplies (not merchandise) purchased on October 6 for credit		
16	Cash	500	
	Sales		500
	Sold merchandise for cash		
22	Accounts Payable	1,600	
	Cash		1,600
	Made payment on account to Ruland Company $1,900 − $300 = $1,600		
23	Cash	900	
	Accounts Receivable		900
	Received payment on account of Ernie Devlin $1,050 − $150 = $900		

2. Perpetual Inventory System *(continued)*

Date	Account	Debit	Credit
Oct. 2	Freight In	145	
	Cash		145
	Freight on previous purchase		
6	Store Supplies	318	
	Accounts Payable		318
	Purchase of store supplies on account from Arizin Supply House, terms n/30		
9	Merchandise Inventory	1,700	
	Freight In	100	
	Accounts Payable		1,800
	Purchase on account from LNP Company, terms n/30, FOB shipping point, freight paid by supplier		
11	Sales Returns and Allowances	150	
	Accounts Receivable		150
	Return of merchandise from Ernie Devlin		
	Merchandise Inventory	90	
	Cost of Goods Sold		90
	To transfer cost of merchandise returned to Merchandise Inventory		
14	Accounts Payable	300	
	Merchandise Inventory		300
	Return of portion of merchandise purchased from Ruland Company		
15	Accounts Payable	100	
	Store Supplies		100
	Return of store supplies (not merchandise) purchased on October 6 for credit		
16	Cash	500	
	Sales		500
	Sale of merchandise for cash		
	Cost of Goods Sold	300	
	Merchandise Inventory		300
	To transfer cost of merchandise sold to Cost of Goods Sold account		
22	Accounts Payable	1,600	
	Cash		1,600
	Payment on account to Ruland Company $1,900 − $300 = $1,600		
23	Cash	900	
	Accounts Receivable		900
	Receipt on account of Ernie Devlin $1,050 − $150 = $900		

CHAPTER ASSIGNMENTS

QUESTIONS

1. What four issues must be faced by managers of merchandising businesses?
2. What is the operating cycle of a merchandising business and why is it important?
3. What is the primary difference between the operations of a merchandising concern and those of a service concern, and how is it reflected on the income statement?
4. Is freight in an operating expense? Explain your answer.
5. Define *gross margin*. Why is it important?
6. During its first year in operation, Kumler Nursery had a cost of goods sold of $64,000 and a gross margin equal to 40 percent of sales. What was the dollar amount of the company's sales?
7. Could Kumler Nursery (in Question 6) have a net loss for the year? Explain your answer.
8. What is the difference between the periodic inventory system and the perpetual inventory system?
9. Under the periodic inventory system, how must the amount of inventory at the end of the year be determined?
10. What are the principal differences in the handling of merchandise inventory in the accounting records under the periodic inventory system and the perpetual inventory system?
11. Discuss this statement: "The perpetual inventory system is the best system because management always needs to know how much inventory it has."
12. What is the difference between a trade discount and a sales discount?
13. The following prices and terms on 50 units of product were quoted by two companies.

	Price	Terms
Supplier A	$20 per unit	FOB shipping point
Supplier B	$21 per unit	FOB destination

Which supplier is quoting the better deal? Explain your answer.
14. What is the principal difference in accounting for the purchase and sale of merchandise under the perpetual inventory system and the periodic inventory system?
15. Hornberger Hardware purchased the following items: (a) a delivery truck, (b) two dozen hammers, (c) supplies for its office workers, and (d) a broom for the janitor. Which items should be debited to the Purchases account under the periodic inventory system?
16. Under which inventory system is a Cost of Goods Sold account maintained? Why?
17. Why is it advisable to maintain a Sales Returns and Allowances account when the same result could be obtained by debiting each return or allowance to the Sales account?
18. Why is special treatment of the Merchandise Inventory account at the end of the accounting period of particular importance in the determination of net income under the periodic inventory system? What must be achieved in the account?
19. What are the principal differences between the work sheet for a merchandising company and that for a service company? Discuss in terms of the periodic and the perpetual inventory systems.
20. What are the principal differences in closing entries between a merchandising company using the periodic inventory system and one using the perpetual inventory system?
21. What is the normal balance of the Sales Discounts account? Is it an asset, a liability, an expense, or a contra-revenue account?

SHORT EXERCISES

SE 1. *Identification of*
L O 1 *Management Issues*
Check Figures: d, b, a, c

Identify each of the following decisions as most directly related to (a) cash flow management, (b) profitability management, (c) choice of inventory systems, or (d) control of merchandising operations.

1. Determination of how to protect cash from theft or embezzlement
2. Determination of the selling price of goods for sale
3. Determination of policies governing sales of merchandise on credit
4. Determination of whether to use the periodic or the perpetual inventory system

SE 2. *Merchandising*
L O 2 *Income Statement*
Check Figure: Net income: $5,000

Using the following data, prepare an income statement for Taylor Dry Goods for the month ending February 28.

Cost of Goods Sold	$30,000
General and Administrative Expenses	8,000
Net Sales	50,000
Selling Expenses	7,000

SE 3. *Cost of Goods Sold:*
L O 2 *Periodic Inventory*
System
Check Figure: Cost of Goods Sold: $91,000

Using the following data, prepare the cost of goods sold section of a merchandising income statement (periodic inventory system) for the month of July.

Freight In	$ 3,000
Merchandise Inventory, June 30, 19xx	25,000
Merchandise Inventory, July 31, 19xx	29,000
Purchases	97,000
Purchases Returns and Allowances	5,000

SE 4. *Cost of Goods Sold:*
L O 2 *Periodic Inventory*
System
Check Figure: Purchases: $238,000

Using the following data and assuming cost of goods sold is $230,000, prepare the cost of goods sold section of a merchandising income statement (periodic inventory system), including computation of the amount of purchases for the month of October.

Freight In	$12,000
Merchandise Inventory, Sept. 30, 19xx	33,000
Merchandise Inventory, Oct. 31, 19xx	44,000
Purchases	?
Purchases Returns and Allowances	9,000

SE 5. *Purchases of*
L O 4 *Merchandise:*
Periodic Inventory
System
No check figure

Record each of the following transactions, assuming the periodic inventory system is used.

Aug. 2 Purchased merchandise on credit from Gear Company, invoice dated August 1, terms n/10, FOB shipping point, $2,300.

3 Received bill from State Shipping Company for transportation costs on August 2 shipment, invoice dated August 1, terms n/30, $210.

7 Returned damaged merchandise received from Gear Company on August 2 for credit, $360.

10 Paid in full the amount due to Gear Company for the purchase of August 2, part of which was returned on August 7.

SE 6. *Purchases of*
L O 4 *Merchandise:*
Perpetual Inventory
System
No check figure

Record the transactions in SE 5 above, assuming the perpetual inventory system is used.

SE 7. *Sales of*
L O 4 *Merchandise:*
Periodic Inventory
System
No check figure

Record each of the following transactions, assuming the periodic inventory system is used.

Aug. 4 Sold merchandise on credit to Kwai Corporation, terms n/30, FOB destination, $1,200.

5 Paid transportation costs for sale of August 4, $110.

9 Merchandise sold on August 4 was accepted back from Kwai Corporation for full credit and returned to the merchandise inventory, $350.

Sept. 4 Received payment in full from Kwai Corporation for merchandise sold on August 4, less the return on August 9.

SE 8. *Sales of*
L O 4 *Merchandise:*
Perpetual Inventory
System

No check figure

Record the transactions in SE 7 using the perpetual inventory system, assuming that the merchandise sold on August 4 cost $720 and the merchandise returned on August 9 cost $210.

SE 9. *Merchandise*
S O 5, 6 *Inventory on the*
Work Sheet and in
Closing Entries

No check figure

Bowers Company had beginning merchandise inventory of $14,800 and ending merchandise inventory of $19,200. Where would these numbers appear on the work sheet and in the closing entries under (1) the periodic inventory system and (2) the perpetual inventory system?

SE 10. *Sales and Purchases*
S O 7 *Discounts*

No check figure

On April 15, the Sural Company sold merchandise to Astor Company for $1,500 on terms of 2/10, n/30. Record the entries in both Sural's and Astor's records for (1) the sale, (2) a return of merchandise on April 20 of $300, and (3) payment in full on April 25. Assume both companies use the periodic inventory system.

EXERCISES

E 1. *Management Issues*
L O 1 *and Decisions*
Check Figures: d, a, c, b, d, b (also a)

The decisions and actions below were undertaken by the management of Byrne Shoe Company. Indicate whether each action pertains primarily to (a) cash flow management, (b) profitability management, (c) choice of inventory system, or (d) control of merchandise operations.

1. Decided to mark each item of inventory with a magnetic tag that sets off an alarm if the tag is removed from the store before being deactivated.
2. Decided to reduce the credit terms offered to customers from thirty days to twenty days to speed up collection of accounts.
3. Decided that the benefits of keeping track of each item of inventory as it is bought and sold would exceed the costs of such a system and acted to implement the decision.
4. Decided to raise the price of each item of inventory to achieve a higher gross margin to offset an increase in rent expense.
5. Decided to purchase a new type of cash register that can be operated only by a person who knows a predetermined code.
6. Decided to switch to a new cleaning service that will provide the same service at a lower cost.

E 2. *Parts of the Income*
L O 2 *Statement: Missing*
Data
Check Figures: a. $60,000;
b. $85,000; c. $28,000; d. $168,000;
e. $114,000; f. $9,000; g. $180,000;
h. $51,000; i. $250,000; j. $230,000;
k. $160,000

Compute the dollar amount of each item indicated by a letter in the following table. Treat each horizontal row of numbers as a separate problem.

Sales	Beginning Inventory	Net Purchases	Ending Inventory	Cost of Goods Sold	Gross Margin	Operating Expenses	Net Income (or Loss)
$125,000	$ a	$ 35,000	$10,000	$ b	$40,000	$ c	$12,000
d	12,000	e	18,000	108,000	60,000	40,000	20,000
230,000	22,000	167,000	f	g	50,000	h	(1,000)
390,000	40,000	i	60,000	j	k	120,000	40,000

E 3. *Gross Margin from*
L O 2 *Sales Computation:*
Missing Data
Check Figure: Purchases: $166,500

Determine the amount of gross purchases by preparing a partial income statement under the periodic inventory system and showing the calculation of gross margin from the following data: freight in, $13,000; cost of goods sold, $188,500; sales, $275,000; beginning inventory, $25,000; purchases returns and allowances, $4,000; ending inventory, $12,000.

E 4. *Preparation of the*
L O 2 *Income Statement:*
Periodic Inventory
System
Check Figure: Net income: $75,700

Using the selected year-end account balances at December 31, 19x2 for the Mill Pond General Store shown at the top of the next page, prepare a 19x2 income statement.

Account Name	Debit	Credit
Sales		$297,000
Sales Returns and Allowances	$ 15,200	
Purchases	114,800	
Purchases Returns and Allowances		4,000
Freight In	5,600	
Selling Expenses	48,500	
General and Administrative Expenses	37,200	

The company uses the periodic inventory system. Beginning merchandise inventory was $26,000; ending merchandise inventory is $22,000.

E 5. *Preparation of the*
L O 4 *Income Statement: Perpetual Inventory System*

Check Figure: Net income: $28,000

Using the selected account balances at December 31, 19xx for Nature's Adventure Store that follow, prepare an income statement for the year ended December 31, 19xx.

Account Name	Debit	Credit
Sales		$475,000
Sales Returns and Allowances	$ 23,500	
Cost of Goods Sold	280,000	
Freight In	13,500	
Selling Expenses	43,000	
General and Administrative Expenses	87,000	

The company uses the perpetual inventory system, and Freight In has not been included in Cost of Goods Sold.

E 6. *Merchandising*
L O 2 *Income Statement: Missing Data, Multiple Years*

Check Figures: (o) $10; (v) $12

Determine the missing data for each letter in the following three income statements for Belden Wholesale Paper Company (in thousands).

	19x3	19x2	19x1
Gross Sales	$ p	$ h	$286
Sales Returns and Allowances	24	19	a
Net Sales	q	317	b
Merchandise Inventory, Beginning	r	i	38
Purchases	192	169	c
Purchases Returns and Allowances	31	j	17
Freight In	s	29	22
Net Cost of Purchases	189	k	d
Goods Available for Sale	222	212	182
Merchandise Inventory, Ending	39	l	42
Cost of Goods Sold	t	179	e
Gross Margin	142	m	126
Selling Expenses	u	78	f
General and Administrative Expenses	39	n	33
Total Operating Expenses	130	128	g
Net Income	v	o	27

E 7. *Recording*
L O 4 *Purchases: Periodic and Perpetual Inventory Systems*

No check figure

Give the entries to record each of the following transactions (1) under the periodic inventory system and (2) under the perpetual inventory system.

a. Purchased merchandise on credit, terms n/30, FOB shipping point, $7,500.
b. Paid freight on the shipment in transaction **a,** $405.
c. Purchased merchandise on credit, terms n/30, FOB destination, $4,200.

d. Purchased merchandise on credit, terms n/30, FOB shipping point, $7,800, which includes freight paid by the supplier of $600.

e. Returned part of the merchandise purchased in transaction **c,** $1,500.

f. Paid the amount owed on the purchase in transaction **a.**

g. Paid the amount owed on the purchase in transaction **d.**

h. Paid the amount owed on the purchase in transaction **c** less the return in **e.**

E 8. *Recording Sales:*
L O 4 *Periodic and Perpetual Inventory Systems*

No check figure

On June 15, the Jackson Company sold merchandise for $2,600 on terms of n/30 to Clement Company. On June 20, Clement Company returned some of the merchandise for a credit of $600, and on June 25, Clement paid the balance owed. Give Jackson's entries to record the sale, return, and receipt of payment (1) under the periodic inventory system and (2) under the perpetual inventory system. The cost of the merchandise sold on June 15 was $1,500, and the cost of the merchandise returned to inventory on June 20 was $350.

E 9. *Purchases and Sales*
S O 7 *Involving Discounts*

No check figure

The Fellini Company purchased $9,200 of merchandise, terms 2/10, n/30, from the Vance Company and paid for the merchandise within the discount period. Give the entries (1) by the Fellini Company to record the purchase and payment and (2) by the Vance Company to record the sale and receipt of payment. Both companies use the periodic inventory system.

E 10. *Preparation of*
S O 5 *Closing Entries: Periodic Inventory System*

No check figure

Selected account balances of the Shady Corner Grocery Store for the year ended December 31, 19xx follow.

Account Name	Debit	Credit
Sales		$297,000
Sales Returns and Allowances	$ 11,000	
Sales Discounts	4,200	
Purchases	114,800	
Purchases Returns and Allowances		1,800
Purchases Discounts		2,200
Freight In	5,600	
Selling Expenses	48,500	
General and Administrative Expenses	37,200	

Beginning merchandise inventory was $26,000, and ending merchandise inventory is $22,000. Prepare closing entries, assuming that the owner of Shady Corner Grocery, Stella Warren, withdrew $34,000 for personal expenses during the year.

E 11. *Preparation of*
S O 6 *Closing Entries: Perpetual Inventory System*

No check figure

Selected account balances of Certin Company for the year ended December 31, 19xx follow.

Account Name	Debit	Credit
Sales		$297,000
Sales Returns and Allowances	$ 15,200	
Cost of Goods Sold	113,000	
Freight In	5,600	
Selling Expenses	48,500	
General and Administrative Expenses	37,200	

Prepare closing entries, assuming that the owner of Certin Company, Roger Certin, withdrew $40,000 for personal expenses during the year.

E 12. *Sales Involving*
S O 7 *Discounts*
No check figure

Give the entries to record the following transactions engaged in by Westland Company, which uses the periodic inventory system.

Mar. 1 Sold merchandise on credit to Grano Company, terms 2/10, n/30, FOB shipping point, $500.
3 Accepted a return from Grano Company for full credit, $200.
10 Received payment from Grano Company for the sale, less the return and discount.
11 Sold merchandise on credit to Grano Company, terms 2/10, n/30, FOB destination, $800.
31 Received payment for amount due from Grano Company for the sale of March 11.

E 13. *Purchases Involving*
S O 7 *Discounts*
No check figure

Give the entries to record the following transactions engaged in by Westland Company, which uses the periodic inventory system.

July 2 Purchased merchandise on credit from Matts Company, terms 2/10, n/30, FOB destination, invoice dated July 1, $800.
6 Returned merchandise to Matts Company for full credit, $100.
11 Paid Matts Company for purchase less return and discount.
14 Purchased merchandise on credit from Matts Company, terms 2/10, n/30, FOB destination, invoice dated July 12, $900.
31 Paid amount owed to Matts Company for purchase of July 14.

SKILLS DEVELOPMENT EXERCISES

Conceptual Analysis

SDE 1. *Merchandising*
L O 2 *Income Statement*

No check figure

Village TV and **TV Warehouse** sell television sets and other video equipment in the Phoenix area. Village TV gives each customer individual attention, with employees explaining the features, advantages, and disadvantages of each video component. When a customer buys a television set or video system, Village provides free delivery, installs and adjusts the equipment, and teaches the family how to use it. TV Warehouse sells the same video components through showroom display. If a customer wants to buy a video component or a system, he or she fills out a form and takes it to the cashier for payment. After paying, the customer drives to the back of the warehouse to pick up the component, which he or she then takes home and installs. Village TV charges higher prices than TV Warehouse for the same components. Discuss how you would expect the income statements of Village TV and TV Warehouse to differ. Is it possible to tell which approach is more profitable?

SDE 2. *Periodic versus*
L O 3 *Perpetual Inventory*
Systems

No check figure

The Book Nook is a well-established chain of twenty bookstores in eastern Michigan. In recent years the company has grown rapidly, adding five new stores in regional malls. Management has relied on the manager of each store to place orders keyed to the market in his or her neighborhood, selected from a master list of available titles provided by the central office. Every six months, a physical inventory is taken, and financial statements are prepared using the periodic inventory system. At that time, books that have not sold well are placed on sale or, whenever possible, returned to the publisher. As a result of the company's fast growth, management has found that the newer store managers do not have the same ability to judge the market as do managers of the older, established stores. Thus, management is considering a recommendation to implement a perpetual inventory system and carefully monitor sales from the central office. Do you think The Book Nook should switch to the perpetual inventory system or stay with the periodic inventory system? Discuss the advantages and disadvantages of each system.

Ethical Dilemma

SDE 3. *Ethics and Timely*
S O 7 *Payments*
No check figure

Files, Folders & Clips, with five branch stores, is the area's largest office supply chain. Francesca Gonzales, a new accountant in charge of accounts payable, is told by her supervisor that many of the company's suppliers allow a 2 percent discount if payment for a purchase is made within ten days. She is instructed to write all checks for

the net amount after deducting the amount of the discount, and to date them ten days following the invoice date. The checks are not to be mailed until there is enough money in the bank to pay them. The supervisor says that, although most checks must be held a week or more after the discount date, suppliers usually allow the discount because they do not want to lose business. He tells Gonzales, "This is business as usual and just good cash management. Last year we got discounts of $30,000." Gonzales wonders if this is true and, more importantly, whether or not the practice is ethical. Is this practice ethical? Would anyone be harmed by it? What other courses of action are available to Gonzales?

Research Activity

SDE 4.
L O 3

Inventory Systems

No check figure

Identify three retail businesses in your local shopping area or a local shopping mall. Choose three different types of retail concerns, such as a bookstore, a clothing shop, a gift shop, a grocery, a hardware store, or a car dealership. In each business, ask to speak to someone who is knowledgeable about the store's inventory methods. Find out the answers to the following questions: How is each item of inventory identified? Does the business have a computerized or a manual inventory system? Which inventory system—periodic or perpetual—is used? How often do employees take a physical inventory? What procedures are followed in taking a physical inventory? What kinds of inventory reports are prepared or received? Create a table that summarizes your findings. In the table, use columns to represent the types of businesses and rows to represent the questions. Be prepared to discuss your findings in class.

Decision-Making Practice

SDE 5.
L O 2

Analysis of Merchandising Income Statement

No check figure

In 19x3 Paul Diamond opened a small retail store in a suburban mall. Called *Diamond Apparel Company*, the shop sold designer jeans. Paul worked fourteen hours a day and controlled all aspects of the operation. All sales were for cash or bank credit card. The business was such a success that in 19x4 Paul decided to open a second store in another mall. Because the new shop needed his attention, he hired a manager to work in the original store with two sales clerks. During 19x4 the new store was successful, but the operations of the original store did not match the first year's performance.

Concerned about this turn of events, Paul compared the two years' results for the original store. The figures are as follows:

	19x4	19x3
Net Sales	$650,000	$700,000
Cost of Goods Sold	450,000	450,000
Gross Margin	$200,000	$250,000
Operating Expenses	150,000	100,000
Net Income	$ 50,000	$150,000

In addition, Paul's analysis revealed that the cost and selling price of jeans were about the same in both years and that the level of operating expenses was roughly the same in both years, except for the new manager's $50,000 salary. Sales returns and allowances were insignificant amounts in both years.

Studying the situation further, Paul discovered the following facts about the cost of goods sold.

	19x4	19x3
Gross purchases	$400,000	$542,000
Total purchases allowances	30,000	40,000
Freight in	38,000	54,000
Physical inventory, end of year	64,000	106,000

Still not satisfied, Paul went through all the individual sales and purchase records for the year. Both sales and purchases were verified. However, the 19x4 ending inventory should have been $114,000, given the unit purchases and sales during the year. After puzzling over all this information, Paul comes to you for accounting help.

Accounting for Merchandising Operations

1. Using Paul's new information, recompute the cost of goods sold for 19x3 and 19x4, and account for the difference in net income between 19x3 and 19x4.
2. Suggest at least two reasons for the difference. (Assume that the new manager's salary is correct.) How might Paul improve the management of the original store?

PROBLEM SET A

A 1.
L O 1, 2
Merchandising Income Statement: Periodic Inventory System

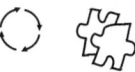

Check Figure: Net income: $47,882

The data below come from the Dubinsky Lighting Shop's adjusted trial balance as of the fiscal year ended September 30, 19x5.

The company's beginning inventory was $162,444; ending merchandise inventory is $153,328.

Dubinsky Lighting Shop
Partial Adjusted Trial Balance
September 30, 19x5

Sales		867,824
Sales Returns and Allowances	22,500	
Purchases	442,370	
Purchases Returns and Allowances		60,476
Freight In	20,156	
Store Salaries Expense	215,100	
Office Salaries Expense	53,000	
Advertising Expense	36,400	
Rent Expense	28,800	
Insurance Expense	5,600	
Utilities Expense	37,520	
Store Supplies Expense	928	
Office Supplies Expense	1,628	
Depreciation Expense, Store Equipment	3,600	
Depreciation Expense, Office Equipment	3,700	

REQUIRED

1. Prepare an income statement for the Dubinsky Lighting Shop. Store Salaries Expense; Advertising Expense; Store Supplies Expense; and Depreciation Expense, Store Equipment are selling expenses. The other expenses are general and administrative expenses.
2. Based on your knowledge at this point in the course, how would you use Dubinsky's income statement to evaluate the company's profitability?

A 2.
L O 2, 4
Merchandising Income Statement: Perpetual Inventory System

Check Figure: Net income: $5,261

At the end of the fiscal year, June 30, 19x3, selected accounts from the adjusted trial balance for Rafi's Camera Store appeared as shown on the next page.

REQUIRED

Prepare an income statement for Rafi's Camera Store. Freight In should be combined with Cost of Goods Sold. Store Salaries Expense; Advertising Expense; Store Supplies Expense; and Depreciation Expense, Store Equipment are selling expenses. The other expenses are general and administrative expenses.

Rafi's Camera Store
Partial Adjusted Trial Balance
June 30, 19x3

Sales		433,912
Sales Returns and Allowances	11,250	
Cost of Goods Sold	221,185	
Freight In	10,078	
Store Salaries Expense	107,550	
Office Salaries Expense	26,500	
Advertising Expense	18,200	
Rent Expense	14,400	
Insurance Expense	2,800	
Utilities Expense	8,760	
Store Supplies Expense	2,464	
Office Supplies Expense	1,814	
Depreciation Expense, Store Equipment	1,800	
Depreciation Expense, Office Equipment	1,850	

A 3.
L O 4

Merchandising Transactions: Periodic and Perpetual Inventory Systems

No check figure

Nakayama Company engaged in the following transactions in July.

July 1 Sold merchandise to Bernice Wilson on credit, terms n/30, FOB shipping point, $2,100 (cost, $1,260).
    3 Purchased merchandise on credit from Simic Company, terms n/30, FOB shipping point, $3,800.
    5 Paid Banner Freight for freight charges on merchandise received, $290.
    6 Purchased store supplies on credit from Hayes Supply Company, terms n/20, $636.
    8 Purchased merchandise on credit from Salinas Company, terms n/30, FOB shipping point, $3,600, which includes $200 freight costs paid by Salinas Company.
    12 Returned some of the merchandise received on July 3 for credit, $600.
    15 Sold merchandise on credit to Marc Singer, terms n/30, FOB shipping point, $1,200 (cost, $720).
    16 Returned some of the store supplies purchased on July 6 for credit, $200.
    17 Sold merchandise for cash, $1,000 (cost, $600).
    18 Accepted for full credit a return from Bernice Wilson and returned merchandise to inventory, $200 (cost, $120).
    24 Paid Simic Company for purchase of July 3 less return of July 12.
    25 Received full payment from Bernice Wilson for her July 1 purchase less the return on July 18.

REQUIRED

1. Prepare general journal entries to record the transactions, assuming use of the periodic inventory system.
2. Prepare general journal entries to record the transactions, assuming use of the perpetual inventory system.

A 4.
S O 5

Work Sheet, Financial Statements, and Closing Entries for a Merchandising Company: Periodic Inventory System

Check Figures: Net income: $23,812; Total assets: $66,336

The trial balance shown at the top of the next page was taken from the ledger of Conner Bookstore at the end of its annual accounting period.

Conner Bookstore
Trial Balance
June 30, 19x2

Cash	$ 6,025	
Accounts Receivable	9,280	
Merchandise Inventory	29,450	
Store Supplies	1,911	
Prepaid Insurance	1,600	
Store Equipment	37,200	
Accumulated Depreciation, Store Equipment		$ 15,600
Accounts Payable		12,300
Judy Conner, Capital		41,994
Judy Conner, Withdrawals	12,000	
Sales		102,250
Sales Returns and Allowances	987	
Purchases	63,200	
Purchases Returns and Allowances		21,011
Freight In	2,261	
Sales Salaries Expense	21,350	
Rent Expense	3,600	
Other Selling Expenses	2,614	
Utilities Expense	1,677	
	$193,155	$193,155

REQUIRED

1. Assuming the company uses the periodic inventory system, enter the trial balance on a work sheet, and complete the work sheet using the following information: ending merchandise inventory, $33,227; ending store supplies inventory, $304; unexpired prepaid insurance, $200; estimated depreciation on store equipment, $4,300; sales salaries payable, $80; and accrued utilities expense, $150.
2. Prepare an income statement, a statement of owner's equity, and a balance sheet. Sales Salaries Expense; Other Selling Expenses; Store Supplies Expense; and Depreciation Expense, Store Equipment are all selling expenses.
3. From the work sheet, prepare the closing entries.

A 5.
S O 6
Work Sheet,
Financial
Statements, and
Closing Entries for a
Merchandising
Company: Perpetual
Inventory System

Check Figures: Net income, $67,480;
Total assets, $244,530

The year-end trial balance that follows was taken from the ledger of the Kirby Party Costumes Company at the end of its annual accounting period on June 30, 19x2.

Kirby Party Costumes Company
Trial Balance
June 30, 19x2

Cash	$ 7,050	
Accounts Receivable	24,830	
Merchandise Inventory	88,900	
Store Supplies	3,800	
Prepaid Insurance	4,800	
Store Equipment	151,300	
Accumulated Depreciation, Store Equipment		$ 25,500
Accounts Payable		38,950
Mark Kirby, Capital		161,350
Mark Kirby, Withdrawals	24,000	
Sales		475,250
Sales Returns and Allowances	4,690	
Cost of Goods Sold	231,840	
Freight In	10,400	
Sales Salaries Expense	64,600	
Rent Expense	48,000	
Other Selling Expenses	32,910	
Utilities Expense	3,930	
	$701,050	$701,050

1. Assuming the company uses the perpetual inventory system, enter the trial balance on a work sheet, and complete the work sheet using the following information: ending store supplies inventory, $550; expired insurance, $2,400; estimated depreciation on store equipment, $5,000; sales salaries payable, $650; and accrued utilities expense, $100.
2. Prepare an income statement, a statement of owner's equity, and a balance sheet. Sales Salaries Expense; Other Selling Expenses; Store Supplies Expense; and Depreciation Expense, Store Equipment are all selling expenses.
3. From the work sheet, prepare closing entries.

A 6. *Journalizing*
L O 4 *Merchandising*
S O 7 *Transactions,*
Including Discounts

No check figure

Below is a list of transactions for the Reynolds Structures Company for the month of January 19xx.

Jan. 2 Purchased merchandise on credit from DEF Company, terms 2/10, n/30, FOB destination, $7,400.
3 Sold merchandise on credit to A. Molina, terms 1/10, n/30, FOB shipping point, $1,000.
5 Sold merchandise for cash, $700.
6 Purchased and received merchandise on credit from Stockton Company, terms 2/10, n/30, FOB shipping point, $4,200.
7 Received freight bill from Eastline Express for shipment received on January 6, $570.
9 Sold merchandise on credit to C. Parish, terms 1/10, n/30, FOB destination, $3,800.
10 Purchased merchandise from DEF Company, terms 2/10, n/30, FOB shipping point, $2,650, including freight costs of $150.
11 Received freight bill from Eastline Express for sale to C. Parish on January 9, $291.
12 Paid DEF Company for purchase of January 2.
13 Received payment in full for A. Molina's purchase of January 3.
14 Paid Stockton Company half the amount owed on the January 6 purchase. A discount is allowed on partial payment.
15 Returned faulty merchandise worth $300 to DEF Company for credit against purchase of January 10.
16 Purchased office supplies from Quaker Co. for $478, terms n/10.
17 Received payment from C. Parish for half of the purchase of January 9. A discount is allowed on partial payment.
18 Paid DEF Company in full for amount owed on purchase of January 10, less return on January 15.
19 Sold merchandise to D. Healy on credit, terms 2/10, n/30, FOB shipping point, $780.
20 Returned for credit several items of office supplies purchased on January 16, $128.
22 Issued a credit to D. Healy for returned merchandise, $180.
25 Paid for purchase of January 16, less return on January 20.
26 Paid freight company for freight charges for January 7 and 11.
27 Received payment of amount owed by D. Healy for purchase of January 19, less credit of January 22.
28 Paid Stockton Company for balance of January 6 purchase.
31 Sold merchandise for cash, $973.

Prepare general journal entries to record the transactions, assuming that the periodic inventory method is used.

PROBLEM SET B

B 1. *Merchandising*
L O 1, 2 *Income Statement:*
Periodic Inventory
System

Check Figure: Net income: $6,870

Selected accounts from the adjusted trial balance for Helen's New Styles Shop for the end of the fiscal year, March 31, 19x4, are shown at the top of the next page.

The merchandise inventory for Helen's New Styles Shop was $76,400 at the beginning of the year and $58,800 at the end of the year.

Helen's New Styles Shop
Partial Adjusted Trial Balance
March 31, 19x4

Sales		330,000
Sales Returns and Allowances	4,000	
Purchases	140,400	
Purchases Returns and Allowances		5,200
Freight In	4,600	
Store Salaries Expense	65,250	
Office Salaries Expense	25,750	
Advertising Expense	48,600	
Rent Expense	4,800	
Insurance Expense	2,400	
Utilities Expense	3,120	
Store Supplies Expense	5,760	
Office Supplies Expense	2,350	
Depreciation Expense, Store Equipment	2,100	
Depreciation Expense, Office Equipment	1,600	

REQUIRED

1. Using the information given, prepare an income statement for Helen's New Styles Shop. Store Salaries Expense; Advertising Expense; Store Supplies Expense; and Depreciation Expense, Store Equipment are selling expenses. The other expenses are general and administrative expenses.
2. Based on your knowledge at this point in the course, how would you use the income statement for Helen's New Styles Shop to evaluate the company's profitability?

B 2. *Merchandising*
L O 2, 4 *Income Statement:*
Perpetual Inventory
System

Check Figures: Net income: $15,435; Total assets: $533,590

At the end of the fiscal year, August 31, 19x2, selected accounts from the adjusted trial balance for Irma's Fashion Shop appeared as follows:

Irma's Fashion Shop
Partial Adjusted Trial Balance
August 31, 19x2

Sales		162,000
Sales Returns and Allowances	2,000	
Cost of Goods Sold	61,400	
Freight In	2,300	
Store Salaries Expense	32,625	
Office Salaries Expense	12,875	
Advertising Expense	24,300	
Rent Expense	2,400	
Insurance Expense	1,200	
Utilities Expense	1,560	
Store Supplies Expense	2,880	
Office Supplies Expense	1,175	
Depreciation Expense, Store Equipment	1,050	
Depreciation Expense, Office Equipment	800	

REQUIRED

Using the information given, prepare an income statement for Irma's Fashion Shop. Combine Freight In with Cost of Goods Sold. Store Salaries Expense; Advertising Expense; Store Supplies Expense; and Depreciation Expense, Store Equipment are selling expenses. The other expenses are general and administrative expenses.

B 3.
L O 4
Merchandising Transactions: Periodic and Perpetual Inventory Systems

No check figure

Heritage Company engaged in the following transactions in October.

Oct. 7 Sold merchandise on credit to Larry Hill, terms n/30, FOB shipping point, $3,000 (cost, $1,800).
   8 Purchased merchandise on credit from Tower Company, terms n/30, FOB shipping point, $6,000.
   9 Paid Kendall Company for shipping charges on merchandise purchased on October 8, $254.
   10 Purchased merchandise on credit from Center Company, terms n/30, FOB shipping point, $9,600, including $600 freight costs paid by Center.
   13 Purchased office supplies on credit from Phelan Company, terms n/10, $2,400.
   14 Sold merchandise on credit to Mary Walton, terms n/30, FOB shipping point, $2,400 (cost, $1,440).
   14 Returned damaged merchandise received from Tower Company on October 8 for credit, $600.
   17 Received check from Larry Hill for his purchase of October 7.
   18 Returned a portion of the office supplies received on October 13 for credit because the wrong items were sent, $400.
   19 Sold merchandise for cash, $1,800 (cost, $1,080).
   20 Paid Center Company for purchase of October 10.
   21 Paid Tower Company the balance from transactions of October 8 and October 14.
   24 Accepted from Mary Walton a return of merchandise, which was put back in inventory, $200 (cost, $120).

REQUIRED

1. Prepare general journal entries to record the transactions, assuming the periodic inventory system is used.
2. Prepare general journal entries to record the transactions, assuming the perpetual inventory system is used.

B 4.
S O 5
Work Sheet, Financial Statements, and Closing Entries for a Merchandising Company: Periodic Inventory System

Check Figure: Net income: $2,440

The year-end trial balance below was taken from the ledger of Le Bere Office Supplies Company at the end of its annual accounting period, on September 30, 19x4.

Le Bere Office Supplies Company
Trial Balance
September 30, 19x4

Cash	$ 21,150	
Accounts Receivable	74,490	
Merchandise Inventory	214,200	
Store Supplies	11,400	
Prepaid Insurance	14,400	
Store Equipment	253,900	
Accumulated Depreciation, Store Equipment		$ 76,500
Accounts Payable		116,850
Grace Le Bere, Capital		484,050
Grace Le Bere, Withdrawals	72,000	
Sales		1,225,750
Sales Returns and Allowances	25,440	
Purchases	754,800	
Purchases Returns and Allowances		18,150
Freight In	31,200	
Sales Salaries Expense	193,800	
Rent Expense	144,000	
Other Selling Expenses	98,730	
Utilities Expense	11,790	
	$1,921,300	$1,921,300

1. Assuming the company uses the periodic inventory system, enter the trial balance on a work sheet, and complete the work sheet using the following information: ending merchandise inventory, $266,700; ending store supplies inventory, $1,650; expired insurance, $7,200; estimated depreciation on store equipment, $15,000; sales salaries payable, $1,950; and accrued utilities expense, $300.
2. Prepare an income statement, a statement of owner's equity, and a balance sheet. Sales Salaries Expense; Other Selling Expenses; Store Supplies Expense; and Depreciation Expense, Store Equipment are selling expenses.
3. From the work sheet, prepare the closing entries.

B 5.
S O 6

Work Sheet, Financial Statements, and Closing Entries for a Merchandising Company: Perpetual Inventory System

Check Figures: Net income: $30,105; Total assets: $199,008

The following trial balance was taken from the ledger of Metzler Music Store at the end of its annual accounting period.

Metzler Music Store
Trial Balance
November 30, 19x4

Cash	$ 18,075	
Accounts Receivable	27,840	
Merchandise Inventory	99,681	
Store Supplies	5,733	
Prepaid Insurance	4,800	
Store Equipment	111,600	
Accumulated Depreciation, Store Equipment		$ 46,800
Accounts Payable		36,900
Susan Metzler, Capital		167,313
Susan Metzler, Withdrawals	36,000	
Sales		306,750
Sales Returns and Allowances	2,961	
Cost of Goods Sold	156,567	
Freight In	6,783	
Sales Salaries Expense	64,050	
Rent Expense	10,800	
Other Selling Expenses	7,842	
Utilities Expense	5,031	
	$557,763	$557,763

1. Assuming the company uses the perpetual inventory system, enter the trial balance on a work sheet, and complete the work sheet using the following information: ending store supplies inventory, $912; unexpired prepaid insurance, $600; estimated depreciation on store equipment, $12,900; sales salaries payable, $240; and accrued utilities expense, $450.
2. Prepare an income statement, a statement of owner's equity, and a balance sheet. Sales Salaries Expense; Other Selling Expenses; Store Supplies Expense; and Depreciation Expense, Store Equipment are all selling expenses.
3. From the work sheet, prepare the closing entries.

B 6. *Journalizing*
L O 4 *Merchandising*
S O 7 *Transactions,*
Including Discounts

No check figure

Following is a list of transactions for the Attention Promotions Company for the month of June 19xx.

June 1 Sold merchandise on credit to B. Holder, terms 2/10, n/60, FOB shipping point, $1,100.
2 Purchased merchandise on credit from Eagle Company, terms 2/10, n/30, FOB shipping point, $6,400.
3 Received freight bill for shipment received on June 2, $450.
4 Sold merchandise for cash, $550.
5 Sold merchandise on credit to T. Kuo, terms 2/10, n/60, $1,200.
6 Purchased merchandise from Reliable Company, terms 1/10, n/30, FOB shipping point, $3,090, including freight costs of $200.
7 Sold merchandise on credit to A. Rodriguez, terms 2/10, n/20, $2,200.
8 Received check from B. Holder for payment in full for sale of June 1.
9 Purchased merchandise from Eagle Company, terms 2/10, n/30, FOB shipping point, $8,200.
10 Received freight bill for shipment of June 9, $730.
11 Paid Eagle Company for purchase of June 2.
12 Returned merchandise from the June 6 shipment that was the wrong size and color for credit, $290.
13 A. Rodriguez returned some of merchandise sold to him on June 7 for credit, $200.
15 Received payment from T. Kuo for half of his purchase on June 5. A discount is allowed on partial payment.
16 Paid Reliable Company balance due on account from transactions on June 6 and 12.
17 In checking the purchase of June 9 from Eagle Company, the accounting department found an overcharge of $400. Eagle agreed to issue a credit.
20 Paid freight company for freight charges of June 3 and 10.
22 Purchased cleaning supplies on credit from Goldman Company, terms n/5, $250.
23 Discovered that some of the cleaning supplies purchased on June 22 were items that had not been ordered. Returned them to Goldman Company for credit, $50.
25 Sold merchandise for cash, $800.
26 Paid Goldman Company for the June 22 purchase, less the June 23 return.
27 Received payment in full from A. Rodriguez for transactions on June 7 and 13.
28 Paid Eagle Company for purchase of June 9, less allowance of June 17.
30 Received payment for balance of amount owed from T. Kuo for transactions of June 5 and 15.

REQUIRED

Prepare general journal entries to record the transactions, assuming that the periodic inventory method is used.

FINANCIAL REPORTING AND ANALYSIS CASES

Interpreting Financial Reports

FRA 1. *Contrast of*
L O 2 *Operating*
Philosophies and
Income Statements

Check Figures: Wal-Mart net income: $2,988,000,000; Kmart net income: $1,458,000,000

Wal-Mart Stores, Inc. and *Kmart Corp.*, two of the largest and most successful retailers in the United States, have different approaches to retailing. You can see the difference by analyzing their respective income statements and merchandise inventories. Selected information from their annual reports for the year ended January 31, 1993 is presented below. (All amounts are in millions.)

Wal-Mart: Net Sales, $55,484; Cost of Goods Sold, $44,175; Operating Expenses, $8,321; Ending Inventory, $9,268

Kmart: Net Sales, $37,724; Cost of Goods Sold, $28,485; Operating Expenses, $7,781; Ending Inventory, $8,752

REQUIRED

1. Prepare a schedule computing the gross margin and net income for both companies as dollar amounts and as percentages of net sales. Also, compute inventory as a percentage of the cost of goods sold.
2. From what you know about the different retailing approaches of these two companies, do the gross margins and net incomes you computed in item **1** seem compatible with these approaches? What is it about the nature of Wal-Mart's operations that produces lower gross margin from sales and lower operating expenses in percentages in comparison to Kmart? Which company's approach was more successful in 1993? Explain your answer.
3. Both companies have chosen a fiscal year that ends on January 31. Why do you suppose they made this choice? How realistic do you think the inventory figures are as indicators of inventory levels during the rest of the year?

International Company

FRA 2.
L O 4
Terminology for Merchandising Transactions in England

No check figure

Marks & Spencer is a large English retailer with department stores throughout England and in other European countries, especially France. The company also owns Brooks Brothers, the business clothing stores, in the United States. Merchandising terms in England differ from those in the United States. For instance, in England, the income statement is called the profit and loss account, sales is called turnover, merchandise inventory is called stocks, accounts receivable is called debtors, and accounts payable is called creditors. Of course, the amounts are stated in terms of pounds (£). In today's business world, it is important to understand and use terminology employed by professionals from other countries. Explain in your own words why the English may use the terms *profit and loss account, turnover, stocks, debtors,* and *creditors* in place of the American terms. Show that you can use these terms by recording in general journal form the following transactions that Marks & Spencer would engage in, using the English terminology (ignore credit terms and assume use of the perpetual inventory system).

a. Sold merchandise on credit, £230 (cost, £120).
b. Received payment for merchandise sold in **a**.
c. Purchased merchandise on credit, £190.
d. Paid for merchandise purchased in **c**.

Toys "R" Us Annual Report

FRA 3.
L O 1

Operating Cycle

No check figure

Refer to the appendix on Toys "R" Us. Is merchandise inventory or accounts receivable a more important component of the Toys "R" Us operating cycle? Explain your answer. In the "To Our Stockholders" section, a part titled "Operational Highlights" refers to the opening of an automated state-of-the-art distribution center in Germany and to the building of two state-of-the-art automated distribution centers in the United States. The enhanced inventory and distribution systems increased inventory productivity and improved the company's ability to replenish inventory. What effects are these actions intended to have on the operating cycle and the profitability of Toys "R" Us?

Financial Reporting and Analysis

1. State the objectives of financial reporting.
2. State the qualitative characteristics of accounting information and describe their interrelationships.
3. Define and describe the use of the conventions of *comparability* and *consistency, materiality, conservatism, full disclosure,* and *cost-benefit.*
4. Explain management's responsibility for ethical financial reporting and define *fraudulent financial reporting.*
5. Identify and describe the basic components of a classified balance sheet.
6. Prepare multistep and single-step classified income statements.
7. Evaluate liquidity and profitability using classified financial statements.

8. Identify the major components of a corporate annual report.

The Gap, Inc.

Corporations issue annual reports to distribute their financial statements and communicate other relevant information to stockholders and others outside the business. Because these users have no direct access to the accounting records, they must depend on the information contained in the report. Beyond the financial statements and accompanying notes and text, management must devise its own methods to help readers understand the data in the statements. What are some ways in which management can accomplish this objective?

The management of The Gap, Inc., one of the most successful U.S. specialty retailers of casual and active wear for men, women, and children, helps readers of its annual report by presenting on the first page a series of statistics called "Financial Highlights." Most of the statistics in the series are based on figures from the financial statements for the preceding three years. Along with such important information as net sales, net earnings, and total assets, a number of ratios appear, including working capital, current ratio, debt to equity, net earnings as a percentage of net sales, and return on average stockholders' equity. Of course, these ratios are meaningless unless the reader understands financial statements and generally accepted accounting principles, on which the statements are based. Because learning how to read and interpret financial statements is so important, this chapter describes the categories and classifications used in balance sheets and income statements and explains some of the most important ratios for financial statement analysis. The chapter begins by describing the objectives, characteristics, and conventions that underlie the preparation of financial statements. It ends with an overview of the Toys "R" Us, Inc. annual report.

OBJECTIVES OF FINANCIAL INFORMATION

OBJECTIVE

1 *State the objectives of financial reporting*

The United States has a highly developed exchange economy. In this kind of economy, most goods and services are exchanged for money or claims to money instead of being used or bartered by their producers. Most business is carried on through corporations, including many extremely large firms that buy, sell, and obtain financing in U.S. and world markets.

By issuing stocks and bonds that are traded in the financial market, businesses can raise capital for production and marketing activities. Investors are interested mainly in returns from dividends and increases in the market price of their investments. Creditors want to know if the business can repay a loan plus interest according to required terms. Thus, investors and creditors both need to know if a company can generate favorable cash flows. Financial statements are important to both groups in making that judgment. They offer valuable information that helps investors and creditors judge a company's ability to pay dividends and repay debts with interest. In this way, the market puts scarce resources to work in the companies that can use them most efficiently.

The needs of users and the general business environment are the basis for the Financial Accounting Standards Board's (FASB) three objectives of financial reporting:[1]

1. *To furnish information useful in making investment and credit decisions* Financial reporting should offer information that can help present and potential investors and creditors make rational investment and credit decisions. The reports should be in a form that makes sense to those who have some understanding of business and are willing to study the information carefully.
2. *To provide information useful in assessing cash flow prospects* Financial reporting should supply information to help present and potential investors and creditors judge the amounts, timing, and risk of expected cash receipts from dividends or interest and the proceeds from the sale, redemption, or maturity of stocks or loans.
3. *To provide information about business resources, claims to those resources, and changes in them* Financial reporting should give information about the company's assets, liabilities, and owner's equity, and the effects of transactions on the company's assets, liabilities, and owner's equity.

Financial statements are the most important way of periodically presenting to parties outside the business the information that has been gathered and processed in the accounting system. For this reason, the financial statements—the balance sheet, the income statement, the statement of owner's equity, and the statement of cash flows—are the most important output of the accounting system. They are "general purpose" because they serve a wide audience. They are "external" because their users are outside the business. Because of a potential conflict of interest between managers, who must prepare the statements, and investors or creditors, who invest in or lend money to the business, the financial statements are often audited by outside accountants to increase confidence in their reliability.

QUALITATIVE CHARACTERISTICS OF ACCOUNTING INFORMATION

OBJECTIVE

2 *State the qualitative characteristics of accounting information and describe their interrelationships*

It is easy for students in their first accounting course to get the idea that accounting is 100 percent accurate. This idea is reinforced by the fact that all the problems in this and other introductory books can be solved. The numbers all add up; what is supposed to equal something else does. Accounting seems very much like mathematics in its precision. In this course, the basics of accounting are presented in a simple form to help you understand them. In

---

1. "Objectives of Financial Reporting by Business Enterprises," *Statement of Financial Accounting Concepts No. 1* (Stamford, Conn.: Financial Accounting Standards Board, 1978), pars. 32–54.

practice, however, accounting information is neither simple nor precise, and it rarely satisfies all criteria. The FASB emphasizes this fact in the following statement.

> The information provided by financial reporting often results from approximate, rather than exact, measures. The measures commonly involve numerous estimates, classifications, summarizations, judgments and allocations. The outcome of economic activity in a dynamic economy is uncertain and results from combinations of many factors. Thus, despite the aura of precision that may seem to surround financial reporting in general and financial statements in particular, with few exceptions the measures are approximations, which may be based on rules and conventions, rather than exact amounts.[2]

The goal of accounting information—to provide the basic data that different users need to make informed decisions—is an ideal. The gap between the ideal and the actual provides much of the interest and controversy in accounting. To facilitate interpretation, the FASB has described the qualitative characteristics of accounting information, which are standards for judging that information. In addition, there are generally accepted conventions for recording and reporting that simplify interpretation. The relationships among these concepts are shown in Figure 1.

The most important qualitative characteristics are understandability and usefulness. Understandability depends on both the accountant and the decision maker. The accountant prepares the financial statements in accordance with accepted practices, generating important information that is believed to be understandable. But the decision maker must interpret the information and use it in making decisions. The decision maker must judge what information to use, how to use it, and what it means.

Figure 1. Qualitative Characteristics and the Conventions of Accounting Information

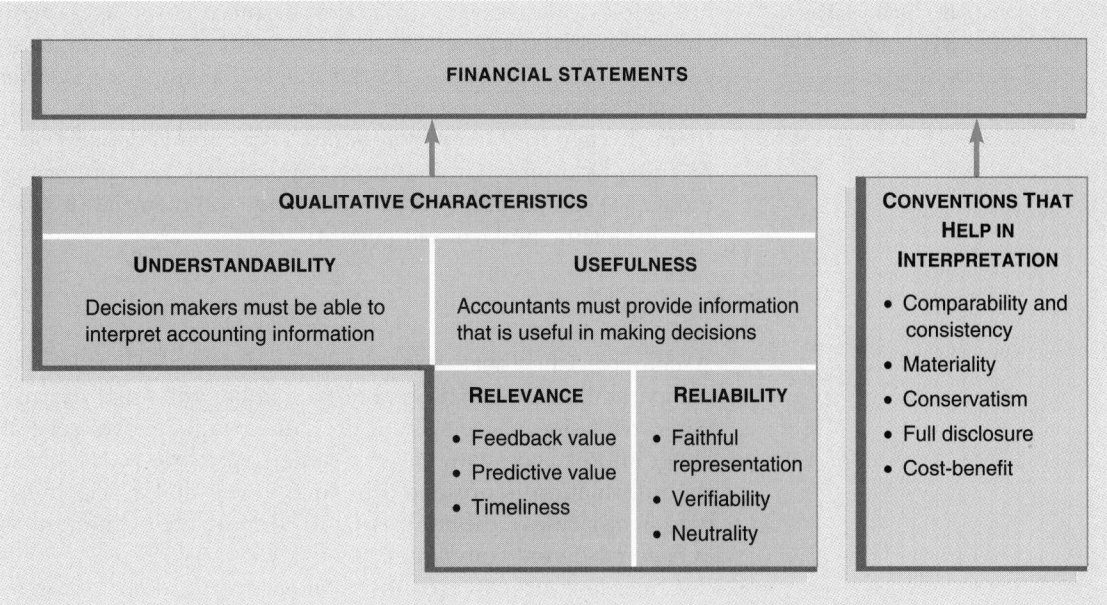

---

2. "Qualitative Characteristics of Accounting Information," *Statement of Financial Accounting Concepts No. 1* (Stamford, Conn.: Financial Accounting Standards Board, 1980), par. 20.

For accounting information to meet the standard of usefulness, it must have two major qualitative characteristics: relevance and reliability. Relevance means that the information can make a difference in the outcome of a decision. In other words, another decision would be made if the relevant information were not available. To be relevant, information must provide feedback, help predict future conditions, and be timely. For example, the income statement provides information about how a company did over the past year (feedback), and it helps in planning for the next year (prediction). To be useful, however, the information must also be communicated soon enough after the end of the accounting period to enable the reader to make decisions (timeliness).

In addition to being relevant, accounting information must have reliability. In other words, the user must be able to depend on the information. It must represent what it is meant to represent. It must be credible and verifiable by independent parties using the same methods of measuring. It must also be neutral. Accounting should convey business activity as faithfully as possible without influencing anyone in a specific direction. For example, the balance sheet should represent the economic resources, obligations, and owner's equity of a business as faithfully as possible in accordance with generally accepted accounting principles, and the balance sheet should be verifiable by an auditor.

CONVENTIONS THAT HELP IN THE INTERPRETATION OF FINANCIAL INFORMATION

OBJECTIVE

3 *Define and describe the use of the conventions of* **comparability** *and* **consistency, materiality, conservatism, full disclosure,** *and* **cost-benefit**

To a large extent, financial statements are based on estimates and arbitrary accounting rules of recognition and allocation. In this book, we point out a number of difficulties with financial statements. One is failing to recognize the changing value of the dollar caused by inflation. Another is treating intangibles, like research and development costs, as assets if they are purchased outside the company and as expenses if they are developed within the company. Such problems do not mean that financial statements are useless; the statements are essential. However, users must know how to interpret them. To help in this interpretation, accountants depend on five conventions, or rules of thumb, in recording transactions and preparing financial statements: (1) comparability and consistency, (2) materiality, (3) conservatism, (4) full disclosure, and (5) cost-benefit.

COMPARABILITY AND CONSISTENCY

A characteristic that increases the usefulness of accounting information is comparability. Information about a company is more useful if it can be compared with similar facts about the same company over several time periods or about another company for the same time period. Comparability means that the information is presented in such a way that a decision maker can recognize similarities, differences, and trends over different time periods or between different companies.

Consistent use of accounting measures and procedures is important in achieving comparability. The consistency convention requires that an accounting procedure, once adopted by a company, remain in use from one period to the next unless users are informed of the change. Thus, without a note to the contrary, users of financial statements can assume that there has been no arbitrary change in the treatment of a particular transaction, account, or item that would affect the interpretation of the statements.

If management decides that a certain procedure is no longer appropriate and should be changed, generally accepted accounting principles require that the change and its dollar effect be described in the notes to the financial statements.

> The nature of and justification for a change in accounting principle and its effect on income should be disclosed in the financial statements of the period in which the change is made. The justification for the change should explain clearly why the newly adopted accounting principle is preferable.[3]

For example, in its 1992 annual report, Rubbermaid Incorporated stated that it changed its method of accounting for inventories in 1992 because management felt the new method improved the matching of resources and costs.

MATERIALITY

The term materiality refers to the relative importance of an item or event. If an item or event is material, it is probably relevant to the users of financial statements. In other words, an item is material if users would have done something differently if they had not known about the item. Accountants are often faced with decisions about small items or events that make little difference to users no matter how they are handled. For example, a large company may decide that expenditures for durable items of less than $500 should be charged as expenses rather than recorded as long-term assets and depreciated.

In general, an item is material if there is a reasonable expectation that knowing about it would influence the decisions of users of financial statements. The materiality of an item normally is determined by relating its dollar value to an element of the financial statements, such as net income or total assets. Some accountants feel that when an item is 5 percent or more of net income, it is material. However, materiality also depends on the nature of the item, not just its value. For example, in a multimillion-dollar company, a mistake in recording an item of $5,000 may not be important, but the discovery of a $5,000 bribe or theft can be very important. Also, many small errors can combine into a material amount. Accountants judge the materiality of many things, and the users of financial statements depend on their judgments being fair and accurate.

CONSERVATISM

Accountants try to base their decisions on logic and evidence that lead to the fairest report of what happened. In judging and estimating, however, accountants often are faced with uncertainties. In such cases, they look to the convention of conservatism. This convention means that when accountants face major uncertainties about which accounting procedure to use, they generally choose the one that is least likely to overstate assets and income.

One of the most common applications of the conservatism convention is the use of the lower-of-cost-or-market method in accounting for inventories. Under this method, if the market value of an item is greater than its cost, the

---

3. Accounting Principles Board, "Accounting Changes," *Opinion No. 20* (New York: American Institute of Certified Public Accountants, 1971), par. 17.

more conservative cost figure is used. If the market value falls below the cost, the more conservative market value is used. The latter situation often occurs in the computer industry.

Conservatism can be a useful tool in doubtful cases, but its abuse leads to incorrect and misleading financial statements. Suppose that someone incorrectly applies the conservatism convention by expensing a long-term asset in the period of purchase. In this case, there is no uncertainty. Income and assets for the current period would be understated, and income in future periods would be overstated. For this reason, accountants depend on the conservatism convention only when there is uncertainty about which accounting procedure to use.

FULL DISCLOSURE

The convention of full disclosure requires that financial statements and their notes present all information that is relevant to the users' understanding of the company's financial condition. In other words, the statements should offer any explanation that is needed to keep them from being misleading. Explanatory notes are considered an integral part of the financial statements. For instance, as mentioned earlier, a change from one accounting procedure to another should be reported. In general, the form of the financial statements can affect their usefulness in making certain decisions. Also, certain items, such as the amount of depreciation expense on the income statement and the accumulated depreciation on the balance sheet, are essential to the readers of financial statements.

Other examples of disclosures required by the Financial Accounting Standards Board and other official bodies are the accounting procedures used in preparing the statements, important terms of the company's debt, commitments and contingencies, and important events taking place after the date of the statements. However, there is a point at which the statements become so cluttered that notes impede rather than help understanding. Beyond required disclosures, the application of the full-disclosure convention is based on the judgment of management and of the accountants who prepare the financial statements.

In recent years, the principle of full disclosure has also been influenced by users of accounting information. To protect investors and creditors, independent auditors, the stock exchanges, and the SEC have made more demands for disclosure by publicly owned companies. The SEC has been pushing especially hard for the enforcement of full disclosure. As a result, more and better information about corporations is available to the public today than ever before.

COST-BENEFIT

The cost-benefit convention underlies all the qualitative characteristics and conventions. It holds that the benefits to be gained from providing accounting information should be greater than the costs of providing it. Of course, minimum levels of relevance and reliability must be reached for accounting information to be useful. Beyond the minimum levels, however, it is up to the FASB and the SEC, which require the information, and the accountant, who provides the information, to judge the costs and benefits in each case. Most of the costs of providing information fall at first on the preparers; the benefits are reaped by both preparers and users. Finally, both the costs and the benefits are passed on to society in the form of prices and social benefits from more efficient allocation of resources.

The costs and benefits of a particular requirement for accounting disclosure are both direct and indirect, immediate and deferred. For example, it is hard to judge the final costs and benefits of a far-reaching and costly regulation. The FASB, for instance, allows certain large companies to make a supplemental disclosure in their financial statements of the effects of changes on current costs. Most companies choose not to present such information because they believe the costs of producing and providing it exceed its benefits to the readers of their financial statements. Cost-benefit is a question faced by all regulators, including the FASB and the SEC. Even though there are no definitive ways of measuring costs and benefits, much of an accountant's work deals with these concepts.

MANAGEMENT'S RESPONSIBILITY FOR ETHICAL REPORTING

OBJECTIVE

4 *Explain management's responsibility for ethical financial reporting and define* **fraudulent financial reporting**

The users of financial statements depend on the good faith of those who prepare the statements. Their dependence places a duty on a company's management and its accountants to act ethically in the reporting process. That duty is often expressed in the report of management's responsibilities that accompanies financial statements. For example, the report of the management of Quaker Oats Company, a company known for strong financial reporting and controls, states

> Management is responsible for the preparation and integrity of the Company's financial statements. The financial statements have been prepared in accordance with generally accepted accounting principles and necessarily include some amounts that are based on management's estimates and judgment.[4]

Quaker Oats's management also tells how it meets this responsibility.

> To fulfill its responsibility, management maintains a strong system of internal controls, supported by formal policies and procedures that are communicated throughout the Company. Management also maintains a staff of internal auditors who evaluate the adequacy of and investigate the adherence to these controls, policies, and procedures.[5]

The intentional preparation of misleading financial statements is called fraudulent financial reporting.[6] It can result from the distortion of records (the manipulation of inventory records), falsified transactions (fictitious sales or orders), or the misapplication of accounting principles (treating as an asset an item that should be expensed). There are many possible motives for fradulent reporting—for instance, to obtain a higher price in the sale of a company, to meet the expectations of stockholders, or to obtain a loan. Other times, the incentive is personal gain, such as additional compensation, promotion, or avoidance of penalties for poor performance. The personal costs of such actions can be high—individuals who authorize or prepare fraudulent financial statements may face criminal penalties and financial loss. Others, including investors and lenders to the company, employees, and customers, suffer from fraudulent financial reporting as well.

---

4. Quaker Oats Company, *Annual Report,* 1992.

5. Ibid.

6. National Commission of Fraudulent Financial Reporting, *Report of the National Commission on Fraudulent Financial Reporting* (Washington, D.C., 1987), p. 2.

Incentives for fraudulent financial reporting exist to some extent in every company. It is management's responsibility to insist on honest financial reporting, but it is also the company accountants' responsibility to maintain high ethical standards. Ethical reporting demands that accountants apply financial accounting concepts to present a fair view of the company's operations and financial position and to avoid misleading readers of the financial statements.

BUSINESS BULLETIN: ETHICS IN PRACTICE

 There is a difference between management's choosing to follow accounting principles that are favorable to its actions and fraudulent financial reporting. For example, a company may choose to recognize revenue as soon as possible after a sale is made; however, when Oracle Corporation, a software company, inflated its revenues and earnings by double-billing customers and failing to record product returns, it engaged in fraudulent financial reporting. The company agreed to settle charges brought by the Securities and Exchange Commission by paying a $100,000 fine. Management said the company's explosive growth in sales exceeded the ability of its internal control systems to detect accounting errors.

CLASSIFIED BALANCE SHEET

OBJECTIVE

5 *Identify and describe the basic components of a classified balance sheet*

The balance sheets you have seen in the chapters thus far categorize accounts as assets, liabilities, and owner's equity. Because even a fairly small company can have hundreds of accounts, simply listing accounts in such broad categories is not particularly helpful to a statement user. Setting up subcategories within the major categories often makes financial statements much more useful. Investors and creditors study and evaluate the relationships among the subcategories. General-purpose external financial statements that are divided into useful subcategories are called classified financial statements.

The balance sheet presents the financial position of a company at a particular time. The subdivisions of the classified balance sheet shown in Exhibit 1 are typical of most companies in the United States. The subdivisions under owner's equity, of course, depend on the form of business.

ASSETS

A company's assets are often divided into four categories: (1) current assets; (2) investments; (3) property, plant, and equipment; and (4) intangible assets. For simplicity, some companies group investments, intangible assets, and other miscellaneous assets into a category called "other assets." The categories are listed in the order of their presumed ease of conversion into cash. For example, current assets are usually more easily converted to cash than are property, plant, and equipment.

Exhibit 1. Classified Balance Sheet for Shafer Auto Parts Company

Shafer Auto Parts Company
Balance Sheet
December 31, 19xx

Assets

Current Assets

Cash	$10,360	
Short-Term Investments	2,000	
Notes Receivable	8,000	
Accounts Receivable	35,300	
Merchandise Inventory	60,400	
Prepaid Insurance	6,600	
Store Supplies	1,060	
Office Supplies	636	
Total Current Assets		$124,356

Investments

Land Held for Future Use		5,000

Property, Plant, and Equipment

Land		$ 4,500	
Building	$20,650		
Less Accumulated Depreciation	8,640	12,010	
Delivery Equipment	$18,400		
Less Accumulated Depreciation	9,450	8,950	
Office Equipment	$ 8,600		
Less Accumulated Depreciation	5,000	3,600	
Total Property, Plant, and Equipment			29,060

Intangible Assets

Trademark		500
Total Assets		$158,916

Liabilities

Current Liabilities

Notes Payable	$15,000	
Accounts Payable	23,883	
Salaries Payable	2,000	
Current Portion of Mortgage Payable	1,800	
Total Current Liabilities		$ 42,683

Long-Term Liabilities

Mortgage Payable		17,800
Total Liabilities		$ 60,483

Owner's Equity

Fred Shafer, Capital		98,433
Total Liabilities and Owner's Equity		$158,916

Current Assets   Current assets are cash or other assets that are reasonably expected to be realized in cash, sold, or consumed within the next year or within the normal operating cycle of the business, whichever is longer. The normal operating cycle of a company is the average time needed to go from cash to cash. For example, cash is used to buy merchandise inventory, which is sold for cash or for a promise of cash if the sale is made on account. If a sale is made on account, the resulting receivable must be collected before the cycle is completed.

The normal operating cycle for most companies is less than one year, but there are exceptions. Tobacco companies, for example, must cure their tobacco for two or three years before it can be sold. The tobacco inventory is nonetheless considered a current asset because it will be sold within the normal operating cycle. Another example is a company that sells on the installment basis. The payments for a television set or stove can be extended over twenty-four or thirty-six months, but such receivables are still considered current assets.

Cash is obviously a current asset. Temporary investments, notes and accounts receivable, and inventory are also current assets because they are expected to be converted to cash within the next year or during the normal operating cycle. On the balance sheet, they are listed in the order of their ease of conversion into cash.

Prepaid expenses, such as rent and insurance paid for in advance, and inventories of supplies bought for use rather than for sale should also be classified as current assets. Such assets are current in the sense that if they had not been bought earlier, a current outlay of cash would be needed to obtain them.[7]

In deciding whether an asset is current or noncurrent, the idea of "reasonable expectation" is important. For example, Short-Term Investments is an account used for temporary investments of idle cash, or cash that is not immediately required for operating purposes. Management can reasonably expect to sell those securities as cash needs arise over the next year or operating cycle. Investments in securities that management does not expect to sell within the next year and that do not involve the temporary use of idle cash should be shown in the investments category of a classified balance sheet.

Investments   The investments category includes assets, usually long term, that are not used in the normal operation of the business and that management does not plan to convert to cash within the next year. Items in that category are securities held for long-term investment, long-term notes receivable, land held for future use, plant or equipment not used in the business, and special funds established to pay off a debt or buy a building. Also included are large permanent investments in another company for the purpose of controlling that company.

Property, Plant, and Equipment   The property, plant, and equipment category includes long-term assets used in the continuing operation of the business. They represent a place to operate (land and buildings) and equipment to produce, sell, deliver, and service the company's goods. Consequently, they may also be called *operating assets* or, sometimes, *fixed assets, tangible assets, long-lived assets,* or *plant assets.* Through depreciation, the costs of such assets (except land) are spread over the periods they benefit. Past depreciation is

---

7. *Accounting Research and Terminology Bulletin,* final ed. (New York: American Institute of Certified Public Accountants, 1961), p. 20.

recorded in the Accumulated Depreciation accounts. The exact order in which property, plant, and equipment are listed on the balance sheet is not the same everywhere. In practice, accounts are often combined to make the financial statements less cluttered. For example:

Property, Plant, and Equipment

Land		$ 4,500
Buildings and Equipment	$47,650	
Less Accumulated Depreciation	23,090	24,560
Total Property, Plant, and Equipment		$29,060

Many companies simply show a single line with a total for property, plant, and equipment and provide the details in a note to the financial statements.

Property, plant, and equipment also includes natural resources owned by the company, such as forest lands, oil and gas properties, and coal mines. Assets that are not used in the regular course of business are listed in the investments category, as noted above.

Intangible Assets   Intangible assets are long-term assets that have no physical substance but that have a value based on the rights or privileges that belong to their owner. Examples are patents, copyrights, goodwill, franchises, and trademarks. An intangible asset is recorded at cost, which is spread over the expected life of the right or privilege.

Other Assets   Some companies use the category other assets to group all owned assets other than current assets and property, plant, and equipment. Other assets can include investments and intangible assets.

LIABILITIES

Liabilities are divided into two categories: current liabilities and long-term liabilities.

Current Liabilities   The category current liabilities consists of obligations due to be paid or performed within one year or within the normal operating cycle of the business, whichever is longer. Current liabilities are typically paid from current assets or by incurring new short-term liabilities. They include notes payable, accounts payable, the current portion of long-term debt, salaries and wages payable, taxes payable, and customer advances (unearned revenues).

Long-Term Liabilities   The debts of a business that fall due more than one year in the future or beyond the normal operating cycle, or that are to be paid out of noncurrent assets, are long-term liabilities. Mortgages payable, long-term notes, bonds payable, employee pension obligations, and long-term lease liabilities generally fall in the category of long-term liabilities.

OWNER'S EQUITY

The terms *owner's equity, proprietorship, capital,* and *net worth* are used interchangeably to denote the owner's interest in a company. The first three terms are preferred to *net worth* because most assets are recorded at original cost rather than at current value. Consequently, the ownership section does not represent "worth." It really represents a claim against the assets of the company.

The accounting treatment of assets and liabilities is not usually affected by the form of business organization. However, the equity section of the balance sheet differs depending on whether the business is a sole proprietorship, a partnership, or a corporation.

Sole Proprietorship   You already are familiar with the owner's equity section of a sole proprietorship, like the one shown in the balance sheet for Shafer Auto Parts Company in Exhibit 1:

Owner's Equity

Fred Shafer, Capital	$98,433

Partnership   The equity section of the balance sheet for a partnership is called partners' equity and is much like that of the sole proprietorship. It might appear as follows:

Partners' Equity

A. J. Martin, Capital	$21,666	
R. C. Moore, Capital	35,724	
Total Partners' Equity		$57,390

Corporation   Corporations are by law separate, legal entities that are owned by their stockholders. The equity section of a balance sheet for a corporation is called stockholders' equity and has two parts: contributed, or paid-in, capital and retained earnings. It might appear like this:

Stockholders' Equity

Contributed Capital		
Common Stock—$10 par value, 5,000 shares authorized, issued, and outstanding	$50,000	
Paid-in Capital in Excess of Par Value	10,000	
Total Contributed Capital		$60,000
Retained Earnings		37,500
Total Stockholders' Equity		$97,500

Remember that owner's equity accounts show the sources of and claims on assets. Of course, the claims are not on any particular asset but on the assets as a whole. It follows, then, that a corporation's contributed and earned capital accounts measure its stockholders' claims on assets and also indicate the sources of the assets. The contributed capital accounts reflect the amounts of assets invested by stockholders. Generally, contributed capital is shown on corporate balance sheets by two amounts: (1) the face, or par, value of issued stock and (2) the amounts paid in, or contributed, in excess of the par value per share. In the illustration above, stockholders invested amounts equal to par value of the outstanding stock (5,000 × $10) plus $10,000 more.

The Retained Earnings account is sometimes called *Earned Capital* because it represents the stockholders' claim to the assets earned from operations and reinvested in corporate operations. Distributions of assets to shareholders, called *dividends,* reduce the Retained Earnings account balance just as withdrawals of assets by the owner of a business lower the Capital account balance. Thus, the Retained Earnings account balance, in its simplest form, represents the earnings of the corporation less dividends paid to stockholders over the life of the business.

BUSINESS BULLETIN: BUSINESS PRACTICE

Accounting can be an issue even in the movies. Despite worldwide receipts of $300 million and additional millions in merchandise sales, Warner Bros. Inc. says the original *Batman* has not made a profit and may never do so. However, a lawsuit by two executive producers says that the studio's accounting is fraudulent and unconscionable. At issue is the measurement of "net profits," a percentage of which the producers are to receive. The problem is that the top actors, like Jack Nicholson, the director, and others receive a share of every dollar that the movie generates and, as a result, have earned millions of dollars. Because of those shares, it is impossible for the movie ever to earn a "net profit." Thus, while others are paid handsomely, the two executive producers receive nothing. It pays to know accounting before signing a movie contract.

FORMS OF THE INCOME STATEMENT

OBJECTIVE

6 *Prepare multistep and single-step classified income statements*

For internal management, a detailed income statement is helpful in analyzing the company's performance. But for external reporting purposes, the income statement is usually presented in condensed form. Condensed financial statements present only the major categories of the detailed financial statements. There are two common forms of the condensed income statement, the multistep form and the single-step form. The multistep form, illustrated in Exhibit 2, derives net income in the same step-by-step fashion as a detailed income statement would, except that only the totals of significant categories are given. Usually, some breakdown is shown for operating expenses, such as the totals for selling expenses and for general and administrative expenses. In the Shafer statement, gross margin less operating expenses is called income from operations, and a new section, other revenues and expenses, has been added to include nonoperating revenues and expenses. The latter section includes revenues from investments (such as dividends and interest from stocks, bonds, and savings accounts) and interest earned on credit or notes extended to customers. It also includes interest expense and other expenses that result from borrowing money or from credit extended to the company. If the company has other revenues and expenses that are not related to normal business operations, they too are included in this part of the income statement. Thus, an analyst who wants to compare two companies independent of their financing methods—that is, before considering other revenues and expenses—would focus on income from operations.

Exhibit 2. Condensed Multistep Income Statement for Shafer Auto Parts Company

Shafer Auto Parts Company Income Statement For the Year Ended December 31, 19xx		
Net Sales		$289,656
Cost of Goods Sold		181,260
Gross Margin		$108,396
Operating Expenses		
Selling Expenses	$54,780	
General and Administrative Expenses	34,504	
Total Operating Expenses		89,284
Income from Operations		$ 19,112
Other Revenues and Expenses		
Interest Income	$ 1,400	
Less Interest Expense	2,631	
Excess of Other Expenses over Other Revenues		1,231
Net Income		$ 17,881

The single-step form of income statement, illustrated in Exhibit 3, derives net income in a single step by putting the major categories of revenues in the first part of the statement and the major categories of costs and expenses in the second part. The multistep form and the single-step form each have advantages. The multistep form shows the components that are used in deriving net income; the single-step form has the advantage of simplicity. Approximately an equal number of large U.S. companies use each form in their public reports.

Net income from the income statement becomes an element of the statement of owner's equity.

USING CLASSIFIED FINANCIAL STATEMENTS

OBJECTIVE

7 *Evaluate liquidity and profitability using classified financial statements*

Earlier in this chapter, you learned that financial reporting, according to the Financial Accounting Standards Board, seeks to provide information that is useful in making investment and credit decisions, in judging cash flow prospects, and in understanding business resources, claims to those resources, and changes in them. That is related to two of the more important goals of management—maintaining adequate liquidity and achieving satisfactory profitability—because investors and creditors base their decisions largely on their assessment of a company's potential liquidity and profitability. The following analysis focuses on those two important goals.

In this section a series of charts shows average ratios for six industries based on data obtained from *Industry Norms and Ratios*, a publication of Dun

Exhibit 3. Condensed Single-Step Income Statement for Shafer Auto Parts Company

Shafer Auto Parts Company Income Statement For the Year Ended December 31, 19xx		
Revenues		
Net Sales		$289,656
Interest Income		1,400
Total Revenues		$291,056
Costs and Expenses		
Cost of Goods Sold	$181,260	
Selling Expenses	54,780	
General and Administrative Expenses	34,504	
Interest Expense	2,631	
Total Costs and Expenses		273,175
Net Income		$ 17,881

and Bradstreet. There are two examples from service industries, advertising agencies and interstate trucking; two examples from merchandising industries, auto and home supply and grocery stores; and two examples from manufacturing, pharmaceuticals and household appliances. Shafer Auto Parts Company, the example that is used in this chapter, falls into the auto and home supply industry.

EVALUATING LIQUIDITY

Liquidity means having enough money on hand to pay bills when they are due and to take care of unexpected needs for cash. Two measures of liquidity are working capital and the current ratio.

Working Capital   The first measure, working capital, is the amount by which total current assets exceed total current liabilities. This is an important measure of liquidity because current liabilities are debts that must be paid within one year and current assets are assets that will be realized in cash or used up within one year or one operating cycle, whichever is longer. By definition, current liabilities are paid out of current assets. So the excess of current assets over current liabilities is the net current assets on hand to continue business operations. It is the working capital that can be used to buy inventory, obtain credit, and finance expanded sales. Lack of working capital can lead to a company's failure.

For Shafer Auto Parts Company, working capital is computed as follows:

Current assets	$124,356
Less current liabilities	42,683
Working capital	$ 81,673

Current Ratio   The second measure of liquidity, the current ratio, is closely related to working capital and is believed by many bankers and other creditors to be a good indicator of a company's ability to pay its bills and to repay outstanding loans. The current ratio is the ratio of current assets to current liabilities. For Shafer Auto Parts Company, it would be computed like this:

$$\text{Current ratio} = \frac{\text{current assets}}{\text{current liabilities}} = \frac{\$124{,}356}{\$42{,}683} = 2.9$$

Thus, Shafer has $2.90 of current assets for each $1.00 of current liabilities. Is that good or bad? The answer requires the comparison of this year's ratio with those of earlier years and with similar measures for successful companies in the same industry. The average current ratio varies widely from industry to industry, as shown in Figure 2. For interstate trucking companies, which have no merchandise inventory, the current ratio is 1.4. In contrast, auto and home supply companies, which carry large merchandise inventories, have an average current ratio of 2.3. Shafer Auto Parts Company, with a ratio of 2.9, exceeds the average for its industry. A very low current ratio, of course, can be unfavorable, but so can a very high one. The latter may indicate that a company is not using its assets effectively.

EVALUATING PROFITABILITY

Just as important as paying bills on time is profitability—the ability to earn a satisfactory income. As a goal, profitability competes with liquidity for managerial attention because liquid assets, although important, are not the best profit-producing resources. Cash, for example, means purchasing power, but a satisfactory profit can be made only if purchasing power is used to buy

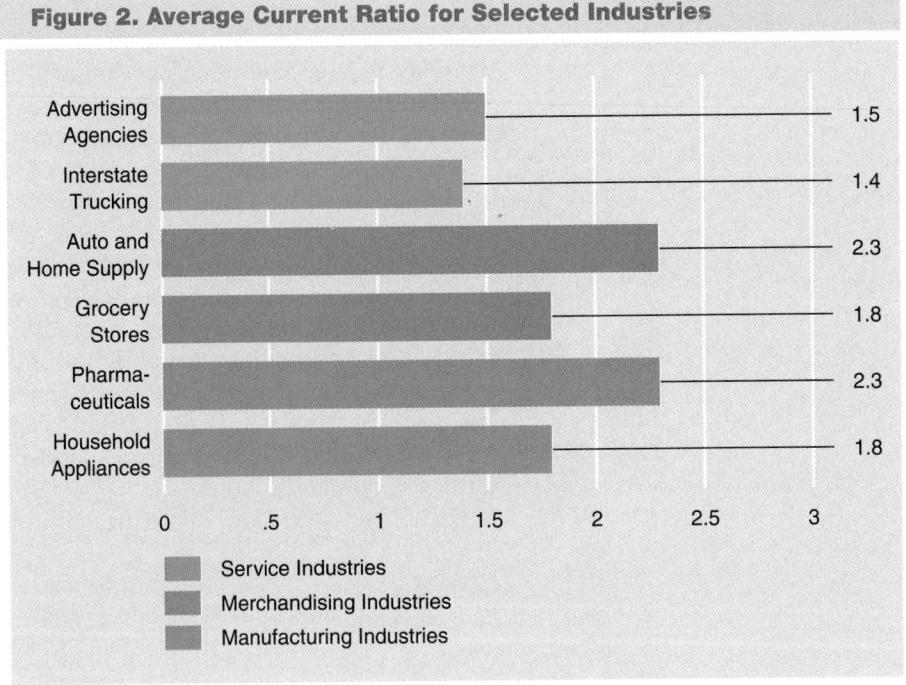

Figure 2. Average Current Ratio for Selected Industries

Source: Data from Dun and Bradstreet, *Industry Norms and Ratios*, 1993–94.

profit-producing (and less liquid) assets, such as inventory and long-term assets.

Among the common measures of a company's ability to earn income are (1) profit margin, (2) asset turnover, (3) return on assets, (4) debt to equity, and (5) return on equity. To evaluate a company meaningfully, one must relate its profit performance to its past performance and prospects for the future as well as to the averages for other companies in the same industry.

Profit Margin   The profit margin shows the percentage of each sales dollar that results in net income. It is figured by dividing net income by net sales. It should not be confused with gross margin, which is not a ratio but rather the amount by which revenues exceed the cost of goods sold.

Shafer Auto Parts Company has a profit margin of 6.2 percent:

$$\text{Profit margin} = \frac{\text{net income}}{\text{net sales}} = \frac{\$17,881}{\$289,656} = .062 \ (6.2\%)$$

On each dollar of net sales, Shafer Auto Parts Company made 6.2 cents. A difference of 1 or 2 percent in a company's profit margin can mean the difference between a fair year and a very profitable one.

Asset Turnover   Asset turnover measures how efficiently assets are used to produce sales. Computed by dividing net sales by average total assets, it shows how many dollars of sales were generated by each dollar of assets. A company with a higher asset turnover uses its assets more productively than one with a lower asset turnover. Average total assets is computed by adding total assets at the beginning of the year to total assets at the end of the year and dividing by 2.

Assuming that total assets for Shafer Auto Parts Company were $148,620 at the beginning of the year, its asset turnover is computed as follows:

$$\text{Asset turnover} = \frac{\text{net sales}}{\text{average total assets}}$$

$$= \frac{\$289,656}{(\$148,620 + \$158,916)/2}$$

$$= \frac{\$289,656}{\$153,768} = 1.9 \text{ times}$$

Shafer Auto Parts Company produces $1.90 in sales for each $1.00 invested in average total assets. This ratio shows a meaningful relationship between an income statement figure and a balance sheet figure.

Return on Assets   Both the profit margin and the asset turnover ratios have some limitations. The profit margin ratio does not take into consideration the assets necessary to produce income, and the asset turnover ratio does not take into account the amount of income produced. The return on assets ratio overcomes those deficiencies by relating net income to average total assets. It is computed like this:

$$\text{Return on assets} = \frac{\text{net income}}{\text{average total assets}}$$

$$= \frac{\$17,881}{(\$148,620 + \$158,916)/2}$$

$$= \frac{\$17,881}{\$153,768} = .116 \ (\text{or } 11.6\%)$$

Figure 3. Average Profit Margin for Selected Industries

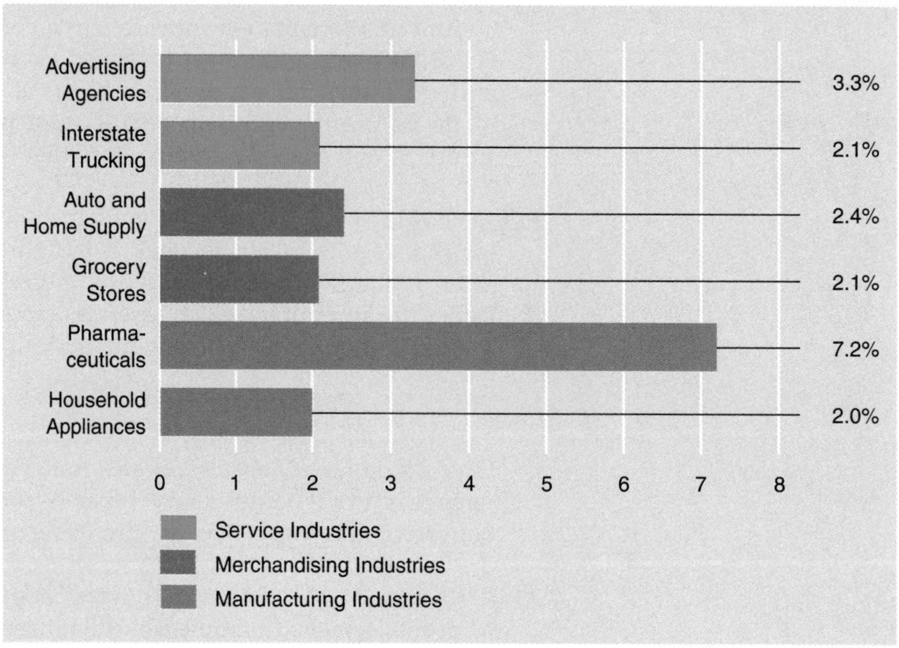

Source: Data from Dun and Bradstreet, *Industry Norms and Ratios*, 1993–94.

For each dollar invested, Shafer Auto Parts Company's assets generated 11.6 cents of net income. This ratio indicates the income-generating strength (profit margin) of the company's resources and how efficiently the company is using all its assets (asset turnover).

Return on assets, then, combines profit margin and asset turnover:

Profit margin × asset turnover = return on assets

6.2% × 1.9 times = 11.8%*

*The slight difference between 11.6 and 11.8 is due to rounding.

Thus, a company's management can improve overall profitability by increasing the profit margin, the asset turnover, or both. Similarly, in evaluating a company's overall profitability, the financial statement user must consider the interaction of both ratios to produce return on assets.

Careful study of Figures 3, 4, and 5 shows the different ways in which the selected industries combine profit margin and asset turnover to produce return on assets. For instance, grocery stores and advertising agencies have a similar return on assets, but they achieve it in very different ways. Grocery stores have a very small profit margin, 2.1 percent, which when multiplied by a high asset turnover, 5.6 times, gives a return on assets of 11.8 percent. Advertising agencies, on the other hand, have a higher margin, 3.3 percent and a lower asset turnover, 4.1 times, and produce a higher return on assets of 13.5 percent. Pharmaceutical companies have the lowest return on assets, 5.0 percent, despite a high profit margin, 7.2 percent, because of a very low asset turnover, .7 times.

Shafer Auto Parts Company's profit margin of 6.2 percent is well above the auto and home supply industry average of 2.4 percent, but its turnover of 1.9 times lags behind the industry average of 2.8 times. Shafer is sacrificing asset turnover to achieve a high profit margin. It is clear that the strategy is

Financial Reporting and Analysis

Figure 4. Asset Turnover for Selected Industries

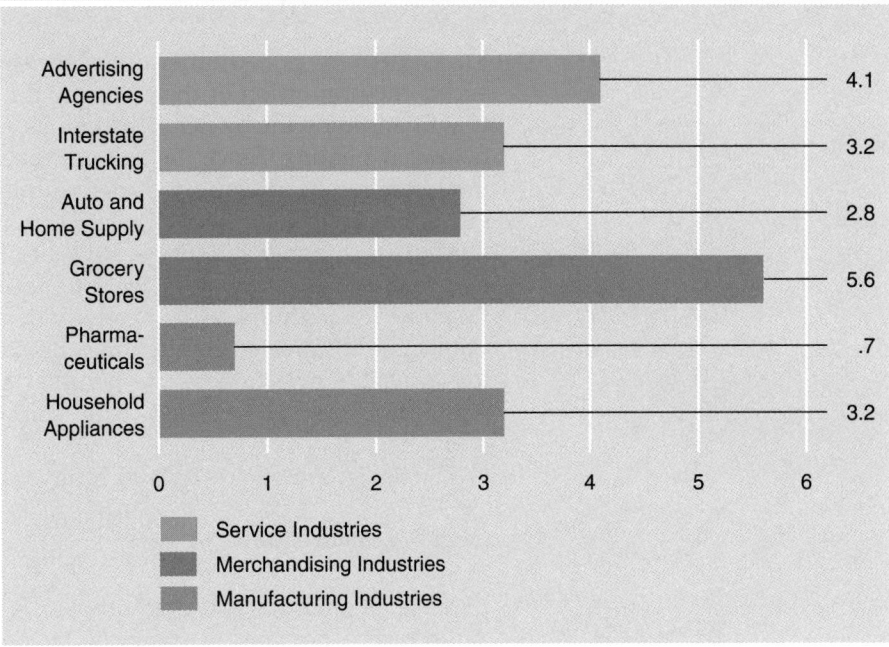

Source: Data from Dun and Bradstreet, *Industry Norms and Ratios,* 1993–94.

Figure 5. Return on Assets for Selected Industries

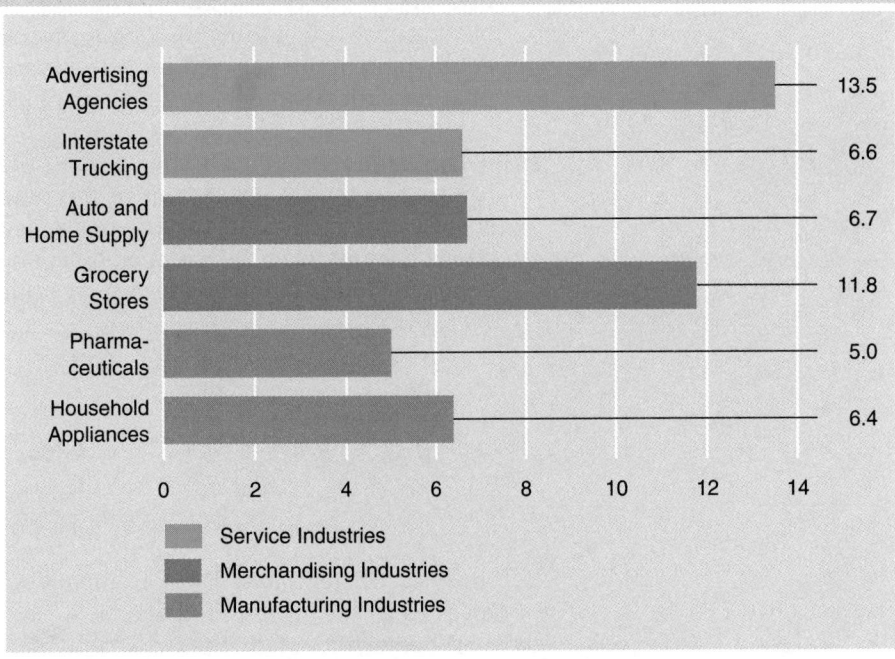

Source: Data from Dun and Bradstreet, *Industry Norms and Ratios,* 1993–94.

working, because Shafer's return on assets of 11.6 percent exceeds the industry average of 6.7 percent.

Debt to Equity   Another useful measure is the debt to equity ratio, which shows the proportion of the company financed by creditors in comparison to that financed by the owner. This ratio is computed by dividing total liabilities by owner's equity. Since the balance sheets of many companies do not show total liabilities, a short way of determining total liabilities is to deduct owner's equity from total assets. A debt to equity ratio of 1.0 means that total liabilities equal owner's equity—that half of the company's assets are financed by creditors. A ratio of .5 would mean that one-third of the assets are financed by creditors. A company with a high debt to equity ratio is more vulnerable in poor economic times because it must continue to repay creditors. Owner's investments, on the other hand, do not have to be repaid, and withdrawals can be deferred if the company is suffering because of a poor economy.

The Shafer Auto Parts debt to equity ratio is computed as follows:

$$\text{Debt to equity} = \frac{\text{total liabilities}}{\text{owner's equity}} = \frac{\$60,483}{\$98,433} = .614 \text{ (or 61.4\%)}$$

Because its ratio of debt to equity is 61.4 percent, about 38 percent of Shafer Auto Parts Company is financed by creditors and roughly 62 percent is financed by Fred Shafer.

The debt to equity ratio does not fit neatly into either the liquidity or the profitability category. It is clearly very important to liquidity analysis because it relates to debt and its repayment. However, the debt to equity ratio is also relevant to profitability for two reasons. First, creditors are interested in the proportion of the business that is debt financed because the more debt a company has, the more profit it must earn to protect the payment of interest to its creditors. Second, an owner is interested in the proportion of the business that is debt financed. The amount of interest that must be paid on the debt affects the amount of profit that is left to provide a return on the owner's investment. The debt to equity ratio also shows how much expansion is possible by borrowing additional long-term funds. Figure 6 shows that the debt to equity ratio in our selected industries varies from a low of 71.2 percent in the pharmaceutical industry to a high of 148.8 percent in household appliances.

Return on Equity   Of course, Fred Shafer is interested in how much he has earned on his investment in the business. His return on equity is measured by the ratio of net income to average owner's equity. Taking the ending owner's equity from the balance sheet and assuming that beginning owner's equity is $100,552, Shafer's return on equity is computed as follows:

$$\text{Return on equity} = \frac{\text{net income}}{\text{average owner's equity}}$$

$$= \frac{\$17,881}{(\$100,552 + \$98,433)/2}$$

$$= \frac{\$17,881}{\$99,492.50} = .180 \text{ (or 18.0\%)}$$

In 19x2, Shafer Auto Parts Company earned 18.0 cents for every dollar invested by the owner, Fred Shafer.

Whether or not this is an acceptable return depends on several factors, such as how much the company earned in prior years and how much other companies in the same industry earned. As measured by return on equity

Financial Reporting and Analysis

(Figure 7), advertising agencies are the most profitable of our sample industries, with a return on equity of 30.1 percent. Shafer Auto Parts Company's average return on equity of 18.0 percent exceeds the average of 13.5 percent for the auto and home supply industry.

Figure 6. Average Debt to Equity for Selected Industries

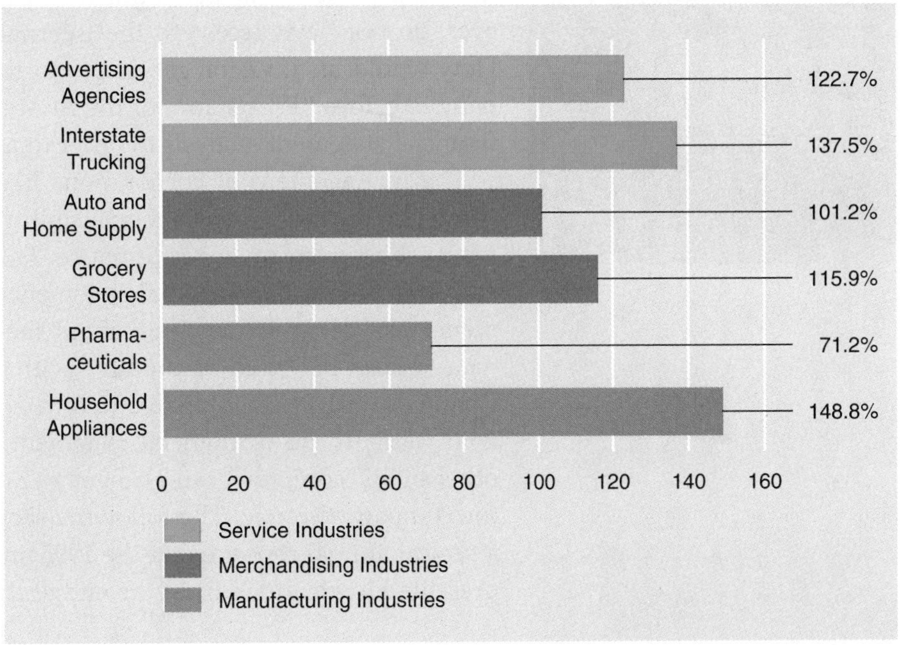

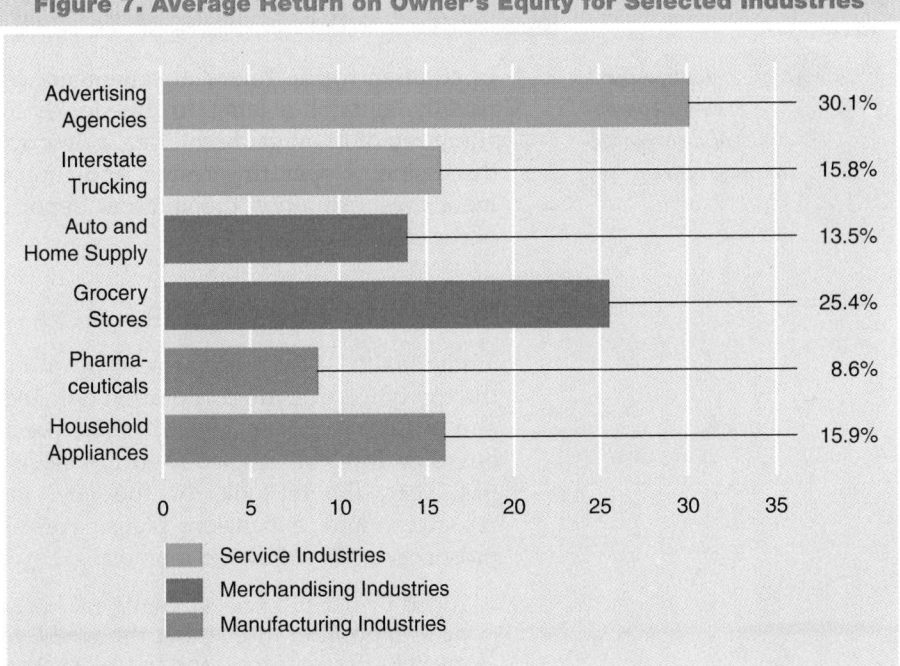

Source: Data from Dun and Bradstreet, *Industry Norms and Ratios,* 1993–94.

Figure 7. Average Return on Owner's Equity for Selected Industries

Source: Data from Dun and Bradstreet, *Industry Norms and Ratios,* 1993–94.

Toys "R" Us

Financial statement analysis, as presented in the previous sections, is a useful tool for management to assess its progress in achieving the goals of liquidity and profitability. It is also a useful tool to help investors make decisions about investing in companies. Investors, however, do not have access to the internal reports that management does. How would an investor get access to the financial statements of a company like Toys "R" Us, one of the most successful retailers today, to do a financial statement analysis in order to make an investment decision?

The management of corporations like Toys "R" Us, whose shares are owned by the public, has a responsibility each year to report to stockholders on their company's performance. This report, called the annual report, contains the annual financial statements, the notes to the financial statements, and other information about the company. This report and other data must be filed annually with the Securities and Exchange Commission and are available to anyone who asks for them. An investor who wants to do a financial statement analysis of Toys "R" Us, or any other public company, can also get an annual report by writing or calling the company directly. The following sections illustrate the components of a typical annual report using the 1995 annual report of Toys "R" Us that is presented in an appendix at the end of this book. :::::

COMPONENTS OF A CORPORATE ANNUAL REPORT

Supplemental OBJECTIVE

8 *Identify the major components of a corporate annual report*

In addition to the financial statements and related notes, the annual report usually contains a letter to the stockholders (or shareholders), a multiyear summary of financial highlights, a description of the business, management's discussion of operating results and financial condition, a report of management's responsibility, the auditors' report, and a list of directors and officers of the company.

LETTER TO THE STOCKHOLDERS

Traditionally, at the beginning of the annual report, there is a letter in which the top officers of the corporation tell stockholders about the performance of and prospects for the company. The president and the vice chairman of the board of Toys "R" Us wrote to the stockholders about the highlights of the past year, the outlook for the new year, corporate citizenship, human resources, and expansion plans. For example, they reported on future prospects in the following manner:

> Aided by our financial strength, we intend to capitalize on our strong competitive position throughout the world, by continued expansion to achieve greater sales, earnings, and market share gains.

FINANCIAL HIGHLIGHTS

The financial highlights section of the annual report presents key financial statistics for a ten-year period and is often accompanied by graphs. The Toys "R" Us annual report, for example, gives key figures for operations, financial position, and number of stores at year end and uses a graph to illustrate the total number of stores for the last ten years. Other key figures are also shown graphically at appropriate points in the report. Note that the financial highlights section often includes nonfinancial data, such as number of stores. In addition to financial highlights, an annual report contains a detailed description of the company's products and divisions. Some analysts scoff at this section of the annual report because it often contains glossy photographs and other image-building material, but it should not be overlooked because it may provide useful information about past results and future plans.

FINANCIAL STATEMENTS

All companies present four basic financial statements. Toys "R" Us presents statements of earnings, balance sheets, statements of stockholders' equity, and statements of cash flows. Refer to these statements in the Toys "R" Us appendix during the following discussion.

All the Toys "R" Us financial statements are preceded by the word *consolidated.* A corporation issues consolidated financial statements when the corporation consists of several companies and has combined their data for reporting purposes. For example, Toys "R" Us also operates Kids "R" Us and has combined that company's financial data with those of the Toys "R" Us stores.

Toys "R" Us also provides several years of data for each financial statement: two years for the balance sheet and three years for the others. Financial statements presented in this fashion are called comparative financial statements. Such statements are in accordance with generally accepted accounting principles and help readers to assess the company's performance over several years.

You may notice that the fiscal year for Toys "R" Us, instead of ending on the same date each year, ends on the Saturday nearest the end of January. This arrangement is convenient because it allows the company to always take its annual physical inventory on a weekend.

In a footnote at the bottom of each page of the financial statements, the company reminds the reader that the accompanying notes are an integral part of the statements and must be consulted in interpreting the data.

Consolidated Statements of Earnings   Toys "R" Us uses a single-step form of income statement and so includes all costs and expenses as a deduction from net sales to arrive at Earnings Before Taxes on Income.

Consolidated Balance Sheets   Toys "R" Us has a typical balance sheet for a merchandising company. Several items in the stockholders' equity section need further explanation. Common Stock represents the number of shares outstanding at par value. Additional Paid-in Capital represents amounts invested by stockholders in excess of the par value of the common stock. Foreign Currency Translation Adjustments occur because Toys "R" Us has foreign operations. Treasury Shares is a contra-stockholders' equity account that represents the cost of previously issued shares that have been bought back by the company.

Consolidated Statements of Stockholders' Equity   Instead of using a simple statement of retained earnings, Toys "R" Us presents a statement of stockholders' equity, which explains the changes in each of the six components of stockholders' equity.

Consolidated Statements of Cash Flows   Whereas the income statement reflects a company's profitability, the statement of cash flows reflects its liquidity. The statement provides information about a company's cash receipts, cash payments, and investing and financing activities during an accounting period.

Refer to the consolidated statements of cash flows in the Toys "R" Us appendix. The first section shows cash flows from operating activities. It begins with the net earnings (income) from the consolidated statements of earnings and adjusts that figure, which is based on accrual accounting, to a figure that represents the net cash flows provided by operating activities. Among the adjustments are increases for depreciation and amortization, which are expenses that do not require the use of cash, and increases and decreases for the changes in the working capital accounts. In the year ended January 28, 1995, Toys "R" Us had net earnings of $531,767,000, and its net cash inflow from those operations was $589,493,000. Added to net income are expenses that do not require a current outlay of cash, such as depreciation and amortization ($161,406,000). An increase of $17,380,000 in accounts and other receivables had a negative effect on cash flow. Cash was also used to increase inventories ($221,579,000) and prepaid expenses and other operating assets ($31,668,000). A large increase of $183,506,000 in accounts payable, accrued expenses, and taxes had the most significant positive effect on cash flows.

The second major section of the consolidated statements of cash flows is cash flows from investing activities. The main item in this category is capital expenditures, net, of $585,702,000. It shows that Toys "R" Us is a growing company.

The third major section of the consolidated statements of cash flows is cash flows from financing activities. You can see here that the primary sources of cash from financing activities are long-term borrowings of $34,648,000, and exercise of stock options of $25,998,000, which was helpful in paying for part of the capital expenditures in the investing activities section. Cash was used to reduce short-term borrowing by $117,201,000, and the amount of $469,714,000 was spent to repurchase the company stock. In total, financing activities during the year had a negative effect on cash flows of $365,738,000.

At the bottom of the consolidated statements of cash flows, the net effect of the operating, investing, and financing activities on the Cash balance may be seen. Toys "R" Us had a decrease in cash (and short-term equivalents) during the year of $422,060,000 and ended the year with $369,833,000 of cash (and short-term equivalents) on hand.

The supplemental disclosures of cash flow information explain that Toys "R" Us intends the word *cash* to include not only cash but also highly liquid short-term investments called *cash equivalents*. The section also explains other significant investing and financing transactions.

NOTES TO CONSOLIDATED FINANCIAL STATEMENTS

To meet the requirements of full disclosure, the company must add notes to the financial statements to help users interpret some of the more complex items. The notes are considered an integral part of the financial statements. In recent years, the need for explanation and further details has become so great that the notes often take more space than the statements themselves. The notes to the financial statements can be put into three broad groups: summary of significant accounting policies, explanatory notes, and supplementary information.

Summary of Significant Accounting Policies   In its *Opinion No. 22*, the Accounting Principles Board requires that the financial statements include a summary of significant accounting policies. In most cases, the summary is presented in the first note to the financial statements or as a separate section just before the notes. In the summary, the company tells which generally accepted accounting principles it has followed in preparing the statements. For example, in the Toys "R" Us annual report, the company states the principles followed for property and equipment:

> Property and equipment are recorded at cost. Depreciation and amortization are provided using the straight-line method over the estimated useful lives of the assets, or, where applicable, the terms of the respective leases, whichever is shorter.

Other important accounting policies listed in the summary by Toys "R" Us deal with fiscal year, principles of consolidation, merchandise inventories, preopening costs, capitalized interest, financial instruments, and forward foreign exchange contracts.

Explanatory Notes   Other notes explain some of the items in the financial statements. For example, Toys "R" Us showed the details of its Property and Equipment account in a table in the second note, as follows:

(In thousands)	Useful Life (In years)	January 28, 1995	January 29, 1994
Land		$ 764,808	$ 693,737
Buildings	45–50	1,627,145	1,446,277
Furniture and Equipment	5–20	1,177,909	953,360
Leaseholds and Leasehold Improvements	12½–50	809,365	658,191
Construction in Progress		55,730	41,855
Leased Property under Capital Leases		24,881	24,360
		$4,459,838	$3,817,780
Less Accumulated Depreciation and Amortization		791,033	633,313
		$3,668,805	$3,184,467

Other explanatory notes have to do with seasonal financing and long-term debt, leases, stockholders' equity, taxes on income, the profit-sharing plan, stock options, and foreign operations.

Supplementary Information In recent years, the FASB and the SEC have ruled that certain supplemental information must be presented with financial statements. An example is the quarterly reports that most companies make to their stockholders and to the Securities and Exchange Commission. The quarterly reports, which are called interim financial statements, are in most cases reviewed but not audited by the company's independent CPA firm. In its annual report, Toys "R" Us presented unaudited quarterly financial data from its 1995 quarterly statements, which are shown in the following table (for the year ended January 28, 1995; dollars in thousands, except per share amounts):

	First Quarter	Second Quarter	Third Quarter	Fourth Quarter
Net Sales	$1,461,933	$1,452,117	$1,631,345	$4,200,191
Cost of Sales	1,001,203	982,892	1,097,236	2,926,627
Net Earnings	37,580	38,014	47,367	408,806
Net Earnings per Share	$.13	$.13	$.17	$1.46

Interim data were presented for 1994 as well. Toys "R" Us also provides supplemental information on the market price of its common stock during the year. Other companies that engage in more than one line or type of business may present information for each business segment.

REPORT OF MANAGEMENT'S RESPONSIBILITIES

A statement of management's responsibility for the financial statements and the internal control structure may accompany the financial statements. The management report of Toys "R" Us acknowledges management's responsibility for the integrity and objectivity of the financial information and for the system of internal controls. It mentions the company's internal audit program and its distribution of policies to employees. It also states that the financial statements have been audited.

MANAGEMENT'S DISCUSSION AND ANALYSIS

Management also presents a discussion and analysis of financial conditions and results of operations. In this section, management explains the difference from one year to the next. For example, the management of Toys "R" Us describes the company's sales performance in the following way:

> The Company has experienced sales growth in each of its last three years; sales were up 10.1% in 1994, 10.8% in 1993, and 17.1% in 1992. Part of the growth is attributable to the opening of 121 new U.S.A. toy stores, 167 international toy stores and 39 children's clothing stores during the three-year period, and a portion of the increase is due to comparable U.S.A. toy store sales increases of 2.1%, 3.3%, and 6.9% in 1994, 1993 and 1992, respectively.

Its management of cash flows is described as follows:

> The seasonal nature of the business (approximately 48% of sales take place in the fourth quarter) typically causes cash to decline from the beginning of

the year through October as inventory increases for the holiday season and funds are used for land purchases and construction of new stores which usually open in the first ten months of the year.

REPORT OF CERTIFIED PUBLIC ACCOUNTANTS

The independent auditors' report addresses the credibility of the financial statements. Prepared by independent certified public accountants, it gives the accountants' opinion about how fairly the statements have been presented. Using financial statements prepared by managers without an independent audit would be like having a judge hear a case in which he or she was personally involved. Management, through its internal accounting system, is logically responsible for recordkeeping because it needs similar information for its own use in operating the business. The certified public accountants, acting independently, add the necessary credibility to management's figures for interested third parties. They report to the board of directors and the stockholders rather than to management.

In form and language, most auditors' reports are like the one shown in Figure 8. Usually such a report is short, but its language is very important. The report is divided into three parts.

1. The first paragraph identifies the financial statements subject to the auditors' report. It also identifies responsibilities. Company management is responsible

Figure 8. Auditors' Report for Toys "R" Us, Inc.

REPORT OF INDEPENDENT AUDITORS

To the Board of Directors and Stockholders
Toys"R"Us, Inc.

① We have audited the accompanying consolidated balance sheets of Toys"R"Us, Inc. and subsidiaries as of January 28, 1995 and January 29, 1994, and the related consolidated statements of earnings, stockholders' equity and cash flows for each of the three years in the period ended January 28, 1995. These financial statements are the responsibility of the Company's management. Our responsibility is to express an opinion on these financial statements based on our audits.

② We conducted our audits in accordance with generally accepted auditing standards. Those standards require that we plan and perform the audit to obtain reasonable assurance about whether the financial statements are free of material misstatement. An audit includes examining, on a test basis, evidence supporting the amounts and disclosures in the financial statements. An audit also includes assessing the accounting principles used and significant estimates made by management,

as well as evaluating the overall financial statement presentation. We believe that our audits provide a reasonable basis for our opinion.

③ In our opinion, the financial statements referred to above present fairly, in all material respects, the consolidated financial position of Toys"R"Us, Inc. and subsidiaries at January 28, 1995 and January 29, 1994, and the consolidated results of their operations and their cash flows for each of the three years in the period ended January 28, 1995, in conformity with generally accepted accounting principles.

Ernst & Young LLP

New York, New York
March 8, 1995

Reprinted courtesy of Toys "R" Us, Inc. The footnotes to the financial statement, which are an integral part of the report, are not included.

for the financial statements, and the auditor is responsible for expressing an opinion on the financial statements based on the audit.

2. The second paragraph, or scope section, states that the examination was made in accordance with generally accepted auditing standards. Those standards call for an acceptable level of quality in ten areas established by the American Institute of Certified Public Accountants. The scope section also contains a brief description of the objectives and nature of the audit.

3. The third paragraph, or opinion section, states the results of the auditors' examination. The use of the word *opinion* is very important because the auditors do not certify or guarantee that the statements are absolutely correct. To do so would go beyond the truth, since many items, such as depreciation, are based on estimates. Instead, the auditors simply give an opinion about whether, overall, the financial statements "present fairly," in all material respects, the financial position, results of operations, and cash flows. Such an opinion means that the statements are prepared in accordance with generally accepted accounting principles. If, in the auditors' opinion, the statements do not meet accepted standards, the auditors must explain why and to what extent.

CHAPTER REVIEW

REVIEW OF LEARNING OBJECTIVES

1. **State the objectives of financial reporting.** The objectives of financial reporting are (1) to furnish the information needed to make investment and credit decisions, (2) to provide information that can be used to assess cash flow prospects, and (3) to provide information about business resources, claims to those resources, and changes in them.

2. **State the qualitative characteristics of accounting information and describe their interrelationships.** Understandability depends on the knowledge of the user and the ability of the accountant to provide useful information. Usefulness is a function of two primary characteristics, relevance and reliability. Information is relevant when it affects the outcome of a decision. Information that is relevant has feedback value and predictive value and is timely. To be reliable, information must represent what it is supposed to represent, must be verifiable, and must be neutral.

3. **Define and describe the use of the conventions of *comparability* and *consistency*, *materiality*, *conservatism*, *full disclosure*, and *cost-benefit*.** Because accountants' measurements are not exact, certain conventions have come to be applied in current practice to help users interpret financial statements. One of these conventions is consistency, which requires the use of the same accounting procedures from period to period and enhances the comparability of financial statements. The second is materiality, which has to do with the relative importance of an item. The third is conservatism, which entails using the procedure that is least likely to overstate assets and income. The fourth is full disclosure, which means including all relevant information in the financial statements. The fifth is cost-benefit, which suggests that above a minimum level of information, additional information should be provided only if the benefits derived from the information exceed the costs of providing it.

4. **Explain management's responsibility for ethical financial reporting and define *fraudulent financial reporting*.** Management is responsible for the preparation of financial statements in accordance with generally accepted accounting principles and for the internal controls that provide assurance that this objective is achieved. Fraudulent financial reporting is the intentional preparation of misleading financial statements.

5. **Identify and describe the basic components of a classified balance sheet.** A classified balance sheet is subdivided as follows:

Assets	**Liabilities**
Current Assets	Current Liabilities
Investments	Long-Term Liabilities
Property, Plant, and Equipment	**Owner's Equity**
Intangible Assets	(Content depends on
(Other Assets)	the form of business)

A current asset is an asset that can reasonably be expected to be realized in cash or consumed during the next year or the normal operating cycle, whichever is longer. Investments are long-term assets that are not usually used in the normal operation of a business. Property, plant, and equipment are long-term assets that are used in day-to-day operations. Intangible assets are long-term assets whose value stems from the rights or privileges they extend to the owner. A current liability is a liability that can reasonably be expected to be paid or performed during the next year or the normal operating cycle, whichever is longer. Long-term liabilities are debts that fall due more than one year in the future or beyond the normal operating cycle. The equity section for a corporation differs from that of a proprietorship in that it has subdivisions of contributed capital (the value of assets invested by stockholders) and retained earnings (stockholders' claim to assets earned from operations and reinvested in operations).

6. **Prepare multistep and single-step classified income statements.** Condensed income statements for external reporting can be in multistep or single-step form. The multistep form arrives at net income through a series of steps; the single-step form arrives at net income in a single step. There is usually a separate section in the multistep form for other revenues and expenses.

7. **Evaluate liquidity and profitability using classified financial statements.** One important use of classified financial statements is to evaluate a company's liquidity and profitability. Two simple measures of liquidity are working capital and the current ratio. Five simple measures of profitability are profit margin, asset turnover, return on assets, debt to equity, and return on equity.

SUPPLEMENTAL OBJECTIVE

8. **Identify the major components of a corporate annual report.** In its annual report, a corporation's management reports to stockholders on the company's financial results for the year. An annual report has the following principal components: letter to the stockholders, financial highlights, the four basic financial statements, notes to the financial statements, report of management's responsibilities, management's discussion and analysis of earnings, and the report of the certified public accountants.

REVIEW OF CONCEPTS AND TERMINOLOGY

The following concepts and terms were introduced in this chapter:

S O 8 **Annual report:** The medium in which the general-purpose external financial statements of a business are communicated once a year to stockholders and other interested parties.

L O 7 **Asset turnover:** A measure of profitability that shows how efficiently assets are used to produce sales; net sales divided by average total assets.

L O 5 **Classified financial statements:** General-purpose external financial statements divided into useful subcategories.

L O 3 **Comparability:** The convention of presenting information in a way that enables decision makers to recognize similarities, differences, and trends over different time periods or between different companies.

S O 8 **Comparative financial statements:** Financial statements in which data for two or more years are presented in adjacent columns.

L O 6   **Condensed financial statements:** Financial statements for external reporting that present only the major categories of information.

L O 3   **Conservatism:** The convention that mandates that, when faced with equally acceptable alternatives, accountants must choose the one least likely to overstate assets and income.

L O 3   **Consistency:** The convention that requires that an accounting procedure, once adopted, not be changed from one period to another unless users are informed of the change.

S O 8   **Consolidated financial statements:** The combined financial statements of a parent company and its subsidiaries.

L O 5   **Contributed capital:** The accounts that reflect the stockholders' investment in a corporation. Also called *paid-in capital*.

L O 3   **Convention:** A rule of thumb or customary way of recording transactions or preparing financial statements.

L O 3   **Cost-benefit:** The convention that holds that benefits gained from providing accounting information should be greater than the costs of providing that information.

L O 5   **Current assets:** Cash or other assets that are reasonably expected to be realized in cash, sold, or consumed within one year or within the normal operating cycle, whichever is longer.

L O 5   **Current liabilities:** Obligations due to be paid or performed within one year or within the normal operating cycle, whichever is longer.

L O 7   **Current ratio:** A measure of liquidity; current assets divided by current liabilities.

L O 7   **Debt to equity:** A ratio that measures the relationship of assets provided by creditors to those provided by owners; total liabilities divided by owner's equity.

L O 4   **Fraudulent financial reporting:** The intentional preparation of misleading financial statements.

L O 3   **Full disclosure:** The convention that requires that financial statements and their notes present all information relevant to the users' understanding of the company's financial condition.

L O 6   **Income from operations:** Gross margin less operating expenses.

S O 8   **Independent auditors' report:** The section of an annual report in which the independent certified public accountants describe the nature of the audit (scope section) and state an opinion about how fairly the financial statements have been presented (opinion section).

L O 5   **Intangible assets:** Long-term assets that have no physical substance but that have a value based on rights or privileges that belong to their owner.

S O 8   **Interim financial statements:** Financial statements prepared for an accounting period of less than one year.

L O 5   **Investments:** Assets, usually long term, that are not used in the normal operation of a business and that management does not intend to convert to cash within the next year.

L O 7   **Liquidity:** Having enough money on hand to pay bills when they are due and to take care of unexpected needs for cash.

L O 5   **Long-term liabilities:** Debts that fall due more than one year in the future or beyond the normal operating cycle, or that are to be paid out of noncurrent assets.

L O 3   **Materiality:** The convention that requires that an item or event in a financial statement be important to the users of financial statements.

L O 6   **Multistep form:** A form of condensed income statement that arrives at net income in the same steps as a detailed income statement.

S O 8   **Notes to the financial statements:** The section of a corporate annual report containing information that aids users in interpreting the financial statements.

S O 8   **Opinion section:** The part of the auditors' report that states the results of the auditors' examination.

L O 5   **Other assets:** The balance sheet category that may include various types of assets other than current assets and property, plant, and equipment.

L O 6   **Other revenues and expenses:** The section of a multistep income statement that includes nonoperating revenues and expenses.

L O 7   **Profitability:** The ability of a business to earn a satisfactory income.

L O 7   **Profit margin:** A measure of profitability that shows the percentage of each sales dollar that results in net income; net income divided by net sales.

L O 5   **Property, plant, and equipment:** Tangible long-term assets used in the continuing operation of a business. Also called *operating assets, fixed assets, tangible assets, long-lived assets,* or *plant assets.*

L O 2   **Qualitative characteristics:** Standards for judging the information that accountants give to decision makers.

L O 2   **Relevance:** The qualitative characteristic of bearing directly on the outcome of a decision.

L O 2   **Reliability:** The qualitative characteristic of being representationally faithful, verifiable, and neutral.

L O 5   **Retained Earnings:** The account that reflects the stockholders' claim to the assets earned from operations and reinvested in corporate operations. Also called *earned capital.*

L O 7   **Return on assets:** A measure of profitability that shows how efficiently a company uses its assets to produce income; net income divided by average total assets.

L O 7   **Return on equity:** A measure of profitability that relates the amount earned by a business to the owner's investments in the business; net income divided by average owner's equity.

S O 8   **Scope section:** The part of the auditors' report that states that the examination was made in accordance with generally accepted auditing standards.

L O 6   **Single-step form:** A form of condensed income statement that arrives at net income in a single step.

S O 8   **Statement of stockholders' equity:** A financial statement that shows the same basic information as the statement of retained earnings, but also shows the changes in all stockholders' equity accounts.

S O 8   **Summary of significant accounting policies:** The section of a corporate annual report that discloses which generally accepted accounting principles the company has followed in preparing the financial statements.

L O 2   **Understandability:** The qualitative characteristic of communicating an intended meaning.

L O 2   **Usefulness:** The qualitative characteristic of being relevant and reliable.

L O 7   **Working capital:** A measure of liquidity equal to the current assets on hand to continue business operations; total current assets minus total current liabilities.

REVIEW PROBLEM
ANALYZING LIQUIDITY AND PROFITABILITY USING RATIOS

L O 7   Flavin Shirt Company has faced increased competition from overseas shirtmakers in recent years. Key information for the last two years is as follows:

	19x2	19x1
Current Assets	$ 200,000	$ 170,000
Total Assets	880,000	710,000
Current Liabilities	90,000	50,000
Long-Term Liabilities	150,000	50,000
Owner's Equity	640,000	610,000
Sales	1,200,000	1,050,000
Net Income	60,000	80,000

Total assets and owner's equity at the beginning of 19x1 were $690,000 and $590,000, respectively.

REQUIRED Use (1) liquidity analysis and (2) profitability analysis to document the declining financial position of Flavin Shirt Company.

Answer to Review Problem

1. Liquidity analysis

	Current Assets	Current Liabilities	Working Capital	Current Ratio
19x1	$170,000	$50,000	$120,000	3.4
19x2	200,000	90,000	110,000	2.2
Increase (decrease) in working capital			($ 10,000)	
Decrease in current ratio				1.2

Both working capital and the current ratio declined because, although current assets increased by $30,000 ($200,000 − $170,000), current liabilities increased by a greater amount, $40,000 ($90,000 − $50,000), from 19x1 to 19x2.

2. Profitability analysis

	Net Income	Sales	Profit Margin	Average Total Assets	Asset Turnover	Return on Assets	Average Owner's Equity	Return on Equity
19x1	$80,000	$1,050,000	7.6%	$700,000[1]	1.50	11.4%	$600,000[3]	13.3%
19x2	60,000	1,200,000	5.0%	795,000[2]	1.51	7.5%	625,000[4]	9.6%
Increase (decrease)	($20,000)	$ 150,000	(2.6%)	$ 95,000	0.01	(3.9%)	$ 25,000	(3.7%)

[1]($690,000 + $710,000) ÷ 2   [3]($590,000 + $610,000) ÷ 2
[2]($710,000 + $880,000) ÷ 2   [4]($610,000 + $640,000) ÷ 2

Net income decreased by $20,000 despite an increase in sales of $150,000 and an increase in average total assets of $95,000. The results were decreases in profit margin from 7.6 percent to 5.0 percent and in return on assets from 11.4 percent to 7.5 percent. Asset turnover showed almost no change and so did not contribute to the decline in profitability. The decrease in return on equity from 13.3 percent to 9.6 percent was not as great as the decrease in return on assets because the growth in total assets was financed by debt instead of owner's equity, as shown by the capital structure analysis on the next page.

Total liabilities increased by $140,000 while owner's equity increased by $30,000. As a result, the amount of the business financed by debt in relation to the amount of the business financed by owner's equity increased from 16.4 percent to 37.5 percent.

	Total Liabilities	Owner's Equity	Debt to Equity Ratio
19x1	$100,000	$610,000	16.4%
19x2	240,000	640,000	37.5%
Increase	$140,000	$ 30,000	21.1%

CHAPTER ASSIGNMENTS

QUESTIONS

1. What are the three objectives of financial reporting?
2. What are the qualitative characteristics of accounting information, and what is their significance?
3. What are the accounting conventions? How does each help in the interpretation of financial information?
4. Who is responsible for preparing reliable financial statements, and what is a principal way of fulfilling the responsibility?
5. What is the purpose of classified financial statements?
6. What are four common categories of assets?
7. What criteria must an asset meet to be classified as current? Under what condition is an asset considered current even though it will not be realized as cash within a year? What are two examples of assets that fall into this category?
8. In what order should current assets be listed?
9. What is the difference between a short-term investment in the current assets section and a security in the investments section of the balance sheet?
10. What is an intangible asset? Give at least three examples.
11. Name the two major categories of liabilities.
12. What are the primary differences between the equity section of the balance sheet for a sole proprietorship or partnership and the corresponding section for a corporation?
13. Explain the difference between contributed capital and retained earnings.
14. Explain how the multistep form of income statement differs from the single-step form. What are the relative merits of each?
15. Why are other revenues and expenses separated from operating revenues and expenses in the multistep income statement?
16. Define *liquidity* and name two measures of liquidity.
17. How is the current ratio computed and why is it important?
18. Which is the more important goal—liquidity or profitability? Explain your answer.
19. Name five measures of profitability.
20. Evaluate the following statement: "Return on assets is a better measure of profitability than profit margin."
21. Why are notes to financial statements necessary? What are three types of notes to the financial statements?
22. What is an independent auditors' report and why is it important?

SHORT EXERCISES

SE 1.
L O 3
*Accounting
Conventions*

No check figure

State which of the accounting conventions—comparability and consistency, materiality, conservatism, full disclosure, or cost-benefit—is being followed in each case below:

1. Management provides detailed information about the company's long-term debt in the notes to the financial statements.
2. A company does not account separately for discounts received for prompt payment of accounts payable because few such transactions occur and the total amount of the discounts is small.
3. Management eliminates a weekly report on property, plant, and equipment acquisitions and disposals because no one finds it useful.
4. A company follows the policy of recognizing a loss on inventory when the market value of an item falls below its cost but does nothing if the market value rises.
5. When several accounting methods are acceptable, management chooses a single method and follows that method from year to year.

SE 2.
L O 5
*Classification of
Accounts: Balance
Sheet*

No check figure

Tell whether each of the following accounts is a current asset; an investment; property, plant, and equipment; an intangible asset; a current liability; a long-term liability; owner's equity; or not on the balance sheet.

1. Delivery Trucks   PPE
2. Accounts Payable   CL
3. Note Payable (due in ninety days)   CL
4. Delivery Expense   Not B/S
5. S. Seig, Capital   OE
6. Prepaid Insurance   CA
7. Trademark   IA
8. Investment to Be Held Six Months   CA
9. Interest Payable   CL
10. Factory Not Used in Business   ?. I

SE 3.
L O 5
*Classified Balance
Sheet*

Check Figure: Total assets: $2,950

Using the following accounts, prepare a classified balance sheet at May 31 year end: Accounts Payable, $400; Accounts Receivable, $550; Accumulated Depreciation, Equipment, $350; Cash, $100; Equipment, $2,000; Franchise, $100; Investments (long-term), $250; Merchandise Inventory, $300; Notes Payable (long-term), $200; R. Riggs, Capital, ?; and Wages Payable, $50.

SE 4.
L O 6
*Classification of
Accounts: Income
Statement*

No check figure

Tell whether each of the following accounts is part of net sales, cost of goods sold, operating expenses, other revenues and expenses, or not on the income statement.

1. Delivery Expense
2. Interest Expense
3. Unearned Revenue
4. Sales Returns and Allowances
5. Purchases
6. Depreciation Expense
7. Investment Income
8. Withdrawals

SE 5.
L O 6
*Single-Step Income
Statement*

Check Figure: Net income: $145

Using the following accounts, prepare a single-step income statement at May 31 year end: Cost of Goods Sold, $280; General Expenses, $150; Interest Expense, $70; Interest Income, $30; Net Sales, $800; and Selling Expenses, $185.

SE 6.
L O 6
*Multistep Income
Statement*

Check Figure: Income from
Operations: $185

Using the accounts presented in SE 5, prepare a multistep income statement.

SE 7. *Liquidity Ratios*

L O 7

Check Figures: Working capital: $21,000; Current ratio: 4.0

Using the following information from a year-end balance sheet, compute working capital and the current ratio.

Accounts Payable	$ 7,000
Accounts Receivable	10,000
Cash	4,000
J. Hanks, Capital	20,000
Marketable Securities	2,000
Merchandise Inventory	12,000
Notes Payable in Three Years	13,000
Property, Plant, and Equipment	40,000

SE 8. *Profitability Ratios*

L O 7

No check figure

Using the following information from a balance sheet and an income statement, compute the (1) profit margin, (2) asset turnover, (3) return on assets, (4) debt to equity, and (5) return on equity. (The previous year's total assets were $100,000 and owner's equity was $70,000.)

Total Assets	$120,000
Total Liabilities	30,000
Total Owner's Equity	90,000
Net Sales	130,000
Cost of Goods Sold	70,000
Operating Expenses	45,000

SE 9. *Components of an*

S O 8 *Annual Report*

No check figure

Tell whether the following information typically included in an annual report would be found in (a) the letter to the stockholders, (b) the financial highlights, (c) the financial statements, (d) the summary of significant accounting policies, (e) the explanatory notes, (f) the supplementary information, (g) the report of management's responsibilities, (h) management's discussion and analysis, or (i) the report of certified public accountants.

1. Detailed information about an account on the balance sheet
2. A statement about the company's method of revenue recognition
3. A comment about whether or not the statements are fairly presented in accordance with generally accepted accounting principles
4. A ten-year summary of financial data
5. The company president's description of future plans
6. Data about cash flows from operations
7. Management's analysis of cash flows from operations
8. Quarterly financial results
9. A statement that management is responsible for the financial statements

EXERCISES

E 1. *Accounting*

L O 3 *Concepts and*

Conventions

No check figure

Each of the statements below violates a convention in accounting. State which of the following concepts or conventions is violated: comparability and consistency, materiality, conservatism, full disclosure, or cost-benefit.

1. A series of reports that are time-consuming and expensive to prepare is presented to the board of directors each month even though the reports are never used.
2. A company changes its method of accounting for depreciation.
3. The company in **2** does not indicate in the financial statements that the method of depreciation was changed, nor does it specify the effect of the change on net income.
4. A new office building next to the factory is debited to the Factory account because it represents a fairly small dollar amount in relation to the factory.
5. The asset account for a pickup truck still used in the business is written down to what the truck could be sold for even though the carrying value under conventional depreciation methods is higher.

E 2. *Financial*
L O 1, 2, 3 *Accounting*
Concepts

Check Figures: 1. g; 2. f; 3. h; 4. g;
5. f; 6. d; 7. g; 8. f; 9. b; 10. g; 11. g;
12. c; 13. b; 14. d; 15. a; 16. f; 17. e;
18. d; 19. a; 20. f; 21. f; 22. c

The lettered items below represent a classification scheme for the concepts of financial accounting. Match each numbered term with the letter of the category in which it belongs.

a. Decision makers (users of accounting information)
b. Business activities or entities relevant to accounting measurement
c. Objectives of accounting information
d. Accounting measurement considerations
e. Accounting processing considerations
f. Qualitative characteristics
g. Accounting conventions
h. Financial statements

1. Conservatism
2. Verifiability
3. Statement of cash flows
4. Materiality
5. Reliability
6. Recognition
7. Cost-benefit
8. Understandability
9. Business transactions
10. Consistency
11. Full disclosure
12. Furnishing information that is useful to investors and creditors
13. Specific business entities
14. Classification
15. Management
16. Neutrality
17. Internal accounting control
18. Valuation
19. Investors
20. Timeliness
21. Relevance
22. Furnishing information that is useful in assessing cash flow prospects

E 3. *Classification of*
L O 5 *Accounts: Balance*
Sheet

Check Figures: 1. d; 2. b; 3. a; 4. e;
5. f; 6. c; 7. b; 8. a; 9. a; 10. h; 11. a;
12. h; 13. e; 14. a; 15. c; 16. g

The lettered items below represent a classification scheme for a balance sheet, and the numbered items are account titles. Match each account with the letter of the category in which it belongs.

a. Current assets
b. Investments
c. Property, plant, and equipment
d. Intangible assets
e. Current liabilities
f. Long-term liabilities
g. Owner's equity
h. Not on balance sheet

1. Patent
2. Building Held for Sale
3. Prepaid Rent
4. Wages Payable
5. Note Payable in Five Years
6. Building Used in Operations
7. Fund Held to Pay Off Long-Term Debt
8. Inventory
9. Prepaid Insurance
10. Depreciation Expense
11. Accounts Receivable
12. Interest Expense
13. Unearned Revenue
14. Short-Term Investments
15. Accumulated Depreciation
16. M. Cepeda, Capital

withdrawl — equity

E 4. *Classified Balance*
L O 5 *Sheet Preparation*
Check Figure: Total assets: $352,000

The following data pertain to AMAX Company: Accounts Payable, $51,000; Accounts Receivable, $38,000; Accumulated Depreciation, Building, $14,000; Accumulated Depreciation, Equipment, $17,000; Bonds Payable, $60,000; Building, $70,000; Cash, $31,200; Copyright, $6,200; Equipment, $152,000; Inventory, $40,000; Investment in Corporate Securities (long term), $20,000; Investment in Six-Month Government Securities, $16,400; Land, $8,000; P. Arnold, Capital, $238,200; Prepaid Rent, $1,200; and Revenue Received in Advance, $2,800.

Prepare a classified balance sheet at December 31, 19xx.

E 5. *Classification of*
L O 6 *Accounts: Income Statement*

Check Figures: 1. b; 2. a; 3. b; 4. e; 5. c; 6. d; 7. c; 8. f; 9. c or d; 10. c; 11. c or d; 12. b; 13. b; 14. c; 15. f; 16. e

Using the classification scheme below for a multistep income statement, match each account with the letter of the category in which it belongs.

a. Net sales
b. Cost of goods sold
c. Selling expenses
d. General and administrative expenses
e. Other revenues and expenses
f. Not on income statement

1. Purchases
2. Sales Discounts
3. Merchandise Inventory (beginning)
4. Interest Income
5. Advertising Expense
6. Office Salaries Expense
7. Freight Out Expense
8. Prepaid Insurance
9. Utilities Expense
10. Sales Salaries Expense
11. Rent Expense
12. Purchases Returns and Allowances
13. Freight In
14. Depreciation Expense, Delivery Equipment
15. Taxes Payable
16. Interest Expense

E 6. *Preparation of*
L O 6 *Income Statements*

Check Figure: Net income: $68,000

The following data pertain to a sole proprietorship: Net Sales, $810,000; Cost of Goods Sold, $440,000; Selling Expenses, $180,000; General and Administrative Expenses, $120,000; Interest Expense, $8,000; and Interest Income, $6,000.

1. Prepare a condensed single-step income statement.
2. Prepare a condensed multistep income statement.

E 7. *Condensed*
L O 6 *Multistep Income Statement*

Check Figures: Gross Margin, $210,026; Income from Operations, $57,812

A condensed single-step income statement appears below. Present the information in a condensed multistep income statement, and tell what insights can be obtained from the multistep form as opposed to the single-step form.

Abdel Furniture Company
Income Statement
For the Year Ended December 31, 19xx

Revenues		
Net Sales	$598,566	
Interest Income	2,860	
Total Revenues		$601,426
Costs and Expenses		
Cost of Goods Sold	$388,540	
Selling Expenses	101,870	
General and Administrative Expenses	50,344	
Interest Expense	6,780	
Total Costs and Expenses		547,534
Net Income		$ 53,892

E 8. *Liquidity Ratios*

L O 7

Check Figures: Working capital: $32,000; Current ratio: 1.7

The following accounts and balances are taken from the general ledger of West Hills Company.

Accounts Payable	$16,600
Accounts Receivable	10,200
Cash	1,500
Current Portion of Long-Term Debt	10,000
Long-Term Investments	10,400
Marketable Securities	12,600
Merchandise Inventory	25,400
Notes Payable, 90 days	15,000
Notes Payable, 2 years	20,000
Notes Receivable, 90 days	26,000
Notes Receivable, 2 years	10,000
Prepaid Insurance	400
Property, Plant, and Equipment	60,000
R. Rawlings, Capital	28,300
Salaries Payable	850
Supplies	350
Property Taxes Payable	1,250
Unearned Revenue	750

Compute the (1) working capital and (2) current ratio.

E 9. *Profitability Ratios*

L O 7

Check Figure: Return on assets: 24.2%

The following end-of-year amounts are taken from the financial statements of Kopoulos Company: Total Assets, $426,000; Total Liabilities, $172,000; Owner's Equity, $254,000; Net Sales, $782,000; Cost of Goods Sold, $486,000; Operating Expenses, $202,000; and Withdrawals, $40,000. During the past year, total assets increased by $75,000. Total owner's equity was affected only by net income and withdrawals.

Compute the (1) profit margin, (2) asset turnover, (3) return on assets, (4) debt to equity, and (5) return on equity.

E 10. *Computation of*

L O 7 *Ratios*

Check Figures: Current ratio: 2.5; Return on assets: 12.5%

The simplified balance sheet and income statement for a sole proprietorship appear as follows:

Balance Sheet
December 31, 19xx

Assets		Liabilities	
Current Assets	$100,000	Current Liabilities	$ 40,000
Investments	20,000	Long-Term Liabilities	60,000
Property, Plant, and		Total Liabilities	$100,000
Equipment	293,000		
Intangible Assets	27,000	**Owner's Equity**	
Total Assets	$440,000	S. Korabik, Capital	$340,000
		Total Liabilities and	
		Owner's Equity	$440,000

Income Statement
For the Year Ended December 31, 19xx

Net Sales	$820,000
Cost of Goods Sold	500,000
Gross Margin	$320,000
Operating Expenses	270,000
Net Income	$ 50,000

Total assets and owner's equity at the beginning of 19xx were $360,000 and $280,000, respectively.

1. Compute the following liquidity measures: (a) working capital and (b) current ratio.
2. Compute the following profitability measures: (a) profit margin, (b) asset turnover, (c) return on assets, (d) debt to equity, and (e) return on equity.

SKILLS DEVELOPMENT EXERCISES

Conceptual Analysis

SDE 1. *Accounting*
L O 3 *Conventions*

No check figure

Mason Parking, which operates a seven-story parking building in downtown Chicago, has a calendar year end. It serves daily and hourly parkers, as well as monthly parkers who pay a fixed monthly rate in advance. The company traditionally has recorded all cash receipts as revenues when received. Most monthly parkers pay in full during the month prior to that in which they have the right to park. The company's auditors have said that beginning in 1996, the company should consider recording the cash receipts from monthly parking on an accrual basis, crediting Unearned Revenues. Total cash receipts for 1996 were $2,500,000, and the cash receipts received in 1996 and applicable to January 1997 were $125,000. Discuss the relevance of the accounting conventions of consistency, materiality, and full disclosure to the decision to record the monthly parking revenues on an accrual basis.

SDE 2. *Materiality*
L O 3

No check figure

Mackey Electronics, Inc. operates a chain of consumer electronics stores in the Atlanta area. This year the company achieved annual sales of $50 million, on which it earned a net income of $2 million. Until this year, the company used the periodic inventory system for financial reporting. At the beginning of the year, management implemented a new inventory system that enabled it to track all purchases and sales. At the end of the year, a physical inventory revealed that the actual inventory was $80,000 below what the new system indicated it should be. The inventory loss, which probably resulted from shoplifting, is reflected in a higher cost of goods sold. The problem concerns management but seems to be less important to the company's auditors. What is materiality? Why might the inventory loss concern management more than it does the auditors? Do you think the amount is material?

Ethical Dilemma

SDE 3. *Ethics and Financial*
L O 4 *Reporting*

No check figure

Salem Software, located outside Boston, develops computer software and licenses it to financial institutions. The firm uses an aggressive accounting method that records revenues from the software it has sold on a percentage of completion basis. Consequently, revenue for partially completed projects is recognized based on the proportion of the project that is completed. If a project is 50 percent completed, then 50 percent of the contracted revenue is recognized. In 19x2, preliminary estimates for a $5 million project are that the project is 75 percent complete. Because the estimate of completion is a matter of judgment, management asks for a new report showing the project to be 90 percent complete. The change will enable senior managers to meet their financial goals for the year and thus receive substantial year-end bonuses. Do you think management's action is ethical? If you were the company controller and were asked to prepare the new report, would you do it? What action would you take?

SDE 4. *Ethics and Financial*
L O 4 *Reporting*

No check figure

Treon Microsystems, Inc., a Silicon Valley manufacturer of microchips for personal computers, has just completed its year-end physical inventory in advance of preparing financial statements. To celebrate, the entire accounting department goes out for a New Year's Eve party at a local establishment. As senior accountant, you join the fun. At the party, you fall into conversation with an employee of one of your main competitors. After a while, the employee reveals that the competitor plans to introduce a new product in sixty days that will make Treon's principal product obsolete.

On Monday morning, you go to the financial vice president with this information, stating that the inventory may have to be written down and net income reduced. To your surprise, the financial vice president says that you were right to come to her, but urges you to say nothing about the problem. She says, "It is probably a rumor, and even if it is true, there will be plenty of time to write down the inventory in sixty days." You wonder if this is the appropriate thing to do. You feel confident that your source knew what he was talking about. You know that the salaries of all top managers, including the financial vice president, are tied to net income. What is fraudulent financial reporting? Is this an example of fraudulent financial reporting? What action would you take?

Research Activity

SDE 5.   *Annual Reports and*
L O 7   *Financial Analysis*
S O 8

No check figure

Most college and public libraries file annual reports of major public corporations. In some libraries, the annual reports are on microfiche. Go to the library and obtain the annual report for a company that you recognize. In the annual report, identify the four basic financial statements and the notes to the financial statements. Perform a liquidity analysis, including the calculation of working capital and the current ratio. Perform a profitability analysis, calculating profit margin, asset turnover, return on assets, debt to equity, and return on equity. Be prepared to present your findings in class.

Decision-Making Practice

SDE 6.   *Financial Analysis*
L O 7   *for Loan Decision*

No check figure

Steve Sulong was recently promoted to loan officer at the *First National Bank.* He has authority to issue loans up to $50,000 without approval from a higher bank official. This week two small companies, Handy Harvey, Inc. and Sheila's Fashions, Inc., have each submitted a proposal for a six-month $50,000 loan. To prepare financial analyses of the two companies, Steve has obtained the information summarized below.

Handy Harvey, Inc. is a local lumber and home improvement company. Because sales have increased so much during the past two years, Handy Harvey has had to raise additional working capital, especially as represented by receivables and inventory. The $50,000 loan is needed to assure the company of enough working capital for the next year. Handy Harvey began the year with total assets of $740,000 and stockholders' equity of $260,000, and during the past year the company had a net income of $40,000 on net sales of $760,000. The company's current unclassified balance sheet appears as follows:

Assets		Liabilities and Stockholders' Equity	
Cash	$ 30,000	Accounts Payable	$200,000
Accounts Receivable (net)	150,000	Notes Payable (short term)	100,000
Inventory	250,000	Notes Payable (long term)	200,000
Land	50,000	Common Stock	250,000
Buildings (net)	250,000	Retained Earnings	50,000
Equipment (net)	70,000	Total Liabilities and	
Total Assets	$800,000	Stockholders' Equity	$800,000

Sheila's Fashions, Inc. has for three years been a successful clothing store for young professional women. The leased store is located in the downtown financial district. Sheila's loan proposal asks for $50,000 to pay for stocking a new line of women's suits during the coming season. At the beginning of the year, the company had total assets of $200,000 and total stockholders' equity of $114,000. Over the past year, the company earned a net income of $36,000 on net sales of $480,000. The firm's unclassified balance sheet at the current date appears as follows:

Assets		Liabilities and Stockholders' Equity	
Cash	$ 10,000	Accounts Payable	$80,000
Accounts Receivable (net)	50,000	Accrued Liabilities	10,000
Inventory	135,000	Common Stock	50,000
Prepaid Expenses	5,000	Retained Earnings	100,000
Equipment (net)	40,000	Total Liabilities and	
Total Assets	$240,000	Stockholders' Equity	$240,000

1. Prepare a financial analysis of each company's liquidity before and after receiving the proposed loan. Also, compute profitability ratios before and after, as appropriate. Write a brief summary of the effect of the proposed loan on each company's financial position.
2. To which company do you suppose Steve would be more willing to make a $50,000 loan? What positive and negative factors could affect each company's ability to pay back the loan in the next year? What other information of a financial or nonfinancial nature would be helpful for making a final decision?

PROBLEM SET A

A 1. *Accounting*
L O 3 *Conventions*
No check figure

In each case below, accounting conventions may have been violated.

1. Figuero Manufacturing Company uses the cost method for computing the balance sheet amount of inventory unless the market value of the inventory is less than the cost, in which case the market value is used. At the end of the current year, the market value is $77,000 and the cost is $80,000. Figuero uses the $77,000 figure to compute net income because management feels it is the more cautious approach.
2. Margolis Company has annual sales of $5,000,000. It follows the practice of charging any items costing less than $100 to expenses in the year purchased. During the current year, it purchased several chairs for the executive conference rooms at $97 each, including freight. Although the chairs were expected to last for at least ten years, they were charged as an expense in accordance with company policy.
3. Choi Company closed its books on December 31, 19x3, before preparing its annual report. On December 30, 19x3, a fire destroyed one of the company's two factories. Although the company had fire insurance and would not suffer a loss on the building, a significant decrease in sales in 19x4 was expected because of the fire. The fire damage was not reported in the 19x3 financial statements because the operations for that year were not affected by the fire.
4. Shumate Drug Company spends a substantial portion of its profits on research and development. The company has been reporting its $2,500,000 expenditure for research and development as a lump sum, but management recently decided to begin classifying the expenditures by project even though the recordkeeping costs will increase.
5. During the current year, McMillan Company changed from one generally accepted method of accounting for inventories to another method.

REQUIRED

In each case, state the convention that applies, tell whether or not the treatment is in accord with the convention and generally accepted accounting principles, and briefly explain why.

A 2. *Forms of the Income*
L O 6 *Statement*
Check Figure: Net income: $63,626

The income statement accounts from the June 30, 19x2 year-end adjusted trial balance of Tasheki Hardware Company appear at the top of the next page. Beginning merchandise inventory was $175,200 and ending merchandise inventory is $157,650. The company is a sole proprietorship.

REQUIRED

From the information provided, prepare the following:

1. A detailed income statement.
2. A condensed income statement in multistep form.
3. A condensed income statement in single-step form.

Account Name	Debit	Credit
Sales		$541,230
Sales Returns and Allowances	$ 15,298	
Purchases	212,336	
Purchases Returns and Allowances		6,159
Freight In	11,221	
Sales Salaries Expense	102,030	
Sales Supplies Expense	1,642	
Rent Expense, Selling Space	18,000	
Utilities Expense, Selling Space	11,256	
Advertising Expense	21,986	
Depreciation Expense, Selling Fixtures	6,778	
Office Salaries Expense	47,912	
Office Supplies Expense	782	
Rent Expense, Office Space	4,000	
Depreciation Expense, Office Equipment	3,251	
Utilities Expense, Office Space	3,114	
Postage Expense	626	
Insurance Expense	2,700	
Miscellaneous Expense	481	
Interest Expense	3,600	
Interest Income		800

A 3. *Classified Balance*
L O 5 *Sheet*

Check Figure: Total assets: $397,143

The following information was taken from the June 30, 19x2 post-closing trial balance of Tasheki Hardware Company.

Account Name	Debit	Credit
Cash	$ 24,000	
Short-Term Investments	13,150	
Notes Receivable	45,000	
Accounts Receivable	76,570	
Merchandise Inventory	156,750	
Prepaid Rent	2,000	
Prepaid Insurance	1,200	
Sales Supplies	426	
Office Supplies	97	
Land Held for Future Expansion	11,500	
Selling Fixtures	72,400	
Accumulated Depreciation, Selling Fixtures		$ 22,000
Office Equipment	24,100	
Accumulated Depreciation, Office Equipment		12,050
Trademark	4,000	
Accounts Payable		109,745
Salaries Payable		787
Interest Payable		600
Notes Payable (due in three years)		36,000
Thomas Tasheki, Capital		250,011

REQUIRED

From the information provided, prepare a classified balance sheet.

A 4. *Ratio Analysis:*
L O 7 *Liquidity and*
Profitability

Check Figures: Current ratio: 2.0, 2.6;
Return on assets: 14.8%, 13.2%

Below is a summary of data taken from the income statements and balance sheets for Heard Construction Supply for the past two years.

	19x4	19x3
Current Assets	$ 183,000	$ 155,000
Total Assets	1,160,000	870,000
Current Liabilities	90,000	60,000
Long-Term Liabilities	300,000	200,000
Owner's Equity	670,000	520,000
Net Sales	2,300,000	1,740,000
Net Income	150,000	102,000

Total assets and owner's equity at the beginning of 19x3 were $680,000 and $420,000, respectively.

REQUIRED

1. Compute the following liquidity measures for 19x3 and 19x4: (a) working capital and (b) current ratio. Comment on the differences between the years.
2. Compute the following measures of profitability for 19x3 and 19x4: (a) profit margin, (b) asset turnover, (c) return on assets, (d) debt to equity, and (e) return on equity. Comment on the change in performance from 19x3 to 19x4.

A 5. *Classified Financial*
L O 5, 6, 7 *Statement*
Preparation and
Evaluation

Check Figures: Net income: $29,130;
Total assets: $367,740

The following accounts (in alphabetical order) and amounts were taken or calculated from the December 31, 19x4 year-end adjusted trial balance of Blossom Lawn Equipment Center: Accounts Payable, $36,300; Accounts Receivable, $84,700; Accumulated Depreciation, Building, $26,200; Accumulated Depreciation, Equipment, $17,400; Building, $110,000; Cash, $10,640; Cost of Goods Sold, $246,000; Dividend Income, $1,280; Equipment, $75,600; General and Administrative Expenses, $60,600; Nancy Gregorio, Capital, $211,210; Nancy Gregorio, Withdrawals, $23,900; Interest Expense, $12,200; Inventory, $56,150; Land (used in operations), $29,000; Land Held for Future Use, $20,000; Mortgage Payable, $90,000; Notes Payable (short term), $25,000; Notes Receivable, $12,000; Sales (net), $448,000; Selling Expenses, $101,350; Short-Term Investment (100 shares of General Motors), $6,500; and Trademark, $6,750. Total assets on December 31, 19x3 were $343,950.

REQUIRED

1. From the information above, prepare (a) an income statement in condensed multistep form, (b) a statement of owner's equity, and (c) a classified balance sheet.
2. Calculate the following measures of liquidity: (a) working capital and (b) current ratio.
3. Calculate the following measures of profitability: (a) profit margin, (b) asset turnover, (c) return on assets, (d) debt to equity, and (e) return on equity.

PROBLEM SET B

B 1. *Accounting*
L O 3 *Conventions*
No check figure

In each case below, accounting conventions may have been violated.

1. After careful study, Hawthorne Company, which has offices in forty states, has determined that in the future its method of depreciating office furniture should be changed. The new method is adopted for the current year, and the change is noted in the financial statements.
2. In the past, Regalado Corporation has recorded operating expenses in general accounts for each classification (for example, Salaries Expense, Depreciation Expense, and Utilities Expense). Management has determined that despite the additional recordkeeping costs, the company's income statement should break down each operating expense into its components of selling expense and administrative expense.
3. Callie Watts, the auditor of Burleson Corporation, discovered that an official of the company may have authorized the payment of a $1,000 bribe to a local official. Management argued that because the item was so small in relation to the size of the company ($1,000,000 in sales), the illegal payment should not be disclosed.

4. Kuberski's Bookstore built a small addition to its main building to house a new computer games section. Because no one could be sure that the computer games section would succeed, the accountant took a conservative approach and recorded the addition as an expense.

5. Since its origin ten years ago, Hsu Company has used the same generally accepted inventory method. Because there has been no change in the inventory method, the company does not declare in its financial statements what inventory method it uses.

REQUIRED

In each case, state the convention that applies, tell whether or not the treatment is in accord with the convention and generally accepted accounting principles, and briefly explain why.

B 2. *Forms of the Income*
L O 6 *Statement*
Check Figure: Net income (loss): ($860)

The March 31, 19x3 year-end income statement accounts that follow are for O'Dell Hardware Company. Beginning merchandise inventory was $86,400 and ending merchandise inventory is $72,500. O'Dell Hardware Company is a sole proprietorship.

Account Name	Debit	Credit
Sales		$461,100
Sales Returns and Allowances	$ 26,900	
Purchases	224,500	
Purchases Returns and Allowances		11,920
Freight In	17,400	
Sales Salaries Expense	62,160	
Sales Supplies Expense	1,640	
Rent Expense, Selling Space	7,200	
Utilities Expense, Selling Space	2,960	
Advertising Expense	16,800	
Depreciation Expense, Delivery Equipment	4,400	
Office Salaries Expense	29,240	
Office Supplies Expense	9,760	
Rent Expense, Office Space	2,400	
Utilities Expense, Office Space	1,000	
Postage Expense	2,320	
Insurance Expense	2,680	
Miscellaneous Expense	1,440	
General Management Salaries Expense	42,000	
Interest Expense	5,600	
Interest Income		420

REQUIRED

From the information provided, prepare the following:

1. A detailed income statement.
2. A condensed income statement in multistep form.
3. A condensed income statement in single-step form.

B 3. *Classified Balance*
L O 5 *Sheet*
Check Figure: Total assets: $297,800

The information at the top of the next page was taken from the March 31, 19x3 post-closing trial balance of O'Dell Hardware Company.

REQUIRED

From the information provided, prepare a classified balance sheet.

Account Name	Debit	Credit
Cash	$ 15,500	
Short-Term Investments	16,500	
Notes Receivable	5,000	
Accounts Receivable	138,000	
Merchandise Inventory	72,500	
Prepaid Rent	800	
Prepaid Insurance	2,400	
Sales Supplies	640	
Office Supplies	220	
Deposit for Future Advertising	1,840	
Building, Not in Use	24,800	
Land	11,200	
Delivery Equipment	20,600	
Accumulated Depreciation, Delivery Equipment		$ 14,200
Franchise Fee	2,000	
Accounts Payable		57,300
Salaries Payable		2,600
Interest Payable		420
Long-Term Notes Payable		40,000
Bill O'Dell, Capital		197,480

B 4. *Ratio Analysis:*
L O 7 *Liquidity and Profitability*

Check Figures: Current ratio: 2.3, 3.5; Return on assets: 12.5%, 11.0%

Sambito Products Company has been disappointed with its operating results for the past two years. As the accountant for the company, you have the following information available to you:

	19x4	19x3
Current Assets	$ 90,000	$ 70,000
Total Assets	290,000	220,000
Current Liabilities	40,000	20,000
Long-Term Liabilities	40,000	—
Owner's Equity	210,000	200,000
Net Sales	524,000	400,000
Net Income	32,000	22,000

Total assets and owner's equity at the beginning of 19x3 were $180,000 and $160,000, respectively.

REQUIRED

1. Compute the following measures of liquidity for 19x3 and 19x4: (a) working capital and (b) current ratio. Comment on the differences between the years.
2. Compute the following measures of profitability for 19x3 and 19x4: (a) profit margin, (b) asset turnover, (c) return on assets, (d) debt to equity, and (e) return on equity. Comment on the change in performance from 19x3 to 19x4.

B 5. *Classified Financial*
L O 5, 6, 7 *Statement Preparation and Evaluation*

Check Figures: Net income: $36,130; Total assets: $541,900

Wedman Company sells outdoor sports equipment. At the 19x2 year end, the following financial information was available from the income statement: Administrative Expenses, $87,800; Cost of Goods Sold, $350,420; Interest Expense, $22,640; Interest Income, $2,800; Net Sales, $714,390; and Selling Expenses, $220,200.

The following information was available from the balance sheet (after closing entries): Accounts Payable, $32,600; Accounts Receivable, $104,800; Accumulated Depreciation, Delivery Equipment, $17,100; Accumulated Depreciation, Store Fixtures, $42,220; Cash, $28,400; Delivery Equipment, $88,500; Inventory, $136,540; Investment in Securities (long term), $56,000; Investment in U.S. Government Securities (short term), $39,600; Long-Term Notes Payable, $100,000; Short-Term Notes Payable, $50,000; Short-Term Prepaid Expenses, $5,760; Store Fixtures, $141,620; and Charles Wedman, Capital, $359,300.

Total assets at December 31, 19x1 were $524,400 and withdrawals during 19x2 were $60,000.

REQUIRED

1. From the information above, prepare (a) an income statement in single-step form, (b) a statement of owner's equity, and (c) a classified balance sheet.
2. From the two statements you have prepared, compute the following measures: (a) working capital and current ratio (for liquidity); and (b) profit margin, asset turnover, return on assets, debt to equity, and return on equity (for profitability).

FINANCIAL REPORTING AND ANALYSIS CASES

Interpreting Financial Reports

FRA 1. *Profitability*
L O 7 *Analysis*

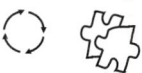

Check Figures: Asset turnover: Albertson's 3.9 times; American Stores: 2.8 times

Two of the largest chains of grocery/drug stores in the United States are *Albertson's, Inc.* and *American Stores Co.* (Jewel, Lucky, Acme, Osco, Sav-on, and others). In its fiscal year ending in January 1993, Albertson's had net income of $269.2 million, and in its fiscal year ending in December 1992, American had net income of $206.4 million. It is difficult to judge which company is more profitable from those figures alone because they do not take into account the relative sales, sizes, and investments of the companies. Data (in millions) are presented below to complete a financial analysis of the two companies.[8]

	Albertson's	American Stores
Net sales	$10,173.7	$19,051.2
Ending total assets	2,945.6	6,545.0
Beginning total assets	2,216.2	6,954.6
Ending total liabilities	1,557.2	4,853.0
Beginning total liabilities	1,016.7	3,439.0
Ending stockholders' equity	1,388.4	1,692.0
Beginning stockholders' equity	1,199.5	1,515.6

REQUIRED

1. Determine which company was more profitable by computing profit margin, asset turnover, return on assets, debt to equity, and return on equity for the two companies. Comment on the relative profitability of the two companies. For industry data, refer to Figures 3 through 7.
2. What do the ratios tell you about the factors that go into achieving an adequate return on assets in the grocery industry?
3. How would you characterize the use of debt financing in the grocery industry and the use of debt by the two companies?

International Company

FRA 2. *Interpretation and*
L O 5, 7 *Analysis of British Financial Statements*

No check figure

Presented on the next page is the classified balance sheet for the British company *Wellcome plc,* a major pharmaceutical firm with marketing and manufacturing operations in eighteen countries.[9]

8. Albertson's, Inc. and American Stores Co., *Annual Reports,* January 31, 1993 and December 31, 1992, respectively.
9. Wellcome plc, *Annual Report,* 1992.

Wellcome plc
Group Company Balance Sheets
as at 1 September 1992

	1992 £m	1991 £m
FIXED ASSETS		
Tangible assets	818.0	811.0
Investments	2.2	3.1
	820.2	814.1
CURRENT ASSETS		
Stocks	196.6	228.1
Debtors	366.5	367.9
Investments	569.7	362.1
Cash	23.3	33.4
	1,156.1	991.5
CREDITORS—AMOUNTS FALLING DUE WITHIN ONE YEAR:		
Loans and overdrafts	(89.7)	(80.5)
Other	(430.0)	(375.8)
NET CURRENT ASSETS	636.4	535.2
TOTAL ASSETS LESS CURRENT LIABILITIES	1,456.6	1,349.3
Creditors—amounts falling due after more than one year:		
Loans	(93.2)	(117.2)
Other	(4.3)	(3.9)
Provisions for liabilities and charges	(155.1)	(100.6)
Minority interests	(26.6)	(26.9)
TOTAL NET ASSETS	1,177.4	1,100.7
CAPITAL AND RESERVES		
Called up share capital	215.2	214.3
Share premium account	64.5	54.5
Profit and loss account	897.7	831.9
SHAREHOLDERS' FUNDS	1,177.4	1,100.7

In the United Kingdom, the format used for classified financial statements is usually different from that used in the United States. To compare the financial statements of companies in different countries, it is important to develop the ability to interpret a variety of formats.

REQUIRED

1. For each line on Wellcome plc's balance sheet, indicate the corresponding term that would be found on a U.S. balance sheet. (For this exercise, consider Provisions for Liabilities and Charges and Minority Interests to be long-term liabilities.) What is the focus or rationale behind the format of the U.K. balance sheet?
2. Assuming that Wellcome plc earned a net income of £250.5 million and £258.2 million in 1991 and 1992, respectively, compute the current ratio, debt to equity, return on assets, and return on equity for 1991 and 1992. (Use year-end amounts to compute ratios.)

Toys "R" Us Annual Report

FRA 3.
L O 5, 6, 7

Reading and
Analyzing an
Annual Report

REQUIRED

No check figure

Refer to the appendix on Toys "R" Us to answer the following questions. (Note that 1995 refers to the year ended January 28, 1995, and 1994 refers to the year ended January 29, 1994.)

1. Consolidated balance sheets: (a) Did the amount of working capital increase or decrease from 1994 to 1995? By how much? (b) Did the current ratio improve from 1994 to 1995? (c) Does the company have long-term investments or intangible assets? (d) Did the capital structure of Toys "R" Us change from 1994 to 1995? (e) What is the contributed capital for 1995? How does it compare with retained earnings?

2. Consolidated statements of earnings: (a) Did Toys "R" Us use a multistep or a single-step form of income statement? (b) Is it a comparative statement? (c) What is the trend of net earnings? (d) How significant are income taxes for Toys "R" Us? (e) Did the profit margin increase from 1994 to 1995? (f) Did asset turnover improve from 1994 to 1995? (g) Did the return on assets increase from 1994 to 1995? (h) Did the return on equity increase from 1994 to 1995? Total assets and total stockholders' equity for 1993 may be obtained from the financial highlights or the notes.

3. Consolidated statements of cash flows: (a) Compare net income in 1995 with cash provided by operating activities in 1995. Why is there a difference? (b) What were the most important investing activities in 1995? (c) What were the most important financing activities in 1995? (d) How did these investing and financing activities compare with those in prior years? (e) Where did Toys "R" Us get cash to pay for the capital expenditures? (f) How did the change in Cash and Cash Equivalents in 1995 compare to that in other years?

4. Auditors' report: (a) What was the name of Toys "R" Us's independent auditor? (b) Who was responsible for the financial statements? (c) What was the auditor's responsibility? (d) Did the auditor examine all the company's records? (e) Did the accountants think that the financial statements presented fairly the financial situation of the company? (f) Did the company comply with generally accepted accounting principles?

CHAPTER 7

Accounting Information Systems and Internal Control

LEARNING OBJECTIVES

1. Identify the principles of accounting systems design.
2. Identify the basic elements of mainframe and microcomputer systems.
3. Explain the objectives and uses of special-purpose journals.
4. Explain the purposes and relationships of controlling accounts and subsidiary ledgers.
5. Construct and use a sales journal, purchases journal, cash receipts journal, cash payments journal, and other special-purpose journals as needed.
6. Define *internal control* and identify the three elements of the internal control structure, including seven examples of control procedures.
7. Describe the inherent limitations of internal control.
8. Apply control procedures to common merchandising transactions.

Boston Chicken, Inc.

Boston Chicken, Inc. is one of the fastest-growing restaurant chains in the United States. Boston Market™ and Boston Chicken® stores serve rotisserie chicken, turkey, ham, and meat loaf with a variety of hot and cold side dishes. In 1993, the company was still doing inventory by hand, tabulating data on a clipboard. As the company grew, the numbers were entered into computerized spreadsheets to eliminate math errors. Functions such as labor scheduling and preparation of the chicken were also computerized. After going public, the company planned to more than double the number of its stores. What does the company need to do to continue to grow profitably?

In early 1994, the company spent $8 to $12 million on systems integration. The new system saves store managers an average of 16 to 30 hours per month by centralizing accounting and payroll. A prototype store was designed in which cooking, customer feedback, and sales are linked by computer. As a result, accurate data are available to everyone instantly. Boston Chicken's experience is not unusual. Many small companies start with small manual systems and gradually convert to computerized systems as they grow.[1]

PRINCIPLES OF ACCOUNTING SYSTEMS DESIGN

OBJECTIVE

1 *Identify the principles of accounting systems design*

Accounting systems gather data from all parts of a business, put them into useful form, and communicate the results to management. Management uses system output to make all kinds of business decisions. As businesses have grown larger and more complicated, the role of accounting systems has also grown. Today, the need for a total information system with accounting as its base has become more pressing. For this reason, accountants must understand all phases of their company's operations as well as the latest developments in systems design and technology.

Accountants may also have a voice in choosing their firm's processing system. Data processing is the means by which an accounting system gathers data, organizes them into useful form, and issues the resulting information to users. The two extremes of data processing systems are computerized systems and manual systems, both of which do the same job. In this chapter, we

1. Scott Collins, "Boston Chicken," *Crain's Chicago Business,* May 9, 1994.

examine the main features of computer systems and their use in data processing, as well as the basic ways of handling a large amount of data using manual data processing. First, however, we discuss the four general principles of accounting systems design: (1) the cost-benefit principle, (2) the control principle, (3) the compatibility principle, and (4) the flexibility principle.

COST-BENEFIT PRINCIPLE

The most important systems principle, the cost-benefit principle, holds that the benefits derived from an accounting system and the information it generates must be equal to or greater than its cost. Beyond certain routine tasks—preparing payroll and tax reports and financial statements, and maintaining internal control—management may want or need other information. That information must be reliable, timely, and useful. The benefits of additional information must be weighed against both the tangible and the intangible costs of gathering it. Among the tangible costs are those for personnel, forms, and equipment. One of the intangible costs is the cost of wrong decisions stemming from the lack of good information. For instance, wrong decisions can lead to loss of sales, production stoppages, or inventory losses. Some companies have spent thousands of dollars on computer systems that do not offer enough benefits. On the other hand, some managers have failed to realize important benefits that could be gained from investing in more advanced systems. It is the job of the accountant and the systems analyst to weigh the costs and benefits.

CONTROL PRINCIPLE

The control principle requires that an accounting system provide all the features of internal control needed to protect the firm's assets and ensure that data are reliable. For example, expenditures should be approved by a responsible member of management before they are made.

COMPATIBILITY PRINCIPLE

The compatibility principle holds that the design of an accounting system must be in harmony with the organizational and human factors of the business. The organizational factors have to do with the nature of a firm's business and the formal roles its units play in meeting business objectives. For example, a company can organize its marketing efforts by region or by product. If a company is organized by region, its accounting system should report revenues and expenses by region. On the other hand, if a company is organized by product, its system should report revenues and expenses first by product and then by region.

The human factors of business have to do with the people within the organization and their abilities, behaviors, and personalities. The interest, support, and competence of a firm's employees are very important to the success or failure of systems design. In changing systems or installing new ones, the accountant must deal with the people presently carrying out or supervising existing procedures. Such people must understand, accept, and, in many cases, be trained in the new procedures. The new system cannot succeed unless the system and the people in the organization are compatible.

FLEXIBILITY PRINCIPLE

The flexibility principle holds that an accounting system must be flexible enough to allow the volume of transactions to grow and organizational changes to be made. Businesses do not stay the same. They grow, offer new products, add new branch offices, sell existing divisions, or make other changes that require adjustments in the accounting system. A carefully designed system allows a business to grow and change without making major alterations. For example, the chart of accounts should be designed to allow the addition of new asset, liability, owner's equity, revenue, and expense accounts.

COMPUTERIZED DATA PROCESSING

Most data processing in business today is done by computer. Computers are able to process large volumes of data very quickly. The development of mainframe computer systems has allowed the largest companies to centralize their accounting operations and eliminate much of the work that used to be done by hand. And the development of minicomputers and microcomputers has made it possible for even the smallest company to keep its accounting records on a computer.

OBJECTIVE

2 *Identify the basic elements of mainframe and microcomputer systems*

ELEMENTS OF A COMPUTER SYSTEM

Regardless of its size, a computerized data processing system consists of three basic elements: hardware, software, and personnel.

Hardware Hardware is all the equipment needed to operate a computerized data processing system. Figure 1 shows the hardware in a typical mainframe computer system; Figure 2 shows the hardware in a typical microcomputer system. Both contain devices that help input data to the system, process and store data, and output information. In a mainframe system, for example, a remote data entry device (a terminal) may be used to input data about a purchase transaction to the central processor, where it is recorded for future processing on a magnetic tape using a magnetic disk drive or on a disk using a disk drive. After the data are processed, accounting reports can be prepared on an output device, such as a printer. In a microcomputer system, the day's transactions can be input through the keyboard and monitor onto a floppy disk or a hard disk. A daily transaction report can then be printed. In today's business environment, it is becoming increasingly common to link microcomputers in a network that enables the computers to communicate with each other.

Software In a manual system, someone actually records transactions in a journal, posts to a ledger, and then prepares a trial balance and financial statements. The computer performs these steps internally, following a set of instructions called a program. Programs are known collectively as software. Several programs are needed to instruct the computer to record and post transactions and to prepare financial statements. On a mainframe computer, programs are written in languages the computer uses, such as COBOL, PL/1, or FORTRAN. Programs for microcomputers often are written in

Figure 1. Mainframe Computer System

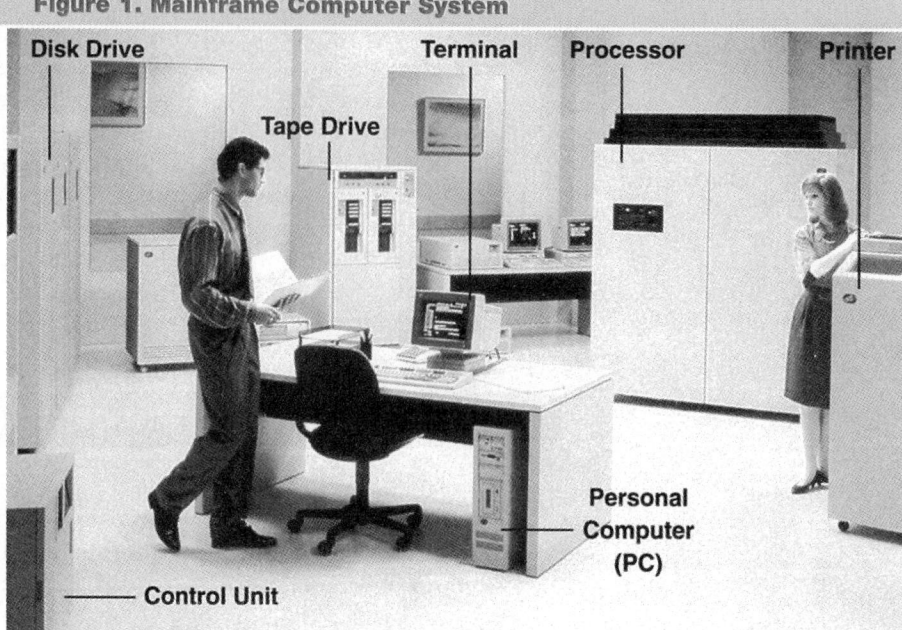

Source: Courtesy of IBM.

BASIC or PASCAL. In addition, many programs are available commercially to do specialized accounting tasks, such as LOTUS® 1-2-3 and Excel for financial analysis and spreadsheet applications; dBASE and Fourth Dimension for organizing, storing, and retrieving large quantities of data; and general ledger accounting systems for keeping records and preparing financial statements.

Personnel   The important personnel in a computer system are the systems analyst, the programmer, and the computer operator. The systems analyst designs the system on the basis of information needs, the programmer writes instructions for the computer, and the computer operator runs the computer. In large organizations, the accountant works closely with the systems analyst to make sure that the accounting data processing system is designed in accordance with the specific needs of users of financial information. In smaller organizations that use a microcomputer system and that do not have computer experts for all these positions, the company's owners or management often work with a certified public accounting firm to purchase and install commercial software that meets the company's needs.

MAINFRAME ACCOUNTING SYSTEMS

The parts of a computerized data processing system can be put together in many different ways, and companies use their computers for many purposes besides accounting. The company's overall goal is to meet all its computing needs at the lowest cost. For the accounting system, it is important to coordinate all tasks to provide management with the reports and statements it needs on a timely basis.

Most mainframe computer systems take two approaches to processing business transactions and preparing financial reports. The first is called batch processing, in which processing tasks are scheduled sequentially. For example, similar transactions for a day or a week are processed together (as a batch).

Figure 2. Microcomputer System

Source: Courtesy of IBM.

Later, a separate program is run to update the ledger and prepare the trial balance and financial statements. The processing of employees' time cards, preparation of payroll, and printing of paychecks on a specific day each week or month are examples of batch processing.

Most mainframe systems also allow on-line processing, in which remote terminals are linked to the central processor and files are updated virtually as transactions occur. For example, when a credit sale takes place, it can be entered into a remote terminal that records and posts the amounts in the appropriate accounts and updates the subsidiary ledger.

MICROCOMPUTER ACCOUNTING SYSTEMS

Most small businesses purchase commercial accounting systems that are already programmed to perform accounting functions. Most of these systems are organized so that each part of the software performs a major task of the accounting system. Although the configuration of such systems, often called general ledger software, differs from system to system, a typical configuration appears in Figure 3. Notice that there is a software program for each major accounting function—sales/accounts receivable, purchases/accounts payable, cash receipts, cash disbursements, payroll, and general journal. If these software packages interact with one another, they are called *integrated programs*.

The transactions for these functions are based on source documents, the written evidence that supports each transaction. Source documents verify that a transaction occurred and provide the details of the transaction. For example, a customer's invoice should support each sale on account, and a vendor's invoice should support each purchase. Even though the transactions are recorded by the computer in a file (on floppy disks or hard disks), the documents should be kept so that they can be examined at a later date if a question arises about the accuracy of the accounting records. The source documents for each function are gathered in a batch and processed in order

Figure 3. Microcomputer Accounting System Using General Ledger Software

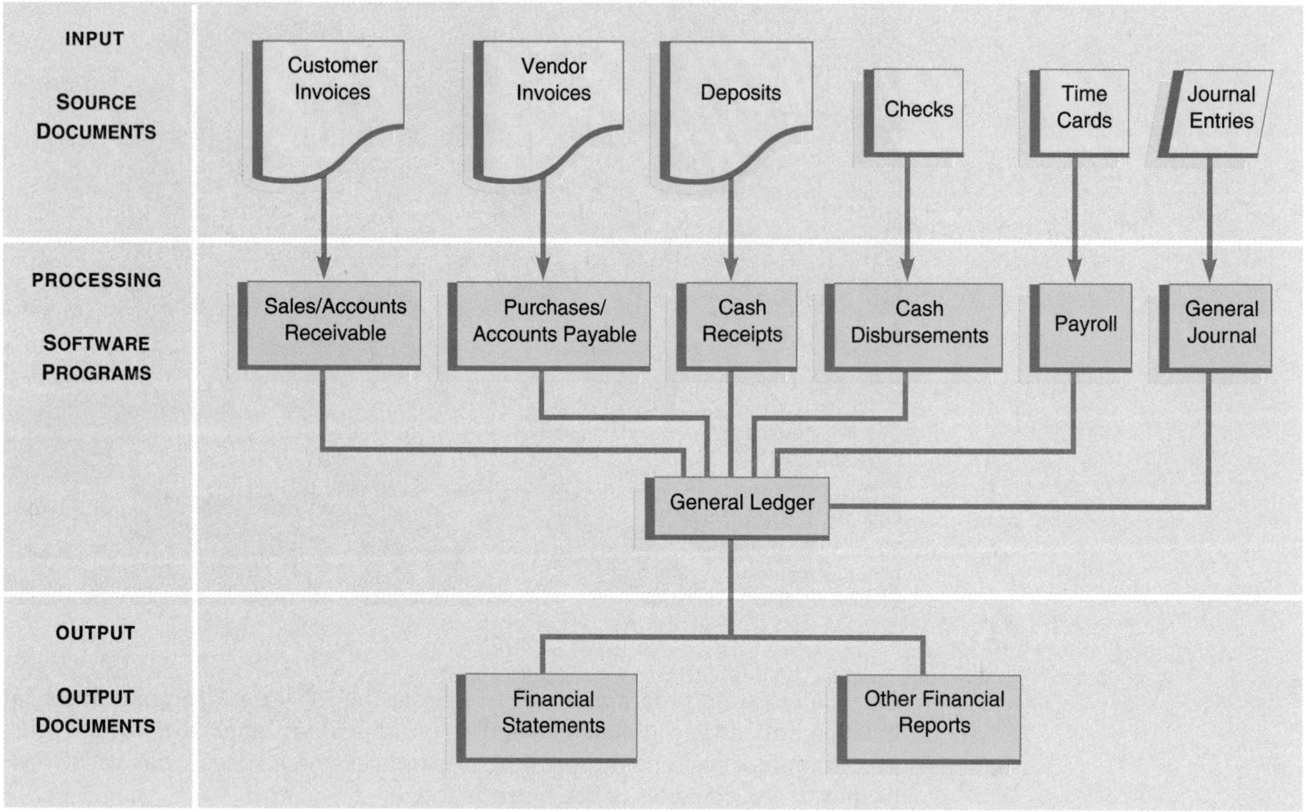

INPUT SOURCE DOCUMENTS	Customer Invoices	Vendor Invoices	Deposits	Checks	Time Cards	Journal Entries

PROCESSING SOFTWARE PROGRAMS	Sales/Accounts Receivable	Purchases/ Accounts Payable	Cash Receipts	Cash Disbursements	Payroll	General Journal

General Ledger

OUTPUT OUTPUT DOCUMENTS	Financial Statements	Other Financial Reports

with the appropriate program. The scheduling of the programs depends on the function. For example, cash transactions and sales are usually processed daily; payroll may be processed only once every week or two weeks.

After the transactions are processed, a procedure is followed to post to and update the ledgers and to prepare the trial balance. Finally, the financial statements and other accounting reports are prepared.

The batch processing systems used in microcomputer accounting systems very closely resemble the manual accounting systems using special-purpose journals that have been in existence for decades. In fact, their basic goal is to computerize existing accounting systems to make them less time consuming and more accurate and dependable. However, it is important to understand, in principle, just what the computer is accomplishing. Knowledge of the underlying accounting process helps ensure that the accounting records are accurate, helps protect the assets of the business, and helps in the analysis of financial statements.

MANUAL DATA PROCESSING: JOURNALS AND PROCEDURES

OBJECTIVE

3 *Explain the objectives and uses of special-purpose journals*

The system of accounting described so far in this book, and presented in Figure 4, is a form of manual data processing. It has been a useful way to present basic accounting theory and practice in small businesses. Data are fed into the system manually by entering each transaction from a source document to the general journal (which parallels the input device in a computer system). Then, each debit and credit is posted to the correct ledger account (parallel to the processor and memory device). A work sheet (output device) is used as a tool to prepare the financial statements (output devices) that are distributed to users. This system, although useful for explaining the basic concepts of accounting, is actually used in only the smallest of companies.

Companies involved in more transactions, perhaps hundreds or thousands every week or every day, must have a more efficient and economical way of recording transactions in the journal and posting entries to the ledger. The easiest approach is to group typical transactions into common categories and use an input device, called a special-purpose journal, for each category. The objectives of special-purpose journals are efficiency, economy, and control. Although manual special-purpose journals are used by companies that have not yet computerized their systems, the concepts underlying special-purpose journals also underlie the programs that drive computerized accounting systems.

Most business transactions—90 to 95 percent—fall into one of the following four categories. Each kind of transaction can be recorded in a special-purpose journal.

Transaction	Special-Purpose Journal	Posting Abbreviation
Sale of merchandise on credit	Sales journal	S
Purchase on credit	Purchases journal	P
Receipt of cash	Cash receipts journal	CR
Disbursement of cash	Cash payments journal	CP

Notice that these special-purpose journals correspond to the accounting functions shown in the microcomputer system in Figure 3, except for payroll.

The general journal is used to record transactions that do not fall into any of the special categories. For example, purchase returns, sales returns, and adjusting and closing entries are recorded in the general journal. (When transactions are posted from the general journal to the ledger accounts, the posting abbreviation is **J.**)

Using special-purpose journals greatly reduces the work involved in entering and posting transactions. For example, instead of posting every debit and credit for each transaction, in most cases only column totals—the sum of many transactions—are posted. In addition, labor can be divided, with each journal assigned to a different employee. This division of labor is important in establishing good internal control.

Figure 4. Steps and Devices in a Manual Accounting System

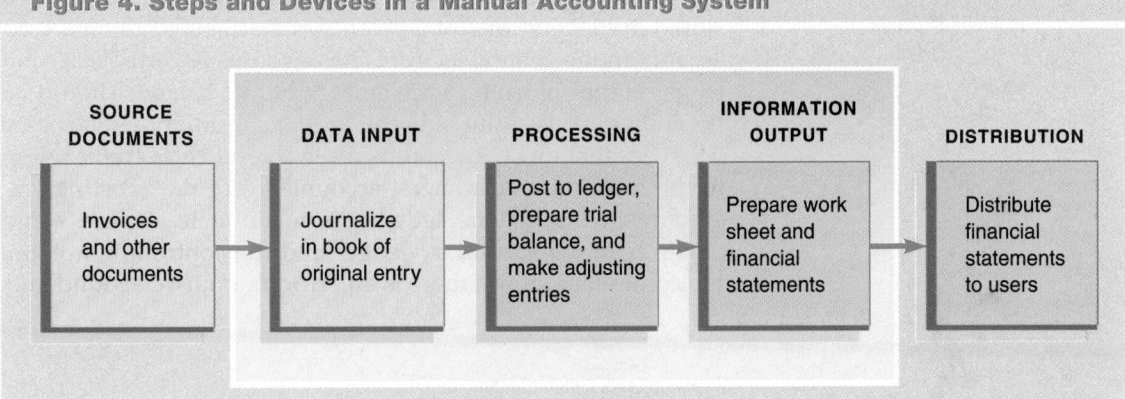

Accounting information systems are obviously important for financial reporting, but they are increasingly becoming a means of providing good customer service as well. For instance, Walgreens, the world's largest prescription pharmacy company, has established direct communications with the insurance companies, employers, and government agencies who pay the bills of Walgreens' customers. From an accounting perspective, such links enhance Walgreens' profitability by eliminating rejected prescriptions, facilitating billing, and speeding collections. From the customers' point of view, instant communication with payers means faster service and immediate confirmation of payments—no forms, no paperwork, and no-hassle service.[2]

CONTROLLING ACCOUNTS AND SUBSIDIARY LEDGERS

OBJECTIVE

4 *Explain the purposes and relationships of controlling accounts and subsidiary ledgers*

Controlling accounts and subsidiary ledgers contain important details about the figures in special-purpose journals and other books of original entry. A controlling account, also called a *control account*, is an account in the general ledger that maintains the total balance of all subsidiary ledgers. A subsidiary ledger is a ledger separate from the general ledger that contains a group of related accounts; the total of the balances in the subsidiary ledger accounts equals or ties in with the balance in the corresponding controlling account. For example, up to this point a single Accounts Receivable account has been used. But the balance in the single Accounts Receivable account does not tell how much each customer bought and paid and how much each customer owes. Consequently, in practice, all companies that sell on credit keep an individual accounts receivable record for each customer. If a company has 6,000 credit customers, it has 6,000 accounts receivable. Including all those accounts with the other asset, liability, and owner's equity accounts would make the ledger very bulky. Therefore, companies take the individual customers' accounts out of the general ledger and place them in a separate, subsidiary ledger. In the accounts receivable subsidiary ledger, customers' accounts are filed either alphabetically or numerically (if account numbers are used).

When individual customers' accounts are put in an accounts receivable subsidiary ledger, the total balance is maintained in one Accounts Receivable account in the general ledger. The Accounts Receivable account in the general ledger is the controlling account in that its balance should equal the total of the individual account balances in the subsidiary ledger, as shown in Figure 5. Entries that involve accounts receivable, such as credit sales, must be posted to the individual customers' accounts every day. Postings to the controlling account in the general ledger are made at least once a month. When the amounts in the subsidiary ledger and the controlling account do not match, the accountant knows there is an error that must be found and corrected.

2. Walgreens, *Annual Report*, 1993.

**Figure 5. Relationship of Subsidiary Accounts to the
Controlling Account**

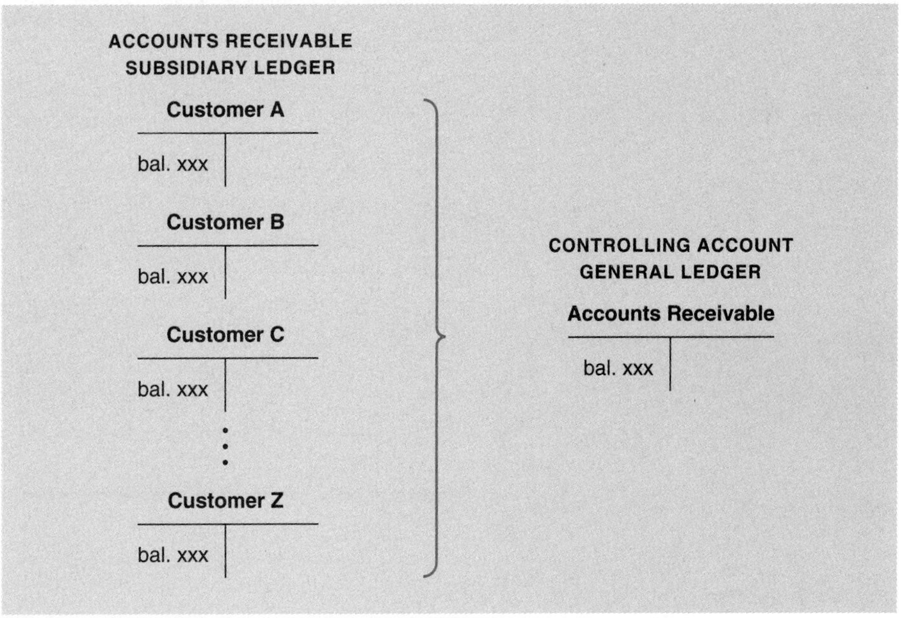

Most companies use an accounts payable subsidiary ledger as well. It is possible to use a subsidiary ledger for almost any account in the general ledger when management wants specific information for individual items, such as Notes Receivable, Short-Term Investments, and Equipment.

OBJECTIVE

5 *Construct and use a sales journal, purchases journal, cash receipts journal, cash payments journal, and other special-purpose journals as needed*

SALES JOURNAL

Special-purpose journals are designed to record particular kinds of transactions. Thus, all transactions in a special-purpose journal result in debits and credits to the same accounts. The sales journal, for example, is designed to handle all credit sales, and only credit sales. Cash sales are recorded in the cash receipts journal.

Exhibit 1 illustrates a page from a typical sales journal. It shows the recording of six sales transactions involving five customers. As each sale takes place, several copies of the sales invoice are made. The seller's accounting department uses one copy to make the entry in the sales journal. The date, the customer's name, the invoice number, and the amount of the sale are recorded. The credit terms are usually also copied from the invoice to the Terms column, but this step (and the Terms column) may be omitted when all the sales are made on the same terms. The columns of the sales journal correspond to those data.

Notice how the sales journal saves time:

1. Only one line is needed to record each transaction. Each entry consists of a debit to a customer's account in Accounts Receivable and a corresponding credit to Sales.
2. The account names do not have to be written out because each entry automatically is debited to Accounts Receivable and credited to Sales.
3. No explanations are necessary because the function of the special-purpose journal is to record just one type of transaction. Only credit sales are recorded in the sales journal. Sales for cash are recorded in the cash receipts journal.

Exhibit 1. Sales Journal and Related Ledger Accounts

	Sales Journal				Page 1
Date	Account Debited	Invoice Number	Terms	Post. Ref.	Amount (Debit/Credit Accounts Receivable/Sales)
July 1	Peter Clark	721	2/10, n/30	✓	750
5	Georgetta Jones	722	2/10, n/30	✓	500
8	Eugene Cumberland	723	2/10, n/30	✓	335
12	Maxwell Gertz	724	2/10, n/30	✓	1,165
18	Peter Clark	725	1/10, n/30	✓	1,225
25	Michael Powers	726	2/10, n/30	✓	975
					4,950
					(114/411)

Post total at end of month.

Accounts Receivable 114

Date	Post. Ref.	Debit	Credit	Balance Debit	Balance Credit
July 31	S1	4,950		4,950	

Sales 411

Date	Post. Ref.	Debit	Credit	Balance Debit	Balance Credit
July 31	S1		4,950		4,950

4. Only one amount—the total credit sales for the month—has to be posted to the general ledger accounts. It is posted twice: once as a debit to Accounts Receivable and once as a credit to Sales. You can see the time this saves in Exhibit 1, with just six transactions. Imagine the time saved when there are hundreds of sales transactions.

Summary of the Sales Journal Procedure Exhibit 2 shows the relationships between the sales journal, the accounts receivable subsidiary ledger, and the general ledger accounts. It also illustrates the procedure for using a sales journal, the steps of which are outlined in the list that follows.

1. Enter each sales invoice in the sales journal on a single line. Record the date, the customer's name, the invoice number, and the amount. Other columns, such as one for credit terms, can be added to the sales journal. No column is needed for the terms if the terms on all sales are the same. The nature of the company's business determines whether additional columns are needed.
2. At the end of each day, post each individual sale to the customer's account in the accounts receivable ledger. As each sale is posted, place a checkmark (or customer account number, if used) in the Post. Ref. (posting reference) column of the sales journal to indicate that it has been posted. In the Post. Ref. column

Exhibit 2. Relationship of Sales Journal, General Ledger, and Accounts Receivable Subsidiary Ledger and the Posting Procedure

	Sales Journal					Page 1
Date	Account Debited	Invoice Number	Terms	Post. Ref.	Amount (Debit/Credit Accounts Receivable/Sales)	
July 1	Peter Clark	721	2/10, n/30	✓	750	
5	Georgetta Jones	722	2/10, n/30	✓	500	
8	Eugene Cumberland	723	2/10, n/30	✓	335	
12	Maxwell Gertz	724	2/10, n/30	✓	1,165	
18	Peter Clark	725	1/10, n/30	✓	1,225	
25	Michael Powers	726	2/10, n/30	✓	975	
					4,950	
					(114/411)	

Post individual amounts **daily** to subsidiary ledger accounts.

Post total at **end of month** to general ledger accounts.

Accounts Receivable Subs. Ledger

Peter Clark

Date	Post. Ref.	Debit	Credit	Balance
July 1	S1	750		750
18	S1	1,225		1,975

Eugene Cumberland

Date	Post. Ref.	Debit	Credit	Balance
July 8	S1	335		335

Continue posting to Maxwell Gertz, Georgetta Jones, and Michael Powers.

General Ledger

Accounts Receivable   114

Date	Post. Ref.	Debit	Credit	Balance Debit	Balance Credit
July 31	S1	4,950		4,950	

Sales   411

Date	Post. Ref.	Debit	Credit	Balance Debit	Balance Credit
July 31	S1		4,950		4,950

of each customer's account, place an **S** and the sales journal page number (**S1** means Sales Journal—Page 1) to indicate the source of the entry.

3. At the end of the month, sum the Amount column in the sales journal to determine the total credit sales and post that total to the general ledger accounts (debit Accounts Receivable and credit Sales). Place the numbers of the accounts debited and credited beneath the total in the sales journal to indicate that this step has been completed. In the general ledger, indicate the source of the entry in the Post. Ref. column of each account.

Exhibit 3. Schedule of Accounts Receivable

Mitchell's Used Car Sales
Schedule of Accounts Receivable
July 31, 19xx

Peter Clark	$1,975
Eugene Cumberland	335
Maxwell Gertz	1,165
Georgetta Jones	500
Michael Powers	975
Total Accounts Receivable	$4,950

4. Verify the accuracy of the posting by adding the individual account balances of the accounts receivable ledger and by matching the total with the Accounts Receivable controlling account balance in the general ledger. You can do this by listing the accounts in a schedule of accounts receivable. As shown in Exhibit 3, the accounts are listed in the order they are maintained. This step is performed after collections on account in the cash receipts journal have been posted.

The single controlling Accounts Receivable account in the general ledger summarizes all the individual accounts in the subsidiary ledger. Because the individual accounts are recorded daily and the controlling account is posted monthly, the total of the individual accounts in the accounts receivable ledger equals the controlling account only after the monthly posting. The monthly trial balance is prepared using only the general ledger accounts.

Sales Taxes   Many retailers are required to collect a sales tax from their customers and periodically remit the total collected to the city or state. In such cases, an additional column is needed in the sales journal to record the credit to Sales Tax Payable on credit sales. The form of the entry is shown in Exhibit 4. The procedure for posting to the ledger is exactly the same as described above, except that the total of the Sales Tax Payable column must be posted as a credit to the Sales Tax Payable account at the end of the month.

Most companies also make cash sales. Cash sales are usually recorded in a column of the cash receipts journal, as discussed later in the chapter.

Exhibit 4. Section of a Sales Journal with a Column for Sales Tax Payable

	Sales Journal							Page 7
						Debit	Credits	
Date		Account Debited	Invoice Number	Terms	Post. Ref.	Accounts Receivable	Sales Tax Payable	Sales
Sept.	1	Ralph P. Hake	727	2/10, n/30	✓	206	6	200

PURCHASES JOURNAL

The purchases journal is used to record purchases on credit. It can take the form of either a single-column journal or a multicolumn journal. In a single-column journal, shown in Exhibit 5, only credit purchases of merchandise for resale to customers are recorded. This kind of transaction is recorded with a debit to Purchases and a credit to Accounts Payable. When a single-column

Exhibit 5. Relationship of Single-Column Purchases Journal to the General Ledger and the Accounts Payable Subsidiary Ledger

					Purchases Journal	Page 1
Date	**Account Credited**	**Date of Invoice**	**Terms**	**Post. Ref.**		**Amount (Debit/Credit Purchases/ Accounts Payable)**
July 1	Jones Chevrolet	7/1	2/10, n/30	✓		2,500
2	Marshall Ford	7/2	2/15, n/30	✓		300
3	Dealer Sales	7/3	n/30	✓		700
12	Thomas Auto	7/11	n/30	✓		1,400
17	Dealer Sales	7/17	2/10, n/30	✓		3,200
19	Thomas Auto	7/17	n/30	✓		1,100
						9,200
						(511/212)

Post individual amounts **daily.**   Post total at **end of month.**

Accounts Payable Subs. Ledger

Dealer Sales

Date	Post. Ref.	Debit	Credit	Balance
July 3	P1		700	700
17	P1		3,200	3,900

Jones Chevrolet

Date	Post. Ref.	Debit	Credit	Balance
July 1	P1		2,500	2,500

Continue posting to Marshall Ford and Thomas Auto.

General Ledger

Accounts Payable   212

				Balance	
Date	Post. Ref.	Debit	Credit	Debit	Credit
July 31	P1		9,200		9,200

Purchases   511

				Balance	
Date	Post. Ref.	Debit	Credit	Debit	Credit
July 31	P1	9,200		9,200	

purchases journal is used, credit purchases of things other than merchandise are recorded in the general journal. Cash purchases are never recorded in the purchases journal; they are recorded in the cash payments journal, which will be explained later.

Like Accounts Receivable, the Accounts Payable account in the general ledger is commonly used as a controlling account. To know how much is owed each supplier, the company keeps a separate account for each supplier in an accounts payable subsidiary ledger. The process described above for using the accounts receivable subsidiary ledger and the general ledger control account also applies to the accounts payable subsidiary ledger and the general ledger control account. Thus, the total of the separate accounts in the accounts payable subsidiary ledger should equal the balance of the Accounts Payable controlling account in the general ledger. Here, too, the monthly total of the credit purchases posted to the individual accounts each day must equal the total credit purchases posted to the controlling account each month.

The procedure for using the purchases journal is much like that for using the sales journal.

1. Enter each purchase invoice in the purchases journal on a single line. Record the date, the supplier's name, the invoice date, the terms (if given), and the amount. It is not necessary to record the shipping terms in the Terms column because they do not affect the payment date.
2. At the end of each day, post each individual purchase to the supplier's account in the accounts payable subsidiary ledger. As each purchase is posted, place a checkmark in the Post. Ref. column of the purchases journal to show that it has been posted. Also place a **P** and the page number in the purchases journal (**P1** stands for Purchases Journal—Page 1) in the Post. Ref. column of each supplier's account to show the source of the entry.
3. At the end of the month, sum the Amount column and post the total to the general ledger accounts (a debit to Purchases and a credit to Accounts Payable). Place the numbers of the accounts debited and credited beneath the total in the purchases journal to show that this step has been carried out.
4. Check the accuracy of the posting by adding the balances of the individual accounts payable ledger accounts and matching the total with the balance of the Accounts Payable controlling account in the general ledger. This step can be carried out by preparing a schedule of accounts payable.

The single-column purchases journal can be expanded to record credit purchases of things other than merchandise by adding a separate debit column for other accounts that are used often. For example, the multicolumn purchases journal in Exhibit 6 has columns for Freight In, Store Supplies, Office Supplies, and Other Accounts. Here, the total credits to Accounts Payable ($9,637) equal the total debits to Purchases, Freight In, Store Supplies, Office Supplies, and Other Accounts ($9,200 + $50 + $145 + $42 + $200). Again, the individual transactions in the Accounts Payable column are posted regularly to the accounts payable subsidiary ledger, and the totals of each named account column in the journal are posted monthly to the correct general ledger accounts. Entries in the Other Accounts column are posted individually to the named accounts; the column total is not posted.

CASH RECEIPTS JOURNAL

All transactions involving receipts of cash are recorded in the cash receipts journal. Examples of such transactions are cash from cash sales, cash from credit customers in payment of their accounts, and cash from other sources.

Exhibit 6. A Multicolumn Purchases Journal

| | | | | | | | Credit | Debits | | | | | | |
| | | | | | | | | | | | | Other Accounts | | |
Date		Account Credited	Date of Invoice	Terms	Post. Ref.	Accounts Payable	Purchases	Freight In	Store Supplies	Office Supplies	Account	Post. Ref.	Amount
July	1	Jones Chevrolet	7/1	2/10, n/30	✓	2,500	2,500						
	2	Marshall Ford	7/2	2/15, n/30	✓	300	300						
	2	Shelby Car Delivery	7/2	n/30	✓	50		50					
	3	Dealer Sales	7/3	n/30	✓	700	700						
	12	Thomas Auto	7/11	n/30	✓	1,400	1,400						
	17	Dealer Sales	7/17	2/10, n/30	✓	3,200	3,200						
	19	Thomas Auto	7/17	n/30	✓	1,100	1,100						
	25	Osborne Supply	7/21	n/10	✓	187			145	42			
	28	Auto Supply	7/28	n/10	✓	200					Parts	120	200
						9,637	9,200	50	145	42			200
						(212)	(511)	(514)	(132)	(133)			(✓)

The cash receipts journal must have several columns because, although all cash receipts are alike in that they require a debit to Cash, they differ in that they require a variety of credit entries. Note the use of an Other Accounts column, the use of account numbers in the Post. Ref. column, and the daily posting of the credits to other accounts.

The cash receipts journal illustrated in Exhibit 7 is based on the following selected transactions for July.

July   1   Henry Mitchell invested $20,000 in a used-car business.
    5   Sold a used car for $1,200 cash.
    8   Collected $500 less a 2 percent sales discount from Georgetta Jones.
  13   Sold a used car for $1,400 cash.
  16   Collected $750 from Peter Clark.
  19   Sold a used car for $1,000 cash.
  20   Sold some store supplies not needed in the business at cost for $500 cash.
  24   Signed a note at the bank for a loan of $5,000.
  26   Sold a used car for $1,600 cash.
  28   Collected partial payment of $600 less a 2 percent sales discount from Peter Clark.

The cash receipts journal shown in Exhibit 7 has three debit columns and three credit columns. The three debit columns are as follows:

1. *Cash*   Each entry must have an amount in this column because each transaction must be a receipt of cash.
2. *Sales Discounts*   This company allows a 2 percent discount for prompt payment. Therefore, it is useful to have a column for sales discounts. Notice that in the transactions of July 8 and 28, the total of debits to Cash and Sales Discounts equals the credit to Accounts Receivable.
3. *Other Accounts*   The Other Accounts column (sometimes called *Sundry Accounts*) is used for transactions that involve both a debit to Cash and a debit to some other account besides Sales Discounts.

Exhibit 7. Relationship of the Cash Receipts Journal to the General Ledger and the Accounts Receivable Subsidiary Ledger

Cash Receipts Journal — Page 1

Date		Account Debited/Credited	Post. Ref.	Debits — Cash	Debits — Sales Discounts	Debits — Other Accounts	Credits — Accounts Receivable	Credits — Sales	Credits — Other Accounts
July	1	Henry Mitchell, Capital	311	20,000					20,000
	5	Sales		1,200				1,200	
	8	Georgetta Jones	✓	490	10		500		
	13	Sales		1,400				1,400	
	16	Peter Clark	✓	750			750		
	19	Sales		1,000				1,000	
	20	Store Supplies	132	500					500
	24	Notes Payable	213	5,000					5,000
	26	Sales		1,600				1,600	
	28	Peter Clark	✓	588	12		600		
				32,528	22		1,850	5,200	25,500
				(111)	(412)		(114)	(411)	(✓)

Post individual amounts in the Accounts Receivable ledger column **daily**.

Post totals at end of month.

Total not posted.

Post individual amounts in Other Accounts column **daily**.

General Ledger

Cash   111

Date	Post. Ref.	Debit	Credit	Balance Debit	Balance Credit
July 31	CR1	32,528		32,528	

Accounts Receivable   114

Date	Post. Ref.	Debit	Credit	Balance Debit	Balance Credit
July 31	S1	4,950		4,950	
31	CR1		1,850	3,100	

Store Supplies   132

Date	Post. Ref.	Debit	Credit	Balance Debit	Balance Credit
Bal.					500
July 20	CR1		500	—	

Accounts Receivable Subsidiary Ledger

Peter Clark

Date	Post. Ref.	Debit	Credit	Balance
July 1	S1	750		750
16	CR1		750	—
18	S1	1,225		1,225
28	CR1		600	625

Georgetta Jones

Date	Post. Ref.	Debit	Credit	Balance
July 5	S1	500		500
8	CR1		500	—

Continue posting to Notes Payable and Henry Mitchell, Capital.

Continue posting to Sales and Sales Discounts.

These are the credit columns:

1. *Accounts Receivable* This column is used to record collections on account from customers. The customer's name is written in the Account Debited/Credited column so that the payment can be entered in the corresponding account in the accounts receivable subsidiary ledger. Postings to the individual accounts receivable accounts are usually done daily so that each customer's account balance is up-to-date.
2. *Sales* This column is used to record all cash sales during the month. Retail firms that use cash registers would make an entry at the end of each day for the total sales from each cash register for that day. The debit, of course, is in the Cash debit column.
3. *Other Accounts* This column is used for the credit portion of any entry that is neither a cash collection from accounts receivable nor a cash sale. The name of the account to be credited is indicated in the Account Debited/Credited column. For example, the transactions of July 1, 20, and 24 involve credits to accounts other than Accounts Receivable or Sales. These individual postings should be done daily (or weekly if there are just a few of them). If a company finds that it is consistently crediting a certain account in the Other Accounts column, it can add another credit column to the cash receipts journal for that particular account.

The procedure for posting the cash receipts journal, shown in Exhibit 7, is as follows:

1. Post the Accounts Receivable column daily to each individual account in the accounts receivable subsidiary ledger. The amount credited to the customer's account is the same as that credited to Accounts Receivable. A checkmark in the Post. Ref. column of the cash receipts journal indicates that the amount has been posted, and a **CR1** (Cash Receipts Journal—Page 1) in the Post. Ref. column of each ledger account indicates the source of the entry.
2. Post the debits/credits in the Other Accounts columns daily, or at convenient short intervals during the month, to the general ledger accounts. As the individual items are posted, write the account number in the Post. Ref. column of the cash receipts journal to indicate that the posting has been done, and write **CR** and the page number of the cash receipts journal in the Post. Ref. column of each ledger account to indicate the source of the entry.
3. At the end of the month, total the columns in the cash receipts journal. The sum of the Debits column totals must equal the sum of the Credits column totals. This step is called *crossfooting*.

Debits Column Totals		**Credits Column Totals**	
Cash	$32,528	Accounts Receivable	$ 1,850
Sales Discounts	22	Sales	5,200
Other Accounts	0	Other Accounts	25,500
Total Debits	$32,550	Total Credits	$32,550

4. Post the Debits column totals as follows:
   a. Post the total amount of the Cash column as a debit to the Cash account.
   b. Post the total of the Sales Discounts column as a debit to the Sales Discounts account.
5. Post the Credits column totals as follows:
   a. Post the total of the Accounts Receivable column as a credit to the Accounts Receivable controlling account.
   b. Post the total of the Sales column as a credit to the Sales account.
6. Write the account numbers below each column in the cash receipts journal as the totals are posted to indicate that this step has been completed. A **CR** and the page number of the cash receipts journal are written in the Post. Ref. column of each account to indicate the source of the entry.

7. Notice that the totals of the Other Accounts columns are not posted to general ledger accounts, because each entry is posted separately when the transaction occurs. The individual accounts are posted in step **2.** Place a checkmark (✓) below the total in an Other Accounts column to show that postings in that column have been made and that the total is not posted.

CASH PAYMENTS JOURNAL

All transactions involving payments of cash are recorded in the cash payments journal (also called the *cash disbursements journal*). Examples of these transactions are cash purchases and payments of obligations resulting from earlier purchases on credit. The form of the cash payments journal is much like that of the cash receipts journal.

The cash payments journal illustrated in Exhibit 8 is based on the following selected transactions of Mitchell's Used Car Sales in July.

July 2 Issued check no. 101 for merchandise (a used car) from Sondra Tidmore, $400.
     6 Issued check no. 102 for newspaper advertising in the *Daily Journal,* $200.
     8 Issued check no. 103 for one month's land and building rent to Siviglia Agency, $250.
    11 Issued check no. 104 to Jones Chevrolet for July 1 invoice (recorded in the purchases journal in Exhibit 5), $2,500 less 2 percent purchases discount.
    16 Issued check no. 105 to Charles Kuntz, a salesperson, for his salary, $600.
    17 Issued check no. 106 to Marshall Ford for July 2 invoice (recorded in the purchases journal in Exhibit 5), $300 less 2 percent purchases discount.
    24 Issued check no. 107 to Grabow & Company for a two-year insurance policy, $480.
    27 Issued check no. 108 to Dealer Sales for July 17 invoice (recorded in the purchases journal in Exhibit 5), $3,200 less 2 percent purchases discount.
    30 Purchased office equipment for $400 and service equipment for $500 from A&B Equipment Company. Issued check no. 109 for the total amount.
    31 Purchased land for $15,000 from Burns Real Estate. Issued check no. 110 for $5,000 and a note payable for $10,000.

The cash payments journal shown in Exhibit 8 has three credit columns and two debit columns. The credit columns for the cash payments journal are as follows:

1. *Cash* Each entry must have an amount in this column because each transaction must involve a payment of cash.
2. *Purchases Discounts* When purchases discounts are taken, they are recorded in this column.
3. *Other Accounts* This column is used to record credits to accounts other than Cash or Purchases Discounts. Notice that the July 31 transaction shows a purchase of land for $15,000, with a check for $5,000 and a note payable for $10,000.

The debit columns are as follows:

1. *Accounts Payable* This column is used to record payments to suppliers that have extended credit to the company. Each supplier's name is written in the Payee column so that the payment can be entered in its account in the accounts payable subsidiary ledger.
2. *Other Accounts* Cash can be expended for many reasons. Thus, an Other Accounts or Sundry Accounts column is necessary in the cash payments

Exhibit 8. Relationship of the Cash Payments Journal to the General Ledger and the Accounts Payable Subsidiary Ledger

Cash Payments Journal

Page 1

	Ck. No.	Payee	Account Credited/Debited	Post. Ref.	Credits			Debits	
Date					Cash	Purchases Discounts	Other Accounts	Accounts Payable	Other Accounts
July 2	101	Sondra Tidmore	Purchases	511	400				400
6	102	Daily Journal	Advertising Expense	612	200				200
8	103	Siviglia Agency	Rent Expense	631	250				250
11	104	Jones Chevrolet		✓	2,450	50		2,500	
16	105	Charles Kuntz	Salary Expense	611	600				600
17	106	Marshall Ford		✓	294	6		300	
24	107	Grabow & Company	Prepaid Insurance	119	480				480
27	108	Dealer Sales		✓	3,136	64		3,200	
30	109	A&B Equipment Company	Office Equipment Service Equipment	144 146	900				400 500
31	110	Burns Real Estate	Notes Payable Land	213 141	5,000		10,000		15,000
					13,710	120	10,000	6,000	17,830
					(111)	(512)	(✓)	(212)	(✓)

Post individual amounts in Other Accounts column **daily**.

Post individual amounts in Accounts Payable column **daily**.

Post totals at **end of month**.

Totals not posted.

General Ledger

Cash   111

Date	Post. Ref.	Debit	Credit	Balance Debit	Balance Credit
July 31	CR1	32,528		32,528	
31	CP1		13,710	18,818	

Prepaid Insurance   119

Date	Post. Ref.	Debit	Credit	Balance Debit	Balance Credit
July 24	CP1	480		480	

Continue posting to Land, Office Equipment, Service Equipment, Notes Payable, Purchases, Salary Expense, Advertising Expense, and Rent Expense.

Continue posting to Purchases Discounts and Accounts Payable.

Accounts Payable Subsidiary Ledger

Dealer Sales

Date	Post. Ref.	Debit	Credit	Balance
July 3	P1		700	700
17	P1		3,200	3,900
27	CP1	3,200		700

Jones Chevrolet

Date	Post. Ref.	Debit	Credit	Balance
July 1	P1		2,500	2,500
11	CP1	2,500		—

Marshall Ford

Date	Post. Ref.	Debit	Credit	Balance
July 2	P1		300	300
17	CP1	300		—

journal. The title of the account to be debited is written in the Account Credited/Debited column, and the amount is entered in the Other Accounts debit column. If a company finds that a particular account appears often in the Other Accounts column, it can add another debit column to the cash payments journal.

The procedure for posting the cash payments journal, shown in Exhibit 8, is as follows:

1. Post the Accounts Payable column daily to each individual account in the accounts payable subsidiary ledger. Place a checkmark in the Post. Ref. column of the cash payments journal to indicate that the posting has been made.
2. Post the debits/credits in the Other Accounts debit/credit columns to the general ledger daily or at convenient short intervals during the month. As the individual items are posted, write the account number in the Post. Ref. column of the cash payments journal to indicate that the posting has been completed and **CP1** (Cash Payments Journal—Page 1) in the Post. Ref. column of each ledger account.
3. At the end of the month, the columns are footed and crossfooted. That is, the sum of the Credits column totals must equal the sum of the Debits column totals, as follows:

Credits Column Totals		Debits Column Totals	
Cash	$13,710	Accounts Payable	$ 6,000
Purchases Discounts	120	Other Accounts	17,830
Other Accounts	10,000	Total Debits	$23,830
Total Credits	$23,830		

4. Post the column totals for Cash, Purchases Discounts, and Accounts Payable at the end of the month to their respective accounts in the general ledger. Write the account number below each column in the cash payments journal as the total is posted to indicate that this step has been completed and a **CP1** in the Post. Ref. column of each ledger account. Place a checkmark under the total of each Other Accounts column in the cash payments journal to indicate that the postings in the column have been made and that the total is not posted.

GENERAL JOURNAL

Transactions that do not involve sales, purchases, cash receipts, or cash payments should be recorded in the general journal. Usually, there are only a few such transactions. The two examples that follow require entries that do not fit in a special-purpose journal; they are a return of merchandise and an allowance from a supplier for credit. Adjusting and closing entries are also recorded in the general journal.

July 25 Returned one of the two used cars purchased on credit from Thomas Auto on July 12, $700 credit.
   26 Agreed to give Maxwell Gertz a $35 allowance on his account because a tire blew out on the car he purchased.

These entries are shown in Exhibit 9. Notice that the entries include a debit or a credit to a controlling account (Accounts Payable or Accounts Receivable). The name of the customer or supplier is also given. When this kind of debit or credit is made to a controlling account in the general journal, the entry must be posted twice: once in the controlling account and once in the individual account in the subsidiary ledger. This procedure keeps the subsidiary ledger equal to the controlling account as far as entries from the gen-

Exhibit 9. Transactions Recorded in the General Journal

Date		Description	Post. Ref.	Debit	Credit
July	25	Accounts Payable, Thomas Auto	212/✓	700	
		Purchases Returns and			
		Allowances	513		700
		Returned used car for			
		credit; invoice date 7/11			
	26	Sales Returns and Allowances	413	35	
		Accounts Receivable, Maxwell			
		Gertz	114/✓		35
		Allowance for faulty tire			

eral journal are concerned. Notice that the July 26 transaction is posted by a debit to Sales Returns and Allowances in the general ledger (shown by the account number 413), by a credit to the Accounts Receivable controlling account in the general ledger (account number 114), and by a credit to the Maxwell Gertz account in the accounts receivable subsidiary ledger (checkmark).

Audio Trak

DECISION POINT

Audio Trak, a specialty retailer of customized audio systems for automobiles, installed a perpetual inventory system in the second quarter of 1995. The new system improved the firm's ability to adjust its merchandise inventories to sales patterns and to prepare monthly financial statements. Although the system led to improved sales and income, the monthly income statements showed that the gross margin was falling below both management's expectations and the industry average. At the end of 1996, a physical inventory revealed that actual merchandise inventory was considerably lower than the perpetual inventory records indicated. The merchandise inventories of some stores were off more than others, but all had deficiencies. What could have caused those losses, and what steps could be taken to prevent them in the future?

The merchandise inventory losses were probably due to shoplifting and embezzlement. Management must carefully review its controls at the individual stores and install a system that will protect its merchandise inventory from those forms of theft. As you will see in the next section, theft can be minimized through an internal control structure that creates an environment that encourages compliance with a company's policies, a good accounting system, and specific procedures designed to safeguard the merchandise inventory. ⦂⦂⦂⦂⦂

THE FLEXIBILITY OF SPECIAL-PURPOSE JOURNALS

Special-purpose journals reduce and simplify the work in accounting and allow for the division of labor. Such journals should be designed to fit the business in which they are used. As noted earlier, if certain accounts show up often in the Other Accounts column of a journal, it is a good idea to add a column for them when a new page of a special-purpose journal is prepared.

Also, if certain transactions appear repeatedly in the general journal, it is a good idea to set up a new special-purpose journal. For example, if Mitchell's Used Car Sales finds that it often gives allowances to customers, it may want to set up a sales returns and allowances journal specifically for such transactions. Sometimes, a purchases returns and allowances journal is in order. In short, special-purpose journals should be designed to take care of the kinds of transactions a company commonly encounters.

INTERNAL CONTROL STRUCTURE: BASIC ELEMENTS AND PROCEDURES

A merchandising company can have high losses of cash and inventory if it does not take steps to protect its assets. The best way to do this is to set up and maintain a good internal control structure.

OBJECTIVE

6 *Define* internal control *and identify the three elements of the internal control structure, including seven examples of control procedures*

INTERNAL CONTROL DEFINED

Internal control has traditionally been defined as all the policies and procedures management uses to protect the firm's assets and to ensure the accuracy and reliability of the accounting records. It also includes controls that promote operating efficiency and encourage adherence to management's policies. In other words, management wants not only to safeguard assets and have reliable records, but also to maintain an efficient operation and ensure employees' compliance with its policies and procedures. To this end, management establishes an internal control structure that consists of three elements: the control environment, the accounting system, and control procedures.[3]

The control environment is created by the overall attitude, awareness, and actions of management. It includes management's philosophy and operating style, organizational structure, methods of assigning authority and responsibility, and personnel policies and practices. Personnel should be qualified to handle responsibilities, which means that employees must be trained and informed. For example, the manager of a retail store should train employees to follow prescribed procedures for handling cash sales, credit card sales, and returns and refunds. It is clear that an accounting system, no matter how well designed, is only as good as the people who run it. The control environment also includes regular reviews for compliance with procedures. For example, large companies often have a staff of internal auditors who review the company's system of internal control to see that it is working properly and that procedures are being followed. In smaller businesses, owners and managers should conduct these reviews.

---

3. *Professional Standards*, Vol. 1 (New York: American Institute of Certified Public Accountants, June 1, 1989), Sec. AU 319.06–11.

As mentioned earlier, the accounting system consists of the methods and records established by management to identify, assemble, analyze, classify, record, and report a company's transactions, and to ensure that the goals of internal control are being met.

Finally, management uses control procedures to safeguard the company's assets and to ensure the reliability of the accounting records. These include:

1. **Authorization** All transactions and activities should be properly authorized by management. In a retail store, for example, some transactions, such as normal cash sales, are authorized routinely; others, such as issuing a refund, may require a manager's approval.

2. **Recording transactions** To facilitate preparation of financial statements and to establish accountability for assets, all transactions should be recorded. In a retail store, for example, the cash register records sales, refunds, and other transactions internally on a paper tape or computer disk so that the cashier can be held responsible for the cash received and the merchandise removed during his or her shift.

3. **Documents and records** The design and use of adequate documents help ensure the proper recording of transactions. For example, to ensure that all transactions are recorded, invoices and other documents should be prenumbered and all numbers should be accounted for.

4. **Limited access** Access to assets should be permitted only with management's authorization. For example, retail stores should use cash registers, and only the cashier responsible for the cash in the register should have access to it. Other employees should not be able to open the cash drawer if the cashier is not present. Likewise, warehouses and storerooms should be accessible only to authorized personnel. Access to accounting records, including company computers, should also be controlled.

5. **Periodic independent verification** The records should be checked against the assets by someone other than the persons responsible for those records and assets. For example, at the end of each shift or day, the owner or store manager should count the cash in the cash drawer and compare the amount to the amounts recorded on the tape or computer disk in the cash register. Other examples of independent verification are the monthly bank reconciliation and periodic counts of physical inventory.

6. **Separation of duties** The organizational plan should separate functional responsibilities. Within a department, no one person should be in charge of authorizing transactions, operating the department, handling assets, and keeping records of assets. For example, in a stereo store, each employee should oversee only a single part of a transaction. A sales employee takes the order and writes out an invoice. Another employee receives the customer's cash or credit card payment and issues a receipt. Once the customer has a paid receipt, and only then, a third employee obtains the item from the warehouse and gives it to the customer. A person in the accounting department subsequently records the sales from the tape in the cash register, comparing them with the sales invoices and updating the inventory in the records. The separation of duties means that a mistake, careless or not, cannot be made without being seen by at least one other person.

7. **Sound personnel procedures** Sound practices should be followed in managing the people who carry out the functions of each department. Among those practices are supervision, rotation of key people among different jobs, insistence that employees take vacations, and bonding of personnel who handle cash or inventories. Bonding is the process of carefully checking an employee's background and insuring the company against theft by that person. Bonding

does not guarantee the prevention of theft, but it does prevent or reduce economic loss if theft occurs. Prudent personnel procedures help ensure that employees know their jobs, are honest, and will find it difficult to carry out and conceal embezzlement over time.

LIMITATIONS OF INTERNAL CONTROL

OBJECTIVE

7 *Describe the inherent limitations of internal control*

No system of internal control is without weaknesses. As long as control procedures are performed by people, the internal control system is vulnerable to human error. Errors may arise from misunderstandings, mistakes in judgment, carelessness, distraction, or fatigue. Separation of duties can be defeated through collusion by employees who secretly agree to deceive the company. Also, established procedures may be ineffective against employees' errors or dishonesty. Or, controls that may have initially been effective may later become ineffective because conditions have changed.[4] In some cases, the costs of establishing and maintaining elaborate systems may exceed the benefits. In a small business, for example, active involvement by the owner can be a practical substitute for separation of some duties.

INTERNAL CONTROL OVER MERCHANDISING TRANSACTIONS

OBJECTIVE

8 *Apply control procedures to common merchandising transactions*

Sound internal control procedures are needed in all aspects of a business, but particularly when assets are involved. Assets are especially vulnerable when they enter or leave a business. When sales are made, for example, cash or other assets enter the business, and goods or services leave the business. Procedures must be set up to prevent theft during those transactions.

Likewise, purchases of assets and payments of liabilities must be controlled. The majority of those transactions can be safeguarded by adequate purchasing and payroll systems. In addition, assets on hand, such as cash, investments, inventory, plant, and equipment, must be protected.

In this section, you will see how internal control procedures are applied to such merchandising transactions as cash sales, receipts, purchases, and cash payments. Similar procedures are applicable to service and manufacturing businesses.

INTERNAL CONTROL AND MANAGEMENT GOALS

When a system of internal control is applied effectively to merchandising transactions, it can achieve important management goals. For example, two key goals for the success of a business are:

1. To prevent losses of cash or inventory from theft or fraud
2. To provide accurate records of merchandising transactions and account balances

Three broader goals for management are:

1. To keep enough inventory on hand to sell to customers without overstocking
2. To keep enough cash on hand to pay for purchases in time to receive discounts

---

4. Ibid., Sec. AU 320.35.

3. To keep credit losses as low as possible by making credit sales only to customers who are likely to pay on time

One control used in meeting broad management goals is the cash budget, which projects future cash receipts and disbursements. By maintaining adequate cash balances, a company is able to take advantage of discounts on purchases, prepare to borrow money when necessary, and avoid the damaging effects of being unable to pay bills when they are due. And by investing excess cash, the company can earn interest until the cash is needed.

A more specific accounting control is the separation of duties that involve the handling of cash. Such separation makes theft without detection extremely unlikely, unless two or more employees conspire. The separation of duties is easier in large businesses than in small ones, where one person may have to carry out several duties. The effectiveness of internal control over cash varies, depending on the size and nature of the company. Most firms, however, should use the following procedures.

1. Separate the functions of authorization, recordkeeping, and custodianship of cash.
2. Limit the number of people who have access to cash.
3. Designate specific people who are responsible for handling cash.
4. Use banking facilities as much as possible, and keep the amount of cash on hand to a minimum.
5. Bond all employees who have access to cash.
6. Physically protect cash on hand by using cash registers, cashiers' cages, and safes.
7. Have a person who does not handle or record cash make unannounced audits of the cash on hand.
8. Record all cash receipts promptly.
9. Deposit all cash receipts promptly.
10. Make payments by check rather than by currency.
11. Have a person who does not authorize, handle, or record cash transactions reconcile the Cash account.

Notice that each of the foregoing procedures helps safeguard cash by making it more difficult for any one person who has access to cash to steal or misuse it undetected.

CONTROL OF CASH SALES RECEIPTS

Cash payments for sales of goods and services can be received by mail or over the counter in the form of checks or currency. Whatever the source of the payments, cash should be recorded immediately upon receipt. This is usually done by making an entry in a cash receipts journal. Such a journal establishes a written record of cash receipts that should prevent errors and make theft more difficult.

Control of Cash Received Through the Mail   Cash receipts that arrive by mail are vulnerable to theft by the employees who handle them. Payment by mail is increasing, however, because of the expansion of mail order sales. To control mailed receipts, customers should be urged to pay by check instead of with currency.

Cash that comes in through the mail should be handled by two or more employees. The employee who opens the mail should make a list in triplicate of the money received. The list should contain each payer's name, the purpose for which the money was sent, and the amount. One copy goes with the cash to the cashier, who deposits the money. The second copy goes to the accounting department for recording. The third copy is kept by the person who opens the mail. Errors can be easily caught because the amount deposited by the cashier must agree with the amount received and the amount recorded in the cash receipts journal.

Control of Cash Received over the Counter   Two common means of controlling cash sales receipts are the use of cash registers and prenumbered sales tickets. The amount of a cash sale should be rung up on a cash register at the time of the sale. The cash register should be placed so that the customer can see the amount recorded. Each cash register should have a locked-in tape on which it prints the day's transactions. At the end of the day, the cashier counts the cash in the cash register and turns it in to the cashier's office. Another employee takes the tape out of the cash register and records the cash receipts for the day in the cash receipts journal. The amount of cash turned in and the amount recorded on the tape should agree; if not, any differences must be accounted for. Large retail chains commonly monitor cash receipts by having each cash register tied directly into a computer that records each transaction as it occurs. Whether performed manually or by computer, separating responsibility for cash receipts, cash deposits, and recordkeeping is necessary to ensure good internal control.

In some stores, internal control is further strengthened by the use of prenumbered sales tickets and a central cash register or cashier's office, where all sales are rung up and collected by a person who does not participate in the sale. The salesperson completes a prenumbered sales ticket at the time of sale, giving one copy to the customer and keeping a copy. At the end of the day, all sales tickets must be accounted for, and the sales total computed from the sales tickets should equal the total sales recorded on the cash register.

BUSINESS BULLETIN: TECHNOLOGY IN PRACTICE

One of the more difficult challenges facing computer programmers is to build good internal controls into computerized accounting programs. Such computer programs must include controls that prevent unauthorized access and tampering as well as unintentional errors. The programs typically use passwords and questions about randomly selected personal data to prevent unauthorized access to computer records. They prevent errors through reasonableness checks that may not allow the entry of a date beyond the current date, limit checks that allow no transactions over a specified amount, mathematical checks that verify the arithmetic of transactions, and sequence checks that require documents and transactions to be in proper order. ===

CONTROL OF PURCHASES AND CASH DISBURSEMENTS

Cash disbursements are particularly vulnerable to fraud and embezzlement. In one recent case, the treasurer of one of the nation's largest jewelry retailers was charged with having stolen over $500,000 by systematically overpaying federal income taxes and pocketing the refund checks as they came back to the company.

To avoid such theft, cash should be paid only after the receipt of specific authorization supported by documents that establish the validity and amount of the claim. In addition, maximum possible use should be made of the principle of separation of duties in the purchase of goods and services and the payment for them. The degree of separation of duties varies, depending on the size of the business. Figure 6 shows how separation of duties can be maximized in large companies. In the figure, five internal units (the requesting department, the purchasing department, the accounting department, the receiving department, and the treasurer) and two external contacts (the supplier and the banking system) all play a role in the internal control plan. Notice that business documents are also crucial components of the plan.

As summarized in Table 1, every action is documented and subject to verification by at least one other person. For instance, the requesting department cannot work out a kickback scheme with the supplier because the receiving department independently records receipts and the accounting department verifies prices. The receiving department cannot steal goods because the receiving report must equal the invoice. For the same reason, the supplier cannot bill for more goods than it ships. The accounting department's work is verified by the treasurer, and the treasurer ultimately is checked by the accounting department.

Figures 7 through 11, which show typical documents used in this internal control plan, follow the purchase of twenty boxes of FAX paper rolls. To begin, the credit office (requesting department) of Martin Maintenance Company

Figure 6. Internal Control for Purchasing and Paying for Goods and Services

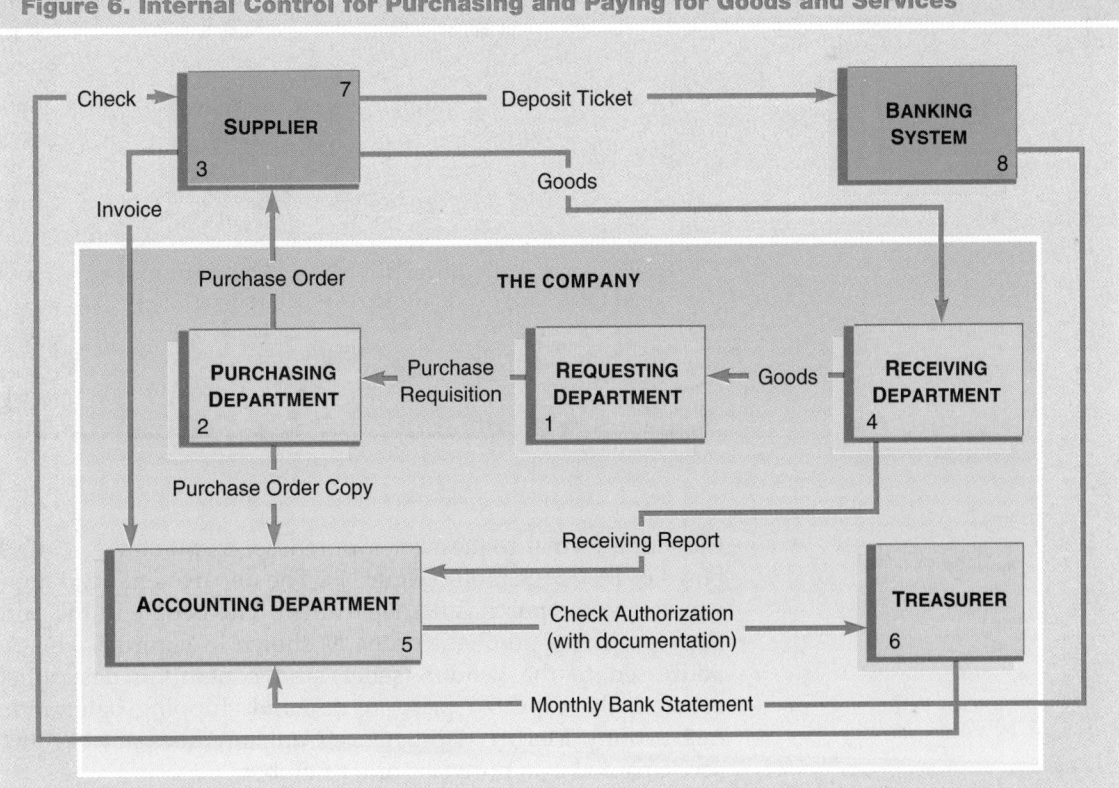

Table 1. Internal Control Plan for Purchases and Cash Disbursements

Business Document	Prepared by	Sent to	Verification and Related Procedures
1. Purchase requisition	Requesting department	Purchasing department	Purchasing verifies authorization.
2. Purchase order	Purchasing department	Supplier	Supplier sends goods or services in accordance with purchase order.
3. Invoice	Supplier	Accounting department	Accounting receives invoice from supplier.
4. Receiving report	Receiving department	Accounting department	Accounting compares invoice, purchase order, and receiving report. Accounting verifies prices.
5. Check authorization	Accounting department	Treasurer	Accounting attaches check authorization to invoice, purchase order, and receiving report.
6. Check	Treasurer	Supplier	Treasurer verifies all documents before preparing check.
7. Deposit ticket	Supplier	Supplier's bank	Supplier compares check with invoice. Bank deducts check from buyer's account.
8. Bank statement	Buyer's bank	Accounting department	Accounting compares amount and payee's name on returned check with check authorization.

fills out a formal request for a purchase, or purchase requisition, for twenty boxes of FAX paper rolls (Figure 7). The department head approves it and forwards it to the purchasing department. The people in the purchasing department prepare a purchase order, as shown in Figure 8. The purchase order is addressed to the vendor (seller) and contains a description of the items ordered; the expected price, terms, and shipping date; and other shipping instructions. Martin Maintenance Company does not pay any bill that is not accompanied by a purchase order number.

Figure 7. Purchase Requisition

Figure 7. Purchase Requisition

PURCHASE REQUISITION   No. 7077

Martin Maintenance Company

From: Credit Office   Date: _September 6, 19xx_

To: Purchasing Department   Suggested Vendor: _Henderson Supply_

Please purchase the following items: _Company_

Quantity	Number	Description
20 boxes	X 144	FAX paper rolls

Reason for Request	To be filled in by Purchasing Department
Six months' supply for office	
	Date ordered _9/8/xx_ P.O. No. _J 102_
Approved _B.M._	

Figure 8. Purchase Order

PURCHASE ORDER   No. J 102

Martin Maintenance Company
8428 Rocky Island Avenue
Chicago, Illinois 60643

To: Henderson Supply Company   Date _September 8, 19xx_
    2525 25th Street
    Mesa, Illinois 61611   FOB _Destination_

                                    Ship by _September 12, 19xx_
Ship to: Martin Maintenance Company
         Above Address   Terms _2/10, n/30_

Please ship the following:

Quantity	✓	Number	Description	Price	Per	Amount
20 boxes		X 144	FAX paper rolls	12.00	box	$240.00

Purchase order number must appear on all shipments and invoices.	Ordered by _Marsha Owen_

Figure 9. Invoice

INVOICE					No. 0468

Henderson Supply Company
2525 25th Street
Mesa, Illinois 61611

Date _September 12, 19xx_

Your Order No. _J 102_

Sold to:

Martin Maintenance Company
8428 Rocky Island Avenue
Chicago, Illinois 60643

Ship to:

Same

Sales Representative: Joe Jacobs

Quantity		Description	Price	Per	Amount
Ordered	Shipped				
20	20	X 144 FAX paper rolls	12.00	box	$240.00

FOB Destination	Terms: 2/10, n/30	Date Shipped: 9/12/xx	Via: Self

After receiving the purchase order, the vendor, Henderson Supply Company, ships the goods and sends an invoice or bill (Figure 9), to Martin Maintenance Company. The invoice gives the quantity and description of the goods delivered and the terms of payment. If goods cannot all be shipped immediately, the estimated date for shipment of the remainder is indicated.

When the goods reach the receiving department of Martin Maintenance Company, an employee writes the description, quantity, and condition of the goods on a form called a receiving report. The receiving department does not receive a copy of the purchase order or invoice, so its employees do not know what should be received. Thus, they are not tempted to steal any excess that may be delivered.

The receiving report is sent to the accounting department, where it is compared with the purchase order and the invoice. If all is correct, the accounting department completes a check authorization and attaches it to the three supporting documents. The check authorization form shown in Figure 10 has a space for each item to be checked off as it is examined. Notice that the accounting department has all the documentary evidence for the transaction but does not have access to the assets purchased. Nor does it write the check for payment. This means that the people performing the accounting function cannot gain by falsifying documents in an effort to conceal fraud.

Finally, the treasurer examines all the documents and issues an order to the bank for payment, called a check (Figure 11), for the amount of the invoice less any appropriate discount. In some systems, the accounting department fills out the check so that all the treasurer has to do is inspect and sign it. The check is then sent to the supplier, with a remittance advice that shows what the check is for. A supplier who is not paid the proper amount

Figure 10. Check Authorization

CHECK AUTHORIZATION

	NO.	CHECK
Requisition	7077	✓
Purchase Order	J 102	✓
Receiving Report	JR 065	✓
INVOICE	0468	
Price		✓
Calculations		✓
Terms		✓

Approved for Payment ___ *J. Joseph*

will complain, of course, thus providing a form of outside control over the payment. The supplier deposits the check in the bank, which returns the canceled check with Martin Maintenance Company's next bank statement. If the treasurer has made the check out for the wrong amount (or altered a pre-filled-in check), the problem shows up in the bank reconciliation.

There are many variations of the system just described. This example is offered as a simple system that provides adequate internal control.

Figure 11. Check with Attached Remittance Advice

Martin Maintenance Company
8428 Rocky Island Avenue
Chicago, Illinois 60643

NO. 2570
61-153/313

9/21 19 XX

PAY TO THE ORDER OF Henderson Supply Company $ 235.20

Two hundred thirty-five and 20/100 — — — — — — — — — Dollars

THE LAKE PARK NATIONAL BANK
Chicago, Illinois

Martin Maintenance Company

by *Arthur Martin*

Remittance Advice

Date	P.O. No.	DESCRIPTION	AMOUNT
9/21/xx	J 102	20 X 144 FAX paper rolls Supplier Inv. No. 0468 Less 2% discount	$240.00 4.80
		Net	$235.20
		Martin Maintenance Company	

CHAPTER REVIEW

REVIEW OF LEARNING OBJECTIVES

1. **Identify the principles of accounting systems design.** The developers of an accounting system must keep in mind the four principles of systems design: the cost-benefit principle, the control principle, the compatibility principle, and the flexibility principle.

2. **Identify the basic elements of mainframe and microcomputer systems.** Computerized data processing systems are the most advanced type of data processing system, in which recording, posting, and other bookkeeping tasks are done with the help of a computer. The typical computer system consists of hardware, software, and personnel. The internal processing is specified in the form of programs, which can be designed to allow batch processing (grouping of similar transactions to be done at a specified time) or on-line processing (recording transactions as they occur). Commercial accounting packages for microcomputer systems are structured according to the major tasks of the accounting system.

3. **Explain the objectives and uses of special-purpose journals.** The typical manual data processing system consists of several special-purpose journals, each designed to record one kind of transaction. Recording only one kind of transaction in each journal reduces and simplifies the accounting task and allows for the division of labor. The division of labor is important for internal control.

4. **Explain the purposes and relationships of controlling accounts and subsidiary ledgers.** Subsidiary ledgers contain individual accounts of a specific kind, such as customers' accounts (accounts receivable) or suppliers' accounts (accounts payable). The individual account records are kept separately in a subsidiary ledger to avoid making the general ledger too bulky. The total of the balances of the subsidiary accounts should equal the balance of the controlling account in the general ledger after all the postings have been made (individual items are posted daily to the subsidiary accounts and column totals are posted to the general ledger account monthly from the special-purpose journal).

5. **Construct and use a sales journal, purchases journal, cash receipts journal, cash payments journal, and other special-purpose journals as needed.** A special-purpose journal is constructed by devoting a single column to a particular account (for example, debits to Cash in the cash receipts journal and credits to Cash in the cash payments journal). Other columns in the journal depend on the kinds of transactions in which the company normally engages. Special-purpose journals also have columns for transaction dates, explanations or subsidiary account names, and posting references.

6. **Define *internal control* and identify the three elements of the internal control structure, including seven examples of control procedures.** Internal controls are the policies and procedures management uses to protect the organization's assets and to ensure the accuracy and reliability of accounting records. They also work to maintain efficient operations and compliance with management's policies. The internal control structure consists of three elements: the control environment, the accounting system, and control procedures. Examples of control procedures are proper authorization of transactions; recording transactions to facilitate preparation of financial statements and to establish accountability for assets; use of well-designed documents and records; limited access to assets; periodic independent comparison of records and assets; separation of duties into the functions of authorization, operations, custody of assets, and recordkeeping; and use of sound personnel policies.

7. **Describe the inherent limitations of internal control.** A system of internal control relies on the people who implement it. Thus, the effectiveness of internal control is limited by the people involved. Human error, collusion, and the failure to recognize changed conditions all can contribute to a system's failure.

8. **Apply control procedures to common merchandising transactions.** Certain procedures strengthen internal control over sales, cash receipts, purchases, and cash disbursements. First, the functions of authorization, recordkeeping, and custody should be kept separate. Second, the accounting system should provide for physical protection of assets (especially cash and merchandise inventory), use of banking services, prompt recording and deposit of cash receipts, and payment by check. Third, the people who have access to cash and merchandise inventory should be specifically designated and their number limited. Fourth, employees who have access to cash or merchandise inventory should be bonded. Fifth, the Cash account should be reconciled each month, and unannounced audits of cash on hand should be made by an individual who does not authorize, handle, or record cash transactions.

REVIEW OF CONCEPTS AND TERMINOLOGY

The following concepts and terms were introduced in this chapter.

L O 1 **Accounting systems:** The process that gathers data, puts them into useful form, and communicates the results to management; it includes analyzing and recording transactions, posting entries, adjusting and closing the accounts, and preparing financial statements.

L O 2 **Batch processing:** The form of data processing in which processing tasks are scheduled sequentially.

L O 6 **Bonding:** The process of carefully checking an employee's background and insuring the company against theft by that person.

L O 5 **Cash payments journal:** A multicolumn special-purpose journal used to record payments of cash; also called the *cash disbursements journal.*

L O 5 **Cash receipts journal:** A multicolumn special-purpose journal used to record transactions involving the receipt of cash.

L O 8 **Check:** A written order to a bank to pay the amount specified from funds on deposit.

L O 8 **Check authorization:** A form prepared by the accounting department after it has compared the receiving report for goods received with the purchase order and the invoice.

L O 1 **Compatibility principle:** The principle that holds that the design of an accounting system must be in harmony with the organizational and human factors of the business.

L O 2 **Computer operator:** The person who runs a computer.

L O 6 **Control environment:** The overall attitude, awareness, and actions of the owners and management of a business, as reflected in philosophy and operating style, organizational structure, methods of assigning authority and responsibility, and personnel policies and practices.

L O 4 **Controlling account:** An account in the general ledger that summarizes the total balance of a group of related accounts in a subsidiary ledger; also called a *control account.*

L O 1 **Control principle:** The principle that holds that an accounting system must provide all the features of internal control needed to protect the firm's assets and ensure that data are reliable.

L O 6 **Control procedures:** Procedures and policies established by management to ensure that the objectives of internal control are met.

L O 1 **Cost-benefit principle:** The principle that holds that the benefits derived from an accounting system and the information it generates should equal or exceed its cost.

L O 1 **Data processing:** The means by which an accounting system gathers data, organizes them into useful forms, and issues the resulting information to users.

L O 1 **Flexibility principle:** The principle that holds that the design of an accounting system must be flexible enough to allow the volume of transactions to grow and organizational changes to be made.

L O 2   **General ledger software:** A group of programs that directs the computer to carry out the major accounting functions.

L O 2   **Hardware:** The equipment needed to operate a computerized data processing system.

L O 6   **Internal control:** All the policies and procedures a company uses to safeguard its assets, check the accuracy and reliability of its accounting data, promote operational efficiency, and encourage adherence to its policies.

L O 6   **Internal control structure:** A structure established to safeguard the assets of a business and provide reliable accounting records; consists of the control environment, the accounting system, and control procedures.

L O 8   **Invoice:** A form sent to the purchaser by the vendor that describes the quantity and price of the goods or services delivered and the terms of payment.

L O 3   **Manual data processing:** A system of accounting in which data for each transaction are entered manually from a source document into the general journal (input device) and each debit and credit is posted manually to the correct ledger account (processor and memory device) for the eventual preparation of financial statements (output devices).

L O 2   **Network:** The linking of two or more microcomputers to enable them to communicate with each other.

L O 2   **On-line processing:** The form of data processing in which remote terminals are linked to a central processor and files are updated virtually as transactions occur.

L O 2   **Program:** The set of instructions and steps that bring about the desired results in a computerized data processing system.

L O 2   **Programmer:** The person who writes instructions for a computer.

L O 8   **Purchase order:** A form prepared by a company's purchasing department and sent to a vendor, it describes the items ordered; their expected price, terms, and shipping date; and other shipping instructions.

L O 8   **Purchase requisition:** A formal written request for a purchase, prepared by the requesting department in an organization and sent to the purchasing department.

L O 5   **Purchases journal:** A single-column or multicolumn special-purpose journal used to record all purchases on credit.

L O 8   **Receiving report:** A form prepared by the receiving department of a company; describes the quantity and condition of goods received.

L O 5   **Sales journal:** A type of special-purpose journal used to record credit sales.

L O 2   **Software:** The programs in a computerized data processing system.

L O 2   **Source documents:** The written evidence that supports the transactions for each major accounting function.

L O 3   **Special-purpose journal:** An input device in an accounting system that is used to record a single type of transaction.

L O 4   **Subsidiary ledger:** A ledger separate from the general ledger that contains a group of related accounts; the total of the balances in the subsidiary ledger accounts must equal the balance of a controlling account in the general ledger.

L O 2   **Systems analyst:** The person who designs a computerized data processing system on the basis of an organization's information needs.

REVIEW PROBLEM

PURCHASES JOURNAL

L O 1, 3, 5   Caraban Company is a retail seller of hiking and camping gear. The company is installing a system of special-purpose journals and the accountant is trying to decide whether to use a single-column or a multicolumn purchases journal. On the following page is a list of several transactions related to purchases in January.

Jan. 5 Received a shipment of merchandise from Simons Corporation, terms 2/10, n/30, FOB shipping point, invoice dated January 4, $2,875.

10 Received a bill from Allied Freight for the freight charges on the January 5 shipment, terms n/30, invoice dated January 4, $416.

15 Returned some of the merchandise received from Simons Corporation because it was not what was ordered, $315.

20 Purchased store supplies of $56 and office supplies of $117 from Mason Company, terms n/30, invoice dated January 20.

25 Received a shipment from Thomas Manufacturing, $1,882, which included supplier-paid freight charges of $175, terms n/30, FOB shipping point, invoice dated January 23.

REQUIRED

1. Record the transactions using a single-column purchases journal and a general journal. Show the posting reference for each journal entry and for the purchases journal total. Use the following accounts: Store Supplies (116), Office Supplies (117), Accounts Payable (211), Purchases (611), Purchases Returns and Allowances (612), and Freight In (613).

2. Record the transactions using a multicolumn purchases journal and a general journal, total the purchases journal, and show the posting reference for each entry.

3. Using the principles of systems design, compare the single-column and multicolumn systems in terms of the number of journal entries and postings.

Answer to Review Problem

1. Record the transactions in a single-column purchases journal and a general journal. Show the posting references.

Purchases Journal						Page 1
Date	Account Credited	Date of Invoice	Terms	Post. Ref.		Amount
Jan. 5	Simons Corporation	1/4	2/10, n/30	✓		2,875
						(211/611)

General Journal					Page 1
Date	Description	Post. Ref.	Debit	Credit
Jan. 10	Freight In	613	416	
	Accounts Payable, Allied Freight	211/✓		416
	Freight charges on Simons Corporation shipment, terms n/30, invoice dated January 4			
15	Accounts Payable, Simons Corporation	211/✓	315	
	Purchases Returns and Allowances	612		315
	Returned merchandise not ordered			
20	Store Supplies	116	56	
	Office Supplies	117	117	
	Accounts Payable, Mason Company	211/✓		173
	Purchased supplies, terms n/30, invoice dated January 20			

(continued)

Jan.	25	Purchases	611	1,707	
		Freight In	613	175	
		Accounts Payable, Thomas Manufacturing	211/✔		1,882
		Purchased merchandise, terms n/30; supplier paid shipping, invoice dated January 23			

2. Record the transactions in a multicolumn purchases journal and a general journal. Total the purchases journal and show posting references.

Purchases Journal   Page 1

Date		Account Credited	Date of Invoice	Terms	Post. Ref.	Credit	Debits			
						Accounts Payable	Purchases	Freight In	Store Supplies	Office Supplies
Jan.	5	Simons Corporation	1/4	2/10, n/30	✔	2,875	2,875			
	10	Allied Freight	1/4	n/30	✔	416		416		
	20	Mason Company	1/20	n/30	✔	173			56	117
	25	Thomas Manufacturing	1/23	n/30	✔	1,882	1,707	175		
						5,346	4,582	591	56	117
						(211)	(611)	(613)	(116)	(117)

> Each of these amounts is posted **daily** to the appropriate account in the subsidiary ledger.

> Each of these totals is posted **monthly** to the applicable general ledger account.

General Journal   Page 1

Date		Description	Post. Ref.	Debit	Credit
Jan.	15	Accounts Payable, Simons Corporation	211/✔	315	
		Purchases Returns and Allowances	612		315
		Returned merchandise not ordered			

> This amount is posted to both the controlling account and the subsidiary account.

> This amount is posted to the general ledger account.

3. The single-column purchases journal requires four general journal entries plus one purchases journal entry, or twenty separate lines, including explanations. In addition, fifteen postings to the general ledger and the accounts payable subsidiary ledger are necessary. Also, the total of the purchases journal must be posted twice at the end of the month: once as a credit to Accounts Payable and once as a debit to

Purchases. The multicolumn purchases journal calls for just one general journal entry and four purchases journal entries. Only eight lines need to be written, and only seven postings must be made for the journal entries. In addition, the column totals in the purchases journal must be posted at the end of the month.

In applying the cost-benefit principle, the benefits of the multicolumn purchases journal in terms of journalizing and posting time saved are clear from this analysis. In addition, there are fewer chances for error when using the multicolumn purchases journal. So the control principle is better achieved under the second system. It is not possible to decide which system better meets the compatibility principle because we do not know the relative proportion of transaction types. For instance, if the number of transactions like the one for January 5 exceeds all the others by ten to one, the first system may be more compatible with the needs of the company. On the other hand, if there are many transactions like those for January 10, 20, and 25, the second system may be more compatible. Finally, in terms of the flexibility principle, the multicolumn purchases journal is obviously more flexible because it can handle more kinds of transactions and can be expanded to include columns for other accounts if necessary.

CHAPTER ASSIGNMENTS

QUESTIONS

1. What is the relationship of accounting systems to data processing?
2. What is the function of data processing?
3. Describe the four principles of accounting systems design.
4. What are the three basic elements of a computerized data processing system?
5. What is the difference between hardware and software?
6. What is the purpose of a computer program?
7. What is the difference between batch processing and on-line processing?
8. Data are the raw material of a computer system. Trace the flow of data through the different parts of a microcomputer accounting system.
9. How do special-purpose journals save time in entering and posting transactions?
10. What is the purpose of the Accounts Receivable controlling account? What is its relationship to the accounts receivable subsidiary ledger?
11. Long Transit had 1,700 sales on credit during the current month.
    a. If the firm uses a two-column general journal to record sales, how many times will the word *Sales* be written?
    b. How many postings to the Sales account will have to be made?
    c. If the firm uses a sales journal, how many times will the word *Sales* be written?
    d. How many postings to the Sales account will have to be made?
12. Why are the cash receipts journal and cash payments journal crossfooted? When is this step performed?
13. A company has the following accounts with balances: 18 asset accounts, including the Accounts Receivable account but not the individual customers' accounts; 200 customer accounts; 8 liability accounts, including the Accounts Payable account but not the individual creditors' accounts; 100 creditor accounts; and 35 owner's equity accounts, including income statement accounts—a total of 361 accounts. How many accounts in total would appear in the general ledger?
14. Most people think of internal control as a means of making fraud harder to commit and easier to detect. What are some other important purposes of internal control?
15. What are the three elements of the internal control structure?
16. What are some examples of control procedures?

17. Why is the separation of duties necessary to ensure sound internal control? What does this principle assume about the relationships of employees in a company and the possibility of two or more of them stealing from the company?

18. In a small business, it is sometimes impossible to separate duties completely. What are three other practices that a small business can follow to achieve the objectives of internal control over cash?

19. At Thrifty Variety Store, each sales clerk counts the cash in his or her cash drawer at the end of the day and then removes the cash register tape and prepares a daily cash form, noting any discrepancies. The information is checked by an employee in the cashier's office, who counts the cash, compares the total with the form, and then gives the cash to the cashier. What is the weakness in this system of internal control?

20. How does a movie theater control cash receipts?

21. For each of the following business documents, tell what department or person prepares it and what department or person receives it: purchase requisition, purchase order, invoice, receiving report, check authorization, check, deposit ticket, and bank statement.

SHORT EXERCISES

SE 1. *Principles of*
L O 1 *Accounting Information System Design*
Check Figures: b, d, a, c

Indicate whether each of the following situations in a newly installed accounting information system is most closely related to the (a) cost-benefit principle, (b) control principle, (c) compatibility principle, or (d) flexibility principle.

1. Procedures are put in place to ensure that the data entered into the system are reliable.
2. The system allows for growth in the number and types of transactions entered into by the company.
3. The system was installed after careful weighing of the additional costs in relation to the improved decision making that will result.
4. The system takes into account the various operations of the business and the capabilities of the people who will interact with the system.

SE 2. *Microcomputer*
L O 2 *Accounting System*
Check Figures: c, e, b, d, a, f

Assuming that a company uses a general ledger package for a microcomputer accounting system, indicate whether each source document listed below would provide input to (a) sales/accounts receivable, (b) purchases/accounts payable, (c) cash receipts, (d) cash disbursements, (e) payroll, or (f) the general journal.

1. Deposit slips
2. Time cards
3. Vendor invoices
4. Checks issued
5. Customer invoices
6. Documents for other journal entries

SE 3. *Transactions and*
L O 3 *Special-Purpose Journals*
Check Figures: c, e, a, b, c, d

Indicate whether each transaction listed below should be recorded in the (a) sales journal, (b) multicolumn purchases journal, (c) cash receipts journal, (d) cash payments journal, or (e) general journal.

1. Receipt on account
2. Purchase return on account
3. Sale on account
4. Purchase on account
5. Sale for cash
6. Payment on account

SE 4. *Sales Journal*
L O 5 *Transactions*
No check figure

Using Exhibit 1 as a model, show how each of the following transactions would be entered in a sales journal. All terms are 2/10, n/30. If a transaction should not appear in the sales journal, tell where it should be recorded.

Oct. 1 Sold merchandise to S. Ruiz on credit, invoice no. 301, $350.
      8 Sold merchandise to J. Sizemore for cash, $150.
     15 Sold merchandise to F. Thomas on credit, invoice no. 302, $200.

Total and rule the journal.

SE 5. *Sales Journal*
L O 4, 5 *Postings and*
              Subsidiary Ledger
No check figure

Assuming the transactions in SE 4 are the only sales transactions for the month of October, describe all the postings that would be made from the sales journal to the general ledger and the accounts receivable subsidiary ledger.

SE 6. *Cash Receipts*
L O 4, 5 *Journal*
No check figure

Using Exhibit 7 as a model, show how each of the following transactions would be entered in the cash receipts journal. If a transaction should not appear in this journal, tell where it should be recorded.

Oct. 8 Sold merchandise for cash to J. Sizemore, $150.
      9 Received payment on account from S. Ruiz, $350 less 2 percent discount.
     17 F. Thomas returned purchase of October 15 for full credit, $200.

Describe the postings that are required for each transaction.

SE 7. *Elements of*
L O 6 *Internal Control*
Check Figures: c, a, b

Fell Company is a men's clothing store. Indicate whether each of the following elements of internal control is part of the (a) control environment, (b) accounting system, or (c) control procedures.

1. An organization plan calls for separation of duties in the handling of cash sales.
2. Charles Fell emphasizes to employees the importance of following specific procedures in the handling of cash.
3. All cash transactions are recorded automatically in the company's computer when the sales are rung up on the cash register.

SE 8. *Internal Control*
L O 6, 8 *Procedures*
Check Figures: f, d, g, e, a, c, b

Match each of the following control procedures to the appropriate check-writing policy for a small business listed below.

a. Authorization
b. Recording transactions
c. Documents and records
d. Limited access
e. Periodic independent verification
f. Separation of duties
g. Sound personnel policies

1. The person who writes the checks to pay bills is different from the persons who authorize the payments and who keep the records of the payments.
2. The checks are kept in a locked drawer. The only person who has the key is the person who writes the checks.
3. The person who writes the checks is bonded.
4. Once each month the owner compares and reconciles the amount of money shown in the accounting records with the amount in the bank account.
5. Each check is approved by the owner of the business before it is mailed.
6. A check stub recording pertinent information is completed for each check.
7. Every day, all checks are recorded in the accounting records, using the information on the check stubs.

SE 9. *Limitations of*
L O 7 *Internal Control*
Check Figures: d, b, a, c

Internal control is subject to several inherent limitations. Indicate whether each of the following situations is an example of (a) human error, (b) collusion, (c) changed conditions, or (d) cost-benefit considerations.

1. Effective separation of duties in a restaurant is impractical because the business is too small.
2. The cashier and the manager of a retail shoe store work together to circumvent the internal controls for the purpose of embezzling funds.
3. The cashier in a pizza shop does not understand the procedures for operating the cash register and thus fails to ring up all sales and to count the cash at the end of the day.

4. At a law firm, computer supplies were mistakenly delivered to the reception area instead of the receiving area because the supplier began using a different means of shipment. As a result, the receipt of the supplies was not recorded.

SE 10. *Internal Control*
L O 8 *Documents for*
Purchases and
Payments
Check Figures: a, b; c, d; f, d; d, e; e, f

Indicate the letter of where each of the following documents would be prepared and the letter of where it would be sent.

a. Requesting department
b. Purchasing department
c. Receiving department
d. Accounting department
e. Treasurer
f. Supplier

1. Purchase requisition
2. Receiving report
3. Invoice
4. Check authorization
5. Check

EXERCISES

E 1. *Matching*
L O 3 *Transactions*
to Special-Purpose
Journals
No check figure

A company uses a single-column sales journal, a single-column purchases journal, a cash receipts journal, a cash payments journal, and a general journal. In which journal would each of the following transactions be recorded?

1. Sold merchandise on credit
2. Sold merchandise for cash
3. Gave a customer credit for merchandise purchased on credit and returned
4. Paid a creditor
5. Paid office salaries
6. Received a customer's payment for merchandise previously purchased on credit
7. Recorded adjusting and closing entries
8. Purchased merchandise on credit
9. Purchased sales department supplies on credit
10. Purchased office equipment for cash
11. Returned merchandise purchased on credit
12. Paid income taxes

E 2. *Characteristics*
L O 3, 4, 5 *of Special-Purpose*
Journals
No check figure

Sanchez Corporation uses a single-column sales journal, a single-column purchases journal, a cash receipts journal, a cash payments journal, and a general journal.

1. In which of the journals listed above would you expect to find the fewest transactions recorded?
2. At the end of the accounting period, to which account or accounts should the total of the sales journal be posted as a debit and/or credit?
3. At the end of the accounting period, to which account or accounts should the total of the purchases journal be posted as a debit and/or credit?
4. What two subsidiary ledgers would probably be associated with the journals listed above? From which journals would postings normally be made to each of the two subsidiary ledgers?
5. In which of the journals are adjusting and closing entries made?

E 3. *Identifying the*
L O 5 *Content of a Special-*
Purpose Journal
No check figure

Shown on the next page is a page from a special-purpose journal.

1. What kind of journal is this?
2. Explain each transaction.
3. Explain the following: (a) the numbers under the double rule, (b) the checkmarks entered in the Post. Ref. column, (c) the numbers 115 and 715 in the Post. Ref. column, and (d) the checkmark below the Other Accounts credit column.

Date		Account Credited	Post. Ref.	Debits			Credits	
				Cash	Sales Discounts	Accounts Receivable	Sales	Other Accounts
		Balance Forward	✓	39,799	787	10,204	4,282	26,100
Aug.	27	Betsy McCray	✓	490	10	500		
	28	Notes Receivable	115	1,120				1,000
		Interest Income	715					120
	29	Sales		960			960	
	30	Michael Harper	✓	200		200		
				42,569	797	10,904	5,242	27,220
				(111)	(412)	(114)	(411)	(✓)

E 4. *Multicolumn*
L O 5 *Purchases Journal*
Check Figure: Accounts Payable total: $4,270

Jablonski Company uses a multicolumn purchases journal similar to the one illustrated in Exhibit 6. During the month of October, Jablonski made the following purchases.

Oct. 1 Purchased merchandise from Cowen Company on account, invoice dated October 1, terms 2/10, n/30, $2,700.

2 Received freight bill dated October 1 from Riker Freight for above merchandise, terms n/30, $175.

23 Purchased supplies from Zimmer, Inc. for $120; allocated one-half each to store and office; invoice dated October 20, terms n/30.

27 Purchased merchandise from Fleming Company on account, invoice dated October 25, terms n/30, FOB shipping point, $987, including freight in of $87.

30 Purchased office supplies from Zimmer, Inc. for $48, invoice dated October 30, terms n/30.

31 Purchased a one-year insurance policy from Greenspan Agency, $240, invoice dated October 30, terms n/30.

1. Draw a multicolumn purchases journal similar to the one in Exhibit 6.
2. Enter the above transactions in the purchases journal. Then foot and crossfoot the columns.

E 5. *Finding Errors*
L O 4, 5 *in Special-Purpose Journals*
No check figure

A company records purchases in a single-column purchases journal and records purchases returns in its general journal. During the past month, an accounting clerk made each of the errors described below. Explain how each error might be discovered.

1. Correctly recorded an $86 purchase in the purchases journal but posted it to the creditor's account as a $68 purchase.
2. Made an addition error in totaling the Amount column of the purchases journal.
3. Posted a purchases return from the general journal to the Purchases Returns and Allowances account and the Accounts Payable account but did not post it to the creditor's account.
4. Made an error in determining the balance of a creditor's account.
5. Posted a purchases return to the Accounts Payable account but did not post it to the Purchases Returns and Allowances account.

E 6. *Posting from a*
L O 4, 5 *Sales Journal*
No check figure

Grammas Corporation began business on September 1. The company maintains a sales journal. The sales journal at the end of the month is shown on the next page.

1. Open general ledger accounts for Accounts Receivable (112) and Sales (411) and an accounts receivable subsidiary ledger with an account for each customer. Make the appropriate postings from the sales journal and in the ledger accounts as you work. Describe the posting references in the sales journal.
2. Prove the accounts receivable subsidiary ledger by preparing a schedule of accounts receivable.

Sales Journal				Page 1
Date	Account Debited	Invoice Number	Post. Ref.	Amount (Debit/Credit Accounts Receivable/ Sales)
Sept. 4	Yung Moon	1001		172
10	Stacy Kravitz	1002		317
15	Arthur Hillman	1003		214
17	Yung Moon	1004		97
25	Juan Robles	1005		433
				1,233

E 7.
L O 4, 5
No check figure

Identification of Transactions

Herrera Company uses a manual accounting system with a sales journal, purchases journal, cash receipts journal, cash payments journal, and general journal similar to those illustrated in the text. On October 31, the Sales account in the general ledger looked like this:

Sales					Account No. 411	
					Balance	
Date	Item	Post. Ref.	Debit	Credit	Debit	Credit
Oct. 31		S11		74,842		74,842
31		CR7		42,414		117,256
31		J17	117,256			—

On October 31, the J. Tanner account in the accounts receivable subsidiary ledger looked like this:

J. Tanner					Account No. 10012
Date	Item	Post. Ref.	Debit	Credit	Balance
Oct. 8		S10	4,216		4,216
12		J14		564	3,652
18		CR6		1,000	2,652

1. Write an explanation of each entry in the Sales account; include the journal from which the entry was posted.
2. Write an explanation of each entry in the J. Tanner accounts receivable subsidiary ledger; include the journal from which the entry was posted.

E 8.
L O 4, 5
No check figure

Identification of Transactions

Medina Company uses a sales journal, single-column purchases journal, cash receipts journal, cash payments journal, and general journal similar to those shown in the text. On April 30, the D. Peters account in the accounts receivable subsidiary ledger appeared as shown at the top of the next page.

D. Peters

Date		Item	Post. Ref.	Debit	Credit	Balance
Mar.	31		S4	2,448		2,448
Apr.	7		J7		192	2,256
	12		CR5		600	1,656
	17		S6	684		2,340

On April 30, the Yung Company account in the accounts payable subsidiary ledger appeared as follows:

Yung Company

Date		Item	Post. Ref.	Debit	Credit	Balance
Apr.	18		P7		6,078	6,078
	20		J9	636		5,442
	25		CP8	5,442		—

1. Write an explanation of each entry that affected the D. Peters accounts receivable, including the journal from which the entry was posted.
2. Write an explanation of each entry that affected the Yung Company account payable, including the journal from which the entry was posted.

E 9. *Use of Accounting*
L O 6 *Records in*
Internal Control

No check figure

Careful scrutiny of accounting records and financial statements can lead to the discovery of fraud or embezzlement. Each of the following situations may indicate a breakdown in internal control. Indicate the nature of the possible fraud or embezzlement in each situation.

1. Wages expense for a branch office was 30 percent higher in 19x2 than in 19x1, even though the office was authorized to employ only the same four employees and raises were only 5 percent in 19x2.
2. Sales returns and allowances increased from 5 percent to 20 percent of sales in the first two months of 19x2, after record sales in 19x1 resulted in large bonuses being paid to the sales staff.
3. Gross margin decreased from 40 percent of net sales in 19x1 to 30 percent in 19x2, even though there was no change in pricing. Ending inventory was 50 percent less at the end of 19x2 than it was at the beginning of the year. There is no immediate explanation for the decrease in inventory.
4. A review of daily records of cash register receipts shows that one cashier consistently accepts more discount coupons for purchases than do the other cashiers.

E 10. *Control Procedures*
L O 6

Check Figures: c, a, b, d

Sean O'Mara, who operates a small grocery store, has established the following policies with regard to the check-out cashiers.

1. Each cashier has his or her own cash drawer, to which no one else has access.
2. Each cashier may accept checks for purchases under $50 with proper identification. Checks over $50 must be approved by O'Mara before they are accepted.
3. Every sale must be rung up on the cash register and a receipt given to the customer. Each sale is recorded on a tape inside the cash register.
4. At the end of each day O'Mara counts the cash in the drawer and compares it to the amount on the tape inside the cash register.

Identify by letter which of the following conditions for internal control applies to each of the policies listed on the previous page.

a. Transactions are executed in accordance with management's general or specific authorization.
b. Transactions are recorded as necessary to permit preparation of financial statements and maintain accountability for assets.
c. Access to assets is permitted only as allowed by management.
d. At reasonable intervals, the records of assets are compared with the existing assets.

E 11. *Internal Control*
L O 6 *Procedures*
Check Figures: 1. g; 2. e; 3. a, c, f; 4. g; 5. b, c

Ruth's Video Store maintains the following policies with regard to purchases of new videotapes at each of its branch stores.

1. Employees are required to take vacations, and duties of employees are rotated periodically.
2. Once each month a person from the home office visits each branch to examine the receiving records and to compare the inventory of tapes with the accounting records.
3. Purchases of new tapes must be authorized by purchase order in the home office and paid for by the treasurer in the home office. Receiving reports are prepared in each branch and sent to the home office.
4. All new personnel receive one hour of training in how to receive and catalogue new tapes.
5. The company maintains a perpetual inventory system that keeps track of all tapes purchased, sold, and on hand.

Indicate by letter which of the following control procedures apply to each of the above policies. (Some may have several answers.)

a. Authorization
b. Recording transactions
c. Documents and records
d. Limited access
e. Periodic independent verification
f. Separation of duties
g. Sound personnel policies

E 12. *Internal Control*
L O 6 *Evaluation*
No check figure

Developing a convenient means of providing sales representatives with cash for their incidental expenses, such as entertaining a client at lunch, is a problem many companies face. Under one company's plan, the sales representatives receive advances in cash from the petty cash fund. Each advance is supported by an authorization from the sales manager. The representative returns the receipt for the expenditure and any unused cash, which is replaced in the petty cash fund. The cashier of the petty cash fund is responsible for seeing that the receipt and the cash returned equal the advance. When the petty cash fund is reimbursed, the amount of the representative's expenditure is debited to Direct Sales Expense.

What is the weak point in this system? What fundamental principle of internal control is being ignored? What improvement in the procedure can you suggest?

E 13. *Internal Control*
L O 6 *Evaluation*
No check figure

An accountant is responsible for the following procedures: (1) receiving all cash; (2) maintaining the general ledger; (3) maintaining the accounts receivable subsidiary ledger that includes the individual records of each customer; (4) maintaining the journals for recording sales, purchases, and cash receipts; and (5) preparing monthly statements to be sent to customers. As a service to customers and employees, the company allows the accountant to cash checks of up to $50 with money from the cash receipts. When deposits are made, the checks are included in place of the cash receipts.

What weaknesses in internal control exist in this system?

SKILLS DEVELOPMENT EXERCISES

Conceptual Analysis

SDE 1.
L O 6, 7, 8

System for Control of Supplies

No check figure

Industrial Services Company provides maintenance services to factories located in the West Bend, Wisconsin, area. The company, which buys large amounts of cleaning supplies, has consistently been over budget in its expenditures for those items. In the past, supplies were left open in the warehouse so that the on-site supervisors could take them as needed. Periodically, a clerk in the accounting department ordered additional supplies from a long-time supplier. The only records maintained were records of purchases. Once a year, an inventory of supplies was made for the preparation of the financial statements.

To solve the budgetary problem, management recently implemented a new system for controlling and purchasing supplies. Under the new system, the cleaning supplies were placed in a secured storeroom overseen by a supplies clerk. Supplies are requisitioned by the supervisors of specific jobs. Each job receives a predetermined amount of supplies based on a study of the needs of that job. In the storeroom, the supplies clerk notes the levels of supplies and completes a purchase requisition when supplies are needed. The purchase requisition goes to the purchasing clerk, a new position, who is solely responsible for authorizing purchases and who prepares the purchase orders for suppliers. The prices of several suppliers are constantly monitored to ensure that the lowest price is obtained. When supplies are received from a vendor, the supplies clerk checks them in and prepares a receiving report, which is sent to accounting, where each payment to a supplier is documented by the purchase requisition, the purchase order, and the receiving report. The accounting department also maintains a record of supplies inventory, supplies requisitioned by supervisors, and supplies received. Once each month, a physical inventory of cleaning supplies in the storeroom is made by the warehouse manager and compared against the supplies inventory records maintained by the accounting department.

Demonstrate how the new system applies or does not apply to each of the seven control procedures described in this chapter. Is each new control procedure an improvement over the old system?

Ethical Dilemma

SDE 2.
L O 2

Confidentiality of Accounting Records

No check figure

Frank Santino is the accounting manager at the Ford and Toyota dealership in Petersburg, Texas, a town with a population of 50,000. At a Friday evening barbecue, José Martinez, a close friend, mentions that he is planning to sell some land to Louis Johnson for $20,000 and will allow Johnson to pay him over a five-year period. Santino, who happened to be reviewing the delinquent accounts at the dealership earlier in the day, knows that Johnson has a poor payment history and that his car may have to be repossessed. Martinez asks Santino what he thinks about the sale. What ethical issue is involved here? If you were Santino, would you warn Martinez about Johnson's credit record?

Research Activity

SDE 3.
L O 6, 7, 8

Internal Control Systems

No check figure

Visit a local outlet of a national retail chain—a fast-food restaurant, a music store, or a store selling jeans or other clothing. Observe for one hour and record as much as you can about the company's internal control structure. It is usually best to conduct the observation at a busy time of day. How would you go about assessing the control environment? Are any aspects of the company's accounting system apparent? What control procedures, including authorization, recording transactions, documents and records, limited access, periodic independent verification, separation of duties, and sound personnel policies, can you observe? Be prepared to discuss your observations in class.

Decision-Making Practice

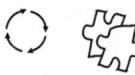
RW Finer Foods Company, owned by Robert Washington, is a neighborhood grocery store that accepts cash or checks in payment for food. Known for its informality, the store has been very successful and has grown with the community. Along with that growth, however, has come an increase in the number of bad checks customers have written for purchases. Washington is concerned about the difficulty of accounting for these returned checks, so he has asked you to look into the problem.

In addition to a purchases journal and a cash payments journal, the company has a combination single-column sales and cash receipts journal. The combination journal has worked in the past because all sales are for cash (including checks), and almost all cash receipts represent sales transactions. Thus, the single column represents a debit to Cash and a credit to Sales.

The bad checks are recorded individually in the general journal by debiting Accounts Receivable and crediting Cash for the amount of the check and returned check revenue for the amount of $10, which represents reimbursement of the service charge by the bank. When a customer pays off a bad check, another entry is made in the general journal debiting Cash and crediting Accounts Receivable. Washington keeps the returned checks in an envelope. When a customer comes in to pay one off, Washington gives the check back. No other records of the returned checks are maintained.

In studying the problem, you discover that the company is averaging ten returned checks a day, totaling $1,000. As part of the solution, you recommend that Washington issue check-cashing cards to customers whose credit is approved in advance. The card must be presented when a customer offers a check in payment for groceries. You recommend further that a special-purpose journal be established for the returned checks and returned check revenue, that a subsidiary ledger be maintained, and that the combination sales/cash receipts journal be expanded.

1. Draw and label the columns for the new returned checks journal and the expanded sales/cash receipts journal.
2. Assume that there are 300 returned checks and 280 collections per month and that the records are closed each month. How many written lines can be saved each month by recording returned checks and subsequent collections in the special journals? How many postings can be saved each month? (Ignore the effect of the subsidiary ledger.)
3. Describe the nature and use of the subsidiary ledger. What advantages do you see in having a subsidiary ledger?
4. Assuming that it takes approximately two and a half minutes to make each entry and related postings under the old system of recording bad checks and one minute to make each entry and related postings under the new system, what are the monthly savings if the cost is $20 an hour? What further, and possibly more significant, savings may be realized by using the new system?

PROBLEM SET A

Sachs Company, a small retail business, uses a manual accounting system similar to the one illustrated in this chapter. At the end of May 19xx, the accounts in the accounts receivable and accounts payable subsidiary ledgers showed the following balances.

Accounts Receivable		Accounts Payable	
T. Bakof	$ 870	Cellcor, Inc.	$2,900
R. Banz	650	Visidyne Company	460
Total accounts receivable	$1,520	Total accounts payable	$3,360

During June, the company engaged in the transactions listed on the next page.

June 2 Sold merchandise on credit to R. Banz, terms 2/10, n/30, invoice no. 4001, $920.
4 Received payment in full from R. Banz for the amount due at the beginning of June less a 2 percent discount.
5 Paid Cellcor, Inc. the full amount owed less a 2 percent discount, check no. 501.
8 Agreed to accept a return of merchandise from R. Banz, $220.
9 Paid Visidyne Company the full amount owed, no discount allowed, check no. 502.
12 Received payment from R. Banz for the amount due less the return and a 2 percent discount.
15 Received partial payment from T. Bakof, no discount allowed, $300.
22 Purchased merchandise from Visidyne Company, terms 2/10, n/30, FOB destination, invoice dated June 21, $1,700.
23 Sold merchandise on credit to F. Younger, terms 2/10, n/30, invoice no. 4002, $2,450.
26 Purchased merchandise from Cellcor, Inc., terms 2/10, n/30, FOB destination, invoice dated June 24, $1,500.
30 Returned merchandise to Visidyne Company for full credit, $600.

REQUIRED

1. Prepare a sales journal, a single-column purchases journal, a cash receipts journal, a cash payments journal, and a general journal similar to the ones illustrated in the chapter. Use Page 1 for all references.
2. Open general ledger accounts for Accounts Receivable (112) and Accounts Payable (211).
3. Open accounts receivable subsidiary ledger accounts for T. Bakof, R. Banz, and F. Younger.
4. Open accounts payable subsidiary ledger accounts for Cellcor, Inc. and Visidyne Company.
5. Enter the transactions in the journals and post to the appropriate subsidiary ledger and general ledger accounts.
6. Foot and crossfoot the journals, and make the end-of-month postings applicable to Accounts Receivable and Accounts Payable.
7. Prove the control balances of Accounts Receivable and Accounts Payable by preparing schedules of accounts receivable and accounts payable.

A 2.
L O 5
Cash Receipts and Cash Payments Journals

Check Figures: Cash total in cash receipts journal: $66,968; Cash total in cash payments journal: $28,644

Baylor Company engaged in the following cash transactions during July. The company uses multicolumn cash receipts and cash payments journals similar to those illustrated in the chapter.

July 1 The owner, Eugene Baylor, invested $50,000 cash and $24,000 in equipment in the business.
2 Paid rent to Leonard Agency with check no. 75, $600.
3 Cash sales, $2,200.
6 Purchased store equipment from Gilmore Company with check no. 76, $5,000.
7 Purchased merchandise from Pascual Company with check no. 77, $6,500.
8 Paid Audretti Company invoice with check no. 78, $1,800, less 2 percent discount. (Assume that a payable has already been recorded.)
9 Paid advertising bill to WOSU with check no. 79, $350.
10 Cash sales, $3,910.
12 Received payment on account from B. Erring, $800.
13 Purchased used truck from Pettit Company with check no. 80, $3,520.
19 Received payment from Monroe Company in settlement of a $4,000 note plus interest, $4,180.
20 Received payment from Young Lee, $1,100, less $22 cash discount.
21 Issued Eugene Baylor check no. 81 for personal use, $2,000.
23 Paid Dautley Company invoice with check no. 82, $2,500, less 2 percent discount.
26 Paid Haywood Company with check no. 83 for freight on merchandise received, $60.

July 27 Cash sales, $4,800.

    28 Paid C. Murphy for monthly salary with check no. 84, $1,400.

    31 Purchased land from N. Archibald for $20,000, paying $5,000 with check no. 85 and signing a note payable for $15,000.

REQUIRED

1. Enter the preceding transactions in the cash receipts and cash payments journals.
2. Foot and crossfoot the journals.

A 3. *Purchases and*
L O 4, 5 *General Journals*

Check Figure: Accounts Payable total: $16,464

Below are the credit transactions for McGarry Company during the month of August. The company uses a multicolumn purchases journal and a general journal similar to those illustrated in the text.

Aug. 2 Purchased merchandise from Alvarez Company, $1,400.

     5 Purchased a truck to be used in the business from Meriweather Company, $8,000.

     8 Purchased office supplies from Dandridge Company, $400.

   12 Purchased filing cabinets from Dandridge Company, $550.

   14 Purchased merchandise, $1,400, and store supplies, $200, from Petrie Company.

   17 Purchased store supplies from Alvarez Company, $100, and office supplies from Hollins Company, $50.

   20 Purchased merchandise from Petrie Company, $1,472.

   24 Purchased merchandise from Alvarez Company, $2,452; the $2,452 invoice total included shipping charges, $232.

   26 Purchased office supplies from Dandridge Company, $150.

   30 Purchased merchandise from Petrie Company, $290.

   31 Returned for full credit defective merchandise purchased from Petrie Company on August 20, $432.

REQUIRED

1. Enter the preceding transactions in the purchases journal and the general journal. Assume that all terms are n/30 and that invoice dates are the same as the transaction dates. Use Page 1 for all references.
2. Foot and crossfoot the purchases journal.
3. Open the following general ledger accounts: Store Supplies (116), Office Supplies (117), Trucks (142), Office Equipment (144), Accounts Payable (211), Purchases (611), Purchases Returns and Allowances (612), and Freight In (613). Open accounts payable subsidiary ledger accounts as needed. Post from the journals to the ledger accounts.

A 4. *Comprehensive Use*
L O 4, 5 *of Special-Purpose*
        Journals

Check Figure: Trial balance: $42,292

The following transactions were completed by Lezcano's Men's Wear during the month of July, its first month of operation.

July   2 Carlos Lezcano deposited $20,000 cash in the new company's bank account.

     3 Issued check no. 101 to Rollins Realty for one month's rent, $1,200.

     4 Received merchandise from Garnett Company, invoice dated July 3, terms 2/10, n/60, FOB shipping point, $7,000.

     5 Received from Wiggins Company freight bill on merchandise purchased, terms n/20, $964.

     6 Issued check no. 102 to Bagley Company for store equipment, $7,400.

     7 Signed a 90-day, 9 percent note for a bank loan and received $8,000 in cash.

     8 Cash sales for the first week, $1,982. (To shorten this problem, cash sales are recorded weekly instead of daily, as they would be in actual practice.)

   10 Sold merchandise to Midlands School, terms 2/10, n/30, invoice no. 1001, $900.

   11 Sold merchandise to Charlotte Soo, terms n/20, invoice no. 1002, $300.

   12 Purchased advertising in the *Journal-Citizen,* terms n/15, $150.

   13 Issued check no. 103 for purchase of July 4 less discount.

   14 Issued a credit memorandum for merchandise returned by Charlotte Soo, $30.

   15 Cash sales for the second week, $3,492.

   17 Received merchandise from Garnett Company, invoice dated July 16, terms 2/10, n/60, FOB shipping point, $1,900.

   18 Received from Wiggins Company freight bill on merchandise purchased, terms n/20, $262.

July 19 Received merchandise from Law Company, invoice dated July 17, terms 1/10, n/60, FOB destination, $1,400.

20 Received payment in full less discount from Midlands School.

21 Received a credit memorandum from Garnett Company for merchandise returned, $100.

22 Cash sales for third week, $2,912.

24 Issued check no. 104 for total amount owed Wiggins Company.

25 Sold merchandise to Midlands School, terms 2/10, n/30, invoice no. 1003, $684.

26 Issued check no. 105 in payment of amount owed Garnett Company less discount.

27 Sold merchandise to Al Kaiser, terms n/20, invoice no. 1004, $372.

28 Issued check no. 106 for amount owed the *Journal-Citizen*.

29 Cash sales for the fourth week, $1,974.

31 Issued check no. 107 to Payroll for sales salaries for the month of July, $3,600.

REQUIRED

1. Prepare a sales journal, a multicolumn purchases journal, a cash receipts journal, a cash payments journal, and a general journal. Use Page 1 for all journal references.
2. Open the following general ledger accounts: Cash (111); Accounts Receivable (112); Store Equipment (141); Accounts Payable (211); Notes Payable (212); Carlos Lezcano, Capital (311); Sales (411); Sales Discounts (412); Sales Returns and Allowances (413); Purchases (511); Purchases Discounts (512); Purchases Returns and Allowances (513); Freight In (514); Sales Salaries Expense (611); Advertising Expense (612); and Rent Expense (613).
3. Open accounts receivable subsidiary ledger accounts for Al Kaiser, Midlands School, and Charlotte Soo.
4. Open accounts payable subsidiary ledger accounts for Garnett Company, the *Journal-Citizen*, Law Company, and Wiggins Company.
5. Enter the transactions in the journals and post as appropriate.
6. Foot and crossfoot the journals, and make the end-of-month postings.
7. Prepare a trial balance of the general ledger and prove the control balances of Accounts Receivable and Accounts Payable by preparing schedules of accounts receivable and accounts payable.

A 5. *Internal Control*
L O 6, 8 *Procedures*
No check figure

Langley Printers makes printers for personal computers and maintains a factory outlet showroom through which it sells its products to the public. The company's management has set up a system of internal controls over the inventory of printers to prevent theft and to ensure the accuracy of the accounting records.

All printers in inventory at the factory outlet are kept in a secured warehouse behind the showroom, except for the sample printers on display. Only authorized personnel may enter the warehouse. When a customer buys a printer, a sales invoice is written in triplicate by the cashier and is marked "paid." The sales invoices are sequentially numbered, and all must be accounted for. The cashier sends the pink copy of the completed invoice to the warehouse, gives the blue copy to the customer, and keeps the green copy. The customer drives around to the warehouse entrance. The warehouse attendant takes the blue copy of the invoice from the customer and gives the customer the printer and the pink copy of the invoice.

The company maintains a perpetual inventory system for the printers at the outlet. The warehouse attendant at the outlet signs an inventory transfer sheet for each printer received. An accountant at the factory is assigned responsibility for maintaining the inventory records based on copies of the inventory transfer sheets and the sales invoices. The records are updated daily and may be accessed by computer but not modified by the sales personnel and the warehouse attendant. The accountant also sees that all prenumbered inventory transfer sheets are accounted for and compares copies of them with the ones signed by the warehouse attendant. Once every three months the company's internal auditor takes a physical count of the printer inventory and compares the results with the perpetual inventory records.

All new employees are required to read a sales and inventory manual and receive a two-hour training session about the internal controls. They must demonstrate that they can perform the functions required of them.

REQUIRED Give an example of how each of the following internal control procedures is applied to the printer inventory at Langley Printers's outlet showroom: authorization, recording transactions, documents and records, limited access, periodic independent verification, separation of duties, and sound personnel procedures. Do not address controls over cash.

PROBLEM SET B

B 1. *Special-Purpose*
L O 4, 5 *Journals and Subsidiary Ledgers*

Check Figures: May 31 Accounts Receivable debit balance: $870; May 31 Accounts Payable credit balance: $2,100

Manner Company is a small retail business that uses a manual accounting system similar to the one described in this chapter. At the end of April 19xx, the firm's accounts receivable and accounts payable subsidiary ledgers showed the following balances.

Accounts Receivable		Accounts Payable	
A. Barlett	$430	Baylor Company	$1,300
L. Lozowich	330	Gentrol Company	890
Total Accounts Receivable	$760	Total Accounts Payable	$2,190

During May, the company engaged in the following transactions.

May 2 Sold merchandise on credit to R. Wood, a new customer, terms 2/10, n/30, invoice no. 1001, $570.
4 Received payment in full from L. Lozowich, no discount allowed.
5 Paid Baylor Company the full amount owed less a 2 percent discount, check no. 201.
8 Agreed to accept a return of merchandise for credit from R. Wood, $170.
9 Paid Gentrol Company the full amount owed, no discount allowed, check no. 202.
12 Received payment from R. Wood for amount due less discount.
15 Received partial payment from A. Barlett, no discount allowed, $230.
22 Purchased merchandise from Baylor Company, terms 2/10, n/30, FOB destination, invoice dated May 22, $1,200.
23 Sold merchandise on credit to L. Lozowich, terms 2/10, n/30, invoice no. 1002, $670.
26 Purchased merchandise from Gentrol Company, terms 2/10, n/30, FOB destination, invoice dated May 23, $1,500.
31 Returned merchandise to Gentrol Company for full credit, $600.

REQUIRED

1. Prepare a single-column sales journal, a single-column purchases journal, a cash receipts journal, a cash payments journal, and a general journal similar to the ones illustrated in the chapter. Use Page 1 for all references.
2. Open general ledger accounts for Accounts Receivable (112) and Accounts Payable (211).
3. Open accounts receivable subsidiary ledger accounts for A. Barlett, L. Lozowich, and R. Wood.
4. Open accounts payable subsidiary ledger accounts for Baylor Company and Gentrol Company.
5. Enter the transactions in the journals and post to the appropriate subsidiary ledger and general ledger accounts.
6. Foot and crossfoot the journals, and make the end-of-month postings applicable to Accounts Receivable and Accounts Payable.
7. Prove the control balances of Accounts Receivable and Accounts Payable by preparing schedules of accounts receivable and accounts payable.

B 2. *Cash Receipts*
L O 5 *and Cash Payments Journals*

Horton Company is a small retail business that uses a manual data processing system similar to the one illustrated in the chapter. Among its special-purpose journals are multicolumn cash receipts and cash payments journals. The cash transactions for Horton Company during the month of June are listed on the next page.

June 1 Paid June rent to P. Nguyen with check no. 782, $500.
    2 Paid Moritz Wholesale on account with check no. 783, $1,150 less a 2 percent discount.
    3 Received payment on account from B. Fischer, $500 less a 2 percent discount.
    4 Cash sales, $1,316.
    7 Paid Jarvis Freight on account with check no. 784, $299.
    8 The owner, Willis Horton, invested an additional $5,000 in cash and a truck valued at $7,000 in the business.
    10 Paid Clear Supply on account with check no. 785, $142.
    11 Cash sales, $1,417.
    14 Paid Jarvis Freight with check no. 786 for freight on shipment of merchandise received today, $155.
    15 Paid Marks Company on account with check no. 787, $800 less a 2 percent discount.
    16 Received payment on account from G. Derby, $60.
    19 Cash sales, $987.
    20 Received payment on a note receivable, $900 plus $18 interest.
    21 Purchased office supplies from Clear Supply, with check no. 788, $54.
    22 Paid a note payable in full to Midwest Bank, with check no. 789, $2,050, including $50 interest.
    26 Cash sales, $1,482.
    27 Paid Moritz Wholesale on account with check no. 790, $250 less a 2 percent discount.
    28 Paid Mary Dillard, a sales clerk, her monthly salary, with check no. 791, $550.
    29 Purchased equipment from Sands Corporation for $8,000, paying $2,000 with check no. 792 and signing a note payable for the difference.
    30 Issued Willis Horton check no. 793 for personal use, $600.

REQUIRED

1. Enter the preceding transactions in the cash receipts and cash payments journals.
2. Foot and crossfoot the journals.

B 3. *Purchases and*
L O 4, 5 *General Journals*
Check Figure: Accounts Payable total: $11,209

Milner Lawn Supply Company uses a multicolumn purchases journal and general journal similar to those illustrated in the text. The company also maintains an accounts payable subsidiary ledger. Below are the company's credit transactions for the month of October.

Oct. 3 Purchased merchandise from Hong Fertilizer Company, $1,320.
    4 Purchased office supplies of $83 and store supplies of $104 from Ferrara Supply, Inc.
    7 Purchased cleaning equipment from Sinclair Company, $928.
    10 Purchased display equipment from Ferrara Supply, Inc., $2,350.
    14 Purchased lawn mowers from Medina Lawn Equipment Company, for resale, $4,200 (which included transportation charges of $175).
    15 Purchased merchandise from Hong Fertilizer Company, $1,722.
    19 Purchased a lawn mower from Medina Lawn Equipment Company to be used by the business, $475 (which included transportation charges of $35).
    24 Purchased store supplies from Ferrara Supply, Inc., $27.
    25 Returned a defective lawn mower purchased on October 14 for full credit, $375.

REQUIRED

1. Enter the preceding transactions in a multicolumn purchases journal and the general journal. Assume that all terms are n/30 and that invoice dates are the same as the transaction dates. Use Page 2 for the page numbers of all journals.
2. Foot and crossfoot the purchases journal.
3. Open the following general ledger accounts: Store Supplies (116), Office Supplies (117), Lawn Equipment (142), Display Equipment (144), Cleaning Equipment (146), Accounts Payable (211), Purchases (611), Purchases Returns and Allowances (612), and Freight In (613). Open accounts payable subsidiary ledger accounts as needed. Post from the journals to the ledger accounts.

B 4. *Comprehensive Use*
L O 4, 5 *of Special-Purpose*
Journals
Check Figure: Trial balance: $45,808

Scott Bookstore opened its doors for business on September 1. During September, the following transactions took place.

Sept. 1 Cynthia Scott started the business by depositing $21,000 cash in the new company's bank account.

2 Issued check no. C001 to Page Rentals for one month's rent, $500.

3 Received a shipment of books from Gray Books, Inc., invoice dated September 2, terms 5/10, n/60, FOB shipping point, $7,840.

4 Received a bill for freight from All Points Shippers for the previous day's shipment, terms n/30, $395.

5 Received a shipment from Choice Books, invoice dated September 5, terms 2/10, n/30, FOB shipping point, $5,650.

6 Issued check no. C002 to Selby Freight, Inc. for transportation charges on the previous day's shipment, $287.

8 Issued check no. C003 to Urban Equipment Company for store equipment, $5,200.

9 Sold books to Spectrum Center, terms 5/10, n/30, invoice no. 1001, $782.

10 Returned books to Gray Books, Inc. for credit, $380.

11 Issued check no. C004 to WBNS for radio commercials, $235.

12 Issued check no. C005 to Gray Books, Inc., for balance of amount owed less discount.

13 Cash sales for the first two weeks, $2,009. (To shorten this problem, cash sales are recorded every two weeks instead of daily, as they would be in actual practice.)

15 Issued check no. C006 to Choice Books, $3,000 less discount.

16 Signed a 90-day, 10 percent note for a bank loan and received $10,000 in cash.

17 Sold books to Joe Prokop, terms n/30, invoice no. 1002, $130.

18 Issued a credit memorandum to Spectrum Center for returned books, $62.

19 Received payment in full from Spectrum Center for balance owed less discount.

20 Sold books to Joyce Monsoya, terms n/30, invoice no. 1003, $97.

22 Received a shipment from Temple Publishing Company, invoice dated September 21, terms 5/10, n/60, $2,302.

23 Returned additional books purchased on Sept. 3 to Gray Books, Inc., for credit at gross price, $718.

24 Sold books to Spectrum Center, terms 5/10, n/30, invoice no. 1004, $817.

25 Received a shipment from Gray Books, Inc., invoice dated September 22, terms 5/10, n/60, FOB shipping point, $1,187.

26 Issued check no. C007 to All Points Shippers for balance owed on account plus shipping charges of $97 on previous day's shipment.

27 Cash sales for the second two weeks, $3,744.

29 Issued check no. C008 to Payroll for sales salaries for first four weeks of the month, $700.

30 Cash sales for the last two days of the month, $277.

REQUIRED

1. Prepare a sales journal, a multicolumn purchases journal, a cash receipts journal, a cash payments journal, and a general journal. Use Page 1 for all journal references.

2. Open the following general ledger accounts: Cash (111); Accounts Receivable (112); Store Equipment (141); Accounts Payable (211); Notes Payable (212); Cynthia Scott, Capital (311); Sales (411); Sales Discounts (412); Sales Returns and Allowances (413); Purchases (511); Purchases Discounts (512); Purchases Returns and Allowances (513); Freight In (514); Sales Salaries Expense (611); Advertising Expense (612); and Rent Expense (613).

3. Open accounts receivable subsidiary ledger accounts for Joyce Monsoya, Joe Prokop, and Spectrum Center.

4. Open accounts payable subsidiary ledger accounts for All Points Shippers; Choice Books; Gray Books, Inc.; and Temple Publishing Company.

5. Enter the transactions in the journals and post as appropriate.

6. Foot and crossfoot the journals, and make the end-of-month postings.

7. Prepare a trial balance of the general ledger, and prove the control balances of Accounts Receivable and Accounts Payable by preparing schedules of accounts receivable and accounts payable.

B 5. *Internal Control*
L O 6, 8 *Procedures*
No check figure

Maris Sports Shop is a small neighborhood sporting goods store. The shop's owner, Robert Maris, has set up a system of internal control over sales to prevent theft and to ensure the accuracy of the accounting records.

When a customer buys a product, the cashier writes up a sales invoice that describes the purchase, including the total price. All sales invoices are prenumbered sequentially.

If the sale is by credit card, the cashier runs the credit card through a scanner that verifies the customer's credit. The scanner prints out a receipt and a slip for the customer to sign. The signed slip is put in the cash register, and the customer is given the receipt and a copy of the sales invoice.

If the sale is by cash or check, the cashier rings it up on the cash register and gives change, if appropriate. Checks must be written for the exact amount of the purchase and must be accompanied by identification. The sale is recorded on a tape inside the cash register that cannot be accessed by the cashier. The cash register may be locked with a key. The cashier is the only person other than Maris who has a key. The cash register must be locked when the cashier is not present. Refunds are made only with the approval of the owner, are recorded on prenumbered credit memorandum forms, and are rung up on the cash register.

At the end of each day, Maris counts the cash and checks in the cash register and compares the total with the amount recorded on the tape inside the register. Maris totals all the signed credit card slips and ensures that the total equals the amount recorded by the scanner. Maris also makes sure that all sales invoices and credit memoranda are accounted for. Maris prepares a bank deposit ticket for the cash, checks, and signed credit card slips, less $40 in change to be put in the cash register the next day, and removes the record of the day's credit card sales from the scanner. All the records are placed in an envelope that is sealed and sent to the company's accountant for verification and recording in the company records. On the way home, Maris places the bank deposit in the night deposit box.

The company hires experienced cashiers who are bonded. The owner spends the first half-day with new cashiers, showing them the procedures and overlooking their work.

REQUIRED

Give an example of how each of the following control procedures is applied to internal control over sales and cash at Maris Sports Shop: authorization, recording transactions, documents and records, limited access, periodic independent verification, separation of duties, and sound personnel procedures. Do not address controls over inventory.

FINANCIAL REPORTING AND ANALYSIS CASES

Interpreting Financial Reports

FRA 1. *Computerized*
L O 1, 2 *Inventory*
System Design

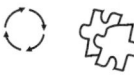

No check figure

In the mid-1960s, a new and tempting mass market was emerging. Americans were becoming better educated and more affluent. Also, the increasing number of shopping centers provided the perfect setting for a chain of national bookstores. Taking advantage of this opportunity, Minneapolis-based Dayton-Hudson Corporation launched its *B. Dalton Bookseller,* and Los Angeles-based Carter Hawley Hale began expanding its *Waldenbooks* division. By 1982, these two chains were by far the biggest book retailers in the country and were very competitive with each other. Dalton had 575 stores and planned to add 556 more by 1987. Waldenbooks had 750 outlets and planned to add 80 to 90 more each year.

Forbes magazine reported that although Waldenbooks had more outlets, Dalton "looks like the leader in the fight." Each chain had roughly $250 million in sales in 1980, but Dalton sold an estimated $132 worth of books per square foot of store space to Waldenbooks' $114. *Forbes* stated that "a computerized inventory system installed in 1966 is what gives Dalton its edge—and is a key to why its 10% pretax profits are well above Walden's." In the book business today, "Success depends far more on fast, high efficiency distribution than on any fundamental appreciation of literature. . . .

Order a little of everything and remain secure in your capabilities to restock quickly those titles the computer says are selling fast."[5]

1. Describe how you believe the four principles of systems design would have been applied to the design of Dalton's computerized inventory system in 1966 so that Dalton could grow rapidly and become more profitable than Waldenbooks.
2. Describe how the following parts of a computerized inventory system would allow Dalton to restock fast-selling books quickly: source documents, data input, processing, information output, and distribution.

International Company

FRA 2.
L O 6
Internal Control and Accounting Education in a Developing Country

No check figure

Zambia, a country in southern Africa, has 8.5 million inhabitants. It has an elected government and is moving toward capital markets through privatization of government-owned business. For example, the government-owned beer company was recently sold to private interests for $13 million. One national priority calls for the training of competent professional accountants, and the *Zambian Centre for Accountancy Studies* has been established with the assistance of the World Bank. There are only about 250 native-born certified accountants in all of Zambia. A state with a comparable population in the United States would have more than 20,000 certified public accountants. One reason for placing a priority on the training of accountants is the importance of good internal controls to the development of a country like Zambia. What are the purposes of internal control, and what are some ways in which such controls would aid the development of a country like Zambia? What are some other reasons for making accounting education a high national priority?

Toys "R" Us Annual Report

FRA 3.
L O 1, 6, 8
Principles of Accounting Systems Design and Internal Control

No check figure

Part One:

Refer to the annual report for Toys "R" Us in the appendix. In the Operational Highlights portion of the To the Stockholders section, management states that its goal is "to provide the best selection of merchandise, stocked in depth with everyday low prices while expanding customer service and maintaining one of the lowest expense structures in the industry." To do this, the company uses satellite technology in North America that instantaneously links stores with headquarters' computer databases to make ordering, inventory control, and customer transaction authorization more cost efficient. Explain how this computer technology and centralized databases complies with the principles of cost-benefit, control, compatibility, and flexibility.

Part Two:

How many stores did Toys "R" Us operate on January 28, 1995 in the United States and abroad? The typical Toys "R" Us store is a large building that contains a showroom where customers wheel grocery carts down aisles to select toys and other products for purchase, a warehouse where larger items may be picked up after purchase, a bank of cash registers, and a service desk where returns and other unusual transactions can be authorized. Identify the main activities or transactions for which Toys "R" Us management would need to establish internal control in each new store. Discuss in general terms the objectives of internal control in each case.

---

5. Jeff Blyskal, "Dalton, Walden and the Amazing Money Machine," *Forbes*, January 18, 1982, p. 47.

PART THREE

Measuring and Reporting Assets and Current Liabilities

CHAPTER 8
Short-Term Liquid Assets

focuses on the management and accounting issues associated with the major types of short-term liquid assets: cash and short-term investments, accounts receivable, and notes receivable.

CHAPTER 9
Inventories

presents the management issues and accounting concepts and techniques associated with inventories and discusses their importance to income measurement. Emphasis is placed on the methods of pricing inventory.

CHAPTER 10
Long-Term Assets

discusses the management and accounting issues associated with the acquisition of property, plant, and equipment and the concept and methods of depreciation. It also presents the management and accounting issues associated with the disposal of depreciable assets and with other long-term assets such as natural resources and intangible assets.

CHAPTER 11
Current Liabilities

deals with the management and accounting issues associated with current liabilities, contingent liabilities, and payroll accounting.

CHAPTER 8

Short-Term Liquid Assets

LEARNING OBJECTIVES

1. Identify and explain the management issues related to short-term liquid assets.
2. Define *cash* and *cash equivalents*.
3. Account for short-term investments.
4. Define *accounts receivable* and apply the allowance method of accounting for uncollectible accounts, using both the percentage of net sales method and the accounts receivable aging method.
5. Define and describe a *promissory note*, and make calculations and journal entries involving promissory notes.

SUPPLEMENTAL OBJECTIVE

6. Account for credit card transactions.

Bell Atlantic Corporation

DECISION POINT

A company must use its assets to maximize income earned while maintaining liquidity. Bell Atlantic Corporation, a leading provider of voice and data communications, mobile telephone services, computer maintenance services, and equipment leasing and financing products, manages almost $3 billion in short-term liquid assets. Short-term liquid assets are financial assets that arise from cash transactions, the investment of cash, and the extension of credit. What is the composition of these assets? Why are they important to Bell Atlantic's management?

As reported on the balance sheet in the company's 1992 annual report, short-term liquid assets (in millions) were:[1]

Cash and Cash Equivalents	$ 296.0
Short-Term Investments	33.7
Accounts Receivable, Net of Allowances of $123.9	2,023.8
Notes Receivable, Net	605.0
Total Short-Term Liquid Assets	$2,958.5

These assets make up only a little more than 10 percent of Bell Atlantic's total assets, yet they are very important to the company's strategy for meeting its goals. Effective asset management techniques ensure that these assets remain liquid and usable for the company's operations.

A commonly used ratio for measuring the adequacy of short-term liquid assets is the quick ratio. The quick ratio is the ratio of short-term liquid assets to current liabilities. Since Bell Atlantic's current liabilities are $5,872,200,000, its quick ratio is .5, computed as follows:

$$\text{Quick ratio} = \frac{\text{quick assets}}{\text{current liabilities}} = \frac{\$2,958,500,000}{\$5,872,200,000} = .5$$

A quick ratio of about 1.0 is a common benchmark, but it is more important to look at industry characteristics and at the trends for a particular company to see if the ratio is improving or not. Bell Atlantic has maintained a quick ratio of .5 over several years. Through good cash management, the company has gotten by with fewer funds tied up in quick assets relative to current liabilities. This chapter emphasizes management of, and accounting for, short-term liquid assets to achieve liquidity. : : : : :

1. Bell Atlantic Corporation, *Annual Report,* 1992.

1 *Identify and explain the management issues related to short-term liquid assets*

MANAGEMENT ISSUES RELATED TO SHORT-TERM LIQUID ASSETS

The management of short-term liquid assets is critical to the goal of providing adequate liquidity. In dealing with short-term liquid assets, management must address three key issues: managing cash needs during seasonal cycles, setting credit policies, and financing receivables.

MANAGING CASH NEEDS DURING SEASONAL CYCLES

Most companies experience seasonal cycles of business activity during the year. These cycles involve some periods when sales are weak and other periods when sales are strong. There are also periods when expenditures are greater and periods when expenditures are smaller. In some companies, such as toy companies, college publishers, amusement parks, construction companies, and sports equipment companies, the cycles are dramatic, but all companies experience them to some degree.

Seasonal cycles require careful planning of cash inflows, outflows, borrowing, and investing. For example, Figure 1 might represent the seasonal cycles for a home improvement company like The Home Depot. As you can see, cash receipts from sales are highest in the late spring, summer, and fall because that is when most people make home improvements. Sales are relatively low in the winter months. On the other hand, cash expenditures are highest in late winter and spring as the company builds up inventory for spring and summer selling. During the late summer, fall, and winter, the company has excess cash on hand that it needs to invest in a way that will earn a return yet permit access as needed. During the late spring and early summer, the company needs to plan for short-term borrowing to tide it over until cash receipts pick up later in the year. The discussion of accounting for cash, cash equivalents, and short-term investments in this chapter is directly related to managing for the seasonal cycles of a business.

Figure 1. Seasonal Cycles and Cash Requirements for a Home Improvement Company

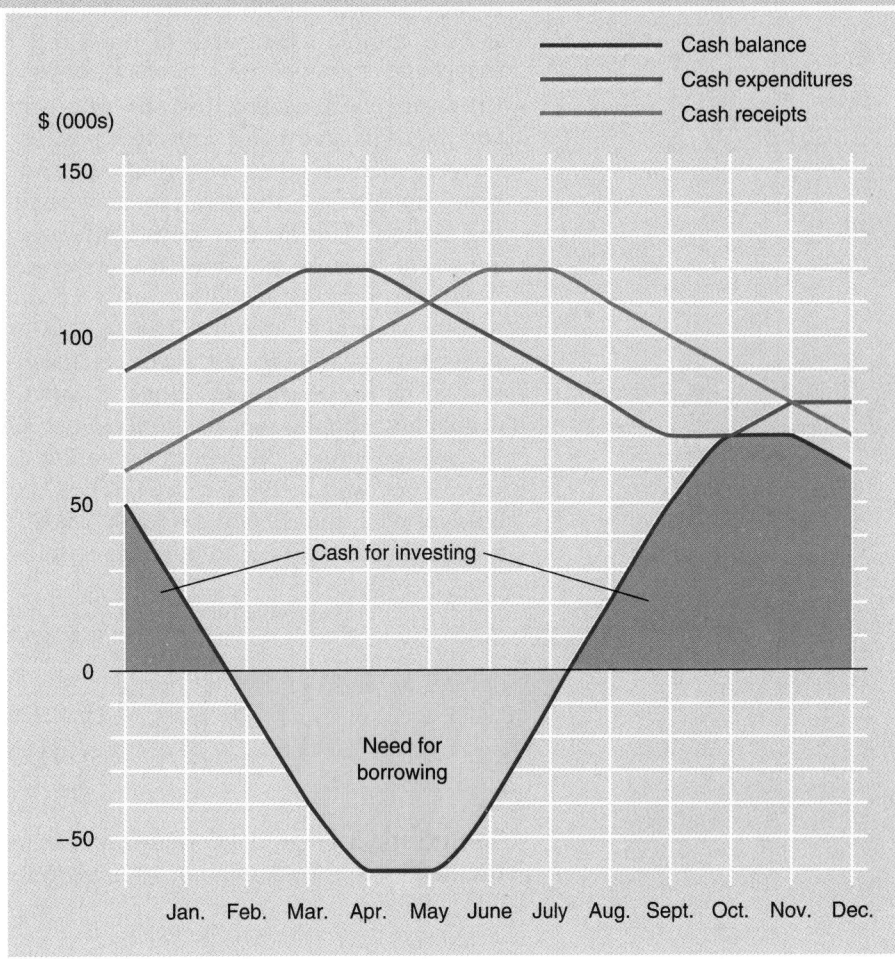

crunch forced the company to close down. When the shopping network finally paid for the big order six months later, it was too late to revive Earthly Elements.[2]

SETTING CREDIT POLICIES

Companies that sell on credit do so to be competitive and to increase sales. In setting credit terms, management must keep in mind both the terms their competitors are offering and the needs of their customers. Obviously, companies that sell on credit want customers who will pay the debts they incur. To increase the likelihood of selling only to customers who will pay when they are supposed to, most companies develop control procedures and maintain a credit department. The credit department's responsibilities include the examination of each person or company that applies for credit and the approval or rejection of a credit sale to that customer. Typically, the credit department will ask for information about the customer's financial resources and debts. It

2. Michael Selz, "Big Customers' Late Bills Choke Small Suppliers," *Wall Street Journal*, June 22, 1994.

may also check personal references and credit bureaus for further information. Then, based on the information it has gathered, the credit department will decide whether to extend credit to the customer.

Two common measures of the effect of a company's credit policies are receivable turnover and average days' sales uncollected. The receivable turnover reflects the relative size of a company's accounts receivable and the success of its credit and collection policies. It may also be affected by external factors, such as seasonal conditions and interest rates. It shows how many times, on average, the receivables were turned into cash during the accounting period. The average days' sales uncollected is a related measure that shows, on average, how long it takes to collect accounts receivable.

Turnover ratios usually consist of one balance sheet account and one income statement account. The receivable turnover is computed by dividing net sales by average net accounts receivable. Theoretically, the numerator should be net credit sales, but the amount of net credit sales is rarely made available in public reports, so total net sales is used. American Greetings is the second largest producer of greeting cards in the United States. The company's net sales in 1993 were $1,671,692,000, and its net trade accounts receivable in 1992 and 1993 were $264,125,000 and $276,932,000, respectively.[3] Its receivable turnover is computed as follows:

$$\text{Receivable turnover} = \frac{\text{net sales}}{\text{average net accounts receivable}}$$

$$= \frac{\$1,671,692,000}{(\$264,125,000 + \$276,932,000) \div 2}$$

$$= \frac{\$1,671,692,000}{\$270,528,500} = 6.2 \text{ times}$$

To find the average days' sales uncollected, the number of days in a year is divided by the receivable turnover, as follows:

$$\text{Average days' sales uncollected} = \frac{365 \text{ days}}{\text{receivable turnover}} = \frac{365 \text{ days}}{6.2} = 58.9 \text{ days}$$

American Greetings turns its receivables 6.2 times a year, for an average of every 58.9 days. While this turnover period is longer than those of many companies, it is not unusual for greeting card companies because their credit terms allow retail outlets to receive and sell cards for various holidays, such as Easter, Thanksgiving, and Christmas, before paying for them. This example demonstrates the need to interpret ratios in light of the specific industry's practice. As may be seen from Figure 2, the receivable turnover ratio varies substantially from industry to industry. Grocery stores, for example, have a high turnover because that type of business has few receivables; the turnover in interstate trucking is about 12 times because the typical credit term in that industry is thirty days. Manufacturers' turnover is lower because those industries tend to have longer credit terms.

FINANCING RECEIVABLES

Financial flexibility is important to most companies. Companies that have significant amounts of assets tied up in accounts receivable may be unwilling or unable to wait until the receivables are collected to receive the cash they

---

3. American Greetings, *Annual Report*, 1993.

Figure 2. Receivable Turnover for Selected Industries

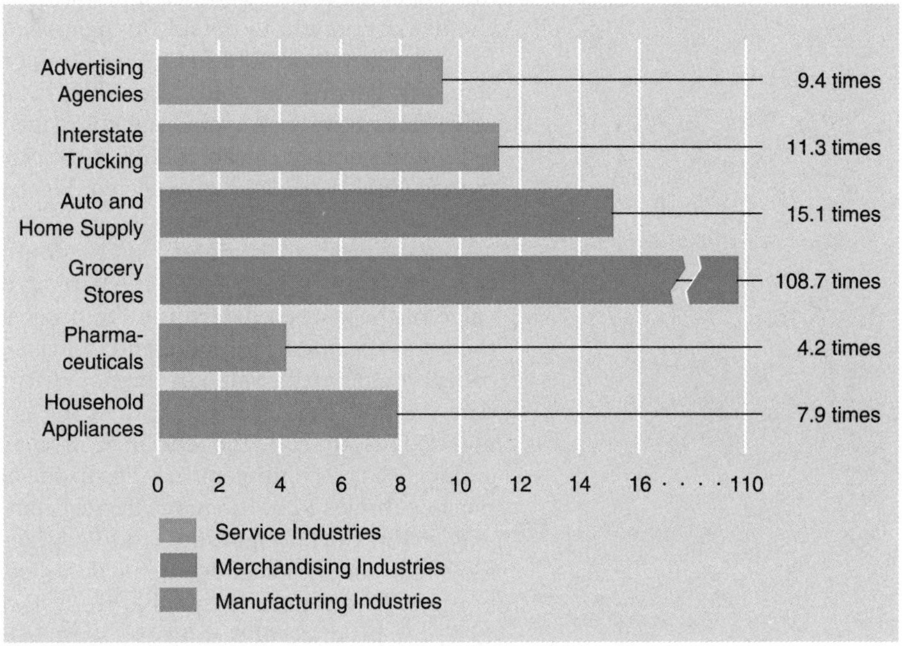

Advertising Agencies	9.4 times
Interstate Trucking	11.3 times
Auto and Home Supply	15.1 times
Grocery Stores	108.7 times
Pharmaceuticals	4.2 times
Household Appliances	7.9 times

0 2 4 6 8 10 12 14 16 · · · ·110

■ Service Industries
■ Merchandising Industries
■ Manufacturing Industries

Source: Data from Dun and Bradstreet, *Industry Norms and Ratios,* 1993–94.

represent. Many companies have set up finance companies to help their customers finance the purchase of their products. For example, Ford Motor Co. has Ford Motor Credit Company (FMCC), General Motors Corp. has General Motors Acceptance Corporation (GMAC), and Sears, Roebuck & Co. has Sears Roebuck Acceptance Corporation (SRAC). Some companies borrow funds by pledging their accounts receivable as collateral. If a company does not pay back its loan, the creditor can take the collateral, in this case the accounts receivable, and convert it to cash to satisfy the loan.

Companies can also raise funds by selling or transferring accounts receivable to another entity, called a factor. The sale or transfer of accounts receivable, called factoring, can be done with or without recourse. *Without recourse* means that the factor that buys the accounts receivable bears any losses from uncollectible accounts. A company's acceptance of credit cards like VISA, MasterCard, or American Express is an example of factoring without recourse because the credit card issuers accept the risk of nonpayment.

With recourse means that the seller of the receivables is liable to the purchaser if the receivable is not collected. The factor, of course, charges a fee for its service. The fee for sales with recourse is usually about 1 percent of the accounts receivable. The fee is higher for sales without recourse because the factor's risk is greater. In accounting terminology, the seller of the receivables with recourse is said to be contingently liable. A contingent liability is a potential liability that can develop into a real liability if a possible subsequent event occurs. In this case, the subsequent event would be nonpayment of the receivable by the customer.

Fleetwood Enterprises, Inc., the nation's leading producer of recreational vehicles and manufactured homes, provides an example of the selling of receivables. The company established Fleetwood Credit Corporation to finance sales of its RVs and by 1990 financed over 35 percent of all Fleetwood sales. Since buyers of RVs can take several years to pay, Fleetwood's management decided to sell significant amounts of the receivables held by Fleetwood Credit Corporation to obtain financial flexibility and funds for future growth. In 1993, Fleetwood sold $111.9 million of receivables to investors, and its outstanding balance of sold receivables was $393.3 million. Even though the receivables have been sold, the company has a contingent liability of up to $31.5 million for receivables sold with recourse that have not yet been paid.[4] If the receivables are paid as expected, Fleetwood will have no further liability.

Another method of financing receivables is through the discounting, or selling, of promissory notes held as notes receivable. Selling notes receivable is called discounting because the bank deducts the interest from the maturity value of the note to determine the proceeds. The holder of the note (usually the payee) endorses the note and delivers it to the bank. The bank expects to collect the maturity value of the note (principal plus interest) on the maturity date but also has recourse against the endorser or seller of the note. If the maker fails to pay, the endorser is liable to the bank for payment. The endorser has a contingent liability in the amount of the discounted notes that must be disclosed in the notes to the financial statements.

Marriott Corporation, the world's largest operator of hotels and a leader in food and services management, is an example of a company that has sold portions of the notes receivable from its various affiliates to obtain cash. In 1989, for instance, the company sold $61 million of its notes receivable. At December 29, 1989, the aggregate unpaid balance of notes receivable sold with recourse was $55 million. This $55 million represented a contingent liability for Marriott.

CASH AND CASH EQUIVALENTS

OBJECTIVE

2 *Define* **cash** *and* **cash equivalents**

The annual report of Bell Atlantic Corporation refers to *cash and cash equivalents.* Of the two terms, *cash* is the easier to understand. It is the most liquid of all assets and the most readily available to pay debts. On the balance sheet, cash normally consists of coins and currency on hand, checks and money orders from customers, and deposits in bank checking accounts. Cash may also include a compensating balance, an amount that is not entirely free to be spent. A compensating balance is a minimum amount that a bank requires a company to keep in its bank account as part of a credit-granting arrangement. Such an arrangement restricts cash and may reduce a company's liquidity. Therefore, the SEC requires companies to disclose the amount of any compensating balances in a note to the financial statements.

The term *cash equivalents* is a little harder to understand. At times a company may find that it has more cash on hand than it needs to pay current obligations. Excess cash should not remain idle, especially during periods of high interest rates. Thus, management may periodically invest its idle funds in time deposits or certificates of deposit at banks and other financial institutions, in government securities such as U.S. Treasury notes, or in other securities. Such actions are rightfully called investments. However, if the investments have a term of less than ninety days when they are purchased, they are called cash equivalents because the funds revert to cash so quickly that they are regarded as cash on the balance sheet. Bell Atlantic follows this

---

4. Fleetwood Enterprises, *Annual Report,* 1993.

practice. Its policy is stated as follows: "The Company considers all highly liquid investments with a maturity of 90 days or less when purchased to be cash equivalents. Cash equivalents are stated at cost, which approximates market value." A survey of the practices of 600 large U.S. corporations found that 96 of them, or 16 percent, used the term *cash* as the balance sheet caption and 425, or 71 percent, used the phrase *cash and cash equivalents* or *cash and equivalents.* Sixty-six companies, or 11 percent, combined cash with marketable securities.[5] The average amount of cash held can also vary by industry.

Most companies need to keep some currency and coins on hand. Currency and coins are needed for cash registers and for paying expenses that are impractical to pay by check. A company may need to advance cash to sales representatives for travel expenses, to divisions to cover their payrolls, and to individual employees to cash their paychecks.

BUSINESS BULLETIN: ETHICS IN PRACTICE

To combat the laundering of money by drug dealers, U.S. law requires banks to report cash transactions in excess of $10,000. Not to be deterred, money launderers began to sidestep the regulation by electronically transferring funds from overseas to banks, money exchanges, and brokerage firms. In response, the Treasury Department has set new rules that require those institutions to keep records about the sources and recipients of all electronic transfers. Given the widespread use of electronic transfers in today's business world, it is questionable how much effect this action will have in the ongoing battle against drugs. Looking for drug money by combing the millions of transfers that occur every day is "like looking for a needle in a haystack."[6]

SHORT-TERM INVESTMENTS

OBJECTIVE

3 *Account for short-term investments*

When investments have a maturity of more than ninety days but are intended to be held only until cash is needed for current operations, they are called short-term investments or marketable securities. Bell Atlantic states its policy on short-term investments as follows: "Short-term investments consist of investments that mature in 91 days to 12 months from the date of purchase."

Investments intended to be held for more than one year are called long-term investments. Long-term investments are classified in an investments section of the balance sheet, not in the current assets section. Although long-term investments may be just as marketable as short-term assets, management intends to hold them for an indefinite period of time.

Securities that may be held as short-term or long-term investments fall into three categories, as specified by the Financial Accounting Standards Board:

5. *Accounting Trends & Techniques* (New York: American Institute of CPAs, 1992), p. 125.

6. Jeffrey Taylor, "Rules on Electronic Transfers of Money Are Being Tightened by U.S. Treasury," *Wall Street Journal,* September 26, 1994.

held-to-maturity securities, trading securities, and available-for-sale securities.[7] Trading securities are classified as short-term investments. Held-to-maturity securities and available-for-sale securities, depending on their length of maturity or management's intent to hold them, may be classified as either short-term or long-term investments. The three categories of securities when held as short-term investments are discussed here.

HELD-TO-MATURITY SECURITIES

Held-to-maturity securities are debt securities that management intends to hold to their maturity date and whose cash value is not needed until that date. Such securities are recorded at cost and valued on the balance sheet at cost adjusted for the effects of interest. For example, suppose that on December 1, 19x1, Lowes Corporation pays $97,000 for U.S. Treasury bills, which are short-term debt of the federal government. The bills will mature in 120 days at $100,000. The following entry would be made by Lowes.

19x1			
Dec. 1	Short-Term Investments	97,000	
	Cash		97,000
	Purchase of U.S. Treasury bills that mature in 120 days		

At Lowes' year end on December 31, the entry to accrue the interest income earned to date would be as follows:

19x1			
Dec. 31	Short-Term Investments	750	
	Interest Income		750
	Accrual of interest on U.S. Treasury bills $3,000 \times 30/120 = \$750$		

On December 31, the U.S. Treasury bills would be shown on the balance sheet as a short-term investment at its amortized cost of $97,750 ($97,000 + $750). When Lowes receives the maturity value on March 31, 19x2, the entry is as follows:

19x2			
Mar. 31	Cash	100,000	
	Short-Term Investments		97,750
	Interest Income		2,250
	Receipt of cash at maturity of U. S. Treasury bills and recognition of related income		

TRADING SECURITIES

Trading securities are debt and equity securities bought and held principally for the purpose of being sold in the near term. Such securities are frequently bought and sold to generate profits on short-term changes in their prices. Trading securities are classified as current assets on the balance sheet and valued at fair value, which is usually the same as market value, for example, when securities are traded on a stock exchange or in the over-the-counter

7. *Statement of Financial Accounting Standards No. 115,* "Accounting for Certain Investments in Debt and Equity Securities" (Stamford, Conn.: Financial Accounting Standards Board, 1993).

market. An increase or decrease in the total trading portfolio (the group of securities held for trading purposes) is included in net income in the accounting period in which the increase or decrease occurs. For example, assume that Franklin Corporation purchases 10,000 shares of Mobil Corporation for $700,000 ($70 per share) and 5,000 shares of Texaco, Inc., for $300,000 ($60 per share) on October 25, 19x1. The purchase is made for trading purposes; that is, management intends to realize a gain by holding the shares for only a short period. The entry to record the investment at cost is as follows:

19x1
Oct. 25 Short-Term Investments   1,000,000
          Cash   1,000,000
          Investment in stocks for trading
          ($700,000 + $300,000 = $1,000,000)

Assume that at year end Mobil's stock price has decreased to $60 per share and Texaco's has risen to $64 per share. The trading portfolio may now be valued at $920,000

Security	Cost	Market Value
Mobil (10,000 shares)	$ 700,000	$600,000
Texaco (5,000 shares)	300,000	320,000
Totals	$1,000,000	$920,000

Since the current fair value of the portfolio is $80,000 less than the original cost of $1,000,000, an adjusting entry is needed, as follows:

19x1
Dec. 31 Unrealized Loss on Investments   80,000
          Allowance to Adjust Short-Term   80,000
          Investments to Market
          Recognition of unrealized loss
          on trading portfolio

The unrealized loss will appear on the income statement as a reduction in income. (The loss is unrealized because the securities have not been sold.) The Allowance to Adjust Short-Term Investments to Market account appears on the balance sheet as a contra-asset, as follows:

Short-Term Investments (at cost)	$1,000,000
Less Allowance to Adjust Short-Term Investments to Market	80,000
Short-Term Investments (at market)	$ 920,000

or more simply,

Short-Term Investments (at market value, cost is $1,000,000)	$ 920,000

If Franklin sells its 5,000 shares of Texaco for $70 per share on March 2, 19x2, a realized gain on trading securities is recorded as follows:

19x2
Mar. 2 Cash   350,000
          Short-Term Investments   300,000
          Realized Gain on Investments   50,000
          Sale of 5,000 shares of Texaco
          for $70 per share; cost was $60 per share

The realized gain will appear on the income statement. Note that the realized gain is unaffected by the adjustment for the unrealized loss at the end of 19x1. The two transactions are treated independently. If the stock had been sold for less than cost, a realized loss on investments would have been recorded. Realized losses also appear on the income statement.

Let's assume that during 19x2 Franklin buys 2,000 shares of Exxon Corporation at $64 per share and has no transactions involving Mobil. Also, assume that by December 31, 19x2, the price of Mobil's stock has risen to $75 per share, or $5 per share more than the original cost, and that Exxon's stock price has fallen to $58, or $6 less than the original cost. The trading portfolio now can be analyzed as follows:

Security	Cost	Market Value
Mobil (10,000 shares)	$700,000	$750,000
Exxon (2,000 shares)	128,000	116,000
Totals	$828,000	$866,000

The market value of the portfolio now exceeds the cost by $38,000 ($866,000 − $828,000). This amount represents the targeted ending balance for the Allowance to Adjust Short-Term Investments to Market account. Recall that at the end of 19x1, that account had a credit balance of $80,000, meaning that the market value of the trading portfolio was less than the cost. The account has no entries during 19x2 and thus retains its balance until adjusting entries are made at the end of the year. The adjustment for 19x2 must be $118,000—enough to result in a debit balance of $38,000 in the allowance account.

19x2
Dec. 31 Allowance to Adjust Short-Term
              Investments to Market   118,000
                 Unrealized Gain on Investments   118,000
                    Recognition of unrealized gain
                    on trading portfolio
                    ($80,000 + $38,000 = $118,000)

The 19x2 ending balance of the allowance account may be determined as follows:

Allowance to Adjust Short-Term Investments to Market

Dec. 31, 19x2 adj.	118,000	Dec. 31, 19x1 bal.	80,000
Dec. 31, 19x2 bal.	38,000		

The balance sheet presentation of short-term investments is as follows:

Short-Term Investments (at cost)	$828,000
Allowance to Adjust Short-Term Investments to Market	38,000
Short-Term Investments (at market)	$866,000

or, more simply,

Short-Term Investments (at market value, cost is $828,000)	$866,000

If the company also holds held-to-maturity securities, they are included in short-term investments at cost adjusted for the effects of interest.

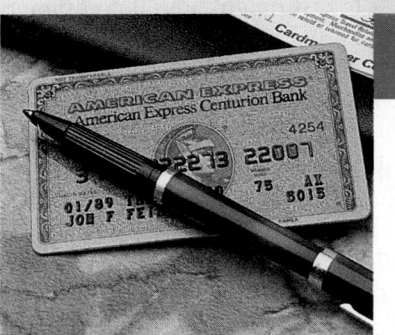

American Express

DECISION POINT

In recent years, American Express's green, gold, and platinum credit cards have lost market share to the rapidly growing VISA, MasterCard, and Discover cards. One reason may be that American Express has traditionally required its cardholders to pay their total account balance every month, whereas its competitors allow cardholders to pay a small amount and carry the balance forward.

In order to regain market share, American Express has introduced the Optima True Grace card, which allows cardholders to carry their balances forward. In addition, while other credit cards charge interest from the date of purchase, True Grace offers an interest-free "grace period" of twenty-five days before interest begins to accrue. The current annual interest rate after twenty-five days is about 18 percent. How does this plan motivate the consumer to use the True Grace card, and what are the costs and benefits to American Express? What factors might affect the chance for success?

Since twenty-five days is almost one month, and an annual interest rate of 18 percent is 1½ percent per month, the consumer will save almost 1½ percent on each purchase. So if a consumer purchases $400 in a given month, the savings in interest over other credit cards is about $6 ($400 × .015). American Express forgoes the $6 in interest, but if the customer chooses not to pay off a portion of the $400, American Express will continue to earn 1½ percent interest in future months on the unpaid balance. Since American Express can borrow money for much less than this rate, it stands to earn much more than the original cost of enticing the customer to use its credit card. Whether or not the plan will be a success depends on the value consumers place on the interest savings in light of the fact that other credit cards also offer inducements such as rebates, frequent flyer miles, and other premiums. ⦂⦂⦂⦂⦂

AVAILABLE-FOR-SALE SECURITIES

Available-for-sale securities are debt and equity securities that do not meet the criteria for either held-to-maturity or trading securities. They are accounted for in exactly the same way as trading securities, except that the unrealized gain or loss is not reported on the income statement, but is reported as a special item in the stockholders' equity section of the balance sheet.

DIVIDEND AND INTEREST INCOME

Dividend and interest income for all three categories of investments is shown in the Other Income and Expenses section of the income statement.

4 *Define* accounts receivable *and apply the allowance method of accounting for uncollectible accounts, using both the percentage of net sales method and the accounts receivable aging method*

ACCOUNTS RECEIVABLE

The other major types of short-term liquid assets are accounts receivable and notes receivable. Both result from credit sales to customers. Retail companies such as Sears, Roebuck and Co. have made credit available to nearly every responsible person in the United States. Every field of retail trade has expanded by allowing customers to make payments a month or more after the date of sale. What is not so apparent is that credit has expanded even more in the wholesale and manufacturing industries than at the retail level. The levels of accounts receivable in several industries are shown in Figure 3.

Accounts receivable are short-term liquid assets that arise from sales on credit to customers by wholesalers or retailers. This type of credit is often called trade credit. Terms on trade credit usually range from five to sixty days, depending on industry practice. For some companies that sell to consumers, installment accounts receivable constitute a significant portion of accounts receivable. Installment accounts receivable arise from the sale of goods on terms that allow the buyer to make a series of time payments. Department stores, appliance stores, furniture stores, used car companies, and other retail businesses often offer installment credit. Retailers such as J. C. Penney Company, Inc. and Sears, Roebuck and Co. have millions of dollars in installment accounts receivable. Although the payment period may be twenty-four months or more, installment accounts receivable are classified as current assets if such credit policies are customary in the industry.

On the balance sheet, the title Accounts Receivable is reserved for sales made to regular customers in the ordinary course of business. If loans or sales that do not fall into this category are made to employees, officers of the corporation, or owners, they should be shown separately with an asset title such as Receivables from Employees.

Normally, individual customer accounts receivable have debit balances, but sometimes customers overpay their accounts by mistake or in anticipation of future purchases. When individual customer accounts show credit balances, the total of the credits should be shown on the balance sheet as a current liability because the amounts must be refunded if future sales are not made to those customers.

UNCOLLECTIBLE ACCOUNTS AND THE DIRECT CHARGE-OFF METHOD

A company will always have some customers who cannot or will not pay their debts. The accounts owed by such customers are called uncollectible accounts, or *bad debts*, and are a loss or an expense of selling on credit. Why does a company sell on credit if it expects that some of its accounts will not be paid? The answer is that the company expects to sell much more than it would if it did not sell on credit, thereby increasing its earnings.

Some companies recognize the loss from an uncollectible account receivable at the time it is determined to be uncollectible. Assume that management determines on March 15 that it will not be able to collect $300 that is owed by an individual. Under the direct charge-off method, the loss is recognized in an entry similar to the following:

Mar. 15	Uncollectible Accounts Expense	300	
	Accounts Receivable		300
	To write off an account deemed to be uncollectible		

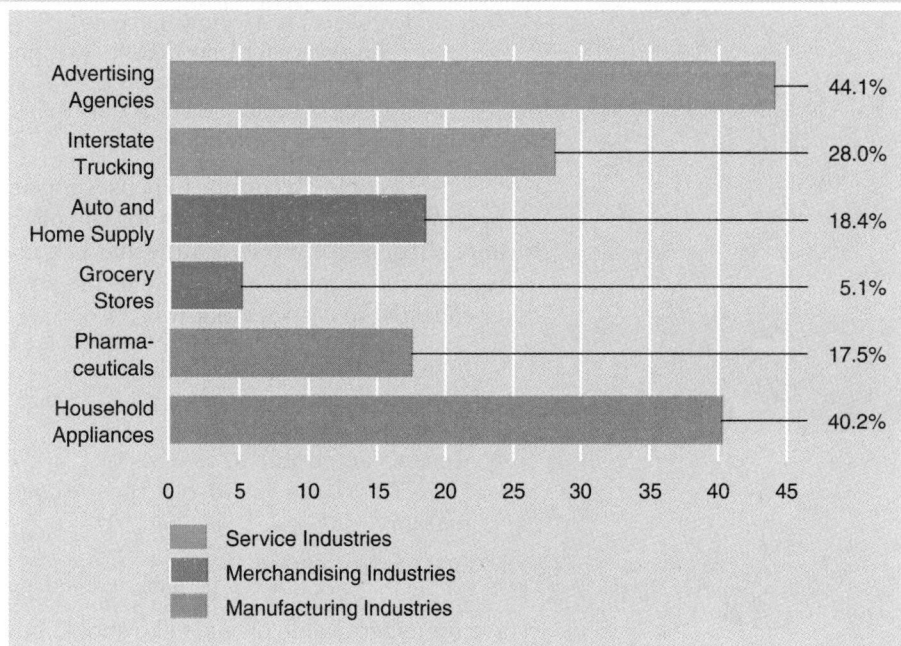

Figure 3. Accounts Receivable as a Percentage of Total Assets for Selected Industries

Source: Data from Dun and Bradstreet, *Industry Norms and Ratios*, 1993–94.

Many small companies use this method because it is required in computing taxable income under federal tax regulations. However, companies that follow generally accepted accounting principles do not use the direct charge-off method in their financial statements because it makes no attempt to match revenues and expenses. They prefer the allowance method, which is explained in the next section.

UNCOLLECTIBLE ACCOUNTS AND THE ALLOWANCE METHOD

Under the allowance method of accounting for uncollectible accounts, bad debt losses are matched against the sales they help to produce. As mentioned earlier, when management extends credit to increase sales, it knows that it will incur some losses from uncollectible accounts. Those losses are expenses that occur at the time sales on credit are made and should be matched to the revenues they help to generate. Of course, at the time the sales are made, management cannot identify which customers will not pay their debts, nor can it predict the exact amount of money that will be lost. Therefore, to observe the matching rule, losses from uncollectible accounts must be estimated, and the estimate becomes an expense in the fiscal year in which the sales are made.

For example, let us assume that Cottage Sales Company made most of its sales on credit during its first year of operation. At the end of the year, accounts receivable amounted to $100,000. On that date, management reviewed the collectible status of the accounts receivable. Approximately $6,000 of the $100,000 of accounts receivable were estimated to be uncollectible. Therefore, the uncollectible accounts expense for the first year of operation was estimated to be $6,000. The following adjusting entry would be made on December 31 of that year.

Dec. 31 Uncollectible Accounts Expense   6,000
              Allowance for Uncollectible Accounts   6,000
                  To record the estimated
                  uncollectible accounts expense
                  for the year 19x1

Uncollectible Accounts Expense appears on the income statement as an operating expense. Allowance for Uncollectible Accounts appears on the balance sheet as a contra account that is deducted from Accounts Receivable.[8] It reduces the accounts receivable to the amount that is expected to be realized, or collected in cash, as follows:

Current Assets
  Cash $ 10,000
  Short-Term Investments   15,000
  Accounts Receivable $100,000
    Less Allowance for Uncollectible Accounts   6,000   94,000
  Inventory   56,000

  Total Current Assets $175,000

Accounts receivable may also be shown on the balance sheet as follows:

Accounts Receivable (net of allowance for uncollectible
  accounts of $6,000) $94,000

Or they may be shown at "net," with the amount of the allowance for uncollectible accounts identified in a note to the financial statements. The estimated uncollectible amount cannot be credited to the account of any particular customer. Nor can it be credited to the Accounts Receivable controlling account because that would cause the controlling account to be out of balance with the total customers' accounts in the subsidiary ledger. The estimated uncollectible amount is therefore credited to a separate contra-asset account—Allowance for Uncollectible Accounts.

The allowance account will often have other titles, such as Allowance for Doubtful Accounts or Allowance for Bad Debts. Once in a while, the older phrase Reserve for Bad Debts will be seen, but in modern practice it should not be used. Bad Debts Expense is another title often used for Uncollectible Accounts Expense.

ESTIMATING UNCOLLECTIBLE ACCOUNTS EXPENSE

As noted, it is necessary to estimate the expense to cover the expected losses for the year. Of course, estimates can vary widely. If management takes an optimistic view and projects a small loss from uncollectible accounts, the resulting net accounts receivable will be larger than if management takes a

8. The purpose of Allowance for Uncollectible Accounts is to reduce the gross accounts receivable to the amount estimated to be collectible (net realizable value). The purpose of another contra account, Accumulated Depreciation, is *not* to reduce the gross plant and equipment accounts to realizable value. Rather, its purpose is to show how much of the cost of the plant and equipment has been allocated as an expense to previous accounting periods.

pessimistic view. The net income will also be larger under the optimistic view because the estimated expense will be smaller. The company's accountant makes an estimate based on past experience and current economic conditions. For example, losses from uncollectible accounts are normally expected to be greater in a recession than during a period of economic growth. The final decision, made by management, on the amount of the expense will depend on objective information, such as the accountant's analyses, and on certain qualitative factors, such as how investors, bankers, creditors, and others may view the performance of the company. Regardless of the qualitative considerations, the estimated losses from uncollectible accounts should be realistic.

The accountant may choose from two common methods for estimating uncollectible accounts expense for an accounting period: the percentage of net sales method and the accounts receivable aging method.

Percentage of Net Sales Method

The percentage of net sales method asks the question, How much of this year's net sales will not be collected? The answer determines the amount of uncollectible accounts expense for the year.

For example, the following balances represent the ending figures for Hassel Company for the year 19x9:

Sales		Sales Returns and Allowances	
	Dec. 31 645,000	Dec. 31 40,000	

Sales Discounts		Allowance for Uncollectible Accounts	
Dec. 31 5,000			Dec. 31 3,600

The actual losses from uncollectible accounts for the past three years have been as follows:

Year	Net Sales	Losses from Uncollectible Accounts	Percentage
19x6	$ 520,000	$10,200	1.96
19x7	595,000	13,900	2.34
19x8	585,000	9,900	1.69
Total	$1,700,000	$34,000	2.00

In many businesses, net sales is understood to approximate net credit sales. If there are substantial cash sales, then net credit sales should be used. Management believes that uncollectible accounts will continue to average about 2 percent of net sales. The uncollectible accounts expense for the year 19x9 is therefore estimated to be

$$.02 \times (\$645,000 - \$40,000 - \$5,000) = .02 \times \$600,000 = \$12,000$$

The entry to record this estimate is

Dec. 31	Uncollectible Accounts Expense	12,000	
	Allowance for Uncollectible Accounts		12,000
	To record uncollectible accounts expense at 2 percent of $600,000 net sales		

After the above entry is posted, Allowance for Uncollectible Accounts will have a balance of $15,600.

Allowance for Uncollectible Accounts

	Dec. 31	3,600
	Dec. 31 adjustment	12,000
	Dec. 31 balance	15,600

The balance consists of the $12,000 estimated uncollectible accounts receivable from 19x9 sales and the $3,600 estimated uncollectible accounts receivable from previous years.

Accounts Receivable Aging Method   The accounts receivable aging method asks the question, How much of the year-end balance of accounts receivable will not be collected? Under this method, the year-end balance of Allowance for Uncollectible Accounts is determined directly by an analysis of accounts receivable. The difference between the amount determined to be uncollectible and the actual balance of Allowance for Uncollectible Accounts is the expense for the year. In theory, this method should produce the same result as the percentage of net sales method, but in practice it rarely does.

The aging of accounts receivable is the process of listing each accounts receivable customer according to the due date of the account. If the customer's account is past due, there is a possibility that the account will not be paid. And the further past due an account is, the greater that possibility. The aging of accounts receivable helps management evaluate its credit and collection policies and alerts it to possible problems. The aging of accounts receivable for Myer Company is shown in Exhibit 1. Each account receivable is classified as being not yet due or as 1–30 days, 31–60 days, 61–90 days, or over 90 days past due. The estimated percentage uncollectible in each category is

Exhibit 1. Analysis of Accounts Receivable by Age

Myer Company
Analysis of Accounts Receivable by Age
December 31, 19xx

Customer	Total	Not Yet Due	1–30 Days Past Due	31–60 Days Past Due	61–90 Days Past Due	Over 90 Days Past Due
A. Arnold	$ 150		$ 150			
M. Benoit	400			$ 400		
J. Connolly	1,000	$ 900	100			
R. DiCarlo	250				$ 250	
Others	42,600	21,000	14,000	3,800	2,200	$1,600
Totals	$44,400	$21,900	$14,250	$4,200	$2,450	$1,600
Estimated percentage uncollectible		1.0	2.0	10.0	30.0	50.0
Allowance for Uncollectible Accounts	$ 2,459	$ 219	$ 285	$ 420	$ 735	$ 800

multiplied by the amount in each category to determine the estimated, or target, balance of Allowance for Uncollectible Accounts. In total, it is estimated that $2,459 of the $44,400 accounts receivable will not be collected.

Once the target balance for Allowance for Uncollectible Accounts has been found, it is necessary to determine how much the adjustment is. The amount of the adjustment depends on the current balance of the allowance account. Let us assume two cases for the December 31 balance of Myer Company's Allowance for Uncollectible Accounts: (1) a credit balance of $800 and (2) a debit balance of $800.

In the first case, an adjustment of $1,659 is needed to bring the balance of the allowance account to $2,459, calculated as follows:

Targeted Balance for Allowance for Uncollectible Accounts	$2,459
Less Current Credit Balance of Allowance for Uncollectible Accounts	800
Uncollectible Accounts Expense	$1,659

The uncollectible accounts expense is recorded as follows:

Dec. 31	Uncollectible Accounts Expense	1,659	
	Allowance for Uncollectible Accounts		1,659
	To record the allowance for		
	uncollectible accounts to the		
	level of estimated losses		

The resulting balance of Allowance for Uncollectible Accounts is $2,459, as shown below:

Allowance for Uncollectible Accounts

	Dec. 31	800
	Dec. 31 adjustment	1,659
	Dec. 31 balance	2,459

In the second case, since Allowance for Uncollectible Accounts has a debit balance of $800, the estimated uncollectible accounts expense for the year will have to be $3,259 to reach the targeted balance of $2,459. This is shown in the calculation that follows.

Targeted Balance for Allowance for Uncollectible Accounts	$2,459
Plus Current Debit Balance of Allowance for Uncollectible Accounts	800
Uncollectible Accounts Expense	$3,259

The uncollectible accounts expense is recorded as follows:

Dec. 31	Uncollectible Accounts Expense	3,259	
	Allowance for Uncollectible Accounts		3,259
	To record the allowance for		
	uncollectible accounts to the		
	level of estimated losses		

After this entry, Allowance for Uncollectible Accounts has a credit balance of $2,459, as shown below:

Allowance for Uncollectible Accounts

Dec. 31	800	Dec. 31 adjustment	3,259
		Dec. 31 balance	2,459

Comparison of the Two Methods   Both the percentage of net sales method and the accounts receivable aging method estimate the uncollectible accounts expense in accordance with the matching rule, but they do so in different ways, as shown in Figure 4. The percentage of net sales method is an income statement approach. It assumes that a certain proportion of sales will not be collected, and this proportion is the *amount of Uncollectible Accounts Expense* for the year. The accounts receivable aging method is a balance sheet approach. It assumes that a certain proportion of accounts receivable outstanding will not be collected. This proportion is the *targeted balance of the Allowance for Uncollectible Accounts account.* The expense for the year is the difference between the targeted balance and the current balance of the allowance account.

Why Accounts Written Off Will Differ from Estimates   Regardless of the method used to estimate uncollectible accounts, the total of accounts receivable written off in any given year will rarely equal the estimated uncollectible amount. The allowance account will show a credit balance when the total of accounts written off is less than the estimated uncollectible amount. The allowance account will show a debit balance when the total of accounts written off is greater than the estimated uncollectible amount.

WRITING OFF AN UNCOLLECTIBLE ACCOUNT

When it becomes clear that a specific account receivable will not be collected, the amount should be written off to Allowance for Uncollectible Accounts. Remember that the uncollectible amount was already accounted for as an expense when the allowance was established. For example, assume that on January 15, R. Deering, who owes Myer Company $250, is declared bankrupt by a federal court. The entry to *write off* this account is as follows:

Jan. 15	Allowance for Uncollectible Accounts	250	
	Accounts Receivable		250
	To write off receivable from		
	R. Deering as uncollectible;		
	Deering declared bankrupt		
	on January 15		

Although the write-off removes the uncollectible amount from Accounts Receivable, it does not affect the estimated net realizable value of accounts receivable. The write-off simply reduces R. Deering's account to zero and reduces Allowance for Uncollectible Accounts by a similar amount, as the following table shows:

	Balances Before Write-off	Balances After Write-off
Accounts Receivable	$44,400	$44,150
Less Allowance for Uncollectible Accounts	2,459	2,209
Estimated Net Realizable Value of Accounts Receivable	$41,941	$41,941

Figure 4. Two Methods of Estimating Uncollectible Accounts

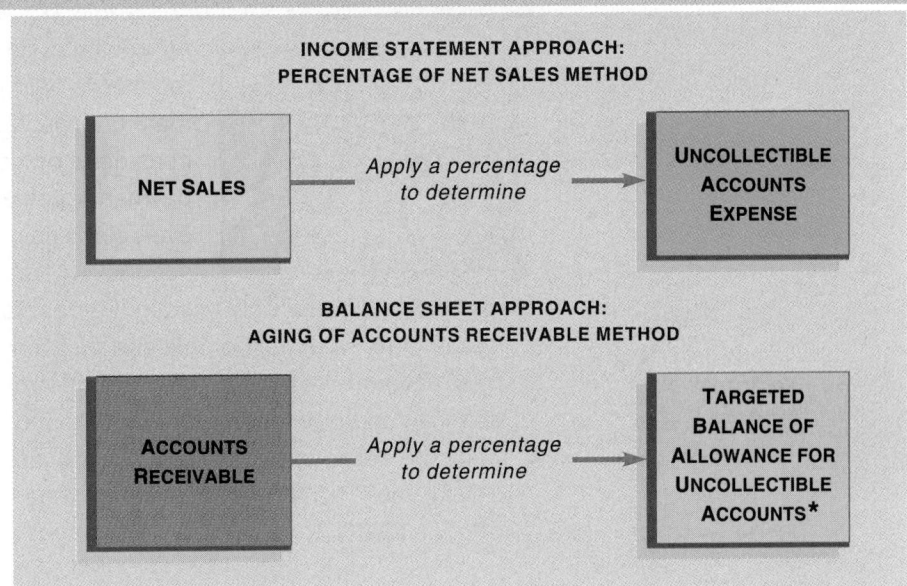

*Add current debit balance or subtract current credit balance to determine uncollectible accounts expense.

Recovery of Accounts Receivable Written Off   Sometimes a customer whose account has been written off as uncollectible will later be able to pay some or all of the amount owed. When this happens, two journal entries must be made: one to reverse the earlier write-off (which is now incorrect) and another to show the collection of the account.

For example, assume that on September 1, R. Deering, after his bankruptcy on January 15, notified the company that he would be able to pay $100 of his account and sent a check for $50. The entries to record this transaction are as follows:

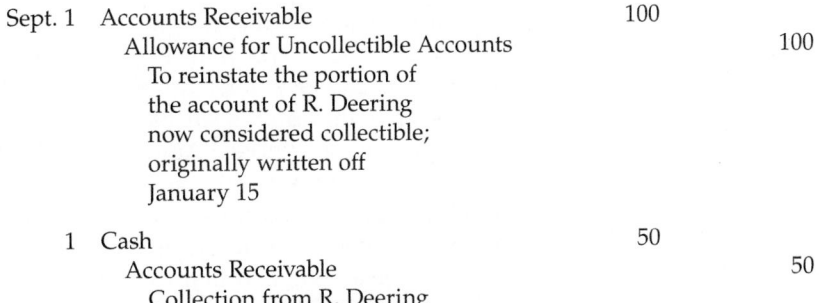

Sept. 1	Accounts Receivable	100	
	Allowance for Uncollectible Accounts		100
	To reinstate the portion of the account of R. Deering now considered collectible; originally written off January 15		
1	Cash	50	
	Accounts Receivable		50
	Collection from R. Deering		

The collectible portion of R. Deering's account must be restored to his account and credited to Allowance for Uncollectible Accounts for two reasons. First, it turned out to be wrong to write off the full $250 on January 15 because only $150 was actually uncollectible. Second, the accounts receivable subsidiary account for R. Deering should reflect his ability to pay a portion of the money he owed despite his declaration of bankruptcy. Documentation of this action will give a clear picture of R. Deering's credit record for future credit action.

Accountants generally believe that the accounts receivable aging method is the best way to estimate uncollectible accounts because it takes into consideration current circumstances, such as payment rates and economic conditions. However, since it is time-consuming to do an aging of accounts manually, the percentage of net sales method was commonly used in the past for preparing interim financial statements, such as monthly and quarterly reports. Now that most companies' accounts receivable are computerized, the aging of accounts receivable can be done much more quickly and easily. Indeed, many companies track the collection and aging of accounts receivables on a weekly or even a daily basis. As a result, the percentage of net sales method is used less often. ▬▬

NOTES RECEIVABLE

OBJECTIVE

5 *Define and describe a* **promissory note,** *and make calculations and journal entries involving promissory notes*

A promissory note is an unconditional promise to pay a definite sum of money on demand or at a future date. The entity who signs the note and thereby promises to pay is called the *maker* of the note. The entity to whom payment is to be made is called the *payee*. The promissory note in Figure 5 is dated May 20, 19x1, and is an unconditional promise by the maker, Samuel Mason, to pay a definite sum, or principal ($1,000), to the payee, Cook County Bank & Trust Company, at the future date of August 18, 19x1. The promissory note bears an interest rate of 8 percent. The payee regards all promissory notes it holds that are due in less than one year as notes receivable in the current assets section of the balance sheet. The maker regards them as notes payable in the current liability section of the balance sheet.

This portion of the chapter is concerned primarily with notes received from customers. The nature of a business generally determines how frequently promissory notes are received from customers. Firms selling durable goods of high value, such as farm machinery and automobiles, will often accept promissory notes. Among the advantages of promissory notes are that they produce interest income and represent a stronger legal claim against a creditor than do accounts receivable. In addition, selling promissory notes to banks is a common financing method. Almost all companies will occasionally receive a note, and many companies obtain notes receivable in settlement of past-due accounts.

COMPUTATIONS FOR PROMISSORY NOTES

In accounting for promissory notes, several terms are important to remember. These terms are (1) maturity date, (2) duration of note, (3) interest and interest rate, and (4) maturity value.

Maturity Date The maturity date is the date on which the note must be paid. This date must either be stated on the promissory note or be deter-

Figure 5. A Promissory Note

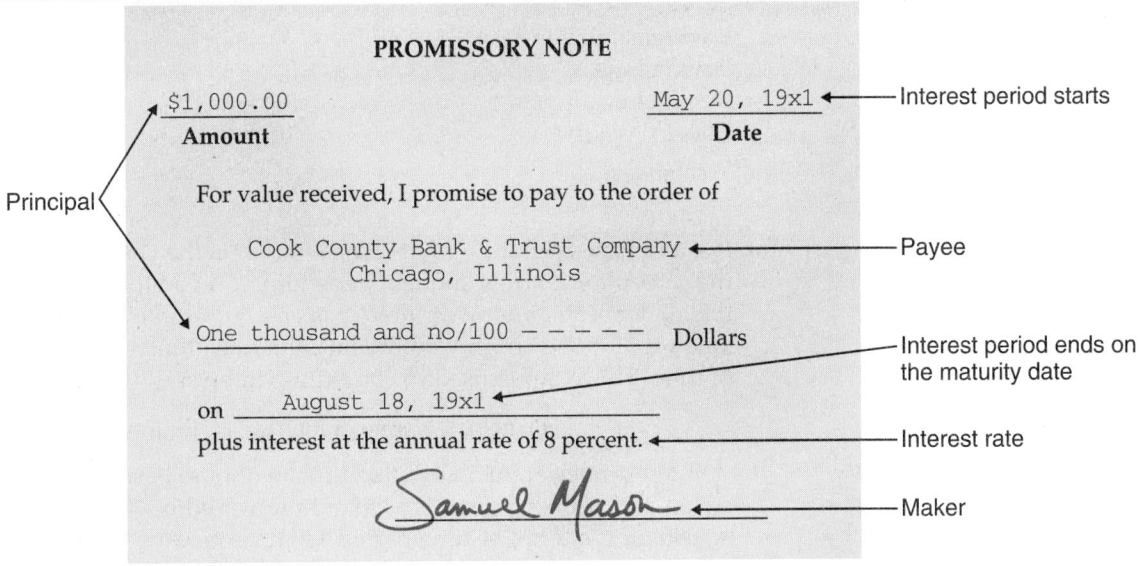

PROMISSORY NOTE

$1,000.00   May 20, 19x1 ← Interest period starts

Amount   **Date**

For value received, I promise to pay to the order of

Cook County Bank & Trust Company ← Payee
Chicago, Illinois

One thousand and no/100 — — — — — Dollars ← Interest period ends on the maturity date

on ____ August 18, 19x1 ____ ← Interest period ends on the maturity date

plus interest at the annual rate of 8 percent. ← Interest rate

Samuel Mason ← Maker

Principal

minable from the facts stated on the note. Among the most common statements of maturity date are the following:

1. A specific date, such as "November 14, 19xx"
2. A specific number of months after the date of the note, for example, "3 months after date"
3. A specific number of days after the date of the note, for example, "60 days after date"

The maturity date is obvious when a specific date is stated. And when the maturity date is a number of months from the date of the note, one simply uses the same day in the appropriate future month. For example, a note that is dated January 20 and that is due in two months would be due on March 20.

When the maturity date is a specific number of days from the date of the note, however, the exact maturity date must be determined. In computing the maturity date, it is important to exclude the date of the note. For example, a note dated May 20 and due in 90 days would be due on August 18, computed as follows:

Days remaining in May (31 − 20)	11
Days in June	30
Days in July	31
Days in August	18
Total days	90

Duration of Note   The duration of note is the length of time in days between a promissory note's issue date and its maturity date. Knowing the duration of the note is important because interest is calculated for the exact number of days. Identifying the duration is easy when the maturity date is stated as a specific number of days from the date of the note because the two numbers are the same. However, if the maturity date is stated as a specific date, the exact number of days must be determined. Assume that a note issued on May 10 matures on August 10. The duration of the note is 92 days, determined as follows:

Days remaining in May (31 − 10)	21
Days in June	30
Days in July	31
Days in August	10
Total days	92

Interest and Interest Rate The interest is the cost of borrowing money or the return for lending money, depending on whether one is the borrower or the lender. The amount of interest is based on three factors: the principal (the amount of money borrowed or lent), the rate of interest, and the loan's length of time. The formula used in computing interest is as follows:

$$\text{Principal} \times \text{rate of interest} \times \text{time} = \text{interest}$$

Interest rates are usually stated on an annual basis. For example, the interest on a $1,000, one-year, 8 percent note would be $80 ($1,000 × 8/100 × 1 = $80). If the term, or time period, of the note were three months instead of a year, the interest charge would be $20 ($1,000 × 8/100 × 3/12 = $20).

When the term of a note is expressed in days, the exact number of days must be used in computing the interest. To keep the computation simple, let us compute interest on the basis of 360 days per year.[9] Therefore, if the term of the above note were 45 days, the interest would be $10, computed as follows: $1,000 × 8/100 × 45/360 = $10.

Maturity Value The maturity value is the total proceeds of a note at the maturity date. Maturity value is the face value of the note plus interest. The maturity value of a 90-day, 8 percent, $1,000 note is computed as follows:

$$
\begin{aligned}
\text{Maturity value} &= \text{principal} + \text{interest} \\
&= \$1,000 + (\$1,000 \times 8/100 \times 90/360) \\
&= \$1,000 + \$20 \\
&= \$1,020
\end{aligned}
$$

There are also so-called non-interest-bearing notes. The maturity value is the face value, or principal amount. In this case, the principal includes an implied interest cost.

ILLUSTRATIVE ACCOUNTING ENTRIES

The accounting entries for promissory notes receivable fall into four groups: (1) recording receipt of a note, (2) recording collection on a note, (3) recording a dishonored note, and (4) recording adjusting entries.

Recording Receipt of a Note Assume that on June 1 a 12 percent, 30-day note is received from a customer, J. Halsted, in settlement of an existing account receivable of $4,000. The entry for this transaction is as follows:

June 1 Notes Receivable	4,000	
Accounts Receivable		4,000
Received 12 percent, 30-day note in payment of account of J. Halsted		

9. Practice varies on the computation of interest. Most banks use a 365-day year for all loans, but some use a 360-day year for commercial loans. In Europe, use of a 360-day year is common. In this book, we use a 360-day year to keep the computations simple.

Recording Collection on a Note

When the note plus interest is collected 30 days later, the entry is as follows:

July 1	Cash	4,040	
	Notes Receivable		4,000
	Interest Income		40
	Collected 12 percent, 30-day		
	note from J. Halsted		

Recording a Dishonored Note

When the maker of a note does not pay the note at maturity, the note is said to be dishonored. The holder, or payee, of a dishonored note should make an entry to transfer the total amount due from Notes Receivable to an account receivable from the debtor. If J. Halsted dishonors her note on July 1, the following entry would be made.

July 1	Accounts Receivable	4,040	
	Notes Receivable		4,000
	Interest Income		40
	12 percent, 30-day note		
	dishonored by J. Halsted		

The interest earned is recorded because, although J. Halsted did not pay the note, she is still obligated to pay both the principal and the interest.

Two things are accomplished by transferring a dishonored note receivable into an Accounts Receivable account. First, it leaves the Notes Receivable account with only notes that have not matured and are presumably negotiable and collectible. Second, it establishes a record in the borrower's accounts receivable account that he or she has dishonored a note receivable. Such information may be helpful in deciding whether to extend future credit to the customer.

Recording Adjusting Entries

A promissory note received in one period may not be due until a following accounting period. Because the interest on a note accrues by a small amount each day of the note's duration, it is necessary, according to the matching rule, to apportion the interest earned to the period in which it belongs. For example, assume that on August 31 a 60-day, 8 percent, $2,000 note was received and that the company prepares financial statements monthly. The following adjusting entry is necessary on September 30 to show how the interest earned for September has accrued.

Sept. 30	Interest Receivable	13.33	
	Interest Income		13.33
	To accrue 30 days' interest		
	earned on a note receivable		
	$2,000 \times 8/100 \times 30/360 = \$13.33$		

The account Interest Receivable is a current asset on the balance sheet. When payment of the note plus interest is received on October 30, the following entry is made.[10]

Oct. 30	Cash	2,026.67	
	Notes Receivable		2,000.00
	Interest Receivable		13.33
	Interest Income		13.34
	Receipt of note receivable		
	plus interest		

10. Some firms may follow the practice of reversing the September 30 adjusting entry. Here we assume that a reversing entry is not made.

As seen from these transactions, both September and October receive the benefit of one-half the interest earned.

6 *Account for credit card transactions*

CREDIT CARD SALES

Many retailers allow customers to charge their purchases to a third-party company that the customer will pay later. These transactions are normally handled with credit cards. Five of the most widely used credit cards are American Express, Discover Card, Diners Club, MasterCard, and VISA. The customer establishes credit with the lender (the credit card issuer) and receives a plastic card to use in making charge purchases. If the seller accepts the card, an invoice is prepared and signed by the customer at the time of the sale. The seller then sends the invoice to the lender and receives cash. Because the seller does not have to establish the customer's credit, collect from the customer, or tie money up in accounts receivable, the seller receives an economic benefit provided by the lender. As payment, the lender takes a discount of 2 to 6 percent on the credit card sales invoices rather than paying 100 percent of their total amount.

One of two procedures is used in accounting for credit card sales, depending on whether the seller must wait for collection from the lender or may immediately deposit the sales invoices in a checking account. The following example illustrates the first procedure. Assume that, at the end of the day, a restaurant has American Express invoices totaling $1,000 and that the discount charged by American Express is 4 percent. The sales are recorded as follows:

Accounts Receivable	960	
Credit Card Discount Expense	40	
Sales		1,000
Sales made on American Express cards; discount fee is 4 percent		

The seller sends the invoices to American Express and later receives payment for them at 96 percent of their face value. When cash is received, the entry is as follows:

Cash	960	
Accounts Receivable		960
Receipt of payment from American Express for invoices at 96 percent of face value		

The second procedure is typical of sales made through bank credit cards such as VISA and MasterCard. Assume that the restaurant made sales of $1,000 on VISA credit cards and that VISA takes a 4 percent discount on the sales. Assume also that the sales invoices are deposited in a special VISA bank account in the name of the company, in much the same way that checks from cash sales are deposited. The sales are recorded as follows:

Cash	960	
Credit Card Discount Expense	40	
Sales		1,000
Sales on VISA cards		

CHAPTER REVIEW

REVIEW OF LEARNING OBJECTIVES

1. **Identify and explain the management issues related to short-term liquid assets.** In managing short-term liquid assets, management must (1) consider the effects of seasonal cycles on the need for short-term investing and borrowing as the business's balance of cash fluctuates, (2) establish credit policies that balance the need for sales with the ability to collect, and (3) assess the need for additional cash flows through the financing of receivables.

2. **Define *cash* and *cash equivalents*.** Cash consists of coins and currency on hand, checks and money orders received from customers, and deposits in bank accounts. Cash equivalents are investments that have a term of less than ninety days.

3. **Account for short-term investments.** Short-term investments may be classified as held-to-maturity securities, trading securities, and available-for-sale securities. Held-to-maturity securities are debt securities that management intends to hold to the maturity date; they are valued on the balance sheet at cost adjusted for the effects of interest. Trading securities are debt and equity securities bought and held principally for the purpose of being sold in the near term; they are valued at fair value or at market value. Unrealized gains or losses on trading securities appear on the income statement. Available-for-sale securities are debt and equity securities that do not meet the criteria for either held-to-maturity or trading securities. They are accounted for in the same way as trading securities, except that an unrealized gain or loss is reported as a special item in the stockholders' equity section of the balance sheet.

4. **Define *accounts receivable* and apply the allowance method of accounting for uncollectible accounts, using both the percentage of net sales method and the accounts receivable aging method.** Accounts receivable are amounts still to be collected from credit sales to customers. The amounts still owed by individual customers are found in the subsidiary ledger.

    Because credit is offered to increase sales, uncollectible accounts associated with credit sales should be charged as expenses in the period in which the sales are made. However, because of the time lag between the sales and the time the accounts are judged uncollectible, the accountant must estimate the amount of bad debts in any given period.

    Uncollectible accounts expense is estimated by either the percentage of net sales method or the accounts receivable aging method. When the first method is used, bad debts are judged to be a certain percentage of sales during the period. When the second method is used, certain percentages are applied to groups of accounts receivable that have been arranged by due dates. A third method, the direct charge-off method, is used by some small companies because it is required in computing taxable income under federal tax regulations. However, companies that follow generally accepted accounting principles do not use the direct charge-off method in their financial statements because it does not follow the matching rule.

    Allowance for Uncollectible Accounts is a contra-asset account to Accounts Receivable. The estimate of uncollectible accounts is debited to Uncollectible Accounts Expense and credited to the allowance account. When an individual account is determined to be uncollectible, it is removed from Accounts Receivable by debiting the allowance account and crediting Accounts Receivable. If the written-off account should later be collected, the earlier entry should be reversed and the collection recorded in the normal way.

5. **Define and describe a *promissory note*, and make calculations and journal entries involving promissory notes.** A promissory note is an unconditional promise to pay a definite sum of money on demand or at a future date. Companies selling durable goods of high value, such as farm machinery and automobiles, often accept promissory notes, which can be sold to banks as a financing method.

    In accounting for promissory notes, it is important to know how to calculate the maturity date, duration of note, interest and interest rate, and maturity value. The accounting entries for promissory notes receivable fall into four groups: recording receipt of a note, recording collection on a note, recording a dishonored note, and recording adjusting entries.

SUPPLEMENTAL OBJECTIVE

6. **Account for credit card transactions.** The use of third-party credit cards allows a company to sell on credit without incurring the cost of a credit department, keeping records of the account, and absorbing losses from bad debts. In return, the company pays a fee, which is recorded as an expense at the time of the sale. Some credit card companies allow the merchant to deposit the credit card receipts in the bank immediately, while others require the merchant to wait for payment.

REVIEW OF CONCEPTS AND TERMINOLOGY

The following concepts and terms were introduced in this chapter.

L O 4   **Accounts receivable:** Short-term liquid assets that arise from sales on credit at the wholesale or retail level.

L O 4   **Accounts receivable aging method:** A method of estimating uncollectible accounts based on the assumption that a predictable proportion of each dollar of accounts receivable outstanding will not be collected.

L O 4   **Aging of accounts receivable:** The process of listing each accounts receivable customer according to the due date of the account.

L O 4   **Allowance for Uncollectible Accounts:** A contra-asset account that reduces accounts receivable to the amount that is expected to be collected in cash; also called *allowance for bad debts*.

L O 4   **Allowance method:** A method of accounting for uncollectible accounts by expensing estimated uncollectible accounts in the period in which the related sales take place.

L O 3   **Available-for-sale securities:** Debt and equity securities that do not meet the criteria for either held-to-maturity or trading securities.

L O 1   **Average days' sales uncollected:** A ratio that shows on average how long it takes to collect accounts receivable; 365 days divided by receivable turnover.

L O 2   **Cash:** Coins and currency on hand, checks and money orders from customers, and deposits in bank checking accounts.

L O 2   **Cash equivalents:** Short-term investments that will revert to cash in less than ninety days from when they are purchased.

L O 2   **Compensating balance:** A minimum amount that a bank requires a company to keep in its account as part of a credit-granting arrangement.

L O 1   **Contingent liability:** A potential liability that can develop into a real liability if a possible subsequent event occurs.

L O 4   **Direct charge-off method:** A method of accounting for uncollectible accounts by directly debiting an expense account when bad debts are discovered instead of using the allowance method; this method violates the matching rule but is required for federal income tax computations.

L O 1   **Discounting:** A method of selling notes receivable in which the bank deducts the interest from the maturity value of the note to determine the proceeds.

L O 5   **Dishonored note:** A promissory note that the maker cannot or will not pay at the maturity date.

L O 5   **Duration of note:** Length of time in days between a promissory note's issue date and its maturity date.

L O 1   **Factor:** An entity that buys accounts receivable.

L O 1   **Factoring:** The selling or transferring of accounts receivable.

L O 3   **Held-to-maturity securities:** Debt securities that management intends to hold to their maturity or payment date and whose cash value is not needed until that date.

L O 4   **Installment accounts receivable:** Accounts receivable that are payable in a series of time payments.

L O 5   **Interest:** The cost of borrowing money or the return for lending money, depending on whether one is the borrower or the lender.

L O 3   **Marketable securities:** Short-term investments intended to be held until needed to pay current obligations. Also called *short-term investments.*

L O 5   **Maturity date:** The due date of a promissory note.

L O 5   **Maturity value:** The total proceeds of a promissory note, including principal and interest, at the maturity date.

L O 5   **Notes payable:** Collective term for promissory notes owed by the entity (maker) who promises payment to other entities.

L O 5   **Notes receivable:** Collective term for promissory notes held by the entity to whom payment is promised (payee).

L O 4   **Percentage of net sales method:** A method of estimating uncollectible accounts based on the assumption that a predictable proportion of each dollar of sales will not be collected.

L O 5   **Promissory note:** An unconditional promise to pay a definite sum of money on demand or at a future date.

L O 1   **Quick ratio:** A ratio for measuring the adequacy of short-term liquid assets; quick assets divided by current liabilities.

L O 1   **Receivable turnover:** A ratio for measuring the average number of times receivables were turned into cash during an accounting period; net sales divided by average net accounts receivable.

L O 3   **Short-term investments:** Temporary investments of excess cash, intended to be held until needed to pay current obligations. Also called *marketable securities.*

L O 1   **Short-term liquid assets:** Financial assets that arise from cash transactions, the investment of cash, and the extension of credit.

L O 4   **Trade credit:** Credit granted to customers by wholesalers or retailers.

L O 3   **Trading securities:** Debt and equity securities bought and held principally for the purpose of being sold in the near term.

L O 4   **Uncollectible accounts:** Accounts receivable owed by customers who cannot or will not pay. Also called *bad debts.*

REVIEW PROBLEM

ENTRIES FOR UNCOLLECTIBLE ACCOUNTS EXPENSE AND NOTES RECEIVABLE TRANSACTIONS

L O 4, 5   The Farm Implement Company sells merchandise on credit and also accepts notes for payment. During the year ended June 30, the company had net sales of $1,200,000, and at the end of the year it had Accounts Receivable of $400,000 and a debit balance in Allowance for Uncollectible Accounts of $2,100. In the past, approximately 1.5 percent of net sales have proved uncollectible. Also, an aging analysis of accounts receivable reveals that $17,000 in accounts receivable appears to be uncollectible.

     The Farm Implement Company sold a tractor to R. C. Sims. Payment was received in the form of a $15,000, 9 percent, 90-day note dated March 16. On June 14, Sims dishonored the note. On June 29, the company received payment in full from Sims plus additional interest from the date of the dishonored note.

REQUIRED   1. Prepare journal entries to record uncollectible accounts expense using (a) the percentage of net sales method and (b) the accounts receivable aging method.

     2. Prepare journal entries relating to the note received from R. C. Sims.

ANSWER TO REVIEW PROBLEM

1. Prepare journal entries to record uncollectible accounts expense.

   a. Percentage of net sales method:

June 30	Uncollectible Accounts Expense	18,000.00	
	Allowance for Uncollectible Accounts		18,000.00
	To record estimated uncollectible accounts expense: 1.5 percent × $1,200,000 = $18,000		

   b. Accounts receivable aging method:

June 30	Uncollectible Accounts Expense	19,100.00	
	Allowance for Uncollectible Accounts		19,100.00
	To record estimated uncollectible accounts expense. The debit balance in the allowance account must be added to the estimated uncollectible accounts: $2,100 + $17,000 = $19,100		

2. Prepare journal entries related to the note.

Mar. 16	Notes Receivable	15,000.00	
	Sales		15,000.00
	Tractor sold to R. C. Sims; terms of note: 9 percent, 90 days		

June 14	Accounts Receivable	15,337.50	
	Notes Receivable		15,000.00
	Interest Income		337.50
	The note was dishonored by R. C. Sims Maturity value: $15,000 + ($15,000 × 9/100 × 90/360) = $15,337.50		

29	Cash	15,395.02	
	Accounts Receivable		15,337.50
	Interest Income		57.52
	Received payment in full from R. C. Sims $15,337.50 + ($15,337.50 × 9/100 × 15/360) $15,337.50 + $57.52 = $15,395.02		

CHAPTER ASSIGNMENTS

QUESTIONS

1. Why does a business need short-term liquid assets? What three issues does management face in managing short-term liquid assets?
2. What is a factor, and what do the terms *factoring with recourse* and *factoring without recourse* mean?
3. What items are included in the Cash account? What is a compensating balance?
4. How do cash equivalents differ from cash? From short-term investments?
5. What are the three kinds of securities held as short-term investments and how are they valued at the balance sheet date?
6. What are unrealized gains and losses on trading securities? On what statement are they reported?

7. Which of the following lettered items should be in Accounts Receivable? If an item does not belong in Accounts Receivable, tell where on the balance sheet it does belong: (a) installment accounts receivable from regular customers, due monthly for three years; (b) debit balances in customers' accounts; (c) receivables from employees; (d) credit balances in customers' accounts; (e) receivables from officers of the company.

8. Why does a company sell on credit if it expects that some of the accounts will not be paid? What role does a credit department play in selling on credit?

9. What accounting rule is violated by the direct charge-off method of recognizing uncollectible accounts? Why?

10. According to generally accepted accounting principles, at what point in the cycle of selling and collecting does a loss on an uncollectible account occur?

11. Are the following terms different in any way: allowance for bad debts, allowance for doubtful accounts, allowance for uncollectible accounts?

12. What is the effect on net income of an optimistic versus a pessimistic view by management of estimated uncollectible accounts?

13. In what ways is Allowance for Uncollectible Accounts similar to Accumulated Depreciation? In what ways is it different?

14. What is the reasoning behind the percentage of net sales method and the accounts receivable aging method of estimating uncollectible accounts?

15. What procedure for estimating uncollectible accounts also gives management a view of the status of collections and the overall quality of accounts receivable?

16. After adjusting and closing entries at the end of the year, suppose that Accounts Receivable is $176,000 and Allowance for Uncollectible Accounts is $14,500. (a) What is the collectible value of Accounts Receivable? (b) If the $450 account of a bankrupt customer is written off in the first month of the new year, what will be the resulting collectible value of Accounts Receivable?

17. Why should an account that has been written off as uncollectible be reinstated if the amount owed is subsequently collected?

18. What is a promissory note? Who is the maker? Who is the payee?

19. What are the maturity dates of the following notes: (a) a 3-month note dated August 16, (b) a 90-day note dated August 16, and (c) a 60-day note dated March 25?

20. Why are merchants willing to pay a fee to credit card companies to be able to accept their cards from customers?

SHORT EXERCISES

SE 1. *Management Issues*
L O 1
Check Figures: c, a, b, a

Indicate whether each of the actions below is related to (a) managing cash needs during seasonal cycles, (b) setting credit policies, or (c) financing receivables.

1. Selling accounts receivable to a factor
2. Borrowing funds for short-term needs during slow periods
3. Conducting thorough checks of new customers' ability to pay
4. Investing cash that is not currently needed for operations

SE 2. *Short-Term*
L O 1 *Liquidity Ratios*
Check Figures: Quick ratio: 1.5; Receivable turnover: 9.0 times; Average days' sales uncollected: 40.6 days

Slater Company has cash of $20,000, short-term investments of $25,000, net accounts receivable of $45,000, inventory of $44,000, accounts payable of $60,000, and net sales of $360,000. Last year's net accounts receivable were $35,000. Compute the following ratios: quick ratio, receivable turnover, and average days' sales uncollected.

SE 3. *Cash and Cash*
L O 2 *Equivalents*
Check Figure: $33,500

Compute the amount of cash and cash equivalents on Quay Company's balance sheet if, on the balance sheet date, it has coins and currency on hand of $500, deposits in checking accounts of $3,000, U.S. Treasury bills due in 80 days of $30,000, and U.S. Treasury bonds due in 200 days of $50,000.

SE 4. *Held-to-Maturity*
L O 3 *Securities*

No check figure

On May 31, Renata Company invested $49,000 in U.S. Treasury bills. The bills mature in 120 days at $50,000. Prepare entries to record the purchase on May 31; the adjustment to accrue interest on June 30, which is the end of the fiscal year; and the receipt of cash at the maturity date of September 28.

SE 5. *Trading Securities*
L O 3

Check Figure: Dec. 31 unrealized gain: $85,000

Monika Corporation began investing in trading securities this year. At the end of 19x1, the following trading portfolio existed.

Security	Cost	Market Value
Sara Lee (10,000 shares)	$220,000	$330,000
Skyline (5,000 shares)	100,000	75,000
Totals	$320,000	$405,000

Prepare the necessary year-end adjusting entry on December 31 and the entry for the sale of all the Skyline shares on the following March 23 for $95,000.

SE 6. *Percentage of Net*
L O 4 *Sales Method*

Check Figure: Uncollectible Accounts Expense: $27,700

At the end of October, Mafa Company management estimates the uncollectible accounts expense to be 1 percent of net sales of $2,770,000. Give the entry to record the uncollectible accounts expense, assuming that the Allowance for Uncollectible Accounts has a debit balance of $14,000.

SE 7. *Accounts Receivable*
L O 4 *Aging Method*

Check Figure: Uncollectible Accounts Expense: a. $34,000; b. $50,000

An aging analysis on June 30 of the accounts receivable of Texbar Corporation indicates uncollectible accounts of $43,000. Give the entry to record uncollectible accounts expense under each of the following independent assumptions: (a) Allowance for Uncollectible Accounts has a credit balance of $9,000 before adjustment, and (b) Allowance for Uncollectible Accounts has a debit balance of $7,000 before adjustment.

SE 8. *Write-off of*
L O 4 *Accounts Receivable*

No check figure

Key Company, which uses the allowance method, has an account receivable from Sandy Burgess of $4,400 that it deems to be uncollectible. Prepare the entries on May 31 to write off the account and on August 13 to record an unexpected receipt from Burgess of $1,000. The company does not expect to collect more from Burgess.

SE 9. *Note Receivable*
L O 5 *Calculations*

Check Figures: Maturity date: September 13; Maturity value: $5,075

On June 15, Rostin Company received a 90-day, 6 percent note in the amount of $5,000. What are the maturity date and the maturity value of the note?

SE 10. *Notes Receivable*
L O 5 *Entries*

No check figure

On August 25, Rostin Company received a 90-day, 9 percent note in settlement of an account receivable in the amount of $10,000. Record the receipt of the note, the accrual of interest at fiscal year end on September 30, and collection of the note on the due date.

EXERCISES

E 1. *Management Issues*
L O 1

Check Figures: 1. a, 2. b, 3. b, 4. c, 5. a, 6. b, 7. c or a, 8. b

Indicate whether each of the following actions is primarily related to (a) managing cash needs during seasonal cycles, (b) setting credit policies, or (c) financing receivables.

1. Buying a U.S. Treasury bill with cash that is not needed for a few months
2. Comparing receivable turnovers for two years
3. Setting policy on which customers may buy on credit
4. Selling notes receivable to a financing company
5. Borrowing funds for short-term needs during the period of the year when sales are low
6. Changing the terms for credit sales in an effort to reduce the average days' sales uncollected
7. Using a factor to provide operating funds
8. Establishing a department whose responsibility is to approve customers' credit

E 2. *Short-Term*
L O 1 *Liquidity Ratios*

Check Figures: Quick ratio: 1.4;
Receivable turnover: 8.4 times;
Average days' sales uncollected:
43.5 days

Using the following information selected from the financial statements of Li Company, compute the quick ratio, the receivable turnover, and the average days' sales uncollected.

Current Assets	
Cash	$ 35,000
Short-Term Investments	85,000
Notes Receivable	120,000
Accounts Receivable, net	100,000
Inventory	250,000
Prepaid Assets	25,000
Total Current Assets	$615,000
Current Liabilities	
Notes Payable	$150,000
Accounts Payable	75,000
Accrued Liabilities	10,000
Total Current Liabilities	$235,000
Net Sales	$800,000
Last Period's Accounts Receivable, net	$ 90,000

E 3. *Cash and Cash*
L O 2 *Equivalents*

Check Figure: $129,800

At year end, Prosac Company had coins and currency in cash registers of $2,800, money orders from customers of $5,000, deposits in checking accounts of $32,000, U.S. Treasury bills due in ninety days of $90,000, certificates of deposits at the bank that mature in six months of $100,000, and U.S. Treasury bonds due in one year of $50,000. Calculate the amount of cash and cash equivalents that will be shown on the company's year-end balance sheet.

E 4. *Held-to-Maturity*
L O 3 *Securities*

No check figure

Swick Company experiences heavy sales in the summer and early fall, after which time it has excess cash to invest until the next spring. On November 1, 19x1, the company invested $194,000 in U.S. Treasury bills. The bills mature in 180 days at $200,000. Prepare entries to record the purchase on November 1; the adjustment to accrue interest on December 31, which is the end of the fiscal year; and the receipt of cash at the maturity date of April 30.

E 5. *Trading Securities*
L O 3

Check Figure: June 30 unrealized
gain: $34,000

Saito Corporation began investing in trading securities and engaged in the following transactions.

Jan. 6   Purchased 7,000 shares of Chemical Bank stock, $30 per share.
Feb. 15 Purchased 9,000 shares of EG&G, $22 per share.

At June 30 year end, Chemical Bank was trading at $40 per share and EG&G was trading at $18 per share. Record the entries for the purchases. Then record the necessary year-end adjusting entry. (Include a schedule of the trading portfolio cost and market in the explanation.) Also record the entry for the sale of all the EG&G shares on August 20 for $16 per share. Is the last entry affected by the June 30 adjustment?

E 6. *Percentage of Net*
L O 4 *Sales Method*

Check Figure: Uncollectible Accounts
Expense: $70,700

At the end of the year, Marin Enterprises estimates the uncollectible accounts expense to be .7 percent of net sales of $10,100,000. The current credit balance of Allowance for Uncollectible Accounts is $17,200. Give the general journal entry to record the uncollectible accounts expense. What is the balance of Allowance for Uncollectible Accounts after this adjustment?

E 7. *Accounts Receivable*
L O 4 *Aging Method*

Check Figures: Uncollectible
Accounts Expense: a. $5,900;
b. $7,500

Accounts Receivable of Herrera Company shows a debit balance of $104,000 at the end of the year. An aging analysis of the individual accounts indicates estimated uncollectible accounts to be $6,700.

Give the general journal entry to record the uncollectible accounts expense under each of the following independent assumptions: (a) Allowance for Uncollectible Accounts has a credit balance of $800 before adjustment and (b) Allowance for Uncollectible Accounts has a debit balance of $800 before adjustment. What is the balance of Allowance for Uncollectible Accounts after each of these adjustments?

E 8. *Aging Method and*
L O 4 *Net Sales Method*
Contrasted

Check Figures: Net Accounts
Receivable: a. $1,220,400;
b. $1,212,600

At the beginning of 19xx, the balances for Accounts Receivable and Allowance for Uncollectible Accounts were $860,000 and $62,800, respectively. During the current year, credit sales were $6,400,000 and collections on accounts were $5,900,000. In addition, $70,000 in uncollectible accounts were written off.

Using T accounts, determine the year-end balances of Accounts Receivable and Allowance for Uncollectible Accounts. Then, make the year-end adjusting entry to record the uncollectible accounts expense, and show the year-end balance sheet presentation of Accounts Receivable and Allowance for Uncollectible Accounts under each of the following conditions:

a. Management estimates the percentage of uncollectible credit sales to be 1.2 percent of total credit sales.
b. Based on an aging of accounts receivable, management estimates the end-of-year uncollectible accounts receivable to be $77,400.

Post the results of each entry to the T account for Allowance for Uncollectible Accounts.

E 9. *Aging Method and*
L O 4 *Net Sales Method*
Contrasted

Check Figures: Balance of Allowance
for Uncollectible Accounts: a. $30,750;
b. $35,000

During 19x1, General Road Company had net sales of $2,850,000. Most of the sales were on credit. At the end of 19x1, the balance of Accounts Receivable was $350,000 and Allowance for Uncollectible Accounts had a debit balance of $12,000. Management has two methods of estimating uncollectible accounts expense: (a) The percentage of uncollectible sales is 1.5 percent, and (b) based on an aging of accounts receivable, the end-of-year uncollectible accounts total $35,000. Make the end-of-year adjusting entry for uncollectible accounts expense under each method and tell what the balance of Allowance for Uncollectible Accounts will be after each adjustment. Why are the results different, and which method is likely to be more reliable?

E 10. *Entries for*
L O 4 *Uncollectible*
Accounts Expense

Check Figures: Uncollectible
Accounts Expense: a. $32,200;
b. $33,400

The Schumacker Office Supply Company sells merchandise on credit. During the fiscal year ended December 31, the company had net sales of $2,300,000. At the end of the year, it had Accounts Receivable of $600,000 and a debit balance in Allowance for Uncollectible Accounts of $3,400. In the past, approximately 1.4 percent of net sales have proved uncollectible. Also, an aging analysis of accounts receivable reveals that $30,000 of the receivables appear to be uncollectible. Prepare journal entries to record uncollectible accounts expense using (a) the percentage of net sales method and (b) the accounts receivable aging method.

What is the resulting balance of Allowance for Uncollectible Accounts under each method? How would your answers under each method change if Allowance for Uncollectible Accounts had a credit balance of $3,400 instead of a debit balance? Why do the methods result in different balances?

E 11. *Accounts Receivable*
L O 4 *Transactions*

No check figure

Assuming that the allowance method is being used, prepare journal entries to record the following transactions.

May 17, 19x4 Sold merchandise to Holly Fox for $900, terms n/10.
Sept. 20, 19x4 Received $300 from Holly Fox on account.
June 25, 19x5 Wrote off as uncollectible the balance of the Holly Fox account when she was declared bankrupt.
July 27, 19x5 Unexpectedly received a check for $100 from Holly Fox. No additional amount is expected to be collected from Fox.

E 12. *Interest*
L O 5 *Computations*

Check Figures: a. $570; b. $320;
c. $135; d. $1,500; e. $108

Determine the interest on the following notes.

a. $22,800 at 10 percent for 90 days
b. $16,000 at 12 percent for 60 days
c. $18,000 at 9 percent for 30 days
d. $30,000 at 15 percent for 120 days
e. $10,800 at 6 percent for 60 days

E 13. *Notes Receivable*
L O 5 *Transactions*

No check figure

Prepare general journal entries to record the following transactions.

Jan. 16 Sold merchandise to Brighton Corporation on account for $36,000, terms n/30.
Feb. 15 Accepted a $36,000, 10 percent, 90-day note from Brighton Corporation in lieu of payment of account.

May 16 Brighton Corporation dishonored the note.

June 15 Received payment in full from Brighton Corporation, including interest at 10 percent from the date the note was dishonored.

E 14. *Adjusting Entries:*
L O 5 *Interest Expense*

No check figure

Prepare journal entries (assuming reversing entries are not made) to record the following transactions.

Dec. 1 Received a 90-day, 12 percent note for $5,000 from a customer for the sale of merchandise.

31 Made end-of-year adjustment for interest income.

Mar. 1 Received payment in full for note and interest.

E 15. *Notes Receivable*
L O 5 *Transactions*

No check figure

Prepare general journal entries to record these transactions.

Jan. 5 Accepted a $2,400, 60-day, 10 percent note dated this day in granting a time extension on the past-due account of A. Jones.

Mar. 6 A. Jones paid the maturity value of his $2,400 note.

9 Accepted a $1,500, 60-day, 12 percent note dated this day in granting a time extension on the past-due account of S. Smith.

May 8 When asked for payment, S. Smith dishonored his note.

June 7 S. Smith paid in full the maturity value of the note plus interest at 12 percent for the period since May 8.

E 16. *Credit Card Sales*
S O 6 *Transactions*

No check figure

Prepare journal entries to record the following transactions for Toni's Novelties Store.

Apr. 8 A tabulation of invoices at the end of the day showed $2,200 in American Express invoices and $1,200 in Diners Club invoices. American Express takes a discount of 4 percent, and Diners Club takes a 5 percent discount.

15 Received payment from American Express at 96 percent of face value and from Diners Club at 95 percent of face value.

19 A tabulation of invoices at the end of the day showed $800 in VISA invoices, which are deposited in a special bank account at full value less 5 percent discount.

SKILLS DEVELOPMENT EXERCISES

Conceptual Analysis

SDE 1. *Management of*
L O 1 *Cash*

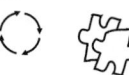

No check figure

Academia Publishing Company publishes college textbooks in the sciences and humanities. More than 50 percent of the company's sales occur in July, August, and December. Its cash balances are largest in August, September, and January. During the rest of the year, its cash receipts are low. The corporate treasurer keeps the cash in a bank checking account earning little or no interest and pays bills from this account as they come due. To survive, the company has borrowed money during some slow sales months. The loans were repaid in the months when cash receipts were largest. A management consultant has suggested that the company institute a new cash management plan under which cash would be invested in marketable securities as it is received and securities would be sold when the funds are needed. In this way, the company will earn income on the cash and may realize a gain through an increase in the value of the securities, thus reducing the need for borrowing. What are the accounting implications of this cash management plan? Are there any disadvantages to the plan?

SDE 2. *Role of Credit Sales*
L O 1

No check figure

Mitsubishi Electric Corp.,[11] a broadly diversified Japanese corporation, instituted a credit plan called Three Diamonds for customers who buy its major electronic products, such as large-screen televisions and videotape recorders, from specified retail dealers. Under the plan, approved customers who make purchases in November 1994 do not have to make any payments until January 1996 and pay no interest for the

11. Information based on promotional brochures received from Mitsubishi Electric Corp.

intervening months. Mitsubishi pays the dealer the full amount less a small fee, sends the customer a Mitsubishi credit card, and collects from the customer at the specified time. What is Mitsubishi's motivation for establishing such generous credit terms? What costs are involved? What are the accounting implications?

SDE 3. *Asset Financing*

L O 1

No check figure

Siegel Appliances, Inc. is a small manufacturer of washing machines and dryers located in central Michigan. Siegel sells most of its appliances to large, established discount retail companies that market the appliances under their own names. Siegel sells the appliances on trade credit terms of n/60. If a customer wants a longer term, however, Siegel will accept a note with a term of up to nine months. At present, the company is having cash flow troubles and needs $5 million immediately. Its cash balance is $200,000, its accounts receivable balance is $2.3 million, and its notes receivable balance is $3.7 million. How might Siegel's management use its accounts receivable and notes receivable to raise the cash it needs? What are the company's prospects for raising the needed cash?

SDE 4. *Percentage of Net*

L O 4 *Sales and Aging*
Methods Contrasted

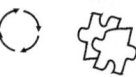

No check figure

All companies that sell on credit face the risk of bad debt losses. For example, in 1992, ***L.A. Gear Inc.,*** the well-known maker of athletic footwear, had an allowance for uncollectible accounts of $6.9 million on accounts receivable of $63.0 million. Its 1992 sales were $430.2 million.[12] What two methods are available to L.A. Gear Inc. for estimating uncollectible accounts expense? Contrast the two methods, including their relationships to the financial statements. Which method would you expect L.A. Gear Inc. to use? Why?

Ethical Dilemma

SDE 5. *Ethics, Uncollectible*

L O 1, 4 *Accounts, and*
Short-Term
Objectives

No check figure

Fitzsimmons Designs, a successful retail furniture company, is located in an affluent suburb where a major insurance company has just announced a restructuring that will lay off 4,000 employees. Fitzsimmons sells quality furniture, usually on credit. Accounts Receivable represents one of the major assets of the company and, although the company's annual uncollectible accounts losses are not out of line, they represent a sizable amount. The company depends on bank loans for its financing. Sales and net income in the past year have declined, and some customers are falling behind in paying their accounts. George Fitzsimmons, owner of the business, knows that the bank's loan officer likes to see a steady performance. Therefore, he has instructed the controller to underestimate the uncollectible accounts this year to show a small growth in earnings. Fitzsimmons believes the short-term action is justified because future successful years will average out the losses, and since the company has a history of success, the adjustments are meaningless accounting measures anyway. Are Fitzsimmons's actions ethical? Would any parties be harmed by his actions? How important is it to try to be accurate in estimating losses from uncollectible accounts?

Research Activity

SDE 6. *Stock and Treasury*

L O 1 *Investments*

No check figure

Find a recent issue of the *Wall Street Journal* in your school library. Turn to the third, or C, section, entitled "Money & Investing." From the index at the top of the page, locate the listing of New York Stock Exchange (NYSE) stocks and turn to that page. From the listing of stocks, find five companies you have heard of. They may be companies like IBM, Deere, McDonald's, or Ford. Copy down the range of each company's stock price for the last year and the current closing price. Also, copy down the dividend, if any, per share. How much did the market values of the common stocks you picked vary in the last year? Do these data demonstrate the need to value short-term investments of this type at market? How does accounting for short-term investments in these common stocks differ from accounting for short-term investments in U.S. Treasury bills? How are dividends received on investments in these common stocks accounted for? Be prepared to hand in your notes and to discuss the results of your investigation in class.

12. L.A. Gear Inc., *Annual Report*, 1992.

Decision-Making Practice

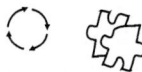
The ***Bates Christmas Tree Company***'s business—the growing and selling of Christmas trees—is seasonal. By January 1, after a successful season, the company has cash on hand that will not be needed for several months. The company has minimal expenses from January to October and heavy expenses during the harvest and shipping months of November and December. The company's management follows the practice of investing the idle cash in marketable securities, which can be sold as the funds are needed for operations. The company's fiscal year ends on June 30. On January 10 of the current year, the company has cash of $373,300 on hand. It keeps $20,000 on hand for operating expenses and invests the rest as follows:

$100,000 3-month Treasury bill	$ 97,800
1,000 shares of Ford Motor Co. ($40 per share)	40,000
2,500 shares of McDonald's ($40 per share)	100,000
2,100 shares of IBM ($55 per share)	115,500
Total short-term investments	$353,300

During the next few months, the company receives two quarterly cash dividends from each company (assume February 10 and May 10): $1 per share from Ford, $.125 per share from McDonald's, and $1.10 per share from IBM. The Treasury bill is redeemed at face value on April 10. On June 1 management sells 500 shares of McDonald's at $45 per share. On June 30 the market values of the investments are:

Ford Motor Co.	$51 per share
McDonald's	$36 per share
IBM	$50 per share

Another quarterly dividend is received from each company (assume August 10). All the remaining shares are sold on November 1 at the following prices:

Ford Motor Co.	$45 per share
McDonald's	$34 per share
IBM	$60 per share

1. Record the investment transactions that occurred on January 10, February 10, April 10, May 10, and June 1. Prepare the required adjusting entry on June 30, and record the investment transactions on August 10 and November 1.
2. Explain how the short-term investments would be shown on the balance sheet on June 30.
3. After November 1, what is the balance of the Allowance to Reduce Short-Term Investments to Market account, and what will happen to this account next June?
4. What is your assessment of Bates Christmas Tree Company's strategy with regard to idle cash?

PROBLEM SET A

F&M Distributors, Inc. follows a policy of investing excess cash until it is needed. During 19x1 and 19x2, the company engaged in the following transactions.

19x1
Feb. 1   Invested $97,000 in 120-day U.S. Treasury bills that had a maturity value of $100,000.
Mar. 30   Purchased 20,000 shares of Dataflex Company common stock at $16 per share and 12,000 shares of Gates Aviation, Inc. common stock at $10 per share as trading securities.
June 1   Received maturity value of U.S. Treasury bills in cash.
     10   Received dividends of $0.50 per share from Dataflex Company and $0.25 per share from Gates Aviation, Inc.
     30   Made year-end adjusting entry for trading securities. Market price of Dataflex Company shares is $13 per share and of Gates Aviation, Inc. is $12 per share.
Dec. 3   Sold all the shares of Dataflex Company for $12 per share.

19x2

Mar. 17 Purchased 15,000 shares of Biotech, Inc., for $9 per share.

May 31 Invested $116,000 in 120-day U.S. Treasury bills that had a maturity value of $120,000.

June 10 Received dividends of $0.30 per share from Gates Aviation, Inc.

30 Made year-end adjusting entry for held-to-maturity securities.

30 Made year-end adjusting entry for trading securities. Market price of Gates Aviation, Inc. shares is $6 per share and of Biotech, Inc. is $11 per share.

REQUIRED

1. Prepare journal entries to record these transactions, assuming that F&M Distributors, Inc.'s fiscal year ends on June 30.
2. Show the balance sheet presentation of short-term investments on June 30, 19x2.

A 2. *Percentage of Net*
L O 4 *Sales Method*

Check Figure: Uncollectible Accounts Expense: $24,965

Chappell Company had an Accounts Receivable balance of $320,000 and a credit balance in Allowance for Uncollectible Accounts of $16,700 at January 1, 19xx. During the year, the company recorded the following transactions.

a. Sales on account, $1,052,000

b. Sales returns and allowances by credit customers, $53,400

c. Collections from customers, $993,000

d. Worthless accounts written off, $19,800

e. and f. Written-off accounts collected, $4,200

The company's past history indicates that 2.5 percent of net credit sales will not be collected.

REQUIRED

1. Open ledger accounts for the Accounts Receivable controlling account (112) and Allowance for Uncollectible Accounts (113). Then enter the beginning balances in those accounts.
2. Record separate general journal entries for each of the six items listed above, summarizing the year's activity.
3. Record the general journal entry on December 31 for the estimated uncollectible accounts expense for the year.
4. Post the appropriate parts of the transactions in **2** and **3** to Accounts Receivable and Allowance for Uncollectible Accounts.

A 3. *Accounts Receivable*
L O 4 *Aging Method*

Check Figure: Amount of adjustment: $73,413

The DiPalma Jewelry Store uses the accounts receivable aging method to estimate uncollectible accounts. The balance of the Accounts Receivable controlling account was a debit of $446,341 and the balance of Allowance for Uncollectible Accounts was a credit of $43,000 at February 1, 19x1. During the year, the store had sales on account of $3,724,000, sales returns and allowances of $63,000, worthless accounts written off of $44,300, and collections from customers of $3,214,000. As part of the end-of-year (January 31, 19x2) procedures, an aging analysis of accounts receivable is prepared. The totals of the analysis, which is partially complete, follow.

Customer Account	Total	Not Yet Due	1–30 Days Past Due	31–60 Days Past Due	61–90 Days Past Due	Over 90 Days Past Due
Balance Forward	$793,791	$438,933	$149,614	$106,400	$57,442	$41,402

The following accounts remain to be classified to finish the analysis.

Account	Amount	Due Date
H. Caldwell	$10,977	January 15
D. Carlson	9,314	February 15 (next fiscal year)
M. Guokas	8,664	December 20
F. Javier	780	October 1
B. Loo	14,810	January 4
S. Qadri	6,316	November 15
A. Rosenthal	4,389	March 1 (next fiscal year)
	$55,250	

From past experience, the company has found that the following rates are realistic to estimate uncollectible accounts.

Time	Percentage Considered Uncollectible
Not yet due	2
1–30 days past due	5
31–60 days past due	15
61–90 days past due	25
Over 90 days past due	50

REQUIRED

1. Complete the aging analysis of accounts receivable.
2. Determine the end-of-year balances (before adjustments) of Accounts Receivable and Allowance for Uncollectible Accounts.
3. Prepare an analysis computing the estimated uncollectible accounts.
4. Prepare a general journal entry to record the estimated uncollectible accounts expense for the year (round the adjustment to the nearest whole dollar).

A 4. *Notes Receivable*
L O 5 *Transactions*

No check figure

Sharman Manufacturing Company sells truck beds. The company engaged in the following transactions involving promissory notes.

Jan. 10 Sold beds to Hudson Company for $30,000, terms n/10.
     20 Accepted a 90-day, 12 percent promissory note in settlement of the account from Hudson.
Apr. 20 Received payment from Hudson Company for the note and interest.
May 5 Sold beds to Monroe Company for $20,000, terms n/10.
     15 Received $4,000 cash and a 60-day, 13 percent note for $16,000 in settlement of the Monroe account.
July 14 When asked to pay, Monroe dishonored the note.
Aug. 2 Wrote off the Monroe account as uncollectible after receiving news that the company declared bankruptcy.
     5 Received a 90-day, 11 percent note for $15,000 from Circle Company in settlement of an account receivable.
Nov. 3 When asked to pay, Circle dishonored the note.
     9 Received payment in full from Circle, including 15 percent interest for the 6 days since the note was dishonored.

REQUIRED

Prepare general journal entries to record the transactions.

A 5. *Notes Receivable*
L O 5 *Transactions*

No check figure

The Alvarado Company accepts notes as payment for sales to key customers. The transactions involving notes for August and October follow.

Aug. 6 Accepted a $9,000, 60-day, 10 percent note from Cronin Company in payment for merchandise.
     8 Accepted a $7,000, 60-day, 11 percent note from La Russo's Electronics in payment for merchandise.
     28 Accepted a $21,000, 60-day, 9 percent note from Ramsey Company in payment for purchase of merchandise.
     30 Accepted a $14,000, 60-day, 12 percent note from Lee Company in payment for merchandise.
Oct. 5 Received payment from Cronin Company for the note and interest.
     7 When asked to pay, La Russo's Electronics dishonored its note.
     27 Received payment from Ramsey Company for its note and interest.
     29 When asked to pay, Lee Company dishonored its note.
     30 Wrote off La Russo's Electronics account because it was deemed to be uncollectible.

REQUIRED

Prepare general journal entries to record these transactions.

PROBLEM SET B

B 1. *Held-to-Maturity*
L O 3 *and Trading*
Securities

Check Figure: Short-Term
Investments (at market): $903,875

During certain periods, Nicks Company invests its excess cash until it is needed. During 19x1 and 19x2, the company engaged in the following transactions.

19x1

Jan. 16 Invested $146,000 in 120-day U.S. Treasury bills that had a maturity value of $150,000.

Apr. 15 Purchased 10,000 shares of Goodrich Paper common stock at $40 per share and 5,000 shares of Keuron Power Company common stock at $30 per share as trading securities.

May 16 Received maturity value of U.S. Treasury bills in cash.

June 2 Received dividends of $2.00 per share from Goodrich Paper and $1.50 per share from Keuron Power.

30 Made year-end adjusting entry for trading securities. Market price of Goodrich Paper shares is $32 per share and of Keuron Power is $35 per share.

Nov. 14 Sold all the shares of Goodrich Paper for $42 per share.

19x2

Feb. 15 Purchased 9,000 shares of Beacon Communications for $50 per share.

Apr. 1 Invested $195,500 in 120-day U.S. Treasury bills that had a maturity value of $200,000.

June 1 Received dividends of $2.20 per share from Keuron Power.

30 Made year-end adjusting entry for held-to-maturity securities.

30 Made year-end adjusting entry for trading securities. Market price of Keuron Power shares is $33 per share and of Beacon Communications is $60 per share.

REQUIRED

1. Prepare journal entries to record the preceding transactions, assuming that Nicks Company's fiscal year ends on June 30.

2. Show the balance sheet presentation of short-term investments on June 30, 19x2.

B 2. *Percentage of Net*
L O 4 *Sales Method*

Check Figure: Uncollectible Accounts
Expense: $17,952

On December 31 of last year, the balance sheet of Marzano Company had Accounts Receivable of $298,000 and a credit balance in Allowance for Uncollectible Accounts of $20,300. During the current year, the company's records included the following selected activities: (a) sales on account, $1,195,000; (b) sales returns and allowances, $73,000; (c) collections from customers, $1,150,000; (d) accounts written off as worthless, $16,000; (e and f) written-off accounts unexpectedly collected, $2,000. In the past, the company had found that 1.6 percent of net sales would not be collected.

REQUIRED

1. Open ledger accounts for the Accounts Receivable controlling account (112) and Allowance for Uncollectible Accounts (113). Then enter the beginning balances in those accounts.

2. Give separate journal entries to record in summary form each of the six activities listed above.

3. Give the general journal entry on December 31 of the current year to record the estimated uncollectible accounts expense for the year.

4. Post the appropriate parts of the transactions in **2** and **3** to the accounts opened in **1**.

B 3. *Accounts Receivable*
L O 4 *Aging Method*

Check Figure: Amount of adjustment:
$9,533

Pokorny Company uses the accounts receivable aging method to estimate uncollectible accounts. The Accounts Receivable controlling account and Allowance for Uncollectible Accounts had balances of $88,430 (debit) and $7,200 (credit), respectively, at the beginning of the year. During the year, the company had sales on account of $473,000, sales returns and allowances of $4,200, worthless accounts written off of $7,900, and collections from customers of $450,730. At the end of the year (December 31), a junior accountant for the company was preparing an aging analysis of accounts receivable. At the top of page 6 of his report, the following totals appeared.

Customer Account	Total	Not Yet Due	1–30 Days Past Due	31–60 Days Past Due	61–90 Days Past Due	Over 90 Days Past Due
Balance Forward	$89,640	$49,030	$24,110	$9,210	$3,990	$3,300

The following accounts remained to finish the analysis.

Account	Amount	Due Date
K. Foust	$ 930	Jan. 14 (next year)
K. Groth	620	Dec. 24
R. Mejias	1,955	Sept. 28
C. Polk	2,100	Aug. 16
M. Spears	375	Dec. 14
J. Yong	2,685	Jan. 23 (next year)
A. Zorr	295	Nov. 5
	$8,960	

The company has found from past experience that the following rates are realistic to estimate the uncollectible accounts.

Time Past Due	Percentage Considered Uncollectible
Not yet due	2
1–30 days	4
31–60 days	20
61–90 days	30
Over 90 days	50

REQUIRED

1. Complete the aging analysis of accounts receivable.
2. Determine the year-end balances (before adjustments) of the Accounts Receivable controlling account and Allowance for Uncollectible Accounts.
3. Prepare an analysis computing the estimated uncollectible accounts.
4. Prepare a general journal entry to record the estimated uncollectible accounts expense for the year (round adjustment to the nearest dollar).

B 4. *Notes Receivable*
L O 5 *Transactions*
No check figure

Hopson Manufacturing Company engaged in the following transactions involving promissory notes.

Jan. 14 Sold merchandise to Barbara Reid Company for $18,500, terms n/30.
Feb. 13 Received $4,200 in cash from Barbara Reid Company and received a 90-day, 8 percent promissory note for the balance of the account.
May 14 Received payment in full from Barbara Reid Company.
     15 Received a 60-day, 12 percent note from Ralph Sarkis Company in payment of a past-due account, $6,000.
July 14 When asked to pay, Ralph Sarkis Company dishonored the note.
     20 Received a check from Ralph Sarkis Company for payment of the maturity value of the note and interest at 12 percent for the six days beyond maturity.
     25 Sold merchandise to James Flowers Company for $18,000, with payment of $3,000 cash down and the remainder on account.
     31 Received a $15,000, 45-day, 10 percent promissory note from James Flowers Company for the outstanding account receivable.
Sept. 14 When asked to pay, James Flowers Company dishonored the note.
     25 Wrote off the James Flowers Company account as uncollectible following news that the company had been declared bankrupt.

REQUIRED

Prepare general journal entries to record the preceding transactions.

B 5. *Notes Receivable*
L O 5 *Transactions*
No check figure

Roman's Auto Store engaged in the following transactions.

Jan. 2 Accepted a $9,400, 90-day, 14 percent note from Willis Daniels as an extension on his past-due account.
     5 Accepted a $2,900, 90-day, 12 percent note from Sharon Kelly in payment of a past-due account receivable.
     10 Accepted a $4,500, 90-day, 10 percent note from Charles Suggs as an extension of a past-due account.
     30 Accepted a $5,200, 90-day, 12 percent note from Linda Pate in lieu of payment of a past-due account.

Apr. 2 When asked to pay, Willis Daniels dishonored his note.
     5 When asked to pay, Sharon Kelly dishonored her note.
    10 Received payment from Charles Suggs for note and interest.
    22 Received payment from Willis Daniels for the total amount owed including maturity value plus interest at 15 percent for the twenty days past maturity.
    25 Wrote off the Sharon Kelly account as uncollectible because she could not be located.
    30 Received payment from Linda Pate for her note and interest.

REQUIRED   Prepare general journal entries to record the transactions.

FINANCIAL REPORTING AND ANALYSIS CASES

Interpreting Financial Reports

FRA 1.
L O 1, 3, 4
Short-Term Liquid Assets in Classic Government Bailout

Check Figures: Quick ratios, 1983: .39; 1990: .51

The automobile industry, especially **Chrysler Corporation,** had serious financial problems in the early 1980s. Chrysler incurred operating losses of over $1 billion in both 1979 and 1980. At that time, it received U.S. government loan guarantees of $1 billion and more. Chrysler's short-term liquid assets for 1979 and 1980 were presented in its annual report as follows (in millions of dollars).[13]

	1980	1979
Cash	$101.1	$ 188.2
Time Deposits	2.6	120.8
Marketable Securities—at lower of cost or market	193.6	165.3
Accounts Receivable (less allowance for doubtful accounts: 1980—$40.3 million; 1979—$34.9 million)	476.2	610.3
Total Short-Term Liquid Assets	$773.5	$1,084.6

The company also reported current liabilities of $3,231.6 million in 1979 and $3,029.3 million in 1980. Sales totaled $12,001.9 million in 1979 and $9,225.3 million in 1980. In management's discussion and analysis of financial conditions and results of operations, it was noted that "Chrysler had to defer paying its major suppliers until it received the proceeds from the additional $400 million of federally guaranteed debt. Chrysler's liquidity and its long-term viability are predicated on a return to sustained profitable operations."

Epilogue: At the end of 1983, Lee A. Iacocca, chief executive officer of Chrysler, could state in the annual report, "We repaid the $1.2 billion in loans guaranteed by the Federal Government. This action was taken seven years early." At the end of 1983, Chrysler had total short-term liquid assets of $1,360.6 million, consisting of Cash and Time Deposits of $111.6 million; Marketable Securities of $957.8 million; and Accounts Receivable (less allowance for uncollectible accounts of $25.5 million) of $291.2. Current liabilities were $3,453.9 million, and sales for 1983 were $13,240.4 million. By 1990, short-term liquid assets were $3,597 million, consisting of Cash and Time Deposits of $1,491 million, Marketable Securities of $1,473 million, and Accounts Receivable of $633 million. Current liabilities were $7,096 million, and sales for 1990 were $26,965 million. For comparison purposes, 1990 figures are shown for Chrysler operations without the finance and rental subsidiaries included. A separate allowance for uncollectible accounts was not disclosed for Chrysler operations.

REQUIRED   1. Compute Chrysler's quick ratios for 1979 and 1980. Did Chrysler's short-term liquidity position improve or deteriorate from 1979 to 1980? What apparent effect did the 1980 federally guaranteed loan of $400 million have on Chrysler's balance sheet and liquidity position?
2. It is important to Chrysler's survival that its customers pay their debts, and pay them on time. Compute for 1979 and 1980 the ratio of the allowance for doubtful

13. Chrysler Corporation, *Annual Report*, 1980, 1983, and 1990.

accounts to *gross* accounts receivable and the ratio of *net* accounts receivable to sales. What do your computations tell about Chrysler's ability to collect from its customers?

3. Compute for 1983 the three ratios you computed in questions **1** and **2** for 1979 and 1980; for 1990, compute the first and third ratios. Comment on Chrysler's situation in 1983 and 1990 compared to 1979–1980.

FRA 2.
L O 4
Accounting for
Accounts Receivable

Check Figures: Receivable turnover 1991: 10.4 times; 1992: 9.9 times; 1993: 9.7 times

Winton Sharrer Co. is a major consumer goods company that sells over three thousand products in 135 countries. The company's annual report to the Securities and Exchange Commission presented the following data (in thousands) pertaining to net sales and accounts related to accounts receivable for 1991, 1992, and 1993.

	1993	1992	1991
Net Sales	$4,910,000	$4,865,000	$4,888,000
Accounts Receivable	523,000	524,000	504,000
Allowance for Uncollectible Accounts	18,600	21,200	24,500
Uncollectible Accounts Expense	15,000	16,700	15,800
Uncollectible Accounts Written Off	19,300	20,100	17,700
Recoveries of Accounts Previously Written Off	1,700	100	1,000

REQUIRED

1. Compute the ratios of Uncollectible Accounts Expense to Net Sales and to Accounts Receivable and of Allowance for Uncollectible Accounts to Accounts Receivable for 1991, 1992, and 1993.
2. Compute the receivable turnover and average days' sales uncollected for each year, assuming 1990 net accounts receivable is $465,000.
3. What is your interpretation of the ratios? What appears to be management's attitude with respect to the collectibility of accounts receivable over the three-year period?

International Company

FRA 3.
L O 1
Interpretation of
Ratios

No check figure

Philips Electronics, N.V. and **Heineken, N.V.** are two of the most famous Dutch companies. Philips is a large, diversified electronics, music, and media company, and Heineken makes a popular beer. Philips is about six times bigger than Heineken, with 1992 revenues of 58.5 billion guilders versus 8.9 billion guilders. Ratios can help in comparing and understanding the companies. For example, the receivable turnovers for the companies for two recent years are as follows:

	1992	1991
Philips	3.7 times	3.9 times
Heineken	8.9 times	9.1 times

What do the ratios tell you about the credit policies of the two companies? How long does it take each on average to collect a receivable? What do the ratios tell about the companies' relative needs for capital to finance receivables? Can you tell which company has a better credit policy? Explain your answers.

Toys "R" Us Annual Report

FRA 4.
L O 1, 2, 4
Analysis of Short-
Term Liquid Assets

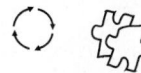

Check Figures: Quick ratio: 1994: .4 times; 1995: .2 times

Refer to the appendix on Toys "R" Us to answer the following questions.

1. How much cash and cash equivalents did Toys "R" Us have in 1995? Do you suppose most of that amount is cash in the bank or cash equivalents?
2. Toys "R" Us does not disclose an allowance for uncollectible accounts. How do you explain the lack of disclosure?
3. Compute the quick ratios for 1994 and 1995 and comment on them.
4. Compute receivable turnover and average days' sales uncollected for 1994 and 1995 and comment on Toys "R" Us credit policies. Accounts Receivable in 1993 were $69,385,000.

Inventories

1. Identify and explain the management issues associated with accounting for inventories.
2. Define *inventory cost* and relate it to goods flow and cost flow.
3. Calculate the pricing of inventory, using the cost basis under the periodic inventory system, according to the (a) specific identification method; (b) average-cost method; (c) first-in, first-out (FIFO) method; and (d) last-in, first-out (LIFO) method.
4. Apply the perpetual inventory system to the pricing of inventories at cost.
5. State the effects of inventory methods and misstatements of inventory on income determination and income taxes.
6. Apply the lower-of-cost-or-market (LCM) rule to inventory valuation.

SUPPLEMENTAL OBJECTIVE

7. Estimate the cost of ending inventory using the (a) retail inventory method and (b) gross profit method.

DECISION POINT

J. C. Penney Company, Inc.

The management of inventory for profit is one of management's most complex and challenging tasks. In terms of dollars, the inventory of goods held for sale is one of the largest assets of a merchandising business. As a major retailer, with department stores in all fifty states and Puerto Rico, J. C. Penney Company, Inc., devotes almost 24 percent, or $3.2 billion, of its $13.6 billion in assets to inventories.[1] What challenges does J. C. Penney's management face in managing its inventory?

Not only must J. C. Penney's management purchase fashions and other merchandise that customers will want to buy, but it must also have the merchandise available in the right locations at the times when customers want to buy it. In addition, it must try to minimize the cost of inventory while maintaining quality. To these ends, J. C. Penney maintains purchasing offices throughout the world, including Hong Kong, Taipei, Osaka, Seoul, Bangkok, Singapore, Bombay, and Florence. Quality assurance experts operate out of twenty-two domestic and fourteen international offices. Further, the amount of money tied up in inventory must be controlled because of the high cost of borrowing funds and storing inventory. Important accounting decisions include what assumptions to make about the flow of inventory costs, what prices to put on inventory, what inventory systems to use, and how to protect inventory against loss. Proper management of inventory helped J. C. Penney earn net income of $777 million in 1992, but small variations in any inventory decision can mean the difference between a net profit and a net loss. ⦂⦂⦂⦂⦂

MANAGEMENT ISSUES ASSOCIATED WITH ACCOUNTING FOR INVENTORIES

OBJECTIVE

1 *Identify and explain the management issues associated with accounting for inventories*

Inventory is considered a current asset because it will normally be sold within a year's time or within a company's operating cycle. For a merchandising business like J. C. Penney or Toys "R" Us, merchandise inventory consists of all goods owned and held for sale in the regular course of business. Inventories are also important for manufacturing companies. Since manufacturers are engaged in the actual making of products, they have three kinds of

1. J. C. Penney Company, Inc., *Annual Report*, 1992.

inventory: raw materials to be used in the production of goods, partially completed products (often called *work in process*), and finished goods ready for sale. For example, in its 1991 annual report, The Goodyear Tire & Rubber Company disclosed the following inventory (in millions):

	1991	1990
Raw materials and supplies	$ 232.0	$ 234.5
Work in process	58.1	67.5
Finished product	1,022.6	1,044.0
Total inventories	$1,312.7	$1,346.0

In manufacturing operations, the costs of the work in process and the finished goods inventories include not only the cost of the raw materials that go into the product, but also the cost of the labor used to convert the raw materials to finished goods and the overhead costs that support the production process. Included in this latter category are such costs as indirect materials (for example, paint, glue, and nails), indirect labor (such as the salaries of supervisors), factory rent, depreciation of plant assets, utilities costs, and insurance costs. The methods for maintaining and pricing inventory explained in this chapter are applicable to manufactured goods, but since the details of accounting for manufacturing companies are usually covered in managerial accounting courses, this chapter focuses on accounting for merchandising firms.

The management issues in this chapter relate to the measurement of income through the allocation of the cost of inventories in accordance with the matching rule; assessing the impact of inventory decisions on such factors as net income, income taxes, and cash flows; and evaluating the level of inventory.

APPLYING THE MATCHING RULE
TO INVENTORIES

The American Institute of Certified Public Accountants states, "A major objective of accounting for inventories is the proper determination of income through the process of matching appropriate costs against revenues."[2] Note that the objective is the proper determination of income through the matching of costs and revenues, not the determination of the most realistic inventory value. As will be shown in this chapter, these two objectives are sometimes incompatible, in which case the objective of income determination takes precedence.

The reason inventory accounting is so important to income measurement is linked to the way income is measured on the merchandising income statement. Recall that gross margin is computed as the difference between net sales and cost of goods sold and that cost of goods sold is measured by deducting ending inventory from the cost of goods available for sale. Because of those relationships, the higher the cost of ending inventory, the lower the cost of goods sold and the higher the resulting gross margin. Conversely, the lower the value assigned to ending inventory, the higher the cost of goods sold and the lower the gross margin. Since the amount of gross margin has a direct effect on the amount of net income, the amount assigned to ending inventory directly affects the amount of net income. *In effect, the value assigned*

---

2. American Institute of Certified Public Accountants, *Accounting Research Bulletin No. 43* (New York: AICPA, 1953), Ch. 4.

to the ending inventory determines what portion of the cost of goods available for sale is assigned to cost of goods sold and what portion is assigned to the balance sheet as inventory to be carried over into the next accounting period.

Figure 1 shows the management choices related to the application of the matching rule to accounting for inventory. In the context of either the periodic inventory system or the perpetual inventory system, the portions of cost of goods available for sale allocated to cost of goods sold and to ending inventory depend on what assumptions are made about the flow of costs into the company as goods are purchased and out of the company as goods are sold. The methods available to management for assigning costs to those flows are the specific identification method; the average-cost method; the first-in, first-out (FIFO) method; and the last-in, first-out (LIFO) method. Further, at the end of the accounting period, the market value of the inventory is calculated to determine whether the inventory must be adjusted through the application of the lower-of-cost-or-market rule. Those choices are described and discussed in this chapter.

ASSESSING THE IMPACT OF INVENTORY DECISIONS

Figure 1 summarizes the management choices with regard to inventory systems and methods. The decisions usually result in different amounts of

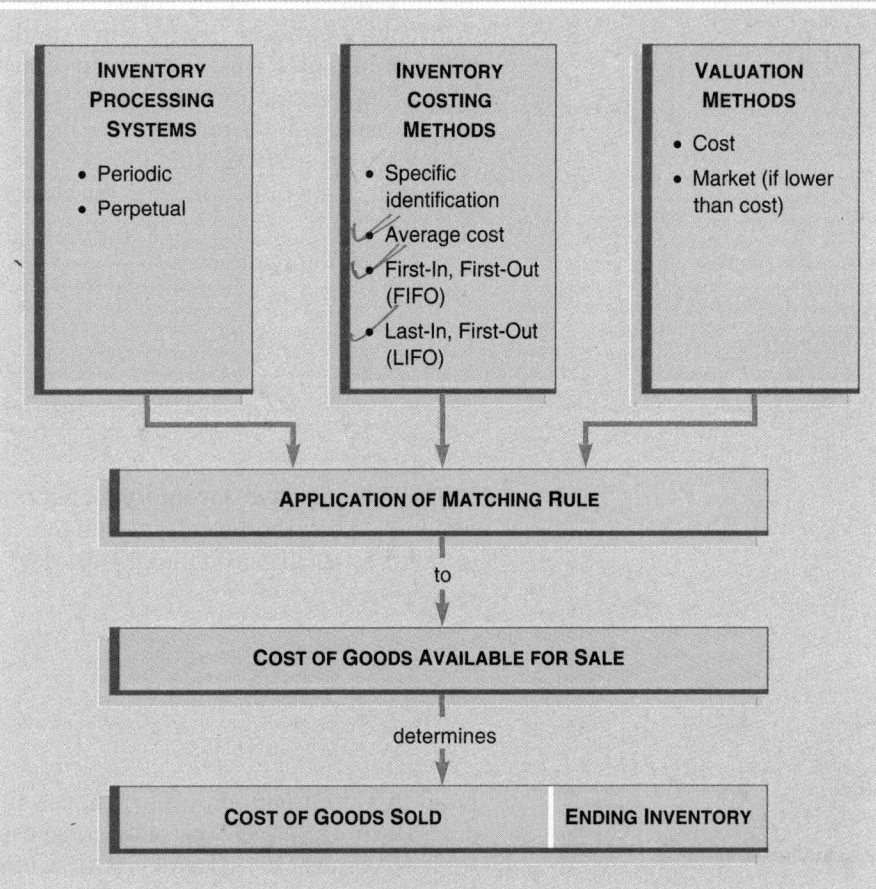

Figure 1. Management Choices in Accounting for Inventories

reported net income and, as a result, affect both the external evaluation of the company by investors and creditors and such internal evaluations as performance reviews, bonuses, and executive compensation. Because income is affected, the valuation of inventory may also have a considerable effect on the amount of income taxes paid. Federal income tax authorities have, therefore, been interested in the effects of various inventory valuation methods and have specific regulations about the acceptability of different methods. As a result, management is sometimes faced with the problem of balancing the goal of proper income determination with that of minimizing income taxes. Another consideration is that since the choice of inventory valuation method affects the amount of income taxes paid, it also affects a company's cash flows. The effects of management's decisions are discussed in more detail in this chapter after the inventory methods are presented.

EVALUATING THE LEVEL OF INVENTORY

Level of inventory has important economic consequences for a company. Ideally, management wants to have a great variety and quantity on hand so that customers have a large choice and do not have to wait. Such an inventory policy is not costless, however. The cost of handling and storage and the interest cost of the funds necessary to maintain high inventory levels are usually substantial. On the other hand, the maintenance of low inventory levels may result in lost sales and disgruntled customers. Common measures used in the evaluation of inventory levels are inventory turnover and its related measure, average days' inventory on hand.

Inventory turnover is a measure similar to receivable turnover. It indicates the number of times a company's average inventory is sold during an accounting period. Inventory turnover is computed by dividing cost of goods sold by average inventory. For example, J. C. Penney's cost of goods sold was $12.04 billion in 1992, and its merchandise inventory was $2.897 billion in 1991 and $3.258 billion in 1992. Its inventory turnover is computed as follows:

$$\text{Inventory turnover} = \frac{\text{cost of goods sold}}{\text{average inventory}}$$

$$= \frac{\$12,040,000,000}{(\$2,897,000,000 + \$3,258,000,000) \div 2}$$

$$= \frac{\$12,040,000,000}{\$3,077,500,000} = 3.9 \text{ times}$$

The average days' inventory on hand indicates the average number of days required to sell the inventory on hand. The average days' inventory on hand is found by dividing the number of days in a year by the inventory turnover, as follows:

$$\text{Average days' inventory on hand} = \frac{\text{number of days in a year}}{\text{inventory turnover}}$$

$$= \frac{365 \text{ days}}{3.9 \text{ times}} = 93.6 \text{ days}$$

From this information, it may be seen that J. C. Penney turned its inventory over 3.9 times in 1992, or on average every 93.6 days. These figures are reasonable because J. C. Penney is in a business where fashions change every season, or about every 90 days. Management would want to sell all of each

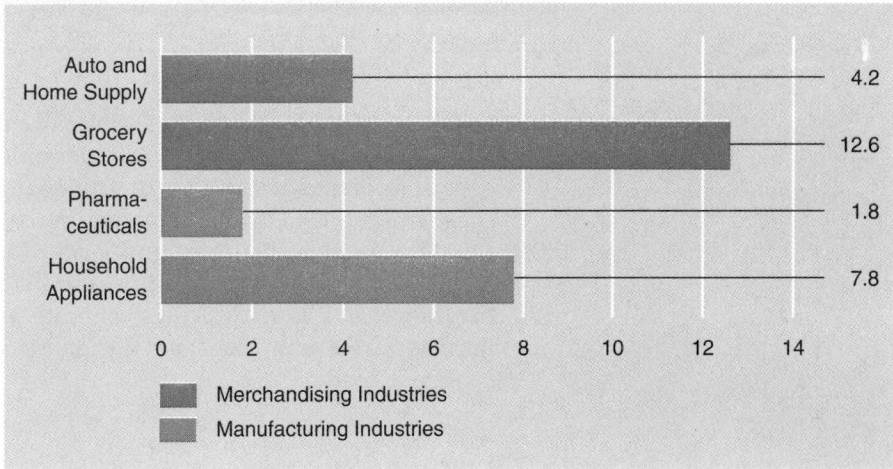

Figure 2. Inventory Turnover for Selected Industries

Source: Data from Dun and Bradstreet, *Industry Norms and Ratios,* 1993–94.

season's inventory within 90 days, even while making purchases for the next season. There are natural levels of inventory in every industry, as shown for selected merchandising and manufacturing industries in Figures 2 and 3. However, companies that are able to maintain their inventories at lower levels and still satisfy customer needs are the most successful.

Many companies, both in merchandising and in manufacturing, are attempting to reduce their inventory assets by changing to a just-in-time operating environment. In such an environment, rather than stockpiling inventories for later use, companies work closely with suppliers to coordinate and schedule shipments so that goods arrive just in time to be used or sold. Less money is thereby tied up in inventories, and the costs associated with carrying inventories are reduced. For example, Pacific Bell has been able to close six warehouses by implementing just-in-time inventory management.

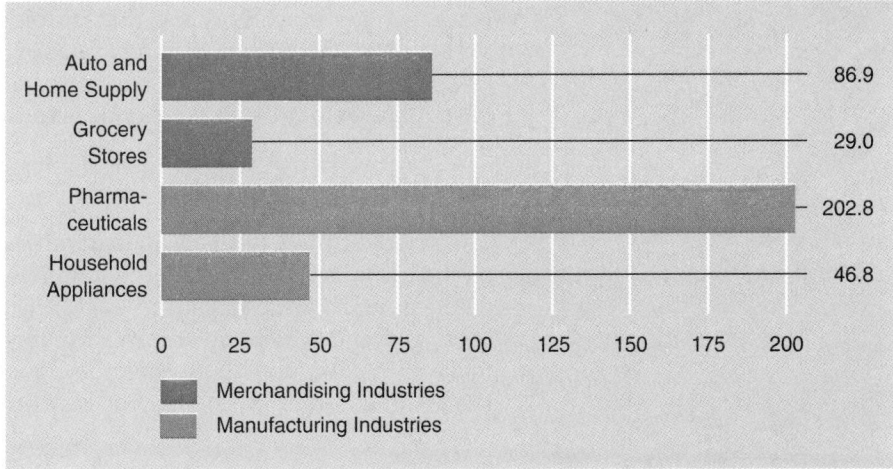

Figure 3. Average Days' Inventory on Hand for Selected Industries

Source: Data from Dun and Bradstreet, *Industry Norms and Ratios,* 1993–94.

OBJECTIVE

2 *Define* **inventory cost** *and relate it to goods flow and cost flow*

PRICING INVENTORY UNDER THE PERIODIC INVENTORY SYSTEM

According to the AICPA, "The primary basis of accounting for inventories is cost, which has been defined generally as the price paid or consideration given to acquire an asset."[3] This definition of inventory cost has generally been interpreted to include the following costs: (1) invoice price less purchases discounts; (2) freight or transportation in, including insurance in transit; and (3) applicable taxes and tariffs. Other costs—for ordering, receiving, and storing—should in principle also be included in inventory cost. In practice, however, it is so difficult to allocate such costs to specific inventory items that they are usually considered expenses of the accounting period instead of inventory costs.

MERCHANDISE IN TRANSIT

Because merchandise inventory includes all items owned by a company and held for sale, the status of any merchandise in transit, either being sold or being purchased by the inventorying company, must be examined to determine if it should be included in the inventory count. The terms of the shipping agreement will indicate whether title has passed. Outgoing goods shipped FOB destination would be included in merchandise inventory, whereas those shipped FOB shipping point would not. Conversely, incoming goods shipped FOB shipping point would be included in merchandise inventory, but those shipped FOB destination would not.

MERCHANDISE ON HAND NOT INCLUDED IN INVENTORY

At the time a physical inventory is taken, there may be merchandise on hand to which the company does not hold title. One category of such goods includes merchandise that has been sold and is awaiting delivery to the buyer. Since the sale has been completed, title to the goods has passed to the buyer, and the merchandise should not be included in the inventory. A second category is goods held on consignment. A consignment is merchandise placed by its owner (known as the *consignor*) on the premises of another company (the *consignee*) with the understanding that payment is expected only when the goods are sold and that unsold items may be returned to the consignor. Title to consigned goods remains with the consignor until the consignee sells the goods. Thus, consigned goods should not be included in the physical inventory of the consignee because they still belong to the consignor.

METHODS OF PRICING INVENTORY AT COST

The prices of most kinds of merchandise vary during the year. Identical lots of merchandise may have been purchased at different prices. Also, when identical items are bought and sold, it is often impossible to tell which have been sold and which are still in inventory. For this reason, it is necessary to make an assumption about the order in which items have been sold. Because the assumed order of sale may or may not be the same as the actual order of

3. American Institute of Certified Public Accountants, *Accounting Research Bulletin No. 43* (New York: AICPA, 1953), Ch. 4.

sale, the assumption is really about the *flow of costs* rather than the *flow of physical inventory.*

Thus, the term goods flow refers to the actual physical movement of goods in the operations of a company, and the term cost flow refers to the association of costs with their *assumed* flow in the operations of a company. The assumed cost flow may or may not be the same as the actual goods flow. The possibility of a difference between cost flow and goods flow may seem strange at first, but it arises because several choices of assumed cost flow are available under generally accepted accounting principles. In fact, it is sometimes preferable to use an assumed cost flow that bears no relationship to goods flow because it gives a better estimate of income, which, as stated earlier, is the main goal of inventory valuation.

Accountants usually price inventory by using one of the following generally accepted methods, each based on a different assumption of cost flow: (1) specific identification method; (2) average-cost method; (3) first-in, first-out (FIFO) method; and (4) last-in, first-out (LIFO) method. The choice of method depends on the nature of the business, the financial effects of the methods, and the costs of implementing them.

To illustrate the four methods under the periodic inventory system, the following data for the month of June will be used.

Inventory Data, June 30

June	1	Inventory	50 units @ $1.00	$ 50
	6	Purchase	50 units @ $1.10	55
	13	Purchase	150 units @ $1.20	180
	20	Purchase	100 units @ $1.30	130
	25	Purchase	150 units @ $1.40	210
Goods Available for Sale			500 units	$625
Sales			280 units	
On hand June 30			220 units	

Notice that there is a total of 500 units available for sale at a total cost of $625. Stated simply, the problem of inventory pricing is to divide the $625 between the 280 units sold and the 220 units on hand. Recall that under the periodic inventory system, the inventory is not updated after each purchase and sale. Thus, it is not necessary to know when the individual sales take place.

OBJECTIVE

3a *Calculate the pricing of inventory, using the cost basis under the periodic inventory system, according to the specific identification method*

Specific Identification Method If the units in the ending inventory can be identified as coming from specific purchases, the specific identification method may be used to price the inventory. For instance, assume that the June 30 inventory consisted of 50 units from the June 1 inventory, 100 units from the purchase of June 13, and 70 units from the purchase of June 25. The cost assigned to the inventory under the specific identification method would be $268, determined as follows:

Periodic Inventory System—Specific Identification Method

50 units @ $1.00	$ 50	Cost of Goods Available	
100 units @ $1.20	120	for Sale	$625
70 units @ $1.40	98	Less June 30 Inventory	268
220 units at a cost of	$268	Cost of Goods Sold	$357

The specific identification method might be used in the purchase and sale of high-priced articles, such as automobiles, heavy equipment, and works of art. Although this method may appear logical, it is not used by many companies because it has two definite disadvantages. First, in many cases, it is difficult and impractical to keep track of the purchase and sale of individual items. Second, when a company deals in items that are identical but were purchased at different costs, deciding which items are sold becomes arbitrary; thus, the company can raise or lower income by choosing to sell the higher- or lower-cost items.

OBJECTIVE

3b *Calculate the pricing of inventory, using the cost basis under the periodic inventory system, according to the average-cost method*

Average-Cost Method   Under the average-cost method, inventory is priced at the average cost of the goods available for sale during the period. Average cost is computed by dividing the total cost of goods available for sale by the total units available for sale. This gives a weighted-average unit cost that is applied to the units in the ending inventory. In our illustration, the ending inventory would be $275, or $1.25 per unit, determined as follows:

Periodic Inventory System—Average-Cost Method

Cost of goods available for sale ÷ units available for sale = Average unit cost

$625 ÷ 500 units = $1.25

Ending inventory: 220 units @ $1.25 = $275

Cost of Goods Available for Sale	$625
Less June 30 Inventory	275
Cost of Goods Sold	$350

The average-cost method tends to level out the effects of cost increases and decreases because the cost for the ending inventory calculated under this method is influenced by all the prices paid during the year and by the beginning inventory price. Some, however, criticize the average-cost method because they believe that recent costs are more relevant for income measurement and decision making.

OBJECTIVE

3c *Calculate the pricing of inventory, using the cost basis under the periodic inventory system, according to the first-in, first-out (FIFO) method*

First-In, First-Out (FIFO) Method   The first-in, first-out (FIFO) method is based on the assumption that the costs of the first items acquired should be assigned to the first items sold. The costs of the goods on hand at the end of a period are assumed to be from the most recent purchases, and the costs assigned to goods that have been sold are assumed to be from the earliest purchases. The FIFO method of determining inventory cost may be adopted by any business, regardless of the actual physical flow of goods, because the assumption is made regarding the flow of costs and not the flow of goods.

In our illustration, the June 30 inventory would be $301 when the FIFO method is used. It is computed as follows:

Periodic Inventory System—First-In, First-Out Method

150 units @ $1.40 from purchase of June 25	$210
70 units @ $1.30 from purchase of June 20	91
220 units at a cost of	$301
Cost of Goods Available for Sale	$625
Less June 30 Inventory	301
Cost of Goods Sold	$324

The effect of the FIFO method is to value the ending inventory at the most recent costs and include earlier ones in cost of goods sold. During periods of consistently rising prices, the FIFO method yields the highest possible amount of net income, since cost of goods sold will show costs closer to the price level at the time the goods were purchased. Another reason for this result is that businesses tend to increase selling prices as costs rise, regardless of the fact that inventories may have been purchased before the price rise. The reverse effect occurs in periods of price decreases. For these reasons a major criticism of FIFO is that it magnifies the effects of the business cycle on income.

OBJECTIVE

3d *Calculate the pricing of inventory, using the cost basis under the periodic inventory system, according to the last-in, first-out (LIFO) method*

Last-In, First-Out (LIFO) Method   The last-in, first-out (LIFO) method of costing inventories is based on the assumption that the costs of the last items purchased should be assigned to the first items used or sold and that the cost of the ending inventory reflects the cost of merchandise purchased earliest.

Under this method, the June 30 inventory would be $249, computed as follows:

Periodic Inventory System—Last-In, First-Out Method

50 units at $1.00 from June 1 inventory		$ 50
50 units at $1.10 from purchase of June 6		55
120 units at $1.20 from purchase of June 13		144
220 units at a cost of		$249
Cost of Goods Available for Sale		$625
Less June 30 Inventory		249
Cost of Goods Sold		$376

The effect of LIFO is to value inventory at the earliest prices and to include in cost of goods sold the cost of the most recently purchased goods. This assumption, of course, does not agree with the actual physical movement of goods in most businesses.

There is a strong logical argument to support LIFO, however, which is based on the fact that a certain size inventory is necessary in a going concern. When inventory is sold, it must be replaced with more goods. The supporters of LIFO reason that the fairest determination of income occurs if the current costs of merchandise are matched against current sales prices, regardless of which physical units of merchandise are sold. When prices are moving either upward or downward, under LIFO, the cost of goods sold will show costs closer to the price level at the time the goods were sold. As a result, the LIFO method tends to show a smaller net income during inflationary times and a larger net income during deflationary times than other methods of inventory valuation. Thus, the peaks and valleys of the business cycle tend to be smoothed out. The important factor to bear in mind in this regard is that in inventory valuation the flow of costs, and hence income determination, is more important than the physical movement of goods and balance sheet valuation.

An argument may also be made against the LIFO method. Because the inventory valuation on the balance sheet reflects earlier prices, it often gives an unrealistic picture of the current value of the inventory. Thus, such balance sheet measures as working capital and current ratio may be distorted and must be interpreted carefully.

A new type of retail business called the "category buster" seems to ignore the tenets of good inventory management. These retailers, such as The Home Depot, Inc., in home improvements, Barnes & Noble in bookstores, Wal-Mart Stores, Inc., in groceries and dry goods, Toys "R" Us, Inc., in toys, and Blockbuster Entertainment, Inc., in videos, maintain huge inventories at such low prices that smaller competitors find it hard to compete. Although these companies do have a large amount of money tied up in inventories, they maintain very sophisticated just-in-time operating environments that require suppliers to meet demanding standards for delivery of products and reduction of inventory costs. Some suppliers are required to stock the shelves and keep track of inventory levels. By minimizing handling and overhead costs and buying at favorably low prices, the category busters achieve great success.

PRICING INVENTORY UNDER THE PERPETUAL INVENTORY SYSTEM

OBJECTIVE

4 *Apply the perpetual inventory system to the pricing of inventories at cost*

The pricing of inventories under the perpetual inventory system differs from pricing under the periodic inventory system. The difference occurs because under the perpetual inventory system, a continuous record of quantities and costs of merchandise is maintained as purchases and sales are made. Under the periodic inventory system, only the ending inventory is counted and priced. Cost of goods sold is determined by deducting the cost of the ending inventory from the cost of goods available for sale. Under the perpetual inventory system, cost of goods sold is accumulated as sales are made and costs are transferred from the inventory account to Cost of Goods Sold. The cost of the ending inventory is the balance of the inventory account. To illustrate pricing methods under the perpetual inventory system, the same data will be used as before, but specific sales dates and amounts will be added, as follows:

Inventory Data—June 30

June 1	Inventory	50 units @ $1.00
6	Purchase	50 units @ $1.10
10	Sale	70 units
13	Purchase	150 units @ $1.20
20	Purchase	100 units @ $1.30
25	Purchase	150 units @ $1.40
30	Sale	210 units
30	Inventory	220 units

Pricing the inventory and cost of goods sold using the specific identification method is the same under the perpetual system as it was under the periodic system because cost of goods sold and ending inventory are based on the cost of the identified items sold and on hand. The perpetual system facilitates the use of the specific identification method because detailed records of purchases and sales are maintained.

Pricing the inventory and cost of goods sold using the average-cost method differs when the perpetual system is used. Under the periodic system, the average cost is computed for all goods available for sale during the month. Under the perpetual system, a moving average is computed after each purchase or series of purchases preceding the next sale, as follows:

Perpetual Inventory System—Average-Cost Method

June 1	Inventory	50 units @ $1.00	$ 50.00
6	Purchase	50 units @ $1.10	55.00
6	Balance	100 units @ $1.05	$105.00
10	Sale	70 units @ $1.05	(73.50)
10	Balance	30 units @ $1.05	$ 31.50
13	Purchase	150 units @ $1.20	180.00
20	Purchase	100 units @ $1.30	130.00
25	Purchase	150 units @ $1.40	210.00
25	Balance	430 units @ $1.28*	$551.50
30	Sale	210 units @ $1.28*	(268.80)
30	Balance	220 units @ $1.28*	$282.70
Cost of Goods Sold		$73.50 + $268.80	$342.30

*Rounded.

The sum of the costs applied to sales becomes the cost of goods sold, $342.30. The ending inventory is the balance, or $282.70.

When pricing the inventory using the FIFO and LIFO methods, it is necessary to keep track of the components of inventory at each step of the way because as sales are made, the costs must be assigned in the proper order. To apply the FIFO method, the approach is as follows:

Perpetual Inventory System—FIFO Method

June 1	Inventory	50 units @ $1.00		$ 50.00
6	Purchase	50 units @ $1.10		55.00
10	Sale	50 units @ $1.00	($50.00)	
		20 units @ $1.10	(22.00)	(72.00)
10	Balance	30 units @ $1.10		$ 33.00
13	Purchase	150 units @ $1.20		180.00
20	Purchase	100 units @ $1.30		130.00
25	Purchase	150 units @ $1.40		210.00
30	Sale	30 units @ $1.10	($33.00)	
		150 units @ $1.20	(180.00)	
		30 units @ $1.30	(39.00)	(252.00)
30	Balance	70 units @ $1.30	$ 91.00	
		150 units @ $1.40	210.00	$301.00
Cost of Goods Sold		$72.00 + $252.00		$324.00

Note that the ending inventory of $301 and the cost of goods sold of $324 are the same as the figures computed earlier under the periodic inventory system. This will always occur because the ending inventory under both systems will always consist of the last items purchased—in this case, the entire purchase of June 25 and 70 units from the purchase of June 20.

To apply the LIFO method, the approach is as follows:

Perpetual Inventory System—LIFO Method

June 1	Inventory	50	units @ $1.00		$ 50.00
6	Purchase	50	units @ $1.10		55.00
10	Sale	50	units @ $1.10	($55.00)	
		20	units @ $1.00	(20.00)	(75.00)
10	Balance	30	units @ $1.00		$ 30.00
13	Purchase	150	units @ $1.20		180.00
20	Purchase	100	units @ $1.30		130.00
25	Purchase	150	units @ $1.40		210.00
30	Sale	150	units @ $1.40	($210.00)	
		60	units @ $1.30	(78.00)	(288.00)
30	Balance	30	units @ $1.00	$ 30.00	
		150	units @ $1.20	180.00	
		40	units @ $1.30	52.00	$262.00
Cost of Goods Sold		$75.00 + $288.00			$363.00

Note that the ending inventory of $262 includes 30 units from the beginning inventory, all units from the purchase of June 13, and 40 units from the purchase of June 20.

BUSINESS BULLETIN: TECHNOLOGY IN PRACTICE

Using the LIFO method under the perpetual inventory system is a very tedious process, especially if done manually. However, the development of faster and less expensive computer systems over the past ten years has made it easier for many companies to switch to LIFO and still use the perpetual inventory system. The availability of better technology may partially account for the increasing use of LIFO in the United States and enable more companies to enjoy LIFO's economic benefits.

COMPARISON AND IMPACT OF INVENTORY DECISIONS AND MISSTATEMENTS

OBJECTIVE

5 *State the effects of inventory methods and misstatements of inventory on income determination and income taxes*

The specific identification, average-cost, FIFO, and LIFO methods of pricing inventory under both the periodic and the perpetual inventory systems have now been illustrated. The effects of the four methods on net income are shown in Exhibit 1, using the same data as before and assuming June sales of $500. Because the specific identification method is based on actual cost, it is the same under both systems.

Keeping in mind that June was a period of rising prices, we can see that LIFO, which charges the most recent and, in this case, the highest prices to cost of goods sold, resulted in the lowest gross margin under both systems. Conversely, FIFO, which charges the earliest and, in this case, the lowest prices to cost of goods sold, produced the highest gross margin. The gross margin under the average-cost method is somewhere between those under LIFO and FIFO. Thus, it is clear that the average-cost method has a less pronounced effect. Note that ending inventory and gross margin under FIFO are always the same under both inventory systems.

During a period of declining prices, the reverse would occur. The LIFO method would produce a higher gross margin than the FIFO method. It is apparent that the method of inventory valuation has the greatest importance during prolonged periods of price changes in one direction, either up or down.

Because the specific identification method depends on the particular items sold, no generalization can be made about the effect of changing prices.

EFFECTS ON THE FINANCIAL STATEMENTS

Each of the four methods of inventory pricing is acceptable for use in published financial statements. The FIFO, LIFO, and average-cost methods are widely used, as can be seen in Figure 4, which shows the inventory cost methods used by six hundred large companies. Each has its advantages and disadvantages, and none can be considered best or perfect. The factors that should be considered in choosing an inventory method are the effects of each method on financial statements, income taxes, and management decisions.

A basic problem in determining the best inventory measure for a particular company stems from the fact that inventory affects both the balance sheet and the income statement. As we have seen, the LIFO method is best suited for the

Exhibit 1. Effects of Inventory Systems and Methods Computed

	Specific Identification Method	Periodic Inventory System			Perpetual Inventory System[†]		
		Average-Cost Method	First-In, First-Out Method	Last-In, First-Out Method	Average-Cost Method	First-In, First-Out Method	Last-In, First-Out Method
Sales	$500	$500	$500	$500	$500	$500	$500
Cost of Goods Sold							
Beginning Inventory	$ 50	$ 50	$ 50	$ 50			
Purchases	575	575	575	575			
Cost of Goods Available for Sale	$625	$625	$625	$625			
Less Ending Inventory	268	275	301	249	283[*]	301	262
Cost of Goods Sold	$357	$350	$324	$376	$342[*]	$324	$363
Gross Margin	$143	$150	$176	$124	$158	$176	$137

[*]Rounded.

[†]Ending inventory under the perpetual inventory system is provided for comparison only. It is not used in the computation of cost of goods sold.

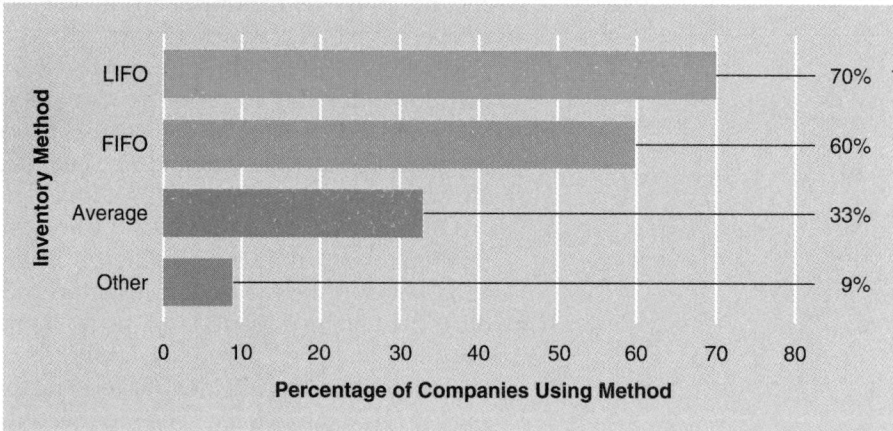

Figure 4. Inventory Costing Methods Used by 600 Large Companies

Total percentage exceeds 100 because some companies used different methods for different types of inventory.

Source: Reprinted with permission from *Accounting Trends and Techniques,* Copyright © 1992 by American Institute of Certified Public Accountants, Inc.

income statement because it matches revenues and cost of goods sold. But it is not the best measure of the current balance sheet value of inventory, particularly during a prolonged period of price increases or decreases. The FIFO method, on the other hand, is best suited to the balance sheet because the ending inventory is closest to current values and thus gives a more realistic view of the current financial assets of a business. Readers of financial statements must be alert to inventory methods and be able to assess their effects.

EFFECTS ON INCOME TAXES

The Internal Revenue Service has developed several rules for valuing inventories for federal income tax purposes. A company has a wide choice of methods, including specific identification, average cost, FIFO, and LIFO, as well as lower of cost or market. But once a method has been chosen, it must be used consistently from one year to the next. The IRS must approve any change in the inventory valuation method for income tax purposes.[4] This requirement agrees with the rule of consistency in accounting, since changes in inventory method may cause income to fluctuate too much and would make income statements hard to interpret from year to year. A company may change its inventory method if there is a good reason for doing so. The nature and effect of the change must be shown on its financial statements.

Many accountants believe that the use of the FIFO and average-cost methods in periods of rising prices causes businesses to report more than their true profit, resulting in the payment of excess income taxes. The profit is overstated because cost of goods sold is understated, relative to current prices. The company must buy replacement inventory at higher prices, but additional funds are also needed to pay income taxes. During the rapid inflation of 1979

---

4. A single exception to this rule is that taxpayers must notify the IRS of a change to LIFO from another method, but do not need to have advance IRS approval.

to 1982, billions of dollars reported as profits and paid in income taxes were believed to be the result of poor matching of current costs and revenues under the FIFO and average-cost methods. Consequently, many companies, encouraged by the belief that prices will continue to rise, have since switched to the LIFO inventory method.

If a company uses the LIFO method in reporting income for tax purposes, the IRS requires that the same method be used in the accounting records. Also, the IRS will not allow the use of the lower-of-cost-or-market rule if LIFO is used to determine inventory cost. In such a case, only the LIFO cost can be used. This rule, however, does not preclude a company from using lower of LIFO cost or market for financial reporting purposes. (The use of lower of cost or market is discussed later in this chapter.)

Over a period of rising prices, a business that uses the LIFO method may find that for balance sheet purposes, its inventory is valued at a cost figure far below what it currently pays for the same items. Management must monitor this situation carefully, because if it should let the inventory quantity at year end fall below the beginning-of-the-year level, the company will find itself paying income taxes on the difference between the current cost and the old LIFO cost in the records. When this occurs, it is called a LIFO liquidation because sales have reduced inventories below the levels established in prior years. A LIFO liquidation may be prevented by making enough purchases prior to year end to restore the desired inventory level. Sometimes a LIFO liquidation cannot be avoided because products are discontinued or supplies are interrupted, as in the case of a strike. In 1992, seventy-three of six hundred large companies reported a LIFO liquidation in which net income was increased because of the matching of older historical cost with present sales dollars.[5]

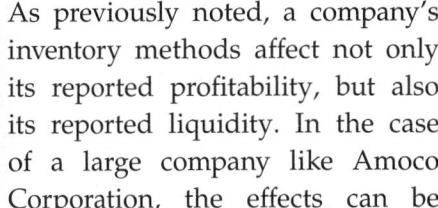

Amoco Corporation

DECISION POINT

As previously noted, a company's inventory methods affect not only its reported profitability, but also its reported liquidity. In the case of a large company like Amoco Corporation, the effects can be complex and material. Like many companies, Amoco uses three of the methods in this chapter to cost its various types of inventory, which in 1992 totaled almost $1 billion. In its statement of accounting policies, management explains its inventory methods: "Cost is determined under the last-in, first-out (LIFO) method for the majority of inventories of crude oil, petroleum products, and chemical products. The costs of remaining inventories are determined under the first-in, first-out (FIFO) or average cost methods." In a subsequent note on inventories, more detail is given.

> Inventories carried under the LIFO method represented approximately 51 percent of total year-end inventory carrying values in 1994 and 47 percent in 1993.

5. American Institute of Certified Public Accountants, *Accounting Trends & Techniques* (New York: AICPA, 1992).

It is estimated that inventories would have been approximately $1,100 million higher than reported on December 31, 1994, and approximately $900 million higher on December 31, 1993, if the quantities valued on the LIFO basis were instead valued on the FIFO basis.

Why was it important for Amoco to include such detail?

The information in the note allows the reader to determine what Amoco's net income for 1994 would have been if FIFO had been used, excluding tax and currency effects and other variables. In this year of increasing oil prices, Amoco's operating income after income taxes of $1,789 million would have increased by $200 million ($1,100 million − $900 million) to $1,989 million, an increase of 11 percent, if FIFO had been used. Finally, in management's discussion and analysis, the following clarifying remark is made.

> Amoco's short-term liquidity position is better than the reported figures indicate since the inventory component of working capital is valued in part under the LIFO method, whereas other elements of working capital are reported at amounts more indicative of their current values. If inventories were valued at current replacement costs, . . . the level of working capital would rise and an increase in the current ratio would result.[6] ◦ ◦ ◦ ◦ ◦

EFFECTS OF MISSTATEMENTS IN INVENTORY MEASUREMENT

The basic problem of separating goods available for sale into two components—goods sold and goods not sold—is that of assigning a cost to the goods not sold, the ending inventory. The portion of the goods available for sale not assigned to the ending inventory is used to determine the cost of goods sold.

Because the figures for ending inventory and cost of goods sold are related, a misstatement in the inventory figure at the end of the period will cause an equal misstatement in gross margin and net income in the income statement. The amount of assets and owner's equity on the balance sheet will also be misstated by the same amount. The consequences of overstatement and understatement of inventory are illustrated in the three simplified examples that follow. In each case, beginning inventory, net purchases, and cost of goods available for sale have been stated correctly. In the first example, ending inventory has been stated correctly. In the second example, inventory is overstated by $6,000; in the third example, inventory is understated by $6,000.

Example 1. Ending Inventory Correctly Stated at $10,000

Cost of Goods Sold for the Year		Income Statement for the Year	
Beginning Inventory	$12,000	Net Sales	$100,000
Net Cost of Purchases	58,000	Cost of Goods Sold	60,000
Cost of Goods Available for Sale	$70,000	Gross Margin	$ 40,000
Ending Inventory	10,000	Operating Expenses	32,000
Cost of Goods Sold	$60,000	Net Income	$ 8,000

6. Amoco Corporation, *Annual Report*, 1994.

Example 2. Ending Inventory Overstated by $6,000

Cost of Goods Sold for the Year		Income Statement for the Year	
Beginning Inventory	$12,000	Net Sales	$100,000
Net Cost of Purchases	58,000	→Cost of Goods Sold	54,000
Cost of Goods Available for Sale	$70,000	Gross Margin	$ 46,000
Ending Inventory	16,000	Operating Expenses	32,000
Cost of Goods Sold	$54,000 ←┘	Net Income	$ 14,000

Example 3. Ending Inventory Understated by $6,000

Cost of Goods Sold for the Year		Income Statement for the Year	
Beginning Inventory	$12,000	Net Sales	$100,000
Net Cost of Purchases	58,000	→Cost of Goods Sold	66,000
Cost of Goods Available for Sale	$70,000	Gross Margin	$ 34,000
Ending Inventory	4,000	Operating Expenses	32,000
Cost of Goods Sold	$66,000 ←┘	Net Income	$ 2,000

In all three examples, the total cost of goods available for sale was $70,000. The difference in net income resulted from how this $70,000 was divided between ending inventory and cost of goods sold.

Because the ending inventory in one period becomes the beginning inventory in the following period, it is important to recognize that a misstatement in inventory valuation affects not only the current period, but also the following period. Note that over a two-year period the errors in net income will offset, or counterbalance, each other. In Example **2** above, for instance, the overstatement of ending inventory in 19x1 caused a $6,000 overstatement of beginning inventory in the following year, resulting in an understatement of income by $6,000 in the second year. This offsetting effect is illustrated in Table 1.

Because the total income for the two years is the same, it may appear that one need not worry about inventory misstatements. However, the misstatements violate the matching rule. In addition, management, creditors, and investors make many decisions on an annual basis and depend on the accountant's determination of net income. The accountant has an obligation to make the net income figure for each year as useful as possible.

Table 1. Ending Inventory Overstated by $6,000

	With Inventory Correctly Stated	With Inventory at Dec. 31, 19x1 Overstated	
		Reported Net Income Will Be	Reported Net Income Will Be Overstated (Understated)
Net Income for 19x1	$ 8,000	$14,000	$6,000
Net Income for 19x2	15,000	9,000	(6,000)
Total Net Income for Two Years	$23,000	$23,000	—

The effects of misstatements in inventory on net income are as follows:

Year 1	Year 2
Ending inventory overstated	**Beginning inventory overstated**
Cost of goods sold understated	Cost of goods sold overstated
Net income overstated	Net income understated
Ending inventory understated	**Beginning inventory understated**
Cost of goods sold overstated	Cost of goods sold understated
Net income understated	Net income overstated

If we assume no income tax effects, a misstatement in inventory results in a misstatement in net income of the same amount. Thus, the measurement of inventory is important.

BUSINESS BULLETIN: ETHICS IN PRACTICE

 Income may be easily manipulated through accounting for inventory. For example, it is easy to misstate the amount of inventory or to overstate or understate inventory by including end-of-the-year purchase and sale transactions in the wrong fiscal year. In one case, the *Wall Street Journal* reported that Leslie Fay Company restated its earnings for three past years to reverse $81 million of pretax earnings. The situation was a "carefully concealed case of fraud" involving many members of the financial accounting staff. "Inventory was overstated, while the cost of making garments was understated in order to enhance profit figures." Such actions are obviously unethical and, in this case, led the company to bankruptcy and ruined the careers of most of its senior officers.[7]

VALUING INVENTORY AT THE LOWER OF COST OR MARKET (LCM)

OBJECTIVE

6 *Apply the lower-of-cost-or-market (LCM) rule to inventory valuation*

Although cost is usually the most appropriate basis for valuation of inventory, there are times when inventory may properly be shown in the financial statements at less than its cost. If by reason of physical deterioration, obsolescence, or decline in price level the market value of inventory falls below its cost, a loss has occurred. This loss may be recognized by writing the inventory down to market. The term market is used here to mean current replacement cost. For a merchandising company, market is the amount that the company would pay at the present time for the same goods, purchased from the usual suppliers and in the usual quantities. It may help in applying the lower-of-cost-or-market (LCM) rule to think of it as the "lower-of-cost-or-replacement-

---

7. Teri Agins, "Report Is Said to Show Pervasive Fraud at Leslie" and "Leslie Fay Co.'s. Profits Restated for Past 3 Years," *Wall Street Journal,* September 27 and 30, 1993.

Table 2. Lower of Cost or Market with Item-by-Item Method

	Quantity	Per Unit Cost	Per Unit Market	Lower of Cost or Market
Category I				
Item a	200	$1.50	$1.70	$ 300
Item b	100	2.00	1.80	180
Item c	100	2.50	2.60	250
Category II				
Item d	300	5.00	4.50	1,350
Item e	200	4.00	4.10	800
Inventory at the lower of cost or market				$2,880

cost" rule.[8] Approximately 90 percent of six hundred large companies report applying the LCM rule to their inventories.[9]

There are three basic methods of valuing inventories at the lower of cost or market: (1) the item-by-item method, (2) the major category method, and (3) the total inventory method. For example, a stereo shop could determine lower of cost or market for each kind of speaker, receiver, and turntable (item by item); for all speakers, all receivers, and all turntables (major categories); or for all speakers, receivers, and turntables together (total inventory).

ITEM-BY-ITEM METHOD

When the item-by-item method is used, cost and market values are compared for each item in inventory. The individual items are then valued at their lower price (see Table 2).

MAJOR CATEGORY METHOD

Under the major category method, the total cost and total market values for each category of items are compared. Each category is then valued at its lower amount (See Table 3).

TOTAL INVENTORY METHOD

Under the total inventory method, the entire inventory is valued at both cost and market, and the lower amount is used to value inventory. Since this method is not acceptable for federal income tax purposes, it is not illustrated here.

8. In some cases, *market value* is determined by the *realizable value* of the inventory—the amount for which the goods can be sold rather than the amount for which the goods can be replaced. The circumstances in which realizable value determines market value are encountered in practice only occasionally, and the valuation procedures are technical enough to be addressed in a more advanced accounting course.

9. American Institute of Certified Public Accountants, *Accounting Trends & Techniques* (New York: AICPA, 1992).

Table 3. Lower of Cost or Market with Major Category Method

		Per Unit		Total		Lower of Cost or Market
	Quantity	Cost	Market	Cost	Market	
Category I						
Item a	200	$1.50	$1.70	$ 300	$ 340	
Item b	100	2.00	1.80	200	180	
Item c	100	2.50	2.60	250	260	
Totals				$ 750	$ 780	$ 750
Category II						
Item d	300	5.00	4.50	$1,500	$1,350	
Item e	200	4.00	4.10	800	820	
Totals				$2,300	$2,170	2,170
Inventory at the lower of cost or market						$2,920

VALUING INVENTORY BY ESTIMATION

It is sometimes necessary or desirable to estimate the value of ending inventory. The methods most commonly used for this purpose are the retail method and the gross profit method.

RETAIL METHOD OF INVENTORY ESTIMATION

Supplemental OBJECTIVE

7a *Estimate the cost of ending inventory using the retail inventory method*

The retail method, as its name implies, is used in retail merchandising businesses to estimate the cost of ending inventory. There are two principal reasons for its use. First, management usually requires that financial statements be prepared at least once a month and, as taking a physical inventory is time-consuming and expensive, the retail method is used instead to estimate the value of inventory on hand. Second, because items in a retail store normally have a price tag or a universal product code, it is a common practice to take the physical inventory at retail from these price tags and codes and reduce the total value to cost through use of the retail method. The term *at retail* means the amount of the inventory at the marked selling prices of the inventory items.

When the retail method is used to estimate ending inventory, the records must show the beginning inventory at cost and at retail. The records must also show the amount of goods purchased during the period both at cost and at retail. The net sales at retail is, of course, the balance of the Sales account less returns and allowances. A simple example of the retail method is shown in Table 4.

Goods available for sale is determined both at cost and at retail by listing beginning inventory and net purchases for the period at cost and at their expected selling price, adding freight to the cost column, and totaling. The

Table 4. Retail Method of Inventory Valuation

	Cost	Retail
Beginning Inventory	$ 40,000	$ 55,000
Net Purchases for the Period (excluding Freight In)	107,000	145,000
Freight In	3,000	
Merchandise Available for Sale	$150,000	$200,000
Ratio of Cost to Retail Price: $\frac{\$150,000}{\$200,000} = 75\%$		
Net Sales During the Period		160,000
Estimated Ending Inventory at Retail		$ 40,000
Ratio of Cost to Retail	75%	
Estimated Cost of Ending Inventory	$ 30,000	

ratio of these two amounts (cost to retail price) provides an estimate of the cost of each dollar of retail sales value. The estimated ending inventory at retail is then determined by deducting sales for the period from the retail price of the goods that were available for sale during the period. The inventory at retail is then converted to cost on the basis of the ratio of cost to retail.

The cost of ending inventory may also be estimated by applying the ratio of cost to retail price to the total retail value of the physical count of the ending inventory. Applying the retail method in practice is often more difficult than this simple example because of such complications as changes in retail price during the year, different markups on different types of merchandise, and varying volumes of sales for different types of merchandise.

Supplemental
OBJECTIVE

7b *Estimate the cost of ending inventory using the gross profit method*

GROSS PROFIT METHOD OF INVENTORY ESTIMATION

The gross profit method assumes that the ratio of gross margin for a business remains relatively stable from year to year. The gross profit method is used in place of the retail method when records of the retail prices of beginning inventory and purchases are not kept. It is considered acceptable for estimating the cost of inventory for interim reports, but it is not acceptable for valuing inventory in the annual financial statements. It is also useful in estimating the amount of inventory lost or destroyed by theft, fire, or other hazards. Insurance companies often use this method to verify loss claims.

The gross profit method is simple to use. First, figure the cost of goods available for sale in the usual way (add purchases to beginning inventory). Second, estimate the cost of goods sold by deducting the estimated gross margin from sales. Finally, deduct the estimated cost of goods sold from the goods available for sale to arrive at the estimated cost of ending inventory. This method is shown in Table 5.

Table 5. Gross Profit Method of Inventory Valuation

1. Beginning Inventory at Cost		$ 50,000
Purchases at Cost (including Freight In)		290,000
Cost of Goods Available for Sale		$340,000
2. Less Estimated Cost of Goods Sold		
Sales at Selling Price	$400,000	
Less Estimated Gross Margin of 30%	120,000	
Estimated Cost of Goods Sold		280,000
3. Estimated Cost of Ending Inventory		$ 60,000

CHAPTER REVIEW

REVIEW OF LEARNING OBJECTIVES

1. **Identify and explain the management issues associated with accounting for inventories.** Included in inventory are goods owned, whether produced or purchased, that are held for sale in the normal course of business. Manufacturing companies also include raw materials and work in process. Among the issues management must face in accounting for inventories are allocating the cost of inventories in accordance with the matching rule, assessing the impact of inventory decisions, and evaluating the levels of inventory. The objective of accounting for inventories is the proper determination of income through the matching of costs and revenues, not the determination of the most realistic inventory value. Because the valuation of inventory has a direct effect on a company's net income, the choice of inventory systems and methods affects not only the amount of income taxes and cash flows, but also the external and internal evaluation of the company. The level of inventory as measured by the inventory turnover and its related measure, average days' inventory on hand, is important to managing the amount of investment needed by a company.

2. **Define *inventory cost* and relate it to goods flow and cost flow.** The cost of inventory includes (1) invoice price less purchases discounts; (2) freight or transportation in, including insurance in transit; and (3) applicable taxes and tariffs. Goods flow relates to the actual physical flow of merchandise, whereas cost flow refers to the assumed flow of costs in the operations of the business.

3. **Calculate the pricing of inventory, using the cost basis under the periodic inventory system, according to the (a) specific identification method; (b) average-cost method; (c) first-in, first-out (FIFO) method; and (d) last-in, first-out (LIFO) method.** The value assigned to ending inventory is the result of two measurements: quantity and price. Quantity is determined by taking a physical inventory. The pricing of inventory is usually based on the assumed cost flow of the goods as they are bought and sold. One of four assumptions is usually made regarding cost flow. These assumptions are represented by four inventory methods. Inventory pricing could be determined by the specific identification method, which associates the

actual cost with each item of inventory, but this method is rarely used. The average-cost method assumes that the cost of inventory is the average cost of goods available for sale during the period. The first-in, first-out (FIFO) method assumes that the costs of the first items acquired should be assigned to the first items sold. The last-in, first-out (LIFO) method assumes that the costs of the last items acquired should be assigned to the first items sold. The inventory method chosen may or may not be equivalent to the actual physical flow of goods.

4. **Apply the perpetual inventory system to the pricing of inventories at cost.** The pricing of inventories under the perpetual inventory system differs from pricing under the periodic system because under the perpetual system a continuous record of quantities and costs of merchandise is maintained as purchases and sales are made. Cost of goods sold is accumulated as sales are made and costs are transferred from the inventory account to Cost of Goods Sold. The cost of the ending inventory is the balance of the inventory account. Under the perpetual inventory system, the specific identification method and the FIFO method will produce the same results as under the periodic method. The results will differ for the average-cost method because a moving average is calculated prior to each sale rather than at the end of the accounting period and for the LIFO method because the cost components of inventory change constantly as goods are bought and sold.

5. **State the effects of inventory methods and misstatements of inventory on income determination and income taxes.** During periods of rising prices, the LIFO method will show the lowest net income; FIFO, the highest; and average cost, in between. The opposite effects occur in periods of falling prices. No generalization can be made regarding the specific identification method. The Internal Revenue Service requires that if LIFO is used for tax purposes, it must also be used for financial statement purposes, and that the lower-of-cost-or-market rule cannot be applied to the LIFO method. If the value of ending inventory is understated or overstated, a corresponding error—dollar for dollar—will be made in net income. Furthermore, because the ending inventory of one period is the beginning inventory of the next, the misstatement affects two accounting periods, although the effects are opposite.

6. **Apply the lower-of-cost-or-market (LCM) rule to inventory valuation.** The lower-of-cost-or-market rule can be applied to the above methods of determining inventory at cost. This rule states that if the replacement cost (market) of the inventory is lower than the inventory cost, the lower figure should be used.

SUPPLEMENTAL OBJECTIVE

7. **Estimate the cost of ending inventory using the (a) retail inventory method and (b) gross profit method.** Two methods of estimating the value of inventory are the retail inventory method and the gross profit method. Under the retail inventory method, inventory is determined at retail prices and is then reduced to estimated cost by applying a ratio of cost to retail price. Under the gross profit method, cost of goods sold is estimated by reducing sales by estimated gross margin. The estimated cost of goods sold is then deducted from cost of goods available for sale to estimate the inventory.

REVIEW OF CONCEPTS AND TERMINOLOGY

The following concepts and terms were introduced in this chapter.

L O 3 **Average-cost method:** An inventory cost method in which the price of inventory is determined by computing the average cost of all goods available for sale during the period.

L O 1 **Average days' inventory on hand:** The average number of days required to sell the inventory on hand; number of days in a year divided by inventory turnover.

L O 2   **Consignment:** Merchandise placed by its owner (the *consignor*) on the premises of another company (the *consignee*) with the understanding that payment is expected only when the merchandise is sold and that unsold items may be returned to the consignor.

L O 2   **Cost flow:** The association of costs with their assumed flow in the operations of a company.

L O 3   **First-in, first-out (FIFO) method:** An inventory cost method based on the assumption that the costs of the first items acquired should be assigned to the first items sold.

L O 2   **Goods flow:** The actual physical movement of goods in the operations of a company.

S O 7   **Gross profit method:** A method of inventory estimation based on the assumption that the ratio of gross margin for a business remains relatively stable from year to year.

L O 2   **Inventory cost:** The price paid or consideration given to acquire an asset; includes invoice price less purchases discounts, plus freight or transportation in and applicable taxes or tariffs.

L O 1   **Inventory turnover:** A ratio indicating the number of times a company's average inventory is sold during an accounting period; cost of goods sold divided by average inventory.

L O 6   **Item-by-item method:** A lower-of-cost-or-market method of valuing inventory in which cost and market are compared for each item in inventory, with each item then valued at its lower price.

L O 1   **Just-in-time operating environment:** An inventory management system in which companies seek to reduce their levels of inventory by working with suppliers to coordinate and schedule deliveries so that goods arrive just at the time they are needed.

L O 3   **Last-in, first-out (LIFO) method:** An inventory cost method based on the assumption that the costs of the last items purchased should be assigned to the first items sold.

L O 5   **LIFO liquidation:** The reduction of inventory below previous levels so that income is increased by the amount current prices exceed the historical cost of the inventory under LIFO.

L O 6   **Lower-of-cost-or-market (LCM) rule:** A method of valuing inventory at an amount below cost if the replacement (market) value is less than cost.

L O 6   **Major category method:** A lower-of-cost-or-market method of valuing inventory in which the total cost and total market values for each category of items are compared, with each category then valued at its lower amount.

L O 6   **Market:** Current replacement cost of inventory.

L O 1   **Merchandise inventory:** All goods owned and held for sale in the regular course of business.

S O 7   **Retail method:** A method of inventory estimation, used in retail businesses, under which inventory at retail value is reduced by the ratio of cost to retail price.

L O 3   **Specific identification method:** An inventory cost method in which the price of inventory is computed by identifying the cost of each item in ending inventory as coming from a specific purchase.

L O 6   **Total inventory method:** A lower-of-cost-or-market method of valuing inventory in which the entire inventory is valued at both cost and market, and the lower price is used to value ending inventory. This is not an acceptable method for federal income tax purposes.

REVIEW PROBLEM

PERIODIC AND PERPETUAL INVENTORY SYSTEMS

L O 3, 4   The table on the next page summarizes the beginning inventory, purchases, and sales of Psi Company's single product during January.

Date		Beginning Inventory and Purchases			Sales Units
		Units	Cost	Total	
Jan. 1	Inventory	1,400	$19	$26,600	
4	Sale				300
8	Purchase	600	20	12,000	
10	Sale				1,300
12	Purchase	900	21	18,900	
15	Sale				150
18	Purchase	500	22	11,000	
24	Purchase	800	23	18,400	
31	Sale				1,350
Totals		4,200		$86,900	3,100

REQUIRED

1. Assuming that the company uses the periodic inventory system, compute the cost that should be assigned to ending inventory and to cost of goods sold using (a) the average-cost method, (b) the FIFO method, and (c) the LIFO method.
2. Assuming that the company uses the perpetual inventory system, compute the cost that should be assigned to ending inventory and to cost of goods sold using (a) the average-cost method, (b) the FIFO method, and (c) the LIFO method.

ANSWER TO REVIEW PROBLEM

	Units	Dollars
Beginning Inventory	1,400	$26,600
Purchases	2,800	60,300
Available for Sale	4,200	$86,900
Sales	3,100	
Ending Inventory	1,100	

1. Periodic inventory system

   a. Average-cost method

Cost of goods available for sale	$86,900
Ending inventory consists of	
1,100 units at $20.69*	22,760[†]
Cost of goods sold	$64,140

   *$86,900 ÷ 4,200 = $20.69.
   [†]Rounded.

   b. FIFO method

Cost of goods available for sale		$86,900
Ending inventory consists of		
January 24 purchase (800 × $23)	$18,400	
January 18 purchase (300 × $22)	6,600	25,000
Cost of goods sold		$61,900

   c. LIFO method

Cost of goods available for sale	$86,900
Ending inventory consists of	
Beginning inventory (1,100 × $19)	20,900
Cost of goods sold	$66,000

2. Perpetual inventory system

a. Average-cost method

Date		Units	Cost*	Amount*
Jan. 1	Inventory	1,400	$19.00	$26,600
4	Sale	(300)	19.00	(5,700)
4	Balance	1,100	19.00	$20,900
8	Purchase	600	20.00	12,000
8	Balance	1,700	19.35	$32,900
10	Sale	(1,300)	19.35	(25,155)
10	Balance	400	19.36	$7,745
12	Purchase	900	21.00	18,900
12	Balance	1,300	20.50	$26,645
15	Sale	(150)	20.50	(3,075)
15	Balance	1,150	20.50	$23,570
18	Purchase	500	22.00	11,000
24	Purchase	800	23.00	18,400
24	Balance	2,450	21.62	$52,970
31	Sale	(1,350)	21.62	(29,187)
31	Inventory	1,100	21.62	$23,783

Cost of Goods Sold: $5,700 + $25,155 + $3,075 + $29,187 = $63,117

*Rounded.

b. FIFO method

Date		Units	Cost	Amount
Jan. 1	Inventory	1,400	$19	$26,600
4	Sale	(300)	19	(5,700)
4	Balance	1,100	19	$20,900
8	Purchase	600	20	12,000
8	Balance	1,100	19	
		600	20	$32,900
10	Sale	(1,100)	19	
		(200)	20	(24,900)
10	Balance	400	20	$ 8,000
12	Purchase	900	21	18,900
12	Balance	400	20	
		900	21	$26,900
15	Sale	(150)	20	(3,000)
15	Balance	250	20	
		900	21	$23,900
18	Purchase	500	22	11,000
24	Purchase	800	23	18,400
24	Balance	250	20	
		900	21	
		500	22	
		800	23	$53,300
31	Sale	(250)	20	
		(900)	21	
		(200)	22	(28,300)
31	Inventory	300	22	
		800	23	$25,000

Cost of Goods Sold: $5,700 + $24,900 + $3,000 + $28,300 = $61,900

c. LIFO method

Date			Units	Cost	Amount
Jan.	1	Inventory	1,400	$19	$26,600
	4	Sale	(300)	19	(5,700)
	4	Balance	1,100	19	$20,900
	8	Purchase	600	20	12,000
	8	Balance	1,100	19	
			600	20	$32,900
	10	Sale	(600)	20	
			(700)	19	(25,300)
	10	Balance	400	19	$ 7,600
	12	Purchase	900	21	18,900
	12	Balance	400	19	
			900	21	$26,500
	15	Sale	(150)	21	(3,150)
	15	Balance	400	19	
			750	21	$23,350
	18	Purchase	500	22	11,000
	24	Purchase	800	23	18,400
	24	Balance	400	19	
			750	21	
			500	22	
			800	23	$52,750
	31	Sale	(800)	23	
			(500)	22	
			(50)	21	(30,450)
	31	Inventory	400	19	
			700	21	$22,300

Cost of Goods Sold: $5,700 + $25,300 + $3,150 + $30,450 = $64,600

CHAPTER ASSIGNMENTS

QUESTIONS

1. What is merchandise inventory, and what is the primary objective of inventory measurement?
2. How does inventory for a manufacturing company differ from that for a merchandising company?
3. Why is the level of inventory important, and what are two common measures of inventory level?
4. What items are included in the cost of inventory?
5. Fargo Sales Company is very busy at the end of its fiscal year on June 30. There is an order for 130 units of product in the warehouse. Although the shipping department tries, it cannot ship the product by June 30, and title has not yet passed. Should the 130 units be included in the year-end count of inventory? Why or why not?
6. What is the difference between goods flow and cost flow?
7. Do the FIFO and LIFO inventory methods result in different quantities of ending inventory?

8. Under which method of cost flow are (a) the earliest costs assigned to inventory, (b) the latest costs assigned to inventory, and (c) the average costs assigned to inventory?

9. What are the relative advantages and disadvantages of FIFO and LIFO from management's point of view?

10. Why do you think it is more expensive to maintain a perpetual inventory system?

11. In periods of steadily rising prices, which inventory method—average cost, FIFO, or LIFO—will give the (a) highest ending inventory cost, (b) lowest ending inventory cost, (c) highest net income, and (d) lowest net income?

12. May a company change its inventory cost method from year to year? Explain.

13. What is the relationship between income tax rules and inventory valuation methods?

14. If the merchandise inventory is mistakenly overstated at the end of 19x8, what is the effect on the (a) 19x8 net income, (b) 19x8 year-end balance sheet value, (c) 19x9 net income, and (d) 19x9 year-end balance sheet value?

15. In the phrase *lower of cost or market,* what is meant by the word *market*?

16. What methods can be used to determine the lower of cost or market?

17. Does using the retail inventory method mean that inventories are measured at retail value on the balance sheet? Explain.

18. For what reasons might management use the gross profit method of estimating inventory?

19. Which of the following inventory systems do not require the taking of a physical inventory: (a) perpetual, (b) periodic, (c) retail, and (d) gross profit?

SHORT EXERCISES

SE 1. *Management Issues*
L O 1
Check Figures: c, c, b, a

Indicate whether each item listed below is associated with (a) allocating the cost of inventories in accordance with the matching rule, (b) assessing the impact of inventory decisions, or (c) evaluating the level of inventory.

1. Calculating the average number of days' inventory on hand
2. Ordering a supply of inventory to satisfy customer needs
3. Calculating the income tax effect of an inventory method
4. Deciding the price to place on ending inventory

SE 2. *Inventory Turnover*
L O 1 *and Average Days'*
Inventory on Hand
Check Figure: Inventory turnover: 4.2 times

During 19x1, Certeen Clothiers had beginning inventory of $240,000, ending inventory of $280,000, and cost of goods sold of $1,100,000. Compute the inventory turnover and average days' inventory on hand.

SE 3. *Specific*
L O 3 *Identification*
Method
Check Figure: Ending inventory: $1,260

Assume the following data with regard to inventory for Alexis Company.

Aug.					
	1	Inventory	80 units @ $10 per unit	$ 800	
	8	Purchase	100 units @ $11 per unit	1,100	
	22	Purchase	70 units @ $12 per unit	840	
Goods Available for Sale			250 units	$2,740	
Aug.	15	Sale	90 units		
	28	Sale	50 units		
Inventory, August 31			110 units		

Assuming that the inventory consists of 60 units from the August 8 purchase and 50 units from the purchase of August 22, calculate the cost of ending inventory and cost of goods sold.

SE 4.
L O 3
Average-Cost Method—Periodic Inventory System
Check Figure: Ending inventory: $1,206

Using the data in SE 3, calculate the cost of ending inventory and cost of goods sold according to the average-cost method under the periodic inventory system.

SE 5.
L O 3
FIFO Method— Periodic Inventory System
Check Figure: Ending inventory: $1,280

Using the data in SE 3, calculate the cost of ending inventory and cost of goods sold according to the FIFO method under the periodic inventory system.

SE 6.
L O 3
LIFO Method— Periodic Inventory System
Check Figure: Ending inventory: $1,130

Using the data in SE 3, calculate the cost of ending inventory and cost of goods sold according to the LIFO method under the periodic inventory system.

SE 7.
L O 4
Average-Cost Method—Perpetual Inventory System
Check Figure: Ending inventory: $1,230

Using the data in SE 3, calculate the cost of ending inventory and cost of goods sold according to the average-cost method under the perpetual inventory system.

SE 8.
L O 4
FIFO Method— Perpetual Inventory System
Check Figure: Ending inventory: $1,280

Using the data in SE 3, calculate the cost of ending inventory and cost of goods sold according to the FIFO method under the perpetual inventory system.

SE 9.
L O 4
LIFO Method— Perpetual Inventory System
Check Figure: Ending inventory: $1,150

Using the data in SE 3, calculate the cost of ending inventory and cost of goods sold according to the LIFO method under the perpetual inventory system.

SE 10.
L O 5
Effects of Methods and Changing Prices
No check figure

Following the pattern of Exhibit 1, prepare a table with seven columns that shows the ending inventory and cost of goods sold for each of the results from your calculations in SE 3 through SE 9. Comment on the results, including the effects of the different prices at which the merchandise was purchased. Which method(s) would result in the lowest income taxes?

SE 11.
L O 6
Lower of Cost or Market
Check Figures: Item-by-item: $13,640; Major category: $13,910

The following schedule is based on a physical inventory and replacement costs for one product line of men's shirts.

Item	Quantity	Cost per Unit	Market per Unit
Short sleeve	280	$24	$20
Long sleeve	190	28	29
Extra-long sleeve	80	34	35

Determine the value of this category of inventory at the lower of cost or market using (1) the item-by-item method and (2) the major category method.

EXERCISES

E 1.
L O 1
Management Issues Related to Inventory
Check Figures: c, c, b, a, b, a

Indicate whether each item listed below is associated with (a) allocating the cost of inventories in accordance with the matching rule, (b) assessing the impact of inventory decisions, or (c) evaluating the level of inventory.

1. Computing inventory turnover
2. Application of the just-in-time operating environment

3. Determining the effects of inventory decisions on cash flows
4. Apportioning the cost of goods available for sale to ending inventory and cost of goods sold
5. Determining the effects of inventory methods on income taxes
6. Determining the assumption about the flow of costs into and out of the company

E 2. *Inventory Ratios*
L O 1

Check Figures: Average days' inventory on hand: 19x2, 60.8 days; 19x3, 67.6 days

Costco Discount Stores is assessing its levels of inventory for 19x2 and 19x3 and has gathered the following data.

	19x3	19x2	19x1
Ending inventory	$ 64,000	$ 54,000	$46,000
Cost of goods sold	320,000	300,000	

Compute the inventory turnover and average days' inventory on hand for 19x2 and 19x3 and comment on the results.

E 3. *Inventory Costing*
L O 3 *Methods*

Check Figures: Ending inventory: (1) $9,150; (2) $9,475; (3) $10,200; (4) $8,350

Helen's Farm Store had the following purchases and sales of fertilizer during the year.

Jan. 1	Beginning inventory	250 cases @ $23	$ 5,750
Feb. 25	Purchase	100 cases @ $26	2,600
June 15	Purchase	400 cases @ $28	11,200
Aug. 15	Purchase	100 cases @ $26	2,600
Oct. 15	Purchase	300 cases @ $28	8,400
Dec. 15	Purchase	200 cases @ $30	6,000
	Total Goods Available for Sale	1,350	$36,550
	Total Sales	1,000 cases	
Dec. 31	Ending inventory	350 cases	

Assume that the ending inventory included 50 cases from the beginning inventory, 100 cases from the February 25 purchase, 100 cases from the August 15 purchase, and 100 cases from the October 15 purchase.

Determine the costs that should be assigned to ending inventory and cost of goods sold under each of the following assumptions: (1) costs are assigned by the specific identification method; (2) costs are assigned by the average-cost method; (3) costs are assigned by the FIFO method; and (4) costs are assigned by the LIFO method. What conclusions can be drawn about the effect of each method on the income statement and the balance sheet of Helen's Farm Store? Round your answers to the nearest whole number.

E 4. *Inventory Costing*
L O 3 *Methods*

Check Figures: (1) Cost of goods sold, year 3, FIFO: $144,000; (2) Cost of goods sold, year 3, LIFO: $150,000

During its first year of operation, Jefferson Company purchased 5,600 units of a product at $21 per unit. During the second year, it purchased 6,000 units of the same product at $24 per unit. During the third year, it purchased 5,000 units at $30 per unit. Jefferson Company managed to have an ending inventory each year of 1,000 units. The company sells goods at a 100 percent markup over cost.

Prepare cost of goods sold statements that compare the value of ending inventory and the cost of goods sold for each of the three years using (1) the FIFO method and (2) the LIFO method. From the resulting data, what conclusions can you draw about the relationships between changes in unit price and changes in the value of ending inventory?

E 5. *Periodic Inventory*
L O 3 *System and*
Inventory Costing
Methods

Check Figures: Gross margin: Average-cost method: $23,958; FIFO method: $24,700; LIFO method: $23,000

In chronological order, the inventory, purchases, and sales of a single product for a recent month are as follows:

		Units	Amount per Unit
June 1	Beginning Inventory	300	$10
4	Purchase	800	11
8	Sale	400	20
12	Purchase	1,000	12
16	Sale	700	20
20	Sale	500	22

		Units	Amount per Unit
June 24	Purchase	1,200	$13
28	Sale	600	22
29	Sale	400	22

Using the periodic inventory system, compute the cost of ending inventory, cost of goods sold, and gross margin. Use the average-cost, FIFO, and LIFO inventory costing methods. Explain the differences in gross margin produced by the three methods. Round unit costs to cents and totals to dollars.

E 6. *Perpetual Inventory*
L O 4 *System and*
Inventory Costing
Methods

Check Figures: Gross margin: Average-cost method: $24,382; FIFO method: $24,700; LIFO method: $23,400

Using the data provided in E 5 and assuming the perpetual inventory system, compute the cost of ending inventory, cost of goods sold, and gross margin. Use the average-cost, FIFO, and LIFO inventory costing methods. Explain the reasons for the differences in gross margin produced by the three methods. Round unit costs to cents and totals to dollars.

E 7. *Inventory Costing*
L O 3, 4 *Methods: Periodic*
and Perpetual
Systems

Check Figures: (1) Gross margin: Specific identification method: $1,220; Average-cost method: $1,102; FIFO method: $1,440; LIFO method: $750; (2) Gross margin: Average-cost method: $1,325; FIFO method: $1,440; LIFO method: $1,180

During July 19x2, Servex, Inc. sold 250 units of its product Dervex for $2,000. The following units were available.

	Units	Cost
Beginning Inventory	100	$1
Purchase 1	40	2
Purchase 2	60	3
Purchase 3	70	4
Purchase 4	80	5
Purchase 5	90	6

A sale of 100 units was made after purchase 1, and a sale of 150 units was made after purchase 4. Of the units sold, 100 came from beginning inventory and 150 from purchases 3 and 4.

Determine cost of goods available for sale and ending inventory in units. Then determine the costs that should be assigned to cost of goods sold and ending inventory under each of the following assumptions: (1) Costs are assigned under the periodic inventory system using (a) the specific identification method, (b) the average-cost method, (c) the FIFO method, and (d) the LIFO method. (2) Costs are assigned under the perpetual inventory system using (a) the average-cost method, (b) the FIFO method, and (c) the LIFO method. For each alternative, show the gross margin. Round unit costs to cents and totals to dollars.

E 8. *Effects of Inventory*
L O 5 *Methods on Cash*
Flows

Check Figures: Net income (after purchase): FIFO method: $238,000; LIFO method: $154,000

Ross Products, Inc. sold 120,000 cases of glue at $40 per case during 19x1. Its beginning inventory consisted of 20,000 cases at a cost of $24 per case. During 19x1, it purchased 60,000 cases at $28 per case and later 50,000 cases at $30 per case. Operating expenses were $1,100,000, and the applicable income tax rate was 30 percent.

Using the periodic inventory system, compute net income using the FIFO method and the LIFO method for costing inventory. Which alternative produces the larger cash flow? The company is considering a purchase of 10,000 cases at $30 per case just before the year end. What effect on net income and on cash flow will this proposed purchase have under each method? (**Hint:** What are the income tax consequences?)

E 9. *Inventory Costing*
L O 3, 5 *Method*
Characteristics

Check Figures: d, a, c, c, d, c, c, d, b, a

The lettered items in the list below represent inventory costing methods. Write the letter of the method that each of the following statements *best* describes.

a. Specific identification
b. Average cost
c. First-in, first-out (FIFO)
d. Last-in, first-out (LIFO)

1. Matches recent costs with recent revenues
2. Assumes that each item of inventory is identifiable
3. Results in the most realistic balance sheet valuation

4. Results in the lowest net income in periods of deflation
5. Results in the lowest net income in periods of inflation
6. Matches the oldest costs with recent revenues
7. Results in the highest net income in periods of inflation
8. Results in the highest net income in periods of deflation
9. Tends to level out the effects of inflation
10. Is unpredictable as to the effects of inflation

E 10. *Effects of Inventory*
L O 5 *Errors*

Check Figures: Net income: 19x4, $12,000; 19x3, $30,000

Condensed income statements for Hamlin Company for two years are shown below.

	19x4	19x3
Sales	$126,000	$105,000
Cost of Goods Sold	75,000	54,000
Gross Margin	$ 51,000	$ 51,000
Operating Expenses	30,000	30,000
Net Income	$ 21,000	$ 21,000

After the end of 19x4, the company discovered that an error had resulted in a $9,000 understatement of the 19x3 ending inventory.

Compute the corrected net income for 19x3 and 19x4. What effect will the error have on net income and owner's equity for 19x5?

E 11. *Lower-of-Cost-or-*
L O 6 *Market Rule*

Check Figures: (1) $7,560; (2) $7,608

Tillman Company values its inventory, shown below, at the lower of cost or market. Compute Tillman's inventory value using (1) the item-by-item method and (2) the major category method.

Exerm

	Quantity	Per Unit Cost	Per Unit Market
Category I			
Item aa	200	$1.00	$0.90
Item bb	240	2.00	2.20
Item cc	400	4.00	3.75
Category II			
Item dd	300	6.00	6.50
Item ee	400	9.00	9.10

E 12. *Retail Method*
S O 7

Check Figures: Estimated cost of ending inventory: $20,400; Estimated cost of inventory shrinkage: $8,160

Jamie's Dress Shop had net retail sales of $250,000 during the current year. The following additional information was obtained from the accounting records.

	At Cost	At Retail
Beginning Inventory	$ 40,000	$ 60,000
Net Purchases (excluding Freight In)	140,000	220,000
Freight In	10,400	

1. Using the retail method, estimate the company's ending inventory at cost.
2. Assume that a physical inventory taken at year end revealed an inventory on hand of $18,000 at retail value. What is the estimated amount of inventory shrinkage (loss due to theft, damage, and so forth) at cost using the retail method?

E 13. *Gross Profit Method*
S O 7

Check Figure: $68,700

Dale Nolan was at home watching television when he received a call from the fire department. His business was a total loss from fire. The insurance company asked him to prove his inventory loss. For the year, until the date of the fire, Dale's company had sales of $450,000 and purchases of $280,000. Freight In amounted to $13,700, and the beginning inventory was $45,000. It was Dale's custom to price goods to achieve a gross margin of 40 percent.

Compute Dale's estimated inventory loss.

SKILLS DEVELOPMENT EXERCISES

Conceptual Analysis

SDE 1.
L O 1

Evaluation of Inventory Levels

No check figure

The Gap, Inc. is one of the most important retailers of casual clothing for all members of the family. *Business Week* reports, "The Gap, Inc. is hell-bent on becoming to apparel what McDonald's is to food." With more than 1,100 stores already open, the company plans to open about 150 new stores per year for the next half decade. How does the company stay ahead of the competition? "One way is through frequent replenishment of mix-and-match inventory. That enables the company to clear out unpopular items fast—which prompts shoppers to check in on the new selections more often. . . . The Gap replaces inventory 7.5 times a year. That compares with 3.5 times at other specialty apparel stores."[10] One way in which The Gap controls inventory is by applying a just-in-time operating environment. How many days of inventory does The Gap have on hand on average compared to the competition? Discuss why those comparisons are important to The Gap. (Think of as many business and financial reasons as you can.) What is a just-in-time operating environment? Why is it important to achieving a favorable inventory turnover?

SDE 2.
L O 5

LIFO Inventory Method

No check figure

In 1992, 95 percent of paper companies used the LIFO inventory method for the costing of inventories, whereas only 19 percent of electronic equipment companies used LIFO.[11] Describe the LIFO inventory method. What effects does it have on reported income and income taxes during periods of price changes? Discuss why the paper industry would use LIFO, but most of the electronics industry would not.

SDE 3.
L O 5

Inventory Methods, Income Taxes, and Cash Flows

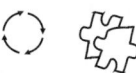

No check figure

The **Kyoto Trading Company** began business in 19x1 for the purpose of importing and marketing an electronics component used widely in digital appliances. It is now December 20, 19x1, and management is considering its options. Among its considerations is which inventory method to choose. It has decided to choose either the FIFO or the LIFO method. Under the periodic inventory system, the effects on net income of using the two methods are as follows:

	FIFO Method	LIFO Method
Sales: 500,000 units × $6	$3,000,000	$3,000,000
Cost of Goods Sold		
Purchases		
200,000 × $2	$ 400,000	$ 400,000
400,000 × $3	1,200,000	1,200,000
Total Purchases	$1,600,000	$1,600,000
Less Ending Inventory		
FIFO: 100,000 × $3	(300,000)	
LIFO: 100,000 × $2		(200,000)
Cost of Goods Sold	$1,300,000	$1,400,000
Gross Margin	$1,700,000	$1,600,000
Operating Expenses	1,200,000	1,200,000
Income Before Income Taxes	$ 500,000	$ 400,000
Income Taxes	150,000	120,000
Net Income	$ 350,000	$ 280,000

Also, management has an option to purchase an additional 100,000 units of inventory before year end at a price of $4 per unit, the price that is expected to prevail during 19x2. The income tax rate applicable to the company in 19x1 is 30 percent.

10. "Everybody's Falling into The Gap," *Business Week,* September 23, 1991, p. 36.

11. American Institute of Certified Public Accountants, *Accounting Trends & Techniques* (New York: AICPA, 1993), p. 146.

Business conditions are expected to be favorable in 19x2, as they were in 19x1. Management has asked you for advice. Analyze the effects of making the additional purchase. Then prepare a memorandum to Kyoto management in which you compare cash outcomes under the four alternatives and advise which inventory method to choose and whether to order the additional inventory. Be prepared to discuss your recommendations.

Ethical Dilemma

SDE 4.
L O 1, 5

Inventories, Income Determination, and Ethics

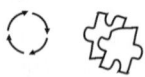

No check figure

Flare, Inc., which has a December 31 year end, designs and sells fashions for young professional women. Sandra Mason, president of the company, feared that the forecasted 1995 profitability goals would not be reached. She was pleased when Flare received a large order on December 30 from The Executive Woman, a retail chain of upscale stores for business women. Mason immediately directed the controller to record the sale, which represented 13 percent of Flare's annual sales, but directed the inventory control department not to separate the goods for shipment until after January 1. Separated goods are not included in inventory because they have been sold. On December 31, the company's auditors arrived to observe the year-end taking of the physical inventory under the periodic inventory system. What will be the effect of Mason's action on Flare's 1995 profitability? What will be the effect on 1996 profitability? Is Mason's action ethical?

Research Activity

SDE 5.
L O 2, 4

Retail Business Inventories

No check figure

Make an appointment to visit a local retail business—a grocery, clothing, book, music, or appliance store, for example—and interview the manager for thirty minutes about the company's inventory accounting system. The store may be a branch of a larger company. Find out answers to the following questions, summarize your findings in a paper to be handed in, and be prepared to discuss your results in class.

What is the physical flow of merchandise into the store, and what documents are used in connection with this flow?

What documents are prepared when merchandise is sold?

Does the store keep perpetual inventory records? If so, does it keep the records in units only or does it keep track of cost as well? If not, what system does the store use?

How often does the company take a physical inventory?

How are financial statements generated for the store?

What method does the company use to price its inventory for financial statements?

Decision-Making Practice

SDE 6.
L O 3, 5

FIFO versus LIFO Analysis

No check figure

Refrigerator Truck Sales Company (RTS Company) buys large refrigerator trucks from the manufacturer and sells them to companies and independent truckers who haul perishable goods for long distances. RTS has been successful in this specialized niche of the industry because it provides a unique product and service. Because of the high cost of the trucks and of financing inventory, RTS tries to maintain as small an inventory as possible. In fact, at the beginning of March the company had no inventory or liabilities, as shown by the balance sheet on the next page.

On March 5, RTS took delivery of a truck at a price of $150,000. On March 15, an identical truck was delivered to the company at a price of $160,000. On March 25, the company sold one of the trucks for $195,000. During March, operating expenses totaled $15,000. All transactions were paid in cash.

**RTS Company
Balance Sheet
March 1, 19xx**

Assets		Owner's Equity	
Cash	$400,000	Robert Trinker, Capital	$400,000
Total Assets	$400,000	Total Owner's Equity	$400,000

1. Prepare income statements and balance sheets for RTS on March 31 using (a) the FIFO method of inventory valuation and (b) the LIFO method of inventory valuation. Explain the effects that each method has on the financial statements.
2. Assume that Robert Trinker, the owner of RTS Company, follows the policy of withdrawing an amount of cash each period that is exactly equal to net income. What effects does this action have on the balance sheets prepared in **1,** and how do these balance sheets compare with the balance sheet at the beginning of the month? Which inventory method, if either, do you feel is more realistic in representing RTS's income?
3. Assume that RTS receives notice of another price increase of $10,000 on refrigerator trucks, to take effect on April 1. How does this information relate to the owner's withdrawal policy, and how will it affect next month's operations?

PROBLEM SET A

A 1. *Inventory Costing*
L O 3 *Methods*

Check Figures: 2. Net income: (a) $829,900; (b) $863,200; (c) $740,000

Palaggi Company merchandises a single product called Compak. The following data represent beginning inventory and purchases of Compak during the past year: January 1 inventory, 68,000 units at $11.00; February purchases, 80,000 units at $12.00; March purchases, 160,000 units at $12.40; May purchases, 120,000 units at $12.60; July purchases, 200,000 units at $12.80; September purchases, 160,000 units at $12.60; and November purchases, 60,000 units at $13.00. Sales of Compak totaled 786,000 units at $20 per unit. Selling and administrative expenses totaled $5,102,000 for the year, and Palaggi Company uses a periodic inventory system.

REQUIRED

1. Prepare a schedule to compute the cost of goods available for sale.
2. Prepare an income statement under each of the following assumptions: (a) costs are assigned to inventory using the average-cost method; (b) costs are assigned to inventory using the FIFO method; and (c) costs are assigned to inventory using the LIFO method.

A 2. *Periodic Inventory*
L O 3 *System and*
Inventory Methods

Check Figures: 1. Cost of goods sold: April, $9,660; May, $22,119

The inventory of Product M and data on purchases and sales for a two-month period follow. The company closes its books at the end of each month. It uses a periodic inventory system.

Apr.	1	Inventory	50 units @ $102
	5	Sale	30 units
	10	Purchase	100 units @ $110
	17	Sale	60 units
	30	Inventory	60 units
May	2	Purchase	100 units @ $108
	8	Sale	110 units
	14	Purchase	50 units @ $112
	18	Sale	40 units
	22	Purchase	60 units @ $117
	26	Sale	30 units
	30	Sale	20 units
	31	Inventory	70 units

1. Compute the cost of ending inventory of Product M on April 30 and May 31 using the average-cost method. In addition, determine cost of goods sold for April and May. Round unit costs to cents and totals to dollars.
2. Compute the cost of the ending inventory on April 30 and May 31 using the FIFO method. In addition, determine cost of goods sold for April and May.
3. Compute the cost of the ending inventory on April 30 and May 31 using the LIFO method. In addition, determine cost of goods sold for April and May.

A 3. *Perpetual Inventory*
L O 4 *System and*
Inventory Methods

Check Figures: 1. Cost of goods sold: April, $9,580; May, $21,991

Use the data provided in A 2, but assume that the company uses the perpetual inventory system. (**Hint:** In preparing the solutions required below, it is helpful to determine the balance of inventory after each transaction, as shown in the Review Problem for this chapter.)

REQUIRED

1. Determine the cost of ending inventory and cost of goods sold for April and May using the average-cost method. Round unit costs to cents and totals to dollars.
2. Determine the cost of ending inventory and cost of goods sold for April and May using the FIFO method.
3. Determine the cost of ending inventory and cost of goods sold for April and May using the LIFO method.

A 4. *Lower-of-Cost-or-*
L O 6 *Market Rule*
Check Figures: (1) $34,480; (2) $35,690

After taking the physical inventory, the accountant for McFarlane Company prepared the inventory schedule that follows.

	Quantity	Per Unit Cost	Per Unit Market
Product line 1			
Item 11	190	$ 9	$10
Item 12	270	4	5
Item 13	210	8	7
Product line 2			
Item 21	160	15	17
Item 22	400	21	20
Item 23	70	18	20
Product line 3			
Item 31	290	26	20
Item 32	310	30	28
Item 33	120	34	39

REQUIRED

Determine the value of the inventory at the lower of cost or market using (1) the item-by-item method and (2) the major category method.

A 5. *Retail Inventory*
S O 7 *Method*
Check Figures: Estimated inventory shortage: At cost, $6,052; At retail, $8,900

Ramirez Company operates a large discount store and uses the retail inventory method to estimate the cost of ending inventory. Management suspects that in recent weeks there have been unusually heavy losses from shoplifting or employee pilferage. To estimate the amount of the loss, the company has taken a physical inventory and will compare the results with the estimated cost of inventory. Data from the accounting records of Ramirez Company are as follows:

	At Cost	At Retail
October 1 Beginning Inventory	$51,488	$ 74,300
Purchases	71,733	108,500
Purchases Returns and Allowances	(2,043)	(3,200)
Freight In	950	
Sales		109,183
Sales Returns and Allowances		(933)
October 31 Physical Inventory at Retail		62,450

REQUIRED

1. Using the retail method, prepare a schedule to estimate the dollar amount of the store's month-end inventory.
2. Use the store's cost ratio to reduce the retail value of the physical inventory to cost.
3. Calculate the estimated amount of inventory shortage at cost and at retail.

A 6. *Gross Profit Method*
S O 7

Check Figure: Estimated loss of inventory in fire: $653,027

Holmes Brothers is a large retail furniture company that operates in two adjacent warehouses. One warehouse is a showroom, and the other is used to store merchandise. On the night of April 22, a fire broke out in the storage warehouse and destroyed the merchandise stored there. Fortunately, the fire did not reach the showroom, so all the merchandise on display was saved.

Although the company maintained a perpetual inventory system, its records were rather haphazard, and the last reliable physical inventory was taken on December 31. In addition, there was no control of the flow of the goods between the showroom and the warehouse. Thus, it was impossible to tell what goods should have been in either place. As a result, the insurance company required an independent estimate of the amount of loss. The insurance company examiners were satisfied when they were provided with the following information.

Merchandise Inventory on December 31	$ 727,400
Purchases, January 1 to April 22	1,206,100
Purchases Returns, January 1 to April 22	(5,353)
Freight In, January 1 to April 22	26,550
Sales, January 1 to April 22	1,979,525
Sales Returns, January 1 to April 22	(14,900)
Merchandise inventory in showroom on April 22	201,480
Average gross margin	44 percent

REQUIRED

Prepare a schedule that estimates the amount of the inventory lost in the fire.

PROBLEM SET B

B 1. *Inventory Costing*
L O 3 *Methods*

Check Figures: 2. Net Income: (a) $103,417; (b) $104,180; (c) $101,850

The Highland Door Company sold 2,200 doors during 19x2 at $160 per door. Its beginning inventory on January 1 was 130 doors at $56. Purchases made during the year were as follows:

February	225 doors @ $62
April	350 doors @ $65
June	700 doors @ $70
August	300 doors @ $66
October	400 doors @ $68
November	250 doors @ $72

The company's selling and administrative costs for the year were $101,000, and the company uses the periodic inventory system.

REQUIRED

1. Prepare a schedule to compute the cost of goods available for sale.
2. Prepare an income statement under each of the following assumptions: (a) costs are assigned to inventory using the average-cost method; (b) costs are assigned to inventory using the FIFO method; and (c) costs are assigned to inventory using the LIFO method.

B 2. *Periodic Inventory*
L O 3 *System*
Check Figures: 1. Cost of goods sold: August, $4,578; September, $15,457

The inventory, purchases, and sales of Product SLT for August and September follow. The company closes its books at the end of each month and uses a periodic inventory system.

Aug.	1	Inventory	60 units @ $49
	7	Sale	20 units
	10	Purchase	100 units @ $52
	19	Sale	70 units
	31	Inventory	70 units
Sept.	4	Purchase	120 units @ $53
	11	Sale	110 units
	15	Purchase	50 units @ $54
	23	Sale	80 units
	25	Purchase	100 units @ $55
	27	Sale	100 units
	30	Inventory	50 units

REQUIRED

1. Compute the cost of the ending inventory on August 31 and September 30 using the average-cost method. In addition, determine cost of goods sold for August and September. Round unit costs to cents and totals to dollars.
2. Compute the cost of the ending inventory on August 31 and September 30 using the FIFO method. In addition, determine cost of goods sold for August and September.
3. Compute the cost of the ending inventory on August 31 and September 30 using the LIFO method. In addition, determine cost of goods sold for August and September.

B 3. *Perpetual Inventory*
L O 4 *System and Inventory Methods*
Check Figures: 1. Cost of goods sold: Aug., $4,560; Sept., $15,424

Use the data provided in B 2, but assume that the company uses the perpetual inventory system. (**Hint:** In preparing the solutions required below, it is helpful to determine the balance of inventory after each transaction, as shown in the Review Problem for this chapter.)

REQUIRED

1. Determine the cost of ending inventory and cost of goods sold for August and September using the average-cost method. Round unit costs to cents and totals to dollars.
2. Determine the cost of ending inventory and cost of goods sold for August and September using the FIFO method.
3. Determine the cost of ending inventory and cost of goods sold for August and September using the LIFO method.

B 4. *Lower-of-Cost-or-*
L O 6 *Market Rule*
Check Figures: (1) $177,900; (2) $184,900

The employees of Garland's Shoes completed their physical inventory as follows:

	Pairs of Shoes	Per Unit Cost	Per Unit Market
Men			
Black	400	$ 88	$ 96
Brown	325	84	84
Blue	100	100	92
Tan	200	76	40
Women			
White	300	104	128
Red	150	92	80
Yellow	100	120	100
Blue	250	100	132
Brown	100	80	120
Black	150	80	100

Determine the value of inventory at the lower of cost or market using (1) the item-by-item method and (2) the major category method.

B 5.   *Retail Inventory*
S O 7   *Method*

Steelcraft Company recently switched to the retail inventory method of estimating the cost of ending inventory. To test this method, the company took a physical inventory one month after its implementation. Cost, retail, and the physical inventory data are as follows:

	At Cost	At Retail
March 1 Beginning Inventory	$236,066	$311,400
Purchases	375,000	504,200
Purchases Returns and Allowances	(12,600)	(17,400)
Freight In	4,175	
Sales		530,000
Sales Returns and Allowances		(14,000)
March 31 Physical Inventory		254,100

1. Using the retail method, prepare a schedule to estimate the dollar amount of Steelcraft's March 31 inventory.
2. Use Steelcraft's cost ratio to reduce the retail value of the physical inventory to cost.
3. Calculate the estimated amount of inventory shortage at cost and at retail.

B 6.   *Gross Profit Method*
S O 7

Raleigh Oil Products stores its oil field products in a West Texas warehouse. The warehouse and most of its inventory were completely destroyed by a tornado on May 11. The company found some of its records, but it does not keep perpetual inventory records. The warehouse manager must estimate the amount of the loss. She found the following information in the records.

Beginning Inventory, January 1	$660,000
Purchases, January 2 to May 11	390,000
Purchases Returns, January 2 to May 11	(15,000)
Freight In since January 2	8,000
Sales, January 2 to May 11	920,000
Sales Returns, January 2 to May 11	(20,000)

Inventory costing $210,000 was recovered and could be sold. The manager remembers that the average gross margin on oil field products is 48 percent.

Prepare a schedule to estimate the inventory destroyed by the tornado.

FINANCIAL REPORTING AND ANALYSIS CASES

Interpreting Financial Reports

FRA 1.   *LIFO, FIFO, and*
L O 2, 5   *Income Taxes*

Hershey Foods Corp. is famous for its chocolate and confectionery products. A portion of the company's income statements for 1992 and 1991 follows (in thousands).[12]

	1992	1991
Net Sales	$3,219,805	$2,899,165
Cost of Goods Sold	1,833,388	1,694,404
Gross Margin	$1,386,417	$1,204,761
Selling, General, and Administrative Expense	958,189	814,459
Income from Operations	$ 428,228	$ 390,302
Interest Expense, Net	27,240	26,845
Income Before Income Taxes	$ 400,988	$ 363,457
Provision for Income Taxes	158,390	143,929
Net Income	$ 242,598	$ 219,528

12. Hershey Foods Corp., *Annual Report,* 1992.

In a note on supplemental balance sheet information, Hershey indicated that most of its inventories are maintained using the last-in, first-out (LIFO) method. The company also reported that inventories using the LIFO method were $436,917 in 1991 and $457,179 in 1992. In addition, it reported that if valued using the first-in, first-out (FIFO) method, inventories would have been $494,290 in 1991 and $505,521 in 1992.

REQUIRED

1. Prepare a schedule comparing net income for 1992 under the LIFO method with what it would have been under FIFO. Use a corporate income tax rate of 39 percent (Hershey's average tax rate in 1992).
2. Why do you suppose Hershey's management chooses to use the LIFO inventory method? On what economic conditions, if any, do those reasons depend? Given your calculations in **1,** do you believe the economic conditions relevant to Hershey were advantageous for using LIFO in 1992? Explain your answer.

FRA 2.
LO 5
Misstatement of Inventory

Check Figure: $45 million

The *Wall Street Journal* reported on November 20, 1987, that **Crazy Eddie Inc.,** a discount consumer electronics chain, seemed to be missing $45 million in merchandise inventory. "It was a shock," Elias Zinn, the new president and chief executive officer, was quoted as saying.[13]

The article went on to say that Mr. Zinn headed a management team that took control of Crazy Eddie after a new board of directors was elected at a shareholders' meeting on November 6. A count on November 9 turned up only $75 million in inventory, compared with $126.7 million reported by the old management on August 30. Net sales could account for only $6.7 million of the difference. Mr. Zinn said he didn't know whether bookkeeping errors or an actual physical loss created the shortfall, although at least one store manager felt it was a bookkeeping error, because security is strong. "It would be hard for someone to steal anything," he said.

REQUIRED

1. What has been the effect of the misstatement of inventory on Crazy Eddie's reported earnings in prior accounting periods?
2. Is this a situation you would expect in a company that is experiencing financial difficulty? Explain.

International Company

FRA 3.
LO 1, 5
Inventory Levels and Methods

Check Figures: Inventory turnover:
Pioneer, 4.4 times; Yamaha, 4.3 times

Two large Japanese diversified electronics companies are **Pioneer Electronic Corporation** and **Yamaha Motor Co., Ltd.** Both companies use the average-cost method and the lower-of-cost-or-market rule to account for inventories. The following data are for their 1992 fiscal years (in millions of yen).

	Pioneer	Yamaha
Beginning Inventory	¥76,324	¥123,768
Ending Inventory	93,148	113,766
Cost of Goods Sold	376,739	506,863

Compare the inventory efficiency of Pioneer and Yamaha by computing the inventory turnover and average days' inventory on hand for both companies in 1992. Comment on the results. Most companies in the United States use the LIFO inventory method. How would inventory method affect your evaluation if you were to compare Pioneer and Yamaha to a U.S. company? What could you do to make the results comparable?

13. Based on Ann Hagedorn, "Crazy Eddie Says About $45 Million of Goods Missing,"*Wall Street Journal,* November 20, 1987, p. 47.

Toys "R" Us Annual Report

FRA 4.   *Retail Method and*
L O 3, 6   *Inventory Ratios*
S O 7

No check figure

Refer to the note related to inventories in the appendix on Toys "R" Us to answer the following questions: What inventory method(s) does Toys "R" Us use? Why do you think that if LIFO inventories had been valued at FIFO, there would be no difference? Do you think many of the company's inventories are valued at market? Even though few companies use the retail inventory method, why do you think Toys "R" Us uses this method? Compute and compare the inventory turnover and average days' inventory on hand for Toys "R" Us for 1994 and 1995.

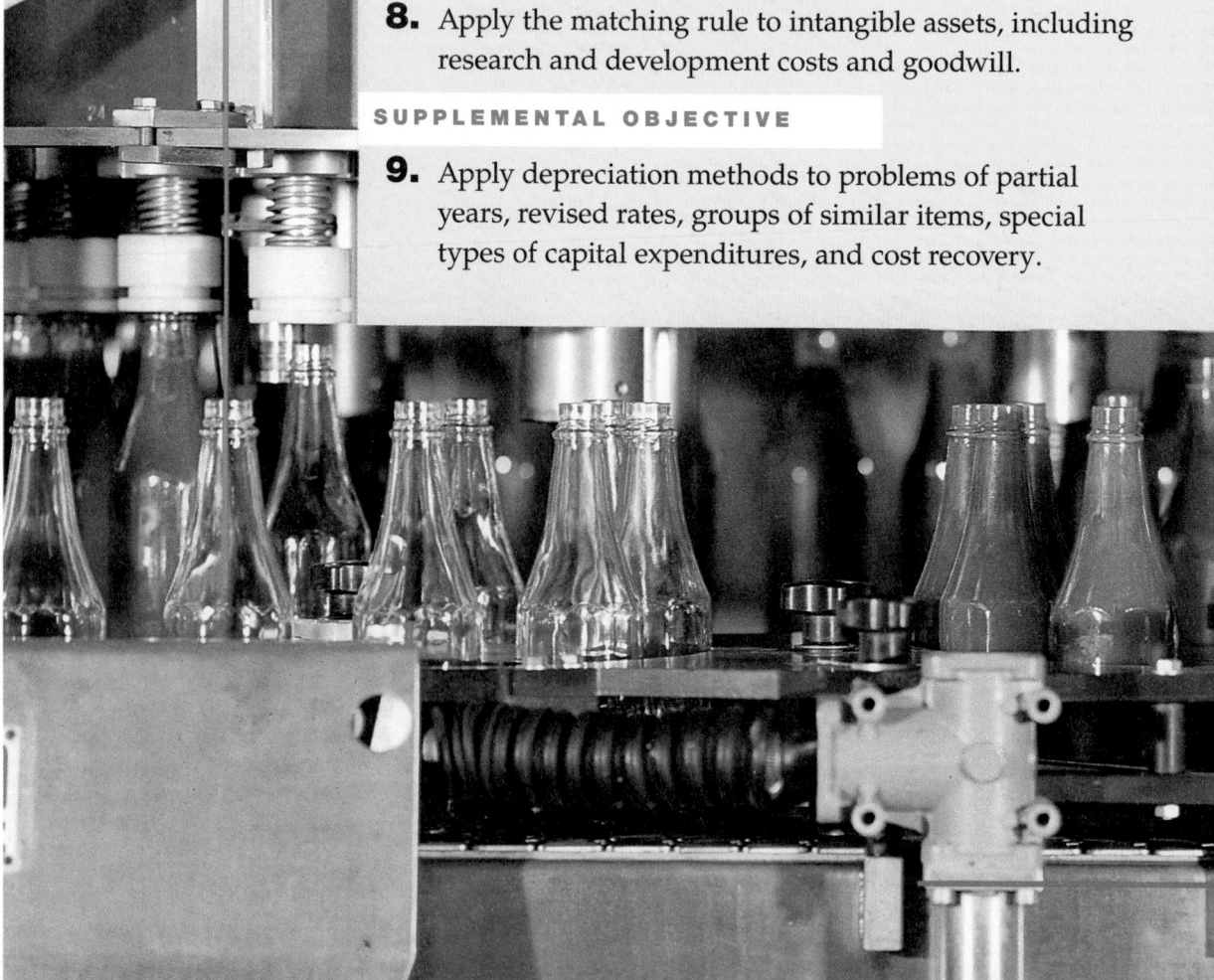

1. Identify the types of long-term assets and explain the management issues related to accounting for them.

2. Distinguish between capital and revenue expenditures, and account for the cost of property, plant, and equipment.

3. Define *depreciation*, state the factors that affect its computation, and show how to record it.

4. Compute periodic depreciation under the (a) straight-line method, (b) production method, and (c) declining-balance method.

5. Account for the disposal of depreciable assets not involving exchanges.

6. Account for the disposal of depreciable assets involving exchanges.

7. Identify the issues related to accounting for natural resources and compute depletion.

8. Apply the matching rule to intangible assets, including research and development costs and goodwill.

9. Apply depreciation methods to problems of partial years, revised rates, groups of similar items, special types of capital expenditures, and cost recovery.

H. J. Heinz Company

DECISION POINT

The effects of management's decisions regarding long-term assets are most apparent in the areas of reported total assets and net income. How does one learn about the significance of those items to a company?

An idea of the extent of a company's long-term assets and their importance can be gained from the financial statements. For example, the following list of assets is taken from the 1992 annual report of H. J. Heinz Company, one of the world's largest food companies (in thousands).

	1992	1991
Property, Plant, and Equipment:		
Land	$ 44,988	$ 39,918
Buildings and leasehold improvements	655,323	529,041
Equipment, furniture, and other	2,279,471	2,195,511
	$2,979,782	$2,764,470
Less accumulated depreciation	1,067,673	1,041,729
Total property, plant, and equipment, net	$1,912,109	$1,722,741
Other Noncurrent Assets:		
Investments, advances and other assets	$ 560,144	$ 343,526
Goodwill (net of amortization: 1992—$88,892 and 1991—$67,553)	822,100	498,029
Other intangibles (net of amortization: 1992—$63,197 and 1991—$44,285)	357,236	251,301
Total other noncurrent assets	$1,739,480	$1,092,856

Of the company's almost $6 billion in total assets, about one-third consists of property, plant, and equipment, and another 20 percent is goodwill and other intangibles. On the income statement, depreciation and amortization expenses associated with those assets are $212 million, or about one-third of net income, and on the statement of cash flows, more than $331 million was spent on new long-term assets. This chapter deals with the long-term assets of property, plant, and equipment and intangible assets.[1] : : : : :

1. H. J. Heinz Company, *Annual Report,* 1992.

MANAGEMENT ISSUES RELATED TO ACCOUNTING FOR LONG-TERM ASSETS

OBJECTIVE

1 *Identify the types of long-term assets and explain the management issues related to accounting for them*

Long-term assets are assets that (1) have a useful life of more than one year, (2) are acquired for use in the operation of a business, and (3) are not intended for resale to customers. For many years, it was common to refer to long-term assets as *fixed assets,* but use of this term is declining because the word *fixed* implies that they last forever. The relative importance of long-term assets to various industries is shown in Figure 1. Long-term assets range from 19.4 percent of total assets in household appliances to 52.4 percent in interstate trucking.

Although an asset need not have a strict minimum useful life to be classified as long term, the most common criterion is that the asset must be capable of repeated use for a period of at least a year. Included in this category is equipment used only in peak or emergency periods, such as generators.

Assets not used in the normal course of business should not be included in this category. Thus, land held for speculative reasons or buildings no longer used in ordinary business operations should not be included in the property, plant, and equipment category. Instead, they should be classified as long-term investments.

Finally, if an item is held for resale to customers, it should be classified as inventory—not plant and equipment—no matter how durable it is. For example, a printing press that is held for sale by a printing press manufacturer would be considered inventory, whereas the same printing press would be considered plant and equipment for a printing company that buys it for use in operations.

Long-term assets and their related expenses are customarily divided into the following categories:

Asset	Expense
Tangible Assets	
Land	None
Plant, buildings, and equipment (plant assets)	Depreciation
Natural resources	Depletion
Intangible Assets	Amortization

Tangible assets have physical substance. Land is a tangible asset, and because it has an unlimited life, it is the only tangible asset not subject to depreciation or other expense. Plant, buildings, and equipment (referred to hereafter as *plant assets*) are subject to depreciation. Depreciation is the periodic allocation of the cost of a tangible long-lived asset (other than land and natural resources) over its estimated useful life. The term applies to manufactured assets only. Note that accounting for depreciation is an allocation process, not a valuation process. This point is discussed in more detail later in the chapter.

Natural resources differ from land in that they are purchased for the economic value that can be taken from the land and used up rather than for the value associated with the land's location. Among natural resources are ore from mines, oil and gas from oil and gas fields, and lumber from forests. Natural resources are subject to depletion rather than to depreciation. The term depletion refers to the exhaustion of a natural resource through mining, cutting, pumping, or other extraction, and to the way in which the cost is allocated.

Figure 1. Long-Term Assets as a Percentage of Total Assets for Selected Industries

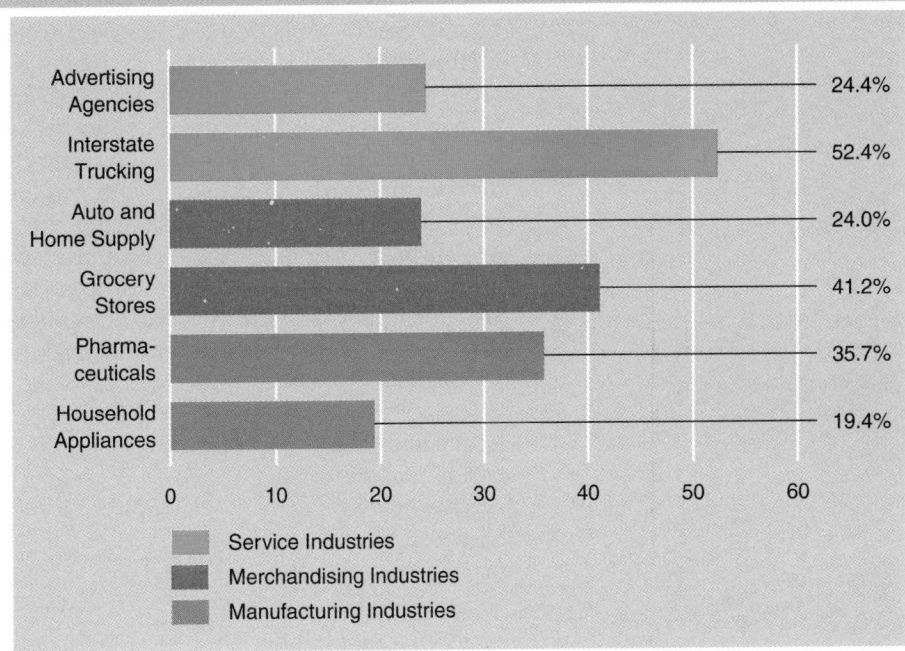

Source: Data from Dun and Bradstreet, *Industry Norms and Ratios, 1993–94.*

Intangible assets are long-term assets that have no physical substance and in most cases relate to legal rights or advantages held. Intangible assets include patents, copyrights, trademarks, franchises, organization costs, lease-holds, leasehold improvements, and goodwill. The allocation of the cost of an intangible asset to the periods it benefits is called amortization. Although the current assets Accounts Receivable and Prepaid Expenses do not have physical substance, they are not considered intangible assets because they are not long term.

The unexpired part of the cost of an asset is generally called its *book value*, or carrying value. The latter term is used in this book when referring to long-term assets. The carrying value of plant assets, for instance, is cost less accumulated depreciation.

Long-term assets differ from current assets in that they support the operating cycle instead of being a part of it. They are also expected to benefit the business for a longer period than do current assets. Current assets are expected to be realized within one year or during the operating cycle, whichever is longer. Long-term assets are expected to last beyond that period. For example, Wickes Furniture, Inc., a retailer, purchases furniture as inventory to sell to customers. Because the company expects to sell the furniture during its operating cycle, the furniture is a current asset. Wickes also owns buildings, which are expected to last for thirty years or more, to store and showcase its inventory. And it owns trucks, which should last for five years or more, to deliver furniture to customers' homes. Because the buildings and trucks have useful lives that will extend well beyond a single operating cycle, they are classified as long-term assets. The management issues related to long-term assets revolve around the decision to acquire such assets, the means of financing them, and the methods of accounting for them.

DECIDING TO ACQUIRE LONG-TERM ASSETS

The decision to acquire a long-term asset involves a complex process. Methods of evaluating data to make rational decisions in this area are grouped under a topic called capital budgeting, which is usually covered in a managerial accounting course. However, an awareness of the general nature of the problem is helpful in understanding the accounting issues related to long-term assets. To illustrate the acquisition decision, let us assume that Irena Markova, M.D., is considering the purchase of a $5,000 computer for her office. By purchasing the computer, she estimates that she can reduce the hours of a part-time employee sufficiently to save net cash flows of $3,000 per year for four years and that the computer will be worth $1,000 at the end of that period. These data are summarized as follows:

	19x1	19x2	19x3	19x4
Acquisition cost	($5,000)			
Net annual savings in cash flows	$3,000	$3,000	$3,000	$3,000
Disposal price				1,000
Net cash flows	($2,000)	$3,000	$3,000	$4,000

To reach a rational decision, Dr. Markova must compare the negative cash outflow required by the purchase with the positive cash flows to be received over a period of years. Such a comparison is not always as obvious as it may seem because the dollars that will be saved in future years are not as valuable as the dollars that must be expended today for the acquisition. Other important factors in the decision process are the costs of training and maintenance, and the possibility that, because of unforeseen circumstances, the savings may not be as great as expected. In Dr. Markova's case, the decision to purchase is likely to be a good one because the positive cash flows from the acquisition are substantially more than the purchase price.

Information about a company's acquisitions of long-term assets may be found under investing activities in the statement of cash flows. For example, in referring to this section of its annual report, the management of Bausch & Lomb, one of the largest makers of health care products, makes the following statement:

> Cash flows used in investing activities reflect payments for purchases of property, plant, and equipment, which increased $30.7 million or 35% to $119.3 million in 1992.[2]

FINANCING LONG-TERM ASSETS

In addition to deciding whether or not to acquire a long-term asset, management must decide how to finance the asset if it is acquired. Some companies are profitable enough to pay for long-term assets out of cash flows from operations, but when financing is needed, some form of long-term arrangement related to the life of the asset is usually most appropriate. For example, an automobile loan generally spans four or five years, whereas a mortgage loan on a house may span thirty years. For a major long-term acquisition, a company may issue capital stock, long-term notes, or bonds. A good place to

---

2. Bausch & Lomb, Inc., *Annual Report*, 1992.

Figure 2. Issues of Accounting for Long-Term Assets

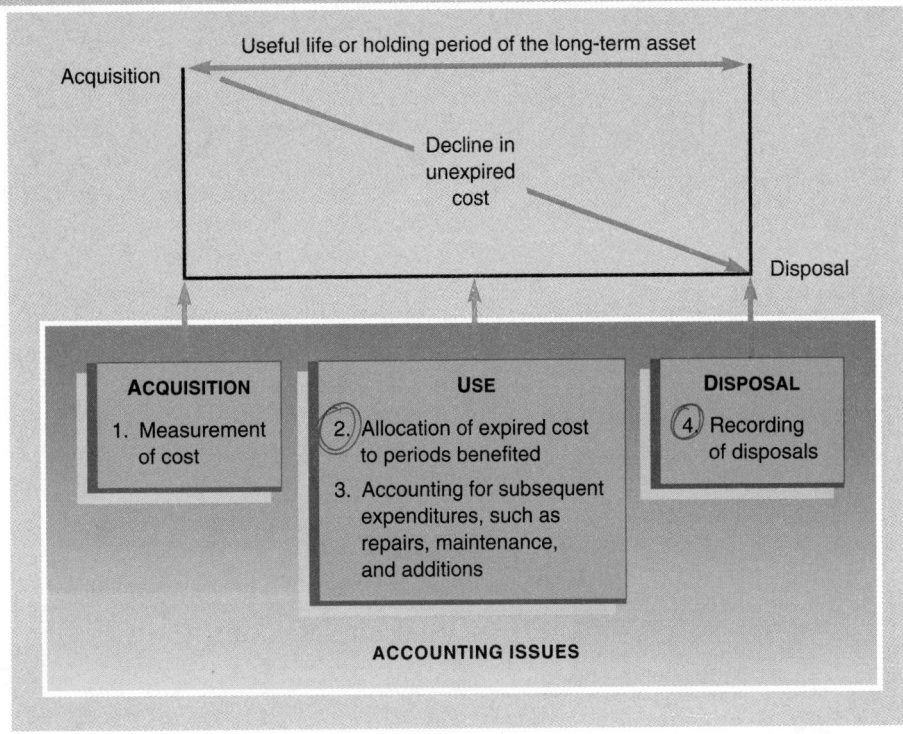

study a company's long-term financing is in the financing activities section of the statement of cash flows. For instance, in discussing this section, Bausch & Lomb's management states that the company's increase in borrowings "was attributable to the higher level of capital spending."[3] Another option a company may have is to lease long-term assets instead of buying them.

APPLYING THE MATCHING RULE TO LONG-TERM ASSETS

Accounting for long-term assets requires the proper application of the matching rule through the resolution of two important issues. The first is how much of the total cost to allocate to expense in the current accounting period. The second is how much to retain on the balance sheet as an asset to benefit future periods. To resolve these issues, four important questions about the acquisition, use, and disposal of each long-term asset, as illustrated in Figure 2, must be answered.

1. How is the cost of the long-term asset determined?
2. How should the expired portion of the cost of the long-term asset be allocated against revenues over time?
3. How should subsequent expenditures, such as repairs and additions, be treated?
4. How should disposal of the long-term asset be recorded?

Because of the long life of long-term assets and the complexity of the transactions involving them, management is faced with many choices and

3. Ibid.

estimates. For example, acquisition cost may be complicated by group purchases, trade-ins, or construction costs. In addition, to allocate the cost of the asset to future periods effectively, management must estimate how long the asset will last and what it will be worth at the end of its use. In making such estimates, it is helpful to think of a long-term asset as a bundle of services to be used in the operation of the business over a period of years. A delivery truck may provide 100,000 miles of service over its life. A piece of equipment may have the potential to produce 500,000 parts. A building may provide shelter for 50 years. As each of those assets is purchased, the company is paying in advance for 100,000 miles, the capacity to produce 500,000 parts, or 50 years of service. In essence, each asset is a type of long-term prepaid expense. The accounting problem is to spread the cost of the services over the useful life of the asset. As the services benefit the company over the years, the cost becomes an expense rather than an asset.

The remainder of this chapter will address the issues raised in Figure 2 as they relate to property, plant, and equipment, natural resources, and intangible assets.

ACQUISITION COST OF PROPERTY, PLANT, AND EQUIPMENT

OBJECTIVE

2 *Distinguish between capital and revenue expenditures, and account for the cost of property, plant, and equipment*

The term expenditure refers to a payment or an obligation to make future payment for an asset, such as a truck, or a service, such as a repair. Expenditures may be classified as capital expenditures or revenue expenditures. A capital expenditure is an expenditure for the purchase or expansion of a long-term asset. Capital expenditures are recorded in the asset accounts because they benefit several future accounting periods. A revenue expenditure is an expenditure related to the maintenance and operation of a long-term asset. Revenue expenditures are recorded in the expense accounts because their benefits are realized in the current period.

Careful distinction between capital and revenue expenditures is important to the proper application of the matching rule. For example, if the purchase of an automobile is mistakenly recorded as a revenue expenditure, the expense for the current period is overstated on the income statement. As a result, current net income is understated, and in future periods net income will be overstated. If, on the other hand, a revenue expenditure, such as the painting of a building, were charged to an asset account, the expense of the current period would be understated. Current net income would be overstated by the same amount, and the net income of future periods would be understated.

Determining when a payment is an expense and when it is an asset is a matter of judgment in which management takes a leading role. Such latitude, however, does not permit distortion of the financial results. For example, in 1991, after an investigation by the Securities and Exchange Commission, Amre, Inc., a maker of aluminum siding and kitchen cabinets, announced that it had overstated its profits in 1987 and 1988 and understated its losses in 1989. Results for 1990 were also restated, and the company's two top officers resigned. According to reports in the *Wall Street Journal*, a primary reason for the adjustments was that Amre improperly recorded its marketing costs, such as the cost of purchasing mailing lists, as assets instead of as expenses. Because the costs were treated as assets, they appeared on Amre's balance sheet and the company was able to spread them over time, thereby improving its profits. For example, if Amre had properly recorded its marketing costs, its 1988 net income would have been $2.9 million, not the reported $7.3 million.[4]

GENERAL APPROACH TO ACQUISITION COSTS

The acquisition cost of property, plant, and equipment includes all expenditures reasonable and necessary to get the asset in place and ready for use. For example, the cost of installing and testing a machine is a legitimate cost of the machine. However, if the machine is damaged during installation, the cost of repairs is an operating expense and not an acquisition cost.

Cost is easiest to determine when a transaction is made for cash. In that case, the cost of the asset is equal to the cash paid for the asset plus expenditures for freight, insurance while in transit, installation, and other necessary related costs. If a debt is incurred in the purchase of the asset, the interest charges are not a cost of the asset but a cost of borrowing the money to buy the asset. They are therefore an operating expense. An exception to this principle is that interest costs during the construction of an asset are properly included as a cost of the asset.[5]

Expenditures such as freight, insurance while in transit, and installation are included in the cost of the asset because they are necessary if the asset is to function. Following the matching rule, they are allocated to the useful life of the asset rather than charged as expenses in the current period.

For practical purposes many companies establish policies defining when an expenditure should be recorded as an expense or an asset. For example, small expenditures for items that would normally be treated as assets may be treated as expenses because the amounts involved are not material in relation to net income. Thus, a wastebasket, which might last for years, would be recorded as a supplies expense rather than as a depreciable asset.

Some of the problems of determining the cost of a long-lived asset are demonstrated in the illustrations for land, buildings, equipment, land improvements, and group purchases presented in the next few sections.

Land   There are often expenditures in addition to the purchase price of land that should be debited to the Land account. Some examples are commissions to real estate agents; lawyers' fees; accrued taxes paid by the purchaser; costs of preparing the land to build on, such as draining, tearing down old buildings, clearing, and grading; and assessments for local improvements, such as streets and sewage systems. The cost of landscaping is usually debited to the Land account because such improvements are relatively permanent. Land is not subject to depreciation because it does not have a limited useful life.

Let us assume that a company buys land for a new retail operation. It pays a net purchase price of $170,000, pays brokerage fees of $6,000 and legal fees of $2,000, pays $10,000 to have an old building on the site torn down, receives $4,000 salvage from the old building, and pays $1,000 to have the site graded. The cost of the land will be $185,000, determined as shown on the next page.

4. Karen Blumenthal, "Amre Overstated Financial Results for Three Fiscal Years," *Wall Street Journal,* August 7, 1991, p. B8.

5. "Capitalization of Interest Cost," *Statement of Financial Accounting Standards No. 34* (Stamford, Conn.: Financial Accounting Standards Board, 1979), par. 9–11.

Net purchase price		$170,000
Brokerage fees		6,000
Legal fees		2,000
Tearing down old building	$10,000	
Less salvage	4,000	6,000
Grading		1,000
Total cost		$185,000

Land Improvements   Improvements to real estate, such as driveways, parking lots, and fences, have a limited life and are thus subject to depreciation. They should be recorded in an account called Land Improvements rather than in the Land account.

Buildings   When an existing building is purchased, its cost includes the purchase price plus all repairs and other expenses required to put it in usable condition. Buildings are subject to depreciation because they have a limited useful life. When a business constructs its own building, the cost includes all reasonable and necessary expenditures, such as those for materials, labor, part of the overhead and other indirect costs, architects' fees, insurance during construction, interest on construction loans during the period of construction, lawyers' fees, and building permits. If outside contractors are used in the construction, the net contract price plus other expenditures necessary to put the building in usable condition are included.

Equipment   The cost of equipment includes all expenditures connected with purchasing the equipment and preparing it for use. Those expenditures include the invoice price less cash discounts; freight or transportation, including insurance; excise taxes and tariffs; buying expenses; installation costs; and test runs to ready the equipment for operation. Equipment is subject to depreciation.

Group Purchases   Sometimes land and other assets are purchased for a lump sum. Because land is a nondepreciable asset that has an unlimited life, it must have a separate ledger account, and the lump-sum purchase price must be apportioned between the land and the other assets. For example, assume that a building and the land on which it is situated are purchased for a lump-sum payment of $85,000. The apportionment can be made by determining the price of each if purchased separately and applying the appropriate percentages to the lump-sum price. Assume that appraisals yield estimates of $10,000 for the land and $90,000 for the building, if purchased separately. In that case, 10 percent of the lump-sum price, or $8,500, would be allocated to the land and 90 percent, or $76,500, would be allocated to the building, as shown below.

	Appraisal	Percentage	Apportionment
Land	$ 10,000	10 ($10,000 ÷ $100,000)	$ 8,500 ($85,000 × 10%)
Building	90,000	90 ($90,000 ÷ $100,000)	76,500 ($85,000 × 90%)
Totals	$100,000	100	$85,000

BUSINESS BULLETIN: ETHICS IN PRACTICE

Determining the acquisition price of a long-term asset is not always as clear-cut as some might imagine, especially in the case of constructed assets. Management has considerable leeway, but choices that are questioned can sometimes be costly. The *Wall Street Journal* reported that Chambers Development Co., a waste-disposal company, wrote off nearly $50 million when it decided to stop deferring costs related to the development of landfills. Previously, Chambers had been including certain indirect costs, such as executives' salaries and travel, legal, and public relations fees, as capital expenditures to be written off over the life of the landfill. The *Wall Street Journal* stated, "Accounting experts consider the practice unorthodox and aggressive, but not necessarily outside generally accepted accounting principles." Further write-offs may follow because of the large amount of interest the company is capitalizing as a cost of the landfill. On news of the accounting change, the company's stock price dropped 63 percent in one day.[6]

ACCOUNTING FOR DEPRECIATION

OBJECTIVE

3 *Define* depreciation, *state the factors that affect its computation, and show how to record it*

Depreciation accounting is described by the AICPA as follows:

> The cost of a productive facility is one of the costs of the services it renders during its useful economic life. Generally accepted accounting principles require that this cost be spread over the expected useful life of the facility in such a way as to allocate it as equitably as possible to the periods during which services are obtained from the use of the facility. This procedure is known as depreciation accounting, a system of accounting which aims to distribute the cost or other basic value of tangible capital assets, less salvage (if any), over the estimated useful life of the unit . . . in a systematic and rational manner. It is a process of allocation, not of valuation.[7]

This description contains several important points. First, all tangible assets except land have a limited useful life. Because of this limited useful life, the costs of these assets must be distributed as expenses over the years they benefit. Physical deterioration and obsolescence are the major causes of the limited useful life of a depreciable asset. The physical deterioration of tangible assets results from use and from exposure to the elements, such as wind and sun. Periodic repairs and a sound maintenance policy may keep buildings and equipment in good operating order and extract the maximum useful life from them, but every machine or building at some point must be discarded.

6. Gabriella Stern, "Chambers Development Co. May Face Further Write-offs Over Accounting," *Wall Street Journal*, April 10, 1992.

7. *Financial Accounting Standards: Original Pronouncements as of July 1, 1977* (Stamford, Conn.: Financial Accounting Standards Board, 1977), ARB No. 43, Ch. 9, Sec. C, par. 5.

The need for depreciation is not eliminated by repairs. Obsolescence is the process of becoming out of date. With fast-changing technology as well as fast-changing demands, machinery and even buildings often become obsolete before they wear out. Accountants do not distinguish between physical deterioration and obsolescence because they are interested in the length of an asset's useful life regardless of what limits that useful life.

Second, the term *depreciation,* as used in accounting, does not refer to an asset's physical deterioration or decrease in market value over time. Depreciation means the allocation of the cost of a plant asset to the periods that benefit from the services of that asset. The term is used to describe the gradual conversion of the cost of the asset into an expense.

Third, depreciation is not a process of valuation. Accounting records are kept in accordance with the cost principle; they are not indicators of changing price levels. It is possible that, through an advantageous purchase and specific market conditions, the market value of a building may rise. Nevertheless, depreciation must continue to be recorded because it is the result of an allocation, not a valuation, process. Eventually the building will wear out or become obsolete regardless of interim fluctuations in market value.

FACTORS THAT AFFECT THE COMPUTATION OF DEPRECIATION

Four factors affect the computation of depreciation. They are (1) cost, (2) residual value, (3) depreciable cost, and (4) estimated useful life.

Cost   As explained earlier in the chapter, cost is the net purchase price plus all reasonable and necessary expenditures to get the asset in place and ready for use.

Residual Value   The residual value of an asset is its estimated net scrap, salvage, or trade-in value as of the estimated date of disposal. Other terms often used to describe residual value are *salvage value* and *disposal value.*

Depreciable Cost   The depreciable cost of an asset is its cost less its residual value. For example, a truck that costs $12,000 and has a residual value of $3,000 would have a depreciable cost of $9,000. Depreciable cost must be allocated over the useful life of the asset.

Estimated Useful Life   Estimated useful life is the total number of service units expected from an asset. Service units may be measured in terms of years the asset is expected to be used, units expected to be produced, miles expected to be driven, or similar measures. In computing the estimated useful life of an asset, an accountant should consider all relevant information, including (1) past experience with similar assets, (2) the asset's present condition, (3) the company's repair and maintenance policy, (4) current technological and industry trends, and (5) local conditions such as weather.

Depreciation is recorded at the end of the accounting period by an adjusting entry that takes the following form.

```
Depreciation Expense, Asset Name                        xxx
    Accumulated Depreciation, Asset Name                        xxx
        To record depreciation for the period
```

METHODS OF COMPUTING DEPRECIATION

Many methods are used to allocate the cost of plant assets to accounting periods through depreciation. Each is proper for certain circumstances. The most common methods are (1) the straight-line method, (2) the production method, and (3) an accelerated method known as the declining-balance method.

Straight-Line Method   When the straight-line method is used to calculate depreciation, the depreciable cost of the asset is spread evenly over the estimated useful life of the asset. The straight-line method is based on the assumption that depreciation depends only on the passage of time. The depreciation expense for each period is computed by dividing the depreciable cost (cost of the depreciating asset less its estimated residual value) by the number of accounting periods in the asset's estimated useful life. The rate of depreciation is the same in each year. Suppose, for example, that a delivery truck costs $10,000 and has an estimated residual value of $1,000 at the end of its estimated useful life of five years. The annual depreciation would be $1,800 under the straight-line method, calculated as follows:

$$\frac{\text{Cost} - \text{residual value}}{\text{Estimated useful life}} = \frac{\$10,000 - \$1,000}{5} = \$1,800$$

The depreciation for the five years would be as follows:

Depreciation Schedule, Straight-Line Method

	Cost	Yearly Depreciation	Accumulated Depreciation	Carrying Value
Date of purchase	$10,000	—	—	$10,000
End of first year	10,000	$1,800	$1,800	8,200
End of second year	10,000	1,800	3,600	6,400
End of third year	10,000	1,800	5,400	4,600
End of fourth year	10,000	1,800	7,200	2,800
End of fifth year	10,000	1,800	9,000	1,000

There are three important points to note from the depreciation schedule for the straight-line depreciation method. First, the depreciation is the same each year. Second, the accumulated depreciation increases uniformly. Third, the carrying value decreases uniformly until it reaches the estimated residual value.

Production Method   The production method of depreciation is based on the assumption that depreciation is solely the result of use and that the passage of time plays no role in the depreciation process. If we assume that the delivery truck from the previous example has an estimated useful life of 90,000 miles, the depreciation cost per mile would be determined as follows:

$$\frac{\text{Cost} - \text{residual value}}{\text{Estimated units of useful life}} = \frac{\$10,000 - \$1,000}{90,000 \text{ miles}} = \$.10 \text{ per mile}$$

If we assume that the use of the truck was 20,000 miles for the first year, 30,000 miles for the second, 10,000 miles for the third, 20,000 miles for the fourth, and 10,000 miles for the fifth, the depreciation schedule for the delivery truck would appear as shown on the next page.

Depreciation Schedule, Production Method

	Cost	Miles	Yearly Depreciation	Accumulated Depreciation	Carrying Value
Date of purchase	$10,000	—	—	—	$10,000
End of first year	10,000	20,000	$2,000	$2,000	8,000
End of second year	10,000	30,000	3,000	5,000	5,000
End of third year	10,000	10,000	1,000	6,000	4,000
End of fourth year	10,000	20,000	2,000	8,000	2,000
End of fifth year	10,000	10,000	1,000	9,000	1,000

There is a direct relation between the amount of depreciation each year and the units of output or use. Also, the accumulated depreciation increases each year in direct relation to units of output or use. Finally, the carrying value decreases each year in direct relation to units of output or use until it reaches the estimated residual value.

Under the production method, the unit of output or use employed to measure the estimated useful life of each asset should be appropriate for that asset. For example, the number of items produced may be an appropriate measure for one machine, but the number of hours of use may be a better measure for another. The production method should be used only when the output of an asset over its useful life can be estimated with reasonable accuracy.

OBJECTIVE

4c *Compute periodic depreciation under the declining-balance method*

Declining-Balance Method

An accelerated method of depreciation results in relatively large amounts of depreciation in the early years of an asset's life and smaller amounts in later years. Such a method, which is based on the passage of time, assumes that many kinds of plant assets are most efficient when new, and so provide more and better service in the early years of their useful life. It is consistent with the matching rule to allocate more depreciation to earlier years than to later years if the benefits or services received in the earlier years are greater.

An accelerated method also recognizes that changing technologies make some equipment lose service value rapidly. Thus, it is realistic to allocate more to depreciation in earlier years than in later years. New inventions and products result in obsolescence of equipment bought earlier, making it necessary to replace equipment sooner than if technology changed more slowly.

Another argument in favor of an accelerated method is that repair expense is likely to be greater in later years than in earlier years. Thus, the total of repair and depreciation expense remains fairly constant over a period of years. This result naturally assumes that the services received from the asset are roughly equal from year to year.

The declining-balance method is the most common accelerated method of depreciation. Under this method, depreciation is computed by applying a fixed rate to the carrying value (the declining balance) of a long-lived asset, resulting in higher depreciation charges during the early years of the asset's life. Though any fixed rate might be used, the most common rate is a percentage equal to twice the straight-line percentage. When twice the straight-line rate is used, the method is usually called the double-declining-balance method.

In our earlier example, the delivery truck had an estimated useful life of five years. Consequently, under the straight-line method, the depreciation rate for each year was 20 percent (100 percent ÷ 5 years).

Under the double-declining-balance method, the fixed rate is 40 percent (2 × 20 percent). This fixed rate is applied to the *remaining carrying value* at the end of each year. Estimated residual value is not taken into account in figuring depreciation except in the last year of an asset's useful life, when depreciation is limited to the amount necessary to bring the carrying value down to the estimated residual value. The depreciation schedule for this method is as follows:

Depreciation Schedule, Double-Declining-Balance Method

	Cost	Yearly Depreciation		Accumulated Depreciation	Carrying Value
Date of purchase	$10,000	—		—	$10,000
End of first year	10,000	(40% × $10,000)	$4,000	$4,000	6,000
End of second year	10,000	(40% × $6,000)	2,400	6,400	3,600
End of third year	10,000	(40% × $3,600)	1,440	7,840	2,160
End of fourth year	10,000	(40% × $2,160)	864	8,704	1,296
End of fifth year	10,000		296*	9,000	1,000

*Depreciation limited to amount necessary to reduce carrying value to residual value:
$296 = $1,296 (previous carrying value) − $1,000 (residual value).

Note that the fixed rate is always applied to the carrying value at the end of the previous year. The depreciation is greatest in the first year and declines each year after that. Finally, the depreciation in the last year is limited to the amount necessary to reduce carrying value to residual value.

Comparing the Three Methods   A visual comparison may provide a better understanding of the three depreciation methods described above. Figure 3 compares yearly depreciation and carrying value under the three methods. In the left-hand graph, which shows yearly depreciation, straight-line depreciation is uniform at $1,800 per year over the five-year period. However, the

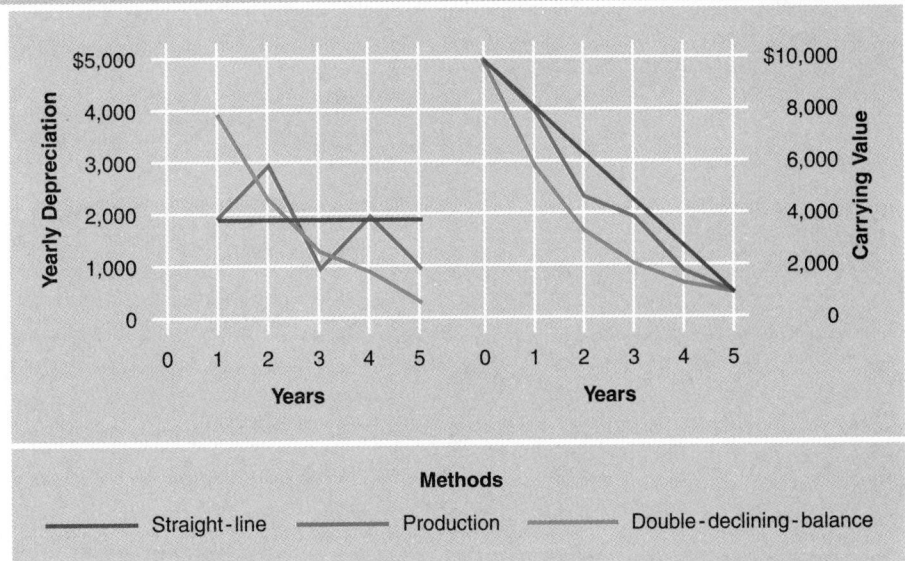

Figure 3. Graphical Comparison of Three Methods of Determining Depreciation

Methods
——— Straight-line   ——— Production   ——— Double-declining-balance

double-declining-balance method begins at an amount greater than straight-line ($4,000) and decreases each year to amounts that are less than straight-line (ultimately, $296). The production method does not generate a regular pattern because of the random fluctuation of the depreciation from year to year. The three yearly depreciation patterns are reflected in the graph of carrying value. In that graph, each method starts in the same place (cost of $10,000) and ends at the same place (residual value of $1,000). It is the patterns during the useful life of the asset that differ for each method. For instance, the carrying value under the straight-line method is always greater than that under the double-declining-balance method, except at the beginning and end of useful life.

BUSINESS BULLETIN: BUSINESS PRACTICE

Most companies choose the straight-line method of depreciation for financial reporting purposes, as shown in Figure 4. Only about 17 percent use some type of accelerated method and 8 percent use the production method. These figures tend to be misleading about the importance of accelerated depreciation methods, however, especially when it comes to income taxes. Federal income tax laws allow either the straight-line method or an accelerated method, and for tax purposes, according to *Accounting Trends and Techniques,* about 75 percent of the six hundred large companies studied preferred an accelerated method. Companies use different methods of depreciation for good reason. The straight-line method can be advantageous for financial reporting because it can produce the highest net income, and an accelerated method can be beneficial for tax purposes because it can result in lower income taxes.

Figure 4. Depreciation Methods Used by 600 Large Companies

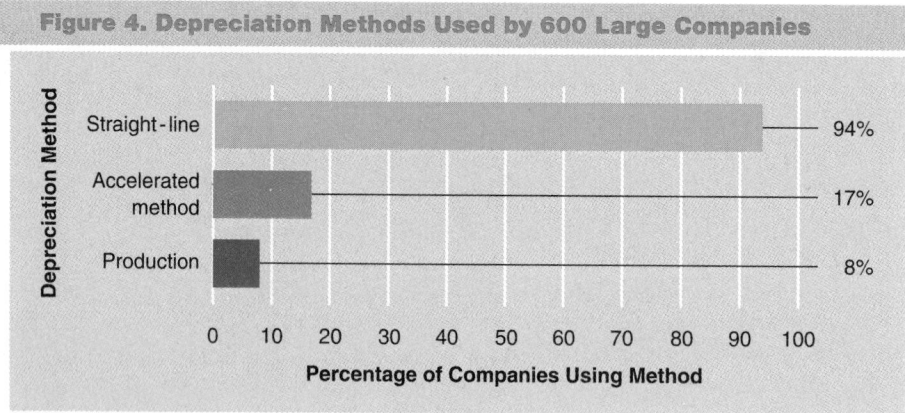

Total percentage exceeds 100 because some companies used different methods for different types of depreciable assets.

Source: Reprinted with permission from *Accounting Trends & Techniques,* Copyright © 1993 by American Institute of Certified Public Accountants, Inc.

OBJECTIVE

DISPOSAL OF DEPRECIABLE ASSETS

OBJECTIVE

5 *Account for the disposal of depreciable assets not involving exchanges*

When plant assets are no longer useful because they are worn out or obsolete, they may be discarded, sold, or traded in on the purchase of new plant and equipment. A comprehensive illustration will be used to show how such disposals are recorded in the accounting records.

ASSUMPTIONS FOR THE COMPREHENSIVE ILLUSTRATION

For accounting purposes, a plant asset may be disposed of in three different ways: It may be (1) discarded, (2) sold for cash, or (3) exchanged for another asset. To illustrate how each of these cases is recorded, assume that MGC Corporation purchased a machine on January 1, 19x0 for $6,500 and depreciated it on a straight-line basis over an estimated useful life of ten years. The residual value at the end of ten years was estimated to be $500. On January 1, 19x7, the balances of the relevant accounts in the plant asset ledger appear as follows:

Machinery		Accumulated Depreciation, Machinery	
6,500			4,200

On September 30, 19x7, management disposes of the asset. The next few sections illustrate the accounting treatment to record depreciation for the partial year and the disposal under several assumptions.

DEPRECIATION FOR PARTIAL YEAR PRIOR TO DISPOSAL

When a plant asset is discarded or disposed of in some other way, it is first necessary to record depreciation expense for the partial year up to the date of disposal. This step is required because the asset was used until that date and, under the matching rule, the accounting period should receive the proper allocation of depreciation expense.

In this comprehensive illustration, MGC Corporation disposes of the machinery on September 30. The entry to record the depreciation for the first nine months of 19x7 (nine-twelfths of a year) is as follows:

Sept. 30	Depreciation Expense, Machinery	450	
	Accumulated Depreciation, Machinery		450
	To record depreciation up to date of disposal		

$$\frac{\$6,500 - \$500}{10} \times \frac{9}{12} = \$450$$

The relevant accounts in the plant asset ledger appear as follows after the entry is posted:

Machinery		Accumulated Depreciation, Machinery	
6,500			4,650

RECORDING DISCARDED PLANT ASSETS

A plant asset rarely lasts exactly as long as its estimated life. If it lasts longer than its estimated life, it is not depreciated past the point at which its carrying value equals its residual value. The purpose of depreciation is to spread the depreciable cost of an asset over the estimated life of the asset. Thus, the total accumulated depreciation should never exceed the total depreciable cost. If an asset remains in use beyond the end of its estimated life, its cost and accumulated depreciation remain in the ledger accounts. Proper records will thus be available for maintaining control over plant assets. If the residual value is zero, the carrying value of a fully depreciated asset is zero until the asset is disposed of. If such an asset is discarded, no gain or loss results.

In the comprehensive illustration, however, the discarded equipment has a carrying value of $1,850 at the time of disposal. The carrying value from the ledger account on the previous page is computed as machinery of $6,500 less accumulated depreciation of $4,650. A loss equal to the carrying value should be recorded when the machine is discarded.

Sept. 30	Accumulated Depreciation, Machinery	4,650	
	Loss on Disposal of Machinery	1,850	
	Machinery		6,500
	Discarded machine no longer used		
	in the business		

Gains and losses on disposals of plant assets are classified as other revenues and expenses on the income statement.

RECORDING PLANT ASSETS SOLD FOR CASH

The entry to record a plant asset sold for cash is similar to the one just illustrated except that the receipt of cash should also be recorded. The following entries show how to record the sale of a machine under three assumptions about the selling price. In the first case, the $1,850 cash received is exactly equal to the $1,850 carrying value of the machine; therefore, no gain or loss results.

Sept. 30	Cash	1,850	
	Accumulated Depreciation, Machinery	4,650	
	Machinery		6,500
	Sale of machine for carrying value;		
	no gain or loss		

In the second case, the $1,000 cash received is less than the carrying value of $1,850, so a loss of $850 is recorded.

Sept. 30	Cash	1,000	
	Accumulated Depreciation, Machinery	4,650	
	Loss on Sale of Machinery	850	
	Machinery		6,500
	Sale of machine at less than carrying		
	value; loss of $850 ($1,850 − $1,000)		
	recorded		

In the third case, the $2,000 cash received exceeds the carrying value of $1,850, so a gain of $150 is recorded.

Sept. 30	Cash	2,000	
	Accumulated Depreciation, Machinery	4,650	
	Gain on Sale of Machinery		150
	Machinery		6,500
	Sale of machine at more than the		
	carrying value; gain of $150		
	($2,000 − $1,850) recorded		

RECORDING EXCHANGES OF PLANT ASSETS

OBJECTIVE

6 *Account for the disposal of depreciable assets involving exchanges*

Businesses also dispose of plant assets by trading them in on the purchase of other plant assets. Exchanges may involve similar assets, such as an old machine traded in on a newer model, or dissimilar assets, such as a machine traded in on a truck. In either case, the purchase price is reduced by the amount of the trade-in allowance.

The basic accounting for exchanges of plant assets is similar to accounting for sales of plant assets for cash. If the trade-in allowance received is greater than the carrying value of the asset surrendered, there has been a gain. If the allowance is less, there has been a loss. There are special rules for recognizing these gains and losses, depending on the nature of the assets exchanged.

Exchange	Losses Recognized	Gains Recognized
For financial accounting purposes		
Of dissimilar assets	Yes	Yes
Of similar assets	Yes	No
For income tax purposes		
Of dissimilar assets	Yes	Yes
Of similar assets	No	No

Both gains and losses are recognized when a company exchanges dissimilar assets. Assets are dissimilar when they perform different functions or do not meet specific monetary and type of business criteria to be considered similar assets. For financial accounting purposes, most exchanges are considered to be exchanges of dissimilar assets. In rare cases, when exchanges meet the specific criteria for them to be considered exchanges of similar assets, the gains are not recognized. In these cases, you could think of the trade-in as an extension of the life and usefulness of the original machine. Instead of recognizing a gain at the time of the exchange, the company records the new machine at the sum of the book value of the older machine plus any cash paid.[8]

For income tax purposes, similar assets are defined as those performing the same function. Neither gains nor losses on exchanges of these assets are recognized in computing a company's income tax liability. Thus, in practice, accountants face cases where both gains and losses are recognized (exchanges of dissimilar assets), where losses are recognized and gains are not

---

8. Accounting Principles Board, *Opinion No. 29*, "Accounting for Nonmonetary Transactions" (New York: American Institute of Certified Public Accountants, 1973) and Emerging Issues Task Force, *EITF Issue Summary 86-29*, "Nonmonetary Transactions: Magnitude of Boot and the Exceptions to the Use of Fair Value" (Stamford, CT: Financial Accounting Standards Board, 1986). The specific criteria for similar assets are the subject of more advanced courses.

recognized (exchanges of similar assets), and where neither gains nor losses are recognized (exchanges of similar assets for income tax purposes). Since all these options are used in practice, they are all illustrated in the following paragraphs.

Loss Recognized on the Exchange   A loss is recognized for financial accounting purposes on all exchanges in which a material loss occurs. To illustrate the recognition of a loss, let us assume that the firm in our comprehensive example exchanges the machine for a newer, more modern machine on the following terms:

List price of new machine	$12,000
Trade-in allowance for old machine	(1,000)
Cash payment required	$11,000

In this case the trade-in allowance ($1,000) is less than the carrying value ($1,850) of the old machine. The loss on the exchange is $850 ($1,850 − $1,000). The following journal entry records this transaction under the assumption that the loss is to be recognized.

Sept. 30	Machinery (new)	12,000	
	Accumulated Depreciation, Machinery	4,650	
	Loss on Exchange of Machinery	850	
	Machinery (old)		6,500
	Cash		11,000
	Exchange of machines—cost		
	of old machine and its accumulated		
	depreciation removed from the		
	records; new machine recorded		
	at list price; loss recognized		

Loss Not Recognized on the Exchange   In the previous example, in which a loss was recognized, the new asset was recorded at the purchase price of $12,000 and a loss of $850 was recorded. If the transaction is for similar assets and is to be recorded for income tax purposes, the loss should not be recognized. In this case, the cost basis of the new asset will reflect the effect of the unrecorded loss. The cost basis is computed by adding the cash payment to the carrying value of the old asset:

Carrying value of old machine	$ 1,850
Cash paid	11,000
Cost basis of new machine	$12,850

Note that no loss is recognized in the entry to record this transaction.

Sept. 30	Machinery (new)	12,850	
	Accumulated Depreciation, Machinery	4,650	
	Machinery (old)		6,500
	Cash		11,000
	Exchange of machines—cost of		
	old machine and its accumulated		
	depreciation removed from the		
	records; new machine recorded at		
	amount equal to carrying value of		
	old machine plus cash paid; no		
	loss recognized		

Note that the new machinery is reported at the purchase price of $12,000 plus the unrecognized loss of $850. The nonrecognition of the loss on the exchange is, in effect, a postponement of the loss. Since depreciation of the new machine will be computed based on a cost of $12,850 instead of $12,000, the "unrecognized" loss results in more depreciation each year on the new machine than if the loss had been recognized.

Gain Recognized on the Exchange   Gains on exchanges are recognized for accounting purposes when dissimilar assets are involved. To illustrate the recognition of a gain, we continue with our example, assuming the following terms in which the machines being exchanged serve different functions:

List price of new machine	$12,000
Trade-in allowance for old machine	(3,000)
Cash payment required	$ 9,000

Here the trade-in allowance ($3,000) exceeds the carrying value ($1,850) of the old machine by $1,150. Thus, there is a gain on the exchange, assuming that the price of the new machine has not been inflated to allow for an excessive trade-in value. In other words, a gain exists if the trade-in allowance represents the fair market value of the old machine. Assuming that this condition is true, the entry to record the transaction is as follows:

Sept. 30	Machinery (new)	12,000	
	Accumulated Depreciation, Machinery	4,650	
	Gain on Exchange of Machinery		1,150
	Machinery (old)		6,500
	Cash		9,000
	Exchange of machines—cost of old machine and its accumulated depreciation removed from the records; new machine recorded at list price; gain recognized		

Gain Not Recognized on the Exchange   When assets meeting the criteria for similar assets are exchanged, gains are not recognized for accounting or income tax purposes. The cost basis of the new machine must indicate the effect of the unrecorded gain. This cost basis is computed by adding the cash payment to the carrying value of the old asset.

Carrying value of old machine	$ 1,850
Cash paid	9,000
Cost basis of new machine	$10,850

The entry to record the transaction is as follows:

Sept. 30	Machinery (new)	10,850	
	Accumulated Depreciation, Machinery	4,650	
	Machinery (old)		6,500
	Cash		9,000
	Exchange of machines—cost of old machine and its accumulated depreciation removed from the records; new machine recorded at amount equal to carrying value of old machine plus cash paid; no gain recognized		

As with the nonrecognition of losses, the nonrecognition of the gain on an exchange is, in effect, a postponement of the gain. In the previous illustration, when the new machine is eventually discarded or sold, its cost basis will be $10,850 instead of its original price of $12,000. Since depreciation will be computed on the cost basis of $10,850, the "unrecognized" gain is reflected in lower depreciation each year on new equipment than if the gain had been recognized.

ACCOUNTING FOR NATURAL RESOURCES

OBJECTIVE

7 *Identify the issues related to accounting for natural resources and compute depletion*

Natural resources are also known as *wasting assets*. Examples of natural resources are standing timber, oil and gas fields, and mineral deposits. The distinguishing characteristic of these wasting assets is that they are converted into inventory by cutting, pumping, or mining. In terms of two of our examples, an oil field is a reservoir of unpumped oil, and a coal mine is a deposit of unmined coal.

Natural resources are shown on the balance sheet as long-term assets with such descriptive titles as Timber Lands, Oil and Gas Reserves, and Mineral Deposits. When the timber is cut, the oil is pumped, or the coal is mined, it becomes an inventory of the product to be sold. Natural resources are recorded at acquisition cost, which may also include some costs of development. As the resource is converted through the process of cutting, pumping, or mining, the asset account must be proportionally reduced. The carrying value of oil reserves on the balance sheet, for example, is reduced by a small amount for each barrel of oil pumped. As a result, the original cost of the oil reserves is gradually reduced, and depletion is recognized by the amount of the decrease.

DEPLETION

The term *depletion* is used to describe not only the exhaustion of a natural resource but also the proportional allocation of the cost of a natural resource to the units extracted. The costs are allocated in a way that is much like the production method used to calculate depreciation. When a natural resource is purchased or developed, there must be an estimate of the total units that will be available, such as barrels of oil, tons of coal, or board-feet of lumber. The depletion cost per unit is determined by dividing the cost of the natural resource (less residual value, if any) by the estimated number of units available. The amount of the depletion cost for each accounting period is then computed by multiplying the depletion cost per unit by the number of units pumped, mined, or cut and sold. For example, for a mine having an estimated 1,500,000 tons of coal, a cost of $1,800,000, and an estimated residual value of $300,000, the depletion charge per ton of coal is $1. Thus, if 115,000 tons of coal are mined and sold during the first year, the depletion charge for the year is $115,000. This charge is recorded as follows:

Dec. 31   Depletion Expense, Coal Deposits   115,000
                Accumulated Depletion, Coal Deposits   115,000
                To record depletion of coal mine:
                $1 per ton for 115,000 tons mined
                and sold

On the balance sheet, the mine would be presented as follows:

Coal Deposits	$1,800,000	
Less Accumulated Depletion	115,000	$1,685,000

Sometimes a natural resource that is extracted in one year is not sold until a later year. It is important to note that it would then be recorded as a depletion *expense* in the year it is *sold*. The part not sold is considered inventory.

DEPRECIATION OF CLOSELY RELATED PLANT ASSETS

Natural resources often require special on-site buildings and equipment, such as conveyors, roads, tracks, and drilling and pumping devices that are necessary to extract the resource. If the useful life of those assets is longer than the estimated time it will take to deplete the resource, a special problem arises. Because such long-term assets are often abandoned and have no useful purpose once all the resources have been extracted, they should be depreciated on the same basis as the depletion is computed. For example, if machinery with a useful life of ten years is installed on an oil field that is expected to be depleted in eight years, the machinery should be depreciated over the eight-year period, using the production method. That way, each year's depreciation will be proportional to the year's depletion. If one-sixth of the oil field's total reserves is pumped in one year, then the depreciation should be one-sixth of the machinery's cost minus the residual value. If the useful life of a long-term asset is less than the expected life of the depleting asset, the shorter life should be used to compute depreciation. In such cases, or when an asset will not be abandoned when the reserves are fully depleted, other depreciation methods, such as straight-line or declining-balance, are appropriate.

DEVELOPMENT AND EXPLORATION COSTS IN THE OIL AND GAS INDUSTRY

The costs of exploration and development of oil and gas resources can be accounted for under either of two methods. Under successful efforts accounting, successful exploration—for example, the cost of a producing oil well—is a cost of the resource. This cost should be recorded as an asset and depleted over the estimated life of the resource. An unsuccessful exploration—such as the cost of a dry well—is written off immediately as a loss. Because of these immediate write-offs, successful efforts accounting is considered the more conservative method and is used by most large oil companies.

Exploration-minded independent oil companies, on the other hand, argue that the cost of dry wells is part of the overall cost of the systematic development of an oil field and thus a part of the cost of producing wells. Under this full-costing method, all costs, including the cost of dry wells, are recorded as assets and depleted over the estimated life of the producing resources. This method tends to improve earnings performance in the early years for companies using it. Either method is permitted by the Financial Accounting Standards Board.[9]

9. *Statement of Financial Accounting Standards No. 25,* "Suspension of Certain Accounting Requirements for Oil and Gas Producing Companies" (Stamford, Conn.: Financial Accounting Standards Board, 1979).

Historically, intangible assets have not been considered very significant for either financial reporting or income taxes. Whether or not the amortization of intangibles was deductible in determining a company's income tax liability was not considered important. Write-offs of the costs of most intangibles have not been allowed for income tax purposes. However, in recent years, the U.S. Congress has been considering a change that would allow the write-off of most intangible assets over a period of fourteen years. Why is there a sudden interest in intangible assets?

Interest in the tax deductibility of the amortization of intangible assets has grown because companies are paying more for such assets. In the past the value of trademarks and other intangible assets tended to rise gradually as a company grew and prospered. Today, many intangible assets are purchased for high prices. This includes not only traditional intangible assets, such as trademarks and copyrights, but also newer assets, such as customer lists for mail order companies, takeoff and landing rights at busy airports, and cellular telephone licenses. During the 1980s, companies became more aggressive in writing off such expensive intangible assets, which led to numerous challenges by the Internal Revenue Service. The write-offs taxpayers claimed for intangible assets grew from $45 billion in 1980 to $262 billion in 1987.[10] The growing financial significance of intangibles has increased their importance as an accounting issue, as shown in the following section. ⦂ ⦂ ⦂

ACCOUNTING FOR INTANGIBLE ASSETS

The purchase of an intangible asset is a special kind of capital expenditure. An intangible asset is long term, but it has no physical substance. Its value comes from the long-term rights or advantages it offers to its owner. Among the most common examples are patents, copyrights, leaseholds, leasehold improvements, trademarks and brand names, franchises, licenses, formulas, processes, and goodwill. Some current assets, such as accounts receivable and certain prepaid expenses, have no physical substance, but they are not classified as intangible assets because they are short term. Intangible assets are both long term and nonphysical.

Intangible assets are accounted for at acquisition cost, that is, the amount paid for them. Some intangible assets, such as goodwill and trademarks, may be acquired at little or no cost. Even though they may have great value and be needed for profitable operations, they should not appear on the balance sheet unless they have been purchased from another party at a price established in the marketplace.

10. Paul Merrion, "The Taxing Battle Over Intangibles," *Crain's Chicago Business*, October 14, 1991, p. 3.

The accounting issues connected with intangible assets are the same as those connected with other long-lived assets. The Accounting Principles Board, in its *Opinion No. 17,* lists them as follows:

1. Determining an initial carrying amount
2. Accounting for that amount after acquisition under normal business conditions—that is, through periodic write-off or amortization—in a manner similar to depreciation
3. Accounting for that amount if the value declines substantially and permanently[11]

Besides these three problems, an intangible asset has no physical substance and, in some cases, may be impossible to identify. For these reasons, its value and its useful life may be quite hard to estimate.

The Accounting Principles Board has decided that a company should record as assets the costs of intangible assets acquired from others. However, the company should record as expenses the costs of developing intangible assets. Also, intangible assets that have a determinable useful life, such as patents, copyrights, and leaseholds, should be written off through periodic amortization over that useful life in much the same way that plant assets are depreciated. Even though some intangible assets, such as goodwill and trademarks, have no measurable limit on their lives, they should also be amortized over a reasonable length of time (not to exceed forty years).

To illustrate these procedures, assume that Soda Bottling Company purchases a patent on a unique bottle cap for $18,000. The entry to record the patent would be as follows:

Patent	18,000	
Cash		18,000
Purchase of bottle cap patent		

Note that if Soda Bottling Company had developed the bottle cap internally instead of purchasing it from a third party, the costs of developing the cap, such as salaries of researchers, supplies used in testing, and costs of equipment, would have been expensed as incurred.

Assume now that Soda's management determines that, although the patent for the bottle cap will last for seventeen years, the product using the cap will be sold only for the next six years. The entry to record the annual amortization would be as follows:

Amortization Expense	3,000	
Patent		3,000
Annual amortization of patent		
$18,000 \div 6$ years $= \$3,000$		

Note that the Patent account is reduced directly by the amount of the amortization expense. This is in contrast to the treatment of other long-term asset accounts, for which depreciation or depletion is accumulated in separate contra accounts.

If the patent becomes worthless before it is fully amortized, the remaining carrying value is written off as a loss. For instance, assume that after the first year Soda Bottling Company's chief competitor offers a bottle with a new type of cap that makes Soda's cap obsolete. The entry to record the loss is shown on the next page.

11. Adapted from Accounting Principles Board, *Opinion No. 17,* "Intangible Assets" (New York: American Institute of Certified Public Accountants, 1970), par. 2.

Loss on Patent	15,000	
Patent		15,000

> Loss resulting from patent's
> becoming worthless

Accounting for several different types of intangible assets is outlined in Table 1.

Table 1. Accounting for Intangible Assets

Type	Description	Accounting Treatment
Patent	An exclusive right granted by the federal government for a period of seventeen years to make a particular product or use a specific process.	The cost of successfully defending a patent in a patent infringement suit is added to the acquisition cost of the patent. Amortize over the useful life, which may be less than the legal life of seventeen years.
Copyright	An exclusive right granted by the federal government to the possessor to publish and sell literary, musical, or other artistic materials for a period of the author's life plus fifty years; includes computer programs.	Record at acquisition cost and amortize over the useful life, which is often much shorter than the legal life, but not to exceed forty years. For example, the cost of paperback rights to a popular novel would typically be amortized over a useful life of two to four years.
Leasehold	A right to occupy land or buildings under a long-term rental contract. For example, Company A, which owns but does not want to use a prime retail location, sells Company B the right to use it for ten years in return for one or more rental payments. Company B has purchased a leasehold.	Debit Leasehold for the amount of the rental payment, and amortize it over the remaining life of the lease. Payments to the lessor during the life of the lease should be debited to Lease Expense.
Leasehold improvements	Improvements to leased property that become the property of the lessor (the person who owns the property) at the end of the lease.	Debit Leasehold Improvements for the cost of improvements, and amortize the cost of the improvements over the remaining life of the lease.
Trademark, brand name	A registered symbol or name that can be used only by its owner to identify a product or service.	Debit Trademark or Brand Name for the acquisition cost, and amortize it over a reasonable life, not to exceed forty years.
Franchise, license	A right to an exclusive territory or market, or to exclusive use of a formula, technique, process, or design.	Debit Franchise or License for the acquisition cost, and amortize it over a reasonable life, not to exceed forty years.
Goodwill	The excess of the cost of a group of assets (usually a business) over the fair market value of the net assets if purchased individually.	Debit Goodwill for the acquisition cost, and amortize it over a reasonable life, not to exceed forty years.

BUSINESS BULLETIN: BUSINESS PRACTICE

One of the most valuable intangible assets some companies have is a list of subscribers. For example, the Newark Morning Ledger Co., a newspaper chain, purchased a chain of Michigan newspapers whose list of 460,000 subscribers was valued at $68 million. In a 1993 decision, the U.S. Supreme Court upheld the company's right to amortize the value of the subscribers list because the company showed that the list had a limited useful life. The Internal Revenue Service had argued that the list had an indefinite life and therefore could not provide tax deductions through amortization. This ruling will benefit other types of businesses that purchase everything from bank deposits to pharmacy prescription files.[12] ═══════

RESEARCH AND DEVELOPMENT COSTS

Most successful companies carry out activities, possibly within a separate department, involving research and development. Among these activities are development of new products, testing of existing and proposed products, and pure research. In the past, some companies would record as assets those costs of research and development that could be directly traced to the development of specific patents, formulas, or other rights. Other costs, such as those for testing and pure research, were treated as expenses of the accounting period and deducted from income.

The Financial Accounting Standards Board has stated that all research and development costs should be treated as revenue expenditures and charged to expense in the period when incurred.[13] The board argues that it is too hard to trace specific costs to specific profitable developments. Also, the costs of research and development are continuous and necessary for the success of a business and so should be treated as current expenses. To support this conclusion, the board cites studies showing that 30 to 90 percent of all new products fail and that three-fourths of new-product expenses go to unsuccessful products. Thus, their costs do not represent future benefits.

COMPUTER SOFTWARE COSTS

Many companies develop computer programs or software to be sold or leased to individuals and companies. The costs incurred in creating a computer software product are considered research and development costs until the product has been proved to be technologically feasible. As a result, costs incurred to that point in the process should be charged to expense as incurred. A product is deemed to be technologically feasible when a detailed working program has been designed. After the working program has been developed,

---

12. "What's In a Name?" *Time*, May 3, 1993.

13. *Statement of Financial Accounting Standards No. 2*, "Accounting for Research and Development Costs" (Stamford, Conn.: Financial Accounting Standards Board, 1974), par. 12.

all software production costs are recorded as assets and amortized over the estimated economic life of the product using the straight-line method. If at any time the company cannot expect to realize from a software product the amount of its unamortized costs on the balance sheet, the asset should be written down to the amount expected to be realized.[14]

BUSINESS BULLETIN: BUSINESS PRACTICE

 Research and development expenditures can be substantial for many companies. For example, General Motors and IBM spent $5.9 billion and $5.1 billion, respectively, on research and development in 1992. Those amounts are about 5 percent of the companies' revenues. Research and development can be even costlier in high-tech fields like biotechnology, where Genentech and Biogen spent 54.4 percent and 48.8 percent, respectively, of revenues.[15] The pharmaceutical industry also invests heavily in research and development. It is estimated that bringing a new drug to market can cost from $125 million to $500 million before taxes.[16] Which of these costs are capitalized and amortized and which must be expensed immediately are obviously important questions for both the management and the stockholders of these companies.

GOODWILL

The term goodwill is widely used by business people, lawyers, and the public to mean different things. In most cases goodwill is taken to mean the good reputation of a company. From an accounting standpoint, goodwill exists when a purchaser pays more for a business than the fair market value of the net assets if purchased separately. Because the purchaser has paid more than the fair market value of the physical assets, there must be intangible assets. If the company being purchased does not have patents, copyrights, trademarks, or other identifiable intangible assets of value, the excess payment is assumed to be for goodwill. Goodwill exists because most businesses are worth more as going concerns than as collections of assets. Goodwill reflects all the factors that allow a company to earn a higher-than-market rate of return on its assets, including customer satisfaction, good management, manufacturing efficiency, the advantages of holding a monopoly, good locations, and good employee relations. The payment above and beyond the fair market value of the tangible assets and other specific intangible assets is properly recorded in the Goodwill account.

In *Opinion No. 17*, the Accounting Principles Board states that the benefits arising from purchased goodwill will in time disappear. It is hard for a com-

---

14. *Statement of Financial Accounting Standards No. 86,* "Accounting for the Costs of Computer Software To Be Sold, Leased, or Otherwise Marketed" (Stamford, Conn.: Financial Accounting Standards Board, 1985).

15. "R & D's Biggest Spenders," *Business Week,* June 28, 1993.

16. George Anders, "Vital Statistic: Disputed Cost of Creating a Drug," *Wall Street Journal,* November 9, 1993.

pany to keep having above-average earnings unless new factors of goodwill replace the old ones. For this reason, goodwill should be amortized or written off by systematic charges to income over a reasonable number of future time periods. The total time period should in no case be more than forty years.[17]

Goodwill, as stated, should not be recorded unless it is paid for in connection with the purchase of a whole business. The amount to be recorded as goodwill can be determined by writing the identifiable net assets up to their fair market values at the time of purchase and subtracting the total from the purchase price. For example, assume that the owners of Company A agree to sell the company for $11,400,000. If the net assets (total assets − total liabilities) are fairly valued at $10,000,000, then the amount of the goodwill is $1,400,000 ($11,400,000 − $10,000,000). If the fair market value of the net assets is later determined to be more or less than $10,000,000, an entry is made in the accounting records to adjust the assets to the fair market value. The goodwill would then represent the difference between the adjusted net assets and the purchase price of $11,400,000.

Supplemental OBJECTIVE

9 *Apply depreciation methods to problems of partial years, revised rates, groups of similar items, special types of capital expenditures, and cost recovery*

SPECIAL PROBLEMS OF DEPRECIATING PLANT ASSETS

The illustrations used so far in this chapter have been simplified to explain the concepts and methods of depreciation. In actual business practice, there is often a need to (1) calculate depreciation for partial years, (2) revise depreciation rates based on new estimates of useful life or residual value, (3) group like items when calculating depreciation, (4) account for special types of capital expenditures, and (5) use the accelerated cost recovery method for tax purposes. The next sections discuss these five cases.

DEPRECIATION FOR PARTIAL YEARS

So far, the illustrations of depreciation methods have assumed that plant assets were purchased at the beginning or end of an accounting period. However, businesses do not often buy assets exactly at the beginning or end of an accounting period. In most cases, they buy assets when they are needed and sell or discard them when they are no longer useful or needed. The time of year is normally not a factor in the decision. Consequently, it is often necessary to calculate depreciation for partial years.

For example, assume that a piece of equipment is purchased for $3,500 and that it has an estimated useful life of six years and an estimated residual value of $500. Assume also that it is purchased on September 5 and that the yearly accounting period ends on December 31. Depreciation must be recorded for four months, September through December, or four-twelfths of the year. This factor is applied to the calculated depreciation for the entire year. The four months' depreciation under the straight-line method is calculated as follows:

$$\frac{\$3,500 - \$500}{6 \text{ years}} \times 4/12 = \$167$$

For the other depreciation methods, most companies will compute the first year's depreciation and then multiply by the partial year factor. For example,

---

17. Accounting Principles Board, *Opinion No. 17*, par. 29.

if the company used the double-declining-balance method on the preceding equipment, the depreciation on the asset would be computed as follows:

$$\$3,500 \times .33 \times 4/12 = \$385$$

Typically, the depreciation calculation is rounded off to the nearest whole month because a partial month's depreciation is rarely material and the calculation is easier. In this case, depreciation was recorded from the beginning of September even though the purchase was made on September 5. If the equipment had been purchased on or after September 16, depreciation would be charged beginning October 1, as if the equipment were purchased on that date. Some companies round off all partial years to the nearest one-half year for ease of calculation (half-year convention).

For all methods, the remainder (eight-twelfths) of the first year's depreciation is recorded in the next annual accounting period together with four-twelfths of the second year's depreciation.

REVISION OF DEPRECIATION RATES

Because a depreciation rate is based on an estimate of an asset's useful life, the periodic depreciation charge is seldom precise. Sometimes it is very inadequate or excessive. This situation may result from an underestimate or overestimate of the asset's useful life or from a wrong estimate of the residual value. What action should be taken when it is found, after several years of use, that a piece of equipment will last less time—or longer—than originally thought? Sometimes it is necessary to revise the estimate of useful life so that the periodic depreciation expense increases or decreases. Then, to reflect the revised situation, the remaining depreciable cost of the asset is spread over the remaining years of useful life.

With this technique, the annual depreciation expense is increased or decreased to reduce the asset's carrying value to its residual value at the end of its remaining useful life. To illustrate, assume that a delivery truck was purchased for $7,000 and has a residual value of $1,000. At the time of the purchase, the truck was expected to last six years, and it was depreciated on the straight-line basis. However, after two years of intensive use, it is determined that the truck will last only two more years, but that its estimated residual value at the end of the two years will still be $1,000. In other words, at the end of the second year, the truck's estimated useful life is reduced from six years to four years. At that time, the asset account and its related accumulated depreciation account would appear as follows:

Delivery Truck		Accumulated Depreciation, Delivery Truck	
Cost 7,000			Depreciation, year 1 1,000
			Depreciation, year 2 1,000

The remaining depreciable cost is computed as follows:

cost	minus	depreciation already taken	minus	residual value		
$7,000	−	$2,000	−	$1,000	=	$4,000

The new annual periodic depreciation charge is computed by dividing the remaining depreciable cost of $4,000 by the remaining useful life of two years. Therefore, the new periodic depreciation charge is $2,000. The annual adjusting entry for depreciation for the next two years would be as follows:

Dec. 31   Depreciation Expense, Delivery
        Truck   2,000
          Accumulated Depreciation, Delivery
             Truck   2,000
             To record depreciation expense for the year

This method of revising depreciation is used widely in industry. It is also supported by the Accounting Principles Board of the AICPA in Accounting Principles Board *Opinion No. 9* and *Opinion No. 20*.

GROUP DEPRECIATION

To say that the estimated useful life of an asset, such as a piece of equipment, is six years means that the average piece of equipment of that type is expected to last six years. In reality, some pieces may last only two or three years, and others may last eight or nine years, or longer. For this reason, and for reasons of convenience, large companies will group similar items, such as trucks, power lines, office equipment, or transformers, to calculate depreciation. This method is called group depreciation. Group depreciation is widely used in all fields of industry and business. A survey of large businesses indicated that 65 percent used group depreciation for all or part of their plant assets.[18]

SPECIAL TYPES OF CAPITAL EXPENDITURES

In addition to the acquisition of plant assets, natural resources, and intangible assets, capital expenditures also include additions and betterments. An addition is an enlargement to the physical layout of a plant asset. If a new wing is added to a building, the benefits from the expenditure will be received over several years, and the amount paid for it should be debited to the asset account. A betterment is an improvement that does not add to the physical layout of an asset. Installation of an air-conditioning system is an example of a betterment that will offer benefits over a period of years, so its cost should be charged to an asset account.

Among the more usual kinds of revenue expenditures for plant equipment are the repairs, maintenance, lubrication, cleaning, and inspection necessary to keep an asset in good working condition. Repairs fall into two categories: ordinary repairs and extraordinary repairs. Ordinary repairs are expenditures that are necessary to maintain an asset in good operating condition. Trucks must have periodic tune-ups, their tires and batteries must be regularly replaced, and other routine repairs must be made. Offices and halls must be painted regularly, and broken tiles or woodwork must be replaced. Such repairs are a current expense.

Extraordinary repairs are repairs of a more significant nature—they affect the estimated residual value or estimated useful life of an asset. For example, a boiler for heating a building may be given a complete overhaul, at a cost of several thousand dollars, that will extend its useful life by five years. Typically, extraordinary repairs are recorded by debiting the Accumulated

18. Edward P. McTague, "Accounting for Trade-Ins of Operational Assets," *National Public Accountant* (January 1986), p. 39.

Depreciation account, under the assumption that some of the depreciation previously recorded has now been eliminated. The effect of this reduction in the Accumulated Depreciation account is to increase the carrying value of the asset by the cost of the extraordinary repair. Consequently, the new carrying value of the asset should be depreciated over the new estimated useful life.

Let us assume that a machine that cost $10,000 had no estimated residual value and an original estimated useful life of ten years. After eight years, the accumulated depreciation under the straight-line method was $8,000, and the carrying value was $2,000 ($10,000 − $8,000). At that point, the machine was given a major overhaul costing $1,500. This expenditure extended the machine's useful life three years beyond the original ten years. The entry for the extraordinary repair would be as follows:

Jan. 4	Accumulated Depreciation, Machinery	1,500	
	Cash		1,500
	Extraordinary repair		
	to machinery		

The annual periodic depreciation for each of the five years remaining in the machine's useful life would be calculated as follows:

Carrying value before extraordinary repairs	$2,000
Extraordinary repairs	1,500
Total	$3,500

$$\text{Annual periodic depreciation} = \frac{\$3,500}{5 \text{ years}} = \$700$$

If the machine remains in use for the five years expected after the major overhaul, the total of the five annual depreciation charges of $700 will exactly equal the new carrying value, including the cost of the extraordinary repair.

COST RECOVERY FOR FEDERAL INCOME TAX PURPOSES

In 1986, Congress passed the Tax Reform Act of 1986, arguably the most sweeping revision of federal tax laws since the original enactment of the Internal Revenue Code in 1913. The new **Modified Accelerated Cost Recovery System (MACRS)** discards the concepts of estimated useful life and residual value. Instead, it requires that a cost recovery allowance be computed (1) on the unadjusted cost of property being recovered, and (2) over a period of years prescribed by the law for all property of similar types. The accelerated method prescribed under MACRS for most property other than real estate is 200 percent declining balance with a half-year convention (only one half-year's depreciation is allowed in the year of purchase, and one half-year's depreciation is taken in the last year). In addition, the period over which the cost may be recovered is specified. Recovery of the cost of property placed in service after December 31, 1986, is calculated as prescribed in the 1986 law.

Congress hoped that MACRS would encourage businesses to invest in new plant and equipment by allowing them to write off such assets rapidly. MACRS accelerates the write-off of these investments in two ways. First, the prescribed recovery periods are often shorter than the estimated useful lives used for calculating depreciation for the financial statements. Second, the accelerated method allowed under the new law enables businesses to recover most of the cost of their investments early in the depreciation process.

Tax methods of depreciation are not usually acceptable for financial reporting under generally accepted accounting principles because the recovery periods are shorter than the depreciable assets' estimated useful lives.

CHAPTER REVIEW

REVIEW OF LEARNING OBJECTIVES

1. **Identify the types of long-term assets and explain the management issues related to accounting for them.** Long-term assets are assets that are used in the operation of a business, are not intended for resale, and have a useful life of more than one year. Long-term assets are either tangible or intangible. In the former category are land, plant assets, and natural resources. In the latter are trademarks, patents, franchises, goodwill, and other rights. The accounting issues associated with long-term assets relate to the decision to acquire the assets, the means of financing the assets, and the methods of accounting for the assets.

2. **Distinguish between capital and revenue expenditures, and account for the cost of property, plant, and equipment.** It is important to distinguish between capital expenditures, which are recorded as assets, and revenue expenditures, which are recorded as expenses. The error of classifying one as the other will have an important effect on net income. The acquisition cost of property, plant, and equipment includes all expenditures that are reasonable and necessary to get such an asset in place and ready for use. Among these expenditures are purchase price, installation cost, freight charges, and insurance.

3. **Define *depreciation*, state the factors that affect its computation, and show how to record it.** Depreciation is the periodic allocation of the cost of a plant asset over its estimated useful life. It is recorded by debiting Depreciation Expense and crediting a related contra-asset account called Accumulated Depreciation. Factors that affect the computation of depreciation are cost, residual value, depreciable cost, and estimated useful life.

4. **Compute periodic depreciation under the (a) straight-line method, (b) production method, and (c) declining-balance method.** Depreciation is commonly computed by the straight-line method, the production method, or an accelerated method. The straight-line method is related directly to the passage of time, whereas the production method is related directly to use. An accelerated method, which results in relatively large amounts of depreciation in earlier years and reduced amounts in later years, is based on the assumption that plant assets provide greater economic benefit in their earlier years than in later years. The most common accelerated method is the declining-balance method.

5. **Account for the disposal of depreciable assets not involving exchanges.** Long-term assets may be disposed of by being discarded, sold, or exchanged. When long-term assets are disposed of, it is necessary to record the depreciation up to the date of disposal and to remove the carrying value from the accounts by removing the cost from the asset account and the depreciation to date from the accumulated depreciation account. If a long-term asset is sold at a price that differs from its carrying value, there is a gain or loss that should be recorded and reported on the income statement.

6. **Account for the disposal of depreciable assets involving exchanges.** In recording exchanges of similar plant assets, a gain or loss may arise. According to the Accounting Principles Board, losses, but not gains, should be recognized at the time of the exchange. When a gain is not recognized, the new asset is recorded at the carrying value of the old asset plus any cash paid. For income tax purposes,

neither gains nor losses are recognized in the exchange of similar assets. When dissimilar assets are exchanged, gains and losses are recognized under both accounting and income tax rules.

7. **Identify the issues related to accounting for natural resources and compute depletion.** Natural resources are wasting assets that are converted to inventory by cutting, pumping, mining, or other forms of extraction. Natural resources are recorded at cost as long-term assets. They are allocated as expenses through depletion charges as the resources are sold. The depletion charge is based on the ratio of the resource extracted to the total estimated resource. A major issue related to this subject is accounting for oil and gas reserves.

8. **Apply the matching rule to intangible assets, including research and development costs and goodwill.** The purchase of an intangible asset should be treated as a capital expenditure and recorded at acquisition cost, which in turn should be amortized over the useful life of the asset. The FASB requires that research and development costs be treated as revenue expenditures and charged as expenses in the periods of expenditure. Software costs are treated as research and development costs and expensed until a feasible working program is developed, after which time the costs may be capitalized and amortized over a reasonable estimated life. Goodwill is the excess of the amount paid over the fair market value of the net assets in the purchase of a business and is usually related to the superior earning potential of the business. It should be recorded only if paid for in connection with the purchase of a business, and it should be amortized over a period not to exceed forty years.

SUPPLEMENTAL OBJECTIVE

9. **Apply depreciation methods to problems of partial years, revised rates, groups of similar items, special types of capital expenditures, and cost recovery.** In actual business practice, many factors affect depreciation calculations. It may be necessary to calculate depreciation for partial years because assets are bought and sold throughout the year, or to revise depreciation rates because of changed conditions. Because it is often difficult to estimate the useful life of a single item, and because it is more convenient, many large businesses group similar items for purposes of depreciation. Companies must also consider certain special capital expenditures when calculating depreciation. For example, expenditures for additions and betterments are capital expenditures. Extraordinary repairs, which increase the residual value or extend the life of an asset, are also treated as capital expenditures, but ordinary repairs are revenue expenditures. For income tax purposes, rapid write-offs of depreciable assets are allowed through the Modified Accelerated Cost Recovery System. Such rapid write-offs are not usually acceptable for financial accounting because the shortened recovery periods violate the matching rule.

REVIEW OF CONCEPTS AND TERMINOLOGY

The following concepts and terms were introduced in this chapter.

L O 4 **Accelerated method:** A method of depreciation that allocates relatively large amounts of the depreciable cost of an asset to earlier years and reduced amounts to later years.

S O 9 **Addition:** An enlargement to the physical layout of a plant asset.

L O 1 **Amortization:** The periodic allocation of the cost of an intangible asset to the periods it benefits.

S O 9 **Betterment:** An improvement that does not add to the physical layout of a plant asset.

L O 8 **Brand name:** A registered name that can be used only by its owner to identify a product or service.

L O 2 **Capital expenditure:** An expenditure for the purchase or expansion of a long-term asset, recorded in the asset accounts.

LO1 **Carrying value:** The unexpired part of the cost of an asset; also called *book value.*

LO8 **Copyright:** An exclusive right granted by the federal government to the possessor to publish and sell literary, musical, or other artistic materials for a period of the author's life plus fifty years; includes computer programs.

LO4 **Declining-balance method:** An accelerated method of depreciation in which depreciation is computed by applying a fixed rate to the carrying value (the declining balance) of a tangible long-lived asset.

LO1 **Depletion:** The exhaustion of a natural resource through mining, cutting, pumping, or other extraction, and the way in which the cost is allocated.

LO3 **Depreciable cost:** The cost of an asset less its residual value.

LO1 **Depreciation:** The periodic allocation of the cost of a tangible long-lived asset (other than land and natural resources) over its estimated useful life.

LO4 **Double-declining-balance method:** An accelerated method of depreciation in which a fixed rate equal to twice the straight-line percentage is applied to the carrying value of a tangible long-term asset.

LO3 **Estimated useful life:** The total number of service units expected from a long-term asset.

LO2 **Expenditure:** A payment or an obligation to make future payment for an asset or a service.

SO9 **Extraordinary repairs:** Repairs that affect the estimated residual value or estimated useful life of an asset.

LO8 **Franchise:** The right to an exclusive territory or market.

LO7 **Full-costing:** A method of accounting for the costs of exploration and development of oil and gas resources in which all costs are recorded as assets and depleted over the estimated life of the producing resources.

LO8 **Goodwill:** The excess of the cost of a group of assets (usually a business) over the fair market value of the net assets if purchased individually.

SO9 **Group depreciation:** The grouping of similar items to calculate depreciation.

LO1 **Intangible assets:** Long-term assets that have no physical substance but have a value based on rights or advantages accruing to the owner.

LO8 **Leasehold:** A right to occupy land or buildings under a long-term rental contract.

LO8 **Leasehold improvements:** Improvements to leased property that become the property of the lessor at the end of the lease.

LO8 **License:** An exclusive right to a formula, technique, process, or design.

LO1 **Long-term assets:** Assets that (1) have a useful life of more than one year, (2) are acquired for use in the operation of a business, and (3) are not intended for resale to customers; less commonly called *fixed assets.*

SO9 **Modified Accelerated Cost Recovery System (MACRS):** A mandatory system of depreciation for income tax purposes, enacted by Congress in 1986, that requires a cost recovery allowance to be computed (1) on the unadjusted cost of property being recovered, and (2) over a period of years prescribed by the law for all property of similar types.

LO1 **Natural resources:** Long-term assets purchased for the economic value that can be taken from the land and used up rather than for the value associated with the land's location; also called *wasting assets.*

LO3 **Obsolescence:** The process of becoming out of date; a contributor, with physical deterioration, to the limited useful life of tangible assets.

SO9 **Ordinary repairs:** Expenditures, usually of a recurring nature, that are necessary to maintain an asset in good operating condition.

LO8 **Patent:** An exclusive right granted by the federal government for a period of seventeen years to make a particular product or use a specific process.

LO3 **Physical deterioration:** Limitations on the useful life of a depreciable asset resulting from use and from exposure to the elements.

L O 4   **Production method:** A method of depreciation that assumes that depreciation is solely the result of use and that allocates depreciation based on the units of output or use during each period of an asset's useful life.

L O 3   **Residual value:** The estimated net scrap, salvage, or trade-in value of a tangible asset at the estimated date of disposal; also called *salvage value* or *disposal value.*

L O 2   **Revenue expenditure:** An expenditure for repairs, maintenance, or other services needed to maintain or operate a plant asset, recorded by a debit to an expense account.

L O 4   **Straight-line method:** A method of depreciation that assumes that depreciation depends only on the passage of time and that allocates an equal amount of depreciation to each accounting period in an asset's useful life.

L O 7   **Successful efforts accounting:** A method of accounting for oil and gas resources in which successful exploration is recorded as an asset and depleted over the estimated life of the resource and all unsuccessful efforts are immediately written off as losses.

L O 1   **Tangible assets:** Long-term assets that have physical substance.

L O 8   **Trademark:** A registered symbol that can be used only by its owner to identify a product or service.

REVIEW PROBLEM

COMPARISON OF DEPRECIATION METHODS

L O 3, 4   Norton Construction Company purchased a cement mixer on January 1, 19x1, for $14,500. The mixer was expected to have a useful life of five years and a residual value of $1,000. The company engineers estimated that the mixer would have a useful life of 7,500 hours. It was used 1,500 hours in 19x1, 2,625 hours in 19x2, 2,250 hours in 19x3, 750 hours in 19x4, and 375 hours in 19x5. The company's year end is December 31.

REQUIRED

1. Compute the depreciation expense and carrying value for 19x1 to 19x5, using the following three methods: (a) straight-line, (b) production, and (c) double-declining-balance.
2. Prepare the adjusting entry to record the depreciation for 19x1 calculated in **1 (a).**
3. Show the balance sheet presentation for the cement mixer after the entry in **2** on December 31, 19x1.
4. What conclusions can you draw from the patterns of yearly depreciation?

ANSWER TO REVIEW PROBLEM

1. Depreciation computed:

Depreciation Method	Year	Computation	Depreciation	Carrying Value
a. Straight-line	19x1	$13,500 × 1/5	$2,700	$11,800
	19x2	13,500 × 1/5	2,700	9,100
	19x3	13,500 × 1/5	2,700	6,400
	19x4	13,500 × 1/5	2,700	3,700
	19x5	13,500 × 1/5	2,700	1,000
b. Production	19x1	$13,500 × $\frac{1,500}{7,500}$	$2,700	$11,800
	19x2	13,500 × $\frac{2,625}{7,500}$	4,725	7,075
	19x3	13,500 × $\frac{2,250}{7,500}$	4,050	3,025
	19x4	13,500 × $\frac{750}{7,500}$	1,350	1,675
	19x5	13,500 × $\frac{375}{7,500}$	675	1,000

Depreciation Method	Year	Computation	Depreciation	Carrying Value
c. Double-declining-balance	19x1	$14,500 × .4	$5,800	$8,700
	19x2	8,700 × .4	3,480	5,220
	19x3	5,220 × .4	2,088	3,132
	19x4	3,132 × .4	1,253*	1,879
	19x5		879*†	1,000

*Rounded.
†Remaining depreciation to reduce carrying value to residual value ($1,879 − $1,000 = $879).

2. Adjusting entry prepared—straight-line method:

```
19x1
Dec. 31   Depreciation Expense, Cement Mixer          2,700
               Accumulated Depreciation, Cement Mixer          2,700
                  To record depreciation expense,
                  straight-line method
```

3. Balance sheet presentation for 19x1 shown:

Cement Mixer	$14,500
Less Accumulated Depreciation	2,700
	$11,800

4. Conclusions drawn from depreciation patterns: The pattern of depreciation for the straight-line method differs significantly from that for the double-declining-balance method. In the early years, the amount of depreciation under the double-declining-balance method is significantly greater than the amount under the straight-line method. In the later years, the opposite is true. The carrying value under the straight-line method is greater than that under the double-declining-balance method in all years except at the end of the fifth year. Depreciation under the production method differs from that under the other methods in that it follows no regular pattern. It varies with the amount of use. Consequently, depreciation is greatest in 19x2 and 19x3, which are the years of greatest use. Use declined significantly in the last two years.

CHAPTER ASSIGNMENTS

QUESTIONS

1. What are the characteristics of long-term assets?
2. Which of the following items would be classified as plant assets on the balance sheet? (a) A truck held for sale by a truck dealer, (b) an office building that was once the company headquarters but is now to be sold, (c) a typewriter used by a secretary of the company, (d) a machine that is used in manufacturing operations but is now fully depreciated, (e) pollution-control equipment that does not reduce the cost or improve the efficiency of a factory, (f) a parking lot for company employees.
3. Why is land different from other long-term assets?
4. What do accountants mean by the term *depreciation,* and what is its relationship to depletion and amortization?
5. How do cash flows relate to the decision to acquire a long-term asset, and how does the useful life of an asset relate to the means of financing it?
6. Why is it useful to think of a plant asset as a bundle of services?
7. What is the distinction between revenue expenditures and capital expenditures, and what in general is included in the cost of a long-term asset?

8. Which of the following expenditures stemming from the purchase of a computer system would be charged to the asset account? (a) The purchase price of the equipment, (b) interest on the debt incurred to purchase the equipment, (c) freight charges, (d) installation charges, (e) the cost of special communications outlets at the computer site, (f) the cost of repairing a door that was damaged during installation, (g) the cost of adjustments to the system during the first month of operation.

9. Hale's Grocery obtained bids on the construction of a receiving dock at the back of its store. The lowest bid was $22,000. The company decided to build the dock itself, however, and was able to do so for $20,000, which it borrowed. The activity was recorded as a debit to Buildings for $22,000 and credits to Notes Payable for $20,000 and Gain on Construction for $2,000. Do you agree with the entry?

10. A firm buys a piece of technical equipment that is expected to last twelve years. Why might the equipment have to be depreciated over a shorter period of time?

11. A company purchased a building five years ago. The market value of the building is now greater than it was when the building was purchased. Explain why the company should continue depreciating the building.

12. Evaluate the following statement: "A parking lot should not be depreciated because adequate repairs will make it last forever."

13. Is the purpose of depreciation to determine the value of equipment? Explain your answer.

14. Contrast the assumptions underlying the straight-line depreciation method with the assumptions underlying the production depreciation method.

15. What is the principal argument supporting an accelerated depreciation method?

16. If a plant asset is sold during the year, why should depreciation be computed for the partial year prior to the date of the sale?

17. If a plant asset is discarded before the end of its useful life, how is the amount of loss measured?

18. When similar assets are exchanged, at what amount is the new asset recorded for federal income tax purposes?

19. When an exchange of similar assets occurs in which there is an unrecorded loss, is the taxpayer ever able to deduct or receive federal income tax credit for the loss?

20. Old Stake Mining Company computes the depletion rate of ore to be $2 per ton. During 19xx the company mined 400,000 tons of ore and sold 370,000 tons. What is the total depletion for the year?

21. Under what circumstances can a mining company depreciate its plant assets over a period of time that is less than their useful lives?

22. Because accounts receivable have no physical substance, can they be classified as intangible assets?

23. Under what circumstances can a company have intangible assets that do not appear on the balance sheet?

24. When the Accounting Principles Board indicates that accounting for intangible assets involves the same issues as accounting for tangible assets, what issues is it referring to?

25. How does the Financial Accounting Standards Board recommend that research and development costs be treated?

26. After spending three years developing a new software program for designing office buildings, Archi Draw Company recently completed the detailed working program. How does accounting for the costs of software development differ before and after the completion of a successful working program?

27. How is accounting for software development costs similar to and different from accounting for research and development costs?

28. Under what conditions should goodwill be recorded? Should it remain in the records permanently once it is recorded?

29. What basic procedure should be followed in revising a depreciation rate?

30. On what basis can depreciation be taken on a group of assets rather than on individual items?
31. What will be the effect on future years' income of charging an addition to a building to repair expense?
32. In what ways do an addition, a betterment, and an extraordinary repair differ?
33. How does an extraordinary repair differ from an ordinary repair? What is the accounting treatment for each?
34. What is the difference between depreciation for accounting purposes and the Modified Accelerated Cost Recovery System for income tax purposes?

SHORT EXERCISES

SE 1. *Management Issues*
L O 1
Check Figures: 1. b; 2. a; 3. c; 4. b; 5. c

Indicate whether each of the following actions is primarily related to (a) acquisition of long-term assets, (b) financing of long-term assets, or (c) choosing methods and estimates related to long-term assets.

1. Deciding between common stock and long-term notes for the raising of funds
2. Relating the acquisition cost of a long-term asset to cash flows generated by the asset
3. Determining how long an asset will benefit the company
4. Deciding to use cash flows from operations to purchase long-term assets
5. Determining how much an asset will sell for when it is no longer useful to the company

SE 2. *Determining Cost of*
L O 2 *Long-Term Assets*
Check Figures: 1. b; 2. c; 3. a; 4. a; 5. c; 6. b; 7. c; 8. c

Haines Auto, Inc. purchased a neighboring lot for a new building and parking lot. Indicate whether each of the following expenditures is properly charged to (a) Land, (b) Land Improvements, or (c) Buildings.

1. Paving costs
2. Architects' fee for building design
3. Cost of clearing the property
4. Cost of the property
5. Structure construction costs
6. Lights around the property
7. Building permit
8. Interest on the construction loan

SE 3. *Group Purchase*
L O 2
Check Figure: Building Apportionment: $468,750

Rezaki Company purchased property with a warehouse and parking lot for $750,000. An appraiser valued the components of the property if purchased separately as follows:

Land	$200,000
Land improvements	100,000
Building	500,000
Total	$800,000

Determine the cost to be assigned to each component.

SE 4. *Straight-Line*
L O 4 *Method*
Check Figure: $1,250 each year

Hubbard Woods Fitness Center, Inc. purchased a new step machine for $5,500. The apparatus is expected to last four years and have a residual value of $500. What will be the depreciation expense for each year under the straight-line method?

SE 5. *Production Method*
L O 4
Check Figure: Depreciation for Year 1: $1,500

Assuming that the step machine in SE 4 has an estimated useful life of 8,000 hours and was used for 2,400 hours in year 1, for 2,000 hours in year 2, for 2,200 hours in year 3, and for 1,400 hours in year 4, how much would depreciation expense be in each year?

SE 6. *Double-Declining-*
L O 4 *Balance Method*
Check Figure: Depreciation for Year 2: $1,375

Assuming that the step machine in SE 4 is depreciated using the declining-balance method at double the straight-line rate, how much would depreciation expense be in each year?

SE 7. *Disposal of Plant*
L O 5 *Assets: No Trade-In*

Check Figures: 1. Loss on Disposal of Equipment: $3,600; 2. Loss on Sale of Equipment: $2,100; 3. Gain on Sale of Equipment: $400

Shanequa Printing, Inc. has a piece of equipment that cost $8,100 and on which $4,500 of accumulated depreciation had been recorded. The equipment was disposed of on January 4, the first day of business of the current year. Give the journal entries to record the disposal under each of the following assumptions.

1. It was discarded as having no value.
2. It was sold for $1,500 cash.
3. It was sold for $4,000 cash.

SE 8. *Disposal of Plant*
L O 6 *Assets: Trade-In*

Check Figures: 1. Gain on Exchange of Equipment: $200; 2. Loss on Exchange of Equipment: $1,850; 3. No loss recognized

Give the journal entries to record the disposal referred to in SE 7 under each of the following assumptions:

1. The equipment was traded in on dissimilar equipment that had a list price of $12,000. A $3,800 trade-in was allowed, and the balance was paid in cash. Gains and losses are to be recognized.
2. The equipment was traded in on dissimilar equipment that had a list price of $12,000. A $1,750 trade-in was allowed, and the balance was paid in cash. Gains and losses are to be recognized.
3. Same as **2,** except that the items are similar and gains and losses are not to be recognized.

SE 9. *Natural Resources*
L O 7

Check Figure: Depletion expense for the first year: $1,020,000

Tulsa Corp. purchased land containing an estimated 4,000,000 tons of ore for $8,000,000. The land will be worth $1,200,000 without the ore after eight years of active mining. Although the equipment needed for the mining will have a useful life of twenty years, it is not expected to be usable and will have no value after the mining on this site is complete. Compute the depletion charge per ton and the amount of depletion expense for the first year of operation, assuming that 600,000 tons of ore were mined and sold. Also, compute the first-year depreciation on the mining equipment using the straight-line method, assuming a cost of $9,600,000 with no residual value.

SE 10. *Intangible Assets:*
L O 8 *Computer Software*

Check Figure: Software: $280,000

Beta-Micro created a new software application for PCs. Its costs during research and development were $500,000, and its costs after the working program was developed were $350,000. Although the copyright lasts forty years, management believes that the product will be viable for five years. How should the costs be accounted for? At what value will the software appear on the balance sheet after one year?

EXERCISES

E 1. *Management Issues*
L O 1

Check Figures: 1. c; 2. a; 3. c; 4. b; 5. a; 6. a

Indicate whether each of the following actions is primarily related to (a) acquisition of long-term assets, (b) financing of long-term assets, or (c) choosing methods and estimates related to long-term assets.

1. Deciding to use the production method of depreciation
2. Allocating costs on a group purchase
3. Determining the total units a machine will produce
4. Deciding to borrow funds to purchase equipment
5. Estimating the savings a new machine will produce and comparing the amount to cost
6. Deciding whether to rent or buy a piece of equipment

E 2. *Determining Cost of*
L O 2 *Long-Term Assets*

Check Figures: Total cost of land: $84,600; Total cost of land improvements: $19,600

Rosemond Manufacturing purchased land next to its factory to be used as a parking lot. Expenditures incurred by the company were as follows: purchase price, $75,000; broker's fees, $6,000; title search and other fees, $550; demolition of a shack on the property, $2,000; general grading of property, $1,050; paving of parking lot, $10,000; lighting for parking lot, $8,000; and signs for parking lot, $1,600. Determine the amounts that should be debited to the Land account and the Land Improvements account.

E 3. *Group Purchase*
L O 2

Check Figure: Equipment: $84,000

Ellen Briggs purchased a car wash for $240,000. If purchased separately, the land would have cost $60,000, the building $135,000, and the equipment $105,000. Determine the amount that should be recorded in the new business's records for land, building, and equipment.

E 4. *Cost of Long-Term*
L O 2, 4 *Asset and*
Depreciation

Check Figures: Total cost: $20,000;
First year's depreciation: $3,000

Jason Farm purchased a used tractor for $17,500. Before the tractor could be used, it required new tires, which cost $1,100, and an overhaul, which cost $1,400. Its first tank of fuel cost $75. The tractor is expected to last six years and have a residual value of $2,000. Determine the cost and depreciable cost of the tractor and calculate the first year's depreciation under the straight-line method.

E 5. *Depreciation*
L O 3, 4 *Methods*

Check Figures: 1. $7,500; 2. $9,000;
3. $10,800

Logan Oil Corporation purchased a drilling truck for $45,000. The company expected the truck to last five years or 200,000 miles, with an estimated residual value of $7,500 at the end of that time. During 19x5, the truck was driven 48,000 miles. The company's year end is December 31.

Compute the depreciation for 19x5 under each of the following methods, assuming that the truck was purchased on January 13, 19x4: (1) straight-line, (2) production, and (3) double-declining-balance. Using the amount computed in **3**, prepare the general journal entry to record depreciation expense for the second year and show how Drilling Truck would appear on the balance sheet.

E 6. *Declining-Balance*
L O 4 *Method*

Check Figures: Year 3: $560; Year 4:
$80

Quadri Burglar Alarm Systems Company purchased a word processor for $4,480. It has an estimated useful life of four years and an estimated residual value of $480. Compute the depreciation charge for each of the four years under the double-declining-balance method.

E 7. *Disposal of Plant*
L O 5, 6 *Assets*

Check Figures: 1. Loss on Disposal of
Equipment: $14,400; 2. Loss on Sale
of Equipment: $8,400; 3. Gain on Sale
of Equipment: $3,600

A piece of equipment that cost $32,400 and on which $18,000 of accumulated depreciation had been recorded was disposed of on January 2, the first day of business of the current year. Give general journal entries to record the disposal under each of the following assumptions.

1. It was discarded as having no value.
2. It was sold for $6,000 cash.
3. It was sold for $18,000 cash.
4. It was traded in on dissimilar equipment having a list price of $48,000. A $15,600 trade-in was allowed, and the balance was paid in cash. Gains and losses are to be recognized.
5. It was traded in on dissimilar equipment having a list price of $48,000. A $7,200 trade-in was allowed, and the balance was paid in cash. Gains and losses are to be recognized.
6. Same as **5** except that the items are similar and gains and losses are not to be recognized.

E 8. *Disposal of Plant*
L O 6 *Assets*

Check Figures: 1. $1,300; 2. $5,100;
3. $300; 4a. $6,100; 4b. $6,400

A commercial vacuum cleaner costing $4,900, with accumulated depreciation of $3,600, was traded in on a new model that had a list price of $6,100. A trade-in allowance of $1,000 was given.

1. Compute the carrying value of the old vacuum cleaner.
2. Determine the amount of cash required to purchase the new vacuum cleaner.
3. Compute the amount of loss on the exchange.
4. Determine the cost basis of the new vacuum cleaner, assuming (a) the loss is recognized and (b) the loss is not recognized.
5. Compute the yearly depreciation on the new vacuum cleaner for both assumptions in **4**, assuming a useful life of five years, a residual value of $1,600, and straight-line depreciation.

E 9. *Disposal of Plant*
L O 5, 6 *Assets*

Check Figures: 1. Loss on Disposal of
Computer: $1,850; 2. Loss on Sale
of Computer: $1,050; 3. Gain on
Sale of Computer: $350; 4. Loss on
Exchange of Computer: $650; 5. No
gain recognized

A microcomputer was purchased by Juniper Company on January 1, 19x1, at a cost of $5,000. It is expected to have a useful life of five years and a residual value of $500. Assuming that the computer is disposed of on July 1, 19x4, record the partial year's depreciation for 19x4 using the straight-line method, and record the disposal under each of the following assumptions.

1. The microcomputer is discarded.
2. The microcomputer is sold for $800.
3. The microcomputer is sold for $2,200.
4. The microcomputer is exchanged for a new microcomputer with a list price of $9,000. A $1,200 trade-in is allowed on the cash purchase. The accounting approach to gains and losses is followed.

5. Same as **4** except a $2,400 trade-in is allowed.
6. Same as **4** except the income tax approach is followed.
7. Same as **5** except the income tax approach is followed.
8. Same as **4** except the microcomputer is exchanged for dissimilar office equipment.
9. Same as **5** except the microcomputer is exchanged for dissimilar office equipment.

E 10. *Natural Resource*
L O 7 *Depletion and Depreciation of Related Plant Assets*

Check Figures: 1. $.72; 2. $576,000; 3. $64,000; 4a. $96,000; 4b. $76,800

Church Mining Corporation purchased land containing an estimated 10 million tons of ore for a cost of $8,800,000. The land without the ore is estimated to be worth $1,600,000. The company expects that all the usable ore can be mined in ten years. Buildings costing $800,000 with an estimated useful life of thirty years were erected on the site. Equipment costing $960,000 with an estimated useful life of ten years was installed. Because of the remote location, neither the buildings nor the equipment has an estimated residual value. During its first year of operation, the company mined and sold 800,000 tons of ore.

1. Compute the depletion charge per ton.
2. Compute the depletion expense that Church Mining Corporation should record for the year.
3. Determine the annual depreciation expense for the buildings, making it proportional to the depletion.
4. Determine the annual depreciation expense for the equipment under two alternatives: (a) using the straight-line method and (b) making the expense proportional to the depletion.

E 11. *Amortization of*
L O 8 *Copyrights and Trademarks*

Check Figures: 1. $5,000; 2. $4,000

1. Fortunato Publishing Company purchased the copyright to a basic computer textbook for $20,000. The usual life of a textbook is about four years. However, the copyright will remain in effect for at least another fifty years. Calculate the annual amortization of the copyright.
2. Guzman Company purchased a trademark from a well-known supermarket for $160,000. The management of the company argued that because the trademark value would last forever and might even increase, no amortization should be charged. Calculate the minimum amount of annual amortization that should be charged, according to guidelines of the appropriate Accounting Principles Board opinion.

E 12. *Depreciation*
S O 9 *Methods: Partial Years*

Check Figures: 1. $7,500; 2. $9,000; 3. $14,400

Using the same data given for Logan Oil Corporation in E 5, compute the depreciation for calendar year 19x5 under each of the following methods, assuming that the truck was purchased on July 1, 19x4: (1) straight-line, (2) production, and (3) double-declining-balance.

E 13. *Straight-Line*
S O 9 *Method: Partial Years*

Check Figures: Machine 1: $275; Machine 2: $833; Machine 3: $900

Strauss Manufacturing Corporation purchased three machines during the year:

February 10	Machine 1	$ 1,800
July 26	Machine 2	12,000
October 11	Machine 3	21,600

Each machine is expected to last six years and have no residual value. The company's fiscal year corresponds to the calendar year. Using the straight-line method, compute the depreciation charge for each machine for the year.

E 14. *Revision of*
S O 9 *Depreciation Rates*

Check Figure: Third-year depreciation: $22,400

Eastmoor Hospital purchased a special x-ray machine for its operating room. The machine, which cost $155,780, was expected to last ten years, with an estimated residual value of $15,780. After two years of operation (and depreciation charges using the straight-line rate), it became evident that the x-ray machine would last a total of only seven years. The estimated residual value, however, would remain the same. Given this information, determine the new depreciation charge for the third year on the basis of the estimated useful life.

E 15. *Special Types of*
L O 2, *Capital Expenditures*
S O 9

Check Figures: 1. RE, OR; 2. CE, B; 3. CE, A; 4. CE, N; 5. CE, ER; 6. RE, N

Tell whether each of the following transactions related to an office building is a revenue expenditure (RE) or a capital expenditure (CE). In addition, indicate whether each transaction is an ordinary repair (OR), an extraordinary repair (ER), an addition (A), a betterment (B), or none of these (N).

1. The hallways and ceilings in the building are repainted at a cost of $8,300.
2. The hallways, which have tile floors, are carpeted at a cost of $28,000.
3. A new wing is added to the building at a cost of $175,000.
4. Furniture is purchased for the entrance to the building at a cost of $16,500.
5. The air-conditioning system is overhauled at a cost of $28,500. The overhaul extends the useful life of the air-conditioning system by ten years.
6. A cleaning firm is paid $200 per week to clean the newly installed carpets.

E 16. *Extraordinary*
S O 9 *Repairs*
Check Figure: 2. New book value: $97,200

Regalado Manufacturing has an incinerator that originally cost $187,200 and now has accumulated depreciation of $132,800. The incinerator just completed its fifteenth year of service in an estimated useful life of twenty years. At the beginning of the sixteenth year, the company spent $42,800 repairing and modernizing the incinerator to comply with pollution-control standards. Therefore, the incinerator is now expected to last ten more years instead of five more years. It will not, however, have more capacity than it did in the past or a residual value at the end of its useful life.

1. Prepare the entry to record the cost of the repair.
2. Compute the book value of the incinerator after the entry.
3. Prepare the entry to record the straight-line depreciation for the current year.

SKILLS DEVELOPMENT EXERCISES

Conceptual Analysis

SDE 1. *Nature of*
L O 1, 3 *Depreciation and Amortization and Estimated Useful Lives*

No check figure

In its 1987 annual report, **General Motors Corp.** states, "In the third quarter of 1987, the Corporation revised the estimated service lives of its plants and equipment and special tools retroactive to January 1, 1987. These revisions, which were based on 1987 studies of actual useful lives and periods of use, recognized current estimates of service lives of the assets and had the effect of reducing 1987 depreciation and amortization charges by $1,236.6 million or $2.53 per share of $1⅔ par value common stock."[19] In 1987, General Motors' income before income taxes was $2,005.4 million. Discuss the purpose of depreciation and amortization. What is the estimated service life, and on what basis did General Motors change the estimates of the service lives of plants and equipment and special tools? What was the effect of this change on the corporation's income before income taxes? Is it likely that the company is in better condition economically as a result of the change? Does the company have more cash at the end of the year as a result? (Ignore income tax effects.)

SDE 2. *Choice of*
L O 3, 4 *Depreciation Methods*

No check figure

Ford Motor Co., one of the nation's largest manufacturers of automobiles, does not use the straight-line depreciation method for financial reporting purposes even though, as shown in Figure 4, most companies do. As noted in Ford's 1992 annual report:

> Depreciation is computed using an accelerated method that results in accumulated depreciation of approximately two-thirds of asset cost during the first half of the asset's estimated useful life.[20]

What reasons can you give for Ford's choosing an accelerated method of depreciation over the straight-line method? What is the role of the matching rule? Discuss which of the two methods is the more conservative.

SDE 3. *Trademarks*
L O 8

No check figure

The **Quaker Oats Company's** advertising campaign, "Gatorade is thirst aid for that deep down body thirst," infringed on a trademark held by **Sands Taylor & Wood** of Norwich, Vermont, according to a 1990 ruling by a federal judge.[21] Sands Taylor & Wood had acquired the trademark "thirst aid" in a 1973 acquisition but was not using it at the time of the 1990 ruling. The judge determined that Gatorade had produced $247.3 million in income over the previous six years and reasoned that the advertising

19. General Motors Corp., *Annual Report*, 1987.

20. Ford Motor Co., *Annual Report*, 1992.

21. James P. Miller, "Quaker Oats Loses Trademark Battle Over Gatorade Ad," *Wall Street Journal*, December 19, 1990.

campaign was responsible for 10 percent of the product's sales. As a result, he awarded Sands Taylor & Wood $24.7 million plus legal fees and interest from 1984. He also prohibited Quaker Oats from further use of the phrase "thirst aid" in any advertising campaign for Gatorade, its largest-selling product.

What is a trademark, and why is it considered an intangible asset? Why does a trademark have value? For whom does a trademark have value? Be prepared to discuss how your answers apply to the case of Quaker Oats Company's use of "thirst aid."

Ethical Dilemma

SDE 4. *Ethics and*
L O 2 *Allocation of Acquisition Costs*

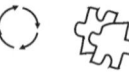

No check figure

Signal Corporation has purchased land and a warehouse for $18,000,000. The warehouse is expected to last twenty years and to have a salvage value equal to 10 percent of its cost. The chief financial officer (CFO) and controller are discussing the allocation of the purchase price. The CFO believes most of the cost should be assigned to the land because this action will improve reported net income in the future. Depreciation expense will be lower because land is not depreciated. He suggests allocating one-third, or $6,000,000, of the cost to the land. This results in depreciation expense each year of $540,000 [($12,000,000 − $1,200,000) ÷ 20 years]. The controller disagrees, arguing that the smallest amount possible, say one-fifth of the purchase price, should be allocated to the land, thereby saving income taxes, since the depreciation, which is tax deductible, will be greater. Under this plan, annual depreciation would be $648,000 [($14,400,000 − $1,440,000) ÷ 20 years]. The annual tax savings at a 30 percent tax rate is $32,400 [($648,000 − $540,000) × .30]. How will this decision affect the company's cash flows? Ethically speaking, how should the purchase cost be allocated? Who will be affected by the decision?

Research Activity

SDE 5. *SEC and Form 10-K*
L O 5, 6

No check figure

Public corporations are required not only to communicate with their stockholders by means of an annual report, but also to submit an annual report to the Securities and Exchange Commission (SEC). The annual report to the SEC is called a 10-K and contains information in addition to that provided to stockholders. Most college and university libraries provide access to at least a selected number of 10-Ks. These 10-Ks may be on microfiche or on file with the companies' annual reports to stockholders. In your school's library, find the 10-K for a single company. In that 10-K, Schedule 5 will contain information about the company's dispositions and acquisitions of property, plant, and equipment at carrying value. Schedule 6 will show the increases and decreases in the accumulated depreciation accounts. In the statement of cash flows, under investing activities, the cash proceeds from dispositions of property, plant, and equipment will be shown. Using the information from the statement of cash flows and the two related schedules, determine whether the company had a gain or loss from dispositions of property, plant, and equipment during the year. Be prepared to discuss your results in class.

Decision-Making Practice

SDE 6. *Natural Resource*
L O 4, 7 *Accounting*

Check Figures: 2. Depletion Expense: $1,365,000; 3. Net Loss: $105,000

Billy Bob Daniels is in the gravel business in Oklahoma and has engaged you to assist in evaluating his company, ***Daniels Gravel Company.*** Your first step is to collect the facts about the company's operations. On January 3, 19x2, Billy Bob purchased a piece of property with gravel deposits for $6,310,000. He estimated that the gravel deposits contained 4,700,000 cubic yards of gravel. The gravel is used for making roads. After the gravel is gone, the land, which is in the desert, will be worth only about $200,000.

The equipment required to extract the gravel cost $1,452,000. In addition, Billy Bob had to build a small frame building to house the mine office and a small dining hall for the workers. The building cost $152,000 and will have no residual value after its estimated useful life of ten years. It cannot be moved from the mine site. The equipment has an estimated useful life of six years (with no residual value) and also cannot be moved from the mine site.

Trucks for the project cost $308,000 (estimated life, six years; residual value, $20,000). The trucks, of course, can be used at a different site.

Billy Bob estimated that in five years all the gravel would be mined and the mine would be shut down. During 19x2, 1,175,000 cubic yards of gravel were mined. The average selling price during the year was $2.66 per cubic yard, and at the end of the year 125,000 cubic yards remained unsold. Operating expenses were $852,000 for labor and $232,000 for other expenses.

1. Prepare general journal entries to record the purchase of the property and the building and equipment associated with the mine. Assume purchases are made with cash on January 3.
2. Prepare adjusting entries to record depletion and depreciation for the first year of operation (19x2). Assume that the depreciation rate is equal to the percentage of the total gravel mined during the year, unless the asset is movable. For movable assets, use the straight-line method.
3. Prepare an income statement for 19x2 for Daniels Gravel Company.
4. What is your evaluation of the company's operations? What are the reasons for your evaluation? Ignore income tax effects.

PROBLEM SET A

A 1. *Determining Cost of*
L O 2 *Assets*

Check Figures: 1. Totals: Land: $426,212; Land Improvements: $166,560; Buildings: $833,940; Machinery: $1,262,640; Losses: $18,120

Flair Corporation began operation on January 1 of the current year. At the end of the year, Flair's auditor discovered that all expenditures involving long-term assets had been debited to an account called Fixed Assets. An analysis of the account, with a year-end balance of $2,644,972, disclosed that it contained the following items.

The timber that was cleared from the land was sold to a firewood dealer for $5,000. This amount was credited to Miscellaneous Income. During the construction period, two supervisors devoted their full time to the construction project. These people earn annual salaries of $48,000 and $42,000, respectively. They spent two months on the purchase and preparation of the land, six months on the construction of the building (approximately one-sixth of which was devoted to improvements on the grounds), and one month on installation of machinery. The plant began operation on October 1, and the supervisors returned to their regular duties. Their salaries were debited to Factory Salary Expense.

Cost of land	$ 316,600
Surveying costs	4,100
Transfer of title and other fees required by the county	920
Broker's fees	21,144
Attorney's fees associated with land acquisition	7,048
Cost of removing unusable timber from land	50,400
Cost of grading land	4,200
Cost of digging building foundation	34,600
Architect's fee for building and land improvements (80 percent building)	64,800
Cost of building	710,000
Cost of sidewalks	11,400
Cost of parking lots	54,400
Cost of lighting for grounds	80,300
Cost of landscaping	11,800
Cost of machinery	989,000
Shipping cost on machinery	55,300
Cost of installing machinery	176,200
Cost of testing machinery	22,100
Cost of changes in building due to safety regulations required because of machinery	12,540
Cost of repairing building that was damaged in the installation of machinery	8,900
Cost of medical bill for injury received by employee while installing machinery	2,400
Cost of water damage to building during heavy rains prior to opening the plant for operation	6,820
Account balance	$2,644,972

REQUIRED

1. Prepare a schedule with the following column headings: Land, Land Improvements, Buildings, Machinery, and Losses. List the items and place each in the proper account. Negative amounts should be shown in parentheses. Total the columns.
2. Prepare an entry to adjust the accounts based on all the information given, assuming that the company's accounts have not been closed at the end of the year.

A 2.
L O 3, 4
Comparison of Depreciation Methods

Riggio Construction Company purchased a new crane for $360,500 at the beginning of year 1. The crane has an estimated residual value of $35,000 and an estimated useful life of six years. The crane is expected to last 10,000 hours. It was used 1,800 hours in year 1; 2,000 in year 2; 2,500 in year 3; 1,500 in year 4; 1,200 in year 5; and 1,000 in year 6.

REQUIRED

Check Figures: 1. Depreciation, Year 3:
a. $54,250; b. $81,375; c. $53,407

1. Compute the annual depreciation and carrying value for the new crane for each of the six years (round to the nearest dollar where necessary) under each of the following methods: (a) straight-line, (b) production, and (c) double-declining-balance.
2. Prepare the adjusting entry that would be made each year to record the depreciation calculated under the straight-line method.
3. Show the balance sheet presentation for the crane after the adjusting entry in year 2 using the straight-line method.
4. What conclusions can you draw from the patterns of yearly depreciation and carrying value in 1?

A 3.
L O 5, 6
Recording Disposals

Robles Construction Company purchased a road grader for $29,000. The road grader is expected to have a useful life of five years and a residual value of $2,000 at the end of that time.

REQUIRED

Check Figures: a. Gain on Sale of Road Grader: $1,800; b. Loss on Sale of Road Grader: $2,200; c. Gain on Exchange of Road Grader: $1,800; d. Loss on Exchange of Road Grader: $2,200; e. No gain recognized

Prepare journal entries to record the disposal of the road grader at the end of the second year, after the depreciation is recorded, assuming that the straight-line method is used and making the following separate assumptions.

a. The road grader is sold for $20,000 cash.
b. It is sold for $16,000 cash.
c. It is traded in on a dissimilar piece of machinery costing $33,000, a trade-in allowance of $20,000 is given, the balance is paid in cash, and gains or losses are recognized.
d. It is traded in on a dissimilar piece of machinery costing $33,000, a trade-in allowance of $16,000 is given, the balance is paid in cash, and gains or losses are recognized.
e. Same as **c,** except it is traded for a similar road grader and Robles Construction Company follows accounting rules for the recognition of gains or losses.
f. Same as **d,** except it is traded for a similar road grader and Robles Construction Company follows accounting rules for the recognition of gains or losses.
g. Same as **c,** except it is traded for a similar road grader and gains or losses are not recognized for income tax purposes.
h. Same as **d,** except it is traded for a similar road grader and gains or losses are not recognized for income tax purposes.

A 4.
L O 7
Comprehensive Natural Resources Entries

Check Figures: 2. Depletion Expense: $2,001,000; Total Depreciation Expense: $812,300

On January 3, 19x2, the Green Company purchased a piece of property with sand deposits for $7,500,000. Green estimated that the deposits contained 3,000,000 cubic yards of sand, which is used for making concrete. After the sand is gone, the land will be worth only about $600,000. The equipment required to extract the sand cost $2,184,000. In addition, Green decided to build a small frame building to house the mine office and a small dining hall for the workers. The building cost $286,000 and will have no residual value after its estimated useful life of ten years. It cannot be moved from the site. The equipment, which has an estimated useful life of six years, has no residual value and cannot be removed from the site. Trucks for the project cost $626,000 (estimated life, six years; residual value, $50,000). The trucks, of course, can be used at a different site. Green estimated that in five years all the sand would be removed and the site would be shut down. During 19x2, 870,000 cubic yards of sand were extracted and sold.

REQUIRED

1. Prepare general journal entries to record the purchase on January 3 of the property and the building and equipment associated with the site. Assume purchases are made with cash.

2. Prepare adjusting entries to record depletion and depreciation for the first year of operation (19x2). Assume that the depreciation rate is equal to the percentage of the total sand sold during the year, unless the asset is movable. For movable assets, use the straight-line method.

A 5. *Amortization of*
L O 8 *Exclusive License, Leasehold, and Leasehold Improvements*

Check Figures: c. Amortization Expense: $492,000; d. Loss on Exclusive License: $1,476,000

REQUIRED

Part 1

On January 1, Future Play, Inc. purchased the exclusive license to make dolls based on the characters in a new hit series on television called "Sky Pirates." The exclusive license cost $2,100,000, and there was no termination date on the rights. Immediately after signing the contract, the company sued a rival firm that claimed it had already received the exclusive license to the series characters. Future Play successfully defended its rights at a cost of $360,000. During the first year and the next, Future Play marketed toys based on the series. Because a successful television series lasts about five years, the company felt it could market the toys for three more years. However, before the third year of the series could get under way, a controversy arose between its two stars and its producer. As a result, the stars refused to work the third year and the show was canceled, rendering exclusive rights worthless.

Prepare journal entries to record the following: (a) purchase of the exclusive license; (b) successful defense of the license; (c) amortization expense, if any, for the first year; and (d) write-off of the license as worthless.

Check Figures: d. Leasehold Amortization Expense: $1,575; e. Leasehold Improvements Amortization Expense: $2,500

REQUIRED

Part 2

Pamela Newell purchased a six-year sublease on a building from the estate of the former tenant, who had died suddenly. It was a good location for her business, and the annual rent of $3,600, which had been established ten years before, was low for such a good location. The cost of the sublease was $9,450. To use the building, Newell had to make certain alterations. First she moved some panels at a cost of $1,700 and installed others for $6,100. Then she added carpet, lighting fixtures, and a sign at costs of $2,900, $3,100, and $1,200, respectively. All items except the carpet would last for at least twelve years. The expected life of the carpet was six years. None of the improvements would have a residual value at the end of those times.

Prepare general journal entries to record the following: (a) the payment for the sublease; (b) the payments for the alterations, panels, carpet, lighting fixtures, and sign; (c) the lease payment for the first year; (d) the amortization expense, if any, associated with the sublease; and (e) the amortization expense, if any, associated with the alterations, panels, carpet, lighting fixtures, and sign.

A 6. *Depreciation*
L O 4, *Methods and Partial*
S O 9 *Years*

Check Figures: Total Depreciation Expense: 19x5: $71,820; 19x6: $103,092; 19x7: $84,072

Wu Corporation operates three types of equipment. Because of the equipment's varied functions, company accounting policy requires the application of three different depreciation methods. Data on this equipment are summarized in the table below. Equipment 3 was used 2,000 hours in 19x5; 4,200 hours in 19x6; and 3,200 hours in 19x7.

Equipment	Date Purchased	Cost	Installation Cost	Estimated Residual Value	Estimated Life	Depreciation Method
1	1/12/x5	$171,000	$ 9,000	$18,000	10 years	Double-declining-balance
2	7/9/x5	191,100	15,900	21,000	10 years	Straight-line
3	10/2/x5	290,700	8,100	33,600	20,000 hours	Production

REQUIRED

Assuming that the fiscal year ends December 31, compute the depreciation expense on each type of equipment and the total depreciation expense for 19x5, 19x6, and 19x7 by filling in a table with the headings shown below.

		Depreciation		
Equipment No.	Computations	19x5	19x6	19x7

PROBLEM SET B

B 1. *Determining Cost of*
L O 2 *Assets*

Check Figures: 1. Totals: Land: $361,950; Land Improvements: $71,000; Building: $691,800; Furniture and Equipment: $105,400

Moline Computers, Inc. constructed a new training center in 19x2. You have been hired to manage the training center. A review of the accounting records lists the following expenditures debited to the Training Center account.

Attorney's fee, land acquisition	$ 17,450
Cost of land	299,000
Architect's fee, building design	51,000
Contractor's cost, building	510,000
Contractor's cost, parking lot and sidewalk	67,800
Electrical wiring, building	82,000
Landscaping	27,500
Costs of surveying land	4,600
Training equipment, tables, and chairs	68,200
Contractor's cost, installing training equipment	34,000
Cost of grading the land	7,000
Cost of changes in building to soundproof rooms	29,600
Total account balance	$1,198,150

During the center's construction, someone from Moline Computers, Inc. worked full time on the project. She spent two months on the purchase and preparation of the site, six months on the construction, one month on land improvements, and one month on equipment installation and training room furniture purchase and set-up. Her salary of $32,000 during this ten-month period was charged to Administrative Expense. The training center was placed in operation on November 1.

REQUIRED

1. Prepare a schedule with the following four column (account) headings: Land, Land Improvements, Building, and Furniture and Equipment. Place each item in the appropriate column. Total the columns.
2. Prepare an entry on December 31 to correct the accounts associated with the training center, assuming that the company's accounts have not yet been closed at the end of the year.

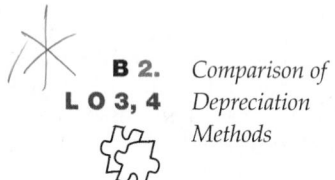

B 2. *Comparison of*
L O 3, 4 *Depreciation*
Methods

Hoekstra Manufacturing Company purchased a robot for its manufacturing operations at a cost of $720,000 at the beginning of year 1. The robot has an estimated useful life of four years and an estimated residual value of $60,000. The robot, which is expected to last 20,000 hours, was operated 6,000 hours in year 1; 8,000 hours in year 2; 4,000 hours in year 3; and 2,000 hours in year 4.

REQUIRED

Check Figures: 1. Depreciation, Year 3: a. $165,000; b. $132,000; c. $90,000

1. Compute the annual depreciation and carrying value for the robot for each year, assuming the following depreciation methods: (a) straight-line, (b) production, and (c) double-declining-balance.
2. Prepare the adjusting entry that would be made each year to record the depreciation calculated under the straight-line method.
3. Show the balance sheet presentation for the robot after the adjusting entry in year 2 using the straight-line method.
4. What conclusions can you draw from the patterns of yearly depreciation and carrying value in **1**?

B 3. *Recording Disposals*
L O 5, 6

Ingram Designs, Inc. purchased a computer that will be used in designing factory layouts. The computer cost $47,000, and its expected useful life is six years. The company can probably sell the computer for $5,000 at the end of six years.

REQUIRED

Check Figures: a. Gain on Sale of Computer: $12,000; b. Loss on Sale of Computer: $6,000; c. Gain on Exchange of Computer: $9,000; d. Loss on Exchange of Computer: $4,000; e. No gain recognized

Prepare journal entries to record the disposal of the computer at the end of the third year, assuming that it was depreciated using the straight-line method and making the following separate assumptions.

a. The computer is sold for $38,000.
b. It is sold for $20,000.
c. It is traded in on a dissimilar piece of equipment costing $72,000, a trade-in allowance of $35,000 is given, the balance is paid in cash, and gains and losses are recognized.

d. Same as **c**, except the trade-in allowance is $22,000.

e. Same as **c**, except it is traded for a similar computer and accounting rules are followed for the recognition of gains or losses.

f. Same as **d**, except it is traded for a similar computer and accounting rules are followed for the recognition of gains or losses.

g. Same as **c**, except it is traded for a similar computer and gains and losses are not recognized for income tax purposes.

h. Same as **d**, except it is traded for a similar computer and gains and losses are not recognized for income tax purposes.

B 4.   *Comprehensive*
L O 7   *Natural Resources*
          Entries

Check Figures: 2. Depletion Expense, Coal Property: $1,300,000; Depreciation Expense, Equipment: $137,500

The Munoz Coal Company purchased property that is estimated to contain 50,000,000 tons of coal. Munoz paid $6,000,000 for the property on January 2, 19x3. The property should be worth $1,000,000 after all the coal is extracted. At the same time Munoz purchased equipment costing $1,196,000 to extract the coal. The equipment has an eight-year estimated useful life with a residual value of $96,000 and can be moved to a new site when this site is depleted. Also, an on-site office had to be constructed for $120,000. The office has an estimated useful life of ten years with no residual value. The office will be abandoned when the site is depleted. The coal extracted from this site will be sold to retail companies that will load and deliver the coal directly from Munoz's property. Munoz's management estimates that all the coal will be mined in four years and that the mine will then be closed. During 19x3, 13,000,000 tons of coal were mined and sold.

REQUIRED

1. Prepare general journal entries to record the purchase of the property, equipment, and office construction. Assume purchases are made with cash.
2. Prepare adjusting entries to record depreciation and depletion for 19x3. Assume that the depreciation rate is equal to the percentage of the total coal mined during the year, unless the asset is movable, and that the straight-line method of depreciation is used for the movable assets.

B 5.   *Leasehold, Leasehold*
L O 8   *Improvements, and*
          Amortization of
          Patent

Check Figures: d. Leasehold Amortization Expense: $3,000; e. Leasehold Improvements Amortization Expense: $6,750

Part 1

At the beginning of the fiscal year, Dempsey Company purchased an eight-year sublease on a warehouse in Nashville for $24,000. Dempsey will also pay rent of $1,000 a month. Dempsey Company paid for the following improvements to the warehouse:

Lighting fixtures	$ 9,000
Replacement of a wall	12,500
Office carpet	7,200
Heating system	15,000
Break room	6,100
Loading dock	4,200

The expected life of the loading dock and carpet is eight years. The other items are expected to last ten years. None of the improvements will have a residual value.

REQUIRED

Prepare general journal entries to record the following: (a) payment for the sublease; (b) the first-year lease payment; (c) payments for the improvements; (d) amortization of the leasehold for the year; and (e) leasehold improvement amortization for the year.

Check Figures: c. Amortization Expense: $74,000; d. Loss on Write-off of Patent: $592,000

Part 2

At the beginning of the fiscal year, Fellner Company paid $515,000 for a patent that applies to the manufacture of a unique tamper-proof lid for medicine bottles. During the first year, Fellner incurred legal costs of $225,000 to successfully defend its patented lid from use by a competitor. Fellner estimated that the patent would be valuable for at least ten years. During the first two years of operation, Fellner successfully marketed the lid. At the beginning of the third year, a study appeared in a consumers' magazine showing that the lid could, in fact, be removed by children. As a result, all orders for the lids were canceled, and the patent was rendered worthless.

REQUIRED

Prepare journal entries to record the following: (a) purchase of the patent; (b) successful defense of the patent; (c) amortization expense for the first year; and (d) write-off of the patent as worthless.

B 6. *Depreciation*
L O 4, *Methods and Partial*
S O 9 *Years*

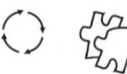

Ada Pinkston purchased a laundry company that caters to college students. In addition to the washing machines, Pinkston installed a tanning machine and a refreshment center. Because each type of asset performs a different function, she has decided to use different depreciation methods. Data on each type of asset are summarized in the table below.

The tanning machine was operated 2,100 hours in 19x5, 3,000 hours in 19x6, and 2,400 hours in 19x7.

Asset	Date Purchased	Cost	Installation Cost	Residual Value	Estimated Life	Depreciation Method
Washing machines	3/5/x5	$15,000	$2,000	$2,600	4 years	Straight-line
Tanning machine	4/1/x5	34,000	3,000	1,000	7,500 hours	Production
Refreshment center	10/1/x5	3,400	600	600	10 years	Double-declining-balance

REQUIRED

Check Figures: Total Depreciation Expense: 19x5: $13,280; 19x6: $18,760; 19x7: $15,728

Assuming that the fiscal year ends December 31, compute the depreciation expense for each item and the total depreciation expense for 19x5, 19x6, and 19x7. Round your answers to the nearest dollar and present them by filling in a table with the headings shown below.

		Depreciation		
Asset	Computations	19x5	19x6	19x7

FINANCIAL REPORTING AND ANALYSIS CASES

Interpreting Financial Reports

FRA 1. *Effects of Change in*
L O 3, 4, *Accounting Method*
S O 9

No check figure

Depreciation expense is a significant expense for companies in which plant assets are a high proportion of assets. The amount of depreciation expense in a given year is affected by estimates of useful life and choice of depreciation method. In 1995, *Century Steelworks Company*, a major integrated steel producer, changed the estimated useful lives for its major production assets. It also changed the method of depreciation for other steel-making assets from straight-line to the production method.

The company's 1995 annual report states, "A recent study conducted by management shows that actual years-in-service figures for our major production equipment and machinery are, in most cases, higher than the estimated useful lives assigned to these assets. We have recast the depreciable lives of such assets so that equipment previously assigned a useful life of 8 to 26 years now has an extended depreciable life of 10 to 32 years." The report goes on to explain that the new production method of depreciation "recognizes that depreciation of production equipment and machinery correlates directly to both physical wear and tear and the passage of time. The production method of depreciation, which we have now initiated, more closely allocates the cost of these assets to the periods in which products are manufactured."

The report summarized the effects of both actions on the year 1995 as follows:

Incremental Increase in Net Income	In Millions	Per Share
Lengthened lives	$11.0	$ .80
Production method		
Current year	7.3	.53
Prior years	2.8	.20
Total increase	$21.1	$1.53

During 1995, Century Steelworks reported a net loss of $83,156,500 ($6.03 per share). Depreciation expense for 1995 was $87,707,200.

In explaining the changes, the controller of Century Steelworks was quoted in an article in *Business Journal* as follows: "There is no reason for Century Steelworks to continue to depreciate our assets more conservatively than our competitors do." But the article quotes an industry analyst who argues that by slowing its method of depreciation, Century Steelworks could be viewed as reporting lower-quality earnings.

REQUIRED

1. Explain the accounting treatment when there is a change in the estimated lives of depreciable assets. What circumstances must exist for the production method to produce the effect it did in relation to the straight-line method? What would have been Century Steelworks' net income or loss if the changes had not been made? What may have motivated management to make the changes?

2. What does the controller of Century Steelworks mean when he says that Century had been depreciating "more conservatively than our competitors do"? Why might the changes at Century Steelworks indicate, as the analyst asserts, "lower-quality earnings"? What risks might Century face as a result of its decision to use the production method of depreciation?

International Company

FRA 2.
L O 8

Accounting for Trademarks: U.S. and British Rules

No check figure

When the British company **Grand Metropolitan** (Grand Met) purchased **Pillsbury** in 1989, it adopted British accounting policies with regard to intangibles. Many analysts feel this gives British companies advantages over U.S. companies, especially in buyout situations.[22] There are two major differences in accounting for intangibles between U.S. accounting standards and British accounting standards. First, under the U.S. rules, as discussed in this chapter, intangible assets such as trademarks are recorded at their acquisition cost, which is often nominal, and the cost is amortized over a reasonable life. Under British accounting standards, on the other hand, firms are able to record the value of trademarks for the purpose of increasing the total assets on their balance sheets. Further, they do not have to amortize the value if management can show that the value can be preserved through extensive brand support. Grand Met, therefore, elected to record such famous Pillsbury trademarks as the Pillsbury Doughboy, Green Giant vegetables, Haagen Dazs ice cream, and Van de Kamp fish at an estimated value and not to amortize them. Second, when one company purchases another company for more than the market value of the assets if purchased individually, under U.S. rules the excess is recorded as the asset Goodwill, which must be amortized over a period not to exceed forty years. Although companies are required to show the expense, they cannot, under U.S. income tax laws, deduct the goodwill amortization for tax purposes. Under British accounting rules, any goodwill resulting from a purchase lowers stockholders' equity directly, rather than being recorded as an asset and lowering net income through amortization over a number of years. Analysts say that these two rules made Pillsbury more valuable to Grand Met than to Pillsbury stockholders and thus led to Pillsbury's being bought by the British firm. Write a one- or two-page paper that addresses the following questions: What is the rationale behind the argument that the British company has an advantage due to the differences between U.S. and British accounting principles? Do you agree with U.S. or British accounting rules regarding intangibles and goodwill? Defend your answers.

Toys "R" Us Annual Report

FRA 3.
L O 2, 3, 4

Long-Term Assets

Check Figures: 55.8%; Real estate; Land, $764,808,000 and buildings, $1,627,145,000

1. Refer to the consolidated balance sheets and to the note on property and equipment in the notes to consolidated financial statements in the appendix on Toys "R" Us to answer the following questions: What percentage of total assets in 1995 was property and equipment? What is the most significant type of property and equipment? Does Toys "R" Us have a significant investment in land? What kinds of things are included in the "Other, net" category? (Ignore leased property under capital leases for now.)

2. Refer to the summary of significant accounting policies and to the note on property and equipment in the appendix on Toys "R" Us. What method of depreciation does Toys "R" Us use? How is interest on construction of long-term assets accounted for? How long does management estimate its buildings to last as compared to furniture and equipment? What does this say about the need for remodeling?

3. Refer to the statement of cash flows in the appendix on Toys "R" Us. How much did Toys "R" Us spend on property and equipment (capital expenditures, net) during 1995? Is this an increase or a decrease from prior years?

22. Joanne Lipman, "British Value Brand Names—Literally," *Wall Street Journal*, February 9, 1989, p. B4; and "Brand Name Policy Boosts Assets," *Accountancy*, October 1988, pp. 38–39.

Current Liabilities

1. Identify the management issues related to recognition, valuation, classification, and disclosure of current liabilities.

2. Identify, compute, and record definitely determinable current liabilities.

3. Identify, compute, and record estimated current liabilities.

4. Define *contingent liability*.

SUPPLEMENTAL OBJECTIVE

5. Compute and record the liabilities associated with payroll accounting.

USAir, Inc.

DECISION POINT

Liabilities are one of the three major parts of the balance sheet. They are legal obligations for the future payment of assets or the future performance of services that result from past transactions. For example, the current and long-term liabilities of USAir, Inc., which has total assets of almost $6.6 billion, are as follows (in millions):[1]

	1992	1991
Current Liabilities		
Current Maturities of Long-Term Debt	$ 250,019	$ 104,508
Accounts Payable	390,583	392,995
Traffic Balances Payable and Unused Tickets	622,428	513,356
Accrued Expenses	1,169,632	927,970
Total Current Liabilities	2,432,662	1,938,829
Long-Term Debt, Net of Current Maturities	2,264,944	2,114,902

Current Maturities of Long-Term Debt, Accounts Payable, and Accrued Expenses for the most part will require an outlay of cash in the next year. Traffic Balances Payable will require payments to other airlines, but those may be partially offset by amounts owed from other airlines. Unused Tickets are tickets already paid for by passengers and represent services that must be performed. Long-Term Debt will require cash outlays in future years. Altogether these liabilities represent more than 70 percent of total assets. How does the decision of USAir, Inc.'s management to incur so much debt relate to the goals of the business?

Liabilities are important because they are closely related to the goals of profitability and liquidity. Liabilities are sources of cash for operating, investing, and financing activities when they are incurred, but they are also obligations that use cash when they are paid as required. Achieving the appropriate level of liabilities is critical to business success. A company that has too few liabilities may not be earning up to its potential. A company that has too many liabilities, however, may be incurring excessive risks. This chapter focuses on the management and accounting issues involving current liabilities, including payroll liabilities and contingent liabilities. ∶∶∶∶∶

1. USAir, Inc., *Annual Report*, 1992.

OBJECTIVE

1 *Identify the management issues related to recognition, valuation, classification, and disclosure of current liabilities*

The primary reason for incurring current liabilities is to meet needs for cash during the operating cycle. The operating cycle is the process of converting cash to purchases, to sales, to accounts receivable, and back to cash. Most current liabilities arise in support of this cycle, as when accounts payable arise from purchases of inventory, accrued expenses arise from operating costs, and unearned revenues arise from customers' advance payments. Short-term debt is used to raise cash during periods of inventory build-up or while waiting for collection of receivables. Sometimes cash is used to pay current maturities of long-term debt, to make investments in long-term assets, or to pay cash dividends.

Failure to manage the cash flows related to current liabilities can have serious consequences for a business. For instance, if suppliers are not paid on time, they may withhold shipments that are vital to a company's operations. Continued failure to pay current liabilities can lead to bankruptcy. To evaluate a company's ability to pay its current liabilities, three measures of liquidity—working capital, the current ratio, and the quick ratio—are often used. Current liabilities are a key component of each of these measures. They typically equal from 25 to 50 percent of total assets, as may be seen in Figure 1. The proper identification and management of current liabilities requires an understanding of how they are recognized, valued, classified, and disclosed.

RECOGNITION OF LIABILITIES

Timing is important in the recognition of liabilities. The failure to record a liability in an accounting period very often goes along with the failure to record an expense. The two errors lead to an understatement of expense and an overstatement of income.

A liability is recorded when an obligation occurs. This rule is harder to apply than it might appear. When a transaction obligates a company to make future payments, a liability arises and is recognized, as when goods are bought on credit. However, current liabilities are often not represented by direct transactions. One of the key reasons for making adjusting entries at the end of an accounting period is to recognize unrecorded liabilities. Among these accrued liabilities are salaries payable and interest payable. Other liabilities that can only be estimated, such as taxes payable, must also be recognized through adjusting entries.

On the other hand, companies often enter into agreements for future transactions. For instance, a company may agree to pay an executive $50,000 a year for a period of three years, or a public utility may agree to buy an unspecified quantity of coal at a certain price over the next five years. Such contracts, though they are definite commitments, are not considered liabilities because they are for future—not past—transactions. As there is no current obligation, no liability is recognized.

VALUATION OF LIABILITIES

On the balance sheet, a liability is generally valued at the amount of money needed to pay the debt or at the fair market value of goods or services to be delivered. For most liabilities the amount is definitely known, but for some it

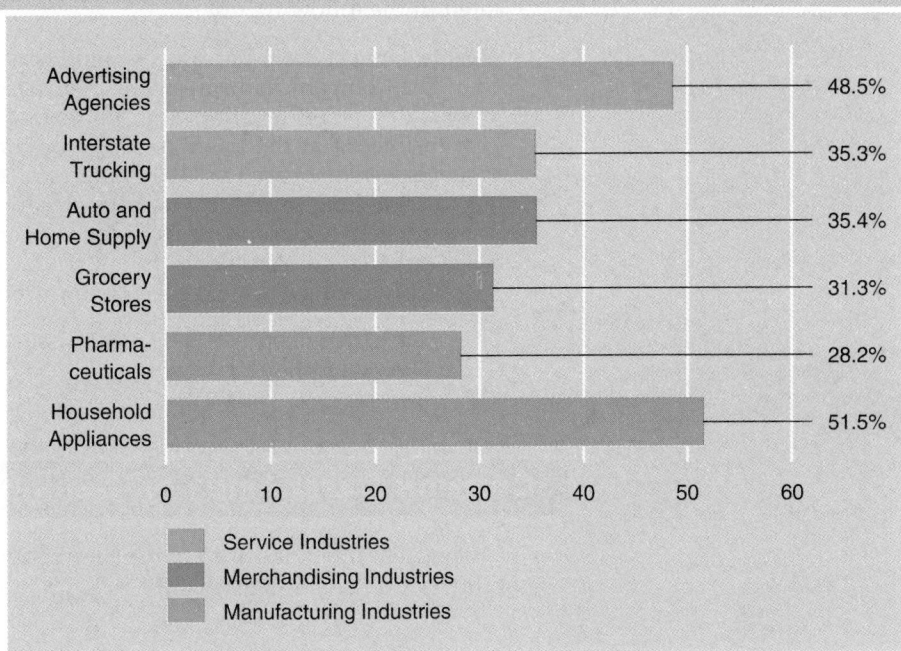

Figure 1. Current Liabilities as a Percentage of Total Assets for Selected Industries

Industry	Percentage
Advertising Agencies	48.5%
Interstate Trucking	35.3%
Auto and Home Supply	35.4%
Grocery Stores	31.3%
Pharmaceuticals	28.2%
Household Appliances	51.5%

Service Industries
Merchandising Industries
Manufacturing Industries

Source: Data from Dun and Bradstreet, *Industry Norms and Ratios,* 1993–94.

must be estimated. For example, an automobile dealer who sells a car with a one-year warranty must provide parts and service during the year. The obligation is definite because the sale of the car has occurred, but the amount of the obligation can only be estimated. Such estimates are usually based on past experience and anticipated changes in the business environment. Additional disclosures of the fair value of liabilities may be required in the notes to the financial statements, as explained below.

CLASSIFICATION OF LIABILITIES

The classification of liabilities directly matches the classification of assets. Current liabilities are debts and obligations expected to be satisfied within one year or within the normal operating cycle, whichever is longer. Such liabilities are normally paid out of current assets or with cash generated from operations. Long-term liabilities, which are liabilities due beyond one year or beyond the normal operating cycle, have a different purpose. They are used to finance long-term assets, such as aircraft in the case of USAir, Inc. The distinctions between current and long-term liabilities are important because they affect the evaluation of a company's liquidity.

DISCLOSURE OF LIABILITIES

To explain some accounts, supplemental disclosure may be required in the notes to the financial statements. For example, if a company has a large amount of notes payable, an explanatory note may disclose the balances, maturities, interest rates, and other features of the debts. Any special credit arrangements, such as issues of commercial paper and lines of credit, should also be disclosed. For example, Lowe's Companies, Inc., a large home center and consumer durables company, disclosed its credit arrangements as indicated in the following note.

> **Note 4, Short-Term Borrowings and Lines of Credit:**
> The Company had agreements with a group of banks at January 31, 1992, which provided for short-term unsecured borrowings of up to $60 million with interest at the lower of prime or bank transaction rate. These agreements were increased to $100 million effective February 1, 1992.
> In addition, several banks have extended lines of credit aggregating $75 million for the purpose of issuing documentary letters of credit and standby letters of credit. Another $240 million is available for the purpose of short-term borrowings on a bid basis from various banks.[2]

This type of disclosure is helpful in assessing whether a company has additional borrowing power.

COMMON CATEGORIES OF CURRENT LIABILITIES

Current liabilities fall into two major groups: (1) definitely determinable liabilities and (2) estimated liabilities.

OBJECTIVE

2 *Identify, compute, and record definitely determinable current liabilities*

DEFINITELY DETERMINABLE LIABILITIES

Current liabilities that are set by contract or by statute and can be measured exactly are called definitely determinable liabilities. The related accounting problems are to determine the existence and amount of each such liability and to see that it is recorded properly. Definitely determinable liabilities include accounts payable, bank loans and commercial paper, notes payable, accrued liabilities, dividends payable, sales and excise taxes payable, current portions of long-term debt, payroll liabilities, and unearned or deferred revenues.

Accounts Payable Accounts payable, sometimes called trade accounts payable, are short-term obligations to suppliers for goods and services. The amount in the Accounts Payable account is generally supported by an accounts payable subsidiary ledger, which contains an individual account for each person or company to whom money is owed.

Bank Loans and Commercial Paper Management will often establish a line of credit from a bank; this arrangement allows the company to borrow funds when they are needed to finance current operations. For example, Nordstrom, Inc., a chain of quality department stores, reported in its 1993 annual report that the finance division had "a $150 [million] unsecured line of credit with a group of commercial banks which is available as liquidity support for short-term debt."[3] A promissory note for the full amount of the line of credit is signed when the credit is granted, but the company has great flexibility in using the available funds. The company can increase its borrowing up to the limit when it needs cash and reduce the amount borrowed when it generates enough cash of its own. Both the amount borrowed and the inter-

---

2. Lowe's Companies, Inc., *Annual Report*, 1992.

3. Nordstrom, Inc., *Annual Report*, 1993.

Figure 2. Two Promissory Notes: One with Interest Stated Separately; One with Interest in the Face Amount

---

CASE 1: INTEREST STATED SEPARATELY

Chicago, Illinois   August 31, 19xx

Sixty days after date I promise to pay First Federal Bank the sum of $5,000 with interest at the rate of 12% per annum.

Sandra Caron
Caron Corporation

CASE 2: INTEREST IN FACE AMOUNT

Chicago, Illinois   August 31, 19xx

Sixty days after date I promise to pay First Federal Bank the sum of $5,000.

Sandra Caron
Caron Corporation

---

est rate charged by the bank may change daily. The bank may require the company to meet certain financial goals (such as maintaining specific profit margins, current ratios, or debt to equity ratios) to retain the line of credit. Companies with excellent credit ratings may borrow short-term funds by issuing commercial paper, unsecured loans sold to the public, usually through professionally managed investment firms. The portion of a line of credit currently borrowed and the amount of commercial paper issued are usually combined with notes payable in the current liabilities section of the balance sheet. Details are disclosed in a note to the financial statements.

Notes Payable   Short-term notes payable, which also arise out of the ordinary course of business, are obligations represented by promissory notes. These notes may be used to secure bank loans, to pay suppliers for goods and services, and to secure credit from other sources.

The interest may be stated separately on the face of the note (Case 1 in Figure 2), or it may be deducted in advance by discounting it from the face value of the note (Case 2). The entries to record the note in each case are as follows:

Case 1—Interest stated separately				Case 2—Interest in face amount		
Aug. 31	Cash	5,000		Aug. 31	Cash	4,900	
	Notes Payable		5,000		Discount on Notes Payable	100	
	Issued 60-day, 12% promissory note with interest stated separately				Notes Payable		5,000
					Issued 60-day promissory note with $100 interest included in face amount		

Note that in Case 1 the money received equaled the face value of the note, whereas in Case 2 the money received ($4,900) was less than the face value ($5,000) of the note. The amount of the discount equals the amount of the interest for sixty days. Although the dollar amount of interest on each of these notes is the same, the effective interest rate is slightly more in Case 2 because the amount received is slightly less ($4,900 in Case 2 versus $5,000 in Case 1). Discount on Notes Payable is a contra account to Notes Payable and is deducted from Notes Payable on the balance sheet.

On October 30, when the note is paid, each alternative is recorded as follows:

	Case 1—Interest stated separately					Case 2—Interest in face amount		
Oct. 30	Notes Payable	5,000			Oct. 30	Notes Payable	5,000	
	Interest Expense	100				Cash		5,000
	Cash		5,100			Payment of note with interest included in face amount		
	Payment of note with interest stated separately				30	Interest Expense	100	
	$5,000 \times \dfrac{60}{360} \times .12 = \$100$					Discount on Notes Payable		100
						Interest expense on note payable		

Accrued Liabilities   A key reason for making adjusting entries at the end of an accounting period is to recognize and record liabilities that are not already in the accounting records. This practice applies to any type of liability. As you will see, accrued liabilities can also include estimated liabilities.

Here the focus is on interest payable, a definitely determinable liability. Interest accrues daily on interest-bearing notes. At the end of the accounting period, an adjusting entry should be made in accordance with the matching rule to record the interest obligation up to that point in time. Let us again use the example of the two notes presented earlier in this chapter. If we assume that the accounting period ends on September 30, or thirty days after the issuance of the sixty-day notes, the adjusting entries for each case would be as follows:

	Case 1—Interest stated separately					Case 2—Interest in face amount		
Sept. 30	Interest Expense	50			Sept. 30	Interest Expense	50	
	Interest Payable		50			Discount on Notes Payable		50
	To record interest expense for 30 days on note with interest stated separately					To record interest expense for 30 days on note with interest included in face amount		
	$5,000 \times \dfrac{30}{360} \times .12 = \$50$					$100 \times \dfrac{30}{60} = \$50$		

In Case 2, Discount on Notes Payable will now have a debit balance of $50, which will become interest expense during the next thirty days.

Dividends Payable   Cash dividends are a distribution of earnings by a corporation. The payment of dividends is solely the decision of the corporation's board of directors. A liability does not exist until the board declares the dividends. There is usually a short time between the date of declaration and the date of payment of dividends. During that short time, the dividends declared are current liabilities of the corporation.

Sales and Excise Taxes Payable   Most states and many cities levy a sales tax on retail transactions. There is a federal excise tax on some products, such as automobile tires. A merchant who sells goods subject to these taxes must collect the taxes and forward them periodically to the appropriate government agency. The amount of tax collected represents a current liability until it is remitted to the government. For example, assume that a merchant makes a $100 sale that is subject to a 5 percent sales tax and a 10 percent excise tax. Assuming that the sale takes place on June 1, the entry to record the sale is as follows:

June 1	Cash	115	
	Sales		100
	Sales Tax Payable		5
	Excise Tax Payable		10
	Sale of merchandise and collection of sales and excise taxes		

The sale is properly recorded at $100, and tax collections are recorded as liabilities to be remitted at the proper times to the appropriate government agencies.

Current Portions of Long-Term Debt   If a portion of long-term debt is due within the next year and is to be paid from current assets, then that current portion is properly classified as a current liability. For example, suppose that a $500,000 debt is to be paid in installments of $100,000 per year for the next five years. The $100,000 installment due in the current year should be classified as a current liability. The remaining $400,000 should be classified as a long-term liability. Note that no journal entry is necessary. The total debt of $500,000 is simply reclassified when the financial statements are prepared, as follows:

Current Liabilities	
Current Portion of Long-Term Debt	$100,000
Long-Term Liabilities	
Long-Term Debt	400,000

Payroll Liabilities   For most companies, the cost of labor and related payroll taxes is a major expense. In some industries, such as banking and airlines, payroll costs represent more than half of all operating costs. Payroll accounting is important because complex laws and significant liabilities are involved. The employer is liable to employees for wages and salaries and to various agencies for amounts withheld from wages and salaries and for related taxes. The term wages refers to payment for the services of employees at an hourly rate. The term salaries refers to the compensation of employees who are paid at a monthly or yearly rate.

Because payroll accounting applies only to the employees of a company, it is important to distinguish between employees and independent contractors. Employees are paid a wage or salary by the company and are under its direct supervision and control. Independent contractors are not employees of the company, so they are not accounted for under the payroll system. They offer services to the firm for a fee, but they are not under its direct control or supervision. Some examples of independent contractors are certified public accountants, advertising agencies, and lawyers.

Figure 3 provides an illustration of payroll liabilities and their relation to employee earnings and employer taxes and other costs. Two important observations may be made. First, the amount payable to employees is less than the amount of earnings. This occurs because employers are required by law or are requested by employees to withhold certain amounts from wages and send them directly to government agencies or other organizations. Second, the total employer liabilities exceed employee earnings because the employer must pay additional taxes and make other contributions, such as for pensions and medical care, that increase the cost. The most common withholdings, taxes, and other payroll costs are described below.

Federal Income Taxes Federal income taxes are collected on a "pay as you go" basis. Employers are required to withhold appropriate taxes from employees' paychecks and pay them to the Internal Revenue Service.

State and Local Income Taxes Most states and some local governments have income taxes. In most cases, the procedures for withholding are similar to those for federal income taxes.

Social Security (FICA) Tax The social security program (the Federal Insurance Contribution Act) offers retirement and disability benefits and survivor's benefits. About 90 percent of the people working in the United States fall under the provisions of this program. The 1994 social security tax rate of 6.20 percent was paid by *both* employee and employer on the first $61,200 earned by an employee during the calendar year. Both the rate and the base to which it applies are subject to change in future years.

Medicare Tax A major extension of the social security program is Medicare, which provides hospitalization and medical insurance for persons over age 65. In 1994, the Medicare tax rate was 1.45 percent of gross income, with no limit, paid by *both* employee and employer.

Medical Insurance Many companies provide medical benefits to employees. Often, the employee contributes a portion of the cost through withholdings from income and the employer pays the rest, usually a greater amount, to the insurance company. Some proposals for national health-care reform, if they become law, could change substantially the way medical insurance is funded and provided in this country.

Pension Contributions Many companies also provide pension benefits to employees. In a manner similar to medical insurance, a portion of the pension contribution is withheld from the employee's income and the rest is paid by the company to the pension fund.

Federal Unemployment Insurance (FUTA) Tax This tax, abbreviated FUTA after the Federal Unemployment Tax Act, is intended to pay for programs to help unemployed workers. It is paid *only* by employers and recently was 6.2 percent of the first $9,000 earned by each employee. Against this federal tax, however, the employer is allowed a credit for unemployment taxes paid to the state. The maximum credit is 5.4 percent of the first $9,000 earned by each employee. Most states set their rate at this maximum. Thus, the FUTA tax most often paid is .8 percent (6.2 percent − 5.4 percent) of the taxable wages.

State Unemployment Insurance Tax All state unemployment programs provide for unemployment compensation to be paid to eligible unemployed workers. This compensation is paid out of the fund provided by the 5.4 percent of the first $9,000 earned by each employee. In some states, employers with favorable employment records may be entitled to pay less than 5.4 percent.

Figure 3. Illustration of Payroll Liabilities

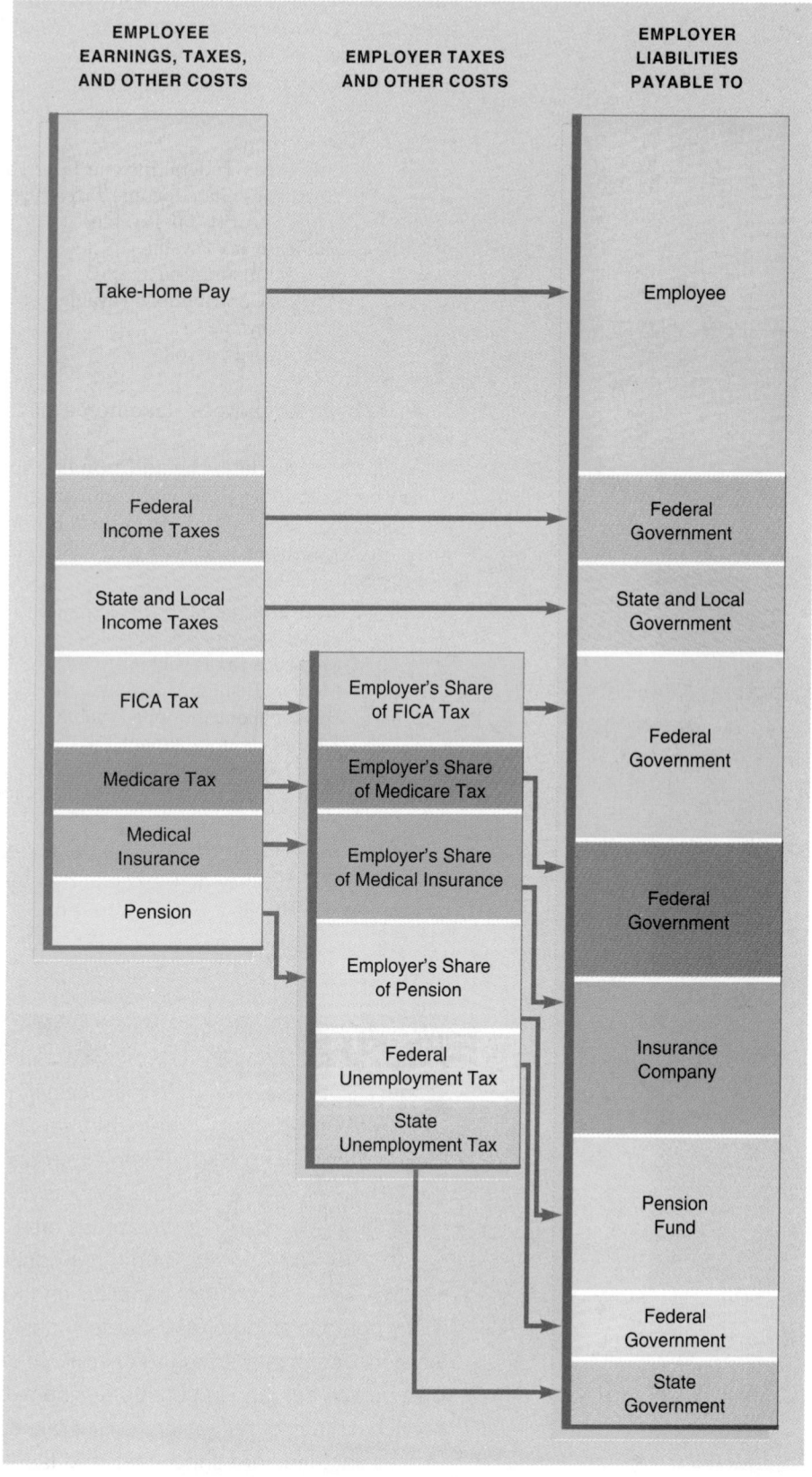

To illustrate the recording of the payroll, assume that on February 15 total employee wages are $32,500, with withholdings of $5,400 for federal income taxes, $1,200 for state income taxes, $2,015 for social security tax, $471 for Medicare tax, $900 for medical insurance, and $1,300 for pension contributions. The entry to record this payroll is

Feb. 15	Wages Expense	32,500	
	Employees' Federal Income Taxes Payable		5,400
	Employees' State Income Taxes Payable		1,200
	Social Security Tax Payable		2,015
	Medicare Tax Payable		471
	Medical Insurance Payable		900
	Pension Contributions Payable		1,300
	Wages Payable		21,214
	To record payroll		

Note that the employees' take-home pay is only $21,214, although $32,500 was earned.

Using the same data, the additional employer taxes and other benefits costs would be recorded as follows, assuming that the payroll taxes correspond to the discussion above and that the employer pays 80 percent of the medical insurance premiums and half of the pension contributions.

Feb. 15	Payroll Taxes and Benefits Expense	9,401	
	Social Security Tax Payable		2,015
	Medicare Tax Payable		471
	Medical Insurance Payable		3,600
	Pension Contributions Payable		1,300
	Federal Unemployment Tax Payable		260
	State Unemployment Tax Payable		1,755
	To record payroll taxes and other costs		

Note that the payroll taxes increase the total cost of the payroll to $41,901 ($9,401 + $32,500), which exceeds by almost 29 percent the amount earned by employees. This is a typical situation.

BUSINESS BULLETIN: TECHNOLOGY IN PRACTICE

The processing of payroll is an ideal application of computers because it is a very routine and complex procedure that must be done with absolute accuracy: Employees want to be paid exactly what they are owed, and failure to pay the taxes and other costs as required can result in severe penalties and high interest charges. Consequently, many companies purchase carefully designed and tested computer software for use in preparing the payroll. Other companies do not process their own payroll but rely on outside businesses that specialize in providing such services. Many of these service suppliers, such as Automatic Data Processing, Inc., are successful and fast growing.

Unearned Revenues   Unearned revenues represent obligations for goods or services that the company must provide or deliver in a future accounting period in return for an advance payment from a customer. For example, a publisher of a monthly magazine who receives annual subscriptions totaling $240 would make the following entry.

Cash	240	
Unearned Subscriptions		240
Receipt of annual subscriptions		
in advance		

The publisher now has a liability of $240 that will be reduced gradually as monthly issues of the magazine are mailed.

Unearned Subscriptions	20	
Subscription Revenues		20
Delivery of monthly magazine issues		

Many businesses, such as repair companies, construction companies, and special-order firms, ask for a deposit or advance from a customer before they will begin work. Such advances are also current liabilities until the goods or services are delivered.

DECISION POINT

American Airlines, Inc.

In the early 1980s American Airlines, Inc. developed a frequent-flyer program that gave free trips and other awards to customers based on the number of miles they flew on the airline. Since then, the number of similar programs offered by other airlines has mushroomed, and it is estimated that 30 million people now belong to the airlines' frequent-flyer programs. Today, U.S. airlines have 1.4 trillion miles outstanding, which is estimated to be enough for 70 million domestic trips. Almost half the "miles" have been earned on purchases from hotel, car rental, and telephone companies and from the use of credit cards. The airlines claim a strong belief in these programs because they build customer loyalty. But some are questioning whether or not they are worth the cost. For example, it is estimated that at the end of 1993, American Airlines owed $380 million of awards to frequent flyers, or 9 percent of its total liabilities. Frequent-flyer awards accounted for 9.5 percent of the miles flown on American in 1993.[4] Are these figures good estimates of the true costs, and is the program worth the costs to the company?

This is a complex question for both business and accounting reasons. For example, competition from low-priced no-frills competitors is threatening the major airlines. On KIWI International, which has no frequent-flyer program, an unrestricted ticket from Newark to Chicago costs $208,

---

4. Julie Schmit, "Cost Cutters Want Frequent Fliers Downed," *USA Today,* June 9, 1994.

but on American, a similar ticket costs over $800. To get one free trip on American, a flyer would have to spend $12,400 for flights that would cost just $3,000 on KIWI. Eliminating or reducing the frequent-flyer programs would save costs for the major air carriers and make them more competitive. But it could also cost them loyal customers. Although many businesses want their employees to fly the low-cost airlines, the employees prefer to fly the majors because of the free tickets they may earn. American and the other majors do not want to alienate their loyal customers, but they also need to compete.

A key component of American's decision-making process is the accounting estimate of the potential cost and resulting liability of its frequent-flyer program. Estimation of the true cost is difficult because it depends on projections of future actions. For example, it is estimated that only 25 percent of frequent-flyer miles are ever redeemed. If this ratio changes, it will affect the projected costs. Airlines also say that the cost is not significant because only 64 percent of domestic airline seats are filled, leaving plenty of room for free travelers. If a free traveler occupies a seat that would otherwise have been empty, the incremental cost is minimal. Estimated liabilities such as those associated with frequent-flyer plans are becoming an important consideration when evaluating an airline's financial position. ⦂ ⦂ ⦂

OBJECTIVE

3 *Identify, compute, and record estimated current liabilities*

ESTIMATED LIABILITIES

Estimated liabilities are definite debts or obligations of which the exact dollar amount cannot be known until a later date. Since there is no doubt about the existence of the legal obligation, the primary accounting problem is to estimate and record the amount of the liability. Examples of estimated liabilities are income taxes, property tax, product warranties, and vacation pay.

Income Taxes   The income of a corporation is taxed by the federal government, most state governments, and some cities and towns. The amount of income taxes liability depends on the results of operations. Often the results are not known until after the end of the year. However, because income taxes are an expense in the year in which income is earned, an adjusting entry is necessary to record the estimated tax liability. The entry is as follows:

Dec. 31	Federal Income Taxes Expense	53,000	
	Estimated Federal Income Taxes Payable		53,000
	To record estimated federal income taxes		

Remember that sole proprietorships and partnerships do *not* pay income taxes. Their owners must report their share of the firm's income on their individual tax returns.

Property Tax Payable   Property taxes are levied on real property, such as land and buildings, and on personal property, such as inventory and equipment. Property taxes are a main source of revenue for local governments. They are usually assessed annually against the property involved. Because the fiscal years of local governments and their assessment dates rarely correspond to a firm's fiscal year, it is necessary to estimate the amount of property tax that applies to each month of the year. Assume, for instance, that a local government has a fiscal year of July 1 to June 30, that its assessment date is November 1 for the current fiscal year, and that its payment date is December 15. Assume also that on July 1, Janis Corporation estimates that its property tax assessment for the coming year will be $24,000. The adjusting entry to be made on July 31, which would be repeated on August 31, September 30, and October 31, would be as follows:

July 31	Property Tax Expense	2,000	
	Estimated Property Tax Payable		2,000
	To record estimated property tax		
	expense for the month		
	$24,000 \div 12$ months $= \$2,000$		

On November 1, the firm receives a property tax bill for $24,720. The estimate made in July was too low. The charge should have been $2,060 per month. Because the difference between the actual assessment and the estimate is small, the company decides to absorb in November the amount undercharged in the previous four months. Therefore, the property tax expense for November is $2,300 [$2,060 + 4($60)] and is recorded as follows:

Nov. 30	Property Tax Expense	2,300	
	Estimated Property Tax Payable		2,300
	To record estimated property tax		

The Estimated Property Tax Payable account now has a balance of $10,300. The entry to record payment on December 15 would be as follows:

Dec. 15	Estimated Property Tax Payable	10,300	
	Prepaid Property Tax	14,420	
	Cash		24,720
	Payment of property tax		

Beginning December 31 and each month afterward until June 30, property tax expense is recorded by a debit to Property Tax Expense and a credit to Prepaid Property Tax in the amount of $2,060. The total of these seven entries will reduce the Prepaid Property Tax account to zero on June 30.

Product Warranty Liability   When a firm places a warranty or guarantee on its product at the time of sale, a liability exists for the length of the warranty. The cost of the warranty is properly debited to an expense account in the period of sale because it is a feature of the product or service sold and thus is included in the price paid by the customer for the product. On the basis of experience, it should be possible to estimate the amount the warranty will cost in the future. Some products or services will require little warranty service; others may require much. Thus, there will be an average cost per product or service.

For example, assume that a muffler company guarantees that it will replace free of charge any muffler it sells that fails during the time the buyer owns the car. The company charges a small service fee for replacing the muffler. This guarantee is an important selling feature for the firm's mufflers. In the past, 6 percent of the mufflers sold have been returned for replacement under the guarantee. The average cost of a muffler is $25. Assume that during July, 350 mufflers were sold. The accrued liability would be recorded as an adjustment at the end of July as shown at the top of the next page.

July 31	Product Warranty Expense	525	
	Estimated Product Warranty Liability		525
	To record estimated product warranty expense:		
	Number of units sold	350	
	Rate of replacement under warranty	× .06	
	Estimated units to be replaced	21	
	Estimated cost per unit	× $ 25	
	Estimated liability for product warranty	$525	

When a muffler is returned for replacement under the warranty, the cost of the muffler is charged against the Estimated Product Warranty Liability account. For example, assume that on December 5 a customer returns with a defective muffler and pays a $10 service fee to have the muffler replaced. Assume that this particular muffler cost $20. The entry is as follows:

Dec. 5	Cash	10	
	Estimated Product Warranty Liability	20	
	Service Revenue		10
	Merchandise Inventory		20
	Replacement of muffler under warranty		

BUSINESS BULLETIN: BUSINESS PRACTICE

Many companies promote their products by issuing coupons that offer "cents off" or other enticements for purchasers. Since four out of five shoppers use coupons, companies are forced by competition to distribute them. The total value of unredeemed coupons, each of which represents a potential liability for the issuing company, is truly staggering. NCH Promotional Services, a company owned by Dun and Bradstreet, estimates that more than 300 billion coupons were issued in 1993. Of course, the liability depends on how many of the coupons will actually be redeemed. NCH estimates that number at approximately 7 billion, or about 2.3 percent. That is not a large percentage, but the value of the redeemed coupons is estimated to be more than $4 billion.[5]

Vacation Pay Liability   In most companies, employees earn the right to paid vacation days or weeks as they work during the year. For example, an employee may earn two weeks of paid vacation for each fifty weeks of work. Therefore, the person is paid fifty-two weeks' salary for fifty weeks' work. Theoretically, the cost of the two weeks' vacation should be allocated as an expense over the whole year so that month-to-month costs will not be distorted. The vacation pay represents 4 percent (two weeks' vacation divided by fifty weeks) of a worker's pay. Every week worked earns the employee a small

5. "Coupons Show Less Redeeming Value," *Chicago Tribune,* July 16, 1993.

fraction (4 percent) of vacation pay. Vacation pay liability can amount to a substantial amount of money. For example, Delta Airlines reported at its 1992 year end a vacation pay liability of $192,198,000.[6]

Suppose that a company with a vacation policy of two weeks of paid vacation for each fifty weeks of work has a payroll of $21,000, of which $1,000 was paid to employees on vacation for the week ended April 20. Since not all employees in every company will collect vacation pay because of turnover and rules regarding term of employment, it is assumed that 75 percent of employees will ultimately collect vacation pay. The computation of vacation pay expense based on the payroll of employees not on vacation ($21,000 − $1,000) is as follows: $20,000 × 4 percent × 75 percent = $600. The entry to record vacation pay expense for the week ended April 20 is as follows:

Apr. 20 Vacation Pay Expense	600	
Estimated Liability for Vacation Pay		600
Estimated vacation pay expense		

At the time employees receive their vacation pay, an entry is made debiting Estimated Liability for Vacation Pay and crediting Cash or Wages Payable. For example, the entry to record the $1,000 paid to employees on vacation is as follows:

Aug. 31 Estimated Liability for Vacation Pay	1,000	
Cash (or Wages Payable)		1,000
Wages of employees on vacation		

The treatment presented in this example for vacation pay may also be applied to other payroll costs, such as bonus plans and contributions to pension plans.

BUSINESS BULLETIN: BUSINESS PRACTICE

Estimated liabilities are presenting greater challenges to accountants as many companies attempt to mimic the success of frequent-flyer programs. For example, if you frequently stay at Holiday Inns, you can earn a three-day tour of castles in the Bavarian Alps, a Magnavox computer, or a Canon Camcorder. Rent cars from Avis or Thrifty and earn points to stay at Sheraton Hotels. Rent cars from Dollar or General and earn a $1,000 U. S. savings bond. If you have a MasterCard issued by General Motors, for every dollar you spend, you receive a nickel credit toward a new car, up to $500 per year. Buy from vendors like MCI, Club Med, Hertz, General Electric Capital, Eddie Bauer, and Spiegel and earn credits toward a retirement account. In each company, accountants must estimate how and when consumers will redeem their points as well as the costs of providing the premiums.[7]

6. Delta Airlines, *Annual Report*, 1992.

7. Brigid McMenamin, "The Great Giveaway," *Forbes*, January 18, 1993.

CONTINGENT LIABILITIES

OBJECTIVE

4 *Define* contingent liability

A contingent liability is not an existing liability. Rather, it is a potential liability because it depends on a future event arising out of a past transaction. For instance, a construction company that built a bridge may have been sued by the state for using poor materials. The past transaction is the building of the bridge under contract. The future event is the outcome of the lawsuit, which is not yet known.

Two conditions have been established by the FASB for determining when a contingency should be entered in the accounting records: (1) the liability must be probable and (2) it must be reasonably estimated.[8] Estimated liabilities such as the estimated income taxes liability, warranty liability, and vacation pay liability that were described earlier in this chapter meet those conditions. Therefore, they are accrued in the accounting records. Potential liabilities that do not meet both conditions (probable and reasonably estimated) are reported in the notes to the financial statements. Losses from such potential liabilities are recorded when the conditions set by the FASB are met. The following example comes from the notes in an annual report of Humana, Inc., one of the largest health services organizations.

Management continually evaluates contingencies based upon the best available evidence. In addition, allowances for loss are provided currently for disputed items that have continuing significance, such as certain third-party reimbursements and deductions that continue to be claimed in current cost reports and tax returns.

Management believes that allowances for loss have been provided to the extent necessary and that its assessment of contingencies is reasonable. To the extent that resolution of contingencies results in amounts that vary from management's estimates, earnings will be charged or credited.

Hospitals' principal contingencies are described below:

Revenues—Certain third-party payments are subject to examination by agencies administering the programs. Management is contesting certain issues raised in audits of prior year cost reports.

Professional Liability Risks—Hospitals has provided for loss for professional liability risks based upon actuarially determined estimates. Actual settlements and expenses incident thereto may differ from the provisions for loss. See Note 5.

Interest Rate Agreements—Hospitals has entered into agreements which reduce the impact of changes in interest rates on its floating rate long-term debt. In the event of nonperformance by other parties to these agreements, Hospitals may incur a loss based on the difference between market rates and the contract rates.

Income Taxes—Management is contesting adjustments proposed by the Internal Revenue Service for years 1988 and 1989.

Litigation—Various suits and claims arising in the ordinary course of business are pending against Hospitals.[9]

Contingent liabilities may also arise from failure to follow government regulations, from discounted notes receivable, and from guarantees of the debt of other companies.

---

8. *Statement of Financial Accounting Standards No. 5,* "Accounting for Contingencies" (Stamford, Conn.: Financial Accounting Standards Board, 1975).

9. Humana, Inc., *Annual Report,* 1992.

**Supplemental
OBJECTIVE**

5 *Compute and
record the liabili-
ties associated with
payroll accounting*

PAYROLL ACCOUNTING ILLUSTRATED

Earlier in this chapter, the liabilities associated with payroll accounting were identified and discussed. This section will focus on the calculations, records, and control requirements of payroll accounting. To demonstrate the concepts, the illustrations are shown in manual format, but, in actual practice, most businesses (including small businesses) use a computer to process payroll.

COMPUTATION OF AN EMPLOYEE'S TAKE-HOME PAY

Besides setting minimum wage levels, the federal Fair Labor Standards Act (also called the Wages and Hours Law) regulates overtime pay. Employers who take part in interstate commerce must pay overtime to employees who work beyond forty hours a week or more than eight hours a day. This pay must be at least one and one-half times the regular rate. Work on Saturdays, Sundays, or holidays may also call for overtime or some sort of premium pay under separate wage agreements. Overtime pay under union or other employment contracts may exceed these minimums.

For example, suppose that the employment contract of Robert Jones calls for a regular wage of $8 an hour, one and one-half times the regular rate for work over eight hours in any weekday, and twice the regular rate for work on Saturdays, Sundays, or holidays. He works the following days and hours during the week of January 18, 19xx.

Day	Total Hours Worked	Regular Time	Overtime
Monday	10	8	2
Tuesday	8	8	0
Wednesday	8	8	0
Thursday	9	8	1
Friday	10	8	2
Saturday	2	0	2
	47	40	7

Jones's wages would be calculated as follows:

Regular time	40 hours × $8	$320
Overtime, weekdays	5 hours × $8 × 1.5	60
Overtime, weekend	2 hours × $8 × 2	32
Total wages		$412

Once Jones's wages are known, his take-home pay can be calculated. Since his total earnings for the week of January 18 are $412.00, his social security tax is 6.2 percent, or $25.54 (he has not earned over $61,200), and his Medicare tax is 1.45 percent, or $5.97. The amount to be withheld for federal income taxes depends in part on Jones's earnings and on the number of his exemptions. All employees are required by law to indicate exemptions by filing a Form W-4 (Employee's Withholding Exemption Certificate). Every employee is entitled to one exemption for himself or herself and one for each dependent. Based on the information in the Form W-4, the amount of withholding is determined by referring to a withholding table provided by the Internal Revenue Service. For example, the withholding table in Figure 4 shows that for Jones, a married employee who has a total of four exemptions

Figure 4. Sample Withholding Table

		WEEKLY PAYROLL PERIOD—EMPLOYEE MARRIED										
		And the number of withholding allowances claimed is—										
And the wages are—		0	1	2	3	4	5	6	7	8	9	10 or more
At least	But less than	The amount of income tax to be withheld will be—										
$300	$310	$37	$31	$26	$20	$14	$ 9	$ 3	$ 0	$ 0	$0	$0
310	320	38	33	27	22	16	10	5	0	0	0	0
320	330	40	34	29	23	17	12	6	1	0	0	0
330	340	41	36	30	25	19	13	8	2	0	0	0
340	350	43	37	32	26	20	15	9	4	0	0	0
350	360	44	39	33	28	22	16	11	5	0	0	0
360	370	46	40	35	29	23	18	12	7	1	0	0
370	380	47	42	36	31	25	19	14	8	2	0	0
380	390	49	43	38	32	26	21	15	10	4	0	0
390	400	50	45	39	34	28	22	17	11	5	0	0
400	410	52	46	41	35	29	24	18	13	7	1	0
410	420	53	48	42	37	31	25	20	14	8	3	0
420	430	55	49	44	38	32	27	21	16	10	4	0

and is paid weekly, the withholding on total wages of $412 is $31. Actual withholding tables change periodically to reflect changes in tax rates and laws. Assume also that Jones's union dues are $2.00, his medical insurance premiums are $7.60, his life insurance premium is $6.00, he places $15.00 per week in savings bonds, and he contributes $1.00 per week to United Charities. His net (take-home) pay is computed as follows:

Total earnings		$412.00
Deductions		
Federal income taxes withheld	$31.00	
Social security tax	25.54	
Medicare tax	5.97	
Union dues	2.00	
Medical insurance	7.60	
Life insurance	6.00	
Savings bonds	15.00	
United Charities contribution	1.00	
Total deductions		94.11
Net (take-home) pay		$317.89

PAYROLL REGISTER

The payroll register, which is prepared each pay period, is a detailed listing of the firm's total payroll. A payroll register is presented in Exhibit 1. Note that the name, hours, earnings, deductions, and net pay of each employee are listed. Compare the entry for Robert Jones in the payroll register with the January 18 entry in the employee earnings record of Robert Jones presented

Exhibit 1. Payroll Register

Payroll Register   **Pay Period: Week ended January 18**

Employee	Total Hours	Regular	Overtime	Gross	Federal Income Taxes	Social Security Tax	Medicare Tax	Union Dues	Medical Insurance	Life Insurance	Savings Bonds	Other: A—United Charities	Net Earnings	Check No.	Sales Wages Expense	Office Wages Expense
Linda Duval	40	160.00		160.00	11.00	9.92	2.32		5.80				130.96	923		160.00
John Franks	44	160.00	24.00	184.00	14.00	11.41	2.67	2.00	7.60			A 10.00	136.32	924	184.00	
Samuel Goetz	40	400.00		400.00	53.00	24.80	5.80		10.40	14.00		A 3.00	289.00	925	400.00	
Robert Jones	47	320.00	92.00	412.00	31.00	25.54	5.97	2.00	7.60	6.00	15.00	A 1.00	317.89	926	412.00	
Billie Matthews	40	160.00		160.00	14.00	9.92	2.32		5.80				127.96	927		160.00
Rosaire O'Brien	42	200.00	20.00	220.00	22.00	13.64	3.19	2.00	5.80				173.37	928	220.00	
James Van Dyke	40	200.00		200.00	20.00	12.40	2.90		5.80				158.90	929		200.00
		1,600.00	136.00	1,736.00	165.00	107.63	25.17	6.00	48.80	20.00	15.00	14.00	1,334.40		1,216.00	520.00

in Exhibit 2. Except for the first column, which lists the employee names, and the last two columns, which show the wage or salary as either sales or office expense, the columns are the same. The columns help employers record the payroll in the accounting records and meet legal reporting requirements. The last two columns in Exhibit 1 are needed to divide the expenses in the accounting records into selling and administrative categories.

Exhibit 2. Employee Earnings Record

Employee Earnings Record

Employee's Name Robert Jones   **Social Security Number** 444-66-9999

Address 777 20th Street   **Sex** Male   **Employee No.** 705

Marshall, Michigan 52603   **Single** ___ **Married** X   **Weekly Pay Rate** ___

Date of Birth September 20, 1962   **Exemptions (W-4)** 4   **Hourly Rate** $8

Position Sales Assistant   **Date of Employment** July 15, 1988   **Date Employment Ended** ___

Period Ended	Total Hours	Regular	Overtime	Gross	Social Security Tax	Medicare Tax	Federal Income Taxes	Union Dues	Medical Insurance	Life Insurance	Savings Bonds	Other: A—United Charities	Net Earnings	Check No.	Cumulative Gross Earnings
Jan 4	40	320.00	0	320.00	19.84	4.64	17.00	2.00	7.60	6.00	15.00	A 1.00	246.92	717	320.00
11	44	320.00	48.00	368.00	22.82	5.34	23.00	2.00	7.60	6.00	15.00	A 1.00	285.24	822	688.00
18	47	320.00	92.00	412.00	25.54	5.97	31.00	2.00	7.60	6.00	15.00	A 1.00	317.89	926	1,100.00

Payroll fraud is a common form of financial wrongdoing because there are strong motivations for both the employee and the employer to cheat. Some employees want to be paid cash "under the table" to avoid income, social security, and Medicare taxes. Some employers may wish to avoid paying their share of social security and Medicare taxes as well as other payroll taxes and employee benefits. Therefore, the Internal Revenue Service cracks down on cheaters. It investigates, for example, the relationships between restaurants' revenues and the tip income that employees report on their tax returns. Severe penalties, including prison terms, can result from false reporting. Good accounting records and controls over payroll help ensure compliance with the law. ═══

RECORDING THE PAYROLL

The journal entry for recording the payroll is based on the column totals from the payroll register. The journal entry to record the January 18 payroll follows. Note that each account debited or credited is a total from the payroll register. If the payroll register is considered a special-purpose journal, the column totals can be posted directly to the ledger accounts, with the correct account numbers shown at the bottom of each column.

Jan. 18	Sales Wages Expense	1,216.00	
	Office Wages Expense	520.00	
	Employees' Federal Income Taxes Payable		165.00
	Social Security Tax Payable		107.63
	Medicare Tax Payable		25.17
	Union Dues Payable		6.00
	Medical Insurance Premiums Payable		48.80
	Life Insurance Premiums Payable		20.00
	Savings Bonds Payable		15.00
	United Charities Payable		14.00
	Wages Payable		1,334.40
	To record payroll		

EMPLOYEE EARNINGS RECORD

Each employer must keep a record of earnings and withholdings for each employee. Many companies today use computers to maintain such records, but some small companies may still use manual records. The manual form of employee earnings record for Robert Jones is shown in Exhibit 2. This form is designed to help the employer meet legal reporting requirements. Each deduction must be shown to have been paid to the proper agency and the employee must receive a report of the deductions made each year. Most columns are self-explanatory. Note, however, the column on the far right for cumulative gross earnings (total earnings to date). This record helps the employer comply with the rule of applying social security and unemployment taxes only up to the maximum wage levels. At the end of the year, the employer reports to the employee on Form W-2, the Wage and Tax Statement, the total earnings and tax deductions for the year, which the employee uses to complete his or her individual tax return. The employer sends a copy of the W-2 to the Internal Revenue Service. Thus, the IRS can check whether the employee has reported all income earned from that employer.

RECORDING PAYROLL TAXES

According to Exhibit 1, the gross payroll for the week ended January 18 was $1,736.00. Because it was the first month of the year, all employees had accumulated less than the $61,200 and $9,000 maximum taxable salaries. Therefore, the total social security tax was $107.63 and the total Medicare tax was $25.17 (equal to tax on employees); the total FUTA tax was $13.89 (.008 $\times$ $1,736.00); and the total state unemployment tax was $93.74 (.054 $\times$ $1,736.00). The entry to record this expense and related liability in the general journal is as follows:

Jan. 18	Payroll Taxes Expense	240.43	
	Social Security Tax Payable		107.63
	Medicare Tax Payable		25.17
	Federal Unemployment Tax Payable		13.89
	State Unemployment Tax Payable		93.74
	To record payroll taxes		

PAYMENT OF PAYROLL AND PAYROLL TAXES

After the weekly payroll is recorded, as illustrated earlier, a liability of $1,334.40 exists for wages payable. How this liability will be paid depends on the system used by the company. Many companies use a special payroll account against which payroll checks are drawn. Under this system, a check must first be drawn on the regular checking account for total net earnings for this payroll ($1,334.40) and deposited in the special payroll account before the payroll checks are issued to the employees. If a voucher system is combined with a special payroll account, a voucher for the total wages payable is prepared and recorded in the voucher register as a debit to Payroll Bank Account and a credit to Vouchers Payable.

The combined social security and Medicare taxes (both employees' and employer's shares) and the federal income taxes must be paid at least quarterly. More frequent payments are required when the total liability exceeds $500. The federal unemployment insurance tax is paid yearly if the amount is less than $100. If the liability for FUTA tax exceeds $100 at the end of any quarter, a payment is necessary. Payment dates vary among the states. Other payroll deductions must be paid in accordance with the particular contracts or agreements involved.

CHAPTER REVIEW

REVIEW OF LEARNING OBJECTIVES

1. **Identify the management issues related to recognition, valuation, classification, and disclosure of current liabilities.** Liabilities represent legal obligations for future payment of assets or future performance of services. They result from past transactions and should be recognized when a transaction obligates the company to make future payments. Liabilities are valued at the amount of money necessary to satisfy the obligation or the fair value of goods or services that must be delivered. Liabilities are classified as current or long term. Supplemental disclosure is required when the nature or details of the obligations would help in understanding the liability.

2. **Identify, compute, and record definitely determinable current liabilities.** Two principal categories of current liabilities are definitely determinable liabilities and estimated liabilities. Although the amounts of definitely determinable liabilities, such as accounts payable, notes payable, dividends payable, accrued liabilities, payroll liabilities, and the current portion of long-term debt, can be measured exactly, the accountant must still be careful to identify all existing liabilities in those categories. For most companies, the cost of labor and related payroll taxes is a significant expense. The employer is liable to employees for wages and salaries and to various agencies for amounts withheld from wages and salaries and for related taxes. The most common payroll withholdings are social security and Medicare taxes, federal and state income taxes, and employee-requested withholdings. The principal employer-paid taxes are social security and Medicare (amounts equal to those of the employee) and federal and state unemployment compensation taxes.

3. **Identify, compute, and record estimated current liabilities.** Estimated liabilities are definite obligations of the business. However, their exact dollar amount is more difficult to determine than the amount of definitely determinable liabilities because they depend on future events. Examples include liabilities for income taxes, property taxes, and product warranties. The accountant must estimate the probable amount of each such liability and record appropriate adjusting entries when the actual amounts are known.

4. **Define *contingent liability*.** A contingent liability is a potential liability arising from a past transaction and dependent on a future event. Examples are lawsuits, income tax disputes, discounted notes receivable, guarantees of debt, and the potential cost of changes in government regulations.

SUPPLEMENTAL OBJECTIVE

5. **Compute and record the liabilities associated with payroll accounting.** Computations for payroll liabilities must be made for the compensation to each employee, for withholdings from each employee's total pay, and for the employer portion of payroll taxes. The salary and deductions for each employee are recorded each pay period in the payroll register. From the payroll register the details of each employee's earnings are transferred to the employee's earnings record. The column totals of the payroll register are used to prepare a general journal entry that records the payroll and accompanying liabilities. The employer's share of social security and Medicare taxes and the federal and state unemployment taxes as well as any liabilities for other fringe benefits must then be recorded.

REVIEW OF CONCEPTS AND TERMINOLOGY

The following concepts and terms were introduced in this chapter.

L O 2 **Commercial paper:** A means of borrowing funds by using unsecured short-term loans sold directly to the public, usually through professionally managed investment firms.

L O 4 **Contingent liability:** A potential liability that depends on a future event arising out of a past transaction.

L O 1 **Current liabilities:** Debts and obligations expected to be satisfied within one year or within the normal operating cycle, whichever is longer.

L O 2 **Definitely determinable liabilities:** Current liabilities that are set by contract or by statute and can be measured exactly.

S O 5 **Employee earnings record:** A record of earnings and withholdings for an individual employee.

L O 3 **Estimated liabilities:** Definite debts or obligations of which the exact dollar amount cannot be known until a later date.

L O 1 **Liabilities:** Legal obligations for the future payment of assets or the future performance of services that result from past transactions.

L O 2 **Line of credit:** A preapproved arrangement with a commercial bank that allows a company to borrow funds as needed.

L O 1 **Long-term liabilities:** Debts or obligations due beyond one year or beyond the normal operating cycle.

S O 5 **Payroll register:** A detailed listing of a firm's total payroll that is prepared each pay period.

L O 2 **Salaries:** Compensation to employees who are paid at a monthly or yearly rate.

L O 2 **Unearned revenues:** Revenues received in advance for which the goods will not be delivered or the services not performed during the current accounting period.

L O 2 **Wages:** Payment for services of employees at an hourly rate.

REVIEW PROBLEM
NOTES PAYABLE TRANSACTIONS AND END-OF-PERIOD ENTRIES

L O 2 McLaughlin, Inc., whose fiscal year ends June 30, completed the following transactions involving notes payable.

May 11 Purchased a small crane by issuing a 60-day, 12 percent note for $54,000. The face of the note does not include interest.
16 Obtained a $40,000 loan from the bank to finance a temporary increase in receivables by signing a 90-day, 10 percent note. The face value includes interest.
June 30 Made the end-of-year adjusting entry to accrue interest expense.
30 Made the end-of-year adjusting entry to recognize interest expired on the note.
30 Made the end-of-year closing entry pertaining to interest expense.
July 10 Paid the note plus interest on the crane purchase.
Aug. 14 Paid off the note to the bank.

REQUIRED
1. Prepare general journal entries for the above transactions (journal Page 36).
2. Open general ledger accounts for Notes Payable (212), Discount on Notes Payable (213), Interest Payable (214), and Interest Expense (721). Post the relevant portions of the entries to those general ledger accounts.

ANSWER TO REVIEW PROBLEM

1. Prepare general journal entries.

		General Journal			Page 36
Date		**Description**	**Post. Ref.**	**Debit**	**Credit**
19xx					
May	11	Equipment		54,000	
		Notes Payable	212		54,000
		Purchase of crane with 60-day, 12% note			
	16	Cash		39,000	
		Discount on Notes Payable	213	1,000	
		Notes Payable	212		40,000
		Loan from bank obtained by signing 90-day, 10% note; discount $40,000 \times .10 \times 90/360 = \$1,000$			
June	30	Interest Expense	721	900	
		Interest Payable	214		900
		To accrue interest expense $54,000 \times .12 \times 50/360 = \$900$			
	30	Interest Expense	721	500	
		Discount on Notes Payable	213		500
		To recognize interest on note $1,000 \times 45/90 = \$500$			
	30	Income Summary		1,400	
		Interest Expense	721		1,400
		To close interest expense			
July	10	Notes Payable	212	54,000	
		Interest Payable	214	900	
		Interest Expense	721	180	
		Cash			55,080
		Payment of note on equipment $54,000 \times .12 \times 60/360 = \$1,080$			
Aug.	14	Notes Payable	212	40,000	
		Cash			40,000
		Payment of bank loan			
	14	Interest Expense	721	500	
		Discount on Notes Payable	213		500
		Interest expense on matured note $1,000 - \$500 = \$500$			

2. Open general ledger accounts and post the relevant amounts.

Notes Payable   Account No. 212

Date		Item	Post. Ref.	Debit	Credit	Balance Debit	Balance Credit
May	11		J36		54,000		54,000
	16		J36		40,000		94,000
July	10		J36	54,000			40,000
Aug.	14		J36	40,000			—

Discount on Notes Payable   Account No. 213

Date		Item	Post. Ref.	Debit	Credit	Balance Debit	Balance Credit
May	16		J36	1,000		1,000	
June	30	Adjustment	J36		500	500	
Aug.	14		J36		500	—	

Interest Payable   Account No. 214

Date		Item	Post. Ref.	Debit	Credit	Balance Debit	Balance Credit
June	30	Adjustment	J36		900		900
July	10		J36	900			—

Interest Expense   Account No. 721

Date		Item	Post. Ref.	Debit	Credit	Balance Debit	Balance Credit
June	30	Adjustment	J36	900		900	
	30	Adjustment	J36	500		1,400	
	30	Closing entry	J36		1,400	—	
July	10		J36	180		180	
Aug.	14		J36	500		680	

CHAPTER ASSIGNMENTS

QUESTIONS

1. What are liabilities?
2. Why is the timing of liability recognition important in accounting?
3. At the end of the accounting period, Janson Company had a legal obligation to accept delivery and pay for a truckload of hospital supplies the following week. Is this legal obligation a liability?
4. Ned Johnson, a star college basketball player, received a contract from the Midwest Blazers to play professional basketball. The contract calls for a salary of $300,000 a year for four years, dependent on his making the team in each of those years. Should this contract be considered a liability and recorded on the books of the basketball team?
5. What is the rule for classifying a liability as current?
6. What are a line of credit and commercial paper? Where do they appear on the balance sheet?
7. A bank is offering Diane Wedge two alternatives for borrowing $2,000. The first alternative is a $2,000, 12 percent, 30-day note. The second alternative is a $2,000, 30-day note discounted at 12 percent. (a) What entries are required by Diane Wedge to record the two loans? (b) What entries are needed by Diane to record the payment of the two loans? (c) Which alternative favors Diane, and why?
8. Where should the Discount on Notes Payable account appear on the balance sheet?
9. When can a portion of long-term debt be classified as a current liability?
10. What are three types of employer-related payroll liabilities?
11. How does an employee differ from an independent contractor?
12. Who pays social security and Medicare taxes?
13. Why are unearned revenues classified as liabilities?
14. What is definite about an estimated liability?
15. Why are income taxes payable considered to be estimated liabilities?
16. When does a company incur a liability for a product warranty?
17. What is a contingent liability, and how does it differ from an estimated liability?
18. What are some examples of contingent liabilities? For what reason is each a contingent liability?
19. What role does the W-4 form play in determining the withholding for estimated federal income taxes?
20. How can the payroll register be used as a special-purpose journal?
21. Why is an employee earnings record necessary and how does it relate to the W-2 form?

SHORT EXERCISES

SE 1. *Issues in Accounting*
L O 1 *for Liabilities*
Check Figures: c, b, d, a

Indicate whether each of the following actions relates to (a) recognition of liabilities, (b) valuation of liabilities, (c) classification of liabilities, or (d) disclosure of liabilities.

1. Determining that a liability will be paid in less than one year
2. Estimating the amount of a liability
3. Providing information about when liabilities are due and the interest rate that they carry
4. Determining when a liability arises

SE 2. *Types of Liabilities*

L O 2, 3, 4

Check Figures: a, c, b, a, b, c

Indicate whether each of the following is (a) a definitely determinable liability, (b) an estimated liability, or (c) a contingent liability.

1. Dividends Payable
2. Pending litigation
3. Income Taxes Payable
4. Current portion of long-term debt
5. Vacation Pay Liability
6. Guaranteed loans of another company

SE 3. *Interest Expense:*

L O 2 *Interest Not Included in Face Value of Note*

No check figure

On the last day of August, Gross Company borrowed $60,000 on a bank note for 60 days at 10 percent interest. Assume that interest is stated separately. Prepare the following general journal entries: (1) August 31, recording of note; and (2) October 30, payment of note plus interest.

SE 4. *Interest Expense:*

L O 2 *Interest Included in Face Value of Note*

No check figure

Assume the same facts as in SE 3, except that interest of $1,000 is included in the face amount of the note and the note is discounted at the bank on August 31. Prepare the following general journal entries: (1) August 31, recording of note; and (2) October 30, payment of note and recording of interest expense.

SE 5. *Payroll*

L O 2 *Withholdings, Taxes, and Other Costs*

Check Figures: W: 1, 8; WE: 3, 4, 5, 7; E: 2, 6

Tell whether each of the following payroll withholdings, taxes, and other costs is generally a withholding only from the employee's wages (W), both a withholding from the employee's wages and a tax or cost to the employer (WE), or a tax or cost only to the employer (E).

1. Employee's federal income taxes
2. State unemployment insurance tax
3. Social security (FICA) tax
4. Medicare tax
5. Medical insurance
6. Federal unemployment insurance (FUTA) tax
7. Pension contributions
8. Employee's state and local income taxes

SE 6. *Payroll Entries*

L O 2

No check figure

The following payroll totals for the month of April were taken from the payroll register of Coover Corporation: salaries, $223,000.00; federal income taxes withheld, $31,440.00; social security tax withheld, $13,826.00; Medicare tax withheld, $3,233.50; medical insurance deductions, $6,580.00; and salaries subject to unemployment taxes, $156,600.00. Prepare general journal entries to record (1) accrual of the monthly payroll and (2) accrual of employer's payroll expense, assuming social security and Medicare taxes equal to the amounts for employees, a federal unemployment insurance tax of .8 percent, a state unemployment tax of 5.4 percent, and medical insurance premiums, for which the employer pays 80 percent of the cost.

SE 7. *Product Warranty*

L O 3 *Liability*

Check Figure: Estimated liability: $65,000

Rainbow Corp. manufactures and sells travel clocks. Each clock costs $25 to produce and sells for $50. In addition, each clock carries a warranty that provides for free replacement if it fails for any reason during the two years following the sale. In the past, 5 percent of the clocks sold have had to be replaced under the warranty. During October, Rainbow sold 52,000 clocks, and 2,800 clocks were replaced under the warranty. Prepare general journal entries to record the estimated liability for product warranties during the month and the clocks replaced under warranty during the month.

SE 8. *Vacation Pay*

L O 3 *Liability*

Check Figures: Vaction pay expense: $3,864; Estimated Liability for Vacation Pay, ending balance: $7,864

The employees of Chan Services receive two weeks of paid vacation each year. Seventy percent of the employees qualify for vacation. Assuming the September payroll is $150,000, including $12,000 paid to employees on vacation, how much is the vacation pay expense for September? What is the ending balance of the Estimated Liability for Vacation Pay account, assuming a beginning balance of $16,000?

SE 9. *Payroll Taxes*
S O 5

Check Figures: Payroll taxes: Employees, $178; Employers, $240

Kristof Company and its employees are subject to a 6.2 percent social security tax on wages up to $61,200 and a 1.45 percent Medicare tax with no limit. The company is subject to a 5.4 percent state unemployment tax and a .8 percent federal unemployment tax up to $9,000 per employee. The company has two employees: A. Burns, who has cumulative earnings of $77,000 and earned $7,000 in the month of December, and C. Dunn, who has cumulative earnings of $5,000 and earned $1,000 during December. Compute the total payroll taxes for the employees and the employer for December.

SE 10. *Payroll Earnings,*
S O 5 *Withholdings, and*
Taxes

Check Figure: Total cost: $570.19

Last week, Manuel Kardo worked 44 hours. He is paid $10 per hour and receives one and one-half times his regular rate for hours worked over 40. Kardo has withholdings of $45 for federal income taxes, $10 for state income taxes, $23 for health insurance, 6.2 percent for social security tax, and 1.45 percent for Medicare tax. Compute Kardo's take-home pay. Also compute the total cost of Kardo to his employer, assuming Kardo's cumulative wages are over the limit for unemployment taxes and that the company makes a health-care contribution of $75.

EXERCISES

E 1. *Issues in Accounting*
L O 1 *for Liabilities*

Check Figures: b, c, a, d, b, c

Indicate whether each of the following actions relates to (a) recognition of liabilities, (b) valuation of liabilities, (c) classification of liabilities, or (d) disclosure of liabilities.

1. Setting a liability at the fair market value of goods to be delivered
2. Relating the payment date of a liability to the length of the operating cycle
3. Recording a liability in accordance with the matching rule
4. Providing information about financial instruments on the balance sheet
5. Estimating the amount of "cents off" coupons that will be redeemed
6. Categorizing a liability as long-term debt

E 2. *Interest Expense:*
L O 2 *Interest Not*
Included in Face
Value of Note

No check figure

On the last day of October, Gross Company borrowed $15,000 on a bank note for 60 days at 12 percent interest. Assume that interest is not included in the face amount. Prepare the following general journal entries: (1) October 31, recording of note; (2) November 30, accrual of interest expense; and (3) December 30, payment of note plus interest.

E 3. *Interest Expense:*
L O 2 *Interest Included in*
Face Value of Note

No check figure

Assume the same facts as in E 2, except that the $300 in interest is included in the face amount of the note and the note is discounted at the bank on October 31. Prepare the following general journal entries: (1) October 31, recording of note; (2) November 30, recognition of interest accrued on note; and (3) December 30, payment of note and recording of interest expense.

E 4. *Sales and Excise*
L O 2 *Taxes*

Check Figure: 1. Service Revenues: $430,000

Quik Dial Service billed its customers a total of $490,200 for the month of May, including 9 percent federal excise tax and 5 percent sales tax.

1. Determine the proper amount of revenue to report for the month.
2. Prepare a general journal entry to record the revenue and related liabilities for the month.

E 5. *Payroll Entries*
L O 2

Check Figure: 2. Payroll Taxes and Benefits Expense: $41,705.19

At the end of October, the payroll register for Mejias Corporation contained the following totals: wages, $185,500; social security tax withheld, $11,501; federal income taxes withheld, $47,442; state income taxes withheld, $7,818; Medicare tax withheld, $2,689.75; medical insurance deductions, $6,435; and wages subject to unemployment taxes, $28,620.

Prepare general journal entries to record (1) accrual of the monthly payroll and (2) accrual of employer payroll expenses, assuming social security and Medicare taxes equal to the amount for employees, a federal unemployment insurance tax of .8 percent, a state unemployment tax of 5.4 percent, and medical insurance premiums for which the employer pays 80 percent of the cost.

E 6. *Product Warranty*
L O 3 *Liability*

Check Figure: 1. Estimated liability: $182,000

Rainbow Company manufactures and sells electronic games. Each game costs $50 to produce and sells for $90. In addition, each game carries a warranty that provides for free replacement if it fails for any reason during the two years following the sale. In the past, 7 percent of the games sold had to be replaced under the warranty. During July, Rainbow sold 52,000 games and 2,800 games were replaced under the warranty.

1. Prepare a general journal entry to record the estimated liability for product warranties during the month.
2. Prepare a general journal entry to record the games replaced under warranty during the month.

E 7. *Vacation Pay*
L O 3 *Liability*
Check Figure: 1. Estimated employee benefit for July vacation: $11,102

Outland Corporation currently allows each employee three weeks' paid vacation after one year of employment. Based on studies of employee turnover and previous experience, management estimates that 65 percent of the employees will qualify for vacation pay this year.

1. Assume that Outland's July payroll is $300,000, of which $20,000 is paid to employees on vacation. Figure the estimated employee vacation benefit for the month.
2. Prepare a general journal entry to record the employee benefit for July.
3. Prepare a general journal entry to record the pay to employees on vacation.

E 8. *Estimated Liability*
L O 3
Check Figure: Estimated liability, 19x1: $160,000,000

Southeast Airways has initiated a frequent-flyer program in which enrolled passengers accumulate miles of travel that may be redeemed for rewards such as free trips or upgrades from coach to first class. Southeast estimates that approximately 2 percent of its passengers are traveling for free as a result of this program. During 19x1, Southeast Airways had total revenues of $8,000,000,000.

In January 19x2, the tickets of passengers who flew free were valued at $150,000. Prepare the December 19x1 year-end adjusting entry to record the estimated liability for this program and the January 19x2 entry for the free tickets used. Can you suggest how these transactions would be recorded if the estimate of the free tickets were to be considered a deferred revenue (revenue received in advance) rather than an estimated liability? How is each treatment an application of the matching rule?

E 9. *Social Security,*
S O 5 *Medicare, and*
Unemployment
Taxes
Check Figure: Cumulative Earnings, total: $320,701

Ultra Company is subject to a 5.4 percent state unemployment insurance tax and a .8 percent federal unemployment insurance tax after credits. Currently, both federal and state unemployment taxes apply to the first $9,000 earned by each employee. Social security and Medicare taxes in effect at this time are 6.20 and 1.45 percent, respectively. The social security tax is levied for both employee and employer on the first $61,200 earned by each employee during the year. During the current year, the cumulative earnings for each employee of the company are as follows:

Employee	Cumulative Earnings	Employee	Cumulative Earnings
Brown, E.	$28,620	Lavey, M.	$16,760
Caffey, B.	5,260	Lehmann, L.	6,420
Evett, C.	32,820	Massie, M.	51,650
Harris, D.	30,130	Neal, M.	32,100
Hester, J.	70,000	Pruesch, R.	36,645
Jordan, P.	5,120	Widmer, J.	5,176

1. Prepare and complete a schedule with the following columns: Employee Name, Cumulative Earnings, Earnings Subject to Social Security Tax, Earnings Subject to Medicare Tax, and Earnings Subject to Unemployment Taxes. Total the columns.
2. Compute the social security and Medicare taxes and the federal and state unemployment taxes for Ultra Company for the year.

E 10. *Net Pay Calculation*
S O 5 *and Payroll Entries*
Check Figure: 1d. Net pay: $273.68

Lynn Karas is an employee whose overtime pay is regulated by the Fair Labor Standards Act. Her hourly rate is $8, and during the week ended July 11, she worked 42 hours. Lynn claims two exemptions on her W-4 form. So far this year she has earned $8,650. Each week $12 is deducted from her paycheck for medical insurance.

1. Compute the following items related to the pay for Lynn Karas for the week of July 11: (a) total pay, (b) federal income taxes withholding (use Figure 4), (c) social security and Medicare taxes (assume rates of 6.2 percent and 1.45 percent, respectively) and (d) net pay.
2. Prepare a general journal entry to record the wages expense and related liabilities for Lynn Karas for the week ended July 11.

E 11. *Payroll Transactions*

S O 5

Check Figure: 3. Total cost of employing Howard: $81,330.20

Monroe Howard earns a salary of $70,000 per year. Social security and Medicare taxes are 6.2 percent on salary up to $61,200 and 1.45 percent on total salary. Federal unemployment insurance taxes are 6.2 percent of the first $9,000; however, a credit is allowed equal to the state unemployment insurance taxes of 5.4 percent on the $9,000. During the year, $15,000 was withheld for federal income taxes, $3,000 for state income taxes, and $1,500 for medical insurance.

1. Prepare a general journal entry summarizing the payment of $70,000 to Howard during the year.
2. Prepare a general journal entry summarizing the employer payroll taxes and other costs on Howard's salary for the year. Assume the company pays 80 percent of the total premiums for medical insurance.
3. Determine the total cost paid by Monroe Howard's employer to employ Howard for the year.

SKILLS DEVELOPMENT EXERCISES

Conceptual Analysis

SDE 1. *Identification of Current Liabilities*

L O 2, 3

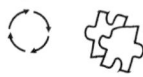

No check figure

Several businesses and organizations and a current liability from the balance sheet of each are listed below. Discuss the nature of each current liability (definitely determinable or estimated), how each arose, and how the obligation is likely to be fulfilled.

Institute of Management Accountants: Deferred Revenues—Membership Dues
The Foxboro Company: Advances on Sales Contracts
UNC Incorporated: Current Portion of Long-Term Debt
Hurco Companies, Inc.: Accrued Warranty Expense
Affiliated Publications, Inc.: Deferred Subscription Revenues
Geo. A Hormel & Company: Accrued Advertising

SDE 2. *Frequent-Flyer Plan*

L O 3

No check figure

America South Airways instituted a frequent-flyer program under which passengers accumulate points based on the number of miles they fly on the airline. One point is awarded for each mile flown, with a minimum of 750 miles given for any flight. Because of competition and a drop in passenger air travel in 1994, the company began a triple mileage bonus plan under which passengers received triple the normal mileage points. In the past, about 1.5 percent of passenger miles were flown by passengers who had converted points to free flights. Under the triple mileage program, it is expected that a 2.5 percent rate will be more appropriate for future years. During 1994 the company had passenger revenues of $966.3 million and passenger transportation operating expenses of $802.8 million before depreciation and amortization. Operating income was $86.1 million. The AICPA is considering requiring airline companies to recognize frequent-flyer plans in their accounting records. What is the appropriate rate to use to estimate free miles? What would be the effect of the estimated liability for free travel by frequent flyers on 1994 net income? Describe several ways to estimate the amount of this liability. Be prepared to discuss the arguments for and against recognizing this liability.

Ethical Dilemma

SDE 3. *Known Legal Violations*

L O 2

No check figure

Tower Restaurant is a large seafood restaurant in the suburbs of Chicago. Last summer, Joe Murray, an accounting student at the local college, secured a full-time accounting job at the restaurant. Joe felt fortunate to have a good job that accommodated his class schedule because the local economy was very bad. After a few weeks on the job, Joe realized that his boss, the owner of the business, was paying the kitchen workers in cash and was not withholding federal and state income taxes or social security and Medicare taxes. Joe understands that federal and state laws require these taxes to be withheld and paid in a timely manner to the appropriate agency. Joe also realizes that if he raises this issue, he may lose his job. What alternatives are available to Joe? What action would you take if you were in Joe's position? Why did you make this choice?

Research Activity

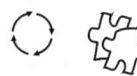
Your school library has indexes for business periodicals in which you can look up articles on topics of interest. Three of the most important of these indexes are the *Business Periodicals Index*, the *Wall Street Journal Index*, and the *Accountants' Index*. Using one or more of these indexes, locate and photocopy two articles related to bank financing, commercial paper, product warranties, airline frequent-flyer plans, or contingent liabilities. Keep in mind that you may have to look under related topics to find an article. For example, to find articles about contingent liabilities, you might look under litigation, debt guarantees, environmental losses, or other topics. For each of the two articles, write a short summary of the situation and tell how it relates to accounting for the topic as described in the text. Be prepared to discuss your results in class.

Decision-Making Practice

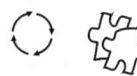
Jerry Highland opened a small television repair shop, ***Highland Television Repair***, on January 2, 19xx. He also sold a small line of television sets. Highland's wife was the sole salesperson for the television sets, and Highland was the only person doing repairs. (Highland had worked for another television repair store for twenty years, where he was the supervisor of six repairpersons.) The new business was such a success that he hired two assistants on March 1, 19xx. In October, Highland realized that he had failed to file any tax reports for his business since its inception and therefore probably owed a considerable amount of taxes. Since Highland has limited experience in running a business, he has brought all his business records to you for help. The records include a checkbook, canceled checks, deposit slips, invoices from his suppliers, a notice of annual property taxes of $4,620 due to the city on November 1, 19xx, and a promissory note to his father-in-law for $5,000. He wants you to determine what his business owes the government and other parties.

    You analyze all his records and determine the following:

Unpaid supplies invoices	$ 3,160
Sales (excluding sales tax)	88,540
Workers' salaries	20,400
Repair revenues	120,600

    You learn that the company has deducted $952 from the two employees' salaries for federal income taxes owed to the government. The current social security tax is 6.2 percent on maximum earnings of $61,200 for each employee, and the current Medicare tax is 1.45 percent (no maximum earnings). The FUTA tax is 5.4 percent to the state and .8 percent to the federal government on the first $9,000 earned by each employee, and each employee earned more than $9,000. Highland has not filed a sales tax report to the state (5 percent of sales).

1. Given these limited facts, determine Highland Television Repair's current liabilities as of October 31, 19xx.
2. What additional information would you want from Highland to satisfy yourself that all current liabilities have been identified?

PROBLEM SET A

Prentiss Paper Company, whose fiscal year ends December 31, completed the following transactions involving notes payable.

19x1

Nov. 25   Purchased a new loading cart by issuing a 60-day, 10 percent note for $21,600.

Dec. 16   Borrowed $25,000 from the bank to finance inventory by signing a 90-day note. The face value of the note includes interest of $750. Proceeds received were $24,250.

       31   Made the end-of-year adjusting entry to accrue interest expense.

       31   Made the end-of-year adjusting entry to recognize the interest expired on the note.

19x2
Jan. 24 Paid off the loading cart note.
Mar. 16 Paid off the inventory note to the bank.

REQUIRED

Prepare general journal entries for these transactions.

A 2. *Payroll Entries*
L O 2

No check figure

At the end of October, the payroll register for Lindos Corporation contained the following totals: sales salaries, $176,220; office salaries, $80,880; administrative salaries, $113,900; federal income taxes withheld, $94,884; state income taxes withheld, $15,636; social security tax withheld, $23,002; Medicare tax withheld, $5,379.50; medical insurance deductions, $12,870; life insurance deductions, $11,712; union dues deductions, $1,368; and salaries subject to unemployment taxes, $57,240.

REQUIRED

Prepare general journal entries to record the (1) accrual of the monthly payroll, (2) payment of the net payroll, (3) accrual of employer's payroll taxes (assuming social security and Medicare taxes equal to the amount for employees, a federal unemployment insurance tax of .8 percent, and a state unemployment tax of 5.4 percent), and (4) payment of all liabilities related to the payroll (assuming that all are paid at the same time).

A 3. *Property Tax and*
L O 3 *Vacation Pay*
          Liabilities

No check figure

Chin Corporation accrues estimated liabilities for property taxes and vacation pay. The company's and the local government's fiscal years end June 30, 19x1. The property tax for the year ended June 30, 19x1 was $36,000, and it is expected to increase 6 percent for the year ended June 30, 19x2. Two weeks' vacation pay is given to each employee after one year of service. Chin management estimates that 75 percent of its employees will qualify for this benefit in the current year.

In addition, the following information is available: The property tax bill of $39,552 for the June 30, 19x2 fiscal year was received in September and paid on November 1. Total payroll for July was $98,200, which includes $9,016 paid to employees on paid vacations.

REQUIRED

1. Prepare the monthly journal entries to record accrued property tax for July through November and actual property tax paid.
2. a. Prepare a general journal entry to record the vacation accrual expense for July. (Round to the nearest dollar.)
   b. Prepare a general journal entry to record the wages of employees on vacation in July. (Ignore payroll deductions and taxes.)

A 4. *Product Warranty*
L O 3 *Liability*

Check Figure: 1b. Estimated liability: $10,080

The Citation Company manufactures and sells food processors. The company guarantees the processors for five years. If a processor fails, it is replaced free, but the customer is charged a service fee for handling. In the past, management has found that only 3 percent of the processors sold required replacement under the warranty. The average food processor costs the company $120. At the beginning of September, the account for estimated liability for product warranties had a credit balance of $104,000. During September, 250 processors were returned under the warranty. Service fees of $4,930 were collected for handling. During the month, the company sold 2,800 food processors.

REQUIRED

1. Prepare general journal entries to record (a) the cost of food processors replaced under warranty and (b) the estimated liability for product warranties for processors sold during the month.
2. Compute the balance of the Estimated Product Warranty Liability account at the end of the month.

A 5. *Payroll Register and*
S O 5 *Related Entries*

Check Figure: 1. Net Pay, total: $7,087.43

Huff Manufacturing Company employs seven people in the Drilling Division. All employees are paid an hourly wage except the supervisor, who receives a monthly salary. Hourly employees are paid once a week and receive a set hourly rate for regular hours plus time-and-a-half for overtime. The employees and employer are subject to social security tax of 6.2 percent on the first $61,200 earned by each employee and Medicare tax of 1.45 percent. The unemployment insurance tax rates are 5.4 percent for the state and .8 percent for the federal government. The unemployment insurance tax applies to the first $9,000 earned by each employee and is levied only on the employer.

Each employee qualifies for the Huff Manufacturing Profit Sharing Plan. Under this plan each employee may contribute up to 10 percent of his or her gross income as a payroll withholding, and Huff Manufacturing Company matches each amount. The data for the last payday of October are presented below:

Employee	Hours Regular	Hours Overtime	Pay Rate	Cumulative Gross Pay Excluding Current Pay Period	Percentage Contribution to Profit Sharing Plan	Federal Income Taxes To Be Withheld
Branch, W.	40	4	$ 9.00	$14,350.00	2	$ 40.00
Choy, T.	40	2	8.50	6,275.00	5	48.00
Duran, P.	40	5	12.70	16,510.00	7	35.00
Finnegan, M.*	Salary	—	6,500.00	58,500.00	9	760.00
Patel, B.	40	—	12.50	15,275.00	3	60.00
Sammuals, J.	40	7	9.00	11,925.00	—	23.00
Tobin, R.	40	3	7.50	10,218.00	—	20.00

*Supervisor M. Finnegan was paid a bonus of $2,000 earlier in the year that is included in his cumulative gross pay.

REQUIRED

1. Prepare a payroll register for the pay period ended October 31. The payroll register should have the following columns:

Employee	Deductions	Net Pay
Total Hours	Federal Income Taxes	Distribution
Earnings	Social Security Tax	Drilling Wages Expense
Regular	Medicare Tax	Supervisory Salaries Expense
Overtime	Profit Sharing Plan	
Gross		
Cumulative		

2. Prepare a general journal entry to record the payroll and related liabilities for deductions for the period ended October 31.
3. Prepare general journal entries to record the expenses and related liabilities for the employer's payroll taxes (social security, Medicare, and federal and state unemployment) and contribution to the profit sharing plan.
4. Prepare the October 31 entries for the transfer of sufficient cash from the company's regular checking account to a special payroll disbursement account and for the subsequent payment of employees.

PROBLEM SET B

B 1.
L O 2

Notes Payable Transactions and End-of-Period Entries

No check figure

Fairbrooks Corporation, whose fiscal year ends June 30, completed the following transactions involving notes payable.

19xx
May 11 Signed a 90-day, $132,000 note payable to Village Bank for a working capital loan. The face value included interest of $3,960. Proceeds received were $128,040.
21 Obtained a 60-day extension on a $36,000 trade account payable owed to a supplier by signing a 60-day, $36,000 note. Interest is in addition to the face value, at the rate of 14 percent.
June 30 Made the end-of-year adjusting entry to accrue interest expense.
30 Made the end-of-year adjusting entry to recognize prepaid interest expense.
July 20 Paid off the note plus interest due the supplier.
Aug. 9 Paid the amount due to the bank on the 90-day note.

REQUIRED

Prepare general journal entries for the notes payable transactions.

B 2. *Payroll Entries*
L O 2

Check Figure: Payroll Tax Expense: $13,384.35

The following payroll totals for the month of April were taken from the payroll register of Tobias Corporation: sales salaries, $58,200; office salaries, $28,500; general salaries, $24,800; federal income taxes withheld, $15,720; social security tax withheld, $6,913; Medicare tax withheld, $1,616.75; medical insurance deductions, $3,290; life insurance deductions, $1,880; and salaries subject to unemployment taxes, $78,300.

REQUIRED

Prepare general journal entries to record the (1) accrual of the monthly payroll, (2) payment of the net payroll, (3) accrual of employer payroll taxes (assuming social security and Medicare taxes equal to the amounts for employees, a federal unemployment insurance tax of .8 percent, and a state unemployment tax of 5.4 percent), and (4) payment of all liabilities related to the payroll (assuming that all are paid at the same time).

B 3. *Property Tax and*
L O 3 *Vacation Pay*

No check figure

Brett Corporation prepares monthly financial statements and ends its fiscal year on June 30, the same as the local government. In July 19x1, your first month as accountant for the company, you find that the company has not previously accrued estimated liabilities. In the past, the company, which has a large property tax bill, has charged the property tax to the month in which the bill is paid. The tax bill for the year ended June 30, 19x1 was $36,000, and it is estimated that the tax will increase by 8 percent for the year ending June 30, 19x2. The tax bill is usually received on September 1, to be paid November 1.

You also discover that employees who have worked for the company for one year are allowed to take two weeks' paid vacation each year. The cost of the vacations has been charged to expense in the month of payment. Approximately 80 percent of the employees qualify for this benefit. You suggest to management that the proper accounting treatment of these expenses is to spread their cost over the entire year. Management agrees and asks you to make the necessary adjustments.

REQUIRED

1. Figure the proper monthly charge to property tax expense and prepare general journal entries for the following:

   July 31   Accrual of property tax expense
   Aug. 31   Accrual of property tax expense
   Sept. 30   Accrual of property tax expense (assume the actual bill is $40,860)
   Oct. 31   Accrual of property tax expense
   Nov. 1   Payment of property tax
        30   Accrual of property tax expense

2. Assume that the total payroll for July is $568,000. This amount includes $21,300 paid to employees on paid vacations.
   a. Compute the vacation pay expense for July.
   b. Prepare a general journal entry on July 31 to record the accrual of vacation pay expense for July.
   c. Prepare a general journal entry, dated July 31, to record the wages of employees on vacation in July (ignore payroll deductions and taxes).

B 4. *Product Warranty*
L O 3 *Liability*

Check Figure: 1b. Estimated liability: $7,200

Lighthouse Company is engaged in the retail sale of washing machines. Each machine has a twenty-four-month warranty on parts. If a repair under warranty is required, a charge for the labor is made. Management has found that 20 percent of the machines sold require some work before the warranty expires. Furthermore, the average cost of replacement parts has been $80 per repair. At the beginning of June, the account for the estimated liability for product warranties had a credit balance of $14,300. During June, 112 machines were returned under the warranty. The cost of the parts used in repairing the machines was $8,765, and $9,442 was collected as service revenue for the labor involved. During the month, Lighthouse Company sold 450 new machines.

REQUIRED

1. Prepare general journal entries to record (a) the warranty work completed during the month, including related revenue, and (b) the estimated liability for product warranties for machines sold during the month.
2. Compute the balance of the Estimated Product Warranty Liability account at the end of the month.

B 5. *Payroll Register and*
S O 5 *Related Entries*

Check Figure: 1. Net Pay, total: $8,176.32

DiGregorio Pasta Company has seven employees. Employees paid hourly receive a set rate for regular hours plus one-and-one-half times their hourly rate for overtime hours. They are paid every two weeks. The salaried employees are paid monthly on the last biweekly payday of each month. The employees and company are subject to social security tax of 6.2 percent up to a maximum of $61,200 for each employee and Medicare tax of 1.45 percent. The unemployment insurance tax rates are 5.4 percent for the state and .8 percent for the federal government. The unemployment insurance tax applies to the first $9,000 earned by each employee and is levied only on the employer.

The company maintains a supplemental benefits plan that includes medical insurance, life insurance, and additional retirement funds for employees. Under the plan, each employee contributes 4 percent of her or his gross income as a payroll withholding, and the company matches the amount. Data for the November 30 payroll, the last payday of November, follow.

	Hours			Cumulative Gross Pay Excluding Current Pay Period	Federal Income Taxes To Be Withheld
Employee	Regular	Overtime	Pay Rate		
Antonelli, J.	80	5	$ 8.00	$ 4,867.00	$ 71.00
Bertelli, A.	80	4	6.50	3,954.00	76.00
DiGregorio, G.*	Salary	—	5,000.00	55,000.00	985.00
Falcone, P.	80	—	5.00	8,250.00	32.00
Greco, P.*	Salary	—	2,000.00	20,000.00	294.00
Parilli, T.	80	20	10.00	12,000.00	103.00
Rosario, A.*	Salary	—	1,500.00	15,000.00	210.00

*Denotes administrative personnel; the rest are sales. G. DiGregorio's cumulative gross pay includes a $5,000 bonus paid early in the year.

REQUIRED

1. Prepare a payroll register for the pay period ended November 30. The payroll register should have the following columns:

Employee	Deductions	Net Pay
Total Hours	Federal Income Taxes	Distribution
Earnings	Social Security Tax	Sales Wages Expense
Regular	Medicare Tax	Administrative Salaries Expense
Overtime	Supplemental Benefits Plan	
Gross		
Cumulative		

2. Prepare a general journal entry to record the payroll and related liabilities for deductions for the period ended November 30.
3. Prepare general journal entries to record the employer's payroll taxes and contribution to the supplemental benefits plan.
4. Prepare the November 30 entries (a) to transfer sufficient cash from the company's regular checking account to a special payroll disbursement account and (b) to pay the employees.

FINANCIAL REPORTING AND ANALYSIS CASES

Interpreting Financial Reports

FRA 1.
L O 1, 2, 3

*Analysis of Current
Liabilities for a
Bankrupt Company*

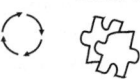

No check figure

Trans World Airlines, Inc. is a major airline that experienced financial difficulties in 1988 and 1989. In TWA's 1989 annual report, management referred to the company's deteriorating liquidity as follows:[10]

> TWA's net working capital deficit was $55.5 million at December 31, 1989, representing a reduction of $82.6 million from net working capital of $27.1 million at December 31, 1988. Working capital deficits are not unusual in the airline industry because of the large advance ticket sales current liability account.

In 1991, the company declared bankruptcy. By 1993, the company had reorganized and was planning to come out of bankruptcy. The company's current liabilities and current assets at December 31 for 1989 and 1992 were as follows (in thousands):

	1992	1989
Current liabilities:		
Short-term notes payable	$ 75,000	—
Current maturities of long-term debt	252,023	$ 127,301
Current obligations under capital leases	228	93,194
Advance ticket sales	151,221	276,549
Accounts payable, principally trade	114,467	387,256
Accounts payable to affiliated companies	22,815	8,828
Securities sold, not yet purchased	—	82,302
Accrued expenses:		
Employee compensation and vacations earned	100,013	148,175
Contributions to retirement and pension trusts	4,583	14,711
Interest on debt and capital leases	6,543	86,761
Taxes	17,069	33,388
Other accrued expenses	148,714	122,295
Total	$892,676	$1,380,760
Current assets:		
Cash and cash equivalents	$ 42,389	$ 454,415
Marketable securities	—	10,355
Receivables, less allowance for doubtful accounts, $13,432 in 1989 and $10,361 in 1992	311,915	435,061
Receivables from affiliated companies	2,925	15,506
Due from brokers	—	70,636
Spare parts, materials, and supplies, less allowance for obsolescence, $38,423 in 1989 and $47,872 in 1992	175,235	227,098
Prepaid expenses and other	44,047	112,232
Total	$576,511	$1,325,303

REQUIRED

1. Identify any current liabilities that did not require a current outlay of cash and identify any current estimated liabilities for 1989 and 1992. Why was management not worried about the cash flow consequences of advance ticket sales?
2. For 1989 and 1992, which current assets would not generate cash inflow, and which would most likely be available to pay for the remaining current liabilities? Compare the amount of these current assets to the amount of current liabilities other than those identified in **1** as not requiring a cash outlay.
3. In light of the calculations in **2,** comment on TWA's liquidity for 1989 and 1992 and its ability to operate successfully after bankruptcy. Identify several alternative sources of additional cash.

---

10. Trans World Airlines, Inc., *Annual Report,* 1989 and 1992.

FRA 2. *Contingent*
L O 4 *Liabilities*

No check figure

Texaco, Inc., one of the largest integrated oil companies in the world, reported its loss of the largest damage judgment in history in its 1986 annual report as follows:[11]

Note 17. Contingent Liabilities
Pennzoil Litigation

State Court Action. On December 10, 1985, the 151st District Court of Harris County, Texas entered judgment for Pennzoil Company of $7.5 billion actual damages, $3 billion punitive damages, and approximately $600 million prejudgment interest in *Pennzoil Company v. Texaco, Inc.,* an action in which Pennzoil claims that Texaco, Inc. tortiously interfered with Pennzoil's alleged contract to acquire a ⅜ths interest in Getty. Interest began accruing on the judgment at the simple rate of 10% per annum from the date of judgment. Texaco, Inc. believes that there is no legal basis for the judgment, which it believes is contrary to the evidence and applicable law. Texaco, Inc. is pursuing all available remedies to set aside or to reverse the judgment.

* * *

The outcome of the appeal on the preliminary injunction and the ultimate outcome of the Pennzoil litigation are not presently determinable, but could have a material adverse effect on the consolidated financial position and the results of the consolidated operations of Texaco, Inc.

At December 31, 1986, Texaco's retained earnings were $12.882 billion, and its cash and marketable securities totaled $3.0 billion. The company's net income for 1986 was $.725 billion.

After a series of court reversals and filing for bankruptcy in 1987, Texaco announced in December 1987 an out-of-court settlement with Pennzoil for $3.0 billion. Although less than the original amount, it is still the largest damage payment in history.

REQUIRED

1. The FASB has established two conditions that a contingent liability must meet before it is recorded in the accounting records. What are the two conditions? Does the situation described in "Note 17. Contingent Liabilities" meet those conditions? Explain your answer.
2. Do the events of 1987 change your answer to **1**? Explain your response.
3. What will be the effect of the settlement on Texaco's retained earnings, cash and marketable securities, and net income?

International Company

FRA 3. *Classification and*
L O 1, 2, *Disclosure of*
3, 4 *Current Liabilities*
     and Contingent
     Liabilities

No check figure

The German company *Volkswagen AG* is one of the largest automobile companies in the world. Accounting in Germany differs in some respects from that in the United States. A good example of the difference is the placement and classification of liabilities. On the balance sheet, Volkswagen places liabilities below a detailed stockholders' equity section. Volkswagen does not distinguish between current and long-term liabilities; however, a note to the financial statements does disclose the amount of the liabilities due within one year. Those liabilities are primarily what we call *definitely determinable liabilities,* such as loans, accounts and notes payable, and unearned revenues. Estimated liabilities do not seem to appear in this category. In contrast, there is an asset category called *current assets,* which is similar to that found in the United States. In another note to the financial statements, the company lists what it calls *contingent liabilities,* which have not been recorded and do not appear on the balance sheet. These include liabilities for notes that have been discounted, 299 million DM; guarantees of loans of other companies, 140 million DM; and warranties on automobiles, 200 million DM.[12] What do you think of the idea of combining all liabilities, whether short term or long term, as a single item on the balance sheet? Do you think any of the contingent liabilities should be recorded and shown on the balance sheet?

11. Texaco, Inc., *Annual Report,* 1986.
12. Volkswagen AG, *Annual Report,* 1992.

Toys "R" Us Annual Report

FRA 4. *Short-Term*
L O 1 *Liabilities and*
Seasonality

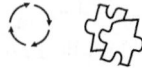

Check Figure: 29.8 percent

Refer to the balance sheet and the liquidity and capital resources section of Management's Discussion—Results of Operations and Financial Condition in the annual report in the appendix on Toys "R" Us to answer the following questions. What percentage of total liabilities and stockholders' equity are current liabilities for Toys "R" Us, and how does this percentage compare to that in other industries, as represented by Figure 1? Toys "R" Us is a seasonal business. Would you expect short-term borrowings and accounts payable to be unusually high or unusually low at the balance sheet date of January 28, 1995? How does management use short-term financing to meet its needs for cash during the year?

Accounting for

Corporations

Contributed Capital

LEARNING OBJECTIVES

1. Define *corporation* and state the advantages and disadvantages of the corporate form of business.
2. Account for organization costs.
3. Identify the components of stockholders' equity.
4. Account for cash dividends.
5. Identify the characteristics of preferred stock, including the effect on distribution of dividends.
6. Account for the issuance of stock for cash and other assets.
7. Account for treasury stock.
8. Account for the exercise of stock options.

DECISION POINT

General Motors Corporation

One way in which corporations raise new capital is by issuing stock. In the spring of 1992, General Motors Corporation, a major automobile maker, successfully issued 55 million shares of common stock at $39 per share, raising more than $2.1 billion.[1] It was the fourth time in two years that the company had raised funds by issuing stock. What are some of the possible reasons why General Motors Corporation would have preferred to choose a stock issue over other ways of raising capital?

There are definite advantages to financing with common stock. First, financing with common stock issues is less risky than financing with bonds, because dividends on common stock are not paid unless management and the board of directors decide to pay them. In contrast, if the interest on bonds is not paid, a company can be forced into bankruptcy. Second, when a company does not pay a cash dividend, the cash generated by profitable operations can be invested in the company's operations. Third, and most important for General Motors, a company may need the proceeds of a common stock issue to improve the balance between liabilities and stockholders' equity. The company had lost more than $4.5 billion in the previous year, drastically reducing its stockholders' equity. However, by issuing common stock, the company improved its debt to equity ratio and its credit rating.

On the other hand, issuing common stock also has certain disadvantages. Unlike the interest expense on bonds, dividends paid on stock are not tax deductible. Furthermore, when it issues more stock, the corporation dilutes its ownership. This means that the current shareholders must yield some control to the new stockholders. It is important for accountants to understand the nature and characteristics of corporations as well as the process of accounting for a stock issue and other types of stock transactions.

1. Susan Antilla, "Big G.M. Issue Lands and Price Holds Up," *New York Times,* May 21, 1992.

OBJECTIVE

1 *Define corporation and state the advantages and disadvantages of the corporate form of business*

THE CORPORATION

A corporation is defined as "a body of persons granted a charter legally recognizing them as a separate entity having its own rights, privileges, and liabilities distinct from those of its members."[2] In other words, a corporation is a legal entity separate and distinct from its owners. Although there are fewer corporations than sole proprietorships and partnerships in the United States, the corporate form of business dominates the economy in total dollars of assets and output of goods and services. Corporations are well suited to today's trends toward large organizations, international trade, and professional management. Figure 1 illustrates the corporation's ability to amass large amounts of capital by showing the amount and sources of new funds raised by corporations over the last five years for which data are available. There were dramatic increases in the amount of funds raised in 1991 and 1992. By 1992, the amount of new corporate capital reached $846.1 billion, of which $744.5 billion, or 88 percent, came from new bond issues; $72.4 billion, or 8.6 percent, came from new common stock issues; and $29.2 billion, or 3.4 percent, came from preferred stock issues.

FORMING A CORPORATION

To form a corporation most states require individuals, called incorporators, to file an application with the proper state official. The application contains the articles of incorporation. If approved by the state, the articles become, in effect, a contract, called the *corporate charter*, between the state and the incorporators. The company is then authorized to do business. The incorporators (usually the initial stockholders) hold a meeting to elect a board of directors and pass a set of bylaws to guide the company's operations. The board of directors then holds a meeting to elect the officers of the corporation. Finally, after beginning capital is raised through the issuance of shares of stock, the corporation is ready to start operating.

ORGANIZING A CORPORATION

The authority to manage a corporation is given by the stockholders to the board of directors, and by the board of directors to the corporate officers (Figure 2). That is, the stockholders elect the board of directors, which sets company policies and chooses the corporate officers. The officers, in turn, carry out corporate policies by managing the business.

Stockholders   A unit of ownership in a corporation is called a share of stock. To invest in a corporation, a stockholder transfers cash or other resources to the corporation. In return, the stockholder receives shares of stock representing a proportionate share of ownership in the corporation. The stockholder can transfer these shares at will.

Individual stockholders do not normally take part in the day-to-day management of a corporation. A stockholder can serve as a member of the board if elected or as an officer of the company if appointed. But, in general, stockholders participate in management only by electing the board of directors and voting on particular issues at stockholders' meetings.

Figure 1. Sources of Capital Raised by Corporations in the United States

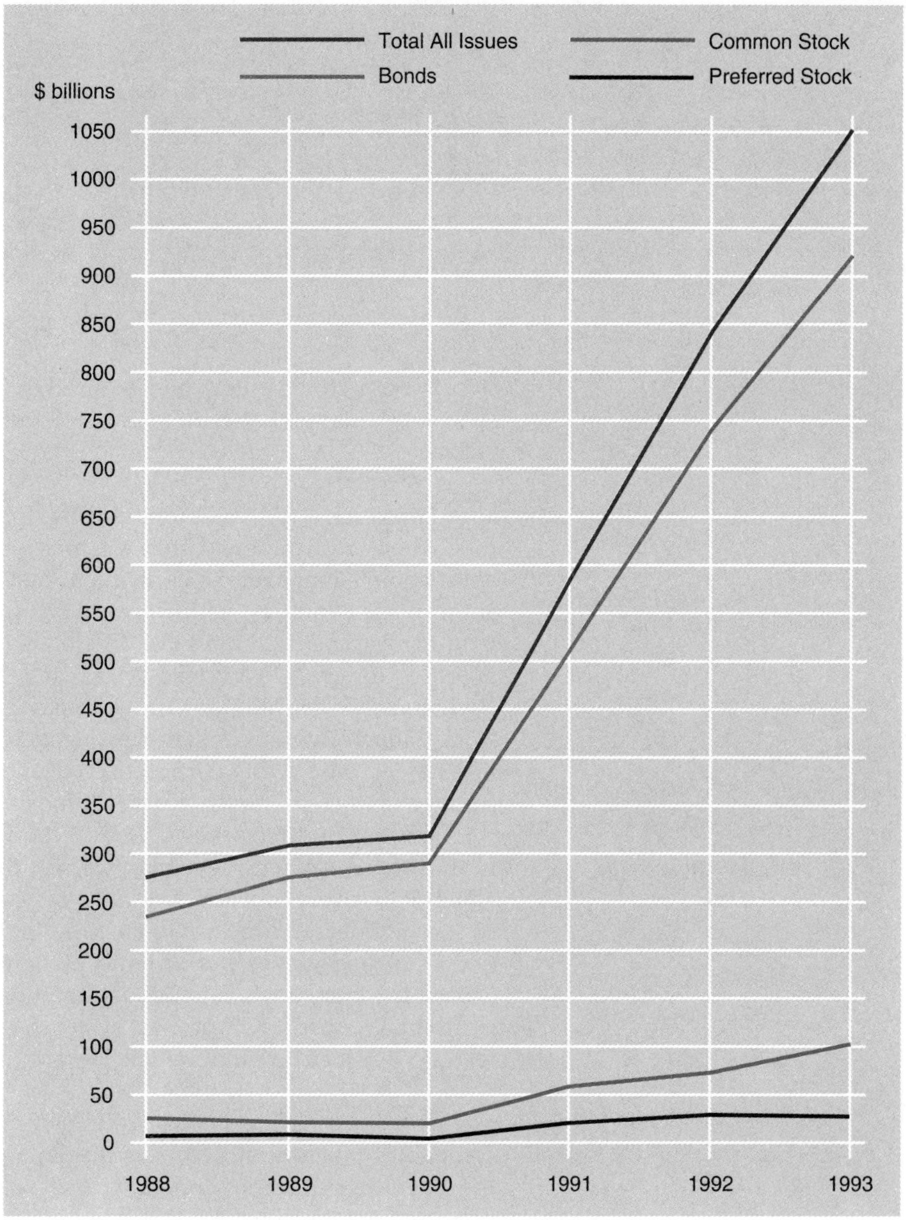

Source: Data from *Securities Industry Yearbook 1994–1995* (New York: Securities Industry Association, 1995), p. 947.

Stockholders usually meet once a year to elect directors and carry on other business as provided in the company's bylaws. Business transacted at those meetings can include the election of auditors; the review of proposed mergers and acquisitions, changes in the charter, or stock option plans; and the decision to issue additional stock or incur long-term debt. Each stockholder has one vote for each share of voting stock held. Today, ownership of large corporations is spread over the entire world. As a result, only a few stockholders may be able to attend an annual stockholders' meeting. A stockholder who cannot attend the meeting can vote by proxy. A proxy is a legal document,

Figure 2. The Corporate Form of Business

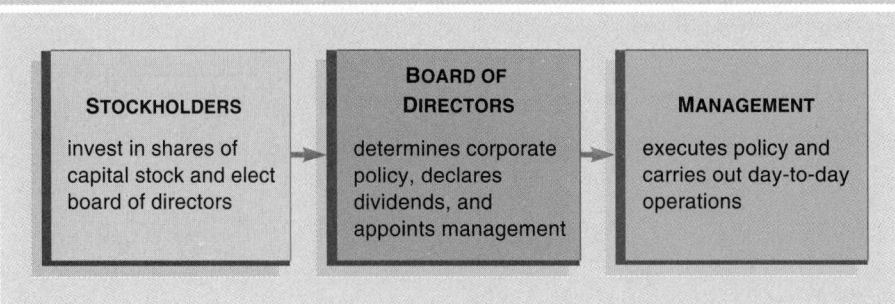

signed by a stockholder, giving another party the right to vote his or her shares. Normally, that right is given to the current management of the corporation.

Board of Directors As noted, the stockholders elect the board of directors, which in turn determines the major business policies of the corporation and appoints managers to carry them out. Among the duties of the board are authorizing contracts, setting executive salaries, and arranging major loans with banks. The declaration of dividends is also an important function of the board of directors. Only the board has the authority to declare dividends. Dividends are distributions of resources, generally in the form of cash, to the stockholders. Paying dividends is one way of rewarding stockholders for their investment when the corporation has earned a profit. (Another way is through an increase in the market value of the stock.)

The board of directors will vary in composition from company to company. In most cases, though, several officers of the corporation will sit on the board along with several outsiders. Today, it is common to form an audit committee of several outside directors to ensure that the board is objective in its evaluation of management's performance. One of the audit committee's tasks is to engage the company's independent auditors and review their work. Another is to make sure that proper systems exist to safeguard the company's resources and ensure that reliable accounting records are kept.

Management The board of directors appoints managers to carry out the company's policies and run day-to-day operations. Management consists of the operating officers—generally, the president, vice presidents, controller, treasurer, and secretary. Besides being responsible for running the business, management has the duty of reporting the financial results of its administration to the board of directors and the stockholders. Although management must, at a minimum, make a comprehensive annual report, it may and generally does report more often. The annual reports of large public corporations are available to the public. Excerpts from many of them appear throughout this book.

ADVANTAGES OF A CORPORATION

The corporate form of business organization has several advantages over the sole proprietorship and the partnership. Among them are existence as a separate legal entity, limited liability, ease of capital generation, ease of transfer of ownership, lack of mutual agency, continuous existence, centralized authority and responsibility, and professional management.

Separate Legal Entity   A corporation is a separate legal entity that has most of the rights of a person except those of voting and marrying. As such, it can buy, sell, or own property; sue and be sued; enter into contracts; hire and fire employees; and be taxed.

Limited Liability   Because a corporation is a separate legal entity, it is responsible for its own actions and liabilities. This means that a corporation's creditors can satisfy their claims only against the assets of the corporation, not against the personal property of the owners. Because the owners are not responsible for the corporation's debts, their liability is limited to the amount of their investment. The personal property of sole proprietors and partners, however, generally is available to creditors.

Ease of Capital Generation   It is fairly easy for a corporation to raise capital because shares of ownership in the business are available to a great number of potential investors for a small amount of money. As a result, a single corporation can be owned by many people.

Ease of Transfer of Ownership   A share of stock, a unit of ownership in a corporation, is a transferable unit. A stockholder can normally buy and sell shares of stock without affecting the activities of the corporation or needing the approval of other owners.

Lack of Mutual Agency   There is no mutual agency in the corporate form of business. If a stockholder, acting as an owner, tries to enter into a contract for the corporation, the corporation is not bound by the contract. But in a partnership, because of mutual agency, all the partners can be bound by one partner's actions.

Continuous Existence   Another advantage of the corporation's existence as a separate legal entity is that an owner's death, incapacity, or withdrawal does not affect the life of the corporation. The life of a corporation is set by its charter and regulated by state laws.

Centralized Authority and Responsibility   The board of directors represents the stockholders and delegates the responsibility and authority for the day-to-day operation of the corporation to a single person, usually the president. Operating power is not divided among the many owners of the business. The president may delegate authority for certain segments of the business to others, but he or she is held accountable to the board of directors. If the board is dissatisfied with the performance of the president, they can replace him or her.

Professional Management   Large corporations are owned by many people, the vast majority of whom are unequipped to make timely decisions about business operations. So, in most cases, management and ownership are separate. This allows a corporation to hire the best talent available to manage the business.

DISADVANTAGES OF A CORPORATION

The corporate form of business also has disadvantages. Among the more important ones are government regulation, taxation, limited liability, and separation of ownership and control.

Government Regulation   Corporations must meet the requirements of state laws. As "creatures of the state," corporations are subject to greater control and regulation by the state than are other forms of business. Corporations must file many reports with the state in which they are chartered. Also, corporations that are publicly held must file reports with the Securities and Exchange Commission and with the stock exchanges. Meeting those requirements is very costly.

Taxation   A major disadvantage of the corporate form of business is double taxation. Because a corporation is a separate legal entity, its earnings are subject to federal and state income taxes, which may be as much as 35 percent of corporate earnings. If any of the corporation's after-tax earnings are then paid out as dividends, the earnings are taxed again as income to the stockholders. In contrast, the earnings of sole proprietorships and partnerships are taxed only once, as personal income to the owners.

Limited Liability   Above, we cited limited liability as an advantage of incorporation, but it also can be a disadvantage. Limited liability restricts the ability of a small corporation to borrow money. Because creditors can lay claim only to the assets of the corporation, they limit their loans to the level secured by those assets or ask stockholders to guarantee the loans personally.

Separation of Ownership and Control   Just as limited liability can be a drawback, so can the separation of ownership and control. Sometimes management makes decisions that are not good for the corporation as a whole. Poor communication can also make it hard for stockholders to exercise control over the corporation or even to recognize that management's decisions are harmful.

ORGANIZATION COSTS

OBJECTIVE

2 *Account for organization costs*

The costs of forming a corporation are called organization costs. Such costs, which are incurred before the corporation begins operation, include state incorporation fees and attorneys' fees for drawing up the articles of incorporation. They also include the cost of printing stock certificates, accountants' fees for services rendered in registering the firm's initial stock, and other expenditures necessary for forming the corporation.

Theoretically, organization costs benefit the entire life of the corporation. For that reason, a case can be made for recording them as intangible assets and amortizing them over the years of the life of the corporation. However, the life of a corporation normally is not known, so accountants amortize organization costs over the early years of a corporation's life. Because federal income tax regulations allow organization costs to be amortized over five years or more, most companies amortize them over a five-year (sixty-month) period.[3] Organization costs normally appear as other assets or as intangible assets on the balance sheet.

To show how organization costs are accounted for, we assume that a corporation pays a lawyer $5,000 for services rendered in July 19x0 to prepare the

---

3. The FASB allows organization costs to be amortized over a period of up to forty years.

application for a charter with the state. The entry to record this cost would be as follows:

```
19x0
July 31    Organization Costs                           5,000
               Cash                                                5,000
                   Lawyer's fee for services rendered
                   in corporate organization
```

If the corporation amortizes the organization costs over a five-year period, the entry to record the amortization at the end of the fiscal year, June 30, 19x1, would look like this:

```
19x1
June 30    Amortization Expense, Organization Costs     1,000
               Organization Costs                              1,000
                   To amortize organization costs
                   for one year
                   $5,000 ÷ 5 years = $1,000
```

COMPONENTS OF STOCKHOLDERS' EQUITY

OBJECTIVE

3 *Identify the components of stockholders' equity*

On the balance sheet, the assets and liabilities of a corporation are handled like the assets and liabilities of other forms of business. The main difference between accounting for corporations and accounting for sole proprietorships lies in the treatment of owners' equity. In a corporation's balance sheet, the owners' claims to the business are called stockholders' equity and are presented on the balance sheet as shown below.

Stockholders' Equity		
Contributed Capital		
Preferred Stock—$50 par value, 1,000 shares		
authorized, issued, and outstanding		$ 50,000
Common Stock—$5 par value, 30,000 shares		
authorized, 20,000 shares issued and outstanding	$100,000	
Paid-in Capital in Excess of Par Value, Common	50,000	150,000
Total Contributed Capital		$200,000
Retained Earnings		60,000
Total Stockholders' Equity		$260,000

Notice that the equity section of the corporate balance sheet is divided into two parts: (1) contributed capital and (2) retained earnings. Contributed capital represents the investments made by the stockholders in the corporation. Retained earnings are the earnings of the corporation since its inception, less any losses, dividends, or transfers to contributed capital. Retained earnings are not a pool of funds to be distributed to the stockholders; they represent, instead, earnings reinvested in the corporation.

In keeping with the convention of full disclosure, the contributed-capital part of the stockholders' equity section of the balance sheet gives a great deal of information about the corporation's stock: the kinds of stock; their par value; and the number of shares authorized, issued, and outstanding.

CAPITAL STOCK

A share of stock is a unit of ownership in a corporation. A stock certificate is issued to the owner. It shows the number of shares of the corporation's stock owned by the stockholder. Stockholders can transfer their ownership at will. When they do, they must sign their stock certificate and send it to the corporation's secretary. In large corporations that are listed on the organized stock exchanges, stockholders' records are hard to maintain. Such companies can have millions of shares of stock, several thousand of which change ownership every day. Therefore, they often appoint independent registrars and transfer agents (usually banks and trust companies) to help perform the secretary's duties. The outside agents are responsible for transferring the corporation's stock, maintaining stockholders' records, preparing a list of stockholders for stockholders' meetings, and paying dividends. To help with the initial issue of capital stock, called an initial public offering (IPO), a corporation often uses an underwriter—an intermediary between the corporation and the investing public. For a fee—usually less than 1 percent of the selling price—the underwriter guarantees the sale of the stock. The corporation records the amount of the net proceeds of the offering—what the public paid less the underwriter's fee, legal and printing expenses, and any other direct costs of the offering—in its capital stock and additional paid-in capital accounts.

Authorized Stock When a corporation applies for a charter, the articles of incorporation specify the maximum number of shares of stock the corporation is allowed to issue. This number represents authorized stock. Most corporations are authorized to issue more shares of stock than are necessary at the time of organization, which allows for future stock issues to raise additional capital. For example, if a corporation plans to expand in the future, it will be able to sell the unissued shares of stock that were authorized in its charter. If a corporation immediately issues all of its authorized stock, it cannot issue more stock unless it applies to the state for a change in charter.

The charter also shows the par value of the stock that has been authorized. Par value is an arbitrary amount printed on each share of stock. It must be recorded in the capital stock accounts and constitutes the legal capital of a corporation. Legal capital equals the number of shares issued times the par value; it is the minimum amount that can be reported as contributed capital. Par value usually bears little if any relationship to the market value or book value of the shares. When a corporation is formed, a memorandum entry can be made in the general journal giving the number and description of authorized shares.

Issued and Outstanding Stock The issued stock of a corporation is the shares sold or otherwise transferred to stockholders. For example, a corporation can be authorized to issue 500,000 shares of stock but may choose to issue only 300,000 shares when the company is organized. The holders of those 300,000 shares own 100 percent of the corporation. The remaining 200,000 shares of stock are unissued shares. No rights or privileges are associated with them until they are issued.

Outstanding stock is stock that has been issued and is still in circulation. A share of stock is not outstanding if the issuing corporation has repurchased it or if a stockholder has given it back to the company that issued it. So, a company can have more shares issued than are currently outstanding. Issued shares that are bought back and held by the corporation are called treasury stock, which we discuss in detail later in this chapter.

COMMON STOCK

A corporation can issue two basic types of stock: common stock and preferred stock. If only one kind of stock is issued by the corporation, it is called common stock. Common stock is the company's residual equity. This means that all other creditors' and preferred stockholders' claims to the company's assets rank ahead of those of the common stockholders in case of liquidation. Because common stock is generally the only stock that carries voting rights, it represents the means of controlling the corporation.

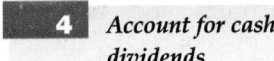

OBJECTIVE

4 *Account for cash dividends*

DIVIDENDS

A dividend is the distribution of a corporation's assets to its stockholders. Each stockholder receives assets, usually cash, in proportion to the number of shares of stock held. The board of directors has sole authority to declare dividends.

Dividends can be paid quarterly, semiannually, annually, or at other times decided on by the board. Most states do not allow the board to declare a dividend that exceeds retained earnings. When a dividend that exceeds retained earnings is declared, the corporation is, in essence, returning to the stockholders part of their contributed capital. It is called a liquidating dividend and is usually paid when a company is going out of business or reducing its operations. Having sufficient retained earnings in itself does not justify the distribution of a dividend. If cash or other readily distributed assets are not available for distribution, the company might have to borrow money to pay a dividend—an action most boards of directors want to avoid.

There are three important dates associated with dividends. In order of occurrence, they are (1) the date of declaration, (2) the date of record, and (3) the date of payment. The *date of declaration* is the date the board of directors formally declares that a dividend is going to be paid. The *date of record* is the date on which ownership of the stock of a company, and therefore of the right to receive a dividend, is determined. Individuals who own the stock on the date of record will receive the dividend. Between that date and the date of payment, the stock is said to be ex-dividend: If one person sells the shares of stock to another, the right to the cash dividend remains with the first person; it does not transfer with the shares to the second person. The *date of payment* is the date on which the dividend is paid to the stockholders of record.

To illustrate the accounting for cash dividends, we assume that the board of directors has decided that sufficient cash is available to pay a $56,000 cash dividend to the common stockholders. The process has two steps. First, the board declares the dividend as of a certain date. Second, the dividend is paid. Assume that the dividend is declared on February 21, 19xx, for stockholders of record on March 1, 19xx, to be paid on March 11, 19xx. Here are the entries to record the declaration and payment of the cash dividend.

Date of Declaration

Feb. 21	Cash Dividends Declared	56,000	
	Cash Dividends Payable		56,000
	Declaration of a cash dividend		
	to common stockholders		

Date of Record

Mar. 1 No entry is required. This date is used simply to determine the owners of the stock who will receive the dividends. After this date (starting March 2), the shares are ex-dividend.

Date of Payment

Mar. 11	Cash Dividends Payable	56,000	
	Cash		56,000
	Payment of cash dividends declared February 21		

Notice that the liability for the dividend is recorded on the date of declaration because the legal obligation to pay the dividend is established on that date. No entry is required on the date of record. The liability is liquidated, or settled, on the date of payment. The Cash Dividends Declared account is a temporary stockholders' equity account that is closed at the end of the accounting period by debiting Retained Earnings and crediting Cash Dividends Declared. Retained Earnings are thereby reduced by the total dividends declared during the period.

Some companies do not pay dividends very often. A company may not have any earnings. Or, a corporation may need the assets generated by the earnings kept in the company for business purposes, perhaps expansion of the plant. Investors in growth companies expect a return on their investment in the form of an increase in the market value of their stock.

OBJECTIVE

5 *Identify the characteristics of preferred stock, including the effect on distribution of dividends*

PREFERRED STOCK

The second kind of stock a company can issue is called preferred stock. Both common stock and preferred stock are sold to raise money. But investors in preferred stock have different investment goals from investors in common stock. In fact, a corporation may offer several different classes of preferred stock, each with distinctive characteristics to attract different investors. Preferred stock has preference over common stock in one or more areas. Most preferred stock has one or more of the following characteristics: preference as to dividends, preference as to assets of the business in liquidation, convertibility, and a callable option.

DECISION POINT

J.C. Penney Company, Inc.

Management can use preferred stock issues to accomplish its objectives. For instance, an article in the *Wall Street Journal* reported that J.C. Penney Company, the large retailer, planned to sell an issue of preferred stock to its newly created Employee Stock Ownership Plan (ESOP) and use the $700 million in proceeds to buy back up to 11 percent of its outstanding common stock. As a result, employees would own about 24 percent of the company. The new preferred stock would pay a dividend of 7.9 percent and would be convertible into common shares at $60 per share. The stock market reacted positively to the plan; the company's common stock rose almost $2 per share to $48 on the date of the announcement. How would this elaborate plan benefit the company?

As reported by the *Wall Street Journal*, "Analysts said the move should make the company less attractive as a takeover candidate by increasing its share price and per share earnings as well as by putting more shares in employees' hands."[4] Further, the company feels that its common stock is undervalued and that because there will be less common stock outstanding after the plan is put into effect, the market value of the stock will be enhanced. ⦂⦂⦂⦂⦂

Preference as to Dividends   Preferred stocks ordinarily have a preference over common stock in the receipt of dividends; that is, the holders of preferred shares must receive a certain amount of dividends before the holders of common shares can receive dividends. The amount that preferred stockholders must be paid before common stockholders can be paid is usually stated in dollars per share or as a percentage of the face value of the preferred shares. For example, a corporation can issue a preferred stock and pay an annual dividend of $4 per share, or it might issue a preferred stock at $50 par value and pay a yearly dividend of 8 percent of par value, also $4 per share.

Preferred stockholders have no guarantee of ever receiving dividends: The company must have earnings and the board of directors must declare dividends on preferred shares before any liability arises. The consequences of not declaring a dividend to preferred stockholders in the current year vary according to the exact terms under which the shares were issued. In the case of noncumulative preferred stock, if the board of directors fails to declare a dividend to preferred stockholders in a given year, the company is under no obligation to make up the missed dividend in future years. In the case of cumulative preferred stock, however, the fixed dividend amount per share accumulates from year to year, and the whole amount must be paid before any common dividends can be paid. Dividends not paid in the year they are due are called dividends in arrears.

Assume that a corporation has been authorized to issue 10,000 shares of $100 par value, 5 percent cumulative preferred stock, and that the shares have been issued and are outstanding. If no dividends were paid in 19x1, at the end of the year there would be preferred dividends of $50,000 (10,000 shares × $100 × .05 = $50,000) in arrears. If dividends are paid in 19x2, the preferred stockholders' dividends in arrears plus the 19x2 preferred dividends must be paid before any dividends on common stock can be paid.

Dividends in arrears are not recognized as liabilities because no liability exists until the board declares a dividend. A corporation cannot be sure it is going to make a profit. So, of course, it cannot promise dividends to stockholders. However, if a company has dividends in arrears, the amount should be reported either in the body of the financial statements or in a footnote. The following footnote appeared in a steel company's annual report a few years ago.

> On January 1, 19xx, the company was in arrears by $37,851,000 ($1.25 per share) on dividends to its preferred stockholders. The company must pay all dividends in arrears to preferred stockholders before paying any dividends to common stockholders.

Suppose that on January 1, 19x1, a corporation issued 10,000 shares of $10 par, 6 percent cumulative preferred stock and 50,000 shares of common stock. The first year's operations resulted in income of only $4,000. The corporation's board of directors declared a $3,000 cash dividend to the preferred stockholders. The dividend picture at the end of 19x1 was as follows.

4. Karen Blumenthal, "J.C. Penney Plans to Buy Back Stock with ESOP Gains," *Wall Street Journal*, August 31, 1988.

19x1 dividends due preferred stockholders ($100,000 × .06)	$6,000
Less 19x1 dividends declared to preferred stockholders	3,000
19x1 preferred stock dividends in arrears	$3,000

Now, suppose that in 19x2 the company earned income of $30,000 and wanted to pay dividends to both the preferred and the common stockholders. Because the preferred stock is cumulative, the corporation must pay the $3,000 in arrears on the preferred stock, plus the current year's dividends on its preferred stock, before it can distribute a dividend to the common stockholders. For example, assume that the corporation's board of directors declared a $12,000 dividend to be distributed to preferred and common stockholders. The dividend would be distributed as follows:

19x2 declaration of dividends	$12,000	
Less 19x1 preferred stock dividends in arrears	3,000	
Available for 19x2 dividends		$9,000
Less 19x2 dividends due preferred stockholders ($100,000 × .06)		6,000
Remainder available to common stockholders		$3,000

And this is the journal entry when the dividend is declared:

Dec. 31	Cash Dividends Declared	12,000	
	Cash Dividends Payable		12,000
	Declaration of a $9,000 cash dividend to preferred stockholders and a $3,000 cash dividend to common stockholders		

Preference as to Assets   Many preferred stocks have preference in terms of the assets of the corporation in the case of liquidation. If the corporation's existence is terminated, the preferred stockholders have a right to receive the par value of their stock or a larger stated liquidation value per share before the common stockholders receive any share of the company's assets. This preference can also include any dividends in arrears owed to the preferred stockholders.

Convertible Preferred Stock   A corporation can make its preferred stock more attractive to investors by adding convertibility. People who hold convertible preferred stock can exchange their shares of preferred stock for shares of the company's common stock at a ratio stated in the preferred stock contract. Convertibility appeals to investors for two reasons. First, like all preferred stockholders, owners of convertible stock are more likely to receive regular dividends than are common stockholders. Second, if the market value of a company's common stock rises, the conversion feature allows the preferred stockholders to share in the increase. The rise in value would come either through equal increases in the value of the preferred stock or through conversion to common stock.

For example, suppose that a company issues 1,000 shares of 8 percent, $100 par value convertible preferred stock for $100 per share. Each share of stock can be converted into five shares of the company's common stock at any time. The market value of the common stock is now $15 per share. In the past, an owner of the common stock could expect dividends of about $1 per share per year. The owner of one share of preferred stock, on the other hand, now holds an investment that is approaching a worth of $100 on the market and is more likely to receive dividends than is the owner of common stock.

Assume that in the next several years, the corporation's earnings increase and that the dividends paid to common stockholders also increase to $3 per share. In addition, the market value of a share of common stock rises from $15 to $30. Preferred stockholders can convert each of their preferred shares into five common shares and increase their dividends from $8 on each preferred share to the equivalent of $15 ($3 on each of five common shares). Furthermore, the market value of each share of preferred stock will be close to the $150 value of the five shares of common stock because each share can be converted into five shares of common stock.

Callable Preferred Stock   Most preferred stocks are callable preferred stocks. That is, they can be redeemed or retired at the option of the issuing corporation at a price stated in the preferred stock contract. A stockholder must surrender nonconvertible preferred stock to the corporation when asked to do so. If the preferred stock is convertible, the stockholder can either surrender the stock to the corporation or convert it into common stock when the corporation calls the stock. The *call price,* or redemption price, is usually higher than the par value of the stock. For example, a $100 par value preferred stock might be callable at $103 per share. When preferred stock is called and surrendered, the stockholder is entitled to (1) the par value of the stock, (2) the call premium, (3) any dividends in arrears, and (4) a portion of the current period's dividend, prorated by the proportion of the year to the call date.

A corporation may call its preferred stock for several reasons. First, the company may want to force conversion of the preferred stock to common stock because the cash dividend paid on the equivalent common stock is lower than the dividend paid on the preferred shares. Second, it may be possible to replace the outstanding preferred stock on the current market with a preferred stock at a lower dividend rate or with long-term debt, which can have a lower after-tax cost. Third, the company may simply be profitable enough to retire the preferred stock.

BUSINESS BULLETIN: BUSINESS PRACTICE

To bolster their debt to equity ratios, which had deteriorated because of operating losses in recent years, General Motors Corporation and Ford Motor Company issued $1.5 to $2.5 billion dollars of preferred stocks.[5] A popular new twist on traditional preferred stock is a hybrid form called PERCs, or preferred equity redemption convertible stock. Citicorp issued $1 billion in PERCs to improve its equity capital ratio. Citicorp's PERCs are popular with investors because they pay a higher dividend, 8.25 percent, than equivalent bonds and they have a mandatory retirement at the end of three years by conversion into common stock at a maximum 37.49 percent premium. PERCs are favored by

5. Joseph B. White, "GM to Double Offer of Preference Stock to $1.5 Billion," *Wall Street Journal,* December 5, 1991.

companies like Citicorp because they provide flexibility through a redemption or call feature. In the event that the financial condition of the company improves, it can substitute a cheaper form of financing by calling and retiring the PERCs.[6] ═══

RETAINED EARNINGS

Retained earnings, the other component of stockholders' equity, represent stockholders' claims to the assets of the company resulting from profitable operations.

OBJECTIVE

6 *Account for the issuance of stock for cash and other assets*

ACCOUNTING FOR STOCK ISSUANCE

A share of capital stock may be either par or no-par. The value of par stock is stated in the corporate charter and must be printed on each share of stock. Par value can be $.10, $1, $5, $100, or any other amount set by the organizers of the corporation. The par values of common stocks tend to be lower than those of preferred stocks.

Par value is the amount per share that is entered into the corporation's capital stock accounts and that makes up the legal capital of the corporation. A corporation cannot declare a dividend that would cause stockholders' equity to fall below the legal capital of the firm. Therefore, the par value is a minimum cushion of capital that protects creditors. Any amount in excess of par value received from the issuance of stock is recorded in the Paid-in Capital in Excess of Par Value account and represents a portion of the company's contributed capital.

No-par stock is capital stock that does not have a par value. There are several reasons for issuing stock without a par value. One is that some investors confuse par value with the market value of stock instead of recognizing it as an arbitrary figure. Another reason is that most states do not allow an original stock issue below par value and thereby limit a corporation's flexibility in obtaining capital.

No-par stock can be issued with or without a stated value. The board of directors of a corporation issuing no-par stock may be required by state law to place a stated value on each share of stock or may choose to do so as a matter of convenience. The stated value can be any value set by the board, although some states specify a minimum amount. The stated value can be set before or after the shares are issued if the state law is not specific.

If a company issues no-par stock without a stated value, all proceeds are recorded in the Capital Stock account. That amount becomes the corporation's legal capital unless a different amount is specified by state law. Because additional shares of the stock can be issued at different prices, the per-share credit to the Capital Stock account will not be uniform. This is a key way in which no-par stock without a stated value differs from par value stock or no-par stock with a stated value.

When no-par stock with a stated value is issued, the shares are recorded in the Capital Stock account at the stated value. Any amount received in excess of the stated value is recorded in the Paid-in Capital in Excess of Stated Value

6. Steven Lipin, "Citicorp Sells Over $1 Billion of Hybrid Stock," *Wall Street Journal,* October 15, 1992.

account. The amount in excess of the stated value is part of the corporation's contributed capital. However, the stated value is normally considered to be the legal capital of the corporation.

PAR VALUE STOCK

When par value stock is issued, the appropriate capital stock account (usually Common Stock or Preferred Stock) is credited for the par value regardless of whether the proceeds are more or less than the par value. For example, assume that Bradley Corporation is authorized to issue 20,000 shares of $10 par value common stock and actually issues 10,000 shares at $10 per share on January 1, 19xx. The entry to record the stock issue at par value would be as follows:

Jan. 1	Cash	100,000	
	Common Stock		100,000
	Issued 10,000 shares of $10 par value common stock for $10 per share		

Cash is debited for $100,000 (10,000 shares $\times$ $10), and Common Stock is credited an equal amount because the stock was sold for par value.

When stock is issued for a price greater than par, the proceeds in excess of par are credited to a capital account called Paid-in Capital in Excess of Par Value, Common. For example, assume that the 10,000 shares of Bradley common stock sold for $12 per share on January 1, 19xx. The entry to record the issuance of the stock at the price in excess of par value would be as follows:

Jan. 1	Cash	120,000	
	Common Stock		100,000
	Paid-in Capital in Excess of Par Value, Common		20,000
	Issued 10,000 shares of $10 par value common stock for $12 per share		

Cash is debited for the proceeds of $120,000 (10,000 shares $\times$ $12), and Common Stock is credited for the total par value of $100,000 (10,000 shares $\times$ $10). Paid-in Capital in Excess of Par Value, Common is credited for the difference of $20,000 (10,000 shares $\times$ $2). The amount in excess of par value is part of the corporation's contributed capital and will be included in the stockholders' equity section of the balance sheet. The stockholders' equity section for Bradley Corporation immediately following the stock issue would appear as follows:

Contributed Capital	
Common Stock—$10 par value, 20,000 shares authorized, 10,000 shares issued and outstanding	$100,000
Paid-in Capital in Excess of Par Value, Common	20,000
Total Contributed Capital	$120,000
Retained Earnings	—
Total Stockholders' Equity	$120,000

If a corporation issues stock for less than par, an account called Discount on Capital Stock is debited for the difference. The issuance of stock at a discount rarely occurs because it is illegal in many states.

NO-PAR STOCK

As mentioned earlier, stock can be issued without a par value. However, most states require that all or part of the proceeds from the issuance of no-par stock be designated as legal capital, which cannot be withdrawn except in liquidation. The purpose of this requirement is to protect the corporation's assets for creditors. Assume that the Bradley Corporation's capital stock is no-par common and that 10,000 shares are issued on January 1, 19xx at $15 per share. The $150,000 (10,000 shares × $15) in proceeds would be recorded as shown in the following entry.

Jan. 1	Cash	150,000	
	Common Stock		150,000
	Issued 10,000 shares of no-par		
	common stock for $15 per share		

Because the stock does not have a stated or par value, all proceeds of the issue are credited to Common Stock and are part of the company's legal capital.

Most states allow the board of directors to put a stated value on no-par stock, and that value represents the corporation's legal capital. Assume that Bradley's board puts a $10 stated value on its no-par stock. The entry to record the issue of 10,000 shares of no-par common stock with a $10 stated value for $15 per share would appear as follows:

Jan. 1	Cash	150,000	
	Common Stock		100,000
	Paid-in Capital in Excess of		
	Stated Value, Common		50,000
	Issued 10,000 shares of no-par		
	common stock of $10 stated value		
	for $15 per share		

Notice that the legal capital credited to Common Stock is the stated value decided by the board of directors. Notice also that the account Paid-in Capital in Excess of Stated Value, Common is credited for $50,000. The $50,000 is the difference between the proceeds ($150,000) and the total stated value ($100,000). Paid-in Capital in Excess of Stated Value is presented on the balance sheet in the same way as Paid-in Capital in Excess of Par Value.

ISSUANCE OF STOCK FOR NONCASH ASSETS

Stock can be issued for assets or services other than cash. The problem is to determine the dollar amount that should be recorded for the exchange. The generally preferred rule is to record the transaction at the fair market value of what the corporation is giving up—in this case, the stock. If the fair market value of the stock cannot be determined, the fair market value of the assets or services received can be used. Transactions of this kind usually involve the use of stock to pay for land or buildings or for the services of attorneys and others who helped organize the company.

When there is an exchange of stock for noncash assets, the board of directors has the right to determine the fair market value of the property. Suppose that when the Bradley Corporation was formed on January 1, 19xx, its attorney agreed to accept 100 shares of its $10 par value common stock for services rendered. At the time the stock was issued, its market value could not be determined. However, for similar services the attorney would have billed the company $1,500. The entry to record the noncash transaction is as follows:

Jan. 1	Organization Costs	1,500	
	Common Stock		1,000
	Paid-in Capital in Excess of		
	Par Value, Common		500
	Issued 100 shares of $10 par		
	value common stock for attorney's		
	services		

Now suppose that two years later the Bradley Corporation exchanged 1,000 shares of its $10 par value common stock for a piece of land. At the time of the exchange, the stock was selling on the market for $16 per share. The entry to record the exchange would be as follows:

Jan. 1	Land	16,000	
	Common Stock		10,000
	Paid-in Capital in Excess of		
	Par Value, Common		6,000
	Issued 1,000 shares of $10 par value		
	common stock with a market value		
	of $16 per share for a piece of land		

BUSINESS BULLETIN: BUSINESS PRACTICE

The year 1993 proved to be a hot year for initial public offerings (IPOs); such offerings reached an unprecedented $40 billion as small companies took advantage of all-time record highs in the stock market. IPOs are common stock issues of companies that are selling their stock to the public for the first time, or "going public," and they are very popular with investors. For example, when Gateway 2000, a North Sioux City, South Dakota, mail-order computer marketer, offered 10.9 million shares at $15 dollars per share, the price rose to above $20 per share on the first day of trading.[7] The stock of another company, Boston Chicken, a midwestern fast-food company, more than doubled in price on the first day, climbing from $20 to over $48 per share. Some analysts note that the good fortune of Gateway and Boston Chicken will continue only as long as the companies maintain fast sales growth. Disappointing sales could cause the stocks to plunge.[8]

OBJECTIVE

7 *Account for treasury stock*

TREASURY STOCK

Treasury stock is capital stock, either common or preferred, that has been issued and reacquired by the issuing company and has not subsequently been resold or retired. The company normally gets the stock back by purchasing the shares on the market.

---

7. Kyle Pope and Warren Getler, "Gateway 2000's New Shares Jump 28% Amid Keen Interest in Computer Issues," *Wall Street Journal,* December 9, 1993.

8. William Power, "Boston Chicken Soars by 143% on Its IPO Day," *Wall Street Journal,* November 10, 1993.

It is common for companies to buy and hold their own stock. In 1992, 382, or 64 percent, of six hundred large companies held treasury stock.[9] A company may purchase its own stock for several reasons:

1. It may want stock to distribute to employees through stock option plans.
2. It may be trying to maintain a favorable market for its stock.
3. It may want to increase its earnings per share.
4. It may want to have additional shares of stock available for such activities as purchasing other companies.
5. It may want to prevent a hostile takeover.

A treasury stock purchase reduces the assets and stockholders' equity of the company. It is not considered a purchase of assets, as the purchase of shares in another company would be. Treasury stock is capital stock that has been issued but is no longer outstanding. Treasury shares can be held for an indefinite period of time, reissued, or retired. Like unissued stock, treasury stock has no rights until it is reissued. Treasury stock does not have voting rights, rights to cash dividends and stock dividends, or rights to share in assets during liquidation of the company, and it is not considered to be outstanding in the calculation of book value. However, there is one major difference between unissued shares and treasury shares: A share of stock that originally was issued at par value or greater and fully paid for, and that then was reacquired as treasury stock, can be reissued at less than par value without negative consequences.

Purchase of Treasury Stock   When treasury stock is purchased, it is normally recorded at cost. The transaction reduces both the assets and the stockholders' equity of the firm. For example, assume that on September 15 the Caprock Corporation purchases 1,000 shares of its common stock on the market at a price of $50 per share. The purchase would be recorded as follows:

Sept. 15	Treasury Stock, Common	50,000	
	Cash		50,000
	Acquired 1,000 shares of the company's common stock for $50 per share		

The treasury shares are recorded at cost. The par value, stated value, or original issue price of the stock is ignored.

The stockholders' equity section of Caprock's balance sheet shows the cost of the treasury stock as a deduction from the total of contributed capital and retained earnings.

Contributed Capital	
Common Stock—$5 par value, 100,000 shares authorized, 30,000 shares issued, 29,000 shares outstanding	$ 150,000
Paid-in Capital in Excess of Par Value, Common	30,000
Total Contributed Capital	$ 180,000
Retained Earnings	900,000
Total Contributed Capital and Retained Earnings	$1,080,000
Less Treasury Stock, Common (1,000 shares at cost)	50,000
Total Stockholders' Equity	$1,030,000

9. American Institute of Certified Public Accountants, *Accounting Trends & Techniques* (New York: AICPA, 1993), p. 260.

Notice that the number of shares issued, and thus the legal capital, has not changed, although the number of outstanding shares has decreased as a result of the transaction.

Sale of Treasury Stock   Treasury shares can be sold at cost, above cost, or below cost. For example, assume that on November 15 the 1,000 treasury shares of the Caprock Corporation are sold for $50 per share. This entry records the transaction:

Nov. 15	Cash	50,000	
	Treasury Stock, Common		50,000
	Reissued 1,000 shares of treasury stock for $50 per share		

When treasury shares are sold for an amount greater than their cost, the excess of the sales price over cost should be credited to Paid-in Capital, Treasury Stock. No gain should be recorded. For example, suppose that on November 15 the 1,000 treasury shares of the Caprock Corporation are sold for $60 per share. The entry for the reissue would be as follows:

Nov. 15	Cash	60,000	
	Treasury Stock, Common		50,000
	Paid-in Capital, Treasury Stock		10,000
	Sale of 1,000 shares of treasury stock for $60 per share; cost was $50 per share		

If treasury shares are sold below their cost, the difference is deducted from Paid-in Capital, Treasury Stock. When this account does not exist or its balance is insufficient to cover the excess of cost over the reissue price, Retained Earnings absorbs the excess. No loss is recorded. For example, suppose that on September 15, the Caprock Corporation bought 1,000 shares of its common stock on the market at a price of $50 per share. The company sold 400 shares of its stock on October 15 for $60 per share and the remaining 600 shares on December 15 for $42 per share. The entries for these transactions follow:

Sept. 15	Treasury Stock, Common	50,000	
	Cash		50,000
	Purchase of 1,000 shares of treasury stock at $50 per share		
Oct. 15	Cash	24,000	
	Treasury Stock, Common		20,000
	Paid-in Capital, Treasury Stock		4,000
	Sale of 400 shares of treasury stock for $60 per share; cost was $50 per share		
Dec. 15	Cash	25,200	
	Paid-in Capital, Treasury Stock	4,000	
	Retained Earnings	800	
	Treasury Stock, Common		30,000
	Sale of 600 shares of treasury stock for $42 per share; cost was $50 per share		

In the entry for the December 15 transaction, Retained Earnings is debited for $800 because the 600 shares were sold for $4,800 less than cost. That amount is $800 greater than the $4,000 of paid-in capital generated by the sale of the 400 shares of treasury stock on October 15.

Retirement of Treasury Stock

If a company determines that it will not reissue stock it has purchased, with the approval of its stockholders it can retire the stock. When shares of stock are retired, all items related to those shares are removed from the related capital accounts. When stock that cost less than the original contributed capital is retired, the difference is recognized in Paid-in Capital, Retirement of Stock. However, when stock that cost more than was received when the shares were first issued is retired, the difference is a reduction in stockholders' equity and is debited to Retained Earnings. For instance, suppose that instead of selling the 1,000 shares of treasury stock it purchased for $50,000, Caprock decides to retire the shares on November 15. Assuming that the $5 par value common stock was originally issued at $6 per share, this entry records the retirement:

Nov. 15	Common Stock	5,000	
	Paid-in Capital in Excess of		
	Par Value, Common	1,000	
	Retained Earnings	44,000	
	Treasury Stock, Common		50,000
	Retirement of 1,000 shares that		
	cost $50 per share and were		
	issued originally at $6 per share		

BUSINESS BULLETIN: INTERNATIONAL PRACTICE

In the United States, it is accepted practice that a company does not report profits from trading in its own stock on the income statement, but this is not the case in other countries. Only if foreign companies raise money in the United States or are listed on a major U.S. stock exchange must they comply with U.S. accounting rules. Because more and more Americans are investing in emerging markets, investors need to realize that U.S. accounting and disclosure rules may not apply. For example, in Mexico a company can record a gain from reselling its own treasury stock. *Forbes* reported that Cemex, a huge Mexican cement company, customarily reports nonoperating items with little explanation. Only by searching in the footnotes does one discover that one-third of Cemex's $495 million in 1991 pretax profits came from gains on treasury stock transactions.[10]

EXERCISING STOCK OPTIONS

Many companies encourage the ownership of their common stock through a stock option plan, which is an agreement to issue stock to employees according to specified terms. Under some plans, the option to purchase stock applies to all employees equally, and the stock is purchased at a price close to its market value at the time of purchase. In such situations, the stock issue is recorded in the same way as a stock issue to an outsider. If, for example, we assume that on March 30 the employees of a company purchased 2,000 shares

---

10. Roula Khalaf, "Free-Style Accounting," *Forbes*, March 1, 1993.

of $10 par value common stock at the current market value of $25 per share, the entry would be as follows:

Mar. 30	Cash	50,000	
	Common Stock		20,000
	Paid-in Capital in Excess of Par		
	Value, Common		30,000
	Issued 2,000 shares of $10 par value common stock under employee stock option plan		

In other cases, the stock option plan gives employees the right to purchase stock in the future at a fixed price. This type of plan, which is usually offered only to management personnel, both compensates and motivates employees because the market value of a company's stock is tied to its performance. As the market value of the stock goes up, the difference between the option price and the market price grows, which increases the employee's compensation. When an option eventually is exercised and the stock is issued, the entry is similar to the one above. For example, assume that on July 1, 19x1, a company grants its key management personnel the option to purchase 50,000 shares of $10 par value common stock at its then-current market value of $15 per share. Suppose that one of the firm's vice presidents exercises the option to purchase 2,000 shares on March 30, 19x2, when the market price is $25 per share. This entry would record the issue:

19x2

Mar. 30	Cash	30,000	
	Common Stock		20,000
	Paid-in Capital in Excess of Par		
	Value, Common		10,000
	Issued 2,000 shares of $10 par value common stock under the employee stock option plan		

Although the vice president has a gain of $20,000 (the $50,000 market value less the $30,000 option price), no compensation expense is recorded. Compensation expense would be recorded only if the option price is less than the $15 market price on July 1, 19x1, the date of grant. Methods of handling compensation in this situation are covered in more advanced courses.[11] Information pertaining to employee stock option plans should be discussed in the notes to the financial statements.

BUSINESS BULLETIN: BUSINESS PRACTICE

Stock options are also used to attract top managers to a company. When Eastman Kodak Company hired George Fisher away from Motorola, the company gave him options to purchase 750,000 shares of Kodak stock. Compensation consultants put a value of between $13 million and $17 million on the package and said that such

---

11. Stock options are discussed here in the context of employee compensation. They can also be important features of complex corporate capitalization arrangements.

compensation was appropriate for an executive hired to turn a company around, as Fisher was charged to do at Kodak. Fisher has options to purchase 742,000 shares at $57.97 per share and 7,910 shares at $63.19 per share. The average price per share at the time the options were granted was $63.19. Thus, if Fisher can increase the price of the shares by improving the company's profitability, he will stand to gain. When Fisher left Motorola, he gave up unexercised options worth $6.4 million.[12] ═══

CHAPTER REVIEW

REVIEW OF LEARNING OBJECTIVES

1. **Define *corporation* and state the advantages and disadvantages of the corporate form of business.** A corporation is a separate legal entity that has its own rights, privileges, and liabilities distinct from its owners. The owners are the firm's stockholders. They elect the board of directors and have the right to vote on key policies. The board determines company policies and appoints managers who are charged with the firm's day-to-day operations. Among the advantages of the corporate form of business are that (a) a corporation is a separate legal entity, (b) stockholders have limited liability, (c) it is easy to generate capital for a corporation, (d) stockholders can buy and sell shares of stock easily, (e) there is a lack of mutual agency, (f) the corporation has a continuous existence, (g) authority and responsibility are centralized, and (h) the corporation is run by a professional management team. The disadvantages of corporations include (a) much government regulation, (b) double taxation, (c) difficulty of raising funds because of limited liability, and (d) separation of ownership and control.

2. **Account for organization costs.** The costs of organizing a corporation are recorded at cost. The costs are usually amortized over five years.

3. **Identify the components of stockholders' equity.** Stockholders' equity consists of contributed capital and retained earnings. Contributed capital includes two basic types of stock: common stock and preferred stock. When only one type of security is issued, it is common stock. Common stockholders have voting rights; they also share in the earnings of the corporation and in its assets in case of liquidation.

    Retained earnings, the other component of stockholders' equity, represents the claim of stockholders to the assets of the company resulting from profitable operations. These are earnings that have been invested in the corporation.

4. **Account for cash dividends.** The liability for payment of cash dividends arises on the date of declaration by the board of directors. The declaration is recorded with a debit to Cash Dividends Declared and a credit to Cash Dividends Payable. The date of record, on which no entry is required, establishes the stockholders who will receive the cash dividend on the date of payment. Payment is recorded with a debit to Cash Dividends Payable and a credit to Cash.

5. **Identify the characteristics of preferred stock, including the effect on distribution of dividends.** Preferred stock, like common stock, is sold to raise capital. But the investors in preferred stock have different objectives. To attract such investors, corporations usually give them a preference—in terms of receiving dividends and assets—over common stockholders. The dividend on preferred stock is generally figured first; then the remainder goes to common stock. If the preferred stock is cumulative and in arrears, the amount in arrears must be allocated to preferred stockholders before any allocation is made to common stockholders. In addition, certain preferred stock is convertible. Preferred stock is often callable at the option of the corporation.

12. Wendy Bounds, "Kodak Gives Fisher Options to Purchase 750,000 of Its Shares," *Wall Street Journal*, December 20, 1993.

6. **Account for the issuance of stock for cash and other assets.** A corporation's stock is normally issued for cash and other assets. The majority of states require that stock be issued at a minimum value called legal capital. Legal capital is represented by the par or stated value of the stock.

   When stock is issued for cash at par or stated value, Cash is debited and Common Stock or Preferred Stock is credited. When stock is sold at an amount greater than par or stated value, the excess is recorded in Paid-in Capital in Excess of Par or Stated Value.

   Sometimes stock is issued for noncash assets. Then, the accountant must decide how to value the stock. The general rule is to record the stock at its market value. If this value cannot be determined, the fair market value of the asset received is used to record the transaction.

7. **Account for treasury stock.** Treasury stock is stock that a company has issued and reacquired but not resold or retired. A company may acquire its own stock to create stock option plans, maintain a favorable market for the stock, increase earnings per share, or purchase other companies. Treasury stock is similar to unissued stock in that it does not have rights until it is reissued. However, treasury stock can be resold at less than par value without incurring a discount liability. The accounting treatment for treasury stock is as follows:

Treasury Stock Transaction	Accounting Treatment
Purchase of treasury stock	Debit Treasury Stock and credit Cash for the cost of the shares.
Sale of treasury stock at the same price as the cost of the shares	Debit Cash and credit Treasury Stock for the cost of the shares.
Sale of treasury stock at an amount greater than the cost of the shares	Debit Cash for the reissue price of the shares, and credit Treasury Stock for the cost of the shares and Paid-in Capital, Treasury Stock for the excess.
Sale of treasury stock at an amount less than the cost of the shares	Debit Cash for the reissue price; debit Paid-in Capital, Treasury Stock for the difference between the reissue price and the cost of the shares; and credit Treasury Stock for the cost of the shares. If Paid-in Capital, Treasury Stock does not exist or its balance is not large enough to cover the difference, Retained Earnings should absorb the difference.

8. **Account for the exercise of stock options.** Companywide stock option plans are used to encourage employees to own a part of the company. Other plans are offered only to management personnel, both to compensate and to motivate them. Usually, the issue of stock to employees under stock option plans is recorded like the issue of stock to any outsider.

REVIEW OF CONCEPTS AND TERMINOLOGY

The following concepts and terms were introduced in this chapter.

L O 1 **Articles of incorporation:** A contract between the state and the incorporators forming a corporation; also called *corporate charter*.

L O 1 **Audit committee:** A committee of the board of directors of a corporation, usually made up of outside directors, whose responsibility is to ensure that the board is objective in its evaluation of management's performance.

L O 3 **Authorized stock:** The maximum number of shares a corporation can issue without changing its charter with the state.

L O 5 **Callable preferred stock:** Preferred stock that can be redeemed or retired at a price stated at the option of the corporation.

L O 3   **Common stock:** Shares of stock that carry voting rights but that rank below preferred stock in terms of dividends and the distribution of assets.

L O 5   **Convertible preferred stock:** Preferred stock that can be exchanged for common stock at the option of the holder.

L O 1   **Corporation:** A separate legal entity having its own rights, privileges, and liabilities distinct from those of its owners.

L O 5   **Cumulative preferred stock:** Preferred stock on which unpaid dividends accumulate over time and must be satisfied in any given year before a dividend can be paid to common stockholders.

L O 4   **Dividend:** The distribution of a corporation's assets (usually cash) to its stockholders.

L O 5   **Dividends in arrears:** Dividends on cumulative preferred stock that remain unpaid in the year they were due.

L O 1   **Double taxation:** The act of taxing corporate earnings twice—once as the net income of the corporation and once as the dividends distributed to stockholders.

L O 4   **Ex-dividend:** A description of capital stock between the date of record and the date of payment when the right to a dividend already declared on the stock remains with the person who sells the stock and does not transfer to the person who buys it.

L O 3   **Initial public offering (IPO):** Common stock issue of a company that is selling its stock to the public for the first time.

L O 3   **Issued stock:** The shares of stock sold or otherwise transferred to stockholders.

L O 3   **Legal capital:** The number of shares of stock issued times the par value; the minimum amount that can be reported as contributed capital.

L O 4   **Liquidating dividend:** A dividend that exceeds retained earnings; usually paid when a corporation goes out of business or reduces its operations.

L O 5   **Noncumulative preferred stock:** Preferred stock that does not oblige the issuer to pay a missed dividend in a subsequent year when a dividend is paid.

L O 6   **No-par stock:** Capital stock that does not have a par value.

L O 2   **Organization costs:** The costs of forming a corporation.

L O 3   **Outstanding stock:** Stock that has been issued and is still in circulation.

L O 3   **Par value:** The arbitrary amount printed on each share of stock; used to determine the legal capital of a corporation.

L O 5   **Preferred stock:** Stock that has preference over common stock in terms of dividends and the distribution of assets.

L O 1   **Proxy:** A legal document, signed by the stockholder, giving another party the right to vote his or her shares.

L O 3   **Residual equity:** The common stock of a corporation.

L O 1   **Share of stock:** A unit of ownership in a corporation.

L O 6   **Stated value:** A value assigned by the board of directors of a corporation to no-par stock.

L O 3   **Stock certificate:** A document issued to a stockholder indicating the number of shares of stock the stockholder owns.

L O 8   **Stock option plan:** An agreement to issue stock to employees according to specified terms.

L O 7   **Treasury stock:** Capital stock, either common or preferred, that has been issued and reacquired by the issuing company but has not been resold or retired.

L O 3   **Underwriter:** An intermediary between the corporation and the public who facilitates an issue of stock or other securities for a fee.

REVIEW PROBLEM

STOCK JOURNAL ENTRIES AND STOCKHOLDERS' EQUITY

L O 2, 3, 4,
5, 6, 7   The Beta Corporation was organized in 19x1 in the state of Arizona. Its charter authorized the corporation to issue 1,000,000 shares of $1 par value common stock and an

additional 25,000 shares of 4 percent, $20 par value cumulative convertible preferred stock. Here are the transactions that related to the company's stock during 19x1.

Feb. 12 Issued 100,000 shares of common stock for $125,000.

  20 Issued 3,000 shares of common stock for accounting and legal services. The services were billed to the company at $3,600.

Mar. 15 Issued 120,000 shares of common stock to Edward Jackson in exchange for a building and land that had appraised values of $100,000 and $25,000, respectively.

Apr. 2 Purchased 20,000 shares of common stock for the treasury at $1.25 per share from an individual who changed his mind about investing in the company.

July 1 Issued 25,000 shares of preferred stock for $500,000.

Sept. 30 Sold 10,000 of the shares in the treasury for $1.50 per share.

Dec. 31 The company reported net income of $40,000 for 19x1, and the board declared dividends of $25,000, payable on January 15 to stockholders of record on January 8. Dividends included preferred stock cash dividends for one-half year.

REQUIRED

1. Prepare the journal entries necessary to record these transactions. Then close the Income Summary and Cash Dividends Declared accounts to Retained Earnings. Following the December 31 entry to record dividends, show dividends payable for each class of stock.
2. Prepare the stockholders' equity section of the Beta Corporation balance sheet as of December 31, 19x1.

ANSWER TO REVIEW PROBLEM

1. Prepare the journal entries.

19x1			
Feb. 12	Cash	125,000	
	Common Stock		100,000
	Paid-in Capital in Excess of Par Value, Common		25,000
	Sale of 100,000 shares of $1 par value common stock for $1.25 per share		
20	Organization Costs	3,600	
	Common Stock		3,000
	Paid-in Capital in Excess of Par Value, Common		600
	Issue of 3,000 shares of $1 par value common stock for billed accounting and legal services of $3,600		
Mar. 15	Building	100,000	
	Land	25,000	
	Common Stock		120,000
	Paid-in Capital in Excess of Par Value, Common		5,000
	Issue of 120,000 shares of $1 par value common stock for a building and land appraised at $100,000 and $25,000, respectively		
Apr. 2	Treasury Stock, Common	25,000	
	Cash		25,000
	Purchase of 20,000 shares of common stock for the treasury at $1.25 per share		

19x1

July 1	Cash		500,000	
	Preferred Stock			500,000
	Sale of 25,000 shares of $20 par value preferred stock for $20 per share			
Sept. 30	Cash		15,000	
	Treasury Stock, Common			12,500
	Paid-in Capital, Treasury Stock			2,500
	Sale of 10,000 shares of treasury stock at $1.50 per share; original cost was $1.25 per share			
Dec. 31	Cash Dividends Declared		25,000	
	Cash Dividends Payable			25,000
	Declaration of a $25,000 cash dividend to preferred and common stockholders			

Total dividend	$25,000
Less preferred stock cash dividend:	
$500,000 $\times$ .04 $\times$ 6/12	10,000
Common stock cash dividend	$15,000

31	Income Summary		40,000	
	Retained Earnings			40,000
	To close the Income Summary account to Retained Earnings			
31	Retained Earnings		25,000	
	Cash Dividends Declared			25,000
	To close the Cash Dividends Declared account to Retained Earnings			

2. Prepare the stockholders' equity section of the balance sheet.

Beta Corporation
Balance Sheet
December 31, 19x1

Stockholders' Equity

Contributed Capital			
Preferred Stock—4% cumulative convertible, $20 par value, 25,000 shares authorized, issued, and outstanding			$500,000
Common Stock—$1 par value, 1,000,000 shares authorized, 223,000 shares issued, and 213,000 shares outstanding		$223,000	
Paid-in Capital in Excess of Par Value, Common		30,600	
Paid-in Capital, Treasury Stock		2,500	256,100
Total Contributed Capital			$756,100
Retained Earnings			15,000
Total Contributed Capital and Retained Earnings			$771,100
Less Treasury Stock, Common (10,000 shares, at cost)			12,500
Total Stockholders' Equity			$758,600

CHAPTER ASSIGNMENTS

QUESTIONS

1. What is a corporation, and how is it formed?
2. What is the role of the board of directors in a corporation, and how does it differ from the role of management?
3. Who are the typical officers in the management of a corporation, and what are their duties?
4. Identify and explain several advantages of the corporate form of business.
5. Identify and explain several disadvantages of the corporate form of business.
6. What are the organization costs of a corporation?
7. What is the proper accounting treatment of organization costs?
8. What is the legal capital of a corporation, and what is its significance?
9. Describe the significance of the following dates as they relate to dividends: (a) date of declaration, (b) date of record, and (c) date of payment.
10. Explain the accounting treatment of cash dividends.
11. What are dividends in arrears, and how should they be disclosed in the financial statements?
12. Define the terms *cumulative, convertible,* and *callable* as they apply to preferred stock.
13. How is the value of stock determined when stock is issued for noncash assets?
14. Define *treasury stock* and explain why a company would purchase its own stock.
15. What is the proper classification of the following accounts on the balance sheet? Indicate whether stockholders' equity accounts are contributed capital, retained earnings, or contra stockholders' equity. (a) Organization Costs; (b) Common Stock; (c) Treasury Stock; (d) Paid-in Capital, Treasury Stock; (e) Paid-in Capital in Excess of Par Value, Common; (f) Paid-in Capital in Excess of Stated Value, Common; and (g) Retained Earnings.
16. What is a stock option plan and why does a company have one?

SHORT EXERCISES

SE 1. *Advantages and*
L O 1 *Disadvantages of the*
Corporation
Check Figure: Advantages: 1, 3, 4, 6

Identify whether each of the following characteristics is an advantage or a disadvantage of the corporate form of business.

1. Ease of transfer of ownership
2. Taxation
3. Separate legal entity
4. Lack of mutual agency
5. Government regulation
6. Continuous existence

SE 2. *Journal Entries for*
L O 2 *Organization Costs*
No check figure

At the beginning of 19x1, Scotch Company incurred two organization costs: (1) attorney's fees with a market value of $5,000, paid with 3,000 shares of $1 par common stock, and (2) incorporation fees paid to the state of $3,000. Prepare the separate journal entries necessary to record those transactions and to amortize organization costs for the first year, assuming that the company elects to write off organization costs over five years.

SE 3. *Stockholders' Equity*
L O 3
Check Figure: Total Stockholders'
Equity: $615,000

Prepare the stockholders' equity section of Aguilar Corporation's balance sheet from the following accounts and balances on December 31, 19xx.

Account Name	Balance Debit	Credit
Common Stock—$10 par value, 60,000 shares authorized, 40,000 shares issued, and 39,000 shares outstanding		$400,000
Paid-in Capital in Excess of Par Value, Common		200,000
Retained Earnings		30,000
Treasury Stock, Common (1,000 shares, at cost)	$15,000	

SE 4. *Cash Dividends*
L O 4
No check figure

Thai Corporation has authorized 100,000 shares of $1 par value common stock, of which 80,000 are issued and 70,000 are outstanding. On May 15, the board of directors declared a cash dividend of $.10 per share payable on June 15 to stockholders of record on June 1. Prepare the entries, as necessary, for each of the three dates.

SE 5. *Preferred Stock Dividends with Dividends in Arrears*
L O 5
Check Figures: Common stock dividends: 19x2, $4,000; 19x3, $32,000

The Timonium Corporation has 1,000 shares of its $100, 8 percent cumulative preferred stock outstanding and 20,000 shares of its $1 par value common stock outstanding. In its first three years of operation, the board of directors of Timonium Corporation paid cash dividends as follows: 19x1, none; 19x2, $20,000; and 19x3, $40,000.

Determine the total cash dividends and dividends per share paid to the preferred and common stockholders during each of the three years.

SE 6. *Issuance of Stock*
L O 6
No check figure

Carlotta Company is authorized to issue 100,000 shares of common stock. The company sold 5,000 shares at $12 per share. Prepare journal entries to record the sale of stock for cash under each of the following independent alternatives: (1) The stock has a par value of $5, and (2) the stock has no par value but a stated value of $1 per share.

SE 7. *Issuance of Stock for Noncash Assets*
L O 6
No check figure

Malaysia Corporation issued 8,000 shares of its $1 par value common stock for some land. The land had a fair market value of $50,000.

Prepare the journal entries necessary to record the issuance of the stock for the land under each of the following independent conditions: (1) The stock was selling for $7 per share on the day of the transaction, and (2) management attempted to place a value on the common stock but could not do so.

SE 8. *Treasury Stock Transactions*
L O 7
No check figure

Prepare the journal entries necessary to record the following stock transactions of the Curry Company during 19xx.

Oct. 5   Purchased 1,000 shares of its own $2 par value common stock for $20, the current market price.
   17   Sold 250 shares of treasury stock purchased on Oct. 5 for $25 per share.
   21   Sold 400 shares of treasury stock purchased on Oct. 5 for $18 per share.

SE 9. *Retirement of Treasury Stock*
L O 7
No check figure

On October 28, 19xx, the Curry Company (SE 8) retired the remaining 350 shares of treasury stock. The shares were originally issued at $5 per share. Prepare the necessary journal entry.

SE 10. *Exercise of Stock Options*
L O 8
No check figure

On June 6, George Jensen exercised his option to purchase 10,000 shares of Marsalis Company $1 par value common stock at an option price of $4. The market price per share was $4 on the grant date and $18 on the exercise date. Record the transaction on Marsalis's books.

EXERCISES

E 1. *Journal Entries for*
L O 2, 6 *Organization Costs*
No check figure

The Korman Corporation was organized during 19x7. At the beginning of the fiscal year, the company incurred the following organization costs: (1) attorney's fees with a market value of $3,000, paid with 2,000 shares of $1 par common stock; (2) incorporation fees paid to the state, $2,500; and (3) accountant's services that normally would be billed at $1,500, paid with 1,100 shares of $1 par value common stock.

Prepare the separate journal entries necessary to record those transactions and to amortize organization costs for the first year, assuming that the company elects to write off organization costs over five years.

E 2. *Stockholders' Equity*
L O 3, 7
Check Figure: Total Stockholders'
Equity: $1,098,000

The following accounts and balances were taken from the records of Narim Corporation on December 31, 19xx.

	Balance	
Account	**Debit**	**Credit**
Preferred Stock—$100 par value, 9% cumulative, 10,000 shares authorized, 6,000 shares issued and outstanding		$600,000
Common Stock—$12 par value, 45,000 shares authorized, 30,000 shares issued, and 27,500 shares outstanding		360,000
Paid-in Capital in Excess of Par Value, Common		170,000
Retained Earnings		23,000
Treasury Stock, Common (2,500 shares, at cost)	$55,000	

Prepare a stockholders' equity section for Narim Corporation's balance sheet.

E 3. *Characteristics of*
L O 3 *Common and*
Preferred Stock
Check Figure: Preferred: 1, 3, 4,
6, 8, 9

Indicate whether each characteristic listed below is more closely associated with common stock (C) or preferred stock (P).

1. Often receives dividends at a set rate
2. Is considered the residual equity of a company
3. Can be callable
4. Can be convertible
5. More likely to have dividends that vary in amount from year to year
6. Can be entitled to receive dividends not paid in past years
7. Likely to have full voting rights
8. Receives assets first in liquidation
9. Generally receives dividends before other classes of stock

E 4. *Stock Journal Entries*
L O 3, 6 *and Stockholders'*
Equity
Check Figure: 2. Total Stockholders'
Equity: $1,700,000

The Winkler Hospital Supply Corporation was organized in 19xx. The company was authorized to issue 100,000 shares of no-par common stock with a stated value of $5 per share, and 20,000 shares of $100 par value, 6 percent noncumulative preferred stock. On March 1, the company sold 60,000 shares of its common stock for $15 per share and 8,000 shares of its preferred stock for $100 per share.

1. Prepare the journal entries to record the sale of the stock.
2. Prepare the stockholders' equity section of the company's balance sheet immediately after the common and preferred stock was issued.

E 5. *Cash Dividends*
L O 4
No check figure

Downey Corporation has secured authorization from the state for 200,000 shares of $10 par value common stock. There are 140,000 shares issued and outstanding. On June 5, the board of directors declared a $.50 per share cash dividend to be paid on June 25 to stockholders of record on June 15. Prepare the journal entries necessary to record these events.

E 6. *Cash Dividends*
L O 4
No check figure

Gayle Corporation has 500,000 authorized shares of $1 par value common stock, of which 400,000 are issued and 360,000 are outstanding. On October 15, the board of directors declared a cash dividend of $.25 per share payable on November 15 to stockholders of record on November 1. Prepare the entries, as necessary, for each of the three dates.

E 7. *Cash Dividends with*
L O 5 *Dividends in*
 Arrears
Check Figures: Total preferred dividends: 19x2, $120,000; 19x3, $90,000; 19x4, $70,000

The Matsuta Corporation has 10,000 shares of its $100 par value, 7 percent cumulative preferred stock outstanding, and 50,000 shares of its $1 par value common stock outstanding. In its first four years of operation, the board of directors of Matsuta Corporation paid cash dividends as follows: 19x1, none; 19x2, $120,000; 19x3, $140,000; 19x4, $140,000.

Determine the dividends per share and total cash dividends paid to the preferred and common stockholders during each of the four years.

E 8. *Preferred and*
L O 5 *Common Cash*
 Dividends
Check Figures: 1. Total preferred dividends: 19x1, $40,000; 19x2, $30,000; 19x3, $60,000

The Goss-Carterly Corporation pays dividends at the end of each year. The dividends paid for 19x1, 19x2, and 19x3 were $40,000, $30,000, and $90,000, respectively.

Calculate the total amount of dividends paid each year to the common and preferred stockholders under each of the following independent capital structures: (1) 10,000 shares of $100 par, 6 percent noncumulative preferred stock and 30,000 shares of $10 par common stock. (2) 5,000 shares of $100 par, 7 percent cumulative preferred stock and 30,000 shares of $10 par common stock. There were no dividends in arrears at the beginning of 19x1.

E 9. *Issuance of Stock*
L O 6
No check figure

Foth Company is authorized to issue 200,000 shares of common stock. On August 1, the company sold 10,000 shares at $25 per share. Prepare journal entries to record the sale of stock for cash under each of the following independent alternatives.

1. The stock has a par value of $25.
2. The stock has a par value of $10.
3. The stock has no par value.
4. The stock has a stated value of $1 per share.

E 10. *Journal Entries:*
L O 6 *Stated Value Stock*
No check figure

The Sayre Corporation is authorized to issue 100,000 shares of no-par stock. The company recently sold 40,000 shares for $13 per share.

1. Prepare the journal entry to record the sale of the stock assuming there is no stated value.
2. Prepare the journal entry if a $10 stated value is authorized by the company's board of directors.

E 11. *Issuance of Stock for*
L O 6 *Noncash Assets*
No check figure

On July 1, 19xx, Wayside, a new corporation, issued 20,000 shares of its common stock to obtain a corporate headquarters building. The building has a fair market value of $300,000 and a book value of $200,000. Because the corporation is new, it is not possible to establish a market value for the common stock.

Record the issuance of stock for the building, assuming each of the following independent conditions: (1) The par value of the stock is $5 per share; (2) the stock is no-par stock; and (3) the stock has a stated value of $2 per share.

E 12. *Issuance of Stock for*
L O 6 *Noncash Assets*
No check figure

The Probst Corporation issued 2,000 shares of its $10 par value common stock for some land. The land had a fair market value of $30,000.

Prepare the journal entries necessary to record the stock issue for the land under each of the following conditions: (1) The stock was selling for $14 per share on the day of the transaction; and (2) management attempted to place a market value on the common stock but could not do so.

E 13. *Treasury Stock*
L O 7 *Transactions*
No check figure

Prepare the journal entries necessary to record the following stock transactions of the Henderson Company during 19xx.

May 5 Purchased 400 shares of its own $1 par value common stock for $10 per share, the current market price.
 17 Sold 150 shares of treasury stock purchased on May 5 for $11 per share.
 21 Sold 100 shares of treasury stock purchased on May 5 for $10 per share.
 28 Sold the remaining 150 shares of treasury stock purchased on May 5 for $9.50 per share.

E 14. *Treasury Stock*
L O 7 *Transactions*
Including
Retirement

No check figure

Prepare the journal entries necessary to record the following stock transactions of Nakate Corporation, which represent all treasury stock transactions entered into by the company.

June 1 Purchased 2,000 shares of its own $15 par value common stock for $35 per share, the current market price.
    10 Sold 500 shares of treasury stock purchased on June 1 for $40 per share.
    20 Sold 700 shares of treasury stock purchased on June 1 for $29 per share.
    30 Retired the remaining shares purchased on June 1. The original issue price was $21 per share.

E 15. *Exercise of Stock*
L O 8 *Options*

Check Figure: Cash: $120,000

Record the following equity transaction of the Evans Company in 19xx.

May 5 Walter Evans exercised his option to purchase 10,000 shares of $1 par value common stock at an option price of $12. The market price per share on the grant date was $12, and it was $25 on the exercise date.

SKILLS DEVELOPMENT EXERCISES

Conceptual Analysis

SDE 1. *Reasons for Issuing*
L O 3, 6 *Common Stock*

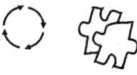

No check figure

For decades *Allstate Corporation,* one of the largest automobile, home, and life insurance companies in the United States, was a division of *Sears, Roebuck & Co.* In June 1993, the company had an initial public offering that raised $2.5 billion, as the public bought 19.9 percent of Allstate common shares for $27 per share. Sears retained 80.1 percent of the shares. The company had paid an estimated $2.5 billion in claims as a result of Hurricane Andrew in Florida the previous year, but it expected to return to profitable operations in 1993 and 1994. Allstate's chief executive officer was quoted as saying, "Going public really focused us."[13] What advantages are there to Sears and Allstate in raising money by issuing common stock rather than bonds? Why would the chief executive officer say that going public "really focused us"?

SDE 2. *Effect of the*
L O 5 *Omission of*
Preferred Dividends

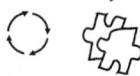

No check figure

Tucson Electric Company omitted all its preferred stock dividends indefinitely in an effort to improve liquidity. All of the company's cumulative preferred stock was affected. According to the *Wall Street Journal,* "Some interpreted the drastic action as a requisite for the cash-strapped utility to secure a new credit agreement. . . . If the credit agreement falls through, the omission of preferred-stock dividends would suggest Tucson Electric is perilously close to filing for bankruptcy."[14] What are cumulative preferred shares? Why is the omission of dividends on those shares a drastic action? If new bank financing is not obtained, why would the company have to consider declaring bankruptcy?

SDE 3. *Reasons for Issuing*
L O 5 *Preferred Stock*

No check figure

Preferred stock is a hybrid security that has some of the characteristics of stock and some of the characteristics of bonds. Historically, preferred stock has not been a popular means of financing. In the last few years, however, it has become more attractive to companies and individual investors alike, and investors are buying large amounts because of high yields. Large preferred stock issues have been made by banks such as *Chase Manhattan, Citicorp, Republic New York,* and *Wells Fargo,* as well as other companies. The dividend yields on these stocks are over 9 percent, higher than the interest rates on comparable bonds.[15] Especially popular are preferred equity redemption convertible stocks, or PERCs, which are automatically convertible into common stock after three years if the company does not redeem or call them first and retire them. What

13. Hillary Durgin, "A New Hand Dealt to 1990s Allstate," *Crain's Chicago Business,* December 20, 1993.

14. Rick Wartzman, "Tucson Electric Omits Dividends on Preferred Stock," *Wall Street Journal,* December 10, 1990.

15. Tom Herman, "Preferreds' Rich Yields Blind Some Investors to Risks," *Wall Street Journal,* March 24, 1992.

reasons can you give for the popularity of preferred stock, and of PERCs in particular, when the tax-deductible interest on bonds is less costly? Discuss both the company's and the investor's standpoints.

SDE 4. *Purposes of Treasury*
L O 7 *Stock*

No check figure

This chapter discusses the recent popularity of issuing common and preferred stock. However, some companies have recently bought back their common stock. For example, because its stock had declined under the uncertainty of possible health care reforms, **Bristol-Myers Squibb** bought 25 million of its own shares. Other companies are awash in cash because of the decline in interest rates, layoffs to cut costs, and decreased need to make new investments. **Quaker Oats** has purchased 4.8 million of its own shares for $323 million and plans to purchase 5 million more. The Quaker Oats treasurer is quoted as saying, "We spend on new products, we make acquisitions, we raise the dividend, and we still can't soak up the cash." **Sun Microsystems** has cut its outstanding shares by 9 percent with an aggressive buyback program, and **PepsiCo** has purchased 50 million shares at a cost of $1.8 billion. For what reasons would a company buy back its own shares?

Ethical Dilemma

SDE 5. *Ethics of*
L O 1 *Incorporating an*
         Accounting Firm

No check figure

Traditionally, accounting firms have organized as partnerships or as professional corporations, a form of corporation that in many ways resembles a partnership. In recent years, some accounting firms have suffered large judgments as a result of lawsuits by investors who lost money when they invested in companies that went bankrupt. Because of the increased risk of large losses from malpractice suits, there is a movement to allow accounting firms to incorporate as long as they maintain a minimum level of partners' capital and carry malpractice insurance. Some accounting practitioners feel that incorporating would be a violation of their responsibility to the public. What features of the corporate form of business would be most advantageous to the partners of an accounting firm? Do you think it would be a violation of the public trust for an accounting firm to incorporate?

Research Activity

SDE 6. *Reading Corporate*
L O 4, 5, *Annual Reports*
   6, 8

No check figure

In your library, select the annual reports of three corporations. You can choose them from the same industry or at random, at the direction of your instructor. (**Note:** You may be asked to use these companies again in the Research Activities in later chapters.) Prepare a table with a column for each corporation. Then answer the following questions for each corporation: Does the corporation have preferred stock? If so, what are the par value and the indicated dividend, and is the preferred stock cumulative or convertible? Is the common stock par value or no-par? What is the par value or stated value? What cash dividends, if any, were paid in the past year? From the notes to the financial statements, determine whether the company has an employee stock option plan. What are some of its provisions? Be prepared to discuss the characteristics of the stocks and dividends for your selected companies in class.

Decision-Making Practice

SDE 7. *Analysis of*
L O 3 *Alternative*
         Financing Methods

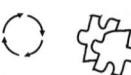

Check Figures: 1. Debt to Equity
Ratio: A, 100%; B, 5.9%; C, 5.9%

Companies offering services to the computer technology industry are growing quickly. Participating in this growth, **Northeast Servotech Corporation** has expanded rapidly in recent years. Because of its profitability, the company has been able to grow without obtaining external financing. This fact is reflected in its current balance sheet, which contains no long-term debt. The liability and stockholders' equity sections of the balance sheet on March 31, 19xx follow.

Northeast Servotech Corporation
Partial Balance Sheet
March 31, 19xx

Liabilities

Current Liabilities	$ 500,000

Stockholders' Equity

Common Stock—$10 par value, 500,000 shares authorized, 100,000 shares issued and outstanding	$1,000,000	
Paid-in Capital in Excess of Par Value, Common	1,800,000	
Retained Earnings	1,700,000	
Total Stockholders' Equity		4,500,000
Total Liabilities and Stockholders' Equity		$5,000,000

The company now has the opportunity to double its size by purchasing the operations of a rival company for $4,000,000. If the purchase goes through, Northeast Servotech will become the top company in its specialized industry in the northeastern part of the country. The problem for management is how to finance the purchase. After much study and discussion with bankers and underwriters, management has prepared three financing alternatives to present to the board of directors, which must authorize the purchase and the financing.

Alternative A: The company could issue $4,000,000 of long-term debt. Given the company's financial rating and the current market rates, management believes the company will have to pay an interest rate of 17 percent on the debt.

Alternative B: The company could issue 40,000 shares of 12 percent, $100 par value preferred stock.

Alternative C: The company could issue 100,000 additional shares of $10 par value common stock at $40 per share.

Management explains to the board that the interest on the long-term debt is tax-deductible and that the applicable income tax rate is 40 percent. The board members know that a dividend of $.80 per share of common stock was paid last year, up from $.60 and $.40 per share in the two years before that. The board has had a policy of regular increases in dividends of $.20 per share. The board feels that each of the three financing alternatives is feasible and now wants to study the financial effects of each alternative.

1. Prepare a schedule to show how the liabilities and stockholders' equity sections of Northeast Servotech's balance sheet would look under each alternative, and compute the debt to equity ratio (total liabilities ÷ total stockholders' equity) for each.
2. Compute and compare the cash needed to pay the interest or dividends for each kind of new financing net of income taxes in the first year.
3. How might the cash needed to pay for the financing change in future years?
4. Evaluate the alternatives, giving arguments for and against each one.

PROBLEM SET A

A 1. *Organization Costs,*
L O 2, 3, *Stock and Dividend*
4, 6 *Journal Entries, and*
Stockholders' Equity

Check Figure: 2. Total Stockholders'
Equity: $252,700

On March 1, 19xx, Benson Corporation began operations with a charter from the state that authorized 100,000 shares of $2 par value common stock. Over the next quarter, the firm engaged in the following transactions.

Mar. 1 Issued 30,000 shares of common stock, $100,000.
2 Paid fees associated with obtaining the charter and organizing the corporation, $12,000.
10 Issued 30,000 shares of stock for land and a building with a fair market value of $19,000 and $64,000, respectively.
Apr. 10 Issued 13,000 shares of common stock, $65,000.
May 31 Closed the Income Summary account. Net income earned during the first quarter, $12,000.
31 The board of directors declared a $.10 per share cash dividend to be paid on June 15 to shareholders of record on June 10.
31 Closed Cash Dividends Declared to Retained Earnings.

REQUIRED

1. Prepare general journal entries to record the transactions and closing entries indicated above.
2. Prepare the stockholders' equity section of Benson Corporation's balance sheet on May 31, 19xx.
3. Assuming that the payment for organization costs on March 2 was going to be amortized over five years, what adjusting entry was made on May 31 to record three months' amortization?
4. How does the adjusting entry in **3** affect the firm's balance sheet, including the resulting amount of organization costs?

A 2. *Preferred and*
L O 5 *Common Stock*
Dividends

Check Figures: 1. 19x3 total dividends:
Preferred, $60,000; Common, $34,000

The Sabatino Corporation had the following stock outstanding from 19x1 through 19x4.

Preferred stock: $50 par value, 8 percent cumulative, 10,000 shares authorized, issued, and outstanding
Common stock: $5 par value, 200,000 shares authorized, issued, and outstanding

The company paid $30,000, $30,000, $94,000, and $130,000 in dividends during 19x1, 19x2, 19x3, and 19x4, respectively.

REQUIRED

1. Determine the dividend per share and the total dividends paid to common stockholders and preferred stockholders in 19x1, 19x2, 19x3, and 19x4.
2. Perform the same computations, with the assumption that the preferred stock was noncumulative.

A 3. *Treasury Stock*
L O 7 *Transactions*

No check figure

The Dwyer Company was involved in the following treasury stock transactions during 19xx.

a. Purchased 52,000 shares of its $1 par value common stock on the market for $20 per share.
b. Sold 16,000 shares of the treasury stock for $21 per share.
c. Sold 12,000 shares of the treasury stock for $19 per share.
d. Sold 20,000 shares of the treasury stock remaining for $17 per share.
e. Purchased an additional 8,000 shares for $18 per share.
f. Retired all the remaining shares of treasury stock. All shares originally were issued at $8 per share.

REQUIRED

Record these transactions in general journal form.

A 4. *Comprehensive*
L O 2, 3, 4, *Stockholders' Equity*
5, 6, 7 *Transactions*

Check Figure: 2. Total Stockholders'
Equity: $475,040

Cabrini, Inc. was organized and authorized to issue 10,000 shares of $100 par value, 9 percent preferred stock and 100,000 shares of no-par, $5 stated value common stock on July 1, 19xx. Stock-related transactions for Cabrini were as follows:

July 1 Issued 20,000 shares of common stock at $11 per share.
1 Issued 1,000 shares of common stock at $11 per share for services rendered in connection with the organization of the company.
2 Issued 2,000 shares of preferred stock at par value for cash.

July 10 Issued 5,000 shares of common stock for land on which the asking price was $60,000. Market value of the stock was $12. Management wishes to record the land at full market value of the stock.

31 Closed the Income Summary account. Net income earned during July was $13,000.

Aug. 2 Purchased 3,000 shares of common stock for the treasury at $13 per share.

10 Declared a cash dividend for one month on the outstanding preferred stock and $.02 per share on common stock outstanding, payable on August 22 to stockholders of record on August 12.

12 Date of record for cash dividends.

22 Paid cash dividends.

31 Closed the Income Summary and Cash Dividends Declared accounts. Net income during August was $12,000.

REQUIRED

1. Prepare general journal entries to record the transactions.
2. Prepare the stockholders' equity section of the balance sheet as it would appear on August 31, 19xx.

A 5. *Comprehensive*
L O 2, 3, 4, *Stockholders' Equity*
6, 7, 8 *Transactions*

Check Figure: 2. Total Stockholders' Equity: $330,375

In January 19xx, the Abelman Corporation was organized and authorized to issue 2,000,000 shares of no-par common stock and 50,000 shares of 5 percent, $50 par value, noncumulative preferred stock. The stock-related transactions for the first year's operations follow.

Jan. 19 Sold 15,000 shares of the common stock for $31,500. State law requires a minimum of $1 stated value per share.

21 Issued 5,000 shares of common stock to attorneys and accountants for services valued at $11,000 and provided during the organization of the corporation.

Feb. 7 Issued 30,000 shares of common stock for a building that had an appraised value of $78,000.

Mar. 22 Purchased 10,000 shares of common stock for the treasury at $3 per share.

June 30 Closed the Income Summary account. Reported $80,000 net income for the first six months of operations ended June 30.

July 15 Issued 5,000 shares of common stock to employees under a stock option plan that allows any employee to buy shares at the current market price, which today is $3 per share.

Aug. 1 Sold 2,500 shares of treasury stock for $4 per share.

Sept. 1 Declared a cash dividend of $.15 per common share to be paid on September 25 to stockholders of record on September 15.

15 Cash dividend date of record.

25 Paid cash dividend to stockholders of record on September 15.

Oct. 30 Issued 4,000 shares of common stock for a piece of land. The stock was selling for $3 per share, and the land had a fair market value of $12,000.

Dec. 15 Issued 2,200 shares of preferred stock for $50 per share.

31 Closed the Income Summary and Cash Dividends Declared accounts. Reported $20,000 net income for the past six months of operations.

REQUIRED

1. Prepare the journal entries to record all transactions above.
2. Prepare the stockholders' equity section of Abelman Corporation's balance sheet as of December 31, 19xx.

PROBLEM SET B

B 1. *Organization Costs,*
L O 2, 3, *Stock and Dividend*
4, 6 *Journal Entries, and*
Stockholders' Equity

Check Figure: 2. Total Stockholders' Equity: $864,200

Forsyth Corporation began operations on September 1, 19xx. The corporation's charter authorized 300,000 shares of $4 par value common stock. Forsyth Corporation engaged in the following transactions during its first quarter.

Sept. 1 Issued 50,000 shares of common stock, $250,000.

1 Paid an attorney $16,000 for work done to organize the corporation and obtain the corporate charter from the state.

Oct. 2 Issued 80,000 shares of common stock, $480,000.

24 Issued 24,000 shares of common stock for land and a warehouse. The land and warehouse had a fair market value of $25,000 and $100,000, respectively.

Nov. 30   The board of directors declared a cash dividend of $.20 per share to be paid on December 15 to stockholders of record on December 10.

30   Closed the Income Summary and Cash Dividends Declared accounts for the first quarter. Revenues were $210,000 and expenses $170,000. (Assume revenues and expenses already have been closed to Income Summary.)

REQUIRED

1. Prepare general journal entries to record the first-quarter transactions and the closing entries.
2. Prepare the stockholders' equity section of Forsyth Corporation's November 30, 19xx, balance sheet.
3. Assuming that the payment to the attorney on September 1 was going to be amortized over five years, what adjusting entry was made on November 30?
4. How does the adjusting entry in **3** affect the balance sheet, including the resulting amount of organization costs?

B 2.   *Preferred and*
L O 5   *Common Stock*
Dividends

Check Figures: 1. 19x5 total dividends: Preferred, $210,000; Common, $190,000

The Jefferson Corporation had both common stock and preferred stock outstanding from 19x4 through 19x6. Information about each stock for the three years is as follows:

Type	Par Value	Shares Outstanding	Other
Preferred	$100	20,000	7% cumulative
Common	10	600,000	

The company paid $70,000, $400,000, and $550,000 in dividends for 19x4 through 19x6, respectively.

REQUIRED

1. Determine the dividend per share and total dividends paid to the common and preferred stockholders each year.
2. Repeat the computations performed in **1,** with the assumption that the preferred stock was noncumulative.

B 3.   *Treasury Stock*
L O 7   *Transactions*

No check figure

The Spivy Corporation was involved in the following treasury stock transactions during 19x7.

a. Purchased 80,000 shares of its $1 par value common stock at $2.50 per share.
b. Purchased 16,000 shares of its common stock at $2.80 per share.
c. Sold 44,000 shares purchased in **a** for $131,000.
d. Sold the other 36,000 shares purchased in **a** for $72,000.
e. Sold 6,000 of the remaining shares of treasury stock for $1.60 per share.
f. Retired all the remaining shares of treasury stock. All shares originally were issued at $1.50 per share.

REQUIRED

Record the treasury stock transactions in general journal form.

B 4.   *Comprehensive*
L O 2, 3, 4,   *Stockholders' Equity*
5, 6, 7   *Transactions*

Check Figure: 2. Total Stockholders' Equity: $728,325

The Specialty Plastics Corporation was chartered in the state of Wisconsin. The company was authorized to issue 10,000 shares of $100 par value, 6 percent preferred stock and 100,000 shares of no-par common stock. The common stock has a $1 stated value. The stock-related transactions for March and April 19xx were as follows:

Mar. 3   Issued 10,000 shares of common stock for $60,000 worth of services rendered in organizing and chartering the corporation.

15   Issued 16,000 shares of common stock for land, which had an asking price of $100,000. The common stock had a market value of $6 per share.

22   Issued 5,000 shares of preferred stock for $500,000.

31   Closed the Income Summary account. Net income for March was $9,000.

Apr. 4   Issued 10,000 shares of common stock for $60,000.

10   Purchased 2,500 shares of common stock for the treasury for $6,500.

15   Declared a cash dividend for one month on the outstanding preferred stock and $.05 per share on common stock outstanding, payable on April 30 to stockholders of record on April 25.

25   Date of record for cash dividends.

30   Paid cash dividends.

30   Closed the Income Summary and Cash Dividends Declared accounts. Net income for April was $14,000.

1. Prepare general journal entries for March and April.
2. Prepare the stockholders' equity section of the company's balance sheet as of April 30, 19xx.

B 5. *Comprehensive*
L O 2, 3, 4, *Stockholders' Equity*
6, 7, 8 *Transactions*
Check Figure: 2. Total Stockholders' Equity: $4,403,600

The Sun Lighting Corporation was organized and authorized to issue 100,000 shares of 6 percent, $100 par value, noncumulative preferred stock and 3,000,000 shares of $5 par value common stock. The stock-related transactions for the first six months of 19xx operations were as follows:

Apr. 3 Issued 12,000 shares of common stock for legal and other organization fees valued at $60,000.

29 Issued 40,000 shares of common stock for a building and land appraised at $150,000 and $80,000, respectively.

May 5 Sold 300,000 shares of common stock for $6 per share.

June 30 Closed the Income Summary account for the first quarter of operations. Net income for the first quarter was $200,000. (Assume that revenues and expenses already have been closed to Income Summary.)

July 10 Issued 2,000 shares of common stock to employees under a stock option plan. The plan allows employees to purchase the stock at the current market price, $6 per share.

17 Issued 200,000 shares of common stock for $8 per share.

Aug. 8 Purchased 20,000 shares of common stock for the treasury at $7.50 per share.

Sept. 11 Declared a cash dividend of $.10 per common share to be paid on September 25 to stockholders of record on September 18.

18 Cash dividend date of record.

25 Paid the cash dividend to stockholders of record on September 18.

26 Issued 5,000 shares of preferred stock at par value.

29 Sold 8,000 shares held in the treasury for $10 per share.

30 Closed the Income Summary and Cash Dividends Declared accounts for the second quarter of operations. Net income for the second quarter was $125,000.

1. Prepare general journal entries to record the stock-related transactions of the Sun Lighting Corporation.
2. Prepare the stockholders' equity section of Sun Lighting Corporation's balance sheet as of September 30, 19xx.

FINANCIAL REPORTING AND ANALYSIS CASES

Interpreting Financial Reports

FRA 1. *Effect of Stock Issue*
L O 3, 6

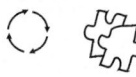

Check Figure: 2. Total Stockholders' Equity (in thousands): $2,037,816

UAL Corporation is a holding company whose primary subsidiary is United Airlines, which provides passenger and cargo air transportation to 141 airports worldwide. On March 21, 1991, UAL announced a common stock issue in a tombstone ad in the *Wall Street Journal:*

1,500,000 Shares
UAL Corporation
Common Stock
($5 par value)
Price $146 per share

In fact, UAL sold 1,733,100 shares of stock at $146, for net proceeds of $247.2 million.

Shown at the top of the next page is a portion of the stockholders' equity section of the balance sheet from UAL's 1990 annual report.

	1990	1989
	(in thousands)	
Common Stock, $5 par value; authorized 125,000,000 shares; issued 23,467,880 shares in 1990 and 23,419,953 shares in 1989	117,339	117,100
Additional Paid-in Capital	52,391	47,320
Retained Earnings	1,620,885	1,526,534

REQUIRED

1. Assuming that all the shares were issued at the price indicated and that UAL received the net proceeds, prepare the entry in UAL's accounting records to record the stock issue.
2. Prepare the portion of the stockholders' equity section of the balance sheet shown above after the issue of the common stock, based on the information given. Round all answers to the nearest thousand.
3. Based on your answer in **2,** did UAL have to increase its authorized shares to undertake this stock issue?
4. What amount per share did UAL receive and how much did UAL's underwriter receive to help in issuing the stock if investors paid $146 per share? What does the underwriter do to earn his or her fee?

FRA 2.   *Preferred Stock*
L O 5, 6, 8   *Characteristics and*
          Stock Options

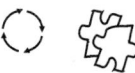

No check figure

At the beginning of fiscal 1986, **Navistar International,** a manufacturer of medium- and heavy-duty diesel trucks, had 685,000 shares of Series A no-par, callable, convertible, cumulative preferred stock outstanding.[16] During fiscal 1986, 16,000 shares were called at $25.67 per share and retired. In addition, 669,000 shares were converted to 2,500,000 shares of no-par common stock. The total carrying value of the preferred stock converted was $17,600,000. The same year, employees exercised employee stock options on 56,000 shares of no-par common stock at $3.60 per share.

REQUIRED

1. Four adjectives are used to describe Navistar's Series A preferred stock. Explain what each means.
2. Prepare journal entries to record the call and the conversion of preferred shares.
3. Prepare the entry to record the exercise of stock options.
4. In 1986 Navistar had a net loss of $12,240,000 and a deficit in Retained Earnings of $1,889,168,000. The company has not paid a cash dividend since 1981. Why would the preferred stockholders and the employees want to own Navistar common stock?

FRA 3.   *Purpose of Treasury*
L O 7   *Stock and Its*
        Retirement

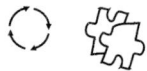

Check Figure: Average cost of treasury stock: $69.44

In its 1989 annual report, **Atlantic Richfield Company** indicated that the number of common shares held in the treasury decreased from 45,546,171 in 1988 to 3,397,381 in 1989. The following also was reported.

> By Board authorization, effective December 31, 1989 the Company cancelled 50 million shares of common stock held in treasury. As a result of the cancellation, common stock decreased by $125 million, capital in excess of par value of stock decreased by $228 million, and retained earnings decreased by $3,119 million.[17]

The shares canceled or retired represent almost 25 percent of the shares of common stock issued by Atlantic Richfield. Explain the accounting for the treasury shares by Atlantic Richfield. Did the company buy any treasury shares during the year? What journal entry was made to record the cancellation or retirement of the treasury shares? At what average price were the treasury shares purchased, and at what average price were they originally issued? What do you think was management's reason for purchasing the treasury shares?

16. Navistar International Corporation, *Annual Report,* 1986.
17. Atlantic Richfield Company, *Annual Report,* 1989.

International Company

FRA 4. *Stockholders' Equity*
L O 3, 4, *Transactions*
6, 8

No check figure

Peugeot S.A. is France's largest automobile maker. Its brands are Peugeot and Citroen. The stockholders' equity section of the company's balance sheet appears as follows:[18]

	1992	1991
Stockholders' Equity (in millions of French francs)		
Common stock (par value FF35 a share, 49,992,620 and 49,964,000 shares issued and outstanding)	1,750	1,749
Capital in excess of par value of stock	5,214	5,203
Reserves	46,180	44,766
Total stockholders' equity	53,144	51,718

Reserves are similar to retained earnings in U.S. financial statements. During 1992, the company paid FF648 million in dividends. The changes in common stock and capital in excess of par value of stock represent stock issued to employees in connection with the exercise of employee stock options. Prepare the journal entries to record the declaration and issue of dividends in 1992 and the issue of stock in connection with the employee stock options. Assuming that dividends and net income were the only factors that affected reserves during 1992, how much did Peugeot earn in 1992 in U.S. dollars (use an exchange rate of 5.8 French francs to the dollar)?

Toys "R" Us Annual Report

FRA 5. *Stockholders' Equity*
L O 3, 4, 8

REQUIRED

No check figure

Refer to the annual report in the appendix on Toys "R" Us to answer the following questions.

1. What type of capital stock does Toys "R" Us have? What is the par value? How many shares are authorized, issued, and outstanding at the end of 1995?
2. What is the policy of Toys "R" Us with regard to dividends? Does the company rely mostly on stock or earnings for its stockholders' equity?
3. What is management's policy with regard to treasury stock as stated in the letter to stockholders? Why do you think this policy was adopted?
4. Does the company have a stock option plan? To whom do the stock options apply? Do employees have significant stock options? Given the market price of the stock shown in the notes to the consolidated financial statements, do these options represent significant value to the executives?

18. Peugeot, S.A., *Annual Report*, 1992.

CHAPTER 13   *Retained Earnings and Corporate Income Statements*

LEARNING OBJECTIVES

1. Define *retained earnings* and prepare a statement of retained earnings.

2. Account for stock dividends and stock splits.

3. Describe the disclosure of restrictions on retained earnings.

4. Prepare a statement of stockholders' equity.

5. Calculate book value per share and distinguish it from market value.

6. Prepare a corporate income statement.

7. Show the relationships among income taxes expense, deferred income taxes, and net of taxes.

8. Describe the disclosure on the income statement of discontinued operations, extraordinary items, and accounting changes.

9. Compute earnings per share.

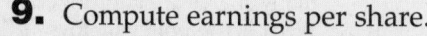

DECISION POINT

General Electric Company

At a board meeting in December 1993, the directors of General Electric Company raised the quarterly cash dividend on common stock by 14 percent and proposed a 2-for-1 stock split. The stock split was to be voted on by stockholders on April 27, 1994. In addition, the board recommended an increase from 1.1 billion authorized common shares to 2.2 billion. General Electric had about 926.5 million shares outstanding, and the current market price of the company's stock was $105 per share.[1] How does a stock split differ from a stock dividend and a cash dividend? Why would the board of directors take these actions? What are the implications for the stockholders?

These are important questions for internal management and external investors in the company. A 2-for-1 stock split gives stockholders one additional share of common stock for each share they own. Stock dividends also give stockholders additional shares based on the value of their holdings, but they have a different effect on the stockholders' equity section of the balance sheet, as will be explained in this chapter. A cash dividend is a distribution of cash based on the number of shares owned. In this case, the board of directors had to recommend increasing the number of authorized shares because there were not enough authorized shares available to give each stockholder another share. General Electric's prosperity is the probable reason for the proposal, as many companies view stock splits as symbols of success. By doubling the number of shares outstanding, the General Electric stock split will reduce the market value per share; this will make the stock more readily tradable and more easily available to the ordinary investor. The benefit to the stockholders is that although the market value per share will be about half of $105 per share, they will own twice as many shares. Transactions involving stock dividends and stock splits affect the financial structure of a company and are important strategic actions that both managers and investors should understand. This chapter examines those actions and their effects, and shows how to read and interpret the statement of stockholders' equity and the corporate income statement.

1. "GE's Directors Raise Quarterly Dividend, Propose Stock Split," *Wall Street Journal*, December 20, 1993.

RETAINED EARNINGS TRANSACTIONS

OBJECTIVE

1 *Define* **retained earnings** *and prepare a statement of retained earnings*

Stockholders' equity has two parts: contributed capital and retained earnings. The retained earnings of a company are the part of stockholders' equity that represents claims to assets arising from the earnings of the business. Retained earnings equal a company's profits since the date of its inception, less any losses, dividends to stockholders, or transfers to contributed capital. Exhibit 1 shows a statement of retained earnings for Caprock Corporation for 19x2. The beginning balance of retained earnings of $854,000 is increased by net income of $76,000 and decreased by cash dividends of $30,000. The ending balance is $900,000. The statement of retained earnings may also disclose other transactions explained in this chapter.

It is important to remember that retained earnings are not the assets themselves. The existence of retained earnings means that assets generated by profitable operations have been kept in the company to help it grow or to meet other business needs. A credit balance in Retained Earnings is *not* directly associated with a specific amount of cash or designated assets. Rather, such a balance means that assets as a whole have been increased.

Retained Earnings can carry a debit balance. Generally, this happens when a company's dividends and subsequent losses are greater than its accumulated profits from operations. In such a case, the firm is said to have a deficit (debit balance) in Retained Earnings. A deficit is shown in the stockholders' equity section of the balance sheet as a deduction from contributed capital.

Accountants use various terms to describe the retained earnings of a business. One is *surplus*, which implies that there are excess assets available for dividends. This usage is poor because the existence of retained earnings carries no connotation of "excess" or "surplus." Because of possible misinterpretation, the American Institute of Certified Public Accountants recommends more fitting terms, such as *retained income, retained earnings, accumulated earnings,* or *earnings retained for use in the business.*[2]

Prior period adjustments are events or transactions that relate to earlier accounting periods but that could not be determined in those earlier periods. When they occur, they are shown on the statement of retained earnings as adjustments to the beginning balance. The Financial Accounting Standards Board identifies only two kinds of prior period adjustments. The first is used to correct an error in the financial statements of a prior year. The second is needed if a company realizes an income tax gain from carrying forward a preacquisition operating loss of a purchased company.[3] Prior period adjustments are rare.

OBJECTIVE

2 *Account for stock dividends and stock splits*

STOCK DIVIDENDS

A stock dividend is a proportional distribution of shares of a corporation's stock to its shareholders. A stock dividend does not change the firm's assets and liabilities because there is no distribution of assets, as there is when a cash dividend is distributed.

2. Committee on Accounting Terminology, *Accounting Terminology Bulletin No. 1,* "Review and Resume" (New York: American Institute of Certified Public Accountants, 1953), par. 69.

3. *Statement of Financial Accounting Standards No. 16,* "Prior Period Adjustments" (Stamford, Conn.: Financial Accounting Standards Board, 1977), par. 11.

Exhibit 1. A Statement of Retained Earnings

Caprock Corporation
Statement of Retained Earnings
For the Year Ended December 31, 19x2

Retained Earnings, December 31, 19x1	$854,000
Net Income, 19x2	76,000
Subtotal	$930,000
Less Cash Dividends, Common	30,000
Retained Earnings, December 31, 19x2	$900,000

A board of directors may declare a stock dividend for several reasons:

1. It may want to give stockholders some evidence of the company's success without paying a cash dividend, which would affect working capital.
2. It may seek to reduce the stock's market price by increasing the number of shares outstanding, although this goal is more often met by stock splits.
3. It may want to make a nontaxable distribution to stockholders. Stock dividends that meet certain conditions are not considered income, so they are not taxed.
4. It may wish to increase the company's permanent capital by transferring an amount from retained earnings to contributed capital.

The total stockholders' equity is not affected by a stock dividend. The effect of a stock dividend is to transfer a dollar amount from retained earnings to the contributed capital section on the date of declaration. The amount transferred is the fair market value (usually, the market price) of the additional shares to be issued. The laws of most states specify the minimum value of each share transferred under a stock dividend, which is normally the minimum legal capital (par or stated value). However, generally accepted accounting principles state that market value reflects the economic effect of small stock distributions (less than 20 to 25 percent of a company's outstanding common stock) better than par or stated value does. For this reason, market price should be used to account for small stock dividends.[4]

To illustrate the accounting for a stock dividend, let us assume that Caprock Corporation has the following stockholders' equity structure.

Contributed Capital	
Common Stock—$5 par value, 100,000 shares	
authorized, 30,000 shares issued and outstanding	$ 150,000
Paid-in Capital in Excess of Par Value, Common	30,000
Total Contributed Capital	$ 180,000
Retained Earnings	900,000
Total Stockholders' Equity	$1,080,000

Suppose that the corporation's board of directors declares a 10 percent stock dividend on February 24, distributable on March 31 to stockholders of record on March 15, and that the market price of the stock on February 24 is

---

4. *Accounting Research Bulletin No. 43* (New York: American Institute of Certified Public Accountants, 1953), chap. 7, sec. B, par 10.

$20 per share. The entries to record the declaration and distribution of the stock dividend are shown below.

Date of Declaration

Feb. 24	Stock Dividends Declared	60,000	
	Common Stock Distributable		15,000
	Paid-in Capital in Excess of Par		
	Value, Common		45,000

> Declared a 10% stock dividend
> on common stock, distributable on
> March 31 to stockholders of record
> on March 15:
> 30,000 shares $\times$ .10 = 3,000 shares
> 3,000 shares $\times$ \$20/share = \$60,000
> 3,000 shares $\times$ \$5/share = \$15,000

Date of Record

Mar. 15   No entry required.

Date of Distribution

Mar. 31	Common Stock Distributable	15,000	
	Common Stock		15,000

> Distribution of a stock dividend of
> 3,000 shares

The effect of this stock dividend is to permanently transfer the market value of the stock, $60,000, from retained earnings to contributed capital and to increase the number of shares outstanding by 3,000. The Stock Dividends Declared account is used to record the total amount of the stock dividend. Retained Earnings is reduced by the amount of the stock dividend when the Stock Dividends Declared account is closed to Retained Earnings at the end of the accounting period. Common Stock Distributable is credited for the par value of the stock to be distributed (3,000 $\times$ \$5 = \$15,000). In addition, when the market value is greater than the par value of the stock, Paid-in Capital in Excess of Par Value, Common must be credited for the amount by which the market value exceeds the par value. In this case, the total market value of the stock dividend ($60,000) exceeds the total par value ($15,000) by $45,000. No entry is required on the date of record. On the distribution date, the common stock is issued by debiting Common Stock Distributable and crediting Common Stock for the par value of the stock ($15,000).

Common Stock Distributable is not a liability account because there is no obligation to distribute cash or other assets. The obligation is to distribute additional shares of capital stock. If financial statements are prepared between the date of declaration and the distribution of stock, Common Stock Distributable should be reported as part of contributed capital.

Contributed Capital	
Common Stock—$5 par value, 100,000 shares	
authorized, 30,000 shares issued and outstanding	$ 150,000
Common Stock Distributable, 3,000 shares	15,000
Paid-in Capital in Excess of Par Value, Common	75,000
Total Contributed Capital	$ 240,000
Retained Earnings	840,000
Total Stockholders' Equity	$1,080,000

Three points can be made from this example. First, the total stockholders' equity is the same before and after the stock dividend. Second, the assets of the corporation are not reduced as in the case of a cash dividend. Third, the proportionate ownership in the corporation of any individual stockholder is the same before and after the stock dividend. To illustrate these points, assume that a stockholder owns 1,000 shares before the stock dividend. After the 10 percent stock dividend is distributed, this stockholder would own 1,100 shares, as illustrated below.

Stockholders' Equity	Before Dividend	After Dividend
Common Stock	$ 150,000	$ 165,000
Paid-in Capital in Excess of Par Value, Common	30,000	75,000
Total Contributed Capital	$ 180,000	$ 240,000
Retained Earnings	900,000	840,000
Total Stockholders' Equity	$1,080,000	$1,080,000
Shares Outstanding	30,000	33,000
Stockholders' Equity per Share	$ 36.00	$ 32.73

Stockholders' Investment

Shares owned	1,000	1,100
Shares outstanding	30,000	33,000
Percentage of ownership	3⅓%	3⅓%
Proportionate investment ($1,080,000 × .03⅓)	$36,000	$36,000

Both before and after the stock dividend, the stockholders' equity totals $1,080,000 and the stockholder owns 3⅓ percent of the company. The proportionate investment (stockholders' equity times percentage ownership) stays at $36,000.

All stock dividends have an effect on the market price of a company's stock. But some stock dividends are so large that they have a material effect. For example, a 50 percent stock dividend would cause the market price of the stock to drop about 33 percent because there is a one-third increase in the number of shares outstanding. The AICPA has decided that large stock dividends, those greater than 20 to 25 percent, should be accounted for by transferring the par or stated value of the stock on the date of declaration from retained earnings to contributed capital.[5]

STOCK SPLITS

A stock split occurs when a corporation increases the number of issued shares of stock and reduces the par or stated value proportionally. A company may plan a stock split when it wants to lower the stock's market value per share and increase its liquidity. This action may be necessary if the market value per share has become so high that it hinders the trading of the stock. An example of this strategy is shown in the Decision Point on General Electric Company that introduced this chapter.

5. Ibid., par. 13.

To illustrate a stock split, suppose that Caprock Corporation has 30,000 shares of $5.00 par value stock outstanding. The market value is $70.00 per share. The corporation plans a 2-for-1 split. This split will lower the par value to $2.50 and increase the number of shares outstanding to 60,000. A stockholder who previously owned 400 shares of the $5.00 par stock would own 800 shares of the $2.50 par stock after the split. When a stock split occurs, the market value tends to fall in proportion to the increase in outstanding shares of stock. For example, a 2-for-1 stock split would cause the price of the stock to drop by approximately 50 percent, to about $35.00. It would also halve earnings per share and cash dividends per share (if the board does not increase the dividend). The lower price plus the increase in shares tend to promote the buying and selling of shares.

A stock split does not increase the number of shares authorized. Nor does it change the balances in the stockholders' equity section of the balance sheet. It simply changes the par value and the number of shares issued, both shares outstanding and shares held as treasury stock. Therefore, an entry is not necessary. However, it is appropriate to document the change by making a memorandum entry in the general journal.

July 15   The 30,000 shares of $5 par value common stock that are issued and outstanding were split 2 for 1, resulting in 60,000 shares of $2.50 par value common stock issued and outstanding.

The change for the Caprock Corporation is as follows:

Before Stock Split (from page 545)

Contributed Capital	
Common Stock—$5 par value, 100,000 shares authorized, 30,000 shares issued and outstanding	$ 150,000
Paid-in Capital in Excess of Par Value, Common	30,000
Total Contributed Capital	$ 180,000
Retained Earnings	900,000
Total Stockholders' Equity	$1,080,000

After Stock Split

Contributed Capital	
Common Stock—$2.50 par value, 100,000 shares authorized, 60,000 shares issued and outstanding	$ 150,000
Paid-in Capital in Excess of Par Value, Common	30,000
Total Contributed Capital	$ 180,000
Retained Earnings	900,000
Total Stockholders' Equity	$1,080,000

Although the amount of stockholders' equity per share would be half as much, each stockholder's proportionate interest in the company would remain the same.

If the number of split shares will exceed the number of authorized shares, the board of directors must secure state approval before it can issue additional shares.

OBJECTIVE

3 *Describe the disclosure of restrictions on retained earnings*

RESTRICTIONS ON RETAINED EARNINGS

A corporation may be required or may want to restrict all or a portion of its retained earnings. A restriction on retained earnings means that dividends can be declared only to the extent of the *unrestricted* retained earnings. The following are several reasons a company might restrict retained earnings.

1. *A contractual agreement.* For example, bond indentures may place a limitation on the dividends the company can pay.
2. *State law.* Many states do not allow a corporation to distribute dividends or purchase treasury stock if doing so impairs the legal capital of the company.
3. *Voluntary action by the board of directors.* Often a board decides to retain assets in the business for future needs. For example, the company may be planning to build a new plant and may want to show that dividends will be limited to save enough money for the building. A company might also restrict retained earnings to show a possible future loss of assets resulting from a lawsuit.

A restriction on retained earnings can be reported to readers of financial statements in two ways: It can be shown in the stockholders' equity section of the balance sheet, or it can be disclosed in a note to the financial statements.

A restriction on retained earnings does not change the total retained earnings or stockholders' equity of the company. It simply divides retained earnings into two parts, restricted and unrestricted. Assets in the restricted part cannot be used to pay dividends. The unrestricted amount represents earnings kept in the business that the company can use for dividends and other purposes.

Assume that Caprock's board of directors has decided to restrict $300,000 in retained earnings because of plans for plant expansion. The disclosure in Caprock's stockholders' equity section would be as follows:

Contributed Capital		
Common Stock—$5 par value, 100,000 shares authorized, 30,000 shares issued and outstanding		$ 150,000
Paid-in Capital in Excess of Par Value, Common		30,000
Total Contributed Capital		$ 180,000
Retained Earnings		
Restricted for Plant Expansion	$300,000	
Unrestricted	600,000	
Total Retained Earnings		900,000
Total Stockholders' Equity		$1,080,000

The same facts about restricted retained earnings also could be presented by reference to a note to the financial statements. For example:

Retained Earnings (Note 15) $900,000

Note 15:
Because of plans to expand the capacity of the clothing division, the board of directors has restricted retained earnings available for dividends by $300,000.

Notice that the restriction of retained earnings does not restrict cash or other assets in any way. It simply explains to the readers of the financial statements that a certain amount of assets generated by earnings will remain in the business for the purpose stated. It is still management's job to make sure that there is enough cash or assets on hand to fulfill the purpose. Also, the removal of a restriction does not necessarily mean that the board of directors is then able to declare a dividend.

BUSINESS BULLETIN: INTERNATIONAL PRACTICE

Restrictions on retained earnings, called *reserves*, are much more common in some foreign countries than in the United States. In Sweden, for instance, reserves are used to respond to fluctuations in the economy. The Swedish tax code allows companies to set up contingency reserves for the purpose of maintaining financial stability. Appropriations to those reserves reduce taxable income and income taxes. The reserves become taxable when they are reversed, but they are available to absorb losses should they occur. For example, although Skandia Group, a large Swedish insurance company, incurred a net loss of SK2.4 billion in 1992, the unrestricted retained earnings increased from SK1 billion to SK1.8 billion because the company reduced its restricted reserves. Skandia Group paid its customary cash dividend and still had SK4.2 billion in restricted reserves.[6]

THE STATEMENT OF STOCKHOLDERS' EQUITY

OBJECTIVE

4 *Prepare a statement of stockholders' equity*

The statement of stockholders' equity, also called the *statement of changes in stockholders' equity*, summarizes the changes in the components of the stockholders' equity section of the balance sheet. More and more companies are using this statement in place of the statement of retained earnings because it reveals much more about the year's stockholders' equity transactions. In the statement of stockholders' equity in Exhibit 2, for example, the first line shows the beginning balance of each account in the stockholders' equity section. Each subsequent line discloses the effects of transactions on those accounts. It is possible to determine from the statement that during 19x2 Tri-State Corporation issued 5,000 shares of common stock for $250,000, had a conversion of $100,000 of preferred stock into common stock, declared and issued a 10 percent stock dividend on common stock, had a net purchase of treasury shares of $24,000, earned net income of $270,000, and paid cash dividends on both preferred and common stock. Notice that the Retained Earnings column has the same components as would the statement of retained earnings. The ending balances of the accounts are presented at the bottom of the statement. Those accounts and balances make up the stockholders' equity section of Tri-State's balance sheet on December 31, 19x2, as shown in Exhibit 3.

---

6. Skandia Group, *Annual Report*, 1992.

Exhibit 2. A Statement of Stockholders' Equity

Tri-State Corporation
Statement of Stockholders' Equity
For the Year Ended December 31, 19x2

	Preferred Stock $100 Par Value 8% Convertible	Common Stock $10 Par Value	Paid-in Capital in Excess of Par Value, Common	Retained Earnings	Treasury Stock	Total
Balance, December 31, 19x1	$400,000	$300,000	$300,000	$600,000	—	$1,600,000
Issuance of 5,000 Shares of Common Stock		50,000	200,000			250,000
Conversion of 1,000 Shares of Preferred Stock into 3,000 Shares of Common Stock	(100,000)	30,000	70,000			—
10 Percent Stock Dividend on Common Stock, 3,800 Shares		38,000	152,000	(190,000)		—
Purchase of 500 Shares of Treasury Stock					($24,000)	(24,000)
Net Income				270,000		270,000
Cash Dividends						
Preferred Stock				(24,000)		(24,000)
Common Stock				(47,600)		(47,600)
Balance, December 31, 19x2	$300,000	$418,000	$722,000	$608,400	($24,000)	$2,024,400

Exhibit 3. Stockholders' Equity Section of a Balance Sheet

Tri-State Corporation
Stockholders' Equity
December 31, 19x2

Contributed Capital		
Preferred Stock—$100 par value, 8% convertible, 10,000 shares authorized, 3,000 shares issued and outstanding		$ 300,000
Common Stock—$10 par value, 100,000 shares authorized, 41,800 shares issued, 41,300 shares outstanding	$418,000	
Paid-in Capital in Excess of Par Value, Common	722,000	1,140,000
Total Contributed Capital		$1,440,000
Retained Earnings		608,400
Total Contributed Capital and Retained Earnings		$2,048,400
Less Treasury Stock, Common (500 shares, at cost)		24,000
Total Stockholders' Equity		$2,024,400

STOCK VALUES

The word *value* is associated with shares of stock in several ways. The terms *par value* and *stated value* are each values per share that establish the legal capital of a company. Par value or stated value is set when the stock is authorized. Neither par value nor stated value has any relationship to a stock's book value or market value.

BOOK VALUE

The book value of a company's stock represents the total assets of the company less its liabilities. It is simply the stockholders' equity of the company or, to look at it another way, the company's net assets. The book value per share, therefore, represents the equity of the owner of one share of stock in the net assets of the corporation. That value, of course, does not necessarily equal the amount the shareholder would receive if the company were sold or liquidated. It differs in most cases because assets are usually recorded at historical cost, not at the current value at which they could be sold.

To determine the book value per share when a company has only common stock outstanding, divide the total stockholders' equity by the total common shares outstanding. In computing the shares outstanding, common stock distributable is included. Treasury stock, however, (shares previously issued and now held by the company) is not included. For example, suppose that Caprock Corporation has total stockholders' equity of $1,030,000 and 29,000 shares outstanding after recording the purchase of treasury shares. The book value per share of Caprock's common stock is $35.52 ($1,030,000 ÷ 29,000 shares).

If a company has both preferred and common stock, the determination of book value per share is not so simple. The general rule is that the call value (or par value, if a call value is not specified) of the preferred stock plus any dividends in arrears are subtracted from total stockholders' equity to determine the equity pertaining to common stock. As an illustration, refer to the stockholders' equity section of Tri-State Corporation's balance sheet in Exhibit 3. Assuming that there are no dividends in arrears and that the preferred stock is callable at $105, the equity pertaining to common stock is calculated as follows:

Total stockholders' equity	$2,024,400
Less equity allocated to preferred shareholders	
(3,000 shares × $105)	315,000
Equity pertaining to common shareholders	$1,709,400

There are 41,300 shares of common stock outstanding (41,800 shares issued less 500 shares of treasury stock). The book values per share are computed as follows:

Preferred Stock: $315,000 ÷ 3,000 shares = $105 per share
Common Stock: $1,709,400 ÷ 41,300 shares = $41.39 per share

If we assume the same facts except that the preferred stock is 8 percent cumulative and that one year of dividends is in arrears, the stockholders' equity would be allocated as follows:

Total stockholders' equity		$2,024,400
Less: Call value of outstanding preferred shares	$315,000	
Dividends in arrears ($300,000 × .08)	24,000	
Equity allocated to preferred shareholders		339,000
Equity pertaining to common shareholders		$1,685,400

The book values per share are then as follows:

Preferred Stock: $339,000 ÷ 3,000 shares = $113 per share
Common Stock: $1,685,400 ÷ 41,300 shares = $40.81 per share

Undeclared preferred dividends fall into arrears on the last day of the fiscal year (the date when the financial statements are prepared). Also, dividends in arrears do not apply to unissued preferred stock.

BUSINESS BULLETIN: BUSINESS PRACTICE

In a dramatic demonstration that investor expectations drive the market value of a company's stock, Eastman Kodak's stock price plunged nearly 12 percent in one day, from $63 to $55.50 per share, after the new chairman, George Fisher, warned financial analysts that their 1994 earnings estimates were too high. Fisher said that cost cutting alone would not overcome Kodak's poor showing in recent years and that the company would have to build a foundation for growth. Analysts had thought the new chairman would move faster to improve earnings. They then revised their earnings estimates downward, which negatively affected the stock price.[7] Eastman Kodak's stock dropped as low as $40 in 1994 and was still only $48 in early 1995.

MARKET VALUE

Market value is the price that investors are willing to pay for a share of stock on the open market. Whereas book value is based on historical cost, market value is usually determined by investors' expectations for the particular company and general economic conditions. That is, people's expectations about the company's future profitability and dividends per share, their perceptions of the risk attached to the company and of its current financial condition, and the state of the money market all play a part in determining the market value of a corporation's stock. Although book value per share often bears little relationship to market value per share, some investors use the relationship between the two as a rough indicator of the relative value of the stock. For example, in early 1991, the stock of Chrysler Corporation had a book value per share of $31 and a market value per share of $14. By early 1995, the book value per share had dropped to $26 because of losses, but the market value of

7. Joan E. Rigdon, "Kodak's Stock Plunges After Chairman Says Analysts' 1994 Forecasts Are High," *Wall Street Journal*, December 16, 1993.

the stock had climbed to $47. Other factors being equal, investors were more optimistic about Chrysler's prospects in 1995 than they were in 1991.

THE CORPORATE INCOME STATEMENT

OBJECTIVE

6 *Prepare a corporate income statement*

Accounting organizations have not specified the format of the income statement because they have considered flexibility more important than a standard format. Either the single-step or the multistep form can be used. However, the accounting profession has taken the position that income for a period should be all-inclusive, comprehensive income.[8] This means that the income or loss for a period should include all revenues, expenses, gains, and losses over the period, except for prior period adjustments. As a result, several items must be added to the income statement, among them discontinued operations, extraordinary items, and accounting changes. In addition, earnings per share figures must be disclosed. Exhibit 4 illustrates a corporate income statement and the required disclosures. The following sections discuss the components of the corporate income statement, beginning with income taxes expense.

INCOME TAXES EXPENSE

OBJECTIVE

7 *Show the relationships among income taxes expense, deferred income taxes, and net of taxes*

Corporations determine their taxable income (the amount on which taxes are paid) by subtracting allowable business deductions from includable gross income. The federal tax laws determine which business expenses may be deducted and which must be included in taxable gross income.[9]

The tax rates that apply to a corporation's taxable income are shown in Table 1. A corporation with taxable income of $70,000 would have a federal income tax liability of $12,500: $7,500 (the tax on the first $50,000 of taxable income) plus $5,000 (25 percent of the $20,000 earned in excess of $50,000).

Income taxes expense is the expense recognized in the accounting records on an accrual basis to be applied to income from continuing operations. This expense may or may not equal the amount of taxes actually paid by the corporation and recorded as income taxes payable in the current period. The amount payable is determined from taxable income, which is measured according to the rules and regulations of the income tax code. For convenience, most small businesses keep accounting records on the same basis as tax records so that the income taxes expense on the income statement equals the income taxes liability to be paid to the Internal Revenue Service (IRS). This practice is acceptable when there is no material difference between the income on an accounting basis and the income on an income tax basis. However, the purpose of accounting is to determine net income in accordance with generally accepted accounting principles, not to determine taxable income and tax liability.

Management has an incentive to use methods that minimize the firm's tax liability, but accountants, who are bound by accrual accounting and the materiality concept, cannot let tax procedures dictate their method of preparing financial statements if the result would be misleading. As a consequence,

8. *Statement of Financial Accounting Concepts No. 6,* "Elements of Financial Statements" (Stamford, Conn.: Financial Accounting Standards Board, 1985), pars. 70–77.

9. Rules for calculating and reporting taxable income in specialized industries such as banking, insurance, mutual funds, and cooperatives are highly technical and may vary significantly from those discussed in this chapter.

Exhibit 4. A Corporate Income Statement

Junction Corporation
Income Statement
For the Year Ended December 31, 19xx

Revenues		$925,000
Less Costs and Expenses		500,000
Income from Continuing Operations Before Taxes		$425,000
Income Taxes Expense		144,500
Income from Continuing Operations		$280,500
Discontinued Operations		
Income from Operations of Discontinued Segment		
(net of taxes, $35,000)	$90,000	
Loss on Disposal of Segment (net of taxes, $42,000)	(73,000)	17,000
Income Before Extraordinary Items and		
Cumulative Effect of Accounting Change		$297,500
Extraordinary Gain (net of taxes, $17,000)		43,000
Subtotal		$340,500
Cumulative Effect of a Change in Accounting		
Principle (net of taxes, $5,000)		(6,000)
Net Income		$334,500
Earnings per Common Share:		
Income from Continuing Operations		$ 2.81
Discontinued Operations (net of taxes)		.17
Income Before Extraordinary Items and		
Cumulative Effect of Accounting Change		$ 2.98
Extraordinary Gain (net of taxes)		.43
Cumulative Effect of Accounting Change		
(net of taxes)		(.06)
Net Income		$ 3.35

Table 1. Tax Rate Schedule for Corporations, 1995*

Taxable Income		Tax Liability	
Over	But Not Over		Of the Amount Over
—	$ 50,000	0 + 15%	—
$ 50,000	75,000	$ 7,500 + 25%	$ 50,000
75,000	100,000	13,750 + 34%	75,000
100,000	335,000	22,250 + 39%	100,000
335,000	10,000,000	113,900 + 34%	335,000
10,000,000	15,000,000	3,496,650 + 35%	10,000,000
15,000,000	18,333,333	5,246,650 + 38%	15,000,000
18,333,333	—	6,513,317 + 35%	18,333,333

*Tax rates are subject to change by Congress.

there can be a material difference between accounting and taxable incomes, especially in larger businesses. This discrepancy can result from differences in the timing of the recognition of revenues and expenses under the two accounting methods. Some possible variations are shown below.

	Accounting Method	**Tax Method**
Expense recognition	Accrual or deferral	At time of expenditure
Accounts receivable	Allowance	Direct charge off
Inventories	Average cost	FIFO
Depreciation	Straight line	Modified Accelerated Cost Recovery System

BUSINESS BULLETIN: ETHICS IN PRACTICE

Generally accepted accounting principles allow companies considerable latitude in reporting certain gains and losses, but that latitude should not be used to mask the true situation. Rodman & Renshaw Capital Group Inc., a large Chicago brokerage firm was involved in negotiations to sell its business and needed to report good earnings. Although the company was rumored to have had a large loss in the fourth quarter ended June 25, 1993, it reported that its earnings would be $854,000 for the period, including a gain on the sale of its London-based futures and options business. It turned out that the firm's auditors would not allow the company to record the gain because the sale had not been closed at the end of the quarter. In the final analysis, the company reported a net loss of $375,000 for the period.[10]

DEFERRED INCOME TAXES

Accounting for the difference between income taxes expense based on accounting income and the actual income taxes payable based on taxable income is accomplished by a technique called income tax allocation. The amount by which income taxes expense differs from income taxes payable is reconciled in an account called Deferred Income Taxes. For example, suppose Junction Corporation shows income taxes expense of $119,000 on its income statement but has actual income taxes payable to the IRS of $92,000. The entry to record the estimated income taxes expense applicable to income from continuing operations using the income tax allocation procedure would appear as follows:

Dec. 31	Income Taxes Expense	119,000	
	Income Taxes Payable		92,000
	Deferred Income Taxes		27,000
	To record estimated current and deferred income taxes		

10. "Timing Is Everything," *Crain's Chicago Business,* October 16, 1993.

In other years, it is possible for Income Taxes Payable to exceed Income Taxes Expense, in which case the same entry is made except that Deferred Income Taxes is debited.

The Financial Accounting Standards Board has issued specific rules for recording, measuring, and classifying deferred income taxes.[11] When the Deferred Income Taxes account has a credit balance, which is its normal balance, it is classified as a liability on the balance sheet. Whether it is classified as a current or long-term liability depends on when the timing difference is expected to reverse. For instance, if an income tax deferral is caused by an expenditure that is deducted for income tax purposes in one year but is not an expense for accounting purposes until the next year, the deferral that is present in the first year will reverse in the second year. In this case, the income tax deferral in the first year is classified as a current liability. On the other hand, if the deferral is not expected to reverse for more than one year, Deferred Income Taxes is classified as a long-term liability. Such a situation can occur when the income tax deferral is caused by a difference in depreciation methods for items of plant and equipment that have useful lives of more than one year. In other words, an income tax liability is classified as short term or long term based on the nature of the transactions that gave rise to the deferral and the expected date of reversal.

The Deferred Income Taxes account can have a debit balance, in which case it should be classified as an asset. In this situation, the company has prepaid its income taxes because total income taxes paid exceed income taxes expensed. Classification of the debit balance as a current asset or as a long-term asset follows the same rules as those for liabilities, but the amount of the asset is subject to certain limitations, which are covered in more advanced courses.

Each year, the balance of the Deferred Income Taxes account is evaluated to determine whether it still accurately represents the expected asset or liability in light of legislated changes in income tax laws and regulations. If changes have occurred, an adjusting entry is required to bring the account balance into line with current laws. For example, a decrease in corporate income tax rates, like the one that occurred in 1987, means that a company with deferred income tax liabilities will pay less taxes in future years than indicated by the credit balance of its Deferred Income Taxes account. As a result, the company would debit Deferred Income Taxes to reduce the liability and credit Gain from Reduction in Income Taxes Rates. This credit increases the reported income on the income statement. If the tax rate increases in future years, a loss would be recorded and the deferred income tax liability would be increased.

In any given year, the amount a company pays in income taxes is determined by subtracting (or adding, as the case may be) the deferred income taxes for that year, as reported in the notes to the financial statements, from (or to) income taxes expense, which is also reported in the notes to the financial statements. In subsequent years, the amount of deferred income taxes can vary based on changes in tax laws and rates.

Some understanding of the importance of deferred income taxes to financial reporting can be gained from studying a survey of the financial statements of six hundred large companies. About 75 percent reported deferred

---

11. *Statement of Financial Accounting Standards No. 96,* "Accounting for Income Taxes" (Stamford, Conn.: Financial Accounting Standards Board, 1987).

income taxes with a credit balance in the long-term liability section of the balance sheet.[12]

NET OF TAXES

The phrase net of taxes, as used in Exhibit 4, means that the effect of applicable taxes (usually income taxes) has been considered in determining the overall effect of an item on the financial statements. The phrase is used on the corporate income statement when a company has items that must be disclosed in a separate section. Each such item should be reported net of the applicable income taxes to avoid distorting the net operating income.

For example, assume that a corporation with operating income of $120,000 before taxes has a total tax liability of $66,000 based on taxable income and that the taxable income is high because it includes a gain of $100,000 on which a tax of $30,000 is due. Also assume that the gain is not part of normal operations and must be disclosed separately on the income statement as an extraordinary item (explained later). This is how the tax liability would be reported on the income statement.

Operating Income Before Taxes	$120,000
Income Taxes Expense (actual taxes are $66,000, of which $30,000 is applicable to extraordinary gain)	36,000
Income Before Extraordinary Item	$ 84,000
Extraordinary Gain (net of taxes) ($100,000 − $30,000)	70,000
Net Income	$154,000

If all the taxes payable were deducted from operating income before taxes, both the income before extraordinary items and the extraordinary gain would be distorted.

A company follows the same procedure in the case of an extraordinary loss. For example, assume the same facts as before except that the total tax liability is only $6,000 because of a $100,000 extraordinary loss. The result is a $30,000 tax saving, as shown below.

Operating Income Before Taxes	$120,000
Income Taxes Expense (actual taxes of $6,000 as a result of an extraordinary loss)	36,000
Income Before Extraordinary Item	$ 84,000
Extraordinary Loss (net of taxes) ($100,000 − $30,000)	(70,000)
Net Income	$ 14,000

In Exhibit 4, the total of the income tax items is $149,500. That amount is allocated among five statement components, as follows:

Income taxes expense on income from continuing operations	$144,500
Income tax on income from a discontinued segment	35,000
Income tax saving on the loss on the disposal of the segment	(42,000)
Income tax on the extraordinary gain	17,000
Income tax saving on the cumulative effect of a change in accounting principle	(5,000)
Total income taxes expense	$149,500

12. American Institute of Certified Public Accountants, *Accounting Trends & Techniques* (New York: AICPA, 1993), p. 233.

Pennzoil Company

DECISION POINT

Someone who does not understand the structure and use of corporate income statements may be confused by corporate earnings reports in the financial press. Pennzoil Company, a major oil and gas producer, reported net income of $21 million in 1991 and $128 million in 1992. Despite this seemingly tremendous rise in net income, the company's income from operations actually declined from $40 million to $17 million.[13] How could Pennzoil Company have both a large increase in net income and a large decrease in operating income? What approach should a user take to analyze a corporate income statement?

As will be explained in the following sections, a corporate income statement has several components. On closer examination, a user would find that in 1991 Pennzoil had a negative $49 million cumulative effect of change in accounting principle stemming from a change in accounting for postretirement benefits other than pensions. It also experienced a positive $116 million cumulative effect from a change in accounting for income taxes. In addition, in 1992 the company experienced an extraordinary loss of almost $17 million and a gain on the sale of certain operations of $1.5 million.[14] Because of the complexity of the corporate income statement, analysts have learned to look beyond the bottom line and to carefully study all components of a corporate income statement to discover the long-term outlook for a company. ⦂⦂⦂⦂⦂

OBJECTIVE

8 *Describe the disclosure on the income statement of discontinued operations, extraordinary items, and accounting changes*

DISCONTINUED OPERATIONS

Large companies in the United States usually have many segments. Each segment may be a separate major line of business or serve a separate class of customer. For example, a company that makes heavy drilling equipment may also have another line of business, such as the manufacture of mobile homes. A large company may discontinue or otherwise dispose of certain segments of its business that do not fit its future plans or are not profitable. Discontinued operations are segments of a business that are no longer part of its ongoing operations. Generally accepted accounting principles require that gains and losses from discontinued operations be reported separately in the income statement. Such separation makes it easier to evaluate the ongoing activities of the business.

In Exhibit 4, the disclosure of discontinued operations has two parts. One part shows that the income from operations of the segment that has been disposed of after the date of the decision to discontinue was $90,000 (net of $35,000 taxes). The other part shows that the loss from the disposal of the segment was $73,000 (net of $42,000 tax savings). Computation of the gains or losses is covered in more advanced accounting courses. The disclosure has been described, however, to give a complete view of the corporate income statement.

---

13. Pennzoil Company, *Annual Report*, 1992.
14. Ibid.

EXTRAORDINARY ITEMS

The Accounting Principles Board, in its *Opinion No. 30*, defines extraordinary items as "events or transactions that are distinguished by their unusual nature *and* by the infrequency of their occurrence."[15] Unusual and infrequent occurrences are explained in the opinion as follows:

> Unusual Nature—the underlying event or transaction should possess a high degree of abnormality and be of a type clearly unrelated to, or only incidentally related to, the ordinary and typical activities of the entity, taking into account the environment in which the entity operates.

> Infrequency of Occurrence—the underlying event or transaction should be of a type that would not reasonably be expected to recur in the foreseeable future, taking into account the environment in which the entity operates.[16]

If an item is both unusual and infrequent (and material in amount), it should be reported separately from continuing operations on the income statement. The disclosure allows readers to identify gains or losses in income that would not be expected to happen again soon. Items usually treated as extraordinary include (1) an uninsured loss from flood, earthquake, fire, or theft; (2) a gain or loss resulting from the passage of a new law; (3) the expropriation (taking) of property by a foreign government; and (4) a gain or loss from the early retirement of debt. Gains or losses from extraordinary items should be reported on the income statement after discontinued operations. And they should be shown net of applicable taxes. In a recent year, eighty-one (14 percent) of six hundred large companies reported extraordinary items on their income statements.[17] In Exhibit 4, the extraordinary gain was $43,000 after applicable taxes of $17,000.

ACCOUNTING CHANGES

Consistency, one of the basic conventions of accounting, means that companies must apply the same accounting principles from year to year. However, a company is allowed to make accounting changes if current procedures are incorrect or inappropriate. For example, a change from the FIFO to the LIFO inventory method can be made if there is adequate justification for the change. Adequate justification usually means that if the change occurs, the financial statements will better show the financial activities of the company. A company's desire to lower the amount of income taxes it pays is not adequate justification for an accounting change. If justification does exist and an accounting change is made, generally accepted accounting principles require the disclosure of the change in the financial statements.

The cumulative effect of an accounting change is the effect that the new accounting principle would have had on net income in prior periods if it had been applied instead of the old principle. This effect is shown on the income statement immediately after extraordinary items.[18] For example, assume that in the five years previous to 19xx, the Junction Corporation had used the straight-line method to depreciate its machinery. This year, the company

---

15. Accounting Principles Board, *Opinion No. 30*, "Reporting the Results of Operations" (New York: American Institute of Certified Public Accountants, 1973), par. 20.

16. Ibid.

17. American Institute of Certified Public Accountants, *Accounting Trends & Techniques* (New York: AICPA, 1992), p. 377.

18. Accounting Principles Board, *Opinion No. 20*, "Accounting Changes" (New York: American Institute of Certified Public Accountants, 1971), par. 20.

changed to the double-declining balance method of depreciation. The following cumulative effect of the change in depreciation charges (net of taxes) was arrived at by the controller.

Cumulative, 5-year double-declining balance depreciation	$16,000
Less Cumulative, 5-year straight-line depreciation	10,000
Cumulative effect of accounting change	$ 6,000

Relevant information about the accounting change is shown in the notes to the financial statements. The change results in $6,000 of depreciation expense for prior years being deducted in the current year in addition to the current year's depreciation costs included in the $500,000 costs and expenses section of the income statement. This expense must be shown in the current year's income statement as a reduction in income (see Exhibit 4). In a recent year, 166, or 28 percent of 600 large companies reported changes in accounting procedures.[19] Further study of accounting changes is left to more advanced accounting courses.

OBJECTIVE

9 *Compute earnings per share*

EARNINGS PER SHARE

Readers of financial statements use earnings per share information to judge a company's performance and to compare it with the performance of other companies. Because such information is so important, the Accounting Principles Board concluded that earnings per share of common stock should be presented on the face of the income statement.[20] As shown in Exhibit 4, the information is usually disclosed just below the net income.

An earnings per share amount is always shown for (1) income from continuing operations, (2) income before extraordinary items and the cumulative effect of accounting changes, (3) the cumulative effect of accounting changes, and (4) net income. If the statement shows a gain or loss from discontinued operations or a gain or loss on extraordinary items, earnings per share amounts can also be presented for them. The following per share data from the income statement of Bally Manufacturing Corporation show why it is a good idea to study the components of earnings per share.[21] Note that the net income reported by Bally in 1991 and 1992 resulted from special items and that the company had losses from continuing operations.

	Years ended December 31		
	1992	**1991**	**1990**
Per Common Share:			
Loss from continuing operations	($.05)	($1.79)	($10.22)
Discontinued operations—			
Income (loss) from operations		.16	(.35)
Gain on disposal of businesses		.53	
Extraordinary items—			
Credit for utilization of tax loss carryforwards	.26		
Gain on extinguishment of debt	.01	1.65	.42
Net income (loss)	$.22	$ .55	($10.15)

---

19. American Institute of Certified Public Accountants, *Accounting Trends & Techniques* (New York: AICPA, 1992), p. 546.

20. Accounting Principles Board, *Opinion No. 15*, "Earnings per Share" (New York: American Institute of Certified Public Accountants, 1969), par. 12.

21. Bally Manufacturing Corporation, *Annual Report*, 1992.

A basic earnings per share amount can be computed when a company has only common stock and has the same number of shares outstanding throughout the year. For example, Exhibit 4 tells us that Junction Corporation, with a net income of $334,500, had 100,000 shares of common stock outstanding for the entire year. The earnings per share of common stock were computed as follows:

$$\text{Earnings per share} = \frac{\text{net income}}{\text{shares outstanding}}$$

$$= \frac{\$334,500}{100,000 \text{ shares}}$$

$$= \$3.35 \text{ per share}$$

If the number of shares outstanding changes during the year, it is necessary to figure the weighted-average number of shares outstanding for the year. Suppose that Junction Corporation had the following amounts of common shares outstanding during various periods of the year: January–March, 100,000 shares; April–September, 120,000 shares; and October–December, 130,000 shares. The weighted-average number of common shares outstanding and earnings per share would be found this way:

100,000 shares × ¼ year	25,000
120,000 shares × ½ year	60,000
130,000 shares × ¼ year	32,500
Weighted-average shares outstanding	117,500

$$\text{Earnings per share} = \frac{\$334,500}{117,500 \text{ shares}}$$

$$= \$2.85 \text{ per share}$$

If a company has nonconvertible preferred stock outstanding, the dividend for that stock must be subtracted from net income before earnings per share for common stock are computed. Suppose that Junction Corporation has preferred stock on which the annual dividend is $23,500. Earnings per share on common stock would be $2.65 [($334,500 − $23,500) ÷ 117,500 shares].

Companies with a capital structure in which there are no bonds, stocks, or stock options that could be converted into common stock are said to have a simple capital structure. The earnings per share for these companies are computed as shown at the top of this page. Some companies, however, have a complex capital structure, which includes convertible stock and bonds. Those convertible securities have the potential of diluting the earnings per share of common stock. *Potential dilution* means that a stockholder's proportionate share of ownership in a company could be reduced through the conversion of stocks or bonds or the exercise of stock options, which would increase the total shares outstanding.

For example, suppose that a person owns 10,000 shares of a company, which equals 2 percent of the outstanding shares of 500,000. Now, suppose that holders of convertible bonds convert the bonds into 100,000 shares of stock. The person's 10,000 shares would then equal only 1.67 percent (10,000 ÷ 600,000) of the outstanding shares. In addition, the added shares outstanding would lower earnings per share and would most likely lower market price per share.

Because stock options and convertible preferred stocks or bonds have the potential to dilute earnings per share, they are referred to as potentially dilutive securities. A special subset of these convertible securities is called common stock equivalents because they are considered to be similar to common stock. A convertible stock or bond is considered a common stock equivalent if its conversion feature plays a key role in determining its original issue price. Special rules are applied to determine if a convertible stock or bond is a common stock equivalent. A stock option, on the other hand, is by definition a common stock equivalent. Common stock equivalents are significant because when they exist, they are used in the earnings per share calculations.

When a company has a complex capital structure, it must report two earnings per share figures: primary earnings per share and fully diluted earnings per share. Primary earnings per share are calculated by including the sum of the weighted-average common shares outstanding and the common stock equivalents in the denominator. Fully diluted earnings per share are calculated by adding the other potentially dilutive securities that are not common stock equivalents to the denominator. The latter figure shows stockholders the maximum potential effect of dilution of their ownership in the company. Here is an example of this type of disclosure for the Tribune Company, a leading newspaper, broadcasting, and entertainment company:[22]

Net Income (Loss) Per Share	1992	1991
Primary:		
Before cumulative effects of changes in accounting principles	$1.82	$1.94
Cumulative effects of accounting changes, net	(.26)	—
Net income (loss)	$1.56	$1.94
Fully diluted:		
Before cumulative effects of changes in accounting principles	$1.70	$1.83
Cumulative effects of accounting changes, net	(.24)	—
Net income (loss)	$1.46	$1.83

The computation of these figures is a complex process reserved for more advanced courses.

BUSINESS BULLETIN: BUSINESS PRACTICE

Sometimes a change in accounting principle is mandated by the Financial Accounting Standards Board. For many companies, such a change has a dramatic effect on reported earnings. In 1992, Xerox Corporation, a major document-processing company, reported a one-time mandated charge of $606 million for adopting SFAS No. 106 to account for postretirement benefits other than pensions and a charge of $158 million for adopting SFAS No. 109 to account for income taxes. The total was reported on the income statement as a negative $764 million cumulative effect of a change in accounting principle, which, combined with the company's loss from operations of $256 million, gave a total net loss of $1.02 billion.[23]

---

22. Tribune Company, *Annual Report*, 1992.

23. Xerox Corporation, *Annual Report*, 1992.

CHAPTER REVIEW

REVIEW OF LEARNING OBJECTIVES

1. **Define *retained earnings* and prepare a statement of retained earnings.** Retained earnings are the part of stockholders' equity that comes from retaining assets earned in business operations. They represent the claims of the stockholders against the assets of the company that arise from profitable operations. Retained earnings are different from contributed capital, which represents the claims against assets arising from the initial and later investments by the stockholders. Both are claims against the general assets of the company, not against any specific assets that have been set aside. It is important not to confuse the assets themselves with the claims against them. The statement of retained earnings always shows the beginning and ending balance of retained earnings, net income or loss, and cash dividends. It also can show prior period adjustments, stock dividends, and other transactions that affect retained earnings.

2. **Account for stock dividends and stock splits.** A stock dividend is a proportional distribution of shares of the company's stock by a corporation to its stockholders. Here is a summary of the key dates and accounting treatment of stock dividends.

Key Date	Stock Dividend
Date of declaration	Debit Stock Dividends Declared for the market value of the stock to be distributed (if it is a small stock dividend), and credit Common Stock Distributable for the stock's par value and Paid-in Capital in Excess of Par Value, Common for the excess of the market value over the stock's par value.
Date of record	No entry.
Date of distribution	Debit Common Stock Distributable and credit Common Stock for the par value of the stock that has been distributed.

    A stock split is usually undertaken to reduce the market value and improve the liquidity of a company's stock. Because there is normally a decrease in the par value of the stock in proportion to the number of additional shares issued, a stock split has no effect on the dollar amounts in the stockholders' equity accounts. The split should be recorded in the general journal by a memorandum entry only.

3. **Describe the disclosure of restrictions on retained earnings.** A restriction on retained earnings means that dividends can be declared only to the extent of unrestricted retained earnings. A corporation may be bound by contractual agreement or state law to restrict retained earnings, or it may do so voluntarily, to retain assets in the business for a plant expansion or a possible loss in a lawsuit. A restriction on retained earnings can be disclosed in two ways: in the stockholders' equity section of the balance sheet or, more commonly, as a note to the financial statements. Once a restriction is removed, its disclosure can be removed from the financial statements.

4. **Prepare a statement of stockholders' equity.** A statement of stockholders' equity shows changes over the period in each component of the stockholders' equity section of the balance sheet. This statement reveals much more about the transactions that adjust stockholders' equity than does the statement of retained earnings.

5. **Calculate book value per share and distinguish it from market value.** Book value per share is the stockholders' equity per share. It is calculated by dividing stockholders' equity by the number of common shares outstanding plus shares distributable. When a company has both preferred and common stock, the call or par value of the preferred stock plus any dividends in arrears is deducted from total stockholders' equity before dividing by the common shares outstanding. Market

value per share is the price investors are willing to pay based on their expectations about the future earning ability of the company and general economic conditions.

6. **Prepare a corporate income statement.** The corporate income statement shows comprehensive income—all revenues, expenses, gains, and losses for the accounting period, except for prior period adjustments. The top part of the corporate income statement includes all revenues, costs and expenses, and income taxes that pertain to continuing operations. The bottom part of the statement contains any or all of the following: discontinued operations, extraordinary items, and the cumulative effect of a change in accounting principle. Earnings per share data should be shown at the bottom of the statement, below net income.

7. **Show the relationships among income taxes expense, deferred income taxes, and net of taxes.** Income taxes expense is the taxes applicable to income from operations on an accrual basis. Income tax allocation is necessary when differences between accrual-based accounting income and taxable income cause a material difference between income taxes expense as shown on the income statement and actual income tax liability. The difference between income taxes expense and income taxes payable is debited or credited to an account called Deferred Income Taxes. *Net of taxes* is a phrase used to indicate that the effect of taxes has been considered when showing an item on the income statement.

8. **Describe the disclosure on the income statement of discontinued operations, extraordinary items, and accounting changes.** Because of their unusual nature, a gain or loss on discontinued operations and on extraordinary items, and the cumulative effect of accounting changes must be disclosed separately from continuing operations and net of income taxes on the income statement. Relevant information about any accounting change is shown in the notes to the financial statements.

9. **Compute earnings per share.** Stockholders and other readers of financial statements use earnings per share data to evaluate a company's performance and to compare it with the performance of other companies. Therefore, earnings per share data are presented on the face of the income statement. The amounts are computed by dividing the income applicable to common stock by the number of common shares outstanding for the year. If the number of shares outstanding has varied during the year, then the weighted-average shares outstanding should be used in the computation. When the company has a complex capital structure, both primary and fully diluted earnings per share must be disclosed on the face of the income statement.

REVIEW OF CONCEPTS AND TERMINOLOGY

The following concepts and terms were introduced in this chapter.

L O 5 **Book value:** The total assets of a company less its liabilities; stockholders' equity.

L O 9 **Common stock equivalents:** Convertible stocks or bonds whose conversion feature plays a key role in determining their original issue price.

L O 9 **Complex capital structure:** A capital structure that includes preferred stocks, bonds, or other stock equivalents that can be converted into common stock.

L O 6 **Comprehensive income:** The concept of income or loss for a period that includes all revenues, expenses, gains, and losses, except prior period adjustments.

L O 8 **Cumulative effect of an accounting change:** The effect that a different accounting principle would have had on the net income of prior periods if it had been used instead of the old principle.

L O 7 **Deferred Income Taxes:** The account used to record the difference between the Income Taxes Expense and the Income Taxes Payable accounts.

L O 1 **Deficit:** A debit balance in the Retained Earnings account.

L O 8 **Discontinued operations:** Segments of a business that are no longer part of its ongoing operations.

L O 8 Extraordinary items: Events or transactions that are both unusual in nature and infrequent in occurrence.

L O 9 Fully diluted earnings per share: The net income applicable to common stock divided by the sum of the weighted average of common shares outstanding, common stock equivalents, and other potentially dilutive securities.

L O 7 Income tax allocation: An accounting method used to accrue income taxes expense on the basis of accounting income whenever there are differences between accounting and taxable income.

L O 5 Market value: The price investors are willing to pay for a share of stock on the open market.

L O 7 Net of taxes: Taking into account the effect of applicable taxes (usually income taxes) on an item to determine the overall effect of the item on the financial statements.

L O 9 Potentially dilutive securities: Stock options and convertible preferred stocks or bonds, which have the potential to dilute earnings per share.

L O 9 Primary earnings per share: The net income applicable to common stock divided by the sum of the weighted average of common shares outstanding and common stock equivalents.

L O 1 Prior period adjustments: Events or transactions that relate to earlier accounting periods but that could not be determined in the earlier periods.

L O 3 Restriction on retained earnings: The required or voluntary restriction of a portion of retained earnings that cannot be used to pay dividends.

L O 1 Retained earnings: Stockholders' claims to assets arising from the earnings of the business; the accumulated earnings of a corporation from its inception, minus any losses, dividends, or transfers to contributed capital.

L O 8 Segments: Distinct parts of business operations, such as lines of business or classes of customer.

L O 9 Simple capital structure: A capital structure in which there are no stocks, bonds, or stock options that can be converted into common stock.

L O 4 Statement of stockholders' equity: A financial statement that summarizes changes in the components of the stockholders' equity section of the balance sheet; also called *statement of changes in stockholders' equity*.

L O 2 Stock dividend: A proportional distribution of shares of a corporation's stock to its stockholders.

L O 2 Stock split: An increase in the number of outstanding shares of stock accompanied by a proportionate reduction in the par or stated value.

REVIEW PROBLEM
COMPREHENSIVE STOCKHOLDERS' EQUITY TRANSACTIONS

L O 1, 2, 3, 4, 5 The stockholders' equity of the Szatkowski Company on June 30, 19x5, is shown below.

Contributed Capital
Common Stock—no par value, $6 stated value, 1,000,000 shares authorized, 250,000 shares issued and outstanding ... $1,500,000
Paid-in Capital in Excess of Stated Value, Common ... 820,000

Total Contributed Capital ... $2,320,000
Retained Earnings ... 970,000
Total Stockholders' Equity ... $3,290,000

Stockholders' equity transactions for the next fiscal year were as follows:

a. The board of directors declared a 2-for-1 stock split.
b. The board of directors obtained authorization to issue 50,000 shares of $100 par value, 6 percent noncumulative preferred stock, callable at $104.
c. Issued 12,000 shares of common stock for a building appraised at $96,000.
d. Purchased 8,000 shares of the company's common stock for $64,000.
e. Issued 20,000 shares of preferred stock for $100 per share.
f. Sold 5,000 shares of treasury stock for $35,000.
g. Declared cash dividends of $6 per share on preferred stock and $.20 per share on common stock.
h. Date of record.
i. Paid the preferred and common stock cash dividends.
j. Declared a 10 percent stock dividend on common stock. The market value was $10 per share. The stock dividend is distributable after the end of the fiscal year.
k. Net income for the year was $340,000.
l. Closed the Cash Dividends Declared and Stock Dividends Declared accounts to Retained Earnings.

Because of a loan agreement, the company is not allowed to reduce retained earnings below $100,000. The board of directors determined that this restriction should be disclosed in the notes to the financial statements.

REQUIRED

1. Prepare the general journal entries to record the preceding transactions.
2. Prepare the company's statement of retained earnings for the year ended June 30, 19x6.
3. Prepare the stockholders' equity section of the company's balance sheet on June 30, 19x6, including appropriate disclosure of the restriction on retained earnings.
4. Compute the book values per share of common stock on June 30, 19x5 and 19x6, and of preferred stock on June 30, 19x6.

ANSWER TO REVIEW PROBLEM

1. Prepare the journal entries.

a. Memorandum entry: 2-for-1 stock split, common, resulting in 500,000 shares issued and outstanding of no par value common stock with a stated value of $3

b. No entry required.

c. Building	96,000	
Common Stock		36,000
Paid-in Capital in Excess of Stated Value, Common		60,000
Issued 12,000 shares of common stock for a building appraised at $96,000		
d. Treasury Stock, Common	64,000	
Cash		64,000
Purchased 8,000 shares of common stock for the treasury for $8 per share		
e. Cash	2,000,000	
Preferred Stock		2,000,000
Sold 20,000 shares of $100 par value preferred stock at $100 per share		
f. Cash	35,000	
Retained Earnings	5,000	
Treasury Stock, Common		40,000
Sold 5,000 shares of treasury stock for $35,000, originally purchased for $8 per share		

g. Cash Dividends Declared | 221,800 |
   Cash Dividends Payable | | 221,800

      Declaration of cash dividends of $6 per share
      on 20,000 shares of preferred stock and $.20
      per share on 509,000 shares of common stock:

      20,000 $\times$ $6   = $120,000
      509,000 $\times$ $.20 =   101,800
                         $221,800

h. No entry required.

i. Cash Dividends Payable | 221,800 |
   Cash | | 221,800
      Paid cash dividend to preferred and
      common stockholders

j. Stock Dividends Declared | 509,000 |
   Common Stock Distributable | | 152,700
   Paid-in Capital in Excess of Stated Value,
     Common | | 356,300
      Declaration of a 50,900-share stock
      dividend (509,000 $\times$ .10) on $3 stated
      value common stock at a market value
      of $509,000 (50,900 $\times$ $10)

k. Income Summary | 340,000 |
   Retained Earnings | | 340,000
      To close the Income Summary account
      to Retained Earnings

l. Retained Earnings | 730,800 |
   Cash Dividends Declared | | 221,800
   Stock Dividends Declared | | 509,000
      To close the Cash Dividends Declared
      and Stock Dividends Declared accounts
      to Retained Earnings

2. Prepare a statement of retained earnings.

Szatkowski Company
Statement of Retained Earnings
For the Year Ended June 30, 19x6

Retained Earnings, June 30, 19x5		$ 970,000
Net Income, 19x6		340,000
Subtotal		$1,310,000
Less: Cash Dividends		
Preferred	$120,000	
Common	101,800	
Stock Dividends	509,000	
Treasury Stock Transaction	5,000	735,800
Retained Earnings, June 30, 19x6 (Note x)		$ 574,200

3. Prepare the stockholders' equity section of the balance sheet.

Szatkowski Company
Stockholders' Equity
June 30, 19x6

Contributed Capital		
Preferred Stock—$100 par value, 6% noncumulative, 50,000 shares authorized, 20,000 shares issued and outstanding		$2,000,000
Common Stock—no par value, $3 stated value, 1,000,000 shares authorized, 512,000 shares issued, 509,000 shares outstanding	$1,536,000	
Common Stock Distributable, 50,900 shares	152,700	
Paid-in Capital in Excess of Stated Value, Common	1,236,300	2,925,000
Total Contributed Capital		$4,925,000
Retained Earnings (Note x)		574,200
Total Contributed Capital and Retained Earnings		$5,499,200
Less Treasury Stock, Common (3,000 shares at cost)		24,000
Total Stockholders' Equity		$5,475,200

Note x: The board of directors has restricted retained earnings available for dividends by the amount of $100,000 as required under a loan agreement.

4. Compute the book values.

June 30, 19x5
Common Stock: $3,290,000 ÷ 250,000 shares = $13.16 per share
June 30, 19x6
Preferred Stock: Call price of $104 per share equals book value per share
Common Stock:
($5,475,200 − $2,080,000) ÷ (509,000 shares + 50,900 shares) =
$3,395,200 ÷ 559,900 shares = $6.06 per share

CHAPTER ASSIGNMENTS

QUESTIONS

1. What are retained earnings, and how do they relate to the assets of a corporation?
2. When does a company have a deficit in retained earnings?
3. What items are identified by generally accepted accounting principles as prior period adjustments?
4. Explain how the accounting treatment of stock dividends differs from that of cash dividends.
5. What is the difference between a stock dividend and a stock split? What is the effect of each on the capital structure of the corporation?
6. What are the purposes of restricting retained earnings?
7. What is the difference between the statement of stockholders' equity and the stockholders' equity section of the balance sheet?

8. Would you expect a corporation's book value per share to equal its market value per share? Why or why not?

9. "Accounting income should be geared to the concept of taxable income because the public understands that concept." Comment on this statement, and tell why income tax allocation is necessary.

10. Exxon Corporation had about $11.1 billion of deferred income taxes in 1992, equal to about 20 percent of total liabilities. This percentage has risen or remained steady for many years. Given management's desire to put off the payment of taxes as long as possible, the long-term growth of the economy and inflation, and the definition of a liability (probable future sacrifices of future benefits arising from present obligations), make an argument for not accounting for deferred income taxes.

11. Why should a gain or loss on discontinued operations be disclosed separately on the income statement?

12. Explain the two major criteria for extraordinary items. How should extraordinary items be disclosed in the financial statements?

13. When an accounting change occurs, what disclosures must be made in the financial statements?

14. How are earnings per share disclosed in financial statements?

15. When does a company have a simple capital structure? A complex capital structure?

16. What is the difference between primary and fully diluted earnings per share?

SHORT EXERCISES

SE 1. *Statement of*
L O 1 *Retained Earnings*
Check Figure: Retained Earnings, Dec. 31, 19x2: $356,000

The Snadhu Corporation had a balance in Retained Earnings on December 31, 19x1, of $260,000. During 19x2, the company reported a profit of $112,000 after taxes. During 19x2, the company declared cash dividends totaling $16,000. Prepare the company's statement of retained earnings for the year ended December 31, 19x2.

SE 2. *Stock Dividends*
L O 2
No check figure

On February 15, Oak Plaza Corporation's board of directors declared a 2 percent stock dividend applicable to the outstanding shares of its $10 par value common stock, of which 200,000 shares are authorized, 130,000 are issued, and 20,000 are held in the treasury. The stock dividend was distributable on March 15 to stockholders of record on March 1. On February 15, the market value of the common stock was $15 per share. On March 30, the board of directors declared a $.50 per share cash dividend. No other stock transactions have occurred. Record the necessary transactions on February 15, March 1, March 15, and March 30.

SE 3. *Stock Split*
L O 2
No check figure

On August 10, the board of directors of Nicolau International declared a 3-for-1 stock split of its $9 par value common stock, of which 800,000 shares were authorized and 250,000 were issued and outstanding. The market value on that date was $60 per share. On the same date, the balance of Paid-in Capital in Excess of Par Value, Common was $6,000,000, and the balance of Retained Earnings was $6,500,000. Prepare the stockholders' equity section of the company's balance sheet after the stock split. What journal entry, if any, is needed to record the stock split?

SE 4. *Restriction of*
L O 3 *Retained Earnings*
No check figure

Thorne Company has a lawsuit filed against it. The board took action to restrict retained earnings in the amount of $2,500,000 on May 31, 19x1, pending the outcome of the suit. On May 31, the company had retained earnings of $3,725,000. Show two ways in which the restriction on retained earnings can be disclosed.

SE 5. *Effects of*
L O 2, 3, 4 *Stockholders' Equity*
Actions
Check Figures: Total Stockholders' Equity: No effect 1, 3, 4; Decrease 2, 5

Tell whether each of the following actions will increase, decrease, or have no effect on total assets, total liabilities, and total stockholders' equity.

1. Declaration of a stock dividend
2. Declaration of a cash dividend
3. Stock split
4. Restriction of retained earnings
5. Purchase of treasury stock

SE 6. *Statement of*
L O 4 *Stockholders' Equity*
Check Figures: 1. $50; 2. $33.33;
3. $50; 4. $48

Refer to the statement of stockholders' equity for Tri-State Corporation in Exhibit 2 to answer the following questions: (1) At what price per share were the 5,000 shares of common stock sold? (2) What was the conversion price per share of the common stock into preferred stock? (3) At what price was the common stock selling on the date of the stock dividend? (4) At what price per share was the treasury stock purchased?

SE 7. *Book Value for*
L O 5 *Preferred and*
Common Stock
Check Figures: Preferred: $112 per share; Common: $29.625 per share

Given the stockholders' equity section of the Giszter Corporation's balance sheet shown below, what is the book value per share for both the preferred and the common stock?

Contributed Capital
    Preferred Stock—$100 per share, 8 percent
    cumulative, 10,000 shares authorized,
        500 shares issued and outstanding* $ 50,000
    Common Stock—$10 par value, 100,000 shares
    authorized, 40,000 shares issued and
        outstanding $400,000
    Paid-in Capital in Excess of Par Value, Common   516,000   916,000
    Total Contributed Capital $ 966,000
Retained Earnings   275,000
Total Stockholders' Equity $1,241,000

*The preferred stock is callable at $104 per share, and one year's dividends are in arrears.

SE 8. *Corporate Income*
L O 6 *Statement*
Check Figure: Net Income (Loss): ($110,000)

Assume that the Diah Company's chief financial officer gave you the following information: Net Sales, $720,000; Cost of Goods Sold, $350,000; Loss from Discontinued Operations (net of income tax benefit of $70,000), $200,000; Loss on Disposal of Discontinued Operations (net of income tax benefit of $16,000), $50,000; Operating Expenses, $130,000; Income Taxes Expense on Continuing Operations, $100,000. From this information, prepare the company's income statement for the year ended June 30, 19xx. (Ignore earnings per share information.)

SE 9. *Use of Corporate*
L O 7 *Income Tax Rate*
Schedule
Check Figures: 1. $136,000;
2. $7,096,650

Using the corporate tax rate schedule in Table 1, compute the income tax liability for taxable income of (1) $400,000 and (2) $20,000,000.

SE 10. *Earnings per Share*
L O 9
Check Figures: 19x1 and 19x2: $1.45 earnings per share

During 19x1, the Junifer Corporation reported a net income of $669,200. On January 1, Junifer had 360,000 shares of common stock outstanding. The company issued an additional 240,000 shares of common stock on August 1. In 19x1, the company had a simple capital structure. During 19x2, there were no transactions involving common stock, and the company reported net income of $870,000. Determine the weighted-average number of common shares outstanding for 19x1 and 19x2. Also, compute earnings per share for 19x1 and 19x2.

EXERCISES

E 1. *Statement of*
L O 1 *Retained Earnings*
Check Figure: Retained Earnings, Dec. 31, 19x2: $312,000

The Drennan Corporation had a balance in Retained Earnings on December 31, 19x1, of $260,000. During 19x2, the company reported a net income of $112,000 after taxes. In addition, the company located a $44,000 (net of taxes) error that resulted in an overstatement of prior years' income and meets the criteria for a prior period adjustment. During 19x2, the company declared cash dividends totaling $16,000.

Prepare the company's statement of retained earnings for the year ended December 31, 19x2.

E 2. *Journal Entries:*

L O 2 *Stock Dividends*

Check Figures: Stock Dividends
Declared: $15,000; Cash Dividends
Declared: $16,500

The Geyer Company has 30,000 shares of its $1 par value common stock outstanding. Record the following transactions as they relate to the company's common stock.

July 17 Declared a 10 percent stock dividend on common stock to be distributed on August 10 to stockholders of record on July 31. Market value of the stock was $5 per share on this date.

 31 Record date.

Aug. 10 Distributed the stock dividend declared on July 17.

Sept. 1 Declared a $.50 per share cash dividend on common stock to be paid on September 16 to stockholders of record on September 10.

E 3. *Journal Entries:*

L O 2 *Stock Dividends*

Check Figures: Stock Dividends
Declared: $28,800; Cash Dividends
Declared: $24,480

On August 26, Shipley Corporation's board of directors declared a 2 percent stock dividend applicable to the outstanding shares of its $5 par value common stock, of which 150,000 shares are authorized, 130,000 are issued, and 10,000 are held in the treasury. The stock dividend was distributable on September 25 to stockholders of record on September 10. On August 26, the market value of the common stock was $12 per share. On November 26, the board of directors declared a $.20 per share cash dividend. No other stock transactions have occurred. Record the transactions on August 26, September 10, September 25, and November 26. Make the December 31 entry to close Cash Dividends Declared and Stock Dividends Declared to Retained Earnings.

E 4. *Stock Split*

L O 2

Check Figures: After split: 400,000 shares issued and outstanding; Total Stockholders' Equity: $920,000

The Colson Company currently has 500,000 shares of $1 par value common stock authorized with 200,000 shares outstanding. The board of directors declared a 2-for-1 split on May 15, when the market value of the common stock was $2.50 per share. The Retained Earnings balance on May 15 was $700,000. Paid-in Capital in Excess of Par Value, Common on this date was $20,000.

Prepare the stockholders' equity section of the company's balance sheet before and after the stock split. What journal entry, if any, would be necessary to record the stock split?

E 5. *Stock Split*

L O 2

Check Figures: After split: 600,000 shares issued and outstanding; Total Stockholders' Equity: $14,400,000

On January 15, the board of directors of Fuquat International declared a 3-for-1 stock split of its $12 par value common stock, of which 800,000 shares were authorized and 200,000 were issued and outstanding. The market value on that date was $45 per share. On the same date, the balance of Paid-in Capital in Excess of Par Value, Common was $4,000,000, and the balance of Retained Earnings was $8,000,000.

Prepare the stockholders' equity section of the company's balance sheet before and after the stock split. What journal entry, if any, is needed to record the stock split?

E 6. *Restriction of*

L O 3 *Retained Earnings*

No check figure

The board of directors of the Hollander Company has approved plans to acquire another company during the coming year. The acquisition should cost approximately $550,000. The board took action to restrict retained earnings of the company in the amount of $550,000 on July 17, 19x1. On July 31, the company had retained earnings of $975,000.

1. Show two ways the restriction on retained earnings can be disclosed.
2. Assuming the purchase takes place as planned, what effect will it have on retained earnings and future disclosures?

E 7. *Statement of*

L O 4 *Stockholders' Equity*

Check Figure: Total Stockholders' Equity, Dec. 31, 19x3: $3,917,240

The stockholders' equity section of Network Corporation's balance sheet on December 31, 19x2, appears as follows:

Contributed Capital	
Common Stock—$1 par value, 500,000 shares authorized, 400,000 issued and outstanding	$ 400,000
Paid-in Capital in Excess of Par Value, Common	600,000
Total Contributed Capital	$1,000,000
Retained Earnings	2,100,000
Total Stockholders' Equity	$3,100,000

Prepare a statement of stockholders' equity for the year ended December 31, 19x3, assuming the following transactions occurred in sequence during 19x3.

a. Issued 5,000 shares of $100 par value, 9 percent cumulative preferred stock at par after obtaining authorization from the state.

b. Issued 40,000 shares of common stock in connection with the conversion of bonds having a carrying value of $300,000.

c. Declared and issued a 2 percent common stock dividend. The market value on the date of declaration was $7 per share.

d. Purchased 10,000 shares of common stock for the treasury at a cost of $8 per share.

e. Earned net income of $230,000.

f. Declared and paid the full year's dividend on preferred stock and a dividend of $.20 per share on common stock outstanding at the end of the year.

E 8.
L O 5
Book Value for Preferred and Common Stock

Check Figures: Preferred: $111 per share; Common: $17.31 per share

The stockholders' equity section of the Colombus Corporation's balance sheet is shown below.

Contributed Capital
  Preferred Stock—$100 par value, 6 percent
  cumulative, 10,000 shares authorized,
    200 shares issued and outstanding* $ 20,000
  Common Stock—$5 par value, 100,000 shares
  authorized, 10,000 shares issued, 9,000 shares
    outstanding $50,000
  Paid-in Capital in Excess of Par Value, Common   28,000   78,000

  Total Contributed Capital $ 98,000
Retained Earnings   95,000

Total Contributed Capital and Retained Earnings $193,000
Less Treasury Stock, Common (1,000 shares, at cost)   15,000

Total Stockholders' Equity $178,000

*The preferred stock is callable at $105 per share, and one year's dividends are in arrears.

Determine the book value per share for both the preferred and the common stock.

E 9.
L O 6
Corporate Income Statement

Check Figure: Net income: $387,500

Assume that the Shortall Furniture Company's chief financial officer gave you the following information: Net Sales, $1,900,000; Cost of Goods Sold, $1,050,000; Extraordinary Gain (net of income taxes of $3,500), $12,500; Loss from Discontinued Operations (net of income tax benefit of $30,000), $50,000; Loss on Disposal of Discontinued Operations (net of income tax benefit of $13,000), $35,000; Selling Expenses, $50,000; Administrative Expenses, $40,000; Income Taxes Expense on Continuing Operations, $300,000.

From this information, prepare the company's income statement for the year ended June 30, 19xx. (Ignore earnings per share information.)

E 10.
L O 7
Use of Corporate Income Tax Rate Schedule

Check Figures: Situation A: $12,500; Situation B: $17,150; Situation C: $108,050

Using the corporate tax rate schedule in Table 1, compute the income tax liability for each of the following situations.

Situation	Taxable Income
A	$ 70,000
B	85,000
C	320,000

E 11.
L O 7
Income Tax Allocation

Check Figures: Income taxes paid: 19x2, $24,950; 19x3, $53,550

The Theus Corporation reported the following accounting income before income taxes, income taxes expense, and net income for 19x2 and 19x3.

	19x3	19x2
Accounting income before taxes	$140,000	$140,000
Income taxes expense	44,150	44,150
Net income	$ 95,850	$ 95,850

Also, on the balance sheet, deferred income taxes liability increased by $19,200 in 19x2 and decreased by $9,400 in 19x3.

1. How much did Theus Corporation actually pay in income taxes for 19x2 and 19x3?
2. Prepare journal entries to record income taxes expense for 19x2 and 19x3.

E 12. *Earnings per Share*
L O 9

Check Figures: Weighted-average shares: 19x1, 805,000; 19x2, 1,120,000

During 19x1, the Heath Corporation reported a net income of $1,529,500. On January 1, Heath had 700,000 shares of common stock outstanding. The company issued an additional 420,000 shares of common stock on October 1. In 19x1, the company had a simple capital structure. During 19x2, there were no transactions involving common stock, and the company reported net income of $2,016,000.

1. Determine the weighted-average number of common shares outstanding each year.
2. Compute earnings per share for each year.

E 13. *Corporate Income*
L O 6, 7, *Statement*
8, 9

Check Figure: Income from Continuing Operations: $78,750

The following items are components in the income statement of Cohen Corporation for the year ended December 31, 19x1.

Net Sales	$500,000
Cost of Goods Sold	(275,000)
Operating Expenses	(112,500)
Total Income Taxes Expense for Period	(82,350)
Income from Operations of a Discontinued Segment	80,000
Gain on Disposal of Segment	70,000
Extraordinary Gain on Retirement of Bonds	36,000
Cumulative Effect of a Change in Accounting Principle	(24,000)
Net Income	$192,150
Earnings per share	$ .96

Recast the 19x1 income statement in proper multistep form, including allocating income taxes to appropriate items (assume a 30 percent income tax rate) and showing earnings per share figures (200,000 shares outstanding).

SKILLS DEVELOPMENT EXERCISES

Conceptual Analysis

SDE 1. *Motivation for Stock*
L O 2 *Dividends*

No check figure

In recent years, **Athey Products Corporation,** a small maker of industrial products for the waste management industry, has followed the practice of issuing a 10 percent stock dividend annually. Although the company's net income has been almost $4 million in each of the last three years, retained earnings have declined from about $10 million to about $6 million.[24] What is the probable motivation for management's decision to issue an annual 10 percent stock dividend? What is the most likely explanation for the decrease in retained earnings? Given your explanation, would stockholders' equity also decrease by a like amount?

SDE 2. *Interpretation of*
L O 6, 8, 9 *Corporate Income Statement*

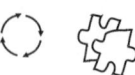

No check figure

Westinghouse Electric Corporation is a major technology company whose main businesses are power systems, electronic systems, environmental services, transport temperature control, and broadcasting. In recent years, the company has faced difficult restructurings, including the sale of several of its businesses, and changes in accounting principles, indicated as follows in the report of the company's independent auditors, Price Waterhouse:[25]

> As discussed in Note 1 to these financial statements, the Corporation adopted Statement of Financial Accounting Standards (SFAS) No. 106, "Employers' Accounting for Postretirement Benefits Other Than Pensions," and SFAS No. 109, "Accounting for Income Taxes," in 1992. As discussed in Note 2 to these financial statements, the Corporation adopted a comprehensive plan in November 1992 that entails exiting the financial services business and certain other non-strategic businesses. These businesses have been accounted for as discontinued operations.

---

24. Athey Products Corporation, *Annual Report,* 1989.
25. Westinghouse Electric Corporation, *Annual Report,* 1992.

These changes are reflected in the company's 1991 and 1992 income statements, a portion of which appears below (amounts in millions of dollars except per share data):[26]

	1992	1991
Income from Continuing Operations	$ 348	$ 265
Discontinued Operations, net of income taxes (note 2):		
Loss from operations	(21)	(1,351)
Estimated loss on disposal of Discontinued Operations	(1,280)	—
Loss from Discontinued Operations	(1,301)	(1,351)
Income (loss) before cumulative effect of changes in accounting principles	(953)	(1,086)
Cumulative effect of changes in accounting principles:		
Postretirement benefits other than pensions (notes 1 and 4)	(742)	—
Income taxes (notes 1 and 5)	404	—
Net income (loss)	($1,291)	($1,086)
Earnings (loss) per common share (note 15):		
From Continuing Operations	$ .93	$ .84
From Discontinued Operations	(3.76)	(4.30)
From cumulative effect of changes in accounting principles	(.98)	—
Earnings (loss) per common share	($3.81)	($3.46)
Cash dividends per common share (note 15)	$ .72	$ 1.40

1. Identify the amounts in the partial income statement for each item mentioned in the independent auditors' report.
2. Define discontinued operations and explain the difference between loss from operations and estimated loss on disposal of discontinued operations. Why are discontinued operations shown separately on the income statement?
3. Define the cumulative effect of changes in accounting principles. Were those changes instigated by management, or were they mandated by outside authorities? If mandated, by whom?
4. Why are several figures given for earnings per common share? Which earnings (loss) per common share figure would you say is most relevant to future operations? Why is it the most relevant?

SDE 3. *Interpretation of*
L O 6, 8 *Earnings Reports*

No check figure

McDonnell Douglas Corporation, the large aerospace and defense company based in St. Louis, was the subject of an article in the *Wall Street Journal* reporting on its third-quarter 1990 results of operations. The following are excerpts from that article.

> McDonnell Douglas Corp. posted a sharp rise in third-quarter net income after an accounting adjustment, but financial problems related to its C-17 military transport program raised questions about the strength of operating results.
>
> Net soared to $248 million, or $6.46 a share, from $38 million, or $.98 a share, in the year-earlier period on a 13% rise in revenue to $4.18 billion from $3.71 billion.
>
> The accounting adjustment, which stems from the settlement of certain pension fund obligations announced in September, contributed $234 million, or $6.11 a share, leaving operating profit of only $14 million, or $.35 a share.
>
> While McDonnell Douglas hailed its "improved performance," some Wall Street analysts weren't quite so upbeat. They took particular issue with the company's effort to paint a $58 million reversal of earnings on the C-17 program as a one-time, nonoperating adjustment, when in fact far more serious write-downs remain possible.
>
> "I would consider the C-17 adjustment an operational issue because it stemmed from cost problems," said Lawrence Harris, an analyst.

26. Ibid.

. . . In making the C-17 adjustment, the company wiped out profit recorded on the program between 1985 and the first quarter of this year, indicating that it expects to bump against the $6.6 billion cost ceiling when the project is completed in the 1990s. Should it pierce that ceiling, things would get much worse. At that point, the company could begin absorbing all expenses with the federal government no longer obliged to reimburse it.[27]

Is the increase shown by McDonnell Douglas's net income misleading? Why or why not? Defend your position by explaining the structure of McDonnell Douglas's income statement as suggested by the excerpt.

Ethical Dilemma

SDE 4. *Ethics and Stock*
L O 2 *Dividends*

No check figure

For twenty years **Bass Products Corporation,** a public corporation, has followed the practice of paying a cash dividend every quarter and has promoted itself to investors as a stable, reliable company. Recent competition from Asian companies has negatively affected its earnings and cash flows. As a result, Sandra Bass, president of the company, is proposing that the board of directors declare a stock dividend of 5 percent this year instead of a cash dividend. She says, "This will maintain our consecutive dividend record and will not require any cash outflow." What is the difference between a cash dividend and a stock dividend? Why does a corporation usually distribute either kind of dividend, and how does each affect the financial statements? Is the action proposed by Bass ethical?

Research Activity

SDE 5. *Stockholders' Equity*
L O 2, 4, 5, *and Book Value*
6, 7, 8 *Versus Market Price*

No check figure

In your library, select the annual reports of three corporations. You may choose them from the same industry or at random, at the direction of your instructor. (If you completed the related research activity in the chapter on contributed capital, use the same three companies.) Prepare a table with a column for each corporation. Then, for any year covered by the balance sheet, the statement of stockholders' equity, and the income statement, answer the following questions: Does the company own treasury stock? Was any treasury stock bought or retired? Did the company declare a stock dividend or a stock split? What other transactions appear in the statement of stockholders' equity? Has the company deferred any income taxes? Were there any discontinued operations, extraordinary items, or accounting changes? Compute the book value per common share for the company. In the *Wall Street Journal* or the financial section of another daily newspaper, find the current market price of each company's common stock and compare it to the book value you computed. Should there be any relationship between the two values? Be prepared to discuss your answers to these questions in class.

Decision-Making Practice

SDE 6. *Analyzing Effects of*
L O 2, 5 *Stockholders' Equity*
Transactions

Check Figure: Total Stockholders'
Equity: $72,340,000

Metzger Steel Corporation (MSC) is a small specialty steel manufacturer located in northern Alabama that has been owned by the Metzger family for several generations. Arnold Metzger is a major shareholder in MSC by virtue of having inherited 200,000 shares of common stock in the company. Arnold has not shown much interest in the business because of his enthusiasm for archaeology, which takes him to far parts of the world. However, when he received the minutes of the last board of directors meeting, he questioned a number of transactions involving stockholders' equity. He asks you, as a person with a knowledge of accounting, to help him interpret the effect of these transactions on his interest in MSC.

You begin by examining the stockholders' equity section of MSC's December 31, 19x1, balance sheet.

27. Rick Wartzman, "McDonnell's Net Rose in 3rd Period; Special Items Cited," *Wall Street Journal,* October 24, 1990.

Metzger Steel Corporation
Stockholders' Equity
December 31, 19x1

Contributed Capital	
Common Stock—$10 par value, 5,000,000 shares	
authorized, 1,000,000 shares issued and outstanding	$10,000,000
Paid-in Capital in Excess of Par Value, Common	25,000,000
Total Contributed Capital	$35,000,000
Retained Earnings	20,000,000
Total Stockholders' Equity	$55,000,000

Then you read the relevant parts of the minutes of the December 15, 19x2, meeting of the firm's board of directors:

Item A: The president reported the following transactions involving the company's stock during the last quarter.

October 15. Sold 500,000 shares of authorized common stock through the investment banking firm of T. R. Kendall at a net price of $50 per share.
November 1. Purchased 100,000 shares for the corporate treasury from Lucy Metzger at a price of $55 per share.

Item B: The board declared a 2-for-1 stock split (accomplished by halving the par value and doubling each stockholder's shares), followed by a 10 percent stock dividend. The board then declared a cash dividend of $2 per share on the resulting shares. All these transactions are applicable to stockholders of record on December 20 and are payable on January 10. The market value of MSC stock on the board meeting date after the stock split was estimated to be $30.

Item C: The chief financial officer stated that he expected the company to report net income for the year of $4,000,000.

1. Prepare a stockholders' equity section of MSC's balance sheet as of December 31, 19x2, that reflects the transactions above. (**Hint:** Use T accounts to analyze the transactions. Also, use a T account to keep track of the shares of common stock outstanding.)
2. Compute the book value per share and Arnold's percentage of ownership of the company at the beginning and end of the year. Explain the differences. Would you say that Arnold's position has improved during the year? Why or why not?

PROBLEM SET A

A 1.
L O 2
Stock Dividend and
Stock Split
Transactions

Check Figure: Total Stockholders'
Equity, Dec. 31, 19x3: $1,157,000

The stockholders' equity section of Linden Cotton Mills, Inc. as of December 31, 19x2, was as follows:

Contributed Capital	
Common Stock—$6 par value, 500,000 shares	
authorized, 80,000 shares issued and outstanding	$ 480,000
Paid-in Capital in Excess of Par Value, Common	150,000
Total Contributed Capital	$ 630,000
Retained Earnings	480,000
Total Stockholders' Equity	$1,110,000

A review of the stockholders' equity records of Linden Cotton Mills, Inc. disclosed the following transactions during 19x3.

Mar. 25 The board of directors declared a 5 percent stock dividend to stockholders of record on April 20 to be distributed on May 1. The market value of the common stock was $11 per share.

Apr. 20 Date of record for the stock dividend.

May 1 Issued the stock dividend.

Sept. 10 Declared a 3-for-1 stock split.

Dec. 15 Declared a 10 percent stock dividend to stockholders of record on January 15 to be distributed on February 15. The market price on this date is $3.50 per share.

31 Closed Stock Dividends Declared to Retained Earnings.

REQUIRED

1. Record the transactions for Linden Cotton Mills, Inc. in general journal form.
2. Prepare the stockholders' equity section of the company's balance sheet as of December 31, 19x3. Assume net income for 19x3 is $47,000. (**Hint:** Use T accounts to keep track of transactions.)

A 2.
L O 1, 2, 3

Dividend and Stock Split Transactions, Retained Earnings, and Stockholders' Equity

Check Figures: Retained Earnings: $231,500; Total Stockholders' Equity: $1,321,500

The balance sheet of the Shimer Clothing Company disclosed the following stockholders' equity as of September 30, 19x1.

Contributed Capital		
Common Stock—$2 par value, 1,000,000 shares		
authorized, 300,000 shares issued and outstanding	$ 600,000	
Paid-in Capital in Excess of Par Value, Common	370,000	
Total Contributed Capital	$ 970,000	
Retained Earnings	350,000	
Total Stockholders' Equity	$1,320,000	

The following stockholders' equity transactions were completed during the next fiscal year in the order presented.

19x1

Dec. 17 Declared a 10 percent stock dividend to be distributed January 20 to stockholders of record on January 1. The market value per share on the date of declaration was $4.

19x2

Jan. 1 Date of record.

20 Distributed the stock dividend.

Apr. 14 Declared a $.25 per share cash dividend. The cash dividend is payable May 15 to stockholders of record on May 1.

May 1 Date of record.

15 Paid the cash dividend.

June 17 Split its stock 2 for 1.

Sept. 15 Declared a cash dividend of $.10 per share payable October 10 to stockholders of record on October 1.

30 Closed Income Summary with a credit balance of $150,000 to Retained Earnings.

30 Closed Cash Dividends Declared and Stock Dividends Declared to Retained Earnings.

On September 14, the board of directors restricted retained earnings for plant expansion in the amount of $150,000. The restriction should be shown in the financial statements.

REQUIRED

1. Record the above transactions in general journal form.
2. Prepare a statement of retained earnings, including disclosure of the restriction.
3. Prepare the stockholders' equity section of the company's balance sheet as of September 30, 19x2, with an appropriate disclosure of the restriction on retained earnings.

A 3. *Corporate Income*
L O 6, 7, *Statement*
8, 9

Check Figure: Income Before
Extraordinary Items and Cumulative
Effect of Accounting Change:
$205,000

Information concerning operations of the Daniels Shoe Corporation during 19xx is as follows:

a. Administrative expenses, $90,000.
b. Cost of goods sold, $420,000.
c. Cumulative effect of an accounting change in depreciation methods that increased income (net of taxes, $20,000), $42,000.
d. Extraordinary loss from an earthquake (net of taxes, $36,000), $60,000.
e. Sales (net), $900,000.
f. Selling expenses, $80,000.
g. Income taxes expense applicable to continuing operations, $105,000.

REQUIRED

Prepare the corporation's income statement for the year ended December 31, 19xx, including earnings per share information. Assume a weighted average of 100,000 common shares outstanding during the year.

A 4. *Corporate Income*
L O 6, 7, 8 *Statement and*
Evaluation of
Business Operations

Check Figure: Income from
Continuing Operations: $275,625

During 19x4 Clever Corporation engaged in a number of complex transactions to restructure the business—selling off a division, retiring bonds, and changing accounting methods. The company has always issued a simple single-step income statement, and the accountant has accordingly prepared the following December 31 year-end income statements for 19x3 and 19x4.

Clever Corporation
Income Statements
For the Years Ended December 31, 19x4 and 19x3

	19x4	19x3
Net Sales	$1,750,000	$2,100,000
Cost of Goods Sold	(962,500)	(1,050,000)
Operating Expenses	(393,750)	(262,500)
Income Taxes Expense	(288,225)	(236,250)
Income from Operations of a Discontinued Segment	280,000	
Gain on Disposal of Discontinued Segment	245,000	
Extraordinary Gain on Retirement of Bonds	126,000	
Cumulative Effect of a Change in Accounting Principle	(84,000)	
Net Income	$ 672,525	$ 551,250
Earnings per share	$ 3.36	$ 2.76

The president of the company, Thomas Clever, is pleased to see that both net income and earnings per share increased by 22 percent from 19x3 to 19x4 and intends to announce to the stockholders that the restructuring is a success.

REQUIRED

1. Recast the 19x4 income statement in proper multistep form, including allocating income taxes to appropriate items (assume a 30 percent income tax rate) and showing earnings per share figures (200,000 shares outstanding).
2. What is your assessment of the restructuring plan and business operations in 19x4?

A 5. *Comprehensive*
L O 1, 2, *Stockholders' Equity*
3, 5 *Transactions*

Check Figure: Total Stockholders'
Equity: $1,401,400

On December 31, 19x1, the stockholders' equity section of the Skolnick Company's balance sheet appeared as follows:

Contributed Capital	
Common Stock—$4 par value, 200,000 shares	
authorized, 60,000 shares issued and outstanding	$ 240,000
Paid-in Capital in Excess of Par Value, Common	640,000
Total Contributed Capital	$ 880,000
Retained Earnings	412,000
Total Stockholders' Equity	$1,292,000

Selected transactions involving stockholders' equity in 19x2 are as follows: On January 4, the board of directors obtained authorization for 20,000 shares of $20 par value non-cumulative preferred stock that carried an indicated dividend rate of $2 per share and was callable at $21 per share. On January 14, the company sold 12,000 shares of the preferred stock at $20 per share and issued another 2,000 in exchange for a building valued at $40,000. On March 8, the board of directors declared a 2-for-1 stock split on the common stock. On April 20, after the stock split, the company purchased 3,000 shares of common stock for the treasury at an average price of $6 per share; 1,000 of these shares subsequently were sold on May 4 at an average price of $8 per share. On July 15, the board of directors declared a cash dividend of $2 per share on the preferred stock and $.20 per share on the common stock. The date of record was July 25. The dividends were paid on August 15. The board of directors declared a 15 percent stock dividend on November 28, when the common stock was selling for $10. The record date for the stock dividend was December 15, and the dividend was to be distributed on January 5. Net loss for 19x2 was $109,000. On December 31, Income Summary, Cash Dividends Declared, and Stock Dividends Declared were closed. The board of directors noted that note disclosure must be made of a bank loan agreement that requires minimum retained earnings. No cash dividends can be declared or paid if retained earnings fall below $50,000.

REQUIRED

1. Prepare journal entries to record the transactions above.
2. Prepare the company's statement of retained earnings for the year ended December 31, 19x2, including disclosure of restriction.
3. Prepare the stockholders' equity section of the company's balance sheet as of December 31, 19x2, including an appropriate disclosure of the restrictions on retained earnings. (**Hint:** Use T accounts to keep track of transactions.)
4. Compute the book value per share for preferred and common stock (including common stock distributable) on December 31, 19x1 and 19x2.

PROBLEM SET B

B 1. *Stock Dividend and*
L O 2 *Stock Split*
Transactions

Check Figure: Total Stockholders'
Equity, Dec. 31, 19x7: $1,554,000

The stockholders' equity section of the balance sheet of Packer Corporation as of December 31, 19x6, was as follows:

Contributed Capital	
Common Stock—$2 par value, 500,000 shares authorized,	
200,000 shares issued and outstanding	$ 400,000
Paid-in Capital in Excess of Par Value, Common	500,000
Total Contributed Capital	$ 900,000
Retained Earnings	600,000
Total Stockholders' Equity	$1,500,000

The following transactions occurred in 19x7 for Packer Corporation.

Feb. 28 The board of directors declared a 10 percent stock dividend to stockholders of record on March 25 to be distributed on April 5. The market value of the stock was $8.

Mar. 25 Date of record for the stock dividend.

Apr. 5 Issued the stock dividend.

Aug. 3   Declared a 2-for-1 stock split.
Dec. 31   Declared a 5 percent stock dividend to stockholders of record on January 25 to be distributed on February 5. The market value per share was $4.50.
     31   Closed Stock Dividends Declared to Retained Earnings.

REQUIRED

1. Record the transactions for Packer Corporation in general journal form.
2. Prepare the stockholders' equity section of the company's balance sheet as of December 31, 19x7. Assume net income for 19x7 is $54,000. (**Hint:** Use T accounts to keep track of transactions.)

B 2.   *Dividend and Stock*
L O 1, 2, 3   *Split Transactions,*
Retained Earnings,
and Stockholders'
Equity

Check Figures: Retained Earnings: $207,500; Total Stockholders' Equity: $1,257,500

The stockholders' equity section of the Hughes Blind and Awning Company's balance sheet as of December 31, 19x6, was as follows:

Contributed Capital		
Common Stock—$1 par value, 3,000,000 shares authorized, 500,000 shares issued and outstanding		$ 500,000
Paid-in Capital in Excess of Par Value, Common		200,000
Total Contributed Capital		$ 700,000
Retained Earnings		540,000
Total Stockholders' Equity		$1,240,000

The following stockholders' equity transactions occurred during 19x7.

Mar. 5   Declared a $.20 per share cash dividend to be paid on April 6 to stockholders of record on March 20.
     20   Date of record.
Apr. 6   Paid the cash dividend.
June 17   Declared a 10 percent stock dividend to be distributed August 17 to stockholders of record on August 5. The market value of the stock was $7 per share.
Aug. 5   Date of record.
     17   Distributed the stock dividend.
Oct. 2   Split its stock 3 for 1.
Dec. 27   Declared a cash dividend of $.05 payable January 27, 19x8, to stockholders of record on January 14, 19x8.
     31   Closed Income Summary with a credit balance of $200,000 to Retained Earnings.
     31   Closed Cash Dividends Declared and Stock Dividends Declared to Retained Earnings.

On December 9, the board of directors restricted retained earnings for a pending lawsuit in the amount of $100,000. The restriction should be shown on the firm's financial statements.

REQUIRED

1. Record the 19x7 transactions in general journal form.
2. Prepare a statement of retained earnings, with appropriate disclosure of the restriction.
3. Prepare the stockholders' equity section of the company's balance sheet as of December 31, 19x7, with an appropriate disclosure of the restriction on retained earnings.

B 3.   *Corporate Income*
L O 6, 7,   *Statement*
8, 9

Check Figure: Income Before Extraordinary Items and Cumulative Effect of Accounting Change: $108,000

Income statement information for the Walker Corporation during 19x1 is as follows:

a. Administrative expenses, $110,000.
b. Cost of goods sold, $440,000.
c. Cumulative effect of a change in inventory methods that decreased income (net of taxes, $28,000), $60,000.
d. Extraordinary loss from a storm (net of taxes, $10,000), $20,000.
e. Income taxes expense, continuing operations, $42,000.
f. Net sales, $890,000.
g. Selling expenses, $190,000.

REQUIRED

Prepare Walker Corporation's income statement for the year ended December 31, 19x1, including earnings per share information. Assume a weighted average of 200,000 shares of common stock outstanding for 19x1.

B 4. *Corporate Income*
L O 6, 7, 8 *Statement and*
Evaluation of
Business Operations

Check Figure: Income from
Continuing Operations: $157,500

During 19x3 Dasbol Corporation engaged in a number of complex transactions to restructure the business—selling off a division, retiring bonds, and changing accounting methods. The company has always issued a simple single-step income statement, and the accountant has accordingly prepared the following December 31 year-end income statements for 19x2 and 19x3.

Dasbol Corporation
Income Statements
For the Years Ended December 31, 19x3 and 19x2

	19x3	19x2
Net Sales	$1,000,000	$1,200,000
Cost of Goods Sold	(550,000)	(600,000)
Operating Expenses	(225,000)	(150,000)
Income Taxes Expense	(164,700)	(135,000)
Income from Operations of a Discontinued Segment	160,000	
Gain on Disposal of Discontinued Segment	140,000	
Extraordinary Gain on Retirement of Bonds	72,000	
Cumulative Effect of a Change in Accounting Principle	(48,000)	
Net Income	$ 384,300	$ 315,000
Earnings per share	$ 1.92	$ 1.58

The president of the company, Joanna Dasbol, is pleased to see that both net income and earnings per share increased by 22 percent from 19x2 to 19x3 and intends to announce to the stockholders that the restructuring is a success.

REQUIRED

1. Recast the 19x3 income statement in proper multistep form, including allocating income taxes to appropriate items (assume a 30 percent income tax rate) and showing earnings per share figures (200,000 shares outstanding).
2. What is your assessment of the restructuring plan and business operations in 19x3?

B 5. *Comprehensive*
L O 1, 2, *Stockholders' Equity*
3, 5 *Transactions*

Check Figure: Total Stockholders'
Equity: $3,085,200

The stockholders' equity on June 30, 19x5, of the Roper Company is shown below:

Contributed Capital
  Common Stock—no par value, $2 stated value,
   500,000 shares authorized, 200,000 shares issued
    and outstanding $ 400,000
    Paid-in Capital in Excess of Stated Value, Common   640,000
    Total Contributed Capital $1,040,000
Retained Earnings   420,000
Total Stockholders' Equity $1,460,000

Stockholders' equity transactions for the next fiscal year are as follows:

a. The board of directors declared a 2-for-1 split.
b. The board of directors obtained authorization to issue 100,000 shares of $100 par value, $4 noncumulative preferred stock, callable at $105.
c. Issued 10,000 shares of common stock for a building appraised at $22,000.
d. Purchased 6,000 shares of the company's common stock for $15,000.
e. Issued 15,000 shares, $100 par value, of preferred stock for $100 per share.
f. Sold 4,000 shares of treasury stock for $9,000.
g. Declared cash dividends of $4 per share on preferred stock and $.10 per share on common stock.
h. Date of record.
i. Paid the preferred and common stock cash dividends.

j. Declared a 5 percent stock dividend on common stock. The market value was $9 per share. The stock dividend was distributable after the end of the fiscal year.

k. Net income for the year was $210,000.

l. Closed the Cash Dividends Declared and Stock Dividends Declared accounts to Retained Earnings.

Because of a loan agreement, the company is not allowed to reduce retained earnings below $100,000. The board of directors determined that this restriction should be disclosed in the notes to the financial statements.

REQUIRED

1. Make the appropriate general journal entries to record the transactions.
2. Prepare the company's statement of retained earnings for the year ended June 30, 19x6, including disclosure of the restriction.
3. Prepare the stockholders' equity section of the company's balance sheet on June 30, 19x6, including an appropriate disclosure of the restriction on retained earnings. (**Hint:** Use T accounts to keep track of transactions.)
4. Compute the book values per share of preferred and common stock (including common stock distributable) on June 30, 19x5 and 19x6.

FINANCIAL REPORTING AND ANALYSIS CASES

Interpreting Financial Reports

FRA 1.
L O 6, 8
Interpretation of Earnings Report in Financial Press

Check Figure: Net Loss: ($289)

Presented below are several excerpts from an article that appeared in the February 2, 1982, *Wall Street Journal* entitled "Lockheed Had Loss in 4th Quarter, Year; $396 Million TriStar Write-Off Is Cited."

As expected, **Lockheed Corp.** took a $396 million write-off to cover expenses of its production phase-out of L-1011 TriStar commercial jets, resulting in a net loss of . . . $289 million for the year.

Roy A. Anderson, Lockheed Chairman, said he believed the company had "recognized all costs, including those yet to be incurred, that are associated with the phase-out of the TriStar program." He said he thinks the company now is in a sound position to embark on a program of future growth and earnings improvement.

Included in the $396 million net write-off are remaining deferred production start-up costs, adjustments for redundant inventories, and provisions for losses and other costs expected to be incurred while TriStar production is completed. In addition to the write-off, discontinued operations include a $70 million after-tax loss associated with 1981 L-1011 operations. The comparable 1980 L-1011 loss was $108 million.

The $289 million net loss in 1981 consists of the TriStar losses, reduced by the previously reported [extraordinary after-tax] gain of $23 million from the exchange of debentures.

For the year, Lockheed had earnings from continuing operations of $154 million, a 14% gain from $135 million in 1980. In 1981 the company had a $466 million loss from discontinued operations, resulting in a net loss of $289 million. A year earlier, the concern had a $108 million loss from discontinued operations, resulting in a net profit of $28 million.[28]

REQUIRED

1. Interpret the financial information from the *Wall Street Journal* by preparing a partial income statement for Lockheed for 1981, beginning with income from continuing operations. Be prepared to explain the nature of each item on the income statement.
2. How do you explain the fact that on the New York Stock Exchange, Lockheed common stock closed at $50 per share, up $.75 on the day after the quoted announcement of a net loss of $289 million and up from $41 per share two months earlier?

28. "Lockheed Had Loss in 4th Quarter, Year; $396 Million TriStar Write-Off Is Cited," *Wall Street Journal,* February 2, 1982. Reprinted by permission of *The Wall Street Journal,* © 1982 Dow Jones & Company, Inc. All Rights Reserved Worldwide.

FRA 2.
L O 4

Interpretation of Statement of Stockholders' Equity

The consolidated statements of stockholders' equity for *Jackson Electronics, Inc.,* a manufacturer of a broad line of electrical components, appear as presented below.

Jackson Electronics, Inc.
Consolidated Statements of Stockholders' Equity
(in thousands)

	Preferred Stock	Common Stock	Paid-in Capital in Excess of Par Value, Common	Retained Earnings	Common Stock in Treasury	Total
Balance at September 30, 1994	$2,756	$3,902	$14,149	$119,312	($ 942)	$139,177
Year Ended September 30, 1995						
Net income	—	—	—	18,753	—	18,753
Redemption and retirement of Preferred Stock (27,560 shares)	(2,756)	—	—	—	—	(2,756)
Stock options exercised (89,000 shares)	—	89	847	—	—	936
Purchases of Common Stock for treasury (501,412 shares)	—	—	—	—	(12,552)	(12,552)
Issuance of Common Stock (148,000 shares) in exchange for convertible subordinated debentures	—	148	3,635	—	—	3,783
Issuance of Common Stock (715,000 shares) for cash	—	715	24,535	—	—	25,250
Issuance of 500,000 shares of Common Stock in exchange for investment interest in Electrix Company	—	500	17,263	—	—	17,763
Cash dividends—Common Stock ($.80 per share)	—	—	—	(3,086)	—	(3,086)
Balance at September 30, 1995	$ —	$5,354	$60,429	$134,979	($13,494)	$187,268

REQUIRED

No check figure

Jackson Electronics, Inc.'s statement of stockholders' equity has eight summary transactions. Show that you understand this statement by preparing a general journal entry with an explanation for each. In each case, if applicable, determine the average price per common share. Sometimes you will also have to make assumptions about an offsetting part of the entry. For example, assume that debentures (long-term bonds) are recorded at face value and that employees pay cash for stock purchased under Jackson Electronics, Inc.'s employee incentive plans.

International Company

FRA 3.
L O 3

Restriction of Retained Earnings

No check figure

In some countries, including Japan, the availability of retained earnings for the payment of dividends is restricted. The following disclosure appeared in the annual report of *Mazda Motor Corporation,* the Japanese automobile manufacturer:[29]

> Under the Commercial Code of Japan, the Company is required to appropriate to legal reserve an amount equal to at least 10% of cash dividends paid in each period through March 31, 1991, and at least 10% of the total amount of cash dividends paid and bonuses to directors and statutory auditors in the period ended March 31, 1992, until the reserve equals 25% of common stock.

29. Mazda Motor Corporation, *Annual Report,* 1992.

This reserve is not available for dividends but may be used to reduce a deficit by resolution of the shareholders or may be capitalized by resolution of the Board of Directors.

For Mazda, this legal reserve amounted to a substantial sum, ¥14 billion, or $105 million. How does this practice differ from that in the United States? Why do you think it is government policy in Japan? Do you think it is a good idea?

Toys "R" Us Annual Report

FRA 4.
L O 4, 5, 6
Corporate Income Statement, Statement of Stockholders' Equity, and Book Value per Share

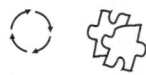

Check Figures: Book value per share: 1994, $10.87; 1995, $12.26

Refer to the annual report in the appendix on Toys "R" Us to answer the following questions.

1. Does Toys "R" Us have discontinued operations, extraordinary items, or cumulative changes in accounting principles? Would you say the income statement for Toys "R" Us is relatively simple or relatively complex?
2. What transactions most commonly affect the stockholders' equity section of the balance sheet of Toys "R" Us?
3. Compute the book value of Toys "R" Us stock in 1995 and 1994 and compare it to the market price. What interpretation do you place on these relationships?

LEARNING OBJECTIVES

1. Explain the advantages and disadvantages of issuing long-term debt.
2. Identify and contrast the major characteristics of bonds.
3. Record the issuance of bonds at face value and at a discount or premium.
4. Use present values to determine the value of bonds.
5. Use the straight-line and effective interest methods to amortize (a) bond discounts and (b) bond premiums.
6. Account for bonds issued between interest dates and make year-end adjustments.
7. Account for the retirement of bonds and the conversion of bonds into stock.
8. Explain the basic features of mortgages payable, installment notes payable, long-term leases, and pensions and other postretirement benefits as long-term liabilities.

RJR Nabisco

DECISION POINT

During the 1980s, there was an explosion in the amount of long-term debt issued by companies either to refinance their own operations or to finance takeovers of other companies. Much of this financing was accomplished through so-called junk bonds, unsecured, high-risk, long-term bonds that carry high rates of interest. Carrying a large amount of debt is risky for a company, and interest charges on junk bonds are especially high in relation to earnings and cash flows. If a company is unable to pay the interest on its bonds, it can be forced to declare bankruptcy. Even if a company can pay the interest, its ability to improve and expand operations can be limited severely.

A record was set in the takeover of RJR Nabisco by Kohlberg Kravis Roberts & Co. when $26 billion in junk bonds was issued. The heavy debt load proved to be a burden to RJR Nabisco. The biggest problem the company faced involved bonds whose interest rate had to be increased if the bonds' prices on the open market declined, as they did in 1990. Some interest rates would have had to be reset at 20 percent or higher, more than double the interest rates on less risky bonds. What could management do to alleviate the situation and avoid potential bankruptcy or the breakup of the company?

As reported in the *Asian Wall Street Journal*, after six months of intense negotiations, RJR Nabisco's management resolved its immediate problems through a $6.9 billion refinancing plan.[1] This large refinancing package was designed to strengthen the balance sheet and ward off a potential financial crisis. Louis Gerstner, the company's chief financial officer, called the refinancing package "a comprehensive, creative program." Under the plan, RJR Nabisco would have billions of dollars at its disposal. Among the components of the plan were new long-term bonds, adjusted interest rates on existing bonds, new issues of capital stock, new bank loans, and expansion of existing bank lines of credit. Although this financing plan is among the most complex in history, it can be understood using the concepts described in this chapter. ⋮ ⋮ ⋮

---

1. George Anders, "RJR Nabisco Moves to Retire Most Troublesome Junk Bonds," *Asian Wall Street Journal*, July 17, 1990.

1 *Explain the advantages and disadvantages of issuing long-term debt*

REASONS FOR ISSUING LONG-TERM DEBT

A corporation has many sources of funds to finance operations and expansion. For example, corporations can acquire cash and other assets from profitable operations and short-term credit. Those sources, however, are seldom sufficient for a growing business that must invest in long-term assets, research and development, and other assets or activities that will produce income in future years. For such assets and activities, the company requires funds that will be available for longer periods of time. Two key sources of long-term funds are the issuance of common stock and the issuance of long-term debt in the form of bonds, notes, mortgages, and leases. Although some companies carry amounts of long-term debt that exceed 50 percent of their total assets, the average company carries less, as can be seen from Figure 1, which shows the ratio of average long-term debt to total assets for selected industries.

Since long-term debts represent financial commitments that must be paid at maturity and interest or other payments that must be paid periodically, common stock would seem to have two advantages over long-term debt: it does not have to be paid back, and dividends on common stock are usually paid only if the company earns sufficient income. However, long-term debt has some advantages over common stock.

1. **Stockholder control.** Since bondholders or other creditors do not have voting rights, common stockholders do not relinquish any control of the company.
2. **Tax effects.** The interest on debt is tax deductible, whereas dividends on common stock are not. For example, if a corporation pays $100,000 in interest and the income tax rate is 30 percent, the net cost to the corporation is $70,000 because it will save $30,000 on its income taxes. To pay $100,000 in dividends, the company would have to earn $142,857 before taxes ($100,000 ÷ .70).
3. **Financial leverage.** If a corporation is able to earn more on its assets than it pays in interest on debt, all of the excess will increase its earnings for stockholders. This concept is called financial leverage, or *trading on the equity*. For example, if a company is able to earn 12 percent, or $120,000, on a $1,000,000 investment financed by long-term 10 percent notes, it will earn $20,000 before taxes ($120,000 − $100,000). Financial leverage makes heavily debt-financed investments in office buildings and shopping centers attractive to investors: They hope to earn a return that exceeds the cost of the interest on the underlying debt. The debt to equity ratio is considered an overall measure of the financial leverage of a company.

Despite these advantages, using debt financing is not always in a company's best interest. First, since cash is required to make periodic interest payments and to pay back the principal amount of the debt at the maturity date, a company whose plans for earnings do not pan out, whose operations are subject to ups and downs, or whose cash flow is weak can be in danger. If it fails to meet its obligations, it can be forced into bankruptcy by creditors. In other words, a company may become overcommitted. Consider, for example, the heavily debt-financed airline industry in recent years. Companies such as TWA, Inc. and Continental Airlines became bankrupt because they could not make payments on their long-term debt and other liabilities. Second, financial leverage can work against a company if the earnings from its investments do not exceed its interest payments. This happened during the savings and loan crisis of a few years ago, when long-term debt was used to finance the construction of office buildings that subsequently could not be leased for enough money to cover interest payments.

Figure 1. Average Long-Term Debt as a Percentage of Total Assets for Selected Industries

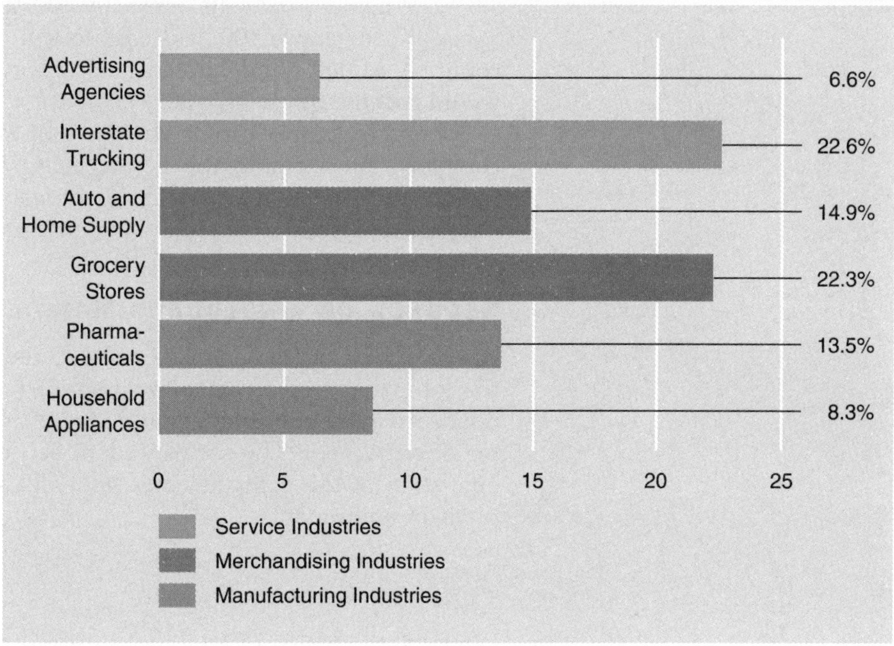

Industry	Percentage
Advertising Agencies	6.6%
Interstate Trucking	22.6%
Auto and Home Supply	14.9%
Grocery Stores	22.3%
Pharmaceuticals	13.5%
Household Appliances	8.3%

Service Industries
Merchandising Industries
Manufacturing Industries

Source: Data from Dun and Bradstreet, *Industry Norms and Ratios, 1993–94.*

THE NATURE OF BONDS

OBJECTIVE

2 *Identify and contrast the major characteristics of bonds*

A bond is a security, usually long term, representing money borrowed by a corporation from the investing public. (Other kinds of bonds are issued by the U.S. government, state and local governments, and foreign companies and countries to raise money.) A bond must be repaid at a specified time and requires periodic payments of interest.[2] Interest is usually paid semiannually (twice a year). Bonds must not be confused with stocks. Because stocks are shares of ownership, stockholders are owners. Bondholders are creditors. Bonds are promises to repay the amount borrowed, called the *principal,* and interest at a specified rate on specified future dates.

A bondholder receives a bond certificate as evidence of the company's debt. In most cases, the face value (denomination) of the bond is $1,000 or some multiple of $1,000. A bond issue is the total number of bonds issued at one time. For example, a $1,000,000 bond issue could consist of a thousand $1,000 bonds. Because a bond issue can be bought and held by many investors, the corporation usually enters into a supplementary agreement called a bond indenture. The bond indenture defines the rights, privileges, and limitations of the bondholders. It generally describes such things as the maturity date of the bonds, interest payment dates, interest rate, and characteristics of the bonds, such as call features. Repayment plans and restrictions also may be covered.

2. At the time this chapter was written, the market interest rates on corporate bonds were volatile. Therefore, the examples and problems in this chapter use a variety of interest rates to demonstrate the concepts.

The prices of bonds are stated in terms of a percentage of face value. A bond issue quoted at 103½ means that a $1,000 bond costs $1,035 ($1,000 × 1.035). When a bond sells at exactly 100, it is said to sell at face or par value. When it sells above 100, it is said to sell at a premium; below 100, at a discount. A $1,000 bond quoted at 87.62 would be selling at a discount and would cost the buyer $876.20.

A bond indenture can be written to fit the financing needs of an individual company. As a result, the bonds being issued by corporations in today's financial markets have many different features. Several of the more important ones are described in the following paragraphs.

SECURED OR UNSECURED BONDS

Bonds can be either secured or unsecured. If issued on the general credit of the company, they are unsecured bonds (also called *debenture bonds*). Secured bonds give the bondholders a pledge of certain company assets as a guarantee of repayment. The security identified by a secured bond can be any specific asset of the company or a general category of asset, such as property, plant, or equipment.

TERM OR SERIAL BONDS

When all the bonds of an issue mature at the same time, they are called term bonds. For instance, a company may issue $1,000,000 worth of bonds, all due twenty years from the date of issue. If the bonds in an issue mature on several different dates, the bonds are serial bonds. An example of serial bonds would be a $1,000,000 issue that calls for retiring $200,000 of the principal every five years. This arrangement means that after the first $200,000 payment is made, $800,000 of the bonds would remain outstanding for the next five years. In other words, $1,000,000 is outstanding for the first five years, $800,000 for the second five years, and so on. A company may issue serial bonds to ease the task of retiring its debt.

REGISTERED OR COUPON BONDS

Most bonds issued today are registered bonds. The names and addresses of the owners of such bonds must be recorded with the issuing company. The company keeps a register of the owners and pays interest by check to the bondholders of record on the interest payment date. Coupon bonds generally are not registered with the corporation; instead, they bear interest coupons stating the amount of interest due and the payment date. The bondholder removes the coupons from the bonds on the interest payment dates and presents them at a bank for collection.

ACCOUNTING FOR BONDS PAYABLE

OBJECTIVE

3 *Record the issuance of bonds at face value and at a discount or premium*

When the board of directors decides to issue bonds, it customarily presents the proposal to the stockholders. If the stockholders agree to the issue, the company prints the certificates and draws up an appropriate legal document. The bonds are then authorized for issuance. It is not necessary to make a journal entry for the authorization, but most companies prepare a memorandum in the Bonds Payable account describing the issue. This note lists the number and value of bonds authorized, the interest rate, the interest payment dates, and the life of the bonds.

Once the bonds are issued, the corporation must pay interest to the bondholders over the life of the bonds (in most cases, semiannually) and the principal of the bonds at maturity.

BALANCE SHEET DISCLOSURE OF BONDS

Bonds payable and either unamortized discounts or premiums (which we explain later) are typically shown on a company's balance sheet as long-term liabilities. However, if the maturity date of the bond issue is one year or less and the bonds will be retired using current assets, Bonds Payable should be listed as a current liability. If the issue is to be paid with segregated assets or replaced by another bond issue, the bonds should still be shown as a long-term liability.

Important provisions of the bond indenture are reported in the notes to the financial statements. Often reported with them is a list of all bond issues, the kinds of bonds, interest rates, any securities connected with the bonds, interest payment dates, maturity dates, and effective interest rates.

BONDS ISSUED AT FACE VALUE

Suppose that the Vason Corporation has authorized the issuance of $100,000 of 9 percent, five-year bonds on January 1, 19x0. According to the bond indenture, interest is to be paid on January 1 and July 1 of each year. Assume that the bonds are sold on January 1, 19x0, for their face value. The entry to record the issuance is as follows:

19x0			
Jan. 1	Cash	100,000	
	Bonds Payable		100,000
	Sold $100,000 of 9%, 5-year bonds at face value		

As stated above, interest is paid on January 1 and July 1 of each year. Therefore, the corporation would owe the bondholders $4,500 interest on July 1, 19x0:

$$\text{Interest} = \text{principal} \times \text{rate} \times \text{time}$$
$$= \$100,000 \times .09 \times {}^{6}/_{12} \text{ year}$$
$$= \$4,500$$

The interest paid to the bondholders on each semiannual interest payment date (January 1 or July 1) would be recorded as follows:

Bond Interest Expense	4,500	
Cash (or Interest Payable)		4,500
Paid (or accrued) semiannual interest to bondholders of 9%, 5-year bonds		

FACE INTEREST RATE AND MARKET INTEREST RATE

When issuing bonds, most companies try to set the face interest rate as close as possible to the market interest rate. The face interest rate is the rate of interest paid to bondholders based on the face value, or principal, of the bonds. The rate and amount are fixed over the life of the bond. A company must decide in advance what the face interest rate will be to allow time to file with regulatory bodies, publicize the issue, and print the certificates.

The market interest rate is the rate of interest paid in the market on bonds of similar risk. It is also referred to as the *effective interest rate*. The market interest rate fluctuates daily. Because a company has no control over the market interest rate, there is often a difference between the market interest rate and the face interest rate on the issue date. The result is that the issue price of the bonds does not always equal their face value. If the market interest rate is higher than the face interest rate, the issue price will be less than the face value and the bonds are said to be issued at a discount. The discount equals the excess of the face value over the issue price. On the other hand, if the market interest rate is lower than the face interest rate, the issue price will be more than the face value and the bonds are said to be issued at a premium. The premium equals the excess of the issue price over the face value.

BONDS ISSUED AT A DISCOUNT

Suppose that the Vason Corporation issues $100,000 of 9 percent, five-year bonds at 96.149 on January 1, 19x0, when the market interest rate is 10 percent. In this case, the bonds are being issued at a discount because the market interest rate exceeds the face interest rate. The following entry records the issuance of the bonds at a discount.

19x0				
Jan. 1	Cash		96,149	
	Unamortized Bond Discount		3,851	
	Bonds Payable			100,000
	Sold $100,000 of 9%, 5-year bonds at 96.149			
	Face amount of bonds	$100,000		
	Less purchase price of bonds ($100,000 × .96149)	96,149		
	Unamortized bond discount	$ 3,851		

In the entry, Cash is debited for the amount received ($96,149), Bonds Payable is credited for the face amount ($100,000) of the bond liability, and the difference ($3,851) is debited to Unamortized Bond Discount. If a balance sheet is prepared right after the bonds are issued at a discount, the liability for bonds payable is reported as follows:

Long-Term Liabilities		
9% Bonds Payable, due 1/1/x5	$100,000	
Less Unamortized Bond Discount	3,851	$96,149

Unamortized Bond Discount is a contra-liability account: Its balance is deducted from the face amount of the bonds to arrive at the carrying value, or present value, of the bonds. The bond discount is described as unamortized because it will be amortized (written off) over the life of the bonds.

BONDS ISSUED AT A PREMIUM

When bonds have a face interest rate above the market rate for similar investments, they are issued at a price above the face value, or at a premium. For example, assume that the Vason Corporation issues $100,000 of 9 percent, five-year bonds for $104,100 on January 1, 19x0, when the market interest rate is 8 percent. This means that investors will purchase the bonds at 104.1 percent of their face value. The issuance would be recorded as follows:

19x0			
Jan. 1	Cash	104,100	
	Unamortized Bond Premium		4,100
	Bonds Payable		100,000
	Sold $100,000 of 9%, 5-year		
	bonds at 104.1		
	($100,000 × 1.041)		

Right after this entry is made, bonds payable would be presented on the balance sheet as follows:

Long-Term Liabilities		
9% Bonds Payable, due 1/1/x5	$100,000	
Unamortized Bond Premium	4,100	$104,100

The carrying value of the bonds payable is $104,100, which equals the face value of the bonds plus the unamortized bond premium. The cash received from the bond issue is also $104,100. This means that the purchasers were willing to pay a premium of $4,100 to buy these bonds because their face interest rate was higher than the market interest rate.

BOND ISSUE COSTS

Most bonds are sold through underwriters, who receive a fee for taking care of the details of marketing the issue or for taking a chance on receiving the selling price. Such costs are connected with the issuance of bonds. Because bond issue costs benefit the whole life of a bond issue, it makes sense to spread the costs over that period. It is generally accepted practice to establish a separate account for bond issue costs and to amortize them over the life of the bonds. However, issue costs decrease the amount of money a company receives from a bond issue. They have the effect, then, of raising the discount or lowering the premium on the issue. As a result, bond issue costs can be spread over the life of the bonds through the amortization of a discount or premium. Because this method simplifies recordkeeping, we assume in the text and problems of this book that all bond issue costs increase the discounts or decrease the premiums of bond issues.

USING PRESENT VALUE TO VALUE A BOND

OBJECTIVE

4 *Use present values to determine the value of bonds*

Present value is relevant to the study of bonds because the value of a bond is based on the present value of two components of cash flow: (1) a series of fixed interest payments and (2) a single payment at maturity.[3] The amount of interest a bond pays is fixed over its life. However, the market interest rate varies from day to day. Thus, the amount investors are willing to pay for a bond changes as well.

Assume, for example, that a particular bond has a face value of $10,000 and pays fixed interest of $450 every six months (a 9 percent annual rate). The

---

3. A knowledge of present value concepts, as presented in the appendix on future value and present value tables, is necessary to an understanding of this section.

bond is due in five years. If the market interest rate today is 14 percent, what is the present value of the bond?

To determine the present value of the bond, we use Table 4 in the appendix on future value and present value tables to calculate the present value of the periodic interest payments of $450, and we use Table 3 to calculate the present value of the single payment of $10,000 at maturity. Since interest payments are made every six months, the compounding period is half a year. Because of this, it is necessary to convert the annual rate to a semiannual rate of 7 percent (14 percent divided by two six-month periods per year) and to use ten periods (five years multiplied by two six-month periods per year). Using this information, we compute the present value of the bond.

Present value of 10 periodic payments at 7%
  (from Table 4 in the appendix on future value
  and present value tables): $450 × 7.024   = $3,160.80
Present value of a single payment at the end of
  10 periods at 7% (from Table 3 in the appendix
  on future value and present value tables):
  $10,000 × .508   = 5,080.00
Present value of $10,000 bond   = $8,240.80

The market interest rate has increased so much since the bond was issued (from 9 percent to 14 percent) that the value of the bond is only $8,240.80 today. That amount is all investors would be willing to pay at this time for a bond that provides income of $450 every six months and a return of the $10,000 principal in five years.

If the market interest rate falls below the face interest rate, say to 8 percent (4 percent semiannually), the present value of the bond will be greater than the face value of $10,000.

Present value of 10 periodic payments at 4%
  (from Table 4 in the appendix on future value
  and present value tables): $450 × 8.111   = $ 3,649.95
Present value of a single payment at the end of
  10 periods at 4% (from Table 3 in the appendix
  on future value and present value tables):
  $10,000 × .676   = 6,760.00
Present value of $10,000 bond   = $10,409.95

BUSINESS BULLETIN: BUSINESS PRACTICE

In 1993, interest rates on long-term debt were at historically low levels, which induced some companies to attempt to lock in those low costs for long periods. One of the most aggressive companies in that regard was The Walt Disney Company, which issued $150 million of 100-year bonds at a yield of only 7.5 percent. It was the first time since 1954 that 100-year bonds had been issued. Some analysts wondered if even Mickey Mouse could survive 100 years. Investors who purchase these bonds are taking a financial risk because if interest rates rise, which they are likely to do, then the market value of the bonds will decrease.[4] ═══

AMORTIZING A BOND DISCOUNT

5a *Use the straight-line and effective interest methods to amortize bond discounts*

In the example on page 592, Vason Corporation issued $100,000 of five-year bonds at a discount because the market interest rate of 10 percent exceeded the face interest rate of 9 percent. The bonds were sold for $96,149, resulting in an unamortized bond discount of $3,851. Because this discount affects interest expense in each year of the bond issue, the bond discount should be amortized (reduced gradually) over the life of the issue. This means that the unamortized bond discount will decrease gradually over time, and that the carrying value of the bond issue (face value less unamortized discount) will increase gradually. By the maturity date of the bond, the carrying value of the issue will equal its face value, and the unamortized bond discount will be zero.

CALCULATION OF TOTAL INTEREST COST

When bonds are issued at a discount, the effective interest rate paid by the company is greater than the face interest rate on the bonds. The reason is that the interest cost to the company is the stated interest payments *plus* the amount of the bond discount. That is, although the company does not receive the full face value of the bonds on issue, it still must pay back the full face value at maturity. The difference between the issue price and the face value must be added to the total interest payments to arrive at the actual interest expense. The full cost to the corporation of issuing the bonds at a discount is as follows:

Cash to be paid to bondholders		
Face value at maturity	$100,000	
Interest payments ($100,000 × .09 × 5 years)	45,000	
Total cash paid to bondholders	$145,000	
Less cash received from bondholders	96,149	
Total interest cost	$ 48,851	←
Or, alternatively:		
Interest payments ($100,000 × .09 × 5 years)	$ 45,000	
Bond discount	3,851	
Total interest cost	$ 48,851	←

The total interest cost of $48,851 is made up of $45,000 in interest payments and the $3,851 bond discount, so the bond discount increases the interest paid on the bonds from the stated interest rate to the effective interest rate. The *effective interest rate* is the real interest cost of the bond over its life.

---

4. Thomas T. Vogel, Jr., "Disney Amazes Investors With Sale of 100-Year Bonds," *Wall Street Journal*, July 21, 1993.

For each year's interest expense to reflect the effective interest rate, the discount must be allocated over the remaining life of the bonds as an increase in the interest expense each period. The process of allocation is called *amortization of the bond discount*. Thus, interest expense for each period will exceed the actual payment of interest by the amount of the bond discount amortized over the period.

Some companies and governmental units issue bonds that do not require periodic interest payments. These bonds, called zero coupon bonds, are simply a promise to pay a fixed amount at the maturity date. They are issued at a large discount because the only interest earned by the buyer or paid by the issuer is the discount. For example, a five-year, $100,000 zero coupon bond issued at a time when the market rate is 14 percent, compounded semiannually, would sell for only $50,800. That amount is the present value of a single payment of $100,000 at the end of five years. The discount of $49,200 ($100,000 − $50,800) is the total interest cost; it is amortized over the life of the bond.

METHODS OF AMORTIZING A BOND DISCOUNT

There are two ways of amortizing bond discounts or premiums: the straight-line method and the effective interest method.

Straight-Line Method   The straight-line method is the easier of the two, with equal amortization of the discount for each interest period. Suppose that the interest payment dates for the Vason Corporation bond issue are January 1 and July 1. The amount of the bond discount amortized and the interest cost for each semiannual period are calculated in four steps.

1. Total interest payments = interest payments per year × life of bonds

$$= 2 \times 5$$

$$= 10$$

2. Amortization of bond discount per interest period $= \dfrac{\text{bond discount}}{\text{total interest payments}}$

$$= \dfrac{\$3,851}{10}$$

$$= \$385*$$

3. Regular cash interest payment = face value × face interest rate × time

$$= \$100,000 \times .09 \times {}^{6}/_{12}$$

$$= \$4,500$$

4. Total interest cost per interest period = interest payment + amortization of bond discount

$$= \$4,500 + \$385$$

$$= \$4,885$$

*Rounded.

On July 1, 19x0, the first semiannual interest date, the entry would be as follows:

```
19x0
July 1   Bond Interest Expense                          4,885
              Unamortized Bond Discount                         385
              Cash (or Interest Payable)                      4,500
                  Paid (or accrued) semiannual interest
                  to bondholders and amortized the
                  discount on 9%, 5-year bonds
```

Notice that the bond interest expense is $4,885, but the amount paid to the bondholders is the $4,500 face interest payment. The difference of $385 is the credit to Unamortized Bond Discount. This lowers the debit balance of the Unamortized Bond Discount account and raises the carrying value of the bonds payable by $385 each interest period. Assuming that no changes occur in the bond issue, this entry will be made every six months for the life of the bonds. When the bond issue matures, there will be no balance in the Unamortized Bond Discount account, and the carrying value of the bonds will be $100,000—exactly equal to the amount due the bondholders.

The straight-line method has long been used, but it has a certain weakness. Because the carrying value goes up each period and the bond interest expense stays the same, the rate of interest falls over time. Conversely, when the straight-line method is used to amortize a premium, the rate of interest rises over time. Therefore, the Accounting Principles Board has ruled that the straight-line method can be used only when it does not lead to a material difference from the effective interest method.[5] As we discuss below, the effective interest method presupposes a constant rate of interest over the life of the bonds. It is constant because the total interest expense changes a little each interest period in response to the changing carrying value of the bonds.

Effective Interest Method   To compute the interest and amortization of a bond discount for each interest period under the effective interest method, a constant interest rate is applied to the carrying value of the bonds at the beginning of the interest period. This constant rate equals the market rate, or effective rate, at the time the bonds are issued. The amount to be amortized each period is the difference between the interest computed by using the effective rate and the actual interest paid to bondholders.

As an example, we use the same facts presented earlier—a $100,000 bond issue at 9 percent, with a five-year maturity and interest to be paid twice a year. The market, or effective, interest rate at the time the bonds were issued was 10 percent. The bonds were sold for $96,149, a discount of $3,851. The interest and amortization of the bond discount are shown in Table 1.

The amounts in the table (using period 1) were computed as follows:

Column A: The carrying value of the bonds is their face value less the unamortized bond discount ($100,000 − $3,851 = $96,149).

Column B: The interest expense to be recorded is the effective interest. It is found by multiplying the carrying value of the bonds by the effective interest rate for one-half year ($96,149 $\times$ .10 $\times$ $\%_2$ = $4,807).

Column C: The interest paid in the period is a constant amount computed by multiplying the face value of the bonds by their face interest rate by the interest time period ($100,000 $\times$ .09 $\times$ $\%_2$ = $4,500).

---

5. Accounting Principles Board, *Opinion No. 21*, "Interest on Receivables and Payables" (New York: American Institute of Certified Public Accountants, 1971), par. 15.

Table 1. Interest and Amortization of a Bond Discount: Effective Interest Method

	A	B	C	D	E	F
Semiannual Interest Period	Carrying Value at Beginning of Period	Semiannual Interest Expense at 10% to Be Recorded* (5% 3 A)	Semiannual Interest to Be Paid to Bondholders (4¹/₂% 3 $100,000)	Amortization of Discount (B 2 C)	Unamortized Bond Discount at End of Period	Carrying Value at End of Period (A 1 D)
0					$3,851	$ 96,149
1	$96,149	$4,807	$4,500	$307	3,544	96,456
2	96,456	4,823	4,500	323	3,221	96,779
3	96,779	4,839	4,500	339	2,882	97,118
4	97,118	4,856	4,500	356	2,526	97,474
5	97,474	4,874	4,500	374	2,152	97,848
6	97,848	4,892	4,500	392	1,760	98,240
7	98,240	4,912	4,500	412	1,348	98,652
8	98,652	4,933	4,500	433	915	99,085
9	99,085	4,954	4,500	454	461	99,539
10	99,539	4,961†	4,500	461	—	100,000

*Rounded to nearest dollar.   †Discrepancy due to rounding.

Column D: The discount amortized is the difference between the effective interest expense to be recorded and the interest to be paid on the interest payment date ($4,807 − $4,500 = $307).

Column E: The unamortized bond discount is the balance of the bond discount at the beginning of the period less the current period amortization of the discount ($3,851 − $307 = $3,544). The unamortized discount decreases each interest payment period because it is amortized as a portion of interest expense.

Column F: The carrying value of the bonds at the end of the period is the carrying value at the beginning of the period plus the amortization during the period ($96,149 + $307 = $96,456). Notice that the sum of the carrying value and the unamortized discount (Column F + Column E) always equals the face value of the bonds ($96,456 + $3,544 = $100,000).

The entry to record the interest expense is exactly like the one used when the straight-line method is applied. However, the amounts debited and credited to the various accounts are different. Using the effective interest method, the entry for July 1, 19x0, would be as follows:

```
19x0
July 1   Bond Interest Expense                      4,807
              Unamortized Bond Discount                          307
              Cash (or Interest Payable)                       4,500
                  Paid (or accrued) semiannual
                  interest to bondholders and
                  amortized the discount on 9%,
                  5-year bonds
```

Figure 2. Carrying Value and Interest Expense—Bonds Issued at a Discount

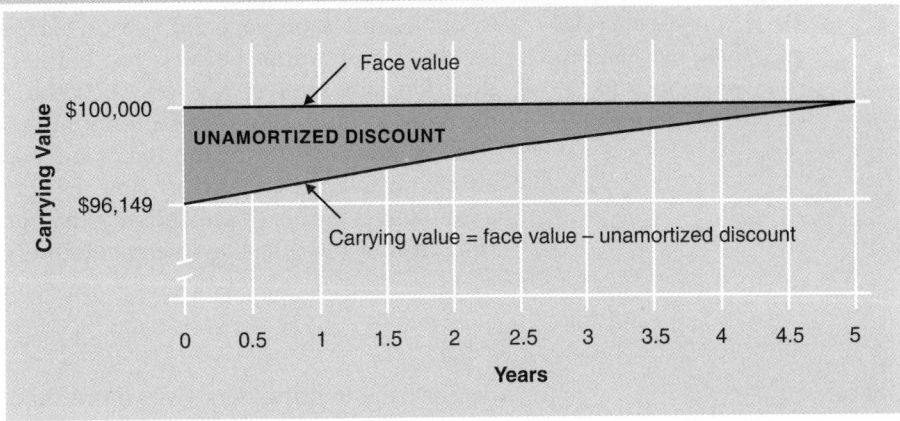

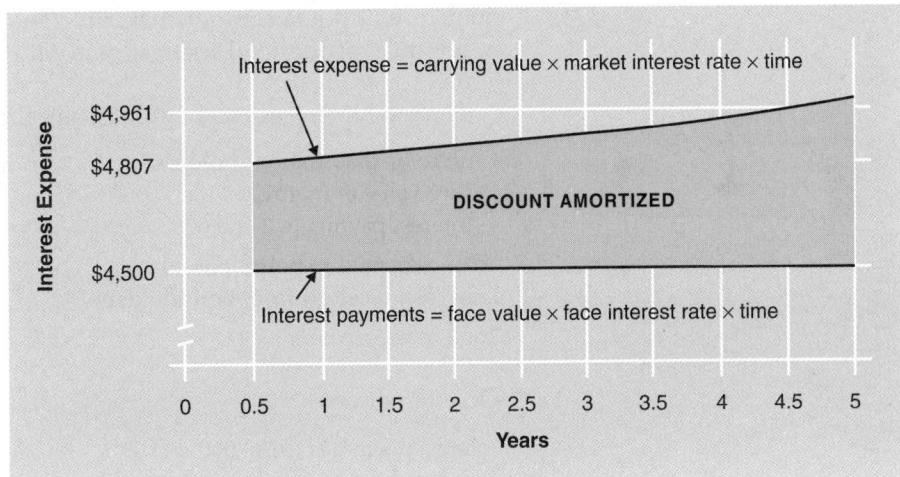

Notice that it is not necessary to prepare an interest and amortization table to determine the amortization of a discount for any one interest payment period. It is necessary only to multiply the carrying value by the effective interest rate and subtract the interest payment from the result. For example, the amount of discount to be amortized in the seventh interest payment period is $412 calculated as follows: ($98,240 × .05) − $4,500.

Visual Summary of the Effective Interest Method   The effect of the amortization of a bond discount using the effective interest method on carrying value and interest expense can be seen in Figure 2 (based on the data from Table 1). Notice that initially the carrying value (issue price) is less than the face value, but that it gradually increases toward the face value over the life of the bond issue. Notice also that interest expense exceeds interest payments by the amount of the discount amortized. Interest expense increases gradually over the life of the bond because it is based on the gradually increasing carrying value (multiplied by the market interest rate).

AMORTIZING A BOND PREMIUM

In our example on page 592, Vason Corporation issued $100,000 of five-year bonds at a premium because the market interest rate of 8 percent was less than the face interest rate of 9 percent. The bonds were sold for $104,100, resulting in an unamortized premium of $4,100. Like a discount, a premium must be amortized over the life of the bonds so that it can be matched to its effects on interest expense during that period. In the following sections, the total interest cost is calculated and the bond premium is amortized using the straight-line and effective interest methods.

CALCULATION OF TOTAL INTEREST COST

Because the bondholders paid more than face value for the bonds, the premium of $4,100 ($104,100 − $100,000) represents an amount that the bondholders will not receive at maturity. The premium is in effect a reduction, in advance, of the total interest paid on the bonds over the life of the bond issue.

The total interest cost over the issue's life can be computed as follows:

Cash to be paid to bondholders	
Face value at maturity	$100,000
Interest payments ($100,000 × .09 × 5 years)	45,000
Total cash paid to bondholders	$145,000
Less cash received from bondholders	104,100
Total interest cost	$ 40,900

Or, alternatively:

Interest payments ($100,000 × .09 × 5 years)	$ 45,000
Less bond premium	4,100
Total interest cost	$ 40,900

Notice that the total interest payments of $45,000 exceed the total interest costs of $40,900 by $4,100, the amount of the bond premium.

METHODS OF AMORTIZING A BOND PREMIUM

The two methods of amortizing a bond premium are the straight-line method and the effective interest method.

Straight-Line Method   Under the straight-line method, the bond premiums are spread evenly over the life of the bond issue. As with bond discounts, the amount of the bond premium amortized and the interest cost for each semiannual period are computed in four steps.

1. Total interest payments = interest payments per year × life of bonds

$$= 2 \times 5$$

$$= 10$$

2. Amortization of bond premium per interest period $= \dfrac{\text{bond premium}}{\text{total interest payments}}$

$$= \dfrac{\$4,100}{10}$$

$$= \$410$$

3. Regular cash interest payment $=$ face value $\times$ face interest rate $\times$ time

$$= \$100,000 \times .09 \times {}^{6}\!/_{12}$$

$$= \$4,500$$

4. Total interest cost per interest period $=$ interest payment $-$ amortization of bond premium

$$= \$4,500 - \$410$$

$$= \$4,090$$

On July 1, 19x0, the first semiannual interest date, the entry would be:

```
19x0
July 1   Bond Interest Expense                    4,090
           Unamortized Bond Premium                 410
             Cash (or Interest Payable)                        4,500
               Paid (or accrued) semiannual interest
               to bondholders and amortized the
               premium on 9%, 5-year bonds
```

Notice that the bond interest expense is $4,090, but the amount received by the bondholders is the $4,500 face interest payment. The difference of $410 is the debit to Unamortized Bond Premium. This lowers the credit balance of the Unamortized Bond Premium account and the carrying value of the bonds payable by $410 each interest period. Assuming that the bond issue remains unchanged, the same entry will be made on every semiannual interest date over the life of the bond issue. When the bond issue matures, there will be no balance in the Unamortized Bond Premium account, and the carrying value of the bonds payable will be $100,000, exactly equal to the amount due the bondholders.

As noted earlier in this chapter, the straight-line method should be used only when it does not lead to a material difference from the effective interest method.

Effective Interest Method   Under the straight-line method, the effective interest rate changes constantly, even though the interest expense is fixed, because the effective interest rate is determined by comparing the fixed interest expense with a carrying value that changes as a result of amortizing the discount or premium. To apply a fixed interest rate over the life of the bonds based on the actual market rate at the time of the bond issue requires the use of the effective interest method. Under this method, the interest expense decreases slightly each period (see Table 2, Column B) because the amount of the bond premium amortized increases slightly (Column D). This occurs because a fixed rate is applied each period to the gradually decreasing carrying value (Column A).

Table 2. Interest and Amortization of a Bond Premium: Effective Interest Method

Semiannual Interest Period	A Carrying Value at Beginning of Period	B Semiannual Interest Expense at 8% to Be Recorded* (4% × A)	C Semiannual Interest to Be Paid to Bondholders (4½% × $100,000)	D Amortization of Premium (C − B)	E Unamortized Bond Premium at End of Period	F Carrying Value at End of Period (A − D)
0					$4,100	$104,100
1	$104,100	$4,164	$4,500	$336	3,764	103,764
2	103,764	4,151	4,500	349	3,415	103,415
3	103,415	4,137	4,500	363	3,052	103,052
4	103,052	4,122	4,500	378	2,674	102,674
5	102,674	4,107	4,500	393	2,281	102,281
6	102,281	4,091	4,500	409	1,872	101,872
7	101,872	4,075	4,500	425	1,447	101,447
8	101,447	4,058	4,500	442	1,005	101,005
9	101,005	4,040	4,500	460	545	100,545
10	100,545	3,955†	4,500	545	—	100,000

*Rounded to nearest dollar.   †Discrepancy due to rounding.

The first interest payment is recorded as follows:

```
19x0
July 1   Bond Interest Expense                           4,164
             Unamortized Bond Premium                     336
                 Cash (or Interest Payable)                        4,500
                     Paid (or accrued) semiannual interest
                     to bondholders and amortized the
                     premium on 9%, 5-year bonds
```

Notice that the unamortized bond premium (Column E) decreases gradually to zero as the carrying value decreases to the face value (Column F). To find the amount of premium amortized in any one interest payment period, subtract the effective interest expense (the carrying value times the effective interest rate, Column B) from the interest payment (Column C). In semiannual interest period 5, for example, the amortization of premium is $393, calculated as follows: $4,500 − ($102,674 × .04).

Visual Summary of the Effective Interest Method   The effect of the amortization of a bond premium using the effective interest method on carrying value and interest expense can be seen in Figure 3 (based on data from Table 2). Notice that initially the carrying value (issue price) is greater than the face value, but that it gradually decreases toward the face value over the life of the bond issue. Notice also that interest payments exceed interest expense by the amount of the premium amortized, and that interest expense decreases gradually over the life of the bond because it is based on the gradually decreasing carrying value (multiplied by the market interest rate).

Figure 3. Carrying Value and Interest Expense—Bonds Issued at a Premium

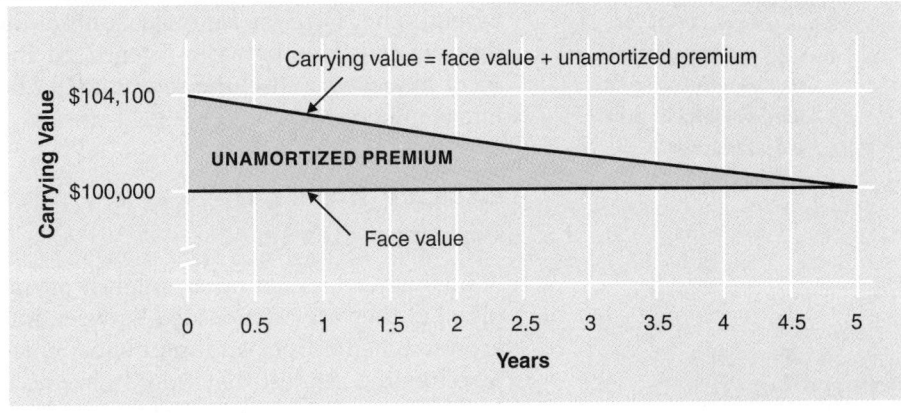

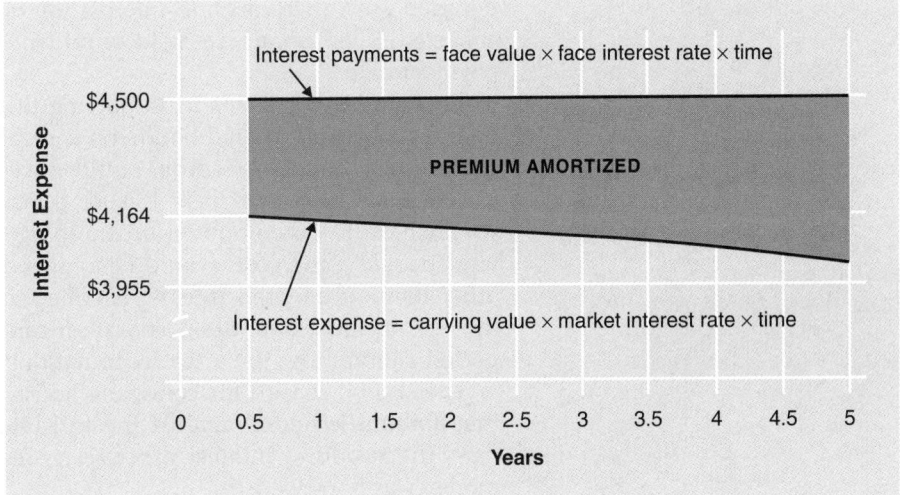

Interest and amortization tables like those in Tables 1 and 2 provide ideal applications for computer spreadsheet software such as Lotus 1-2-3 and Microsoft Excel. Once the tables have been constructed with the proper formula in each cell, only five variables must be entered to produce the entire table. The five variables are the face value of the bonds, the selling price, the life of the bonds, the face interest rate, and the effective interest rate.

OTHER BONDS PAYABLE ISSUES

Several other issues arise in accounting for bonds payable. Among them are the sale of bonds between interest payment dates, the year-end accrual of bond interest expense, the retirement of bonds, and the conversion of bonds into common stock.

SALE OF BONDS BETWEEN INTEREST DATES

Bonds may be issued on an interest payment date, as in the previous examples, but they are often issued between interest payment dates. The generally accepted method of handling bonds issued in this manner is to collect from investors the interest that would have accrued for the partial period preceding the issue date. Then, when the first interest period is completed, the corporation pays investors the interest for the entire period. Thus, the interest collected when bonds are sold is returned to investors on the next interest payment date.

There are two reasons for following this procedure. The first is a practical one. If a company issued bonds on several different days and did not collect the accrued interest, records would have to be maintained for each bondholder and date of purchase. In such a case, the interest due each bondholder would have to be computed on the basis of different time periods. Clearly, large bookkeeping costs would be incurred under this kind of system. On the other hand, if accrued interest is collected when the bonds are sold, on the interest payment date the corporation can pay the interest due for the entire period, eliminating the extra computations and costs.

The second reason for collecting accrued interest in advance is that when that amount is netted against the full interest paid on the interest payment date, the resulting interest expense represents the amount for the time the money was borrowed.

For example, assume that the Vason Corporation sold $100,000 of 9 percent, five-year bonds for face value on May 1, 19x0, rather than on January 1, 19x0, the issue date. The entry to record the sale of the bonds is as follows:

19x0		
May 1 Cash	103,000	
Bond Interest Expense		3,000
Bonds Payable		100,000
Sold 9%, 5-year bonds at face value		
plus 4 months' accrued interest		
$100,000 \times .09 \times \frac{4}{12} = \$3,000$		

As shown, Cash is debited for the amount received, $103,000 (the face value of $100,000 plus four months' accrued interest of $3,000). Bond Interest Expense is credited for the $3,000 of accrued interest, and Bonds Payable is credited for the face value of $100,000.

When the first semiannual interest payment date arrives, the following entry is made:

19x0		
July 1 Bond Interest Expense	4,500	
Cash (or Interest Payable)		4,500
Paid (or accrued) semiannual interest		
$100,000 \times .09 \times \frac{6}{12} = \$4,500$		

Figure 4. Effect on Bond Interest Expense When Bonds Are Issued Between Interest Dates

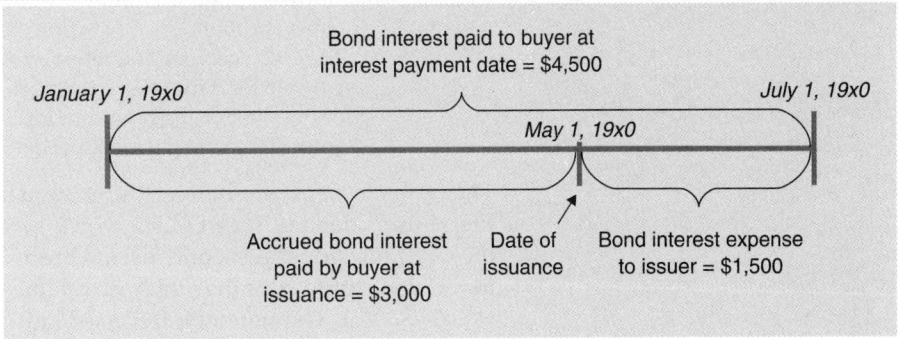

Notice that the entire half-year interest is both debited to Bond Interest Expense and credited to Cash because the corporation pays bond interest only once every six months, in full six-month amounts. This process is illustrated in Figure 4. The actual interest expense for the two months that the bonds were outstanding is $1,500. This amount is the net balance of the $4,500 debit to Bond Interest Expense on July 1 less the $3,000 credit to Bond Interest Expense on May 1. You can see these steps clearly in the posted entries in the ledger account for Bond Interest Expense below.

Bond Interest Expense						Account No. 723	
						Balance	
Date		**Item**	**Post. Ref.**	**Debit**	**Credit**	**Debit**	**Credit**
19x0							
May	1				3,000		3,000
July	1			4,500		1,500	

YEAR-END ACCRUAL FOR BOND INTEREST EXPENSE

Bond interest payment dates rarely correspond with a company's fiscal year. Therefore, an adjustment must be made at the end of the accounting period to accrue the interest expense on the bonds from the last payment date to the end of the fiscal year. Further, if there is any discount or premium on the bonds, it must also be amortized for the fractional period.

Remember that in an earlier example, Vason Corporation issued $100,000 in bonds on January 1, 19x0, at 104.1 (see page 592). Suppose the company's fiscal year ends on September 30, 19x0. In the period since the interest payment and amortization of the premium on July 1, three months' worth of interest has accrued, and the following adjusting entry under the effective interest method must be made.

19x0

Sept. 30	Bond Interest Expense	2,075.50	
	Unamortized Bond Premium	174.50	
	Interest Payable		2,250.00
	To record accrual of interest on 9% bonds payable for 3 months and amortization of one-half of the premium for the second interest payment period		

This entry covers one-half of the second interest period. Unamortized Bond Premium is debited for $174.50, which is one-half of $349, the amortization of the premium for the second period from Table 2. Interest Payable is credited for $2,250, three months' interest on the face value of the bonds ($100,000 × .09 × 3/12). The net debit figure of $2,075.50 ($2,250 − $174.50) is the bond interest expense for the three-month period.

When the January 1, 19x1, payment date arrives, the entry to pay the bondholders and amortize the premium is as follows:

19x1

Jan. 1	Bond Interest Expense	2,075.50	
	Interest Payable	2,250.00	
	Unamortized Bond Premium	174.50	
	Cash		4,500.00
	Paid semiannual interest including interest previously accrued, and amortized the premium for the period since the end of the fiscal year		

As shown here, one-half ($2,250) of the amount paid ($4,500) was accrued on September 30. Unamortized Bond Premium is debited for $174.50, the remaining amount to be amortized for the period ($349.00 − $174.50). The resulting bond interest expense is the amount that applies to the three-month period from October 1 to December 31.

Bond discounts are recorded at year end in the same way as bond premiums. The difference is that the amortization of a bond discount increases interest expense instead of decreasing it, as a premium does.

OBJECTIVE

7 *Account for the retirement of bonds and the conversion of bonds into stock*

RETIREMENT OF BONDS

Most bond issues give the corporation a chance to buy back and retire the bonds at a specified call price, usually above face value, before maturity. Such bonds are known as callable bonds, and give the corporation flexibility in financing its operations. For example, if bond interest rates drop, the company can call its bonds and reissue debt at a lower interest rate. A company might also call its bonds if the company has earned enough to pay off the debt, the reason for having the debt no longer exists, or the company wants to restructure its debt to equity ratio. The bond indenture states the time period and the prices at which the bonds can be redeemed. The retirement of a bond issue before its maturity date is called early extinguishment of debt.

Let's assume that Vason Corporation can call or retire the $100,000 of bonds issued at a premium (page 592) at 105, and that it decides to do so on July 1, 19x3. (To simplify the example, the retirement is made on an interest payment date.) Because the bonds were issued on January 1, 19x0, the retirement takes place on the seventh interest payment date. Assume that the entry for the required interest payment and the amortization of the premium has been made. The entry to retire the bonds is as follows:

19x3
July 1 Bonds Payable 100,000
          Unamortized Bond Premium 1,447
          Loss on Retirement of Bonds 3,553
              Cash 105,000
                  Retired 9% bonds at 105

In this entry, the cash paid is the face value times the call price ($100,000 × 1.05 = $105,000). The unamortized bond premium can be found in Column E of Table 2. The loss on retirement of bonds occurs because the call price of the bonds is greater than the carrying value ($105,000 − $101,447 = $3,553). The loss, if material, is presented as an extraordinary item on the income statement.

Sometimes a rise in the market interest rate can cause the market value of bonds to fall considerably below their face value. If it has the cash to do so, the company may find it advantageous to purchase the bonds on the open market and retire them, rather than wait and pay them off at face value. An extraordinary gain is recognized for the difference between the purchase price of the bonds and the face value of the retired bonds. For example, assume that because of a rise in interest rates, Vason Corporation is able to purchase the $100,000 bond issue on the open market at 85, making it unnecessary to call the bonds at the higher price of 105. Then, the entry would be as follows:

19x3
July 1 Bonds Payable 100,000
          Unamortized Bond Premium 1,447
              Cash 85,000
              Gain on Retirement of Bonds 16,447
                  Purchased and retired
                  9% bonds at 85

Inco Limited

DECISION POINT

On March 20, 1991, the *Wall Street Journal* reported that Inco Limited was issuing that day $172.5 million in 7¾ percent convertible debentures due in 2016. The debentures, which are callable, could be converted into the company's common stock at a conversion price of $38.25. In other words, a holder of a $1,000 bond could convert it into 26.14 ($1,000 ÷ $38.25) shares of common stock.[6] On the previous day, March 19, the company's common stock had sold on the New York Stock Exchange for $31.50. What advantages and disadvantages did Inco's management weigh in deciding to issue convertible bonds rather than another security, such as nonconvertible bonds or common stock?

Several factors are favorable to the issuance of convertible bonds. First, the interest rate of 7¾ percent is less than the company would have to offer if the bonds were not convertible. An investor is willing to give up some

6. "$172,500,000 Inco Limited 7¾% Convertible Debentures Due 2016," *Wall Street Journal,* March 20, 1991.

current interest for the prospect that the value of the stock will increase, and therefore the value of the bonds will also increase. For example, if the common stock rises from $31.50 to more than $38.25 per share, the value of the bond will begin to rise based on changes in the price of the common stock, not on changes in interest rates. If the common stock were to rise to $50, the market value of a $1,000 bond would rise to $1,307 (26.14 shares × $50). A second advantage is that Inco does not have to give up any current control of the company. Unlike stockholders, bondholders do not have voting rights. A third benefit is tax savings. Interest paid on bonds is fully deductible for income tax purposes, whereas cash dividends on common stock are not. Fourth, the company's income will be affected favorably if the company earns a return that exceeds the interest cost of the debentures. For example, if the company uses the funds for a purpose that earns 16 percent, the return will be more than twice the interest cost of 7¾ percent. Finally, the convertible feature offers financial flexibility. If the price of the stock rises above $38.25, management can avoid repaying the bonds by calling them for redemption, thereby forcing the bondholders to convert their bonds into common stock. The bondholders will agree to convert because the common stock they will receive will be worth more than they would receive if the bonds were redeemed.

One major disadvantage of debentures is that interest must be paid semiannually. Inability to make an interest payment could force the company into bankruptcy. Common stock dividends are declared and paid only when the board of directors decides to do so. Another disadvantage is that when the bonds are converted, they become new outstanding common stock and no longer have the features of bonds. Inco's management obviously felt that the advantages of its choice outweighed the disadvantages. ⦂⦂⦂⦂⦂

CONVERSION OF BONDS INTO COMMON STOCK

Bonds that can be exchanged for other securities of the corporation (in most cases, common stock) are called convertible bonds. Convertibility enables an investor to make more money because if the market price of the common stock rises, the value of the bonds rises. However, if the common stock price does not rise, the investor still holds the bonds and receives both the periodic interest payments and the principal at the maturity date.

When a bondholder wishes to convert bonds into common stock, the common stock is recorded at the carrying value of the bonds. The bond liability and the associated unamortized discount or premium are written off the books. For this reason, no gain or loss is recorded on the transaction. For example, suppose that Vason Corporation's bonds are not called on July 1, 19x3. Instead, the corporation's bondholders decide to convert all the bonds to $8 par value common stock under a convertible provision of 40 shares of common stock for each $1,000 bond. The entry would be as follows:

```
19x3
July  1  Bonds Payable                         100,000
            Unamortized Bond Premium            1,447
               Common Stock                                    32,000
               Paid-in Capital in Excess of Par
                  Value, Common                                69,447
                  Converted 9% bonds payable into
                  $8 par value common stock at a rate
                  of 40 shares for each $1,000 bond
```

The unamortized bond premium is found in Column E of Table 2. At a rate of 40 shares for each $1,000 bond, 4,000 shares will be issued at a total par value of $32,000 (4,000 × $8). The Common Stock account is credited for the amount of the par value of the stock issued. And Paid-in Capital in Excess of Par Value, Common is credited for the difference between the carrying value of the bonds and the par value of the stock issued ($101,447 − $32,000 = $69,447). No gain or loss is recorded.

OTHER LONG-TERM LIABILITIES

OBJECTIVE

8 *Explain the basic features of mortgages payable, installment notes payable, long-term leases, and pensions and other postretirement benefits as long-term liabilities*

A company may have other long-term liabilities besides bonds. The most common are mortgages payable, installment notes payable, long-term leases, and pensions and other postretirement benefits.

MORTGAGES PAYABLE

A mortgage is a long-term debt secured by real property. It is usually paid in equal monthly installments. Each monthly payment includes interest on the debt and a reduction in the debt. Table 3 shows the first three monthly payments on a $50,000, 12 percent mortgage. The mortgage was obtained on June 1, and the monthly payments are $800. According to the table, the entry to record the July 1 payment would be as follows:

```
July  1  Mortgage Payable                       300
            Mortgage Interest Expense            500
               Cash                                            800
               Made monthly mortgage payment
```

Notice from the entry and from Table 3 that the July 1 payment represents interest expense of $500 ($50,000 × .12 × ¹⁄₁₂) and a reduction in the debt of $300 ($800 − $500). Therefore, the unpaid balance is reduced by the July payment to $49,700. August's interest expense is slightly less than July's because of the decrease in the debt.

INSTALLMENT NOTES PAYABLE

A long-term note can be paid at its maturity date by making a lump-sum payment that includes the amount borrowed plus the interest. Often, however, the terms of a note will call for a series of periodic payments. Such a note is called an installment note payable because each payment includes the interest

Table 3. Monthly Payment Schedule on a $50,000, 12 Percent Mortgage

	A	B	C	D	E
Payment Date	Unpaid Balance at Beginning of Period	Monthly Payment	Interest for 1 Month at 1% on Unpaid Balance* (1% × A)	Reduction in Debt (B − C)	Unpaid Balance at End of Period (A − D)
June 1					$50,000
July 1	$50,000	$800	$500	$300	49,700
Aug. 1	49,700	800	497	303	49,397
Sept. 1	49,397	800	494	306	49,091

*Rounded to nearest dollar.

to date plus a repayment of part of the amount that was borrowed. For example, let's assume that on December 31, 19x1, $100,000 is borrowed on a 15 percent installment note, to be paid annually over five years. The entry to record the note is as follows:

19x1			
Dec. 31	Cash	100,000	
	Notes Payable		100,000
	Borrowed $100,000 at 15% on a 5-year installment note		

Payments of Accrued Interest Plus Equal Amounts of Principal   Installment notes most often call for payments consisting of accrued interest plus equal amounts of principal repayment. The amount of each installment decreases because the amount of principal on which the accrued interest is owed decreases by the amount of the previous principal payment. Banks use installment notes to finance equipment purchases by businesses; such notes are also common for other kinds of purchases when payment is spread over several years. They can be set up on a revolving basis whereby the borrower can borrow additional funds as the installments are paid. Moreover, the interest rate charged on installment notes may be adjusted periodically as market interest rates change.

On our sample installment note for $100,000, the principal declines by an equal amount each year for five years, or by $20,000 per year ($100,000 ÷ 5 years). The interest is calculated on the balance of the note that remains each year. Because the balance of the note declines each year, the amount of interest also declines. For example, the entries for the first two payments of the installment note are as follows:

19x2			
Dec. 31	Notes Payable	20,000	
	Interest Expense	15,000	
	Cash		35,000
	Made first installment payment on note		
	$100,000 × .15 = $15,000		

19x3
Dec. 31 Notes Payable   20,000
         Interest Expense   12,000
             Cash   32,000
                 Made second installment payment
                 on note
                 $80,000 × .15 = $12,000

Notice that the amount of the payment decreases from $35,000 to $32,000 because the amount of interest accrued on the note has decreased from $15,000 to $12,000. The difference of $3,000 is the interest on the $20,000 that was repaid in 19x2. Each subsequent payment decreases by $3,000, as the note itself decreases by $20,000 each year until it is fully paid. This example assumes that the repayment of principal and the interest rate remain the same from year to year.

Payments of Accrued Interest Plus Increasing Amounts of Principal   Less commonly, the terms of an installment note, like those used for leasing equipment, may call for equal periodic (monthly or yearly) payments of accrued interest plus increasing amounts of principal. Under this method, the interest is deducted from the equal payments to determine the amount by which the principal will be reduced each year. This procedure, presented in Table 4, is very similar to that for mortgages, shown in Table 3. Each equal payment of $29,833 is allocated between interest and principal reduction. Each year the interest is calculated on the remaining principal. As the principal decreases, the annual interest also decreases, and because the payment remains the same, the amount by which the principal decreases becomes larger each year. The entries for the first two years, with data taken from Table 4, are as follows:

19x2
Dec. 31 Notes Payable   14,833
         Interest Expense   15,000
             Cash   29,833
                 Made first installment payment on note

19x3
Dec. 31 Notes Payable   17,058
         Interest Expense   12,775
             Cash   29,833
                 Made second installment payment on note

Similar entries will be made for the next three years.

How is the equal annual payment calculated? Because the $100,000 borrowed is the present value of the five equal annual payments at 15 percent interest, present value tables can be used to calculate the annual payments. Using Table 4 from the appendix on future value and present value tables, the calculation is made as follows:

Periodic payment × factor (Table 4 in the present
                            value appendix: 15%, 5 periods) = present value

Periodic payment × 3.352   = $100,000

Periodic payment = $100,000 ÷ 3.352 = $29,833

Table 4 shows that five equal annual payments of $29,833 at 15 percent will reduce the principal balance to zero (except for the discrepancy due to rounding).

Table 4. Payment Schedule on a $100,000, 15 Percent Installment Note

	A	B	C	D	E
Payment Date	Unpaid Principal at Beginning of Period	Equal Annual Payment	Interest for 1 Year at 15% on Unpaid Principal* (15% × A)	Reduction in Principal (B 2 C)	Unpaid Principal at End of Period (A 2 D)
					$100,000
19x2	$100,000	$29,833	$15,000	$14,833	85,167
19x3	85,167	29,833	12,775	17,058	68,109
19x4	68,109	29,833	10,216	19,617	48,492
19x5	48,492	29,833	7,274	22,559	25,933
19x6	25,933	29,833	3,900†	25,933	—

*Rounded to the nearest dollar.
†The last year's interest equals the installment payment minus the remaining unpaid principal ($29,833 − $25,933 = $3,900); it does not exactly equal $3,890 ($25,933 × .15) because of the cumulative effect of rounding.

LONG-TERM LEASES

There are several ways for a company to obtain new operating assets. One way is to borrow money and buy the asset. Another is to rent the equipment on a short-term lease. A third way is to obtain the equipment on a long-term lease. The first two methods do not create accounting problems. In the first case, the asset and liability are recorded at the amount paid, and the asset is subject to periodic depreciation. In the second case, the lease is short term or cancelable, and the risks of ownership lie with the lessor. This type of agreement is called an operating lease. It is proper accounting to treat operating lease payments as an expense and to debit the amount of each monthly payment to Rent Expense.

The third case, a long-term lease, is one of the fastest-growing ways of financing operating equipment in the United States today. It has several advantages. For instance, a long-term lease requires no immediate cash payment, the rental payment is deducted in full for tax purposes, and it costs less than a short-term lease. Acquiring the use of plant assets under long-term leases does cause several accounting problems, however. Often, such leases cannot be canceled. Also, their duration may be about the same as the useful life of the asset. Finally, they may provide for the lessee to buy the asset at a nominal price at the end of the lease. The lease is much like an installment purchase because the risks of ownership lie with the lessee. Both the lessee's available assets and its legal obligations (liabilities) increase because it must make a number of payments over the life of the asset.

The Financial Accounting Standards Board has described this kind of long-term lease as a capital lease. The term reflects the provisions of such a lease, which make the transaction more like a purchase or sale on installment. The FASB has ruled that in the case of a capital lease, the lessee must record an asset and a long-term liability equal to the present value of the total lease payments during the lease term. In doing so, the lessee must use the present

Table 5. Payment Schedule on a 16 Percent Capital Lease*

Year	A Lease Payment	B Interest (16%) on Unpaid Obligation (D × 16%)	C Reduction of Lease Obligation (A − B)	D Balance of Lease Obligation (D − C)
Beginning				$14,740
1	$ 4,000	$2,358	$ 1,642	13,098
2	4,000	2,096	1,904	11,194
3	4,000	1,791	2,209	8,985
4	4,000	1,438	2,562	6,423
5	4,000	1,028	2,972	3,451
6	4,000	549	3,451	—
	$24,000	$9,260	$14,740	

*Computations are rounded to the nearest dollar.

value at the beginning of the lease.[7] Much like a mortgage payment, each lease payment consists partly of interest expense and partly of repayment of debt. Further, depreciation expense is figured on the asset and entered on the records of the lessee.

Suppose, for example, that Isaacs Company enters into a long-term lease for a machine used in its manufacturing operations. The lease terms call for an annual payment of $4,000 for six years, which approximates the useful life of the machine (see Table 5.) At the end of the lease period, the title to the machine passes to Isaacs. This lease is clearly a capital lease and should be recorded as an asset and a liability according to FASB *Statement No. 13*.

A lease is a periodic payment for the right to use an asset or assets. Present value techniques can be used to place a value on the asset and on the corresponding liability associated with a capital lease. If Isaacs's interest cost is 16 percent, the present value of the lease payments can be computed as follows:

Periodic payment × factor (Table 4 in the present
value appendix: 16%, 6 periods) = present value

$4,000 × 3.685 = $14,740

The entry to record the lease contract is as follows:

Equipment Under Capital Lease	14,740	
Obligations Under Capital Lease		14,740
To record capital lease on machinery		

Equipment Under Capital Lease is classified as a long-term asset; Obligations Under Capital Lease is classified as a long-term liability. Each year, Isaacs must record depreciation on the leased asset. Using straight-line depreciation, a six-year life, and no salvage value, the following entry would record the depreciation.

---

7. *Statement of Financial Accounting Standards No. 13*, "Accounting for Leases" (Stamford, Conn.: Financial Accounting Standards Board, 1976), par. 10.

```
Depreciation Expense, Leased Equipment          2,457
    Accumulated Depreciation, Leased
      Equipment Under Capital Lease                       2,457
        To record depreciation expense on capital lease
```

The interest expense for each year is computed by multiplying the interest rate (16 percent) by the amount of the remaining lease obligation. Table 5 shows these calculations. Using the data in the table, the first lease payment would be recorded as follows:

```
Interest Expense (Column B)                     2,358
Obligations Under Capital Lease (Column C)      1,642
    Cash                                                 4,000
      Made payment on capital lease
```

PENSIONS

Most employees who work for medium- and large-sized companies are covered by some sort of pension plan. A pension plan is a contract between a company and its employees in which the company agrees to pay benefits to the employees after they retire. Most companies contribute the full cost of the pension, but sometimes the employees also pay part of their salary or wages toward their pension. The contributions from both parties are typically paid into a pension fund, from which benefits are paid to retirees. In most cases, pension benefits consist of monthly payments to retired employees and other payments on disability or death.

There are two kinds of pension plans. Under a *defined contribution plan*, the employer is required to contribute an annual amount specified by an agreement between the company and its employees or a resolution of the board of directors. Retirement payments depend on the amount of pension payments the accumulated contributions can support. Under a *defined benefit plan*, the employer's annual contribution is the amount required to fund pension liabilities arising from employment in the current year, but the exact amount will not be determined until the retirement and death of the current employees. Under a defined benefit plan, the amount of future benefits is fixed, but the annual contributions vary depending on assumptions about how much the pension fund will earn. Under a defined contribution plan, each year's contribution is fixed, but the benefits vary depending on how much the pension fund earns.

Accounting for annual pension expense under a defined contribution plan is simple. After the required contribution is determined, Pension Expense is debited and a liability (or Cash) is credited.

Accounting for annual expense under a defined benefit plan is one of the most complex topics in accounting; thus, the intricacies are reserved for advanced courses. In concept, however, the procedure is simple. First, the amount of pension expense is determined. Then, if the amount of cash contributed to the fund is less than the pension expense, a liability results, which is reported on the balance sheet. If the amount of cash paid to the pension plan exceeds the pension expense, a prepaid expense arises and appears on the asset side of the balance sheet. For example, the December 31, 1991, annual report for Westinghouse Electric Corporation included among assets on the balance sheet a prepaid pension contribution of $864 million.

In accordance with the FASB's *Statement No. 87,* all companies should use the same actuarial method to compute pension expense.[8] However, because of the need to estimate many factors, such as the average remaining service life of active employees, the expected long-run return on pension plan assets, and expected future salary increases, the computation of pension expense is not simple. In addition, actuarial terminology further complicates pension accounting. In nontechnical terms, the pension expense for the year includes not only the cost of the benefits earned by people working during the year but interest costs on the total pension obligation (which are calculated on the present value of future benefits to be paid) and other adjustments. Those costs are reduced by the expected return on the pension fund assets.

Since 1989, all employers whose pension plans do not have sufficient assets to cover the present value of their pension benefit obligations (on a termination basis) must record the amount of the shortfall as a liability on their balance sheets. The investor no longer has to read the notes to the financial statements to learn whether the pension plan is fully funded. However, if a pension plan does have sufficient assets to cover its obligations, then no balance sheet reporting is required or permitted.

BUSINESS BULLETIN: BUSINESS PRACTICE

Lower interest rates—as have occurred in recent years—are usually good news for businesses. This is not the case, however, when it comes to accounting for pension plans. The amount of the pension liabilities reported on the balance sheet depends on the assumed rate of return on the pension fund in the future. The lower the assumed rate, the higher the resulting liability will be. The *Wall Street Journal* reported that the Securities and Exchange Commission (SEC) was pressuring companies to revise their assumptions about future interest rates. The SEC was concerned that many companies had minimized their obligations to retirees by using high assumed interest rates to calculate their current pension liability. To better reflect 1993 rates, the SEC urged companies to reduce the rate to about 7 percent, which approximated the current yield on long-term, high-grade corporate bonds. Companies such as General Electric, McDonnell Douglas, Rockwell International, Merck & Co., and Abbott Laboratories were then using rates of 9 percent. Lowering the interest rate by even 1 percent would have increased the pension liabilities of those companies by 10 to 25 percent.[9] The companies argued that the low rates were temporary. And indeed they were, for interest rates rose back above 8.5 percent in 1995. ═════

---

8. *Statement of Financial Accounting Standards No. 87,* "Employers' Accounting for Pensions" (Stamford, Conn.: Financial Accounting Standards Board, 1985).

9. Laura Jereski, "SEC Is Challenging Funding for Plans," *Wall Street Journal,* November 17, 1993.

OTHER POSTRETIREMENT BENEFITS

In addition to pensions, many companies provide health care and other benefits to employees after retirement. In the past, these other postretirement benefits were accounted for on a cash basis; that is, they were expensed when the benefits were paid, after an employee had retired. The FASB has concluded, however, that those benefits are earned by the employee, and that, in accordance with the matching rule, they should be estimated and accrued while the employee is working.[10] The estimates must take into account assumptions about retirement age, mortality, and, most significantly, future trends in health care benefits. Like pension benefits, such future benefits should also be discounted to the current period. In a field test conducted by the Financial Executives Research Foundation, it was determined that the change to accrual accounting increased postretirement benefits by two to seven times the amount recognized on a cash basis. Although the new requirement was not effective for businesses until 1993, some companies elected to implement it early. For example, IBM Corporation reported its first quarterly loss ever in the first quarter of 1991, when it recorded a one-time $2.26 billion charge associated with the adoption of *Statement No. 106.*[11] The charge covered the costs of bringing all postretirement benefits previously earned by employees up to date. Future quarters would bear only the costs associated with earnings in those quarters.

BUSINESS BULLETIN: ETHICS IN PRACTICE

Accounting sometimes has a profound impact on our lives. When the FASB adopted SFAS No. 106, which requires companies to account for postretirement medical benefits on an accrual basis in accordance with the matching rule rather than on a cash basis in a distant year when the benefits are paid, companies had to face up to the cost of promising such benefits. Because the management of many companies, including Unisys Corporation, McDonnell Douglas Corporation, and Navistar International Corporation, had not realized the magnitude of the promises they had made, they were compelled to reduce health care benefits to retirees. As a result, many retirees are finding that they have lost benefits they had counted on receiving. According to one study, almost two-thirds of U.S. companies will have scaled back or eliminated benefits.[12] By making companies aware of the real cost of health care, accounting has played a significant role in making health care reform a key political issue. Some people think the FASB should have left well enough alone and not required companies to report these costs. What do you think? ▀▀▀

10. *Statement of Financial Accounting Standards No. 106,* "Employers' Accounting for Postretirement Benefits Other Than Pensions" (Stamford, Conn.: Financial Accounting Standards Board, 1990).

11. "Earnings Drop and One-Time Charge Produce $1.7 Billion Loss at IBM," *International Herald Tribune,* April 13–14, 1991.

12. Larry Light, Kelly Holland, and Kevin Kelly, "Honest Balance Sheets, Broken Promises," *Business Week,* November 23, 1992.

CHAPTER REVIEW

REVIEW OF LEARNING OBJECTIVES

1. **Explain the advantages and disadvantages of issuing long-term debt.** Long-term debt is used to finance long-term assets and business activities that have long-run earnings potential, such as research and development. Among the advantages of long-term debt financing are (1) common stockholders do not relinquish any control, (2) interest on debt is tax deductible, and (3) financial leverage may increase earnings. Disadvantages of long-term financing are (1) interest and principal must be repaid on schedule, and (2) financial leverage can work against a company if a project is not successful.

2. **Identify and contrast the major characteristics of bonds.** A bond is a security that represents money borrowed from the investing public. When a corporation issues bonds, it enters into a contract, called a bond indenture, with the bondholders. The bond indenture identifies the major conditions of the bonds. A corporation can issue several types of bonds, each having different characteristics. For example, a bond issue may or may not require security (secured versus unsecured bonds). It may be payable at a single time (term bonds) or at several times (serial bonds). And the holder may receive interest automatically (registered bonds) or may have to return coupons to receive interest payable (coupon bonds). Bonds may be callable or convertible into other securities.

3. **Record the issuance of bonds at face value and at a discount or premium.** When bonds are issued, the bondholders pay an amount equal to, less than, or greater than the bonds' face value. Bondholders pay face value for bonds when the interest rate on the bonds approximates the market rate for similar investments. The issuing corporation records the bond issue at face value as a long-term liability in the Bonds Payable account.

   Bonds are issued at an amount less than face value when their face interest rate is lower than the market rate for similar investments. The difference between the face value and the issue price is called a discount and is debited to Unamortized Bond Discount.

   When the face interest rate on bonds is greater than the market interest rate on similar investments, investors are willing to pay more than face value for the bonds. The difference between the issue price and the face value is called a premium and is credited to Unamortized Bond Premium.

4. **Use present values to determine the value of bonds.** The value of a bond is determined by summing the present values of (a) the series of fixed interest payments of the bond issue and (b) the single payment of the face value at maturity. Tables 3 and 4 in the appendix on future value and present value tables should be used in making these computations.

5. **Use the straight-line and effective interest methods to amortize (a) bond discounts and (b) bond premiums.** When bonds are sold at a discount or a premium, the interest rate is adjusted from the face rate to an effective rate that is close to the market rate when the bonds were issued. Therefore, bond discounts or premiums have the effect of increasing or decreasing the interest expense on the bonds over their life. Under these conditions, it is necessary to amortize the discount or premium over the life of the bonds by using either the straight-line method or the effective interest method.

   The straight-line method allocates a fixed portion of the bond discount or premium each interest period to adjust the interest payment to interest expense. The effective interest method, which is used when the effects of amortization are material, results in a constant rate of interest on the carrying value of the bonds. To find interest and the amortization of discounts or premiums, the effective interest rate is applied to the carrying value of the bonds (face value minus the discount or plus the premium) at the beginning of the interest period. The amount of the discount or premium to be amortized is the difference between the interest figured by using the effective rate and that obtained by using the face rate. The results of using the effective interest method on bonds issued at a discount or a premium are summarized below and compared with issuance at face value.

	Bonds Issued at		
	Face Value	**Discount**	**Premium**
Trend in carrying value over bond term	Constant	Increasing	Decreasing
Trend in interest expense over bond term	Constant	Increasing	Decreasing
Interest expense versus interest payments	Interest expense = interest payments	Interest expense > interest payments	Interest expense < interest payments
Classification of bond discount or premium	Not applicable	Contra-liability (deducted from Bonds Payable)	Liability (added to Bonds Payable)

6. **Account for bonds issued between interest dates and make year-end adjustments.** When bonds are sold on dates between the interest payment dates, the issuing corporation collects from investors the interest that has accrued since the last interest payment date. When the next interest payment date arrives, the corporation pays the bondholders interest for the entire interest period.

   When the end of a corporation's fiscal year does not fall on an interest payment date, the corporation must accrue bond interest expense from the last interest payment date to the end of the company's fiscal year. This accrual results in the inclusion of the interest expense in the year incurred.

7. **Account for the retirement of bonds and the conversion of bonds into stock.** Callable bonds can be retired before maturity at the option of the issuing corporation. The call price is usually an amount greater than the face value of the bonds, so the corporation usually recognizes a loss on the retirement of bonds. An extraordinary gain can be recognized on the early extinguishment of debt, when a company purchases its bonds on the open market at a price below face value. This happens when a rise in the market interest rate causes the market value of the bonds to fall.

   Convertible bonds allow the bondholder to convert bonds to stock in the issuing corporation. In this case, the common stock issued is recorded at the carrying value of the bonds being converted. No gain or loss is recognized.

8. **Explain the basic features of mortgages payable, installment notes payable, long-term leases, and pensions and other postretirement benefits as long-term liabilities.** A mortgage is a long-term debt secured by real property. It usually is paid in equal monthly installments. Each payment is partly interest expense and partly debt repayment. Installment notes payable are long-term notes that are paid in a series of payments. Part of each payment is interest, and part is repayment of principal. If a long-term lease is a capital lease, the risks of ownership lie with the lessee. Like a mortgage payment, each lease payment is partly interest and partly a reduction of debt. For a capital lease, both an asset and a long-term liability should be recorded. The liability should be equal to the present value at the beginning of the lease of the total lease payments over the lease term. The recorded asset is subject to depreciation. Pension expense must be recorded in the current period. Other postretirement benefits should be estimated and accrued while the employee is still working.

REVIEW OF CONCEPTS AND TERMINOLOGY

The following concepts and terms were introduced in this chapter.

L O 2   **Bond:** A security, usually long term, representing money borrowed by a corporation from the investing public.

L O 2   **Bond certificate:** Evidence of a company's debt to a bondholder.

L O 2   **Bond indenture:** A supplementary agreement to a bond issue that defines the rights, privileges, and limitations of bondholders.

L O 2   **Bond issue:** The total value of bonds issued at one time.

L O 7   **Callable bonds:** Bonds that a corporation can buy back and retire at a call price before maturity.

L O 7   **Call price:** A specified price, usually above face value, at which a corporation may, at its option, buy back and retire bonds before maturity.

L O 8   **Capital lease:** A long-term lease in which the risk of ownership lies with the lessee and whose terms resemble a purchase or sale on installment.

L O 7   **Convertible bonds:** Bonds that can be exchanged for other securities of the corporation, usually its common stock.

L O 2   **Coupon bonds:** Bonds that are usually not registered with the issuing corporation but instead bear interest coupons stating the amount of interest due and the payment date.

L O 3   **Discount:** The amount by which the face value of a bond exceeds the issue price; occurs when the market interest rate is higher than the face interest rate.

L O 7   **Early extinguishment of debt:** The retirement of a bond issue before its maturity date.

L O 5   **Effective interest method:** A method of amortizing bond discounts or premiums that applies a constant interest rate, the market rate at the time the bonds were issued, to the carrying value of the bonds at the beginning of each interest period.

L O 3   **Face interest rate:** The rate of interest paid to bondholders based on the face value of the bonds.

L O 1   **Financial leverage:** The ability to increase earnings for stockholders by earning more on assets than is paid in interest on debt incurred to finance the assets; also called *trading on the equity.*

L O 8   **Installment note payable:** A long-term note paid off in a series of payments, of which part is interest and part is repayment of principal.

L O 3   **Market interest rate:** The rate of interest paid in the market on bonds of similar risk; also called *effective interest rate.*

L O 8   **Mortgage:** A long-term debt secured by real property; usually paid in equal monthly installments, of which part is interest and part is repayment of principal.

L O 8   **Operating lease:** A short-term or cancelable lease in which the risks of ownership lie with the lessor, and whose payments are recorded as a rent expense.

L O 8   **Other postretirement benefits:** Health care and other nonpension benefits paid to a worker after retirement but earned while the employee is still working.

L O 8   **Pension fund:** A fund established through contributions from an employer (and, sometimes, employees) from which payments are made to employees after retirement or on disability or death.

L O 8   **Pension plan:** A contract between a company and its employees under which the company agrees to pay benefits to the employees after they retire.

L O 3   **Premium:** The amount by which the issue price of a bond exceeds its face value; occurs when the market interest rate is lower than the face interest rate.

L O 2   **Registered bonds:** Bonds for which the names and addresses of bondholders are recorded with the issuing company.

L O 2   **Secured bonds:** Bonds that give the bondholders a pledge of certain company assets as a guarantee of repayment.

L O 2 **Serial bonds:** A bond issue with several different maturity dates.

L O 5 **Straight-line method:** A method of amortizing bond discounts or premiums that allocates a discount or premium equally over each interest period of the life of a bond.

L O 2 **Term bonds:** Bonds of a bond issue that all mature at the same time.

L O 2 **Unsecured bonds:** Bonds issued on the general credit of a company; also called *debenture bonds.*

L O 5 **Zero coupon bonds:** Bonds that do not pay periodic interest but that promise to pay a fixed amount on the maturity date.

REVIEW PROBLEM

INTEREST AND AMORTIZATION OF A BOND DISCOUNT, BOND RETIREMENT, AND BOND CONVERSION

L O 3, 5, 7   When the Merrill Manufacturing Company was expanding its metal window division, it did not have enough capital to finance the expansion. So, management sought and received approval from the board of directors to issue bonds. The company planned to issue $5,000,000 of 8 percent, five-year bonds in 19x1. Interest would be paid on June 30 and December 31 of each year. The bonds would be callable at 104, and each $1,000 bond would be convertible into 30 shares of $10 par value common stock.

On January 1, 19x1, the bonds were sold at 96 because the market rate of interest for similar investments was 9 percent. The company decided to amortize the bond discount by using the effective interest method. On July 1, 19x3, management called and retired half the bonds, and investors converted the other half into common stock.

REQUIRED   1. Prepare an interest and amortization schedule for the first five interest payment dates.

2. Prepare the journal entries to record the sale of the bonds, the first two interest payments, the bond retirement, and the bond conversion.

ANSWER TO REVIEW PROBLEM

1. Prepare a schedule for the first five interest periods.

Interest and Amortization of Bond Discount

Semiannual Interest Payment Date	Carrying Value at Beginning of Period	Semiannual Interest Expense* $(9\% \times \frac{1}{2})$	Semiannual Interest Paid per Period $(8\% \times \frac{1}{2})$	Amortiza-tion of Discount	Unamortized Bond Discount at End of Period	Carrying Value at End of Period
Jan. 1, 19x1					$200,000	$4,800,000
June 30, 19x1	$4,800,000	$216,000	$200,000	$16,000	184,000	4,816,000
Dec. 31, 19x1	4,816,000	216,720	200,000	16,720	167,280	4,832,720
June 30, 19x2	4,832,720	217,472	200,000	17,472	149,808	4,850,192
Dec. 31, 19x2	4,850,192	218,259	200,000	18,259	131,549	4,868,451
June 30, 19x3	4,868,451	219,080	200,000	19,080	112,469	4,887,531

*Rounded to the nearest dollar.

2. Prepare the journal entries.

```
19x1
Jan.   1   Cash                                      4,800,000
               Unamortized Bond Discount              200,000
                   Bonds Payable                                   5,000,000
                   Sold $5,000,000 of 8%,
                   5-year bonds at 96
```

```
19x1
June 30  Bond Interest Expense                    216,000
             Unamortized Bond Discount                        16,000
             Cash                                            200,000
                 Paid semiannual interest and
                 amortized the discount on 8%,
                 5-year bonds

Dec. 31  Bond Interest Expense                    216,720
             Unamortized Bond Discount                        16,720
             Cash                                            200,000
                 Paid semiannual interest and
                 amortized the discount on 8%,
                 5-year bonds

19x3
July  1  Bonds Payable                          2,500,000
         Loss on Retirement of Bonds              156,235
             Unamortized Bond Discount                        56,235
             Cash                                          2,600,000
                 Called $2,500,000 of 8% bonds
                 and retired them at 104
                 $112,469 × ¹/₂ = $56,235*

      1  Bonds Payable                          2,500,000
             Unamortized Bond Discount                        56,234
             Common Stock                                    750,000
             Paid-in Capital in Excess of Par
               Value, Common                              1,693,766
                 Converted $2,500,000 of 8% bonds
                 into common stock:
                 2,500 × 30 shares = 75,000 shares
                 75,000 shares × $10 = $750,000
                 $112,469 − $56,235 = $56,234*
                 $2,500,000 − ($56,234 + $750,000)
                 = $1,693,766
```

*Rounded.

CHAPTER ASSIGNMENTS

QUESTIONS

1. What are the advantages and disadvantages of issuing long-term debt?
2. What are a bond certificate, a bond issue, and a bond indenture? What information is found in a bond indenture?
3. What are the essential differences between (a) secured and debenture bonds, (b) term and serial bonds, and (c) registered and coupon bonds?
4. Napier Corporation sold $500,000 of 5 percent $1,000 bonds on the interest payment date. What would the proceeds from the sale be if the bonds were issued at 95, at 100, and at 102?
5. If you were buying bonds on which the face interest rate was less than the market interest rate, would you expect to pay more or less than par value for the bonds?
6. Why does the amortization of a bond discount increase interest expense to an amount greater than interest paid? Why does the amortization of a premium have the opposite effect?
7. When the effective interest method of amortizing a bond discount or premium is used, why does the amount of interest expense change from period to period?

8. When bonds are issued between interest dates, why is it necessary for the issuer to collect an amount equal to accrued interest from the buyer?

9. Why would a company want to exercise the callable provision of a bond when it can wait to pay off the debt?

10. What are the advantages of convertible bonds to the company issuing them and to the investor?

11. What are the two components of a uniform monthly mortgage payment?

12. What are the two methods of repaying an installment note?

13. Under what conditions is a long-term lease called a capital lease? Why should an accountant record both an asset and a liability in connection with this type of lease? What items should appear on the income statement as the result of a capital lease?

14. What is a pension plan? What assumptions must be made to account for the expenses of such a plan?

15. What is the difference between a defined contribution plan and a defined benefit plan? In general, how is expense determined under each plan?

16. What are other postretirement benefits, and how does the matching rule apply?

SHORT EXERCISES

SE 1.
L O 1
Bond Versus Common Stock Financing

Check Figures: Advantages: 1, 4, 5

Indicate whether each of the following is an advantage or a disadvantage of using long-term bond financing rather than issuing common stock.

1. Interest paid on bonds is tax deductible.
2. Sometimes projects are not as successful as planned.
3. Financial leverage can have a negative effect when investments do not earn as much as the interest payments on the related debt.
4. Bondholders do not have voting rights in a corporation.
5. Positive financial leverage may be achieved.

SE 2.
L O 3, 5
Journal Entries for Interest Using the Straight-Line Method

Check Figure: Bond Interest Expense: $178,000

On April 1, 19x1, Taylor Corporation issued $4,000,000 in 8.5 percent, five-year bonds at 98. The semiannual interest payment dates are April 1 and October 1. Prepare journal entries for the issue of the bonds by Taylor on April 1, 19x1, and the first two interest payments on October 1, 19x1, and April 1, 19x2. Use the straight-line method and ignore year-end accruals.

SE 3.
L O 3, 5
Journal Entries for Interest Using the Effective Interest Method

Check Figure: August 31 Bond Interest Expense: $4,717

On March 1, 19xx, River Front Freight Company sold $100,000 of its 9.5 percent, twenty-year bonds at 106. The semiannual interest payment dates are March 1 and September 1. The effective interest rate is approximately 8.9 percent. The company's fiscal year ends August 31. Prepare journal entries to record the sale of the bonds on March 1, the accrual of interest and amortization of premium on August 31, and the first interest payment on September 1. Use the effective interest method to amortize the premium.

SE 4.
L O 4
Valuing Bonds Using Present Value

Check Figures: PV of Choice A: $520,272; PV of Choice B: $482,550

Mine-Mart, Inc. is considering two bond issues. Choice A is a $400,000 bond issue that pays semiannual interest of $32,000 and is due in twenty years. Choice B is a $400,000 bond issue that pays semiannual interest of $30,000 and is due in fifteen years. Assume that the market rate of interest for each bond is 12 percent. Calculate the amount that Mine-Mart, Inc. will receive if both bond issues occur. (Calculate the present value of each bond issue and sum.)

SE 5.
L O 3, 6
Journal Entries for Bond Issues

Check Figures: a. Cash: $918,000; b. Cash: $927,000

Macrofilm Company is authorized to issue $900,000 in bonds on June 1. The bonds carry a face interest rate of 8 percent, which is to be paid on June 1 and December 1. Prepare journal entries for the issue of the bonds under the independent assumptions that (a) the bonds are issued on September 1 at 100 and (b) the bonds are issued on June 1 at 103.

SE 6.
L O 6
Sales of Bonds Between Interest Dates

Tripp Corporation sold $200,000 of 9 percent, ten-year bonds for face value on September 1, 19xx. The issue date of the bonds was May 1, 19xx. The company's fiscal year ends on December 31, and this is its only bond issue. Record the sale of the

Check Figure: Bond Interest Expense: $6,000

bonds on September 1 and the first semiannual interest payment on November 1, 19xx. What is the bond interest expense for the year ending December 31, 19xx?

SE 7. *Year-End Accrual of*
L O 3, 5, 6 *Bond Interest*
Check Figure: December 31 Bond Interest Expense: $12,000

On October 1, 19x1, Alexus Corporation issued $500,000 of 9 percent bonds at 96. The bonds are dated October 1 and pay interest semiannually. The market rate of interest is 10 percent, and the company's year end is December 31. Prepare the entries to record the issuance of the bonds, the accrual of the interest on December 31, 19x1, and the payment of the first semiannual interest on April 1, 19x2. Assume that the company does not use reversing entries and uses the effective interest method to amortize the bond discount.

SE 8. *Journal Entry for*
L O 7 *Bond Retirement*
Check Figure: Loss on Retirement of Bonds: $31,800

The Falstaf Corporation has outstanding $800,000 of 8 percent bonds callable at 104. On December 1, immediately after the payment of the semiannual interest and the amortization of the bond discount were recorded, the unamortized bond discount equaled $21,000. On that date, $480,000 of the bonds were called and retired. Prepare the entry to record the retirement of the bonds on December 1.

SE 9. *Journal Entry for*
L O 7 *Bond Conversion*
No check figure

The Degas Corporation has $1,000,000 of 6 percent bonds outstanding. There is $20,000 of unamortized discount remaining on the bonds after the March 1, 19x2, semiannual interest payment. The bonds are convertible at the rate of 20 shares of $10 par value common stock for each $1,000 bond. On March 1, 19x2, bondholders presented $600,000 of the bonds for conversion. Prepare the journal entry to record the conversion of the bonds.

SE 10. *Mortgage Payable*
L O 8
Check Figure: Unpaid balance at end of month 3: $298,792

Sternberg Corporation purchased a building by signing a $300,000 long-term mortgage with monthly payments of $2,400. The mortgage carries an interest rate of 8 percent. Prepare a monthly payment schedule showing the monthly payment, the interest for the month, the reduction in debt, and the unpaid balance for the first three months. (Round to the nearest dollar.)

EXERCISES

✳ E 1. *Journal Entries for*
L O 3, 5 *Interest Using the Straight-Line Method*
Check Figure: Bond Interest Expense: $101,000

On February 1, 19x1, Plantation Corporation issued $2,000,000 in 10.5 percent, ten-year bonds at 104. The semiannual interest payment dates are February 1 and August 1.

Prepare journal entries for the issue of bonds on February 1, 19x1, and the first two interest payments on August 1, 19x1, and February 1, 19x2. Use the straight-line method and ignore year-end accruals.

✳ E 2. *Journal Entries for*
L O 3, 5 *Interest Using the Straight-Line Method*
Check Figure: Bond Interest Expense: $186,000

On March 1, 19x1, Brennan Corporation issued $4,000,000 in 8.5 percent, five-year bonds at 96. The semiannual interest payment dates are March 1 and September 1.

Prepare journal entries for the issue of the bonds on March 1, 19x1, and the first two interest payments on September 1, 19x1, and March 1, 19x2. Use the straight-line method and ignore year-end accruals.

E 3. *Journal Entries for*
L O 3, 5 *Interest Using the Effective Interest Method*
Check Figure: Bond Interest Expense: $23,585

On April 1, 19xx, the Mayfair Drapery Company sold $500,000 of its 9.5 percent, twenty-year bonds at 106. The semiannual interest payment dates are April 1 and October 1. The effective interest rate is approximately 8.9 percent. The company's fiscal year ends September 30.

Prepare journal entries to record the sale of the bonds on April 1, the accrual of interest and amortization of premium on September 30, and the first interest payment on October 1. Use the effective interest method to amortize the premium.

E 4. *Journal Entries for*
L O 3, 5 *Interest Using the Effective Interest Method*
Check Figure: Sept. 1 Bond Interest Expense: $31,662

On March 1, 19x1, the Clayton Corporation issued $600,000 of 10 percent, five-year bonds. The semiannual interest payment dates are March 1 and September 1. Because the market rate for similar investments was 11 percent, the bonds had to be issued at a discount. The discount on the issuance of the bonds was $24,335. The company's fiscal year ends February 28.

Prepare journal entries to record the bond issue on March 1, 19x1; the payment of interest and the amortization of the discount on September 1, 19x1; the accrual of interest and the amortization of the discount on February 28, 19x2; and the payment of interest on March 1, 19x2. Use the effective interest method. (Round answers to the nearest dollar.)

E 5. *Valuing Bonds Using*
L O 4 *Present Value*
Check Figures: PV of Choice A: $1,040,544; PV of Choice B: $965,100

Lakeshore, Inc. is considering two bond issues: Choice A is an $800,000 bond issue that pays semiannual interest of $64,000 and is due in twenty years. Choice B is an $800,000 bond issue that pays semiannual interest of $60,000 and is due in fifteen years. Assume that the market interest rate for each bond is 12 percent.

Calculate the amount that Lakeshore, Inc. will receive if both bond issues are made. (**Hint:** Calculate the present value of each bond issue and sum.)

E 6. *Valuing Bonds Using*
L O 4 *Present Value*
Check Figures: a. $525,288; b. $689,472; c. $681,300; d. $509,580; e. $877,650

Use the present value tables in the appendix on future value and present value tables to calculate the issue price of a $600,000 bond issue in each of the following independent cases, assuming that interest is paid semiannually.

a. A ten-year, 8 percent bond issue; the market interest rate is 10 percent.
b. A ten-year, 8 percent bond issue; the market interest rate is 6 percent.
c. A ten-year, 10 percent bond issue; the market interest rate is 8 percent.
d. A twenty-year, 10 percent bond issue; the market interest rate is 12 percent.
e. A twenty-year, 10 percent bond issue; the market interest rate is 6 percent.

E 7. *Zero Coupon Bonds*
L O 4
No check figure

The Commonwealth of Kentucky needs to raise $50,000,000 for highway repairs. Officials are considering issuing zero coupon bonds, which do not require periodic interest payments. The current market interest rate for the bonds is 10 percent. What face value of bonds must be issued to raise the needed funds, assuming the bonds will be due in thirty years and compounded annually? How would your answer change if the bonds were due in fifty years? How would both answers change if the market interest rate were 8 percent instead of 10 percent?

E 8. *Journal Entries for*
L O 5 *Interest Payments*
Using the Effective
Interest Method
Check Figure: Dec. 31 Bond Interest Expense: $23,150

The long-term debt section of the Discovery Corporation's balance sheet at the end of its fiscal year, December 31, 1994, was as follows:

Long-Term Liabilities
  Bonds Payable—8%, interest payable
    1/1 and 7/1, due 12/31/06 $500,000
  Less Unamortized Bond Discount   40,000 $460,000

Prepare the journal entries relevant to the interest payments on July 1, 1995, December 31, 1995, and January 1, 1996. Assume there is an effective interest rate of 10 percent.

E 9. *Journal Entries for*
L O 3, 6 *Bond Issue*
Check Figure: b. Cash: $945,000

Graphic World, Inc. is authorized to issue $900,000 in bonds on June 1. The bonds carry a face interest rate of 9 percent, which is to be paid on June 1 and December 1.

Prepare journal entries for the issue of the bonds by Graphic World, Inc. under the assumptions that (a) the bonds are issued on September 1 at 100 and (b) the bonds are issued on June 1 at 105.

E 10. *Sale of Bonds*
L O 6 *Between Interest*
Dates
No check figure

Reese Corporation sold $200,000 of 12 percent, ten-year bonds at face value on September 1, 19xx. The issue date of the bonds was May 1, 19xx.

1. Record the sale of the bonds on September 1 and the first semiannual interest payment on November 1, 19xx.
2. The company's fiscal year ends on December 31 and this is its only bond issue. What is the bond interest expense for the year ending December 31, 19xx?

E 11. *Year-End Accrual of*
L O 3, 5, 6 *Bond Interest*
Check Figure: Dec. 31 Bond Interest Expense: $12,000

On October 1, 19x1, Rex Corporation issued $500,000 of 9 percent bonds at 96. The bonds are dated October 1 and pay interest semiannually. The market interest rate is 10 percent, and the company's fiscal year ends on December 31.

Prepare the entries to record the issuance of the bonds, the accrual of the interest on December 31, 19x1, and the first semiannual interest payment on April 1, 19x2. Assume the company does not use reversing entries and uses the effective interest method to amortize the bond discount.

E 12. *Time Value of*
L O 4, 7 *Money and Early*
Extinguishment of
Debt

Check Figures: 1. $850,808; 2. Gain
on Retirement of Bonds: $549,192

Feldman, Inc. has a $1,400,000, 8 percent bond issue that was issued a number of years ago at face value. There are now ten years left on the bond issue, and the market interest rate is 16 percent. Interest is paid semiannually.

1. Using present value tables, figure the current market value of the bond issue.
2. Record the retirement of the bonds, assuming the company purchases the bonds on the open market at the calculated value.

E 13. *Journal Entry for*
L O 7 *Bond Retirement*

Check Figure: Loss on Retirement of
Bonds: $73,500

The Figaro Corporation has outstanding $1,600,000 of 8 percent bonds callable at 103. On September 1, immediately after the payment of the semiannual interest and the amortization of the discount were recorded, the unamortized bond discount equaled $50,000. On that date, $1,200,000 of the bonds were called and retired.

Prepare the entry to record the retirement of the bonds on September 1.

E 14. *Journal Entry for*
L O 7 *Bond Conversion*

No check figure

The Gallery Corporation has $400,000 of 6 percent bonds outstanding. There is $20,000 of unamortized discount remaining on the bonds after the July 1, 19x8, semiannual interest payment. The bonds are convertible at the rate of 40 shares of $5 par value common stock for each $1,000 bond. On July 1, 19x8, bondholders presented $300,000 of the bonds for conversion.

Prepare the journal entry to record the conversion of the bonds.

E 15. *Mortgage Payable*
L O 8

Check Figure: Month 2, Mortgage
Interest Expense: $1,495

Inland Corporation purchased a building by signing a $150,000 long-term mortgage with monthly payments of $2,000. The mortgage carries an interest rate of 12 percent.

1. Prepare a monthly payment schedule showing the monthly payment, the interest for the month, the reduction in debt, and the unpaid balance for the first three months. (Round to the nearest dollar.)
2. Prepare journal entries to record the purchase and the first two monthly payments.

E 16. *Recording Lease*
L O 8 *Obligations*

Check Figure: 1. $116,552

Profile Corporation has leased a piece of equipment that has a useful life of twelve years. The terms of the lease are $21,500 per year for twelve years. Profile currently is able to borrow money at a long-term interest rate of 15 percent. (Round answers to the nearest dollar.)

1. Calculate the present value of the lease.
2. Prepare the journal entry to record the lease agreement.
3. Prepare the entry to record depreciation of the equipment for the first year using the straight-line method.
4. Prepare the entries to record the lease payments for the first two years.

E 17. *Installment Notes*
L O 8 *Payable: Unequal*
Payments

Check Figures: Interest Expense,
Dec. 31, 19x2: $4,800; Dec. 31, 19x3:
$3,600

Assume that on December 31, 19x1, $40,000 is borrowed on a 12 percent installment note, to be paid annually over four years. Prepare the entry to record the note and the first two annual payments, assuming that the principal is paid in equal annual installments and the interest on the unpaid balance accrues annually. How would your answer change if the interest rate rose to 13 percent in the second year?

E 18. *Installment Notes*
L O 8 *Payable: Equal*
Payments

Check Figure: Cash: $13,171

Assume that on December 31, 19x1, $40,000 is borrowed on a 12 percent installment note, to be paid in equal annual payments over four years. Calculate to the nearest dollar the amount of each equal payment, using Table 4 from the appendix on future value and present value tables. Prepare a payment schedule table similar to Table 4, and record the first two annual payments.

SKILLS DEVELOPMENT EXERCISES

Conceptual Analysis

SDE 1. *Bond Interest Rates*
L O 3 *and Market Prices*

No check figure

RJR Nabisco's debt restructuring was the subject of the Decision Point that appeared at the beginning of this chapter. The following statement relates to the plan.

> The refinancing plan's chief objective is to purge away most of the reset bonds of 2007 and 2009. These bonds have proved to be an immense headache for RJR.

. . . That's because the bonds' interest rate must be reset so that they trade at full face value. The bonds had sunk to a deep discount earlier this year, raising the prospect that RJR might have to accept a painfully high reset rate of 20% or more to meet its reset obligations.[13]

What is a "deep discount," and what causes bonds to sell at a deep discount? Who loses when they do? What does "the bonds' interest rate must be reset so that they trade at full face value" mean? Why would this provision in the covenant be "an immense headache" to RJR Nabisco?

SDE 2. *Nature of Zero*
L O 5 *Coupon Notes*

No check figure

The *Wall Street Journal* reported, "Financially ailing **Trans World Airlines** has renegotiated its agreement to sell its 40 landing and takeoff slots and three gates at O'Hare International Airport to **American Airlines.**" Instead of receiving a lump-sum cash payment in the amount of $162.5 million, TWA elected to receive a zero coupon note from American that would be paid off in monthly installments over a twenty-year period. Since the 240 monthly payments total $500 million, TWA placed a value of $500 million on the note and indicated that the bankruptcy court would not have accepted the lower lump-sum cash payment. How does this zero coupon note differ from the zero coupon bonds described earlier in this chapter? Explain the difference between the $162.5 million cash payment and the $500 million. Is TWA right in placing a $500 million price on the sale?[14]

SDE 3. *Lease Financing*
L O 8

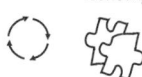

No check figure

FedEx Corporation, known for overnight delivery and distribution of high-priority goods and documents throughout the world, has an extensive fleet of aircraft and vehicles. In its 1993 annual report, the company stated that it "utilizes certain aircraft, land, facilities, and equipment under capital and operating leases which expire at various dates through 2021. In addition, supplemental aircraft are leased under agreements which generally provide for cancellation upon 60 days' notice." The annual report further stated that the minimum commitments for capital leases and noncancelable operating leases for 1994 were $18,635,000 and $458,112,000, respectively.[15] What is the difference between a capital lease and an operating lease? How do the accounting procedures for the two types of leases differ? How do you interpret management's reasoning in placing some aircraft under capital leases and others under operating leases? Why do you think the management of FedEx leases most of its aircraft instead of buying them?

SDE 4. *Issuance of Long-*
L O 1, 2, 8 *Term Bonds Versus*
Leasing

No check figure

The **Coniglio Chemical Corporation** plans to build a new plant that will produce liquid fertilizer for the agricultural market. The plant is expected to cost $400,000,000 and will be located in the southwestern United States. The company's chief financial officer, Terry Coniglio, has spent the last several weeks studying different means of financing the plant's construction. From her talks with bankers and other financiers, she has decided that there are two basic choices: The plant can be financed through the issuance of a long-term bond or a long-term lease. Details for the two options are given below.

a. Issue a $400,000,000, twenty-five-year, 16 percent bond secured by the new plant. Interest on the bonds would be payable semiannually.
b. Sign a twenty-five-year lease calling for lease payments of $32,700,000 on a semiannual basis.

Coniglio wants to know what the effect of each choice will be on the company's financial statements. She estimates that the useful life of the plant is twenty-five years, at which time it is expected to have an estimated residual value of $40,000,000.

Coniglio plans a meeting to discuss the alternatives. Prepare a short memorandum to her identifying the issues that should be considered in making this decision. (**Note:** You are not asked to discuss the factors or to recommend an action.)

13. George Anders, "RJR Nabisco Moves to Retire Most Troublesome Junk Bonds," *Asian Wall Street Journal,* July 17, 1990.

14. Stanley Ziemba, "TWA, American Revise O'Hare Gate Agreement," *Wall Street Journal,* May 13, 1992.

15. FedEx Corporation, *Annual Report,* 1993.

Ethical Dilemma

SDE 5. *Bond Indenture and*
L O 2 *Ethical Reporting*

No check figure

Xetol Corporation, a biotech company, has a $12,000,000 bond issue outstanding that has several restrictive provisions in its bond indenture. Among them are requirements that current assets exceed current liabilities by a ratio of 2 to 1 and that income before income taxes exceed the annual interest on the bonds by a ratio of 3 to 1. If those requirements are not met, the bondholders can force the company into bankruptcy. The company is still awaiting Food and Drug Administration (FDA) approval of its new product XTL-14, a cancer treatment drug. Management had been counting on sales of XTL-14 in 19x4 to meet the provisions of the bond indenture. As the end of the fiscal year approaches, the company does not have sufficient current assets or income before taxes to meet the requirements. Serge Sokolov, the chief financial officer, proposes, "Since we can assume that FDA approval will occur in early 19x5, I suggest we book sales and receivables from our major customers now in anticipation of next year's sales. This action will increase our current assets and our income before taxes. It is essential that we do this to save the company. Look at all the people who will be hurt if we don't do it." Is Sokolov's proposal acceptable accounting? Is it ethical? Who could be harmed by it? What steps might management take?

Research Activity

SDE 6. *Reading the Bond*
L O 3 *Markets*

No check figure

From your school or local library, obtain a copy of a recent issue of the *Wall Street Journal.* In the newspaper, find Section C, "Money & Investing," and turn to the page where the New York Exchange Bonds are listed. Notice, first, the Dow Jones Bond Averages of twenty bonds, ten utilities, and ten industrials. Are the averages above or below 100? Is this a premium or a discount? Is the market interest rate above or below the face rate of the average bond? Now, identify three bonds from those listed. Choose one that sells at a discount, one that sells at a premium, and one that sells for approximately 100. For each bond, write the name of the company, the face interest rate, the year the bond is due, the current yield, and the current closing market price. (Some bonds have the letters *cv* in the Yield column. This means the bonds are convertible into common stock and the yield may not be meaningful.) For each bond, explain the relationships between the face interest rate, the current yield, and the closing price. What other factors affect the current yield of a bond? Be prepared to discuss.

Decision-Making Practice

SDE 7. *Contrasting Types of*
L O 3, 4 *Bonds*

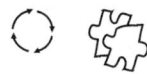

Check Figures: J. C. Penney: 14.8%; Transamerica: 14%; Greyhound: 14.25%

A bond or note with no periodic interest payments sounds like a car with no motor. But some large companies are issuing such bonds. For example, in 1981, **J.C. Penney Company, Inc.** advertised in the business press and sold $200,000,000 of zero coupon bonds due in 1989. The price, however, was not $200,000,000 but only 33.247 percent of $200,000,000. In other words, the investor paid about $332,470 initially and in eight years collected $1,000,000. The advantage to J.C. Penney was that it did not have to pay a cent of interest for eight years. It did, of course, have to produce the full face value of the notes at the maturity date. For the investor, a return would be guaranteed regardless of the market interest rate over the eight years, as long as J.C. Penney was able to pay off the notes at the maturity date. The J.C. Penney zero coupon bonds can be contrasted with the financing transactions that occurred at about the same time at two other companies of similar quality: **Transamerica Corporation** and **Greyhound Corporation.** Transamerica sold $200,000,000 (face value) of thirty-year bonds with a 6.5 percent coupon at a price of $480.67 per $1,000 bond. Greyhound issued $75,000,000 of ten-year notes carrying an interest rate of 14.25 percent at 100.

1. Using Tables 3 and 4 in the appendix on future value and present value tables, compute the effective interest rates for the three debt issues. Which issue would have been the most attractive to investors?
2. Federal tax laws require the payment of income taxes on amortized interest income from low-coupon bonds and notes as well as on interest that is actually paid. In light of this, would your answer to **1** change? What factors other than the effective interest rate and income taxes would you consider important in deciding which of these bonds was the best investment?

PROBLEM SET A

A 1.
L O 3, 5, 6
Bond Transactions—
Straight-Line
Method

REQUIRED

No check figure

Marconi Corporation has $10,000,000 of 10.5 percent, twenty-year bonds dated June 1, with interest payment dates of May 30 and November 30. The company's fiscal year ends December 31, and it uses the straight-line method to amortize bond premiums or discounts.

1. Assume the bonds are issued at 103 on June 1. Prepare general journal entries for June 1, November 30, and December 31.
2. Assume the bonds are issued at 97 on June 1. Prepare general journal entries for June 1, November 30, and December 31.
3. Assume the bonds are issued at face value plus accrued interest on August 1. Prepare general journal entries for August 1, November 30, and December 31.

A 2.
L O 3, 5, 6
Bond Transactions—
Effective Interest
Method

REQUIRED

No check figure

Aparicio Corporation has $8,000,000 of 9.5 percent, twenty-five-year bonds dated March 1, with interest payable on March 1 and September 1. The company's fiscal year ends on November 30. It uses the effective interest method to amortize bond premiums or discounts. (Round amounts to the nearest dollar.)

1. Assume that on March 1 the bonds are issued at 102.5 to yield an effective interest rate of 9.2 percent. Prepare general journal entries for March 1, September 1, and November 30.
2. Assume that on March 1 the bonds are issued at 97.5 to yield an effective interest rate of 9.8 percent. Prepare general journal entries for March 1, September 1, and November 30.
3. Assume the bonds are issued on June 1 at face value plus accrued interest. Prepare general journal entries for June 1, September 1, and November 30.

A 3.
L O 3, 5, 6
Bonds Issued at a
Discount and a
Premium

Check Figures: Bond Interest Expense: June 30, 19x2: $144,666; Sept. 1, 19x2: $93,290

Chambliss Corporation sold bonds twice during 19x2. A summary of the transactions involving the bonds follows.

19x2
Jan.   1   Issued $3,000,000 of 9.9 percent, ten-year bonds dated January 1, 19x2, with interest payable on December 31 and June 30. The bonds were sold at 102.6, resulting in an effective interest rate of 9.4 percent.
Mar.   1   Issued $2,000,000 of 9.2 percent, ten-year bonds dated March 1, 19x2, with interest payable March 1 and September 1. The bonds were sold at 98.2, resulting in an effective interest rate of 9.5 percent.
June 30   Paid semiannual interest on the January 1 issue and amortized the premium.
Sept. 1   Paid semiannual interest on the March 1 issue and amortized the discount.
Dec. 31   Paid semiannual interest on the January 1 issue and amortized the premium.
       31   Made a year-end adjusting entry to accrue the interest on the March 1 issue and to amortize one-third of the discount applicable to the second interest period.

19x3
Mar.   1   Paid semiannual interest on the March 1 issue and amortized the remainder of the discount applicable to the second interest period.

REQUIRED

Prepare general journal entries to record the bond transactions. Use the effective interest method to amortize premiums and discounts. (Round amounts to the nearest dollar.)

A 4.
L O 3, 5,
6, 8
Bond and Mortgage
Transactions
Contrasted

Check Figure: Bond Interest Expense, Dec. 31: $124,788

Munson Grocery Stores, Inc. is expanding its operations by buying a chain of four outlets in another city. To finance the purchase of land and buildings, Munson has obtained a $2,000,000 mortgage that carries an interest rate of 12 percent and requires monthly payments of $27,000. To finance the rest of the purchase, Munson is issuing $2,000,000 of 12.5 percent unsecured bonds due in twenty years, with interest payable December 31 and June 30.

The company's fiscal year ends March 31. Selected transactions related to the two financing activities are as follows:

Jan.   1   Issued the bonds for cash at 104 to yield an effective rate of 12 percent.
Feb.   1   Issued the mortgage in exchange for land and buildings. The land represents 15 percent of the purchase price.

Mar. 1 Made first mortgage payment.
   31 Made the year-end adjusting entry to accrue interest on the bonds and amortize the premium, using the effective interest method.
Apr. 1 Made second mortgage payment.
May 1 Made third mortgage payment.
June 1 Made fourth mortgage payment.
   30 Made the first semiannual interest payment on the bonds and amortized the premium for the time period since the end of the fiscal year.
July 1 Made fifth mortgage payment.
Dec. 1 Made tenth mortgage payment.
   31 Made the second semiannual interest payment on the bonds and amortized the premium for the time period since the last payment.

REQUIRED

1. Prepare a ten-month mortgage-payment schedule using these headings: Payment Date, Unpaid Balance at Beginning of Period, Monthly Payment, Interest for One Month at 1 percent on Unpaid Balance, Reduction in Debt, and Unpaid Balance at End of Period. (Round amounts to the nearest dollar.)
2. Prepare the journal entries for the selected transactions. (Ignore the mortgage payments for August 1 through November 1.)

A 5.
L O 3, 5, 7
Bond Interest and Amortization Table and Bond Retirements

Check Figure: Bond Interest Expense, Sept. 30: 19x1: $168,731

In 19x1, Sharif Corporation was authorized to issue $3,000,000 of unsecured bonds, due March 31, 19x6. The bonds carried a face interest rate of 11.6 percent, payable semiannually on March 31 and September 30, and were callable at 104 any time after March 31, 19x4. All the bonds were issued on April 1, 19x1, at 102.261, a price that yielded an effective interest rate of 11 percent.

On April 1, 19x4, Sharif Corporation called one-half of the outstanding bonds and retired them.

REQUIRED

1. Prepare a table similar to Table 2 to show the interest and amortization of the bond premium for ten interest-payment periods, using the effective interest method. (Round results to the nearest dollar.)
2. Prepare general journal entries for the bond issue, interest payments and amortization of the bond premium, and the bond retirement on the following dates: April 1, 19x1; September 30, 19x1; March 31, 19x4; April 1, 19x4; and September 30, 19x4.

A 6.
L O 3, 5, 6, 7
Comprehensive Bond Transactions

No check figure

Over a period of three years, Henley Corporation, a company whose fiscal year ends on December 31, engaged in the following transactions involving two bond issues.

19x1
July 1 Issued $10,000,000 of 12 percent convertible bonds at 96. The bonds are convertible into $20 par value common stock at the rate of 20 shares of stock for each $1,000 bond. Interest is payable on June 30 and December 31, and the market interest rate is 13 percent.
Dec. 31 Made the semiannual interest payment and amortized the bond discount.

19x2
June 1 Issued $20,000,000 of 9 percent bonds at face value plus accrued interest. Interest is payable on February 28 and August 31. The bonds are callable at 105.
   30 Made the semiannual interest payment on the 12 percent bonds and amortized the bond discount.
Aug. 31 Made the semiannual interest payment on the 9 percent bonds.
Dec. 31 Made the semiannual interest payment and amortized the discount on the 12 percent bonds, and accrued interest on the 9 percent bonds.

19x3
Feb. 28 Made the semiannual interest payment on the 9 percent bonds.
June 30 Made the semiannual interest payment and amortized the bond discount on the 12 percent bonds.
July 1 Accepted all the 12 percent bonds for conversion into common stock.
   31 Called and retired all of the 9 percent bonds, including accrued interest.

REQUIRED

Prepare general journal entries to record the bond transactions, making all necessary accruals and using the effective interest method. (Round all calculations to the nearest dollar.)

PROBLEM SET B

B 1.
L O 3, 5, 6
*Bond Transactions—
Straight-Line
Method*

Dunston Corporation has $4,000,000 of 9.5 percent, twenty-five-year bonds dated March 1, with interest payable on March 1 and September 1. The company's fiscal year ends on November 30. It uses the straight-line method to amortize bond premiums or discounts.

REQUIRED

No check figure

1. Assume the bonds are issued at 103.5 on March 1. Prepare general journal entries for March 1, September 1, and November 30.
2. Assume the bonds are issued at 96.5 on March 1. Prepare general journal entries for March 1, September 1, and November 30.
3. Assume the bonds are issued on June 1 at face value plus accrued interest. Prepare general journal entries for June 1, September 1, and November 30.

B 2.
L O 3, 5, 6
*Bond Transactions—
Effective Interest
Method*

Marino Corporation has $10,000,000 of 10.5 percent, twenty-year bonds dated June 1, with interest payment dates of May 30 and November 30. The company's fiscal year ends December 31. It uses the effective interest method to amortize bond premiums or discounts. (Round amounts to the nearest dollar.)

REQUIRED

No check figure

1. Assume that on June 1 the bonds are issued at 103 to yield an effective interest rate of 10.1 percent. Prepare general journal entries for June 1, November 30, and December 31.
2. Assume that on June 1 the bonds are issued at 97 to yield an effective interest rate of 10.9 percent. Prepare general journal entries for June 1, November 30, and December 31.
3. Assume the bonds are issued at face value plus accrued interest on August 1. Prepare general journal entries for August 1, November 30, and December 31.

B 3.
L O 3, 5, 6
*Bonds Issued at a
Discount and a
Premium*

Check Figures: Bond Interest Expense, June 30, 19x1: $46,598; Sept. 30, 19x1: $96,900

Perennial Corporation issued bonds twice during 19x1. The transactions were as listed below.

19x1
Jan. 1 Issued $1,000,000 of 9.2 percent, ten-year bonds dated January 1, 19x1, with interest payable on June 30 and December 31. The bonds were sold at 98.1, resulting in an effective interest rate of 9.5 percent.

Apr. 1 Issued $2,000,000 of 9.8 percent, ten-year bonds dated April 1, 19x1, with interest payable on March 31 and September 30. The bonds were sold at 102, resulting in an effective interest rate of 9.5 percent.

June 30 Paid semiannual interest on the January 1 issue and amortized the discount.

Sept. 30 Paid semiannual interest on the April 1 issue and amortized the premium.

Dec. 31 Paid semiannual interest on the January 1 issue and amortized the discount.

31 Made an end-of-year adjusting entry to accrue interest on the April 1 issue and to amortize half the premium applicable to the second interest period.

19x2
Mar. 31 Paid semiannual interest on the April 1 issue and amortized the premium applicable to the second half of the second interest period.

REQUIRED

Prepare general journal entries to record the bond transactions. Use the effective interest method to amortize premiums and discounts. (Round amounts to the nearest dollar.)

B 4.
L O 3, 5,
6, 8
*Bond and Mortgage
Transactions
Contrasted*

Check Figure: Bond Interest Expense, March 31, 19x2: $552,115

Shah Manufacturing Company, whose fiscal year ends on June 30, is expanding its operations by building and equipping a new plant. It is financing the building and land with a $10,000,000 mortgage, which carries an interest rate of 12 percent and requires monthly payments of $118,000. The company is financing the equipment and working capital for the new plant with a $10,000,000 twenty-year bond that carries a face interest rate of 11 percent, payable semiannually on March 31 and September 30. To date, selected transactions related to these two issues have been as follows:

19x1
Jan. 1 Signed mortgage in exchange for land and building. Land represents 10 percent of total price.

19x1
Feb. 1 Made first mortgage payment.
Mar. 1 Made second mortgage payment.
31 Issued bonds for cash at 96, resulting in an effective interest rate of 11.5 percent.
Apr. 1 Made third mortgage payment.
May 1 Made fourth mortgage payment.
June 1 Made fifth mortgage payment.
30 Made end-of-year adjusting entry to accrue interest on bonds and to amortize the discount, using the effective interest method.
July 1 Made sixth mortgage payment.
Aug. 1 Made seventh mortgage payment.
Sept. 1 Made eighth mortgage payment.
30 Made first interest payment on bonds and amortized the discount for the time period since the end of the fiscal year.

19x2
Mar. 31 Made second interest payment on bonds and amortized the discount for the time period since the last interest payment.

REQUIRED

1. Prepare a ten-month mortgage-payment schedule using these headings: Payment Due, Unpaid Balance at Beginning of Period, Monthly Payment, Interest for One Month at 1 percent on Unpaid Balance, Reduction in Debt, and Unpaid Balance at End of Period. (Round amounts to the nearest dollar.)
2. Prepare the journal entries for the selected transactions. (Ignore mortgage payments made after September 1, 19x1.)

B 5. *Bond Interest and*
L O 3, 5, 7 *Amortization Table and Bond Retirements*

Check Figure: Bond Interest Expense, Dec. 31, 19x1: $1,433,520

In 19x1, the Vallejo Corporation was authorized to issue $30,000,000 of six-year unsecured bonds. The bonds carried a face interest rate of 9 percent, payable semiannually on June 30 and December 31. The bonds were callable at 105 any time after June 30, 19x4. All of the bonds were issued on July 1, 19x1, at 95.568, a price yielding an effective interest rate of 10 percent. On July 1, 19x4, the company called and retired half the outstanding bonds.

REQUIRED

1. Prepare a table similar to Table 1 to show the interest and amortization of the bond discount for twelve interest-payment periods. Use the effective interest method. (Round results to the nearest dollar.)
2. Prepare general journal entries for the bond issue, interest payments and amortization of the bond discount, and bond retirement on the following dates: July 1, 19x1; December 31, 19x1; June 30, 19x4; July 1, 19x4; and December 31, 19x4.

B 6. *Comprehensive*
L O 3, 5, *Bond Transactions*
6, 7
No check figure

The Ozaki Corporation, a company whose fiscal year ends on June 30, engaged in the following long-term bond transactions over a three-year period.

19x5
Nov. 1 Issued $20,000,000 of 12 percent debenture bonds at face value plus accrued interest. Interest is payable on January 31 and July 31, and the bonds are callable at 104.

19x6
Jan. 31 Made the semiannual interest payment on the 12 percent bonds.
June 30 Made the year-end accrual of interest payment on the 12 percent bonds.
July 31 Issued $10,000,000 of 10 percent, fifteen-year convertible bonds at 105 plus accrued interest. Interest is payable on June 30 and December 31, and each $1,000 bond is convertible into 30 shares of $10 par value common stock. The market rate of interest is 9 percent.
31 Made the semiannual interest payment on the 12 percent bonds.
Dec. 31 Made the semiannual interest payment on the 10 percent bonds and amortized the bond premium.

19x7
Jan. 31 Made the semiannual interest payment on the 12 percent bonds.
Feb. 28 Called and retired all of the 12 percent bonds, including accrued interest.
June 30 Made the semiannual interest payment on the 10 percent bonds and amortized the bond premium.
July 1 Accepted all the 10 percent bonds for conversion into common stock.

REQUIRED Prepare general journal entries to record the bond transactions, making all necessary accruals and using the effective interest method. (Round all calculations to the nearest dollar.)

FINANCIAL REPORTING AND ANALYSIS CASES

Interpreting Financial Reports

FRA 1. *Lease Financing*

L O 8

No check figure

UAL Corporation, owner of United Airlines, stated in its 1992 annual report that it had leased 271 of its aircraft, 43 of which were capital leases.[16] United had leased many of these planes for terms of ten to twenty-two years. Some leases carried the right of first refusal to purchase the aircraft at fair market value at the end of the lease term and others set the price at fair market value or a percentage of cost.

On United's December 31, 1992, balance sheet, the following accounts appeared (in thousands):

Owned—Flight Equipment	$7,790,100
Capital Leases—Flight Equipment	959,200
Current Obligations Under Capital Leases	53,700
Long-Term Obligations Under Capital Leases	812,400

Expected payments in 1993 were $1,106,600 for operating leases and $135,900 for capital leases.

REQUIRED

1. How would you characterize the differences in the aircraft leases described in the first paragraph as operating leases and those descrbed as capital leases? Explain your answer.
2. Explain in general the difference in accounting for (a) operating and capital leases and (b) Owned—Flight Equipment and Capital Leases—Flight Equipment.

International Company

FRA 2. *Pros and Cons of*

L O 7 *Convertible Bonds*

No check figure

Sumitomo Corporation, a Japanese company that is one of the world's leading merchandisers of commodities, industrial goods, and consumer goods, has a number of issues of long-term debt. Among them are almost ¥20,000 million ($15.9 million) of 1.6% convertible bonds payable in Japanese yen in the year 2002.[17] (The interest rate illustrates the historically low rates in Japan.) The bonds are unsecured and are convertible into common stock at ¥1,193 per share. Since Japanese practice for issuing convertible debt is similar to that in the United States, what reasons can you suggest for the company's issuing bonds that are convertible into common stock rather than simply issuing nonconvertible bonds or issuing common stock directly? Are there any disadvantages to this approach?

Toys "R" Us Annual Report

FRA 3. *Business Practice,*

L O 1, 8 *Long-Term Debt,*
and Leases

No check figure

Refer to Management's Discussion, the Financial Statements, and the Notes to Consolidated Financial Statements in the appendix on Toys "R" Us and answer the following questions.

1. Is it the practice of Toys "R" Us to own or lease most of its property and buildings?
2. What proportion of total assets is financed with long-term debt? What proportion of long-term debt is classified as current obligations due within the next year?
3. In what countries has Toys "R" Us incurred long-term debt? Which maturity date is farthest in the future?
4. Does Toys "R" Us lease property predominantly under capital leases or operating leases? Compare the amount to be paid out for operating leases in 1996 with the total obligations under capital leases.

16. UAL Corporation, *Annual Report*, 1992.

17. Sumitomo Corporation, *Annual Report*, 1992.

Fundamentals of Management Accounting

describes the field of management accounting, compares management accounting with financial accounting, and focuses on the analysis of nonfinancial data, a common activity of management accountants. The effects of global competition on management accounting practices are discussed, as are ethical standards for management accountants.

introduces the concept of product costing and discusses the basic terminology used in accounting for internal operations. The reporting of manufacturing costs is highlighted and illustrated. The chapter concludes with an examination of cost allocation principles and practices.

describes the first of two approaches to product costing. After discussing absorption costing and predetermined overhead rates, the chapter focuses on product costing in the job order cost system.

continues the discussion of product costing by analyzing cost assignment within a process cost system.

Introduction to Management Accounting

Caterpillar Inc.[1]

Caterpillar Inc., headquartered in Peoria, Illinois, makes large construction and earth-moving equipment. The accounting staff is responsible for the company's information needs and differentiates between financial accounting (providing information for external financial reporting purposes) and managerial accounting (providing relevant decision information to internal managers). The function of reliable financial reporting and its related controls, records, and systems is a profound responsibility requiring technical accounting skills, a deep knowledge base, and expertise.

In the new globally competitive environment of the 1990s, these financial reporting duties have not changed at Caterpillar. But the role of the accountant has evolved dramatically to embrace managerial as well as financial obligations. The company must still generate reliable external financial reports, but managers depend on accountants for more than financial statements: They need information that can be used internally to manage and improve the business. How can Caterpillar's management accountants make business-enhancing decisions in addition to deriving the data supporting the decisions?

Caterpillar's management accountants provide specific, focused data that help the organization pinpoint areas requiring change and improvement. They view the company's value chain (all activities that add value and generate revenue and profit) as one continuous customer delivery system—from product design and development, through production, marketing, and distribution, to customer service and support. They recognize that it is just as important to have a cost-effective product distribution system as it is to have a cost-effective production process. They know that all key business systems, processes, and activities across the customer delivery system must be well managed, tightly controlled, and continuously improved. To ensure this, Caterpillar's management accountants identify critical success factors, establish accountability for results, set targets for improvement, and provide feedback through cost systems, performance measurements, and business analyses. ∶∶∶∶∶

---

1. *Source:* Lou Jones, Cost Management and Business Resources Manager, Caterpillar Inc., Peoria, Illinois. Reprinted by permission of the author.

WHAT IS MANAGEMENT ACCOUNTING?

OBJECTIVE

1 *Define* manage-
ment accounting
*and identify the princi-
pal types of information
managers need*

Management accounting consists of accounting techniques and procedures for gathering and reporting financial, production, and distribution data to meet management's information needs. The management accountant is expected to provide timely, accurate information—including budgets, standard costs, variance analyses, support for day-to-day operating decisions, and analyses of capital expenditures. The Institute of Management Accountants defines management accounting as

> the process of identification, measurement, accumulation, analysis, preparation, interpretation, and communication of financial [as well as nonfinancial] information used by management to plan, evaluate, and control within the organization and to assure appropriate use and accountability for its resources.[2]

The information that management accountants gather and analyze is used to support the actions of management. All business managers need accurate, timely information to support pricing, planning, operating, and many other types of decisions. Managers of production, merchandising, government, and service enterprises all depend on management accounting information. Multidivisional corporations need large amounts of information and more complex accounting and reporting systems than do small businesses. But small- and medium-sized businesses make use of certain types of financial and operating information as well. The types of data needed to ensure efficient operating conditions do not depend entirely on an organization's size.

MEETING NEEDS FOR FINANCIAL INFORMATION

Companies need three types of financial information to operate effectively. First, manufacturing and service companies need product and service costing information. They use cost accounting techniques to gather production information, assign specific costs to batches of products, and calculate unit costs.

Second, to accomplish their objectives, all companies need data to plan and control operations. In a manufacturing company, as production takes place and costs are incurred, formal control procedures are used to compare planned and actual costs. In this way, the effectiveness of operations and of management can be measured.

Third, managers need special reports and financial analyses to support their decisions. All management decisions should be supported by analyses of alternative courses of action. The management accountant is expected to supply the information for such decisions.

MEETING CHANGING NEEDS

Management accounting is constantly evolving to meet the changing needs of management. Strong international competition has generated new management philosophies that have pushed management accountants in new directions. Quality is no longer taken for granted, and the cost of scrap and rework

---

2. Institute of Management Accountants, *Statement No. 1A* (New York, 1982). Since this definition was prepared, the importance of nonfinancial information has increased significantly. Words in brackets were added by the authors.

is no longer factored into product cost. New operating methods—like the just-in-time (JIT) operating environment and total quality management (TQM)—are causing companies to revamp production processes and develop new approaches to cost assignment and product costing. Totally integrated information systems are placing new pressures on the management accounting system. The role of budgeting is changing. New strategies and approaches to making decisions about capital expenditures are generating new forms of analysis.

As a result of all of these changes, management accounting has become a very dynamic discipline. Small- and medium-sized companies still use many of the established practices and procedures of management accounting. But large, global companies are moving rapidly into a new operating environment that demands new management accounting techniques and analyses. We will focus on these new approaches following our discussion of the more traditional methods of product costing, cost planning and control techniques, and decision support analyses.

BUSINESS BULLETIN: BUSINESS PRACTICE

Companies commonly stress product quality in their advertising and marketing efforts. Is this a new practice? The following advertisement was taken from a Sears, Roebuck and Co. catalogue published in the late 1800s.

**The Economy Chief Cream Separator—
Our $1,000 Challenge Offer**

We will give $1,000 in gold to the separator manufacturer who can produce a machine that will out skim the Economy Chief at temperatures of 50, 60, 70, 80, and 90 degrees. We make this offer to the makers of the DeLaval, Sharples, Empire, and every other machine sold in the United States. We have tested them all and we know what we are talking about. The Economy Chief ranks first. The best of the others is a poor second.

At the time of this marketing effort, a new horse-drawn buggy, the then-current mode of transportation, cost less than $100. ===

LINKS BETWEEN MANAGEMENT ACCOUNTING, FINANCIAL ACCOUNTING, AND THE MANAGEMENT INFORMATION SYSTEM

OBJECTIVE

2 *Identify the links between management accounting, financial accounting, and the management information system*

Management accounting and financial accounting are linked by their responsibilities for summarizing and reporting information for interested parties, yet the two differ in many ways. Financial accounting includes all the principles that regulate the accounting for and reporting of financial information that must be disclosed to people outside a company, such as stockholders, bankers, creditors, and investment brokers. In contrast, management accounting exists primarily for the benefit of managers inside a company, the people who are responsible for day-to-day operations.

Before we look at the differences between the two parts of the accounting profession, it is important to look at their links. Both financial accounting and management accounting are part of and use data from a company's management information system. Much of the financial data generated by a company's events, activities, and actions are used for both financial and management accounting purposes. The financial accountant concentrates on using the data for external reporting, and the management accountant is interested in developing reports and analyses for internal use.

For example, consider the costs of marketing a product. Following financial accounting procedures, such costs are reported on the company's income statement as sales or marketing expenses and are deducted from revenues to determine net income. The same costs are analyzed by the management accountant to see if they were within budgeted, or planned, amounts. If not, management accounting helps to determine why actual expenses exceeded budgeted amounts. In addition, marketing costs can be traced to the products they helped to sell so that accurate prices can be established. In fact, all revenues and expenses shown on the income statement are scrutinized by the management accountant to determine if corrective action is needed to make products more profitable and to help project budgeted amounts for the next accounting period.

One of the most important links between financial and management accounting involves the cost of inventories. The costs of the goods a company produces and holds in inventory are developed through product cost systems within the management accounting function. Such amounts enable the financial accountant to report accurate inventory costs on the company's balance sheet. The interaction between the two parts of the accounting discipline is greatest in the area of inventory costing.

Figure 1 illustrates additional links between management accounting, financial accounting, and the management information system. A management information system (MIS) is a system that gathers comprehensive data, organizes and summarizes them into a form that is of value to functional managers, and then provides those same managers with the information that they need to do their work.[3] An organization's data base feeds information through the MIS to several information systems operating concurrently within the firm. The financial information system is only one of many information systems. Product design and engineering personnel have information needs unique to their efforts and thus need their own information system, as do personnel in production, inventory control, marketing, distribution, and customer service. Much of the information is nonfinancial in nature and is not disclosed in the financial statements, so financial accountants deal primarily with the financial information system when developing external reports and financial statements.

The management accountant, on the other hand, interacts with all the different information systems to supply managers with the information necessary for their work. The management accountant is also responsible for interpreting financial information as it pertains to other functions within the company. For such analyses, the management accountant deals with both financial and nonfinancial data. For example, consider the kinds of information involved in product distribution. The supervisor of product distribution is responsible for delivering accurate amounts of goods to customers on a timely basis and accomplishing the delivery within budgeted cost constraints.

---

3. Ricky W. Griffin, *Management*, 4th ed. (Boston: Houghton Mifflin Company, 1993), p. 555.

Figure 1. Links Between Management Accounting, Financial Accounting, and the Management Information System

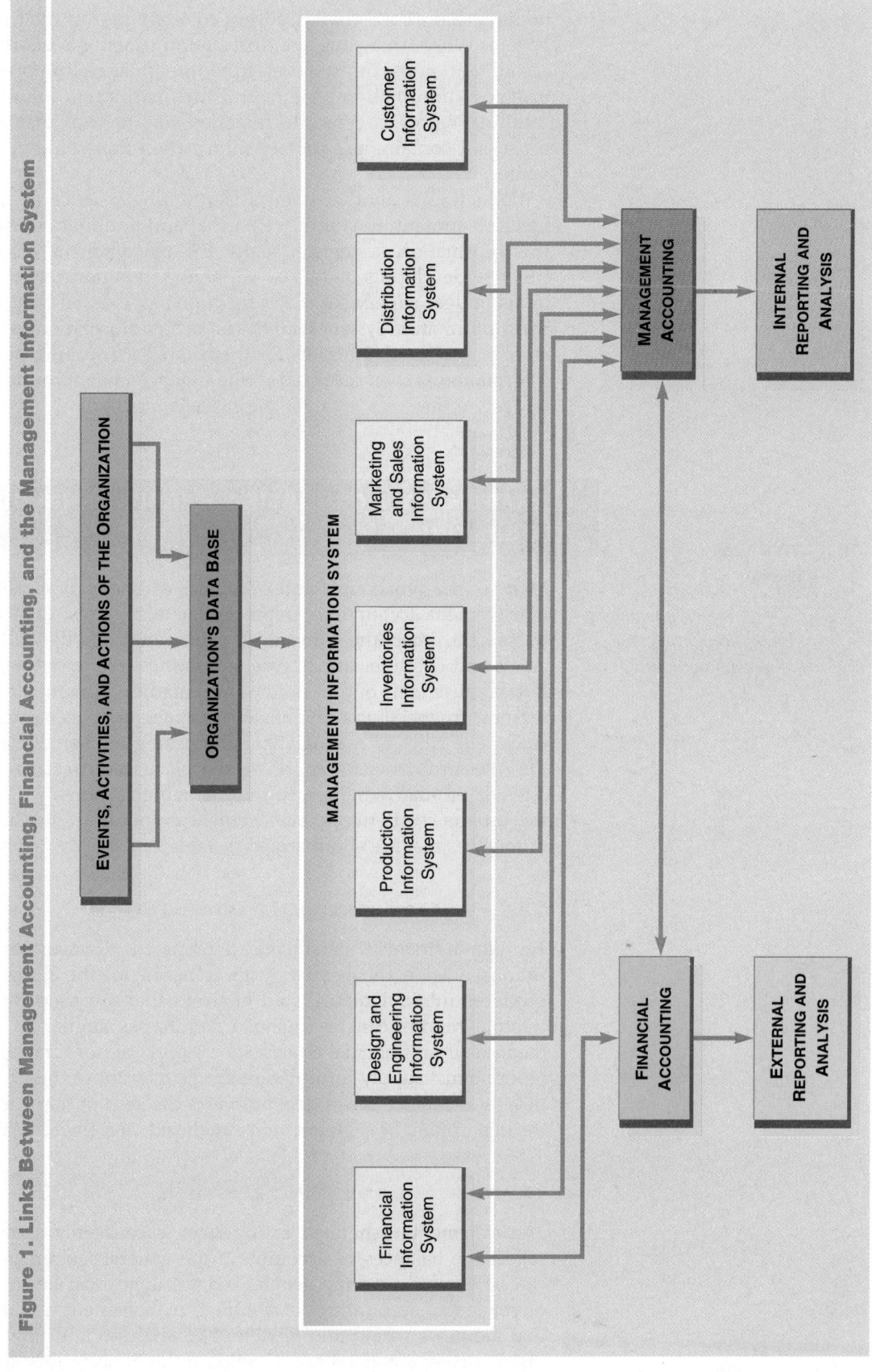

The quantity of goods delivered and the amount of time taken for delivery are nonfinancial information. Delivery costs are part of the financial information system. When analyzing the distribution function's efforts, the management accountant pulls information from the financial information system, the inventory information system, and the distribution information system. The resulting report is typically intended for internal management's use only because it contains proprietary information that could be valuable to a competitor.

Budgeting is another internal accounting practice for which the management accountant must utilize financial and nonfinancial information from all the information systems. Usually the management accountant helps each function develop its budget by supplying the financial information requested by its budget supervisor. Each function's personnel then combine data from their information system with the financial information to develop their budgeted, or projected, amounts for the coming accounting period. The projected information is then returned to the management accountant, who prepares a budget, or one-year plan, for the entire company.

MANAGEMENT ACCOUNTING VERSUS FINANCIAL ACCOUNTING

OBJECTIVE

3 *Distinguish between management accounting and financial accounting*

Many of the procedures and principles of financial accounting also apply to management accounting. Depreciation techniques, cash collection and disbursement procedures, inventory valuation methods, and the recognition of assets and liabilities are all essential to the study of management accounting. But, because their output is communicated to different audiences for different reasons, financial accountants and management accountants follow different rules. The rules of management accounting are somewhat less defined than the rules of financial accounting and place fewer restrictions on the accountant's day-to-day activities. In the following sections, we take a closer look at the differences between management accounting and financial accounting, differences that are summarized in Table 1.

THE PRIMARY USERS OF INFORMATION

Traditional financial statements are prepared primarily for people and organizations outside the company. In comparison, the management accountant produces internal reports and analyses that are used by all managers. The internal reports can be financial summaries similar to the financial statements, special financial analyses, or reports of nonfinancial data. Because the reports must supply information that is relevant to their users' specific activities, their content varies depending on the level of management being served, the department or segment being analyzed, and the report's purpose.

TYPES OF ACCOUNTING SYSTEMS

The statements generated by financial accountants show dollar totals that reflect the balances of accounts in the general ledger. Before financial data can be entered into the general ledger, they must be in a form suitable for double-entry accounting. In contrast, management accounting uses systems that are more varied and flexible. The analyses and flow of accounting data inside a company need not depend on the double-entry format. Management

Table 1. Comparison of Financial and Management Accounting

Areas of Comparison	Financial Accounting	Management Accounting
1. Primary users of information	Persons and organizations outside the business entity	Various levels of internal management
2. Types of accounting systems	Double-entry system	Any useful system; not restricted to double-entry system
3. Restrictive guidelines	Adherence to generally accepted accounting principles	No formal guidelines or restrictions; only criterion is usefulness
4. Units of measure	Historical dollar	Any useful monetary or physical measure, such as machine hours or labor hours; if dollars are used, can be historical or future dollars
5. Focal point for analysis	Business entity as a whole	Various segments of the business entity
6. Frequency of reporting	Periodically on a regular basis	Whenever needed; may not be on a regular basis
7. Degree of objectivity	Demands objectivity; historical in nature	Heavily subjective for planning purposes, but objective data are used when relevant; futuristic in nature

accountants may gather data for small segments or large divisions, and they may express the data in units of measure other than historical dollars. The information need not be organized in general ledger accounts, and special reports can be prepared for a particular manager's use. To support the many activities of management accounting, the information storage and retrieval system must be flexible and have broad capabilities.

RESTRICTIVE GUIDELINES

Financial accounting is concerned with analyzing, classifying, recording, and reporting a company's financial activities. Financial accountants must adhere to generally accepted accounting principles that govern the measuring, recording, and reporting of financial information. Such principles are necessary to ensure the accuracy and reliability of information, but they limit accountants to a finite number of accounting practices.

Usually, much more information is available to managers than to people outside the company. The presentation and analysis of that information are not limited by a set of rigid rules. Management accounting has one primary guideline: The accounting practice or technique must produce *useful* information. Before tackling a problem, the management accountant must decide what information will be useful to the recipient of the report, and then must choose concepts, procedures, and techniques to generate that information. As always, the benefits of preparing each report should outweigh the costs of preparation.

UNITS OF MEASURE

The fourth area of comparison between financial and management accounting is the unit of measure used in reports and analyses. Financial accounting generates financial information about events in the past. The common unit of measure in financial accounting is the historical dollar. Management accountants, on the other hand, are not restricted to using only the historical dollar; they can employ any useful unit of measure. Historical dollars may be used for cost control analyses and for measuring trends for routine planning. However, most management decisions require forecasts and projections that rely on estimates of future dollar flows. In addition to monetary units, the management accountant uses such nonfinancial measures as machine hours, labor hours, and product or service units.

FOCAL POINT FOR ANALYSIS

Typically, financial accounting records and reports information on the assets, liabilities, equities, and net income of a company as a whole. Financial statements summarize the transactions of an entire organization. Management accounting, in contrast, usually focuses on segments of a business—cost centers, profit centers, divisions, or departments—or some specific aspect of operations. Reports can range from an analysis of revenues and expenses for an entire division to an examination of the materials used by one machine.

FREQUENCY OF REPORTING

Financial statements for external use are usually prepared on a regular basis: monthly, quarterly, or annually. Periodic reporting at regular intervals is a basic concept of financial accounting. Management accounting reports can be prepared monthly, quarterly, or annually on a regular basis, but they also can be requested daily or on an irregular basis. What is important is that each report be useful and be prepared whenever it is needed.

DEGREE OF OBJECTIVITY

Financial statements consist of data about transactions that have already happened. As a result, the information is determined objectively and is verifiable. In contrast, management accounting is concerned primarily with planning and controlling internal operations—activities that are often future-related. Past revenue and expense transactions, although useful for establishing trends, are not used directly for planning purposes. Thus, the information prepared by management accountants typically consists of subjective estimates of future events.

THE INFORMATION NEEDS OF MANAGEMENT

It is customary to talk about manufacturing operations when discussing management accounting, but any manager in any business, from a conglomerate to a family grocery store, relies daily on management accounting information. Service organizations, such as banks, hotels, public accounting firms, insurance companies, and attorneys' offices, need internal accounting information to determine the costs of providing their services and the prices to charge. Retail organizations, such as Sears, Roebuck and Co. and Neiman Marcus Group, use management accounting reports to manage operations and maximize profits. Not-for-profit and government agencies use internal accounting information to develop budgets and performance reports.

Management accounting principles and procedures are not just for accountants. Financial analysts, real estate brokers, insurance agents, bankers, market researchers, and economists are just a few of the managers who make decisions based on the information supplied by management accountants. Every person employed in a management-related job should help develop and should rely on management accounting information.

To illustrate the widespread use of management accounting information, we look at three business enterprises: a manufacturing company, a bank, and a department store.

A MANUFACTURING COMPANY

A manufacturer takes raw materials, such as wood, steel, and rubber, and transforms them into finished products, such as furniture, automobiles, and tires. Product cost information is an important contribution management accounting makes to a manufacturing company. Product cost information allows managers to identify weak production areas, control costs, support pricing decisions, and set inventory values.

The information used to make operating decisions is also extremely important to manufacturing managers. A manager must be knowledgeable and able to respond to questions about pricing and delivery dates when special orders are received. If a company manufactures several products, constant monitoring of the different production operations is important. Often a manufacturer must decide whether to make a part or to purchase it. If two or more products are derived from a common raw material—for example, as gasoline and motor oil are derived from crude oil—the manufacturer must decide which product will be more salable and profitable—the one that is derived first or the one that requires further processing.

Managers in a manufacturing company need other information in addition to that related to product costing and operating decisions. They need budgets for both planning and control. They also need current information about production planning and scheduling, product-line management and development, cash management, capital expenditures, product quality levels, customer satisfaction, and selling and distribution. And they need information for external reporting and computing taxes.

A SERVICE BUSINESS—A BANK

A bank provides financial services for a fee. When it makes loans, it charges interest for the service. To maintain a customer's checking account, a bank usually requires either a monthly fee or a minimum balance so that it can lend the money to another party and earn interest income. It also charges fees for certified checks and safe deposit boxes. Large banks provide other services as well.

In a bank, the accounting system plays a key role in the management of resources. The balancing and monitoring of cash reserves are critical activities. Managers are responsible for customers' savings accounts and the federal deposit reserves required by the Federal Reserve Board and other government agencies.

Although operating decisions in banks and manufacturing companies differ in many ways, the bank manager must continually analyze the services provided and the optimal service mix, just as the manufacturing manager must continually analyze the products manufactured and the optimal product mix. Budgets must be prepared, and capital expenditure decisions made. Loan activities require a system for verifying credit. And monitoring loan payments and delinquent loans is very important. Recently, banks have started to adopt product cost procedures. Because a bank's products are its services, it has to determine if its services are operating efficiently and are cost-effective. This means that information on the cost of maintenance per loan, per savings transaction, and per checking account is increasingly important to bank managers.

A MERCHANDISING BUSINESS— A DEPARTMENT STORE

A department store's most important asset is its merchandise. The store's manager is responsible for (1) ordering merchandise in optimal quantities, (2) safely storing merchandise once it is received, (3) displaying items to attract customers, (4) marketing merchandise, and (5) distributing items to customers. To manage these areas of responsibility, a store manager needs an accounting information system that can generate reports, requisitions, controls, and analyses. Market surveys and other research often support purchase decisions. Knowing the most economical quantity to order helps control costs. And inventory records are critical once merchandise has been received. These documents give the manager information about merchandise quality, deterioration, obsolescence, losses caused by theft, quantity on hand, reorder points, and current demand. Obviously, store managers need internal accounting information to control merchandise.

But store managers are involved in other areas as well, including (1) budgeting; (2) cash management; (3) product-line sales analyses; (4) capital expenditure analyses; (5) product selling cost analyses; (6) report preparation for all levels of management and tax authorities; and (7) operating decisions about sales mix, special orders, and personnel. The information reported by management accountants helps store managers in these areas.

HOW TO PREPARE A MANAGEMENT ACCOUNTING REPORT OR ANALYSIS

At all business levels, managers are required to prepare and interpret reports and analyses. Each company may have a preferred style, but the specific format and structure are usually decided by the person developing the report

OBJECTIVE

5 *Identify the important questions a manager must consider before requesting or preparing a managerial report*

and by the time constraints of the project. The keys to successful report preparation are the four W's: Why? What? Who? and When?

Why? The response to the question "Why is this report being prepared?" establishes the report's characteristics and helps in answering the other three questions. Therefore, a manager should write down the purpose of a report before creating it. Many reports prepared without this step are unfocused and do not fulfill their original need.

What? After stating the purpose of the report, the manager must decide what information will satisfy that purpose and what method of presentation will be most effective. The information should be relevant to the decision and easy to read and understand. Cluttered reports do not communicate clearly. A report should address the purpose directly.

Who? There are several "who" questions: For whom is the report being prepared? To whom should the report be distributed? Who will read it? The answers to all three questions will dictate the report's format. If the report is prepared for only one manager, it may be less structured than one that is distributed to a dozen managers or sent to stockholders. Widely distributed reports normally contain concise, summarized information, whereas reports prepared for a company's president or for a particular manager are more detailed.

When? When is the report due? Timing is crucial to effective reporting. A report is useful only when its information is timely. Preparation time is often limited by a report's urgency. Quick reports often lack accuracy. The tradeoff between accuracy and urgency is a normal constraint, one that the report maker must become accustomed to and master.

ANALYSIS OF NONFINANCIAL DATA

OBJECTIVE

6 *Recognize the need for, and prepare an analysis of, nonfinancial data*

Most people associate accounting with the analysis of resources and their monetary equivalents. As noted earlier, however, management accountants prepare analyses expressed not only in dollars but also in nonfinancial units of measure. Today's globally competitive operating environment has created additional demand for nonfinancial data analysis. Management has four primary concerns: (1) increasing the quality of the firm's products or services, (2) increasing efficiency by reducing the time it takes to create and deliver products or services, (3) achieving total customer satisfaction, and (4) reducing costs.

To measure increased quality, management needs information about and trend analysis of the number of items that require rework, the amount of scrapped materials and products, the total time devoted to inspection, and the time spent on product development, design, and testing. Improvements in production and delivery can be measured by trends in throughput time (the total production time per unit per product type), total delivery time by customer and geographic location, raw materials spoilage and scrap rates, machine setup time rates, production bottlenecks (slowdowns), and completed production. Customer satisfaction can be measured by trends in the number of product warranty claims and the number of products returned (analyzed by product line and by customer), retention of customers, product reorders by customers, and time spent on product repairs and adjustments in the field.

These analyses of nonfinancial data also measure how well management has been able to reduce operating costs. Reducing or eliminating the need to

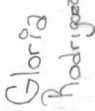

rework defective units or the incurrence of scrap also reduces the cost of a product. If throughput time is reduced, the costs connected with the time saved—such as storage costs, inspection labor time costs, and product moving costs—are also reduced. Improved product quality reduces or eliminates warranty claims and service work, thus reducing product costs.

Notice that all of these performance measures are nonfinancial and are critical in today's operating environment. In addition, all are part of the decision-supporting data management needs and are expected to be supplied by the management accounting information system.

Accountants are often confronted with problems that require such nonfinancial measures as machine hours, labor hours, units of output, number of employees, and number of requests for a particular service. The following case illustrates a situation in which a manager requires nonfinancial data to make an informed decision.

CASE EXAMPLE: KINGS BEACH NATIONAL BANK

Lynda Babb supervises tellers at Kings Beach National Bank. The bank has three drive-up windows, each with a full-time teller. Historically, each teller served an average of thirty customers per hour. However, on November 1, 19x7, management implemented a new check-scanning procedure that has cut back the number of customers served per hour.

Data on the number of customers served for the three-month period ending December 31, 19x7, are shown in Part A of Exhibit 1. Each teller works an average of 170 hours per month. Window 1 is always the busiest; Windows 2 and 3 receive progressively less business. The October figure of thirty customers per hour is derived from the averages for all three windows.

Ms. Babb is preparing a report for management on the effects of the new procedure. To help her, you have been asked to calculate a new average for customers served per hour for both November and December.

Analysis of Nonfinancial Data   Part B of Exhibit 1 shows an analysis of the number of customers served over the three months by each teller window. Using the monthly average hours worked per teller (170), you can compute the number of customers served per hour by dividing the number of customers served by 170. By averaging the customer service rates for the three tellers, you get 28.43 for November and 28.83 for December. As you can see, the service rate has decreased. But December's average is higher than November's, which means the tellers, as a whole, are becoming more accustomed to the new procedure.

MEETING THE DEMANDS OF GLOBAL COMPETITION

OBJECTIVE

7 *Describe the new needs for management information caused by global competition*

During the 1970s and 1980s, the United States lost its dominance in the world marketplace. Countries such as Japan, Germany, Great Britain, and Korea successfully entered many product markets with high-quality, low-cost goods. Customers around the world were pleased with the quality of the new products and purchased them in large numbers. Most affected by the emergence of foreign competition were the automobile, television and VCR equipment, appliance, steel, and audio equipment industries. These industries repre-

Exhibit 1. Analysis of Nonfinancial Data—Bank

Kings Beach National Bank
Summary of Number of Customers Served
For the Quarter Ended December 31, 19x7

Part A	Number of Customers Served			
Window	October	November	December	Quarter Totals
1	5,428	5,186	5,162	15,776
2	5,280	4,820	4,960	15,060
3	4,593	4,494	4,580	13,667
Totals	15,301	14,500	14,702	44,503

Part B	Number of Customers Served per Hour			
Window	October	November	December	Quarter Averages
1	31.93	30.51	30.36	30.93
2	31.06	28.35	29.18	29.53
3	27.02	26.44	26.94	26.80
Totals	90.01	85.30	86.48	87.26
Average per hour per window	30.00	28.43	28.83	29.09

sented a significant portion of the United States' manufacturing sector, and hundreds of companies were affected. American management had to develop the means to cope with this world-class competition.

For American industries to become globally competitive again, management needed information to strengthen six areas of performance: product quality, delivery, inventory control, materials/scrap control, machine maintenance, and product cost. To improve product quality, management had to identify customer needs, expectations, reactions, and complaints about products and services. They also needed accurate records of vendors of quality materials and timely reports summarizing the costs of improving product quality.

Timely product delivery is vital to customer satisfaction. Therefore, analyses had to be developed for on-time delivery records, throughput time (the time it takes to move a product through the entire production process), machine setup times, and wasted time within each production process. Carrying large amounts of inventory, a safety device to ensure satisfaction of customer needs, had become a financial burden. To monitor this area, new measures of inventory reduction were created, including new turnover rates for all categories of inventory showing how many times each product was produced and sold during a given year, continuous tracking of the financial value of each type of inventory, and the reduction in storage space needed for inventories.

Some level of scrap incurrence has always been anticipated and included in the cost of a product. However, scrap must be controlled if a product is to be globally competitive in quality and price. So scrap incurrence is now monitored closely and reduced or eliminated, if possible. Machine breakdowns also cause poor product quality and increase throughput time. The management accountant is expected to keep records of routine machine maintenance so that unexpected breakdowns are minimized. In addition, machine utilization is closely managed.

Finally, product costs needed to be traced more accurately. In the past, costs were traced to departments. Today, all activities of a company are identified and costs are traced to each activity. This new practice is called activity-based costing (ABC). In addition to production costs, a company needs to measure and manage engineering design costs, marketing and sales costs, distribution costs, and even the costs of correcting defects after an item has been purchased or sold.

All of these performance measures are new and still in various stages of development in industry.

BUSINESS BULLETIN: BUSINESS PRACTICE

People do not usually think of management accounting as applicable to the banking industry. Banking is a service industry and a bank's services are its products. To be profitable and to price its services appropriately, a bank must be able to determine the costs incurred to provide each service. Nonetheless, until recently, few banks actually tracked the costs of services. Now, because competition has increased significantly, banks have begun adopting activity-based costing practices and automating their management accounting systems. By applying state-of-the-art technology and costing procedures, bank managers have been able to increase the profitability of most services they offer. Unprofitable services have been identified and eliminated, thanks to this new approach to resource management. ▭▭▭

NEW MANAGEMENT PHILOSOPHIES AND MANAGEMENT ACCOUNTING

OBJECTIVE

8 *Identify the new management philosophies stemming from the world-class operating environment and define the concept of continuous improvement*

Three significant new management philosophies evolved in the United States to deal with expanding global competition: just-in-time operating techniques, total quality management, and activity-based management. In addition, flexible manufacturing systems have been developed to assist in improving quality and reducing throughput time. The just-in-time (JIT) operating environment is an organizational environment in which personnel are hired and raw materials and facilities are purchased and used only as needed; emphasis is on the elimination of waste. Workers are trained to be multiskilled, and production processes are consolidated to allow workers to operate several different machines or processes. Raw materials and parts are scheduled to be delivered when they are needed in the production process, so materials inventories are reduced significantly. Products are produced continuously, so work in process inventories are very small. Goods are usually pro-

duced only when an order is received and are shipped when completed, so inventories of finished goods are reduced. Adopting the JIT operating environment results in reduced production time, reduced materials waste, higher-quality goods, and reduced production costs.

Total quality management (TQM) is an organizational environment in which all functions work together to build quality into the firm's product or service. TQM has many of the same characteristics as the JIT operating philosophy. Workers function as team members and are empowered to make operating decisions that improve both the product and their work environment. TQM focuses on improved product quality by identifying and reducing or eliminating the waste of resources caused by poor product quality. Emphasis is placed on using resources efficiently and effectively to prevent poor quality and examining current operations to spot possible causes of poor quality. Improved quality of both the work environment and the product is the goal of TQM. Like JIT, TQM results in reduced waste of materials, higher-quality goods, and lower production costs.

The development of flexible manufacturing systems has paralleled the spread of the just-in-time operating environment and total quality management. A flexible manufacturing system (FMS) is a single, multifunctional machine or an integrated set of computerized machines or systems designed to complete a series of operations automatically. The number of operations performed by a flexible manufacturing system is determined by the process itself, as is the configuration of the system. Several benefits result from developing or purchasing an FMS. Both the number of machine setups and the amount of time spent on each setup are significantly reduced; production consistency and product quality are enhanced; products with similar shapes and sizes can be produced with minimal downtime for setups; labor costs are reduced because the process is partially or fully automated; and scrap incurrence is reduced or eliminated.

Activity-based management (ABM) is an approach to managing a business that identifies all major operating activities, determines what resources are consumed by each activity, identifies what causes resource usage of each activity, and categorizes the activities as either adding value to a product or being nonvalue-adding. ABM is an extension of a new management accounting practice called activity-based costing. Activity-based costing (ABC) is a system that identifies all of a company's major operating activities (both production and nonproduction), traces costs to those activities, and then determines which products use the resources and services supplied by those activities. Activities that add value to a product, as perceived by the customer, are known as value-adding activities. Such activities are enhanced to improve product quality and customer satisfaction. All other activities are called nonvalue-adding activities. Nonvalue-adding activities that are needed because they support the business are focal points for cost reduction. Nonvalue-adding activities that do not support the business are eliminated. ABM results in reduced product costs, reduced waste of resources, increased processing efficiency, and increased customer satisfaction.

THE GOAL: CONTINUOUS IMPROVEMENT

One of the most valuable lessons to be gained from the emergence of stiff global competition is never to become complacent. While the United States rested on it laurels as the world's most productive nation, countries around the globe were perfecting their productive capabilities. Because our industry had been lulled into self-satisfaction, other countries equaled and surpassed our levels of quality and productivity. What followed was a period of catch-up by American companies.

The concept of continuous improvement evolved during this period. Companies that adhere to continuous improvement are never satisfied with what is; they constantly seek a better method, product, process, or resource. Their goal is perfection in everything they do.

JIT, TQM, FMS, and ABM all have perfection by means of continuous improvement as their goal. Figure 2 illustrates how each approach attempts to accomplish its goal. In the just-in-time operating environment, management wages a relentless war on waste: wasted time, wasted space, and wasted use of materials. All employees are encouraged to continuously look for ways to improve processes and save time. Total quality management focuses on improving the quality of the product and the work environment. It pursues continuous improvement by reducing the number of defective products and the amount of wasted time.

Flexible manufacturing systems are designed to reduce, and in many cases completely eliminate, machine setup time. Teams are trained to make setups

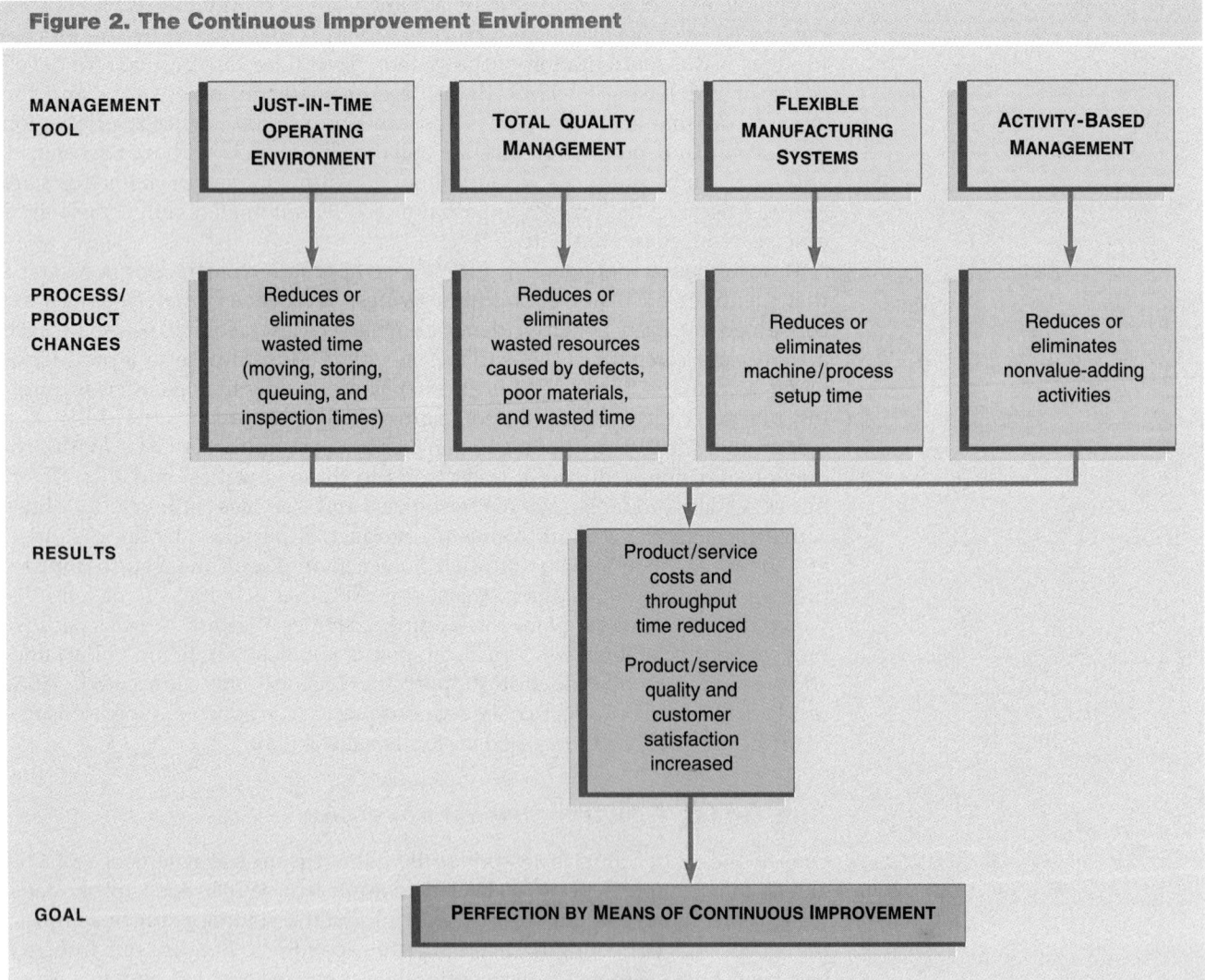

Figure 2. The Continuous Improvement Environment

in minimal time, and employees are rewarded for suggestions that will reduce setup time. Automating part or all of the production process significantly reduces the generation of defective units, thereby reducing waste. These systems are continuously fine-tuned to improve their process. Activity-based management focuses on the ongoing reduction or elimination of non-value-adding activities as its way of seeking continuous improvement.

Each of these new management tools can be used as an individual system, or parts of them can be combined to create a new operating environment. Some aspects of them can be employed in service industries, such as banking, as well as in manufacturing. By continuously trying to improve and fine-tune operations, these new management tools contribute to the same basic results for any company: Product/service costs and throughput time are reduced, and product/service quality and customer satisfaction are increased. If American businesses continuously improve upon all these results, the United States will catch up with and then surpass its competition.

DECISION POINT

Acme Printing Co., Inc.[4]

Continuous improvement is the end result of all the new management philosophies of the 1990s. The concept takes into account improvements in product design, product quality, processing, and even management techniques. The president of Acme Printing Co., Inc. decided to pursue a continuous improvement program after reading materials written by Dr. W. Edwards Deming about how various companies, including Acme's direct competitors, were implementing new quality programs. Continuous improvement requires that everyone in an organization take a critical look at operations to try to detect areas where improvements are needed. Acme management targeted employee training as the first step in their implementation of continuous improvement. To show their commitment to the program, management offered every employee in the company the opportunity to attend training sessions on company time. Only two employees out of a work force of ninety declined the training offer.

Acme's approach to continuous quality improvement focused on the production process, rather than on the products. Management felt that improvements to the process would result in improved product quality. Employee teams were formed, and each team was charged with investigating a particular segment of the process. But before the teams could begin their activities, they needed to understand the concept of internal supplier and internal customer. An internal supplier is a department that supplies an area of the process with raw materials or services; an internal customer is a department that uses the materials or services of another

4. Dennis D. Sissel, "Continuous Quality Improvement at Acme Printing," *Management Accounting*, Institute of Management Accountants, May 1994, pp. 53–55.

department. Why is the concept of internal supplier and customer important to the continuous improvement program at Acme Printing Company?

Quality means exceeding a customer's needs and expectations. The needs and expectations of internal customers must be viewed in the same terms as the needs and expectations of external customers if a quality process is to be established. Internal suppliers of raw materials and services must view receiving departments as customers and must seek to exceed their needs and expectations. Receiving departments, or internal customers, must communicate their needs and expectations to internal suppliers if they expect to have their needs satisfied. In a traditional business setting, internal departments are not viewed as suppliers and customers. Therefore, special training is required to help employees adopt the new perspective. Once the new mindset has been established, it becomes possible to identify necessary changes in the internal process and take corrective action. ⦂⦂⦂⦂⦂

MERCHANDISING VERSUS MANUFACTURING COMPANIES

OBJECTIVE

9 *Compare accounting for inventories and cost of goods sold in merchandising and manufacturing companies*

Much of what you have learned about accounting has centered on the merchandising organization. But all businesses—especially manufacturing companies—need cost information. This section looks at how the computation of the cost of goods sold differs between merchandising and manufacturing organizations.

A merchandising company normally buys a product that is ready for resale when it is received. Nothing needs to be done to the product to make it salable, except possibly to prepare a special package or display. As shown in Figure 3, total beginning merchandise inventory plus net purchases is the basis for computing both the cost of goods sold and the ending merchandise inventory. Costs assigned to unsold items make up the ending inventory balance. The difference between the cost of goods available for sale and the ending inventory balance is the cost of goods sold during the period.

Beginning merchandise inventory	$ 2,000
Add net purchases	8,000
Cost of goods available for sale	$10,000
Less ending merchandise inventory	2,700
Cost of goods sold	$ 7,300

Computing the cost of goods sold for a manufacturing company is more complex. As shown in Figure 4, instead of one inventory account, a manufacturer maintains three inventory accounts: Materials Inventory, Work in Process Inventory, and Finished Goods Inventory. Purchased materials unused during the production process make up the Materials Inventory balance. The cost of materials used plus the costs of labor services and factory overhead (utility costs, depreciation of factory machinery and building, supplies) are transferred to the Work in Process Inventory account once the materials, labor services, and overhead items are used in the production process.

These three types of costs often are called simply *materials, labor,* and *overhead.* These costs are accumulated in the Work in Process Inventory account

Figure 3. Cost of Goods Sold: A Merchandising Company

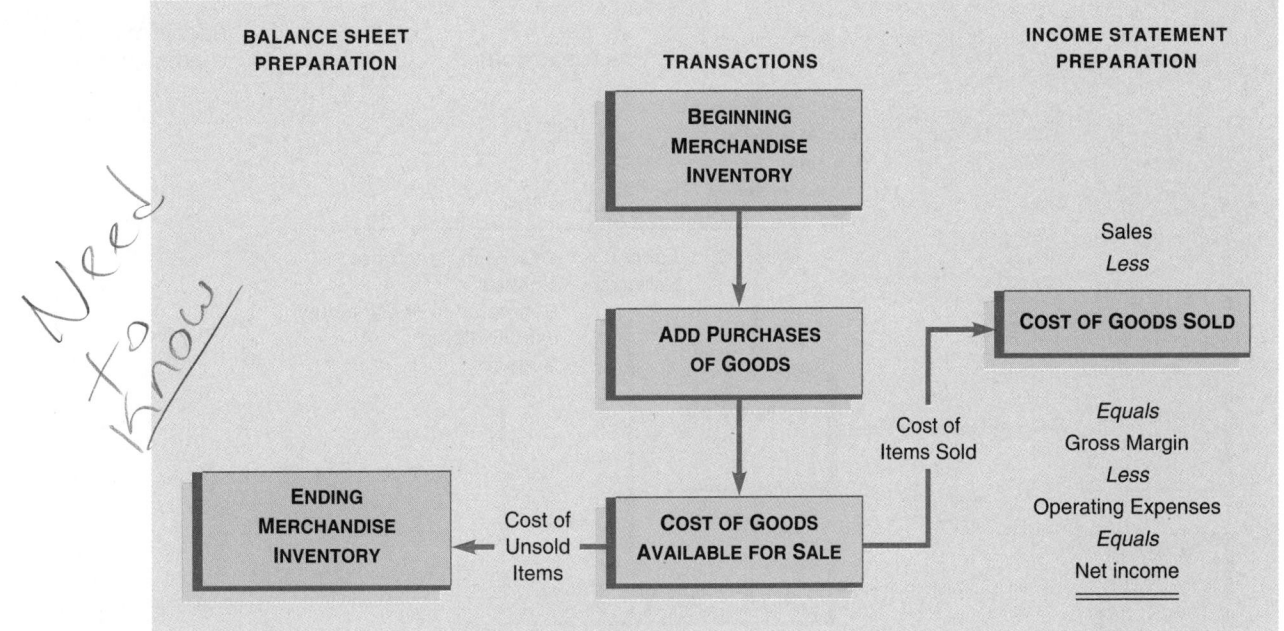

Need to know

BALANCE SHEET PREPARATION | TRANSACTIONS | INCOME STATEMENT PREPARATION

BEGINNING MERCHANDISE INVENTORY

ADD PURCHASES OF GOODS

ENDING MERCHANDISE INVENTORY ← Cost of Unsold Items — COST OF GOODS AVAILABLE FOR SALE

Cost of Items Sold → COST OF GOODS SOLD

Sales
Less
COST OF GOODS SOLD
Equals
Gross Margin
Less
Operating Expenses
Equals
Net income

during an accounting period. When a batch or order is completed, all manufacturing costs assigned to the completed units are moved to the Finished Goods Inventory account. The costs that remain in the Work in Process Inventory account belong to partly completed units. These costs make up the ending balance in the Work in Process Inventory account.

The Finished Goods Inventory account is set up in much the same way as the ending Merchandise Inventory account in Figure 3. The costs of completed goods are entered into the Finished Goods Inventory account. As shown in Figure 4, costs attached to unsold items at year end make up the ending balance in the Finished Goods Inventory account. All costs related to units sold are transferred to the Cost of Goods Sold account and reported on the income statement.

BUSINESS BULLETIN:

What constitutes ethical conduct in business is open to many interpretations. Each of us has developed a viewpoint about ethical conduct in our lives as well as in our school work and business efforts. Stories of insider trading in the stock market and misuse of funds by government officials drive home the importance of ethical conduct. But the differences between ethical and unethical behavior are not always the same as the differences between legal and illegal activities. Today, students and employees are frequently given increased responsibilities and asked to work in teams. If one member of a team sits back and allows the other members to cover his or her responsibilities, that member

Figure 4. Cost of Goods Sold: A Manufacturing Company

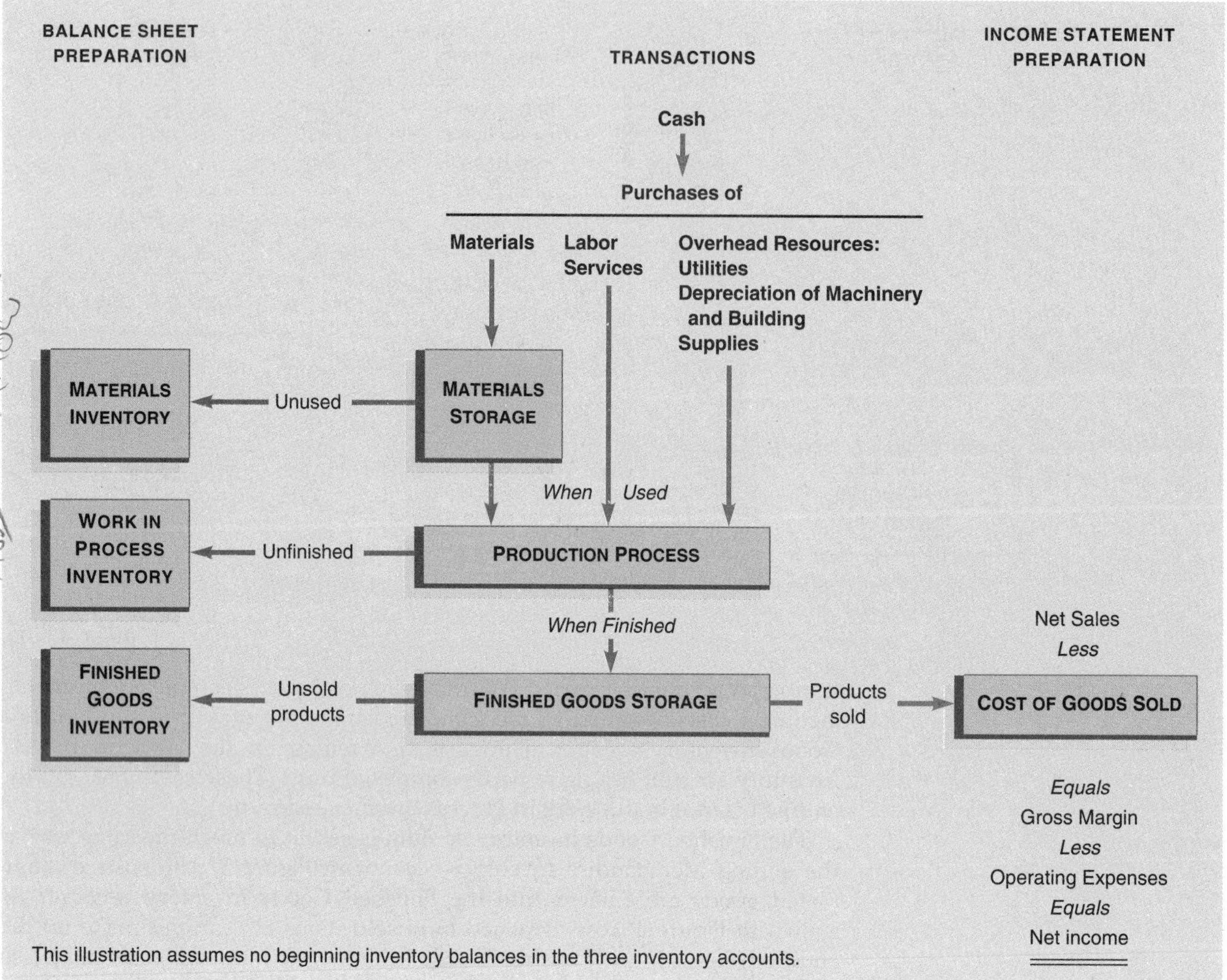

This illustration assumes no beginning inventory balances in the three inventory accounts.

is behaving unethically. Each of us has an ethical responsibility to put forth our best efforts in everything we do, including our educational and business activities. Being a contributing team member is part of that obligation.

STANDARDS OF ETHICAL CONDUCT FOR MANAGEMENT ACCOUNTANTS

OBJECTIVE

10 *Identify the standards of ethical conduct for management accountants and recognize activities that are not ethical*

Credibility is crucial to the accounting profession. And that credibility demands that accountants, both financial and management, adhere to high standards of ethical conduct. On June 1, 1983, the Institute of Management Accountants, formerly called the National Association of Accountants, formally adopted standards of ethical conduct for management accountants.[5]

5. Institute of Management Accountants, *Statement No. 1C*, "Standards of Ethical Conduct for Management Accountants" (Montvale, N.J., June 1, 1983).

These standards specify responsibilities for competence, confidentiality, integrity, and objectivity.

COMPETENCE

To act ethically, management accountants first of all must be competent. In our rapidly changing world, a professional's skills can become obsolete very quickly. To keep current with management accounting issues and skills, management accountants should attend professional development and continuing education programs on an ongoing basis.

The competence required of management accountants is also far-reaching. Accountants must understand and follow all laws, regulations, and technical standards that pertain to their duties. They must maintain professional competence at all times when dealing with their own company, outside entities (customers, vendors, and contractors) associated with that company, and the world marketplace in general. Furthermore, to develop information and reports, management accountants must research relevant information and approaches. Reports, financial analyses, and statements must reveal all necessary information, follow current reporting standards, and clearly state the accountants' findings.

CONFIDENTIALITY

Management accountants are entrusted with information that is confidential and proprietary. In many cases, management accountants generate reports that have direct bearing on a company's profitability. Leaks of such information could give competitors an unfair advantage. Therefore, management accountants should not communicate information to anyone, inside or outside the organization, who is not authorized to receive it, except when disclosure is required by law.

In the conduct of their responsibilities, management accountants often supervise other accountants. These subordinates should be informed whenever they are dealing with confidential or restricted information. Furthermore, management accountants must monitor subordinates' actions to ensure that confidentiality is maintained.

Disclosure, of course, is not the only way of breaking confidentiality. It is also unethical to use confidential information, directly or through third parties, for personal gain or to cause harm to the company, again unless the law requires that the information be disclosed.

INTEGRITY

Management accountants must be impartial. To meet this obligation, they must avoid all actual or apparent conflicts of interest. For example, owning stock in a company that is competing with other vendors for business with the management accountant's company is a potential conflict of interest if the accountant has direct input into the selection of vendors. The management accountant is responsible for informing all appropriate parties of the potential conflict.

Management accountants should refrain from relationships with individuals or organizations that could cause possible conflicts of interest or compromise the accountants' work. Gifts, favors, or special hospitality from an individual or organization should not be accepted.

Realistic (not blind) loyalty to one's company, industry, and country is an important aspect of integrity. Performing or encouraging an act that threatens the organization's legitimate and ethical objectives is not ethical. If a management accountant gains information about disloyal, incompetent, or illegal acts that threaten the company in any way, the accountant must communicate that information to management.

Management accounting reports must be accurate and truthful, regardless of whether their findings have a positive or a negative impact on the company. It is not ethical to alter a report to make it appear that targets have been met or expectations have been exceeded when in fact they have not.

OBJECTIVITY

Accountants are responsible for all financial and many nonfinancial reports to management. Management relies on accountants' reports to make operating decisions, and so, indirectly, do outsiders—investors, creditors, vendors, and customers. All of these people have a right to expect objective information, and accountants must supply it.

Internal managers in particular depend on the information generated by management accountants. Following ethical standards is critical to carrying out these reporting responsibilities. Familiarity with ethical standards and the ability to recognize unethical actions and avoid compromising situations should be an integral part of the management accountant's knowledge and skills.

CHAPTER REVIEW

REVIEW OF LEARNING OBJECTIVES

1. **Define *management accounting* and identify the principal types of information managers need.** Management accounting is the process of identifying, measuring, accumulating, analyzing, preparing, interpreting, and communicating information used by management to plan, evaluate, and control an organization and to ensure that its resources are used and accounted for appropriately. The financial and production data generated by management accountants help managers assign costs to products or services, calculate unit costs, plan and control operations, and support decisions.

2. **Identify the links between management accounting, financial accounting, and the management information system.** Management accountants and financial accountants use data from the same financial information system. The main difference is that financial accountants prepare financial information for use by people external to the company, whereas management accountants prepare reports and analyses for internal management use. In many cases, both financial and management accountants work with the same revenue, cost, and expense categories. However, financial accountants deal almost exclusively with the financial information system, whereas management accountants interact with the information systems of all functions within the organization. Management accountants compute the product costs financial accountants use to determine the ending inventory balances that appear on a manufacturer's balance sheet.

3. **Distinguish between management accounting and financial accounting.** There are seven areas in which the differences between management accounting and financial accounting can be compared. (1) People and organizations outside the business unit are the primary users of financial accounting information, whereas managers at all levels within the organization use management accounting information.

(2) There is no restriction on the types of accounting systems that can be used in management accounting, but financial accounting centers on the double-entry system. (3) Restrictive guidelines for financial accounting are defined by generally accepted accounting principles; management accounting's only restriction is that the information be useful. (4) The historical dollar is the primary unit of measure in financial accounting; any useful unit of measure can be used in management accounting. (5) The business unit as a whole is the focal point of analysis in financial accounting; a management accounting analysis can focus on a division, a department, or even a machine. (6) Financial accountants prepare financial statements on a regular, periodic basis; management accountants prepare reports on an as-needed basis. (7) Financial accounting deals with data about transactions that have happened and therefore demands objectivity; management accounting often focuses on the future and can be highly subjective.

4. **Compare the information needs of the managers of a manufacturing company, a bank, and a department store.** All managers need certain types of information to prepare budgets, make operating decisions, manage cash, and plan for capital expenditures. But the nature of a business also creates special information needs. For example, a manufacturer needs product cost information to help control various types of inventory. A banker relies on special analyses to manage and control depositors' funds. And a department store manager needs merchandise control information.

5. **Identify the important questions a manager must consider before requesting or preparing a managerial report.** Report preparation depends on the four W's: Why? What? Who? and When? The why question is answered by stating the purpose of the report. Once that has been stated, the report maker must determine what information the report should contain to satisfy that purpose. The who question can take several forms: For whom is the report being prepared? To whom should the report be distributed? Who will read it? Finally, there is the question of when. When is the report due?

6. **Recognize the need for, and prepare an analysis of, nonfinancial data.** Management accountants have always been responsible for analyzing nonfinancial data. Today's globally competitive operating environment has created additional demand for nonfinancial analyses centered on increasing the quality of a firm's products or services, reducing production and delivery time, and satisfying customers. Among the performance measures used in these analyses are units of output, time measures, and scrap incurrence rates.

7. **Describe the new needs for management information caused by global competition.** To meet global competition, management must track six areas to strengthen performance: product quality, delivery, inventory control, materials/scrap control, machine maintenance, and product cost. To closely monitor areas of weakness, new measures have been developed that focus on such factors as customers' needs and expectations (product quality), throughput time (delivery), space reduction (inventory control), quality of incoming materials (materials/scrap control), machine availability and downtime (machine maintenance), and engineering design costs (product cost).

8. **Identify the new management philosophies stemming from the world-class operating environment and define the concept of continuous improvement.** The new approaches to management include the just-in-time (JIT) operating environment, total quality management (TQM), and activity-based management (ABM). The use of flexible manufacturing systems (FMS) with any of these new philosophies significantly reduces setup times and increases the likelihood of product consistency. All of these approaches are designed to increase product quality, reduce resource waste, and reduce cost.

   Continuous improvement is the goal of each of the new approaches. Continuous improvement means never being satisfied with what is; there is always a better method, product, process, or resource to be found. Through the concept of continuous improvement, management strives for perfection.

9. **Compare accounting for inventories and cost of goods sold in merchandising and manufacturing companies.** A merchandising firm purchases a product that is ready for resale when it is received. Only one account, Merchandise Inventory,

is used to record and account for items in inventory. And the cost of goods sold is simply the difference between the cost of goods available for sale and ending merchandise inventory. A manufacturing company, because it creates a product, maintains three inventory accounts: Materials Inventory, Work in Process Inventory, and Finished Goods Inventory. Manufacturing costs flow through all three inventory accounts. At the end of the accounting period, the cost of completed products is transferred to the Finished Goods Inventory account; the cost of units that have been sold is transferred to the Cost of Goods Sold account.

10. **Identify the standards of ethical conduct for management accountants and recognize activities that are not ethical.** Standards of ethical conduct govern management accountants' competence, confidentiality, integrity, and objectivity. These standards help management accountants recognize and avoid situations and activities that compromise their honesty, loyalty, and ability to supply management with accurate and relevant information.

REVIEW OF CONCEPTS AND TERMINOLOGY

The following concepts and terms were introduced in this chapter.

L O 8 **Activity-based costing (ABC):** A system that identifies all of a company's major operating activities (both production and nonproduction), traces costs to those activities, and then determines which products use the resources and services supplied by those activities.

L O 8 **Activity-based management (ABM):** An approach to managing a business that identifies all major operating activities, determines what resources are consumed by each activity, identifies what causes resource usage of each activity, and categorizes the activities as either adding value to a product or being nonvalue-adding; emphasis is on the reduction or elimination of nonvalue-adding activities.

L O 8 **Continuous improvement:** The management concept that one should never be satisfied with what is; one should always seek a better method, product, process, or resource.

L O 8 **Flexible manufacturing system (FMS):** A single, multifunctional machine or an integrated set of computerized machines or systems designed to complete a series of operations automatically.

L O 8 **Just-in-time (JIT) operating environment:** An organizational environment in which personnel are hired and raw materials and facilities are purchased and used only as needed; emphasis is on the elimination of waste.

L O 1 **Management accounting:** The process of identification, measurement, accumulation, analysis, preparation, interpretation, and communication of financial and nonfinancial information used by management to plan, evaluate, and control the organization and to assure appropriate use and accountability for its resources.

L O 2 **Management information system (MIS):** A system that gathers comprehensive data, organizes and summarizes them into a form that is of value to functional managers, and then provides those same managers with the information they need to do their work.

L O 8 **Nonvalue-adding activity:** A production- (or service-) related activity that adds cost to a product, but, from a customer's perspective, does not increase its value.

L O 8 **Total quality management (TQM):** An organizational environment in which all functions work together to build quality into the firm's product or service.

L O 8 **Value-adding activity:** A production- (or service-) related activity that adds cost to a product, but, from a customer's perspective, also increases its value.

REVIEW PROBLEM

NONFINANCIAL DATA

L O 6 Ingvar Ullén Surfaces, Inc. is a house-painting company located in Stockholm, Sweden. The company employs twelve painters. Mr. Ullén manages the operation and does all of the estimating and billing work. Two painters specialize in interior painting, three painters are exterior trim specialists, and the remaining seven are semi-skilled, all-purpose painters. Mr. Ullén prepared the following projection of work hours for the month of June.

	Projected Hours to Be Worked				
	Week #1	Week #2	Week #3	Week #4	Totals
Gaten Apartments:					
Interior	60	60	48	32	200
Exterior trim	100	60	48	24	232
General painting	180	160	120	60	520
Vagen Building:					
Interior	20	20	32	48	120
Exterior trim	20	60	72	96	248
General painting	100	120	160	220	600
Totals	480	480	480	480	1,920

On July 2, Mr. Ullén assembled the actual hour data shown below.

	Actual Hours Worked				
	Week #1	Week #2	Week #3	Week #4	Totals
Gaten Apartments:					
Interior	72	76	68	52	268
Exterior trim	88	56	44	20	208
General painting	220	180	144	76	620
Vagen Building:					
Interior	24	32	48	64	168
Exterior trim	16	52	64	88	220
General painting	116	136	184	260	696
Totals	536	532	552	560	2,180

Mr. Ullén is concerned about the excess labor hours worked during June. The July forecast needs to be developed, but he needs further analysis of June's data before proceeding.

REQUIRED

1. Prepare an analysis that shows the number of hours over or under projected hours for each job assignment in June.
2. From your analysis in part **1,** what trouble areas would you point out to Mr. Ullén? Suggest some solutions.

ANSWER TO REVIEW PROBLEM

1.

	Hours Worked (Over) or Under Projected Hours				
	Week #1	Week #2	Week #3	Week #4	Totals
Gaten Apartments:					
Interior	(12)	(16)	(20)	(20)	(68)
Exterior trim	12	4	4	4	24
General painting	(40)	(20)	(24)	(16)	(100)
Vagen Building:					
Interior	(4)	(12)	(16)	(16)	(48)
Exterior trim	4	8	8	8	28
General painting	(16)	(16)	(24)	(40)	(96)
Totals	(56)	(52)	(72)	(80)	(260)

2. Both the interior and the semiskilled painters are taking more time to complete the jobs than was anticipated by Mr. Ullén. Either his estimates were wrong, the quality of the painting materials was poor, or some of the painters need to be reprimanded or dismissed.

CHAPTER ASSIGNMENTS

QUESTIONS

1. What is management accounting?
2. What effect does the size of a business have on the amount or type of financial information needed by management?
3. What are the three areas in which management needs information?
4. How is management accounting similar to financial accounting?
5. How is management accounting linked to a company's management information system?
6. How do financial accounting and management accounting differ in terms of primary users, types of accounting systems, and restrictive guidelines?
7. How do financial accounting and management accounting differ in terms of units of measure, focal point of analysis, frequency of reporting, and degree of objectivity?
8. What types of information are important to a manager in a manufacturing company?
9. How are the information needs of a bank manager (a) different from those of a manager in a department store and (b) similar to those of a manager in a department store?
10. What are the four W's of report preparation? Explain the importance of each.
11. Why are nonfinancial data analyses important to management accountants?
12. Explain how the new globally competitive marketplace has increased the demand for nonfinancial data analyses. Give examples of such analyses.
13. What areas of performance had to be strengthened for American industries to compete effectively with foreign manufacturers?
14. What four new management philosophies or approaches have developed in response to global competition?

15. How does each of the new management philosophies affect a company's operating environment?
16. What are the desired results of adopting any one of the four new management approaches?
17. What is the difference between a merchandising company and a manufacturing company, and how does it affect accounting for inventories?
18. Why are ethical standards of competence so important to the work of management accountants?
19. Why is integrity so important for management accountants to maintain?

SHORT EXERCISES

SE 1.
L O 1
No check figure

Information Needs of Managers

All managers need accurate, timely information to operate their businesses. Tell which of the following management actions require information from management accountants.

1. Decide to increase the selling price of a product
2. Decide to increase advertising costs
3. Decide to buy a new, technologically advanced piece of equipment
4. Control the disposal of waste from the production process
5. Measure the performance of the sales manager
6. Plan next year's operating activities

SE 2.
L O 2
No check figure

Management Accounting Versus Financial Accounting

Similarities and differences exist between management accounting and financial accounting. Tell whether each of the following descriptions reflects management accounting (MA), financial accounting (FA), or both (B).

1. Includes all principles that regulate accounting for and reporting information to a banker
2. Uses accounting information about revenues and expenses
3. Benefits people responsible for the day-to-day operations of a business
4. Uses accounting information about inventory costs
5. Uses nonfinancial quantitative data, such as number of pounds of wasted materials, number of customer complaints, or number of orders to change a product's design

SE 3.
L O 3
No check figure

Management Accounting Versus Financial Accounting

Management accounting differs from financial accounting in a number of ways. Tell whether each of the following characteristics relates to management accounting (MA) or financial accounting (FA).

1. Focuses on various segments of the business entity
2. Demands objectivity
3. Relies on the criterion of usefulness rather than formal guidelines or restrictions for gathering information
4. Measures units in historical dollars
5. Reports information periodically on a regular basis
6. Uses monetary measures for reports
7. Adheres to generally accepted accounting principles
8. Prepares reports whenever needed

SE 4.
L O 4
No check figure

Information Needs of Companies

Cash is very important to any kind of business, but the uses of cash vary depending on the type of venture. Think about the ways cash is used in a manufacturing company, a department store, and a bank. What uses of cash would be similar in all three kinds of operations? What uses of cash would be specific to each type of company? Give an example of a control measure that all three companies could use to avoid the misuse of cash.

SE 5.
L O 5
No check figure

Managerial Report Preparation

Anne Taylor, president of Taylor Industries, asked controller Rick Carr to prepare a report on the use of electricity by each of the company's five divisions. Increases in electricity costs had ranged from 20 to 35 percent at the divisions over the past year. What questions should Rick ask before he begins his analysis?

SE 6. *Analysis of*
L O 6 *Nonfinancial Data*

No check figure

Spectrum Technologies has been having a problem with the computerized welding operation in its dialogic extractor product line. The extractors are used to sift through and separate various types of metal shavings into piles of individual metals for recycling and scrap sales. The time for each welding operation has been increasing at an erratic rate. Management has asked that the time intervals be analyzed to see if the cause of the problem can be determined. The number of parts welded per shift during the previous week is reported below. What can you deduce from the information that may help management solve the welding operation problem?

	Machine Number	Monday	Tuesday	Wednesday	Thursday	Friday
First shift:						
Kovacs	1	642	636	625	617	602
Abington	2	732	736	735	729	738
Geisler	3	745	726	717	694	686
Second shift:						
Deragon	1	426	416	410	404	398
Berwager	2	654	656	661	664	670
Grass	3	526	524	510	504	502

SE 7. *Monitoring Product*
L O 7 *Quality*

No check figure

In a globally competitive environment, one of management's most critical needs is for accurate and timely information about product quality. Why is tracking product quality so important? What types of information would management use to monitor product quality?

SE 8. *JIT and Continuous*
L O 8 *Improvement*

No check figure

The just-in-time operating environment focuses on reducing or eliminating the waste of resources. Resources include physical assets such as machinery and buildings, labor time, and materials and parts used in the production process. Choose one of these resources and tell how it could be wasted. How can a company prevent the waste of that resource? How can the concept of continuous improvement be implemented to reduce the waste of that resource?

SE 9. *Merchandising*
L O 9 *Versus*
Manufacturing

No check figure

Based on the following information, decide whether the Vikram Company is a merchandising firm or a manufacturing firm. List reasons for your answer.

Beginning Work in Process Inventory	$3,800
Materials Used	2,350
Overhead Costs	4,250
Direct Labor Costs	1,500
Cost of Goods Sold	9,340
Ending Materials Inventory	2,430
Beginning Finished Goods Inventory	4,800
Ending Finished Goods Inventory	7,250

SE 10. *Ethical Conduct*
L O 10

No check figure

Gary Louskip, a management accountant for Pegstone Cosmetics Company, has lunch every day with his good friend Joe Blaik, a management accountant for Shepherd Cosmetics, Inc., a competitor of Pegstone. Last week, Gary couldn't decide how to treat some information in a report he was preparing, so he discussed the information with Joe. Is Gary adhering to the ethical standards of management accountants? Defend your answer.

EXERCISES

E 1. *Definitions of*
L O 1 *Management*
Accounting

No check figure

There are many definitions and descriptions of management accounting. The Institute of Management Accountants, in *Statement No. 1A* in its series *Statements on Management Accounting*, defined management accounting as

the process of identification, measurement, accumulation, analysis, preparation, interpretation, and communication of financial information used by management to plan, evaluate, and control within the organization and to assure appropriate use and accountability for its resources. Management accounting also comprises the preparation of financial reports for nonmanagement groups such as shareholders, creditors, regulatory agencies, and tax authorities.[6]

In *The Modern Accountant's Handbook,* management (managerial) accounting is described as follows:

> Managerial accounting, although generally anchored to the financial accounting framework, involves a broader information-processing system. It deals in many units of measure and produces a variety of reports designed for specific purposes. Its scope encompasses the past, the present, and the future. Its purposes include short- and long-range planning, cost determination, control of activities, assessment of objectives and program performance, and provision of basic information for decision making.[7]

1. Compare these two statements about management accounting.
2. Explain this statement: "It is impossible to distinguish the point at which financial accounting ends and management accounting begins."

E 2. *Management*
L O 2 *Information Systems*

No check figure

Members of the board of directors of Goldwater, Ltd. were discussing the cost and other considerations connected with the expansion of the company's information network. Director Charmayne Kelliher questioned the cost item entitled Expansion of Management Accounting Information System. She asked, "Mr. Goldwater, what is the difference between the management accounting information system and the management information system? Aren't they the same thing?" Paul Goldwater replied, "That's a very good question, Charmayne, but I don't know the answer. Let's ask our controller, Arleta Judd, to clarify the issue for us." Assuming that you are Arleta Judd, how would you respond to the president? (**Hint:** The response should be based around Figure 1.)

E 3. *Types of Accounting*
L O 3 *Systems*

No check figure

Many management accounting analyses are not limited by the double-entry accounting system. Two such analyses are shown below.

a. Budgeted materials purchases for March

Aluminum ingots	$ 80,000
Copper ingots	140,000
Silver ingots	500,000
Total estimated materials costs	$720,000

b. Determining an appropriate selling price for a new product

Estimated manufacturing costs per unit	$51.00
Operating expenses	
(40% of manufacturing costs)	20.40
Profit factor	
(25% of manufacturing and operating costs)	17.85
Projected selling price	$89.25

1. Do the above analyses require a journal entry to become effective?
2. When will the above information enter the general ledger?

E 4. *Management*
L O 4 *Information Needs*

No check figure

The following statement was overheard by Ann Trione, the newly appointed senior budget analyst for the Classique Corporation. The statement was made by the vice president of sales in a conversation with the controller.

> Budgets are guesswork and don't apply to salespeople. Because budgets restrict our freedom, they inhibit our sales efforts and hold down sales. Budgets should apply only to production people, who need to keep their costs down and concentrate on efficient operating plans and procedures.

Do you agree with the vice president? Defend your answer, basing your arguments on the information needs of managers.

---

6. Institute of Management Accountants, *Statement No. 1A* (New York, 1982).
7. James Don Edwards and Homer A. Black, *The Modern Accountant's Handbook* (Homewood, Ill.: Dow Jones-Irwin, 1976), p. 830.

E 5. *Report Preparation*
L O 5
No check figure

Jim Morris is the sales manager for All-Occasions Greeting Cards, Inc. At the beginning of the year, the company introduced a new line of humorous wedding cards into the U.S. market. Now management is holding a strategic planning meeting to plan next year's operating activities. One item on the agenda is to review the success of the new wedding card line and the need to change the selling price or stimulate sales volume in the five sales territories. For the October 31 meeting, Jim was asked to prepare a report addressing these issues. His report was to include profits generated in each sales territory for the wedding card line only.

On October 31 Jim arrived late at the meeting and immediately distributed his report to the members of the strategic planning team. The report consisted of comments made by seven of Jim's leading sales representatives. The comments were broad in scope and touched only lightly on the success of the new card line. Jim was pleased that he had met the deadline to distribute the report, but the other team members were disappointed in the information he had provided.

Using the four W's for report presentation, comment on Jim's effectiveness in preparing a report for the strategic planning team.

E 6. *Nonfinancial Data*
L O 6 *Analysis*
No check figure

Fairfield Landscapes, Inc. specializes in lawn installations requiring California bluegrass sod. The sod comes in 1-yard squares. The company uses the guideline of 500 square yards per person per hour to evaluate the performance of its sod layers.

During the first week of March, the following actual data were collected.

Employee	Hours Worked	Square Yards of Sod Planted
R. Crump	38	18,240
G. W. Churchill	45	22,500
J. B. Spry	40	19,800
E. E. Ma	42	17,640
H. P. Palmettos	44	22,880
F. L. Probyn	45	21,500

Evaluate the performance of the six employees.

E 7. *Classifying*
L O 7 *Performance Information*
No check figure

Mendels Company manufactures inexpensive women's clothing. Management uses numerous measures of operating efficiency to closely monitor product and process quality. An intern in the Management Accounting Department has collected the information listed below. Identify in which of the following performance areas each piece of information would be useful: product quality, product delivery, inventory control, materials/scrap control, machine maintenance, or product cost.

1. Production line workers wasted or scrapped 4,000 yards of fabric during February.
2. A dress remains unsold in finished goods inventory for an average of 60 days.
3. Sewing machines were idle a total of 300 hours in February.
4. The production process required 1 machine hour to complete each dress.
5. The sewing activity added $5 in value to each dress.
6. The cotton cloth vendor sent 200 yards of defective materials to the Atlanta plant in February.
7. Production management eliminated the need for 1,000 square feet of inventory storage space.
8. The Maintenance Department spent 70 hours repairing machines in February.
9. The company paid $70,000 to a private fashion design firm to create next year's dress lines.
10. The company received complaints about product durability from 117 customers.

E 8. *New Management*
L O 8 *Philosophies*
No check figure

Recently, you were dining with four chief financial officers who were attending a seminar on new management tools and approaches to improving operations. During dinner, they shared information about their companies' current operating environments. Excerpts from the dinner conversation are presented below. Tell whether each excerpt describes activity-based management (ABM), flexible manufacturing systems (FMS), just-in-time operations (JIT), or total quality management (TQM).

CFO #1: Our company is interested in achieving quality by focusing on the production process. We have a variety of products to manufacture, so we achieve quality by having an adaptable production process that minimizes setup downtime for products of similar size and shape.

CFO #2: Well, we also believe that quality can be achieved through carefully designed production processes. However, we have an environment in which the time to move, store, queue, and inspect materials and products is greatly reduced. We have reduced inventories by purchasing and using materials only as needed.

CFO #3: Both of your approaches are good. However, we are more concerned with our total operating environment, so we have a strategy that asks all employees to contribute to the achievement of quality, both for our products and for our production processes. We focus on eliminating poor product quality by targeting and reducing waste and inefficiencies in our current operating methods.

CFO #4: Our company has adopted a strategy for quality products that incorporates many of your approaches. We also want to manage our resources effectively, but we do so by monitoring operating activities. All activities are analyzed, and the ones that do not add value to products are reduced or eliminated.

E 9. *Balance Sheet*
L O 9 *Interpretation*
No check figure

Dosmann Corporation is located in Houston, Texas. The corporation's balance sheet at July 31 is shown below.

Dosmann Corporation
Balance Sheet
July 31, 19x7

Assets

Current Assets			
Cash		$ 16,400	
Accounts Receivable		290,000	
Materials Inventory		18,700	
Work in Process Inventory		50,600	
Finished Goods Inventory		40,400	
Prepaid Factory Insurance		23,100	
Small Tools		24,000	
Total Current Assets			$ 463,200
Machinery and Equipment			
Factory Machinery	$720,000		
Less Accumulated Depreciation	132,000	$588,000	
Office Equipment	$ 94,000		
Less Accumulated Depreciation	47,000	47,000	
Total Machinery and Equipment			635,000
Total Assets			$1,098,200

Liabilities and Stockholders' Equity

Liabilities			
Accounts Payable		$ 52,500	
Employee's Payroll Taxes Payable		36,100	
Federal Income Taxes Payable		14,000	
Total Liabilities			$ 102,600
Stockholders' Equity			
Common Stock		$750,000	
Retained Earnings, July 31, 19x7		245,600	
Total Stockholders' Equity			995,600
Total Liabilities and Stockholders' Equity			$1,098,200

1. Is Dosmann Corporation a merchandising firm or a manufacturing company?
2. Identify at least five reasons for your answer to **1**.

E 10. *Professional Ethics*
L O 10

No check figure

Kim Wallenski went to work for Vegas Industries five years ago. She was recently promoted to cost accounting manager and now has a new boss, Ted Wilcox, corporate controller. Last week, Kim and Ted went to a two-day professional development program on accounting changes in the new manufacturing environment. During the first hour of the first day's program, Ted disappeared and Kim didn't see him again until the cocktail hour. The same thing happened on the second day. During the trip home, Kim asked Ted if he enjoyed the conference. He replied:

> Kim, the golf course was excellent. You play golf. Why don't you join me during the next conference? I haven't sat in on one of those sessions in ten years. This is my R&R time. Those sessions are for the new people. My experience is enough to keep me current. Plus, I have excellent people to help me as we adjust our accounting system to the changes being implemented on the production floor.

Does Kim have an ethical dilemma? If so, what is it? What are her options? How would you solve her problem? Be prepared to defend your answer.

SKILLS DEVELOPMENT EXERCISES

Conceptual Analysis

SDE 1. *Continuous*
L O 8 *Improvement*

No check figure

Achieving high quality requires high standards of performance. And to maintain high standards of quality, individuals and companies must continuously improve their performance. To illustrate this, select your favorite sport or hobby.

1. Answer the following questions:
    a. What standards would you establish to assess your actual performance?
    b. What process would you design to achieve high quality in your performance?
    c. When do you know you have achieved high quality in your performance?
    d. Once you know you perform well, how easy would it be for you to maintain that level of expertise?
    e. What can you do to continuously improve your performance?
2. If you owned a business, which of the questions in **1** would be important to answer?
3. Answer the questions in **1,** assuming you own a business.

Ethical Dilemma

SDE 2. *Professional Ethics*
L O 10

No check figure

Roy Simons is controller for the **Atlanta Corporation.** Roy has been with the company for seventeen years and is being considered for the job of chief financial officer (CFO). His boss, the current CFO, will be Atlanta Corporation's new president. Roy has just discussed the year-end closing with his boss, who made the following statement during the conversation:

> Roy, why are you so inflexible? I'm only asking you to postpone the write-off of the $2,500,000 obsolete inventory for ten days so that it won't appear on this year's financial statements. Ten days! Do it. Your promotion is coming up, you know. Make sure you keep all the possible outcomes in mind as you complete your year-end work. Oh, and keep this conversation confidential—just between you and me. OK?

Identify the ethical issue or issues involved and state the appropriate solution to the problem. Be prepared to defend your answer.

Research Activity

SDE 3. *Management*
L O 5 *Reports*

No check figure

The registrar's office is responsible for maintaining a record of each student's grades and credits for use by students, instructors, and administrators.

1. Assume that you are a manager in the registrar's office and that you recently joined a team of managers to review the grade-reporting process. State how you would

prepare a grade report for students and a grade report for instructors by answering the following questions.

   a. Who will read the grade report?
   b. Why must the registrar's office prepare the grade report?
   c. What information should the grade report contain?
   d. When is the grade report due?

2. Why do differences exist between the information in a grade report for students and the information in a grade report for instructors?

3. Obtain a copy of your grade report and a copy of the forms the registrar's office uses to report grades to instructors at your school. Compare the information on the actual grade report forms to the information you listed in **1** above. Explain any differences.

4. What can the registrar's office do to make sure that grade reports present all necessary information in a manner that communicates effectively to users?

Decision-Making Practice

SDE 4. *Nonfinancial Data*
L O 6 *Analysis*

Check Figures: 1. Machine 1, Week 4: 46,800 lbs., 131.31%

As a subcontractor in the jet aircraft industry, *Song Street Manufacturing Company* specializes in the production of housings for landing gears on jet airplanes. Production begins on Machine 1, which bends pieces of metal into cylinder-shaped housings and trims off the rough edges. Machine 2 welds the seam of the cylinder and pushes the entire piece into a large die to mold the housing into its final shape.

Sara Mondragon, the production supervisor, believes that too much scrap (wasted metal) is created in the current process. To help her, James Deacon began preparing an analysis by comparing the amounts of actual scrap generated with the amounts of expected scrap for production in the last four weeks. His incomplete reports follows.

Song Street Manufacturing Company
Comparison of Actual Scrap and Expected Scrap
Four-Week Period

	Scrap in Pounds		Difference	
	Actual	**Expected**	**Pounds**	**Percentage**
Machine 1				
Week 1	36,720	36,720		
Week 2	54,288	36,288		
Week 3	71,856	35,856		
Week 4	82,440	35,640		
Machine 2				
Week 1	43,200	18,180		
Week 2	39,600	18,054		
Week 3	7,200	18,162		
Week 4	18,000	18,108		

Because of a death in his family, James is unable to complete the analysis. Sara asks you to complete the following tasks and submit a recommendation to her.

1. Complete the analysis by calculating the difference between the actual and the expected scrap in pounds per machine per week. Also calculate the difference as a percentage (divide the difference in pounds by the expected pounds of scrap for each week). If the actual poundage of scrap is less than the expected poundage, record the difference as a negative. (This means there is less scrap than expected.)

2. Examine the differences for the four weeks for each machine and determine which machine operation is creating excessive scrap.

3. What could cause these problems?

4. What could Sara do to identify the specific cause of such problems sooner?

PROBLEM SET A

A 1. *Approach to Report*
L O 4, 5 *Preparation*
No check figure

George Bird recently purchased Lawn & Garden Supplies, Inc., a wholesale distributor of lawn- and garden-care equipment and supplies. The company, headquartered in Baltimore, Maryland, has four distribution centers: Boston, Massachusetts; Rye, New York; Reston, Virginia; and Lawrenceville, New Jersey. The distribution centers service fourteen eastern states. Company profits were $225,400, $337,980, and $467,200 for 19x7, 19x8, and 19x9, respectively.

Shortly after purchasing the company, Mr. Bird appointed people to fill the following positions: vice president, marketing; vice president, distribution; corporate controller; and vice president, research and development. Mr. Bird has called a meeting of his management group. He wishes to create a deluxe retail lawn and garden center that would include a large, fully landscaped plant and tree nursery. The purposes of the retail center would be (1) to test equipment and supplies before selecting them for sales and distribution and (2) to showcase the effects of using the company's products. The retail center must also make a profit on sales.

REQUIRED

1. What types of information will Mr. Bird need before deciding whether to create the retail lawn and garden center?
2. One of the reports Mr. Bird needs to support his decision is an analysis of all possible plants and trees that could be planted and their ability to grow in the possible locations for the new retail center. The report would be prepared by the vice president of research and development. How would each of the four W's pertain to this report?
3. Design a format for the report in **2.**

A 2. *Nonfinancial Data*
L O 6 *Analysis:*
Manufacturing
Check Figure: 1. Cutting/Lining, average hours per pair on Monday: .25 hours

Shepherd Enterprises makes shoes for every major sport. The Awesome Shoe, one of the company's leading products, is lightweight, long wearing, and inexpensive. Production of the Awesome Shoe involves five different departments: (1) the Cutting/Lining Department, where cloth tops are cut and lined; (2) the Molding Department, where the shoe's rubber base is formed; (3) the Bonding Department, where the cloth top is bonded to the rubber base; (4) the Soling Department, where the sole is attached to the rubber base; and (5) the Finishing Department, where the shoe is trimmed, stitched, and laced.

Recently, manufacturing costs have increased for the Awesome Shoe. Controller Larry Cabby has been investigating the production process to determine the problems. Everything points to the labor hours required to make the shoe. Actual labor hours worked in a recent week are as follows.

	Actual Hours Worked					
Operation	Monday	Tuesday	Wednesday	Thursday	Friday	Total
Cutting/Lining	300	310	305	300	246	1,461
Molding	144	186	183	200	246	959
Bonding	456	434	488	450	492	2,320
Soling	408	434	366	400	492	2,100
Finishing	600	620	549	625	615	3,009

The company has estimated that the following labor hours for each department should be needed to complete a pair of Awesome Shoes: Cutting/Lining, .2 hour; Molding, .1 hour; Bonding, .4 hour; Soling, .3 hour; and Finishing, .5 hour. During the week under review, the number of Awesome Shoes produced was 1,200 pairs on Monday; 1,240 pairs on Tuesday; 1,220 pairs on Wednesday; 1,250 pairs on Thursday; and 1,230 pairs on Friday.

REQUIRED

1. Prepare an analysis to determine the average actual labor hours worked per day per pair of Awesome Shoes for each operation in the production process.
2. By comparing the average actual labor hours worked from **1** with the expected labor hours per pair of shoes per department, prepare an analysis showing the differences in each operation for each day. Identify reasons for the differences.

A 3. *Nonfinancial Data*
L O 6 *Analysis: Airport*

Check Figures: Average traffic flow: March 6–12, 21,984.14; March 13–15, 24,447.32

The Winnebago County Airport in Rockford, Illinois, has experienced increased air traffic over the past year. How passenger traffic flow is handled is important to airport management. Because of the requirement that all passengers be checked for possible weapons, passenger flow has slowed significantly. Winnebago County Airport uses eight metal detectors to screen passengers. The airport is open from 6:00 A.M. to 10:00 P.M. daily, and present machinery allows a maximum of 45,000 passengers to be checked each day.

Four of the metal detectors have been selected for special analysis to determine if additional equipment is needed or if a passenger traffic director could solve the problem. The passenger traffic director would be responsible for guiding people to different machines and instructing them on the detection process. This solution would be less expensive than acquiring new machines, so it has been decided that a suitable person will be assigned to this function on a trial basis. Management hopes this procedure will speed up passenger traffic flow by at least 10 percent. Manufacturers of the machinery have stated that each machine can handle an average of 400 passengers per hour. Data on passenger traffic through the four machines for the past ten days is shown below.

Passengers Checked by Metal Detectors

Date	Machine 1	Machine 2	Machine 3	Machine 4	Totals
March 6	5,620	5,490	5,436	5,268	21,814
March 7	5,524	5,534	5,442	5,290	21,790
March 8	5,490	5,548	5,489	5,348	21,875
March 9	5,436	5,592	5,536	5,410	21,974
March 10	5,404	5,631	5,568	5,456	22,059
March 11	5,386	5,667	5,594	5,496	22,143
March 12	5,364	5,690	5,638	5,542	22,234
March 13	5,678	6,248	6,180	6,090	24,196
March 14	5,720	6,272	6,232	6,212	24,436
March 15	5,736	6,324	6,372	6,278	24,710

In the past, passenger traffic flow at the airport has favored Machine 1 because of its location. Overflow traffic goes to Machine 2, Machine 3, and Machine 4, in that order.

The passenger traffic director, Lynn Hedlund, began her duties on March 13. If her work results in at least a 10 percent increase in passengers handled, management plans to hire a second traffic director for the remaining four machines rather than purchase additional metal detectors.

REQUIRED

1. Calculate the average daily traffic flow for the period March 6–12 and then calculate management's traffic flow goal.
2. Calculate the average traffic flow for the period March 13–15. Did the passenger traffic director pass the minimum test set by management, or should airport officials purchase additional metal detectors?
3. Is there anything unusual in the analysis of passenger traffic flow that management should look into? Explain your answer.

A 4. *Manufacturing*
L O 9 *Company Balance Sheet*

Check Figure: Total assets: $952,230

Hincks Industries, Inc. manufactures racing hubs specially designed for sports car enthusiasts. The company's balance sheet accounts at year end are shown at the top of the next page.

Closing entries have been made, but net income has been separated so that year-end financial statements can be prepared.

REQUIRED

Using the information given and the proper form, prepare a balance sheet for Hincks Industries, Inc. at December 31, 19x6. (**Hint:** Production Supplies and Small Tools are considered current assets. Patents are classified as Other Assets.)

Ledger Accounts	Debit	Credit
Cash	$ 34,000	
Accounts Receivable	27,000	
Materials Inventory, 12/31/x6	31,000	
Work in Process Inventory, 12/31/x6	47,900	
Finished Goods Inventory, 12/31/x6	54,800	
Production Supplies	5,700	
Small Tools	9,330	
Land	160,000	
Factory Building	575,000	
Accumulated Depreciation, Building		$ 199,000
Factory Equipment	310,000	
Accumulated Depreciation, Factory Equipment		137,000
Patents	33,500	
Accounts Payable		26,900
Insurance Premiums Payable		6,700
Income Taxes Payable		41,500
Mortgage Payable, due within one year		18,000
Mortgage Payable		325,000
Common Stock		200,000
Retained Earnings, 1/1/x6		196,000
Net Income for 19x6		138,130
	$1,288,230	$1,288,230

PROBLEM SET B

B 1. *Approach to Report*
L O 4, 5 *Preparation*
No check figure

St. Lawrence Industries, Inc. is deciding whether to expand its Jeans by Susette line of women's clothing. Sales in units of this product were 22,500, 28,900, and 36,200 in 19x6, 19x7, and 19x8, respectively. The product has been very profitable, averaging 35 percent profit (above cost) over the three-year period. St. Lawrence has ten sales representatives covering seven states in the Northeast. Present production capacity is about 40,000 pairs of jeans per year. There is adequate plant space for additional equipment, and the labor needed can be easily hired and trained.

The company's management is made up of four vice presidents: vice president of marketing, vice president of production, vice president of finance, and vice president of data processing. Each vice president is directly responsible to the president, Susette St. Lawrence.

REQUIRED

1. What types of information will Ms. St. Lawrence need before she can decide whether to expand the Jeans by Susette product line?
2. Assume one of the reports needed to support Ms. St. Lawrence's decision is an analysis of sales over the past three years. This analysis should be broken down by sales representative. How would each of the four W's pertain to this report?
3. Design a format for the report in **2**.

B 2. *Nonfinancial Data*
L O 6 *Analysis:*
Manufacturing
Check Figure: Molding First Shift, Week 1, hours per board: 3.50

Bathsheba Surfboards, Inc. manufactures state-of-the-art surfboards and related equipment. Chuck Russell is manager of the West Indies branch. The production process involves the following departments and tasks: (1) the Molding Department, where the board's base is molded; (2) the Sanding Department, where the base is sanded after being taken out of the mold; (3) the Fiber-Ap Department, where a fiberglass coating is applied; and (4) the Finishing Department, where a finishing coat of fiber glass is applied and the board is inspected. After the molding process, all functions are performed by hand.

Mr. Russell is concerned about the hours being worked by his employees. The West Indies branch utilizes a two-shift labor force. The actual hours worked for the past four weeks are summarized below.

Actual Hours Worked—First Shift

Department	Week #1	Week #2	Week #3	Week #4	Totals
Molding	420	432	476	494	1,822
Sanding	60	81	70	91	302
Fiber-Ap	504	540	588	572	2,204
Finishing	768	891	952	832	3,443

Actual Hours Worked—Second Shift

Department	Week #1	Week #2	Week #3	Week #4	Totals
Molding	360	357	437	462	1,616
Sanding	60	84	69	99	312
Fiber-Ap	440	462	529	506	1,937
Finishing	670	714	782	726	2,892

Expected labor hours per product for each operation are Molding, 3.4 hours; Sanding, .5 hour; Fiber-Ap, 4.0 hours; and Finishing, 6.5 hours. Actual units completed were as follows:

Week	First Shift	Second Shift
1	120	100
2	135	105
3	140	115
4	130	110

REQUIRED

1. Prepare an analysis of each week to determine the average labor hours worked per board for each phase of the production process and for each shift.
2. Using the information from **1** and the expected labor hours per board for each department, prepare an analysis showing the differences in each phase of each shift. Identify reasons for the differences.

B 3. *Nonfinancial Data*
LO 6 *Analysis: Bank*

Check Figure: Using the attachment, Machine BD sorts 42,871 more checks than average in Week 8

Colbert State Bank was founded in 1869. It has had a record of slow, steady growth since inception. Management has always kept the processing of information as current as technology allows. Leslie Oistins, manager of the Paynes Bay branch, is upgrading the check-sorting equipment in her office. There are ten check-sorting machines in operation. Information on the number of checks sorted by machine for the past eight weeks is summarized below.

	Weeks							
Machine	One	Two	Three	Four	Five	Six	Seven	Eight
AA	89,260	89,439	89,394	90,288	90,739	90,658	90,676	90,630
AB	91,420	91,237	91,602	91,969	91,950	92,502	92,446	92,816
AC	94,830	95,020	94,972	95,922	96,401	96,315	96,334	96,286
AD	91,970	91,786	92,153	92,522	92,503	93,058	93,002	93,375
AE	87,270	87,445	87,401	88,275	88,716	88,636	88,654	88,610
BA	92,450	92,265	92,634	93,005	92,986	93,544	93,488	93,862
BB	91,910	92,094	92,048	92,968	93,433	93,349	93,368	93,321
BC	90,040	89,860	90,219	90,580	90,562	91,105	91,051	91,415
BD	87,110	87,190	87,210	130,815	132,320	133,560	134,290	135,770
BE	94,330	94,519	94,471	95,416	95,893	95,807	95,826	95,778

The Paynes Bay branch has increased its checking business significantly over the past two years. Ms. Oistins must decide whether to purchase additional check-sorting machines or attachments for the existing machines to increase productivity. Five weeks ago the Colonnade Company convinced her to experiment with one such attachment, and it was placed on Machine BD. Ms. Oistins is impressed with the attachment but has yet to decide between the two courses of action.

REQUIRED

1. If the Colonnade Company attachment costs about the same as a new check-sorting machine, which alternative should Ms. Oistins choose?
2. Would you change your recommendation if two attachments could be purchased for the price of one check-sorting machine?
3. If three attachments could be purchased for the price of one check-sorting machine, what action would you recommend?

(Show computations to support your answers.)

B 4.
L O 9
Manufacturing Company Balance Sheet

Check Figure: Total assets: $995,000

The analysis below shows the balance sheet accounts at Harrison Manufacturing Company after closing entries were made. Net income for the year is identified for the purposes of report preparation.

Ledger Accounts	Debit	Credit
Cash	$ 26,000	
Accounts Receivable	30,000	
Materials Inventory, 12/31/x7	42,000	
Work in Process Inventory, 12/31/x7	27,400	
Finished Goods Inventory, 12/31/x7	52,700	
Production Supplies and Tools	8,600	
Land	200,000	
Factory Building	400,000	
Accumulated Depreciation, Building		$ 110,000
Factory Equipment	250,000	
Accumulated Depreciation, Equipment		72,000
Sales Warehouse	148,000	
Accumulated Depreciation, Warehouse		35,000
Patents	27,300	
Accounts Payable		29,800
Property Taxes Payable		12,000
Income Taxes Payable		60,000
Mortgage Payable, due in one year		20,000
Mortgage Payable		380,000
Common Stock		260,000
Retained Earnings, 1/1/x7		100,000
Net Income for 19x7		133,200
	$1,212,000	$1,212,000

REQUIRED

Using the information in the analysis and proper form, prepare a balance sheet for the Harrison Manufacturing Company at December 31, 19x7. (**Hint:** Production Supplies and Tools is a current asset. Patents is classified as Other Assets.)

MANAGERIAL REPORTING AND ANALYSIS CASES

Interpreting Management Reports

MRA 1.
L O 7
Management Information Needs

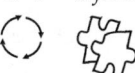

No check figure

Obtain a copy of a recent annual report for a publicly held company in which you have a particular interest. (Copies of annual reports are available at your campus library, a local public library, or by direct request to a company.) Assume that you have just been appointed to a middle-management position in a division of the company you have chosen. You are interested in obtaining information that will help you better manage the activities of your division and have decided to thoroughly review the contents of the annual report in an attempt to learn as much as possible. You particularly want to know about:

1. Size of inventory maintained
2. Ability to earn income
3. Reliance on debt financing
4. Types, volume, and prices of products sold
5. Type of production process used
6. Management's long-range strategies
7. Success (profitability) of the division's various product lines
8. Efficiency of operations
9. Operating details of your division

REQUIRED

1. Write a brief description of the company and its products, services, or activities.
2. From a review of the financial statements and the accompanying disclosure footnotes, prepare a written summary of the information you found that pertained to items **1** through **9** above.
3. Is any of the information you seek in other sections of the annual report? If so, which information, and where is it found?
4. The annual report also includes other types of information you may find helpful in your new position. In outline form, summarize the additional information you think will help you.

Formulating Management Reports

MRA 2.
L O 5, 7
Management Information Needs

No check figure

In MRA 1, you examined your new employer's annual report and noted some useful information. You still wish to find out if your new division's products are competitive, but cannot find the necessary information in the annual report.

REQUIRED

1. What kinds of information do you want to know about your competition?
2. Why is this information relevant? (Link your response to a particular decision about your company's products. For example, you might seek information to help you determine a new selling price.)
3. From what sources could you obtain the information you need?
4. When would you want to obtain this information?
5. Create a report that will communicate your findings to your superior.

International Company

MRA 3.
L O 5, 6, 7
Management Information Needs

No check figure

McDonald's is the leading competitor in the fast-food restaurant business. Forty percent of McDonald's restaurants are located outside the United States. One component of McDonald's marketing strategy is to increase sales by expanding its foreign markets. The company uses financial and nonfinancial as well as quantitative and qualitative information in making decisions about new restaurant locations in foreign markets. For example, the following types of information would be important to such a decision: the cost of a new building (financial quantitative information), the estimated number of hamburgers to be sold in the first year (nonfinancial quantitative information), and site desirability (qualitative information).

REQUIRED

You are a member of a management team that must decide whether or not to open a new restaurant in France. Identify at least two examples each of the (a) financial quantitative, (b) nonfinancial quantitative, and (c) qualitative information you will need before you can make a decision.

CHAPTER 16 — *Operating Costs and Cost Allocation*

LEARNING OBJECTIVES

1. Distinguish between the cost of a manufactured versus a purchased product and state how managers use product costs.

2. Define and give examples of the three elements of manufacturing cost—direct materials costs, direct labor costs, and factory overhead costs—and identify the source documents used to collect information about those costs.

3. Compute a product's unit cost.

4. Describe the contents of and the flow of costs through the Materials Inventory, Work in Process Inventory, and Finished Goods Inventory accounts.

5. Identify various approaches to cost classification and show how the purpose of a cost analysis can change the classification of a single cost item.

6. Prepare a statement of cost of goods manufactured and an income statement for a manufacturing company.

7. Apply costing concepts to a service business.

8. Define *cost allocation* and state the role of cost objectives in the cost allocation process.

9. Allocate common costs to joint products.

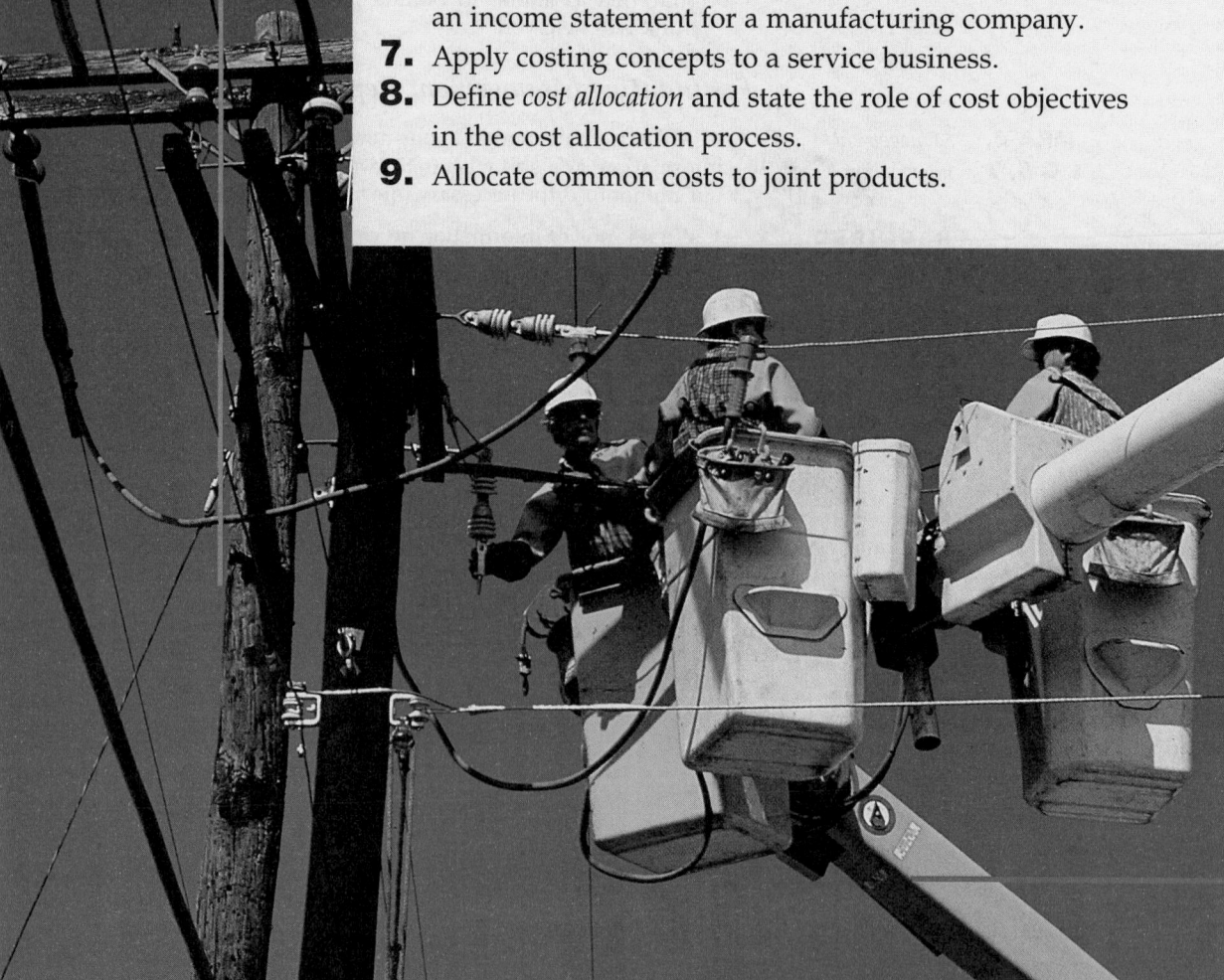

DECISION POINT Southwestern Bell Telephone Co.[1]

The telecommunications industry has had cost allocation problems since the National Bell Company was formed by Alexander Graham Bell in 1879. Even the 1984 breakup of the Bell System into many smaller local companies did not solve the cost allocation problems. Allocating the costs of basic telephone equipment to the categories of service provided by the Bell companies is the focus of the problems. Such costs are indirect and are common to two or more categories of service. In most cases, they have been allocated arbitrarily. Because rates are based on cost of service, accurately allocating indirect costs to the various telephone services is very important.

Telecommunications costs are classified as either nontraffic-sensitive (NTS) or traffic-sensitive (TS). NTS costs include the costs of the subscriber lines running between the telephone user and the local Bell exchange company's switching equipment that transfer calls between customers. Also included are the costs of executive compensation, business office costs, and general accounting. NTS costs behave like fixed costs. TS costs are incurred by providing services that have a direct relationship to the number of messages or volume of traffic handled by a local or regional network. TS costs are either variable or semivariable and can be traced directly to the three service classifications—interstate toll, intrastate toll, and local service—that generate the costs. How would you allocate NTS costs to the three services?

Because costs should be allocated fairly—not arbitrarily—based on benefits received, NTS costs should be linked with the three service categories by a benefits-received connection. Southwestern Bell Telephone Co., for example, uses minutes of line usage. The company determines the number of minutes a subscriber uses the telecommunications equipment and then divides the total into the minutes of usage for each of the three service categories. If, for instance, 10 percent of usage is traced to interstate toll calls, 10 percent of NTS costs would be allocated to that service category.

1. Based on J. Patrick Cardello and Richard A. Moellenberndt, "The Cost Allocation Problem in a Telecommunications Company," *Management Accounting*, Institute of Management Accountants, September 1987, pp. 39–44.

PRODUCTS AND THEIR COSTS

1 *Distinguish between the cost of a manufactured versus a purchased product and state how managers use product costs*

To make a profit means to sell something for more than its total cost. This fundamental principle underlies the free-enterprise system and the profit objective. Without knowing the accurate cost of a product or service, management has difficulty in establishing prices that will yield a profit and still be attractive to customers. But computing the accurate cost of a product is not an easy task. Over the past century, accountants have used several methods of tracking costs of products and services, and each new method has increased the accuracy of the results. New approaches continue to be developed and tested as management accounting pushes for continuous improvement in this important area. As you begin your study of product costing, keep in mind that it is not a precisely defined technique but a dynamic process that is continuously changing.

Computing the cost of a purchased product should be an easy task. The company buys a product and pays the vendor the agreed purchase price. The cost of that product has been established . . . or has it? For example, Gray Furniture Store recently purchased 48 recliners for resale in its downtown New Orleans store. A check for $4,560 was issued to the vendor. The cost of each chair was $95 ($4,560 ÷ 48). But the process of computing the total cost of the chairs goes beyond the initial purchase price. True, the $95 will be used to value the chairs in inventory when financial statements are prepared. But there are a number of supporting costs incurred by Gray Furniture to market the chairs: salespersons' commissions, rent or mortgage payments, display cases and showrooms, warehouse costs, office employees' salaries, delivery costs, advertising costs, and display area cleaning costs. Before the company can make a profit, all those costs have to be recovered through the selling price of the furniture. The total cost of a purchased product includes its purchase price plus a portion of the cost of all supporting services needed to market and deliver the product and keep the business running effectively. Product costing techniques are used for this purpose.

The cost of a manufactured product is even more difficult to compute. Instead of purchasing a product ready for resale, a manufacturing company purchases raw materials, parts used in assembly operations, and labor services from employees. Using specially designed machinery and manufacturing processes, the employees shape and assemble a finished product. The cost of the manufactured product includes the prices paid for the raw materials and parts, wages paid to the factory workers, costs of the machinery, supervisory costs, product design costs, and the cost of utilities used within the factory. In addition, as was the case with the purchased product, costs of marketing, distribution, and customer service must be included in the product's total cost. The process of tracking all those costs to specific products is difficult and can vary depending on the product, industry, plant location, and management structure.

Managers use product costing information in several important ways. We have already touched on two of them—the pricing of a product or service and inventory valuation. Managers use product costs as one method of establishing the price for a product. A profit is made only when the selling price exceeds the total cost of the product. Accurate product or service costs lead to realistic prices. The inventory valuation of a purchased product is the actual amount paid for the product. The costs of marketing and delivery are not included in the inventoried amount. For a manufactured product, all costs incurred to get a finished product ready for sale are included in the inventory value of unsold products.

Public utilities, such as San Diego Electric & Gas Company, are regulated by a state agency and use product cost information to establish rates. The electric and gas rates they charge their customers must be within specific guidelines set by that agency. The companies have a right to recover all their costs plus earn a certain percentage for profit. If their cost data understate the amount of a product's cost, their rates will be too low and they will not earn the desired profit. Excessive rates, if detected by the agency, will result in fines and penalties. Therefore, public utilities track all costs very carefully.

Managers also use product costs of the current period to plan for future production of similar products and to help in the design of new product lines. Accurate product costs help in cost control too. If competition is high and the market is driving prices down, the required price may fall below a company's current cost levels. To stay competitive, management will direct the accountant to analyze every cost being incurred to see where costs can be cut without hurting product quality.

Determining the accurate cost of a product or service is difficult in almost any business setting. But without accurate costing information, a company's profits can be seriously eroded and losses can arise. If a company experiences continued losses, it will eventually go bankrupt. The remainder of this chapter will introduce important concepts and techniques used in product costing.

ELEMENTS OF MANUFACTURING COST

OBJECTIVE

2 *Define and give examples of the three elements of manufacturing cost—direct materials costs, direct labor costs, and factory overhead costs—and identify the source documents used to collect information about those costs*

Manufacturing costs include all costs related to the production process. They can be classified in many ways. The most common scheme groups them into one of three classes: (1) direct materials costs, (2) direct labor costs, or (3) indirect manufacturing costs, which often are called *factory overhead.* Direct costs can be easily traced to specific products. Indirect costs must be assigned to products by a cost assignment method.

DIRECT MATERIALS COSTS

All manufactured products are made from basic direct materials. The basic material may be iron ore for steel, sheet steel for automobiles, or flour for bread. Direct materials are materials that become part of a finished product and can be conveniently and economically traced to specific product units. The costs of such materials are direct costs. In some cases, however, even though a material becomes part of a finished product, the expense of actually tracing its cost is too great. Some examples include nails in furniture, bolts in automobiles, and rivets in airplanes. Minor materials and other production supplies that cannot be conveniently or economically traced to specific products are accounted for as indirect materials. Indirect materials costs are part of factory overhead costs, which are discussed later in this chapter.

The way a company buys, stores, and uses materials is important. Timely purchasing is important because if the company runs out of materials, the manufacturing process will be forced to shut down. Shutting down production results in no products, unhappy customers, and loss of sales and profits. Buying too many direct materials, on the other hand, can lead to high storage costs.

Proper storage of materials will avoid waste and spoilage. Adequate storage space and orderly storage procedures are essential. Materials must be handled and stored properly to guarantee their satisfactory use in production. Proper records make it possible to find goods easily. Such records reduce problems caused by lost or misplaced items.

Direct Materials Purchases   Direct materials are a sizable expenditure each year, so special care must be taken in purchasing them. A company should buy proper amounts and ensure that it receives quality goods. An efficient purchasing system uses several important documents to account for direct materials purchases. The purchase requisition (or *purchase request*) is used to begin the materials purchasing process. The requisition describes the items to be purchased and the quantities needed. It must be approved by a qualified manager or supervisor.

From the information on the purchase requisition, the purchasing department prepares a formal purchase order. Some copies of the purchase order are sent to the vendor or supplier; the remaining copies are kept for internal use. When the ordered goods are received, a receiving report is prepared and matched against the descriptions and quantities listed on the purchase order. Usually, the materials are inspected for inferior quality or damage as soon as they arrive. The purchasing process is complete when the company gets an invoice from the vendor and approves it for payment.

Direct Materials Usage   Controlling direct materials costs does not end with the receipt and inspection of purchased goods. The materials must be stored in a safe place. It is important to keep the materials storage areas clean and orderly and to lock up valuable items. Regular physical counts are necessary to see how many units are on hand and to test the inventory accounting system. Materials should be issued to production only when an approved materials requisition form is presented to the storeroom clerk. The materials requisition form, shown in Figure 1, is essential for controlling direct materials. Besides providing the supervisor's approval signature, the materials requisition describes the types and quantities of goods needed and received.

DIRECT LABOR COSTS

Labor services are, in essence, purchased from employees working in the factory. In addition, other types of labor are purchased from people and organizations outside the company. The labor costs in a manufacturing operation are usually associated with machine operators; maintenance workers; managers and supervisors; support personnel; and people who handle, inspect, and store materials. Because these people are all connected in some way with the production process, their wages and salaries must be accounted for as production costs and, finally, as costs of products. However, tracing many of these costs directly to individual products is difficult.

To help overcome this problem, the wages of machine operators and other workers involved in actually shaping the product are classified as direct labor costs. Direct labor costs include all labor costs for specific work that can be conveniently and economically traced to an end product. Labor costs for production-related activities that cannot be conveniently and economically traced to an end product are called indirect labor costs. These costs include the wages and salaries of such workers as machine helpers, supervisors, and other support personnel. Like indirect materials costs, indirect labor costs are accounted for as factory overhead costs.

Figure 1. A Materials Requisition Form

Benton Publishing Company
Boston, Massachusetts

Materials Requisition

No. 49621

Charge to Job No. __14-629__

Requested by __Jim MacKenzie__ Date __4/27/x7__

Department __Binding__

Part Number	Description	Quantity Requested	Quantity Issued	Unit Cost	Total Cost
16T	Glue	140 gallons	60 gallons	$12.40	$744.00

Issued by __L. Yates__
Approved by __A. Bailey__
Received by __Jim MacKenzie__   Date Received __5/1/x7__

Labor Documentation   Records of labor time are important to both the employee and the company. The employee wants to be paid at the correct rate for all hours worked. The company does not want to underpay or overpay its employees. In addition, management wants a record of hours worked on products or batches of products made during the period. For these reasons, accounting for wages and salaries requires careful attention.

The basic record of time is called an employee time card. A time card shows an employee's daily starting and finishing times as recorded by the supervisor or a time clock. Normally, a company uses another set of cards to help verify the time recorded on the time cards and to keep track of labor costs per job or batch of goods produced. These documents, called job cards, record the time spent by an employee on a particular job. Each eight-hour period recorded on a time card may be supported by several job cards. Special job cards also record machine downtime, which may stem from machine repair or product design changes. Job cards verify the time worked by each employee and help control labor time per job.

Gross Versus Net Payroll   Accounting for direct and indirect labor costs often causes misunderstanding. People sometimes confuse gross payroll with net payroll. For internal accounting, gross wages and salaries are used. Net payroll is the amount paid to employees after all payroll deductions have been subtracted from gross wages. Payroll deductions, such as those for federal income taxes and social security tax, are paid by the employee. The employer just withholds them and pays them to the government and other organizations for the employee. Gross payroll is the total wages and salaries earned by employees, including payroll deductions. Gross payroll is used to compute total manufacturing costs and must be accounted for as a cost of production and assigned to products or jobs. The following example shows the difference between the gross and net payroll for an individual.

Gross wages earned		
40 hours at $10/hour		$400.00
Less deductions		
Federal income taxes withheld	$82.50	
FICA and Medicare taxes withheld	26.00	
U.S. government savings bond	37.50	
Union dues	12.50	
Insurance premiums	21.00	
Total deductions		179.50
Net wages paid (amount of check)		$220.50

The employee receives net wages of only $220.50, even though the company pays $400.00 in wages and deductions. The amounts withheld from the employee's gross wages are paid by the company to the taxing agencies, savings plan, union, and insurance companies.

Labor-Related Costs   Other labor-related manufacturing costs fall into two categories: employee benefits and employer payroll taxes. Employee benefits are considered part of an employee's compensation package. They may include paid vacations, holiday and sick pay, and a pension plan. Other benefits might be life and medical insurance, performance bonuses, profit sharing, and recreational facilities.

Besides the payroll taxes paid by the employee, there are payroll-related taxes paid by the employer. For every dollar of social security tax withheld from an employee's paycheck, the employer usually pays an equal amount. The company must also pay state and federal unemployment compensation taxes. Agreements between management and labor as well as government regulations are sources of some labor-related costs. Management may voluntarily spend other money for the benefit of its employees.

Most labor-related costs are incurred in direct proportion to wages and salaries earned by employees. As much as possible, labor-related costs that are dependent on direct labor costs and conveniently traceable to them should be accounted for as part of direct labor. All other labor-related costs should be classified as factory overhead. However, because of the size and complexity of payroll systems, most labor-related costs are not traced to individual employees. Such costs are normally calculated from wages and salaries by means of a predetermined rate based on past experience. For instance, a company may incur twelve cents of labor-related costs for every dollar of wages and salaries earned by employees. In this case labor-related costs average 12 percent of labor costs. Therefore, if direct labor totaled $6,000 for a period of time, the total direct labor cost would be $6,720 ($6,000 plus 12 percent, or $720, in labor-related costs). The total indirect labor cost could be computed in the same manner.

FACTORY OVERHEAD

The third element of manufacturing cost includes all manufacturing costs that cannot be classified as direct materials or direct labor costs. Factory overhead costs are a varied collection of production-related costs that cannot be practically or conveniently traced directly to an end product. This collection of costs is also called *manufacturing overhead, factory burden,* or *indirect manufacturing costs.* Examples of the major classifications of factory overhead costs are:

Indirect materials and supplies: nails, rivets, lubricants, and small tools

Indirect labor costs: lift-truck driver's wages, maintenance and inspection labor, engineering labor, machine helpers, and supervisors

Other indirect factory costs: building maintenance, machinery and tool maintenance, property taxes, property insurance, pension costs, depreciation on plant and equipment, rent expense, and utilities expense

Overhead Cost Behavior   Cost behavior is an important concept in management accounting. Manufacturing costs tend either to rise and fall with the volume of production or to stay the same within certain ranges of output. Variable manufacturing costs increase or decrease in direct proportion to the number of units produced. Examples include direct materials costs, direct labor costs, indirect materials and supply costs, most indirect labor costs, and small-tool costs.

Production costs that stay fairly constant during the accounting period are called fixed manufacturing costs. Even with changes in output, these costs tend to stay the same. Examples of fixed manufacturing costs are fire insurance premiums, factory rent, supervisors' salaries, and depreciation on machinery. Some costs are called *semivariable* because part of the cost is fixed and part varies with usage. Telephone charges (basic charge plus long-distance charges) and utility charges are generally semivariable.

Overhead Cost Allocation   A cost is classified as a factory overhead cost when it cannot be directly traced to an end product. Yet a product's total cost must include factory overhead costs. Somehow factory overhead costs must be identified with and assigned to specific products or jobs. Because direct materials and direct labor costs are traceable to products, assigning their costs to units of output is relatively easy. Factory overhead costs, however, must be assigned to products by some cost allocation method. Cost allocation methods are explained later in this chapter.

COST ELEMENTS, DOCUMENTS, AND THE ACCOUNTING SYSTEM

Looking at the way the three elements of manufacturing cost and their source documents relate to the accounting system provides an excellent opportunity to again compare and contrast the financial accounting and management accounting systems. Table 1 identifies the transactions and documents for each of the three cost elements and shows how each corresponding group of events is reflected in both the financial and the management accounting systems. The purchase of materials starts with the preparation of a purchase requisition, which must be approved by a designated manager before the purchase order is prepared and sent to the vendor. This series of events is not recorded in the financial accounting system because a financial transaction has not occurred. The management accountant, however, must update the purchase order file. When the goods arrive, they are counted, a receiving report is completed, and the quantities are checked against the original purchase order and the vendor's packing list. Subsequently, the vendor's invoice is received. These events affect the financial accounting system because the increase in materials inventory and the increase in accounts payable must be

Table 1. Manufacturing Cost Elements, Their Documents, and the Accounting System

Transaction and Document	Financial Accounting System	Management Accounting System
Materials		
Purchase requisition approval Purchase order (PO) to vendor	No input to system	Purchase order file updated
Goods arrive Receiving report prepared Report checked against PO Vendor invoice received	Recorded in Materials Inventory; recorded in Accounts Payable	Inventory quantities file updated
Materials requisition approval Materials put into production	Recorded out of Materials Inventory; recorded in Work in Process Inventory	Quantities and costs tracked to job, activity, or process
Labor		
Time card preparation Worker and manager payroll preparation Checks issued	Worker payment recorded as direct labor; manager payment recorded as factory overhead; all accruals recorded	Labor time records updated
Job card preparation Job cards verified against time cards	Direct labor charged to Work in Process Inventory; indirect labor charged to Factory Overhead	Direct labor hours and cost identified with job, activity, or process; indirect labor applied to job, activity, or process
Factory Overhead		
Vendors' invoices for items in factory overhead for utilities, outside labor, supplies, rent, etc.	Checks issued; amounts recorded in respective subsidiary accounts; amounts recorded in Factory Overhead account	Costs assigned to job, activity, or process

recorded. At the same time, the inventory quantities file is updated in the management accounting system.

Nothing that has happened thus far has directly affected the manufacturing process. When materials are requisitioned into production, however, the manufacturing cost flow begins through the Work in Process Inventory account. The materials requisition is prepared, approved by a designated manager, and used to support the movement of materials from storage into the production process. This transaction generates an entry that reduces the Materials Inventory account and increases the Work in Process Inventory account. In the management accounting system, the quantities and costs of materials are tracked to the appropriate job, activity, or process.

Labor involves two different groups of transactions: (1) those that provide payment to the workers and managers and (2) those that link the direct and indirect labor costs to the proper work effort. In the first group, a time card is prepared by each worker, workers' and managers' wages and salaries are computed, and paychecks are issued. This group of transactions is recorded in the financial accounting system by charging the Direct Labor account for the direct labor costs, charging the Factory Overhead account for the indirect labor amounts, and recording all employee deductions in the accrued liability accounts. These transactions do not require any input into the management accounting system. Each worker prepares job cards to identify the jobs on which they worked. The number of hours reported by the workers is verified by comparing the job cards with the respective time cards. In the financial accounting system, the direct labor is transferred to the Work in Process Inventory account and the indirect labor is charged to the Factory Overhead account. The management accounting system identifies and traces the direct and indirect labor costs to specific jobs, activities, or processes.

Factory overhead costs that require cash payments usually begin with the receipt of a supply or service and a vendor's invoice. Examples given in Table 1 include costs of utilities, outside labor, supplies, and rent. Such amounts are paid by check, recorded in their respective subsidiary accounts, and recorded as factory overhead in the financial accounting system. In the management accounting system, the factory overhead costs are assigned to specific jobs, activities, or processes. All of the preceding transactions that affect the production process will be illustrated in the cost flow section of this chapter.

OBJECTIVE

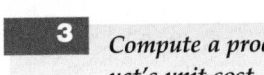

Compute a product's unit cost

DETERMINING UNIT COST

Direct materials costs, direct labor costs, and factory overhead costs constitute total manufacturing costs for a period of time or batch of products. The product unit cost for each completed job is computed by dividing the total cost of direct materials, direct labor, and factory overhead for that job by the total units produced. For example, assume that Howard Products, Inc., produced 3,000 units of output for Job 12K. Costs for Job 12K included direct materials, $3,000; direct labor, $5,400; and factory overhead, $2,700. The product unit cost for Job 12K is $3.70.

Direct materials ($3,000 ÷ 3,000 units)	$1.00
Direct labor ($5,400 ÷ 3,000 units)	1.80
Factory overhead ($2,700 ÷ 3,000 units)	.90
Product unit cost ($11,100 ÷ 3,000 units)	$3.70

In this case, the unit cost was computed when the job ended, when all information was known. What if a company needs this information a month before a job starts, perhaps because it is pricing a proposed product for a customer? Here, unit cost figures have to be estimated. Assume that accounting personnel have developed the following estimates for another product: $2.50 per unit for direct materials, $4.50 per unit for direct labor, and 50 percent of direct labor costs for factory overhead. The estimated unit cost would be $9.25.

Direct materials	$2.50
Direct labor	4.50
Factory overhead ($4.50 × 50%)	2.25
Product unit cost	$9.25

The $9.25 unit cost is an estimate, but it is still useful for job costing and as a starting point for product pricing decisions.

BUSINESS BULLETIN: TECHNOLOGY IN PRACTICE

Technology and new manufacturing processes of the 1990s have produced entirely new patterns of product costs. The three elements of product cost are still materials, labor, and factory overhead. However, the percentage of each element to the total cost of a product has changed.

During the 1950s, 1960s, and 1970s, labor was the dominant cost element, making up over 40 percent of total product cost. Direct materials contributed 35 percent and factory overhead around 25 percent of total cost. Seventy-five percent of total product cost was a direct cost, traceable to the product. Improved production technology caused a dramatic shift in the three product cost elements. People were replaced by machines, and direct labor was reduced significantly. Today, only 50 percent of the cost of a product is directly traceable to the product; the other 50 percent is factory overhead, an indirect cost.

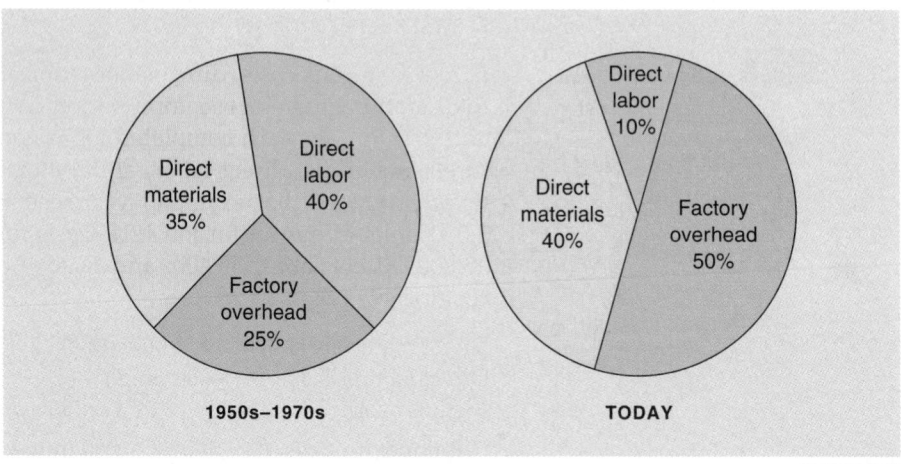

MANUFACTURING INVENTORY ACCOUNTS

OBJECTIVE

4 *Describe the contents of and the flow of costs through the Materials Inventory, Work in Process Inventory, and Finished Goods Inventory accounts*

Most manufacturing companies use the perpetual inventory system. In the remainder of this book, you should assume that a company uses the perpetual inventory system unless otherwise indicated. Accounting for inventories is more complicated in manufacturing accounting than in merchandising accounting. Instead of dealing with one inventory account—Merchandise Inventory—manufacturing accounting traditionally uses three accounts: Materials Inventory, Work in Process Inventory, and Finished Goods Inventory.

MATERIALS INVENTORY

The Materials Inventory account, also called the *Stores, Raw Materials Inventory,* or *Materials Inventory Control* account, is made up of the balances of materials, parts, and supplies on hand. This account is maintained in much the same way as the Merchandise Inventory account. The main difference is in the way the costs of items in inventory are assigned. For a manufacturing company, materials, parts, and supplies are purchased for use in the production of a product; they are not purchased for direct resale. When a direct material is taken out of materials inventory and requisitioned into production, its cost is transferred to the Work in Process Inventory account. Figure 2 shows how the transfer works. On January 1, 19xx, the Materials Inventory account had a beginning balance of $17,500. Over the year, purchases totaled $142,600; this amount was debited to the account. During 19xx, goods costing $139,700 were requisitioned into production. This transaction was accounted for by debiting the Work in Process Inventory account and crediting the Materials Inventory account for the amount requisitioned. At the end of the period, the balance in the Materials Inventory account was $20,400 ($17,500 + $142,600 − $139,700).

WORK IN PROCESS INVENTORY

All manufacturing costs incurred and assigned to products being produced are transferred to the Work in Process Inventory account. This inventory account has no counterpart in merchandise accounting. Figure 3 shows activity in the account over the year.

The beginning balance in the account was $21,200. The production process begins as materials are requisitioned into production. The materials must be cut, molded, assembled, or in some other way changed into a finished product. To do this, people, machines, and other factory resources (buildings, electricity, supplies, and so on) are used. The use of resources results in the three kinds of manufacturing costs, which are accumulated in the

Figure 2. Accounting for Materials Inventory

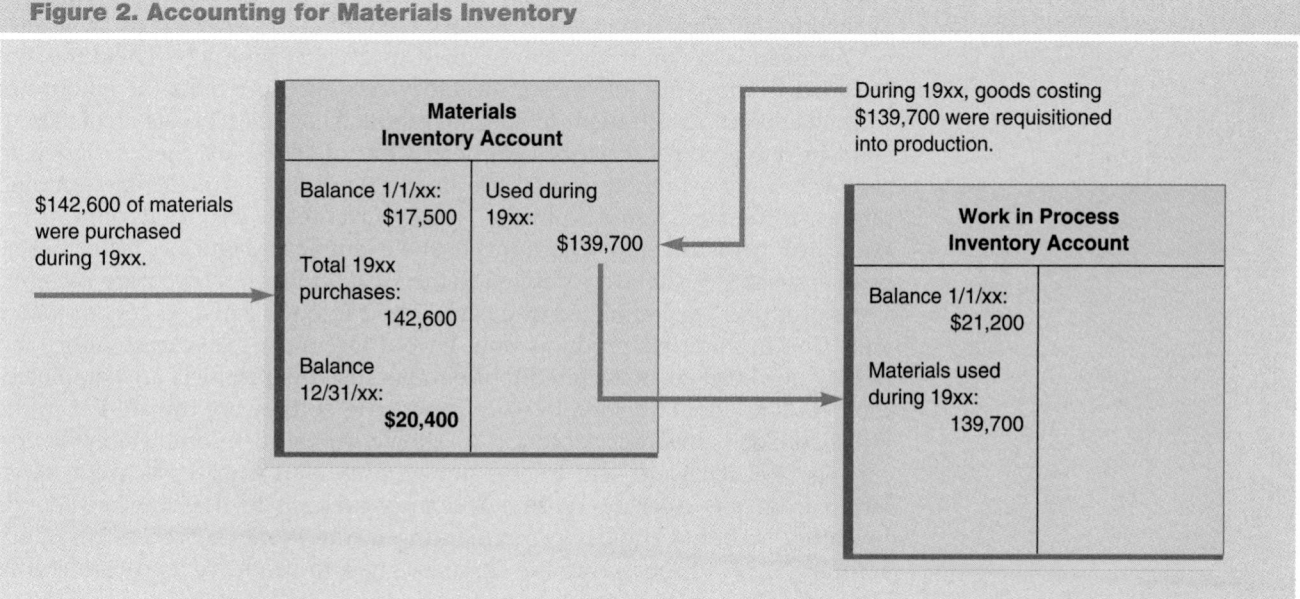

Figure 3. Accounting for Work in Process Inventory

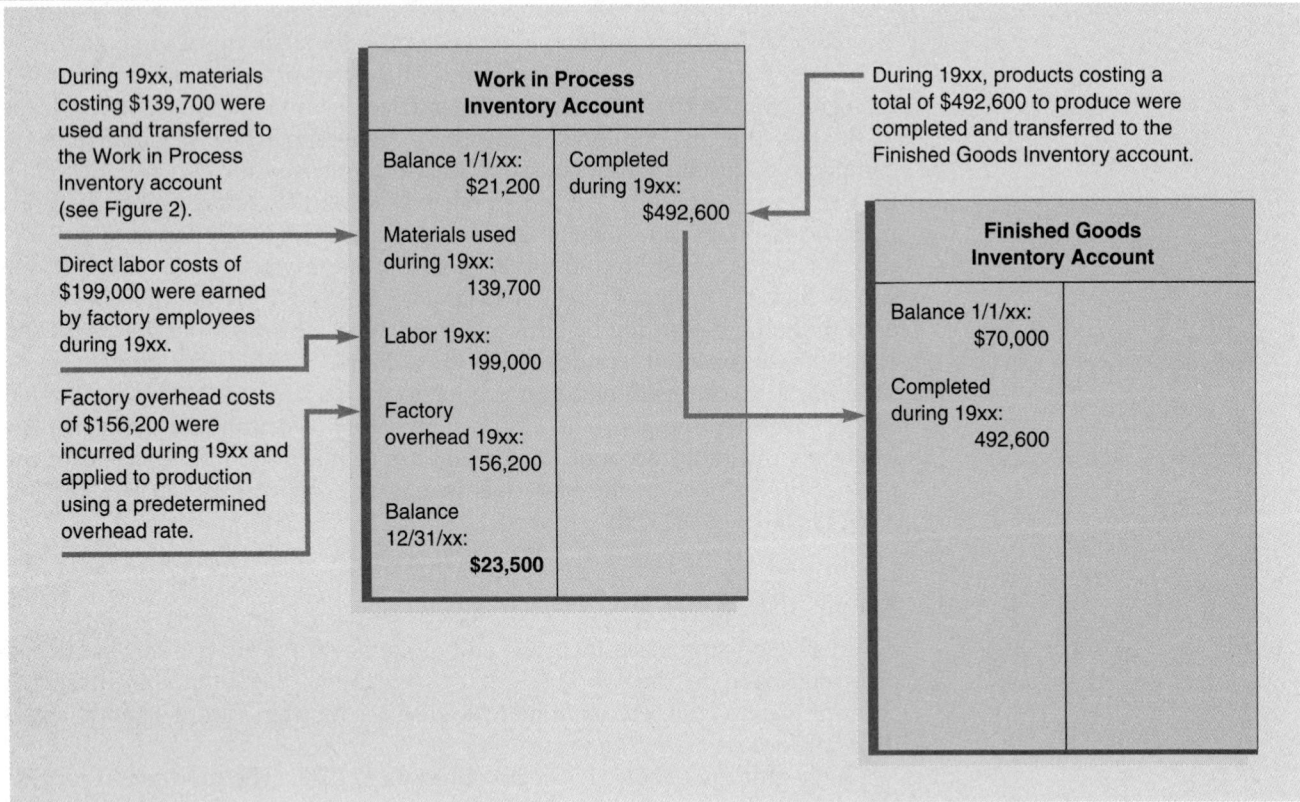

During 19xx, materials costing $139,700 were used and transferred to the Work in Process Inventory account (see Figure 2).

Direct labor costs of $199,000 were earned by factory employees during 19xx.

Factory overhead costs of $156,200 were incurred during 19xx and applied to production using a predetermined overhead rate.

Work in Process Inventory Account

Balance 1/1/xx: $21,200	Completed during 19xx: $492,600
Materials used during 19xx: 139,700	
Labor 19xx: 199,000	
Factory overhead 19xx: 156,200	
Balance 12/31/xx: **$23,500**	

During 19xx, products costing a total of $492,600 to produce were completed and transferred to the Finished Goods Inventory account.

Finished Goods Inventory Account

| Balance 1/1/xx: $70,000 | |
| Completed during 19xx: 492,600 | |

Work in Process Inventory account. The materials cost flow, a total of $139,700, was debited to the Work in Process Inventory account as shown in Figure 3.

Direct labor dollars earned by factory employees are also product costs. Because the employees work on specific products, their labor costs are assigned to those products by including the labor dollars earned as part of the Work in Process Inventory account. As shown in Figure 3, direct labor costs of $199,000 were earned by factory employees during 19xx and were debited to the Work in Process Inventory account.

Overhead costs must also be assigned to specific products. They, too, are included in the Work in Process Inventory account. To reduce the amount of work needed to assign them to specific products, overhead costs are accumulated in one account, Factory Overhead Control. They are then assigned to products using a predetermined overhead rate. Based on the predetermined rate, costs are transferred from the Factory Overhead Control account to the Work in Process Inventory account. In the example in Figure 3, factory overhead costs of $156,200 were debited to the Work in Process Inventory account.

As products are completed, they are moved into the finished goods storage area. The inventoried products now have direct materials, direct labor, and factory overhead costs assigned to them. Because the products are completed, their costs no longer belong to work in process, so they are transferred to the Finished Goods Inventory account. As shown in Figure 3, completed products costing $492,600 were sent to the storage area, and their costs were transferred from the Work in Process Inventory account to the Finished Goods Inventory account. The balance remaining in the Work in Process Inventory account ($23,500) represents the costs assigned to products that were still in process at the end of the period.

Figure 4. Accounting for Finished Goods Inventory

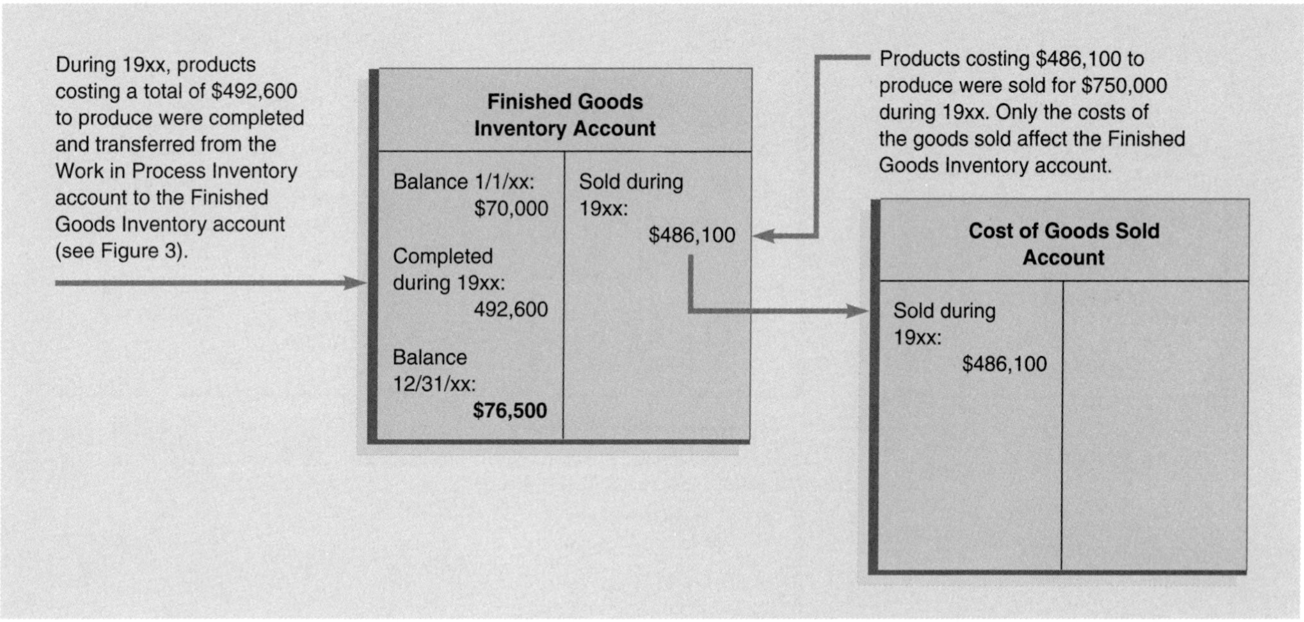

During 19xx, products costing a total of $492,600 to produce were completed and transferred from the Work in Process Inventory account to the Finished Goods Inventory account (see Figure 3).

Finished Goods Inventory Account

Balance 1/1/xx: $70,000	Sold during 19xx: $486,100
Completed during 19xx: 492,600	
Balance 12/31/xx: **$76,500**	

Products costing $486,100 to produce were sold for $750,000 during 19xx. Only the costs of the goods sold affect the Finished Goods Inventory account.

Cost of Goods Sold Account

| Sold during 19xx: $486,100 | |

FINISHED GOODS INVENTORY

The Finished Goods Inventory account holds the costs assigned to all completed products that have not been sold. This account, like Materials Inventory, shares some characteristics with the Merchandise Inventory account. When goods or products are sold, their costs are transferred to the Cost of Goods Sold account. During 19xx, products costing $486,100 to produce were sold for $750,000. As shown in Figure 4, these costs were debited to Cost of Goods Sold and credited to Finished Goods Inventory. At the end of the accounting period, the balance in the Finished Goods Inventory account ($76,500) equaled the cost of products completed but unsold as of that date.

THE MANUFACTURING COST FLOW

A defined, structured flow of manufacturing costs is the foundation for product costing, inventory valuation, and financial reporting. We outlined this manufacturing cost flow in our discussion of the three manufacturing inventory accounts. Figure 5 summarizes the entire cost-flow process as it relates to accounts in the general ledger.

COST CLASSIFICATIONS AND THEIR USES

OBJECTIVE

5 *Identify various approaches to cost classification and show how the purpose of a cost analysis can change the classification of a single cost item*

One of the most confusing concepts for beginning students of management accounting is that a single cost can be classified and used in several different ways, depending on the purpose of the analysis. Let's look at an example—depreciation expense. In financial accounting, Depreciation Expense is listed as an account in the expense section of the general ledger and recorded in the expense section of the income statement when financial statements are prepared. No other classification is associated with depreciation expense. In management accounting, depreciation can be classified as (1) a product cost

Figure 5. Manufacturing Cost Flow: An Example

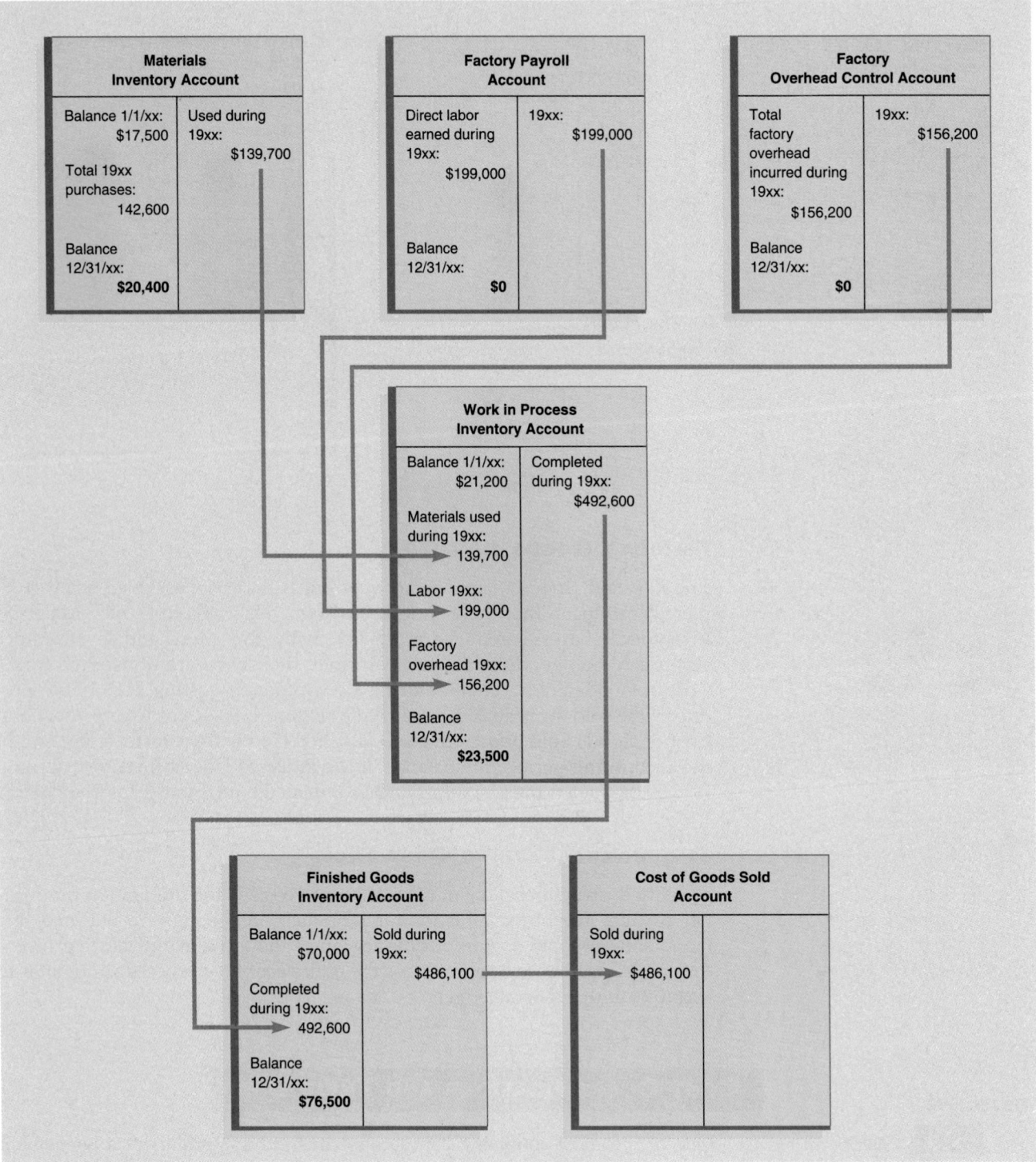

or a period cost, (2) an inventoriable cost or a noninventoriable cost, (3) a direct cost or an indirect cost, (4) a variable cost or a fixed cost, (5) a value-adding cost or a nonvalue-adding cost, and (6) a budgeted cost or an actual cost. In fact, the very same cost can be classified in these six different ways at the same time, if, for various purposes, management requires six different cost analyses using all of the cost classifications. In other words, in management accounting, cost categories have different meanings for different purposes and costs are not rigidly classified when incurred, as they are in financial accounting. Direct and indirect costs were discussed earlier in this chapter, so the remaining cost classification schemes will now be discussed.

PRODUCT COSTS VERSUS PERIOD COSTS

Costs are classified as product or period costs for many reasons, among them (1) to determine unit manufacturing costs so that inventories can be valued and selling prices created and verified, (2) to report production costs on the income statement, and (3) to analyze costs for control purposes. Product costs consist of the three elements of manufacturing cost: direct materials, direct labor, and factory overhead. They are incurred as a product is made and can be inventoried. That is, product costs flow through the materials, work in process, and finished goods inventory accounts before becoming part of the cost of goods sold. They are used to compute ending inventory balances as well as the cost of goods sold. Product costs can also be considered unexpired costs because, as inventory balances, they are assets of the company and are expected to benefit future operations. As will be shown in the section about manufacturing and reporting, product costs alone make up the statement of cost of goods manufactured.

Both product costs and period costs are found on the income statement. Period costs are the costs of resources consumed during the current period; they cannot be inventoried. For example, selling and administration expenses are period costs because selling and administrative resources are used up in the same period in which they originate; they cannot be stored. Period costs are not used to determine a product's unit cost when establishing ending inventory balances.

INVENTORIABLE COSTS VERSUS NONINVENTORIABLE COSTS

Inventoriable cost is another term for *product cost*, a cost that is incurred to make or buy a salable product. Noninventoriable cost is a synonym for *period cost*, a cost that is incurred during the period to support the activities of the company, is not connected with the production process, and stems from the purchase of something that was consumed during the period and cannot be used to value inventory.

VARIABLE COSTS VERSUS FIXED COSTS

Costs behave in defined or predictable ways and can be anticipated based on their behavior patterns. Knowledge of such patterns helps managers develop budgets, make short-run and capital expenditure decisions, and establish benchmarks for controlling costs. The two primary types of cost behavior are variable and fixed. Variable and fixed manufacturing costs were discussed earlier in this chapter, but other costs besides manufacturing costs can be classified in this manner. Variable costs are costs that change in direct proportion to changes in productive output (or any other measure of volume). For example, direct labor cost should vary in direct proportion to units produced. And sales commissions based on a percentage of selling price vary in direct proportion to sales. Fixed costs, on the other hand, remain constant within a defined range of activity or time period. Depreciation of machinery is constant for a time period if there is no change in the amount of machinery owned. Rent costs based on time are fixed, but rental costs based on usage are variable because the more the rented item is used, the greater the rental cost.

VALUE-ADDING COSTS VERSUS NONVALUE-ADDING COSTS

Another cost classification that has developed recently is based on whether a cost adds market value to a product or service or is incurred with no apparent effect on market value or customer satisfaction. A value-adding cost is the cost of an operating activity that increases the market value of a product or service. A nonvalue-adding cost is the cost of an operating or support activity that adds cost to a product or service but does not increase its market value. The depreciation of a machine that shapes a part assembled into the final product is a value-adding cost; depreciation of a sales department automobile is a nonvalue-adding cost. Costs incurred to improve the quality of a product are value-adding costs if the customer is willing to pay more for the higher-quality product; if not, they are nonvalue-adding costs because they do not increase the product's market value. The costs of administrative activities such as accounting and personnel are nonvalue-adding costs; they are necessary for the operation of the business, but they do not add value to the product.

BUDGETED COSTS VERSUS ACTUAL COSTS

The management accountant deals with both predicted, or budgeted, costs and actual costs, or costs that have already been incurred. It is therefore necessary to distinguish between these two cost classifications. A budgeted cost is an anticipated or projected cost for a future period, whereas an actual cost is a cost that has already been incurred and is verifiable. Budgeted costs are used to formulate a complete budget for the company for a future period and are also used to measure performance through comparison with actual costs. Actual costs are used to formulate financial statements as well as various internal reports.

COST CLASSIFICATIONS AND THEIR PURPOSES

A single cost can be classified in many different ways, depending on the purpose of a cost analysis. To illustrate different cost classifications for different purposes, we will look at three examples—cost of raw materials, depreciation cost of machinery, and advertising cost—and identify their cost classifications for six different types of analyses.

Table 2 summarizes these relationships. If a decision depends on accurate tracing of product costs, direct versus indirect cost classifications are important. Raw materials costs are directly traceable to the product, whereas depre-

Table 2. Cost Classification and Cost Analyses

Purpose of Cost Analysis	Cost Type and Classification		
	Raw Materials	Depreciation of Machinery	Advertising
Traceability	Direct	Indirect	Indirect
Financial reporting	Product	Product	Period
Behavior	Variable	Fixed	Fixed
Value	Value-adding	Value-adding	Nonvalue-adding
Planning	Budgeted	Budgeted	Budgeted
Cost control	Budgeted compared to actual	Budgeted compared to actual	Budgeted compared to actual

ciation of machinery and advertising costs are indirect costs. For purposes of inventory valuation and financial reporting, a cost must be classified as either a product cost (inventoriable cost) or a period cost (noninventoriable cost). Raw materials and depreciation of machinery are product costs, whereas advertising is a period cost.

When decisions require knowledge of cost behavior, variable versus fixed cost classifications are used. The costs of raw materials vary with the number of products produced, but both depreciation of machinery and advertising costs are usually fixed for a period of time. Product value is analyzed by distinguishing between value-adding and nonvalue-adding costs. Both raw materials and depreciation add value to a product, but advertising adds cost without adding value. Planning and control of costs deal with budgeted and actual costs. Planning activities focus on budgeted costs, and decisions about cost control require comparisons of budgeted and actual costs.

In summary, the concept of cost classification is an integral part of management accounting. As you continue your study of the subject, it is important to remember that cost classifications change depending on the decision and the type of analysis required.

BUSINESS BULLETIN: BUSINESS PRACTICE

In the mid-1800s, the industrial revolution in Europe upset long-established patterns of life. Skilled workers were replaced by machines, leaving them with no ability to compete. Their living conditions were reduced to the poverty level. Demand for factory workers pulled peasants from the farms into the slums of the cities. Capitalism caused a permanent change in society, a force that Karl Marx felt would lead to its downfall.

Well, capitalism has survived and communism has fallen. Yet, today we are experiencing another revolution—a technological revolution. Instead of being centered in a particular country or region, it is worldwide. New industries are replacing old ones. Again, skilled workers are being replaced—by robots and automated machinery. Workers whose jobs were abolished by technology are having difficulty finding new jobs. Retraining is required if these people expect to return to the work force. This new global environment is continuously influenced by new approaches to management, new quality standards, and new production processes. And capitalism lives on.[2] ===

MANUFACTURING AND REPORTING

OBJECTIVE

6 *Prepare a statement of cost of goods manufactured and an income statement for a manufacturing company*

The financial statements of manufacturing companies differ very little from those of merchandising companies. Account titles on the balance sheet of manufacturers are similar to those used by merchandisers. The primary difference between the balance sheets is the use of three inventory accounts by manufacturing companies versus only one by merchandising companies. Even the income statements for a merchandiser and a manufacturer are similar. However, manufacturers use the heading Cost of Goods Manufactured in place of the Purchases account. Also, the Merchandise Inventory account is replaced by the Finished Goods Inventory account. Notice these differences in the income statement shown in Exhibit 1.

The key to preparing an income statement for a manufacturing company is to determine the cost of goods manufactured. This dollar amount is calculated on the statement of cost of goods manufactured. This special statement is based on the classification of costs as either product costs or period costs.

STATEMENT OF COST OF GOODS MANUFACTURED

The flow of manufacturing costs, shown in Figures 2 through 5, provides the basis for accounting for manufacturing costs. In this process, all manufacturing costs incurred are considered product costs. They are used to compute ending inventory balances and the cost of goods sold. In Figures 2 through 5, the costs flowing from one account to another during the year are combined into one number to show the basic idea. In fact, hundreds of transactions occur during a year, and each transaction affects part of the cost flow process. At the end of the year, the flow of all manufacturing costs incurred during the year is summarized in the statement of cost of goods manufactured. This statement gives the dollar amount of costs for products completed and moved to finished goods inventory during the year. The cost of goods manufactured should be the same as the amount transferred from the Work in Process Inventory account to the Finished Goods Inventory account during the year.

---

2. Adapted from Walter Mead, "Two Cheers for Karl Marx," *Worth Financial Intelligence,* Capital Publishing Company, July–August, 1994, pp. 43–46.

Exhibit 1. Income Statement for a Manufacturing Company

Windham Company
Income Statement
For the Year Ended December 31, 19xx

Net Sales		$750,000
Cost of Goods Sold		
Finished Goods Inventory, Jan. 1, 19xx	$ 70,000	
Cost of Goods Manufactured (Exhibit 2)	492,600	
Total Cost of Finished Goods Available for Sale	$562,600	
Less Finished Goods Inventory, Dec. 31, 19xx	76,500	
Cost of Goods Sold		486,100
Gross Margin		$263,900
Operating Expenses		
Selling Expenses		
Salaries and Commissions	$46,500	
Advertising	19,500	
Other Selling Expenses	7,400	
Total Selling Expenses	$ 73,400	
General and Administrative Expenses		
Administrative Salaries	$65,000	
Franchise and Property Taxes	72,000	
Other General and Administrative Expenses	11,300	
Total General and Administrative Expenses	148,300	
Total Operating Expenses		221,700
Income from Operations		$ 42,200
Less Interest Expense		4,600
Income Before Income Taxes		$ 37,600
Less Income Taxes Expense		11,548
Net Income		$ 26,052

The statement of cost of goods manufactured is shown in Exhibit 2. The statement is complex, so we piece it together in three steps. The first step is to compute the cost of materials used. To do so, we add the materials purchases for the period to the beginning balance in the Materials Inventory account. The subtotal represents the cost of materials available for use during the period. Then, we subtract the ending balance of Materials Inventory from the cost of materials available for use. The difference is the cost of materials used during the accounting period.

Exhibit 2. Statement of Cost of Goods Manufactured

Windham Company
Statement of Cost of Goods Manufactured
For the Year Ended December 31, 19xx

Step One	Materials Used		
	Materials Inventory, Jan. 1, 19xx	$ 17,500	
	Materials Purchases (net)	142,600	
	Cost of Materials Available for Use	$160,100	
	Less Materials Inventory, December 31, 19xx	20,400	
	Cost of Materials Used		$139,700
Step Two	Direct Labor Costs		199,000
	Factory Overhead Costs		
	Indirect Labor	$ 46,400	
	Power	25,200	
	Depreciation, Machinery and Equipment	14,800	
	Depreciation, Factory Building	16,200	
	Small Tools	2,700	
	Factory Insurance	1,600	
	Supervision	37,900	
	Other Factory Costs	11,400	
	Total Factory Overhead Costs		156,200
	Total Manufacturing Costs		$494,900
Step Three	Add Work in Process Inventory, January 1, 19xx		21,200
	Total Cost of Work in Process During the Year		$516,100
	Less Work in Process Inventory, December 31, 19xx		23,500
	Cost of Goods Manufactured		$492,600

Computation of Cost of Materials Used

Beginning Balance Materials Inventory	$ 17,500
Add Materials Purchases (net)	142,600
Cost of Materials Available for Use	$160,100
Less Ending Balance Materials Inventory	20,400
Cost of Materials Used	$139,700

Before going on to the next step, trace the numbers back to the Materials Inventory account in Figure 2 (page 685) to see how that account is related to the statement of cost of goods manufactured.

Calculating total manufacturing costs for the year is the second step. As shown in Figure 3, the costs of materials used and direct labor are added to total factory overhead costs incurred during the year.

Computation of Total Manufacturing Costs

Cost of Materials Used	$139,700
Add Direct Labor Costs	199,000
Add Total Factory Overhead Costs	156,200
Total Manufacturing Costs	$494,900

The third step shown in Exhibit 2 adjusts total manufacturing costs to determine the total cost of goods manufactured for the period. The beginning Work in Process Inventory balance is added to total manufacturing costs for the period to arrive at the total cost of work in process during the period. From this amount, the ending Work in Process Inventory balance is subtracted to get the cost of goods manufactured.

Computation of Cost of Goods Manufactured

Total manufacturing costs	$494,900
Add beginning balance Work in Process Inventory	21,200
Total cost of work in process during the year	$516,100
Less ending balance Work in Process Inventory	23,500
Cost of goods manufactured	$492,600

The term *total manufacturing costs* should not be confused with the cost of goods manufactured. Total manufacturing costs are the total costs of materials, direct labor, and factory overhead incurred and charged to production during an accounting period. The cost of goods manufactured consists of the total manufacturing costs attached to units of a product *completed* during an accounting period. To understand the difference between these two dollar amounts, look again at the computations above. Total manufacturing costs of $494,900 incurred during the year are added to the beginning balance in Work in Process Inventory. Costs of $21,200 in the beginning balance are, by definition, costs from an earlier period. The costs of two accounting periods are now being mixed to arrive at the total cost of work in process during the year, $516,100. The costs of products still in process ($23,500) are then subtracted from the total cost of work in process during the year. The remainder, $492,600, is the cost of goods manufactured (completed) during the current year. It is assumed that the items in beginning inventory were completed first. The costs attached to the ending balance of Work in Process Inventory are part of the current period's total manufacturing costs. But they will not become part of the cost of goods manufactured until the next accounting period, when the products are completed.

COST OF GOODS SOLD AND THE INCOME STATEMENT

Exhibits 1 and 2 demonstrate the relationship between the income statement and the statement of cost of goods manufactured. The total amount of the cost of goods manufactured during the period is carried over to the income statement. There, it is used to compute the cost of goods sold. The cost of goods manufactured is added to the beginning balance of Finished Goods Inventory to get the total cost of finished goods available for sale during the period. The cost of goods sold is then computed by subtracting the ending balance in Finished Goods Inventory (the cost of goods completed but not sold) from the total cost of finished goods available for sale. The cost of goods sold is considered an expense in the period in which the related products are sold.

Computation of Cost of Goods Sold

Beginning balance Finished Goods Inventory	$ 70,000
Add cost of goods manufactured	492,600
Total cost of finished goods available for sale	$562,600
Less ending balance Finished Goods Inventory	76,500
Cost of goods sold	$486,100

Notice that this computation is similar to the computation of the cost of goods sold in the income statement in Exhibit 1. The other parts of the income statement in Exhibit 1 should be familiar from financial accounting.

Stolle Corporation

DECISION POINT

Ralph Stolle founded a small chrome and cadmium plating company in Cincinnati, Ohio, in 1923. Through several mergers and acquisitions, the company, now located in Sidney, Ohio, became a major player in the computer hard disk market. However, antiquated production methods threatened the company's ability to compete in such a high-tech, fast-changing industry.

Recently, management of the company's Memory Products Division decided to pursue world-class manufacturing (WCM) stature for the company. Cultural as well as physical changes were necessary to attain the goal. Achieving total employee involvement was the most important obstacle between the present work environment and WCM. To meet the challenge, management devoted special resources and time to the program, including workshops for all employees on the just-in-time operating environment. A steering committee was created to oversee the program. The final phase of training included the formation of the Polish Center Team, whose charge was to develop a set of objectives that would lead to WCM. The team produced the following objectives:

1. Minimize such nonvalue-adding steps as scrap, defective work, and idle time.
2. Reduce distance between operations.
3. Minimize handling damage.
4. Decrease work in process inventory.
5. Improve process flow.

What performance measures could the team use to support their objectives and achieve WCM status?

The team identified and used three performance measures to help establish a WCM environment: (1) reduction of throughput time, (2) reduction in the amount of work in process inventory, and (3) reduction of the percentage of product damage caused by handling errors. An essential element of the team's efforts was the elimination of nonvalue-adding work. The result was the elimination of several nonvalue-adding testing steps, the standardization of and improvement in some maintenance procedures, and significant improvements in many parts of the manufacturing process. As a result, Stolle Corporation has reached WCM status. Management commitment and employee dedication made the achievement of the goal possible. And by eliminating many nonvalue-adding aspects of the production process, significant product cost reduction was accomplished.[3] ⁞ ⁞ ⁞ ⁞ ⁞

PRODUCT COSTS IN A SERVICE BUSINESS

OBJECTIVE

7 *Apply costing concepts to a service business*

Costs are classified as product or period costs for many reasons, including: (1) to determine unit manufacturing costs so that inventories can be valued and selling prices created and verified; (2) to report production costs on the income statement; and (3) to analyze costs for control purposes. When we shift from a manufacturing environment to a service environment, the only major difference is that we are no longer dealing with a physical product that can be assembled, stored, and valued. Services are rendered and cannot be held in inventory.

Processing loans, representing people in courts of law, selling insurance policies, and computing people's income taxes are typical services performed by professionals. Because no products are manufactured in the course of providing such services, service businesses have no materials costs. Nonetheless, specific costs arise that must be included when computing the cost of providing a service.

The most important cost in a service business would be the professional labor involved, and the usual standard is applicable; that is, the direct labor cost must be traceable to the service rendered. In addition to the labor cost, any type of business, whether manufacturing, service, or not-for-profit, incurs overhead costs. In a service business the overhead costs associated with and incurred for the purpose of offering a service are classified as service overhead (like factory overhead) and, along with professional labor costs, are considered service costs (like product costs) rather than period costs.

For example, assume that the Loan Department at the Seminole Bank of Commerce wants to determine the total costs incurred in processing a typical loan application. Its policy for the past five years has been to charge a $150 fee for processing a home-loan application. Barbara Hasegawa, the chief loan officer, thinks the fee is far too low. Considering the way operating costs have

---

3. Nabil Hassan, Herbert E. Brown, Paula M. Saunders, and Nick Koumoutzis, "Stolle Puts World Class into Memory," *Management Accounting*, Institute of Management Accountants, January 1993, pp. 22–25.

soared in the past five years, she proposes that the fee be doubled. You have been asked to compute the cost of processing a typical home-loan application.

The following information concerning the processing of loan applications has been given to you.

Direct professional labor:
  Loan processors' monthly salaries:
    4 people at $3,000 each $12,000

Indirect monthly loan department overhead costs:
  Chief loan officer's salary $ 4,500
  Telephone   750
  Depreciation, building   2,800
  Depreciation, equipment   1,750
  Depreciation, automobiles   1,200
  Legal advice   2,460
  Legal forms/supplies   320
  Customer relations   640
  Credit check function   1,980
  Advertising   440
  Internal audit function   2,400
  Utilities   1,690
  Clerical personnel   3,880
  Miscellaneous   290
  Total overhead costs $25,100

In addition, you discover that all appraisals and title searches are performed by people outside the bank, and their fees are treated as separate loan costs. One hundred home-loan applications are usually processed each month.

The Loan Department performs several other functions in addition to processing home-loan applications. Roughly one-half of the department is involved in loan collection. After determining how many of the processed loans were not home loans, you conclude that only 25 percent of the overhead costs of the Loan Department were applicable to the processing of home-loan applications. The cost of processing one home-loan application can be computed as follows:

Direct professional labor cost:
  $12,000 ÷ 100 $120.00
Service overhead cost:
  $25,100 × 25% ÷ 100   62.75
Total processing cost per loan $182.75

Finally, you conclude that the chief loan officer was correct; the present fee does not cover the current costs of processing a typical home-loan application. However, doubling the loan fee seems inappropriate. To allow for a profit margin, the loan fee could be raised to $225 or $250.

COST ALLOCATION

Some costs (direct costs) can be easily traced and assigned to products or services, but other costs (indirect costs) must be assigned using an allocation method. The concept of cost allocation underlies every financial report a

OBJECTIVE

8 *Define* cost allo- cation *and state the role of cost objec- tives in the cost alloca- tion process*

business prepares and uses—budgets, production cost forecasts, and decision support analyses. So cost allocation is important to every aspect of manage- ment, not just to the work of management accountants.

The terms *cost allocation* and *cost assignment* often are used interchangeably, although *cost allocation* is the more popular of the two. Cost allocation is the process of assigning a specific cost to a specific cost objective.[4] A cost objec- tive is the destination of an assigned or allocated cost.[5] If the purpose of a cost analysis is to evaluate the operating performance of a division or depart- ment, the cost objective is that department or division. But if product costing is the reason for accumulating costs, a specific product or order, or an entire contract, could be the cost objective. The important point to remember is that the outcome of cost allocation depends on the cost objective being analyzed.

To understand cost allocation, you also need to understand the terms *cost center*, *direct cost*, and *indirect cost*. A cost center is any segment of an organiza- tion or area of activity for which there is a reason to accumulate costs. Examples of cost centers include the company as a whole, corporate divisions, specific operating plants, departments, and even specific machines or work areas. No accounting report about a cost center can be prepared until all the proper cost allocation procedures have been carried out.

Finally, we need to expand the definitions of direct and indirect costs that we introduced earlier. A direct cost is any cost that can be conveniently and economically traced to a specific cost objective. Direct materials costs and direct labor costs are usually thought of as direct costs. However, direct costs vary with individual cost objectives. When the cost objective is a division of a company, electricity, maintenance, and special tooling costs of the division are classified as direct costs. But when the cost objective is one of several products manufactured by the division, electricity, maintenance, and special tooling costs are indirect costs that must be allocated to that product. An indirect cost is any cost that cannot be conveniently or economically traced to a specific cost objective. Any production cost not classified as a direct cost is an indirect cost.

THE ALLOCATION OF MANUFACTURING COSTS

All manufacturing costs can be traced, or allocated, to a company's divisions, departments, or units of productive output. Direct costs, such as the cost of direct materials, can be assigned to specific jobs, products, or departments. Many manufacturing costs, however, are indirect costs that are incurred for the benefit of more than one product or department. Such costs must be allo- cated to the products and departments that benefit from them. For example, a portion of the total electricity cost for a month is incurred for the benefit of all of a company's departments. The cost must be allocated to all the work done during the month. We have already discussed the fact that depreciation is actually an allocation process: A portion of the item's original depreciable

4. *Cost Accounting Standard 402*, promulgated by the Cost Accounting Standards Board in 1972, defined the term *allocate* as follows: "To assign an item of cost, or group of items of cost, to one or more cost objectives. This term includes both direct assignment of cost and the reassign- ment of a share from an indirect cost pool."

5. *Cost Accounting Standard 402*, promulgated by the Cost Accounting Standards Board in 1972, defined the term *cost objective* as follows: "A function, organizational subdivision, contract or other work unit for which cost data are desired and for which provision is made to accumulate and measure the cost to processes, products, jobs, capitalized projects, etc."

cost is allocated to each period in which the item is used by the company. A similar process is used to allocate manufacturing costs.

The cost allocation process is shown in Figure 6. All three cost elements are included: materials, labor, and factory overhead. In this example, the cost objective is the product. The costs of lumber and the cabinetmaker's wages are direct costs of the product. The factory overhead costs include depreciation of the table saw, cleanup and janitorial services, and nails. All factory overhead costs are indirect costs of the product and must be assigned by means of an allocation method.

To summarize, the allocation of production costs calls for assigning direct and indirect manufacturing costs to specific cost objectives. The method of cost allocation depends on the specific cost objective being analyzed. A cost can be a direct cost to a large cost objective (a division) but an indirect cost to a smaller cost objective (a product). In general, the number of costs classified as direct costs increases with the size of the cost objective.

THE ROLE OF COST ASSIGNMENT IN CORPORATE REPORTING

Accounting reports are prepared for all levels of management, from the president down to the department manager or supervisor. The president is responsible for all of the company's costs. A department manager, on the other hand, is responsible only for the costs connected to that one department. Reports must be prepared for all cost centers, including the company as a whole, each division, and all of the departments within each division. The same costs shown in departmental reports appear again in divisional and corporate reports, but perhaps in summary form.

Figure 6. Cabinetmaking: Assigning Manufacturing Costs to a Product

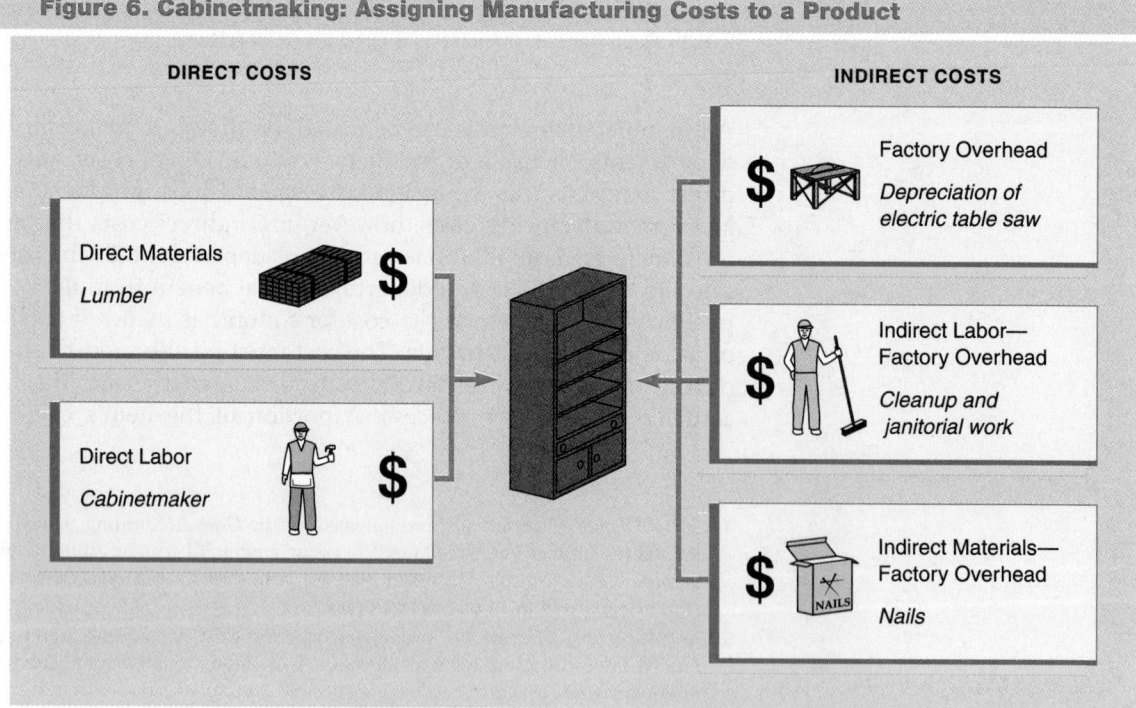

As the focus changes from one cost center or cost objective to another, so does the ease with which costs can be traced. Here is where cost allocation comes into the picture. As costs are reclassified and assigned to smaller cost centers or cost objectives, they become more difficult to trace. When the cost objective is reduced to a single product, only direct materials and direct labor costs can be traced directly. All other costs are classified as indirect and must be assigned to the product.

Table 3 shows how three manufacturing costs are traced as their cost objectives change. Direct materials costs can be traced directly to any level of cost objective shown. They are a direct cost at the divisional, departmental, and product levels. All 40,000 pounds of sugar were issued to Division A, so they can be traced directly to that division. Only half (20,000 pounds) was used by Department XZ, so only half can be traced directly to that department. At the product level, every unit of Product AB requires one-half pound of sugar. The cost of that one-half pound is a direct cost that can be traced to the product.

Depreciation costs of Machine 201 can be traced directly to both Division A and Department XZ. When Product AB is the cost objective, however, the depreciation of the machine is considered an indirect manufacturing cost and

Table 3. Manufacturing Cost Classification and Traceability

Costs	Cost Objectives		
	Division A	**Department XZ**	**Product AB**
Direct Materials	*Direct cost:* 40,000 pounds of sugar were issued from inventory specifically for Division A.	*Direct cost:* 20,000 of the 40,000 pounds of sugar issued from inventory were used by Department XZ.	*Direct cost:* Every unit of Product AB requires one-half pound of sugar.
Depreciation of Machine 201	*Direct cost:* Machine 201 is located within Department XZ and is used exclusively by Division A. Depreciation on the machine, then, can be traced directly to Division A.	*Direct cost:* Machine 201 is used only by Department XZ. Therefore, its depreciation charges can be traced directly to Department XZ.	*Indirect cost:* The depreciation of Machine 201 cannot be traced directly to the individual products it produces. Depreciation charges are accounted for as part of factory overhead costs.
Depreciation of Factory Building G	*Direct cost:* Factory Building G is used entirely by Division A. Therefore, all depreciation expenses from the use of Factory Building G can be traced directly to Division A.	*Indirect cost:* Department XZ is one of four departments in Factory Building G. Depreciation of Factory Building G is allocated to the four departments according to the square footage used by each department.	*Indirect cost:* Depreciation of Factory Building G is an indirect product cost. It is allocated to individual products as part of factory overhead charges applied to products, using machine hours as a base.

is accounted for as a factory overhead cost. Factory overhead costs are accumulated and then allocated to the products produced in Department XZ.

Finally, the depreciation of Factory Building G, which is used entirely by Division A, can be traced directly to Division A. For smaller cost objectives, though, it becomes an indirect cost. Building depreciation must be shared by the various cost centers in the building. The costs of building depreciation must be allocated to departmental cost objectives using an allocation base such as space occupied. It is then reallocated to products.

The principles of classifying and tracing costs that we have discussed here play a part in the preparation of all internal accounting reports. In accounting for operating costs, each cost must be assigned to products, services, jobs, or departments before reports can be prepared. Without proper cost allocation techniques, management accountants cannot (1) determine product or service unit costs, (2) develop cost budgets and cost control measures for management, or (3) prepare reports and analyses to help management make and support its decisions. Each of these tasks depends on cost allocation procedures.

ASSIGNING THE COSTS OF SUPPORTING SERVICE FUNCTIONS

Every business depends on the help of supporting service functions or departments to carry on the activities of the company. Although not directly involved in actually producing the product or creating the service, a supporting service function is an operating unit, activity, or department that supports a company's producing operations. Examples include a repair and maintenance department, a production scheduling department, a central computer facility, or materials storage and handling activities. The costs of these service functions are incurred for the purpose of supporting the production of a product or service, so they are product costs. They must be included in the costs assigned to products or services as overhead.

Many approaches have been devised to assign supporting service functions to production departments and then to products. A new technique focusing on activities as a basis for assigning these costs is rapidly gaining acceptability. We have already studied how all activities of a company can be separated into those that add value to a product or service and those that do not. Even though the nonvalue-adding activities do not directly add value to a product, many are still necessary for the overall operation of the business. Thus for a company to make a profit, the company's costs must still be covered by the prices of goods sold.

Supporting service functions are nonvalue-adding, but necessary, activities. Under activity-based costing, costs are accumulated for each service activity, and a basis for cost assignment is identified. The assignment basis is usually related to service usage. Examples include engineering hours for assigning the costs of the Design and Engineering activity, and minutes of usage for assigning the costs of the Central Computer activity. When activities and their respective cost assignment bases or drivers are the focal point, the usage cost of each supporting service activity is charged to the process or product using the service. For example, assume that the total cost of running the Central Computer activity for March was $325,440 and that a total of 28,800 minutes of operating time was available during the month. Each minute of operating time costs $11.30 ($325,440 ÷ 28,800). If the manufacture of Product CVT used 1,450 minutes of computer time, a total of $16,385

(1,450 minutes × \$11.30) would be charged by the Central Computer activity to Product CVT.

This new cost assignment approach, based on the costs and usage of activities, has two significant advantages. First, the supporting service costs are assigned to products based on usage, providing an accurate basis for cost assignment. Second, when the usage of a supporting service is the basis for cost assignment, management can quickly determine which of these non-value-adding activities are in demand and required by the production process and which can be reduced or eliminated because they are not in high demand.

ACCOUNTING FOR JOINT PRODUCT COSTS

OBJECTIVE

9 *Allocate common costs to joint products*

Joint, or common, costs are a special case in cost allocation. A joint cost (or *common cost*) is a cost that relates to two or more products or services produced from a common raw material or input and that can be assigned only by an arbitrary method after the products or services become identifiable. *Joint products* cannot be identified as separate products during some or all of the production process. Only at a particular point, called the split-off point, do separate products or services evolve from a common processing unit.

Petroleum refining, wood processing, and meat packing often result in joint products. In other words, more than one end product arises from a single material input. In beef processing, for example, the final cuts of meat (steaks, roasts, hamburger) do not appear until the end of the process. However, the cost of the steer and the costs of transportation, storage, hanging, and labor have been incurred to get the side of beef ready for final butchering. Figure 7 shows the accounting problem presented by joint costs. We will outline the two most commonly used methods for solving it.

PHYSICAL VOLUME METHOD

One way to allocate joint costs to specific products or services is the physical volume method, which uses a measure of physical volume (units, pounds, liters, grams) as the basis for allocating joint costs.

Figure 7. Joint Product Cost Allocation: The Fuentes Company

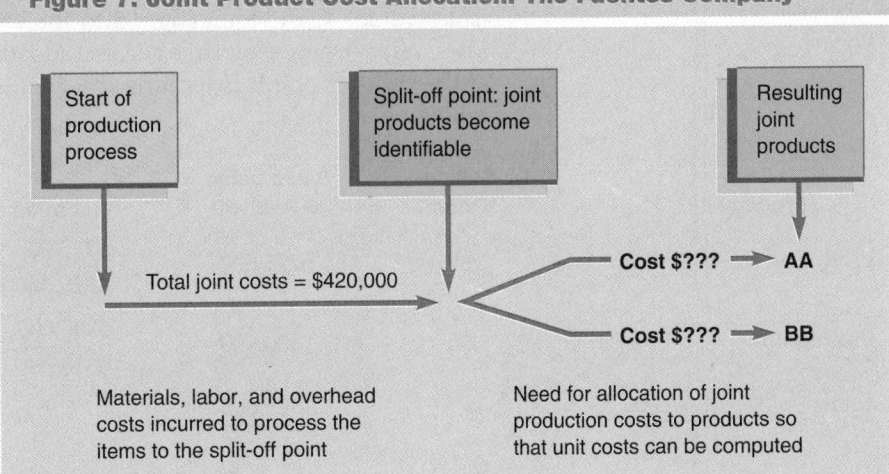

Assume that the Fuentes Company makes two grades of paint from the same mixture of substances. During August, 75,000 liters of ingredients were put into the production process. The final output for the month was 25,000 liters of Product AA and 50,000 liters of Product BB. Total joint production costs for August were $420,000: $210,000 for direct materials, $115,000 for direct labor, and $95,000 for factory overhead. The two products cannot be identified until the end of the production process. Product AA sells for $9 per liter and Product BB for $6 per liter. Taking total liters as the allocation basis, we apply a ratio of the physical volume of each product to the total physical volume.

	Total Liters	Allocation Ratio	Joint Cost Allocation
Product AA	25,000	$\frac{25,000}{75,000}$ or ⅓	$140,000 ($420,000 × ⅓)
Product BB	50,000	$\frac{50,000}{75,000}$ or ⅔	280,000 ($420,000 × ⅔)
Totals	75,000		$420,000

Note that Product AA will generate $225,000 in net sales (25,000 liters at $9 per liter). Thus, the gross margin for this product line will be $85,000. (We compute this by subtracting $140,000 of assigned joint costs from the net sales of $225,000.) Product BB will sell for a total of $300,000 (50,000 liters at $6 per liter) and will show only a $20,000 gross margin ($300,000 minus $280,000 of assigned joint costs). Product BB's gross margin suffers because its high-volume content attracts two-thirds of the production costs, even though its selling price is much less than that of Product AA.

This example demonstrates the key strength and weakness of the physical volume method of allocating joint costs. It is easy to use, but it often seriously distorts gross margin, because the physical volume of joint products may not be proportionate to each product's ability to generate revenue.

RELATIVE SALES VALUE METHOD

Another way to allocate joint production costs depends on the relative sales value of the products. The relative sales value method allocates joint costs to products or services in proportion to each one's revenue-producing ability (sales value). Costs are assigned to the joint products based on their relative sales value when they first become identifiable as specific products—that is, at the split-off point. Extending the Fuentes Company data, we can make the following analysis:

	Liters Produced	×	Selling Price	=	Sales Value at Split-off	Allocation Ratio	Joint Cost Allocation
Product AA	25,000		$9		$225,000	$\frac{\$225,000}{\$525,000}$ or 3/7	$180,000 ($420,000 × 3/7)
Product BB	50,000		$6		300,000	$\frac{\$300,000}{\$525,000}$ or 4/7	240,000 ($420,000 × 4/7)
Totals	75,000				$525,000		$420,000

Product AA has a relative sales value of $225,000 at split-off; Product BB, $300,000. The resulting cost allocation ratios are 3/7 and 4/7, respectively.

Applying those ratios to the total joint cost of $420,000, we assign $180,000 to Product AA and $240,000 to Product BB.

If we compare these results with those of the physical volume method, we see a wide difference in gross margin for the two product lines.

	Product AA		Product BB	
	Physical Volume Method	Relative Sales Value Method	Physical Volume Method	Relative Sales Value Method
Net sales	$225,000	$225,000	$300,000	$300,000
Cost of goods sold	140,000	180,000	280,000	240,000
Gross margin	$ 85,000	$ 45,000	$ 20,000	$ 60,000
Gross margin as percent of sales	37.8%	20.0%	6.7%	20.0%

The principal advantage of the relative sales value method is that it allocates joint costs according to a product's ability to absorb the cost. For this reason, gross margin percentages will always be equal at the split-off point, as the example shows. Under the relative sales value method, gross margin as a percentage of sales is 20% for both products.

As mentioned earlier, these approaches to assigning joint production costs are arbitrary. They are used because it is difficult to determine just how the end products (cost objectives) benefited from the incurrence of the cost. Both the physical volume method and the relative sales value method should be used only in those cases where it is impossible to tell how the cost benefited the cost objective.

CHAPTER REVIEW

REVIEW OF LEARNING OBJECTIVES

1. **Distinguish between the cost of a manufactured versus a purchased product and state how managers use product costs.** The total cost of a purchased product includes its purchase price plus a portion of the cost of all the supporting services needed to market and deliver the product and keep the business running effectively. The product's inventoriable cost usually includes only its purchase price.

    The cost of a manufactured product is more difficult to compute. Its cost includes the prices paid for the raw materials and parts, wages paid to the factory workers, cost of depreciation of the machinery, supervisory costs, product design costs, and the cost of utilities used within the factory. These costs would also be used to establish the product's inventoriable cost. In addition, as with purchased products, the costs of marketing, distribution, and customer service must be included in the product's total cost.

    Managers use product costs to support the pricing of a product or service and to value inventory. Public utilities are regulated by a state agency and use product cost information to establish rates. The electric and gas rates they charge their customers must be within specific guidelines set by that agency. Managers also use the product costs of the current period to plan for future production of similar products or to help in the design of new product lines. Accurate product costs help in cost control too.

2. **Define and give examples of the three elements of manufacturing cost—direct materials costs, direct labor costs, and factory overhead costs—and identify**

the source documents used to collect information about those costs. Direct materials are materials that become part of the finished product and that can be conveniently and economically traced to specific product units. The sheet metal used to manufacture cars is an example of a direct material. Direct labor costs include all labor costs for specific work that can be conveniently and economically traced to end products. A machine operator's wages are a direct labor cost. All other production-related costs—for utilities, depreciation on equipment, and operating supplies, for example—are classified and accounted for as factory overhead costs. These costs cannot be conveniently or economically traced to end products, so they are assigned to products by a cost allocation method.

Purchase requisitions list the items or materials needed by the production departments. The purchasing department then uses purchase orders to order the items. When the items or materials come in from vendors, receiving reports are used to identify the items and to match them against the purchase orders and the vendors' packing lists to ensure that the correct items were received. Materials requisitions are used to request items and to prove that items or materials were issued in the production process. Time cards record each employee's daily starting and finishing times. Job cards record time spent by each employee on each job. Job cards are matched against time cards to verify the time worked by each employee and to control labor time per job.

3. **Compute a product's unit cost.** The unit cost of a product is made up of the costs of direct materials, direct labor, and factory overhead. These three cost elements are accumulated for a batch of products as they are produced. When the batch has been completed, the number of units produced is divided into the total costs incurred to determine the product's unit cost.

4. **Describe the contents of and the flow of costs through the Materials Inventory, Work in Process Inventory, and Finished Goods Inventory accounts.** The flow of costs through the inventory accounts begins when costs are incurred for direct materials, direct labor, and factory overhead. Materials costs flow first into the Materials Inventory account, which is used to record the costs of materials when they are received and again when they are issued for use in a production process. All manufacturing-related costs—direct materials, direct labor, and factory overhead—are recorded in the Work in Process Inventory account as the production process begins. When products are completed, their costs are transferred from the Work in Process Inventory account to the Finished Goods Inventory account. Costs remain in the Finished Goods Inventory account until the products are sold, at which time they are transferred to the Cost of Goods Sold account.

5. **Identify various approaches to cost classification and show how the purpose of a cost analysis can change the classification of a single cost item.** In management accounting, a single cost can be classified as (1) a product cost or a period cost, (2) an inventoriable cost or a noninventoriable cost, (3) a direct cost or an indirect cost, (4) a variable cost or a fixed cost, (5) a value-adding cost or a nonvalue-adding cost, and (6) a budgeted cost or an actual cost. For financial reporting, a cost must be classified as either a product cost (inventoriable cost) or a period cost (noninventoriable cost). If tracing costs is the focal point of the analysis, direct versus indirect cost classifications are important. When cost behavior is being analyzed, variable versus fixed cost classifications are used. Product value is analyzed by distinguishing between value-adding and nonvalue-adding costs. Planning and control of costs deals with budgeted and actual costs.

6. **Prepare a statement of cost of goods manufactured and an income statement for a manufacturing company.** The cost of goods manufactured is a key component of the income statement for a manufacturing company. Determining the cost of goods manufactured involves three steps: (1) computing the cost of materials used, (2) computing total manufacturing costs for the period, and (3) computing the cost of goods manufactured. This last figure, taken from the statement of cost of goods manufactured, is used in the income statement to compute the cost of goods sold.

7. **Apply costing concepts to a service business.** Most types of costs incurred by a manufacturer and called product costs are also incurred by a service company. The only important difference is that a service business does not deal with a physical

product that can be assembled, stored, and valued. Services are rendered and cannot be held in inventory. Because no products are manufactured in the course of providing services, service businesses have no materials costs. To determine the cost of performing a particular service, professional labor and service-related overhead costs are included in the analysis.

8. **Define *cost allocation* and state the role of cost objectives in the cost allocation process.** Cost allocation is the process of assigning a specific cost to a specific cost objective. A cost objective is the destination of an assigned cost. It varies with the focus of a report and may range from an entire company or division down to a particular cost center, machine, or product.

   A supporting service function is an operating unit or department that supports the activities of a company's production facilities. The costs incurred by supporting service departments are accounted for as indirect operating costs. Supporting service functions are accounted for as nonvalue-adding activities because they support the production process rather than being a direct part of the process. They do not directly add value to the product, but they are necessary to ensure smooth operations. Assigning the cost of a supporting service activity involves determining the total cost of the activity, identifying an appropriate assignment base, and computing the cost for each element of the base. Costs are then charged to the production process and to units of product based on their usage of the supporting service function.

9. **Allocate common costs to joint products.** Joint products evolve from a common processing unit. They cannot be identified as specific products until the split-off point in the process. All manufacturing costs incurred prior to the split-off point are shared by all the products. After the split-off point, joint costs are assigned to individual products using either the physical volume method or the relative sales value method.

REVIEW OF CONCEPTS AND TERMINOLOGY

The following concepts and terms were introduced in this chapter.

L O 5   **Actual cost:** A cost that has already been incurred and is verifiable.

L O 5   **Budgeted cost:** An anticipated or projected cost for a future period.

L O 8   **Cost allocation:** The process of assigning a specific cost to a specific cost objective. Also called *cost assignment.*

L O 8   **Cost center:** Any segment of an organization or area of activity for which there is a reason to accumulate costs.

L O 8   **Cost objective:** The destination of an assigned or allocated cost.

L O 6   **Cost of goods manufactured:** The total manufacturing costs attached to units of a product completed during an accounting period.

L O 2   **Direct cost:** Any cost that can be conveniently and economically traced to a specific cost objective; a manufacturing cost that is easily traced to a specific product.

L O 2   **Direct labor costs:** All labor costs for specific work that can be conveniently and economically traced to an end product.

L O 2   **Direct materials:** Materials that become part of a finished product and can be conveniently and economically traced to specific product units.

L O 2   **Factory overhead costs:** A varied collection of production-related costs that cannot be practically or conveniently traced to an end product. Also called *manufacturing overhead, factory burden,* and *indirect manufacturing costs.*

L O 4   **Finished Goods Inventory account:** An inventory account unique to manufacturing operations that holds the costs assigned to all completed products that have not been sold.

L O 5   **Fixed costs:** Costs that remain constant within a defined range of activity or time period.

L O 2   **Fixed manufacturing costs:** Production costs that stay fairly constant during the accounting period.

L O 2 **Gross payroll:** The total wages and salaries earned by employees, including payroll deductions.

L O 2 **Indirect cost:** Any cost that cannot be conveniently and economically traced to a specific cost objective; a manufacturing cost that is not easily traced to a specific product and must be assigned using an allocation method.

L O 2 **Indirect labor costs:** Labor costs for production-related activities that cannot be connected with or conveniently and economically traced to an end product.

L O 2 **Indirect materials:** Minor materials and other production supplies that cannot be conveniently and economically traced to specific products.

L O 5 **Inventoriable cost:** A cost incurred to make or buy a salable product. Another term for *product cost*.

L O 2 **Job card:** A record of the time spent by each employee on a particular job.

L O 9 **Joint cost:** A cost that relates to two or more products or services produced from a common input or raw material and that can be assigned only by means of arbitrary cost allocation after the products or services become identifiable. Also called *common cost*.

L O 4 **Manufacturing cost flow:** The flow of manufacturing costs (direct materials, direct labor, and factory overhead) from their incurrence through the Materials, Work in Process, and Finished Goods inventory accounts to the Cost of Goods Sold account.

L O 4 **Materials Inventory account:** An inventory account made up of the balances of materials, parts, and supplies on hand at a given time. Also called the *Stores, Raw Materials Inventory,* or *Materials Inventory Control* account.

L O 2 **Materials requisition:** A form used within a company to authorize the use of stored materials and parts in the production operation; it describes the types and quantities of goods needed and received, and requires an authorized signature.

L O 2 **Net payroll:** The amount paid to employees after all payroll deductions have been subtracted from gross wages.

L O 5 **Noninventoriable cost:** A cost that is incurred during the period to support the activities of the company, is not connected with the production process, and stems from the purchase of something that was consumed during the period. Another term for *period cost*.

L O 5 **Nonvalue-adding cost:** The cost of an operating or support activity that adds cost to a product but does not increase its market value.

L O 5 **Period costs:** The costs of resources consumed during an accounting period; they cannot be inventoried.

L O 9 **Physical volume method:** An approach to allocating joint costs to specific products or services that uses a measure of physical volume (units, pounds, liters, grams) as the basis for allocation.

L O 5 **Product costs:** Inventoriable production costs consisting of the three elements of manufacturing cost: direct materials, direct labor, and factory overhead.

L O 3 **Product unit cost:** The manufacturing costs of a single unit of product; total cost of direct materials, direct labor, and factory overhead for a job divided by the total units produced.

L O 2 **Purchase order:** A form used to communicate a company's raw materials or parts needs to a supplier; it specifies the items and quantities to be purchased and any other pertinent information.

L O 2 **Purchase requisition:** A form that begins the purchasing process by identifying a need for raw materials or parts; it describes the items and quantities needed, and must be approved by a qualified manager or supervisor. Also called *purchase request*.

L O 2 **Receiving report:** A form used to confirm receipt of goods from a supplier; its data are compared to data on the purchase order.

L O 9 **Relative sales value method:** The use of revenue-producing ability (sales value) as the basis for allocating joint costs to specific products or services.

LO 9 **Split-off point:** A point in the production or development process at which joint products or services separate and become identifiable.

LO 6 **Statement of cost of goods manufactured:** A formal statement summarizing the flow of all manufacturing costs incurred during an accounting period.

LO 8 **Supporting service function:** An operating unit, activity, or department that supports the activities of a company's production facilities.

LO 2 **Time card:** The basic record of time maintained for each employee; it shows the employee's daily starting and finishing times as recorded by the supervisor or a time clock.

LO 6 **Total manufacturing costs:** The total costs of materials, direct labor, and factory overhead incurred and charged to production during an accounting period.

LO 5 **Value-adding cost:** The cost of an operating activity that increases the market value of a product or service.

LO 5 **Variable costs:** Costs that vary in direct proportion to changes in productive output (or any other measure of volume).

LO 2 **Variable manufacturing costs:** Costs that increase or decrease in direct proportion to the number of units produced.

LO 4 **Work in Process Inventory account:** An inventory account in which all manufacturing costs incurred and assigned to products being produced are recorded.

REVIEW PROBLEM

COST OF GOODS MANUFACTURED— THREE FUNDAMENTAL STEPS

LO 6 In addition to the year-end balance sheet and income statement, the management of Mison Company requires the controller to prepare a statement of cost of goods manufactured. During 19x4, $361,920 of materials were purchased. Operating cost data and inventory account balances for 19x4 follow:

Account	Balance
Direct Labor (10,430 hours at $9.50 per hour)	$ 99,085
Plant Supervision	42,500
Indirect Labor (20,280 hours at $6.25 per hour)	126,750
Factory Insurance	8,100
Utilities, Factory	29,220
Depreciation, Factory Building	46,200
Depreciation, Factory Equipment	62,800
Manufacturing Supplies	9,460
Repair and Maintenance	14,980
Selling and Administrative Expenses	76,480
Materials Inventory, January 1, 19x4	26,490
Work in Process Inventory, January 1, 19x4	101,640
Finished Goods Inventory, January 1, 19x4	148,290
Materials Inventory, December 31, 19x4	24,910
Work in Process Inventory, December 31, 19x4	100,400
Finished Goods Inventory, December 31, 19x4	141,100

REQUIRED

1. Compute the cost of materials used during the year.
2. Given the cost of materials used, compute the total manufacturing costs for the year.
3. Given the total manufacturing costs for the year, compute the cost of goods manufactured during the year.

ANSWER TO REVIEW PROBLEM

1. Compute the cost of materials used.

Beginning Balance Materials Inventory	$ 26,490
Add Materials Purchases (net)	361,920
Cost of Materials Available for Use	$388,410
Less Ending Balance Materials Inventory	24,910
Cost of Materials Used	$363,500

2. Compute the total manufacturing costs.

Cost of Materials Used		$363,500
Add Direct Labor Costs		99,085
Add Total Factory Overhead Costs		
Plant Supervision	$ 42,500	
Indirect Labor	126,750	
Factory Insurance	8,100	
Utilities, Factory	29,220	
Depreciation, Factory Building	46,200	
Depreciation, Factory Equipment	62,800	
Manufacturing Supplies	9,460	
Repair and Maintenance	14,980	
Total Factory Overhead Costs		340,010
Total Manufacturing Costs		$802,595

3. Compute the cost of goods manufactured.

Total Manufacturing Costs	$802,595
Add Beginning Balance Work in Process Inventory	101,640
Total Cost of Work in Process During the Year	$904,235
Less Ending Balance Work in Process Inventory	100,400
Cost of Goods Manufactured	$803,835

CHAPTER ASSIGNMENTS

QUESTIONS

1. How do managers use product costing information?
2. What are the three kinds of manufacturing cost included in a product's cost?
3. How is a direct cost different from an indirect cost?
4. Define *direct materials.*
5. Describe the following: purchase requisition, purchase order, and receiving report.
6. How is direct labor different from indirect labor?
7. What are the two categories of labor-related costs? Discuss each one.
8. What characteristics identify a cost as part of factory overhead?
9. What is meant by the term *cost behavior?*
10. Identify and describe the three inventory accounts that are used by a manufacturing company.
11. What is meant by the term *manufacturing cost flow?*
12. What is the difference between a period cost and a product cost?
13. State six purposes for analyzing costs.
14. Describe how to compute the cost of direct materials used.

15. Describe how total manufacturing costs differ from the total cost of goods manufactured.

16. How is the cost of goods manufactured used in computing the cost of goods sold?

17. "The concept of product costs is not applicable to service companies." Is this statement correct? Defend your answer.

18. Since service companies do not maintain materials and finished goods inventories, what use do they have for unit cost information? Explain your answer.

19. Identify two types of service companies, state their primary services, and discuss methods that could control the costs of these services.

20. What is *cost allocation* and why is it important to every aspect of management?

21. What is a cost objective, and what is its role in management accounting?

22. "The smaller the cost center or cost objective, the more difficult it is to trace costs and revenues to it." Explain this statement.

23. What is a joint cost?

24. Describe the physical volume method of allocating joint costs to products. Identify the main advantage and disadvantage of the physical volume method.

25. Should joint costs be allocated to a product on the basis of the product's ability to generate revenue? Explain your answer.

SHORT EXERCISES

SE 1. *Distinguishing the*
L O 1 *Costs of a Product*
No check figure

Ray Christopher, owner of Candlelight, Inc., was given the following list of costs he incurs in his candle business. Examine the list and identify the costs that Ray should *not* include in the total cost of making and selling candles.

1. Salary of Mary, the office employee
2. Cost of delivering candles to Candles Plus, a buyer
3. Cost of wax
4. Sales commission on a sale to Candles Plus
5. Cost to custom-design Christmas candles

SE 2. *Elements of*
L O 2 *Manufacturing Cost*
Check Figure: 5. FO

Flora Rose, the bookkeeper at Candlelight, Inc., must group the costs to manufacture candles. Tell whether each of the following items should be classified as direct materials (DM), direct labor (DL), factory overhead (FO), or none of the three (N).

1. Cost of vats to hold melted wax
2. Cost of wax
3. Rent on the factory where candles are made
4. Cost of George's time to dip the wicks into the wax
5. Cost of coloring for candles
6. Cost of Ray's time to design candles for Halloween
7. Sam's commission to sell candles to Candles Plus

SE 3. *Computing Product*
L O 3 *Unit Cost*
Check Figure: Product unit cost: $52

What is the product unit cost for Job 14, which consists of 300 units and has total manufacturing costs of direct materials, $4,500; direct labor, $7,500; and factory overhead, $3,600?

SE 4. *Manufacturing Cost*
L O 4 *Flow*
Check Figure: Work in Process, ending balance: $108,750

Given the following information, compute the ending balances of the Materials Inventory, Work in Process Inventory, and Finished Goods Inventory accounts.

Materials Inventory, beginning balance	$ 23,000
Work in Process Inventory, beginning balance	25,750
Finished Goods Inventory, beginning balance	38,000
Materials purchased	85,000
Materials placed into production	74,000
Direct labor costs	97,000
Factory overhead costs	35,000
Cost of goods completed	123,000
Cost of goods sold	93,375

SE 5. *Cost Classification*
L O 5
No check figure

Indicate whether each of the following is a product (PR) or a period (PER) cost and a variable (V) or a fixed (F) cost. Also indicate whether each adds value (VA) or does not add value (NVA) to the product.

1. Production supervisor's salary
2. Sales commission
3. Wages of a production line worker

SE 6. *Income Statement*
L O 6 *for a Manufacturing Company*
Check Figure: Net income: $36,300

Using the following information from C.L.I.N.T. Company, prepare an income statement for 19x7.

Net Sales	$900,000
Finished Goods Inventory, January 1, 19x7	45,000
Cost of Goods Manufactured	585,000
Finished Goods Inventory, December 31, 19x7	60,000
Operating Expenses	270,000
Interest Expense	5,000
Tax Rate	34%

SE 7. *Unit Costs in a*
L O 7 *Service Business*
Check Figure: Cost per acre: $10.40

Pickerson's Picking Services provides inexpensive, high-quality labor for farmers growing vegetable and fruit crops. In June, Pickerson paid laborers $4,000 to pick 500 acres of winter-grown onions. Pickerson incurred overhead costs of $2,400 for onions and lettuce picking services in June. This included the costs of transporting the laborers to the various fields; providing facilities, food, and beverages for the laborers; and scheduling, billing, and collecting from the farmers. Of this amount, 50 percent was related to picking onions. Compute the cost per acre to pick onions.

SE 8. *Cost Allocation and*
L O 8 *Cost Objectives*
Check Figure: 3. Indirect

Given a chair as the cost objective, indicate whether the following are direct or indirect costs.

1. Wood
2. Depreciation of saws
3. Electricity for the plant
4. Chair assembler's wages
5. Wood glue used in chair assembly
6. Clean-up crew's wages

SE 9. *Assigning Costs of*
L O 8 *Supporting Service Functions*
Check Figure: Allocated to Filling Department: $6,000

At the Findley Bottling Co., the services of the Production and Scheduling Department are allocated to two production departments based on the number of service requests. The Filling Department made 40 service requests in April, and the Bottling Department made 60 requests. If the Production and Scheduling Department's costs were $15,000 for April, how much of the service department's costs would be allocated to the Filling Department? How much would be allocated to the Bottling Department?

SE 10. *Allocating Common*
L O 9 *Costs to Joint Products*
Check Figure: Allocated to Product M: $36,000

Using the relative sales value method, allocate joint costs to Products M and N, given the following information:

Product M has a relative sales value of $20 per jar at the split-off point.

Product N has a relative sales value of $15 per jar at the split-off point.

2,250 jars of Product M were produced.

7,000 jars of Product N were produced.

Total joint costs for the month were $120,000.

EXERCISES

E 1. *Distinguishing the*
L O 1 *Costs of Products*
No check figure

Identify each of the following as a cost of a manufactured product (M), a cost of a purchased product (P), or both (B).

1. Warehouse costs for merchandise
2. Cost of utilities used in the factory
3. Advertising costs
4. Building rent

5. Product design costs
6. Cost of raw materials
7. Delivery costs
8. Display cases for merchandise
9. Parts in assembly operations
10. Production supervisor's salary

E 2. *Documentation*
L O 2
No check figure

St. Paul Company manufactures a complete line of music boxes. Seventy percent of its products are standard items and are produced in long production runs. The remaining 30 percent of the music boxes are special orders involving specific requests for tunes. The special order boxes cost from three to six times as much as the standard product because of the use of additional materials and labor.

Erin Townsend, controller, recently received a complaint memorandum from V. Johnson, the production supervisor, because of the new network of source documents added to the existing cost accounting system. The new documents include a purchase requisition, a purchase order, a receiving report, and a materials requisition. Mr. Johnson claims that the forms represent extra busy work and interrupt the normal flow of production.

Prepare a written response from Ms. Townsend that fully explains the purpose of each type of document.

E 3. *Unit Cost*
L O 3 *Determination*
Check Figure: 1. Unit Cost: $9.10

The Greer Winery is one of the finest and oldest wineries in the country. One of its most famous products is a red table wine called Olen Millot. The wine is made from Olen Millot grapes grown in Missouri's Ozark region. Recently, management has become concerned about the increasing cost of making Olen Millot and needs to find out if the current $10 per bottle selling price is adequate. The following information is given to you for analysis.

Batch size	10,550 bottles

Costs	
Materials	
Olen Millot grapes	$22,155
Chancellor grapes	9,495
Bottles	5,275
Labor	
Pickers/loaders	2,110
Crusher	422
Processors	8,440
Bottler	1,688
Storage and racking	11,605
Production overhead	
Depreciation, equipment	2,743
Depreciation, building	5,275
Utilities	1,055
Indirect labor	6,330
Supervision	7,385
Supplies	3,165
Storage fixtures	2,532
Chemicals	4,220
Repairs	1,477
Miscellaneous	633
Total production costs	$96,005

1. Compute the unit cost per bottle for materials, labor, and production overhead.
2. What would you advise company management regarding the price per bottle of Olen Millot wine? Defend your answer.

E 4. *Manufacturing Cost*
L O 4 *Flow*
No check figure

Using the ideas illustrated in Figure 5 and discussed in this chapter, describe in detail the flow of materials costs through the recording process of a management accounting system. Include in your answer all general ledger accounts affected and all recording documents used.

E 5. *Cost Classification*
L O 5
No check figure

The typical costs incurred by a garment maker include (a) gasoline and oil for the salesperson's automobile, (b) factory telephone charges, (c) dyes for the fabric, (d) the seamstresses' regular hourly labor, (e) thread, (f) the president's subscription to the *Wall Street Journal,* (g) sales commissions, (h) business forms used in the office, (i) buttons and zippers, (j) depreciation of the sewing machines, (k) property taxes on the factory, (l) advertising, (m) brand labels, (n) administrative salaries, (o) interest on business loans, (p) starch and fabric conditioners, (q) patterns, (r) the hourly workers' vacation pay, (s) roof repairs on the office, and (t) packaging.

1. At the time the above costs are incurred, which ones will be classified as period costs? Which ones will be treated as product costs?
2. Of the costs identified as product costs, which are direct costs? Which are indirect costs?

E 6. *Total Manufacturing*
L O 6 *Costs*
Check Figure: Total Manufacturing Costs: $831,200

The partial trial balance of Dorfman Millinery, Inc. appears below. Inventory accounts reflect balances at the beginning of the period. Period-end balances are $77,000, $95,800, and $46,200 for the Materials Inventory, Work in Process Inventory, and Finished Goods Inventory accounts, respectively. From this information, prepare a schedule showing the computation of total manufacturing costs for the period ending May 31, 19x8.

Account	Debit	Credit
Accounts Receivable	$ 97,420	
Materials Inventory *beginning*	78,400	
Work in Process Inventory	84,400	
Finished Goods Inventory	51,400	
Accounts Payable		$ 99,250
Sales		891,940
Materials Purchases	421,600	
Direct Labor	161,200	
Operating Supplies, Factory	31,700	
Depreciation, Machinery	74,100	
Fire Loss	82,000	
Insurance, Factory	9,700	
Indirect Labor	56,900	
Supervisory Salaries, Factory	38,700	
President's Salary	39,900	
Property Tax, Factory	9,400	
Other Indirect Manufacturing Costs	26,500	

E 7. *Statement of Cost of*
L O 6 *Goods Manufactured*
Check Figure: Cost of Goods Manufactured: $211,450

The following information about the manufacturing costs incurred by the Goodsell Company for the month ended August 31, 19x9, is available.

Purchases of materials during August totaled $139,000.

Direct labor was 3,400 hours at $8.75 per hour.

The following factory overhead costs were incurred: utilities, $5,870; supervision, $16,600; indirect supplies, $6,750; depreciation, $6,200; insurance, $1,830; and miscellaneous, $1,100.

Inventory accounts on August 1 were as follows: Materials, $48,600; Work in Process, $54,250; and Finished Goods, $38,500. Inventory accounts on August 31 were as follows: Materials, $50,100; Work in Process, $48,400; and Finished Goods, $37,450.

From the information given, prepare a statement of cost of goods manufactured.

E 8. *Unit Costs in a*
L O 7 *Service Business*
Check Figure: Cost per bale: $.33

Hector Franco provides custom farming services to owners of five-acre alfalfa fields. In July, he earned $2,400 by cutting, turning, and baling 3,000 bales of alfalfa. He incurred the following costs: gas, $150; annual tractor depreciation, $1,500; tractor maintenance, $115; and labor, $600. What was Franco's cost per bale? What was his revenue per bale? Should he increase the amount he charges the owners for his custom farming services?

E 9.   *Cost Allocation—*
L O 8   *Direct Versus*
          Indirect

No check figure

Classifying a cost as direct or indirect depends on the cost objective. Depreciation of a factory building is a direct cost when the plant is the cost objective. But when the cost objective is a product, depreciation cost is indirect.

For the following costs, indicate for each cost objective—division, department, or product—whether the cost would be indirect (I) or direct (D). Defend your answers.

	Cost Objective		
Cost	**Division**	**Department**	**Product**
1. Department repairs and maintenance	D	D	I
2. Direct materials	D	D	D
3. Division manager's salary	D	I	I
4. Property taxes, division plant	D	I	D
5. Direct labor	D	D	D
6. Departmental supplies	D	D	I
7. President's salary	I	I	I
8. Fire insurance on a specific machine	D	D	I

E 10.   *Joint Cost*
L O 9   *Allocation—Relative*
          Sales Value Method

Check Figure: Joint costs allocated to Grade B pulp: $106,800

In the processing of paper, two distinct grades of wood pulp emerge from a common crushing and mixing process. Fleener Paper Products, Inc. produced 88,000 liters of pulp during January. Direct materials used during the month cost the company $172,000. Labor and overhead costs for the month were $72,000 and $112,000, respectively. Output for the month was as follows:

Product	Quantity	Market Value at Split-off
Grade A pulp	28,000 liters	$14.00 per liter
Grade B pulp	16,000 liters	$10.50 per liter

Using the relative sales value method, allocate the common production costs to Grade A pulp and Grade B pulp.

SKILLS DEVELOPMENT EXERCISES

Conceptual Analysis

SDE 1.   *Product Costs and*
L O 1   *Continuous*
          Improvement

No check figure

As a manager at *Bakerstrat Motor Company,* you have been invited to serve on a planning team. The team's task is to improve next year's model of the Goldenhawk Sedan while minimizing the product costs. The Goldenhawk Sedan is currently a budget-priced car with few standard features. Bakerstrat always redesigns its cars to meet the current and anticipated mandates of the federal and state governments and to satisfy consumers' wants and needs.

1. To meet the demands of governments and consumers, recommend three changes that could be made to the design of the Goldenhawk Sedan. Identify the product costs that would be affected by each change and explain how those costs would be affected.
2. Assume that your suggested changes would increase the car's product costs. What recommendations would your team make to control such costs?

Ethical Dilemma

SDE 2.   *Preventing Pollution*
L O 2, 7 *and the Costs of*
          Waste Disposal

No check figure

Preston Power Plant currently provides power to a metropolitan area of 4 million people. Joan Peters, the controller for the plant, just returned from a conference about the Environmental Protection Agency's regulations concerning pollution prevention. She met with Jake Simpson, the president of the company, to discuss the impact of the EPA's regulations on the plant.

"Jake, I'm really concerned. We haven't been monitoring the disposal of the radioactive material we send to the Derrick Disposal Plant. If Derrick is disposing of our waste material improperly, we could be sued," said Joan. "We also haven't been recording the costs of the waste as part of our product cost. Ignoring that cost will have a negative impact on our decision about the next rate hike."

"Hey, Joan, don't worry. I don't think we need to concern ourselves with the waste we send to Derrick. We pay them to dispose of it. They take it off of our hands, and it's their responsibility to manage its disposal. As for the cost of waste disposal, I think we would have a hard time justifying a rate increase based on a requirement to record the full cost of waste as a cost of producing power. Let's just forget about waste and its disposal as a component of our power cost. We can get our rate hike without mentioning waste disposal," replied Jake.

What responsibility does Preston Power Plant have to monitor the condition of the waste at the Derrick Disposal Plant? Should Joan take Jake's advice to ignore waste disposal costs in calculating the cost of power? Be prepared to discuss your response.

Research Activity

SDE 3. *Variable and Fixed*
L O 5 *Costs*

No check figure

Make a trip to a local fast-food restaurant. Observe all aspects of the operation and take notes on the entire process. Describe the procedures used to take, process, and fill an order and get the food to the customer. Based on your observations, make a list of the costs incurred by the owner. Then identify at least three fixed costs and three costs that vary based on the number of sandwiches sold. Bring your notes to class and report your findings.

Decision-Making Practice

SDE 4. *Unit Costs for a*
L O 3, 7 *Service Business*

Check Figures: 1. Total cost per patient day: $2,772; 3. Industry Average Billing Approach: $3,984

Payson Municipal Hospital relies heavily on cost data to keep its pricing structures in line with those of competitors. The hospital provides a wide range of services, including nursing care in intensive care units, intermediate care units, the neonatal (newborn) nursery, and nursing administration.

Jerry Snyder, the hospital's controller, is concerned about the profits being generated from the thirty-bed intensive care unit (ICU), so he is reviewing current billing procedures. The focus of Jerry's analysis is Payson's billing per patient day. The billing per patient day equals the cost of a patient day in the ICU plus a markup of an additional 40 percent of cost to cover other operating costs and to generate a profit.

ICU patient costs include the following:

Doctors' care	2 hours per day @ $360 per hour (actual)
Special nursing care	4 hours per day @ $85 per hour (actual)
Regular nursing care	24 hours per day @ $28 per hour (average)
Medications	$237 per day (average)
Medical supplies	$134 per day (average)
Room rental	$350 per day (average)
Food and services	$140 per day (average)

One other significant cost is equipment, which costs about $185,000 per room. Jerry has determined that the cost per patient day for the equipment is $179.

Ralph Pope, the hospital director, has asked Jerry to review the current billing procedure and compare it to another procedure using industry averages to determine the billing per patient day.

1. Compute the cost per patient per day.
2. Compute the billing per patient day using the hospital's existing markup rate. Round answers to whole dollars.
3. Many hospitals use separate markup rates for each cost when preparing billing statements. Industry averages revealed the following markup rates:

Equipment	30 percent
Doctors' care	50
Special nursing care	40
Regular nursing care	50
Medications	50

Medical supplies	50 percent
Room rental	30
Food and services	25

Using these rates, recompute the billing per patient day in the ICU. Round answers to whole dollars.
4. Based on your findings in **2** and **3,** which billing procedure would you recommend to the hospital's director? Why? Be prepared to discuss your response.

PROBLEM SET A

A 1. *Factory Overhead:*
L O 2 *Cost Flow*

Check Figure: 5. Total variable costs: $53,140

A working knowledge of the makeup of factory overhead is essential to understanding the elements, purpose, and operation of a management accounting system.

REQUIRED

1. Identify the characteristics of factory overhead.
2. Are factory overhead costs always indirect costs? Why or why not? Explain your answer.
3. List three examples of a factory overhead cost.
4. Diagram the flow of factory overhead costs in a manufacturing environment. List the documents used to record those costs, and link the documents to specific parts of the cost flow diagram.
5. Lafite Industries in Hermann, Missouri, produces oak wine barrels. The oak wood is purchased in large slabs and milled to size. Metal barrel rings are purchased from an outside vendor. The following factory overhead costs were incurred in June: indirect mill labor, $32,620; indirect assembly labor, $16,910; supervisory salaries, $9,200; depreciation, equipment, $2,800; factory rent, $4,500; utilities, $2,200; and small tools, $1,410. Identify each of the above costs as either a variable cost or a fixed cost and compute a total for each classification.

A 2. *Computation of Unit*
L O 3 *Cost*

Check Figure: 2. Total unit cost: $6.86

Maestro Industries, Inc. manufactures video discs for several of the leading recording studios in the United States and Europe. Department 85 is responsible for the electronic circuitry within each disc. Department 82 applies the plastic-like surface to the discs and packages them for shipment. Some of the materials are purchased from outsiders, and other materials are produced internally. A recent order for 4,000 discs from the ERV Company was produced during July. For this job, the departments incurred the following costs to complete and ship the goods in July.

	Department	
	85	82
Direct materials used:		
Purchased from outside vendors	$7,920	$ —
Produced internally	6,800	1,960
Direct labor	3,400	1,280
Factory overhead	3,680	2,400

REQUIRED

1. Compute the unit cost for each of the two departments.
2. Compute the total unit cost for the ERV Company order.
3. The selling price for this order was $7 per unit. Was the selling price adequate? List the assumptions and/or computations upon which you based your answer. What suggestions would you make to Maestro Industries' management concerning the pricing of future orders?

A 3. *Cost of Goods*
L O 6 *Manufactured: Three*
Fundamental Steps

Check Figure: 3. Cost of Goods Manufactured: $755,120

Triad Company manufactures a line of aquatic equipment, including a new gill-like device that produces oxygen from water and replaces large, cumbersome pressurized air tanks. Management requires that a statement of cost of goods manufactured be prepared quarterly, along with an income statement. As the company's accountant, you have determined the following account balances for the quarter ended October 31, 19x9.

718

Chapter 16

Account	Balance
Materials Purchases During Quarter	$328,000
Small Tools	18,240
Factory Insurance	3,690
Factory Utilities	7,410
Depreciation, Building	16,240
Depreciation, Equipment	12,990
Selling Expenses	42,600
Plant Supervisor's Salary	16,250
Direct Labor	194,700
Indirect Labor	81,400
Repairs and Maintenance, Factory	21,200
Miscellaneous Factory Overhead	14,120
Indirect Materials and Supplies, Factory	39,400
Materials Inventory, August 1, 19x9	55,600
Materials Inventory, October 31, 19x9	56,240
Work in Process Inventory, August 1, 19x9	44,020
Work in Process Inventory, October 31, 19x9	41,900
Finished Goods Inventory, August 1, 19x9	39,200
Finished Goods Inventory, October 31, 19x9	40,200

REQUIRED

Perform the three basic steps used in preparing the statement of cost of goods manufactured, as follows:

1. Prepare a schedule showing the computation of the cost of materials used during the quarter.
2. Using the amount calculated in **1**, prepare a schedule that determines the total manufacturing costs for the quarter.
3. From the amount computed in **2**, prepare a final schedule that derives cost of goods manufactured for the quarter.

A 4. *Statement of Cost of*
L O 6 *Goods Manufactured*

Check Figure: Cost of Goods Manufactured: $1,171,150

Svengan Manufacturing Company produces a line of Viking ship replicas that is sold at Scandinavian gift shops throughout the world. Inventory account balances on May 1, 19x7 were Materials, $190,400; Work in Process, $96,250; and Finished Goods, $52,810. April 30, 19x8 inventory account balances were Materials, $186,250; Work in Process, $87,900; and Finished Goods, $56,620.

During the 19x7–x8 fiscal year $474,630 of materials were purchased, and payroll records indicated that direct labor costs totaled $215,970. Overhead costs for the period included indirect materials and supplies, $77,640; indirect labor, $192,710; depreciation, building, $19,900; depreciation, equipment, $14,240; heating, $19,810; electricity, $8,770; repairs and maintenance, $12,110; liability and fire insurance, $2,980; property taxes, building, $3,830; design and rework, $23,770; and supervision, $92,290. Other costs for the period included selling costs, $41,720, and administrative salaries, $102,750.

REQUIRED

Prepare a statement of cost of goods manufactured for the fiscal year ended April 30, 19x8.

A 5. *Joint Cost Allocation*
L O 9

Check Figure: 1. Costs allocated to gasoline, physical volume method: $757,500.00

The processing of crude oil produces three joint products: gasoline, motor oil, and kerosene. Patterson Petroleum Products, Inc. is a Chicago-based processor. During April, the company used 1,950,000 gallons of crude oil at a cost of $.40 per gallon, paid $315,000 in direct labor wages, and applied $420,000 of factory overhead to the crude oil processing department. Production during the period yielded 950,000 gallons of gasoline, 350,000 gallons of motor oil, and 600,000 gallons of kerosene. Evaporation caused the loss of 50,000 gallons; the amount lost was normal, and its cost should be included in the cost of good units produced. Selling prices for the joint products are $.80 per gallon of gasoline, $.95 per quart of motor oil, and $.50 per gallon of kerosene. Assume there were no beginning or ending work in process inventories, and that everything produced was sold during the period. (Note: four quarts equal one gallon.)

REQUIRED	
	1. Using the physical volume method, allocate the joint costs to each of the three joint products.
	2. Using the relative sales value method, allocate the joint costs to each of the three joint products.
	3. Prepare a schedule that compares the gross margin at the split-off point using the two methods of allocation. Compute gross margin both in total dollars and as a percentage of sales.

(Round answers to three decimal places where appropriate.)

PROBLEM SET B

B 1. *Direct Materials:*
L O 2 *Cost Flow*

No check figure

A good working knowledge of direct materials cost is important for understanding the elements, purpose, and operation of a management accounting system.

REQUIRED

1. Name the characteristics associated with (a) direct materials and (b) indirect materials.
2. Give at least two examples for each cost category listed in **1.**
3. Prepare a diagram of the flow of all materials costs, both direct and indirect, for a manufacturing concern. Show which documents are used to record materials costs, and relate those documents to specific parts of the cost flow diagram.
4. If a direct materials invoice for $600 is dated September 2, terms 2/10, n/30, how much should be paid if the invoice is paid on September 8? On September 29?

B 2. *Unit Cost*
L O 3 *Computation*
Check Figure: 2. Total unit cost: $1.348

Grand Industries has recently finished production of Job Sb-15 for 41,480 units of product. Each unit was processed through three departments: F-14, G-12, and H-15. The corporation's management accountant is ready to calculate the unit cost for this order. Relevant information for the month ended March 31, 19x7, is as follows:

Direct Materials Used
Department F-14	4,410 liters @ $3.00 per liter
Department G-12	850 liters @ $5.57 per liter
Department H-15	1,980 liters @ $5.00 per liter

Direct Labor Used
Department F-14	152 hours @ $8.50 per direct labor hour
Department G-12	510 hours @ $7.80 per direct labor hour
Department H-15	620 hours @ $8.00 per direct labor hour

Overhead Incurred
Department F-14	$3,514
Department G-12	7,470
Department H-15	6,810

There was no ending balance in the Work in Process Inventory account as of March 31, 19x7.

REQUIRED

1. Compute the unit cost for each of the three departments, rounding to three decimal places.
2. Compute the total unit cost.
3. Order Sb-15 was specially made for the Ishton Company for a selling price of $57,125. Determine whether the selling price was appropriate. List the assumptions or computations on which you base your answer. What advice, if any, would you offer to the management of Grand Industries on the pricing of future orders?

B 3. *Cost of Goods*
L O 6 *Manufactured: Three Fundamental Steps*
Check Figure: 3. Cost of Goods Manufactured: $1,549,230

Lowe Metallurgists, Inc. is a large manufacturing firm that prepares financial statements quarterly. Assume that you work in the firm's accounting department and that preparing a statement of cost of goods manufactured is one of your regular quarterly duties. Account balances for the quarter ended March 31, 19x9, are listed at the top of the next page.

Account	Balance
Office Supplies	$ 4,870
Depreciation, Plant and Equipment	25,230
President's Salary	36,000
Property Taxes, Office	1,950
Equipment Repairs, Factory	4,290
Plant Supervisors' Salaries	16,750
Insurance, Plant and Equipment	2,040
Direct Labor	248,310
Utilities, Plant	6,420
Indirect Labor	16,000
Manufacturing Supplies	4,760
Small Tools	2,900
Materials Inventory, January 1, 19x9	397,950
Materials Inventory, March 31, 19x9	415,030
Work in Process Inventory, January 1, 19x9	529,840
Work in Process Inventory, March 31, 19x9	515,560
Finished Goods Inventory, January 1, 19x9	375,010
Finished Goods Inventory, March 31, 19x9	402,840
Materials Purchases During the Quarter	1,225,330

REQUIRED

Perform the three basic steps in preparing the statement of cost of goods manufactured, as follows:

1. Prepare a schedule showing the computation of the cost of materials used during the quarter.
2. Using the amount calculated in **1**, prepare a schedule that determines the total manufacturing costs for the quarter.
3. From the amount derived in **2**, prepare a final schedule that calculates the cost of goods manufactured for the quarter.

B 4. *Statement of Cost of*
L O 6 *Goods Manufactured*

Check Figure: Cost of Goods
Manufactured: $10,163,200

Plano Vineyards operates a large winery in Texas that produces a full line of varietal wines. The company, whose fiscal year begins on November 1, has just completed a record-breaking year. The vineyard's inventory and production data for the year are as follows:

Account	Oct. 31, 19x9	Nov. 1, 19x8
Materials Inventory	$1,803,800	$2,156,200
Work in Process Inventory	2,764,500	3,371,000
Finished Goods Inventory	1,883,200	1,596,400

Materials purchased during the year amounted to $6,750,000. Direct labor hours incurred totaled 142,500, at an average labor rate of $8.20 per hour. The following factory overhead costs were incurred during the year: depreciation, plant and equipment, $685,600; operating supplies, $207,300; property tax, plant and equipment, $94,200; material handlers' labor, $83,700; small tools, $42,400; utilities, $96,500; and employee benefits, $76,100.

REQUIRED

Using proper form, prepare a statement of cost of goods manufactured.

B 5. *Joint Cost Allocation*
L O 9

Check Figure: 1. Costs allocated to
regular product, physical volume
method: $261,888

Three distinct grades of chocolate sauce are made by Mona's Toppings, Inc. The ingredients for all three grades are first blended together. Then other ingredients are added to produce the three separate grades. The Extra-Rich blend sells for $8.20 per pound. The Quality blend sells for $6.60 per pound. And the Regular blend sells for $5.00 per pound. In July, 383,000 pounds of ingredients were put into production, with output of 94,218 pounds of Extra-Rich blend, 153,966 pounds of Quality blend, and 134,816 pounds of Regular blend. Joint costs for the period were $401,200 for direct materials, $146,000 for direct labor, and $196,800 for factory overhead. Assume no beginning or ending inventories and no loss of input during production.

REQUIRED

1. Using the physical volume method, allocate the joint costs to the three different blends.
2. Using the relative sales value method, allocate the joint costs to the three blends.
3. Prepare a schedule that compares the gross margin at split-off point using the two methods of allocation. Compute gross margin both in total dollars and as a percentage of sales.

(Round allocation ratios to four decimal places where appropriate.)

MANAGERIAL REPORTING AND ANALYSIS CASES

Interpreting Management Reports

MRA 1.
L O 6
Analyzing Financial Statements

Check Figure: 1. a. Ratio of materials to total manufacturing costs, 19x7: 48.3%

Rudolph Manufacturing Company makes sheet metal products for heating and air conditioning installations. For the past several years, the income of the company has been declining, and this past year, 19x7, was particularly poor. The company's statement of cost of goods manufactured and its income statement for 19x6 and 19x7 are shown below and on the following page.

Rudolph Manufacturing Company
Statements of Cost of Goods Manufactured
For the Years Ended December 31, 19x7 and 19x6

	19x7		19x6	
Materials Used				
Materials Inventory, January 1	$ 91,240		$ 93,560	
Materials Purchases (net)	987,640		959,940	
Cost of Materials Available for Use	$1,078,880		$1,053,500	
Less Materials Inventory, December 31	95,020		91,240	
Cost of Materials Used		$ 983,860		$ 962,260
Direct Labor Costs		571,410		579,720
Factory Overhead Costs				
Indirect Labor	$ 182,660		$ 171,980	
Power	34,990		32,550	
Insurance	22,430		18,530	
Supervision	125,330		120,050	
Depreciation	75,730		72,720	
Other Factory Costs	41,740		36,280	
Total Factory Overhead Costs		482,880		452,110
Total Manufacturing Costs		$2,038,150		$1,994,090
Add Work in Process Inventory, January 1		148,875		152,275
Total Cost of Work in Process During the Year		$2,187,025		$2,146,365
Less Work in Process Inventory, December 31		146,750		148,875
Cost of Goods Manufactured		$2,040,275		$1,997,490

Rudolph Manufacturing Company
Income Statements
For the Years Ended December 31, 19x7 and 19x6

	19x7		19x6	
Net Sales		$2,942,960		$3,096,220
Cost of Goods Sold				
Finished Goods Inventory,				
January 1	$ 142,640		$ 184,820	
Cost of Goods Manufactured	2,040,275		1,997,490	
Total Cost of Finished Goods				
Available for Sale	$2,182,915		$2,182,310	
Less Finished Goods				
Inventory, December 31	186,630		142,640	
Cost of Goods Sold		1,996,285		2,039,670
Gross Margin		$ 946,675		$1,056,550
Operating Expenses				
Sales Salary and				
Commission Expense	$ 394,840		$ 329,480	
Advertising Expense	116,110		194,290	
Other Selling Expenses	82,680		72,930	
Administrative Expenses	242,600		195,530	
Total Operating Expenses		836,230		792,230
Income from Operations		$ 110,445		$ 264,320
Other Revenues and Expenses				
Interest Expense		54,160		56,815
Income Before Income Taxes		$ 56,285		$ 207,505
Less Income Taxes Expense (34%)		19,137		87,586
Net Income		$ 37,148		$ 119,919

You have been asked to comment on why the company's profitability has deteriorated.

REQUIRED

1. In preparing your comments on the decline in income, compute the following ratios for each year:
   a. Ratios of cost of materials used to total manufacturing costs, direct labor costs to total manufacturing costs, and total factory overhead costs to total manufacturing costs. Round to one decimal place.
   b. Ratios of gross margin to net sales, total operating expenses to net sales, and net income to net sales. Round to one decimal place.
2. From your evaluation of the ratios computed in **1**, state the probable causes of the decline in net income.
3. What other factors or ratios do you believe should be considered in determining the cause of the company's decreased income?

Formulating Management Reports

MRA 2. *Management*
L O 5, 7 *Decision for a*
Supporting Service
Function

As the manager of grounds maintenance for *PICA,* a large insurance company in Texas, you are responsible for maintaining the grounds surrounding the three buildings, the six entrances to the property, and the recreational facilities, which include a golf course, a soccer field, jogging and bike paths, and tennis, basketball, and volleyball courts. Maintenance activities include gardening (watering, mowing, trimming, sweeping, and removing debris) and upkeep of land improvements (repairing concrete and gravel areas and replacing damaged or worn recreational equipment).

No check figure

Yesterday you received a memo from the president requesting information about the cost of operating your department for the last twelve months. She has received a bid from Fantastic Landscapes, Inc. to perform the gardening activities you now perform. You are to prepare a cost report that will help the president in deciding whether to continue gardening activities within the company or to outsource the work to another company.

REQUIRED

1. Before preparing your report, answer the following questions.
   a. What kinds of information do you need about your department?
   b. Why is this information relevant?
   c. Where would you go to obtain this information (sources)?
   d. When would you want to obtain this information?
2. Prepare a draft of the cost report that would best communicate the costs of your department. Show only headings and line items. How would you change your report if the president asked you to reduce the costs of operating your department?
3. One of your department's costs is Maintenance Expense, Garden Equipment.
   a. Is it a direct or indirect cost for the Grounds Maintenance Department?
   b. Is it a product or a period cost?
   c. Is it a variable or a fixed cost?
   d. Does the activity add value to the provision of insurance services?
   e. Is it a budgeted or an actual cost in your report?

International Company

MRA 3. *Management*
L O 5, 6 *Information Needs*

Check Figure: 1. Net income:
$469,128

The *Datil Pharmaceuticals Corporation* manufactures the majority of its three pharmaceutical products in Indonesia. Inventory information for April 19x9 was as follows:

Account	April 30	April 1
Direct Materials	$228,100	$258,400
Work in Process	127,200	138,800
Finished Goods	114,100	111,700

Purchases of materials for April were $612,600, which included natural materials, basic organic compounds, catalysts, and suspension agents. Direct labor costs were $160,000, and actual factory overhead costs were $303,500. Net sales for the company's three pharmaceutical products for April were $2,188,400. General and administrative expenses were $362,000. Income is taxed at a rate of 34 percent.

REQUIRED

1. Prepare a statement of cost of goods manufactured and an income statement for the month ended April 30.
2. Explain why the total manufacturing costs do not equal the cost of goods manufactured.
3. What additional information would you need to determine the profitability of each pharmaceutical product line?
4. Tell whether each of the following is a product cost or a period cost:
   a. Import duties for suspension agent materials
   b. Shipping expenses to deliver manufactured products to the United States
   c. Rent on manufacturing facilities in Jakarta
   d. Salary of the American production line manager working at the Indonesian manufacturing facilities
   e. Training costs for an Indonesian accountant

Product Costing: The Job Order Cost System

LEARNING OBJECTIVES

1. Identify the types of product costing systems and state the uses managers make of product costing information.
2. Compare the characteristics of the job order and process cost systems.
3. Describe the concept of absorption costing.
4. Compute a predetermined overhead rate and use it to apply overhead costs to products in process.
5. Dispose of underapplied or overapplied overhead.
6. Describe the cost flow in a job order cost system.
7. Journalize transactions in a job order cost system.
8. Compute the product unit cost for a specific job order.

DECISION POINT

FMI Forms Manufacturers[1]

FMI Forms Manufacturers is a medium-sized printing company that produces all types of business forms. During the 1970s and early 1980s, the company had no formal cost structure on which to base bids for proposed jobs. In the mid-1980s, management implemented a traditional job order cost system that traced direct costs of materials and labor to each job and then applied overhead based on those direct costs.

With competition increasing in the 1990s, FMI found itself operating at full capacity but continually losing money. Management realized that its cost system was still not supplying accurate information for the bidding process. Since direct labor costs were set by contract and employees were not shifted between different work classifications, labor cost was constant (fixed) per month. Only the cost of materials (paper) was a variable cost of the jobs. Management decided to adopt an activity-based job order product costing system that traced costs to products by type of cost driver (size of form, type of paper, and the like). To replace the single factory overhead pool and single overhead rate, costs were categorized by activity, and the cost drivers of each activity were used to apply costs to products.

Did the decision to integrate an activity-based approach to labor and overhead cost assignment make the existing job order cost system obsolete? Did a new product costing system need to be implemented?

The type of business usually identifies the product costing system that should be used. FMI produces unique, made-to-order business forms according to the requirements of specific job orders. Their type of business has not changed, so they still use a job order cost system. What has changed is the way labor and overhead costs are assigned to each job order. In the 1980s, labor was traced directly to job orders, but now it is charged to individual activity cost pools. Overhead costs are also assigned to activity cost pools. The costs of each activity are then assigned to job orders based on the usage of the corresponding cost driver. The accuracy of FMI's product costing information produced by the system has improved significantly as has the effectiveness and profitability of FMI's bidding process. ⦂⦂⦂⦂⦂

1. Jacci L. Rodgers, S. Mark Comstock, and Karl Pritz, "Customize Your Costing System," *Management Accounting,* Institute of Management Accountants, May 1993, pp. 31–32.

TYPES OF PRODUCT COSTING SYSTEMS AND THEIR USES

OBJECTIVE

1 *Identify the types of product costing systems and state the uses managers make of product costing information*

One important reason for having a management accounting system is to determine the cost of manufacturing an individual product or batch of products or of constructing a large product, such as a bridge or a jet airplane. Such management accounting systems differ widely from one company to another, but each system is designed to provide information that management believes is important. To determine the cost of producing or constructing something, two basic product costing systems have been developed, the job order cost system and the process cost system. A job order cost system is a product costing system used by companies that make large, unique, or special-order products. Under such a system, the costs of direct materials, direct labor, and factory overhead are traced to and assigned to specific job orders or batches of products. A process cost system is a product costing system used by companies that produce large amounts of similar products or liquids, or that have a continuous production flow. Under such a system, the costs of direct materials, direct labor, and factory overhead are first traced to a process or work cell and then assigned to the products produced by that process or work cell.

These two product costing systems are each designed for a specific type of production activity. But few actual production processes fit either of the production environments described. As discussed in the Decision Point about FMI Forms Manufacturers, the production process dictates the type of product costing system a company needs. As the production process changes, so does the product costing system. The typical product costing system in actual use incorporates parts of both the job order and the process cost systems to create a hybrid system designed specifically for a particular production process. It would be impossible to study all actual systems because they number in the thousands. However, by learning the terms and procedures connected with the basic job order and process cost systems, managers can adapt to any operating environment and help design product costing systems that fit their specific information needs.

The role of the product costing system is illustrated in Figure 1. First, costs of all types are incurred and recorded in various accounting records, including the general ledger. Period costs, once recorded, are used directly in developing the income statement. They are not used to develop product unit costs. All product costs, those of direct materials, direct labor, and factory overhead, are routed through the product costing system, where they are assigned to the products produced. Product costing information is used to compute the ending balances of both the work in process and the finished goods inventories on the balance sheet. Product costs are also used to compute the costs of the goods sold during the period, an important amount shown on the income statement.

Business success depends on product costing information in several ways. First, product unit cost is an important element in determining an adequate, fair, and competitive selling price for a product. Although product unit cost is not the only information used to arrive at a price, if a product's costs are not covered by its price, the company will not make a profit. Second, product costing information is often the basis for forecasting future costs. Managers are asked to prepare budgets for the next operating period as a means of planning for the effective use of resources. Product unit costs of previous periods are often used to help develop these budgets. Controlling current operations and costs is also facilitated by product cost information. If operat-

Figure 1. The Role of the Product Costing System

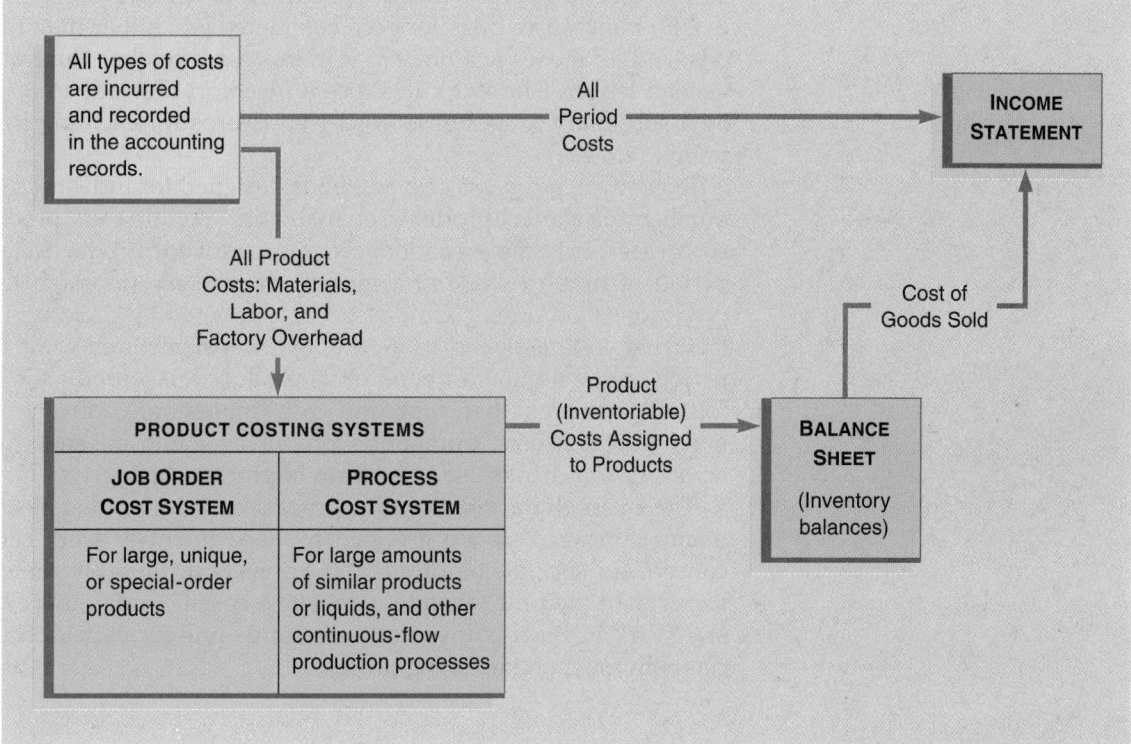

ing costs are too high and must be cut, the product cost can be broken down into its many parts to find places where costs can be decreased. Finally, product unit costs are used to determine inventory balances on the balance sheet and the cost of goods sold on the income statement, so they also assist in financial reporting.

JOB ORDER VERSUS PROCESS COSTING

OBJECTIVE

2 *Compare the characteristics of the job order and process cost systems*

The job order cost system and the process cost system both have the same objective: to account for a company's product costs and provide unit cost information for pricing, cost planning and control, inventory valuation, and income statement preparation. As is illustrated in Figure 1, the product costing system provides end-of-period values for the Cost of Goods Sold account on the income statement and the Work in Process Inventory and Finished Goods Inventory accounts on the balance sheet.

A job order cost system is used by industries that make large, unique, or made-to-order products. A job order is a customer order for a specific number of specially designed, made-to-order products. In computing unit costs, the total manufacturing costs for each job are accumulated and divided by the number of good units produced. Users of job order cost systems include manufacturers of ships, airplanes, large machines, bridges, and buildings. Job order costing may also be used when producing a set quantity of a product for inventory replenishment, such as a production run of 500 identical lawn mowers.

The primary characteristics of a job order cost system are that (1) it collects all manufacturing costs and assigns them to specific jobs or batches of product; (2) it measures costs for each completed job, rather than for set time periods; and (3) it uses just one Work in Process Inventory Control account in the general ledger. The Work in Process Inventory Control account is supported by a subsidiary ledger of job order cost cards for each job in process at any point in time.

In contrast, a process cost system is designed for industries that make large numbers of similar products or maintain a continuous production flow. In such cases, it is more economical to account for product-related costs for a period of time (a week or a month) than to try to assign them to specific products or job orders. Unit costs are computed by dividing the total manufacturing costs assigned to a particular department or work center during a period by the number of good units produced. If a product is routed through four departments, then four unit cost amounts are added to find the product's total unit cost. Companies producing paint, oil and gas, automobiles, bricks, or soft drinks use some form of process costing system.

The main characteristics of a process cost accounting system are that (1) manufacturing costs are grouped by department or work center, with little concern for specific job orders; (2) a weekly or monthly time period is used rather than the time taken to complete a specific order; and (3) there are several Work in Process Inventory accounts—one for each department or work center in the manufacturing process.

THE CONCEPT OF ABSORPTION COSTING

OBJECTIVE

3 *Describe the concept of absorption costing*

Product costing is possible only when the accounting system can define the types of manufacturing costs to be included in the analysis. For instance, should all factory overhead costs be considered costs of making a product, or only the variable factory overhead costs? Usually, we assume that product costing is governed by the concept of absorption costing. Absorption costing is an approach to product costing that assigns a representative portion of *all* types of manufacturing costs—direct materials, direct labor, variable factory overhead, and fixed factory overhead—to individual products. The product costing systems we discuss here apply the absorption costing concept.

Direct materials and direct labor costs are not difficult to handle in product costing because they can be conveniently and economically traced to products. Factory overhead costs, on the other hand, are not as easy to trace directly to products. For example, for a company making lawn and garden equipment, how much machine depreciation should be assigned to a single lawnmower? How about the costs of electrical power and indirect labor? One solution would be to wait until the end of the accounting period, add all the variable and fixed factory overhead costs incurred and divide the total by the number of units produced during the period. This procedure would be acceptable only if all products were alike (and required the same manufacturing operations) and managers could wait until the end of the period to determine the product unit costs. Such a situation is seldom found in industry. In practice, a company usually makes many different products, and managers need product costing information to set prices before the goods are produced. Therefore management accountants use a predetermined overhead rate to allocate factory overhead costs to products.

Xerox Corporation had a problem with errors in its customer billing process. In fact, an analysis revealed that each billing error cost the company an average of $106. The cost per billing error was computed using the salaries of the people answering customer complaints about billing errors and the costs of related postage, computer time, and clerical support. A quality improvement team of Xerox employees created a series of Captain Zero cartoons illustrating typical billing bloopers. The result was a significant decrease in billing errors and a steady rise in customer satisfaction with the billing process. This simple change in business practice saved Xerox over $110,000 in the six-month period under review—and cost only about $7,000.[2]

PREDETERMINED OVERHEAD RATES

OBJECTIVE

4 *Compute a predetermined overhead rate and use it to apply overhead costs to products in process*

Factory overhead costs are a problem for the management accountant. Actual overhead costs fluctuate from month to month because of the timing of fixed overhead costs and the changing patterns and amounts of variable costs. The need to price new products and to evaluate production performance prevents management from waiting until the end of the accounting period to account for these costs.

The most common way of estimating and assigning costs to products or jobs before the end of an accounting period is to use a predetermined overhead rate for each department or operating unit. The predetermined overhead rate is a factor used to assign factory overhead costs to specific products or jobs. It is based on *estimated* overhead costs and production levels for the period.

The predetermined overhead rate is computed in three steps.

1. Estimate factory overhead costs. Using management accounting tools and analyses, estimate all factory overhead costs. Do so for each service and production department for the coming accounting period. (Cost behavior analysis is especially useful for this procedure.) Allocate the service department costs, and then add the totals for all the production departments. For example, assume that the total estimated factory overhead costs assigned to the Heading/Slotting Department at Mahla Industries were $561,600.
2. Select a basis for allocating costs and estimate its amount. Overhead costs must be connected to products using some measure of production activity—machine hours, labor hours, dollars of direct labor costs, or units of output, for example. The basis chosen should link the overhead costs to the products in a meaningful way. For instance, if an operation is more machine-hour than labor-hour intensive, then machine hours would be a good basis for overhead allocation. Suppose that this is the basis Mahla Industries decides to use to allocate factory overhead costs in its Heading/Slotting Department and that management

2. David M. Buehlmann and Donald Stover, "How Xerox Solves Quality Problems," *Management Accounting*, Institute of Management Accountants, September 1993, pp. 33–36.

estimates that the department will generate 124,800 machine hours during the year.

3. Divide the total estimated overhead costs for the period by the total estimated basis (hours, dollars, or units). The result is the predetermined overhead rate. At Mahla Industries, the computation for the Heading/Slotting Department is as follows:

$$\frac{\text{Predetermined overhead rate}}{\text{per machine hour}} = \frac{\text{total estimated overhead costs}}{\text{total estimated machine hours}}$$

$$= \frac{\$561,600}{124,800 \text{ machine hours}}$$

$$= \underline{\underline{\$4.50}} \text{ of overhead per machine hour}$$

Overhead costs are then applied to each product using the predetermined overhead rate. For example, suppose that it takes 0.5 machine hour to produce one unit. Because the overhead rate is $4.50 per machine hour, that unit is assigned $2.25 of factory overhead costs. This amount is added to the direct materials and direct labor costs already assigned to the product, and their sum is the total unit cost.

Table 1 summarizes the process of allocating overhead costs. In Phase I, the predetermined overhead rate is computed. To do so, the total overhead costs and total production activity are estimated. In Phase II, the predetermined overhead rate is used to compute the amount of overhead costs to be applied to products or jobs during the period—a process described in a later section.

THE IMPORTANCE OF GOOD ESTIMATES

The successful allocation of overhead costs depends on two factors. One is a careful estimate of total overhead. The other is a good forecast of the production activity used as the allocation basis.

Estimating total overhead costs is critical. If the estimate is wrong, the overhead rate will be wrong: Either too much or too little overhead will be assigned to the products. Therefore, in developing this estimate, the management accountant must be careful to include all factory overhead items and to forecast their costs accurately.

Overhead costs generally are estimated as part of the normal budgeting process. Expected overhead costs are gathered from all departments involved either directly or indirectly with the production process. The accounting department receives and totals each department's cost estimates. As we have seen, the costs of supporting service departments, such as the Repair and Maintenance Department, are connected only indirectly to the products, and their costs are distributed among the production departments. In this way, they are included as part of a total factory overhead when computing the predetermined overhead rate for the period.

Forecasting production activity is also critical to the success of overhead cost allocation. Once the appropriate base (machine hours, direct labor hours, direct labor cost, or units of output) has been determined, the estimated total activity base for the coming period must be computed. Assume that the activity base is machine hours. How do we estimate total machine hours for a future period? Machine hours are a function of the number of products to be produced. Each product requires a certain amount of machine time. The first step, then, is to find out how many units the manufacturing departments are planning to produce. Once this number has been determined, total estimated

Table 1. Overhead Cost Allocation

Phase I: Computing the Predetermined Overhead Rate

Develop Overhead Cost Estimates
Estimate total overhead costs for each production department.

Develop Allocation (Activity) Basis Estimates
1. For each production department, select an allocation basis with a causal or beneficial relationship to the costs being assigned to the end product or job.
2. Carefully estimate the activity level for each department for the coming period.

$$\frac{\text{total estimated overhead costs}}{\text{total estimated activity basis}} = \text{predetermined overhead rate}$$

Phase II: Using the Rate to Assign Overhead Costs

Predetermined overhead rate × actual amount of activity per job order = overhead cost assigned to that job order or batch of products

machine hours can be computed by multiplying total units to be produced by the number of machine hours required per unit.

USING A PREDETERMINED OVERHEAD RATE

A predetermined overhead rate has two primary uses. First, it enables a management accountant to provide cost information to sales personnel to support pricing decisions for a new product or job order. Price is influenced by many factors, including the item's cost, and price is usually determined before an item is produced. Factory overhead can consist of dozens, even hundreds, of types of costs, and estimating these costs every time a price must be determined would be difficult. A predetermined overhead rate significantly simplifies the price-setting process. Second, a predetermined overhead rate allows a company to attach overhead costs to items as they are worked on and completed, instead of at the end of an accounting period. Factory overhead is "applied" to a product as it moves through the production process.

Using a predetermined overhead rate changes the recordkeeping process. To this point in your study of accounting, a separate account has been maintained for each type of overhead cost incurred. When electricity or factory insurance costs were incurred, we debited the individual accounts for the amounts. With a predetermined overhead rate, we introduce a new account into the recording process. The Factory Overhead Control account is a general ledger account that contains the cumulative total of all types of factory overhead costs; it also is used to accumulate all overhead costs applied to products produced. As with all control accounts, a subsidiary ledger is maintained to account for all of the individual types of costs charged to the Factory Overhead Control account. Each time an overhead cost is incurred, both the Factory Overhead Control account and the individual account are debited.

Factory overhead is applied to products by debiting an amount to the Work in Process Inventory Control account. The amount is determined by multiplying the predetermined overhead rate by the amount of the basis used by the production process. (This computation is shown at the bottom of Table 1.) Each time the Work in Process Inventory Control account is debited for overhead costs applied, the Factory Overhead Control account is credited for the same amount. At the end of the accounting period, all overhead costs actually incurred have been debited to the Factory Overhead Control account, and all overhead costs applied to the products produced have been credited to the same account.

For example, assume that the Heading/Slotting Department of Mahla Industries incurred the following overhead costs during March.

Mar. 5 Recorded usage of indirect materials and supplies, $11,890 (transferred from Materials Inventory Control account).
    10 Paid indirect labor wages, $14,220.
    15 Paid property taxes on factory building, $7,540, and utility bill, $5,200.
    31 Recorded expiration of prepaid insurance premiums, $2,820, and depreciation of machinery for the month, $4,430.

These transactions resulted in the following entries.

Mar. 5	Factory Overhead Control	11,890	
	Materials Inventory Control		11,890
	Usage of indirect		
	materials and supplies		
10	Factory Overhead Control	14,220	
	Factory Payroll		14,220
	Distribution of indirect labor costs		
	from the Factory Payroll account		
15	Factory Overhead Control	12,740	
	Cash		12,740
	Payment of property taxes of $7,540		
	and utilities of $5,200		
31	Factory Overhead Control	7,250	
	Prepaid Insurance		2,820
	Accumulated Depreciation, Machinery		4,430
	To record the expiration of prepaid		
	insurance premiums and depreciation		
	on machinery for March		

These entries record actual overhead costs of $46,100 debited to the Factory Overhead Control account. However, they neither assign the costs to products nor transfer the costs to the Work in Process Inventory Control account. This transfer must take place before factory overhead costs can be added to the costs of direct materials and direct labor so that product unit costs can be computed. This is when the predetermined overhead rate is used. Remember that the predetermined overhead rate for Mahla's Heading/Slotting Department for the period is $4.50 per machine hour. The following list of jobs completed during March shows the number of machine hours required for each job and the overhead costs applied to each job.

Job	Machine Hours	×	Rate	=	Overhead Applied
16–2	3,238		$4.50		$14,571
18–6	3,038		4.50		13,671
21–5	3,884		4.50		17,478
	10,160				$45,720

The following journal entry records the application of factory overhead to Job 16–2 (a similar entry would be made for each job worked on during March).

Work in Process Inventory Control	14,571	
Factory Overhead Control		14,571
Application of overhead costs to Job 16–2		

This entry transfers the estimated overhead costs from the Factory Overhead Control account to the Work in Process Inventory Control account. Normally, the entry is made when production data are recorded because overhead costs can be applied only after the number of machine hours used is known.

After posting all of the overhead transactions discussed above, the applied overhead costs (the amounts credited to the Factory Overhead Control account) are compared with the actual overhead costs incurred (the amounts debited to the account). As shown below, fewer costs were applied than were incurred, so overhead costs are underapplied.

Factory Overhead Control

3/5	11,890	Job 16–2	14,571
3/10	14,220	Job 18–6	13,671
3/15	12,740	Job 21–5	17,478
3/31	7,250		45,720
	46,100		
Bal.	**380**		

ACCOUNTING FOR UNDERAPPLIED OR OVERAPPLIED OVERHEAD

OBJECTIVE

5 *Dispose of under-applied or over-applied overhead*

Although companies expend much time and effort on estimating and allocating factory overhead costs, actual overhead costs and actual production activities seldom agree with the estimates. Because of changes in either the overhead costs or the activity-related allocation base, assigned factory overhead is either *underapplied* or *overapplied*—that is, the amount applied is less than or greater than the actual overhead costs incurred. These differences are accounted for by making a monthly, quarterly, or annual adjusting entry, depending on the company policy.

For example, the records at Mahla Industries show that at month's end, overhead costs have been underapplied by $380 ($46,100 − $45,720). The predetermined overhead rate was low, and, as a result, all of the overhead costs incurred were not applied to the products produced. To account for all actual costs, the $380 must be added to the production costs for the period. Assuming that most of the goods worked on during the period have been sold or that the amount is immaterial, the adjusting entry at the end of the month would charge the amount underapplied to the Cost of Goods Sold account.

Mar. 31	Cost of Goods Sold	380	
	Factory Overhead Control		380
	To record charge of underapplied		
	overhead to the Cost of Goods Sold		
	account		

The company should investigate any significant differences between the amount applied and the actual overhead costs incurred; the rate may have to be recomputed if large differences persist.

Wattie Frozen Foods Limited of New Zealand[3]

The corporate headquarters of Wattie Frozen Foods (WFF) is located in Auckland, New Zealand. The company processes frozen and dehydrated foods and sells its products in New Zealand, Australia, and other Pacific Rim countries. Company management recently initiated a new operating philosophy that focuses on the work center and empowers work-center managers to make most decisions about daily operations. Management and staff were specially trained for the transition to this new approach, and continuous improvement became the driving force behind the system. One of the unique aspects of the new operating environment is that physical measures rather than financial measures are used for daily control of operations. Products and processes are tracked by looking at physical measures of productivity. Resource usage is traced to products by means of activity measures. WFF managers call this approach "costing without dollars." Why would physical measures be better barometers of work-center operations than financial measures? Would the new approach mean that the importance of financial information has been downgraded?

Physical measures have not replaced dollars at WFF. However, physical measures are used in place of dollars at the work-center level because they are easier to use in planning and controlling the food-processing operations, and because combining dollars with physical measures at the work-center level was adding confusion to the interpretation and analysis of production data. Under the new operating philosophy, dollars are later attached to the physical measures so that product costs can be computed and the financial consequences of operations can be determined. Financial measures are still important overall, but, at the operating level, they can cloud the issues and problems being analyzed. ⦂⦂⦂⦂⦂

THE JOB ORDER COST SYSTEM

Remember that a job order cost system is designed to gather manufacturing costs for a specific order or batch of products to help determine product unit costs. Price setting, production scheduling, and other management tasks related to job orders depend on information from the management account-

3. William D. J. Cotton, "Relevance Regained Down Under," *Management Accounting*, Institute of Management Accountants, May 1994, pp. 38–42.

ing system. This is why it is necessary to maintain a system that gives timely, correct data about product costs. Here, we see how the three main cost elements—materials, labor, and factory overhead—are accounted for in a job order cost system. Notice that all inventory balances in a job order cost system are kept on a perpetual basis, and, following the absorption costing approach, all production costs are included in the analysis.

INCURRING MATERIALS, LABOR, AND FACTORY OVERHEAD COSTS

A basic part of a job order cost system is the set of procedures, accounts, and journal entries used when the company incurs materials, labor, and factory overhead costs. To help control such costs, businesses use various documents to support each transaction. The effective use of procedures and documents generates timely, accurate information for managers and facilitates the smooth and continuous flow of information through the accounting records.

Materials Careful use of materials improves a company's overall efficiency and profitability by conserving productive resources and saving their related costs. At the same time, good records ensure accountability. So, controlling the physical materials used in production and keeping good records increase the opportunity to earn a profit.

To help record and control materials costs, accountants rely on a series of documents, including purchase requisitions, purchase orders, receiving reports, inventory records, and materials requisitions. Through these documents, direct materials are ordered, received, stored, and issued into production. Information from purchase requisitions enables the tracing of direct materials costs to specific jobs or batches of product, and identifies the amount of indirect materials to be charged to factory overhead.

Labor Labor is one production resource that cannot be stored and used later, so it must be accounted for carefully. Labor time cards and job cards are used to record labor costs as they are incurred. Time cards keep track of the total time each employee works per day, and job cards track the amount of time each employee works on a particular job or other labor classification. Labor costs that can be traced directly to a job or batch of products are debited to the Work in Process Inventory Control account, and all indirect labor costs flow through the Factory Overhead Control account.

Factory Overhead All indirect manufacturing costs are classified as factory overhead. Like direct materials and direct labor costs, factory overhead costs require documents to support their recording and payment. As described above, materials requisitions support the use of indirect materials and supplies, and labor job cards track indirect labor; vendors' bills support most of the other indirect costs. In a job order cost system, all factory overhead costs are debited to the Factory Overhead Control account, and separate subsidiary accounts are maintained to keep track of the individual kinds of overhead costs. Using a predetermined overhead rate, factory overhead costs are charged to individual jobs by crediting the Factory Overhead Control account and debiting the Work in Process Inventory Control account.

THE WORK IN PROCESS INVENTORY CONTROL ACCOUNT

Job order costing focuses on the flow of costs through the Work in Process Inventory Control account. All manufacturing costs incurred and charged to production are routed through this account. Figure 2 summarizes the cost flow in a job order cost system.

The costs of direct materials and indirect materials and supplies are debited to Materials Inventory Control when purchased. When used, direct materials are debited to the Work in Process Inventory Control account, and indirect materials and supplies are debited to the Factory Overhead Control account. All labor costs that can be traced to specific jobs are debited to the Work in Process Inventory Control account, and indirect labor costs are charged to the Factory Overhead Control account. Using a predetermined overhead rate, overhead costs are applied to specific jobs by debiting the Work

Figure 2. Job Order Cost Flow

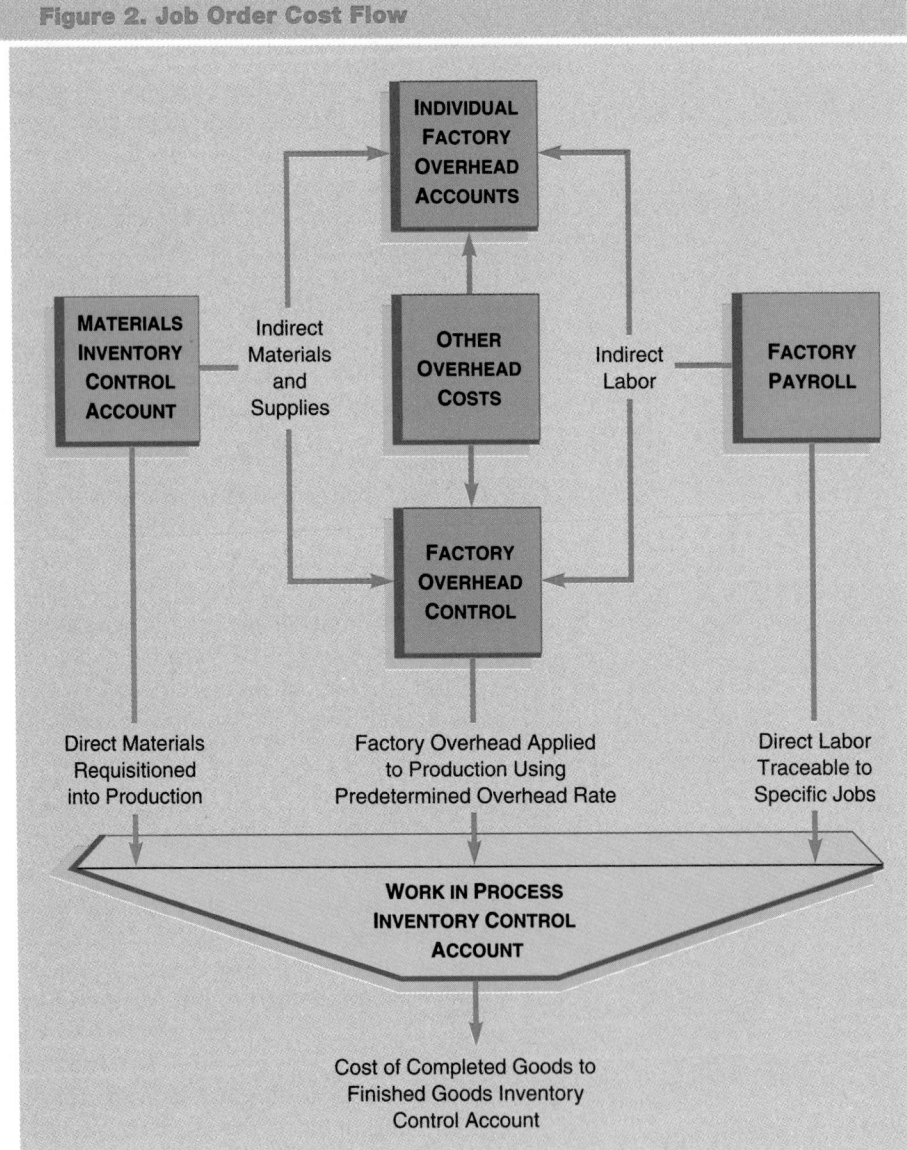

in Process Inventory Control account and crediting the Factory Overhead Control account.

Because all manufacturing costs are debited to the Work in Process Inventory Control account, a separate accounting procedure is needed to link those costs to specific jobs. The solution is a subsidiary ledger made up of job order cost cards. For each job being worked on, there is a job order cost card on which all costs of that job are recorded. As costs are debited to Work in Process Inventory Control, they are reclassified by job and recorded on the appropriate job order cost cards.

A typical job order cost card is shown in Figure 3. Each card has space for direct materials, direct labor, and factory overhead costs. It also includes the job order number, product specifications, the name of the customer, the date of the order, the projected completion date, and a cost summary. As each department incurs materials and labor costs, the individual job order cost cards are updated. Factory overhead, as applied, is also posted to the job order cost cards. Job order cost cards for incomplete jobs make up the subsidiary ledger for the Work in Process Inventory Control account. To ensure correctness, the ending balance in the Work in Process Inventory Control account is compared with the total of the costs shown on the job order cost cards. (We illustrate this process later in this section, when we examine a specific example in detail.)

Figure 3. Job Order Cost Card

Job Order	Wasa Boat Company	
No. *16F*	New Port Richey, Florida	

Product Specs: *Model GB30-Mark I: 30 foot fiberglass sailing sloop with full galley*

Customer:	Materials:	
Hinds Yachts, Inc.	Dept. 1	*$96,500*
	Dept. 2	*23,700*
Date of Order:	Dept. 3	*-0-*
February 10, 19x7	Total	*$120,200*
Date of Completion:		
October 28, 19x7	Direct Labor:	
	Dept. 1	*$43,440*
Cost Summary:	Dept. 2	*60,960*
Materials *$120,200*	Dept. 3	*40,400*
Direct Labor *144,800*	Total	*$144,800*
Factory Overhead *123,080*		
Total *$388,080*	Applied Factory Overhead:	
Units Completed *11*	Dept. 1	*$36,924*
(eleven)	Dept. 2	*51,816*
Cost per Unit	Dept. 3	*34,340*
$35,280	Total	*$123,080*

ACCOUNTING FOR FINISHED GOODS

When a job has been completed, all costs assigned to it are transferred to the Finished Goods Inventory Control account by debiting the Finished Goods Inventory Control account and crediting the Work in Process Inventory Control account. Once this entry is made, the job order cost card is removed from the subsidiary ledger file. It is then used to update the Finished Goods Inventory Control account.

When goods are shipped, the order for them is recorded as a sale. Accounts Receivable is debited and Sales is credited for the entire selling price. Under the perpetual inventory system, the cost of the goods shipped must also be accounted for. The proper procedure is to debit Cost of Goods Sold and credit Finished Goods Inventory Control for the cost of the goods shipped.

BUSINESS BULLETIN: INTERNATIONAL PRACTICE

The auto maker Daihatsu Motor Company, of Osaka, Japan, employs a system called Kaizen costing to help control product costs. Although not a product costing system in itself, Kaizen costing supports the continuous improvement environment adopted by Daihatsu management. Kaizen costing is a cost-reduction technique that aims at reducing actual costs below anticipated or budgeted costs. So instead of trying to meet budgeted goals, managers at Daihatsu try to meet or exceed budgeted output targets at below budgeted costs. Improvements in product design, production techniques, marketing, and distribution channels all help the company reduce product costs below budget. Kaizen costing is one way of introducing continuous improvement into the operating and product costing systems of a company.[4]

OBJECTIVE

7 *Journalize transactions in a job order cost system*

ANALYSIS OF JOURNAL ENTRIES

Because a job order cost system emphasizes cost flow, it is important to understand the journal entries that record the various costs as they are incurred and to recognize the entries used to transfer costs from one account to another. These entries, along with job order cost cards and subsidiary ledgers for materials and finished goods inventories, are a major part of the job order cost system.

The journal entries are illustrated in the step-by-step example below. As each entry is discussed, trace its number and related debits or credits to Exhibit 1. Also, keep in mind the cost flow shown in Figure 2.

Recording the Purchase of Materials   The Wasa Boat Company bought Material 5X for $57,200 and Material 14Q for $34,000. Materials purchases are recorded at cost in the Materials Inventory Control account.

---

4. Yasuhiro Monden and John Lee, "How a Japanese Auto Maker Reduces Costs," *Management Accounting,* Institute of Management Accountants, August 1993, pp. 22–26.

Entry 1: Materials Inventory Control   91,200
      Accounts Payable (or Cash)   91,200
          Purchase of $57,200 of Material 5X
          and $34,000 of Material 14Q

Notice that the debit is to an inventory account, not a purchases account. Because a perpetual inventory system is used, all materials costs flow through the inventory account, which is a control account. Some companies have hundreds of items in inventory. To keep a separate account for each item in the general ledger would make the ledger bulky and hard to work with. When entry **1** is posted to the general ledger, the individual accounts in the subsidiary materials ledger also are updated, as Exhibit 1 shows.

Recording the Purchase of Supplies   The company purchased $8,200 of operating supplies for the manufacturing process.

Entry 2: Materials Inventory Control   8,200
      Accounts Payable (or Cash)   8,200
          Purchase of operating supplies

The procedures used to account for the purchase of supplies are much like those used for the purchase of direct materials. Operating Supplies Inventory is one of the subsidiary accounts that makes up the Materials Inventory Control account. If the supplies inventory is large, a separate general ledger account can be used. Regardless of which method is selected, the accountant should be able to justify the approach taken and should follow it consistently.

Requisitioning Materials and Supplies   On receipt of a properly prepared materials requisition form, the following direct materials and supplies are issued from inventory to production: Material 5X, $124,000; Material 14Q, $64,000; and operating supplies, $9,600.

Entry 3: Work in Process Inventory Control   188,000
      Factory Overhead Control   9,600
          Materials Inventory Control   197,600
          Issuance of $124,000 of Material 5X,
          $64,000 of Material 14Q, and $9,600
          of operating supplies into production

This entry shows that $188,000 of direct materials and $9,600 of indirect materials were issued. The debit to the Work in Process Inventory Control account records the cost of the direct materials issued to production. These costs can be traced directly to specific job orders. As the direct materials costs are charged to work in process, the amounts for individual jobs are entered on the job order cost cards. As shown in Exhibit 1, $103,800 of direct materials were used on Job 16F and $84,200 of direct materials were used on Job 23H. Indirect materials costs (supplies) are debited to the Factory Overhead Control account.

Recording Labor Costs   Recording labor costs for a manufacturing company requires three journal entries. The first records the total payroll liability of the company. Let's assume that payroll liability for the period consists of total direct labor wages, $164,000; total indirect labor wages, $76,000; total administrative salaries, $72,000; social security and Medicare taxes withheld, $18,720; and federal income taxes withheld, $78,000. Although only $215,280 of net earnings is to be paid to employees, total direct and indirect labor costs are used for product and job costing.

Exhibit 1. The Job Order Cost System—Wasa Boat Company

Materials Inventory Control

Beg. Bal.	123,000	Requisitions:		
(1) Purchases	91,200	Materials	188,000 (3)	
(2) Purchases	8,200	Supplies	9,600 (3)	
End. Bal.	24,800			

Work in Process Inventory Control

Beg. Bal.	40,080	Completed	388,080 (10)
(3) Materials Used	188,000		
(6) Direct Labor	164,000		
(9) Overhead	139,400		
End. Bal.	143,400		

Factory Payroll

(4) Wages Earned	240,000	Direct Labor	164,000 (6)
		Indirect Labor	76,000 (6)

Factory Overhead Control

(3) Supplies Used	9,600	Applied	139,400 (9)
(6) Indirect Labor	76,000		
(7) Other	29,500		
(8) Adjustment	24,000		
	139,100		139,400
(13) To close	300		
	—		

SUBSIDIARY LEDGERS

MATERIALS LEDGER

Material 5X

Beg. Bal.	83,000	Used	124,000 (3)
(1) Purchases	57,200		
End. Bal.	16,200		

Material 14Q

Beg. Bal.	37,000	Used	64,000 (3)
(1) Purchases	34,000		
End. Bal.	7,000		

Operating Supplies Inventory

Beg. Bal.	3,000	Used	9,600 (3)
(2) Purchases	8,200		
End. Bal.	1,600		

JOB ORDER COST CARDS

Job 16F

Costs from the previous period	40,080
Materials	103,800
Direct Labor	132,000
Factory Overhead	112,200
Completed Cost	388,080

Job 23H

Materials	84,200
Direct Labor	32,000
Factory Overhead	27,200
Ending Balance	143,400

moved production cost to accounts

Entry 4:	Factory Payroll	240,000	
	Administrative Salaries Expense	72,000	
	Social Security and Medicare Taxes Payable		18,720
	Federal Income Tax Payable		78,000
	Wages and Salaries Payable		215,280
	Payroll liability for the period		

Exhibit 1. The Job Order Cost System—Wasa Boat Company *(continued)*

Finished Goods Inventory Control					Cost of Goods Sold			
Beg. Bal.	—				(12) Sold		Adjustment	300 (13)
(10) Completed During Period	388,080	Sold	352,800 (12)		During Period	352,800		
End. Bal.	35,280				End. Bal.	352,500		

FINISHED GOODS LEDGER

Product F

Beg. Bal.	—	Sold	352,800 (12)
(10) Completed	388,080		
End. Bal.	35,280		

Product H

Beg. Bal.	—	

Entry 5 records the payment of the payroll liability established in entry **4**. Following the preparation of payroll checks for the period, this entry records their distribution to the employees.

Entry 5:	Wages and Salaries Payable	215,280	
	Cash		215,280
	Payment of payroll		

A third entry is needed to account for the labor costs. The $240,000 debited to the Factory Payroll account must be moved to the production accounts. Total direct labor costs are debited to Work in Process Inventory Control, and total indirect wages (including factory supervisory salaries) are debited to Factory Overhead Control. Factory Payroll is credited to show that the total amount has been distributed to the production accounts.

Entry 6:	Work in Process Inventory Control	164,000	
	Factory Overhead Control	76,000	
	Factory Payroll		240,000
	Distribution of factory payroll		
	to the production accounts		

In addition, the direct labor costs are recorded by job on the individual job order cost cards. This distribution of $132,000 to Job 16F and $32,000 to Job 23H is shown in Exhibit 1.

Accounting for Other Factory Overhead Costs

The sum of factory overhead costs other than indirect materials and indirect labor costs is charged (debited) to the Factory Overhead Control account. Each cost is identified in the journal entry explanation. In our example, factory overhead costs were electricity, $6,300; maintenance and repair, $16,900; insurance, $2,800; and property taxes, $3,500.

Entry 7:	Factory Overhead Control	29,500	
	Accounts Payable (or Cash)		29,500
	Incurrence of the following		
	overhead costs: electricity, $6,300;		
	maintenance and repair, $16,900;		
	insurance, $2,800; and property		
	taxes, $3,500		

The individual subsidiary ledger accounts also are updated. Because of space limitations, Exhibit 1 does not show the subsidiary ledger for the Factory Overhead Control account. However, the subsidiary ledger would include a separate account for each type of factory overhead cost. The costs would be accounted for in much the same way that costs are accounted for in the materials ledger and job order cost cards.

The next transaction is an adjusting entry to record the depreciation of factory equipment for the period.

Entry 8:	Factory Overhead Control	24,000	
	Accumulated Depreciation, Equipment		24,000
	To record the depreciation of		
	factory equipment for the period		

Adjusting entries are usually prepared after all transactions for the period have been recorded. We introduce the topic at this point because depreciation of factory equipment is a part of total factory overhead cost. The actual depreciation expense account is part of the factory overhead subsidiary ledger.

Applying Factory Overhead

Factory overhead is applied using a predetermined overhead rate and an appropriate allocation base (machine hours, direct labor hours, direct labor dollars, or units of output). In this example, factory overhead costs are applied to production using a rate of 85 percent of direct labor dollars.

Entry 9:	Work in Process Inventory Control	139,400	
	Factory Overhead Control		139,400
	Application of factory overhead		
	costs to production		

The amount of overhead charged to production is found by multiplying the measurement units of the base by the predetermined overhead rate. In the example, the direct labor dollars ($164,000) are multiplied by 85 percent, which equals $139,400 ($164,000 × .85). This amount is debited to the Work in Process Inventory Control account. Because the application of overhead is related to direct labor dollars, the job order cost cards can be updated using the same procedure. Job 16F is assigned $112,200 of overhead costs ($132,000 × .85), and Job 23H is assigned $27,200 ($32,000 × .85). These amounts have been posted to the job order cost cards in Exhibit 1.

Accounting for Completed Units   As job orders are completed, their costs are moved to the Finished Goods Inventory Control account. In this case, goods costing $388,080 for Job 16F were completed and transferred to Finished Goods Inventory Control (see the job order cost card for Job 16F in Exhibit 1).

Entry 10: Finished Goods Inventory Control	388,080	
Work in Process Inventory Control		388,080
Transfer of completed goods for		
Job 16F from Work in Process		
Inventory Control to Finished Goods		
Inventory Control		

When a job is completed, its job order cost card is pulled from the work in process subsidiary ledger. It is then used to update the finished goods subsidiary ledger. Specifically, costs recorded on the job order cost card are used to figure unit costs and to determine the amount of the transfer entry.

Accounting for Units Sold   The final phase of the manufacturing cost flow is the transfer of costs from the Finished Goods Inventory Control account to the Cost of Goods Sold account. At this point, ten sailing sloops from Job 16F have been shipped to the customer. The selling price for the goods shipped was $520,000. The total cost of manufacturing these products was $352,800.

Entry 11: Accounts Receivable	520,000	
Sales		520,000
Sale of a portion of Job 16F		

Entry 12: Cost of Goods Sold	352,800	
Finished Goods Inventory Control		352,800
Transfer of the cost of the shipped		
goods for Job 16F from Finished		
Goods Inventory Control to Cost of		
Goods Sold		

Both the entry to record the sale and the entry to establish the cost of the goods sold are shown here. Entry **12** is made at the time the sale is recorded. When the costs of the products sold are transferred out of the Finished Goods Inventory Control account, the finished goods subsidiary ledger should also be updated, as shown in Exhibit 1.

Disposing of Underapplied or Overapplied Overhead   At the end of the accounting period, both sides of the Factory Overhead Control account are totaled to determine if the appropriate amount of factory overhead costs has been applied to the jobs and products worked on during the period. As shown on the next page, $139,100 of factory overhead costs were actually incurred during the period, but $139,400 was applied, a difference of $300.

Factory Overhead Control

(3)	9,600	(9)		139,400
(6)	76,000			
(7)	29,500			
(8)	24,000			
	139,100			**139,400**
		Bal.		300

overapplied *×*
underapplied —

Now an entry must be made to close this account and dispose of the overapplied factory overhead. During the period, $300 too much was applied to jobs worked on, so a credit of $300 must be made to Cost of Goods Sold to reduce the costs of jobs completed. The debit of $300 to the Factory Overhead Control account returns the balance to zero.

Entry 13:	Factory Overhead Control	300	
	Cost of Goods Sold		300
	To dispose of the overapplied balance and close out the Factory Overhead Control account		

OBJECTIVE

8 *Compute the product unit cost for a specific job order*

COMPUTING PRODUCT UNIT COSTS

The process of computing product unit costs is fairly simple in a job order cost system. All costs of direct materials, direct labor, and factory overhead are recorded on the job order cost card as the job progresses toward completion. When the job is finished, the costs on the job order cost card are totaled. The unit cost is computed by dividing the total costs for the job by the number of good units produced.

The cost data for completed Job 16F are shown on the job order cost card in Figure 3. Eleven sailing sloops were produced at a total cost of $388,080. This worked out to a cost of $35,280 per sloop before adjustments. Notice in Exhibit 1 that only ten of the sloops were actually shipped during the year. The entire $300 of overapplied overhead was credited to the ten sloops sold. One still remains in Finished Goods Inventory Control at the unadjusted cost.

FULLY AND PARTLY COMPLETED PRODUCTS

In a job order costing system, manufacturing costs are accumulated, classified, and reclassified several times. All manufacturing costs are linked to products as the products are produced. These costs follow the products to the Finished Goods Inventory Control account and then to the Cost of Goods Sold account. Exhibit 1 illustrates the accounting procedures and cost flows of units worked on during the period. The dollar amounts in Exhibit 1 come from posting the journal entries just discussed.

At the end of the period, some costs remain in the Work in Process Inventory Control account and the Finished Goods Inventory Control account. The ending balance of $143,400 in the Work in Process Inventory Control account is from costs attached to partly completed units from Job 23H. These costs are traceable to the job order cost card in the subsidiary ledger (see Exhibit 1). The Finished Goods Inventory Control account also has an ending balance. Of all the units completed during the accounting period, one sloop from Job 16F has not been sold or shipped. Its cost, $35,280, now appears as the ending balance in the Finished Goods Inventory Control account.

CHAPTER REVIEW

REVIEW OF LEARNING OBJECTIVES

1. **Identify the types of product costing systems and state the uses managers make of product costing information.** Two basic product costing systems have been developed to determine the cost of producing or constructing something. A job order cost system is used by companies that make large, unique, or special-order products. Under such a system, the costs of direct materials, direct labor, and factory overhead are traced to and assigned to specific job orders or batches of products. A process cost system is used by companies that produce large amounts of similar products or liquids or that have a continuous production flow. Under such a system, the costs of direct materials, direct labor, and factory overhead are first traced to processes or work cells and then assigned to the products produced by that process or work cell.

   Managers use product costing information in many ways. First, product unit cost is an important element in determining an adequate, fair, and competitive selling price for a product. Second, product costing information often forms the basis for forecasting future costs. Controlling current operations and costs is also facilitated by product cost information. Finally, product unit costs are used to determine inventory balances reported on the balance sheet and the cost of goods sold reported on the income statement, so they also assist in financial reporting.

2. **Compare the characteristics of the job order and process cost systems.** Both the job order cost system and the process cost system are basic, traditional approaches to management accounting. However, they have different characteristics. In a job order cost system: (1) manufacturing costs are assigned to specific jobs or batches of product; (2) costs are measured for each completed job, rather than for set time periods; and (3) one Work in Process Inventory Control account appears in the general ledger. In determining unit costs, the total manufacturing costs assigned to each job are divided by the number of good units produced. In a process cost system: (1) manufacturing costs are grouped by department or work center; (2) costs are measured in terms of a weekly or monthly time period; and (3) several Work in Process Inventory accounts appear in the general ledger. Unit costs are found by dividing total manufacturing costs for a department or work center during the week or month by the number of good units produced.

3. **Describe the concept of absorption costing.** Absorption costing is an approach to product costing in which a representative portion of *all* manufacturing costs is assigned to individual products. Thus, direct materials, direct labor, variable factory overhead, and fixed factory overhead costs are all assigned to products.

4. **Compute a predetermined overhead rate and use it to apply overhead costs to products in process.** A predetermined overhead rate is a factor used to assign factory overhead costs to specific products or jobs. It is computed by dividing total estimated overhead costs for a period by the total expected activity basis (machine hours, labor hours, dollars of direct labor costs, units of output) for that period. Factory overhead costs are applied to a job or product by multiplying the predetermined overhead rate by the actual amount of the activity base used to produce that job or product.

5. **Dispose of underapplied or overapplied overhead.** If, at the end of a period, there is a difference between the debit and credit sides of the Factory Overhead Control account, factory overhead has been either underapplied or overapplied. When the difference is small or when most of the products worked on during the period have been sold, the underapplied or overapplied amount is eliminated with an adjusting entry that transfers the balance to the Cost of Goods Sold account.

6. **Describe the cost flow in a job order cost system.** A job order cost system presumes an absorption costing approach and use of the perpetual inventory system. The costs of materials and supplies are first debited to the Materials Inventory Control account. Labor costs are debited to the Factory Payroll account. The various factory overhead costs are debited to the Factory Overhead Control account. As products are manufactured, the costs of direct materials and direct labor are transferred to

the Work in Process Inventory Control account. Factory overhead costs are applied and charged to the Work in Process Inventory Control account using a predetermined overhead rate. The charges are credited to the Factory Overhead Control account. When products or jobs are completed, the costs assigned to them are transferred to the Finished Goods Inventory Control account. Then, when the products are sold and shipped, their assigned costs are transferred to the Cost of Goods Sold account.

7. **Journalize transactions in a job order cost system.** A job order cost system requires journal entries for each of the following transactions: (a) purchase of materials, (b) purchase of operating supplies, (c) requisition of materials and supplies into production, (d) recording of payroll liability, (e) payment of payroll to employees, (f) distribution of factory payroll to production accounts, (g) cash payment of overhead costs, (h) recording of noncash overhead costs such as depreciation of factory and equipment, (i) application of factory overhead costs to production, (j) transfer of costs of completed jobs from the Work in Process Inventory Control account to the Finished Goods Inventory Control account, (k) sale of products and transfer of related costs from the Finished Goods Inventory Control account to the Cost of Goods Sold account, and (l) disposition of underapplied or overapplied factory overhead.

8. **Compute the product unit cost for a specific job order.** Product costs are computed by first totaling all the manufacturing costs accumulated on a particular job order cost card. This amount is then divided by the number of good units produced to find the individual unit cost for the order. The unit cost information is entered on the job order cost card and used to value inventory.

REVIEW OF CONCEPTS AND TERMINOLOGY

The following concepts and terms were introduced in this chapter.

L O 3 **Absorption costing:** An approach to product costing that assigns a representative portion of all types of manufacturing costs—direct materials, direct labor, variable factory overhead, and fixed factory overhead—to individual products.

L O 4 **Factory Overhead Control account:** A general ledger account that contains the cumulative total of all types of factory overhead costs incurred as well as factory overhead costs applied to the products produced.

L O 2 **Job order:** A customer order for a specific number of specially designed, made-to-order products.

L O 6 **Job order cost card:** A document on which all costs incurred in the production of a particular job order are recorded; part of the subsidiary ledger for the Work in Process Inventory Control account.

L O 1 **Job order cost system:** A product costing system used by companies that make large, unique, or special-order products; the costs of direct materials, direct labor, and factory overhead are traced to and assigned to specific job orders or batches of products.

L O 4 **Predetermined overhead rate:** A factor used to assign factory overhead costs to specific products or jobs.

L O 1 **Process cost system:** A product costing system used by companies that produce large amounts of similar products or liquids, or that have a continuous production flow; the costs of direct materials, direct labor, and factory overhead are first traced to a process or work cell and then assigned to the products produced by that process or work cell.

REVIEW PROBLEM

THE JOB ORDER COST CARD—CONSTRUCTION COMPANY

L O 6   Avery Construction Co., located in Lakeland Hills, Georgia, designs and builds large multiple-apartment housing units. The company uses cost-plus profit contracts, and the profit factor used is 20 percent of total job cost. Costs are accumulated for three primary activities: Building Design, Building Construction, and Surface Prep and Inspection. Direct materials and construction labor are traceable to each job. The following are current construction overhead rates based on labor hours: Building Design, $8 per hour; Building Construction, $15 per hour; and Surface Prep and Inspection, $10 per hour. Two large apartment complexes were in process at the end of November, 19x7. During December, the costs related to these projects were as follows:

	Busch Apartments	Salter Housing, Inc.
Beginning Balances		
Building Design	$ 31,400	$ 47,900
Building Construction	196,200	246,100
Surface Prep and Inspection	8,600	10,540
Work during December		
Building Design		
Direct materials	$ 0	$ 1,200
Labor: hours	10	30
dollars	$ 200	$ 600
Building Construction		
Direct materials	$140,900	$172,300
Labor: hours	1,540	730
dollars	$ 24,640	$ 11,680
Surface Prep and Inspection		
Direct materials	$ 36,220	$ 8,450
Labor: hours	760	80
dollars	$ 13,680	$ 1,440

REQUIRED
1. Create the job order cost cards for the two construction projects.
2. The Busch Apartments project was completed by the end of December. What will be the billing amount for this job?
3. What is Avery Construction Co.'s December ending Construction-in-Process account balance?

ANSWER TO REVIEW PROBLEM

1. Create the job order cost cards (see next two pages).
2. Customer billing amount:
   Busch Apartments $579,144

3. Ending Construction-in-Process account balance:
   Ending balance = $512,200

JOB ORDER COST CARD
Avery Construction Co.
Lakeland Hills, Georgia

Customer: Busch Apartments   Date Completed: December 31, 19x7

Costs Charged to Job	Previous Period	Current Month	Total
Building Design			
Beginning balance	$ 31,400		
Current month's costs			
Direct materials		$ 0	
Direct labor		200	
Construction overhead		80	
Totals	$ 31,400	$ 280	$ 31,680
Building Construction			
Beginning balance	$196,200		
Current month's costs			
Direct materials		$140,900	
Direct labor		24,640	
Construction overhead		23,100	
Totals	$196,200	$188,640	$384,840
Surface Prep and Inspection			
Beginning balance	$ 8,600		
Current month's costs			
Direct materials		$ 36,220	
Direct labor		13,680	
Construction overhead		7,600	
Totals	$ 8,600	$ 57,500	$ 66,100

Cost Summary to Date:	Total Cost	Percent of Total Cost
Building Design	$ 31,680	6.56%
Building Construction	384,840	79.74%
Surface Prep and Inspection	66,100	13.70%
Totals	$482,620	100.00%
Profit margin	96,524	
Construction revenue	$579,144	

JOB ORDER COST CARD
Avery Construction Co.
Lakeland Hills, Georgia

Customer: Salter Housing, Inc.   Date Completed: _____

Costs Charged to Job	Previous Period	Current Month	Total
Building Design			
Beginning balance	$ 47,900		
Current month's costs			
Direct materials		$ 1,200	
Direct labor		600	
Construction overhead		240	
Totals	$ 47,900	$ 2,040	$ 49,940
Building Construction			
Beginning balance	$246,100		
Current month's costs			
Direct materials		$172,300	
Direct labor		11,680	
Construction overhead		10,950	
Totals	$246,100	$194,930	$441,030
Surface Prep and Inspection			
Beginning balance	$ 10,540		
Current month's costs			
Direct materials		$ 8,450	
Direct labor		1,440	
Construction overhead		800	
Totals	$ 10,540	$ 10,690	$ 21,230

Cost Summary to Date:	Total Cost	Percent of Total Cost
Building Design	$ 49,940	9.75%
Building Construction	441,030	86.11%
Surface Prep and Inspection	21,230	4.14%
Totals	$512,200	100.00%
Profit margin	_____	
Construction revenue		

CHAPTER ASSIGNMENTS

QUESTIONS

1. Identify four ways in which managers use product costing information.
2. Because the public is more familiar with the output of financial accounting, that area of accounting often overshadows cost and management accounting. Describe the importance of a product costing system to (a) the preparation of financial statements and (b) profitability.
3. What is a job order cost system? What types of companies use this kind of system?
4. What are the main similarity and the main difference between a job order cost system and a process cost system? (Focus on the characteristics of each system.)

5. Explain the concept of absorption costing.

6. Describe the steps used to arrive at a predetermined overhead rate based on machine hours.

7. What are the keys to successfully applying overhead to products and job orders?

8. What are the two primary uses of a predetermined overhead rate?

9. What is the nature of the Factory Overhead Control account? How does the use of this account change the recordkeeping process?

10. Define *control account* and *subsidiary ledger*. How are the two related?

11. How does an accountant "apply" factory overhead to a product? How is the amount to be applied determined?

12. What is meant by underapplied or overapplied overhead?

13. Describe how to adjust for underapplied or overapplied overhead.

14. How does materials usage influence a company's efficiency and profitability?

15. "Purchased labor services cannot be stored." Discuss this statement.

16. In what way is timely purchasing a "do or die" function?

17. Why are subsidiary ledgers maintained for Materials Inventory, Work in Process Inventory, and Finished Goods Inventory?

18. Discuss the role of the Work in Process Inventory Control account in a job order cost system.

19. What is the purpose of a job order cost card? Identify the types of information recorded on such a card.

20. What transactions are recorded in a job order cost system to reflect the manufacturing, completion, and sale of a product?

21. Explain the process of computing product unit costs in a job order cost system. How are the necessary data accumulated?

SHORT EXERCISES

SE 1.
L O 1
No check figure

Uses of Product Costing Information

Kerri's Kennel provides boarding for dogs and cats. Kerri must make several decisions soon. Write *yes* or *no* to indicate whether knowing the cost to board one animal per day (i.e., the product unit cost) can help Kerri answer the following questions.

1. Is the boarding fee high enough to cover my costs?
2. How much profit will I make if I board an average of ten dogs per day for fifty weeks?
3. What costs can I reduce so that I can compete with the boarding fee charged by my competitor?

SE 2.
L O 1
No check figure

Industries Using a Job Order Cost System

Write *yes* or *no* to indicate whether each of the following industries would normally use a job order cost system for product costing.

1. Soft drink producer
2. Jeans manufacturer
3. Submarine contractor

4. Office building contractor
5. Stuffed toy maker

SE 3.
L O 2
No check figure

Job Order Versus Process Cost Systems

State whether a job order cost system or a process cost system would normally be used to account for the costs of producing the following:

1. Dog collars
2. Custom-designed fencing for outdoor breeding kennels
3. Pet grooming

4. Aquariums
5. Dog food
6. Veterinary services

SE 4.
L O 3
No check figure

Concept of Absorption Costing

Write *yes* or *no* to indicate whether each of the following costs is included in the product unit cost when absorption costing is used. Then explain your answers.

1. Direct materials costs
2. Fixed factory overhead costs
3. Variable selling costs

4. Fixed administrative costs
5. Direct labor costs
6. Variable factory overhead costs

SE 5. *Computation of*
L O 4 *Predetermined*
Overhead Rate

Check Figure: Predetermined overhead rate: $5.90

Compute the predetermined overhead rate per service request for the Maintenance Department if estimated overhead costs are $18,290 and the number of estimated service requests is 3,100.

SE 6. *Disposition of*
L O 5 *Underapplied or*
Overapplied
Overhead

Check Figure: Factory overhead overapplied by $3,130

At year end, records show actual factory overhead costs incurred were $23,870 and the amount of factory overhead costs applied to production was $27,000. Identify the amount of under- or overapplied factory overhead and prepare the entry to dispose of it.

SE 7. *Documentation for a*
L O 6 *Job Order Cost*
System

No check figure

Identify the document needed to support each of the following transactions.

1. Placing an order for raw materials with a supplier
2. Recording direct labor time at the beginning and end of each work shift
3. Receiving raw materials at the shipping dock
4. Producing a job requiring materials, labor, and overhead
5. Issuing direct materials into production
6. Using water and electricity in the production process
7. A request from the Production Scheduling Department for the purchase of raw materials

SE 8. *Transactions in a Job*
L O 7 *Order Cost System*

No check figure

For each of the following transactions, tell which account would be debited in a job order cost system.

1. Purchased materials, $12,890.
2. Charged direct labor to production, $3,790.
3. Requisitioned indirect materials into production, $6,800.
4. Applied factory overhead to jobs in process, $3,570.

SE 9. *Transactions in a Job*
L O 7 *Order Cost System*

No check figure

Journalize the following transactions.

1. Requisitioned $34,000 of Material X, $18,000 of Material Y, and $7,000 of assembly supplies into production.
2. Applied factory overhead based on 12,680 machine hours @ $6.50 per machine hour.

SE 10. *Computation of*
L O 8 *Product Unit Cost*

Check Figure: Cost per unit: $2,625

Complete the following job order cost card for six custom-built computer systems.

Job Order No. 168		Gatekeeper 3000 Apache City, North Dakota	
Customer: Robert Arthur		Materials:	
		Dept. 1	$ 3,540
		Dept. 2	2,820
Date of Order: April 4, 19x7		Total	$_____
Date of Completion: June 18, 19x7		Direct Labor:	
		Dept. 1	$ 2,340
		Dept. 2	1,620
Cost Summary:		Total	$_____
Materials	$_____		
Direct Labor	_____	Applied Factory Overhead:	
Factory Overhead	_____	Dept. 1	$ 2,880
Total	$_____	Dept. 2	2,550
Units Completed	_____	Total	$_____
Cost per Unit	$_____		

EXERCISES

E 1. *Product Versus*
L O 1 *Period Costs*
No check figure

Paula's Printing Company specializes in wedding invitations. Paula needs information to budget next year's activities. Write *yes* or *no* to indicate whether each piece of information listed below is likely to be available in the company's product costing system.

1. Cost of paper and envelopes
2. Printing machine setup costs
3. Depreciation of printing machinery
4. Advertising costs
5. Repair costs for printing machinery
6. Costs to deliver stationery to customers
7. Office supplies costs
8. Costs to design a wedding invitation
9. Cost of ink
10. Sales commissions

E 2. *Cost System:*
L O 2 *Industry Linkage*
No check figure

Which of the following products would normally be accounted for using a job order cost system? Which would be accounted for using a process cost system? (a) paint, (b) automobiles, (c) jet aircraft, (d) bricks, (e) large milling machines, (f) liquid detergent, (g) aluminum compressed-gas cylinders of standard size and capacity, (h) aluminum compressed-gas cylinders with a special fiber-glass overwrap for a Mount Everest expedition, (i) standard nails produced from wire, (j) television sets, (k) printed wedding invitations, (l) a limited edition of lithographs, (m) flea collars for pets, (n) high-speed lathes with special-order thread drills, (o) breakfast cereal, and (p) an original evening gown.

E 3. *Concept of*
L O 3 *Absorption Costing*
Check Figure: $1.551 per unit

Using the absorption costing concept, determine product unit cost from the following costs incurred during March: liability insurance, factory, $2,500; rent, sales office, $2,900; depreciation, factory equipment, $6,100; materials used, $32,650; indirect labor, factory, $3,480; factory supplies, $1,080; heat, light, and power, factory, $1,910; fire insurance, factory, $2,600; depreciation, sales equipment, $4,250; rent, factory, $3,850; direct labor, $18,420; manager's salary, factory, $3,100; president's salary, $5,800; sales commissions, $8,250; and advertising expenses, $2,975. The Inspection Department reported that 48,800 good units were produced during March. Carry your answer to three decimal places.

E 4. *Computation of*
L O 4 *Predetermined*
Overhead Rate
Check Figure: 2. 19x9 predetermined overhead rate: $7.683 per machine hour

The overhead costs used by Baylor Industries, Inc., to compute its predetermined overhead rate for 19x8 are listed below.

A total of 45,600 machine hours was used as the 19x8 allocation base. In 19x9, all overhead costs except depreciation, property taxes, and miscellaneous factory overhead are expected to increase by 10 percent. Depreciation should increase by 12 percent, and a 20 percent increase in property taxes and miscellaneous factory overhead is expected. Plant capacity in terms of machine hours used will increase by 4,400 hours in 19x9.

Indirect materials and supplies	$ 79,200
Repairs and maintenance	14,900
Outside service contracts	17,300
Indirect labor	79,100
Factory supervision	42,900
Depreciation, machinery	85,000
Factory insurance	8,200
Property taxes	6,500
Heat, light, and power	7,700
Miscellaneous factory overhead	5,760
	$346,560

1. Compute the 19x8 predetermined overhead rate. (Carry your answer to three decimal places.)
2. Compute the predetermined overhead rate for 19x9. (Carry your answer to three decimal places.)

E 5.
L O 4

Computation and Application of Overhead Rate

Check Figure: 3. Total factory overhead applied: $152,385.60

Foster Compumatics specializes in the analysis and reporting of complex inventory costing projects. Materials costs are minimal, consisting entirely of operating supplies (data processing cards, inventory sheets, and other recording tools). Labor is the highest single expense item, totaling $693,000 for 75,000 hours of work in 19x7. Factory overhead costs for 19x7 were $916,000 and were applied to specific jobs on the basis of labor hours worked. In 19x8 the company anticipates a 25 percent increase in overhead costs. Labor costs will increase by $130,000, and the number of hours worked is expected to increase 20 percent.

1. Determine the total amount of factory overhead anticipated by the company in 19x8.
2. Compute the predetermined overhead rate for 19x8. (Round your answer to the nearest penny.)
3. During April 19x8, the following jobs were completed in the following times: Job 16–A4, 2,490 hours; Job 21–C2, 5,220 hours; and Job 17–H3, 4,270 hours. Prepare the journal entry required to apply overhead costs to the jobs completed in April.

E 6.
L O 5

Disposition of Overapplied Overhead (Extension of E 5)

Check Figure: 2. Overapplied overhead: $382.40

At the end of 19x8, Foster Compumatics had compiled a total of 89,920 hours worked. The actual overhead incurred was $1,143,400.

1. Using the predetermined overhead rate computed in E 5, determine the total amount of overhead applied to operations during 19x8.
2. Compute the amount of overapplied overhead for the year.
3. Prepare the journal entry needed to close out the overhead account and dispose of the overapplied overhead for 19x8. Assume that the amount is not significant.

E 7.
L O 5

Disposition of Underapplied Overhead

No check figure

The Tunnell Manufacturing Company ended the year with a total of $750 of underapplied overhead. Ending account balances were as follows: Materials Inventory Control, $214,740; Work in Process Inventory Control, $312,500; Finished Goods Inventory Control, $250,000; Cost of Goods Sold, $687,500; and Factory Overhead Control, $750. Close out the Factory Overhead Control account and dispose of the underapplied overhead. Show your work in journal entry form.

E 8.
L O 6

Job Order Cost Flow

No check figure

The three manufacturing cost elements—direct materials, direct labor, and factory overhead—flow through a job order cost system in a structured, orderly fashion. Specific general ledger accounts, subsidiary ledgers, and source documents are used to verify and record cost information. In both paragraph and diagram form, describe the cost flow in a job order cost system.

E 9.
L O 7

Work in Process Inventory Control Account: Journal Entry Analysis

Check Figure: 2. Ending balance, Work in Process Inventory Control: $27,320

On July 1, Schadle Specialty Company's Work in Process Inventory Control account showed a beginning balance of $29,400. Production activity for July was as follows: (a) Direct materials costing $238,820, along with $28,400 of operating supplies, were requisitioned into production. (b) Schadle Specialty Company's total factory payroll for July was $140,690, of which $52,490 was used to pay for indirect labor. (Assume that payroll has been recorded but not distributed to production accounts.) (c) Factory overhead was applied at a rate of 150 percent of direct labor costs.

1. Prepare journal entries to record the materials, labor, and factory overhead costs for July.
2. Compute the ending balance in the Work in Process Inventory Control account. Assume a transfer of $461,400 to the Finished Goods Inventory Control account during the period.

E 10. *Computation of Unit*
L O 8 *Cost*

Check Figure: 2. Unit cost, Job B–14: $75.10

Walton Corporation manufactures a full line of women's apparel. During February, Walton Corporation worked on three special orders: A–25, A–27, and B–14. Cost and production data for each order are shown in the following table.

	Job A–25	Job A–27	Job B–14
Direct materials:			
Fabric Q	$10,840	$12,980	$17,660
Fabric Z	11,400	12,200	13,440
Fabric YB	5,260	6,920	10,900
Direct labor:			
Garmentmaker	8,900	10,400	16,200
Layout	6,450	7,425	9,210
Packaging	3,950	4,875	6,090
Factory overhead:			
120% of direct labor dollars	?	?	?
Number of units produced	700	775	1,482

1. Compute the total cost associated with each job. Show the subtotals for each cost category.
2. Compute the unit cost for each job. (Round your computations to the nearest penny.)

E 11. *Job Order Cost Card*
L O 6, 8 *Preparation and*
Computation of Unit
Cost

Check Figure: Cost per unit: $1,195

During the month of January, the Cable Cabinet Company worked on six different orders for specialty kitchen cabinets. Job A–62, manufactured for T. J. Products, Inc., was begun and completed during the month. Partial data from Job A–62's job order cost card are summarized in the following table.

	Costs	Machine Hours Used
Direct materials:		
Cedar	$7,900	
Pine	6,320	
Hardware	2,930	
Assembly supplies	988	
Direct labor:		
Sawing Department	$2,840	120
Shaping Department	2,200	220
Finishing Department	2,250	180
Assembly Department	2,890	50

A total of thirty-four cabinets was included in Job A–62. The current predetermined factory overhead rate is $21.60 per machine hour. From the information given, prepare a job order cost card similar to Figure 3. The cedar and pine are placed into production in the Sawing Department. The hardware and supplies are placed into production in the Assembly Department. (Round to whole dollars where appropriate.)

SKILLS DEVELOPMENT EXERCISES

Conceptual Analysis

SDE 1. *Computation of*
L O 4, 5 *Predetermined*
Overhead Rates

No check figure

Both **Jones Company** and **Proctor Corporation** use predetermined overhead rates for product costing, inventory pricing, and sales quotations. The two businesses are about the same size, and they compete in the corrugated box industry. Jones Company's management believes that because the predetermined overhead rate is an estimated measure, the controller's department should spend little effort in developing it. The company computes the rate once a year based on a trend analysis of the previous year's costs. No one monitors its accuracy during the year.

Proctor Corporation takes a much more sophisticated approach. One person in the controller's office is responsible for developing predetermined overhead rates on a monthly basis. All cost estimates are checked carefully to make sure they are realistic. Accuracy checks are done routinely during each monthly closing analysis, and forecasts of changes in business activity are taken into account.

Assume you are a consultant who has been hired by the **Bullock Corporation,** a West Coast manufacturer of corrugated boxes. Janelle Bullock wants you to recommend the best approach for developing overhead rates. Based on your knowledge of the practices described above, write a memo to Janelle Bullock that will answer the following questions.

1. What are the advantages and disadvantages of each company's approach to developing predetermined overhead rates?
2. Which company has taken the more cost-effective approach to developing predetermined overhead rates? Defend your answer.
3. Is an accurate overhead rate most important for product costing, inventory valuation, or sales quotations? Why?

Ethical Dilemma

SDE 2.
L O 6
Ethical Job Order Costs

No check figure

Dean Porter, production manager for **Stitts Metal Products Company**, entered the office of controller Ed Grissom and asked, "Ed, what gives here? I was charged for 330 direct labor hours on Job AD22 and my records show that we only spent 290 hours on that job. That 40-hour difference caused the total cost of labor and factory overhead for the job to increase by over $5,500. Are my records wrong or was there an error in the labor assigned to the job?" Ed responded, "Don't worry about it, Dean. This job won't be used in your quarterly performance evaluation. Job AD22 was a federal government job, a cost-plus-fixed-fee contract, so the more costs we assign to it, the more profit we make. We decided to add a few hours to the job in case there is some follow-up work to do. You know how fussy the feds are with their close tolerances."

What should Dean Porter do? Discuss Ed Grissom's costing procedure.

Research Activity

SDE 3.
L O 6
Job Order Costing

No check figure

Many businesses accumulate costs for each job performed. Examples of businesses that use a job order cost system include print shops, car repair shops, health clinics, and kennels. Visit a local business that uses job order costing, and interview the owner, manager, or accountant about the process and the documents the business uses to accumulate product costs. Write a paper that summarizes the information you obtained. Include the following items in your written summary:

1. The name of the business and the type of business performed
2. The name and position of the individual you interviewed
3. A description of the process of starting and completing a job
4. A description of the accounting process and the documents used to track a job
5. Your response to the following questions:
   a. Did the person you interviewed know the *actual* amount of materials, labor, and overhead charged to a particular job? If the job includes some estimated costs, how are the estimates calculated? Is the determination of the selling price of the product or service affected by the product costs?
   b. Compare the documents discussed in the chapter to the documents used in the company that you visited. How are they similar, and how are they different?
   c. In your opinion, does the business record and accumulate its product costs effectively? Explain.

Decision-Making Practice

SDE 4. *Analysis of Job*
L O 4, 6, 8 *Order Cost Systems*

Check Figure: 1. Unit cost, Job Order
K–2: $28.40

Pearson Manufacturing Company is a small family-owned business that makes specialty plastic products. Since it was started three years ago, the company has grown quickly and now employs ten production people. Because of its size, the company uses a job order cost system that was designed around a periodic inventory system. Work sheets and special analyses are used to account for manufacturing costs and inventory valuations.

Two months ago, in May 19x7, the company's accountant quit. You have been called in to help management. The following information has been given to you.

Beginning inventory balances (1/1/19x7):

Materials	$50,420
Work in Process (Job K–2)	59,100
Finished Goods (Job K–1)	76,480

Direct materials requisitioned into production during 19x7:

Job K–2	$33,850
Job K–4	53,380
Job K–6	82,400

Direct labor for the year:

Job K–2	$25,300
Job K–4	33,480
Job K–6	45,600

The company purchased materials only once (in February), for $126,500. All jobs use the same materials. For the current year, the company has been using an overhead application rate of 150 percent of direct labor dollars. So far, two jobs, K–2 and K–4, have been completed, and Jobs K–1 and K–2 have been shipped to customers. Job K–1 contained 3,200 units; Job K–2, 5,500 units; and Job K–4, 4,600 units.

1. Calculate the unit costs for jobs K–1, K–2, and K–4, and the costs so far for job K–6.
2. From the information given, prepare a T account analysis, and compute the current balances in the three inventory accounts and the Cost of Goods Sold account.
3. The president has asked you to analyze the current job order cost system. Should the system be changed? How? Why? Prepare an outline of your response to the president.

PROBLEM SET A

A 1. *Application of*
L O 4, 5 *Factory Overhead*
Check Figure: 2. Overhead applied to
Job 2214: $29,717

Charisma Cosmetics Company applies factory overhead costs on the basis of machine hours. The current predetermined overhead rate is computed by using data from the two prior years, in this case 19x7 and 19x8, adjusted to reflect expectations for the current year, 19x9. The controller prepared the overhead rate analysis for 19x9 using the following information.

	19x7	19x8
Machine hours	47,800	57,360
Factory overhead costs:		
Indirect labor	$ 18,100	$ 23,530
Employee benefits	22,000	28,600
Manufacturing supervision	16,800	18,480
Utilities	10,350	14,490
Factory insurance	6,500	7,800
Janitorial services	11,000	12,100
Depreciation, factory and machinery	17,750	21,300
Miscellaneous	5,750	7,475
Total overhead	$108,250	$133,775

Utilities are expected to increase by 40 percent over the previous year; indirect labor, employee benefits, and miscellaneous factory overhead are expected to increase by 30 percent; insurance and depreciation are expected to increase by 20 percent; and supervision and janitorial services are expected to increase by 10 percent. Machine hours are expected to total 68,832.

REQUIRED

1. Compute the projected costs and the predetermined overhead rate for 19x9. (Carry your answer to three decimal places.)
2. Assume that the company actually surpassed its sales and operating expectations in 19x9. Jobs completed during the year and the related machine hours used were as follows:

Job No.	Machine Hours
2214	12,300
2215	14,200
2216	9,800
2217	13,600
2218	11,300
2219	8,100

Total machine hours were 69,300. Determine the amount of factory overhead to be applied to each job and to total production during 19x9. (Round answers to whole dollars.)
3. Prepare the journal entry needed to close the overhead accounts and dispose of the underapplied or overapplied overhead for 19x9. Assume that $165,845 of factory overhead was incurred during the year. Also assume that the difference between actual overhead costs and applied overhead costs was insignificant.

A 2.
L O 4, 5, 7

*Job Order Costing:
Journal Entry
Analysis and T
Accounts*

Check Figure: 1. Overhead applied, January 15: $108,000

Geraldi Manufacturing, Inc. produces electric golf carts. The carts are special-order items, so the company uses a job order cost system. Factory overhead is applied at the rate of 90 percent of direct labor cost. Following is a list of events and transactions for January.

Jan. 1   Direct materials costing $215,400 were purchased on account.
    2   Operating supplies were purchased on account, $49,500.
    4   Production personnel requisitioned direct materials costing $193,200 (all used on Job X) and operating supplies costing $38,100 into production.
    10   The following overhead costs were paid: utilities, $4,400; factory rent, $3,800; and maintenance charges, $3,900.
    15   Payroll was distributed to employees. Gross wages and salaries were as follows: direct labor, $120,000 (all for Job X); indirect labor, $60,620; sales commissions, $32,400; and administrative salaries, $38,000.
    15   Overhead was applied to production.
    19   Operating supplies costing $27,550 and direct materials listed at $190,450 were purchased on account.
    21   Direct materials costing $214,750 (Job X, $178,170; Job Y, $18,170; Job Z, $18,410) and operating supplies costing $31,400 were requisitioned into production.
    31   The following gross wages and salaries were paid to employees: direct labor, $132,000 (Job X, $118,500; Job Y, $7,000; Job Z, $6,500); indirect labor, $62,240; sales commissions, $31,200; and administrative salaries, $38,000.
    31   Overhead was applied to production.
    31   Jobs X and Y were completed and transferred to Finished Goods Inventory Control; total cost was $855,990.
    31   Job X was shipped to the customer. The total production cost was $824,520 and the sales price was $996,800.
    31   The following overhead costs (adjusting entries) were recorded: prepaid insurance expired, $3,700; property taxes (payable at year end), $3,400; and depreciation, machinery, $15,500.

REQUIRED

1. Record the journal entries for all transactions and events in January. In the payroll entries, concern yourself only with the distribution of factory payroll to the production accounts.
2. Post the entries prepared in **1** to T accounts, and determine the partial account balances. Include T accounts for Jobs X, Y, and Z. Assume no beginning inventory balances. Also assume that entries made when the payroll was recorded were posted to the Factory Payroll account.
3. Compute the amount of underapplied or overapplied overhead as of January 31.

A 3. *The Job Order Cost*
L O 6 *Card: Service*
Company

Check Figure: 1. Contract revenue, Job order P-12: $28,990

Central Engineering Co. specializes in designing automated characters and displays for theme parks. Cost-plus profit contracts are used, and the company's profit factor is 30 percent of total cost. A job order cost system is used to track the costs associated with the development of each project. Costs are accumulated for three primary activities: Bid and Proposal; Design; and Prototype Development. Current service overhead rates based on engineering hours are as follows: Bid and Proposal, $18 per hour; Design, $22 per hour; and Prototype Development, $20 per hour. Supplies are treated as direct materials, traceable to each job. Three projects, P-12, P-15, and P-19, were worked on during January. The following table contains the costs for these projects.

	P-12	P-15	P-19
Beginning balances:			
Bid and Proposal	$2,460	$2,290	$ 940
Design	1,910	460	0
Prototype Development	2,410	1,680	0
Work during January:			
Bid and Proposal			
Supplies	0	$ 280	$2,300
Labor: hours	12	20	68
dollars	$ 192	$ 320	$1,088
Design			
Supplies	$ 400	$ 460	$ 290
Labor: hours	64	42	26
dollars	$1,280	$ 840	$ 520
Prototype Development			
Special materials	$6,744	$7,216	$2,400
Labor: hours	120	130	25
dollars	$2,880	$3,120	$ 600

REQUIRED

1. Using the format shown in the chapter's review problem, create the job order cost cards for the three projects.
2. Projects P-12 and P-15 were completed and the customers approved of the prototype products. Customer A plans to produce 12 special characters using the design and specifications created by Project P-12. Customer B plans to make 18 displays from the design developed by Project P-15. What dollar amount will each customer use as the cost of design for each of their products? (Round to the nearest dollar.)
3. What is Central Engineering Co.'s January ending Contract-in-Process Inventory balance?

A 4. *Job Order Costing:*
L O 6 *Unknown Quantity*
Analysis

Check Figures: b. Factory overhead applied, June: $58,512; h. Factory overhead applied, July: $65,448

Partial operating data for the Primo Picture Company are presented below. Management has decided the predetermined overhead rate for the current year is 120 percent of direct labor dollars.

Account/Transaction	June	July
Beginning Materials Inventory Control	$ a	$ e
Beginning Work in Process Inventory Control	89,605	f
Beginning Finished Goods Inventory Control	79,764	67,660
Direct Materials Requisitioned	59,025	g
Materials Purchased	57,100	60,216

Account/Transaction	June	July
Direct Labor Costs	48,760	54,540
Factory Overhead Applied	b	h
Cost of Units Completed	c	231,861
Cost of Goods Sold	166,805	i
Ending Materials Inventory Control	32,014	27,628
Ending Work in Process Inventory Control	d	j
Ending Finished Goods Inventory Control	67,660	30,515

REQUIRED

Using the data provided, compute the unknown values. Show all your computations.

A 5. *Job Order Cost Flow*

L O 7, 8

Check Figure: 2. Cost of goods completed and transferred: $185,073

The three September 1 inventory balances of Randolph House, a manufacturer of high-quality children's clothing, were as follows:

Account	Balance
Materials Inventory Control	$21,360
Work in Process Inventory Control	15,112
Finished Goods Inventory Control	17,120

Job order cost cards for jobs in process as of September 30, 19x9, revealed the following totals.

Job No.	Direct Materials	Direct Labor	Factory Overhead
24–A	$1,596	$1,290	$1,677
24–B	1,492	1,380	1,794
24–C	1,984	1,760	2,288
24–D	1,608	1,540	2,002

Materials purchased and received in September:

September 4	$33,120
September 16	28,600
September 22	31,920

Direct labor costs for September:

September 15 payroll	$23,680
September 29 payroll	25,960

Predetermined overhead rate:
130 percent of direct labor dollars

Direct materials requisitioned into production during September:

September 6	$37,240
September 23	38,960

Finished goods with a 75 percent markup over cost were sold during September for $320,000.

REQUIRED

1. Using T accounts, reconstruct the transactions for September.
2. Compute the cost of units completed during the month.
3. What was the total cost of units sold during September?
4. Determine the ending inventory balances.
5. Jobs 24–A and 24–C were completed during the first week of October. No additional materials costs were incurred, but Job 24–A required $960 more direct labor, and Job 24–C needed additional direct labor of $1,610. Job 24–A was composed of 1,200 pairs of trousers; Job 24–C, 950 shirts. Compute the unit cost for each job. (Round your answers to three decimal places.)

PROBLEM SET B

Power Products, Inc. uses a predetermined overhead rate in its production, assembly, and testing departments. One rate is used for the entire company and is based on machine hours. The current rate was determined by analyzing data from the previous two years and projecting figures for the current year, adjusted for expected changes. Mr. Hinnen is about to compute the rate to be used in 19x8 using the following data.

	19x6	19x7
Machine hours	38,000	41,800
Factory overhead costs:		
Indirect materials	$ 44,500	$ 57,850
Indirect labor	21,200	25,440
Supervision	37,800	41,580
Utilities	9,400	11,280
Labor-related costs	8,200	9,020
Depreciation, factory	9,800	10,780
Depreciation, machinery	22,700	27,240
Property taxes	2,400	2,880
Insurance	1,600	1,920
Miscellaneous	4,400	4,840
Total overhead	$162,000	$192,830

Indirect materials are expected to increase by 30 percent over the previous year. Indirect labor, factory utilities, machinery depreciation, property taxes, and insurance are expected to increase by 20 percent. All other expenses are expected to increase by 10 percent. Machine hours are estimated to be 45,980 for 19x8.

REQUIRED

1. Compute the projected costs and the predetermined overhead rate for 19x8. (Round your answer to three decimal places.)
2. During 19x8, Power Products, Inc. produced the following jobs using the machine hours shown.

Job No.	Machine Hours	Job No.	Machine Hours
H–142	7,840	H–201	10,680
H–164	5,260	H–218	12,310
H–175	8,100	H–304	2,460

Determine the amount of factory overhead applied to each job in 19x8. What was the total overhead applied during the year? (Round answers to the nearest dollar.)
3. Prepare the journal entry needed to close the overhead account and dispose of the under- or overapplied overhead. Actual factory overhead for 19x8 was $234,485.

Riley Industries, Inc., the finest name in parking attendant apparel, has been in business for over thirty years. Its colorful and stylish uniforms are special-ordered by exclusive hotels and country clubs all over the world. During April 19x7, Riley completed the following transactions.

Apr. 1 Materials costing $59,400 were purchased on account.
   3 Materials costing $26,850 were requisitioned into production (all used on Job A).
   4 Operating supplies were purchased for cash, $22,830.
   8 The company issued checks for the following factory overhead costs: utilities, $4,310; factory insurance, $1,925; and repairs, $4,640.
   10 The Cutting Department manager requisitioned $29,510 of materials (all used on Job A) and $6,480 of operating supplies into production.
   15 Payroll was distributed to the employees. Gross wages and salaries were as follows: direct labor, $62,900 (all for Job A); indirect labor, $31,610; factory supervision, $26,900; and sales commissions, $32,980.

Apr. 15 Overhead was applied to production.

22 Factory overhead costs were paid: utilities, $4,270; maintenance, $3,380; and rent, $3,250.

23 The Receiving Department recorded the purchase on account and receipt of $31,940 of materials and $9,260 of operating supplies.

27 Production requisitioned $28,870 of materials (Job A, $2,660; Job B, $8,400; Job C, $17,810) and $7,640 of operating supplies.

30 The following gross wages and salaries were paid to employees: direct labor, $64,220 (Job A, $44,000; Job B, $9,000; Job C, $11,220); indirect labor, $30,290; factory supervision, $28,520; and sales commissions, $36,200.

30 Factory overhead was applied to production.

30 Jobs A and B were completed and transferred to Finished Goods Inventory Control; the total cost was $322,400.

30 Job A was shipped to the customer. The total production cost was $294,200 and the sales price was $418,240.

30 Adjusting entries for the following were recorded: $2,680 for depreciation, factory equipment; $1,230 for property taxes, factory, payable at month end.

Factory overhead was applied at a rate of 120 percent of direct labor cost.

REQUIRED

1. Record the journal entries for all transactions and events in April. In the payroll entries, concern yourself only with the distribution of factory payroll to the production accounts.
2. Post the entries prepared in **1** to T accounts, and determine the partial account balances. Include T accounts for Jobs A, B, and C. Assume no beginning inventory balances. Assume that entries made when payroll was recorded also were posted to the Factory Payroll account. (Round your answers to the nearest whole dollar.)
3. Compute the amount of underapplied or overapplied overhead for April.

B 3. *The Job Order Cost*
L O 6 *Card—Service*
Company

Check Figure: 1. Audit revenue, Brodahl Bakeries: $37,163

Galley & Associates is a CPA firm located in Rock Island, Illinois. The firm deals primarily in tax and audit work. For billing of major audit engagements, the firm uses cost-plus profit agreements and the profit factor used is 25 percent of total job cost. Costs are accumulated for three primary activities: Preliminary Analysis; Field Work; and Report Development. Current service overhead rates based on billable hours are: Preliminary Analysis, $12 per hour; Field Work, $20 per hour; and Report Development, $16 per hour. Supplies are treated as direct materials, traceable to each engagement. Audits for three clients, Adams, Inc., Brodahl Bakeries, and Hill House Restaurants, are currently in process. During March, costs related to these audits were:

	Adams, Inc.	Brodahl Bakeries	Hill House Restaurants
Beginning balances:			
Preliminary Analysis	$1,160	$2,670	$2,150
Field Work	710	1,980	3,460
Report Development	0	1,020	420
Work during March:			
Preliminary Analysis			
Supplies	$ 710	$ 430	$ 200
Labor: hours	60	10	12
dollars	$1,200	$ 200	$ 240
Field Work			
Supplies	$ 450	$1,120	$ 890
Labor: hours	120	240	230
dollars	$4,800	$9,600	$9,200
Report Development			
Supplies	$ 150	$ 430	$ 390
Labor: hours	30	160	140
dollars	$ 900	$4,800	$4,200

1. Using the format shown in the chapter's review problem, create the job order cost cards for the three audit engagements.
2. The Brodahl Bakeries and Hill House Restaurants audits were completed by the end of March. What will be the billing amount for each of these audit engagements?
3. What is Galley & Associates' March ending Audit-in-Process account balance?

B 4.
L O 6

Job Order Costing: Unknown Quantity Analysis

Check Figures: b. Direct labor costs, May: $66,500; i. Factory overhead applied, June: $57,800

Tyler Enterprises makes an assortment of computer support equipment. Dana Josephs, the new controller for the organization, can find only partial information from the past two months, which is presented below.

Account/Transaction	May	June
Materials Inventory Control, Beginning	$ 36,240	$ e
Work in Process Inventory Control, Beginning	56,480	f
Finished Goods Inventory Control, Beginning	44,260	g
Materials Purchased	a	96,120
Direct Materials Requisitioned	82,320	h
Direct Labor Costs	b	72,250
Factory Overhead Applied	53,200	i
Cost of Units Completed	c	221,400
Cost of Units Sold	209,050	j
Materials Inventory Control, Ending	38,910	41,950
Work in Process Inventory Control, Ending	d	k
Finished Goods Inventory Control, Ending	47,940	51,180

The current year's predetermined overhead rate is 80 percent of direct labor dollars.

Using the information given, compute the unknown values. Show your computations.

B 5.
L O 7, 8

Job Order Cost Flow

Check Figure: 3. Cost of units sold: $89,647

Gilbert Johnston is the chief financial officer for Marion Industries, a company that makes special-order printers for personal computers. His records for February 19x9 revealed the following information.

Beginning inventory balances:

Materials Inventory Control	$27,450
Work in Process Inventory Control	22,900
Finished Goods Inventory Control	19,200

Direct materials purchased and received:

February 6	$ 7,200
February 12	8,110
February 24	5,890

Direct labor costs:

February 14	$13,750
February 28	13,230

Direct materials requisitioned into production:

February 4	$ 9,080
February 13	5,940
February 25	7,600

Job order cost cards for jobs in process on February 28 showed the following totals.

Job No.	Direct Materials	Direct Labor	Factory Overhead
AJ–10	$3,220	$1,810	$2,534
AJ–14	3,880	2,110	2,954
AJ–30	2,980	1,640	2,296
AJ–16	4,690	2,370	3,318

The predetermined overhead rate for the month was 140 percent of direct labor dollars. Sales for February totaled $152,400, which represented a 70 percent markup over the cost of production.

REQUIRED

1. Using T accounts, reconstruct the transactions for February.
2. Compute the cost of units completed during the month.
3. What was the total cost of units sold during February?
4. Determine the ending inventory balances.
5. During the first week of March, Jobs AJ–10 and AJ–14 were completed. No additional materials costs were incurred, but Job AJ–10 needed $720 more direct labor, and Job AJ–14 required additional direct labor of $1,140. Job AJ–10 was 40 units; Job AJ–14, 55 units. Compute the unit cost for each completed job.

MANAGERIAL REPORTING AND ANALYSIS

Interpreting Management Reports

MRA 1.   *Interpreting*
L O 1   *Nonfinancial Data*

No check figure

Maynard Manufacturing supplies engine parts to *Ralston Cycle Company*, a major U.S. manufacturer of motorcycles. Maynard, like all parts suppliers for Ralston, has always added a healthy profit margin to its cost when calculating its selling price to Ralston. Recently, however, several new suppliers have offered to provide parts to Ralston for lower prices than Maynard has been charging.

Because Maynard wants to keep Ralston's business, a team of managers analyzed the company's production costs and decided to make minor changes in the company's production process. No new equipment was purchased, and no additional labor was required. Instead, the machines were rearranged and some of the work was reassigned.

To monitor the effectiveness of the changes, Maynard introduced four new performance measures to its information system: square feet of floor space used in production, inventory levels, lead time (total time required for a part to move through the production process), and productivity (number of parts manufactured per person per day). Maynard's goal was to reduce the quantities of the first three performance measures and to increase the quantity of the fourth.

A section of a recent management report, shown below, summarizes the quantities for each performance measure before and after the changes were made to the production process.

Measure	Before	After	Improvement
Floor space in square feet	198	97	51%
Inventory in dollars	$21,444	$10,772	50%
Lead time in minutes	17	11	35%
Productivity			
(parts/person/day)	515	1,152	124%

REQUIRED

1. Do you believe Maynard improved the quality of its production process and the quality of its engine parts? Explain your answer.
2. Do you believe Maynard was able to lower its selling price to Ralston? Explain your answer.
3. Was the design of the product costing system affected by the introduction of the new measures? Explain your answer.
4. Do you believe that the new measures caused a change in Maynard's cost per engine part? In what way?
5. What impact did the introduction of these new measures have on Maynard's income statement and balance sheet?

Formulating Management Reports

MRA 2.
L O 1, 6

Product Costing
Systems and
Nonfinancial Data

No check figure

Refer to the information in MRA 1. Bertha Riley, who is the president of *Maynard Manufacturing,* wants to improve the quality of the company's operations and products. She believes waste exists in the design and manufacture of standard engine parts. To begin the improvement process, she has asked you to (1) identify sources of waste, (2) develop performance measures to account for the waste, and (3) estimate the current costs associated with such waste. She has asked you to write a memo presenting your findings within two weeks so that she can begin strategic planning to revise the selling price for engine parts to Ralston.

You have identified two sources of costly waste. The Production Department is redoing work that was not done correctly the first time, and the Engineering Design Department is redesigning products that were not designed according to customer specifications the first time. Having improper designs has caused the company to buy parts that are not used in production. You have also obtained the following information from the product costing system:

Direct labor costs	$673,402
Engineering design costs	124,709
Indirect labor costs	67,200
Depreciation on production equipment	84,300
Supervisors' salaries	98,340
Direct materials costs	432,223
Indirect materials costs	44,332

REQUIRED

1. In preparation for writing your memo, answer the following questions.
   a. For whom are you preparing the memo? What is the appropriate length of the memo?
   b. Why are you preparing the memo?
   c. What information is needed for the memo? Where can you get such information? What performance measure would you suggest for each activity? Is the accounting information sufficient for your memo?
   d. When is the memo due? What can be done to provide accurate and timely information?
2. Prepare an outline of the sections you would want in your memo.

International Company

MRA 3.
L O 4

Overhead Allocation/
Comparative
Analysis

No check figure

Kensington Pharmaceutical Products, Ltd. operates four manufacturing facilities in eastern Canada. The company manufactures a wide variety of products. Few materials are needed to produce plaster, bandages, and gloves, but numerous materials are required to manufacture pharmaceutical products for the ears, eyes, nose, and throat.

John Moore, the president of Kensington, is concerned that selling prices for plaster, bandages, and gloves are not competitive. In reviewing activities that support the production process, Marie Des Jardins, the company's management accountant, found that costs are not being applied proportionately to the products. To illustrate her point, she prepared an analysis of the costs of storing materials.

Storage activities include receiving materials from suppliers, warehousing materials, and issuing materials from the warehouse to the factory. Marie found that if materials storage costs were applied to gloves based on direct labor hours, each pair of gloves would be charged $0.17. However, if materials storage costs were applied based on the number of materials requisitions, each pair of gloves would be charged only $.05.

Realizing that other production-related activities may not be properly charged to the company's products, John wants to know the "real" production costs for each product.

REQUIRED

1. Would it be wise to apply factory overhead costs using bases other than direct labor hours? Explain.
2. Assume that John asks Marie to use the number of requisition forms as a base for allocating materials storage costs.
   a. What will be the impact of this change on the product cost per pair of gloves?
   b. Will the change affect the selling price?
3. If Kensington manufactured only gloves, would Marie want to use more than one base to apply overhead to production?

Product Costing: The Process Cost System

LEARNING OBJECTIVES

1. Describe the process cost system and identify the reasons for its use.

2. Compare and contrast the characteristics of the process and job order cost systems.

3. Explain the role of the Work in Process Inventory account(s) in a process cost system.

4. Diagram the product flow and cost flow through a process cost system.

5. Compute equivalent production for situations with and without units in beginning Work in Process Inventory.

6. Use a unit cost analysis schedule to compute product unit cost for a specific time period.

7. Prepare a cost summary schedule that assigns costs to units completed and transferred out during the period, and find the ending Work in Process Inventory balance.

8. Prepare the journal entry(ies) needed to transfer costs of completed units out of the Work in Process Inventory account.

9. Analyze a process costing situation involving two production processes in a series.

SUPPLEMENTAL OBJECTIVE

10. Compute equivalent units, product unit cost, and the ending Work in Process Inventory balance in a process cost system that uses the average costing approach.

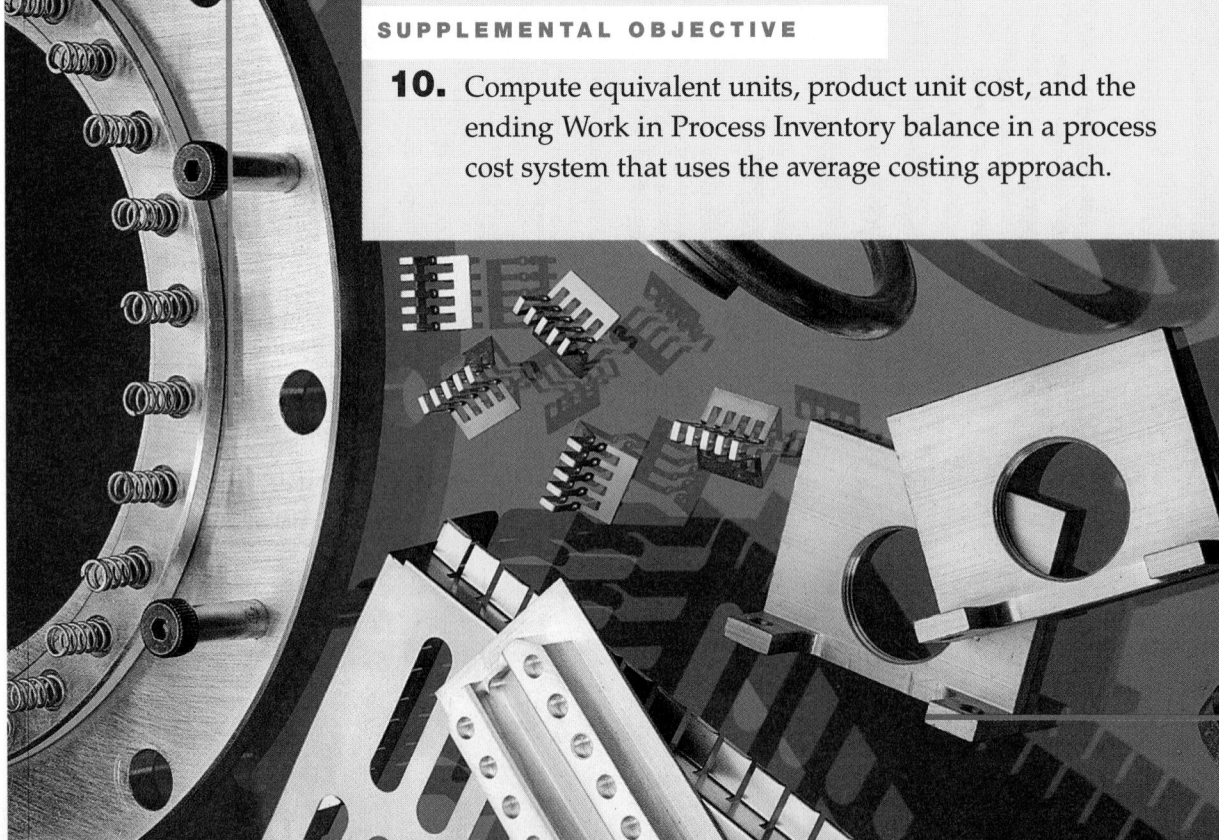

Banyon Industries

DECISION POINT

In the book *Crossroads: A JIT Success Story*,[1] Banyon Industries is a job-shop manufacturer that produces counters, count controls, and programmable controls. Although the company's name is fictitious, the story about implementing a new system based on work cells rather than departments is taken from an actual case. Main characters Ben and Julie systematically create a new plantwide operating environment. Starting with the conversion of a single product line into a continuous flow production work cell, the story takes the reader through a complete transformation of the plant's physical layout, an improvement in employees' attitudes, a revision of the employee incentive plan, and the installation of a new accounting and performance evaluation system.

The existing job order cost system was found to be inappropriate for the new operating environment. As stated by the plant's manager,

> We identified eight major areas where changes were needed to match accounting results to plant performance. After looking at the problem, John [the controller] suggested that we change our basic cost model from job order to process cost. This was a major shift, resulting in a de-emphasis on labor and material reporting and an emphasis on good units produced.

What major operating system characteristic changed and thus required management to shift from a job order cost approach to the process cost system?

Because of the shift to a continuous product flow through production work cells, a process cost system fit management's needs perfectly. With the transition to the new operating environment, it became much easier to trace production costs to work cells than to job orders. Direct labor decreased significantly as automation was introduced. Production-related overhead costs, both fixed and variable, became traceable to the cells. Emphasis was placed on product throughput time, which meant lowering the time it took to get a product through the production process. In addition, high product quality levels, low scrap and rework levels, and an emphasis on good units produced were important elements of the new operating system. :::::

1. Robert Stasey and Carol J. McNair, *Crossroads: A JIT Success Story,* from the Coopers & Lybrand Performance Solutions Series (Homewood, Ill.: Dow Jones–Irwin, 1990).

THE PROCESS COST SYSTEM

A product cost system is expected to provide unit cost information, supply cost data to support management decisions, and generate ending values for the materials, work in process, and finished goods inventory accounts. The job order cost system is one approach to satisfying those objectives. Using a process cost system is a second approach to product costing. A process cost system is a product costing system used by companies that produce large amounts of similar products or have a continuous production flow. In a process cost system, the costs of materials, labor, and factory overhead are traced to processes or work cells and then assigned to the products produced by those processes or work cells. Companies that adopt the just-in-time operating philosophy usually employ process costing procedures, because a continuous flow work cell or process is central to a JIT operation.

The continuous flow of a production process signals the need for a process cost system. In a continuous flow environment, liquid products or large numbers of similar products are produced. Tracking individual costs to individual products is too difficult and too expensive and does not result in significantly different product costs. One gallon of green paint is identical to the next gallon. One brick looks just like the next brick. Each product is similar to the next and should cost the same amount to produce. A process cost system accumulates the costs of materials, labor, and factory overhead for each process or work cell and assigns those costs equally to the products produced during a particular time period. Industries that produce paint, beverages, bricks, canned foods, milk, and paper are typical users of the process cost system.

COMPARISON OF PROCESS COSTING AND JOB ORDER COSTING

The process cost system and the job order cost system both provide product unit cost information for pricing, cost control, inventory valuation, and the preparation of financial statements. The two systems differ in key ways, however, because they are designed to serve two different environments. Process costing is intended for use in high-volume, continuous-flow production facilities, and job order costing is devised for special-order operations.

The main characteristics of the process cost and job order cost systems may be summarized as follows:

Process Cost System	Job Order Cost System
1. Collects manufacturing costs and groups them by department, work center, or work cell.	1. Collects manufacturing costs and assigns them to specific jobs or batches of product.
2. Measures costs in terms of units completed in specific time periods.	2. Measures costs for each completed job.
3. Utilizes several Work in Process Inventory accounts, one for each department, work center, or work cell.	3. Utilizes one Work in Process Inventory Control account supported by a subsidiary ledger of job order cost cards.

The process cost system depends on three schedules: a schedule of equivalent production, a unit cost analysis schedule, and a cost summary schedule.

From the information in those three schedules, costs are traced or assigned to units completed and transferred out of a department or work center. A journal entry then transfers those costs out of the department's Work in Process Inventory account. The costs remaining in the Work in Process Inventory account belong to units still in process at the period's end.

COST FLOW THROUGH WORK IN PROCESS INVENTORY ACCOUNTS

OBJECTIVE

3 *Explain the role of the Work in Process Inventory account(s) in a process cost system*

Accounting for the costs of materials, direct labor, and factory overhead is similar for job order costing and process costing. Under both systems, costs must be recorded and eventually charged to production. Materials and supplies must be purchased and requisitioned into production. Direct labor wages must be paid to employees and charged to production accounts. Finally, factory overhead costs must be assigned to production. Journal entries record these transactions and events. Therefore the flow of costs *into* the Work in Process Inventory account is very similar in the two product costing systems.

The major difference between job order costing and process costing is the way in which costs are assigned to products. In a job order cost system, costs are traced to specific jobs and products. In a process cost system, an averaging technique is used. All products worked on during a specific time period (a week or a month) are used as the output base for computing unit cost. Total costs of materials, direct labor, and factory overhead accumulated in the Work in Process Inventory account (or accounts) are divided by the equivalent units for products worked on during the period. Though technical factors can complicate the process costing procedure, the concept of accumulating costs by work cell or process and assigning them to good units produced supports the system's basic tenet.

WORK IN PROCESS INVENTORY ACCOUNTS

The Work in Process Inventory account is the focal point of process costing. Unlike a job order cost system, a process cost system is not limited to one Work in Process Inventory account. In fact, process costing uses as many Work in Process Inventory accounts as there are departments or steps in the production process. The process shown in Figure 1 involves two departments. The three cost elements flow into the Work in Process Inventory account of Department 1. When the processed units move from Department 1 to Department 2, the total costs accumulated for those units also move from Department 1 to Department 2. In Department 2, the units from Department 1 are processed further. No more materials are needed, but as shown in the figure, more labor is added and factory overhead is assigned.

When the products are completed, they are transferred from the work in process inventory of Department 2 to the finished goods inventory. At that point each unit's cost is made up of five cost inputs, three from Department 1 and two from Department 2. A breakdown of costs, using hypothetical dollar amounts, could be detailed as shown on the next page.

Figure 1. Cost Elements and Process Cost Accounts

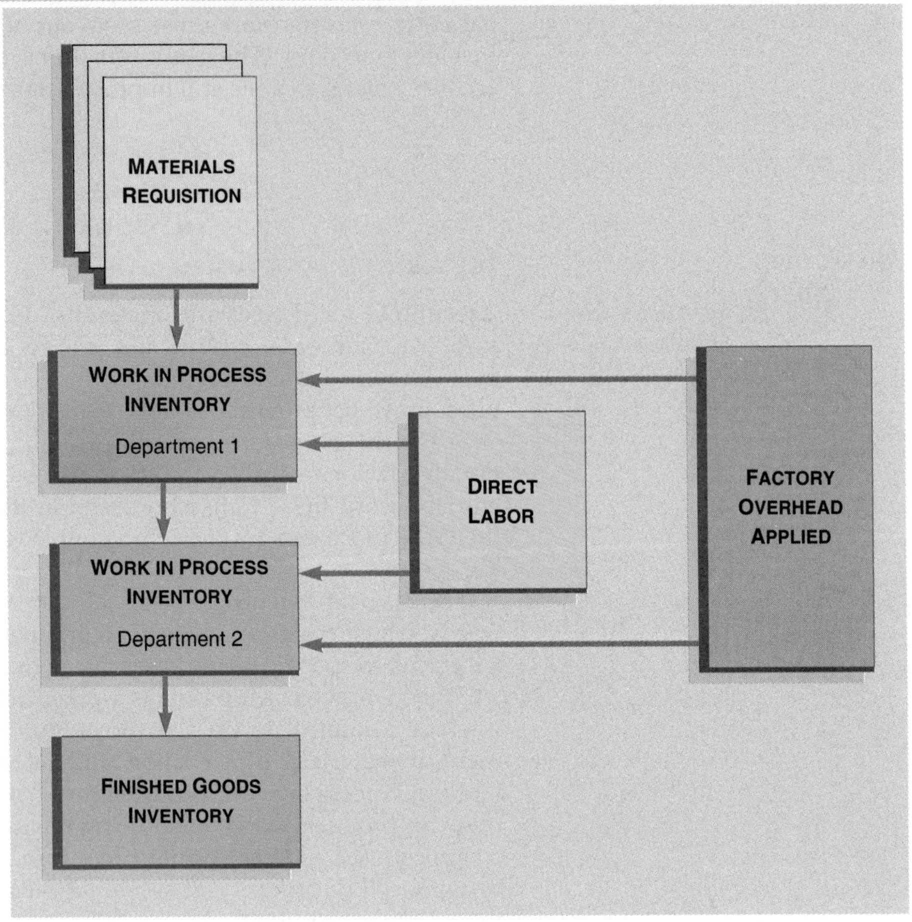

Total Unit Cost

Department 1		
Materials	$2.55	
Direct labor	.90	
Factory overhead	.75	
Total, Department 1		$4.20
Department 2		
Direct labor	$1.20	
Factory overhead	2.05	
Total, Department 2		3.25
Total unit cost (to finished goods inventory)		$7.45

OBJECTIVE

4 *Diagram the product flow and cost flow through a process cost system*

PRODUCTION FLOW COMBINATIONS

Product flows can combine with department production processes in hundreds of ways. Two basic structures are illustrated in Figure 2. Example 1 shows a series of three processes, or departments. The completed product from one department becomes the direct materials input in the next depart-

Figure 2. Cost Flow for Process Costing

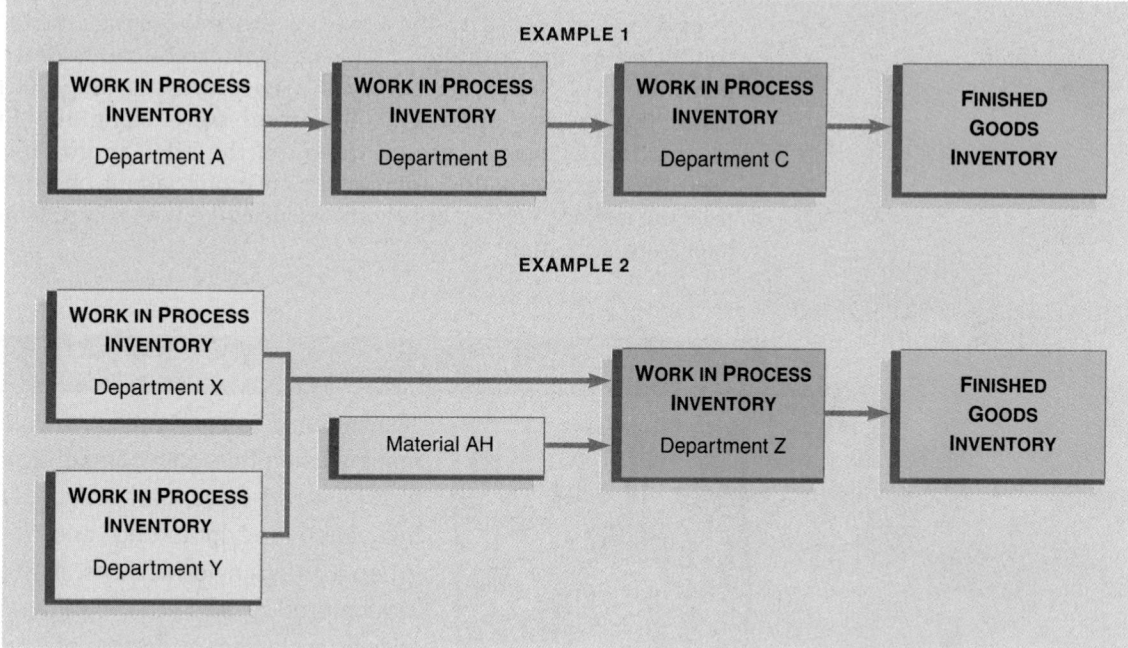

ment. A department series can include from two to a dozen or more departments, or processes. The product unit cost is the sum of the cost elements in all departments.

Example 2 in Figure 2 shows a different kind of production flow. Again there are three departments, but the product does not flow through all departments in a simple 1-2-3 order. Instead, two separate products are developed, one in Department X and the other in Department Y. Both products then go to Department Z, where they are joined with a third direct materials input, Material AH. The unit cost transferred to the Finished Goods Inventory account when the products are completed includes cost elements from Departments X, Y, and Z.

COST FLOW ASSUMPTIONS

As products are developed, the costs of the necessary production activities are accumulated and assigned to those products. Because of the nature of a process industry, products flow in a first-in, first-out (FIFO) pattern. The first item entering the process must be the first one completed. If not, the production flow must have been interrupted by an unforeseen event or work stoppage. The product flows diagrammed in Figures 1 and 2 are based on a FIFO product flow.

In process costing, costs may be assigned to products based on either the FIFO method or a weighted average. The FIFO costing approach is a process costing method in which cost flow follows product flow; the first products to be introduced into the production process are the first products to be completed. Costs assigned to the first products are the first costs to be transferred out of the production center or department. We have elected to use the FIFO costing method in our analysis of the process cost system for two reasons.

First, since products flow through the process in a FIFO manner, it is easier to learn how to account for the costs if the same cost flow approach is used. The second reason relates to the usage of process costing in industry. A study conducted by the Institute of Management Accountants determined that 52 percent of 112 companies surveyed used process costing. Of the companies using the process approach, 58 percent were using the FIFO cost flow assumption, 21 percent used a variant of the FIFO approach, and 21 percent used the average costing approach.[2] Since only about one in five companies uses the average costing approach, we describe it as a Supplemental Objective later in this chapter.

BUSINESS BULLETIN: ETHICS IN PRACTICE

"Downsizing" is one tactic American management is using to regain competitiveness in today's world-class marketplace. Other terms for this action are "rightsizing" and "re-engineering." When a company downsizes, it attempts to reduce product and other operating costs by dismissing a significant portion of its workforce. In the process, life-long, dedicated workers are often replaced by automated manufacturing and other operating systems. Such wholesale firings have caused employees to question their loyalty to their employers, loyalty that has been the backbone of American success in world markets. Is it ethical to fire a person who has been a productive employee for fifteen or twenty years or more? In Japan, a productive employee becomes a part of the company family and is given a life-long job. If a task is replaced by an automated process, the company retrains the employee for another task. American businesses need to recognize that retraining is another way to enhance competitiveness. Because productive and loyal employees are hard to replace, such workers should be given the chance to gain new skills and continue to serve their companies. =====

THE CONCEPT OF EQUIVALENT PRODUCTION

OBJECTIVE

5 *Compute equivalent production for situations with and without units in beginning Work in Process Inventory*

A key feature of a process cost system is the computation of equivalent units of production for each department or process for each accounting period. This computation is needed before product unit costs can be computed. Remember that in process costing, an averaging approach is used. No attempt is made to associate costs with particular job orders. Instead, all manufacturing costs incurred in a department or process are divided by the units produced during the period. There are, however, several important questions to answer in connection with the number of units produced. Exactly how many

---

2. Rex C. Hunter, Frank R. Urbancic, and Donald E. Edwards, "Process Costing: Is It Relevant?" *Management Accounting*, Institute of Management Accountants, December 1989, p. 53.

units were produced? Do we count only those units completed during the period? What about partly completed units in the beginning work in process inventory? Do we count them even if only part of the work needed to complete them was done during the period? And what about products in the ending work in process inventory? Is it proper to focus only on those units started and completed during the period?

The answers to all these questions are linked to the concept of equivalent production. Equivalent production (also called *equivalent units*) is a measure of the number of equivalent whole units produced in a period of time. That is, partly completed units are restated in terms of equivalent whole units. The number of equivalent units produced is equal to the sum of (1) total units started and completed during the period and (2) an amount representing the work done on partially completed products in both the beginning and the ending work in process inventories. A percentage of completion factor is applied to partially completed units to calculate the number of equivalent whole units.

Figure 3 illustrates the computation of equivalent units. One automobile was in process at the beginning of the month, three were started and completed during February, and one was still in process at period end. Actually, one-half (.5) of Car A and three-quarters (.75) of Car E were completed during February. The total equivalent units for the month are found by adding together the units started and completed (3.0) and the units partly completed (.5 and .75). Therefore, equivalent production for February is 4.25 units.

The foregoing method is used for determining equivalent production for direct labor and factory overhead, commonly called conversion costs. Conversion costs are the combined total of direct labor and factory overhead costs incurred by a production department. Because the two costs are often

Figure 3. Equivalent Unit Computation

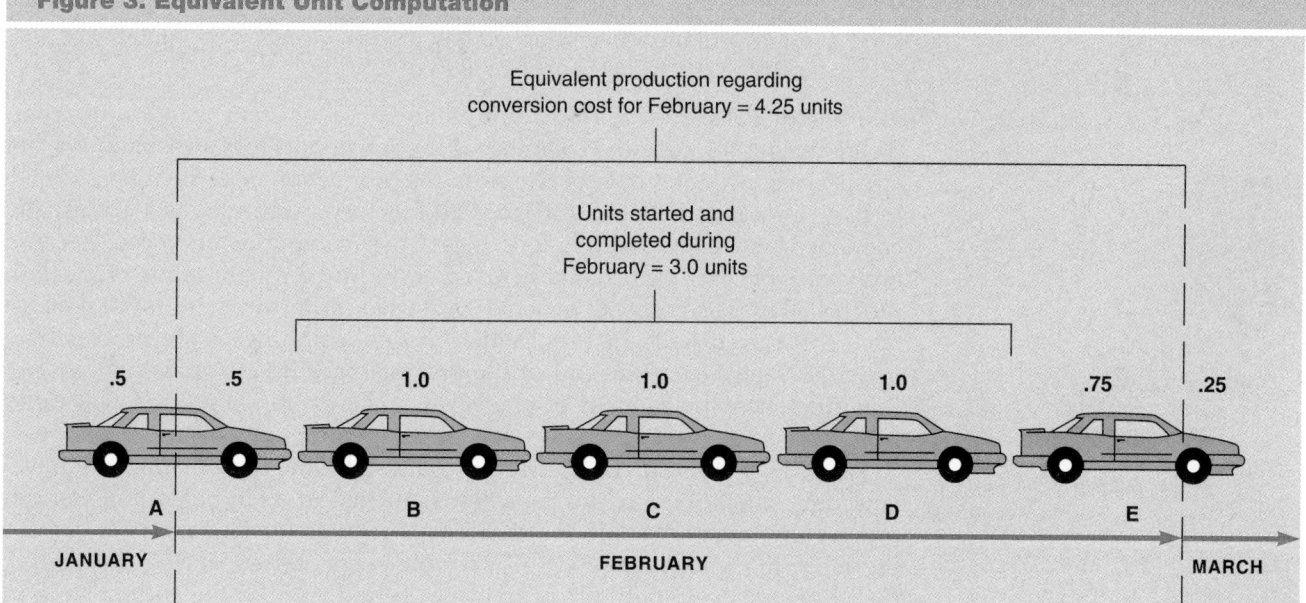

Conversion costs (those for direct labor and factory overhead) are incurred uniformly as each car moves through production. Equivalent production for February is 4.25 units as to conversion costs. But materials costs are all added to production at the beginning of the process. Since four cars entered production in February (cars B, C, D, and E), equivalent production for the month is 4.0 units as to material costs.

incurred uniformly throughout the production process, it is convenient to combine them when determining unit cost.

Raw materials are usually added at the beginning of a process, however, so equivalent units for *materials* costs are computed in a different manner. As shown in Figure 3, materials for Car A were added in January and therefore do not influence equivalent units for materials in February. However, materials for Car E were *all* added to production in February. So, 3.0 (units started and completed—Cars B, C, and D) is added to 1.0 (unit started but not completed—Car E) to get the equivalent units for materials for February, 4.0 units.

Once you know the number of equivalent units produced, you can compute unit costs for materials and conversion costs for each department or work cell in the production process. The equations for computing the unit cost amounts are as follows (note the role of equivalent units):

$$\text{Unit cost for materials} = \frac{\text{total materials costs}}{\text{equivalent units—materials costs}}$$

$$\text{Unit cost for conversion costs} = \frac{\text{total labor and factory overhead costs}}{\text{equivalent units—conversion costs}}$$

EQUIVALENT PRODUCTION: NO BEGINNING WORK IN PROCESS INVENTORY

To begin the analysis for computing equivalent production, we will assume that there are no units in beginning work in process inventory. In such a case, we need to consider only (1) units started and completed during the period, and (2) units started but not completed. By definition, the number of units started but not completed equals the balance of units in the ending Work in Process Inventory. Equivalent production is computed in parts as follows:

Part 1: Units started and completed = (number of units) × 100 percent

Part 2: Equivalent units in ending work in process inventory = (number of units) × (percentage of completion)

The *sum* of these two amounts represents the equivalent whole units completed during the period. Percentage of completion factors are obtained from engineering estimates or supervisors in the production departments.

Earlier we noted that direct labor and factory overhead costs are usually combined and called conversion costs when computing unit cost because both types of costs are usually incurred uniformly throughout the production process. Materials costs are generally not used uniformly within the process. Such costs are usually incurred either at the beginning of the process (raw materials input) or at the end of the process (packing materials). Because of this difference, the number of equivalent units for raw materials will differ from the number for conversion costs. Separate computations are necessary.

We will use Karlsson Clothing, Inc. to illustrate the computation of equivalent units when there are no partially completed units in beginning work in process inventory. Assume that Karlsson's records for January 19xx contain the following information: (1) 47,500 units were started during the period; (2) 6,200 units were partially complete at period end; (3) the ending work in process inventory was 60 percent completed; (4) raw materials were added at the beginning of the process, and conversion costs were incurred uniformly throughout the process; (5) no units were lost or spoiled during the month.

Exhibit 1. Equivalent Units: No Beginning Inventory

Karlsson Clothing, Inc.
Schedule of Equivalent Production
For the Month Ended January 31, 19xx

Units—Stage of Completion	Units to Be Accounted For	Equivalent Units	
		Materials Costs	Conversion Costs
Beginning inventory—units started last period but completed in this period	—	—	—
Units started and completed in this period	41,300	41,300	41,300
Ending inventory—units started but not completed in this period	6,200		
(Materials costs—100% complete)		6,200	
(Conversion costs—60% complete)			3,720
Totals	47,500	47,500	45,020

The schedule of equivalent production, in which the period's equivalent units are computed for both materials costs and conversion costs, is shown in Exhibit 1. Because there were no units in beginning work in process inventory, dashes are entered in the appropriate columns. All 41,300 units started and completed during the period (47,500 units started − 6,200 units not completed) have received 100 percent of the materials, labor, and overhead needed to complete them. Therefore, 41,300 equivalent units are recorded in both the Materials Costs and Conversion Costs columns.

The next step is to account for the equivalent units in ending inventory. The 6,200 units have received all raw materials inputs because materials were added to each product as it entered the production process. Therefore, 6,200 equivalent units are entered in the Materials Costs column. However, conversion costs (direct labor and factory overhead) are added uniformly as the products move through the process. The 6,200 units in ending inventory are only 60 percent complete. Equivalent whole units are determined by multiplying the number of units by the percentage completed. In Exhibit 1, the amount of equivalent units for conversion costs of ending inventory is computed as follows:

6,200 units × 60% completion = 3,720 equivalent units

The computations show that, for January, there were 47,500 equivalent units for materials costs and 45,020 equivalent units for conversion costs.

EQUIVALENT PRODUCTION: WITH BEGINNING WORK IN PROCESS INVENTORY

A situation where there is no beginning work in process inventory is very seldom found in industry. By definition, process costing techniques are used in industries where production flows continuously or where there are long runs of identical products. Because there is usually something in process at month end, there are always units in beginning work in process inventory in the following period. Thus, we turn our analysis to such a situation, expanding the previous example.

During February 19xx, unit production results for Karlsson Clothing, Inc. were as follows: (1) the 6,200 units in beginning work in process inventory (60 percent complete at the beginning of February) were finished during the month; and (2) 57,500 units were started during the period, of which 5,000 units were partially complete (45 percent) at period end and constituted the ending work in process inventory.

February operations of Karlsson Clothing, Inc. involve both beginning and ending balances in Work in Process Inventory. To compute equivalent units for February, we must be careful to account only for the work done in February. The computation of equivalent units is illustrated in Exhibit 2. Units in beginning inventory were 60 percent complete as to conversion costs

Exhibit 2. Equivalent Units: With Beginning Inventory

Karlsson Clothing, Inc.
Schedule of Equivalent Production
For the Month Ended February 28, 19xx

Units—Stage of Completion	Units to Be Accounted For	Equivalent Units Materials Costs	Equivalent Units Conversion Costs
Beginning inventory—units started last period but completed in this period	6,200		
(Materials costs—100% complete)		—	
(Conversion costs—60% complete)			2,480
Units started and completed in this period	52,500	52,500	52,500
Ending inventory—units started but not completed in this period	5,000		
(Materials costs—100% complete)		5,000	
(Conversion costs—45% complete)			2,250
Totals	63,700	57,500	57,230

before the period began, and 100 percent complete as to materials costs. All materials were added during the preceding period (January). Therefore, for those units, no equivalent units of materials costs were applicable to February, and only 40 percent of the conversion costs were needed to complete the units. As shown in Exhibit 2, equivalent units of conversion costs are 2,480 (6,200 units × 40 percent, the remaining percentage of completion).

Computations involving units started and completed, as well as ending inventory computations, are similar to those for January. Units started and completed receive the full amount of raw materials and conversion costs. Therefore, the resulting equivalent units equal 52,500 (57,500 started − 5,000 not completed) for both materials and conversion costs. Ending inventory is 100 percent complete as to materials (5,000 units) and 45 percent complete as to conversion costs (5,000 × 45 percent = 2,250 units). The end result is that February produced 57,500 equivalent units that used raw materials and 57,230 equivalent units that received conversion costs.

Note that these illustrations of the computation of equivalent units cover only two of the hundreds of possible process costing situations with varying percentages of completion. These examples, however, establish the procedures necessary to solve all process costing problems utilizing the FIFO product and cost flows.

COST ANALYSIS SCHEDULES

Thus far we have focused on accounting for *units* of productive output. In the schedule of equivalent production, we have computed totals for units to be accounted for and equivalent units for materials costs and conversion costs. Once the unit information has been sorted out and equivalent unit figures have been generated, we can turn to the dollar information. Accounting for manufacturing costs, cost per equivalent unit, and inventory costing can now be brought into our analysis.

UNIT COST ANALYSIS SCHEDULE

OBJECTIVE

6 *Use a unit cost analysis schedule to compute product unit cost for a specific time period*

A unit cost analysis schedule is a process costing statement used to (1) accumulate all costs charged to the Work in Process Inventory account of each department or production process, and (2) compute cost per equivalent unit for materials costs and conversion costs. Unit cost analysis schedules are illustrated in Exhibits 3 and 5. Exhibit 3 shows the calculations when there is no beginning work in process inventory and Exhibit 5 shows the calculations when there are units in beginning work in process inventory.

A unit cost analysis schedule has two parts: total cost analysis and computation of equivalent unit costs. All costs for the period are accumulated in the unit cost analysis schedule, and the Total Costs to Be Accounted For column serves as a check figure for the final distribution of costs to inventories in the third schedule, the cost summary schedule. The costs in the Total Costs to Be Accounted For column may become part of ending Work in Process Inventory and remain in the account, or they may be part of the costs of completed goods transferred to the next department or to Finished Goods Inventory. The amount of total costs to be accounted for consists of materials costs and conversion costs incurred during the current period plus the costs included in the beginning balance of Work in Process Inventory.

The second part of the unit cost analysis schedule is the computation of costs per equivalent unit. For both materials costs and conversion costs, *only current period costs* are divided by the respective equivalent unit amounts. Costs attached to units in beginning inventory are *not* included in the computation of equivalent unit costs. Under the FIFO cost flow assumption, separate costing analyses are used for each accounting period, and costs of different periods are not averaged. Therefore, costs attached to beginning inventory are isolated and treated separately.

OBJECTIVE

7 *Prepare a cost summary schedule that assigns costs to units completed and transferred out during the period, and find the ending Work in Process Inventory balance*

COST SUMMARY SCHEDULE

The final phase of the process costing analysis is the distribution of total costs accumulated during the period to the units in ending Work in Process Inventory or to the units completed and transferred out of the department. This is done using the cost summary schedule. Information in this schedule originates in either the schedule of equivalent production or the unit cost analysis schedule. Using hypothetical amounts, the following analysis illustrates the computation of total costs transferred out of the department during the period.

Units in beginning inventory	
Costs attached to units in beginning inventory	$ 4,460
Costs necessary to complete units in beginning inventory	2,910
Total cost of units in beginning inventory	$ 7,370
Costs of units started and completed during the period	46,880
Total cost of completed units	$54,250

The computation of each of these amounts is illustrated in the next section. All costs remaining in Work in Process Inventory after costs of completed units have been transferred out represent the cost of ending units in process.

To complete the cost summary schedule, we add the total cost of completed units transferred and the costs attached to ending Work in Process Inventory, and compare their total with the total costs to be accounted for in the unit cost analysis schedule. The two totals should be equal; if they are not equal, the difference may be due to rounding or a computational error.

ILLUSTRATIVE ANALYSIS

To fully explain the form and use of the cost schedules, we will expand the Karlsson Clothing, Inc. example. In addition to the equivalent unit information analyzed earlier, the company disclosed the following cost data.

January 19xx	
Beginning Work in Process Inventory	—
Materials costs	$154,375
Conversion costs for the month	258,865
February 19xx	
Materials costs	$189,750
Conversion costs for the month	320,488

From these data, we will compute equivalent unit costs, total costs transferred to Finished Goods Inventory, and the ending balance in Work in Process Inventory for January and February 19xx.

Exhibit 3. Unit Cost Determination: No Beginning Inventories

Karlsson Clothing, Inc.
Unit Cost Analysis Schedule
For the Month Ended January 31, 19xx

Total Cost Analysis	Costs from Beginning Inventory	Costs from Current Period	Total Costs to Be Accounted For
Materials costs	—	$154,375	$154,375
Conversion costs	—	258,865	258,865
Totals	—	$413,240	$413,240

Computation of Equivalent Unit Costs	Current Period Cost	÷	Equivalent Units	=	Cost per Equivalent Unit
Materials costs	$154,375		47,500		$3.25
Conversion costs	258,865		45,020		5.75
Totals	$413,240				$9.00

January   Cost analysis schedules for January are shown in Exhibits 3 and 4. Total costs to be accounted for are $413,240, as depicted in the unit cost analysis schedule in Exhibit 3. Dividing the January materials costs of $154,375 and the conversion costs of $258,865 by the equivalent unit amounts computed in Exhibit 1, we obtain costs per equivalent unit of $3.25 ($154,375 ÷ 47,500) for materials costs and $5.75 ($258,865 ÷ 45,020) for conversion costs. These per unit amounts are used in the cost summary schedule to compute costs transferred to Finished Goods Inventory and the cost of ending Work in Process Inventory.

The cost summary schedule for January is shown in Exhibit 4. No units were in process at the beginning of January, so no costs are entered for beginning inventory. Units transferred to Finished Goods Inventory in January are made up entirely of units started and completed because there were no units in beginning inventory. Those 41,300 units cost $9 each to produce (total cost per equivalent unit), so $371,700 must be transferred to Finished Goods Inventory.

Since $413,240 was debited to Work. in Process Inventory during January and $371,700 of that amount was transferred to Finished Goods Inventory, the $41,540 remaining in the account is the ending inventory balance. The amount of $41,540 is verified in Exhibit 4. Using the ending inventory amounts from the schedule of equivalent production in Exhibit 1 and the costs per equivalent unit from the cost analysis schedule in Exhibit 3, we make the following computations.

Materials costs: 6,200 equivalent units × $3.25 per unit	$20,150
Conversion costs: 3,720 equivalent units × $5.75 per unit	21,390
Ending Work in Process Inventory balance	$41,540

Exhibit 4. Ending Inventory Computation: No Beginning Inventories

Karlsson Clothing, Inc.
Cost Summary Schedule
For the Month Ended January 31, 19xx

	Cost of Goods Transferred to Finished Goods Inventory	Cost of Ending Work in Process Inventory
Beginning inventory*		
Costs from preceding period	—	
Costs to complete this period	—	
Units started and completed*		
41,300 units × $9.00 per unit	$371,700	
Ending inventory*		
Materials costs: 6,200 units × $3.25		$ 20,150
Conversion costs: 3,720 units × $5.75		21,390
Totals	$371,700	$ 41,540
Computational check:		
Costs to Finished Goods Inventory		$371,700
Costs in ending Work in Process Inventory		41,540
Total costs to be accounted for (see unit cost analysis schedule)		$413,240

*Note: Unit figures come from the schedule of equivalent production for January (Exhibit 1).

Exhibit 5. Unit Cost Determination: With Beginning Inventories

Karlsson Clothing, Inc.
Unit Cost Analysis Schedule
For the Month Ended February 28, 19xx

Total Cost Analysis	Costs from Beginning Inventory	Costs from Current Period	Total Costs to Be Accounted For
Materials costs	$20,150	$189,750	$209,900
Conversion costs	21,390	320,488	341,878
Totals	$41,540	$510,238	$551,778

Computation of Equivalent Unit Costs	Current Period Cost	÷	Equivalent Units	=	Cost per Equivalent Unit
Materials costs	$189,750		57,500		$3.30
Conversion costs	320,488		57,230		5.60
Totals	$510,238				$8.90

The computational check at the bottom of Exhibit 4 verifies that all calculations are correct.

February The cost analysis for February must consider units and costs in beginning Work in Process Inventory. February operating results are analyzed in Exhibits 5 and 6. Total costs to be accounted for in February are $551,778. Included in this amount are the beginning inventory balance of $41,540 (see January computation in Exhibit 4) plus current period costs of $189,750 for materials costs and $320,488 for conversion costs.

Even though February has a beginning balance in Work in Process Inventory, the procedure to compute costs per equivalent unit is similar to the technique used in the January analysis. As shown in Exhibit 5, only current period costs are used. February materials costs of $189,750 and conversion costs of $320,488 are divided by the equivalent unit figures computed in Exhibit 2. February's $8.90 cost per equivalent unit includes $3.30 per unit for raw materials ($189,750 ÷ 57,500) and $5.60 per unit for conversion costs ($320,488 ÷ 57,230).

Exhibit 6. Ending Inventory Computation: With Beginning Inventories

Karlsson Clothing, Inc.
Cost Summary Schedule
For the Month Ended February 28, 19xx

	Cost of Goods Transferred to Finished Goods Inventory	Cost of Ending Work in Process Inventory
Beginning inventory*		
Costs from preceding period	$ 41,540	
Costs to complete this period		
Materials costs: none	—	
Conversion costs: 2,480		
units × $5.60	13,888	
Subtotal	$ 55,428	
Units started and completed*		
52,500 units × $8.90 per unit	467,250	
Ending inventory*		
Materials costs: 5,000 units × $3.30		$ 16,500
Conversion costs: 2,250 units × $5.60		12,600
Totals	$522,678	$ 29,100
Computational check:		
Costs to Finished Goods Inventory		$522,678
Costs in ending Work in Process		
Inventory		29,100
Total costs to be accounted for		
(see unit cost analysis schedule)		$551,778

*Note: Unit figures come from the schedule of equivalent production for February (Exhibit 2).

The February cost analysis concludes with the preparation of the cost summary schedule, illustrated in Exhibit 6. Costs transferred to Finished Goods Inventory include costs of $41,540 attached to the 6,200 units in beginning inventory from January, the costs of completing the units in beginning inventory, and the costs of producing the 52,500 units started and completed during February. January costs of $41,540 were carried forward to February as the beginning balance in the Work in Process Inventory account. In addition, as shown in Exhibit 2, 2,480 equivalent units of conversion costs were required to complete the 6,200 units. Because the equivalent unit conversion cost for February is $5.60, $13,888 (2,480 units × $5.60 per unit) of additional costs were required to complete units in beginning inventory. The 52,500 units started and completed in February cost $8.90 each to produce. This total of $467,250 is added to the $55,428 cost to produce the 6,200 units in beginning inventory to arrive at the $522,678 of costs transferred to Finished Goods Inventory during February.

The ending Work in Process Inventory balance of $29,100 is made up of $16,500 of materials costs (5,000 units × $3.30 per unit) and $12,600 of conversion costs (5,000 units × 45 percent × $5.60 per unit). The extensions of these amounts are shown in Exhibit 6. At the conclusion of the cost summary schedule, the computational check reveals that no calculation errors were made in the February cost analysis.

ANALYSIS OF JOURNAL ENTRIES

OBJECTIVE

8 *Prepare the journal entry(ies) needed to transfer costs of completed units out of the Work in Process Inventory account*

The study of process costing focuses on the preparation of the schedules for equivalent production, unit cost analysis, and cost summary. All computations within those schedules involve the Work in Process Inventory account. The objective is to compute the dollar totals for goods completed and transferred to Finished Goods Inventory and for partially completed products that remain in the Work in Process Inventory account. However, the three schedules alone do not cause costs to flow through accounts in the general ledger. They only provide the information needed. Journal entries are required to effect the flow of costs from one account to another.

The culmination of a process costing analysis, then, is the preparation of a journal entry to transfer costs of completed products out of Work in Process Inventory. Remember that all entries analyzed in earlier chapters are also necessary in a process cost system. Only one entry is highlighted here, however, because it is directly involved in transferring the cost of completed goods. To transfer the costs of units completed, Finished Goods Inventory (or Work in Process Inventory of a subsequent department) is debited and Work in Process Inventory is credited for the amount of the cost transfer computed in the cost summary schedule.

In the example of Karlsson Clothing, Inc., the following entries would be made at the end of each time period.

Jan. 31 Finished Goods Inventory	371,700	
Work in Process Inventory		371,700
To transfer cost of units		
completed in January to		
Finished Goods Inventory		

Feb. 28 Finished Goods Inventory   522,678
       Work in Process Inventory   522,678
       To transfer cost of units
       completed in February to
       Finished Goods Inventory

On February 28, 19xx, after the entries are posted, the Work in Process Inventory account would appear as follows:

Work in Process Inventory

Balance	—	Transferred to Finished	
Jan. materials costs	154,375	Goods in Jan.	371,700
Jan. conversion costs	258,865		
Balance 1/31/xx 41,540			
Feb. materials costs	189,750	Transferred to Finished	
Feb. conversion costs	320,488	Goods in Feb.	522,678
Balance 2/28/xx 29,100*			

*This amount is confirmed by the cost summary schedule in Exhibit 6.

DECISION POINT

Kunde Estate Winery[3]

Kunde Estate Winery is a typical small wine producer located in California's Sonoma Valley. Kunde is considered an estate winery because it either grows or controls the growth of at least 95 percent of the grapes it uses in its wines. The wine-making process differs for red wines and white wines, but both begin with the freshly picked grapes being first put into a hopper and then fed into the crusher-stemmer machine. The resulting solution of crushed, destemmed grapes, called a *must*, comprises skins, seeds, and juice. Red wines gain their color from the skins, so they are fermented with the skins still in the must. Following fermentation, the must is pressed to extract the wine liquid. It is then aged for up to eighteen months in oak barrels before being bottled. The must of white wines is pressed soon after the grapes are crushed, and fermentation takes place in stainless steel tanks or oak barrels. White wines are aged for up to eight months before being bottled. Because red wines continue to develop in the bottle, they are usually held by the winery for one or two years before being released. White wines are released the year after processing.

Determining the product cost of a bottle of wine creates special problems and requires the blending of the job order and process costing approaches into a hybrid system. The process of taking the picked grapes

3. John Y. Lee and Brian G. Jacobs, "Kunde Estate Winery: A Case Study in Cost Accounting," *CMA Magazine,* The Society of Management Accountants (Canada), April 1993, pp. 15–19.

and turning them into a fermented solution requires a process costing approach. But once the wine maker begins to work with the fermented solutions, blending other types of grapes with varietals such as Cabernet Sauvignon or Chardonnay, the uniqueness of the resulting wines suggests the need for a job order system. Tracing production and aging costs to specific lots of wine involves many allocations, but tracking the cost of blending and refining the wine requires a different kind of attention. What types of problems do wineries encounter in this critical costing area? How could Kunde Estate Winery overcome this problem?

Blending takes place during the aging process and usually begins about three months after the initial must was produced. The wine maker experiments with different combinations of grapes at different stages in the eight- to eighteen-month aging process. Taking a joint costing approach to allocating costs based on gallons of wine, an approach used by several wineries, does not reflect where and how the wine maker's time was spent. Some white varietals can be easily developed, whereas some red varietals are very complex and take months to develop. The controller at Kunde Winery created a tracking system that records the activities of the wine maker. The time spent on each batch of each varietal wine is recorded. Then, all costs connected with the wine maker's activities are assigned to a batch or lot of wine based on the amount of time the wine maker took to produce it. The new approach is a version of activity-based costing applied to a hybrid product cost system. ⁚⁚⁚⁚⁚

PROCESS COSTING FOR TWO PROCESSES IN A SERIES

OBJECTIVE

9 *Analyze a process costing situation involving two production processes in a series*

Karlsson Clothing, Inc. employed only one production department, and the analysis centered on two consecutive monthly accounting periods. Because only one production department was used, only one Work in Process Inventory account was needed.

The following illustrative problem deals with two production departments in a series. The product passes from the first to the second department and then to Finished Goods Inventory and is similar to the situation depicted in Example 1 of Figure 2. When the production process requires two departments, the accounting system must maintain two separate Work in Process Inventory accounts, one for each department. This situation does entail more work but does not complicate the computational aspects of the process cost system. The key point to remember is to treat *each* department and its related Work in Process Inventory account as a separate analysis. The three schedules must be prepared for *each* department. Departments should be analyzed in the order in which they contribute to the process.

ILLUSTRATIVE PROBLEM:
TWO PRODUCTION DEPARTMENTS

Jens-Lena Manufacturing Company produces a liquid chemical compound used in converting salt water to fresh water. The production process involves the Mixing Department and the Cooling Department. Every unit produced must be processed by both departments, with cooling as the final operation.

In the Mixing Department, a chemical powder (Material BP) is blended with water, heated to 88° Celsius, and mixed for two hours. Material BP is added at the beginning of the process, and no evaporation takes place. Conversion costs are incurred uniformly throughout the process. Operating data for the Mixing Department for April 19xx are as follows:

Beginning Work in Process Inventory
Units (40% complete as to conversion costs)	1,450 liters
Costs: Materials costs	$ 13,050
Conversion costs	$ 1,760

Ending Work in Process Inventory
All units 70% complete as to conversion costs

April operations
Units started	55,600 liters
Costs: Materials costs	$489,280
Conversion costs	$278,975
Units completed and transferred to the Cooling Department	54,800 liters

1. Prepare (a) a schedule of equivalent production, (b) a unit cost analysis schedule, and (c) a cost summary schedule for the Mixing Department.
2. Using information in the cost summary schedule, prepare the journal entry to transfer costs of completed units for April from the Mixing Department to the Cooling Department.

Before constructing the three schedules and preparing the journal entry, it is necessary to make a special analysis of the units (liters) worked on during April. To complete the schedule of equivalent production, we must first calculate the number of units started and completed and the number of units in ending work in process inventory. These amounts were not stated explicitly in the data given but can be easily computed.

Units started and completed:
	Units completed and transferred (given)	54,800 liters
Less:	Units in beginning inventory (given)	1,450 liters
Equals:	Units started and completed	53,350 liters

Units in ending inventory:
	Units started during April (given)	55,600 liters
Less:	Units started and completed (above)	53,350 liters
Equals:	Units in ending inventory	2,250 liters

Once we know the number of units started and completed and the number of units in ending work in process inventory, we can prepare the three schedules in the cost analysis.

1. The FIFO solution is shown in Exhibit 7. Carefully review each of the three schedules. If you have any problems following the computations, refer to Exhibits 1 through 6 for explanations.
2. The costs of completed units for April are now ready to be transferred from the Mixing Department to the Cooling Department. The required journal entry would be as follows:

Work in Process Inventory—Cooling Department	755,390	
Work in Process Inventory—Mixing Department		755,390
To transfer cost of units completed in April from Mixing Department to Cooling Department		

Exhibit 7. FIFO Costing Approach for Process Cost Analysis

Jens-Lena Manufacturing Company
Mixing Department—FIFO Process Cost Analysis
For the Month Ended April 30, 19xx

A. Schedule of Equivalent Production

Units—Stage of Completion	Units to Be Accounted For	Equivalent Units Materials Costs	Equivalent Units Conversion Costs
Beginning inventory—units started last period but completed in this period (Materials costs—100% complete) (Conversion costs—40% complete)	1,450	—	870 (60% of 1,450)
Units started and completed in this period	53,350	53,350	53,350
Ending inventory—units started but not completed in this period (Materials costs—100% complete) (Conversion costs—70% complete)	2,250	2,250	1,575 (70% of 2,250)
Totals	57,050	55,600	55,795

B. Unit Cost Analysis Schedule

	Costs from Beginning Inventory (1)	Costs from Current Period (2)	Total Costs to Be Accounted For (3)	Equivalent Units (4)	Cost per Equivalent Unit (2 ÷ 4)
Materials costs	$13,050	$489,280	$502,330	55,600	$ 8.80
Conversion costs	1,760	278,975	280,735	55,795	5.00
Totals	$14,810	$768,255	$783,065		$13.80

C. Cost Summary Schedule

	Cost of Goods Transferred to Cooling Department	Cost of Ending Work in Process Inventory
Beginning inventory		
Beginning balance	$ 14,810	
Cost to complete: 870 units (1,450 units × 60%) × $5.00 per unit	4,350	
Total beginning inventory	$ 19,160	
Units started and completed: 53,350 units × $13.80 per unit	736,230	
Ending inventory		
Materials costs: 2,250 units × $8.80 per unit		$ 19,800
Conversion costs: 1,575 units × $5.00 per unit		7,875
Totals	$755,390	$ 27,675
Computational check:		
Costs to Cooling Department		$755,390
Costs in ending Work in Process Inventory		27,675
Total costs to be accounted for (see unit cost analysis schedule)		$783,065

In the preceding entry, the $755,390 is being transferred from one Work in Process Inventory account to another. The $755,390 attached to the units transferred into the Cooling Department during April would be accounted for in the same way as raw materials used in the Mixing Department. All other procedures and schedules illustrated in the Mixing Department example would be used again for the Cooling Department. See the Review Problem at the end of this chapter for the accounting treatment of the Cooling Department.

Rounding of Numerical Answers   Unlike the problems discussed so far in this chapter, most real-world unit costs do not work out to even-numbered dollars and cents. They must be rounded. Remember these three simple rules: (1) Round unit cost computations to three decimal places where appropriate. (2) Round cost summary data to the nearest dollar. (3) On the cost summary schedule, any difference caused by rounding should be added to or subtracted from the amount being transferred out of the department before the journal entry is prepared.

BUSINESS BULLETIN: BUSINESS PRACTICE

Thus far, our study of product costs has involved tracing actual costs incurred to the products produced. Costs of materials, direct labor, and factory overhead were either those actually incurred or, for factory overhead, an applied amount that was based on previous actual costs. Such traditional costing approaches were developed during a time when efficiency was the focal point. Comparing product costs of different time periods was a useful way of analyzing changes in production efficiency. Scrap and rework were anticipated, and costs of machine and worker downtime were part of the product cost. Significant managerial time and dollars were spent tracking those costs and analyzing differences between actual and budgeted costs.

Today, defects in the production process are not tolerated. Scrap and rework have been minimized. Many companies are using "engineered" costs to cost out their products. Engineered costs are computed by determining the resources needed to produce a product and assigning anticipated costs to those resources. All similar products are given the same product cost. Since downtime and other production inefficiencies have been minimized, management believes that costs for similar products should be constant. Using engineered costs frees management accountants to focus on analyzing new production measures, such as product throughput time and costs of quality, rather than trying to trace costs to products.

**Supplemental
OBJECTIVE**

THE AVERAGE COSTING APPROACH TO PROCESS COSTING

10 *Compute equivalent units, product unit cost, and the ending Work in Process Inventory balance in a process cost system that uses the average costing approach*

Figure 3 illustrates how products flow through a production process in a first-in, first-out (FIFO) order. But cost flow and accountability do not have to follow the same assumptions that support the flow of products. Such is the case with the average costing approach to process costing. The average costing method is very similar to the FIFO costing method in that the same three schedules are used in both methods. The primary difference between the two methods is that the average costing approach assumes that the items in beginning work in process inventory were started and completed during the current period. Although less accurate than the FIFO approach, the average costing method is a bit easier to work with.

The procedures used to complete the three process costing schedules under the average costing approach differ from those under the FIFO method. The changes are described and illustrated below. The data found in this chapter's illustrative problem, the Jens-Lena Manufacturing Company, form the basis for the schedules that follow.

SCHEDULE OF EQUIVALENT PRODUCTION

No Beginning Work in Process Inventory   When there is no beginning work in process inventory, the computation of equivalent units is exactly the same under the average costing approach as it is under the FIFO method. The two approaches generate different equivalent unit amounts only when a beginning inventory is involved.

With Beginning Work in Process Inventory   The first difference between the FIFO costing and average costing methods is found in the computation of equivalent units when there is a beginning work in process inventory. Remember that under the average costing approach, all units in beginning inventory are treated as if they were started and completed in the current period. However, equivalent units can still be calculated in three parts (or the first two parts can be combined, since they require similar calculations):

Part 1:   Units in beginning inventory = number of units × 100 percent

Part 2:   Units started and completed = number of units × 100 percent

Part 3:   Equivalent units in ending work in process inventory:
Materials costs = number of units × percentage of completion
Conversion costs = number of units × percentage of completion

Notice that the computation of parts 2 and 3 is the same under both costing approaches.

Exhibit 8 (part **A**) illustrates the computation of equivalent units for Jens-Lena Manufacturing Company, using the average costing approach when beginning inventory items must be accounted for. For April 19xx, there were 1,450 units in beginning Work in Process Inventory, 100 percent complete as to materials costs and 40 percent complete as to conversion costs. In addition, 53,350 units were started and completed during the month. Ending Work in Process Inventory contained 2,250 units, 100 percent complete as to materials costs and 70 percent complete regarding conversion costs. As shown in Exhibit 8, the 1,450 units in beginning inventory are extended at their full amount to both the Materials Costs and Conversion Costs columns. This is

Exhibit 8. Average Costing Approach for Process Cost Analysis

Jens-Lena Manufacturing Company
Mixing Department—Process Cost Analysis Using Average Costing
For the Month Ended April 30, 19xx

A. Schedule of Equivalent Production

Units—Stage of Completion	Units to Be Accounted For	Equivalent Units	
		Materials Costs	Conversion Costs
Beginning inventory	1,450	1,450	1,450
Units started and completed in this period	53,350	53,350	53,350
Ending inventory—units started but not completed in this period	2,250		
(Materials costs—100% complete)		2,250	
(Conversion costs—70% complete)			1,575 (70% of 2,250)
Totals	57,050	57,050	56,375

B. Unit Cost Analysis Schedule

	Total Costs			Equivalent Unit Costs	
	Costs from Beginning Inventory (1)	Costs from Current Period (2)	Total Costs to Be Accounted For (3)	Equivalent Units (4)	Cost per Equivalent Unit (3 ÷ 4)
Materials costs	$13,050	$489,280	$502,330	57,050	$ 8.805
Conversion costs	1,760	278,975	280,735	56,375	4.980
Totals	$14,810	$768,255	$783,065		$13.785

C. Cost Summary Schedule

	Cost of Goods Transferred to Cooling Department	Cost of Ending Work in Process Inventory
Beginning inventory: 1,450 units × $13.785 per unit	$ 19,988	
Units started and completed: 53,350 units × $13.785 per unit	735,430	
Ending inventory		
Materials costs: 2,250 units × $8.805		$ 19,811
Conversion costs: 1,575 units × $4.980		7,844
Totals	$755,418	$ 27,655
Computational check:		
Costs to Cooling Department		$755,418
Costs in ending Work in Process Inventory		27,655
Difference due to rounding		(8)
Total costs to be accounted for (see unit cost analysis schedule)		$783,065

the same treatment given to the 53,350 units started and completed during April. Units started and completed receive the full amount of materials costs and conversion costs. Ending inventory is 100 percent complete as to materials, so 2,250 equivalent units are extended to the Materials Costs column. Since these units are only 70 percent complete, 1,575 equivalent units (2,250 × 70 percent) are entered in the Conversion Costs column. The end result is a monthly total of 57,050 equivalent units for materials costs and 56,375 equivalent units for conversion costs for the Mixing Department at Jens-Lena Manufacturing Company.

UNIT COST ANALYSIS SCHEDULE

At first glance, the unit cost analysis schedule computed under the average costing method looks just like the one prepared using the FIFO method. There is, however, one significant difference between the two schedules. Following the FIFO approach, we divide the amount in the Costs from Current Period column by the respective amount in the Equivalent Units column to compute the cost per equivalent unit. Under the average costing approach, we divide the amount in the Total Costs to Be Accounted For column by the respective amount in the Equivalent Units column. Following the average costing method, the costs in beginning inventory and the costs of the current period are added together and treated as current costs (averaged), just as beginning inventory units are treated as if they were started and completed during the period.

As shown in part **B** of Exhibit 8, total unit cost computed under the average costing approach is $13.785 (rounded to three decimal places). Materials costs per unit are $8.805 (found by dividing the total materials costs to be accounted for, $502,330, by equivalent units of 57,050). To compute the conversion costs per unit, the total conversion costs to be accounted for—$280,735—are divided by 56,375 equivalent units to arrive at $4.980 per unit.

COST SUMMARY SCHEDULE

Under the average costing method, the cost summary schedule sets out the cost of goods completed and transferred to the next department, process, or Finished Goods Inventory. Because beginning Work in Process Inventory is treated as if it were started and completed during the current period, the units in beginning inventory and the units actually started and completed this period are treated alike. Both are costed out at the total unit cost computed in the unit cost analysis schedule. Costs of units in ending Work in Process Inventory are computed in exactly the same way as they were under the FIFO costing approach. The units in ending inventory are multiplied by the respective percentages of completion and cost per equivalent unit for materials costs and conversion costs to compute the ending balance of Work in Process Inventory.

Part **C** of Exhibit 8, shows the completed cost summary schedule for the Jens-Lena Manufacturing Company. To compute the cost of goods completed and transferred to the Cooling Department during April, both the units in beginning Work in Process Inventory (1,450) and the units started and completed in April (53,350) are multiplied by the $13.785 cost per equivalent unit. The 1,450 units in beginning inventory are valued at $19,988 (1,450 × $13.785), and the 53,350 units started and completed are costed out at $735,430 (53,350 × $13.785). The total costs transferred out in April are $755,410 ($755,418 − $8).

The final step needed to complete the cost summary schedule is to compute the dollar amount of the units in ending Work in Process Inventory. Since all materials are added at the beginning of the process, the 2,250 units are multiplied by a 100 percent completion factor and by $8.805 to arrive at the $19,811 for total materials costs. Conversion costs of $7,844 are computed by multiplying 2,250 units times the 70 percent completion factor (equals 1,575 equivalent units) times $4.980 per unit. Total cost of the units in ending Work in Process Inventory of $27,655 is found by adding $19,811 and $7,844.

The check of computations at the bottom of Exhibit 8 shows that an $8 difference due to rounding arose in the analysis. The unit costs computed in the unit cost analysis schedule were rounded up, so too much money has been attached to the units worked on during the month. When preparing the entry to account for the costs of units completed and transferred, this small amount should be merged with the total costs transferred. In our example, the $8 overage is subtracted from the $755,418. The adjusted total cost of the 54,800 units transferred to the Cooling Department is thus $755,410. The journal entry needed to record this transfer is as follows:

Work in Process Inventory—Cooling Department	$755,410	
Work in Process Inventory—Mixing Department		$755,410
To transfer costs of completed units from the Mixing Department to the Cooling Department		

CHAPTER REVIEW

REVIEW OF LEARNING OBJECTIVES

1. **Describe the process cost system and identify the reasons for its use.** A process cost system is a product costing system used by companies that produce large amounts of similar products or have a continuous production flow. In a process cost system, the costs of materials, labor, and factory overhead are traced to processes or work cells and then assigned to the products produced by those processes or work cells. In a continuous flow environment, tracking individual costs to individual products is too difficult and too expensive and does not result in significantly different product costs. So, a process cost system accumulates the costs of materials, labor, and factory overhead for each process or work cell and assigns the costs equally to the products produced during a particular time period. Industries that produce paint, beverages, bricks, canned foods, milk, and paper are typical users of the process cost system.

2. **Compare and contrast the characteristics of the process and job order cost systems.** Both process costing and job order costing are basic, traditional approaches to product costing. The two systems differ in key ways, however, because they are designed to serve two different environments. A job order costing system is used for unique or special-order products. In such a system, materials, direct labor, and factory overhead costs are assigned to specific job orders or batches of products. In determining unit costs, the total manufacturing cost assigned to each job order is divided by the number of good units produced for that order. A process costing system is used by companies that produce a large number of similar products or have a continuous production flow. Such companies find it more economical to account for product-related costs for a period of time (a week or month) than to

assign them to specific products or job orders. In a process costing system, unit costs are found by dividing total manufacturing costs for a department or work center during the week or month by the number of good units produced.

3. **Explain the role of the Work in Process Inventory account(s) in a process cost system.** The Work in Process Inventory account is the heart of the process cost system. Each production department or operating unit has its own Work in Process Inventory account. All costs charged to that department flow into this inventory account. Special analysis, using three schedules, is needed at period end to determine the costs flowing out of the account. All special analyses in process costing are related to costs in the Work in Process Inventory account.

4. **Diagram the product flow and cost flow through a process cost system.** Process costing is used to account for the production of liquids or long, continuous production runs of identical products. Thus, products flow in a FIFO fashion (first in, first out). Once a product is started into production, it flows on to completion. In a process cost system, manufacturing costs are handled differently than in a job order cost system. Following a FIFO costing approach, unit costs are computed using only current period cost and unit data. Costs in beginning Work in Process Inventory are treated separately. The unit costs are assigned to completed units and to units in ending Work in Process Inventory.

5. **Compute equivalent production for situations with and without units in beginning Work in Process Inventory.** Equivalent units are computed from unit information including (1) units in, and percent completion of, beginning Work in Process Inventory; (2) units started and completed during the period; and (3) units in, and percent completion of, ending Work in Process Inventory. If materials are added at the beginning of the process, no materials are added to the units in beginning inventory during the current period, so they are not included in the computation of equivalent units. All units started during the period receive the full amount of materials. Equivalent units for costs added uniformly throughout the process are computed by multiplying the percentage completed in the current period by the total units in the respective categories mentioned above.

6. **Use a unit cost analysis schedule to compute product unit cost for a specific time period.** Unit costs are found by using a unit cost analysis schedule. Materials costs for units in beginning inventory and materials costs of the current period are added. The same procedure is followed for conversion costs. Total costs to be accounted for are found by adding the total materials costs and conversion costs. Following FIFO costing procedures, the unit cost for materials is found by dividing the materials costs for the current period by the equivalent unit amount for materials. The same procedure is followed for conversion costs. Then the unit costs for materials and conversion costs are added to yield the total unit cost for the period.

7. **Prepare a cost summary schedule that assigns costs to units completed and transferred out during the period, and find the ending Work in Process Inventory balance.** The first part of the cost summary schedule centers on computing the costs assigned to units completed and transferred out during the period. This part is done in two steps: (1) costs needed to complete units in beginning inventory are added to costs assigned from the previous period, and (2) units started and completed during the current period are assigned the full amount of production costs. The total of these two calculations represents costs assigned to units completed and transferred during the period. The second part of the cost summary schedule assigns costs to units still in process at period end. Unit costs for materials and conversion costs are multiplied by their respective equivalent units. The total of the two dollar amounts represents the balance in the Work in Process Inventory account at the end of the period.

8. **Prepare the journal entry(ies) needed to transfer costs of completed units out of the Work in Process Inventory account.** After the first part of the cost summary schedule (the part that assigns costs to units completed and transferred out during the period) is completed, a journal entry is prepared to transfer costs out of the Work in Process Inventory account. In the journal entry, Finished Goods Inventory (or the Work in Process Inventory account of a subsequent department) is debited and the transferring department's Work in Process Inventory account is credited for the amount of the cost transfer computed in the cost summary schedule.

9. **Analyze a process costing situation involving two production processes in a series.** In a process costing situation involving two production processes in a series, the product passes from the first process to the second and then to finished goods inventory. Two separate Work in Process Inventory accounts are maintained, one for each process. Each process and its related Work in Process Inventory account must be treated in a separate analysis. The three schedules are prepared for each process. Processes should be analyzed in the order they follow in the production process because the costs assigned to the completed goods in the first process are transferred to the second process.

SUPPLEMENTAL OBJECTIVE

10. **Compute equivalent units, product unit cost, and the ending Work in Process Inventory balance in a process cost system that uses the average costing approach.** The average costing approach to process costing is an alternative method of accounting for production costs in a continuous flow production environment. The same three schedules—schedule of equivalent production, unit cost analysis schedule, and cost summary schedule—must be completed for each process, as they were under the FIFO method. The only difference between the FIFO and average costing approaches is that the latter assumes that the items in beginning work in process inventory were started and completed during the current period. Costs in beginning inventory are averaged with current period costs to compute product unit costs used to value the ending balance in Work in Process Inventory and goods completed and transferred out of the process or work cell.

REVIEW OF CONCEPTS AND TERMINOLOGY

The following concepts and terms were introduced in this chapter.

S O 10 **Average costing approach:** A process costing method in which unit costs are computed based on the assumption that the items in beginning work in process inventory were started and completed during the current period.

L O 5 **Conversion costs:** The combined total of direct labor and factory overhead costs incurred by a production department.

L O 7 **Cost summary schedule:** A process costing schedule that facilitates the distribution of all production costs incurred and accumulated during the period among the units of output, either those completed and transferred out of the department or those still in process at period end.

L O 5 **Equivalent production:** A measure of the number of equivalent whole units produced in a period of time. Also called *equivalent units.*

L O 4 **FIFO costing approach:** A process costing method in which cost flow follows product flow; the first products to be introduced into the production process are the first products to be completed. Costs assigned to those first products are the first costs to be transferred out of the production center or department.

L O 1 **Process cost system:** A product costing system used by companies that produce large amounts of similar products or have a continuous production flow; the costs of materials, labor, and factory overhead are traced to processes or work cells and then assigned to the products produced by those processes or work cells.

L O 5 **Schedule of equivalent production:** A process costing schedule in which a period's equivalent units are computed for both materials costs and conversion costs.

L O 6 **Unit cost analysis schedule:** A process costing statement used to (1) accumulate all costs charged to the Work in Process Inventory account of each department or production process and (2) compute cost per equivalent unit for materials costs and conversion costs.

REVIEW PROBLEM
COSTS TRANSFERRED IN

L O 3, 6, 7, 8   This problem reviews the three-schedule analysis used in process costing. It also introduces a new situation common in process costing, which is how to deal with costs transferred in. Accounting for the second department's costs in a series of Work in Process Inventory accounts is very much like accounting for the first department's costs. The only difference is that instead of (or in addition to) accounting for current materials and conversion costs, we are dealing with *costs transferred in* during the period. All procedures used to account for costs transferred in are exactly the same as those used for materials costs and units. *When accounting for costs and units transferred in, treat them as you would materials added at the beginning of the process.*

This Review Problem illustrates the accounting approach for the second in a series of production departments. We will continue with the example of the Jens-Lena Manufacturing Company, concentrating this time on the Cooling Department. No new materials are added in this department; only conversion costs are added during the cooling process. Operating data for the Cooling Department for April 19xx are:

Beginning Work in Process Inventory	
Units	2,100 liters
Costs: Transferred in	$ 29,200
Conversion costs	$ 4,610
Units in beginning inventory 70% complete as to conversion costs	
Ending Work in Process Inventory	
All units 60% complete as to conversion costs	
April Operations	
Units transferred in	54,800 liters
Costs: Transferred in	$755,390
Conversion costs	$169,884
Units completed and transferred to Finished Goods Inventory	54,450 liters

REQUIRED

1. Using the FIFO costing method, prepare (a) a schedule of equivalent production, (b) a unit cost analysis schedule, and (c) a cost summary schedule.
2. From the cost summary schedule, prepare the journal entry to transfer costs of completed units for April to the Finished Goods Inventory account.

ANSWER TO REVIEW PROBLEM

1. Before preparing the three-schedule analysis, we must determine the following unit information.

Units started and completed:	
Units completed and transferred (given)	54,450 liters
Less units in beginning inventory (given)	2,100 liters
Units started and completed	52,350 liters
Units in ending inventory:	
Units transferred in during April (given)	54,800 liters
Less units started and completed (above)	52,350 liters
Units in ending inventory	2,450 liters

With this unit information, we can prepare the schedules, shown on the next page.

2. The costs of completed units for April are now ready to be transferred from the Cooling Department to the Finished Goods Inventory account. The journal entry is:

Finished Goods Inventory ($920,700 + $27)	920,727	
Work in Process—Cooling Department		920,727
To transfer cost of units completed in April to Finished Goods Inventory		

Jens-Lena Manufacturing Company
Cooling Department—FIFO Process Cost Analysis
For the Month Ended April 30, 19xx

A. Schedule of Equivalent Production

Units—Stage of Completion	Units to Be Accounted For	Equivalent Units	
		Transferred-in Costs	Conversion Costs
Beginning inventory—units started last period but completed in this period	2,100		
(Transferred-in costs—100% complete)		—	
(Conversion costs—70% complete)			630 (30% of 2,100)
Units started and completed in this period	52,350	52,350	52,350
Ending inventory—units started but not completed in this period	2,450		
(Transferred-in costs—100% complete)		2,450	
(Conversion costs—60% complete)			1,470 (60% of 2,450)
Totals	56,900	54,800	54,450

B. Unit Cost Analysis Schedule

	Total Costs			Equivalent Unit Costs	
	Costs from Beginning Inventory (1)	Costs from Current Period (2)	Total Costs to Be Accounted For (3)	Equivalent Units (4)	Cost per Equivalent Unit (2 ÷ 4)
Transferred-in costs	$29,200	$755,390	$784,590	54,800	$13.784
Conversion costs	4,610	169,884	174,494	54,450	3.120
Totals	$33,810	$925,274	$959,084		$16.904

C. Cost Summary Schedule

	Cost of Goods Transferred to Finished Goods Inventory	Cost of Ending Work in Process Inventory
Beginning inventory		
Beginning balance	$ 33,810	
Cost to complete: 2,100 units × 30% × $3.120 per unit	1,966	
Total beginning inventory	$ 35,776	
Units started and completed		
52,350 units × $16.904 per unit	884,924	
Ending inventory		
Transferred-in costs: 2,450 units × $13.784 per unit		$ 33,771
Conversion costs: 1,470 units × $3.120 per unit		4,586
Totals	$920,700	$ 38,357
Computational check:		
Costs to Finished Goods Inventory		$920,700
Costs in ending Work in Process Inventory		38,357
Difference due to rounding		27
Total costs to be accounted for (see unit cost analysis schedule)		$959,084

CHAPTER ASSIGNMENTS

QUESTIONS

1. What is a process cost system?
2. What types of production are best suited to a process cost system?
3. "In job order costing, one Work in Process Inventory account is used for all jobs. In process costing, several Work in Process Inventory accounts are used." Explain these statements.
4. What three schedules are used in process costing analysis?
5. Explain the similarity between job order and process cost systems in accounting for the costs of materials, labor, and overhead.
6. Explain the difference between job order and process cost systems in accounting for the costs of materials, labor, and overhead.
7. What are the two ways in which costs may be assigned to products in a process cost system?
8. Explain the FIFO costing approach for assigning costs to products in a process cost system.
9. Define the term *equivalent production* (or *equivalent units*).
10. Why do actual unit data need to be changed to equivalent unit data for product costing purposes in a process cost system?
11. Define the term *conversion costs*. Why are conversion costs used in process costing computations?
12. Why is it easier to compute equivalent units without units in beginning inventory than with units in beginning inventory?
13. What are the purposes of the unit cost analysis schedule?
14. What two important dollar amounts come from the cost summary schedule? How do they relate to the year-end financial statements?
15. Describe the procedures to check the accuracy of the results in the cost summary schedule.
16. What is the significance of the journal entry used to transfer costs of completed products out of the Work in Process Inventory account?
17. Why is it necessary to make a special analysis of the number of units started and completed in a production period and of the number of units in ending work in process inventory at the end of the production period?
18. Explain the average costing approach to assigning costs to products in a process cost system.
19. How are the FIFO costing and average costing approaches similar in assigning costs to products in a process cost system?
20. What is a *transferred-in cost*? Where does it come from? Why is it handled like materials added at the beginning of the process?

SHORT EXERCISES

SE 1. *Process Versus Job*
L O 1 *Order Costing*
No check figure

Indicate whether the manufacturer of each of the following products should use a job order cost system or a process cost system to accumulate product costs.

1. Plastics
2. Ocean cruise ships
3. Cereal
4. Medical drugs for veterinary practices

SE 2. *Process Versus Job*
L O 2 *Order Costing*
No check figure

Indicate whether each of the following is a characteristic of job order costing or of process costing.

1. Several Work in Process Inventory accounts are used, one for each department or part in the process.
2. Costs are grouped by department, work center, or work cell.
3. Costs are measured for each completed job.
4. Only one Work in Process Inventory account is used.
5. Costs are measured in terms of units completed in specific time periods.
6. Costs are assigned to specific jobs or batches of product.

SE 3. *Process Costing and*
L O 3 *the Work in Process*
Inventory Account
Check Figure: Units Completed and Transferred: 6,500

BioCo Chemical uses an automated mixing machine to combine three raw materials into a product called Triogo. On the average, each unit of Triogo contains $3 of Material X, $6 of Material Y, $9 of Material Z, $2 of direct labor, and $12 of factory overhead. Total costs charged to the Work in Process Inventory account during the month were $208,000. There were no units in beginning or ending Work in Process Inventory. How many units were completed and transferred to Finished Goods Inventory during the month?

SE 4. *Product Flow*
L O 4 *Diagram*
No check figure

Draw a diagram showing the flow of production for product A. Product A goes through Department 1, Department 2, Department 4, and Department 5. Materials are added in Departments 1 and 4, and direct labor and factory overhead are added in every department.

SE 5. *Equivalent*
L O 5 *Production: No*
Beginning Inventory
Check Figure: Equivalent Units for Materials Costs: 17,000

Given the following information from Blue Blaze's records for July 19x7, compute the equivalent units of production.

Beginning inventory	—
Units started during the period	17,000
Units partially completed	2,500
Percentage of completion of ending Work in Process Inventory	70%

Raw materials are added at the beginning of the process, and conversion costs are added uniformly throughout the process.

SE 6. *Equivalent*
L O 5 *Production:*
Beginning Inventory
Check Figure: Equivalent Units for Conversion Costs: 18,050

Assume the same information as in SE 5, except that there were 3,000 units in beginning Work in Process Inventory, 100 percent complete as to materials and 40 percent complete as to conversion costs. Compute the equivalent units of production for the month.

SE 7. *Unit Cost*
L O 6 *Determination*
Check Figure: Total Cost per Equivalent Unit: $3.20

Using the information from SE 5 and the following information, compute the total cost per equivalent unit.

Costs for the period	
Materials costs	$20,400
Conversion costs	32,500

SE 8. *Cost Summary*
L O 7 *Schedule*
Check Figure: Cost of ending work in process inventory: $6,500

Using the information from SE 5 and SE 7 and the FIFO method, prepare a cost summary schedule.

SE 9. *Journal Entry to*
L O 8 *Transfer Costs*
No check figure

From the information obtained in SE 8, prepare the journal entry(ies) to transfer costs of completed goods to the Finished Goods Inventory account.

SE 10. *Average Costing*
S O 10 *Method*
Check Figure: Equivalent Units, Materials Costs: 102,300

The cost summary schedule on the next page is based on the average costing method and was prepared for the Berino Pasta Company for the year ended July 31, 19x9.

Berino Pasta Company
Cost Summary Schedule
For the Year Ended July 31, 19x9

	Cost of Goods Transferred to Finished Goods Inventory	Cost of Ending Work in Process Inventory
Beginning inventory		
3,140 units at $4.60	$ 14,444	
Units started and completed		
94,960 units at $4.60	436,816	
Ending inventory		
Materials costs: 4,200 units at $3.20		$13,440
Conversion costs: 2,100 units at $1.40		2,940
Totals	$451,260	$16,380

1. From the information given, prepare the journal entry for July 31, 19x9.
2. Prepare the company's schedule of equivalent production. Assume that materials are added at the beginning of the process.

EXERCISES

E 1.
L O 1
Process Versus Job Order Costing

No check figure

Indicate whether the manufacturer of each of the following products should use a job order cost system or a process cost system to accumulate product costs.

1. Paint
2. Fruit juices
3. Tailor-made suits
4. Milk
5. Coffee cups printed with your school insignia
6. Paper
7. Roller coaster for a theme park
8. Posters for a fund-raising event

E 2.
L O 2
Use of Process Costing Information

No check figure

Dana's Delight makes a variety of cakes, cookies, and pies for distribution to five major grocery store chains in the Tri-City area. A standard process is used to manufacture all items, except the special-order birthday cakes. Dana wants to know if the process cost system currently used in the company can help her find some crucial information. Which of the following questions can be answered using information extracted from a process cost system? Which of the following questions can be best answered using a job order cost system? Explain.

1. How much does it cost to make one chocolate cheesecake?
2. Did the cost of making special-order birthday cakes exceed the cost budgeted for this month?
3. What is the value of the pie inventory at the end of June?
4. What were the costs of the cookies sold during June?
5. At what price should we sell our famous brownies to the grocery store chains?
6. Did we exceed our planned production costs of $3,000 for making pies in June?

E 3.
L O 3
Work in Process Inventory Accounts in Process Cost Systems

Check Figure: Transferred to Finished Goods Inventory: $18,600

Birgit, Inc. makes a chemical used as a food preservative during a manufacturing process involving Departments A and B. The company had the following total costs and unit costs for completed production last month during which 10,000 pounds of chemicals were manufactured.

	Total Cost	Unit Cost
Department A		
Materials	$10,000	$1.00
Direct labor	2,600	.26
Factory overhead	1,300	.13
Totals, Dept. A	$13,900	$1.39
Department B		
Materials	$ 3,000	$ .30
Direct labor	700	.07
Factory overhead	1,000	.10
Totals, Dept. B	$ 4,700	$ .47
Totals	$18,600	$1.86

1. How many Work in Process Inventory Accounts would Birgit use?
2. What dollar amount of the chemical's production cost was transferred from Department A to Department B last month?
3. What dollar amount was transferred from Department B to Finished Goods Inventory?
4. What dollar amount is useful in estimating a selling price for one pound of the chemical?

E 4. *Product Flow*
L O 4 *Diagram*
No check figure

Pines Paint Company uses a process cost system to analyze the costs incurred in making paint. Production of Superior Brand starts in the Blending Department, where materials SM and HA are added to a water base. The solution is heated to 70° Celsius and transferred to the Mixing Department, where it is mixed for one hour. Then the paint goes to the Settling/Canning Department, where it is cooled and put into 4-liter cans. Direct labor and factory overhead charges are incurred uniformly throughout each part of the paint-making process.

In diagram form, show the product flow for Superior Brand paint.

E 5. *Equivalent Units:*
L O 5 *No Beginning*
Inventories
Check Figure: Equivalent Units, Materials Costs: 580,500

Jacquin Stone Company produces slumpstone bricks. Though it has been in operation for only twelve months, the company already enjoys a good reputation. During its first year, materials for 580,500 bricks were put into production; 576,900 were completed and transferred to finished goods inventory. The remaining bricks were still in process at year end, 60 percent complete. In the company's process cost system, all materials are added at the beginning of the process. Conversion costs are incurred uniformly throughout the production process.

From this information, prepare a schedule of equivalent production for the year ending December 31, 19x8. Use the FIFO costing approach.

E 6. *Equivalent Units:*
L O 5 *Beginning*
Inventories—FIFO
Method
Check Figure: Equivalent Units, Conversion Costs: 211,940

Kerle Enterprises makes So-Soft Shampoo for professional hair stylists. On January 1, 19x8, 6,200 liters of shampoo were in process, 80 percent complete as to conversion costs and 100 percent complete as to materials costs. During the month, 212,500 liters of materials were put into production. Data for work in process inventory on January 31, 19x8 were as follows: shampoo, 4,500 liters; stage of completion, 60 percent of conversion costs and 100 percent of materials content.

From this information, prepare a schedule of equivalent production for the month. Use the FIFO costing approach.

E 7. *Equivalent Units:*
L O 5 *Beginning*
Inventories—FIFO
Method
Check Figure: Equivalent Units, Materials Costs: 170,000

The Sardonia Company, a major producer of liquid vitamins, uses a process cost system. During February 19x9, 130,000 gallons of Material CIA and 40,000 gallons of Material CMA were put into production. Beginning work in process inventory was 15,000 gallons of product, 70 percent complete as to labor and overhead. Ending work in process inventory was made up of 12,000 gallons, 45 percent complete as to conversion costs. All materials are added at the beginning of the process.

From this information, prepare a schedule of equivalent production for February using the FIFO costing approach.

E 8. *Work in Process*
L O 6 *Inventory Accounts:*
Total Unit Cost

Check Figure: Total Unit Cost: $105.70

Scientists at Baca Laboratories, Inc. have just perfected a liquid substance called D. K. Rid, which dissolves tooth decay. The substance, which is generated from a complex process involving five departments, is very expensive. Cost and equivalent unit data for the latest week are as follows (units are in ounces).

Dept.	Materials Costs Dollars	Materials Costs Equivalent Units	Conversion Costs Dollars	Conversion Costs Equivalent Units
A	$12,500	1,000	$34,113	2,055
B	23,423	1,985	13,065	1,005
C	24,102	1,030	20,972	2,140
D	—	—	22,086	2,045
E	—	—	15,171	1,945

From these data, compute the unit cost for each department and the total unit cost of producing one ounce of D. K. Rid.

E 9. *Unit Cost*
L O 6 *Determination*

Check Figure: Cost per Equivalent Unit: $27.54

Krause Kitchenwares, Inc. manufactures sets of heavy-duty cookware. Production has just been completed for July 19x7. At the beginning of July, the Work in Process Inventory account showed materials costs of $31,700 and conversion costs of $29,400. Cost of materials used in July was $273,728; conversion costs were $176,689. During the month, 15,190 sets were started and completed. A schedule of equivalent production for July has already been prepared. It shows a total of 16,450 equivalent sets as to materials costs and 16,210 equivalent sets as to conversion costs.

With this information, prepare a unit cost analysis schedule for July. Use the FIFO costing approach.

E 10. *Cost Summary*
L O 7 *Schedule*

Check Figure: Cost of goods transferred to Finished Goods Inventory: $32,239

The Ammons Bakery produces Kringle coffee bread. It uses a process cost system for internal recordkeeping. In August 19x8, beginning inventory was 450 units, 100 percent complete as to materials costs and 10 percent as to conversion costs, and had a value of $675. Units started and completed during the month totaled 14,200. Ending inventory was 420 units, 100 percent complete as to materials costs and 70 percent as to conversion costs. Unit costs per equivalent unit for August were materials costs, $1.40, and conversion costs, $.80.

Using the information given, compute the cost of goods transferred to the Finished Goods Inventory account, the cost remaining in the Work in Process Inventory account, and the total costs to be accounted for. Use the FIFO costing approach.

E 11. *Journal Entry to*
L O 8 *Transfer Costs*

Check Figure: 12,000 equivalent units

The accountant is preparing to transfer the cost of units completed during the month. Department X is the last of five production departments in the company's manufacturing process. The following information is provided:

Work in Process Inventory, Department X	
January 1	$ 40,200
January 31	86,300
Costs incurred during the month	
Transferred in	
from Department H	163,000
Materials	74,300
Direct labor	18,700
Factory overhead	10,300

Prepare the journal entry to transfer costs of completed units from Department X to the Finished Goods Inventory account. If the cost per equivalent unit was $18.35, what number of equivalent units were completed and transferred?

E 12. *Average Costing*
S O 10 *Method*

Check Figure: Total Cost per Equivalent Unit: $4.45

Adler Corporation produces children's toys using a liquid plastic formula and a continuous production process. In the Toy Truck Work Cell, the plastic is heated and fed into a molding machine. The molded toy trucks are then cooled and trimmed and sent to the Packaging Work Cell. All raw materials are added at the beginning of the process. In July, the Work in Process Inventory account had a beginning balance of 420 units, 40 percent complete; its ending balance was 400 units, 70 percent complete.

During the month, 15,000 units were started into production. Beginning Work in Process Inventory contained $937 of materials costs and $370 of conversion costs. During July, $35,300 of materials were added to the process and $31,760 of conversion costs were assigned to the Toy Truck Work Cell. Using the average costing method, compute the equivalent units for July, the unit cost for the toy trucks, and the ending balance in Work in Process Inventory.

SKILLS DEVELOPMENT EXERCISES

Conceptual Analysis

SDE 1.
L O 3

Changing the Accounting System

No check figure

International Commcable produces several types of communications cable for a worldwide market. Since the manufacturing process is continuous, a process cost system is used to develop product costs. Until recently, costs were accumulated monthly, and revised product costs were made available to management by the tenth of the following month. With the installation of a computer-integrated manufacturing system, cost information is now available as soon as each production run is finished. The production superintendent has asked the controller to change the accounting system so that product unit costs are available the day following production.

The controller must prepare a memorandum to the corporate vice president justifying the proposed accounting system change. Identify reasons that the controller can use to support the production superintendent's request. What benefits would be obtained from the proposed modification? Be prepared to share your ideas with your classmates.

Ethical Dilemma

SDE 2.
L O 2

Continuing Professional Education

No check figure

Paula Espolar is head of the Information Systems Department at **Cortez Manufacturing Company.** Tom Phillips, the company's controller, is meeting with Paula to discuss changes in data gathering connected with the company's new automated flexible manufacturing system. Paula opened the conversation by saying, "Tom, the old job order cost methods just will not work for the new flexible manufacturing system. The new system is based on continuous product flow, not batch processing. We need to change to a process cost system for both data gathering and product costing. Otherwise, our product costs will be way off and it will affect our pricing decisions. I found out about the need for this change at a professional seminar I attended last month. You should have been there with me." Phillips responded, "Paula, who is the accounting expert here? I know what product costing approach is best for this situation. Job order costing has provided accurate information for this product line for more than fifteen years. Why should we change just because we've purchased a new machine? We've purchased several machines for this line over the years. And as for your seminar, I don't need to learn about costing methods. I was exposed to them all when I studied management accounting back in the late 1970s."

Is Tom's behavior ethical? If not, what has he done wrong? What can Paula do if Tom continues to refuse to update the product costing system? Prepare a dialogue or develop a role play with your classmates that is a follow-up to this conversation.

Research Activity

SDE 3.
L O 1

Process Costing Systems

No check figure

Look up a current issue of the periodical *Production and Inventory Management* at your campus library. Review the articles, paying particular attention to the types of products and production processes described. Find an example of a company that would most likely be using a process cost system. Prepare a short report that includes the company's name, its product(s), and a description of its production process. Bring this information to class to share with your classmates. Be sure to acknowledge the title, author(s), and publication date of the magazine.

Decision-Making Practice

SDE 4. *Setting a Selling*
L O 5, 6 *Price*

Check Figure: Equivalent Units, Bottle
Costs: 458,900

For the past four years, three companies have dominated the soft drink industry, holding a combined 85 percent of market share. ***King Cola, Inc.*** ranks second nationally in soft drink sales; the company attained gross revenues last year of $27,450,000. Management is thinking about introducing a new low-calorie drink called Slimit Cola.

King soft drinks are processed in a single department. All materials (ingredients) are added at the beginning of the process. The beverages are bottled at the end of the process in bottles costing one cent each. Direct labor and factory overhead costs are applied uniformly throughout the process.

Corporate controller Samantha Robbins believes that costs for the new cola will be very much like those for the company's Cola Plus drink. Last year, she collected the following data about Cola Plus.

	Units	Costs
Work in Process Inventory		
January 1, 19x7*	2,400	
Materials costs		$ 2,160
Conversion costs		610
December 31, 19x7†	2,800	
Materials costs		2,520
Conversion costs		840
Units started during the year	459,300	
Costs for 19x7		
Liquid materials added		413,370
Direct labor and factory overhead		229,690
Bottles		110,136

*50% complete.   †60% complete.   *Note:* Each unit is a twenty-four–bottle case.

The company's variable general administrative and selling costs are $1.10 per unit. Fixed administrative and selling costs are assigned to products at the rate of $.50 per unit. King's two major competitors have already introduced a diet cola in the marketplace. Company A's product sells for $4.10 per unit, Company B's for $4.05. All costs are expected to increase by 10 percent from 19x7 to 19x8. The company tries to earn a profit of at least 15 percent on the total unit cost.

1. What factors should the company consider in setting a selling price for Slimit Cola?
2. Using the FIFO costing approach, compute (a) equivalent units for materials, bottle, and conversion costs; (b) the total production cost per unit; and (c) the total cost per unit of Cola Plus for 19x7.
3. What is the expected total cost per unit of Slimit Cola for 19x8?
4. Recommend a unit selling price range for Slimit Cola for 19x8 and give the reason(s) for your choice.

PROBLEM SET A

A 1. *Process Costing: No*
L O 5, 6, *Beginning*
7, 8 *Inventories*
Check Figure: Cost of ending work in process inventory: $7,225

Daily Industries specializes in making Slik, a high-moisture, low-alkaline wax used to protect and preserve skis. Production of a new, improved brand of Slik began January 1, 19x7. To make the new product, Materials A-14 and C-9 are introduced at the beginning of the production process, along with a wax base. During January, 640 pounds of A-14, 1,860 pounds of C-9, and 12,800 pounds of wax base were used at costs of $15,300, $29,070, and $2,295, respectively. Direct labor of $17,136 and factory overhead costs of $25,704 were incurred uniformly throughout the month. By January 31, 13,600 pounds of Slik had been completed and transferred to the finished goods inventory. Since no spoilage occurred, the leftover materials remained in production, 40 percent complete on the average.

REQUIRED

1. Prepare (a) a schedule of equivalent production, (b) a unit cost analysis schedule, and (c) a cost summary schedule for January.
2. From the cost summary schedule, prepare the journal entry to transfer costs of completed units for January to Finished Goods Inventory.

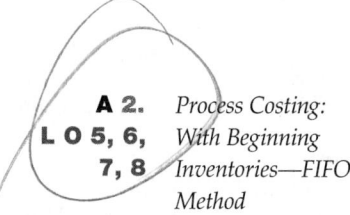

A 2. *Process Costing:*
L O 5, 6, *With Beginning*
7, 8 *Inventories—FIFO Method*

Check Figure: Cost per Equivalent Unit: $2.00

Likert Liquid Extracts Company produces a line of fruit extracts for use in making homemade products such as wines, jams and jellies, pies, and meat sauces. Fruits are introduced into the production process in pounds; the product emerges in quarts (one pound of input equals one quart of output). On June 1, 19x8, 4,250 units were in process. All materials had been added and the units were 70 percent complete as to conversion costs. Materials costs of $4,607 and conversion costs of $3,535 were attached to the units in beginning work in process inventory. During June, 61,300 pounds of fruit were added: apples, 23,500 pounds costing $20,915; grapes, 22,600 pounds costing $28,153; and bananas, 15,200 pounds costing $22,040. Direct labor for the month totaled $19,760, and overhead costs applied were $31,375. On June 30, 19x8, 3,400 units remained in process. All materials had been added, and 50 percent of conversion costs had been incurred.

REQUIRED

1. Using the FIFO costing approach, prepare for June (a) a schedule of equivalent production, (b) a unit cost analysis schedule, and (c) a cost summary schedule.
2. From the cost summary schedule, prepare the journal entry to transfer costs of completed units to the Finished Goods Inventory account.

A 3. *Process Costing:*
L O 5, 6, *One Process/Two*
7, 8 *Time Periods—FIFO Method*

Check Figures: Cost per Equivalent Unit, July: $3.78; Cost per Equivalent Unit, August: $3.74

Palomino Laboratories produces liquid detergents that leave no soap film. All elements are biodegradable. The production process has been automated, so that the product can now be produced in one operation instead of a series of heating, mixing, and cooling operations. All materials are added at the beginning of the process, and conversion costs are incurred uniformly throughout the process. Operating data for July and August 19x7 are as follows:

	July	August
Beginning Work in Process Inventory		
Units (pounds)	2,300	?
Costs: Materials costs	$ 4,699	?
Conversion costs	$ 1,219	?
Production during the period		
Units started (pounds)	31,500	32,800
Current period costs:		
Materials costs	$65,520	$66,912
Conversion costs	$54,213	$54,774
Ending Work in Process Inventory		
Units (pounds)	3,050	3,600

Beginning Work in Process Inventory was 30 percent complete as to conversion costs. The point of completion for ending work in process inventories was July, 60 percent, and August, 50 percent. Assume that the loss from spoilage and evaporation was negligible.

REQUIRED

1. Using the FIFO costing approach, prepare for July (a) a schedule of equivalent production, (b) a unit cost analysis schedule, and (c) a cost summary schedule.
2. From the cost summary schedule, prepare a journal entry to transfer costs of units completed in July to the Finished Goods Inventory account.
3. Repeat parts **1** and **2** for August.

A 4. *Process Costing*
L O 6, 7, *With Beginning*
8, 9 *Inventories/Two Departments—FIFO Method*

Check Figures: 1c. Cost of goods transferred to Conditioning Department: $465,376; 3c. Cost of goods transferred to Canning Department: $725,499

Ray Enterprises produces dozens of products for the housing construction industry. Its most successful product is called Sta-Soft Plaster, a mixture that is used to finish wall surfaces after dry-wall sheets have been positioned. The product's unique quality is that it will not harden until it comes into contact with the dry-wall. Sta-Soft is produced using three processes: blending, conditioning, and canning. All materials are introduced at the beginning of the blending operation, except for the can, which is added in the canning process. Direct labor and factory overhead costs are applied to the products uniformly throughout each process. Production and cost information for September 19x8 follow.

Blending Department: Beginning Work in Process Inventory contained 22,920 pounds of Sta-Soft, 60 percent complete as to conversion costs. Costs of $38,900 were assigned to those units, $28,600 of which was for materials. During September, 242,280 pounds of materials costing $302,850 were put into production. Direct labor for the month was $88,203, and an equal amount of factory overhead costs were charged to Work in Process. Ending Work in Process Inventory contained 32,480 pounds, 50 percent complete as to conversion costs.

Conditioning Department: During September, 232,720 pounds of Sta-Soft were received from the Blending Department. Beginning Work in Process Inventory consisted of 10,500 pounds of Sta-Soft, 40 percent complete, costing $30,250 ($21,000 worth of Sta-Soft was transferred-in costs). Direct labor costs incurred during September totaled $115,625, and factory overhead costs applied were $138,751. Ending Work in Process Inventory contained 8,900 pounds, 70 percent complete as to conversion costs. Assume no measurable loss due to spoilage or waste. (**Hint:** Before completing this problem, refer to the Review Problem in the Chapter Review section in this chapter.)

REQUIRED

1. Using the FIFO costing approach, prepare for the Blending Department for September (a) a schedule of equivalent production, (b) a unit cost analysis schedule, and (c) a cost summary schedule.
2. From the cost summary schedule, prepare the journal entry to transfer costs of completed units for September from the Blending Department to the Conditioning Department.
3. Prepare the same schedules as in **1**, but for the Conditioning Department.
4. Prepare the journal entry to transfer costs of completed units from the Conditioning Department to the Canning Department.

A 5. *Process Costing:*
S O 10 *With Beginning Inventories— Average Costing Method*

Check Figure: 1c. Cost of goods transferred to Finished Goods Inventory: $5,463,040

Many of the products made by Perriet Plastics Company are standard replacement parts for telephones and require long production runs. One of the parts, a wire clip, is produced continuously. During April 19x7, materials for 25,250 units of wire clips were put into production (1 unit contains 500 clips). Total cost of materials used during April was $2,273,000. Direct labor costs totaled $1,135,000, and factory overhead was $2,043,000. The beginning work in process inventory contained 1,600 units, 100 percent complete as to materials costs and 60 percent complete as to conversion costs. Costs attached to the units in beginning inventory totaled $232,515, including $143,500 of materials costs. At month end there were 1,250 units in ending inventory; all materials had been added, and the units were 70 percent complete as to conversion costs.

REQUIRED

1. Assuming an average costing approach and no loss due to spoilage, prepare (a) a schedule of equivalent production, (b) a unit cost analysis schedule, and (c) a cost summary schedule.
2. From the cost summary schedule, prepare the journal entry to transfer costs of units completed in April to the Finished Goods Inventory account.

PROBLEM SET B

B 1. *Process Costing:*
L O 5, 6, *No Beginning*
7, 8 *Inventories*

Check Figure: 1c. Cost of ending work in process inventory: $20,520

The Chang Chewing Gum Company, which produces several flavors of bubble gum, began production of a new kumquat-flavored gum on June 1, 19x9. Two basic materials, gum base and kumquat-flavored sweetener, are blended at the beginning of the process. Direct labor and factory overhead costs are incurred uniformly throughout the blending process. During June, 135,000 kilograms of gum base and 270,000 kilograms of kumquat additive were used at costs of $162,000 and $81,000, respectively. Direct labor charges were $360,310, and factory overhead costs applied during June were $184,010. The ending work in process inventory was 21,600 kilograms. All materials have been added to those units, and 25 percent of the conversion costs have been assigned.

REQUIRED

1. Prepare (a) a schedule of equivalent production, (b) a unit cost analysis schedule, and (c) a cost summary schedule for the Blending Department for June.

2. Using information from the cost summary schedule, prepare the journal entry to transfer costs of completed units for June from the Blending Department to the Forming and Packing Department.

B 2.
L O 5, 6,
7, 8

Process Costing:
With Beginning
Inventories—FIFO
Method

Check Figure: Cost per Equivalent Unit: $.59

Topper Bottling Company manufactures and sells several different kinds of soft drinks. Materials (sugar syrup and artificial flavor) are added at the beginning of production in the Mixing Department. Direct labor and factory overhead costs are applied to products throughout the process. During August 19x7, beginning inventory for the citrus flavor was 2,400 gallons, 80 percent complete. Ending inventory was 3,600 gallons, 50 percent complete. Production data showed 240,000 gallons started during August. A total of 238,800 gallons was completed and transferred to the Bottling Department. Beginning inventory costs were $600 for materials and $676 for conversion costs. Current period costs were $57,600 for materials and $83,538 for conversion costs.

REQUIRED

1. Using the FIFO costing approach, prepare for the Mixing Department for August (a) a schedule of equivalent production, (b) a unit cost analysis schedule, and (c) a cost summary schedule.
2. From the cost summary schedule, prepare the journal entry to transfer the cost of completed units to the Bottling Department.

B 3.
L O 5, 6,
7, 8

Process Costing:
One Process/Two
Time Periods—FIFO
Method

Check Figures: 1b. Cost per Equivalent Unit, April: $1.25; 3b. Cost per Equivalent Unit, May: $1.28

The Flowers Products Company produces organic honey for sale to health food stores and restaurants. The company owns thousands of beehives. No materials other than the honey are used. The production operation is a simple one in which the impure honey is added at the beginning of the process. A series of filterings follows, leading to a pure finished product. Costs of labor and factory overhead are incurred uniformly throughout the filtering process. Production data for April and May 19x8 are shown below:

	April	May
Beginning Work in Process Inventory		
Units (liters)	7,100	?
Costs: Materials costs	$ 2,480	?
Conversion costs	$ 5,110	?
Production during the period		
Units started (liters)	288,000	310,000
Current period costs		
Materials costs	$100,800	$117,800
Conversion costs	$251,550	$277,281
Ending Work in Process Inventory		
Units (liters)	12,400	16,900

April beginning inventory was 80 percent complete as to conversion costs, and ending inventory was 20 percent complete. Ending inventory for May was 30 percent complete as to conversion costs. Assume that there was no loss from spoilage or evaporation.

REQUIRED

1. Using the FIFO approach, prepare for April (a) a schedule of equivalent production, (b) a unit cost analysis schedule, and (c) a cost summary schedule.
2. From the cost summary schedule, prepare the journal entry to transfer costs of units completed in April to the Finished Goods Inventory account.
3. Repeat parts **1** and **2** for May.

B 4.
L O 6, 7,
8, 9

Process Costing:
With Beginning
Inventories/Two
Departments—FIFO
Method

Check Figure: 1c. Cost of goods transferred to Cooking Department: $600,302

Canned fruits and vegetables are the main products made by Bravo Foods, Inc. All basic materials are added at the beginning of the Mixing Department's process. When the ingredients have been mixed, they go to the Cooking Department. There the mixture is heated to 100° Celsius and simmered for twenty minutes. When cooled, the mixture goes to the Canning Department for final processing. Throughout the operations, direct labor and factory overhead costs are incurred uniformly. No materials are added in the Cooking Department stage of production.

Cost data and other information for January 19x7 were as follows:

Production Cost Data	Materials Costs	Conversion Costs
Mixing Department		
Beginning inventory	$ 28,760	$ 5,030
Current period costs	$432,000	$182,608

	Transferred-In Costs	Conversion Costs
Cooking Department		
Beginning inventory	$ 61,380	$ 13,320
Current period costs	?	$671,040

Work in Process Inventories
Beginning inventories

Mixing Department (40% complete)	6,000 liters
Cooking Department (20% complete)	9,000 liters

Ending inventories

Mixing Department (60% complete)	8,000 liters
Cooking Department (70% complete)	10,000 liters

Unit Production Data	Mixing Department	Cooking Department
Units started during January	90,000 liters	88,000 liters
Units transferred out during January	88,000 liters	87,000 liters

Assume that no spoilage or evaporation loss took place during January. (**Hint:** Before completing this problem, refer to the Review Problem in the Chapter Review section in this chapter.)

1. Using the FIFO costing approach, prepare for the Mixing Department for January (a) a schedule of equivalent production, (b) a unit cost analysis schedule, and (c) a cost summary schedule.
2. Using information from the cost summary schedule, prepare the journal entry to transfer costs of completed units for January from the Mixing Department to the Cooking Department.
3. Prepare the same schedules as in **1,** this time for the Cooking Department.
4. Prepare the journal entry to transfer costs of completed units from the Cooking Department to the Canning Department.

B 5.
S O 10

Process Costing: With Beginning Inventories— Average Costing Method

Check Figure: 1c. Cost of goods transferred to Finished Goods Inventory: $552,720

Energy Food Products, Inc. makes high-vitamin, calorie-packed wafers used by professional sports teams to supply quick energy to players. The thin white wafers are produced in a continuous product flow. The company, which uses a process cost system based on the average costing approach, recently purchased several automated machines so that the wafers can be produced in a single department. Materials are all added at the beginning of the process. The costs for the machine operators' labor and production-related overhead are incurred uniformly throughout the process.

In February 19x8, a total of 231,200 liters of materials was put into production at a cost of $294,780. Two liters of materials were used to produce one unit of output (one unit = 144 wafers). Labor costs for February were $60,530. Factory overhead was $181,590. Beginning Work in Process Inventory on February 1 was 14,000 units, 100 percent complete as to materials and 20 percent complete as to conversion costs. The total cost of those units was $55,000, with $48,660 assigned to the cost of materials. The ending Work in Process Inventory of 12,000 units was fully complete as to materials, but only 30 percent complete as to conversion costs.

1. Assuming an average costing approach and no loss due to spoilage, prepare (a) a schedule of equivalent production, (b) a unit cost analysis schedule, and (c) a cost summary schedule.
2. From the cost summary schedule you prepared in **1** above, prepare the journal entry to transfer costs of completed units in February to the Finished Goods Inventory account.

MANAGERIAL REPORTING AND ANALYSIS CASES

Interpreting Management Reports

MRA 1. *Analysis of Product*
L O 6 *Cost*

Check Figure: 2. Cost per Equivalent
Unit: $49.221

Troy Tire Corporation makes several lines of automobile and truck tires. The company operates in a competitive marketplace, so it relies heavily on cost data from its FIFO process cost system. It uses that information to set prices for its most competitive tires. The company's Blue Radial line has lost some of its market share during each of the past four years. Management believes price breaks allowed by the three competitors are the major reason for the decline in sales.

The company controller, Karen Jones, has been asked to review the product costing information that supports price decisions on the Blue Radial line. In preparing her report, she collected the following data related to 19x7, the last full year of operations.

		Units	Dollars
Equivalent units:	Materials costs	84,200	
	Conversion costs	82,800	
Manufacturing costs:	Materials		$1,978,700
	Direct Labor		800,400
	Factory overhead applied		1,600,800
Unit cost data:	Materials costs		23.50
	Conversion costs		29.00
Work in Process Inventory:	Beginning (70% complete)	4,200	
	Ending (30% complete)	3,800	

Units started and completed during 19x7 totaled 80,400. The costs attached to the beginning Work in Process Inventory account were materials costs of $123,660 and conversion costs of $57,010. Jones found that little spoilage had occurred. The proper cost allowance for spoilage was included in the predetermined overhead rate of $2.00 per direct labor dollar. The review of direct labor cost revealed, however, that $90,500 was charged twice to the production account, the second time in error. This resulted in too much labor and applied overhead costs being charged to the above accounts.

So far in 19x8, the Blue Radial has been selling for $92 per tire. This price was based on the 19x7 unit data plus a 75 percent markup to cover operating costs and profit. During 19x8, the three competitors' prices for comparable tires have been about $87 per tire. In the company's process cost system, all materials are added at the beginning of the process, and conversion costs are incurred uniformly throughout.

REQUIRED

1. Explain how the cost-charging error is affecting the company.
2. Prepare a revised unit cost analysis schedule for 19x7.
3. What should have been the minimum selling price per tire in 19x8?
4. Suggest ways of preventing such errors in the future.

Formulating Management Reports

MRA 2. *Using the Process*
L O 9 *Cost System*

No check figure

You are the production manager for **Great Plains Corp.**, a manufacturer of four cereal products. The company's leading product in the market is Smackaroos, a sugar-coated puffed rice cereal. Yesterday, Jana Springer, the controller, reported that the production cost for each box of Smackaroos has increased approximately 22 percent in the last four months. Since the company is unable to increase the selling price for a box of Smackaroos, the increased production costs will reduce profits significantly.

Today you received a memo from John Williams, the company president, asking you to review your production process to identify inefficiencies or waste that can be eliminated. Once you have completed your analysis, you are to write a memo presenting your findings and suggesting ways to reduce or eliminate the problems. The president will use your information during a meeting with the top management team in ten days.

You are aware of previous problems in the Baking Department and the Packaging Department. Upon your request, Jana has provided you with schedules of equivalent production, unit cost analysis schedules, and cost summary schedules for the two departments. She has also given you the following detailed summary of the cost per equivalent unit for a box of cereal.

	April	May	June	July
Baking Department				
Direct materials	$1.25	$1.26	$1.24	$1.25
Direct labor	.50	.61	.85	.90
Factory overhead	.25	.31	.34	.40
Department totals	$2.00	$2.18	$2.43	$2.55
Packaging Department				
Direct materials	$ .35	$ .34	$ .33	$ .33
Direct labor	.05	.05	.04	.06
Factory overhead	.10	.16	.15	.12
Department totals	$ .50	$ .55	$ .52	$ .51
Total cost per equivalent unit	$2.50	$2.73	$2.95	$3.06

REQUIRED

1. In preparation for writing your memo, answer the following questions.
   a. For whom are you preparing the memo? Does this affect the length of the memo? Explain.
   b. Why are you preparing the memo?
   c. What actions should you take to gather information for the memo? What information is needed? Is the information provided by Jana sufficient for analysis and reporting?
   d. When is the memo due? What can be done to provide accurate and timely information?
2. Based on your analysis of the information provided by Jana, where is the major problem in the production process?
3. Prepare an outline of the sections you would want in your memo.

International Company

MRA 3.
L O 1, 2

Design of a Product Costing System

No check figure

The **El-Dahshan Corporation**'s copper mines hold 63 percent of the 23.2 million tons of copper in Saudi Arabia. The owners of the mining operation are willing to invest millions of dollars in the latest pyrometallurgical copper extraction processes. The production managers are currently examining both batch and continuous methods of the new copper extraction process. The method they choose will replace the hydrometallurgical process now in use.

What impact will the method selected by the production managers have on the design of the product costing system? What impact would changing from hydrometallurgical to pyrometallurgical processing have on the design of the product costing system, if both processes use continuous methods of extraction?

CHAPTER 19 — *Cost-Volume-Profit Analysis and Responsibility Accounting*

LEARNING OBJECTIVES

1. Define the concept of cost behavior and explain how managers make use of this concept.
2. Identify specific types of variable and fixed cost behavior, and compute the changes in variable and fixed costs caused by changes in operating activity.
3. Define *semivariable cost* and *mixed cost,* and separate their variable and fixed cost components.
4. Analyze cost behavior patterns in a service business.
5. Illustrate how changes in cost, volume, or price affect the profit formula.
6. Compute a breakeven point in units of output and in sales dollars, and prepare a breakeven graph.
7. Define *contribution margin* and use the concept to determine a company's breakeven point.
8. Apply contribution margin analysis to estimated levels of future sales and compute projected profit.
9. Define *responsibility accounting* and identify the elements of a responsibility accounting system.
10. Identify the cost and revenue classifications controllable by a particular manager.

DECISION POINT

Carey Construction Company[1]

Carey Construction Company is a medium-sized construction firm located in Lexington, Kentucky. The company specializes in road-building and paving projects and uses a variety of heavy construction equipment. The costs of all the equipment are considered fixed because the equipment can be used over a long period of time and on many different projects. The costs of the equipment are assigned to projects based on the extent of its usage and the duration (in weeks or months) of the project.

But equipment does not last forever. Fixed-cost equipment deteriorates, and some pieces become outdated by new, more productive models. Management must decide when to replace equipment as well as when to purchase additional heavy equipment so that the business can expand. What factors should management consider when it makes these decisions? Does the relationship of fixed costs to the company's volume and profit play a role in the decision process?

Carey Construction tracks the performance of each piece of equipment. Data are recorded about (1) productive run time (time the equipment is in use on the job), (2) travel time (time in transit from one construction site to another), (3) downtime (time in repair), and (4) idle time (time not in use). A computer program analyzes equipment usage to see whether the expected productivity of each piece is being maintained. If not, replacement is considered.

When making plans to expand, Carey Construction Company's management must first estimate the projected size and types of contracts (volume of business), the costs involved, and the projected profit. With those projections in mind, management can decide how much new equipment it needs to meet the company's goals. ⋮⋮⋮⋮⋮

1. C. Douglas Poe, Gadis J. Dillion, and Kenneth Day, "Replacing Fixed Costs in the Construction Industry," *Management Accounting*, Institute of Management Accountants, August 1988, pp. 39–43.

COST BEHAVIOR PATTERNS

Before analyzing past performance, estimating a future cost, or preparing a budget, a manager must understand how costs behave. Cost behavior is the way costs respond to changes in volume or activity. Some costs vary with volume or operating activity; others remain fixed as volume changes. Between these two extremes are costs that exhibit characteristics of both.

Managers use information about cost behavior in almost every decision they make. Before introducing a new product, managers project its anticipated costs. Cost behavior underlies this estimating process. Before changing an existing product or service, managers perform a cost analysis based on estimates and cost behavior patterns. And before buying an existing business, managers estimate both revenue and cost results. Whenever managers are asked to make a decision, they must always deal with cost ramifications, and they must understand and anticipate cost behavior patterns if they are to decide correctly.

In our discussion, we focus on cost behavior as it relates to production. But some costs are not measured according to production volume. Sales commissions, for example, depend on the number of units sold or total sales revenue, not production measures. Another important point to be made is that costs behave in much the same way in service businesses as they do in manufacturing enterprises. We look specifically at the costs of service businesses later in the chapter.

THE BEHAVIOR OF VARIABLE COSTS

OBJECTIVE

2 *Identify specific types of variable and fixed cost behavior, and compute the changes in variable and fixed costs caused by changes in operating activity*

Total costs that change in direct proportion to changes in productive output (or any other measure of volume) are called variable costs. To explore an example of how variable costs work, consider an auto maker. Each new car has four tires, and each tire costs $48. The total cost of tires, then, is $192 for one car, $384 for two, $576 for three, $768 for four, $960 for five, $1,920 for ten, and $19,200 for one hundred. In the production of automobiles, the total cost of tires is a variable cost. On a per unit basis, however, a variable cost remains constant. In this case, the cost of tires per automobile is $192 ($48 × 4) whether one car or one hundred cars are produced. True, the cost of tires varies depending on the number purchased, and purchases discounts are available for purchases of large quantities. But once the purchase has been made, the cost per tire is established.

Table 1 lists other examples of variable costs. A manufacturing company's variable costs include direct materials costs, hourly direct labor costs, hourly indirect labor costs, operating supplies, and small tools costs. Among the variable costs a bank incurs are the leasing expense for computer equipment (based on usage), the hourly wages of computer operators, and the costs of operating supplies and data storage disks. A department store incurs such variable costs as the cost of merchandise, sales commissions, and the hourly wages of shelf stockers. All of these costs—whether incurred by a manufacturer, a service business, or a merchandiser—are variable based on either productive output or total sales.

Operating Capacity Because variable costs increase or decrease in direct proportion to volume or output, it is important to know a company's operating capacity. Operating capacity is the upper limit of a company's productive output capability, given its existing resources. It describes just what a com-

Table 1. Examples of Variable, Fixed, and Semivariable Costs

Costs	Manufacturing Company	Service Company— Bank	Merchandising Company— Department Store
Variable	Direct materials Direct labor (hourly) Indirect labor (hourly) Operating supplies Small tools cost	Computer equipment leasing (based on usage) Computer operators (hourly) Operating supplies Data storage disks	Cost of merchandise Sales commissions Shelf stockers (hourly)

Fixed	Depreciation, machinery and building
	Insurance premiums
	Labor (salaried)
	Supervisory salaries
	Property taxes
		Depreciation, furniture and fixtures
		Insurance premiums
		Salaries:
		  Programmers
		  Systems designers
		  Bank administrators
		Rent, buildings
			Depreciation, building
			Insurance premiums
			Buyers (salaried)
			Supervisory salaries
			Property taxes (on equipment and building)

Semivariable	Electrical power Telephone Heat	Electrical power Telephone Heat	Electrical power Telephone Heat

pany can accomplish in a given time period. Operating capacity, or volume, can be expressed in several ways, including total labor hours, total machine hours, and total units of output. Any increase in volume or activity over operating capacity requires additional expenditures for building, machinery, personnel, and operations. In our discussion of cost behavior patterns, we assume that operating capacity is constant and that all activity occurs within the limits of current operating capacity. Cost behavior patterns can change when additional operating capacity is added.

There are three common measures, or types, of operating capacity: theoretical, or ideal, capacity; practical capacity; and normal capacity. Theoretical (ideal) capacity is the maximum productive output for a given period, assuming all machinery and equipment are operating at optimum speed, without interruption. Theoretical (ideal) capacity is useful in estimating maximum production levels, but a company never operates at ideal capacity. In fact, the concept had little relationship to actual operations until the advent of the just-in-time operating environment. The concept that drives the just-in-time environment is the continuous improvement of operations, with the long-term goal of approaching ideal capacity.

Practical capacity is theoretical capacity reduced by normal and expected work stoppages. Production is interrupted by machine breakdowns and downtime for retooling, repairs and maintenance, and employees' work breaks. Such normal interruptions and the resulting reductions in output are considered when measuring practical capacity.

Most companies do not operate at either ideal or practical capacity. Both measures include excess capacity, extra machinery and equipment kept on standby. This extra equipment is used when regular equipment is being repaired. Also, during a slow season, a company may use only part of its equipment, or it may work just one or two shifts instead of around the clock.

Because it is necessary to consider so many different circumstances, managers often use a measure called normal capacity, rather than practical capacity, when planning operations. Normal capacity is the average annual level of operating capacity needed to meet expected sales demand. The sales demand figure is adjusted for seasonal changes and business and economic cycles. Therefore, normal capacity is a realistic measure of what a company is likely to produce, not what it can produce.

Each variable cost should be related to an appropriate measure of capacity, but, in many cases, more than one measure of capacity applies. Operating costs can be related to machine hours used or total units produced. Sales commissions, on the other hand, usually vary in direct proportion to total sales dollars.

There are two reasons for carefully selecting the basis for measuring the activity of variable costs. First, an appropriate activity base simplifies cost planning and control. Second, the management accountant must combine (aggregate) many variable costs with the same activity base so that the costs can be analyzed in a reasonable way. Such aggregation also provides information that allows management to predict future costs.

The general guide for selecting an activity base is to relate costs to their most logical or causal factor. For example, machinery setup costs should be considered variable in relation to the number of setup operations needed for a particular job or function. This approach allows machinery setup costs to be budgeted and controlled more effectively.

Linear Relationships and the Relevant Range   The traditional definition of a variable cost assumes that there is a linear relationship between cost and volume, that costs go up or down as volume increases or decreases. You saw that relationship in our tire example earlier. Figure 1 shows another linear relationship. Here, each unit of output requires $2.50 of labor cost. Total labor costs grow in direct proportion to the increase in units of output: For two units, total labor costs are $5.00; for six units, the company incurs $15.00 in labor costs.

Figure 1. A Common Variable-Cost Behavior Pattern: A Linear Relationship

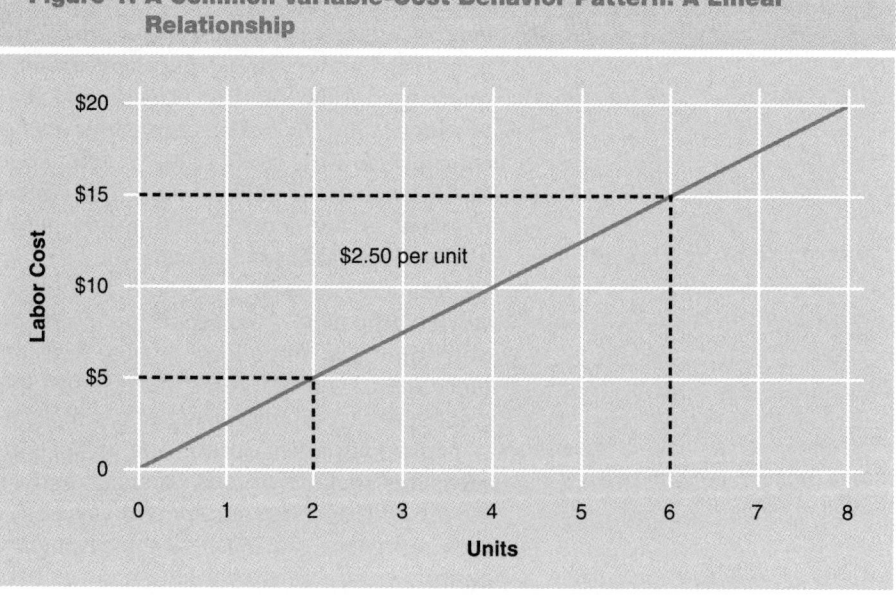

Figure 2. Other Variable-Cost Behavior Patterns: Nonlinear Relationships

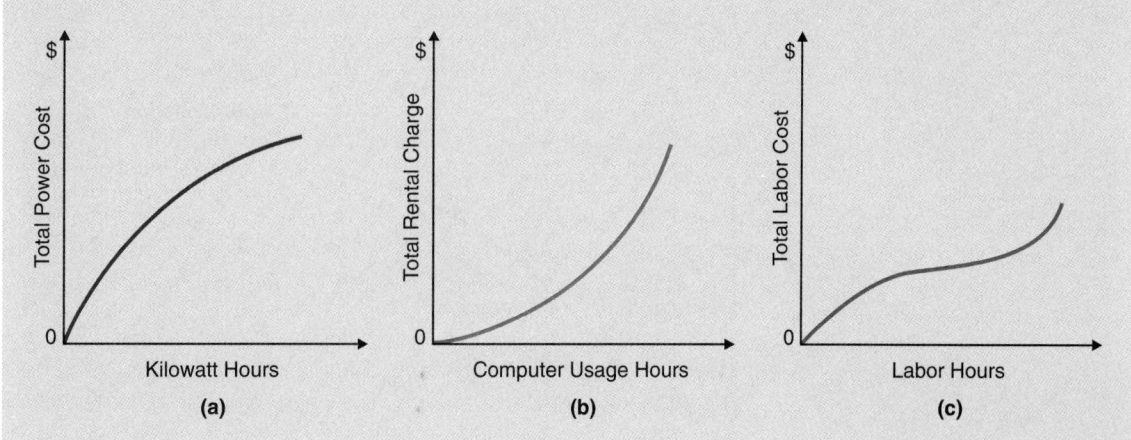

Many costs, however, vary with operating activity in a nonlinear fashion. In Figure 2, part (a) shows the behavior of power costs as usage increases and the unit cost of power consumption falls. Part (b) shows the behavior of rental costs when each additional hour of computer usage costs more than the previous hour. And part (c) shows how labor costs vary as efficiency increases and decreases. These three nonlinear cost patterns are variable in nature, but they differ from the straight-line variable-cost pattern shown in Figure 1.

Variable costs with linear relationships to a volume measure are easy to analyze and project for cost planning and control. Nonlinear variable costs are not easy to use. But all costs must be included in an analysis if the results are to be useful to management. To simplify cost analysis procedures and make variable costs easier to use, accountants have developed a method of converting nonlinear variable costs into linear variable costs. This method is called *linear approximation* and relies upon the concept of relevant range. Relevant range is the span of activity in which a company expects to operate. Within that range, many nonlinear costs can be estimated using the straight-line linear approximation approach illustrated in Figure 3. Those estimated costs can then be treated as part of the other variable costs.

A linear approximation of a nonlinear variable cost is not a precise measure, but it allows the inclusion of nonlinear variable costs in cost behavior analysis, and the loss of accuracy is usually not significant. The goal is to help management estimate costs and prepare budgets, and linear approximation helps accomplish that goal.

THE BEHAVIOR OF FIXED COSTS

Fixed costs behave much differently from variable costs. Fixed costs remain constant within a relevant range of volume or activity. Remember that a relevant range of activity is the range in which actual operations are likely to occur.

Look back at Table 1 for examples of fixed costs. The manufacturing company, the bank, and the department store all incur depreciation costs and fixed annual insurance premiums. In addition, all salaried personnel have fixed earnings for a particular period. The manufacturing company and the department store own their buildings and must pay annual property taxes.

Figure 3. The Relevant Range and Linear Approximation

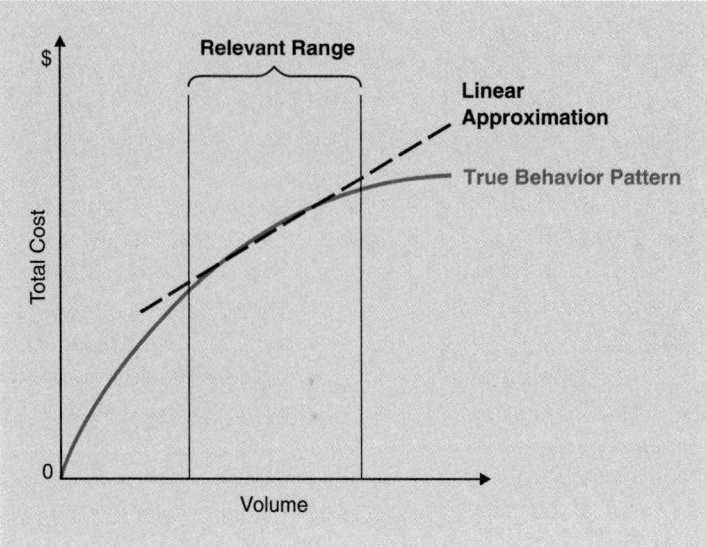

The bank, on the other hand, pays an annual fixed rental charge for the use of its building.

As the examples in Table 1 suggest, reference to a particular time period is essential to the concept of fixed costs because, according to economic theory, all costs tend to be variable in the long run. Altering plant capacity, machinery, labor requirements, and other production factors causes fixed costs to increase or decrease. Thus, a cost is fixed only within a limited time period. For planning purposes, management usually considers an annual time period: Fixed costs are expected to be constant within this period.

Of course, fixed costs change when activity exceeds the relevant range. For example, assume that a local manufacturing company needs one supervisor for an eight-hour work shift. Production can range from zero to 500,000 units per month per shift; the relevant range, then, is from zero to 500,000 units. The supervisor's salary is $4,000 per month. The cost behavior analysis is as follows:

Units of Output per Month	Total Supervisory Salaries per Month
0–500,000	$4,000
Over 500,000	$8,000

If a maximum of 500,000 units can be produced per month per shift, any output above 500,000 units calls for another work shift and another supervisor. Like all fixed costs, this fixed cost remains constant in total within the new relevant range.

What about unit costs? Remember that the fixed costs per unit change as volume increases or decreases. *Unit fixed costs vary inversely with activity or volume.* On a per unit basis, fixed costs go down as volume goes up. That pattern holds true as long as the firm is operating within the relevant range of activity. Look at how supervisory costs per unit fall as the volume of activity increases in the relevant range.

Volume of Activity	Cost per Unit
100,000 units	$4,000 ÷ 100,000 = $.0400
200,000 units	$4,000 ÷ 200,000 = $.0200
300,000 units	$4,000 ÷ 300,000 = $.0133
400,000 units	$4,000 ÷ 400,000 = $.0100
500,000 units	$4,000 ÷ 500,000 = $.0080
600,000 units	**$8,000 ÷ 600,000 = $.0133**

The per unit cost increases at the 600,000-unit level because that activity level is above the relevant range, which means another shift must be added and another supervisor must be hired.

Figure 4 shows this behavior pattern. The fixed supervisory costs for the first 500,000 units of production are $4,000. Those costs hold steady at $4,000 for any level of output within the relevant range. But if output goes above 500,000 units, another supervisor must be hired, pushing fixed supervisory costs to $8,000.

OBJECTIVE

3 *Define* semivari-able cost *and* mixed cost, *and sepa-rate their variable and fixed cost components*

SEMIVARIABLE AND MIXED COSTS

Some costs cannot be classified as either variable or fixed. A **semivariable cost** has both variable and fixed cost components. Part of the cost changes with volume or usage, and part of the cost is fixed over the period. Telephone cost is an example. Monthly telephone cost is made up of charges for long-distance calls, and a service charge plus charges for extra telephones. The

Figure 4. A Common Fixed-Cost Behavior Pattern

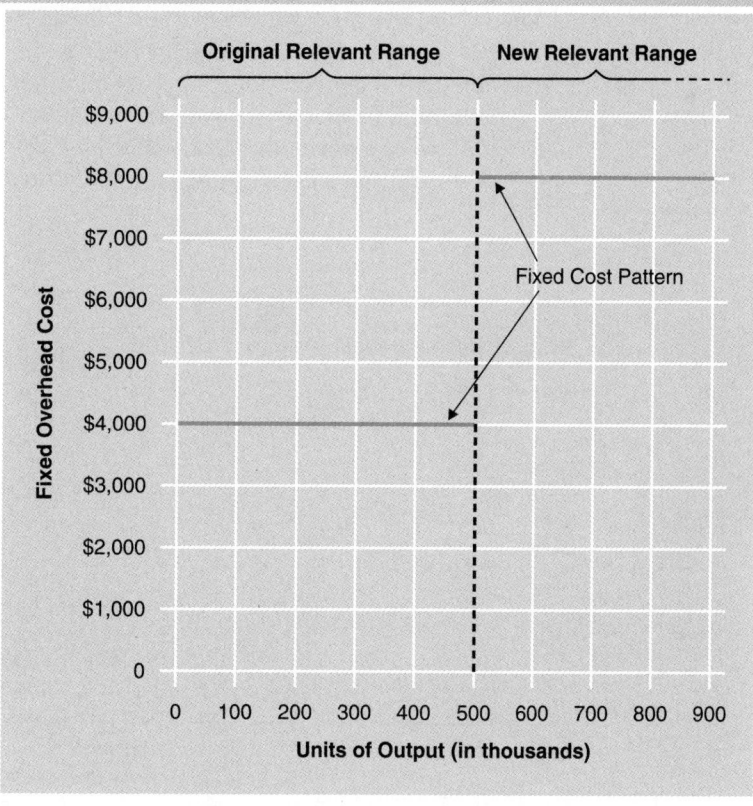

long-distance charges are variable because they depend on the amount of use; the service charge and the cost of the additional telephones are fixed costs.

Mixed costs are also made up of variable and fixed costs. Mixed costs result when both variable and fixed costs are charged to the same general ledger account. The Repairs and Maintenance account is a good example of an account that holds mixed costs. Labor charges to this account can vary in proportion to the amount of repairs done. However, only one repair and maintenance worker may be employed on a full-time basis (a fixed cost if he or she is salaried), with extra help hired only when needed (a variable cost). Depreciation costs for machinery used in repair and maintenance are also fixed costs, but costs of repair supplies depend on use.

Examples of Semivariable Costs   Many costs demonstrate both variable and fixed behavior characteristics. Utilities costs often fall in this category. Like telephone costs, electricity and gas heat costs normally consist of a fixed base amount and additional charges based on usage. Figure 5 shows just three of the many types of semivariable-cost behavior patterns. Part (a) depicts the total telephone cost for a factory. The monthly bill begins with a fixed charge for the service and increases as long-distance calls are made. Part (b) shows a special rent-labor incentive agreement found in contracts with municipalities. Factory rent has a fixed basis for the year, but as labor hours are paid, it is reduced to a minimum annual guaranteed rental charge. Part (c) also depicts a special contractual arrangement: The cost of annual equipment maintenance by an outside company is variable per maintenance hour worked, up to a maximum per period. After the maximum is reached, additional maintenance is done at no cost.

The High-Low Method of Separating Costs   For cost planning and control, semivariable and mixed costs must be divided into their respective variable and fixed components. This allows them to be grouped with other variable and fixed costs for analysis. When there is doubt about the behavior pattern of a particular cost, especially a semivariable cost, it helps to plot past costs and related measures of volume in a scatter diagram. A scatter diagram

Figure 5. Semivariable-Cost Behavior Patterns

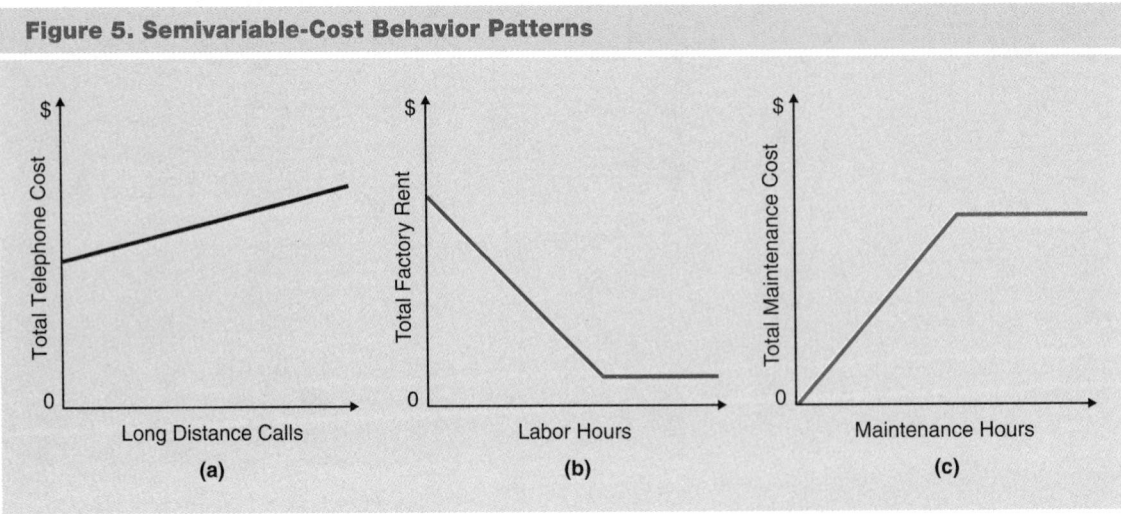

is a chart of plotted points that helps determine if a linear relationship exists between a cost item and its related activity measure. It is a form of linear approximation. If the diagram suggests that a linear relationship exists, a cost line can be imposed on the data by either visual means or statistical analysis.

For example, last year, the Evelio Corporation's Winter Park Division incurred the following machine hours and electricity costs.

Month	Machine Hours	Electricity Costs
January	6,250	$ 24,000
February	6,300	24,200
March	6,350	24,350
April	6,400	24,600
May	6,300	24,400
June	6,200	24,300
July	6,100	23,900
August	6,050	23,600
September	6,150	23,950
October	6,250	24,100
November	6,350	24,400
December	6,450	24,700
Totals	75,150	$290,500

Figure 6 shows a scatter diagram of these data. The diagram suggests that there is a linear relationship between machine hours and the cost of electricity. To determine the variable and fixed components of this cost, we apply the high-low method, a common, simple approach to separating variable and fixed costs. This method identifies a linear relationship between activity level and cost by analyzing the highest and lowest volumes in a period and their related costs. The change in cost between the two sets of data is divided by the change in volume to find the variable cost component of the semivariable or mixed cost. This amount, in turn, is used to compute the fixed costs at each level of activity.

We begin by determining the periods of high and low activity within the accounting period. In our example, the Winter Park Division experienced high machine-hour activity in December and low machine-hour activity in August. Now, we want to find the difference between the high and low amounts for both machine hours and the related electricity costs.

Volume	Month	Activity Level	Cost
High	December	6,450 machine hours	$24,700
Low	August	6,050 machine hours	23,600
Difference		400 machine hours	$ 1,100

To determine the variable cost per machine hour, we divide the cost difference by the machine-hour difference.

$$\text{Variable cost per machine hour} = \$1,100 \div 400 \text{ machine hours}$$
$$= \$2.75 \text{ per machine hour}$$

Then we compute the fixed cost for a month (remember that fixed costs stay the same each month) by multiplying the machine hours times the variable rate and subtracting the amount from the total cost.

$$\text{Fixed cost for December} = \$24,700 - (6,450 \times \$2.75) = \$6,962.50$$
$$\text{Fixed cost for August} = \$23,600 - (6,050 \times \$2.75) = \$6,962.50$$

Figure 6. Scatter Diagram of Machine Hours and Electricity Costs

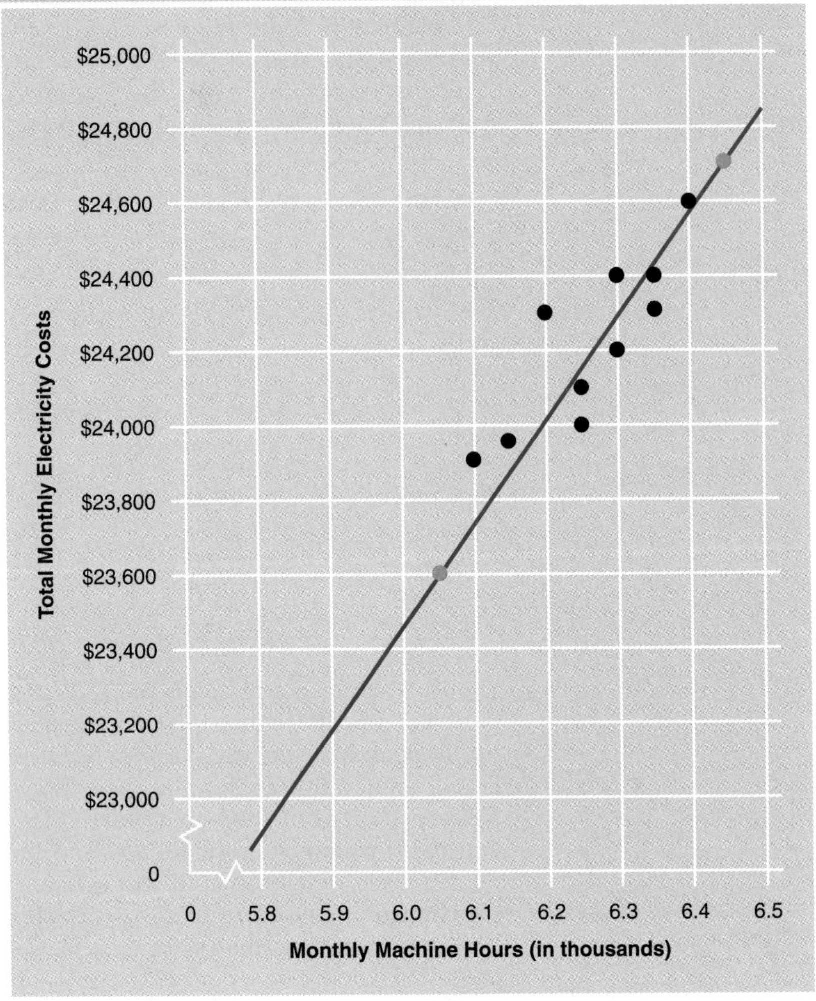

Here's the breakdown of total costs for the year.

Variable costs (75,150 × $2.75)	$206,662.50
Fixed costs [$290,500 − (75,150 × $2.75)]	83,837.50
	$290,500.00

And this is the linear relationship of the data for the Winter Park Division.

Total cost per month = $6,962.50 + $2.75 per machine hour

SPECIAL NOTE

Cost behavior depends on whether the focus is on total costs or cost per unit. Variable costs vary in total: They increase in direct proportion to increases in volume or activity. But variable costs per unit remain constant as long as there are no changes in the price of materials and services consumed. Fixed costs, in contrast, react just the opposite. Total fixed costs remain constant as volume increases. But on a per unit basis, fixed costs decrease as volume increases. Because total fixed costs are constant, the more units produced, the lower the fixed cost per unit.

Consider the business of producing women's jeans. Let's say the material in the jeans costs $2 per pair. This is a constant per pair amount, but the more jeans you manufacture, the higher the total *variable* costs. That is, the total variable cost of materials for five pairs of jeans is $10; for ten pairs of jeans, it's $20. Now, think about the sewing machines used to sew the jeans together. The depreciation on those machines is a *fixed* cost. Let's say that total depreciation is $400 a month. The firm records $400 whether it manufactures one hundred pairs of jeans or one thousand. But at one hundred pairs of jeans, the fixed cost per pair is $4; at one thousand pairs, the fixed cost per pair drops to $.40.

These principles underlie the concepts of variable and fixed costs. It is important that you understand this pattern of cost behavior. *Variable costs vary in total as volume or activity changes but are constant per unit; fixed costs are fixed in total but vary per unit as volume changes.*

COST BEHAVIOR IN A SERVICE BUSINESS

OBJECTIVE

4 *Analyze cost behavior patterns in a service business*

The need to account for and control costs is fundamental to all business organizations: manufacturers, merchandisers, and service providers. But there is an important difference between the service company and the other organizations: In a service business, no physical product is produced, assembled, stored, or valued. Services are rendered; they cannot be accumulated or held in inventory. Examples include processing loans, representing people in courts of law, selling insurance policies, and computing people's income taxes.

The difference affects cost behavior patterns in only two areas. A service business has no materials or merchandise costs. In computing the unit cost of a service, the primary cost component is the professional labor involved. It is this direct labor cost that must be traced to the service rendered. Like other businesses, service providers also incur overhead costs. Service overhead costs are a varied collection of costs (excluding direct labor costs) incurred specifically to develop and provide services. Some service overhead costs vary with the number of services performed, and some are fixed in nature. Along with professional labor costs, service overhead costs are used to compute the cost per service rendered.

Assume that the manager of the Appraisal Department of Valencia Mortgage Company wants to assess the current fee the company is charging for a typical home appraisal in connection with each mortgage loan application. The company has been charging $400 for this service. To evaluate the adequacy of the fee, we compute the total cost of appraising a home, including a breakdown of the variable and fixed costs incurred. The following information has been collected for the past six-month period.

Direct professional labor: $160 per appraisal

Monthly service overhead: January, $20,305; February, $20,018; March, $20,346; April, $20,182; May, $20,100; and June, $20,223

Actual number of home appraisals: January, 105; February, 98; March, 106; April, 102; May, 100; and June, 103

County survey map fee: $99 per appraisal

Estimated average home appraisals per month next year: 100

With this information, we can compute the cost of appraising a single home. The first step is to determine the variable and fixed cost components of the Service Overhead account using the high-low method.

Volume	Month	Number of Appraisals	Cost
High	March	106	$20,346
Low	February	98	20,018
Difference		8	$ 328

Next, we determine the variable overhead costs per appraisal and the fixed overhead costs per month.

Variable overhead costs per appraisal = $328 ÷ 8 = $41 per appraisal

Fixed overhead costs for March = $20,346 − (106 appraisals × $41) = $16,000

Fixed overhead costs for February = $20,018 − (98 appraisals × $41) = $16,000

Now we can compute the cost per appraisal:

Variable costs per appraisal	
Direct professional labor	$160
County survey map fee	99
Variable service overhead	41
Fixed costs per appraisal:	
Monthly fixed service overhead ($16,000 ÷ 100 appraisals)	160
Estimated total cost per appraisal	$460

Based on this information, the manager found that the present fee does not cover the actual costs of a typical home appraisal. To cover costs and allow for some profit, the fee should be raised to around $525.

COST-VOLUME-PROFIT ANALYSIS

OBJECTIVE

5 *Illustrate how changes in cost, volume, or price affect the profit formula*

Suppose Ford Motor Company wants to plan operations for the upcoming model year. How do managers know the correct amounts of materials and parts to purchase? Will additional workers need to be hired? Will there be enough space on existing assembly lines or must new facilities be constructed? What should the cars sell for to meet the company's target profit for the year? These questions cannot be answered until an estimate of the anticipated volume for the year is made. Once a target volume has been developed, the costs of production for the period and product pricing can be computed using cost-volume-profit analysis.

Cost-volume-profit (C-V-P) analysis is an analysis of the cost behavior patterns that underlie the relationships between cost, volume of output, and profit. C-V-P analysis is a tool for both planning and control. The process involves a number of techniques and problem-solving procedures based on understanding a company's cost behavior patterns. The techniques express relationships between revenue, sales mix, cost, volume, and profits, and include breakeven analysis and profit planning. These relationships provide a general model of financial activity that management can use for short-range planning, evaluating performance, and analyzing alternatives.

How does C-V-P analysis in Japan, Germany, Great Britain, or Canada differ from the same analysis in the United States? The only difference is in the measures used. The procedures and formulas remain the same. Instead of expressing volume in pounds or gallons, these countries use metric measures such as grams and liters. Whereas our cost and profit amounts are expressed in dollars, Japan's amounts would be in yen, Germany's in German marks, Great Britain's in British pounds, and Canada's in Canadian dollars. Most management accounting procedures and analyses are appropriate for use by companies in any free economy. All that changes are the units of measurement. ═══

BASIC C-V-P ANALYSIS

Cost-volume-profit relationships can be expressed through the use of graphs or formulas. Suppose that a company sells its product for $20, that total annual fixed costs for production and distribution are expected to be $96,000, and that variable costs for manufacturing and selling are $8 per unit.

Figure 7 shows the basic C-V-P relationships for this company. Total revenues and total costs are plotted by locating two points for each element and drawing a straight line through the two points. The total revenue line begins at zero dollars (no sales) and extends through $200,000 at sales of 10,000 units ($20 × 10,000 units). The total cost line begins at zero units and $96,000, the fixed costs that would be incurred if no units are sold. At the 6,000-unit mark, $144,000 of costs would be incurred ($96,000 of fixed costs plus 6,000 × $8, or $48,000 of variable costs). The point at which the two lines intersect, where total revenues equal total costs, is called the *breakeven point*. We discuss the breakeven point later in this chapter.

(The 10,000 units used to help plot the total revenue line and the 6,000 units used in identifying the total cost line in Figure 7 are arbitrary expressions of volume. Any number of units could have been used.)

HOW MANAGERS USE C-V-P ANALYSIS

The graph in Figure 7 is a basic C-V-P model. It shows revenues, costs, volume, and profit or loss. The model is based on a set of fixed relationships. If unit prices, costs, operating efficiency, or other operating circumstances change, the model must be revised to fit the new C-V-P relationships. Similar analyses can be applied to multiproduct divisions or companies as long as a given mix of products is assumed.

The C-V-P model is useful because it gives a general overview of a company's financial operations. For planning, managers can use C-V-P analysis to calculate profit when sales volume is known. Or, through C-V-P analysis,

Figure 7. Cost-Volume-Profit Relationships

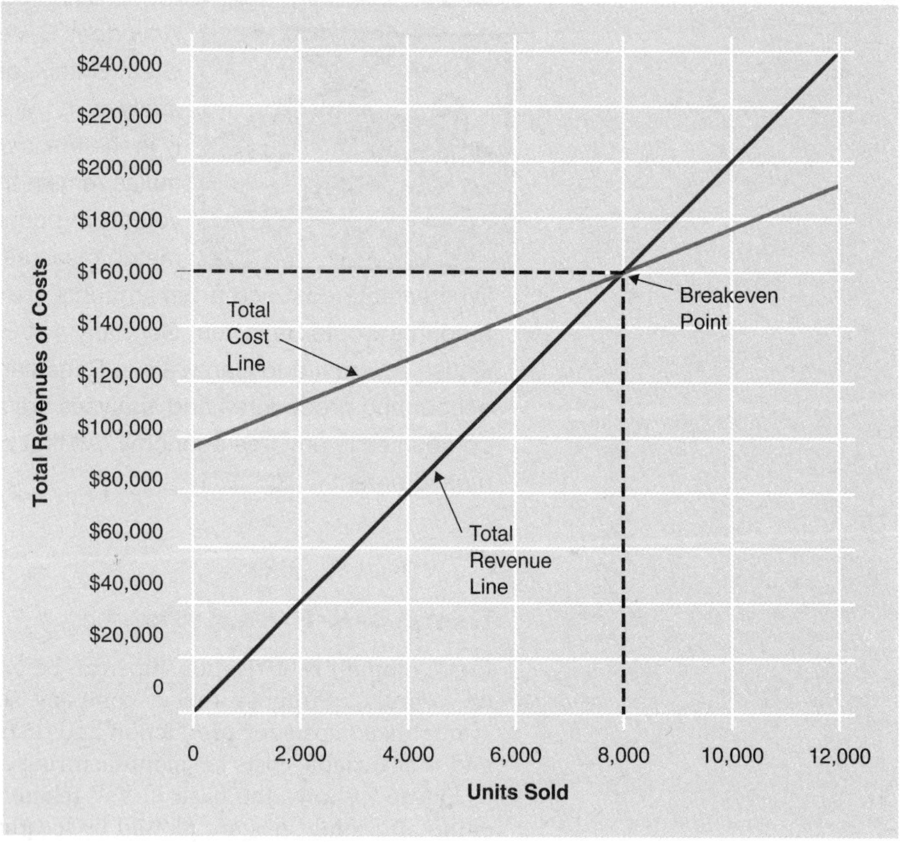

management can decide the level of sales needed to reach a target profit. C-V-P analysis is also used extensively in budgeting.

The C-V-P relationship is expressed in a simple profit planning equation.

$$\text{Sales revenue} = \text{variable costs} + \text{fixed costs} + \text{profit}$$

Or,

$$S = VC + FC + P$$

Cost-volume-profit analysis is a way of measuring how well the departments in a company are doing. At the end of a period, sales volume and related actual costs are analyzed to find actual profit. A department's performance is measured by comparing actual costs with expected costs, costs that have been computed by applying C-V-P analysis to actual sales volume. The result is a performance report on which management can base the control of operations.

Basic C-V-P analysis can also be applied to measure the effects of alternative choices: changes in variable and fixed costs, expansion or contraction of sales volume, increases or decreases in selling prices, or other changes in operating methods or policies. Cost-volume-profit analysis is useful for problems of product pricing, sales mix analysis (when a company produces more than one product or offers more than one service), adding or deleting a product line, and accepting special orders. There are many types of applications of

C-V-P analysis, and all are used by managers to plan and control operations effectively.

BREAKEVEN ANALYSIS

Breakeven analysis utilizes the basic elements of cost-volume-profit relationships. As shown in Figure 7, the breakeven point is the point at which total revenues equal total costs. Breakeven, then, is the point at which a company begins to earn a profit. When new ventures or product lines are being planned, the likelihood of success can be measured quickly by finding the project's breakeven point. If, for instance, breakeven is 50,000 units and the total market is only 25,000 units, the idea should be abandoned promptly.

The objective of breakeven analysis is to find the level of activity at which revenues from sales equal the sum of all variable and fixed costs. There is no net profit when a company just breaks even. Thus, only sales (S), variable costs (VC), and fixed costs (FC) are used to compute the breakeven point. The breakeven point can be stated in terms of sales units or sales dollars. The general equation for finding the breakeven point is:

$$S = VC + FC$$

Here is an example of how this equation can be used to find breakeven units and dollars. Keller Products, Inc. makes special wooden stands for portable compact disc players; the stands have a protective storage compartment for the discs. Variable costs are $50 per unit, and fixed costs average $20,000 per year. Each wooden stand sells for $90. Given this information, we can compute the breakeven point for this product in sales units (x equals sales units):

$$
\begin{aligned}
S &= VC + FC \\
\$90x &= \$50x + \$20,000 \\
\$40x &= \$20,000 \\
x &= 500 \text{ units}
\end{aligned}
$$

and in sales dollars:

$$\$90 \times 500 \text{ units} = \$45,000$$

We can also make a rough estimate of the breakeven point using a graph. This method is less exact, but it does yield meaningful data. Figure 8 shows a breakeven graph for Keller Products, Inc. This graph, like the standard breakeven chart, has five parts.

1. A horizontal axis in volume or units of output
2. A vertical axis in dollars
3. A line running horizontally from the vertical axis at the level of fixed costs
4. A total cost line that begins at the point where the fixed cost line crosses the vertical axis and slopes upward to the right (The slope of the line depends on the variable cost per unit.)
5. A total revenue line that begins at the origin of the vertical and horizontal axes and slopes upward to the right (The slope depends on the selling price per unit.)

At the point where the total revenue line crosses the total cost line, revenues equal total costs. The breakeven point, stated in either units or dollars of sales, is found by extending broken lines from this point to the axes. As Figure 8 shows, Keller Products, Inc. will break even when 500 wooden stands have been made and sold for $45,000.

Figure 8. Graphic Breakeven Analysis: Keller Products, Inc.

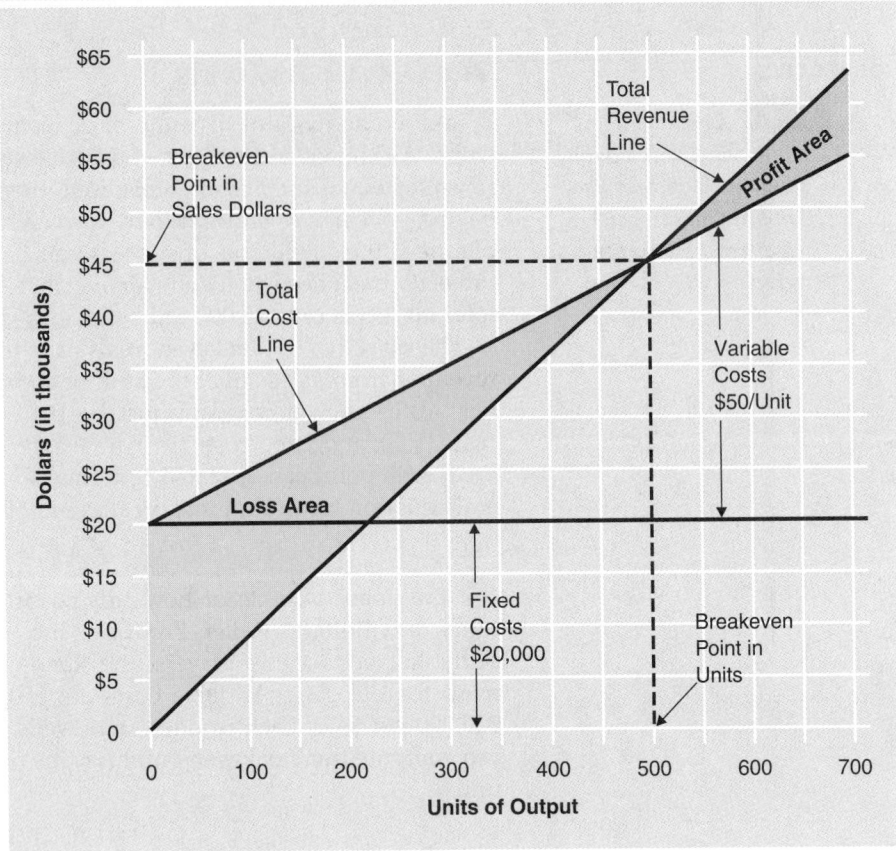

Mobay Chemical Corp.

DECISION POINT

Mobay Chemical Corp. uses breakeven analysis in a special way, consolidating breakeven figures for its product lines and divisions into one companywide analysis. From this analysis, the controller's staff develops a single graph, which the firm calls *profit geometry*, that portrays the entire company's breakeven history and plans. According to Howard Martin, the corporation's manager of strategic planning, consolidating standard breakeven analysis enables the controller, financial analyst, or planning professional to answer questions like:

How did last year's profit compare with the last time we experienced this level of capacity utilization (actual production levels relative to maximum possible production levels)?

How much have our so-called fixed costs actually increased with volume over recent years?

What level of profitability as a percent of sales and/or investment can we expect at "full" utilization of capacity?

What confidence level can we have that a recent actual or forecast future change in profitability is really significant (i.e., more than just normal variability)?[2]

How are answers to these questions useful to a manager?

Breakeven analysis can be used to examine the profitability of a new product line or an existing plant or division. A companywide analysis from a historical perspective gives management valuable direction. The analysis provides a broad view of costs that enables managers to see if costs really behave as variable or fixed. This approach also allows capacity utilization to become part of the measurement of operating performance. :::::

<table>
<tr><td>OBJECTIVE</td></tr>
<tr><td>7   *Define* contribu-
tion margin *and
use the concept to deter-
mine a company's
breakeven point*</td></tr>
</table>

CONTRIBUTION MARGIN

A simpler method of determining the breakeven point uses contribution margin. Contribution margin is the excess of revenues over all variable costs related to a particular sales volume. A product line's contribution margin represents its net contribution to paying off fixed costs and earning profits. In other words, the contribution margin (CM) is what remains after variable costs are subtracted from total sales.

$$S - VC = CM$$

And what remains after fixed costs are paid and subtracted from the contribution margin is profit.

$$CM - FC = P$$

The following example uses contribution margin to determine the profitability of Keller Products, Inc.

		Units Produced and Sold		
Symbols		**250**	**500**	**750**
S	Sales revenue ($90 per unit)	$22,500	$45,000	$67,500
VC	Less variable costs ($50 per unit)	12,500	25,000	37,500
CM	Contribution margin	$10,000	$20,000	$30,000
FC	Less fixed costs	20,000	20,000	20,000
P	Profit (loss)	($10,000)	—	$10,000

The breakeven point (BE) can be expressed as the point at which contribution margin minus total fixed costs equals zero (or the point at which contribution margin equals fixed costs). In terms of units of product, the breakeven point equation looks like this:

$$(CM \text{ per unit} \times BE \text{ units}) - FC = 0$$

At this point, we need to develop an equation that isolates the expression *BE units*. The equation can be rearranged as shown on the next page.

2. Howard Martin, "Breaking Through the Breakeven Barriers," *Management Accounting,* Institute of Management Accountants, May 1985, p. 31.

1. Move fixed costs to the right side of the equation.

$$\text{CM per unit} \times \text{BE units} = \text{FC}$$

2. Divide both sides of the equation by contribution margin per unit.

$$\frac{\text{CM per unit} \times \text{BE units}}{\text{CM per unit}} = \frac{\text{FC}}{\text{CM per unit}}$$

3. After canceling terms, the result is:

$$\text{BE units} = \frac{\text{FC}}{\text{CM per unit}}$$

To show how the equation works, we use the data for Keller Products, Inc.

$$\text{BE units} = \frac{\text{FC}}{\text{CM per unit}} = \frac{\$20,000}{\$90 - \$50} = \frac{\$20,000}{\$40} = 500 \text{ units}$$

PROFIT PLANNING

The primary goal of a business venture is not to break even; it is to make a profit. Breakeven analysis adjusted for a profit factor can be used to estimate the profitability of a venture. In fact, the approach is excellent for "what if" analysis, in which the accountant selects several scenarios and computes the anticipated profit for each. For instance, what if the number of units sold is increased by 17,000 items? What effect will the increase have on anticipated profits? What if the increase in units sold is only 6,000? What if fixed costs are reduced by $14,500? What if the variable unit cost increases by $1.40? All these scenarios generate different amounts of profit or loss.

To illustrate how breakeven analysis can be applied to profit planning, assume that the president of Keller Products, Inc., Don Chico, has set $10,000 in profit as the goal for the year. If all the data in our earlier example stay as they were, how many compact disc stands must Keller Products, Inc. make and sell to reach the target profit? The answer is 750 units. (Again, x equals the number of units.)

$$
\begin{aligned}
S &= VC + FC + P \\
\$90x &= \$50x + \$20,000 + \$10,000 \\
\$40x &= \$30,000 \\
x &= 750 \text{ units}
\end{aligned}
$$

To check the accuracy of the answer, insert all known data into the equation:

$$
\begin{aligned}
S - VC - FC &= P \\
(750 \text{ units} \times \$90) - (750 \times \$50) - \$20,000 &= \$10,000 \\
\$67,500 - \$37,500 - \$20,000 &= \$10,000
\end{aligned}
$$

The contribution margin approach can also be used for profit planning. To do so, we simply add target profit to the numerator of the contribution margin breakeven equation:

$$\text{Target sales units} = \frac{\text{FC} + \text{P}}{\text{CM per unit}}$$

Using the data from the Keller Products, Inc. example, the number of sales units needed to generate a $10,000 profit is computed this way:

$$\text{Target sales units} = \frac{\text{FC} + \text{P}}{\text{CM per unit}} = \frac{\$20,000 + \$10,000}{\$40} = \frac{\$30,000}{\$40} = 750 \text{ units}$$

To compute the target sales in dollars for the example on the preceding page, divide the fixed costs plus profit by the contribution margin percentage. The CM percentage is computed by dividing the contribution margin per unit by the unit selling price:

$$\text{CM percent} = \frac{\$40}{\$90} = .44444 = 44.444 \text{ percent}$$

$$\text{Target sales dollars} = \frac{FC + P}{\text{CM percent}} = \frac{\$30,000}{.44444} = \$67,500$$

APPLICATIONS OF COST-VOLUME-PROFIT ANALYSIS

Almost every type of business uses cost-volume-profit analysis. Manufacturing companies, service companies, and merchandisers all use C-V-P relationships for forecasting and controlling operations. As an example, let's look at the year-end planning activities of the Kalmar Corporation. The information for the current year is presented in the contribution income statement below. Notice that the contribution income statement focuses on cost behavior, not cost function. Variable costs in all the functional areas—production, sales, and administration—are subtracted from sales to arrive at the contribution margin.

Kalmar Corporation Contribution Income Statement For the Year Ended December 31, 19x7		
Total Sales (66,000 units at $11.00 per unit)		$726,000
Less: Variable Production Costs		
(66,000 units at $4.40 per unit)	$290,400	
Variable Selling Costs		
(66,000 units at $2.80 per unit)	184,800	
Total Variable Costs		475,200
Contribution Margin		$250,800
Less: Fixed Production Costs	$130,500	
Fixed Selling and Administrative Costs	48,200	
Total Fixed Costs		178,700
Income Before Taxes		$ 72,100

Carl Nilsson, the company's controller, has asked several members of the executive committee to describe their expectations of the business environment for the coming year. Each person was asked to write up his or her personal outlook, including changes in selling prices, product demand, variable production costs, variable selling costs, fixed production costs, and fixed selling and administrative costs. In the following sections, we examine those projections and their implications.

Changes in Production Costs Only   The vice president of production believes that variable production costs will increase by 10 percent and that fixed production costs will rise by 5 percent. With no other anticipated changes, what is the projected profit for the coming year?

SOLUTION

Total sales (66,000 units at $11.00 per unit)		$726,000
Less: Variable production costs		
[66,000 units at $4.84 ($4.40 × 1.10) per unit]	$319,440	
Variable selling costs		
(66,000 units at $2.80 per unit)	184,800	
Total variable costs		504,240
Contribution margin		$221,760
Less: Fixed production costs ($130,500 × 1.05)	$137,025	
Fixed selling and administrative costs	48,200	
Total fixed costs		185,225
Projected income before taxes		$ 36,535

As shown, if the variable and fixed production costs do change and no adjustments to selling price or volume are made, the corporation's profit will decrease by $35,565 (from $72,100 to $36,535). Because both variable and fixed production costs are projected to increase, management may want to increase the selling price to offset the rise in costs. Increasing the number of units produced and sold would also help offset the higher fixed costs. Because the vice president of production has commented only on production costs, the controller should try to augment the forecast by having other managers develop projections in their areas of expertise.

Changes in All Cost Areas   All costs will change, according to the vice president of data processing. She believes that all variable costs will go up by 10 percent, and that all fixed costs will rise by 5 percent. She does not anticipate any other changes.

SOLUTION

Total sales (66,000 units at $11.00 per unit)		$726,000
Less: Variable production costs		
(66,000 units at $4.84 per unit)	$319,440	
Variable selling costs		
[66,000 units at $3.08 ($2.80 × 1.10) per unit]	203,280	
Total variable costs		522,720
Contribution margin		$203,280
Less: Fixed production costs ($130,500 × 1.05)	$137,025	
Fixed selling and administrative costs		
($48,200 × 1.05)	50,610	
Total fixed costs		187,635
Projected income before taxes		$ 15,645

Like the vice president of production, the vice president of data processing has concentrated only on projected costs. In this scenario, all costs are expected to increase. Profit suffers even more, pushed down to $15,645, a decrease of $56,455 ($72,100 − $15,645). Again, the controller may want to adjust this projection to include changes in volume and selling price.

Changes in Demand and in All Cost Areas   The vice president of finance anticipates volume changes as well as changes in all cost areas. He believes that unit demand in 19x8 will increase by 8 percent, all variable costs will go up by 20 percent, and all fixed costs will decrease by 10 percent.

SOLUTION

Total sales [71,280 (66,000 × 1.08) units at $11.00 per unit]		$784,080
Less: Variable production costs [71,280 units at $5.28 ($4.40 × 1.20) per unit]	$376,358	
Variable selling costs [71,280 units at $3.36 ($2.80 × 1.20) per unit]	239,501	
Total variable costs		615,859
Contribution margin		$168,221
Less: Fixed production costs ($130,500 × .9)	$117,450	
Fixed selling and administrative costs ($48,200 × .9)	43,380	
Total fixed costs		160,830
Projected income before taxes		$ 7,391

This projection is the most pessimistic. The vice president of finance believes not only that all variable costs are going to increase but that volume also will increase. The $82,579 decrease in contribution margin far outweighs the positive aspects of lower fixed costs being spread over more units. If these projections prove correct, something should be done to increase the selling price.

Changes in Selling Price, Product Demand, and Selling Costs   According to the vice president of sales, the corporation should increase the selling price by 10 percent, which will cause demand to fall by 8 percent. In addition, variable selling costs will go down by 5 percent, and fixed selling and administrative costs will go up by 10 percent.

SOLUTION

Total sales [60,720 (66,000 × .92) units at $12.10 ($11 × 1.10) per unit]		$734,712
Less: Variable production costs (60,720 units at $4.40 per unit)	$267,168	
Variable selling costs [60,720 units at $2.66 ($2.80 × .95) per unit]	161,515	
Total variable costs		428,683
Contribution margin		$306,029
Less: Fixed production costs	$130,500	
Fixed selling and administrative costs ($48,200 × 1.10)	53,020	
Total fixed costs		183,520
Projected income before taxes		$122,509

The vice president of sales has the most optimistic outlook. Overall, in this scenario, profits increase by $50,409 ($122,509 − $72,100). Although the increase in selling price reduces demand, total revenue increases by $8,712. The increase in fixed selling costs is countered by an even larger decrease in variable selling costs.

Comparative Summary   A comparative summary of the four executives' predictions is presented in Exhibit 1. The controller would use a document like the one in Exhibit 1 as a basis for discussing predictions for the coming

Exhibit 1. Comparative C-V-P Analysis

Kalmar Corporation
Summary of Projected Income Before Taxes
For the Year Ended December 31, 19x7

	VP Production	VP Data Processing	VP Finance	VP Sales
Total Sales	$726,000	$726,000	$784,080	$734,712
Less: Variable Production Costs	$319,440	$319,440	$376,358	$267,168
Variable Selling Costs	184,800	203,280	239,501	161,515
Total Variable Costs	$504,240	$522,720	$615,859	$428,683
Contribution Margin	$221,760	$203,280	$168,221	$306,029
Less: Fixed Production Costs	$137,025	$137,025	$117,450	$130,500
Fixed Selling and Administrative Costs	48,200	50,610	43,380	53,020
Total Fixed Costs	$185,225	$187,635	$160,830	$183,520
Projected Income Before Taxes	$ 36,535	$ 15,645	$ 7,391	$122,509

year. From the executives' predictions and a discussion of their views, the controller can develop a portrait of the expected environment, and from that he can develop the budget for 19x8.

BUSINESS BULLETIN: TECHNOLOGY IN PRACTICE

As competition in the world marketplace has increased, world-class companies have relied on new technologies to maintain or improve their competitiveness. Such companies have used technology to transform their production processes into computer-based systems that focus on increasing process efficiency and product quality while holding costs to a minimum. Many of the management accounting analyses supporting the new processes employ nonfinancial measures. Time is the focal point, not dollars. The theory is that if product throughput time can be reduced, cost reduction will automatically follow. The less time a product spends in production and inventory storage, the less overhead cost it will cause. So time is an important factor in the cost-volume-profit analyses of world-class companies. Profit is as much a result of time efficiencies as it is of increases in volume or cost reduction programs.

ASSUMPTIONS UNDERLYING
C-V-P ANALYSIS

Cost-volume-profit analysis is useful only under certain conditions and only when certain assumptions hold true. These assumptions and conditions are as follows:

1. The behavior of variable and fixed costs can be measured accurately.
2. Costs and revenues have a close linear approximation. For example, if costs rise, revenues rise proportionately.
3. Efficiency and productivity hold steady within the relevant range of activity.
4. Cost and price variables also hold steady during the period being planned.
5. The product sales mix does not change during the period being planned.
6. Production and sales volume are roughly equal.

If one or more of these conditions and assumptions are absent, the C-V-P analysis may be misleading.

RESPONSIBILITY ACCOUNTING

OBJECTIVE

9 *Define responsibility accounting and identify the elements of a responsibility accounting system*

Responsibility accounting is an information reporting system that (1) classifies financial data according to areas of responsibility in an organization, and (2) reports each area's activities by including only the revenue and cost categories that the assigned manager can control. Also called *profitability accounting,* a responsibility accounting system personalizes accounting reports. Such a system emphasizes responsibility centers. A responsibility center is an organizational unit, within a responsibility accounting system, for which reports are generated. Cost/expense centers, profit centers, and investment centers are all responsibility centers. By concentrating on responsibility centers, a responsibility accounting system classifies and reports cost and revenue information according to responsibility areas assigned to managers or management positions.

Even though a company uses a responsibility accounting system, it still needs to collect the usual cost and revenue data. To do so, a company must use the usual recording methods and make the usual accounting entries. A general ledger, special journals, and a defined chart of accounts are also used. Responsibility accounting focuses on the reporting—not the recording—of operating cost and revenue data. Once the financial data from daily operations have been recorded in the accounting system, specific costs and revenues can be reclassified and reported for specific areas of managerial responsibility.

ORGANIZATIONAL STRUCTURE
AND REPORTING

A responsibility accounting system is made up of several responsibility centers. There is a responsibility center for each area or level of managerial responsibility, and a report is generated for each center. The report for a responsibility center includes only those cost and revenue items the manager of that center can control. If a manager cannot control a cost or revenue item, it is either not included in the manager's report or classified separately. This

Figure 9. Organization Chart Emphasizing the Manufacturing Area

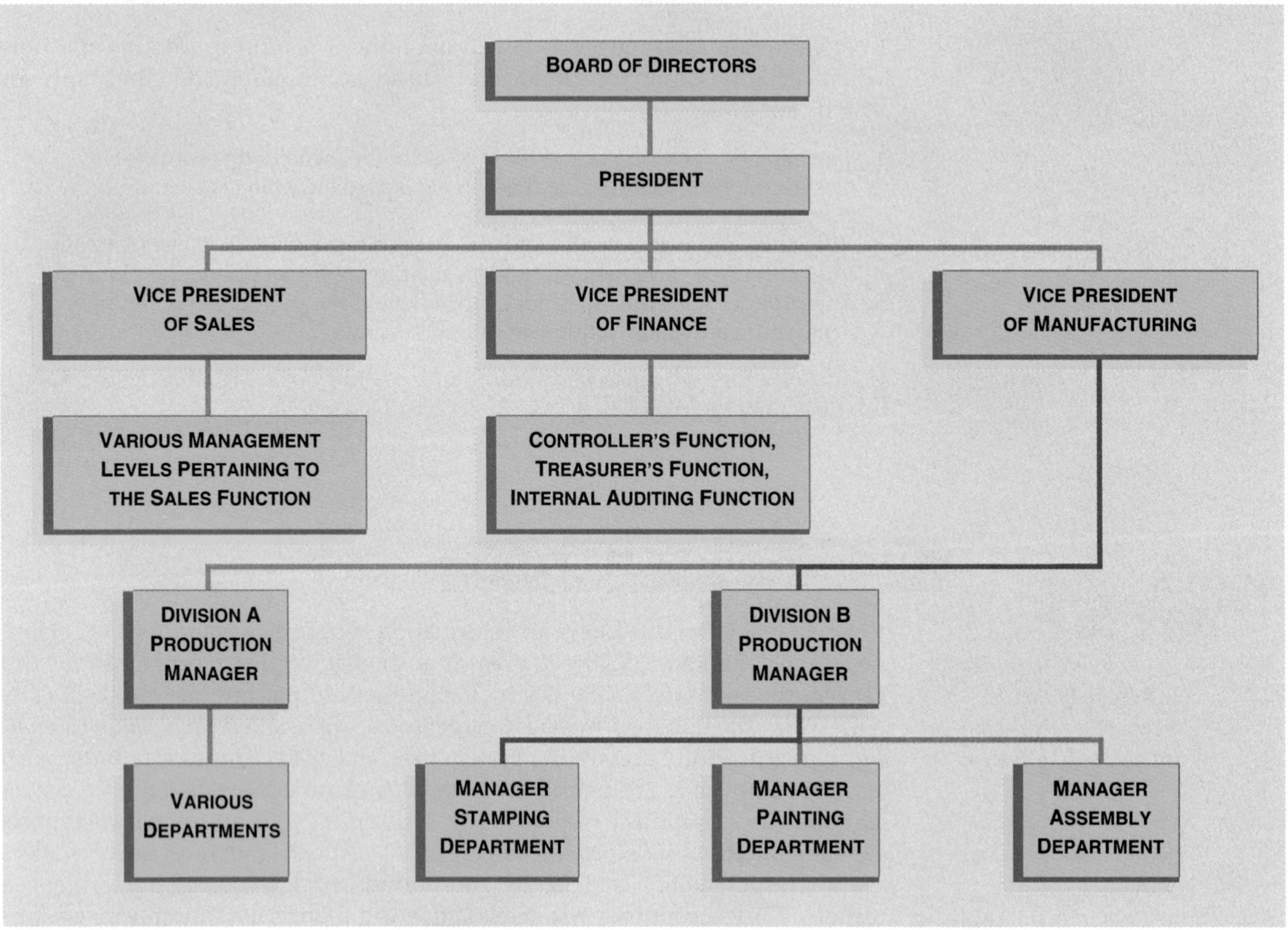

classification treatment prevents the item from influencing the manager's performance evaluation. Cost and revenue controllability is discussed in the next section.

By examining a corporate organization chart and a series of related managerial reports, you can see how a responsibility accounting system works. Figure 9 shows a typical management hierarchy, with the three vice presidents reporting to the corporate president. The sales and finance areas are condensed, however, to emphasize the manufacturing area. The production managers of Divisions A and B report to the vice president of manufacturing. In Division B, the managers of the Stamping Department, Painting Department, and Assembly Department report to the division's production manager.

In a responsibility accounting system, operating reports for each level of management are tailored to individual needs. Because a responsibility accounting system provides a report for every manager and because lower-level managers report to higher-level managers, the same costs and revenues may appear in several reports. When lower-level operating data are included in higher-level reports, the data are summarized.

Based on the managerial hierarchy presented in Figure 9, Exhibit 2 illustrates how the responsibility reporting network is tied together. At the department level, the report lists cost items under the manager's control and compares expected (or budgeted) costs with actual costs. This comparison is a

Exhibit 2. Reporting Within a Responsibility Accounting System

Manufacturing: Vice President — Monthly Report: November

Amount Budgeted	Controllable Cost	Actual Amount	Over (Under) Budget
$ 281,400	Central production scheduling	$ 298,100	$16,700
179,600	Office expenses	192,800	13,200
19,800	Operating expenses	26,200	6,400
339,500	Division A	348,900	9,400
426,200	Division B	399,400	(26,800)
$1,246,500	Totals	$1,265,400	$18,900

Division B: Production Manager — Monthly Report: November

Amount Budgeted	Controllable Cost	Actual Amount	Over (Under) Budget
	Division expenses		
$101,800	Salaries	$ 96,600	($ 5,200)
39,600	Utilities	39,900	300
25,600	Insurance	21,650	(3,950)
	Departments		
46,600	Stamping	48,450	1,850
69,900	Painting	64,700	(5,200)
142,700	Assembly	128,100	(14,600)
$426,200	Totals	$399,400	($26,800)

Stamping Department: Manager — Monthly Report: November

Amount Budgeted	Controllable Cost	Actual Amount	Over (Under) Budget
$22,500	Direct materials	$23,900	$1,400
14,900	Factory labor	15,200	300
2,600	Small tools	1,400	(1,200)
5,100	Maintenance salaries	6,000	900
1,000	Supplies	1,200	200
500	Other costs	750	250
$46,600	Totals	$48,450	$1,850

measure of operating performance. The manager who receives the report on the Stamping Department should be particularly concerned with direct materials costs and maintenance salaries, for they are significantly over budget. Also, the underutilization of small tools may signal problems with productivity in that department.

The production manager of Division B is responsible for the three operating departments plus controllable divisionwide costs. The production manager's report includes a summary of results from the Stamping Department as well as from the other areas of responsibility. At the division level, the report does not present detailed data on each department; only department totals appear. As shown in Exhibit 2, the data are even more condensed in the vice president's report. Only corporate and summarized divisional data about costs controllable by the vice president are included. Notice that the $1,200 for supplies, shown in the Stamping Department report, is part of the vice president's report. The cost is included in the $399,400. But like all costs reported at higher levels, specific identity has been lost.

OBJECTIVE

10 *Identify the cost and revenue classifications controllable by a particular manager*

COST AND REVENUE CONTROLLABILITY

Management wants to incur the lowest possible costs while still producing a quality product or providing a useful service. Profit-oriented businesses want to maximize their profits. Not-for-profit organizations, such as government units or charitable associations, seek to accomplish a mission while operating within their appropriations or budgets. To achieve those goals, management must know the origin of a cost or revenue item and be able to identify the person who controls it.

A manager's controllable costs and revenues are those that result from his or her actions, influence, and decisions. If a manager can regulate or influence a cost or revenue item, the item is controllable at that level of operation. Or if a manager has the authority to acquire or supervise the use of a resource or service, he or she controls its cost.

Determining controllability is the key to a successful responsibility accounting system. In theory, it means that every dollar of a company's incurred costs or earned revenue is traceable to and controllable by at least one manager. However, identifying controllable costs at lower management levels is often difficult because those managers seldom have full authority to acquire or supervise the use of resources and services. For example, if resources are shared with another department, a manager has only partial control and influence over such costs. For this reason, managers should help identify the costs for which they will be held accountable in their performance reviews. If cost and revenue items can be controlled by the person responsible for the area in which they originate, then it is possible to design an efficient, meaningful reporting system that highlights operating performance.

The activity of a responsibility center dictates the extent of the manager's responsibility. If a responsibility center involves only costs or expenditures, it is called a cost or expense center. On the other hand, if a manager is responsible for both revenues and costs, the department is called a profit center. Finally, if a manager is involved in decisions to invest in plant, equipment, and other capital resources and is also responsible for revenues and costs, the unit is called an investment center. A responsibility accounting reporting system establishes a communications network within the company that is ideal for gathering information about operations.

CHAPTER REVIEW

REVIEW OF LEARNING OBJECTIVES

1. **Define the concept of cost behavior and explain how managers make use of this concept.** Cost behavior is the way costs respond to changes in volume or activity. Some costs vary in relation to volume or operating activity; other costs remain fixed as volume changes. Cost behavior depends on whether the focus is total costs or cost per unit. Variable costs vary in total as volume changes but are fixed per unit; fixed costs are fixed in total as volume changes but vary per unit. Managers use information about cost behavior in almost every decision they make. Whenever managers are asked to make a decision, they must always deal with cost ramifications, and they must understand and anticipate cost behavior patterns if they are to decide correctly.

2. **Identify specific types of variable and fixed cost behavior, and compute the changes in variable and fixed costs caused by changes in operating activity.** Total costs that change in direct proportion to changes in productive output (or any other volume measure) are called variable costs. Hourly wages, the cost of operating supplies, direct materials costs, and the cost of merchandise are all variable costs. Total fixed costs remain constant within a relevant range of volume or activity. They change only when activity exceeds the anticipated relevant range, when new equipment or new buildings must be purchased, higher insurance premiums and property taxes must be paid, or additional supervisory personnel must be hired to accommodate the increased activity.

3. **Define *semivariable cost* and *mixed cost*, and separate their variable and fixed cost components.** A semivariable cost, such as the cost of electricity, has both variable and fixed cost components. Mixed costs result when both variable and fixed costs are charged to the same general ledger account. The balance in the Repairs and Maintenance account is an example of a mixed cost. The high-low method, which identifies a linear relationship between activity level and cost, is the easiest way to separate variable costs from fixed costs in semivariable or mixed costs.

4. **Analyze cost behavior patterns in a service business.** A service business's primary costs are professional labor and service overhead. Both types of costs are used to compute the cost per service rendered.

5. **Illustrate how changes in cost, volume, or price affect the profit formula.** Profit equals sales minus variable costs minus fixed costs. If sales, variable costs, or fixed costs change, profit changes.

6. **Compute a breakeven point in units of output and in sales dollars, and prepare a breakeven graph.** The breakeven point is the point at which total revenues equal total costs, the point at which net sales equal variable costs plus fixed costs. Once the number of units needed to break even is known, it can be multiplied by the product's selling price to determine the breakeven point in sales dollars.

    A breakeven graph is made up of a horizontal axis (units) and a vertical axis (dollars). Three lines are plotted: The fixed cost line runs horizontally from the point on the vertical axis representing total fixed cost. The total cost line begins at the intersection of the fixed cost line and the vertical axis and runs upward to the right. The total revenue line runs from the intersection of the two axes upward to the right. The slope of the total cost line is determined by the variable cost per unit; the slope of the total revenue line is determined by the selling price per unit. The point at which the total cost and the total revenue lines cross determines the breakeven point in units and in dollars.

7. **Define *contribution margin* and use the concept to determine a company's breakeven point.** Contribution margin is the excess of revenues over all variable costs related to a particular sales volume. A product line's contribution margin represents its net contribution to paying off fixed costs and earning a profit. The breakeven point in units can be computed by dividing total fixed costs by the contribution margin per unit.

8. **Apply contribution margin analysis to estimated levels of future sales and compute projected profit.** The addition of projected profit to the breakeven equation makes it possible to plan levels of operation that yield target profits. The formula in terms of contribution margin is

$$\text{Target sales units} = \frac{FC + P}{CM \text{ per unit}}$$

9. **Define *responsibility accounting* and identify the elements of a responsibility accounting system.** Responsibility accounting is an information reporting system that (1) classifies financial data according to areas of responsibility in an organization, and (2) reports each area's activities by including only revenue and cost categories that the assigned manager can control. A responsibility accounting system personalizes accounting reports. It is composed of a series of reports, one for each person with responsibility for cost control in a company's organization chart.

10. **Identify the cost and revenue classifications controllable by a particular manager.** A manager's controllable costs and revenues are those that result from his or her actions, influence, and decisions. If managers can regulate or influence a cost or revenue item, it is controllable at that level of operation. If managers have the authority to acquire or supervise the use of a resource or service, they control its cost.

REVIEW OF CONCEPTS AND TERMINOLOGY

The following concepts and terms were introduced in this chapter.

L O 6   **Breakeven point:** The point at which total revenues equal total costs.

L O 7   **Contribution margin:** The excess of revenues over all variable costs related to a particular sales volume.

L O 10   **Controllable costs:** Operating costs that result from a particular manager's actions, influence, and decisions.

L O 1   **Cost behavior:** The way costs respond to changes in volume or activity.

L O 10   **Cost or expense center:** A responsibility center, such as a department or division, whose manager is responsible only for the costs or expenditures incurred by that center.

L O 5   **Cost-volume-profit (C-V-P) analysis:** An analysis of the cost behavior patterns that underlie the relationships between cost, volume of output, and profit.

L O 2   **Excess capacity:** Machinery and equipment kept on standby.

L O 2   **Fixed costs:** Cost totals that remain constant within a relevant range of volume or activity.

L O 3   **High-low method:** A method that identifies the linear relationship between activity level and cost; used to separate variable from fixed costs in a semivariable or mixed cost.

L O 10   **Investment center:** A responsibility center whose manager is responsible for profit generation and, in addition, can make significant decisions about the assets the center uses.

L O 3   **Mixed costs:** Costs that result when both variable and fixed costs (for example, repairs and maintenance costs) are charged to the same general ledger account.

L O 2   **Normal capacity:** The average annual level of operating capacity needed to meet expected sales demand.

L O 2   **Operating capacity:** The upper limit of a company's productive output capability, given its existing resources.

L O 2   **Practical capacity:** Theoretical capacity reduced by normal and expected work stoppages.

L O 10   **Profit center:** A responsibility center whose manager is responsible for revenues, costs, and resulting profits.

L O 2   **Relevant range:** The span of activity in which a company expects to operate.

L O 9 **Responsibility accounting:** An information reporting system that (1) classifies financial data according to areas of responsibility in an organization, and (2) reports each area's activities by including only the revenue and cost categories that the assigned manager can control. Also called *profitability accounting*.

L O 9 **Responsibility center:** An organizational unit, within a responsibility accounting system, for which reports are generated. This includes, but is not limited to, cost/expense centers, profit centers, and investment centers.

L O 3 **Scatter diagram:** A chart of plotted points that helps determine if a linear relationship exists between a cost item and its related activity measure.

L O 3 **Semivariable costs:** Costs that have both variable and fixed cost components.

L O 4 **Service overhead costs:** A varied collection of costs (excluding direct labor costs) incurred specifically to develop and provide services.

L O 2 **Theoretical capacity:** The maximum productive output for a given period, assuming all machinery and equipment are operating at optimum speed, without interruption. Also called *ideal capacity*.

L O 2 **Variable costs:** Total costs that change in direct proportion to changes in productive output or any other measure of volume.

REVIEW PROBLEM

BREAKEVEN/PROFIT PLANNING ANALYSIS

L O 6, 7, 8   Instrument City, Inc. is a major producer of pipe organs. Its Model D14 is a double-manual organ with a large potential market. Here is a summary of data from 19x8 operations for Model D14.

Variable costs per unit	
Direct materials	$ 2,300
Direct labor	800
Factory overhead	600
Selling expense	500
Total fixed costs	
Factory overhead	195,000
Advertising	55,000
Administrative expense	68,000
Selling price per unit	9,500

REQUIRED

1. Compute the 19x8 breakeven point in units.
2. Instrument City sold sixty-five D14 models in 19x8. How much profit did the firm realize?
3. Management is pondering alternative courses of action for 19x9. (Treat each alternative independently.)
   a. Calculate the number of units that must be sold to generate a profit of $95,400. Assume that costs and selling price remain constant.
   b. Calculate income before taxes if the company increases the number of units sold by 20 percent and cuts the selling price by $500 per unit.
   c. Determine the number of units that must be sold to break even if advertising is increased by $47,700.
   d. If variable costs are cut by 10 percent, find the number of units that must be sold to generate a profit of $125,000.

ANSWER TO REVIEW PROBLEM

1. Compute the breakeven point in units for 19x8.

$$\text{Breakeven units} = \frac{\text{FC}}{\text{CM per unit}} = \frac{\$318,000}{\$9,500 - \$4,200} = \frac{\$318,000}{\$5,300} = 60 \text{ units}$$

2. Calculate income before taxes from sales of sixty-five units.

Units sold	65
Units required to break even	60
Units over breakeven	5

19x8 income before taxes = $5,300 per unit × 5 = $26,500

Contribution margin equals sales minus all variable costs. Contribution margin per unit equals the amount of sales dollars remaining, after variable costs have been subtracted, to cover fixed costs and earn a profit. If all fixed costs have been absorbed by the time breakeven is reached, the entire contribution margin of each unit sold in excess of breakeven represents profit.

3. a. Calculate the number of units that must be sold to generate a given profit.

$$\text{Target sales units} = \frac{FC + P}{\text{CM per unit}}$$

$$= \frac{\$318,000 + \$95,400}{\$5,300} = \frac{\$413,400}{\$5,300} = 78 \text{ units}$$

b. Calculate income before taxes under specified conditions.

Total sales [78 (65 × 1.20) units at $9,000 per unit]	$702,000
Less variable costs (78 units × $4,200)	327,600
Contribution margin	$374,400
Less fixed costs	318,000
Projected income before taxes	$ 56,400

c. Determine the number of units needed to break even under specified conditions.

$$\text{BE units} = \frac{FC}{\text{CM per unit}}$$

$$= \frac{\$318,000 + \$47,700}{\$5,300} = \frac{\$365,700}{\$5,300} = 69 \text{ units}$$

d. Calculate the number of units that must be sold to generate a given profit under specified conditions.

CM per unit = $9,500 − ($4,200 × .9) = $9,500 − $3,780 = $5,720

$$\text{Target sales units} = \frac{FC + P}{\text{CM per unit}}$$

$$= \frac{\$318,000 + \$125,000}{\$5,720} = \frac{\$443,000}{\$5,720} = 77.45 \text{ or } 78 \text{ units}$$

CHAPTER ASSIGNMENTS

QUESTIONS

1. Define *cost behavior*.
2. Why is an understanding of cost behavior useful to managers?
3. What is the difference between theoretical capacity and practical capacity?
4. Why does a company never operate at theoretical capacity?
5. Define *excess capacity*.

6. What is normal capacity? Why is normal capacity considered more relevant and useful than either theoretical or practical capacity?

7. What does *relevant range of activity* mean?

8. What makes variable costs different from fixed costs?

9. "Fixed costs remain constant in total but decrease per unit as productive output increases." Explain this statement.

10. Why is the cost of telephone usage usually considered a semivariable cost?

11. What is a mixed cost? Give an example.

12. Describe the high-low method of separating costs.

13. "The concept of product cost is not applicable to service companies." Is this statement correct? Defend your answer.

14. Service companies do not maintain work in process and finished goods inventories. Why, then, do they need unit cost information?

15. Define *cost-volume-profit analysis*.

16. Identify two uses of C-V-P analysis and explain their significance to management.

17. Define *breakeven point*. Why is information about the breakeven point important to managers?

18. Define *contribution margin* and describe its use in breakeven analysis.

19. State the equation that determines target sales units using the elements of fixed costs, target profit, and contribution margin per unit.

20. What conditions must be met for C-V-P computations to be accurate?

21. Define *responsibility accounting*.

22. Describe a responsibility accounting system.

23. How does a company's organizational structure affect its responsibility accounting system?

24. What role does controllability play in a responsibility accounting system?

25. Compare and contrast a cost or expense center, a profit center, and an investment center.

SHORT EXERCISES

SE 1. *Concept of Cost*
L O 1 *Behavior*
Check Figures: Hat maker A: Variable cost per derby, $4.50; Fixed cost per derby, $16.67

Patrick's Hat Makers is in the business of designing specialty hats. The material that goes into producing a derby costs $4.50 per unit, and Patrick's pays each of its two full-time hat makers $250 per week. If hat maker A makes 15 derbies in one week, what is the variable cost per derby, and what is this worker's fixed cost per derby? If hat maker B makes only 12 derbies in one week, what are this worker's variable and fixed costs per derby? (Round to two decimal places where necessary.)

SE 2. *Identification of*
L O 2, 3 *Variable, Fixed, and*
Semivariable Costs
No check figure

Identify the following as either fixed costs, variable costs, or semivariable costs.

1. Direct materials
2. Telephone expense
3. Operating supplies
4. Personnel manager's salary
5. Factory building rent payment

SE 3. *Semivariable Costs:*
L O 3 *High-Low Method*
Check Figures: Variable cost per telephone hour: $40; Total fixed cost: $510

Using the high-low method and the following information, compute the monthly variable costs per telephone hour and fixed costs for Saulding Corporation.

Month	Business Telephone Hours	Telephone Expenses
April	96	$4,350
May	93	4,230
June	105	4,710

SE 4. *Cost Behavior in a*
L O 4 *Service Business*
Check Figure: Variable cost per case: $275

Eye Spy, a private investigation firm, has the following costs for December.

Direct labor: $190 per case
Service overhead, December

Salary for director of investigations	$ 4,800
Telephone	930
Depreciation	8,300
Legal advice	2,300
Supplies	590
Advertising	360
Utilities	1,560
Wages for clerical personnel	2,000
Total service overhead	$20,840

Service overhead for October: $21,150
Service overhead for November: $21,350

The number of cases investigated during October, November, and December was 93, 97, and 91, respectively.

Compute the variable and fixed cost components of service overhead. Then determine the variable and fixed costs per case for December. (Round to nearest dollar where necessary.)

SE 5. *Cost-Volume-Profit*
L O 5 *Analysis*
Check Figure: Sales price per unit: $88

Dante, Inc. wishes to make a $20,000 profit. The company has variable costs of $80 per unit and fixed costs of $12,000. How much must Dante charge per unit if 4,000 units are sold?

SE 6. *Computing the*
L O 6 *Breakeven Point*
Check Figure: Breakeven point: 900 units

How many units must Marshand sell to break even if the selling price per unit is $8.50, variable costs are $4.30 per unit, and fixed costs are $3,780?

SE 7. *Contribution*
L O 7 *Margin*
Check Figure: Breakeven point: 1,100

Using the contribution margin approach, find the breakeven point in units for Douglas Consumer Products if the selling price per unit is $11, the variable cost per unit is $6, and the fixed costs are $5,500.

SE 8. *Contribution*
L O 8 *Margin and*
Projected Profit
Check Figure: Profit: $5,000

If Sanford Watches sells 300 watches at $48 per watch, has variable costs of $18 per watch and fixed costs of $4,000, what is the projected profit on this sale?

SE 9. *Identification of*
L O 10 *Controllable Costs*
No check figure

Bill Faries is the manager of the Paper Cutting Department in Division A of Warren Paper Products. From the following list, identify the costs that are controllable by Bill.

1. Salaries of cutting machine workers
2. Cost of cutting machine parts
3. Cost of electricity for Division A
4. Lumber Department hauling costs
5. Vice president's salary

SE 10. *Cost or Expense*
L O 10 *Centers, Profit*
Centers, and
Investment Centers
No check figure

Identify the following as either a cost or expense center, a profit center, or an investment center.

1. In business unit A, the manager is responsible for generating cash inflows and incurring costs with the goal of making the most money for the company. The manager has no responsibility for assets.
2. Business unit B produces a component that is not sold to an external party.

EXERCISES

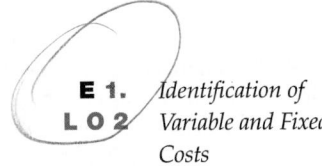

E 1. *Identification of*
L O 2 *Variable and Fixed*
Costs

No check figure

Indicate whether each of the following costs of productive output is usually considered variable or fixed: (1) packing materials for stereo components, (2) real estate taxes, (3) gasoline for a delivery truck, (4) property insurance, (5) depreciation expense of buildings (straight-line method), (6) supplies, (7) indirect materials, (8) bottles used to package liquids, (9) license fees for company cars, (10) wiring used in radios, (11) machine helper's wages, (12) wood used in bookcases, (13) city operating license, (14) machine depreciation based on machine hours of usage, (15) machine operator's hourly wages, and (16) cost of required outside inspection of each unit produced.

E 2. *Variable Cost*
L O 2 *Analysis*

Check Figure: 1. Three-month total cost: $1,776

Pronto Oil Change has been in business for six months. Each oil change requires an average of four quarts of oil. The cost of oil to Pronto Oil Change is $.50 per quart. The estimated number of cars that will be serviced in the next three months is 240, 288, and 360.

1. Compute the cost of oil for each of the three months and the total cost for all three months. Fill in the blanks in the following table.

Month	Cars to Be Serviced	Required Quarts/Car	Cost/Quart	Total Cost/Month
1	240	4	$.50	_____
2	288	4	.50	_____
3	360	4	.50	_____
Three-month total	888			_____

2. Complete the following sentences by choosing the words that best describe the cost behavior at Pronto Oil Change.

   Cost per unit (increased, decreased, remained constant). Total variable cost per month (increased, decreased) as the quantity of oil used (increased, decreased).

E 3. *Semivariable Costs:*
L O 3 *High-Low Method*

Check Figure: 2. Fixed cost per month: $18,000

Langtry Electronics Company manufactures major appliances. The company just had its most successful year because of increased interest in its refrigerator line. While preparing the budget for next year, Lynn Dobson, the company's controller, came across the following data.

Month	Volume in Machine Hours	Electricity Costs
July	6,000	$60,000
August	5,000	53,000
September	4,500	49,500
October	4,000	46,000
November	3,500	42,500
December	3,000	39,000

Using the high-low method, determine (1) the variable electricity cost per machine hour, (2) the monthly fixed electricity cost, and (3) the total variable electricity costs and fixed electricity costs for the six-month period.

E 4. *Cost Behavior in a*
L O 4 *Service Business*

Check Figure: Estimated total cost per tax return: $72.12

Armando Slater, CPA, provides tax services in Lakewood. To prepare standard short-form tax returns, he incurred the following costs for the previous three months.

Direct professional labor: $50 per tax return

Service overhead (included telephone, depreciation on equipment and building, tax forms, office supplies, wages of clerical personnel, and utilities): January, $18,500; February, $20,000; March, $17,000.

Number of tax returns prepared: January, 850; February, 1,000; March, 700.

Determine the variable and fixed cost components of the Service Overhead account. What would be the estimated total cost per tax return if Armando's CPA firm prepares 825 standard short-form tax returns in April?

E 5. *Breakeven Analysis*
L O 6, 7

Check Figure: 1. Breakeven point in sales units: 34,755

Parker Manufacturing Company makes head covers for golf clubs. The company expects to make a profit next year. It anticipates fixed manufacturing costs of $126,500 and fixed general and administrative expenses of $82,030 for the year. Variable manufacturing and selling costs per set of head covers will be $4.65 and $2.75, respectively. Each set will sell for $13.40.

1. Compute the breakeven point in sales units.
2. Compute the breakeven point in sales dollars.
3. If the selling price were increased to $14 per unit and fixed general and administrative expenses were cut by $33,465, what would the new breakeven point be in units?
4. Prepare a graph to illustrate the breakeven point found in **2.**

E 6. *Graphical Analysis*
L O 6

No check figure

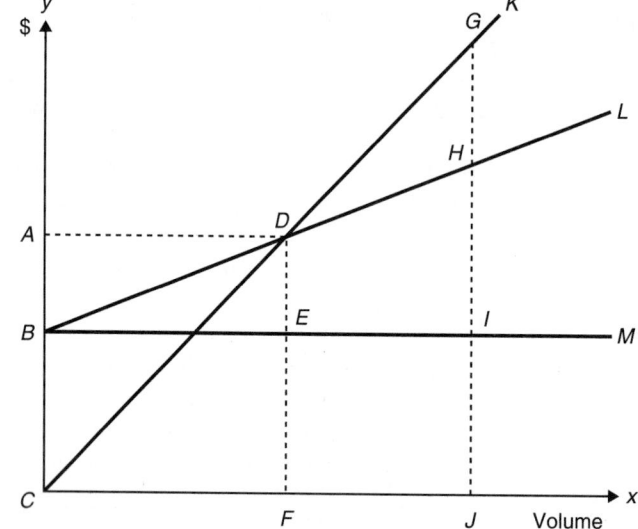

Identify the letter of the point, line segment, or area of the breakeven graph that correctly completes each of the following statements.

1. The maximum possible operating loss is
  a. *A.*   c. *B.*
  b. *D.*   d. *F.*
2. The breakeven point in sales dollars is
  a. *C.*   c. *A.*
  b. *D.*   d. *G.*
3. At volume *F,* total contribution margin is
  a. *C.*   c. *E.*
  b. *D.*   d. *G.*
4. Profits are represented by area
  a. *KDL.*   c. *BDC.*
  b. *KCJ.*   d. *GCJ.*
5. At volume *J,* total fixed costs are represented by
  a. *H.*   c. *I.*
  b. *G.*   d. *J.*
6. If volume increases from *F* to *J,* the change in total costs is
  a. *HI* minus *DE.*   c. *BC* minus *DF.*
  b. *DF* minus *HJ.*   d. *AB* minus *DE.*

E 7. *Profit Planning*
L O 4, 8

Check Figure: 3. Total rental revenue: $301,875

Short-term automobile rentals are the specialty of Boyd Auto Rentals, Inc. Average variable operating costs have been $12.50 per day per automobile. The company owns sixty cars. Fixed operating costs for the next year are expected to be $145,500. Average daily rental revenue per automobile is expected to be $34.50. Management would like to earn $47,000 during the year.

1. Calculate the total number of daily rentals the company must have during the year to earn the target profit.
2. On the basis of your answer to **1**, determine the number of days on the average that each automobile must be rented.
3. Find the total rental revenue for the year needed to earn the $47,000 profit.
4. What would the total rental revenue be if fixed operating costs could be lowered by $5,180 and target earnings increased to $70,000?

E 8.
L O 7, 8

Contribution Margin/Profit Planning

Check Figure: 3. Additional units: 20

Ikard Systems, Ltd. makes undersea missiles for nuclear submarines. Management has just been offered a government contract that may generate a profit for the company. The contract purchase price is $130,000 per unit, but the number of units to be purchased has not yet been decided. The company's fixed costs are budgeted at $3,973,500, and the variable costs are $68,500 per unit.

1. Compute the number of units the company should agree to make at the stated contract price to earn a target income of $1,500,000.
2. Using a lighter material, the variable unit cost can be reduced by $1,730, but total fixed overhead will increase by $27,500. How many units must be produced to make $1,500,000 in profit?
3. Using the figures in **2**, how many additional units must be produced to increase profit by $1,264,600?

E 9.
L O 9

Responsibility Accounting: Organizational Structure

No check figure

The O'Malley Company uses the following job titles.

Purchasing agent	Vice president, administration
Vice president, sales	Treasurer
Production supervisor	Personnel manager
Controller	Engineering research manager
Cashier	Marketing manager
President	Warehouse manager
Vice president, manufacturing	Supervisor, repairs and maintenance
Sales manager	Internal auditor

1. Design an organization chart using these job titles.
2. List some possible costs for which the person holding each position would be responsible.

E 10.
L O 2, 3, 10

Identification of Controllable Costs

No check figure

Kastner Corporation produces computer equipment. Production has a three-tier management structure, as follows:

Vice-president, production

Plant superintendent

Production supervisors

Identify each cost item below as variable (V), fixed (F), or semivariable (SV). Then identify the manager responsible for that cost.

1. Repair and maintenance costs
2. Material handling costs
3. Direct labor
4. Supervisors' salaries
5. Maintenance of plant grounds
6. Depreciation, equipment
7. Superintendent's salary
8. Materials usage costs
9. Storage, finished goods inventory
10. Property taxes, plant
11. Depreciation, plant

SKILLS DEVELOPMENT EXERCISES

Conceptual Analysis

SDE 1. *Concept of Cost*
L O 1, 2 *Behavior*

No check figure

Gulf Coast Shrimp Company is a very small company. It owns an ice house and shrimp preparation building, a refrigerated van, and three shrimp boats. Steven Raven inherited the company from his father three months ago. The company employs three boat crews of four people each and five processing workers. Willman and Stevens, a local accounting firm, has kept the company's financial records for many years.

In her last analysis of operations, Lisa Willman stated that the company's fixed-cost base of $100,000 is satisfactory for this type and size of business. However, variable costs have averaged 70 percent of sales over the last two years, a percentage that is too high for the volume of business. For example, last year only 30 percent of the company's sales revenue of $300,000 contributed toward covering the fixed costs. As a result, the company reported a $10,000 operating loss.

Raven wants to improve the company's profits, but he is confused by Willman's explanation of the fixed and variable costs. Prepare a response to Raven from Willman in which you explain the concept of cost behavior as it relates to Gulf Coast's operations. Include ideas for improving the company's profits based on changes in fixed and variable costs.

Ethical Dilemma

SDE 2. *Breaking Even and*
L O 6 *Ethics*

No check figure

Matt Stokowski is the supervisor of the new product division of **Fricker Corp.**, located in Jackson, Wyoming. Stokowski's annual bonus is based on the success of new products and is computed on the amount of sales over and above each product's projected breakeven point. In reviewing the computations supporting his most recent bonus, he found that a large order for 7,500 units of product WR4, which had been refused by a customer and returned to the company, had been included in the calculations. He later found out that the company's accountant had labeled the return as an overhead expense and had charged the entire cost of the returned order to the plantwide factory overhead account. The result was that product WR4 exceeded breakeven by more than 5,000 units and Matt's bonus from that product amounted to over $800. What actions should Stokowski take? Be prepared to discuss your response.

Research Activity

SDE 3. *Projecting Revenues*
L O 7, 8 *and Costs*

No check figure

During profit planning, the primary difficulty is the development of accurate projections of future revenues and costs. If the projections are wrong, the planned profit will be wrong. At the library, search through issues of the periodical *Management Accounting* for the past three years and locate an article related to profit or operational planning. Prepare a written analysis that includes the date of the publication, the title and author(s) of the article, the name of the company being discussed, and the techniques used by the company to improve the accuracy of projected revenues and costs in its planning activities. Be prepared to present your findings to the class.

Decision-Making Practice

SDE 4. *Mixed Costs*
L O 2, 3

Check Figures: 2. Total fixed cost for electricity: $27,000; for repair and maintenance: $18,600

Officials of the **Rio Bravo Golf and Tennis Club** are putting together a budget for the year ending December 31, 19x9. A problem has caused the budget to be delayed by more than four weeks. Ray Landberg, the club treasurer, indicated that two expense items were creating the problem. The items were difficult to account for because they were called "semivariable or mixed costs," and he did not know how to break them down into their variable and fixed components. An accountant friend and golfing partner told him to use the high-low method to divide the costs into their variable and fixed parts.

The two cost categories are Electricity Expense and Repairs and Maintenance Expense. Information pertaining to last year's spending patterns and the measurement activity connected with each cost are as shown on the next page.

Month	Electricity Expense		Repairs and Maintenance	
	Amount	Kilowatt Hours	Amount	Labor Hours
January	$ 7,500	210,000	$ 7,578	220
February	8,255	240,200	7,852	230
March	8,165	236,600	7,304	210
April	8,960	268,400	7,030	200
May	7,520	210,800	7,852	230
June	7,025	191,000	8,126	240
July	6,970	188,800	8,400	250
August	6,990	189,600	8,674	260
September	7,055	192,200	8,948	270
October	7,135	195,400	8,674	260
November	8,560	252,400	8,126	240
December	8,415	246,600	7,852	230
Totals	$92,550	2,622,000	$96,416	2,840

1. Using the high-low method, compute the variable cost rates used last year for each expense. What was the monthly fixed cost for electricity and repairs and maintenance?
2. Compute the total variable cost and total fixed cost for each expense category for last year.
3. Landberg believes that for the coming year the electricity rate will increase by $.005 and the repairs rate will rise by $1.20. Usage of all items and their fixed cost amounts will remain constant. Compute the projected total cost for each category. How will these increases in costs affect the club's profits and cash flow?

PROBLEM SET A

A 1. *Cost Behavior and*
L O 2, 3, 4 *Projection*
Check Figure: 4. Unit cost per job: $81.56

Glowing Auto, Inc., which opened for business on March 1, 19x8, specializes in revitalizing automobile exteriors. *Detailing* is the term used to describe the process. The objective is to detail an automobile until it looks like it just rolled off the showroom floor. Area market research indicates that a full exterior detail should cost about $100. The company has just completed its first year of business and has asked its accountants to analyze the operating results. Management wants costs divided into variable, fixed, and semivariable components and would like them projected for the coming year. Anticipated volume for next year is 1,100 jobs.

The process used to detail a car's exterior is as follows:

1. One $20-per-hour employee spends twenty minutes cleaning the car's exterior.
2. One can per car of Tars-Off, a cleaning compound, is used on the trouble spots.
3. A chemical compound called Buff Glow 7 is used to remove oxidants from the paint surface and restore the natural oils to the paint.
4. Poly Wax is applied by hand, allowed to sit for ten minutes, and then buffed off.
5. The final step is an inspection to see that all wax and debris have been removed.

On average, two hours are spent on each car, including the cleaning time and wait time for the wax. The following first-year operating information for Glowing Auto is provided to the accountant.

Number of automobiles detailed	840
Labor per auto	2 hours at $20.00 per hour
Containers of Tars-Off consumed	840 at $3.50 per can
Pounds of Buff Glow 7 consumed	105 pounds at $32.00 per pound
Pounds of Poly Wax consumed	210 pounds at $8.00 per pound
Rent	$1,400.00 per month

Here are the utilities costs for the fiscal year.

Month	Cost	Number of Jobs
March, 19x8	$ 800	40
April	850	50
May	900	65
June	1,000	85
July	1,600	105
August	1,801	110
September	1,300	90
October	850	65
November	900	75
December	925	60
January, 19x9	890	50
February	880	45
Totals	$12,696	840

REQUIRED

1. Classify the costs as variable, fixed, or semivariable.
2. Using the high-low method, separate the semivariable costs into their variable and fixed components. Use number of jobs as the basis.
3. Project the same costs for next year, assuming that the anticipated increase in activity will occur and that fixed costs will remain constant.
4. Compute the unit cost per job for next year.
5. Based on your answer to **4**, should the price remain at $100 per job?

A 2. *Breakeven Analysis*
LO 6, 7
Check Figure: 1. Breakeven point: 7,500 billable hours

Smith & Watson, a law firm in downtown San Diego, is considering the development of a legal clinic for middle- and low-income clients. Paraprofessional help would be employed, and a billing rate of $18 per hour would be used. The paraprofessionals would be law students who would work for only $9 per hour. Other variable costs are anticipated to be $5.40 per hour, and annual fixed costs are expected to total $27,000.

REQUIRED

1. Compute the breakeven point in billable hours.
2. Compute the breakeven point in total billings.
3. Find the new breakeven point in total billings if fixed costs should go up by $2,340.
4. Using the original figures, compute the breakeven point in total billings if the billing rate is decreased by $1 per hour, variable costs are decreased by $.40 per hour, and fixed costs go down by $3,600.

A 3. *Profit Planning:*
LO 8 *Contribution*
Margin Approach
Check Figure: 3. Unit price: $255

Lenny Financial Corporation is a subsidiary of Harpo Enterprises. Processing loan applications is the main task of the corporation. Last year, Nancy Bar, manager of the Loan Department, established a policy of charging a $250 fee for every loan application processed. Next year's variable costs have been projected as follows: loan consultant's wages, $15.50 per hour (a loan application takes five hours to process); supplies, $2.40 per application; and other variable costs, $5.60 per application. Annual fixed costs include depreciation of equipment, $8,500; building rental, $14,000; promotional costs, $12,500; and other fixed costs, $8,099.

REQUIRED

1. Using the contribution margin approach, compute the number of loan applications the company must process to (a) break even and (b) earn a profit of $14,476.
2. Continuing the same approach, compute the number of applications the company must process to earn a target profit of $20,000 if promotional costs increase by $5,662.
3. Assuming the original information and the processing of 500 applications, compute the loan application fee the company must charge if the target profit is $41,651.
4. Bar believes that 750 loan applications is the maximum number her staff can handle. How much more can be spent on promotional costs if the highest fee tolerable to the customer is $280, if variable costs cannot be reduced, and if the target net income for such an application load is $50,000?

A 4. *Profit Planning*

L O 7, 8

Check Figure: 2. Target sales units: 190,000

REQUIRED

Vogel Company has a maximum capacity of 200,000 units per year. Variable manufacturing costs are $12 per unit. Fixed factory overhead is $600,000 per year. Variable selling and administrative costs are $5 per unit, and fixed selling and administrative costs are $300,000 per year. The current sales price is $23 per unit.

1. What is the breakeven point in (a) sales units and (b) sales dollars?
2. How many units must be sold to earn a target net income of $240,000 per year?
3. A strike at a major supplier has caused a material shortage, so the current year's production and sales is limited to 160,000 units. Top management is planning to reduce fixed costs to $841,000 to partially offset the effect on profits of the reduced sales. Variable cost per unit is the same as last year. The company already has sold 30,000 units at the regular selling price of $23 per unit.
   a. How much of the fixed costs was covered by the total contribution margin of the first 30,000 units sold?
   b. What contribution margin per unit will be needed on the remaining 130,000 units to cover the remaining fixed costs and to earn a $210,000 profit this year?

A 5. *Allocation and*

L O 9, 10 *Responsibility of Overhead*

Check Figure: 2a. Costs allocated to central receiving based on total costs incurred: $36,390

A division of Vilnius Enterprises makes special-order horse saddles for customers in the Southeast. Seven responsibility centers are used to manage the production operation: cutting, trimming, inspection, packing, storage/shipping, central receiving, and scheduling. Management has asked you to make a comparative analysis of the allocation methods that assign corporate overhead costs to the seven centers. The following data were developed for your use.

Department	Total Costs Incurred	Labor Hours	Labor Dollars
Cutting	$ 385,308	3,360	$ 46,080
Trimming	535,150	3,120	37,440
Inspection	214,060	2,400	31,680
Packing	149,842	840	11,520
Storage/Shipping	428,120	1,080	8,640
Central Receiving	321,090	720	5,760
Scheduling	107,030	480	2,880
Totals	$2,140,600	12,000	$144,000

During July, $242,600 in corporate overhead was assigned to the Saddle Production Division for distribution to the responsibility centers.

REQUIRED

1. Define *responsibility accounting*.
2. Allocate the balance of corporate overhead charges to the seven departments, using as a basis (a) total costs incurred, (b) labor hours, and (c) labor dollars.
3. For performance evaluation, which of the overhead distributions computed in **2** most effectively controls costs? Defend your answer.

PROBLEM SET B

B 1. *Cost Behavior and*

L O 2, 3, 4 *Projection*

Check Figure: 3. Average cost per job: $806.60

Howard Painting Company, located in Summer Haven, specializes in refurbishing exterior painted surfaces on homes and other buildings. In the humid South, exterior surfaces are hit hard with insect debris during the summer months. A special refurbishing technique, called *pressure cleaning*, is needed before the surface can be primed and repainted.

The technique involves the following steps:

1. Unskilled laborers trim trees and bushes two feet away from the structure.
2. Skilled laborers clean the building with a high-pressure cleaning machine, using about six gallons of Debris-Luse per job.
3. Unskilled laborers apply a coat of primer.
4. Skilled laborers apply oil-based exterior paint to the entire surface.

On average, skilled laborers work twelve hours per job, and unskilled laborers work eight hours.

The special pressure-cleaning and refurbishing process generated the following operating results during 19x9.

Number of structures refurbished	628
Skilled labor	$20.00 per hour
Unskilled labor	$8.00 per hour
Gallons of Debris-Luse used	3,768 gallons at $5.50 per gallon
Paint primer	7,536 gallons at $15.50 per gallon
Paint	6,280 gallons at $16.00 per gallon
Paint spraying equipment	$600.00 per month depreciation
Two leased vans	$800.00 per month total
Rent for storage building	$450.00 per month

The utilities costs for the year were as follows:

Month	Number of Jobs	Cost	Hours Worked
January	42	$ 3,950	840
February	37	3,550	740
March	44	4,090	880
April	49	4,410	980
May	54	4,720	1,080
June	62	5,240	1,240
July	71	5,820	1,420
August	73	5,890	1,460
September	63	5,370	1,260
October	48	4,340	960
November	45	4,210	900
December	40	3,830	800
Totals	628	$55,420	12,560

REQUIRED

1. Classify the cost items as variable, fixed, or semivariable costs.
2. Using the high-low method, separate semivariable costs into their variable and fixed components. Use total hours worked as a basis.
3. Compute the average cost per job for 19x9. (**Hint:** Divide 19x9's total cost for all cost items by the number of jobs completed.)

B 2. *Breakeven Analysis*
L O 6, 7
Check Figure: 1. Breakeven point: 740 systems

At the beginning of each year, the accounting department at Alder Lighting, Ltd., must find the point at which projected sales revenue will equal total budgeted variable and fixed costs. The company makes custom-made, low-voltage outdoor lighting systems. Each system sells for an average of $435. Variable costs per unit are $210. Total fixed costs for the year are estimated to be $166,500.

REQUIRED

1. Compute the breakeven point in sales units.
2. Compute the breakeven point in sales dollars.
3. Find the new breakeven point in sales units if the fixed costs should go up by $10,125.
4. Using the original figures, compute the breakeven point in sales units if the selling price decreases to $425 per unit, fixed costs go up by $15,200, and variable costs decrease by $15 per unit.

B 3. *Profit Planning:*
L O 8 *Contribution*
Margin Approach
Check Figure: 1a. Breakeven: 3,500 units

George Faber is president of the UNM Plastics Division of Land Industries. Management is considering a new product line featuring a dashing medieval knight posed on a beautiful horse. Called Chargin' Knight, this product is expected to have global market appeal and become the mascot for many high school and university athletic teams. Expected variable unit costs are as follows: direct materials, $18.50; direct labor, $4.25; production supplies, $1.10; selling costs, $2.80; and other, $1.95. The following are annual fixed costs: depreciation, building and equipment, $36,000; advertising, $45,000; and other, $11,400. Land Industries plans to sell the product for $55.00.

REQUIRED

1. Using the contribution margin approach, compute the number of products the company must sell to (a) break even and (b) earn a profit of $70,224.
2. Using the same data, compute the number of products that must be sold to earn a target profit of $139,520 if advertising costs rise by $40,000.
3. Assuming the original information and sales of 10,000 units, compute the new selling price the company must use to make a profit of $131,600.

4. According to the vice president of marketing, Wally Rice, the most optimistic annual sales estimate for the product would be 15,000 items. How much more can be spent on fixed advertising costs if the highest possible selling price the company can charge is $52.00, if the variable costs cannot be reduced, and if the target net income for 15,000 unit sales is $251,000?

B 4. *Profit Planning*
L O 7, 8
Check Figure: 2. Breakeven units: 12,000

Baker Company, a manufacturer of quality handmade pipes, has experienced a steady growth in sales over the last five years. However, increased competition has led Alice Baker, the company president, to believe that an aggressive advertising campaign will be necessary in 19x8 to maintain the company's present growth. To prepare for the 19x8 advertising campaign, the company's accountants have presented Baker with the data in the table below, based on 19x7 operations.

Variable Cost per Pipe		Annual Fixed Costs	
Direct labor	$ 8.00	Manufacturing	$ 25,000
Direct materials	3.25	Selling	40,000
Variable overhead	2.50	Administrative	70,000
	$13.75		$135,000

Sales volume in 19x7 was 20,000 units at $25 per pipe. Target sales volume for 19x8 is $550,000, or 22,000 units. Assume a 34 percent tax rate.

REQUIRED

1. Compute the 19x7 after-tax net income.
2. Compute the breakeven volume in units for 19x7.
3. Baker believes an additional selling expense of $11,250 for advertising in 19x8, with all other costs remaining constant, will be necessary to achieve the sales target. Compute the after-tax net income for 19x8, assuming the target sales volume and expenditure for advertising occur as planned.
4. Compute the breakeven volume in sales dollars for 19x8, assuming the additional $11,250 is spent for advertising.
5. If the additional $11,250 is spent for advertising in 19x8, what is the 19x8 dollar sales volume required to earn the 19x7 after-tax net income?
6. At a 19x8 sales level of 22,000 units, what is the maximum additional amount that can be spent on advertising to earn an after-tax profit of $60,000?

(CMA adapted)

B 5. *Allocation and*
L O 9, 10 *Responsibility of*
Overhead
Check Figure: 2a. Amount allocated to storage department based on square footage: $191,200

Augusta Manufacturing Company operates as a decentralized enterprise. There are seven responsibility centers in the factory area: molding, finishing, storage, receiving, shipping, scheduling, and inspection. During February, the Factory Overhead account was charged with $764,800 of indirect management-related expenses. Management wants those costs allocated to the responsibility centers. It is considering three allocation bases: square footage, total costs incurred, and labor hours. The following information was provided to support the allocation analysis.

Department	Square Footage	Total Costs Incurred	Labor Hours
Molding	7,000	$ 435,060	1,024
Finishing	5,250	188,526	3,840
Storage	8,750	72,510	896
Receiving	3,150	145,020	2,304
Shipping	1,750	217,530	1,536
Scheduling	3,500	101,514	640
Inspection	5,600	290,040	2,560
Totals	35,000	$1,450,200	12,800

REQUIRED

1. Define *responsibility accounting*.
2. Allocate the balance in the Factory Overhead account to the seven departments, using as a basis (a) square footage, (b) total costs incurred, and (c) labor hours.
3. For performance evaluation, which of the factory overhead distributions computed in **2** leads to the most effective control of costs? Defend your answer.

MANAGERIAL REPORTING AND ANALYSIS CASES

Interpreting Management Reports

MRA 1. *Cost-Volume-Profit*
L O 6, 7 *Analysis*

Check Figure: 2. Breakeven point in units: 11,475 sets

Nambe-Baca, Ltd. is an international importer-exporter of fine china. The company was formed in 1963 in Albuquerque, New Mexico. The company has distribution centers in the United States, Europe, and Australia. Although very successful in its early years, the company's profitability has steadily declined. As a member of a management team selected to gather information for the next strategic planning meeting, you are asked to review the most recent income statement for the company. Sales in 19x8 were 15,000 sets of fine china.

Nambe-Baca, Ltd.
Contribution Income Statement
For the Year Ended December 31, 19x8

Sales		$13,500,000
Less: Variable Costs		
Purchases	$6,000,000	
Distribution	2,115,000	
Sales Commissions	1,410,000	
Total Variable Costs		9,525,000
Contribution Margin		$ 3,975,000
Less: Fixed Costs		
Distribution	$ 985,000	
Selling	1,184,000	
General and Administrative	871,875	
Total Fixed Costs		3,040,875
Income Before Taxes		$ 934,125

REQUIRED

1. For each set of fine china, calculate the (a) selling price, (b) variable purchases cost, (c) variable distribution cost, (d) variable sales commission, and (e) contribution margin.
2. Calculate the breakeven point in units and in sales dollars.
3. Historically, variable costs should be about 60 percent of sales. What was the ratio of variable costs to sales for 19x8? List three actions Nambe-Baca could take to correct the difference.
4. What would have been the impact on fixed costs if Nambe-Baca had sold only 14,000 sets of fine china?

Formulating Management Reports

MRA 2. *Cost-Volume-Profit*
L O 8, 9 *Analysis*

Check Figure: 1. Income Before Taxes: $775,225

Refer to the information in MRA 1. In January 19x9, Laura Baca, president and chief executive officer, conducted a strategic planning meeting with her officers. Below is a summary of the information provided by two of the officers.

Carol Clayburn, vice president of sales: A review of the competitors indicates that the selling price of a set of china should be lowered to $890. We plan to sell 15,000 sets of fine china again in 19x9. To encourage increased sales, we should raise sales commissions to 12 percent of the selling price.

Maurice Harwood, vice president of distribution: We have signed a contract with a new shipping line for foreign shipments. We will be able to reduce the fixed distribution costs by 10 percent and reduce variable distribution costs by 4 percent.

Laura needs your help. She is concerned that the changes may not improve income before taxes sufficiently in 19x9. If income before taxes does not increase by at least 10 percent, she will want to find other ways to reduce the company's costs. Since the new year has already started and changes need to be made quickly, she requests your report within five days.

REQUIRED

1. Prepare a contribution income statement for 19x9. Your report should show the budgeted (estimated) income before taxes based on the information provided above and in MRA 1. Will the changes improve income before taxes sufficiently? Explain.
2. In preparation for writing your report, answer the following questions:
   a. Who needs the report?
   b. Why are you preparing the report?
   c. What were the sources of information for your report?
   d. When is the report due?
3. Carol recently told Laura that the company's distribution activities in Europe are generating an operating loss of $500,000. How can a responsibility accounting system help Laura examine the distribution activities?

International Company

MRA 3.
L O 5
C-V-P Analysis and Decision Making

No check figure

The *Schmidt Corporation* cuts stones used in the construction and restoration of cathedrals throughout Europe. Granite, marble, and sandstone are cut into a variety of dimensions for walls, ceilings, and floors. The German-based company has operations in Italy and Switzerland. Edgar Neuman, the controller, recently determined that the breakeven point was $325,000 in sales. In preparation for a quarterly planning meeting, Edgar must provide information for the following six proposals, which will be discussed individually by the planning team.

a. Increase the selling price of marble slabs by 10 percent.
b. Change the sales mix to respond to the increased sales demand for marble slabs. As a result, the company would increase production of marble slabs and decrease the production and sales of sandstone, the least profitable product.
c. Increase fixed production costs by $40,000 annually for the depreciation of new stone-cutting equipment.
d. Increase the variable costs by 1 percent for increased export duties on foreign sales.
e. Decrease the sales volume of the sandstone slabs because of political upheavals in eastern Europe.
f. Decrease the number of days that a customer can wait before paying without being charged interest.

REQUIRED

1. For each proposal, determine if cost-volume-profit (C-V-P) analysis would provide useful financial information.
2. Indicate whether each proposal that lends itself to C-V-P analysis would show an increase, decrease, or no impact on the profit formula. Consider each decision separately.

The Budgeting Process

1. Identify managers' needs for, and uses of, a budget.
2. State the objectives underlying the creation of a budget.
3. Define the concept of *budgetary control*.
4. Name the five groups of budgeting principles, and explain the principles in each group.
5. Identify and explain the components of a master budget.
6. Prepare a period budget.
7. Combine the information from the period budgets into a forecasted income statement.
8. State the purposes of, and prepare, a cash budget.
9. Prepare a forecasted balance sheet.

Lord Corporation[1]

DECISION POINT

Lord Corporation is a privately held, medium-sized manufacturing and research company located in Erie, Pennsylvania. The firm sells metal parts and chemical products to equipment manufacturers in aerospace, automotive, and industrial companies. The company computerized its budgeting process so that its 250 budget centers are defined according to reporting and functional responsibility. The computerized system contains the following transaction screens to help each segment's budget manager make all budgets consistent within the company.

1. An hourly personnel screen, which determines how many labor hours and how many personnel it will take to operate a department in the upcoming year.
2. A salaries detail screen, which presents a work sheet of all employees' pay and work classification data in each budget center.
3. A salaries summary and personnel head count screen, which displays a projection of labor cost based on extensions of information on the first two screens.
4. A budget screen by account, which contains projections of all budgeted accounts in each budget center.
5. A variable overhead rate screen, which is used to create the variable overhead budgets for each budget center.

Why would a company wish to computerize its budgeting process? What benefits and costs would be analyzed to support such a decision?

Speed in preparation, consistency of budget format, and reduction in errors are three primary reasons (benefits) supporting the computerization of the budgeting process. Errors made at the budget center level are compounded when combined with upper-level reporting summaries. On the cost side, the initial cost of a special computer program and hardware for all 250 budget centers was offset by the reduction in managers' time devoted to the budgeting process. With the possibility of mathematical errors eliminated, Lord Corporation found that the on-line feature of the budget system, allowing budgets prepared in outlying locations to be printed at world headquarters as soon as they were finalized, improved both the accuracy and usefulness of its planning function.

---

1. Keith C. Gourley and Thomas R. Blecki, "Computerizing Budgeting at Lord Corporation," *Management Accounting,* Institute of Management Accountants, August 1986, pp. 37–40.

MANAGERS AND THEIR BUDGETS

Budgets are synonymous with managing an organization. The term *organization* is important because budgets are used in nonprofit organizations as well as profit-oriented businesses. All types of organizations rely on plans to help them accomplish their objectives. All types of organizations have managers whose responsibilities are determined by top management or a board of directors; budgets are used to plan for and assess these areas of responsibility and to measure managers' performance. All organizations need cash to purchase resources to help accomplish their goals. Whenever cash needs to be managed and accounted for, budgets come into play. Budgets establish (1) minimum desired or target levels of cash receipts and (2) limits on the spending of cash for particular purposes. The primary difference between nonprofit and profit-oriented organizations is that a profit-oriented company sells a product or service for the purpose of making a profit. Profit-oriented companies often call their budgeting function a profit-planning activity.

The budgeting process pushes managers to take time to create strategies, targets, and goals *before* activity begins. Budget preparation helps managers focus on the next month or the entire coming year. The budgeting process forces managers to assess current operating conditions and aids in forecasting and implementing needed changes. Budget preparation is also an excellent vehicle with which to work with all supervised personnel by requesting their input and suggestions. Once developed, budgets provide operating targets for managers and their staffs. At the end of a period, the budget helps managers evaluate performance, locate problem areas and bottlenecks, and provide solutions to these problems. Budget analysis should be a regular and ongoing part of managers' duties because it helps chart the course of operations and provides a means to evaluate performance once the task has been completed. If realistic goals have been established, comparing the actual results with budgeted targets can help management assess how well the organization performed.

The budgeting process is as important in today's globally competitive operating environment as in more traditional settings. In fact, budgeting becomes even more important when just-in-time (JIT) or total quality management (TQM) concepts and techniques are applied and when computers and other electronic operating and data accumulation devices are used. In these new operating settings, actual operating data are made available quickly, and budgets are updated continuously to accommodate management's need for performance evaluation. The principles of budgeting do not change in these new environments, only the speed and timing with which they are applied.

THE BUDGETING PROCESS

Establishing an effective budgeting process is the key to a successful business venture. Without a fully coordinated budgeting system, management has only a vague idea of where the company is headed financially. An effective budgeting system can supply such information as monthly cash needs, raw materials requirements, peak labor demand seasons, and timing of capital facility expenditures. At the end of an accounting period, budgets help determine areas of strength and weakness within the company through comparisons of actual operating results with budgeted amounts. These comparisons assist managers in identifying reasons why profit expectations were or were not attained.

WHAT IS A BUDGET AND WHAT DOES IT LOOK LIKE?

OBJECTIVE

2 *State the objectives underlying the creation of a budget*

Almost everyone uses the word *budget* as if it were a cure-all for the financial problems of an enterprise. However, a budget is simply a plan, and specific management actions are needed to make it a reality. A budget is a planning document created before anticipated transactions occur. Often called a plan of action, a budget can be made up of financial data, nonfinancial operating data, or a combination of both. These data are projected for a series of events that have yet to occur. The *primary objective* of a budget is to forecast future financial and nonfinancial transactions and events.

Other misconceptions about budgets are obvious in innumerable reports on television and in newspapers regarding our federal budget and deficit spending by the federal government. The cure for this deficit spending, it is said, is to "balance the budget." This statement is misleading because spending processes alone cannot be used to balance the budget. To reduce or reverse the current deficit, one must ensure that revenues are greater than expenditures. There is only one way to operate within a balanced budget, and that is by first preparing a document in which planned revenues equal planned expenditures and then by operating within these constraints.

A budget can have an infinite number of shapes and forms. The structure depends on what is being budgeted, the size of the organization, the degree to which the budgeting process is integrated into the financial structure of the organization, and the preparer's background. Unlike the formal income statement or the balance sheet, a budget does *not* have a standard form that can be memorized. A budget can be as simple as the projected sales and costs of a corner soft drink stand or as complicated as the financial projections of Exxon Corporation or Ford Motor Company.

The actual format of the budget is developed by the budget preparer. A company may develop its own format for budgets used on a regular basis. But if a new product or service requires budget information, the document need not follow the structure or format of other budgets.

The *second objective* of a budget is to develop information that is as accurate and as meaningful to the recipient as possible. To accomplish this objective, a budget should present information in an orderly manner. Too much information clouds the meaning and accuracy of the data. Too little information may result in over- or underspending because the reader did not understand the limits suggested by the document. A budget need not contain both revenues and expenses, nor does it have to be balanced. A materials purchase/usage budget, for example, contains only projected expenditures for, and usage of, raw materials and parts. A budget can also be made up entirely of nonfinancial data, such as hours or number of units.

Exhibit 1 contains two simple budgets prepared for diverse purposes. Example A shows the revenues and expenditures budget for a homecoming football celebration; Example B contains projections of hotel occupancy for a resort. Note that in Example B, the budget contains no dollar information and is not balanced.

The examples in Exhibit 1 are for illustrative purposes only and should not be considered official guidelines. Common sense, however, suggests two very

Exhibit 1. Examples of Budgets

Example A

State University Knights
Alumni Club
Revenues and Expenditures Budget
Homecoming Activities—19x4

Budgeted Revenues		
Football Concession Sales	$32,500	
Homecoming Dance Tickets		
(1,200 at $20)	24,000	
Parking Fees	1,425	
Total Budgeted Revenues		$57,925
Budgeted Expenditures		
Dance Music Group	$ 7,500	
Hall Rental	2,000	
Refreshments	2,600	
Printing Costs	1,450	
Concession Purchases	12,200	
Clean-up Costs	4,720	
Miscellaneous	800	
Total Budgeted Expenditures		31,270
Excess of Revenues Over Expenditures*		$26,655

*To be contributed to State University's Scholarship Fund.

Example B

Scottsdale Resort
Room Occupancy Budget
For the Year Ending December 31, 19x5

	Projected Occupancy							
	Singles (50)		Doubles (80)		Mini Suites (10)		Luxury Suites (6)	
Month	Rooms	%	Rooms	%	Rooms	%	Rooms	%
January	20	40.0	30	37.5	2	20.0	1	16.7
February	24	48.0	36	45.0	3	30.0	1	16.7
March	28	56.0	42	52.5	4	40.0	2	33.3
April	32	64.0	50	62.5	5	50.0	2	33.3
May	44	88.0	60	75.0	6	60.0	2	33.3
June	46	92.0	74	92.5	7	70.0	3	50.0
July	50	100.0	78	97.5	9	90.0	4	66.7
August	50	100.0	80	100.0	10	100.0	5	83.3
September	48	96.0	78	97.5	10	100.0	6	100.0
October	34	68.0	60	75.0	8	80.0	5	83.3
November	30	60.0	46	57.5	2	20.0	3	50.0
December	34	68.0	50	62.5	4	40.0	4	66.7

basic rules to follow when presenting a budget. First, make sure you begin the document with a clearly stated title or heading that includes the time period under consideration. Second, label the budget's components, and list the unit and financial data in an orderly manner.

OBJECTIVE

3 *Define the concept of* **budgetary control**

THE NEED FOR BUDGETARY CONTROL

Planning and control of operations and related resources and their costs are the keys to good management. Profit planning is important to all successful profit-oriented companies as part of the budgeting program. The process of developing plans for a company's expected operations and controlling operations to help carry out those plans is known as budgetary control. The objectives of budgetary control are:

1. To aid in establishing procedures for preparing a company's planned revenues and costs.
2. To aid in coordinating and communicating these plans to various levels of management.
3. To formulate a basis for effective revenue and cost control.

In this chapter, we deal mainly with the planning element.

A business does not benefit from budgetary control by operating haphazardly. The company must first set quantitative goals, define the roles of individuals, and establish operating targets. Short-term or one-year plans are generally formulated in a set of period budgets (also known as detailed operating budgets). A period budget is a forecast of operating results for a segment or function of a company for a specific period of time. It is a quantitative expression of planned activities and requires timely information and careful coordination. This process converts unit sales and production forecasts into revenue and cost estimates for each of the many operating segments of the company.

Preparing period budgets requires several management accounting tools. In particular, knowledge of responsibility accounting reporting systems, cost behavior patterns, and the use of cost-volume-profit analyses help management project revenues and costs for departments or products. Profit planning, in itself, is possible only after all cost behavior patterns have been identified. These tools, together with the concepts of cost allocation and cost accumulation, provide the foundation for preparing an organization's budget.

OBJECTIVE

4 *Name the five groups of budgeting principles, and explain the principles in each group*

BASIC PRINCIPLES OF BUDGETING

The preparation of an organization's budget is important to its success for three reasons. First, preparing a budget forces management to look ahead and plan both long-range and short-range goals and events. Second, the entire management team must work together to make and carry out the plans. Third, by comparing the budget with actual results, it is possible to review performance at all levels of management. Underlying the budgeting process is a set of principles, summarized in Table 1, that provides the foundation for an effective planning function. Each group of principles will be explained further to show its connection to the entire budgeting process.

Long-Range Goals Principles Annual operating plans cannot be made unless those preparing the budget know the direction that top management expects for the organization. Long-range goals, projections covering a five- to ten-year period, must be set by top management. In doing so, management

Table 1. Principles of Effective Budgeting

Group A: Long-Range Goals Principles

1. Develop long-range goals for the organization.
2. Convert the long-range goals into statements about plans for product lines or services offered and associated profit plans in broad quantitative terms.

Group B: Short-Range Goals and Strategies Principles

3. Restate the long-range plan in terms of short-range plans for product lines or services offered and a detailed profit plan.
4. Prepare a set of budget development plans and a specific timetable for the whole period.

Group C: Human Responsibilities and Interaction Principles

5. Identify the budget director and staff.
6. Identify all participants involved in the budget development process.
7. Practice participative budgeting.
8. Obtain the full support of top management and communicate this support to budget participants.
9. Practice full communication during the entire budgeting process.

Group D: Budget Housekeeping Principles

10. Practice realism in the preparation of budgets.
11. Require that all deadlines be met.
12. Use flexible application procedures.

Group E: Budget Follow-up Principles

13. Maintain a continuous budgeting process and monitor the budget at frequent points throughout the period.
14. Develop a system of periodic performance reports that are linked to assigned responsibilities.
15. Review problem areas before further planning takes place.

should consider economic and industry forecasts, employee-management relationships, and the structure and role of management in leading the organization. The long-range goals themselves should include statements about the expected quality of products or services, percentage-of-market targets, and growth rates.

Vague aims are not sufficient. The long-term goals should set actual targets and expected timetables and name those responsible for achieving the goals. For example, assume that the Ramos Corporation has, as one of its long-term goals, the control of 15 percent of its product's market. At present the company holds only 4 percent of the market. The company's long-term goals may state that the vice president of marketing is to develop plans and strategies so that the company controls 10 percent of the market in five years and increases its share to 15 percent by the end of ten years.

Once all of the organization's goals have been developed, they should be compiled in a total long-range plan. This plan should state a spectrum of targets and goals, and it should give direction to the company's efforts to achieve those goals. The long-range plan should include future profit projections. It should spell out in general terms new product lines and services. Enlarging the scope of the company's marketplace may be a consideration.

Specific statements about long-range goals, then, are the basis for preparing the annual budget.

Short-Range Goals and Strategies Principles

With long-range goals as a basis, management prepares yearly operating plans and targets. The short-range plan or budget involves every part of the organization, and it is much more detailed than the long-range goals.

First, the long-range goals must be restated in terms of what should be accomplished during the next year. Decisions must be made about sales and profit targets by product or service line, personnel needs and expected changes, and plans for introducing new products or services. Budget statements must also cover needs for materials and supplies; labor needs; forecasts of overhead costs such as electric power, property taxes, and insurance; and all capital expenditures such as new buildings, machinery, and equipment. These short-range targets and goals form the basis for the organization's operating budget for the year.

Once management has set the short-range goals, the controller or budget director takes charge of preparing the budget. This person designs a complete set of budget development plans and a timetable with deadlines for all levels and parts of the year's operating plan. Specific people must be named to carry out each part of the budget's development and their responsibilities, targets, and deadlines must be described clearly.

Human Responsibilities and Interaction Principles

Budgeting success or failure is, in large part, determined by how well the human aspects of the process are handled. From top management down through the organization, all appropriate people must take part actively and honestly in the budgeting process. This kind of cooperation will occur only if each person realizes that he or she is important to the process. More specifically, the principles discussed below, related to responsibilities and interaction, underlie effective budgeting.

First, the selection of a budget director (and staff, if necessary) is very important to an effective budgeting system. This person must be able to communicate well with the people both above and below in the organization's hierarchy. Top management gives the budget targets and organizational goals to the budget director. He or she in turn assigns those targets and goals to managers at various levels. If the managers detect problem areas, they communicate this to the budget director, who analyzes and passes the information on to top management. The targets and goals are then reassessed, restructured, and passed back to the budget director, and the process begins all over again. In short, the budget director acts as an information-gathering center and clearing-house, coordinating all the different budgeting activities.

Second, we have mentioned that all participants in the budget development process should be identified and informed of their responsibilities. The identification process begins with high-level managers. These people must choose managers who will actually prepare the data under their supervision. Since the organization's main activities—whether they are forecasts for production, sales, health care, or employee training—take place at the lower levels, information must flow from the managers of these activities through the supervisory levels to top management. Each one of these people plays a part in developing the budget and implementing it. Effective budgeting, then, requires participative budgeting, which means that all levels of personnel take part in the budgeting process in a meaningful, active way. If every manager has significant input in setting the goals for his or her unit, then every manager will be personally motivated to ensure the success of the budgeting process.

Top management's role is also very important to the budgeting process. If targets and goals are simply dictated and sent down for implementation, participative budgeting is not being practiced. Such dictated targets are often difficult to attain and do not motivate lower-level managers to try to reach them. If top management lets the budget director handle all aspects of the process, others may feel that budgeting has a low priority and may not take it seriously. To have an effective budgeting program, top management must communicate its support and allow managers to play a meaningful role in the process.

Full communication throughout the budgeting process is our final interaction principle. In particular, the budget must be communicated clearly to the participants. After all, each participant in the budgeting process has another job in the organization. The production supervisor, for instance, is most interested in what is happening on the production floor, not in next year's activities. A key part of the budget director's job is fostering open communication, to make sure each participant knows what he or she is expected to do and when it must be done.

Budget Housekeeping Principles

Effective budgeting also requires good "housekeeping," which means that three guidelines should be followed. First, a realistic approach must be taken by the participants. Second, deadlines must be met. Third, the organization must use flexible procedures for implementing the budget.

Realism is a two-way street. Top management must first suggest attainable targets and goals. Then each manager must provide realistic information and not place departmental goals ahead of the goals of the whole organization. Inflated expenditure plans or deflated sales targets may make life easier for a manager's unit, but they can cause the entire budget to be inaccurate and difficult to use as a guide and control mechanism for the organization.

Deadlines are important because budget preparation depends on the timely cooperation of many people. If one or two people ignore a deadline for submitting information, the budget might not be ready on time. Management should communicate the importance of the timetable to all participants and should review timely submission of budget data as part of each manager's performance evaluation.

Our final principle of budget housekeeping calls for flexibility. Budgets should always be treated as guides and not as absolute truths. Budgets are important guides to the actions of management; but participants must remember that budgets are often prepared almost a year before the actual operating cycle. During that time, unexpected changes may take place. A manager cannot ignore these changes just because they were not a part of the original budget. Instead, dealing with changes in operating capacities, customer desires, and revenues and expenditures should be part of budget implementation. Each company should establish a procedure for notifying the budget director of a change and receiving approval from him or her for it. Through flexible implementation, a company can deal with change without disrupting performance.

Budget Follow-up Principles

Since the budget consists of projections and estimates, it is important that it be checked and corrected continuously. It makes more sense to correct an error than to work with an inaccurate guide.

Budget follow-up and data feedback are part of the control aspect of budgeting costs.

Organizational or departmental expectations can also be unrealistic. Such problems are detected when performance reports compare actual results with budgeted results. These reports are the backbone of the responsibility accounting system. The budgeting cycle is completed after solutions to problems are identified from the performance reports and the data are restructured to become targets or goals of the next budgeting cycle.

BUSINESS BULLETIN: BUSINESS PRACTICE

Professor Kenneth Merchant has conducted research on the behavioral effects challenging but achievable profit budget targets have on managers. The respondents to the study identified the following advantages of using highly achievable profit budget targets.

1. Managers' commitment to achieve the budgeted targets is increased.
2. Managers' confidence remains high.
3. Organizational control costs decrease.
4. The risk of managers engaging in harmful earnings management practices (manipulation) is reduced.
5. Effective managers are allowed greater operating flexibility.
6. The corporation is somewhat protected against the costs of optimistic projections.
7. The predictability of corporate earnings is increased.[2]

There are risks, too. Of primary concern is that managers may not be challenged to perform at their top levels if budgeted profit targets are perceived to be too high.

THE MASTER BUDGET

A master budget is a set of period budgets that have been consolidated into forecasted financial statements for the entire company. Each period budget supplies the projected costs and revenues for a part of the company. When combined, these budgets show all anticipated transactions of the company for a future accounting period. With this information, the anticipated results of the company's operations can be put together with the beginning general ledger balances to prepare forecasted statements of the company's net income and financial position.

---

2. Kenneth A. Merchant, "How Challenging Should Profit Budget Targets Be?" *Management Accounting*, Institute of Management Accountants, November 1990, pp. 46–48.

Three steps lead up to the completed master budget. They are: (1) The period budgets are prepared. (2) The forecasted income statement is prepared. (3) The forecasted balance sheet is prepared. After describing each of these components and illustrating the types of period budgets, we will show how the budgets are prepared.

DETAILED PERIOD BUDGETS

Period budgets generally are prepared for each departmental or functional segment that produces costs and revenues. Data usually are developed and transmitted to the budget director in departmental form; then they are consolidated into the following functional budgets: (1) sales budget (in units and dollars), (2) selling cost budget, (3) production budget (in units), (4) materials purchase/usage budget (in units and dollars), (5) labor budget (in hours and dollars), (6) factory overhead budget, (7) general and administrative (G&A) expense budget, and (8) capital expenditures budget.

To facilitate your understanding of the budget development process, we now introduce the Taylor Piano Company. The company assembles and sells three piano models. As each part of the master budget is discussed, the comparable budget for the Taylor Piano Company will be created. When all of the company's period budgets have been developed, we will complete the master budget process by putting together the company's forecasted income statement and balance sheet. The company's beginning balance sheet on January 1, 19x8, is shown in Exhibit 2. You will note that there is no balance in Work in Process Inventory at year end. The reason is that the company follows a policy of closing the plant for two weeks during the year-end holidays, and all units in process are completed before the break begins. The Materials Inventory balance is comprised of the materials and parts needed for January 19x8 operations. The company always purchases materials and parts one month in advance. Finished Goods Inventory contains five units of each of the three models, a level that the company tries to maintain. Costs flow through inventory on a FIFO basis.

Sales Budget   The unit sales forecast is the starting point of the budgeting process and probably the most critical component. The company's sales target is developed by top management with input from the marketing and production areas. This forecast provides the basis for the entire cost portion of the master budget.

A sales budget is a detailed plan, expressed in both units and dollars, that identifies expected product (or service) sales for a future period. A sales budget for the Taylor Piano Company is shown in Exhibit 3. Sales information for the three piano models is stated in both units and dollar revenue amounts for the year under review. In addition, unit and dollar information for the current year is shown for comparison. Once the unit sales target has been agreed upon, all of the other period budgets can be prepared.

Selling Cost Budget   Information from the sales budget and the sales staff provides the basis for the selling cost budget. This budget details all anticipated costs related to the selling function of the business for a future period. Selling costs may be variable, such as sales commissions and automobile costs, or they may be fixed, such as advertising costs and supervisory

Exhibit 2. Beginning Balance Sheet

Taylor Piano Company
Balance Sheet
January 1, 19x8

Assets

Current Assets			
Cash		$ 27,440	
Accounts Receivable		28,800	
Materials Inventory		23,259	
Work in Process Inventory		0	
Finished Goods Inventory		27,990	
Total Current Assets			$107,489
Property, Plant, and Equipment			
Land		$ 50,000	
Plant and Equipment	$260,000		
Less Accumulated Depreciation	45,200	214,800	
Total Property, Plant, and Equipment			264,800
Total Assets			$372,289

Liabilities and Stockholders' Equity

Current Liabilities			
Accounts Payable		$ 23,259	
Income Taxes Payable		11,430	
Total Current Liabilities			$ 34,689
Long-Term Liabilities			
Notes Payable			70,000
Total Liabilities			$104,689
Stockholders' Equity			
Common Stock		$200,000	
Retained Earnings		67,600	
Total Stockholders' Equity			267,600
Total Liabilities and Stockholders' Equity			$372,289

salaries. The selling cost budget is the responsibility of the sales department and can be prepared as soon as the sales budget has been completed.

The selling cost budget for the Taylor Piano Company is shown in Exhibit 4. Two major cost categories are used: Selling Commissions, which are 5 percent of sales; and Travel Expenses, Brochures, and Other Selling Support Materials, which are 3 percent of sales. Every company will have its own approach to developing the selling cost budget, so understand that these cost categories are unique to the Taylor Piano Company.

Exhibit 3. Sales Budget

Taylor Piano Company
Sales Budget
For the Year Ended December 31, 19x7 and the Year Ending December 31, 19x8

Units

	Actual Results For the Year Ended December 31, 19x7		Budgeted Results For the Year Ended December 31, 19x8	
	Units	Selling Price	Units	Selling Price
Piano Models				
Model J–12	70	$1,800	75	$1,840
Model E–23	40	1,940	50	1,990
Model N–45	100	3,400	120	3,600

Total Revenue

	Actual Sales	Percent of Total Sales	Budgeted Sales	Percent of Total Sales
Piano Models				
Model J–12	$126,000*	23.18%	$138,000	20.61%
Model E–23	77,600	14.28%	99,500	14.86%
Model N–45	340,000	62.55%	432,000	64.53%
Totals	$543,600	100.00%**	$669,500	100.00%

*Computed by multiplying the number of units by the selling price per unit:
70 units $\times$ $1,800 = $126,000.
**Rounded.

Production Budget   Once the sales target in units has been established, the units needed from the production area (production budget) can be computed. The production budget is a detailed schedule that identifies the products or services that must be produced or provided to meet budgeted sales and inventory needs. Management must first determine if the finished goods inventory level should remain the same or be increased or decreased. The unit sales forecast, along with the desired changes in finished goods inventory, is then used to determine the unit production schedule.

Exhibit 5 illustrates the production budget for the Taylor Piano Company. In addition to quarterly and annual production schedules, it shows a detailed view of the production schedules for the first three months of the budgeted year. Projected unit production for January 19x9 is also included so that the December 19x8 purchases can be computed.

Materials Purchase/Usage Budget   The production budget and anticipated changes in materials inventory levels determine materials usage. This information will generate the units of materials to be purchased. Multiplying

Exhibit 4. Selling Cost Budget

Taylor Piano Company
Selling Cost Budget
For the Year Ending December 31, 19x8

	January	February	March	April–December	Totals
Selling Commissions (5% of Sales)					
Piano Models					
Model J–12	$ 552*	$ 828	$ 460	$ 5,060	$ 6,900
Model E–23	398	597	199	3,781	4,975
Model N–45	2,700	1,440	2,160	15,300	21,600
Totals	$3,650	$2,865	$2,819	$24,141	$33,475
Travel Expenses, Brochures, and Other Selling Support Materials (3% of Sales)					
Piano Models					
Model J–12	$ 331	$ 497	$ 276	$ 3,036	$ 4,140
Model E–23	239	358	119	2,269	2,985
Model N–45	1,620	864	1,296	9,180	12,960
Totals	$2,190	$1,719	$1,691	$14,485	$20,085

Note: All amounts are rounded to the nearest dollar. Because of no changes in inventoried units, sales units are the same as production units in Exhibit 5. The selling prices of the units are found in Exhibit 3.

*Computed by multiplying the number of sales units (see *Note* above) by the selling price per unit by the selling commission:
6 units × $1,840 per unit × 5% = $552.

the number of units to be purchased by the estimated purchase prices for those materials will yield the materials purchase budget. The statement of materials purchase and usage needs can be given in separate schedules or in the same document. We prefer to group these two categories in the same document. Thus, a materials purchase/usage budget is a detailed plan that identifies the numbers and timing of raw materials and parts to be purchased and used to meet production demands. (A merchandise purchasing budget is a similar document used by retail businesses.) The materials purchase/usage budget for the Taylor Piano Company is developed in the illustrative problem at the end of this section.

Labor Budget The labor budget identifies the labor needs for a future period and the labor costs associated with those needs. Like plans for materials purchase and usage, the forecasted labor hours and dollars can be structured in separate schedules or in one comprehensive schedule. Labor hours can be determined as soon as the unit production budget has been set.

Exhibit 5. Production Budget

Taylor Piano Company
Production Budget
For the Year Ending December 31, 19x8

Production Schedule

Piano Models	First Quarter	Second Quarter	Third Quarter	Fourth Quarter	19x8 Totals	Projected Production for January 19x9
Model J–12	20	16	22	17	75*	7
Model E–23	12	10	15	13	50	5
Model N–45	35	25	20	40	120	18
Totals	67	51	57	70	245	30

Detailed Production Schedule for First Quarter of 19x8 and
Projected Production for January 19x9

	First Quarter 19x8			Total Production for First Quarter
	January	February	March	
Piano Models				
Model J–12	6	9	5	20
Model E–23	4	6	2	12
Model N–45	15	8	12	35
Totals	25	23	19	67

*Taylor Piano Company follows a policy of minimizing finished goods inventory and maintains a five-unit stock of each model in inventory for unexpected customer demand. Therefore, changes in finished goods inventory do not affect the budgeted production numbers. Unit production plans equal projected sales amounts. The cost of finished goods inventory will change as production costs change.

Multiplying labor hours needed per unit by the anticipated units of production gives the labor hour requirements for the budget period. These labor hours, when multiplied by the various hourly labor rates, yield the labor dollar budget.

As shown for the Taylor Piano Company in Exhibit 6, quarterly and annual data can be summarized in the labor budget. First the labor hours per unit and the labor rate per hour for each operation are identified. The total labor cost per model is then computed by multiplying the rates times the hours for each operation and adding the three amounts. To compute the labor budget, the labor cost per unit is multiplied by the units for each model from the production budget. Some companies prefer to prepare a separate budget for direct labor only and to account for indirect labor only in the factory overhead budget. Because Taylor's production manager prefers to have all labor shown in the labor budget, indirect labor costs are included here as well as in the factory overhead budget.

Exhibit 6. Labor Budget

Taylor Piano Company
Labor Budget
For the Year Ending December 31, 19x8

Direct Labor Hours and Rate Schedule

	Sound System Assembly		Wood Cabinet Assembly		Final Piano Assembly		Total Direct Labor Cost per Model
	Hours per Unit	Rate	Hours per Unit	Rate	Hours per Unit	Rate	
Piano Models							
Model J–12	5.6	$10.50	5.8	$11.50	12.8	$12.50	$285.50
Model E–23	6.2	10.50	6.0	11.50	13.6	12.50	304.10
Model N–45	8.2	10.50	7.4	11.50	22.4	12.50	451.20

Direct Labor Budget

	First Quarter	Second Quarter	Third Quarter	Fourth Quarter	Totals
Piano Models					
Model J–12	$ 5,710*	$ 4,568	$ 6,281	$ 4,854	$ 21,413
Model E–23	3,649	3,041	4,562	3,953	15,205
Model N–45	15,792	11,280	9,024	18,048	54,144
Total direct labor	$25,151	$18,889	$19,867	$26,855	$ 90,762
Budgeted Indirect Labor (50% of direct labor)	12,576	9,445	9,933	13,427	45,381
Total Labor Budget	$37,727	$28,334	$29,800	$40,282	$136,143

Note: Totals may vary because of rounding.

*Computed by multiplying the number of pianos to be produced from the production budget by the total labor cost per model from the three assembly operations: 20 units × $285.50 = $5,710.

Factory Overhead Budget   The factory overhead budget is a detailed schedule of anticipated manufacturing costs, other than direct materials and direct labor costs, that must be incurred to meet the production expectations of a future period. The budget for factory overhead has two purposes: (1) to integrate the overhead cost budgets developed by the managers of production and service departments; and (2) by accumulating this information, to compute factory overhead rates for the forthcoming accounting period.

The Taylor Piano Company's factory overhead budget is illustrated in Exhibit 7, and again, shows quarterly as well as annual forecasts. Data from each of the three assembly operations (Sound System Assembly, Wood Cabinet Assembly, and Final Piano Assembly) are combined in the budget shown. A more detailed breakdown of this information, which may be needed to help control costs, can be supplied later. The year's predetermined factory overhead rate is computed at the bottom of Exhibit 7. The projected overhead costs of $224,914 come from this exhibit. The projected direct labor

Exhibit 7. Factory Overhead Budget

Taylor Piano Company
Factory Overhead Budget
For the Year Ending December 31, 19x8

	First Quarter	Second Quarter	Third Quarter	Fourth Quarter	Totals
Factory Overhead Costs:*					
Indirect Materials and Supplies	$ 5,847	$ 4,330	$ 4,258	$ 6,370	$ 20,805
Indirect Labor	12,576	9,445	9,933	13,427	45,381
Employee Benefits	7,545	5,667	5,960	8,056	27,228
Factory Supervision	15,000	15,000	15,000	15,000	60,000
Utilities	2,880	3,000	3,050	3,150	12,080
Small Tools	1,200	1,200	1,200	1,200	4,800
Insurance and Property Taxes	1,080	1,080	3,180	3,180	8,520
Depreciation, Plant and Machinery	5,100	5,100	5,100	5,100	20,400
Machinery Rentals	3,000	3,000	3,000	3,000	12,000
Repairs and Maintenance	3,300	3,400	3,500	3,500	13,700
Totals	$57,528	$51,222	$54,181	$61,983	$224,914

*The amounts in the factory overhead budget were derived from several sources.
   Indirect materials and supplies: percentage of materials used
   Indirect labor: the labor budget
   Employee benefits: percentage of total labor costs
   The remainder of the items are cumulative totals from managers in the factory and are based on estimates using the results of the previous year.

Predetermined Factory Overhead Rate for 19x8:

$$\text{Rate} = \frac{\text{Projected Overhead Costs}}{\text{Projected Direct Labor Dollars}} = \frac{\$224,914}{\$90,762} = \$2.478 \text{ per direct labor dollar}$$

dollars come from Exhibit 6. The factory overhead rate for 19x8 is $2.478 per direct labor dollar.

General and Administrative Expense Budget   A general and administrative (G&A) expense budget is a detailed plan of operating expenses, other than those of the manufacturing and selling functions, needed to support the overall operations of the business for a future period. In preparing a master budget, general and administrative expenses must be projected to provide information included in the cash budget (which is discussed later in this chapter). The G&A expense budget also serves as a means of controlling these costs. Many elements of this budget are fixed costs. General and administrative expenses for Taylor Piano Company for 19x8 are projected as follows. These expenses will be paid in the month incurred.

January	$ 6,063
February	5,159
March	5,290
April–December	46,540
Total	$63,052

Capital Expenditures Budget

A capital expenditures budget is a detailed plan outlining the amount and timing of anticipated capital expenditures for a future period. Information regarding capital facility investment could influence the cash budget, the interest expense on the forecasted income statement, and the plant and equipment account balance on the forecasted balance sheet. Therefore, these decisions must be anticipated and integrated into the master budget.

During 19x8, Taylor Piano Company plans to purchase a second piano cabinet assembly layout for model N–45. The total cost is expected to be $30,000, payable $15,000 in February at the time the order is placed, and $15,000 when the equipment is received in May.

Relationships Among the Period Budgets

From our discussion, it should be apparent that the period budgets are closely related to each other. The sales unit forecast is the first step in the budgeting process. Once it is completed, the selling cost budget can be prepared. The production budget also depends on the sales forecast. The production budget in turn provides information regarding requirements for direct materials purchases and usage, as well as information for the labor and factory overhead budgets. In most cases, plans for general and administrative expenses and capital expenditures are made by top management, although much of this information may be gathered at the departmental level and included in the period budgets.

Figure 1 shows how the period budgets fit into the process of preparing a master budget. The key point to remember is that the whole budgeting process begins with the sales unit forecast. The following illustrative problem takes you step by step through the preparation of one of the detailed period budgets—the materials purchase/usage budget. We will then follow with the development of the forecasted income statement, the cash budget, and finally the forecasted balance sheet for Taylor Piano Company.

BUSINESS BULLETIN: INTERNATIONAL PRACTICE

Christina Simons, managing director of Simons Communications in the United Kingdom, started a new public relations company called the Journalism Training Centre, in February 1993. Based on what she thought was a carefully constructed budget totaling £80,000, she applied for and received a £20,000 loan from Lloyds Bank. Soon after the loan was approved, she began to experience unexpected costs in addition to those planned and covered by the loan. These unexpected costs included bank loan fees, a computer maintenance contract, an extra up-front lease payment on the copier, installation of more powerful electrical outlets, a large rent deposit, costs for security alarms and sensors, and telecommunications installation costs. Total hidden costs amounted to £20,688 or over 25 percent of the budgeted start-up costs.[3] What can we learn from Ms. Simons's experience? Budgeting is a serious

3. Steven Sonsino, "Expect the Unexpected—Hidden Costs Can Mean the Difference Between Success and Failure," *Financial Times,* September 6, 1994, p. 10.

Figure 1. Preparation of a Master Budget

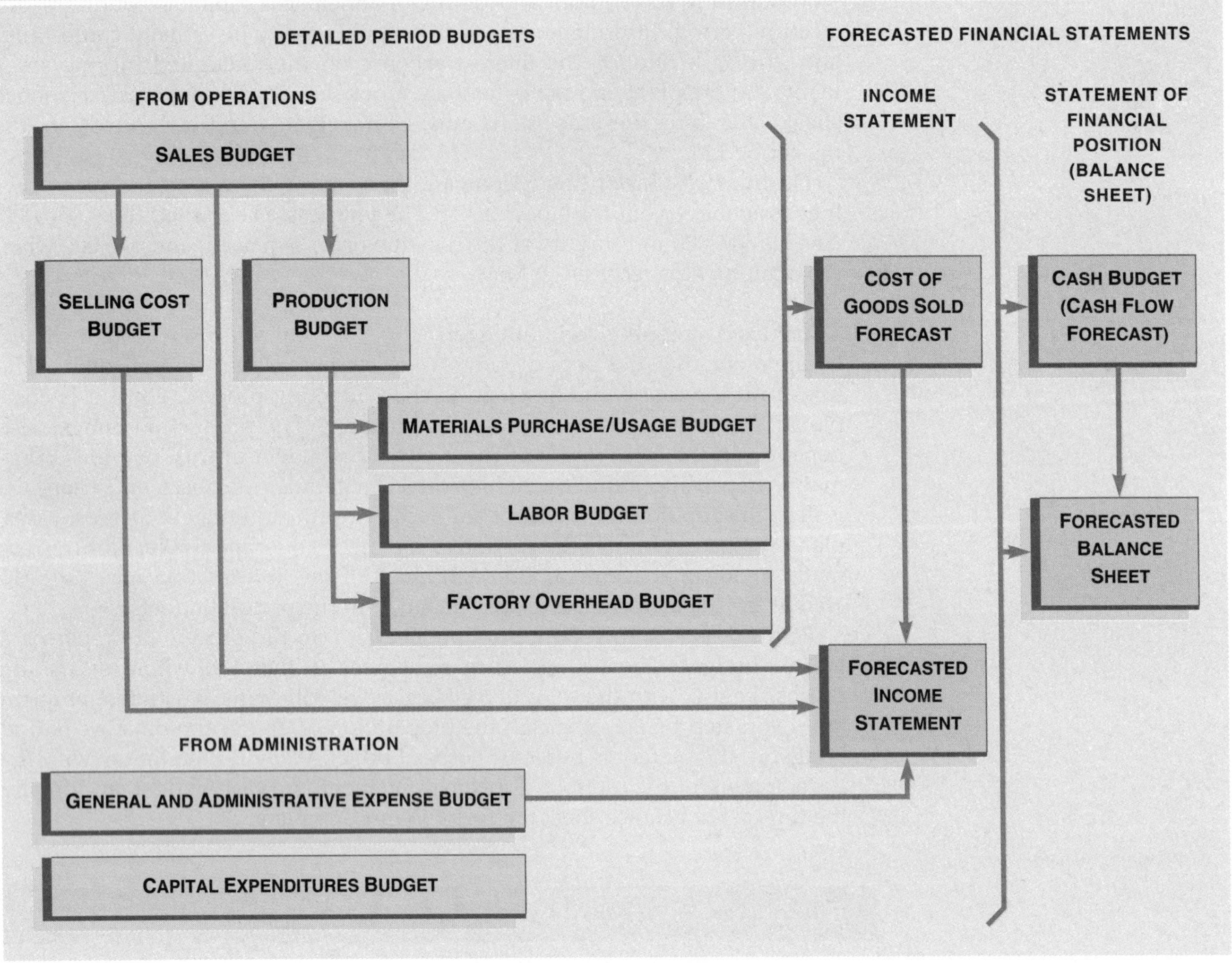

DETAILED PERIOD BUDGETS   FORECASTED FINANCIAL STATEMENTS

FROM OPERATIONS

| SALES BUDGET |

INCOME STATEMENT

STATEMENT OF FINANCIAL POSITION (BALANCE SHEET)

| SELLING COST BUDGET | | PRODUCTION BUDGET |

| COST OF GOODS SOLD FORECAST | | CASH BUDGET (CASH FLOW FORECAST) |

| MATERIALS PURCHASE/USAGE BUDGET |

| LABOR BUDGET |

| FORECASTED BALANCE SHEET |

| FACTORY OVERHEAD BUDGET |

| FORECASTED INCOME STATEMENT |

FROM ADMINISTRATION

| GENERAL AND ADMINISTRATIVE EXPENSE BUDGET |

| CAPITAL EXPENDITURES BUDGET |

endeavor and should be researched carefully. Ask questions to determine if all costs have been included. Contact people with recent, similar experiences of starting a new business to find out about possible hidden costs. In most cases, it is better to overbudget than to find that you have run out of funds before you have accomplished your objective. ▬▬▬

ILLUSTRATIVE PROBLEM:
PERIOD BUDGET PREPARATION

OBJECTIVE

6 *Prepare a period budget*

Procedures for preparing period budgets and building a master budget vary from one company to another. Since it is impossible to cover all procedures found in actual practice, the following problem illustrates one approach to preparing a period budget. Remember that by applying the tools of cost behavior and C-V-P analysis, and by working with a particular product costing method, you can prepare any kind of budget. We have already stated that there is no standard format to use for budget preparation; your only guidelines are that the budget be clear and understandable and that it communicate the intended information to the reader.

Continuing with the Taylor Piano Company example, we will develop the materials purchase/usage budget for the year ending December 31, 19x8. The company assembles and sells three piano models, each with a different quality level and market segment. The price of the purchased parts varies according to the model's quality level, and all materials and parts are purchased from outside vendors. The amounts of materials and parts to be purchased and used are derived from data found in the production budget. The company purchases such items monthly and attempts to limit its materials inventory to the monthly amounts. A list of parts needed for each of the three assembly operations, along with purchase prices applicable to both 19x7 and 19x8 follows.

Parts Listing and Related Costs per Piano	Model J–12	Model E–23	Model N–45
Sound System Assembly			
Wire strings	$ 14	$ 16	$ 37
Keyboard assembly	47	52	123
Sound chamber	94	103	245
Wire adjusters/connectors	9	10	25
Wood Cabinet Assembly			
Piano body	118	130	305
Keyboard frame	37	42	98
Top, including brace	56	62	147
Leg sets (3 per set)	42	47	110
Final Piano Assembly			
Fastener set	8	9	22
Varnishes	28	31	74
Wheel sets (3 per set)	15	17	39
	$468	$519	$1,225

REQUIRED

1. Prepare an analysis of Materials Inventory balances and makeup at December 31, 19x7 and December 31, 19x8.
2. Prepare a materials purchase/usage budget for 19x8.

SOLUTION

1. Exhibit 8 contains an analysis of the ending Materials Inventory balances for 19x7 and 19x8. These balances, which are relevant to the preparation of the materials purchase/usage budget, are used to convert projected materials usage figures to materials purchase amounts. That computation is illustrated in Exhibit 9.

Since the company follows a policy of stocking materials and parts for the subsequent month's production levels, December items in ending Materials Inventory will equal the January production needs. According to the production plans shown in Exhibit 5, in January 19x8, the company plans to produce 6, 4, and 15 units of Models J–12, E–23, and N–45, respectively. December 19x7 materials and parts inventory levels must reflect these plans. Similarly, January 19x9 production estimates are used to purchase the materials and parts on hand at the end of 19x8. These inventory amounts are described in Exhibit 8.

Exhibit 8. Analysis of Materials Inventory Balances

Taylor Piano Company
Materials Inventory
At December 31, 19x7 and December 31, 19x8

	Unit Costs			Model J-12		Model E-23		Model N-45		Total December Purchases and Year-End Materials Inventory Balances	
	J-12	E-23	N-45	December 19x7	December 19x8	December 19x7	December 19x8	December 19x7	December 19x8	December 19x7	December 19x8
Number of Units to Be Assembled in the Following Month				6	7	4	5	15	18		
Sound System Assembly											
Wire strings	$ 14	$ 16	$ 37	$ 84*	$ 98	$ 64	$ 80	$ 555	$ 666	$ 703	$ 844
Keyboard assembly	47	52	123	282	329	208	260	1,845	2,214	2,335	2,803
Sound chamber	94	103	245	564	658	412	515	3,675	4,410	4,651	5,583
Wire adjusters/ connectors	9	10	25	54	63	40	50	375	450	469	563
Wood Cabinet Assembly											
Piano body	118	130	305	708	826	520	650	4,575	5,490	5,803	6,966
Keyboard frame	37	42	98	222	259	168	210	1,470	1,764	1,860	2,233
Top, including brace	56	62	147	336	392	248	310	2,205	2,646	2,789	3,348
Leg sets (3 per set)	42	47	110	252	294	188	235	1,650	1,980	2,090	2,509
Final Piano Assembly											
Fastener set	8	9	22	48	56	36	45	330	396	414	497
Varnishes	28	31	74	168	196	124	155	1,110	1,332	1,402	1,683
Wheel sets (3 per set)	15	17	39	90	105	68	85	585	702	743	892
	$468	$519	$1,225	$2,808	$3,276	$2,076	$2,595	$18,375	$22,050	$23,259	$27,921

Note: Materials and parts purchased in December make up the ending balance in the Materials Inventory account.

*Computed by multiplying the number of units to be assembled in the month following December 19x7 by the cost per wire string set shown in the list of parts and related costs: 6 units × $14 = $84.

Exhibit 9. Materials Purchase/Usage Budget

Taylor Piano Company
Materials Purchase/Usage Budget
For the Year Ending December 31, 19x8

	Unit Costs			Model J-12		Model E-23		Model N-45		Total Budget	
	J-12	E-23	N-45	First Quarter	All of 19x8	First Quarter	All of 19x8	First Quarter	All of 19x8	First Quarter	All of 19x8
Number of Units to Be Produced				20	75	12	50	35	120	67	245
Sound System Assembly											
Wire strings	$ 14	$ 16	$ 37	$ 280*	$ 1,050	$ 192	$ 800	$ 1,295	$ 4,440	$ 1,767	$ 6,290
Keyboard assembly	47	52	123	940	3,525	624	2,600	4,305	14,760	5,869	20,885
Sound chamber	94	103	245	1,880	7,050	1,236	5,150	8,575	29,400	11,691	41,600
Wire adjusters/connectors	9	10	25	180	675	120	500	875	3,000	1,175	4,175
Wood Cabinet Assembly											
Piano body	118	130	305	2,360	8,850	1,560	6,500	10,675	36,600	14,595	51,950
Keyboard frame	37	42	98	740	2,775	504	2,100	3,430	11,760	4,674	16,635
Top, including brace	56	62	147	1,120	4,200	744	3,100	5,145	17,640	7,009	24,940
Leg sets (3 per set)	42	47	110	840	3,150	564	2,350	3,850	13,200	5,254	18,700
Final Piano Assembly											
Fastener set	8	9	22	160	600	108	450	770	2,640	1,038	3,690
Varnishes	28	31	74	560	2,100	372	1,550	2,590	8,880	3,522	12,530
Wheel sets (3 per set)	15	17	39	300	1,125	204	850	1,365	4,680	1,869	6,655
Total Direct Materials and Parts to Be Used in 19x8				$9,360	$35,100	$6,228	$25,950	$42,875	$147,000	$58,463	$208,050
Deduct Materials and Parts Purchased in December 19x7					2,808		2,076		18,375		23,259
Add Materials and Parts Purchased in December 19x8					3,276		2,595		22,050		27,921
Total Direct Materials and Parts to Be Purchased in 19x8					$35,568		$26,469		$150,675		$212,712

*Computed by multiplying the number of units to be produced in the first quarter by the cost per wire string set shown on the schedule of parts listing and related costs: 20 units × $14 = $280.

2. The materials purchase/usage budget for the Taylor Piano Company for the year ending December 31, 19x8 is shown in Exhibit 9. The units to be produced for the year and the first quarter were taken from the production budget in Exhibit 5. Each dollar amount is computed by multiplying the units by the costs per item or set described previously. The company anticipates spending $208,050 on materials and parts to produce 245 pianos during 19x8, and $58,463 will be needed to pay for the first quarter's usage.

THE FORECASTED INCOME STATEMENT

OBJECTIVE

7 *Combine the information from the period budgets into a forecasted income statement*

Once the period budgets have been prepared, the budget director or the company controller can prepare the forecasted income statement for the period. A forecasted income statement projects the amount of revenues that will be earned and the expenses that will be incurred by a business for a future period. Information about projected sales and costs come from several period budgets. Taylor Piano Company's forecasted income statement for 19x8 is shown in Exhibit 10. Note that the sources of each element of the statement are identified on the right side of the exhibit so you can trace the development of the income statement from the budgets and schedules involved. The cost of goods manufactured is computed in a separate schedule at the bottom of Exhibit 10.

The only amount on the income statement that cannot be found on other exhibits or described thus far in the text is the Finished Goods Inventory at December 31, 19x8. The following analysis provides that information.

Computation of Finished Goods Inventory Balances

	J–12		E–23		N–45	
	19x7	19x8	19x7	19x8	19x7	19x8
Total Cost of Each Model						
Materials	$ 468	$ 468	$ 519	$ 519	$1,225	$1,225
Labor	273	286	291	304	432	451
Factory Overhead	655	709	698	753	1,037	1,118
Totals	$1,396	$1,463	$1,508	$1,576	$2,694	$2,794

Finished Goods Inventory

19x7
J–12	5 × $1,396 =	$ 6,980
E–23	5 × $1,508 =	7,540
N–45	5 × $2,694 =	13,470
Total		$27,990

19x8
J–12	5 × $1,463 =	$ 7,315
E–23	5 × $1,576 =	7,880
N–45	5 × $2,794 =	13,970
Total		$29,165

Exhibit 10. Forecasted Income Statement

Taylor Piano Company
Forecasted Income Statement
For the Year Ending December 31, 19x8

			Source of Data
Net Sales		$669,500	Exhibit 3
Cost of Goods Sold			
Finished Goods Inventory, Jan. 1, 19x8	$ 27,990		Exhibit 2
Cost of Goods Manufactured	523,726		Analysis below
Total Cost of Goods Available for Sale	$551,716		
Less Finished Goods Inventory, Dec. 31, 19x8	29,165		From chapter
Cost of Goods Sold		522,551	
Gross Margin		$146,949	
Operating Expenses			
Selling Commissions	$33,475		Exhibit 4
Other Selling Expenses	20,085		Exhibit 4
General and Administrative Expenses	63,052		From chapter
Total Operating Expenses		116,612	
Income from Operations		$ 30,337	
Less Interest Expense		5,600	8% of $70,000
Income Before Income Taxes		$ 24,737	(See cash budget)
Less Income Taxes Expense (35%)		8,658	
Projected Net Income		$ 16,079	
Cost of Goods Manufactured:			
Materials Used			
Materials Inventory, Jan. 1, 19x8	$ 23,259		Exhibit 2
Purchases for 19x8	212,712		Exhibit 9
Cost of Materials Available for Use	$235,971		
Less Materials Inventory, Dec. 31, 19x8	27,921		Exhibit 8
Cost of Materials Used During 19x8		$208,050	
Direct Labor Costs		90,762	Exhibit 6
Factory Overhead Costs		224,914	Exhibit 7
Total Manufacturing Costs and			
Cost of Goods Manufactured*		$523,726	

*It is company policy to have no units in process at year end.

The process of developing the forecasted income statement follows the process diagrammed in Figure 1. To fully understand the steps taken to develop the forecasted income statement, compare the sources listed on the right side of Exhibit 10 with the diagram in Figure 1.

Cardinal Industries, Inc.[4]

Cardinal Industries, Inc. is a privately held manufacturing company and the nation's largest manufacturer of modular shelter products. Founded in 1954, its headquarters is in Columbus, Ohio, and its manufacturing facilities are located in Atlanta, Orlando, Baltimore, Dallas, and Columbus. The company also owns and operates a motel chain, six retirement villages, apartments, single-family homes, student housing, office buildings, and rehabilitation centers located in eighteen states. Thus, although Cardinal Industries operates primarily as a manufacturer, it also serves as a construction company, mortgage financier, securities broker, real estate developer, landscape designer, and property manager.

The company grew rapidly and in many areas simultaneously. Cash budgeting was a sideline function, updated monthly at the division level. Each geographic location utilized up to four different banks and no use was made of the banks' daily balance reporting services. When an account was budgeted to be low, loans were made at the individual location. The divisions reported effective cash budgeting because low cash situations were always covered by immediate credit line transactions. But management began to be concerned about the way cash was managed. Should the company change its approach to cash management? What is wrong with the present system? What suggestions would you make to improve cash management at Cardinal Industries, Inc.?

The company decided to centralize its cash management. Instead of doing business with twenty banks at five locations, the company used only six banks. Five regional banks were selected to handle all receipts from each bank's particular region. One main bank was chosen to transact all company disbursements, and money was transferred from the location banks to the main bank daily. The need for short-term loans to cover cash shortfalls disappeared. Net annual savings from this shift in cash management was over $2 million per year. :::::

CASH BUDGETING

OBJECTIVE

8 *State the purposes of, and prepare, a cash budget*

Cash flow is one of the most important aspects of a company's operating cycle. Without cash, a business cannot function. But if cash balances are very large, funds may not earn the best possible rate of return. Low cash reserves, however, may indicate that the company cannot pay current liabilities. To prevent either of these problems, careful cash planning is necessary. The cash budget is the essential tool for this planning.

---

4. Royce L. Gentzel and Mary Ann Swepston, "The Cardinal Difference in Cash Management," *Management Accounting*, Institute of Management Accountants, February 1988, pp. 43–47.

A cash budget (or cash flow forecast) is a projection of the cash receipts and cash payments for a future period. It summarizes the cash flow results of planned transactions in all phases of a master budget. Generally, a cash budget shows the company's projected ending cash balance and the cash position for each month of the year.

The cash budget serves two purposes. First, it provides the ending cash balance for the period, which is needed to complete the forecasted balance sheet in the master budget (see Figure 1). Thus, the cash budget holds a key position in the master budget preparation cycle. Second, the cash budget highlights periods of excess cash reserves or cash shortages. As a result, the budget director can advise financial executives of times when the company will need extra short-term financing because of cash shortages, and times when it will have excess cash available for short-term investments.

THE ELEMENTS OF A CASH BUDGET

The cash budget is developed after all period budgets are final and the forecasted income statement is complete. It combines information from several period budgets and brings together all elements of cash flow, both inflows (receipts) and outflows (payments). Since the master budget summarizes the expected transactions for a future period, it also includes expected cash transactions. To prepare the cash budget, then, one must analyze the master budget in terms of cash inflows and outflows.

The person preparing the cash budget must also know how the direct materials, labor, and other goods and services are going to be purchased. That is, will they be paid for immediately with cash, or will they be purchased on account, with the cash payment delayed for a time? Besides regular operating costs, cash is also used to buy equipment and pay off loans and other long-term liabilities. All of this information must be available before an accurate cash budget can be prepared.

The elements of a cash budget, examples of the cash receipts and cash payments, and their relationships with the master budget are depicted in Table 2. Cash receipts information comes from several sources, including the sales budget, cash collection records and trends, the forecasted income statement, and the cash budgets of previous periods. Monthly sales on account must be converted to monthly cash flows before being entered in the cash budget.

Cash payment data are found by analyzing the period budgets supporting the master budget. Cash payment policies are also important. If the company holds all invoices for thirty days, the cash outflow for such items as the purchases of materials and supplies will lag the budgeted usage by a month. Cash payments information is found in the materials purchase/usage budget, factory overhead budget, labor budget, selling cost budget, general and administrative expense budget, capital expenditures budget, previous year's balance sheet (income tax payments), loan records, and forecasted income statement. Each must be reviewed thoroughly to ensure that all cash payments have been included in the cash budget.

PREPARING A CASH BUDGET

The cash budget for the Taylor Piano Company for the year ending December 31, 19x8 is shown in Exhibit 11. Detailed cash inflows and outflows are presented for January, February, and March; the remaining nine months of the year are combined. It is good practice to continually update the cash budget

Table 2. Master Budget and Cash Budget Interrelationships

Elements of the Cash Budget	Sources of the Information
Cash Receipts	
Cash sales	Sales budget (cash sales)
Cash collections of previous sales	Sales budget (credit sales) plus collection records—percent collected in the first month, second month, etc.
Proceeds from sale of assets	Forecasted income statement and capital expenditures budget
Loan proceeds	Previous month's information on cash budget
Cash Payments	
Direct materials	Materials purchase/usage budget
Operating supplies	Factory overhead budget and materials purchase/usage budget
Direct labor	Labor budget
Factory overhead	Factory overhead budget
Selling expenses	Selling cost budget
General and administrative expenses	General and administrative expense budget
Capital expenditures	Capital expenditures budget
Income taxes	Estimated from previous year's income statement and current year's projections
Interest expense	Forecasted income statement
Loan payments	Loan records

Note: Other sources of cash receipts and cash payments exist. The above analysis covers only the most common types of cash inflows and outflows.

so that as one month is completed, a new month is added to the detailed section. In our example, at the end of January, the column for January would be dropped and a new column for April added. This gives management a continuous three-month view of its cash flow projections.

To assist you in understanding how the Taylor Piano Company's cash budget was developed, we will explain each line item in Exhibit 11. First let us analyze cash receipts. For the upcoming year, the company expects cash receipts from sales only; no other source is anticipated. Note that 60 percent of all sales generate cash in the month of sale. Forty percent are credit sales collected in the following month. Most of the necessary cash inflow information comes from the sales budget in Exhibit 3 and the production budget in Exhibit 5. There is a waiting list for the company's pianos and, as a result, its pianos are shipped as soon as they are completed. So that you can determine

Exhibit 11. Cash Budget

Taylor Piano Company
Cash Budget
For the Year Ending December 31, 19x8

	January	February	March	April–December	Totals	Source of Data
Cash Receipts						
Sales from previous month (40%)	$28,800	$29,200	$22,920	$ 22,552	$103,472	Exhibits 2, 3, and 5
Sales from current month (60%)	43,800	34,380	33,828	454,260*	566,268	
Total cash receipts	$72,600	$63,580	$56,748	$476,812	$669,740	
Cash Payments						
Direct materials and parts	$23,259	$17,126	$18,078	$149,587	$208,050†	Exhibits 5 and 9
Indirect materials and supplies	2,326	1,713	1,808	14,958	20,805	10% of materials and parts
Direct labor	9,697	8,004	7,450	65,611	90,762	Exhibits 5 and 6
Indirect labor	4,849	4,002	3,725	32,805	45,381	50% of direct labor
Other factory overhead**	11,729	11,221	11,055	104,323	138,328	Exhibit 7
Selling commissions	3,650	2,865	2,819	24,141	33,475	Exhibit 4
Other selling costs	2,190	1,719	1,691	14,485	20,085	Exhibit 4
General and administrative expenses	6,063	5,159	5,290	46,540	63,052	From chapter
Capital expenditures	0	15,000	0	15,000	30,000	From chapter
Income taxes	0	0	11,430	0	11,430	Exhibit 2
Interest expense	1,400	0	0	4,200	5,600	8% of note, payable quarterly
Total cash payments	$65,163	$66,809	$63,346	$471,650	$666,968	
Cash Increase (Decrease)	$ 7,437	($ 3,229)	($ 6,598)	$ 5,162	$ 2,772	
Beginning Cash Balance	27,440	34,877	31,648	25,050	27,440	
Ending Cash Balance	$34,877	$31,648	$25,050	$ 30,212	$ 30,212	

*Computed by multiplying the number of units of each model sold in the last three quarters by the selling prices of each model and subtracting 40% of December sales:

[(55 × $1,840) + (38 × $1,990) + (85 × $3,600)] − (40% × $71,400) = $454,260.

**Noncash items (depreciation) are not included.

†Cash payments for materials and parts equal amounts used, not amounts purchased, because materials and parts are paid for one month after purchase, during the month when they are being used.

the cash credit collections for January, you need to know that the December 19x7 sales were $72,000. December 19x8 sales are projected to be $71,400.

Information supporting cash payments comes from several sources. Every company should have an established policy about payment on account as part of its cash management approach. If the policy is to pay the total within the discount period, and the terms are 2/10, net/30, cash flow would take place in ten days. If, however, the company wishes to hold its cash for the discount period, cash payments would not be made for thirty days. The Taylor Piano Company's policy is to pay invoices for all items, except materials and parts, in the month received. All direct materials and parts purchases are paid for in the month following the purchase. Cash used to purchase materials and parts is determined from the materials purchase/usage budget in Exhibit 9 and the detailed unit figures in the production budget.

Direct labor cash payments are derived from data in the labor budget in Exhibit 6 and from the detailed unit data in the production budget. Indirect materials and indirect labor are part of the factory overhead budget in Exhibit 7, but the company prefers to list them separately in its cash budget. They are computed using a rate based on materials and parts dollars and direct labor dollars, respectively. The remaining costs in the factory overhead budget also are assigned to time periods using a rate based on direct labor dollars. The allocation of selling commissions and other selling expenses to time periods is accomplished using data from the sales budget in Exhibit 3, the selling cost budget in Exhibit 4, and the unit data in the production budget in Exhibit 5. All sources of information are listed on the right side of the cash budget in Exhibit 11.

Once the cash receipts and cash payments have been established, the cash increase or decrease for the period is computed. The resulting increase or decrease is added to the period's beginning balance to arrive at the projected cash balance at period end. In the Taylor Piano Company example in Exhibit 11, you can see that the beginning cash balance for January (taken from Exhibit 2) was $27,440. Then each month's projected ending balance is the next month's beginning balance. In the case of the Taylor Piano Company, February and March will cut into cash reserves, but positive cash flow is expected to return during the last nine months of the year. The company seems to have a favorable cash position for the year. Depending on what the company's policy is on maximum cash reserves, a $30,212 projected cash balance at year end may be too much extra cash. At that time, management may want to make plans for investing part of this money in short-term securities.

The cash budget usually is the final budget to be developed because, to create it, all other budgets must have been completed first. When the cash budget's ending balance is determined, the forecasted balance sheet can be completed.

THE FORECASTED BALANCE SHEET

OBJECTIVE

9 *Prepare a fore-
casted balance
sheet*

The final step in the master budget development process is to prepare a forecasted balance sheet for the company. A forecasted balance sheet projects the financial position of a business for a future period. As shown in Figure 1, all budgeted data are used in this process. The forecasted balance sheet at December 31, 19x8, for the Taylor Piano Company is illustrated in Exhibit 12. To assist you in following the development of this statement, the sources for all information are listed on the right side of the exhibit. The cash budget

Exhibit 12. Forecasted Balance Sheet

			Source of Data
Taylor Piano Company **Forecasted Balance Sheet** **December 31, 19x8**			
Assets			
Current Assets			
Cash		$ 30,212	**Exhibit 11**
Accounts Receivable		28,560	**40% of $71,400**
Materials Inventory		27,921	**Exhibit 8**
Work in Process Inventory		0	
Finished Goods Inventory		29,165	**From chapter**
Total Current Assets		$115,858	
Property, Plant, and Equipment			
Land		$ 50,000	**Exhibit 2**
Plant and Equipment	$290,000		**Exhibits 2 and 11**
Less Accumulated Depreciation	65,600	224,400	**Exhibits 2 and 7**
Total Property, Plant, and Equipment		274,400	
Total Assets		$390,258	
Liabilities and Stockholders' Equity			
Current Liabilities			
Accounts Payable		$ 27,921	**Exhibit 8**
Income Taxes Payable		8,658	**Exhibit 10**
Total Current Liabilities		$ 36,579	
Long-term Liabilities			
Notes Payable		70,000	**Exhibit 2**
Total Liabilities		$106,579	
Stockholders' Equity			
Common Stock		$200,000	**Exhibit 2**
Retained Earnings			
Beginning Balance	$ 67,600		**Exhibit 2**
Net Income for 19x8	16,079		**Exhibit 10**
Retained Earnings, Dec. 31, 19x8		83,679	
Total Stockholders' Equity		283,679	
Total Liabilities and Stockholders' Equity		$390,258	

(Exhibit 11) yields the ending Cash balance for the company. The ending Accounts Receivable balance is 40 percent of December sales of $71,400. The ending Materials Inventory balance was computed in Exhibit 8, and the ending Finished Goods Inventory was computed in conjunction with the preparation of the forecasted income statement. Property, plant, and equipment balances started with the beginning balance sheet in Exhibit 2. Equipment purchases were identified in the cash budget and depreciation expense for the period was shown in the factory overhead budget (Exhibit 7).

Regarding the liabilities and stockholders' equity balances, Accounts Payable should equal the Materials Inventory balance. (Inventory items are ordered one month in advance and are paid for in the month following purchase.) The income taxes payable amount comes from the forecasted income statement (Exhibit 10). Notes Payable is not expected to change during the year so that balance comes from Exhibit 2, as does the Common Stock balance. Ending Retained Earnings is computed by adding the projected net income from the forecasted income statement to the beginning balance in Exhibit 2.

The forecasted financial statements are the end product of the budgeting process. At this point, management must decide whether to accept the proposed master budget, as well as the planned operating results, or ask the budget director to change the plans and do parts of the budget over again.

BUDGET IMPLEMENTATION

Budget implementation is the responsibility of the budget director. Two elements discussed earlier, communication and support, determine the success of this process. Proper communication of expectations and targets to all key people in the company is essential. All employees involved in the operations of the business must know what is expected of them, and they must receive directions on how to achieve their goals. Equally important, top management must support the budgeting process and encourage implementation of the budget. The process will succeed only if middle- and lower-level managers can see that top management is truly interested in the outcome and willing to reward people for meeting the budget goals.

CHAPTER REVIEW

REVIEW OF LEARNING OBJECTIVES

1. **Identify managers' needs for, and uses of, a budget.** The budgeting process pushes managers to take time to create strategies, targets, and goals before activity begins. Budget preparation helps managers focus on the next month or the entire coming year. The budgeting process forces managers to assess current operating conditions and aids in forecasting and implementing needed changes. Budget preparation is also an excellent vehicle with which to work with all supervised personnel by requesting their input and suggestions. Once developed, budgets provide operating targets for managers and their staffs. At the end of a period, the budget helps managers evaluate performance, locate problem areas and bottlenecks, and provide solutions to these problems. Budget analysis should be a regular and ongoing part of managers' duties because it helps chart the course of operations and provides a means to evaluate performance once the task has been completed. If realistic goals have been established, comparing the actual results with budgeted targets can help management assess how well the organization performed.

2. **State the objectives underlying the creation of a budget.** The primary objective of a budget is to forecast future financial and nonfinancial transactions and events of the organization. The second objective is to develop projected information that is as accurate and as meaningful to the recipient as possible.

3. **Define the concept of *budgetary control.*** The budgetary control process includes cost planning and cost control. It is the total process of developing plans for a company's expected operations and controlling operations to help carry out those plans.

4. **Name the five groups of budgeting principles, and explain the principles in each group.** The five groups of budgeting principles apply to: (1) long-range goals, (2) short-range goals and strategies, (3) human responsibilities and interaction, (4) budget housekeeping, and (5) follow-up. Every organization needs to set long-range goals and convert them into plans for product line or service offerings. These must be restated in terms of short-range goals and strategies, which provide plans for the annual product line or service offerings and associated profit plans. The budget development plans and timetable must also be set up. Principles regarding the human side of effective budgeting include identifying a budget director, staff, and participants. These people must be informed of their duties and responsibilities. Furthermore, it is essential to practice participative budgeting, obtain the full support of top management, and ensure full and open communication among all participants. Being realistic, requiring that all deadlines be met, and using flexible application procedures are the housekeeping principles of budgeting. Finally, budget follow-up should provide for a continuous budgeting process, a system of periodic reports to measure performance of the operating segments, and identification of problems for analysis and inclusion in the next period's planning activities.

5. **Identify and explain the components of a master budget.** A master budget is a set of period budgets that have been consolidated into forecasted financial statements for the whole company. First the detailed period budgets are prepared. These are the sales budget, selling cost budget, production budget, materials purchase/usage budget, labor budget, factory overhead budget, general and administrative expense budget, and capital expenditures budget. The selling cost budget and the production budget are computed from the sales budget data. Materials purchase/usage, labor, and factory overhead budgets arise from the production budget. Materials purchases can be determined only after materials needs are known. General and administrative expenses and proposed capital expenditures are determined by top management. Once these budgets have been prepared, a forecasted income statement, a cash budget, and a forecasted balance sheet can be prepared.

6. **Prepare a period budget.** A period budget, also known as an *operating budget,* is a forecast of a year's operating results for a segment of a company. It is a quantitative expression of planned activities. The period budgeting process converts forecasts of unit sales and production into revenue and cost estimates for each of the many operating segments of the company.

7. **Combine the information from the period budgets into a forecasted income statement.** Once the period budgets have been prepared, the forecasted income statement can be developed. Information about projected sales and costs come from several period budgets. Information from the beginning balance sheet, sales budget, selling cost budget, production budget, materials purchase/usage budget, labor budget, factory overhead budget, and general and administrative expense budget are integrated into the forecasted income statement.

8. **State the purposes of, and prepare, a cash budget.** The cash budget's purposes are (1) to disclose the firm's projected ending cash balance and (2) to show the cash position for each month of the year so that periods of cash excesses or shortages can be anticipated. A cash budget (or cash flow forecast) is a projection of the cash receipts and cash payments for a future period. It summarizes the cash results of planned transactions in all parts of a master budget.

   The preparation of a cash budget begins with the projection of all expected sources of cash (cash receipts). Next, all expected cash payments are found by analyzing all other period budgets within the master budget. The difference between these two totals is the cash increase or decrease anticipated for the period. This total, combined with the period's beginning cash balance, yields the ending cash balance.

9. **Prepare a forecasted balance sheet.** The final step in the master budget development process is to prepare a forecasted balance sheet for the company. All budgeted data are used in this process.

REVIEW OF CONCEPTS AND TERMINOLOGY

The following concepts and terms were introduced in this chapter.

L O 2   **Budget:** A planning document created before anticipated transactions occur.

L O 3   **Budgetary control:** The process of developing plans for a company's expected operations and controlling operations to help carry out those plans.

L O 5   **Capital expenditures budget:** A detailed plan outlining the amount and timing of anticipated capital expenditures for a future period.

L O 8   **Cash budget (or cash flow forecast):** A projection of cash receipts and cash payments for a future period.

L O 5   **Factory overhead budget:** A detailed schedule of anticipated manufacturing costs, other than direct materials and direct labor costs, that must be incurred to meet the production expectations of a future period.

L O 9   **Forecasted balance sheet:** A document that projects the financial position of a business for a future period.

L O 7   **Forecasted income statement:** A document that projects the amount of revenues that will be earned and the expenses that will be incurred by a business for a future period.

L O 5   **General and administrative (G&A) expense budget:** A detailed plan of operating expenses, other than those of the manufacturing and selling functions, needed to support the overall operations of the business for a future period.

L O 5   **Labor budget:** A detailed schedule that identifies the labor needs for a future period and the labor costs associated with those needs.

L O 5   **Master budget:** A set of departmental or functional period budgets that have been consolidated into forecasted financial statements for the entire company.

L O 5   **Materials purchase/usage budget:** A detailed plan developed from information on the production budget and anticipated changes in the materials inventory levels that identifies the numbers and timing of raw materials and parts to be purchased and used to meet production needs. (A merchandise purchasing budget is used by retail businesses.)

L O 4   **Participative budgeting:** A managerial budget preparation process in which all levels of personnel take part in creating budgets in a meaningful, active way.

L O 3   **Period budget:** A forecast of operating results for a particular segment or function of a company for a specific period of time.

L O 5   **Production budget:** A detailed schedule that identifies the products or services that must be produced or provided to meet budgeted sales and inventory needs.

L O 5   **Sales budget:** A detailed plan, expressed in both units and dollars, that identifies the expected product (or service) sales for a future period.

L O 5   **Selling cost budget:** A schedule developed from information on the sales budget and from the sales staff that details all anticipated costs related to the selling function of the business for a future period.

REVIEW PROBLEM

CASH BUDGET PREPARATION

L O 8   Millson Information Processing Company provides word processing services for its clients. Millson uses state-of-the-art equipment and employs five keyboard operators, who each average 160 hours of work a month. The following table sets out information developed by the budget officer.

	Actual—19x7		Forecast—19x8		
	November	**December**	**January**	**February**	**March**
Client billings (sales)	$25,000	$35,000	$25,000	$20,000	$40,000
Selling costs	4,500	5,000	4,000	4,000	5,000
General and administrative expenses	7,500	8,000	8,000	7,000	7,500
Operating supplies purchased	2,500	3,500	2,500	2,500	4,000
Processing overhead	3,200	3,500	3,000	2,500	3,500

The company has a bank loan of $12,000 at a 12 percent annual interest rate. Interest is paid monthly, and $2,000 of the principal of the loan is due on February 28, 19x8. No capital expenditures are anticipated for the first quarter of the coming year. Income taxes of $4,550 for calendar year 19x7 are due and payable on March 15, 19x8. The company's five employees earn $8.50 an hour, and all payroll-related labor benefit costs are included in processing overhead. For the items included in the table, assume the following conditions.

Client billings	60% are cash sales collected during the current period 30% are collected in the first month following the sale 10% are collected in the second month following the sale
Operating supplies	Paid for in the month purchased
Selling costs, general and administrative expenses, and processing overhead	Paid in the month following the cost's incurrence

The beginning cash balance on January 1, 19x8, is expected to be $13,840.

REQUIRED Prepare a monthly cash budget for Millson Information Processing Company for the three-month period ending March 31, 19x8.

ANSWER TO REVIEW PROBLEM

Details supporting the individual computations within the cash budget are as follows:

	January	February	March
Cash from client billings			
Current month = 60%	$15,000	$12,000	$24,000
Previous month = 30%	10,500	7,500	6,000
Month before last = 10%	2,500	3,500	2,500
	$28,000	$23,000	$32,500
Operating supplies			
All paid in the month purchased	$2,500	$2,500	$4,000
Direct labor			
5 employees × 160 hours a month × $8.50 an hour	6,800	6,800	6,800
Processing overhead			
Paid in the month following incurrence	3,500	3,000	2,500
Selling costs			
Paid in the month following incurrence	5,000	4,000	4,000
General and administrative expenses			
Paid in the month following incurrence	8,000	8,000	7,000

	January	February	March
Interest expense			
January and February = 1% of $12,000	$120	$ 120	
March = 1% of $10,000			$ 100
Loan payment	—	2,000	—
Income tax payment	—	—	4,550

The ending cash balances of $15,920, $12,500, and $16,050 for January, February, and March 19x8, respectively, appear to be comfortable but not too large for the company.

Here is the three-month cash budget for Millson Information Processing Company:

Millson Information Processing Company
Monthly Cash Budget
For the Three-Month Period Ending March 31, 19x8

	January	February	March	Totals
Cash Receipts				
Client billings	$28,000	$23,000	$32,500	$83,500
Cash Payments				
Operating supplies	$ 2,500	$ 2,500	$ 4,000	$ 9,000
Direct labor	6,800	6,800	6,800	20,400
Processing overhead	3,500	3,000	2,500	9,000
Selling costs	5,000	4,000	4,000	13,000
General and administrative				
expenses	8,000	8,000	7,000	23,000
Interest expense	120	120	100	340
Loan payment	—	2,000	—	2,000
Income tax payment	—	—	4,550	4,550
Total cash payments	$25,920	$26,420	$28,950	$81,290
Cash Increase (Decrease)	$ 2,080	($ 3,420)	$ 3,550	$ 2,210
Beginning Cash Balance	13,840	15,920	12,500	13,840
Ending Cash Balance	$15,920	$12,500	$16,050	$16,050

CHAPTER ASSIGNMENTS

QUESTIONS

1. How does a manager benefit from the preparation of budgets?
2. Define a *budget.* What is a budget composed of, and what is its primary objective?
3. Describe the concept of budgetary control. Why is it important?
4. What are the budgeting principles related to long-range goals?
5. Distinguish between long-range plans and yearly operating plans.
6. What is the purpose of the following budgeting principle? "Restate the long-range plans in terms of short-range plans for product lines or services and a detailed profit plan."
7. In what ways does a well-defined organizational structure help in the preparation of budgets?
8. State the budget housekeeping principles.

9. Describe participative budgeting. Why is it necessary to identify all participants involved in budget development?

10. Why use a continuous budgeting process?

11. What is the connection between periodic performance reports and the budgeting process?

12. What is a master budget? What is its purpose?

13. Define a *period budget.*

14. What are the three main phases of the budget preparation cycle?

15. Describe the contents of a materials purchase/usage budget.

16. Identify and discuss relationships among detailed operating budgets.

17. Does a labor budget always contain projections of both direct labor and indirect labor costs? What are the advantages of including both categories?

18. Identify the period budgets that must be completed before the forecasted income statement can be prepared.

19. Why is the preparation of a cash budget so important to a company?

20. In the budget preparation process, what period budgets must precede the preparation of the cash budget?

21. How are sales and purchases on account handled when drawing up the cash budget?

22. Why is it important to complete the cash budget before completing the forecasted balance sheet, the final step in the budgeting process?

Short Exercises

SE 1. *Manager's Budget*
L O 1 *Uses*
No check figure

Jim Gray is the manager of a shoe department in a local discount department store. His supervisor has indicated that Jim's goal is to increase the number of pairs of shoes sold by 20 percent. The department sold 8,000 pairs of shoes last year. Two shoe salespersons currently work for Jim. What type of budgets should Jim use to help achieve his sales goal? What kinds of information should these budgets provide?

SE 2. *Budget Objectives*
L O 2
No check figure

Janice Linnet was told by her manager that the primary objective of a budget "is to put pressure on your subordinates—to get as much work out of them as possible." She was told to make her budget forecasts as tight as possible so that her employees have difficult goals to achieve. Is the manager correct? If not, what is the problem? What should the budget development objectives be?

SE 3. *Budgetary Control*
L O 3
No check figure

Max Greenwood likes to analyze the results of his tree nursery operations by comparing the actual operating results with budgeted figures from the beginning of the year. If the business generated large profits, he often overlooks the differences between actual and budgeted data. But if profits are low, he spends many hours analyzing those differences. If you were Max, would you approach budgetary control in a similar manner? If not, what changes would you make to his approach?

SE 4. *Budgeting Principles*
L O 4
No check figure

The basic principles of budgeting have just been discussed with the dashboard assembly team at the Rockford Automobile Company. The team is participating in the company's budgeting process for the first time. One team member asked the controller to explain how the long-range goals principles relate to the short-range goals and strategies principles. How should the controller respond?

SE 5. *Master Budget*
L O 5 *Components*
No check figure

The master budget is a compilation of many departmental or functional forecasts for the coming year or operating cycle. What is the most important forecast made in relation to the master budget? List the reasons for your answer. Which budgets must be prepared before you can develop a materials purchase/usage budget?

SE 6. *Period Budget*
L O 6 *Preparation*
Check Figure: Total budgeted selling costs: $209,500

Lockwood Company expects to sell 50,000 units of its product in the coming year. Each unit sells for $45. Sales brochures and supplies are expected to cost $7,000 for the year. Three sales representatives cover the southeast region. Their individual base salary is $20,000, and they earn a sales commission of 5 percent of the units they sell.

The sales representatives supply their own means of transportation and they are reimbursed for travel at a rate of $.40 per mile. Based on the current year's mileage, the sales representatives are expected to drive a total of 75,000 miles next year. From the information provided, prepare a selling cost budget for the coming year.

SE 7. *Period Budget*
L O 6 *Preparation*
Check Figure: May cash collections, Total: $61,704

BK Insurance Co. specializes in term life insurance contracts. Cash collection experience shows that 20 percent of billed premiums are collected in the month prior to being due, 60 percent are paid in the month they are due, and 16 percent are paid in the month following their due date. Four percent of the billed premiums are paid late (in the second month following their due date) and include a 10 percent penalty payment. Total billing notices were: January, $58,000; February, $62,000; March, $66,000; April, $65,000; May, $60,000; and June, $62,000. How much cash does the company expect to collect in May?

SE 8. *Forecasted Income*
L O 7 *Statement*
Check Figure: Gross Margin: $150,900

Period budgets for the Constantine Company revealed the following information: net sales, $450,000; beginning materials inventory, $23,000; materials purchased, $185,000; beginning work in process inventory, $64,700; beginning finished goods inventory, $21,600; direct labor costs, $34,000; factory overhead applied, $67,000; ending work in process inventory, $61,200; ending materials inventory, $18,700; and ending finished goods inventory, $16,300. Compute the company's forecasted gross margin.

SE 9. *Cash Budget*
L O 8
Check Figure: Total Cash Payments: $258,000

The following materials purchase projections are for the Martinson Corp. Experience has shown that the company pays 60 percent of the purchases on account in the month of purchase and 40 percent in the month following the purchase. Prepare a cash payments budget for the first quarter of 19x7.

	Purchases on Account	Cash Purchases
December 19x6	$40,000	$20,000
January 19x7	60,000	30,000
February 19x7	50,000	25,000
March 19x7	70,000	35,000

SE 10. *Forecasted Balance*
L O 9 *Sheet*
Check Figure: Beginning retained earnings: $900,400

Shadow Corporation's budgeted data showed total projected assets for the coming year of $4,650,000. Total liabilities were expected to be $1,900,000. Common stock and retained earnings make up the entire stockholders' equity section of the balance sheet. Common stock remains at its beginning balance of $1,500,000. The projected net income for the year is $349,600. What was the balance of retained earnings at the beginning of the budget period?

EXERCISES

E 1. *Budget Objectives*
L O 2
No check figure

You recently attended a workshop on budgeting and overheard the following comments as you moved to the refreshment table.

1. "Budgets look the same regardless of the size of a company and the role of the budget process in management."
2. "Budgets can include financial or nonfinancial data. At our company, we plan the number of hours to be worked and the number of customer contacts we want our salespeople to make."
3. "All budgets are complicated. You have to be an expert to prepare one."
4. "Budgets do not need to be highly accurate or very meaningful. No one stays within a budget at our company."

Do you agree or disagree with each comment? Explain.

E 2. *Budgeting Principles*
L O 4
No check figure

The managers of Colorado Calendars, Inc. recently held a planning meeting to develop goals for the company. The company's success has been influenced by the managers' willingness to effectively follow budgeting principles. These principles include long-range goals, short-range goals, human responsibilities and interaction, budget housekeeping principles, and budget follow-up. Identify the budgeting principle accomplished by each of the following actions taken by the management team.

1. At the end of each month, the management team met to consider making changes to the budget. They reviewed significant variances between actual and budgeted activities that were presented in performance reports.
2. The management team considered economic and industry forecasts, employee-management relationships, and the structure and role of management in forecasting the next ten-year period.
3. The management team decided to be as realistic as possible by establishing attainable goals for the operations of the company. They reminded everyone that deadlines must be met and that budgets act as a flexible guide for managers.
4. Decisions were made about next year's sales and profit targets by calendar line and sales territory based on the forecast for the next ten years.
5. The management team selected a budget director and planned a workshop that would encourage the participation of all managers in developing the budget each year.

E 3. *Budgeting Principles*
L O 4
No check figure

Assume that you work in the accounting department of a small wholesale warehousing business. After attending a seminar on the values of a budgeting system at an industry association meeting, the president wants to develop a budgeting system and has asked you to direct it.

State the points that you should communicate to the president about the initial development steps of the process. Concentrate on long-range goals principles and short-range goals and strategies principles.

E 4. *Components of a*
L O 5 *Master Budget*
No check figure

Identify the order in which the following budgets are prepared within the master budget process. Use the letters *a* through *g*, with the first budget to be prepared as *a*.

1. Production budget
2. Labor budget
3. Materials purchase/usage budget
4. Sales budget
5. Forecasted balance sheet
6. Cash budget
7. Forecasted income statement

E 5. *Production Budget*
L O 5, 6 *Preparation*
Check Figure: Production needs for February: 5,000 doors

Bob Walsh, the controller for the Walton Specialty Door Company, is preparing a production budget for 19x8. The company's policy is to maintain a finished goods inventory equal to one-half of the following month's sales. Complete the following production budget for the first quarter using the information provided.

	January	February	March
Desired sales in units	5,000	4,000	6,000
Desired ending finished goods inventory	2,000	?	?
	7,000		
Less desired beginning finished goods inventory	2,500	?	?
Production needs	4,500	?	?

Budgeted sales for April is 7,000 doors.

E 6. *Materials*
L O 5, 6 *Purchase/Usage*
Budget
Check Figure: Total purchases for the first quarter: $4,056,000

The Walton Specialty Door Company manufactures garage door units. These units include hinges, door panels, and other hardware. Prepare a materials purchase/usage budget for the first quarter of 19x8 based on budgeted production of 16,000 garage door units. Bob Walsh, the controller, has provided the following information.

Hinges	4 sets per door	$11.00 a set
Door panels	4 panels per door	$27.00 a panel
Other hardware	1 lock per door	$31.00 a lock
	1 handle per door	$22.50 a handle
	2 roller tracks per door	$16.00 for a set of 2 roller tracks
	8 rollers per door	$4.00 a roller

Mickie Runner, controller for Parks Cosmetics Corporation, is in the process of putting together the 19x8 master budget. The sales and production budgets have been assembled and Ms. Runner is now in the process of preparing the materials purchase/usage budget for the first quarter of 19x8. The company produces three main product lines—A-1, C-3, and E-5—and each product requires different mixtures of four raw material compounds. Planned production of the three products for January–March 19x8 is as follows:

Product	Batches to Be Produced
A-1	15,000
C-3	20,000
E-5	40,000

The mixture of raw material compounds per batch of product is shown below.

Product	Raw Material Compounds per Batch (in gallons)			
	BB	**DD**	**FF**	**HH**
A-1	4	3	—	2
C-3	2	—	6	4
E-5	5	2	3	8

Inventory level requirements and raw material compound unit costs are as follows:

	BB	**DD**	**FF**	**HH**
Inventory level (gallons):				
January 1, 19x8	2,000	1,600	900	3,000
March 31, 19x8	1,000	800	500	1,500
Projected 19x8 cost/gallon	$6	$7	$8	$10

Prepare a budget for the purchase of materials for the first quarter of 19x8 that details the total gallons to be purchased for each compound and the total cost per compound.

Miller Metals Company manufactures three products in a single plant with four departments: Cutting, Grinding, Polishing, and Packing. The company has estimated costs for products T, M, and B and is currently analyzing direct labor hour requirements for the budget year 19x7. The routing sequence and departmental data follow.

Unit of Product	Estimated Hours per Unit				Total Estimated Direct Labor Hours/Unit
	Cutting	**Grinding**	**Polishing**	**Packing**	
T	.8	1.1	.5	.3	2.7
M	1.2	—	2.9	.7	4.8
B	1.8	3.2	—	.5	5.5
Hourly labor rate	$10	$9	$7	$6	
Annual direct labor hour capacity	1,100,000	1,200,000	1,248,000	460,000	

The annual direct labor hour capacity for each department at Miller Metals is based on a normal two-shift operation. Hours of labor in excess of capacity are provided by overtime labor at 150 percent of normal hourly rates. Budgeted unit production in 19x7 for the products is 210,000 of T, 360,000 of M, and 300,000 of B.

Prepare a direct labor budget for 19x7 showing annual and monthly costs. Assume that direct labor hour capacity is the same each month. Production should be close to constant each month.

Sales for 19x8 for the Carlson Manufacturing Company are shown on the next page. The data are presented in quarterly figures because management monitors its business activity in this manner.

Carlson Manufacturing Company
Actual Sales Revenue
For the Year Ended December 31, 19x8

Product Class	January–March	April–June	July–September	October–December	Annual Totals	Estimated 19x9 Percent Increases by Product Class
Marine Products	$ 44,500	$ 45,500	$ 48,200	$ 47,900	$ 186,100	10%
Mountain Products	36,900	32,600	34,100	37,200	140,800	5%
River Products	29,800	29,700	29,100	27,500	116,100	30%
Hiking Products	38,800	37,600	36,900	39,700	153,000	15%
Running Products	47,700	48,200	49,400	49,900	195,200	25%
Biking Products	65,400	65,900	66,600	67,300	265,200	20%
Totals	$263,100	$259,500	$264,300	$269,500	$1,056,400	

Prepare the 19x9 sales budget for the company. Show both quarterly and annual totals for each product class.

E 10. *Factory Overhead*
L O 5, 6 *Budget*
Check Figure: Totals: $861,161

George Smith is chief financial officer of the London division for Isadora Corporation, a multinational company operating with three divisions. As part of the budgeting process, Smith's staff is developing the factory overhead budget for 19x8. Data from the current year as well as projections for 19x8 are as follows:

Isadora Corporation
Factory Overhead Cost Summary Analysis: London Division
For the Year Ended December 31, 19x7

Cost Category	19x7 Amount	Projected 19x8 Increase
Indirect Materials	$ 86,900	12%
Indirect Labor	104,600	9%
Factory Supervision	180,000	13%
Employee Benefits	76,400	20%
Insurance		
Casualty	4,650	4%
Flood	6,800	5%
Liability	5,200	12%
Taxes		
Property	34,700	24%
Other	3,300	20%
Depreciation, Machinery	82,200	2%
Depreciation, Building	71,500	2%
Repairs and Maintenance	26,300	8%
Supplies	10,600	4%
Special Tools	45,600	25%
Electricity	29,800	10%
Miscellaneous	3,780	5%
Totals	$772,330	

From the data given, prepare the 19x8 factory overhead budget for the division. Round to whole dollar amounts.

E 11. *Cash Budget*
L O 8 *Preparation—*
Revenues

Check Figure: Totals, November: $696,200

Fishe Car Care, Inc. is an automobile maintenance and repair organization with outlets throughout the midwestern United States. Cynthia Sears, budget director for the home office, is beginning to assemble next quarter's operating cash budget. Sales are projected as follows:

	On Account	Cash
October 19x9	$452,000	$196,800
November 19x9	590,000	214,000
December 19x9	720,500	218,400

Sears's past collection results for sales on account indicate the following pattern.

Month of sale	40%
1st month following sale	30%
2nd month following sale	28%
Uncollectible	2%

Sales on account during the months of August and September were $346,000 and $395,000, respectively.

What are the purposes of preparing a cash budget? Compute the amount of cash to be collected from sales during each month of the last quarter.

E 12. *Cash Budget*
L O 8 *Preparation—*
Expenditures

Check Figure: Total Cash Outflow, August: $24,304

Gryder Corporation relies on its cash budget to predict periods of high or low cash. The company considers proper cash management to be a primary short-range strategy for achieving higher profits. All materials and supplies are purchased on account, with terms of either 2/10, n/30 or 2/30, n/60. Discounts are taken whenever possible, but payment is not made until the final day of the discount period. Purchases for the next quarter of 19x7 are expected to be as follows:

Date	Terms	Gross Amount	Date	Terms	Gross Amount
July 10	2/10, n/30	$ 7,400	Aug. 31	2/10, n/30	$5,800
16	2/30, n/60	9,200	Sept. 4	2/10, n/30	8,400
24	2/30, n/60	8,400	9	2/10, n/30	7,100
Aug. 6	2/10, n/30	7,200	18	2/10, n/30	6,500
12	2/30, n/60	11,400	20	2/10, n/30	9,400
18	2/30, n/60	12,500	24	2/30, n/60	8,300
30	2/10, n/30	13,600	29	2/10, n/30	3,900

Three purchases in June affect July cash flow: June 6, 2/30, n/60, $13,200; June 21, 2/30, n/60, $11,400; and June 24, 2/10, n/30, $5,400.

From the information given, compute total cash outflow for July, August, and September resulting from the purchases identified above.

SKILLS DEVELOPMENT EXERCISES

Conceptual Analysis

SDE 1. *The Art of*
L O 4 *Budgeting Profit*
Targets

No check figure

University of Southern California Professor Kenneth A. Merchant conducted a field research study of twelve corporations in which he specifically looked at the levels at which profit budgets (targets) should be set.[5] Should the budget targets be easy to reach, should their attainment be very difficult, or should the targets be set somewhere in between these extremes? Between the two extremes, literally hundreds of levels could be selected. The Merchant study showed that profit budgets influence manager behavior and that the setting of budget targets is an art as well as a science. According to Merchant, profit budget targets should be set to be "challenging but achievable." Write a statement explaining what you believe Professor Merchant meant by this statement.

5. Kenneth A. Merchant, "How Challenging Should Profit Budget Targets Be?" *Management Accounting*, Institute of Management Accountants, November 1990, pp. 46–48.

Ethical Dilemma

SDE 2.

L O 3

Ethical Considerations in the Budgeting Process

No check figure

Doug Togo is manager of the Repairs and Maintenance (R&M) Department, a cost center at *Phoenix Industries.* Mr. Togo is responsible for preparing the annual budget for his department. For 19x8, he turned in the following budgeted information to the company's budget director. The 19x8 figures are 20 percent above the 19x7 budget figures. Most managers in the company inflate their budget numbers by at least 10 percent because their bonuses depend upon how much below budget they operate.

Cost Category	Budget 19x7	Actual 19x7	Budget 19x8
Supplies	$ 20,000	$ 16,000	$ 24,000
Labor	80,000	82,000	96,000
Utilities	8,500	8,000	10,200
Tools	12,500	9,000	15,000
Hand-carried equipment	25,000	16,400	30,000
Cleaning materials	4,600	4,200	5,520
Miscellaneous	2,000	2,100	2,400
Totals	$152,600	$137,700	$183,120

The director has questioned some of the numbers. Mr. Togo defended them by saying that he expects a significant increase in repairs and maintenance activity in 19x8.

What are the real reasons for the increased budgeted data? What are the ethical considerations of this situation?

Research Activity

SDE 3.

L O 2, 3

Actual Budget Practices

No check figure

Budgets are used by every kind of enterprise, including both profit-oriented and not-for-profit concerns. Select a store, church, company, or charity that you are familiar with. Set up a meeting with the owner or manager and ask questions pertaining to the organization's use of budgets. Determine from your conversation if the person relies on budgets heavily, only once a year at preparation time, or never. Make notes on the types of budgets used. Prepare your findings in outline form for presentation to the class.

Decision-Making Practice

SDE 4.

L O 4, 6, 7

Effective Budgeting Procedures

Check Figure: Income Before Income Taxes, 12/31/x8: $130,150

During the past ten years, *Banta Enterprises* has practiced participative budgeting all the way from the maintenance personnel to the president's staff. Gradually, however, the objectives of honesty and decisions made in the best interest of the company as a whole have given way to division-benefiting decisions. Mr. Coffman, corporate controller, has asked Ms. Rodriguez, budget director, to carefully analyze this year's divisional budgets before incorporating them into the company's master budget.

The Motor Division was the first of six divisions to submit its 19x9 budget request to the corporate office. Its summary income statement and notes are on the next page.

1. Recast the Motor Division's forecasted income statement into the following format (round percentages to two places):

	Budget—12/31/x8		Budget—12/31/x9	
Account	Amount	Percent of Sales	Amount	Percent of Sales

2. Actual results for 19x8 revealed the following information about revenues and cost of goods sold.

	Amount	Percent of Sales
Net Sales		
Radios	$ 780,000	43.94%
Appliances	640,000	36.06%
Telephones	280,000	15.77%
Miscellaneous	75,000	4.23%
Net Sales	$1,775,000	100.00%
Less Cost of Goods Sold	763,425	43.01%
Gross Margin	$1,011,575	56.99%

On the basis of this information and your analysis in **1,** what should the budget director say to the managers of the Motor Division? Mention specific areas of the budget that need to be revised.

Banta Enterprises
Motor Division
Forecasted Income Statement
For the Years Ending December 31, 19x8 and 19x9

	Budget 12/31/x8	Budget 12/31/x9	Increase (Decrease)
Net Sales			
Radios	$ 850,000	$ 910,000	$ 60,000
Appliances	680,000	740,000	60,000
Telephones	270,000	305,000	35,000
Miscellaneous	84,400	90,000	5,600
Net Sales	$1,884,400	$2,045,000	$160,600
Less Cost of Goods Sold	750,960	717,500[1]	(33,460)
Gross Margin	$1,133,440	$1,327,500	$194,060
Operating Expenses			
Wages			
Warehouse	$ 94,500	$ 102,250	$ 7,750
Purchasing	77,800	84,000	6,200
Delivery/Shipping	69,400	74,780	5,380
Maintenance	42,650	45,670	3,020
Salaries			
Supervisory	60,000	92,250	32,250
Executive	130,000	164,000	34,000
Purchases, Supplies	17,400	20,500	3,100
Merchandise Moving Equipment			
Maintenance	72,400	82,000	9,600
Depreciation	62,000	74,750[2]	12,750
Building Rent	96,000	102,500	6,500
Sales Commissions	188,440	204,500	16,060
Insurance			
Fire	12,670	20,500	7,830
Liability	18,200	20,500	2,300
Utilities	14,100	15,375	1,275
Taxes			
Property	16,600	18,450	1,850
Payroll	26,520	41,000	14,480
Miscellaneous	4,610	10,250	5,640
Total Operating Expenses	$1,003,290	$1,173,275	$169,985
Income Before Income Taxes	$ 130,150	$ 154,225	$ 24,075

1. Less expensive merchandise will be purchased in 19x9 to boost profits.
2. Depreciation is increased because of a need to buy additional equipment to handle increased sales.

PROBLEM SET A

A 1. *Budget Preparation*

L O 6

📁

Check Figure: 1. Total production budget for November: $578,500

The main product of Thompson Enterprises, Inc., is a multipurpose hammer that carries a lifetime guarantee. The steps in the manufacturing process have been combined by using modern, automated equipment. A list of cost and production information for the Thompson hammer follows.

Direct materials
  Anodized steel: 2 kilograms per hammer at $1.60 per kilogram
  Leather strapping for the handle: .5 square meter per hammer at $4.40 per square meter
  (Packing materials are returned to the manufacturer and thus are not included as part of cost of goods sold.)

Direct labor
  Forging operation: $12.50 per labor hour; 6 minutes per hammer
  Leather-wrapping operation: $12.00 per direct labor hour; 12 minutes per hammer

Factory overhead
  Forging operation: rate equals 70 percent of department's direct labor dollars
  Leather-wrapping operation: rate equals 50 percent of department's direct labor dollars

For the three months ending December 31, 19x9, Thompson's management expects to produce 54,000 hammers in October, 52,000 hammers in November, and 50,000 hammers in December.

REQUIRED

1. For the three-month period ending December 31, 19x9, prepare monthly production cost information for the manufacture of the Thompson hammer. In your budget analysis, show a detailed breakdown of all costs involved and the computation methods used.
2. Prepare a quarterly production cost budget for the hammer. Show monthly cost data and combined totals for the quarter for each cost category.

A 2. *General and*

L O 6 *Administrative*

📁 *Expense Budget*

Check Figure: 1. Totals, 19x9 Expense: $786,200

Cordova Metal Products, Inc. has four divisions and a centralized management structure. The home office is located in Kansas City, Missouri. General and administrative expenses of the corporation for 19x8 and expected percentage increases for 19x9 are as follows:

Expense Categories	19x8 Expenses	Expected Increase In 19x9
Administrative salaries	$160,000	20%
Facility depreciation	47,000	10%
Operating supplies	34,500	20%
Insurance and taxes	26,000	10%
Computer services	250,000	40%
Clerical salaries	85,000	15%
Miscellaneous	22,500	10%
Total	$625,000	

To determine divisional profitability, all general and administrative expenses except for computer services are allocated to divisions on a total labor dollar basis. Computer service costs are charged directly to divisions on the basis of percent of total usage charges. Computer usage charges and direct labor costs in 19x8 were as follows:

	Computer Charges	Direct Labor
Division A	$ 60,000	$150,000
Division B	54,000	100,000
Division C	46,000	150,000
Division D	40,000	200,000
Home Office	50,000	—
Total	$250,000	$600,000

REQUIRED

1. Prepare the general and administrative expense budget for Cordova Metal Products, Inc. for 19x9.
2. Prepare a schedule of budgeted computer service charges to each division and the home office, assuming that percent of usage time and cost distribution in 19x9 will be the same as in 19x8.
3. Determine the amount of general and administrative expense to be allocated to each division in 19x9, using the same direct labor cost distribution percentages as in 19x8.

A 3. *Basic Cash Budget*
L O 8
Check Figure: 1. Ending Cash Balance, August: $3,600

Produce Mart, Inc. is the creation of Leo Rubio. Rubio's dream was to develop the biggest produce store with the widest selection of fresh fruits and vegetables in the northern Illinois area. In three years, he accomplished his objective. Eighty percent of his business is conducted on credit with area retail enterprises, and 20 percent of the produce sold is to walk-in customers at his retail outlet on a cash only basis.

Collection experience has shown that 50 percent of all credit sales are collected during the month of sale, 30 percent are received in the month following the sale, and 20 percent are collected in the second month after the sale. Rubio has asked you to prepare a cash budget for the quarter ending September 30, 19x9.

Operating data for the period are as follows: Total sales in May were $132,000, and in June, $135,000. Anticipated sales include July, $139,000; August, $152,500; and September, $168,500. Purchases for the quarter are expected to be $87,400 in July; $97,850 in August; and $111,450 in September. All purchases are for cash.

Other projected costs for the quarter include salaries and wages of $36,740 in July, $38,400 in August, and $40,600 in September; and monthly costs of $2,080 for heat, light, and power; $750 for bank collection fees; $3,850 for rent; $2,240 for supplies; $3,410 for depreciation of equipment; $2,570 for equipment repairs; and $950 for miscellaneous expenses. The corporation's cash balance at June 30, 19x9, was $5,490.

REQUIRED

1. Prepare a cash budget by month for the quarter ending September 30, 19x9.
2. Should Produce Mart, Inc. anticipate taking out a loan during the quarter? How much should be borrowed? When? (**Note:** Management has a $3,000 minimum monthly cash balance policy.)

A 4. *Forecasted Financial*
L O 7, 9 *Statements*
Check Figure: 1. Projected Net Income: $101,812

The Bank of Wagner County has asked the president of Gutherie Products, Inc. for a forecasted income statement and balance sheet for the quarter ending June 30, 19x7. These documents will be used to support the company's request for a loan. A quarterly master budget is prepared on a routine basis by the company, so the president indicated that the requested documents would be forwarded to the bank.

To date (April 2), the following period budgets have been developed. Sales: April, $220,400, May, $164,220, and June, $165,980; materials purchases for the period, $96,840; materials usage, $102,710; labor expenses, $71,460; factory overhead, $79,940; selling expenses for the quarter, $82,840; general and administrative expenses, $60,900; capital expenditures, $125,000 (to be spent on June 29); cost of goods manufactured, $252,880; and cost of goods sold, $251,700.

Balance sheet account balances at March 31, 19x7 were: Cash, $28,770; Accounts Receivable, $26,500; Materials Inventory, $23,910; Work in Process Inventory, $31,620; Finished Goods Inventory, $36,220; Prepaid Expenses, $7,200; Plant, Furniture, and Fixtures, $498,600; Accumulated Depreciation, Plant, Furniture, and Fixtures, $141,162; Patents, $90,600; Accounts Payable, $39,600; Notes Payable, $105,500; Common Stock, $250,000; and Retained Earnings, $207,158.

Monthly cash balances for the quarter are projected to be: April 30, $20,490; May 31, $35,610; and June 30, $45,400. During the quarter, accounts receivable are supposed to increase by 30 percent, patents will go up by $6,500, prepaid expenses will remain constant, accounts payable will go down by 10 percent, and the company will make a $5,000 payment on the note payable ($4,100 is principal reduction). The federal income tax rate is 34 percent and the second quarter's tax is paid in July. Depreciation for the quarter will be $6,420, which was already included in the factory overhead budget.

REQUIRED

1. Prepare a forecasted income statement for the quarter ending June 30, 19x7. Round answers to the nearest dollar.
2. Prepare a forecasted balance sheet as of June 30, 19x7.

A 5. *Cash Budget*
L O 8 *Preparation:*
Comprehensive

Check Figure: Ending Cash Balance, February: $919,400

Ruidoso Mountain Ski Resort, Inc. has been in business for twenty-two years. Although the skiing season is difficult to predict, the company operates under the assumption that all of its revenues will be generated during the first three months of the calendar year. Routine maintenance and repair work are done during the remaining nine-month period. The following projections for 19x9 were developed by Sandy Regal, company budget director.

Cash Receipts

Lift tickets: January, 16,800 people @ $22; February, 17,400 people @ $23; and March, 17,800 people @ $24
Food sales: January, $62,000; February, $56,000; and March, $62,000
Skiing lessons: January, $158,000; February, $134,000; and March, $158,000
Equipment sales and rental: January, $592,000; February, $496,000; and March, $592,000
Liquor sales: January, $124,000; February, $92,000; and March, $104,000

Cash Payments

Salaries:
  Ski area:
    Lift operators: 12 people @ $2,500 per month for January, February, and March (first quarter)
    Instruction and equipment rental: 24 people @ $2,700 per month for first quarter
  Maintenance: $35,000 per month for first quarter, and a total of $96,000 for the rest of the year
  Customer service: Shuttle bus drivers, 10 people @ $1,400 per month for first quarter
  Medical: 8 people @ $6,400 per month for first quarter
  Food service: 24 people @ $1,800 per month for first quarter
Purchases:
  Food: $30,000 per month for the first quarter
  Ski equipment: Purchases of $340,000 in both January and February plus a $700,000 purchase anticipated in December 19x9
  Liquor: $50,000 in each month of the first quarter
  Tickets and supplies: $50,000 in January, $40,000 in February, and $80,000 in December 19x9
Advertising: $40,000 in January, $30,000 in February, and a total of $90,000 from April through the end of the year
Fire and liability insurance: January and June premium payments of $8,000
Medical facility costs: $15,000 per month during first quarter
Utilities: $5,000 per month for the first quarter and $1,000 per month for the rest of the year
Lift maintenance: $25,000 per month for the first quarter and $10,000 per month for the rest of the year
Property taxes: $180,000 due in June
Federal income taxes: 19x8 taxes of $364,000 due in March

The beginning cash balance for 19x9 is anticipated to be $10,000.

REQUIRED

Prepare a cash budget for Ruidoso Mountain Ski Resort, Inc. for 19x9, using the following column headings.

Item	January	February	March	April–December	Total

PROBLEM SET B

B 1. *Budget Preparation*
L O 6, 7

Check Figure: 1. Projected Net Income: $930,415

Bryan Burns is budget director for Highland Spectaculars, Inc., a multinational company based in Maryland. Highland Spectaculars, Inc. organizes and coordinates art shows and auctions throughout the world. Budgeted and actual costs and expenses for 19x8 are compared in the following schedule.

	19x8 Amounts	
Expense Item	**Budget**	**Actual**
Salaries expense, staging	$ 240,000	$ 256,400
Salaries expense, executive	190,000	223,600
Travel costs	320,000	326,010
Auctioneer services	270,000	224,910
Space rental costs	125,500	123,290
Printing costs	96,000	91,250
Advertising expense	84,500	91,640
Insurance, merchandise	42,400	38,650
Insurance, liability	32,000	33,550
Home office costs	104,600	109,940
Shipping costs	52,500	56,280
Miscellaneous	12,500	12,914
Total expenses	$1,570,000	$1,588,434
Net receipts	$3,100,000	$3,184,600

For 19x9, the following fixed costs have been budgeted: executive salaries, $220,000; advertising expense, $95,000; merchandise insurance, $40,000; and liability insurance, $34,000. Additional information follows.

a. Net receipts are expected to be $3,200,000 in 19x9.
b. Staging salaries will increase 20 percent over 19x8 actual figures.
c. Travel costs are expected to be 11 percent of net receipts.
d. Auctioneer services will be billed at 9.5 percent of net receipts.
e. Space rental costs will go up 20 percent from 19x8 budgeted amounts.
f. Printing costs are expected to be $95,000 in 19x9.
g. Home office costs are budgeted for $115,000 in 19x9.
h. Shipping costs are expected to rise 20 percent over 19x8 budgeted amounts.
i. Miscellaneous expenses for 19x9 will be budgeted at $14,000.

REQUIRED

1. Prepare the company's forecasted income statement for 19x9. Assume that only services are being sold and that there is no cost of sales. (Net receipts equal gross margin.) Use a 34 percent federal income tax rate.
2. Should the budget director be worried about the trend in the company's operations? Be specific.

B 2. *Factory Overhead*
L O 6 *Expense Budget*

Check Figure: 3. Totals, All Divisions: $576,925

Luarkie Manufacturing Company has a home office and three operating divisions. The home office houses the top management personnel, including all accounting functions. The factory overhead costs incurred during 19x8 are summarized in the table below.

Expected percentage increases for 19x9 are shown for all categories except computer services. These services will increase by different amounts for each division: East Division, 25%; West Division, 30%; and Central Division, 40%. In 19x8, the home office was charged $55,000 for computer service costs. This amount is expected to rise by 25% in 19x9. During 19x9, the company will rent a new software package at an annual cost of $90,000.

Expense Categories	East Division	West Division	Central Division	All Divisions	Expected Increase In 19x9
Indirect labor	$ 34,500	$ 30,600	$ 39,200	$104,300	10%
Indirect materials	12,800	13,200	14,000	40,000	20%
Supplies	11,900	12,900	12,000	36,800	10%
Utilities	14,200	15,400	11,100	40,700	10%
Computer services	32,500	35,800	37,700	106,000	—
Insurance	11,400	12,500	13,600	37,500	10%
Repairs and Maintenance	11,600	16,000	14,400	42,000	20%
Miscellaneous	10,100	12,200	11,300	33,600	10%
Totals	$139,000	$148,600	$153,300	$440,900	

REQUIRED

1. Find the total expected cost for computer services for 19x9 for the three divisions and the home office.
2. Assume that the new software package rental charge is allocated to computer service users on the basis of their normal computer use costs as a percentage of total computer service charges. Allocate the rental charges to the three divisions and the home office. (Use the 19x9 amounts computed in **1** above, and round to one percentage decimal place.)
3. Prepare the divisional factory overhead expense budget for Luarkie Manufacturing Company for 19x9.

B 3. *Basic Cash Budget*
L O 8

Check Figure: 1. Ending Cash Balance, February: ($1,450)

Jim Shannon is president of Rocky Mountain Nurseries of Utah, Inc. This corporation has four locations and has been in business for six years. Each retail outlet offers over 300 varieties of plants and trees. Mary Ritter, the controller, has been asked to prepare a cash budget for the Southern Division for the first quarter of 19x7.

Projected data supporting the budget are summarized as follows. Collection history for the accounts receivable has shown that 30 percent of all credit sales are collected in the month of sale, 60 percent in the month following the sale, and 8 percent in the second month following the sale. Two percent of the credit sales are uncollectible. Purchases are all paid for in the month following the purchase. As of December 31, 19x6, the Southern Division had a cash balance of $4,800.

Sales (60 percent on credit)		Purchases	
November 19x6	$ 80,000	December 19x6	$43,400
December 19x6	100,000	January 19x7	62,350
January 19x7	60,000	February 19x7	49,720
February 19x7	80,000	March 19x7	52,400
March 19x7	70,000		

Salaries and wages are projected to be $12,600 in January; $16,600 in February; and $10,600 in March. Monthly costs are estimated to be: utilities, $2,110; collection fees, $850; rent, $2,650; equipment depreciation, $2,720; supplies, $1,240; small tools, $1,570; and miscellaneous, $950.

REQUIRED

1. Prepare a cash budget by month for the Southern Division for first quarter 19x7.
2. Should Rocky Mountain Nurseries of Utah, Inc. anticipate taking out a loan for the Southern Division during the quarter? How much should be borrowed? When? (**Note:** Management maintains a $3,000 minimum cash balance at each location.)

B 4. *Forecasted Financial*
L O 7, 9 *Statements*

Check Figure: 1. Projected Net Income: $52,404

Giles Video Company, Inc. produces and markets two popular video games, "Fifth Avenue" and "Young Adventures." The company's closing balance sheet account balances for 19x7 are as follows: Cash, $18,735; Accounts Receivable, $19,900; Materials Inventory, $18,510; Work in Process Inventory, $24,680; Finished Goods Inventory, $21,940; Prepaid Expenses, $3,420; Plant and Equipment, $262,800; Accumulated Depreciation, Plant and Equipment, $55,845; Other Assets, $9,480; Accounts Payable, $52,640; Mortgage Payable, $70,000; Common Stock, $90,000; and Retained Earnings, $110,980.

Period budgets for the first quarter of 19x8 revealed the following: materials purchases, $58,100; materials usage, $62,400; labor expense, $42,880; factory overhead expense, $51,910; selling expenses, $35,820; general and administrative expenses, $60,240; capital expenditures, $0; ending cash balances by month: January, $34,610; February, $60,190; March, $54,802; cost of goods manufactured, $163,990; and cost of goods sold, $165,440.

Sales per month are projected to be $125,200 for January, $105,100 for February, and $112,600 for March. Accounts receivable will double during the quarter, and accounts payable will decrease by 20 percent. Mortgage payments for the quarter will total $6,000, of which $2,000 is interest expense. Prepaid expenses are expected to go up by $20,000, and other assets are projected to increase 50 percent over the budget period. Depreciation for plant and equipment (already included in the factory overhead budget) averages 5 percent of total Plant and Equipment per year. Federal income taxes (34 percent of profits) are payable in April. No dividends were paid.

REQUIRED

1. Prepare a forecasted income statement for the quarter ending March 31, 19x8.
2. Prepare a forecasted balance sheet as of March 31, 19x8.

B 5. *Cash Budget*
L O 8 *Preparation:*
Comprehensive

Check Figure: Ending Cash Balance, January: $455

Thomas's Wellness Centers, Inc. operates three fully equipped personal health facilities in Scottsdale, Arizona. In addition to the health facilities, the corporation maintains a complete medical center specializing in preventive medicine. Emphasis is placed on regular workouts and medical examinations. The following projections have been made for 19x8.

Cash Receipts: First Quarter, 19x8

Membership dues:
    Memberships: December, 19x7, 870; January, 19x8, 880; February, 910; and March, 1,030
    Dues: $90 per month, payable on the 10th (80 percent collected on time, 20 percent collected one month late)
Medical examinations: January, $35,610; February, $41,840; and March, $45,610
Special aerobics classes: January, $4,020; February, $5,130; and March, $7,130
High-protein food sales: January, $4,890; February, $5,130; and March, $6,280

Cash Payments: First Quarter, 19x8

Salaries and wages:
    Corporate officers: $24,000 per month
    Medical doctors: 2 @ $7,000 per month
    Nurses: 3 @ $2,900 per month
    Clerical staff: 2 @ $1,500 per month
    Aerobics instructors: 3 @ $1,100 per month
    Clinic staff: 6 @ $1,700 per month
    Maintenance staff: 3 @ $900 per month
    Health food servers: 3 @ $750 per month
Purchases:
    Muscle-tone machines: January, $14,400; February, $13,800; and March, $0
    Pool supplies: $520 per month
    Health food: January, $3,290; February, $3,460; and March, $3,720
    Medical supplies: January, $10,400; February, $11,250; and March, $12,640
    Medical clothing: January, $7,410; February, $3,900; and March, $3,450
    Medical equipment: January, $11,200; February, $3,400; and March $5,900
Advertising: January, $2,250; February, $1,190; and March, $2,450
Utilities expense: January, $5,450; February, $5,890; and March, $6,090
Insurance:
    Fire: January, $3,470
    Liability: March, $3,980
Property taxes: $3,760 due in January
Federal income taxes: 19x7 taxes of $21,000 due in March 19x8
Miscellaneous: January, $2,625; February, $2,800; and March, $1,150

The beginning cash balance for 19x8 is anticipated to be $9,840.

REQUIRED

Prepare a cash budget for Thomas's Wellness Centers, Inc. for the first quarter of 19x8. Use the following column headings:

Item	January	February	March	Total

MANAGERIAL REPORTING AND ANALYSIS CASES

Interpreting Management Reports

MRA 1. *Interpreting Budget*
L O 2, 4 *Formulation Policies*

No check figure

Husin Corporation is a manufacturing company with annual sales of $25,000,000. The controller, Victor Subroto, appointed Yolanda Alvillar as budget director. She created the following budget formulation policy based on a calendar-year accounting period.

May 19x8   Meeting of corporate officers and budget director to discuss corporate plans for 19x9.

June 19x8   Meeting(s) of division managers, department heads, and budget director to communicate 19x9 corporate objectives. At this time, relevant background data are distributed to all managers and a time schedule is established for development of 19x9 budget data.

July 19x8 — Managers and department heads continue to develop budget data. Complete 19x9 monthly sales forecasts by product line and receive final sales estimates from sales vice president.

Aug. 19x8 — Complete 19x9 monthly production activity and anticipated inventory level plans. Division managers and department heads should communicate preliminary budget figures to budget director for coordination and distribution to other operating areas.

Sept. 19x8 — Development of preliminary 19x9 master budget. Revised budget data from all functional areas to be received. Budget director will coordinate staff activities, integrating labor requirements, direct materials and supplies requirements, unit cost estimates, cash requirements, and profit estimates, and prepare preliminary 19x9 master budget.

Oct. 19x8 — Meeting with corporate officers to discuss preliminary 19x9 master budget; any corrections, additions, or deletions to be communicated to budget director by corporate officers; all authorized changes to be incorporated into the 19x9 master budget.

Nov. 19x8 — Submit final draft of 19x9 master budget to corporate officers for approval. Publish approved budget and distribute to all corporate officers, division managers, and department heads.

REQUIRED

1. Comment on the proposed budget formulation policy.
2. What changes in the policy would you recommend?

Formulating Management Reports

MRA 2.
L O 2, 5
Forecasted Financial Statement Preparation

No check figure

Assume that you have just signed a partnership agreement with your cousin Eddie to open a bookstore near the college campus. You believe that you will be able to provide excellent services at prices lower than your local competition. In order to begin operations, Eddie and you have decided to apply for a small business loan from the Small Business Administration (SBA). Part of the application requires that you submit financial statements that will forecast the bookstore's first two years of operating activity and its financial position at the end of the second year. The application is due within six weeks. Because of your expertise in accounting and business, Eddie has asked you to develop the forecasted financial statements.

REQUIRED

1. List the forecasted financial statements and supporting schedules you believe you must prepare.
2. Who needs the forecasted financial statements?
3. Why are you preparing forecasted financial statements?
4. What information do you need to develop on the forecasted financial statements? How will you obtain the information?
5. When must you have the forecasted financial statements prepared?
6. In what ways can Eddie and you use the forecasted financial statements you have prepared?

International Company

MRA 3.
L O 8
Goals and the Budgeting Process

No check figure

3M manufactures a variety of products ranging from office supplies to household sponges and laser imagers for CAT scanners to reflective materials for roads. Because of the company's aggressive research and development activities, many of these products have been redesigned to satisfy the needs of Asian customers. Business has been so successful that sales in the Asia-Pacific division of 3M have doubled in the past five years. Facilities are in Malaysia, South Korea, India, Thailand, and Taiwan.[6]

Based on 3M's strategic plan for next year, two goals for the Asia-Pacific division have been developed. These goals include a 25 percent growth in sales volume and construction of a $14 million manufacturing plant in Shanghai that will begin operations in the third quarter of the year.

REQUIRED

The manager for the Asia-Pacific division is preparing the cash budget for next year's operations. How would the forecasted cash receipts and cash payments on the cash budget be affected by these two goals?

6. "3M: Business Booms in Asia," *Asian Business*, Vol. 29, No. 22, February 1993, pp. 9–10.

Standard Costing and Variance Analysis

1. Define *standard costs* and describe how managers use standard costs to plan for, and control, costs.

2. State the purposes for using standard costs.

3. Identify the six elements of, and compute, a standard unit cost.

4. Define and prepare a *flexible budget*.

5. Describe the concept of management by exception.

6. Compute and analyze (a) direct materials, (b) direct labor, and (c) factory overhead variances.

7. Prepare journal entries to record transactions involving variances in a standard costing system.

8. Evaluate managers' performance using variances.

9. Compute and evaluate factory overhead variances using a three-variance analysis.

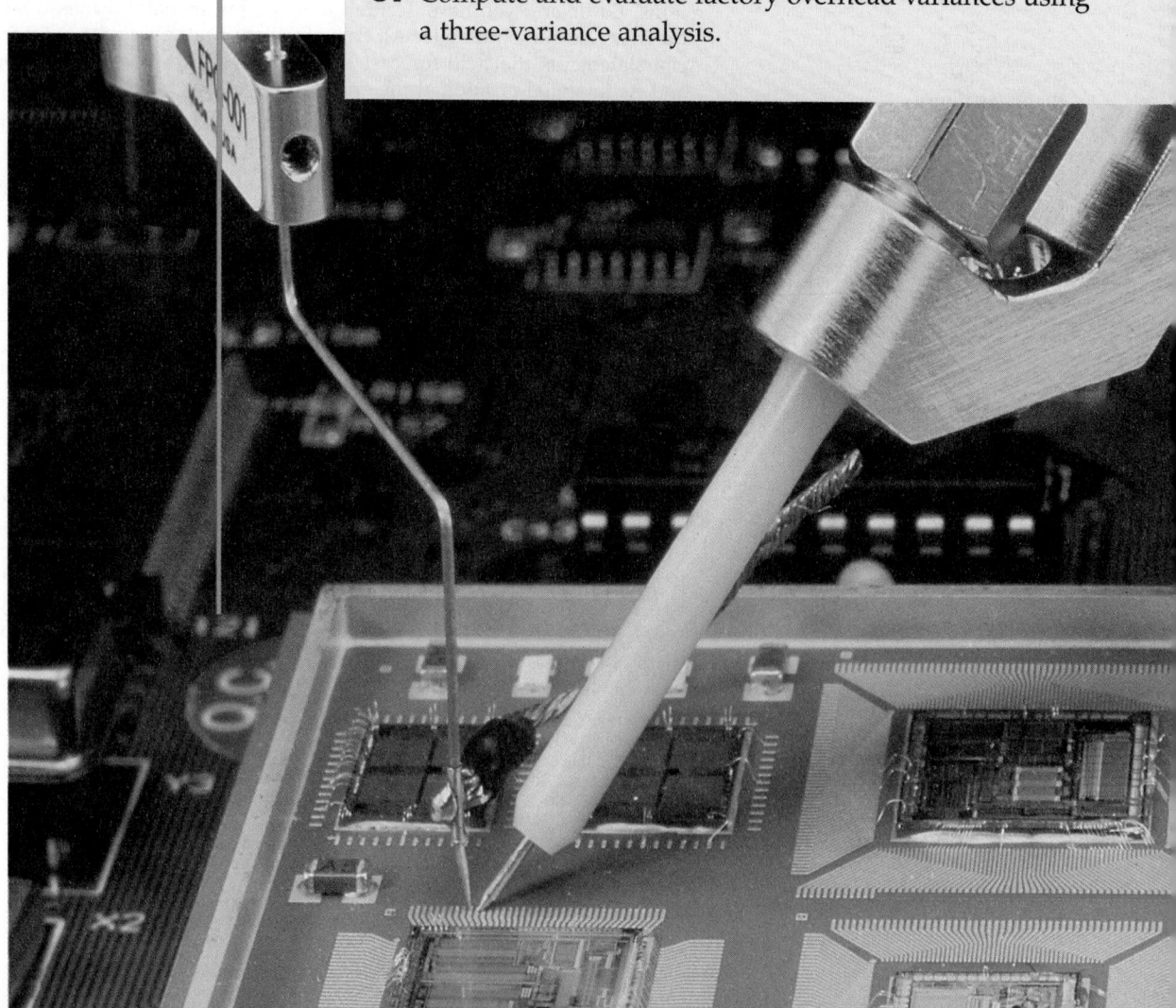

Hewlett-Packard

Hewlett-Packard has experimented with replacing standard costs with historical costs as a basis for recording and cost control in its new manufacturing environment.[1] Hewlett-Packard was one of the first companies to successfully update and automate its production facilities and to significantly reduce its product processing time. In a study of the Hewlett-Packard case, a group of researchers questioned the use of historical costs for cost control purposes. The researchers were concerned that historical costs may have been incurred during periods of poor performance and would therefore not be a fitting measure when trying to control costs in a constantly changing environment. The researchers sought to answer the question: Should Hewlett-Packard shift from using standard costs to using historical costs as a basis for cost control analyses?

The researchers found that in the new globally competitive environment, operating conditions promote the use of standard costs. This is because an automated manufacturing environment decreases labor costs significantly, which reduces the emphasis on labor standard costs and variances. Hewlett-Packard's new system reduces the number of suppliers and advocates higher-quality goods and the use of long-term purchase contracts, all of which increases the importance of price and quality of raw materials. Updated standard costs allow materials prices and quality differences to be measured and evaluated.

Automated machinery results in a standardized, repetitive operation and a reduction of overhead costs related to scrap and rework. The use of machinery and equipment capacity must be measured through variance analysis, because in Hewlett-Packard's new manufacturing environment, inventories are kept small and facilities are idle if no orders are being processed. Factory overhead standards and variances measure these areas. The researchers concluded that these facts support an *increase* in the use of standard costs, rather than their elimination.

1. Richard V. Calvasina, Eugene J. Calvasina, and Gerald E. Calvasina, "Beware of New Accounting Myths," *Management Accounting*, Institute of Management Accountants, December 1989, pp. 41–45.

STANDARD COSTS IN TODAY'S BUSINESS ENVIRONMENT

1 *Define* standard costs *and describe how managers use standard costs to plan for, and control, costs*

Standard cost accounting is a budgetary control technique. In a standard cost system, standard costs for materials, labor, and factory overhead flow through the inventory accounts and eventually into Cost of Goods Sold. Instead of using actual costs for product costing purposes, standard costs are used in their place. Standard costs are realistically predetermined costs that are developed from analyses of both past operating costs, quantities, and times and future resource costs and operating conditions.

Once standard costs have been developed, managers use them as tools for planning and budgeting activities. After projected sales and production unit targets for the upcoming year are established, planned materials purchase costs, labor costs, and variable factory overhead costs can be computed using standard costs. These costs serve as targets or goals for product costing purposes; they can also be used in the product distribution and selling cost areas. Standard costs not only aid in the development of budgets, they also serve as yardsticks for evaluating actual expenditure amounts. If a vendor charges a price different from the anticipated standard price, the manager should question the difference.

At the end of an accounting period—whether weekly, monthly, or quarterly—the actual costs incurred are compared with standard costs, and the differences are computed. The difference between a standard cost and an actual cost is called a variance. Variances provide measures of performance that can be used to control costs. The amount of the variance provides one measure of the significance of the variance. But managers should look beyond the amount of a variance and try to determine its cause or causes. By analyzing the causes of the variances, managers are able to separate efficient functions from inefficient areas within departments or work cells in order to concentrate on problem areas needing improvement. In this way, standard costs aid in controlling operating costs.

Standard costing has traditionally been used to measure and evaluate operating performance in manufacturing settings. Today, standard costing is being applied by managers in service businesses. The only difference between using standard costs in a manufacturing company and in a service company is that there are no materials costs in a service environment. But labor and overhead costs are very much a part of a service business and must be planned and controlled. Therefore, managers in service businesses, such as banks and hospitals, can also use standard costs and measure performance through variance analysis.

Today, a globally competitive manufacturing environment has evolved with new approaches to performance evaluation. Instead of concentrating exclusively on production efficiency and cost control, managers in the new manufacturing environment are also concerned with reducing processing time and improving quality, customer satisfaction, and the number of on-time deliveries. This environment requires new measures of performance that track processing time, quality, customer responses, and delivery results. The importance of standard costs and variances relating to labor has been reduced because the amount of direct labor cost has dropped significantly. However, standard costs and variance analysis of materials and factory overhead costs are still very much in use. The Hewlett-Packard Decision Point illustrates this change in standard cost usage.

NATURE AND PURPOSE OF STANDARD COST ACCOUNTING

OBJECTIVE

2 *State the purposes for using standard costs*

Accountants do not build a full cost accounting system from standard costs alone. Standard costs are used with existing job order or process costing systems. When a company uses standard costs, all costs affecting the inventory accounts and the Cost of Goods Sold account are recorded using standard or predetermined costs rather than actual costs incurred. In this section, we examine the nature and purpose of standard costs—their components, their development, their use in product costing, and their related journal entries. Later in the chapter we concentrate on the way they are used, primarily as a tool for cost control.

Standard costs are predetermined costs for direct materials, direct labor, and factory overhead. They usually are expressed as cost per unit of finished product or process. Standard costs share two very important characteristics with predetermined overhead costs: both forecast the dollar amounts to be used in product costing, and both depend on projected costs for budgeted items. But that is where the similarity ends.

Unlike the predetermined overhead rate, standard costing focuses on *total* unit cost, which includes all three manufacturing cost elements. The computation of standard costs is more detailed than that of predetermined overhead costs. Whereas predetermined overhead rates usually depend on projections based on past costs, standard costs are based on engineering estimates, forecasted demand, worker input, time and motion studies, and type and quality of direct materials. One drawback to standard costing is that it is expensive to use. Since the predetermined overhead rate does provide some of the same data as the standard overhead rate, a company that cannot afford to add standard costing to its cost system should continue to use predetermined overhead rates.

Standard costing is a total cost concept. In a fully integrated standard cost system, standard cost data replace all actual manufacturing cost data. Accounts such as Materials Inventory, Work in Process Inventory, Finished Goods Inventory, and Cost of Goods Sold are reported in terms of standard costs. All debits and credits to these accounts are in terms of standard costs, not actual costs. All inventory balances are computed using standard unit costs. The management accountant keeps separate records of actual costs to compare what should have been spent (the standard costs) with the actual costs incurred.

There are, then, several reasons for introducing standard costs into a cost accounting system. They are useful in preparing operating budgets. They make it easier to pinpoint production costs that must be controlled and to evaluate the performance of managers and workers. They help in setting realistic prices, and they simplify cost accounting procedures for inventories and product costing. Although expensive to set up and maintain, a standard cost accounting system can save a company money by helping to reduce waste and inefficiency.

DEVELOPMENT OF STANDARD COSTS

A standard unit cost for a manufactured product has six parts: (1) direct materials price standard, (2) direct materials quantity standard, (3) direct labor time standard, (4) direct labor rate standard, (5) standard variable factory overhead rate, and (6) standard fixed factory overhead rate. To develop a standard unit cost, we must identify and analyze each of these elements. For service companies, only the last four apply because those companies do not use raw materials or parts in their operations.

Standard Direct Materials Cost   The standard direct materials cost is found by multiplying the standard price for direct materials by the standard quantity for direct materials. If the standard price for a certain item is $2.75 and a specific job calls for a standard quantity of 8 of the items, the standard direct materials cost for that job is $22.00 (8 × $2.75).

The direct materials price standard is a careful estimate of the cost of a certain type of direct material in the next accounting period. The purchasing agent is responsible for developing price standards for all direct materials. When estimating the direct materials price standard, the purchasing agent must take into account all possible price increases, changes in available quantities, and new sources of supply. The purchasing agent also makes the actual purchases.

The standard quantity of direct materials is one of the most difficult standards to forecast. The direct materials quantity standard is an estimate of the expected quantity to be used. It is influenced by product engineering specifications, the quality of direct materials, the age and productivity of machinery, and the quality and experience of the work force. Some scrap and waste may be unavoidable and anticipated when computing the standard quantity amount. Production managers or cost accountants usually establish and police direct materials quantity standards, although engineers, purchasing agents, and machine operators may provide input into the development of these standards.

Standard Direct Labor Cost   The standard direct labor cost for a product, task, or job order is calculated by multiplying the standard hours of direct labor by the standard wage for direct labor. If a product takes 1.5 standard direct labor hours to produce and the standard direct labor rate is $8.40 per hour, then the product's standard direct labor cost is $12.60 ($8.40 × 1.5).

The direct labor time standard is the expected time required for each department, machine, or process to complete the production of one unit or one batch of output. Current time and motion studies of workers and machines as well as past employee and machine performance are the basic input for the development of this standard. In many cases, standard time per unit is a small fraction of an hour. The direct labor time standard should be revised whenever a machine is replaced or the quality of the labor force changes. Meeting time standards is the responsibility of the department manager or supervisor.

Standard labor rates are fairly easy to develop because labor rates are either set by a labor contract or defined by the company. Direct labor rate standards are the hourly labor costs that are expected to prevail during the next accounting period for each function or job classification. Although rate ranges are established for each type of worker and rates vary within these ranges based on experience and length of service, an average standard rate is developed for each task. Even if the person actually making the product is paid more or less than the standard rate, the standard rate is used to calculate the standard direct labor cost.

| **Standard Factory Overhead Cost** | The standard factory overhead cost is the sum of the estimates for variable and fixed factory overhead in the next accounting period. It is based on standard rates computed in much the same way as the predetermined overhead rate discussed earlier. One major difference, however, is that the standard overhead rate is made up of two parts, one for variable costs and one for fixed costs. The reason for computing the standard variable and fixed overhead rates separately is that different application bases are generally required. The standard variable overhead rate is total budgeted variable factory overhead costs divided by an expression of capacity, such as the expected number of standard machine hours or direct labor hours. (Other bases may be used if machine hours or direct labor hours are not good measures of variable overhead costs.) Using standard machine hours as the basis, the formula is:

$$\frac{\text{Standard variable}}{\text{overhead rate}} = \frac{\text{total budgeted variable overhead costs}}{\text{expected number of standard machine hours}}$$

The standard fixed overhead rate is total budgeted fixed factory overhead costs divided by an expression of capacity, usually normal capacity in terms of standard hours or units. The denominator is expressed in the same terms (direct labor hours, machine hours, and so forth) as that used to compute the variable overhead rate. The formula is:

$$\frac{\text{Standard fixed}}{\text{overhead rate}} = \frac{\text{total budgeted fixed overhead costs}}{\text{normal capacity in terms of standard machine hours}}$$

Using normal capacity as the application basis ensures that all fixed overhead costs have been applied to units produced by the time normal capacity is reached.

USING STANDARDS FOR PRODUCT COSTING

Using standard costs eliminates the need to calculate unit costs from actual cost data every week or month or for each batch produced. Once standard costs are developed for direct materials, direct labor, and factory overhead, a total standard unit cost can be computed at any time.

With standard cost elements, the following amounts are determined: (1) cost of purchased direct materials entered into Materials Inventory, (2) cost of goods requisitioned out of Materials Inventory and into Work in Process Inventory, (3) cost of direct labor charged to Work in Process Inventory, (4) cost of factory overhead applied to Work in Process Inventory, (5) cost of goods completed and transferred to Finished Goods Inventory, and (6) cost of units sold and charged to Cost of Goods Sold. In other words, all transactions (and related journal entries) affecting the three inventory accounts and Cost of Goods Sold are expressed in terms of standard costs, no matter what the amount of actual costs incurred. An illustrative problem shows how standard costing works.

ILLUSTRATIVE PROBLEM:
USE OF STANDARD COSTS

Bokinski Industries, Inc. uses a standard cost accounting system. Recently, the company updated the standards for its line of automatic pencils. New standards include the following: Direct materials price standards are $9.20 per square foot for casing materials and $2.25 for each movement mechanism.

Direct materials quantity standards are .025 square foot of casing materials per pencil and one movement mechanism per pencil. Direct labor time standards are .01 hour per pencil for the Stamping Department and .05 hour per pencil for the Assembly Department. Direct labor rate standards are $8.00 per hour for the Stamping Department and $10.20 per hour for the Assembly Department. Standard factory overhead rates are $12.00 per total direct labor hours for the standard variable overhead rate and $9.00 per total direct labor hours for the standard fixed overhead rate.

REQUIRED   Compute the standard manufacturing cost of one automatic pencil.

SOLUTION

Direct materials costs	
Casing ($9.20/sq. ft. × .025 sq. ft.)	$ .23
One movement mechanism	2.25
Direct labor costs	
Stamping Department (.01 hour/pencil × $8.00/hour)	.08
Assembly Department (.05 hour/pencil × $10.20/hour)	.51
Factory overhead	
Variable overhead (.06 hour/pencil × $12.00/hour)	.72
Fixed overhead (.06 hour/pencil × $9.00/hour)	.54
Total standard cost of one pencil	$4.33

JOURNAL ENTRY ANALYSIS

Recording standard costs is much like recording actual cost data. The major difference is that amounts for direct materials, direct labor, and factory overhead entered into the Work in Process Inventory account are recorded at standard cost. This means that any transfer of units to Finished Goods Inventory or to the Cost of Goods Sold account will automatically be stated at standard unit cost. When actual costs for direct materials, direct labor, and factory overhead differ from standard costs, the difference is recorded in a variance account. (We discuss variance accounts in the next section.) In the following journal entry analysis, it is assumed that all costs incurred are at standard cost, so no variances are shown in the entries. Again, Bokinski Industries' standard costs, which were given previously, are used in the examples.

Sample Transaction: Purchased 500 square feet of casing materials at standard cost on account.

Entry:	Materials Inventory	4,600	
	Accounts Payable		4,600
	Purchase of 500 sq. ft. of casing material @ $9.20/sq. ft.		

Here it does not matter if the actual purchase price differs from the standard price. The standard cost only is entered into the Materials Inventory account.

Sample Transaction: Requisitioned 60 square feet of casing material and 240 movement mechanisms into production.

Entry:	Work in Process Inventory	1,092	
	Materials Inventory		1,092
	Requisition of 60 sq. ft. of casing material (@ $9.20/sq. ft.) and 240 movement mechanisms (@ $2.25 each) into production		

Sample Transaction: During the period, 600 pencils were completed and transferred to Finished Goods Inventory.

Entry: Finished Goods Inventory   2,598
              Work in Process Inventory   2,598
                 Transfer of 600 completed units to
                 finished goods inventory (600 pencils
                 × $4.33/pencil)

These entries show that when a standard cost accounting system is used, standard costs, not actual costs, flow through the production and inventory accounts. Examples later in this chapter combine the recording of standard cost information with the analysis of variances.

BUSINESS BULLETIN: INTERNATIONAL PRACTICE[2]

To the Japanese, a standard operation is the combination of workers and machines carrying out production in the most efficient way. The standard operation is made up of "takt time," work sequence procedures, and standard amounts of work in process within the work cell. Takt time is the key element in achieving a standard operation. *Takt* is the Japanese word for "baton." The baton is used by a band leader to set the pace or the beat of the music of an orchestra. In the factory, takt time is the "beat" that the factory must follow. It is computed as follows: Takt time = time available ÷ sold units. Sold units—those units that have actually been ordered—reinforces the concept that production is driven by demand and that there will be no overproduction. A JIT cell with a takt time of five minutes must complete one unit every five minutes.

COST CONTROL THROUGH VARIANCE ANALYSIS

Managers of manufacturing operations, as well as those responsible for selling and service functions, constantly compare what did happen with what was expected to happen. The difference—or variance—between actual and standard costs provides information needed to evaluate managers' performance. If the variance is too great, managers can implement cost control measures. Our discussion now focuses on the differences between actual costs and budgeted or standard costs. Before budgeted data can be used to analyze performance, they must be adjusted to reflect actual productive output. The flexible budget is the management accounting tool used for this purpose.

2. Mark C. DeLuzio, "The Tools of Just-In-Time," *Journal of Cost Management,* A Warren Gorham Lamont Publication, Summer 1993, pp. 13–20.

Exhibit 1. Performance Analysis: Comparison of Actual and Budgeted Data

Rockford Industries, Inc.
Performance Report—Eastern Division
For the Year Ended December 31, 19x8

Cost Item	Budget*	Actual†	Difference Under (Over) Budget
Direct materials	$ 42,000	$ 46,000	($ 4,000)
Direct labor	68,250	75,000	(6,750)
Factory overhead			
Variable			
Indirect materials	10,500	11,500	(1,000)
Indirect labor	14,000	15,250	(1,250)
Utilities	7,000	7,600	(600)
Other	8,750	9,750	(1,000)
Fixed			
Supervisory salaries	19,000	18,500	500
Depreciation	15,000	15,000	—
Utilities	4,500	4,500	—
Other	10,900	11,100	(200)
Totals	$199,900	$214,200	($14,300)

*Budget based on expected productive output of 17,500 units.

†Actual cost of producing 19,100 units.

THE FLEXIBLE BUDGET

The type of budget used determines the accuracy of performance measurement. *Static,* or fixed, *budgets* describe just one level of expected sales and production activity. The master budget, including all the period budgets, is usually prepared for a single expected or normal level of output. For budgeting or planning, a set of static budgets based on a single level of output is adequate. These budgets show the desired operating results and provide a target for use in developing monthly and weekly operating plans.

Such budgets, however, are often inadequate for evaluating operating results. Exhibit 1 presents data for Rockford Industries, Inc. As you can see, actual costs exceed budgeted costs by $14,300, or 7.2 percent. Most managers would consider such an overrun to be significant. But was there really a cost overrun? The budgeted amounts are based on an expected output of 17,500 units, but actual output was 19,100 units. Thus, the static budget for 17,500 units is inadequate for evaluating performance. Before analyzing the performance of the Eastern Division, we must change the budgeted data to reflect an output of 19,100 units.

Unlike a static budget, a flexible budget provides forecasted data that can be adjusted automatically for changes in the level of output. A flexible budget is a summary of expected costs for a *range* of activity levels, geared to changes in the level of productive output. The flexible budget (also called a *variable budget*) is primarily a cost control tool used in evaluating performance.

Exhibit 2. Flexible Budget Preparation

Rockford Industries, Inc.
Flexible Budget Analysis—Eastern Division
For the Year Ended December 31, 19x8

Cost Item	Unit Levels of Activity			Variable Cost per Unit*
	15,000	17,500	20,000	
Direct materials	$ 36,000	$ 42,000	$ 48,000	$2.40
Direct labor	58,500	68,250	78,000	3.90
Variable factory overhead				
Indirect materials	9,000	10,500	12,000	.60
Indirect labor	12,000	14,000	16,000	.80
Utilities	6,000	7,000	8,000	.40
Other	7,500	8,750	10,000	.50
Total variable costs	$129,000	$150,500	$172,000	$8.60
Fixed factory overhead				
Supervisory salaries	$ 19,000	$ 19,000	$ 19,000	
Depreciation	15,000	15,000	15,000	
Utilities	4,500	4,500	4,500	
Other	10,900	10,900	10,900	
Total fixed costs	$ 49,400	$ 49,400	$ 49,400	
Total costs	$178,400	$199,900	$221,400	

Flexible budget formula:
(variable cost per unit × number of units produced) + budgeted fixed costs
= ($8.60 × units produced) + $49,400

Note: Activity expressed in units was used as the basis for this analysis. When units are used, direct material and direct labor costs are included in the analysis. Flexible budgets commonly are restricted to overhead costs. In such a situation, machine hours or direct labor hours are often used in place of units produced.

*Computed by dividing the dollar amount in any column by the respective level of activity.

Exhibit 2 presents a flexible budget for Rockford Industries, Inc., with budgeted data for 15,000, 17,500, and 20,000 units of output. The important part of this illustration is the flexible budget formula shown at the bottom. The flexible budget formula is an equation that determines the correct budgeted cost for any level of productive activity. It consists of a per unit amount for variable costs and a total amount for fixed costs. In Exhibit 2, the $8.60 variable cost per unit is computed in the right-hand column, and the $49,400 is found in the fixed cost section of the analysis. Using this formula, you can draw up a budget for the Eastern Division at any level of output.

Exhibit 3 shows a performance report prepared using the flexible budget data in Exhibit 2. Unit variable cost amounts have been multiplied by 19,100 units to arrive at the total budgeted figures. Fixed overhead information has been carried over from the flexible budget developed in Exhibit 2. As the new performance report shows, costs exceeded budgeted amounts during the year

Exhibit 3. Performance Analysis Using Flexible Budget Data

Rockford Industries, Inc.
Performance Report—Eastern Division
For the Year Ended December 31, 19x8

Cost Item (Variable Unit Cost)	Budget Based on 19,100 Units Produced	Actual Costs at 19,100-Unit Level	Difference Under (Over) Budget
Direct materials ($2.40)	$ 45,840	$ 46,000	$(160)
Direct labor ($3.90)	74,490	75,000	(510)
Factory overhead			
Variable			
Indirect materials ($.60)	11,460	11,500	(40)
Indirect labor ($.80)	15,280	15,250	30
Utilities ($.40)	7,640	7,600	40
Other ($.50)	9,550	9,750	(200)
Fixed			
Supervisory salaries	19,000	18,500	500
Depreciation	15,000	15,000	—
Utilities	4,500	4,500	—
Other	10,900	11,100	(200)
Totals	$213,660	$214,200	$(540)

by only $540, or less than three-tenths of one percent. In other words, using a flexible budget, we find that the performance of the Eastern Division is almost on target. Performance has now been measured and analyzed accurately. In addition to being a tool for overall performance measurement, a flexible budget is also used in analyzing factory overhead cost variances.

Analog Devices, Inc.[3]

DECISION POINT

Analog Devices, Inc. (ADI) produces high-quality electronic components that interface between analog and digital computer systems.[4] The company was founded in 1965 and had grown to a point where, by 1990, it employed 5,500 people in seven manufacturing facilities around the world. Its primary product line is precision, high-performance, linear integrated circuits.

3. Robert A. Howell, John K. Shank, Stephen R. Soucy, and Joseph Fisher, "The Analog Devices, Inc. Case," *Cost Management for Tomorrow: Seeking the Competitive Edge* (Morristown, N.J.: Financial Executives Research Foundation, 1992), pp. 127–149.

4. In an analog computer, numerical data are represented by measurable physical variables, such as electronic signals; a digital computer performs calculations and logical operations with quantities represented as digits, usually in a binary number system. *Source: The American Heritage Dictionary,* Third Edition, (Boston: Houghton Mifflin Company, 1992), pp. 65 and 521.

ADI used a standard cost system that employed cost standards for materials, labor, and variable factory overhead that were developed with the help of line managers. These standards were based on an anticipated level of product output. If a department spent more on materials and labor than the projected number and type of products, spending variances arose. Managers were held accountable for these variances.

However, one manager complained about the system saying:

> I receive stacks of variance reports every month, but they just aren't useful for me in trying to manage plant operations. And it is not because these reports are slow in arriving on my desk. They would not be any more useful if I got them every day! The problem is that they don't help me in understanding what is going wrong, or right, with my operations.

Another manager agreed, saying:

> The cost accounting system at ADI does not add value to my operations or to my customers. It is the nonfinancial, real-time data, such as process yields, that tell me where there are problems in my plant. The financial reports simply tell me 90 days later how much the problem cost me.

What adjustments needed to be made to the company's performance measurement system to make it more useful to the managers?

Financial performance measures provided managers with one view of their operations, but they did not identify specific operating problems—and they were usually not produced in a timely manner. In response to its managers' comments, ADI developed a separate performance measurement system called the Quality Improvement Program (QIP). This system tracks three areas using specific measures: high-quality products are measured by looking at the product defect rate; reliable suppliers are measured by tracking on-time deliveries; and responsive supplier performance is measured by delivery lead time. QIP teams continually try to improve performance by finding ways to improve the measured areas. Variances and financial reports are still issued to ADI managers, but managers' performance is now judged by looking at both the QIP measures and the financial results of operations. :::::

VARIANCE DETERMINATION AND ANALYSIS

We can evaluate operating performance by comparing actual results with either budgeted data or standard cost data. Budgeted data tend to be less precise than standard cost data, so we will focus on measuring performance using standard costs.

The first step in measuring performance is to find out if a cost variance exists. Variance determination helps to locate areas of efficiency or inefficiency. But the key to effective control of operations is not just finding the amount of the variance, but finding the reason for the variance. Once the cause is known, managers can take steps to correct the problem.

OBJECTIVE

5 *Describe the concept of management by exception*

The process of computing the amount of and isolating the causes of differences between actual costs and standard costs is called variance analysis. It is employed selectively. Many companies are so big that it is impossible to review all areas of operations in detail. Only the areas of unusually good or unusually bad performance are examined, a practice called management by exception. Let's assume that management decides that performance within ± 4 percent of budget or target is acceptable. When reviewing performance reports, they examine only those cost areas where differences exceed these limits. In Figure 1, for example, only direct materials C and E are outside the 4 percent limit, so only their costs will be analyzed.

Management accountants can compute variances for whole categories, such as total direct materials cost, or for any item in a category. The more refined and detailed the analysis, the more effective it is in cost control. This chapter presents a simplified example of standard cost variance analysis. In practice, variance analyses are much more complex, taking into account all facets of production and distribution.

Management accountants compute three types of variances: direct materials variances, direct labor variances, and factory overhead variances. Although materials variances are unique to manufacturing companies, labor and overhead variances may be computed for service enterprises as well as manufacturing companies. The term *service overhead* replaces factory overhead in service companies.

OBJECTIVE

6a *Compute and analyze direct materials variances*

Direct Materials Variances   The total direct materials cost variance is the difference between the actual direct materials cost incurred and the standard cost of those items. Let us assume, for example, that Collins Company makes leather chairs. Each chair should use 4 yards of leather (standard quantity), and the standard price of leather is $6.00 per yard. During August, Collins Company purchased 760 yards of leather costing $5.90 per yard and used the leather to produce 180 chairs. The total direct materials cost variance is as follows:

Actual cost
  Actual quantity × actual price =
    760 yd. × $5.90/yd. = $4,484

Less standard cost
  Standard quantity × standard price =
    (180 chairs × 4 yd./chair) × $6.00/yd. =
      720 yd. × $6.00/yd. = 4,320

Total direct materials cost variance $ 164 (U)

Here actual cost exceeds standard cost. The situation is unfavorable, as indicated by the U placed in parentheses after the dollar amount. An F designates a favorable situation.

To find the area or people responsible for the variance, the total direct materials cost variance must be broken down into two parts: the direct materials price variance and the direct materials quantity variance. The direct materials price variance is the difference between the actual price and the standard price, multiplied by the actual quantity purchased. For Collins Company, the direct materials price variance is computed as follows:

Actual price	$5.90
Less standard price	6.00
Difference	$ .10 (F)

Figure 1. The Management-by-Exception Technique

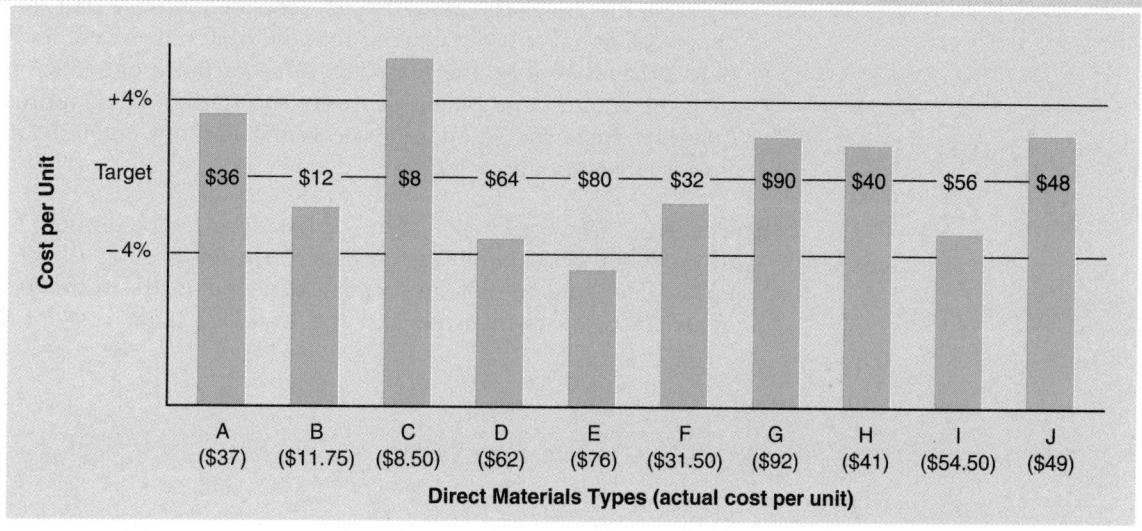

Direct materials price variance = (actual price − standard price) × actual quantity
= $.10 (F) × 760 yards
= $76 (F)

Because the materials purchased cost less than the standard cost, the variance is favorable.

The direct materials quantity variance is the difference between the actual quantity used and the standard quantity, multiplied by the standard price.

Actual quantity	760 yd.
Less standard quantity (180 × 4 yd./chair)	720 yd.
Difference	40 yd. (U)

Direct materials quantity variance = (actual quantity − standard quantity) × standard price
= 40 yd. (U) × $6/yd.
= $240 (U)

Because more material than prescribed was used, the direct materials quantity variance is unfavorable.

If the results of these calculations are correct, the sum of the price variance and the quantity variance should equal the total direct materials cost variance, as follows:

Direct materials price variance	$ 76 (F)
Direct materials quantity variance	240 (U)
Total direct materials cost variance	$164 (U)

Normally, the purchasing agent is responsible for price variances and the production department supervisors are accountable for quantity variances. In cases like this one, however, the cheaper materials may have been of such poor quality that higher-than-expected spoilage rates resulted, creating the unfavorable quantity variance. Each situation must be evaluated according to specific circumstances and not in terms of general guidelines.

Sometimes cost relationships are easier to interpret in diagram form. Figure 2 illustrates the analysis just described. Notice that materials are purchased at actual cost but entered into the Materials Inventory account at standard price; therefore, the materials price variance of $76 (F) is known when costs are entered into Materials Inventory. As shown in Figure 2, the standard quantity times the standard price is the amount entered into the Work in Process Inventory account.

Direct Labor Variances   The procedure for finding variances in direct labor costs parallels the procedure for finding direct materials variances. The total direct labor cost variance is the difference between the actual labor costs incurred and the standard labor cost for the good units

Figure 2. Materials Variance Analysis

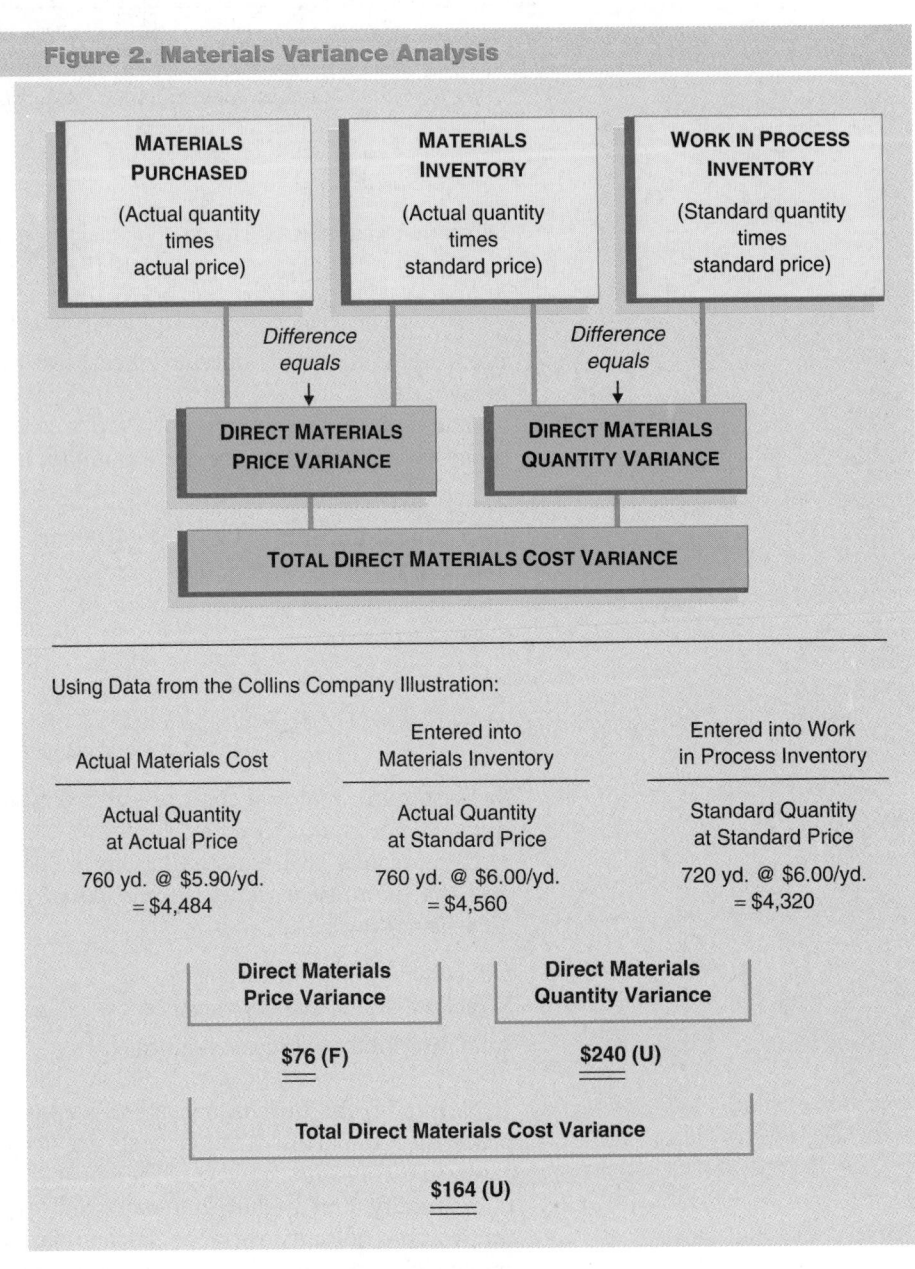

produced. (Good units are the total units produced less those units scrapped or needing rework.) In the Collins Company example, each chair requires 2.4 standard labor hours, and the standard labor rate is $8.50 per hour. During August, 450 direct labor hours were used to make 180 chairs at an average pay rate of $9.20 per hour. The total direct labor cost variance is computed as follows:

Actual cost
Actual hours × actual rate = 450 hr. × $9.20 = $4,140

Less standard cost
   Standard hours allowed × standard rate =
   (180 chairs × 2.4 hr./chair) × $8.50/hr. =
   432 hr. × $8.50/hr.   = 3,672

Total direct labor cost variance $ 468 (U)

Both the actual direct labor hours per chair and the actual direct labor rate varied from the standard. For effective performance evaluation, management must know how much of the total cost arose from differing labor rates and how much from varying labor hours. This information is found by computing the direct labor rate variance and the direct labor efficiency variance.

The **direct labor rate variance** is the difference between the actual labor rate and the standard labor rate, multiplied by the actual labor hours worked.

Actual rate $9.20
Less standard rate   8.50
Difference $ .70 (U)

Direct labor rate variance = (actual rate − standard rate) × actual hours
                           = $.70 (U) × 450 hr.
                           = $315 (U)

The **direct labor efficiency variance** is the difference between actual hours worked and standard hours allowed for the good units produced, multiplied by the standard labor rate.

Actual hours worked   450 hr.
Less standard hours allowed (180 chairs × 2.4 hr./chair)   432 hr.
Difference   18 hr. (U)

Direct labor
efficiency variance = (actual hours − standard hours allowed) × standard rate
                    = 18 hr. (U) × $8.50/hr.
                    = $153 (U)

The following check shows that the direct labor rate and the efficiency variances have been computed correctly.

Direct labor rate variance $315 (U)
Direct labor efficiency variance   153 (U)
Total direct labor cost variance $468 (U)

Direct labor rate variances are generally the responsibility of the personnel department. A rate variance can occur when a person is hired at a rate higher or lower than expected or performs the duties of a higher- or lower-paid employee. Direct labor efficiency variances can be traced to departmental supervisors. Problems in controlling labor costs arise when the wrong worker steps in to cover another's task. An example would be when a highly paid worker performs a lower-level task. For instance, a machine operator making $9.25 per hour may actually perform the work of a set-up person earning $6.50 per hour. Here, the actual cost for the work will be at variance with the standard direct labor rate. An unfavorable labor efficiency variance can also occur if an inexperienced, lower-paid person is assigned to a task requiring greater skill. Management should judge each situation according to the circumstances.

Figure 3 summarizes the direct labor variance analysis. Unlike materials variances, the labor rate and efficiency variances are usually computed and recorded at the same time, because labor is not stored in an inventory account before use. Data from Collins Company in the lower portion of Figure 3 illustrate this approach to labor variance analysis.

OBJECTIVE

6c *Compute and analyze factory overhead variances*

Factory Overhead Variances Controlling overhead costs is more difficult than controlling direct materials and direct labor costs because responsibility for overhead costs is hard to assign. Most fixed overhead costs are not controlled by specific department managers. But if variable overhead costs can be linked to operating departments, some control is possible.

Analyses of factory overhead variances differ in sophistication. The basic approach is to first compute the total overhead variance, which is the difference between actual overhead costs incurred and the standard overhead costs applied to production using the standard variable and fixed overhead rates. The total overhead variance is then divided into two parts: the controllable overhead variance and the overhead volume variance.

In our example, Collins Company budgeted standard variable overhead costs of $5.75 per direct labor hour plus $1,300 of fixed overhead costs for the month of August (flexible budget formula). Normal capacity was set at 400 direct labor hours per month. The company incurred $4,100 of actual overhead costs in August.

Before finding the overhead variances, the total standard overhead rate must be calculated. The total standard overhead rate has two parts. One is the variable rate of $5.75 per direct labor hour. The other is the standard fixed overhead rate, which is found by dividing budgeted fixed overhead ($1,300) by normal capacity. The result is $3.25 per direct labor hour ($1,300 ÷ 400 hours). So, the total standard overhead rate is $9.00 per direct labor hour ($5.75 + $3.25). The total budgeted fixed overhead costs divided by normal capacity provides a rate that assigns fixed overhead costs to products in a way that is consistent with expected output. The total overhead variance is computed as follows:

Actual overhead costs incurred	$4,100
Less standard overhead costs applied to good units produced	
$9.00/direct labor hour × (180 chairs × 2.4 hr./chair)	3,888
Total overhead variance	$ 212 (U)

This amount can be divided into two parts: the controllable overhead variance and the overhead volume variance. The controllable overhead variance is the difference between the actual overhead costs incurred and the factory overhead costs budgeted for the level of production reached. Thus, the controllable overhead variance for Collins Company for August is as follows:

Figure 3. Direct Labor Variance Analysis

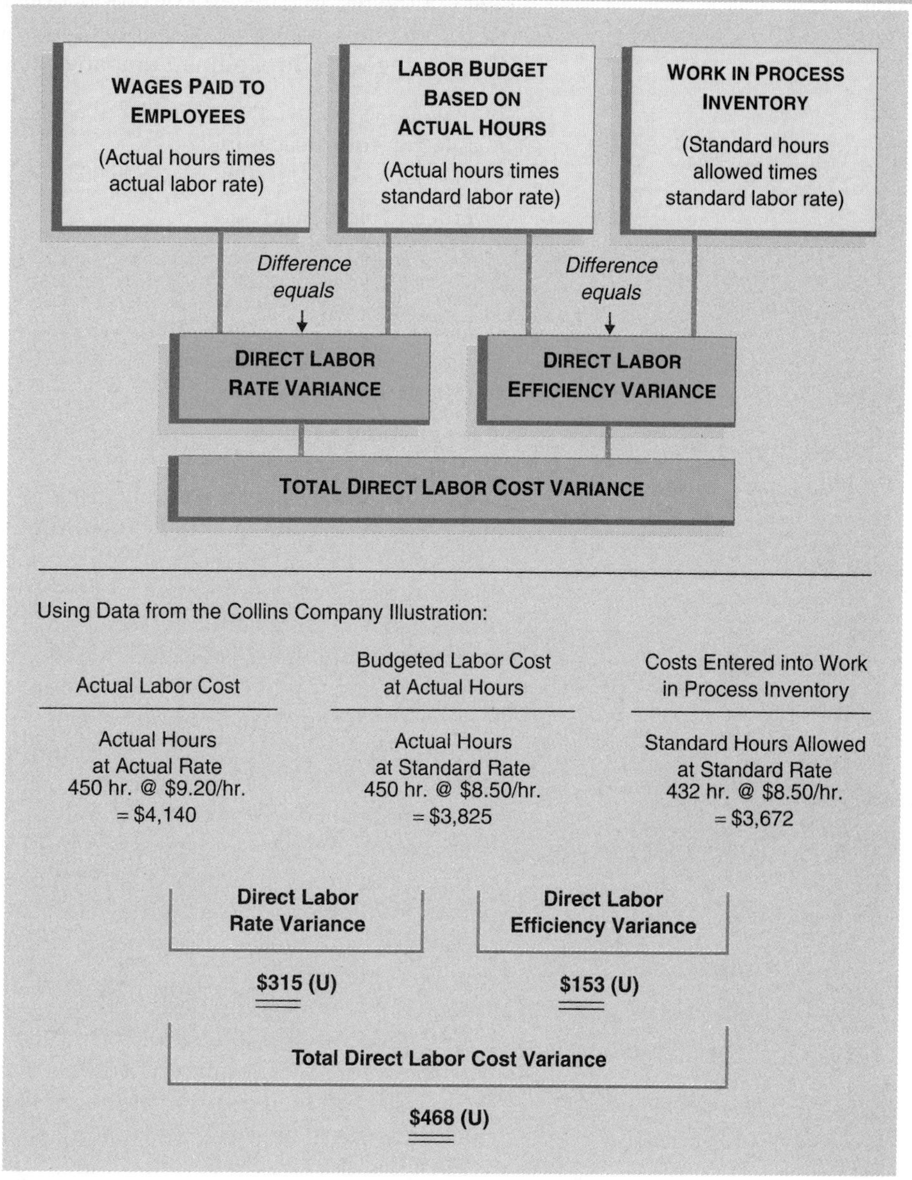

WAGES PAID TO EMPLOYEES	LABOR BUDGET BASED ON ACTUAL HOURS	WORK IN PROCESS INVENTORY
(Actual hours times actual labor rate)	(Actual hours times standard labor rate)	(Standard hours allowed times standard labor rate)

Difference equals → **DIRECT LABOR RATE VARIANCE**

Difference equals → **DIRECT LABOR EFFICIENCY VARIANCE**

TOTAL DIRECT LABOR COST VARIANCE

Using Data from the Collins Company Illustration:

Actual Labor Cost	Budgeted Labor Cost at Actual Hours	Costs Entered into Work in Process Inventory
Actual Hours at Actual Rate 450 hr. @ $9.20/hr. = $4,140	Actual Hours at Standard Rate 450 hr. @ $8.50/hr. = $3,825	Standard Hours Allowed at Standard Rate 432 hr. @ $8.50/hr. = $3,672

Direct Labor Rate Variance

Direct Labor Efficiency Variance

$315 (U)

$153 (U)

Total Direct Labor Cost Variance

$468 (U)

Actual overhead costs incurred		$4,100
Less budgeted factory overhead (flexible budget) for 180 chairs:		
Variable overhead cost (180 chairs × 2.4 hr./chair) × $5.75/direct labor hour	$2,484	
Budgeted fixed overhead cost	1,300	
Total budgeted factory overhead		3,784
Controllable overhead variance		$ 316 (U)

In this example, the controllable variance is unfavorable; the company spent more than had been budgeted.

The overhead volume variance is the difference between the factory overhead budgeted for the level of production achieved and the overhead applied to production using the standard variable and fixed overhead rates. Continuing with the Collins Company example, we have the following:

Budgeted factory overhead (see detail above)	$3,784
Less factory overhead applied	
(180 chairs × 2.4 hr./chair) × $9.00/direct labor hour	3,888
Overhead volume variance	$ 104 (F)

Checking the computations, we find that the two variances do equal the total overhead variance.

Controllable overhead variance	$316 (U)
Overhead volume variance	104 (F)
Total overhead variance	$212 (U)

Because the overhead volume variance gauges the use of existing facilities and capacity, a volume variance will occur if more or less capacity than normal is used. In this example, 400 direct labor hours is considered normal use of facilities. Fixed overhead costs are applied on the basis of standard hours allowed. So in the example, overhead was applied on the basis of 432 hours, even though the fixed overhead rate was computed using 400 hours (normal capacity). Thus, more fixed costs would be applied to products than were budgeted. Because the products can absorb no more than actual costs incurred, this level of production would tend to lower unit cost. Thus, when capacity exceeds the expected amount, the result is a favorable overhead volume variance. When capacity does not meet the normal level, not all of the fixed overhead costs will be applied to units produced. It is then necessary to add the amount of underapplied fixed overhead to the cost of the good units produced, thereby increasing their unit cost. This condition is unfavorable.

Figure 4 summarizes the analysis of overhead variance. As explained earlier, to determine the controllable overhead variance, the management accountant subtracts the budgeted overhead amount (using a flexible budget for the level of output achieved) from the actual overhead costs incurred. A positive result means an unfavorable variance, because actual costs were greater than budgeted costs. The controllable overhead variance is favorable if the difference is negative. Subtracting total overhead applied from budgeted overhead at the level of output achieved yields the overhead volume variance. Again, a positive result means an unfavorable variance; a negative result, a favorable variance. The data from the Collins Company example are shown in the lower part of Figure 4. Carefully check the solution in the figure with that computed above.

VARIANCES IN THE ACCOUNTING RECORDS

OBJECTIVE

7 *Prepare journal entries to record transactions involving variances in a standard costing system*

Special journal entries are needed to record variances from standard costs. Three simple rules make this recording process easy to remember.

1. *All* inventory balances are recorded at standard cost.
2. Separate general ledger accounts are created for each type of variance.
3. *Unfavorable* variances are *debited* to their accounts; *favorable* variances are *credited*.

With these rules in mind, let us record all the transactions of the Collins Company described earlier.

Figure 4. Overhead Variance Analysis

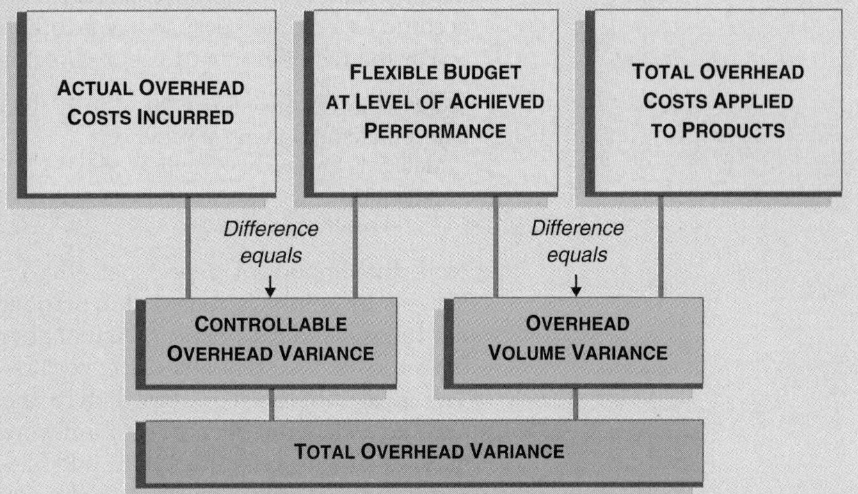

Using Data from the Collins Company Illustration:

Actual Overhead Costs Incurred	Flexible Budget at Level of Achieved Performance		Total Overhead Costs Applied to Products	
(Given in example)	Variable rate times standard hours allowed*	$5.75 × 432 hours = $2,484	Variable:	$5.75 × 432 hours = $2,484
			Fixed:	
	Plus budgeted fixed costs	1,300		$3.25 × 432 hours = 1,404
$4,100		**$3,784**		**$3,888**

Controllable Overhead Variance —— $316 (U) ——

Overhead Volume Variance —— $104 (F) ——

Total Overhead Variance = $212 (U)

*Standard hours allowed (achieved performance level) is computed by multiplying good units produced times required standard direct labor time per unit. The computation is as follows:

180 chairs produced × 2.4 hours per chair = 432 standard hours allowed

Direct Materials Transactions   First, consider the following entry for Collins' purchase of direct materials (described earlier).

Materials Inventory (760 yd. @ $6/yd.)	4,560	
Direct Materials Price Variance		76
Accounts Payable (actual cost) (760 × $5.90)		4,484
Purchase of direct materials on account		
and resulting variance		

There are two key points to note about this transaction: (1) The increase in Materials Inventory is recorded at the actual quantity purchased, but priced at the standard cost. (2) Accounts Payable is stated at the actual cost (actual quantity purchased times actual price per unit) in order to record the proper liability. The $76 difference is recorded in the Direct Materials Price Variance account as a credit, because it is favorable.

For the requisition and use of direct materials, the entry would be:

Work in Process Inventory (720 yd. @ $6/yd.)	4,320	
Direct Materials Quantity Variance	240	
Materials Inventory (760 yd. @ $6/yd.)		4,560
Requisition and usage of direct materials and resulting variance		

Note the important aspects of this entry: (1) Everything in the Work in Process Inventory is recorded at standard cost, which means standard quantity times standard price. (2) Actual quantity must be removed from Materials Inventory at the standard price, because it was entered at the standard price. The $240 difference is recorded in the Direct Materials Quantity Variance account as a debit, because it is unfavorable. Remember that materials may be used in smaller quantities than purchased. In the example, the entire amount of the purchase was used during the period.

Direct Labor Transactions   When recording labor costs, the same rules hold true as for the requisition of materials. (1) Work in Process Inventory is charged with standard labor cost—standard direct labor hours allowed times the standard labor rate. (2) Factory Payroll must be credited for the actual labor cost of the workers—actual hours worked times the actual labor rate earned. The variances, if computed properly, will balance out the difference between the two amounts. The journal entry for recording labor costs for Collins Company is shown below.

Work in Process Inventory (432 hr. @ $8.50/hr.)	3,672	
Direct Labor Rate Variance	315	
Direct Labor Efficiency Variance	153	
Factory Payroll (450 hr. @ $9.20/hr.)		4,140
Charged labor costs to work in process and identified the resulting variances		

Application of Factory Overhead   Recording factory overhead variances differs in timing and technique from recording direct materials and direct labor variances. First, total factory overhead is charged to Work in Process Inventory at standard cost (standard labor hours allowed times the standard variable and fixed rates). The variances are identified later, when the Factory Overhead Control account is closed out at period end. The journal entries to record factory overhead for Collins Company are:

Work in Process Inventory (432 direct labor hours @ $9/direct labor hour)	3,888	
Factory Overhead Control		3,888
Applied factory overhead costs to work in process at standard cost		

Since the company incurred $4,100 in overhead costs and applied only $3,888 of those costs to units produced, factory overhead has been underapplied by $212. The following entry is needed to account for the $212.

Controllable Overhead Variance	316	
Overhead Volume Variance		104
Factory Overhead Control		212
To close out Factory Overhead Control and record resulting variances		

Transfer of Completed Units to Finished Goods Inventory   There are now $11,880 of standard costs recorded in the Work in Process Inventory account (direct materials, $4,320; direct labor, $3,672; and factory overhead, $3,888). Assuming that the 180 chairs have been completed, the following entry would be made.

Finished Goods Inventory		
(180 chairs @ $66/chair)	11,880	
Work in Process Inventory		11,880
Transferred completed units to Finished Goods Inventory		

The standard unit price of $66 is computed as follows:

Direct materials: 4 yd. @ $6/yd.	$24.00
Direct labor: 2.4 hr. @ $8.50/hr.	20.40
Factory overhead: 2.4 hr. @ $9/hr.	21.60
Total standard unit cost	$66.00

All costs that were entered into the Work in Process Inventory account were at standard cost, so standard cost must be used when they are transferred out of the account.

BUSINESS BULLETIN: BUSINESS PRACTICE[5]

The new globally competitive business environment has caused managers in many companies to revise their costing systems, in particular their standard costing systems. Tracking product quality and avoiding inventory buildups are major concerns today. Variance analysis in traditional systems focuses on the efficient usage of materials and labor inputs. Defects and product rework are expected and anticipated amounts are incorporated into the standards. Excess production that built inventories was not penalized in the past. Revised standard costing systems track product quality and rates of production as well as the efficient usage of resources. Quality variances are computed to indicate the production costs wasted by generating defective units. One approach to calculating a quality variance is: (Total units produced − good units produced) × standard cost per unit. Overproduction is also frowned upon in

5. Carole Cheatham, "Updating Standard Cost Systems," *Journal of Accountancy*, American Institute of Certified Public Accountants, December 1990, pp. 57–60.

the new global operating environment. To help track overproduction, a production variance can be computed as follows: (Good units produced − scheduled units) × standard cost per unit. These variances should be incorporated into an existing standard cost system to monitor product defects and to prevent overproduction. Materials price and quantity variances and labor rate and efficiency variances are still necessary to help measure the efficiency of resource usage. ▬▬▬

Transfer Cost of Units Sold to Cost of Goods Sold Account The 180 chairs completed were sold on account for $169 per chair and shipped to a customer. The resulting journal entries would be as shown below.

Accounts Receivable (180 chairs @ $169/chair)	30,420	
Sales		30,420
Sold 180 chairs on account		
Cost of Goods Sold (180 chairs @ $66 standard cost)	11,880	
Finished Goods Inventory		11,880
Transferred standard cost of units sold to Cost of Goods Sold account		

Disposal of End-of-Period Variance Account Balances As with over- or underapplied overhead, the balances in variance accounts at the end of the period are disposed of in one of two ways. First, if all units worked on were completed and sold, a period-end journal entry is made to close all variances to Cost of Goods Sold. Using the data from Collins Company, the entry to close out the variance account balances is:

Cost of Goods Sold	844	
Direct Materials Price Variance	76	
Overhead Volume Variance	104	
Direct Materials Quantity Variance		240
Direct Labor Rate Variance		315
Direct Labor Efficiency Variance		153
Controllable Overhead Variance		316
To close all variance account balances to Cost of Goods Sold		

In contrast, if at period end significant balances still exist in Work in Process Inventory and Finished Goods Inventory from work performed during the period, the net amount of the variances ($844 here) should be divided among Work in Process Inventory, Finished Goods Inventory, and Cost of Goods Sold, in proportion to their balances.

PERFORMANCE EVALUATION

OBJECTIVE

8 *Evaluate managers' performance using variances*

Effective performance evaluation of managers depends on both human factors and company policies. Introducing variances from standard costs into the performance report lends a degree of accuracy to the evaluation process. The human factor is the key to meeting corporate goals. People do the planning, people perform the manufacturing operations, and people evaluate or are evaluated. Management should develop appropriate policies and get direct input from managers and employees when setting up a performance evaluation process.

More specifically, a company should establish policies or procedures for (1) preparing operational plans, (2) assigning responsibility for performance, (3) communicating operational plans to key personnel, (4) evaluating each area of responsibility, and (5) if variances exist, learning the causes and making the necessary corrections.

Variance analysis tends to pinpoint efficient and inefficient operating areas better than simple comparisons between actual and budgeted data. The key to preparing a performance report based on standard costs and related variances is to follow company policies by (1) identifying those responsible for each variance, (2) determining the causes for each variance, (3) establishing a system of management by exception, and (4) developing a reporting format suited to the task. Performance reports should be tailored to a manager's responsibilities. They should be clear and accurate and should contain only those cost items that can be controlled by the manager receiving the report.

Exhibit 4 shows a performance report compiled using data that pertain only to the production manager at Collins Company. This person is responsible for direct materials used (and the related direct materials quantity variance), for direct labor hours used (and the related direct labor efficiency variance), and for the costs included in the controllable overhead variance. Note that space was provided at the bottom for the manager to explain the reasons for the variances.

Exhibit 4. Performance Report Using Variance Analysis

Collins Company
Production Department Performance Report—Cost Variance Analysis
For the Month Ended August 31, 19x8

400 hours: Normal capacity (direct labor hours)
432 hours: Capacity performance level achieved (standard hours allowed)
180 chairs: Good units produced

Cost Analysis

	Cost		Variance	
	Budgeted	Actual	Amount	Type
Direct materials used (leather)	$ 4,320	$ 4,560	$240 (U)	Quantity variance
Direct labor used	3,672	3,825	153 (U)	Efficiency variance
Factory overhead	3,784	4,100	316 (U)	Controllable over-head variance
Totals	$11,776	$12,485	$709 (U)	

Reasons for Variances

Direct materials quantity variance: (1) inferior quality-control inspection; (2) cheaper grade of direct materials
Direct labor efficiency variance: (1) inferior direct materials; (2) new, inexperienced employee
Controllable overhead variance: (1) excessive indirect labor usage; (2) changes in employee overtime;
 (3) unexpected price changes

The report in Exhibit 4 is simpler than most. Normally such a report would show several items of direct materials, two or more direct labor classifications, and many overhead cost items. The report has been simplified to allow you to more easily focus on its purposes and uses.

THREE-VARIANCE APPROACH TO FACTORY OVERHEAD VARIANCE ANALYSIS

9 *Compute and evaluate factory overhead variances using a three-variance analysis*

The three-variance approach to overhead variance analysis divides the total overhead variance into three parts instead of the two parts shown earlier in the chapter. Remember, the purpose of variance analysis is to break down variations from budgeted information so that reasons for changes from planned operations can be determined. The three-variance approach to overhead variance analysis breaks the controllable overhead variance into two parts and identifies an *overhead spending variance* and an *overhead efficiency variance*. The overhead volume variance is the third overhead variance, and it is identical to its counterpart in the two-variance analysis.

The overhead spending variance is the difference between the actual overhead costs incurred and the amount that should have been spent, based on actual hours worked or other productive input measures. Therefore actual overhead costs incurred are compared with the costs of a flexible budget based on actual hours worked. When the Collins Company example is expanded, the spending variance is computed as follows:

Actual overhead costs incurred		$4,100.00
Less budgeted factory overhead (flexible budget) for 450 hours worked		
Variable overhead cost		
450 hours × $5.75 per direct labor hour	$2,587.50	
Budgeted fixed overhead cost	1,300.00	
Total budgeted factory overhead		3,887.50
Overhead spending variance		$ 212.50 (U)

Note that the total overhead spending variance can be broken down into its variable and fixed components. In the example, actual overhead incurred was given in total and details were not provided. If the actual variable and fixed cost components were given, however, it would be easy to generate a variable overhead spending variance and a fixed overhead spending variance. This further breakdown would give the supervisor additional information. If most of the spending variance involved fixed costs, much of the variance would be difficult for the manager to control. If, on the other hand, most of the spending variance were caused by noncompliance with variable cost targets, those responsible should be held accountable for the differences.

The overhead efficiency variance is linked directly with the labor efficiency variance. An efficiency variance occurs when actual hours worked differ from standard hours allowed for good units produced. The overhead efficiency variance is the difference between actual direct labor hours worked and standard labor hours allowed multiplied by the standard variable overhead rate. Computing the overhead efficiency variance involves comparing two flexible budgets, one based on actual hours worked and the other on standard hours allowed for good units produced. Collins Company's overhead efficiency variance is computed as follows:

Budgeted factory overhead (flexible budget) for actual hours worked		
Variable overhead cost		
450 hours $\times$ $5.75 per direct labor hour	$2,587.50	
Budgeted fixed overhead cost	1,300.00	
Total budgeted overhead for actual hours worked		$3,887.50
Budgeted factory overhead (flexible budget) for standard hours allowed		
Variable overhead cost (180 chairs $\times$ 2.4 hours per chair) $\times$ $5.75 per direct labor hour	$2,484.00	
Budgeted fixed overhead cost	1,300.00	
Total budgeted overhead for standard hours allowed		3,784.00
Overhead efficiency variance		$ 103.50 (U)

Note that by design the overhead efficiency variance is the difference between variable costs only. When two flexible budgets are compared, the fixed cost component is identical for each budget. The difference must come from the variable costs.

The overhead efficiency variance identifies the portion of the total overhead variance that occurs automatically when a labor efficiency variance develops. If the labor efficiency variance is unfavorable, the overhead efficiency variance will also be unfavorable. The person responsible for the labor efficiency variance is also responsible for the overhead efficiency variance.

As stated earlier, the overhead volume variance is computed in the same manner as in the two-variance approach. To review the computation of the two-variance approach to overhead variance analysis, refer to Figure 4.

In the upper part of Figure 5, the total overhead variance is broken down into the three variances: (1) spending, (2) efficiency, and (3) volume variances. In addition, the cost totals that must be compared to arrive at each variance are identified. Note that the difference between Figures 4 and 5 is the introduction of the flexible budget for effort expended. Using this flexible budget, one can break down the controllable overhead variance into overhead spending variance and overhead efficiency variance.

In the bottom portion of Figure 5, the actual computation of the three variances is summarized. To check your answers to the three variances, perform the following calculation:

Overhead spending variance	$212.50 (U)
Overhead efficiency variance	103.50 (U)
Overhead volume variance	104.00 (F)
Total overhead variance	$212.00 (U)

The journal entry used to record the overhead variances in the three-variance approach is shown on the next page. The primary difference between this entry and the one shown earlier for the two-variance approach is that the Controllable Overhead Variance account has been replaced by the Overhead Spending Variance and the Overhead Efficiency Variance accounts.

Figure 5. Three-Variance Approach to Overhead Variance Analysis

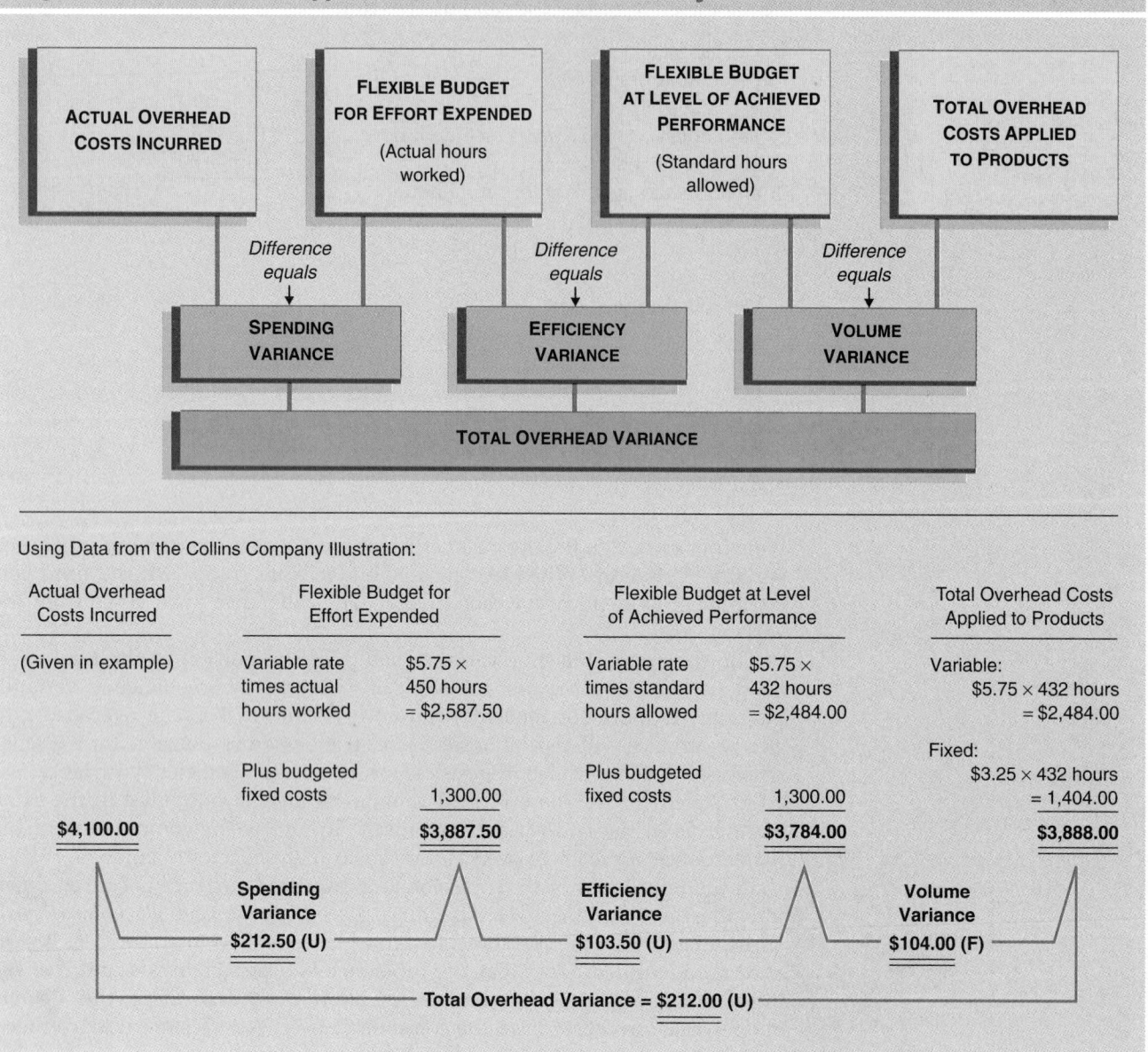

Using Data from the Collins Company Illustration:

Three-Variance Analysis: Journal Entry to Record Variances

Overhead Spending Variance	212.50	
Overhead Efficiency Variance	103.50	
Overhead Volume Variance		104.00
Factory Overhead Control		212.00
To close out Factory Overhead Control and record resulting variances		

CHAPTER REVIEW

REVIEW OF LEARNING OBJECTIVES

1. **Define** *standard costs* **and describe how managers use standard costs to plan for, and control, costs.** Standard costs are realistically predetermined costs that are developed from analyses of both past costs, quantities, and times and future resource costs and operating conditions. In a standard cost system, standard costs for materials, labor, and factory overhead flow through the inventory accounts and eventually into Cost of Goods Sold. Instead of using actual costs for product costing purposes, standard costs are used in their place.

    Once standard costs have been developed, managers use them as tools for planning and budgeting activities. Once the projected sales and production unit targets for the upcoming year are established, planned materials purchase costs, labor costs, and variable factory overhead costs can be computed using standard costs. These costs serve as targets or goals for product costing purposes; they can also be used in the product distribution and selling cost areas as well. At the end of an accounting period, actual costs incurred are compared with standard costs and the differences are computed. These differences, called variances, provide measures of performance that can be used to control costs.

2. **State the purposes for using standard costs.** Standard costs are predetermined costs for direct materials, direct labor, and factory overhead that are usually expressed as a cost per unit of finished product. Standard costs are introduced into a cost accounting system to help in the budgetary control process because they are useful for preparing operating budgets and for evaluating performance. They help in identifying parts of the production process that require cost control measures, in establishing realistic prices, and in simplifying cost accounting procedures for inventories and product costing.

3. **Identify the six elements of, and compute, a standard unit cost.** The six elements of a standard unit cost are (1) the direct materials price standard, (2) the direct materials quantity standard, (3) the direct labor time standard, (4) the direct labor rate standard, (5) the standard variable factory overhead rate, and (6) the standard fixed factory overhead rate. The direct materials price standard is found by carefully considering expected price increases, changes in available quantities, and possible new sources of supply. The direct materials quantity standard expresses the expected quantity to be used. It is affected by product engineering specifications, quality of direct materials used, age and productivity of the machines used, and the quality and experience of the work force. The direct labor time standard is based on current time and motion studies of workers and machines and by past employee and machine performance. Labor union contracts and company personnel policies influence direct labor rate standards. Standard variable and fixed factory overhead rates are found by dividing total budgeted variable and fixed factory overhead costs by an appropriate application base.

    A product's total standard unit cost is computed by adding the following costs: (1) direct materials cost (equals direct materials price standard times direct materials quantity standard), (2) direct labor cost (equals direct labor time standard times direct labor rate standard), and (3) factory overhead cost (equals standard variable and standard fixed factory overhead rate times standard direct labor hours allowed per unit).

4. **Define and prepare a** *flexible budget.* A flexible budget is a summary of anticipated costs for a range of activity levels, geared to changes in productive output. Variable, fixed, and total costs are given for several levels of capacity or output. From those data the management accountant derives the flexible budget formula. This formula, which can be applied to any level of productive output, allows management to evaluate the performance of individuals, departments, or processes.

5. **Describe the concept of management by exception.** Management by exception is the practice of analyzing only significant variances. Variances within specific limits set by management are not analyzed. This technique is especially useful in companies that control many cost centers or cost categories.

6. **Compute and analyze (a) direct materials, (b) direct labor, and (c) factory overhead variances.** The direct materials price and quantity variances help explain differences between actual and standard direct materials costs. A direct materials price variance is computed by finding the difference between the actual price and the standard price per unit and multiplying it by the actual quantity purchased. The direct materials quantity variance is the difference between the actual quantity used and the standard quantity, multiplied by the standard price. Actual and standard direct labor cost differences are analyzed by computing the direct labor rate variance and the direct labor efficiency variance. A direct labor rate variance is computed by determining the difference between the actual labor rate and the standard labor rate and multiplying it by the actual labor hours worked. The direct labor efficiency variance is the difference between actual hours worked and standard hours allowed for good units produced, multiplied by the standard labor rate. The controllable overhead variance and the overhead volume variance help explain differences in overhead costs. Computing the controllable overhead variance is done by finding the difference between actual overhead costs incurred and the factory overhead costs budgeted for the level of production achieved (flexible budget based on standard hours allowed). The overhead volume variance is the difference between the factory overhead budgeted for the level of production achieved and the total overhead costs applied to production using the standard variable and fixed overhead rates.

7. **Prepare journal entries to record transactions involving variances in a standard costing system.** Journal entries are used to integrate standard cost variances into the accounting records. Unfavorable variances create debit balances, and favorable variances create credit balances. General ledger accounts are maintained for the direct materials price variance, direct materials quantity variance, direct labor rate variance, direct labor efficiency variance, controllable overhead variance, and overhead volume variance. At the close of an accounting period, balances in these accounts are disposed of by either (1) closing them to Cost of Goods Sold, if the variance balances are small or if most of the goods produced during the period were sold, or (2) dividing the net balance among Work in Process Inventory, Finished Goods Inventory, and Cost of Goods Sold, in proportion to their balances.

8. **Evaluate managers' performance using variances.** Introducing variances from standard costs into the performance report lends accuracy to the evaluation. Variances tend to pinpoint efficient and inefficient operating areas better than comparisons between actual and static budget data. The keys to preparing a performance report based on standard costs and related variances are to (1) identify those responsible for each variance, (2) determine the causes for each variance, (3) establish a system of management by exception, and (4) develop a reporting format suited to the task.

SUPPLEMENTAL OBJECTIVE

9. **Compute and evaluate factory overhead variances using a three-variance analysis.** If more information is desired concerning the differences in overhead costs, a more detailed analysis can be made. Using the three-variance approach, the controllable overhead variance is broken down into an overhead spending variance and an overhead efficiency variance. The overhead volume variance is the third component of the total overhead variance. Using the three-variance approach, management can determine how much of the total overhead variance was caused by unanticipated spending activities (higher or lower prices or changes in purchases) and how much was caused by changes in the level of labor or machine hour efficiency.

REVIEW OF CONCEPTS AND TERMINOLOGY

The following concepts and terms were introduced in this chapter.

L O 6 **Controllable overhead variance:** The difference between actual overhead costs incurred and the factory overhead costs budgeted for the level of production reached.

L O 6   **Direct labor efficiency variance:** The difference between actual hours worked and standard hours allowed for the good units produced, multiplied by the standard labor rate.

L O 3   **Direct labor rate standards:** The hourly labor costs that are expected to prevail during the next accounting period for each function or job classification.

L O 6   **Direct labor rate variance:** The difference between the actual labor rate and the standard labor rate, multiplied by the actual labor hours worked.

L O 3   **Direct labor time standard:** The expected time that it takes each department, machine, or process to complete production on one unit or one batch of output.

L O 3   **Direct materials price standard:** A careful estimate of the cost of a certain type of direct material in the next accounting period.

L O 6   **Direct materials price variance:** The difference between the actual price and the standard price, multiplied by the actual quantity purchased.

L O 3   **Direct materials quantity standard:** An estimate of expected quantity usage that is influenced by product engineering specifications, quality of direct materials, age and productivity of machinery, and quality and experience of the work force.

L O 6   **Direct materials quantity variance:** The difference between the actual quantity used and the standard quantity, multiplied by the standard price.

L O 4   **Flexible budget:** A summary of expected costs for a range of activity levels, geared to changes in the level of productive output; also called *variable budget.*

L O 4   **Flexible budget formula:** An equation that determines the correct budgeted cost for any level of productive output; the equation is: (variable costs per unit $\times$ the number of units produced) + total budgeted fixed costs.

L O 5   **Management by exception:** The practice of locating and analyzing only the areas of unusually good or unusually bad performance.

S O 9   **Overhead efficiency variance:** The difference between actual direct labor hours worked and standard labor hours allowed, multiplied by the standard variable overhead rate.

S O 9   **Overhead spending variance:** The difference between the actual overhead costs incurred and the amount that should have been spent, based on actual hours worked or other productive input measures.

L O 6   **Overhead volume variance:** The difference between the factory overhead budgeted for the level of production achieved and the overhead applied to production using the standard variable and fixed overhead rates.

L O 1   **Standard costs:** Realistically predetermined costs that are developed from analyses of both past operating costs, quantities, and times and future resource costs and operating conditions.

L O 3   **Standard direct labor cost:** The standard hours of direct labor multiplied by the standard wage for direct labor.

L O 3   **Standard direct materials cost:** The standard price for direct materials multiplied by the standard quantity for direct materials.

L O 3   **Standard factory overhead cost:** The sum of the estimates for variable and fixed factory overhead in the next accounting period.

L O 3   **Standard fixed overhead rate:** Total budgeted fixed factory overhead costs divided by an expression of capacity, usually normal capacity in terms of standard hours or units.

L O 3   **Standard variable overhead rate:** Total budgeted variable factory overhead costs divided by an expression of capacity, such as the expected number of standard direct labor hours or standard machine hours.

L O 6   **Total direct labor cost variance:** The difference between actual labor costs incurred and the standard labor cost for the good units produced.

L O 6   **Total direct materials cost variance:** The difference between the actual materials cost incurred and the standard cost of those same items.

L O 6 **Total overhead variance:** The difference between actual overhead costs incurred and the standard overhead costs applied to production using the standard variable and fixed overhead rates.

L O 1 **Variance:** The difference between a standard cost and an actual cost.

L O 5 **Variance analysis:** The process of computing the amount of and isolating the causes of differences between actual costs and standard costs.

REVIEW PROBLEM
VARIANCE ANALYSIS

L O 3, 6
SO 9 Mecca Manufacturing Company has a standard cost system and keeps all cost standards up to date. The company's main product is heating pipe, which is made in a single department. The standard variable costs for one unit of finished pipe are:

Direct materials (3 sq meters @ $12.50/sq meter)	$37.50
Direct labor (1.2 hours @ $9.00/hour)	10.80
Variable overhead (1.2 hr. @ $5.00/direct labor hour)	6.00
Standard variable cost per unit	$54.30

Normal capacity is 15,000 direct labor hours, and budgeted fixed overhead costs for the year were $54,000. During the year, the company produced and sold 12,200 units. Related transactions and actual cost data for the year were as follows: Direct materials consisted of 37,500 sq meters purchased and used; unit purchase cost was $12.40 per sq meter. Direct labor consisted of 15,250 direct labor hours worked at an average labor rate of $9.20 per hour. Actual factory overhead costs incurred for the period consisted of variable overhead costs of $73,200 and fixed overhead costs of $55,000.

REQUIRED Using the data given, compute the following:

1. Standard hours allowed
2. Standard fixed overhead rate
3. Direct materials price variance
4. Direct materials quantity variance
5. Direct labor rate variance
6. Direct labor efficiency variance
7. Overhead spending variance (if SO 9 was assigned)
8. Overhead efficiency variance (if SO 9 was assigned)
9. Controllable overhead variance
10. Overhead volume variance

ANSWER TO REVIEW PROBLEM

1. Standard hours allowed = good units produced × standard direct labor hours per unit

   12,200 units × 1.2 direct labor hours/unit = 14,640 hours

2. Standard fixed overhead rate = $\frac{\text{budgeted fixed overhead cost}}{\text{normal capacity}}$

   = $\frac{\$54,000}{15,000 \text{ direct labor hours}}$

   = $3.60 per direct labor hour

3. Direct materials price variance:

Price difference:	Actual price paid	$12.40 /sq meter
	Less standard price	12.50 /sq meter
	Difference	$ .10 (F)

Direct materials price variance = (actual price − standard price) × actual quantity
= $.10 (F) × 37,500 sq meters
= $3,750 (F)

4. Direct materials quantity variance:

Quantity difference:	Actual quantity used	37,500 sq meters
	Less standard quantity (12,200 units × 3 sq meters)	36,600 sq meters
	Difference	900 (U)

Direct materials quantity variance = (actual quantity − standard quantity) × standard price
= 900 (U) × $12.50/sq meter
= $11,250 (U)

5. Direct labor rate variance:

Rate difference:	Actual labor rate	$9.20 /hour
	Less standard labor rate	9.00 /hour
	Difference	$ .20 (U)

Direct labor rate variance = (actual rate − standard rate) × actual hours
= $.20 (U) × 15,250 hours
= $3,050 (U)

6. Direct labor efficiency variance:

Difference in hours:	Actual hours worked	15,250 hours
	Less standard hours allowed	14,640 hours*
	Difference	610 (U)

Direct labor efficiency variance = (actual hours − standard hours allowed) × standard rate
= 610 hours (U) × $9.00/hour
= $5,490 (U)

*12,200 units produced × 1.2 hours per unit = 14,640 hours

7. Overhead spending variance:

Overhead costs incurred		
Variable	$73,200	
Fixed	55,000	$128,200
Less flexible budget for effort expended		
Actual hours worked × variable overhead rate		
15,250 labor hours × $5.00/hour	$76,250	
Plus budgeted fixed costs	54,000	130,250
Overhead spending variance		$ 2,050 (F)

8. Overhead efficiency variance:

Flexible budget for effort expended (see computation in **7** above)		$130,250
Less flexible budget at level of achieved performance		
Standard hours allowed × variable overhead rate		
14,640 labor hours × $5.00/hour	$73,200	
Plus budgeted fixed costs	54,000	127,200
Overhead efficiency variance		$ 3,050 (U)

9. Controllable overhead variance

Actual overhead incurred		$128,200
Less budgeted factory overhead for 14,640 hours:		
Variable overhead cost (14,640 labor hours × $5.00/hour)	$73,200	
Budgeted fixed factory overhead	54,000	
Total budgeted factory overhead		127,200
Controllable overhead variance		$ 1,000 (U)

10. Overhead volume variance

Total budgeted factory overhead (see computation in **9**)		$127,200
Less factory overhead applied:		
Variable: 14,640 labor hours × $5.00/hour	$73,200	
Fixed: 14,640 labor hours × $3.60/hour	52,704	
Total factory overhead applied		125,904
Overhead volume variance		$ 1,296 (U)

CHAPTER ASSIGNMENTS

QUESTIONS

1. What are standard costs?
2. Can standard costing be used by a service business? Explain your answer.
3. What do predetermined overhead costing and standard costing have in common? How are they different?
4. "Standard costing is a total cost concept, in that standard unit costs are determined for direct materials, direct labor, and factory overhead." Explain this statement.
5. Name the six elements used to compute a standard unit cost.
6. What three factors could affect a direct materials price standard?
7. What general ledger accounts are affected by a standard cost system?
8. "Performance is evaluated or measured by comparing what did happen with what should have happened." What is meant by this statement? Relate your comments to the budgetary control process.
9. What is a variance?
10. How can variances help management achieve effective control of operations?
11. What is a flexible budget? What is its purpose?
12. What are the two parts of the flexible budget formula? How are they related to each other?
13. What is variance analysis? How is it related to management by exception?
14. What is the formula for computing a direct materials price variance?
15. How would you interpret an unfavorable direct materials price variance?
16. Distinguish between the controllable overhead variance and the overhead volume variance.
17. If standard hours allowed exceed normal hours, will the period's overhead volume variance be favorable or unfavorable? Explain your answer.
18. Can an unfavorable direct materials quantity variance be caused, at least in part, by a favorable direct materials price variance? Explain.

19. What are the three rules that underlie the recording of standard cost variances?
20. What is the key to preparing a performance report based on standard costs and related variances?
21. What is the difference between the three-variance approach and the two-variance approach to factory overhead variance analysis?

SHORT EXERCISES

SE 1. *Uses of Standard*
L O 1 *Costs*
No check figure

Jensen Corporation is considering the installation of a standard costing system. Bill Bondeson, manager of the Missouri Division, attended the corporate meeting where Cheryl Emerson, the controller, discussed the proposal. Bill asked, "Cheryl, how will this new system benefit me? How will I use the new system?" Prepare Cheryl's response to Bill.

SE 2. *Purposes of Standard*
L O 2 *Costs*
No check figure

You are a consultant and a client asks you why companies augment their cost accounting systems with standard costs. Prepare your response, listing several purposes for introducing standard costs into a cost accounting system.

SE 3. *Standard Unit*
L O 3 *Cost Computation*
Check Figure: Total standard unit cost: $91.30

Given the following information, compute the standard unit cost of Product JLT.

Direct materials quantity standard:	5 pounds/unit
Direct materials price standard:	$10.20/pound
Direct labor hours standard:	.4 hours/unit
Direct labor price standard:	$10.75/hour
Variable overhead rate standard:	$7.00/machine hour
Fixed overhead rate standard:	$11.00/machine hour
Machine hour standard:	2 hours/unit

SE 4. *Flexible Budget*
L O 4 *Preparation*
Check Figure: Total costs, 12,000 Units of Output: $279,200

Prepare a flexible budget for 10,000, 12,000, and 14,000 units of output, given the following information.

Variable costs	
Direct materials	$8.00/unit
Direct labor	$2.50/unit
Variable factory overhead	$6.00/unit
Total budgeted fixed factory overhead	$81,200

SE 5. *Management by*
L O 5 *Exception*
No check figure

DeHoyes Metal Works produces sculptures for lawn beautification. The company follows a practice of analyzing only variances that differ by more than 5 percent from the standard cost. The controller computed the following labor efficiency variances for March.

	Labor Efficiency Variance	Standard Labor Cost
Product 4	$1,240 (U)	$26,200
Product 6	3,290 (F)	41,700
Product 7	2,030 (U)	34,300
Product 9	1,620 (F)	32,560
Product 12	2,810 (U)	59,740

Identify those variances that should be analyzed for cause. Round to two decimal places.

SE 6. *Direct Materials*
L O 6 *and Direct Labor*
Variances
Check Figure: Direct materials price variance: $11,000 (F)

Given the standard costs in SE 3 and the following actual costs, compute the direct materials price and quantity variances and the direct labor rate and efficiency variances for the period. (The number of good units produced was 11,000.)

Direct materials purchased and used:	55,000 pounds
Direct materials price paid:	$10.00/pound
Direct labor hours used:	4,950 hours
Direct labor cost:	$53,460

SE 7. *Factory Overhead*
L O 6 *Variances: Two-*
Variance Approach

Check Figure: Controllable overhead
variance: $12,560 (F)

Roberta Products uses a standard costing system. The following information relating to factory overhead was generated during August:

Standard variable overhead rate	$2/machine hour
Standard fixed overhead rate	$3/machine hour
Actual variable overhead costs	$443,200
Actual fixed overhead costs	$698,800
Budgeted fixed overhead costs	$700,000
Standard machine hours per unit	12
Good units produced	18,940
Actual machine hours	228,400

Compute the controllable overhead variance and the overhead volume variance.

SE 8. *Standards, Variances,*
L O 7 *and Journal Entries*

No check figure

Prepare the journal entries to record the information provided in SE 6, including the variances for materials and labor.

SE 9. *Evaluating*
L O 8 *Managerial*
Performance

No check figure

Herb Billings, production manager, received a report containing the following information from Zena Meth, the company controller.

	Actual	Standard	Variance
Materials	$38,200	$36,600	$1,600 (U)
Labor	19,450	19,000	450 (U)
Factory overhead	62,890	60,000	2,890 (U)

She asked for a response. If you were Herb, what would you do? What additional information does Herb need in order to prepare his response?

SE 10. *Factory Overhead*
S O 9 *Variances: Three-*
Variance Approach

Check Figure: Overhead spending
variance: $14,800 (F)

Using the same information from Roberta Products in SE 7, compute the overhead spending variance, the overhead efficiency variance, and the overhead volume variance.

EXERCISES

E 1. *Development of*
L O 3 *Standard Costs*

Check Figure: Direct materials price
standard: $3.51 per sq. yd.

Siempre Corp. maintains a complete standard costing system and is in the process of updating its materials and labor standards for Product 20B. The following data have been accumulated.

Materials
In the previous period, 20,500 units were produced and a total of 32,800 square yards of material was used to produce them.
Three suppliers of material will be used in the coming period: Supplier A will provide 20 percent of the material at a cost of $3.40 per sq. yd.; Supplier B will be responsible for 50 percent at a cost of $3.50 per sq. yd.; and Supplier C will ship 30 percent at a cost of $3.60 per sq. yd.

Labor
During the previous period, 57,400 direct labor hours were worked, 34,850 hours on machine H and 22,550 hours on machine K.
Machine H operators earned $8.90 per hour and machine K operators earned $9.20 per hour last period. The new labor contract calls for a 10 percent increase in labor rates for the coming period.

From the information above, compute the direct materials quantity and price standards and the direct labor time and rate standards for each machine listed for the coming accounting period.

E 2. *Standard Unit*
L O 3 *Cost Computation*

Check Figure: Total standard manufacturing cost: $3,159.50

Griselda Aerodynamics, Inc. makes electronically equipped weather-detecting balloons for university meteorological departments. Recent nationwide inflation has caused the company management to order that standard costs be recomputed. New direct materials price standards are $620.00 per set for electronic components and $13.40 per square meter for heavy-duty canvas. Direct materials quantity standards include one set of electronic components and 95 square meters of heavy-duty canvas per balloon. Direct labor time standards are 16 hours per balloon for the Electronics Department and 19 hours per balloon for the Assembly Department. Direct labor rate standards are $11.00 per hour for the Electronics Department and $9.50 per hour for the Assembly Department. Standard factory overhead rates are $16.00 per direct labor hour for the standard variable overhead rate and $10.00 per direct labor hour for the standard fixed overhead rate.

Using the production standards provided, compute the standard manufacturing cost of one weather balloon.

E 3. *Flexible Budget*
L O 4 *Preparation*

Check Figures: Total costs, 18,000
Units of Output: $829,100; 20,000
Units of Output: $898,500

Fixed overhead costs for the Kara Kostume Company for 19x9 are expected to be as follows: depreciation, $72,000; supervisory salaries, $92,000; property taxes and insurance, $26,000; and other fixed overhead, $14,500. Total fixed overhead is thus expected to be $204,500. Variable costs per unit are expected to be as follows: direct materials, $16.50; direct labor, $8.50; operating supplies, $2.50; indirect labor, $4.00; and other variable overhead costs, $3.20.

Prepare a flexible budget for the following levels of production: 18,000 units, 20,000 units, and 22,000 units. What is the flexible budget formula for 19x9?

E 4. *Management by*
L O 5 *Exception*

No check figure

Green Instruments, Inc. produces scientific apparatus for food inspection. More than five hundred types of materials and the labor skills of more than eighty different specialists are used in the production process. During the past five years, the corporation has grown from sales of $2,800,000 to a current level of over $25,000,000. The company's rapid growth has caused numerous variances, which the controller's department has not had time to investigate. A standard cost accounting system was introduced two years ago, but it has proven impractical for analyzing all the variances. The controller has been asked by the vice president of finance to develop an improved method of controlling costs.

1. Describe the concept of management by exception.
2. Discuss how the concept could prove useful to the controller of Green Instruments, Inc.

E 5. *Direct Materials*
L O 6 *Price and Quantity*
Variances

Check Figure: Direct materials price variance: $594 (F)

The Lohman Elevator Company manufactures small hydroelectric elevators with a maximum capacity of ten passengers. One of the direct materials used by the Production Department is heavy-duty carpeting for the floor of the elevator. The direct materials quantity standard used for the month ended April 30, 19x7 was 6 square yards per elevator. During April, the purchasing agent purchased this carpeting at $11 per square yard; standard price for the period was $12. Ninety elevators were completed and sold during April; the Production Department used an average of 6.6 square yards of carpet per elevator.

Calculate Lohman Elevator Company's direct materials price and quantity variances for carpet for April 19x7.

E 6. *Direct Labor*
L O 6 *Rate and Efficiency*
Variances

Check Figure: 1. Direct labor rate variance: $14,950 (U)

Joy Park Foundry, Inc. manufactures castings used by other companies in the production of machinery. For the past two years, the largest selling product has been a casting for an eight-cylinder engine block. Standard direct labor hours per engine block are 1.8 hours. The labor contract requires that $17.00 per hour be paid to all direct labor employees. During June, 16,500 engine blocks were produced. Actual direct labor hours and costs for June were 29,900 hours and $523,250, respectively.

1. Compute the direct labor rate variance for the engine block product line during June.
2. Using the same data, compute the direct labor efficiency variance for the engine block product line during June. Check your answer, assuming that the total direct labor variance is $18,350 (U).

E 7. *Factory Overhead*
L O 6 *Variances*

Check Figure: Controllable overhead variance: $1,930.00 (U)

Peterson Company produces handmade clamming pots that are sold to distributors along the Atlantic coast of North Carolina. The company incurred $11,100 of actual overhead costs in May. Budgeted standard overhead costs for May were $4 of variable overhead costs per direct labor hour plus $1,250 in fixed overhead costs. Normal capacity was set at 2,000 direct labor hours per month. In May, the company was able to produce 9,900 clamming pots. The time standard is .2 direct labor hours per clamming pot.

Compute the total overhead variance, the controllable overhead variance, and the overhead volume variance for May.

E 8. *Factory Overhead*
L O 6 *Variances*
Check Figure: 1. Overapplied overhead: $24,300

Karlson Industries uses a standard cost accounting system that includes flexible budgeting for cost planning and control. The 19x8 monthly flexible budget for factory overhead costs is $200,000 of fixed costs plus $4.80 per machine hour. Monthly normal capacity of 100,000 machine hours is used to compute the standard fixed overhead rate. During December 19x8, plant workers recorded 105,000 actual machine hours. The standard machine hours allowed for good production during December was only 98,500. Actual factory overhead costs incurred during December totaled $441,000 of variable costs and $204,500 of fixed costs.

Compute (1) the under- or overapplied overhead during December and (2) the controllable overhead variance and the overhead volume variance.

E 9. *Standard Cost*
L O 7 *Journal Entries*
Check Figure: 3. Direct Materials Quantity Variance: $32 (U)

Dane Battery Company produces batteries for automobiles, motorcycles, and mopeds. Transactions for direct materials and direct labor for March were as follows:

1. Purchased 1,000 type A battery casings for $6.50 each, on account; standard cost, $7.00 per casing.
2. Purchased 5,000 type 10C lead battery plates for $2.40 each, on account; standard cost, $2.25 per plate.
3. Requisitioned 32 type A battery casings and 248 type 10C lead plates into production. Order no. 674 called for 30 batteries, each using a standard quantity of 8 plates per casing.
4. Direct labor costs for order no. 674 were as follows:

Department H
    Actual labor   26 hours @ $10.00/hour
    Standard labor   24 hours @ $11.00/hour

Department J
    Actual labor   10 hours @ $13.00/hour
    Standard labor   12 hours @ $14.00/hour

Prepare journal entries for these four transactions.

E 10. *Three-Variance*
S O 9 *Analysis of Overhead*
Check Figure: Overhead spending variance: $1,085 (U)

Signal Corporation generated the following data for November.

Standard variable overhead rate	$8.50/machine hour
Standard fixed overhead rate	$7.50/machine hour
Actual variable overhead costs	$35,200
Actual fixed overhead costs	$31,500
Budgeted fixed overhead costs	$30,000
Actual machine hours	4,190 machine hours
Standard machine hours allowed	4,230 machine hours

Compute the overhead spending variance, overhead efficiency variance, and overhead volume variance.

SKILLS DEVELOPMENT EXERCISES

Conceptual Analysis

SDE 1. *Variances and*
L O 3, 6 *the Factory of the Future Concept*

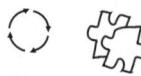

No check figure

The **United States Air Force,** with the assistance of Price Waterhouse, has developed a model of an advanced cost management system (ACMS) that will enable companies with newly automated factories to develop more accurate cost measures. The Electronics Systems Division of the USAF initiated the study.[6] The conceptual design features include tracking future costs, focusing on parts costs (rather than labor costs), and separating the tracking of the production process from the tracking of product costs. Variances, called planning gaps, compare the differences between predeter-

6. Daniel P. Keegan, Robert G. Eiler, and Joseph V. Anania, "An Advanced Cost Management System for the Factory of the Future," *Management Accounting,* Institute of Management Accountants, December 1988, pp. 31–37.

mined estimates and actual results. Variances are classified by various causing factors and are generated for scrap, machine utilization, labor efficiency, labor utilization, set-up usage, lot size, spending, and volume. On a work sheet, separate these variance categories into two groups, those related to (1) production process control (nonfinancial data) and (2) product cost control. Be prepared to discuss in class your variance classification approach and the reasons supporting your position.

Ethical Dilemma

SDE 2.
L O 2, 6, 8

An Ethical Question Involving Standard Costs

No check figure

Chris Shoucair is manager of standard costing systems at **Richard Industries, Inc.** Standard costs are developed for all product-related materials, labor, and factory overhead costs and are used for pricing products, for costing all inventories, and for performance evaluation of all purchasing and production line managers. The company updates standard costs whenever costs, prices, or rates change by 3 percent or more; in addition, all standard costs are reviewed and updated annually in December. This practice provided currently attainable standards that were appropriate for use in valuing year-end inventories on Richard Industries' financial statements.

On November 30, 19x8, Chris Shoucair received a memo from the company's chief financial officer. The memo said that the company was considering a major purchase of another company and that Chris and his staff were to concentrate their full effort on analyzing the proposed transaction and ignore adjusting the standards until February or March. In late November, prices on over twenty raw materials were reduced by 10 percent or more and a new labor contract reduced several categories of labor rates. Lower standard costs would result in lower inventories, higher cost of goods sold due to inventory write-downs, and lower net income for the year. Chris believed that the company was facing an operating loss and that the assignment to evaluate the proposed major purchase was designed primarily to keep his staff from revising and lowering the standards. Chris questioned the CFO about the assignment and reiterated the need for updating the standard costs, but he was told again to ignore the update procedure and concentrate on the major purchase. The proposed major purchase never materialized and Chris and his staff were removed from the assignment in early February.

Assess Chris's actions regarding this situation. Did he follow all ethical paths to solve the problem? What are the consequences of not adjusting the standard costs?

Research Activity

SDE 3.
L O 1, 2

The Relevance of Standard Costing

No check figure

Standard costs and the materials, labor, and factory overhead variances generated by a standard costing system have been used as cost control and performance evaluation mechanisms for many years. Standard costs are also used to assist in the pricing of new products. In recent years, the standard costing approach has been criticized for being irrelevant as an operating measurement device. Locate an article written on this topic within the last five years in the periodical *Management Accounting*, published monthly by the Institute of Management Accountants. Identify the issues addressed by the author(s). Is the article positive or negative toward standard costs? What role does the globally competitive environment play in the points being made by the author(s)? Prepare a formal two-page summary of the article. Also prepare an outline that you would use if called upon to report on the assignment to your classmates.

Decision-Making Practice

SDE 4.
L O 3, 6, 8

Annuity Life Insurance Company—Standard Costing in a Service Industry

Check Figures: 1. Policy developers, Standard hours allowed: 795 hours; 3. Labor rate variance, Policy salespeople: $450.50 (F)

The **Annuity Life Insurance Company** (ALIC) markets several types of life insurance policies, but its permanent, twenty-year life annuity policy (P20A) is the company's most desired product. The P20A policy sells in $10,000 increments and features variable percentages of whole life insurance and single-payment annuity, depending on the potential policyholder's needs and age. There is an entire department devoted to developing and marketing the P20A policy. ALIC has determined that both the policy developer and the policy salesperson contribute to creating each policy, so ALIC categorizes these people as direct labor for variance analysis, cost control, and performance evaluation purposes. For unit costing purposes, each $10,000 increment is considered 1 unit. Thus, a $90,000 policy is counted as 9 units.

Standard unit cost information for the period is as follows:

Direct labor
  Policy developer
    3 hours at $12.00/hour $ 36.00
  Policy salesperson
    8.5 hours at $14.20/hour   120.70

Operating overhead
  Variable overhead
    11.5 hours at $26.00/hour   299.00
  Fixed overhead
    11.5 hours at $18.00/hour   207.00
Standard unit cost $662.70

Actual costs incurred during January for the 265 units sold were as follows:

Direct labor
  Policy developers
    848 hours at $12.50/hour $10,600.00
  Policy salespeople
    2,252.5 hours at $14.00/hour   31,535.00

Operating overhead
  Variable operating overhead   78,440.00
  Fixed operating overhead   53,400.00

Normal monthly capacity was 260 units, and the budgeted fixed operating overhead for the month was $53,820.

1. Compute the standard hours allowed in January for policy developers and policy salespeople.
2. What were the total actual costs incurred for January? What should the total standard costs for that period have been?
3. Compute the labor rate and efficiency variances for policy developers and policy salespeople.
4. Compute the overhead variances for January.
5. Identify possible causes for each variance, and develop possible solutions.

PROBLEM SET A

A 1.
L O 3
Development of Standards: Direct Labor

Check Figure: 1. Standard direct labor cost: $86.53

Because of a planned change in labor structure, Cee Salt Company must develop a new standard direct labor cost for its product. Standard direct labor costs per 1,000 pounds of salt in 19x8 were 3.5 hours in the Sodium Preparation Department at $10.00 per hour; 2.6 hours in the Chloride Mixing Department at $12.50 per hour; and 2.2 hours in the Cleaning and Packaging Department at $8.50 per hour. Labor rates are expected to increase in 19x9 by 10 percent in the Sodium Preparation Department and 20 percent in the Chloride Mixing Department, and to decrease by 10 percent in the Cleaning and Packaging Department. New machinery in the Chloride Mixing Department will lower the direct labor time standard by 20 percent per 1,000 pounds of salt. All other time standards are expected to remain the same.

REQUIRED

1. Compute the standard direct labor cost per 1,000 pounds of salt for 19x9.
2. Management has a plan to improve productive output in the Sodium Preparation Department by 20 percent. If such results are achieved in 19x9, determine (a) the effect on the direct labor time standard and (b) the resulting total standard direct labor cost per 1,000 pounds of salt. Round to three decimal places.
3. Unskilled labor can be hired to staff all departments in 19x9, with the result that all labor rates paid in 19x8 would be cut by 30 percent in the new year. Such a change in labor skill would cause the direct labor time standards to increase by 50 percent over their 19x8 levels, based on skilled labor. Compute the standard direct labor cost per 1,000 pounds of salt if this change takes place. (Round to three decimal places.)

A 2. *Developing and*
L O 3, 7 *Using Standard*
Costs

Check Figure: 2. Total standard unit cost per umbrella: $141.80

The Zima Supply Company manufactures swimming pool equipment and accessories. To make high-quality umbrellas for poolside tables, waterproof canvas is first sent to the Cutting Department. In the Assembly Department, the canvas is stretched over the umbrella's ribs and attached to the center pole and opening mechanism. Then the umbrella, along with a heavy mounting base, is packed for shipment.

The company uses a standard cost accounting system. Direct labor and factory overhead standards for each umbrella for 19x7 are as follows: direct labor consists of .6 hour charged to the Cutting Department at $11.00 per hour and .8 hour charged to the Assembly Department at $12.50 per hour. Variable overhead is 120 percent and fixed overhead 140 percent of total direct labor dollars.

During 19x6, the company used the following direct materials standards: waterproof canvas at $8.60 per square yard for 4 square yards per umbrella; a unit consisting of pole, ribs, and opening mechanism at $30.50 per unit; and an umbrella mounting base at $10.40 per unit.

Quantity standards are expected to remain the same during 19x7, but price changes are likely. The cost of waterproof canvas is expected to increase by 10 percent. The poles, ribs, and opening mechanism will be purchased from three vendors. Vendor A will provide 20 percent of the total supply at $31.00 per unit; Vendor B, 50 percent at $30.80; and Vendor C, 30 percent at $32.00. The cost of each umbrella mounting base is expected to increase 25 percent.

REQUIRED

1. Compute the total standard direct materials cost per umbrella for 19x7.
2. Using your answer from **1** and information from the problem, compute the standard manufacturing cost of one umbrella for 19x7.
3. Using your answers from **1** and **2,** prepare journal entries for the following transactions in 19x7.

Jan. 20 Purchased 4,500 square yards of waterproof canvas at $9.50 per square yard, on account.
Feb. 1 Requisitioned 810 pole, rib, and opening mechanism assemblies into production to complete a job calling for 800 umbrellas.
Mar. 15 Transferred 600 completed umbrellas to finished goods inventory.

A 3. *Materials and*
L O 6 *Labor Variances*

Check Figures: 1. Direct materials price variance—Liquid plastic: $0; Direct materials quantity variance—Liquid plastic: $24 (U)

The Kawalski Packaging Company makes plastic walnut baskets for food wholesalers. Each Type R basket is made of .8 gram of liquid plastic and .5 gram of an additive that includes color and hardening agents. The standard prices are $.12 per gram of liquid plastic and $.09 per gram of additive.

Three kinds of labor are required: molding, trimming, and packing. The labor time and rate standards per 100-basket batch are as follows: molding, .8 hour per batch at an hourly rate of $12; trimming, .6 hour per batch at an hourly rate of $10; and packing, .2 hour per batch at $9 per hour.

During 19x9, the company produced 48,000 Type R walnut baskets. Actual materials used were 38,600 grams of liquid plastic at a total cost of $4,632 and 23,950 grams of additive at a cost of $2,395. Actual direct labor included 380 hours for molding, at a total cost of $4,484; 290 hours for trimming, at $2,929; and 96 hours for packing, at $864.

REQUIRED

1. Compute the direct materials price and quantity variances for both the liquid plastic and the additive.
2. Compute the direct labor rate and efficiency variances for the molding, trimming, and packing processes.

A 4. *Direct Materials,*
L O 6 *Direct Labor,*
and Factory
Overhead Variances

Check Figures: 1. Direct materials price variance: $2,520 (F); 2. Direct materials quantity variance: $3,600 (U)

Schroeder Shoe Company has a sandal division that produces a line of all-vinyl thongs. Each pair of thongs calls for .4 meters of vinyl material that costs $3.00 per meter. Standard direct labor hours and cost per pair of thongs are .2 hour and $1.80 (.2 hour × $9.00 per hour), respectively. The division's current standard variable overhead rate is $1.50 per direct labor hour, and the standard fixed overhead rate is $.80 per direct labor hour.

In August the sandal division manufactured and sold 60,000 pairs of thongs. During the month, 25,200 meters of vinyl material were used up, at a total cost of $73,080. The total actual overhead costs for August were $28,200, of which $18,200 were variable. The total number of direct labor hours worked was 10,800, and factory payroll for direct labor for August was $95,040. Normal monthly capacity for the year has been set at 58,000 pairs of thongs. Budgeted fixed factory overhead for the period was $9,280.

Compute (1) the direct materials price variance, (2) the direct materials quantity variance, (3) the direct labor rate variance, (4) the direct labor efficiency variance, (5) the controllable overhead variance, and (6) the overhead volume variance.

A 5. *Standard Cost*
L O 3, 6, 7 *Journal Entry*
 Analysis
Check Figure: 2. March 16, direct labor rate variance: $413 (U)

Brannigan Bottle Company makes wine bottles for many of the major wineries in California's Napa and Sonoma valleys, as well as for wineries in the grape-growing regions around Cupertino and Santa Cruz, California. Paul Sega, controller of the company, has installed the following cost, quantity, and time standards for 19x9.

Direct materials: 4 five-gallon pails of a special silicon dioxide and phosphorus pentoxide-based compound per one gross (144) of bottles; cost, $10.00 per pail.

Direct labor: Forming Department, .2 hour per gross at $12.80 per direct labor hour; Finishing/Polishing Department, .1 hour per gross at $9.40 per direct labor hour.

Factory overhead: variable, $3.20 per direct labor hour; fixed, $2.80 per direct labor hour.

All direct materials are added at the beginning of the bottle-forming process. Much of Brannigan Bottle Company's machinery is automated, and the compound is heated, mixed, and poured into molds in a short time. Once cooled, the new bottles move via conveyor belt to the Finishing/Polishing Department. Again the process is highly automated. Machines scrape off excess material on the bottles and then polish all the outside and inside surfaces. After polishing, the bottles are fed into large cartons for shipping to customers.

During March 19x9, the following selected transactions took place.

Mar. 2 Purchased 14,000 pails of compound at $9.80 per pail, on account.
3 Requisitioned 13,240 pails of compound into production for an order calling for 3,300 gross of wine bottles.
6 Requisitioned 11,200 pails of compound into production for an order of 2,900 gross of wine bottles.
12 Transferred 5,400 gross of bottles to finished goods inventory.
15 Requisitioned 9,240 pails of compound into production for an order calling for 2,300 gross of wine bottles.
16 For the two-week period ending March 14, actual labor costs included 1,660 direct labor hours in the Forming Department at $13.00 per hour and 810 direct labor hours in the Finishing/Polishing Department at $9.50 per hour. During the pay period, 8,200 gross of good bottles were produced.
16 Factory overhead was applied to units worked on during the previous two weeks.
18 Purchased 19,000 pails of compound at $10.25 per pail, on account.
20 Requisitioned 13,960 pails of compound into production for an order of 3,500 gross of wine bottles.
28 Transferred 9,600 gross of bottles to finished goods inventory.
30 For the two-week period ending March 28, actual labor costs included 1,420 direct labor hours in the Forming Department at $12.60 per hour and 750 direct labor hours in the Finishing/Polishing Department at $9.20 per hour. During the pay period, 7,300 gross of good bottles were produced.
30 Factory overhead was applied to units worked on during the two-week period.
31 During March, 9,800 gross of wine bottles were sold on account and shipped to customers. The selling price for these bottles was $76 per gross.

Actual factory overhead for March was $14,500 of variable and $13,300 of fixed overhead. These amounts have been recorded in the Factory Overhead Control account. Budgeted fixed factory overhead for March was $12,600. Beginning inventory information included: Materials Inventory, $42,100; Work in Process Inventory, $30,064; and Finished Goods Inventory, $146,772.

REQUIRED

1. Compute the standard cost per gross of wine bottles.
2. Prepare the entries necessary to record the above transactions (show calculations for each variance). For the direct labor entries, assume that everything except the distribution of direct labor to Work in Process Inventory has already been recorded.
3. Analyze the factory overhead accounts and compute the controllable overhead and overhead volume variances. (Assume that actual overhead incurred has already been debited to the control account.)
4. Prepare the entry to dispose of the balance in the Factory Overhead account and record the overhead variances.
5. Close all variance account balances to the Cost of Goods Sold account.

A 6.
S O 9
*Variance Review:
Missing Information—
Three-Variance
Approach*

Check Figures: (b) Koenig Company, Budgeted fixed overhead: $17,160; (i) Shukitt Corporation, Total overhead costs applied: $65,600

Overhead variances are interrelated. The Koenig Company and the Shukitt Corporation both use standard costing systems. These systems depend on a standard overhead rate when overhead costs are applied to units produced.

	Koenig Company	Shukitt Corporation
Actual machine hours	7,500	8,400
Standard machine hours allowed	(a)	8,200
Normal capacity in machine hours	(c)	(k)
Total overhead rate per machine hour	$ 3.20	(j)
Standard variable overhead rate	$ 1.00	$ 4.00
Actual variable and fixed overhead	$26,200	(l)
Total overhead costs applied	$25,600	(i)
Budgeted fixed overhead	(b)	$24,000
Total overhead variance	(d)	$ 600 (F)
Overhead spending variance	(e)	(m)
Overhead efficiency variance	(f)	$ 800 (U)
Overhead volume variance	$ 440 (F)	(h)
Controllable overhead variance	(g)	$ 8,200 (U)

REQUIRED

Fill in the unknown amounts by analyzing the data given for each company. Capacities are expressed in machine hours. (**Hint:** Use the structure of Figure 5 in this chapter as a guide for your analysis.)

PROBLEM SET B

B 1.
L O 3
*Development of
Standards: Direct
Materials*

Check Figure: 1. Total standard direct materials cost per unit: $167.52

Tick & Tock, Ltd. assembles clock movements for grandfather clocks. Each movement has four components to assemble: the clock facing, the clock hands, the time movement, and the spring assembly. For the current year, 19x8, the company used the following standard costs: clock facing, $15.90; clock hands, $12.70; time movement, $66.10; and spring assembly, $52.50.

Prices and sources of materials are expected to change in 19x9. Sixty percent of the facings will be supplied by Company A at $18.50 each, and the remaining 40 percent will be purchased from Company B at $18.80 each. The hands are produced for Tick & Tock, Ltd. by Brown Hardware, Inc., and will cost $15.50 per set in 19x9. Time movements will be purchased from three Swiss sources: Company Q, 30 percent of total need at $68.50 per movement; Company R, 20 percent at $69.50; and Company S, 50 percent at $71.90. Spring assemblies will be purchased from a French company and are expected to increase in cost by 20 percent.

REQUIRED

1. Determine the total standard direct materials cost per unit for 19x9.
2. If the company could guarantee the purchase of 2,500 sets of hands from Brown Hardware, Inc., the unit cost would be reduced by 20 percent. Find the resulting standard direct materials unit cost.

3. Substandard spring assemblies can be purchased at $50.00, but 20 percent of them will be unusable and cannot be returned. Compute the standard direct materials unit cost if the company follows this procedure, assuming the original facts of the case for the remaining data. The cost of the defective materials will be spread over good units produced.

B 2. *Developing and*
L O 3, 7 *Using Standard*
Costs

Check Figure: 2. Total standard cost of front entrance, 19x7: $7,463

Prefabricated houses are the specialty of Hardin Homes, Inc., of Plano, Texas. Although Hardin Homes produces many models, and customers can even special-order a home, 60 percent of the company's business comes from the sale of the Citadel, a three-bedroom, 1,400 square foot home with an impressive front entrance. The six basic materials used to manufacture the entrance with their standard costs for 19x6 are as follows: wood framing materials, $1,820; deluxe front door, $480; door hardware, $260; exterior siding, $710; electrical materials, $580; and interior finishing materials, $1,250.

Three types of labor are used to build this section: carpenter, 20 hours at $12.00 per hour; door specialist, 4 hours at $14.00 per hour; and electrician, 8 hours at $16.00 per hour. In 19x6, the company used an overhead rate of 30 percent of total materials cost.

During 19x7, wood framing materials costs are expected to increase by 20 percent. The deluxe front door will need two suppliers: Supplier A will produce 40 percent of the company's needs at $490 per door; Supplier B, 60 percent at $500 per door. Door hardware cost will increase by 10 percent; electrical materials cost, by 20 percent. Exterior siding cost should decrease by $10 per unit. Interior finishing materials costs are expected to remain the same. Carpenter's wages will increase by $1 per hour, while the door specialist's wages should remain the same. Electrician's wages will increase by $.50 per hour. Finally, the factory overhead rate will decrease to 25 percent of total materials cost.

REQUIRED

1. Compute the total standard cost per front entrance for 19x6.
2. Using your answer to **1** and other information given, compute the 19x7 standard manufacturing cost for the Citadel's entrance.
3. From the information given, prepare journal entries for the following transactions for 19x7.

Jan. 6 Purchased 120 front doors from Supplier A for $57,120.
14 Requisitioned 60 sets of hardware into production to complete a job calling for 56 entrance units.
30 Transferred the 56 completed front entrances to finished goods inventory.

B 3. *Materials and*
L O 6 *Labor Variances*

Check Figures: 1. Direct materials quantity variances, Metal: $1,430 (U); Plastic, $340 (U); Wood, $50 (U)

Lambert Trophy Company produces a variety of athletic awards, most in the form of trophies or mounted replicas of athletes in action. Lisa Lambert, president of the company, is in the process of developing a standard cost accounting system. Lambert produces six standard sizes. The deluxe trophy stands three feet tall above the base. Materials standards include one pound of metal and six ounces of plastic supported by an 8-ounce wooden base. Standard prices for 19x8 were $3.25 per pound of metal, $.40 per ounce of plastic, and $.25 per ounce of wood.

Direct labor is used in both the Molding and the Trimming/Finishing Departments. Deluxe trophies require labor standards of .2 hours of direct labor in the Molding Department and .4 hours in the Trimming/Finishing Department. Standard labor rates for deluxe trophies are $10.75 per hour in the Molding Department and $12.00 per hour in the Trimming/Finishing Department.

During January 19x8, 16,400 deluxe trophies were made. Actual production data were as follows:

Materials
Metal	16,840 pounds @ $3.25/pound
Plastic	99,250 ounces @ $.38/ounce
Wood	131,400 ounces @ $.28/ounce

Labor
Molding	3,420 hours @ $10.60/hour
Trimming/Finishing	6,540 hours @ $12.10/hour

REQUIRED

1. Compute the direct materials price and quantity variances for metal, plastic, and wood.

2. Compute the direct labor rate and efficiency variances for the Molding and the Trimming/Finishing Departments.

B 4.

L O 6

Direct Materials, Direct Labor, and Factory Overhead Variances

Check Figures: 1. Direct materials price variances, Chemicals: $15,250 (F), Packages: $0; 2. Direct materials quantity variances, Chemicals: $5,000 (U), Packages: $240 (U)

During 19x8, Brightland Laboratories, Inc. researched and perfected a cure for the common cold. Called Cold-Gone, the product consists of a series of five tablets and sells for $28.00 per package. Standard unit costs for this product were developed in late 19x8 for use in 19x9. Per package, the standard unit costs were: chemical ingredients, 6 ounces at $1.00 per ounce; packaging, $1.20; direct labor, .8 hour at $14.00 per hour; standard variable factory overhead, $4.00 per direct labor hour; and standard fixed factory overhead, $6.00 per direct labor hour.

In the first quarter of 19x9, the peak season for colds, demand for the new product rose beyond even the wildest expectations of management. During these three months, the company produced and sold 4 million packages of Cold-Gone. During the first week in April, 50,000 packages were produced using materials for 50,200 packages costing $60,240. Chemical use was 305,000 ounces costing $289,750. Direct labor was 40,250 direct labor hours at a total cost of $571,550. Total variable factory overhead was $161,100 and total fixed factory overhead, $242,000. Budgeted fixed factory overhead for the period was $240,000.

REQUIRED

Compute (1) all direct materials price variances, (2) all direct materials quantity variances, (3) the direct labor rate variance, (4) the direct labor efficiency variance, (5) the controllable overhead variance, and (6) the overhead volume variance.

B 5.

L O 3, 6, 7

Standard Cost Journal Entry Analysis

Check Figure: 1. Total standard unit cost: $151.70

Michael Francis Lamp Company manufactures several lines of home and business lights and lighting systems. Mahogany table lamps are one of its most popular product lines. Since the wood is very difficult to work with, Michael Francis employs skilled wood carvers. Fannie Newton, controller, has developed the following cost, quantity, and time standards for one table lamp for the current year.

Materials: wood, 10 × 8 × 18-inch block of mahogany, $14.00; electrical fixture and cord, $5.50; and shade and mounting, $9.20.

Direct labor: wood carvers, 6 hours at $14.50 per hour; assemblers and packers, 1.2 hours at $9.00 per hour.

Factory overhead: variable rate, $1.40 per direct labor hour; fixed rate, $2.10 per direct labor hour.

Mahogany table lamps sell for $250 each.

Selected transactions for August 19x8 are as follows:

Aug. 3   Purchased 800 blocks of mahogany for $11,280, on account.

4   Requisitioned 70 blocks of wood into production for order 16, calling for 65 lamps.

5   Purchased 500 electrical fixture kits for $2,700 and 600 lamp shades and mountings for $5,580, on account.

7   Requisitioned 68 electrical fixture kits and 66 lamp shades and mountings into production for order 16.

14   Semimonthly payroll was paid, including the following wages for order 16: wood carvers, 400 hours, $5,760; assemblers and packers, 80 hours, $720. These labor efforts completed order 16.

14   Factory overhead was applied to units worked on during the payroll period. (Assume order 16 represents the only units worked on during the pay period.)

16   Requisitioned 74 blocks of wood into production for order 26, calling for 70 lamps.

19   Requisitioned 78 electrical fixture kits and 75 lamp shades and mountings into production for order 26.

30   Semimonthly payroll was paid. Labor costs associated with order 26 included: wood carvers, 434 hours, $6,293; assemblers and packers, 90 hours, $846. These labor efforts completed order 26.

Aug. 30 Factory overhead was applied to the work performed during the last two weeks. (Assume order 26 represents the only units worked on during the pay period.)

    30 Orders 16 and 26 were transferred to Finished Goods Inventory.

    31 Orders 16 and 26 were shipped to customers at the contracted price.

During August, actual factory overhead incurred for orders 16 and 26 was variable, $1,420, and fixed, $2,160. All actual overhead costs have already been recorded in the Factory Overhead Control account. Assume that budgeted fixed factory overhead was $2,697 for these two orders.

REQUIRED

1. Compute the standard cost for one mahogany table lamp.
2. Prepare the entries necessary to record the month's transactions (show calculations for each variance). For the direct labor entries, assume that everything has been recorded except the distribution of direct labor to Work in Process Inventory. Round answers to the nearest dollar.
3. Analyze the factory overhead accounts by computing the controllable overhead and overhead volume variances. Round amounts to the nearest dollar.
4. Prepare the entry to dispose of the overhead control account and record the overhead variances. (Assume that actual overhead incurred has already been debited to the control account.)
5. Close all variance account balances to the Cost of Goods Sold account. (Round answers to the nearest dollar.)

B 6.   *Variance Review:*
S O 9   *Missing Information—*
        Three-Variance
        Approach

Check Figures: (c) Casey Corporation, Total overhead variance: $3,450 (F); (h) Andrews Company, Budgeted fixed overhead: $28,800

Over- or underapplied overhead is the reason for analyzing overhead variances. These variances are interrelated. Casey Corporation and Andrews Company have standard costing systems. Each firm uses the three-variance approach to overhead variance analysis.

	Casey Corporation	Andrews Company
Actual machine hours	8,550	(i)
Standard machine hours allowed	8,750	8,800
Normal capacity in machine hours	(f)	9,000
Total overhead rate per machine hour	(e)	(g)
Standard variable overhead rate	$ 2.50	$ 1.80
Actual variable and fixed overhead	(a)	$43,850
Total overhead costs applied	(d)	$44,000
Budgeted fixed overhead	$76,500	(h)
Total overhead variance	(c)	(j)
Overhead spending variance	$ 700 (F)	(k)
Overhead efficiency variance	(b)	$ 360 (F)
Overhead volume variance	$ 2,250 (F)	(l)

REQUIRED

Fill in the unknown amounts by analyzing the data for each organization. Capacities are expressed in machine hours. (**Hint:** Use the structure of Figure 5 in this chapter as a guide for your analysis.)

MANAGERIAL REPORTING AND ANALYSIS CASES

Interpreting Management Reports

MRA 1.
L O 4, 8
Flexible Budgets and Performance Evaluation

Check Figure: 2. Budgeted variable costs per home resale: $10,922.50

Sid Realtors, Inc. specializes in home resales. Revenue is earned from selling fees. Commissions for salespersons, listing agents, and listing companies are the major costs for the company. Business has improved steadily over the last ten years. As usual, Bonnie Sid, the managing partner of Sid Realtors, Inc. received a report summarizing the performance for the most recent year.

Sid Realtors, Inc.
Performance Report
For the Year Ended December 31, 19x9

	Budget*	Actual**	Difference Under (Over) Budget
Total Selling Fees	$2,052,000	$2,242,200	($190,200)
Less Variable Costs			
Sales Commissions	$1,102,950	$1,205,183	($102,233)
Automobile	36,000	39,560	(3,560)
Advertising	93,600	103,450	(9,850)
Home Repairs	77,400	89,240	(11,840)
General Overhead	656,100	716,970	(60,870)
	$1,966,050	$2,154,403	($188,353)
Less Fixed Costs			
General Overhead	60,000	62,300	(2,300)
Total Costs	$2,026,050	$2,216,703	($190,653)
Income Before Income Taxes	$ 25,950	$ 25,497	$ 453

* Budgeted data based on 180 home resales.

** Actual selling fees and operating costs of 202 home resales.

REQUIRED

1. Analyze the performance report. What does it say about the performance of the company? Is the performance report reliable? Explain.
2. Calculate the budgeted selling fee and budgeted variable costs per home resale.
3. Prepare a performance report using a flexible budget based on the actual number of home resales.
4. Analyze the report you prepared in **3.** What does it say about the performance of the company? Is the performance report reliable? Explain.
5. What recommendations would you make to improve next year's performance?

Formulating Management Reports

MRA 2.
L O 6, 8
Preparing Performance Reports

Check Figure: 2. Labor rate variance: $675 (U)

Rita Worthington, president of *Sun Valley Spa,* is concerned about the spa's operating performance in March 19x8. She carefully budgeted her costs so that she could reduce the 19x8 membership fees. Now she needs to monitor these costs to make sure that the spa's profits are at the level she expected.

She has asked you, as the controller for the spa, to prepare a performance report for the labor and overhead costs. She also wants you to analyze the report and suggest possible causes for any problems you find. She needs your work immediately so that any problems can be solved.

The following information was made available:

	Standard	Actual
Variable costs		
Operating labor	$12,160	$13,500
Utilities	2,880	3,360
Repairs and maintenance	5,760	7,140
Fixed costs		
Depreciation, equipment	2,600	2,680
Rent	3,280	3,280
Other	1,704	1,860
Totals	$28,384	$31,820

Normal operating hours call for eight operators, working 160 hours each per month. During March, nine operators worked an average of 150 hours each.

REQUIRED

1. Answer the following questions about preparing performance reports.
   a. Who needs the performance report?
   b. Why are you preparing the performance report?
   c. What information do you need to develop the performance report? How will you obtain that information?
   d. When must you have the performance report and analysis prepared?
2. With this limited information, compute the labor rate variance, the labor efficiency variance, and the factory overhead controllable variance.
3. Prepare a performance report for the month. Analyze the report and suggest possible causes for any problems that you find.

International Company

MRA 3.
LO 6, 8

Variance Analysis

No check figure

Edmund Yu recently became the controller of a joint venture in Hong Kong. Edmund created a standard costing system to help plan for and control the company's activities. After completing the first quarter of operating activities using standard costing, Edmund met with the budget team, which included managers from purchasing, engineering, production, and personnel. He asked them to share any problems that occurred during the quarter. He planned to use the information to analyze the variances that his staff would calculate.

REQUIRED

For each of the following situations, identify the variance or variances for materials and labor that could be affected and indicate the direction (favorable or unfavorable) of these variances.

a. The production department used highly skilled, higher-paid workers.
b. Machines were improperly adjusted.
c. Direct labor personnel worked more carefully to manufacture the product.
d. The product design engineer substituted a raw material that was less expensive and of lesser quality.
e. The Purchasing Department bought higher-quality materials at a higher price.
f. A major supplier delivered the raw materials using a less expensive mode of transportation.
g. Work was halted for two hours due to a power disruption.

Accounting for Management Decision Making

exposes the difficulties of setting an accurate price for a good or a service. External as well as internal factors are used in the price setting process. Target costing is a new approach to pricing within a highly competitive market environment. Transfer pricing involves internally created prices that can be either cost- or market-based. If not applied properly, transfer prices can cause internal employee problems when used to evaluate performance.

introduces the concepts of relevant decision information, variable costing, contribution margin reporting, and incremental decision analysis. Examples of short-run decisions include make-or-buy, special order, scarce resource/sales mix, elimination of unprofitable segments, and sell or process-further considerations.

first looks at the steps in the capital expenditure decision process. Then the techniques of accounting rate of return, payback period, and net present value are discussed. The concept of the time value of money and income tax influences on the capital expenditure decision analysis conclude the chapter.

Pricing Decisions, Including Transfer Pricing

Maison & Jardin Restaurant

Maison & Jardin is a gourmet restaurant in Altamonte Springs, Florida. Among its selections of red wine is a 1989 Cabernet Sauvignon from California's Shafer Vineyards. The restaurant's normal list price for a bottle of this wine served at tableside is $18.50. However, in March, the restaurant's manager featured it as "the special selection of the month" at a price of $16.75 per bottle.

The restaurant is unique because it also has a license to sell wine for take-home trade. So in addition to the prices mentioned above, the wine list contained the following prices relating to this same bottle of wine.

	Price per Bottle
Purchased by the glass, $5.25 (4 glasses per bottle)	$21.00
Purchased by the bottle to take home	13.70
Purchased by the case to take home ($144.00 ÷ 12)	12.00

So the wine list has five different prices for the same bottle of wine. What factors did the manager consider when setting these prices?

The $18.50 price is based on the cost of the bottle; reputation of the vineyard; and prices of wines of comparable quality, vintage (1989), and mixture of varietal grapes. To promote a specific product, many businesses run special sales. A restaurant is no different. In March, the manager decided to reduce the bottle's price by $1.75 to lure customers into trying the product with their meal.

Once a bottle of quality red wine has been opened, the wine begins to oxidize and spoils in a few hours. Therefore, the restaurant risks losing part of the bottle to spoilage when it is sold by the glass. Thus, the $5.25 price per glass seems reasonable under the circumstances. Although the take-home feature is unusual, the pricing is appropriate. Part of the cost for a bottle of wine served with a meal is the cost of serving it. Since the restaurant manager reduced the price of a take-home bottle by $4.80 from its regular price, the cost of serving a bottle of wine plus the restaurant's profit margin is somewhere around $5.00 per bottle. Finally, the take-home case price is $1.70 per bottle less than the single-bottle price. This reduction is known as quantity discounting, a concept widely followed in the free enterprise system. Reduced handling costs support the use of quantity discount pricing. :::::

THE PRICING DECISION AND THE MANAGER

1 *State the objectives managers use, and the rules they follow, to establish prices of goods and services*

The process of establishing a correct price is more of an art than a science. There are many mechanical approaches to price setting, and each produces a price. Six pricing approaches to the same product or service may very well produce six different prices. The art of price setting stems from the manager's ability to read the marketplace and anticipate customer reaction to a product and its price. Pricing methods do not provide a manager with the ability to react to the market. Market savvy is developed through experience in dealing with customers and products in an industry. Intuition also plays a major role in price setting. These managerial traits were shown in the Maison & Jardin Restaurant Decision Point.

Deciding on an appropriate price is one of a manager's most difficult day-to-day decisions. Such decisions affect the long-term life of any profit-oriented enterprise. The long-run objectives of a company should include a pricing policy. Such a policy is one way to differentiate one company from another; for example, Mercedes-Benz from Ford or Neiman-Marcus from Kmart. All four companies are successful, but their pricing policies are quite different. Of primary importance in setting company pricing objectives is identifying the market being served and meeting the needs of that market. Possible pricing policy objectives include:

1. Identifying and adhering to both short-run and long-run pricing strategies
2. Maximizing profits
3. Maintaining or gaining market share
4. Setting socially responsible prices
5. Maintaining a minimum rate of return on investment targets
6. Being customer driven

Pricing strategies depend on many factors and conditions. Companies producing standard items for a competitive marketplace will have different pricing strategies from firms making custom-designed items. In a competitive market, prices can be reduced to gain market share by displacing sales of competing companies. Continuous upgrading of a product or service can help in this area. The company making custom-designed items can be more conservative in its pricing strategy.

Maximizing profits has always been considered the underlying objective of any pricing policy. Maintaining or gaining market share is closely related to pricing strategies. However, market share is important only if sales are profitable. To increase market share by reducing prices below cost can be disastrous unless this move is accompanied by other compensating objectives and goals.

Although still a dominant factor in price setting, profit maximization has been tempered in recent years by other, more socially acceptable goals. Prices have a social effect, and companies are concerned about their public image. We just mentioned Mercedes-Benz, Ford, Neiman-Marcus, and Kmart. Does not each company have an individual image in your mind? And are the prices not a part of that image? Other social concerns, such as legal constraints and ethical considerations, also affect many companies' pricing policies.

Other pricing policy objectives include maintaining a minimum return on investment and being customer driven. Return on investment involves markup percentages designed to provide a buffer between costs and prices and is linked closely with the profit maximization objective. Being customer driven, which occurs when the needs of customers influence prices, is important for several reasons. First, it is basic to continuous sales growth. Second, customer acceptance is key to being successful in a competitive market. Finally, prices should reflect the value that is added by the respective company, which is another way of saying that prices are customer driven.

In summary, to stay in business, a company's selling price must (1) be equal to or lower than the competition's price, (2) be acceptable to the customer, (3) recover all costs incurred in bringing the product or service to a marketable condition, and (4) return a profit. If a manager deviates from any of these four selling rules, there must be a specific short-run objective that accounts for the change. Breaking these pricing rules for a long period will force a company into bankruptcy.

The methods discussed below illustrate the process of developing a specific price under defined circumstances or objectives. Some of the methods provide the manager with the minimum price he or she can charge and still make a profit. Other prices are based on competition and market conditions. The concept of setting prices according to "whatever the market will bear" will produce still another figure. In making a final pricing decision, the manager must consider all these projected prices. The more data the manager has, the more he or she will be able to make a well-informed decision. But remember, pricing methods and approaches yield only decision support data. The manager must still select the appropriate price and be evaluated on that decision.

TRADITIONAL ECONOMIC PRICING CONCEPTS

OBJECTIVE

2 *Describe traditional economic pricing concepts*

The traditional approach to pricing is based on microeconomic theory. Pricing has a major role in the concepts underlying the theory as it is practiced at each individual firm. At the base of this concept, every firm is in business to maximize profits. Although each product has its own set of revenues and costs, microeconomic theory states that profit will be maximized when the difference between total revenue and total cost is the greatest. In breakeven analysis, a graphical representation is used to analyze each breakeven situation. A company will lose money when total costs exceed total revenues; profit will be realized when total revenues are greater than total costs. But where is the point at which profits are maximized, and what is the role of pricing in this discussion?

Total Revenue and Total Cost Curves   When looking at a graphic breakeven analysis, the outlook for profits can be a bit misleading. The profit area can seem to increase significantly as more and more products are sold. Therefore, it could seem that if the company could produce an infinite number of products, maximum profit would be realized. But this situation is untrue, and microeconomic theory explains why.

Figure 1A shows the economist's view of a breakeven chart. On it there are two breakeven points, between which is a large space labeled *profit area.* Notice that the total revenue line is curved rather than straight. The theory is that as one markets a product, price reductions due to competition and other factors will be necessary to sell additional units. Total revenue will continue to increase, but the rate of increase will diminish as more units are sold. Therefore, the total revenue line curves toward the right.

Costs react in an opposite fashion. Over the assumed relevant range, variable and fixed costs are fairly predictable, with fixed costs remaining constant

Figure 1. Microeconomic Pricing Theory

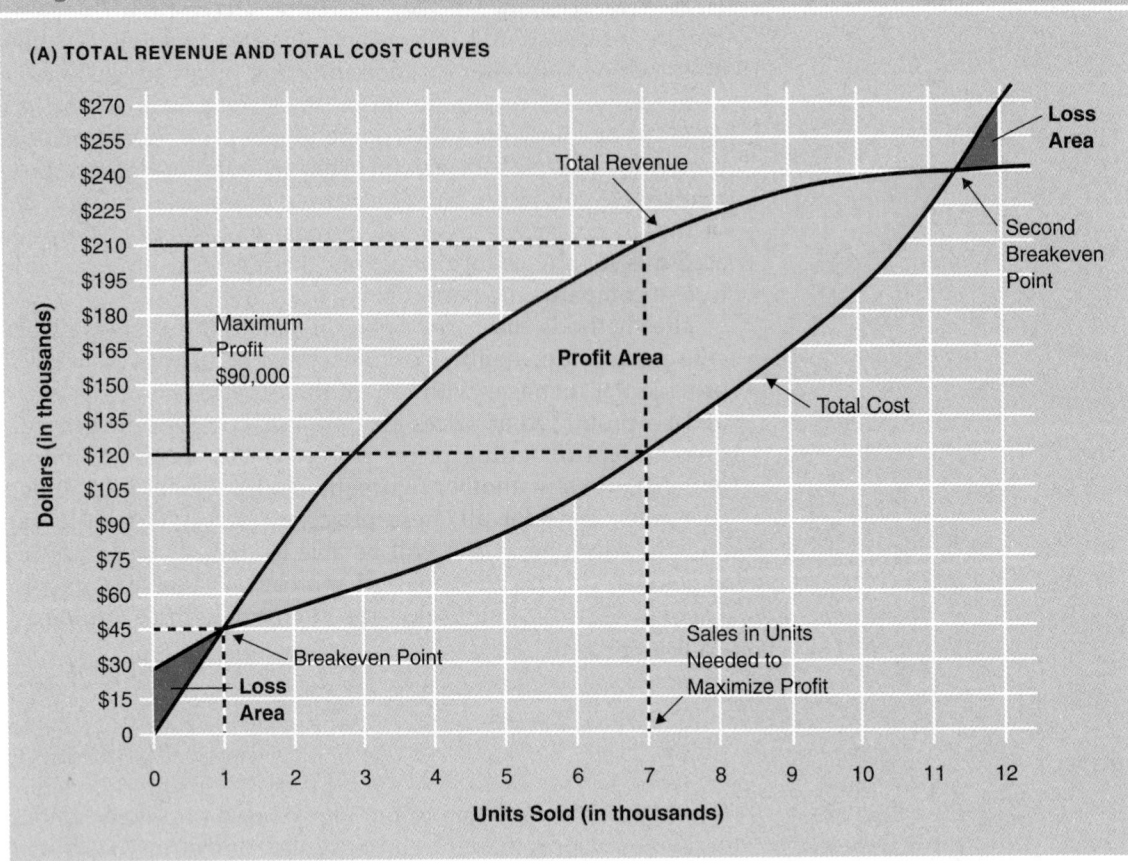

(A) TOTAL REVENUE AND TOTAL COST CURVES

y-axis: Dollars (in thousands) — $270, $255, $240, $225, $210, $195, $180, $165, $150, $135, $120, $105, $90, $75, $60, $45, $30, $15, 0

x-axis: Units Sold (in thousands) — 0, 1, 2, 3, 4, 5, 6, 7, 8, 9, 10, 11, 12

Labels: Loss Area, Total Revenue, Second Breakeven Point, Maximum Profit $90,000, Profit Area, Total Cost, Breakeven Point, Loss Area, Sales in Units Needed to Maximize Profit

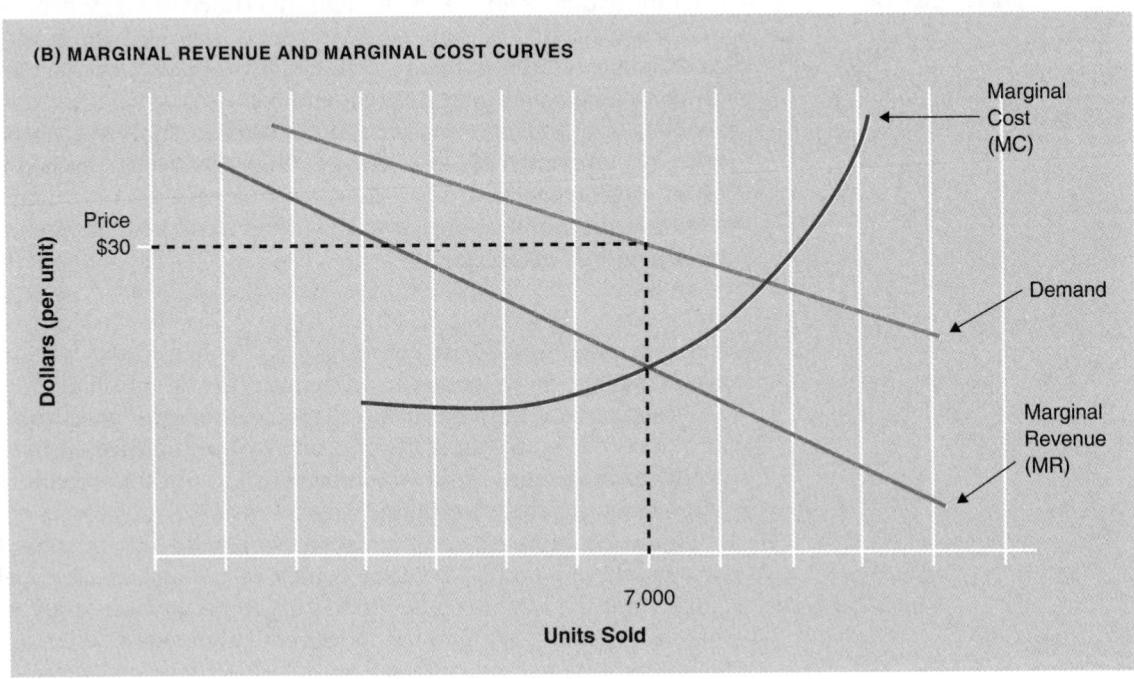

(B) MARGINAL REVENUE AND MARGINAL COST CURVES

y-axis: Dollars (per unit)

Price $30

Labels: Marginal Cost (MC), Demand, Marginal Revenue (MR)

x-axis: Units Sold — 7,000

and variable costs being the same per unit. The result is a straight line for total costs. Following microeconomic theory, costs per unit will increase over time, since fixed costs will change. As one moves into different relevant ranges, such fixed costs as supervision and depreciation increase. In addition, as the company pushes for more and more products from limited facilities, repair and maintenance costs increase. And as the push from management increases, total costs rise at an accelerating rate per unit. The result is that the total cost line in Figure 1A begins curving upward. The total revenue line and the total cost line then cross again, beyond which point the company suffers a loss on additional sales.

Profits are maximized at the point at which the difference between total revenue and total cost is the greatest. In Figure 1A, this point is 7,000 units of sales. At that sales level, total revenue will be $210,000; total cost, $120,000; and profit, $90,000. In theory, if one additional unit is sold, profit per unit will drop, because total cost is rising at a faster rate than total revenues. As you can see, if the company sells 11,000 units, total profits will be almost entirely depleted by the rising costs. Therefore, in the example, 7,000 sales units is the optimum operating level, and the price charged at that level is the optimal price.

Marginal Revenue and Marginal Cost Curves   Economists use the concepts of marginal revenue and marginal cost to help determine the optimum price for a good or service. Marginal revenue is the change in total revenue caused by a one-unit change in output. Marginal cost is the change in total cost caused by a one-unit change in output. Graphic curves for marginal revenue and marginal cost are derived by measuring and plotting the rate of change in total revenue and total cost at various activity levels. Were you to compute marginal revenue and marginal cost for each unit sold in the example and plot them onto a graph, the lines would resemble those in Figure 1B. Notice that the marginal cost line crosses the marginal revenue line at 7,000 units. After that point, total profits will decrease as additional units are sold. Marginal cost will exceed marginal revenue for each unit sold over 7,000. Profit will be maximized when the marginal revenue and marginal cost lines intersect. By projecting this point onto the product's demand curve, you can locate the optimal price, which is $30 per unit.

If all information used in microeconomic theory were certain, picking the optimal price would be fairly easy. But most information used in the previous analysis relied on projected amounts for unit sales, product costs, and revenues. Just computing total demand for a product or service from such data is difficult. And projecting repair and maintenance costs is usually done by using unsupported estimates. Nevertheless, developing such an analysis usually makes the analyst aware of cost patterns and the unanticipated influences of demand. For this reason it is important for management to consider the microeconomic approach to pricing when setting product prices. But information from this type of analysis should not be the only data relied on.

FACTORS INFLUENCING THE PRICING DECISION

OBJECTIVE

3 *Identify the external and internal factors on which prices are based*

A manager must consider many factors when creating the best price for a product or service. Therefore, before exploring the methods used to compute a selling price, we will analyze those influential factors. Some of those factors are external to the company; others are internal.

External Factors   Each product or service has a targeted market that determines demand. Strong consideration should be given to this market before choosing a final price. External factors to be considered in setting a price are summarized in Table 1. They include the following considerations:

1. What is total demand for the item?
2. Are there one or several competing products in the marketplace?
3. What prices are being charged by others already selling the item?
4. Do customers want the least expensive product or are they more interested in quality than in price?
5. Is the product unique or so new that the company is the only source in the marketplace?

All these questions should be answered by the person developing the price. If competition is keen and the quality is similar, market price will set the ceiling for any new entry into the market. If, however, a product is unique, a more flexible pricing environment exists. Customers' needs and desires are important for any new product. If quality is of primary importance, as is the case for top-of-the-line automobiles, then emphasis should be placed on using quality inputs. The price will be adjusted upward accordingly.

In summary, it is important to know the marketplace, including customers' needs and the competition, before determining a final price.

Internal Factors   Several internal factors also influence the price of a good or service; these are summarized in Table 1 as well. Basic among these factors is an item's cost. What cost basis should be considered when determining price—variable costs, full absorption costs, or total costs? Should the price be based on a desired rate of return on assets? Is the product a loss leader, created to lure customers into considering additional, more expensive products?

Table 1. Factors to Consider When Setting a Price

External Factors:

Total demand for product or service
Number of competing products or services
Quality of competing products or services
Current prices of competing products or services
Customers' preferences for quality versus price
Sole source versus heavy competition
Seasonal demand or continual demand
Life of product or service

Internal Factors:

Cost of product or service
   Variable costs
   Full absorption costs
   Total costs
Price geared toward return on investment
Loss leader or main product
Quality of materials and labor inputs
Labor intensive or automated process
Markup percentage updated
Usage of scarce resources

Where should one draw the line on the quality of materials and supplies? Is the product labor intensive or can it be produced using automated equipment? If markup percentages are used to establish prices, were they updated to reflect current operating conditions? Are the company's scarce resources being overtaxed by introducing an additional product or service, and does the price reflect this use of scarce resources?

As with external factors, each of these questions should be answered before a manager establishes a price for a product or service. Underlying every pricing decision is the fact that all costs incurred must be recovered in the long run or the company will no longer be in business.

COST-BASED PRICING METHODS

OBJECTIVE

4 *Create prices by applying the methods and tools of price determination*

There are many pricing methods used in business. Although managers may use one or two traditional approaches, at some point they also deviate from those approaches and use their experience. Several pricing methods are available that can be adopted by managers. A good starting point is for a manager to develop a price based on the cost of producing a good or service. Here, three methods based on cost will be discussed: (1) gross margin pricing, (2) profit margin pricing, and (3) return on assets pricing. Remember that in a competitive environment, market prices and conditions also influence price; however, if prices do not cover a company's costs, the company will eventually fail.

To illustrate the three methods of cost-based pricing, our example uses data from the Johnson Company. The Johnson Company assembles parts purchased from outside vendors into an electric car-wax buffer. Total costs and unit costs incurred in the previous accounting period to produce 14,750 wax buffers were as follows:

	Total Costs	Unit Costs
Variable production costs		
Materials and parts	$ 88,500	$ 6.00
Direct labor	66,375	4.50
Variable factory overhead	44,250	3.00
Total variable production costs	$199,125	$13.50
Fixed factory overhead	$154,875	$10.50
Selling, general, and administrative expenses		
Selling expenses	$ 73,750	$ 5.00
General expenses	36,875	2.50
Administrative expenses	22,125	1.50
Total selling, general, and administrative expenses	$132,750	$ 9.00
Total costs and expenses	$486,750	$33.00

No changes in unit costs are expected this period. Desired profit for the period is $110,625. The company uses assets totaling $921,875 in producing the wax buffers and a 12 percent return on these assets is expected.

GROSS MARGIN PRICING

One cost-based approach to determining a selling price is known as gross margin pricing. Gross margin is the difference between sales and total production costs of those sales. The markup percentage under the gross margin method is designed to include all costs other than those used in the computation of gross margin in the computation of the selling price. The gross margin markup percentage is composed of selling, general, and administrative expenses and desired profit. Because an accounting system often provides management with unit production cost data, both variable and fixed, this method of determining selling price can be easily applied. The formulas used are as follows:

$$\text{Markup percentage} = \frac{\substack{\text{desired profit} \\ + \text{ total selling, general, and} \\ \text{administrative expenses}}}{\text{total production costs}}$$

Gross-margin-based price = total production costs per unit
+ (markup percentage × total production costs per unit)

The numerator in the markup percentage formula contains desired profit plus total selling, general, and administrative expenses. As you can see, this numerator is divided by total production costs to arrive at the markup factor.

For the Johnson Company, the markup percentage and selling price are computed as follows:

$$\text{Markup percentage} = \frac{\$110,625 + \$132,750}{\$199,125 + \$154,875}$$

$$= \frac{\$243,375}{\$354,000}$$

$$= 68.75\%$$

Gross-margin-based price = $13.50 + $10.50 + (68.75% × $24.00)
= $40.50

The numerator in the markup percentage formula is the sum of the desired profit ($110,625) and the total selling, general, and administrative expenses ($132,750). The denominator contains all production costs—variable costs of $199,125 and fixed production costs of $154,875. Gross margin markup is 68.75 percent of total production costs, or $16.50. Adding $16.50 to the total production cost base yields a selling price of $40.50.

PROFIT MARGIN PRICING

When using an approach known as profit margin pricing, the markup percentage includes only the desired profit factor. For this method to be effective, all costs and expenses must be broken down into unit cost data. Since selling, general, and administrative costs tend to be more difficult to allocate to products or services than variable and fixed production costs, only arbitrary assignments can be used. However, arbitrary allocations can be misleading and may result in poor price setting. As long as market and competition factors are accounted for before establishing a final price, profit margin pricing can be used as a starting point in any price-setting decision analysis.

In the following markup percentage computation, all costs have shifted from the numerator to the denominator.

$$\text{Markup percentage} = \frac{\text{desired profit}}{\text{total costs and expenses}}$$

Profit-margin-based price = total costs and expenses per unit
+ (markup percentage × total costs and expenses per unit)

As shown, only desired profit remains in the numerator. The denominator contains all production and operating costs related to the product or service being priced. In the profit margin pricing formula, total costs and expenses per unit are multiplied by the markup percentage to obtain the appropriate profit margin. The selling price is computed by adding profit margin to total unit costs.

Refer again to the data for the Johnson Company. The markup percentage and the unit selling price using the profit margin pricing approach are computed as follows:

$$\text{Markup percentage} = \frac{\$110,625}{\$199,125 + \$154,875 + \$132,750}$$

$$= \frac{\$110,625}{\$486,750}$$

$$= 22.73\%$$

$$\begin{aligned}\text{Profit-margin-based price} &= \$13.50 + \$10.50 + \$9.00 \\ &\quad + (22.73\% \times \$33.00) \\ &= \$40.50\end{aligned}$$

Only the $110,625 in desired profit margin remains in the numerator, whereas the denominator increased to $486,750. The denominator represents total costs and expenses to be incurred. Markup percentage for this situation is 22.73 percent. The selling price is again $40.50. However, in this computation the markup percentage of 22.73 percent is applied to the total cost of $33.00 to obtain the profit margin of $7.50 per unit ($33.00 + $7.50 = $40.50).

BUSINESS BULLETIN: TECHNOLOGY IN PRACTICE[1]

In the traditional approach to management accounting, costs of technology are treated as part of overhead and allocated to products or services. In a cost-based pricing model, these costs are part of fixed factory overhead. But the business environment has changed and new accounting practices have emerged, including the practice of "technology accounting." Proponents say that technology accounting embodies the concept that technology costs, which can include special buildings, computer hardware, and information systems software, should be treated as direct costs, equivalent to direct labor and material.

Traditional accounting methods link plant and equipment with productive output through a time-based amortization approach—that is, depreciation. As time passes, these costs are charged to the units produced during that time period. There is no relationship between the use of technology and the allocation of its cost. Many technology costs, however, are incurred for a specific product line or venture and can be traced directly to specific products. In addition, many of these costs can be treated as an activity center

---

1. Dennis E. Peavey, "Battle at the GAAP? It's Time for a Change," *Management Accounting,* Institute of Management Accountants, February 1990, pp. 31–35.

and charged to products based on the actual usage of the technology. If cost is going to continue to be used as a basis for price-setting, then direct traceability of costs to the maximum extent possible should be the objective. Arbitrary allocations or time-based depreciation approaches do not yield accurate costs. If cost tracking is not accurate, cost-based prices will not reflect accurate product profitability. ▬▬

RETURN ON ASSETS PRICING

Return on assets pricing changes the objective of the price determination process. Earning a profit margin on total costs is replaced by earning a profit equal to a specified rate of return on assets employed in the operation. Since a business's primary objective should be earning a minimum desired rate of return, the return on assets pricing approach has great appeal and support.

Assuming a company has a stated minimum desired rate of return, you can use the following formula to calculate the return-on-assets-based price.

$$\text{Return-on-assets-based price} = \text{total costs and expenses per unit} + [\text{desired rate of return} \times (\text{total costs of assets employed} \div \text{anticipated units to be produced})]$$

The return-on-assets-based price is computed by first dividing the cost of assets employed by the projected units to be produced. This number is then multiplied by the rate of return to obtain desired earnings per unit. Desired earnings per unit plus total costs and expenses per unit yields the unit selling price.

For the Johnson Company, the selling price per unit needed to earn a 12 percent return on the $921,875 asset base when estimated production is 14,750 units is calculated as follows.

$$\text{Return-on-assets-based price} = \$13.50 + \$10.50 + \$9.00 + [12\% \times (\$921,875 \div 14,750)]$$
$$= \$40.50$$

The desired profit amount has been replaced by an overall company rate of return on assets. By dividing cost of assets employed by projected units of output and multiplying the result by the minimum desired rate of return, one obtains a unit profit factor of $7.50 [12% × ($921,875 ÷ 14,750)]. Adding this profit factor to total unit costs and expenses determines the selling price of $40.50.

SUMMARY OF THE COST-BASED PRICING METHODS

The three cost-based pricing methods are summarized in Figure 2. All three methods—gross margin pricing, profit margin pricing, and return on assets pricing—will yield the same selling price if applied to the same data. Therefore, companies select their methods based on their degree of trust in a cost base. The cost bases from which they can choose are (1) total product costs per unit or (2) total costs and expenses per unit. Often, total product costs per unit are readily available, which makes gross margin pricing a good benchmark on which to compute selling prices. Return on assets pricing is also a good pricing method if the cost of the assets used on a product can be identi-

Figure 2. Cost-Based Pricing Methods: Johnson Company

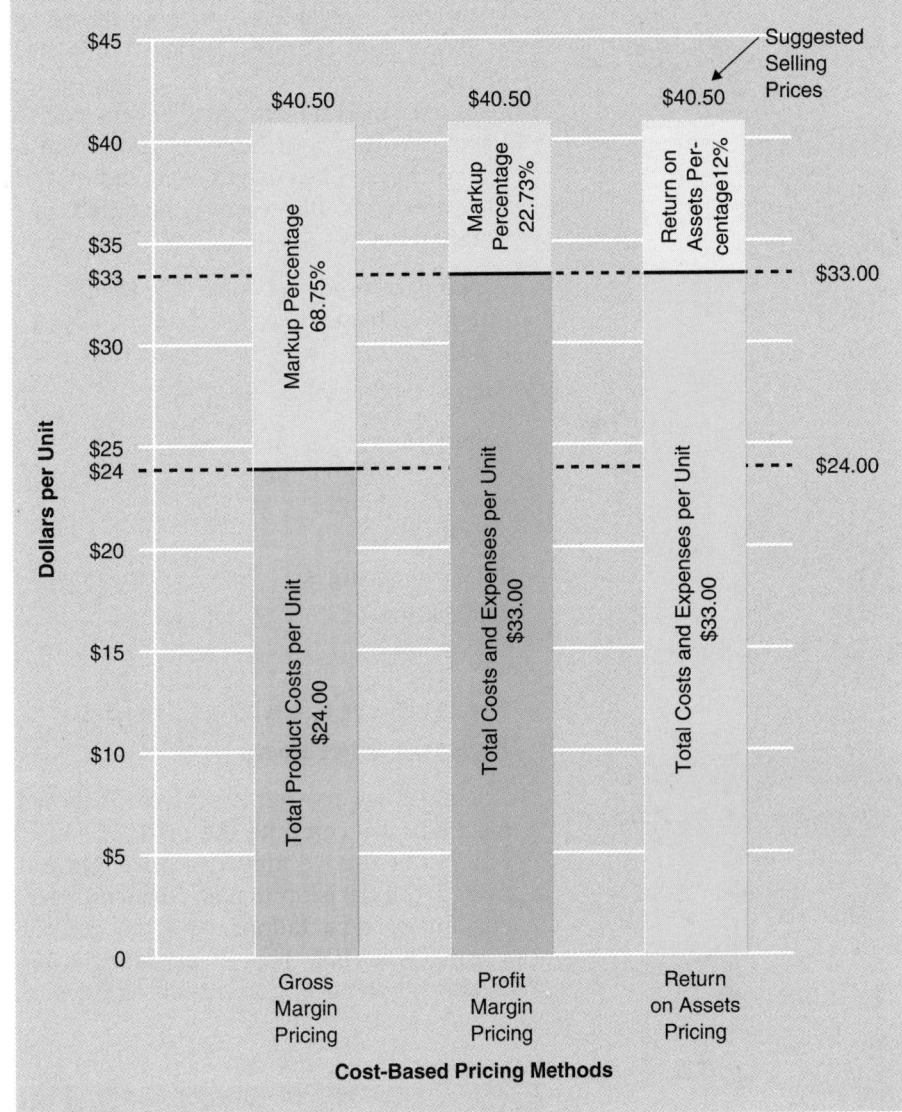

fied and a cost amount determined. If not, the method yields inaccurate results.

PRICING OF SERVICES

Service businesses take a different approach to pricing their products. Although a service has no physical existence, it must still be priced and billed to the customer. Most service organizations use a form of time and materials pricing to arrive at the price of a service. Service companies, such as appliance repair shops, home-addition specialists, pool cleaners, and automobile repair businesses, arrive at prices by using two computations, one for labor and one for materials and parts. As with the cost-based approaches, a markup percentage is used to add the cost of overhead and a profit factor to the direct costs of labor, materials, and parts. If materials and parts are not a component of the service being performed, then only direct labor costs are used as a basis for developing price. For professionals, such as attorneys, accountants, and consultants, a factor representing all overhead costs is applied to the base labor costs to establish a price for the services.

Twins Auto Pampering just completed working on Ms. Burgess's 1988 Jaguar XJS. Parts used to repair the vehicle cost $840. The company's 40 percent markup rate on parts covers parts-related overhead costs and profit. Labor involved four hours of time from a Jaguar specialist whose wages are $35 per hour. The current overhead markup rate on labor is 80 percent. To see how much Ms. Burgess will be billed for these auto repairs, review the computation below.

Repair parts used	$840	
Overhead charges		
$840 × 40%	336	
Total parts charges		$1,176
Labor charges		
4 hours @ $35/hour	$140	
Overhead charges		
$140 × 80%	112	
Total labor charges		252
Total billing		$1,428

FINAL NOTES ON COST-BASED PRICING METHODS

Pricing is an art, not a science. Although one can use several methods to mechanically compute the price of something, many factors external to the product or service influence price. Once the cost-based price has been determined, the decision maker must consider such factors as competitors' prices, customers' expectations, and the cost of substitute products and services. Pricing is a risky part of operating a business, and care must be taken to establish that all-important selling price.

BUSINESS BULLETIN: BUSINESS PRACTICE[2]

Culp, Inc. is a textile manufacturer for the home furnishings industry. The company now bases its pricing decisions on the target costing approach. Prior to this change, the company's price-setting objective was to cover all costs and then add a profit factor. Why this shift in pricing methods? Because target costing aims to reduce costs before they are incurred. According to John Brausch, the company's former cost accounting manager, "Target costing is a strategic management tool that seeks to reduce a product's cost over its lifetime. Target costing presumes interaction between cost accounting and the rest of the firm, well-

2. John M. Brausch, "Beyond ABC: Target Costing for Profit Enhancement," *Management Accounting,* Institute of Management Accountants, November 1994, pp. 45–49.

executed long-range profit planning, and a commitment to continuous cost reduction. . . . it is used to understand costs better and to enhance long-term profitability."

Management at Culp, Inc. looks at accurate product costing as being necessary for accurate financial reporting but not as a tool for controlling costs. Target costing is not a product costing approach, it is a pricing method that emphasizes cost control. Cost control begins at the product design stage by placing cost limits on a product or service. Cost reduction is engineered into the product. Target costing represents a significant change in management philosophy as well. Managers at Culp, Inc. are now more interested in the long-run profitability of their products rather than with maximizing their quarterly net income.

PRICING USING TARGET COSTING

OBJECTIVE

5 *Analyze pricing decisions using target costing*

The concept of target costing, which was developed by the Japanese to compete successfully in the global marketplace, is a product pricing variant of the cost-based models described earlier in this chapter. Instead of first determining the cost of an item and then adding a profit factor to identify a product's price, target costing reverses the procedure. Target costing is a pricing method that (1) identifies the price at which a product will be competitive in the marketplace, (2) defines the minimum desired profit to be made on that product, and (3) computes a target cost for the product by subtracting the desired profit from the competitive market price. This target cost is then given to the engineers and product design people and is used as a maximum cost for the materials, methods, and procedures needed to design and produce the product. It is the responsibility of these people to design the product at or below its target cost.

What happens if the engineers determine that the product cannot be produced at or below its target cost? First, its design should be re-evaluated and attempts made to improve the production approach. But if it still cannot come close to its target cost, the company should understand that its current productive equipment and facilities prevent it from competing in that particular marketplace. Either the company should invest in new equipment and procedures or abandon its plans for producing the product.

In a highly competitive market, product quality and price determine the winners in the quest to lure customers. Customers will purchase the product that has the highest quality at the lowest price. These two customer-decision determinants—quality and price—go together; one is not sacrificed for the other. Target costing is a very useful pricing tool in such an environment because it allows the company to critically analyze the potential for success of a product before committing resources to its production. If the company first produces a product and then finds out its cost-based price is not competitive, the company will lose money because of the resources already used to produce the product. In most cases, the target costing approach can identify the potential success or failure of a product.

Target costing should not be confused with the cost-based methods used for pricing decisions. In cost-based situations, if the product does not produce a desired profit, production procedures are analyzed to find areas in which costs can be cut and controlled. This approach is based on guesswork until the product hits the marketplace. A target cost is not an anticipated cost to be achieved by some midway point in a product's life cycle. The product is expected to produce a profit as soon as it is marketed. Improvements can still be made in a product's design and production methods that will reduce its cost below its target cost, but profitability is built into the selling price from the beginning.

Even though the management accountant is not directly involved in the process of designing a product to meet its target cost, the accountant does supply cost information to the designers during a product's development stages. In addition, the accountant is responsible for tracking the costing experience of a new product and advising the engineers of their success or failure to meet the target costs.

ILLUSTRATIVE PROBLEM:
TARGET COSTING

To illustrate pricing using target costing, consider the approach to new product decisions that is used by Beck Products Company. A salesperson has indicated that a customer is seeking price quotations on two electronic components: a special-purpose battery charger (Product AA4) and a small transistorized machine computer (Product CC6). Competition for these parts comes from one German company and two firms in Sweden. Current market price ranges are as follows:

Product AA4	$320–$380 per unit
Product CC6	$750–$850 per unit

The salesperson feels that if Beck could quote prices of $300 for Product AA4 and $725 for Product CC6, the company would get this order and probably gain a significant share of the global market for these goods. Beck's normal profit markup is 25 percent of total unit cost. The company's design engineers and accountants put together the following specifications and costs for the new products:

Overhead cost rates

Materials handling activity	$1.30	per dollar of raw materials and purchased parts cost
Production activity	$3.50	per machine hour
Product delivery activity	$24.00	per unit of AA4
	$30.00	per unit of CC6

	Product AA4	Product CC6
Anticipated unit demand	26,000	18,000
per unit data		
Raw materials cost	$25.00	$65.00
Purchased parts cost	$15.00	$45.00
Manufacturing labor		
Hours	2.6	4.8
Hourly labor rate	$12.00	$15.00
Assembly labor		
Hours	3.4	8.2
Hourly labor rate	$14.00	$16.00
Machine hours	12.8	28.4

REQUIRED

1. Compute the target cost for each product.
2. Compute the anticipated total unit cost of production and delivery.
3. Using the target costing approach, should the company produce the products?

SOLUTION

1. Target cost for each product:

$$\text{Product AA4} = \$300.00 \div 1.25 = \$240.00$$

$$\text{Product CC6} = \$725.00 \div 1.25 = \$580.00$$

2. Anticipated total unit cost of production and delivery:

	Product AA4	Product CC6
Raw materials cost	$ 25.00	$ 65.00
Purchased parts cost	15.00	45.00
Total cost of raw materials and parts	$ 40.00	$110.00
Manufacturing labor		
AA4 (2.6 hours × $12.00)	31.20	
CC6 (4.8 hours × $15.00)		72.00
Assembly labor		
AA4 (3.4 hours × $14.00)	47.60	
CC6 (8.2 hours × $16.00)		131.20
Overhead costs		
Materials handling activity		
AA4 ($40.00 × $1.30)	52.00	
CC6 ($110.00 × $1.30)		143.00
Production activity		
AA4 (12.8 machine hours × $3.50)	44.80	
CC6 (28.4 machine hours × $3.50)		99.40
Product delivery activity		
AA4	24.00	
CC6		30.00
Total anticipated unit cost	$239.60	$585.60

3. Production decision:

	Product AA4	Product CC6
Target unit cost	$240.00	$580.00
Less anticipated unit cost	239.60	585.60
Difference	$ 0.40	$ (5.60)

Product AA4 can be produced below its target cost, so it should be produced. As currently designed, Product CC6 cannot be produced at or below its target cost; it either needs to be redesigned or the company should discontinue plans to produce it.

TRANSFER PRICING

OBJECTIVE

6 *Define and discuss transfer pricing*

A decentralized organization is an organization having several operating segments; operating control of each segment's activities is the responsibility of the segment's manager. Cost/expense centers and profit centers are important to a decentralized organization because they help alleviate some of the difficulty of controlling diverse operations. Responsibility for a company's functions is placed with its managers, and their performance is measured by comparing actual results with budgeted or projected results.

Profit measurement and return on investment are important gauges of performance in decentralized divisions. But in cost/expense centers where only costs are involved, profitability and performance are difficult to measure. The problem becomes more complicated when divisions within a company exchange goods or services and assume the role of customer or supplier to another division. As a result, transfer prices are used. A transfer price is the price at which goods and services are charged and exchanged between a company's divisions. Such prices allow intracompany transactions to be measured and accounted for. These prices also affect the revenues and costs of the divisions involved. Furthermore, since a transfer price contains an estimated amount of profit, a cost/expense center manager's ability to meet a targeted profit can be measured. Although often called artificial or created prices, company transfer prices as well as related policies are closely connected with performance evaluation.

DECISION POINT

American Transtech, Inc.[3]

American Transtech, Inc., of Jacksonville, Florida, was created in the early 1980s during the divestiture of the Bell System. Formerly AT&T's Stocks and Bonds Division, the new company's primary objectives were to issue stock certificates for the seven Regional Holding Companies (RHCs) and to service the RHC shareholders. When the new company was formed, its responsibility centers were transformed from cost centers to profit centers, since management felt that by stressing profit, the company's resources would be better managed. Because the company is a service organization and each internal segment provides service to the others, pricing of service transfers within the company is a significant part of American Transtech's management control system. Therefore the company required an accounting system that would (1) track usage of all internal services so that the costs of services provided to clients could be computed and (2) create incentives for internal segments to control their usage of intracompany services.

The cost of computer operations accounts for about one-third of the company's total cost and is one of many operating units within the company. These units are called Lines of Service (LOSs) and are evaluated as profit centers. In the case of Computer Operations, twenty-five computer service-related cost pools or activities have been identified and are used in charging other internal LOSs for services provided. Examples of these

---

3. Robert J. Fox and Thomas L. Barton, "A System Is Born: Management Control at American Transtech," *Management Accounting*, Institute of Management Accountants, September 1986, pp. 37–47; and Thomas L. Barton and Robert J. Fox, "Evolution at American Transtech," *Management Accounting*, Institute of Management Accountants, April 1988, pp. 49–52.

activities include CPU minutes, tapes mounted, disk storage space (in megabytes), and lines printed.

The Dividend Payment LOS is responsible for the issuance of dividend checks for all of AT&T's Regional Holding Companies and uses a significant amount of Computer Operations' services. From the examples of activities discussed above, how would the Dividend Payment LOS be charged for its computer service usage? How does the system of internal transfer prices safeguard the use of the company's resources?

Since the company established usage rates for each of the Computer Operations' twenty-five activities, the Dividend Payment LOS is billed at the standard rates for each service used. Because each LOS is evaluated as a profit center, managers want to minimize the charges received from Computer Operations without reducing the quality of services. Since each is a profit center too, minimizing costs helps maximize profits. Monitoring the level of internal service usage accomplishes this objective and also helps conserve the company's resources. $\vdots\,\vdots\,\vdots\,\vdots\,\vdots$

TRANSFER PRICING CHARACTERISTICS

Transfer pricing is somewhat controversial. Some people believe in the benefits of using transfer prices. Others believe they should never be used because they are not real prices. To illustrate how transfer prices are used and to help explain their difficult operational and behavioral aspects, we will analyze two situations requiring such prices. Figure 3 shows how products flow at the Barker Pulp Company. This company is composed of three divisions: the Pulp Division, the Cardboard Division, and the Box Division. Example I shows the Pulp Division transferring wood pulp to the Cardboard Division for use in making cardboard. The Cardboard Division also has the option of purchasing the pulp from an outside supplier. The cost of making the pulp, including materials, labor, variable overhead, and fixed overhead, is $12.90 per pound. By adding a 10 percent factor to cover miscellaneous divisional overhead expenses as well as a small profit, the proposed transfer price is $14.19 per pound. The outside supplier will sell the pulp to the company for $14.10 per pound. What should the manager of the Cardboard Division do?

Clearly, pressure is on the manager of the Pulp Division to lower the transfer price to an amount equal to or less than $14.10, the market price. If this action is taken, however, the $.09 per pound reduction will directly affect profits of the Pulp Division. In turn, that situation will affect the manager's performance. On the other hand, if the manager of the Cardboard Division agrees or is forced to pay the $14.19 price to benefit overall company operating results, that person's profit and performance will be negatively affected. Thus, the question arises: is either amount a fair price? Such a problem would not occur if costs were simply accumulated as the product travels through the production process. The Pulp Division could be treated as a cost/expense center and the manager's performance evaluated on the basis of only budgeted and actual costs. But then the Pulp Division's return on investment could not be measured. These are the conflicting objectives of performance evaluation in a decentralized organization.

A second common situation is shown in Example II of Figure 3. Instead of an outside supplier's influencing an internal transfer price, the Cardboard

Figure 3. Intracompany Transfer Pricing Examples: Barker Pulp Company

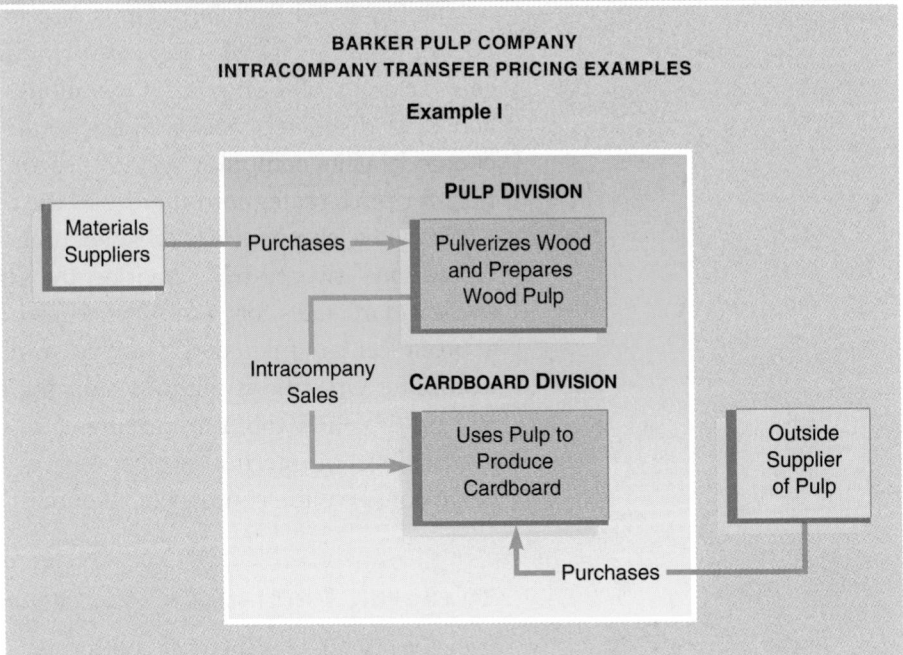

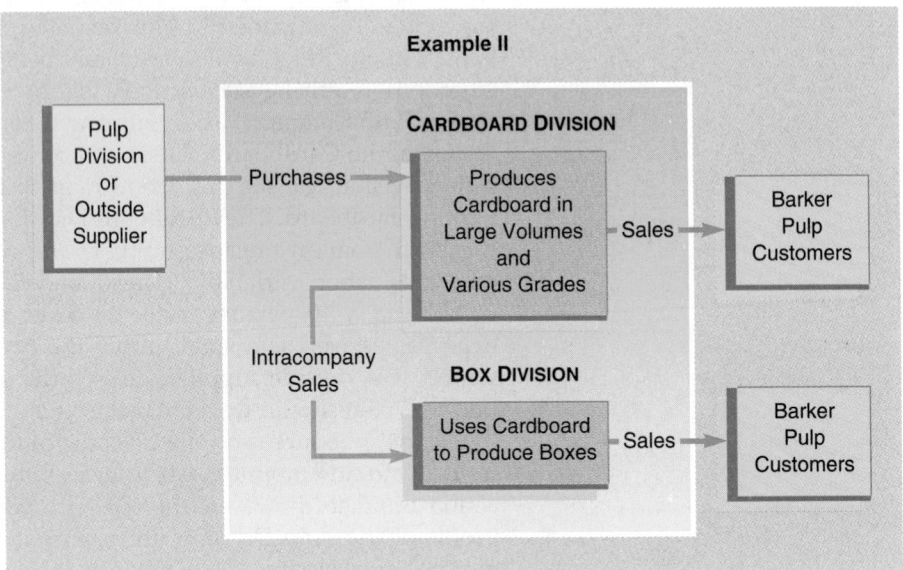

Division has an outside customer. The manager of the Cardboard Division must decide whether to sell cardboard to the outside customer for $28.10 per pound or supply the Box Division at $27.90 per pound. (The $27.90 covers all costs plus a profit margin.)

Several possible problems must be considered here. Is the outside customer going to make boxes that compete with those of the company's Box Division? Should the Box Division pay a market value transfer price so the Cardboard Division's manager can be evaluated properly? What about the Box Division? Should that manager suffer because all profits were siphoned off by managers of the Pulp and Cardboard divisions?

These are but a few of the problems involved in using transfer prices. So, perhaps you can now better understand why there are both proponents and opponents of this concept. From the example, it is easy to understand why transfer prices often cause internal bickering between managers. But measuring a manager's performance is still a major objective of decentralized companies. And the use of transfer prices is one approach to that objective.

OBJECTIVE

7 *Distinguish between a cost-based transfer price and a market-based transfer price*

TRANSFER PRICING METHODS

There are two primary approaches to developing a transfer price.

1. The price may be based on the cost of the item until its transfer to the next department or process.
2. A market value may be used if the item has an existing external market when transferred.

Both of these pricing situations were present in the Barker Pulp Company example. There, the Pulp Division would be inclined to use the cost method, since no apparent outside market exists for the pulp product. The only user of pulp is the Cardboard Division. However, the Box Division will probably have to pay a market-related price for the cardboard, since the Cardboard Division can either sell its product outside or transfer it to the Box Division.

In a situation in which no external markets are involved, division managers in a decentralized company may agree on a *cost-plus transfer price* or a *negotiated transfer price*. A cost-plus transfer price is the sum of costs incurred by the producing division plus an agreed-on profit percentage. The weakness of the cost-plus pricing method is that cost recovery is guaranteed to the selling division. And guaranteed cost recovery fails to detect inefficient operating conditions as well as excessive cost incurrence.

A negotiated transfer price, on the other hand, is bargained for by the managers of the buying and selling divisions. From the cost-plus side, a transfer price may be based on an agreement to use a standard cost plus a profit percentage. This approach emphasizes cost control through the use of standard costs while still allowing the selling division to return a profit even though it is a cost center. A negotiated transfer price may also be based on a market price that was reduced in the bargaining process.

Market transfer prices are based on the prices that could be charged if a segment could buy from or sell to an external party. They are discussed but seldom used without being subjected to negotiations between managers. Using market prices may cause the selling division to ignore negotiation attempts from the buying division manager and sell directly to outside customers. If this causes an internal shortage of materials and forces the buying division to purchase materials from the outside, overall company profits may be lowered even when the selling division makes a profit. Such use of market prices works against a company's overall operating objectives. Therefore, when market prices are used to develop transfer prices, they are normally used only as a basis for negotiation.

OBJECTIVE

8 *Develop a transfer price*

DEVELOPING A TRANSFER PRICE

Many of the normal pricing considerations introduced earlier in this chapter are also present in the development of a transfer price. The first step is to compute the unit cost of the item being transferred. Next, management must determine the appropriate profit markup. If the semifinished product (1) has an existing external market for the selling division to consider or (2) can be purchased in similar condition by the buying division from an outside source, then the market price must be included in the analysis used to develop a transfer price. The final step is to have the managers negotiate a compromise between the two prices.

Now, look again at the Barker Pulp Company example. The division manager's computations supporting the $14.19 cost-plus transfer price are shown in Exhibit 1. This one-year budget is based on the expectation that the Cardboard Division will require 480,000 pounds of pulp. Unit costs are stated in the right column. Notice that allocated corporate overhead is not included in the computation of the transfer price. Only costs related to the Pulp Division are included. The profit markup percentage of 10 percent adds $1.29 to the final transfer price of $14.19.

At this point, management could dictate that the $14.19 price be used. On the other hand, the manager of the Cardboard Division could bring the outside purchase price of $14.10 per pound to the attention of management. Usually, such situations end up being negotiated to determine the final transfer price. Each side has a position and strong arguments to support a price. And each manager's performance will be compromised by adopting the other's price.

In this example, both managers brought their concerns to the attention of top management. A unique settlement was reached. Since internal profits must be erased before financial statements are prepared, management allowed the Pulp Division to use the $14.19 price and the Cardboard Division the $14.10 price for purposes of performance evaluation. Obviously, the company did not want the Cardboard Division buying pulp from another company. At the same time, the Pulp Division had the right to a 10 percent profit.

Exhibit 1. Transfer Price Computation

Barker Pulp Company
Pulp Division—Transfer Price Computation

Cost Category	Budgeted Costs	Cost per Unit
Materials		
Wood	$1,584,000	$ 3.30
Scrap wood	336,000	0.70
Labor		
Shaving/cleaning	768,000	1.60
Pulverizing	1,152,000	2.40
Blending	912,000	1.90
Overhead		
Variable	936,000	1.95
Fixed	504,000	1.05
Subtotals	$6,192,000	$12.90
Costs allocated from corporate office	144,000	
Target profit, 10% of division's costs	619,200	1.29
Total costs and profit	$6,955,200	
Cost-plus transfer price		$14.19

Such approaches are often used to maintain harmony within a corporation. In this case, it allowed top management to measure the managers' performance while avoiding behavioral issues. After the period was over, all fictitious profits were canceled by using adjusting entries before preparing end-of-year financial statements. The final product, in this case the boxes, had a profit factor that took into account all operations of the business.

MEASURING PERFORMANCE BY USING TRANSFER PRICES

OBJECTIVE

9 *Measure a manager's performance by using transfer prices*

When transfer prices are used, the performance reports on the managers of cost/expense centers will contain the revenue and income figures used in the evaluation. The Pulp Division performance report in Exhibit 2 is a good example.

The Pulp Division supplied 500 more pounds of pulp than anticipated for the month. Sales were priced at $14.19 per pound. The variable costs per unit shown earlier were used to extend budgeted and actual amounts for materials, labor, and variable overhead. The result was that the manager of the Pulp Division earned a March profit of $43,350, which was $1,170 over budget. The

Exhibit 2. Performance Report Using Transfer Prices

Barker Pulp Company
Pulp Division—Performance Report
For March 19x0

	Budget (42,000 pounds)	Actual (42,500 pounds)	Difference Over/(Under) Budget
Costs Controllable by Supervisor			
Sales to Cardboard Division	$595,980	$603,075	$7,095
Cost of goods sold			
Materials			
Wood	$138,600	$140,250	$1,650
Scrap wood	29,400	29,750	350
Labor			
Shaving/cleaning	67,200	68,000	800
Pulverizing	100,800	102,000	1,200
Blending	79,800	80,750	950
Overhead			
Variable	81,900	82,875	975
Fixed	44,100	44,100	—
Total cost of goods sold	$541,800	$547,725	$5,925
Gross margin from sales	$ 54,180	$ 55,350	$1,170
Costs Uncontrollable by Supervisor			
Cost allocated from corporate office	12,000	12,000	—
Division's income	$ 42,180	$ 43,350	$1,170

transfer price made it possible for the division to be evaluated as if it were a profit center, even though the division does not sell to outside customers. Were the Pulp Division still accounted for as a cost/expense center, the manager would have to explain costs being $5,925 over budget instead of divisional income being over target.

(**Note:** Management may want the budget column restated at 42,500 pounds for evaluation purposes.)

FINAL NOTE ON TRANSFER PRICES

Problems in transfer price policy arise when buying divisions elect to purchase from outside suppliers. A selling division with adequate capacity to fulfill the buying division's demands should sell to that division at any price that recovers incremental costs. The incremental costs of intracompany sales include all variable costs of production and distribution plus any fixed costs directly traceable to intracompany sales. If a buying division can acquire products from outside suppliers at an annual cost that is less than the supplying division's incremental costs, then purchases should be made from the outside supplier because overall company profits will be enhanced. A thorough analysis of the supplying division's operations should also be conducted.

CHAPTER REVIEW

REVIEW OF LEARNING OBJECTIVES

1. **State the objectives managers use, and the rules they follow, to establish prices of goods and services.** The long-run objectives of a company should include statements on pricing policy. Possible pricing policy objectives include: (a) identifying and adhering to both short-run and long-run pricing strategies, (b) maximizing profits, (c) maintaining or gaining market share, (d) setting socially responsible prices, (e) maintaining a minimum rate of return on investment targets, and (f) being customer driven. For a company to stay in business, a product's or service's selling price must adhere to the following selling rules: (a) be equal to or lower than the competition's price, (b) be acceptable to the customer, (c) recover all costs incurred in bringing the product or service to a marketable condition, and (d) return a profit. If a manager deviates from these four selling rules, there must be a specific short-run objective that accounts for the change. Breaking these pricing rules for a long period will force a company into bankruptcy.

2. **Describe traditional economic pricing concepts.** The traditional approach to pricing is based on microeconomic theory. Microeconomic theory states that profits will be maximized at the point at which the difference between total revenue and total cost is greatest. Total revenue then tapers off, since as a product is marketed, price reductions are necessary to sell more units. Total cost increases when large quantities are produced because fixed costs change. To locate the point of maximum profit, marginal revenue and marginal cost must be computed and plotted. Profit is maximized at the point at which the marginal revenue and marginal cost curves intersect.

3. **Identify the external and internal factors on which prices are based.** Many factors influence the process of determining a selling price. Factors external to a company include: (a) total demand for the product or service, (b) number of competing products or services, (c) competitor's quality and price, (d) customer preference, (e) seasonal demand, and (f) life of the product. Internal factors are: (a) costs of producing the product or service, (b) purpose and quality of the product, (c) type

of process used–labor intensive versus automated, (d) markup percentage procedure, and (e) amount of scarce resources used.

4. **Create prices by applying the methods and tools of price determination.** Several cost-based pricing methods can be adopted by the pricing manager. However, experience in pricing a product often leads to adjustments in the formula used. Pricing methods include: (a) gross margin pricing, (b) profit margin pricing, and (c) return on assets pricing. A pricing method often used by service businesses is time and materials pricing.

5. **Analyze pricing decisions using target costing.** Target costing is an approach to pricing developed by the Japanese to compete successfully in the global marketplace. Instead of being cost-based and letting total costs dictate a product's price, target costing is price-based. First, the maximum competitive price is determined. Then the company's normal profit margin is subtracted to yield the maximum allowable production and distribution costs the company can incur and still remain competitive and earn a normal profit on the product.

6. **Define and discuss transfer pricing.** A transfer price is the price at which goods and services are charged and exchanged between a company's divisions. Since a transfer price contains an amount of estimated profit, a manager's ability to meet a profit target can be measured, even for a typical cost/expense center. Although often called artificial or created prices, company transfer prices and related policies are closely connected with performance evaluation.

7. **Distinguish between a cost-based transfer price and a market-based transfer price.** There are two primary approaches to developing transfer prices: (a) the price may be based on the cost of the item up to the point at which it is transferred to the next department or process or (b) a market value may be used if an item has an existing external market. A cost-plus transfer price is the sum of costs incurred by the producing division plus an agreed-on profit percentage. A market-based transfer price is geared to external market prices. In most cases, a negotiated transfer price is used; that is, one that was bargained for between the managers of the selling and buying divisions.

8. **Develop a transfer price.** Many of the normal pricing considerations are also present in the development of a transfer price. The first step is to compute the unit cost of the item being transferred. Next, management must determine the appropriate profit markup. Then, those involved in the intracompany transfer must discuss any relevant market prices before negotiating a final transfer price.

9. **Measure a manager's performance by using transfer prices.** When transfer prices are used, the performance reports for the managers of the cost centers must contain revenue, cost, and income figures used in the evaluation process. Actual performance reports for cost centers will look just like those used for profit centers. Evaluation procedures will also be similar in that the manager of the cost/expense center will have to explain any differences between budgeted and actual revenues, costs, and income.

REVIEW OF CONCEPTS AND TERMINOLOGY

The following concepts and terms were introduced in this chapter.

L O 7 **Cost-plus transfer price:** A transfer price computed as the sum of costs incurred by the producing division plus an agreed-on percentage markup for profit.

L O 6 **Decentralized organization:** An organization having several operating segments; operating control of each segment's activities is the responsibility of the segment's manager.

L O 4 **Gross margin pricing:** An approach to cost-based pricing in which the price is computed using the percentage of a product's total production costs.

L O 2 **Marginal cost:** The change in total cost caused by a one-unit change in output.

L O 2 **Marginal revenue:** The change in total revenue caused by a one-unit change in output.

L O 7 **Market transfer price:** A transfer price based on the prices that could be charged if a segment could buy from or sell to an external party.

L O 7 **Negotiated transfer price:** A transfer price that is arrived at through bargaining between the managers of the buying and selling divisions or segments.

L O 4 **Profit margin pricing:** An approach to cost-based pricing in which the price is computed using the percentage of a product's total costs and expenses.

L O 4 **Return on assets pricing:** A pricing method in which the objective of price determination is to earn a profit equal to a specific rate of return on assets employed in the operation.

L O 5 **Target costing:** A pricing method that (1) identifies the price at which a product will be competitive in the marketplace, (2) defines the minimum desired profit to be made on the product, and (3) computes a target cost for the product by subtracting the desired profit from the competitive market price.

L O 4 **Time and materials pricing:** An approach to pricing used by service businesses in which the total billing is composed of actual materials cost and actual labor cost plus a percentage markup of each to cover overhead costs and a profit factor.

L O 6 **Transfer price:** The price at which goods and services are charged and exchanged between a company's divisions or segments.

REVIEW PROBLEM
COST-BASED PRICING

L O 3, 4 The Valley Toy Company makes a complete line of toy vehicles, including three types of trucks: a pickup, a dumpster, and a flatbed. These toy trucks are produced in assembly line fashion beginning with the Stamping Department and continuing through the Welding, Painting, and Detailing departments. Projected costs of each toy truck and allocation percentages for fixed and common costs are as follows:

Cost Categories		Total Projected Costs	Toy Pickup Truck	Toy Dumpster Truck	Toy Flatbed Truck
Materials:	Metal	$137,000	$62,500	$29,000	$45,500
	Axles	5,250	2,500	1,000	1,750
	Wheels	9,250	3,750	2,000	3,500
	Paint	70,500	30,000	16,000	24,500
Labor:	Stamping	53,750	22,500	12,000	19,250
	Welding	94,000	42,500	20,000	31,500
	Painting	107,500	45,000	24,000	38,500
	Detailing	44,250	17,500	11,000	15,750
Indirect labor		173,000	77,500	36,000	59,500
Operating supplies		30,000	12,500	7,000	10,500
Variable production costs		90,500	40,000	19,000	31,500
Fixed production costs		120,000	45%	25%	30%
Distribution costs		105,000	40%	20%	40%
Variable marketing costs		123,000	$55,000	$26,000	$42,000
Fixed marketing costs		85,400	40%	25%	35%
General and administrative costs		47,600	40%	25%	35%

Valley Toy's policy is to earn a minimum of 30 percent over total cost on each type of toy produced. Expected sales for 19x9 are: pickup, 50,000 units; dumpster, 20,000 units; and flatbed, 35,000 units. Assume no change in inventory levels, and round all answers to two decimal places.

REQUIRED

1. Compute the selling price for each toy truck using the gross margin pricing method.
2. Check your answers in **1** by computing the selling prices using the profit margin pricing method.
3. If the competition's selling price for a similar pickup truck is around $14.00, would this influence Valley Toy's pricing decision? Give reasons defending your answer.

ANSWER TO REVIEW PROBLEM

Before the various selling prices are computed, the cost analysis must be completed and restructured to supply the information needed for the pricing computations.

Cost Categories		Total Projected Costs	Toy Pickup Truck	Toy Dumpster Truck	Toy Flatbed Truck
Materials:	Metal	$ 137,000	$ 62,500	$ 29,000	$ 45,500
	Axles	5,250	2,500	1,000	1,750
	Wheels	9,250	3,750	2,000	3,500
	Paint	70,500	30,000	16,000	24,500
Labor:	Stamping	53,750	22,500	12,000	19,250
	Welding	94,000	42,500	20,000	31,500
	Painting	107,500	45,000	24,000	38,500
	Detailing	44,250	17,500	11,000	15,750
Indirect labor		173,000	77,500	36,000	59,500
Operating supplies		30,000	12,500	7,000	10,500
Variable production costs		90,500	40,000	19,000	31,500
Fixed production costs		120,000	54,000	30,000	36,000
Total production costs		$ 935,000	$410,250	$207,000	$317,750
Distribution costs		$ 105,000	$ 42,000	$ 21,000	$ 42,000
Variable marketing costs		123,000	55,000	26,000	42,000
Fixed marketing costs		85,400	34,160	21,350	29,890
General and administrative costs		47,600	19,040	11,900	16,660
Total selling, general, and administrative costs		$ 361,000	$150,200	$ 80,250	$130,550
Total costs		$1,296,000	$560,450	$287,250	$448,300
Desired profit		$ 388,800	$168,135	$ 86,175	$134,490

1. Pricing using the gross margin approach.

   Markup percentage formula:

   $$\text{Markup percentage} = \frac{\text{desired profit} + \text{total selling, general, and administrative costs}}{\text{total production costs}}$$

   Gross margin pricing formula:

   Gross-margin-based price = total production costs per unit + (markup percentage × total production costs per unit)

Pickup truck:

$$\text{Markup percentage} = \frac{\$168,135 + \$150,200}{\$410,250} = 77.60\%$$

$$\text{Gross-margin-based price} = (\$410,250 \div 50,000) + [(\$410,250 \div 50,000) \times 77.6\%] = \$14.58$$

Dumpster truck:

$$\text{Markup percentage} = \frac{\$86,175 + \$80,250}{\$207,000} = 80.40\%$$

$$\text{Gross-margin-based price} = (\$207,000 \div 20,000) + [(\$207,000 \div 20,000) \times 80.4\%] = \$18.67$$

Flatbed truck:

$$\text{Markup percentage} = \frac{\$134,490 + \$130,550}{\$317,750} = 83.41\%$$

$$\text{Gross-margin-based price} = (\$317,750 \div 35,000) + [(\$317,750 \div 35,000) \times 83.41\%] = \$16.65$$

2. Pricing using the profit margin approach.

Markup percentage formula:

$$\text{Markup percentage} = \frac{\text{desired profit}}{\text{total costs and expenses}}$$

Profit margin pricing formula:

Profit-margin-based price = total costs and expenses per unit + (markup percentage × total costs and expenses per unit)

Pickup truck:

$$\text{Markup percentage} = \frac{\$168,135}{\$560,450} = 30.00\%$$

$$\text{Profit-margin-based price} = (\$560,450 \div 50,000) + [(\$560,450 \div 50,000) \times 30\%] = \$14.57$$

Dumpster truck:

$$\text{Markup percentage} = \frac{\$86,175}{\$287,250} = 30.00\%$$

$$\text{Profit-margin-based price} = (\$287,250 \div 20,000) + [(\$287,250 \div 20,000) \times 30\%] = \$18.67$$

Flatbed truck:

$$\text{Markup percentage} = \frac{\$134,490}{\$448,300} = 30.00\%$$

$$\text{Profit-margin-based price} = (\$448,300 \div 35,000) + [(\$448,300 \div 35,000) \times 30\%] = \$16.65$$

3. Competition's influence on price.

If the competition's toy pickup truck was similar in quality as well as design and looks, then Valley Toy's management would have to consider the $14.00 price range. At $14.58, they have a 30 percent profit factor built into their price. Break even is at $11.22 ($14.58 ÷ 1.3). Therefore, they have the ability to reduce the price below the competition and still make a significant profit.

CHAPTER ASSIGNMENTS

QUESTIONS

1. If a manager's pricing strategy is to price products so that total market share will increase, what considerations should go into selecting a price?
2. Identify six possible pricing policy objectives. Discuss each one briefly.
3. Do prices have a social effect? How or in what way?
4. Identify some considerations a decision maker must allow for when setting a price of a product or service.
5. Discuss the concept of making pricing decisions based on whatever the market will bear.
6. In the traditional economic pricing concept, what role does total revenue play in maximizing profit?
7. Why is profit maximized at the point where marginal revenue equals marginal cost?
8. List four external factors to consider when establishing an item's price.
9. Identify four internal factors one should use to gauge pricing decisions.
10. What is the gross margin pricing method? How is the markup percentage calculated under this method?
11. Differentiate the profit margin pricing method from the return on assets pricing method.
12. In the pricing of services, what is meant by time and materials pricing?
13. Describe the pricing approach based on target costing.
14. Why is the target costing approach to pricing considered more useful in a competitive marketplace than the cost-based pricing methods?
15. What is a transfer price?
16. Why are transfer prices associated with decentralized corporations?
17. Why is a transfer price often referred to as an artificial or created price?
18. Describe the cost-plus approach to setting transfer prices.
19. How are market prices used to develop a transfer price? Under what circumstances are market prices relevant to a transfer pricing decision?
20. "Most transfer prices are negotiated prices." Explain this statement.

SHORT EXERCISES

SE 1.
L O 1
Rules to Follow When Establishing Prices

No check figure

Ronny Owens is planning to open a pizza restaurant next month in Birmingham, Alabama. He plans to sell his large pizzas for a base price of $18 plus $2 for each topping selected. When asked how he arrived at the base price, he said that his cousin developed that price for his pizza restaurant in New York City. What pricing rules has Ronny not followed?

SE 2.
L O 2
Traditional Economic Pricing Concept

No check figure

You are to decide the total demand for a particular product. Assume that the product you are evaluating has the same total cost and total revenue curves as those pictured in Figure 1A in this chapter. Also assume that the difference between total revenue and total cost is the same at the 4,000 and 9,000 unit levels. If you had to choose between these two levels of activity as goals for total sales over the life of the product, which would you choose as a target? Why?

SE 3.
L O 3
External Factors That Influence Prices

No check figure

Your client is about to introduce a very high-quality product that will remove Spanish moss from trees in the southern United States. Marketing has established a price of $37 per gallon and the company controller has projected total production, selling, and distribution costs at $26 per gallon. What other factors should be considered before the product is introduced into the marketplace?

SE 4. *Cost-Based Price*
L O 4 *Setting*
Check Figure: Gross-margin-based price: $80

The Margate Company has collected the following data for one of its product lines: total production costs, $300,000; total selling, general, and administrative expenses, $112,600; desired profit, $67,400; and production costs per unit, $50. Using the gross margin pricing method, compute a suggested selling price for this product that would yield the desired profit.

SE 5. *Pricing a Service*
L O 4
Check Figure: Total billing price for this job: $1,302

Ben Alvarez runs a home repair business. Recently he gathered the following information on the repair of a client's pool deck: Replacement wood, $650; deck screws and supplies, $112; and labor, 12 hours at $14 per hour. Ben uses a 40 percent overhead rate that he applies to all direct costs of a job. Compute the total billing price for this job.

SE 6. *Pricing Using*
L O 5 *Target Costing*
No check figure

Hirioto Furniture is considering a new product line and must make a go-or-no-go decision before tomorrow's planning team meeting. The following data have been collected: unit selling price agreeable to potential customers, $1,600, and normal profit markup, 22 percent. The design engineer's preliminary estimates of the product's design, production, and distribution costs is $1,380 per unit. Using the target costing approach, determine whether there will be a go-or-no-go decision on the product.

SE 7. *Decision to Use*
L O 6 *Transfer Prices*
No check figure

Bucknell Castings uses a production process that includes eight work cells, each of which is currently treated as a cost center with a specific set of operations to perform on each casting produced. Following the fourth work cell's operations, the rough castings have an external market. The fourth work cell must also supply the fifth work cell with its raw materials. Management wants to develop a new approach to measuring work cell performance. Is Bucknell a candidate for using transfer prices? Explain your answer.

SE 8. *Cost-Based Versus*
L O 7 *Market-Based*
Transfer Prices
No check figure

Refer to the information in SE 7. Should Bucknell Castings use cost-based or market-based transfer prices?

SE 9. *Developing a*
L O 8 *Negotiated Transfer*
Price
No check figure

The Molding Work Cell at Montelena Plastic Products has been treated as a cost center since the company was founded in 1968. Recently, management decided to change the performance evaluation approach and treat its work cells as profit centers. Each cell is expected to earn a 20 percent profit on its total production costs. One of Montelena's products is a plastic base for a tool storage chest. Molding supplies this base to the Cabinet Work Cell and it also sells the base to another company. Molding's total production cost for the base is $27.40. It sells the base to the other company for $38.00. What should the transfer price for the plastic base be?

SE 10. *Measuring*
L O 9 *Performance Using*
Transfer Prices
No check figure

Refer to the information in SE 9. For the month of November, the Molding Work Cell produced 780 plastic bases at a total cost of $24,570. Of the total units produced, 680 were "sold" to the Cabinet Work Cell for $22,780. The remaining 100 bases were sold to the external company at the agreed price. Did the Molding Work Cell meet management's expectations for November?

EXERCISES

E 1. *Pricing Policy*
L O 1 *Objectives*
No check figure

Silken, Ltd. is an international clothing company specializing in retailing medium-priced goods. Retail outlets are located throughout the United States, France, Germany, and Great Britain. Management is interested in creating an image of giving the customer the most quality for the dollar. Selling prices are developed to draw customers away from competitors' stores. First-of-the-month sales are a regular practice of all stores, and customers are accustomed to this practice. Company buyers are carefully trained to seek out quality goods at inexpensive prices. Sales are targeted to increase a minimum of 5 percent per year. All sales should yield a 15 percent return on assets. Sales personnel are expected to wear Silken clothing while working, and all personnel can purchase clothing at 10 percent above cost. Cleanliness and an orderly appearance are required at all stores. Competitors' prices are checked daily.

Identify the pricing policy objectives of Silken, Ltd.

E 2. *Traditional Economic*
L O 2 *Pricing Theory*
Check Figure: 2. $34.09 per unit

Bullock & Foster are product designers. The firm has just completed a contract to develop a portable telephone. The telephone must be recharged only once a week and can be used up to one mile from the receiver. Initial fixed costs for this product are $4,000. The designers estimate the product will break even at the $5,000/100-unit mark. Total revenues will again equal total costs at the $25,000/900-unit point. Marginal cost is expected to equal marginal revenue when 550 units are sold.

1. Sketch total revenue and total cost curves for this product. Mark the vertical axis at each $5,000 increment and the horizontal axis at each 100-unit increment.
2. From your total revenue and total cost curves in 1, at what unit selling price will profits be maximized?

E 3. *External and*
L O 3 *Internal Pricing*
Factors
Check Figure: 1. Unit selling price, Roadster, One tire: $109

Lieberman's Tire Outlet features more than a dozen brands of tires in many sizes. Two of the brands are Gripper and Roadster, both imports. The tire size, 205/70–VR15, is available in both brands. The following information on the two brands was obtained:

	Gripper	Roadster
Selling price		
Single tire, installed	$145	$124
Set of four tires, installed	520	460
Cost per tire	90	60

As shown, selling prices include installation costs. Each Gripper tire costs $20 to mount and balance; each Roadster tire, $15 to mount and balance.

1. Compute each brand's unit selling price for both a single tire and a set of four.
2. Was cost the major consideration in supporting these prices?
3. What other factors could have influenced these prices?

E 4. *Price Determination*
L O 4
Check Figure: 2. Gross-margin-based price: $10.00

Anthony Industries has just patented a new product called "Shine-O," an automobile wax for lasting protection against the elements. Annual information developed by the company's controller for use in price determination meetings is as follows:

Variable production costs	$1,130,000
Fixed factory overhead	540,000
Selling expenses	213,000
General and administrative expenses	342,000
Desired profit	275,000

Annual demand for the product is expected to be 250,000 cans.

1. Compute the projected unit cost for one can of Shine-O.
2. Using the gross margin pricing method, compute the markup percentage and selling price for one can.
3. To check your answer to 2, compute the markup percentage and selling price of one can of Shine-O using the profit margin pricing method.

E 5. *Pricing a Service*
L O 4
Check Figure: 1. Total cost per head: $10.50

The state of Nevada has just passed a law making it mandatory to have every head of cattle inspected at least once a year for a variety of communicable diseases. Baca Enterprises is considering entering this inspection business. After extensive studies, Mr. Baca has developed the following annual projections.

Direct service labor	$625,000
Variable service overhead costs	150,000
Fixed service overhead costs	237,500
Selling expenses	142,500
General and administrative expenses	157,500
Minimum desired profit	125,000
Cost of assets employed	781,250

Mr. Baca believes his company would inspect 125,000 head of cattle per year. On average, Baca Enterprises now earns a 16 percent return on assets.

1. Compute the projected cost of inspecting each head of cattle.
2. Determine the price to charge for inspecting each head of cattle. Use the gross margin pricing method.
3. Using the return on assets method, compute the unit price to charge for this inspection service.

E 6. *Time and Materials*
L O 4 *Pricing*
Check Figure: Total price for job: $40,860

Floyd's Home Remodeling Service specializes in refurbishing older homes. Last week Floyd was asked to bid on a remodeling job for the town's mayor. His list of materials and labor needed to complete the job is as follows:

Materials		Labor	
Lumber	$6,380	Carpenter	$2,060
Nails/bolts	160	Floor specialist	1,300
Paint	1,420	Painter	2,000
Glass	2,890	Supervisor	1,920
Doors	730	Helpers	1,680
Hardware	610	Total	$8,960
Supplies	400		
Total	$12,590		

The company uses an overhead markup percentage for both materials (60 percent) and labor (40 percent). These markups cover all operating costs of the business. In addition, Floyd expects to make at least a 25 percent profit on all jobs. Compute the price that Floyd should quote for the mayor's job.

E 7. *Target Costing*
L O 5 *and Pricing*
Check Figure: Target cost: $64.58

Hoodfire Company has determined that its new fireplace heat shield would gain widespread customer acceptance if the company could price it at or under $77.50. Anticipated labor hours and costs for each unit of this new product are:

Direct materials cost	$11.00
Direct labor cost	
Manufacturing labor	
Hours	1.2
Hourly labor rate	$12.00
Assembly labor	
Hours	1.5
Hourly labor rate	$10.00
Machine hours	2

The company currently uses three factory and delivery overhead rates as follows:

Materials handling overhead	$1.70 per dollar of materials
Production overhead	$3.20 per machine hour
Product delivery overhead	$7.50 per unit

The company's minimum desired profit is 20 percent over total production and delivery cost. Compute the target cost for this product and determine if it should be marketed by the company.

E 8. *Transfer Price*
L O 6, 8 *Comparison*
Check Figure: 1. Cost-plus transfer price: $13.68

Jane Hearron is developing a transfer price for the housing section of an automatic pool-cleaning device. The housing for the device is made in Department AA. It is then passed on to Department DG, where final assembly occurs. Unit costs for the housing are as follows:

Cost Categories	Unit Costs
Materials	$4.20
Direct labor	3.30
Variable factory overhead	2.30
Fixed factory overhead	1.60
Profit markup, 20% of cost	?

An outside supplier can supply the housing for $13.60 per unit.

1. Develop a cost-plus transfer price for the housing.
2. What should the transfer price be? Support your answer.

E 9. *Develop a Cost-Plus*
L O 8 *Transfer Price*
Check Figure: 2. Cost-plus transfer price per unit: $62.21

Management at Bullseye Industries has just decided to use a set of transfer prices for intracompany transfers between departments. Management's objective is to include return on assets in the performance evaluation of managers at its cost centers. Data from the Molding Department for the past six months are as follows:

Account	Total Costs	Expected Increases/Decreases
Raw plastic	$637,300	+10%
Direct labor	507,600	− 5%
Variable factory overhead	92,300	+20%
Fixed factory overhead	125,900	—

During the six-month period, 26,250 plastic units were produced. The same number of units is expected to be completed during the next six-month period. The company uses a 15 percent profit markup percentage.

1. Compute estimated total costs for the Molding Department for the next six months.
2. Develop a cost-plus transfer price for the plastic unit. Round your answer to the nearest cent.

E 10. *Transfer Prices*
L O 9 *and Performance Evaluation*

Check Figure: Divisional income, Difference Under Budget: $1,497

The Kalore Fireplace Accessories Company uses transfer prices when evaluating division managers. Data from the Forging Department for April 19x9 are as follows:

	Budget	Actual
Direct materials	$309,960	$311,580
Direct labor	235,340	236,570
Variable factory overhead	74,620	75,010
Fixed factory overhead	34,440	34,440
Corporate selling expenses	17,410	18,700
Corporate administrative expenses	18,200	19,100

The division's transfer price is $13.11 per unit. It includes a 15 percent profit factor. During April the budget called for 57,400 units, and 57,700 units were actually produced and transferred. Prepare a performance report for the Forging Department.

SKILLS DEVELOPMENT EXERCISES

Conceptual Analysis

SDE 1. *Product*
L O 3 *Differentiation and Pricing*

No check figure

Maytag Corporation can price its products higher than any other company in the home appliance industry and still maintain and even increase market share. How can the company do this? Are its costs higher, resulting in higher prices than those of its competitors? No. Will customers shop around for products with lower price tags? No. Will competitors single Maytag products out in comparative ad campaigns and try to exploit the higher prices? No. Think about the Maytag repairman television commercials that you have seen over the past ten years. They feature a very lonely person who never gets a call to repair a Maytag product. The ads say nothing about price. They do not attack competitors' products. But the commercials do inspire customers to purchase Maytag products through what is known in the marketing area as product differentiation. Prepare a two-page paper explaining how Maytag Corporation differentiated its products from the competition. Is product cost a factor in Maytag's pricing strategy?

Ethical Dilemma

SDE 2. *Ethics in Pricing*
L O 3

No check figure

Dowling Company has been doing business with mainland China for the last three years. The company produces leather handbags that are in great demand in the cities of China. On a recent trip to Hong Kong, Yu-Ling Chen, purchasing agent for Liu Enterprises, approached Dowling salesperson Bill Weiser to arrange for a purchase of 2,500 handbags. Dowling's normal price is $75 per bag. Yu-Ling Chen wanted to purchase the handbags at $65 per bag. After an hour of haggling, the two people agreed to a final price of $68 per item. When Weiser returned to his hotel room after dinner, he found an envelope containing five new $100 bills and a note that said "Thank you for agreeing to our order of 2,500 handbags at $68 per bag. My company's president wants you to have the enclosed gift for your fine service." Weiser later learned that

Yu-Ling Chen was following her company's normal business practice. What should Bill Weiser do? Is the gift his to keep? Write a note to Yu-Ling, either accepting or returning the gift. Be prepared to justify the note's contents.

Research Activity

SDE 3. *Transfer Pricing*
L O 6

No check figure

One reason that companies use transfer prices is to allow cost/expense centers to function and be evaluated as profit centers. Transfer prices are fictitious prices charged to one department by another for internally manufactured parts and products that are used by the "purchasing" department. Transfer pricing policies and methods have generated much controversy in recent years. Using *The Accountant's Index*, the *Business Periodicals Index*, and the *Wall Street Journal Index*, locate an article about transfer prices. Prepare a one-page summary of the article and use it as a basis for a classroom presentation. Include in your summary the name and date of the publication, the article's title and author(s), a list of the issues being discussed, and a brief statement about the conclusions reached by the author(s).

Decision-Making Practice

SDE 4. *Pricing Decisions*
L O 4

Check Figure: 1b. Gross-margin-based price: $30

The *Forrest Company* manufactures office equipment for retail stores. Cara Reed, vice president of marketing, has proposed that Forrest introduce two new products: an electric stapler and an electric pencil sharpener.

Reed has requested that the Profit Planning Department develop preliminary selling prices for the two new products for her review. Profit Planning is to follow the company's standard policy for developing potential selling prices. It is to use all data available on each product. Data accumulated by Profit Planning on the two new products are reproduced as follows:

	Electric Stapler	Electric Pencil Sharpener
Estimated annual demand in units	12,000	10,000
Estimated unit manufacturing costs	$12.00	$18.00
Estimated unit selling and administrative expenses	$5.00	Not available
Assets employed in manufacturing	$180,000	Not available

Forrest plans to use an average of $2,400,000 in assets to support operations in the current year. The condensed pro forma operating income statement that follows represents Forrest's planned costs and return on assets for the entire company for all products.

Forrest Company
Pro Forma Operating Income Statement
For the Year Ended May 31, 19x9
($000 omitted)

Revenue	$4,800
Cost of goods sold, manufacturing costs	2,880
Gross profit	$1,920
Selling and administrative expenses	1,440
Operating profit	$ 480

1. Calculate a potential selling price for the:
   a. electric stapler, using return on assets pricing.
   b. electric pencil sharpener, using gross margin pricing.
2. Could a selling price for the electric pencil sharpener be calculated using return on assets pricing? Explain your answer.

3. Which of the two pricing methods—return on asset pricing or gross margin pricing—is more appropriate for decision analysis? Explain your answer.
4. Discuss the additional steps Cara Reed is likely to take after she receives the potential selling prices for the two new products (as calculated in **1**) to set an actual selling price for each of the two products.

(CMA adapted)

PROBLEM SET A

A 1. *Pricing Decision*

L O 3, 4

Check Figure: 1. Gross-margin-based price: $276.80

Aranda & Hart, Ltd. designs and assembles handguns for police departments across the country. Only four other companies compete in this specialty market. The most popular police handgun is the Aranda & Hart .357-caliber magnum, model 87, made of stainless steel. Aranda & Hart estimates there will be 23,500 requests for this model in 19x9.

Estimated costs related to this product for 19x9 are shown in the following table. The budget is based on the demand previously stated. The company wants to earn a $846,000 profit in 19x9.

Description	Budgeted Costs
Gun casing	$ 432,400
Ammunition chamber	545,200
Trigger mechanism	1,151,500
Direct labor	1,598,000
Variable indirect assembly costs	789,600
Fixed indirect assembly costs	338,400
Selling expenses	493,500
General operating expenses	183,300
Administrative expenses	126,900

Last week the four competitors released their wholesale prices for the next year.

Gunsmith A	$256.80
Gunsmith B	245.80
Gunsmith C	239.60
Gunsmith D	253.00

Aranda & Hart handguns are known for their high quality. They compete with handguns at the top of the price range. Despite the high quality, however, every $10 price increase above the top competitor's price causes a 5,500-unit drop in demand from what was originally estimated. (Assume all price changes are in $10 increments.)

REQUIRED

1. Compute the anticipated selling price. Use the gross margin pricing method.
2. Based on competitors' prices, what should the Aranda & Hart handgun sell for in 19x9 (assume a constant unit cost)? Defend your answer. (**Hint:** Determine the total profit at various sales levels.)
3. Would your pricing structure in **2** above change if the company had only limited competition at this quality level? If so, in what direction? Explain why.

A 2. *Time and Materials*

L O 4 *Pricing*

Check Figure: 2. Total billing: $14,812.71

Krutis-Storr Maintenance, Inc. repairs heavy construction equipment and vehicles. Recently, the Cantu Construction Company had one of its giant earthmovers overhauled and its tires replaced. Repair work for a vehicle of this size usually takes from one week to ten days. The vehicle must be lifted enough to gain access to the engine. Parts are normally so large that a crane must be used to put them into place.

Krutis-Storr uses the time and materials pricing method for billing. A markup percentage, based on data from the previous year, is applied to the cost of parts and materials to cover materials-related overhead. A similar approach is used for labor-related overhead costs. During the previous year the company incurred $535,590 in materials-related overhead costs and paid $486,900 for materials and parts. During that same time period, direct labor employees earned $347,200, and labor-related overhead of $416,640 was incurred. A factor of 20 percent is added to markup percentages to cover desired profit.

A summary of the materials and parts used and the labor needed to repair the giant earthmover is as follows:

Quantity		Unit Price		Hours		Hourly Rate
Materials and parts				Labor		
24	Spark plugs	$ 3.40		42	Mechanic	$18.20
20	Oil, quarts	2.90		54	Assistant Mechanic	12.00
12	Hoses	11.60				
1	Water pump	764.00				
30	Coolant, quarts	6.50				
18	Clamps	5.90				
1	Distributor cap	128.40				
1	Carburetor	214.10				
4	Tires	820.00				

REQUIRED

1. Compute a markup percentage for overhead and profit for (a) materials and parts and (b) labor.
2. Prepare a complete billing for this job. Include itemized amounts for each type of material, part, and labor. Follow the time and materials pricing approach and show the total price for the job.

A 3. *Cost-Based Pricing*
L O 3, 4
Check Figure: 2. Keri book, Profit-margin-based price: $20.56

Hennessey Publishing Company specializes in health awareness books. Because the field of health awareness is very competitive, Jay Dufty, the company's president, maintains a strict policy about selecting manuscripts to publish. Dufty wants to publish only books whose projected earnings are 20 percent above total projected costs. Three titles were accepted for publication during 19x8. The authors of these books are Tracy, Todd, and Keri. Projected costs for each book and allocation percentages for fixed and common costs are shown below.

Cost Categories	Total Projected Costs	Tracy Book	Todd Book	Keri Book
Labor	$487,500	$146,250	$243,750	$97,500
Royalty costs	120,000	36,000	60,000	24,000
Printing costs	248,600	74,580	124,300	49,720
Supplies	34,200	10,260	17,100	6,840
Variable production costs	142,000	42,600	71,000	28,400
Fixed production costs	168,000	35%	40%	25%
Distribution costs	194,000	30%	50%	20%
Marketing costs	194,000	$61,670	$90,060	$42,270
General and administrative costs	52,400	35%	40%	25%

Expected sales for 19x8 are as follows: Tracy, 26,000 copies; Todd, 32,000 copies; and Keri, 20,000 copies.

REQUIRED

1. Compute the selling price for each book. Use the gross margin pricing method.
2. Check your answers in **1** by computing selling prices under the profit margin pricing method.
3. If the competition's average selling price for a book on the same subject as Keri's is $22, should this influence Dufty's pricing decision? State your reasons.

(**Hint:** In **1** and **2**, treat royalty costs as production costs.)

Weber Machine Tool Company designs and produces a line of high-quality machine tools and markets them throughout the world. The company's main competition comes from companies in France, Great Britain, and Korea. Two highly specialized machine tools, Y14 and Z33, have recently been introduced by five competing firms. The prices charged for these products are in the following ranges: Y14, $625–$675 per tool, and Z33, $800–$840 per tool. The company is contemplating entering the market for these two products. Market research has indicated that if Weber can sell Y14 for $600 per tool and Z33 for $780 per tool, the company will be successful in marketing these products worldwide. The company's normal profit markup is 20 percent over all costs to produce and deliver a product. Current factory overhead rates are:

Materials handling activity	$1.20 per dollar of raw materials and purchased parts cost
Production activity	$4.20 per machine hour
Product delivery activity	$34.00 per unit of Y14
	$40.00 per unit of Z33

Design engineering and accounting estimates for the production of the two new products are as follows:

	Product Y14	Product Z33
Anticipated unit demand	74,000	90,000
Per unit data		
Raw materials cost	$56.00	$62.00
Purchased parts cost	$65.00	$70.00
Manufacturing labor		
Hours	6.4	7.2
Hourly labor rate	$10.00	$14.00
Assembly labor		
Hours	4.6	9.2
Hourly labor rate	$12.00	$15.00
Machine hours	15	18

REQUIRED

1. Compute the target cost for each product.
2. Compute the anticipated total unit cost of production and delivery.
3. Using the target costing approach, decide whether or not the products should be produced.

Seven years ago Darla Logan formed the Logan Corporation and began producing sound equipment for home use. Because of the highly technical and competitive nature of the industry, Logan established the Research and Development Division. That division is responsible for continually evaluating and updating critical electronic parts used in the corporation's products. The R & D staff has been very successful, contributing to the corporation's ranking as America's leader in the industry.

Two years ago, R & D took on the added responsibility of producing all microchip circuit boards for Logan's sound equipment. One of Logan's specialties is a sound dissemination board (SDB) used in videocassette recorders (VCRs). The SDB greatly enhances the sound quality of Logan's VCRs.

Demand for the SDB has increased significantly in the past year. As a result, R & D has increased its production and assembly labor force. Three outside customers want to purchase the SDB for their sound products. To date, R & D has been producing SDBs for internal use only.

The controller of the R & D Division wants to create a transfer price for the SDBs applicable to all intracompany transfers. The following data show cost projections for the next six months.

Materials	
Boards	$325,350
Chips	867,600
Wire posts	397,650
Wire	289,200
Electronic glue	433,800

Direct labor	
Board preparation	$ 759,150
Assembly	1,265,250
Testing	1,012,200
Supplies	90,375
Indirect labor	524,175
Other variable overhead costs	180,750
Fixed overhead, SDBs	397,650
Other fixed overhead, corporate	506,100
Variable selling expenses, SDBs	1,337,550
Fixed selling expenses, corporate	469,950
General corporate operating expenses	795,300
Corporate administrative expenses	614,550

A profit factor of at least 25 percent must be added to total unit cost for internal transfer purposes. Outside customers are willing to pay $36 for each SDB. Estimated demand over the next six months is 235,000 SDBs for internal use and 126,500 SDBs for external customers.

REQUIRED

1. Compute the cost of producing and distributing one SDB.
2. What transfer price should R & D use? Explain the factors that influenced your decision.

PROBLEM SET B

B 1. *Pricing Decision*

L O 3, 4

Check Figure: 1. Gross-margin-based price: $23.04

Rivera & Company is an assembly jobber specializing in home appliances. One division, Boyd Operations, focuses most of its efforts on assembling a standard bread toaster. Projected costs on this product for 19x8 are as follows:

Cost Description	Budgeted Costs
Toaster casings	$ 960,000
Electrical components	2,244,000
Direct labor	3,648,000
Variable indirect assembly costs	780,000
Fixed indirect assembly costs	1,740,000
Selling expenses	1,536,000
General operating expenses	840,000
Administrative expenses	816,000

Estimated annual demand for the toaster is 600,000 per year. The above budgeted amounts were geared to this demand. The company wants to make a $1,260,000 profit.

Competitors have just published their wholesale prices for the coming year. They range from $21.60 to $22.64 per toaster. The Rivera toaster is known for its high quality, and it competes with products at the top end of the price range. Even with its reputation, however, every $.20 increase above the top competitor's price causes a drop in demand of 60,000 units below the original estimate. Assume that all price changes are in $.20 increments.

REQUIRED

1. Compute the anticipated selling price. Use the gross margin pricing method.
2. Based on competitors' prices, what should the Rivera toaster sell for in 19x8 (assume a constant unit cost)? Defend your answer. (**Hint:** Determine the total profit at various sales levels.)
3. Would your pricing structure in **2** change if the company had only limited competition at their quality level? If so, in what direction? Explain why.

B 2. *Time and Materials*

L O 4 *Pricing*

Check Figure: 2. Total billing: $8,041.35

Machande Construction Company specializes in additions to custom homes. Last week a potential customer called for a quote on a two-room addition to the family home. After visiting the site and taking all relevant measurements, Dan Machande returned to the office to work on drawings for the addition. As part of the process of preparing a bid, a total breakdown of costs is required.

The company follows the time and materials pricing system and uses data from the previous six months to compute markup percentages for overhead. Separate rates are used for materials and supplies and for labor. During the past six months, $35,625 of materials and supplies-related overhead was incurred and $142,500 of materials and supplies were billed. Labor cost for the six-month period was $341,600. Labor-related overhead was $170,800. Add 20 percent to each markup percentage to cover desired profit. According to Mr. Machande's design, the following materials, supplies, and labor are needed to complete the job.

Quantity		Unit Price
Materials		
150	2" × 4" × 8' cedar	$ 1.30
50	2" × 6" × 8' cedar	2.20
14	2" × 8" × 8' cedar	4.50
25	4' × 8' sheets, ½" plywood	10.40
6	Framed windows	80.00
3	Framed doors	110.00
30	4' × 8' sheets, siding	14.00
	Supplies	65.00

Hours		Hourly Rate
Labor		
120	Laborers/helpers	$10.50
80	Semiskilled carpenters	12.00
60	Carpenters	14.50

REQUIRED

1. Compute a markup percentage for overhead and profit for (a) materials and supplies and (b) labor.
2. Prepare a complete billing for this job. Include itemized amounts for each type of materials, supplies, and labor. Follow the time and materials pricing approach and show total price for the job.

B 3. *Cost-Based Pricing*
L O 3, 4
Check Figure: 1. Mint Blend, Gross-margin-based price: $5.51

Bailey Coffee Company produces special types of blended coffee. Its products are used in exclusive restaurants throughout the world. Quality is the primary objective of the company. A team of consultants is employed to continuously assess the quality of the purchased coffee beans and of the blending procedures and ingredients used. The company's controller is in the process of determining prices for the coming year. Three blends are currently produced: Regular Blend, Mint Blend, and Choco Blend. Expected profit on each blend is 20 percent above costs. Expected production for 19x9 is: 360,000 pounds of Regular Blend, 150,000 pounds of Mint Blend, and 90,000 pounds of Choco Blend.

Total anticipated costs and percentages of total costs per blend for 19x9 follow.

Cost Categories	Percentage of Total Costs			Total Projected Costs
	Regular Blend	Mint Blend	Choco Blend	
Coffee beans	60%	25%	15%	$770,000
Chocolate	0%	10%	90%	45,000
Mint leaf	10%	80%	10%	32,000
Direct labor				
Cleaning	60%	25%	15%	148,000
Blending	40%	30%	30%	372,000
Roasting	60%	25%	15%	298,000
Indirect labor	60%	25%	15%	110,000
Supplies	30%	40%	30%	36,500
Other variable factory overhead	60%	25%	15%	280,000
Fixed factory overhead	60%	25%	15%	166,000
Selling expenses	40%	30%	30%	138,500
General and administrative expenses	34%	33%	33%	146,000

1. Compute the selling price for each blend, using the gross margin pricing method.
2. Check your answers in **1** by computing selling prices using the profit margin pricing method.
3. If the competition's selling price for the Choco Blend averaged $7.20 per pound, should this influence the controller's pricing decision? Explain.

B 4. *Pricing Using*
L O 5 *Target Costing*
Check Figure: 2. Anticipated total unit cost, Speed-Calc #4: $77.50

Tomshew Hi-Tech Corp. is considering marketing two new high-speed desk calculators and has named them Speed-Calc #4 and Speed-Calc #5. The two products will surpass current competition in both speed and quality and would be welcomed into the market, according to a recent market research study. Customers would be willing to pay $99 for Speed-Calc #4 and $109 for Speed-Calc #5, based on their projected design capabilities. Both products have numerous uses but the primary market interest comes from the payroll activity of all types of businesses. Current production capacity exists for the manufacture and assembly of these two products. The company has a minimum desired profit of 25 percent above all costs for all of its products. Current activity-based factory overhead rates are:

Materials/parts handling activity	$1.30 per dollar of raw materials and purchased parts cost
Production activity	$7.80 per machine hour
Marketing/delivery activity	$4.40 per unit of Speed-Calc #4
	$6.20 per unit of Speed-Calc #5

Design engineering and accounting estimates for the production of the two new products are as follows:

	Speed-Calc #4	Speed-Calc #5
Anticipated unit demand	94,000	65,000
Per unit data		
Raw materials cost	$5.40	$7.30
Computer chip cost	$10.60	$11.70
Production labor		
Hours	1.4	1.5
Hourly labor rate	$15.00	$14.00
Assembly labor		
Hours	0.6	0.5
Hourly labor rate	$12.50	$16.00
Machine hours	1	1.2

1. Compute the target costs for each product.
2. Compute the anticipated total unit cost of production and delivery.
3. Using the target costing approach, decide whether or not the products should be produced.

B 5. *Developing Transfer*
L O 6, 8 *Prices*

Check Figure: 1. Cost-plus transfer price: $19.20

Lemelin Company has two divisions, Stacy Division and Matt Division. For several years Stacy Division has manufactured a special glass container, which it sells to the Matt Division at the prevailing market price of $20. Stacy produces the glass containers only for Matt and does not sell the product to outside customers. Annual production and sales volume is 20,000 containers. A unit cost analysis for Stacy showed the following.

Cost Categories	Costs per Container
Direct materials	$ 3.40
Direct labor, ¼ hour	2.20
Variable factory overhead	7.60
Traceable fixed costs	
$30,000 ÷ 20,000	1.50
Corporate overhead, $18 per direct labor hour	4.50
Variable shipping costs	1.30
Unit cost	$20.50

Corporate overhead represents such allocated joint fixed costs of production as building depreciation, property taxes, fire insurance, and salaries of production executives. A normal profit allowance of 20 percent is used in determining transfer prices.

REQUIRED

1. What would be the appropriate transfer price for Stacy Division to use in billing its transactions with Matt Division?
2. If Stacy Division decided to sell some containers to outside customers, would your answer to 1 change? Defend your answer.

MANAGERIAL REPORTING AND ANALYSIS CASES

Interpreting Management Reports

MRA 1. *Transfer Pricing*
L O 7, 8

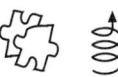

No check figure

Two major operating divisions, the Cabinet Division and the Electronics Division, make up **Bynum Industries, Inc.** The company's major products are deluxe console television sets. The TV cabinets are manufactured by the Cabinet Division, while the Electronics Division produces all electronic components and assembles the sets. The company uses a decentralized organizational structure.

The Cabinet Division not only supplies cabinets to the Electronics Division, but also sells cabinets to other TV manufacturers. Based on a normal sales order of 40 cabinets, the following unit cost breakdown for a deluxe television cabinet was developed.

Materials	$ 22.00
Direct labor	25.00
Variable factory overhead	14.00
Fixed factory overhead	16.00
Variable selling expenses	9.00
Fixed selling expenses	6.00
Fixed general and administrative expenses	8.00
Total unit cost	$100.00

The Cabinet Division's normal profit margin is 20 percent, and the regular selling price of a deluxe cabinet is $120. Divisional management recently decided that $120 will also be the transfer price used for all intracompany transactions.

Managers at the Electronics Division are unhappy with that decision. They claim the Cabinet Division will show superior performance at the expense of the Electronics Division. Competition recently forced the company to lower prices. Because of a newly established transfer price for the cabinet, Electronics' portion of the profit margin on deluxe television sets was lowered to 18 percent. To counteract the new intracompany transfer price, management at the Electronics Division announced that, effective immediately, all cabinets will be purchased from an outside supplier. They will be purchased in lots of 200 cabinets at a unit price of $110 per cabinet.

The corporate president, Marc Lilley, has called a meeting of both divisions in order to negotiate a fair intracompany transfer price. The following prices were listed as possible alternatives.

Current market price	$120 per cabinet
Current outside purchase price (This price is based on a large-quantity purchase discount. It will cause increased storage costs for the Electronics Division.)	$110 per cabinet
Total unit manufacturing costs plus a normal 20 percent profit margin: $77.00 + $15.40	$92.40 per cabinet
Total unit costs, excluding variable selling expenses, plus a normal 20 percent profit margin: $91.00 + $18.20	$109.20 per cabinet

REQUIRED

1. What price should be established for intracompany transactions? Defend your answer by showing the shortcomings of each alternative.
2. Were there an outside market for all units produced by the Cabinet Division at the $120 price, would you change your answer to 1? Why?

Formulating Management Reports

"That Noble Division is robbing us blind!" This statement by the director of the Platt Division was heard during the board of directors meeting at *June Company*. The company produces umbrellas in a two-step process. The Noble Division prepares the fabric tops and transfers them to the Platt Division. The Platt Division produces the ribs and handles, secures the tops, and packs all finished umbrellas for shipment.

Because of the director's concern, the company controller gathered data on the past year, as shown in the table below.

	Noble Division	Platt Division	Company Totals
Sales			
Regular	$700,000	$1,720,000	$2,420,000
Deluxe	900,000	3,300,000	4,200,000
Materials			
Fabric tops (from Noble Division)	—	1,600,000	1,600,000
Cloth	360,000	—	360,000
Aluminum	—	660,000	660,000
Closing mechanisms	—	1,560,000	1,560,000
Direct labor	480,000	540,000	1,020,000
Variable factory overhead	90,000	240,000	330,000
Fixed divisional overhead	150,000	210,000	360,000
Selling and general operating expenses	132,000	372,000	504,000
Company administrative expenses	84,000	108,000	192,000

During the year, 200,000 regular umbrellas and 150,000 deluxe umbrellas were completed and transferred or shipped by the two divisions. Transfer prices used by the Noble Division were:

Regular $3.50
Deluxe 6.00

The regular umbrella wholesales for $8.60; the deluxe model, for $22.00. Company administrative costs are allocated to divisions by a predetermined formula.

Management has indicated the transfer price should include a 20 percent profit factor on total division costs.

REQUIRED

1. Prepare a performance report on the Noble Division.
2. Prepare a performance report on the Platt Division.
3. Compute each division's rate of return on controllable and on total division costs.
4. Do you agree with the director's statement?
5. What procedures would you recommend to the board of directors?

International Company

HPI, Inc. is an international corporation manufacturing and selling home care products. Today, a meeting is being held at corporate headquarters in New York City. The purpose of the meeting is to discuss changing the price of laundry detergent manufactured and sold in Brazil. During the meeting, a conflict develops between Robert Hendricks, corporate sales manager, and Enrique Soledad, the Brazilian Division's sales manager.

Hendricks insists that the selling price of the laundry detergent should be increased to the equivalent of $3 U.S. This increase is necessary because the Brazilian Division's costs are higher than those of other international divisions. The Brazilian

Division is paying high interest rates on notes payable for the acquisition of the new manufacturing plant. In addition, a stronger, more expensive, ingredient has been introduced into the laundry detergent, which has caused the product cost to increase by $.20.

Soledad believes that the laundry detergent's selling price should remain at $2.50 for several reasons. Soledad argues that the market for laundry detergent in Brazil is highly competitive. Labor costs are low and the costs of distribution are small since the target market is the Rio de Janeiro metropolitan area. Inflation is significantly high in Brazil, and the Brazilian government continues to impose a policy to control inflation. Because of these controls, Soledad insists that the buyers will be resistant to any price hikes.

REQUIRED

1. What selling price do you believe HPI, Inc. should set for the laundry detergent? Explain your answer. Do you believe HPI, Inc. should let the division set the selling price for laundry detergent in the future? When should corporate headquarters set prices?
2. Based on the information given above, should cost-plus pricing or target costing be used to set the selling price for laundry detergent in Brazil? Explain your answer.

LEARNING OBJECTIVES

1. Explain how managers obtain and use decision support information.
2. Identify the steps in the management decision cycle.
3. Define and identify *relevant decision information.*
4. Calculate product costs using variable costing procedures.
5. Prepare an income statement using the contribution margin reporting format.
6. Develop decision data using incremental analysis.
7. Prepare decision alternative evaluations for (a) make-or-buy decisions, (b) special order decisions, (c) sales mix analyses, (d) decisions to eliminate unprofitable segments, and (e) sell or process-further decisions.

Solectron, Inc.[1]

Solectron, Inc. is a manufacturing company known as a contract producer. Contract producers, which are a viable and growing segment of companies in the United States, produce the goods of other companies. Many of these goods are brand names associated with world-class enterprises such as Apple Computers. Solectron's plant in Milpitas, California, produces and assembles the Apple PowerPC. The company specializes in producing and assembling the computer's key element—its circuit board. Besides making these "motherboards," the company also produces smaller boards for disk drives. Solectron then purchases monitors and keyboards from outside suppliers, assembles the computers, packs them in cardboard boxes bearing the Apple logo, and ships them to Apple's customers. And Apple is only one of more than eighty companies being served by Solectron. The company's thirty-two different production lines provide the flexibility to shift end products in response to market demands. Why have these contract producers become so successful? Why would a large company like Apple allow an outside company to take over the production, assembly, and shipment of its product?

Apple has discovered that it is more economical to have someone else produce its products than to manufacture its own computers. Contract producers like Solectron rely on their customers for engineering design, marketing, and sales activities. The contract producers concentrate on production, thus avoiding the overhead costs from the other areas of business activity. Apple, on the other hand, avoids all costs (and headaches) associated with production. It can concentrate its efforts on new product design and marketing. Both sides are able to focus their abilities on their areas of specialty. Typical manufacturing companies with large amounts of capital invested in plant and equipment are lucky if their sales are four or five times total asset value. Many companies that rely on contract producers experience sales that are fifty or sixty times total asset value. This extremely high utilization of assets usually translates into high profits. Deciding to use a contract producer is the ultimate make-or-buy decision but it still involves projecting the total costs on each side of the decision and selecting the most profitable alternative. ⦂⦂⦂⦂⦂

1. Shawn Tully, "You'll Never Guess Who Really Makes . . .," *Fortune*, October 3, 1994, pp. 124–128.

MANAGERS, DECISIONS, AND INFORMATION

Managers need information to fulfill their responsibilities. These information needs may be financial in nature or they may involve nonfinancial data such as number of hours worked, product or service throughput time, or units of product produced and sold. In addition to being used to value inventories on the balance sheet, product costs are used by managers to help set prices for existing products and to aid in decisions regarding the development of new product lines or the discontinuance of unprofitable ones. Making long-range plans and annual budget decisions are an integral part of the managers' role in an organization and result in the proactive involvement of their peers and subordinates, the setting of realistic targets for operating personnel, and the establishment of performance measuring points for the managers.

Managers face other types of decisions, both on a regular and a periodic basis. Examples of some of these decisions are as follows:

1. Should a product be sold as is or processed further, if two markets exist?
2. Should a company buy parts from an outside vendor or make them internally?
3. Which products or divisions are not profitable? When should they be discontinued?
4. Which products in a diverse product environment are the most profitable? Can their markets be expanded?
5. If alternatives exist in a decision to purchase a machine, which alternative should be selected?
6. Should a process be automated? If so, what alternatives does the company have for retraining the dislodged employees?

The Solectron, Inc. Decision Point is a good example of the use of a make-or-buy decision model. The next Decision Point in this chapter, which is about the Fireman's Fund Insurance Company, will focus on the third and fourth decision types above and relate them to a service business.

Each area of uncertainty requires information upon which to support the actual decision. Information sources are numerous. Managers should always be aware of their environment and identify, remember, and record relevant information whenever it surfaces. Managers get information from sources that are both internal and external to their organizations. Internal sources include regular company reports, observations of practices and processes, company meetings, specific information requests from other functions and departments, direct involvement in company activities, and results and actions related to past decisions. External sources include attending professional meetings and conferences, participating in training and professional development seminars, reading journals and business publications, and analyzing competing organizations to determine the reasons for their successes and failures.

Decisions usually involve the selection of the best of two or more alternatives. In many cases, one of those alternatives is to do nothing. Even doing nothing can alter financial measures. For example, sales will decrease if customers want new products and a manager elects not to purchase a machine designed to expand the product line. Before selecting an alternative, a manager will have his or her staff gather as much information on all alternatives as time permits. Some of this information will focus on details of the particular alternative, such as productivity estimates of various machines, while other information will spell out the financial consequences of each alternative. The manager must analyze the information supporting each alternative, use intuitive instincts to identify the most likely alternatives, project the results of each alternative, and then make the final decision. Mathematical formulas and computer programs are useful in projecting, organizing, and analyzing decision support information. But the final decision is a judgment made by the manager.

THE DECISION-MAKING PROCESS

The management accountant is part of an organization's decision-making team. As background to the discussion of the types of analyses an accountant prepares and the techniques used to identify potential investments, this section describes the steps in the management decision cycle and the kinds of information that are valuable in evaluating alternatives.

OBJECTIVE

2 *Identify the steps in the management decision cycle*

MANAGEMENT DECISION CYCLE

Although many decisions are unique and are not made according to strict rules, steps, or timetables, certain events occur frequently in the analysis of the kinds of problems facing managers. These events form a pattern called the management decision cycle (Figure 1).

The first step in the cycle is the discovery of a problem or a need. Then in step **2**, the accountant seeks out all reasonable courses of action that will solve the problem or meet the need. In step **3**, the accountant prepares a complete analysis of each action, identifying its total cost, cost savings, or financial

Figure 1. The Management Decision Cycle

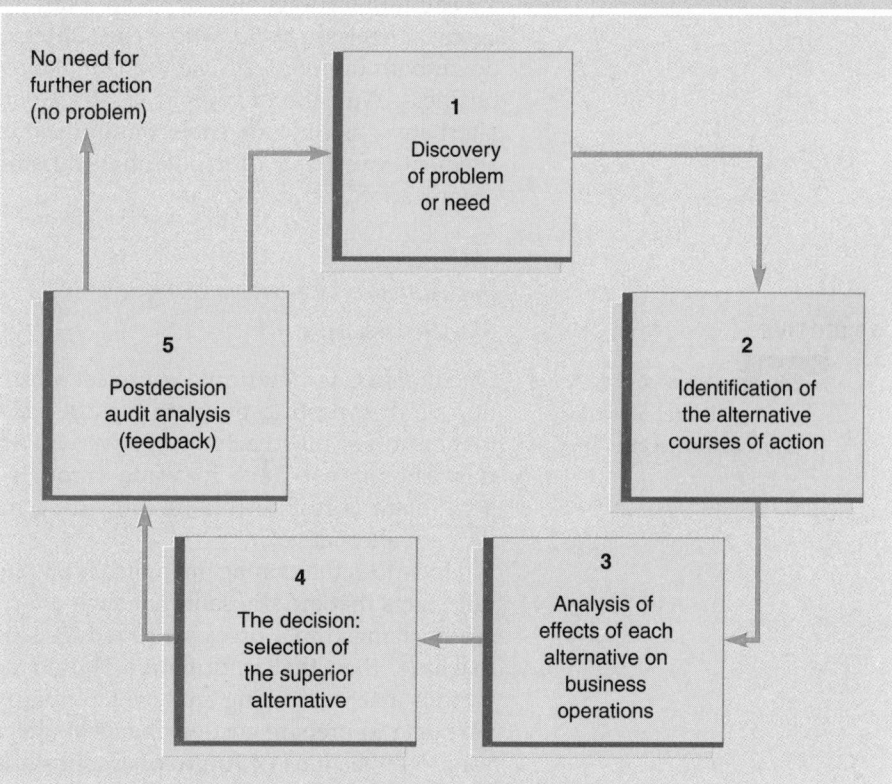

effects on business expectations. Each alternative may require different cost information. In step **4,** after studying the information the accountant has gathered and organized in a meaningful way, management selects the best course of action. In step **5,** after the decision has been carried out, the account- ant prepares a postdecision audit to give management feedback about the results of the decision. If the solution is not completely satisfactory or if prob- lems remain, the decision cycle begins again. If the solution solved the prob- lem, then this decision process is complete.

DECISIONS AND STRATEGIC PLANNING

Managers are responsible for short- and long-range planning and for develop- ing an overall strategy that determines the company's general course of action over several years. Strategic plans give direction to management's daily or monthly actions. The strategic plan specifies the company's objectives, its organizational structure, and its policies about growth and product or service lines. Identifying markets is part of the strategic plan, as are any other actions that affect the organization's structure. These strategic plans often determine the projects that managers are willing to consider.

To demonstrate how strategic planning influences the management deci- sion cycle, consider the actions of the managers at the DataRite Corporation. DataRite markets quality computer equipment—diskettes, tape drives, and hard disk drives. In its current strategic plan, DataRite's management decided to expand operations and profitability potential by moving into new product lines. One such business venture identified in the planning process was telecommunications. After developing this strategic plan, DataRite had the option of purchasing a company specializing in telecommunications devices or upgrading an existing product line using a special, potentially high-profit telecommunications memory chip. Both projects were studied using the man- agement decision cycle. Before the strategic plan, DataRite would have turned down both options because the company was not in the telecommunications business. With the change in its strategic plan, each option became a viable alternative, as did other telecommunications projects. Any project that man- agement investigates for potential investment should be consistent with the organization's strategic plan.

OBJECTIVE

3 *Define and iden- tify* relevant deci- sion information

RELEVANT INFORMATION FOR MANAGEMENT

Once managers determine a project worthy of consideration, what informa- tion do they need to evaluate the alternatives? Managers need enough infor- mation to see how each alternative will affect the company's operations, but they should not have to wade through reams of data. The management accountant is responsible for providing managers with relevant information for each alternative.

How does the management accountant decide what is relevant and what is not? Facts that are the same for each alternative are not relevant. If total sales are unchanged in a proposal to reduce labor costs by installing an automated machine, then that information should not appear in the evaluation of the various machines being analyzed. Similarly, although the accountant may use past data to prepare cost estimates of alternatives, historical data are not rele- vant to projections of future operations and do not guide managers in choosing between alternatives. The accountant should include only those cost projections or estimates that are relevant to the decision. Relevant decision information is comprised of future cost, revenue, and resource usage data that are different for each alternative. The analyses and reports accountants use to present decision data to management should include relevant information and omit past data or data that are common to each alternative under study.

BUSINESS BULLETIN: ETHICS IN PRACTICE

Roger B. Smith, the former chairman and CEO of General Motors, was interviewed on the subject of ethics and he had the following to say. ". . . the world is not neat and orderly, and arriving at an ethical decision can be difficult. It has been wisely observed that 'It is easy to do what is right; it is hard to know what is right.' . . . In the final analysis, each of us must exercise individual judgment and answer to our own conscience. As General Motors employees, we should never do anything we would be ashamed to explain to our family or afraid to see on the front page of the local newspaper.

Ethical conduct in business goes beyond this, however. For example, one of the basic needs top management has is to receive reliable data and honest opinions from people throughout the organization. Management needs to hear bad news as well as good news. Too often, subordinates are reluctant to tell all of the details of a project or assignment that has failed or is in trouble. This very human trait occurs in all walks of life, whether personal, business, or government, and contributes to the making of bad decisions. In short, ethics is an essential element of success in business."[2]

ACCOUNTING TOOLS AND REPORTS FOR DECISION ANALYSIS

The accountant's role in the decision-making process is to provide information that is accurate, timely, refined, and readable. To accomplish this, the accountant must gather the appropriate information and report it in a way that is meaningful to management. Two common decision tools that help accountants generate this information and the accompanying reports are variable costing and incremental analysis. Each technique helps to identify information relevant to a particular decision and each provides a special decision reporting format based on a specific decision model.

2. From Roger B. Smith, "Ethics in Business: An Essential Element of Success," *Management Accounting,* June 1990, p. 50. Reprinted by permission of Institute of Management Accountants.

DECISION MODELS IN MANAGEMENT ACCOUNTING

When numerous alternatives are to be evaluated, the decision-making process becomes complex. In addition, many decisions are nonrecurring and cannot be resolved by relying on past experience. To facilitate a complex analysis, a decision model is developed. A decision model is a symbolic or numerical representation of the variables and parameters affecting a decision. Decision variables are factors controlled by management. Decision parameters are uncontrollable factors and operating constraints and limitations. As an example, suppose you need to develop a decision model to evaluate new product lines. Your analysis would involve such decision parameters as customer demand, market growth, competitors' actions, and production capacity limitations. Decision variables in this decision model include product selling prices, production costs, and manufacturing methods. The key to developing such a model is to identify relevant decision variables and parameters and put the information together in an informative manner.

Figure 2 outlines the steps in the model-building process. Decision parameters affecting the project are first defined, then possible alternatives are identified. In steps **3** and **4,** appropriate cost and revenue information are developed and analyzed. After the irrelevant information has been eliminated, the relative benefits of each alternative are summarized and presented to management. The output of the decision model is a comparative analysis, using the measurement criterion selected for the particular decision problem. This analysis is a formal report to management, and it should include the following:

1. A brief description of the project or problem situation
2. A comparative financial analysis of each alternative
3. A summary of the relative advantages and disadvantages of each alternative

OBJECTIVE

4 *Calculate product costs using variable costing procedures*

VARIABLE COSTING

Variable costing (also called direct costing) is a method management accountants use to calculate product costs. The income statement generated by a variable costing system shows the contribution margin of the goods produced, information that is helpful in decision making. To understand why the contribution margin format is so useful, we first calculate and compare product costs under a variable costing system and under absorption costing (also known as full costing). We then prepare income statements under both costing procedures and observe the benefits of the contribution margin format.

Unlike absorption costing, which assigns all manufacturing costs to products, variable costing uses only the variable manufacturing costs for product costing and inventory valuation. Direct materials costs, direct labor costs, and variable factory overhead costs are the only cost elements used to compute product costs. Fixed factory overhead costs are considered costs of the current accounting period.

The rationale for variable costing is that a company has fixed operating costs whether it operates or not. Proponents of variable costing argue that such costs do not have a direct relationship to the product and should not be included in the product's unit cost. Fixed manufacturing costs are linked more closely with time than with productive output. Opponents of variable costing say that without fixed manufacturing costs, production would stop. They are, therefore, an integral part of a product's costs.

Figure 2. Steps in Developing a Decision Model

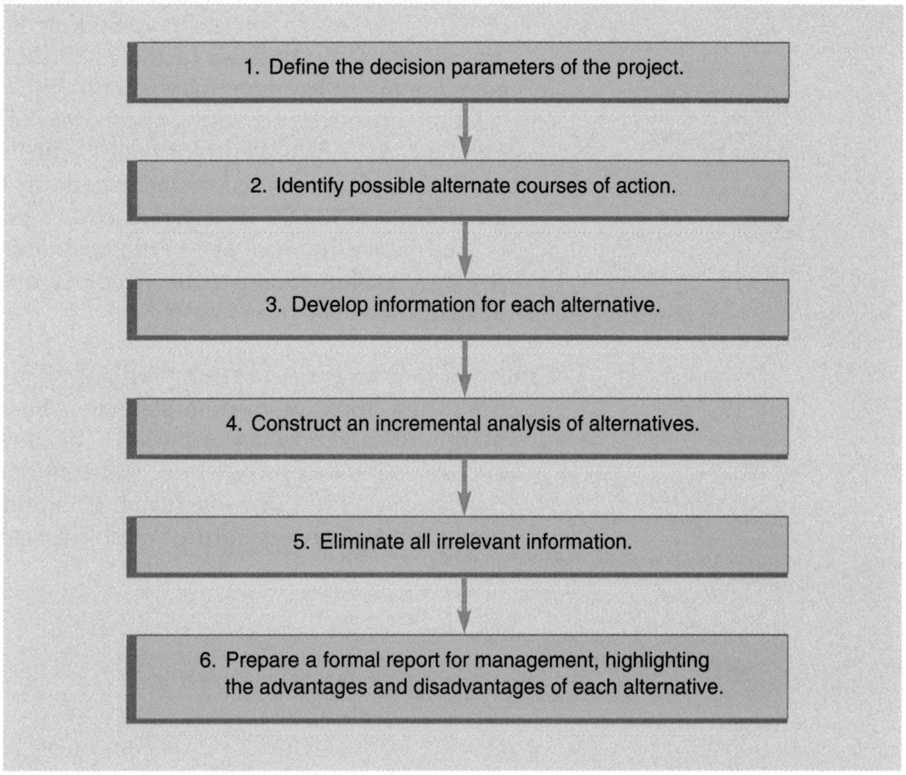

1. Define the decision parameters of the project.

2. Identify possible alternate courses of action.

3. Develop information for each alternative.

4. Construct an incremental analysis of alternatives.

5. Eliminate all irrelevant information.

6. Prepare a formal report for management, highlighting the advantages and disadvantages of each alternative.

Whichever argument you accept, two points are certain. First, neither the Internal Revenue Service nor the public accounting profession accepts variable costing for external reporting purposes. They reject it because fixed costs are not included in inventory and cost of goods sold. Therefore variable costing cannot be used for computing federal income taxes or for reporting the results of operations and financial position to stockholders and others outside the company. Second, even with its limitations regarding financial reporting, variable costing is useful for internal management decisions and is used in many types of decision analyses, some of which are discussed later in this chapter.

Product Costing   For purposes of product costing, variable costing treats fixed manufacturing costs differently from production costs that vary with output. Notice, too, that fixed manufacturing costs are left out of all inventories, which is why the value of inventories found using variable costing is lower than the value of those computed under absorption costing.

The following example explains the differences between these two product costing methods. Atkins Industries, Inc. produces grills for outdoor cooking. During 19x7, the company produced a new, disposable grill. A summary of 19x7 cost and production data for the grill is: direct materials, $76,384; direct labor, $59,136; variable factory overhead, $44,352; and fixed factory overhead, $36,960. There were 24,640 units completed and 22,000 units sold during 19x7. There were no beginning or ending work in process inventories.

Using these data, the unit cost as well as the ending inventory and cost of goods sold amounts for 19x7 can be determined under variable costing and under absorption costing. This information is summarized in Exhibit 1. Unit production cost under variable costing is $7.30 per grill, whereas unit cost is $8.80 using absorption costing. Ending Finished Goods Inventory balances are not the same because of the $1.50 difference in unit cost. Because fewer costs remain in inventory at year end with variable costing amounts, it is logical that greater costs will appear on the income statement. As shown in Exhibit 1, $197,560 of current manufacturing costs are considered costs of the period, to be subtracted from revenue in the variable costing income statement. Only $193,600 is shown as cost of goods sold when absorption costing is used. The difference of $3,960 (2,640 units in inventory × $1.50 fixed costs per unit) is shown as part of inventory under absorption costing ($23,232 − $19,272).

Contribution Margin Reporting Format   Variable costing produces an entirely new form of income statement because it measures the contribution margin of each product or period. This new form emphasizes cost variability and segment or product-line contributions to income. Costs are no longer classified as either manufacturing or nonmanufacturing costs. Instead, attention is focused on separating variable costs from fixed costs.

Exhibit 1. Variable Costing Versus Absorption Costing

Atkins Industries, Inc.
Unit Costs and Ending Inventory Values
For the Year Ended December 31, 19x7

	Variable Costing	Absorption Costing
Unit cost		
Direct materials ($76,384 ÷ 24,640 units)	$ 3.10	$ 3.10
Direct labor ($59,136 ÷ 24,640 units)	2.40	2.40
Variable factory overhead ($44,352 ÷ 24,640 units)	1.80	1.80
Fixed factory overhead ($36,960 ÷ 24,640 units)	—	1.50
Total unit cost	$ 7.30	$ 8.80
Total manufacturing costs to be accounted for	$216,832	$216,832
Less costs charged against income		
Cost of goods sold for 19x7		
22,000 units at $7.30	$160,600	
22,000 units at $8.80		$193,600
Fixed factory overhead	36,960	—
Costs appearing on the 19x7 income statement	$197,560	$193,600
Ending Finished Goods Inventory		
2,640 units at $7.30	$ 19,272	
2,640 units at $8.80		$ 23,232

OBJECTIVE

5 *Prepare an income statement using the contribution margin reporting format*

Referring again to the Atkins Industries, Inc. example, assume the following additional information for 19x7: selling price per grill is $24.50; variable selling costs per grill are $4.80; fixed selling expenses are $48,210; and fixed administrative expenses are $82,430. Exhibit 2 compares income before income taxes under variable costing and absorption costing. The contribution margin format is presented first. Note that the term *gross margin* is replaced by the term *contribution margin* and that only variable costs (including variable selling costs) are subtracted from sales to calculate the contribution margin. Contribution margin is the amount that each segment or product line is contributing to the company's payment of fixed costs and earning of profits. Income before income taxes calculated in the conventional

Exhibit 2. The Income Statement: Contribution Margin Versus Conventional Format

Atkins Industries, Inc.
Disposable Grill Division
Income Statement
For the Year Ended December 31, 19x7

Contribution Margin Format

Sales (22,000 units at $24.50)		$539,000
Variable Cost of Goods Sold		
Variable Cost of Goods Available for Sale		
(24,640 units at $7.30)	$179,872	
Less Ending Inventory	19,272*	
Variable Cost of Goods Sold	$160,600*	
Plus Variable Selling Costs		
(22,000 units at $4.80)	105,600	266,200
Contribution Margin		$272,800
Less Fixed Costs		
Fixed Manufacturing Costs	$ 36,960	
Fixed Selling Expenses	48,210	
Fixed Administrative Expenses	82,430	167,600
Income Before Income Taxes		$105,200

Conventional Format

Sales		$539,000
Cost of Goods Sold		
Cost of Goods Manufactured	$216,832*	
Less Ending Inventory	23,232*	193,600*
Gross Margin		$345,400
Selling Expenses		
Variable	$105,600	
Fixed	48,210	
Administrative Expenses	82,430	236,240
Income Before Income Taxes		$109,160

*Detailed computations are in Exhibit 1.

statement appears in the lower part of Exhibit 2. Note that income before income taxes is different under the two methods. This difference, $3,960, is the same amount noted earlier. It is the part of fixed manufacturing overhead cost that is inventoried when absorption costing is used.

Contribution Reporting and Decisions   Variable costing and the contribution margin format of income reporting are used a great deal in decision analysis, most commonly in deciding whether to continue a segment, division, or product line. Other uses are in the evaluation of new product lines and in sales mix studies. Decisions about the contribution of sales territories also use the contribution margin approach to income reporting. These uses are explained in detail later in this chapter when we look at specific kinds of decisions.

OBJECTIVE

6 *Develop decision data using incremental analysis*

INCREMENTAL ANALYSIS

Incremental analysis is a technique used to compare alternative projects by focusing on the differences in their projected revenues and costs. The accountant organizes relevant information to determine which alternative contributes the most to profits or incurs the least costs. Only relevant decision information appears in the report.

To illustrate how incremental analysis identifies the best alternative, consider the following situation. The management accountant is preparing a report to help the management of the Lewis Company decide which of two mill blade grinders—C or W—to buy. The accountant has collected the following annual sales and operating cost estimates for the two machines.

	Grinder C	Grinder W
Increase in revenue	$16,200	$19,800
Increase in annual operating costs		
Direct materials	4,800	4,800
Direct labor	2,200	4,100
Variable factory overhead	2,100	3,050
Fixed factory overhead		
(depreciation included)	5,000	5,000

An incremental analysis shows increases or decreases in revenues and costs that arise from each alternative. Since direct materials and fixed factory overhead costs are the same for each alternative, they are not included in the analysis.

If you assume that the purchase price and the useful life of the two grinders are the same, the incremental analysis in Exhibit 3 shows that Grinder W generates $750 more in income than Grinder C. Thus, the decision based on this report is to purchase Grinder W.

Since the incremental analysis focuses on the differences between alternatives, it isolates the benefits or drawbacks of each. A report based on incremental analysis makes the evaluation easier for the decision maker and reduces the time needed to decide on the best course of action.

SPECIAL DECISION REPORTS

Income statements in the contribution margin format and incremental analyses work best when comparing quantitative information. In some cases, however, managers might be considering many alternatives, each of which is best

Exhibit 3. Incremental Decision Analysis

Lewis Company
Incremental Decision Analysis

	Grinder C	Grinder W	Difference in Favor of Grinder W
Increase in revenues	$16,200	$19,800	$3,600
Increased operating costs that differ between alternatives			
Direct labor	$ 2,200	$ 4,100	$1,900
Variable factory overhead	2,100	3,050	950
Total relevant operating costs	$ 4,300	$ 7,150	$2,850
Resulting changes in net revenues	$11,900	$12,650	$ 750

in certain circumstances. One may generate more profits, while another diversifies the company's product line. A third alternative may prevent a huge layoff, bolstering the company's goodwill. Even though several equally good alternatives may be available, management must choose only one. In such cases, qualitative information must support or replace the quantitative analyses, and the accountant must use imagination to prepare the special decision report that demonstrates which alternative is best under the circumstances.

For most special decision reports, there is no one correct, set structure. Experienced accountants prepare these reports to fit individual situations. For the purpose of this course, you can solve most of the problems by following the examples in the text. But remember that in practice, management accountants must create formats appropriate to existing circumstances. Such challenges contribute to the dynamic role of the management accountant.

DECISION POINT

Fireman's Fund Insurance Company[3]

Fireman's Fund Insurance Company is one of the top twenty property/casualty insurance companies in the United States. Fifty major field offices service the needs of the company's 6,000 independent insurance agents and brokers. Eighty percent of the company's business is commercial and the remainder is personal insurance. The company offers hundreds of different types of policies and has had trouble tracking the profitability of its numerous product lines. To set appropriate premium rates, knowledge of both policy costs and claims experience is necessary.

3. Michael Crane and John Meyer, "Focusing on True Costs in a Service Organization," *Management Accounting,* Institute of Management Accountants, February 1993, pp. 41–45.

Fireman's Fund developed a system for tracking policy and claims costs. Based on specific activities of company personnel, operating costs are accumulated and traced to policies utilizing those services. Claims are also monitored by policy type and by geographic location. How does such a cost tracking system aid in managing the company's numerous types of insurance policies?

The new accounting system allows the company to determine the profitability of insurance policies by type as well as by geographic location. Once identified, unprofitable policy types and locations can be analyzed before deciding whether or not they should be eliminated. If operating costs are too high, controls may be instituted to limit them.

Analysis of claims procedures and geographic claims experience may point to higher premiums or to policy type elimination. By improving its cost tracking ability, the company can determine the sources of its profits and can manage its resources more effectively. $:::::$

OPERATING DECISIONS OF MANAGEMENT

Many business decisions can be made using income statements generated by a variable costing system and incremental analysis. In this section, those tools will be used to select the best alternative when managers face (1) make-or-buy decisions, (2) special order decisions, (3) sales mix analyses, (4) decisions to eliminate unprofitable segments, and (5) sell or process-further decisions.

OBJECTIVE

7a *Prepare decision alternative evaluations for make-or-buy decisions*

MAKE-OR-BUY DECISIONS

A common problem facing managers of manufacturing companies is whether to make or to buy some or all of the parts used in product assembly. The goal of make-or-buy decision analysis is to identify the costs involved in making or buying some or all of the parts used in product assembly operations, and to select the more profitable choices. Listed below are the factors to be considered in this type of analysis.

To Make	To Buy
Need for additional machinery	Purchase price of item
Variable costs of making the item	Rent or net cash flow to be generated
Incremental fixed costs	from vacated space in factory
	Salvage value of unused machinery

The case of the Sedona Electronics Company illustrates a make-or-buy decision. For the past five years, the firm has purchased a small transistor casing from an outside supplier at a cost of $1.25 per casing. The supplier just informed Sedona Electronics that it is raising the price 20 percent, effective immediately. Sedona has idle machinery that could be adjusted to produce the casings. Sedona estimates the cost of direct materials at $84 per 100 casings, the amount of direct labor at three minutes of labor per casing at a rate of $8 per direct labor hour, and the cost of variable factory overhead at $4 per direct labor hour. Fixed factory overhead includes $4,000 of depreciation per year and $6,000 of other fixed costs. Annual production and usage would be 20,000 casings, the space and machinery to produce the casing

Exhibit 4. Incremental Analysis: Make-or-Buy Decision

Sedona Electronics Company
Incremental Analysis
Current Year—Annual Usage

	Make	Buy	Difference in Favor of Make
Raw materials			
(20,000 ÷ 100 × $84)	$16,800	—	$(16,800)
Direct labor			
(20,000 ÷ 20 × $8)	8,000	—	(8,000)
Variable factory overhead			
(20,000 ÷ 20 × $4)	4,000	—	(4,000)
To purchase completed casings			
(20,000 × $1.50)	—	$30,000	30,000
Totals	$28,800	$30,000	$ 1,200

would be idle if the part were purchased. Should Sedona Electronics Company make or buy the casings?

Incremental analysis enables the accountant to organize the relevant data in a make-or-buy decision. From a review of decision data, management can quickly analyze all relevant costs or revenues and use that information to select the best alternative.

Exhibit 4 presents an incremental analysis of the two alternatives. All relevant costs are listed. Because the machinery has already been purchased and neither the machinery nor the required factory space has any other use, the depreciation costs and other fixed factory overhead costs are the same for both alternatives, so they are not relevant to the decision. The cost of making the needed casings is $28,800. The cost of buying 20,000 casings will be $30,000 at the increased purchase price. The company saves $1,200 by making the casings, and it should do so.

BUSINESS BULLETIN: BUSINESS PRACTICE

Outsourcing is a new business term that means going outside the company to obtain resources and services. The make-or-buy decision is really an insourcing versus outsourcing decision regarding a part or product. But many outsourcing decisions are linked to labor and services. Should the company retain a staff of people for repair and maintenance duties or should an outside company be hired to provide these services? Is it necessary to fund an internal computer systems department or can these services be supplied more economically by an outside computer contractor? These decisions are cost-based. But in addition to the purchase prices of these services and the costs that will be eliminated if the outsourcing is pursued, there are people involved that may have been employed by the company for many years. Should these people be retrained or should they be laid off? Decisions about people are always more complicated than decisions regarding replacing machines or buying different raw materials. If the various staff changes are permanent, employees may be dismissed. But if there are other areas of employee need in the company, retraining should be provided. These retraining costs are relevant to the outsourcing decision. ═══

OBJECTIVE

7b *Prepare decision alternative evaluations for special order decisions*

SPECIAL ORDER DECISIONS

Management is often faced with special order decisions, that is, whether to accept or reject special product orders at prices below normal market prices. These orders usually contain large numbers of similar products to be sold in bulk (packaged in large containers). Because management did not expect the orders, they are not included in annual cost or sales estimates. And, since these orders are one-time events, they should not be included in revenue or cost estimates for subsequent years. The company should consider them only if unused capacity exists.

Before a firm accepts a special order, it must be sure that the products produced under the special order contract are sufficiently different from its regular product line to avoid violating federal price discrimination laws.

Bjorklund Sporting Goods, Inc. manufactures a complete line of sporting equipment. Lange Enterprises operates a large chain of discount stores. Lange has approached Bjorklund with a special order calling for 30,000 deluxe baseballs to be shipped in bulk packaging of 500 baseballs per box. Lange is willing to pay $2.45 per baseball.

The Bjorklund accounting department collected the following data: annual expected production, 400,000 baseballs; current year's production, 410,000 baseballs; and maximum production capacity, 450,000 baseballs. Additional data are:

Standard unit cost data	
Direct materials	$ .90
Direct labor	.60
Factory overhead	
Variable	.50
Fixed ($100,000 ÷ 400,000)	.25
Packaging per unit	.30
Advertising ($60,000 ÷ 400,000)	.15
Other fixed selling and administrative	
costs ($120,000 ÷ 400,000)	.30
Total	$ 3.00
Unit selling price	$ 4.00
Total estimated bulk packaging costs	
(30,000 baseballs: 500 per box)	$2,500

Should Bjorklund Sporting Goods, Inc. accept Lange's offer?

A comparative analysis in the contribution margin reporting format appears in Exhibit 5. The report shows income before income taxes for the Base-

Exhibit 5. Contribution Margin Reporting: Special Product Order

Bjorklund Sporting Goods, Inc.
Comparative Decision Analysis
Special Product Order—Baseball Division

	Without Lange Order (410,000 products)	With Lange Order (440,000 products)
Sales	$1,640,000	$1,713,500
Less variable costs		
Direct materials	$ 369,000	$ 396,000
Direct labor	246,000	264,000
Variable factory overhead	205,000	220,000
Packaging costs	123,000	125,500
Total variable costs	$ 943,000	$1,005,500
Contribution margin	$ 697,000	$ 708,000
Less fixed costs		
Factory overhead	$ 100,000	$ 100,000
Advertising	60,000	60,000
Selling and administrative	120,000	120,000
Total fixed costs	$ 280,000	$ 280,000
Income before income taxes	$ 417,000	$ 428,000

ball Division's operations both with and without the Lange offer. The only costs affected by the order are for direct materials, direct labor, variable factory overhead, and packaging. Packaging costs will increase, but only by the amount of the added bulk packaging. All other costs will remain the same. The net result of accepting the special order is an $11,000 increase in contribution margin (and income before income taxes). This amount is verified by the following computation.

$$\text{Net gain} = [(\text{unit selling price} - \text{unit variable mfg. costs}) \times \text{units}]$$
$$- \text{ bulk packaging costs}$$
$$= [(\$2.45 - \$2.00) \times 30,000] - \$2,500$$
$$= \$13,500 - \$2,500$$
$$= \$11,000$$

Thus, the analysis reveals that Bjorklund should accept the special order from Lange Enterprises.

For special order analysis, both comparative contribution margin reporting and incremental analysis can be used. In this case, we used contribution margin reporting because the fixed cost data in the problem were misleading. Contribution margin reporting highlights the effect of changes in variable costs on contribution margin and income before income taxes.

Fixed costs of existing facilities would normally not change if the special orders were accepted and are, therefore, usually irrelevant to the decision. If, on the other hand, additional fixed costs are incurred to facilitate the transaction, they would be relevant to the decision. Examples of relevant fixed costs include purchase of additional machinery, increase in supervisory help, or increase in insurance premiums resulting from extra control of resources.

SALES MIX ANALYSIS

Profit analysis and maximization are possible only when the profitability of all product lines is known. The question is, Which product or products contribute the most to company profitability in relation to the amount of capital assets or other scarce resources needed to produce the item(s)? To answer this question, the accountant must measure the contribution margin of each product. The next step is to determine a set of ratios of contribution margin to the required capital equipment or other resources. Once this step is completed, management should request a marketing study to set the upper limits of demand on the most profitable products. If product profitability can be computed and market demand exists for these products, management should shift production to the more profitable products.

Many kinds of decisions can be related to the approach described here. Sales mix analysis involves determining the most profitable combination of product sales when a company produces more than one product or offers more than one service. Closely connected with sales mix analysis is the product line profitability study designed to discover which products are losing money for the company. The same decision approach is used, but the goal is to eliminate the unprofitable product line(s). The Fireman's Fund Decision Point involved a problem to be analyzed using the sales mix approach.

Another decision area using the sales mix approach is that of corporate segment analysis. The contribution margin analysis is again used, with the goal of isolating production costs to identify the unprofitable segment(s). If corrective action is not possible, management should eliminate the noncontributing segment(s). Even though not all of these decision areas will be discussed, it is important to remember that the same kind of analysis can be used for product line profitability studies and corporate segment analyses.

An example of this kind of analysis will aid understanding. The management of Bradley Enterprises is in the process of analyzing its sales mix. The company manufactures three products—C, S, and F—using the same production equipment for all three. The total productive capacity is being used. The product line statistics are as follows:

	Product C	Product S	Product F
Current production and sales (units)	20,000	30,000	18,000
Machine hours per product	2	1	2.5
Selling price per unit	$24.00	$18.00	$32.00
Unit variable manufacturing costs	$12.50	$10.00	$18.75
Unit variable selling costs	$6.50	$5.00	$6.25

Should the company try to sell more of one product and less of another?

Because total productive capacity is being used, the only way to expand the production of one product is to reduce the production of another. The sales mix analysis of Bradley Enterprises is shown in Exhibit 6. Though contribution reporting is used here, contribution margin per product is not the important figure for a decision about shifts in sales mix. In the analysis, Product F has the highest contribution margin. However, all products use the same machinery and all machine hours are being used. So machine hours become the scarce resource.

Exhibit 6. Contribution Margin Reporting: Sales Mix Analysis

Bradley Enterprises
Sales Mix Analysis
Contribution Margin Reporting Format

	Product C	Product S	Product F
Unit sales price	$24.00	$18.00	$32.00
Variable costs			
Manufacturing	$12.50	$10.00	$18.75
Selling	6.50	5.00	6.25
Total variable costs	$19.00	$15.00	$25.00
Contribution margin per unit (A)	$ 5.00	$ 3.00	$ 7.00
Machine hours required per unit (B)	2	1	2.5
Contribution margin per machine hour (A ÷ B)	$ 2.50	$ 3.00	$ 2.80

The analysis in Exhibit 6 goes one step beyond the computation of contribution margin per unit. A sales mix decision such as this one should use two decision variables: contribution margin per unit and machine hours required per unit. For instance, Product C requires two machine hours to generate $5 of contribution margin. But Product S would generate $6 of contribution margin using the same two machine hours. For this reason, we have calculated contribution margin per machine hour. Based on this information, management can readily see that it should produce and sell as much of Product S as possible. Next, it should push Product F. If any productive capacity remains, it should produce Product C.

Product-line profitability studies are similar to sales mix analyses. They are designed to discover if any products are losing money for the company. The contribution margin format is also used in this analysis, but the goal of the analysis is to eliminate unprofitable product lines or services. Identification of unprofitable corporate divisions or segments also relies on the contribution margin approach.

DECISIONS TO ELIMINATE UNPROFITABLE SEGMENTS

OBJECTIVE

7d *Prepare decision alternative evaluations for decisions to eliminate unprofitable segments*

Whether to eliminate an unprofitable product, service, division, or other corporate segment is another type of operating decision management may face. The unprofitable segment decision analysis prepared for this type of decision is an extension of the normal performance evaluation of the segment. As an overview, the analysis of unprofitable segments compares (1) operating results of the corporation with the segment in question included against (2) operating results for the same period that do not include data from that segment. The key to this analysis is to be able to isolate the segment, product, or service in question. Variable costs associated with a product or segment are easy to identify and account for. But each product or segment also has fixed

costs associated with and traceable to it that will usually be eliminated if the segment is discontinued. These fixed costs are commonly referred to as trace-able fixed costs

To analyze the financial consequences of eliminating a segment, one must concentrate on the incremental effect of the decision on profits. The decision analysis consists of comparing contribution margin income statements for the company. One statement includes the segment under review, and the second excludes this information. The basic decision is a problem of choosing to keep the product, service, or segment or to eliminate it.

Assume management at Randolph Corporation wants to determine if Division B should be eliminated. Exhibit 7 provides basic cost and revenue data and illustrates a format for evaluating alternate decisions. This analysis requires that an income statement be prepared for each alternative and that profits be compared. All traceable fixed costs of Division B are assumed to be avoidable. Avoidable costs are costs that will be eliminated if a particular product, service, or operating segment is discontinued. As shown in Exhibit 7A, the profits of Randolph Corporation would have increased by $9,000 if Division B had been eliminated.

Exhibit 7. Divisional Profit Summary and Decision Analysis

Randolph Corporation
Divisional Profit Summary and Decision Analysis
Contribution Margin Format

A. Income Statements	Divisions D and E	Division B	Total Company
Sales	$135,000	$15,000	$150,000
Less variable costs	52,500	7,500	60,000
Contribution margin	$ 82,500	$ 7,500	$ 90,000
Less traceable fixed costs	55,500	16,500	72,000
Divisional income	$ 27,000	$ (9,000)	$ 18,000
Less unallocated fixed costs			12,000
Income before income taxes			$ 6,000

	Company Profitability if It Elects to		Benefit or (Cost) to	
B. Incremental Decision Analysis	Keep Division B	Eliminate Division B	Eliminate Division B	
Sales	$150,000	$135,000	$(15,000)	Sales decrease
Less variable costs	60,000	52,500	7,500	Cost reduction
Contribution margin	$ 90,000	$ 82,500	$ (7,500)	CM decrease
Less total fixed costs	84,000	67,500	16,500	Cost reduction
Income before income taxes	$ 6,000	$ 15,000	$ 9,000	Profit increase

Another way of looking at this decision is to concentrate on the third column in Exhibit 7B. Revenue and cost factors that are different under each alternative can be analyzed to explain the profit difference of $9,000. The incremental factors are analyzed in Exhibit 8. If all fixed costs traceable to Division B are avoidable, then the operating loss of $9,000 is also avoidable if the division is eliminated. The primary concept is to isolate avoidable costs, which may not always correspond with traceable costs. Avoidable costs are incremental costs since these amounts are incurred only if the division exists.

In trying to understand the significance of determining an accurate amount of avoidable costs, assume you discover that executives and supervisors in Division B will be reassigned to other divisions if Division B is eliminated. Included in the $16,500 of traceable fixed costs for Division B are salaries of $12,000 for these people. This assumption now changes the profit effect of eliminating Division B, as shown below.

Advantage of eliminating Division B
Reduction of variable expenses $ 7,500
Reduction of fixed expenses ($16,500 − $12,000)   4,500
Total benefits $12,000

Disadvantage of eliminating Division B
Reduction in sales $15,000

Decrease in profit as a result of eliminating
Division B ($15,000 − $12,000) $ 3,000

By following these revised assumptions, you compute that avoidable fixed costs for Division B are $4,500 (traceable fixed costs of $16,500 less the

Exhibit 8. Incremental Revenue and Cost Analysis

Randolph Corporation
Incremental Revenue and Cost Analysis

Advantage of Eliminating Division B	Amount
Increase in sales	—
Decrease in costs ($7,500 + $16,500)	$24,000
Total advantage	$24,000

Disadvantage of Eliminating Division B	Amount
Decrease in sales	$15,000
Increase in costs	—
Total disadvantage	$15,000
Incremental profit from eliminating Division B advantage less disadvantage	$ 9,000

unavoidable $12,000 cost of people to be reassigned to other divisions). Generally, it is unprofitable to eliminate any segment for which contribution margin exceeds avoidable fixed costs. This rule is actually a condensed version of the incremental profit analysis.

If you apply this rule to the Randolph Corporation example, the analysis would be as follows:

Division B

Contribution margin	$7,500
Less avoidable fixed costs	4,500
Profit contribution	$3,000

In such an analysis, corporate profits would actually decrease by $3,000 if Division B were eliminated. This conclusion is valid even though operating reports for Division B disclose a loss of $9,000.

As shown in Exhibit 7, the decision analysis used to decide about eliminating an unprofitable segment (product line, service, or division) requires two decision analysis tools: (1) contribution margin reporting and (2) incremental analysis. Contribution margin reporting helped identify traceable and avoidable fixed costs relevant to the decision, whereas incremental analysis assisted in comparing the operating results with and without the segment.

OBJECTIVE

7e *Prepare decision alternative evaluations for sell or process-further decisions*

SELL OR PROCESS-FURTHER DECISIONS

The sell or process-further decision is the choice between selling a joint product at the split-off point or processing it further. The decision to process a joint product beyond the split-off point requires an analysis of incremental revenues and costs of the two alternate courses of action. Additional processing adds value to a product and increases its selling price above the amount it may have been sold for at split-off. The decision to process further depends on whether the increase in total revenue exceeds additional costs for processing beyond split-off. *Joint costs incurred before split-off do not affect the decision.* These costs are incurred regardless of the point at which the products are sold. Thus they are irrelevant to the decision. Only future costs differing between alternatives are relevant to the decision.

Maximizing company profits is the objective of sell or process-further decisions. For example, assume that Hilbrich Gardening Supplies, Inc. produces various products to enhance plant growth. In one process, three products—Gro-Pow, Gro-Pow II, and Gro-Supreme—emerge from the joint initial phase. For each 20,000-pound batch of materials converted into products, $120,000 in joint production costs are incurred. At split-off, 50 percent of the output becomes Gro-Pow, 30 percent becomes Gro-Pow II, and 20 percent becomes Gro-Supreme. Each product must be processed beyond split-off, and the following additional variable costs are incurred.

Product	Pounds	Additional Processing Costs
Gro-Pow	10,000	$24,000
Gro-Pow II	6,000	38,000
Gro-Supreme	4,000	33,500
Totals	20,000	$95,500

Exhibit 9. Incremental Analysis: Sell or Process-Further Decision

Hilbrich Gardening Supplies, Inc.
Incremental Analysis—Sell or Process-Further Decision

Unit selling price data

Product	If Sold at Split-Off	If Sold After Additional Processing
Gro-Pow	$ 8	$12
Gro-Pow II	24	30
Gro-Supreme	40	50

Incremental analysis per 20,000-pound batch

Product	(1) Pounds	(2) Total Revenue if Sold at Split-Off	(3) Total Revenue if Sold After Processing Further	(4) Incremental Revenue (3) − (2)	(5) Incremental Costs	(6) Effect on Overall Profit (4) − (5)
Gro-Pow	10,000	$ 80,000	$120,000	$40,000	$24,000	$16,000
Gro-Pow II	6,000	144,000	180,000	36,000	38,000	(2,000)
Gro-Supreme	4,000	160,000	200,000	40,000	33,500	6,500

Linda & Parks Landscapers has offered to purchase any or all joint products at split-off for the following prices per pound: Gro-Pow, $8; Gro-Pow II, $24; and Gro-Supreme, $40. To help decide whether to sell at split-off or process the products further, Hilbrich management requested an incremental analysis. This analysis is to compare increases in revenue and increases in processing costs for each alternative.

Exhibit 9 reveals the selling prices of the three products at split-off and if processed further. This exhibit also contains the incremental analysis. As illustrated, products Gro-Pow and Gro-Supreme should be processed further since each will cause a significant increase in overall company profit. If Gro-Pow II can be sold to Linda & Parks Landscapers, the company will avoid a $2,000 loss from further processing. Note that the $120,000 in joint processing costs are irrelevant to the decision since they will be incurred with either alternative.

Measuring incremental costs for additional processing beyond split-off can create problems. Additional costs of materials, labor, and variable overhead are incremental since these costs are caused by additional processing. However, supervisors' salaries, property taxes, insurance, and other fixed costs incurred regardless of the production decision are not incremental costs. Incremental processing costs should include only production costs if a product is processed beyond split-off. Fixed overhead costs common to other production activity must be excluded from a sell or process-further incremental analysis.

CHAPTER REVIEW

REVIEW OF LEARNING OBJECTIVES

1. **Explain how managers obtain and use decision support information.** Managers need information to fulfill their responsibilities. These information needs may be financial in nature or they may involve nonfinancial data such as number of hours worked, product or service throughput time, or units of product produced and sold. Managers get information from sources that are both internal and external to their organizations. Managers must analyze the information supporting each alternative, use intuitive instincts to identify the most likely alternatives, project the results of each alternative, and then make the final decision.

2. **Identify the steps in the management decision cycle.** The management decision cycle begins with discovery of a problem or resource need. Then alternative courses of action to solve the problem or meet the need are identified. Next, a complete analysis to determine the effects of each alternative on business operations is prepared. With these supporting data, the decision maker chooses the best alternative. After the decision has been carried out, the accountant conducts a postdecision review to see if the decision was correct or if other needs have arisen.

3. **Define and identify *relevant decision information*.** Any data that relate to future cost, revenue, or use of resources and that will be different for alternative courses of action are considered relevant decision information. Projected sales or estimated costs, such as materials or direct labor, that are different for each decision alternative are examples of relevant information.

4. **Calculate product costs using variable costing procedures.** Variable costing uses only variable manufacturing costs for product costing and inventory valuation. Direct materials, direct labor, and variable factory overhead costs are the only cost elements used to compute product costs. Fixed factory overhead costs are considered costs of the current period and are not included in inventories.

5. **Prepare an income statement using the contribution margin reporting format.** In an income statement in the contribution margin format, costs are categorized as variable or fixed. Variable costs of goods sold and variable selling expenses are subtracted from sales to arrive at contribution margin. All fixed costs, including those from manufacturing, selling, and administrative activities, are subtracted from contribution margin to determine income before income taxes.

6. **Develop decision data using incremental analysis.** In incremental analysis, alternatives are compared by their information differences. After identifying the potential increases or decreases in revenues and costs that result from each alternative, the accountant highlights the relevant data. They are the values that differ among the alternatives. Only these values are included in the analysis.

7. **Prepare decision alternative evaluations for (a) make-or-buy decisions, (b) special order decisions, (c) sales mix analyses, (d) decisions to eliminate unprofitable segments, and (e) sell or process-further decisions.** Make-or-buy decision analysis helps managers decide whether to buy a part used in product assembly or to make the part inside the company. An incremental analysis of the expected costs and revenues for each alternative identifies the best alternative. To analyze special orders, the accountant must determine if there is unused capacity and must find the lowest acceptable selling price of a product. Generally, fixed costs are irrelevant to the decision since these costs were covered by regular operations. Contribution margin reporting shows whether the special order increases net income. Sales mix analysis is used to find the most profitable combination of product sales when a company makes more than one product using a common scarce resource. (A similar approach may be used for decisions based on the profitability of sales territo-

ries, service lines, or corporate segments.) The analysis uses the contribution margin reporting format but goes beyond computation of the contribution margin to examine the contribution margin per unit of scarce resource.

The decision to eliminate unprofitable products, services, or company segments requires an incremental analysis. This analysis should compare operating results that include the questionable segment against operating results without the segment's traceable and avoidable revenues and costs. Both income statements are prepared by following the contribution margin reporting format. Sell or process-further decisions are also based on comparisons of incremental revenues and costs of the two alternatives. Joint processing costs are irrelevant to the decision since they are identical for either alternative.

REVIEW OF CONCEPTS AND TERMINOLOGY

The following concepts and terms were introduced in this chapter.

L O 7   **Avoidable costs:** Costs that will be eliminated if a particular product, service, or operating segment is discontinued.

L O 3   **Decision model:** A symbolic or numerical representation of the variables and parameters affecting a decision.

L O 3   **Decision parameters:** The uncontrollable factors and the operating constraints and limitations within a decision model.

L O 3   **Decision variables:** Factors within a decision model that are controlled by management.

L O 6   **Incremental analysis:** A technique used in decision analysis that compares alternatives by focusing on the differences in their projected revenues and costs.

L O 7   **Make-or-buy decision analysis:** A decision analysis that helps management choose the more profitable option by identifying the costs involved in making or buying some or all of the parts used in product assembly operations.

L O 3   **Relevant decision information:** Future cost, revenue, and resource usage data that differ for the decision alternatives being evaluated.

L O 7   **Sales mix analysis:** A special analysis prepared to determine the most profitable combination of product sales when a company produces more than one product or offers more than one service.

L O 7   **Sell or process-further decision:** A decision analysis designed to help management determine whether to sell a joint product at the split-off point or process it further to increase its market price and profits.

L O 7   **Special order decision:** A decision analysis designed to help management determine whether to accept or reject unexpected special product orders at prices below normal market prices.

L O 7   **Traceable fixed costs:** Fixed costs that are traceable to a division, department, or other operating unit or product line.

L O 7   **Unprofitable segment decision analysis:** A decision analysis designed to help management decide whether to continue operating a segment or to discontinue its operations.

L O 4   **Variable costing:** A costing method that uses only the variable manufacturing costs for product costing and inventory valuation purposes (as contrasted with absorption costing, which uses all product costs).

REVIEW PROBLEM
SHORT-RUN OPERATING DECISION ANALYSIS

L O 3, 7 Ten years ago, Dale Bandy formed Home Services, Inc., a company specializing in repair and maintenance services for the home and its surroundings. To date, Home Services has six offices in major cities across the country. Fourteen services, ranging from plumbing repair to appliance repair to lawn care, are available to the home owner. During the past two years, the company's profitability has decreased, and Bandy wants to determine which service lines are not meeting the company's profit targets. Once the unprofitable service lines are identified, he will either eliminate them or set higher prices. If higher prices are set, all variable and fixed operating, selling, and general administration costs will be covered by the price structure. The data from the most recent year-end closing shown below were available for the analysis. Four service lines are under serious review.

Home Services, Inc.
Service Profit and Loss Summary
For the Year Ended December 31, 19x5

	Auto Repair Service	Boat Repair Service	Tile Floor Repair Service	Tree Trimming Service	Total Company Impact
Net sales	$297,500	$114,300	$126,400	$97,600	$635,800
Less variable costs					
Direct labor	$119,000	$ 40,005	$ 44,240	$34,160	$237,405
Operating supplies	14,875	5,715	6,320	4,880	31,790
Small tools	11,900	4,572	5,056	7,808	29,336
Replacement parts	59,500	22,860	25,280	—	107,640
Truck costs	—	11,430	12,640	14,640	38,710
Selling costs	44,625	17,145	18,960	9,760	90,490
Other variable costs	5,950	2,286	2,528	1,952	12,716
Total	$255,850	$104,013	$115,024	$73,200	$548,087
Contribution margin	$ 41,650	$ 10,287	$ 11,376	$24,400	$ 87,713
Less traceable fixed costs	74,200	29,600	34,700	28,400	166,900
Service margin	($ 32,550)	($ 19,313)	($ 23,324)	($ 4,000)	($ 79,187)
Less nontraceable joint fixed costs ·					32,100
Income before income taxes					($111,287)
Avoidable fixed costs included in traceable fixed costs above	$ 35,800	$ 16,300	$ 24,100	$ 5,200	$ 81,400

REQUIRED

1. Analyze the performance of the four services being reviewed.
2. Should Bandy eliminate any of the service lines? Why?
3. Identify some possible causes for poor performance by the services.
4. What factors would lead you to raise the fee for a service rather than eliminate the service?

ANSWER TO REVIEW PROBLEM

1. When analyzing the performance of four service lines for possible elimination, you should concentrate on the revenues and costs to be eliminated if the service is eliminated. You should start your analysis with contribution margin because all sales and variable costs will be eliminated. By subtracting the avoidable fixed costs from contribution margin, you will find the profit or loss that will be eliminated if the service is eliminated. These calculations are shown below.

	Auto Repair Service	Boat Repair Service	Tile Floor Repair Service	Tree Trimming Service	Total Company Impact
Contribution margin	$41,650	$10,287	$11,376	$24,400	$87,713
Less avoidable fixed costs	35,800	16,300	24,100	5,200	81,400
Profit (loss) reduced if service is eliminated	$ 5,850	($ 6,013)	($12,724)	$19,200	$ 6,313

2. From the analysis in **1,** you can see that the company will improve by $18,737 ($6,013 + $12,724) if the Boat Repair Service and the Tile Floor Repair Service are eliminated.

3. There are several possible causes for poor performance by the four services, including
   a. Low service fees being charged
   b. Inadequate advertising of the service
   c. High direct labor costs
   d. Other variable costs too high
   e. Poor management of fixed cost levels
   f. Excessive management costs

4. To judge the adequacy of the service fees being charged, you should first look at the contribution margin percentages. This additional information will help support pricing decisions for the four services.

	Auto Repair Service	Boat Repair Service	Tile Floor Repair Service	Tree Trimming Service
Sales	$297,500	$114,300	$126,400	$97,600
Contribution margin	$ 41,650	$ 10,287	$ 11,376	$24,400
Contribution margin percentage	14.00%	9.00%	9.00%	25.00%

Only 9 percent of the selling price is available to cover fixed costs and earn a profit from the Boat Repair and Tile Floor Repair services. This is a thin margin with which to work. An increase in fees seems appropriate. Even fees for the Auto Repair Service may need to be increased.

Also, remember that there were large amounts of unavoidable and nontraceable fixed costs reported. These costs may need to be analyzed too. Although they may or may not be avoidable, these costs must be covered by fees if the company is to remain profitable.

CHAPTER ASSIGNMENTS

QUESTIONS

1. Give six examples of decisions that are made on either a regular or a periodic basis.

2. Identify three internal and three external sources of information used by managers to support their decisions.

3. "Strategic planning provides the basic framework for applying short-run period planning." Do you agree with this statement? If so, why?

4. Describe the five steps of the management decision cycle.

5. What is meant by relevant decision information? What are the two important characteristics of such information?

6. Describe variable costing. In what ways does variable costing differ from absorption costing?

7. Is variable costing widely used for financial reporting? Defend your answer.

8. What is the connection between variable costing and the contribution margin approach to reporting?

9. Are variable costs always relevant? Defend your response.

10. Identify and discuss the steps required to build a decision model.

11. What are the objectives of incremental analysis? What types of decision analyses depend on the incremental approach?

12. Illustrate and discuss some qualitative inputs into decision analysis.

13. How does one determine which data are relevant to a make-or-buy decision?

14. When pricing a special order, what justifies excluding fixed overhead costs from the analysis? Under what circumstances are fixed costs relevant to the pricing decision?

15. What questions must be answered in trying to make the most of product line profitability? Give examples of approaches to the solution of this question.

16. For sales mix decisions, what criteria can be used to select products that will maximize income before income taxes?

17. Why is the term *avoidable cost* used in connection with alternatives to eliminating a segment?

18. Distinguish between the terms *avoidable cost* and *traceable cost*.

19. Why are joint processing costs irrelevant to the decision to sell a product at split-off or process it further?

20. Is incremental analysis important to the sell or process-further decision? If so, why?

SHORT EXERCISES

SE 1. *Information Sources*
L O 1 *for Decision Support*
No check figure

Darryl Burns is the manager of an electrical repair department in a large appliance assembly company. His employees are responsible for the repair of over thirty machines as well as the repair of customers' appliances that are still under warranty. Darryl is planning to attend a national conference on warranty repair work, and one of the seminars he plans to attend focuses on using outside contract repair companies that specialize in warranty work. What types of information is Darryl likely to pick up from attending this seminar?

SE 2. *Planning and*
L O 2 *Management*
Decisions
No check figure

The corporate officers of the Holcumb Company have just returned from their annual planning retreat. Four of their planning statements were:

1. Gain 10 percent market share in five years.
2. Sales target for next year's new product is $16,400,000.
3. Cut the number of products needing rework by 20 percent a year for the next five years.
4. Reduce production costs by 15 percent to meet competition's prices.

Which of these statements represent long-term strategic plans and which represent directives for the company's annual budget for the coming year?

SE 3. *Identifying Relevant*
L O 3 *Information*
No check figure

From the following decision support information, identify which of the items are relevant to the decision analysis. Why are the other items irrelevant?

	Alternative 1	Alternative 2
Expected sales increase	$300,000	$325,000
Purchase price of machine	75,000	80,000
Cost of needed materials	40,000	40,000
Machine operator labor	25,000	25,000
Machine maintenance costs	14,000	12,000

SE 4. *Variable Costing*
L O 4
Check Figure: Unit cost: $106

Costs associated with producing and selling a 100-pound bag of Dergonite, a chemical designed to reduce pollution in large lakes, are listed below. Compute the unit cost using the variable costing method.

Raw materials	$40
Direct labor	20
Variable factory overhead	46
Fixed factory overhead	29
Variable selling costs	18

SE 5. *Contribution*
L O 5 *Margin Reporting*
Check Figure: Income Before Income Taxes: $70,200

Jardin Corp. generated the following information for November: Net sales, $890,000; raw materials cost, $220,000; direct labor cost, $97,000; variable factory overhead, $150,000; fixed factory overhead, $130,000; variable selling expenses, $44,500; fixed selling expenses, $82,300; and general and administrative expenses, $96,000. There were no beginning or ending inventories.

Using this information, prepare an income statement using the contribution margin format. How much contribution margin was generated during the month?

SE 6. *Using Incremental*
L O 6 *Analysis*
Check Figure: Resulting change in net income, Difference in Favor of Vogle Machine: $3,300

Forlands Corporation has assembled information related to the decision to purchase a new automated degreasing machine. This information is shown on the next page. Using incremental analysis and only relevant information, compute the difference in favor of the Vogle machine.

	Harvey Machine	Vogle Machine
Increase in revenue	$43,200	$49,300
Increase in annual operating costs		
Direct materials	12,200	12,200
Direct labor	10,200	10,600
Variable factory overhead	24,500	26,900
Fixed factory overhead (including depreciation)	12,400	12,400

SE 7. *Make-or-Buy*
L O 7 *Decision*
Check Figure: Totals, Difference in Favor of Make: $1,250

Walters Company markets products that it assembles from a group of interconnecting parts. Some of the parts are produced by the company and some are purchased from outside vendors. The vendor for Part 23X has just increased its price by 35 percent, to $10 per unit for the first 5,000 and then $9 per unit for additional orders each year. The company uses 7,500 units of Part 23X each year. Unit costs to make and sell the part are:

Direct materials	$3.50
Direct labor	1.75
Variable factory overhead	4.25
Variable selling costs for the assembled product	3.75

Using the information presented, should the company continue to purchase the part or should it begin making the part?

SE 8. *Special Order*
L O 7 *Decision*
Check Figure: Total variable costs to produce: $20.60

Beuret Company has received a special order for Product YTZ at a selling price of $20 per unit. This order is over and above normal production, and budgeted production and sales targets have already been exceeded for the year. Capacity exists to satisfy the special order. No selling costs will be incurred in connection with this order. Unit costs to manufacture and sell Product YTZ are as follows: Direct materials, $7.60; direct labor, $3.75; variable factory overhead, $9.25; fixed manufacturing costs, $4.85; variable selling costs, $2.75; and fixed general and administrative costs, $6.75. Should Beuret Company accept the order?

SE 9. *Decision to*
L O 7 *Eliminate Unprofitable Segment*
Check Figure: Divisional income, West Division: $110,000

Allis Company is evaluating its two divisions, West Division and East Division. Data for the West Division include sales of $530,000, variable costs of $290,000, and fixed costs of $260,000, 50 percent of which are traceable to the division. East Division's efforts for the same time period include sales of $610,000, variable costs of $340,000, and fixed costs of $290,000, 60 percent of which are traceable to the division. Should either of the divisions be considered for elimination? Is there any other problem that needs attention?

SE 10. *Sell or Process-*
L O 7 *Further Decision*
No check figure

Palmer Industries produces three products from a single operation. Product A sells for $3 per unit, Product B sells for $6 per unit, and Product C sells for $9 per unit. When B is processed further, there are additional unit costs of $3, and its new selling price is $10 per unit. Each product is allocated $2 of joint costs from the initial production operation. Should Product B be processed further, or should it be sold at the end of the initial operation?

EXERCISES

E 1. *Information Sources*
L O 1 *for Decision Support*
No check figure

Peter Morrisson, owner of Laguna Cement Company, must make a decision to replace the current cement production process with a process using the newest technology. Indicate whether each of the following information sources is internal or external to the organization.

1. Presentation at the national conference on the use of current technology for the manufacture of cement
2. Observation of the current production activities at the plant
3. A report of production output from the current production process
4. A summary of information from the leading trade journals about the latest techniques used by competitors
5. A presentation by sales representatives of the company that manufactures the machines that process cement

E 2.
L O 2
Steps in the Management Decision Cycle

No check figure

Bobby Latham owns Latham's Department Store in Kansas City. Bobby is concerned that profits for the store have declined because one or more departments are no longer profitable. Apply the management decision cycle to Latham's decision process by ranking actions 1 through 5 listed below in the order in which the actions would occur.

1. Bobby decided to close the Cosmetics Department.
2. Bobby realized that the declining profits of the store may be due to the poor sales performance of one or more departments in the store.
3. Bobby believes that he must decide to keep or drop an unprofitable department.
4. Bobby gathered monthly sales and expense information directly related to each department in the department store. He noticed that the Cosmetics Department was operating at a loss.
5. Bobby subsequently reviewed the profitability in each department and found that profits in the Women's Clothing Department had dropped. The sales clerks suggested that closing the Cosmetics Department had reduced the flow of traffic into their department.

E 3.
L O 3
Relevant Costs and Revenues

Check Figure: 1. Net revenue from sale: $61,700

Medallion Enterprises manufactures household metal products, such as window frames, light fixtures, and doorknobs. In 19x8, the company produced 10,000 special oblong doorknobs but sold only 1,000 doorknobs at $20.00 each. The remaining 9,000 units cannot be sold through Medallion's normal channels.

For inventory purposes, December 31, 19x8 data included the following costs on unsold units:

Direct materials	$ 6.00
Direct labor	3.00
Variable factory overhead	1.00
Fixed factory overhead	4.00
Cost per knob	$14.00

The 9,000 oblong knobs can be sold to a scrap dealer in another state for $7.00 each. A license for doing business in this state will cost Medallion $400. Shipping expenses will average $0.10 per knob.

1. Identify the relevant costs and revenues for the scrap sale alternative.
2. Assume the oblong knobs can be reprocessed to produce round knobs that normally have the same $14.00 unit cost components and sell for $16.00 each. Rework costs will be $9.00 per unit. Determine the most profitable alternative: (a) doing nothing, (b) reprocessing the knobs (assuming a market exists for the reworked knobs), or (c) selling them as scrap.

E 4.
L O 4
Variable Costing: Unit Cost Computation

Check Figure: 1. Total unit cost, Variable Costing: $1,025,985

E-Tracker Corporation produces a full line of energy-tracking devices. These devices can detect and track all forms of thermochemical energy-emitting space vehicles.

The following cost data are provided: Direct materials cost $1,185,000 for 2 units. Direct labor for assembly is 4,590 hours per unit at $26.50 per hour. Variable factory overhead is $48.00 per direct labor hour, and fixed factory overhead is $2,796,000 per month (based on an average production of 30 units per month). This amount includes fixed packaging overhead. Packaging materials come to $127,200 for 2 units, and packaging labor per unit is 420 hours per unit at $18.50 per hour. The variable factory overhead rate for packaging is the same as for production. Advertising and marketing cost $196,750 per month, and other fixed selling and administrative costs are $287,680 per month.

1. From the cost data given, find the unit production cost, using both the variable costing and the absorption costing methods.
2. Assume that the current month's ending inventory is 8 units. Compute the inventory valuation under both variable and absorption costing methods.

E 5. *Income Statement:*
L O 5 *Contribution Reporting Format*

Check Figure: Income Before Income Taxes: $49,650

The income statement in the conventional reporting format for Bonsai Products, Inc. for the year ended December 31, 19x0, appeared as shown below.

Bonsai Products, Inc.
Income Statement
For the Year Ended December 31, 19x0

Net Sales		$296,400
Less Cost of Goods Sold		
Cost of Goods Available for Sale	$125,290	
Less Ending Inventory	12,540	112,750
Gross Margin		$183,650
Less Operating Expenses		
Selling Expenses		
Variable	$ 69,820	
Fixed	36,980	
Administrative Expenses	27,410	134,210
Income Before Income Taxes		$ 49,440

Fixed manufacturing costs of $17,600 and $850 are included in Cost of Goods Available for Sale and Ending Inventory, respectively. Total fixed manufacturing costs for 19x0 were $16,540. There were no beginning or ending work in process inventories. All administrative expenses are considered to be fixed.

Using this information, prepare an income statement for Bonsai Products, Inc. for the year ended December 31, 19x0, using the contribution reporting format.

E 6. *Relevant Data*
L O 3, 6 *and Incremental Analysis*

Check Figure: Resulting increase in net income, Difference in Favor of Model A: $180

Carla Cordova, business manager for Orlando Industries, must select a new computer and word processing package for her secretary. Rental of Model A, which is similar to the model now being used, is $2,200 per year. Model B is a deluxe computer with Windows support for its word processing software. It rents for $2,900 per year, but will require a new desk for the secretary. The annual desk rental charge is $750. The secretary's salary of $1,200 per month will not change. If Model B is rented, $280 in annual software training costs will be incurred. Model B has greater capacity and is expected to save $1,550 per year in part-time secretarial wages. Upkeep and operating costs will not differ between the two models.

1. Identify the relevant data in this problem.
2. Prepare an incremental analysis for the business manager to assist her in this decision.

E 7. *Make-or-Buy*
L O 7 *Decision*

Check Figure: Totals, Difference in Favor of Make: $10,500

One of the parts for a radio assembly being produced by St. Rudolph Audio Systems, Inc. is currently being purchased for $225 per 100 parts. Management is studying the possibility of manufacturing the part. Cost and production data being examined are as follows: Annual production (usage) is 70,000 units; fixed costs (all of which remain unchanged whether the part is made or purchased) are $38,500; and variable costs are

$.95 per unit for direct materials, $.55 per unit for direct labor, and $.60 per unit for manufacturing overhead.

Using incremental decision analysis, decide whether St. Rudolph Audio Systems, Inc. should manufacture the part or continue to purchase it from an outside vendor.

E 8. *Special Order*
L O 7 *Decision*
Check Figure: Contribution margin from order: $18,000

Igor Antiquities, Ltd. produces antique-looking lampshades. Management has just received a request for a special-design order and must decide whether or not to accept it. The special order calls for 9,000 shades to be shipped in a total of 300 bulk-pack cartons. Shipping costs of $180 per carton will replace normal packing and shipping costs. Frandsen Furniture Company, the purchasing company, is offering to pay $22 per shade plus packing and shipping expenses.

The following company data have been provided by the accounting department: Annual expected production is 350,000 shades, and the current year's production (before special order) is 360,000 shades. Maximum production capacity is 380,000 shades. Unit cost data include $9.20 for direct materials, $4.00 for direct labor, variable factory overhead of $6.80, and fixed factory overhead of $2.50 ($875,000 ÷ 350,000). Normal packaging and shipping costs per unit come to $1.50, and advertising is $.30 per unit ($105,000 ÷ 350,000). Other fixed administrative costs are $1.30 per unit ($455,000 ÷ 350,000). Total normal cost per unit is $25.60, with per unit selling price set at $38.00. Total estimated bulk packaging and shipping costs are $54,000 ($180 per carton × 300 cartons).

Determine whether this special order should be accepted by Igor Antiquities, Ltd.

E 9. *Scarce-Resource*
L O 7 *Usage*
Check Figure: 2. Contribution Margin: $2,600,000

Blazek, Inc. manufactures two products that require both machine processing and labor operations. Although there is unlimited demand for both products, Blazek could devote all its capacities to a single product. Unit prices, cost data, and processing requirements are:

	Product A	Product M
Unit selling price	$80	$220
Unit variable costs	$40	$ 90
Machine hours per unit	.4	1.4
Labor hours per unit	2	6

In 19x9 the company will be limited to 160,000 machine hours and 120,000 labor hours.

1. Compute the most profitable combination of products to be produced in 19x9.
2. Prepare an income statement for the product volume computed in **1.**

E 10. *Elimination of*
L O 7 *Unprofitable*
Segment
Check Figure: Loss reduction if eliminated, Nio Division: $8,000; Eliminate the Nio Division

Skye Glass, Inc. has three divisions: Atta, Nio, and Tio. The divisional income summaries for 19x8 revealed the following:

Skye Glass, Inc.
Divisional Profit Summary and Decision Analysis

	Atta Division	Nio Division	Tio Division	Total Company
Sales	$290,000	$533,000	$837,000	$1,660,000
Variable Costs	147,000	435,000	472,000	1,054,000
Contribution Margin	$143,000	$ 98,000	$365,000	$ 606,000
Less Traceable Fixed Costs	166,000	114,000	175,000	455,000
Divisional Income	($ 23,000)	($ 16,000)	$190,000	$ 151,000
Less Unallocated Fixed Costs				82,000
Income Before Income Taxes				$ 69,000

A detailed analysis of the traceable fixed costs revealed the following information:

	Atta Division	Nio Division	Tio Division
Avoidable Fixed Costs	$124,000	$106,000	$139,000
Unavoidable Fixed Costs	42,000	8,000	36,000
Totals	$166,000	$114,000	$175,000

Based on the 19x8 income summaries, determine whether it would be profitable for the company to eliminate one or more of its segments. Identify which division(s) should be eliminated, and compute how much the resulting increase in total company income would be before income taxes.

E 11. *Sell or Process-*
L O 7 *Further Decision*
Check Figure: 1. Total costs, All Parts: $102,400

Maya Marketeers, Inc. has developed a promotional program for a large shopping center in Tempe, Arizona. After investing $360,000 in developing the original promotion campaign, the firm is ready to present its client with an add-on contract offer that includes the original promotion areas of (1) TV advertising program, (2) series of brochures for mass mailing, and (3) special rotating BIG SALE schedule for 10 of the 28 tenants in the shopping center. Following are the revenue terms from the original contract with the shopping center and the offer for an add-on contract, which extends the original contract terms.

	Contract Terms	
	Original Contract Terms	Extended Contract Including Add-On Terms
TV advertising program	$520,000	$ 580,000
Brochure package	210,000	230,000
Rotating BIG SALE schedule	170,000	190,000
Totals	$900,000	$1,000,000

Maya estimates that the following additional costs will be incurred by extending the contract.

	TV Program	Brochures	BIG SALE Schedule
Direct labor	$30,000	$ 9,000	$7,000
Variable overhead costs	22,000	14,000	6,000
Fixed overhead costs*	12,000	4,000	2,000

*20 percent are unavoidable fixed costs applied to this contract.

1. Compute the costs that will be incurred for each part of the add-on portion of the contract.
2. Should Maya Marketeers, Inc. offer the add-on contract or should it ask for a final settlement check based on the original contract only? Defend your answer.
3. If management of the shopping center indicated the terms of the add-on contract were negotiable, how should Maya respond?

SKILLS DEVELOPMENT EXERCISES

Conceptual Analysis

SDE 1. *Management*
L O 2 *Decision Cycle*

No check figure

Last week your cousin Loretta wrote asking for your help in making a purchase decision. Two weeks ago she moved from New York City to Houston. She found that she needs a car to drive to work and to run her errands. She has no personal experience in selecting a car.

Using the management decision cycle presented in this chapter, write her a letter explaining how she can approach making this decision. How would your response change if the president of your company asked you to help make a decision about acquiring a fleet of cars for use by the sales personnel?

Ethical Dilemma

SDE 2. *Make or Purchase*
L O 6 *Parts*

No check figure

Michelle Pinto is assistant controller for *Bannister Corp.*, a leading producer of home appliances. Her friend, Eddie Mason, is supervisor of the Cookware Department. Mason has the authority to decide whether parts are purchased from outside vendors or manufactured in his department. Pinto recently conducted an internal audit of the parts being manufactured in the Cookware Department, including doing a check of the prices currently being charged by vendors for similar parts. She found over a dozen parts that could be purchased for less money than they cost the company to produce. In her discussion with Mason, she was told that if those parts were purchased from outside vendors, two automated machines would be idled for several hours a week. This action would negatively influence Mason's performance evaluation and could reduce his yearly bonus. He told Pinto that he was in charge of the decision to make or purchase these parts and asked her not to pursue the matter any further.

What should Pinto do in this situation? Discuss her options.

Research Activity

SDE 3. *Identifying Relevant*
L O 3 *Decision Information*

No check figure

You need relevant information in order to make good decisions. Assume you want to take a two-week vacation. Select two destinations for your vacation and gather information from travel brochures, magazines, and travel agents. Using your personal experiences and the information you have gathered, list in order of importance the quantitative information and qualitative information that would be relevant in making your decision. Analyze this information and select a destination. What factors were the most important to your decision? Why? What factors were the least important to your decision? Why? How would the process of identifying relevant decision information differ if you were asked by the president of your company to prepare a budget for the next training meeting to be held at a location of your choice?

Decision-Making Practice

SDE 4. *Decision to Add*
L O 7 *a New Department*

Check Figure: 1. Incremental profit from adding Department III: $45,000

Management at *Tingle Company* is considering a proposal to install a third production department within its factory building. With the company's present production setup, raw material is processed through Department I to produce materials A and B in equal proportions. Material A is then processed through Department II to yield Product C. Material B is sold as-is at $20.25 per pound. Product C has a selling price of $100.00 per pound. Current per-pound standard costs used by Tingle Company are shown on the next page.

	Department I (Materials A & B)	Department II (Product C)	(Material B)
Prior department's cost	—	$53.03**	$13.47**
Direct materials	$20.00	—	—
Direct labor	6.00	9.00	—
Variable overhead	4.00	8.00	—
Fixed overhead			
Traceable	2.25	2.25	—
Allocated (⅔, ⅓)	1.00	1.00	—
	$33.25*	$73.28	$13.47

*Cost to produce each A and B product.

**Department I costs ($33.25 + $33.25) assigned based on relative sales value at split-off point:

$66.50 x 77.95% = $53.03

$66.50 x 20.25% = $13.47

These standard costs were developed by using an estimated production volume of 200,000 pounds of raw material as the standard volume. The company assigns Department I costs to materials A and B in proportion to their net sales values at the point of separation. These values are computed by deducting subsequent standard production costs from sales prices. The $300,000 in common fixed overhead costs are allocated to the two producing departments on the basis of the space used by the departments.

Department III is being proposed to be used to process Material B into Product D. It is expected that any quantity of Product D can be sold for $30 per pound. Standard costs per pound under this proposal were developed by using 200,000 pounds of raw material as the standard volume. Those costs are as shown below.

	Department I (Materials A & B)	Department II (Product C)	Department III (Product D)
Prior department's cost	—	$52.80	$13.20
Direct materials	$20.00	—	—
Direct labor	6.00	9.00	3.50
Variable overhead	4.00	8.00	4.00
Fixed overhead			
Traceable	2.25	2.25	1.80
Allocated (½, ¼, ¼)	.75	.75	.75
	$33.00	$72.80	$23.25

1. If (a) sales and production levels are expected to remain constant in the foreseeable future and (b) there are no foreseeable alternate uses for the factory space, should Tingle Company install Department III and produce Product D? Show calculations to support your answer.
2. List at least two qualitative reasons why Tingle Company may *not* want to install Department III and produce Product D, even if it appears that this decision is profitable.
3. List at least two qualitative reasons why Tingle Company may want to install Department III and produce Product D, even if it appears that this decision is *un*profitable.

(CMA adapted)

PROBLEM SET A

A 1.
L O 4, 5
Variable Costing: Contribution Approach to Income Statement

Roofing tile is the major product of the Zygo Corporation. The company had a particularly good year in 19x9, as shown by the following operating data.

It produced 92,600 cases (units) of tile and sold 88,400 cases. Direct materials used cost $384,290; direct labor was $208,350; variable factory overhead was $296,320; fixed factory overhead was $166,680; variable selling expenses were $132,600; fixed selling expenses were $152,048; and fixed administrative expenses were $96,450. Selling price was $18 per case. There were no partially completed jobs in process at the beginning or the end of the year. Finished goods inventory had been used up at the end of the previous year.

REQUIRED

1. Compute the unit cost, cost of goods sold for 19x9, and ending finished goods inventory value, using (a) variable costing procedures and (b) absorption costing procedures.
2. Prepare the year-end income statement for the Zygo Corporation, using (a) the contribution format based on variable costing data and (b) the conventional format based on absorption costing data.

A 2. *Make-or-Buy*
L O 7 *Decision*

The Freezaire Refrigerator Company purchases and installs defrost clocks in its products. The clocks cost $138 per case, and each case contains twelve clocks. The supplier recently gave advance notice that, effective in thirty days, the price will rise by 50 percent. The company has idle equipment which, with only a few minor changes, could be used to produce similar defrost clocks.

The following cost estimates have been prepared under the assumption that the company could make the product itself. Direct materials would cost $100.80 per twelve clocks. Direct labor required would be ten minutes per clock at a labor rate of $18.00 per hour. Variable factory overhead would be $4.60 per clock. Fixed factory overhead, which would be incurred under either decision alternative, would be $32,420 a year for depreciation and $234,000 a year for other costs. Production and usage are estimated at 75,000 clocks a year. (Assume that any idle equipment cannot be used for any other purpose.)

REQUIRED

1. Prepare an incremental decision analysis to determine whether the defrost clocks should be made within the company or purchased from the outside supplier at the higher price.
2. Compute the unit cost to make one clock and to buy one clock.

A 3. *Special-Order*
L O 7 *Decision*

Berino Resorts, Ltd. has approached PRO Technical Printers, Inc. with a special order to produce 300,000 two-page brochures. Most of PRO Technical's work consists of recurring short-run orders. Berino Resorts is offering a one-time order, and PRO Technical does have the capacity to handle the order over a two-month period.

Berino's management has stated that the company would be unwilling to pay more than $48 per 1,000 brochures. The following cost data were assembled by PRO Technical's controller for this decision analysis: direct materials (paper) would be $26.50 per 1,000 brochures. Direct labor costs would be $6.80 per 1,000 brochures. Direct materials (ink) would be $4.40 per 1,000 brochures. Variable production overhead would be $6.20 per 1,000 brochures. Machine maintenance (fixed cost) is $1.00 per direct labor dollar. Other fixed production overhead amounts to $2.40 per direct labor dollar. Variable packing costs would be $4.30 per 1,000 brochures. Also, the share of general and administrative expenses (fixed costs) to be allocated would be $5.25 per direct labor dollar.

REQUIRED

1. Prepare an analysis for PRO Technical's management to use in deciding whether to accept or reject Berino Resort's offer. What decision should be made?
2. What is the lowest possible price PRO Technical can charge per thousand and still make a $6,000 profit on the order?

A 4. *Sales Mix Decision*
L O 7

Management at Morehart Chemical Company is evaluating its product mix in an attempt to maximize profits. For the past two years, Morehart has produced four products, and all have a large market in which to expand market share. Cindi Heinz, Morehart's controller, has gathered data from current operations and wants you to analyze it for her. Sales and operating data are shown on the next page.

	Product AZ1	Product BY7	Product CX5	Product DW9
Variable production costs	$ 71,000	$ 91,000	$ 91,920	$ 97,440
Variable selling costs	$ 10,200	$ 5,400	$ 12,480	$ 30,160
Fixed production costs	$ 20,400	$ 21,600	$ 29,120	$ 18,480
Fixed administrative costs	$ 3,400	$ 5,400	$ 6,240	$ 10,080
Total sales	$122,000	$136,000	$156,400	$161,200
Units produced and sold	85,000	45,000	26,000	14,000
Machine hours used*	17,000	18,000	20,800	16,800

*Morehart's scarce resource, machine hours, is operating at full capacity.

REQUIRED

1. Compute the machine hours needed to produce one unit of each product.
2. Determine the contribution margin per machine hour for each product.
3. Which product line(s) should be targeted for market share expansion?

A 5. *Analysis to Eliminate*
L O 7 *an Unprofitable*
Segment

Wright Sporting Goods, Inc. is a nationwide distributor of sporting equipment. The home office is located in Las Vegas, Nevada, and four branch distributorships are in Tuba City, Alabama; Cherry Valley, Illinois; Orange, California; and Bozeman, Montana. Operating results for 19x9 (all amounts in the summary are in thousands of dollars) are as follows:

Wright Sporting Goods, Inc.
Segment Profit and Loss Summary
For the Year Ended December 31, 19x9

	Tuba City Branch	Cherry Valley Branch	Orange Branch	Bozeman Branch	Total Company
Sales	$6,008	$6,712	$6,473	$8,059	$27,252
Less variable costs					
Purchases	$3,471	$4,119	$3,970	$5,246	$16,806
Wages and salaries	694	702	687	841	2,924
Sales commissions	535	610	519	881	2,545
Selling expenses	96	102	79	127	404
Total variable costs	$4,796	$5,533	$5,255	$7,095	$22,679
Contribution margin	$1,212	$1,179	$1,218	$ 964	$ 4,573
Less traceable fixed costs	972	1,099	808	1,059	3,938
Branch margin	$ 240	$ 80	$ 410	($ 95)	$ 635
Less nontraceable joint costs					325
Income before income taxes					$ 310

The corporate president, Mr. Hegel, is upset with overall corporate operating results, particularly those of the Bozeman branch. He has requested the controller to work up a complete profitability analysis of the four branch operations and to study the possibility of closing the Bozeman branch. The controller needed the following additional information before the analysis could be completed.

1. Shipping costs were 20 percent of the cost of goods purchased by the Bozeman branch.
2. Of the fixed costs traceable to the branch operations, the following were avoidable.

Tuba City	$782,000	Orange	$648,000
Cherry Valley	$989,000	Bozeman	$849,000

3. An analysis of sales revealed the following:

	Average Growth, Last Five Years	Growth, 19x9	Future Average Growth Rate
Tuba City	8%	7%	5%
Cherry Valley	7	5	6
Orange	10	13	8
Bozeman	22	20	10

REQUIRED

1. Analyze the performance of each branch. (**Hint:** Convert the segment profit and loss summary to a common-size statement and state percentages using three decimal places.
2. Should the corporation eliminate the Bozeman branch?
3. Are there other branches Hegel should be concerned about? Why?
4. List possible causes for the corporation's poor performance.

PROBLEM SET B

B 1.
L O 4, 5

Variable Costing: Contribution Approach to Income Statement

Check Figure: 2a. Income Before Income Taxes, contribution format: $418,555

Interior designers often utilize the deluxe carpet products of Sierra Mills, Inc. The Maricopa blend is the company's top product line. In March 19x8, Sierra produced 187,500 square yards and sold 174,900 square yards of Maricopa blend. Factory operating data for the month included: direct materials used of $1,209,375; direct labor of .5 direct labor hours per square yard at $14.50 per hour; variable factory overhead of $243,750; and fixed factory overhead of $346,875. Other expenses included: variable selling expenses, $166,155; fixed selling expenses, $148,665; and fixed general and administrative expenses, $231,500. Total sales revenue equaled $3,935,250. All production took place in March and there was no work in process at month end. Goods are usually shipped when completed but at the end of March, 12,600 square yards still await shipment.

REQUIRED

1. Compute the unit cost, cost of goods sold for March 19x8, and ending finished goods inventory value, using (a) variable costing, and (b) absorption costing procedures.
2. Prepare the month-end income statement for Sierra Mills, Inc., using (a) the contribution format based on variable costing data, and (b) the conventional format based on absorption costing data.

B 2.
L O 7

Make-or-Buy Decision

Check Figure: 1. Difference in Favor of Buy: $459,200

The Kokopelli Furniture Company of Santa Fe, New Mexico, is famous for its dining room furniture. One full department is engaged in the production of the Cottonwood line, an elegant but affordable dining room set. To date, the company has been manufacturing all pieces of the set, including the six chairs.

Management has just received word that a company in Pueblo, Colorado, is willing to produce the chairs for Kokopelli Furniture Company at a total purchase price of $2,688,000 for the annual demand. Company records show that the following costs have been incurred in the production of the chairs: wood materials, $2,250 per 100 chairs; cloth materials, $850 per 100 chairs; direct labor, 1.2 hours per chair at $14.00 per hour; variable factory overhead, $7.00 per direct labor hour; fixed factory overhead, depreciation, $135,000; and fixed factory overhead, other, $109,400. Fixed factory overhead would continue whether or not the chairs are produced. Assume that idle facilities cannot be used for any other purpose and that annual usage is 56,000 chairs.

REQUIRED

1. Prepare an incremental decision analysis to determine whether the chairs should be made by the company or purchased from the outside supplier in Pueblo.
2. Compute the unit cost to make one chair and to buy one chair.

B 3.
L O 7

Special-Order Decision

Check Figure: 2. Lowest price: $640.17 (rounded)

On March 26, the San Mateo Boat Division of Rio Grande Industries received a special order request for 120 ten-foot aluminum fishing boats. Operating on a fiscal year ending May 31, the division already has orders that will allow them to produce at budget levels for the period. However, extra capacity exists to produce the 120 additional boats.

Terms of the special order call for a selling price of $625 per boat and the customer will pay all shipping costs. No sales personnel were involved in soliciting this order.

The ten-foot fishing boat has the following cost estimates: direct materials, aluminum, two 4' × 8' sheets at $145 per sheet; direct labor, 14 hours at $14.50 per hour; variable factory overhead, $5.75 per direct labor hour; fixed factory overhead, $4.50 per direct labor hour; variable selling expenses, $46.50 per boat; and variable shipping expenses, $57.50 per boat.

REQUIRED

1. Prepare an analysis for management of the San Mateo Boat Division to use in deciding whether to accept or reject the special order. What decision should be made?
2. To make an $8,000 profit on this order, what would be the lowest possible price that the San Mateo Boat Division could charge per boat?

B 4. *Sales Mix Analysis*
L O 7

Check Figure: 2. CK1, Contribution margin per machine hour: $5.50

The vice president of finance for Dolby Machine Tool, Inc. is evaluating the profitability of the company's four product lines. During the current year, the company will operate at full machine-hour capacity. The following production data have been compiled for the vice president's use.

Product	Current Year's Production (Units)	Total Machine Hours Used
FR2	30,000	75,000
BL7	50,000	100,000
SN5	20,000	20,000
CK1	90,000	45,000

Sales and operating cost data are as follows:

	Product FR2	Product BL7	Product SN5	Product CK1
Selling price per unit	$20.00	$25.00	$30.00	$35.00
Unit variable manufacturing cost	8.00	17.00	21.00	29.00
Unit fixed manufacturing cost	4.00	3.00	2.50	2.00
Unit variable selling cost	2.00	2.00	4.50	3.25
Unit fixed administrative cost	3.00	2.00	3.00	1.75

REQUIRED

1. Compute the machine hours needed to produce one unit of each product type.
2. Determine the contribution margin per machine hour of each product type.
3. Which product line(s) should be pushed by the company's sales force? Why?

B 5. *Analysis to Eliminate*
L O 7 *an Unprofitable Product*

Check Figure: 1. Short-run contribution, Jones book: $22,050

Seven years ago, Wright & Smith Publishing Company produced its first book. Since then, the company has added four more books to its product list. Management is considering proposals for three more new books, but editorial capacity limits the company to producing only seven books. Before deciding which of the proposed books to publish, management wants you to evaluate the performance of its present book list. The revenue and cost data for the most recent year (each book is identified by the author) are given on the next page.

Projected data for the proposed new books are Book J, sales, $450,000, contribution margin, $45,000; Book K, sales, $725,000, contribution margin, $25,200; and Book L, sales, $913,200, contribution margin, $115,500.

REQUIRED

1. Analyze the performance of the five books currently being published.
2. Should the company eliminate any of its present products? If so, which one(s)?
3. Identify the new books you would use to replace those eliminated. Justify your answer. (**Hint:** Consider contribution margin as a percentage of sales on all books.)

Wright & Smith Publishing Company
Product Profit and Loss Summary
For the Year Ended December 31, 19x5

	Jones	Lee	Samson	Byrd	Logan	Company Totals
Sales	$813,800	$782,000	$634,200	$944,100	$707,000	$3,881,100
Less variable costs						
Materials and binding	$325,520	$312,800	$190,260	$283,230	$212,100	$1,323,910
Editorial services	71,380	88,200	73,420	57,205	80,700	370,905
Author royalties	130,208	125,120	101,472	151,056	113,120	620,976
Sales commissions	162,760	156,400	95,130	141,615	141,400	697,305
Other selling costs	50,682	44,740	21,708	18,334	60,700	196,164
Total variable costs	$740,550	$727,260	$481,990	$651,440	$608,020	$3,209,260
Contribution margin	$ 73,250	$ 54,740	$152,210	$292,660	$ 98,980	$ 671,840
Less traceable fixed costs	97,250	81,240	89,610	100,460	82,680	451,240
Product margin	($ 24,000)	($ 26,500)	$ 62,600	$192,200	$ 16,300	$ 220,600
Less nontraceable joint fixed costs						82,400
Income before income taxes						$ 138,200
Avoidable fixed costs included in traceable fixed costs above	$ 51,200	$ 55,100	$ 49,400	$ 69,100	$ 58,800	$ 283,600

MANAGERIAL REPORTING AND ANALYSIS CASES

Interpreting Management Reports

MRA 1. *Special Order*
L O 7 *Decision*

Check Figure: 1. Contribution margin, Order 1: $543,750

Roscoe Can Opener Company is a subsidiary of Boedigheimer Appliances, Inc. The can opener Roscoe produces is in strong demand. Sales during the present year, 19x8, are expected to hit the 1,000,000 mark. Full plant capacity is 1,150,000 units, but the 1,000,000-unit mark was considered normal capacity for the current year. The unit price and cost breakdown shown on the next page is applicable in 19x8.

During November, the company received three special-order requests from large chain-store companies. These orders are not part of the budgeted 1,000,000-unit sales for 19x8, but company officials think that sufficient capacity exists for one order to be accepted. Orders received and their terms are:

Order 1: 75,000 can openers @ $20.00/unit, deluxe packaging
Order 2: 90,000 can openers @ $18.00/unit, plain packaging
Order 3: 125,000 can openers @ $15.75/unit, bulk packaging

Since these orders were made directly to company officials, no variable selling costs will be incurred.

REQUIRED

1. Analyze the profitability of each of the three special orders.
2. Which special order should be accepted?

	Per Unit
Sales price	$22.50
Less manufacturing costs	
Direct materials	$ 6.00
Direct labor	2.50
Overhead: Variable	3.50
Fixed	1.50
Total manufacturing costs	$13.50
Gross margin	$ 9.00
Less selling and administrative expenses	
Selling: Variable	$ 1.50
Fixed	1.00
Administrative, fixed	1.25
Packaging, variable*	.75
Total selling and administrative expenses	$ 4.50
Income before income taxes	$ 4.50

*Three types of packaging are available: deluxe, $.75/unit; plain, $.50/unit; and bulk pack, $.25/unit.

Formulating Management Reports

MRA 2.
L O 5

Formulating an Income Statement Using the Contribution Format

Carmen Melgoza recently purchased the **Picacho Country Club** in Tucson, Arizona. The club offers swimming, golfing, and tennis activities as well as dining services for its members. Melgoza is unfamiliar with the actual operating activity of these areas. As the controller for the country club's operations, you are requested to formulate a report that reflects how each of these activities or services has contributed to the profitability of the country club for the year ended December 31, 19x9. The information you provide will assist Melgoza in her decision to keep or eliminate one or more of these areas.

REQUIRED

No check figure

1. To help you prepare this report, answer the following questions.
   a. What kinds of information do you need about each area?
   b. Why is this information relevant?
   c. Where would you go to obtain this information (sources)?
   d. When would you want to obtain this information?
2. Prepare a draft of your report omitting the actual numbers. Show only the headings and line items.
3. Assume that Melgoza wants to increase the membership of the country club and will invest a large sum of money to promote membership sales. How would you structure the report differently to address this decision?

International Company

MRA 3.
L O 3

Define and Identify Relevant Information

No check figure

Arthur's Burger N' Fries is a competitor in the fast-food restaurant business. One component of its marketing strategy is to increase growth in sales by expanding its foreign markets. The company uses both financial and nonfinancial quantitative information, as well as qualitative information, upon which to base its decisions to open a restaurant in a foreign market.

Arthur's decided to open a restaurant in Saudi Arabia five years ago. The following information assisted the managers in making that decision.

Financial Quantitative Information

Operating information

Estimated food, labor, and other operating costs (for example, taxes, insurance, utilities, and supplies)

Estimated selling price for each food item

Capital investment information

Cost of land, building, equipment, and furniture

Financing options and amounts

Nonfinancial Quantitative Information

Estimated daily number of customers, hamburgers to be sold, employees to work

High traffic time periods

Income of people living in the area

Ratio of population to number of restaurants in the market area

Traffic counts in front of similar restaurants in the area

Qualitative Information

Government regulations, taxes, duties, tariffs, political involvement in business operations

Property ownership restrictions

Site visibility

Accessibility of store location

Training process for local managers

Hiring process for employees

Local customs and practices

As an owner of five Arthur's franchise restaurants in the Middle East, you received an income statement comparing the net income for each of the five restaurants. You notice that the Saudi Arabia location is operating at a loss (including unallocated fixed costs). You must decide whether or not to close this restaurant.

REQUIRED

Review the information used to make the decision to open the restaurant. Identify the types of information that would also be relevant to decide whether or not to close this restaurant. What period or periods of time should be reviewed in making your decision? What additional information would be relevant in making your decision?

Capital Expenditure Decisions

LEARNING OBJECTIVES

1. Identify the steps in the capital expenditure decision cycle and describe the manager's role in the decision process.

2. State the purpose of the minimum desired rate of return and identify the methods used to arrive at this rate.

3. Identify the types of projected costs and revenues used to evaluate capital expenditure decision alternatives.

4. Evaluate capital expenditure proposals using the (a) accounting rate-of-return method and (b) payback period method.

5. Apply the concept of the time value of money.

6. Evaluate capital expenditure proposals using the net present value method.

7. Analyze capital expenditure decision alternatives that incorporate the effects of income taxes.

8. Rank proposals competing for limited capital expenditure funds.

9. Identify qualitative information designed to improve the capital expenditure decision process in today's globally competitive business environment.

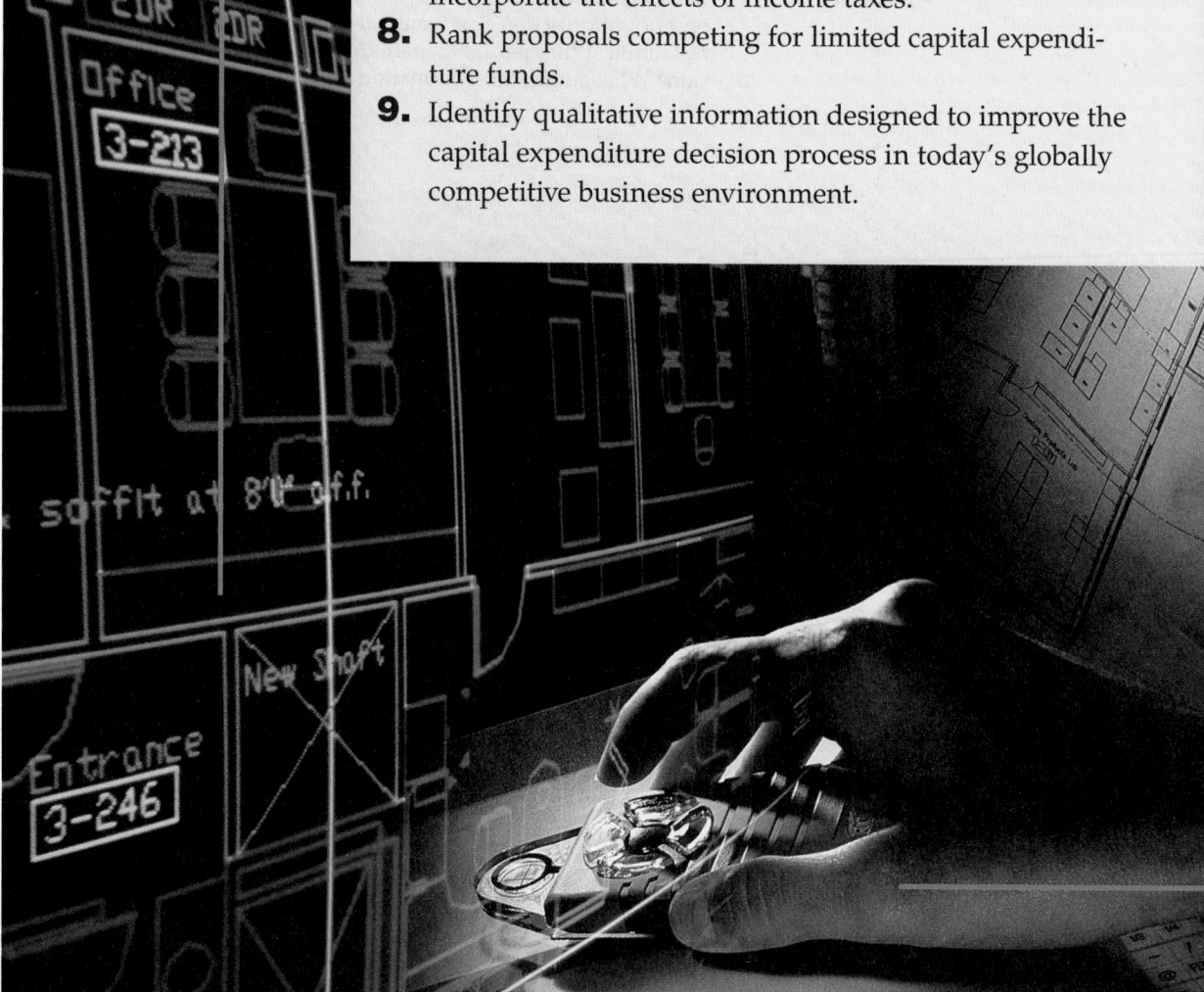

DECISION POINT

United Architects, Inc.[1]

United Architects, Inc., founded in Los Angeles in 1965, is a medium-sized architectural firm with expertise in designing and developing buildings, parking garages, and other commercial structures. Like most service organizations, United Architects is labor intensive, and labor cost is a major component of each project's total cost. The company allocates service overhead to projects based on labor hours.

United Architects must make capital expenditures for its office space and furniture as well as for computer drafting equipment. The company's capital expenditure decision analyses have not changed much in the past two or three decades. United Architects uses standard practices of computing the accounting rate of return or the payback period. In addition, it uses the net present value method to account for the time value of money. But remaining competitive in the world's marketplace means staying on the cutting edge in the use and mastery of the latest technology in the field, and standard capital budgeting decision practices do not always yield optimal results. United Architects recently experienced such a problem when it purchased a new computer-aided design system. The company opted initially to purchase an inexpensive model of computer-aided design and drafting equipment, a stand-alone personal computer system. Standard capital expenditure analyses yielded positive decision numbers because of the equipment's low cost. But competitors purchased top-of-the-line equipment, mainframe systems that had state-of-the-art programming capabilities. These companies began winning major contracts that UAI was also bidding for. Why? Because the potential customers were very impressed with the competitors' computer technology, especially their ability to render three-dimensional structural designs. What change in the capital expenditure decision analysis would support a decision to purchase the more advanced technology?

New technology is expensive and most standard capital expenditure analyses do not identify such projects as good investments because it is difficult to quantify a "competitive edge." Controller Pete Lone at United Architects, Inc. found a solution to this problem. He incorporated a factor

---

1. John Y. Lee, "Investing in New Technology to Stay Competitive," *Management Accounting*, Institute of Management Accountants, June 1991, pp. 45–48.

for business gained by purchasing the equipment into his capital budgeting model. He measured this factor by the estimated increase in the contribution margin that the new piece of equipment would generate. In addition to all of the normal cash inflows and outflows, Lone added a cash inflow representing competitiveness into the net present value model. His management accepted this solution, and UAI again is in the running for major architectural contracts.

The new globally competitive business environment has changed capital expenditure decisions. When evaluating investments that enable a firm to challenge its competition, the question managers must ask is: Do we make this major investment or do we go out of business? Meeting a target rate of return means little when you cannot afford to pay your employees. Because no decision formula should be followed blindly, the health and sometimes the survival of a company depend on people like Pete Lone who adjust existing decision models to incorporate current business conditioning. He made a difference and probably saved his company's future. ⦂⦂⦂⦂⦂

THE CAPITAL EXPENDITURE DECISION PROCESS

OBJECTIVE

1 *Identify the steps in the capital expenditure decision cycle and describe the manager's role in the decision process*

Among the most significant decisions facing management are those called capital expenditure decisions. These are decisions about when and how much to spend on capital facilities. A capital facility could include machinery, systems, or processes; building additions, renovations, or new structures; or entire new divisions or product lines. Thus, decisions about installing new equipment, replacing old equipment, expanding the production area by adding to a building, buying or building a new factory, or acquiring another company are all examples of capital expenditure decisions. Spending on capital assets is expensive. A new factory or production system may cost millions of dollars and require several years to implement. Managers must make capital expenditure decisions carefully to select the alternative that contributes the most to profits.

CAPITAL BUDGETING: A COOPERATIVE VENTURE

The process of making decisions about capital expenditures is called capital budgeting, or *capital expenditure decision analysis*. It consists of identifying the need for a capital facility, analyzing courses of action to meet the need, preparing reports for managers, choosing the best alternative, and rationing capital expenditure funds among competing needs. People in every part of the organization participate in capital budgeting. Financial analysts supply a target cost of capital or desired rate of return and an estimate of how much money can be spent annually on capital facilities. Marketing specialists predict sales trends and new product demands. This identifies operations that need expansion or new equipment. Management personnel at all levels help identify facility needs and often prepare preliminary cost estimates of the desired capital expenditure. These same people implement the project selected and try to keep results within revenue and cost estimates.

The management accountant gathers and organizes the decision information into a workable, readable form. Generally, he or she applies one or more decision evaluation methods to the information gathered for each alternative. The most common of these methods are (1) the accounting rate-of-return method, (2) the payback period method, and (3) the net present value method. Once these methods have been applied, management can make a choice based on the criteria used for the decision. But before we can focus on the evaluation of capital expenditure proposals using each of these methods, we must explore the decision cycle, desired rate-of-return measures, and cost and revenue measures relevant to this decision process.

THE CAPITAL EXPENDITURE DECISION CYCLE

The capital expenditure decision process involves the evaluation of alternate proposals for large capital expenditures, including considerations for financing the projects. Referred to earlier as capital budgeting, capital expenditure decision analyses affect both short-term and long-term planning activities of management. Figure 1 illustrates the time span of the capital expenditure planning process. Most companies have developed a long-term plan, either a five- or ten-year projection of operations. Large capital expenditures should be an integral part of a long-term strategic plan. Anticipated additions or changes to a product line, replacements of equipment, and acquisitions of other companies are examples of items to be included in long-term capital expenditure plans. In addition, capital expenditure needs may arise from changes in current operations.

One of the period budgets in the master budget is a capital expenditure budget. The capital expenditure budget must fit into the planning process

Figure 1. Time Span of Capital Expenditure Planning Process

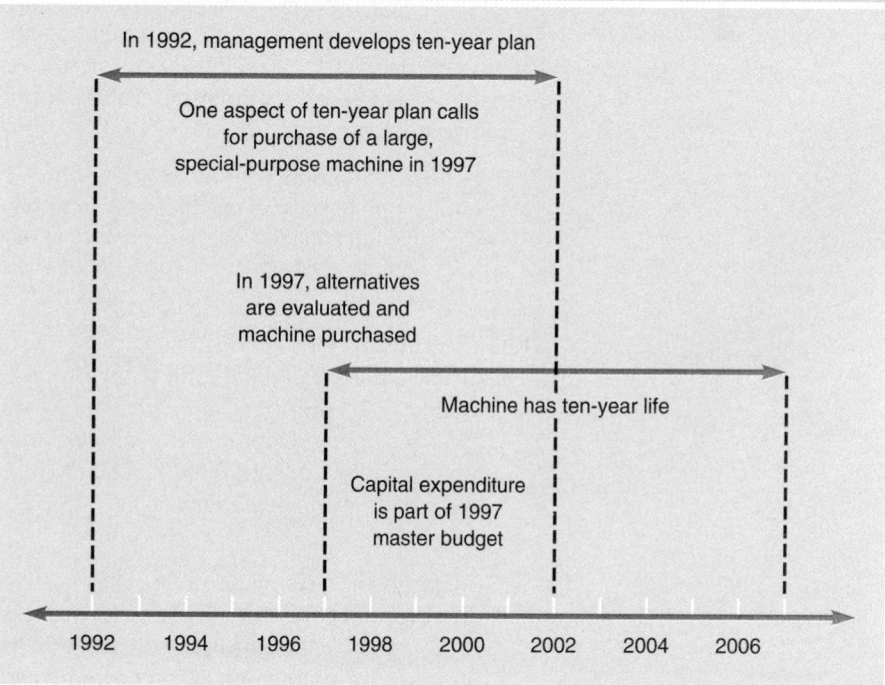

and the capital expenditure decision process. Long-term plans are not very specific; they are expressed in broad, goal-oriented terms. Each annual budget must help accomplish long-term plans. Look again at Figure 1. In 1997, the company plans to purchase a large, special-purpose machine. When the ten-year plan was developed, only a broad statement about a plan to purchase the machine was included. There was nothing in the ten-year plan concerning the cost of the machine or the anticipated operating details and costs. The annual master budget for 1997 contains this detailed information. And it is in 1997 that the capital expenditure decision analysis will occur. So, even though capital expenditure decisions that will affect the company for many years are discussed and estimates of future revenues and expenditures are made, the analysis is for the current period. This point is often confusing and needs to be emphasized here so the remainder of the chapter can be studied in the proper perspective.

Evaluating capital expenditure proposals, deciding on proposals to be authorized, and implementing capital expenditures are long, involved procedures. The management accountant's primary responsibilities in the decision process center on three functions: (1) evaluation of proposals, (2) methods of evaluation, and (3) postcompletion audit. The most important components of the capital expenditure decision cycle, as illustrated in Figure 2, are discussed below.

Environmental Factors   The capital expenditure decision cycle occurs within a defined time period and under constraints imposed by economic policies, conditions, and objectives originating at corporate, industry, and/or national levels. Coordinating short- and long-term capital investment plans within this dynamic environment is the manager's responsibility, and it is vital to profitable operations.

Detection of Capital Facility Needs   Identifying the need for a new capital facility is the starting point of the decision process. Managers identify capital investment opportunities from past sales experience, changes in sources and quality of raw materials, subordinates' suggestions, production bottlenecks caused by obsolete equipment, new production or distribution methods, or customer complaints. In addition, capital facility needs are identified through proposals to

1. Add new products to the product line
2. Expand capacity in existing product lines
3. Reduce production costs of existing products without altering operating levels
4. Automate existing production processes

Request for Capital Expenditure   To facilitate control over capital expenditures, the appropriate manager prepares a formal request for a new capital facility. The proposed request should include a complete description of the facility under review, reasons a new facility is needed, alternate means of satisfying the need, estimated costs and related cost savings for each alternative, and engineering specifications.

Preliminary Analysis of Request   In a large company with a highly developed capital expenditure decision process, information contained in a request for a capital expenditure is often verified before the initial screening of proposals. The management accountant assists the manager in this activity by

Figure 2. The Capital Expenditure Decision Cycle

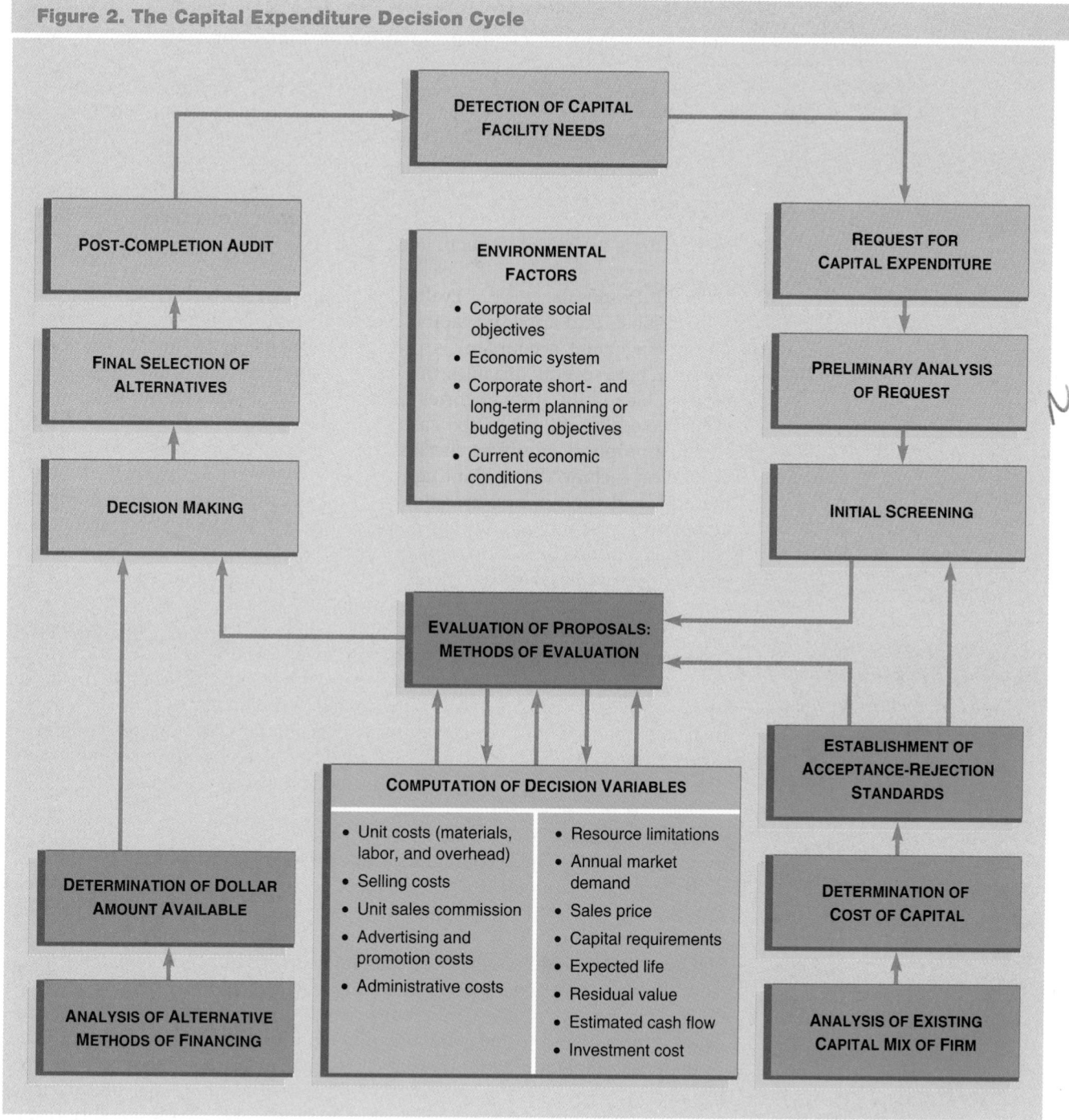

helping to identify undesirable or nonqualifying proposals, computational errors, and deficiencies in request information.

Initial Screening   Initial screening processes are used by companies with several branch plants and a highly developed program for capital expenditures. The objective of initial screening is to ensure that the only proposals going forward for further review are those meeting both company objectives and the minimum desired rate of return established by management.

Establishment of Acceptance-Rejection Standards   When there are many requests for capital expenditures and limited funds for capital investment, a company establishes an acceptance-rejection standard. Such a standard may be expressed as a minimum desired rate of return or as a minimum cash-flow payback period. As shown in Figure 2, acceptance-rejection standards are used in the screening processes to identify projects expected to yield inadequate or marginal returns. This step also identifies proposed projects with high demand and return expectations. Cost of capital information is often used to establish minimum desired rates of return on investment. Developing these rates is discussed in detail later in this chapter.

Evaluation of Proposals   Evaluation of proposals involves verifying decision variables and applying capital expenditure proposal evaluation methods. The management accountant is primarily responsible for these procedures. Figure 2 lists several variables that may be relevant to a capital expenditure request. Generally, the categories of variables in capital facility decisions are (1) expected life, (2) estimated cash flow, and (3) investment cost. Each variable in a proposal should be checked for accuracy. Methods used for proposal evaluation include the accounting rate-of-return method, the payback period method, and the net present value method. Using management's minimum acceptance-rejection standard as a cut-off point, the management accountant evaluates all proposals, using one or more evaluation methods. The approach selected should be used consistently to facilitate project comparison.

Final Selection of Alternatives   After passing through the evaluation process, acceptable capital expenditure requests are given to the appropriate manager for final review. Before deciding which requests to implement, the manager must consider the funds available for capital expenditures. Requests that have made it through screening and evaluation are ranked in order of profitability or payback potential. The final capital expenditure budget is then prepared by allocating funds to the selected proposals.

Postcompletion Audit   The decision process does not end when the facility is operational. The accountant should perform a postcompletion audit for each project to evaluate the accuracy of forecasted results. Any weakness found in the decision process should be corrected to avoid the same problem in future decisions.

    The postcompletion audit is a difficult decision step. To isolate how a decision affects a company's overall operating results requires extensive analysis. Only when an entire new plant is constructed can one isolate and identify relevant information and measure a facility's performance. The main problems in the postcompletion audit are that (1) long-term projects must be evaluated by concentrating on cash flows over the project's life, (2) a particular decision may influence the operations of existing facilities, and (3) profitability resulting from a decision may be difficult to isolate and identify.

Summary   The capital expenditure decision cycle is vital to managing a company. By making correct decisions about capital expenditures, the manager provides for the continued existence of the company. A series of incorrect decisions on capital expenditures could cause a company to fail. The role of the manager in this very involved decision process is to identify and explain capital investment needs; the management accountant's role is to provide information useful to the manager in support of the capital investment decisions. In the remaining parts of this chapter, we look at aspects of a decision that are the responsibility of the management accountant, including the development of a minimum desired rate of return on investment, proposal evaluation methods, and ranking of acceptable proposals.

DESIRED RATE OF RETURN ON INVESTMENT

Choosing the best capital expenditure alternative is not always the approach taken in the decision-making process. Most companies have a set minimum rate of return, below which the expenditure request is automatically refused. If none of the capital expenditure requests is expected to meet the minimum desired rate of return, all requests will be turned down.

Why do companies use such a cutoff point? The idea is that if an expenditure request falls below the minimum rate of return, the funds can be used more profitably in another part of the company. Supporting poor-return proposals will lower the company's profitability later.

Deciding a company's minimum desired rate of return is not a simple task. Each measure that can be used to set a cutoff point has certain advantages. The most common measures used are (1) cost of capital, (2) corporate return on investment, (3) industry's average return on investment, and (4) federal bank interest rates. How to find the cost of capital is described in some detail, and then the use of other measures is briefly explained.

Cost of Capital Measures Of all the measures for desired rates of return listed previously, cost of capital measures is the most widely used and discussed. The goal is to find the cost of financing the company's activities. However, to finance its activities, a company borrows funds and issues preferred and common stock. At the same time the company tries to operate at a profit. Each of these financing alternatives has a different cost rate. And each company uses a different mix of these sources to finance current and future operations.

To set a desired cutoff rate of return, management can use cost of debt, cost of preferred stock, cost of equity capital, or cost of retained earnings. In many cases a company will average these cost results to establish an average cost of capital measure. Sophisticated methods are used to compute these financial return measures.[2] But the purpose here is simply to identify measures used, so we present only a brief description of each type of cost of financing.

Cost of debt is the ratio of loan charges to net proceeds of the loan. The effects of income taxes and the present value of interest charges must be taken into account, but the rate is essentially the ratio of costs to loan proceeds. Cost of preferred stock is the stated dividend rate of the individual stock issue. Tax effects are unimportant in this case because dividends, unlike interest charges, are a nondeductible expense. Cost of equity capital is the rate of return to the investor and is computed by calculating net income as a percentage of invested capital. It is not just the dividend rate to the stockholder because management can raise or lower the dividend rate almost at will. This concept is very complex, but it has sound authoritative financial support.[3] Cost of retained earnings is the opportunity cost, or the dividends given up by the stockholder. Such a cost is linked closely with the cost of equity capital

2. See David F. Scott, Jr., John D. Martin, J. William Petty, and Arthur J. Keown, "Cost of Capital," *Basic Financial Management*, 6th Edition (Englewood Cliffs, N.J.: Prentice-Hall, 1993), Chapter 8, pp. 265–281.

3. Ibid.

just described. The point is that a firm's cost of capital is hard to compute because it is a weighted average of the cost of various financing methods. However, this figure is the best estimate of a minimum desired rate of return.

Weighted average cost of capital is computed by first finding the cost rate for each source or class of capital-raising instrument. The second part of the computation is to figure the percentage of each source of capital to the company's total debt and equity financing. Weighted average cost of capital is the sum of the products of each financing source's percentage multiplied by its cost rate. For example, assume the Gramercy Company's financing structure is as follows:

Cost Rate (Percentage)	Source of Capital	Amount	Capital Mix (Percentage of Each to Total)
10	Debt financing	$150,000	30
8	Preferred stock	50,000	10
12	Common stock	200,000	40
14	Retained earnings	100,000	20
	Totals	$500,000	100

The weighted average cost of capital of 11.4 percent would be computed as follows:

Source of Capital	Cost Rate	×	Ratio of Capital Mix	=	Portion of Weighted Average Cost of Capital
Debt financing	.10		.30		.030
Preferred stock	.08		.10		.008
Common stock	.12		.40		.048
Retained earnings	.14		.20		.028
Weighted average cost of capital					.114

Other Cutoff Measures　　If cost of capital information is unavailable, management can use one of three less accurate but still useful amounts as the minimum desired rate of return. The first is average total corporate return on investment. The reasoning used to support such a measure is that any capital investment that produced a return lower than an amount earned historically by the company would negatively affect future operations. A second method is to use an industry's averages of the cost of capital. Most sizable industry associations supply such information. As a last resort, a company might use the current bank lending rate. But because most companies are both debt and equity financed, this rate seldom reflects an accurate rate of return.

COST AND REVENUE MEASURES USED IN CAPITAL BUDGETING

OBJECTIVE

3 *Identify the types of projected costs and revenues used to evaluate capital expenditure decision alternatives*

When evaluating a proposed capital expenditure, the management accountant must predict how the new asset will perform and how it will benefit the company. Various measures of costs and revenues are used to estimate the benefits to be derived from these projects. In this section we identify these measures and explain their relevance to the capital expenditure decision process. We also reveal measures that are not relevant to capital budgeting decision analysis but that are often incorporated into the decision process in error.

BUSINESS BULLETIN: INTERNATIONAL PRACTICE⁴

Lego Systems AS, the Danish toy company known worldwide for its tiny toy building blocks, is planning to construct a theme park in the United States similar to its Legoland park in Billund, Denmark. Like Legoland, which has a replica of the Statue of Liberty built entirely out of Lego blocks, the U.S. park will feature Lego attractions. Initial plans call for a capital investment of between $100 million and $200 million. The key to the decision is to find a location that will have little or no competition from existing theme parks and yet draw at least 1.5 million people a year. Studies of the U.S. market revealed that the average visitor spends $26 per visit, $14 for admission and $12 for food, merchandise, and games. The estimated average cost per visitor to operate the park is projected to be $20. The $6 margin will not be sufficient to justify the initial capital outlay. So to compete and to justify the capital investment, the company also needs a partner to build shops, restaurants, and hotels around the proposed park. By joining in such a partnership, the company would receive royalties from the revenue of the partner, thereby justifying the capital investment. =====

Net Income and Cash Flow   Each capital expenditure analysis must include a measure of the expected benefit from an investment project. For the accounting rate-of-return method, this measure is net income, calculated in the normal fashion. Increases in net income resulting from the capital expenditure must be determined for each alternative. All other methods of evaluating capital expenditure proposals use projected cash flows. Net cash inflow, the balance of increases in cash receipts over increases in cash payments resulting from the capital expenditure, is used in evaluating capital projects when either the payback period or the net present value method is employed. In some cases, equipment replacement decisions involve alternatives that do not increase current revenue. In these cases, cost savings measure the benefits resulting from the proposed capital investments. Both net cash flow and cost savings can be used as a basis for the evaluation, but you should not confuse one with the other. Each of the alternatives must be measured and evaluated consistently.

Equal Versus Unequal Cash Flows   Projected cash flows may be the same for each year of the asset's life or they may vary from year to year. Unequal cash flows are common and must be analyzed for each year of the asset's life. Proposed projects with equal annual cash flows require less detailed analysis. Evaluations for projects with both equal and unequal cash flows are illustrated and explained later in this chapter.

Book Value of Assets   Book value (also called carrying value) is the undepreciated portion of the original cost of a fixed asset. When evaluating a

4. Joseph Pereira, "Denmark's Lego Blocks Out Plans for U.S. Theme Park," *Wall Street Journal*, Monday, March 25, 1991, p. B1.

decision to replace an asset, the book value of the old asset is irrelevant since it is a past, or historical, cost and will not be altered by the decision. Net proceeds from the asset's sale or disposal are relevant, however, because the proceeds affect cash flows and may differ for each alternative. Gains or losses incurred in an exchange or sale of an old asset are also relevant, but only to the extent of their tax consequences. Gains or losses themselves (the difference between sales price and book value) do not involve cash but they do affect cash paid out in income taxes and are discussed in a later section.

Depreciation Expense Since depreciation is a noncash expense requiring no cash outlay during the period, it is irrelevant to decision analyses based on cash flow. But, because depreciation expense reduces net income and income tax expense, the tax-related cash saving *is* relevant to cash-flow–based evaluations.

Disposal or Salvage Values Proceeds from the sale of an old asset are current cash inflows and are relevant to evaluating capital expenditure decisions. Projected disposal or salvage values of replacement equipment are also relevant because these values represent future cash inflows and usually differ among alternatives. Remember, these salvage values will be received at the end of the asset's estimated life.

CAPITAL EXPENDITURE EVALUATION METHODS

Although many methods are used to evaluate capital expenditure proposals, the most common are (1) the accounting rate-of-return method, (2) the payback period method, and (3) the net present value approach, which is the most common discounted cash flow method.

OBJECTIVE

4a *Evaluate capital expenditure proposals using the accounting rate-of-return method*

ACCOUNTING RATE-OF-RETURN METHOD

The accounting rate-of-return method is a crude but easy way to measure estimated performance of a capital investment. With this method, expected performance is measured using two variables: (1) estimated annual after-tax net income from the project and (2) average investment cost. The basic equation is as follows:

$$\text{Accounting rate of return} = \frac{\text{project's average annual after-tax net income}}{\text{average investment cost}}$$

To compute average annual after-tax net income, use the revenue and expense data prepared for evaluating the project. Average investment in the proposed capital facility is figured as follows:[5]

$$\text{Average investment} = \frac{\text{total investment} + \text{salvage value}}{2}$$

---

5. The procedure of adding salvage value to the numerator may seem illogical. However, a fixed asset is never depreciated below its salvage value. Average investment is computed by determining the midpoint of the depreciable portion of the asset and adding back the salvage value. Another way of stating the above formula is

$$\text{Average investment} = \frac{\text{total investment} - \text{salvage value}}{2} + \text{salvage value}$$

Such a statement reduces to the formula used above.

To demonstrate how this equation is used in a capital expenditure decision, assume the Gordon Company is interested in purchasing a new bottling machine. The company's management will consider only those projects that promise to yield more than a 16 percent return. Estimates for the proposal include revenue increases of $17,900 a year and operating cost increases of $8,500 a year (including depreciation). The cost of the machine is $51,000. Its salvage value is $3,000. The company's income tax rate is 34 percent. Should the company invest in the machine? To answer the question, compute the accounting rate of return as follows:

$$\text{Accounting rate of return} = \frac{(\$17,900 - \$8,500) \times .66}{(\$51,000 + \$3,000) \div 2}$$

$$= \frac{\$6,204}{\$27,000}$$

$$= 22.98\%$$

The projected rate of return is higher than the 16 percent minimum desired rate, so management should think seriously about making the investment.

This method is widely used because it is easy to understand and apply. It does have several disadvantages, however. First, because net income is averaged over the life of the investment, actual net income may vary and produce errors in earnings estimates. Second, the method is unreliable if estimated annual income differs from year to year. Finally, the time value of money is not considered in the computations. Thus, future and present dollars are treated as equal.

CASH FLOW AND THE PAYBACK PERIOD METHOD

OBJECTIVE

4b *Evaluate capital expenditure proposals using the payback period method*

Instead of measuring the rate of return on investments, many managers estimate the cash flow generated by a capital investment. Their goal is to determine the minimum time it will take to recover the initial investment. If two investment alternatives are being studied, management should choose the investment that pays back its initial cost in the shortest time. This period of time is known as the payback period, and the method of evaluation is called the payback period method. The payback period is calculated as follows:

$$\text{Payback period} = \frac{\text{cost of investment}}{\text{annual net cash inflows}}$$

To apply the payback period method to the proposed capital investment of the Gordon Company, determine the net cash flow. To do so, first find and eliminate the effects of all noncash revenue and expense items included in the analysis of net income. In this case, the only noncash expense or revenue is machine depreciation. To calculate this amount, you must know the asset's life and the depreciation method. Suppose the Gordon Company uses the straight-line method of depreciation, and the new bottling machine will have a 10-year estimated service life. Using this information and the facts given earlier, the payback period is computed as follows:

$$\text{Annual depreciation} = \frac{\text{cost} - \text{salvage value}}{10 \text{ (years)}}$$

$$= \frac{\$51,000 - \$3,000}{10}$$

$$= \$4,800 \text{ per year}$$

$$\text{Payback period} = \frac{\text{cost of machine}}{\text{cash revenue} - \text{cash expenses} - \text{taxes}}$$

$$= \frac{\$51,000}{\$17,900 - (\$8,500 - \$4,800) - \$3,196^*}$$

$$= \frac{\$51,000}{\$11,004}$$

$$= 4.6347 \text{ years}$$

*($17,900 − $8,500) × .34

If the company's desired payback period is five years or less, this proposal would be approved.

If a proposed capital expenditure has unequal annual net cash inflows, the payback period is determined by subtracting each annual amount (in chronological order) from the cost of the capital facility. When a zero balance is reached, you have determined the payback period. Often this will occur in the middle of a year. The portion of the final year is computed by dividing the amount needed to reach zero into the entire year's cash inflow.

Like the accounting rate of return, the payback method is widely used because it is easy to compute and understand. However, the disadvantages of this approach far outweigh its advantages. First, the method does not measure profitability. Second, it ignores differences in the present values of cash flows from different periods; thus, it does not adjust cash flows for the time value of money. Finally, the payback method emphasizes the time it takes to recoup the investment rather than the long-run return on the investment.

OBJECTIVE

5 *Apply the concept of the time value of money*

TIME VALUE OF MONEY

Today there are many options for investing capital besides buying fixed assets. Consequently, management expects an asset to yield a reasonable return during its useful life. Capital expenditure decision analysis involves the evaluation of estimates of cash flows for several future time periods. It is unrealistic for cash flows from different periods to have the same values when measured in current dollars, so treating all future cash flows alike ignores the time value of money. Both the accounting rate-of-return and the payback period methods have this disadvantage.

The time value of money implies that cash flows of equal dollar amounts separated by an interval of time have different values. The values differ because of the effect of compound interest. For example, assume that Debbie Shewman was awarded a $20,000 settlement in a lawsuit over automobile damages from an accident. The terms of the settlement dictate that the first payment of $10,000 is to be paid on December 31, 1996. The second $10,000 installment is due on December 31, 2000. What is the current (present) value of the total settlement on December 31, 1996? Assume that Shewman could earn 10 percent interest on her current funds. To compute the present value of the settlement, you must go to Table 3 in the appendix on future value and present value tables. There you will find the multiplier for four years at 10 percent, which is .683. The settlement's present value is computed as:

Present value of first payment on Dec. 31, 1996	$10,000
Present value of second payment to be received on Dec. 31, 2000	
($10,000 × .683)	6,830
Present value of the total settlement	$16,830

If Shewman had the choice of (1) accepting the $20,000 settlement as offered or (2) receiving $16,830 today as total compensation for the lawsuit, she would be indifferent.

As seen, the $10,000 to be received in four years is not worth $10,000 today. If funds can be invested to earn 10 percent interest, then each $1 to be received in four years is worth only $.683 today. To prove the indifference statement above, look at the value of the total settlement to Shewman on December 31, 2000 for each choice. In this analysis, Table 1 in the appendix on future value and present value tables is used because this example deals with future values based on compounding of interest.

(1) Accepting the $20,000 settlement as offered
　　　　December 31, 1996 payment after earning four
　　　　years of interest income @ 10% annual rate
　　　　　　($10,000 × 1.464)　　　　　　　　　　　　　　　$14,640.00
　　　　December 31, 2000 payment　　　　　　　　　　　　 10,000.00
　　　　　　　Total amount at December 31, 2000　　　　　$24,640.00

(2) Receiving $16,830 on December 31, 1996 as total
　　　compensation for the lawsuit
　　　　December 31, 1996 payment after earning
　　　　four years of interest income @ 10% annual
　　　　rate ($16,830 × 1.464)　　　　　　　　　　　　　　$24,639.12*

*Difference due to rounding.

The analysis above was based on single payments received either today or on a future date. Now, assume that Thomas Gregor was just told that he won the lottery. His winnings are $1,000,000, to be paid in $50,000 amounts at the end of each of the next twenty years. If he could choose to receive the value of the winnings today and earn 9 percent interest on his savings, how much should he settle for? Since a series of payments is being dealt with, use Table 4 in the appendix on future value and present value tables to locate the applicable multiplier of 9.129, which represents the discounting of twenty future payments back to the present assuming a 9 percent rate-of-return factor.

Present value of twenty annual future payments
　of $50,000 commencing one year from now
　assuming a 9% interest factor is used
　($50,000 × 9.129)　　　　　　　　　　　　　　　　　　　$456,450

In other words, Gregor would be indifferent if given the choice of (1) receiving $1,000,000 in twenty future annual installments of $50,000 each or (2) receiving $456,450 today. To prove this point, determine the future value of the two alternatives by using data from Table 2 in the appendix on future value and present value tables. Such data are used because this example deals with a series of future payments and the compounding of interest on those payments.

(1) Receiving $1,000,000 in twenty future annual
　　　installments of $50,000 each
　　　　($50,000 × 51.16)　　　　　　　　　　　　　　　$2,558,000.00

(2) Receiving $456,450 today, using Table 1
　　　because you are dealing with a single payment
　　　　($456,450 × 5.604)　　　　　　　　　　　　　　$2,557,945.80*

*Difference due to rounding.

When dealing with the time value of money, use compounding to find the future value of an amount now held. To find the present value of an amount to be received, use discounting. When determining future values, refer to Tables 1 and 2, in the appendix on future value and present value tables. To determine present values of future amounts of money, use Tables 3 and 4 in the appendix on future value and present value tables. Also, remember that Tables 1 and 3 deal with a single payment or amount, whereas Tables 2 and 4 are used for a series of equal annual amounts.

BUSINESS BULLETIN: TECHNOLOGY IN PRACTICE[6]

Starting with a lone machine that is numerically controlled by computer, today's manufacturing companies quickly graduate to flexible manufacturing systems (FMS) and plantwide computer-integrated manufacturing (CIM) environments. To justify the purchase of these very large and expensive systems, new evaluation techniques are required, as explained by the following three statements.

1. CIM projects do not have a finite life; they are ongoing. Parts of the process will be replaced as new technology is developed, but the environment changes with continuous improvement. How do you quantify this long-term change?
2. The success of a CIM environment depends on how the parts of the system integrate and work for the good of the whole organization. This synergism is required but cannot be dictated. How do you quantify the cost of gaining this synergism?
3. Installing a CIM system improves process flexibility, reduces process throughput time, hastens delivery of new products to customers, improves product design and quality, and optimizes customer service. How can these intangibles be reflected in capital expenditure decisions?

These points illustrate the difficulty of evaluating decisions involving new technology. Using only traditional project evaluation methods can lead to incorrect decisions. In the new globally competitive environment, long-term vision is as important as financial statistics when evaluating a proposed capital investment. ▬▬▬

OBJECTIVE

6 *Evaluate capital expenditure proposals using the net present value method*

NET PRESENT VALUE METHOD

Managers expect a capital asset to yield returns for its entire useful life. Capital budgeting techniques that treat cash flows in each period as if they have the same value in current dollars do not properly value the returns from the investment. In other words, capital budgeting techniques like the accounting

6. Joel C. Polakoff, "Computer Integrated Manufacturing: A New Look at Cost Justification," *Journal of Accountancy,* American Institute of Certified Public Accountants, March 1990, pp. 24–29.

rate-of-return method and the payback period method ignore the time value of money.

The net present value method helps overcome the disadvantages of the accounting rate-of-return and payback period methods in evaluating capital investment alternatives. By using the present value tables in the appendix on future value and present value tables, you can discount future cash flows back to the present. This approach to capital investment analysis is called the net present value method. Multipliers used to find the present value of a future cash flow are in the present value tables. Which multipliers to use is determined by connecting the minimum desired rate of return and the life of the asset or length of time for which the amount is being discounted. Each cash inflow and cash outflow to be realized over the life of the asset is discounted back to the present. If the present value of all expected future net cash inflows is greater than the amount of the current investment, the expenditure meets the minimum desired rate of return, and the project should be carried out.

The net present value method is used differently depending on whether annual cash flows are equal or unequal. If all annual net cash flows (inflows less outflows) are equal, the discount factor to be used comes from Table 4 of the appendix on future value and present value tables. This table gives multipliers for the present value of $1 received each period for a given number of periods. One computation will cover the cash flows of all periods involved. If, however, expected cash inflows and outflows differ from one year to the next, each year's cash flow amount must be individually discounted back to the present. Discount factors used in this kind of analysis are found in Table 3 of the appendix on future value and present value tables. Multipliers in this table are used to find the present value of $1 to be received (or paid out) at the end of a given number of periods.

The following example shows the difference in the present value analysis of expenditures with equal and unequal cash flows. Suppose the Major Metal Products Company is deciding which of two stamping machines to buy. The blue machine has equal expected annual net cash inflows and the black machine has unequal annual amounts. Information on the two machines is given in the table below.

	Blue Machine	**Black Machine**
Purchase price: January 1, 19x7	$16,500	$16,500
Salvage value	—	—
Expected life	5 years	5 years
Estimated net cash inflows		
19x7	$5,000	$6,000
19x8	$5,000	$5,500
19x9	$5,000	$5,000
20x0	$5,000	$4,500
20x1	$5,000	$4,000

The company's minimum desired rate of return is 16 percent. Which—if either—of the two alternatives should be chosen?

The evaluation process is shown in Exhibit 1. The analysis of the blue machine is easier to prepare because it generates equal annual cash flows. Present value of net cash inflows for the five-year period for the blue machine is found by first locating the appropriate multiplier in Table 4 of the appendix on future value and present value tables, using the 16 percent minimum desired rate of return and a five-year life. The factor of 3.274 is then multi-

Exhibit 1. Net Present Value Analysis: Equal Versus Unequal Cash Flows

Major Metal Products Company
Capital Expenditure Analysis
19x7

Blue Machine

Present value of cash inflows: ($5,000 × 3.274)	$16,370.00
Less purchase price of machine	16,500.00
Negative net present value	($ 130.00)

Black Machine

Present value of cash inflows:	
19x7 ($6,000 × .862)	$ 5,172.00
19x8 ($5,500 × .743)	4,086.50
19x9 ($5,000 × .641)	3,205.00
20x0 ($4,500 × .552)	2,484.00
20x1 ($4,000 × .476)	1,904.00
Total	$16,851.50
Less purchase price of machine	16,500.00
Positive net present value	$ 351.50

Note: If a piece of equipment has a salvage value at the end of its useful life, the present value of that amount needs to be computed in order to determine the present value of all future net cash inflows.

plied by $5,000, yielding $16,370, the present value of the total cash inflows from the blue machine. Comparing this figure with the $16,500 purchase price results in a negative net present value of $130.

Analysis of the black machine gives a different result. Multipliers for this part of the analysis are found by using the same 16 percent rate. But five multipliers must be used, one for each year of the asset's life. Table 3 in the appendix on future value and present value tables applies here since each annual amount must be discounted back to the present. For the black machine, the $16,851.50 present value of net cash inflows is more than the $16,500.00 purchase price of the machine. Thus, there is a positive net present value of $351.50.

A positive net present value means the return on the asset exceeds the 16 percent minimum desired rate of return. A negative figure means the rate of return is below the minimum cutoff point. In the Major Metal Products case, the right decision would be to purchase the black machine.

Incorporating the time value of money into the evaluation of capital expenditure proposals is the major advantage of the net present value method. This method also measures total cash flows from the investment over its useful life, so total profitability can be brought into the analysis as well. The major disadvantage of the net present value method is that the computations are more difficult than those made for the payback period or the rate-of-return methods.

INCOME TAXES AND BUSINESS DECISIONS

TAX EFFECTS ON CAPITAL EXPENDITURE DECISIONS

OBJECTIVE

7 *Analyze capital expenditure decision alternatives that incorporate the effects of income taxes*

The capital budgeting techniques discussed compare the relative benefits of proposed capital expenditures by measuring the cash receipts and payments for a project. Income taxes alter the amount and timing of cash flows of projects under consideration by for-profit companies. To assess the benefits of a capital project, a company must include the effects of taxes in capital expenditure analyses.

Corporate income tax rates, shown below, range from 15 percent on income under $50,000 to 35 percent on income of more than $18,333,333.

Taxable Income	Tax Rate
$0 to $50,000	15%
$50,000 to $75,000	$7,500 + 25% of amount over $50,000
$75,000 to $100,000	$13,750 + 34% of amount over $75,000
$100,000 to $335,000	$22,250 + 39% of amount over $100,000
$335,000 to $10,000,000	$113,900 + 34% of amount over $335,000
$10,000,000 to $15,000,000	$3,496,650 + 35% of amount over $10,000,000
$15,000,000 to $18,333,333	$5,246,650 + 38% of amount over $15,000,000
Over $18,333,333	$6,513,317 + 35% of amount over $18,333,333

Tax rates change yearly. To demonstrate the effect of taxes on capital expenditure decision analysis, we assume a tax rate of 34 percent on taxable income.

Suppose a project makes the following annual contribution to net income:

Cash revenues	$ 400,000
Cash expenses	(200,000)
Depreciation	(100,000)
Income before income taxes	$ 100,000
Income taxes at 34%	(34,000)
Income after income taxes	$ 66,000

Annual cash flow for this project can be determined by two procedures:

1. Cash flow—receipts and disbursements

Revenues (cash inflow)	$ 400,000
Cash expenses (outflow)	(200,000)
Income taxes (outflow)	(34,000)
Net cash inflow	$ 166,000

2. Cash flow—income adjustment procedure

Income after income taxes	$ 66,000
Add noncash expenses (depreciation)	100,000
Less noncash revenues	—
Net cash inflow	$ 166,000

In both computations the net cash inflow is $166,000, and the total effect of income taxes is to lower the net cash flow by $34,000.

A closer look at income taxes reveals their two-sided effect on cash flows. First, income taxes reduce cash inflows from the receipt of revenues and proceeds from the sale of assets. Second, income taxes have the effect of reducing the amounts of potential expenses (cash outflows). Analyses of capital expenditures must include both effects.

Consider first the relationship between income taxes and cash inflows. Revenues and gains from the sale of equipment increase taxable income and tax payments. When evaluating cash inflows, you must distinguish between a gain on the sale of an asset and the proceeds received from the sale. *Gains* are the amount received over and above the book value of the asset; *proceeds* include the whole sales price and represent the cash inflow. Gains are not cash-flow items, but they do raise tax payments. If a company sells equipment with a book value of $80,000 for $180,000 in cash, it realizes a gain of $100,000. Assuming that this gain is taxable at 34 percent, the cash flow is analyzed as follows:

Proceeds from sale		$180,000
Gain on sale	$100,000	
Corporate tax rate	× .34	
Cash outflow (tax increase)		(34,000)
Net cash inflow		$146,000

The relationship among income taxes, expenses, and cash flow is less obvious. Cash expenses lower net income and result in cash outflows only to the extent that they exceed related tax reductions. This generalization is true for both cash operating expenses and losses on the sale of fixed assets. The following examples show the cash-flow effects of increases in both cash and noncash expenses and of losses on the sale of equipment.

Cash expenses		
Increase in cash operating expenses	$100,000	
Less tax reduction at 34%	34,000	
Net increase in cash outflow	$ 66,000	
Noncash expenses		
Annual depreciation expense	$200,000	
Corporate tax rate	× .34	
Tax reduction = cash savings	$ 68,000	
Loss on the sale of an asset		
Proceeds from sale		$150,000
Loss on sale	$100,000	
Corporate tax rate	× .34	
Reduction of taxes and cash outflow		34,000
Total cash inflow resulting from sale		$184,000

Notice that depreciation expense is not a cash-flow item, but it does provide a cash benefit equal to the amount of the reduction in taxes. Losses on the sale of fixed assets are also not cash-flow items, but they provide a cash benefit by reducing the amount of taxes to be paid in cash. For illustrations of the above ideas, see the Review Problem at the end of this chapter.

Income taxes affect the results of all capital expenditure analyses. Gains from the sale of assets increase taxes; noncash expenditures (depreciation) and losses from the sale of assets decrease taxes. Therefore, the tax impact must be analyzed for all capital investment decision variables.

MINIMIZING TAXES THROUGH PLANNING

Businesses can minimize their tax liability in several ways. Taxation rates can be reduced in some instances by timing transactions so they fall in a given year. A corporation that is nearing a change in tax brackets for the year may elect to delay an income-producing job until after year end to avoid the higher tax rate. Or the timing of certain expenditures may be changed for the same reason. The timing of transactions involving depreciable business assets may also reduce tax liability.

A second way of minimizing tax liability is to take advantage of provisions in the tax law that give preferential treatment to certain investments and spending. The tax law often is used to encourage investment in industries important for national goals. Because these goals change over the years, the tax law has been used to promote everything from emergency war equipment to pollution-control devices. Special credits are also allowed for spending that lowers unemployment or encourages the hiring of such underemployed groups as the handicapped. Therefore, business owners or managers should keep up with current tax laws so that they can maximize their return on investment.

RANKING CAPITAL EXPENDITURE PROPOSALS

OBJECTIVE

8 *Rank proposals competing for limited capital expenditure funds*

Generally, a company's requests for capital funds exceed the amount of dollars available for capital expenditures. Even after proposals have been evaluated and selected under minimum desired acceptance-rejection standards, there are normally too many to fund adequately. At that point the proposals must be ranked according to their rates of return or profitability. A second selection process is then imposed.

Assume that five acceptable proposals are competing for the same limited capital expenditure funds. Brooklyn Enterprises has $4,500,000 to spend this year for capital improvements. It currently uses an 18 percent minimum desired rate of return. The following proposals are under review.

Project	Rate of Return (Percentage)	Capital Expenditure
A	32	$1,460,000
B	30	1,890,000
C	28	460,000
D	24	840,000
E	22	580,000
Total		$5,230,000

How would you go about selecting the capital expenditure proposals to be implemented for the year? Projects A, B, and C are obvious contenders, and their combined dollar needs total $3,810,000. There are $690,000 in capital funds remaining. Project D should be examined to see if it can be implemented for $150,000 less. If not, then Project E should be selected. The selection of projects A, B, C, and E means there will be $110,000 in uncommitted capital expenditure funds for the year.

DECISION POINT

Monsanto Chemical Company[7]

The Fibers Division of the Monsanto Chemical Company produces its products using a continuous flow process. The division's main products are nylon yarn for tires and carpeting, fine denier for hosiery, nonwoven fibers for filters, and artificial turf products. In the mid-1980s, the company experienced a significant increase in competition. Management decided that it needed to decrease product throughput time (the time it takes to produce a completed product) to reduce labor costs and meet the prices of the competition. Automating the production process seemed to be the answer, and management focused on the idea of purchasing a computer-integrated manufacturing (CIM) system. Top-level management required that the capital expenditure be justified by showing how much the new system would increase the company's overall competitive advantage and overall profits. The controller's group launched an analysis of product unit cost, anticipating that a savings from direct labor cost could be computed and used to justify the purchase.

But the analysis did not yield the expected results. A thorough study of the employee needs with and without the new system revealed that the CIM system would only eliminate some of the direct labor cost. Although the direct labor savings may have been adequate to justify the purchase, further studies were conducted and the controller's group identified several additional areas of savings resulting from the installation of the system. The projected cost savings exceeded management's expectations and the system was purchased. What kinds of cost-savings-related areas were found that helped justify the purchase decision?

The analysis revealed that the new CIM system would provide a far superior flow of information between various activities of the division. As a result, significant cost savings were experienced from reduced scrap and waste, lower inventory levels, an increase in the quality of products, and lower indirect labor costs. All of these factors increased the division's ability to compete in the new global market place and led to the positive decision. ⁞⁞⁞⁞⁞

CAPITAL EXPENDITURE DECISIONS IN A GLOBALLY COMPETITIVE BUSINESS ENVIRONMENT

In the capital expenditure evaluation methods described earlier in this chapter, the objective underlying the decision was to either meet or surpass a stated target rate of return on the investment or to meet or surpass a stated period of time needed to recoup the initial investment. The only factors used in the decision were those that could be quantified and used in the evaluation

7. Raymond C. Cole, Jr., and H. Lee Hales, *CIM Justification in the Process Industry: A Case Study* (Montvale, N.J.: Institute of Management Accountants, 1991).

OBJECTIVE

> **9** *Identify qualitative information designed to improve the capital expenditure decision process in today's globally competitive business environment*

process. Companies have begun to question the reliability of these traditional capital expenditure evaluation methods. Managers have turned down proposed investments in new technology and computer-integrated manufacturing systems because the projects could not meet the desired minimum cutoff rates of return. Yet, without this new technology, these same companies will become less competitive because other companies in their industry are able to make the investment.

The objective of a capital expenditure decision process has changed along with the technological changes in equipment. Companies now want to identify an optimal set of activities and resources that allow them to meet their strategic goals. They are striving to eliminate waste and to inject an atmosphere of continuous improvement within their organizations. As revealed in the United Architects, Inc. Decision Point at the beginning of this chapter, buying a less expensive model because it meets an estimated rate of return on investment is not always the correct decision. The managers at United Architects found out the hard way that pleasing the customer is far more important than just meeting a target rate of return. Satisfying a customer means producing a quality product or service in a timely fashion and meeting projected delivery dates. To do this, a company must establish a high level of quality throughout the organization, be flexible so as to meet customer demand, and minimize throughput times. Yet when it comes to making capital expenditure decisions, how does one quantify decision elements such as quality, flexibility, and throughput time?

As illustrated in the Monsanto Chemical Company Decision Point, capital investment decision analysis in today's globally competitive business environment should include both quantitative and qualitative factors. Each capital expenditure should be evaluated by its ability to meet the organization's total set of objectives, not just one objective such as the project's estimated rate of return on investment. Each decision should include an analysis of the proposed project's contributions to an increase in product or process quality, a decrease in the waste of resources or time, a decrease in production and delivery time, and an increase in customer satisfaction. Although more difficult, making capital expenditure decisions that include qualitative factors as well as quantitative factors will help ensure the company's competitive market position.

CHAPTER REVIEW

REVIEW OF LEARNING OBJECTIVES

1. **Identify the steps in the capital expenditure decision cycle and describe the manager's role in the decision process.** Capital expenditure decisions are concerned with when and how much to spend on a company's capital facilities. The capital expenditure decision-making process, often referred to as capital budgeting, consists of identifying the need for a facility, analyzing courses of action to meet that need, preparing reports for management, choosing the best alternative, and rationing capital expenditure funds among competing resource needs.

The capital expenditure decision cycle begins with detecting a facility's need. A proposal or request is then prepared and analyzed before being subjected to one or two screening processes, depending on the size of the business involved. Using various evaluation methods and a minimum desired rate of return, the proposal is determined to be either acceptable or unacceptable. If acceptable, the proposal is ranked with all other acceptable proposals. Total dollars available for capital investment are used to determine which of the ranked proposals to authorize and implement. The final step is a postcompletion audit to determine the accuracy of the forecasted data used in the decision cycle and to find out if some of the projections need corrective action.

The role of the manager in this decision process is to identify and explain capital investment needs; the management accountant's role is to provide information useful to managers in support of capital investment decisions.

2. **State the purpose of the minimum desired rate of return and identify the methods used to arrive at this rate.** The minimum desired rate of return acts as a screening mechanism by eliminating from further consideration capital expenditure requests with anticipated low returns. By using such an approach to decision making, many unprofitable requests are turned away or discouraged without a great deal of wasted executive time. The most common measures used to compute minimum desired rates of return include (1) cost of capital, (2) corporate return on investment, (3) industry's average return on investment, and (4) federal and bank interest rates. The weighted average cost of capital and average return on investment are the most widely used measures.

3. **Identify the types of projected costs and revenues used to evaluate capital expenditure decision alternatives.** The accounting rate-of-return method requires measures of net income. Other methods of evaluating capital expenditures evaluate net cash inflow or cash savings. The analysis process must estimate whether the cash flows are equal in each period or unequal. Book values and depreciation expense of assets awaiting replacement are irrelevant. Net proceeds from the sale of an old asset and estimated salvage value of a new facility represent future cash flows and must be part of the estimated benefit of a project. Gains and losses on the sale of old assets and depreciation expense on replacement equipment change future cash flows because they affect cash payments for income taxes.

4. **Evaluate capital expenditure proposals using the (a) accounting rate-of-return method and (b) payback period method.** When using the accounting rate-of-return method to evaluate two or more capital expenditure proposals, the alternative that yields the highest ratio of net income after taxes to average cost of investment is chosen. When using the payback period method to evaluate a capital expenditure proposal, emphasis is on the shortest time period needed to recoup in cash the original amount of the investment.

5. **Apply the concept of the time value of money.** Time value of money implies that cash flows of equal dollar amounts at different times have different values because of the effect of compound interest. Of the evaluation methods discussed in this chapter, only the net present value method is based on the concept of the time value of money.

6. **Evaluate capital expenditure proposals using the net present value method.** The net present value method of evaluating capital expenditures depends on the time value of money. Present values of future cash flows are computed to see if they are greater than the current cost of the capital expenditure being evaluated.

7. **Analyze capital expenditure decision alternatives that incorporate the effects of income taxes.** Income taxes affect the results of all capital expenditure analyses. Gains on the sale of assets increase taxes. Noncash expenditures (depreciation) and losses from the sale of assets decrease taxes. So, the impact of gains, losses, and noncash expenditures on the cash flows of the project must be examined in light of their tax consequences.

8. **Rank proposals competing for limited capital expenditure funds.** When ranking capital expenditure proposals, acceptable projects are listed in their order of estimated rate of return. They are then authorized in their order of ranking until all capital expenditure funds appropriated for the year have been taken. If funds remain because the selection process was halted by a project too large to be funded, a smaller proposal, lower in priority, may be authorized.

9. **Identify qualitative information designed to improve the capital expenditure decision process in today's globally competitive business environment.** Qualitative information relating a capital investment's impact on product and process quality, production flexibility, customer satisfaction, and the reduction in time needed to complete the production and distribution cycles should be analyzed and incorporated into the capital expenditure decision analysis in addition to the relevant quantitative decision variables.

REVIEW OF CONCEPTS AND TERMINOLOGY

The following concepts and terms were introduced in this chapter.

L O 4 **Accounting rate-of-return method:** A capital investment evaluation method designed to measure the benefit of a potential capital project. It is calculated by dividing the project's average annual after-tax net income by the average cost of the investment.

L O 2 **Average cost of capital:** A minimum desired rate of return on invested capital that is computed by taking an average of the cost of debt, the cost of preferred stock, the cost of equity capital, and the cost of retained earnings.

L O 3 **Book value:** The undepreciated portion of the original cost of a fixed asset.

L O 1 **Capital budgeting:** The process of making decisions about capital expenditures. It includes identifying the need for a capital facility, analyzing different courses of action to meet that need, preparing the reports for management, choosing the best alternative, and rationing capital expenditure funds among the competing capital projects. Also called *capital expenditure decision analysis*.

L O 1 **Capital expenditure decisions:** Management decisions about when and how much to spend on capital facilities for the company.

L O 2 **Cost of debt:** A minimum desired rate of return on invested capital that is computed as the ratio of loan charges to net proceeds of the loan.

L O 2 **Cost of equity capital:** A minimum desired rate of return on invested capital that is computed by calculating net income as a percentage of invested capital.

L O 2 **Cost of preferred stock:** A minimum desired rate of return on invested capital that is the stated dividend rate of the individual preferred stock issues.

L O 2 **Cost of retained earnings:** A minimum desired rate of return on invested capital that is the opportunity cost, or the dividends given up by the common stockholders.

L O 3 **Net cash inflow:** The balance of increases in cash receipts over increases in cash payments resulting from a proposed capital expenditure.

L O 6 **Net present value method:** A capital investment evaluation method based on future cash flows that are discounted back to their present value before being used to support a capital expenditure decision; the net present value of the future cash flows is compared with the amount of the proposed expenditure to determine if the investment should or should not be made.

L O 3 **Noncash expense:** An expense of the period that did not require a cash outlay during the period under review.

L O 4 **Payback period method:** A capital investment evaluation method that bases the decision to invest in capital equipment on the minimum length of time it will take to get back in cash the amount of the initial investment.

L O 5 **Time value of money:** The concept that cash flows of equal dollar amounts that are separated by a time interval have different present values because of the effect of compound interest.

REVIEW PROBLEM

TAX EFFECTS ON A CAPITAL EXPENDITURE DECISION

L O 3, 4, 5, 6, 7 Howard Construction Company specializes in building large shopping centers. The company is considering the purchase of a new earth-moving machine and has gathered the following information.

Purchase price	$600,000
Salvage value	$100,000
Useful life	4 years
Effective tax rate*	34 percent
Depreciation method	Straight-line
Desired before-tax payback period	3 years
Desired after-tax payback period	4 years
Minimum before-tax desired rate of return	15%
Minimum after-tax desired rate of return	9%

*All company operations combined result in a 34 percent tax rate. Because of this, do not use specific tax rates from the tax schedule.

The before-tax cash flow estimates are as follows:

Year	Revenues	Costs	Net Cash Flow
1	$ 500,000	$260,000	$240,000
2	450,000	240,000	210,000
3	400,000	220,000	180,000
4	350,000	200,000	150,000
Totals	$1,700,000	$920,000	$780,000

REQUIRED 1. Using before-tax information, analyze the Howard Construction Company's investment in the new earth-moving machine. In your analysis, use (a) the accounting rate-of-return method, (b) the payback period method, and (c) the net present value method.
2. Repeat **1** using after-tax information.
3. Summarize your findings from **1** and **2**.

ANSWER TO REVIEW PROBLEM

1. Before-tax calculations

The increase in net income is as follows:

Year	Before-Tax Net Cash Flow	Depreciation	Income Before Taxes
1	$240,000	$125,000	$115,000
2	210,000	125,000	85,000
3	180,000	125,000	55,000
4	150,000	125,000	25,000
Totals	$780,000	$500,000	$280,000

1a. (Before-tax) Accounting rate-of-return method

$$\text{Accounting rate of return} = \frac{\text{average annual income before income taxes}}{\text{average investment cost}}$$

$$= \frac{\$280,000 \div 4}{(\$600,000 + \$100,000) \div 2} = \frac{\$70,000}{\$350,000}$$

$$= 20\%$$

1b. (Before-tax) Payback period method

Total cash investment		$600,000
Less cash-flow recovery		
Year 1	$240,000	
Year 2	210,000	
Year 3 (⅚ of $180,000)	150,000	(600,000)
Unrecovered investment		0

Payback period: 2.833 (2⅚) years, or 2 years 10 months

1c. (Before-tax) Net present value method (multipliers are from Table 3 of the appendix on future value and present value tables)

Year	Net Cash Flow	Present-Value Multiplier	Present Value
1	$240,000	.870	$208,800
2	210,000	.756	158,760
3	180,000	.658	118,440
4	150,000	.572	85,800
4	100,000 (salvage)	.572	57,200
Total present value			$629,000
Less cost of original investment			600,000
Positive net present value			$ 29,000

2. After-tax calculations

The increase in net income after taxes is:

Year	Before-Tax Net Cash Flow	Depreciation	Income Before Taxes	Taxes (34%)	Income After Taxes
1	$240,000	$125,000	$115,000	$39,100	$ 75,900
2	210,000	125,000	85,000	28,900	56,100
3	180,000	125,000	55,000	18,700	36,300
4	150,000	125,000	25,000	8,500	16,500
Totals	$780,000	$500,000	$280,000	$95,200	$184,800

The after-tax cash flow is as follows:

Year	Net Cash Flow Before Taxes	Taxes	Net Cash Flow After Taxes
1	$240,000	$39,100	$200,900
2	210,000	28,900	181,100
3	180,000	18,700	161,300
4	150,000	8,500	141,500
Totals	$780,000	$95,200	$684,800

2a. (After-tax) Accounting rate-of-return method

$$\text{Accounting rate of return} = \frac{\text{average annual after-tax net income}}{\text{average investment cost}}$$

$$= \frac{\$184,800 \div 4}{(\$600,000 + \$100,000) \div 2} = \frac{\$46,200}{\$350,000}$$

$$= 13.2\%$$

2b. (After-tax) Payback period method

Total cash investment		$600,000
Less cash-flow recovery		
Year 1	$200,900	
Year 2	181,100	
Year 3	161,300	
Year 4 (40.1% of $141,500)	56,700	(600,000)
Unrecovered investment		0

Payback period: 3.401 years

2c. (After-tax) Net present value method (multipliers are from Table 3 of the appendix on future value and present value tables)

Year	Net Cash Inflow After Taxes	Present-Value Multiplier	Present Value
1	$200,900	.917	$184,225
2	181,100	.842	152,486
3	161,300	.772	124,524
4	141,500	.708	100,182
4	100,000 (salvage)	.708	70,800
Total present value			$632,217
Less cost of original investment			600,000
Positive net present value			$ 32,217

3. Howard Construction Company: Summary of Decision Analysis

	Before-Tax		After-Tax	
	Desired	Predicted	Desired	Predicted
Accounting rate of return	15%	20%	9%	13.2%
Payback period	3 years	2.833 years	4 years	3.401 years
Net present value	—	$29,000	—	$32,217

Based on the calculations in **1** and **2,** Howard Construction Company's proposed investment in the earth-moving machine meets all company criteria for such investments. Given these results, the company should invest in the machine.

CHAPTER ASSIGNMENTS

QUESTIONS

1. What is a capital expenditure? Give examples of some types of capital expenditures.
2. Define *capital budgeting*.
3. Discuss the interrelationship of the following steps in the capital expenditure decision cycle:
   a. Determination of dollar amount available
   b. Final selection of alternatives
   c. Final evaluation of proposals
4. What are some difficulties encountered in trying to implement the postcompletion audit step in the capital expenditure decision cycle?
5. Describe some approaches used by companies in arriving at a minimum desired rate of return for their acceptance-rejection standards in capital expenditure decision making.

6. What is the importance of equal versus unequal cash flows in capital expenditure decisions? Are they relevant to the accounting rate-of-return method? The payback period method? The net present value method?

7. What is a crude but easy method for evaluating capital expenditures? List the advantages and disadvantages of this method.

8. What is the formula used for determining payback period? Is this decision-measuring technique accurate? Defend your answer.

9. Distinguish between cost savings and net cash flow.

10. Discuss the statement, "To treat all future income flows alike ignores the time value of money."

11. Explain the relationship of compound interest to determination of present value.

12. What is the objective of using discounted cash flows?

13. "In using discounted cash-flow methods, the book value of an asset is irrelevant, whereas current and future salvage values are relevant." Is this statement valid? Defend your answer.

14. Why is depreciation of the old equipment ignored when evaluating equipment replacement decisions under the net present value method?

15. What is the role of cost of capital when using the net present value method to evaluate capital expenditure proposals?

16. Why is it important to consider income taxes when evaluating a capital expenditure proposal?

17. When selecting capital expenditure proposals for implementation, final ranking of proposals may not follow the order in which they were presented. Why?

18. "Satisfying a customer means producing a quality product or service in a timely fashion and meeting a projected delivery date." What relationship does this statement have with the capital expenditure decision process?

SHORT EXERCISES

SE 1. *Manager's Role*
L O 1 *in Capital Expenditure Decisions*

No check figure

Joe Goodman, supervisor of the Drilling Department, has suggested to Christine Atkins, the plant manager, that a new machine costing $185,000 be purchased to improve drilling operations for the plant's newest product line. How should the plant manager proceed with this request?

SE 2. *Minimum Desired*
L O 2 *Rate of Return*

Check Figure: Average Cost of Capital: 10 percent

Gilmore Industries has three sources of funds for its planned $1 million plant expansion: a mortgage loan of $700,000 at 9 percent interest, a bank loan of $250,000 at 12 percent using existing machinery as collateral, and a second trust deed loan from a major stockholder of $50,000 at 14 percent interest. What is Gilmore's average cost of capital for this investment?

SE 3. *Capital Budgeting*
L O 3 *Cost and Revenue Measures*

No check figure

Miles Corp. is analyzing a proposal to purchase a computer-integrated boring mill. The machine will be able to produce an entire product line in a single operation. Projected annual net cash inflow from the machine is $180,000 and projected net income is $120,000. Why is projected net income lower than projected net cash inflow? Identify possible causes for the $60,000 difference.

SE 4. *Capital Expenditure*
L O 4 *Decision: Payback Period Method*

Check Figure: Payback period: 3.478 years

Swanson Communications, Inc. is considering the purchase of a new piece of computerized data transmission equipment. Estimated annual net cash inflow for the new equipment is $575,000. The equipment costs $2 million, it has a five-year life, and it will have no salvage value at the end of the five years. The company uses the following capital expenditure decision guidelines: maximum payback period of four years; minimum desired rate of return of 12 percent. Compute the before-tax payback period of the piece of equipment. Should the company purchase it?

SE 5. *Time Value of*
L O 5 *Money*
Check Figure: Present value at 8 percent: $196,360

Your Aunt Martha recently inherited a trust fund from a distant relative. On January 2, the bank managing the trust fund notified Aunt Martha that she has the option of receiving a lump-sum check for $175,500 or leaving the money in the trust fund and receiving an annual year-end check for $20,000 for each of the next twenty years. Aunt Martha likes to earn at least an 8 percent return on her investments. What should Aunt Martha do?

SE 6. *Capital Expenditure*
L O 6 *Decision: Net*
Present Value
Method
Check Figure: Net present value: $72,875

Using the information from Swanson Communications, Inc., in SE 4, compute the before-tax net present value of the piece of equipment. Does this method yield a positive or negative solution to the decision to buy the equipment?

SE 7. *Tax Considerations*
L O 7 *in Capital*
Expenditure
Decisions
No check figure

Which of the following has a direct tax effect on cash flow? Which directly influences the amount of cash flow but has no tax effect on cash flow?

Gain on sale of equipment
Proceeds from sale of equipment
Loss on sale of building

SE 8. *Computing Tax*
L O 3, 7 *Liability and*
Cash Flow
Check Figure: Total tax liability: $24,850

Finlay Company replaced a machine on January 2, 1996. During that year, the machine generated net cash inflows from operations of $63,000 and noncash expenditures (depreciation) of $12,000. The sale of the old machine netted $54,000 in proceeds and involved a $20,000 capital gain. Using a 35 percent tax rate for income and capital gains, compute the company's tax liability and net cash flow for the year.

SE 9. *Ranking Capital*
L O 8 *Expenditure*
Proposals
No check figure

Mahoney Corp. has the following capital expenditure requests pending from its three divisions: Request 1, $60,000, 11 percent projected return; Request 2, $110,000, 14 percent projected return; Request 3, $130,000, 16 percent projected return; Request 4, $160,000, 13 percent projected return; Request 5, $175,000, 12 percent projected return; and Request 6, $230,000, 15 percent projected return. The company's minimum desired rate of return is 10 percent and $700,000 is available for capital investment this year. Which requests will be honored and in what order?

SE 10. *Qualitative Capital*
L O 9 *Expenditure Decision*
Measures
No check figure

Donel Company has just completed a special analysis for the purchase of a flexible manufacturing system for its tractor transmission casing division. The analysis, which was based on the payback period and net present value methods, turned out negative. Donel is trying to increase its market share in a very competitive environment. The production manager strongly believes that the company needs the new system to meet competition. What other factors should be considered before a final decision is made regarding this capital investment?

EXERCISES

E 1. *Capital Expenditure*
L O 1 *Decision Cycle*
No check figure

Christina Maxwell was just promoted to supervisor of building maintenance for the Larson Hills Theatre complex in Okemah, Oklahoma. The complex comprises seventeen buildings. Lakes Entertainment, Inc., Maxwell's employer, uses an integral system for evaluating capital expenditure requests from its twenty-two supervisors. Maxwell has approached you, the corporate controller, for advice on preparing her first proposal. She would also like to become familiar with the entire decision cycle.

1. What advice would you give Maxwell before she prepares her first capital expenditure request proposal?
2. Explain the capital expenditure decision cycle to Maxwell.

E 2. *Minimum Desired*
L O 2 *Rate of Return*
Check Figure: Weighted average cost of capital: 9.85 percent

The controller of Heath Corporation wants to establish a minimum desired rate of return and would like to use a weighted average cost of capital. Current data about the corporation's financing structure are as follows: debt financing, 50 percent; preferred stock, 20 percent; common stock, 20 percent; and retained earnings, 10 percent. After-tax cost of debt is 9½ percent. Dividend rates on the preferred and common stock issues are 7½ and 12 percent, respectively. Cost of retained earnings is 12 percent.
Compute the weighted average cost of capital.

E 3. *Analysis of Relevant*
L O 3 *Information*
Check Figure: 2. Difference: $4,400

Higgins & Co., a scrap-metal company, supplies area steel companies with recycled materials. The company collects scrap metal, sorts and cleans the material, and compresses it into one-ton blocks for easy handling. Increased demand for recycled metals has caused Mr. Higgins to consider purchasing an additional metal-compressing machine. He has narrowed the choice to two models. The company's management accountant has gathered the following information related to each model.

	Model One	Model Two
Purchase price	$100,000	$120,000
Salvage value	12,000	20,000
Annual depreciation*	8,800	10,000
Resulting increases in annual sales	172,000	200,000
Annual operating costs		
Materials	60,000	70,000
Direct labor	40,000	40,000
Operating supplies	3,600	4,000
Indirect labor	24,000	36,000
Insurance and taxes	1,600	2,000
Plant rental	8,000	8,000
Electricity	1,000	1,120
Other overhead	5,000	5,680

*Computed using the straight-line method.

1. Identify the costs and revenues relevant to the decision.
2. Prepare an incremental cash-flow analysis for year 1.

E 4. *Capital Expenditure*
L O 4 *Decision: Accounting*
Rate-of-Return
Method
Check Figure: Accounting rate of
return: 15.22 percent

Sharpstown Corporation manufactures metal hard hats for on-site construction workers. Recently, management has tried to raise productivity to meet the growing demand from the real estate industry. The company is now thinking about a new stamping machine. Management has decided that only capital expenditures that yield a 16 percent return before taxes will be accepted. The following projections for the proposal are given: the new machine will cost $325,000; revenue will increase $98,400 per year; the salvage value of the new machine will be $32,500; and operating cost increases (including depreciation) will be $71,200.

Using the accounting rate-of-return method, decide whether the company should invest in the machine. (Show all computations to support your decision, and ignore income tax effects.)

E 5. *Capital Expenditure*
L O 4 *Decision: Payback*
Period Method
Check Figure: Payback period: 4.746
years

Stereo Sounds, Inc., a manufacturer of stereo speakers, is thinking about adding a new injection molding machine. This machine can produce speaker parts that the company now buys from outsiders. The machine has an estimated useful life of fourteen years and will cost $415,000. Gross cash revenue from the machine will be about $397,500 per year, and related cash expenses should total $265,000. Taxes on income are estimated at $45,050 a year. The payback period should be five years or less.

On the basis of the data given, use the payback period method to determine whether the company should invest in this new machine. Show your computations to support your answer.

E 6. *Using the Present*
L O 6 *Value Tables*
Check Figure: 6. $27,360

For each of the following situations, identify the correct multiplier to use from the tables in the appendix on future value and present value tables. Also, compute the appropriate present value.

1. Annual net cash inflow of $30,000 for five years, discounted at 16%
2. An amount of $25,000 to be received at the end of ten years, discounted at 12%
3. The amount of $21,000 to be received at the end of two years, and $15,000 to be received at the end of years four, five, and six, discounted at 10%
4. Annual net cash inflow of $22,500 for twelve years, discounted at 14%
5. The following five years of cash inflows, discounted at 10%:

Year 1	$25,000	Year 4	40,000
Year 2	20,000	Year 5	50,000
Year 3	30,000		

6. The amount of $60,000 to be received at the beginning of year 7, discounted at 14%

E 7. *Present-Value*
L O 6 *Computations*

Check Figure: 1. Present value,
Machine K: $106,823

Three machines (Machine J, Machine K, and Machine L) are being considered in a replacement decision. All three machines have about the same purchase price and an estimated ten-year life. The company uses a 12 percent minimum desired rate of return as its acceptance-rejection standard. Following are the estimated net cash inflows for each machine.

Year	Machine J	Machine K	Machine L
1	$18,000	$12,000	$17,500
2	20,000	12,000	17,500
3	24,000	14,000	17,500
4	23,000	19,000	17,500
5	22,000	20,000	17,500
6	19,000	22,000	17,500
7	16,000	23,000	17,500
8	14,000	24,000	17,500
9	8,000	25,000	17,500
10	4,000	20,000	17,500
Salvage value	1,000	20,000	10,000

1. Compute the present value of future cash flows for each machine.
2. Which machine should the company purchase, assuming they all involve the same capital expenditure?

E 8. *Capital Expenditure*
L O 6 *Decision: Net*
Present Value
Method

Check Figure: Positive net present value: $3,088

Pierre St. James and Associates wants to buy an automatic extruding machine. This piece of equipment would have a useful life of six years, would cost $219,500, and would increase annual after-tax net cash inflows by $57,250. Assume there is no salvage value at the end of six years. The company's minimum desired rate of return is 14 percent.

Using the net present value method, prepare an analysis to determine whether the company should purchase the machine.

E 9. *Ranking Capital*
L O 8 *Expenditure*
Proposals

No check figure

Managers of the Sheepshead Bay Furniture Company have all capital expenditure proposals for the year, and they are ready to make their final selections. The following proposals and related rate-of-return amounts were all received during the period.

Project	Amount of Investment	Rate of Return (Percentage)
AB	$ 450,000	19
CD	500,000	28
EF	654,000	12
GH	800,000	32
IJ	320,000	23
KL	240,000	18
MN	180,000	16
OP	400,000	26
QR	560,000	14
ST	1,200,000	22
UV	1,600,000	20

Assume the company's minimum desired rate of return is 15 percent and $5,000,000 is available for capital expenditures during the year.

1. List the acceptable capital expenditure proposals in order of profitability.
2. Which proposals will be selected for this year?

E 10. *Capital Investments*
L O 9 *in Computer-*
Integrated
Manufacturing

No check figure

Hurco, Inc. is a manufacturer of computer-controlled milling machines and other automated equipment.[8] Based in Indianapolis, Indiana, the company recently revamped its production facility and invested in a flexible computer-integrated manufacturing (FCIM) system. Investing in FCIM equipment creates a unique set of prob-

8. Thornton Parker and Theodore Lettes, "Is Accounting Standing in the Way of Flexible Computer-Integrated Manufacturing?" *Management Accounting*, Institute of Management Accountants, January 1991, pp. 34–38.

lems involving capital expenditure decisions. These systems, costing millions of dollars, provide the company with high-quality, state-of-the-art production capability and are essential if the company is to remain competitive. Key elements in the FCIM capital expenditure decision process include: quality, life cycle cost, just-in-time operations and customer delivery, and the ability to change from one product to the next rapidly. These are intangible considerations that are not easily quantifiable and, as a result, are virtually ignored by traditional accounting practices. Focusing on the quality element, prepare a one-page paper describing how increased product quality will lead to increased cash flow and profitability for the company. Explain how quality can be included in the net present value approach to capital expenditure decision analysis. Be prepared to share your views with the class.

SKILLS DEVELOPMENT EXERCISES

Conceptual Analysis

SDE 1.
L O 1
Capital Expenditures for Hazardous Waste

No check figure

The **Upjohn Company** is a leading pharmaceutical company that uses thousands of chemicals considered to be hazardous.[9] The Superfund Amendments and Reauthorization Act of 1986 (SARA) requires companies to report their operating environmental discharges, and the Upjohn Company is in compliance. Assume that Chemical XOC, a hazardous material, requires a special building for its storage. In addition, the company must regularly monitor the chemical's condition and report it to government officials. (Some chemicals must be monitored as long as thirty years.) In groups of three or four people, decide how to account for the cost of (1) the special building and (2) tracking the chemical's condition. Should these costs be capitalized or expensed in the period incurred? Can they be traced to specific products for costing purposes or should they be included in factory overhead and divided among all products? Select a spokesperson who will report the group's findings to the class and defend your position.

Ethical Dilemma

SDE 2.
L O 6, 9
Ethics, Capital Expenditure Decisions, and the New Globally Competitive Business Environment

No check figure

Marvin Ditmer is controller of **Belstar Corporation,** a globally competitive producer of standard and custom-designed window units for the housing industry. As part of the corporation's move to become automated, Ditmer was asked to prepare a capital expenditure decision analysis for a robot-guided aluminum extruding and stamping machine. This machine would automate the entire window-casing manufacturing line. He had just returned from a national seminar on the subject of qualitative inputs into the capital expenditure decision process and was anxious to incorporate these new ideas into the decision analysis. In addition to the normal net present value analysis (which produced a significant negative result), Ditmer factored in figures for customer satisfaction, scrap reduction, reduced inventory needs, and quality reputation. With the additional information included, the analysis produced a positive response to the decision question.

When the chief financial officer finished reviewing Ditmer's work, he threw the papers on the floor and said, "What kind of garbage is this? You know it's impossible to quantify such things as customer satisfaction and quality reputation. How do you expect me to go to the board of directors and explain your work? I want you to redo the entire analysis and follow only the traditional approach to net present value. Get it back to me in two hours!"

Write a short paper outlining Marvin's options and the possible consequences of each.

---

9. Gale E. Newell, Jerry G. Kreuze, and Stephen J. Newell, "Accounting for Hazardous Waste," *Management Accounting*, Institute of Management Accountants, May 1990, pp. 58–61.

Research Activity

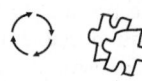
Computers are important in today's business world. Every business can benefit from the capabilities of these electronic devices, which include rapid data processing, timely report generation, automated accounting systems, and the use of specialized software packages for such areas as payroll, accounts receivable, accounts payable, and tax return preparation. Make a trip to a local computer retailer. Inquire about the various types of computers available and identify one that would be useful to a local nursery selling landscape plants and gardening supplies and equipment. Find out the cost of this computer. Make notes of the model name, its special features and capabilities, and its cost. After gathering this data, identify the benefits that the nursery's controller would include in the analysis to justify the purchase of the computer. For each benefit, describe its effect on cash flow and profitability. Be prepared to discuss your findings in class.

Decision-Making Practice

The **Rio Hotel Syndicate** owns four resort hotels in Hawaii. Because the Maui operation (Hotel 1) has been booming over the past five years, management has decided to build an addition to the hotel. This addition will increase the hotel's capacity by 20 percent. A construction company has offered to build the addition at a cost of $29,000,000. The building will have a salvage value of $2,900,000 and will be depreciated on a straight-line basis over its twenty-year life.

Rhonda Dodson, controller, has started an analysis of the net present value for this project. She has calculated the annual before-tax cash flow by subtracting the increase in cash operating expenses from the increase in cash inflows from room rentals. She calculated the income taxes (based on a 34 percent tax rate) on the net income from the room rentals for this addition. Her partially completed schedule follows.

Year	Annual Before-Tax Cash Inflows	Income Taxes
1–7 (each year)	$ 5,100,000	$ 1,290,300
8	5,400,000	1,392,300
9	6,200,000	1,664,300
10–20 (each year)	6,500,000	1,766,300

Capital investment projects must generate a 12 percent after-tax minimum desired rate of return to qualify for consideration.

Calculate the annual after-tax cash flow. Evaluate the proposal using net present value analysis, and make a recommendation to management.

PROBLEM SET A

Capital investment analysis is the main function of Gary Woods, special assistant to the controller of Winkler Manufacturing Company. During the previous twelve-month period, the company's capital mix and respective costs (after tax) were as follows:

	Percentage of Total Financing	Cost of Capital (Percentage)
Debt financing	25	7
Preferred stock	15	9
Common stock	50	12
Retained earnings	10	12

Plans for the current year call for a 10 percent shift in total financing, from common stock financing to debt financing. Also, debt financing is expected to increase to 8 percent, although the cost of the other types of financing will remain the same.

Woods has already analyzed several proposed capital expenditures. He expects the after-tax return on investment for each capital expenditure to be as follows: 9.5 percent on Project A; 8.5 percent on Equipment Item B; 15.0 percent on Product Line C; 6.9 percent on Project D; 10.5 percent on Product Line E; 11.9 percent on Equipment Item F; and 11.0 percent on Project G.

REQUIRED

1. Using the expected adjustments to cost and capital mix, compute the weighted average cost of capital for the current year.
2. Identify the proposed capital expenditures that should be implemented based on the minimum desired rate of return calculated in **1**.

A 2. *Accounting Rate-of-*
LO 4 *Return and Payback Period Methods*

Check Figure: 3. Payback period, Heinrich Machine: 5.435 years

The Lasso Company is expanding its production facilities to include a new product line, a sporty automotive tire rim. Because of a new computerized machine, tire rims can be produced with little labor cost. The controller has advised management about two machines that could do the job. Following are the details about each machine.

	Heinrich Machine	Morgen Machine
Estimated annual increase in revenue	$282,010	$279,250
Purchase price	490,000	510,000
Salvage value	49,000	51,000
Traceable annual costs		
Materials	75,400	60,800
Direct labor	21,200	36,900
Factory overhead (excluding depreciation)	77,200	84,730
Estimated useful life in years	8	12

The company uses the straight-line depreciation method and is in the 34 percent tax bracket. The minimum desired after-tax rate of return is 12 percent. The maximum payback period is six years. (Where necessary, round calculations to the nearest dollar.)

REQUIRED

1. From the information given, compute the change in the company's net income after taxes arising from each alternative.
2. For each machine, compute the projected accounting rate of return.
3. Compute the payback period for each machine.
4. From the information generated in **2** and **3**, which machine should be purchased? Why?

A 3. *Net Present Value*
LO 6, 7 *Method*

Check Figure: 2. Negative net present value: ($31,342)

Baeza and Carpenter, Inc. owns and operates a group of apartment buildings. Management wants to sell one of its older four-family buildings and buy a new structure. The old building, which was purchased twenty-five years ago for $100,000, has a forty-year estimated useful life. The current market value is $70,000. Annual net cash inflows before taxes on the old building are expected to average $16,000 for the remainder of its estimated useful life.

The new building being considered will cost $350,000. It has an estimated useful life of twenty-five years. Net cash inflows before taxes are expected to be $50,000 annually.

Assume that (1) all cash flows occur at year end, (2) the company uses straight-line depreciation, (3) the buildings will have a salvage value equal to 10 percent of their purchase price, (4) the minimum desired rate of return after taxes is 14 percent, and (5) the company is in the 34 percent tax bracket. Round to the nearest dollar.

REQUIRED

1. Compute the net present value of future cash flows from the old building.
2. What will be the net present value of cash flows if the new building is purchased?
3. Should the company keep the old building or purchase the new one?

A 4. *Capital Expenditure*
LO 6, 7 *Decision: Net Present Value Method*

Check Figure: 1. Positive net present value: $9,760

The management of Pluto Plastics has recently been looking at a proposal to purchase a new plastic injection-style molding machine. With the new machine, the company would not have to buy small plastic parts to use in production. The estimated useful life of the machine is fifteen years, and the purchase price, including all set-up charges, is $395,000. Salvage value is estimated to be $39,500. The net addition to the company's cash inflow due to the savings from making the parts is estimated to be $65,000 a year. Pluto Plastic's management has decided on a minimum desired before-tax rate of return of 14 percent.

1. Using the net present value method to evaluate this capital expenditure, determine whether the company should purchase the machine. Support your answer. Ignore taxes.

2. If management had decided on a minimum desired before-tax rate of return of 16 percent, should the machine be purchased? Show all computations to support your answer.

3. Assuming straight-line depreciation, a 34 percent tax rate, and an after-tax minimum desired rate of return of 8 percent, should the company purchase the machine? Show your computations.

A 5.
L O 4, 6, 7
Capital Expenditure Decision: Comprehensive

Check Figure: 1b. Payback period: 3.4 years

The Plains Manufacturing Company, based in Platte, Colorado, is one of the fastest-growing companies in its industry. According to Mr. Lisec, the company's production vice president, keeping up-to-date with technological changes is what makes the company successful.

Mr. Lisec feels that a machine introduced recently would fill an important need of the company. The machine has an estimated useful life of four years, a purchase price of $225,000, and a salvage value of $22,500. The company controller's estimated operating results, using the new machine, follow.

Cash Flow Estimates

Year	Cash Revenues	Cash Expenses	Net Cash Inflow
1	$305,000	$250,000	$55,000
2	315,000	250,000	65,000
3	325,000	250,000	75,000
4	325,000	250,000	75,000

The company uses straight-line depreciation for all its machinery. Mr. Lisec uses a 12 percent minimum desired rate of return and a three-year payback period for capital expenditure evaluation purposes (before-tax decision guidelines).

1. Ignoring income taxes, analyze the data on the machine and decide if the company should purchase it. Use the following evaluation approaches in your analysis: (a) the accounting rate-of-return method, (b) the payback method, and (c) the net present value method.

2. Rework **1**, assuming a 34 percent tax rate, after-tax guidelines of an 8 percent minimum desired rate of return, and a 3.5-year payback period. Does the decision change when after-tax information is used?

PROBLEM SET B

B 1.
L O 2, 8
Minimum Desired Rate of Return

Check Figure: Weighted average cost of capital: 10.9 percent

Lillian Woon, controller of the Bundrant Corporation, is developing her company's minimum desired rate of return for the year. This measure will be used as an acceptance-rejection standard in capital expenditure decision analyses during the coming year. As in the past, this rate will be based on the company's weighted average cost of capital. Capital mix and respective costs (after tax) for the previous twelve months were as follows:

	Percentage of Total Financing	Cost of Capital (Percentage)
Debt financing	30	9
Preferred stock	10	11
Common stock	40	10
Retained earnings	20	12

The company will soon convert one-third of its debt financing into common stock, reducing debt financing to 20 percent of total financing and increasing common stock to 50 percent of total financing. Changes in the cost of capital are anticipated only in debt financing, where the rate is expected to increase to 12 percent.

Several capital expenditure proposals have been submitted for consideration for the current year. Those projects and their projected rates of return are as follows: Project A, 13 percent; Project B, 10 percent; Capital Equipment C, 12 percent; Project D, 9 percent; Capital Equipment E, 8 percent; and Project F, 14 percent.

1. Using the anticipated adjustments to capital cost and mix, compute the weighted average cost of capital for the current year.
2. Identify the proposed capital expenditures that should be implemented on the basis of the minimum desired rate of return calculated in **1**.

B 2. *Accounting Rate-of-*
L O 4 *Return and Payback*
Period Methods
Check Figure: 3. Payback period, Bailey Machine: 4.348 years

Cicero Corporation wants to buy a new rubber-stamping machine. The machine will provide the company with a new product line: pressed rubber food trays for kitchens. Two machines are being considered by Cicero Corporation; the data applicable to each machine are as follows:

	Bailey Machine	**Metro Machine**
Estimated annual increase in revenue	$470,000	$500,000
Purchase price	280,000	320,000
Salvage value	28,000	32,000
Traceable annual costs		
Materials	181,670	157,500
Direct labor	65,250	92,300
Factory overhead (excluding depreciation)	138,480	149,500
Estimated useful life in years	10	12

Depreciation is computed using the straight-line method net of salvage value. Assume a 34 percent income tax rate. The company's minimum desired after-tax rate of return is 16 percent, and the maximum allowable payback period is 5 years.

1. From the information given, compute how the company's net income after taxes will change by each alternative.
2. For each machine, compute the projected accounting rate of return.
3. Compute the payback period for each machine.
4. From the information generated in **2** and **3**, decide which machine should be purchased. Why?

B 3. *Even Versus Uneven*
L O 6, 7 *Cash Flows*
Check Figure: 2. Positive net present value: $54,980.32

Tarry Entertainment, Ltd. operates a tour and sightseeing business in southern California. Its trademark is the use of trolley buses. Each vehicle has its own identity and is specially made for the company. Jenny, the oldest bus, was purchased fifteen years ago and has five years of its estimated useful life remaining. The company paid $25,000 for Jenny, whose current market value is $15,000. Jenny is expected to generate an average annual net cash inflow of $24,000 before taxes for the remainder of its estimated useful life.

Management wants to replace Jenny with a modern-looking vehicle called Sean. Sean has a purchase price of $140,000 and an estimated useful life of twenty years. Net cash inflows before taxes are projected to be as follows for Sean:

Years	Annual Net Cash Inflows
1–5	$40,000
6–10	45,000
11–20	50,000

Assume that (1) all cash flows occur at year end, (2) the company uses straight-line depreciation, (3) the vehicles' salvage value equals 10 percent of their purchase price, (4) the minimum desired after-tax rate of return is 16 percent, and (5) the company is in the 34 percent income tax bracket.

1. Compute the net present value of the future cash flows from Jenny.
2. What would be the net present value of cash flows if Sean were purchased?
3. Should the company keep Jenny or purchase Sean?

B 4. *Capital Expenditure*
L O 6, 7 *Decision: Net*
Present Value
Method

The Twelfth of Leo is a famous restaurant in the New Orleans French Quarter. "Bouillabaisse Kathryn" is the house specialty. Management is currently considering the purchase of a machine that would prepare all the ingredients, mix them automatically, and cook the dish to the restaurant's specifications. The machine will function for an estimated twelve years, and the purchase price, including installation, is

$246,000. Estimated salvage value is $24,600. This labor-saving device is expected to increase cash flows by an average of $42,000 per year during its estimated useful life. For purposes of capital expenditure decisions, the restaurant uses a 12 percent minimum desired before-tax rate of return.

REQUIRED

1. Using the net present value method to evaluate this capital expenditure, determine whether the company should purchase the machine. Support your answer. Ignore taxes.
2. If management had decided on a minimum desired before-tax rate of return of 14 percent, should the machine be purchased? Show all computations to support your answer.
3. Assuming straight-line depreciation, a 34 percent tax rate, and an after-tax minimum desired rate of return of 7 percent, should the company purchase the machine? Show your computations.

B 5. *Capital Expenditure*
L O 6, 7 *Decision: Net Present Value Method*

Memorial Medical Center provides medical services to communities in southern Idaho. Management has decided to add new equipment for pediatric care. The new equipment will cost $1,750,000 and will have a salvage value of $130,000 at the end of a nine-year life. The company uses straight-line depreciation. The new equipment is expected to generate the following annual cash flows:

Year	Increase in Cash Inflows from Equipment	Increase in Cash Operating Expenses
1–7 (each year)	$5,500,000	$4,600,000
8	6,000,000	5,000,000
9	6,500,000	5,400,000

Capital investment projects must generate a 12 percent after-tax minimum desired rate of return to qualify for consideration. Assume a 34 percent tax rate. Round your answers to the nearest dollar.

REQUIRED

Using net present value analysis, make a recommendation to management.

MANAGERIAL REPORTING AND ANALYSIS CASES

Interpreting Management Reports

MRA 1. *Capital Expenditure*
L O 6, 7 *Analysis*

Automatic teller machines (ATMs) have rapidly become a common element of the banking industry. **Santa Cruz Federal Bank** is planning to replace some old machines and has decided on the York Machine. Ms. Liu, the controller, has prepared the decision analysis shown on the next page. She has recommended the purchase of the machine based on the positive net present value shown in the analysis.

The York Machine has an estimated useful life of five years and an expected salvage value of $35,000. Its purchase price would be $385,000. Two existing ATMs, each having a book value of $25,000, would be sold for a total of $85,000 to a neighboring bank. Annual operating cash inflow is expected to increase in the following manner:

Year 1	$55,000
Year 2	80,000
Year 3	85,000
Year 4	90,000
Year 5	95,000

The bank uses straight-line depreciation. Before-tax minimum desired rate of return is 16 percent, and a 10 percent rate is used for interpreting after-tax data. Assume a 34 percent tax rate for normal operating and capital gains items.

REQUIRED

1. Analyze the work of Ms. Liu. What changes need to be made in her capital expenditure decision analysis?
2. What would be your recommendation to bank management about the York Machine purchase?

Santa Cruz Federal Bank
Capital Expenditure Decision Analysis
Before-Tax Net Present Value Approach
March 2, 19x7

Year	Net Cash Inflow	Present Value Multipliers	Present Value
1	$ 55,000	.909	$ 49,995
2	80,000	.826	66,080
3	85,000	.751	63,835
4	90,000	.683	61,470
5	95,000	.621	58,995
5 (salvage)	35,000	.621	21,735
Total Present Value			$322,110
Initial Investment	$385,000		
Less Proceeds from the Sale of Existing Teller Machines	85,000		
Net Capital Investment			(300,000)
Net Present Value			$ 22,110

Formulating Management Reports

MRA 2.
L O 4, 6, 7

Evaluating a
Capital Expenditure
Proposal

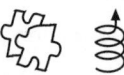

Check Figure: 2a. Accounting rate of
return: 22.39 percent

Quality work and timely output are the benchmarks upon which **River Photo, Inc.** was organized. River Photo is a nationally franchised company with over fifty outlets located in the southern states. Part of the franchise agreement promises a centralized photo developing process with overnight delivery to the outlets.

Because of the tremendous increase in demand for its photo processing, Jules Jacquin, the corporation's president, is considering the purchase of a new, deluxe processing machine by the end of this month. Jacquin wants you to formulate a report showing your evaluation. Your report will be presented to the board of directors' meeting next week.

You have gathered the following information. The new machine will cost $320,000. The machine will function for an estimated five years and should have a $32,000 salvage value. All capital expenditures are expected to produce a 20 percent before-tax minimum rate of return, and the investment should be recouped in three years or less. All fixed assets are depreciated using the straight-line method. The forecasted increases in operating results of the new machine are as follows:

Cash Flow Estimates

Year	Cash Revenues	Cash Expenses
1	$310,000	$210,000
2	325,000	220,000
3	340,000	230,000
4	300,000	210,000
5	260,000	180,000

REQUIRED

1. To help you prepare your report, answer the following questions.
   a. What kinds of information do you need to prepare this report?
   b. Why is this information relevant?
   c. Where would you go to obtain this information (sources)?
   d. When would you want to obtain this information?
2. Ignoring income taxes, analyze the purchase of the machine and decide if the company should purchase it. Use the following evaluation approaches to your analysis:

(a) the accounting rate-of-return method; (b) the payback period method; and (c) the net present value method.

3. Rework **2,** assuming a 34 percent tax rate, after-tax guidelines of a 10 percent minimum desired rate of return, and a four-year payback period. How does the decision change when after-tax information is used?

International Company

MRA 3.
L O 9
Using Qualitative Information in Capital Expenditure Decisions

No check figure

The board of directors of the ***Tsuji Corporation*** met to review a number of proposals involving the use of capital to improve the quality of the products manufactured at Tsuji. A proposal submitted by a production line manager requested the purchase of new computer-integrated machines to replace the older machines in one of the ten production departments at the Tokyo plant. Although the manager had presented quantitative information to support the purchase of the new machines, the board members asked the following important questions related to the proposal:

1. Why do we want to replace the old machines? Have they deteriorated or are they obsolete?
2. Will the new machines require less cycle time?
3. Can we reduce inventory levels or save floor space by replacing the old machines?
4. How expensive is the software used with the new machines?
5. Will we be able to find highly skilled employees to maintain the new machines? Or can we find workers who are trainable? What would be the costs to train these workers? Would the training disrupt the staff by causing relocations?
6. Would the implementation of the machines be delayed because of the time required to recruit new workers?
7. What is the impact of the new machines on the other parts of the manufacturing systems? Would the company lose some of the flexibility in its manufacturing systems if it introduced these new machines?

The board members believe that the qualitative information needed to answer these questions could lead to the rejection of a project that would have been accepted based on the quantitative information.

REQUIRED

1. Identify the questions that can be answered with quantitative information. Give an example of the quantitative information that could be used.
2. Identify the questions that can be answered with qualitative information. Explain why this information could negatively influence the capital expenditure decision that would otherwise be approved because of the quantitative information presented.

PART EIGHT

Management Accounting, Global Competition, and Continuous Improvement

focuses on the just-in-time operating environment. The JIT approach is defined, described, and illustrated. In addition, process automation is explored. Accounting methods used in the JIT environment are discussed and applied.

examines the new cost management systems area, focusing on the activity-based costing approach to cost management. The concept of total quality management is introduced and both financial and nonfinancial measures of quality are analyzed and applied. The chapter closes with a look at performance reporting in the new operating environment.

The Just-in-Time Operating Environment and Automation

1. State the strategies necessary to compete in a globally competitive business environment, define the just-in-time management philosophy, and link JIT to these strategies.

2. Describe how changes in managers' information needs cause management accounting systems to change.

3. Identify the elements of a JIT operating environment.

4. Compare traditional manufacturing with just-in-time operations.

5. Identify the changes in product costing that result when firms adopt a JIT operating environment.

6. Apply process costing procedures to compute JIT product costs.

7. Record transactions involving the Raw in Process Inventory account.

8. Identify the unique aspects of product costing in an automated manufacturing process.

9. Compute a product unit cost using data from a flexible manufacturing system.

DECISION POINT

Grand Rapids Spring & Wire Company[1]

Grand Rapids Spring & Wire Company (GRS&W) opened its doors in 1960 in Grand Rapids, Michigan. The company's 125 employees manufacture compression, extension, and torsion springs and specialty wire products. In 1987, in order to compete in the world marketplace, the company changed from a traditional production process to a total quality management/just-in-time operating environment. Changing procedures was the easy part of the transition; changing employees' attitudes and gaining their support and trust was much more difficult. Yet, without employee involvement and trust, shifting to a new manufacturing environment is virtually impossible. What steps should management take to involve employees in a new operating environment?

GRS&W succeeded in implementing a JIT operating environment because managers broke down autocratic barriers and replaced them with full employee involvement. First, the president adamantly supported the program. Second, employee teams were formed to identify the major constraints to production in the plant. Third, employees were asked to identify and make suggestions about how to eliminate the five biggest problem areas. Fourth, management acted immediately on employees' suggestions. And, finally, employees participated in creating a group bonus plan to reward quality work. The last two steps convinced workers that management had changed and that employees' suggestions mattered. The entire culture of the organization changed over a ten-month period. :::::

THE NEW MANUFACTURING ENVIRONMENT AND JIT OPERATIONS

Companies face more challenges today than they ever have. Once, companies in the United States simply had to produce products or supply services to be assured of a reasonable share of the world market. But over the last twenty years, changes in technology and communications and the growing expertise of foreign companies have forced U.S. companies to reorganize in order to

1. Harper A. Roehm, Donald J. Klein, and Joseph F. Castellano, "Springing to World-Class Manufacturing," *Management Accounting*, Institute of Management Accountants, March 1991, p. 44.

OBJECTIVE

1 *State the strategies necessary to compete in a globally competitive business environment, define the just-in-time management philosophy, and link JIT to these strategies*

compete successfully with foreign firms in the world market. Foreign firms, most notably Asian and European companies, have challenged U.S. firms by producing high-quality products at prices below those charged by many U.S. businesses for comparable goods. To gain a foothold in world markets, foreign companies had to look for ways to streamline their manufacturing processes and to improve productivity. Their strategies were to: (1) eliminate waste of raw materials, labor, space, and production time; (2) reduce resources (inventories) that tied up working capital; and (3) simplify measurement approaches and recordkeeping.

These same strategies have become the objectives of U.S. companies participating in the globally competitive marketplace. These companies have had to revamp their production processes and rethink their basic operating methods. Many companies that relied on traditional production processes are changing to new operating and managing approaches, particularly the just-in-time (JIT) operating environment. Companies that adopt the JIT approach to production must redesign their manufacturing facilities and the events that trigger the production process. Just-in-time (JIT) is an overall operating philosophy of management in which all resources, including raw materials and parts, personnel, and facilities, are used only as needed. The objectives are to improve productivity and reduce waste. JIT is based on the concept of continuous production flow and requires that each part of the production process work in concert with the other components. Direct labor workers in a JIT environment are empowered with expanded responsibilities, contributing to the reduction of waste in labor cost, space, and production time. JIT production methods require virtually no materials inventory because materials and parts are scheduled to arrive from suppliers as needed. JIT can also reduce work in process and finished goods inventories by as much as 90 percent, significantly reducing the level of working capital devoted to inventories.

Redesigning the plant layout—moving machines and processes closer together to reduce throughput time—is the initial step in attaining JIT operating efficiencies. But the Japanese took the process one step further, by automating these new processes. Automated JIT operations moved Japanese industry into world prominence. Japanese manufacturers were able to improve product quality while reducing waste. The result was significant cost savings that were reflected in reduced prices. Furthermore, they increased the productivity of their factories as they approached total capacity. Their success has prompted manufacturers in other countries to change from traditional production methods to these new automated JIT environments. And you will see a continued movement toward automated JIT operations as more and more companies enter world markets.

MANAGING IN A CHANGING ENVIRONMENT

OBJECTIVE

2 *Describe how changes in managers' information needs cause management accounting systems to change*

Businesses that cannot adjust to changing conditions will fail, forced from the marketplace by competition. Companies and their managers must be able to change as conditions dictate. A change involving a new method, technique, or machine that influences the productivity of a process but does not involve a change in the way things are managed is easy to adjust to and implement. Trend analyses of various process measurements and newly introduced technology improvements identify the need for such changes, and managers can be trained to monitor these approaches. A change involving employee empowerment, a new quality work environment, or team management means that managers must change their approach to, and their attitude about, the way they manage.

The existing management accounting system can also contribute to the difficulty managers have in adapting to change. Managers' information needs change whenever there is a change in management philosophy. Yet, in many cases, accountants have tried to use the same reports and analyses provided in traditional management settings to satisfy managers' information needs in the new operating environments.

The management accounting system must change as the information needs of managers change. Two examples will demonstrate the need for such a change. The first example involves managing the production process. The traditional approach to monitoring process efficiency focused on the effective use of direct labor. Direct labor was watched closely, and the management accounting system tracked and reported to managers the *units per direct labor hour* for each worker and department. The goal was to continuously increase units per hour without increasing the resources used in the process. In a JIT environment, the focus is on throughput time, the time it takes to start and complete a product. The JIT manager needs information on *total processing time per unit.* If the accounting system still focuses on units per direct labor hour, however, it is impossible for the JIT manager to monitor throughput time. The change in management philosophy caused a change in the information needs of the manager; the management accounting system should change too.

A second example focuses on inventory management. In a traditional system, the focus was on unit and product cost accuracy. The management accounting system tracked the number of units on hand, and those numbers were verified at least once a year with a physical count. The primary emphasis was on *inventory accuracy* as a means of inventory management. In a JIT environment, the emphasis is on reducing or eliminating inventories. Managers are interested in trends in *inventory size reduction, inventory turnover,* and the *reduction of space needed to store inventory.* Inventory accuracy is much less important when there is very little inventory to account for. Again, the management accounting system must refocus its tracking and reporting approaches if it is to supply relevant information to managers.

As we study the new operating methods that result from global competition and technological advances, keep in mind that with each change in operating philosophy come changes that ripple through the entire organization. Managers have to adjust to changes in managerial approaches. Management accountants have to develop new ways to measure business processes and to assess the productivity and profitability of the company. Top management has to become receptive to ideas from the workers. Everyone in the organization has to concentrate on continuously improving the work environment. As was pointed out in the Grand Rapids Spring & Wire Company Decision Point, changing employee attitudes and gaining their respect and trust is not easy, but by working together managers and workers can make it happen.

IMPLEMENTING A JIT OPERATING ENVIRONMENT

OBJECTIVE

3 *Identify the elements of a JIT operating environment*

Companies that want to adopt a JIT operating environment must reevaluate their current operations and implement new ways of manufacturing products. Underlying these new methods are several basic concepts.

Simple is better.

Product quality is critical.

The work environment must emphasize continuous improvement.

Maintaining inventories wastes resources and may hide bad work.

Any activity or function that does not add value to the product should be eliminated or reduced.

Goods should be produced only when needed.

Workers must be multiskilled and must participate in improving efficiency and product quality.

To implement a JIT operating environment—an environment based on these concepts—a company must develop an operating system that can:[2]

1. Maintain minimum inventory levels.
2. Develop pull-through production planning and scheduling.
3. Purchase materials and produce products as needed, in smaller lot sizes.
4. Perform quick, inexpensive machine setups.
5. Create flexible manufacturing work cells.
6. Develop a multiskilled work force.
7. Maintain high levels of product quality.
8. Enforce a system of effective preventive maintenance.
9. Encourage continuous improvement of the work environment.

This section describes each element and its impact on costs, product quality, and productivity.

MAINTAIN MINIMUM INVENTORY LEVELS

One objective of a JIT operating environment is to maintain minimum inventory levels. In contrast to the traditional environment, in which parts, materials, and supplies are purchased far in advance and stored until the production department needs them, in a JIT environment raw materials and parts are purchased and received only when needed. The system reduces costs by reducing (a) the space needed for inventory storage, (b) the amount of material handling, and (c) the amount of inventory obsolescence. There is less need for inventory control facilities, personnel, and recordkeeping. The amount of work in process inventory waiting to be processed, as well as the amount of working capital tied up in all inventories, is reduced significantly.

DEVELOP PULL-THROUGH PRODUCTION PLANNING AND SCHEDULING

Pull-through production is a system in which a customer order triggers the purchase of materials and the scheduling of production for the required products. In contrast, traditional manufacturing operations use the push-through method, whereby products are manufactured in long production runs and stored in anticipation of customers' orders. With pull-through production, the company purchases materials and parts and schedules work only as needed.

---

2. James B. Dilworth, *Operations Management,* 5th ed. (New York: McGraw-Hill, Inc., 1992), pp. 495–500.

PURCHASE MATERIALS AND PRODUCE PRODUCTS AS NEEDED, IN SMALLER LOT SIZES

With pull-through production, the size of customers' orders determines the size of production runs. Low inventory levels are maintained, but machines have to be set up more frequently, resulting in more work stoppages. Long production runs, previously thought to be more cost-effective, are no longer the rule in a JIT environment; in this environment products are not manufactured to be inventoried.

PERFORM QUICK, INEXPENSIVE MACHINE SETUPS

One reason that traditional production processes relied on long production runs was to reduce the number of machine setups. In the past, managers felt that it was more cost-effective to produce large inventories rather than to produce small lot sizes, which increase the number of machine setups. The success of JIT over the last twenty years has disproved this belief. By placing machines in more efficient locations and scheduling similar products on common machine groupings, setup time can be minimized. In addition, set-up specialists and JIT cell workers become more experienced and more efficient with frequent setups.

CREATE FLEXIBLE MANUFACTURING WORK CELLS

In a traditional factory layout, all similar machines are grouped together, forming functional departments. Products are routed through each department in sequence, so that all necessary operations are completed in order. This process can take several days or weeks, depending on the size and complexity of the job.

By changing the factory layout, the JIT operating environment cuts the manufacturing time of a product from days to hours, or from weeks to days. In many cases, time can be reduced more than 80 percent by rearranging the machinery so that machines that are needed for sequential processing are placed together. This cluster of machinery forms a flexible work cell or island, an autonomous production line that can perform all required operations efficiently and continuously. The flexible work cell handles work on products of similar shape or size, often called a "family" of products. Product families require minimum setup changes as workers move from one job to the next. The more flexible the work cell, the greater the minimization of total production time.

DEVELOP A MULTISKILLED WORK FORCE

In the flexible work cells of a JIT environment, workers may be required to operate several types of machines simultaneously. Therefore, they must learn new operating skills. Many work cells are run by only one operator, who, for example, may have to set up and retool several machines, inspect the products, and even perform routine maintenance on equipment. In addition, workers are encouraged to identify inefficiencies and make recommendations for improvement. In short, a JIT operating environment requires a multi-skilled work force.

Multiskilled workers have been very effective in contributing to the high levels of productivity experienced by Japanese companies. In the United States, union contracts often restrict workers to a single skill. Companies that honor these labor contracts may encounter difficulties in retraining workers to run work cells.

MAINTAIN HIGH LEVELS OF PRODUCT QUALITY

JIT operations produce high-quality products because products are produced from high-quality raw materials and because inspections are made continuously throughout the production process. Unlike traditional manufacturing methods, inspection is viewed as an activity that does not add value to the product, so the JIT environment incorporates inspection into the continuous production operation. JIT machine operators inspect the products as they pass through the production process. An operator who detects a flaw determines its cause. The operator even may help the engineer or quality control person find a way to correct the problem. Once an operator finds a defect, he or she shuts down the production cell and fixes the problem to prevent the production of similarly flawed products. This integrated inspection procedure, combined with quality raw materials, produces high-quality finished goods.

ENFORCE A SYSTEM OF EFFECTIVE PREVENTIVE MAINTENANCE

When a company rearranges its machinery into flexible manufacturing cells, each machine in the work cell becomes an integral part of that cell. If one machine breaks down, the entire cell stops functioning. Because the product cannot be routed easily to another machine while the malfunctioning machine is repaired, continuous JIT operations require an effective system of preventive maintenance. Preventing machine breakdowns is considered more important and more cost-effective than keeping machines running continuously. Machine operators are trained to perform minor repairs on machines as they detect problems. Machines are serviced regularly—much like an automobile—to help guarantee continued operation. The machine operator conducts routine maintenance during periods of machine downtime (caused by a lack of orders). Remember that in a JIT setting, the work cell does not operate unless there is a customer order for the product. Machine operators take advantage of downtime to perform maintenance.

ENCOURAGE CONTINUOUS IMPROVEMENT OF THE WORK ENVIRONMENT

The JIT environment fosters loyalty among workers, who are likely to see themselves as part of a team because they are so deeply involved in the production process. Machine operators must have the skills to run several types of machines, be able to detect defective products, suggest measures to correct problems, and maintain the machinery within their work cell. Japanese companies receive thousands of employee suggestions and implement a high percentage of them. And workers are rewarded for suggestions that improve the process. This kind of environment supports workers' initiative and benefits the company.

To sum up, a JIT operating environment does more than just lower inventory levels or cut production time. JIT operations produce high-quality products efficiently. Every action taken by machine operators, setup people, repair and maintenance personnel, and company management is dedicated to building high-quality products. Every person who participates in the production of the product is working to perform at maximum capacity.

BUSINESS BULLETIN: BUSINESS PRACTICE

Worker empowerment is a key factor in a company's move toward an environment of continuous improvement. Creating an atmosphere that encourages employee creativity is an important step in this process. The Grand Rapids Spring & Wire Company[3] (GRS&W), discussed in the first Decision Point in this chapter, took special steps to make this change happen. In addition to encouraging workers' participation in operating decisions, management implemented special training programs and rewarded employees for making sound suggestions. GRS&W established tuition rebates and an apprenticeship program for tool and die making to encourage continuing education among its work force. The company even created family health programs for weight loss, nutrition, and smoking cessation. All of these programs significantly improved employee involvement and cooperation; on-time shipments improved from 60 percent to 97 percent, the costs associated with achieving product quality decreased from 6 percent to just 2.7 percent of sales, and parts defects were virtually eliminated. But the real proof came at the end of the day. No longer were there lines waiting to punch the time clock; instead, workers stayed to complete their tasks before going home.

TRADITIONAL VERSUS JUST-IN-TIME PRODUCTION

OBJECTIVE

4 *Compare traditional manufacturing with just-in-time operations*

The most effective way to differentiate between traditional and JIT operating environments is to analyze and compare product flow and plant layout. The traditional manufacturing process can be broken down into five parts, or time frames: (1) actual processing time, (2) inspection time, (3) moving time, (4) queue time, and (5) storage time. Traditional manufacturing and assembly operations incorporate dozens of nonvalue-adding activities. JIT operations reduce or eliminate all nonvalue-adding activities from production and product distribution. Of the five time frames listed, JIT operations attempt to eliminate all but the actual processing time because inspection time, moving time, queue time, and storage time are activities that usually do not add value to a product. In this section, the two manufacturing environments are compared.

3. Roehm, Klein, and Castellano, p. 44.

Figure 1. The Plant Layout of a Factory Using Traditional Manufacturing Operations

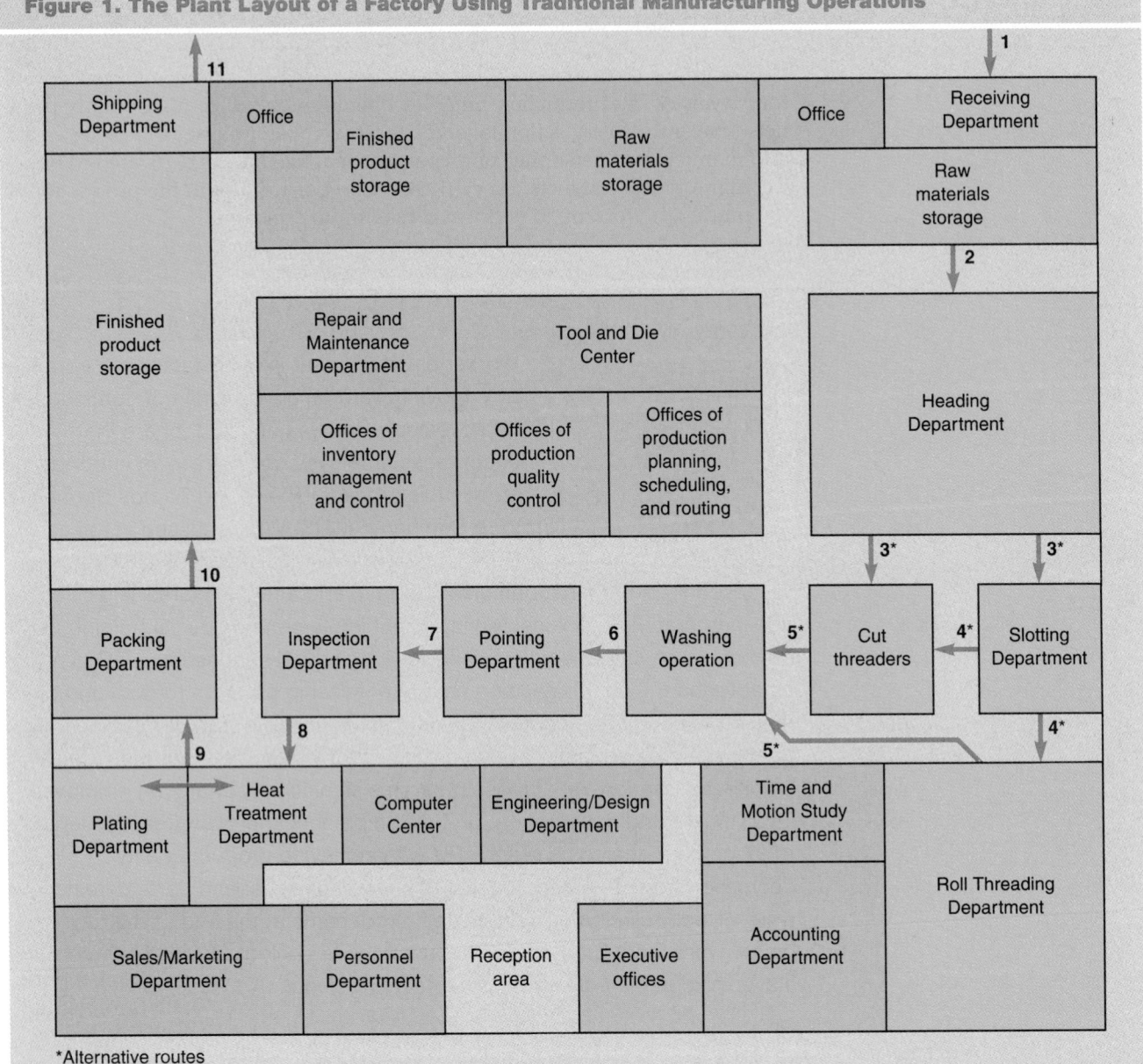

*Alternative routes

The JIT manufacturing environment is examined to see how it redesigns both manufacturing facilities and the work force to eliminate nonvalue-adding activities, enabling JIT operations to produce higher-quality goods more efficiently than the traditional manufacturing process does.

THE TRADITIONAL MANUFACTURING ENVIRONMENT

The traditional manufacturing process will be studied in terms of the production methods of a fastener company. In its factory, the company produces screws, bolts, and specialty fasteners. Figure 1 shows the plant layout, and Figure 2 shows the operations needed to produce a fastener.

Figure 2. Steps in the Production of a Fastener

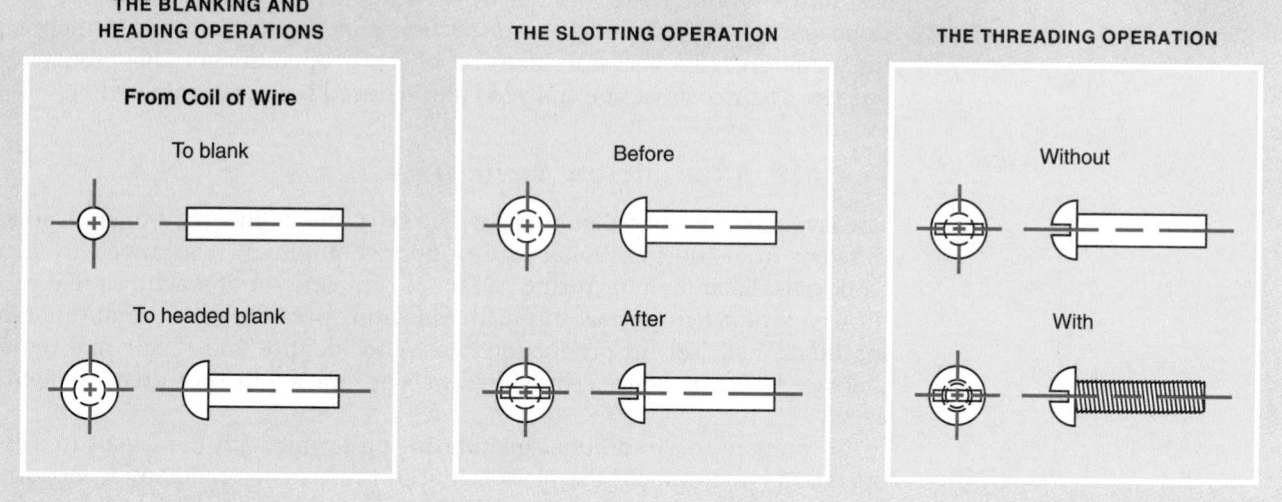

The arrows and numbers in Figure 1 indicate the sequence of events in the manufacturing process. Raw materials arrive at the plant as coils of wire of various thicknesses. The wire is fed into a heading machine, which cuts the wire to length and forms the head. Headed blanks then are collected in large movable bins for temporary storage, until they are transported to the next department. If the headed blank needs a slot, it is added in the Slotting Department. Then the products again are collected in movable bins. The next operation is threading the fastener, either by cutting away the excess metal or by rolling the headed blank between two dies to form the thread (similar to rolling a pencil between your hands).

At this point, although the product looks like a screw or bolt, it needs additional operations before it becomes a finished product. These are operations **5** through **9** in Figure 1. The fastener may need to be pointed, and all fasteners must be washed to remove excess oils and foreign materials. Inspection is necessary to determine if the product meets specifications. Some fasteners require heat treatment and plating, and some batches need special packaging.

Throughout the process, the products are stored and moved in large bins from one operation to the next. Finally, they are transported to the finished goods storage area to await sale and shipment.

Figure 1 also shows the location of several support services in the traditional plant. Notice that production support services—tool and die, repair and maintenance, inventory control, quality control, and scheduling and routing functions—are located in the middle of the factory. The lower part of Figure 1 shows other common support services. Accounting, time and motion study, engineering, computer services, sales, personnel, and executive activity functions all support the production, sale, or distribution of the company's products.

There are several nonvalue-adding activities in the layout in Figure 1. The most obvious are the raw materials and finished product storage areas and activities. Much of the aisle space is filled with bins of work in process inventory. The time taken to move the products in process between departments and the resulting queue time are also nonvalue-adding activities. Finally, the

Inspection Department adds no value to the product, although it does contribute to the cost. Many support functions are costly to maintain and add cost to the product without increasing its market value. But, unlike the non-value-adding activities such as inspection and product movement, support functions are still necessary for the effective operation of the production process. Their costs can be analyzed and reduced but not eliminated.

THE JIT PRODUCTION ENVIRONMENT

The layout of a factory that operates in a JIT production environment is quite different from the traditional factory floor. Equipment is arranged to form work cells. Each manufacturing cell has a complete set of machines that produces a product from start to finish. Machine operators run several different machines, help set up production runs, and identify and repair machinery that needs maintenance. And they are encouraged to spot areas of inefficiency.

To compare the traditional manufacturing layout with the layout in a JIT operating environment, the plant layout of the fastener company in Figure 1 was converted to the hypothetical JIT plant layout in Figure 3. Instead of large departments containing dozens of similar machines (like the Heading Department in Figure 1), small operating cells start and complete a product in minimal time, with minimal movement and storage. Each of the six headers, which are identified as #1, #2, etc., begins a separate operating cell.

In Subplant A, existing machinery is relocated to form JIT work cells. Raw materials are received as they are needed, and are unloaded in the materials storage area adjacent to the header scheduled to fill that order. Each of the six work cells includes heading, slotting, threading, and pointing machines, as necessary. Each cell is designed to work on different sizes and types of fasteners. Instead of work in process inventory sitting in travel bins as it moves from one department to the next, wire is fed into the header automatically. The headed blanks move on a conveyer belt to subsequent operations. If order specifications call for additional processing, such as heat treatment or plating, the computerized routing system moves the products to those locations. Packaging is the final phase; then, the goods are shipped to the customer. The fastener order is completed in a matter of hours, as compared to the days or weeks necessary when an order is moved and queued for each departmental operation.

Subplant B in Figure 3 shows three flexible manufacturing systems. A flexible manufacturing system (FMS) is a single multifunctional machine or an integrated set of computerized machines and systems designed to complete a series of operations automatically. An FMS often completes a product from beginning to end without the product being touched or moved by hand. Raw materials are fed in at one end of the FMS machine, and a finished product emerges at the other end.

Assume that FMS #1 in Subplant B makes a special type of fastener called a "sems screw." To manufacture a sems screw, a locking washer is placed on the screw blank before the threading operation. Once the threads have been rolled on, the washer becomes part of the finished product; it cannot be removed. This FMS cell produces all types and sizes of sems fasteners from start to finish. Each part of the cell represents a different operation—heading, slotting, lock washer fitting, threading, and pointing. All operations are computerized, and the manufacturing process is continuous. When the sems fasteners have been packaged, they are sent to the finished goods area to be shipped out to the customer.

Figure 3. The Plant Layout of a Factory with a JIT Production Environment

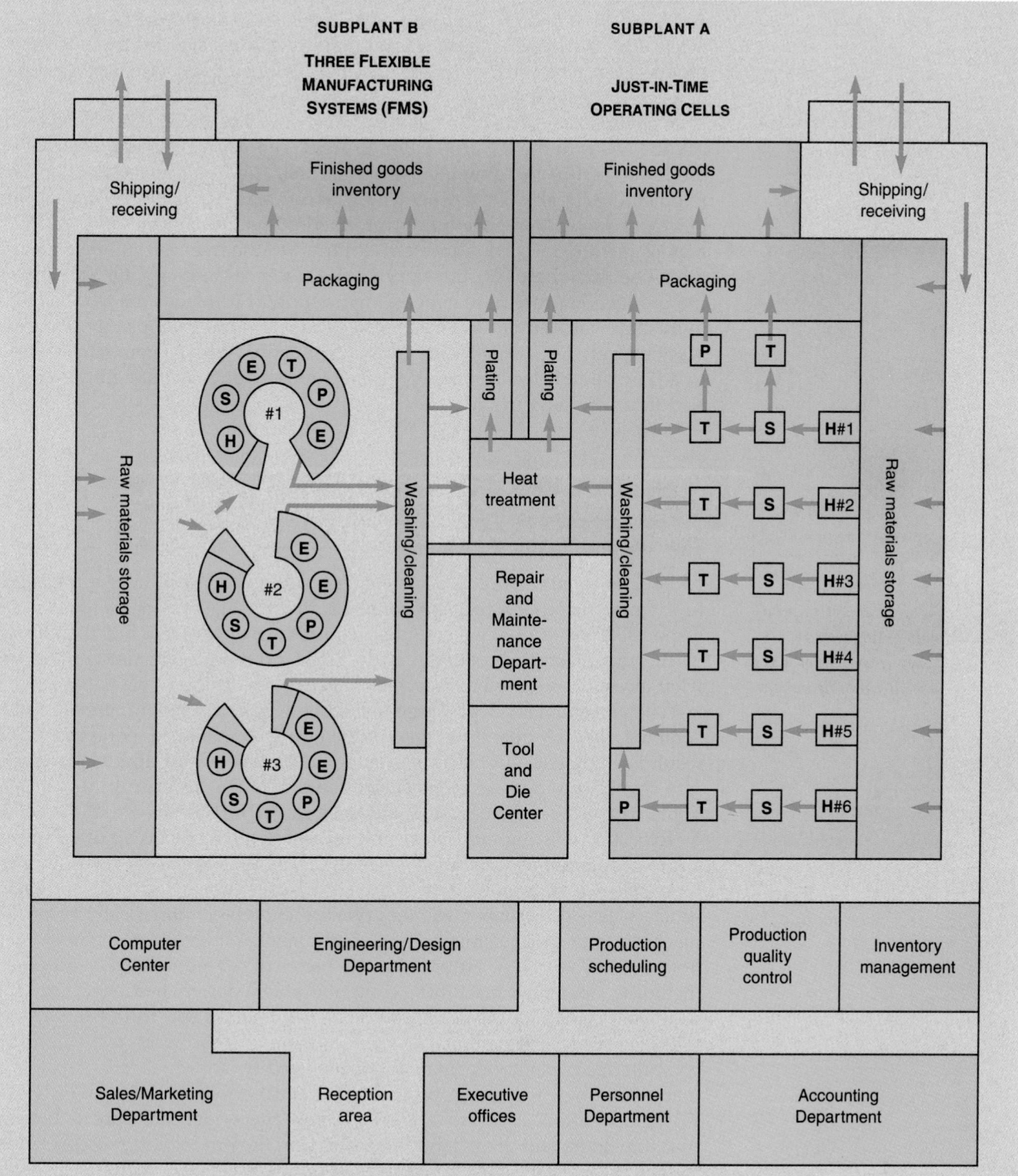

Key: **H** = Header   **S** = Slotter   **T** = Threader   **P** = Pointer   **E** = Extra operations for specialized fasteners

Some aspects of the plant layout in Figure 3 are similar to the traditional arrangement in Figure 1. For example, supporting services such as the Tool and Die Center and the Repair and Maintenance Department remain close to the manufacturing operation. Heat-treating facilities are very expensive and products are still batch-processed, so both subplant layouts share the same heat-treating furnaces.

The remaining parts of the factory in Figure 3 have been redesigned to satisfy the needs of the JIT production process. The support functions located in the lower part of the drawing are similar, but the Computer Center and the Engineering/Design Department have been enlarged in the JIT layout. The offices of production scheduling, production quality control, and inventory management have been reduced and moved to the managerial office area; in the JIT setting, these functions need to be closer to the computer area than to the production process. In general, many support functions are too expensive to maintain and simply add cost to the product. In our example, the Time and Motion Study Department falls into this category. When a company switches to a JIT operating environment, several support functions are either reduced significantly or eliminated.

ACCOUNTING FOR PRODUCT COSTS IN THE NEW MANUFACTURING ENVIRONMENT

OBJECTIVE

5 *Identify the changes in product costing that result when firms adopt a JIT operating environment*

Although the production process changes when firms shift from a traditional to the new manufacturing environment, the management accountant is still responsible for evaluating costs and controlling operations. But the changes in the manufacturing operations do affect how costs are determined and what measures are used to monitor performance.

When companies adopt a new manufacturing environment, they normally combine the JIT operating environment with automated equipment. The result is an increase in machine hours and a reduction in direct labor hours. The size of the increase in machine hours and the decrease in direct labor hours depends on the degree of automation. JIT operations are implemented by relocating existing machinery and equipment; JIT practices can be applied without automating operations. More commonly, however, firms increase their reliance on automation. Many companies use a partially automated setup, where direct labor workers operate computer numerically controlled machines and other semiautomatic equipment. Computer numerically controlled (CNC) machines are stand-alone pieces of computer-driven equipment, including operating machines, computer-aided design hardware and software, and robots. At the other end of the automation spectrum from a single CNC machine is a computer-integrated manufacturing (CIM) system, a fully computerized, plantwide manufacturing facility, in which all parts of the manufacturing process are programmed and performed automatically. The closer operations come to a CIM system, the wider the spread between machine hours and direct labor hours used in the production process.

In addition to the shift from direct labor hours to machine hours caused by work cell configurations and automated operations, the characteristics of labor change as a company adopts the new manufacturing environment. Direct labor workers no longer just help shape the product; they are responsible for many tasks that used to be categorized as indirect labor. Examples of tasks that are performed by direct labor workers are machine setup, machine maintenance, and product inspection.

Many traditional management accounting procedures depend on measures of direct labor. For example, accountants use direct labor to allocate factory overhead costs, find standard cost variances, and estimate the costs of potential projects. Most important, accountants have relied heavily on direct labor to compute product unit costs. Because of the significant reduction in direct labor hours and dollars in a JIT environment, many believe that costs should be assigned differently. They argue that traditional product costing techniques have become obsolete, and they cite three reasons: (1) JIT operations have changed many of the relationships and cost patterns associated with traditional manufacturing; (2) automation has replaced direct labor hours with machine hours; and (3) computerized processes and systems have increased the ability to trace costs to the specific activities that generate them.[4]

This section looks at ways accountants can change their product costing procedures to develop more accurate costs for products manufactured in the new manufacturing environment. After looking at changes in the way costs are categorized and assigned, the FIFO process costing method is used to compute product costs in an automated JIT setting.

CLASSIFYING COSTS

The JIT work cell and the goal of reducing or eliminating nonvalue-adding activities change the assignment of costs in a JIT operating environment from those in a traditional manufacturing environment. To see how costs are assigned in JIT operations, we again start with the five time frames that make up the traditional production process and compare JIT operations with them.

Processing time	The actual amount of time that a product is being worked on
Inspection time	The time spent either looking for product flaws or reworking defective units
Moving time	The time spent moving a product from one operation or department to another
Queue time	The time a product spends waiting to be worked on once it arrives at the next operation or department
Storage time	The time a product is in materials storage, work in process inventory, or finished goods inventory

In product costing under JIT, costs associated with actual processing time are grouped as either materials costs or conversion costs. Direct labor cost is generally small and does not need to be accounted for separately. Conversion costs include the total of direct labor and factory overhead costs incurred by and/or traceable to a production department, JIT/FMS work cell, or other work center.

The costs associated with and traceable to the other four time classifications are not necessary to the production process and are either reduced or eliminated through process and cost control measures. Inspection costs, for instance, are reduced significantly because the cell operator performs this function. The costs associated with moving the work in process inventory from department to department are reduced because of the reconfiguration of the factory layout. Many of the costs of queue time are reduced or eliminated

4. Several of the ideas in this section are from Robert D. McIlhattan, "How Cost Management Systems Can Support the JIT Philosophy," *Management Accounting,* Institute of Management Accountants, September 1987, pp. 20–26.

because of the continuous flow of products through the work cells. Storage costs also are reduced significantly or eliminated. When the JIT production process operates optimally, raw materials and parts arrive from vendors just in time to be used in the work cells, goods flow continuously through the work cells, and finished products are packaged and shipped immediately to customers. Thus, a large percentage of the old costs of storage are eliminated under JIT. Indirect product costs that are not eliminated must still be treated as factory overhead and charged to work cells as part of conversion costs.

Accounting for product costs under JIT is not a complicated procedure; it is summarized in Table 1. A product cost is classified as either a materials cost or a conversion cost. Product costs are traced to work cells. The process costing method then is used to determine product unit costs. The illustrative problem later in the chapter demonstrates this approach to product costing.

COST ALLOCATION

In a traditional manufacturing company, direct labor hours or dollars are a common basis for allocating factory overhead costs to products. Direct labor is usually a large cost component of finished goods and thought to be the primary cause of factory overhead costs. Therefore, most factory overhead costs are allocated to products based on direct labor hours or dollars.

Because flexible automated work cells significantly decrease the reliance on direct labor, other measures must replace direct labor in assigning costs to finished goods produced in the new manufacturing environment. Two cost allocation changes are: (1) replacing the work order with other measures of production and (2) merging direct labor and factory overhead, and accounting only for conversion costs.

The work order is a key document in a traditional manufacturing system. Labor time is accumulated as the order moves from one operation to the next. When the job is complete, the work order contains a record of all labor time required for the job. This information enables the accountant to determine the cost of direct labor and to apply factory overhead costs. Work cells and continuous production eliminate the need for work orders. Daily production schedules are maintained, and costs are assigned to the work completed dur-

Table 1. Product Costing Under JIT

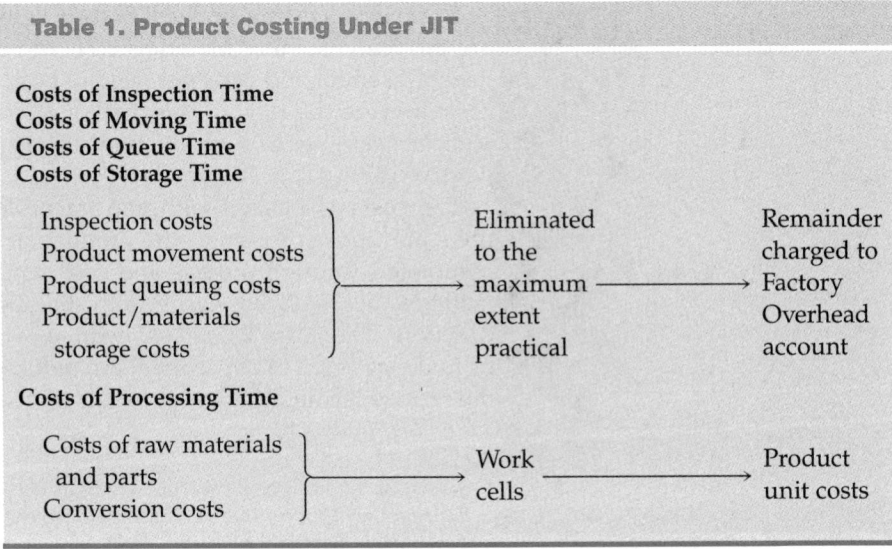

Table 2. Changes Caused by JIT: Direct Versus Indirect Costs

Traditional Environment		JIT Environment
Direct	Materials and parts	Direct
Direct	Direct labor	Direct
Indirect	Repairs and maintenance	Direct to work cell
Indirect	Materials handling	Direct to work cell
Indirect	Operating supplies	Direct to work cell
Indirect	Utility costs	Direct to work cell
Indirect	Supervision	Direct to work cell
Indirect	Depreciation	Direct to work cell
Indirect	Supporting service functions	Mostly direct
Indirect	Building occupancy	Indirect
Indirect	Insurance and taxes	Indirect

ing the day. Detailed reporting, such as completing documents like the work order, is not a part of the simplified JIT process.

In the JIT operating environment, indirect costs have little correlation with direct labor hours. The key measure is throughput time, the time it takes to get a product through the entire production process. Machine hours become more important than labor hours. Product velocity measures, such as throughput time, are used to apply conversion costs to products via process costing. In addition, practical or even theoretical capacity is used to establish conversion cost application rates.

Sophisticated computer monitoring of the work cells allows many costs to be traced directly to the cells where products are being manufactured. As Table 2 shows, several costs that used to be treated as indirect costs and applied to products using a labor base are now treated as direct costs of a work cell. They are directly traceable to the JIT production cell. If standard costs are used, products are costed using predetermined rates for materials and conversion costs. In the JIT operating environment, each cell manufactures similar products to minimize setup time. Therefore, conversion costs should be nearly uniform per product per cell. The costs of materials handling, utilities, operating supplies, and supervision can be traced directly to work cells as they are incurred. Depreciation is charged on units of output, not on a time basis, so depreciation also can be charged directly to work cells based on the number of units produced. Building occupancy costs, property and casualty insurance premiums, and property taxes remain indirect costs and must be allocated to the production cells for inclusion in the conversion cost category.

OBJECTIVE

6 *Apply process costing procedures to compute JIT product costs*

JIT AND PROCESS COSTING

The process costing method can be adapted easily to compute product unit costs in a JIT manufacturing setting. First, every manufacturing cost is classified as either materials costs (including materials-related costs) or conversion costs. After all costs have been categorized and allocated, process costing can be used to calculate product costs for the period. The illustrative problem on the next page shows how JIT product costs are developed.

In order for the just-in-time operating environment to work, a company and its materials suppliers must work together closely to ensure on-time delivery of quality parts and materials. JIT II, the 1990s version of JIT inventory control, goes one step further. Suppliers' sales representatives have desks next to the production process on the company's factory floor.[5] The sales representatives monitor materials stock as they are used and, using on-line computers, replenish them as needed. Lance Dixon, director of purchasing at Bose Corp. in Framingham, Massachusetts, created the idea but warns that it can cause problems if not implemented properly. Trust is key to the concept. Until the partnership between the company and supplier becomes strong, most managers are uncomfortable with outsiders roaming around the production floor. Meetings between production managers and suppliers' personnel will help to develop the trust needed for the process to work. Once implemented, JIT II saves money and reduces wasted time and effort for both the company and the supplier. It is a win-win concept. ▬▬

ILLUSTRATIVE PROBLEM:
JIT PROCESS COSTING

Lewis Company produces automobile steering wheels for all of the major car manufacturers in the United States. Three JIT operating cells are used in the process: One cell produces leather steering wheels, a second produces air-bag models, and a third makes special wood-grained wheels. The day-shift operator of each cell prepares the equipment so that the machines can run automatically during the two night shifts. Only indirect labor is used during the night shifts.

During the week ended June 15, 19x8, the JIT air-bag wheel cell produced the following data:

Units
Beginning work in process inventory (60 percent complete)	30
Units completed during week	4,600
Ending work in process inventory (80 percent complete)	35

Hours worked
Direct labor—40 hours
Machine hours
  Nine machines in cell
  JIT air-bag wheel cell ran 110 hours during week

Costs in beginning Work in Process Inventory
Materials costs	$1,080
Conversion costs	378

---

5. Fred R. Bleakley, "Strange Bedfellows—Some Companies Let Suppliers Work on Site and Even Place Orders," *Wall Street Journal*, January 13, 1995, p. A–1.

Direct costs incurred for and traced directly to air-bag wheel cell

Raw materials (added at beginning of process)	$138,150
Direct labor (40 hours at $14 per hour)	560
Power costs	3,056
Cell machinery depreciation	2,420
Engineering design costs	4,963
Indirect labor	11,970
Lubricants, supplies, and fasteners	7,015

Overhead rates used

Materials handling overhead (to be added to and included
  as part of materials cost in process costing analysis)
    20 percent of raw materials costs
Factory overhead not traceable directly to cell
    $6.50 per machine hour worked

REQUIRED

1. Compute the total materials costs and total conversion costs for the week.
2. Using good form and the FIFO process costing approach, prepare a cost of production report, including
  a. Schedule of equivalent production
  b. Unit cost analysis schedule
  c. Cost summary schedule
3. From the cost summary schedule, prepare a journal entry to transfer the costs of completed units to the Finished Goods Inventory account.

SOLUTION

1. Before preparing the cost of production report for the Lewis Company, first compute the costs of the period. Remember that two cost categories are used in a JIT operating environment: materials costs and conversion costs. These same categories also are used in process costing.

Raw materials costs	
In beginning work in process inventory	$ 1,080
Materials used in production during week	138,150
Materials handling overhead for week	
$138,150 × 20%	27,630
Total materials costs	$166,860
Conversion costs	
In beginning inventory	$ 378
Charged to FMS cell during period	
Directly traceable costs	
Direct labor (40 hours at $14 per hour)	560
Power costs	3,056
Cell machinery depreciation	2,420
Engineering design costs	4,963
Indirect labor	11,970
Lubricants, supplies, and fasteners	7,015
Indirect factory overhead	
110 hours × 9 machines × $6.50/machine hour	6,435
Total conversion costs	$ 36,797

2. The cost of production report is shown in Exhibit 1.

3. Prepare a journal entry to transfer the costs of completed units to Finished Goods Inventory.

Exhibit 1. Cost of Production Report

Lewis Company
Cost of Production Report—FIFO Method
For the Week Ended June 15, 19x8

A. Schedule of Equivalent Production

Units—Stage of Completion	Units to Be Accounted For	Equivalent Units Materials Costs	Equivalent Units Conversion Costs
Beginning inventory (units started last period but completed this period)	30		
(Materials costs—100% complete)		0	
(Conversion costs—60% complete)			12 (40% of 30)
Units started and completed in this period (4,600 − 30)	4,570	4,570	4,570
Ending inventory (units started but not completed in this period)	35		
(Materials costs—100% complete)		35	
(Conversion costs—80% complete)			28 (80% of 35)
Totals	4,635	4,605	4,610

B. Unit Cost Analysis Schedule

	Total Costs — Costs from Beginning Inventory (1)	Total Costs — Costs from Current Period (2)	Total Costs — Total Costs to Be Accounted For (1 + 2)	Equivalent Unit Costs — Equivalent Units (3)	Equivalent Unit Costs — Cost per Equivalent Unit (2 ÷ 3)
Materials costs	$1,080	$165,780	$166,860	4,605	$36.00
Conversion costs	378	36,419	36,797	4,610	7.90
Totals	$1,458	$202,199	$203,657		$43.90

C. Cost Summary Schedule

	Cost of Goods Transferred to Finished Goods Inventory	Cost of Ending Work in Process Inventory
Beginning inventory		
Beginning balance	$ 1,458	
Cost to complete: 30 units × 40% × $7.90 per unit	95*	
Total beginning inventory	$ 1,553	
Units started and completed: 4,570 units × $43.90 per unit	200,623	
Ending inventory		
Materials costs: 35 units × $36.00 per unit		$ 1,260
Conversion costs: 35 units × 80% × $7.90 per unit		221*
Totals	$202,176	$ 1,481
Check on computations:		
Costs to Finished Goods Inventory		$202,176
Costs in ending Work in Process Inventory		1,481
Total costs to be accounted for (see unit cost analysis schedule)		$203,657

*Rounded.

Finished Goods Inventory	202,176	
Work in Process Inventory		202,176
Transferred the cost of units completed		
to Finished Goods Inventory		

THE RAW IN PROCESS INVENTORY ACCOUNT

OBJECTIVE

7 *Record transactions involving the Raw in Process Inventory account*

One of the most basic accounting changes caused by the JIT environment is the use of the Raw in Process Inventory account. This new inventory account replaces both the Materials Inventory and the Work in Process Inventory accounts. Because raw materials are ordered and received immediately prior to use, there is no need to debit them to a Materials Inventory account; they are debited directly to the Raw in Process Inventory account.

Raw in Process Inventory	50,000	
Accounts Payable		50,000
Purchased raw materials		

In process costing situations, as goods were completed by one department and transferred to another department, the cumulative cost of the products had to be transferred from one Work in Process Inventory account to another. This is also changed in the JIT environment. There is no need for numerous Work in Process Inventory accounts because the products flow continuously through the flexible manufacturing cell. All conversion costs (direct labor and factory overhead costs) are debited to the single Raw in Process Inventory account. When the goods have been completed, the following entry is made as follows:

Finished Goods Inventory	185,600	
Raw in Process Inventory		185,600
Transferred completed		
products to Finished Goods		
Inventory		

If adjustments have to be made at the end of an accounting period because of over- or underapplied factory overhead, the debits or credits are made only to the Raw in Process Inventory and Finished Goods Inventory accounts. For example, assume that factory overhead was overapplied by $1,600 and that $100 should be taken back from goods in process and $500 from finished goods; the remaining $1,000 are in Cost of Goods Sold. The entry would be made as follows:

Factory Overhead Control	1,600	
Raw in Process Inventory		100
Finished Goods Inventory		500
Cost of Goods Sold		1,000
To adjust for overapplied factory overhead		

One last example helps clarify the Raw in Process Inventory account. Assume that $17,500 of raw materials were purchased and the accountant discovered that these goods were priced $1,500 over their standard cost. The following entry would be made to record the purchase.

Raw in Process Inventory	16,000	
Materials Price Variance	1,500	
Accounts Payable		17,500
To record the purchase of raw materials		
and the related price variance		

Using the Raw in Process Inventory account is an easy adjustment to make. Remember that this new account is used in every situation in which either Materials Inventory or Work in Process Inventory was used in the past.

DECISION POINT

American Telephone & Telegraph

American Telephone & Telegraph (AT&T) has incorporated the just-in-time (JIT) operating philosophy at its New River Valley Works in Radford, Virginia. This AT&T division is composed of different shops making microelectronic components for the communications industry. The company had used standards and standard costing to measure efficiency through variance analysis for many years. With the new operating environment in place, the company shifted its accounting emphasis from efficiency measures based on variances to a simple cost ratio called "incurred-to-standard."[6] Each shop now receives a monthly report of all costs, including both directly traceable costs and allocated costs. This total is divided by the total standard cost for units produced (number of units produced multiplied by the standard cost per unit). When the incurred-to-standard ratio is less than or equal to 1, the shop is assumed to have operated at a full cost recovery level. If the ratio is greater than 1, too much cost was incurred for the units of output generated, and an analysis is necessary to determine why performance was not up to standard. Why did the managers at AT&T decide to abandon efficiency measures based on variance analysis and adopt a single, simple measure of operating performance? Do you approve of the change?

The new incurred-to-standard measure is appropriate for the new manufacturing environment based on the JIT philosophy. Many companies using JIT have found that the traditional measures of efficiency—essential when 30–50 percent of operating costs were related to direct labor and labor efficiency was extremely important—are no longer very useful. The new environment is highly automated and labor cost can be as low as 2 percent of total product cost. Operating costs are made up mostly of materials and factory overhead costs. A measure to indicate when these costs are being covered by units produced at standard cost seems very appropriate. In addition, one of the elements of the JIT operating philosophy is that performance measurements be expressed in simple terms to be understood by everyone involved in the production team. AT&T's new measure meets this objective. ⦙⦙⦙⦙⦙

6. F. B. Green, Felix Amenkhienan, and George Johnson, "Performance Measures and JIT," *Management Accounting*, Institute of Management Accountants, February 1991, pp. 50–53.

How JIT and Automation Are Changing Management Accounting

Significant changes are underway in the management accounting systems of companies that have adopted the JIT philosophy and that are employing automated manufacturing processes. These changes stem from three new areas of accounting emphasis created by the move to JIT and automated production facilities: (1) a macro versus a micro approach to control of operations, (2) the increasing importance of nonfinancial data, and (3) using theoretical capacity to evaluate actual performance.

Macro versus Micro Approach

The management accountant approaches the control of JIT operations by looking at the entire production process rather than small parts or segments of the process. Profit is maximized by supplying customers with a quality product on a timely basis at a reasonable price. With the more traditional approach, profits are thought to be increased by cutting labor time, buying large quantities of raw materials to take advantage of quantity discounts, or applying fixed overhead costs over an increased number of units of output. In a JIT setting, profitability is enhanced when the entire operation is running in a just-in-time fashion. Nonvalue-adding aspects such as storage time, inspection time, moving time, and queue time are the primary focus: If these wasted time periods are minimized or eliminated, profitability will increase.

Nonfinancial Data

A major part of the reporting and measurement aspects of the JIT operating environment involves nonfinancial considerations, which are linked closely with the macro approach to control of operations. Rather than being interested in labor efficiency or overhead volume variances, the management accountant must focus on time reduction, helping to determine (1) causes for excess storage time, (2) information sources that will reduce the need for separate inspection activities, (3) reporting methods that will help reduce the moving time associated with product flow through the process, and (4) causes for excessive queue time. All these analyses are nonfinancial in nature and require studies of time periods, distance factors or measures, and numbers of people involved.

The JIT environment also emphasizes product distribution and customer satisfaction. Analyses leading to control in these areas require information from such reports as number and causes of customer complaints, average delivery time, and ability to meet promised delivery dates. All these analyses involve nonfinancial data.

Emphasis on Theoretical Capacity

To measure performance in a traditional work environment, actual productive output is compared with expected output based on normal capacity. Variances resulting from differences between these two amounts are reported. One major objective of the JIT philosophy is to minimize nonproductive time in the total delivery cycle, which means that the company is expected to operate at or near theoretical or ideal capacity. This goal may not be attained, but the philosophy is to work toward that ideal level. Machine operators, engineers, product designers, supervisors, salespeople, and management accountants are expected to continuously look for ways to cut nonvalue-adding time and related costs. The JIT environment exists when everyone involved in the operation of the company actively participates in a relentless effort of continuous improvement.

AUTOMATION: PRODUCT COSTING ISSUES

OBJECTIVE

8 *Identify the unique aspects of product costing in an automated manufacturing process*

Earlier, product costing procedures related to the just-in-time philosophy were introduced and illustrated. In addition to JIT, automated manufacturing facilities have also influenced the computation of a product's cost. This section takes a more detailed look at product costing in a JIT/FMS environment, an operating environment created by a flexible manufacturing system functioning within the just-in-time operating philosophy. Product costing methods must change as the manufacturing environment changes. And yet many companies that have automated their production facilities try to use traditional methods to cost products. In a study titled *Cost Accounting for Factory Automation* sponsored by the Institute of Management Accountants (IMA), researchers Robert E. Bennett, James A. Hendricks, David E. Keys, and Edward J. Rudnicki found that product costing problems and solutions differed with the degree of automation in the production process. These problems concern the allocation of factory overhead, the classification of costs as variable or fixed, and the changing nature of costs involving their direct versus indirect characteristics. The report was organized according to four levels of computer integration, from low to high, as follows:

1. Computer numerically controlled (CNC) machines — Stand-alone computer-controlled machines

2. Computer-aided design/ computer-aided manufacturing (CAD/CAM) — Using computers in product design work, planning and controlling production, and in linking CNC machines and flexible manufacturing systems to the engineering design function

3. Flexible manufacturing systems (FMS) — A computer-controlled production system comprised of a single, multifunctional machine or several types of machines that perform a series of operations and/or assemble a number of parts in a flexible and automatic fashion

4. Automated material handling system (AMHS) — A necessary component of a computer-integrated manufacturing (CIM) system in which the raw materials and partially completed product handling function is automatic, providing a continuous product flow through the entirely automated process

COMPUTER NUMERICALLY CONTROLLED MACHINES

Automating the production process begins with the introduction of computer numerically controlled (CNC) machines to reduce the dependency on labor and to increase efficiency. Even after introducing the CNC machines, most companies continue to allocate factory overhead based on direct labor dollars or hours for product costing purposes. This problem was a primary finding of the IMA research team's study of factory automation. They determined that there are four reasons why inaccurate factory overhead allocation exists in a CNC machine environment: (1) use of inappropriate allocation bases, (2) allocation of irrelevant costs, (3) use of inappropriate activity levels, and (4) use of plant or companywide overhead rates rather than FMS work cell rates.

Inappropriate Allocation Base   Direct labor is not an appropriate allocation base in an automated production setting because there is very little connection between overhead costs incurred in a CNC machine environment and direct labor hours or cost. Most of the overhead costs are associated with and caused by the operation of the machines. Machine hours differ from labor hours because of setup time, idle machine time, and the fact that one person can operate several machines simultaneously. Three machine time expressions can be used as a basis for factory overhead cost allocation: actual machine hours, run time (total machine hours needed less setup time), and engineered time (standard or predicted machine time for the product). Each expression of machine hours has advantages and disadvantages regarding cost and accuracy, but each is a better factory overhead allocation base than direct labor hours or dollars.

Relevance of Costs Being Allocated   There is still an argument that allocating fixed factory overhead costs to products tends to introduce inaccuracy into the computation of product cost. These costs tend to be unrelated to the activity levels that are often used to assign costs to work cells or products. Building occupancy costs such as building depreciation, insurance costs, and property taxes are included in this category. Even with improved cost traceability, these costs must still be considered indirect. Variable costing procedures are one answer to this concern, but to date few companies have adopted them.

Selection of Activity Levels   The selection of activity levels to be used for allocating factory overhead costs should be a primary concern for the management accountant because it is the activities within the factory that cause costs to be incurred. Therefore costs should be categorized by type of activity, and the activity itself should be used as a base for allocating those costs to the work cell or product. Approaching cost allocation from this direction will allow, for example, computer-related costs to be allocated using a computer-usage base.

Use of Work Cell Versus Plantwide Rates   Fixed factory overhead can be more closely related to production if a company converts from a companywide or plantwide overhead rate to FMS work cell overhead rates. The closer the factory overhead costs are brought to the product, the more accurate the resulting product cost. Many costs can be directly traced to a particular FMS work cell, which further aids the product costing process.

COMPUTER-AIDED DESIGN/ COMPUTER-AIDED MANUFACTURING

Most computer-aided design/computer-aided manufacturing (CAD/CAM) costs should be assigned to specific products. But the traditional methods used to accomplish this task do not usually yield accurate cost assignments.

Many companies simply charge these costs to overhead pools and then distribute them to products through the use of predetermined factory overhead rates. Yet many of these costs are traceable directly to specific orders; for instance, drafting/design costs incurred in connection with specifications for a particular order are traceable to and should be charged directly to that individual order. Because of sophisticated computer monitoring equipment, many CAD/CAM related costs can be easily traced to the order needing the design work. Routing these costs through plantwide or departmental overhead rates will distort product costs.

FLEXIBLE MANUFACTURING SYSTEMS

Product costing within a flexible manufacturing system (FMS) further changes the characteristics of some common variable costs, fixed costs, and direct costs. The FMS cell itself becomes the cost center. Variable costs of an FMS include direct materials, direct labor, and some indirect materials, tooling, and power costs.

Many fixed costs can be traced directly to FMS cost centers. Costs of machine depreciation, FMS computer depreciation, computer programmers and other computer backup people working only on FMS maintenance, product line supervision, and selected off-line inspection labor can be traced to specific FMS work cells. The work and time of setup personnel and machine operators who are trouble-shooters and who move from one work cell to another can also be traced directly to specific FMS cost centers. The IMA researchers recommended that separate FMS factory overhead application rates be used because each FMS cell is usually a self-contained operating unit.

Other fixed costs are not traceable and must be allocated to the FMS cost centers. Common computer center costs may be allocated to cost centers based on some expression of usage. In addition, building occupancy costs such as plant depreciation, building maintenance, taxes, and insurance are usually pooled and allocated based on square footage.

AUTOMATED MATERIAL HANDLING SYSTEM

An automated material handling system (AMHS) adds the final dimension to a fully integrated computerized production process. Traditional material handling systems required manual movement of materials and parts through the manufacturing layout, and the paperwork needed to track the materials and product in process was also done manually. According to the *Cost Accounting for Factory Automation* study, companies today rely on automatic storage/retrieval systems (AS/RS) and AMHSs to move products within a computer-integrated manufacturing process.[7] Hand-pushed carts, operator-directed forklifts, and manual conveyors are being replaced by power-rolled conveyors, shuttles, and raised track, towline, or computer-guided vehicles. Computer-controlled production scheduling and material handling trace and account for all product and parts movement, replacing the old punched card and off-line tracking systems.

Traditionally, material handling costs have been included in the factory overhead cost pool and allocated to products based on direct labor. In the

7. Robert E. Bennett, James A. Hendricks, David E. Keys, and Edward J. Rudnicki, *Cost Accounting for Factory Automation* (Montvale, N.J.: Institute of Management Accountants, 1987), p. 59.

new manufacturing environment, there is little relationship between the amount of labor cost incurred and the amount of material handling a process or FMS work cell needs. A suggested approach for today's automated JIT environment is to account for the material handling and purchasing functions as a separate cost center. Costs associated with these functions are grouped into a cost pool and allocated as part of the materials charged to production. Materials quantity, cost, or weight may be used as the allocation basis, depending on the relationship between the costs involved and the size and complexity of the products being produced.

UNIT COST ANALYSIS IN AN AUTOMATED FMS ENVIRONMENT

OBJECTIVE

9 *Compute a product unit cost using data from a flexible manufacturing system*

In a globally competitive environment, accurate product costs are key to correct pricing and to a company's overall profitability. A two or three percent error in pricing a product may result in the loss of customers and market share. In practice, although production processes have shifted from being labor-intensive to machine- or capital-intensive operations, direct labor hours and dollars are still the most commonly used overhead allocation bases. The traditional approach to product costing traces direct materials and direct labor costs to the products but relies heavily on cost allocation when assigning factory overhead costs. A single factory overhead cost pool is often used to accumulate these costs, which are then assigned to products based on direct labor hours or dollars.

Even as automation begins to dominate production lines, accountants continue to use direct labor cost allocation bases. Many existing allocation systems are at a point where there is little relationship between the factory overhead costs being incurred and the amount of direct labor being used. The keys to accurate product costing are to (1) maximize the direct tracing of costs to the product and (2) break down the indirect costs into as many cost pools as possible and assign costs based on the cost drivers that cause the costs to be incurred. In an automated environment, direct labor no longer drives or causes overhead costs, machines do.

The impact of the change from using one overhead cost allocation rate to using several rates is a bit difficult to comprehend when you first begin to use multiple rates. The objective is to improve product costing, and the more one breaks down the overhead assignment process, the more accurate the tracking of product cost becomes. As companies integrate JIT into their processes, the focus on activities increases. The end result is a need for activity-based costing systems, which accumulate costs by activity and develop cost assignment rates for each activity. As a job or product batch uses the resources of an activity, costs are assigned based on resource usage.

Computing a product unit cost for an FMS cell consists of determining the unit cost of materials; materials handling cost overhead; and conversion costs per unit, including all traceable indirect costs and other factory overhead allocations. Costs such as electricity, machine depreciation, indirect labor, supplies, and repairs and maintenance, which used to be charged to a plantwide overhead pool, can now be traced directly to the FMS cell activity. These costs are then reassigned to the units being processed by the cell as part of conversion costs. Although an overhead cost such as electricity cannot be directly traced to a product, the ability to trace it directly to the FMS cell enables the costing system to more accurately charge units of product with such a cost.

The review problem, Lawrence Corporation, at the end of this chapter, illustrates how making only a few changes in the cost assignment process can have significant results. A company can easily change from using one companywide overhead pool to using separate FMS cell overhead rates. A significant difference in product cost can arise when an automated company simply shifts from a direct labor dollar allocation basis to one based on machine hours. Even with only minor adjustments, individual product cost changes can be dramatic.

CHAPTER REVIEW

REVIEW OF LEARNING OBJECTIVES

1. **State the strategies necessary to compete in a globally competitive business environment, define the just-in-time management philosophy, and link JIT to these strategies.** The strategies needed to compete in the globally competitive marketplace are to (1) eliminate waste of raw materials, labor, space, and production time; (2) reduce resources (inventories) that tie up working capital; and (3) simplify measurement approaches and recordkeeping.

    Just-in-time (JIT) is an overall operating philosophy of management in which all resources, including raw materials and parts, personnel, and facilities, are used only as needed. The objectives are to improve productivity and reduce waste. JIT is based on the concept of continuous production flow and requires that each part of the production process work in concert with the others. Direct labor workers in a JIT environment are empowered with expanded responsibilities, contributing to the reduction of waste in labor cost, space, and production time. Redesigning the plant layout, moving machines and processes closer together to reduce throughput time, is the initial step to attaining JIT operating efficiencies.

2. **Describe how changes in managers' information needs cause management accounting systems to change.** The management accounting system must change as the information needs of managers change. The following example demonstrates the need for such a change. The traditional approach to monitoring process efficiency focused on the effective use of direct labor. Direct labor was watched closely, and the management accounting system tracked and reported units per direct labor hour information to managers for each worker and department. The goal was to continuously increase units per hour without increasing the resources used in the process. In a JIT environment, the focus is on throughput time, which is the time it takes to start and complete a product. The JIT manager needs to have total processing time per unit tracked and reported. If the accounting system still focuses on units per direct labor hour, the JIT manager will not be able to monitor throughput time.

3. **Identify the elements of a JIT operating environment.** The elements that comprise a JIT operating environment are (1) maintain minimum inventory levels; (2) develop pull-through production planning and scheduling; (3) purchase materials and produce parts as needed, in smaller lot sizes; (4) perform quick, inexpensive machine setups; (5) create flexible manufacturing work cells; (6) develop a multiskilled work force; (7) maintain high levels of product quality; (8) enforce a system of effective preventive maintenance; and (9) encourage continuous improvement of the work environment.

4. **Compare traditional manufacturing with just-in-time operations.** Traditional manufacturing plants are divided into functional departments, with similar machines grouped in each department. Products flow from department to department. Raw materials are ordered well in advance and stored until needed. Work in process and finished goods inventories are usually large. And long production runs are scheduled to reduce setup costs and to lower fixed costs per product.

Just-in-time manufacturing operations are organized in work cells: All machines necessary for the production of a product line are grouped together to reduce the distance between operations and the time it takes to produce a product. Raw materials and parts are ordered as needed. Goods are pulled through the work cell based on actual orders received. And the size of production runs is based on the size of orders. Work in process inventories are almost nonexistent, and finished products are shipped when completed.

5. **Identify the changes in product costing that result when firms adopt a JIT operating environment.** In the JIT operating environment, as firms increase their reliance on automation, machine hours replace direct labor hours as the dominant source of costs. This means that measures of direct labor are no longer a reliable means of determining product costs. In product costing under JIT, processing costs are grouped as either materials costs or conversion costs. The costs associated with inspection time, moving time, queue time, and storage time are reduced or eliminated. The shift to automation also affects the allocation of factory overhead costs. Other measures of production replace the work order, and direct labor and factory overhead costs are merged into conversion costs. At work here are computerized facilities that improve cost tracking, so that many costs considered indirect costs in traditional manufacturing settings, such as electricity and factory supplies, can be traced directly to work cells. Only costs associated with building occupancy, insurance, and property taxes remain indirect costs and must be allocated to work cells.

6. **Apply process costing procedures to compute JIT product costs.** Because manufacturing costs are classified as either materials costs or conversion costs, the process costing method can be adapted easily to compute product costs in a JIT environment. Remember that there usually is very little beginning inventory in a JIT operation. So, it is easy to determine the stage of completion of goods. Unit cost analysis is used to compute product unit costs.

7. **Record transactions involving the Raw in Process Inventory account.** The Raw in Process Inventory account has taken the place of both the Materials Inventory and the Work in Process Inventory accounts. Because raw materials are received as needed and the products flow continuously through the process, only one inventory account is needed in these areas.

8. **Identify the unique aspects of product costing in an automated manufacturing process.** With automation, machine hours replace direct labor hours or dollars and become the primary basis for overhead allocation. The use of several overhead cost pools and appropriate cost drivers (allocation bases) is also encouraged. More costs are treated as direct costs because of their traceability to operating cells. Departmental or operating cell overhead rates are preferred over plantwide rates.

9. **Compute a product unit cost using data from a flexible manufacturing system.** Computing a product unit cost for an FMS cell consists of determining the unit cost of materials; materials handling cost overhead; and conversion costs per unit, including all traceable indirect costs and other factory overhead allocations.

REVIEW OF CONCEPTS AND TERMINOLOGY

The following concepts and terms were introduced in this chapter.

L O 8 **Automated material handling system (AMHS):** A necessary component of a computer-integrated manufacturing system in which the raw materials and partially completed product handling function is automatic, providing a continuous product flow through the entirely automated process.

L O 8 **Computer-aided design/computer-aided manufacturing (CAD/CAM):** The use of computers in product design work, planning and controlling production, and in linking CNC machines and flexible manufacturing systems to the engineering design function.

L O 5 **Computer-integrated manufacturing (CIM) system:** A fully computerized, plantwide manufacturing facility, in which all parts of the manufacturing process are programmed and performed automatically.

L O 5 **Computer numerically controlled (CNC) machines:** Stand-alone pieces of computer-driven equipment, including operating machines, computer-aided design hardware and software, and robots.

L O 8 **Engineered time:** Standard or predicted machine time for the product.

L O 4 **Flexible manufacturing system (FMS):** A single, multifunctional machine or an integrated set of computerized machines and systems designed to complete a series of operations automatically.

L O 5 **Inspection time:** The time spent either looking for product flaws or reworking defective units.

L O 1 **Just-in-time (JIT):** An overall operating philosophy of management in which all resources, including raw materials and parts, personnel, and facilities, are used only as needed.

L O 8 **JIT/FMS environment:** An operating environment created by a flexible manufacturing system functioning within the just-in-time operating philosophy.

L O 5 **Moving time:** The time spent moving a product from one operation or department to another.

L O 5 **Processing time:** The actual amount of time that a product is being worked on.

L O 3 **Pull-through production:** A production system in which a customer order triggers the purchase of materials and the scheduling of production for the required products.

L O 3 **Push-through method:** A production system in which products are manufactured in long production runs and stored in anticipation of customers' orders.

L O 5 **Queue time:** The time a product spends waiting to be worked on once it arrives at the next operation or department.

L O 7 **Raw in Process Inventory:** An inventory account in the just-in-time operating environment that combines the Raw Materials Inventory and the Work in Process Inventory accounts.

L O 8 **Run time:** Total machine hours needed less setup time.

L O 5 **Storage time:** The time a product is in materials storage, work in process inventory, or finished goods inventory.

L O 5 **Throughput time:** The time it takes to get a product through the entire production process.

L O 3 **Work cell (island):** An autonomous production line that can perform all required operations efficiently and continuously.

REVIEW PROBLEM

PRODUCT COSTING IN AN AUTOMATED ENVIRONMENT

L O 5, 9 Lawrence Corporation's Gardner Division produces three products: J12, K14, and L16. Four years ago the company renovated its manufacturing facilities and installed automated flexible manufacturing systems. Each product is produced in its own FMS cell, but the allocation of factory overhead continues to be based on direct labor dollars. The following information has been made available.

	Product J12	Product K14	Product L16
Unit information			
Raw materials cost	$3	$4	$10
Direct labor hours	.5 hours	.8 hours	.2 hours
Direct labor cost per hour	$16	$16	$16
Machine hours	3.2 hours	4 hours	5 hours
Total annual unit demand	30,000	50,000	10,000
Total factory overhead	$1,680,000	$4,480,000	$1,568,000

Gardner Division's policy is to set the selling price at 140 percent of the unit's production cost.

REQUIRED

1. Compute the division's plantwide factory overhead rate using total direct labor dollars as a basis.
2. Compute each product's total production cost and selling price using the application rate computed in **1.**
3. Compute a new factory overhead application rate assuming that
   a. Materials storage and handling overhead of 20 percent of the cost of raw materials is subtracted from the factory overhead cost totals.
   b. Machine hours (MH) is the overhead application basis.
   c. Product line overhead rates rather than a single plantwide rate are used.
4. Compute each product's total production cost and selling price using the application rates disclosed or computed in **3.**
5. Compare product selling prices. Is there a problem?

ANSWER TO REVIEW PROBLEM

1. Factory overhead rate based on direct labor dollars computed.

	Total Factory Overhead Cost	Total Direct Labor Cost
Product J12		
Factory overhead cost	$1,680,000	
Direct labor cost		
.5 hours × $16 × 30,000 units		$240,000
Product K14		
Factory overhead cost	4,480,000	
Direct labor cost		
.8 hours × $16 × 50,000 units		640,000
Product L16		
Factory overhead cost	1,568,000	
Direct labor cost		
.2 hours × $16 × 10,000 units		32,000
Totals	$7,728,000	$912,000

Factory overhead application rate
$7,728,000 ÷ $912,000 = 847.37% of direct labor cost

2. Each product's unit cost and selling price based on plantwide overhead rate computed.

	Product J12	Product K14	Product L16
Unit cost information			
Raw materials cost	$ 3.00	$ 4.00	$10.00
Direct labor cost			
.5 hr. at $16/hr.	8.00		
.8 hr. at $16/hr.		12.80	
.2 hr. at $16/hr.			3.20
Factory overhead cost			
$8 × 8.4737	67.79		
$12.80 × 8.4737		108.46	
$3.20 × 8.4737			27.12
Total unit cost	$ 78.79	$125.26	$40.32
Unit selling price			
J12: $78.79 × 140%	$110.31		
K14: $125.26 × 140%		$175.36	
L16: $40.32 × 140%			$56.45

3. Product line factory overhead rates based on machine hours computed.

	Net Factory Overhead Cost	Total Machine Hours Required
Product J12:		
Factory overhead cost	$1,680,000	
Less materials handling cost		
$3 × 30,000 units × 20%	18,000	
Net factory overhead cost	$1,662,000	
Machine hours required		
3.2 hours × 30,000 units		96,000
Product K14:		
Factory overhead cost	$4,480,000	
Less materials handling cost		
$4 × 50,000 units × 20%	40,000	
Net factory overhead cost	$4,440,000	
Machine hours required		
4 hours × 50,000 units		200,000
Product L16:		
Factory overhead cost	$1,568,000	
Less materials handling cost		
$10 × 10,000 units × 20%	20,000	
Net factory overhead cost	$1,548,000	
Machine hours required		
5 hours × 10,000 units		50,000

Product line FMS factory overhead application rates per machine hour
J12: $1,662,000 ÷ 96,000 MH = $17.3125/MH
K14: $4,440,000 ÷ 200,000 MH = $22.20/MH
L16: $1,548,000 ÷ 50,000 MH = $30.96/MH

4. Each product's unit cost and selling price based on product line overhead rates computed.

	Product J12	Product K14	Product L16
Unit cost information			
Raw materials cost	$ 3.00	$ 4.00	$ 10.00
Materials handling overhead cost at 20%	0.60	0.80	2.00
Direct labor cost			
.5 hour at $16/hour	8.00		
.8 hour at $16/hour		12.80	
.2 hour at $16/hour			3.20
Factory overhead cost			
3.2 hours × $17.3125	55.40		
4 hours × $22.20		88.80	
5 hours × $30.96			154.80
Total unit cost	$67.00	$106.40	$170.00
Unit selling price			
J12: $67.00 × 140%	$93.80		
K14: $106.40 × 140%		$148.96	
L16: $170.00 × 140%			$238.00

5. Selling prices compared and analyzed.

	Product J12	Product K14	Product L16
Selling prices using direct labor cost allocation basis and a plantwide rate	$110.31	$175.36	$ 56.45
Selling prices using machine hours basis and product line FMS rates	93.80	148.96	238.00
Differences	$ 16.51	$ 26.40	($181.55)

Conclusion: Products J12 and K14 are overpriced, and product L16 is extremely underpriced.

CHAPTER ASSIGNMENTS

QUESTIONS

1. Briefly describe the just-in-time operating environment.
2. What role does the elimination of waste play in the development of the just-in-time operating environment?
3. Why do changes in the information needs of managers cause changes in the management accounting system?
4. Describe the pull-through production concept.
5. What is a flexible manufacturing system (FMS) work cell?
6. "Preventive maintenance of machinery is critical to the operation of a flexible manufacturing system work cell." Explain this statement.
7. What are the changes in the responsibilities of the direct labor worker in the JIT operating environment?
8. How has the movement to JIT operations and automated manufacturing facilities affected the role of direct labor in management accounting practices?
9. Contrast the traditional manufacturing layout and the JIT production layout.
10. Name and describe the five time frames included in the traditional manufacturing process.
11. How has the inspection function changed in a JIT environment?
12. What is a nonvalue-adding activity?
13. Differentiate between a flexible manufacturing system and a computer-integrated manufacturing system.
14. What role does computer-integrated manufacturing play in JIT operations?
15. Why is the process costing method useful for computing the product unit costs of a JIT/FMS work cell?
16. Explain the meaning and use of the Raw in Process Inventory account.
17. Why is the analysis of nonfinancial data so important in a JIT environment?
18. Which level of capacity, normal or theoretical, is more important in analyzing a JIT/FMS operating cell? Why?
19. Give three examples of costs treated as indirect costs in a traditional manufacturing environment but accounted for as direct costs in a JIT setting. Explain the reasons for the three changes.
20. An automatic storage/retrieval system (AS/RS) is the key reason for the decrease in the levels of work in process inventories in a JIT/FMS environment. Why?

SHORT EXERCISES

SE 1. *New Manufacturing*
L O 1 *Environment*
Objectives

No check figure

Steve Taylor has just purchased a new machine that automates one entire product line. In order to implement a JIT operating environment, Steve has contracted with two local vendors to deliver raw materials only when needed. No raw materials inventory will be maintained. Has Steve accomplished the objectives of the new operating environment? Provide supporting evidence for your answer.

SE 2. *A Changing Work*
L O 2 *Environment and*
Managers' Behavior

No check figure

Wagner Industries has recently adopted a total quality management operating philosophy. Part of this new work environment involves the managing of process operations and support functions using employee teams as decision makers. Before this new environment was introduced, Mary Scott was manager of the design engineering function. Today, Mary's responsibilities are to help manage the function's decision team and to provide managerial support and encouragement. Mary feels that she has been demoted. Was she? What advice would you offer to Mary?

SE 3. *Elements of a JIT*
L O 3 *Operating*
Environment

No check figure

Maintaining minimum inventory levels, developing pull-through production planning and scheduling, and purchasing materials and product parts as needed in smaller lot sizes are three elements of a just-in-time operating environment. How does the pull-through production element and the producing-as-needed element help to accomplish the objective of minimizing inventories?

SE 4. *Traditional Versus*
L O 4 *JIT Operating*
Environment

No check figure

When changing from a traditional operating environment to a just-in-time operating environment, what are the primary objectives? What are some of the benefits that a company can expect to experience from such a change? Does such a change always pertain to a manufacturing company or does the JIT concept also apply to service businesses? If service businesses can utilize JIT elements, give an example of one type that would benefit from its adoption.

SE 5. *Product Costing*
L O 5 *Changes in a*
JIT Environment

No check figure

Crosson Tool Products Company is in the process of adopting the just-in-time operating philosophy for its tool-making operations. From the following list of factory overhead costs, identify those that are nonvalue-adding costs (NVA) and those that can be traced directly to the new tool-making work cell (D).

Storage barrels for work in process inventory
Inspection labor
Machine electricity
Machine repairs
Depreciation of the storage barrel movers
Machine setup labor

SE 6. *JIT and Process*
L O 6 *Costing*

Check Figure: Total unit cost: $213

Delisi Motor Corporation uses a JIT motor parts insertion work cell to assemble its main product line. During the first week in February, the following data were generated by the cell.

Beginning work in process inventory	
Materials and parts costs	$ 6,420
Conversion costs	4,280
Equivalent units	
Materials and parts costs	2,890
Conversion costs	2,640
Cost of materials used	$161,840
Cost of purchased parts used	196,520
Direct labor	39,600
Cell depreciation	68,640
Indirect labor and supplies	95,040
Other cell overhead	31,680

Assuming that the company uses the FIFO process costing method, compute the unit cost for the week.

SE 7. *Raw in Process*
L O 7 *Inventory*
Check Figure: Total cost of goods completed: $44,650

Dumler Products Corporation recently switched its production process to a just-in-time operating environment. Raw materials now arrive as needed and immediately enter the production process. A Raw in Process Inventory account is used to record all costs of production. During March, materials costing $17,400 were received, direct labor workers were paid $7,200, and $19,650 of factory overhead was applied to production activities. The beginning balance in the Raw in Process Inventory account was $1,850 and the ending balance was $1,450. Reconstruct the T account for the Raw in Process Inventory account and compute the cost of goods completed during March.

SE 8. *Product Costing*
L O 8 *and Automation*
No check figure

Castle Company has purchased its first computer numerically controlled (CNC) boring mill and the boring activity's supervisor is concerned about how the controller is going to assign factory overhead to the work of the boring activity. Direct labor hours has been the allocation basis. With the purchase of the CNC machine, three of the five direct labor boring machine workers were reassigned to other areas. What is the problem with continuing to use direct labor hours to allocate factory overhead? What alternative methods can be used? Why would the new methods result in improved product costing?

SE 9. *FMS and Product*
L O 9 *Unit Cost*
Check Figure: Total unit cost: $143.20

Shortly after installing its new flexible manufacturing system, Ranton Industries restructured its process of computing product unit cost. In addition to the costs of materials and labor, costs are assigned to products for materials handling, at a rate of 30 percent of the costs of materials used, and factory overhead, at a rate of $9 per machine hour. Product A78 generated the following data on a recent production run: Raw materials, $24 per unit; direct labor, $4 per unit; machine hours, 12 hours per unit. Compute the unit cost of Product A78.

EXERCISES

E 1. *JIT and Global*
L O 1 *Competition*
No check figure

Noyes Corporation has been losing money for the past two years and management has determined that foreign competition is the reason for the company's troubles. Foreign companies are making similar, higher-quality products and selling them at lower prices. Competitors have superior production methods and much lower product scrap rates. Noyes's management has decided to adopt a just-in-time operating philosophy. How will the JIT operating environment help the company become more profitable? Give specific examples of changes that will increase profits.

E 2. *JIT, Synchronous*
L O 2 *Manufacturing*
⟳ *Techniques, and*
Performance
Measurement
No check figure

General Motors Company's plant in Oshawa, Canada, has changed its production process from a traditional departmental structure into nine individually focused mini-factories, one for each major product line.[8] Each minifactory is a set of synchronous manufacturing work stations organized in a cell formation. Synchronous manufacturing is an offshoot of the JIT operating environment—all production is demand driven. To be synchronous, products from one station cannot be moved to the next until the receiving work station is ready to work on them. This system cuts lead times, improves quality, and reduces unit costs—all benefits of any JIT-based system.

GM's new performance measurement system has been named QUILS, which stands for quality, unit cost, inventory, lead time, and schedule. These five measures are used to monitor the plant's operating performance. Operating results are graphically displayed on large boards for easy viewing by all employees of a particular work cell. Quality is monitored using graphs of the trend of defects per million parts. Unit cost includes the cost of major components as well as the total manufacturing cost of products in a work cell. Progress in the inventory area is measured by the trend in inventory turnover. The lead-time graphs summarize the cycle time of the products through the work cell, breaking the cycle time down into its constituent components. Schedule is depicted on a graph describing the percentage of production that was completed on time.

Prepare a short paper about GM's new performance measurement system. Respond to the following questions as part of your report: What do you think of the QUILS system? What is unique about it? Does it measure operating performance?

8. Anthony A. Atkinson, "GM's Innovation for Performance," *CMA Magazine*, The Society of Management Accountants of Canada, June 1990, pp. 10–14.

E 3.
L O 4
*Old Versus New
Manufacturing
Environment*

No check figure

Irving Industries manufactures computer keyboard casings. The following machines and operations are involved in the production process.

Mixing machines   The Mixing Department has three machines that mix various chemicals to develop the raw materials used in the molding operation.

Molding machines   The Molding Department uses six molding machines. Each machine can be set up to make any keyboard casing sold by the company.

Trimming machines   In the Trimming Department, casings removed from the molds are trimmed of all excess materials. Six trimming machines are used.

Packing machines   Packing machines wrap and individually box each completed computer keyboard casing. Each of the two packing machines can keep pace with three trimming machines.

Products are moved from the mixing operation to the molding machines in 200-gallon drums. The drums usually sit one to three days before they are used. Sometimes the mixture must be remixed before it can be used by the Molding Department. From molding to trimming, the casings are stacked on wooden skids and moved by small lift trucks. The same moving procedure is used from trimming to the packing operation. Total production time can range from two weeks to three months, depending on the urgency of the order. Bill Loomis, CEO, is not happy with this rate of output. Suggest a plant layout that would change the manufacturing operation into a JIT production operation without the purchase of new equipment.

E 4.
L O 5
*Computer-Integrated
Manufacturing—
Definition*

No check figure

Morris Plastics, Inc. has had trouble competing in world markets for the past five years. Every time the company attempts to reduce costs to maintain a price advantage, the quality of its products suffers. As the overall quality has decreased, so has the company's market share. Mal Morris, founder and president of the company, has asked the production consulting firm of Sams & Colby to develop a strategic plan that would make the company competitive again and improve the quality of its products.

Jean Sams did the fieldwork for the consulting firm before preparing the plan. Sams spent two weeks at the Morris facilities in New Jersey and obtained information from the plastics industry trade association regarding recent trends and changes in production. The latest manufacturing equipment was reviewed and compared to existing machinery. Product flow was observed. Inventory storage and management were studied. And customer complaints were analyzed.

Sams & Colby's recommendations included the following statements.

1. Adopt the just-in-time operating environment.
2. Purchase two flexible manufacturing systems to replace existing functional production lines.
3. Purchase enough computer support to enable overall production setup to be linked in a computer-integrated manufacturing system.

Explain these three statements to Mal Morris.

E 5.
L O 5
*Direct Versus
Indirect Costs*

No check figure

The cost categories in the following list are common in a manufacturing and assembly operation.

Raw materials   Operating supplies
  Sheet steel   Small tools
  Iron castings   Depreciation, plant
Assembly parts   Depreciation, machinery
  Part 24RE6   Supervisory salaries
  Part 15RF8   Electrical power
Direct labor   Insurance and taxes, plant
Engineering labor   President's salary
Indirect labor   Employee benefits

Identify each type of cost as being either direct or indirect, assuming the cost was incurred in (1) a traditional manufacturing setting and (2) a JIT/FMS environment. State the reasons for any classification changes noted.

E 6. *Raw in Process*
L O 7 *Inventory*
No check figure

DePaul Manufacturing Company installed a JIT/FMS environment in its Shovel Division, and the system has been operating at near capacity for about eight months. Transactions related to the JIT/FMS are recorded when incurred. The following transactions took place last week.

Sept. 5 Wooden handles for jobs 12A, 14N, and 13F were ordered and received, $3,670.
    6 Sheet metal costing $5,630 received from vendor B.
    7 Work begun on job 14N.
    8 Job 12A completed and shipped to the customer; total cost, $13,600. (Company uses a 40 percent markup to establish selling price.)
    9 Spoiled goods with a net realizable value of $1,200 were moved to the shipping dock to be sold as scrap.

Using good journal entry form, record these transactions.

E 7. *The Changing*
L O 8 *Management*
    Accounting
    Environment
No check figure

Bill Cross, president and CEO of Curling Products, Inc., has just called controller Ray Horst into his office. "Ray, I don't understand several parts of this request for a new management accounting system that you submitted yesterday. I thought that we already had a very modern, up-to-date system. Why this sudden request for a major change? Is your request in any way connected with our new flexible manufacturing system? If so, why does a new manufacturing system require a complete revamping of an accounting system? Can't existing accounting practices and procedures handle the new equipment?"

Prepare Ray Horst's reply to Bill Cross.

E 8. *Product Costing*
L O 8 *Changes Caused by*
    JIT and Automation
No check figure

Berg Manufacturing Company produces high-tempered drill bits used by steel and aluminum products companies. The management accounting system uses standard costs. Cost control is accomplished by carefully computing and analyzing a series of price, rate, and efficiency variances. One factory overhead cost pool is used, and a plantwide overhead rate is the main aspect of the system. Direct labor hours is the base used to allocate factory overhead to products. Only raw materials and machinist labor are considered direct costs of the system.

Last week, the company installed its first FMS operating cell. The vice president of finance has asked the controller to identify specific changes to the management accounting system that have become necessary because of the new flexible manufacturing system.

Prepare a summary of the information that should be included in the controller's response to the vice president of finance.

E 9. *JIT's Influence on*
L O 8 *Product Unit Cost*
No check figure

Dafne Corporation has just installed a fully automated just-in-time production system. The entire manufacturing function comprises eight automated production cells that complete a product from beginning to end in less than two hours. Some products complete the production cycle in less than an hour. The production cycle time on the old, traditional processes took from three to five weeks. Now product orders are completed in two to three days.

What predictable effect will this production system change have on the following (give examples where appropriate)?

1. Total cost of raw materials and cost of raw materials per unit
2. Total cost of direct labor and cost of direct labor per unit
3. Total cost of factory overhead and cost of overhead per unit

E 10. *Product Costing*
L O 9 *in a Flexible*
    Manufacturing
    System
Check Figure: Manufacturing cost per tray: $9.53

Juris Enterprises, Inc. manufactures wooden serving trays using an FMS work cell. The wood is shaped and the trays assembled in one continuous operation. September's output totaled 42,300 units. Each unit requires two machine hours of effort. Materials handling cost is allocated to the product based on unit materials cost; engineering design costs are allocated based on units produced; and FMS cell overhead and building occupancy costs are allocated based on machine hours. Operating data for September follow.

Materials: Wood and hardware	$148,050
Total materials handling costs	50,337
Direct labor: Machinists	46,530
Engineering design costs	19,458
FMS cell overhead	87,984
Building occupancy overhead	50,760
Total costs	$403,119

The following allocation rates were computed:

Materials handling cost allocation rate per dollar of materials
$50,337 \div \$148,050 = 34\%$

Engineering design cost allocation rate per unit
$19,458 \div 42,300 = \$.46$

FMS overhead allocation rate per machine hour
$87,984 \div 84,600 = \$1.04$

Building occupancy allocation rate per machine hour
$50,760 \div 84,600 = \$.60$

Compute the unit cost of one wooden serving tray. Identify the six elements of the computation as part of your answer.

SKILLS DEVELOPMENT EXERCISES

Conceptual Analysis

SDE 1. *JIT in a Service*
L O 3 *Business*

No check figure

You are attending the installation banquet for new initiates into your business fraternity. The banquet is being held at an excellent restaurant. You are sitting next to Sally Nordstrum, a sophomore marketing major. In discussing her experiences in the accounting course she is taking, Sally mentions that she is having difficulty understanding the just-in-time (JIT) concept. She has read that a company's JIT operating system contains elements that support the concepts of simplicity, continuous improvement, waste reduction, timeliness, and efficiency. She realizes that before she can begin to understand JIT in a complex manufacturing environment, she must first understand JIT in a simpler context. She asks you to explain the term and provide an example.

Briefly explain the just-in-time philosophy. Using the elements of a JIT operating system that are presented in this chapter, apply these elements to the restaurant where your banquet is being held. Do you believe the JIT philosophy applies in all restaurant operations? Explain.

Ethical Dilemma

SDE 2. *Ethics and JIT*
L O 3 *Implementation*

No check figure

For almost a year, **Barineau Company** has been undergoing a change from a traditional to a JIT approach to its manufacturing process. Management has asked for employee assistance in the transition and has offered bonuses for suggestions that cut time from the production operation. Darby Lindsay and Todd Burks each identified a time-saving opportunity and, independently, turned in their suggestions to their manager, Sean McKinney.

McKinney sent the suggestions to the vice president of production and, inadvertently, they were identified as being his own. After careful analysis, the company's Production Review Committee decided that the two suggestions were worthy of reward and voted a large bonus to McKinney. When notified by the vice president, McKinney could not bring himself to identify the true authors of the suggestions.

When Lindsay and Burks heard about McKinney's ill-gained bonus, they were both very upset and confronted him with their grievance. He told them that he needed the recognition in order to be eligible for an upcoming promotion opportunity and stated that if they kept quiet about the matter, he would see to it that they both received significant raises. Prepare written responses so that you can discuss the following questions in class.

1. Should Lindsay and Burks keep quiet about the matter? What other avenues are open to them?
2. Having committed the fraudulent act, how should McKinney have dealt with the complaint of Lindsay and Burks?

Research Activity

SDE 3. *Just-in-Time*
L O 4 *Production and*
⟳ *Quality*

No check figure

Your campus library has a collection of annual reports for large, multinational companies as well as for companies in your state and local area. Many of these companies have recently installed automated just-in-time production processes in order to compete for new domestic as well as foreign business. Search through the annual reports of several manufacturers. Choose one that describes the changes made within its plant to increase product quality and to compete as a world-class manufacturer. Prepare a one-page description of those changes. Include in your report the name of the company, its geographic location, the name of the chief executive officer and/or president, and the dollar amount of total sales for the most recent year. Be prepared to present your findings to your classmates.

Decision-Making Practice

SDE 4. *Installing JIT*
L O 3 *Work Cells*
⟳

No check figure

The presidents of three companies have contracted with your consulting firm to help improve profitability, and each wishes to discuss the possible installation of JIT work cells in their plants. You obtain the following descriptions of their production processes.

Company A: This company manufacturers small, executive-type jet airplanes. Their product line consists of four models. Capacity for the company is ten planes per month and they are currently operating at full capacity. World competition exists from ten companies in six foreign countries as well as eight other U.S. firms. The company employs eighteen highly skilled people: three designer engineers, thirteen assembly people, and two test pilots. They would like to double their capacity because of the demand for their products.

Company B: Automobile engine blocks are the specialty of this company. They manufacture engine blocks exclusively for one automobile manufacturer. Their products include 4-, 6-, and 8-cylinder blocks and each category has at least three different models. The engine block castings arrive directly from the foundry. The company must mill, bore, drill, tap, finish, and inspect each engine block. All of these operations are currently performed by different departments.

Company C: This company is a world leader in the manufacture of plastic parts for the personal computer market. The company currently produces over five hundred different parts that it classifies into twenty different groupings. Production runs can range from as few as 20 units to as many as 500,000 units. If the plastic parts are allowed to cool for more than six hours during production, they must be reheated before additional processing can be completed.

Identify the company that you think would benefit most from the installation of JIT work cells. Which company would probably never need to consider the installation of work cells? Prepare a written analysis stating your position on each question and the reasons for your responses. Does one of the companies need to develop a flexible manufacturing system rather than a JIT work cell? If so, identify the company and state the reasons to support your decision.

PROBLEM SET A

A 1. *Production Layout*
L O 4 *Design*

No check figure

Processing and canning vegetables and fruits is a major industry in many countries. Alabama Food Products Company of Huntsville, Alabama, is one of the biggest food processors in the Southeast. The following processing operations for black-eyed peas are common in this industry.

Cooking	Heating peas to a correct temperature so that consumers only have to reheat and serve
Inspecting raw peas	Weeding out inedible peas
Canning	Automatically putting cooked peas into cans
Labeling	Placing labels on processed cans
Shelling	Taking shells off raw peas
Finished goods storage	Storing canned peas while they await shipment
Cleaning	Washing peas before processing
Receiving	Accepting shipments of freshly picked peas
Packing	Placing labeled cans in boxes
Lid sealing	Sealing lids on cans to prevent spoilage or leakage
Shipping	Loading and shipping cartons according to customers' needs
Bin storage	Storing raw peas before processing
Can inspection	Isolating improperly sealed cans
Cooling	Reducing temperature of cooked peas to facilitate canning operation

REQUIRED

1. Arrange these operations in the order they would occur in a traditional production system.
2. Assume that just-in-time operations are going to replace the traditional production process. Identify the
   a. operations or process elements that would be eliminated.
   b. operations that would be automated.
   c. operations that could be combined into operating cells.
3. Is this company a good candidate for the JIT/FMS environment? Be prepared to defend your answer.

A 2.

L O 5, 9

Product Costing in a Flexible Manufacturing System

Check Figure: 1b. Pattern design cost allocation rate: $11.25 per unit

Fletcher Apparel, Inc. specializes in manufacturing business suits for women. The company has three basic suit lines and can produce more than a dozen variations of each basic design. Last year, because of rising backlogs and declining quality, the company installed a flexible manufacturing system for all three suit lines. Operating results to date have been very good, but management would still like to improve its delivery cycle and reduce the cost per unit.

Following are the operating data for October.

Materials		Pattern design	
Cloth material	$233,600	Labor	$22,806
Lining material	94,900	Electrical power	5,475
Sewing supplies	29,200	Pattern design overhead	12,775
Materials handling		FMS overhead	
Labor	4,380	Equipment depreciation	5,840
Equipment depreciation	3,285	Indirect labor	26,280
Electrical power	2,190	Supervision	49,640
Maintenance	2,920	Operating supplies	13,140
Direct labor		Electrical power	8,760
Machinists	80,300	Repairs and maintenance	7,300
		Building occupancy overhead	67,160

October's output totaled 3,650 suits. Each suit requires four machine hours of effort. Materials handling cost is allocated to the product based on unit materials cost; pattern design costs are allocated based on units produced; and FMS overhead is allocated based on machine hours.

REQUIRED

1. Compute the following:
   a. Materials handling cost allocation rate
   b. Pattern design cost allocation rate
   c. FMS overhead allocation rate
2. Compute the unit cost of one business suit. Show details of your computation.

A 3. *JIT Unit Cost*
L O 5 *Computations*

Check Figure: 2. Total unit cost for quarter ended 3/31/x7: $10.39

Drafts Corp. installed an automated just-in-time production cell in its Battery Casings Division at the beginning of the year. Operating data for the first quarter of 19x7 are now available. Prior to the installation of the JIT cell, four operations were performed in functional departments to complete a casing. These departments were: Sheet Metal Cutting, Stamping, Shaping, and Finishing. Now all operations are performed in a single cell run by two highly skilled machine operators. The controller is interested in a unit cost comparison and has selected casing FM20 for the analysis. Data for the last two quarters are summarized below.

	Casing FM20	
	Quarter Ended 3/31/x7	Quarter Ended 12/31/x6
Units produced	39,400	21,700
Raw materials		
Sheet metal	$106,380	$ 56,420
Rivets	2,364	1,519
Direct labor		
Sheet metal cutting		26,040
Stamping		20,615
Shaping		16,275
Finishing		19,964
JIT cell	77,224	
Factory overhead		
Indirect labor	83,528	31,682
Operating supplies	3,152	2,170
Inspection labor	0	1,953
Lift truck labor	4,334	2,604
Electricity	21,276	7,378
Materials scrap costs	5,516	7,812
Small tools expense	37,430	25,606
Machine depreciation	22,064	4,774
Building depreciation	3,940	2,604
Production scheduling costs	3,152	5,208
Repairs and maintenance	9,062	4,774
Supervisory salaries	20,488	15,190
Machine lubricants	7,092	2,821
Storage space costs	2,364	11,935
Total costs incurred	$409,366	$267,344

REQUIRED

1. Compute the unit cost for each cost category listed for the last quarter of 19x6 and the first quarter of 19x7.
2. Compute and compare total units cost for the two quarters.
3. Which unit costs changed the most by installing the JIT cell? Were these anticipated cost changes? State your reasons.

A 4. *JIT and FIFO*
L O 6 *Process Costing*

Check Figure: 1. Total conversion costs: $108,243

The Cheyenne Company is located in Cheyenne, Wyoming, and has been producing sink faucets for the past twelve years. The prices of the seven models of kitchen sink faucets range from $24 to $94. The Grand model is the highest-priced faucet, and its market share has declined steadily over the last four years.

Bothered by the decline in market share, management recently purchased a JIT/FMS cell for the kitchen faucet line. Two day-shift operators prepare the equipment to run automatically during the two evening shifts. Only indirect support labor is needed during the night shifts. For the week ending July 30, 19x7, the Grand model was run and the following data were generated.

Units
  Beginning raw in process inventory
    (60 percent complete as to conversion costs,
    100 percent complete as to materials costs)   45
  Units completed during week   6,295
  Ending raw in process inventory
    (70 percent complete as to conversion costs,
    100 percent complete as to materials costs)   50

Hours worked
  Direct labor—80 hours
  Machine hours
    Fourteen machines in cell
    Each machine in the FMS cell ran 116 hours
      during week

Costs in beginning raw in process inventory

Materials costs	$ 2,410
Conversion costs	765

Direct costs incurred by faucet JIT/FMS cell

Raw materials	$157,458
Direct labor (80 hours at $16 per hour)	1,280
Electricity costs	6,056
JIT cell machinery depreciation	3,890
Engineering design costs	7,934
Indirect labor	12,000
Lubricants, supplies, and fasteners	8,110

Overhead rates used
  Materials handling overhead (included as part of
    raw materials cost in the process costing analysis):
      25 percent of raw materials costs
  Factory overhead not traceable to cell:
    $42 per machine hour worked

REQUIRED

1. Compute the total materials cost and total conversion cost for the week.
2. Using good form and the FIFO process costing approach, prepare (a) a schedule of equivalent production, (b) a unit cost analysis schedule, and (c) a cost summary schedule.
3. From the cost summary schedule, prepare a journal entry to transfer costs of completed units to the Finished Goods Inventory account.
4. Do you think the $94 price is too high for the Grand model? Explain your answer.

A 5. *Machine Hours*
L O 8, 9 *Versus Labor Hours*
Check Figure: 1. Plantwide factory overhead rate: 62.11% of direct labor cost

Fanny's Furniture Company specializes in recreational furniture for all types of outdoor life. Portable tables are the company's best-selling product, and three models have become very popular products: the Mini, Max, and Deluxe models.

To keep up with the competition, the company purchased flexible manufacturing systems for these product lines about eight months ago. But since the purchase, factory overhead rates have been increasing, to the disappointment of the owners of the business, who have asked the controller to prepare a comparative analysis of this situation.

The following data are from the past month's records.

	Mini	Max	Deluxe
Unit information			
Raw materials cost	$21	$32	$46
Direct labor hours	2.2	2.8	3.4
Direct labor cost per hour	$16	$16	$16
Machine hours	3.4	3.2	3
Information totals			
Unit sales during month	120,000	108,000	94,000
Total factory overhead	$2,904,000	$3,024,000	$2,876,400

The company's policy has been to set selling prices at 180 percent of a product's production cost.

REQUIRED

1. Compute the company's plantwide factory overhead rate using total direct labor dollars as a basis.
2. Compute each product's total production costs and selling price using the application rate computed in **1.**
3. Compute a new factory overhead application rate assuming:
   a. Materials storage and handling overhead equal to 10 percent of the cost of raw materials is subtracted from the factory overhead cost totals.
   b. Machine hours is the factory overhead allocation basis.
   c. Product line overhead rates are used rather than a plantwide rate.
4. Compute each product's total production cost and selling price using the allocation rates computed in **3.**
5. Compare the old and new product selling prices and comment on your findings.

PROBLEM SET B

B 1. *Production Layout*
L O 4 *Design*

No check figure

Whatley Automotive Products Company manufactures chrome automobile parts. The following manufacturing operations and functions are part of the production of all types of automobile grills.

Assembly	Connecting devices are put on the completed grill.
Stamping	The grill shape is stamped out of a piece of sheet metal.
Plating	A chrome substance is adhered to the heat-treated product.
Receiving	Sheet metal and assembly parts are received in the central receiving area.
Welding	Connector pads are attached to the heat-treated product before plating.
Washing	Products are cleaned before being inspected for the first time.
Postassembly inspection	Products are inspected just prior to being packaged.
Raw materials storage	Sheet metal and assembly parts are stored before they are used.
Drilling	Holes are drilled into the products before the connector pads are welded.
Bending	Stamped grills are bent into shape.
Heat treating	All products are heat-treated after passing the preassembly inspection point.
Sheet metal inspection	All sheet metal received is inspected.
Polishing	Plated grills are polished before being assembled.
Skid moving	All grills are moved on large wooden skids from operation to operation.
Shipping	Railroad cars are loaded for shipment to automobile manufacturers.
Packing	Grills are packed in large wooden crates.
Preassembly inspection	All grills are inspected after the washing operation.

REQUIRED

1. Arrange these operations in the order they would occur in a traditional manufacturing system.
2. Assume that a just-in-time approach is going to be taken in redesigning this production process. Identify the
   a. operations or process elements that would be eliminated.
   b. operations that would be automated.
   c. operations that could be combined into operating cells.
3. Is this company a good candidate for the JIT/FMS environment? Why or why not?

B 2.
L O 5, 9

Product Costing in a Flexible Manufacturing System

Check Figure: 2. Manufacturing cost per seat: $8.67

Largo Company produces a complete line of bicycle seats in its Flagstaff plant. The four versions of Model J17-21 are made on flexible manufacturing system #2. The four seats have different shapes but identical processing operations and production costs. During July, the following costs were incurred and traced to FMS #2.

Materials
Leather	$23,520
Metal frame	38,220
Bolts	2,940

Materials handling
Labor	7,350
Equipment depreciation	4,410
Electrical power	2,460
Maintenance	5,184

Direct labor
Machinists	13,230

Engineering design
Labor	4,116
Electrical power	1,176
Engineering overhead	7,644

FMS overhead
Equipment depreciation	7,056
Indirect labor	30,870
Supervision	17,640
Operating supplies	4,410
Electrical power	10,584
Repairs and maintenance	21,168
Building occupancy overhead	52,920

July's output totaled 29,400 units. Each unit requires three machine hours of effort. Materials handling costs are allocated to the products based on unit materials cost; engineering design costs are allocated based on units produced; and FMS overhead is allocated based on machine hours.

REQUIRED

1. Compute the following:
   a. Materials handling cost allocation rate
   b. Engineering design cost allocation rate
   c. FMS overhead allocation rate
2. Compute the unit cost of one bicycle seat. Show the details of your computation.

B 3.
L O 5

JIT Unit Cost Computations

Check Figure: 2. Total unit cost for quarter ended 3/31/x8: $2.51

Cabrera Food Products Co. had its first automated just-in-time production cell installed in the fall of 19x7. The cell began producing large frozen pizzas on January 2, 19x8. Before the JIT cell was in operation, the pizzas were processed through four departments: Dough Processing, Meat and Vegetable Preparation, Ingredients Application, and Trimming and Packaging. The new JIT cell performs all of these operations in a continuous process and only one skilled operator is needed to run the cell. The company's general manager is interested in the impact of the new cell on the unit costs of the large pizzas and has asked you to prepare a comparative analysis of these costs. Data for the quarters before and after installation of the cell are summarized on the next page.

REQUIRED

1. Compute the unit cost for each cost category listed for the last quarter of 19x7 and the first quarter of 19x8.
2. Compute and compare total units cost for the two quarters.
3. Which unit costs changed the most by installing the JIT cell? Were these anticipated cost changes? State your reasons.

	Large Pizzas	
	Quarter Ended 3/31/x8	Quarter Ended 12/31/x7
Units produced	65,900	43,200
Raw materials		
Pizza dough	$ 36,245	$ 21,600
Meats, cheese, and vegetables	42,835	30,240
Direct labor		
Dough preparation		12,960
Meat and vegetable preparation		10,800
Ingredients application		17,280
Trimming and packaging		21,600
JIT cell	26,360	
Factory overhead		
Indirect labor	19,770	864
Ingredients waste	6,590	25,920
Inspection labor	0	4,320
Lift truck labor	1,977	5,184
Electricity	3,295	1,296
Spoiled units	1,318	6,912
Production scheduling costs	659	8,640
Machine depreciation	9,885	4,752
Building depreciation	2,636	2,592
Supplies	593	432
Storage space costs	659	5,616
Supervisory salaries	7,908	7,776
Machine lubricants	923	648
Repairs and maintenance	3,954	1,728
Total costs incurred	$165,607	$191,160

B 4.
L O 6

JIT and Process Costing—Average Method

Check Figure: 1. Total conversion costs: $105,448

Engles Corporation has manufactured ladders for both home and business use for more than twenty-five years. Ten years ago the company introduced all-aluminum models, and the Engles Ladder became a very popular brand. But with the recent introduction of several other brands of aluminum ladders into the marketplace, the Engles models have suffered significant sales declines. The company produces two major types of ladders: collapsible stepladders and extension ladders. Three sizes of each type of ladder are produced. Extension ladders come in 8-, 10-, and 12-foot lengths and cost $80, $100, and $125, respectively. The 12-foot model is known as the Primo Ladder.

To improve efficiency and reduce operating costs, the company purchased two JIT/flexible manufacturing systems last year, one for each type of ladder produced. Three direct labor workers run the extension ladder cell, one worker for each of the three eight-hour shifts per day. Most of the operation is run automatically, and several indirect labor support people help with setups and maintenance.

During the week ended August 12, 19x8, the extension ladder work cell produced the following data pertaining to the manufacturing of the Primo Ladder.

Units	
Beginning raw in process inventory	60
Units completed during week	4,280
Ending raw in process inventory (60 percent complete as to conversion costs, 100 percent complete as to materials costs)	40

Hours worked
   Direct labor—120 hours
   Machine hours
     Eleven machines in the cell
     Each machine in the FMS cell ran 112 hours
      during week

Costs in beginning raw in process inventory	
Materials costs	$1,780
Conversion costs	1,450

Direct costs incurred by extension ladder JIT/FMS cell	
Raw materials	$96,994
Direct labor (120 hours at $19 per hour)	2,280
Electrical power costs	8,342
JIT cell machinery depreciation	2,780
Engineering design costs	8,570
Indirect labor	12,320
Lubricants, supplies, and fasteners	4,410

Overhead rates used
   Materials handling overhead (included as part of
    raw materials cost in the process costing analysis):
     30 percent of raw materials costs
   Factory overhead not traceable to cell:
     $53 per machine hour worked

REQUIRED

1. Compute the total materials cost and the total conversion cost for the week.
2. Using good form and the average process costing approach, prepare the following schedules:
   a. schedule of equivalent production
   b. unit cost analysis schedule
   c. cost summary schedule
3. From the cost summary schedule, prepare a journal entry to transfer the costs of completed units to the Finished Goods Inventory account.
4. Do you think the $125 price is too high for the Primo Ladder? Why?

B 5.   *Machine Hours*
L O 8, 9   *Versus Labor Hours*
Check Figure: 1. Plantwide factory overhead rate: 128.684% of direct labor cost

Gene Epstein has been in the manufacturing business for more than twenty years. Four months ago, Epstein Products, Inc. made a major investment in automated machinery. The three new flexible manufacturing systems each have seven operating stations and produce chrome automobile bumpers in one operation. Each FMS specializes in one type of bumper; these products are identified as A-Bump, B-Bump, and C-Bump, with A-Bump being the most complex and C-Bump the least difficult to make. After four months of operation, Epstein began complaining to the controller about the ever-increasing factory overhead rate. Epstein was under the impression that the new automated machinery was going to reduce product costs. A plantwide overhead rate is still being used, but the machinery installation consultant did suggest switching to individual FMS factory overhead rates, with materials handling costs being treated separately. These costs are currently included in the total factory overhead cost pool.

The following data are from the past month's records.

	A-Bump	B-Bump	C-Bump
Unit information			
Raw materials cost	$96	$88	$82
Direct labor hours	1.2	1.5	.8
Direct labor cost per hour	$20	$18	$16
Machine hours	4.2	3.1	3
Information totals			
Unit sales during month	50,000	70,000	100,000
Total factory overhead	$2,950,000	$1,242,500	$1,431,000

Epstein's policy has been to set selling prices at 160 percent of a product's production cost.

REQUIRED

1. Compute the company's plantwide factory overhead rate using total direct labor dollars as a basis.
2. Compute each product's total production costs and selling price using the application rate computed in **1.**
3. Compute a new factory overhead application rate assuming:
   a. Materials storage and handling overhead equal to 5 percent of the cost of raw materials is subtracted from the factory overhead cost totals.
   b. Machine hours is the factory overhead allocation basis.
   c. Product line overhead rates are used rather than a plantwide rate.
4. Compute each product's total production cost and selling price using the allocation rates computed in **3.**
5. Compare the old and new product selling prices and comment on your findings.

MANAGERIAL REPORTING AND ANALYSIS CASES

Interpreting Management Reports

MRA 1. *Cost Allocation*

L O 4, 5

Check Figure: 3. Total costs to be allocated to Job 101: $26,284

The management of *Kingsley Iron Works* has decided to convert its present traditional manufacturing system in the Castings Department to a just-in-time operation. The following tasks have been accomplished.

1. An agreement was signed with a supplier for daily deliveries of iron ingots needed for the department's iron casting products. The department supervisor is responsible for ordering the ingots.
2. Responsibility for machine repairs and maintenance and for product quality control and inspection was shifted to the machine operators in the Castings Department.
3. Three CNC machines were purchased that are capable of melting the ingots, mixing specified alloys, and molding the castings ordered to specific shapes and sizes. In addition, an automated conveyor system was purchased for work in process movement between the new machines. The entire operation is now a flexible manufacturing system and is operated in a just-in-time manner.
4. New electrical power meters were installed in all departments of the plant so that each unit's power usage can be monitored and computed. Each machine's electrical power usage in the Castings Department can be identified.
5. Insurance rates on plant machinery are broken down on a per machine hour usage basis.
6. Due to streamlining, the size of the Castings Department was reduced by 50 percent.
7. There are now eight direct labor workers in the Castings Department; there were twenty-six before the FMS was installed.

Kingsley Iron Works has a second department, the Small Tools Department, that specializes in making over twenty varieties of small iron and steel hand tools for business. The Small Tools Department still operates under the traditional methods and has only one automated machine. Thirty-six direct labor employees are needed to keep the department running. Because products are moved manually, large bins of partially completed tools are everywhere. Individual machine power usage is not metered. Repair and maintenance of machines is done on an as-needed basis. Raw materials are ordered two months in advance so that there is never a stock out.

The following facts relate to last month's operating activities:

	Castings Department	Small Tools Department	Totals
Direct labor hours	1,344	6,336	7,680
Machine hours			
Castings Department			
Machine A	484		484
Machine B	440		440
Machine C	420		420
Small Tools Department			
Semiautomatic machine		176	176
Nonprogrammed machinery*		1,920	1,920
Engineering hours used	640	320	960
Computer time usage (hours)	300	25	325
Cost of raw materials used	$96,000	$120,000	$216,000
Square footage of department (revised)	3,000	9,000	12,000

*When using nonprogrammed machine hours for distribution purposes, they should count one-tenth as much as computer-driven machine hours.

Details for the Castings Department:

	Job 101	Job 105	Job 110	Totals
Direct labor hours	168	672	504	1,344
Machine hours				
Machine A	220	132	132	484
Machine B	264	88	88	440
Machine C	84	210	126	420
Totals	568	430	346	1,344

Plantwide factory overhead costs	
Property taxes, building	$ 2,400
Wages, warehouse	8,640
Depreciation, warehouse equipment	1,296
Depreciation, factory machines	5,992
Depreciation, engineering equipment	1,440
Raw materials handling costs	25,920
Indirect support labor	15,408
Computer center costs, factory	4,030
Salaries, engineering	8,160
Operating supplies, engineering	1,728
Salaries, Accounting Department	5,136
Salaries, Personnel Department	7,104
Cafeteria costs	4,736
Insurance, building	600
Insurance, factory machinery	3,424
Employee benefits	3,552
Repairs and Maintenance Department	2,576
Quality Control Department	3,312
Electrical power, building	10,200
Electrical power, machines	5,136
Purchasing Department costs	3,240
Total	$124,030

REQUIRED

1. Compute the traditional plantwide factory overhead rate based on direct labor hours. Allocate the overhead costs to both departments and to the jobs in the Castings Department using this approach.

2. Recommend changes to Kingsley's management concerning the distribution of traditional indirect costs to both departments. Identify the allocation basis to be used for each cost listed.
3. Distribute the costs to both departments and to the jobs in the Castings Department using the methods you recommended in **2**. Use machine hours as the basis for the distribution of costs to jobs in the Castings Department.
4. Highlight and explain the differences resulting from the two approaches.

Formulating Management Reports

MRA 2.
L O 3, 4

Manufacturing Processes and Management Reporting Systems

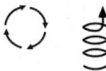

No check figure

Hamby, Inc. manufactures professional golf clubs. Demand for the golf clubs is so great that the company built a special plant that makes only custom-crafted clubs. The clubs are shaped by machines but vary according to the customer's sex, height, weight, and arm length. Ten basic sets of clubs are produced, five for females and five for males. Slight variations in machine setup provide the difference in the club weights and lengths.

In the past six months, several problems have developed at the golf club plant. Even though one computer numerically controlled machine is used in the manufacturing process, the company's backlog is growing rapidly. Customers are complaining that delivery is too slow. Quality is declining because clubs are pushed through the production process without proper inspection. Working capital is wastefully used for space to store excessive amounts of inventory. Workers are complaining about the pressure to produce the backlogged orders. Machine breakdown is increasing. Production control reports are not useful because they are not timely and contain irrelevant information. Hamby's profitability and cash flow is suffering.

You have been hired by Hamby, Inc. as a consultant to define the problem and suggest a possible solution to the current dilemma. Jim Hamby, the president, asks that you complete your work within a month so that he can prepare and present an action plan to the board of directors at the mid-year board meeting.

REQUIRED

1. Prepare a response to Hamby. Include in your analysis specific changes in the manufacturing process and the management accounting system. Defend each change that you suggest.
2. To help you prepare this report, answer the following questions.
   a. What kinds of information do you need to prepare this report?
   b. Why is this information relevant?
   c. Where would you go to obtain this information (sources)?
   d. When would you want to obtain this information?

International Company

MRA 3.
L O 1, 2, 3

Implementing Just-in-Time Principles

No check figure

Sandra Alvarez recently attended a conference on the implementation of just-in-time principles in manufacturing operations. During lunch, she talked with Rick Salcedo, the president of a Mexican corporation that manufactures photographic equipment, and Roland Sims, the chief executive officer of a Tanzanian textile manufacturer.

Salcedo stated that a number of obstacles exist in the implementation of JIT in Mexican plants. He believes that many companies find employees and suppliers unwilling to participate fully in the process of implementing JIT. Also, the managers of many plant operations are integrating only a few components of JIT into traditional manufacturing operations.

Sims agreed that obstacles also exist for manufacturing operations in Tanzania. He says that his company has encountered constraints in obtaining loans for machine acquisitions, inadequate supplies of materials for mills to operate near capacity, delays in deliveries of materials from international sources, inadequate transportation infrastructure, and unreliable product demand forecasts.

REQUIRED

1. Which of these obstacles might also exist for U.S. manufacturing companies that want to implement just-in-time manufacturing principles?
2. What recommendations would you make to help companies change to a just-in-time operating environment?

Cost Management Systems: Activity-Based Costing and Measures of Quality

1. Define *cost management*, describe a cost management system, and identify how this type of system benefits managers.

2. Define and explain *activity-based costing*, and list examples of cost drivers.

3. Identify all activities that comprise a particular operating process, distinguish between value-adding and nonvalue-adding activities, and describe the value chain of a product or service.

4. Define *total quality management* and identify and compute the costs of quality for products and services.

5. Evaluate operating performance using financial and nonfinancial measures of quality.

6. Identify the types of financial and nonfinancial analyses used in a competitive operating environment to evaluate the performance of (a) product delivery, (b) inventory control, (c) materials cost/scrap control, and (d) machine management and maintenance.

7. Define *full cost profit margin* and state the advantages of this measure of profitability.

8. Identify the primary areas of management reporting in a competitive operating environment and give examples of reports needed.

Hughes Aircraft Company

The Product Operations and Quality Systems Division of Hughes Aircraft Company decided to implement its new activity-based costing (ABC) system to improve the accuracy of product cost information.[1] The division's traditional costing system data was found to be inaccurate and did not support management's strategic and operational decisions. The old system's primary purpose was to provide costs for customer billing and financial statement preparation purposes.

The ABC implementation process involved a four-step approach. The first step was a move to multiple burden centers. This was done by breaking down a single, companywide overhead pool (burden center) into major product-line-oriented overhead pools. This move alone improved product costing by avoiding resource subsidies across product lines. Next, central service functions that were shared by all production activities were analyzed to determine the primary causes for the use of their resources. These causes, called cost drivers, were identified for each service function and used to assign costs to activities using a function's services. Examples of service functions, their cost drivers, and the resulting cost assignment rate for each are shown below.

Function	Cost Driver	Rate
Human Resources	Headcount	Dollars per employee
	Hires	Dollars per hire
	Union employees	Dollars per employee
	Training hours	Dollars per training hour
Security	Square footage	Dollars per square foot
Receiving	Number of receivers	Dollars per receipt
Data Processing	Lines printed	Dollars per line
	CPU minutes	Dollars per CPU minute
	Storage	Dollars per storage unit

Third, an activity accounting procedure was implemented to define the activities of the company, examine those activities to make sure each was doing what it was supposed to be doing in a cost-effective manner, and

---

1. Jack Haedicke and David Feil, "In a DOD Environment, Hughes Aircraft Sets the Standard for ABC," *Management Accounting*, Institute of Management Accountants, February 1991, pp. 29–33.

highlight areas needing improvement. The final step was to pull the information from the first three steps together and implement an activity-based costing system. At this point, costs had been grouped by burden center, supporting service costs could be assigned using cost driver rates, and all activities had been identified. Now indirect costs could be assigned to activities and traced to products using cost drivers connected with the activities. This process took over five years to accomplish, an evolutionary rather than a revolutionary approach. Why did the company purposely take five years to implement its ABC system?

Dropping such a massive new system on an unsuspecting work force would have been disastrous. Time was needed to educate people about the system. Government agencies dealing with Hughes Aircraft were brought in early and asked to help design the system. Other Hughes business units were asked to contribute to the system's development. The system was tested at several locations to work out deficiencies. With everyone affected by the ABC system on board, the new system was successfully implemented. ⦂⦂⦂⦂

COST MANAGEMENT SYSTEMS

OBJECTIVE

1 *Define* cost management, *describe a cost management system, and identify how this type of system benefits managers*

Many traditional management accounting techniques and practices do not produce meaningful results when applied to today's globally competitive business environment. Companies have found that traditional cost allocation and product costing approaches generate erroneous unit cost information when used to measure the output of automated just-in-time (JIT) operations. Computerized facilities and computer-aided processes enable the accountant to trace more types of costs directly to work cells or products. Traditional management accounting practices, however, were not designed to identify and eliminate nonvalue-adding activities. Traditional practices do not trace costs adequately; they do not isolate the costs of unnecessary activities; they do not penalize overproduction; and they do not quantify such nonfinancial measures as quality, throughput, and flexibility.[2] Their focus is on costs, not on the activities that generate costs.

These concerns have led to the creation of cost management systems (CMS). According to James Brimson, a partner in Coopers & Lybrand, Deloitte, United Kingdom, cost management is the management and control of *activities* to determine product cost accurately, to improve business processes, to eliminate waste, to identify cost drivers, to plan operations, and to set business strategies.[3] A cost management system (CMS) is a management accounting and reporting system that identifies, monitors, and maintains continuous, detailed analyses of a company's activities and provides managers with timely measures of operating results. A CMS is designed to support new management philosophies including just-in-time operations, activity-based costing (ABC) and activity-based management (ABM) approaches, and total quality management (TQM) environments.

2. Callie Berliner and James A. Brimson, Computer Aided Manufacturing—International, *Cost Management for Today's Advanced Manufacturing* (Boston: Harvard Business School Press, 1988).

3. James A. Brimson, *Activity Accounting* (New York: John Wiley & Sons, 1991).

Rather than take a historical approach to cost control as most accounting systems do, a cost management system is on-line and interactive with current management strategies and decisions. A CMS plays a major role in planning, managing, and reducing costs. Cost cutting is not accomplished by just slashing the amount of existing resources that a department can use to produce a product, as happens in a traditional costing system. A CMS relies on the concept of continuous improvement to reduce costs while still increasing product quality. Continuous improvement means that design engineers are continuously looking for ways to improve the product while still cutting its cost; the production process is watched constantly to find areas for improvement, thereby increasing efficiency and reducing costs; and nonvalue-adding activities are monitored continuously to find activities or resource usage that can be reduced or eliminated. In cost management systems, the primary focus is on the management of activities, not costs, for both product costing and cost control purposes. CMS advocates believe that when activities are managed effectively, a natural consequence is the effective use of money and other resources.

Another trait of a cost management system is the use of target costing. When continuous improvement is employed, a company can increase profits by first designing the product so that its target cost is achieved. It can then make ongoing improvements to reduce costs further. Finally, cost assignment within a cost management system is far superior to that within traditional cost systems. By accumulating costs by activities and then tracing the usage of the activity to specific products or product types, costs can be assigned easily and accurately.

By focusing on activities, a CMS provides managers with improved knowledge of the processes for which they are responsible. Activity-related information needed to trim process operating cycle time or product throughput time is readily available. More accurate product costs lead to improved pricing decisions. Nonvalue-adding activities are highlighted and managers can work to reduce or eliminate them. In addition to product profitability information, a CMS can analyze individual customer profitability by looking at the costs of servicing customers. Overall, the CMS pinpoints resource usage and cost for each activity for managers and fosters managerial decisions that lead to continuous improvement throughout the organization.

OBJECTIVE

2 *Define and explain* **activity-based costing,** *and list examples of cost drivers*

ACTIVITY-BASED COSTING

Because of changes in direct labor, problems arise when traditional cost allocation and product costing methods are used in automated JIT operations. Critics insist that costs assigned to products using direct labor as a basis increasingly distort product costs as direct labor becomes a smaller and smaller factor in production. Even though many nonvalue-adding costs are reduced significantly or eliminated by adopting JIT procedures, the problem of cost traceability remains. Numerous product costing errors can result if all indirect product-related costs are charged to one Factory Overhead account and if those costs are allocated to products based on direct labor hours or dollars.[4]

Cost management systems resolve these problems with a new method of tracing and managing costs, called *activity-based costing.* Activity-based cost-

---

4. Robin Cooper and Robert S. Kaplan, "How Cost Accounting Distorts Product Costs," *Management Accounting,* Institute of Management Accountants, April 1988, p. 21.

ing (ABC) is an approach to cost assignment that identifies all major operating activities, categorizes costs by activity, reduces or eliminates nonvalue-adding activities, and assigns costs using a basis that causes the costs to be incurred. A company that uses activity-based costing allocates product costs by identifying production and distribution activities and the events and circumstances that cause or "drive" those activities. As a result, many smaller cost pools are created, and many different cost assignments are made either directly to a product or job or to a JIT work cell. The costs traced or assigned to a work cell then are allocated to the products produced by that cell.

IDENTIFYING COST DRIVERS

When a company uses activity-based costing, cost drivers are the basis for cost assignment. A cost driver is any activity that causes a cost to be incurred.

The objective of a traditional management accounting system is cost control. Cost allocation procedures assign costs to cost objectives on a causal or beneficial basis. These assigned costs are then compared with budgeted amounts to help control costs. In the new manufacturing environment using activity-based costing, the objective is to identify and eliminate unnecessary costs rather than to just try to reduce them through cost control procedures. But before a cost can be eliminated or accounted for properly, the management accountant must know what causes the cost—what drives it. Once the cost driver has been identified, the indirect costs it generates can be either (1) treated as legitimate product costs and traced directly to a work cell or product or (2) reduced or eliminated by reducing or eliminating the activities that cause the costs to be incurred.

Table 1 lists ten potential cost drivers. Let's look at one—the number of engineering change orders—and develop a list of costs that it generates. Suppose an engineering change is made that leads to the reworking of products already produced as well as those in the production process. The possible costs generated by this engineering change order include the following:

1. Additional engineering time and labor costs
2. Utility and space costs associated with the extra work
3. Machine setup time and costs caused by the change order
4. Product rework time in the work cell
5. Increased conversion costs in the cell

Most engineering change orders occur because the design of the product was not refined before it was introduced into the manufacturing process. The costs associated with engineering change orders are reduced if the number of change orders is reduced. In addition, if an engineering change order is for a specific job, then all costs related to that activity are traceable and chargeable to that job. Following activity-based costing procedures, there is no need to allocate these costs through a single Factory Overhead account to all units produced, as is done by the traditional allocation method. By focusing on cost drivers and their associated costs, management can correct operating inefficiencies and reduce overall product costs. These cost reductions make price reductions possible, which can help increase sales, market share, and profitability.

ASSIGNING COSTS USING ACTIVITY-BASED COSTING

Cost assignment using activity-based costing principles is a two-step procedure. First, the accountant identifies activities and traces all costs attributable

Table 1. Examples of Potential Cost Drivers

Number of labor transactions
Number of material moves
Number of parts received in a month
Number of products
Number of schedule changes
Number of vendors
Number of units reworked
Number of engineering change orders
Number of direct labor employees
Number of new parts added

Source: Robert D. McIlhattan, "How Cost Management Systems Can Support the JIT Philosophy," *Management Accounting,* September 1987, p. 22. Used by permission of Institute of Management Accountants.

to and caused by those activities. Second, the accountant assigns costs to work cells, jobs, or products by the amount of their use of each of the activities. Cost drivers identified with each of the activities are the mechanism for cost assignment. For example, assume that one of the activities of the Flagstaff Company is machine setup, the process of making a machine ready to run a particular product. Four specially trained indirect workers make up the machine setup team. Suppose that the costs generated and traceable to the setup activity for July totaled $17,600 and that a total of 640 setup hours were used. The cost driver is the number of setup hours. If Job AD26 involved three setups requiring a total of 18.4 hours, $506 in setup costs should be assigned to Job AD26 ($17,600 ÷ 640 = $27.50 per setup hour × 18.4 hours = $506). An actual ABC system includes cost assignments for dozens of activities.

PROCESS VALUE ANALYSIS—IDENTIFYING THE ACTIVITIES

OBJECTIVE

3 *Identify all activities that comprise a particular operating process, distinguish between value-adding and non-value-adding activities, and describe the value chain of a product or service*

Identifying the activities in an operating process is an important but difficult task. How detailed should the process be? What exactly is an activity? Is every action taken throughout the company considered an activity? Obviously, the activities identified should be detailed enough so that all essential areas are included; but trying to associate costs with too many areas is not cost-effective. A balanced approach is best.

From a cost management viewpoint, a business is composed of functions, activities, and tasks. Figure 1 is a schematic diagram that shows the relationships among functions, activities, and tasks. A function is a group of activities that have a common purpose or objective. The functions of a manufacturing company include product design, engineering, production, distribution, marketing and sales, and customer service follow-up. An activity is an action that is needed to help accomplish the purpose or objective of a function. As shown in Figure 1, the activities of an engineering department or function might include new-product engineering, developing and maintaining bills (listings) of materials used, developing product routings, filling special orders, conducting capacity studies, implementing engineering change orders, developing ways to improve the process, laboratory testing, and designing tools. Tasks are the work elements or operating steps needed to

Figure 1. Elements Underlying a Cost Management System

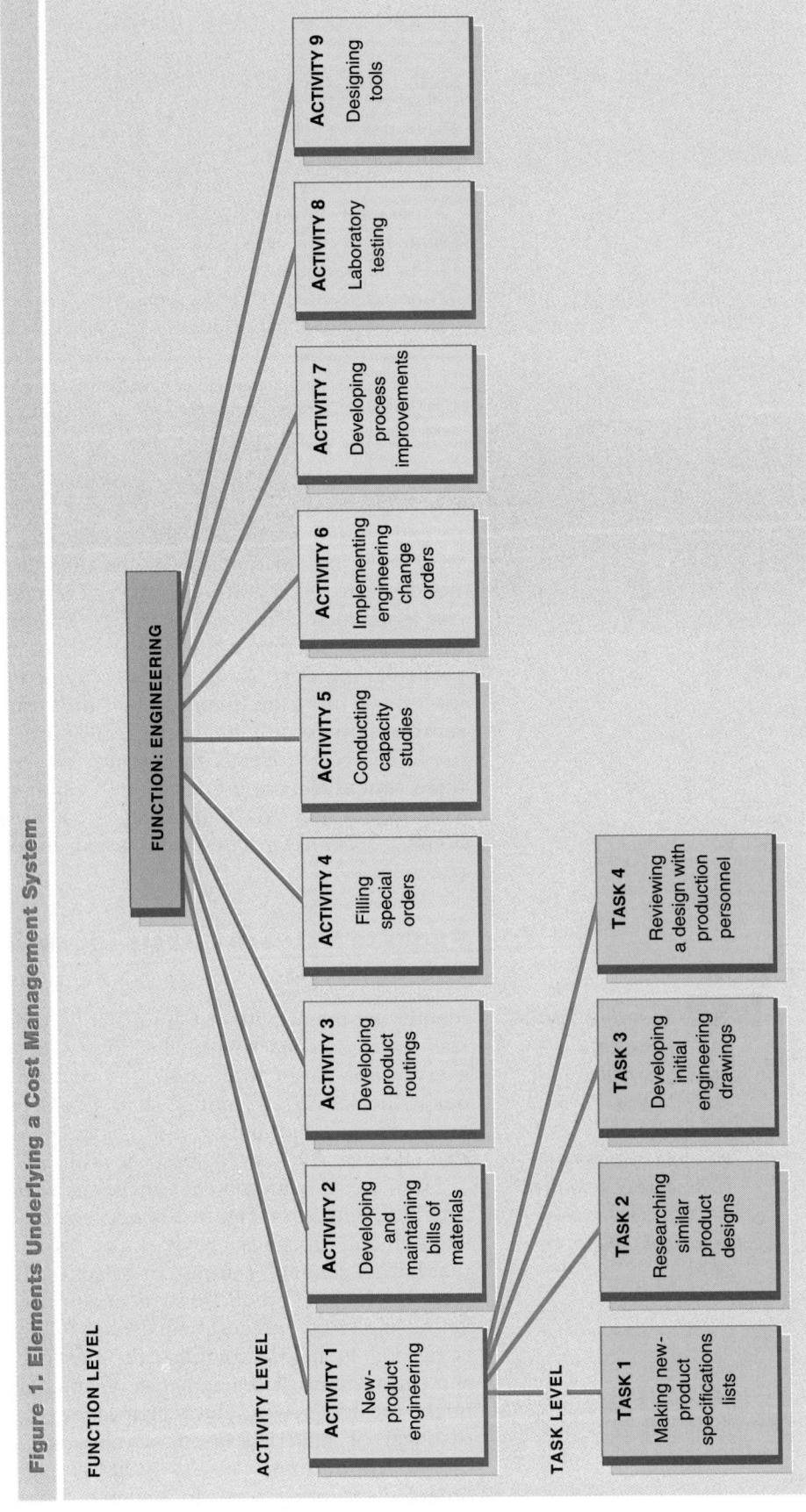

perform and complete an activity. The tasks of a new-product engineering activity might include making up a list of specifications for a new product, researching similar product designs, developing an initial set of engineering drawings, and reviewing the design with production personnel. There can be hundreds of tasks for each activity, and many activities supporting each function.

Activities can be classified as either value-adding activities or nonvalue-adding activities. **Value-adding activities** add value to a product or service as perceived by the customer; they involve resource usage and related costs that customers feel are necessary and important to satisfying their needs. Examples include engineering design of a new automobile, assembly of that automobile, painting the car, and installing seats and airbags. A **nonvalue-adding activity** is a production- or service-related activity that adds cost to a product but does not increase its market value. Examples include repair of machines, shop floor cleanup activities, inventory control, and building maintenance. The **value chain** of a product or service is comprised of all of the activities in its development path that add or contribute to its value and marketability; that is, all of a product's value-adding activities. Value chain analysis is used to monitor the operating process so that continuous improvement of a product's cost, quality, and throughput time can be accomplished.

Activity-based costing matches costs to activities. To use activity-based costing, a company must (1) identify all of the activities in its operating processes, (2) develop methods to trace costs to those activities, and (3) identify the primary causes (cost drivers) of the costs for each activity. **Process value analysis (PVA)** is the process of identifying all activities and relating them to events that create or drive the need for the activities and the resources consumed. In process value analysis, management has a technique to identify those activities that add value to a product and to isolate those that simply add cost.[5] PVA forces managers to look critically at all existing phases of their operations. By reducing or eliminating nonvalue-adding activities and costs and by improving cost traceability, product costs become significantly more accurate, which serves to improve management decisions and increase profitability.

Nonvalue-adding activities are not all wasteful and are not automatically targeted for elimination. Every company maintains support functions, without which the business would not exist. Although support activities are not included in the value chain of activities, they foster the activities of a function. For example, consider the data-processing activity in a manufacturing company, the center of the company's information system. It does not add value to the products produced, but it is a critical activity. Although its costs should be controlled, this support area should not be eliminated. A separate inspection activity, on the other hand, is a support activity of a traditional manufacturing environment that can be eliminated. In a JIT environment, inspection is incorporated into the duties of the work cell operator. The inspection support still exists, but not as a separate activity.

To summarize the steps to a successful activity-based costing system: First, identify the appropriate activities for each function. Second, accumulate costs for each activity. Third, analyze every activity to determine if it is adding value to the product or service. Fourth, analyze all nonvalue-adding activities to determine if they are necessary support areas. If they are, scrutinize their

---

5. Michael R. Ostrenga, "Activities: The Focal Point of Total Cost Management," *Management Accounting,* Institute of Management Accountants, February 1990, p. 43.

costs and reduce them if possible. If they are not, eliminate them. And, finally, assign the costs of each activity to work cells and products that consume the resources of the activities.

ILLUSTRATIVE EXAMPLE: ACTIVITIES AND ACTIVITY-BASED COSTING

TGS Company produces a line of remote control door-opening devices. The company is considering changing from a traditional absorption costing approach for product and order costing purposes to an activity-based cost assignment approach. Management has asked the controller to compute the cost of order no. 1142 using both the old and the proposed new costing approaches so that the two methods can be compared and analyzed. A summary of the data pertaining to order no. 1142 follows.

Raw materials and labor costs

Cost of raw materials	$1,650.00
Direct labor hours	30
Average direct labor pay rate	$14.50

Other operating costs include the following.

Traditional Costing Data:

Factory overhead costs were assigned at a rate of 350 percent of direct labor dollars.

Activity-Based Costing Data:

Activities	Cost Drivers
Engineering design	Engineering hours
Work cell setup	Number of setups
Production work cell	Machine hours
Final tuning	Number of processes
Packaging/shipping work cell	Cell hours

Cost Assignment Rates	Activity Usage for Order No. 1142
$25.00 per engineering hour	12 engineer hours
$28.00 per setup	3 setups
$17.50 per machine hour	24 machine hours
$34.00 per process	3 processes
$38.25 per cell hour	2 cell hours

Building occupancy-related overhead costs are allocated at a rate of $6.50 per production work cell machine hour in the ABC approach.

REQUIRED

1. Compute the total cost of order no. 1142 following the traditional absorption costing approach.
2. Compute the total cost of order no. 1142 following the activity-based costing approach.
3. What was the difference in the amount of cost assigned to order no. 1142 resulting from the shift to the activity-based costing approach?

SOLUTION

1 and 2. Total costs assigned to order no. 1142:

	Traditional Costing Approach	Activity-Based Costing Approach
Raw materials cost	$1,650.00	$1,650.00
Direct labor cost ($14.50 × 30 hours)	435.00	435.00
Factory overhead cost (traditional costing approach)($14.50 per hour × 30 hours × 350%)	1,522.50	
Cost of activities		
Engineering design $25.00 per engineering hour × 12 engineering hours		300.00
Work cell setup $28.00 per setup × 3 setups		84.00
Production work cell $17.50 per machine hour × 24 machine hours		420.00
Final tuning $34.00 per process × 3 processes		102.00
Packaging/shipping work cell $38.25 per cell hour × 2 cell hours		76.50
Building occupancy-related overhead $6.50 × 24 machine hours		156.00
Total costs assigned to order no. 1142	$3,607.50	$3,223.50

3. The change to an activity-based costing approach reduced the amount of costs assigned to this order by $384.00, from $3,607.50 to $3,223.50.

DECISION POINT

Sola Optical Company

Sola Optical Company is a manufacturer of ophthalmic spectacle lenses and is located in Petaluma, California.[6] Until 1988, the company operated in a traditional manner, experiencing continual growth in sales and profitability while holding a constant lens market share. But in 1988, Sola Optical purchased another company. The firm's management now had responsibility for new product lines and divisions that were located in three different geographic regions. Sales volume doubled, as did the number of employees. To help control the new operations and to compete well globally, Sola Optical developed a TQM/JIT operating environment.

After examining the company's approach to product quality, a consultant determined that 20 percent of revenues were being spent either to

6. Richard K. Youde, "Cost of Quality Reporting: How We See It," *Management Accounting,* Institute of Management Accountants, January 1992, pp. 34–38.

create and ensure quality or to rework defective goods. Clearly, management needed a way to control the costs of quality while still ensuring high product quality. The company implemented activity-based costing. For each quality problem area, the activities involved were identified and analyzed. Costs were traced to the activities and reported to the managers and employees in each of the processes under review. The company formed quality teams that created cost-of-quality reports that were posted in each plant. Employees' suggestions were used to improve quality and to reduce quality costs. The result was a dramatic reduction in the costs of quality and an increase in the quality of all product lines.

How did management's decision to use activity-based costing increase overall product quality while significantly reducing the costs of quality?

There are "good" costs of quality and "bad" costs of quality. Good costs of quality are incurred to either prevent or uncover problems with a product or process before the product is manufactured. Bad costs of quality—the costs of poor quality—are incurred after a product is manufactured, to rework entire batches of defective products. By identifying the activities that generated costs of poor quality, Sola Optical's management was able to eliminate unnecessary activities, correct poorly implemented activities, add or modify quality-enhancing activities, and reduce the number of product defects. Although the company incurred additional costs to prevent defects, rework costs and separate inspection costs were reduced because employees began inspecting goods as production took place. The overall effect for Sola Optical was a significant reduction in the total costs of quality, a dramatic increase in product quality, and increased profitability. ⋮⋮⋮⋮⋮

ACCOUNTING FOR PRODUCT AND SERVICE QUALITY

Over the last two decades, the quality of American-made goods has slipped as manufacturers sacrificed or ignored quality in an attempt to lower prices to meet world competition. Over the same period, Japan and other countries increased the quality of their goods while lowering prices. To survive in global markets, American companies must produce quality products at competitive prices. Quality, however, is not something that a company can apply somewhere in the production process or assume will happen automatically. Inspection points can detect bad products, but they do not ensure quality. Managers need reliable measures of quality to help them meet the goal of producing a high-quality, reasonably priced product or service. They need to create a total quality management environment. Total quality management (TQM) is an organizational environment in which all business functions work together to build quality into the firm's products or services. From a management accounting perspective, the first step toward a TQM environment is to identify and manage the costs of quality. The second step is to analyze operating performance using nonfinancial measures and require that all operating processes and products be improved continuously.

COST-BASED MEASURES OF QUALITY[7]

The cost of quality is a cost classification scheme that reflects a company's commitment to quality—to produce quality output and to continuously improve both product and process. Global competition has forced manufacturing and service companies to concentrate on producing high-quality products or services. In the absence of high-quality products or services, companies lose market share to their competitors and eventually go out of business.

To the average person, quality means that one product is better than another—possibly because of design, durability, or some other attribute. In a business setting, however, quality is an operating environment in which a company's product or service meets or conforms to a customer's specifications the first time it is produced or delivered. The costs of quality are the costs specifically associated with the achievement or nonachievement of product or service quality. In other words, total costs of quality include (1) costs of good quality incurred to ensure the successful development of a product or service and (2) costs of poor quality incurred to transform a faulty product or service into one that is acceptable to the customer.

The costs of quality comprise a significant portion of a product's or service's total cost. In his book *Thriving on Chaos*, Tom Peters states that poor-quality costs consume 25 percent of all labor and assets in manufacturing firms; in service firms, the costs of poor quality can run as high as 40 percent of labor and asset costs.[8] Therefore, controlling the costs of quality has a sizable impact on profitability. Today's managers should be able to identify the activities associated with improving quality and should be aware of the cost of resources used to achieve high quality.

The costs of quality have two components: the costs of conformance, which are the costs incurred to produce a quality product or service, and the costs of nonconformance, which are the costs incurred to correct the defects or irregularities of a product or service. Costs of conformance are made up of prevention costs and appraisal costs. Prevention costs are the costs associated with the prevention of defects and failures in products and services. Appraisal costs are the costs of activities that measure, evaluate, or audit products, processes, or services to ensure conformance to quality standards and performance requirements. The costs of nonconformance include internal failure costs and external failure costs. Internal failure costs are the costs incurred as a consequence of the discovery of defects before the product is shipped or the service delivered to the customer. Costs incurred after the delivery of defective goods or services are called external failure costs. Examples of each cost category are shown in Table 2. You should note that there is a trade-off between the two major categories: If a company spends money on the costs of conformance, the costs of nonconformance should be reduced. If, however, little attention is paid to the costs of conformance, then the costs of nonconformance may escalate.

The management accountant is responsible for controlling the costs of quality. The accountant's overall objective is to avoid costs of nonconformance because internal and external failure affects customers' satisfaction as

7. Many of the ideas and thoughts in this section come from John Hawley Atkinson, Jr., Gregory Hohner, Barry Mundt, Richard B. Troxel, and William Winchell, *Current Trends in Cost of Quality: Linking the Cost of Quality and Continuous Improvement*, a joint study of the Institute of Management Accountants, KPMG Peat Marwick, and William Winchell (Montvale, N.J., 1991).

8. Tom Peters, *Thriving on Chaos* (New York: Alfred A. Knopf, 1987), p. 91.

Table 2. Costs of Quality and Quality Measures

Costs of Conformance to Customer Standards

Prevention Costs
- Quality training of employees
- Design review
- Quality planning activities
- Quality engineering
- Preventive maintenance
- Design and development of quality equipment
- Quality improvement projects
- On-line statistical process control

Appraisal Costs
- Sample preparation
- All inspection activities
- Setup for testing
- Product simulation and development
- Vendor audits and sample testing
- Maintenance of test equipment
- Quality audits
- Maintenance of equipment used for quality enhancement

Costs of Nonconformance to Customer Standards

Internal Failure Costs
- Scrap and rework
- Reinspection of rework
- Quality-related downtime
- Losses caused by vendor scrap
- Failure analysis
- Inventory control and scheduling costs
- Downgrading because of defects

External Failure Costs
- Loss of goodwill and future orders
- Warranty claims and adjustments
- Customer complaint processing
- Customer service
- Returned goods
- Investigation of defects
- Product recalls
- Product liability suits

Quality Measures

Total costs of quality as a percentage of net sales
Ratio of conformance costs to total costs of quality
Ratio of nonconformance costs to total costs of quality
Nonconformance costs as a percentage of net sales

---

well as the company's profitability. High initial costs of conformance are justified when they minimize total costs of quality over the life of the product or service. The cost-based measures of quality listed at the bottom of Table 2 are used and explained in the illustrative problem at the end of this section.

OBJECTIVE

5 *Evaluate operating performance using financial and nonfinancial measures of quality*

NONFINANCIAL MEASURES OF QUALITY

Measuring the costs of quality tells a company how much it has spent in its efforts to improve product or service quality. But critics say that tracking historical cost data to account for quality performance does little to help production and engineering personnel enhance quality. What managers need is a measurement and evaluation system that signals poor quality early enough so that they can take steps to correct problems before a product reaches the customer. Implementing a policy of continuous improvement satisfies this need and is part of the second step of total quality management.

Nonfinancial measures of operating performance, identified and reported in a timely manner to engineering and production managers, augment cost-based measures in JIT/TQM operations. Although cost control is still an important consideration, a commitment to ongoing product improvement encourages activities that enhance product quality, from design to delivery. As explained earlier, these activities, or cost drivers, cause costs. By controlling cycle time and using nonfinancial performance measures of production activities to spot bottlenecks and other inefficiencies, managers ultimately maximize the financial return from operations.

Product Design Quality Measures   Problems with quality often are the result of poor design. Most automated production operations utilize computer-aided design (CAD), a computer-based engineering system with a built-in program to detect product design flaws. This computer program automatically identifies faulty design parts or manufacturing processes included in error so that engineers can correct problems before actual production begins. The management accountant is not involved directly in this process but should be aware of the existence and use of product design control measures.

High-Quality Raw Materials Input Measures   One of the most significant changes for a company that is converting to a JIT/TQM operating environment is its relationship with suppliers of raw materials and parts. Instead of dealing with dozens of suppliers, looking for the lowest cost, JIT companies analyze their materials vendors to determine which are most reliable, deal in high-quality goods, have a record of timely deliveries, and charge competitive prices. Once identified, those vendors become an integral part of the production team. A JIT company works closely with its vendors to ensure a continuing supply of high-quality raw materials and parts. Vendors may even contribute to product design to ensure that correct materials and parts are being used. The management accountant should conduct the necessary analyses to identify and monitor reliable vendors so that high-quality, reasonably-priced materials are available when they are needed.

In-Process and Delivery Control Measures   Automated machinery linked into a flexible manufacturing system can be programmed easily with in-process product control mechanisms. Product quality problems are detected by computer-programmed control techniques, and corrective action is taken when a problem is detected. No longer is it necessary to wait for a specified inspection point to detect a product flaw. In-process controls form a continuous inspection system that highlights trouble spots, helps reduce the incidence of scrap significantly, cuts overall product rework machine time, and eliminates the nonvalue-adding product costs of traditional inspection activities. Although the management accountant is not expected to develop and program FMS in-process quality controls, the accountant should understand the control points, maintain records, and prepare reports of the rates of defective parts produced. Product delivery is part of overall quality. The cost management system should maintain records of on-time deliveries to track the performance of the firm's delivery systems.

Customer Acceptance Measures   The sale and shipment of a product no longer marks the end of management's performance measurement duties. Customer follow-up helps evaluate total customer satisfaction. Accounting measures used to determine degree of customer acceptance include (1) the

Table 3. Nonfinancial Measures of Quality Used by Management

High-Quality Raw Materials Input Measures

Vendor quality analysis	An analysis of the quality of materials and parts received; prepared for each vendor used
Vendor delivery analysis	An analysis of timely vendor deliveries; prepared for each vendor used

In-Process and Delivery Control Measures

Production quality level	Defective parts per million; usually tracked by product line
Percentage of on-time deliveries	Percentage of total shipments received by the promised date

Customer Acceptance Measures

Returned-order percentage	Number of shipments returned by customers as a percentage of total shipments
Customer complaints	An analysis of the number and types of customer complaints
Customer acceptance percentage	Number of shipments accepted as a percentage of total shipments, computed for each customer
Warranty claims	An analysis of the number and causes of warranty claims

percentage of shipments returned by customers, (2) the number and types of customer complaints, (3) the percentage of shipments accepted by customers, and (4) an analysis of the number and causes of warranty claims. Several companies have developed their own customer satisfaction indices from these measures so that they can compare different product lines over different time periods.

The nonfinancial measures of quality mentioned above are summarized in Table 3. This list is only a sample of the many nonfinancial measures that are used to monitor quality. These measures help a company move toward its goals of continuously seeking to produce higher-quality products, to improve production processes, and to reduce throughput time and costs.

ILLUSTRATIVE PROBLEM: MEASURING QUALITY

Using many of the examples of the costs of quality identified in Table 2 and the nonfinancial measures of quality listed in Table 3, the following situations demonstrate how a company's progress toward its goal of achieving total quality management is measured and evaluated.

Part A: Evaluating the Costs of Quality As shown in Part A of Exhibit 1, which follows, three companies—Able, Baker, and Cane—have each taken a

Exhibit 1. Measures of Quality—Data Base for Case Scenarios

Part A: Costs of Quality

	Able Co.	Baker Co.	Cane Co.
Annual Sales	$15,000,000	$15,000,000	$15,000,000
Costs of Conformance to Customer Standards			
Prevention Costs			
Quality training of employees	$ 210,000	$ 73,500	$ 136,500
Quality engineering	262,500	115,500	189,000
Design review	105,000	42,000	84,000
Preventive maintenance	157,500	84,000	115,500
Total Prevention Costs	$ 735,000	$ 315,000	$ 525,000
Appraisal Costs			
Setup for testing	$ 126,000	$ 63,000	$ 73,500
Product simulation and development	199,500	31,500	115,500
Quality audits	84,000	21,000	42,000
Vendor audits and sample testing	112,500	52,500	63,000
Total Appraisal Costs	$ 522,000	$ 168,000	$ 294,000
Costs of Nonconformance to Customer Standards			
Internal Failure Costs			
Scrap and rework	$ 21,000	$ 189,000	$ 126,000
Reinspection of rework	15,750	126,000	73,500
Quality-related downtime	42,000	231,000	178,500
Losses caused by vendor scrap	26,250	84,000	52,500
Total Internal Failure Costs	$ 105,000	$ 630,000	$ 430,500
External Failure Costs			
Warranty claims	$ 47,250	$ 94,500	$ 84,000
Returned goods	15,750	68,250	36,750
Investigation of defects	26,250	78,750	57,750
Customer service	120,750	178,500	126,000
Total External Failure Costs	$ 210,000	$ 420,000	$ 304,500

Part B: Nonfinancial Measures of Quality

	Able Co.	Baker Co.	Cane Co.
Vendor Quality Analysis			
19x6	98.20%	94.40%	95.20%
19x7	98.40%	93.20%	95.30%
19x8	98.60%	93.10%	95.20%
Production Quality Level (product defects per million)			
19x6	1,400	4,120	2,710
19x7	1,340	4,236	2,720
19x8	1,210	4,340	2,680
Percentage of On-Time Deliveries			
19x6	94.20%	76.20%	84.10%
19x7	94.60%	75.40%	84.00%
19x8	95.40%	73.10%	83.90%
Order-Return Percentage			
19x6	1.30%	6.90%	4.20%
19x7	1.10%	7.20%	4.10%
19x8	.80%	7.60%	4.00%
Number of Customer Complaints			
19x6	22	189	52
19x7	18	194	50
19x8	12	206	46

different approach to achieving product quality. All three companies are the same size, each generating $15 million in sales last year.

Evaluate each company's approach to quality enhancement by analyzing the costs of quality and by answering the following questions.

Which company is more likely to remain competitive in the global marketplace?

Which company is in serious trouble regarding its product's quality?

What do you feel will happen to the total costs of quality for each company over the next five years? Why?

SOLUTION

The costs of quality have been summarized and analyzed in Exhibit 2. The analysis shows that each company spent between 10.22 and 10.48 percent of its sales dollars on costs of quality. The following statements are based on this analysis.

Which company is more likely to remain competitive in the global marketplace? Able Co. spent the most money on costs of quality. More importantly, however, 80 percent of the money was spent on costs of conformance. These dollars spent now will bring benefits in years to come. The company's focus on the costs of conformance means that only a small amount had to be spent on internal and external failure costs. This also would lead to improved customer satisfaction.

Which company is in serious trouble regarding its product's quality? Baker Co. spent the least on costs of quality but that's not the reason why the company is in serious trouble. Over 68 percent of its costs of quality ($1,050,000 of a total of $1,533,000) was spent on internal and external failure costs. Scrap costs, reinspection costs, the cost of downtime, warranty costs, and customer service costs were all high. Baker's products are very low in quality, and this will mean hard times in future years.

What do you feel will happen to the total costs of quality for each company over the next five years? Why? Money spent on costs of conformance early in a product's life cycle means that quality is integrated into the development and production processes. Once a high level of quality has been established, total costs of quality should be lower in future years. Able seems to be in this position today.

Baker's costs of conformance will have to increase significantly if the company expects to stay in business. Seven percent of its sales revenue is spent on internal and external failure costs. The products are not being accepted by the marketplace, and the company is vulnerable to its competitors. This is not a good situation to be in when a company faces global competition.

Cane is steering down the middle road. The company is spending a little more than half (53 percent) of its cost-of-quality dollars on conformance, so product quality should be increasing. But the company still is incurring high internal and external failure costs. Cane's managers must learn to prevent these costs if they expect to remain competitive.

Part B: Evaluating Nonfinancial Measures of Quality   From the information presented in Part B of Exhibit 1, evaluate each company's experience in its pursuit of total quality management.

SOLUTION

The nonfinancial measures presented in Exhibit 1 identify trends for each company for three years, 19x6, 19x7, and 19x8. Those data tend to support the findings in Part A, the analysis of the costs of quality.

Able Co. For Able Co. in 19x8, 98.6 percent of the raw materials and parts received from suppliers are high quality, and the trend is increasing. The product defect rate, measured in number of defects per million, is decreasing

Exhibit 2. Analysis of Costs of Quality

	Able Co.	Baker Co.	Cane Co.
Annual Sales	$15,000,000	$15,000,000	$15,000,000
Costs of Conformance to Customer Standards			
Prevention costs	$ 735,000	$ 315,000	$ 525,000
Appraisal costs	522,000	168,000	294,000
Total Conformance Costs	$ 1,257,000	$ 483,000	$ 819,000
Costs of Nonconformance to Customer Standards			
Internal failure costs	$ 105,000	$ 630,000	$ 430,500
External failure costs	210,000	420,000	304,500
Total Nonconformance Costs	$ 315,000	$ 1,050,000	$ 735,000
Total Costs of Quality	$ 1,572,000	$ 1,533,000	$ 1,554,000
Total costs of quality as a percentage of sales	10.48%	10.22%	10.36%
Ratio of conformance costs to total costs of quality	.80 to 1	.32 to 1	.53 to 1
Ratio of nonconformance costs to total costs of quality	.20 to 1	.68 to 1	.47 to 1
Nonconformance costs as a percentage of sales	2.10%	7.00%	4.90%

rapidly, proof that the costs of conformance are having a positive effect. The percentage of on-time deliveries is increasing, and both the order-return percentage and the number of customer complaints are decreasing, which means that customer acceptance and satisfaction are increasing.

Baker Co. Baker Co.'s experience is not encouraging. The number of high-quality shipments of materials and parts from vendors is decreasing; the product defect rate is increasing (it seems to be out of control); on-time deliveries were bad to begin with and are getting worse; more goods are being returned each year; and customer complaints are on the rise. All of these signs reflect the company's high nonconformance costs of quality.

Cane Co. Cane Co. is making progress toward higher quality standards, but that progress is very slow. Most of the nonfinancial measures indicate a very slight positive trend. More money needs to be spent on the conformance costs of quality.

MEASURING SERVICE QUALITY

The quality of services rendered can be measured and analyzed. Many of the costs of product conformance and nonconformance also apply to the development and delivery of a service. Service design flaws lead to poor-quality services. Timely service delivery is as important as timely product shipments. Customer satisfaction in a service business can be measured by services accepted or rejected, the number of complaints, and the number of returning customers. Poor service development leads to internal and external failure costs. Many of the costs-of-quality categories and several of the nonfinancial measures of quality can be applied directly to services and can be adopted by any type of service company.

Self-directed work teams (SDWTs) are an important element of total quality management. An SDWT is defined as "a group of employees who have day-to-day responsibilities for managing themselves and a whole work process that delivers a service or a product." Managing such a group of people requires a much different approach from that of traditional autocratic methods. The traditional role of managers changes in an SDWT. Some of the skills necessary to be a successful SDWT manager are listed below.

Leader—Holds an inspiring and motivating vision to which team members can make personal commitments.

Role model—"Walks the walk," demonstrating the desired behaviors.

Coach—Teaches and helps team members realize their potential, ensures accountability, and maintains authority.

Business analyzer—Brings the big picture context to teams, translates changes in business environment into opportunities for the team.

Advocate—Opens doors for teams, manages senior support, challenges status quo and artificial barriers that limit team performance.

Facilitator—Brings together resources, information, technologies, and does whatever it takes to allow the team to be successful.

Customer advocate—Keeps close to the customers, understands their needs, and brings the customer perspective to the team. ══

PERFORMANCE MEASURES FOR JIT/FMS OPERATING CONTROL

As with product costing, many companies have installed a flexible manufacturing system (FMS) or moved to a computer-integrated production system without changing their approaches to the monitoring and measurement of performance. One problem with the adoption of JIT production procedures is relying on an obsolete management accounting system to measure operating performance. Traditional performance evaluation measures are used, but these measures are not designed to track the objectives of automated facilities and thus are not appropriate for the new manufacturing environment. For instance, measures that center on labor efficiency or factory overhead absorption rates do not coincide with the objectives of JIT. Variance analysis based on direct labor hours will have little to measure and evaluate. JIT/FMS emphasizes minimum labor usage and a rapid, automated production process. Because building inventory levels also conflicts with the goals of JIT, measuring performance through lower overhead absorption rates is an antiquated approach.

9. Don Irwin and Victor Rocine, "Self-directed Work Teams," *CMA Magazine,* September 1994, pp. 10–15. Used by permission of The Society of Management Accountants of Canada.

In addition, the management accountant may not be familiar with the production process and thus has a difficult time identifying areas of weakness.[10] The new manufacturing environment has created a need for close cooperation between all parts of the management team. The management accountant must get closer to the actual operations and become familiar with all aspects of the manufacturing process. The accountant, the engineer, and the production manager must work closely to ensure that the production process is being monitored fairly and accurately. Without a knowledge of the production facilities, the management accountant does not know what to measure or which cost drivers are appropriate under the circumstances.

As was shown in the section on measures of quality, many nonfinancial measures have replaced traditional performance measures in a JIT/FMS setting. The primary control areas, in addition to product quality, are product delivery, inventory control, material costs/scrap control, and machine management and maintenance. Although cost control is still an important consideration in these areas, emphasis is on the factors that make an FMS or a product line a successful part of a profitable operation. These factors are what drive or cause the costs to be incurred. The belief is that control of the nonfinancial performance aspects will ultimately maximize the financial return on operations.

OBJECTIVE

6a *Identify the types of financial and nonfinancial analyses used in a competitive operating environment to evaluate the performance of product delivery*

PRODUCT DELIVERY PERFORMANCE

Besides emphasizing product quality and customer satisfaction, a JIT company is also interested in product delivery. The delivery cycle time is the time period between acceptance of the order and final delivery of the product. It is important for the salesperson to be able to promise accurate delivery schedules at the time the sales order is gained; the goal is for product delivery to be 100 percent on time and for the order to be filled 100 percent of the time. To meet this goal, the JIT company must establish and maintain consistency and reliability within the manufacturing process.

JIT companies place heavy importance on the delivery cycle. One company cut its delivery cycle from more than six months to less than five weeks; another company cut its four-week delivery cycle to less than five days. Such reductions in delivery time have a significant impact on income from operations. The delivery cycle is comprised of the purchase order lead time (the time it takes for raw materials and parts to be ordered and received so that production can begin), production cycle time (the time it takes for the production personnel to make the product available for shipment to the customer), and delivery time (the time period between product completion and customer receipt of the item).

The management accountant has several control measures to establish and maintain that help management minimize the delivery cycle. The accountant should provide managers with records and reports that are designed to monitor each product's purchase order lead time, production cycle time, delivery time, and total delivery cycle time. Trends should be highlighted, and the reports should be made available on a daily or weekly basis. Other measures designed to monitor the delivery cycle include an on-time delivery performance record and a daily or weekly report showing percentage of orders filled.

10. Robert A. Howell and Stephen R. Soucy, "Operating Controls in the New Manufacturing Environment," *Management Accounting,* Institute of Management Accountants, October 1987, p. 26.

OBJECTIVE

6b *Identify the types of financial and nonfinancial analyses used in a competitive operating environment to evaluate the performance of inventory control*

INVENTORY CONTROL PERFORMANCE

Within a JIT environment, the objective is to have no inventory. Therefore the management accountant must emphasize zero inventory balances and concentrate on measures that detect why inventory exists, not measures that lead to accurate inventory valuation. As was pointed out earlier, inventory storage is a nonvalue-adding activity and should be reduced or eliminated. Making this shift in accounting for and controlling of inventory cost has been very difficult for accounting personnel. For decades, inventory has been one of the largest asset balances on the balance sheet, and accountants have been trained to verify inventory balances and compute the value of total inventory. JIT has made such concerns obsolete: Emphasis should be on reducing inventory.

The JIT/FMS environment utilizes only two inventory accounts, and both balances are kept at a minimum. The old Materials Inventory and Work in Process Inventory accounts have been merged into the Raw in Process Inventory account. All purchases of raw materials and parts are debited immediately to the Raw in Process Inventory account. Because the goal is to eliminate storage as a cost, materials and parts are received only when needed. All costs of product conversion (labor and factory overhead) are also debited to the Raw in Process Inventory account.

Inventory controls in the new manufacturing environment are designed to reduce or eliminate inventory balances and related nonvalue-adding product costs. Old control measures such as the economic order quantity and reorder point computations are no longer as useful; now the emphasis is on reducing the amount of space used to store raw materials, goods in process, and finished goods. Measures that detect possible product obsolescence are very important. Inventory turnover measures such as the ratio of inventory to total sales have become more important because the number of annual turnovers may double or triple with the adoption of JIT.

The inventory area remains critical to company profitability in a JIT/FMS environment. But there is heavy emphasis on nonfinancial measures to minimize the cost incurred in handling and storing inventory. The management accountant must develop measures that identify unreliable vendors because using fewer vendors who supply quality and timely raw material inputs is an objective of JIT. Another objective is to determine the amount of production time wasted because of engineering change orders and highlight the causes for management. The same approach must be applied to production schedule changes because time wasted here can be significant. Maintaining accurate records of required machine maintenance is an important JIT control measure. Cutting the downtime from machine breakdowns reduces the need for inventory. Every company's production process and inventory needs are different. When developing a set of inventory control measures, each must be tailored to a particular set of operating circumstances. Although most of these measures are nonfinancial, they are critical to gaining market share and remaining profitable.

OBJECTIVE

6c *Identify the types of financial and nonfinancial analyses used in a competitive operating environment to evaluate the performance of materials cost/scrap control*

MATERIALS COST/SCRAP CONTROL PERFORMANCE

In a traditional situation, controlling the cost of raw materials meant seeking the lowest possible price while maintaining some minimum level of quality. Responsibility for this transaction was given to the Purchasing Department. Performance was measured by analyzing the materials price variance (the difference between the standard price and the actual price of the goods purchased). Today, emphasis is on the quality of materials, timeliness of delivery, and reasonableness of price. Because materials cost is the largest single cost element in the new JIT/FMS environment, control in this area is extremely important.

Control of scrap also takes on a different focus in a competitive operating environment. The JIT objective is to incur no scrap in the production process, a significant difference from the traditional approach, which developed a normal scrap level or tolerance at or below which no corrective action was taken. The factory of the future sees scrap as a nonvalue-added series of costs. Each defective product has already cost the company materials costs, labor costs, and materials handling and factory overhead costs. In the new manufacturing environment, specific records are kept regarding scrap, rework, and defective units. Machine operators are expected to detect flaws in the production process and to suggest possible corrective action on the spot. When a flaw is detected, the FMS cell should be stopped, and a solution should be developed immediately. Personnel should work continuously to eradicate bad or defective output.

The management accountant is responsible for developing a set of control measures for the scrap area. Although financial data on the cost of scrap are important and should be computed, nonfinancial measures should also be developed and maintained. Questions such as the following should be analyzed, answered, and reported.

1. Where was the scrap detected?
2. How often does a product flaw occur at each of these locations?
3. Was the flaw detected at the spot of machine or product failure, or were additional manufacturing costs wasted on the defective products? If so, why?
4. Who is responsible for feeding the information regarding scrap incurrence to the management accountant?
5. Who should the scrap control reports go to, and how often should the reports be prepared?

MACHINE MANAGEMENT AND MAINTENANCE PERFORMANCE

OBJECTIVE

6d *Identify the types of financial and nonfinancial analyses used in a competitive operating environment to evaluate the performance of machine management and maintenance*

One of the most challenging areas for the management accountant in the JIT setting is keeping records of machine maintenance and downtime. Automated equipment requires large capital expenditures. For a JIT company, the largest item on the balance sheet is often automated machinery and equipment. Each piece of equipment has a specific capability, above which continuous operation is threatened. The machine management and maintenance measures should have two objectives.

1. Evaluate performance in relation to each piece of equipment's capacity.
2. Evaluate performance of maintenance personnel to keep to a prescribed maintenance program.

Machines must operate within specified tolerances, or damage and downtime could result. Keeping track of proper machine operation is not easy, but electronic surveillance is possible because of the computer network connecting all of the machines in a JIT/FMS cell. These controls should be programmed into the system and tracked as a regular part of the operation. The accountant should help prepare the reporting format for this function and analyze and report the findings to appropriate production personnel.

Because automated equipment requires a heavy investment and unanticipated machine downtime is not tolerated in a JIT/FMS environment,

Table 4. Machine Maintenance Record as of April 30, 19x6—Milling Machine FMS

	January	February	March	April	May	June
Small Mills						
Monthly						
Wash machine	X	X	X	X		
Replace oil	X	X	X	X		
Check bearing	X	X	X	X		
Stone sand ways	X	X	X	X		
Clean moving table	X	X	X	X		
Check cutter grip	X	X	X	X		
Quarterly						
Replace bearing	X			X		
Check wiring	X			X		
Check all motors	X			X		
Replace lights	X			X		
Check scrap removal system	X			X		
Check computer system	X			X		
Materials Conveyor System						
Monthly						
Clean all belts	X	X	X	X		
Oil all parts	X	X	X	X		
Check all motors	X	X	X	X		
Clean electronic contact spots	X	X	X	X		
Quarterly						
Replace small motors	X			X		
Grease gears	X			X		
Check wiring	X			X		
Check computer system	X			X		

machine maintenance is critical. Minor maintenance tasks are part of the machine operator's duties. When the operating cell does not have an order to process, the operator is expected to perform routine maintenance. A regular program of major maintenance should also be implemented. Timing can be flexible, based on work orders, but major maintenance cannot be ignored. Detailed records on machine maintenance should be maintained, similar to the maintenance records required for commercial aircraft. Table 4 is an example of a machine maintenance record.

SUMMARY OF CONTROL MEASURES

Table 5 summarizes control measures in the new manufacturing environment. Quality performance is measured by tracking customer complaints, warranty claims, and vendor quality. Delivery performance is shown by on-time delivery, production backlog, lead time, cycle time, and waste time. Successful inventory performance is identified through turnover rates, space reduction, and automatic production cycle count accuracy. Materials cost/scrap control performance is measured by incoming materials inspection, materials as a percentage of total cost, actual scrap loss, and scrap as a percentage of total cost. Machine management and maintenance performance

Table 5. Control Points in the New Manufacturing Environment

Quality Performance

Customer complaints
Customer surveys
Warranty claims
Vendor quality
Quality audits

Causes of cost of quality:
  Scrap and rework
  Returns and allowances
  Field service
  Warranty claims
  Lost business

Delivery Performance

On-time delivery
Setup time
Production backlog
Lead time (order to shipment)

Order fulfillment rate
Cycle time (materials receipt to
  product shipment)
Waste time (lead time less
  process time)

Inventory Performance

Turnover rates by product
Cycle count accuracy
Space reduction
Number of inventoried items

Turnover rates by location:
  Raw in process
  Finished goods
  Composite

Materials Cost/Scrap Control Performance

Actual scrap loss
Scrap by part, product, and
  operation
Scrap percentage of total cost

Quality—incoming materials
  inspection
Materials cost as a percentage
  of total cost

Machine Management and Maintenance Performance

Availability/downtime
Machine maintenance

Equipment capacity/utilization
Equipment experience

Source: Robert A. Howell and Stephen R. Soucy, "Operating Controls in the New Manufacturing Environment," *Management Accounting,* October 1987. Reprinted by permission of Institute of Management Accountants.

is revealed through machine maintenance records, availability/downtime experience, and equipment capacity/utilization information.

FULL COST PROFIT MARGIN

OBJECTIVE

7 *Define* **full cost profit margin** *and state the advantages of this measure of profitability*

The new manufacturing environment has yet another dimension that must be analyzed when dealing with performance measures. For years, management accountants have been touting the measurement qualities of contribution margin. This number concerns itself with only revenue and those costs that are variable in relation to the products being sold. Fixed costs are excluded from the analysis so that they will not cloud the measurement of the performance of a division or a product.

As a company moves in the direction of a computer-integrated manufacturing (CIM) system, more and more direct labor hours are replaced by machine hours. When a complete JIT/CIM environment is attained, very little direct labor cost is incurred. A major part of the traditional variable product cost has been replaced by costly machinery, a fixed cost. As a result, contribution margins also get larger and less meaningful.

Today, management accountants are turning to full cost profit margins to help measure the performance of a division or a product line. Full costing has always been an alternative for performance evaluation, but a stigma of inaccuracy was associated with the number because fixed costs had to be allocated to the product. Full cost profit margins are more appropriate in a capital-intensive environment. Full cost profit margin is the difference between total revenue and total costs traceable to the work cell or product. The computer has enabled the accountant to more easily trace costs to FMS work cells. A CIM system can provide data that enable most costs to be treated as direct costs of the work cells. If direct traceability is not possible, new cost drivers have been established to more closely link indirect costs with cost objectives such as work cells or products. Only building occupancy costs remain as non-traceable costs to be allocated based on some causal allocation base such as machine hours or square footage occupied. Full cost profit margin, therefore, is a meaningful figure for performance evaluation as well as for new product line decision analysis.

An example points out the differences between contribution margin and full cost profit margin as measures of performance. Exhibit 3 shows operating data for three product lines of the Montvale Manufacturing Company. First, the cost data are summarized as they were before the FMS was installed. Next, the data have been reclassified to reflect the increased traceability aspects of a JIT/FMS environment. The bottom portion of Exhibit 3 contains computations for contribution margins prior to FMS and for full cost profit margins following the installation of the new system.

The Montvale Manufacturing Company example illustrates what is likely to happen with a switch from the contribution margin to the full cost profit margin approach to performance evaluation. Better methods of cost tracing and more direct cost elements provide a more complete picture of which product lines are most profitable. In our example, the most profitable product is 162 before the FMS was installed. Product 214 is the second most profitable, with Product 305 generating the lowest profit. The order of product profitability remains the same after FMS, but look at the percent of revenue for the contribution margins and the full cost profit margins: Costs have generally shifted from Products 162 and 305 to Product 214. This shift often occurs when activity-based costing is introduced. Through ABC, more direct cost relationships are uncovered and better cost tracing is made possible. Under the traditional costing methods, Product 214 had an inflated profit structure, which could have led to some bad decisions on the part of Montvale's management. With full cost profit margins, management receives more accurate decision support and price determination information.

MANAGEMENT REPORTING GUIDELINES IN A COMPETITIVE OPERATING ENVIRONMENT

Reporting the results of operations to management is one of the management accountant's primary responsibilities. This role is amplified in the new manufacturing environment, and an entirely revised set of reports is usually required. The accountant must be careful when selecting reports prepared for

Exhibit 3. Contribution Margin Versus Full Cost Profit Margin

Montvale Manufacturing Company
Product Performance Evaluation

	Product 162	Product 214	Product 305
Total revenue	$2,340,000	$2,400,000	$1,560,000
Before FMS installed:			
Variable costs			
Direct materials	$ 450,000	$ 560,000	$ 270,000
Direct labor	660,000	600,000	420,000
Variable factory overhead	240,000	240,000	150,000
Variable selling expenses	90,000	80,000	60,000
Variable distribution costs	120,000	200,000	180,000
Total variable costs	$1,560,000	$1,680,000	$1,080,000
Allocated costs			
Fixed factory overhead	$ 210,000	$ 360,000	$ 240,000
Fixed selling expenses	60,000	40,000	90,000
Fixed distribution costs	150,000	128,000	135,000
Total fixed costs	$ 420,000	$ 528,000	$ 465,000
After FMS installed:			
Traceable costs			
Direct materials	$ 450,000	$ 560,000	$ 270,000
Materials-related overhead	72,000	88,000	54,000
Direct labor	90,000	128,000	84,000
Indirect labor	108,000	112,000	90,000
Setup labor	66,000	104,000	66,000
Electrical power	54,000	80,000	48,000
Supervision	96,000	120,000	96,000
Repairs and maintenance	78,000	96,000	78,000
Operating supplies/lubricants	36,000	56,000	42,000
Other traceable indirect costs	114,000	168,000	120,000
Traceable selling expenses	102,000	104,000	72,000
Traceable distribution costs	156,000	284,000	204,000
Total traceable costs	$1,422,000	$1,900,000	$1,224,000
Allocated costs			
Nontraceable factory overhead	$ 126,000	$ 244,000	$ 132,000
Nontraceable selling and distribution costs	96,000	112,000	108,000
Total nontraceable costs	$ 222,000	$ 356,000	$ 240,000

(continued)

Exhibit 3. Contribution Margin Versus Full Cost Profit Margin
(continued)

	Product 162	Product 214	Product 305
Product Performance Measures			
Before FMS installed:			
Contribution margin			
Total revenue	$2,340,000	$2,400,000	$1,560,000
Less variable costs	1,560,000	1,680,000	1,080,000
Contribution margin	$ 780,000	$ 720,000	$ 480,000
Less total fixed costs	420,000	528,000	465,000
Operating profit	$ 360,000	$ 192,000	$ 15,000
Contribution margin as a percent of revenue	33.33%	30.00%	30.77%
Operating profit as a percent of revenue	15.38%	8.00%	.96%
After FMS installed:			
Full cost profit margin			
Total revenues	$2,340,000	$2,400,000	$1,560,000
Less total traceable costs	1,422,000	1,900,000	1,224,000
Full cost profit margin	$ 918,000	$ 500,000	$ 336,000
Less total nontraceable costs	222,000	356,000	240,000
Operating profit	$ 696,000	$ 144,000	$ 96,000
Full cost profit margin as a percent of revenue	39.23%	20.83%	21.54%
Operating profit as a percent of revenue	29.74%	6.00%	6.15%

OBJECTIVE

8 *Identify the primary areas of management reporting in a competitive operating environment and give examples of reports needed*

the traditional manufacturing structure. Few are still relevant for automated processes. Studies have shown that well over half the reports prepared for management each month in the traditional environment have little or no relevance and are ignored by the recipients.

The management accountant faces a real challenge in the JIT/FMS management reporting area. As with performance measurement and operations control, emphasis must shift from primarily financial operating reports to a wide range of both financial and nonfinancial data reports. But the need for a responsibility accounting and reporting structure is still present in the JIT/FMS environment for the nonfinancial as well as for the financial operating results of the period. Reporting emphasis must be directed at specific areas of interest, such as customer responsiveness, product line profitability, product contribution, operating effectiveness, and asset management.

Before we discuss JIT/FMS reporting, we must mention one unique aspect of the new manufacturing environment that affects preparation of reports.

For decades, the accountant seldom visited the manufacturing site, and reports were in traditional form, highlighting comparisons between actual and budgeted financial data. Production personnel were seldom asked for input concerning the content or structure of a report. Things have changed in today's environment. Production managers have their own personal computers in the factory and know how to use them. If the accountant does not supply needed information, these managers develop their own reports. Today, management accountants must become very familiar with the production operation and prepare reports that are requested by those responsible for the product line or operating cell.

CUSTOMER RESPONSIVENESS REPORTING

Close contact with the level of customer satisfaction is a critical issue in the new manufacturing environment. Reports prepared for management should reflect this concern. The customer is interested in receiving a quality product on a timely basis. Price is a factor, but usually the price is competitive. Other factors such as customer service and follow-up can make the difference between retaining a customer or losing a sale.

Reporting should concentrate on tracking quality through the (1) number and types of customer complaints and (2) returns and allowances. Records of promised versus actual delivery dates can be important. Continuous records of backlogged orders and delayed delivery dates are critical to maintaining customer satisfaction. A report tracking shipments from the time they leave the plant until the time they arrive at the customer's facility is also a good measure of service performance. Any report that will enhance delivery and service should be prepared. All of these reports involve nonfinancial data.

BUSINESS BULLETIN: INTERNATIONAL PRACTICE

The value of a company's human resources is not shown on its balance sheet but intellectual capital is a company's most important asset.

Because it is an intangible that is very difficult to measure, accountants have shied away from quantifying and reporting its amount. But that is changing. Skandia AFS (Assurance and Financial Services) in Sweden is one of many companies around the world that are beginning to measure and report the value of their human capital.[11] Skandia created a top management position entitled Director of Intellectual Capital and now publishes a supplement to its annual report containing measures of this valuable asset. Examples of new measures include annual comparisons of (1) information technology investments as a percentage of total expenses, (2) information technology employees as a percentage of all employees, (3) innovative business development expenses as a percentage

---

11. Thomas A. Stewart, "Your Company's Most Valuable Asset: Intellectual Capital," *Fortune,* October 3, 1994, pp. 68–74.

of total expenses, and (4) the amount of production from newly launched projects. Also tracked and reported is the amount of gross insurance premiums per employee, a bottom line measure of the impact of human resource utilization and refined business practices on the amount of new business. ═══

PRODUCT LINE PROFITABILITY REPORTING

Reporting on product line profitability should concentrate on manufacturing and selling and delivery costs. Minimizing the cost of production does not guarantee product profitability. Selling and delivery costs could easily make a product line unprofitable if they are not continuously analyzed and controlled. In the manufacturing area, reports should focus on both materials and conversion costs. Materials cost is made up of purchase prices and materials handling costs once the item has been received from the vendor. Nonvalue-adding costs in the materials handling area can be eliminated in part through effective tracking and reporting procedures. Conversion costs must be analyzed continuously using a combination of traditional methods and newly created reports for scrap control, operating cell yield, and the effective use of energy.

Selling and delivery costs must be monitored very closely to ensure that waste does not occur. Reports should be tailored by sales territory, product line, and mode of transportation. This information needs to be supplied to supervisory personnel on a timely basis.

PRODUCT CONTRIBUTION REPORTING

A product's contribution to the absorption of a company's untraceable fixed costs is still important in a JIT/FMS environment, but as pointed out in the section on full cost profit margin, product contribution can include traceable fixed costs. Contribution margin is no longer the only measure of product contribution. If contribution margin is still requested, management accounting reports should also contain information regarding full cost profit margin so that managers have additional information upon which to base their decisions.

OPERATING EFFECTIVENESS REPORTING

Reporting to enhance operating effectiveness concentrates on the nonvalue-adding areas of a traditional system. Reports that focus on product cycle times, including the process time, lead time, and waste time, are especially good for determining operating effectiveness. Reports that track causes of downtime and defective units should be prepared. Reports on inventory turnover and space utilization can lead to significant reductions in nonvalue-adding costs. Special studies on ways to decrease throughput (processing) time of a JIT and/or FMS cell should be prepared on request. Employee suggestions for operating improvement should be encouraged and the results reported to management. Most of the reports in this category are nonfinancial and all help reduce operating costs.

ASSET MANAGEMENT REPORTING

The final report preparation category centers on management of the company's fixed assets. Automation caused huge increases in capital asset expenditures. Special reporting is necessary to help manage this large resource. Machine maintenance must be recorded and tracked. Records of machine time availability or the lack thereof (downtime) is important information to production managers and scheduling personnel. Space utilization must be reported periodically. Equipment capacity and experience must be logged in continuously and reports generated. Again, most of those reports are nonfinancial but are critical to the successful operation of the manufacturing facilities. The management accountant is expected to provide those data.

SUMMARY

Table 6 depicts the reporting network described above. Some reports are primarily financial in nature; others contain only nonfinancial data. A few

Table 6. JIT Management Reporting Guidelines

Operations Reporting Areas	Nonfinancial	Financial
Customer responsiveness		
Number/types of customer complaints	X	
Returns and allowances by customers	X	X
Actual versus promised delivery	X	
Backlogged orders	X	
Product shipment tracking	X	
Product line profitability		
Materials purchasing	X	X
Materials handling costs		X
Conversion costs		X
Selling and delivery costs		X
Product contribution		
Full cost profit margins		X
Contribution margins		X
Operating effectiveness		
Product cycle times	X	
Product lead times	X	
Product waste times	X	
Scrap/defective units	X	
Machine yield rates	X	
Throughput time analyses	X	
Asset management		
Machine maintenance	X	
Machine availability/downtime	X	
Space utilization	X	
Equipment capacity/experience	X	

reporting areas have both financial and nonfinancial information. The important aspect of this analysis is that the management accountant's role and responsibilities have expanded in the new manufacturing environment. The accountant must become familiar with the manufacturing facilities to be able to supply management with relevant, timely data.

CHAPTER REVIEW

REVIEW OF LEARNING OBJECTIVES

1. **Define *cost management*, describe a cost management system, and identify how this type of system benefits managers.** Cost management is the management and control of activities to determine product costs accurately, to improve business processes, to eliminate waste, to identify cost drivers, to plan operations, and to set business strategies. In a cost management system (CMS), the primary focus is on the management of activities, not costs, for both product costing and cost control purposes. A CMS plays a major role in planning, managing, and reducing costs. Cost cutting is not accomplished by just slashing the amount of existing resources that a department can use to produce a product, as happens in a traditional costing system. A CMS relies on the concept of continuous improvement to reduce costs while still increasing product quality. When continuous improvement is employed, a company can increase profits by first designing the product so that its target cost is achieved and then making ongoing improvements to reduce costs further. Finally, cost assignment within a cost management system is far superior to traditional cost systems.

    By focusing on activities, a CMS provides managers with improved knowledge of the processes under their responsibility. The CMS pinpoints resource usage for each activity for managers and fosters managerial decisions that lead to continuous improvement throughout the organization.

2. **Define and explain *activity-based costing*, and list examples of cost drivers.** Activity-based costing is an approach to product cost assignment that identifies all major operating activities, categorizes costs by activity, reduces or eliminates nonvalue-adding activities, and assigns costs using an appropriate basis. This process allows most costs to be traced directly to a work cell or product. Building occupancy-related costs must still be allocated based on either machine hours or some other causal allocation base.

    A cost driver is any activity that causes a cost to be incurred. Before a cost can be eliminated or accounted for properly, we must know what caused the cost—what drives the cost. Once the cost driver has been identified, the indirect costs it causes can either be (a) treated as legitimate product costs and traced directly to a work cell or product, or (b) reduced or eliminated by reducing or eliminating the need for the cost driver. Cost drivers include the number of machine setups, the number of schedule changes, the number of vendors, and the number of units reworked.

3. **Identify all activities that comprise a particular operating process, distinguish between value-adding and nonvalue-adding activities, and describe the value chain of a product or service.** A manufacturing process can be broken down into functions, activities, and tasks. Functions, such as engineering, production, or distribution, are groups of activities that have a common purpose or objective. Activities, such as new-product engineering or engineering change orders, are the actions needed to accomplish a function's purpose or objective. Tasks, such as making up a list of specifications for a new product or researching similar product designs, are the operating steps of an activity. The value chain of a product or service is all of the functions (and related activities) in its development path that add or contribute to its value and marketability. Nonvalue-adding support functions and activities that are necessary for product development are not eliminated, but their costs should be reduced to minimum levels. Many nonvalue-adding activities, among them separate inspection, can be eliminated.

4. **Define *total quality management* and identify and compute the costs of quality for products and services.** Total quality management is an organizational environment in which all business functions work together to build quality into a firm's products or services. The costs of quality are measures of costs specifically related to the achievement or nonachievement of product or service quality. The costs of quality have two components. One is the cost of conforming to a customer's product or service standards, by preventing defects and failures and by appraising quality and performance. The other is the cost of nonconformance—the costs incurred when defects are discovered before a product is shipped and the costs incurred after a defective product or faulty service is delivered.

   The objective here should be to reduce or eliminate the costs of nonconformance, the internal and external failure costs that are associated with customer dissatisfaction. To this end, we can justify high initial costs of conformance if they minimize the total costs of quality over the product's or service's life cycle.

5. **Evaluate operating performance using financial and nonfinancial measures of quality.** Nonfinancial measures of quality are related to product design, raw materials input, in-process and delivery control, and customer acceptance. These measures, together with the costs of quality, help the firm meet its goal of continuously improving product or service quality and the production process.

6. **Identify the types of financial and nonfinancial analyses used in a competitive operating environment to evaluate the performance of (a) product delivery, (b) inventory control, (c) materials cost/scrap control, and (d) machine management and maintenance.** Product delivery performance centers on tracking lead time, process time, cycle time, setup time, production backlog, and on-time deliveries. Inventory control performance looks at turnover rates by product, space reduction for storage, and number of inventoried items. Materials cost/scrap control performance looks at actual scrap loss, scrap as a percentage of total cost, materials cost as a percentage of total cost, and quality of incoming goods. Machine management and maintenance performance considers the performance of each piece of equipment in relation to its capacity and how maintenance personnel follow a prescribed maintenance program.

7. **Define *full cost profit margin* and state the advantages of this measure of profitability.** Full cost profit margin is the difference between total revenue and total costs traceable to the work cell or product. The measure is more meaningful than contribution margin because of the additional costs brought into the analysis. Profitability is measured more accurately using the full cost profit margin.

8. **Identify the primary areas of management reporting in a competitive operating environment and give examples of reports needed.** The primary areas of management reporting in a competitive operating environment are (a) customer responsiveness reporting (number and types of customer complaints, backlogged orders), (b) product line profitability reporting (materials purchasing, materials handling costs), (c) product contribution reporting (full cost profit margins, contribution margins), (d) operating effectiveness reporting (product cycle times, product waste times), and (e) asset management reporting (machine maintenance, machine utilization/downtime).

REVIEW OF CONCEPTS AND TERMINOLOGY

The following concepts and terms were introduced in this chapter.

L O 3 **Activity:** An action that is needed to accomplish the purpose or objective of a function.

L O 2 **Activity-based costing (ABC):** An approach to cost assignment that identifies all major operating activities, categorizes costs by activity, reduces or eliminates nonvalue-adding activities, and assigns costs using a basis that causes the costs to be incurred.

L O 4 **Appraisal costs:** The costs of activities that measure, evaluate, or audit products, processes, or services to ensure conformance to quality standards and performance requirements; a cost of conformance.

L O 5 **Computer-aided design (CAD):** A computer-based engineering system with a built-in program to detect product design flaws.

L O 2 **Cost driver:** Any activity that causes a cost to be incurred.

L O 1 **Cost management:** The management and control of activities to determine product cost accurately, to improve business processes, to eliminate waste, to identify cost drivers, to plan operations, and to set business strategies.

L O 1 **Cost management system (CMS):** A management accounting and reporting system that identifies, monitors, and maintains continuous, detailed analyses of a company's activities and provides managers with timely measures of operating results.

L O 4 **Costs of conformance:** The costs incurred to produce a quality product or service.

L O 4 **Costs of nonconformance:** The costs incurred to correct the defects or irregularities in a product or service.

L O 4 **Costs of quality:** The costs specifically associated with the achievement or non-achievement of product or service quality.

L O 6 **Delivery cycle time:** The time period between acceptance of an order and final delivery of the product.

L O 6 **Delivery time:** The time period between product completion and customer receipt of the item.

L O 4 **External failure costs:** The costs incurred as a consequence of the discovery of defects after a product or service has been delivered to a customer; a cost of nonconformance.

L O 7 **Full cost profit margin:** The difference between total revenue and total costs traceable to the work cell or product.

L O 3 **Function:** A group of activities that have a common purpose or objective.

L O 4 **Internal failure costs:** The costs incurred as a consequence of the discovery of defects before a product is shipped or a service delivered to a customer; a cost of nonconformance.

L O 3 **Nonvalue-adding activity:** A production- or service-related activity that adds cost to a product but does not increase its market value.

L O 4 **Prevention costs:** The costs associated with the prevention of defects and failures in products and services; a cost of conformance.

L O 3 **Process value analysis (PVA):** The process of identifying all activities and relating them to events that cause or drive the need for the activities and the resources consumed.

L O 6 **Production cycle time:** The time it takes for production personnel to make the product available for shipment to the customer.

L O 6 **Purchase order lead time:** The time it takes for raw materials and parts to be ordered and received so that production can begin.

L O 4 **Quality:** An operating environment in which a company's product or service meets or conforms to a customer's specifications the first time it is produced or delivered.

L O 3 **Tasks:** The work elements or operating steps needed to perform and complete an activity.

L O 4 **Total quality management (TQM):** An organizational environment in which all business functions work together to build quality into the firm's products or services.

L O 3 **Value-adding activity:** An activity that adds value to a product or service as perceived by the customer; this activity involves resource usage and related costs that customers feel are necessary and important to satisfying their needs.

L O 3 **Value chain:** All of the activities in the development path of a product or service that add or contribute to its value and marketability; all of a product's value-adding activities.

REVIEW PROBLEM

ANALYSIS OF NONFINANCIAL DATA— DASSIE PRODUCTS, INC.

L O 5, 6, 8 The Baum Motor Division of Dassie Products, Inc. has been in operation for six years. Three months ago a new flexible manufacturing system was installed in the small motors department. A just-in-time approach is followed for everything from ordering materials and parts to product shipment and delivery. The division's superintendent is very interested in the initial results of the venture. The following data have been collected for your analysis.

	Weeks							
	1	2	3	4	5	6	7	8
Warranty claims	2	4	1	1	0	5	7	11
Average setup time (hours)	.3	.25	.25	.3	.25	.2	.2	.15
Average lead time (hours)	2.4	2.3	2.2	2.3	2.35	2.4	2.4	2.5
Average cycle time (hours)	2.1	2.05	1.95	2	2	2.1	2.2	2.3
Average process time (hours)	1.9	1.9	1.85	1.8	1.9	1.95	1.95	1.9
Number of inventoried items	2,450	2,390	2,380	2,410	2,430	2,460	2,610	2,720
Customer complaints	12	12	10	8	9	7	6	4
Times inventory turnover	4.5	4.4	4.4	4.35	4.3	4.25	4.25	4.35
Production backlog (units)	9,210	9,350	9,370	9,420	9,410	8,730	8,310	7,950
Machine downtime (hours)	86.5	83.1	76.5	80.1	90.4	100.6	120.2	124.9
Parts scrapped (units)	112	126	134	118	96	89	78	64
Equipment utilization rate (%)	98.2	98.6	98.9	98.5	98.1	97.3	96.6	95.7
On-time deliveries (%)	93.2	94.1	96.5	95.4	92.1	90.5	88.4	89.3
Machine maintenance time (hours)	34.6	32.2	28.5	22.1	18.5	12.6	19.7	26.4

REQUIRED
1. Analyze the performance of the Baum Motor Division for the eight-week period, centering your analysis on the following areas of performance:
   a. Product quality
   b. Product delivery
   c. Inventory control
   d. Materials cost/scrap control
   e. Machine management and maintenance
2. Summarize your findings in a report to the division's superintendent.

ANSWER TO REVIEW PROBLEM

The data given were reorganized in the following manner, and two additional pieces of information, average waste time and estimated number of units sold, were calculated from the given information.

1. Analysis of performance

	Weeks								Weekly
	1	2	3	4	5	6	7	8	Average
Product quality performance									
Customer complaints	12	12	10	8	9	7	6	4	8.5 cmplt.
Warranty claims	2	4	1	1	0	5	7	11	3.875 claims

(continued)

	Weeks								Weekly Average
	1	**2**	**3**	**4**	**5**	**6**	**7**	**8**	
Product delivery performance									
On-time deliveries (%)	93.2	94.1	96.5	95.4	92.1	90.5	88.4	89.3	92.44 %
Average setup time (hours)	.3	.25	.25	.3	.25	.2	.2	.15	.238 hours
Average lead time (hours)	2.4	2.3	2.2	2.3	2.35	2.4	2.4	2.5	2.356 hours
Average cycle time (hours)	2.1	2.05	1.95	2	2	2.1	2.2	2.3	2.088 hours
Average process time (hours)	1.9	1.9	1.85	1.8	1.9	1.95	1.95	1.9	1.894 hours
Production backlog (units)	9,210	9,350	9,370	9,420	9,410	8,730	8,310	7,950	8,969 units
Average waste time (hours) (average lead time less process time)	.5	.4	.35	.5	.45	.45	.45	.6	.463 hours
Inventory control performance									
Number of inventoried items (units) (a)	2,450	2,390	2,380	2,410	2,430	2,460	2,610	2,720	2,481 units
Times inventory turnover (b)	4.5	4.4	4.4	4.35	4.3	4.25	4.25	4.35	4.35 times
Estimated number of units sold (a × b)	11,025	10,516	10,472	10,484	10,449	10,455	11,093	11,832	10,791 units
Materials cost/scrap control performance									
Parts scrapped (units)	112	126	134	118	96	89	78	64	102.125 units
Machine management and maintenance performance									
Machine downtime (hours)	86.5	83.1	76.5	80.1	90.4	100.6	120.2	124.9	95.288 hours
Equipment utilization rate (%)	98.2	98.6	98.9	98.5	98.1	97.3	96.6	95.7	97.74 %
Machine maintenance time (hours)	34.6	32.2	28.5	22.1	18.5	12.6	19.7	26.4	24.325 hours

2. Memorandum to division superintendent.

My analysis of the operating data for the Baum Motor Division for the last eight weeks revealed the following:

Product quality performance
Product quality seems to be improving, with the number of complaints decreasing rapidly. However, warranty claims rose significantly in the past three weeks, which may be a signal of quality problems ahead.

Product delivery performance
Although the averages for the product delivery measures seem great when compared to our old standards, we are having trouble maintaining the averages established eight weeks ago. Waste time is increasing, which is contrary to our goals. Backlogged orders are decreasing, which is a good sign from a JIT viewpoint but could spell problems in the future. On-time deliveries percentages are slipping. On the positive side, setup time seems to be under control. Emphasis needs to be placed on reducing lead time, cycle time, and process time.

Inventory control performance
This area spells trouble. Inventory size is increasing, and the number of inventory turns is decreasing. The result is increased storage costs and decreased units sold. The last two weeks do show signs of improvement.

Materials cost/scrap control performance

The incidence of scrap has decreased significantly, which is very good. We had to increase cycle time to correct our manufacturing problems, which accounts for the increases in that area. With the scrap problem under control, processing and cycle time may improve in the future.

Machine management and maintenance performance

Machine downtime is increasing, which is consistent with the scrap report. Also, the equipment utilization rate is down. Machine maintenance has also tailed off but has increased in the past two weeks. Department managers should be made aware of these pending problem areas.

Overall, we can see good signs from the new equipment, but we need to stay on top of the pending problem areas mentioned above.

CHAPTER ASSIGNMENTS

QUESTIONS

1. Describe a cost management system.
2. What is activity-based costing?
3. What is a cost driver? What is its role in activity-based costing practices?
4. Explain the two-step procedure accountants use to assign costs using activity-based costing principles.
5. What is the value chain of a product or service?
6. What is process value analysis? How does this form of analysis help management?
7. What is total quality management? How does the management accountant help a company achieve total quality management?
8. How is *quality* defined in business? What are the costs of quality?
9. Identify and describe the cost-of-quality categories.
10. Name five nonfinancial measures of quality and indicate what they are designed to measure in terms of product or service quality.
11. Identify four types of nonfinancial analyses that are used to measure product quality performance. Describe the kind of data used in each analysis.
12. Why is customer satisfaction emphasized in a JIT environment? How is this attention linked to the profitability of a JIT approach?
13. Inventory controls in the JIT manufacturing environment are designed to eliminate inventory balances and nonvalue-adding product costs connected with inventory management. Do you agree? Why is there emphasis on inventory elimination?
14. In a JIT/FMS environment, the formal inspection departments are eliminated but product quality controls are given high priority. How is this accomplished?
15. For what reasons are accurate records of machine maintenance so critical to a JIT/FMS operation?
16. Define full cost profit margin and contrast it with contribution margin.
17. What does customer responsiveness reporting mean? How does it differ from product line profitability reporting?
18. Identify and describe several of the reports needed to monitor an FMS's operating effectiveness.

SHORT EXERCISES

SE 1. *Traits of a Cost*
L O 1 *Management System*
No check figure

Cost management means managing and controlling activities to achieve control of costs. Cost management systems provide the structure to achieve control of activities. Identify three traits of cost management systems that differentiate them from traditional systems. Explain how each trait helps control costs.

SE 2. *Activity-Based*
L O 2 *Costing and Cost Drivers*
Check Figure: Designing activity: $19 per designer hour

Kloezeman Clothiers Company relies on its activity-based costing system for cost support information to set prices for its products. Compute ABC costing rates from the following budgeted data for each of the activity centers.

	Budgeted Cost	Budgeted Cost Driver
Cutting/stitching activity	$5,220,000	145,000 machine hours
Trimming/packing activity	$ 998,400	41,600 operator hours
Designing activity	$1,187,500	62,500 designer hours

SE 3. *Identifying a*
L O 3 *Product's Value Chain*
No check figure

Which of the following activities would be part of the value chain of a manufacturing company?

Product inspection
Machine drilling
Materials storage
Product engineering

Plating/packing
Cost accounting
Moving work in process
Inventory control

SE 4. *Costs of Quality in*
L O 4 *a Service Business*
No check figure

Modesto-Kropp Insurance Agency incurred the following activity costs related to service quality. Identify those that are costs of conformance (CC) and those that are costs of nonconformance (CN).

Policy processing improvements	$76,400
Customer complaints response	34,100
Policy writer training	12,300
Policy error losses	82,700
Policy proofing	39,500

SE 5. *Nonfinancial*
L O 5 *Measures of Quality*
No check figure

For a fast-food restaurant that specializes in deluxe cheeseburgers, identify two nonfinancial measures of good product quality and two nonfinancial measures of poor product quality.

SE 6. *Product Delivery*
L O 6 *Performance Evaluation*
Check Figure: Total delivery cycle time for Week 1: 9.9 days

Alesha Cosmetics, Inc. has developed a set of nonfinancial measures to evaluate on-time product delivery performance for one of its best-selling cosmetics. The following data have been generated for the past four weeks.

Week	Purchase Order Lead Time	Production Cycle Time	Delivery Time
1	2.4 days	3.5 days	4.0 days
2	2.3 days	3.5 days	3.5 days
3	2.4 days	3.3 days	3.4 days
4	2.5 days	3.2 days	3.3 days

Compute total delivery cycle time for each week. Evaluate the product delivery performance. Is there an area that needs management's attention?

SE 7. *Full Cost Profit*
L O 7 *Margin*
Check Figure: Contribution margin for July–September: $950,000

Smith Company hired a consultant to refine its cost management system. One of the changes implemented was a shift in division performance indicators from contribution margin to full cost profit margin. The Southwest Division generated the information summarized below for the last two quarters of the year.

Month	Revenue	Variable Costs	Traceable Fixed Costs
July–September	$1,400,000	$450,000	$630,000
October–December	2,550,000	980,000	680,000

Evaluate the performance of the division by computing the contribution margin the full cost profit margin for each quarter. Also compute the percentages of each to total revenue. How is the division performing?

SE 8. *Cost Management*
L O 8 *System Reporting*
No check figure

Kayprice Corporation installed a new cost management system six months ago. Initially, top management was reluctant to trust the new emphasis on managing activities to facilitate cost control and was hesitant to request reports generated by the CMS. Through the efforts of the controller, the chief executive officer finally warmed up to the system. Those efforts were tied to two new reports from the CMS, the customer responsiveness report and the product line profitability report. Using the content of these reports, explain why the CEO changed her mind about the CMS.

EXERCISES

E 1. *Cost Driver*
L O 2 *Determination*
No check figure

Salesman Hans Klammer just stormed out of the office of controller Rita Milano. When asked what was wrong, Klammer stated that he had just been told to refuse any additional orders for goods that had to circumvent the existing three-week backlog. Milano had just added $2,450 in additional scheduling costs to a recent order from Glazner Corp., one of Klammer's accounts, and this charge turned a $2,200 profit into a $250 loss. (Sales personnel earn commissions on the profits their orders generate.)

Milano used the following analysis to back up her position regarding the Glazner Corp. order.

Costs Associated with Production Schedule Changes

Personnel overtime	$1,940
Extra computer time	1,260
Unanticipated supplies and utility costs	1,080
Communication with affected customers	620
Total costs of schedule changes	$4,900
50 percent traceable to Glazner Corp. order	$2,450

What is a cost driver? Does this case involve a cost driver? Should the cost of schedule changes be spread over all orders worked on or traced to specific orders? Do you agree with Milano's decision? Why or why not?

E 2. *Costs and Their Cost*
L O 2 *Drivers*
No check figure

The following items appeared on the trial balance of the Elsie Corporation in Troy, New York. Company accountants are in the process of establishing an overhead allocation system for factory-related costs. To help ensure accuracy, they have set up the following cost pools, each of which will be allocated using a different cost driver.

Tool and Die Department Cost Pool

Depreciation on equipment	$ 7,270
Operating supplies	1,274
Electrical costs	2,310
Wages	19,740
Total	$30,594

Engineering Department Cost Pool

Salaries	$22,190
Depreciation on equipment	4,260
Electrical costs	1,980
Total	$28,430

Plant Building Cost Pool

Repairs and maintenance	$11,578
Depreciation	8,150
Insurance and taxes	3,520
Total	$23,248

For each pool, identify the cost driver that will distribute the costs fairly. Be prepared to defend your selections. Possible cost drivers include direct labor hours, tool and die orders, engineering change orders, machine hours, engineering hours, tool and die labor hours, direct labor dollars, and square footage.

E 3.   *Activities and*
L O 2, 3   *Activity-Based*
              Costing

Check Figure: Quality control cost
using ABC: $827.00

Yu Enterprises produces antennas for telecommunications equipment. One of the most important parts of the company's new just-in-time production process is quality control. Initially, a traditional cost accounting system was used to assign quality control costs to products. All costs of the Quality Control Department were included in the plant's overhead cost pool and allocated to products based on direct labor dollars. Recently, the firm implemented an activity-based costing system. The activities, cost drivers, and rates for the quality control function are summarized below, along with cost allocation information from the traditional system. Also shown is information related to one order, HQ14, of the Qian model antenna.

Traditional costing approach:
   Quality control costs were assigned at a rate of 12 percent of direct labor dollars. Order HQ14 was charged with $9,350 of direct labor cost.

Activity-based costing approach:
   Quality Control Function

Activities	Cost Drivers	Cost Assignment Rates	Order HQ14 Activity Usage
Incoming materials inspection	Types of materials used	$17.50 per type of material	17 types of materials
In-process inspection	Number of products	$ .06 per product	2,400 products
Tool and gauge control	Number of processes per cell	$26.50 per process	11 processes
Product certification	Per order	$94.00 per order	1 order

Compute the quality control cost that would be assigned to the Qian model order HQ14 under both the traditional approach and the activity-based costing approach.

E 4.   *Measuring Costs of*
L O 4   *Quality*

No check figure

Lasho Corporation operates using two departments that produce two separate product lines. The company has been implementing a total quality management operating philosophy over the past year. Revenue and costs of quality data for that year are presented below.

	Dept. A	Dept. B	Totals
Annual Sales	$7,950,000	$9,650,000	$17,600,000
Costs of Quality			
Prevention costs	$ 185,000	$ 130,000	$ 315,000
Internal failure costs	98,200	205,000	303,200
External failure costs	44,100	159,000	203,100
Appraisal costs	136,700	68,000	204,700
Totals	$ 464,000	$ 562,000	$ 1,026,000

Which department is taking the most serious approach to implementing TQM? Base your answer on the following computations:

a. Total costs of quality as a percentage of sales
b. Ratio of conformance costs to total costs of quality
c. Ratio of nonconformance costs to total costs of quality
d. Nonconformance costs as a percentage of sales

E 5.   *Nonfinancial*
L O 5   *Measures of Quality*
           and TQM

No check figure

"A satisfied customer is the most important goal of this company!" was the opening remark of the corporate president, Jonathan Reilly, at the monthly executive committee meeting of Niederland Company. The company manufactures piping products for customers in sixteen western states. Four divisions, each producing a different type of piping material, make up the company's organizational structure. Reilly, a proponent of total quality management, was reacting to the latest measures of quality data from the four divisions. The data are presented on the next page.

	Brass Division	Plastics Division	Aluminum Division	Copper Division	Company Averages
Vendor on-time delivery	96.20%	92.40%	98.10%	90.20%	94.23%
Production quality rates (defective parts per million)	1,640	2,820	1,270	4,270	2,500
On-time shipments	89.20%	78.40%	91.80%	75.60%	83.75%
Returned orders	1.10%	4.60%	.80%	6.90%	3.35%
Number of customer complaints	24	56	10	62	38.0
Number of warranty claims	7	12	4	14	9.3*

*Rounded.

Why was Reilly upset? Which division or divisions do not appear to have satisfied customers? What criteria did you use to make your decision?

E 6. *Nonfinancial Data*
L O 6 *Analysis*
No check figure

Walsh & Company makes racing bicycle products. Their Royce model is considered top of the line within the industry. Three months ago the company purchased and installed a flexible manufacturing system for the Royce line, with emphasis on improving quality as well as reducing production time. Management is interested in cutting time in all phases of the delivery cycle.

Following are data the controller's office gathered for the past four-week period.

	Weeks			
	1	2	3	4
Average process time (hours)	23.6	23.4	22.8	22.2
Average setup time (hours)	2.4	2.3	2.2	2.1
Customer complaints	6	5	7	8
Delivery time (hours)	34.8	35.2	36.4	38.2
On-time deliveries (%)	98.1	97.7	97.2	96.3
Production backlog (units)	8,230	8,340	8,320	8,430
Production cycle time (hours)	28.5	27.9	27.2	26.4
Purchase order lead time (hours)	38.5	36.2	35.5	34.1
Warranty claims	2	3	3	2

Analyze the performance of the Royce model line for the four-week period, centering your analysis on the following areas of performance: (1) Product quality and (2) Product delivery.

E 7. *Full Cost Profit*
L O 7 *Margin*
Check Figure: Full cost profit margin: $512,616

Baron Enterprises produces all-purpose sports vehicles. The company recently installed a flexible manufacturing system for its AJ-25 product line. The accounting system has been recast to reflect the new operating process. Following are monthly operating data for periods before and after the FMS installation.

	Product AJ-25
Average monthly revenue	$1,378,000
Total operating costs:	
For month before FMS installed	
Direct materials	$ 330,720
Direct labor	454,740
Variable factory overhead	124,020
Variable selling expenses	41,340
Variable distribution costs	55,120
Fixed factory overhead	456,200
Fixed selling expenses	132,300
Fixed distribution costs	189,700

	Product AJ-25
For month after FMS installed	
Direct materials	$ 330,720
Materials-related overhead	48,230
Direct labor	62,010
Indirect labor	99,216
Setup labor	66,144
Electrical power	24,804
Supervision	35,828
Repairs and maintenance	46,852
Operating supplies and lubricants	11,024
Other traceable indirect costs	30,316
Traceable selling expenses	52,364
Traceable distribution costs	57,876
Nontraceable factory overhead	245,300
Nontraceable selling and distribution costs	178,200

Using the after-FMS data, compute the full cost profit margin for product AJ-25. Also include full cost profit margin as a percent of revenue and operating profit as a percent of revenue as part of your answer.

E 8.
L O 8

Measuring Operating Performance

No check figure

Bailey's Bakery produces a variety of breads and desserts for local groceries. Larry Johnson, the controller, recently collected information to help the bakery measure performance and control operations. Determine whether the information listed below measures customer responsiveness, product line profitability, product contribution, operating effectiveness, or efficient asset management. Also indicate if the information is nonfinancial or financial in nature.

1. Space utilization
2. Contribution margin
3. Materials purchasing
4. Product lead times

5. Backlogged orders
6. Product shipment tracking
7. Machine maintenance
8. Conversion costs

SKILLS DEVELOPMENT EXERCISES

Conceptual Analysis

SDE 1.
L O 2

Activity-Based Costing

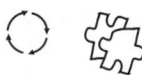

No check figure

Activity-based costing requires that all activities related to a particular function be identified and that costs be traced to those activities. Select your favorite clothing store. Interview the manager or a salesperson to determine what activities take place between the decision to buy a particular line of clothing and the actual sale of an item to a customer. Make a list of all the activities involved in the process. Which of those activities are nonvalue-adding? Select one major activity from your list and identify the costs that could be traced to it. Be prepared to discuss your answers in class.

Ethical Dilemma

SDE 2.
L O 1

Cost Management and Ethics

No check figure

Three months ago, **Townsend Enterprises** hired a consultant, Lisa Swan, to assist in the design and installation of a new cost management system for the company. Tom Granger, one of Townsend's product/systems design engineers, was assigned to work with Swan on the project. During the three-month period, Swan and Granger met six times and developed a tentative design and installation plan for the CMS. Before the plan was to be unveiled to top management, Granger asked his supervisor, Beth Leftwich, to look it over and comment on the design.

Included in the plan is a consolidation of three engineering functions into one. Both of the current supervisors of the other two functions have seniority over Leftwich, so she believes that the design would lead to her losing her management position. She communicates this to Granger and ends her comments with the following statement, "If you don't redesign the system to accommodate all three of the existing engineering functions, I will see to it that you are given an unsatisfactory performance evaluation for this year!"

How should Granger respond to Leftwich's assertion? Should he handle the problem alone, keeping it inside the company or communicate the comment to Swan? Outline Granger's options and be prepared to discuss them in class.

Research Activity

SDE 3. *Cost Drivers*

L O 2

No check figure

Go to the library and find a recent issue of *Management Accounting*. Locate an article that has *cost driver, activity-based costing, ABC,* or *cost management* in its title. From the article, prepare a one-page paper on the topic of cost drivers. Be sure to include examples of cost drivers in your work.

Decision-Making Practice

SDE 4. *Activities, Cost*

L O 2, 3 *Drivers, and JIT*

No check figure

Savannah, Georgia is home of the **Claus Corporation.** Fifteen years ago Sam Claus teamed up with ten financial supporters and created a roller skate manufacturing company. Company design people soon turned the roller skate idea into a riding skateboard. Twelve years and more than 4 million skateboards later, Claus Corporation finds itself an industry leader in both volume and quality.

To retain market share, Claus Corporation has decided to automate its manufacturing process. Flexible manufacturing systems have been ordered for the wheel assembly and the board shaping lines. Manual operations will be retained for the board decorating line because some hand painting is involved. All operations will be converted to a just-in-time environment.

You have been called in as a consultant to Claus, who wants some idea of the impact of the new JIT/FMS approach on the company's product costing practices.

1. Summarize the elements of a JIT environment.
2. What product costing changes should be anticipated when the new automated systems are installed?
3. What are some of the cost drivers that the company should employ? In what situations?
4. Are there any other accounting practices that will be affected? Why?

PROBLEM SET A

A 1. *Activities and*

L O 2, 3 *Activity-Based*

Costing

Check Figure: 1. Total cost of Goodacre order: $70,463.50

Needham Computer Company, which has been in operation for ten years, produces a line of minicomputers. Goodacre Realtors, Ltd. placed an order for eighty minicomputers and the order has just been completed. Needham recently shifted its cost assignment approach to an activity-based system. Sandra Alvarez, the controller, is interested in finding out the impact that the ABC system had on the Goodacre order. Raw materials, purchased parts, and production labor costs for the Goodacre order are as follows:

Cost of raw materials	$36,750.00	Production direct labor hours	220
Cost of purchased parts	21,300.00	Average direct labor pay rate	$15.25

Other operating costs are as follows:

Traditional costing data:
Factory overhead costs were assigned at a rate of 270 percent of direct labor dollars.

Activity-based costing data:

Activities	Cost Drivers	Cost Assignment Rates	Activity Usage for Goodacre Order
Electrical engineering design	Engineering hours	$19.50 per engineering hour	32 engineering hours
Work cell setups	Number of setups	$29.40 per setup	11 setups
Parts production work cell	Machine hours	$26.30 per machine hour	134 machine hours
Product testing cell	Cell hours	$32.80 per cell hour	52 cell hours
Packaging work cell	Cell hours	$17.50 per cell hour	22 cell hours

Building occupancy-related overhead costs are allocated at a rate of $9.80 per production work cell machine hour.

REQUIRED

1. Using the traditional absorption costing approach, compute the total cost of the Goodacre order.
2. Using the activity-based costing approach, compute the total cost of the Goodacre order.
3. What was the difference in the amount of cost assigned to the Goodacre order resulting from the shift to activity-based costing? Does the use of activity-based costing guarantee cost reduction for every product?

A 2. *Costs and*
L O 4, 5 *Nonfinancial*
Measures of Quality

Check Figure: 1. Total costs of quality, Deming Company: $1,713,500

Roswell Enterprises, Inc. operates as three autonomous companies. Each company has a chief executive officer who oversees its operations. At a recent corporate meeting, the company CEOs agreed to adopt total quality management for their operations and to track, record, and analyze their costs and nonfinancial measures of quality. All three companies are operating in a highly competitive worldwide market. Sales and quality-related data for September are summarized below.

	Deming Company	Laredo Company	Hobbs Company
Annual sales	$11,500,000	$13,200,000	$10,900,000
Costs of quality			
Sample preparation	$ 69,000	$ 184,800	$ 130,800
Quality audits	57,500	112,200	141,700
Failure analysis	184,000	92,400	16,350
Design review	80,500	171,600	218,000
Scrap and rework	207,000	158,400	21,800
Quality planning activities	46,000	105,600	239,800
Preventive maintenance	92,000	158,400	163,500
Warranty adjustments	143,750	105,600	49,050
Customer service	201,250	198,000	81,750
Quality training of employees	149,500	237,600	272,500
Product simulation and development	34,500	145,200	207,100
Reinspection of rework	126,500	66,000	27,250
Returned goods	212,750	72,600	16,350
Customer complaint processing	109,250	158,400	38,150
Total costs of quality	$ 1,713,500	$ 1,966,800	$ 1,624,100
Nonfinancial measures of quality			
Number of warranty claims	61	36	12
Customer complaints	107	52	18
Defective parts per million	4,610	2,190	1,012
Returned orders	9.20%	4.10%	.90%

REQUIRED

1. Prepare an analysis of the costs of quality of the three companies. Categorize the costs in the following format: costs of conformance with subsets of prevention costs and appraisal costs, and costs of nonconformance with subsets of internal failure costs and external failure costs. Compute the total costs for each category for each of the three companies.
2. Compute the percentage of sales for each cost-of-quality total for each company.
3. Interpret the cost-of-quality data for each company. Is the company's product of high or low quality? Why? Is each company headed in the right direction to be globally competitive?
4. Evaluate the nonfinancial measures of quality in terms of customer satisfaction. Are the results consistent with your analysis in **3**? Explain your answer.

A 3. *Analysis of*
L O 5, 6 *Nonfinancial Data*

Taylor Enterprises, Inc. manufactures several lines of small machinery. Before automated equipment was installed, the total delivery cycle for the Beki machine models averaged about three weeks. Last year management decided to purchase an FMS for the Beki line. The cost was $17,458,340 and included twelve separate work stations producing the four components needed to assemble a finished product. Each machine is linked to the next via an automated conveyor system. Assembly of the four parts,

Check Figure: 1d. Materials cost/ scrap control for Week 1: 98 parts scrapped

including the machine's entire electrical system, now takes only two hours. Following is a summary of operating data for the past eight weeks for the Beki line.

	Weeks							
	1	2	3	4	5	6	7	8
Average process time (hours)	8.2	8.2	8.1	8.4	8.6	8.2	7.8	7.6
Average setup time (hours)	1.2	1.2	1.1	.9	.9	.8	1.0	.9
Customer complaints	4	5	3	6	5	7	8	8
Delivery time (hours)	36.2	37.4	37.2	36.4	35.9	35.8	34.8	34.2
Equipment utilization rate (%)	99.1	99.2	99.4	99.1	98.8	98.6	98.8	98.8
Machine downtime (hours)	82.3	84.2	85.9	84.3	83.4	82.2	82.8	80.4
Machine maintenance time (hours)	52.4	54.8	51.5	48.4	49.2	47.8	46.8	44.9
Number of inventoried items	5,642	5,820	5,690	5,780	5,630	5,510	5,280	5,080
On-time deliveries (%)	92.4	92.5	93.2	94.2	94.4	94.1	95.8	94.6
Parts scrapped	98.0	96.0	102.0	104.0	100.0	98.2	98.6	100.6
Production backlog (units)	15,230	15,440	15,200	16,100	14,890	13,560	13,980	13,440
Production cycle time (hours)	12.2	12.6	11.9	11.8	12.2	11.6	11.2	10.6
Purchase order lead time (hours)	26.2	26.8	26.5	25.9	25.7	25.3	24.8	24.2
Times inventory turnover	3.2	3.4	3.4	3.6	3.8	3.8	4.2	4.4
Warranty claims	2	2	3	2	3	4	3	3

REQUIRED

1. Analyze the performance of the Beki machine line for the eight-week period, centering your analysis on performance in the following areas:
   a. Product quality
   b. Product delivery
   c. Inventory control
   d. Materials cost/scrap control
   e. Machine management and maintenance
2. Summarize your findings in a report to the company management.

A 4. *Full Cost Profit*
L O 7 *Margin*

Check Figure: 4. Operating profit for Meadow Assembly: $820,260

Sara Vado began producing scrap-iron art works seven years ago. Her business became so profitable that she converted to an assembly line approach two years ago. Concerned about continuously rising labor costs, Vado recently agreed to purchase flexible manufacturing systems for her three largest-selling products: the Meadow, Ridge, and Valley assemblies. Vado is very concerned about the Valley assembly because of its recent poor profitability performance. Following are operating data from before and after the FMS installation.

Vado Metal Products Company
Product Performance Evaluation

	Meadow Assembly	Ridge Assembly	Valley Assembly
Total revenue	$3,972,000	$6,731,000	$4,262,000
Total operating costs			
Before FMS installed			
Direct materials	$ 953,280	$1,750,060	$1,193,360
Direct labor	1,310,760	2,288,540	1,363,840
Variable factory overhead	357,480	336,550	230,148
Variable selling expenses	166,824	289,433	157,694
Variable distribution costs	158,880	403,860	242,934
Fixed factory overhead	461,100	647,700	515,600
Fixed selling expenses	146,100	153,400	166,700
Fixed distribution costs	191,600	299,600	249,800

(continued)

	Meadow Assembly	Ridge Assembly	Valley Assembly
After FMS installed			
Direct materials	$ 953,280	$1,750,060	$1,193,360
Materials-related overhead	206,544	363,474	242,934
Direct labor	285,984	457,708	272,768
Indirect labor	278,040	430,784	315,388
Setup labor	190,656	282,702	187,528
Electrical power	71,496	121,158	68,192
Supervision	103,272	188,468	110,812
Repairs and maintenance	135,048	208,661	157,694
Operating supplies/lubricants	31,776	60,579	34,096
Other traceable indirect costs	87,384	141,351	102,288
Traceable selling expenses	150,936	222,123	161,956
Traceable distribution costs	166,824	262,509	183,266
Nontraceable factory overhead	276,300	341,300	253,400
Nontraceable selling and distribution costs	214,200	297,300	209,700

REQUIRED

1. Recast the information given for the three products into an analysis that reveals total traceable and total nontraceable costs (a) before and (b) after the FMS was installed.
2. Describe and differentiate between full cost profit margin and contribution margin.
3. Using the before-FMS data, prepare an analysis that reveals contribution margin, operating profit, contribution margin as a percentage of revenue, and operating profit as a percentage of revenue.
4. Using the after-FMS data, prepare an analysis that reveals full cost profit margin, operating profit, full cost profit margin as a percentage of revenue, and operating profit as a percentage of revenue.
5. Should the company drop the Valley assembly? Defend your answer.

A 5.
L O 2, 3
Comprehensive View of Cost Allocation Featuring Activity-Based Costing

Check Figure: 3. Unit cost for Job Order A using six activity rates: $5,052

Blackburn Products, Inc. produces transmission housings for large earth-moving equipment. Because of global competition, prices have had to be analyzed to make sure they reflect accurate costs and profit margins. The company has been using a single, plantwide factory overhead rate when applying overhead costs to its products. Management has requested that the controller's office develop three additional approaches to overhead allocation. Data for the past month are summarized in the schedule on the next page. In addition to the current overhead cost allocation approach using a plantwide rate based on direct labor hours (column 1 data), the following approaches are being discussed:

Using two departmental overhead rates (columns 2 and 3 data)

Using three rates, two departmental rates excluding materials handling cost plus a separate rate for materials handling activity costs (columns 4, 5, and 6 data)

Using six overhead allocation rates, one for each of the six activities of the production operation (columns 6 through 11 data)

Note that a cost driver has been identified for each of the eleven columns in the data schedule.

REQUIRED

1. Compute the overhead allocation rates for each column in the schedule using the designated cost drivers as a basis for the rates.
2. Compute the overhead charges per unit for each job order completed. (Round all answers to whole dollars.)
   a. Using a single, plantwide overhead rate.
   b. Using two departmental overhead rates.
   c. Using three overhead rates, two departmental rates that exclude materials handling costs plus a separate rate for materials handling activity usage.
   d. Using an activity-based costing approach with six different activity-related rates.

	(1)	(2)	(3)	(4)	(5)	(6)	(7)	(8)	(9)	(10)	(11)
	Plant Totals	Department One	Department Two	Department One Less Materials Handling Costs	Department Two Less Materials Handling Costs	Materials Handling Activity	Computer Center Activity	Repairs and Maintenance Activity	Tool and Die Activity	Machine Setup Activity	Engineering and Design Activity
Overhead Cost Data											
Building occupancy costs	$ 23,500	$ 9,400	$ 14,100	$ 8,552	$ 12,828	$ 2,120	$ 4,300	$ 5,650	$ 3,950	$ 1,850	$ 5,630
Electrical costs	7,820	2,346	5,474	2,061	4,809	950	1,940	1,020	1,260	240	2,410
Indirect labor	47,260	16,541	30,719	15,432	28,658	3,170	10,400	4,860	7,420	5,110	16,300
Indirect materials	23,240	13,944	9,296	13,410	8,940	890	3,220	1,460	9,280	950	7,440
Employee benefits	18,904	6,616	12,288	6,173	11,463	1,268	4,160	1,944	2,968	2,044	6,520
Janitorial services	7,050	2,115	4,935	1,924	4,490	636	1,290	1,695	1,185	555	1,689
Machine depreciation	19,780	3,956	15,824	3,334	13,336	3,110	3,900	1,800	4,600	1,050	5,320
Supervisor salaries	37,808	24,575	13,233	22,927	12,345	2,536	8,320	3,888	5,936	4,088	13,040
Other utilities	3,128	938	2,190	824	1,924	380	776	408	504	96	964
Leasehold costs	15,000	3,000	12,000	2,812	11,248	940	5,000	200	4,500	0	4,360
	$203,490	$83,431	$120,059	$77,449	$110,041	$16,000	$43,306	$22,925	$41,603	$15,983	$63,673
Cost Driver Used	Direct Labor Hours	Direct Labor Hours	Direct Labor Hours	Direct Labor Hours	Machine Hours	Weight of Materials (lbs)	Computer Hours of Use	Repair Labor Hours	Number of Requests	Number of Setups	Engineering Hours
Cost Driver Data											
Job Order A											
20 units @ 60 DLHs/unit	1,200	840	360	840		9,900	320	110	35	52	60
20 units @ 160 MHs/unit*					2,560						
Job Order B											
50 units @ 30 DLHs/unit	1,500	900	600	900		24,400	120	230	17	94	720
50 units @ 80 MHs/unit*					3,200						
Job Order C											
30 units @ 80 DLHs/unit	2,400	1,200	1,200	1,200		15,700	200	140	28	74	180
30 units @ 40 MHs/unit*					960						
Totals	5,100	2,940	2,160	2,940	6,720	50,000	640	480	80	220	960

*Some of these machine hours are incurred in Department One; these are not shown because they are not used as a cost driver.

3. Complete the unit cost analysis schedule below.

	Using Plantwide Overhead Rate	Using Departmental Overhead Rates	Using Three Different Overhead Rates	Using Six Activity Rates
Job Order A				
Direct materials cost	$1,530	$1,530	$1,530	$1,530
Direct labor cost	720	720	720	720
Factory overhead cost				
Totals				
Job Order B				
Direct materials cost	$3,365	$3,365	$3,365	$3,365
Direct labor cost	360	360	360	360
Factory overhead cost				
Totals				
Job Order C				
Direct materials cost	$2,600	$2,600	$2,600	$2,600
Direct labor cost	960	960	960	960
Factory overhead cost				
Totals				

4. Which of the four overhead cost allocation approaches yields the most accurate product cost data? List the reasons supporting your selection.

PROBLEM SET B

B 1. *Activities and*
L O 2, 3 *Activity-Based*
Costing

Check Figure: 2. Total cost of Jekyl order using ABC: $41,805.60

Hampton Products, Inc. produces a line of FAX machines for wholesale distributors in the Pacific Northwest. Jekyl Company ordered 150 Model 14 FAX machines and Hampton has just completed packaging the order. Before shipping the Jekyl order, the controller has asked for a unit cost analysis, comparing costs determined by the traditional absorption costing system with costs computed under the new activity-based costing system.

Raw materials, purchased parts, and production labor costs for the Jekyl order are as follows:

Cost of raw materials	$17,450.00
Cost of purchased parts	$14,800.00
Production direct labor hours	140
Average direct labor pay rate	$16.50

Other operating costs are as follows:

Traditional costing data:
Factory overhead costs were assigned at a rate of 240 percent of direct labor dollars.

Activity-based costing data:

Activities	Cost Drivers	Cost Assignment Rates	Activity Usage for Jekyl Order
Engineering systems design	Engineering hours	$28.00 per engineering hour	18 engineering hours
Work cell setup	Number of setups	$42.00 per setup	8 setups
Parts production work cell	Machine hours	$37.50 per machine hour	84 machine hours
Product assembly cell	Cell hours	$44.00 per cell hour	36 cell hours
Packaging work cell	Cell hours	$28.50 per cell hour	28 cell hours

Building occupancy-related overhead costs are allocated at a rate of $10.40 per production work cell machine hour.

REQUIRED

1. Use the traditional absorption costing approach to compute the total cost of the Jekyl order.
2. Use the activity-based costing approach to compute the total cost of the Jekyl order.
3. What was the difference in the amount of cost assigned to the Jekyl order resulting from the shift to activity-based costing? Does the use of activity-based costing guarantee cost reduction for every product?

B 2. *Costs and*
L O 4, 5 *Nonfinancial*
Measures of Quality

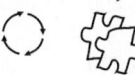

Check Figure: Total costs of quality, Call Division: $1,169,600

The Quail Company operates as three autonomous divisions. Each division has a general manager in charge of product development, production, and distribution. Management recently adopted total quality management, and the divisions now track, record, and analyze their costs and nonfinancial measures of quality. All three divisions are operating in a worldwide, highly competitive marketplace. Sales and quality-related data for April are summarized below.

	Call Division	Davis Division	Ellis Division
Annual sales	$8,600,000	$9,400,000	$12,900,000
Costs of quality			
Setup for testing	$ 51,600	$ 112,800	$ 180,600
Quality audits	17,200	75,200	109,650
Failure analysis	103,200	14,100	90,300
Quality training of employees	60,200	188,000	167,700
Scrap and rework	154,800	18,800	154,800
Quality planning activities	34,400	94,000	103,200
Preventive maintenance	68,800	141,000	141,900
Warranty claims	107,500	42,300	103,200
Customer service	150,500	108,100	154,800
Quality engineering	94,600	235,000	232,200
Product simulation and development	25,800	178,600	141,900
Losses caused by vendor scrap	77,400	23,500	64,500
Returned goods	159,100	14,100	45,150
Product recalls	64,500	32,900	64,500
Total costs of quality	$1,169,600	$1,278,400	$ 1,754,400
Nonfinancial measures of quality			
Defective parts per million	3,410	1,104	1,940
Returned orders	7.40%	1.10%	3.20%
Customer complaints	62	12	30
Number of warranty claims	74	16	52

REQUIRED

1. Prepare an analysis of the costs of quality of the three divisions. Categorize the costs as follows: costs of conformance with subsets of prevention costs and appraisal costs, and costs of nonconformance with subsets of internal failure costs and external failure costs. Compute the total costs for each category for each division.
2. Compute the percentage of sales of each cost-of-quality total for each division.
3. Interpret the cost-of-quality data for each division. Is each division's product of high or low quality? Explain your answers. Are the divisions headed in the right direction to be globally competitive?
4. Evaluate the nonfinancial measures of quality in terms of customer satisfaction. Are these results consistent with your analysis in **3**? Explain your answers.

B 3. *Analysis of*
L O 5, 6 *Nonfinancial Data*

Check Figure: 1d. Materials cost/ scrap control for Week 1: 243 parts scrapped

Henson Electronics Company was formed in 1952. Over the years the company has become known for its high-quality electronics products and its dependability for on-time delivery. Six months ago management decided to install a flexible manufacturing system for its Electronic Components Department. With the new equipment, the entire component is produced by the FMS so the finished product is ready to be shipped when needed. Shown on the next page are data the controller's staff gathered during the past eight-week period.

	Weeks							
	1	2	3	4	5	6	7	8
Average process time (hours)	11.9	12.1	11.6	11.8	12.2	12.8	13.2	14.6
Average setup time (hours)	1.5	1.6	1.6	1.8	1.7	1.4	1.2	1.2
Customer complaints	10	9	22	14	8	6	4	5
Delivery time (hours)	26.2	26.4	26.1	25.9	26.2	26.6	27.1	26.4
Equipment utilization rate (%)	97.2	97.1	97.3	98.2	98.4	97.2	97.4	96.3
Machine downtime (hours)	106.4	108.1	120.2	110.4	112.8	102.2	124.6	136.2
Machine maintenance time (hours)	66.8	68.7	74.6	76.2	78.8	68.6	82.4	90.2
Number of inventoried items	3,450	3,510	3,680	3,790	3,620	3,490	3,560	3,260
On-time deliveries (%)	97.2	97.5	97.6	98.2	98.4	96.4	94.8	92.6
Parts scrapped	243	268	279	245	256	280	290	314
Production backlog (units)	10,246	10,288	10,450	10,680	10,880	11,280	11,350	12,100
Production cycle time (hours)	16.5	16.4	16.3	16.1	16.3	17.6	19.8	21.8
Purchase order lead time (hours)	15.2	15.1	14.9	14.6	14.6	13.2	12.4	12.6
Times inventory turnover	2.1	2.3	2.2	2.4	2.2	2.1	2.1	1.9
Warranty claims	4	8	2	1	6	4	2	3

REQUIRED

1. Analyze the performance of the Electronic Components Department for the eight-week period, centering your analysis on performance in the following areas.
   a. Product quality
   b. Product delivery
   c. Inventory control
   d. Materials cost/scrap control
   e. Machine management and maintenance
2. Summarize your findings in a report to the department's superintendent.

B 4. *Full Cost Profit*
L O 7 *Margin*

Check Figure: 4. Operating profit for Assembly C2: $1,283,980

Kizer Molded Products Company produces three main products, identified as C2, K5, and R4. Two months ago, the company installed three fully automated flexible manufacturing systems for the product lines. The controller is anxious to see how the FMS machinery affects operating costs for the three products. Product K5 has been a low performer for the company and is being outpriced on the market. The line may have to be dropped.

Monthly operating data for before and after the FMS installation are as follows:

Kizer Molded Products Company
Product Performance Evaluation

	Assembly C2	Assembly K5	Assembly R4
Total revenue	$4,590,000	$5,180,000	$3,520,000
Total operating costs			
Before FMS installed			
Direct materials	$1,101,600	$1,346,800	$ 774,400
Direct labor	1,514,700	1,761,200	985,600
Variable factory overhead	413,100	259,000	158,400
Variable selling expenses	137,700	155,400	123,200
Variable distribution costs	183,600	310,800	193,600
Fixed factory overhead	456,200	654,200	432,600
Fixed selling expenses	132,300	103,290	196,700
Fixed distribution costs	189,700	304,520	291,800

(continued)

	Assembly C2	Assembly K5	Assembly R4
After FMS installed:			
Direct materials	$1,101,600	$1,346,800	$774,400
Materials-related overhead	160,650	150,220	112,640
Direct labor	206,550	227,920	147,840
Indirect labor	330,480	331,520	260,480
Setup labor	220,320	217,560	154,880
Electrical power	82,620	93,240	56,320
Supervision	119,340	145,040	91,520
Repairs and maintenance	156,060	160,580	130,240
Operating supplies/lubricants	36,720	46,620	28,160
Other traceable indirect costs	100,980	108,780	84,480
Traceable selling expenses	174,420	170,940	133,760
Traceable distribution costs	192,780	202,020	154,880
Nontraceable factory overhead	245,300	323,100	241,100
Nontraceable selling and distribution costs	178,200	231,400	198,760

REQUIRED

1. Recast the information given for the three products into an analysis that reveals total traceable and total nontraceable costs (a) before and (b) after the FMS was installed.
2. Describe and differentiate between full cost profit margin and contribution margin.
3. Using the before-FMS data, prepare an analysis that reveals contribution margin, operating profit, contribution margin as a percentage of revenue, and operating profit as a percentage of revenue.
4. Using the after-FMS data, prepare an analysis that reveals full cost profit margin, operating profit, full cost profit margin as a percentage of revenue, and operating profit as a percentage of revenue.
5. Should the company drop the K5 product line? Defend your answer.

B 5.
L O 2, 3
Comprehensive View of Cost Allocation Featuring Activity-Based Costing

Check Figure: 3. Unit cost for Job Order 20 using six activity rates: $1,617

Alfonso Industries manufactures turbo-jet engine casings. The company has experienced significant competition from a German company and must realign its pricing structure. For the past thirty years, the company has been using a single, divisionwide factory overhead rate when applying overhead costs to its products. The chief executive officer has requested that the controller's office create three new approaches to overhead allocation for management to consider. Data for the past quarter are summarized in the schedule on the next page. In addition to the current overhead cost allocation approach, which uses a divisionwide rate based on direct labor hours (column 1 data), the following approaches are being discussed:

Using two departmental overhead rates (columns 2 and 3 data)

Using three rates, two departmental rates excluding materials handling cost plus a separate rate for materials handling activity costs (columns 4, 5, and 6 data)

Using six overhead allocation rates, one for each of the six activities of the production operation (columns 6 through 11 data)

Note that a cost driver has been identified for each of the eleven columns in the data schedule.

REQUIRED

1. Compute the overhead allocation rates for each column in the schedule using the designated cost drivers as a basis for the rates.
2. Compute the overhead charges per unit for each job order completed. (Round all answers to whole dollars.)
   a. Using a single, divisionwide overhead rate.
   b. Using two departmental overhead rates.
   c. Using three overhead rates, two departmental rates that exclude materials handling costs plus a separate rate for materials handling activity usage.
   d. Using an activity-based costing approach with six different activity-related rates.

	(1)	(2)	(3)	(4)	(5)	(6)	(7)	(8)	(9)	(10)	(11)
	Division Totals	Forming Department	Assembly Department	Forming Department Less Materials Handling Costs	Assembly Department Less Materials Handling Costs	Materials Handling Activity	Computer Center Activity	Engineering Activity	Tool and Die Activity	Machine Setup Activity	Repairs and Maintenance Activity
Overhead Cost Data											
Machine depreciation	$ 16,870	$ 6,748	$10,122	$ 6,300	$ 9,450	$ 1,120	$ 3,210	$ 4,720	$ 2,990	$ 1,620	$ 3,210
Electrical costs	6,340	1,902	4,438	1,680	3,920	740	1,230	980	960	450	1,980
Indirect labor	37,460	13,111	24,349	12,345	22,926	2,190	9,800	4,710	6,620	4,940	9,200
Supervisor salaries	21,320	12,792	8,528	12,408	8,272	640	2,910	1,370	8,980	870	6,550
Employee benefits	14,984	5,244	9,740	4,938	9,170	876	3,920	1,884	2,648	1,976	3,680
Rental costs	5,061	1,518	3,543	1,418	3,308	336	963	1,416	897	486	963
Janitorial services	17,866	3,573	14,293	3,128	12,512	2,226	3,620	1,640	4,410	990	4,980
Indirect materials	29,968	19,479	10,489	18,340	9,876	1,752	7,840	3,768	5,296	3,952	7,360
Other utilities	2,536	761	1,775	672	1,568	296	492	392	384	180	792
Building occupancy costs	13,195	2,639	10,556	2,534	10,137	524	4,015	220	4,415	636	3,385
	$165,600	$67,767	$97,833	$63,763	$91,139	$10,700	$38,000	$21,100	$37,600	$16,100	$42,100

Cost Driver Used	Direct Labor Hours	Direct Labor Hours	Direct Labor Hours	Machine Hours	Direct Labor Hours	Weight of Materials (lbs)	Computer Hours of Use	Engineering Hours	Number of Requests	Number of Setups	Repairs and Maintenance Hours
Cost Driver Data											
Job Order 20											
300 units @ 3 DLHs/unit	900	270	630		630						
300 units @ 14 MHs/unit*				3,360		4,530	270	180	29	68	230
Job Order 21											
400 units @ 4 DLHs/unit	1,600	640	960		960						
400 units @ 8 MHs/unit*				2,560		13,700	330	340	59	86	630
Job Order 22											
200 units @ 8 DLHs/unit	1,600	800	800		800						
200 units @ 2 MHs/unit*				320		8,520	150	110	12	66	140
Totals	4,100	1,710	2,390	6,240	2,390	26,750	750	630	100	220	1,000

*Some of these machine hours are incurred in the Assembly Department; these are not shown because they are not used as a cost driver.

3. Complete the unit cost analysis schedule below.

	Using Divisionwide Overhead Rate	Using Departmental Overhead Rates	Using Three Different Overhead Rates	Using Six Activity Rates
Job Order 20				
Direct materials cost	$1,240	$1,240	$1,240	$1,240
Direct labor cost	220	220	220	220
Factory overhead cost				
Totals				
Job Order 21				
Direct materials cost	$2,130	$2,130	$2,130	$2,130
Direct labor cost	120	120	120	120
Factory overhead cost				
Totals				
Job Order 22				
Direct materials cost	$1,910	$1,910	$1,910	$1,910
Direct labor cost	640	640	640	640
Factory overhead cost				
Totals				

4. Which of the four overhead cost allocation approaches yields the most accurate product cost data? List the reasons supporting your selection.

MANAGERIAL REPORTING AND ANALYSIS CASES

Interpreting Management Reports

MRA 1. *Cost of Quality*

L O 4

Check Figure: Costs of conformance, Illinois Division: $75,020

Jason Thompson has been appointed chief accountant for *South Bend Industries.* The business has three divisions that manufacture oil well depth gauges. The business is very competitive, and South Bend Industries has lost market share in each of the last four years. Three years ago, management announced a companywide restructuring and the adoption of total quality management. Since that time, each of the divisions has been allowed to chart its own path toward TQM. Mr. Thompson is new to the company and has asked to see summary figures of the costs of quality for each of the divisions. The following data were presented to him for the past six months:

South Bend Industries
Cost of Quality Report
For the six months ended June 30, 19x8

	Illinois Division	Indiana Division	Ohio Division	Company Totals
Sales	$1,849,400	$1,773,450	$1,757,400	$5,380,250
Prevention costs	$ 32,680	$ 48,120	$ 15,880	$ 96,680
Appraisal costs	42,340	32,210	17,980	92,530
Internal failure costs	24,100	21,450	41,780	87,330
External failure costs	32,980	16,450	45,560	94,990
Total costs of quality	$ 132,100	$ 118,230	$ 121,200	$ 371,530

Evaluate the three divisions' quality control programs by first computing the costs of conformance and the costs of nonconformance of each division. Also compute quality costs as a percentage of sales for each division. Identify the division that is developing the strongest quality program. What division has been the slowest to react to the management directive of TQM? Be prepared to explain your answers.

Formulating Management Reports

MRA 2.
L O 4, 5, 6
Reporting Quality Data

No check figure

Zachary Platt is chief executive officer of **Micro Machinery, Inc.** The company adopted a JIT operating environment about five years ago. Since then, each segment of the company has been converted, and a complete computer-integrated manufacturing system operates in all parts of the company's five plants. Processing of Micro's products now averages less than four days once the materials have been placed into production.

Platt is worried about customer satisfaction and has asked you, as the controller, for some advice and help. He also asked the marketing department to perform a quick survey of customers to determine weak areas in customer relations. Here is a summary of four customers' replies.

Customer A
Customer for five years; waits an average of six weeks for delivery; located 1,200 miles from plant; returns an average of 3 percent of products; receives 90 percent on-time deliveries; never hears from salesperson after placing order; likes quality or would go with competitor.

Customer B
Customer for seven years; waits an average of five weeks for delivery; orders usually sit in backlog for at least three weeks; located 50 miles from plant; returns about 5 percent of products; receives 95 percent on-time deliveries; has great rapport with salesperson; salesperson is reason why this customer is loyal.

Customer C
Customer for twelve years; waits an average of seven weeks for delivery; located 1,500 miles from plant; returns about 4 percent of products; receives 92 percent on-time deliveries; salesperson is available but of little help in getting faster delivery; customer is thinking about dealing with another source for its product needs.

Customer D
Customer for fifteen years; very pleased with company's product; still waits almost five weeks for delivery; located 120 miles from plant; returns only 2 percent of goods received; rapport with salesperson very good; follow-up service of salesperson excellent; would like delivery cycle time reduced to equal that of competitors; usually deals with three-week backlog.

REQUIRED

1. Identify the areas of concern and give at least three examples of reports that will provide information to help managers improve the company's response to customer needs.
2. Assume you are asked to prepare a report that will provide information about product quality. To help you prepare this report, answer the following questions.
   a. What kinds of information do you need to prepare this report?
   b. Why is this information relevant?
   c. Where would you find this information (sources)?
   d. When would you want to obtain this information?

International Company

MRA 3.
L O 2
Activity-Based Costing in a Service Business

Ross and Timmons is an accounting firm that has provided audit, tax, and management advisory services to businesses in the London area for over fifty years. Recently, the firm decided to use activity-based costing to allocate its overhead costs to these service functions. John Ross, who is one of the partners, is interested in seeing the difference in the average cost per audit job using the traditional and the activity-based costing approaches to allocating overhead costs. The following information has been provided to assist in the comparison.

Total direct labor costs	£400,000
Other direct costs	120,000
Total direct costs	£520,000

Other overhead costs are as follows:

Traditional overhead costing data:
Overhead costs were assigned using a rate of 120 percent of direct labor cost.

Activity-based costing data:

Activities	Cost Drivers	Cost Assignment Rates	Activity Usage for Audit Function
Professional development	Number of employees	£2,000 per employee	50 employees
Administration	Number of jobs	£1,000 per job	50 jobs
Client development	Number of new clients	£5,000 per new client	29 new clients

REQUIRED

1. Calculate the total costs for the audit function using direct labor cost as the cost driver. What is the average cost per job?
2. Calculate the total costs for the audit function using activity-based costing to allocate overhead. What is the average cost per job?
3. Calculate the difference in average cost per audit job between the two approaches. Why would activity-based costing be a better approach to allocate overhead to the audit function?

PART NINE

Special Reports

and Analyses of

Accounting

Information

presents the statement of cash flows, which explains the major operating, financing, and investing activities of a business. The chapter uses the indirect approach to the statement of cash flows, with the direct approach presented as a supplemental objective. Emphasis is placed on the use and analysis of cash flow information.

explains the objectives and techniques of financial statement analysis from the standpoint of the financial analyst. A comprehensive financial analysis of Apple Computer is illustrated. The ratios are summarized in easy-to-read tables.

LEARNING OBJECTIVES

1. Describe the statement of cash flows, and define *cash* and *cash equivalents*.
2. State the principal purposes and uses of the statement of cash flows.
3. Identify the principal components of the classifications of cash flows, and state the significance of noncash investing and financing transactions.
4. Use the indirect method to determine cash flows from operating activities.
5. Determine cash flows from (a) investing activities and (b) financing activities.
6. Use the indirect method to prepare a statement of cash flows.
7. Analyze the statement of cash flows.

SUPPLEMENTAL OBJECTIVES

8. Prepare a work sheet for the statement of cash flows.
9. Use the direct method to determine cash flows from operating activities and prepare a statement of cash flows.

DECISION POINT

Marriott International, Inc.

Marriott International is a world leader in lodging and contract services. The balance sheet, income statement, and statement of stockholders' equity presented in the company's annual report give an excellent picture of management's philosophy and performance.

Those three financial statements are essential to the evaluation of a company, but they do not tell the entire story. Some information they do not cover is presented in a fourth statement, the statement of cash flows. It tells how much cash was generated by the company's operations during the year and how much was used in or came from investing and financing activities. Marriott feels that maintaining adequate cash flow is important to the future of the company, as shown by the following statement in its annual report.

> Marriott places strong emphasis on maximizing cash flow, and its incentive compensation programs were revised in 1991 to reward managers based on cash flow rather than accounting earnings. In 1992, all nine of the company's major business units generated operating cash flow in excess of their capital expenditures, including outlays for expansion.[1]

Why would Marriott emphasize cash flow to such an extent?

A strong cash flow is essential to management's key goal of liquidity. If cash flow exceeds what is needed for operations and expansion, the company will not have to borrow additional funds. The excess cash flow will be available to reduce the company's debt and improve its financial position by lowering its debt to equity ratio.

The statement of cash flows demonstrates management's commitments for the company in ways that are not readily apparent in the other financial statements. For example, the statement of cash flows can show whether management's focus is on the short term or the long term. This statement is required by the FASB[2] and satisfies the FASB's long-held position that a primary objective of financial statements is to provide investors and creditors with information about a company's cash flows.[3] : : : : :

---

1. Marriott Corporation, *Annual Report*, 1992.

2. *Statement of Financial Accounting Standards No. 95*, "Statement of Cash Flows" (Stamford, Conn.: Financial Accounting Standards Board, 1987).

3. *Statement of Financial Accounting Concepts No. 1*, "Objectives of Financial Reporting for Business Enterprises" (Stamford, Conn.: Financial Accounting Standards Board, 1978), par. 37–39.

OVERVIEW OF THE STATEMENT OF CASH FLOWS

OBJECTIVE

1 *Describe the statement of cash flows, and define* **cash** *and* **cash equivalents**

The statement of cash flows shows how a company's operating, investing, and financing activities have affected cash during an accounting period. It explains the net increase (or decrease) in cash during the accounting period. For purposes of preparing this statement, cash is defined to include both cash and cash equivalents. Cash equivalents are defined by the FASB as short-term, highly liquid investments, including money market accounts, commercial paper, and U.S. Treasury bills. A company maintains cash equivalents to earn interest on cash that would otherwise temporarily lie idle. Suppose, for example, that a company has $1,000,000 that it will not need for thirty days. To earn a return on this sum, the company may place the cash in an account that earns interest (such as a money market account); it may loan the cash to another corporation by purchasing that corporation's short-term note (commercial paper); or it might purchase a short-term obligation of the U.S. government (a Treasury bill). In this context, short-term refers to original maturities of ninety days or less. Since cash and cash equivalents are considered the same, transfers between the Cash account and cash equivalents are not treated as cash receipts or cash payments. In effect, cash equivalents are combined with the Cash account on the statement of cash flows.

Cash equivalents should not be confused with short-term investments or marketable securities, which are not combined with the Cash account on the statement of cash flows. Purchases of marketable securities are treated as cash outflows and sales of marketable securities as cash inflows on the statement of cash flows. In this chapter, cash will be assumed to include cash and cash equivalents.

PURPOSES OF THE STATEMENT OF CASH FLOWS

OBJECTIVE

2 *State the principal purposes and uses of the statement of cash flows*

The primary purpose of the statement of cash flows is to provide information about a company's cash receipts and cash payments during an accounting period. A secondary purpose of the statement is to provide information about a company's operating, investing, and financing activities during the accounting period. Some information about those activities may be inferred by examining other financial statements, but it is on the statement of cash flows that all the transactions affecting cash are summarized.

INTERNAL AND EXTERNAL USES OF THE STATEMENT OF CASH FLOWS

The statement of cash flows is useful internally to management and externally to investors and creditors. Management uses the statement to assess liquidity, to determine dividend policy, and to evaluate the effects of major policy decisions involving investments and financing. In other words, management may use the statement to determine if short-term financing is needed to pay current liabilities, to decide whether to raise or lower dividends, and to plan for investing and financing needs.

Investors and creditors will find the statement useful in assessing the company's ability to manage cash flows, to generate positive future cash flows, to pay its liabilities, to pay dividends and interest, and to anticipate its need for additional financing. Also, they may use the statement to explain the differences between net income on the income statement and the net cash flows generated from operations. In addition, the statement shows both the cash and the noncash effects of investing and financing activities during the accounting period.

OBJECTIVE

3 *Identify the principal components of the classifications of cash flows, and state the significance of noncash investing and financing transactions*

CLASSIFICATION OF CASH FLOWS

The statement of cash flows classifies cash receipts and cash payments into the categories of operating, investing, and financing activities. The components of these activities are illustrated in Figure 1 and summarized below.

1. Operating activities include the cash effects of transactions and other events that enter into the determination of net income. Included in this category as cash inflows are cash receipts from customers for goods and services, interest and dividends received on loans and investments, and sales of trading securities. Included as cash outflows are cash payments for wages, goods and services, expenses, interest, taxes, and purchases of trading securities. In effect, the income statement is changed from an accrual to a cash basis.
2. Investing activities include the acquiring and selling of long-term assets, the acquiring and selling of marketable securities other than trading securities or cash equivalents, and the making and collecting of loans. Cash inflows include the cash received from selling long-term assets and marketable securities and from collecting loans. Cash outflows include the cash expended for purchases of long-term assets and marketable securities and the cash loaned to borrowers.
3. Financing activities include obtaining resources from or returning resources to owners and providing them with a return on their investment, and obtaining resources from creditors and repaying the amounts borrowed or otherwise settling the obligations. Cash inflows include the proceeds from issues of stocks and from short-term and long-term borrowing. Cash outflows include the repayments of loans and payments to owners, including cash dividends. Treasury stock transactions are also considered financing activities. Repayments of accounts payable or accrued liabilities are not considered repayments of loans under financing activities, but are classified as cash outflows under operating activities.

A company will occasionally engage in significant noncash investing and financing transactions involving only long-term assets, long-term liabilities, or stockholders' equity, such as the exchange of a long-term asset for a long-term liability or the settlement of a debt by issuing capital stock. For instance, a company might take out a long-term mortgage for the purchase of land and a building. Or it might convert long-term bonds into common stock. Such transactions represent significant investing and financing activities, but they would not be reflected on the statement of cash flows because they do not involve either cash inflows or cash outflows. However, since one purpose of the statement of cash flows is to show investing and financing activities, and since such transactions will affect future cash flows, the FASB has determined that they should be disclosed in a separate schedule as part of the statement of cash flows. In this way, the reader of the statement will see the company's investing and financing activities clearly.

FORMAT OF THE STATEMENT OF CASH FLOWS

The statement of cash flows, shown in Exhibit 1, is divided into three sections corresponding to the three categories of activities just discussed. The cash flows from operating activities are followed by cash flows from investing

Figure 1. Classification of Cash Inflows and Cash Outflows

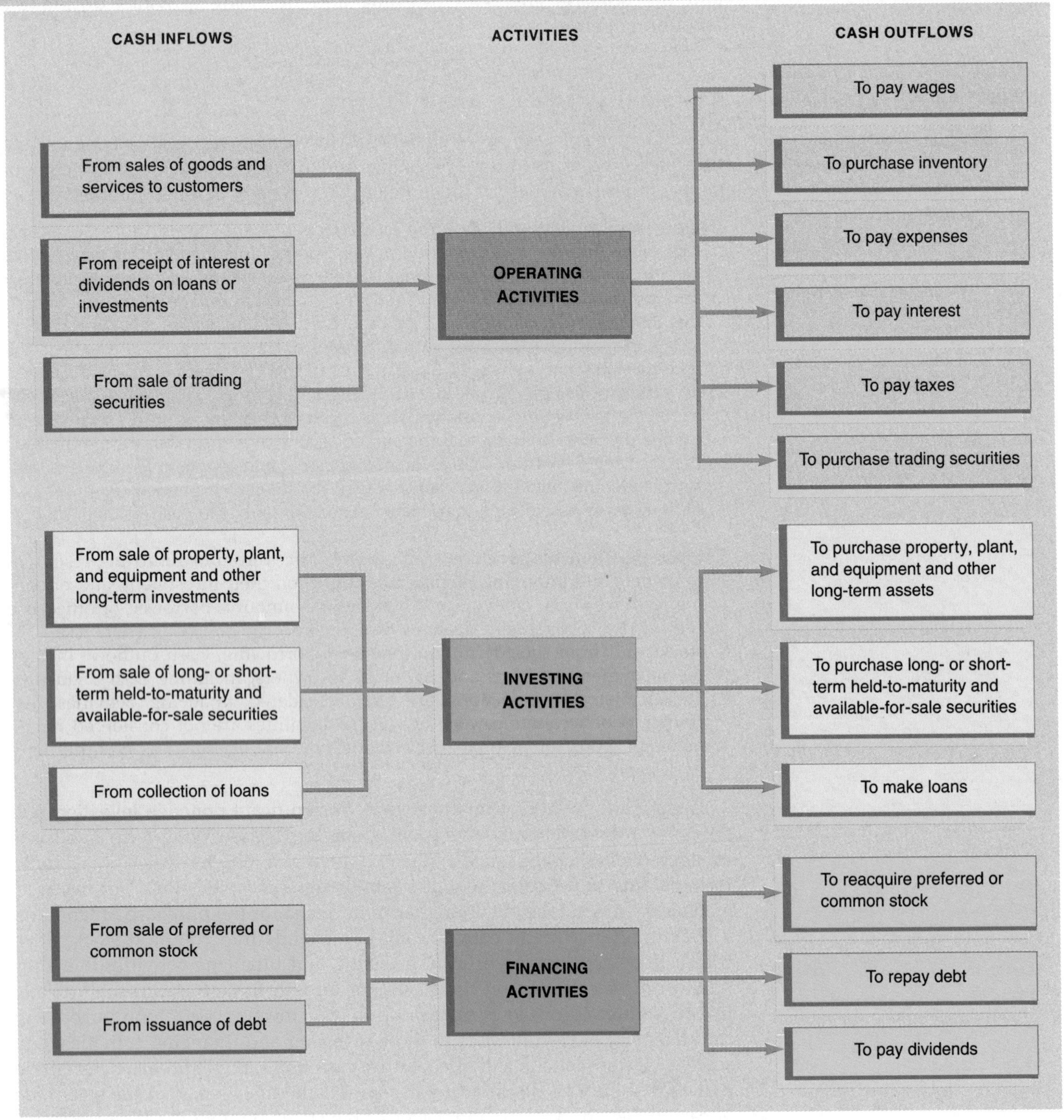

CASH INFLOWS	ACTIVITIES	CASH OUTFLOWS

CASH INFLOWS

From sales of goods and services to customers

From receipt of interest or dividends on loans or investments

From sale of trading securities

ACTIVITIES

OPERATING ACTIVITIES

CASH OUTFLOWS

To pay wages

To purchase inventory

To pay expenses

To pay interest

To pay taxes

To purchase trading securities

From sale of property, plant, and equipment and other long-term investments

From sale of long- or short-term held-to-maturity and available-for-sale securities

From collection of loans

INVESTING ACTIVITIES

To purchase property, plant, and equipment and other long-term assets

To purchase long- or short-term held-to-maturity and available-for-sale securities

To make loans

From sale of preferred or common stock

From issuance of debt

FINANCING ACTIVITIES

To reacquire preferred or common stock

To repay debt

To pay dividends

---

activities and cash flows from financing activities. The individual inflows and outflows from investing and financing activities are usually shown separately in their respective categories. For instance, cash inflows from the sale of property, plant, and equipment are shown separately from cash outflows for the purchase of property, plant, and equipment. Similarly, cash inflows from borrowing are shown separately from cash outflows to retire loans. A reconciliation of the beginning and ending balances of cash is shown at the end of the

Exhibit 1. Format for the Statement of Cash Flows

Company Name
Statement of Cash Flows
Period Covered

Cash Flows from Operating Activities		
(List of individual inflows and outflows)	xxx	
Net Cash Flows from Operating Activities		xxx
Cash Flows from Investing Activities		
(List of individual inflows and outflows)	xxx	
Net Cash Flows from Investing Activities		xxx
Cash Flows from Financing Activities		
(List of individual inflows and outflows)	xxx	
Net Cash Flows from Financing Activities		xxx
Net Increase (Decrease) in Cash		xx
Cash at Beginning of Year		xx
Cash at End of Year		xx
Schedule of Noncash Investing and Financing Transactions		
(List of individual transactions)		xxx

statement. A list of noncash transactions appears in the schedule at the bottom of the statement.

THE INDIRECT METHOD OF PREPARING THE STATEMENT OF CASH FLOWS

OBJECTIVE

4 *Use the indirect method to determine cash flows from operating activities*

To demonstrate the preparation of the statement of cash flows, we will work through an example step by step. The data for this example are presented in Exhibits 2 and 3. Those two exhibits present Ryan Corporation's balance sheets for December 31, 19x1 and 19x2, and its 19x2 income statement, with additional data about transactions affecting noncurrent accounts during 19x2. Since the changes in the balance sheet accounts will be used for analysis, those changes are shown in Exhibit 2. Whether the change in each account is an increase or a decrease is also shown. In addition, Exhibit 3 contains data about transactions that affected noncurrent accounts. Those transactions would be identified by the company's accountants from the records.

There are four steps in preparing the statement of cash flows:

1. Determine cash flows from operating activities.
2. Determine cash flows from investing activities.
3. Determine cash flows from financing activities.
4. Use the information obtained in the first three steps to compile the statement of cash flows.

Exhibit 2. Comparative Balance Sheets with Changes in Accounts Indicated for Ryan Corporation

Ryan Corporation
Comparative Balance Sheets
December 31, 19x2 and 19x1

	19x2	19x1	Change	Increase or Decrease
Assets				
Current Assets				
Cash	$ 46,000	$ 15,000	$ 31,000	Increase
Accounts Receivable (net)	47,000	55,000	(8,000)	Decrease
Inventory	144,000	110,000	34,000	Increase
Prepaid Expenses	1,000	5,000	(4,000)	Decrease
Total Current Assets	$238,000	$185,000	$ 53,000	
Investments	$115,000	$127,000	($ 12,000)	Decrease
Plant Assets				
Plant Assets	$715,000	$505,000	$210,000	Increase
Accumulated Depreciation	(103,000)	(68,000)	(35,000)	Increase
Total Plant Assets	$612,000	$437,000	$175,000	
Total Assets	$965,000	$749,000	$216,000	
Liabilities				
Current Liabilities				
Accounts Payable	$ 50,000	$ 43,000	$ 7,000	Increase
Accrued Liabilities	12,000	9,000	3,000	Increase
Income Taxes Payable	3,000	5,000	(2,000)	Decrease
Total Current Liabilities	$ 65,000	$ 57,000	$ 8,000	
Long-Term Liabilities				
Bonds Payable	$295,000	$245,000	$ 50,000	Increase
Total Liabilities	$360,000	$302,000	$ 58,000	
Stockholders' Equity				
Common Stock, $5 par value	$276,000	$200,000	$ 76,000	Increase
Paid-in Capital in Excess of Par Value, Common	189,000	115,000	74,000	Increase
Retained Earnings	140,000	132,000	8,000	Increase
Total Stockholders' Equity	$605,000	$447,000	$158,000	
Total Liabilities and Stockholders' Equity	$965,000	$749,000	$216,000	

DETERMINING CASH FLOWS FROM OPERATING ACTIVITIES

The first step in preparing the statement of cash flows is to determine cash flows from operating activities. The income statement indicates a business's

Exhibit 3. Income Statement and Other Information on Noncurrent Accounts for Ryan Corporation

Ryan Corporation
Income Statement
For the Year Ended December 31, 19x2

Net Sales		$698,000
Cost of Goods Sold		520,000
Gross Margin		$178,000
Operating Expenses (including Depreciation Expense of $37,000)		147,000
Operating Income		$ 31,000
Other Income (Expenses)		
Interest Expense	($23,000)	
Interest Income	6,000	
Gain on Sale of Investments	12,000	
Loss on Sale of Plant Assets	(3,000)	(8,000)
Income Before Income Taxes		$ 23,000
Income Taxes		7,000
Net Income		$ 16,000

Other transactions affecting noncurrent accounts during 19x2:

1. Purchased investments in the amount of $78,000.
2. Sold investments classified as long-term and available for sale for $102,000. These investments cost $90,000.
3. Purchased plant assets in the amount of $120,000.
4. Sold plant assets that cost $10,000 with accumulated depreciation of $2,000 for $5,000.
5. Issued $100,000 of bonds at face value in a noncash exchange for plant assets.
6. Repaid $50,000 of bonds at face value at maturity.
7. Issued 15,200 shares of $5 par value common stock for $150,000.
8. Paid cash dividends in the amount of $8,000.

success or failure in earning an income from its operating activities, but it does not reflect the inflow and outflow of cash from those activities. The reason is that the income statement is prepared on an accrual basis. Revenues are recorded even though the cash for them may not have been received, and expenses are recorded even though the cash for them may not have been expended. As a result, to arrive at cash flows from operations, the figures on the income statement must be converted from an accrual basis to a cash basis.

There are two methods of converting the income statement from an accrual basis to a cash basis: the direct method and the indirect method. Under the direct method, each item in the income statement is adjusted from the accrual basis to the cash basis. The result is a statement that begins with cash receipts from sales and deducts cash payments for purchases, operating expenses, interest payments, and income taxes to arrive at net cash flows from operating activities. The indirect method, on the other hand, does not require the individual adjustment of each item in the income statement, but lists only those adjustments necessary to convert net income to cash flows from operations. Because the indirect method is more common, it will be used to illustrate the conversion of the income statement to a cash basis in the sections that follow. The direct method is presented in a supplemental objective at the end of the chapter.

The indirect method, as illustrated in Figure 2, focuses on items from the income statement that must be adjusted to reconcile net income to net cash flows from operating activities. The items that require adjustment are those that did not affect net cash flows. They fall into two categories. In the first category are items that appear on the income statement but did not result in a cash outlay or cash receipt. Examples include depreciation expense and gains and losses. In the second category are current asset and current liability accounts with balances that have changed during the accounting period. The reconciliation of Ryan Corporation's net income to net cash flows from operating activities is shown in Exhibit 4. Each adjustment is discussed in the following sections.

Depreciation

Cash payments for plant assets, intangibles, and natural resources occur when the assets are purchased and are reflected as investing activities on the statement of cash flows at that time. When depreciation expense, amortization expense, and depletion expense appear on the income statement, they simply indicate allocations of the costs of the original purchases to the current accounting period; they do not affect net cash flows in the current period.

The amount of such expenses can usually be found by referring to the income statement or a note to the financial statements. For Ryan Corporation, the income statement reveals depreciation expense of $37,000, which would have been recorded as follows:

Depreciation Expense, Plant Assets	37,000	
Accumulated Depreciation, Plant Assets		37,000
To record annual depreciation on plant assets		

The recording of depreciation involved no outlay of cash. Thus, as cash flow was not affected, an adjustment for depreciation is needed to increase net income by the amount of cash recorded.

Figure 2. Indirect Method of Determining Net Cash Flows from Operating Activities

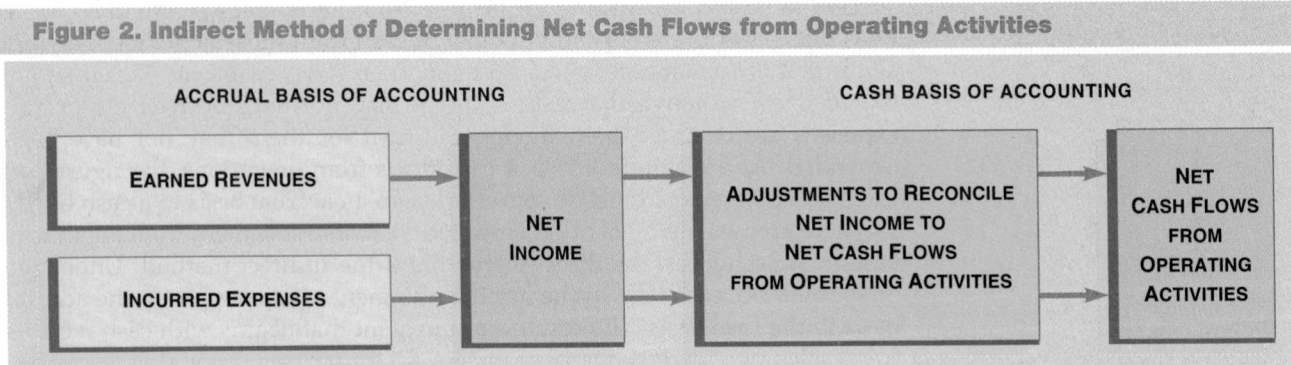

Ryan Corporation
Schedule of Cash Flows from Operating Activities
For the Year Ended December 31, 19x2

Cash Flows from Operating Activities		
Net Income		$16,000
Adjustments to Reconcile Net Income to Net		
Cash Flows from Operating Activities		
Depreciation	$37,000	
Gain on Sale of Investments	(12,000)	
Loss on Sale of Plant Assets	3,000	
Changes in Current Assets and Current Liabilities		
Decrease in Accounts Receivable	8,000	
Increase in Inventory	(34,000)	
Decrease in Prepaid Expenses	4,000	
Increase in Accounts Payable	7,000	
Increase in Accrued Liabilities	3,000	
Decrease in Income Taxes Payable	(2,000)	14,000
Net Cash Flows from Operating Activities		$30,000

Survey of Large Companies

DECISION POINT

The direct method and the indirect method of determining cash flows from operating activities produce the same results. Although it will accept either method, the FASB recommends that the direct method be used. If the direct method of reporting net cash flows from operating activities is used, reconciliation of net income to net cash flows from operating activities is to be provided in a separate schedule (the indirect method). Despite the FASB's recommendations, a survey of large companies in 1992 showed that an overwhelming majority, 97 percent, chose to use the indirect method. Of six hundred companies, only fifteen chose the direct approach.[4] Why did so many choose the indirect approach?

The reasons for choosing the indirect method may vary, but chief financial officers tend to prefer it because it is easier and less expensive to prepare. Moreover, because the FASB requires the reconciliation of net income (accrual) to cash flow (operations) as a supplemental schedule, the indirect method has to be implemented anyway.

4. American Institute of Certified Public Accountants, *Accounting Trends & Techniques* (New York: AICPA, 1993), p. 452.

A knowledge of the direct method helps managers and the readers of financial statements perceive the underlying causes for the differences between reported net income and cash flows from operations. The indirect method is a practical way of presenting the differences. Both methods have merit. ● ● ● ● ●

Gains and Losses   Gains and losses that appear on the income statement also do not affect cash flows and need to be removed in this section of the statement of cash flows. The cash receipts generated from the disposal of the assets that resulted in the gains or losses are shown in the investing section of the statement of cash flows. For example, on the income statement, Ryan Corporation showed a $12,000 gain on the sale of investments that should be subtracted from net income to arrive at net cash flows from operating activities. Also, Ryan Corporation showed a $3,000 loss on the sale of plant assets that should be added to net income to arrive at net cash flows from operating activities. As will be seen below, the cash received from the sale of the investments and the plant assets is included in the statement of cash flows as coming from investing activities.

Changes in Current Assets   Decreases in current assets have positive effects on cash flows and increases in current assets have negative effects on cash flows. For example, refer to the balance sheet and income statement for Ryan Corporation in Exhibits 2 and 3. Note that net sales were $698,000 in 19x2 and that Accounts Receivable decreased by $8,000. Thus, cash received from sales was $706,000, calculated as follows:

$$\$706,000 = \$698,000 + \$8,000$$

Collections were $8,000 more than sales recorded for the year. This relationship may be illustrated as follows:

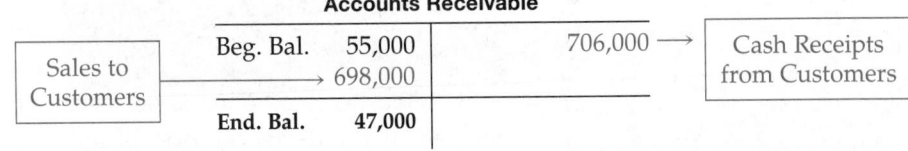

Thus, to reconcile net income to net cash flows from operating activities, the $8,000 decrease in Accounts Receivable is added to net income.

Inventory may be analyzed in the same way. For example, Exhibit 2 shows that Inventory increased by $34,000 from 19x1 to 19x2. This means that Ryan Corporation expended $34,000 more in cash for inventory than was included in cost of goods sold on the income statement. As a result of this expenditure, net income overstates the net cash flows from operating activities, so $34,000 must be deducted from net income.

Using the same logic, the decrease of $4,000 in Prepaid Expenses is added to net income to arrive at net cash flows from operations.

Changes in Current Liabilities   Changes in current liabilities have the opposite effect on cash flows that changes in current assets do. Increases in current liabilities are added to net income and decreases in current liabilities are deducted from net income to arrive at net cash flows from operating activities. For example, note from Exhibit 2 that Ryan Corporation had a $7,000 increase in Accounts Payable from 19x1 to 19x2. This means that Ryan

Corporation paid $7,000 less to creditors than would appear as purchases on the income statement. This relationship may be visualized as follows:

Cash Payments to Suppliers	← 547,000	**Accounts Payable**		
		Beg. Bal.	43,000	
			554,000	← Purchases
		End. Bal.	50,000	

As a result, $7,000 is added to net income to arrive at net cash flows from operating activities.

Using this same logic, the increase of $3,000 in Accrued Liabilities is added to net income and the decrease of $2,000 in Income Taxes Payable is deducted from net income to arrive at net cash flows from operating activities.

Schedule of Cash Flows from Operating Activities   In summary, Exhibit 4 shows that, using the indirect method, net income of $16,000 has been adjusted by reconciling items totaling $14,000 to arrive at net cash flows from operating activities of $30,000. This means that although net income was $16,000, Ryan Corporation actually has net cash flows available from operating activities of $30,000 to use for purchasing assets, reducing debts, or paying dividends.

Summary of Adjustments   The effects of items on the income statement that do not affect cash flows may be summarized as follows:

	Add to or Deduct from Net Income
Depreciation Expense	Add
Amortization Expense	Add
Depletion Expense	Add
Losses	Add
Gains	Deduct

The adjustments for increases and decreases in current assets and current liabilities may be summarized as follows:

	Add to Net Income	Deduct from Net Income
Current Assets		
Accounts Receivable (net)	Decrease	Increase
Inventory	Decrease	Increase
Prepaid Expenses	Decrease	Increase
Current Liabilities		
Accounts Payable	Increase	Decrease
Accrued Liabilities	Increase	Decrease
Income Taxes Payable	Increase	Decrease

DETERMINING CASH FLOWS FROM INVESTING ACTIVITIES

OBJECTIVE

5a *Determine cash flows from investing activities*

The second step in preparing the statement of cash flows is to determine cash flows from investing activities. Each account involving cash receipts and cash payments from investing activities is examined individually. The objective is to explain the change in each account balance from one year to the next.

Investing activities center on the long-term assets shown on the balance sheet, but they also include transactions affecting short-term investments from the current asset section of the balance sheet and investment income from the income statement. The balance sheet in Exhibit 2 shows that Ryan Corporation has long-term assets of investments and plant assets, but no short-term investments. The income statement in Exhibit 3 shows that Ryan has investment income in the form of interest income, a gain on the sale of investments, and a loss on the sale of plant assets. The schedule at the bottom of Exhibit 3 lists the following five items pertaining to investing activities in 19x2:

1. Purchased investments in the amount of $78,000.
2. Sold investments that cost $90,000 for $102,000, resulting in a gain of $12,000.
3. Purchased plant assets in the amount of $120,000.
4. Sold plant assets that cost $10,000 with accumulated depreciation of $2,000 for $5,000, resulting in a loss of $3,000.
5. Issued $100,000 of bonds at face value in a noncash exchange for plant assets.

The following paragraphs analyze the accounts related to investing activities to determine their effects on Ryan Corporation's cash flows.

Investments   The objective here is to explain the corporation's $12,000 decrease in investments, all of which are classified as available-for-sale securities. This is accomplished by analyzing the increases and decreases in the Investments account to determine the effects on the Cash account. Purchases increase investments and sales decrease investments. Item **1** in Ryan's list of investing activities shows purchases of $78,000 during 19x2. The transaction would have been recorded as follows:

Investments	78,000	
Cash		78,000
Purchase of investments		

The entry shows that the effect of this transaction is a $78,000 decrease in cash flows.

Item **2** in the list shows a sale of investments at a gain. This transaction was recorded as follows:

Cash	102,000	
Investments		90,000
Gain on Sale of Investments		12,000
Sale of investments for a gain		

The effect of this transaction is a $102,000 increase in cash flows. Note that the gain on sale of investments is included in the $102,000. This is the reason it was excluded earlier in computing cash flows from operations. If it had been included in that section, it would have been counted twice.

The $12,000 decrease in the Investments account during 19x2 has now been explained, as may be seen in the following T account.

Investments

Beg. Bal.	127,000	Sales	90,000
Purchases	78,000		
End. Bal.	115,000		

The cash flow effects from these transactions are shown under the Cash Flows from Investing Activities section on the statement of cash flows as follows:

| Purchase of Investments | ($ 78,000) |
| Sale of Investments | 102,000 |

Notice that purchases and sales are disclosed separately as cash outflows and cash inflows. They are not netted against each other into a single figure. This disclosure gives readers of the statement a more complete view of investing activity.

If Ryan Corporation had short-term investments or marketable securities, the analysis of cash flows would be the same.

Plant Assets   In the case of plant assets, it is necessary to explain the changes in both the asset account and the related accumulated depreciation account. According to Exhibit 2, Plant Assets increased by $210,000 and Accumulated Depreciation increased by $35,000. Purchases increase plant assets and sales decrease plant assets. Accumulated depreciation is increased by the amount of depreciation expense and decreased by the removal of the accumulated depreciation associated with plant assets that are sold. Three items listed in Exhibit 3 affect plant assets. Item **3** in the list on the previous page indicates that Ryan Corporation purchased plant assets totaling $120,000 during 19x2, as shown by this entry:

Plant Assets	120,000	
Cash		120,000
Purchase of plant assets		

This transaction results in a cash outflow of $120,000.

Item **4** states that Ryan Corporation sold for $5,000 plant assets that had cost $10,000 and had accumulated depreciation of $2,000. The entry to record this transaction is as follows:

Cash	5,000	
Accumulated Depreciation	2,000	
Loss on Sale of Plant Assets	3,000	
Plant Assets		10,000
Sale of plant assets at a loss		

Note that in this transaction the positive cash flow is equal to the amount of cash received, or $5,000. The loss on the sale of plant assets is considered here rather than in the operating activities section. The amount of a loss or gain on the sale of an asset is determined by the amount of cash received and does not represent a cash outflow or inflow.

The disclosure of these two transactions in the investing activities section of the statement of cash flows is as follows:

| Purchase of Plant Assets | ($120,000) |
| Sale of Plant Assets | 5,000 |

As with investments, cash outflows and cash inflows are not netted, but are presented separately to give full information to the statement reader.

Item **5** on the list of Ryan's investing activities is a noncash exchange that affects two long-term accounts, Plant Assets and Bonds Payable. It was recorded as follows:

Plant Assets	100,000	
Bonds Payable		100,000
Issued bonds at face value		
for plant assets		

Although this transaction does not involve an inflow or outflow of cash, it is a significant transaction involving both an investing activity (the purchase of plant assets) and a financing activity (the issue of bonds payable). Because one purpose of the statement of cash flows is to show important investing and financing activities, the transaction is listed in a separate schedule, either at the bottom of the statement of cash flows or accompanying the statement, as follows:

Schedule of Noncash Investing and Financing Transactions

Issue of Bonds Payable for Plant Assets	$100,000

Through our analysis of the preceding transactions and the depreciation expense for plant assets of $37,000, all the changes in the plant assets accounts have now been accounted for, as shown in the following T accounts:

Plant Assets

Beg. Bal.	505,000	Sale	10,000
Cash Purchase	120,000		
Noncash Purchase	100,000		
End. Bal.	**715,000**		

Accumulated Depreciation

Sale	2,000	Beg. Bal.	68,000
		Dep. Exp.	37,000
		End. Bal.	**103,000**

If the balance sheet had included specific plant asset accounts, such as Buildings and Equipment and their related accumulated depreciation accounts, or other long-term asset accounts, such as intangibles or natural resources, the analysis would have been the same.

DETERMINING CASH FLOWS FROM FINANCING ACTIVITIES

OBJECTIVE

5b *Determine cash flows from financing activities*

The third step in preparing the statement of cash flows is to determine cash flows from financing activities. The procedure is similar to the analysis of investing activities, including treatment of related gains or losses. The only difference is that the accounts to be analyzed are the short-term borrowings, long-term liabilities, and stockholders' equity accounts. Cash dividends from the statement of stockholders' equity must also be considered. Since Ryan Corporation does not have short-term borrowings, only long-term liabilities and stockholders' equity accounts are considered here. The following items from Exhibit 3 pertain to Ryan Corporation's financing activities in 19x2.

5. Issued $100,000 of bonds at face value in a noncash exchange for plant assets.
6. Repaid $50,000 of bonds at face value at maturity.
7. Issued 15,200 shares of $5 par value common stock for $150,000.
8. Paid cash dividends in the amount of $8,000.

Bonds Payable   Exhibit 2 shows that Bonds Payable increased by $50,000 in 19x2. This account is affected by items **5** and **6**. Item **5** was analyzed in connection with plant assets. It is reported on the schedule of noncash investing and financing transactions (see Exhibit 5 on page 1197), but it must be remembered here in preparing the T account for Bonds Payable. Item **6** results in a cash outflow, a point that can be seen in the following transaction.

Bonds Payable	50,000	
Cash		50,000
Repayment of bonds at face value		
at maturity		

This cash outflow is shown in the financing activities section of the statement of cash flows as follows:

Repayment of Bonds ($50,000)

From these transactions, the change in the Bonds Payable account can be explained as follows:

Bonds Payable

Repayment	50,000	Beg. Bal.	245,000
		Noncash Issue	100,000
		End. Bal.	**295,000**

If Ryan Corporation had notes payable, either short-term or long-term, the analysis would be the same.

Common Stock   As with plant assets, related stockholders' equity accounts should be analyzed together. For example, Paid-in Capital in Excess of Par Value, Common should be examined with Common Stock. In 19x2 Ryan Corporation's Common Stock account increased by $76,000 and Paid-in Capital in Excess of Par Value, Common increased by $74,000. Those increases are explained by item **7**, which states that Ryan Corporation issued 15,200 shares of stock for $150,000. The entry to record the cash inflow was as follows:

Cash	150,000	
Common Stock		76,000
Paid-in Capital in Excess of Par Value, Common		74,000
Issued 15,200 shares of $5 par		
value common stock		

The cash inflow is shown in the financing activities section of the statement of cash flows as follows:

Issue of Common Stock $150,000

The analysis of this transaction is all that is needed to explain the changes in the two accounts during 19x2, as follows:

Common Stock			Paid-in Capital in Excess of Par Value, Common		
	Beg. Bal.	200,000		Beg. Bal.	115,000
	Issue	76,000		Issue	74,000
	End. Bal.	**276,000**		End. Bal.	**189,000**

Retained Earnings   At this point in the analysis, several items that affect retained earnings have already been dealt with. For instance, in the case of Ryan Corporation, net income was used as part of the analysis of cash flows from operating activities. The only other item affecting the retained earnings of Ryan Corporation is the payment of $8,000 in cash dividends (item **8** on the list on page 1194), as reflected by the following transaction.

Retained Earnings	8,000	
Cash		8,000
Cash dividends for 19x2		

Ryan Corporation would have declared the dividend before paying it and debited the Cash Dividends Declared account instead of Retained Earnings, but after paying the dividend and closing the Cash Dividends Declared account to Retained Earnings, the effect is as shown. Cash dividends are displayed in the financing activities section of the statement of cash flows:

Dividends Paid ($8,000)

The following T account shows the change in the Retained Earnings account.

Retained Earnings

Dividends	8,000	Beg. Bal.	132,000
		Net Income	16,000
		End. Bal.	**140,000**

COMPILING THE STATEMENT OF CASH FLOWS

OBJECTIVE

6 *Use the indirect method to prepare a statement of cash flows*

At this point in the analysis, all income statement items have been analyzed, all balance sheet changes have been explained, and all additional information has been taken into account. The resulting information may now be assembled into a statement of cash flows for Ryan Corporation, as presented in Exhibit 5. The Schedule of Noncash Investing and Financing Transactions is presented at the bottom of the statement.

ANALYZING THE STATEMENT OF CASH FLOWS

OBJECTIVE

7 *Analyze the statement of cash flows*

Like the other financial statements, the statement of cash flows can be analyzed to reveal significant relationships. Two areas analysts examine when studying a company are cash-generating efficiency and free cash flow.

CASH-GENERATING EFFICIENCY

Cash-generating efficiency is the ability of a company to generate cash from its current or continuing operations. Three ratios are helpful in measuring cash-generating efficiency: cash flow yield, cash flows to sales, and cash flows to assets. These ratios are computed and discussed below for Ryan Corporation. Data for the computations are obtained from Exhibits 2, 3, and 5.

Cash flow yield is the ratio of net cash flows from operating activities to net income, as follows:

$$\text{Cash flow yield} = \frac{\text{net cash flows from operating activities}}{\text{net income}}$$

$$= \frac{\$30,000}{\$16,000}$$

$$= 1.9 \text{ times}$$

Exhibit 5. Statement of Cash Flows: Indirect Method

Ryan Corporation
Statement of Cash Flows
For the Year Ended December 31, 19x2

Cash Flows from Operating Activities		
Net Income		$ 16,000
Adjustments to Reconcile Net Income to Net		
Cash Flows from Operating Activities		
Depreciation	$ 37,000	
Gain on Sale of Investments	(12,000)	
Loss on Sale of Plant Assets	3,000	
Changes in Current Assets and Current Liabilities		
Decrease in Accounts Receivable	8,000	
Increase in Inventory	(34,000)	
Decrease in Prepaid Expenses	4,000	
Increase in Accounts Payable	7,000	
Increase in Accrued Liabilities	3,000	
Decrease in Income Taxes Payable	(2,000)	14,000
Net Cash Flows from Operating Activities		$ 30,000
Cash Flows from Investing Activities		
Purchase of Investments	($ 78,000)	
Sale of Investments	102,000	
Purchase of Plant Assets	(120,000)	
Sale of Plant Assets	5,000	
Net Cash Flows from Investing Activities		(91,000)
Cash Flows from Financing Activities		
Repayment of Bonds	($ 50,000)	
Issue of Common Stock	150,000	
Dividends Paid	(8,000)	
Net Cash Flows from Financing Activities		92,000
Net Increase (Decrease) in Cash		$ 31,000
Cash at Beginning of Year		15,000
Cash at End of Year		$ 46,000
Schedule of Noncash Investing and Financing Transactions		
Issue of Bonds Payable for Plant Assets		$100,000

Ryan Corporation provides a good cash flow yield of 1.9 times. This means that operating activities are generating almost twice as much cash flow as net income. If special items that are material appear on the income statement, such as discontinued operations, income from continuing operations should be used as the denominator.

Cash flows to sales is the ratio of net cash flows from operating activities to sales, as shown on the next page.

The FASB in the United States is not the only body that makes changes in accounting standards that significantly affect financial reporting. A change in accounting standards in England caused consternation on the part of Saatchi & Saatchi, a British company that is one of the largest advertising agencies in the world. The chief executive announced that in 1992 the company had the highest pretax loss—£595.1 million—in its history. According to the chief executive, the 1992 figures were caused by a £600 million writedown of assets, reflecting the fall in value of a large group of companies purchased by Saatchi & Saatchi during the 1980s. He explained that it was entirely a paper item that did not affect cash flows and described the new accounting standard as "a typical accounting trick which I do not understand."[5]

In fact, the new rule is understandable as good accounting practice. The writedowns are not a cash outflow in the *current* year because the companies were purchased in *prior* years; however, they are appropriately deducted in determining net income because if the values of the purchased companies have declined, as all agree they have, *future* cash flows will be negatively affected. A purpose of net income is to provide information about future cash flows. The net loss reported by Saatchi & Saatchi reflects reduced future cash flows.

$$\text{Cash flows to sales} = \frac{\text{net cash flows from operating activities}}{\text{net sales}}$$

$$= \frac{\$30,000}{\$698,000}$$

$$= 4.3\%$$

Ryan Corporation generates cash flows to sales of only 4.3 percent. This means that the company is not generating much cash from sales.

Cash flows to assets is the ratio of net cash flows from operating activities to average total assets, as follows:

$$\text{Cash flows to assets} = \frac{\text{net cash flows from operating activities}}{\text{average total assets}}$$

$$= \frac{\$30,000}{(\$749,000 + \$965,000) \div 2}$$

$$= 3.5\%$$

The cash flows to assets is even lower than cash flows to sales because Ryan Corporation has a poor asset turnover ratio (sales ÷ average total assets) of less than 1.0 times. Cash flows to sales and cash flows to assets are closely related to the profitability measures profit margin and return on assets. They exceed those measures by the amount of the cash flow yield ratio because cash flow yield is the ratio of net cash flows from operating activities to net income.

5. Martin Waller, "Writedown Condemns Saatchi to £595m Loss," *The Times*, March 10, 1993.

Although Ryan Corporation's cash flow yield is relatively strong, the other two ratios show that its efficiency at generating cash flows from operating activities is low.

FREE CASH FLOW

It would seem logical for the analysis to move along to investing and financing activities. For example, because there is a net cash outflow of $91,000 in the investing activities section, it is apparent that the company is expanding. However, that figure mixes net capital expenditures for plant assets, which reflect management's expansion of operations, with purchases and sales of investments. Also, cash flows from financing activities were a positive $92,000, but that figure combines financing activities associated with bonds and stocks with dividends paid to stockholders. While something can be learned by looking at those broad categories, many analysts find it more fruitful to go beyond them and focus on a computation called free cash flow.

Free cash flow is the amount of cash that remains after deducting the funds the company must commit to continue operating at its planned level. The commitments must cover current or continuing operations, interest, income taxes, dividends, and net capital expenditures. Cash requirements for current or continuing operations, interest, and income taxes must be paid or the company's creditors and the government can bring action. Although the payment of dividends is not strictly required, dividends normally represent a commitment to stockholders. If they are reduced or eliminated, stockholders will be unhappy and the price of the company's stock will suffer. Net capital expenditures represent management's plans for the future.

If free cash flow is positive, it means that the company has met all of its planned cash commitments and has cash available to reduce debt or expand. A negative free cash flow means that the company will have to sell investments, borrow money, or issue stock in the short term to continue at its planned levels. If free cash flow remains negative for several years, a company may not be able to raise cash by selling investments or issuing stock or bonds.

Since cash commitments for current or continuing operations, interest, and income taxes are incorporated in cash flows from current operations, free cash flow for Ryan Corporation is computed as follows:

$$
\begin{aligned}
\text{Free cash flow} &= \text{net cash flows from operating activities} \ - \ \text{dividends} \\
&\quad - \ \text{purchases of plant assets} \ + \ \text{sales of plant assets} \\
&= \$30{,}000 \ - \ \$8{,}000 \ - \ \$120{,}000 \ + \ \$5{,}000 \\
&= (\$93{,}000)
\end{aligned}
$$

Purchases and sales of plant assets appear in the investing activities section of the statement of cash flows. Many companies provide this number as a net amount, using terms such as "net capital expenditures." Dividends are found in the financing activities section. Ryan Corporation has negative free cash flow of $93,000 and must make up the difference from sales of investments and from financing activities. Net sales from investments provided $24,000 ($102,000 − $78,000). Looking at the financing activities section, it may be seen that the company repaid debt of $50,000 and issued common stock in the amount of $150,000, providing more than enough cash to overcome the negative free cash flow. Also, reducing debt while increasing equity is a wise action in light of the negative free cash flow. Unless the company improves its free cash flow, it may have difficulty meeting future debt repayments.

Cash flows can vary from year to year; it is best to look at trends in cash flow measures over several years when analyzing a company's cash flows.

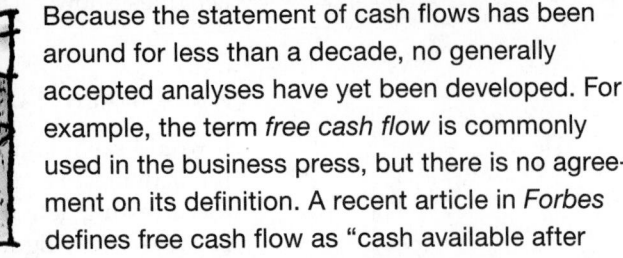

BUSINESS BULLETIN: BUSINESS PRACTICE

Because the statement of cash flows has been around for less than a decade, no generally accepted analyses have yet been developed. For example, the term *free cash flow* is commonly used in the business press, but there is no agreement on its definition. A recent article in *Forbes* defines free cash flow as "cash available after paying out capital expenditures and dividends, *but before taxes and interest*"[6] [emphasis added]. In the *Wall Street Journal*, free cash flow was defined as "operating income less maintenance-level capital expenditures."[7] The definition with which we are most in agreement is the one used in *Business Week*, which is net cash flows from operating activities less net capital expenditures and dividends. This "measures truly discretionary funds—company money that an owner could pocket without harming the business."[8] ====

PREPARING THE WORK SHEET

Supplemental OBJECTIVE

8 *Prepare a work sheet for the statement of cash flows*

Previous sections illustrated the preparation of the statement of cash flows for Ryan Corporation, a relatively simple company. To assist in preparing the statement of cash flows for more complex companies, accountants have developed a work sheet approach. The work sheet approach employs a special format that allows for the systematic analysis of all the changes in the balance sheet accounts to arrive at the statement of cash flows. In this section, the work sheet approach is demonstrated using the statement of cash flows for Ryan Corporation. The work sheet approach uses the indirect method of determining cash flows from operating activities because of its basis in changes in the balance sheet accounts.

PROCEDURES IN PREPARING THE WORK SHEET

The work sheet for Ryan Corporation is presented in Exhibit 6. The work sheet has four columns, labeled as follows:

Column A: Description
Column B: Account balances for the end of the prior year (19x1)
Column C: Analysis of transactions for the current year
Column D: Account balances for the end of the current year (19x2)

Five steps are followed in preparing the work sheet. As you read each one, refer to Exhibit 6.

6. Gary Slutsker, "Look at the Birdie and Say: 'Cash Flow,'" *Forbes*, October 25, 1993.
7. Jonathan Clements, "Yacktman Fund Is Bloodied but Unbowed," *Wall Street Journal*, November 8, 1993.
8. Jeffrey Laderman, "Earnings, Schmearnings—Look at the Cash," *Business Week*, July 24, 1989.

Exhibit 6. Work Sheet for the Statement of Cash Flows

Ryan Corporation
Work Sheet for Statement of Cash Flows
For the Year Ended December 31, 19x2

Description	Account Balances 12/31/x1	Analysis of Transactions				Account Balances 12/31/x2
			Debit		Credit	
Debits						
Cash	15,000	(x)	31,000			46,000
Accounts Receivable (net)	55,000			(b)	8,000	47,000
Inventory	110,000	(c)	34,000			144,000
Prepaid Expenses	5,000			(d)	4,000	1,000
Investments	127,000	(h)	78,000	(i)	90,000	115,000
Plant Assets	505,000	(j)	120,000	(k)	10,000	715,000
		(l)	100,000			
Total Debits	817,000					1,068,000
Credits						
Accumulated Depreciation	68,000	(k)	2,000	(m)	37,000	103,000
Accounts Payable	43,000			(e)	7,000	50,000
Accrued Liabilities	9,000			(f)	3,000	12,000
Income Taxes Payable	5,000	(g)	2,000			3,000
Bonds Payable	245,000	(n)	50,000	(l)	100,000	295,000
Common Stock	200,000			(o)	76,000	276,000
Paid-in Capital	115,000			(o)	74,000	189,000
Retained Earnings	132,000	(p)	8,000	(a)	16,000	140,000
Total Credits	817,000		425,000		425,000	1,068,000
Cash Flows from Operating Activities						
Net Income		(a)	16,000			
Decrease in Accounts Receivable		(b)	8,000			
Increase in Inventory				(c)	34,000	
Decrease in Prepaid Expenses		(d)	4,000			
Increase in Accounts Payable		(e)	7,000			
Increase in Accrued Liabilities		(f)	3,000			
Decrease in Income Taxes Payable				(g)	2,000	
Gain on Sale of Investments				(i)	12,000	
Loss on Sale of Plant Assets		(k)	3,000			
Depreciation Expense		(m)	37,000			
Cash Flows from Investing Activities						
Purchase of Investments				(h)	78,000	
Sale of Investments		(i)	102,000			
Purchase of Plant Assets				(j)	120,000	
Sale of Plant Assets		(k)	5,000			
Cash Flows from Financing Activities						
Repayment of Bonds				(n)	50,000	
Issue of Common Stock		(o)	150,000			
Dividends Paid				(p)	8,000	
			335,000		304,000	
Net Increase in Cash				(x)	31,000	
			335,000		335,000	

1. Enter the account names from the balance sheet (Exhibit 2) in column A. Note that all accounts with debit balances are listed first, followed by all accounts with credit balances.
2. Enter the account balances for 19x1 in column B and the account balances for 19x2 in column D. In each column, total the debits and the credits. The total debits should equal the total credits in each column. (This is a check of whether all accounts were correctly transferred from the balance sheet.)
3. Below the data entered in step **2,** insert the captions Cash Flows from Operating Activities, Cash Flows from Investing Activities, and Cash Flows from Financing Activities, leaving several lines of space between each one. As you do the analysis in step **4,** write the results in the appropriate categories.
4. Analyze the changes in each balance sheet account using information from both the income statement (see Exhibit 3) and other transactions affecting non-current accounts during 19x2. (The procedures for this analysis are presented in the next section.) Enter the results in the debit and credit columns. Identify each item with a letter. On the first line, identify the change in cash with an (*x*). In a complex situation, these letters will refer to a list of explanations on another working paper.
5. When all the changes in the balance sheet accounts have been explained, add the debit and credit columns in both the top and the bottom portions of column C. The debit and credit columns in the top portion should equal each other. They should *not* be equal in the bottom portion. If no errors have been made, the difference between columns in the bottom portion should equal the increase or decrease in the Cash account, identified with an (*x*) on the first line of the work sheet. Add this difference to the lesser of the two columns, and identify it as either an increase or a decrease in cash. Label the change with an (*x*) and compare it with the change in Cash on the first line of the work sheet, also labeled (*x*). The amounts should be equal, as they are in Exhibit 6, where the net increase in cash is $31,000. Also, the new totals from the debit and credit columns should be equal.

When the work sheet is complete, the statement of cash flows may be prepared using the information in the lower half of the work sheet.

ANALYZING THE CHANGES IN BALANCE SHEET ACCOUNTS

The most important step in preparing the work sheet is the analysis of the changes in the balance sheet accounts (step **4**). Although a number of transactions and reclassifications must be analyzed and recorded, the overall procedure is systematic and not overly complicated. It is as follows:

1. Record net income.
2. Account for changes in current assets and current liabilities.
3. Use the information about other transactions to account for changes in noncurrent accounts.
4. Reclassify any other income and expense items not already dealt with.

In the following explanations, the identification letters refer to the corresponding transactions and reclassifications in the work sheet.

a. Net Income　　Net income results in an increase in Retained Earnings. Under the indirect method, it is the starting point for determining cash flows from operating activities. Under this method, additions and deductions are made to net income to arrive at cash flows from operating activities. Work sheet entry **a** is as follows:

| (a) Cash Flows from Operations: Net Income | 16,000 | |
| Retained Earnings | | 16,000 |

b–g. *Changes in Current Assets and Current Liabilities*

Entries **b** to **g** record the effects of the changes in current assets and current liabilities on cash flows. In each case, there is a debit or credit to the current asset or current liability to account for the change in the year and a corresponding debit or credit in the operating activities section of the work sheet. Recall that in the prior analysis, each item on the accrual-based income statement was adjusted for the change in the related current assets or current liabilities to arrive at the cash-based figure. The same reasoning applies in recording these changes in accounts as debits or credits in the operating activities section. For example, work sheet entry **b** records the decrease in Accounts Receivable as a credit (decrease) to Accounts Receivable and as a debit in the operating activities section because the decrease has a positive effect on cash flows, as follows:

(b) Cash Flows from Operating Activities:		
Decrease in Accounts Receivable	8,000	
Accounts Receivable		8,000

Work sheet entries **c–g** reflect the effects of the changes in the other current assets and current liabilities on cash flows from operating activities. As you study these entries, note how the effects of each entry on cash flows are automatically determined by debits or credits reflecting changes in the balance sheet accounts.

(c) Inventory	34,000	
Cash Flows from Operating Activities:		
Increase in Inventory		34,000
(d) Cash Flows from Operating Activities:		
Decrease in Prepaid Expenses	4,000	
Prepaid Expenses		4,000
(e) Cash Flows from Operating Activities:		
Increase in Accounts Payable	7,000	
Accounts Payable		7,000
(f) Cash Flows from Operating Activities:		
Increase in Accrued Liabilities	3,000	
Accrued Liabilities		3,000
(g) Income Taxes Payable	2,000	
Cash Flows from Operating Activities:		
Decrease in Income Taxes Payable		2,000

h–i. *Investments*

Among the other transactions affecting noncurrent accounts during 19x2 (see Exhibit 3), two pertain to investments. One is the purchase for $78,000 and the other is the sale at $102,000. The purchase is recorded on the work sheet as a cash flow in the investing activities section, as follows:

(h) Investments	78,000	
Cash Flows from Investing Activities:		
Purchase of Investments		78,000

Note that instead of crediting Cash, a credit entry with the appropriate designation is made in the appropriate section in the lower half of the work sheet. The sale transaction is more complicated because it involves a gain that appears on the income statement and is included in net income. The work sheet entry accounts for this gain as follows:

(i) Cash Flows from Investing Activities:
    Sale of Investments   102,000
      Investments   90,000
      Cash Flows from Operating Activities:
        Gain on Sale of Investments   12,000

This entry records the cash inflow in the investing activities section, accounts for the remaining difference in the Investments account, and removes the gain on sale of investments from net income.

j–m. Plant Assets and Accumulated Depreciation

Four transactions affect plant assets and the related accumulated depreciation. They are the purchase of plant assets, the sale of plant assets at a loss, the noncash exchange of bonds for plant assets, and the depreciation expense for the year. Because these transactions may appear complicated, it is important to work through them systematically when preparing the work sheet. First, the purchase of plant assets for $120,000 is entered (entry **j**) in the same way the purchase of investments was entered in entry **h:**

(j) Plant Assets   120,000
    Cash Flows from Investing Activities:
      Purchase of Plant Assets   120,000

Second, the sale of plant assets is similar to the sale of investments, except that a loss is involved, as follows:

(k) Cash Flows from Investing Activities:
    Sale of Plant Assets   5,000
    Cash Flows from Operating Activities:
      Loss on Sale of Plant Assets   3,000
      Accumulated Depreciation   2,000
        Plant Assets   10,000

The cash inflow from this transaction is $5,000. The rest of the entry is necessary to add the loss back into net income in the operating activities section of the statement of cash flows (since it was deducted to arrive at net income and no cash outflow resulted) and to record the effects on plant assets and accumulated depreciation.

The third transaction (entry **l**) is the noncash issue of bonds for the purchase of plant assets, as follows:

(l) Plant Assets   100,000
    Bonds Payable   100,000

Note that this transaction does not affect Cash. Still, it needs to be recorded because the objective is to account for all changes in the balance sheet accounts. It is listed at the end of the statement of cash flows (Exhibit 5) in the schedule of noncash investing and financing transactions.

At this point the increase of $210,000 ($715,000 − $505,000) in plant assets has been explained by the two purchases less the sale ($120,000 + $100,000 − $10,000 = $210,000), but the change in Accumulated Depreciation has not been completely explained. The depreciation expense for the year needs to be entered, as follows:

(m) Cash Flows from Operating Activities:
    Depreciation Expense   37,000
      Accumulated Depreciation   37,000

The debit is to the operating activities section of the work sheet because, as explained earlier in the chapter, no current cash outflow is required for depreciation expense. The effect of this debit is to add the amount for depreciation expense back into net income. The $35,000 increase in Accumulated Depreciation has now been explained by the sale transaction and the depreciation expense (−$2,000 + $37,000 = $35,000).

n. Bonds Payable   Part of the change in Bonds Payable was explained in entry l when a noncash transaction, a $100,000 issue of bonds in exchange for plant assets, was entered. All that remains is to enter the repayment, as follows:

(n) Bonds Payable	50,000	
Cash Flows from Financing Activities:		
Repayment of Bonds		50,000

o. Common Stock and Paid-in Capital in Excess of Par Value, Common   One transaction affects both these accounts. It is an issue of 15,200 shares of $5 par value common stock for a total of $150,000. The work sheet entry is as follows:

(o) Cash Flows from Financing Activities:		
Issue of Common Stock	150,000	
Common Stock		76,000
Paid-in Capital in Excess of Par Value, Common		74,000

p. Retained Earnings   Part of the change in Retained Earnings was recognized when net income was entered (entry **a**). The only remaining effect to be recognized is the $8,000 in cash dividends paid during the year, as follows:

(p) Retained Earnings	8,000	
Cash Flows from Financing Activities:		
Dividends Paid		8,000

x. Cash   The final step is to total the debit and credit columns in the top and bottom portions of the work sheet and then to enter the net change in cash at the bottom of the work sheet. The columns in the upper half equal $425,000. In the lower half, the debit column totals $335,000 and the credit column totals $304,000. The credit difference of $31,000 (entry **x**) equals the debit change in cash on the first line of the work sheet.

THE DIRECT METHOD OF PREPARING THE STATEMENT OF CASH FLOWS

Supplemental OBJECTIVE

9 *Use the direct method to determine cash flows from operating activities and prepare a statement of cash flows*

To this point in the chapter, the indirect method of preparing the statement of cash flows has been emphasized. In this section, the direct method is presented. First, the use of the direct method to determine net cash flows from operating activities is covered. Then the statement of cash flows under the direct method is illustrated.

DETERMINING CASH FLOWS FROM OPERATING ACTIVITIES

The principal difference between the indirect and the direct methods appears in the cash flows from operating activities section of the statement of cash flows. As you have seen, the indirect method starts with net income from the

Figure 3. Direct Method of Determining Net Cash Flows from Operating Activities

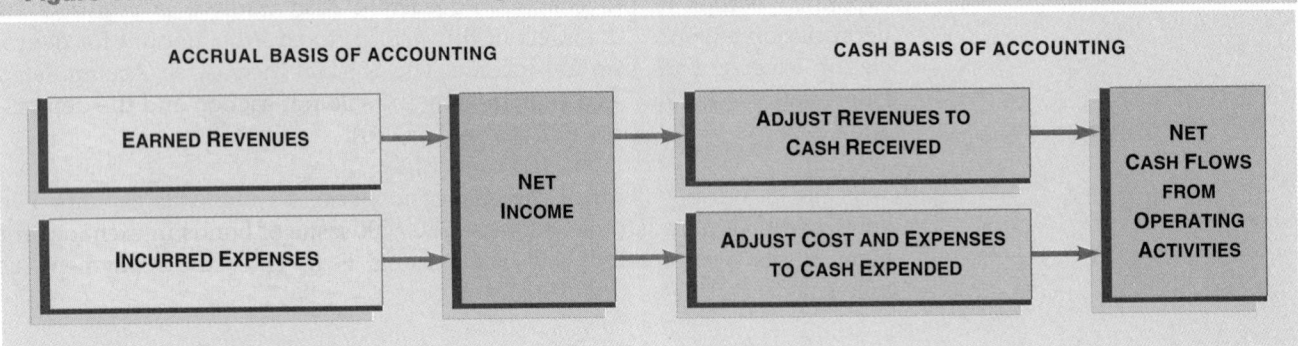

income statement and converts it to net cash flows from operating activities by adding or subtracting items that do not affect net cash flows. The direct method takes a different approach. It converts each item on the income statement to its cash equivalent, as illustrated in Figure 3. For instance, sales are converted to cash receipts from sales, and purchases are converted to cash payments for purchases. Exhibit 7 shows the schedule of cash flows from operating activities under the direct method for Ryan Corporation. The conversion of the components of Ryan Corporation's income statement to those figures is explained in the following paragraphs.

Cash Receipts from Sales   Sales result in a positive cash flow for a company. Cash sales are direct cash inflows. Credit sales are not, because they are originally recorded as accounts receivable. When they are collected, they become cash inflows. You cannot, however, assume that credit sales are automatically inflows of cash, because the collections of accounts receivable in any one accounting period are not likely to equal credit sales. Receivables may be uncollectible, sales from a prior period may be collected in the current period, or sales from the current period may be collected next period. For example, if accounts receivable increase from one accounting period to the next, cash receipts from sales will not be as great as sales. On the other hand, if accounts receivable decrease from one accounting period to the next, cash receipts from sales will exceed sales.

The relationships among sales, changes in accounts receivable, and cash receipts from sales are reflected in the following formula:

$$\text{Cash Receipts from Sales} = \text{Sales} \begin{cases} + \text{ Decrease in Accounts Receivable} \\ \qquad\qquad\qquad \text{or} \\ - \text{ Increase in Accounts Receivable} \end{cases}$$

Refer to the balance sheets and income statement for Ryan Corporation in Exhibits 2 and 3. Note that sales were $698,000 in 19x2 and that accounts receivable decreased by $8,000. Thus, cash received from sales is $706,000:

$$\$706,000 = \$698,000 + \$8,000$$

Collections were $8,000 more than sales recorded for the year.

Cash Receipts from Interest and Dividends   Although interest and dividends received are most closely associated with investment activity and are often called investment income, the FASB has decided to classify the cash received from these items as operating activities. To simplify the examples in

**Exhibit 7. Schedule of Cash Flows from Operating Activities:
Direct Method**

**Ryan Corporation
Schedule of Cash Flows from Operating Activities
For the Year Ended December 31, 19x2**

Cash Flows from Operating Activities		
Cash Receipts from		
Sales	$706,000	
Interest Received	6,000	$712,000
Cash Payments for		
Purchases	$547,000	
Operating Expenses	103,000	
Interest	23,000	
Income Taxes	9,000	682,000
Net Cash Flows from Operating Activities		$ 30,000

this text, it is assumed that interest income equals interest received and that dividend income equals dividends received. Thus, based on Exhibit 3, interest received by Ryan Corporation is assumed to equal $6,000, which is the amount of interest income.

Cash Payments for Purchases   Cost of goods sold (from the income statement) must be adjusted for changes in two balance sheet accounts to arrive at cash payments for purchases. First, cost of goods sold must be adjusted for changes in Inventory to arrive at net purchases. Then, net purchases must be adjusted for the change in Accounts Payable to arrive at cash payments for purchases. If Inventory has increased from one accounting period to another, net purchases will be greater than cost of goods sold because net purchases during the period have exceeded the dollar amount of the items sold during the period. If Inventory has decreased, net purchases will be less than cost of goods sold. Conversely, if Accounts Payable has increased, cash payments for purchases will be less than net purchases; if accounts payable has decreased, cash payments for purchases will be greater than net purchases.

These relationships may be stated in equation form as follows:

$$\text{Cash Payments for Purchases} = \text{Cost of Goods Sold} \begin{cases} + \text{ Increase in Inventory} \\ \text{or} \\ - \text{ Decrease in Inventory} \end{cases} \begin{cases} + \text{ Decrease in Accounts Payable} \\ \text{or} \\ - \text{ Increase in Accounts Payable} \end{cases}$$

From Exhibits 2 and 3, cost of goods sold is $520,000, inventory increased by $34,000, and accounts payable increased by $7,000. Thus, cash payments for purchases is $547,000, as the following calculation shows:

$$\$547,000 = \$520,000 + \$34,000 - \$7,000$$

In this example, Ryan Corporation purchased $34,000 more inventory than it sold and paid out $7,000 less in cash than it made in purchases. The net result is that cash payments for purchases exceeded cost of goods sold by $27,000 ($547,000 − $520,000).

Cash Payments for Operating Expenses

Just as cost of goods sold does not represent the amount of cash paid for purchases during an accounting period, operating expenses do not match the amount of cash paid to employees, suppliers, and others for goods and services. Three adjustments must be made to operating expenses to arrive at the cash outflows. The first adjustment is for changes in prepaid expenses, such as prepaid insurance or prepaid rent. If prepaid assets increase during the accounting period, more cash will have been paid out than appears on the income statement as expenses. If prepaid assets decrease, the expenses shown on the income statement will exceed the cash spent.

The second adjustment is for changes in liabilities resulting from accrued expenses, such as wages payable and payroll taxes payable. If accrued liabilities increase during the accounting period, operating expenses on the income statement will exceed the cash spent. And if accrued liabilities decrease, operating expenses will fall short of cash spent.

The third adjustment is made because certain expenses do not require a current outlay of cash; those expenses must be subtracted from operating expenses to arrive at cash payments for operating expenses. The most common expenses in this category are depreciation expense, amortization expense, and depletion expense. For example, Ryan Corporation recorded 19x2 depreciation expense of $37,000. No cash payment was made in this transaction. Therefore, to the extent that operating expenses include depreciation and similar items, an adjustment is needed to reduce operating expenses to the amount of cash expended.

The three adjustments to operating expenses are summarized in the following equation.

$$
\begin{array}{l}
\text{Cash Payments} \\
\text{for Operating} \\
\text{Expenses}
\end{array}
=
\begin{array}{l}
\text{Operating} \\
\text{Expenses}
\end{array}
\left\{
\begin{array}{l}
+ \text{ Increase in} \\
\text{Prepaid} \\
\text{Expenses} \\
\text{or} \\
- \text{ Decrease in} \\
\text{Prepaid} \\
\text{Expenses}
\end{array}
\right.
\left\{
\begin{array}{l}
+ \text{ Decrease in} \\
\text{Accrued} \\
\text{Liabilities} \\
\text{or} \\
- \text{ Increase in} \\
\text{Accrued} \\
\text{Liabilities}
\end{array}
\right.
\left\{
\begin{array}{l}
- \text{ Depreciation} \\
\text{and Other} \\
\text{Noncash} \\
\text{Expenses}
\end{array}
\right.
$$

According to Exhibits 2 and 3, Ryan's operating expenses (including depreciation of $37,000) were $147,000; prepaid expenses decreased by $4,000; and accrued liabilities increased by $3,000. As a result, Ryan Corporation's cash payments for operating expenses are $103,000, computed as follows:

$$\$103,000 = \$147,000 - \$4,000 - \$3,000 - \$37,000$$

If there are prepaid expenses and accrued liabilities that are *not* related to specific operating expenses, they are not included in these computations. One example is income taxes payable, which is the accrued liability related to income taxes expense. The cash payment for income taxes will be discussed shortly.

Cash Payments for Interest

The FASB classifies cash payments for interest as operating activities, although some authorities argue that they should be considered financing activities because of their association with loans incurred to finance the business. The FASB feels that interest expense is a cost of operating a business, and this is the position followed in this text. Also, for the sake of simplicity, all examples in this text assume that interest payments are equal to interest expense on the income statement. Thus, based on

Exhibit 3, Ryan Corporation's interest payments are assumed to be $23,000 in 19x2.

Cash Payments for Income Taxes

The amount of income taxes expense that appears on the income statement rarely equals the amount of income taxes actually paid during the year. To determine cash payments for income taxes, Income Taxes Expense (from the income statement) is adjusted by the change in Income Taxes Payable. If Income Taxes Payable increased during the accounting period, cash payments for taxes will be less than the expense shown on the income statement. If Income Taxes Payable decreased, cash payments for taxes will exceed income taxes on the income statement. In other words, the following equation is applicable:

$$\text{Cash Payments for Income Taxes} = \text{Income Taxes} \begin{cases} + \text{ Decrease in Income Taxes Payable} \\ \qquad\qquad\text{or} \\ - \text{ Increase in Income Taxes Payable} \end{cases}$$

In 19x2, Ryan Corporation showed income taxes of $7,000 on its income statement and a decrease of $2,000 in Income Taxes Payable on its balance sheets (see Exhibits 2 and 3). As a result, cash payments for income taxes during 19x2 were $9,000, calculated as follows:

$$\$9,000 = \$7,000 + \$2,000$$

COMPILING THE STATEMENT OF CASH FLOWS

The Ryan Corporation's statement of cash flows under the direct method is presented in Exhibit 8. The only differences between that statement of cash flows and the one based on the indirect method shown in Exhibit 5 occur in the first and last sections. The middle sections, which present cash flows from investing activities and financing activities, net increases or decreases in cash, and the schedule of noncash investing and financing activities, are the same under both methods.

The first section of the statement in Exhibit 8 shows the net cash flows from operating activities on a direct basis, as presented in Exhibit 7. The last section is the same as the cash flows from operating activities section of the statement of cash flows under the indirect method (see Exhibits 4 and 5). The FASB believes that when the direct method is used, a schedule should be provided that reconciles net income to net cash flows from operating activities. Thus, the statement of cash flows under the direct method includes a section that accommodates the main difference between it and the indirect method.

Exhibit 8. Statement of Cash Flows: Direct Method

Ryan Corporation
Statement of Cash Flows
For the Year Ended December 31, 19x2

Cash Flows from Operating Activities

Cash Receipts from		
Sales	$706,000	
Interest Received	6,000	$712,000
Cash Payments for		
Purchases	$547,000	
Operating Expenses	103,000	
Interest	23,000	
Income Taxes	9,000	682,000
Net Cash Flows from Operating Activities		$ 30,000

Cash Flows from Investing Activities

Purchase of Investments	($ 78,000)	
Sale of Investments	102,000	
Purchase of Plant Assets	(120,000)	
Sale of Plant Assets	5,000	
Net Cash Flows from Investing Activities		(91,000)

Cash Flows from Financing Activities

Repayment of Bonds	($ 50,000)	
Issue of Common Stock	150,000	
Dividends Paid	(8,000)	
Net Cash Flows from Financing Activities		92,000
Net Increase (Decrease) in Cash		$ 31,000
Cash at Beginning of Year		15,000
Cash at End of Year		$ 46,000

Schedule of Noncash Investing and Financing Transactions

Issue of Bonds Payable for Plant Assets	$100,000

Reconciliation of Net Income to Net Cash Flows from Operating Activities

Net Income		$ 16,000
Adjustments to Reconcile Net Income to Net		
Cash Flows from Operating Activities		
Depreciation	$ 37,000	
Gain on Sale of Investments	(12,000)	
Loss on Sale of Plant Assets	3,000	
Changes in Current Assets and Current Liabilities		
Decrease in Accounts Receivable	8,000	
Increase in Inventory	(34,000)	
Decrease in Prepaid Expenses	4,000	
Increase in Accounts Payable	7,000	
Increase in Accrued Liabilities	3,000	
Decrease in Income Taxes Payable	(2,000)	14,000
Net Cash Flows from Operating Activities		$ 30,000

CHAPTER REVIEW

REVIEW OF LEARNING OBJECTIVES

1.   **Describe the statement of cash flows, and define *cash* and *cash equivalents*.** The statement of cash flows explains the changes in cash and cash equivalents from one accounting period to the next by showing cash inflows and cash outflows from the operating, investing, and financing activities of a company for an accounting period. For purposes of preparing the statement of cash flows, *cash* is defined to include cash and cash equivalents. *Cash equivalents* are short-term (ninety days or less), highly liquid investments, including money market accounts, commercial paper, and U.S. Treasury bills.

2.   **State the principal purposes and uses of the statement of cash flows.** The primary purpose of the statement of cash flows is to provide information about a company's cash receipts and cash payments during an accounting period. Its secondary purpose is to provide information about a company's operating, investing, and financing activities. The statement is useful to management as well as to investors and creditors in assessing the liquidity of a business, including its ability to generate future cash flows and to pay debts and dividends.

3.   **Identify the principal components of the classifications of cash flows, and state the significance of noncash investing and financing transactions.** Cash flows may be classified as stemming from (1) operating activities, which include the cash effects of transactions and other events that enter into the determination of net income; (2) investing activities, which include the acquiring and selling of long- and short-term marketable securities, property, plant, and equipment, and the making and collecting of loans, excluding interest; or (3) financing activities, which include the obtaining and returning or repaying of resources, excluding interest, to owners and creditors. Noncash investing and financing transactions are also important because they are exchanges of assets and/or liabilities that are of interest to investors and creditors when evaluating the financing and investing activities of a business.

4.   **Use the indirect method to determine cash flows from operating activities.** Under the indirect method, net income is adjusted for all noncash effects to arrive at a cash flow basis, as follows:

Cash Flows from Operating Activities		
Net Income		xxx
Adjustments to Reconcile Net Income to Net Cash		
Flows from Operating Activities		
(List of individual items)	xxx	xxx
Net Cash Flows from Operating Activities		xxx

5.   **Determine cash flows from (a) investing activities and (b) financing activities.** Cash flows from investing activities are determined by identifying the cash flow effects of the transactions that affect each account relevant to investing activities. Such accounts include all long-term assets and short-term marketable securities. The same procedure is followed for financing activities, except that the accounts involved are short-term notes payable, long-term liabilities, and stockholders' equity. The effects of gains and losses reported on the income statement must also be considered. When the change in a balance sheet account from one accounting period to the next has been explained, all the cash flow effects should have been identified.

6.   **Use the indirect method to prepare a statement of cash flows.** The statement of cash flows lists cash flows from operating activities, investing activities, and financing activities, in that order. The sections on investing and financing activities are prepared by examining individual accounts involving cash receipts and cash payments to explain year-to-year changes in the account balances. Significant noncash transactions are included in a schedule of noncash investing and financing transactions that accompanies the statement of cash flows.

7. **Analyze the statement of cash flows.** In analyzing a company's statement of cash flows, analysts tend to focus on cash-generating efficiency and free cash flow. Cash-generating efficiency is a company's ability to generate cash from its current or continuing operations. Three ratios used in measuring cash-generating efficiency are cash flow yield, cash flows to sales, and cash flows to assets. Free cash flow is the cash that remains after deducting funds a company must commit to continue operating at its planned level. Such commitments must cover current or continuing operations, interest, income taxes, dividends, and net capital expenditures.

SUPPLEMENTAL OBJECTIVES

8. **Prepare a work sheet for the statement of cash flows.** A work sheet is useful in preparing the statement of cash flows for complex companies. The basic procedures are to analyze the changes in the balance sheet accounts for their effects on cash flows (in the top portion of the work sheet) and to classify those effects according to the format of the statement of cash flows (in the lower portion of the work sheet). When all changes in the balance sheet accounts have been explained and entered on the work sheet, the change in the Cash account will also be explained, and all necessary information will be available to prepare the statement of cash flows. The work sheet approach lends itself to the indirect method of preparing the statement of cash flows.

9. **Use the direct method to determine cash flows from operating activities and prepare a statement of cash flows.** The principal difference between a statement of cash flows prepared under the direct method and one prepared under the indirect method appears in the cash flows from operating activities section. Instead of beginning with net income and making additions and subtractions, as is done under the indirect method, the direct method converts each item on the income statement to its cash equivalent by adjusting for changes in the related current asset or current liability accounts and for other items such as depreciation. The rest of the statement of cash flows is the same under the direct method, except that a schedule that reconciles net income to net cash flows from operating activities should be included.

REVIEW OF CONCEPTS AND TERMINOLOGY

The following concepts and terms were introduced in this chapter.

L O 1   **Cash:** For purposes of the statement of cash flows, both cash and cash equivalents.

L O 1   **Cash equivalents:** Short-term (ninety days or less), highly liquid investments, including money market accounts, commercial paper, and U.S. Treasury bills.

L O 7   **Cash flows to assets:** The ratio of net cash flows from operating activities to average total assets.

L O 7   **Cash flows to sales:** The ratio of net cash flows from operating activities to sales.

L O 7   **Cash flow yield:** The ratio of net cash flows from operating activities to net income.

L O 7   **Cash-generating efficiency:** The ability of a company to generate cash from its current or continuing operations.

L O 4   **Direct method:** The procedure for converting the income statement from an accrual basis to a cash basis by separately adjusting each item in the income statement.

L O 3   **Financing activities:** Business activities that involve obtaining resources from or returning resources to owners and providing them with a return on their investment, and obtaining resources from creditors and repaying the amounts borrowed or otherwise settling the obligations.

L O 7   **Free cash flow:** The amount of cash that remains after deducting the funds a company must commit to continue operating at its planned level; net cash flows from operating activities minus dividends minus net capital expenditures.

L O 4   **Indirect method:** The procedure for converting the income statement from an accrual basis to a cash basis by adjusting net income for items that do not affect cash flows, including depreciation, amortization, depletion, gains, losses, and changes in current assets and current liabilities.

L O 3   **Investing activities:** Business activities that include the acquiring and selling of long-term assets, the acquiring and selling of marketable securities other than cash equivalents, and the making and collecting of loans.

L O 3   **Noncash investing and financing transactions:** Significant investing and financing transactions that do not involve an actual cash inflow or outflow but involve only long-term assets, long-term liabilities, or stockholders' equity, such as the exchange of a long-term asset for a long-term liability or the settlement of a debt by the issue of capital stock.

L O 3   **Operating activities:** Business activities that include the cash effects of transactions and other events that enter into the determination of net income.

L O 1   **Statement of cash flows:** A primary financial statement that shows how a company's operating, investing, and financing activities have affected cash during an accounting period.

REVIEW PROBLEM
THE STATEMENT OF CASH FLOWS

L O 4, 5, 6, S O 9   The 19x7 income statement for Northwest Corporation is presented below and the comparative balance sheets for the years 19x7 and 19x6 are shown on the following page.

Northwest Corporation
Income Statement
For the Year Ended December 31, 19x7

Net Sales		$1,650,000
Cost of Goods Sold		920,000
Gross Margin		$ 730,000
Operating Expenses (including Depreciation Expense of $12,000 on Buildings and $23,100 on Equipment, and Amortization Expense of $4,800)		470,000
Operating Income		$ 260,000
Other Income (Expense)		
Interest Expense	($55,000)	
Dividend Income	3,400	
Gain on Sale of Investments	12,500	
Loss on Disposal of Equipment	(2,300)	(41,400)
Income Before Income Taxes		$ 218,600
Income Taxes		52,200
Net Income		$ 166,400

Northwest Corporation
Comparative Balance Sheets
December 31, 19x7 and 19x6

	19x7	19x6	Change	Increase or Decrease
Assets				
Cash	$ 115,850	$ 121,850	($ 6,000)	Decrease
Accounts Receivable (net)	296,000	314,500	(18,500)	Decrease
Inventory	322,000	301,000	21,000	Increase
Prepaid Expenses	7,800	5,800	2,000	Increase
Long-Term Investments	36,000	86,000	(50,000)	Decrease
Land	150,000	125,000	25,000	Increase
Buildings	462,000	462,000	—	—
Accumulated Depreciation, Buildings	(91,000)	(79,000)	(12,000)	Increase
Equipment	159,730	167,230	(7,500)	Decrease
Accumulated Depreciation, Equipment	(43,400)	(45,600)	2,200	Decrease
Intangible Assets	19,200	24,000	(4,800)	Decrease
Total Assets	$1,434,180	$1,482,780	($ 48,600)	
Liabilities and Stockholders' Equity				
Accounts Payable	$ 133,750	$ 233,750	($100,000)	Decrease
Notes Payable (current)	75,700	145,700	(70,000)	Decrease
Accrued Liabilities	5,000	—	5,000	Increase
Income Taxes Payable	20,000	—	20,000	Increase
Bonds Payable	210,000	310,000	(100,000)	Decrease
Mortgage Payable	330,000	350,000	(20,000)	Decrease
Common Stock—$10 par value	360,000	300,000	60,000	Increase
Paid-in Capital in Excess of Par Value	90,000	50,000	40,000	Increase
Retained Earnings	209,730	93,330	116,400	Increase
Total Liabilities and Stockholders' Equity	$1,434,180	$1,482,780	($ 48,600)	

The following additional information was taken from the company's records:

a. Long-term investments (available-for-sale securities) that cost $70,000 were sold at a gain of $12,500; additional long-term investments were made in the amount of $20,000.

b. Five acres of land were purchased for $25,000 to build a parking lot.

c. Equipment that cost $37,500 with accumulated depreciation of $25,300 was sold at a loss of $2,300; new equipment costing $30,000 was purchased.

d. Notes payable in the amount of $100,000 were repaid; an additional $30,000 was borrowed by signing notes payable.

e. Bonds payable in the amount of $100,000 were converted into 6,000 shares of common stock.

f. The Mortgage Payable account was reduced by $20,000 during the year.

g. Cash dividends declared and paid were $50,000.

REQUIRED

1. Prepare a schedule of cash flows from operating activities using the (a) direct method and (b) indirect method.
2. Prepare a statement of cash flows using the indirect method.

ANSWER TO REVIEW PROBLEM

1. (a) Prepare a schedule of cash flows from operating activities using the direct method.

Northwest Corporation
Schedule of Cash Flows from Operating Activities
For the Year Ended December 31, 19x7

Cash Flows from Operating Activities		
Cash Receipts from		
Sales	$1,668,500[1]	
Dividends Received	3,400	$1,671,900
Cash Payments for		
Purchases	$1,041,000[2]	
Operating Expenses	427,100[3]	
Interest	55,000	
Income Taxes	32,200[4]	1,555,300
Net Cash Flows from Operating Activities		$ 116,600

1. $1,650,000 + $18,500 = $1,668,500
2. $920,000 + $100,000 + $21,000 = $1,041,000
3. $470,000 + $2,000 − $5,000 − ($12,000 + $23,100 + $4,800) = $427,100
4. $52,200 − $20,000 = $32,200

1. (b) Prepare a schedule of cash flows from operating activities using the indirect method.

Northwest Corporation
Schedule of Cash Flows from Operating Activities
For the Year Ended December 31, 19x7

Cash Flows from Operating Activities		
Net Income		$166,400
Adjustments to Reconcile Net Income to		
Net Cash Flows from Operating Activities		
Depreciation Expense, Buildings	$ 12,000	
Depreciation Expense, Equipment	23,100	
Amortization Expense, Intangible Assets	4,800	
Gain on Sale of Investments	(12,500)	
Loss on Disposal of Equipment	2,300	
Changes in Current Assets		
and Current Liabilities		
Decrease in Accounts Receivable	18,500	
Increase in Inventory	(21,000)	
Increase in Prepaid Expenses	(2,000)	
Decrease in Accounts Payable	(100,000)	
Increase in Accrued Liabilities	5,000	
Increase in Income Taxes Payable	20,000	(49,800)
Net Cash Flows from Operating Activities		$116,600

2. Prepare a statement of cash flows using the indirect method.

Northwest Corporation
Statement of Cash Flows
For the Year Ended December 31, 19x7

Cash Flows from Operating Activities

Net Income		$166,400
Adjustments to Reconcile Net Income to		
Net Cash Flows from Operating Activities		
Depreciation Expense, Buildings	$ 12,000	
Depreciation Expense, Equipment	23,100	
Amortization Expense, Intangible Assets	4,800	
Gain on Sale of Investments	(12,500)	
Loss on Disposal of Equipment	2,300	
Changes in Current Assets and		
Current Liabilities		
Decrease in Accounts Receivable	18,500	
Increase in Inventory	(21,000)	
Increase in Prepaid Expenses	(2,000)	
Decrease in Accounts Payable	(100,000)	
Increase in Accrued Liabilities	5,000	
Increase in Income Taxes Payable	20,000	(49,800)
Net Cash Flows from Operating Activities		$116,600

Cash Flows from Investing Activities

Sale of Long-Term Investments	$ 82,500[1]	
Purchase of Long-Term Investments	(20,000)	
Purchase of Land	(25,000)	
Sale of Equipment	9,900[2]	
Purchase of Equipment	(30,000)	
Net Cash Flows from Investing Activities		17,400

Cash Flows from Financing Activities

Repayment of Notes Payable	($ 100,000)	
Issuance of Notes Payable	30,000	
Reduction in Mortgage	(20,000)	
Dividends Paid	(50,000)	
Net Cash Flows from Financing Activities		(140,000)

Net Increase (Decrease) in Cash		($ 6,000)
Cash at Beginning of Year		121,850
Cash at End of Year		$115,850

Schedule of Noncash Investing and Financing Transactions

Conversion of Bonds Payable into Common Stock	$100,000

---

1. $70,000 + $12,500 (gain) = $82,500
2. $37,500 − $25,300 = $12,200 (book value) − $2,300 (loss) = $9,900

CHAPTER ASSIGNMENTS

QUESTIONS

1. In the statement of cash flows, what is the term *cash* understood to include?
2. To earn a return on cash on hand during 19x3, Sallas Corporation transferred $45,000 from its checking account to a money market account, purchased a $25,000 Treasury bill, and invested $35,000 in common stocks. How will each of these transactions affect the statement of cash flows?
3. What are the purposes of the statement of cash flows?
4. Why is the statement of cash flows needed when most of the information in it is available from a company's comparative balance sheets and the income statement?
5. What are the three classifications of cash flows? Give some examples of each.
6. Why is it important to disclose certain noncash transactions? How should they be disclosed?
7. What are the essential differences between the direct method and the indirect method of determining cash flows from operations?
8. What are the effects of the following items on net income to arrive at net cash flows from operating activities (assuming the indirect method is used): (a) an increase in accounts receivable, (b) a decrease in inventory, (c) an increase in accounts payable, (d) a decrease in wages payable, (e) depreciation expense, and (f) amortization of patents?
9. Cell-Borne Corporation has a net loss of $12,000 in 19x1 but has positive cash flows from operations of $9,000. What conditions may have caused this situation?
10. What is the proper treatment on the statement of cash flows of a transaction in which a building that cost $50,000 with accumulated depreciation of $32,000 is sold for a loss of $5,000?
11. What is the proper treatment on the statement of cash flows of (a) a transaction in which buildings and land are purchased by the issuance of a mortgage for $234,000 and (b) a conversion of $50,000 in bonds payable into 2,500 shares of $6 par value common stock?
12. Define *cash-generating efficiency* and identify three ratios that measure cash-generating efficiency.
13. Define *free cash flow* and identify its components. What does it mean to have a positive or a negative free cash flow?
14. Why is the work sheet approach considered to be more compatible with the indirect method than with the direct method of determining cash flows from operations?
15. Assuming in each of the following independent cases that only one transaction occurred, what transactions would be likely to cause (a) a decrease in investments and (b) an increase in common stock? How would each case be treated on the work sheet for the statement of cash flows?
16. Glen Corporation has the following other income and expense items: interest expense, $12,000; interest income, $3,000; dividend income, $5,000; and loss on the retirement of bonds, $6,000. How does each of these items appear on or affect the statement of cash flows, assuming the direct method is used?

SHORT EXERCISES

SE 1. *Classification of*
L O 3 *Cash Flow Transactions*
Check Figures: 1. b; 2. c; 3. a; 4. d; 5. c; 6. c

Turandot Corporation engaged in the transactions below. Identify each as (a) an operating activity, (b) an investing activity, (c) a financing activity, (d) a noncash transaction, or (e) none of the above.

1. Sold land for a gain.
2. Declared and paid a cash dividend.
3. Paid interest.
4. Issued common stock for plant assets.
5. Issued preferred stock.
6. Borrowed cash on a bank loan.

SE 2. *Computing Cash*
L O 4 *Flows from Operating Activities: Indirect Method*

Check Figure: Net Cash Flows from Operating Activities: $41,000

Grand Services Corporation had a net income of $33,000 during 19x1. During the year the company had depreciation expense of $14,000. Accounts receivable increased by $11,000 and accounts payable increased by $5,000. Those were the company's only current assets and current liabilities. Use the indirect method to determine cash flows from operating activities.

SE 3. *Computing Cash*
L O 4 *Flows from Operating Activities: Indirect Method*

Check Figure: Net Cash Flows from Operating Activities: $74,950

During 19x1, Akabah Corporation had a net income of $72,000. Included on the income statement was depreciation expense of $8,000 and amortization expense of $900. During the year, accounts receivable decreased by $4,100, inventories increased by $2,700, prepaid expenses decreased by $500, accounts payable decreased by $7,000, and accrued liabilities decreased by $850. Use the indirect method to determine cash flows from operating activities.

SE 4. *Cash Flows from*
L O 5 *Investing Activities and Noncash Transactions*

Check Figure: Net Cash Flows from Investing Activities: ($60,000)

During 19x1, Maryland Company purchased land for $750,000. It paid $250,000 in cash and signed a $500,000 mortgage for the rest. The company also sold a building that had originally cost $180,000, on which it had $140,000 of accumulated depreciation, for $190,000 cash and a gain of $150,000. Prepare the cash flows from investing activities and schedule of noncash investing and financing transactions sections of the statement of cash flows.

SE 5. *Cash Flows from*
L O 5 *Financing Activities*

Check Figure: Net Cash Flows from Financing Activities: $760,000

During 19x1, Maryland Company issued $1,000,000 in long-term bonds at 96, repaid $150,000 of bonds at face value, paid interest of $80,000, and paid dividends of $50,000. Prepare the cash flows from financing activities section of the statement of cash flows.

SE 6. *Identifying*
L O 6 *Components of the Statement of Cash Flows*

Check Figures: 1. c; 2. e; 3. a; 4. b; 5. a; 6. d; 7. c; 8. a

Assuming the indirect method is used to prepare the statement of cash flows, tell whether each item below would (a) appear as cash flows from operating activities, (b) appear as cash flows from investing activities, (c) appear as cash flows from financing activities, (d) appear in the schedule of noncash investing and financing transactions, or (e) not appear at all.

1. Dividends paid
2. Cash receipts from sales
3. Decrease in accounts receivable
4. Sale of plant assets

5. Gain on sale of investment
6. Issue of stock for plant assets
7. Issue of common stock
8. Net income

SE 7. *Cash-Generating*
L O 7 *Efficiency Ratios and Free Cash Flow*

Check Figures: Cash flow yield: 2.0 times; Free cash flow: $40,000

In 19x2, Wong Corporation had year-end assets of $550,000, net sales of $790,000, net income of $90,000, net cash from operations of $180,000, dividends of $40,000, purchases of plant assets of $120,000, and sales of plant assets of $20,000. In 19x1, year-end assets were $500,000. Calculate the cash-generating efficiency ratios of cash flow yield, cash flows to sales, and cash flows to average total assets. Also calculate free cash flow.

SE 8. *Cash Receipts from*
S O 9 *Sales and Cash Payments for Purchases: Direct Method*

Check Figures: Cash receipts from sales: $457,700; Cash payments for purchases: $304,800

During 19x2, Maine Grain Company, a marketer of whole-grain products, had sales of $426,500. The ending balance of Accounts Receivable was $127,400 in 19x1 and $96,200 in 19x2. Also, during 19x2, Maine Grain Company had cost of goods sold of $294,200. The ending balance of Inventory was $36,400 in 19x1 and $44,800 in 19x2. The ending balance of Accounts Payable was $28,100 in 19x1 and $25,900 in 19x2. Using the direct method, calculate cash receipts from sales and cash payments for purchases in 19x2.

SE 9. *Cash Payments for*
S O 9 *Operating Expenses and Income Taxes: Direct Method*

Check Figures: Cash payments for operating expenses: $58,700; Cash payments for income taxes: $13,100

During 19x2, Maine Grain Company had operating expenses of $79,000 and income taxes expense of $12,500. Depreciation expense of $20,000 for 19x2 was included in operating expenses. The ending balance of Prepaid Expenses was $3,600 in 19x1 and $2,300 in 19x2. The ending balance of Accrued Liabilities (excluding Income Taxes Payable) was $3,000 in 19x1 and $2,000 in 19x2. The ending balance of Income Taxes Payable was $4,100 in 19x1 and $3,500 in 19x2. Calculate cash payments for operating expenses and income taxes in 19x2.

SE 10.
S O 9
Preparing a Schedule of Cash Flows from Operating Activities: Direct Method
Check Figure: Net Cash Flows from Operating Activities: $7,400

The income statement for the Trumbull Corporation follows.

Trumbull Corporation
Income Statement
For the Year Ended June 30, 19xx

Net Sales		$60,000
Cost of Goods Sold		30,000
Gross Margin		$30,000
Operating Expenses		
Salaries Expense	$16,000	
Rent Expense	8,400	
Depreciation Expense	1,000	25,400
Income Before Income Taxes		$ 4,600
Income Taxes		1,200
Net Income		$ 3,400

Additional information: (a) All sales were on credit, and accounts receivable increased by $2,000 during the year. (b) All merchandise purchased was on credit. Inventories increased by $3,000, and accounts payable increased by $7,000 during the year. (c) Prepaid rent decreased by $700, and salaries payable increased by $500. (d) Income taxes payable decreased by $200 during the year. Using the direct method, prepare a schedule of cash flows from operating activities.

EXERCISES

E 1.
L O 3
Classification of Cash Flow Transactions
Check Figures: (a) 3, 4, 7, 11; (b) 2, 5, 13; (c) 1, 8, 10; (d) 6, 9; (e) 12

Horizon Corporation engaged in the following transactions. Identify each as (a) an operating activity, (b) an investing activity, (c) a financing activity, (d) a noncash transaction, or (e) none of the above.

1. Declared and paid a cash dividend.
2. Purchased a long-term investment.
3. Received cash from customers.
4. Paid interest.
5. Sold equipment at a loss.
6. Issued long-term bonds for plant assets.
7. Received dividends on securities held.
8. Issued common stock.
9. Declared and issued a stock dividend.
10. Repaid notes payable.
11. Paid employees their wages.
12. Purchased a 60-day Treasury bill.
13. Purchased land.

E 2.
L O 4
Cash Flows from Operating Activities: Indirect Method
Check Figure: Net Cash Flows from Operating Activities: $820,000

The condensed single-step income statement of Union Chemical Company, a distributor of farm fertilizers and herbicides, appears as follows:

Sales		$6,500,000
Less: Cost of Goods Sold	$3,800,000	
Operating Expenses (including depreciation of $410,000)	1,900,000	
Income Taxes	200,000	5,900,000
Net Income		$ 600,000

Selected accounts from the company's balance sheets for 19x1 and 19x2 appear as shown below:

	19x2	19x1	
Accounts Receivable	$1,200,000	$850,000	+ 350
Inventory	420,000	510,000	− 90
Prepaid Expenses	130,000	90,000	+ 40
Accounts Payable	480,000	360,000	+ 120
Accrued Liabilities	30,000	50,000	− 20
Income Taxes Payable	70,000	60,000	+ 10

Use the indirect method to prepare a schedule of cash flows from operating activities.

E 3.
L O 4
Computing Cash Flows from Operating Activities: Indirect Method
Check Figure: Net Cash Flows from Operating Activities: $46,850

During 19x1, Mayfair Corporation had a net income of $41,000. Included on the income statement was depreciation expense of $2,300 and amortization expense of $300. During the year, accounts receivable increased by $3,400, inventories decreased by $1,900, prepaid expenses decreased by $200, accounts payable increased by $5,000, and accrued liabilities decreased by $450. Use the indirect method to determine cash flows from operating activities.

E 4.
L O 4
Preparing a Schedule of Cash Flows from Operating Activities: Indirect Method
Check Figure: Net Cash Flows from Operating Activities: $13,800

For the year ended June 30, 19xx, net income for BJR Corporation was $7,400. The following is additional information: (a) depreciation expense was $2,000; (b) all sales were on credit, and accounts receivable increased by $4,400 during the year; (c) all merchandise purchased was on credit; inventories increased by $7,000, and accounts payable increased by $14,000 during the year; (d) prepaid rent decreased by $1,400, and salaries payable increased by $1,000; and (e) income taxes payable decreased by $600 during the year. Use the indirect method to prepare a schedule of cash flows from operating activities.

E 5.
L O 5
Computing Cash Flows from Investing Activities: Investments
Check Figure: Net cash inflow from sale: $32,500

Krieger Company's T account for long-term available-for-sale investments at the end of 19x3 is shown below.

Investments			
Beg. Bal.	68,500	Sales	39,000
Purchases	58,000		
End. Bal.	**87,500**		

In addition, Krieger's income statement shows a loss on the sale of investments of $6,500. Compute the amounts to be shown as cash flows from investing activities and show how they are to appear on the statement of cash flows.

E 6.
L O 5
Computing Cash Flows from Investing Activities: Plant Assets
Check Figure: Cash inflow from sale of plant assets: $12,700

The T accounts for plant assets and accumulated depreciation for Krieger Company at the end of 19x3 are as follows:

Plant Assets			
Beg. Bal.	65,000	Disposal	23,000
Purchases	33,600		
End. Bal.	**75,600**		

Accumulated Depreciation			
Disposal	14,700	Beg. Bal.	34,500
		19x3	
		Depreciation	10,200
		End. Bal.	**30,000**

In addition, Krieger Company's income statement shows a gain on sale of plant assets of $4,400. Compute the amounts to be shown as cash flows from investing activities and show how they are to appear on the statement of cash flows.

E 7. *Determining Cash*
L O 5 *Flows from Investing and Financing Activities*

Check Figure: Net Cash Flows from Financing Activities: $13,000

All transactions involving Notes Payable and related accounts engaged in by Krieger Company during 19x3 are as follows:

Cash	18,000	
Notes Payable		18,000
Bank loan		
Patent	30,000	
Notes Payable		30,000
Purchase of patent by issuing note payable		
Notes Payable	5,000	
Interest Expense	500	
Cash		5,500
Repayment of note payable at maturity		

Determine the amounts and how these transactions are to be shown in the statement of cash flows for 19x3.

E 8. *Preparing the*
L O 6 *Statement of Cash Flows: Indirect Method*

Check Figures: Net Cash Flows from: Operating Activities, $45,000; Investing Activities, $11,700; Financing Activities, $700

Javier Corporation's 19x2 net income was $17,900. Its comparative balance sheets for June 30, 19x2 and 19x1 follow.

Javier Corporation
Comparative Balance Sheets
June 30, 19x2 and 19x1

	19x2	19x1
Assets		
Cash	$ 69,900	$ 12,500
Accounts Receivable (net)	21,000	26,000
Inventory	43,400	48,400
Prepaid Expenses	3,200	2,600
Furniture	55,000	60,000
Accumulated Depreciation, Furniture	(9,000)	(5,000)
Total Assets	$183,500	$144,500
Liabilities and Stockholders' Equity		
Accounts Payable	$ 13,000	$ 14,000
Income Taxes Payable	1,200	1,800
Notes Payable (long-term)	37,000	35,000
Common Stock—$10 par value	115,000	90,000
Retained Earnings	17,300	3,700
Total Liabilities and Stockholders' Equity	$183,500	$144,500

Additional information: (a) Issued a $22,000 note payable for the purchase of furniture; (b) sold furniture that cost $27,000 with accumulated depreciation of $15,300 at carrying value; (c) recorded depreciation on the furniture during the year, $19,300; (d) repaid a note in the amount of $20,000 and issued $25,000 of common stock at par value; and (e) declared and paid dividends of $4,300. Without using a work sheet, prepare a statement of cash flows for 19x2 using the indirect method.

E 9. *Cash-Generating*
L O 7 *Efficiency Ratios and Free Cash Flow*

Check Figure: Free cash flow: ($140,000)

In 19x2, Kenetics Corporation had year-end assets of $2,400,000, net sales of $3,300,000, net income of $280,000, net cash from operations of $390,000, dividends of $120,000, and net capital expenditures of $410,000. In 19x1, year-end assets were $2,100,000. Calculate the cash-generating efficiency ratios of cash flow yield, cash flows to sales, and cash flows to average total assets. Also calculate free cash flow.

E 10. *Preparing a Work*
L O 6 *Sheet for the State-*
S O 8 *ment of Cash Flows*
Check Figure: Same as E 8

Using the information in E 8, prepare a work sheet for the statement of cash flows for Javier Corporation for 19x2. Based on the work sheet, use the indirect method to prepare a statement of cash flows.

E 11. *Computing Cash*
S O 9 *Flows from*
Operating Activities:
Direct Method
Check Figures: a. $182,300;
b. $135,800; c. $25,100; d. $4,530

Europa Corporation engaged in the following transactions in 19x2. Using the direct method, compute the cash flows from operating activities as required.

a. During 19x2, Europa Corporation had cash sales of $41,300 and sales on credit of $123,000. During the same year, Accounts Receivable decreased by $18,000. Determine the cash received from customers during 19x2.

b. During 19x2, Europa Corporation's cost of goods sold was $119,000. During the same year, Merchandise Inventory increased by $12,500 and Accounts Payable decreased by $4,300. Determine the cash payments for purchases during 19x2.

c. During 19x2, Europa Corporation had operating expenses of $45,000, including depreciation of $15,600. Also during 19x2, related prepaid expenses decreased by $3,100 and relevant accrued liabilities increased by $1,200. Determine the cash payments for operating expenses to suppliers of goods and services during 19x2.

d. Europa Corporation's Income Taxes Expense for 19x2 was $4,300. Income Taxes Payable decreased by $230 that year. Determine the cash payment for income taxes during 19x2.

E 12. *Preparing a Schedule*
S O 9 *of Cash Flows from*
Operating Activities:
Direct Method
Check Figure: Net Cash Flows from Operating Activities: $7,600

The income statement for the Ridge Corporation appears below. The following is additional information: (a) All sales were on credit, and Accounts Receivable increased by $2,200 during the year; (b) all merchandise purchased was on credit; inventories increased by $3,500, and Accounts Payable increased by $7,000 during the year; (c) Prepaid Rent decreased by $700, while Salaries Payable increased by $500; and (d) Income Taxes Payable decreased by $300 during the year. Using the direct method, prepare a schedule of cash flows from operating activities.

Ridge Corporation
Income Statement
For the Year Ended June 30, 19xx

Sales		$61,000
Cost of Goods Sold		30,000
Gross Margin		$31,000
Other Expenses		
Salaries Expense	$16,000	
Rent Expense	8,400	
Depreciation Expense	1,000	25,400
Income Before Income Taxes		$ 5,600
Income Taxes		1,200
Net Income		$ 4,400

SKILLS DEVELOPMENT EXERCISES

Conceptual Analysis

SDE 1. *Direct Versus*
L O 4 *Indirect Method*

No check figure

Compaq Computer Corporation, a leading manufacturer of personal computers, uses the direct method of presenting cash flows from operating activities in its statement of cash flows.[9] As noted in the text, 97 percent of large companies use the indirect method. Explain the difference between the direct and indirect methods of presenting

9. American Institute of Certified Public Accountants, *Accounting Trends & Techniques* (New York: AICPA, 1993), p. 452.

cash flows from operating activities. Then choose either the direct or the indirect method and tell why it is the best way of presenting cash flows from operations. Be prepared to discuss your opinion in class.

SDE 2. *Cash-Generating*
L O 7 *Efficiency and Free*
Cash Flow

⟳ ⬡

Check Figures: Cash flow yield: 1991, 3.2 times; 1992, 0.8 times; Free cash flow: 1991, $426,422; 1992, ($32,780)

The statement of cash flows for **Tandy Corporation,** the owner of Radio Shack and other retail store chains, appears on the next page. For the two years shown, compute the cash-generating efficiency ratios of cash flow yield, cash flows to sales, and cash flows to average total assets. Also compute free cash flow for the two years. Assess Tandy's cash-generating efficiency and evaluate its available free cash flow in light of its financing activities. Were there any special operating circumstances that should be taken into consideration? Is the concept of free cash flow a useful one in light of your evaluation? Be prepared to discuss your analysis in class. The following data come from the supplemental information in Tandy's annual report.

	1992	1991	1990
Net Sales	$4,680,156	$4,561,782	$4,499,604
Total Assets	$3,165,164	$3,078,145	$3,239,980

Ethical Dilemma

SDE 3. *Ethics and Cash*
L O 3 *Flow Classifications*

🏛 ⟳ ⬡

No check figure

Chemical Waste Treatment, Inc. is a fast-growing company that disposes of chemical wastes. The company has an $800,000 line of credit at its bank. One covenant in the loan agreement stipulates that the ratio of cash flows from operations to interest expense must exceed 3.0. If this ratio falls below 3.0, the company must pay down the balance outstanding on its line of credit to one-half if the funds borrowed against the line of credit currently exceed that amount. After the end of the fiscal year, the controller informs the president: "We will not meet the ratio requirements on our line of credit in 19x2 because interest expense was $1.2 million and cash flows from operations were $3.2 million. Also, we have borrowed 100 percent of our line of credit. We do not have the cash to reduce the credit line by $400,000." The president says, "This is a serious situation. To pay our ongoing bills, we need our bank to increase our line of credit, not decrease it. What can we do?" "Do you recall the $500,000 two-year note payable for equipment?" replied the controller. "It is now classified as 'Proceeds from Notes Payable' in cash flows provided from financing activities in the statement of cash flows. If we move it to cash flows from operations and call it 'Increase in Payables,' it would put us over the limit at $3.7 million." "Well, do it," ordered the president. "It surely doesn't make any difference where it is on the statement. It is an increase in both places. It would be much worse for our company in the long term if we failed to meet this ratio requirement." What is your opinion of the president's reasoning? Is the president's order ethical? Who is benefited and who is harmed if the controller follows the president's order? What are management's alternatives? What would you do?

Research Activity

SDE 4. *Basic Research Skills*
L O 7

⟳ ⬡

No check figure

In your library, select the annual reports of three corporations. You may choose them from the same industry or at random, at the direction of your instructor. (If you did a related exercise in a previous chapter, use the same three companies.) Prepare a table with a column for each corporation. Then, for any year covered by the statement of cash flows, answer the following questions: Does the company use the direct or the indirect approach? Is net income more or less than net cash flows from operating activities? What are the major causes of differences between net income and net cash flows from operating activities? Compute cash flow efficiency ratios and free cash flow. Does the dividend appear secure? Did the company make significant capital expenditures during the year? How were the expenditures financed? Do you notice anything unusual about the investing and financing activities of your companies? Do the investing and financing activities provide any insights into management's plan for each company? If so, what are they? Be prepared to discuss your findings in class.

Tandy Corporation
Statements of Cash Flows
Years Ended June 30,
(in thousands)

	1992	1991
Cash flows from operating activities		
Net income...................................	**$183,847**	$195,444
Adjustments to reconcile net income to net cash provided by operating activities:		
Cumulative effect on prior years of change in accounting principle, net of taxes...........	**—**	10,619
Depreciation and amortization..............	**103,281**	99,698
Deferred income taxes and other items......	**9,302**	(29,633)
Provision for credit losses and bad debts	**67,388**	60,643
Gain on sale of subsidiary, assets of which were primarily real estate..................	**(18,987)**	—
Changes in operating assets and liabilities, excluding the effect of businesses acquired:		
Securitization of customer receivables.....	**—**	350,000
Receivables	**(121,719)**	(256,445)
Inventories	**(89,441)**	151,339
Other current assets.......................	**(2,955)**	(2,028)
Accounts payable, accrued expenses and income taxes	**16,066**	37,716
Net cash provided by operating activities	**146,782**	617,353
Investing activities		
Additions to property, plant and equipment, net of retirements............................	**(123,430)**	(139,453)
Proceeds from sale of subsidiary, assets of which were primarily real estate	**20,293**	—
Acquisition of Victor Technologies	**—**	—
Payment received on InterTAN note............	**—**	—
Other investing activities	**947**	(1,046)
Net cash used by investing activities	**(102,190)**	(140,499)
Financing activities		
Purchases of treasury stock....................	**(527,773)**	(83,086)
Sales of treasury stock to employee stock purchase program	**49,590**	50,383
Issuance of Series C PERCS....................	**429,982**	—
Issuance of preferred stock to TESOP	**—**	100,000
Dividends paid, net of taxes	**(56,132)**	(51,478)
Changes in short-term borrowings—net	**57,533**	(598,763)
Additions to long-term borrowings	**21,071**	210,167
Repayments of long-term borrowings..........	**(98,702)**	(52,981)
Net cash provided (used) by financing activities	**(124,431)**	(425,758)
Increase (decrease) in cash and short-term investments	**(79,839)**	51,096
Cash and short-term investments at the beginning of the year	**186,293**	135,197
Cash and short-term investments at the end of the year	**$106,454**	$186,293

Decision-Making Practice

SDE 5. *Analysis of Cash*
L O 6, 7 *Flow Difficulty*

Check Figure: 1. Net Cash Flows from Operating Activities: $16,000

Bernadette Adams, the president of **Adams Print Gallery, Inc.,** is examining the income statement for 19x2, which has just been handed to her by her accountant, Jason Rosenberg, CPA. After looking at the statement, Ms. Adams says to Mr. Rosenberg, "Jason, the statement seems to be well done, but what I need to know is why I don't have enough cash to pay my bills this month. You show that I have earned $60,000 in 19x2, but I only have $12,000 in the bank. I know I bought a building on a mortgage and paid a cash dividend of $24,000, but what else is going on?" Mr. Rosenberg replies, "To answer your question, Bernadette, we have to look at comparative balance sheets and prepare another type of statement. Here, take a look at these balance sheets." The income statement and comparative balance sheets handed to Ms. Adams follow.

Adams Print Gallery, Inc.
Income Statement
For the Year Ended December 31, 19x2

Net Sales	$442,000
Cost of Goods Sold	254,000
Gross Margin	$188,000
Operating Expenses (including Depreciation Expense of $10,000)	102,000
Operating Income	$ 86,000
Interest Expense	12,000
Income Before Income Taxes	$ 74,000
Income Taxes	14,000
Net Income	$ 60,000

Adams Print Gallery, Inc.
Comparative Balance Sheets
December 31, 19x2 and 19x1

	19x2	19x1
Assets		
Cash	$ 12,000	$ 20,000
Accounts Receivable (net)	89,000	73,000
Inventory	120,000	90,000
Prepaid Expenses	5,000	7,000
Building	200,000	—
Accumulated Depreciation	(10,000)	—
Total Assets	$416,000	$190,000
Liabilities and Stockholders' Equity		
Accounts Payable	$ 37,000	$ 48,000
Income Taxes Payable	3,000	2,000
Mortgage Payable	200,000	—
Common Stock	100,000	100,000
Retained Earnings	76,000	40,000
Total Liabilities and Stockholders' Equity	$416,000	$190,000

1. Which statement does Mr. Rosenberg have in mind when he refers to "another type of statement"? From the information given, use the indirect method to prepare the additional statement.
2. Adams Print Gallery, Inc. has a cash problem despite profitable operations. Why?

PROBLEM SET A

A 1. *Classification of*
L O 3 *Transactions*

No check figure

Analyze each transaction in the following schedule and place an *X* in the appropriate columns to indicate its classification and its effect on cash flows when the indirect method is used.

Transaction	Operating Activity	Investing Activity	Financing Activity	Noncash Transaction	Increase	Decrease	No Effect
	Cash Flow Classification				**Effect on Cash**		
1. Incurred a net loss.	1			2 Not on CF Statement		1	2
2. Declared and issued a stock dividend.							
3. Paid a cash dividend.			3			3	
4. Collected accounts receivable.	4				4		
5. Purchased inventory with cash.	5					5	
6. Retired long-term debt with cash.			6			6	
7. Sold available-for-sale securities for a loss. Current Asset	7				7		
8. Issued stock for equipment.				8			8
9. Purchased a one-year insurance policy for cash.	9					9	
10. Purchased treasury stock with cash.			10			10	
11. Retired a fully depreciated truck (no gain or loss).				11 not on CF Statement		12	11
12. Paid interest on note.	12						
13. Received cash dividend on investment.	13				13		
14. Sold treasury stock.			14		14		
15. Paid income taxes.	15					15	
16. Transferred cash to money market account.				16 Not on CF Statement			16
17. Purchased land and building with a mortgage.				17			17

A 2. *Cash Flows from*
L O 4 *Operating Activities:*
Indirect Method

Check Figure: Net Cash Flows from Operating Activities: ($25,900)

Net income for Jefferson Corporation for the year ended December 31, 19xx, was $26,500. The following additional information is available: (a) Depreciation expense is $18,000 and amortization expense (intangible assets) is $1,500; (b) Accounts Receivable (net) increased by $18,000 and Accounts Payable decreased by $26,000 during the year; (c) inventory increased by $30,000 from last year; (d) salaries payable at the end of the year were $7,000 more than last year; (e) the expired amount of prepaid insurance for the year is $500 and equals the decrease in the Prepaid Insurance account; and (f) Income Taxes Payable decreased by $5,400 from last year.

REQUIRED

Using the indirect method, prepare a schedule of cash flows from operating activities.

A 3. *Cash Flows from*
L O 4 *Operating Activities: Indirect Method*

Check Figure: Net Cash Flows from Operating Activities: $59,490

Gardner Electronics, Inc. had net income of $51,400 and depreciation expense of $21,430. The company also had a $12,100 loss on the sale of investments during 19x3. Relevant accounts from the comparative balance sheets for February 28, 19x3 and 19x2 are as follows:

	19x3	19x2
Accounts Receivable (net)	$65,490	$ 48,920
Inventory	98,760	102,560
Prepaid Expenses	10,450	5,490
Accounts Payable	42,380	55,690
Accrued Liabilities	3,560	8,790
Income Taxes Payable	24,630	13,800

16570
- 3800
4960
- 13310
- 5230
10830

REQUIRED

Prepare a schedule of cash flows from operating activities using the indirect method.

A 4. *The Statement of*
L O 6, 7 *Cash Flows: Indirect Method*

Check Figures: 1. Net Cash Flows from: Operating Activities, $63,300; Investing Activities, ($12,900); Financing Activities, $7,000

Meridian Corporation's comparative balance sheets as of December 31, 19x2 and 19x1 and its income statement for the year ended December 31, 19x2 follow.

Meridian Corporation
Comparative Balance Sheets
December 31, 19x2 and 19x1

	19x2	19x1
Assets		
Cash	$ 82,400	$ 25,000 +57400
Accounts Receivable (net)	82,600	100,000 -17400
Merchandise Inventory	175,000	225,000 -50,000
Prepaid Rent	1,000	1,500 - 500
Furniture and Fixtures	74,000	72,000 + 2000
Accumulated Depreciation, Furniture and Fixtures	(21,000)	(12,000) +9000
Total Assets	$394,000	$411,500 -17500
Liabilities and Stockholders' Equity		
Accounts Payable	$ 71,700	$100,200 -28,500
Notes Payable (long-term)	20,000	10,000 + 10,000
Bonds Payable	50,000	100,000 - 50,000
Income Taxes Payable	700	2,200 - 1500
Common Stock—$10 par value	120,000	100,000 + 20,000
Paid-in Capital in Excess of Par Value	90,720	60,720 +30,000
Retained Earnings	40,880	38,380 + 2500
Total Liabilities and Stockholders' Equity	$394,000	$411,500 - 17500

Meridian Corporation
Income Statement
For the Year Ended December 31, 19x2

Net Sales		$804,500
Cost of Goods Sold		563,900
Gross Margin		$240,600
Operating Expenses (including Depreciation		
Expense of $23,400)		224,700
Income from Operations		$ 15,900
Other Income (Expenses)		
Gain on Disposal of Furniture and Fixtures	$ 3,500	
Interest Expense	(11,600)	(8,100)
Income Before Income Taxes		$ 7,800
Income Taxes		2,300
Net Income		$ 5,500

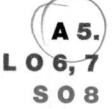

Additional information about 19x2: (a) Furniture and fixtures that cost $17,800 with accumulated depreciation of $14,400 were sold at a gain of $3,500; (b) furniture and fixtures were purchased in the amount of $19,800; (c) a $10,000 note payable was paid and $20,000 was borrowed on a new note; (d) bonds payable in the amount of $50,000 were converted into 2,000 shares of common stock; and (e) $3,000 in cash dividends were declared and paid.

REQUIRED

1. Using the indirect method, prepare a statement of cash flows. Include a supporting schedule of noncash investing and financing transactions. (Do not use a work sheet.)
2. What are the primary reasons for Meridian Corporation's large increase in cash from 19x1 to 19x2, despite its low net income?
3. Compute and assess cash flow yield and free cash flow for 19x2.

A 5.
LO 6, 7
SO 8
The Work Sheet and the Statement of Cash Flows: Indirect Method

Check Figures: 2. Net Cash Flows from: Operating Activities, ($32,600); Investing Activities, ($7,200); Financing Activities, $51,000

The comparative balance sheets for Gregory Fabrics, Inc. for December 31, 19x3 and 19x2 appear on the next page. Additional information about Gregory Fabrics' operations during 19x3: (a) net loss, $28,000; (b) building and equipment depreciation expense amounts, $15,000 and $3,000, respectively; (c) equipment that cost $13,500 with accumulated depreciation of $12,500 sold for a gain of $5,300; (d) equipment purchases, $12,500; (e) patent amortization, $3,000; purchase of patent, $1,000; (f) funds borrowed by issuing notes payable, $25,000; notes payable repaid, $15,000; (g) land and building purchased for $162,000 by signing a mortgage for the total cost; (h) 3,000 shares of $10 par value common stock issued for a total of $50,000; and (i) cash dividend distributed, $9,000.

REQUIRED

1. Prepare a work sheet for the statement of cash flows for Gregory Fabrics.
2. Based on the information in the work sheet, use the indirect method to prepare a statement of cash flows.
3. Why did Gregory Fabrics have an increase in Cash in a year in which it recorded a net loss of $28,000? Discuss and interpret.
4. Compute and assess cash flow yield and free cash flow for 19x3.

Gregory Fabrics, Inc.
Comparative Balance Sheets
December 31, 19x3 and 19x2

	19x3	19x2
Assets		
Cash	$ 38,560	$ 27,360
Accounts Receivable (net)	102,430	75,430
Inventory	112,890	137,890
Prepaid Expenses	—	20,000
Land	25,000	—
Building	137,000	—
Accumulated Depreciation, Building	(15,000)	—
Equipment	33,000	34,000
Accumulated Depreciation, Equipment	(14,500)	(24,000)
Patents	4,000	6,000
Total Assets	$423,380	$276,680
Liabilities and Stockholders' Equity		
Accounts Payable	$ 10,750	$ 36,750
Notes Payable	10,000	—
Accrued Liabilities (current)	—	12,300
Mortgage Payable	162,000	—
Common Stock—$10 par value	180,000	150,000
Paid-in Capital in Excess of Par Value	57,200	37,200
Retained Earnings	3,430	40,430
Total Liabilities and Stockholders' Equity	$423,380	$276,680

A 6. *Cash Flows from*
S O 9 *Operating Activities:*
Direct Method

Check Figure: Net Cash Flows from Operating Activities: ($25,900)

The income statement for Milos Food Corporation is as follows:

Milos Food Corporation
Income Statement
For the Year Ended December 31, 19xx

Net Sales		$490,000
Cost of Goods Sold		
Beginning Inventory	$220,000	
Net Cost of Purchases	400,000	
Goods Available for Sale	$620,000	
Ending Inventory	250,000	
Cost of Goods Sold		370,000
Gross Margin		$120,000
Selling and Administrative Expenses		
Selling and Administrative Salaries Expense	$ 50,000	
Other Selling and Administrative Expenses	11,500	
Depreciation Expense	18,000	
Amortization Expense (Intangible Assets)	1,500	81,000
Income Before Income Taxes		$ 39,000
Income Taxes		12,500
Net Income		$ 26,500

Additional information: (a) Accounts Receivable (net) increased by $18,000 and Accounts Payable decreased by $26,000 during the year; (b) salaries payable at the end of the year were $7,000 more than last year; (c) the expired amount of prepaid insurance for the year is $500 and equals the decrease in the Prepaid Insurance account; and (d) Income Taxes Payable decreased by $5,400 from last year.

REQUIRED

Using the direct method, prepare a schedule of cash flows from operating activities.

A 7. *Statement of Cash*
S O 9 *Flows: Direct Method*

Use the information for Meridian Corporation given in A 4 to complete the following requirements.

REQUIRED

Check Figure: Same as A 4.

1. Use the direct method to prepare a statement of cash flows. Include a supporting schedule of noncash investing and financing transactions. (Do not use a work sheet.)
2. Answer requirements **2** and **3** in A 4 if that problem was not assigned.

PROBLEM SET B

B 1. *Classification of*
L O 3 *Transactions*
No check figure

Analyze each transaction in the following schedule and place an X in the appropriate columns to indicate its classification and its effect on cash flows when the indirect method is used.

	Cash Flow Classification				Effect on Cash		
Transaction	Operating Activity	Investing Activity	Financing Activity	Noncash Transaction	Increase	Decrease	No Effect
1. Earned a net income.							
2. Declared and paid cash dividend.							
3. Issued stock for cash.							
4. Retired long-term debt by issuing stock.							
5. Paid accounts payable.							
6. Purchased inventory with cash.							
7. Purchased a one-year insurance policy with cash.							
8. Purchased a long-term investment with cash.							
9. Sold trading securities at a gain.							
10. Sold a machine at a loss.							
11. Retired fully depreciated equipment.							
12. Paid interest on debt.							
13. Purchased available-for-sale securities (long-term).							
14. Received dividend income.							
15. Received cash on account.							
16. Converted bonds to common stock.							
17. Purchased ninety-day Treasury bill.							

B 2. *Cash Flows from*
L O 4 *Operating Activities:*
Indirect Method

Check Figure: Net Cash Flows from
Operating Activities: $23,800

Net income for Falcone Clothing Store for the year ended June 30, 19xx, was $103,000. The following additional information is available: (a) Depreciation expense was $52,000 and amortization expense was $18,000; (b) inventory was $80,000 more than the previous year; (c) accrued liabilities for salaries were $12,000 less than the previous year and prepaid expenses were $20,000 more than the previous year; and (d) during the year Accounts Receivable (net) increased by $144,000, Accounts Payable increased by $114,000, and Income Taxes Payable decreased by $7,200.

REQUIRED

Using the indirect method, prepare a schedule of cash flows from operating activities.

B 3. *Cash Flows from*
L O 4 *Operating Activities:*
Indirect Method

Check Figure: Net Cash Flows from
Operating Activities: $98,970

Net income for Malamud Greeting Card Company was $69,500, depreciation expense was $21,430, and there was a loss on the sale of investments of $5,800. Relevant accounts from the balance sheet for December 31, 19x2 and 19x1 are as follows:

	19x2	19x1
Accounts Receivable (net)	$18,530	$23,670
Inventory	39,640	34,990
Prepaid Expenses	2,400	8,900
Accounts Payable	34,940	22,700
Accrued Liabilities	4,690	8,830
Income Taxes Payable	4,750	17,600

REQUIRED

Using the indirect method, prepare a schedule of cash flows from operating activities.

B 4. *The Statement of*
L O 6, 7 *Cash Flows: Indirect*
Method

Check Figures: 1. Net Cash Flows from: Operating Activities, $274,000; Investing Activities, $3,000; Financing Activities, ($130,000)

Plath Corporation's comparative balance sheets as of June 30, 19x7 and 19x6 and its 19x7 income statement appear as follows:

Plath Corporation
Comparative Balance Sheets
June 30, 19x7 and 19x6

	19x7	19x6
Assets		
Cash	$167,000	$ 20,000
Accounts Receivable (net)	100,000	120,000
Finished Goods Inventory	180,000	220,000
Prepaid Expenses	600	1,000
Property, Plant, and Equipment	628,000	552,000
Accumulated Depreciation, Property, Plant, and Equipment	(183,000)	(140,000)
Total Assets	$892,600	$773,000
Liabilities and Stockholders' Equity		
Accounts Payable	$ 64,000	$ 42,000
Notes Payable (due in 90 days)	30,000	80,000
Income Taxes Payable	26,000	18,000
Mortgage Payable	360,000	280,000
Common Stock—$5 par value	200,000	200,000
Retained Earnings	212,600	153,000
Total Liabilities and Stockholders' Equity	$892,600	$773,000

Plath Corporation
Income Statement
For the Year Ended June 30, 19x7

Net Sales		$1,040,900
Cost of Goods Sold		656,300
Gross Margin		$ 384,600
Operating Expenses (including Depreciation Expense of $60,000)		189,200
Income from Operations		$ 195,400
Other Income (Expenses)		
Loss on Disposal of Equipment	($ 4,000)	
Interest Expense	(37,600)	(41,600)
Income Before Income Taxes		$ 153,800
Income Taxes		34,200
Net Income		$ 119,600

Additional information about 19x7: (a) Equipment that cost $24,000 with accumulated depreciation of $17,000 was sold at a loss of $4,000; (b) land and building were purchased in the amount of $100,000 through an increase of $100,000 in the mortgage payable; (c) a $20,000 payment was made on the mortgage; (d) the notes were repaid, but the company borrowed an additional $30,000 through the issuance of a new note payable; and (e) a $60,000 cash dividend was declared and paid.

REQUIRED

1. Using the indirect method, prepare a statement of cash flows. Include a supporting schedule of noncash investing and financing transactions. (Do not use a work sheet.)
2. What are the primary reasons for Plath Corporation's large increase in cash from 19x6 to 19x7?
3. Compute and assess cash flow yield and free cash flow for 19x7.

B 5.
L O 6, 7
S O 8
The Work Sheet and the Statement of Cash Flows: Indirect Method

Check Figures: 2. Net Cash Flows from: Operating Activities, ($53,000); Investing Activities, $17,000; Financing Activities, $22,000

The comparative balance sheets for Willis Ceramics, Inc. for December 31, 19x3 and 19x2 are presented on the next page. Additional information about Willis Ceramics' operations during 19x3: (a) Net income was $48,000; (b) building and equipment depreciation expense amounts were $40,000 and $30,000, respectively; (c) intangible assets were amortized in the amount of $10,000; (d) investments in the amounts of $58,000 were purchased; (e) investments were sold for $75,000, on which a gain of $17,000 was made; (f) the company issued $120,000 in long-term bonds at face value; (g) a small warehouse building with the accompanying land was purchased through the issue of a $160,000 mortgage; (h) the company paid $20,000 to reduce mortgage payable during 19x7; (i) the company borrowed funds in the amount of $30,000 by issuing notes payable and repaid notes payable in the amount of $90,000; and (j) cash dividends in the amount of $18,000 were declared and paid.

REQUIRED

1. Prepare a work sheet for the statement of cash flows for Willis Ceramics.
2. Based on the information in the work sheet, use the indirect method to prepare a statement of cash flows. Include a supporting schedule of noncash investing and financing transactions.
3. Why did Willis Ceramics experience a decrease in cash in a year in which it had a net income of $48,000? Discuss and interpret.
4. Compute and assess cash flow yield and free cash flow for 19x3.

Willis Ceramics, Inc.
Comparative Balance Sheets
December 31, 19x3 and 19x2

	19x3	19x2
Assets		
Cash	$ 138,800	$ 152,800
Accounts Receivable (net)	369,400	379,400
Inventory	480,000	400,000
Prepaid Expenses	7,400	13,400
Long-Term Investments (available-for-sale)	220,000	220,000
Land	180,600	160,600
Building	600,000	460,000
Accumulated Depreciation, Building	(120,000)	(80,000)
Equipment	240,000	240,000
Accumulated Depreciation, Equipment	(58,000)	(28,000)
Intangible Assets	10,000	20,000
Total Assets	$2,068,200	$1,938,200
Liabilities and Stockholders' Equity		
Accounts Payable	$ 235,400	$ 330,400
Notes Payable (current)	20,000	80,000
Accrued Liabilities	5,400	10,400
Mortgage Payable	540,000	400,000
Bonds Payable	500,000	380,000
Common Stock	600,000	600,000
Paid-in Capital in Excess of Par Value	40,000	40,000
Retained Earnings	127,400	97,400
Total Liabilities and Stockholders' Equity	$2,068,200	$1,938,200

B 6. *Cash Flows from*
S O 9 *Operating Activities:*
Direct Method

Check Figure: Net Cash Flows from Operating Activities: $23,800

The income statement for Falcone Clothing Store is presented on the next page. Additional information: (a) Other sales and administrative expenses include depreciation expense of $52,000 and amortization expense of $18,000; (b) accrued liabilities for salaries were $12,000 less than the previous year and prepaid expenses were $20,000 more than the previous year; and (c) during the year Accounts Receivable (net) increased by $144,000, Accounts Payable increased by $114,000, and Income Taxes Payable decreased by $7,200.

REQUIRED

Using the direct method, prepare a schedule of cash flows from operating activities.

Falcone Clothing Store
Income Statement
For the Year Ended June 30, 19xx

Net Sales		$2,450,000
Cost of Goods Sold		
Beginning Inventory	$ 620,000	
Net Cost of Purchases	1,520,000	
Goods Available for Sale	$2,140,000	
Ending Inventory	700,000	
Cost of Goods Sold		1,440,000
Gross Margin		$1,010,000
Operating Expenses		
Sales and Administrative Salaries Expense	$ 556,000	
Other Sales and Administrative Expenses	312,000	
Total Operating Expenses		868,000
Income Before Income Taxes		$ 142,000
Income Taxes		39,000
Net Income		$ 103,000

B 7.
S O 9 *The Statement of Cash Flows: Direct Method*

REQUIRED

Check Figure: Same as B 4.

Use the information for Plath Corporation given in Problem B 4 to answer the requirements below.

1. Prepare a statement of cash flows using the direct method. Include a supporting schedule for noncash investing and financing transactions. (Do not use a work sheet.)
2. Answer requirements **2** and **3** in B 4 if that problem was not assigned.

FINANCIAL REPORTING AND ANALYSIS CASES

Interpreting Financial Reports

FRA 1.
L O 7 *Analysis of the Statement of Cash Flows*

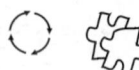

Check Figures: 2. Cash flow yield: 1990, 3.3 times; 1991, 4.3 times; 1992, 20.4 times; 3. Free cash flow: 1990, ($112,925); 1991, ($124,456); 1992, ($154,970)

Airborne Freight Corporation, which is known as Airborne Express, is an air express transportation company that provides next-day, morning delivery of small packages and documents throughout the United States. Airborne Express is one of three major participants, along with FedEx and United Parcel Service, in the air express industry. The following statement appears in "Management's discussion and analysis of results of operations and financial condition" from the company's 1992 annual report: "Capital expenditures and financing associated with those expenditures have been the primary factor affecting the financial condition of the company over the last three years."[10] The company's consolidated statements of cash flows for 1992, 1991, and 1990 appear on the next page. The following data are also available.

	1992	1991	1990	1989
Net Sales	$1,484,316	$1,367,047	$1,181,890	$949,896
Total Assets	964,739	823,647	613,534	470,605

10. Airborne Freight Corporation, *Annual Report*, 1992.

Airborne Freight Corporation and Subsidiaries
Consolidated Statements of Cash Flows
Year Ended December 31
(in thousands)

	1992	1991	1990
Operating Activities			
Net earnings	$ 5,157	$ 29,999	$ 33,577
Adjustments to reconcile net earnings to net cash provided by operating activities:			
Depreciation and amortization	110,206	90,586	69,055
Provision for aircraft engine overhauls	10,426	8,445	6,224
Deferred income taxes	(9,930)	(3,256)	536
Other	5,949	8,125	1,921
Cash Provided by Operations	121,808	133,899	111,313
Change in:			
Receivables	(16,158)	(11,880)	(19,722)
Inventories and prepaid expenses	(5,635)	(7,594)	(6,496)
Accounts payable	16	(3,177)	14,514
Accrued expenses, salaries and taxes payable	5,167	19,229	10,715
Net Cash Provided by Operating Activities	105,198	130,477	110,324
Investing Activities			
Additions to property and equipment	(252,733)	(248,165)	(217,926)
Disposition of property and equipment	1,068	1,674	2,286
Expenditures for engine overhauls	(1,933)	(4,970)	(7,483)
Other	206	1,094	(1,868)
Net Cash Used in Investing Activities	(253,392)	(250,367)	(224,991)
Financing Activities			
Proceeds from bank note borrowings, net	30,700	17,900	(6,800)
Proceeds from debt issuances	132,786	126,479	—
Principal payments on debt	(6,273)	(19,190)	(8,642)
Proceeds from sale-leaseback of aircraft	—	—	28,464
Proceeds from redeemable preferred stock issuance	—	—	40,000
Proceeds from common stock issuance	1,641	2,370	69,461
Dividends paid	(8,503)	(8,442)	(7,609)
Net Cash Provided by Financing Activities	150,351	119,117	114,874
Net Increase (Decrease) in Cash	2,157	(773)	207
Cash at Beginning of Year	8,022	8,795	8,588
Cash at End of Year	$ 10,179	$ 8,022	$ 8,795

REQUIRED

1. Have operations provided significant cash flows over the past three years? What is the role of net earnings in this provision? Other than net earnings, what is the most significant factor in providing the cash flows? Have changes in working capital accounts been a significant factor?
2. Calculate and assess Airborne Express's cash-generating ability for the three years.
3. Calculate free cash flow for the three years. Is management's statement about capital expenditures and associated financing substantiated by the figures? If your answer is yes, what were Airborne Express's primary means of financing the expansion in 1992?

International Company

FRA 2. *Format and*
L O 3, 7 *Interpretation of
Statement of Cash
Flows*

No check figure

The format of the statement of cash flows can differ from country to country. One of the more interesting presentations, as shown below, is that of *Guinness PLC,* a large British liquor company that distributes Johnny Walker Scotch and many other products.[11] (The word *group* means the same as *consolidated* in the United States.) What differences can you identify between this British statement of cash flows and the one used in the United States? In what ways do you find the Guinness format more useful than the format used in the United States? Assume that net cash flow from operating activities is computed similarly in both countries, except for the items shown.

Guinness PLC
Group Cash Flow Statement
For the Years Ended 31 December 1992 and 1991

	1992 £m	1991 £m
NET CASH INFLOW FROM OPERATING ACTIVITIES*	**891**	**833**
Interest received	106	43
Interest paid	(284)	(197)
Dividends received from associated undertakings	58	32
Dividends paid	(221)	(193)
NET CASH OUTFLOW FROM RETURNS ON INVESTMENTS AND SERVICING OF FINANCE	(341)	(315)
United Kingdom corporation tax paid	(72)	(129)
Overseas tax paid	(73)	(56)
TOTAL TAX PAID	(145)	(185)
NET CASH INFLOW BEFORE INVESTING ACTIVITIES	**405**	**333**
Purchase of tangible fixed assets	(218)	(224)
Sale of tangible fixed assets	18	14
Purchase of subsidiary undertakings	(16)	(679)
Other investments	(126)	(46)
Disposals	6	50
NET CASH OUTFLOW FROM INVESTING ACTIVITIES	(336)	(885)
NET CASH INFLOW/(OUTFLOW) BEFORE FINANCING ACTIVITIES	69	(552)
Proceeds of new borrowings	736	1,635
Borrowings repaid	(1,252)	(1,272)
Issue of shares (employee share schemes)	15	20
NET CASH (OUTFLOW)/INFLOW FROM FINANCING ACTIVITIES	(501)	383
(DECREASE) IN CASH AND CASH EQUIVALENTS	(432)	(169)
ANALYSIS OF FREE CASH FLOW		
Net cash inflow before investing activities	405	333
Purchase of tangible fixed assets	(218)	(224)
Sale of tangible fixed assets	18	14
FREE CASH FLOW (AFTER DIVIDENDS)	**205**	**123**
FREE CASH FLOW (BEFORE DIVIDENDS)	**426**	**316**

*The company provides the detail for this item in a note to the financial statements.

11. Guinness PLC, *Annual Report*, 1992.

Toys "R" Us Annual Report

FRA 3.
L O 7
Analysis of the Statement of Cash Flows

Check Figures: 3. Cash flow yield: 1993, 1.3 times; 1994, 1.4 times; 1995, 1.1 times

Refer to the statement of cash flows in the appendix on Toys "R" Us to answer the following questions:

1. Does Toys "R" Us use the direct or the indirect method of reporting cash flows from operating activities? Other than net earnings, what are the three most important factors affecting cash flows from operating activities? Explain the trend of each.

2. Based on the cash flows from investing activities, would you say that Toys "R" Us is a contracting or an expanding company?

3. Calculate the cash flow yield, cash flows to sales, cash flows to average total assets, and free cash flow for the last three years for Toys "R" Us. How would you evaluate the company's cash-generating efficiency? Does Toys "R" Us need external financing? If so, where has it come from?

Financial Statement Analysis

1. Describe and discuss the objectives of financial statement analysis.
2. Describe and discuss the standards for financial statement analysis.
3. State the sources of information for financial statement analysis.
4. Identify the issues related to evaluating the quality of a company's earnings.
5. Apply horizontal analysis, trend analysis, and vertical analysis to financial statements.
6. Apply ratio analysis to financial statements in a comprehensive evaluation of a company's financial situation.

DECISION POINT · *Moody's Investors Service, Inc.*

Moody's Investors Service, Inc. rates the bonds and other indebtedness of companies on the basis of safety, that is, the likelihood of repayment. Investors rely on this service when making investments in bonds and other long-term company debt. The *Wall Street Journal* reported on September 19, 1990, that Moody's was reviewing $40 million of Ford Motor Co.'s debt for possible downgrade.[1] Moody's cited the softness in the U.S. auto market. Ford replied that the action was not warranted and questioned Moody's decision to review its debt, given that the market problem might be short term. One month later, on October 25, 1990, Moody's did in fact lower the rating on Ford's long-term debt. The new rating was still in the high-grade category, but the downgrade meant that Ford would pay higher interest rates because, according to Moody's, its debt was not quite as secure as it had been. On what basis would Moody's decide to upgrade or lower the bond rating of a company?

According to the *Wall Street Journal*, "Moody's said it took the actions because Ford's returns and cash flow are vulnerable to a weaker U.S. economy, softer European sales, and volatile fuel prices. At the same time, Moody's said, Ford has committed to huge capital spending plans."[2] Ford Motor Co. officials, according to the same article, said they were disappointed with the decision, as the reasons given were cyclical and transitional.

This case demonstrates several features of the evaluation of a company's financial prospects. First, the analysis is rooted in the financial statements (for example, returns and cash flow). Second, it is directed toward the future (for example, capital spending plans). Third, the operating environment must be taken into consideration (for example, a weaker U.S. economy, softer European sales, and volatile fuel prices). Fourth, judgment is involved (for example, the disagreement between Moody's and Ford about the seriousness of the situation). ⦂⦂⦂⦂⦂

---

1. "Ford Motor's Debt Reviewed by Moody's; Downgrade Is Possible," *Wall Street Journal*, September 19, 1990.
2. Bradley A. Stertz, "Ratings on Ford and Units' Debt Cut by Moody's," *Wall Street Journal*, October 25, 1990.

OBJECTIVES OF FINANCIAL STATEMENT ANALYSIS

1 *Describe and discuss the objectives of financial statement analysis*

Financial statement analysis comprises all the techniques employed by users of financial statements to show important relationships in the financial statements. Users of financial statements fall into two broad categories: internal and external. Management is the main internal user. However, because those who run a company have inside information on operations, other techniques are available to them. The main focus here is on the external users of financial statements and the analytical techniques they employ.

Creditors make loans in the form of trade accounts, notes, or bonds. They receive interest on the loans and expect them to be repaid according to specified terms. Investors buy capital stock, from which they hope to receive dividends and an increase in value. Both groups face risks. The creditor faces the risk that the debtor will fail to pay back the loan. The investor faces the risk that dividends will be reduced or not paid or that the market price of the stock will drop. For both groups, the goal is to achieve a return that makes up for the risk. In general, the greater the risk taken, the greater the return required as compensation.

Any one loan or any one investment can turn out badly. As a result, most creditors and investors put their funds into a portfolio, or group of loans or investments. The portfolio allows them to average both the returns and the risks. Nevertheless, individual decisions must still be made about the loans and stock in the portfolio. It is in making those individual decisions that financial statement analysis is most useful. Creditors and investors use financial statement analysis in two general ways: (1) to judge past performance and current position and (2) to judge future potential and the risk connected with the potential.

ASSESSMENT OF PAST PERFORMANCE AND CURRENT POSITION

Past performance is often a good indicator of future performance. Therefore, an investor or creditor looks at the trend of past sales, expenses, net income, cash flow, and return on investment not only as a means for judging management's past performance but also as a possible indicator of future performance. In addition, an analysis of current position will tell, for example, what assets the business owns and what liabilities must be paid. It will also tell what the cash position is, how much debt the company has in relation to equity, and what levels of inventories and receivables exist. Knowing a company's past performance and current position is often important in achieving the second general objective of financial analysis.

ASSESSMENT OF FUTURE POTENTIAL AND RELATED RISK

Information about the past and present is useful only to the extent that it bears on decisions about the future. An investor judges the potential earning ability of a company because that ability will affect the market price of the company's stock and the amount of dividends the company will pay. A creditor judges the potential debt-paying ability of the company.

The riskiness of an investment or loan depends on how easy it is to predict future profitability or liquidity. If an investor can predict with confidence that a company's earnings per share will be between $2.50 and $2.60 next year, the investment is less risky than if the earnings per share are expected to fall between $2.00 and $3.00. For example, the potential associated with an investment in an established and stable electric utility, or a loan to it, is relatively easy to predict on the basis of the company's past performance and current position. The potential associated with a small microcomputer manufacturer, on the other hand, may be much harder to predict. For this reason, the investment or loan to the electric utility carries less risk than the investment or loan to the small microcomputer company.

Often, in return for taking a greater risk, an investor in the microcomputer company will demand a higher expected return (increase in market price plus dividends) than will an investor in the utility company. Also, a creditor of the microcomputer company will demand a higher interest rate and possibly more assurance of repayment (a secured loan, for instance) than a creditor of the utility company. The higher interest rate reimburses the creditor for assuming a higher risk.

STANDARDS FOR FINANCIAL STATEMENT ANALYSIS

OBJECTIVE

2 *Describe and discuss the standards for financial statement analysis*

When analyzing financial statements, decision makers must judge whether the relationships they have found are favorable or unfavorable. Three commonly used standards of comparison are (1) rule-of-thumb measures, (2) a company's past performance, and (3) industry norms.

RULE-OF-THUMB MEASURES

Many financial analysts, investors, and lenders employ ideal, or rule-of-thumb, measures for key financial ratios. For example, it has long been thought that a current ratio (current assets divided by current liabilities) of 2:1 is acceptable. The credit-rating firm of Dun and Bradstreet, in its *Key Business Ratios,* offers such rules of thumb as the following:

> Current debt to tangible net worth. Ordinarily, a business begins to pile up trouble when this relationship exceeds 80%.
>
> Inventory to net working capital. Ordinarily, this relationship should not exceed 80%.

Although such measures may suggest areas that need further investigation, there is no proof that the specified levels are the best for any company. A company with a current ratio higher than 2:1 may have a poor credit policy (resulting in accounts receivable being too large), too much inventory, or poor cash management. Another company may have a ratio lower than 2:1 as a result of excellent management in those three areas. Thus, rule-of-thumb measures must be used with great care.

PAST PERFORMANCE OF THE COMPANY

An improvement over rule-of-thumb measures is the comparison of financial measures or ratios of the same company over a period of time. This standard will at least give the analyst some basis for judging whether the measure or ratio is getting better or worse. It may also be helpful in showing possible future trends. However, since trends do reverse at times, such projections must be made with care. Another problem with trend analysis is that the past may not be a useful measure of adequacy. In other words, past performance may not be enough to meet present needs. For example, even if return on total investment improved from 3 percent last year to 4 percent this year, the 4 percent return may in fact not be adequate.

PepsiCo, Inc.

DECISION POINT

Most people think of PepsiCo, Inc. as a maker of soft drinks, but in fact, the company is also involved in diversified food products (Frito-Lay) and restaurants (Pizza Hut, Taco Bell, and KFC). The overall success of PepsiCo as reflected in its financial statements is affected by the relative amounts of investment and earnings in each of its very different businesses. How should a financial analyst assess the impact of each of these three segments on the company's overall financial performance?

In accordance with FASB *Statement No. 14,* PepsiCo reports key information about its three segments in a note to the financial statements in its annual report (see Exhibit 1). The analyst can learn a lot about the company from this information. For example, domestic and international net sales and operating profits for each segment are shown for the past three years. Note that in all three segments, international net sales and operating profits are growing much more rapidly than their counterparts in the United States. Identifiable assets, capital spending, and depreciation and amortization expense are also indicated on the next page of the report. Segment information allows the analyst to see the profitability of each business and to identify where management is investing most for the future. The information about net sales, segment operating profits, and identifiable assets by geographic area is also useful. It is interesting to note, for instance, that although PepsiCo's net sales are increasing in Europe, its operating profits in this region are declining. ⦂⦂⦂⦂⦂

INDUSTRY NORMS

One way of making up for the limitations of using past performance as a standard is to use industry norms. Such norms will tell how the company being analyzed compares with other companies in the same industry. For example, suppose that other companies in an industry have an average rate of return on total investment of 8 percent. In such a case, 3 and 4 percent returns are probably not adequate. Industry norms can also be used to judge trends. Suppose that, because of a downward turn in the economy, a company's profit margin dropped from 12 to 10 percent. A finding that other companies in the same industry had experienced an average drop in profit margin from 12 to 4 percent would indicate that the company being analyzed did relatively well.

There are three limitations to using industry norms as standards. First, two companies that seem to be in the same industry may not be strictly comparable. Consider two companies said to be in the oil industry. The main business of one may be purchasing oil products and marketing them through service stations. The other, an international company, may discover, produce, refine, and market its own oil products. The operations of these two companies cannot be compared because they are different.

Second, most large companies today operate in more than one industry. Some of these diversified companies, or *conglomerates*, operate in many unrelated industries. The individual segments of a diversified company generally have different rates of profitability and different degrees of risk. In analyzing the consolidated financial statements of such companies, it is often impossible to use industry norms as standards. There are simply no other companies that are similar enough. A requirement by the Financial Accounting Standards Board, presented in *Statement No. 14*, provides a partial solution to this problem. It states that diversified companies must report revenues, income from operations, and identifiable assets for each of their operating segments. Depending on specific criteria, segment information may be reported for operations in different industries, in foreign markets, or to major customers.[3]

The third limitation of industry norms is that companies in the same industry with similar operations may use different acceptable accounting procedures. That is, different methods may be used to value inventories, or different methods may be used to depreciate similar assets. Even so, if little information about a company's prior performance is available, industry norms probably offer the best available standards for judging current performance—as long as they are used with care.

SOURCES OF INFORMATION

OBJECTIVE

3 *State the sources of information for financial statement analysis*

The external analyst is often limited to using publicly available information about a company. The major sources of information about publicly held corporations are reports published by the company, SEC reports, business periodicals, and credit and investment advisory services.

REPORTS PUBLISHED BY THE COMPANY

The annual report of a publicly held corporation is an important source of financial information. The main parts of an annual report are (1) management's analysis of the past year's operations, (2) the financial statements, (3) the notes to the statements, including the principal accounting procedures

---

3. *Statement of Financial Accounting Standards No. 14,* "Financial Reporting for Segments of a Business Enterprise" (Stamford, Conn.: Financial Accounting Standards Board, 1976).

Exhibit 1. Segment Information for PepsiCo, Inc.

Industry Segments

(dollars in millions)

		Growth Rate (a) 1989 - 1994	1994	1993	1992	1991	1990
Net Sales							
Beverages:	Domestic	7.2%	$ 6,541.2	$ 5,918.1	$ 5,485.2	$ 5,171.5	$ 5,034.5
	International	22.2%	3,146.3	2,720.1	2,120.4	1,743.7	1,488.5
		10.9%	9,687.5	8,638.2	7,605.6	6,915.2	6,523.0
Snack Foods:	Domestic	9.3%	5,011.3	4,365.3	3,950.4	3,737.9	3,471.5
	International	32.0%	3,253.1	2,661.5	2,181.7	1,512.2	1,295.3
		15.5%	8,264.4	7,026.8	6,132.1	5,250.1	4,766.8
Restaurants:	Domestic	13.2%	8,693.9	8,025.7	7,115.4	6,258.4	5,540.9
	International	26.4%	1,826.6	1,330.0	1,116.9	868.5	684.8
		14.9%	10,520.5	9,355.7	8,232.3	7,126.9	6,225.7
Combined Segments							
	Domestic	10.1%	20,246.4	18,309.1	16,551.0	15,167.8	14,046.9
	International	26.6%	8,226.0	6,711.6	5,419.0	4,124.4	3,468.6
		13.6%	$28,472.4	$25,020.7	$21,970.0	$19,292.2	$17,515.5
By Restaurant Chain							
	Pizza Hut	12.8%	$ 4,474.4	$ 4,128.7	$ 3,603.5	$ 3,258.3	$ 2,949.9
	Taco Bell	18.3%	3,401.4	2,901.3	2,460.0	2,038.1	1,745.5
	KFC	14.7%	2,644.7	2,325.7	2,168.8	1,830.5	1,530.3
		14.9%	$10,520.5	$ 9,355.7	$ 8,232.3	$ 7,126.9	$ 6,225.7
Operating Profits							
Beverages:	Domestic	12.1%	$ 1,022.3	$ 936.9	$ 686.3	$ 746.2	$ 673.8
	International	20.0%	194.7	172.1	112.3	117.1	93.8
		13.2%	1,217.0	1,109.0	798.6	863.3	767.6
Snack Foods:	Domestic	8.9%	1,025.1	900.7	775.5	616.6	732.3
	International	27.1%	351.8	288.9	209.2	140.1	160.3
		12.2%	1,376.9	1,189.6	984.7	756.7	892.6
Restaurants:	Domestic	12.2%	658.8	685.1	597.8	479.4	447.2
	International	4.3%	71.5	92.9	120.7	96.2	75.2
		11.3%	730.3	778.0	718.5	575.6	522.4
Combined Segments							
	Domestic	11.1%	2,706.2	2,522.7	2,059.6	1,842.2	1,853.3
	International	20.6%	618.0	553.9	442.2	353.4	329.3
		12.3%	3,324.2	3,076.6	2,501.8	2,195.6	2,182.6
Equity Income			37.8	30.1	40.1	32.2	30.1
Unallocated Expenses, net			(160.8)	(200.2)	(170.7)	(116.0)	(170.6)
Operating Profit		12.6%	$ 3,201.2	$ 2,906.5	$ 2,371.2	$ 2,111.8	$ 2,042.1
By Restaurant Chain							
	Pizza Hut	7.5%	$ 294.8	$ 372.1	$ 335.4	$ 314.5	$ 245.9
	Taco Bell	18.7%	270.3	253.1	214.3	180.6	149.6
	KFC	9.0%	165.2	152.8	168.8	80.5	126.9
		11.3%	$ 730.3	$ 778.0	$ 718.5	$ 575.6	$ 522.4

Geographic Areas (b)	Net Sales			Segment Operating Profits			Identifiable Assets		
	1994	1993	1992	1994	1993	1992	1994	1993	1992
United States	$20,246.4	$18,309.1	$16,551.0	$2,706.2	$2,522.7	$2,059.6	$14,218.4	$13,589.5	$11,957.0
Europe	2,177.1	1,819.0	1,349.0	16.7	47.4	52.6	3,062.0	2,666.1	1,948.4
Mexico	2,022.8	1,613.4	1,234.6	261.4	223.1	172.1	994.7	1,217.1	1,054.6
Canada	1,244.3	1,206.1	979.6	81.6	101.7	78.9	1,342.1	1,364.0	1,340.6
Other	2,781.8	2,073.1	1,855.8	258.3	181.7	138.6	2,195.6	1,675.1	1,282.0
Combined Segments	$28,472.4	$25,020.7	$21,970.0	$3,324.2	$3,076.6	$2,501.8	21,812.8	20,511.8	17,582.6
Corporate							2,979.2	3,194.0	3,368.6
							$24,792.0	$23,705.8	$20,951.2

(a) Five-year compounded annual growth rate. Operating profit growth rates exclude the impact of previously disclosed 1989 unusual items affecting international beverages and domestic Taco Bell and KFC. There were no unusual items in 1994.

Source: PepsiCo, Inc. *Annual Report,* 1994.

used by the company, (4) the auditors' report, and (5) a summary of operations for a five- or ten-year period. Most publicly held companies also publish interim financial statements each quarter. Those reports present limited information in the form of condensed financial statements, which need not be subjected to a full audit by the independent auditor. The interim statements are watched closely by the financial community for early signs of important changes in a company's earnings trend.

SEC REPORTS

Publicly held corporations must file annual reports, quarterly reports, and current reports with the Securities and Exchange Commission (SEC). All such reports are available to the public at a small charge. The SEC calls for a standard form for the annual report (Form 10-K) that contains more information than the published annual report. Form 10-K is, for that reason, a valuable source of information. It is available free of charge to stockholders of the company. The quarterly report (Form 10-Q) presents important facts about interim financial performance. The current report (Form 8-K) must be filed within a few days of the date of certain significant events, such as the sale or purchase of a division of the company or a change in auditors. It is often the first indicator of important changes that may affect the company's financial performance in the future.

BUSINESS PERIODICALS AND CREDIT AND INVESTMENT ADVISORY SERVICES

Financial analysts must keep up with current events in the financial world. Probably the best source of financial news is the *Wall Street Journal*, which is published every business day and is the most complete financial newspaper in the United States. Some helpful magazines, published every week or every two weeks, are *Forbes, Barron's, Fortune*, and the *Commercial and Financial Chronicle*.

For further details about the financial history of companies, the publications of such services as Moody's Investors Service, Inc. and Standard & Poor's are useful. Data on industry norms, average ratios and relationships, and credit ratings are available from such agencies as The Dun & Bradstreet Corp. Dun & Bradstreet offers an annual analysis using fourteen ratios of 125 industry groups classified as retailing, wholesaling, manufacturing, and construction in its *Key Business Ratios. Annual Statement Studies*, published by Robert Morris Associates, presents many facts and ratios for 223 different industries. Also, a number of private services are available for a yearly fee.

An example of specialized financial reporting readily available to the public is Moody's *Handbook of Dividend Achievers,* which profiles companies that have increased their dividends consistently over the past ten years. A sample listing from that publication—for PepsiCo, Inc.—is shown in Exhibit 2. Within one page, a wealth of information about the company is summarized: the market action of its stock; summaries of its business operations, recent developments, and prospects; earnings and dividend data; annual financial data for the past six or seven years; and other information. From the data contained in those summaries, it is possible to do many of the trend analyses and ratios explained in this chapter.

Exhibit 2. Sample Listing from Moody's *Handbook of Dividend Achievers*

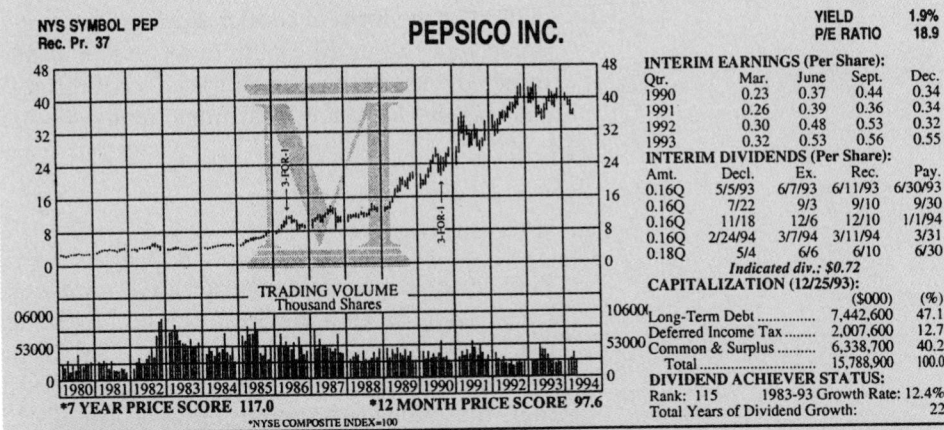

| NYS SYMBOL PEP | | | | | | | PEPSICO INC. | | YIELD | 1.9% |
| Rec. Pr. 37 | | | | | | | | | P/E RATIO | 18.9 |

INTERIM EARNINGS (Per Share):

Qtr.	Mar.	June	Sept.	Dec.
1990	0.23	0.37	0.44	0.34
1991	0.26	0.39	0.36	0.34
1992	0.30	0.48	0.53	0.32
1993	0.32	0.53	0.56	0.55

INTERIM DIVIDENDS (Per Share):

Amt.	Decl.	Ex.	Rec.	Pay.
0.16Q	5/5/93	6/7/93	6/11/93	6/30/93
0.16Q	7/22	9/3	9/10	9/30
0.16Q	11/18	12/6	12/10	1/1/94
0.16Q	2/24/94	3/7/94	3/11/94	3/31
0.18Q	5/4	6/6	6/10	6/30

Indicated div.: $0.72

CAPITALIZATION (12/25/93):

	($000)	(%)
Long-Term Debt	7,442,600	47.1
Deferred Income Tax	2,007,600	12.7
Common & Surplus	6,338,700	40.2
Total	15,788,900	100.0

DIVIDEND ACHIEVER STATUS:
Rank: 115   1983-93 Growth Rate: 12.4%
Total Years of Dividend Growth: 22

*7 YEAR PRICE SCORE 117.0   *12 MONTH PRICE SCORE 97.6
*NYSE COMPOSITE INDEX=100

RECENT DEVELOPMENTS: For the year ended 12/25/93, net income was $1.59 billion compared with $1.30 billion last year. Sales rose 13.9% to $25.02 billion. Worldwide snack food sales increased 15% to $7.03 billion and operating profits rose 21%. International profits increased 16% to $288.9 million. Worldwide beverage sales rose 14% to $8.64 billion, and operating profits rose 18%. Restaurant profits advanced 8%, led by an 18% increase in profits at Taco Bell.

PROSPECTS: The Company's restaurant segment will continue to benefit from expansions in the near term. Although profits at KFC are being affected by soft international results, profits at Pizza Hut and Taco Bell will continue to grow. In the domestic beverage market, contributions from the new line of Lipton products should boost sales and earnings. Market share gains should aid results at Frito-Lay.

BUSINESS

PEPSICO, INC. operates on a worldwide basis within three distinct business segments: soft drinks, snackfoods and restaurants. The soft drinks segment manufactures concentrates, and markets Pepsi-Cola, Diet Pepsi, Mountain Dew, Slice and allied brands worldwide, and 7-up internationally. This segment also operates soft drink bottling businesses principally in the United States. Snack Foods manufactures and markets snack chips through Frito-Lay Inc. Well known brands include: Doritos, Ruffles and Lays. Restaurants consists of Pizza Hut, Taco Bell and Kentucky Fried Chicken.

BUSINESS LINE ANALYSIS

(12/25/93)	Rev(%)	Inc(%)
Beverages	34.5	36.0
Snack Foods	28.1	38.7
Restaurants	37.4	25.3
Total	100.0	100.0

ANNUAL EARNINGS AND DIVIDENDS PER SHARE

	12/25/93	12/26/92	12/28/91	12/29/90	12/30/89	12/31/88	12/28/87
Earnings Per Share	1.96	1.61	1.35	1.37	1.13	0.97	⊡ 0.77
Dividends Per Share	0.58	0.50	0.44	0.367	0.31	0.25	0.22
Dividend Payout %	29.6	31.1	32.6	26.8	27.1	26.2	28.7

⊡ Before disc. oper.

ANNUAL FINANCIAL DATA

RECORD OF EARNINGS (IN MILLIONS):

	12/25/93	12/26/92	12/28/91	12/29/90	12/30/89	12/31/88	12/28/87
Total Revenues	25,020.7	21,970.0	19,607.9	17,802.7	15,242.4	13,007.0	11,485.2
Costs and Expenses	21,810.5	19,332.9	17,276.3	15,558.0	13,309.1	11,017.7	9,778.9
Depreciation & Amort	1,444.2	1,214.9	1,034.5	884.0	772.0	629.3	563.0
Operating Income	2,906.5	2,371.2	2,122.9	2,055.6	1,782.9	1,360.0	1,143.3
Income Bef Income Taxes	2,422.5	1,898.8	1,670.3	1,667.4	1,350.5	1,137.6	960.4
Provision for Inc Taxes	834.6	597.1	590.1	576.8	449.1	375.4	355.3
Net Income	1,587.9	374.3	1,080.2	⊡1,090.6	901.4	762.2	⊡605.1
Aver. Shs. Outstg. (000)	810,100	806,700	802,500	798,700	795,900	790,500	789,300

⊡ Before disc. op. dr$13,700,000. ⊡ Before disc. op. dr$10,300,000.

BALANCE SHEET (IN MILLIONS):

	12/25/93	12/26/92	12/28/91	12/29/90	12/30/89	12/31/88	12/28/87
Tot Cash & Sh-tm Invests	1,856.2	2,058.4	2,036.0	1,815.7	1,533.9	1,617.8	1,352.6
Receivables, Net	1,883.4	1,588.5	1,481.7	1,414.7	1,239.7	979.3	885.6
Inventories	924.7	768.8	661.5	585.8	546.1	442.4	433.0
Gross Property	14,250.0	12,095.2	10,501.7	8,977.7	7,818.4	6,658.4	6,000.6
Accumulated Depreciation	5,394.4	4,653.2	3,907.0	3,266.8	2,688.2	2,195.9	1,883.2
Long-Term Debt	7,442.6	7,964.8	7,806.2	5,600.1	5,777.1	2,356.6	2,150.6
Net Stockholders' Equity	6,338.7	5,355.7	5,545.4	4,904.2	3,891.1	3,161.0	2,508.6
Total Assets	23,705.8	20,951.2	18,775.1	17,143.4	15,126.7	11,135.3	9,022.7
Total Current Assets	5,164.1	4,842.3	4,566.1	4,081.4	3,550.8	3,264.7	2,939.6
Total Current Liabilities	6,574.9	4,324.4	3,722.1	4,770.5	3,691.8	3,873.6	2,722.8
Net Working Capital	d1,410.8	517.9	844.0	d689.1	d141.0	d608.9	216.8
Year End Shs Outstg (000)	798,800	798,800	789,101	788,389	791,057	863,100	781,239

STATISTICAL RECORD:

	12/25/93	12/26/92	12/28/91	12/29/90	12/30/89	12/31/88	12/28/87
Operating Profit Margin %	11.6	10.8	10.8	11.5	11.7	10.5	10.0
Return on Equity %	25.1	24.3	19.5	22.2	23.2	24.1	24.1
Return on Assets %	6.7	6.2	5.8	6.4	6.0	6.8	6.7
Average Yield %	1.5	1.4	1.5	1.6	1.8	2.0	1.9
P/E Ratio	22.3-17.6	26.9-18.9	27.0-17.4	20.3-13.1	19.5-11.2	14.9-10.3	18.3-11.0
Price Range	43⅝-34½	43⅜-30½	36½-23½	27⅞-18	22-12⅝	14½-10	14⅛-8½

Statistics are as originally reported.

OFFICERS:
D.W. Calloway, Chmn. & C.E.O.
R.G. Dettmer, Exec. V.P. & C.F.O.
E.V. Lahey, Jr., Sr. V.P., Couns. & Sec.
R.C. Barnes, Sr. V.P. & Treas.

INCORPORATED: NC, Dec., 1986

PRINCIPAL OFFICE: Purchase, NY 10577

TELEPHONE NUMBER: (914) 253-2000

FAX: (914) 253-2070

NO. OF EMPLOYEES: 118,296

ANNUAL MEETING: In May

SHAREHOLDERS: 67,210

INSTITUTIONAL HOLDINGS:
No. of Institutions: 1,077
Shares Held: 470,494,447

REGISTRAR(S): Chemical Bank, New York, NY

TRANSFER AGENT(S): Chemical Bank, New York, NY

Source: From Moody's *Handbook of Dividend Achievers*, 1994. Used by permission of Moody's Investor Services.

EVALUATING A COMPANY'S QUALITY OF EARNINGS

OBJECTIVE

4 *Identify the issues related to evaluating the quality of a company's earnings*

It is clear from the preceding sections that current and expected earnings play an important role in the analysis of a company's prospects. In fact, a survey of two thousand members of the Association for Investment Management and Research indicated that the two most important economic indicators in evaluating common stocks were expected changes in earnings per share and expected return on equity.[4] Net income is a key component of both measures. Because of the importance of net income, or the "bottom line," in measures of a company's prospects, there is significant interest in evaluating the quality of the net income figure, or the *quality of earnings*. The quality of a company's earnings may be affected by (1) the accounting methods and estimates the company's management chooses and (2) the nature of nonoperating items in the income statement.

CHOICE OF ACCOUNTING METHODS AND ESTIMATES

Two aspects of the choice of accounting methods affect the quality of earnings. First, some accounting methods are by nature more conservative than others because they tend to produce a lower net income in the current period. Second, there is considerable latitude in the choice of the estimated useful life over which assets are written off and in the amount of estimated residual value. In general, an accounting method or estimated useful life or residual value that results in lower current earnings is considered to produce better-quality earnings.

In this text, various acceptable methods have been used in applying the matching rule. Those methods are based on allocation procedures, which in turn are based on certain assumptions. Some of those procedures are listed at the top of the next page.

---

4. Cited in *The Week in Review* (Deloitte Haskins & Sells), February 28, 1985.

1. For estimating uncollectible accounts expense: percentage of net sales method and accounts receivable aging method
2. For costing ending inventory: average-cost method; first-in, first-out (FIFO) method; and last-in, first-out (LIFO) method
3. For estimating depreciation expense: straight-line method, production method, and accelerated depreciation methods
4. For estimating depletion expense: production (extraction) method
5. For estimating amortization of intangibles: straight-line method

All these procedures are designed to allocate the costs of assets to the periods in which their costs contribute to the production of revenue. They are based on a determination of the benefits to the current period (expenses) versus the benefits to future periods (assets). They are estimates, and the period or periods benefited cannot be demonstrated conclusively. They are also subjective, because in practice it is hard to justify one method of estimation over another.

For those reasons, it is important for both the accountant and the financial statement user to understand the possible effects of different accounting procedures on net income and financial position. For example, suppose that two companies have similar operations, but one uses FIFO for inventory costing and the straight-line (SL) method for computing depreciation, and the other uses LIFO for inventory costing and the double-declining-balance (DDB) method for computing depreciation. The income statements of the two companies might appear as follows:

	FIFO and SL	LIFO and DDB
Net Sales	$500,000	$500,000
Goods Available for Sale	$300,000	$300,000
Less Ending Inventory	60,000	50,000
Cost of Goods Sold	$240,000	$250,000
Gross Margin	$260,000	$250,000
Less: Depreciation Expense	$ 40,000	$ 80,000
Other Expenses	170,000	170,000
Total Operating Expenses	$210,000	$250,000
Net Income Before Income Taxes	$ 50,000	$ 0

The $50,000 difference in income before income taxes stems only from the differences in accounting methods. Differences in the estimated lives and residual values of the plant assets could lead to an even greater variation. In practice, of course, differences in net income occur for many reasons, but the user must be aware of the discrepancies that can occur as a result of the methods chosen by management.

The existence of such alternatives could cause problems in the interpretation of financial statements were it not for the conventions of full disclosure and consistency. Full disclosure requires that management explain the significant accounting policies used in preparing the financial statements in a note to the statements. Consistency requires that the same accounting procedures be followed from year to year. If a change in procedure is made, the nature of the change and its monetary effect must be explained in a note.

NATURE OF NONOPERATING ITEMS

The corporate income statement consists of several components. The top of the statement presents earnings from current ongoing operations, called income from operations. The lower part of the statement can contain such nonoperating items as discontinued operations, extraordinary gains and losses, and effects of accounting changes. Those items may drastically affect the bottom line, or net income, of the company.

For practical reasons, the calculations of trends and ratios are based on the assumption that net income and other components are comparable from year to year and from company to company. However, in making interpretations, the astute analyst will always look beyond the ratios to the quality of the components. For example, in a recent year, AT&T wrote off $7 billion for retiree health benefits and another $1.3 billion to cover future disability and severance payments. Despite those huge losses, the company's stock price has been higher because income from operations before those charges was up for the year.[5] Although such write-offs reduce a company's net worth, they do not affect current operations or cash flows and are usually ignored by analysts assessing current performance.

In some cases, a company may boost income by selling assets on which it can report a gain. For example, the *Wall Street Journal* reported that Lotus Development Corporation, the well-known software company, reported a 40 percent increase in net income when earnings from operations actually decreased by 66 percent. Weak sales and earnings were camouflaged by a one-time $33.3 million gain after taxes from the sale of shares Lotus owns in another company.[6] The quality of Lotus's earnings is in fact lower than might appear on the surface. Unless analysts go beyond the "bottom line" in analyzing and interpreting financial reports, they can come to the wrong conclusions.

BUSINESS BULLETIN: ETHICS IN PRACTICE

External users of financial statements depend on management's honesty and openness in disclosing factual information about a company. In the vast majority of cases, management's reports are reliable, but on occasion, employees (called *whistle-blowers*) may publicly disclose wrongdoing on the part of their company. For instance, employees have accused various divisions of Teledyne, Inc., a large defense contractor, of financial misdeeds. The charges include keeping two sets of records, overbilling the government, and making illegal payments to Egyptian officials. Although whistle-blowers are protected by law, their actions often harm their careers. A former Teledyne employee, for example, who complained about poor equipment, improper training, and shipments of untested components claims to have been banished to a dingy corner of the plant. The company is now subject to a possible $1.1 billion in damages and a Congressional hearing.[7] Whether or not those allegations are true, they will have a negative effect on the market's view of Teledyne and must be considered when analyzing the company.

5. "Accounting Rule Change Will Erase AT&T Earnings," *Chicago Tribune*, January 15, 1994.

6. John R. Wilke, "Lotus Net Rises 40% on One-Time Gain While Operating Earnings Plunge 66%," *Wall Street Journal*, October 16, 1992.

7. "At Teledyne, A Chorus of Whistle-blowers," *Business Week*, December 14, 1992.

TOOLS AND TECHNIQUES OF FINANCIAL ANALYSIS

Few numbers mean very much when looked at individually. It is their relationship to other numbers or their change from one period to another that is important. The tools of financial analysis are intended to show relationships and changes. Among the more widely used of those tools are horizontal analysis, trend analysis, vertical analysis, and ratio analysis.

OBJECTIVE

5 *Apply horizontal analysis, trend analysis, and vertical analysis to financial statements*

HORIZONTAL ANALYSIS

Generally accepted accounting principles call for the presentation of comparative financial statements that give the current year's and past year's financial information. A common starting point for studying such statements is horizontal analysis, which begins with the computation of changes in both dollar amounts and percentages from the previous to the current year. The percentage of change must be computed to relate the size of the change to the size of the dollar amounts involved. A change of $1 million in sales is not so drastic as a change of $1 million in net income, because sales is a larger amount than net income.

Exhibits 3 and 4 present the comparative balance sheets and income statements, respectively, for Apple Computer, Inc., with the dollar and percentage changes shown. The percentage change is computed as follows:

$$\text{Percentage change} = 100 \left(\frac{\text{amount of change}}{\text{previous year amount}} \right)$$

The base year in any set of data is always the first year being studied. For example, from 1993 to 1994, Apple's total assets increased by $131 million, from $5,171 million to $5,303 million, or by 2.5 percent. This is computed as follows:

$$\text{Percentage increase} = 100 \left(\frac{\$131 \text{ million}}{\$5,171 \text{ million}} \right) = 2.5\%$$

An examination of the comparative balance sheets shows much change from 1993 to 1994, even though total assets increased by only 2.5 percent. There was an especially large decrease in inventories of 27.8 percent and a decrease in short-term investments of 74.8 percent. The decrease of 22.5 percent in current liabilities was due primarily to a 64.5 percent decrease in short-term borrowing. Accounts payable showed an increase of 18.7 percent. Apple made a substantial issue of long-term debt for the first time and increased its total stockholders' equity by 17.6 percent. Overall, Apple improved its financial position by depending less on short-term debt and relying more on long-term debt and equity financing.

From the income statements in Exhibit 4, the most obvious change is the increase in cost of sales of 30.4 percent in relation to only a 15.2 percent increase in net sales. However, by reducing expenses, management was able to keep the increase in total costs and expenses to 10.2 percent. The result was a very favorable increase in operating income of 373.3 percent. Apple had restructuring adjustments associated with the downsizing of certain operations. Interest and Other Income (Expense), Net is a negative amount in 1994 due to the increase in long-term debt. Overall, the company had a very good year, with net income increasing 258.2 percent.

Care must be taken in the analysis of percentage changes. For example, in Exhibit 3, one might view the 77.9 percent increase in Cash as similar to the 74.8 percent decrease in short-term investments. However, this is not the

Exhibit 3. Comparative Balance Sheets with Horizontal Analysis

Apple Computer, Inc.
Consolidated Balance Sheets
September 30, 1994, and September 24, 1993

	(Dollars in thousands)		Increase (Decrease)	
	1994	1993	Amount	Percentage
Assets				
Current Assets				
Cash and Cash Equivalents	$1,203,488	$ 676,413	$ 527,075	77.9
Short-Term Investments	54,368	215,890	(161,522)	(74.8)
Accounts Receivable, Net of Allowance for				
Doubtful Accounts of 90,992 ($83,776 in 1993)	1,581,347	1,381,946	199,401	14.4
Inventories	1,088,434	1,506,638	(418,204)	(27.8)
Prepaid Income Taxes	293,048	268,085	24,963	9.3
Other Current Assets	255,767	289,383	(33,616)	(11.6)
Total Current Assets	$4,476,452	$4,338,355	$ 138,097	3.2
Property, Plant, and Equipment				
Land and Buildings	$ 484,592	$ 404,688	$ 79,904	19.7
Machinery and Equipment	572,728	578,272	(5,544)	(1.0)
Office Furniture and Equipment	158,160	167,905	(9,745)	(5.8)
Leasehold Improvements	236,708	261,792	(25,084)	(9.6)
Total Property, Plant, and Equipment	$1,452,188	$1,412,657	$ 39,531	2.8
Accumulated Depreciation and Amortization	(785,088)	(753,111)	31,977	4.2
Net Property, Plant, and Equipment	$ 667,100	$ 659,546	$ 7,554	1.1
Other Assets	$ 159,194	$ 173,511	($ 14,317)	(8.3)
Total Assets	$5,302,746	$5,171,412	$ 131,334	2.5
Liabilities and Shareholders' Equity				
Current Liabilities				
Short-Term Borrowings	$ 292,200	$ 823,182	($ 530,982)	(64.5)
Accounts Payable	881,717	742,622	139,095	18.7
Accrued Compensation and Employee Benefits	136,895	144,779	(7,884)	(5.4)
Accrued Marketing and Distribution	178,294	174,547	3,747	2.1
Accrued Restructuring Costs	58,238	307,932	(249,694)	(81.1)
Other Current Liabilities	396,961	315,023	81,938	26.0
Total Current Liabilities	$1,944,305	2,508,085	($ 563,780)	(22.5)
Long-Term Debt	304,472	7,117	297,355	4,178.1
Deferred Liabilities	670,668	629,832	40,836	6.5
Commitments and Contingencies	—	—	—	—
Total Liabilities	$2,919,445	$3,145,034	$ 338,191	10.8
Shareholders' Equity				
Common Stock, no par value; 320,000,000 shares				
authorized; 119,542,527 shares issued and				
outstanding in 1994 (116,147,035 shares in 1993)	$ 297,929	$ 203,613	$ 94,316	46.3
Retained Earnings	2,096,206	1,842,600	253,606	13.8
Accumulated Translation Adjustment	(10,834)	(19,835)	(9,001)	(45.4)
Total Shareholders' Equity	$2,383,301	$2,026,378	$ 356,923	17.6
Total Liabilities and Stockholders' Equity	$5,302,746	$5,171,412	$ 131,334	2.5

Source: Copyright © 1993 and 1994 by Apple Computer, Inc. Used with permission.

15.2

Exhibit 4. Comparative Income Statements with Horizontal Analysis

Apple Computer, Inc.
Consolidated Statements of Income
For the Years Ended September 30, 1994 and September 24, 1993

	(In thousands, except per share amounts)		Increase (Decrease)	
	1994	1993	Amount	Percentage
Net Sales	$9,188,748	$7,976,954	$1,211,794	15.2
Costs and Expenses				
Cost of Sales	$6,844,915	$5,248,834	$1,596,081	30.4
Research and Development	564,303	664,564	(100,261)	(15.1)
Selling, General and Administrative	1,384,111	1,632,362	(248,251)	(15.2)
Restructuring Costs	(126,855)	320,856	(447,711)	(139.5)
Total Costs and Expenses	$8,666,474	$7,866,616	$ 799,858	10.2
Operating Income	$ 522,274	$ 110,338	$ 411,936	373.3
Interest and Other Income (Expense), Net	(21,988)	29,321	(51,309)	(175.0)
Income Before Income Taxes	$ 500,286	$ 139,659	$ 360,627	258.2
Provision for Income Taxes	190,108	53,070	137,038	258.2
Net Income	$ 310,178	$ 86,589	$ 223,589	258.2
Earnings per Common and Common Equivalent Share	$ 2.61	$ 0.73	$ 1.88	257.5
Common and Common Equivalent Shares used in the Calculations of Earnings per Share	118,735	119,125	(390)	(.3)

Source: Copyright © 1993 and 1994 by Apple Computer, Inc. Used with permission.

proper conclusion because, in dollars, the increase of $527 million in Cash is more than three times the decrease of $162 million in Short-Term Investments.

TREND ANALYSIS

A variation of horizontal analysis is trend analysis, in which percentage changes are calculated for several successive years instead of for two years. Trend analysis is important because, with its long-run view, it may point to basic changes in the nature of a business. In addition to comparative financial statements, most companies present a summary of operations and data about other key indicators for five or more years. Domestic and international net sales from Apple's summary of operations together with a trend analysis are presented in Exhibit 5.

Trend analysis uses an index number to show changes in related items over a period of time. For index numbers, one year, the base year, is equal to 100 percent. Other years are measured in relation to that amount. For example, the 1994 index for domestic net sales was figured as follows:

$$\text{Index} = 100 \left(\frac{\text{index year amount}}{\text{base year amount}} \right) = 100 \left(\frac{\$4,987,539}{\$3,241,061} \right) = 153.9$$

Exhibit 5. Trend Analysis

Apple Computer, Inc.
Domestic and International Net Sales
Trend Analysis

	1994	1993	1992	1991	1990
Net Sales (in thousands)					
Domestic Net Sales	$4,987,539	$4,387,674	$3,885,042	$3,484,533	$3,241,061
International Net Sales	$4,201,209	$3,589,280	$3,201,500	$2,824,316	$2,317,374
Trend Analysis (in percentages)					
Domestic Net Sales	153.9	135.4	119.9	107.5	100.0
International Net Sales	181.3	154.9	138.2	121.9	100.0

Source: Copyright © 1992, 1993, and 1994 by Apple Computer, Inc. Used with permission.

An index number of 153.9 means that 1994 sales are 153.9 percent, or 1.539 times, 1990 sales.

A study of the trend analysis in Exhibit 5 clearly shows that Apple's international sales have been rising more rapidly than domestic sales over the past five years. Domestic sales have grown steadily to a five-year index of 153.9. International sales have risen substantially in every year to a five-year index of 181.3. Those contrasting trends are presented graphically in Figure 1.

Figure 1. Trend Analysis Presented Graphically for Apple Computer, Inc.

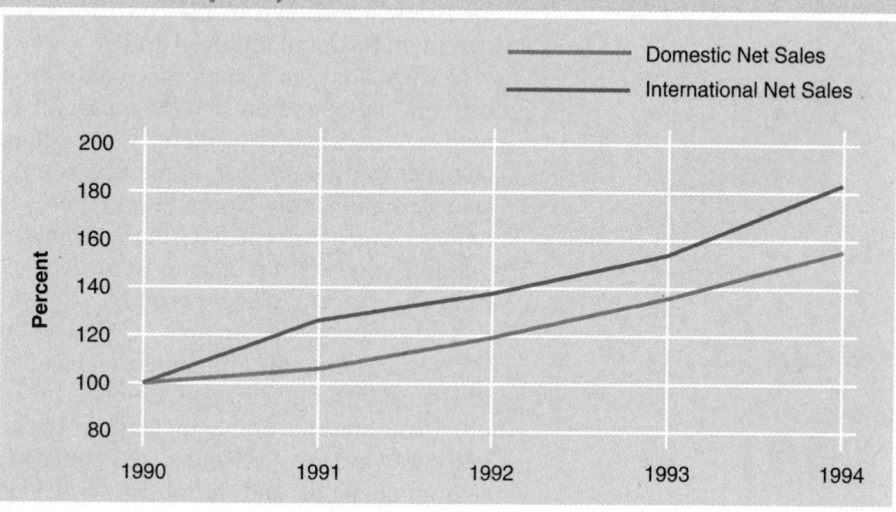

Figure 2. Common-Size Balance Sheets Presented Graphically

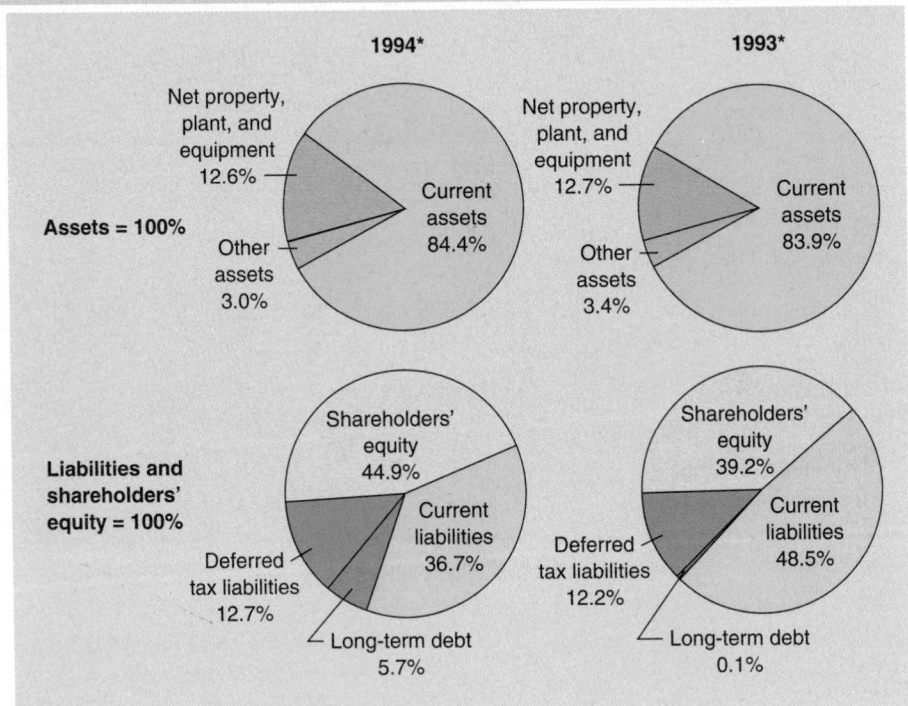

*Rounding causes some additions not to total precisely.

VERTICAL ANALYSIS

In vertical analysis, percentages are used to show the relationship of the different parts to a total in a single statement. The accountant sets a total figure in the statement equal to 100 percent and computes each component's percentage of that total. (The figure would be total assets or total liabilities and stockholders' equity on the balance sheet, and revenues or sales on the income statement.) The statement of percentages that results is called a common-size statement. Common-size balance sheets and income statements for Apple are shown in pie-chart form in Figures 2 and 3, and in financial-statement form in Exhibits 6 and 7.

Vertical analysis is useful for comparing the importance of specific components in the operation of a business. It can also be used in comparative common-size statements to identify important changes in the components from one year to the next. For Apple, the composition of assets in Exhibit 6 did not change significantly from 1993 to 1994. The composition of liabilities shows more change. Current liabilities decreased from 48.5 percent to 36.7 percent due to the new issue of long-term debt. Also, shareholders' equity increased from 39.2 percent to 44.9 percent.

The common-size income statements in Exhibit 7 show the importance of the decrease in costs and expenses from 98.6 to 94.3 percent of sales. Two factors caused that decrease. One was the effects of restructuring costs, but the other was an unfavorable increase in the cost of sales from 65.8 percent to 74.5 percent, which was offset by cost cutting in research and development and in selling, general, and administrative expenses. Those factors were major

Figure 3. Common-Size Income Statements Presented Graphically

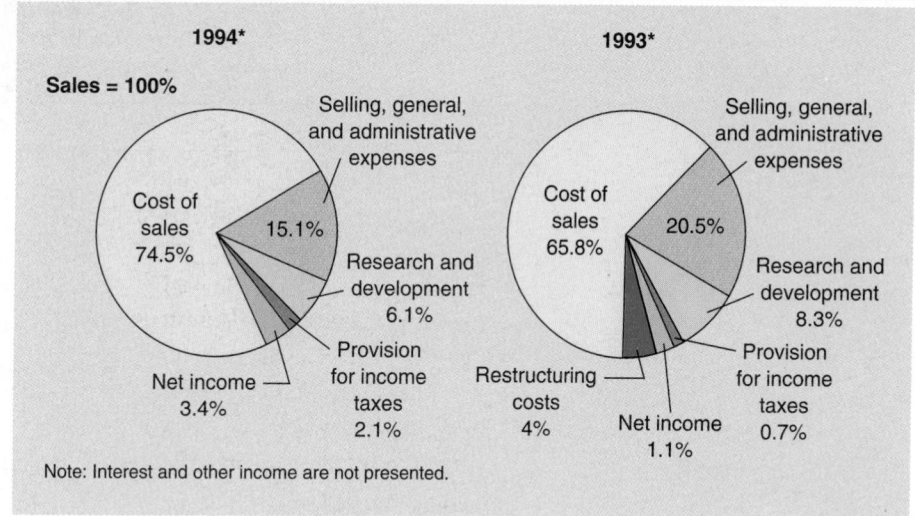

Note: Interest and other income are not presented.

*Rounding causes some additions not to total precisely.

Exhibit 6. Common-Size Balance Sheets

Apple Computer, Inc.
Common-Size Balance Sheets
September 30, 1994 and September 24, 1993

	1994*	1993*
Assets		
Current Assets	84.4%	83.9%
Net Property, Plant, and Equipment	12.6	12.7
Other Assets	3.0	3.4
Total Assets	100.0%	100.0%
Liabilities and Shareholders' Equity		
Current Liabilities	36.7%	48.5%
Long-Term Debt	5.7	.1
Deferred Tax Liabilities	12.7	12.2
Total Liabilities	55.1%	60.8%
Total Shareholders' Equity	44.9	39.2
Total Liabilities and Shareholders' Equity	100.0%	100.0%

*Results are rounded in some cases to equal 100%.

Source: Copyright © 1993 and 1994 by Apple Computer, Inc. Used with permission.

Exhibit 7. Common-Size Income Statements

Apple Computer, Inc.
Common-Size Income Statements
For Years Ended September 30, 1994 and September 24, 1993

	1994*	1993*
Sales	100.0%	100.0%
Costs and Expenses		
Cost of Sales	74.5%	65.8%
Research and Development	6.1	8.3
Selling, General, and Administrative	15.1	20.5
Restructuring Costs	(1.4)	4.0
Total Costs and Expenses	94.3%	98.6%
Operating Income	5.7%	1.4%
Interest and Other Income (Expense), Net	(.2)	.4
Income Before Income Taxes	5.4%	1.8%
Provision for Income Taxes	2.1	.7
Net Income	3.4%	1.1%

*Rounding causes some additions and subtractions not to total precisely.

Source: Copyright © 1993 and 1994 by Apple Computer, Inc. Used with permission.

causes of the increase in operating income from 1.4 to 5.7 percent. Consequently, net income as a percentage of sales increased from 1.1 percent in 1993 to 3.4 percent in 1994.

Common-size statements are often used to make comparisons between companies. They allow an analyst to compare the operating and financing characteristics of two companies of different size in the same industry. For example, the analyst may want to compare Apple to other companies in terms of the percentage of total assets financed by debt or the percentage of general administrative and selling expenses to sales and revenues. Common-size statements would show those and other relationships.

OBJECTIVE

6 *Apply ratio analysis to financial statements in a comprehensive evaluation of a company's financial situation*

RATIO ANALYSIS

Ratio analysis is an important way to state meaningful relationships between the components of the financial statements. To be most meaningful, the interpretation of ratios must include a study of the underlying data. Ratios are guides or shortcuts that are useful in evaluating a company's financial position and operations and making comparisons with results in previous years or with other companies. The primary purpose of ratios is to point out areas needing further investigation. They should be used in connection with a general understanding of the company and its environment.

Ratios may be expressed in several ways. For example, a ratio of net income of $100,000 to sales of $1,000,000 may be stated as (1) net income is 1/10, or 10 percent of sales; (2) the ratio of sales to net income is 10 to 1 (10:1), or 10 times net income; or (3) for every dollar of sales, the company has an average net income of 10 cents.

COMPREHENSIVE ILLUSTRATION OF RATIO ANALYSIS

In prior chapters, financial ratios have been introduced at appropriate points. The purpose of this section is to show a comprehensive ratio analysis of a real company, Apple Computer, Inc., using the ratios that have been introduced and a few new ones. The ratios are used to compare Apple's performance for the years 1993 and 1994 in achieving the following objectives: (1) liquidity, (2) profitability, (3) long-term solvency, (4) cash flow adequacy, and (5) market strength. Most data for the analyses come from the financial statements presented in Exhibits 3 and 4. Other data are presented as needed.

EVALUATING LIQUIDITY

Liquidity is a company's ability to pay bills when they are due and to meet unexpected needs for cash. The ratios that relate to liquidity all have to do with working capital or some part of it, because it is out of working capital that debts are paid. The objective of liquidity is also closely related to the cash flow ratios discussed in a following section.

In 1993, Apple's management predicted a better liquidity position, as follows: "The Company expects that during 1994, its liquidity position will improve from recent levels, as the measures the company has identified to reduce inventory are implemented and take effect."[8] Whether this prediction turned out to be true may be determined by referring to the liquidity ratios for 1993 and 1994 in Exhibit 8. The current ratio and the quick ratio are measures of short-term debt-paying ability. The principal difference between the two is that the numerator of the current ratio includes inventories. Inventories take longer to convert to cash than do the other current assets included in the numerator of the quick ratio. Both ratios increased from 1993 to 1994. The current ratio increased from 1.7 times to 2.3 times, and the quick ratio increased from .9 times to 1.5 times. The primary reason for the improvement was the large decrease in current liabilities. This was the result of management's decision to replace short-term borrowings with long-term debt.

Analysis of two major components of current assets, receivables and inventory, show contrasting trends. The relative size of accounts receivable and the effectiveness of credit policies are measured by the receivable turnover, which showed only a small change from 1993 to 1994 of 6.5 times to 6.2 times. The related ratio of average days' sales uncollected increased from 56.2 days in 1993 to 58.9 days in 1994. The major change in this category is in the inventory turnover, which measures the relative size of inventories. Management achieved its objective of reducing the size of inventory, and this achievement is reflected in the higher inventory turnover of 5.3 times in 1994 versus 5.0 times in 1993. This results in a favorable decrease in average days' inventory on hand from 73.0 days in 1993 to 68.9 days in 1994. When taken together, this result means that Apple's operating cycle, or the time it takes to sell and collect for products sold, decreased from 129.2 days in 1993 (73.0 days + 56.2 days) to 127.8 days in 1994 (68.9 days + 58.9 days). This decrease represents a small improvement in liquidity.

8. Apple Computer, Inc., "Management's Discussion and Analysis of Financial Condition and Results of Operations," *Annual Report,* 1993.

Exhibit 8. Liquidity Ratios of Apple Computer, Inc.

	1994	1993
Current ratio: Measure of short-term debt-paying ability		
$\dfrac{\text{Current assets}}{\text{Current liabilities}}$	$\dfrac{\$4,476,452}{\$1,944,305} = 2.3 \text{ times}$	$\dfrac{\$4,338,355}{\$2,508,085} = 1.7 \text{ times}$
Quick ratio: Measure of short-term debt-paying ability		
$\dfrac{\text{Cash + marketable securities + receivables}}{\text{Current liabilities}}$	$\dfrac{\$1,203,488 + \$54,368 + \$1,581,347}{\$1,944,305}$	$\dfrac{\$676,413 + \$215,890 + \$1,381,946}{\$2,508,085}$
	$= \dfrac{\$2,839,203}{\$1,944,305} = 1.5 \text{ times}$	$= \dfrac{\$2,274,249}{\$2,508,085} = .9 \text{ times}$
Receivable turnover: Measure of relative size of accounts receivable balance and effectiveness of credit policies		
$\dfrac{\text{Net sales}}{\text{Average accounts receivable*}}$	$\dfrac{\$9,188,748}{(\$1,381,946 + \$1,581,347) \div 2}$	$\dfrac{\$7,976,954}{(\$1,087,185 + \$1,381,946) \div 2}$
	$= \dfrac{\$9,188,748}{\$1,481,647} = 6.2 \text{ times}$	$= \dfrac{\$7,976,954}{\$1,234,566} = 6.5 \text{ times}$
Average days' sales uncollected: Measure of average time taken to collect receivables		
$\dfrac{\text{Days in year}}{\text{Receivable turnover}}$	$\dfrac{365 \text{ days}}{6.2 \text{ times}} = 58.9 \text{ days}$	$\dfrac{365 \text{ days}}{6.5 \text{ times}} = 56.2 \text{ days}$
Inventory turnover: Measure of relative size of inventory		
$\dfrac{\text{Cost of goods sold}}{\text{Average inventory*}}$	$\dfrac{\$6,844,915}{(\$1,506,638 + \$1,088,434) \div 2}$	$\dfrac{\$5,248,834}{(\$580,097 + \$1,506,638) \div 2}$
	$= \dfrac{\$6,844,915}{\$1,297,536} = 5.3 \text{ times}$	$= \dfrac{\$5,248,834}{\$1,043,368} = 5.0 \text{ times}$
Average days' inventory on hand: Measure of average days taken to sell inventory		
$\dfrac{\text{Days in year}}{\text{Inventory turnover}}$	$\dfrac{365 \text{ days}}{5.3 \text{ times}} = 68.9 \text{ days}$	$\dfrac{365 \text{ days}}{5.0 \text{ times}} = 73.0 \text{ days}$

*1992 figures are from the eleven-year financial history in Apple Computer's annual report.

Source: Copyright © 1993 and 1994 by Apple Computer, Inc. Used with permission.

EVALUATING PROFITABILITY

The objective of profitability relates to a company's ability to earn a satisfactory income so that investors and stockholders will continue to provide capital to it. A company's profitability is also closely linked to its liquidity because earnings ultimately produce cash flow. For this reason, evaluating profitability is important to both investors and creditors. The profitability ratios and analysis of Apple Computer, Inc. are shown in Exhibit 9.

Exhibit 9. Profitability Ratios of Apple Computer, Inc.

	1994	1993

Profit margin: Measure of net income produced by each dollar of sales

$$\frac{\text{Net income*}}{\text{Net sales}} \qquad \frac{\$310,178}{\$9,188,748} = 3.4\% \qquad \frac{\$86,589}{\$7,976,954} = 1.1\%$$

Asset turnover: Measure of how efficiently assets are used to produce sales

$$\frac{\text{Net sales}}{\text{Average total assets}} \qquad \frac{\$9,188,748}{(\$5,302,746 + \$5,171,412) \div 2} \qquad \frac{\$7,976,954}{(\$5,171,412 + \$4,223,693) \div 2}$$

$$= \frac{\$9,188,748}{\$5,237,079} \qquad\qquad = \frac{\$7,976,954}{\$4,697,553}$$

$$= 1.8 \text{ times} \qquad\qquad = 1.7 \text{ times}$$

Return on assets: Measure of overall earning power or profitability

$$\frac{\text{Net income}}{\text{Average total assets}} \qquad \frac{\$310,178}{\$5,237,079} = 5.9\% \qquad \frac{\$86,589}{\$4,697,553} = 1.8\%$$

Return on equity: Measure of the profitability of stockholders' investments

$$\frac{\text{Net income}}{\text{Average stockholders' equity}} \qquad \frac{\$310,178}{(\$2,383,301 + \$2,026,378) \div 2} \qquad \frac{\$86,589}{(\$2,026,378 + \$2,187,370) \div 2}$$

$$= \frac{\$310,178}{\$2,204,840} \qquad\qquad = \frac{\$86,589}{\$2,106,874}$$

$$= 14.1\% \qquad\qquad = 4.1\%$$

*In comparing companies in an industry, some analysts use net income before income taxes as the numerator to eliminate the effect of differing tax rates among firms.

Source: Copyright © 1993 and 1994 by Apple Computer, Inc. Used with permission.

Apple's profitability improved by all measures from 1993 to 1994 primarily because of the large increase in net income. The reasons for that increase were discussed previously in the sections on horizontal and vertical analysis. Profit margin, which measures the net income produced by each dollar of sales, increased from 1.1 to 3.4 percent, and asset turnover, which measures how efficiently assets are used to produce sales, increased from 1.7 to 1.8 times. The result is an improvement in the overall earning power of the company, or return on assets, from 1.8 to 5.9 percent. These relationships may be illustrated as follows:

	Profit Margin		**Asset Turnover**		**Return on Assets**
	$\dfrac{\text{Net income}}{\text{Net sales}}$	$\times$	$\dfrac{\text{net sales}}{\text{average total assets}}$	$=$	$\dfrac{\text{net income}}{\text{average total assets}}$
1994	3.4%	$\times$	1.8	$=$	6.1%
1993	1.1%	$\times$	1.7	$=$	1.9%

The slight differences in the two sets of return on assets figures result from the rounding of the ratios in the second set of computations.

Finally, the profitability of stockholders' investments or return on equity, increased from an inadequate 4.1 percent to a more favorable 14.1 percent.

BUSINESS BULLETIN: INTERNATIONAL PRACTICE

 Just because a company lists substantial cash and cash equivalents on its balance sheet does not necessarily mean that this cash is available to pay short-term debt in the United States. For example, although Apple showed almost $.7 billion dollars in cash and cash equivalents at the end of 1993, management warned that continued short-term borrowing would be necessary "because a substantial portion of the company's cash, cash equivalents, and short-term investments is held by foreign subsidiaries. . . . Amounts held by foreign subsidiaries would be subject to U.S. income taxation upon repatriation to the United States."[9]

EVALUATING LONG-TERM SOLVENCY

Long-term solvency has to do with a company's ability to survive for many years. The aim of long-term solvency analysis is to detect early signs that a company is on the road to bankruptcy. Studies have shown that accounting ratios can show as much as five years in advance that a company may fail.[10] Declining profitability and liquidity ratios are key indicators of possible business failure. Two other ratios that analysts often consider when assessing long-term solvency are debt to equity and interest coverage. Long-term solvency ratios are shown in Exhibit 10.

Increasing amounts of debt in a company's capital structure mean that the company is becoming more heavily leveraged. This condition negatively affects long-term solvency because it represents increasing legal obligations to pay interest periodically and the principal at maturity. Failure to make those payments can result in bankruptcy. The debt to equity ratio measures capital structure and leverage by showing the amount of a company's assets provided by creditors in relation to the amount provided by stockholders. Apple's capital structure became less leveraged from 1993 to 1994, during which time the debt to equity ratio decreased, from 1.6 times to 1.2 times. At the 1994 level, Apple has more debt than equity. It is especially noteworthy to recall from Exhibit 3 that the company has shifted the balance of short-term and long-term debt by issuing long-term debt and reducing short-term borrowings and that the company has increased the amount of stockholders' equity through increases in both common stock and retained earnings. All of

9. Apple Computers, Inc., "Management's Discussion and Analysis of Financial Condition and Results of Operations," *Annual Report*, 1993.

10. William H. Beaver, "Alternative Accounting Measures as Indicators of Failure," *Accounting Review*, January 1968; and Edward Altman, "Financial Ratios, Discriminant Analysis and the Prediction of Corporate Bankruptcy," *Journal of Finance*, September 1968.

Exhibit 10. Long-Term Solvency Ratios of Apple Computer, Inc.

	1994	1993
Debt to equity ratio: Measure of capital structure and leverage		
$\dfrac{\text{Total liabilities}}{\text{Stockholders' equity}}$	$\dfrac{\$2,919,445}{\$2,383,301} = 1.2$ times	$\dfrac{\$3,145,034}{\$2,026,378} = 1.6$ times
Interest coverage ratio: Measure of creditors' protection from default on interest payments		
$\dfrac{\text{Net income before}}{\text{taxes + interest expense*}}$ $\dfrac{}{\text{Interest expense*}}$	$\dfrac{\$500,286 + \$39,653}{}$ $= 13.6$ times	$\dfrac{\$139,659 + \$11,800}{}$ $= 12.8$ times

*Interest expense was obtained from the notes to the financial statements.

Source: Copyright © 1993 and 1994 by Apple Computer, Inc. Used with permission.

these are positive factors for the company's long-term solvency. As to the future, "The Company expects that it will continue to incur short- and long-term borrowings from time to time to finance U.S. working capital needs and capital expenditures."[11]

If debt is bad, why have any? The answer is that the level of debt is a matter of balance. Despite its riskiness, debt is a flexible means of financing certain business operations. Apple is using debt to finance what management plans to be a temporary increase in inventory. The interest paid on that debt is deductible for income tax purposes, whereas dividends on stock are not. Also, because debt usually carries a fixed interest charge, the cost of financing can be limited and leverage can be used to advantage. If the company is able to earn a return on assets greater than the cost of the interest, it makes an overall profit.[12] However, the company runs the risk of not earning a return on assets equal to the cost of financing those assets, thereby incurring a loss.

The interest coverage ratio measures the degree of protection creditors have from a default on interest payments. That ratio improved by a small amount, from 12.8 times in 1993 to 13.6 times in 1994, despite the increase in interest expense, because of the corresponding increase in net income. An interest coverage ratio of 13.6 times is normally considered adequate, so unless it declines in 1995, it is not a problem for Apple.

EVALUATING CASH FLOW ADEQUACY

Because cash flows are needed to pay debts when they are due, cash flow measures are closely related to the objectives of liquidity and long-term solvency. Apple's cash flow adequacy ratios are presented in Exhibit 11. By all measures, Apple's ability to generate positive operating cash flows increased from 1993 to 1994. Key to those increases is the rise in cash flow yield, or the

11. Apple Computer, Inc., "Management's Discussion and Analysis of Financial Condition and Results of Operations," *Annual Report,* 1994.

12. In addition, there are advantages to being a debtor in periods of inflation because the debt, which is fixed in dollar amount, may be repaid with cheaper dollars.

Exhibit 11. Cash Flow Adequacy Ratios of Apple Computer, Inc.

	1994	1993

Cash flow yield: Measure of a company's ability to generate operating cash flows in relation to net income

Net cash flows from
operating activities / Net income

$$\frac{\$736,995}{\$310,178} = 2.4 \text{ times}$$

$$\frac{(\$651,213)}{\$86,589} = -7.5 \text{ times}$$

Cash flows to sales: Measure of the ability of sales to generate operating cash flows

Net cash flows from
operating activities / Net sales

$$\frac{\$736,995}{\$9,188,748} = 8.0\%$$

$$\frac{(\$651,213)}{\$7,976,954} = -8.2\%$$

Cash flows to assets: Measure of the ability of assets to generate operating cash flows

Net cash flows from
operating activities / Average total assets

$$\frac{\$736,995}{(\$5,302,746 + \$5,171,412) \div 2}$$

$$\frac{(\$651,213)}{(\$5,171,412 + \$4,223,693) \div 2}$$

$$= \frac{\$736,995}{\$5,237,079} = 14.1\%$$

$$= \frac{(\$651,213)}{\$4,697,553} = -13.9\%$$

Free cash flow: Measure of cash generated or cash deficiency after providing for commitments

Net cash flows from operating
activities − dividends − net
capital expenditures

$736,995 − $56,572
− $159,587 = $520,836

($651,213) − $55,593
− $213,118 = $(919,924)

Source: Copyright © 1993 and 1994 by Apple Computer, Inc. Used with permission.

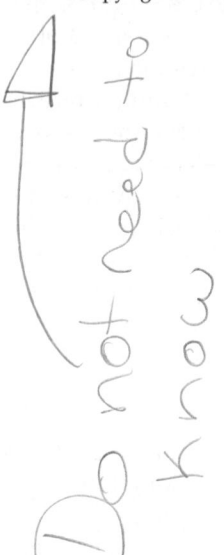
(handwritten notes: "2 of", "4 of", "Do not need to know")

relationship of cash flows from operating activities to net income, from a negative 7.5 times to a positive 2.4 times. This occurred because net cash flows from operating activities, as presented in the statement of cash flows, showed an extraordinary increase from a negative $651,213,000 in 1993 to a positive $736,995,000 in 1994. The principal reasons for the improvement in operating cash flows were the increase in net income and the large decrease in inventories, which we have already discussed. As a result of the increase in cash flow yield, the other cash flow ratios also improved significantly. Cash flows to sales, or the ability of sales to generate operating cash flows, increased from a negative 8.2 percent to a positive 8.0 percent. Cash flows to assets, or the ability of assets to generate operating cash flows, increased from a negative 13.9 percent to a positive 14.1 percent. Overall, Apple's free cash flow, or cash generated after providing for commitments, went from a dangerously negative $919,924,000 to an acceptably positive $520,836,000. Included in those computations are net capital expenditures of $213,118,000 in 1993 and $159,587,000 in 1994, based on the statement of cash flows.

EVALUATING MARKET RATIOS

The market price of a company's stock is of interest to the analyst because it represents what investors as a whole think of the company at a point in time. Market price is the price at which people are willing to buy or sell the stock. It

Exhibit 12. Market Strength Ratios of Apple Computer, Inc.

	1994	1993
Price/earnings ratio: Measure of investor confidence in a company		
$\dfrac{\text{Market price per share*}}{\text{Earnings per share}}$	$= \dfrac{\$31}{\$2.61} = 11.9$ times	$= \dfrac{\$32}{\$.73} = 43.8$ times
Dividends yield: Measure of the current return to an investor in a stock		
$\dfrac{\text{Dividends per share*}}{\text{Market price per share}}$	$= \dfrac{\$.48}{\$31} = 1.5\%$	$= \dfrac{\$.48}{\$32} = 1.5\%$

*Market price and dividends are from Apple's annual report.

Source: Copyright © 1993 and 1994 by Apple Computer, Inc. Used with permission.

provides information about how investors view the potential return and risk connected with owning the company's stock. Market price by itself is not very informative for this purpose, however. Companies differ in number of outstanding shares and amount of underlying earnings and dividends. Thus, market price must be related to earnings by considering the price/earnings ratio and the dividends yield. Those ratios for Apple appear in Exhibit 12 and have been computed using the average market price for Apple's stock during the last quarters of 1993 and 1994.

The price/earnings (P/E) ratio, which measures investor confidence in a company, is the ratio of the market price per share to earnings per share. The P/E ratio is useful in comparing the relative values placed on the earnings of different companies and in comparing the value placed on a company's shares in relation to the overall market. Apple's price/earnings ratio decreased from 43.8 times in 1993 to 11.9 times in 1994 because the earnings per share increased significantly while the market price per share remained stable. This would indicate that investors were justified in their confidence in 1993 that Apple would rebound in profitability in 1994 and beyond. The dividends yield measures a stock's current return to an investor in the form of dividends. Apple's dividends yield was unchanged from 1993 to 1994 because of little or no change in the components of the ratio. Because those are very low dividends yields, it may be concluded that investors expect to earn a greater return from increases in the market value of Apple's stock than from dividends.

SUMMARY OF THE FINANCIAL ANALYSIS OF APPLE COMPUTER, INC.

This ratio analysis clearly shows that Apple's liquidity, profitability, long-term solvency, and cash flow position improved from 1993 to 1994. The primary reasons were the increase in earnings, the decreases in inventories, the shift from short-term to long-term debt, and the increase in operating cash flows. Management points out that Apple faces many challenges, such as product introductions and transitions, fierce competition, global market risks, and other factors. It will be interesting to see whether improvement continues in 1995 and beyond. Based on the market ratios, investors seem willing to give Apple the benefit of the doubt.

CHAPTER REVIEW

REVIEW OF LEARNING OBJECTIVES

1. **Describe and discuss the objectives of financial statement analysis.** Creditors and investors, as well as managers, use financial statement analysis to judge the past performance and current position of a company. In this way they also judge its future potential and the risk associated with it. Creditors use the information gained from their analysis to make reliable loans that will be repaid with interest. Investors use the information to make investments that will provide a return that is worth the risk.

2. **Describe and discuss the standards for financial statement analysis.** Three commonly used standards for financial statement analysis are rule-of-thumb measures, the company's past performance, and industry norms. Rule-of-thumb measures are weak because of the lack of evidence that they can be widely applied. The past performance of a company can offer a guideline for measuring improvement but is not helpful in judging performance relative to other companies. Although the use of industry norms overcomes this last problem, its disadvantage is that firms are not always comparable, even in the same industry.

3. **State the sources of information for financial statement analysis.** The main sources of information about publicly held corporations are company-published reports, such as annual reports and interim financial statements; SEC reports; business periodicals; and credit and investment advisory services.

4. **Identify the issues related to evaluating the quality of a company's earnings.** Current and prospective net income is an important component in many ratios used to evaluate a company. The user should recognize that the quality of reported net income can be influenced by certain choices made by management. First, management exercises judgment in choosing the accounting methods and estimates used in computing net income. Second, discontinued operations, extraordinary gains or losses, and changes in accounting methods may affect net income positively or negatively.

5. **Apply horizontal analysis, trend analysis, and vertical analysis to financial statements.** Horizontal analysis involves the computation of changes in both dollar amounts and percentages from year to year. Trend analysis is an extension of horizontal analysis in that percentage changes are calculated for several years. The changes are usually computed by setting a base year equal to 100 and calculating the results for subsequent years as percentages of that base year. Vertical analysis uses percentages to show the relationship of the component parts to the total in a single statement. The resulting financial statements, which are expressed entirely in percentages, are called common-size statements.

6. **Apply ratio analysis to financial statements in a comprehensive evaluation of a company's financial situation.** A comprehensive ratio analysis includes the evaluation of a company's liquidity, profitability, long-term solvency, cash flow adequacy, and market ratios. The ratios for measuring these characteristics are found in Exhibits 8 to 12.

REVIEW OF CONCEPTS AND TERMINOLOGY

The following concepts and terms were introduced in this chapter.

L O 6 **Asset turnover:** Net sales divided by average total assets. Used to measure how efficiently assets are used to produce sales.

L O 6 **Average days' inventory on hand:** Days in year divided by inventory turnover. Shows the average number of days taken to sell inventory.

L O 6 **Average days' sales uncollected:** Days in year divided by receivable turnover. Shows the speed at which receivables are turned over—literally, the number of days, on average, that a company must wait to receive payment for credit sales.

L O 5 **Base year:** In financial analysis, the first year to be considered in any set of data.

L O 6 **Cash flows to assets:** Net cash flows from operating activities divided by average total assets. Used to measure the ability of assets to generate operating cash flows.

L O 6 **Cash flows to sales:** Net cash flows from operating activities divided by net sales. Used to measure the ability of sales to generate operating cash flows.

L O 6 **Cash flow yield:** Net cash flows from operating activities divided by net income. Used to measure the ability of a company to generate operating cash flows in relation to net income.

L O 5 **Common-size statement:** A financial statement in which the components of a total figure are stated in terms of percentages of that total.

L O 6 **Current ratio:** Current assets divided by current liabilities. Used as an indicator of a company's liquidity and short-term debt-paying ability.

L O 6 **Debt to equity ratio:** Total liabilities divided by stockholders' equity. Used to measure the relationship of debt financing to equity financing, or the extent to which a company is leveraged.

L O 2 **Diversified companies:** Companies that operate in more than one industry; also called *conglomerates*.

L O 6 **Dividends yield:** Dividends per share divided by market price per share. Used as a measure of the current return to an investor in a stock.

L O 1 **Financial statement analysis:** All techniques used to show important relationships among figures in financial statements.

L O 6 **Free cash flow:** Net cash flows from operating activities minus dividends minus net capital expenditures. Used to measure cash generated after providing for commitments.

L O 5 **Horizontal analysis:** A technique for analyzing financial statements that involves the computation of changes in both dollar amounts and percentages from the previous to the current year.

L O 5 **Index number:** In trend analysis, a number against which changes in related items over a period of time are measured. Calculated by setting the base year equal to 100 percent.

L O 6 **Interest coverage ratio:** Net income before taxes plus interest expense divided by interest expense. Used as a measure of the degree of protection creditors have from a default on interest payments.

L O 3 **Interim financial statement:** A financial statement issued for a period of less than one year, usually quarterly or monthly.

L O 6 **Inventory turnover:** The cost of goods sold divided by average inventory. Used to measure the relative size of inventory.

L O 6 **Operating cycle:** The time it takes to sell and collect for products sold; average days' inventory on hand plus average days' sales uncollected.

L O 1 **Portfolio:** A group of loans or investments designed to average the returns and risks of a creditor or investor.

L O 6 **Price/earnings (P/E) ratio:** Market price per share divided by earnings per share. Used as a measure of investor confidence in a company and as a means of comparison among stocks.

L O 6 **Profit margin:** Net income divided by net sales. Used to measure the percentage of each revenue dollar that contributes to net income.

L O 6 **Quick ratio:** The more liquid current assets—cash, marketable securities or short-term investments, and receivables—divided by current liabilities. Used as a measure of short-term liquidity.

L O 6 **Ratio analysis:** A technique of financial analysis in which meaningful relationships are shown between the components of the financial statements.

L O 6 **Receivable turnover:** Net sales divided by average accounts receivable. Used as a measure of the relative size of a company's accounts receivable and the success of its credit and collection policies; shows how many times, on average, receivables were turned into cash during the period.

L O 6 **Return on assets:** Net income divided by average total assets. Used to measure the amount earned on each dollar of assets invested. A measure of overall earning power, or profitability.

L O 6 **Return on equity:** Net income divided by average stockholders' equity. Used to measure how much income was earned on each dollar invested by stockholders.

L O 5 **Trend analysis:** A type of horizontal analysis in which percentage changes are calculated for several successive years instead of for two years.

L O 5 **Vertical analysis:** A technique for analyzing financial statements that uses percentages to show the relationships of the different parts to the total in a single statement.

REVIEW PROBLEM

COMPARATIVE ANALYSIS OF TWO COMPANIES

L O 6 Maggie Washington is considering an investment in one of two fast-food restaurant chains because she believes the trend toward eating out more often will continue. Her choices have been narrowed to Quik Burger and Big Steak, whose income statements and balance sheets follow.

The statement of cash flows shows that net cash flows from operations were $2,200,000 for Quik Burger and $3,000,000 for Big Steak. Net capital expenditures were $2,100,000 for Quik Burger and $1,800,000 for Big Steak. Dividends of $500,000 were paid for Quik Burger and $600,000 for Big Steak. The market prices of the stocks for Quik Burger and Big Steak were $30 and $20, respectively. Financial information pertaining to prior years is not readily available to Maggie Washington. Assume that all notes payable are current liabilities and that all bonds payable are long-term liabilities.

Balance Sheets
(in thousands)

	Quik Burger	Big Steak
Assets		
Cash	$ 2,000	$ 4,500
Accounts Receivable (net)	2,000	6,500
Inventory	2,000	5,000
Property, Plant, and Equipment (net)	20,000	35,000
Other Assets	4,000	5,000
Total Assets	$30,000	$56,000
Liabilities and Stockholders' Equity		
Accounts Payable	$ 2,500	$ 3,000
Notes Payable	1,500	4,000
Bonds Payable	10,000	30,000
Common Stock ($1 par value)	1,000	3,000
Paid-in Capital in Excess of Par Value, Common	9,000	9,000
Retained Earnings	6,000	7,000
Total Liabilities and Stockholders' Equity	$30,000	$56,000

Income Statements
(in thousands, except per share amounts)

	Quik Burger	Big Steak
Net Sales	$53,000	$86,000
Cost of Goods Sold (including restaurant operating expenses)	37,000	61,000
Gross Margin	$16,000	$25,000
General Operating Expenses		
Selling Expenses	$ 7,000	$10,000
Administrative Expenses	4,000	5,000
Interest Expense	1,400	3,200
Income Taxes Expense	1,800	3,400
Total Operating Expenses	$14,200	$21,600
Net Income	$ 1,800	$ 3,400
Earnings per Share	$ 1.80	$ 1.13

REQUIRED

Conduct a comprehensive ratio analysis of Quik Burger and Big Steak and compare the results. The analysis should be performed using the following steps (round all ratios and percentages to one decimal place):

1. Prepare an analysis of liquidity.
2. Prepare an analysis of profitability.
3. Prepare an analysis of long-term solvency.
4. Prepare an analysis of cash flow adequacy.
5. Prepare an analysis of market strength.
6. Compare the two companies by inserting the ratio calculations from the preceding five steps in a table with the following column headings: Ratio Name, Quik Burger, Big Steak, and Company with More Favorable Ratio. Indicate in the last column the company that apparently had the more favorable ratio in each case. (Consider changes of .1 or less to be neutral.)
7. In what ways would having access to prior years' information aid this analysis?

ANSWER TO REVIEW PROBLEM

Ratio Name	Quik Burger	Big Steak
1. Liquidity analysis		
a. Current ratio	$\dfrac{\$2,000 + \$2,000 + \$2,000}{\$2,500 + \$1,500}$	$\dfrac{\$4,500 + \$6,500 + \$5,000}{\$3,000 + \$4,000}$
	$= \dfrac{\$6,000}{\$4,000} = 1.5$ times	$= \dfrac{\$16,000}{\$7,000} = 2.3$ times
b. Quick ratio	$\dfrac{\$2,000 + \$2,000}{\$2,500 + \$1,500}$	$\dfrac{\$4,500 + \$6,500}{\$3,000 + \$4,000}$
	$= \dfrac{\$4,000}{\$4,000} = 1.0$ times	$= \dfrac{\$11,000}{\$7,000} = 1.6$ times
c. Receivable turnover	$\dfrac{\$53,000}{\$2,000} = 26.5$ times	$\dfrac{\$86,000}{\$6,500} = 13.2$ times

Ratio Name	Quik Burger	Big Steak
d. Average days' sales uncollected	$\dfrac{365}{26.5} = 13.8$ days	$\dfrac{365}{13.2} = 27.7$ days
e. Inventory turnover	$\dfrac{\$37,000}{\$2,000} = 18.5$ times	$\dfrac{\$61,000}{\$5,000} = 12.2$ times
f. Average days' inventory on hand	$\dfrac{365}{18.5} = 19.7$ days	$\dfrac{365}{12.2} = 29.9$ days

2. **Profitability analysis**

	Quik Burger	Big Steak
a. Profit margin	$\dfrac{\$1,800}{\$53,000} = 3.4\%$	$\dfrac{\$3,400}{\$86,000} = 4.0\%$
b. Asset turnover	$\dfrac{\$53,000}{\$30,000} = 1.8$ times	$\dfrac{\$86,000}{\$56,000} = 1.5$ times
c. Return on assets	$\dfrac{\$1,800}{\$30,000} = 6.0\%$	$\dfrac{\$3,400}{\$56,000} = 6.1\%$
d. Return on equity	$\dfrac{\$1,800}{\$1,000 + \$9,000 + \$6,000}$ $= \dfrac{\$1,800}{\$16,000} = 11.3\%$	$\dfrac{\$3,400}{\$3,000 + \$9,000 + \$7,000}$ $= \dfrac{\$3,400}{\$19,000} = 17.9\%$

3. **Long-term solvency analysis**

	Quik Burger	Big Steak
a. Debt to equity ratio	$\dfrac{\$2,500 + \$1,500 + \$10,000}{\$1,000 + \$9,000 + \$6,000}$ $= \dfrac{\$14,000}{\$16,000} = .9$ times	$\dfrac{\$3,000 + \$4,000 + \$30,000}{\$3,000 + \$9,000 + \$7,000}$ $= \dfrac{\$37,000}{\$19,000} = 1.9$ times
b. Interest coverage ratio	$\dfrac{\$1,800 + \$1,800 + \$1,400}{\$1,400}$ $= \dfrac{\$5,000}{\$1,400} = 3.6$ times	$\dfrac{\$3,400 + \$3,400 + \$3,200}{\$3,200}$ $= \dfrac{\$10,000}{\$3,200} = 3.1$ times

4. **Cash flow adequacy analysis**

	Quik Burger	Big Steak
a. Cash flow yield	$\dfrac{\$2,200}{\$1,800} = 1.2$ times	$\dfrac{\$3,000}{\$3,400} = .9$ times
b. Cash flows to sales	$\dfrac{\$2,200}{\$53,000} = 4.2\%$	$\dfrac{\$3,000}{\$86,000} = 3.5\%$
c. Cash flows to assets	$\dfrac{\$2,200}{\$30,000} = 7.3\%$	$\dfrac{\$3,000}{\$56,000} = 5.4\%$
d. Free cash flow (in thousands)	$\$2,200 - \$500 - \$2,100$ $= (\$400)$	$\$3,000 - \$600 - \$1,800$ $= \$600$

5. **Market strength analysis**

	Quik Burger	Big Steak
a. Price/earnings ratio	$\dfrac{\$30}{\$1.80} = 16.7$ times	$\dfrac{\$20}{\$1.13} = 17.7$ times
b. Dividends yield	$\dfrac{\$500,000 \div 1,000,000}{\$30} = 1.7\%$	$\dfrac{\$600,000 \div 3,000,000}{\$20} = 1.0\%$

6. Comparative analysis

Ratio Name	Quik Burger	Big Steak	Company with More Favorable Ratio*
1. Liquidity analysis			
a. Current ratio	1.5 times	2.3 times	Big Steak
b. Quick ratio	1.0 times	1.6 times	Big Steak
c. Receivable turnover	26.5 times	13.2 times	Quik Burger
d. Average days' sales uncollected	13.8 days	27.7 days	Quik Burger
e. Inventory turnover	18.5 times	12.2 times	Quik Burger
f. Average days' inventory on hand	19.7 days	29.9 days	Quik Burger
2. Profitability analysis			
a. Profit margin	3.4%	4.0%	Big Steak
b. Asset turnover	1.8 times	1.5 times	Quik Burger
c. Return on assets	6.0%	6.1%	Neutral
d. Return on equity	11.3%	17.9%	Big Steak
3. Long-term solvency analysis			
a. Debt to equity ratio	.9 times	1.9 times	Quik Burger
b. Interest coverage ratio	3.6 times	3.1 times	Quik Burger
4. Cash flow adequacy analysis			
a. Cash flow yield	1.2 times	.9 times	Quik Burger
b. Cash flows to sales	4.2%	3.5%	Quik Burger
c. Cash flows to assets	7.3%	5.4%	Quik Burger
d. Free cash flow	($400)	$600	Big Steak
5. Market strength analysis			
a. Price/earnings ratio	16.7 times	17.7 times	Big Steak
b. Dividends yield	1.7%	1.0%	Quik Burger

*This analysis indicates the company with the apparently more favorable ratio. Class discussion may focus on conditions under which different conclusions may be drawn.

7. Usefulness of prior years' information

Prior years' information would be helpful in two ways. First, turnover, return, and cash flows to assets ratios could be based on average amounts. Second, a trend analysis could be performed for each company.

CHAPTER ASSIGNMENTS

QUESTIONS

1. What are the differences and similarities in the objectives of investors and creditors in using financial statement analysis?
2. What role does risk play in making loans and investments?
3. What standards are commonly used to evaluate financial statements, and what are their relative merits?
4. Why would a financial analyst compare the ratios of Steelco, a steel company, with the ratios of other companies in the steel industry? What factors might invalidate such a comparison?
5. Where may an investor look for information about a publicly held company in which he or she is thinking of investing?

6. What is the basis of the statement "Accounting income is a useless measurement because it is based on so many arbitrary decisions"? Is the statement true?

7. Why would an investor want to see both horizontal and trend analyses of a company's financial statements?

8. What does the following sentence mean: "Based on 1980 equaling 100, net income increased from 240 in 1995 to 260 in 1996"?

9. What is the difference between horizontal and vertical analysis?

10. What is the purpose of ratio analysis?

11. Under what circumstances would a current ratio of 3:1 be good? Under what circumstances would it be bad?

12. In a period of high interest rates, why are receivable turnover and inventory turnover especially important?

13. The following statements were made on page 35 of the November 6, 1978, issue of *Fortune* magazine: "Supermarket executives are beginning to look back with some nostalgia on the days when the standard profit margin was 1 percent of sales. Last year the industry overall margin came to a thin 0.72 percent." How could a supermarket earn a satisfactory return on assets with such a small profit margin?

14. Company A and Company B both have net incomes of $1,000,000. Is it possible to say that these companies are equally successful? Why or why not?

15. Circo Company has a return on assets of 12 percent and a debt to equity ratio of .5. Would you expect return on equity to be more or less than 12 percent?

16. What amount is common to all cash flow adequacy ratios? To what other groups of ratios are the cash flow adequacy ratios most closely related?

17. The market price of Company J's stock is the same as that of Company Q. How might you determine whether investors are equally confident about the future of these companies?

SHORT EXERCISES

SE 1.
L O 1, 2
Objectives and Standards of Financial Statement Analysis

Check Figure: a. 2, 4

Indicate whether each of the following items is (a) an objective or (b) a standard of comparison of financial statement analysis.

1. Industry norms
2. Assessment of the company's past performance
3. The company's past performance
4. Assessment of future potential and related risk
5. Rule-of-thumb measures

SE 2.
L O 3
Sources of Information

Check Figures: 1. c; 2. a; 3. d; 4. b; 5. c

For each piece of information listed below, indicate whether the *best* source would be (a) reports published by the company, (b) SEC reports, (c) business periodicals, or (d) credit and investment advisory services.

1. Current market value of a company's stock
2. Management's analysis of the past year's operations
3. Objective assessment of a company's financial performance
4. Most complete body of financial disclosures
5. Current events affecting the company

SE 3.
L O 5
Trend Analysis

Check Figures: Net sales, 19×3: 141.1%; Accounts receivable, 19×3: 204.8%

Using 19x1 as the base year, prepare a trend analysis for the following data, and tell whether the results suggest a favorable or unfavorable trend. (Round your answers to one decimal place.)

	19x3	19x2	19x1
Net sales	$158,000	$136,000	$112,000
Accounts receivable (net)	$43,000	$32,000	$21,000

SE 4. *Horizontal Analysis*
L O 5
No check figure

Compute the amount and percentage changes for the following income statements, and comment on the changes from 19x1 to 19x2. (Round the percentage changes to one decimal place.)

Nu-Way, Inc.
Comparative Income Statements
For the Years Ended December 31, 19x2 and 19x1

	19x2	19x1
Net Sales	$180,000	$145,000
Cost of Goods Sold	112,000	88,000
Gross Margin	$ 68,000	$ 57,000
Operating Expenses	40,000	30,000
Operating Income	$ 28,000	$ 27,000
Interest Expense	7,000	5,000
Income Before Income Taxes	$ 21,000	$ 22,000
Income Taxes	7,000	8,000
Net Income	$ 14,000	$ 14,000
Earnings per Share	$ 1.40	$ 1.40

SE 5. *Vertical Analysis*
L O 5
No check figure

Express the comparative balance sheets that follow as common-size statements, and comment on the changes from 19x1 to 19x2. (Round computations to one decimal place.)

Nu-Way, Inc.
Comparative Balance Sheets
December 31, 19x2 and 19x1

	19x2	19x1
Assets		
Current Assets	$ 24,000	$ 20,000
Property, Plant, and Equipment (net)	130,000	100,000
Total Assets	$154,000	$120,000
Liabilities and Stockholders' Equity		
Current Liabilities	$ 18,000	$ 22,000
Long-Term Liabilities	90,000	60,000
Stockholders' Equity	46,000	38,000
Total Liabilities and Stockholders' Equity	$154,000	$120,000

SE 6. *Liquidity Analysis*
L O 6
Check Figures: Current ratio, 19x2: 1.3; 19x1: .9; Quick ratio, 19x2: .9; 19x1: .7

Using the information for Nu-Way, Inc. in SE 4 and SE 5, compute the current ratio, quick ratio, receivable turnover, average days' sales uncollected, inventory turnover, and average days' inventory on hand for 19x1 and 19x2. Inventories were $4,000 in 19x0, $5,000 in 19x1, and $7,000 in 19x2. Accounts Receivable were $6,000 in 19x0, $8,000 in 19x1, and $10,000 in 19x2. There were no marketable securities or prepaid assets. Comment on the results. (Round computations to one decimal place.)

SE 7. *Profitability*
L O 6 *Analysis*
Check Figures: Profit margin, 19x2: 7.8%; 19x1: 9.7%

Using the information for Nu-Way, Inc. in SE 4 and SE 5, compute the profit margin, asset turnover, return on assets, and return on equity for 19x1 and 19x2. In 19x0, total assets were $100,000 and total stockholders' equity was $30,000. Comment on the results. (Round computations to one decimal place.)

SE 8. *Long-Term Solvency*
L O 6 *Analysis*
Check Figures: Interest coverage, 19x2: 4.0 times; 19x1: 5.4 times

Using the information for Nu-Way, Inc. in SE 4 and SE 5, compute the debt to equity and interest coverage ratios for 19x1 and 19x2. Comment on the results. (Round computations to one decimal place.)

SE 9. *Cash Flow Adequacy*
L O 6 *Analysis*
Check Figures: Cash flow yield, 19x2: 1.1 times; 19x1: 1.5 times

Using the information for Nu-Way, Inc. in SE 4, SE 5, and SE 7, compute the cash flow yield, cash flows to sales, cash flows to assets, and free cash flow for 19x1 and 19x2. Net cash flows from operating activities were $21,000 in 19x1 and $16,000 in 19x2. Net capital expenditures were $30,000 in 19x1 and $40,000 in 19x2. Cash dividends were $6,000 in both years. Comment on the results. (Round computations to one decimal place.)

SE 10. *Market Strength*
L O 6 *Analysis*
Check Figures: P/E ratio, 19x2: 14.3 times; 19x1: 21.4 times

Using the information for Nu-Way, Inc. in SE 4, SE 5, and SE 9, compute the price/earnings and dividends yield ratios for 19x1 and 19x2. The company had 10,000 shares of common stock outstanding in both years. The price of Nu-Way's common stock was $30 in 19x1 and $20 in 19x2. Comment on the results. (Round computations to one decimal place.)

EXERCISES

E 1. *Effect of Alternative*
L O 4 *Accounting Methods*
Check Figures: 1. $19,500; 2. $15,000

At the end of its first year of operations, a company calculated its ending merchandise inventory according to three different accounting methods, as follows: FIFO, $47,500; average-cost, $45,000; and LIFO, $43,000. If the company uses the average-cost method, net income for the year would be $17,000.

1. Determine net income if the FIFO method is used.
2. Determine net income if the LIFO method is used.
3. Which method is more conservative?
4. Will the consistency convention be violated if the company chooses to use the LIFO method?
5. Does the full-disclosure convention require disclosure of the inventory method selected by management in the financial statements?

E 2. *Effect of Alternative*
L O 4, 6 *Accounting Methods*
Check Figures: 1. Jeans F' All; 2. Jeans 'R' Us; 3. Jeans F' All; 4. Cannot tell

Jeans F' All and Jeans 'R' Us are very similar companies in size and operation. Jeans F' All uses FIFO and the straight-line depreciation method, and Jeans 'R' Us uses LIFO and accelerated depreciation. Prices have been rising during the past several years. Each company has paid its taxes in full for the current year, and each uses the same method for calculating income taxes as for financial reporting. Identify which company will report the greater amount for each of the following ratios.

1. Current ratio
2. Inventory turnover
3. Profit margin
4. Return on assets

If you cannot tell which company will report the greater amount, explain why.

E 3. *Horizontal Analysis*
L O 5
No check figure

Compute the amount and percentage changes for the following balance sheets, and comment on the changes from 19x1 to 19x2. (Round the percentage changes to one decimal place.)

Herrera Company
Comparative Balance Sheets
December 31, 19x2 and 19x1

	19x2	19x1
Assets		
Current Assets	$ 18,600	$ 12,800
Property, Plant, and Equipment (net)	109,464	97,200
Total Assets	$128,064	$110,000
Liabilities and Stockholders' Equity		
Current Liabilities	$ 11,200	$ 3,200
Long-Term Liabilities	35,000	40,000
Stockholders' Equity	81,864	66,800
Total Liabilities and Stockholders' Equity	$128,064	$110,000

E 4. *Trend Analysis*
L O 5

Check Figures: Net sales, 19×5: 116.0; Cost of goods sold, 19×5: 123.0%

Using 19x1 as the base year, prepare a trend analysis of the following data, and tell whether the situation shown by the trends is favorable or unfavorable. (Round your answers to one decimal place.)

	19x5	19x4	19x3	19x2	19x1
Net sales	$12,760	$11,990	$12,100	$11,440	$11,000
Cost of goods sold	8,610	7,700	7,770	7,350	7,000
General and administrative expenses	2,640	2,592	2,544	2,448	2,400
Operating income	1,510	1,698	1,786	1,642	1,600

E 5. *Vertical Analysis*
L O 5

Check Figures: Net Operating Income, 19x2: 3.0%; 19x1: 5.0%

Express the comparative income statements that follow as common-size statements, and comment on the changes from 19x1 to 19x2. (Round computations to one decimal place.)

Herrera Company
Comparative Income Statements
For the Years Ended December 31, 19x2 and 19x1

	19x2	19x1
Net Sales	$212,000	$184,000
Cost of Goods Sold	127,200	119,600
Gross Margin	$ 84,800	$ 64,400
Selling Expenses	$ 53,000	$ 36,800
General Expenses	25,440	18,400
Total Operating Expenses	$ 78,440	$ 55,200
Net Operating Income	$ 6,360	$ 9,200

E 6. *Liquidity Analysis*
L O 6

Partial comparative balance sheet and income statement information for Prange Company follows.

	19x2	19x1
Cash	$ 3,400	$ 2,600
Marketable securities	1,800	4,300
Accounts receivable (net)	11,200	8,900
Inventory	13,600	12,400
Total current assets	$30,000	$28,200
Current liabilities	$10,000	$ 7,050
Net sales	$80,640	$55,180
Cost of goods sold	54,400	50,840
Gross margin	$26,240	$ 4,340

The year-end balances for Accounts Receivable and Inventory in 19x0 were $8,100 and $12,800, respectively. Compute the current ratio, quick ratio, receivable turnover, average days' sales uncollected, inventory turnover, and average days' inventory on hand for each year. (Round computations to one decimal place.) Comment on the change in the company's liquidity position from 19x1 to 19x2.

E 7. *Turnover Analysis*
L O 6

McEnroe's Men's Shop has been in business for four years. Because the company has recently had a cash flow problem, management wonders whether there is a problem with receivables or inventories. Here are selected figures from the company's financial statements (in thousands).

	19x4	19x3	19x2	19x1
Net sales	$144	$112	$96	$80
Cost of goods sold	90	72	60	48
Accounts receivable (net)	24	20	16	12
Merchandise inventory	28	22	16	10

Compute receivable turnover and inventory turnover for each of the four years, and comment on the results relative to the cash flow problem that McEnroe's Men's Shop has been experiencing. (Use ending balances for calculations for 19x1, and round computations to one decimal place.)

E 8. *Profitability*
L O 6 *Analysis*

At year end, Bodes Company had total assets of $320,000 in 19x0, $340,000 in 19x1, and $380,000 in 19x2. In all three years, stockholders' equity equaled 60 percent of total assets. In 19x1, the company had net income of $38,556 on revenues of $612,000. In 19x2, the company had net income of $49,476 on revenues of $798,000. Compute the profit margin, asset turnover, return on assets, and return on equity for 19x1 and 19x2. Comment on the apparent cause of the increase or decrease in profitability. (Round the percentages and other ratios to one decimal place.)

E 9. *Long-Term Solvency*
L O 6 *and Market Test Ratios*

An investor is considering investing in the long-term bonds and common stock of Companies B and C. Both companies operate in the same industry. In addition, both companies pay a dividend per share of $2 and a yield of 10 percent on their long-term bonds. Other data for the two companies follow.

	Company B	Company C
Total assets	$1,200,000	$540,000
Total liabilities	540,000	297,000
Net income before taxes	144,000	64,800
Interest expense	48,600	26,730
Earnings per share	1.60	2.50
Market price of common stock	20	23.75

Compute the debt to equity, interest coverage, price/earnings (P/E), and dividends yield ratios, and comment on the results. (Round computations to one decimal place.)

E 10. *Cash Flow Adequacy*
L O 6 *Analysis*

Using the data on the next page, taken from the financial statements of Furri, Inc., compute the cash flow yield, cash flows to sales, cash flows to assets, and free cash flow.

Net sales	$3,200,000
Net income	352,000
Net cash flows from operating activities	456,000
Total assets, beginning of year	2,890,000
Total assets, end of year	3,120,000
Cash dividends	120,000
Net capital expenditures	298,000

E 11. *Preparation of*
L O 6 *Statements from Ratios and Incomplete Data*

Following are the income statement and balance sheet of Chang Corporation, with most of the amounts missing.

Chang Corporation
Income Statement
For the Year Ended December 31, 19x1
(in thousands of dollars)

Net Sales		$9,000
Cost of Goods Sold		(a)
Gross Margin		(b)
Operating Expenses		
Selling Expenses	$ (c)	
Administrative Expenses	117	
Interest Expense	81	
Income Taxes Expense	310	
Total Operating Expenses		(d)
Net Income		$ (e)

Chang Corporation
Balance Sheet
December 31, 19x1
(in thousands of dollars)

Assets

Cash	$ (f)	
Accounts Receivable (net)	(g)	
Inventories	(h)	
Total Current Assets		$ (i)
Property, Plant, and Equipment (net)		2,700
Total Assets		$ (j)

Liabilities and Stockholders' Equity

Current Liabilities	$ (k)	
Bonds Payable, 9% interest	(l)	
Total Liabilities		$ (m)
Common Stock—$10 par value	$1,500	
Paid-in Capital in Excess of Par Value, Common	1,300	
Retained Earnings	2,000	
Total Stockholders' Equity		4,800
Total Liabilities and Stockholders' Equity		$ (n)

Chang's only interest expense is on long-term debt. Its debt to equity ratio is .5; its current ratio, 3:1; its quick ratio, 2:1; the receivable turnover, 4.5; and its inventory turnover, 4.0. The return on assets is 10 percent. All ratios are based on the current year's information. No averages were available. Using the information presented, complete the financial statements. Show supporting computations.

SKILLS DEVELOPMENT EXERCISES

Conceptual Analysis

SDE 1.
L O 2, 6
Standards for Financial Analysis

No check figure

Helene Curtis is a well-known, publicly owned corporation. "By almost any standard, Chicago-based Helene Curtis rates as one of America's worst-managed personal care companies. In recent years its return on equity has hovered between 10% and 13%, well below the industry average of 18% to 19%. Net profit margins of 2% to 3% are half that of competitors. . . . As a result, while leading names like Revlon and Avon are trading at three and four times book value, Curtis's trades at less than two-thirds book value."[13] Considering that many companies in other industries are happy with a return on equity of 10 percent to 13 percent, why is this analysis so critical of Curtis's performance? Assuming that Curtis could double its profit margin, what other information would be necessary to project the resulting return on stockholders' investment? Why are Revlon's and Avon's stocks trading for more than Curtis's? Be prepared to discuss your answers to these questions in class.

SDE 2.
L O 4
Quality of Earnings

No check figure

On Tuesday, January 19, 1988, *International Business Machines Corp. (IBM)*, the world's largest computer manufacturer, reported greatly increased earnings for the fourth quarter of 1987. Despite this reported gain in earnings, the price of IBM's stock on the New York Stock Exchange declined by $6 per share to $111.75. In sympathy with this move, most other technology stocks also declined.[14]

IBM's fourth-quarter net earnings rose from $1.39 billion, or $2.28 a share, to $2.08 billion, or $3.47 a share, an increase of 49.6 percent and 52.2 percent over the year-earlier period. Management declared that these results demonstrated the effectiveness of IBM's efforts to become more competitive and that, despite the economic uncertainties of 1988, the company was planning for growth.

The apparent cause of the stock price decline was that the huge increase in income could be traced to nonrecurring gains. Investment analysts pointed out that IBM's high earnings stemmed primarily from factors such as a lower tax rate. Despite most analysts' expectations of a tax rate between 40 and 42 percent, IBM's rate was a low 36.4 percent, down from the previous year's 45.3 percent.

In addition, analysts were disappointed in IBM's revenue growth. Revenues within the United States were down, and much of the growth in revenues came through favorable currency translations, increases that might not be repeated. In fact, some estimates of the fourth-quarter earnings attributed $.50 per share to currency translations and another $.25 to tax-rate changes.

Other factors contributing to the rise in earnings were one-time transactions, such as the sale of Intel Corporation stock and bond redemptions, along with a corporate stock buyback program that reduced the amount of stock outstanding in the fourth quarter by 7.4 million shares.

The analysts were concerned about the quality of IBM's earnings. Identify four quality of earnings issues reported in the case and the analysts' concern about each. In percentage terms, what is the impact of the currency changes on fourth-quarter earnings? Comment on management's assessment of IBM's performance. Do you agree with management? (Optional question: What has IBM's subsequent performance been?) Be prepared to discuss your answers to the questions in class.

---

13. *Forbes*, November 13, 1978, p. 154.

14. "Technology Firms Post Strong Earnings But Stock Prices Decline Sharply," *Wall Street Journal*, January 21, 1988; Donald R. Seace, "Industrials Plunge 57.2 Points—Technology Stocks' Woes Cited," *Wall Street Journal*, January 21, 1988.

SDE 3. *Use of Investors*
L O 3 *Service*

Check Figures: Revenue, Beverages: 34.5%; Snack Foods: 28.1%; Restaurants: 37.4%

Refer to Exhibit 2, which contains the listing of *PepsiCo, Inc.* from Moody's *Handbook of Dividend Achievers*. Write a short report that describes:

1. PepsiCo's business segments and their relative importance (In what three business segments does PepsiCo, Inc. operate and what is the relative size of each in terms of sales and operating income? Which business segment appears to be the most profitable?)
2. PepsiCo's earnings history (What generally has been the relationship between PepsiCo's return on assets and its return on equity over the years 1987 to 1993? What does this tell you about the way the company is financed? What figures back up your conclusion?)
3. The trend of PepsiCo's stock price and price/earnings ratio for the seven years shown
4. PepsiCo's prospects, including developments that are likely to affect the future of the company

Ethical Dilemma

SDE 4. *Management of*
L O 4 *Earnings*

No check figure

In 1993, the *Wall Street Journal* reported that *H. J. Heinz Co.*, the famous maker of catsup and many other food products, earned a quarterly income of $.75 per share, including a gain on sale of assets of $.24 per share. Income from continuing operations was only $.51 per share, or 16 percent below the previous year's figure. The paper was critical of Heinz's use of a one-time gain to increase earnings: "In recent years, H. J. Heinz Co. has been spicing up its earnings with special items. The latest quarter is no exception." An analyst was quoted as saying that Heinz had not admitted the slump in its business but had "started including nonrecurring items in the results they were showing. That created an artificially high base of earnings that they can no longer match."[15] Do you think it is unethical for a company's management to increase earnings periodically through the use of one-time transactions, such as sales of assets, on which it has a profit? What potential long-term negative effects might this practice have for Heinz?

Research Activity

SDE 5. *Use of Investors*
L O 3 *Services*

No check figure

In your school library, find either *Moody's Investors Service, Standard & Poor's Industry Guide,* or *The Value Line Investment Survey.* Locate the reports on three corporations. You may choose the corporations at random or choose them from the same industry, if directed to do so by your instructor. (If you did a related exercise in a previous chapter, use the same three companies.) Write a summary of what you learn about each company's financial performance and its prospect for the future and be prepared to discuss your findings in class.

Decision-Making Practice

SDE 6. *Effect of Alternative*
L O 4 *Accounting Methods*
on Executive
Compensation

Check Figures: EPS, 19x3: $1.50; 19x2: $1.80; 19x1: $2.30

At the beginning of 19x1, Ted Lazzerini retired as president and principal stockholder in *Tedtronics Corporation,* a successful producer of personal computer equipment. As an incentive to the new management, Lazzerini supported the board of directors' new executive compensation plan, which provides cash bonuses to key executives for years in which the company's earnings per share equal or exceed the current dividends per share of $2.00, plus a $.20 per share increase in dividends for each future year. Thus, for management to receive the bonuses, the company must earn per-share income of $2.00 the first year, $2.20 the second, $2.40 the third, and so forth. Since Lazzerini owns 500,000 of the 1,000,000 common shares outstanding, the dividend income will provide for his retirement years. He is also protected against inflation by the regular increase in dividends. Earnings and dividends per share for the first three years of operation under the new management were as shown on the next page.

15. "Heinz's 25% Jump in 2nd-Period Profit Masks Weakness," *Wall Street Journal,* December 8, 1993.

	19x3	19x2	19x1
Earnings per share	$2.50	$2.50	$2.50
Dividends per share	2.40	2.20	2.00

During this time, management earned bonuses totaling more than $1 million under the compensation plan. Lazzerini, who had taken no active part on the board of directors, began to worry about the unchanging level of earnings and decided to study the company's annual report more carefully. The notes to the annual report revealed the following information:

a. Management changed from the LIFO inventory method to the FIFO method in 19x1. The effect of the change was to decrease cost of goods sold by $200,000 in 19x1, $300,000 in 19x2, and $400,000 in 19x3.
b. Management changed from the double-declining-balance accelerated depreciation method to the straight-line method in 19x2. The effect of this change was to decrease depreciation by $400,000 in 19x2 and by $500,000 in 19x3.
c. In 19x3, management increased the estimated useful life of intangible assets from five to ten years. The effect of this change was to decrease amortization expense by $100,000 in 19x3.

1. Compute earnings per share for each year according to the accounting methods in use at the beginning of 19x1. (Use common shares outstanding.)
2. Have the executives earned their bonuses? What serious effect has the compensation package apparently had on the net assets of Tedtronics Corporation? How could Lazzerini have protected himself from what has happened?

PROBLEM SET A

A 1.
LO 4, 6
Effect of Alternative Accounting Methods
Check Figure: 2. Difference in net income: $51,667

Sarrafi Company began operations by purchasing $300,000 in equipment that had an estimated useful life of nine years and an estimated residual value of $30,000.

During 19xx, Sarrafi Company purchased inventory as presented in the chart that follows.

January	2,000 units at $25	$ 50,000
March	4,000 units at $24	96,000
May	1,000 units at $27	27,000
July	5,000 units at $27	135,000
September	6,000 units at $28	168,000
November	2,000 units at $29	58,000
December	3,000 units at $28	84,000
Total	23,000 units	$618,000

During the year, the company sold 19,000 units for a total of $910,000 and incurred salaries expense of $170,000 and expenses other than depreciation of $120,000.

Sarrafi's management is anxious to present its income statement fairly in its first year of operation. It realizes that alternative methods are available for accounting for inventory and equipment. Management wants to determine the effect of various alternatives on this year's income. Two sets of alternatives are required.

REQUIRED

1. Prepare two income statements for Sarrafi Company: one using the FIFO and straight-line methods, the other using the LIFO and the double-declining-balance methods.
2. Prepare a schedule accounting for the difference in the two net income figures obtained in **1**.
3. What effect does the choice of accounting methods have on Sarrafi's inventory turnover? What conclusion can you draw?
4. What effect does the choice of accounting methods have on Sarrafi's return on assets? Assume that the company's only assets are cash of $30,000, inventory, and equipment.

Use year-end balances to compute ratios. Round all ratios and percentages to one decimal place. Is your evaluation of Sarrafi's profitability affected by the choice of accounting methods?

A 2. *Horizontal and*
L O 5 *Vertical Analysis*

No check figure

The condensed comparative income statements and balance sheets for Kelso Corporation follow.

Kelso Corporation
Comparative Income Statements
For the Years Ended December 31, 19x2 and 19x1

	19x2	19x1
Net Sales	$800,400	$742,600
Cost of Goods Sold	454,100	396,200
Gross Margin	$346,300	$346,400
Operating Expenses		
Selling Expenses	$130,100	$104,600
Administrative Expenses	140,300	115,500
Interest Expense	25,000	20,000
Income Taxes Expense	14,000	35,000
Total Operating Expenses	$309,400	$275,100
Net Income	$ 36,900	$ 71,300
Earnings per Share	$ 1.23	$ 2.38

Kelso Corporation
Comparative Balance Sheets
December 31, 19x2 and 19x1

	19x2	19x1
Assets		
Cash	$ 31,100	$ 27,200
Accounts Receivable (net)	72,500	42,700
Inventory	122,600	107,800
Property, Plant, and Equipment (net)	577,700	507,500
Total Assets	$803,900	$685,200
Liabilities and Stockholders' Equity		
Accounts Payable	$104,700	$ 72,300
Notes Payable	50,000	50,000
Bonds Payable	200,000	110,000
Common Stock—$10 par value	300,000	300,000
Retained Earnings	149,200	152,900
Total Liabilities and Stockholders' Equity	$803,900	$685,200

REQUIRED

Perform the following analyses. Round all ratios and percentages to one decimal place.

1. Prepare schedules showing the amount and percentage changes from 19x1 to 19x2 for the comparative income statements and the balance sheets.
2. Prepare common-size income statements and balance sheets for 19x1 and 19x2.
3. Comment on the results in **1** and **2** by identifying favorable and unfavorable changes in the components and composition of the statements.

A 3. *Analyzing the Effects*
L O 6 *of Transactions on Ratios*

Estevez Corporation engaged in the transactions listed in the first column of the following table. Opposite each transaction is a ratio and space to mark the effect of each transaction on the ratio.

Transaction	Ratio	Effect		
		Increase	**Decrease**	**None**
a. Issued common stock for cash.	Asset turnover			
b. Declared cash dividend.	Current ratio			
c. Sold treasury stock.	Return on equity			
d. Borrowed cash by issuing note payable.	Debt to equity ratio			
e. Paid salaries expense.	Inventory turnover			
f. Purchased merchandise for cash.	Current ratio			
g. Sold equipment for cash.	Receivable turnover			
h. Sold merchandise on account.	Quick ratio			
i. Paid current portion of long-term debt.	Return on assets			
j. Gave sales discount.	Profit margin			
k. Purchased marketable securities for cash.	Quick ratio			
l. Declared 5% stock dividend.	Current ratio			
m. Purchased a building.	Free cash flow			

REQUIRED

Place an X in the appropriate column to show whether the transaction increased, decreased, or had no effect on the indicated ratio.

A 4. *Ratio Analysis*
L O 6

Additional data for Kelso Corporation in 19x2 and 19x1 follow. These data should be used in conjunction with the data in A 2.

	19x2	19x1
Net cash flows from operating activities	$ 64,000	$99,000
Net capital expenditures	$119,000	$38,000
Dividends paid	$ 31,400	$35,000
Number of common shares	30,000	30,000
Market price per share	$40	$60
Earnings per share	$1.23	$2.38

Selected balances at the end of 19x0 were Accounts Receivable (net), $52,700; Inventory, $99,400; Total Assets, $647,800; and Stockholders' Equity, $376,600. All of Kelso's notes payable were current liabilities; all of the bonds payable were long-term liabilities.

REQUIRED

Perform the following analyses. Round all answers to one decimal place, and consider changes of .1 or less to be neutral. After making the calculations, indicate whether each ratio improved or deteriorated from 19x1 to 19x2 by writing F for favorable or U for unfavorable.

1. Prepare a liquidity analysis by calculating for each year the (a) current ratio, (b) quick ratio, (c) receivable turnover, (d) average days' sales uncollected, (e) inventory turnover, and (f) average days' inventory on hand.
2. Prepare a profitability analysis by calculating for each year the (a) profit margin, (b) asset turnover, (c) return on assets, and (d) return on equity.

Financial Statement Analysis

3. Prepare a long-term solvency analysis by calculating for each year the (a) debt to equity ratio and (b) interest coverage ratio.
4. Conduct a cash flow adequacy analysis by calculating for each year the (a) cash flow yield, (b) cash flows to sales, (c) cash flows to assets, and (d) free cash flow.
5. Conduct a market strength analysis by calculating for each year the (a) price/earnings ratio and (b) dividends yield.

A 5. *Comprehensive*
L O 6 *Ratio Analysis of*
Two Companies
Check Figures: 1b. Quick ratio, Morton: .4; Pound: 1.0; 2d. Return on equity, Morton: 11.8%; Pound: 8.8%

Louise Brown has decided to invest some of her savings in common stock. She feels that the chemical industry has good growth prospects and has narrowed her choice to two companies in that industry. As a final step in making the choice, she has decided to perform a comprehensive ratio analysis of the two companies, Morton and Pound. Income statement and balance sheet data for the two companies appear below.

	Morton	Pound
Net Sales	$9,486,200	$27,287,300
Cost of Goods Sold	5,812,200	18,372,400
Gross Margin	$3,674,000	$ 8,914,900
Operating Expenses		
Selling Expenses	$1,194,000	$ 1,955,700
Administrative Expense	1,217,400	4,126,000
Interest Expense	270,000	1,360,000
Income Taxes Expense	450,000	600,000
Total Operating Expenses	$3,131,400	$ 8,041,700
Net Income	$ 542,600	$ 873,200
Earnings per Share	$ 1.55	$ .88

	Morton	Pound
Assets		
Cash	$ 126,100	$ 514,300
Marketable Securities (at cost)	117,500	1,200,000
Accounts Receivable (net)	456,700	2,600,000
Inventories	1,880,000	4,956,000
Prepaid Expenses	72,600	156,600
Property, Plant, and Equipment (net)	5,342,200	19,356,000
Intangibles and Other Assets	217,000	580,000
Total Assets	$8,212,100	$29,362,900
Liabilities and Stockholders' Equity		
Accounts Payable	$ 517,400	$ 2,342,000
Notes Payable	1,000,000	2,000,000
Income Taxes Payable	85,200	117,900
Bonds Payable	2,000,000	15,000,000
Common Stock—$1 par value	350,000	1,000,000
Paid-in Capital in Excess of Par Value, Common	1,747,300	5,433,300
Retained Earnings	2,512,200	3,469,700
Total Liabilities and Stockholders' Equity	$8,212,100	$29,362,900

During the year, Morton paid a total of $140,000 in dividends, and its current market price per share is $20. Pound paid a total of $600,000 in dividends during the year, and its current market price per share is $9. Morton has net cash flows from operations of $771,500 and net capital expenditures of $450,000. Pound has net cash flows from operations of $843,000 and net capital expenditures of $1,550,000. Information pertaining to prior years is not readily available. Assume that all notes payable are current liabilities and that all bonds payable are long-term liabilities.

REQUIRED

Conduct a comprehensive ratio analysis of Morton and of Pound, using the current end-of-year data. Compare the results. Round all ratios and percentages except earnings per share to one decimal place. This analysis should be done in the following steps:

1. Prepare an analysis of liquidity by calculating for each company the (a) current ratio, (b) quick ratio, (c) receivable turnover, (d) average days' sales uncollected, (e) inventory turnover, and (f) average days' inventory on hand.
2. Prepare an analysis of profitability by calculating for each company the (a) profit margin, (b) asset turnover, (c) return on assets, and (d) return on equity.
3. Prepare an analysis of long-term solvency by calculating for each company the (a) debt to equity ratio and (b) interest coverage ratio.
4. Prepare an analysis of cash flow adequacy by calculating for each company the (a) cash flow yield, (b) cash flows to sales, (c) cash flows to assets, and (d) free cash flow.
5. Prepare an analysis of market strength by calculating for each company the (a) price/earnings ratio and (b) dividends yield.
6. Compare the two companies by inserting the ratio calculations from **1** through **5** in a table with the following column heads: Ratio Name, Morton, Pound, and Company with More Favorable Ratio. Indicate in the right-hand column of the table which company had the more favorable ratio in each case.
7. How could the analysis be improved if information from prior years were available?

PROBLEM SET B

B 1. *Effect of Alternative*
L O 4, 6 *Accounting Methods*
Check Figure: 2. Difference in net income: $48,800

Jewell Company began operations this year. At the beginning of 19xx, the company purchased plant assets of $450,000, with an estimated useful life of ten years and no salvage value. During the year, the company had net sales of $650,000, salaries expense of $100,000, and other expenses of $40,000, excluding depreciation. In addition, Jewell Company purchased inventory as follows:

January 15	400 units at $200	$ 80,000
March 20	200 units at $204	40,800
June 15	800 units at $208	166,400
September 18	600 units at $206	123,600
December 9	300 units at $210	63,000
Total	2,300 units	$473,800

At the end of the year, a physical inventory disclosed 500 units still on hand. The managers of Jewell Company know they have a choice of accounting methods, but are unsure how those methods will affect net income. They have heard of the FIFO and LIFO inventory methods and the straight-line and double-declining-balance depreciation methods.

REQUIRED

1. Prepare two income statements for Jewell Company, one using the FIFO and straight-line methods, the other using the LIFO and double-declining-balance methods.
2. Prepare a schedule accounting for the difference in the two net income figures obtained in **1.**
3. What effect does the choice of accounting method have on Jewell's inventory turnover? What conclusions can you draw?
4. How does the choice of accounting methods affect Jewell's return on assets? Assume the company's only assets are cash of $40,000, inventory, and plant assets.

Use year-end balances to compute the ratios. Is your evaluation of Jewell's profitability affected by the choice of accounting methods?

B 2. *Horizontal and*
L O 5 *Vertical Analysis*
No check figure

The condensed comparative income statements and balance sheets of Jensen Corporation follow. All figures are given in thousands of dollars, except earnings per share.

Jensen Corporation
Comparative Income Statements
For the Years Ended December 31, 19x2 and 19x1

	19x2	19x1
Net Sales	$1,638,400	$1,573,200
Cost of Goods Sold	1,044,400	1,004,200
Gross Margin	$ 594,000	$ 569,000
Operating Expenses		
Selling Expenses	$ 238,400	$ 259,000
Administrative Expenses	223,600	211,600
Interest Expense	32,800	19,600
Income Taxes Expense	31,200	28,400
Total Operating Expenses	$ 526,000	$ 518,600
Net Income	$ 68,000	$ 50,400
Earnings per Share	$ 1.70	$ 1.26

Jensen Corporation
Comparative Balance Sheets
December 31, 19x2 and 19x1

	19x2	19x1
Assets		
Cash	$ 40,600	$ 20,400
Accounts Receivable (net)	117,800	114,600
Inventory	287,400	297,400
Property, Plant, and Equipment (net)	375,000	360,000
Total Assets	$820,800	$792,400
Liabilities and Stockholders' Equity		
Accounts Payable	$133,800	$238,600
Notes Payable	100,000	200,000
Bonds Payable	200,000	—
Common Stock—$5 par value	200,000	200,000
Retained Earnings	187,000	153,800
Total Liabilities and Stockholders' Equity	$820,800	$792,400

REQUIRED

Perform the following analyses. Round all ratios and percentages to one decimal place.

1. Prepare schedules showing the amount and percentage changes from 19x1 to 19x2 for Jensen's comparative income statements and balance sheets.
2. Prepare common-size income statements and balance sheets for 19x1 and 19x2.
3. Comment on the results in **1** and **2** by identifying favorable and unfavorable changes in the components and composition of the statements.

Check Figures for B 3: Increase: a, f, l, m; Decrease g, i, j; None: c, h, k; Depends on assumptions made: b, d, e

B 3. *Analyzing the Effects*
L O 6 *of Transactions on Ratios*

Rader Corporation engaged in the transactions listed in the first column of the following table. Opposite each transaction is a ratio and space to indicate the effect of each transaction on the ratio.

Transaction	Ratio	Increase	Decrease	None
		Effect		
a. Sold merchandise on account.	Current ratio			
b. Sold merchandise on account.	Inventory turnover			
c. Collected on accounts receivable.	Quick ratio			
d. Wrote off an uncollectible account.	Receivable turnover			
e. Paid on accounts payable.	Current ratio			
f. Declared cash dividend.	Return on equity			
g. Incurred advertising expense.	Profit margin			
h. Issued stock dividend.	Debt to equity ratio			
i. Issued bond payable.	Asset turnover			
j. Accrued interest expense.	Current ratio			
k. Paid previously declared cash dividend.	Dividends yield			
l. Purchased treasury stock.	Return on assets			
m. Recorded depreciation expense.	Cash flow yield			

REQUIRED

Place an *X* in the appropriate column to show whether the transaction increased, decreased, or had no effect on the indicated ratio.

B 4. *Ratio Analysis*
L O 6

Check Figures: 1a. Current ratio, 19x2: 1.9 times; 19x1: 1.0 times; 2c. Return on assets, 19x2: 8.4%; 19x1: 6.6%

Additional data for Jensen Corporation in 19x2 and 19x1 follow. This information should be used with the data in B 2.

	19x2	19x1
Net cash flows from operating activities	$106,500,000	$86,250,000
Net capital expenditures	$ 22,500,000	$16,000,000
Dividends paid	$ 22,000,000	$17,200,000
Number of common shares	40,000,000	40,000,000
Market price per share	$9	$15
Earnings per share	$1.70	$1.26

Selected balances (in thousands) at the end of 19x0 were Accounts Receivable (net), $103,400; Inventory, $273,600; Total Assets, $732,800; and Stockholders' Equity, $320,600. All of Jensen's notes payable were current liabilities; all of the bonds payable were long-term liabilities.

REQUIRED

Perform the following analyses. Round percentages and ratios to one decimal place, and consider changes of .1 or less to be neutral. After making the calculations, indicate whether each ratio had a favorable (F) or unfavorable (U) change from 19x1 to 19x2.

1. Conduct a liquidity analysis by calculating for each year the (a) current ratio, (b) quick ratio, (c) receivable turnover, (d) average days' sales uncollected, (e) inventory turnover, and (f) average days' inventory on hand.
2. Conduct a profitability analysis by calculating for each year the (a) profit margin, (b) asset turnover, (c) return on assets, and (d) return on equity.

3. Conduct a long-term solvency analysis by calculating for each year the (a) debt to equity ratio and (b) interest coverage ratio.
4. Conduct a cash flow adequacy analysis by calculating for each year the (a) cash flow yield, (b) cash flows to sales, (c) cash flows to assets, and (d) free cash flow.
5. Conduct a market strength analysis by calculating for each year the (a) price/earnings ratio and (b) dividends yield.

B 5.   *Comprehensive*
L O 6   *Ratio Analysis of*
       Two Companies

Check Figures: 1b. Quick ratio, Kemp: 1.5 times; Russo: 1.2 times; 2d. Return on equity, Kemp: 8.8%; Russo: 4.9%

Charles Tseng is considering an investment in the common stock of a chain of retail department stores. He has narrowed his choice to two retail companies, Kemp Corporation and Russo Corporation, whose income statements and balance sheets are shown below.

	Kemp Corporation	Russo Corporation
Net Sales	$12,560,000	$25,210,000
Cost of Goods Sold	6,142,000	14,834,000
Gross Margin	6,418,000	10,376,000
Operating Expenses		
Selling Expense	$ 4,822,600	$ 7,108,200
Administrative Expense	986,000	2,434,000
Interest Expense	194,000	228,000
Income Taxes Expense	200,000	300,000
Total Operating Expenses	$ 6,202,600	$10,070,200
Net Income	$ 215,400	$ 305,800
Earnings per Share	$ 2.15	$ 5.10

	Kemp Corporation	Russo Corporation
Assets		
Cash	$ 80,000	$ 192,400
Marketable Securities	203,400	84,600
Accounts Receivable (net)	552,800	985,400
Inventories	629,800	1,253,400
Prepaid Expenses	54,400	114,000
Property, Plant, and Equipment (net)	2,913,600	6,552,000
Intangibles and Other Assets	553,200	144,800
Total Assets	$4,987,200	$9,326,600
Liabilities and Stockholders' Equity		
Accounts Payable	$ 344,000	$ 572,600
Notes Payable	150,000	400,000
Income Taxes Payable	50,200	73,400
Bonds Payable	2,000,000	2,000,000
Common Stock—$10 par value	1,000,000	600,000
Paid-in Capital in Excess of Par Value, Common	609,800	3,568,600
Retained Earnings	833,200	2,112,000
Total Liabilities and Stockholders' Equity	$4,987,200	$9,326,600

During the year, Kemp Corporation paid a total of $50,000 in dividends. The market price per share of its stock is currently $30. In comparison, Russo Corporation paid a total of $114,000 in dividends, and the current market price of its stock is $38 per share. Kemp Corporation had net cash flows from operations of $271,500 and net capital expenditures of $625,000. Russo Corporation had net cash flows from operations of $492,500 and net capital expenditures of $1,050,000. Information for prior years is not readily available. Assume that all notes payable are current liabilities and all bonds payable are long-term liabilities.

REQUIRED

Conduct a comprehensive ratio analysis for each company, using the available information. Compare the results. Round percentages and ratios except earnings per share to one decimal place, and consider changes of .1 or less to be indeterminate. This analysis should be done in the following steps:

1. Prepare an analysis of liquidity by calculating for each company the (a) current ratio, (b) quick ratio, (c) receivable turnover, (d) average days' sales uncollected, (e) inventory turnover, and (f) average days' inventory on hand.
2. Prepare an analysis of profitability by calculating for each company the (a) profit margin, (b) asset turnover, (c) return on assets, and (d) return on equity.
3. Prepare an analysis of long-term solvency by calculating for each company the (a) debt to equity ratio and (b) interest coverage ratio.
4. Prepare an analysis of cash flow adequacy by calculating for each company the (a) cash flow yield, (b) cash flows to sales, (c) cash flows to assets, and (d) free cash flow.
5. Prepare an analysis of market strength by calculating for each company the (a) price/earnings ratio and (b) dividends yield.
6. Compare the two companies by inserting the ratio calculations from **1** through **5** in a table with the following column heads: Ratio Name, Kemp Corporation, Russo Corporation, and Company with More Favorable Ratio. Indicate in the right-hand column which company had the more favorable ratio in each case.
7. How could the analysis be improved if information from prior years were available?

FINANCIAL REPORTING AND ANALYSIS CASES

Interpreting Financial Reports

FRA 1.
L O 4

Quality of Earnings

Check Figures: Earnings before write-down and change in accounting principle, 1983: $93.2 million; 1984: $187.8 million

The *Walt Disney Company* is, of course, a famous entertainment company that produces films and operates theme parks, among other things. The company is also well known as a profitable and well-managed business. On November 15, 1984, the *Wall Street Journal* ran the following article by Michael Cieply, under the title "Disney Reports Fiscal 4th-Period Loss After Taking $166 Million Write-Down."

Walt Disney Productions reported a $64 million net loss for its fiscal fourth quarter ended Sept. 30, after writing down a record $166 million in movies and other properties.

In the year-earlier quarter, Disney had net income of $24.5 million, or 70 cents a share. Fourth-quarter revenue this year rose 28% to $463.2 million from $363 million.

In the fiscal year, the entertainment company's earnings rose 5% to $97.8 million, or $2.73 a share, from $93.2 million, or $2.70 a share, a year earlier. Revenue rose 27% to $1.66 billion from $1.31 billion.

The company said it wrote down $112 million in motion picture and television properties. The write-down involves productions that already have been released as well as ones still under development, but Disney declined to identify the productions or projects involved.

"This just reflects the judgment of new management about the ultimate value of projects we had under way," said Michael Bagnall, Disney's executive vice president for finance. . . .

The company also said it charged off $40 million to reflect the "abandonment" of a number of planned projects at its various theme parks. An additional $14 million was charged off as a reserve to cover possible legal obligations resulting from the company's fight to ward off a pair of successive takeover attempts last summer, Mr. Bagnall said.

Disney said its full-year net included a $76 million gain from a change in its method of accounting for investment tax credits. The change was made retroactive to the fiscal first quarter ended Dec. 31, and will boost that quarter's reported net to $85 million, from $9 million.

Mr. Bagnall said the $76 million credit stemmed largely from construction of Disney's Epcot Center theme park in Florida. By switching to flow-through from deferral accounting, the company was able to take the entire credit immediately instead of amortizing it over eighteen years, as originally planned, Mr. Bagnall said. Flow-through accounting is usual in the entertainment industry.[16]

REQUIRED

1. What two categories of issues does the user of financial statements want to consider when evaluating the quality of a company's reported earnings? Did Disney have one or both types of items in fiscal 1984?
2. Compare the fourth-period earnings or losses for 1983 and 1984 and full fiscal 1983 and 1984 earnings or losses before and after adjusting for the item or items described in **1.** Which comparisons do you believe give the best picture of Disney's performance?

International Company

FRA 2. *Analyzing Non-U.S.*
L O 3, 6 *Financial Statements*

Check Figures: a. Current ratio: .9; d. Profit margin: 8.1%; h. Debt to equity: 2.9

When dealing with non-U.S. companies, the analyst is often faced with financial statements that do not follow the same format as the statements of U.S. companies. The 1990 group balance sheet and the group profit and loss account (income statement) for *Maxwell Communication Corporation plc*, a British publishing firm, present such a situation. The statements are on the next two pages.

The following year, Maxwell's chairman was lost at sea, and the company subsequently went into bankruptcy and was sold. In these statements, the word *group* is used in the same way that the word *consolidated* is used in U.S. financial statements. It means that the company's financial statements present the combined results of a number of subsidiary companies.[17]

Show that you can read these British financial statements by computing as many of the following ratios as you can: (a) current ratio, (b) receivable turnover, (c) inventory turnover, (d) profit margin, (e) asset turnover, (f) return on assets, (g) return on equity, and (h) debt to equity. Use year-end figures to compute ratios that normally require averages. Indicate what data are missing for any ratio you are not able to compute. What terms or accounts did you have trouble interpreting? How do you evaluate the usefulness of the formats of the British financial statements compared to the formats of U.S. financial statements?

16. "Disney Reports Fiscal 4th-Period Loss After Taking $166 Million Write-Down," *Wall Street Journal*, November 15, 1984.
17. Maxwell Communication Corporation plc, *Annual Report*, 1990.

Maxwell Communication Corporation plc
Group Balance Sheet
At 31st March

	1990 £ million
Fixed Assets	
Intangible assets	2,162.7
Tangible assets	337.3
Investments in convertible loan notes	—
Partnerships and associated companies	582.5
Investments	188.1
	3,270.6
Current Assets	
Stocks	108.4
Debtors	757.6
Investments	1.3
Cash at bank and in hand	65.3
	932.6
Creditors—amounts falling due within one year	(1,024.5)
Net Current Assets/(Liabilities)	(91.9)
Total Assets Less Current Liabilities	3,178.7
Creditors—amounts falling due after more than one year	(1,679.7)
Provisions for liabilities and charges	(55.1)
Accruals and deferred income	(140.4)
	1,303.5
Capital and Reserves	
Called up ordinary share capital	161.5
Share premium account	60.3
Special reserve	566.7
Capital reserve	59.2
Revaluation reserve	2.7
Profit and loss account	155.9
	1,006.3
Minority shareholders' interests	297.2
	1,303.5

Maxwell Communication Corporation plc
Group Profit and Loss Account
For the Year Ended 31st March 1990

	Year 1990 £ million
Sales	1,242.1
Operating costs	(1,006.1)
Share of profits of partnership and associated companies	25.2
Operating Profit Before Exceptional Item	261.2
Exceptional item	19.2
Total Operating Profit	280.4
Net interest and investment income	(108.1)
Profit Before Taxation	172.3
Taxation on profit on ordinary activities	(34.5)
Profit on Ordinary Activities After Taxation	137.8
Minority shareholders' interests	(11.0)
Extraordinary items less taxation	(25.7)
Profit Attributable to Shareholders	101.1
Dividends paid and proposed	(95.8)
Retained Profit for the Period	5.3
Retained Profits at Beginning of Period	173.3
Transfer of depreciation from revaluation reserve	—
Exchange translation differences	(22.7)
Retained Profits at End of Period	155.9
Earnings per Share	20.0p

Toys "R" Us Annual Report

FRA 3. *Comprehensive*
L O 6 *Ratio Analysis*

Check Figures: Current ratio, 1995: 1.2; 1994: 1.3; Receivable turnover, 1995: 81.6; 1994: 94.6 times

Refer to the Annual Report in the appendix on Toys "R" Us, and conduct a comprehensive ratio analysis that compares data from 1995 and 1994. If you have been computing ratios for Toys "R" Us in previous chapters, you may prepare a table that summarizes the ratios for 1995 and 1994 and show calculations only for the ratios not previously calculated. If this is the first time you are doing a ratio analysis for Toys "R" Us, show all your computations. In either case, after each group of ratios, comment on the performance of Toys "R" Us. Round your calculations to one decimal place. Prepare and comment on the following categories of ratios:

Liquidity analysis: Current ratio, quick ratio, receivable turnover, average days' sales uncollected, inventory turnover, and average days' inventory on hand

Profitability analysis: Profit margin, asset turnover, return on assets, and return on equity

Long-term solvency analysis: Debt to equity and interest coverage

Cash flow adequacy analysis: Cash flow yield, cash flows to sales, cash flows to assets, and free cash flows

Market strength analysis: Price/earnings ratio and dividends yield

Toys "R" Us
Annual Report

ANNUAL REPORT
YEAR ENDED JANUARY 28, 1995

TABLE OF CONTENTS

Toys"R"Us is the world's largest children's specialty retail chain in terms of both sales and earnings. At January 28, 1995, the Company operated 618 toy stores in the United States, 293 international toy stores and 204 Kids"R"Us children's clothing stores.

STORE LOCATIONS

TOYS"R"US UNITED STATES - 618 LOCATIONS

Alabama - 7	Indiana - 12	Nebraska - 3	South Dakota - 2
Alaska - 1	Iowa - 7	Nevada - 3	Tennessee - 12
Arizona - 10	Kansas - 4	New Hampshire - 5	Texas - 50
Arkansas - 2	Kentucky - 7	New Jersey - 21	Utah - 5
California - 77	Louisiana - 8	New Mexico - 3	Virginia - 18
Colorado - 10	Maine - 2	New York - 41	Washington - 11
Connecticut - 9	Maryland - 17	North Carolina - 16	West Virginia - 3
Delaware - 2	Massachusetts - 16	Ohio - 28	Wisconsin - 11
Florida - 39	Michigan - 23	Oklahoma - 4	
Georgia - 14	Minnesota - 11	Oregon - 7	Puerto Rico - 4
Hawaii - 1	Mississippi - 5	Pennsylvania - 29	
Idaho - 2	Missouri - 12	Rhode Island - 1	
Illinois - 34	Montana - 1	South Carolina - 8	

TOYS"R"US INTERNATIONAL - 293 LOCATIONS

Australia - 17	France - 29	Malaysia - 3	Sweden - 3
Austria - 7	Germany - 53	Netherlands - 8	Switzerland - 4
Belgium - 3	Hong Kong - 4	Portugal - 3	Taiwan - 4
Canada - 56	Japan - 24	Singapore - 3	United Arab Emirates - 1
Denmark - 1	Luxembourg - 1	Spain - 20	United Kingdom - 49

KIDS"R"US UNITED STATES - 204 LOCATIONS

Alabama - 1	Indiana - 7	Minnesota - 5	Pennsylvania - 14
California - 25	Iowa - 1	Missouri - 4	Rhode Island - 1
Connecticut - 6	Kansas - 1	Nebraska - 1	Tennessee - 1
Delaware - 1	Maine - 1	New Hampshire - 2	Texas - 7
Florida - 8	Maryland - 8	New Jersey - 17	Utah - 2
Georgia - 4	Massachusetts - 5	New York - 20	Virginia - 7
Illinois - 20	Michigan - 13	Ohio - 19	Wisconsin - 3

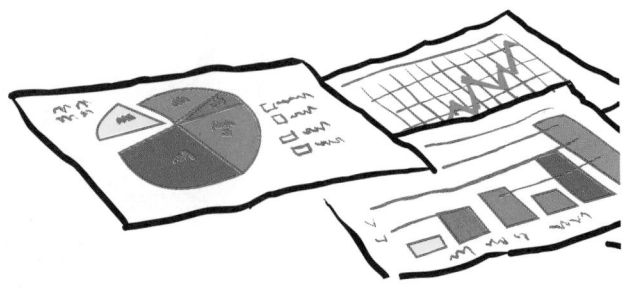

TOYS"R"US, INC. AND SUBSIDIARIES
FINANCIAL HIGHLIGHTS

(Dollars in millions except per share information)   Fiscal Year Ended

	Jan. 28, 1995	Jan. 29, 1994	Jan. 30, 1993	Feb. 1, 1992	Feb. 2, 1991	Jan. 28, 1990	Jan. 29, 1989	Jan. 31, 1988	Feb. 1, 1987	Feb. 2, 1986
OPERATIONS:										
Net Sales...........................	$ 8,746	$ 7,946	$ 7,169	$ 6,124	$ 5,510	$ 4,788	$ 4,000	$ 3,137	$ 2,445	$ 1,976
Net Earnings	532	483	438	340	326	321	268	204	152	120
Earnings Per Share	1.85	1.63	1.47	1.15	1.11	1.09	.91	.69	.52	.41
FINANCIAL POSITION AT YEAR END:										
Working Capital	394	633	797	328	177	238	255	225	155	181
Real Estate-Net..................	2,271	2,036	1,877	1,751	1,433	1,142	952	762	601	423
Total Assets	6,571	6,150	5,323	4,583	3,582	3,075	2,555	2,027	1,523	1,226
Long-Term Obligations.........	785	724	671	391	195	173	174	177	85	88
Stockholders' Equity............	3,429	3,148	2,889	2,426	2,046	1,705	1,424	1,135	901	717
NUMBER OF STORES AT YEAR END:										
Toys"R"Us - United States....	618	581	540	497	451	404	358	313	271	233
Toys"R"Us - International	293	234	167	126	97	74	52	37	24	13
Kids"R"Us - United States....	204	217	211	189	164	137	112	74	43	23

Michael Goldstein,
Vice Chairman and Chief Executive Officer

Robert C. Nakasone,
President and Chief Operating Officer

TO OUR STOCKHOLDERS

FINANCIAL HIGHLIGHTS

We are proud to report another good year for Toys"R"Us. In 1994, we achieved gains in market share and once more reported record results, marking the 16th consecutive year of increased sales and earnings since Toys"R"Us became a public company. Over that period, earnings have grown at an annual compounded rate of 24%.

For the year, sales grew to $8.7 billion, a 10% increase over the $7.9 billion reported in the previous year. Operating earnings increased 11% while net earnings rose to $532 million, a 10% increase over the $483 million reported in 1993. Earnings per share climbed 14% to $1.85 compared to $1.63 a year ago.

Comparable store sales at our U.S.A. toy stores rose 2% for the year, with operating earnings up 7%. Our performance reflected several new marketing and merchandising initiatives: we introduced a new Spring catalog and three Holiday catalogs, which featured more pages, more coupons and received wider distribution; we introduced several initiatives to improve customer service; and expanded our Books"R"Us shops. We also introduced Lego and Stuffed Animal shops and the sale of PC software for children, which was successfully tested as a new Learning Center shop in a number of U.S.A. and European toy stores. However, we experienced a downturn in our video game business in the fall of 1994 as customers awaited new generation 32 and 64 bit video game systems by Sega, Sony and Nintendo, expected in the latter half of 1995. In addition, competition from national and regional discount stores, as well as mall based toy stores, intensified as they increased advertising and more than ever emphasized lower prices. Lastly, new competitors have emerged targeting specific segments of our business. These competitors include juvenile specialty stores, educational toy stores and computer electronic shops with broad offerings of video games.

We now face a number of issues, in our U.S.A. toy store operations, which require us to take significant actions. These steps, while improving our long-term profitability and market share, will adversely impact our ability to achieve our historic earnings growth rate in 1995. Further, until the new video game systems are introduced, the outlook for that category in the first three quarters of 1995 is poor, and it will hurt sales and profits. However, we expect a strong fourth quarter as the new systems and our initiatives create excitement and improved customer traffic.

Our strategies for 1995 include improving our image through a variety of pricing and marketing initiatives, the introduction of new in-store shops that highlight our dominant selection of merchandise and an increased emphasis on customer service. The Toys"R"Us franchise is one of the best in the world and we intend to take aggressive measures to strengthen this franchise over the years to come.

Internationally, our French and Iberian toy stores had comparable store sales increases for the full year. In Japan, our performance improved in the fourth quarter with the introduction of 32 bit video game systems by both Sony and Sega. These gains were offset by lower comparable store sales for our Canadian, Central European and United Kingdom toy stores, reflecting new competition in Canada and a poor retail environment in Central Europe. In spite of this, our International division achieved a 37% increase in operating earnings, by again improving upon inventory management and increasing productivity in both labor and distribution.

Our International franchising division added a third franchisee to the Toys"R"Us family in 1994, which will now enable us to open toy stores in Israel, Saudi Arabia and the United

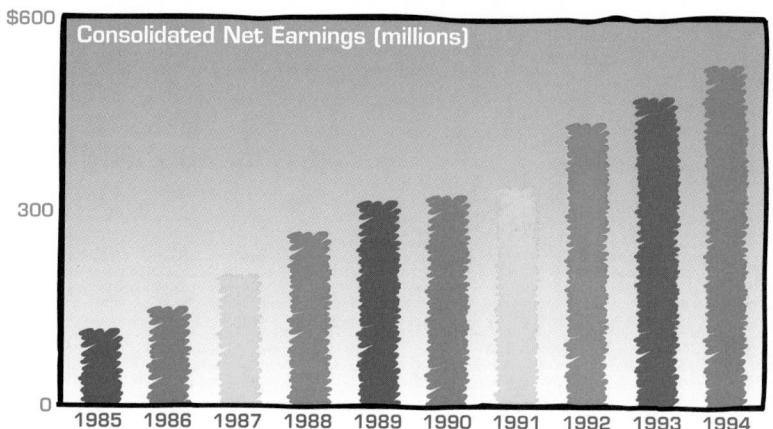

Consolidated Net Earnings (millions)

$600 / 300 / 0

1985 1986 1987 1988 1989 1990 1991 1992 1993 1994

Arab Emirates. Our first franchise store opened in Dubai in January 1995 to tremendous excitement and heavy consumer traffic. We expect to accelerate our franchising program by entering into agreements in additional countries in 1995, with plans to open stores in 1996.

Our Kids"R"Us children's clothing division enjoyed relatively strong comparable store sales despite the continuation of the difficult apparel sales environment. Operating profits rose 16%, our third successive year of strong growth, reflecting improved expense control as well as new marketing and merchandising initiatives. Our greatly expanded private label merchandise program has met with excellent customer response. In addition, Kids"R"Us closed 19 stores in 1994 which were not meeting expectations. Based on the last three years' results, we will expand Kids"R"Us at a faster rate as we enter 1996.

Under our $1 billion stock buyback program, we repurchased 13.1 million shares at a cost of $470 million during 1994. We intend to continue to aggressively buy back stock during 1995. In addition, we completed our transaction with Petrie Stores Corporation at the end of January 1995, which gave us approximately $162 million in cash, net of expenses, and increased our outstanding stock by approximately 2.2 million shares.

OPERATIONAL HIGHLIGHTS

We are proud of our ability to provide the best selection of merchandise, stocked in depth with everyday low prices while expanding customer service and maintaining one of the lowest expense structures in the industry. The following are some of the highlights of 1994 along with our plans for 1995.

In 1994, we significantly expanded our catalog program with a Spring catalog and two new and one expanded Holiday Toy catalogs that provided our customers with over $1,800 in coupon savings. This program allows us to continue to demonstrate the broad selection of merchandise that can be found at Toys"R"Us. Increasingly, customers in our stores use these as shopping

aids. Our International division has also begun to use the catalog program with tremendous success.

We have continued to test various "specialty shops" within our U.S.A. and International toy stores. In 1994, we added 130 Books"R"Us shops bringing our total to over 300 stores. We also added approximately twenty Lego shops, twenty Stuffed Animal shops and five Learning Center shops in our stores. Based on our successful test results, we will implement the Learning Center concept in 100 stores in 1995. These shops will carry a full selection of learning aid products as well as PC software for kids. In addition, by the middle of 1995 we plan to offer an exciting and full selection of PC software for children in all of our U.S.A. toy stores and in several international markets. Our focus will be on children's educational and entertainment software, and we plan to have the most dominant selection anywhere. We also plan to greatly expand our space allocation to large outdoor/indoor playsets to show our dominant selection in this merchandise category.

Enhancing customer service was our single most important operational development in 1994. In conjunction with this initiative, we installed customer friendly in-aisle price scanners and other service oriented

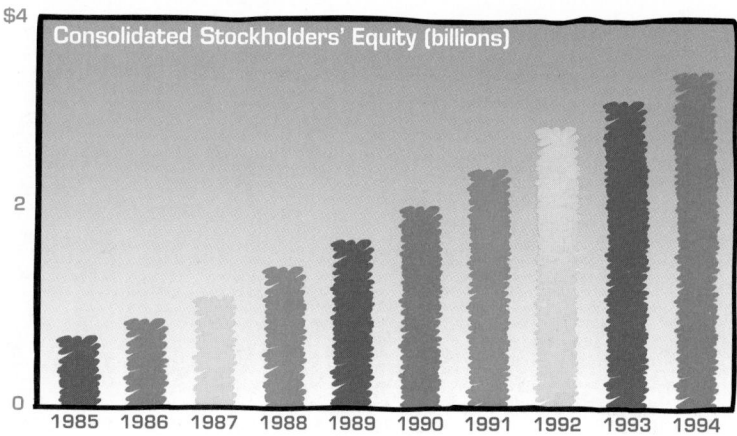

Consolidated Stockholders' Equity (billions)

$4 / 2 / 0

1985 1986 1987 1988 1989 1990 1991 1992 1993 1994

technology in our U.S.A. toy stores. We also tested and intend to install a new automated Baby Registry throughout the entire chain in 1995. Our Geoffrey Helper Program was expanded and we modified some of our store policies and procedures to be more customer friendly and increase employee empowerment and decision-making. In 1995, we will continue to enhance all aspects of customer service, from improving basic store maintenance and housekeeping standards to dedicating additional associate hours to critical customer service needs.

From the beginning of our remodeling program in 1990 through the end of January 1995, we have remodeled over 100 toy stores including 30 stores this past year. These remodeled stores enhance the customer's shopping experience while increasing in-store productivity. We expect to remodel another 15 to 20 toy stores in 1995.

During the year, the U.S.A. toy division continued to increase productivity and improve its ability to replenish stores by building two state-of-the-art automated distribution centers that replaced four older facilities. Further, our International division retrofitted two existing distribution centers with our new automated systems. We are proud of our associates in Japan who were able to continue to

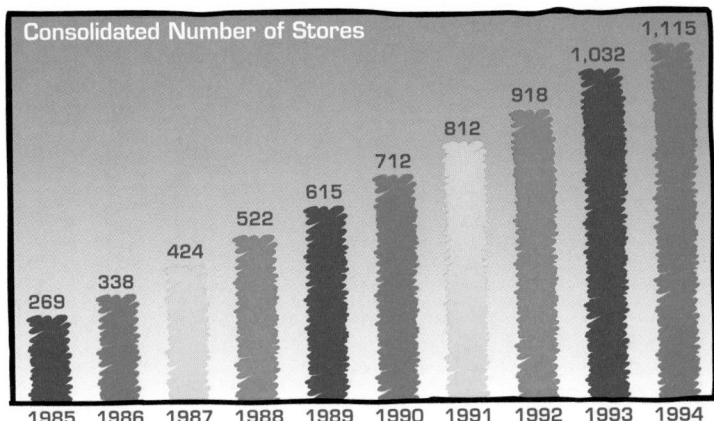

operate successfully following the January earthquake. Our distribution center located in Kobe sustained only minor damage. In 1995, we will be opening our largest distribution center in New Jersey and will also open a state-of-the-art distribution center in Germany.

STORE GROWTH

In 1994, we opened 37 toy stores in the United States. Internationally, 59 stores opened in 17 countries, including our first stores in Denmark, Luxembourg and Sweden and our first franchise store in the United Arab Emirates. For the second year in a row, our International division opened more toy stores than our U.S.A. toy division. We also opened 6 Kids"R"Us stores.

In 1995, we plan to open 40 toy stores in the United States and about 50 toy stores internationally, including franchise stores in the Middle East. We also plan to open about 10 new Kids"R"Us stores. The 1995 stores will capitalize on the existing infrastructure, thereby enhancing the profitability of new and existing stores alike.

Aided by our financial strength, we intend to capitalize on our strong competitive position throughout the world, by continued expansion to achieve greater sales, earnings and market share gains.

CORPORATE CITIZENSHIP

Toys"R"Us maintains a company-wide giving program focused on improving the health-care needs of children by supporting many national and regional children's health care organizations. In 1994, we contributed funds to over 100 children's health care organizations. We also expanded our Hospital Playroom Program, which equips quality children's play centers in hospitals, by opening eight additional playrooms, bringing the total to twenty-six. We expect to expand our program to thirteen additional hospitals in 1995.

Toys"R"Us is a signatory to a Fair Share Agreement with the NAACP and has taken steps to support

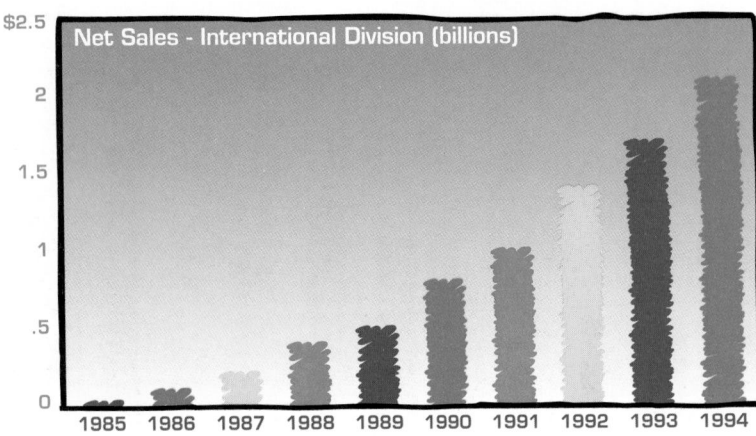

women and minorities in the workplace. We are the leading purchaser of products from several minority-owned toy companies.

Toys"R"Us continues to have a strong toy safety program which includes the inspection of directly imported toys. Furthermore, we continue to take numerous pro-active initiatives, including a leadership position in eliminating the sale of look-alike toy guns. We are proud to be the recent recipient of the Consumer Product Safety Commission Chairman's Commendation For Significant Contributions to Product Safety.

Through our new Books"R"Us shops we are promoting literacy among children by demonstrating that reading is fun.

Lastly, we developed a Toy Guide for differently-abled children, which was carefully designed with their specific abilities and needs in mind.

HUMAN RESOURCES

The talent and high caliber of our management team and of our associates allows Toys"R"Us to expand aggressively and profitably.

We have made the following important promotions within our executive ranks:

Toys"R"Us, United States:
Michael J. Madden,
Group Vice President -
Store Operations

Michael A. Gerety,
Vice President - Store Planning

Kids"R"Us:
James G. Parros,
Senior Vice President - Stores and Distribution Center Operations

Jonathan M. Friedman,
Vice President -
Chief Financial Officer

Number of Countries - Internatonal Division

| 1985 | 1986 | 1987 | 1988 | 1989 | 1990 | 1991 | 1992 | 1993 | 1994 |
| 3 | 4 | 5 | 6 | 8 | 8 | 10 | 11 | 16 | 20 |

SUMMARY

We intend to aggressively pursue all of our strategic initiatives and are committed to building market share and profitability in the years to come. We will work hard to continue being the most trusted store in town.

We value our excellent relationships with our innovative suppliers and commend them for their products, which create an atmosphere of excitement in our stores. Our assessment of the February New York Toy Fair indicates a year of robust sales in basic categories such as fashion dolls and preschool toys, where there is quality product that is reasonably priced.

We recognize the dedication and quality work of our associates around the world who have made this another record year. Our appreciation is also extended to you, our stockholders, for your commitment and loyalty to Toys"R"Us.

Sincerely,

Michael Goldstein
Vice Chairman and
Chief Executive Officer

Robert C. Nakasone
President and
Chief Operating Officer

March 29, 1995

MANAGEMENT'S DISCUSSION-RESULTS OF OPERATIONS AND FINANCIAL CONDITION

RESULTS OF OPERATIONS*

The Company has experienced sales growth in each of its last three years; sales were up 10.1% in 1994, 10.8% in 1993 and 17.1% in 1992. Part of the growth is attributable to the opening of 121 new U.S.A. toy stores, 167 international toy stores and 39 children's clothing stores during the three year period, and a portion of the increase is due to comparable U.S.A. toy store sales increases of 2.1%, 3.3% and 6.9% in 1994, 1993 and 1992, respectively.

Cost of sales as a percentage of sales decreased to 68.7% in 1994 from 69.2% in 1993 and from 69.3% in 1992 due to a more favorable merchandise mix.

Selling, advertising, general and administrative expenses as a percentage of sales increased to 19.0% in 1994 from 18.8% in 1993 and 18.7% in 1992 primarily as a result of increases in such expenses at a rate faster than comparable store sales increases and also due to customer service initiatives implemented in 1994, and start-up costs for the opening of our new market in Australia in 1993.

Interest expense increased in 1994 as compared to 1993 and 1992 due to increased average borrowings and a change in the mix of borrowings and interest rates among countries. Short-term interest income decreased in 1994 as compared to 1993 and increased in 1993 as compared to 1992, principally due to the availability of cash for investments.

The effective tax rate decreased to 37.0% in 1994 from 37.5% in 1993, due to a one-time retroactive adjustment in 1993 for an increase in the U.S. Federal corporate income tax rate. The effective rate increased to 37.5% in 1993 from 36.5% in 1992, due to the rate change and retroactive adjustment discussed above. The Company believes its deferred tax assets, as reported, are fully realizable.

The Company believes that its risks attendant to foreign operations are minimal as it operates in twenty different countries which are politically stable. The Company's foreign exchange risk management objectives are to stabilize cash flow from the effect of foreign currency fluctuations. The Company will, whenever practical, offset local investments in foreign currencies with borrowings denominated in the same currency. The Company also enters into forward foreign exchange contracts or purchase options to eliminate specific transaction currency risk. International sales and operating earnings were favorably impacted by the translation of local currency results into U.S. dollars at higher average exchange rates in 1994 than 1993 and unfavorably impacted by lower average exchange rates in 1993 than in 1992. Inflation has had little effect on the Company's operations in the last three years.

LIQUIDITY AND CAPITAL RESOURCES

The Company continues to maintain a strong financial position as evidenced by its working capital of $394 million at January 28, 1995 and $633 million at January 29, 1994. The long-term debt to equity percentage is 22.9% at January 28, 1995 as compared to 23.0% at January 29, 1994.

In 1995, the Company plans to open approximately 90 toy stores in the United States and internationally, including the new markets of Israel and Saudi Arabia. Additionally, there are plans to open about 10 Kids"R"Us children's clothing stores. The Company opened 96 toy stores in 1994, 108 in 1993 and 84 in 1992 and 6 Kids"R"Us children's clothing stores in 1994, 10 in 1993 and 23 in 1992. The Company closed 19 Kids"R"Us children's clothing stores in 1994 and 4 in 1993, which were not meeting our expectations. These closures did not have a significant impact on the Company's financial position.

For 1995, capital requirements for real estate, store and warehouse fixtures and equipment, leasehold improvements and other additions to property and equipment are estimated at $575 million (including real estate and related costs of $375 million). The Company's policy is to purchase its real estate where appropriate and plans to continue this policy.

The Company has an existing $1 billion share repurchase program, under which it has repurchased 13.7 million shares of its common stock for $493.7 million, since it had announced the program in January of 1994.

The seasonal nature of the business (approximately 48% of sales take place in the fourth quarter) typically causes cash to decline from the beginning of the year through October as inventory increases for the holiday selling season and funds are used for land purchases and construction of new stores, which usually open in the first ten months of the year. The Company has a $1 billion multi-currency unsecured revolving credit facility expiring in February 2000, from a syndicate of financial institutions. Cash requirements for operations, capital expenditures, lease commitments and the share repurchase program will be met primarily through operating activities, borrowings under the revolving credit facility, issuance of short-term commercial paper and bank borrowings for foreign subsidiaries.

*References to 1994, 1993 and 1992 are for the 52 weeks ended January 28, 1995, January 29, 1994 and January 30, 1993, respectively.

TOYS"R"US, INC. AND SUBSIDIARIES
CONSOLIDATED STATEMENTS OF EARNINGS

(In thousands except per share information)   *Year Ended*

	January 28, 1995	January 29, 1994	January 30, 1993
Net sales	$8,745,586	$7,946,067	$7,169,290
Costs and expenses:			
Cost of sales	6,007,958	5,494,766	4,968,555
Selling, advertising, general and administrative	1,664,180	1,497,011	1,342,262
Depreciation and amortization	161,406	133,370	119,034
Interest expense	83,945	72,283	69,134
Interest and other income	(15,970)	(24,116)	(18,719)
	7,901,519	7,173,314	6,480,266
Earnings before taxes on income	844,067	772,753	689,024
Taxes on income	312,300	289,800	251,500
Net earnings	$ 531,767	$ 482,953	$ 437,524
Earnings per share	$ 1.85	$ 1.63	$ 1.47

See notes to consolidated financial statements.

TOYS"R"US, INC. AND SUBSIDIARIES
CONSOLIDATED BALANCE SHEETS

(In thousands)

	January 28, 1995	January 29, 1994
ASSETS		
Current Assets:		
Cash and cash equivalents	$ 369,833	$ 791,893
Accounts and other receivables	115,914	98,534
Merchandise inventories	1,999,148	1,777,569
Prepaid expenses and other	45,818	40,400
Total Current Assets	2,530,713	2,708,396
Property and Equipment:		
Real estate, net	2,270,825	2,035,673
Other, net	1,397,980	1,148,794
Total Property and Equipment	3,668,805	3,184,467
Other Assets	371,675	256,746
	$ 6,571,193	$ 6,149,609
LIABILITIES AND STOCKHOLDERS' EQUITY		
Current Liabilities:		
Short-term borrowings	$ 122,661	$ 239,862
Accounts payable	1,339,081	1,156,411
Accrued expenses and other current liabilities	472,653	471,782
Income taxes payable	202,548	206,996
Total Current Liabilities	2,136,943	2,075,051
Deferred Income Taxes	219,927	202,663
Long-Term Debt	785,448	723,613
Stockholders' Equity:		
Common stock	29,795	29,794
Additional paid-in capital	521,295	454,061
Retained earnings	3,544,573	3,012,806
Foreign currency translation adjustments	(25,121)	(56,021)
Treasury shares, at cost	(641,667)	(292,358)
	3,428,875	3,148,282
	$ 6,571,193	$ 6,149,609

See notes to consolidated financial statements.

TOYS"R"US, INC. AND SUBSIDIARIES
CONSOLIDATED STATEMENTS OF CASH FLOWS

(In thousands)

	January 28, 1995	January 29, 1994	Year Ended January 30, 1993
CASH FLOWS FROM OPERATING ACTIVITIES			
Net earnings	$ 531,767	$ 482,953	$ 437,524
Adjustments to reconcile net earnings to net cash provided by operating activities:			
Depreciation and amortization	161,406	133,370	119,034
Deferred income taxes	(14,545)	36,534	13,998
Changes in operating assets and liabilities:			
Accounts and other receivables	(17,380)	(29,149)	(5,307)
Merchandise inventories	(221,579)	(278,898)	(108,066)
Prepaid expenses and other operating assets	(31,668)	(39,448)	(36,249)
Accounts payable, accrued expenses and other liabilities	183,506	325,165	112,232
Income taxes payable	(2,014)	26,588	40,091
Total adjustments	57,726	174,162	135,733
Net cash provided by operating activities	589,493	657,115	573,257
CASH FLOWS FROM INVESTING ACTIVITIES			
Capital expenditures, net	(585,702)	(555,258)	(421,564)
Other assets	(44,593)	(58,383)	(22,175)
Net cash used in investing activities	(630,295)	(613,641)	(443,739)
CASH FLOWS FROM FINANCING ACTIVITIES			
Short-term borrowings, net	(117,201)	119,090	(170,887)
Long-term borrowings	34,648	40,576	318,035
Long-term debt repayments	(1,111)	(1,335)	(7,926)
Exercise of stock options	25,998	29,879	86,323
Share repurchase program	(469,714)	(183,233)	(27,244)
Sale of stock to Petrie Stores Corporation	161,642	–	–
Net cash (used)/provided by financing activities	(365,738)	4,977	198,301
Effect of exchange rate changes on cash and cash equivalents	(15,520)	(20,279)	(8,691)
CASH AND CASH EQUIVALENTS			
(Decrease)/increase during year	(422,060)	28,172	319,128
Beginning of year	791,893	763,721	444,593
End of year	$ 369,833	$ 791,893	$ 763,721

SUPPLEMENTAL DISCLOSURES OF CASH FLOW INFORMATION

The Company considers its highly liquid investments purchased as part of its daily cash management activities to be cash equivalents. During the years ended January 28, 1995, January 29, 1994, and January 30, 1993 the Company made income tax payments of $318,948, $220,229, and $151,722 and interest payments (net of amounts capitalized) of $123,603, $104,281, and $83,584 respectively.

See notes to consolidated financial statements.

TOYS"R"US, INC. AND SUBSIDIARIES
CONSOLIDATED STATEMENTS OF STOCKHOLDERS' EQUITY

| (In thousands) | Common Stock | | | | |
| | Issued | | In Treasury | Additional paid-in capital | Retained earnings |
	Shares	Amount	Amount		
Balance, February 1, 1992.................................	297,938	$ 29,794	$ (127,717)	$ 384,803	$ 2,092,329
Net earnings for the year...	–	–	–	–	437,524
Share repurchase program (708 Treasury shares).......	–	–	(27,244)	–	–
Exercise of stock options (4,479 Treasury shares)	–	–	4,524	35,301	–
Tax benefit from exercise of stock options	–	–	–	45,390	–
Balance, January 30, 1993.................................	297,938	29,794	(150,437)	465,494	2,529,853
Net earnings for the year...	–	–	–	–	482,953
Share repurchase program (4,940 Treasury shares)....	–	–	(183,233)	–	–
Exercise of stock options (1,394 Treasury shares)	–	–	41,312	(21,464)	–
Tax benefit from exercise of stock options	–	–	–	10,031	–
Balance, January 29, 1994.................................	297,938	29,794	(292,358)	454,061	3,012,806
Net earnings for the year...	–	–	–	–	531,767
Share repurchase program (13,074 Treasury shares)..	–	–	(469,714)	–	–
Exercise of stock options (1,103 Treasury shares)	16	1	41,888	(21,947)	–
Tax benefit from exercise of stock options	–	–	–	6,056	–
Exchange with and sale of stock to Petrie Stores Corporation (2,223 Net treasury shares)..................	–	–	78,517	83,125	–
Balance, January 28, 1995.................................	297,954	$ 29,795	$ (641,667)	$ 521,295	$ 3,544,573

See notes to consolidated financial statements.

TOYS"R"US, INC. AND SUBSIDIARIES
NOTES TO CONSOLIDATED FINANCIAL STATEMENTS

(Amounts in thousands, except per share amounts)

SUMMARY OF SIGNIFICANT ACCOUNTING POLICIES

Fiscal Year
The Company's fiscal year ends on the Saturday nearest to January 31. References to 1994, 1993, and 1992 are for the 52 weeks ended January 28, 1995, January 29, 1994 and January 30, 1993, respectively.

Principles of Consolidation
The consolidated financial statements include the accounts of the Company and its subsidiaries. All material intercompany balances and transactions have been eliminated. Assets and liabilities of foreign operations are translated at current rates of exchange at the balance sheet date while results of operations are translated at average rates in effect for the period. Translation gains or losses are shown as a separate component of stockholders' equity. The increase (decrease) in the foreign currency translation adjustment was $30,900, ($70,338) and ($33,650) for 1994, 1993 and 1992, respectively.

Merchandise Inventories
Merchandise inventories for the U.S.A. toy store operations, which represent over 62% of total inventories, are stated at the lower of LIFO (last-in, first-out) cost or market as determined by the retail inventory method. If inventories had been valued at the lower of FIFO (first-in, first-out) cost or market, inventories would show no change at January 28, 1995 or January 29, 1994. All other merchandise inventories are stated at the lower of FIFO cost or market as determined by the retail inventory method.

Property and Equipment
Property and equipment are recorded at cost. Depreciation and amortization are provided using the straight-line method over the estimated useful lives of the assets or, where applicable, the terms of the respective leases, whichever is shorter.

Preopening Costs
Preopening costs, which consist primarily of advertising, occupancy and payroll expenses, are amortized over expected sales to the end of the fiscal year in which the store opens.

Capitalized Interest
Interest on borrowed funds is capitalized during construction of property and is amortized by charges to earnings over the depreciable lives of the related assets. Interest of $6,926, $7,300 and $8,403 was capitalized during 1994, 1993 and 1992, respectively.

Financial Instruments
The carrying amounts reported in the balance sheets for cash and cash equivalents and short-term borrowings approximate their fair market values.

Forward Foreign Exchange Contracts
The Company enters into forward foreign exchange contracts to eliminate the risk associated with currency movement relating to its short-term intercompany loan program with foreign subsidiaries and inventory purchases denominated in foreign currency. Gains and losses which offset the movement in the underlying transactions are recognized as part of such transactions. Gross deferred unrealized gains and losses on the forward contracts were not material at either January 28, 1995 or January 29, 1994. The related receivable, payable and deferred gain or loss are included on a net basis in the balance sheet. As of January 28, 1995 and January 29, 1994, the Company had approximately $547,000 and $290,000, of outstanding forward contracts maturing in 1995 and 1994, respectively, which are entered into with counterparties that have high credit ratings and with which the Company has the contractual right to net forward currency settlements.

PROPERTY AND EQUIPMENT

	Useful Life (in years)	January 28, 1995	January 29, 1994
Land		$ 764,808	$ 693,737
Buildings	45-50	1,627,145	1,446,277
Furniture and equipment	5-20	1,177,909	953,360
Leaseholds and leasehold improvements	12½-50	809,365	658,191
Construction in progress		55,730	41,855
Leased property under capital leases		24,881	24,360
		4,459,838	3,817,780
Less accumulated depreciation and amortization		791,033	633,313
		$ 3,668,805	$ 3,184,467

SEASONAL FINANCING AND LONG-TERM DEBT

	January 28, 1995	January 29, 1994
Industrial revenue bonds, net of expenses (a)	$ 74,239	$ 74,208
Mortgage notes payable at annual interest rates from 7⅛% to 11% (b)	12,980	13,318
Japanese yen loans payable at annual interest rates from 3.45% to 6.47%, due in varying amounts through 2012	192,910	142,688
British pound sterling 11% Stepped Coupon Guaranteed Bonds, due 2017	206,570	194,415
8¼% sinking fund debentures, due 2017, net of discounts	88,220	88,117
8¾% debentures, due 2021, net of expenses	198,051	197,978
Obligations under capital leases	14,056	14,432
	787,026	725,156
Less current portion	1,578	1,543
	$ 785,448	$ 723,613

(a) Bank letters of credit of $57,135, expiring in 1996, support certain industrial revenue bonds. The Company expects the bank letters of credit expiring in 1996 will be renewed. The bonds have fixed or variable interest rates with an average rate of 3.2% at January 28, 1995.

(b) Mortgage notes payable are collateralized by property and equipment with an aggregate carrying value of $18,330 at January 28, 1995.

The fair market value of the Company's long-term debt at January 28, 1995 is approximately $815,000. The fair market value was estimated using quoted market rates for publicly traded debt and estimated interest rates for non-public debt.

On January 27, 1995, the Company entered into a $1 billion unsecured committed revolving credit facility expiring in five years. This multi-currency facility permits the Company to borrow at the lower of LIBOR plus a fixed spread or a rate set by competitive auction. The facility is available to support domestic commercial paper borrowings and to meet the cash requirements of selected foreign subsidiaries.

Additionally, the Company also has lines of credit with various banks to meet the short-term financing needs of its foreign subsidiaries. The weighted average interest rate on short-term borrowings outstanding at January 28, 1995 and January 29, 1994, was 6.3% and 5.4%, respectively.

The annual maturities of long-term debt at January 28, 1995 are as follows:

Year ending in	
1996	$ 1,578
1997	5,559
1998	8,085
1999	9,740
2000	8,662
2001 and subsequent	753,402
	$ 787,026

LEASES

The Company leases a portion of the real estate used in its operations. Most leases require the Company to pay real estate taxes and other expenses; some require additional amounts based on percentages of sales.

Minimum rental commitments under noncancelable operating leases having a term of more than one year as of January 28, 1995 were as follows:

Year ending in	Gross minimum rentals	Sublease income	Net minimum rentals
1996	$ 258,447	$ 8,461	$ 249,986
1997	256,477	7,265	249,212
1998	255,650	7,091	248,559
1999	256,373	6,215	250,158
2000	254,144	6,036	248,108
2001 and subsequent	3,226,873	37,387	3,189,486
	$ 4,507,964	$ 72,455	$4,435,509

Total rental expense was as follows:

		Year ended	
	January 28, 1995	January 29, 1994	January 30, 1993
Minimum rentals	$ 226,382	$ 180,118	$ 149,027
Additional amounts computed as percentages of sales	6,361	5,604	5,447
	232,743	185,722	154,474
Less sublease income	10,348	7,935	5,788
	$ 222,395	$ 177,787	$ 148,686

STOCKHOLDERS' EQUITY

The common shares of the Company, par value $.10 per share, were as follows:

	January 28, 1995	January 29, 1994
Authorized shares	550,000	550,000
Issued shares	297,954	297,938
Treasury shares	18,164	8,416

Earnings per share is computed by dividing net earnings by the weighted average number of common shares outstanding after reduction for treasury shares and assuming exercise of dilutive stock options computed by the treasury stock method using the average market price during the year.

Weighted average numbers of shares used in computing earnings per share were as follows:

	Year ended		
	January 28, 1995	January 29, 1994	January 30, 1993
Common and common equivalent shares	287,415	296,463	297,718

In April 1994, the Company entered into an agreement with Petrie Stores Corporation ("Petrie"), the then holder of 14% of the Company's outstanding Common Stock. Pursuant to such agreement, the Company consummated a transaction with Petrie on January 24, 1995, wherein 42,076 shares of the Company's common stock were issued from its treasury in exchange for 39,853 shares of the Company's common stock and $165,000 in cash.

TAXES ON INCOME

The provisions for income taxes consist of the following:

	Year ended		
	January 28, 1995	January 29, 1994	January 30, 1993
Current:			
Federal	$ 251,621	$ 200,303	$ 186,013
Foreign	29,221	17,259	15,605
State	46,003	35,704	35,884
	326,845	253,266	237,502
Deferred:			
Federal	8,873	49,961	17,187
Foreign	(24,752)	(16,186)	(6,705)
State	1,334	2,759	3,516
	(14,545)	36,534	13,998
Total	$ 312,300	$ 289,800	$ 251,500

Deferred tax liabilities and deferred tax assets reflect the net tax effects of temporary differences between the carrying amounts of assets and liabilities for financial reporting purposes and the amounts used for income tax purposes. The Company has gross deferred tax liabilities of $270,900 at January 28, 1995 and $251,700 at January 29, 1994, which consist primarily of temporary differences related to fixed assets of $217,000 and $194,000, respectively. The Company had gross deferred tax assets of $129,900 at January 28, 1995 and $92,800 at January 29, 1994, which consist primarily of net operating losses of foreign start-up operations of $94,000 and $60,400, and operating costs not currently deductible for tax purposes of $25,400 and $23,200, respectively. Valuation allowances are not significant.

A reconciliation of the federal statutory tax rate with the effective tax rate follows:

	Year ended		
	January 28, 1995	January 29, 1994	January 30, 1993
Statutory tax rate	35.0%	35.0%	34.0%
State income taxes, net of federal income tax benefit	3.7	3.2	4.0
Foreign	(0.4)	(0.5)	(1.2)
Other, net	(1.3)	(0.2)	(0.3)
	37.0%	37.5%	36.5%

Deferred income taxes were not provided on unremitted earnings of foreign subsidiaries that are intended to be indefinitely invested. Unremitted earnings were approximately $131,000 at January 28, 1995, exclusive of amounts that if remitted would result in little or no tax under current U.S. tax laws. Net income taxes of approximately $46,000 would be due if these earnings were to be remitted.

PROFIT SHARING PLAN

The Company has a profit sharing plan with a 401(k) salary deferral feature for eligible domestic employees. The terms of the plan call for annual contributions by the Company as determined by the Board of Directors, subject to certain limitations. The profit sharing plan may be terminated at the Company's discretion. Provisions of $31,391, $29,961 and $29,824 have been charged to operations in 1994, 1993 and 1992, respectively.

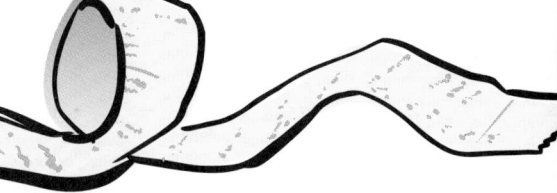

STOCK OPTIONS

The Company has Stock Option Plans (the "Plans") which provide for the granting of options to purchase the Company's common stock to substantially all employees and non-employee directors of the Company. The Plans provide for the issuance of non-qualified options, incentive stock options, performance share options, performance units, stock appreciation rights, restricted shares and unrestricted shares. The majority of the options become exercisable four years and nine months from the date of grant. Certain non-qualified options become exercisable nine years from the date of grant, however the exercise date of all or a portion of such options may be accelerated if the price of the Company's common stock reaches certain target amounts. The options granted to non-employee directors are exercisable 20% each year on a cumulative basis commencing one year from the date of grant.

In addition to the aforementioned plans, 2,862 stock options were granted to certain senior executives during the period from 1988 to 1993 pursuant to individual plans. These options are exercisable 20% each year on a cumulative basis commencing one year from the date of grant.

The exercise price per share of all options granted has been the average of the high and low market price of the Company's common stock on the date of grant. Options must be exercised within ten years from the date of grant.

At January 28, 1995, an aggregate of 28,502 shares of authorized common stock was reserved for all of the Plans noted above; 9,139 of which were available for future grants and 5,390 which were reserved for exercisable options. All outstanding options expire at dates varying from May 1995 to November 2004.

Stock option transactions are summarized as follows:

			Shares Under Option
	Incentive	Non-Qualified	Price Range
Outstanding January 29, 1994 ...	527	16,720	$ 7.68 - 40.94
Granted....................................	–	4,189	34.31 - 38.56
Exercised.................................	(167)	(952)	7.68 - 36.94
Canceled	–	(954)	7.68 - 39.88
Outstanding January 28, 1995 ...	360	19,003	$ 7.68 - 40.94

The exercise of non-qualified stock options results in state and federal income tax benefits to the Company related to the difference between the market price at the date of exercise and the option price. During 1994, 1993 and 1992, $6,056, $10,031 and $45,390, respectively, was credited to additional paid-in capital.

FOREIGN OPERATIONS

Certain information relating to the Company's foreign operations is set forth below. Corporate assets include all cash and cash equivalents and other related assets.

			Year ended
	January 28, 1995	January 29, 1994	January 30, 1993
Sales			
Domestic...................	$ 6,644,799	$ 6,278,591	$ 5,795,119
Foreign.....................	2,100,787	1,667,476	1,374,171
Total...........................	$ 8,745,586	$ 7,946,067	$ 7,169,290
Operating Profit			
Domestic...................	$ 778,659	$ 724,818	$ 647,640
Foreign.....................	140,829	102,923	101,132
General corporate expenses..................	(7,446)	(6,821)	(9,333)
Interest expense, net	(67,975)	(48,167)	(50,415)
Earnings before taxes on income	$ 844,067	$ 772,753	$ 689,024
Identifiable Assets			
Domestic...................	$ 3,950,511	$ 3,630,921	$ 3,277,527
Foreign.....................	2,216,086	1,694,565	1,248,827
Corporate.................	404,596	824,123	796,498
Total...........................	$ 6,571,193	$ 6,149,609	$ 5,322,852

QUARTERLY FINANCIAL DATA

The following table sets forth certain unaudited quarterly financial information.

	First Quarter	Second Quarter	Third Quarter	Fourth Quarter
Year Ended January 28, 1995				
Net Sales.................	$ 1,461,933	$ 1,452,117	$ 1,631,345	$ 4,200,191
Cost of Sales.............	1,001,203	982,892	1,097,236	2,926,627
Net Earnings	37,580	38,014	47,367	408,806
Earnings per Share	$ .13	$ .13	$ .17	$ 1.46
Year Ended January 29, 1994				
Net Sales.................	$ 1,286,479	$ 1,317,012	$ 1,449,118	$ 3,893,458
Cost of Sales.............	882,876	902,414	982,151	2,727,325
Net Earnings	35,436	35,505	37,457	374,555
Earnings per Share	$ .12	$ .12	$ .13	$ 1.27

REPORT OF MANAGEMENT

Responsibility for the integrity and objectivity of the financial information presented in this Annual Report rests with Toys"R"Us management. The accompanying financial statements have been prepared from accounting records which management believes fairly and accurately reflect the operations and financial position of the Company. Management has established a system of internal controls to provide reasonable assurance that assets are maintained and accounted for in accordance with its policies and that transactions are recorded accurately on the Company's books and records.

The Company's comprehensive internal audit program provides for constant evaluation of the adequacy of the adherence to management's established policies and procedures. The Company has distributed to key employees its policies for conducting business affairs in a lawful and ethical manner.

The Audit Committee of the Board of Directors, which is comprised solely of outside directors, provides oversight to the financial reporting process through periodic meetings with our independent auditors, internal auditors and management.

The financial statements of the Company have been audited by Ernst & Young LLP, independent auditors, in accordance with generally accepted auditing standards, including a review of financial reporting matters and internal controls to the extent necessary to express an opinion on the consolidated financial statements.

Michael Goldstein
Vice Chairman and
Chief Executive Officer

Louis Lipschitz
Senior Vice President - Finance
and Chief Financial Officer

MARKET INFORMATION

The Company's common stock is listed on the New York Stock Exchange. The following table reflects the high and low prices (rounded to the nearest one-eighth) based on New York Stock Exchange trading since January 30, 1993.

The Company has not paid any cash dividends, however, the Board of Directors of the Company reviews this policy annually.

The number of stockholders of record of common stock on March 7, 1995 was approximately 27,200.

		High	Low
1993	1st Quarter	42 3/8	36 5/8
	2nd Quarter	39 3/4	32 3/8
	3rd Quarter	40 3/8	33 3/4
	4th Quarter	42 7/8	36
1994	1st Quarter	37 3/8	32 3/8
	2nd Quarter	36 3/4	32 1/4
	3rd Quarter	38 3/4	33
	4th Quarter	39	28 1/4

REPORT OF INDEPENDENT AUDITORS

The Board of Directors and Stockholders
Toys"R"Us, Inc.

We have audited the accompanying consolidated balance sheets of Toys"R"Us, Inc. and subsidiaries as of January 28, 1995 and January 29, 1994, and the related consolidated statements of earnings, stockholders' equity and cash flows for each of the three years in the period ended January 28, 1995. These financial statements are the responsibility of the Company's management. Our responsibility is to express an opinion on these financial statements based on our audits.

We conducted our audits in accordance with generally accepted auditing standards. Those standards require that we plan and perform the audit to obtain reasonable assurance about whether the financial statements are free of material misstatement. An audit includes examining, on a test basis, evidence supporting the amounts and disclosures in the financial statements. An audit also includes assessing the accounting principles used and significant estimates made by management, as well as evaluating the overall financial statement presentation. We believe that our audits provide a reasonable basis for our opinion.

In our opinion, the financial statements referred to above present fairly, in all material respects, the consolidated financial position of Toys"R"Us, Inc. and subsidiaries at January 28, 1995 and January 29,1994, and the consolidated results of their operations and their cash flows for each of the three years in the period ended January 28, 1995, in conformity with generally accepted accounting principles.

Ernst & Young LLP

New York, New York
March 8, 1995

DIRECTORS AND OFFICERS

DIRECTORS

Charles Lazarus
Chairman of the Board
of the Company

Robert A. Bernhard
Real Estate Developer

Michael Goldstein
Vice Chairman and Chief Executive
Officer of the Company

Milton S. Gould
Attorney-at-law;
Of Counsel to LeBoeuf, Lamb,
Greene & MacRae

Shirley Strum Kenny
President, State University of
New York at Stony Brook

Reuben Mark
Chairman and CEO
Colgate-Palmolive Company

Howard W. Moore
Former Executive
Vice President - General
Merchandise Manager of
the Company; Consultant

Robert C. Nakasone
President and Chief Operating
Officer of the Company

Norman M. Schneider
Former Chairman, Leisure Products
Division of Beatrice Foods
Company; Consultant

Harold M. Wit
Managing Director,
Allen & Company Incorporated;
Investment Bankers

OFFICERS - CORPORATE AND ADMINISTRATIVE

Michael Goldstein
Vice Chairman and
Chief Executive Officer

Robert C. Nakasone
President and
Chief Operating Officer

Dennis Healey
Senior Vice President -
Management Information Systems

Louis Lipschitz
Senior Vice President -
Finance and Chief Financial Officer

Michael P. Miller
Senior Vice President - Real Estate

Jeffrey S. Wells
Senior Vice President -
Human Resources

Gayle C. Aertker
Vice President - Real Estate

Michael J. Corrigan
Vice President - Compensation
and Benefits

Richard N. Cudrin
Vice President - Employee and
Labor Relations

Jonathan M. Friedman
Vice President - Controller and
Chief Financial Officer - Kids"R"Us

Eileen C. Gabriel
Vice President -
Information Systems

Jon W. Kimmins
Vice President - Treasurer

Matthew J. Lombardi
Vice President -
Information Technology

Eric A. Swartwood
Vice President -
Architecture and Construction

Michael L. Tumolo
Vice President -
Real Estate Counsel

Peter W. Weiss
Vice President - Taxes

Andre Weiss
Secretary - Attorney-at-law;
Partner-Schulte Roth & Zabel

TOYS"R"US UNITED STATES - OFFICERS AND GENERAL MANAGERS

Roger V. Goddu
Executive Vice President -
General Merchandise Manager

Michael J. Madden
Group Vice President -
Store Operations

Van H. Butler
Senior Vice President -
Divisional Merchandise Manager

Bruce C. Hall
Senior Vice President -
Regional Operations

Thomas J. Reinebach
Senior Vice President - Distribution
and Support Services

Ernest V. Speranza
Senior Vice President -
Advertising/Marketing

Robert J. Weinberg
Senior Vice President -
Divisional Merchandise Manager

Kristopher M. Brown
Vice President - Distribution Operations

Harvey J. Finkel
Vice President - Regional Operations

Martin Fogelman
Vice President -
Divisional Merchandise Manager

Michael A. Gerety
Vice President - Store Planning

Lee Richardson
Vice President - Advertising

John P. Sullivan
Vice President - Divisional
Merchandise Manager

Karl S. Taylor
Vice President - Merchandise
Planning and Allocation

GENERAL MANAGERS

Robert F. Price
Vice President
New York/Northern New Jersey

Thomas A. Drugan
Alabama/Georgia/South
Carolina/Tennessee

Larry D. Gardner
Pacific Northwest/Alaska

Mark H. Haag
Southern California/
Arizona/Nevada/Hawaii

Daniel D. Hlavaty
Central Ohio/Indiana/Kentucky

Debra M. Kachurak
New England

Richard A. Moyer
S. Texas/Louisiana/Mississippi

Gerald S. Parker
Northern California/Utah

John J. Prawlocki
Florida/Puerto Rico

J. Michael Roberts
Pennsylvania/Delaware/
Southern New Jersey

Edward F. Siegler
Colorado/Kansas/Missouri/
Iowa/Nebraska

Carl P. Spaulding
N.E. Ohio/W. Pennsylvania/
N. New York

William A. Stephenson
Illinois/Wisconsin/Minnesota

John P. Suozzo
Maryland/Virginia/North Carolina

Brian L. Voorhees
N. Texas/Oklahoma/Arkansas/
New Mexico

Dennis J. Williams
Michigan/N.W. Ohio

KIDS"R"US - OFFICERS

Richard L. Markee
President

Virginia Harris
Senior Vice President -
General Merchandise Manager

James G. Parros
Senior Vice President - Stores and
Distribution Center Operations

James L. Easton
Vice President -
Divisional Merchandise Manager

Jerel G. Hollens
Vice President -
Merchandise Planning and
Management Information Systems

Debra G. Hyman
Vice President -
Divisional Merchandise Manager

Elizabeth S. Jordan
Vice President - Human Resources

Lorna E. Nagler
Vice President -
Divisional Merchandise Manager

TOYS"R"US INTERNATIONAL - OFFICERS AND COUNTRY MANAGEMENT

Larry D. Bouts
President

Gregory R. Staley
Senior Vice President -
General Merchandise Manager

Lawrence H. Meyer
Vice President -
Chief Financial Officer

Ken Bonning
Vice President - Logistics

Joseph Giamelli
Vice President -
Information Systems

Adam Szopinski
Vice President - Operations

Keith Van Beek
Vice President - Development

COUNTRY MANAGEMENT

Jacques Le Foll
President - Toys"R"Us France

Carl Olsen
Managing Director -
Toys"R"Us Australia

Guillermo Porrati
Managing Director -
Toys"R"Us Central Europe/Iberia

David Rurka
Managing Director - Toys"R"Us
United Kingdom/Scandinavia

Manabu Tazaki
President - Toys"R"Us Japan

Elliott Wahle
President - Toys"R"Us Canada

Keith C. Spurgeon
Vice President -
Toys"R"Us Asia/Australia

Scott Chen
General Manager -
Toys"R"Us Taiwan

David Silber
General Manager -
Toys"R"Us Hong Kong

Michael Yeo
General Manager -
Toys"R"Us Singapore

CORPORATE DATA

ANNUAL MEETING
The Annual Meeting of the
Stockholders of Toys"R"Us will be
held at the offices of the Company
on Wednesday, June 7, 1995 at
10:00 a.m.

THE OFFICE OF THE
COMPANY IS LOCATED AT
461 From Road
Paramus, New Jersey 07652
Telephone: 201-262-7800

GENERAL COUNSEL
Schulte Roth & Zabel
900 Third Avenue
New York, New York 10022

INDEPENDENT AUDITORS
Ernst & Young LLP
787 Seventh Avenue
New York, New York 10019

STOCKHOLDER INFORMATION
The Company will supply to any owner of
Common Stock, upon written request to
Mr. Louis Lipschitz of the Company at the
address set forth herein, and without
charge, a copy of the Annual Report on
Form 10-K for the year ended January
28, 1995, which has been filed with the
Securities and Exchange Commission.

Stockholder information, including
quarterly earnings and other corporate
news releases, can be obtained toll free
by calling 800-785-TOYS. Significant
news releases will be available on the
following dates:

CALL AFTER...	FOR THE FOLLOWING...
May 15, 1995	1st Quarter Results
Aug. 14, 1995	2nd Quarter Results
Nov. 13, 1995	3rd Quarter Results
Jan. 2, 1996	Christmas Sales Results
Mar. 13, 1996	1995 Results

COMMON STOCK LISTED
New York Stock Exchange, Symbol: TOY

REGISTRAR AND TRANSFER AGENT
American Stock Transfer
and Trust Company
40 Wall Street
New York, New York 10005
Telephone: 718-921-8200

 Printed on
recycled paper

The Time Value of Money

LEARNING OBJECTIVES

1. Distinguish between simple and compound interest.

2. Use compound interest tables to compute the future value of a single invested sum at compound interest and of an ordinary annuity.

3. Use compound interest tables to compute the present value of a single sum due in the future and of an ordinary annuity.

4. Apply the concept of present value to simple accounting situations.

Interest is an important cost to the debtor and an important revenue to the creditor. Because interest is a cost associated with time, and "time is money," it is also an important consideration in any business decision. For example, an individual who holds $100 for one year without putting that $100 in a savings account has forgone the interest that could have been earned. Thus, there is a cost associated with holding this money equal to the interest that could have been earned. Similarly, a business person who accepts a noninterest-bearing note instead of cash for the sale of merchandise is not forgoing the interest that could have been earned on that money but is including the interest implicitly in the price of the merchandise. These examples illustrate the point that the timing of the receipt and payment of cash must be considered in making business decisions.

SIMPLE INTEREST AND COMPOUND INTEREST

OBJECTIVE

1 *Distinguish between simple and compound interest*

Interest is the cost associated with the use of money for a specific period of time. Simple interest is the interest cost for one or more periods, under the assumption that the amount on which the interest is computed stays the same from period to period. Compound interest is the interest cost for two or more periods, under the assumption that after each period the interest of that period is added to the amount on which interest is computed in future periods. In other words, compound interest is interest earned on a principal sum that is increased at the end of each period by the interest of that period.

Example: Simple Interest   Joe Sanchez accepts an 8 percent, $30,000 note due in ninety days. How much will he receive in total at that time? Remember that the formula for calculating simple interest is as follows:

$$
\begin{aligned}
\text{Interest} &= \text{principal} \times \text{rate} \times \text{time} \\
&= \$30{,}000 \times 8/100 \times 90/360 \\
&= \$600
\end{aligned}
$$

Therefore, the total that Sanchez will receive is calculated as follows:

$$
\begin{aligned}
\text{Total} &= \text{principal} + \text{interest} \\
&= \$30{,}000 + \$600 \\
&= \$30{,}600
\end{aligned}
$$

Example: Compound Interest   Ann Clary deposits $5,000 in a savings account that pays 6 percent interest. She expects to leave the principal and accumulated interest in the account for three years. How much will her account total at the end of three years? Assume that the interest is paid at the end of the year and is added to the principal at that time and that this total in turn earns interest. The amount at the end of three years is computed as follows:

(1) Year	(2) Principal Amount at Beginning of Year	(3) Annual Amount of Interest (Col. 2 × 6%)	(4) Accumulated Amount at End of Year (Col. 2 + Col. 3)
1	$5,000.00	$300.00	$5,300.00
2	5,300.00	318.00	5,618.00
3	5,618.00	337.08	5,955.08

At the end of three years, Clary will have $5,955.08 in her savings account. Note that the annual amount of interest increases each year by the interest rate times the interest of the previous year. For example, between year 1 and year 2, the interest increased by $18 ($318 − $300), which exactly equals 6 percent times $300.

FUTURE VALUE OF A SINGLE INVESTED SUM AT COMPOUND INTEREST

OBJECTIVE

2 *Use compound interest tables to compute the future value of a single invested sum at compound interest and of an ordinary annuity*

Another way to ask the question in the example of compound interest above is, What is the future value of a single sum ($5,000) at compound interest (6 percent) for three years? Future value is the amount that an investment will be worth at a future date if invested at compound interest. A business person often wants to know future value, but the method of computing the future value illustrated above is too time-consuming in practice. Imagine how tedious the calculation would be if the example were ten years instead of three. Fortunately, there are tables that simplify solving problems involving compound interest. Table 1, showing the future value of $1 after a given number of time periods, is an example. It is actually part of a larger table, Table 1 in the appendix on future value and present value tables. Suppose that we

Table 1. Future Value of $1 after a Given Number of Time Periods

Periods	1%	2%	3%	4%	5%	6%	7%	8%	9%	10%	12%	14%	15%
1	1.010	1.020	1.030	1.040	1.050	1.060	1.070	1.080	1.090	1.100	1.120	1.140	1.150
2	1.020	1.040	1.061	1.082	1.103	1.124	1.145	1.166	1.188	1.210	1.254	1.300	1.323
3	1.030	1.061	1.093	1.125	1.158	1.191	1.225	1.260	1.295	1.331	1.405	1.482	1.521
4	1.041	1.082	1.126	1.170	1.216	1.262	1.311	1.360	1.412	1.464	1.574	1.689	1.749
5	1.051	1.104	1.159	1.217	1.276	1.338	1.403	1.469	1.539	1.611	1.762	1.925	2.011
6	1.062	1.126	1.194	1.265	1.340	1.419	1.501	1.587	1.677	1.772	1.974	2.195	2.313
7	1.072	1.149	1.230	1.316	1.407	1.504	1.606	1.714	1.828	1.949	2.211	2.502	2.660
8	1.083	1.172	1.267	1.369	1.477	1.594	1.718	1.851	1.993	2.144	2.476	2.853	3.059
9	1.094	1.195	1.305	1.423	1.551	1.689	1.838	1.999	2.172	2.358	2.773	3.252	3.518
10	1.105	1.219	1.344	1.480	1.629	1.791	1.967	2.159	2.367	2.594	3.106	3.707	4.046

Source: Excerpt from Table 1 in the appendix on future value and present value tables.

want to solve the problem of Clary's savings account above. We simply look down the 6 percent column in Table 1 until we reach the line for period 3 and find the factor 1.191. This factor, when multiplied by $1, gives the future value of that $1 at compound interest of 6 percent for three periods (years in this case). Thus, we solve the problem as follows:

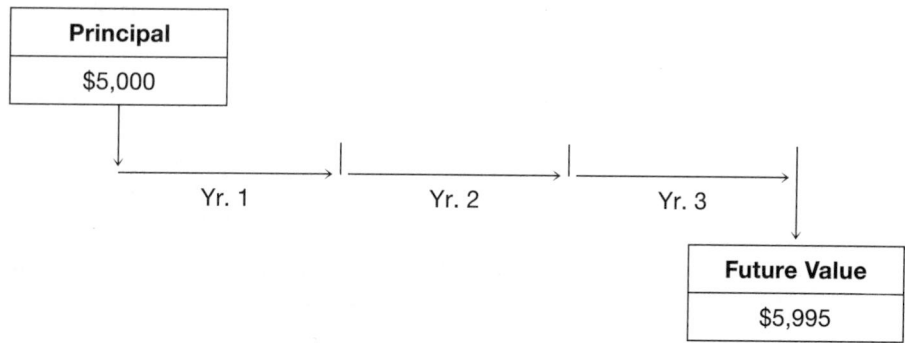

Principal × factor = future value
$5,000 × 1.191 = $5,955

Except for a rounding difference of $.08, the answer is exactly the same as that calculated earlier.

FUTURE VALUE OF AN ORDINARY ANNUITY

Another common problem involves an ordinary annuity, which is a series of equal payments made at the end of equal intervals of time, with compound interest on these payments.

The following example shows how to find the future value of an ordinary annuity. Assume that Ben Katz makes a $200 payment at the end of each of the next three years into a savings account that pays 5 percent interest. How much money will he have in his account at the end of the three years? One way of computing the amount is shown in the following table.

Appendix B

(1) Year	(2) Beginning Balance	(3) Interest Earned (5% × Col. 2)	(4) Periodic Payment	(5) Accumulated at End of Period (Col. 2 + Col. 3 + Col. 4)
1	—	—	$200	$200.00
2	$200.00	$10.00	200	410.00
3	410.00	20.50	200	630.50

Katz would have $630.50 in his account at the end of three years, consisting of $600.00 in periodic payments and $30.50 in interest.

This calculation can also be simplified by using Table 2. We look down the 5 percent column until we reach period 3 and find the factor 3.153. This factor, when multiplied by $1, gives the future value of a series of three $1 payments (years in this case) at compound interest of 5 percent. Thus, we solve the problem as follows:

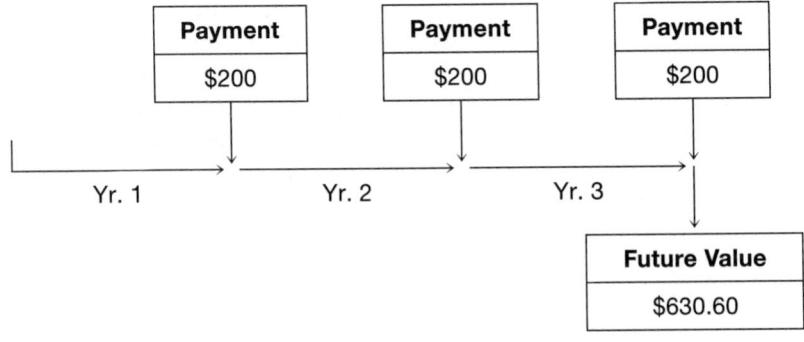

Periodic payment × factor = future value
$200.00 × 3.153 = $630.60

Except for a rounding difference of $.10, this result is the same as the one calculated earlier.

Table 2. Future Value of an Ordinary Annuity of $1 Paid in Each Period for a Given Number of Time Periods

Periods	1%	2%	3%	4%	5%	6%	7%	8%	9%	10%	12%	14%	15%
1	1.000	1.000	1.000	1.000	1.000	1.000	1.000	1.000	1.000	1.000	1.000	1.000	1.000
2	2.010	2.020	2.030	2.040	2.050	2.060	2.070	2.080	2.090	2.100	2.120	2.140	2.150
3	3.030	3.060	3.091	3.122	3.153	3.184	3.215	3.246	3.278	3.310	3.374	3.440	3.473
4	4.060	4.122	4.184	4.246	4.310	4.375	4.440	4.506	4.573	4.641	4.779	4.921	4.993
5	5.101	5.204	5.309	5.416	5.526	5.637	5.751	5.867	5.985	6.105	6.353	6.610	6.742
6	6.152	6.308	6.468	6.633	6.802	6.975	7.153	7.336	7.523	7.716	8.115	8.536	8.754
7	7.214	7.434	7.662	7.898	8.142	8.394	8.654	8.923	9.200	9.487	10.09	10.73	11.07
8	8.286	8.583	8.892	9.214	9.549	9.897	10.26	10.64	11.03	11.44	12.30	13.23	13.73
9	9.369	9.755	10.16	10.58	11.03	11.49	11.98	12.49	13.02	13.58	14.78	16.09	16.79
10	10.46	10.95	11.46	12.01	12.58	13.18	13.82	14.49	15.19	15.94	17.55	19.34	20.30

Source: Excerpt from Table 2 in the appendix on future value and present value tables.

PRESENT VALUE

Suppose that you had the choice of receiving $100 today or one year from today. Intuitively, you would choose to receive the $100 today. Why? You know that if you have the $100 today, you can put it in a savings account to earn interest and will have more than $100 a year from today. Therefore, we can say that an amount to be received in the future (future value) is not worth as much today as an amount to be received today (present value) because of the cost associated with the passage of time. In fact, present value and future value are closely related. Present value is the amount that must be invested now at a given rate of interest to produce a given future value.

For example, assume that Sue Dapper needs $1,000 one year from now. How much should she invest today to achieve that goal if the interest rate is 5 percent? From earlier examples, the following equation may be established.

Present value × (1.0 + interest rate) = future value
Present value ×   1.05   = $1,000.00
Present value   = $1,000.00 ÷ 1.05
Present value   = $952.38

Thus, to achieve a future value of $1,000.00, a present value of $952.38 must be invested. Interest of 5 percent on $952.38 for one year equals $47.62, and these two amounts added together equal $1,000.00

PRESENT VALUE OF A SINGLE SUM DUE IN THE FUTURE

OBJECTIVE

3 *Use compound interest tables to compute the present value of a single sum due in the future and of an ordinary annuity*

When more than one time period is involved, the calculation of present value is more complicated. Consider the following example. Don Riley wants to be sure of having $4,000 at the end of three years. How much must he invest today in a 5 percent savings account to achieve this goal? Adapting the above equation, we compute the present value of $4,000 at compound interest of 5 percent for three years in the future.

Year	Amount at End of Year	Divide by		Present Value at Beginning of Year
3	$4,000.00	÷	1.05 =	$3,809.52
2	3,809.52	÷	1.05 =	3,628.11
1	3,628.11	÷	1.05 =	3,455.34

Riley must invest a present value of $3,455.34 to achieve a future value of $4,000.00 in three years.

This calculation is again made much easier by using the appropriate table. In Table 3, we look down the 5 percent column until we reach period 3 and find the factor .864. This factor, when multiplied by $1, gives the present value of the $1 to be received three years from now at 5 percent interest. Thus, we solve the problem as shown on the next page.

Table 3. Present Value of $1 to Be Received at the End of a Given Number of Time Periods

Periods	1%	2%	3%	4%	5%	6%	7%	8%	9%	10%
1	0.990	0.980	0.971	0.962	0.952	0.943	0.935	0.926	0.917	0.909
2	0.980	0.961	0.943	0.925	0.907	0.890	0.873	0.857	0.842	0.826
3	0.971	0.942	0.915	0.889	0.864	0.840	0.816	0.794	0.772	0.751
4	0.961	0.924	0.888	0.855	0.823	0.792	0.763	0.735	0.708	0.683
5	0.951	0.906	0.863	0.822	0.784	0.747	0.713	0.681	0.650	0.621
6	0.942	0.888	0.837	0.790	0.746	0.705	0.666	0.630	0.596	0.564
7	0.933	0.871	0.813	0.760	0.711	0.665	0.623	0.583	0.547	0.513
8	0.923	0.853	0.789	0.731	0.677	0.627	0.582	0.540	0.502	0.467
9	0.914	0.837	0.766	0.703	0.645	0.592	0.544	0.500	0.460	0.424
10	0.905	0.820	0.744	0.676	0.614	0.558	0.508	0.463	0.422	0.386

Source: Excerpt from Table 3 in the appendix on future value and present value tables.

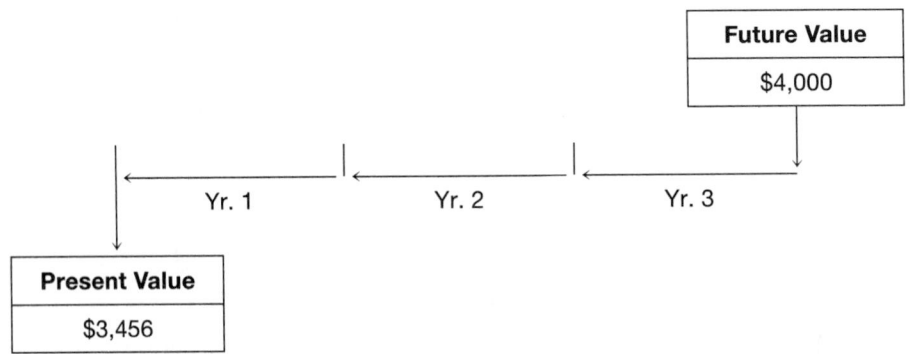

Future value × factor = present value
$4,000 × .864 = $3,456

Except for a rounding difference of $.66, this result is the same as the one above.

PRESENT VALUE OF AN ORDINARY ANNUITY

It is often necessary to compute the present value of a series of receipts or payments. When we calculate the present value of equal amounts equally spaced over a period of time, we are computing the present value of an ordinary annuity.

For example, assume that Kathy Foster has sold a piece of property and is to receive $15,000 in three equal annual payments of $5,000, beginning one year from today. What is the present value of this sale, assuming a current interest rate of 5 percent? This present value may be computed by calculating a separate present value for each of the three payments (using Table 3) and summing the results, as shown in the table at the top of the next page.

The present value of this sale is $13,615. Thus, there is an implied interest cost (given the 5 percent rate) of $1,385 associated with the payment plan that allows the purchaser to pay in three installments.

The Time Value of Money

Future Receipts (Annuity)			Present Value Factor at 5 Percent (from Table 3)		Present Value
Year 1	Year 2	Year 3			
$5,000			× .952	=	$ 4,760
	$5,000		× .907	=	4,535
		$5,000	× .864	=	4,320
Total Present Value					$13,615

We can make this calculation more easily by using Table 4. We look down the 5 percent column until we reach period 3 and find factor 2.723. This factor, when multiplied by $1, gives the present value of a series of three $1 payments (spaced one year apart) at compound interest of 5 percent. Thus, we solve the problem as follows:

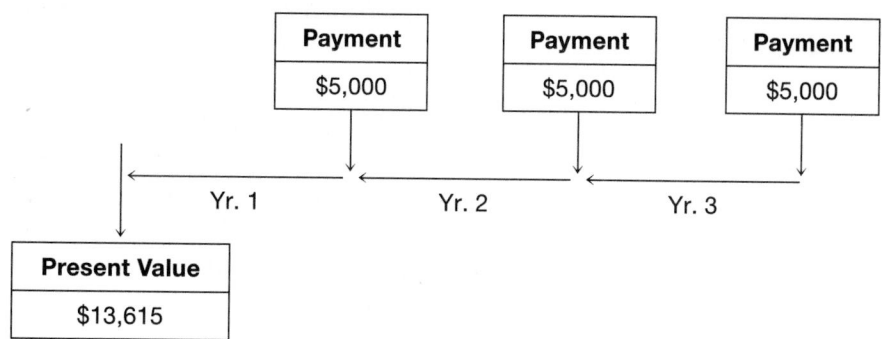

Periodic payment × factor = present value
$5,000 × 2.723 = $13,615

This result is the same as the one computed earlier.

Table 4. Present Value of an Ordinary Annuity of $1 Received Each Period for a Given Number of Time Periods

Periods	1%	2%	3%	4%	5%	6%	7%	8%	9%	10%
1	0.990	0.980	0.971	0.962	0.952	0.943	0.935	0.926	0.917	0.909
2	1.970	1.942	1.913	1.886	1.859	1.833	1.808	1.783	1.759	1.736
3	2.941	2.884	2.829	2.775	2.723	2.673	2.624	2.577	2.531	2.487
4	3.902	3.808	3.717	3.630	3.546	3.465	3.387	3.312	3.240	3.170
5	4.853	4.713	4.580	4.452	4.329	4.212	4.100	3.993	3.890	3.791
6	5.795	5.601	5.417	5.242	5.076	4.917	4.767	4.623	4.486	4.355
7	6.728	6.472	6.230	6.002	5.786	5.582	5.389	5.206	5.033	4.868
8	7.652	7.325	7.020	6.733	6.463	6.210	5.971	5.747	5.535	5.335
9	8.566	8.162	7.786	7.435	7.108	6.802	6.515	6.247	5.995	5.759
10	9.471	8.983	8.530	8.111	7.722	7.360	7.024	6.710	6.418	6.145

Source: Excerpt from Table 4 in the appendix on future value and present value tables.

TIME PERIODS

In all of the previous examples, and in most other cases, the compounding period is one year, and the interest rate is stated on an annual basis. However, in each of the four tables the left-hand column refers, not to years, but to periods. This wording is intended to accommodate compounding periods of less than one year. Savings accounts that record interest quarterly and bonds that pay interest semiannually are cases where the compounding period is less than one year. To use the tables in such cases, it is necessary to (1) divide the annual interest rate by the number of periods in the year, and (2) multiply the number of periods in one year by the number of years.

For example, assume that a $6,000 note is to be paid in two years and carries an annual interest rate of 8 percent. Compute the maturity (future) value of the note, assuming that the compounding period is semiannual. Before using the table, it is necessary to compute the interest rate that applies to each compounding period and the total number of compounding periods. First, the interest rate to use is 4 percent (8% annual rate ÷ 2 periods per year). Second, the total number of compounding periods is 4 (2 periods per year × 2 years). From Table 1, therefore, the maturity value of the note is computed as follows:

$$\text{Principal} \times \text{factor} = \text{future value}$$
$$\$6,000 \quad \times \quad 1.170 = \quad \$7,020$$

The note will be worth $7,020 in two years.

This procedure for determining the interest rate and the number of periods when the compounding period is less than one year may be used with all four tables.

APPLICATIONS OF PRESENT VALUE TO ACCOUNTING

The concept of present value is widely applicable in the discipline of accounting. Here, the purpose is to demonstrate its usefulness in some simple applications. In-depth study of present value is deferred to more advanced courses.

IMPUTING INTEREST ON NONINTEREST-BEARING NOTES

OBJECTIVE

4 *Apply the concept of present value to simple accounting situations*

Clearly there is no such thing as an interest-free debt, regardless of whether the interest rate is explicitly stated. The Accounting Principles Board has declared that when a long-term note does not explicitly state an interest rate (or if the interest rate is unreasonably low), a rate based on the normal interest cost of the company in question should be assigned, or imputed.[1]

The following example applies this principle. On January 1, 19x8, Gato purchased merchandise from Haines by issuing an $8,000 noninterest-bearing note due in two years. Gato can borrow money from the bank at 9 percent interest. Gato paid the note in full after two years.

1. Accounting Principles Board, *Opinion No. 21*, "Interest on Receivables and Payables" (New York: American Institute of Certified Public Accountants, 1971), par. 13.

Note that the $8,000 note represents partly a payment for merchandise and partly a payment of interest for two years. In recording the purchase and sale, it is necessary to use Table 3 to determine the present value of the note. The calculation follows.

Future payment × present value factor (9%, 2 years) = present value
$8,000 × .842 = $6,736

The imputed interest cost is $1,264 ($8,000 − $6,736) and is recorded as a discount on notes payable in Gato's records and as a discount on notes receivable in Haines's records. The entries necessary to record the purchase in the Gato records and the sale in the Haines records are as follows:

Gato Journal			**Haines Journal**		
Purchases	6,736		Notes Receivable	8,000	
Discount on			Discount on		
Notes Payable	1,264		Notes Receivable		1,264
Notes Payable		8,000	Sales		6,736

On December 31, 19x8, the adjustments to recognize the interest expense and interest income are as follows:

Gato Journal			**Haines Journal**		
Interest Expense	606.24		Discount on		
Discount on			Notes Receivable	606.24	
Notes Payable		606.24	Interest Income		606.24

The interest is calculated by multiplying the original purchase by the interest for one year ($6,736.00 × .09 = $606.24). When payment is made on December 31, 19x9, the following entries are made in the respective journals.

Gato Journal			**Haines Journal**		
Interest Expense	657.76		Discount on		
Notes Payable	8,000.00		Notes Receivable	657.76	
Discount on			Cash	8,000.00	
Notes Payable		657.76	Interest Income		657.76
Cash		8,000.00	Notes Receivable		8,000.00

The interest entries represent the remaining interest to be expensed or realized ($1,264 − $606.24 = $657.76). This amount approximates (because of rounding differences in the table) the interest for one year on the purchase plus last year's interest [($6,736 + $606.24) × .09 = $660.80].

VALUING AN ASSET

An asset is recorded because it will provide future benefits to the company that owns it. This future benefit is the basis for the definition of an asset. Usually, the purchase price of the asset represents the present value of these future benefits. It is possible to evaluate a proposed purchase price of an asset by comparing that price with the present value of the asset to the company.

For example, Sam Hurst is thinking of buying a new machine that will reduce his annual labor cost by $700 per year. The machine will last eight years. The interest rate that Hurst assumes for making managerial decisions is 10 percent. What is the maximum amount (present value) that Hurst should pay for the machine?

The present value of the machine to Hurst is equal to the present value of an ordinary annuity of $700 per year for eight years at compound interest of 10 percent. From Table 4, we compute the value as follows:

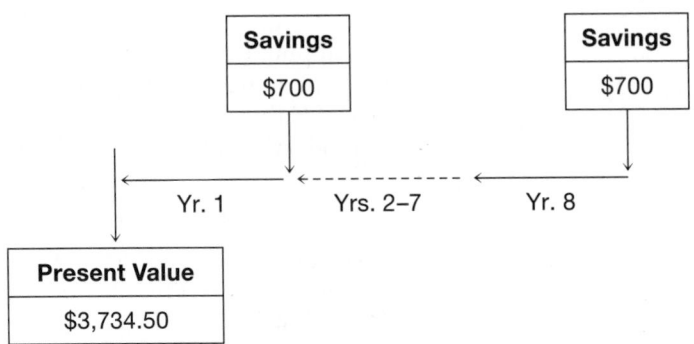

Periodic savings × factor = present value
$700.00   × 5.335 = $3,734.50

Hurst should not pay more than $3,734.50 for the new machine because this amount equals the present value of the benefits that will be received from owning the machine.

DEFERRED PAYMENT

A seller will sometimes agree to defer payment for a sale in order to encourage the buyer to make the purchase. This practice is common, for example, in the farm implement industry, where the farmer needs the equipment in the spring but cannot pay for it until the fall crop is in. Assume that Plains Implement Corporation sells a tractor to Dana Washington for $50,000 on February 1, agreeing to take payment ten months later on December 1. When this type of agreement is made, the future payment includes not only the sales price of the tractor but also an implied (imputed) interest cost. If the prevailing annual interest rate for such transactions is 12 percent compounded monthly, the actual sale (purchase) price of the tractor would be the present value of the future payment, computed according to Table 3 (10 periods, 1 percent), as follows:

Future payment × factor = present value
$50,000   × .905 = $45,250

The purchase in Washington's records and the sale in Plains's records are recorded at the present value, $45,250. The balance consists of interest expense or interest income. The entries necessary to record the purchase in Washington's records and the sale in Plains's records are as follows:

Washington Journal

Feb. 1	Tractor	45,250	
	Accounts Payable		45,250
	Purchase of tractor		

Plains Journal

Accounts Receivable	45,250	
Sales		45,250
Sale of tractor		

When Washington pays for the tractor, the entries are as follows:

Washington Journal

Dec. 1	Accounts Payable	45,250	
	Interest Expense	4,750	
	Cash		50,000
	Payment on account		
	including imputed		
	interest expense		

Plains Journal

Cash	50,000	
Accounts Receivable		45,250
Interest Income		4,750
Receipt on account from		
Washington including		
imputed interest earned		

INVESTMENT OF IDLE CASH

Childware Corporation, a toy manufacturer, has just completed a successful fall selling season and has $10,000,000 in cash to invest for six months. The company places the cash in a money market account that is expected to pay 12 percent annual interest. Interest is compounded monthly and credited to the company's account each month. How much cash will the company have at the end of six months, and what entries will be made to record the investment and the monthly interest? From Table 1, the future value factor is based on six monthly periods of 1 percent (12 percent divided by 12 months), and the future value is computed as follows:

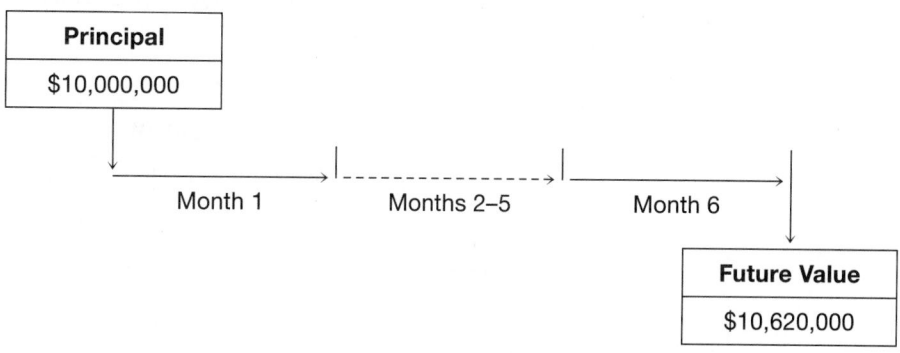

Investment × factor = future value
$10,000,000 × 1.062 = $10,620,000

When the investment is made, the following entry is made.

Short-Term Investments	10,000,000	
Cash		10,000,000
Investment of cash		

After the first month, the interest is recorded by increasing the Short-Term Investments account.

Short-Term Investments	100,000	
Interest Income		100,000
One month's interest income		
$10,000,000 \times .01 = \$100,000$		

After the second month, the interest is earned on the new balance of the Short-Term Investments account.

Short-Term Investments	101,000	
Interest Income		101,000
One month's interest income		
$10,100,000 \times .01 = \$101,000$		

Entries would continue in a similar manner for four more months, at which time the balance of Short-Term Investments would be about $10,620,000. The actual amount accumulated may vary from this total because the interest rate paid on money market accounts can vary over time as a result of changes in market conditions.

ACCUMULATION OF A FUND

When a company owes a large fixed amount due in several years, management would be wise to accumulate a fund with which to pay off the debt at maturity. Sometimes creditors, when they agree to provide a loan, require that such a fund be established. In establishing the fund, management must determine how much cash to set aside each period in order to pay the debt. The amount will depend on the estimated rate of interest the investments will earn. Assume that Vason Corporation agrees with a creditor to set aside cash at the end of each year to accumulate enough to pay off a $100,000 note due in six years. Since the first contribution to the fund will be made in one year, five annual contributions will be made by the time the note is due. Assume also that the fund is projected to earn 8 percent, compounded annually. The amount of each annual payment is calculated from Table 2 (5 periods, 8 percent), as follows:

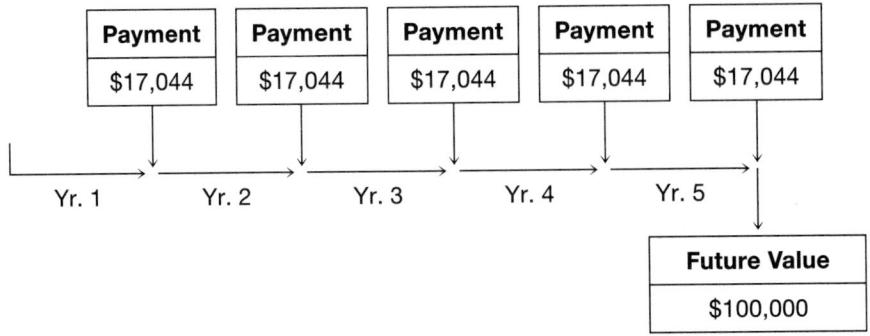

Future value of fund ÷ factor = annual investment
      $100,000   ÷ 5.867 = $17,044 (rounded)

Each year's contribution to the fund is $17,044. This contribution is recorded as follows:

Loan Repayment Fund	17,044	
Cash		17,044
Annual contribution to loan repayment fund		

OTHER ACCOUNTING APPLICATIONS

There are many other applications of present value in accounting, including accounting for installment notes, valuing a bond, and recording lease obligations. Present value is also applied in such areas as pension obligations; premium and discount on debt; depreciation of property, plant, and equipment; capital expenditure decisions; and generally any problem where time is a factor.

QUESTIONS

1. What is the key variable that distinguishes present value from future value?
2. What is an ordinary annuity?
3. How does the use of a compounding period of less than one year affect the computation of present value?
4. Why is present value important to accounting? (Illustrate your answer by giving concrete examples of applications in accounting.)

EXERCISES

Tables 1 to 4 in the appendix on future value and present value tables may be used where appropriate to solve these exercises.

E 1.
L O 2
Future Value
Calculations

Wieland receives a one-year note that carries a 12 percent annual interest rate on $3,000 for the sale of a used car.

Compute the maturity value under each of the following assumptions: (1) The interest is simple interest. (2) The interest is compounded semiannually. (3) The interest is compounded quarterly. (4) The interest is compounded monthly.

E 2.
L O 2
Future Value
Calculations

Find the future value of (1) a single payment of $20,000 at 7 percent for ten years, (2) ten annual payments of $2,000 at 7 percent, (3) a single payment of $6,000 at 9 percent for seven years, and (4) seven annual payments of $6,000 at 9 percent.

E 3.
L O 2
Future Value
Calculations

Assume that $40,000 is invested today. Compute the amount that would accumulate at the end of seven years when the interest rate is (1) 8 percent compounded annually, (2) 8 percent compounded semiannually, and (3) 8 percent compounded quarterly.

E 4.
L O 2
Future Value
Calculations

Calculate the accumulation of periodic payments of $1,000 made at the end of each of four years, assuming (1) 10 percent annual interest compounded annually, (2) 10 percent annual interest compounded semiannually, (3) 4 percent annual interest compounded annually, and (4) 16 percent annual interest compounded quarterly.

E 5.
L O 2
Future Value
Applications

a. Two parents have $20,000 to invest for their child's college tuition, which they estimate will cost $40,000 when the child enters college twelve years from now.

Calculate the approximate rate of annual interest that the investment must earn to reach the $40,000 goal in twelve years. (**Hint:** Make a calculation; then use Table 1 in the appendix on future value and present value tables.)

b. Ted Pruitt is saving to purchase a summer home that will cost about $64,000. He has $40,000 now, on which he can earn 7 percent annual interest.

Calculate the approximate length of time he will have to wait to purchase the summer home. (**Hint:** Make a calculation; then use Table 1 in the appendix on future value and present value tables.)

E 6. *Working Backward*
L O 2 *from a Future Value*

Gloria Faraquez has a debt of $90,000 due in four years. She wants to save money to pay it off by making annual deposits in an investment account that earns 8 percent annual interest.

Calculate the amount she must deposit each year to reach her goal. (**Hint:** Use Table 2 in the appendix on future value and present value tables; then make a calculation.)

E 7. *Determining an*
L O 3 *Advance Payment*

Ellen Saber is contemplating paying five years' rent in advance. Her annual rent is $9,600. Calculate the single sum that would have to be paid now for the advance rent, if we assume compound interest of 8 percent.

E 8. *Present Value*
L O 3 *Calculations*

Find the present value of (1) a single payment of $24,000 at 6 percent for twelve years, (2) twelve annual payments of $2,000 at 6 percent, (3) a single payment of $5,000 at 9 percent for five years, and (4) five annual payments of $5,000 at 9 percent.

E 9. *Present Value of a*
L O 3 *Lump-Sum Contract*

A contract calls for a lump-sum payment of $60,000. Find the present value of the contract, assuming that (1) the payment is due in five years, and the current interest rate is 9 percent; (2) the payment is due in ten years, and the current interest rate is 9 percent; (3) the payment is due in five years, and the current interest rate is 5 percent; and (4) the payment is due in ten years, and the current interest rate is 5 percent.

E 10. *Present Value of an*
L O 3 *Annuity Contract*

A contract calls for annual payments of $1,200. Find the present value of the contract, assuming that (1) the number of payments is seven, and the current interest rate is 6 percent; (2) the number of payments is fourteen, and the current interest rate is 6 percent; (3) the number of payments is seven, and the current interest rate is 8 percent; and (4) the number of payments is fourteen, and the current interest rate is 8 percent.

E 11. *Noninterest-Bearing*
L O 4 *Note*

On January 1, 19x8, Pendleton purchased a machine from Leyland by signing a two-year, noninterest-bearing $32,000 note. Pendleton currently pays 12 percent interest to borrow money at the bank.

Prepare entries in Pendleton's and Leyland's journals to (1) record the purchase and the note, (2) adjust the accounts after one year, and (3) record payment of the note after two years (on December 31, 19x9).

E 12. *Valuing an Asset for*
L O 4 *the Purpose of*
Making a Purchasing
Decision

Oscaro owns a service station and has the opportunity to purchase a car wash machine for $30,000. After carefully studying projected costs and revenues, Oscaro estimates that the car wash will produce a net cash flow of $5,200 annually and will last for eight years. Oscaro feels that an interest rate of 14 percent is adequate for his business.

Calculate the present value of the machine to Oscaro. Does the purchase appear to be a correct business decision?

E 13. *Deferred Payment*
L O 4

Johnson Equipment Corporation sold a precision tool machine with computer controls to Borst Corporation for $800,000 on January 1, agreeing to take payment nine months later on October 1. Assuming that the prevailing annual interest rate for such a transaction is 16 percent compounded quarterly, what is the actual sales (purchase) price of the machine tool, and what journal entries will be made at the time of the purchase (sale) and at the time of the payment (receipt) on the records of both Borst and Johnson?

E 14. *Investment of Idle*
L O 4 *Cash*

Scientific Publishing Company, a publisher of college books, has just completed a successful fall selling season and has $5,000,000 in cash to invest for nine months, beginning on January 1. The company placed the cash in a money market account that is expected to pay 12 percent annual interest compounded monthly. Interest is credited to the company's account each month. How much cash will the company have at the end of nine months, and what entries are made to record the investment and the first two monthly (February 1 and March 1) interest amounts?

E 15. *Accumulation of a*
L O 4 *Fund*

Laferia Corporation borrowed $3,000,000 from an insurance company on a five-year note. Management agreed to set aside enough cash at the end of each year to accumulate the amount needed to pay off the note at maturity. Since the first contribution to the fund will be made in one year, four annual contributions are needed. Assuming that the fund will earn 10 percent compounded annually, how much will the annual contribution to the fund be (round to nearest dollar), and what will be the journal entry for the first contribution?

E 16. *Negotiating the Sale*
L O 4 *of a Business*

Horace Raftson is attempting to sell his business to Ernando Ruiz. The company has assets of $900,000, liabilities of $800,000, and owner's equity of $100,000. Both parties agree that the proper rate of return to expect is 12 percent; however, they differ on other assumptions. Raftson believes that the business will generate at least $100,000 per year of cash flows for twenty years. Ruiz thinks that $80,000 in cash flows per year is more reasonable and that only ten years in the future should be considered. Using Table 4 in the appendix on future value and present value tables, determine the range for negotiation by computing the present value of Raftson's offer to sell and of Ruiz's offer to buy.

PROBLEMS

B 1. *Time Value of Money*
L O 2, 3, 4 *Applications*

Neiman Corporation's management took several actions, each of which was to be effective on January 1, 19x1, and each of which involved an application of the time value of money.

a. Established a new retirement plan to take effect in three years and authorized three annual payments of $500,000 starting January 1, 19x2, to establish the retirement fund.
b. Approved plans for a new distribution center to be built for $1,000,000 and authorized five annual payments, starting January 1, 19x2, to accumulate the funds for the new center.
c. Bought out the contract of a member of top management for a payment of $50,000 per year for four years beginning January 1, 19x2.
d. Accepted a two-year noninterest-bearing note for $100,000 as payment for equipment that the company sold.
e. Set aside $300,000 for possible losses from lawsuits over a defective product. The lawsuits are not expected to be settled for three years.

REQUIRED

Assuming an annual interest rate of 10 percent and using Tables 1, 2, 3, and 4, answer the following questions.

1. In action **a,** how much will the retirement fund accumulate in three years?
2. In action **b,** how much must the annual payment be to reach the goal?
3. In action **c,** what is the cost (present value) of the buy-out?
4. In action **d,** assuming that interest is compounded semiannually, what is the selling price (present value) of the equipment?
5. In action **e,** how much will the fund accumulate to in three years?

B 2. *Time Value of Money*
L O 2, 3, 4 *Applications*

Effective January 1, 19x1, the board of directors of Riordan, Inc. approved the following actions, each of which is an application of the time value of money.

a. Established in a single payment of $100,000 a contingency fund for the possible settlement of a lawsuit. The suit is expected to be settled in two years.
b. Asked for another fund to be established by a single payment to accumulate to $300,000 in four years.
c. Approved purchase of a parcel of land for future plant expansion. Payments are to start January 1, 19x2, at $50,000 per year for 5 years.
d. Determined that a new building to be built on the property in **c** would cost $800,000 and authorized annual payments to be paid starting January 1, 19x2, into a fund for its construction.
e. Purchased Riordan common stock from a stockholder who wanted to be bought out by issuing a four-year noninterest-bearing note for $200,000.

REQUIRED

Assuming an annual interest rate of 8 percent and using Tables 1, 2, 3, and 4, answer the following questions.

1. In action **a,** how much will the fund accumulate to in two years?
2. In action **b,** how much will need to be deposited initially to accumulate the desired amount?
3. In action **c,** what is the purchase price (present value) of the land?
4. In action **d,** how much would the equal annual payments need to be to accumulate enough money to build the building?
5. In action **e,** assuming semiannual compounding of interest, what is the actual purchase price of the stock (present value of the note)?

Table 1 provides the multipliers necessary to compute the future value of a *single* cash deposit made at the *beginning* of year 1. Three factors must be known before the future value can be computed: (1) the time period in years, (2) the stated annual rate of interest to be earned, and (3) the dollar amount invested or deposited.

Example   Determine the future value of $5,000 deposited now that will earn 9 percent interest compounded annually for five years. From Table 1, the necessary multiplier for five years at 9 percent is 1.539, and the answer is

$$\$5,000 \times 1.539 = \$7,695$$

Where r is the interest rate and n is the number of periods, the factor values for Table 1 are

$$FV = PV(1 + r)^n$$

Situations requiring the use of Table 2 are similar to those requiring Table 1 except that Table 2 is used to compute the future value of a *series* of *equal* annual deposits at the end of each period.

Example   What will be the future value at the end of thirty years if $1,000 is deposited each year on January 1, beginning in one year, assuming 12 percent interest compounded annually? The required multiplier from Table 2 is 241.3, and the answer is

$$\$1,000 \times 241.3 = \$241,300$$

The factor values for Table 2 are

$$FVa = \left[\frac{(1 + r)^n - 1}{r} \right]$$

Table 3 is used to compute the value today of a *single* amount of cash to be received sometime in the future. To use Table 3, you must first know: (1) the time period in years until funds will be received, (2) the stated annual rate of interest, and (3) the dollar amount to be received at the end of the time period.

Example   What is the present value of $30,000 to be received twenty-five years from now, assuming a 14 percent interest rate? From Table 3, the required multiplier is .038, and the answer is

$$\$30,000 \times .038 = \$1,140$$

The factor values for Table 3 are

$$PV = FV \times (1 + r)^{-n}$$

Table 1. Future Value of $1 After a Given Number of Time Periods

Periods	1%	2%	3%	4%	5%	6%	7%	8%	9%	10%	12%	14%	15%
1	1.010	1.020	1.030	1.040	1.050	1.060	1.070	1.080	1.090	1.100	1.120	1.140	1.150
2	1.020	1.040	1.061	1.082	1.103	1.124	1.145	1.166	1.188	1.210	1.254	1.300	1.323
3	1.030	1.061	1.093	1.125	1.158	1.191	1.225	1.260	1.295	1.331	1.405	1.482	1.521
4	1.041	1.082	1.126	1.170	1.216	1.262	1.311	1.360	1.412	1.464	1.574	1.689	1.749
5	1.051	1.104	1.159	1.217	1.276	1.338	1.403	1.469	1.539	1.611	1.762	1.925	2.011
6	1.062	1.126	1.194	1.265	1.340	1.419	1.501	1.587	1.677	1.772	1.974	2.195	2.313
7	1.072	1.149	1.230	1.316	1.407	1.504	1.606	1.714	1.828	1.949	2.211	2.502	2.660
8	1.083	1.172	1.267	1.369	1.477	1.594	1.718	1.851	1.993	2.144	2.476	2.853	3.059
9	1.094	1.195	1.305	1.423	1.551	1.689	1.838	1.999	2.172	2.358	2.773	3.252	3.518
10	1.105	1.219	1.344	1.480	1.629	1.791	1.967	2.159	2.367	2.594	3.106	3.707	4.046
11	1.116	1.243	1.384	1.539	1.710	1.898	2.105	2.332	2.580	2.853	3.479	4.226	4.652
12	1.127	1.268	1.426	1.601	1.796	2.012	2.252	2.518	2.813	3.138	3.896	4.818	5.350
13	1.138	1.294	1.469	1.665	1.886	2.133	2.410	2.720	3.066	3.452	4.363	5.492	6.153
14	1.149	1.319	1.513	1.732	1.980	2.261	2.579	2.937	3.342	3.798	4.887	6.261	7.076
15	1.161	1.346	1.558	1.801	2.079	2.397	2.759	3.172	3.642	4.177	5.474	7.138	8.137
16	1.173	1.373	1.605	1.873	2.183	2.540	2.952	3.426	3.970	4.595	6.130	8.137	9.358
17	1.184	1.400	1.653	1.948	2.292	2.693	3.159	3.700	4.328	5.054	6.866	9.276	10.76
18	1.196	1.428	1.702	2.026	2.407	2.854	3.380	3.996	4.717	5.560	7.690	10.58	12.38
19	1.208	1.457	1.754	2.107	2.527	3.026	3.617	4.316	5.142	6.116	8.613	12.06	14.23
20	1.220	1.486	1.806	2.191	2.653	3.207	3.870	4.661	5.604	6.728	9.646	13.74	16.37
21	1.232	1.516	1.860	2.279	2.786	3.400	4.141	5.034	6.109	7.400	10.80	15.67	18.82
22	1.245	1.546	1.916	2.370	2.925	3.604	4.430	5.437	6.659	8.140	12.10	17.86	21.64
23	1.257	1.577	1.974	2.465	3.072	3.820	4.741	5.871	7.258	8.954	13.55	20.36	24.89
24	1.270	1.608	2.033	2.563	3.225	4.049	5.072	6.341	7.911	9.850	15.18	23.21	28.63
25	1.282	1.641	2.094	2.666	3.386	4.292	5.427	6.848	8.623	10.83	17.00	26.46	32.92
26	1.295	1.673	2.157	2.772	3.556	4.549	5.807	7.396	9.399	11.92	19.04	30.17	37.86
27	1.308	1.707	2.221	2.883	3.733	4.822	6.214	7.988	10.25	13.11	21.32	34.39	43.54
28	1.321	1.741	2.288	2.999	3.920	5.112	6.649	8.627	11.17	14.42	23.88	39.20	50.07
29	1.335	1.776	2.357	3.119	4.116	5.418	7.114	9.317	12.17	15.86	26.75	44.69	57.58
30	1.348	1.811	2.427	3.243	4.322	5.743	7.612	10.06	13.27	17.45	29.96	50.95	66.21
40	1.489	2.208	3.262	4.801	7.040	10.29	14.97	21.72	31.41	45.26	93.05	188.9	267.9
50	1.645	2.692	4.384	7.107	11.47	18.42	29.46	46.90	74.36	117.4	289.0	700.2	1,084

Table 3 is the reciprocal of Table 1.

Table 4 is used to compute the present value of a *series* of *equal* annual cash flows.

Example   Arthur Howard won a contest on January 1, 1996, in which the prize was $30,000, payable in fifteen annual installments of $2,000 every December 31, beginning in 1996. Assuming a 9 percent interest rate, what is the present value of Mr. Howard's prize on January 1, 1996? From Table 4, the required multiplier is 8.061, and the answer is:

$$\$2,000 \times 8.061 = \$16,122$$

Table 2. Future Value of $1 Paid in Each Period for a Given Number of Time Periods

Periods	1%	2%	3%	4%	5%	6%	7%	8%	9%	10%	12%	14%	15%
1	1.000	1.000	1.000	1.000	1.000	1.000	1.000	1.000	1.000	1.000	1.000	1.000	1.000
2	2.010	2.020	2.030	2.040	2.050	2.060	2.070	2.080	2.090	2.100	2.120	2.140	2.150
3	3.030	3.060	3.091	3.122	3.153	3.184	3.215	3.246	3.278	3.310	3.374	3.440	3.473
4	4.060	4.122	4.184	4.246	4.310	4.375	4.440	4.506	4.573	4.641	4.779	4.921	4.993
5	5.101	5.204	5.309	5.416	5.526	5.637	5.751	5.867	5.985	6.105	6.353	6.610	6.742
6	6.152	6.308	6.468	6.633	6.802	6.975	7.153	7.336	7.523	7.716	8.115	8.536	8.754
7	7.214	7.434	7.662	7.898	8.142	8.394	8.654	8.923	9.200	9.487	10.09	10.73	11.07
8	8.286	8.583	8.892	9.214	9.549	9.897	10.26	10.64	11.03	11.44	12.30	13.23	13.73
9	9.369	9.755	10.16	10.58	11.03	11.49	11.98	12.49	13.02	13.58	14.78	16.09	16.79
10	10.46	10.95	11.46	12.01	12.58	13.18	13.82	14.49	15.19	15.94	17.55	19.34	20.30
11	11.57	12.17	12.81	13.49	14.21	14.97	15.78	16.65	17.56	18.53	20.65	23.04	24.35
12	12.68	13.41	14.19	15.03	15.92	16.87	17.89	18.98	20.14	21.38	24.13	27.27	29.00
13	13.81	14.68	15.62	16.63	17.71	18.88	20.14	21.50	22.95	24.52	28.03	32.09	34.35
14	14.95	15.97	17.09	18.29	19.60	21.02	22.55	24.21	26.02	27.98	32.39	37.58	40.50
15	16.10	17.29	18.60	20.02	21.58	23.28	25.13	27.15	29.36	31.77	37.28	43.84	47.58
16	17.26	18.64	20.16	21.82	23.66	25.67	27.89	30.32	33.00	35.95	42.75	50.98	55.72
17	18.43	20.01	21.76	23.70	25.84	28.21	30.84	33.75	36.97	40.54	48.88	59.12	65.08
18	19.61	21.41	23.41	25.65	28.13	30.91	34.00	37.45	41.30	45.60	55.75	68.39	75.84
19	20.81	22.84	25.12	27.67	30.54	33.76	37.38	41.45	46.02	51.16	63.44	78.97	88.21
20	22.02	24.30	26.87	29.78	33.07	36.79	41.00	45.76	51.16	57.28	72.05	91.02	102.4
21	23.24	25.78	28.68	31.97	35.72	39.99	44.87	50.42	56.76	64.00	81.70	104.8	118.8
22	24.47	27.30	30.54	34.25	38.51	43.39	49.01	55.46	62.87	71.40	92.50	120.4	137.6
23	25.72	28.85	32.45	36.62	41.43	47.00	53.44	60.89	69.53	79.54	104.6	138.3	159.3
24	26.97	30.42	34.43	39.08	44.50	50.82	58.18	66.76	76.79	88.50	118.2	158.7	184.2
25	28.24	32.03	36.46	41.65	47.73	54.86	63.25	73.11	84.70	98.35	133.3	181.9	212.8
26	29.53	33.67	38.55	44.31	51.11	59.16	68.68	79.95	93.32	109.2	150.3	208.3	245.7
27	30.82	35.34	40.71	47.08	54.67	63.71	74.48	87.35	102.7	121.1	169.4	238.5	283.6
28	32.13	37.05	42.93	49.97	58.40	68.53	80.70	95.34	113.0	134.2	190.7	272.9	327.1
29	33.45	38.79	45.22	52.97	62.32	73.64	87.35	104.0	124.1	148.6	214.6	312.1	377.2
30	34.78	40.57	47.58	56.08	66.44	79.06	94.46	113.3	136.3	164.5	241.3	356.8	434.7
40	48.89	60.40	75.40	95.03	120.8	154.8	199.6	259.1	337.9	442.6	767.1	1,342	1,779
50	64.46	84.58	112.8	152.7	209.3	290.3	406.5	573.8	815.1	1,164	2,400	4,995	7,218

Table 3. Present Value of $1 to be Received at the End of a Given Number of Time Periods

Periods	1%	2%	3%	4%	5%	6%	7%	8%	9%	10%	12%
1	0.990	0.980	0.971	0.962	0.952	0.943	0.935	0.926	0.917	0.909	0.893
2	0.980	0.961	0.943	0.925	0.907	0.890	0.873	0.857	0.842	0.826	0.797
3	0.971	0.942	0.915	0.889	0.864	0.840	0.816	0.794	0.772	0.751	0.712
4	0.961	0.924	0.888	0.855	0.823	0.792	0.763	0.735	0.708	0.683	0.636
5	0.951	0.906	0.863	0.822	0.784	0.747	0.713	0.681	0.650	0.621	0.567
6	0.942	0.888	0.837	0.790	0.746	0.705	0.666	0.630	0.596	0.564	0.507
7	0.933	0.871	0.813	0.760	0.711	0.665	0.623	0.583	0.547	0.513	0.452
8	0.923	0.853	0.789	0.731	0.677	0.627	0.582	0.540	0.502	0.467	0.404
9	0.914	0.837	0.766	0.703	0.645	0.592	0.544	0.500	0.460	0.424	0.361
10	0.905	0.820	0.744	0.676	0.614	0.558	0.508	0.463	0.422	0.386	0.322
11	0.896	0.804	0.722	0.650	0.585	0.527	0.475	0.429	0.388	0.350	0.287
12	0.887	0.788	0.701	0.625	0.557	0.497	0.444	0.397	0.356	0.319	0.257
13	0.879	0.773	0.681	0.601	0.530	0.469	0.415	0.368	0.326	0.290	0.229
14	0.870	0.758	0.661	0.577	0.505	0.442	0.388	0.340	0.299	0.263	0.205
15	0.861	0.743	0.642	0.555	0.481	0.417	0.362	0.315	0.275	0.239	0.183
16	0.853	0.728	0.623	0.534	0.458	0.394	0.339	0.292	0.252	0.218	0.163
17	0.844	0.714	0.605	0.513	0.436	0.371	0.317	0.270	0.231	0.198	0.146
18	0.836	0.700	0.587	0.494	0.416	0.350	0.296	0.250	0.212	0.180	0.130
19	0.828	0.686	0.570	0.475	0.396	0.331	0.277	0.232	0.194	0.164	0.116
20	0.820	0.673	0.554	0.456	0.377	0.312	0.258	0.215	0.178	0.149	0.104
21	0.811	0.660	0.538	0.439	0.359	0.294	0.242	0.199	0.164	0.135	0.093
22	0.803	0.647	0.522	0.422	0.342	0.278	0.226	0.184	0.150	0.123	0.083
23	0.795	0.634	0.507	0.406	0.326	0.262	0.211	0.170	0.138	0.112	0.074
24	0.788	0.622	0.492	0.390	0.310	0.247	0.197	0.158	0.126	0.102	0.066
25	0.780	0.610	0.478	0.375	0.295	0.233	0.184	0.146	0.116	0.092	0.059
26	0.772	0.598	0.464	0.361	0.281	0.220	0.172	0.135	0.106	0.084	0.053
27	0.764	0.586	0.450	0.347	0.268	0.207	0.161	0.125	0.098	0.076	0.047
28	0.757	0.574	0.437	0.333	0.255	0.196	0.150	0.116	0.090	0.069	0.042
29	0.749	0.563	0.424	0.321	0.243	0.185	0.141	0.107	0.082	0.063	0.037
30	0.742	0.552	0.412	0.308	0.231	0.174	0.131	0.099	0.075	0.057	0.033
40	0.672	0.453	0.307	0.208	0.142	0.097	0.067	0.046	0.032	0.022	0.011
50	0.608	0.372	0.228	0.141	0.087	0.054	0.034	0.021	0.013	0.009	0.003

The factor values for Table 4 are

$$PVa = \left[\frac{1 - (1 + r)^{-n}}{r} \right]$$

Table 4 is the columnar sum of Table 3.

Table 4 applies to *ordinary annuities,* in which the first cash flow occurs one time period beyond the date for which the present value is to be computed.

An *annuity due* is a series of equal cash flows for N time periods, but the first payment occurs immediately. The present value of the first payment equals

Table 3. (*continued*)

14%	15%	16%	18%	20%	25%	30%	35%	40%	45%	50%	Periods
0.877	0.870	0.862	0.847	0.833	0.800	0.769	0.741	0.714	0.690	0.667	1
0.769	0.756	0.743	0.718	0.694	0.640	0.592	0.549	0.510	0.476	0.444	2
0.675	0.658	0.641	0.609	0.579	0.512	0.455	0.406	0.364	0.328	0.296	3
0.592	0.572	0.552	0.516	0.482	0.410	0.350	0.301	0.260	0.226	0.198	4
0.519	0.497	0.476	0.437	0.402	0.328	0.269	0.223	0.186	0.156	0.132	5
0.456	0.432	0.410	0.370	0.335	0.262	0.207	0.165	0.133	0.108	0.088	6
0.400	0.376	0.354	0.314	0.279	0.210	0.159	0.122	0.095	0.074	0.059	7
0.351	0.327	0.305	0.266	0.233	0.168	0.123	0.091	0.068	0.051	0.039	8
0.308	0.284	0.263	0.225	0.194	0.134	0.094	0.067	0.048	0.035	0.026	9
0.270	0.247	0.227	0.191	0.162	0.107	0.073	0.050	0.035	0.024	0.017	10
0.237	0.215	0.195	0.162	0.135	0.086	0.056	0.037	0.025	0.017	0.012	11
0.208	0.187	0.168	0.137	0.112	0.069	0.043	0.027	0.018	0.012	0.008	12
0.182	0.163	0.145	0.116	0.093	0.055	0.033	0.020	0.013	0.008	0.005	13
0.160	0.141	0.125	0.099	0.078	0.044	0.025	0.015	0.009	0.006	0.003	14
0.140	0.123	0.108	0.084	0.065	0.035	0.020	0.011	0.006	0.004	0.002	15
0.123	0.107	0.093	0.071	0.054	0.028	0.015	0.008	0.005	0.003	0.002	16
0.108	0.093	0.080	0.060	0.045	0.023	0.012	0.006	0.003	0.002	0.001	17
0.095	0.081	0.069	0.051	0.038	0.018	0.009	0.005	0.002	0.001	0.001	18
0.083	0.070	0.060	0.043	0.031	0.014	0.007	0.003	0.002	0.001		19
0.073	0.061	0.051	0.037	0.026	0.012	0.005	0.002	0.001	0.001		20
0.064	0.053	0.044	0.031	0.022	0.009	0.004	0.002	0.001			21
0.056	0.046	0.038	0.026	0.018	0.007	0.003	0.001	0.001			22
0.049	0.040	0.033	0.022	0.015	0.006	0.002	0.001				23
0.043	0.035	0.028	0.019	0.013	0.005	0.002	0.001				24
0.038	0.030	0.024	0.016	0.010	0.004	0.001	0.001				25
0.033	0.026	0.021	0.014	0.009	0.003	0.001					26
0.029	0.023	0.018	0.011	0.007	0.002	0.001					27
0.026	0.020	0.016	0.010	0.006	0.002	0.001					28
0.022	0.017	0.014	0.008	0.005	0.002						29
0.020	0.015	0.012	0.007	0.004	0.001						30
0.005	0.004	0.003	0.001	0.001							40
0.001	0.001	0.001									50

the face value of the cash flow; Table 4 then is used to measure the present value of $N - 1$ remaining cash flows.

Example   Determine the present value on January 1, 1996, of twenty lease payments; each payment of $10,000 is due on January 1, beginning in 1996. Assume an interest rate of 8 percent.

Present value = immediate payment + { present value of 19 subsequent payments at 8%

= $10,000 + ($10,000 × 9.604) = $106,040

Table 4. Present Value of $1 Received Each Period for a Given Number of Time Periods

Periods	1%	2%	3%	4%	5%	6%	7%	8%	9%	10%	12%
1	0.990	0.980	0.971	0.962	0.952	0.943	0.935	0.926	0.917	0.909	0.893
2	1.970	1.942	1.913	1.886	1.859	1.833	1.808	1.783	1.759	1.736	1.690
3	2.941	2.884	2.829	2.775	2.723	2.673	2.624	2.577	2.531	2.487	2.402
4	3.902	3.808	3.717	3.630	3.546	3.465	3.387	3.312	3.240	3.170	3.037
5	4.853	4.713	4.580	4.452	4.329	4.212	4.100	3.993	3.890	3.791	3.605
6	5.795	5.601	5.417	5.242	5.076	4.917	4.767	4.623	4.486	4.355	4.111
7	6.728	6.472	6.230	6.002	5.786	5.582	5.389	5.206	5.033	4.868	4.564
8	7.652	7.325	7.020	6.733	6.463	6.210	5.971	5.747	5.535	5.335	4.968
9	8.566	8.162	7.786	7.435	7.108	6.802	6.515	6.247	5.995	5.759	5.328
10	9.471	8.983	8.530	8.111	7.722	7.360	7.024	6.710	6.418	6.145	5.650
11	10.368	9.787	9.253	8.760	8.306	7.887	7.499	7.139	6.805	6.495	5.938
12	11.255	10.575	9.954	9.385	8.863	8.384	7.943	7.536	7.161	6.814	6.194
13	12.134	11.348	10.635	9.986	9.394	8.853	8.358	7.904	7.487	7.103	6.424
14	13.004	12.106	11.296	10.563	9.899	9.295	8.745	8.244	7.786	7.367	6.628
15	13.865	12.849	11.938	11.118	10.380	9.712	9.108	8.559	8.061	7.606	6.811
16	14.718	13.578	12.561	11.652	10.838	10.106	9.447	8.851	8.313	7.824	6.974
17	15.562	14.292	13.166	12.166	11.274	10.477	9.763	9.122	8.544	8.022	7.120
18	16.398	14.992	13.754	12.659	11.690	10.828	10.059	9.372	8.756	8.201	7.250
19	17.226	15.678	14.324	13.134	12.085	11.158	10.336	9.604	8.950	8.365	7.366
20	18.046	16.351	14.878	13.590	12.462	11.470	10.594	9.818	9.129	8.514	7.469
21	18.857	17.011	15.415	14.029	12.821	11.764	10.836	10.017	9.292	8.649	7.562
22	19.660	17.658	15.937	14.451	13.163	12.042	11.061	10.201	9.442	8.772	7.645
23	20.456	18.292	16.444	14.857	13.489	12.303	11.272	10.371	9.580	8.883	7.718
24	21.243	18.914	16.936	15.247	13.799	12.550	11.469	10.529	9.707	8.985	7.784
25	22.023	19.523	17.413	15.622	14.094	12.783	11.654	10.675	9.823	9.077	7.843
26	22.795	20.121	17.877	15.983	14.375	13.003	11.826	10.810	9.929	9.161	7.896
27	23.560	20.707	18.327	16.330	14.643	13.211	11.987	10.935	10.027	9.237	7.943
28	24.316	21.281	18.764	16.663	14.898	13.406	12.137	11.051	10.116	9.307	7.984
29	25.066	21.844	19.189	16.984	15.141	13.591	12.278	11.158	10.198	9.370	8.022
30	25.808	22.396	19.600	17.292	15.373	13.765	12.409	11.258	10.274	9.427	8.055
40	32.835	27.355	23.115	19.793	17.159	15.046	13.332	11.925	10.757	9.779	8.244
50	39.196	31.424	25.730	21.482	18.256	15.762	13.801	12.234	10.962	9.915	8.305

Table 4. (continued)

14%	15%	16%	18%	20%	25%	30%	35%	40%	45%	50%	Periods
0.877	0.870	0.862	0.847	0.833	0.800	0.769	0.741	0.714	0.690	0.667	1
1.647	1.626	1.605	1.566	1.528	1.440	1.361	1.289	1.224	1.165	1.111	2
2.322	2.283	2.246	2.174	2.106	1.952	1.816	1.696	1.589	1.493	1.407	3
2.914	2.855	2.798	2.690	2.589	2.362	2.166	1.997	1.849	1.720	1.605	4
3.433	3.352	3.274	3.127	2.991	2.689	2.436	2.220	2.035	1.876	1.737	5
3.889	3.784	3.685	3.498	3.326	2.951	2.643	2.385	2.168	1.983	1.824	6
4.288	4.160	4.039	3.812	3.605	3.161	2.802	2.508	2.263	2.057	1.883	7
4.639	4.487	4.344	4.078	3.837	3.329	2.925	2.598	2.331	2.109	1.922	8
4.946	4.772	4.607	4.303	4.031	3.463	3.019	2.665	2.379	2.144	1.948	9
5.216	5.019	4.833	4.494	4.192	3.571	3.092	2.715	2.414	2.168	1.965	10
5.453	5.234	5.029	4.656	4.327	3.656	3.147	2.752	2.438	2.185	1.977	11
5.660	5.421	5.197	4.793	4.439	3.725	3.190	2.779	2.456	2.197	1.985	12
5.842	5.583	5.342	4.910	4.533	3.780	3.223	2.799	2.469	2.204	1.990	13
6.002	5.724	5.468	5.008	4.611	3.824	3.249	2.814	2.478	2.210	1.993	14
6.142	5.847	5.575	5.092	4.675	3.859	3.268	2.825	2.484	2.214	1.995	15
6.265	5.954	5.669	5.162	4.730	3.887	3.283	2.834	2.489	2.216	1.997	16
6.373	6.047	5.749	5.222	4.775	3.910	3.295	2.840	2.492	2.218	1.998	17
6.467	6.128	5.818	5.273	4.812	3.928	3.304	2.844	2.494	2.219	1.999	18
6.550	6.198	5.877	5.316	4.844	3.942	3.311	2.848	2.496	2.220	1.999	19
6.623	6.259	5.929	5.353	4.870	3.954	3.316	2.850	2.497	2.221	1.999	20
6.687	6.312	5.973	5.384	4.891	3.963	3.320	2.852	2.498	2.221	2.000	21
6.743	6.359	6.011	5.410	4.909	3.970	3.323	2.853	2.498	2.222	2.000	22
6.792	6.399	6.044	5.432	4.925	3.976	3.325	2.854	2.499	2.222	2.000	23
6.835	6.434	6.073	5.451	4.937	3.981	3.327	2.855	2.499	2.222	2.000	24
6.873	6.464	6.097	5.467	4.948	3.985	3.329	2.856	2.499	2.222	2.000	25
6.906	6.491	6.118	5.480	4.956	3.988	3.330	2.856	2.500	2.222	2.000	26
6.935	6.514	6.136	5.492	4.964	3.990	3.331	2.856	2.500	2.222	2.000	27
6.961	6.534	6.152	5.502	4.970	3.992	3.331	2.857	2.500	2.222	2.000	28
6.983	6.551	6.166	5.510	4.975	3.994	3.332	2.857	2.500	2.222	2.000	29
7.003	6.566	6.177	5.517	4.979	3.995	3.332	2.857	2.500	2.222	2.000	30
7.105	6.642	6.234	5.548	4.997	3.999	3.333	2.857	2.500	2.222	2.000	40
7.133	6.661	6.246	5.554	4.999	4.000	3.333	2.857	2.500	2.222	2.000	50